ISBN 978-0-260-66875-2
PIBN 11117848

1 MONTH OF
FREE
READING

at

www.ForgottenBooks.com

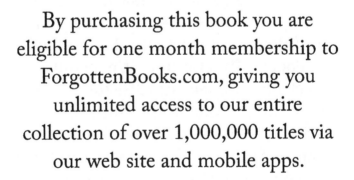

By purchasing this book you are eligible for one month membership to ForgottenBooks.com, giving you unlimited access to our entire collection of over 1,000,000 titles via our web site and mobile apps.

To claim your free month visit:

www.forgottenbooks.com/free1117848

English
Français
Deutsche
Italiano
Español
Português

www.forgottenbooks.com

Mythology Photography **Fiction**
Fishing Christianity **Art** Cooking
Essays Buddhism Freemasonry
Medicine **Biology** Music **Ancient Egypt** Evolution Carpentry Physics
Dance Geology **Mathematics** Fitness
Shakespeare **Folklore** Yoga Marketing
Confidence Immortality Biographies
Poetry **Psychology** Witchcraft
Electronics Chemistry History **Law**
Accounting **Philosophy** Anthropology
Alchemy Drama Quantum Mechanics
Atheism Sexual Health **Ancient History**
Entrepreneurship Languages Sport
Paleontology Needlework Islam
Metaphysics Investment Archaeology
Parenting Statistics Criminology
Motivational

Lincoln Bartlett Co.

Importers of French and English Apparel
For Men and Women

46 Jackson Boulevard

French and English Shirtings

MENS SHIRTS
UNDERWEAR
NECKWEAR
GLOVES --
WAISTS ---

NE VILE VELIS

This Season's Fancy Materials for Shirts and Shirt Waists are in most exquisite colorings ❋ ❋ ❋ Our Samples are now complete and ready for inspection ❋ ❋ ❋ ❋ ❋

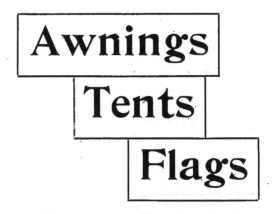

THE DUNDEE NURSERY

Large Shade Trees
with balls of earth a specialty.

A VERY CHOICE LIST OF ORNAMENTAL AND SHADE TREES, ALL SIZES. LARGE FLOWERING SHRUBS, ROSES, FRUIT TREES, EVERGREENS, ETC. PRUNING TREES, SODDING AND LAWN WORK DONE PROMPTLY.

Subdivisions Planted

PORTER & HILL, Office on Sales Grounds, Garfield Boulevard, between State Street and Michigan Avenue, from Fifty-Fifth to Fifty-Sixth Streets . . . . . . CHICAGO.

Proprietors.

PHONE WENTWORTH-596.

THE

CHICAGO BLUE BOOK

OF

SELECTED NAMES

OF

CHICAGO AND SUBURBAN TOWNS

CONTAINING THE

Names and Addresses of Prominent Residents, arranged Alphabetically
and Numerically by Street; also Ladies' Shopping Guide,
Street Directory, and other Valuable Information.

FOR THE YEAR ENDING 1899.

PRICE, FIVE DOLLARS.

THE CHICAGO DIRECTORY COMPANY,
PUBLISHERS,
LAKESIDE PRESS BUILDING, POLK ST., CORNER PLYMOUTH CT

PREFACE.

WE herewith present the Tenth issue of the CHICAGO BLUE BOOK. We wish to thank our lady patrons for the appreciation they have shown our efforts, and trust that this volume will retain the high place in their favor, which we have won, and will endeavor to hold.

Neither time nor money have been spared to make the work as complete and valuable as possible. The difficulty however attending the compiling of such a book can be easily appreciated; and we therefore trust that any omissions will be brought to our notice, that they may be corrected in future. We keep the entire work standing in type, that such corrections can be made promptly ; and in this way we hope to make the Chicago Blue Book as nearly perfect as it is possible to make such a volume.

The title, "BLUE BOOK," is simply a name given the work on account of its *blue* cover. It does not refer to blue blood, as many people suppose. Webster's definition of Blue Book is as follows: "BLUE BOOK—A parliamentary publication, so called from its blue paper cover, such being commonly used ; *also, a book containing a list of fashionable addresses.*"

We do not claim the BLUE BOOK to be either a City Directory or absolutely an Elite Directory ; neither do we pretend to pass upon the social or financial standing of the parties whose names are contained therein. It is simply a compilation of thirty thousand names of the most prominent householders of Chicago, and suburbs within a radius of thirty miles, published in the most convenient form for reference by our lady patrons.

While retaining all the old features, such as Calling Days in the Street List, and Summer Residences in Alphabetical List, we have added very materially to our Miscellaneous Information, Club Lists, Churches, etc.

We shall always be pleased to receive any suggestions from our lady patrons whereby we can enhance the value of this work to them, or any information regarding Social or Literary Clubs and Associations, which we have not already incorporated in our volume. The data of this work have not been compiled from circulars or information out of other Directories, but experienced men, particularly adapted for such work, have been assigned to each locality, and the greatest care has been used in selecting these names. In order to issue the book before the Holidays, it is necessary for us to commence our canvass early in September. We would therefore deem it a great favor if those absent from their homes after October 1st would send us the information which they wish inserted, as it is not safe to take it from servants, or anyone except the parties interested.

THE PUBLISHERS.

17

WHITE STAR LINE

UNITED STATES AND
ROYAL MAIL STEAMERS

NEW YORK, QUEENSTOWN
AND LIVERPOOL

UNSURPASSED FOR EXCELLENCE OF SERVICE.

Disembarking Passengers at Prince's Landing Stage, Liverpool, whence special train to London in 3¾ hours.

"Majestic"   "Teutonic"
"Germanic"   "Brittanic"
"Cymric," 600 feet, 12,552 tons
"Oceanic," 704 feet, over 17,000 tons (building)

S. TENNEY FRENCH, General Western Agent,
244 South Clark Street, Chicago.
Grand Pacific Hotel.

Telephone Express-139.

GENERAL INDEX.

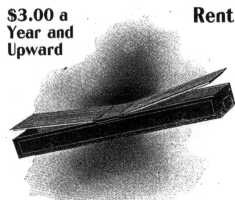

INDEX TO ADVERTISERS.

25

26

28

INDEX TO STREETS.

31

32

ANDERSON GALLERIES

BEECROFT & CO.

40

42

45

MISCELLANEOUS INFORMATION.

CORPORATION OF THE CITY.

Mayor—Carter H. Harrison, office. 2d floor, City Hall.

City Clerk—William Loeffler, office, 3d floor, City Hall.

Comptroller—R. A. Waller, office, 1st floor, City Hall.

Board of Public Works—Lawrence E. McGann, Commissioner, 2d floor, City Hall.

Treasurer—Ernst Hummel, office, 1st floor, City Hall.

Corporation Counsel—Charles Thornton, office, 2d floor, City Hall.

City Attorney—Miles J. Devine, office, 3d floor, City Hall.

Prosecuting Attorney—Howard S. Taylor, office, 3d floor, City Hall.

Health Commissioner—Dr. A. R. Reynolds, office, basement City Hall.

City Physician—D. G. Moore, 677 Jackson boul.

Supt. House of Correction—Adolph Sturm, S. California av. nr. W. Twenty-sixth.

Supt. Public Schools—E. Benjamin Andrews, office, 12th floor, Schiller bldg., 109 Randolph.

School Agent—William A. S. Graham, office, Schiller bldg.

City Sealer of Weights and Measures—Fred E. Eldred, office, 29 City Hall.

Fire Marshal—Denis J. Swenie, office, City Hall, basement.

Gen'l Supt. Police—Joseph Kipley, office, room 32, City Hall.

Gas Inspector—Maurice M. O'Connor, office, basement City Hall.

Inspector of Oils—Robert E. Burke, Wabash av. sw. cor. Randolph

Inspector of Steam Boilers—James Pyne, office, 50 City Hall.

BOARD OF ALDERMEN.

Meets every Monday evening.

First Ward—John J. Coughlin, Dem., Michael Kenna, Dem.

Second Ward—Patrick J. Cook, Dem. Charles F. Gunther, Dem.

Third Ward—Henry S. Fitch, Rep., Charles Alling, jr., Rep.

Fourth Ward—William S. Jackson, Rep., Abraham Ballenberg, Dem.

Fifth Ward—Edward D. Connor, Rep., Frank X. Cloidt, Rep.

Sixth Ward—Charles Martin, Dem., William J. O'Brien, Dem.

Seventh Ward—Henry L. Fick, jr., Dem., William J. Murphy, Ind.

Eighth Ward—John Bennett, Dem., Edward J. Novak, Dem.

Ninth Ward—Edward F. Cullerton, Dem., Rudolph Hurt, Dem.

Tenth Ward—August W. Miller, Rep., Peter Biewer, Dem.

Eleventh Ward—Robert K. Colson, Rep., George Duddleston, Dem.

Twelfth Ward—John F. Neagle, Dem., Joseph H. Francis, Dem.

Thirteenth Ward—William T. Maypole, Dem., Thomas F. Little, Dem.

Fourteenth Ward—Albert W. Beilfuss, Rep., William C. L. Ziehn, Dem.

Fifteenth Ward—Walter J. Raymer, Rep., William A. Tuite, Dem.

Sixteenth Ward—John F. Smulski, Rep., Stanley H. Kunz, Dem.

Seventeenth Ward—James Walsh, Ind., Frank Oberndorf, Rep.

Eighteenth Ward—John J. Brennan, Dem., Michael C. Conlon, Dem.

Nineteenth Ward—Joseph A. Haberkorn, Dem., John Powers, Dem.

Twentieth Ward—Frederick W. Alwart, Dem., Charles F. Brown, Dem.

Twenty-first Ward—William Mangler, Dem., Ernst F. Herrman, Ind.

Twenty-second Ward—Adolphus W. Maltby, Ind., Fred W. Upham, Rep.

Twenty-third Ward—William H. Lyman, Dem., Albert J. Olson, Rep.

Twenty-fourth Ward—Miles E. Barry, Dem., Charles M. Walker, Dem.

Twenty-fifth Ward—Robert Griffith, Rep., James H. Hirsch, Ind.

Twenty-sixth Ward—William E. Schlake, Dem., John C. Cannon, Rep.

Twenty-seventh Ward—Hubert W. Butler, Rep., Spencer S. Kimbell, Rep.

Twenty-eighth Ward—John Bigane, Dem., Frank M. McCarthy, Dem.
Twenty-ninth Ward—Thomas Cary, Dem., Michael McInerney, Dem.
Thirtieth Ward—Charles J. Boyd, Dem., Ernst Reichardt, Dem.
Thirty-first Ward—Joseph Badenoch, Rep., Elliot W. Sproul, Rep.
Thirty-secondWard—William Mavor, Rep., Walter C. Nelson, Ind.
Thirty-third Ward—Hugh T. Darcy, Dem., Martin Wiora, Dem.
Thirty-fourth Ward—John B. Math, Rep., Frank I. Bennett, Rep.

MAYOR'S DEPARTMENT.

2d floor, City Hall.
Mayor—Carter H. Harrison; Secretary, Ed. M. Lahiff.

BOARD OF ELECTION COMMISSIONERS,

3d floor, City Hall.
- Chairman, W. W. Wheelock, Sec., Theodore Stimming, P. H. Keenan. Isaac N. Powell, chief clerk.

BUILDING DEPARTMENT.

122, City Hall.
Commissioner of Buildings—James McAndrews; Secretary, William J. McAllister.

CITY CLERK'S DEPARTMENT.

1st floor, City Hall.
City Clerk—William Loeffler,

CITY COLLECTOR'S DEPARTMENT.

1st floor, City Hall.
Collector—Joseph S. Martin.

CITY TREASURER'S DEPARTMENT.

1st floor, City Hall.
Treasurer—Ernst Hummel.

CIVIL SERVICE COMMISSION.

Room 400 City Hall.
President—Robert Lindblom.
Secretary—T. Corcoran.
Commissioners — Edward Carroll, John W. Ludwig.

COMPTROLLER'S DEPARTMENT.

3d floor, City Hall.
Comptroller—R. A. Waller; Deputy City Comptroller, Edward A. Halsey.

DEPARTMENT OF PUBLIC WORKS.

2d floor, City Hall.
Commissioner—Lawrence E. McGann; Dep. Commissioner—Andrew J. Toolen; City Engineer—John Ericson, 3d floor; Superintendent of Sewerage—Frank J. Davidson; Superintendent of Streets—Michael J. Doherty; Superintendent of Map Dept.—William Raisenegger; Superintendent of Water Dept.—H. O. Nourse; Special Assessments—J. S. Sheahan.

HEALTH DEPARTMENT.

Basement, City Hall.
Commissioner—Arthur R. Reynolds; Asst. Commissioner—Dr. F. W. Reilly; Secretary—E. R. Pritchard; Registrar of Vital Statistics—M. O. Heckard, M.D.

LAW DEPARTMENT.

3d floor, City Hall.
Corporation Counsel—Charles S. Thornton; City Attorney—Miles J. Devine; ProsecutingAttorney—Howard S. Taylor.

PARK COMMISSIONERS.

Lincoln Park—President, Dr. P. M. Woodworth; V. Pres., Joseph E. Dunton; Sec., I. J. Bryan; Auditor, Peter Hand; Treas., H. A. Haugan; Supt. C. W. Andrews. Office, Academy of Sciences bldg., Lincoln Park.
West Chicago Park — President, Joseph W. Suddard; Treasurer, F. M. Blount; Secretary, Ernest G. Schubert; Commissioners, F. M. Blount, William C. Eggert, Andrew J. Graham, Charles B. Pavlicek, Anton Petersen, Joseph W. Suddard. William J. Wilson; gen. supt. Wm. J. Cooke. Office, Union Park,
South Park—Pres., John B. Sherman, Secretary, Edward G. Shumway; Auditor, William Best; Treas., John R. Walsh; John B. Sherman, William Best, Jefferson Hodgkins, Joseph Donnersberger, James W. Ellsworth; gen. supt., J. F. Foster. Office, 57th cor. Cottage Grove av.

POST-OFFICE.

Post-office Building, Michigan av. opp. Washington.
Postmaster—Charles U. Gordon.
Assistant Postmaster—John M. Hubbard.
Private Secretary—Walter B. Getty.
Auditor—John Matter.
Night Superintendent—George Mcgrew, room 5, hours 6 p.m. to 6 a.m.
Cashier—Charles A. Hanna.
Bookkeeper—Thomas R. Melody.
Supt. of City Delivery Division — Maurice J. McGrath.
Supt. of Mailing Division—John A. Montgomery.
Supt. of Money Order Division — Joseph B. Schlossman.

Supt. of Registry Division—William W. Marr.

Supt. Inquiry Division and Bureau of Information—Perry H. Smith jr.

Post Office Inspector — James E. Stuart.

Supt. Railway Mail Service—Lewis L. Troy.

OFFICE HOURS.

Postmaster's office from 9 a. m. to 4 p. m.

Superintendent of Mails, from 9 a. m. to 5 p. m.

Cashier and Accountant, from 9 a. m. to 4 p. m.

Money Order Division, 9 a.m. to 5 p.m.

Registered Letter Division, 8 a..m. to 10 p. m.

Wholesale Stamp Division, 9 a. m. to 4 p. m.

Retail Stamp Division, 7 a.m. to 10 p.m.

Carrier's Division for Delivery of Mail, 7:15 a. m. to 6 p. m.—Sundays, 11:30 a. m. to 12:30 p. m.

General Delivery, open day and night. —Sundays, 11:30 a. m. to 12,30 p. m.

CARRIER STATIONS.

Post Office—Michigan av. opp. Washington
A—575 and 577 N. Clark.
B—1662-1664 N. Clark
C—416 and 418 W. Madison.
D—833-835 W. Madison.
E—2021 W. Madison.
F—291 and 293 N. Carventer.
G—1551 Milwaukee av.
H—(Pilsen) 671-673 N. Carpenter
J—(Armour) 3217 State
K—4193 S. Halsted.
L—2224 Cottage Grove av.
M—Cottage Grove av. cor. 40th
N—(Hyde Park) 324 W. 55th.
O—528 W. 63d.
P—606 W. 79th.
R—1143, 75th.
S—9210 Commercial av.
U—Jackson boul. cor. S. Canal
V—1058 Millard av.
W—3155 Archer av.
X—1250 E. Ravenswood Park
Y—4775 N. Clark.
Chicago Lawn—3520 W. 63d
Elsdon—3553 W. 51st
Hegewisch—13303 Erie av.
Irving Park—1168 W. Byron.
Jefferson—4303 Milwaukee av.
Norwood Park—3470 Avondale av.
Pullman—4 Arcade bldg.
Riverdale—13565 Indiana av.
Sub-Station 56—(Board of Trade) 117-119 Quincy.
Washington Heights—1370 W. 103d.
West Pullman—12005 S. Halsted.

SUB-STATIONS,
1—Larrabee and North av.
2—1072 Lincoln av.
3—104 N. Clark.
4—1249 N, Clark.
5—511 Lincoln av.
6—1061-1063 Milwaukee av.
7—677 Grand av.
8—2601 S. Halsted.
9—409 S. Western av.
10—240 W. Polk.
11—1324 Ogden av.
12—953 W. Lake.
13—525 W. Vanburen.
14—572 W. Madison.
15—1355 Wabash av.
16—5101 State.
17—3112 Cottage Grove av.
18—3859 State.
19—48, 43d.
20—245, 57th.
21—2904 Archer av.
22—360 Ogden av.
23—118, 53d.
24—2358 Wentworth av.
25—1273 W. Vanburen
26—5100 Ashland av.
27—601 Garfield boul.
28—3815 Archer av.
29—200 W. Randolp
30—372, 63d.
31—Masonic Temple.
32—1248 Bryn Mawr av.
33—Lincoln av. cor. W. Foster av., Bowmanville.
34—185 N. Halsted.
35—1168 W. Byron, Irving Park.
36—1840 N. Kedzie av.
37—1403 N. Rockwell
38—1190 Armitage av.
39—1085 N. 42d av.
40—87 N. 48th av., Moreland.
41—6818 S. Chicago av., Park Manor.
42—7111 Cottage Grove av., Brookline Park.
43—126, 75th.
44—7900 Commercial av., Cheltenham
45—8665 Vincennes rd.
46—9332 Cottage Grove av., Burnside.
47—95th and Wood, Rock Isl. Depot Longwood.
48—1360 W. 103d.
49—656, 103d.
50—11110 Michigan av., Roseland.
51—6300 S. Halsted.
52—10554 Torrence av., Cummings.
53—10301 Avenue M, Colehour.
54—W. Lake se. cor. N. 52d av.
55—285 Lincoln av.
56—117 Quincy
57—Monadnock bldg.
58—Dearborn ne. cor. Monroe.
59—1714 E. Ravenswood Park.
60—924, 33d.
61—6600 Wentworth av.

62—1 Ashland boul.
63—1302 W. Madison.
64—410 S. California av.
65—Wabash av. ne. cor. Congress.
66—1352 N. Halsted.
67—Washington sw. cor. Lasalle
68—240 Blue Island av.
69—1248 Argyle.
70—5262 S. Halsted.
71—1713 W. 63d.
72—5900 Wentworth av.
73—887 W. North av.
74—4301 Wabash av.
75—987 Ogden av.
76—744 W. Vanburen.
77—155 W. Taylor.
78—1619 Avondale av.
79—Elston cor. Forest Glen av.

SUB-STATIONS—BRANCH POST-OFFICES.

Dunning—Railroad Station, C.M. & St.P.R.R.
Montclare—Railroad Station, C.M. & St.P.RR.
Clarkdale—S.Central Park av.,near 83d Place.
Forest Hill—7900 S. Robey.

FOREIGN MAILS.

Mails for Great Britain and Ireland, Sundays, Mondays and Thursdays, and Tuesdays during summer via New York, close at 4 and 12 p. m.

For Germany, Denmark, Norway and Sweden, Sundays, Mondays and Thursdays, via New York, close at 4 and 12 p. m.

For China, Japan, New Zealand, Australia, Sandwich Islands, Fiji Islands, Samoa and specially addressed addressed matter for Siam, mails close daily at 2 a. m. sent to San Francisco for dispatch in direct bags from that office.

Note—Mails for countries not named above close daily at 4.30 p.m. and are sent to New York for dispatch in the closed bags from that office.

For Canada—Provinces Ontario and Quebec, close at 9.30 a.m. and 8.30 p. m. daily except Sunday,and Sunday 5 p.m., Hamilton, Toronto, Montreal, London, special dispatch closes daily at 2 a.m., 2:30 and 7:30 p. m.

For Nova Scotia, New Brunswick, Prince Edward's Island and Newfoundland, close daily at 2, 7:45 and 9:45 a.m. and 4:45 and 8:45 p. m. and are dispatched (except for Newfoundland) at 2.30 p. m. daily.

For British Columbia and Manitoba, dispatched via St. Paul, closing daily at 2 a.m.

Foreign postage tables will be found in the public lobbies of the main and branch offices.

For Mexico close daily at 10.30 a. m., and 4.45 and 10.45 p.m.

UNIVERSAL POSTAL UNION.

The rates of postage to the countries and colonies composing the Universal Postal Union (except Canada and Mexico) are as follows:

Letters, per 15 grams (½ ounce,) 5 cents; postal cards each, 2 cents; newspapers and other printed matter, per 2 ounces, 1 cent; commercial papers, packets not in excess of 10 ounces, 5 cents, packets in excess of 10 ounces, for each 2 ounces or fraction thereof, 1 cent; samples of merchandise, packets not in excess of 4 ounces 2 cents, packets in excess of 4 ounces, for each 2 ounces or fraction thereof, 1 cent; registration fee on letters or other articles, 10 cents.

Ordinary letters for countries of the Postal Union (except Canada and Mexico) will be forwarded, whether any postage is prepaid on them or not. All other mailable matter must be prepaid, at least partially.

Argentine Republic, Australia, Austria-Hungary, Bahamas, Barbadoes, W. I., Belgium, Bermudas, Bolivia, Brazil, British Colonies on West coast of Africa and in West Indies, British Guiana, British Honduras, British India, Bulgaria, Canada, Ceylon, Chili, Colombia U. S. of, Congo, Costa Rica, Cyprus, Cuba, Danish Colonies of St. Thomas, St. Croix and St. John; Denmark, Dominica, Ecuador, Egypt, Falkland Islands, Fiji Islands, France, French Colonies, in Asia, Africa, America and Oceanica; Germany, German Protectorates, Great Britain and Ireland, Greece, Greenland, Guatemala, Hawaii, Sandwich Islands; Hayti, Honduras, Hong Kong, Italy, Jamaica, Jap n, Labuan, Liberia, Luxemburg, Malta, Mauritius, Mexico, Montenegro, Netherlands, Netherland Colonies in Asia, Oceanica and America, Newfoundland, New South Wales, New Zealand, Nicaragua, Norway, Paraguay, Persia, Peru, Porto Rico, Portugal, Portuguese Colonies in Asia and Africa, Queensland, Roumania, Russia, Salvador, Servia, Siam, South Australia, Spain, Spanish Colonies in Africa, Oceanica and Asia; Singapore, Penang and Malacca; St. Vincent, W. I., Sweden, Switzerland, Tasmania, Trinidad, W. I., Regency of Tunis, Uruguay, Venezuela, West Australia.

RATES OF POSTAGE.

The letter rate of postage is two cents for each ounce or fraction thereof throughout the United States, Dominion of Canada and Mexico. The postage on letters dropped in the office for delivery in the city is two cents per ounce.

All letters must be fully prepaid by stamps.

The following Classes of Letters are not Advertised: Drop Letters. Box Letters. Letters directed and sent to hotels, and thence returned to the post office as unclaimed. Letters returned from the dead letter office to writers, and card request letters. Circulars, free packets, containing printed documents, speeches and other printed matter. N.B.—A request for the return of a letter to the writer if unclaimed within thirty days or less, written or printed with the writer's name, post-office and State, across the left hand side of the envelope, on the face side, will be complied with. Such letters will be returned to the writer free of postage.

MAIL MATTER OF THE SECOND CLASS.

This class embraces newspapers and other periodical publications, issued not less than four times a year, from a known office of publication, and bearing a date of issue, and which have no cloth, leather, or other substantial binding. Such publications must have a legitimate list of subscribers and must not be designed primarily for advertising purposes or for free circulation. The rate of postage on second-class matter when sent from the office of publication (including sample copies), or when sent from a news agent to actual subscribers, or to other news agents, is one cent per pound or fraction thereof; but if sent by any other than the publisher or a news agent is one cent for each four ounces or fraction thereof.

MAIL MATTER OF THE THIRD CLASS.

This class embraces transient newspapers and periodicals, books (printed), photographs, circulars, proof sheets,and corrected proof sheets with manuscript copy accompanying the same, and all matter of the same general character, as above enumerated. The rate of postage is one cent for each two ounces or fractional part thereof, except on transient newspapers and periodicals of the second-class, which will be one cent for each four ounces or fraction thereof.

MAIL MATTER OF THE FOURTH CLASS.

This class embraces labels, patterns, playing cards, visiting cards, address tags, paper sacks, wrapping paper and blotting pads, with or without printed advertisements thereon, bill heads, letter heads, envelopes with printed addresses thereon, ornamented paper, and all other matter of the same general character. This class also includes merchandise, and samples of merchandise, models, samples of ores, metals, minerals, seeds, etc., and any other matter not included in the first, second, or third classes, and which is not in its form of nature liable to damage the contents of the mail bag, or harm the person. Postage rate thereon, one cent for each ounce or fractional part thereof.

U. S. MONEY ORDER SYSTEM.

FEES FOR MONEY ORDERS.

On orders not exceeding $5 . . 5 cts.
Over $5, and not exceeding $10 . 8 cts.
Over $10 and not exceeding $15, 10 cts.

Over	15	"	"	30,	15 cts.
Over	30	"	"	40,	20 cts.
Over	40	"	"	50,	25 cts.
Over	50	"	"	60,	30 cts.
Over	60	"	"	70,	35 cts.
Over	70	"	"	80,	40 cts.
Over	80	"	"	100,	45 cts.

A charge of two cents is now added to each money order as a war tax.

No fraction of cents to be introduced in the order.

No single orders issued for more than $100.

Parties desiring to remit larger sums must obtain additional money orders.

No applicant, however, can obtain in one day more than three orders payable at the same office and to the same payee.

INTERNATIONAL MONEY ORDER SYSTEM.

Orders can be obtained upon any money order office in Great Britain and Ireland, Germany, Austria, Belgium, Holland, Denmark, Sweden, Norway, Switzerland, Italy, Canada, France, Algeria, Japan, Portugal, The Hawaiian Kingdom, Jamaica, New Zealand, New South Wales, Hungary, Egypt and Hong Kong, India and Tasmania, Queensland, Cape Colony, The Windward Islands and The Leeward Islands, for any sum not exceeding $50 in United States currency.

No single order issued for more than $50.

Parties desiring to remit larger sums must obtain additional money orders.

There is no limit to the number of orders in the International Money Order System.

FEES FOR ALL INTERNATIONAL MONEY ORDERS.

On orders not exceeding $10 . . $ .10
Over $10 and not exceeding $20 . .20
" 20 " " 30 . .30
" 30 " " 40 . .40
" 40 " " 50 . .50
" 50 " " 60 . .60
" 60 " " 70 . .70
" 70 " " 80 . .80
" 80 " " 90 . .90
" 90 " " 100 . 1.00

REGISTRY DEPARTMENT.

Letters can be registered to all parts of the United States upon payment of a fee of eight cents, in addition to the regular postage.

RAILWAY POST-OFFICES.

Railway post-offices are established on all lines from Chicago. These offices run upon nearly all trains, and letters may be mailed at the cars up to the moment prior to the departure of the trains. Stamps of the denominations of two cents may be had at the cars.

ACADEMIES AND SEMINARIES.

ARMOUR INSTITUTE OF TECHNOLOGY—Armour av. sw. cor. 33d

BAPTIST UNION THEOLOGICAL SEMINARY—(Now the Divinity School of the University of Chicago.)

BIBLE INSTITUTE FOR HOME AND FOREIGN MISSIONS OF THE CHICAGO EVANGELIZATION SOCIETY—80 Institute pl. and 228 to 232 and 252 to 254 Lasalle av.

CHICAGO KINDERGARTEN COLLEGE — Director, Mrs. J. N. Crouse; Teachers' dept., Miss Elizabeth Harrison.

CHICAGO MANUAL TRAINING SCHOOL—Michigan av. nw. cor. 12th.

CHICAGO MUSICAL COLLEGE—3d floor Central Music Hall.

CHICAGO THEOLOGICAL SEMINARY—81 Ashland boul.

DE LA SALLE INSTITUTE—Wabash av. ne. cor. 35th

EPHPHETA SCHOOL FOR DEAF AND DUMB—409 S. May.

GARRETT BIBLICAL INSTITUTE—Evanston.

GERMAN LUTHERAN THEOLOGICAL SEMINARY—435 N. Ashland av.

LEWIS INSTITUTE—W. Madison cor. S. Robey.

McCORMICK THEOLOGICAL SEMINARY OF THE PRESBYTERIAN CHURCH—1060 N. Halsted.

NORTHWESTERN UNIVERSITY — Evanston. Henry Wade Rogers, LL.D., Pres.

NORTHWESTERN UNIVERSITY DENTAL SCHOOL—Edgar D. Swain, D.D.S., Dean. Madison sw. cor. Franklin.

NORTHWESTERN UNIVERSITY LAW SCHOOL — Henry Wade Rogers, Pres. 7th floor, Masonic Temple.

NORTHWESTERN UNIVERSITY MEDICAL SCHOOL — N. S. Davis, M.D., LL.D., Dean. 2421 Dearborn.

NORTHWESTERN UNIVERSITY PHARMACY SCHOOL — Oscar Oldberg, Ph.D., Dean. 2421 Dearborn.

NORTHWESTERN UNIVERSITY SCHOOL OF MUSIC—Evanston. Dean, Peter C. Lutkin.

NORTHWESTERN UNIVERSITY WOMAN'S MEDICAL SCHOOL —Isaac N. Danforth, M.D., Dean. 333 Lincoln.

ST. IGNATIUS COLLEGE—413 W· 12th.

ST. PROCOPIUS COLLEGE—704 Allport.

ST. VIATEUR'S COLLEGE— N. 40th av. cor. W. Belmont av.

SECRETARIAL INSTITUTE AND TRAINING SCHOOL OF YOUNG MEN'S CHRISTIAN ASSN. —709, 153 Lasalle, Gen. Sec., John W. Hausel.

THEOLOGICAL SEMINARY OF THE EVANGELICAL LUTHERAN CHURCH—1301-1311 Sheffield av. n. of Addison, Lake View.

UNIVERSITY OF CHICAGO — Located bet. 57th and 59th and Ellis and Lexington avs. W. R. Harper, Pres. of University; Martin A. Ryerson, Pres. of Board; C. L Hutchinson, Treas.; T. W. Goodspeed, Sec.; H. A. Rust, Comptroller; Harry P. Judson, Head Dean; R. D. Salisbury, University Examiner; G. S. Goodspeed Recorder; C. H. Thurber, Dean of Morgan Park Academy; E. J. James, Director Univ. Extension; H. A. Cuppy, Director Univ. Press.

WESTERN THEOLOGICAL SEMINARY OF THE PROTESTANT EPISCOPAL CHURCH—1113 Washington boul.

APARTMENTS.

(See also Public Halls, Blocks and Building.)

Abbotsford Flats — 6310 and 6312 Monroe av.

Abinette Flats—1763 and 1765 Oakdale av.

Addison Flats—1503 and 1505 Addison av.

Alabama Flats—3035 Prairie av.

Alameda Flats—Vincennes av. sw. cor. 40th.

Albemarle Flats—3769 to 3801 Lake av.

Albert Flats—6512 and 6514 Madison av.

Albion Flats—4011 and 4013 Lake av.

Albion Flats—5463 and 5465 Kimbark av.

Alden Flats—684 and 686, 43d.

Alden Flats—4228 Greenwood av.

Alexander Flats—335 to 341 Rush.

Alexander Flats—Bowen av. se. cor. Cottage Grove av.

Algonquin Flats—6236 and 6238 Monroe av.

Alleghany Flats—6047 and 6049 Ellis av.

Allen Flats—143 Oakwood boul.

Alma Flats—4713 and 4715 Indiana av.

Altdorf Flats—4015 and 4017 Lake av.

Alvah Flats—4554 and 4556 Forrestville av.

Alvina Flats—1408 and 1410 N. Clark.

Amelia Flats—4714 Evans av.

Anderson Flats—105 to 109, 37th.

Anita Flats—426 to 430 Superior.

Anita Flats—781 and 783, 43d.

Anna Flats—4800 to 4802 Prairie av.

Arizona Flats—4224 Greenwood av.

Arlington Flats—Grand boul. se. cor. 41st.

Armour Flats—33d cor. Dearborn.

Ashburton Flats—567, 42d.

Ashland Flats—213 Ashland boul.

Aslak Flats—5813 and 5815 Jackson av.

Athena Flats—566 to 576, 43d.

Atlanta Flats—3131 and 3133 Indiana av.

Audubon Flats—6032 to 6038 Monroe av.

Avalon Flats—4000 and 4002 Lake av.

Avergennes Flats — 1801 and 1807 Barry av.

Averill Flats—550 to 560, 55th.

Avon Flats—99, 33d.

Avon Flats—2340 Prairie av.

Balmoral Flats—2968 and 2970 Vernon av.

Banker's Flats—341 to 347, 62d.

Barbara Flats—453 and 455 North av.

Beatrice Flats—342 and 344, 57th.

Belden Flats—295 to 299 Belden av.

Belfort Flats—3739 and 3741 Indiana av.

Bellevue Flats—219 to 225, 64th.

Bellevue Flats—310 to 314 N. State.

Belmont Flats—1452 to 1458 Belmont av.

Belmont Hall Flats—1508 to 1514 Belmont av.

Belmonte Flats—4257 and 4259 Grand boul.

Belvedere Flats—3100 Cottage Grove av.

Belvoir Flats—4740 to 4744 Madison av.

Benton Flats—Ohio sw. cor. Pine.

Berkshire Flats—2505 Michigan av.

Bernard Flats—224 and 226 N. State.

Berwick Flats—1502 to 1512 Cornelia av.

Beveridge Flats—Calumet av. se. cor. 26th.

Binderton Flats—298 and 300 Schiller.

Blair Flats—3004 and 3006 Prairie av.

Bonnie Brae Flats—4810 and 4812 Champlain av.

Boston Flats—615 to 623, 55th.

Braintree Flats—3726 Wabash av.

Brighton Flats—Indiana av. nw. cor. 41st.

Brooks Flats—4142 and 4144 Grand boul.

Brown's Flats—4652 to 4656 State.

Buckingham Flats—1790 N. Clark.

Bucklen Flats—276 Michigan av.

Bunton Flats—6113 to 6125 Madison av.

Burke Flats—6024 and 6026 Ellis av.

Burlingham Flats—281 Oak.

Cadmea Flats—3634 and 3636 Michigan av.

Caldwell Flats—321 and 323 W. 63d.

Calumet Flats—248 Erie.

Cambria Flats—290 and 292 Rush.

Cambridge Flats—39th nw. cor. Ellis av.

Canajoharie Flats—4212 to 4216 Ellis av.

Candee Flats—18 and 20 E. Pearson.

Canterbury Flats—4245 and 4247 Cottage Grove av.

Canterbury Flats — 6034 and 6036 Langley av.

Capel Flats—239 and 241, 66th pl.

Carl Flats—5466 and 5468 Lake av.

Carlota Flats—13 to 20 Stanley Terrace.

Carlyle Flats—3558 Cottage Grove av.

Carnot Flats—Langley av. nw. cor. 48th.

Caroline Flats—43 and 45 Wisconsin.
Carrie Flats—4709 and 4711 Prairie av.
Cartier Flats—494 to 500 Belden av.
Cazenovia Flats—169 and 171 Oakwood boul.
Champlain Flats — 6037 and 6039 Champlain av.
Charles Flats—Wabash av. sw. cor. 23d.
Charlevoix Flats—87 Rush.
Charlotta Flats—4210 and 4212 Evans av.
Chatauqua Flats—4800 to 4806 Champlain av.
Chateau Flats—4417 and 4419 Indiana av.
Chatham Flats—4542 to 4548 Cottage Grove av.
Claremont Flats—N. Clark se. cor. Deming pl.
Cleveland Flats—659 to 665 Cleveland av. and 725 to 731 Fullerton av.
Clinton Flats—1423 to 1429 Michigan av.
Cobden Flats—502 to 508 Belden av.
Colonnade Flats — 6132 and 6134 Prairie av.
Columbian Flats—6042 to 6048 Princeton av.
Concord Flats—Indiana av. nw. cor. 24th.
Cordova Flats—Park av. nw. cor. S. Paulina.
Corinne Flats—4713 and 4715 Prairie av.
Cornell Flats—5538 and 5540 Cornell av.
Coronado Flats—2223 to 2231 Cottage Grove av.
Coronado Flats—801 to 813, 44th.
Crescent Flats—2951 and 2953 Vernon av.
Cristoval Flats—177, 40th.
Crystal Flats—354 and 356 N. Clark.
Cummings Flats—4709 and 4711 Indiana av.
Dagmar Flats—Madison av. sw. cor. 64th.
Dakota Flats—3025 Prairie av.
Darby Flats—16 E. Pearson.
Dayton Flats—4249 to 4253 Cottage Grove av.
Delavan Flats—Vincennes av. sw. cor. 45th.
DeLeon Flats—229 and 231, 42d.
DeLincoln Flats—60 and 62 Wisconsin.
Dell Flats—550 and 552, 46th pl.
Delta Flats—5622 and 5624 Ellis av.
DeMarks Flats—377 and 379, 45th.
DeSota Flats—3667 Wabash av.
Detroit Flats—259 and 261 Lasalle av.
Devonia Flats—604 and 606, 46th.
Devonshire Flats—28th se. cor. Wabash av.

Dorchester Flats—4047 and 4049 Ellis av.
Drexel Flats—250 and 252, 43d.
Drexel Flats—4524 and 4526 Cottage Grove av.
Drexel Flats—5614 and 5616 Drexel av.
Dubuque Flats—60 to 68 Rush.
Duffin Flats—582 and 584, 45th.
Dunton Flats—3850 and 3852 Vincennes av.
DuPage Flats—194 and 196 Cass.
Duquesne Flats—271 and 273 Oakwood boul.
Edgar Flats—10 and 12 Crilly ct.
Edna Flats—4354 and 4356 Berkeley av.
Eleanor Flats—4850 and 4852 Calumet av.
Ellergill Flats—4059 Grand boul.
Ellis Flats—4201 and 4203 Ellis av.
Elmwood Flats—3810 and 3812 Elmwood ct.
Erie Flats—Lake av. sw. cor. 37th.
Erminie Flats—16 and 18 Crilly ct.
Essex Flats—591 to 595 Lasalle av.
Essex Flats—Wabash av. nw. cor. 25th.
Ethel Flats—4058 and 4060 Ellis av.
Eugenie Flats—147 Eugenie.
Eureka Flats—6147 and 6149 Kimbark av.
Evaline Flats—5902 Michigan av.
Evandale Flats—93 and 95 Evanston av.
Evanston Flats—1750 to 1758 York pl.
Everett Flats—272 and 274, 42d.
Exeter Flats—386 and 388 Ashland boul.
Fairfax Flats—402 and 404 Erie.
Fairhaven Flats—495 and 497, 43d.
Falmouth Flats — 5724 and 5726 Drexel av.
Farley Flats—4314 to 4318 Cottage Grove av.
Fleur de Lis Flats—3606 Wabash av.
Florence Flats—16 to 22 Bellevue pl.
Florence Flats—45, 18th.
Florence Flats—764 and 766 North Park av.
Florence Flats—3453 and 3455 Cottage Grove av.
Florence Flats—4714 Calumet av.
Florida Flats—217 to 221 Schiller.
Florimond Flats—66 Florimond.
Follansbee Flats—23d nw. cor. Wabash av.
Forest Flats—3240 and 3242 Forest av.
Forester Flats—453 to 457, 47th.
Foreston Flats—33d ne. cor. Forest av.
Forrestville Flats—4450 to 4458 Cottage Grove av.
Forum, The—595, 43d.
Francis Flats—69 and 71, 34th pl.

Franconia Flats—2220 Wabash av.
Franklin Flats—138 to 142, 38th.
Fremont Flats—281 and 283 Fremont av.
Fremont Flats—4338 to 4342 Cottage Grove av.
Garfield Flats—W. Garfield boul. sw. cor. State.
Garibaldi Flats—59 to 65 Walton pl.
Garrard Flats—381 to 383 Superior.
Genesee Flats—6117 Monroe av.
Geneseo Flats—3351 Calumet av.
Geneva Flats—Madison av. se. cor. 57th.
Genoa Flats—302 and 304, 62d.
Gertrude Flats—528 and 530, 47th.
Glencoe Flats—344 Michigan av.
Gondolier Flats—3917 and 3919 Indiana av.
Gordon Flats—3501 Wabash av.
Gosnold Flats—3951 and 3953 Indiana av.
Graeme Flats—Wabash av. se. cor. 43d.
Grafton Flats—4442 Evans av.
Greenwood Flats—530 to 538, 65th.
Griesbach's Flats—5012 and 5014 Cottage Grove av.
Grosvenor Flats—Grand boul. sw. cor. 47th.
Groveland Flats—3100 Groveland av.
Hamilton Flats—49 and 51, 22d.
Hampden Flats—39th ne. cor. Langley av.
Harcourt Flats—338 and 340, 57th.
Harold Flats—Prairie av. ne. cor. 44th.
Hartford Flats—6030 and 6032 Washington av.
Harvard Flats—2346 and 2348 Calumet av.
Hayden Flats—152 and 154, 36th.
Henrietta Flats—651 to 655 W. 12th.
Hiawatha Flats—6427 and 6429 Jefferson av.
Hiawatha Flats—37th nw. cor. Vernon av.
Holland Flats—4543 Evans av.
Houghton Flats—584 and 586 Dearborn av.
Howard Annex Flats—302 to 308, 61st pl.
Hudson Flats—4353 Berkeley av.
Ibsen Flats—3716 Wabash av.
Ideal Flats—4206 Ellis av.
Ingletide Flats—1 to 5 Park av.
Ingram Flats—300 to 308, 60th.
Inverness Flats—5556 and 5558 Drexel av.
Ionia Flats—6442 to 6448 Stony Island av.
Irene Flats—3837 and 3839 Elmwood ct.
Irving Flats—296 and 304 to 308 N. State.

Irving Flats—Oakenwald av. sw. cor. 44th pl.
Irvington Flats—462 to 470, 55th.
Irvington Flats—1713 and 1715 Barry av.
Isabella Bldg.—48 Vanburen.
Isabella Flats—2 and 4 Crilly ct.
Isabella Flats—4046 and 4048 Indiana av.
Isabella Flats—5475 and 5477 Kimbark av.
Ismond Flats—207 to 213, 41st.
Ivanhoe Flats—1841 and 1843 Aldine av.
Ivanhoe Flats—36th ne. cor. Cottage Grove av.
Jackson Flats—2829 to 2833 Calumet av.
Jaeschke Flats—296 and 298 Ohio.
Jefferson Flats—5029 Jefferson av.
Judson Flats—St. Lawrence av. sw. cor. 44th pl.
Juniata Flats—1006 and 1008 Garfield boul.
Keene Flats—25th nw. cor. Ellis av.
Kenilworth Flats—280 and 282 Erie.
Kenilworth Flats—36th nw. cor. Ellis av.
Kenosha Flats—2976 South Park av.
Kimbark Flats—Kimbark av. sw. cor. 65th.
Kingston Flats—716 and 718, 45th.
Kinzie Flats—144 Pine.
Kirkwood Flats—558 and 560 Division.
Knickerbocker Flats—4160 Ellis av.
Koehsel Flats—755 and 757, 45th.
La Burnum Flats—259 and 261 Lasalle av.
Lafayette Flats—Washington av. ne. cor. 66th pl.
Lakewood Flats — 4407 and 4409 Greenwood av.
Langley Flats—3731 and 3733 Langley av.
Lanita Flats—197 to 203 S. Western av.
LaSalle Flats—204 and 206 Cass.
Lavergne Flats—4727 and 4729 Lake av.
Laveta Flats—3943 and 3945 Indiana av.
Leamington Flats—92 to 98, 37th.
LeChateau—65 and 67, 34th pl.
Le Grand Flats—1043 to 1053, 60th.
Lehman Flats—Surf ne. cor. Evanston av.
Leighton Flats—114 and 116, 31st.
Lemont Flats—6235 to 6241 Monroe av.
Lenham Flats—Calumet av. ne. cor. 37th.
Leroy Flats—1522 to 1528 Cornelia av.
Lester Flats—486 to 496, 48th.

Iles Tours Flats—Indiana av. se. cor.
44t .

Lincoln Park Palace Flats—Diversey nw. cor. Pine Grove av.

Linde Flats—4400 and 4402 Greenwood av.

Lindell Flats—4219 and 4221 Ellis av.

Lindeman Flats—5132 to 5138 Prairie av.

Linne Flats—6051 to 6059 Ellis av.

Livorno Flats—279 and 281 Lasalle av.

Locust Flats—113 and 115 Locust.

Lorraine Flats—36th ne. cor. Ellis av.

Lowell Flats—5717 and 5719 Madison av.

Lowell Flats—Wabash av. ne. cor. 43d

Lucania Flats—Greenwood av. nw. cor. 62d.

Lucano Flats—294 Lasalle av.

Lucile Flats—46th sw. cor. Prairie av.

Lucy Flats—3569 to 3571 Forest av.

Ludgate Flats—1841 and 1843 Wabash av.

Mabel Flats—3001 and 3003 Calumet av.

Maison Du Nord—16 and 18 Astor.

Majestic, The—Walton pl. sw. cor. Rush.

Manhattan Flats—Deming pl. nw. cor. Hampden ct.

Manitou Flats—56th nw. cor. Lexington av.

Marcus Flats—477 to 483, 45th.

Marie Flats 4632 to 4638 Vincennes av.

Marion Flats—248 Ohio.

Marionette Flats — 2341 and 2343 Calumet av.

Marlborough Flats — 4901 to 4903 Calumet av.

Marquette Flats—85 Rush.

Maryland Flats—1211 and 1213, 56th.

Maryland Flats—4320 and 4322 Forrestville av.

May-Netta Flats—2718 and 2720 Indiana av.

McIntosh Flats—377 and 379 Superior.

Mecca Flats—State sw. cor. 34th.

Melrose, The—3756 Ellis av.

Melrose Flats—76 and 78, 50th.

Melvira Flats—1746 and 1748 York pl.

Menetta Flats—4346 Berkeley av.

Menoken Flats—5415 and 5417 Cottage Grove av.

Merrill Flats—4643 Evans av.

Mexican Flats—2958 to 2964 Langley av.

Milano Flats—338 Ohio.

Mineola Flats—69 and 71, 33d.

Minneola Flats—328 and 330 Lasalle av.

Minnetonka Flats—3244 and 3246 Wabash av.

Modjeska Flats—6440 Ellis av.

Monroe Flats—5511 to 5521 Monroe av.

Montclair Flats—5486 to 5494 East End av.

Monterey Flats—161 Oakwood boul.

Montgomery Flats—Indiana av. ne. cor. 31st.

Montreal Flats—6238 to 6246 Madison av.

Montrose Flats—54 and 56 St. James pl.

Morris Flats—1930 and 1932 Dunning.

Morton Flats—203 and 205 Ontario.

Morton Flats—1800 Michigan av.

Needham Flats—49 and 51, 32d.

Nelda Flats—4552 and 4554 Oakenwald av.

Nelson Flats—5425 to 5431 Cottage Grove av.

Netherland Flats—5224 and 5226 Lake av.

Nevada Flats—3830 and 3832 Elmwood ct.

Newberry, The—225 to 231 Dearborn av.

Newport Flats—77 to 83 Erie.

Newport Flats—1945 and 1947 Deming pl.

Newton Flats—3902 to 3906 Calumet av.

Nordica Flats—Fullerton av. ne. cor. N. Clark.

Normandie Flats—287 and 289, 67th.

Normandy Flats—504 to 510 W. Vanburen.

Normandy Flats—2300 Indiana av.

North Entrance Flats—265 to 273, 57th.

Norvin Flats—1255 and 1257, 61st.

Norwood Flats—1517 to 1523 Aldine av.

Norwood Flats—3000 Indiana av.

Norwood Flats—6333 to 6339 Jefferson av.

Nottbohm Flats—5034 to 5040 Cottage Grove av.

Oak Place Flats—1741 to 1747 N. Clark.

Oakdale Flats—1547 and 1549 Oakdale av.

Oakland Flats—3724 to 3732 Cottage Grove av.

Oakley Flats—504 to 508 S. Oakley av.

Ogden Flats—606 and 608 Ogden av.

Ogden Flats—Warren av. sw. cor. Ogden av.

Ohio Flats—344 Ohio.

Olga Flats—3554 Cottage Grove av.

Oliver Flats—6 and 8 Crilly ct.

Omaha Flats—55th nw. cor. Lexington av.

Omara Flats—421 Superior.

Oneida, The—5100 Hibbard av.

Onota Flats—7 to 13, 34th pl.

Oregon Flats—1518 to 1522 Michigan av.
Orient Flats—4826 and 4828 Evans av.
Orleans Flats—354 to 360 Erie.
Orleans Flats—4301 to 4307 Oakenwald av.
Ormond Flats—Lake av. sw.cor. 54th.
Ormonde, The—49 to 55 Astor.
Ornatus Flats—435 and 437, 47th.
Osceola Flats—4716 Lake av.
Ottawa Flats—309 to 315 Chicago av.
Outlook Flats—6124 and 6126 Ingleside av.
Oxford Flats—1454 and 1456 Michigan av.
Palace Flats—28 and 30, 44th pl.
Palace Flats—1955 and 1957 Deming pl.
Palo Allo Flats—State se. cor. 23d.
Palos Flats—215, 31st.
Park Gate Flats—63d nw. cor. Stony Island av.
Park View Flats—240 and 242 Hampden ct.
Passyunk Flats—65th nw. cor. Ellis av.
Pelham Flats—544 to 552 Garfield av.
Persada Flats—4229 and 4231 Lake av.
Peyton Flats—194 and 196 Oakwood boul.
Piasa Flats—4707 and 4709 Calumet av.
Pickwick, The—Michigan av. se. cor. 20th.
Plaisance Flats—578 and 580, 60th.
Plaza, The—N. Clark se. cor. North av.
Plymouth Flats—6341 to 6351 Washington av.
Portland Flats—290 to 296, 60th.
Portumna Flats—419 and 421, 44th.
Potomac Flats—Michigan av. sw.cor. 30th.
Prairie Flats—3031 Prairie av.
Prairie Flats—4515 and 4517 Prairie av.
P e Flats—Lexington av. ne. cor. 62d r ss
Pullman Flats—230 to 252, 55th.
Puan-A-Powit—3737 and 3739 Langley av.
Rainer Flats—33d se. cor. Cottage Grove av.
Ramona Flats—235 and 237, 66th pl.
Ramona Flats—2235 to 2243 Cottage Grove av.
Randle Flats—214 to 224, 40th.
Ravenna Flats—LaSalle av. ne. cor. Division.
Ravenna Flats—Vincennes av. ne. cor. 44th pl.
Raworth Flats—1421 to 1427 N. Clark.
Renfost, The—Cottage Grove av. ne. cor. 52d.

Retford Flats—4601 and 4603 Vincennes av.
Revonoc Flats—4707 and 4709 St. Lawrence av.
Rexham Flats—3955 and 3957 Indiana av.
Reynolds Flats—Greenwood av. ne. cor. 63d.
Richard's Flats—89 and 91 Evanston av.
Richelieu Flats—3806 and 3808 Ellis av.
Rochester Flats—634 and 636, 46th pl.
Rockingham Flats—Michigan av. sw. cor. 59th.
Rosabel Flats—4712 Calumet av.
Rosalie Flats—240 to 248, 57th.
Roxbury Flats—4535 and 4537 St. Lawrence av.
'Roxbury Flats—W. Vanburen sw. cor. S. Sangamon.
Royer Flats—3824 and 3826 Rhodes av.
Russell Flats—2222 to 2226 Wabash av.
Rutland Flats—55th se. cor. Washington av.
St. Agnes Flats—4448 and 4450 St. Lawrence av.
St. Albans Flats—5216 and 5218 Jefferson av.
St. Benedict Flats—Chicago av. ne. cor. Cass.
St. Catherine Flats—4001 Grand boul.
St. Germaine Flats—3500 Ellis av.
St. James Flats—369 Chicago.
St. Lawrence Flats—394 and 396, 43d.
St. Lawrence Flats—3135 and 3137 Indiana av.
Salerno Flats—290 Lasalle av.
San Carlos Flats—404 to 414, 43d.
San Jacinto Flats—1704 to 1708 Oakdale av.
San Marco Flats—900 to 914, 47th
San Salvador Flats—6501 Kimbark av.
Santa Maria Flats—90 Pine.
Saranac Flats—6030 and 6032 Ellis av.
Savoy Flats—165 and 167 Locust
Savoy Flats—257, 66th
Schuyler Flats—45 and 47, 22d.
Seville Flats—159 and 161 Locust.
Shenandoah Flats—97 to 105 Oakwood av.
Sheridan Flats—576 to 582 Lasalle av.
Shibley Flats—4347 and 4349 Oakenwald av.
Shoreham Flats—4458 and 4460 Oakenwald av.
Southern Flats—5516 and 5518 S. Halsted.
Stanley Flats—W. Vanburen nw. cor. Stanley terrace.
Stratford Flats—93, 33d
Strathmore Flats—171 and 173. 55th

Suffield Flats—1723 to 1737 Wabash av
Tawanda Flats—44th se. cor. Wabash av.
Tecumseh Flats—Washington av. se. cor. 56th.
Tisbury Flats—3947 and 3949 Indiana av.
Toledo Flats—5153 and 5155 Cornell av.
Toledo Flats—Minerva av. ne. cor. 65th.
Torino Flats—337 Indiana.
Tudor The—4300 to 4316 Ellis av.
Tulane Flats—1761 Oakdale av.
Turner Flats—Wrightwood av. nw. cor. N. Clark.
Tuxedo Flats—1626 and 1628 Cornelia av.
University Flats—5, 34th pl.
University Flats—444 to 452, 55th
Van Dyke The—3953 Michigan av.
Varsity Flats—6106 Ellis av.
Vendome Flats—Ogden av. ne. cor. W. Madison.
Vermont Flats—51st ne. cor. Cottage Grove av.
Verona Flats—355 to 359 N. Clark
Ville Marie Flats—4508 and 4510 Indiana av.
Vincennes Flats—Vincennes av. se. cor. 36th.
Viola Flats—6034 and 6036 Ingleside av.
Wacousta Flats—275 Erie.
Walden Flats—612 and 614 Orchard
Waldorf Flats—244 to 254, 60th
Walton Flats—212, 40th.
Walton Flats—307 N. Clark.
Washington Park Flats—54th ne. cor. Indiana av.
Waukesha Flats—64th, Washington av. and Jefferson av.
Waveland Flats—1956 to 1970 N. Halsted.
Waverly Flats—530 to 536 W. Lake.
Wellington Flats—3433 to 3437 Wabash av.
Wellsboro Flats—3052 to 3058 Calumet av.
Westchester Flats—5021 Cottage Grove av.
Westminster Flats—6050 and 6052 Langley av.
Wilcox Flats—361 and 363, 43d.
Willows Flats—5618 and 5620 Drexel av.
Wilmar Flats—198 and 200 Oakwood boul.
Winamac, The—Oakwood av. nw. cor. Ellis av.
Winchester Flats—401 to 405, 64th
Winchester Flats—Winchester av. sw. cor. W. Madison.
Winnebago Flats—6443 and 6445 Jefferson av.

Winston Flats—135, 137 and 145 and 147 Pine.
Wisconsin Flats—Ellis av. se. cor. 60th.
Woodlawn Flats—Washington av. sw. cor. 65th pl.
Woodstock, The—2728 Wabash av.
Wrightwood Flats—1818 Wrightwood av.
Wyandank Flats - 6527 and 6529 Kimbark av.
Yale Flats—Yale ne. cor. W. 66th.
Yale Flats—2346 and 2348 Calumet av.
Yorktown Flats—86 Pine.

ASYLUMS.

BETHANY HOME—2948 N. Paulina.
CHICAGO DAILY NEWS FRESH-AIR FUND—City office, 123, 5th av. Sanitarium, foot of Fullerton av., Lincoln Park.
CHICAGO HOME FOR INCURABLES—Ellis av. ne. cor. 56th.
CHICAGO INDUSTRIAL HOME FOR CHILDREN—106 Franklin.
CHICAGO INDUSTRIAL SCHOOL FOR GIRLS—49th and Prairie av.
CHICAGO NURSERY AND HALF ORPHAN ASYLUM—855 N. Halsted and 175 Burling.
CHICAGO ORPHAN ASYLUM—2228 Michigan av.
CHURCH HOME FOR AGED PERSONS—4327 Ellis av.
COOK COUNTY INSANE ASYLUM—Located at Dunning, Ill.
COOK COUNTY POOR HOUSE—Dunning P. O.
DANISH LUTHERAN ORPHANS' HOME—1183 N. Maplewood av.
DANISH MISSION HOME—480 Fulton,
ENGLEWOOD NURSERY OF CHILDREN'S HOME SOCIETY—6516 Perry av.
ENGLEWOOD WORKROOM AND HOME FOR WOMEN—6311 Parnell av.
EPWORTH CHILDREN'S HOME—2410 N. Paulina.
ERRING WOMAN'S REFUGE—5024 Indiana av.
FOUNDLINGS HOME—114 S. Wood nr. W. Madison.
GERMAN BAPTIST OLD PEOPLE'S HOME—1006 N. Spaulding av.

GERMAN OLD PEOPLE'S HOME —Harlem. (Altenheim P.O.) Cook Co.

GUARDIAN ANGEL GERMAN (R.C.) ORPHAN ASYLUM—Located at High Ridge.

HOLY FAMILY ORPHAN ASYLUM—136 W. Division.

HOME FOR AGED JEWS—Drexel av. cor. 62d.

HOME FOR THE AGED—W. Harrison cor. Throop; Sheffield av. sw. cor. Fullerton av., and 5148 Prairie av.

HOME FOR DESTITUTE CRIPPLED CHILDREN—46 Park av.

HOME FOR MISSIONARIES' CHILDREN—Morgan Park.

*HOME FOR OLD WOMEN—4327 and 4329 Ellis av.

HOME FOR SELF-SUPPORTING WOMEN—275 Indiana.

HOME FOR THE FRIENDLESS—Vincennes av. ne. cor. 51st.

HOUSE OF MERCY (for young women)—Adjoining Mercy Hospital, Calumet av. cor. Twenty-sixth.

HOUSE OF PROVIDENCE—Orleans se. cor. Elm.

HOUSE OF THE GOOD SHEPHERD—Orleans cor. Hill

ILLINOIS INDUSTRIAL SCHOOL FOR GIRLS—South Evanston.

ILLINOIS MASONIC ORPHANS' HOME—447 Carroll av. cor. Sheldon.

ILLINOIS SCHOOL OF AGRICULTURE AND MANUAL TRAINING SCHOOL FOR BOYS—Glenwood Ill. Chicago office, 113 Adams.

INDUSTRIAL HOME FOR THE BLIND—W. 19th cor. Southwest boul.

INDUSTRIAL SCHOOL FOR GIRLS (POLISH)—130 W. Division

JEWISH ORPHAN'S HOME—3601 Vernon av.

MARTHA WASHINGTON HOME —Irving Park boul. cor. Western av,, Lake View.

NATIONAL HOME FOR DISABLED VOLUNTEER SOLDIERS —304, 184 Lasalle.

NEWS-BOYS' & BOOT-BLACKS' HOME—1418 Wabash av.

NORWEGIAN OLD PEOPLE'S HOME—Avondale av. sw. cor. Ceylon av.

OLD PEOPLE'S HOME—Indiana av. nw. cor. Thirty-ninth.

REMENSTEINE INDUSTRIAL HOME—82d cor. Seipp av.

SERVITE SISTERS' INDUSTRIAL HOME FOR GIRLS—1418 W. Congress.

SHELTERING HOME FOR CHILDREN—(Under the auspices of the United Hebrew Charities) Calumet av. sw. cor. 31st.

SISTER'S OF CHARITY OF THE IMMACULATE HEART INDUSTRIAL HOME FOR GIRLS—1402 W. Congress.

SOLDIERS' HOME—South Evanston.

ST. ANTHONY'S HOSPITAL AND ORPHANAGE—N. Hoyne av. cor. Homer.

ST. JOSEPH PROVIDENT ORPHAN ASYLUM—N. 40th av. bet. W. Diversey av. and W. Belmont av.

ST. JOSEPH'S HOME FOR WORKING GIRLS AND INDUSTRIAL SCHOOL—409 S. May.

ST. JOSEPH'S ORPHAN ASYLUM —Thirty-fifth cor. Lake av.

ST. MARY'S HOME FOR CHILDREN—209 Washington boul.

ST. MARY'S TRAINING SCHOOL FOR BOYS—Feehanville, Cook Co.,Ill.

ST. VINCENT'S INFANT ASYLUM AND MATERNITY HOSPITAL—191 Lasalle av.

STAR OF HOPE MISSION HOME —110 S. Green.

SWEDISH HOME OF MERCY—W. Foster av. W. Lincoln av.

UHLICH EVANGELICAL LUTHERAN ORPHAN ASYLUM—221 Burling nw. cor. Centre.

WASHINGTONIAN HOME—566 to 572 W. Madison.

WORKING BOYS' HOME AND MISSION OF OUR LADY OF MERCY—363 W. Jackson boul.

WORKING MEN'S HOME AND MEDICAL MISSION—42 Custom House ct.

WORKING WOMAN'S HOME—189 E. Huron.

THE ROSEHILL CEMETERY COMPANY,

ROOM 704, 171 LA SALLE ST., NEW YORK LIFE BLDG.

OFFICERS.

WESLEY DEMPSTER, President.   EUGENE C. LONG, Sec'y and Treas.

AT CEMETERY:

GEO. H. SCOTT,   THOS. WALLIS,
    Supt. and Civil Engineer.   Greenhouse Manager.

WALTER CHADBAND, Lot Salesman, Etc.

BOARD OF MANAGERS.

KILLIAN V. R. LANSINGH.   CHAS. W. DEMSPTER.
HENRY S. OSBORNE.   WM. H. TURNER.
CLANCEY J. DEMPSTER.   HENRY L. PITCHER.
WESLEY DEMPSTER.

TRUSTEES OF THE FUND.

Created for the Perpetual care of the Cemetery after all Lots therein are sold.

FRANCIS LACKNER.   CHAS. F. GREY.   JOHN B. KIRK.

BOARD OF CONSULTATION.

GEORGE SCHNEIDER.   MARVIN HUGHITT.   ANDREW T. SHERMAN.
JOHN E. SCOTT.   REV. CLINTON B. LOCKE. EDWARD G. MASON.
MARSHALL FIELD.   D. R. HOLT.   J. H. KEDZIE.
F. B. TUTTLE.   MOSES L. WENTWORTH.   FRANK H. COOPER.
HON. OLIVER H. HORTON. JOHN J. HERRICK.   JAS. B. BRADWELL.
LAWRENCE PROUDFOOT.   CHAS. B. FARWELL.   ORSON SMITH.

Rosehill Cemetery is situated 7½ miles from Chicago, on the Chicago & North-
Western Railway, and the Clark Street Electric Railway. Good
Carriage Drives from the city to the grounds.

TELEPHONE DIRECTIONS.

If City Office is wanted, ask for Express-615. If Cemetery is wanted,
ask for Lake View-101.

64

CEMETERIES.

BOHEMIAN NATIONAL—N. 40th av. nr. W. Lawrence av.

CALVARY—Ten miles n. of city. Office at Cemetery and 216 Reaper blk.

CONCORDIA—Five miles west of city limits on Madison. Office 621, 56, 5th av.

FOREST HOME CEMETERY— Oak Park. Office 84 Lasalle.

GERMAN LUTHERAN OF ST. PAUL'S AND EMANUEL CHURCHES—N. Clark cor. Graceland av.

GRACELAND—N. Clark ne. cor. Graceland av. five miles n. of court house, on Chicago & Evanston R.R. Open every day (Sundays to lot owners only). Office, 1675 Old Colony bldg.

HEBREW BENEVOLENT SO-CIETY—S. of Graceland cemetery.

HIGHLAND—Turner Junction, C. & N. W. Ry., 28 miles west of city hall.

MOUNT GREENWOOD CEME-TERY—One-half mile w. of Morgan Park. Office, room 202, 185 Dearborn.

MOUNT HOPE CEMETERY— Blue Island Ridge nr. Morgan Park. Office, 311 and 312, 138 Jackson.

MOUNT MAARIV—Dunning.

MOUNT OLIVE CEMETERY— Dunning Station, C. M. & St. P. Ry. 9 miles w. of city hall. Office, 415 Milwaukee av.

MOUNT OLIVET CEMETERY— One-half mile w. of Morgan Park, on Grand Trunk R. R. Office, 216 Reaper blk.

OAKLAND—Proviso, 12 miles west of city hall. Office 400, 160 Washington.

OAKWOODS—Sixty-seventh st. cor. Cottage Grove av., Hyde Park. Office, room 200, 185 Dearborn.

RIDGELAWN CEMETERY— N. 40th av. cor. W. Peterson av. (J.) Office, 844 Unity bldg.

ROSEHILL—Seven miles from city, on Mil. div. C. & N.W.Ry. City office, room 704, 171 Lasalle.

ST.BONIFACE—(German Catholic) N. Clark cor. Lawrence av.

St. MARIA—87th and Grand Trunk Ry.

WALDHEIM—Ten miles from court house, on Galena div. C.H.& B. and C. & Wis. Cent. Ry. Office, 670 W. Chicago av.

ZION CONGREGATION CEME-TERY—Rosehill.

CHURCHES.

Baptist.

AUBURN PARK—Sherman av. cor. 79th. Pastor, Rev. W. A. Waldo.

AUSTIN—Pastor, Rev. J. F.Bartlett.

AUSTIN SWEDISH—Pastor, Rev. J. Samuelson.

BELDEN AVENUE—N. Halsted cor. Belden av. Pastor, Rev. Myron W. Haynes, D.D.

BERWYN—Pastor, Rev. L. L. Turney.

BETHANY—S. Hoyne av. nr. 35th. Pastor, Rev. W. W. Dewey.

BETHESDA(Colored)—34th se. cor. Armour av. Pastor, Rev. J. E. Ford.

BOHEMIAN— Pastor, Rev. John Kejr.

CALVARY—Wabash av. cor. 38th. Pastor, Rev. Homer M. Cook.

CENTENNIAL—Jackson boul. cor. S. Lincoln. Pastor. Rev. Alonzo K. Parker, D.D.

CENTRAL—324 Clark, Pastor, Rev. T. L. Smith.

CHICAGO LAWN—Pastor, Rev. H. A. Stoughton.

CLYDE — Pastor, Rev. David B. Jones.

COLEHOUR GERMAN — Pastor. Rev. A. Peterson.

COVENANT—W. 60th pl. cor. Butler. Pastor, Rev. Gilbert Frederick, D.D.

CRAWFORD—Pastor, Rev. Elmer Hall.

ELSDON—52d cor. S. Ridgway av.

ENGLEWOOD—Englewood av. cor. Stewart av. Pastor, Rev. H. Francis Perry.

ENGLEWOOD SWEDISH— Princeton av. bet. 57th and 58th. Pastor, Rev. C. Rosen.

ENGLEWOOD - ON-THE-HILL— 67th nr. Bishop. Pastor, Rev. A. F Green.

EVANSTON FIRST SWEDISH— Pastor, Rev. Charles Palm.

EVANSTON SECOND (Colored)— Pastor, Rev. G. M. Davis.

EVERGREEN PARK—Pastor,Rev. Charles Firth.

FERNWOOD — Murray st. Fernwood. Pastor, Rev. C. H. Doolittle.

FIRST DANISH—N.Talman av.cor. Lemoyne. Pastor, Rev.C.Henningsen.

FIRST—South Park av. cor. 31st. Pastor, Rev. P. S. Henson, D.D.

FIRST EVANSTON—Pastor, Rev. B. A. Greene, D.D.

FIRST GERMAN—W. Superior cor. N. Paulina. Pastor, Rev. J. L. Meier.

FIRST SWEDISH—Elm cor. Milton av. Pastor, Rev. A. Hjelm.

FOURTH—Ashland boul. cor. W. Monroe. Pastor, Rev. Kittredge Wheeler, D. D.

FOURTH SWEDISH—2537, 111th· Pastor. Rev. E. J. Nordlander.

GALILEE—859 Clybourn av. Pastor, Rev. D. C. Henshaw.

GRACE—Sacramento av. cor. W. Lake. Pastor, Rev. W.Carey MacNaul.

HIGHLAND PARK—Pastor, Rev. Wm. M. Vines.

HUMBOLDT PARK—N. Humboldt cor. Cortland.

HUMBOLDT PARK GERMAN— Pastor, Rev. V. Forkel.

HUMBOLDT PARK SWEDISH— N. Rockwell nr. Wabansia av. Pastor Rev. M. Carlson.

HYDE PARK—Woodlawn av. cor. 46th. Pastor, Rev. J. L. Jackson, D.D.

IMMANUEL—ws. Michigan av. nr. 23d. Pastor, Rev. Johnston Myers,D.D.

IRVING PARK—Pastor, Rev. J. R. Hargreaves.

LAGRANGE—Pastor, Rev. E. S. Tuttle.

LAKE VIEW—Otto nr. Southport av, Pastor, Rev. Geo. H. Brown.

LAKEVIEW SWEDISH—Noble av. nr. Clifton av. Pastor, Rev. C. W. Anderson.

LASALLE AVENUE—439 Lasalle av. Pastor, Rev. J. Q. A. Henry, D.D.

MAPLEWOOD—Maplewood av.cor. W. Dunning av. Pastor, Rev. H. B. Waterman.

MAYWOOD—Pastor, Rev. F. L. Anderson.

MEMORIAL—Oakwood boul. bet. Cottage Grove and Langley avs. Pastor, Rev. L. A. Crandall, D.D.

MESSIAH—Flournoy cor. S.Washtenaw av. Pastor, Rev. Howland Hanson.

MILLARD AVENUE—Millard av. se. cor. W. 24th. Lawndale. Pastor, —.

MORGAN PARK—Crescent av. Pastor, Rev. A. R. E. Wyant.

MOUNT CARMEL—2077 W. Vanburen.

NORMAL PARK—Stewart av. cor. 70th. Pastor, Rev. A. W. Runyan.

OAK PARK—Pastor, Rev. J. W. Conley, D.D.

OLIVET—(Colored) Dearborn cor. 27th. Pastor, J. F. Thomas.

PILGRIM SCANDINAVIAN — 208 N. Carpenter. Pastor, Rev. J. A. Ohrn.

PILGRIM TEMPLE—824 N. Leavitt. Pastor, Rev. J. P. Thoms, LL.D.

PROVIDENCE — (Colored) 26 N. Irving av. Pastor. Rev. A. W. Newsome.

RAVENSWOOD—Pastor, Rev. F. E. Weston.

ROGERS PARK—Pastor, Rev. J. E. Conant.

SALEM SWEDISH—Ambrose cor. S. Lincoln. Pastor, Rev. C. W. Sundmark.

SECOND—S. Morgan sw. cor. W. Monroe. Pastor, Rev. W. M. Lawrence, D.D.

SECOND GERMAN—Burling cor. Willow. Pastor, Rev. Christian Dippel.

SECOND SWEDISH—3020, 5th av. Pastor, Rev. O. John Engstrand.

SOUTH CHICAGO—Houston av. and 90th. Pastor, Rev. A. C. Kelly.

SOUTH CHICAGO GERMAN — Pastor, Rev. C. F. Tiemann.

SOUTH CHICAGO SWEDISH — 4th av. and 98th. Pastor, Rev. A. Xallgren.

SOUTH PARK—South Park av. and 47th. Pastor Rev. Charles Henry.

TABERNACLE SWEDISH—Erie av. and 90th. Pastor, Rev. David Myrhman.

THIRD GERMAN—Johnson cor. W. 14th pl. Pastor, Rev. Jacob Pfeiffer.

TRINITY—W. Ohio nr. N. Robey. Pastor, Rev. R. E. Manning.

WESTERN AVENUE—Warren av. nw. cor. S. Western av. Pastor, —.

WINDSOR PARK — Pastor, Rev. Bruce Kinney.

WOODLAWN PARK — Lexington av. and 62d. Pastor, Rev. Melbourne P. Boynton.

Baptist Missions.

HOPE MISSION—Austin.

RAYMOND MISSION—Poplar av. nr. 30th.

Christian.

CENTRAL—Indiana av. cor. 37th. Pastor, Prof. W. F. Black.

COLORED—2956 State. Supt George Dawson.

DOUGLAS PARK—No. 1298 Ogden av. nr. Kedzie av. Pastor, Rev. Geo. A. Campbell.

ENGLEWOOD — Eggleston cor. 64th. Pastor, Rev. N. S. Haynes.

EVANSTON—807 Davis. Pastor, Rev. E. W. Darst.

GARFIELD PARK—W. Ohio cor. Monticello av. Pastor, Rev. F. G. Strickland.

HUMBOLDT PARK — Armitage and Kedzie aves. Pastor, Rev. F. Nelson Glover.

HYDE PARK—Masonic Hall, 57th e. of Washington. Pastor, Rev. Errett Gates.

KEDZIE AVENUE—Pastor, Rev. Elder Holst.

MONROE STREET—W. Monroe cor. Francisco av. Pastor, Rev. Morrison.

NORTH SIDE—Montana and Sheffield av. Pastor, Rev. W. B. Taylor.

RAVENSWOOD—Wilson av. and Hamilton. Pastor, E. W. Allen.

UNION—People's Institute. Pastor, Rev. J. H. O. Smith.

WEST PULLMAN—Wallace cor. 118th. Pastor, Rev. R. W. Lilly.

WEST SIDE—1010 Jackson boul. Pastor, Rev. Bruce Brown.

Missions.

AUSTIN MISSION—52d av. nr. Lake. Supt., A. Larrabee.

GUIDING STAR MISSION—53 S. Halsted. Pastor, H. E. Luck.

LAKE MISSION—Halsted cor. Garfield boul. Pastor, J. R. McIntyre.

Congregational.

ASBURY AVENUE — Evanston. Pastor, Rev. B. M. Southgate.

AUBURN PARK—77th cor. Butler. Pastor, Rev. A. T. Stone.

AUSTIN—Pastor, Rev. W. L. Demerest.

AUSTIN PARK—Pastor, Rev. J. C. Evans.

BEECHER—Pastor, Rev. T. V. Davies.

BEREA—936 S. Hoyne av. Pastor, Rev. C. L. Fisk.

BETHANY—W. Superior cor. N. Lincoln. Pastor, Rev. J. J. Klopp.

BETHEL — Marquette cor. 77th. Pastor, Rev. M. H. Lyon.

BETHESDA—26 Clybourn av. Pastor, Rev. John John.

BETHLEHEM—709 to 713 Loomis. Pastor, Rev. E. A. Adams.

BETHLEHEM BRANCH — 47th cor. Goodspeed. Pastor, Rev. F. Rybar.

BLUE ISLAND—Pastor, ——.

BOWMANVILLE — Bowmanville. Pastor, Rev. A. W. Safford.

BRAINARD—W. 88th ne. cor. Bishop. Pastor. ——.

BRIDGEPORT (SWEDISH)— S. Hermitage av. cor. 35th.

BRIGHTON—34th pl. cor. S. Lincoln. Pastor, Rev. H. M. Evans.

CALIFORNIA AVENUE—S. California av. cor. W. Monroe. Pastor, Rev. D. F. Fox.

CENTRAL PARK—Park av. cor. S. 40th ct. Pastor, Rev. S. C. Haskin.

CHRIST'S GERMAN—31st pl. cor. S. Center av. Pastor, Rev. Jacob Heim.

COMMERCIAL AV.—98th nr. Commercial av. Pastor, Rev. G. H. Bird.

CORTLAND ST.—83 Cortland. Pastor, Rev. H. B. Harrison.

COVENANT — W. Polk nw. cor S. C e nt av. Pastor, Rev. H. T. Sell. lar mo

CRAGIN—Armitage av. nr. Grand av. Pastor, Rev. Alex. Ericson.

CRAWFORD—S. 42d av. cor. W. 26th. Pastor, Rev. J. J. Kolmos.

DESPLAINES — Pastor, Rev. N. Burgess.

DOREMUS—Butler nr. 31st. Pastor, Rev. J. M. Green.

DOUGLAS PARK—W. 19th cor. S. Spaulding av. Pastor, Rev. F. T. Lee.

EVANSTON—Pastor, Rev. J. F. Loba.

EWING STREET—241 and 243 Ewing. Pastor, Rev. H. M. Lyman.

FELLOWSHIP—Jackson av. cor. 63d. Pastor, Rev. D. D. DeLong.

FIRST—Washington boul. sw. cor. S. Ann. Pastor, Rev. E. P. Goodwin, D.D.

FIRST EVANGELICAL LUTHERAN—Cor. N. Leavitt and

Haddon. Pastor, Rev. C. A. Dettmers.

FIRST EVANGELICAL LUTHERAN—(Branch) 968 Ogden av.

FIRST SCANDINAVIAN — Point cor Channey. Pastor, Rev. C. T. Dyrness.

FOREST AV. (Oak Park)—Pastor, Rev. H. M. Stough.

FOREST GLEN—N. 50th ct. cor. W. Catalpa av. Pastor, Rev. H. A. Hall.

FORESTVILLE—Chaplain av. cor. 46th. Pastor, ——.

GLEN ELLYN—Pastor, Rev. G. W. Jackman.

GLENCOE—Pastor, ——.

GRACE—N. Campbell av. cor. Cherry pl. Pastor, Rev. T. A. Moffatt.

GRAND AV.—Grand and N. Hamlin aves. Pastor, ——.

GREEN STREET — W. 56th cor. S. Green. Pastor, ——.

GROSS PARK — 1844 N. Leavitt. Pastor, Rev. W. H. Hopkins.

GROSSDALE—Pastor, Rev. G. H. Grannis.

HERMOSA—Hermosa. Pastor, ——.

HINSDALE — Pastor, Rev. M. N. Preston.

HUMBOLDT PARK— W. Chicago av. cor. N. Fairfield av. Pastor, Rev. O. C. Johnson.

IMMANUEL—Cor. Drexel av. and 92d pl. Pastor, R. A. Hadden.

JEFFERSON — Jefferson. Pastor, Rev. J. J. G. Graham.

JEFFERSON PARK TRINITY BRANCH (Park Ridge)—Pastor, Rev. John Block.

LA GRANGE—Pastor, Rev. H. A. Bushnell.

LAKE VIEW — Seminary av. cor. Lill av. Pastor, Rev. P. Krohn.

LA VERGNE--Pastor, Rev. J. M. Stevens.

LEAVITT STREET—S. Leavitt sw. cor. W. Adams. Pastor, Rev. J. B. Silcox.

LINCOLN PARK — Fullerton av. nr. Cleveland av. Pastor, Rev. David Beaton.

LOMBARD — Pastor, Rev. J. M. Campbell.

MADISON AVENUE—7117 Madison av. Pastor, Rev. J. H. Simons.

MAPLEWOOD—N. Talman av. nr. Humboldt Park boul. Pastor, Rev. A. E. Beddoes.

MAYFLOWER CHAPEL —Sacramento av. cor. Fillmore. Pastor, Rev. J. J. Brokenshire.

MAYWOOD—Pastor, Rev. S. P. Dunlap.

MILLARD AVENUE — S. Central Park av. se. cor. W. Twenty-third. Pastor Rev. W. A. Waterman.

MIZPAH CHAPEL—575 Washburn av. Pastor, Rev. C. W. Merritt.

MONT CLARE—N. 69th av. cor. Medill av. Pastor, Rev. E. S. Chandler.

MORGAN PARK—Pastor, Rev. W. D. Westervell.

MORTON PARK—Pastor, Rev. J. M. Stevens.

NEW ENGLAND — Dearborn av. cor. Delaware pl. Pastor, ——.

NORTH ENGLEWOOD — Lasalle cor. W. 59th. Pastor, Rev. Chas. Reynolds.

OAK PARK FIRST—Pastor, Rev. P. S. Hulbert.

OAK PARK SECOND — Pastor, Rev. Sidney Strong.

PACIFIC — Cortland cor. Ballou. Pastor, Rev. S. S. Healy.

PARK MANOR—71st and Rhodes av. Pastor, Rev. J. A. Cole.

PARK RIDGE—Pastor, Rev. F. D. Burhans.

PEOPLE'S CHURCH—9855 Avenue K. Pastor, Rev. C. T. Baylis.

PILGRIM—Harvard cor. 64th. Pastor, Rev. G. R. Wallace.

PILGRIM GERMAN—N. Avers av. cor. Thomas. Pastor, Rev. A. H. Vogell.

PILGRIM MAYFLOWER—4357 Wentworth av. · Pastor, Rev. E. A. Marshall.

PLYMOUTH—Michigan av.nr. 26th. Pastor, Rev. J. A. Haines.

PORTER MEMORIAL BRANCH —S. Paulina nr. W. Taylor. Pastor, Rev. W. R. Bennett.

PURITAN—817-819 Grand av. Pastor, Rev. C. E. Burton.

RAVENSWOOD--N. Hermitage av. cor. Montrose av. Pastor, Rev. J. M. Sturtevant.

REDEEMER—School nr. Evanston av. Pastor Rev. W. H. Manss.

ROGERS PARK—Pastor, Rev. P. E. Holp.

ROSEHILL—Rosehill. Pastor, ——.

ST. JAMES' EVANGELICAL GERMAN—N. Park av. cor. Florimond. Pastor, Rev. N. Bolt.

SARDIS WELSH — 143 S. Peoria.

SEDGWICK—388 Sedgwick. Pastor, L. A. Townsend.

SOUTH — Drexel boul. nw. cor. 40th. Pastor, Rev. W. Scott.

SOUTH CHICAGO—Ontario av. nr. 91st. Pastor, Rev. G. H. Bird.

SOUTH CHICAGO WELSH—Cor. 90th & Erie av. Pastor, Rev. W. H. Jones.

STONY ISLAND PARK—Cornell av. cor. 82d. Pastor, Rev. G. H. Bird.

SUMMERDALE—N. Paulina cor. Farragut av. Pastor, Rev. E. B. Wylie.

TABERNACLE—Grand av. se. cor. N. Morgan. Pastor, Prof. Graham Taylor.

TRINITY — Butler cor. 71st. Pastor, Rev. L. G. Kent.

UNION PARK — Cor. S. Ashland av. and Washington boul. Pastor, Rev. Frederick A. Noble, D.D.

UNITED—Archer av. nr. W. 35th. Pastor, Rev. H. E. Mills.

UNIVERSITY—56th and Madison av. Pastor, Rev. N. I. Rubinkam.

WARREN AVENUE — Warren av. sw. cor. S. Albany av. Pastor, Rev. J. W. Fifield.

WASHINGTON PARK—1010, 51st nr. Indiana av. Pastor, Rev. W. E. Danforth.

WAUKEGAN—Pastor, Rev. C. M. Burkholder.

WAUKEGAN, GERMAN, EBEN-EZER—Pastor, Rev. Karl Freitag.

WAVELAND AV.—Waveland and Janssen aves. Pastor,—Rev. A. H. Armstrong.

WEST PULLMAN — Pastor, Rev. H. N. Dascomb.

WHEATON—Pastor, Rev. Edward Anderson.

WILMETTE—Pastor, Rev. E. B. Dean.

WINNETKA—Pastor, Rev. Q. L. Dowd.

MISSIONS.

CHINESE MISSION—Washington boul. sw. cor. Ann.

LOGAN SQUARE MISSION—Diversey cor. Sacramento av. Pastor, Rev. O. C. Grauer.

PLACERDALE MISSION (Branch of West Pullman Church)—Supt., H. J. Kloeppel.

RIVERVIEW MISSION (Branch of Des Plaines Church)—Supt., Roscoe Burgess.

Cumberland Presbyterian.

CHURCH OF PROVIDENCE — Sheffield av. nr. N. Clark, Pastor, Rev. A. H. Stephens.

DREXEL PARK—6330 S. Marshfield av. Pastor, Rev. G. D. Crawford.

FIRST—6623 Stewart av. Pastor, Rev. John Lewis Clark.

FIRST COLORED—Perry av. nr. 62d. Pastor, Rev. Mr. Nichelson.

FOURTH—Alpine Heights. Pastor, ——.

LINCOLN PARK—Pastor, ——.

MEMORIAL—253 Jackson Park terrace. Pastor, Rev. W. C. Logan.

Episcopal.

DIOCESE OF CHICAGO—Bishop, Rt. Rev. William E. McLaren, D.D., D.C.L. Office 510 Masonic Temple; res. Highland Park. Dean, Rev. Clinton Locke, D.D., 2825 Indiana av.; Rev. Luther Pardee, Sec., 90 Pine; F. F. Ainsworth, Treas. Board of Missions, 510 Masonic Temple. Bishop's Sec. Rev. Jos. Rushton.

ALL ANGELS' (for the deaf)— State nr. 20th. Rev. A. W. Mann.

ALL SAINTS'—Ravenswood—Rev. Charles E. Bowles.

ALL SAINTS'—Pullman. Rev. J. M. McGrath.

ANNUNCIATION — Auburn Park. Rev. John S. Cole.

CATHEDRAL SS. PETER AND PAUL—cor. Washington boul. and S. Peoria. Bishop, Rt. Rev. William E. McLaren. D.D., LL.D. Assistant, Jesse H. Dennis.

CALVARY—W. Monroe and Kedzie av. Rector, Rev. W. B. Hamilton.

CHRIST—65th cor. Woodlawn av. Rector, Rev. A. L. Williams.

CHURCH OF ATONEMENT—Edgewater. Rector, Rev. J. M. D. Davidson.

CHURCH OF THE ASCENSION—Lasalle av. se. cor. Elm. Rector, Rev. Edward A. Larrabee.

CHURCH OF THE EPIPHANY—Ashland boul. cor. W. Adams. Rector, Rev. T. N. Morrison.

CHURCH OF THE GOOD SHEPHERD—S. Lawndale av. ne. cor. W. 24th. Reader, F. F. Beckerman.

CHURCH OF THE HOLY COMMUNION—Maywood. Rector, Rev. C. C. Tate.

CHURCH OF THE INCARNATION—10042 Wallace. Priest, Rev. J. M. McGrath.

CHURCH OF THE MEDIATOR—Morgan Park. Rector, Rev. J. M. McGrath.

CHURCH OF THE HOLY TRINITY—Stock Yards. Rector, Rev. H. C. Kinney.

CHURCH OF OUR SAVIOR—702 Fullerton av. Rector, Rev. J. H. Edwards.

CHURCH OF THE REDEEMER—56th cor. Washington av. Rev. Percival McIntire.

CHURCH OF THE TRANSFIGURATION—43d nr. Cottage Grove av. Rector, Rev. Walter Delafield, S. T. D.

EMMANUEL—LaGrange. Rector, Rev. Chas. Scadding.

GRACE—Oak Park. Rector, Rev. C. P. Anderson.

GRACE—1445 Wabash av. nr. 16th. Rector, Rev. E. M. Stires.

GRACE—Hinsdale. Rector, Rev. W. R. Cross.

SEMINARY CHAPEL—1113 Washington boul. Rev. W. J. Gold, assistant, Rev. F. J. Hall.

ST. ALBAN'S—4336 Prairie av. Rector, Rev. Geo. W. Knapp.

ST. ALBAN'S—W. Circle av. ne. cor. Crescent av. Reader, J. K. Ochiai.

ST. ANDREW'S—Washington boul. cor. S. Robey. Rector, Rev. W. C. Dewitt.

ST. ANSGARIUS' — Sedgwick nr. Chicago av. Rector, Rev. Herman Lindskog.

ST. AUGUSTINE—(Wilmette).

ST. BARNABAS' — W. 44th cor. Park av. Rector, Rev. E. J. Randall.

ST. BARTHOLOMEW'S—W. 65th cor. Stewart av. Rector, Rev. B. F. Matrau.

ST. CHRYSOSTOM—544 Dearborn av. Rector, Rev. T. A. Snively.

ST. GEORGE'S—Grand Crossing. Priest, Rev. T. J. O. Curran.

ST. JAMES'—Cor. Cass and Huron. Rector, Rev. James S. Stone, D.D., Assistant, Rev. E. M. Thompson.

ST. JOHN'S—Irving Park. Rev. C. E. Bowles.

ST. JOHN'S—26 Clybourn av. Rector, Rev. H. C. Goodman.

ST. JOSEPH'S — West Pullman. Priest, Rev. J. M. McGrath.

ST. LUKE'S—388 S. Western av. Rector, Rev. T. D. Phillipps.

ST. LUKE'S — Evanston. Rector, Rev. D. F. Smith.

ST. MARGARET—Windsor Park. Rev. E. L. Roland.

ST. MARK'S—Evanston. Rector, Rev. A. W. Little, L.H.D.

ST. MARK'S—Cottage Grove av. cor. 36th. Rector, Rev. W. W. Wilson.

ST. MARY'S—Morton Park. Rector, Rev. Geo. N. Mead.

ST. MATTHEW'S—Evanston.

ST. MICHAEL AND ALL ANGELS — (Berwyn) Rector, Rev. Geo. N. Mead.

ST. PAUL THE APOSTLE—Austin. Rev. L. Pardee.

ST. PAUL'S—4928 Lake av. Rector, Rev. C. H. Bixby, Rev. David W. Howard.

ST. PAUL'S CHURCH—Riverside. Rector, Rev. George D. Adams.

ST. PAUL'S—Rogers' Park. Rector, Rev. H. R. Neely.

ST. PETER'S — 1737 Belmont av. Rector, Rev. S. C. Edsall, Assistant, Rev. H. C. Granger.

ST. PHILIP THE EVANGELIST—Brighton Park. Rector, Rev. Henry J. Brown.

ST. THOMAS'—(colored) 3025 Dearborn. Rector, Rev. A. H. Lealtad.

TRINITY—Michigan av. cor. 26th. Rector, Rev. Harold Morse.

TRINITY—Highland Park. Rector, Rev. P. C. Wolcott.

TRINITY—Wheaton. Rector, Rev. Wm. J. Hawthorne.

Missions and Chapels.

CHAPEL OF CHURCH HOME FOR AGED PERSONS—4327 Ellis av. Chaplain, Rev. Walter Delafield.

CHAPEL OF ST. LUKE'S HOSPITAL—1430 Indiana av. Chaplain, Rev. J. H. Van Ingen.

CITY MISSION TO HOSPITALS AND PRISONS — Rev. J. Rushton, Rev. J. M. Chattin.

HOME FOR INCURABLES—Ellis av. s. of 55th. Supt..F. D. Mitchell.

SISTERS OF ST. MARY CHAPEL —Washington boul. nr. S. Peoria. Superior, Sister Frances.

Episcopal (Reformed).
(Synod of Chicago.)

Bishop, Rt. Rev. Chas. E. Cheney, D.D.

CHRIST—Michigan av. and 24th. Rector, Rt. Rev. Charles E. Cheney, D. D.

EMMANUEL— S. Canal cor. 28th. Rector. Rev. Geo. W. Bowne.

ST. JOHN'S—37th cor. Langley av. Rector, Rev. Thomas J. Mason.

ST. LUKE'S—N. Fairfield av. nr. Wabansia av., Humboldt Park. Minister in charge, Rev. Richard H. Burke.

ST. MARK'S—N. Washtenaw av. nr. W. Dunning, Maplewood. Minister in charge, ——.

ST. MATTHEW'S—Larrabee cor. Glenlake av. Minister in Charge, Rev. E. S. Fairchild.

TRINITY — Yale cor. 70th. Rector, Rev. Fred J. Walton.

TYNG MISSION—Archer av. cor. 21st. Supt., Robert J. Martin.

EPISCOPAL (REFORMED) MISSIONARY JURISDICTION OF THE NORTHWEST AND WEST—Bishop, Rt. Rev. Samuel Fallows, D. D.

ST. PAUL'S—W. Adams sw. cor. S. Winchester av. Rector, Rt. Rev. Samuel Fallows. D. D.

Evangelical Association.

Board of Bishops—Bishop J. J. Esher, 745 Jackson boul.; Bishop Thomas Bowman, 232 Winchester av.; Bishop S. C. Breyfogel, Reading, Pa., Bishop William Horn, Cleveland, O.

CHICAGO DISTRICT—Presiding Elder, Rev. John Wellner, 658 Sheffield av.

CENTENNIAL—W. Harrison sw. cor. Hoyne av. Pastor, Rev. G. C. Knobel.

DOUGLAS PARK—S. Homan av. s. 15th. Pastor, Rev. C. Ott.

EBENEZER—S. Sangamon nr. W. 67th (Englewood). Pastor, Rev. H. F, Ebert.

EMANUEL—Sheffield av. ne. cor. Marianna. Pastor, Rev. Leo Schmitt.

FIRST—35th cor. Dearborn. Pastor, Rev. Carl Hauser.

LANE PARK — Roscoe cor. Bosworth av. Pastor, Rev. Wm. Klingbeil.

NORWOOD PARK—Pastor, Rev. C. Burgi.

OAK PARK—Pastor Rev. M.Hoehn.

SAINT JOHN'S — W. Huron cor. Noble. Pastor, Rev. G. M. Hallwachs.

SALEM—W. 12th cor. S. Union. Pastor, Rev. Wm. Schuman.

SECOND—Wisconsin cor. Sedgwick. Pastor, Rev. H. Hintze.

SOUTH CHICAGO—Avenue J nr. 98th. Pastor, Rev. W. B. Rilling.

Evangelical Lutheran.
ENGLISH.

CHRIST'S—Augusta cor. N. Hoyne av. Pastor, Rev. H. F. G. Bartholomew.

CHURCH OF THE HOLY TRINITY—Lasalle av. cor. Elm. Pastor, Rev. Wm. Evans.

COVENANT — Ohio cor. Noble. Pastor, Rev. Carl Weswig.

GRACE—Belden av. cor. Larrabee. Pastor, Rev. W. S. Hinman, D.D.

ST. JOHN'S—Indiana av. cor. 61st. Pastor, Rev. W. A. Sadtler, Ph.D.

ST. MARK'S—N. Clark cor. Addison. Pastor, Rev. A. T. Clay, Ph.D.

ST. MATTHEW'S—Pastor, Rev. G. Kabele.

ST. PAUL'S — Fairfield av. cor. Hirsch. Pastor, ——.

ST. PETER'S—1184 W. North av. Rev. H. B. Reed.

WICKER PARK—N. Hoyne av. nw. cor. LeMoyne. Pastor, Rev. H. W. Roth, D. D.

GERMAN.

ANDREAS—3650 Honore. Pastor, Rev. W. C. Kohn.

BETHEL—Grand av. cor. N. 40th av. Pastor, Rev. A. E. Pfund.

BETHANIA—Humboldt Park boul. cor. Rockwell. Pastor, Rev. E. Pardieck.

BETHLEHEM—N. Paulina cor. Mc-Reynolds. Pastor, Rev. Augustus Reinke. Asst. Rev. E. Reinke.

BETHLEHEM — 103d cor. Av. G. Pastor, Rev. J. Feiertag.

CHRIST — Cor. N. Humboldt and McLean aves. Pastor, Rev. E. Werfelmann.

CHURCH OF THE HOLY CROSS —S. Centre av. nw. cor. 31st. pl. Pastor, Rev. W. Uffenbeck.

CONCORDIA — Belmont av, cor. Washtenaw av. Pastor, Rev. C. Dietz.

EMANUEL—W. 12th cor. S. Ashland av. Pastor, Rev. L. Hoelter, Asst. E. Hoelter.

EMMAUS — N. California av. cor. Walnut. Pastor, Rev. M. Fuelling.

GETHSEMANE — 49th and Dearborn. Pastor, Rev. J. G. Nuetzel.

MARCUS — 1114 S. California av. Pastor, Rev. Th. Kohn.

MARTINI—W. 51st cor. Ashland av. Pastor, Rev. F. C. Leeb.

ST. JACOBI—Fremont sw. cor. Garfield av. Pastor, Rev. Chas. Schmidt.

ST. JOHANNES—1704 Montrose av. Pastor, Rev. P. Luecke.

ST. JOHN'S—W. Superior cor. Bickerkike. Pastor, Rev. H. H. Succop. Asst. Rev. P. Sauer.

ST. LUKE'S — Belmont av. cor. Perry. Pastor, Rev. J. E. A. Mueller.

ST. MATTHEW'S—S. Hoyne av. bet W. 20th and W. 21st. Pastor, Rev. H. Engelbrecht. Asst. H. Engelbrecht. jr.

ST. PAUL'S — Superior cor. N. Franklin. Pastor, Rev. Henry Wunder. Asst. Rev. J. Baumgartner.

ST. PAUL'S—Madison av. nr. South Chicago av. Pastor, Rev. August Frederking.

ST. PETER'S—Dearborn s. of 39th. Pastor, Rev. F. P. Merbitz.

ST. PHILIP'S—Lawrence av. cor. N. Hoyne av. Pastor, Rev. W. H. Ganske.

ST. STEPHANUS—Englewood av. cor. Union. Pastor, Rev. Adolph Buenger.

TRINITY (U. A. C.)—S. Canal cor. 25th pl. Pastor, Rev. Louis Lochner.

TRINITY—Hegewisch. Pastor, Rev. M. Kaeppel.

WASHINGTON HEIGHTS—Winston av. nr. 99th. Pastor, Rev. R. P. Budach.

ZION—W. 19th ne. cor. Johnson. Pastor, Rev. Anton Wagner.

ZION'S—113th and Curtis av. Pastor, Rev. G. Sievers.

Missions.

MISSION FOR THE DEAF AND DUMB. Pastor, Arthur L. Reinke.

POLISH MISSION — Pastor, Fred Sattelmeier.

SLAVONISH MISSION — Pastor, Ladislaus Boor.

NORWEGIAN.

BETHANIA—W. Indiana se. cor. Carpenter. Pastor, Rev. John Z. Torgersen.

BETHEL—Humboldt nr. Cortland. Pastor, Rev. A. Oeffstedal.

BETHLEHEM—W. Huron cor. N. Centre av. Pastor, Rev. J. N. Kildahl.

EMANUEL—N. Maplewood av. cor. Cherry pl. Pastor, Rev. C. C. Holter.

EMAUS—N. Springfield av. cor. Iowa. Pastor, Rev. John L. Hetland.

NORWEGIAN EVANG. LUTHERAN CHURCH OF CHICAGO (The)—Baxter cor. Roscoe. Pastor, Rev. S. T. Regue.

OUR SAVIOR'S—May cor. W. Erie. Pastor, Rev. Alfred Johnson.

ST. JOHANNES—461 N. Washtenaw av. Pastor, Rev. M. K. Blekem.

ST. PAUL'S—W. North av. bet. Leavitt and Shober. Pastor, Rev. I. B. Torrison.

TRINITY—Grand av. sw. cor. Peoria. Pastor, Rev. N. G. Petersen.

ZION—N. Artesian av. cor. Potomac. Pastor, Rev. J. H. Meyer.

SWEDISH.

AUGUSTANA—Berwyn.

BETHANIA—Houston av. nr. 91st. Pastor, Rev. G. Lundhal.

BETHEL—6607 S. Sangamon. Pastor, Rev. A. S. Becklund.

BETHESDA—Avenue K s. 101st. Pastor, Rev. C. O. Lindell.

BETHLEHEM—W. 58th cor. 5th av. Pastor, Rev. M. Noyd.

EBENEZER—Summerdale av. nr. Ashland av. Pastor, Rev. T. O. Linell.

ELIM—113th cor. Calumet av.

EMAUS—Jefferson.

GETHSEMANE—N. May cor. W. Huron. Pastor, Rev. Matthew C. Ranseen.

GUSTAVUS ADOLPHUS—75th cor. Drexel av. Pastor, C. P. Rydholm.

IMMANUEL—Sedgwick cor. Hobbie. Pastor, Rev. C. A. Evald.

IMMANUEL — Evanston. Pastor, Rev. Carl Solomonson.

LIBANON—Hegewisch. Pastor, Rev. G. Lundahl.

MAYWOOD — Pastor, Rev. T. A. Brandelle.

MESSIAH—Austin. Pastor, Rev. J. Telleen.

SALEM—2819 Princeton av. Pastor, Rev. L. G. Abrahamson.

SARON—N. Humboldt cor. Shakespeare av. Pastor, Rev. Uric J. A. Rosenquist.

SILVA—Blue Island. Pastor, Rev. Carl Granath.

TRINITY—Seminary av. cor. Noble av. Pastor, Rev. S. A. Sandahl.

ZION—S. Irving av. 22d. Pastor. Rev. C. Granath.

ZION — Chicago Heights. Pastor, Rev. C. Rejholm.

Evangelical United.

BETHANY—Irving Park boul. cor. N. Paulina. Pastor, Rev. W. Grotefeld.

BETHLEHEM'S—Diversey cor. Diversey ct. Pastor, Rev. J. G. Kircher.

CHRISTUS — 1502 Lexington av. Pastor, Rev. C. Katerndahl.

CHURCH OF PEACE—52d cor. Justine. Pastor, Rev. K. J. Freitag.

EMANUEL'S—46th cor. Dearborn. Pastor, Rev. W. Hattendorf.

EPIPHANY—Roscoe cor. Claremont av. Pastor, Rev. P. Brauns.

NAZARETH—N. Campbell av. nr. Fullerton av. Pastor, Rev. Glade.

PETRI—103d cor. Av. J. Pastor, Rev. J. Holz.

SALEM—386, 25th. Pastor, Rev. C. Krafft.

ST. ANDREW'S—W. 28th cor. S. 41st av. Pastor, Rev. F. Grorse.

ST. JOHN'S—Moffatt cor. N. Campbell av. Pastor, Rev. H. Stamer.

ST. JOHN'S N. C.—Garfield av. cor. Mohawk. Pastor, Rev. G. A. Zimmerman.

ST. LUKE'S—W. 62d cor. S. Green. Pastor, Rev. A. Schmidt.

ST. MARKUS—35th cor. Union av. Pastor. Rev. Fred Mueller.

ST. MATHEW'S—Iowa cor. N. Washtenaw av. Pastor, Rev. Ed. E. Klimpke.

ST. NICOLAS—Avondale. Pastor, Rev. Edward F. Pinckert.

ST. PAUL'S—Orchard cor. Kemper pl. Pastor, Rev. R. A. John.

ST. PAUL'S—Rose Hill. Pastor, Rev. P. Dietz.

ST. PETER'S—W. Chicago av. cor. Noble. Pastor, Rev. Gotthilf Lambrecht.

TRINITY—S. Robey sw. cor. W. 22d pl. Pastor, Rev. Julius Kircher.

ZION'S—W. 14th cor. S. Union. Pastor, Rev. Paul Foerster.

ZION'S—Auburn Park. Pastor, Rev. G. Schlutius.

ZION'S—Washington Heights. Pastor, Rev. L. Pfeiffer.

Friends.

FRIENDS' MEETING (Orthodox) Indiana av. cor. 44th.

FRIENDS' MEETING — 26 Vanburen.

Free Methodist.

CRAWFORD—N. Crawford av. nr. W. Lake. Pastor, Rev. D. M. Smashey.

FIRST—16 N. May. Pastor, Rev. D. M. Smashey.

HUMBOLDT PARK — Mozart nr. Armitage av. Pastor, Rev. W. P. Ferries.

SEVENTY-SECOND STREET— 72d cor. S. Sangamon. Pastor, Rev. T. H. Marsh.

SECOND—48 Lexington. Pastor, Rev. B. D. Fay.

SOUTH SIDE—5251 Dearborn. Pastor, Rev. T. H. Marsh.

SOUTH CHICAGO—South Chicago. Pastor, Rev. Fred Campbell.

THIRD CHURCH—701 W. Lake. Pastor, Rev. B. J. Brown.

Independent.

ALL SOULS'—Oakwood boul. se. cor. Langley av. Pastor, Rev. Jenkin Lloyd Jones.

CENTRAL—Central Music Hall, State se. cor. Randolph. Pastor, Rev. N. D. Hillis.

CHICAGO AVENUE—Chicago av. nw. cor. Lasalle av. Pastor, Rev. R. A. Torrey.

KIRKLAND MISSION—111 S. Halsted. Morris E. Hulbert, supt.

PEOPLE'S—McVicker's Theatre. Pastor, Rev. H. W. Thomas, 535 W. Monroe.

Jewish.

ANSHE EMETH—349 Sedgwick. Pres. Sol. Levinsohn; Minister, Rev. Dr. S. Bauer.

ANSHE K'NESSETH ISRAEL— W. 12th pl. se. cor. S Clinton. Pres. Sol. Browarsky. Rabbi, Rev. B. Bernstein.

CONGREGATION AGUDAS ACHEM—307 Maxwell. Pres. Mark Gross; Minister, Rev. M. Baloch.

CONGREGATION BEKUR HEILIM BUE JACOB—1218, 61st. Pres. A. Brill.

CONGREGATION BETH HAMEDRASH—134 Pacific av. Pres. J. Robinson; Rabbi, Rev. A. J. G. Lesser.

CONGREGATION BETHEL—N. May nr. W. Huron. Pres., S. Klee.

CONGREGATION B'NAI ABRAHAM—590 Marshfield av. Pres. Ignatz Beck; Minister, Dr. A. R. Levey.

CONGREGATION B'NAI DAVID —618 N. Wood. Pres. G. Roth; Rabbi, A. Stern.

CONGREGATION B'NAI ISRAEL —Aberdeen ne. cor. W. 62d. Pres. I. Goldberg; Minister, Hyman Rosenweig.

CONGREGATION B'NAI SHOLOM—26th cor. Indiana av. Pres. S. Richter; Minister, Rev. A. J. Messing.

CONGREGATION CHOWRE CHOWWE SION—171 Maxwell.

CONGREGATION MIKRO KODESH—76 W. 12th pl.

CONGREGATION MOSES MONTEFIORE — 130 Augusta. Pres. L. Newman; Rabbi, Rev. I. Agat.

CONGREGATION OF THE NORTH SIDE — Lasalle av. cor. Goethe. Pres. A. I. Frank; Minister, Rev. Dr. A. Norden.

CONGREGATION OHAVEH-SHOLOM—582 S. Canal. Pres. J. Berkson; Minister, Charles Alexandrowitz.

CONGREGATION OHAVO AMUNO BETH HAMEDRASH HOCHODOSH—386 Clark. Pres. Philip Drazdowitz; Minister, Rabbi L. Anixter.

CONGREGATION POWALEI ZEDOCK—S. Clinton cor. W. 12th. Pres. M. Richman; Minister, B. Cohn.

CONGREGATION TIFERES YISHROES ANSHE— 174 W. 14th. Pres. A. W. Sandler.

ISAIAH CONGREGATION—Ellis av. cor. 39th. Pres. Henry Greenebaum; Minister, Rev. Joseph Stolz.

KEHILATH ANSHE MAARIV— (Congregation of the Men of the West) —Indiana av. cor. 33d. Pres. Henry N. Hart; Minister, Rev. Moses P. Jacobson.

SINAI CONGREGATION (Reformed)—Indiana av. cor. 21st. Pres. Albert Fishell; Minister, Rev. Dr. E. G. Hirsch.

ZION CONGREGATION OF WEST CHICAGO—Ogden av. se. cor. Washington boul. Pres. Rudolph Gerber; Minister, Rabbi Emeritus Dr. B. Felsenthal.

Methodist Episcopal.

Bishop—Rev. S. M. Merrill, 1138 Washington boul. Office 57 Washington.

Presiding Elders—Chicago District, Rev. Henry G. Jackson; Chicago Northern District, Rev. C. E. Mandeville; Chicago Western District, Rev. J. M. Caldwell.

Cor. Sec. Chicago Home Missionary and Church Extension Society—A. D. Traveller, 57 Washington.

ADA STREET—Ada bet. W. Lake and Fulton. Supply, Rev. C. G. D. Cleworth.

ADAMS STREET—Adams cor. West 42d. Pastor, Rev. W. H. Carwardine.

ASBURY—Parnell av. Pastor, Rev. C. A. Kelley.

ASHLAND BOUL.—Ashland boul. cor. W. Harrison. Pastor, Rev. W. W. Diehl.

AUBURN PARK—Auburn Park. Pastor, Rev. C. A. Van Anda.

AUGUSTA ST. — Washtenaw av. cor. Augusta. Pastor, Rev. O. F. Hall.

AUSTIN—Pastor, Rev. A. M. White.

AVONDALE — Avondale. Pastor, Rev. H. V. Holt.

BERWYN—Pastor, Rev. W. E. McLennan.

BETHANY—W. Jackson ne. cor. Francisco. Pastor, Rev. William Ashford.

BRIGHTON PARK —Washtenaw av. nw. cor. 38th. Supply, Rev. H. B. Haskell.

CENTENARY—295 W. Monroe nr. Morgan. Pastor, Rev. A. C. Hirst.

CENTRAL AVENUE—Evanston. Pastor, Rev. C. P. Sturges.

CHICAGO LAWN—Chicago Lawn. Rev. H. G. Wenz.

CLYDE—Pastor, Rev. E. G. Shutz.

CUYLER—Byron cor. Perry. Pastor, Rev. W. M. Ewing.

DEAF MUTE MISSION — Pastor, Rev. P. J. Hasenstab.

DEERING — Dunning n w. c o r. Ward. Pastor, Rev. T. M. H. Coghlan.

DOUGLAS PARK—624 and 626 S. Washtenaw av. Pastor, Rev. A. C. Wakeman.

EDISON PARK—Pastor Rev. L. A. McCaffree.

ELSMERE—Mead sw. cor. Waubausia av. Pastor, Rev J. H. Alling.

EMMANUEL — Evanston. Pastor, Rev. N. M. Waters.

ENGLEWOOD FIRST—6410 Stewart av. Pastor, Rev. P. H. Swift.

ENGLEWOOD SECOND—62d cor. S. May. Pastor, Rev. E. A. Stickleman.

EPWORTH—Kenmore av. cor. Berwyn av. Pastor, Rev. F. D. Sheets.

ERIE STREET—W. Erie nr. N. Robey. Pastor, Rev. E. W. Akers.

EVANSTON AV.— Pastor, Rev. J. H. Odgers.

FIRST—Cor. Clark and Washington, Methodist Church blk. Pastor, Rev. J. P. Brushingham.

FIRST — Evanston. Pastor, Rev. William Macafee.

FORTY-SEVENTH STREET—W. 47th cor. S. Marshfield av. Pastor, Rev. H. G. Warren.

FOWLER—Millard av. ne. cor. W. 23d. Pastor, Rev. M. M. Bales.

FULTON STREET—891-893 Fulton w. of Oakley av. Pastor, Rev. M. W. Satterfield.

GARFIELD BOUL.—Garfield boul. cor. Emerald av. Pastor, Rev. C. A. Bunker.

GARFIELD PARK — Fulton cor. Hamlin av. Pastor, Rev. James Rowe.

GRACE—Lasalle av. cor. Locust. Pastor, Rev. Fred H. Sheets.

GROSS PARK—Gross Park (L.V.) Supply, Rev. John Thompson.

HALSTED STREET—778 to 784 S. Halsted. Pastor, Rev. J. F. Clancy.

HAMLIN AVENUE—Pastor, Rev. Robert Pate.

HEMENWAY—Evanston. Pastor, Rev. O. F. Mattison.

HERMOSA—Hermosa (J.) Pastor, Rev. A. H. Miller.

HIGHWOOD—Supply, Rev. Clyde L. Hay.

HINSDALE—Pastor, Rev. E. P. Thomas.

HONORE STREET — 47th cor. Honore. Pastor, Rev. E. Harris.

HUMBOLDT PARK—Pastor, Rev. J. B. McGuffin.

HYDE PARK—Pastor, Rev. A. W. Patten.

INGLESIDE AVENUE — Pastor, Rev. W. J. Libberton.

IRVING PARK—Irving Park. Pastor, Rev. A. S. Haskins.

JOYCE—Pastor, Rev. J. K. Shields.

KENSINGTON—Michigan av. cor. Kensington av. Pastor, Rev. F. C. Bruner.

LANGLEY AVENUE — Pastor, Rev. W. H. Head.

LAGRANGE—Pastor, Rev. J. F. Pierce.

LEAVITT AND DEKALB STREETS—nr. Ogden av. Pastor, Rev. C. R. Robinson.

LINCOLN STREET—S. Lincoln se. cor. Ambrose. Pastor, Rev. A. E. Saunders.

LOCK STREET—Pastor, Rev. F. C. Sherman.

LOOMIS STREET—Pastor, Rev. O. E. Murray.

LUKE HITCHCOCK—Homer w. Milwaukee av. Pastor, Rev. M. E. Dix.

MAREY MISSION—Supply, Rev. H. R. DeBra.

MARIE CHAPEL—Pastor, Rev. Joshua Smith.

MAYFAIR — Pastor, Rev. C. D. Wilson.

MAYWOOD—Supply, Rev. J. C. Bigelow.

MELROSE PARK — Pastor, Rev. Raymond T. Cookingham.

MERRILL—S. Ashland av. cor. W. 55th. Pastor, Rev. H. Rood.

METROPOLITAN—W. Chicago av. cor. N. Ada. Supply, Rev. D. M. Farson.

MORELAND — Moreland. Pastor, Rev. R. A. Morley.

MORGAN PARK — Pastor, Rev. N. O. Freeman.

NORMAL PARK—Normal Park. Pastor, Rev. J. S. Bell.

NORWOOD PARK—Supply, Rev. J. F. Peschmann.

OAK PARK—Pastor, Rev. W. H. Burns.

OAK PARK SECOND — Pastor, Rev. J. C. Youker.

OAKLAND—Oakland boul. sw. cor. Langley av. Pastor, Rev. W. O. Shepard.

PARK AVENUE—Park av. se. cor. Robey. Pastor, Rev. William Craven.

PARK RIDGE—Pastor, Rev. J. M. Wheaton.

PARK SIDE — Pastor, Rev. J. F. Boeye.

PAULINA STREET—3342 S. Paulina nr. Archer av. Pastor, Rev. George B. Millar.

PROSPECT AVENUE — Supply, Rev. F. M. Withey.

PULLMAN—Pullman. Pastor, Rev. N. M. Stokes.

RAVENSWOOD—Commercial cor. Sunnyside av. Pastor, Rev. W. E. Tilroe.

RAVINIA — Pastor, ——.

RIVERSIDE — Pastor, Rev. W. C. Scott.

RIVER FOREST—Pastor, Rev. Wm. Fawcett.

ROGERS PARK — Pastor, Rev. Clarence Abel.

SACRAMENTO AVENUE—Sacramento av. head of Adams st. Pastor, Rev. T. K. Gale.

SEVENTY-SEVENTH ST. — Pastor, Rev. J. E. Honeywell.

SHEFFIELD AVENUE—Sheffield av. cor. George. Pastor, Rev. W. B. Norton.

SIMPSON—Lasalle cor. 59th. Pastor, Rev. G. S. Young.

SOUTH CHICAGO—Superior av. ne. cor. 91st. Pastor, Rev. J. A. Matlack.

SOUTH ENGLEWOOD — Murray cor. 87th. Pastor, Rev. L. E. Leseman.

SOUTH PARK AVENUE.— South. Park av. cor. 33d. Pastor, Rev. W. A. Burch.

STATE STREET — 4637 State. Pastor, Rev. R. B. Kester.

ST. JAMES—Ellis av. cor. 46th. Pastor, Rev. Robert McIntyre.

ST. JOHN'S—462 Colorado av. Pastor, Rev. S. H. Wirsching.

ST. PAUL'S — Center av. nr. W. Taylor. Pastor, Rev. J. L. Walker.

TRINITY — Indiana av. nr. 24th. Pastor, Rev. Frank Crane.

UNION AV.—Union av. cor. 44th. Pastor, Rev. H. T. Clendenning.

VINCENT—Dauphin Park. Pastor, Rev. H. E. Clark.

WABASH AVENUE — Cor. 14th and Wabash av. Pastor, Rev. G. K. Flack.

WARREN—Pastor, Rev. L. B. Lott.

WESLEY — 1003-1009 N. Halsted. Pastor, Rev. O. H. Cessna.

WEST PULLMAN — Pastor, Rev. L. A. Rockwell.

WESTERN AVENUE — Cor. W. Monroe and Western av. Pastor, Rev. M. E. Cady.

WHEADON, EVANSTON — Pastor, ——.

WICKER PARK—N. Robey cor. Evergreen av. Pastor, Rev. W. B. Leach.

WILLARD—1787 W. 12th. Pastor, Rev. George H. Studley.

WILMETTE — Pastor, Rev. H. D. Atchison.

WOODLAWN PARK — Woodlawn Park. Supply, Rev. W. F. Atchison.

AFRICAN.

ALLEN CHAPEL—Avondale. Pastor, ——.

BETHEL—Dearborn ne. cor. 30th. Pastor, Rev. R. C. Ranson.

QUINN CHAPEL—Wabash av. se. cor. 24th. Pastor, Rev. A. J. Carey.

ST. JOHN'S—64th cor. S. Halsted. Pastor, Rev. H. S. Graves.

ST. STEPHEN'S — 682 Austin av. Pastor, Rev. H. H. Thompson.

BOHEMIAN.

FIRST — 778 S. Halsted. Pastor, Rev. F. J. Hrejsa.

FOURTH—Pastor, Rev. F Pelikan.

JAN HUSS—24th nw. cor. Sawyer av. Pastor, Rev. F. J. Zavodzky.

SECOND—S. Halsted cor. W. 12th. Pastor, Rev. J. Froula.

GERMAN.

Presiding Elder Chicago District, German Conference—Rev. H. Lemcke.

ASHLAND AVENUE—485 N. Ashland av. Pastor, Rev. A. Peter.

AVONDALE — Avondale. Pastor, Rev. J. Bletsch.

CENTENNIAL CHURCH — Cor. Wellington and Sheffield avs. Pastor, Rev. Peter Rech.

CENTER STREET — Center nw. cor. Dayton. Pastor, Rev. J. A. Mulfinger.

CLYBOURN AVENUE—51 Clybourn av. Pastor, Rev. C. F. Morf.

EBENEZER—S. Center av. sw. cor. 31st. Pastor, Rev. H. Guenther.

FULLERTON AVENUE—W. Fullerton av. ne. cor. N. Western av. Pastor, Rev. F. F. Klenzky.

IMMANUEL—832 W. 22d. Pastor, Rev. A. F. Fuerstenau.

MAXWELL STREET—308 W. 13th pl. Pastor, Rev. Wm. Keller.

MEMORIAL — McLean av. cor. Hancock. Pastor, Rev. F. T. Enderis.

PORTLAND AVENUE — Princeton av. se. cor. 28th. Pastor, Rev. J. Keller.

ROBEY STREET—506 S. Robey. Pastor, Rev. H. C. Apfelbach.

SOUTH MORGAN STREET—54th cor. S. Morgan. Pastor, Rev. H. Wegner.

WENTWORTH AVENUE — 3829 Wentworth av. Pastor, Rev. H. Meyer.

SWEDISH.

Presiding Elder Chicago District, Swedish Conference—Rev. A. Anderson, 2834 N. Ashland av.

BETHANY—N. Paulina cor. Winnemac av. Pastor, Rev. John Bendix.

BRIGHTON PARK—S. Leavitt nr. W. 36th. Pastor, Rev. E. A. Davidson.

EMMANUEL—W. 24th pl. bet. Western and Oakley avs. Pastor, Rev. J. B. Anderson.

ENGLEWOOD — 66th pl. cor. Butler. Pastor, Rev. John Simpson.

FIRST—Orleans cor. Oak. Pastor, Rev. J. O. Nelson.

FOREST GLEN — Jefferson. Pastor, Rev. N. O. Westergreen.

HUMBOLDT PARK—N. Fairfield av. nr. North av. Pastor, Rev. P. M. Alfvin.

LAKE VIEW — Cor. Osgood and Noble av. Pastor, Rev. A. J. Anderson.

MORELAND—W. Indiana nr. N. 48th av. Pastor, Rev. K. Hanson.

PULLMAN—113th cor. Indiana av. Pastor, Rev. F. U. Liljegren.

SECOND—N. May bet. Ohio and Erie. Pastor, Rev. William Swenson.

SOUTH CHICAGO—Exchange av. cor. 91st. Pastor, Rev. Isaac Anderson.

THIRD—5th av. cor. 33d. Pastor, Rev. M. L. Wickman.

UNION AV.— Union av. cor. 60th. Pastor, Rev. Blomquist.

NORWEGIAN AND DANISH.

Presiding Elder Chicago District, Norwegian Conference — Rev. Frederick King, Evanston.

EVANSTON—Pastor, Rev. G. Mathisen.

FIRST—Grand av. se. cor. N. Sangamon. Pastor, Rev. Jas. Sanaker.

IMMANUEL—232 W. Huron. Pastor, Rev. H. C. Munson.

KEDZIE AVENUE—N. Kedzie av. nr. Cortland. Pastor, Rev. Andrew Hansen.

MAPLEWOOD AVENUE—N. Maplewood av. cor. LeMoyne av. Pastor, Rev. L. A. Larson.

MORELAND—Pastor, Rev. O. A. Wierson.

NORTH AVENUE—W. North av. nr. 42d av. Pastor, Rev. B. Carlson.

PARK SIDE AND WEST PULLMAN—Pastor, Rev. Jens J. Petersen.

New Jerusalem (Swedenborgian).

ENGLEWOOD — 70th and Stewart av. Pastor, Rev. Thomas A. King.

KENWOOD—42d cor. Berkeley av. Pastor, Rev. L. P. Mercer.

IMMANUEL—434 Carroll av. Pastor, Rev. N. D. Pendleton.

NORTH SIDE—757 N. Clark. Revs. L. P. Mercer and Thomas A. King.

SECOND NEW CHURCH SOCIETY—1140 W. Division. Pastor, Rev. A. J. Bartels.

Presbyterian.

AUSTIN FIRST—Lake and Central av. Pastor, Rev. Samuel M. Johnson.

AVONDALE — Avondale. Pastor, Rev. C. Boyd Becker.

BELDEN AVENUE — Belden av. cor. Seminary av. Pastor, Rev. Robert D. Scott.

BERWYN — Pastor, Rev. James R. Kay.

BETHANY — Humboldt Park boul. cor. Cortland. Pastor, Rev. C. A. Wilson.

BRIGHTON PARK—38th nr. Sacramento av. Pastor, Rev. James Maclaughlan.

BROOKLINE—73d cor. Jackson av. Pastor, Rev. J. A. Gray.

CALVARY — W. Harrison cor. S. 40th av. Rev. G. A. Mitchell.

CAMPBELL PARK — S. Leavitt sw. cor. Harrison. Pastor, Rev. Philip F. Matzinger.

CENTRAL PARK — Warren av. cor. S. Sacramento av. Pastor, Rev. H. H. Van Vranken.

COVENANT—N. Halsted se. cor. Belden av. Pastor, Rev. W. S. Plummer Bryan.

DOUGLAS PARK—Sawyer av. cor. W. 12th. Pastor, Rev. S. M. Marsh.

EDGEWATER — Winthrop and Hollywood av. Pastor, ——.

EIGHTH — Washington boul. nw. cor. S. Robey. Pastor, Rev. Thos. D. Wallace, D.D.

ELEVENTH—Washtenaw av. cor. Crystal. Pastor, Rev. Robt. H. Westwood.

EMERALD AVENUE — Emerald av. and W. 67th. Pastor, Rev. S. M. Campbell.

ENDEAVOR—Cornelia and N. Paulina. Pastor, Rev. Walter E. Price.

EVANSTON FIRST—Chicago av. and Lake, Evanston. Pastor, Rev. John H. Boyd.

ENGLEWOOD——64th cor. Yale. Pastor, Rev. W. H. Robinson, D.D.

FIFTH—Indiana av. cor. 30th. Pastor, Rev. W. Francis Irwin.

FIRST—Indiana av. cor. 21st. Pastor, Rev. W. J. Chichester.

FIRST GERMAN—Willow cor. Orchard. Pastor, Rev. Daniel Volz.

FORTY-FIRST STREET — Grand boul. cor. 41st. Pastor, Rev. Howard A. Johnston.

FORTY-EIGHTH AVENUE — S. 48th av. cor. Fulton. Pastor, Rev. H. M. Shields.

FOURTH—Rush cor. Superior. Pastor, Rev. ——.

FULLERTON AVENUE—Fullerton av. nw. cor. Larrabee. Pastor, Rev. J. A. Rondthaler, D.D.

GRACE (colored)— 3409 Dearborn Pastor, Rev. M. H. Jackson.

HIGHLAND PARK — Highland Park. Pastor, Rev. A. A. Pfanstiehl.

HINSDALE — Hinsdale. Pastor, Rev. D. S. Johnson.

IMMANUEL — Bonfield cor. 31st. Pastor, Rev. E. B. Hubbell.

ITALIAN—W. Ohio cor. Milwaukee av. Pastor, Rev. Fillipo Grilli.

JEFFERSON PARK—W. Adams cor. Throop. Pastor, Rev. F. DeWitt Talmage.

LAGRANGE — LaGrange. Pastor, Rev. Arthur M. Little.

LAKE FOREST—Lake Forest. Pastor, Rev. J. G. K. McClure.

LAKE VIEW—Evanston av. cor. Addison. Pastor, Rev. Frank M. Carson.

MAYWOOD — Maywood. Pastor, Rev. C. H. Currens.

MILLARD AVENUE—Millard av. cor. W. 22d. Pastor, ——.

MORGAN PARK—Morgan Park. Pastor, W. A. Eisenhart.

NINTH—S. Ashland av. cor. Hastings. Pastor, ——.

NORMAL PARK—W. 69th cor. Yale. Pastor, Rev. H. Atwood Percival.

OAK PARK—Oak Park. Pastor, Rev. Charles S. Hoyt.

OLIVET MEMORIAL—Penn cor. Vedder. Pastor, Rev. Norman B. Barr.

ONWARD—N. Leavitt and W. Ohio. Pastor, Rev. J. H. Collins.

PULLMAN—Pastor, ——.

RIDGEWAY AVENUE—233 N. Ridgeway av. nr. W. Huron. Pastor, Rev. Henry C. Buell.

RIVER FOREST — River Forest. Pastor, Rev. Jos. N. Boyd.

RIVERSIDE — Riverside. Pastor, Rev. Chas. C. Snyder.

SCOTCH WESTMINSTER—S. Sangamon cor. W. Adams. Pastor, Rev. A. Dunlop King.

SECOND—Michigan av. cor. 20th. Pastor, Rev. Simon J. McPherson, D.D.

SEVENTH—South Englewood. Pastor, Rev. H. S. Jenkinson.

SIXTH—Vincennes av. cor. 36th. Pastor, Rev. Wm. P. Merrill.

SIXTIETH STREET—W. 60th cor. Princeton av. Pastor, ——.

SOUTH CHICAGO—Houston av. cor. 92d. Pastor, Rev. Samuel Charles Black.

SOUTH EVANSTON—Main and Hinman av., Evanston. Pastor, Rev. A. W. Ringland.

SOUTH SIDE TABERNACLE—3825 Dearborn. Pastor, Rev. D. A. McWilliams.

TENTH—W. 46th cor. Emerald av. Pastor, Rev. Daniel E. Long.

THIRD—S. Ashland av. cor. Ogden av. Pastor, Rev. Wm. J. McGaughan.

WEST DIVISION STREET—308 W. Division. Pastor, Rev. Geo. B. Laird.

WINDSOR PARK—76th nr. Bond av. Rev. LeRoy Hooker.

WOODLAWN PARK — 64th cor. Kimbark av. Pastor, Rev. Edward H. Curtis.

Reformed Churches.

BETHANY—111th w. of State (Roseland). Pastor, Rev. G. J. Hekhuis.

IRVING PARK—Irving Park. Pastor, Rev. J. W. Brooks, Ph.D.

NORWOOD PARK—Norwood Park. Pastor, Rev. J. N. Hutchinson.

TRINITY— 440 S. Marshfield av. Pastor, Rev. P. Moerdyke.

HOLLAND.

ENGLEWOOD — 62d cor. Peoria. Pastor, Rev. L. Dykstra.

FIRST—Hastings nr. Ashland av. Pastor, Rev. R. H. Joldersma.

FIRST CHURCH OF GANO—Perry av. cor. 117th. Pastor, Rev. J. W. Poot.

FIRST ROSELAND—Michigan av. sw. cor. 107th (Roseland). Pastor, Rev. B. VanEss.

NORTHWESTERN — W. Superior bet. N. Robey and Hoyne av. Pastor, Rev. S. V. Vander Werf.

HOLLAND CHRISTIAN.

HOLLAND CHRISTIAN RE-FORMED—523 W. 14th. Pastor, John Riemersma, D.D.

HOLLAND CHRISTIAN RE-FORMED—948, 71st. Pastor, Rev. L. Van Dellen.

HOLLAND CHRISTIAN RE FORMED (FIRST)—111th, Roseland Pastor, Rev. John Robbert.

HOLLAND CHRISTIAN RE-FORMED (SECOND)—106th, Roseland. Pastor, Rev. K. Kuiper.

Reformed Church in the United States.

BOHEMIAN CHURCH — 561 W. 61st. Pastor, Rev. Charles V. Molnar.

FIRST GERMAN CHURCH—177 and 179 Hastings. Pastor, Rev. Arnold A. K. Heinemann.

GRACE CHURCH—Jackson boul. cor. S. Washtenaw av. Pastor, Rev. John M. Kendig.

HUNGARIAN CHURCH—9231 Houston av. Pastor, Rev. Alexander Harsanyi.

THIRD FRIEDENS CHURCH—1330 Wellington. Pastor, Rev. John Traeger.

Roman Catholic.

Archbishop of Chicago—Most Rev. Patrick A. Feehan, D.D.

Vicar-General—Very Rev. D. M. J. Dowling.

Chancellor and Secretary—Rev. N. J. Mooney.

CATHEDRAL OF THE HOLY NAME—Cor. Superior and N. State. Rector, Rev. M. J. Fitzsimmons.

ALL SAINTS'—Wallace sw. cor. 25th pl. Pastor, Rev. J. C. Gillan.

CHAPEL OF OUR LADY OF MERCY—St. Paul's Home, 363 Jackson boul. Pastor, Rev. D. S. Mahoney.

CHURCH OF NOTRE DAME DE CHICAGO (French)—Vernon Park pl. cor. Sibley. Pastor, Rev. Achille L. Bergeron.

CHURCH OF OUR LADY OF GOOD COUNSEL (Bohemian)—N. Western av. cor. Cornelia. Pastor, Rev. John Hodic.

CHURCH OF OUR LADY OF LOURDES—N. Ashland av. cor Leland av. Pastor, Rev. F. N. Perry.

CHURCH OF OUR LADY OF LOURDES (Bohemian)—S. 42d av. cor. W. 15th. Pastor, Rev. J. C. Oeenezak, O.S.B.

CHURCH OF OUR LADY OF MOUNT CARMEL—859 Bissel. Pastor, Rev. P. D. Gill.

CHURCH OF OUR LADY OF SORROWS—1406 Jackson boul. Pastor, Rev. Hugh Crevier.

CHURCH OF OUR LADY OF THE ANGELS—N. Hamlin av. cor. Iowa. Pastor, Rev. J. A. Hynes.

CHURCH OF THE ANNUNCIATION B. V. M.—N. Paulina sw. cor. Wabansia av. Pastor, Rev. Hugh O'Gara McShane.

CHURCH OF THE ASSUMPTION B. V. M. (Italian)—Illinois nr. Orleans. Rev. Thos. Moreschini, O.S.

CHURCH OF THE BLESSED SACRAMENT—993 S. Central Park av. Pastors, Revs. J. M. Dunne and J. T. Bennett.

CHURCH OF THE HOLY ANGELS—281 Oakwood boul. Pastor, Rev. Dennis A. Tighe.

CHURCH OF THE HOLY CROSS —6604 Jackson av. Rev. D. Hisben and Rev. H. J. Wills.

CHURCH OF THE HOLY FAMILY—W. 12th cor. S. May. Rector, Very Rev. J. Hoeffer, S.J.; Pastor, Rev. M. J. Dowling, S. J.

CHURCH OF THE HOLY GHOST—(German) W. Adams cor. S. 43d av. Pastor, Rev. Joseph Wanner.

CHURCH OF THE HOLY ROSARY—113th sw. cor. South Park av. (Pullman). Pastor, Rev. P. J. Tinan.

CHURCH OF THE IMMACULATE CONCEPTION—North Park av. and Schiller. Pastor, Rev. P. T Butler.

CHURCH OF THE NATIVITY OF OUR LORD—37th cor. Union av. Pastor, Rev. Joseph M. Cartan.

CHURCH OF THE SACRED HEART—se. cor. W. 19th and Johnson. Pastor, Rev. J. A. Dowling, S. J.

CHURCH OF THE SACRED HEART—70th cor. S. May. Pastor, Rev. A. J. Wolfgarten.

CHURCH OF ST. CATHERINE OF SIENNA—Austin. Pastor, Rev. L. Campbell.

CHURCH OF THE VISITATION —Garfield boul. cor. S. Peoria. Pastor, D. F. McGuire.

HOLY TRINITY (German)—S.Lincoln cor. W. Taylor. Pastor, Rev. F. Burelbach.

HOLY TRINITY (Polish) — 540 Noble. Pastor Rev. Casimir Sztuczko.

IMMACULATE CONCEPTION B. V. M. (German)—Bonfield cor. 31st. Pastor, Rev. Peter Faber.

IMMACULATE CONCEPTION B. V. M. (Polish)—Commercial av. nw. cor. 88th. Pastor, Rev. J. M. Wojtalewicz.

ST. ADALBERT'S (Polish)—cor. W. 17th and S. Paulina. Pastor, Rev. J. Radziejewski.

ST. AGATHA—Douglas boul. and S. Kedzie av. Pastor, Rev. M. Bonfield.

ST. AGNES—S. Washtenaw av. nr. 38th, Brighton Park. Pastor, Rev. N. J. Hitchcock.

ST. AILBE—92d and Washington av. Pastor, Rev. W. S. Hennessy.

ST. ALOYSIUS' (German)—247 Le-Moyne. Pastor, Rev. A. J. Thiele.

ST. ALPHONSUS' (German)—Lincoln av. cor. Southport av. Pastor, Rev. Wm. Loewekamp.

ST. ANDREW'S—Addison and N. Paulina. Pastor, Rev. A. Croke.

ST. ANN'S—cor. 55th and Wentworth av. Pastor, Rev. P. M. Flannigan.

ST. ANTHONY OF PADUA (German)—S. Canal se. cor. 24th pl. Pastor, Rev. Peter Fischer.

ST. AUGUSTINE'S (German)— Laflin and 51st. Rev. S. Forstmann, O. S. F.

ST. BERNARD'S—66th and Stewart av. Pastor, Rev. Bernard P. Murray.

ST. BONIFACE'S (German)—Cornell cor. Noble. Pastor, Rev. A. Evers.

ST. BRENDAN'S — W. 67th and Bishop. Rev. M. T. Mackin.

ST. BRIDGET'S—Archer av. cor. Church ct. Pastor, Very Rev. Daniel M. J. Dowling, V. G.

ST. CASIMIR'S (Polish) — 1007 Whipple. Pastor, Rev. A. Furman.

ST. CATHERINE OF GENOA— 118th and Lowe av. Pastor, Rev. W. M. Foley.

ST. CECELIA'S—W. 45th pl. nr. Wentworth av. Pastor, Rev. E. A. Kelly.

ST. CHARLES BORROMEO'S— 91 Cypress. Pastor, Rev. P. J. Muldoon.

ST. CLARA'S—64th cor. Woodlawn av. Pastor, Rev. J. Schikowski.

ST. COLUMBA—133d and Green Bay av. Pastor, Rev. Francis Knoll.

ST. COLUMBKILL'S—Cor. N. Paulina and Grand av. Pastor, Rev. Thomas Burke.

STS. CYRIL AND METHODIUS (Bohemian)—W. 50th cor.S. Hermitage av. Pastor, Rev. Thomas Bobal.

ST. DIONYSIUS'—Hawthorne. Pastor, Rev. Charles A. Erkenswick.

ST. ELIZABETH'S—41st cor. Wabash av. Pastor, Rev. D. J. Riordan.

ST. FRANCIS OF ASSISIUM (German)—W. 12th cor. Newberry av. Pastor, Rev. D. M. Thiele.

ST. FRANCIS DE SALES—Avenue K cor. to2d. Rector, Rev. J. Diekman.

ST. FRANCIS XAVIER (German)—299 Warsaw av. Rev. E. Goldschmidt.

ST. FRANCIS XAVIER—LaGrange. Pastor, Rev. John M. Hagan.

ST. GABRIEL'S—W. 45th se. cor. Wallace. Pastor, Rev. M. J. Dorney.

ST. GEORGE'S (German) — 3924 Wentworth av. Pastor, Rev. J. Dittmers.

ST. GEORGE'S (Lithuanian)—33d cor. 32d pl. Pastor, Rev. M. Krawezunias.

ST. HEDWIG'S (Polish)—W. Webster and N. Hamilton avs. Pastor, Rev. J. Piechowski.

ST. HENRY'S—Ridge and Devon avs. Pastor, Rev. J. Rutershoff.

ST. JAMES'—Wabash av. cor. 29th. Pastor, Rev. Hugh McGuire.

ST. JARLATH'S—S. Hermitage av. cor. Jackson boul. Pastor, Rev. T. F. Cashman.

ST. JEROME'S CHURCH — Lunt av. cor. Forest. Pastor, Rev. A. P. Lonergan.

ST. JOHN BAPTIST (French) — 1041 W. 51st. Pastor, Rev. T. Ouimet.

ST. JOHN THE BAPTIST (Syrian-Arabian) 323 Franklin. Pastor, Rev. B. Souaya.

ST. JOHN'S—18th cor. Clark. Rector, Rev. Alex. J. McGavick.

ST. JOHN'S CHURCH—Turner av. ne. cor. W. 52d. Pastor, Rev. J. C. Lesage.

ST. JOHN CANTIUS (Polish)—Carpenter cor. Front. Pastor, Rev. J. Kasprzycki.

ST. JOHN NEPOMUCENE'S (Bohemian)—25th cor. Princeton av. Pastor, Rev. Francis Bobal.

ST. JOSAPHAT'S (Polish)—Belden av. cor. Southport av. Pastor, Rev. F. Lange.

ST. JOSEPH'S (German Priory)—Orleans cor. Hill. Pastor, Very Rev. C. Strattmann, O.S.B.

ST. JOSEPH'S (French)—2033, 38th pl. Rev. J. C. Lesage.

ST. JOSEPH'S (Polish)—W. 48th and S. Paulina. Rev. M. Pyplatz.

ST. KEVIN'S—105th se.cor. Torrence av. Pastor, Rev. Timothy O'Sullivan.

ST. LAWRENCE—73d cor. Madison av., Grand Crossing. Pastor, Rev. S. Maloney.

ST. LEO'S—Butler cor. 79th pl. Pastor, Rev. P. A. L. Egan.

ST. LOUIS'—Curtis av. sw. cor. 114th. Pastor, Rev. J. B. Bourassa.

ST. LUDMILLA'S—W. 24th cor. S. Albany av. Rev. M. Farnik.

ST. MALACHY'S — Walnut cor. N. Western av. Pastor, Rev. Thomas P. Hodnett.

ST. MARGARETH'S — 99th cor. Vincennes av. Pastor, Rev. S. P. McDonnell.

ST. MARK APOSTLE — N. Campbell av. cor. Thomas. Pastor, Rev. T. Kearns.

ST. MARTIN'S (German)—W. 59th cor. Princeton av. Pastor, Rev. J. Schaefers.

ST. MARY'S—Wabash av. cor. Eldredge pl. Rector, Rev. E. A. Murphy.

ST. MARY'S (German)—Riverdale. Attended from St. Joseph's.

ST. MARY'S OF CZENTOCHOWA—34th cor. Linden av. Pastor, Rev. C. F. Slominski.

ST. MARY'S OF PERPETUAL HELP (Polish)—32d and Mosspratt. Pastor, Rev. S. Nawocki.

ST. MATHIAS—Bowmanville. Pastor, Rev. M. E. Erz.

ST. MATTHEW'S—Walnut cor. N. Francisco av. Pastor, Rev. J. Flood.

ST. MAURITIUS' — 36th and S. Hoyne av. Pastor, Rev. D. Konen.

ST. MEL'S—Washington boul. cor. S. 43d av. Pastor, Rev. P. J. McDonnell.

ST. MICHAEL'S (German)—Eugenie cor. Cleveland av. Pastor, Rev. A. Herz, C.S.S.R.

ST. MICHAEL'S (Polish)—83d cor. Ontario av. Pastor, Rev. Paul Rohde.

ST. MONICA'S—36th cor. Dearborn. Attended from St. Elizabeth's.

ST. NICOLAS' (German) — 113th Place and State. Pastor, Rev. Theodore A. Bonifas.

ST. PATRICK'S—Commercial av. nr. 95th. Pastor, Rev. M. Van de Laar.

ST. PATRICK'S—S. Desplaines cor. W. Adams. Pastor, Rev. Thomas F. Galligan.

ST. PAUL'S (German)—164 W. 22d pl. Pastor, Rev. Geo. Heldman.

ST. PETER'S (German)—Clark cor. Polk. Rev. P. Kohnen, O.S.F.

SS. PETER AND PAUL—91st cor. Exchange av., South Chicago. Pastor, Rev. George J. Blatter.

ST. PHILOMENA'S—Cortland cor. N. 41st ct. Pastor, Rev. P. Faber.

ST. PIUS'—S. Ashland av. se. cor. W. 19th. Pastor, Rev. F. S. Henneberry.

ST. PROCOPIUS' (Bohemian)— Allport cor. W. 18th. Pastor, Rev. Procopius Neuzil.

ST. ROSE OF LIMA—Ashland av. nr. W. 48th. Pastor, Rev. Dennis Hayes.

ST. STANISLAUS KOSTKA'S(Polish)—Noble cor. Ingraham. Superior, Very Rev. Vincent Barzynski, C. R.

ST. STEPHEN'S—N. Sangamon cor. W. Ohio. Pastor, Rev. Dominic Egan.

ST. SYLVESTER'S — 895 N. Humboldt. Pastor, Rev. Michael O'Brien.

ST. TERESA'S (German)—Centre cor. Osgood. Pastor, Rev. Mathias W. Barth.

ST. THOMAS'—55th and Kimbark av. Pastor, Rev. J. J. Carroll.

ST. VIATEUR'S—W. Belmont cor. N. 40th av. Pastor, Very Rev. C. Fournier, P. S. V.

ST. VINCENT DE PAUL'S—Webster av. cor. Osgood. Pastor, Very Rev. T. J. Smith.

ST. VITUS—S. Paulina cor. W. 18th pl. Pastor, Rev. A. Rebec.

ST. WENCESLAUS' (Bohemian) —173 DeKoven. Pastor, Rev. Joseph Molitor.

The Salvation Army.

NORTH WESTERN CHIEF DIVISIONAL HEADQUARTERS — 84 Adams st. Dexter bldg. Lieut.-Colonel Geo. French, chief divisional officer.

CORPS.

WEST SIDE.

558 W. Madison Street.
1026 W. Madison Street.
154 N. 48th Avenue.
53 Desplaines Street.
244 Grand Avenue (Norwegian).

SOUTH SIDE.

3761 Cottage Grove Avenue.
4029 State Street.
3202 State Street.
365, 63d Street.
3515 Jefferson Avenue.
63d and S. Halsted Streets.
315 S. Clark Street.
Corner State and Monroe Streets (open air work).
8931 Buffalo Avenue, Swedish.
2967 Wentworth Avenue, Swedish.
5240 Wentworth Avenue, Swedish.
6116 Aberdeen Street, Swedish.
10957 Michigan Avenue, Swedish.

NORTH SIDE.

501 Lincoln Avenue.
1014 Sheffield av., Swedish.
96 Oak, Swedish.

EDUCATIONAL DEPARTMENT.

MEN'S TRAINING HOME — 558 W. Madison.

WOMEN'S TRAINING HOME— 334 W. Monroe.

SOCIAL DEPARTMENT.

SLUM WORK.

NO. 1 POST—53 Desplaines.
NO. 2 POST—315 S. Clark.
NO. 3 POST—82 W. 15th.

WORKING MEN'S HOTELS.

EVANGELINE—387 S. Clark
HARBOR LIGHT—118 W. Madison.
BEACON LIGHT—515 State.

WORKING WOMEN'S HOTEL.

MINA—544 Wabash av.

SALVAGE DEPARTMENT.

SALVAGE WAREHOUSE — rear 411 Harrison
SALVAGE STORE — 2522 Wentworth av.

RESCUE WORK.

HOME—6201 Wabash av.

MISCELLANEOUS.

LABOR BUREAU—558 W. Madison.

DISPENSARY—3761 Cottage Grove av.

SHOE AND FURNITURE REPAIR SHOP—2522 Wentworth av.

EXPRESS AND LAUNDRY OFFICE—556 W. Madison.

Volunteers of-America.

Western Territorial Headquarters and Training Fort—456 W. Madison, Waverly Theatre. Territorial Com. Brig.-Gen. Edward Fielding.

CHICAGO POST No. 1—456 W. Madison.

CHICAGO POST No. 3—644 W. 63d.

CHICAGO POST No. 4—Evanston.

CHICAGO POST No. 5—3525 State.

CHICAGO POST No. 10—865 North av.

CHICAGO POST No. 11—Rogers Park.

Union Evangelical.

BETHANY UNION—Prospect av· cor 103d. Pastor Rev. Geo. E. Hunt.

BRYN MAWR—7149 Jeffrey av. Pastor, Rev. F. W. Ellis.

KENWOOD EVANGELICAL— Greenwood av. and 46th.

OAKWOODS UNION—Champlain av. and 65th. Pastor, Rev. T.W. Stamp.

ST. PAUL'S EVANGELICAL— Howard ct. cor. 94th. Rev. Columbus Bradford.

Unitarian.

CHURCH OF THE MESSIAH— Michigan boul. se. cor. 23d. Pastor, Rev. W. W. Fenn.

MEMORIAL CHAPEL—57th cor. Woodlawn av. Pastor, Rev. W. W. Fenn.

THIRD—W. Monroe cor. Kedzie av. Pastor, Rev. F. C. Southworth.

UNITY—Dearborn av. se. cor. Walton pl. Pastor, Rev. John S. Thomson

United Evangelical.

Bishop, Rudolph Dubs, D.D., LL.D., 81 S. Robey. Presiding Elder, Rev. F. Busse, 4358 Dearborn av.

ADAMS STREET—W. Adams cor. S. Robey. Pastor, Rev. Edwin Woodring.

DIVERSEY STREET—Diversey nw. cor. Bissell. Pastor, Rev. John G. Fidder.

EMANUEL—4638 Dearborn. Pastor, Rev. C. M. Kaufmann.

NORTH ASHLAND AV.—N. Ashland av. cor. Noble av. Pastor, Rev. Albert Lutz.

SOUTHWEST—Sacramento av. sw. cor. Harvey. Pastor, Rev. C. A. Walz.

ZION'S—N. Hoyne av. cor. Iowa. Pastor, Rev. C. A. Fuessle.

United Presbyterian.

FIRST—W. Monroe sw. cor. S. Paulina. Pastor, Rev. Wm. T. Meloy.

SECOND—Honore cor. 63d. Pastor, Rev. J. A. Duff.

THIRD—43d cor. Champlain av. Pastor, Rev. E. B. Stewart.

FOURTH—1080 W. Polk. Rev. J. A. Collins, D.D.

FIFTH—Ravenswood. Pastor, Rev. Ralph Atkinson.

SIXTH—62d cor. Oglesby av. Pastor, Rev. Riley Little.

SEVENTH—S. Central Park av. cor. W. Congress. Pastor, Rev. T. V. Dugan.

EIGHTH—Garfield boul. cor. Aberdeen. Pastor, Rev. J. B. Courtney.

Universalists.

CHURCH OF THE REDEEMER —Warren av. ne. cor. Robey. Pastor, Rev. T. B. Gregory.

ST. PAUL'S—Prairie av. cor. 30th. Pastor, Rev. A. J. Canfield, D.D.

CHURCH OF OUR FATHER—844 Burling. Pastor, Rev. R. Jardine.

STEWART AVENUE — 65th st. and Stewart av. Pastor, Rev. R. A. White.

RYDER CHAPEL—Woodlawn Park. Rev. F. W. Millar.

UNITY—Oak Park. Pastor, Rev. R. F. Johanet.

Miscellaneous.

APOSTOLIC CATHOLIC—Ss. Locust, w. Franklin. Pastor, Rev. James Grundy.

ARMOUR MISSION—33d se. cor. Armour av. Pastor, Rev. D. C. Milner.

CHICAGO SEVENTH DAY BAPTIST CHURCH—40 Randolph. Pastor, Rev. Lester C. Randolph.

CHURCH OF CHRIST — Pastor, Rev. F. S. Van Eps, 64th cor. Woodlawn av.

CHURCH OF THE SOUL—412 Masonic Temple. Pastor, Mrs. Cora L. V. Richmond.

COTTAGE GROVE AVENUE CHAPEL—2427 Cottage Grove av. Pastor, Rev. John Cordingly.

DISCIPLES OF CHRIST—Meet every First Day at 10:30 a. m. and 7:30 p. m. at 23 and 25 Kendall.

FIRST CHURCH OF CHRIST— (Scientist) 4015 Drexel boul.

GERMAN ADVENT CHURCH—274 Augusta. Pastor, Rev. C. M. Koier.

KIRKLAND MISSION—111 S. Halsted. Pastor, Rev. M. E. Hulbert.

PACIFIC GARDEN MISSION—100 E. Vanburen, Supt. Mrs. Geo. R. Clarke; Asst. Supt. Harry Monroe. Meetings every evening.

PEOPLE'S INSTITUTE—(Undenominational) Vanburen cor.S.Leavitt.

SEAMEN'S BETHEL—East end Randolph street viaduct. Chaplain, Rev. Edward R. Pierce.

THEOSOPHICAL SOCIETY—(Chicago Branch) 424, 26 Van Buren.

UNION GOSPEL MISSION—368 W. Lake. Supt., E. W. Allen.

CONSULS IN CHICAGO.

ARGENTINE REPUBLIC—134 Vanburen. Consul, P. S. Hudson.

AUSTRO-HUNGARIAN — 620 Dearborn av. Acting-Consul, Alexander Nuber.

BELGIUM—940, 108 Lasalle. Consul, Charles Henrotin.

BRAZIL—205, 19 Wabash av. Consul, Stuart R. Alexander.

CHILE—57, 22d, Consul, Mathew J. Steffens.

DENMARK—407, 59 Dearborn. Consul, C. H. Hanson. Vice-Consuls, Villas K. Assens, Wilhelm Weimann.

FRANCE—1511 Ashland blk. Consul, Henri Mernon; V.-Consul-Chancellor, J. Gabriel Viellhomme.

GERMAN EMPIRE—8th floor Schiller bldg. Consul, Karl Buenz; Vice-Consul, Dr. J. A. Lettenbaur; Sec., Carl Schinkel.

GREAT BRITAIN — 630 Pullman bldg. Consul, William Wyndham. V.-Consul, A. R. Getty.

GREECE — Corn Exchange Bank. Consul-General, Charles L.Hutchinson.

ITALY—500, 56, 5th av. Consul, Anthony Rozwadowski.

MEXICO—4009 Drexel boul. Consul, Felipe Berriozabal, jr.

NETHERLANDS—85 Washington. Consul, Geo. Birkhoff, jr.

PERU — 501, 358 Dearborn. Consul, Charles H. Sergel.

PORTUGAL—353, 53d. S. Chapman Simms.

RUSSIA—56, 5th av. Consul, Baron A. A. Schlippenbach.

SWEDEN AND NORWAY — 142 Washington. V.-Consul, John R. Lindgren.

SWITZERLAND—165 Washington. Consul, A. Holinger.

TURKEY — 404, 160 Washington. Consul, Chas. Henrotin.

URUGUAY REPUBLIC—307, 134 Vanburen. Consul, C. C. Turner.

VENEZUELA — 228 N. Franklin. Consul, R. Philip Gormully.

EDUCATIONAL.

BOARD OF EDUCATION.
12th floor, 109 Randolph.
Office open—From 9 a. m. to 5 p. m.
Saturdays from 9 a. m. to 1 p. m.
President—Graham H. Harris.
Vice-President—Thomas Gallagher.
Secretary—W. A. S. Graham.

. MEMBERS OF THE BOARD.

Christian Meier. Term expires 1899.
Thomas Brenan. Term expires 1899.
Daniel R. Cameron. Term expires 1899.
Mrs. Isabella O'Keefe. Term expires 1901.
Graham H. Harris. Term expires 1900.
Je e Sherwood. Term expires 1900.
Bennard F. Rogers. Term expires 1900.
Joseph S. Schwab. Term expires 1900.
Thomas Gallagher. Term expires 1900.
John T. Keating. Term expires 1900.
Alfred S. Trude. Term expires 1901.
Joseph Downey. Term expires 1901.
W. S. Christopher. Term expires 1901.
F. J. Loesch. Term expires 1901.
Mrs. Caroline K. Sherman. Term expires 1900.
C. R. Walleck. Term expires 1901.
Austin J. Sexton. Term expires 1901.
Joseph H. Strong. Term expires 1899.
George E. Adams. Term expires 1899.
Clayton Mark. Term expires 1899.
H. H. Gross. Term expires 1899.
Regular meetings of the Board are held on alternate Wednesday evenings.
Superintendent of Schools — E. Benjamin Andrews.

Assistant Superintendents of Schools—Edward C. Delano, Albert R. Sabin, Ella F. Young, Leslie Lewis, James Hannan, A. F. Nightingale, A. Kirk, W. W. Speer, Albert G. Lane.

Clerk and School Agent—W. A. S. Graham.

Business Manager—John A. Guilford.

Chief Engineer—Thomas J. Waters.

Auditor—George G. Custer.

Superintendent of Supplies — John W. Foster.

Architect—Normand S. Patton.

Free Kindergartens.

CHICAGO FREE KINDERGARTEN ASSOCIATION — Armour av. cor. 33d. H. N. Higinbotham, Pres.; W. E. Kelley, Treas.; Richard Nash, Rec. Sec.; Mrs. L.A. Hagans, Cor. Sec.

NORMAL AND TRAINING DEPARTMENT.

Faculty—Miss Eva B. Whitmore, General Superintendent; Miss Anna E. Bryan, Principal of Normal, and Training Department, Miss Alice Temple, Physical Culture; Mrs. Jessie L. Gaynor, Vocal Music; Mrs. Crosby Adams, Instrumental Music; Lucy S. Silke, Drawing; Prof. Louis C. Monin, History of Education.

THE KINDERGARTENS.

ARMOUR—33d and Armour av.

A. P. KELLEY — N. Morgan cor. Grand av.

CHAS. KOZMINSKI—54th cor. Ingleside av.

DIVISION STREET—308 W. Division.

DOOLITTLE — 35th cor. Cottage Grove av.

ELEANOR REID—2541 Calumet av.

FORRESTVILLE — 45th and St. Lawrence av.

GADSHILL — W. 22d pl. cor. S. Wood.

HALSTED STREET—784 S. Halsted.

KEITH—34th cor. Dearborn.

MARGARET ETTER — 2421 Wabash av.

MARIE CHAPEL—Wentworth av. cor. 23d pl.

PLYMOUTH—3027 Butler.

SIXTH PRESBYTERIAN — Vincennes av. cor. 36th.

SOUTH SIDE TABERNACLE—3825 Dearborn.

ST. PAUL'S—30th and Prairie av.

UNION AV.—Union av. cor. W. 44th.

UNIVERSITY CONGREGATIONAL CHURCH—Madison av. cor. 56th.

WALTER SCOTT—65th cor. Washington av.

Chicago Kindergarten College.

10 Vanburen. Mrs. J. N. Crouse, Director; Elizabeth Harrison, Principal.

HOSPITALS.

ALEXIAN BROTHERS HOSPITAL—Belden and Racine avs.

AUGUSTANA HOSPITAL — 480 Cleveland av.

BENNETT HOSPITAL—Ada nw. cor. Fulton.

CHICAGO BAPTIST HOSPITAL—3400 to 3418 Rhodes av.

CHICAGO CHARITY HOSPITAL—2407 Dearborn.

CHICAGO EYE AND EAR HOSPITAL—3111 Indiana av.

CHICAGO HOMEOPATHIC HOSPITAL—S. Wood se. cor. York.

CHICAGO HOSPITAL — 49th nr. Drexel boul.

CHICAGO LYING-IN HOSPITAL—298 Maxwell.

CHICAGO MATERNITY HOSPITAL—703 N. Clark.

CHICAGO OPHTHALMIC HOSPITAL—607 W. Vanburen.

CHICAGO POLICLINIC AND HOSPITAL—174 and 176 Chicago av.

COLUMBIA HOSPITAL—334 S. Wood.

COOK COUNTY HOSPITAL—W. Harrison cor. S. Wood.

DETENTION HOSPITAL—S. Wood nw. cor. W. Polk.

ENGLEWOOD UNION HOSPITAL—826 to 830 W. 65th

GERMAN HOSPITAL—754 and 756 Larrabee.

HAHNEMANN HOSPITAL—2812 to 2816 Groveland av.

ILLINOIS CHARITABLE EYE AND EAR INFIRMARY—227 W. Adams.

ISOLATION HOSPITAL—S. Lawndale av. cor. W. 35th.

JENNER HOSPITAL—385 Washington boul.

Streeter Hospital

2646 CALUMET AVE.

For the Treatment of Chronic Diseases

The finest Private Hospital in the world. Rooms, board and nursing
from $25.00 to $35.00 per Week.

JOHN W. STREETER, M.D.   **E. H. PRATT, M.D.**

SHELDON LEAVITT, M.D.   **JOSEPH H. LOW, M.D.**

SURGEONS IN ATTENDANCE.

MILDRED R. WINANS, Superintendent

LAKESIDE HOSPITAL — 4147 Lake av.,

LINNÆAN HOSPITAL — 233 Lasalle av.

MARINE HOSPITAL—N. Halsted nr. Graceland av. five miles north of court house, on lake shore. Office, Rand-McNally bldg. rooms 315 to 319.

MARY THOMPSON HOSPITAL OF CHICAGO FOR WOMEN AND CHILDREN—W. Adams nw. cor. S. Paulina.

MAURICE PORTER MEMORIAL FREE HOSPITAL FOR CHILDREN —606 Fullerton av.

MERCY HOSPITAL—Calumet av. cor. 26th.

MICHAEL REESE HOSPITAL— 29th ne. cor. Groveland av.

NATIONAL TEMPERANCE HOSPITAL AND SANITARIUM —1619 Diversey av.

NORWEGIAN LUTHERAN TABITHA HOSPITAL — N. Francisco av. sw. cor. Thomas.

PASSAVANT MEMORIAL HOSPITAL—194 Superior.

POST-GRADUATE HOSPITAL— (Under direction of Post-Graduate Medical School.) Dearborn sw. cor. 24th.

PRESBYTERIAN HOSPITAL—W. Congress s.e. cor. S. Wood.

PROVIDENT HOSPITAL AND TRAINING SCHOOL—2900 Dearborn.

ST. ANTHONY'S HOSPITAL—W. 19th cor. Douglas boul.

ST. ELIZABETH'S HOSPITAL— N. Claremont av. se. cor. Lemoyne.

ST. JOSEPH'S HOSPITAL—360 Garfield av. nw. cor. Burling.

ST. LUKE'S HOSPITAL—1426 to 1436 Indiana av.

ST. MARY'S POLISH HOSPITAL —258 W. Division.

STREETER HOSPITAL—2646 Calumet av.

WESLEY HOSPITAL—2459 Dearborn.

WEST SIDE HOSPITAL—819 to 823 W. Harrison.

WILLIE HIPP HOSPITAL — 1211, 56th.

WOMAN'S HOSPITAL OF CHICAGO—32d nw. cor. Rhodes av.

LIBRARIES AND READING ROOMS.

ARMOUR INSTITUTE OF TECHNOLOGY LIBRARY — 33d sw. cor. Armour av.

CHICAGO HISTORICAL SOCIETY LIBRARY—142 Dearborn av. nw. cor. Ontario.

CHICAGO LAW INSTITUTE— Room 414 County bldg.

CHICAGO PUBLIC LIBRARY— Washington cor. Michigan av. Open week days from 9 a.m. to 10 p.m. Sundays 12 m. to 6 p.m. Regular meetings of the Board 2d and 4th Friday of each month, at 3 p.m.

CHICAGO THEOSOPHICAL SOCIETY LIBRARY—Room 424 Athenæum bldg. 26 Vanburen.

COLUMBUS MEDICAL LIBRARY —1405, 103 State.

HAMMOND LIBRARY — 43 Warren av.

HYDE PARK LYCEUM READING ROOM AND LIBRARY—136, 53d.

JOHN CRERAR LIBRARY—6th fl. 87 Wabash av.

NEWBERRY LIBRARY — Walton pl. bet. N. Clark and Dearborn av.

PULLMAN PUBLIC LIBRARY— 73 and 77 Arcade bldg. (P.)

RAVENSWOOD PUBLIC LIBRARY—2517 Commercial.

SOUTH CHICAGO PUBLIC LIBRARY—Bowen School bldg. 93d cor. Houston av.

TEMPERANCE READING ROOM—5511 S. Halsted.

UNION CATHOLIC LIBRARY ASSOCIATION—Garfield boul. cor. Wentworth av. Open from 12 m. to 5 p.m.

UNIVERSAL BROTHERHOOD LIBRARY—511 Masonic Temple.

UNIVERSITY OF THE TRAVELING LIBRARY—1841 Wabash av.

VIRGINIA LIBRARY—326 Belden av.

WESTERN NEW CHURCH UNION BOOK ROOM — 901 Steinway Hall. Open 9 a.m. to 5 p.m.

YOUNG MEN'S CHRISTIAN ASSOCIATION READING ROOM — Open daily from 9 a.m. to 10 p.m. except Sundays. 153 Lasalle; 542 W. Monroe; 610 Wilson av.; 428 Garfield

boul.; N, Canal, cor. W. Kinzie; 284;
53d; 169-171 Plymouth ct.; N. 41st av.
and W. Kinzie.

YOUNG MEN'S CHRISTIAN AS-
SOCIATION READING ROOM
(Scandinavian)—381 Grand av. Reading room and library open every evening from 7 to 9:30.

MILITARY.

United States Army.

Stationed at Headquarters, Department of the Lakes, Pullman bldg.,
southwest cor. Michigan av. and Adams
st.

Brigadier General John M. Bacon
commanding (St. Paul, Minn.) U. S.
Army, room No. 406,

Colonel Thomas F. Barr, A. G. Dept.,
Acting Adjutant General, room No. 406.

Captain George B. Duncan, Assistant
Adjutant General, room 403.

Major J. M. J. Samo, Acting Inspector General, room No. 611.

Colonel Thomas F. Barr, J. A. G.
Dept., Judge Advocate, room 405.

Major Fred A: Smith, Sub. Dept.,
Chief Commissary, room 417.

Lieut. Colonel Albert Hartsuff, Medical Department, Chief Surgeon, room
No. 404.

Colonel J. G. C. Lee, Assistant Quartermaster General, Chief Quartermaster, room No. 415.

Colonel A. B. Carey, Pay Department, Chief Paymaster, room No. 610.

Captain Charles D. Palmer, Q. M.
Dept., Disbursing Officer, room No.
416.

Major W. F. Tucker, Pay Dept.,
Paymaster, room 506; Major B. B.
Ray, Pay Dept., room 610, Major E.
A. Bigelow, Pay Dept. Paymaster,
room 506.

Major William L. Marshall, Corps
Engineer. In charge of River and
Harbor Improvements, 1637 Indiana av.

Lieutenant Colonel O. M. Smith,
Subsistence Department, Depot Commissary of Subsistence, 250 Illinois.

Captain Richard W. Johnson, Med.
Dept., Attending Surgeon, 602 Pullman
bldg.

Captain P. S. Bomus, 1st Cavalry,
Recruiting Officer, 82 W. Madison.

Illinois First Brigade National Guard.

Stationed at Chicago Headquarters,
Grand Pacific hotel, Brigadier General
Chas FitzSimons, Commanding. Per-
sonal Staff: Aides-de-Camp, Lieuten-

ant C. C. Ames and Lieutenant Ralph
Winston; Brigade Staff: Adjutant Gen-
eral, Colonel Henry B. Maxwell; Lieu-
tenant Colonel E. A. Glenon, Judge Ad-
vocate; Lieutenant Colonel Francis
Riddle, Inspector General; Major Geo.
T. Lovejoy, Commissary. Major F. O.
Bartlett, Quartermaster; Major Chas.
Adams, Surgeon.

First Regiment Infantry.

Armory 1542 Michigan av. Field and
Staff Officers—Majors, Joseph B. San-
born, Edgar B. Tolman and J. M. Ed-
dy, jr.; Surgeon, Capt. William G.
Willard; Assistant Surgeons, Captain
Thomas E. Roberts and Lieutenant C.
B. Walls; Chaplain, Captain Hiram
W. Thomas; Adjutant First Battalion,
First Lieutenant B. E. Patrick, jr.;
Adjutant Second Battalion, First Lieu-
tenant Willis J. Wells; Adjutant Third
Battalion, First Lieutenant Wm. J.
Sanderson.

Company A — Captain Taylor E.
Brown. Company B—Captain Walter
H. McComb. Company C—Captain
Anson L. Bolte. Company D—Captain
Edward J. Simmick. Company E—
———. Company F—Captain Oliver
D. Steele, Company G—Captain
Charles T. Wilt, jr., Company H—
Captain W. H. Whigam. Company
I—Captain Chas. B. Sandham. Com-
pany K—Captain M. L. C. Funk-
houser. Company L—Captain Alex-
ander M. Daniels. Company M—Cap-
tain Edward H. Switzer.

Second Regiment Infantry.

Armories Washington boul. ne. cor.
Curtis. Field and Staff Officers—Col-
onel, George M. Moulton; Lieutenant
Colonel, W. D. Hotchkiss; Majors,
James E. Stuart, W. P. Dusenberry
and Holman G. Purinton; Adjutant,
Captain James P. Sherwin; Inspector
of Small Arms Practice, Captain
Stephen B. Thompson; Surgeon, Ma-
jor Dr. Morris; Assistant Surgeon,
Dr. Porter. Quartermaster, Captain
Fred W. Laas. Adjutant 2d Battalion,
First Lieutenant Frank W. Mechener;
Adjutant 3d Battalion,

Company A—Captain Paul B. Lino.
Company B—Captain Charles P.
Wright. Company C — Captain T.
I. Mair. Company D———. Com-
pany E—Captain F. Nussbaumer.
Company F —Captain James H. Stans-
field. Company G—Captain Willis
McFeely. Company H—Captain John
J. Garrity. Company I — Captain
Henry Koehler. Company K—Cap-

tain A. A. Benning. Company L—
Captain M. J. Swatek. CompanyM
—Captain John McFadden.

Sixth Regiment Infantry.

Headquarters 132 LaSalle. Col. D.
J. Foster, Commanding; Adjutant
Capt. John J. Cairns.

Seventh Regiment Infantry.

Armory Wabash av. cor. Hubbard
pl. Field and Staff Officers: Colonel
Commanding, Marcus Kavanagh;
Lieut. Col. Daniel Moriarity, ; Majors,
Garrett J. Carroll and Lawrence M.
Ennis; Surgeon, Major Thomas J. Sul-
livan; Assistant Surgeon. Captain G.
W. Mahoney; Lieut. Frank P. St.Clair;
Adjutant, Captain Michael E. Cassidy;
Chaplain, Captain Edward A. Kelly;
Quartermaster, Captain Michael H.
Hoey: Adjutant 1st Battalion, First
Lieutenant Thomas M. Kavanagh; Ad-
jutant 2d Battalion, First Lieutenant
Joseph G. Kirwin; Adjutant 3d Bat-
talion, First Lieutenant John F. Ryan.
Company A—Captain W. Edward
Hoinville. Company B—Captain Pat-
rick O'Connor. Company C—Captain
Timothy M. Kennedy. Company D—
Captain Martin Duhig. Company E—
Captain James Kelly. Company F
—Captain J. J. Sisk. Company G—
Captain J. L. Malley. Company H—
Captain William J. Carroll. Company
I—Captain Joseph E. G. Ryan. Com-
pany K—Captain John T. McCormick.
Company L—Captain John M. Clasby,
Company M—Captain James Clark.

Ninth Battalion Infantry (Col-
ored).

Adjutant, Capt. James H. Johnson;
Insp. Rifle Practice, Capt. William A.
Jones; Asst. Surgeon, Capt. James N.
Crocker; Quartermaster, First Lieut.
Daniel M. Jackson; Chaplain, Capt.
John F. Thomas.
Company A—Captain John R. Mar-
shall. Company B—Captain Adolph
Thomas. Company C—Captain Charles
L. Hunt. Company D—Captain Rob-
ert R. Jackson.

Artillery Battalion.

Armory 145 Michigan av. Major Alfred Russell, Commanding; Adjutant,.
Capt. James J. Healy; Quartermaster, First Lieutenant Thos. J. Ford.
Battery D—Captain, William Austin.

Cavalry Squadron.

Headquarters, Michigan av. cor. 16th.
Major Edward C. Young, Commanding; Adjutant, Capt. Pierrepont Isham;

Insp. Rifle Practice, First Lieutenant
Milton J. Foreman; Insp. Small Arms
Practice, Arthur M. Chamberlin; Asst.
Surgeon, Lieut. T. J. Robeson.
Troop A—Captain, Paul B. Lino.
Troop B—Captain, Metellus L. C.
Funkhouser.
Troop C—Captain, Frank B. Alsip.

Columbia Zouaves.

Armory, 192 Washington. Captain,
A. F. Lott; Lieut., E. Bittle.

Illinois Zouaves.

Armory, 40 Clark. Captain, Benj.
A. Case. First Lieut., Louis A. Hugul-
let; Second Lieut., Joseph A. Webber.

Hussar Squadron.

Staff Officers — Major Edwin L.
Brand, 210 Wabash av.
Adjutant, J. J. Murray; Judge Advo-
cate, C. E. Moore; Inspector, A. Mat-
thews; Quartermaster,P. E. Carpenter;
Surgeon, Stuart Johnstone, M.D.;
Chaplain, Rev. R. A. White.
Troop A, Chicago Hussars: Capt. H.
Waldo Howe.
Troop B, Black Hussars: Capt. Sol
Wolfe.

Chicago Ships Crew Naval Militia
of Illinois.

Commander 1st Ship's Crew, E. H.
Harrison; Lieut. Commander, H. A.
Allen; Navigator and Ordnance Officer,
W. J. Wilson; Aide to Commander,
Ensign George H. Thorne; Past Asst.
Surgeon, Norval H. Pierce; Asst. Sur-
geon, L. Blake Baldwin; Chief Engi-
neer, F. W. Strong.
1st Division—Lieut., S. D. Flood; Jr.
Lieut., O. Zillman; Ensign, Warren H.
Purdy; Ensign, Howard Blivin.
2d Division—Lieut., John Ubsdell;
Jr. Lieut., O. T. Warren; Ensign Wal-
ter Aikmen; Ensign, L. C. Roberts.
3d Division—Lieut., D. De Le Fon-
taine; Jr. Lieut., W. H. Quinlan; Ensign, Geo. Hayden; Ensign, J. Jacobs.
4th Division—Lieut., S. W. Stratton.
Jr. Lieut., Claude F. Fitch; Ensign, B.
R. T. Collins.

MUSEUMS.

CHICAGO ACADEMY OF SCI-
ENCES—Matthew Laflin Memorial
Bldg., Lincoln Park. Pres. Prof.
Thomas C. Chamberlain; Sec. Frank
C. Baker; Treas., Chas. F. Gunther.
FIELD COLUMBIAN MUSEUM
—Jackson Park. Pres. Edward E.
Ayer; 1st Vice-Pres. Martin A. Ryer-

son; 2d Vice-Pres. Norman B. Ream; Chairman Executive Committee, Harlow N. Higinbotham; Secretary, George Manierre; Treasurer, Byron L. Smith; Director, Frederick J. V. Skiff.

PARKS.

DOUGLAS—W. 12th, S. Fairfield av. W. Nineteenth and S. Albany avs.

DOUGLAS MONUMENT SQUARE —Foot 35th.

ELLIS—36th, 37th and Langley av.

GARFIELD—W. Madison, S. Homan av. W. Lake.

HUMBOLDT — W. North av. S. California av. W. Division.

JACKSON—The Lake, 56th, Stony Island av. 67th

JEFFERSON—W. Adams, Throop, W. Monroe, Loomis.

LAKE FRONT — Michigan av. fr. Jackson to Lake Park pl.

LINCOLN—The Lake, North av. N. Clark, N. Park av. Diversey av.

MIDWAY PLAISANCE — Cottage Grove av. to Stony Island av. bet. 59th and 60th.

SOUTH—See Jackson and Washington Parks.

UNION—Ogden av. Warren av. Ashland av. W. Lake, Bryan pl.

VERNON—Lytle, Sibley, Gilpin pl. Macalister pl.

WASHINGTON—Cottage Grove av. 51st, South Park av. 60th.

WASHINGTON SQ. — N. Clark, Washington pl. Dearborn av. Walton pl.

WICKER—Park, Fowler, N. Robey.

PUBLIC HALLS, BLOCKS, AND BUILDINGS.

Abel Bldg.—447 to 455 W. 63d.

Adams Express Bldg.—185 to 189 Dearborn.

Allerton Bldg.—South Water ne. cor. State.

American Express Co.'s Bldg—72 to 78 Monroe.

Apollo Hall—5th floor, 69 State.

Arcade Bldg.—156 to 164 Clark.

Arcade Bldg.—Pullman.

Argyle Bldg.— Jackson nw. cor. Michigan av.

Art Institute The—Michigan av. opp. Adams.

Ashland Blk.—53 to 65 Clark.

Association Bldg.—153 and 155 Lasalle.

Athenæum Bldg.—18 to 26 Vanburen.

Athenæum Bldg.—52 Dearborn.

Atlas Blk.—45 to 61 Wabash av.

Atwood Bldg.--Clark nw. cor. Madison.

Auditorium Bldg. — Congress, Michigan av. and Wabash av.

Baltimore Bldg.—17 to 21 Quincy.

Bassett Bldg.—191 and 193, 5th av.

Bay State Bldg.—State sw. cor. Randolph.

Belmont Hall—1682 N. Clark.

Board of Trade—Head of Lasalle.

Borden Blk. — Randolph nw. cor. Dearborn.

Boyce Bldg.—112 and 114 Dearborn.

Boylston Block—265 to 273 Dearborn.

Brand's Hall—160 to 170 N. Clark.

Brother Jonathan Bldg. — 2 and 4 Sherman.

Bryan Blk.—160 to 174 Lasalle.

Building Trades Council Hall—187 and 189 Washington.

Calumet Bldg.—187 to 191 Lasalle.

Caxton Bldg.—328 to 334 Dearborn.

Central Music Hall—State se. cor. Randolph.

Central Union Blk.—Madison nw. cor. Market.

Ceylon Bldg.—15 to 27 Wabash av.

Chamber of Commerce Bldg.—Washington se. cor. Lasalle.

Champlain Bldg.—State nw. cor. Madison

Chicago Opera House Bldg.— Clark sw. cor. Washington.

Chicago Public Library—Washington nw. cor. Michigan av.

Chicago Stock Exch. Bldg. — Lasalle sw. cor. Washington.

Chicago Title and Trust Co. Bldg.— 98 to 102 Washington.

Chronicle Bldg.—166 Washington.

Cisco Bldg.—84 Washington.

City Hall—Washington cor. Lasalle.

Cobb's Bldg.—120 to 128 Dearborn.

Columbia Theatre—104 to 110 Monroe.

Columbus Memorial Bldg. — State se. cor. Washington.

Commerce Bldg.—14 and 16 Pacific av.

Commercial Bldg.—144 to 152 Franklin.

Commercial Nat. Bank Bldg.—Dearborn se. cor. Monroe.

Como Bldg.—323 and 325 Dearborn.

Consolidated Exchange Bldg. — 134 Vanburen.

Continental Bank Bldg.—218 Lasalle.

Counselman Bldg.—Lasalle cor. Jackson.

County Bldg.—Clark cor. Washington.

Crilly Bldg.—163 to 171 Dearborn.

Criminal Ct. Bldg. — Michigan cor. Dearborn av.
Dexter Bldg.—80 and 82 Adams.
Dickey Bldg.—34 to 46 Dearborn.
Donohue & Henneberry's Bldg.—407 to 425 Dearborn.
Douglas Arcade—Cottage Grove av. cor. 36th.
Edison Bldg:—139 Adams.
Electric Blk.—72 to 88 Market.
Ellsworth Bldg.—355 and 357 Dearborn.
Ely Bldg.—Wabash av. sw. cor. Monroe.
Empire Blk.—128 and 130 Lasalle.
Enterprise and Industry Bldgs.—79 to 87, 5th av.
Equitable Bldg.—106 to 110 Dearborn.
Equitable Bldg.—106 to 110 Dearborn.
Exchange Bldg.—Union Stock Yards.
Fairbank Bldg.—58 to 62 Wabash av.
Field Columbian Museum — Jackson Park.
Field Marshall & Co. Bldg.—Wabash av. nw. cor. Washington.
Fine Arts Bldg.—203 to 207 Michigan av.
First Inf. I. N. G. Armory—Michigan av. nw. cor. 16th.
First Nat. Bank Bldg.—Dearborn nw. cor. Monroe.
Fisher Bldg.—Vanburen and Dearborn.
Fort Dearborn Bldg.—Monroe sw. cor. Clark.
Franklin Bldg.—341 to 349 Dearborn.
Freiberg's Opera House—180, 182 and 184, 22d.
Fullerton Blk.—90 to 96 Dearborn.
Fullerton Memorial Hall — Art Institute, Michigan av. opp. Congress.
Gaff Bldg.—230 to 236 Lasalle.
Galbraith Bldg. — Madison ne. cor. Franklin.
Garden City Bldg.—56, 5th av.
Gardner Bldg.—171 and 173 Randolph.
Giles Bldg.—298 to 304 Wabash av.
Girard Bldg.—298 to 306 Dearborn.
Grand Central Depot—Harrison sw. cor. 5th av.
Grand Opera House—87 Clark.
Great Northern Bldg. — 77 Jackson boul.
Greenebaum Bldg.—72 to 82 Fifth av.
Hallet & Davis Bldg.—241 Wabash av.
Hampshire Blk. — Lasalle se. cor. Monroe.
Handel Hall—40 Randolph.
Hartford Bldg.—134 to 146 Dearborn.
Haymarket Theatre.—161 to 169 W. Madison.
Henning & Speed Blk. — 121 to 127 Dearborn.
Henrietta Bldg.—64 and 66 Wabash av.
Herald Bldg.—154 and 156 Washington.

Home Insurance Bldg.—Lasalle ne. cor. Adams.
Howland Blk.—174 to 192 Dearborn.
Huylers Bldg.—155 State.
Hyman Bldg.—146 to 152 South Water.
Illinois Bank Bldg.— 111 to 117 Dearborn.
Imperial Bldg.—252 to 260 Clark.
Industry and Enterprise Bldgs.—79 to 87, 5th av.
Inter Ocean Bldg. — Dearborn nw. cor. Madison.
Isabella Bldg.—48 Vanburen.
Jones John Bldg.—119 Dearborn.
Journal Bldg.—160 and 162 Washington.
Kedzie Bldg.—120 and 122 Randolph.
Kentucky Blk.—195 to 203 Clark.
Kimball Hall.—243 to 249 Wabash av.
Lafayette Bldg.—68 to 74 Lasalle.
Lakeside Bldg. — Clark ' sw. cor. Adams.
LAKESIDE PRESS BLDG.—149 Plymouth ct. cor. Polk.
Lasalle Blk.—Lasalle nw. cor. Madison.
Law Bldg.—318 Dearborn.
Lees Bldg.—147 to 151, 5th av.
LeMoyne Bldg.—40 Randolph.
Lenox Bldg.—88 and 90 Washington.
Lind Bldg.—28 to 34 Market.
Lowell Bldg.—308 to 316 Dearborn.
Ludington Bldg. — Wabash av. cor. Harmon pl.
Mallers Bldg.—226 and 228 Lasalle.
Manhattan Bldg.—307 to 321 Dearborn.
Manufactures Bldg.—18 to 30 W. Randolph.
Marine Bldg.—152 to 158 Lake.
Marquette Bldg. — Dearborn nw. cor. Adams.
Mason Blk.—92 and 94 Washington.
Masonic Temple—State ne. cor. Randolph.
McCormick Blk.—67 to 73 Dearborn.
McVicker's Theatre Bldg.—78 to 84 Madison.
Medinah Temple—Fifth av. ne. cor. Jackson.
Mentor Blk.—163 State.
Merchants' Bldg.—Lasalle nw. cor. Washington.
Methodist Church Blk. — Clark se. cor. Washington.
Metropolitan Blk.—159 to 165 Randolph.
Monadnock Bldg.—Jackson cor. Dearborn.
Monon Bldg.—320 to 326 Dearborn.
Montauk Blk.—111 to 117 Monroe.
National Life Ins. Bldg. — 159 to 163 Lasalle.
National Union Bldg.—70 Adams.
New Era Bldg.—Blue Island av. sw. cor. W. Harrison.

New York Life Ins. Bldg.—Lasalle ne. cor. Monroe.
Ogden Bldg.—Clark sw. cor. Lake.
Old Colony Bldg.—Vanburen se. cor. Dearborn.
Oneonta Bldg.—67 to 73 Clark.
Open Board Bldg.—18 to 24 Pacific av.
Oriental Bldg. and Hall—122 Lasalle.
Otis Bldg.—Madison sw. cor. State.
Otis Blk.—138 to 158 Lasalle.
Owings Bldg.—215 Dearborn.
Oxford Bldg.—84 and 86 Lasalle.
Pontiac Bldg.—Dearborn nw. cor. Harrison, .
Portland Blk.—103 to 109 Dearborn.
Post-Office.—Michigan av. opp. Washington. .
Powers Bldg.—Madison nw. cor. Michigan av.
Produce Exchange Bldg.—South Water ne. cor. Clark.
Pullman Bldg. — Adams sw. cor. Michigan av.
Quincy Bldg.—Clark ne. cor. Adams.
Quinlan Bldg.—81 and 83 Clark.
Rand-McNally Bldg.—162 to 182 Adams.
Rawson Bldg.—149 and 151 State.
Real Estate Board Bldg.—Dearborn ne. cor. Randolph.
Reaper Blk.—Clark ne. cor. Washington. .
Recital Hall—Auditorium Bldg.
Reliance Bldg.—State sw. cor. Washington.
Rialto Bldg. — 135 to 153 Vanburen, rear Board of Trade. .
Roanoke Blk.—139 to 151 Lasalle.
Rookery Bldg. — Lasalle se. cor. Adams.
Rosalie Music Hall—Rosalie ct. sw. cor. 57th. .
Royal Insurance Bldg. — 165 to 173 Jackson and 108 to 116 Quincy.
Ryerson Bldg.—45 to 49 Randolph.
Schiller Bldg.—103 to 109 Randolph.
Schloesser Blk.—200 to 210 Lasalle.
Sears Bldg.—99 and 101 Washington.
Second Regt. Armory. — Washington boul. ne. cor. Curtis.
Security Bldg.—Madison se. cor. 5th av.
Shreve Blk.—91 and 93 Washington.
Sibley Bldg.—2 to 16 N. Clark.
Silversmith's Bldg.—131 to 137 Wabash av.
Sorento—Clark ne. cor. Kinzie.
Sringer Bldg.—195 to 207 S. Canal.
Springer Bldg.—166 to 174 S. Clinton
Staats Zeitung Bldg.—91 to 99 Fifth av.
Star Accident Insurance Bldg.—352 to 356 Dearborn.
Steinway Hall—17 Vanburen.
Stewart Bldg.—State nw. cor. Washington.
Studebaker Bldg.—378 to 388 Wabash av.

Studio Bldg.—N. State, Ohio to Ontario.
Superior Blk.—75 to 79 Clark.
Tacoma Bldg.—Lasalle ne. cor Madison.
Taylor Bldg.—140 to 146 Monroe. .
Telephone Bldg.—203 Washington.
Temple Ct. Bldg.—217 to 225 Dearborn.
Teutonic Bldg.—Washington se. cor. 5th av.
The Temple—Lasalle sw. cor. Monroe.
Times Bldg.—Washington nw. cor. Fifth av.
Title and Trust Bldg.—98 to 102 Washington.
Traders' Bldg.—6 to 12 Pacific av.
Tribune Bldg. — Dearborn se. cor. Madison.
Trude Bldg. — Wabash av. sw. cor. Randolph.
Unity Bldg.—75 to 81 Dearborn. .
University Club Bldg.—116 and 118 Dearborn.
U. S. Express Co.'s Bldg.—87 and 89 Washington.
Venetian Bldg.—34 and 36 Washington.
Wadsworth Bldg.—175 to 181 Madison.
Washington Blk.—104 to 110, 5th av.
Watson Bldg.—123 and 125 Lasalle.
Western Bank Note Bldg.—Madison sw. cor. Michigan av.
Western Union Bldg.—138 Jackson.
Westminster Hotel—462 N. Clark.
Wheeler Bldg.—6 and 8 Sherman.
Williams Bldg.—164 to 176 Wabash av.
Williams Bldg.—Monroe sw. cor. 5th av.
Willoughby Bldg.—Franklin nw. cor. Jackson.
Winnipeg Blk.—Commercial av. ne. cor. 92d.
Young Men's Christian Assn. Bldg. —153 and 155 Lasalle.

THEATRES AND PLACES OF AMUSEMENT.

ACADEMY OF MUSIC — Halsted near Madison.

ADELPHI THEATRE—1840 Wabash av.

ALHAMBRA THEATRE—State cor. 20th.

ARCADE THEATRE—Arcade bldg. (P.)

AUDITORIUM, THE — Congress cor. Wabash av. .

BIJOU THEATRE—169 S. Halsted.

CALUMET THEATRE — 9206 South Chicago av.

CENTRAL MUSIC HALL — State cor. Randolph.

CHICAGO OPERA HOUSE—Washington sw. cor. Clark.

CLIFFORD'S THEATRE—126 Washington.

COLUMBIA THEATRE—106 Monroe.

DEARBORN THEATRE—107 Randolph.

GRAND OPERA HOUSE — 87 Clark.

GREAT NORTHERN THEATRE—22 Quincy.

HAYMARKET THEATRE—Madison east of Halsted.

HOPKINS' THEATRE—337 State.

KIMBALL HALL—243 to 249 Wabash av.

LINCOLN THEATRE — 468 N. Clark.

MARLOWE THEATRE — 6254 Stewart av.

MASONIC TEMPLE ROOF GARDEN—Masonic Temple.

McVICKER'S THEATRE—78 Madison.

POWERS' THEATRE — 149 Randolph.

___

SOCIETIES, CLUBS AND ASSOCIATIONS.

ACACIA CLUB—Pres., Daniel A· Arnold; 1st V. Pres., William Johnston; 2d V. Pres., Sidney G. Many; Treas., Severt T. Gunderson; Sec., C. S. Gurney, 878 W. Monroe.

ÆOLUS CLUB — 174 Evergreen av. Pres., Kickham Scanlon; Sec., R. P. Beygeh; Treas., E. A. Hoeft; Capt. W. F. Hoeft.

ALOHA CLUB—40 Randolph. Pres., Miss Ida Burgess; Cor. Sec,, Mrs. Seymour Stedman; Treas., ·Miss Cora E. Wilson.

ALPHA SOROSIS CLUB — Pres. Mrs. Calvin Stanbaugh; Sec. Mrs. Harriet B. Ellithorpe. 4th floor, 52 Dearborn.

ALTERNATE CLUB — 2714 Kenmore av. Pres., Mrs. C. T. Parkes; V. Pres., Mrs. George J. Reed and Mrs. Lemuel C. Grosvenor; Sec, Mrs. W. H. Layman, 1142 Morse av.; Treas, Miss Lillian Smith.

ALTRUA ART LIBRARY ASSOCIATION, THE, 1223 Masonic Temple. Director, Mrs. J. B. Sherwood.

AMATEUR MUSICAL CLUB — Meets alternate Mondays in Fine Arts bldg. See p. 365.

AMERICAN BAPTIST HOME MISSION SOCIETY —1627 Marquette bldg. Supt. and Dist. Sec., Rev. J. B. Thomas, D.D.

AMERICAN BAPTIST MISSIONARY UNION—49, 69 Dearborn; Dist. Sec. Rev. E. W. Lounsbury, D.D.; Home Sec. Rev.Henry C. Mabie, D.D., Boston, Mass.

AMERICAN BAPTIST PUBLICATION SOCIETY—Chicago Depository 177 Wabash av. Charles M. Roe, Manager; Dist. Sec. of Missionary Dept., Rev. E. S. Stucker.

AMERICAN BOARD OF COMMISSIONERS FOR FOREIGN MISSIONS—1003, 155 Lasalle. Dist. Sec. Rev. A. N. Hitchcock.

AMERICAN HOME-FINDING ASSOCIATION—712, 167 · Dearborn. Pres., Charles Waldo Fareman; Sec., Rev. J..W. Lee; Treas., Finley Ellingwood; Counselor, McKenzie Cleland; Gen. Supt., Geo. K. Hoover.

AMERICAN MISSIONARY ASSOCIATION—1004, 155 Lasalle. Western Sec. Rev. J. E. Roy, D.D.

AMERICAN SUNDAY-SCHOOL UNION—1010, 153 Lasalle. Supt. F. G. Ensign.

AMERICAN TRACT SOCIETY—167-169 Wabash av. Pres., Maj. Gen. O. O. Howard; V. Pres., Rev. Robert S. McArthur, D.D.; Dist. Sec. Rev. Jesse Brooks, D.D.

AMERICAN UNION CLUB OF CHICAGO—213, 323 Dearborn. Pres., Allen A. Wesley; V. Pres., C. R. Johnson; Treas., A. H. Garrett; Sec., M. F. Hussie.

APOLLO MUSICAL CLUB—Meets at Handel Hall, 40 Randolph; Pres. Angus S. Hibbard; Sec. Dana Hull, 4750 Lake av.; Treas. John H. Cameron. Musical Director, Harrison M. Wild.

ARCHÉ CLUB—See p. 366.

ARGONAUTS—Foot of Randolph. See p. 368.

ART STUDENTS' LEAGUE—Art Institute. Pres., L. Beulah Mitchell; V. Pres., F. C. Oswald; Sec., Walter J. Enright, 713 W. Jackson boul.; Treas., Harry H. Osgood.

ASHLAND CLUB.—575 Washington boul. See p. 369.

ATLAN ART CLUB—Columbus Memorial bldg. Pres. Mrs. E. L. Humphrey; V. Pres. Mrs. F. M. Steele; Sec., Miss Eva E. Adams; Treas.,Miss Mary H. Phillips.

AUDUBON CLUB—Meets 2d Tuesday each quarter at Sherman House. J. H. Amberg, pres.; Wm. L. Shepard, sec. and treas. 155 Lasalle.

BANKERS' CLUB—See p. 370.

BAPTIST CITY MISSION SOCIETY—185 and 187 W. Randolph; Pres. Julius A. Johnson; Treas., Frank J. Walsh; Sec., Walter E. Gillespie.

BAPTIST MISSIONARY TRAINING SCHOOL—2411 Indiana av. Preceptress, Mrs. C. D. Morris; Cor. Sec. Miss M.G. Burdette.

BAPTIST PASTORS' CONFERENCE—Meet every Monday, 2d fl. 155 Lasalle, at 10.30 a. m.

BAPTIST THEOLOGICAL UNION—(Now the Divinity School of the University of Chicago.) Dean, Rev. E. B. Hulbert; Pres. Baptist Theological Union, E. Nelson Blake; Treas. Edward Goodman, 69 Dearborn; Sec. T. W. Goodspeed; Fin. Sec. Rev. E. C. Hewitt, D.D., 5535 Lexington av.

BAPTIST YOUNG PEOPLE'S UNION OF AMERICA—Headquarters at 1030, 324 Dearborn. Pres. John H. Chapman; Gen. Sec. Rev. E. E. Chivers; Treas. Frank Moody.

BAPTIST YOUNG PEOPLE'S UNION OF THE CHICAGO ASSN.— Pres. S. H. Bloom, 324 Dearborn; Sec. Charles H. Warren; Treas., W. S. Lindsley.

BOARD OF FOREIGN MISSIONS OF THE PRESBYTERIAN CHURCH IN THE U. S. A.— Field Sec. Rev. Thomas Marshall, D.D., 48 McCormick blk.

BOOK CLUB—304 Warren av. Pres. Robert F. Pettibone; Sec. and Treas., Miss Mary A. Swett, 543 W. Monroe.

BROTHERHOOD OF ST. ANDREW (Chicago Local Council)— Chairman, Geo. W. Waterman, 54 St. Clair; Sec., P. C. Hart, 2952 Cottage Grove av. Meets 2d Thursdays in March, June, September and December at 510 Masonic Temple.

BRYN MAWR CLUB—7149 Jeffery av. See p. 371.

BUILDERS' CLUB — 418 Chamb. Com. bldg. See p. 372.

CALUMET CLUB—Michigan av. ne. cor. 20th. See p. 373.

CALUMET HEIGHTS CLUB— Pres. Dr. A. W. Harlan; V. Pres. Walter Metcalfe; Sec. and Treas. G. C. Lamphere, 43, 221, 5th av. Meets semi-annually at Sherman House.

CASINO AT EDGEWATER. See p. 374.

CATLIN BOAT CLUB—481 Belden av. Pres. Chas. Catlin; Sec. Franklin S. Catlin; Capt., Charles T. Goff.

CENTRAL ART ASSOCIATION OF AMERICA—936, 203 Michigan av. Pres., Halsey C. Ives; V. Pres., Lorado Taft; Ex. Sec., T. Vernette Morse; Treas., Abner Crossman.

CENTURY CLUB—Pres., Harry Hamill; Sec. and Treas., Donald C. Catlin, 4300 Ellis av.

CHICAGO ACADEMY OF SCIENCES—Lincoln Park. Pres. Prof. Thomas C. Chamberlain; Sec. W. K. Higley.

CHICAGO ARCHITECTURAL CLUB—Art Institute. Pres., J. C. Llewellyn; Sec., N. Max Dunning; Treas., August C. Wilmann.

CHICAGO ARMY AND NAVY LEAGUE — 410 Masonic Temple. Pres., Geo. E. Adams; V. Prests., John W. Ela and E. G. Pauling; Sec., E. P. Bicknell; Treas., Elbridge G. Keith.

CHICAGO ART ASSOCIATION— Art Institute. Pres., Judge John Barton Payne; V. Pres., Mrs. John B. Sherwood; Sec., Miss Jessie S. Gardner.

CHICAGO ART INSTITUTE — Michigan av. opposite Adams. Pres. C. L. Hutchinson; V. Pres. James H. Dole; Treas. L. J. Gage; Sec. N. H. Carpenter; Director, W. M. R. French.

CHICAGO ASTRONOMICAL SOCIETY—Pres. Elias Colbert; V. Pres. J. B. Hobbs; Sec. H. C. Ranney, 410 Oak; Treas. Murry Nelson; Director, Prof. G. W. Hough.

CHICAGO ATHENÆUM—18 to 26 Vanburen; Pres. Ferd W. Peck; 1st V. Pres. Wm. R. Page; 2d V. Pres. Harry G. Selfridge; Sec. and Treas. Franklin H. Head.

CHICAGO ATHLETIC ASSOCIATION—Michigan av. bet. Madison and Monroe. See p. 377.

CHICAGO BAPTIST ASSOCIATION — Pres. Rev. Johnston Myers, D.D., 2339 Michigan av.; Sec., H. R. Clissold, 1210 Security bldg.

CHICAGO BAPTIST SOCIAL UNION—Pres. John H. Chapman; Sec. Orren V. Stookey, 75 Metropolitan blk.; Treas. John P. Ahrens.

CHICAGO BAR ASSOCIATION— Meets at 100 Washington. Pres. Henry S. Towle; 1st V. Pres. S. S. Gregory; 2d V. Pres. Arthur D. Eddy; Sec. George Mills Rogers; Treas. Thomas J. Holmes.

CHICAGO BIBLE SOCIETY — Office and Depository, 817 to 820, 155 Lasalle. Gen. Sec. and Agt. Rev. J. A. Mack; Supt. Bible Work, Miss E. Dryer, 49 S. Ada.

CHICAGO BRANCH OF THE WOMAN'S AUXILIARY OF THE BOARD OF MISSIONS—510 Masonic Temple. Pres., Mrs. David B. Lyman; V. Pres., Mrs. Katherine D. Arnold; Treas., Mrs. James T. Hoyne; Cor. Sec., Mrs. C. O. Meacham, 2458 Michigan av.; Rec. Sec., Mrs. S. L. K. Monroe.

CHICAGO BUREAU OF ASSOCIATED CHARITIES—Pres., Franklin MacVeagh; Treas., E. G. Keith; Gen. Supt., Ernest P. Bicknell; Asst. Supt., R. Brickell Holmes. Central office 410 Masonic Temple.

CHICAGO CAT CLUB—4011 Drexel boul. Pres., Mrs. Leland Norton; V. Pres., Dr. E. M. Hale; Cor. Sec., Mrs C. F. Smith; Rec. Sec., Miss Jennie VanAllen; Treas., Mrs. C. H. Lane.

CHICAGO CENTRAL WOMEN'S CHRISTIAN TEMPERANCE UNION—1118 The Temple. Pres. Mrs. Matilda B. Carse; V. Pres. Mrs. Margaret Howell; Sec. Mrs. J. B. Hilton; Treas. Mrs. L. A. Hagans.

CHICAGO CERAMIC ASSOCIATION—Room 7, Fine Arts bldg. Pres., Mrs. N. A. Cross; 1st V. Pres., Miss Olive Barton; 2d V. Pres., Miss Helen Clark; Treas., Mrs. W. L. Glass; Cor. Sec., Mrs. T. M. Wright; Rec. Sec., Mrs. J. B. Ralston.

CHICAGO CHRISTIAN ENDEAVOR UNION—Pres., C. A. Wetzel; 1st V. Pres., R. N. Stewart; 2d V. Pres., Thomas Wainwright; Sec., Miss Mary A. Crane; 1121 Association bldg. Treas., Lincoln Higgins.

CHICAGO CITY MISSIONARY SOCIETY—Supt. Rev. J. C. Armstrong, D.D., 24, 151 Washington.

CHICAGO CLUB — Michigan av. sw. cor. Vanburen. See p. 375.

CHICAGO CONGREGATIONAL CLUB—Regular meetings third Monday in each month, October to May inclusive, at the Palmer House. Pres., Judge Nathaniel C. Sears; Sec., E. B. Case, 198 Lasalle; Treas., Harvey Dean.

CHICAGO CONTINENTAL GUARD, THE—Captain, Samuel E. Gross; Lieutenant, Frederick C. Pierce; Ensign, John C. Long; Adjutant, Paul W. Linebarger, Calumet Club; Paymaster, John S Sargent; Quartermaster, Seymour Morris; Surgeon, Dr. John L. Morris; 1st Sergt., Chas. N. Black.

CHICAGO CULTURE CLUB— See page 385.

CHICAGO CYCLING CLUB—3947 Michigan av. Pres., Geo. K. Barrett; V. Pres., Geo. B. Berry; Sec. and Treas., C. I. Critchett; Captain, Orlando Adams.

CHICAGO DAILY NEWS FRESH-AIR FUND—Pres. Victor F. Lawson; gen. mngr. C. M. Faye; city office, 123, 5th av.; Sanitarium, foot Fullerton av., Lincoln Park.

CHICAGO DEACONESSES' HOME—Sec., N. M. Jones, Tacoma bldg; Supt., Miss Mary Jefferson, 227 Ohio.

CHICAGO EXCHANGE FOR WOMAN'S WORK—187 Wabash av. Pres., Mrs. J. B. Lyon; Cor. Sec., Mrs. A. Courtney Campbell; Rec. Sec., Miss Kate Gerts; Treas., Mrs. S. R. Howell.

CHICAGO FLY CASTING CLUB —Pres. Fred N. Peet; V. Pres. C. G. Ludlow; Sec. and Treas. George A. Murrell, 2; 161 Lasalle.

CHICAGO GOLF CLUB — Club house, Wheaton. See p. 386.

CHICAGO HISTORICAL SOCIETY —142 Dearborn av. Public days, Mondays and Thursdays. Open to members (and to others by introduction or approval of the Secretary) every day from 9 a.m. to 5 p.m. Pres., Edward G. Mason; V. Pres. Geo. W. Smith, A. C. McClurg; Sec. and Librarian, Charles Evans.

CHICAGO HOME MISSIONARY AND CHURCH EXTENSION SOCIETY—Pres. William Deering; V. Pres., James B. Hobbs; Treas., H. A. Goodrich; Sec., R. V. Vasey; Cor. Sec., Rev. A D. Traveller, 35, 57 Washington.

CHICAGO KINDERGARTEN CLUB—Meets at 508, 40 Randolph, 2d Saturday of each month. Pres., Miss Mary Jean Miller.

CHICAGO LITERARY CLUB—200 Michigan av. See p. 388.

CHICAGO MECHANICS' INSTITUTE—239 Wabash av. Pres., J. W. Hosmer; Treas., George C. Prussing; Sec. and Librarian, J. Silvers.

CHICAGO MENDELSSOHN CLUB—Apollo Hall. Pres., George H. Iott; V. Pres., D. A. Clippinger; Sec., W. C. Boorn; Treas., C. H. Strawbridge; Musical Director, Harrison M. Wild.

CHICAGO METHODIST PREACHERS' MEETING—Sessions Mondays 10.30 a. m. in First Methodist Church, Clark se. cor. Washington. Pres. Rev. Wm. Fawcett, D.D.

CHICAGO MUSICAL SOCIETY—4, 83 Madison. Pres., H. H. Thiele; V. Pres., James Kubicek; Sec., Chas. F. Hahn; Treas., H. Schols.

CHICAGO ORCHESTRAL ASSN. —1301 Auditorium Tower. Pres., George E. Adams; V. Pres., Bryan Lathrop; Sec., Philo A. Otis, 10, 152 Lasalle; Treas., F. J. Wessels.

CHICAGO PHOTOGRAPHERS' CLUB—Pres., Chas. E. Smith; Sec. and Treas., John F. Decker. Meets at the Victoria Hotel.

CHICAGO PRAYER BOOK SOCIETY—510 Masonic Temple. Pres. Rt. Rev. W. E. McLaren, D.D.; Sec. Rev. Thaddeus A. Snively; Treas. Charles A. Street.

CHICAGO PRESS LEAGUE—156 Washington; Pres. Mrs. Grace Duffie Boylan; 1st V. Pres., Miss Eve Brodlique; 2d V. Pres., Miss Mary Krout; 3d V. Pres., Miss May Rogers; Rec. Sec., Mrs. Mate Palmer; Cor. Sec. Mrs. Maude Corbett Smith; Treas., Miss Vesta E. Severinghaus, 437 N. Ashland av.

CHICAGO RED CROSS SOCIETY —Pres. Chas. M. Faye, 123, 5th av.

CHICAGO RELIEF AND AID SOCIETY—Central office 51 and 53 Lasalle. Telephone 773. Office hours 8 a. m. to 5 p. m. Wood yard foot of Superior; telephone North-415. Pres. Bryan Lathrop; Chairman Executive Com. H. G. Selfridge; Treas. Ernest A. Hamill; Sec. Geo. D. Rumsey; Gen. Supt. Rev. C. G. Trusdell. Directors meet first Monday of every month.

CHICAGO SOUTH SIDE CLUB— 50th ne. cor. Madison av. See p. 389.

CHICAGO SOUTHERN SOCIETY —Pres., Carlos S. Hardy; 1st V. Pres., Henry Hiden ; 2d V.Pres., George W. Becker; Sec. and Treas., Dr. W. T. Mefford, 423 Washington boul. Meet

first Tuesday of each month at Palmer House club room.

CHICAGO TEACHERS' CLUB— 412 Masonic Temple. Pres. Miss Jennie Goldman; 1st V. Pres. Eva B. Crowe; Treas., Miss Helen J. Bliss; Cor. Sec. Miss Mary E. Marshall; Rec. Sec., Miss Caroline M. Towles.

CHICAGO TRACT SOCIETY—167 and 169 Wabash av. Pres., Joseph N. Barker; V. Pres. Rev. E. A. Adams, D.D.; Sec., Jesse W. Brooks, Ph.D.; Treas., David Vernon.

CHICAGO TRAINING SCHOOL FOR CITY, HOME AND FOREIGN MISSIONS—Harris Hall, 4949 Indiana av. Prin. Mrs. Lucy Rider Meyer, M.D.; Sec. N. M. Jones; Treas. N. W. Harris; Supt. Rev. J. Shelly Meyer.

CHICAGO WHIST CLUB— Chicago Stock Exch. bldg. Pres. John T. Mitchell; V. Pres., Willard C. Coe; Sec., C. C. Broomell; Treas., Geo. W. Keehn.

CHICAGO WOMAN'S CLUB— 203 Michigan av. See p. 391.

CHICAGO YALE ASSOCIATION —116 Dearborn. Pres. David B. Lyman; V. Pres. George W. Meeker; Sec. and Treas. R. T. Crane, jr. 10 N. Jefferson.

CHURCH CLUB OF CHICAGO, THE — 510 Masonic Temple. Pres. George S. McReynolds; Sec. Taylor E. Brown; Treas. E. H. Buehler.

CHURCH HOME FOR AGED PERSONS—4327 Ellis av. Visitor ex-officio, Rt. Rev. Wm. E. McLaren, D.D., D.C.L.; Pres. Rev. Joseph Rushton, D.D.; Treas. F. E. Pettit; Chaplain, Rev. Walter Delafield.

CITIZEN'S ASSOCIATION OF CHICAGO—33 Merchants' bldg. 92 Lasalle. Pres. E. Fletcher Ingals; V. Pres. R. E. Jenkins; Sec. J. C. Ambler; Treas. John C. Black; Executive Committee: R. J. Smith, H. H. Kohlsaat, Melville E. Stone, R. E. Jenkins, Wm. A. Fuller, J Stern, E. Fletcher Ingals, J. Harley Bradley, Christoph Hotz, Murry Nelson, Francis B. Peabody, Eugene E. Prussing, John McLaren, Chas. H. Mulliken, F. W. Burlingham. Office, open daily. Executive committee meet Tuesdays.

CITIZEN'S LEAGUE OF CHICAGO—Room 580 Quincy bldg. Pres, I. P. Rumsey; Cor. and Rec. Sec. Geo. E. Wissler; Treas. A. L. Coe; Gen. Agt. H. J. Hayward; Executive Committee: Ira J. Mason, H. W. Dudley, Thomas

Hood, J. W. Janney, Rev. W. T. Meloy, H. H. Forsyth, Albert L. Coe, H. W. Rogers, F. P. Fisher, A. N. Graves. Executive committee meets first Friday of each month.

CIVIC FEDERATION OF CHICAGO — 215 First Nat. Bank bldg. Josiah L. Lombard, Pres.; John W. Ela, 1st V. Pres.; Jane Addams, 2d V. Pres.; Ralph M. Easley, Sec.; Gertrude Beeks, Asst. Sec.; E. G. Keith, Treas. Executive Committee, Josiah L. Lombard, Chm., Adolph Nathan, Wm. T. Baker, Wm. A. Giles, R. T. Crane, Adolph Moses, W. K. Ackerman, Henry Wade Rogers, Paul O. Stensland, Wm. Vocke, Sigmund Zeisler, E. Burritt Smith, Rev. S. J. McPherson, Sadie American, Wm. R. Harper, Newton A. Partridge, Jane Addams, Thos. C. MacMillan, Franklin MacVeagh, Lucy L. Flower, E. G. Keith, Bernard A. Eckhart, John W. Ela, Wm. J. Onahan, Ralph M. Easley, Sarah Hackett Stevenson.

CIVIL SERVICE REFORM ASSOCIATION OF CHICAGO—Pres. Frank H. Scott; Sec. and Treas., F. W. Bull, 423, 184 Lasalle.

COLONIAL DAMES OF AMERICA IN THE STATE OF ILLINOIS—Meets 1st Thursday in each month 10.30 a.m. in Columbus Memorial bldg. Pres., Mrs. Annie W. I. Kerfoot; 1st V. Pres., Mrs. Adlai E. Stevenson; 2d V. Pres., Mrs. Henry B. Mason; Cor. Sec. Mrs. Henry S. Robbins; Rec. Sec., Mrs. James C. Peasley; Treas., Mrs. Martha G. W. Trippe.

COLUMBUS CLUB—43-45 Monroe. See p. 395.

COMMERCIAL CLUB—Meets last Saturday in each month, October to April inclusive. See p. 396.

CONGREGATIONAL CHURCH BUILDING SOCIETY—Office 25, 151 Washington. Western Sec. Rev. C. H. Taintor.

CONGREGATIONAL S.S. AND PUB. SOCIETY — Business Dept. Mgr. E. Herrick Brown, 175 Wabash av. Missionary Dept. District Sec. Rev. W. F. McMillen, 153 Lasalle.

CONVERSATIONAL, THE —6327 Woodlawn av. Pres. and Sec., Mrs. G. V. Hilton.

COOK COUNTY SUNDAY SCHOOL ASSOCIATION—23, 132 Lasalle. Pres., Herbert L. Hill; Supt. and Statistical Sec. W. B. Jacobs; Treas. R. E. Brownell.

CORNELL UNIVERSITY ALUMNI ASSOCIATION OF CHICAGO —Pres. Louis Carl Ehle; V. Pres., D. O. Barts; Sec. and Treas., Frederick G. Fisher, 427 The Rookery.

CORPORATION FOR RELIEF OF WIDOWS AND ORPHANS OF DECEASED CLERGYMEN OF THE PROTESTANT EPISCOPAL CHURCH—Pres. Calvin T. Wheeler; Sec. Mrs. Lydia B. Hibbard, 1701 Prairie av.

COUNTRY CLUB OF EVANSTON —See p. 396.

DAUGHTERS OF THE AMERICAN REVOLUTION—See p 400.

DEACONESS AID SOCIETY—227 Ohio. Pres. Miss C. Addie Brown; Sec., Mrs. F. F. Andrews; Cor. Sec., Mrs. W. A. Conover; Treas., Miss Helen Robinson, 59 Aberdeen.

DELAWARE BOAT CLUB — Pres. Wm. Sullivan; V. Pres. A. Wiesrock; Treas. Fred J. Ringley; Rec. Sec. John T. Riley, 4 Sherman.

DELTA KAPPA EPSILON NORTHWESTERN ASSN. — Pres. Edgar B. Tolman; V. Pres., A. J. Hirschl, A. B. Pease, C. F. McLean; Sec. and Treas. B. W. Sherman, 1153 Monadnock bldg.

DIOCESAN CHOIR ASSOCIATION — Patron, Rt. Rev. Wm. Edward McLaren, D.D., C.L.; Pres., Rev. S. C. Edsall, D.D.; Sec. Alfred Thompson. 211 Jackson boul.; Choirmaster, Harrison M. Wild.

DOUGLAS CLUB—3518 Ellis av. See p. 403.

EDGEWATER CASINO — Edgewater. See p. 374.

ENGINEERS' CLUB OF CHICAGO—1800 Fisher bldg. Pres. M. O. Kasson; V. Pres., J. H. Harris; Sec.. B. W. Thurtell; Treas., T. J. McMaster.

ENGLEWOOD MEN'S CLUB — 63d cor. Harvard av. Pres. Judge E. C. Field; V. Pres., Chas. A. Nowak; sec. and Treas. J. Grant Teller.

ENGLEWOOD WHEELMEN — 319 W. 65th. Pres. Elery S. Caywood; V. Pres., F. D. Tyler; Sec. W. Earl Creviston; Treas. K. R. Howard; Capt. O. V. Mueller.

EVANSTON BOAT CLUB—Sheridan Road n. of Greenleaf av., Evanston. Pres. Frank N. Winne; Sec. Lewis C. Downs; Treas. Peter Taylor.

EVANSTON CLUB—See p. 404.

FELLOWSHIP CLUB—See p 405.

FIELD COLUMBIAN MUSEUM
—See Museums.

FORTNIGHTLY CLUB—15 Washington. See p. 405.

FORTY CLUB—See p. 407.

FORUM CLUB—Forum Hall, Calumet av. nw. cor. 43d. Sec., Geo. E. Quigley; Treas. Geo. H. Bell, Councilor, Arthur F. Klinetop.

FRIDAY CLUB—See p. 407.

GERMANIA MÆNNERCHOR —
Club Room N. Clark nw. cor. Grant. See p. 408.

GIRLS' FRIENDLY SOCIETY (CHICAGO DIOCESAN ORGANIZATION)—Pres., Miss Fanny Groesbeck; V. Pres., Miss Eleanor P. Wood, 405 Dearborn av.; Sec. and Treas., Mrs. Rudolph Williams, Wilmette.

GLEN VIEW GOLF & POLO CLUB—See page 410.

GNOSIS, THE—Pres., Wm. H. Busbey; Sec. and Treas., Mrs. F. L. Morse, 393 Warren av.

GRANT CLUB—Pres. L. L. Bond; Treas. M. E. Cole; Sec. Dr. Liston H. Montgomery, 504, 92 State.

HAMILTON CLUB—114 Madison. See p. 412.

HIGHLAND PARK CLUB—Highland Park. See p. 414.

HILLSDALE COLLEGE ALUMNI ASSOCIATION—Pres. Rev. L. A. Crandall; Sec. Lorenzo E. Dow, 53 Dearborn.

HINSDALE CLUB—See p. 415.

HOLLAND SOCIETY — Annual banquet April 15th. Pres. Peter Van Schaack; V. Pres., D. J. Schuyler; Sec. Robt. H. Van Schaack, 139 Lake; Treas. Geo. E. Van Woert.

HOME FOR DESTITUTE CRIPPLED CHILDREN— 46 Park av. Pres. Mrs. George Sherwood; Sec. Mrs. E. A. Delano; Supt. Miss Isabella Cochrane.

HOME FOR SELF-SUPPORTING WOMEN—275 and 277 Indiana. Pres. Mrs. James B. Waller, jr.; V. Pres. Mrs. C. D. Hamill; Cor. Sec. Mrs. Henry C. Bannard; Rec. Sec. Mrs. Joseph M. Rogers; Treas. Mrs. John S. Hannah.

HOME MISSIONS COMMITTEE OF THE PRESBYTERY OF CHICAGO—1610, 153 Lasalle. Treas. A. G. Pettibone; Supt. Rev. G. P. Williams.

HULL HOUSE—A Social Settlement. 335 S. Halsted. Head resident, Miss Jane Addams.

HYDE PARK CLUB. Washington av. nw. cor. 51st. See p. 416.

HYDE PARK CLUB—Washington av. nw. cor. 51st. Pres., Will H. Moore; V. Pres., Thos. S. Cruttenden; 2d V. Pres., F. H. Trude; Treas., Edward E. Smith; Sec., David W. Ross.

IDEAL CLUB—531 N. Wells. See p. 417.

ILLINOIS AUDUBON SOCIETY Pres., Ruthven Deane, 30 Michigan av.; Sec. and Treas., Miss Mary Drummond, Wheaton, Ill.

ILLINOIS CHILDREN'S HOME AND AID SOCIETY—36, 115 Monroe. Pres., Rev. R. A. White; Sec., Mrs. D. S. Gross; Treas., F. B. Tobey; Supt., Hastings H. Hart; Asst. Supt., Mrs. M. V. B. VanArsdale.

ILLINOIS CLUB—154 S. Ashland av. See p. 418.

ILLINOIS CYCLING CLUB—1215 Washington boul, Pres., W. H. Arthur; V. Pres., L. C. Jaquish; Sec., Dr. A. D. O'Neill; Treas., W. G. Riggs; Capt., W. D. Jaworski.

ILLINOIS FEDERATION OF WOMEN'S CLUBS—Pres., Mrs. Robert B. Farson, 26 Delaware pl., Chicago; Cor. Sec., Mrs. John A. Lutz, Lincoln; Rec. Sec., Mrs. Virginia B. LeRoy. Streator; Treas., Miss Sarah M. Fairbank, Jacksonville.

ILLINOIS HOME MISSIONARY SOCIETY — Office 1006, 153 Lasalle. Pres. Hon. Thomas C. MacMillan; Supt. Rev. James Tompkins; Treas. A. B. Mead.

ILLINOIS HUMANE SOCIETY— 560 Wabash av. Complaints received at office from 8 to 6. Pres. John G. Shortall; Treas. Charles E. Murison; Asst. Sec., J. C. Forbes.

ILLINOIS SOCIETY SONS OF THE AMERICAN REVOLUTION— See page 420.

ILLINOIS ST. ANDREWS SOCIETY—Meets 1st Thursday in February, May, August and November at Room 13, 81 Clark. Pres., Donald L. Morrill; 1st V. Pres. John Williamson; 2d V. Pres. Joseph Cormack; Treas. William Inglis; Sec. John Thomson; Chairman Board of Managers, George Thomson, 47, 97 Washington.

ILLINOIS STATE SUNDAY SCHOOL ASSOCIATION — 23, 132

Lasalle. Treas., R. W. Hare; Sec. W. B. Jacobs.

ILLINOIS WOMAN'S CHRISTIAN TEMPERANCE UNION — 1114 The Temple. Pres. Mrs. Louise S. Rounds, Chicago; V. Pres. Mrs. Mary E. Metzgar, Moline, Ill.; Cor. Sec. Miss Helen Walker, Barry; Rec. Sec. Mrs. Jessie B. Hilton, Evanston, Ill.; Treas. Mrs. A. E. Sanford, Bloomington, Ill.

ILLINOIS WOMAN'S HOME MISSIONARY UNION—25, 151 Washington. Pres. Mrs. Sydney Strong; Sec., Mrs. C. M. Barnes; Treas., Miss Bessie E. Crosby.

ILLINOIS WOMEN'S PRESS ASSOCIATION—See p. 422.

INTERNATIONAL COMMITTEE YOUNG WOMEN'S CHRISTIAN ASSNS.—1312, 126 State. Sec., Mrs. Frank G. Hall; Treas., Mrs. L. W. Messer.

IROQUOIS CLUB — 110 Monroe. See p. 423.

IRVING CLUB—Irving Park. See p. 424.

KENWOOD CLUB—47th cor. Lake av. See p. 425.

KLIO ASSN. THE—210 Masonic Temple. See p. 427.

LA GRANGE CLUB—See p. 427.

LAKE VIEW ART CLUB—Pres., Mrs. Pauline Palmer; V. Pres., Mrs. Olive C. Howard; Sec., Miss Mary Golden Younglove, 522 Fullerton av.; Treas., Miss Maud M. Tilt.

LAKE VIEW CLUB—1923 Barry av. Pres., Simon Mayer; Sec., John Frederick; Treas., Wm. S. Hanlon.

LAKE VIEW WOMAN'S CLUB—Belmont Hall, 1682 N. Clark. See p. 428.

LAKESIDE CLUB—3138 and 3140 Indiana av. See p. 429.

LEAGUE AMERICAN WHEELMEN, ILLINOIS DIVISION—Chief Consul, William H. Arthur, 1009, 59 Clark.

LE SALON FRANCAIS DE CHICAGO—Pres., Miss Anna Clara Boal; V. Prests., Miss Josephine R. Cooke, Miss Adeline Fargo; Treas., Miss Clara Dixon; Sec., Miss Valentine Smith; Dramatic Director, Miss Maud Peixotto.

LEWIS INSTITUTE—W. Madison cor. Robey. Pres. John A. Roche; V. Pres. Christian C. Kohlsaat; Sec. and Treas. John McLaren.

LINCOLN CLUB — Cor. Ashland and Jackson bouls. See p. 431.

LINCOLN CYCLING CLUB — 390 Dearborn av. Pres., H. C. Beitler; V. Pres., Dr. J. M. Cooke; Sec., J. K. Witzel; Treas., C. Hynson; Quartermaster, E. M. Newman; Captain, Geo. R. Catto.

MARQUETTE CLUB — 365 Dearborn av. See p. 434.

MARGARET ETTER CRECHE—Pres., Mrs. L. J. Lamson; Treas., Mrs. E. F. Robbins; Sec., Mrs. A. K. Brown, 3003 Calumet av.

MARY NOBLE CLUB—Pres., Mrs. E. G. Shumway; V. Pres;, Mrs. E. A. Potter; Sec., Miss Annie Oakley, 4700 Drexel boul.

MARYLAND SOCIETY — Pres., John E. Owens; 1st V. Pres., William Ritchie; 2d V. Pres., Martin Emerich; Sec., Charles G. Snow, care Armour & Co.; Treas., William J. Digges.

MATHEON THE—154 Ashland boul. Pres., Sue W. Archibald; 1st V. Pres., Nelly A. Peters; 2d V. Pres., Harriett G. Curtis; Cor. Sec., Mary Maud Avery, 512 W. Adams; Treas., Janet B. MacDowell.

MAYWOOD CLUB—19th av. Maywood. Pres., Luke T. O'Brien; V. Pres., Wm. G. Taylor; Sec., P. H. Gray; Treas., Wm. M. Hulbert.

MENOKEN CLUB—1196 Washington boul. See p. 436.

MIDLOTHIAN COUNTRY CLUB —See page 438.

MILITARY ORDER OF FOREIGN WARS (ILLINOIS COMMANDERY)—Com. Samuel Eberly Gross; V. Com. John H. Trumbull; Sec. John D. Vandercook, 604 Masonic Temple; Treas. Robert P. Walker; Registrar, Nelson A. McClary.

MORTON PARK CLUB—Morton Park. See p. 439.

NAKAMA THE—115 North Oak av. Oak Park. See p. 439.

NATIONAL CHILDREN'S HOME SOCIETY — 36, 115 Monroe. Pres. Hon. John Woodbridge; Sec. Hon. A. O. Wright; Treas. Hon. F. B. Tobey.

NATIONAL WOMAN'S CHRISTIAN TEMPERANCE UNION—1115 The Temple. Pres. Mrs. Lillian M. N. Stevens; V. Pres., Miss Anna A. Gordon; Cor. Sec., Mrs. S. M. Fry; Treas., Mrs. Helen M. Barker.

NEW ENGLAND SOCIETY—Pres. John S. Runnells; Sec. James G. Cozzens, 44, 97 Washington.

NIKÉ CLUB—All Souls Church, Langley av. and Oakwood boul. Pres., Miss Frances T. McMullen; V. Pres., Mrs. J. M. F. Erwin; Rec. Sec., Miss Jennie A. Mosely; Cor. Sec., Miss Lucy B. Penfield, 849, 72d pl.; Treas., Miss Ella M. Porter.

NORTH SHORE CLUB—1835 Wellington av. Pres. C. N. Holden; 1st V. Pres., L. B. Hitchings; 2d V. Pres., Jesse M. Watkins; Sec., Frank A. Raymond; Treas., Harry F. Ross-Lewin.

NORTH SIDE ART CLUB—Pres.¹ Mrs. C. H. Conover; Rec. Sec., Miss Flershem; Cor. Sec., Mrs. F. H. Starkweather; Treas., Mrs. D. H. Wegg.

NORTHWESTERN BAPTIST EDUCATION SOCIETY—At University of Chicago. Sec. Rev. C. E. Hewitt, D.D.

OAK PARK CLUB—Oak Park, Ill. See p. 440.

OAKLAND CLUB—22 Oakwood av. See p. 441.

OAKS, THE—Austin. See p. 442.

OAKS CULTURE CLUB—Austin. Meets third Tuesdays in each month from October to March inclusive, in Oaks Club House, Austin. Pres. Mrs. W. Franklin Ray; Cor. Sec., Mrs. Louis Falk; Treas., Mrs. R. Traill.

101 CLUB—Fine Arts bldg. Pres. Grace Duffie Boylan; V. Pres., John Vance Cheney; Sec. J. Breckenridge Hodges; Fin. Sec., Marie F. Lennards; Treas., Mrs. Willis Howe.

ONWENTSIA—Lake Forest. See p. 443.

PALETTE AND CHISEL CLUB —Athenæum bldg. Pres., Walter M. Clute; V. Pres., David Hunter: Sec., Troy S. Kinney; Treas., W. H. Irvine.

PIONEERS OF CHICAGO—Pres., Henry W. Blodgett; Cor. Sec., Chas. J. Haines; Rec. Sec., Geo. H. Fergus; Sec., Henry H. Handy, 110 Lasalle.

POLYTECHNICAL SOCIETY OF CHICAGO—Pres. Dr. F. W. Ihne, 920, 237, 5th av.; V. Pres. R. R. Henssgen; Treas. William Raecke; Proc. Sec. W. Beyenbach; Librarian, Martin Asch. Meeting every Saturday evening at 106 Randolph.

PRESBYTERIAN BOARD OF AID FOR COLLEGES AND ACADEMIES—30, 115 Monroe. Sec. and Treas. Rev. E. C. Ray, D.D.

PRESBYTERIAN LEAGUE, THE —1010, 155 Lasalle. Pres. Eugene S. Pike,

PRESBYTERIAN MINISTERIAL ASSOCIATION — Meets Mondays, 10:30 a.m. 201 Atlas blk. Pres., Rev. W. F. Irwin; Sec., Rev. H. C. Buell.

PRESS CLUB—106 Madison. See p. 445.

PROTECTIVE AGENCY FOR WOMEN AND CHILDREN — 818 Chicago Opera House bldg. Mrs. R. R. Baldwin, agt.

PULLMAN ATHLETIC ASSOCIATION — Grounds Athletic Island, Pullman, Ill. Pres. Alex. McLachlan; Sec. John McLachlan, 61 Arcade bldg.

PULLMAN CRICKET CLUB — Grounds Pullman, Ill. Thomas Dunbar, pres.; H. Weldrake, sec.

P. E. O. SOCIETY, CHAPTER A. —Pres., Mrs. Emma R. Pratt; Cor. Sec., Miss Minnie Osgood; Treas. Miss Adah Webber.

QUADRANGLE CLUB — Lexington av. and Fifty-eighth. See p. 447.

QUEEN ISABELLA ASSOCIATION—209, 70 State. Pres. Miss Eliza A. Starr; Sec. Dr. Frances Dickinson; Treas. C. V. Waite.

RAVENSWOOD WOMAN'S CLUB—Library Hall, Montrose boul. cor. N. Hermitage av. Pres., Mrs. Geo. Depew; Rec. Sec., Mrs. M. Washington; Cor. Sec., Mrs. Geo. Grannis; Treas., Mrs. Chas. Truax.

RIDGELAND CRICKET CLUB— E. W. Cross, Pres.; Dr. J. H. Ross, V. Pres,; Sec., Joseph Fletcher; Treas.; J. Rigby. Grounds, Lake & 64th st. Oak Park.

RYDER CLUB—St. Paul's Universalist Church. Pres. W. E. Lamb, Sec. Miss Alice Sollitt; Treas., Miss Francelia Colby.

SALON FRANCAIS OF CHICAGO—Pres., Miss Anna Clara Boal; Sec., Miss Valentine Smith; Treas., Miss Clara Dixon.

SERVICE CLUB—Pres. Miss Annie M. Warren; 1st V. Pres. Miss Ida B. Mosebach; 2d V. Pres., Miss Ellen Shumway; Rec. Sec. Miss Abby M. Raymond; Cor. Sec., Miss Eunice Follansbee; Treas., Miss Kate Lancaster. Club Leader, Mrs. Antoinette Van. H. Wakeman.

SHERIDAN CLUB—4100 Michigan av. See p. 448.

SIGMA CHI FRATERNITY—5716 Kimbark av. Prof. S. W. Clark, Head; Warren McIntire, Sec.

SISTERS OF ST. MARY—Mission houses 215 Washington boul.

SOCIAL ECONOMICS CLUB—See p. 450.

SOCIETY FOR ETHICAL CULTURE — Lectures every Sunday, at 11:15 a. m. at Steinway hall. Pres. Frank B. Tobey; Treas. J. F. Turner; Sec., F. W. Allinson, 5825 Kimbark av.; Lecturer, W. M. Salter.

SOCIETY OF COLONIAL WARS —See p. 450.

SOCIETY OF MAYFLOWER DESCENDENTS—See p. 451.

SOCIETY OF SONS OF THE REVOLUTION — Pres. George Mayhew Moulton; V. Pres., Albert Crane Barnes; Sec. Frank Kimball Root, 307 Wabash av.; Treas., Harrison Kelley; Registrar, Frederick Dickinson; Chaplain, Rev. George DeMing Wright.

SOCIETY OF THE WAR OF 1812 —Pres., Charles Page Bryan; 1st V. Pres., William Porter Adams; Sec., Theron Royal Woodward, 302 Dearborn; Treas., Charles Cromwell; Registrar, Edward Nevers; Historian, Milton Tootle, Jr.

SOCIETY OF WESTERN ARTISTS — 1735 Marquette bldg. Pres., F. C. Steele, Indianapolis, Ind.; V. Pres. Lorado Taft, 203 Michigan av.; Sec. and Treas., Holmes Smith, St. Louis, Mo.

SONS AND DAUGHTERS OF MAINE—Pres., Lorenzo E. Dow; V. Pres., F. J. Berry; 2d V. Pres., Chas. H. Deering; Treas., R. Z. Herrick; Sec., Chas. H. Taylor, 1, 159 Lasalle.

SONS OF NEW YORK — Pres Charles A. Dibble; 1st V. Pres. J. Irving Pearce; 2d V. Pres. Fernando Jones; 3d V. Pres. Benjamin F. Chase; Treas. Howard E. Patterson; Sec. F. Ben Davis, 211 Madison.

SONS OF THE AMERICAN REVOLUTION (NATIONAL SOCIETY)—Sec. Gen., Samuel Eberly Gross, 604 Masonic Temple.

SOUTH SIDE CYCLING CLUB—3800 Vincennes av. Pres. Marson French; V. Pres. L. C. Whitaker; Cor. Sec. A. A. Annewalt; Treas. A. R. Nickell, Capt. Charles Dameier.

ST. GEORGE'S BENEVOLENT ASSOCIATION—Meets at call of the President. Pres. W. B. Jackson; Sec. C. J. Burroughs, 859 Washington boul. Treas. Wm. L. Tapson.

ST. GEORGE'S CRICKET CLUB — Grounds Fullerton av. cor. North Park av. Pres. Bicknell Young; Sec. and Tres., W. J. Terrell.

STANDARD CLUB—Michigan av. sw. cor. Twenty-fourth. See p. 452.

SUNSET CLUB—506 Tacoma bldg. Sec. Howard Leslie Smith.

SUPREME AND ILLUSTRIOUS ASCLEPION OF THE WORLD—Mystic Order Disciples of Æsculapius Dr. Frank C. Hoyt, 504, 92 State; Supreme and Illustrious High Priest, Dr. Liston H. Montgomery, 504, 92 State; Supreme and Illustrious Censor, Dr. Fred C. Zapffe, 925 Warren av.; Supreme and illustrious Registrar and Financier.

SWEDISH GLEE CLUB—470 Lasalle av. Pres. Gus. Lundquist; Sec. G. Wallin.

TOLLESTON CLUB—Sec. George Manierre, 214, 184 Lasalle.

TRUSTEES OF THE ENDOWMENT FUND OF THE DIOCESE OF CHICAGO—Pres. Francis B. Peabody; Treas., Wm. Kelsey Reed, 25 Borden blk.

TWENTIETH CENTURY CLUB —See p. 454.

UM-ZOO-EE CLUB—Pres., Charles A. Nowak; V. Pres., H. S. Culliton; Sec. and Treas., J. H. Crane, 6836 Wentworth av.

UNION CLUB—Washington pl. sw. cor. Dearborn av. See p. 455.

UNION LEAGUE CLUB—Jackson boul. sw. cor. Custom House pl. See p. 457.

UNITED HEBREW CHARITIES —223, 26th. Office hours 8 a.m. to 4 p.m. except Sundays. Pres. I. Greensfelder; V. Pres., H. F. Hahn; Rec. Sec. Julian W. Mack; Fin. Sec. Chas. Hefter; Supt. Francis E. Kiss; Supt. Employment Bureau, S. Bartenstein.

UNITY CLUB—See p. 461.

UNIVERSITY CLUB — 118 Dearborn. See p. 462.

URSULA LUNCH CLUB—64 and 66 Wabash av. Pres., Mrs. W. F. Dummer; Sec., Miss June Mott; Treas., Miss Harriet G. Phillips.

WASHINGTON PARK CLUB — 61st and South park av. See p. 464.

WEST END WOMAN'S CLUB— 542 W. Monroe. See p. 467.

WESTERN NEW CHURCH UN-

ION—901 Steinway Hall. Sec., Rev. L. P. Mercer.

WESTERN SOCIETY ARMY OF THE POTOMAC—Pres., Sergt. H. P. Thompson; Sec., Capt. Bradley Dean, 140 Monroe. Meets second Monday in March, May, September and November in club-room, Sherman House. Annual meeting, January.

WESTWARD HO GOLF CLUB—Oak Park. See p. 469.

WHITE CITY CLUB—Leland Hotel. Pres., Mrs. Sara Steenberg; V. Pres., Mrs. O. A. Wells; Treas., Mrs. E. W. Beadell; Sec., N. C. Martin.

WOMAN'S AUXILIARY OF THE BOARD OF MISSIONS—See Chicago Branch of the.

WOMAN'S BAPTIST FOREIGN MISSION QUARTERLY—Pres., Mrs. E. F. Stearns; V. Pres., Mrs. J. B. Smalley; Sec., Mrs. L. K. Torbet, Hotel Holland, 53d and Lake av.; Treas., Mrs. M. E. Kline.

WOMAN'S BAPTIST FOREIGN MISSIONARY SOCIETY OF THE WEST—1535 Masonic Temple. Pres., Mrs. J. H. Randall, St. Paul, Minn.; Treas., Mrs. Matilda E. Kline, 1535 Masonic Temple.

WOMAN'S BOARD OF MISSIONS OF THE INTERIOR—Room 603, 59 Dearborn. Pres. Mrs. Moses Smith; Rec. Sec. Miss M. D. Wingate; Treas. Mrs. J. B. Leake. Office hours, 9 a. m. to 5 p. m. Illinois branch of W. B. M. I., Pres., Mrs. Oliver C. Ely; Rec. Sec., Miss Mary I. Lyman, 200 Ashland boul.

WOMAN'S CLUB OF AUSTIN—Pres. Mrs. George W. Kretzinger; V. Pres. Mrs. George B. Charles; Sec. Mrs. Henry F. Griffing; Cor. Sec. Mrs. Fred H. Alden; Treas. Mrs. Edwin F. Abbott.

WOMAN'S EXCHANGE—187 Wabash av. See Chicago Exchange for Woman's Work.

WOMAN'S FOREIGN MISSIONARY SOCIETY OF CHICAGO PRESBYTERY—48 McCormick blk. Pres., Mrs. L. H. Mitchell; Cor. Sec. Mrs. James Frothingham, 527 Kenwood Terrace; Treas., Mrs. W. A. Lacy.

WOMAN'S PRESBYTERIAL SOCIETY FOR HOME MISSIONS—Room 817 Association bldg. Pres. Mrs. H. P. Merriman; Gen. Sec. Mrs. C. K. Adams; Treas. Mrs. J. A. Yale.

WOMAN'S PRESBYTERIAN BOARD OF MISSIONS OF THE

NORTHWEST—48 McCormick blk. Rec. Sec. Mrs. W. B. Jacobs, Chicago; Treas. Mrs. C. B. Farwell.

WOMAN'S SOUTH SIDE STUDY CLUB — Pres., Mrs. Edward Roby; Treas;, Mrs. G. E. Eastman; Cor. Sec. Mrs. W. J. Young, 9144 Commercial av.; Rec. Sec., Mrs. Edward Watkins.

WOMEN'S BAPTIST HOME MISSION SOCIETY — 2411 Indiana av. Pres., Mrs. J. N. Crouse; Treas., Mrs. A. H. Barber; Cor. Sec., Miss M. G. Burdette.

WOMEN'S BAPTIST HOME MISSION UNION—2411 Indiana av. Pres. Mrs. J. N. Crouse; Cor. Sec. Miss M. G. Burdette, 2411 Indiana av.; Rec. Sec., Mrs. W. E. Walmsley, Brooklyn; Treas. Mrs. A. H. Barber.

WOMEN'S FOREIGN MISSIONARY SOCIETY of the Methodist Episcopal Church, Northwestern Branch—Meets 2d and 4th Fridays at 35, 57 Washington. Pres. Mrs. W. E. Quine; Cor. Sec. Mrs. F. P. Crandon; Rec. Sec. Mrs. L. H. Jennings.

WOODLAWN MATINEE MUSICALE. See p. 470.

WOODLAWN PARK CLUB—Woodlawn av. cor 64th. See p. 470.

WORKING WOMAN'S HOME ASSOCIATION—21 S. Peoria. Pres. Frank Pearson; V. Pres. Mrs. E. R. Nichols; 2d V. Pres. Mrs. A. Chaiser; Sec., Amelia Stegman; Treas., Geo. P. Bay; Auditor, Frank E. Brown; Medical Supt. Dr. J. J. Thompson; Manager, Laura G. Fixen; Councelor, Chas. S. Williston; Free Fresh Air Summer Cottage, Lake Bluff, Ill.; Free Dispensary, 420 W. Madison.

WYANDOT TENNIS CLUB—Superior and Pine. Pres. Louis V. Le Moyne; V. Pres. Miss Rosalie Sturges; Treas. Frank J. LeMoyne; Sec. Morris L. Johnston, Jr., 1626 Prairie av.; Capt. Everts Wrenn.

YOUNG MEN'S CHRISTIAN ASSOCIATION—General office, 153-155 Lasalle. Board of Trustees: Pres. Albert L. Coe; V. Pres. A. G. Lane; Treas. E. G. Keith; Sec. John V. Farwell Jr.; Board of Managers, Pres. Henry M. Hubbard; 1st V. Pres. John M. Ewen; 2d V. Pres., W. H. Holcomb; Treas. Arthur Heurtley; Rec. Sec. Horace M. Starkey, M. D.; Gen. Sec. L. Wilbur Messer; Asst. Gen. Sec. Walter T. Hart; Committee of Management Central Department, Chairman, John M. Ewen; V. Chairman, John R. Case; Rec. Sec. Frank Milligan; Dept.

Sec. James F. Oates; Educational Director, Walter M. Wood; Physical Director, George W. Ehler. Central Dept. 153 Lasalle; West Side Dept. 542 W. Monroe; Ravenswood Dept. 610 Wilson av.; Garfield Boulevard Railway Dept. Garfield boul. and Shields av.; Intercollegiate Dept. 153 Lasalle; Hyde Park Dept. 5701 Rosalie ct., C. & N. W. Railway, Dept. N. 41st av. and W. Kinzie; Dearborn Station R.R. Dept. 169-171 Plymouth ct.; Grand Trunk Railway Dept., W. 51st cor. S. St. Louis av.

YOUNG MEN'S CHRISTIAN ASSOCIATION—Evanston, 1615 Orrington av. open daily 9 a. m. to 9 p. m. Sundays 3 to 5 p. m. Gen. Sec. Wm. Boyd.

YOUNG WOMEN'S CHRISTIAN ASSOCIATION—288 Michigan av. Pres. Mrs. Leander Stone; V. Pres. Mrs. Irenus K. Hamilton, Mrs. Thomas Corlett, Mrs. Fannie B. Myers; Treas. Miss M. E. True; Cor. Sec. Mrs. J. M. Brodie; Rec. Sec. Mrs. A. S. Chamberlin.

YOUNG WOMEN'S CHRISTIAN ASSOCIATION (INTERNATIONAL COMMITTEE OF) — 1313, 126 State. Chairman, Mrs. H. C. Tillman; Vice Chairman, Mrs. C. M. Howe; Sec. Mrs. Frank G. Hall; Cor. Sec. Mrs. J. W. Dickinson; Treas. Mrs. L. W. Messer.

YOUNG WOMEN'S CHRISTIAN ASSOCIATION (TRANSIENT HOME)—59 Centre av. cor. W. Adams.

SOUTH DIVISION.

ALDINE SQUARE.

2 Mrs. Charles E. Bliven
Receiving day Tuesday
2 Howard Bliven
2 Waite Bliven
2 Miss Sarah M. Horton
3 Mr. & Mrs. Thomas Brown jr. & dr.
3 Everett C. Brown
4 Mrs. Henry E. Meleney & dr.
4 George B. Meleney
4 Miss Katharine C. Innis
5 Mr. & Mrs. Wm. A. Moulton
6 Mr. & Mrs. Thos. E. Milchrist & drs.
7 Mr. & Mrs. Charles H. Hildreth
7 Miss Grace B. Chappelle
8 Mr. & Mrs. Alex. P. Moore
8 Clarence E. Moore
8 Francis S. Moore
9 Mrs. R. H. Kelly
9 Mrs. A. W. Freeman
9 Howard Freeman
9 L. H. Freeman
10 Mr. & Mrs. Geo. R. Walker
10 Mr. & Mrs. Samuel K. Dow
11 Mr. & Mrs. Henry C. F. Zeiss
Receiving day 1st Friday
12 Mrs. John W. Marsh & dr.
12 John P. Marsh
13 Mrs. Wm. H. Alexander
Receiving day Wednesday
13 Henry O. Alexander
14 Mrs. C. C. Logan & dr.
14 Mr. & Mr. Samuel W. Russell
15 Mr. & Mrs. Abner Smith
17 Mr. & Mrs. Daniel C. Osmun
18 Mr. & Mrs. Paul Dana
19 Mr. & Mrs. Geo. C. Lazear
20 Dr. & Mrs. Charles F. Bassett
21 Rev. & Mrs. Wm. White Wilson & dr.
Receiving day Monday

21 Albert E. Wilson
22 George Chainey
25 Mr. & Mrs. John C. Hatch & dr.
25 Edwin H. Hatch
25 Lullus J. Ennis
26 Mrs. Joseph H. Hall
27 Mr. & Mrs. John H. Purdy
27 Charles S. Purdy
28 James P. Black
30 Mrs. Anna R. Mulford & dr.
31 John Wills
31 Mr. & Mrs. John D. Parker & dr.
32 Mr. & Mrs. Augustus O. Hall & dr.
Receiving day Tuesday
32 Newman G. Hall
33 Mrs. Lora McCluer
34 Mr. & Mrs. Joseph W. Helmer & dr.
34 Harry Helmer
35 Mr. & Mrs. Alonzo Blossom & dr.
36 Mr. & Mrs. Mifflin E. Bell & drs.
36 Dillwyn M. Bell
37 Mr. & Mrs. William S. Jackson
37 William C. Jackson
38 Mr. & Mrs. Wm. G. Jerrems & dr.
38 Alex. N. Jerrems
40 Mr. & Mrs. B. G. Robinson
40 Mr. & Mrs. Frank B. Robinson
41 Mrs. Myrtle W. Thayer & dr.
41 Mrs. Myrtilla Wilkins
41 Charles H. Wilkins
41 Edwin P. Wilkins
41 Wm. A. Wilkins
41 Mrs. May W. Arms
41 Frank D. Arms
42 Mr. & Mrs. H. D. Smith
Receive 1st Tuesday in mo.
42 Harry B. Smith

ANTHONY AVENUE.

6848 Mr. & Mrs. F. E. Stevens
     Receiving day Tuesday

BERKELEY AVENUE.

4117 Mrs. & Mrs. Charles T. Daily
4161 Dr. & Mrs. W. A. Fisher
4167 Mr. & Mrs. George G. Yeomans
4169 Mr. & Mrs. Frederick W. Becker
4227 Mr. & Mrs. J. W. Simmons
4315 Mr. & Mrs. James H. Teller
4317 Mr. & Mrs. Henry A. Pope
4319 Mrs. M. E. Magee & dr.
4319 George Magee
4321 Mr. & Mrs. L. D. Wright
4323 Mr. & Mrs. Henry Waixel
     Receiving day Sunday
4323 Sol. H. Waixel
4323 Isaac H. Waixel
4327 Mrs. C. Neuberger
4327 Henry May
4331 Mr. & Mrs. Arthur Schiller
4337 Dr. Eliza R. Morse
4353 Mr. & Mrs. Arthur T. Whitman
4359 Mr. & Mrs. E. A. Calkins
4401 Mrs. M. B. Pitts
4403 Wm. McMillan
4403 Miss Anna McMillan
4409 Mr. & Mrs. Louis Heilprin
4411 Mr. & Mrs. Edward Rector
4413 Mr. & Mrs. Harry Wilkinson
4415 Mr. & Mrs. Hamlin M. Spiegel
4417 Mr. & Mrs. Charles Sittig
     Receiving day Tuesday
4417 Clarence Hirschhorn
4421 Mr. & Mrs. R. L. Van Arsdale
4429 Mr. & Mrs. J. G. Hartigan
4431 Mr. & Mrs. Sol Wolf
4431 Mrs. S. H. Kahn
4433 Mr. & Mrs. Horace Baker
4435 Mr. and Mrs. F. W. Preston
4441 Mr. & Mrs. Charles J. Dodgshun
4445 Mrs. F. Degginger
4445 Sidney Degginger
4453 Mr. & Mrs. Carlos A. W. Platt
4453 Miss Louise J. Haagen
4453 Mrs. A. M. Topping & dr.
4453 Miss Helen M. Topping
4455 Mr. & Mrs. J. N. Hobbs
———
4446 Mrs. S. Friedman
4450 Mr. & Mrs. R. Delos Martyn
     Receiving day Wednesday

4128 Dr. E. R. Carpenter
4128 Mr. & Mrs. W. P. J. DeLand
4130 Mr. & Mrs. C. P. Boorn
4132 Mr. & Mrs. W. H. Duffield
4140 Mrs. C. Webster
4140 Mr. & Mrs. Henry Lawrie
4140 William Lawrie
4156 Mrs. Mary M. Hill & drs.
4156 John H. Hill
4206½ Mr. & Mrs. Geo. N. Pogue
4208½ Mr. & Mrs. Thad. H. Howe
4210 Mrs. Mary S. Foulke & dr.
4216 Mr. & Mrs. G. A. Douglass
4216 Leonard B. Douglass
4322 Mr. & Mrs. H. H. Drew & dr.
4324 Mr. & Mrs. Wm. C. Drew
4328 Mr. & Mrs. Charles H. Smith
4328 W. T. Smith
4332 Mr. & Mrs. Sterling P. Wiley
4332 Miss Vilette Windett
4336 Mr. & Mrs. A. C. Mace
4338 Mr. & Mrs. W. H. Rothermel
4346 Mr. & Mrs. H. F. Leopold
4346 Mr. & Mrs. Charles H. Trego
4356 Mr. & Mrs. Walter S. Jones
     Receiving day Thursday
4356 Mrs. Mary E. Hitchcock
4358 Mr. & Mrs. M. F. Mogg
4400 Mr. & Mrs. Louis K. Fisher
4400 Mrs. H. Nassauer
4402 Mr. & Mrs. Charles Dougherty
4404 Mr. & Mrs. Joel H. Levi
4406 Mr. & Mrs. B. M. Douglas
4408 Mr. & Mrs. C. F. Krebs
4412 Mr. & Mrs. B. F. Patrick jr.
4412 Mr. & Mrs. G. H. McClellan
4416 Mr. & Mrs. W. H. Sills
4416 Mrs. Mary A. Sills
4418 Mr. & Mrs. C. P. Monash
4432 Mr. & Mrs. F. W. Bullock
4434 Mr. & Mrs. Frank Reed
4436 Mr. & Mrs. George F. Schilling
4438 Dr. & Mrs. I. A. Freeman
4440 Mr. & Mrs. A. Hartman
4442 Mr. & Mrs. Frank R. Strauss
4444 Mr. & Mrs. Albert H. Meads
4446 Jacob Friedman

4456 Mr. & Mrs. D. Guthman
4458 Mr. & Mrs. J. J. Wagoner & drs.
4458 Stanley Wagoner

4460 Dr. & Mrs. Carl E. Kurtz
4462 Mr. & Mrs. Frank L. Danforth
4464 Mr. & Mrs. J. B. Pollard

BOWEN AVENUE.

77 Miss Fannie Schwartz
77 Mrs. S Zuckerman & dr.
79 Mr. & Mrs. George W. Ambrose
89 Mr. & Mrs. Charles M. Faye
91 Mr. & Mrs. Frank A. Bingham
93 Mr. & Mrs. David L. Druliner
267 Mr. & Mrs. W. S. Jones
267 Mr. & Mrs. Harry Goodwin
315 Mr. & Mrs. F. C. Seymour
319 Dr. Sarah W. Andrews
319 Mrs. Alvah Perry & dr.
327 Mr. & Mrs. W. W. Wyatt
329 Mr. & Mrs. Stephen VanKirk
     & dr.
339 Mrs. Mary C. Taylor & dr.
343 Mr. & Mrs. R. E. Ismond
363 Mr. & Mrs. F. H. Holden
363 Miss Abbie L. Howe
367 Mr. & Mrs. Wm. Fulghum
371 Mr. & Mrs. M. C. Scobey & drs.
399 Mr. & Mrs. Michael Ash
399 M. L. Ash
403 Mr. & Mrs. J. S. Hartmann
403 Henry S. Hartmann
403 Samuel Hartmann
405 Mr. & Mrs. E. Myer
409 Mr. & Mrs. F. J. Lewis
411 Miss Louise M. Dunning
413 Mr. & Mrs. H. J. Pollak
413 Mrs. Clara Holzner
457 Mr. & Mrs. H. G. Holloway
459 Mr. & Mrs. Thomas Foster & drs
459 Mr. & Mrs. Leon Jacobs
465 Miss Lucille Stevenson
467 Mr. & Mrs. Adolph Shakman
467 Henry A. Shakman

80 Mr. & Mrs. F. E. Makeel
80 William Anderson & dr.
182 Mrs. Frances Klein
184 Mr. & Mrs. C. E. Wilner
186 Mr. & Mrs. James Campbell
186 John G. Campbell
190 Mr. & Mrs. C. J. Shepard
194 Mr. & Mrs. Alfred Daniels
196 Mr. & Mrs. Louis Hasbrouck
320 Dr. & Mrs. Morey L. Reed
378 George J. Cozard
378 Mr. & Mrs. Louis Bergersen
390 Mr. & Mrs. Enoch Harpole
392 Mr. & Mrs. W. A. Schmitt & drs.
400 Mr. & Mrs. Daniel Martin
408 Dr. & Mrs. A. L. Van Patten
410 Mr. & Mrs. J. F. Randolph
410 Miss Ruth F. Randolph
414 Mrs. Kenyon Green
416 Mrs. Ann Green & dr.
444 E. Olmstead & dr.
462 Dr. Marie Louise Hunt
462 Mr. & Mrs. J. E. Strader
464 Mr. & Mrs. Neil McMillan
486 Mr. & Mrs. C. R. Pfeiffer

467 Mr. & Mrs. Aaron Shubart
469 J. C. Considene & drs.
471 Mrs. P. Kohner
471 J. B. Kohner
479 Dr. & Mrs. W. M. Harsha
481 Mr. & Mrs. M. Stern
481 Mr. & Mrs. M. Joseph
485 Mr. & Mrs. John G. Boess
489 Rev. & Mrs. Howard A. John-
     ston

BRYANT AVENUE.

19 John B. Adams
19 Miss Nellie M. Adams
21 Mr. & Mrs. William J. Marks
21 Mrs. Dennis Graham
21 Dennis C. Graham
39 Mrs. Martha A. Walker
39 Mrs. Jessie M. Tucker
47 Mr. & Mrs. J. Pearson Coleman
57 Mr. & Mrs. Elli A. Beach & dr.
57 Henry L. Beach

10 Mr. & Mrs. Wm. R. Everett
12 Mr. & Mrs. David J. Bard
14 Miss Charlotte S. Murch
14 Mrs. Addie S. Cornell
18 Mr. & Mrs. William S. Bates
22 Mr. & Mrs. Albert H. Barber
26 Mr. & Mrs. Frederick Dickinson
26 John R. Dickinson
30 Thomas W. Stillman
30 Herman W. Stillman & dr.

57 Clinton S. Beach
59 Mr. & Mrs. Thomas J. Sutherland
61 Mr. & Mrs. Adolph Klein
65 Mr. & Mrs. Wm. B. Jacobs & drs.
69 Mrs. Caroline H. Cotton & dr.
69 Charles H. Cotton
77 Mr. & Mrs. Herbert V. Richards
81 Mr. & Mrs. Joseph S. Shaw
83 Dr. & Mrs. S. G. Bailey

84 Mrs. James McD. Mulchahey
84 Mrs. Elicia F. Sargeant & dr.
86 Charles H. Low
88 Mr. & Mrs. Wm. F. File

34 Mr. & Mrs. Herman Prenzlauer
40 Mr. & Mrs. T. P. Murray
44 Mr. & Mrs. Benno F. Nell
46 Mr. & Mrs. John L. Jones.
50 Mr. & Mrs. George B. Clason
52 Mr. & Mrs. Julius Loewenthal
52 Milton Loewenthal
54 Mr. & Mrs. W. S. Goodhue & drs.
54 A. Homer Goodhue
62 Mrs. Sarah Marshall & dr.
64 Mr. & Mrs. Walter H. Baldwin
66 Mr. & Mrs. Mark Neuman
68 Mr. & Mrs. Thomas B. Ackers
74 Mr. & Mrs. Orrin S. Cook & dr.
74 Robert S. Cook

BUTLER STREET.

5933 William Roovaart
6401 Mr. & Mrs. James G. Elsdon
7413 Raymond O. Evans
7657 Rev. & Mrs. O. E. Murray
7657 Mrs. William Brush
7659 Mr. & Mrs. G. Huston
7659 Mrs. Hannah Walton
7735 Mr. & Mrs. Jos. B. Mann
7847 Dr. & Mrs. H. H. Mather

7424 Mr. & Mrs. Selim H. Peabody
7732 Mr. & Mrs. W. A. Ebbert
7738 George Weber
7738 Mr. & Mrs. Henry Weber
7740 Mr. & Mrs. H. E. Crouch
7804 Rev. & Mrs. Wm. A. Waldo

5918 Mr. & Mrs. W. H. Dudgeon
6414 Rev. & Mrs. F. A. Hardin
6414 Rev. Raymond A. Hardin
6510 Mr. & Mrs. G. F. Child
6550 Mr. & Mrs. Ira F. Eulette
6556 Samuel R. Moore
6618 Mr. & Mrs. P. S. Hudson & dr.
6638 Mr. & Mrs. Gates A. Ryther
6710 Mr. & Mrs. Geo. A. Gindele
6710 Mrs. H. Long
6756 Mr. & Mrs. Edwin F. Stevens
6802 Mr. & Mrs. Chas. S. Mather
6808 Mr. & Mrs. L. D. Bristol
6950 Mr. & Mrs. Franklin Hess
6950 Mrs. R. D. Meeker & dr.
7020 Dr. & Mrs. Charles D. Camp

CALUMET AVENUE.

1927 Mr. & Mrs. George S. Fleet
1931 Mr. & Mrs. Charles Sumner Holt
2101 Mrs. Moses Gunn
2101 Walter C. Gunn
2101 Dr. Malcolm Gunn
2107 Mr. & Mrs. Arthur B. Meeker & dr.
2119 Mr. & Mrs. Geo. M. Moulton
   Receiving day Friday
2119 Garland Moulton
2119 Mrs. M. A. Garland
   Receiving day Friday
2119 Mr. & Mrs. John H. Murphy
2125 Mr. & Mrs. John A. Markley
2125 Mr. & Mrs. W. Vincent Baker
2129 Mr. & Mrs. William E. Kelley & dr.
   Receiving day Friday

1830 Dr. & Mrs. Wm. E. Casselberry
1832 Mr. & Mrs. John Buckingham
1836 Mr. & Mrs. Norman Williams
1836 Norman Williams jr.
1840 Mr. & Mrs. William Randall Crawford
1910 Mr. & Mrs. Arthur J. Caton
1922 Mr. & Mrs. Henry Dibblee & drs.
1922 Stanley Field
1928 Mrs. H. H. Manierre
1928 Edward Manierre
1928 Benjamin Manierre
1932 Mr. & Mrs. E. P. Whitehead & dr.
2000 Mr. & Mrs. Henry Crawford & dr.
2000 Miss E. L. Kent
2004 Mr. & Mrs. W. H. Mitchell & drs.

2129 Wm. R. Kelley
2129 Mrs. Ellen P. Vail
2131 Mr. & Mrs. John Alling & dr.
2131 John Alling jr.
2133 Mr. & Mrs. John R. Walsh & dr.
2201 Mr. & Mrs. B. F. Jacobs
2201 Mr. & Mrs. Maclay Hoyne
2205 J. A. Cassidy & dr.
2205 Harry C. Cassidy
2209 Mr. & Mrs. Albert H. Farnum
    Receiving day Tuesday
2209 Harry W. Farnum
2213 Mr. & Mrs. Lazarus Silverman
    & dr. *Receiving day Monday*
2217 Mr. & Mrs. M. Bensinger
    Receiving day Tuesday
2217 Mr. & Mrs. B. E. Bensinger
2227 Mr. & Mrs. John C. Richberg
    & dr.
2227 Donald R. Richberg
2229 Mr. & Mrs. Joseph Rosenbaum
    & dr. *Receiving day Friday*
2231 Mr. & Mrs. E. T. Rosenbaum
2233 Mr. & Mrs. O. W. Barrett
2233 Oliver S. Barrett
2233 S. S. Osborne
2235 Judge & Mrs. Kirk Hawes
2239 Mr. & Mrs. C. L. Raymond
2241 Mr. & Mrs. Frank Hall Childs
2241 Miss Clara Hunt
2241 Clement M. Hunt
2241 A. Lucas Hunt
2243 Mrs. Leopold Simon & dr.
    Receiving day Friday
2243 Benjamin F. Simon
2243 Mr. & Mrs. M. S. Greenebaum
2247 Mr. & Mrs. Henry Katz & drs.
    Receiving day Friday
2247 Samuel B. Katz
2249 Mr. & Mrs. A. B. Adam & dr.
    Receiving day Tuesday
2253 Mr. & Mrs. Chas. H. Kingman
2253 Barry Kingman
2301 Mr.&Mrs.Frank H. Follansbee
    Receiving day Friday
2305 Mr. & Mrs. John P. Laflin
2329 Mr. & Mrs. Henry Crawford jr.
2339 Mr. & Mrs. R. J. Walshe & dr.
2419 Mrs. Frederick Espert & dr.
2419 Frederick Espert jr
2611 Frank Burnam
2621 J. H. Streeter
2623 Mrs. Rosa Friendly
2623 Mrs. William Friend
2623 Edward Friend

2008 Mrs. P. C. Hanford & dr.
    Receiving day Friday
2016 Mr. & Mrs. Arthur Meeker
2018 Mr. & Mrs. J. A. Kohn
    Receiving day Saturday
2018 Mr. & Mrs. Harry W. Hahn
2032 Mr. & Mrs. Otto Young
2032 Miss Daisy Marie Young
2032 Miss Catherine Orsburne
    Young
2100 Mrs. D. B. Fisk
2100 Mrs. B. B. Botsford & dr.
2100 Henry E. Fisk
2106 Mr. & Mrs. A. C. Badger
    Receiving day Tuesday
2106 Miss Ada C. Badger
2106 Sheridan S. Badger
2114 Mrs. John B. Drake & drs.
2114 Francis E. Drake
2124 Mr. & Mrs. Theodore A. Shaw
2124 Theodore A. Shaw jr.
2128 Mr. & Mrs. John A. Davidson
2140 Mrs. Daniel A. Jones
    Receiving day Friday
2222 Mrs. A. DeGraff
2222 Robert M. Fair
2222 Miss A. M. Fair
2222 Joseph B. Fair
2222 Charles M. Fair
2230 Mr. & Mrs. Charles W. Drew
    & dr.
2240 Mr. & Mrs. Julius Strauss
2240 Milton H. Kohn
2240 A. H. Kohn
2244 Mrs. Asa P. Kelley
2244 Mr. & Mrs. W. B. E. Shufeldt
2252 Mrs. W. F. Coolbaugh & drs.
    Receiving day Wednesday
2300 Mr. & Mrs. Rudolph Matz
2306 Mr. & Mrs. Augustus W. Green
    & dr. *Receiving day Friday*
2306 Irwin Green
2310 Mr. & Mrs. John S. Gould & dr.
2310 Mr. & Mrs. Edward A. Fargo
2312 Mr. & Mrs. John B. Mayo
    Receiving day Friday
2316 Mrs. Henry L. Hill
2324 Mr.& Mrs.Frank Ogden Magie
    Receiving day Wednesday
2340 Mr. & Mrs. Lewis L. Davis
    Receiving day Thursday
2340 George Townsend
2340 Miss Cornelia Townsend
2340 Rev. & Mrs. Harold Morse
2340 Charles L. Cursham
2342 Mr. & Mrs. Franklin Nichols

2625 Mr. & Mrs. Henry Adler
Receiving day Friday
2633 Mr. & Mrs. Samuel Jackson
2633 Miss Ray Jackson
2729 Mrs. E. Burnham & dr.
2731 Mr. & Mrs. Charles W. Neill
2813 Mrs. M. F. Hopkins & drs.
2941 Mr. & Mrs. Charles P. Miller
2943 Mrs. John F. Temple & drs.
2943 Miss Anna E. Bryan
3001 Mr. & Mrs. Joseph H. Dimery
3001 Mrs. Emma D. Frederick
3005 Mrs. E. P. Burlingham
3005 Frederick W. Burlingham
3005 Mr. & Mrs. Wm. C. Boyden
3015 Mr. & Mrs. D. B. Quinlan
3021 Dr. & Mrs. H. T. Byford
3021 Mr. & Mrs. Wm. G. Jerrems jr.
3023 Mr. & Mrs. Geo. W. Wiley & dr.
3023 James R. Wiley
3023 Benjamin S. Wiley
3105 Mr. & Mrs. J. A. McLennan
3119 Mr. & Mrs. Henry B. Steele
3123 Mr. & Mrs. Samuel B. Steele
Receiving day Friday
3123 Mrs. Bernard Steele
3123 Maurice B. Steele
3127 Mr. & Mrs. Isaac Wedeles
Receiving day Tuesday
3141 Mr. & Mrs. Joseph Deimel
3141 Mr. & Mrs. Rudolph Deimel
3147 Mr. & Mrs. Levi B. Bane & dr.
3147 Joseph W. McKee
3147 Mr. & Mrs. Orville K. Richards
3153 Mr. & Mrs. Charles E. Felton
Receiving day Thursday
3153 Mrs. Mary Felton Grey
3155 Mr. & Mrs. Melvin J. Neahr
3155 George H. Neahr
3157 Mr.&Mrs. Malcolm C. Mitchell
3157 Mr. & Mrs. Chas. B. Brown
3201 Dr. & Mrs. Ernest Lackner
3201 Mr. & Mrs. J. Grossenheider
3203 Mr. & Mrs. Thomas Kent
3203 Miss Isabella E. Westlake
3207 Mrs. Samuel M. Fleishman
3207 Mrs. Jacob May
3211 Mr. & Mrs. John A. Orb
3221 James C. Sinclair
3247 Stephen Healy & drs.
3253 Mrs. Henry Kerber & drs.
3305 Mr. & Mrs. George J. Cooke
3307 Mrs. John E. Wilson & dr.
3307 Luke E. Wilson
3307 Paul E. Wilson

2342 Mr. & Mrs. P. J. Roche & dr.
2346 Dr. & Mrs. Wm. F. Fowler
2600 Mr. & Mrs. H. P. Colegrove
2600 Dr. T. Jay Robeson
2616 Mrs. Jennie Hall Aiken
2616 J. F. Aiken
2616 Frank Hall
2616 Miss Mary J. Carrigan
2624 Charles H. Randall
2624 Mr. & Mrs. T. D. Randall
2624 Mrs. Charlotte Breese
2632 Mrs. W. B. Burbank
2632 E. A. Burbank
2646 Dr. & Mrs. John W. Streeter
2646 Miss Marjorie Streeter
2646 Edward Clark Streeter
2704 Mrs. James Stenson & dr.
2712 Mr. & Mrs. M. C. Hickey & drs.
2712 Charles M. Hickey
2712 Joseph V. Hickey
2716 Mrs. Geo. W. Adams & dr.
2716 Mr. & Mrs. Harry H. Fisher
2718 Mr. & Mrs. Jacob Schroder & drs.
2718 Milton Schroder
2718 Albert Schroder
2728 Mr.&Mrs.William H. Peeke jr.
2804 Mr. & Mrs. John Soames
2804 Arthur F. Soames
2818 Mrs. Margaret S. Perine
2818 Josiah W. Perine
2818 Mr. & Mrs. Henry H. Munger
2920 Mrs. Ransom Dexter & dr.
2950 Mrs. Edwin Sturtevant
2950 Mr. & Mrs. J. H. Whitman
2954 Mr. & Mrs. James E. Taylor
2954 Edward H. Taylor
2954 Mrs. D. W. Sawin
3010 Mr. & Mrs.William S. Edwards
3020 Mr. & Mrs. Edwin Nicodemus
3024 Mr. & Mrs. G. L. Magill
3028 Mr. & Mrs. A. S. Weinsheimer
3028 Warren E. Weinsheimer
3034 Mr. & Mrs. W. F. Senour
Receiving day Thursday
3040 Mrs. J. M. Colwell
3040 Ray M. Colwell
3040 Clyde B. Colwell
3048 Mr. & Mrs. Horace S. Hubbard
3050 Mr. & Mrs. L. D. Doty
3104 Mr. & Mrs. Louis Morris
3104 Henry Morris
3104 Sol C. Moss
3118 William Mueller & dr.
3120 Wm. L. Hagans & drs.

3309 Alexander Barth
3311 Morris Pflaum & dr.
3311 Harry Pflaum
3311 Abram Pflaum
3311 Isaac B. Lipson
3315 Mr. & Mrs. August Binswanger
   & dr.
3315 Alvin Binswanger
3317 Mr. & Mrs. Leopold Seaman
3319 Mr. & Mrs. E. Starr Lloyd
3321 Mr. & Mrs. Morris Cohn
3327 Dr. Geo. Morgenthau
3327 Lewis Morgenthau
3327 Sidney Morgenthau
3327 Milton Morgenthau
3327 Miss Selma Morgenthau
3331 Mr. & Mrs. S. Parliament
3331 Mrs. S. J. Ela
3335 Dr. & Mrs. Mendle A. Cohen
   & drs.
3335 David M. Cohen
3335 Dr. Samuel A. Cohen
3335 Joseph J. Cohen
3341 Mrs. Marion Goldschmidt &
   drs.
3341 Moses Goldschmidt
3351 Mr. & Mrs. Wm. M. Brinkman
   Receiving day Thursday
3359 Miss Annie Dooling
3359 Miss Ellen Dooling
3361 Mrs. Charles Packer
3363 Mr. & Mrs. Samuel Heyman &
   dr. *Receiving day Thursday*
3369 Mr. & Mrs. Thos. M. Hoyne &
   dr.
3369 Thomas Temple Hoyne
3403 Mr.& Mrs.Frank H. Markham
   Receiving day Thursday
3403 Robert Markham
3405 Mr. & Mrs. Jos. C. Manheimer
3405 Wm. S. Manheimer
3407 Mr.& Mrs. Henry Klopfer & dr.
3409 G. H. Lermit
3411 Mr. & Mrs. J. B. Stubbs & dr.
   Receiving day Wednesday
3413 Mr. & Mrs. Fred F. Day
3415 Mr. & Mrs. S. N. Swan
3515 Mrs. Helen Lester Jordan
   Receive Saturday eve.
3515 Mrs. Mary S. Lester
3515 Mrs. Josephine Lester Bruce
3519 Mr. & Mrs. Wm. T. Hall
3523 Prof. & Mrs. Carl Koelling &
   dr.
3523 John Koelling
3525 Mr. & Mrs. Frank T. Beard

3122 Mr. & Mrs. Milton B. Miller
3122 Charles B. Miller
3122 Mrs. James E. Miller
3126 Mr. & Mrs. William H. Russell
3126 Mrs. Elizabeth C. White
3126 Mr. & Mrs. C. B. Scott
3132 Mr. and Mrs. John Willard
   Northrop
   Receive 3 to 6 p. m. Wednesdays
3132 Mr. & Mrs. Robert G. Martin
   & dr.
3132 Mrs. Emma Martin Coon
3142 Mr. & Mrs. William A. Walter
3146 Mrs. Lizette Miller
3146 Mr. & Mrs. Jacob Keim
3150 Mrs. A. Liebenstein & dr.
   Receive 2d and 4th Wednesdays
3150 A. M. Liebenstein
3210 Mr. & Mrs. Leopold Eisenstaedt
3212 Mr. & Mrs. L. B. Dixon
   Receive Tuesdays 3 to 6 p.m.
3212 Lawrence Belmont Dixon
3212 Lawrence B. Dixon jr.
3216 Mrs. Anna Wedeles
3216 Mr. & Mrs. Edward L.Wedeles
3216 Sigmund Wedeles
3218 Mr. & Mrs. Alfred Despres
3218 Alexander Despres
3218 Samuel Despres
3218 Emile Despres
3218 Miss Anaise Despres
   Receiving day Friday
3222 R. H. Countiss & drs.
3222 Fred D. Countiss
3226 Mr. & Mrs. Selden Fish & dr.
3228 Mr. & Mrs. N. W. Lyman & dr.
3228 Eugene W. Lyman
3230 Mr. & Mrs. John R. Barrett
3230 Saxton S. Barrett
3232 Mr. & Mrs. S. W. Wyatt
3236 Mrs. Benjamin W. Root
3236 Mr. & Mrs. John M. Graves
3238 Mr. & Mrs. J. D. Sheahan & dr.
   Receiving day Tuesday
3240 Mr. & Mrs. Geo. S. Blakeslee
   & dr.
3242 Mr. & Mrs. Wm. J. Manning
3242 Ralph C. Manning
3304 Mr. & Mrs. Joseph Beifeld
   Receiving day Monday
3304 Morris Hirsch
3306 Mr. & Mrs. Isa Swabacker
3306 Joseph S. Rosenfield
3312 Mr. & Mrs. B. Lindauer & drs.
   Receive 1st and 2d Wednesdays

3527 Mr. & Mrs. M. D. Markheim & drs.
3527 Joseph Markheim
3529 Mr. & Mrs. Alex Goodman
3529 Mrs. R. Deitsch
3535 Mr. & Mrs. Geo. L. Rood
3833 Mr. & Mrs. Chas. E. Springer
3835 Mrs. M. L. Livingston & drs.
3835 Howard W. Livingston
3835 Thomas Livingston
3841 Mr. & Mrs. E. C. Richardson
4045 Mr. & Mrs. Henry M. Paynter
Receiving day Wednesday
4047 Mrs. William M. Dee & dr.
Receiving day Thursday
4047 Mrs. Catherine White & drs.
Receiving day Tuesday
4101 Mr. & Mrs. James A. Baldwin
4133 Mr. & Mrs. Albert Despres
4207 Mr. & Mrs. J. B. Hall
4209 Herbert A. Pierce
4209 Addison S. Pierce
4211 Mr. & Mrs. William Herbst & dr.
Receiving day 1st Friday
4213 Mr. & Mrs. Ralph M. Leopold
4227 Mr. & Mrs. L. Daube
Receiving day 2d Friday
4229 Dr. J. Harvey Lyons
4229 Mr. & Mrs. Samuel W. Klein
4229 Mrs. E. D. Joel
Receiving day 1st Thursday
4231 Mr. & Mrs. S. Leppel
4231 Mr. & Mrs. D. M. Ottenheimer
4243 Mr. & Mrs. John W. Walsh
4323 Mr. & Mrs. Samuel Eppstein & drs.
4327 Mr. & Mrs. Joseph Hart
4327 Mr. & Mrs. Herman Lehman
4329 Mr. & Mrs. J. S. Wolbach
4339 Mr. & Mrs. N. S. Wertheimer
Receiving day 2d Wednesday
4341 Mr. & Mrs. Sigmund Bachmann
4341 Sidney Klein
4341 Moses Klein
4343 Mr. & Mrs. H. W. Hoffheimer
4343 Edward A. Rosenthal
4351 Mr. & Mrs. Millard J. Sheridan
4351 Mr. & Mrs. J. H. Breckenridge
4355 Mr. & Mrs. Hugo Brady
4405 Mr. & Mrs. J. H. Wilson
4407 Mr. & Mrs. Delos A. Wilkins
4429 Mr. & Mrs. J. A. Loranger
4445 Mr. & Mrs. J. Jacoby
4445 Charles Friend

3312 Julius B. Lindauer
3316 Mrs. L. Loewenstein & dr.
3316 Emanuel L. Loewenstein
3316 Sidney Loewenstein
3320 Mr. & Mrs. J. J. Mullen & drs.
3322 Mr. & Mrs. Clarence A. Knight
3330 Mr. & Mrs. Paul Brown
3332 Mr. & Mrs. Joseph Bond & drs.
3336 Mr. & Mrs. Silas Huntley
3336 Mr. & Mrs. Jas. H. Gilbert & dr.
3338 Henry Clarke
3338 Henry L. Clarke
3338 Mr. & Mrs. Edmund Pendleton
Receive Thursday afternoon
3342 Mr. & Mrs. Bernard Rosenheim
3344 Mrs. Orvil S. Abbott
3344 Mrs. G. A. Farling
3344 Miss Retta Sullivan
3348 Mrs. J. E. Hebard & dr.
3352 Mr. & Mrs. Charles J. Furst
3356 Mr. & Mrs. George A. Gilbert & dr.
3358 Mr. & Mrs. George F. Bunday & dr.
3360 Mr. & Mrs. Chauncey E. Seaton
3360 Mr. & Mrs. Walter A. Frost
3362 Mr. & Mrs. O. S. Caspary
Receive 1st and 3d Thursdays
3366 Mr. & Mrs. Jesse D. Bisbee
3400 Mr. & Mrs. Geo. Atwell Hamlin
3400 Edward Ellis Hamlin
3402 Mr. & Mrs. Louis Eisendrath & dr.
3404 Mr. & Mrs. Albert W. Long
3404 Mr. & Mrs. Isaac Rosenfield
3408 Dr. & Mrs. R. E. Clark
3410 Mr. & Mrs. Samuel H. Rosenthal
3410 Miss Rose E. Rosenthal
3410 Mr. & Mrs. Geo. L. Wicks
3412 Mr. & Mrs. A. S. Lowenthal & dr.
3414 Mrs. B. Kurz & dr.
3414 A. Kurz
3416 Mr. & Mrs. Chas. E. Rothschild
Receiving day Wednesday
3418 Mr. & Mrs. Levi Strouss & drs.
Receiving day Wednesday
3418 Emil Strouss
3418 Ernst Strouss
3420 Mr. & Mrs. Samuel C. Nessler
3424 Mr. & Mrs. Chas. D. Rubel
3426 Mr. & Mrs. L. G. Wolff
Receiving day Thursday

4655 Mr. & Mrs. John A. Heusner
4707 Dr. William Fuller
4725 Dr. Max Cornelius
4749 Mr. & Mrs. D. Cromelien
4749 Mr. & Mrs. Hubert F. Miller
4753 George H. Bell
4759 Mr. & Mrs. Henry S. Wilcox
4843 Mr. & Mrs. Herman Baum
4845 Louis Kiper
4845 Mr.& Mrs. D. H. Salinger & dr.
4907 Mr. & Mrs. Joseph Granick
5041 Mr. & Mrs. Edwin B. Myers
5409 Mr. & Mrs. S. W. Moon
    Receiving day Thursday
5409 Mr. & Mrs. C. J. Wightman
    Receiving day Thursday
5413 Mr. & Mrs. Geo. F. Montgom-
    ery
    Receiving day Thursday
6839 Leon Hornstein

4158 Mr. & Mrs. John A. Doherty
4202 Mr. & Mrs. Simon S. Mendel-
    sohn & drs.
    Receiving day Friday
4202 Jacob S. Mendelsohn
4202 Benjamin E. Mendelsohn
4202 Sigmond Mendelsohn
4212 Arthur Pollak
4214 Mr. & Mrs. Ph. L. Raphael
4216 Mr. & Mrs. Sol H. Shoninger
4218 Adolph Kempner
4226 Mr. & Mrs. Ferdinand Lang-
    bein & drs.
    Receiving day Friday
4228 Mr. & Mrs. Edward J. Queeny
4234 Mr. & Mrs. D. L. Feibelman
    Receiving day Wednesday
4234 Mr. & Mrs. Zadig Levy & dr.
4234 David R. Levy
4236 Dr. & Mrs. A. R. Solenberger
4236 Charles Ruben
4306 Mr. & Mrs. Seymour J. Thurber
4306 Mrs. Evelyn Leckie & drs.
4322 Mr. & Mrs. A. E. Samuel
4352 Mr. & Mrs. Thomas Norton
4356 Mr. & Mrs. Abner Piatt & dr.
4446 Mr. & Mrs. Martin J. Isaacs
4918 Lee Drom
5238 Mr. & Mrs. P. H. Keenan
5238 Mr. & Mrs. Chas. C. Colby
5248 Mr. & Mrs. Harry G. Thomp-
    son
5252 Mr. & Mrs. Winn W. Gill
5252 Mr. & Mrs. Leland G. English
5318 John W. Weston

3426 Maurice B. Wolff
3428 Mr. & Mrs. Lee Mayer
    Receive Saturday afternoon
3428 Harry L. Mayer
3428 Jo. Mayer
3430 Mrs. S. L. Smith & drs.
    Receive 1st and 3d Thursdays
3430 William S. Smith
3430 Samuel H. Smith
3434 Mr. & Mrs. Aaron Straus
3436 Mr. & Mrs. Morris Hecht
    Receiving day Saturday
3436 Mr. & Mrs. W. S. B. Mathews
    & drs.
3436 E. Newman
3518 Mrs. W. M. Baker
3522 Mr. & Mrs. Edward J. Judd
3522 Mrs. N. B. Judd
3532 Mrs. Clara Smith & drs.
3538 Mr. & Mrs. F. W. Campbell
3540 Mr. & Mrs. George W. Anderson
3540 Miss Josephine McLane
3614 Mr. & Mrs. B. H. Jefferson
3616 Mr. & Mrs. R. Jefferson
3636 Mr. & Mrs. R. J. Prins
3652 Joseph B. Schlossman & drs.
3652 Weller D. Bishopp
3732 Mr. & Mrs. G. R. Rockfeller
3734 Mr. & Mrs. James P. Bradley
    & dr.
3804 Mr. & Mrs. George F. Lee
3808 Mr. & Mrs. Geo. S. Crilly
3812 Mr. & Mrs. Charles M. Bradley
3814 Mr. & Mrs. Frank G. Springer
3816 Mr. & Mrs. Wm. M. Knapp
3818 Mr. & Mrs. Frank R. Greene
3822 Mr. & Mrs. Chas. B. Stafford
3828 Mr. & Mrs. D. F. Kelley
3832 Mr. & Mrs. G. K. Harrington
3838 Edward B. Leigh
3844 Mr. & Mrs. J. H. Ingwersen
3910 Mr. & Mrs. Orlo W. Richardson
3910 Mr. & Mrs. Robert E. Richard-
    son
3912 Mr. & Mrs. George E. McHie
3914 Mrs. S. L. Straus
3914 B. F. Straus
3916 Seymour W. Ayers
3916 Frank D. Ayers
3918 Mr. & Mrs. Louis Kesner & drs.
3940 Mr. & Mrs. Nathan Engel
3940 Mr. & Mrs. Sigmund Kline
    Receiving day Friday
3940 Miss Clara Wallerstein
4056 Mr. & Mrs. Harry L. Hettich
4132 Mr. & Mrs. I. D. Richards & dr.

CHAMPLAIN AVENUE.

4227 Mrs. Caroline H. Lutz & dr.
4227 Mrs. Margaret D. Howard
4227 Harry G. Davis
4243 Mr. & Mrs. W. K. Haynes
4315 Mrs. Sarah W. Booth
4317 Mr. & Mrs. George A. Jewett
4319 Mr. & Mrs. J. H. Eastburn
4401 Mr. & Mrs. Charles B. Slade
4419 Mr. & Mrs. W. H. Moore
4421 Mr. & Mrs. A. L. Potter
4421 Augustus E. Potter
4427 Mr. & Mrs. Edward S. Meloy
   Receiving day Wednesday
4427 Mrs. Jenny Mitchell
4427½ Mr. & Mrs. Orren V. Stookey
   Receiving day Friday
4433 Dr. & Mrs. John F. Orr
4437 Mrs. Elizabeth Nash
4437 Samuel S. Nash
4441 Miss Florence Holbrook
4441 Miss Maud Holbrook
4449 Mrs. John M. Haslett
4451 Mr. & Mrs. G. W. Chandler
4455 Mr. & Mrs. O. S. Gaither
4551 Mrs. Minnie Page & dr.
4551 Edgar Pope
4601 Mr. & Mrs. A. S. Core
4623 Mr. & Mrs. N. H. Fairbanks
4715 Mr. & Mrs. Edmund H. Stevens
   Receiving day Wednesday
4715 Mr. & Mrs. J. W. Stevens
4715 Charles N. Stevens
4717 Mr. & Mrs. L. Curtis Ball
4717 Mr. & Mrs. Louis E. Bloch
4729 Mr. & Mrs. W. W. Taberner
4733 Mr. & Mrs. O. H. Bardwell
   Receiving day Thursday
4737 Mr. & Mrs. John J. Van Nostrand & dr.
4743 Mr. & Mrs. G. W. Conover
4747 Mr. & Mrs. C. E. Randall
   Receiving day Wednesday
4751 Maurice T. Rotschild
4753 Mr. & Mrs. M. S. Fleishman
4757 Mr. & Mrs. F. Sydney Hayward
4801 Dr. & Mrs. Wm. H. Ensminger
4921 Mr. & Mrs. P. B. Normoyle
4943 Mr. & Mrs. E. L. Haynes
4949 Mr. & Mrs. Frederick T. Conrad
6019 Horace G. Stone

4804 Mr. & Mrs. Moses Harris
   Receiving day Saturday
4806 Mr. & Mrs. Clarence P. Eyre
   Receiving day Thursday

4218 Albert Kunstadter
4240 Mrs. W. H. Edgar & dr.
4240 William H. Edgar
4240 Mrs. James F. Wallace
   Receiving day Thursday
4400 Arthur W. Cleaver
4404 Mr. & Mrs. Charles E. Lund
4404 John A. Moody & dr.
4418 Mr. & Mrs. J. J. Farrelly
4420 Mr. & Mrs. Orton G. Orr
4420 Mr. & Mrs. C. T. Zahringer
4422 Mr. & Mrs. G. F. Geist
4438 Mr. & Mrs. F. P. Hopkins
4444 Isaac S. Lederer
4518 Mr. & Mrs. G. Felsenthal
4548 Gardiner Chipley
4608 Mr. & Mrs. Robert J. Hill
   Receiving day Thursday
4610 Mr. & Mrs. Daniel Boyle
   Receiving day Wednesday
4614 Mr. & Mrs. Eli Pfaelzer
4626 W. F. Flagg
4714 Mr. & Mrs. David Witkowsky & dr.
4716 Mr. & Mrs. Julius Daniels
4718 Mr. & Mrs. Morris J. Frankland
4718 Mrs. A. E. Frankland
4720 Mr. & Mrs. Montefiore M. Jacobs
   Receive 1st and 3d Wednesdays
4724 Mr. & Mrs. Truman D. Gore
4726 Mr. & Mrs. John E. Day & dr.
   Receiving day Thursday
4730 Mr. & Mrs. P. Noonan
4734 Mr. & Mrs. L. W. Allenberg
4734 Moses E. Greenewald
4736 Mr. & Mrs. Hiram H. Newhall
4736 Horace G. Parkins
4738 Mr. & Mrs. I. Speyer
4740 Mr. & Mrs. Horace L. Cooper
4742 Mr. & Mrs. George O. Gordon
4744 Mr. & Mrs. D. P. Shaw
   Receiving day Thursday
4748 Mr. & Mrs. Willard A. Roberts
4748 Mrs. Sarah C. Whiteman
4750 Mr. & Mrs. John J. Rogers & drs.
   Receiving day Thursday
4752 Mr. & Mrs. Max Friedlander
4754 Dr. & Mrs. L. S. Eastlake
4756 Mr. & Mrs. John Coulter
   Receiving day Tuesday
4760 Mr. & Mrs. M. Philipsborn & dr.
4760 Mrs. R. Gattman
4760 Henry Gattman
4800 Mr. & Mrs. John B. Murphy

4808 Mr. & Mrs. E. C. Shankland
4814 Mr. & Mrs. William H. Hop-
    kins *Receiving day Friday*
4834 Mr. & Mrs. Robert L. Grady
4840 Mr. & Mrs. Henry Lapp
4920 Mr. & Mrs. Jacob F. Doerr

4924 Mr. & Mrs. John P. Doerr
    Receiving day Thursday
4924 William P. Doerr
4926 Mr. & Mrs. Wm. S. Armour
6520 Mr. & Mrs. Albert Labarthe

COLES AVENUE.

7635 Mr. & Mrs. P. M. Stults & dr.

CORNELL AVENUE.

5115 Mr. & Mrs. Edward J. Phelps
    Receiving day Tuesday
5115 Wm. P. Hapgood
5125 Mr. & Mrs. J. S. Carpenter
5125 W. P. Griswold
5127 Dr. Janet Gunn
    Receives Friday, 2 to 5 p. m.
5131 Mr. & Mrs. H. S. Whitcomb
    & dr.
5135 Mr. & Mrs. Wm. S. Keck
5147 Mr. & Mrs. Frederick D. Ware
5149 Charles H. Gibson
5149 William T. Gibson
5149 Mrs. Douglas Gibson
5149 Miss Lilian W. Gibson
5149 Watts C. Gibson
5155 Mr. & Mrs. George R. Mitchell
    Receiving day Tuesday
5155 Mr. & Mrs. R. W. McConn
5155 Mr. & Mrs. Geo. W. Warwick
5313 Mr. & Mrs. Frank M. Wood
5325 Mrs. John H. Nair
5327 Mr. & Mrs. S. L. Underwood
5327 Sidney F. Underwood
5333 Mr. & Mrs. F. W. Root
5335 Mr. & Mrs. Charles Wincote
5401 Mr. & Mrs. J. E. Holden
5401 Mrs. M. E. Holden
5451 Mr. & Mrs. G. L. Paddock
    & dr.
5461 Herbert Driggs
5461 Mrs. George Driggs
5461 Miss Josephine C. Griffing
5461 Frank L. Douglas
5461 Edward S. Elliott
5473 Mr. & Mrs. James S. Cummins
5473 Miss Mary L. Byllesby
5477 Mr. & Mrs. Edward W. Dennis
5495 Mr. & Mrs. R. W. Hyman jr.
    Receiving day Wednesday
5501 Dr. & Mrs. Arno Behr & dr.
5501 Mr. & Mrs. Robt. M. Lovett
5503 Mr. & Mrs. L. Everingham & dr.

5100 Mr. & Mrs. Edward S. Frasher
5106 Mrs. C. D. Larrabee & drs.
5118 Dr. & Mrs. W. Franklin Coleman
5118 Miss Margaret Kinnear
5124 Mr. & Mrs. Benjamin B. Bryan
5130 Miss Julia F. Mulvey
5130 Richard J. Mulvey
5130 Arthur B. Mulvey
5138 Mr. & Mrs. Norton H. Van
    Sicklen
5140 Mr. & Mrs. John A. Bunnell
5200 Mrs. E. T. Root & drs.
5200 Miss Fanny A. Root
5200 Wm. A. Root
5200 George F. Root
5214 Mr. & Mrs. Wm. L. Robinson
5316 John A. Jameson
5316 Mrs. E. D. Jameson & drs.
5316 Franklin Denison
5320 Mr. & Mrs. Wm. V. Kelley
5320 Miss Irene Phelps
5322 Mr. & Mrs. Louis G. Richardson
5326 Mr. & Mrs. Frederick R. Lamb
5326 Walter J. Feron
5326 Bayard T. Bacon
5326 Miss Annie Quigley
5340 Mr. & Mrs. Abram Mitchell
5342 Mr. & Mrs. D. B. Gann
5402 Mr. & Mrs. R. W. Bridge
5402 Miss A. E. Allison
5422 Mrs. M. G. Dow
5422 Miss Nellie Quigg
5422 Mrs. George H. French
5434 Mr. & Mrs. John G. Drennan
5436 Mr. & Mrs. Curtis N. Kimball
5438 Mr. & Mrs. Russell S. Clark
5438 Mr. & Mrs. Wm. B Dunlap
5450 Mr. & Mrs. D. M. Lord & drs.
5450 Arthur D. Lord
5458 Mr. & Mrs. A. E. Dyer
5474 Sandford C. Kirtland
5474 Miss Betty L. Carter
5474 Mr. & Mrs. Abner P. Downer

5503 Edward L. Everingham
5503 H. D. Everingham
5505 Mr. & Mrs. J. C. Fleming
5511 Mr. & Mrs. Henry Phillips
5517 Judge & Mrs. David J. Baker
   & dr.
5517 John W. Baker
5517 Mrs. Maria A. White
5519 Rev. & Mrs. John Henry Barrows
5533 Mrs. M. Rice
5533 Mr. & Mrs. M. G. Sterrett
5535 Mr. & Mrs. John Wooley
5535 Edwin Wooley
5537 Mr. & Mrs. John S. Coonley
5539 Mr. & Mrs. Frank W. Smith
   & dr.
5539 Osborn F. Smith

5476 Mr. & Mrs. H. E. Hubbard
5480 Mr. & Mrs. J. Herbert Ware
   Receiving day Thursday
5480 Mrs. James D. Stevens
5484 Dr. & Mr.James.B. McChesney
5504 Mr. & Mrs. Howard S. Hart
5508 Mr. & Mrs. R. W. Phillips
   Receiving day Thursday
5510 Ernest Hendrickson
5526 Mr. & Mrs. Isaac H. Radford
   & drs.
   Receiving day Wednesday
5530 Mr.& Mrs.Edwin Burritt Smith
5534 Mr. & Mrs. Frank L. Eastman
5538 Mr. & Mrs. Oliver A. Olmsted
5538 Mr. & Mrs. Frank G. Wright
5540 Mr. & Mrs. Elijah P. Ramsay
5540 Mr. & Mrs. John S. Goodwin
   Receiving day Thursday

COTTAGE GROVE AVENUE.

3305 Dr. Charles Todd
3913 Thomas C. Bowen
4313 Mr. & Mrs. Harry D. Hollister
cor. 52d The Renfost
   Mr. & Mrs. J. J. Abercrombie
   Mr. & Mrs. Geo. S. Atterbury
   James H. Ballagh
   Mrs. Lillian Ballagh
   Miss Elizabeth Reynolds
   Mrs. S. A. Sprague & drs.
   Mr.& Mrs. Fernando H. Staud
   Mr. & Mrs. K. E. Valentine
   Dr. & Mrs. A. C. Van Duyn
   Mr. & Mrs. Wm. C. Vierbuchen
5415 Dr. S. V. Clevenger & dr.

3000 Mr. & Mrs. August Newhaus
3300 Dr. J. A. Dinwoody
3638 Dr. Frederick E. Bigelow
3638 Dr. Irving J. Straus
4454 Dr. A. Ralph Johnstone
4458 Evan Lloyd
4834 Dr. & Mrs. Chas. C. Whitmore

5415 Mr. & Mrs. H. P. Simmons
5415 John S. Carter
5417 Dr. & Mrs. M. J. Jones
5425 Mr. & Mrs. J.Grafton Parker jr.
5431 Mrs. Marie Hilgard & drs.
5431 Mr. & Mrs. Jules Girardin

DREXEL AVENUE.

5201 Mr. & Mrs. D. H. S. Tuttle
5701 Mr. & Mrs. J. McGraw
5815 Mr. & Mrs. Chas. F. Pearce
6413 Mr. & Mrs. P. L. Simpson
6413 William Simpson
6413 Joseph T. Simpson
6413 P. L. Simpson jr.
6443 Mr. & Mrs. E. J. Henderson
6501 Mr. & Mrs. I. W. Kelley

5524 Dr. & Mrs. George P. Brady
5524 Miss Ida H. Kollman
5618 Mr. & Mrs. Alfred Shackleton
5822 Mr. & Mrs. Wardner Williams
5822 Alfred Williams
6336 Mrs. Flora D. Porter & dr.
6336 Geo. Rupert Porter
6340 Mr. & Mrs. Augustus Hussey
6352 Mr. & Mrs. Howard N. Ogden

DREXEL BOULEVARD.

3931 Oakland Hotel
   Mr. and Mrs. A. E. Becker
   Mr. & Mrs. Leopold Buxbaum
   & dr.

3960 Mr. & Mrs. Albert B. Wilson
3964 Dr. & Mrs. Albert G. Paine
4000 Dr. & Mrs. D. B. Freeman
4004 Mr. & Mrs. Horace W. Soper

3931 Oakland Hotel (continued.)
Emanuel L. Buxbaum
Dr. Robert Challoner
Mr. & Mrs. Wm. Freschl
Miss Hulda Friedenthal
Mr. & Mrs. Isaac Harris
Mr. & Mrs. J. Hermann
Mr. & Mrs. Joshua Hutchinson
Mrs. H. Joseph & dr.
Henry Joseph
Herbert L. Joseph
Mr. & Mrs. M. Lazarus
Hugo D. Loeb
Mrs. W. W. McCarty
Mr. & Mrs. Leopold Moss
Mrs. Regina Powell & dr.
Mr. & Mrs. Simon N. Silverman
Fred T. Smith
Victor U. Sutter
Dr. Julia C. Whaling
Dr. James W. White
Miss Mary Wilson
3961 Mr. & Mrs. G. M. Reynolds
3963 Mr. & Mrs. George Hackney
3965 Mrs. W. J. Edbrooke
3971 Mr.&Mrs.F.W.Dickerman&dr.
3975 C. A. Howe
3979 Mrs. S. Alshuler
3981 Mr. & Mrs. J. C. Thomas &.dr.
3985 Mr. & Mrs. E. B. Sherman
3985 Mr. & Mrs.B. W. Sherman
3987 Mr. & Mrs. Daniel H.Kochersperger
    Receiving day Friday
3987 Mr. & Mrs. Arthur J. Morrison
3989 Mr. & Mrs. Harding L. Kochersperger
3989 Miss Carrie Russ
3989 Miss Aimee Knowlton
4001 Mr. & Mrs. J. H. McFarland
    Receiving day Wednesday
4001 Dr. & Mrs. J. M. Taylor
4001 Mr. & Mrs. Thos. J. Leavitt
4003 Mrs. R. H. Fleming
4007 Mrs. Ellery C. Spinney & dr.
4009 Mr. & Mrs. Felipe Berriozabal
4011 Mr. & Mrs. Leland.Norten
    Receiving day Thursday
4013 Mr. & Mrs. Arthur J. O'Leary
4025 Mr. & Mrs. William A. Bond
    & dr.
4025 Wm. Scott Bond
4025 Laurence Colton Bond
4033 Mr. & Mrs. N. T. Read

4004 Miss Adaline Carr
4012 Mr. & Mrs. Thos. C. Penington
    & dr.
4012 Walter V. Penington
4014 Mr. & Mrs. J. A. McCartney
4016 Dr. & Mrs. Charles E. Fisher
4024 Mrs. M. F. Coe
4024 Dr. & Mrs. A. H. Hiatt
4112 Mr. & Mrs. P. C. Hoops
4128 Mr. & Mrs. Benjamin F. Head
4128 Harry C. Head
4148 Mr. & Mrs. A. G. Cone
4148 Mrs. W. S. Bond
4166 Mr. & Mrs. John W. Iliff
4166 Mr. & Mrs. G. F. Cram
4168 Dr. & Mrs. Silas T. Yount
4168 Mr. & Mrs. Henry C. Strahorn
4168 Mrs Frank C. Otis
4168 B. Frederick Moon
4200 Mr. & Mrs. Robert E. Jenkins
    & dr.
4200 George R. Jenkins
4200 Mr. & Mrs. Edgar L. Masters
4202 Mr. & Mrs. S. A. Humiston
4202 Mrs. J. C. Salisbury
4204 Mr. and Mrs. Charles C. Landt
4206 Dr. & Mrs. Geo. O. Taylor
4212 Mr. & Mrs. Jno. Blair Robertson & dr.
4238 Mr. & Mrs. Simeon H. Crane
4238 M. L. Barrett
4246 Mr. & Mrs. J. L. Bobo
4250 Mr. & Mrs. Nat A. Mayer
    Receive 1st & 3d Wednesdays
4252 Mr. & Mrs. Simon Bloch
4330 Dr. & Mrs. Edwin J. Kuh
4342 Mr. & Mrs. Geo. W. Champlin
    Receiving day Thursday
4342 Charles P. Champlin
4346 Mr.&Mrs.Wm. H. Keogh & dr.
    Receiving day Thursday
4346 James B. Keogh
4346 Chester H. Keogh
4346 John W. Keogh
4436 Mr. & Mrs. James Stinson
4436 Henry J. Stinson
4436 Miss Cornelia Stinson
4508 Mr. & Mrs. S. T. Fish
    Rec. days 2d and 4th Wednesdays
4512 Mr.& Mrs. Herman Stern & dr.
4512 Joseph Ballin
4516 Mr. & Mrs. Max Frank
4518 Mr.&Mrs. Adolph Kraus & drs.
4520 Mr. & Mrs. Norman W. Harris
    & dr.
4520 N. Dwight Harris

4037 Mr. & Mrs. J. H. Bell
4045 Hiram A. Gooch
4101 Mr. & Mrs. W. H. Starbuck
4101 Mr. & Mrs. Henry W. Cook
4105 Mrs. Thomas Dunne
4105 Mr. & Mrs. William H. Hoops
4109 Mr. & Mrs. Albert H. Thacker
4109 W. F. Cornell
4111 Mr. & Mrs. J. Robert Thacker
4111 Mr. & Mrs. W. H. O'Connell
4111 C. Edward Thacker
4111 Jennes R. Thacker
4115 Geo. L. Pratt
4115 Mr. & Mrs. Clinton B. Pratt
4121 Mr. &. Mrs. Jacob H. Gregory
4121 Miss Mary Hudson
4123 Mrs. W. E. Hennessy
  Receiving day Thursday
4123 W. B. Hennessy
4123 Miss C. M. Hennessy
4125 Dr. & Mrs. Joseph B. Bacon
4127 Dr. & Mrs. Willoughby Walling *Receive Wednesday*
4127 William E. Walling
4129 Mrs. R. Lancaster
4129 Dr. & Mrs. F. A. Emmons
4133 Mrs. S. Stein & drs.
 Receive 1st & 3d Saturday p. m.
4133 Arthur Stein
4135 Mrs. A. Cahn & drs.
  Receiving day Thursday
4139 Mr. & Mrs. Adolph Moses
  Receiving day Wednesday
4201 Dr. John L. Van Valkenburg
4203 Mr. & Mrs. James D. Bradley
4239 Mr. & Mrs. J. G. Goodrich &
  drs.
4239 C. Harry Goodrich
4241 Mr. & Mrs. J. A. Gauger
4243 Mr. & Mrs. S. H. Hunt
4245 Mrs. E. Sidney Lunt
4247 Dr. & Mrs. L. L. McArthur
4247 Mrs. M. A. Walker
4313 Mrs. Luella M. Wilson
4315 Mr. & Mrs. Simon Klein
4319 Mr. & Mrs. S. O. Blair
4325 Mr. & Mrs. M. Reiman
4329 Mr. & Mrs. J. M. Gartside
  Receiving day Friday
4331 Mr.& Mrs. William Best
  Receive 1st & 3d Wednesdays
4337 Mr. & Mrs. D.S. Googins & drs.
4339 Mr. & Mrs. Chas. H. Randle
4345 Mr. & Mrs. George D. Holton
4353 Mr. & Mrs. George A. Fuller
4353 Mr. and Mrs. H. S. Black

4548 A. O. Slaughter & dr.
4548 A. O. Slaughter jr.
4548 Mrs. J. B Tilden
4620 Mr. & Mrs. Delonas W. Potter
4620 Mr. & Mrs. Frank M. Smith
4630 Mr. & Mrs. Edward Iverson
4630 Mr. & Mrs. E. L. Johnson
4650 Mr. & Mrs. H. P. Darlington
  Receiving day Tuesday
4650 Frank Floyd
4650 Darlington De Costa
4700 Mrs. James W. Oakley
4700 Miss Bertha Oakley
4700 Miss Annie Oakley
4724 Geo. T. Williams
4724 Grant Williams
4724 Mr.& Mrs. George S. Williams
  Receiving day Friday
4730 Mr. & Mrs. Caleb H. Marshall
  Receiving day Monday
4730 Benjamin H. Marshall
4730 Miss Carrie L. Phillips
4730 Edmund R. Phillips
4736 Mr. & Mrs. Francis Beidler
4740 Mr. & Mrs. S. B. Walton
4740 Miss Mabel Barnard Walton
4740 Miss M. Elizabeth Walton
4742 Mr. & Mrs. Joseph Schaffner
4742 Miss Rachel Schaffner
4830 Mr. & Mrs. Chauncey J. Blair
  Receiving day Tuesday
4902 Mr. & Mrs. James N. Raymond
4938 Dr. & Mrs. J. A. McGill
4960 Mr. & Mrs. A. S. Trude
  Receive 1st & 3d Thursday
4960 Miss Algenia Trude
4960 Miss Cecelia Trude
4960 George A. Trude
4960 Mr. & Mrs. Alfred Percy Trude
  Receive 1st & 3d Thursday
4960 Daniel P. Trude
4960 Mrs. A. P. Dana
5012 Mr.& Mrs. Siegfried M.Fischer
5016 Mr. and Mrs. Adolph Nathan
  Receive Wednesday evening
5016 Miss Nathan

4415 Mr. & Mrs. Franklin C. Jocelyn
  Receiving day Monday
4415 Robert Mc. Jocelyn
4415 Miss Jocelyn
4419 Mr. & Mrs. John H. Weiss
4425 Mr. & Mrs. Ira N. Morris
4427 Mr. & Mrs. Charles Netcher
4433 Mr. & Mrs. Henry Falker
  Receiving day 1st & 3d Friday

4455 Mr. & Mrs. F. S. Hanson & dr.
4455 Miss Helen Geary
4455 Mr. & Mrs. Edwin B. Harts
4537 Mr. & Mrs. Anthony Schmitt
   Receiving day Thursday
4537 Miss Schmitt
4537 Miss Dora Schmitt
4537 Eugene J. Schmitt
4537 Arthur G. Schmitt
4545 Mrs. Wm. E. Hale
4545 William B. Hale
4545 George W. Hale
4605 Mr. & Mrs. John A. Roche
4605 Prof. & Mrs. George C. Howland
4613 Mr. & Mrs. E. Crane Wilson
   Receiving day Monday
4613 Dr. & Mrs. Luke Hitchcock
4613 Miss Adelaide Wilson

4623 Mr. & Mrs. Everett W. Brooks
4623 Mr. & Mrs. Robert L. Gifford
4637 Mr. & Mrs. C. E. Gifford
4637 Mr. & Mrs. I. C. Gifford
4639 Mr. & Mrs. Harry Hart & dr.
   Receive 2d and 4th Thursday
4639 Mr. & Mrs. Louis H. Kohn
4643 Mr. & Mrs. Max Hart
   Receive 1st and 3d Thursday
4651 Mr. & Mrs. Warren F. Leland
4825 Mr. & Mrs. Albert Wisner
   Receiving day Tuesday
4851 Mr. & Mrs. Martin A. Ryerson
   Receiving day Tuesday
4917 Mr. & Mrs. C. H. Matthiessen & dr.
4941 Mr. & Mrs. John H. Nolan & drs.

EAST END AVENUE.

5110 Mr. & Mrs. H. R. Hobart
5110 Ralph Hastings Hobart
5112 Mr. & Mrs. John McNulta
5126 Mr. & Mrs. W. F. Hunt
5126 Arthur S. Peebles
5126 William S. Peebles
5126 Miss Louise Dart
5132 Mr. & Mrs. A. G. Becker
5132 Oscar J. Friedman
5132 Isaac K. Friedman
5144 Mr. & Mrs. Lucius Clark
5200 Mr. & Mrs. James Morgan
5200 Dr. & Mrs. H. H. Frothingham
5406 Col. & Mrs. R. S. Thompson & dr.
5420 C. B. Wood
5420 Webster Wood
5420 Miss Julia Wood
5420 Miss Harriet B. Wood
5482 Mr. & Mrs. L. Frank Castle
5484 Mr. & Mrs. D. Johnston
5488 Mr. & Mrs. F. H. Atkinson & dr.

5488 Frank H. Atkinson jr.
5488 Mr. & Mrs. Charles C. Dunlap & dr.
5488 Mr. & Mrs. Robert Herrick
5488 John M. Manly
5488 Wm. V. Moody
5490 Mr. & Mrs. Norman P. Cooley
5490 Fred S. Ackerman
5496 Mr. & Mrs. C. W. Smith
5496 Mr. & Mrs. Wm. H. Smith
5498 Mr. & Mrs. L. R. Hall
5518 Mr. & Mrs. W. B. Conkey
5522 Mr. & Mrs. Geo. A. Poole
5522 Geo. A. Poole jr.
5528 Mr. & Mrs. H. H. Peters & drs.
   Receiving day Tuesday
5530 Mr. & Mrs. E. S. Rice
5533 Mr. & Mrs. Henry C. M. Thomson
   Receiving day Tuesday

EGGLESTON AVENUE.

5931 Mr. & Mrs. Wm. Gately
7107 Chas. I. Westerfield
7107 W. E. Hemenover
7111 Mr. & Mrs. Thos. Cossar
7115 Mr. & Mrs. Andrew G. Lyons
7121 Mr. & Mrs. Julius Cole
7125 Mr. & Mrs. F. W. Myrick
7131 Mr. & Mrs. E. W. A. Rowles
7133 Mr. & Mrs. Lory O. Rand & dr.

5944 Joseph H. Schneider & drs.
5944 Henry Schneider
6400 Dr. & Mrs. Solomon Lewin
7024 Mr. & Mrs. Henry H. Davis & dr.
7024 W. F. Davis
7100 Mr. & Mrs. E. J. Hill & dr.
7100 Fred. W. Hill
7100 Albert E. Hill

7137 Mr. & Mrs. M. P. Pennington
7409 Mr. & Mrs. John J. Williams
7529 Mr. & Mrs. George R. Hayden
7601 Rev. & Mrs. C. A. Van Anda
     & drs.

_____

7720 Mr. & Mrs. H. A. Ferguson
7728 Mr. & Mrs. W. Roulet
7728 Miss Florence Spence
7730 Mr. & Mrs. E. R. Ealy
7868 Mrs. Z. D. Scobey

7112 Mrs. Nellie Burt
7120 Mr. & Mrs. Philip Hesse
7120 Miss Marie Hesse
7120 Miss Emma Hesse
7138 Mr. & Mrs. Grove Sackett
7436 Mr. & Mrs. W. N. Abbott
7526 Dr. & Mrs. E. Lathrop
7526 Mr. & Mrs. E. D. Seaton
7526 Mrs. I. F. Dillon
7620 Mr. & Mrs. C. B. Kinney
7648 Mr. & Mrs. S. W. Earle
7716 Mr. & Mrs. J. P. Haynes

EIGHTEENTH STREET.

89 Mr. & Mrs. C. L. Sherlock

ELLIS AVENUE.

3517 Mr. & Mrs. Horace Tucker &
     drs.
3517 Fred W. Tucker
3521 Mr. & Mrs. I. M. Rice
3521 Mrs. Fanny Cahn
3521 Moses Loeb
3523 Mr. & Mrs. George M. Aykroyd
3523 Mr. & Mrs. Chas. C. Swinborne
3523 Charles Wade Swinborne
3523 A. L. Bailhache
3525 Mr. & Mrs. Henry R. Kasson
3529 Mr. & Mrs. W. A. Paulsen
     Receiving day Tuesday
3541 Isaac A. Kohn
3541 Simon A. Kohn
3541 Louis A. Kohn ·
3541 Miss Henrietta Kohn
3543 Mr. & Mrs. Dankmar Adler &
     dr.
3543 A. K. Adler
3543 Sidney J. Adler
3545 Mr. & Mrs. Emanuel Bach
3547 Marcus E. Cooke
3547 Mr. & Mrs. Martin Alvaro
     Fountain
3551 Mr. & Mrs. Richard W. Mor-
     rison
3555 Mr. & Mrs. John S. Snyder
3555 Mr. & Mrs. James W. Tice
3555 Frank M. Bertrand
3601 Mr. & Mrs. T. G. Warden
3603 Mr. & Mrs. Samuel Slade
3603 Mrs. M. K. LaVictoire ·
3605 Mr. & Mrs. Wm. Morris Booth
     Receiving day Tuesday
3607 Mr. & Mrs. James A. Charter
3609 Mr. & Mrs. Stephen Emory
3613 Mr. & Mrs. Thos. Gibson

3500 to 3504 St. Germaine Apart-
     ments
     Mr. & Mrs. Chas. E. Bloch
     Mrs. H. L. Botsford & dr.
     Dr. & Mrs. Albert H. Burr
     Mr. & Mrs. Nathan L. Clement
     Miss Blanche Dingley
     Mr. & Mrs. W. H. Doty ·
     Miss Emma M. Dunlap
         Receiving day Tuesday
     Oscar Eisendrath
     Sam B. Eisendrath
     Simeon B. Eisendrath
     Mrs. Jess Gaynor
         Receiving day Thursday
     Mr. & Mrs. J. K. Gwynn
     Mr. & Mrs. Benj. F. Hutches jr.
         Receiving day Wednesday
     Mr. & Mrs. John Alfred Johnson
     Harry G. Lewis
     Mr. & Mrs. A. L. Lilienthal
     Mr. & Mrs. Earl MacN. Mann
         Receiving day Thursday
     Dr. & Mrs. Chas. Morgan
     Mr. & Mrs. F. W. Neumann
         Receiving day Wednesday
     Mr. & Mrs. Lewis B. Nichols
         Receiving day Wednesday
     Mrs. M. Ross & dr.
         Receiving day Tuesday
     Irving Schoenbrun
     Mr. & Mrs. S. Schoenbrun
3508 Mr. & Mrs. Edward F. Stearns
3528 Mr. & Mrs. Joseph G. Lane
         Receiving day Friday
3528 Richard B. Langdon
3530 Mr. & Mrs. David M. Cochrane
     & drs. *Receiving day Wednesday*

3613 Prof. Edouard LeCroart
3613 Mr. & Mrs. A. C. Stone
3613 Mrs. H. Wheeler
3615 Mr. & Mrs. Jacob Newman jr.
3615 Miss Pauline Bauland
3615 Harry B. Newman
3617 Mr. & Mrs. Eugene Vallens & dr.
3621 Mr. & Mrs. Geo. E. Halsey & dr.
3625 Mr. & Mrs. C. H. Gabriel
3627 Mr. & Mrs. Frederick A. Brodhead & dr.
3633 Mr. & Mrs. A. J. W. Copelin & dr.
3633 Bertram Copelin
3635 Mr. & Mrs. J. N. Buchanan & dr.
3703 Mr. & Mrs. William B. Candee
3705 Mr. & Mrs. Thomas S. Temple
3709 Mrs. Dr. C. E. Weilhart
3709 Mrs. Amelia Meyer
3715 Moses Willner
3725 Mr. & Mrs. Thos. B. Hawson & drs.
3725 Thos. W. Hawson
3725 Louis Hawson
3727 Mrs. Mary Hubbard & drs.
3727 Henry H. Hubbard
3729 Mr. & Mrs. Paul K. Richter ·
3731 Mr. & Mrs. Julius E. Weil
3733 Mr. & Mrs. I. N. Simons & dr.
Receiving day Thursday
3733 Louis E. Simons
3733 Robert I. Simons
3733 Leonard Simons
3735 Mr. & Mrs. Herman Landauer
3737 Thomas C. Sheldon
3743 Judge & Mrs. Wm. G. Ewing & drs.
3745 Mr. & Mrs. Robert A. Scovel
3745 Miss Ella F. Cobb
3747 Mr. & Mrs. Adlai T. Ewing
3753 Mr. & Mrs. Willis J. Wells
3753 Mrs. E. K. Patton
3757 Mr. & Mrs. Anson L. Bolte
3757 Edward M. Endicott
3763 Mr. & Mrs. J. E. Forsyth
3763 Hervey B. Hicks
3767 Mr. & Mrs. Edwin H. Ellett & dr.
3767 Harry L. Ellett
3767 Mrs. Diantha Stockton
3801 Mr. & Mrs. W. L. Hazen
3815 Mr. & Mrs. Frederick M. Steele
3815 Mrs. Roxana Pratt

9

3530 D. K. Cochrane
3532 Mrs. Mary E. Williams
Receiving day Wednesday
3532 Miss Carrie E. Williams
3532 Mrs. Margaret M. Fisher
3532 Wilburn E. Paddock
3534 Mr. & Mrs. Archibald Winne
Receiving day Wednesday
3534 John Winne
3536 Mr. & Mrs. S. D. Ward & drs.
3538 Mrs. Eda Holzheimer ·
3538 Levi A. Eliel ·
3540 Mr. & Mrs. Wm. H. Mooney & dr.
3540 Frank A. Mooney
3544 Mr. & Mrs. Chas. E. Cox & drs.
Receiving day Friday
3544 Eugene R. Cox
3546 Dr. & Mrs. Harry Williamson
3546 Mr. & Mrs. M. J. Garty
3548 Mr. & Mrs. I. H. Mayer
3550 Mr. & Mrs. B. R. Cahn
3552 Mrs. E. A. Houston & dr.
3552 William T. Houston ·
3552 Mrs. Estella Rader
3608 J. W. Rush
3610 Mr. & Mrs. George W. Best
3612 Mr. and Mrs. Wm. R. Bascom
3612 Fred Bascom
3614 Mr. & Mrs. Thomas Tobey
3616 Mrs. John Beers
3618 Mr. & Mrs. Simon Glickauf
3624 Mrs. M. Rider
3624 William H. Rider
3626 Frank H. Dickey
3706 Mrs. G. Newburger & dr.
3706 E. Newton Newburger.
3706 William S. Newburger
3706 Frank D. Newburger ·
3706 James M. Newburger
3708 Mr. & Mrs. Geo. Karnes & dr.
3708 William Karnes
3710 Mr. & Mrs. Ernest D. Owen
3712 Mrs. L. B. Root & dr.
3712 Mr. & Mrs. Willis C. DeMar
3724 Mr. & Mrs. Ward B. Sherman & drs.
3724 Rev. Frank C. Sherman
3724 Miss Annette Cole
3724 Mrs. Phoebe Cole
3726 Miss Julia J. Sweet
3726 Miss Ellen Sweet
3728 Mr. & Mrs. J. S. Bloomingston
3728 John Albert Bloomingston
3736 Mr. & Mrs. Robt. G. Dwen
3742 Mr. & Mrs. Henry S. Tiffany

3819 Mr. & Mrs. M. C. Noyes & drs.
  Receiving day Tuesday
3819 Walter W. Todd
3819 Miss Laura Todd
  Receiving day Tuesday
3821 Mrs. Urilla Clark & dr.
3821 Frank H. Clark
3823 Mr. & Mrs. William K. Sidley
  & dr.
3823 William P. Sidley
3823 Fred K. Sidley
3823 Frank C. Sidley
3827 Mr. & Mrs. Arthur S. Welch
3827 Eugene Welch
3831 Mr. & Mrs. T. C. Williams jr.
3835 Mr. & Mrs. J. B. McGregor
3837 Mr. & Mrs. Fred'k Meyer
3839 Mr. & Mrs. Frank T. Bliss
3845 Mrs. D. W. Gale & drs.
3845 Mr. & Mrs. Henry H. Blake
3845 James H. Neilson
3845 Walter Blake
3845 Miss Edna Calvin Bigelow
3845 Nelson Calvin Bigelow
3847 Mrs. Frederick L. Smith
3849 Mr. & Mrs. John G. Mead
3851 Mr. & Mrs. James D. Fleming
3853 Mr. & Mrs. Aaron S. Nichols
  & drs.
3857 Mr. & Mrs. Jas. E. Wilson
3861 Mrs. Dean Bangs
3861 Mr. & Mrs. John D. Bangs
3861 Harrie L. Bangs
3869 Mr. & Mrs. Jeremiah Leaming
  & drs.
3929 Mr. & Mrs. J. R. Bensley & dr.
3929 John R. Bensley jr.
3929 Miss Kate W. Bensley
3935 Mr. & Mrs. H. G. Hopkins
3935 Mr. & Mrs. C. E. Braden
3937 Mr. & Mrs. F. A. Shoemaker
3939 Mr. & Mrs. A. H. Wolf
3939 Henry M. Wolf
3943 Mr. & Mrs. Simeon Straus
3945 Mr. & Mrs. Leopold Gans
3949 Mr.&Mrs. Wm. N. Eisendrath
3949 Mrs. Helen Eisendrath & dr.
3957 Mrs. Robert Morrisson
3957 James W. Morrisson
3957 Mr. & Mrs. Walter H. Atwater
3959 Mr. & Mrs. Chas. B. Gilbert
3963 Mr. & Mrs. Chas. C. Lay
3963 Frederick C. Lay
3963 Robert D. Lay
3965 Mr. & Mrs. S. S. Whitehouse
3971 Mr. & Mrs. Shea Smith

3742 Mrs. H. C. Tiffany
3744 Mr. & Mrs. John B. Brady
3746 Mr. & Mrs. Samuel L. Joseph
3756 Mr. & Mrs. F. P. Blackman
3806 Mr. & Mrs. W. E. Bailey
3806 Louis E. Replogle
3816 Mr.& Mrs. Theo. A. Gehrmann
3816 Dr. Adolph Gehrmann
3816 Felix Gehrmann
3820 Henry I. Harmon
3822 Mr. & Mrs. Christopher Mc-
  Lennan
3824 Mr.& Mrs. Festus B. Cole &drs.
3834 Wm. S. Ransome
3836 Mr. & Mrs. Alfred D. Eddy
3836 Mr. & Mrs. Edward Silvey
3840 Mr.& Mrs.Frederick W.Sutton
3842 Mrs. T. W. Beal
3844 Rev. & Mrs. Latham A. Crandall & dr.
3844 Bruce V. Crandall
3846 Mr. & Mrs. Jas. Lee Bell
3846 Mr. & Mrs. Thos. B. Hunter
3846 Mr. & Mrs. A. S. Jackson
3848 Mr. & Mrs. John E. Zeltner
3848 Mr. & Mrs. W. S. Rice
3848 Mr. & Mrs. Edward Bliven
3848 Mr. & Mrs. Geo. W. Schultz
3848 Hobart M. Cable
3850 Mr. & Mrs. Thos. B. Hamm
3850 Mr. & Mrs. Wm. M. Pack
3852 Mr. & Mrs. VanBuren Ruth
3852 Mr. & Mrs. Henry Thackray
3908 Mr. & Mrs. Samuel Pike & drs.
3908 Charles S. Pike
3942 Mr. & Mrs. Geo. M. Dugan
3942 Mr. & Mrs. John H. Wilson
3942 Isaac N. Marks jr.
3946 Mr. & Mrs. Dennison F.Groves
3946 Mr. & Mrs. Allan M. Clement
3952 Mr. & Mrs. E. E. Worthington
3960 Mr. & Mrs. E. A. Casey
3982 Mr. & Mrs. Frank E. Barnard
  & dr.
3998 Mr. & Mrs. Alex. C. Soper
3998 Alex. C. Soper jr.
3998 Miss Paulina Pope
4000 Mrs. Marie D. Lawrence
4000 Mrs. M. J. Taylor
4000 Fred O. Taylor
4004 Mr. & Mrs. Frank H. Pitkin
4018 Mr. & Mrs. Charles W. Beeman
  & dr.
4018 Charles H. Beeman
4018 Geo. R. Rommeiss
4020 L. Bernard Kilbourne

3975 Mr. & Mrs. C. W. Merriam
3975 Mrs. I. N. Harmon
3991 Mr.& Mrs. S.W. Lamson & drs.
3995 Mr.& Mrs.Samuel Baker & drs.
3995 James R. Baker
4003 Mr. & Mrs. Chas. A. Stevens
  Receiving day Monday
4013 Mr. & Mrs. C. W. Lapham
4021 Mr. & Mrs. John Roper & dr.
4037 Mr. & Mrs. Alexander Dunlop
  & dr.
4037 Mr. & Mrs. Geo. M. Pennoyer
4043 Mr. & Mrs. Clement L. Clapp
4043 Mrs. C. Payen
4043 Misses Cecile E. & Juliette
  Payen
4043 Dr. & Mrs. T. H. McClure
4043 Dr. & Mrs. Frank E. Cheeseman
4045 Mr. & Mrs. Sumner Hopkins
4045 Mr. & Mrs. Henry R. Vandercook
4045 Mrs. Henry M. Knickerbocker
  & dr.
4045 Charles K. Knickerbocker
4045 Mr. & Mrs. Henry F. Jones
  Receiving day Thursday
4045 Mrs. Jennie Higbee
4045 W. E. Higbee
4049 Mrs. F. H. Baldwin & dr.
4049 Lieut. Merchant Baldwin
4049 Elbert D. Baldwin
4051 Mr.& Mrs. Solon D. Wilson
  Receiving day Monday
4201 Mrs. Elizabeth P. Hill
4201 Miss Helen Hill
4201 Mr. & Mrs. Thornton Ware
4201 Mr. & Mrs. David B. Robbins
4201 Mr. & Mrs. George Hyers
4201 Mr. & Mrs. Orson K. Tyler
4203 Mr. & Mrs. Frank S. Eberhart
4203 Mr. & Mrs. Duff Porter
4203 John Albert Porter
4203 Mr. & Mrs. J. Frank Edwards
4203 Mr. & Mrs. S. A. Harvey
4207 Mr. & Mrs. James F. Waughop
4207 Miss Ella Cassell
4211 Mrs. F. S. Emmons
4211 Mr. & Mrs. Joseph F. Titus
4211 Miss S. M. Titus
4211 Walter K. Hass
4213 Mrs. Mary E. Munger
4213 Frank L. Hume
4215 Mr. & Mrs. Howard Davis
4219 Mr. & Mrs. Horace W. Gleason
4219 Mr. & Mrs. Edward R. Slagle

4020 Mrs. F. A. Kilbourne
4020 Mrs. E. K. Newell
4024 Mr.& Mrs. Charles E. Morrison
4024 Miss Ada Sylvester
4028 Mr. & Mrs. Frank N. Gage
4032 Mrs. J. J. McDermid
4032 Julian McDermid
4032 Ralph McDermid
4032 Ferdinand McDermid
4032 John J. McDermid jr.
4032 Mrs. M. A. Metcalf
4036 Mr. & Mrs. Lucius G. Fisher
4036 Miss Frances M. Eddy
4040 Mrs. Lucy W. Messer
4040 Mr. & Mrs. Geo. W. Lawrence
4040 Paul Messer
4044 Mr. & Mrs. Frank A. Devlin
4050 Mr. & Mrs. R. Kennicott
4050 Mr. & Mrs. Cass L. Kennicott
4050 Lynn S. Kennicott
4050 Donald Kennicott
4058 Mr. & Mrs. Lewis W. Young
4058 Mr. & Mrs. John C. Harmon
4058 Dr. & Mrs. F. H. Blackmarr
4060 Mr. & Mrs. W. C. Boorn
4060 Mr. & Mrs. W. P. Collings
4060 Mr. & Mrs. Gerrit Fort
4060 Mr. & Mrs. Hiram P. Fort
4060 James G. Fort
4102 Mr. & Mrs. Mathias Walker
4106 Dr. Godfrey S. Salomon
4114 Mr. & Mrs. John McIntyre
4114 Edward M. Montgomery
4118 L. C. Moore
4120 Mr. & Mrs. E. R. Rosenthal
4124 Mr. & Mrs. Fred J. Ratsch
4128 Lamont E. Parker
4128 Mrs. E. P. Titcomb
4130 Mr. & Mrs. Frederick Gardner
4130 Mrs. L. C. Upton
4132 Mr. & Mrs. Iver C. Zarbell &
  drs.
  Receive 1st & 3d Wednesday
4136 Mrs. Leretta M. Crandal
4136 Frederick E. Crandal
4136 Mr. & Mrs. William B. Ewing
4138 Mr. & Mrs. Abner C. Fish
4138 Mr. & Mrs. Frank F. Fish
4138 Edwin S. Fish
4138 Arthur C. Fish
4140 Mr. & Mrs. John C. Lewis
4140 Chas. Ray Lewis
4150 Mr. & Mrs. Allen R. Jewett
  Receiving day Wednesday
4154 Mrs. Victorine Wolf
  Receiving day Wednesday

4221 Mr. & Mrs. Wm. V. Geary
4221 Mr. & Mrs. Henry W. Hart
4305 Mr. & Mrs. Chas. F. Thompson
4307 Mr. & Mrs. Thos. A. Bowden
    & dr.
4307 Dr. & Mrs. Frank X. Walls
4311 Mr. & Mrs. David Anderson &
    dr.   *Receiving day Tuesday*
4313 Mr. & Mrs. Nelson Monroe
4315 Mr. & Mrs. J. R. Wettstein
4317 Mr. & Mrs. John F. Wallace
4317 Mr. & Mrs. Thornton M. Orr
4319 Miss E. R. Dater
4319 Mrs. Harriet H. Burleson & dr.
4333 Rev. & Mrs. Walter Delafield
    & dr.
4333 Selwyn Delafield
4333 Herbert Delafield
4335 Mr. & Mrs. Eugene L. Merritt
4335 Mr. & Mrs. F. C. Kenyon
4337 Mr. & Mrs. Gordon McLeod
4337 Mr. & Mrs. John J. Ellsworth
4343 Mr. & Mrs. A. W. Sproehnle
4345 Mr. & Mrs. Wm. H. Bell
4345 Mr. & Mrs. B. S. Wasson
4347 Mr. & Mrs. Francis Watts
4347 Mr. & Mrs. H. H. McDuffee &
    dr.
4347 Mr. & Mrs. Arthur L. Otto
4349 Mr. & Mrs. Edwin O. Excell
4349 Mr. & Mrs. Wm. Alonzo Excell
4401 Mr. & Mrs. L. J. Carter
4403 Mr. & Mrs. Frank R. Pardridge
    Receiving day Tuesday
4403 Mrs. F. L. Dickie
4405 Dr. & Mrs. Edwin C. Williams
4407 Mr. & Mrs. C. V. Banta jr.
4409 Mr. & Mrs. John Sebastian
    Receiving day Tuesday
4409 Don B. Sebastian
4411 Mrs. Bertha Greenhoot & dr.
4413 Mr. & Mrs. Isaac Kuh
4413 Dr. Sydney Kuh
4415 Mr. & Mrs. W. F. Newberry
4417 Mr. & Mrs. C. H. McConnell
    & dr.
4419 Mr. & Mrs. Brice Worley
4419 Mrs. Ira Couch
4419 Ira J. Couch
4421 Mr. & Mrs. J. A. Miner
    Receive Wednesday
4421 Fred M. Miner
4421 Mrs. Minnie M. Brown
    Receives Wednesday
4423 Mr. & Mrs. H. H. Handy
4423 Mrs. C. C. Cole

4156 Mr. & Mrs. Henry H. Dody
4156 Mrs. Esther A. McDougall
    Receiving day Wednesday
4156 Mr. & Mrs. William McDougall
4160 The Knickerbocker
    Mrs. & Mrs. Edmund C. Biden
    Mr. & Mrs. Caleb Clapp
    Mrs. Edwin Clapp
    Mr. & Mrs. M. I. Cohen
    Mrs. Harriet Holmes
    Mr. & Mrs. C. A. Perlbach
    Mr. & Mrs. F. B. Smith
    Mr. & Mrs. Sam H. Williams jr.
4200 Mrs. Rossiter Kehoe
    Receiving day Thursday
4200 Mr. & Mrs. John Blanchfield
    Keogh
    Receiving day Thursday
4200 James Clowry
4202 Mr. & Mrs. John P. Byrne
    Receiving day Thursday
4204 Mr. & Mrs. William S. Thomas
4204 Mr. & Mrs. Edward S. Thomas
4206 Mr. & Mrs. George E. Van
    Hagen
4206 Mr. & Mrs. Wm. A. Bither
4206 Mr. & Mrs. W. P. Elliott
4212 Mrs. Margaretta E. Burnap
4212 A. Nellis
4214 Mr. & Mrs. Harris Russell &
    drs.
4214 James M. Hadley
4214 Edwin M. Hadley
4214 Mr. & Mrs. John H. Cook
4216 Mr. & Mrs. Erastus H. Scott
4220 Mr. & Mrs. John A. Yakel
4220 J. Stephen Soden
4300-4316 The Tudor
    Mr. & Mrs. Charles T. Allyn
    John F. Carnegie
    Mrs. Barbara Carnegie
    Mrs. Annie C. DeVore
    Mr. & Mrs. Harry F. Carson
    Donald C. Catlin
    Mrs. E. S. Chase
    Robert G. Chase
    Mr. & Mrs. Simeon W. Croy
    Miss A. E. Gordon
    Mr. & Mrs. Herbert Hammond
    Mr. & Mrs. Chas. C. Heldmann
    Receiving day Thursday
    Mr. & Mrs. Aaron V. Kline
    Mr. & Mrs. George L. Lavery
    Receiving day Wednesday
    Mr. & Mrs. Frank W. Mat-
    thews

4425 Mr. & Mrs. John D. Besler
 Receiving day Thursday
4425 Mrs. Laura B. Bassett
4427 Mr. & Mrs. Louis Schamberg
 Receiving day Friday
4429 Mr. & Mrs. Theodore Weil
4431 Mr. & Mrs. Christopher J. Hess
 Receiving day Wednesday
4431 Howard A. Hess
4433 Mr. & Mrs. W. P. Johnson & drs.
4435 Mr. & Mrs. Theo. Regensteiner
4439 Mr. & Mrs. William Renshaw
 Receiving day Tuesday
4441 Mr. & Mrs. Richard Walsh & dr.
4443 Mrs. M. Eliel & dr.
4443 Alexander B. Eliel
4443 Walter R. Eliel
4443 Roy A. Eliel
4443 Eugene D. Eliel
4445 Mr. & Mrs. George E. King
4447 Mr. & Mrs. L. Liebensberger
4449 Mr. & Mrs. Edwin Dow Scott
4449 William H. Scott
4449 Mrs. M. B. Scott
4451 Miss Annie M. Boggs
4451 Albert W. Boggs
4451 A. Emmet Bogg
4453 Gen'l & Mrs. C. S. Bentley & dr.
4453 Mr. & Mrs. Morris R. Dial
4457 Mr. & Mrs. Ralph Gates
4459 Mr. & Mrs. Silas Howe & dr.
4461 Mr. & Mrs. D. Jacobson
4463 Mr. & Mrs. Leopold Wolff
4465 Mr. & Mrs. G. E. VanWoert
 Receiving day Wednesday
4503 Mr. & Mrs. John R. Campbell
4505 Mr. & Mrs. Wallace Heckman
4505 Lorenzo E. Dow
4515 Mr. & Mrs. Chas. E. Follansbee
4521 Mr. & Mrs. Isaac Block
 Receiving day 2d & 4th Friday
4523 Mr. & Mrs. R. G. Sykes & dr.
4525 Mr. & Mrs. Burke Stone
4525 Alfred Bates Stone
4527 Mr. & Mrs. Isaac M. Mayer
 Receiving day Friday
4527 Mrs. R. Mayer & dr.
4529 Mr. & Mrs. E. S. Heyman
 Receiving day Thursday
4529 Mrs. R. Feibelman
4531 Mr. & Mrs. A. Hirsch & dr.
4531 Oscar Hirsch
4533 Mr. & Mrs. Magnus Goodman
4535 Mr. & Mrs. F. E. A. Wolcott
4537 Mr. & Mrs. M. J. Spiegel
4539 Rev. & Mrs. L. P. Mercer & dr.

Joseph S. Maynard
William B. Moulton
Mr. & Mrs. D. P. Peck
Mr. & Mrs. H. E. Radeker
Count & Countess Anthony
 Rozwadowski
Hamline P. Rucker
M. E. Sampsell
Mr. & Mrs. Frederic W. Scullin
 Receiving day Thursday
Mr. & Mrs. Clarence L. Smith
Harold Smith
Mrs. J. R. Stow
Mr. & Mrs. Jos. H. Sullivan
Mr. & Mrs. F. M. Swearingen
Dr. & Mrs. Albert H. Wales
Dr. Frederick M. Wales
Henry N. Wales jr.
Mr. & Mrs. Alfred J. Wright
4320 Mr. & Mrs. Henry L. Green
4322 Mr. & Mrs. G. E. Downe
4324 Mr. & Mrs. Myron W. Atwood
4324 Mrs. Arthur Swazey
4330 Mrs. Mary A. Clark
4330 Mr. & Mrs. Arthur R. Clark
4332 Mr. & Mrs. Charles M. Fay
4334 Mr. & Mrs. R. A. DeWees
4334 Mr. & Mrs. John H. Rood
4334 Mr. F. W. C. Hayes
4336 Mr. & Mrs. Jas. Russell Vincent
4338 Mr. & Mrs. Charles B. Sears
4340 Mr. & Mrs. Geo. H. Martin &
 dr.
4342 Mr. & Mrs. Gordon Valentine
4348 Dr. & Mrs. I. H. Rea
4348 Albert Mendel
4356 Mr. & Mrs. Edward S. Jenison
 & drs.
4356 Edward S. Jenison jr.
4400 Mr. & Mrs. J. L. Chance & dr.
4400 M. B. Clancy
4402 Mr. & Mrs. William M. White
4402 Harley C. White
4404 Mr. & Mrs. A. E. Schuten
4406 Mr. & Mrs. J. D. Derby
 Receiving day Monday
4406 Mrs. I. E. Davis
4410 Mr. & Mrs. Moses Baker
4412 Mrs. Julius Bauer & dr.
4412 Richard Bauer
4412 A. O. Mueller
4414 Mr. & Mrs. Wm. H. Keyser &
 dr.
4420 Mr. & Mrs. C. B. Shefler
4422 Mr. & Mrs. G. W. Simpson &
 dr.

4539 Louis P. Mercer jr.
4543 Mr. & Mrs. W. Northup
4543 Mrs. L. T. Kimball
4545 Mr. & Mrs. Frederick M. Smith
          Receiving day Friday
4547 Mr. & Mrs. Jacob Beiersdorf
4547 Arthur Beiersdorf
4547 I. H. Miller
4549 Mr. & Mrs. E. G. Shumway
4551 Mr. & Mrs. E. C. Ferguson
          Receiving day Thursday
4551 William G. Ferguson
4553 Mrs. Gilbert Montague
4553 Miss Belle Dunklee
4555 Mr. & Mrs. Edwin H. Keen
4557 Mrs. C. G. Ortmayer
4559 Mr. & Mrs. M. Gottfried
4611 Rev. & Mrs. Robert McIntyre
          Receiving day Monday
4613 Mr. & Mrs. Harry A. Wheeler
4615 Mr. & Mrs. H. W. Seymour
4617 Mr. & Mrs. Selig Greenbaum
4619 Mr. & Mrs. W. T. Fenton
4619 Miss Fenton
4619 Howard Withrow Fenton
4621 Mr. & Mrs. Wm. H. Brintnall
4623 Mr. & Mrs. Edward G. Mason
4623 Roswell B. Mason
4623 Julian S. Mason
4625 Mr. & Mrs. Milo B. Randall
4625 Benj. G. Randall
4727 Mr. & Mrs. John A. Tolman
4731 O. F. Lindman
4731 Mrs. Harriet Tallmadge
4737 Mr. & Mrs. David N. Hanson
4821 Mr. & Mrs. Caleb H. Canby
4849 Mr. & Mrs. Samuel A. Spry
          Receiving day Thursday
4933 Mr. & Mrs. J. L. Higgie &
          drs.
4933 Noble K. Higgie
4933 Arthur M. Higgie
4933 Miss M. L. Higgie
          Receiving day Wednesday
4933 Archibald A. Higgie
4933 George Wm. Higgie
4945 S. W. Rawson
4945 F. H. Rawson
5401 Mr. & Mrs. Theodore Oehne
5401 Mrs. T. Schell & dr.
5477 Mr. & Mrs. I. G. Levy
cor. 58th University of Chicago
          Miss Julia E. Bulkley
          Joseph E. Raycroft
          Miss Myra Reynolds
          Miss Marion Talbot

4422 John H. Jones
4424 Mr. & Mrs. John R. LeVally
4424 John S. Scoville
4430 Oliver Jackson & drs.
          Receiving day Thursday
4430 Paul Jackson
4430 Oliver A. Jackson
4432 Mrs. M. Palmiter
          Receiving day Thursday
4432 Miss Alta Mae Palmiter
4432 Mr. & Mrs. Charles D. Cox
4434 Mrs. Gardner McGregor & dr.
4436 Mr. & Mrs. Edward B. Lathrop
4438 Mr. & Mrs. Wm. H. Lake
          Receiving day Thursday
4440 Mrs. & Mrs. Arthur Dow
4442 Mr. & Mrs. E. A. Bremner
4442 Mrs. B. Bremner
4444 Mr. & Mrs. J. G. Bodenschatz
4450 Mr. & Mrs. Frank B. Orr
          Receiving day Monday
4452 Mr. & Mrs. Levi Abt & dr.
4452 Herman H. Abt
4454 Mr. & Mrs. J. Dreyfus
4456 Mr. & Mrs. Henry W. Wolseley
4458 Mr. & Mrs. M. Lewis Swift
4500 Mr. & Mrs. Jacob S. Smith
          Receiving day Wednesday
4502 Mr. & Mrs. Henry Kuh
4504 Mrs. M. R. Greeley
          Receiving day Tuesdays
4506 Mr. & Mrs. Percy G. Ullman
          Receive 1st & 3d Friday
4508 Mr. & Mrs. Louis M. Dillman
          Receiving day Thursday
4508 Louis C. Dillman
4510 Mr. & Mrs. Herman Felsen-
          thal & drs.
4510 Herbert Felsenthal
4510 Mrs. Hannah Schwarz
4514 Mr. & Mrs. Theo. Holman
4516 Mr. & Mrs. Marshall W. George
4516 Charles F. Franklin
4516 Mrs. Percy R. Franklin
4520 Mr. & Mrs. Ernest J. Preston
4524 Mr. & Mrs. E. H. Sedgwick
4530 Mr. & Mrs. A. W. Harris
4550 Mr. & Mrs. DeWitt P. Ballard
4552 Mr. & Mrs. Wilber Wait & drs.
4554 Mr. & Mrs. Sam'l A. McClean jr.
4556 Mr. & Mrs. David Lepman & dr.
          Receive 1st & 3d Wednesdays
4556 Horace Lepman
4556 Miss R. Lichtenstein
4558 Mr. & Mrs. Chester D. Cran-
          dall *Receiving day Monday*

cor. 58th Univ. of Chicago (cont'd.)
   Prof. Oliver J. Thatcher
   Oscar L. Triggs
   Camillo Von Klenze
   Miss Elizabeth Wallace
6051 Mr.& Mrs. Sherman H. Bouton
6127 Mr. & Mrs. Frank Brust
6353 Mr. & Mrs. Henry A. Nott

5016 Howard Woodhead
5332 Mr. & Mrs. T. F. Hagan
5332 Thos. F. Hagan jr.
5400 Mr. & Mrs. Wm. J. Moore
5400 Mrs. M. H. Moore
5406 Mr. & Mrs. Elbert S. Young & dr.
5444 Mr. &Mrs. J. R. Hansell
5514 Mr. & Mrs. J. M. Detrick
6024 Sho. Watase
6040 Mr. & Mrs. Jno. E. Sutherland
6042 Mr. & Mrs. Geo B. Engle jr.
6136 Mr. & Mrs. E. A. Buzzell
6136 Mrs. Mary J. Gibson
6320 Mr. & Mrs. G. A. Claussenius
6328 Mr. & Mrs. Geo. W. Hatter
6440 Mr. & Mrs. W. A. Prior
6440 Mrs. M. E. Hayes
6448 Mr. & Mrs. N. J. Weil
6450 Mr. & Mrs. Frank H. Wolford
6500 Mr. & Mrs. W. J. Morgan
6552 Mr. & Mrs. Emil Ufer
6600 Mr. & Mrs. M. Leonard
6618 Mr. & Mrs. John J. Hibler

4600 Mr. & Mrs. E. T. Williams
4600 John R. Williams
4600 Mrs. H. E. Whipple
4628 Mr. & Mrs. James M. Ball
4800 Mr. & Mrs. E. C. Potter
4810 Mr. & Mrs. James C. Hutchins
4822 Mr. & Mrs. A. C. Buttolph
4832 Mr. & Mrs. Alonzo M. Fuller & dr.
4832 Frank Hoyt Fuller
4840 Mr. & Mrs. Henry H. Kennedy
4900 Mr. & Mrs. G. F. Swift
4908 Mr. & Mrs. M. K. Bowen
4918 Mr. & Mrs. C. W. Hodge
4920 S. Wedeles
4920 Mrs. Celia Wedeles
4920 Miss Babetta Wedeles
4924 Mrs. S. Becker & dr.
4924 Benj. F. Becker
4928 Mrs. A. E. Densmore
4928 Mr. & Mrs. J. F. Holland
4938 Mr. & Mrs. Albert R. Bremer
4940 Mr. & Mrs. L. T. Dickason & dr.
4942 Mr. & Mrs. Benjamin Thomas
4942 Mrs. Henry Gaylord
4944 Mr. & Mrs. Ferdinand Gundrum & drs.
4950 Mr. & Mrs. Lauren J. Drake & dr.
5006 Mr. & Mrs. P. B. Palmer
5006 George R. Palmer
5012 Mr. & Mrs. H. W. Harwood
5016 Mr. & Mrs. J. E. Woodhead & dr.

ELLIS PARK.

3601 Mr. & Mrs. T. M. Turner & dr.
3601 J. Lyle Turner
3601 Thomas M. Turner jr.
3605 Mr. & Mrs. Frederick S. Cowles
3607 Mrs. E. Shermer
3615 Mr. & Mrs. Meyer Wheeler & dr.
3615 Leo W. Wheeler

3608 Mr. & Mrs. J. G. Cozzens

3621 Dr. John G. Trine & dr.
3621 Mrs. A. C. Burgess
3623 Mrs. Rose Forrester
3623 Mr. & Mrs. S. E. Davis
3629 Mrs. Marie H. Garrison
3633 Jesse T. Greene

ELMWOOD COURT.

3823 Mr. & Mrs. J. B. Wiggins
3823 A. D. Wiggins
3825 Mr. & Mrs. Julius E. Odelius
3841 Mr. & Mrs. William Pound

3842 Mr. & Mrs. John M. White & dr.
   Receiving day Wednesday

3704 Mr. & Mrs. Wm. M. Morrison
3750 Mr. & Mrs. Simon Rosenheim & dr.
3808 Mr. & Mrs. G. A. M. Liljencrantz & dr.
3842 Augustus J. White

EMERALD AVENUE.

4457 Mr. & Mrs.W.H. Thompson jr.
4515 Mr. & Mrs. Henry Clapp
4515 Mr. & Mrs. Samuel Cozzens
4541 Mr. & Mrs. Harry M. McNair
4601 Mr. & Mrs. Wm. W. Shearer
4605 Mr. & Mrs. Frank W. Tubbs
6749 Dr. Malcolm D. MacNab
7721 Mr. & Mrs. J. D. Tidmarsh
7721 James McMillan
7737 Mr. & Mrs. Chas. E. Baker &
        dr.
7737 Chas. Baker jr.

4436 Dr. & Mrs. W. H. Bohart
4506 Dr. & Mrs. W. R. Parsons
4554 Mr. & Mrs. George Dennis
4612 Mr. & Mrs. Edward Tilden
4624 Mr. & Mrs. D. E. Hartwell
        Receiving day Wednesday
7600 Mr. & Mrs. James B. Galloway
7600 Mr. & Mrs. A. J. Galloway
7624 Mr. & Mrs. Thomas R. Bishop

7751 Mr. & Mrs. W. A. Colvin

ENGLEWOOD AVENUE.

435 Mr. & Mrs. Wm. B. Oxnam &
        drs.
441 Dr. & Mrs. J. P. Webster & drs.
443 Dr. & Mrs. George J. Wilder
445 Mr. & Mrs. Baxter A. Dickinson
447 Mrs. Nellie A. Bryant
453 Mr. & Mrs. Philip C. Miller
457 Mr. & Mrs. Fred G. Thearle jr.
533 Mr. & Mrs. J. C. Kilgore
537 Mr. & Mrs. S. T. Lewis
541 Mr. & Mrs. James E. Farrell
551 Mr. & Mrs. Walter H. Miller
555 W. S. Hancock
613 Mr. & Mrs. Chas. H. Adolph
615 Mr.& Mrs. Wesley W. Wickham
615 Mr. & Mrs. Henry S. Judd
623 Pearce C. Kelley
627 Mr. & Mrs. Wm. W. Schatz
627 Mr. & Mrs. J. Stoltz
629 Mr. & Mrs. John L. Stevens

432 Dr. & Mrs. Mervin B. Rimes
432 Mr. & Mrs. G. W. I. Cole
438 Mr.& Mrs. H. C.Washburn
440 Dr. & Mrs. John S. Hunt
500 Mr. & Mrs. S. M. Sutherland
504 Mr. & Mrs. Frank P. Crane
508 Mr. & Mrs. H. A. Swanzey
512 Mr. & Mrs. H. H. Carpenter
526 Jonathan Periam & drs.
534 Asa B. Kile & dr.
606 Mr. & Mrs. James A. Hinson
610 Mr. & Mrs. John W. Fitch
614 Mr. & Mrs. Edward W. Drew
620 Mr. & Mrs. Edmond A. Wood
634 Mr. & Mrs. W. W. Backman &
        drs.
636 Mr. & Mrs. John A. Morgan
714 George R. Jarvis
750 Mr. & Mrs. G. J. Tatge
752 Mrs. Sophia Tatge & drs.
754 Mr. & Mrs. Louis Rathje

EVANS AVENUE.

4333 Mr. & Mrs. Wm. C. Moore
4337 Mr.& Mrs. Lincoln S. Eastburn
4551 Mr. & Mrs. John K. Yarnell
4551 Mrs. Margaretta Macfall
4557 Mr. & Mrs. Norman A.MacRae
4625 Dr. & Mrs. M. Schycker
4633 Dr. & Mrs. D. S. Satterlee
4643 Dr. John E. Sawyer
4645 Dr. Clarrisa Bigelow
4645 Dr. Marie L. White
4645 Dr. Wm. A. Campbell
4709 Dr. Thomas W. Combs
4709 Dr. Helen Combs

4828 Dr. & Mrs. A. M. Casper

4436 Mr. & Mrs. Wm. C. McClain
4444 Mr. & Mrs. Charles Farquhar
4546 Dr. & Mrs. Alfred Dahlberg
4618 Benjamin S. Paddock
4714 Mr. & Mrs. Harry A. Fritz
4720 Joseph Herz
4720 Arthur Herz
4722 Mr. & Mrs. M. B. Custard & drs.
4724 Mrs. M. L. Graham
4724 R. A. Wells
4724 E. L. Wells
4726 Mr. & Mrs. Moritz Bermann
        & drs.
4730 Mrs. Rose Shore
        Receiving day Wednesday

4846 Mrs. A. M. Kearney & drs.
4848 Mr. & Mrs. Abram B. Stratton
4856 Dr. & Mrs. W. O. Cheeseman
4856 Harry Cheeseman
4858 Mr. & Mrs. Frank Schlegel
Receiving day Wednesday

4738 Mr. & Mrs. E. C. Webster
4740 Mrs. Laura Nathanson & drs.
4744 Mr. & Mrs. Frank M. Trissal
4748 Mrs. Sarah C. Anderson & drs
4808 Dr. & Mrs. Charles A. Hoag
4818 Mrs. Emma McCally & dr.
4826 Mr. & Mrs. George F. Ebert

FIFTIETH STREET.

331 Mrs. Emily L. Wilson
331 Granville M. Wilson
389 Mr. & Mrs. Edward Burnham
397 Mr. & Mrs. B. C. Strehl
733 Mr. & Mrs. Harry L. Irwin
829 Mrs. William A. Foster
829 William Elmore Foster

---

142 Mr. & Mrs. Richard F. Clark
144 Mr. & Mrs. William Lyman
146 Mr. & Mrs. Edward M. Luce
148 Mr. & Mrs. T. M. Bates & dr.
156 Mr. & Mrs. G. H. Lussky & drs.
156 E. A. Lussky
156 Arthur Lussky
188 Mr. & Mrs. Charles E. Murison
198 Mr. & Mrs. Albert C. Barnes
728 Mr. & Mrs. Chas. W. Greenfield
872 Mr. & Mrs. O. G. Brown
878 Mr. & Mrs. W. J. Clizbe

44 Mr. & Mrs. Chas. L. Etheridge
44 Mr. & Mrs. Oswald Lockett
44 Mr. & Mrs. A. D. Warren
46 Mr. & Mrs. John G. Elliott
76 Mr. & Mrs. G. Russell Leonard
76 Rev. Chas. H. Bixby & dr.
76 Mr. & Mrs. Geo. C. Nimmons
78 Dr. & Mrs. W. W. Curtis
Receiving day Wednesday
124 Mr. & Mrs. F. G. Hartwell
126 Mrs. Lyman L. Barbour
128 Mr. & Mrs. J. J. Tobias
128 Mr. & Mrs. Clayton H. Tobias
130 Mr. & Mrs. Wm. Mead Fletcher
134 Mr. & Mrs. Wm. K. Fellows
134 Dr. Antoinette K. Fellows
134 John B. Fellows
136 Dr. & Mrs. R. A. Norris
Receiving day Wednesday
136 Mrs. C. P. Norris
140 Mr. & Mrs. Lucius A. Hine

FIFTIETH PLACE.

613 Mr. & Mrs. Thomas B. Smith

570 Mr. & Mrs. C. C. Richt

FIFTY-FIRST STREET.

95 Mr. & Mrs. S. W. Burnham & drs.
95 A. J. Burnham
95 R. W. Burnham
95 Dr. & Mrs. A. W. Hitt
97 Mr. & Mrs. William H. Spear
97 W. H. Spear jr.
97 Harry E. Spear
97 Mrs. Mary M. Raper
101 Mr. & Mrs. C. C. Shepard
121 Mr. & Mrs. G. B. S. Stewart
121 Mr. & Mrs. James S. Carter
123 Dr. & Mrs. John H. R. Bond
Receiving day Friday
123 Dr. & Mrs. W. J. N. Davis
123 Mr. & Mrs. J. G. Warner
125 Prof. & Mrs. J. J. Schobinger
129 Mr. & Mrs. Barton Sewell

158 Mr. & Mrs. Edward E. Smith
162 Mr. & Mrs. James R. Smith
162 Mrs. Wm. L. Catherwood
166 Mr. & Mrs. B. F. Cummins
166 Mr. & Mrs. A. H. Mulford
166 Mrs. M. A. Mulford
166 Mr. & Mrs. Thomas Allen
166 Edward M. Gage
166 Mr. & Mrs. H. A. Foresman
166 Mr. & Mrs. Thomas Allen
180 Mr. & Mrs. James W. Barrett
180 Mr. & Mrs. Chas. E. White
184 Mr. & Mrs. A. M. Heath
184 Miss Jennie E. Jackman
210 Dr. & Mrs. H. Wernicke Gentles
Receive 1st & 3d Thursdays
212 Mr. & Mrs. J. J. Hattstaedt

135 Mr. & Mrs. J. T. Richards
169 Hon. & Mrs. T. G. Norse
     Recceiving day Friday
171 Mr. & Mrs. Edwin C. Loomis
171 Maj. & Mrs. W. L. Marshall
173 Mr. & Mrs. Egbert W. Leonard
     Receiving day Thursday
171 Mr. & Mrs. Wm. E. Dewey
171 Mrs. B. R. Fisher
171 Dr. H. J. Johnson
171 Mrs. M. A. Bowman & dr.
171 Miss Elizabeth S. Stewart
171 Mrs. Jane Shirra
173 Mrs. O. F. Allen
177 Dr. & Mrs. Filip Kreissl
183 Mr. & Mrs. Frank L. Gordon
185 Alexander Robertson
185 Mr. & Mrs. E. A. Sutter
185 Mr. & Mrs. H. A. Snyder
185 Mr. & Mrs. John V. Berg
     Receiving day Monday
185 Mr. & Mrs. Wm. E. Keepers
185 Leon A. Bell
569 to 575 The Vermont Flats
     Mr. & Mrs. S. L. Bailey & dr.
     Mr. & Mrs. Wm. S. Brewster &
     dr.
     Mr. & Mrs. G. O. Brewster
     Mrs. S. A. Brooks
     Mrs. Dora A. Harris & dr.
     Receiving day Thursday

214 Mr. & Mrs. Joseph H. Coöke &
     dr.
248 Mr. & Mrs. John Allyn Campbell
     Receiving day Thursday
248 Miss Corinne Campbell
250 Mr. & Mrs. John F. Hetherington
252 Mr. & Mrs. James F. May
256 Mr. & Mrs. E. E. Black
264 Arthur C. Jackman
264 Dr. & Mrs. Winthrop Girling
354 Mr. & Mrs. Geo. Caven
     Receiving day Wednesday
546 Mr. & Mrs. Orett L. Munger
     Receiving day Tuesday
546 Miss Laura M. Munger
548 Dr. & Mrs. A. H. Ferguson
550 Dr. & Mrs. Stuart Johnstone
     Receiving day Monday

———

Mrs. A. Reeves Jackson
Mr. & Mrs. James G. McMichael
Mr. & Mrs. D. B. Nash
     Receiving day Monday
Mr. & Mrs. Aaron J. Newby
Mrs. H. S. Pond
Gen. & Mrs. G. B. Raum & dr.
Mrs. M. Raum Littell
Mrs. Nellie M. Rogers
Mr. & Mrs. John C. Sherer

FIFTY-SECOND STREET.

217 Mr. & Mrs. Robert P. Lamont
225 Mr. & Mrs. William A. Burrows
227 Mr. & Mrs. U. Young
273 Mrs. Nellie E. Hunneman

232 Mr. & Mrs. Wm. G. Carlisle

———

275 Mr. & Mrs. Hunter W. Finch

FIFTY-THIRD STREET.

 35 Mr. & Mrs. Calvin C. Taylor
 41 Mr. & Mrs. G. C. Varney
     Receiving day Thursday
 41 Mr. & Mrs. R. P. Donaldson
     Receiving day Thursday
 53 Mrs. Edward F. Utley
 53 Mr. & Mrs. S. A. Brown
 53 Spencer M. Brown
 55 Dr. & Mrs. N. B. Delamater
 55 Mr. & Mrs. S. F. Phelps
 55 G. G. Place
 55 William H. A. Munns
 55 Mrs. Anna E. Wilson & dr.
 55 Fred S. Wilson
205 Mr. & Mrs. James E. Baker

 42 Mr. & Mrs. E. H. Kellogg & dr.
 42 E. B. Kellogg
 42 Guy B. Child
 44 Mr. & Mrs. A. W. Wheeler
 44 Mr. & Mrs. Edwin A. Booth
 46 Mr. & Mrs. Wm. R. Mygatt
 46 Mrs. A. J. Hull
 48 Mr. & Mrs. Geo. W. Binford
 52 Mr. & Mrs. Lester A. Talcott
110 Dr. N. R. Yeager
132 H. D. Jones
186 Miss Jennie Squier
222 Rev. & Mrs. Franklin Johnson
222 Mr. & Mrs. Hugh A Kelso, jr.
224 Mr. & Mrs. John A. Grier & dr.

213 Frederick D. Hills
213 Mrs. A. M. Hunn
217 Dr. Denslow Lewis
241 Mr. & Mrs. Addison Ballard
247 Mrs. John J. Clark & drs.
263 Mr. & Mrs. R. H. Garrigue
271 Mr. & Mrs. John A. Cole & dr.
271 Edward S. Cole
271 Mrs. M. M. Alvord
275 Mr. & Mrs. Charles E. Morrill
279 Mr. & Mrs. Allan M. Hays
289 Mr. & Mrs. J. F. Sanders
289 Miss Ethel J. Magee
293 Mr. & Mrs. C. W. Hotchkiss
293 Mr. & Mrs. Geo. L. Reppert &
    dr.
295 Mr. & Mrs. W. H. Palmer
299 Mr. & Mrs. J. C. Morrison
301 Mr. & Mrs. S. L. Tompkins
    Receiving day Wednesday
307 Mr. & Mrs. Arthur A. Crosby
335 Mrs. Louisa H. Adams & dr.
339 Mr. & Mrs. Edward Allen
339 Mr. & Mrs. Arthur G. Allen
339 Mrs. M. A. Allen
343 Mr. & Mrs. S. Q. Perry & dr.
343 Crooker Perry

226 Mr. & Mrs. Ira W. Howerth
228 Mr. & Mrs. L. T. Damon
228 Dr. Joseph A. Capps
228 Mr. & Mrs. Hollon F. Miles
236 Mr. & Mrs. S. F. Fogg
240 Mr. & Mrs. Charles H. Mifflin
244 Mrs. G. T. McMurray
244 Geo. N. McMurray
244 A. M. McMurray
248 Mr. & Mrs. Albert O. Parker
248 B. M. Parker
248 A. H. Parker
252 Frederick A. Bowles & dr.
252 G. D. Corliss
260 Dr. & Mrs. T. J. Balhatchett
    Receiving day Wednesday
262 Mr. & Mrs. Geo. Willard &
    dr.
264 Mr. & Mrs. Geo. R. Willard
300 Mr. & Mrs. C. H. Evans
316 Mr. & Mrs. Andrew McAdams
506 Mr. & Mrs. Henry E. Weaver
512 Mr. & Mrs. Clinton E. Woods
512 Miss Mary Wells
    Receiving day Thursday
518 Mr. & Mrs. B. W. May

FIFTY-FOURTH STREET.

191 Mr. & Mrs. E. F. Carry
193 Albert A. Dexter & dr.
223 Prof. & Mrs. Chas. O. Whitman
229 Mr. & Mrs. Geo. L. Forester
387 Dr. Samuel J. Jones

146 Mr. & Mrs. Walter Wardrop &
    drs.
188 Mr. & Mrs. W. C. Robinson
304 Mr. & Mrs. Chas. P. Jennings
346 Mr. & Mrs. Joseph W. Errant

FIFTY-FOURTH PLACE.

189 Mrs. Julia Ward

228 Mr. & Mrs. Frank M. Sessions

FIFTY-FIFTH STREET.

446 Mr. & Mrs. J. H. Lewis

FIFTY-SIXTH STREET.

135 Mrs. Mary E. Potter
135 Miss Bessie O. Potter
137 Prof. & Mrs. Frank F. Abbott
137 Mr. & Mrs. Wm. Bates Price
    Receiving day Thursday
301 Prof. & Mrs. James H. Breasted
301 Prof. George F. James
301 Dr. Sarah C. Buckley
    Receiving day Tuesday

226 Mr. & Mrs. Harry G. Lee
230 Mr. & Mrs. Grant Carpenter
636 Mr. & Mrs. W. G. McGee
636 Harry L. McGee

307 Mr. & Mrs. Charles E. Lane
347 Mr. & Mrs. Ephraim Hewitt

WEST FIFTY-SIXTH PLACE.

615 Dr. & Mrs. Willis C. Stone

635 Mr. & Mrs. Archibald Mac Arthur

FIFTY-SEVENTH STREET.

429 Herbert L. Willett
689 Mr. & Mrs. M. F. Pierce & dr.

———

244 Dr. & Mrs. Jay O. Nelson
    Receiving day Thursday
248 Dr. & Mrs. Horatio F. Wood
248 Mrs. O. F. Wood
338 The Harcourt
    Prof. & Mrs. William Hill
    Prof. & Mrs. O. C. Farrington
    Miss Laura T. Brayton

Mrs. Ella F. Young
Dr. & Mrs. J. Truman Clark
344 Mr. & Mrs. H. S. Fiske
344 Bertram K. Hollister
358 Mr. & Mrs. J. G. C. Troop
362 Mr. & Mrs. J. M. Coulter
362 Mr. & Mrs. Frank B. Rae
438 Mrs. Carroll Cutler
440 Dr. & Mrs. G. A. Hadfield
440 Mr. & Mrs. Chas. K. Burton & dr.

FIFTY-EIGHTH STREET.

315 Theophilus W. Hamill & dr.
315 Ernest S. Hamill
357 Prof. & Mrs. George Baur
357 Prof. William M. Wheeler

363 Dr. & Mrs. J. H. Boyd
363 Prof. & Mrs. George S. Goodspeed

FIFTY-NINTH STREET.

ne. cor. Lexington av.
    Mr. & Mrs. Wm. R. Harper
    Receiving day Thursday

1015 Mrs. Mary Cameron & drs.
1015 Gordon Cameron

WEST FIFTY-NINTH STREET.

621 Freeman DeWolfe
621 Miss Eda DeWolfe

138 Mr. & Mrs. James H. Winn
540 Mr. & Mrs. Wm. Whinnery
542 Mr. & Mrs. James E. Plew

WEST FIFTY-NINTH PLACE.

332 Mr. & Mrs. John Mies
334 Rev. & Mrs. Chas. Reynolds

344 Mr. & Mrs. F. B. Virden

FOREST AVENUE.

3107 Mr. & Mrs. Edw. E. Wendell
3107 Mrs. Hattie Boyd
3113 Mr. & Mrs. W. K. Forsyth
3117 Mrs. Philo G. Dodge
3123 Mr. & Mrs. Jerry Knowles
3131 Mr. & Mrs. Wm. W. Crooker & drs.
3131 Miss Elizabeth M. Buckley
3135 Mr. & Mrs. J. G. Slafter
3135 Mrs. Hattie Adams
3139 Mr. & Mrs. Geo. H. Cole & dr.
3145 Edward Frensdorf
3145 Samuel Frensdorf

3122 W. I. Neely
3122 H. M. Dickson
3156 Mr. & Mrs. E. Calamara & dr.
3206 Julius Neumann
3206 I. D. Neumann
3206 Miss Josephine Neumann
3230 Mrs. George F. Harding & drs.
3230 Victor M. Harding
3232 Mr. & Mrs. J. W. Scofield
3240 Mr. & Mrs. Jas. M. Harper
3246 Mr. & Mrs. N. Martin
3258 Mr. & Mrs. S. R. Howell
    Receiving day Friday

3145 Mr. & Mrs. Aaron Kahn
3149 Mrs. T. E. Webb & dr.
3151 Mr. & Mrs. Leon Klein & dr.
3151 Samuel Klein
3151 Nathan Klein
3157 Miss Laura M. Hubbard
3231 Mrs. F. B. Miles & drs.
3233 Mrs. Mary A. Clemmons
3233 Mr. & Mrs. E. T. Shedd
3245 Mrs. W. H. Sanders
3245 Dr. H. B. Sanders
3253 Mr. & Mrs. Clifford Williams
Receiving day Tuesday.
3253 Clifford Hoyne Williams
3301 Dr. & Mrs. Daniel H. Williams
3305 Mr. & Mrs. Maurice Goodman
3305 Mrs. Abraham Newman
3307 Mr. & Mrs. Ambrose Risdon
3311 Mr. & Mrs. George F. Bodwell
3323 Mr. & Mrs. Frederick Crumbaugh
3351 Mr. & Mrs. John D. Stowell & drs.
3351 Miss Louise M. Farnham
3353 Mr. & Mrs. B. F. Chase & dr.
3353 B. F. Chase jr.
3363 Mr. & Mrs. H. F. Brown
3403 Mr. & Mrs. J. Freudenthal
3405 H. H. Heimerdinger
3407 Mrs. M. F. Hine
3409 Mr. & Mrs. Edward H. Banker
3411 Mr. & Mrs. J. Harry Theobald
3413 Mr. & Mrs. F. Rothschild
3419 Mr. & Mrs. Henry Friend
3423 Mr. & Mrs. W. Rosenbaum
3423 Moses Bloom & dr.
3423 Samuel Bloom
3563 Mr. & Mrs. Joseph Lindquist
3569 Mr. & Mrs. Moses Eiseman
3569 Mr. & Mrs. J. E. Simon
3633 Mr. & Mrs. Henry Kahn
3637 Mr. & Mrs. Henry Spitz
Receiving day 2d Thursday
3639 Mr. & Mrs. H. Simons
3641 Mr. & Mrs. M. L. Hefter
3647 Mr. & Mrs. Samuel Flower
3649 Mr. & Mrs. Julius Coné
3725 Mr. & Mrs. J. G. Straus
3725 Mrs. S. Straus
3731 Mr. & Mrs. Wm. O. Stanley
3733 Mr. & Mrs. Thos. W. Wilmarth
3737 Mr. & Mrs. Frederick W. Leé
3805 Mr. & Mrs. Samuel A. Wilson
3813 Matthew E. Magill
3813 Mr. & Mrs. Lorenz Küssner
3813 Albert J. Küssner

3258 Mr. Ida Morey Riley
3258 Miss Mary A. Blood
3342 S. J. Nihlean
3346 Mr. & Mrs. Isaac Lichtstern
3348 Mr. & Mrs. Samuel C. Peiser
3362 Mr. & Mrs. Sigmund Stein
3402 Mr. & Mrs. J. Frank Tenney
Receive Tuesday
3404 Mr. & Mrs. Michael Cohen & drs.
3408 Mrs. H. J. Metz
3408 Mrs. J. Peiser
3518 Mr. & Mrs. Jacob Lindheimer
3524 Mr. & Mrs. Arthur W. Gray
3526 Wm. J. Burdsall
3526 Miss Marion C. Burdsall
3526 Miss Mary J. Burdsall
3530 Mrs. Sarah Frohman & drs.
3530 Fred Frohman
3558 Mr. & Mrs. James A. Hedglin
3650 Mr. & Mrs. M. D. Singer
3700 Mr. & Mrs. Max Ellbogen
3714 Mr. & Mrs. Henry Harris
3716 Mr. & Mrs. Osbourne J. Shannon
3716 Mrs. Mary E. Holt
3722 Mr. & Mrs. Max Eiseman
3722 Mr. & Mrs. S. W. Klein
3726 Mrs. Clara Mandelbaum & drs.
3726 M. H. Mandelbaum
3728 Mr. & Mrs. Marcellus Hopkins & dr.
3730 Mr. & Mrs. C. A. Garcelon
3732 Mrs. Geo. Sunderland
3736 Mr. & Mrs. Edward J. Mitchell
3740 Mr. & Mrs. Sol. H. Eisenstaedt
3742 Mr. & Mrs. James H. Northup
3742½ Mr. & Mrs. R. S. Matheson
3744 Mr. & Mrs. Joseph A. Kramer
3744 Mrs. Julius Rosenberger
3744 Otto J. Rosenberger
3748 Mr. & Mrs. C. H. Ingwersen
3748 Marvin Ingwersen
3800 Mr. & Mrs. E. L. Tufts
Receiving day Wednesday
3800 Melville S. Nichols
3802 Mr. & Mrs. Harry S. Raymond
3804 Mr. & Mrs. Arthur B. Waughop
3806 Mr. & Mrs. Eugene D. Anderson
3810 Mr. & Mrs. Arthur N. Fisher
Receiving day Friday
3810 James E. Goodman
3814 Mr. & Mrs. F. B. Bradley

3813 Miss Louise C. Küssner
3815 Mr. & Mrs. John J. Kenna
3815 P. J. McIntyre

3825 John H. Jones & dr.
3825 Ed. L. Jones
3833 Mr. & Mrs. Edward F. Keebler
Receive Thursday

FORRESTVILLE AVENUE.

4317 Mr. & Mrs. E. L. Pottle & drs.
4319 Mr. & Mrs. A. G. Jewell & drs.
4319 Edwin S. Jewell
4321 Mrs. Fred N. Boughton
4329 Mr. & Mrs. Wm. Watkins
4331 Mr. & Mrs. J. H. Morganroth
4333 Mr. & Mrs. Wm. Wolff & drs.
4333 Dr. H. D. Wolff
4335 Mr. & Mrs. Louis Hartman
4337 Mr. & Mrs. Wm. Taussig
4339 Mr. & Mrs. Leopold Price
4345 Mr. & Mrs. Adolph Hasterlik
4349 Mrs. Jenny G. Myers & dr.
Receiving day 2d & 4th Wednesday
4503 Mrs. H. E. Putnam & dr.
Receiving day Friday
4511 Mr. & Mrs. H. E. Rycroft
4511 Mrs. Margaret Costello
4515 Mr. & Mrs. R. G. Erler
4517 Mr. & Mrs. Moses Goldsmith
4519 Mr. & Mrs. Edward Niles Hill
4523 Mr. & Mrs. J. M. Trainer
4525 Mr. & Mrs. J. M. Wile
4531 Mr. & Mrs. Geo. W. Brown
Receiving day Thursday
4545 Mr. & Mrs. Ralph T. Sollitt
Receiving day Tuesday
4551 Mr. & Mrs. Simon Goldsmith
4553 Dr. & Mrs. J. P. McGill
4555 Mr. & Mrs. Byron M. Fellows
4559 Mr. & Mrs. Theodore Nelson
4649 Mr. & Mrs. J. E. Ullery
4815 Mr. & Mrs. L. D. Powers
4827 Mr. & Mrs. Edmund F. Dodge
4839 Mr. & Mrs. Geo. V. Wells & drs.
4841 Mr. & Mrs. M. O. Tremaine
4845 Mr. & Mrs. Chas. F. Lammert
4845 Mr. & Mrs. Funley Scruggs
4851 Albert Neuberger
4851 Henry Neuberger
4851 Edward Neuberger
4853 Mr. & Mrs. Samuel Weil
4857 Mr. & Mrs. John E. Shields
4859 Mr. & Mrs. Frederick Uhlmann
4909 Mr. & Mrs. Henry Weil
4911 Harry Harlan Doggett
4911 William Francis Doggett
4911 Mrs. Mary E. Doggett
4915 Mr. & Mrs. Jacob Hart

4306 Mr. & Mrs. F. R. Van Hamm
4318 Jerome Hewitt & dr.
4330 Mr. & Mrs. Henry Leopold jr.
4332 Mr. & Mrs. Wm. A. Buttolph
Receive Thursday
4334 Mr. & Mrs. Wm. Moody Smith
4336 Mr. & Mrs. Jacob Floersheim
4338 Mr. and Mrs. William D. Stein
4342 Mr. & Mrs. M. D. Witkowsky
4342 Miss Ernestine Witkowsky
4344 Mr. & Mrs. Fred Messick
Receiving day Thursday
4346 Mr. & Mrs. Charles S. Wilcox
Receive Thursday
4350 Mr. & Mrs. Jacob L. Reiss
4352 Mr. & Mrs. Gustav Hochstadter
4356 Mr. & Mrs. Clement J. Dunlap
4356 William P. Dunlap
4500 Mr. & Mrs. E. Rothschild
4500 Mr. & Mrs. D. Wasserman
4506 Mr. & Mrs. W. C. Crosier
4508 Mr. & Mrs. Frank I. Cordo
4508 Adams A. Goodrich
4514 Mr. & Mrs. Samuel Sholem
Receiving day Friday
4516 Mr. & Mrs. G. M. Woodward
4518 Mr. & Mrs. T. G. Younglove
4520 Mr. & Mrs. Wallace G. Clark
4524 Mr. & Mrs. Chas. R. McLain
4528 Mr. & Mrs. Thos. S. Howell
4538 Mr. & Mrs. F. G. Avers
4548 Mr. & Mrs. James C. Corbet
4552 Mr. & Mrs. H. F. Vehmeyer
4800 Mr. & Mrs. Simon Lederer
4812 Mr. & Mrs. William H. Sutton
4814 Mr. & Mrs. E. D. Friedlander
4816 Mr. & Mrs. Harry Kraus
Receive 2d Friday
4818 Mr. & Mrs. Myer J. Oppenheim
4824 Mr. & Mrs. Chas. H. Swift
4828 Mr. & Mrs. E. A. Weeks
Receive Thursday
4828 Charles D. Weeks
4830 Mr. & Mrs. Harry S. Hyman
4830 Miss Edna Bushnell
4838 Miss M. Maguire
4918 Mr. & Mrs. Wm. B. Ingwersen
4920 Mr. & Mrs. Saul G. Harris
    & drs.

4917 Mr. & Mrs. Wm. T. Rankin
4948 Mr. & Mrs. Samuel J. Howe
4958 Mr. & Mrs. N. P. Cummings

4922 Mr. & Mrs. Sumner Sollitt
   Receive Tuesday
4928 Mr. & Mrs. Max Alber & dr.
4934 Mrs. W. Ward & drs.

FORTIETH STREET.

15 Mr. & Mrs. J. A. Bishop
17 Mr. & Mrs. Walter E. Miller
17 Mrs. W. M. Sage & dr.
17 C. F. Sage
17 G. Kenneth Sage
177 Thomas J. Poston
213 Mr. & Mrs. C. H. Bradley
213 Mrs. Loring Bradley
401 Mr. & Mrs. E. R. Clark
401 Mrs. E. E. Clark

402 Mr. & Mrs. C. Y. Boardman

52 Mr. & Mrs. C. H. Stone
104 Dr. & Mrs. Bayard Holmes
106 Mr. & Mrs. Alfred R. Urion
106 J. Casper Sauer
196 Mr. & Mrs. Wm. D. Clark & dr.
196 Mr. & Mrs. J. A. Root
330 Mr. & Mrs. Frank B. Davis
358 Thomas B. Livingstone & drs.
358 Archie T. Livingstone
376 Mr. & Mrs. Frank F. Conner
398 Mr. & Mrs. A. C. Blayney
398 Mrs. E. F. Hollister
402 Mr. & Mrs. James H. Harris

FORTY-FIRST STREET.

189 Dr. & Mrs. Wm. Cuthbertson
193 Dr. & Mrs. C. H. Buchanan
207 Mr. & Mrs. George M. Cook
207 Mr. & Mrs. Harry W. Adams
207 Mrs. C. F. Huet
207 N. D. Soper
317 Mr. & Mrs. Edward K. Orr
333 Frances Allen
341 Mr. & Mrs. Clark Hayner
343 Mr. & Mrs. A. E. Whitaker
351 Mr. & Mrs. W. A. Lowell & drs.
353 Mrs. A. R. Abbott & drs.
359 Mr. & Mrs. A. E. Crowley
403 Sol. J. Son
407 Mr. & Mrs. W. A. Howe
409 E. Neal & drs.
411 Mr. & Mrs. S. M. Becker
417 Mr. & Mrs. G. S. Calkins
419 Mr. & Mrs. H. E. Caster
427 Mr. & Mrs. John E. O'Brien
439 Mr. & Mrs. T. W. Cole
449 Dr. & Mrs. L. W. Schwab
449 Mr. & Mrs. Granville Kimball
451 Mr. & Mrs. C. J. Lilienthal

178 David S. Geer
184 Mr. & Mrs. L. M. Barber & drs.
186 Mr. & Mrs. June Barrett
188 Frank W. Wood
302 Mr. & Mrs. Clifford N. White
306 Mr. & Mrs. J. H. Smith
326 Mr. & Mrs. James M. Cobham
354 Mr. & Mrs. John Bagley
364 Mr. & Mrs. H. M. Quackenbos
408 Mr. & Mrs. George Fortin
422 Mr. & Mrs. Mark Solomon
424 Mr. & Mrs. H. Griffin
424 Mrs. Wm. Crawford & dr.
426 Mrs. Helen H. Hibben
426 Samuel E. Hibben
426 Heron K. Hibben
426 Mrs. Lucy H. Hodges
426 Mr. & Mrs. A. E. Phillips
438 Mr. & Mrs. Frederick Von Weis-
   enfluh
440 Mr. & Mrs. Max Wertheimer

625 Dr. & Mrs. F. B. Noyes

FORTY-SECOND STREET.

213 Mrs. E. C. Crosby
213 Miss Samuella Crosby
213 Robt. Floyd Ford
215 Mr. & Mrs. H. C. Johnson
229 Mr. & Mrs. Albert G. Mang
229 Mr. & Mrs. Jared Hinkley
229 Mr. & Mrs. Paul Tarbell

164 Mr. & Mrs. Geo. F. Fisher jr.
214 Mr. & Mrs. J. Schnadig
286 Wm. R. Mooney & drs.
   Receiving day Tuesday
286 Mrs. C. E. Banks & dr.
350 Mr. & Mrs. Herman Hefter
414 Mr. & Mrs. Anthony Beck

231 Col. & Mrs. Jacob T. Foster
231 Mr. & Mrs. W. H. Pruyn
231 W. H. Pruyn jr.
231 Samuel R. Pruyn
365 Mr. & Mrs. Henry Strauss
365 Carl Goldman
461 Mr. & Mrs. Morris Mayer
471 Mr. & Mrs. Charles A. Heath
475 Mr. & Mrs. Joseph A. Agee
487 Mr. & Mrs. Amos Lakey
489 Dr. Bertha VanHoosen

420 Mr.&Mrs.L.W.Austermell& drs.
464 Dr. & Mrs. H. S. Tucker
464 Mrs. C. Whitley
472 Mr. & Mrs. T. S. Quincey
472 Miss Franc C. Morrison
484 Mr. & Mrs. C. H. Bunker
484 Dr. R. W. Bishop
496 Mrs. L. A. Palmer
496 C. M. Palmer & dr.
560 Mr. & Mrs. E. F. Hoxey
726 Mr. & Mrs. James H. Wilson

FORTY-SECOND PLACE.

41 Dr. & Mrs. W. B. Hunt
    Receiving day Wednesday
149 Mr. & Mrs. Maurice Cornhauser
151 Mr. & Mrs. Charles Stewart
153 Mr. & Mrs. Louis Stein & dr.
153 Lawrence Stein
155 Mrs. T. M. Humphrey
157 Rabbi & Mrs. J. Stolz
225 Mrs. D. Van Arsdale
477 Mr. & Mrs. M. Eisenberg
479 Dr. & Mrs. J. R. Richardson
481 Mrs. M. Roecker & dr.
481 H. Leon Roecker
481 O. E. Roecker
485 Mr. & Mrs. Jacob Fass
487 Mr. & Mrs. C. A. Hewitt
491 Mr. & Mrs. William R. Parker
493 Mr. & Mrs. Jacob Steiner & drs.
497 Mr. & Mrs. Richard Morgan
    Evans
497 Mr. & Mrs. J. J. Doctor
501 Mr. & Mrs. Emanuel Moyses
————
492 Mrs. Hannah Rubel
500 Mr. & Mrs. J. H. Birmingham
502 Mr. & Mrs. Frank Schoenfeld
504 Mr. & Mrs. Henry Wolf

32 Mr. & Mrs. J. J. Howard
32 Miss Ruth Raymond
32 Frederick A. Ingalls
36 Mr. & Mrs. J. A. Conly
42 Mr. & Mrs. Charles C. King
96 Mr. & Mrs. John H. Bogue
140 Mr. & Mrs. Ira T. Eaton
146 Mr. & Mrs. F. J. Forrest
146 Mr. & Mrs. W. G. Curtis
148 Mr. & Mrs. A. S. Loeb
154 F. A. Menge & dr.
154 Dr. Frederick Menge
162 Mr. & Mrs. Isaiah Danks
164 Mr. & Mrs. G. F. Fisher jr.
166 Dr. & Mrs. G. B. Salter
174 Mr. & Mrs. Arthur D. Black
216 Mr. & Mrs. J. L. Rutherford
220 Mr. & Mrs. Jacob Kahn & dr.
    Receiving day Wednesday
222 Mr. & Mrs. J. J. Healy
228 Mr. & Mrs. Geo. W. Teel & dr.
426 Mr. & Mrs. Edward L. Wall-
    work
428 Mr. & Mrs. T. H. Faulkner
482 Mr. & Mrs. L. Fernbach
490 Mr. & Mrs. Charles Hefter
492 Mr. & Mrs. G. B. Chamberlin

FORTY-THIRD STREET.

13 Dr. & Mrs. W. A. Mann
91 Mr. & Mrs. H. T. White & dr.
245 Dr. & Mrs. T. S. Huffaker
249 Dr. & Mrs. J. G. Berry
277 Monroe T. Moss
419 Carl S. Simon
573 Dr. & Mrs. C. W. Prettyman
573 Mrs. O. J. Ahlenfeld

58 Dr. & Mrs. Robt. H. Harvey
106 Dr. Benjamin F. Kerns
116 Dr. H. R. Wallace
116 Mrs. H. M. Hapgood
396 Dr. & Mrs. John A. Kirkpatrick
404 Dr. Edward Tomlinson
576 Dr. & Mrs. F. Gurney Stubbs
    Receiving day Tuesday
576 Mrs. Thankful Durant

FORTY-FOURTH STREET.

79 Mr. & Mrs. T. W. Blatchford
87 Mr. & Mrs. George Lloyd
89 Mr. & Mrs. C. F. Vent & dr.
89 Fred G. Vent
89 Thomas G. Vent
91 Mr. & Mrs. E. T. Doyle
107 Mr. & Mrs. Frank A. Walker
195 Mr. & Mrs. W. A. Combs
197 Mrs. E. L. Skinner
201 Mr. & Mrs. F. K. Lyon
205 Dr. & Mrs. Garrett Newkirk
349 Mr. & Mrs. Albert D. Long
351 Mr. & Mrs. John Harvey
359 Mr. & Mrs. G. P. Blume
367 Mr. & Mrs. John G. Halsey
369 Mr. & Mrs. H. A. Hoerlein
369 Charles J. Schmidt
369 William D. Schmidt
379 Mr. & Mrs. William R. Parks
531 Mr. & Mrs. John Jacobs
531 Miss Dorothy Jones
535 Mr.& Mrs. John E.Murphy&drs.
539 Dr. & Mrs. H. H. Schuhmann
Receiving day Wednesday
539 Mr.& Mrs. Herman Schuhmann
541 Mr. & Mrs. Emil Hart
Receive 2d and 4th Wednesday
543 Mr. & Mrs. E. B. Huling
545 Mr. & Mrs. Jacob N. Strauss
547 Mr. & Mrs. Isaac H. Foreman
547 David L. Frank

72 Mr. & Mrs. Belton Halley
76 Mr. & Mrs. George E. Farwell
78 Miss Georgiana Springer
78 Miss Adel G. Springer
78 Miss Emily J. Springer
196 Mr. & Mrs. J. Kemper Dering
198 Dr. & Mrs. J. Austin Dunn
198 Mrs. E. M. Cooke
200 Mr. & Mrs. Henry R. Kaiser
204 Mr. & Mrs. John Lee Mahin
334 Mrs. R. G. Stevens & drs.
334 Dr. & Mrs. James Robertson
334 W. H. True
360 James Nellis
458 Mr.& Mrs. Wm. Stevenson
458 Edward N. D'Ancona
460 Mr. & Mrs. J. D. Caldwell
464 Mr. & Mrs. Harry L. Swarts
Receive 2d & 3d Wednesday
466 Mr. & Mrs. Sol L. Abt
470 Dr. & Mrs. G. E. Willard
542 Mr. & Mrs. Joseph N. Friedman
546 Mrs. Wm. Beatty & drs.
548 Mr. & Mrs. A. S. Straus
606 Mrs. O. W. Folsom
608 Mr. & Mrs. J. M. Hoadley
722 Mr. & Mrs. Noble Hill Howe
776 Mr. & Mrs. David P. Ahern

803 Mr. & Mrs. W. Irving Clark

WEST FORTY-FOURTH STREET.

756 Mr. & Mrs. Hiram S. Bunker

FORTY-FOURTH PLACE.

24 Mr. & Mrs. Chas. F. Marlow
24 Col. & Mrs. Harry Marston
24 Mr. & Mrs. W. G. Sheridan
30 Mr. & Mrs. E. J. Fay

486 Mr. & Mrs. Henry A. Sumner
510 Mr. & Mrs. Chas. Gumbiner

515 Mr. & Mrs. Jacob Friedlander

FORTY-FIFTH STREET.

105 Dr. & Mrs. Edgar D. Swain
231 Mr. & Mrs. Samuel H. Harris
231 Mr. & Mrs. I. K. Hamilton jr.
235 Mr. & Mrs. Charles F. Harding
413 Mr. & Mrs. Albert O. McLain
Receiving day Thursday
417 Max Mayer
515 Mr.& Mrs. K. J. W.Featherstone
559 Mrs. Fannie Schaffner & drs.
559 Abe Schaffner

108 Mr. & Mrs. C. B. Shourds
108 James L. Shourds
112 Mr. & Mrs. Anson Low
116 Mr. & Mrs. Wm. P. Smith
116 Ralph S. Smith
168 Mr. & Mrs. B. H. Conkling
172 Mr. & Mrs. C. E. Scribner
180 Mr. & Mrs. D. C. Plummer
182 Mrs. Proctor Smith
182 Mrs. H. B. Jackson

10

559. Abraham J. Schaffner
561 Mr. & Mrs. Julius Kiper

———

190 Mr. & Mrs. Edward B. Ellicott
230 Mr. & Mrs. Frank A. Westover
242 Mr. & Mrs. John Craig

434 Mr. & Mrs. C. G. Thomas
554 Mrs. Florence I: Gardner
566 Mrs. J. Glaser & dr.
Receive 1st & 3d Thursday
566 B. Z. Glaser
568 Mr. & Mrs. Joseph F. Sturdy
584 Mr. & Mrs. Gustav Heller .

FORTY-FIFTH PLACE.

559 Mr. & Mrs. Charles Gross
561 Mr. & Mrs. George A. Blume
561 Mrs. Rebecca Ives
563 Mr. & Mrs. M. L. Goldsmith
Receive last Friday in Mo.
563 Mr. & Mrs. Levy Lebolt & dr.
565 Mr. & Mrs. Harry Falkenau
567 Mr. & Mrs. M. N. Porter
569 Mr. & Mrs. John Thomson
575 Mr. & Mrs. Ben Shoninger
579 Mr. & Mrs. A. Schumacher

558 Mr. & Mrs. Albert Elwell
582 Mr. & Mrs. Clare J. Olmsted
582 Mrs. Jennie E. Reynolds
586 Mr. & Mrs. Eugene V. Doron

579 Miss Camille Baer
581 Mr. & Mrs. Wm. H. Alcock
583 Mr. & Mrs. Frank P. Epps
Receiving day Thursday
585 Mr. & Mrs. Harry E. Harper
587 Mr. & Mrs. Eugene Lewis

FORTY-SIXTH STREET.

15 Mr.&Mrs. Thomas Crouch & dr.
15 Albert W. Crouch
19 Mr. & Mrs. J. A. Coleman & dr.
21 Mr. & Mrs. E. H. Lewis
25 Mr. & Mrs. Lewis K. Scofield
& drs.
25 Mrs. A. S. Morse
29 Mr. & Mrs. I. T. Hartz
33 Mr. & Mrs. H. S. Dale
35 Mr. & Mrs. W. B. Henion
41 Mr. & Mrs. James H. Rhodes
& dr.
45 Mr. & Mrs. Edmund L. Mansure
45 Mrs. Susan T. Forsman
47 Dr. & Mrs. W. V. B. Ames
47 Mr. & Mrs. Charles M. Wilkes
49 Mr. & Mrs. Abel Bliss
49 Mr. & Mrs. Chas. A. Kniskern
49 Frederick B. Buss
203 Mr. & Mrs. T. A. Rittenhouse
205 Mr. & Mrs. Charles F. Baldwin
219 Mr. & Mrs. Dyke Williams
221 Mr. & Mrs. John T. Alexander
& dr.
267 Mr. & Mrs. Silas H. Strawn
269 Mr. & Mrs. Martin Allen Devitt
275 Mr. & Mrs. J. L. Felsenthal
275 Henry Felsenthal
353 Mr. & Mrs. John Boomer & drs.
353 John B. Boomer
353 George A. Boomer
399 Mr. & Mrs. Charles C. Leonard

38 Charles G. DuBois
148 Mr. & Mrs. W. S. Seaverns &
drs.
148 L. H. Ash ˙
206 Mr. & Mrs. Frank H. Baker
220 Mr. & Mrs. T. C. Keller
514 Mr. & Mrs. Adam Ortseifen
594 Mr. & Mrs. E. C. Francis
Receiving day Thursday
604 Mrs. Carrie A. Goodwin
604 Karl H. Goodwin
604 Miss Mabel E. Goodwin
612 Mr. & Mrs. Charles A. Neal
614 Dr. A. J. Brislen
614 Mrs. E. Brislen
614 Mr. & Mrs. Felix Schiff
616 Mr. & Mrs. H. G. Saylor

———

409 Mr. & Mrs. Eugene Marie
437 Mr. & Mrs. C. H. Newbre & drs.
595 Charles H. Eulette
597 Mr. & Mrs. G. St. John Kneller
Receiving day Thursday
599 Mr. & Mrs. Louis Adler
603 Mr. & Mrs. Henry Faurot
603 Mr. & Mrs. David Silverthorne
605 Mr. & Mrs. J. Grabfield
607 Mr. & Mrs. Frank L. Beveridge
609 Mr. & Mrs. C. F. Mitchell
611 Mr. & Mrs. C. W. Allen
619 Mr. & Mrs. Cornelius McAuliff

FORTY-SIXTH PLACE.

569 Mr. & Mrs. Sam'l C. Matthews
573 Alexander S. Houston
575 Mr. & Mrs. C. F. McVeagh
613 Mr. & Mrs. George M. Lovejoy
637 Mr. & Mrs. Louis Daube
637 Mr. & Mrs. Morris B. Rosen-
    heim
639 Mr. & Mrs. Henry J. Schlacks

552 Mr. & Mrs. Henry L. Cook
564 Mr. & Mrs. Walter B. Sherman
568 Mr. & Mrs. Fred P. Sherman
622 Mr. & Mrs. George R. French
624 Edward D. Waters
632 Mr. & Mrs. L. B. Hefter
634 Mr. & Mrs. J. F. Knight
634 Edgar F. Knight
634 John B. Knight

FORTY-SEVENTH STREET.

 25 Dr. John L. Porter
 25 Dr. Otto J. Stein
 81 Mr. & Mrs. Christopher W. Hall
 81 Mr. & Mrs. Frederick L. Fake
 83 Dr.& Mrs. Charles W.Crary&dr.
 85 Mr. & Mrs. Wm. C. Asay
 99 Mr. & Mrs. C. T. Conger
111 Gen. & Mrs. Geo. M. Guion
111 Mr. & Mrs. LeRoy P. Guion
113 Mr. & Mrs. Wm. H. Colvin
125 Mr. & Mrs. William C. Niblack
      Receiving day Tuesday
135 Mr. & Mrs.Milo G. Kellogg& dr.
135 Leroy D. Kellogg
143 E. M. Barton
175 Mr. & Mrs. C. H. Phillips
191 Mr. & Mrs. N. S. Bouton
197 Mr. & Mrs. Alexander Forbes
197 Allen B. Forbes
197 George S. Forbes
197 John A. Forbes
197 Robert R. Forbes
205 Mr. & Mrs. Joseph Gregg & drs.
205 Mrs. L. C. Eastman
221 Mrs. I. N. Ash
227 Mr. & Mrs. Edward A. Turner
      & drs.
267 Mr. & Mrs. L. Pratt
267 Rodney K. Pratt
267 Mr. & Mrs. Foster C. Phelps
299 Mr. & Mrs. Chas. L. Wellington
299 Mrs. F. F. Hammell
299 Miss Fanny F. Campbell
455 Mr. & Mrs. Richard R. Trench
535 Mr. & Mrs. Alfred W. Bensinger
707 Mr. & Mrs. J. Beyerlein

234 J. Solomon Bridges
250 Mr. & Mrs. W. Adolphus
250 Oscar Heineman
254 Dr. & Mrs. Joseph T. Cobb
254 Edmond P. Cobb
530 Miss Caroline C. Crouise

 40 Mrs. Emily W. Butts
 40 Miss Annice E. Butts
 40 Miss M. A. Butts
 40 Miss Kathryn B. Butts
 56 Mr. & Mrs. C. E. Gifford jr.
 56 Mrs. Joseph B. Lewis
 90 Mr. & Mrs. G. R. Thorne
 90 James W. Thorne
 90 Robert J. Thorne
 90 Mr. & Mrs. Reuben H. Don-
      nelley
124 Mr. & Mrs. H. R. Dering
126 Mr. & Mrs. William G. Sage
128 Mr. & Mrs. Clarence Simpson
130 Mr. & Mrs. Wm. S. Shaw
130 Edward R. Shaw
130 Edward Coleman
134 Mr. & Mrs. Harry Mills & dr.
140 Mr. & Mrs. A. C. Thomas & dr.
140 Melville J. Thomas
164 Mr. & Mrs. William C. Thorne
164 Mrs. Letitia MacMurphy
174 Mr. & Mrs. John E. Cowles
174 John T. Cowles
174 Mr. & Mrs. George M. Groves
228 Dr. & Mrs. Moses Furlong
228 Mr. & Mrs. Frank J. Gardner
228 Mr. & Mrs. J. A. Macdonnell
228 Mr. & Mrs. Beckman Graham
230 Mr. & Mrs. Harry L. Wyatt
      Receiving day Thursday
230 Mr. & Mrs. J. Oliver Williams
      Receiving day Thursday
230 Mr. & Mrs. J. H. Macmillan
230 Everett Macmillan
232 Mr. & Mrs. Robert S. Thomp-
      son & dr.
232 Mr.&Mrs.Joseph Evan MacKay
232 Mr. & Mrs. J. H. Churchill Clark
234 Mr. & Mrs. Frederic Clark
234 Mr. & Mrs. Charles A. Has-
      brouck
234 Mr. & Mrs. William T. Solomon

FORTY-SEVENTH PLACE.

9 Mr. & Mrs. Geo. A. Thomas & drs.

FORTY-EIGHTH STREET.

69 Frank E. May
69 H. Howell Kennedy
69 Clarence K. Wooster
211 Mr. & Mrs. Richard Nash
213 Mr. & Mrs. Chas. W. Hubbell
215 Mr. & Mrs. H. C. Whitehead
219 Mrs. A. M. Hess
219 Mr. & Mrs. F. A. Ingalls
221 Mr. & Mrs. Jas. J. Wait
291 Mr. & Mrs. E. J. Harkness & dr.
415 Mr. & Mrs. Staunton B. Peck
419 Mr. & Mrs. M. M. Ritterband
    & drs.
421 Mr. & Mrs. Chas. B. Niblock
671 Mr. & Mrs. Homer A. Stillwell
673 Mr. & Mrs. LeRoy H. McBean
677 Mr. & Mrs. George W. Fretts
679 Mr. & Mrs. F. A. Goodnow

72 Mr. & Mrs. Charles Denham
220 Mr. & Mrs. Edwin F. Simonds
282 Mr. & Mrs. Frederic Ullmann &
    dr.
286 Mr. & Mrs. Henry M. Lane
290 Mr. & Mrs. D. O. Strong & drs.
290 Charles R. Strong
290 Mrs. Mary J. Doty
670 Mr. & Mrs. W. K. Gore
672 Mr. & Mrs. Philip Angsten
674 Mr. & Mrs. R. Eisenstedt
678 Mr. & Mrs. J. J. Burns
        Receiving day Thursday
678 Mr. & Mrs. Warren E. Burns
682 Mr. & Mrs. Wm. C. Adams
688 Mr. & Mrs. Albin P. Gaylord &
    dr.
690 Mr. & Mrs. Geo. W. Ross
        Receiving day Monday
692 Mr. & Mrs. James Todd

FORTY-EIGHTH PLACE.

671 Mr. & Mrs. Frederick W. Gard-
    ner
673 Mr. & Mrs. L. J. Willner
675 Mr. & Mrs. Louis D. Heusner
677 Mr. & Mrs. Franklin R. Wood-
    ruff
677 Mr. & Mrs. Gustavus Austen
681 Mr. & Mrs. J. H. Schmaltz
683 Mr. & Mrs. Chas. Kiper
689 Mr. & Mrs. John C. Ilse
        Receiving day Wednesday

688 Mr. & Mrs. J. L. Harris
690 Dr. & Mrs. Twing B. Wiggin

666 Capt. & Mrs. Jas. B. Aleshire
670 Mr. & Mrs. H. M. Stevenson
672 Mr. & Mrs. Frank E. Willard
        Receiving day Thursday
674 Mr. & Mrs. Maier Neumann
    & dr.
        Receive 2d & 4th Monday
676 C. F. Langdon
678 James B. Watt
678 George R. Skinner
680 Mr. & Mrs. David Sullivan
680 Edward B. Healy
682 Mr. & Mrs. J. H. Stevens & dr.
686 Mr. & Mrs. John P. Williams

FORTY-NINTH STREET.

47 Mrs. A. E. Walker & dr.
99 Mr. & Mrs. N. W. Hacker
        Receiving day Monday
107 Mr. & Mrs. F. C. N. Robertson
111 Mr. & Mrs. Chas. H. Rockwell
    & dr.
111 Edward R. Rockwell
117 Mr. & Mrs. Wm. M. Jones
117 W. Morris Jones
117 Charles J. Jones
117 Mr. & Mrs. C. S. Painter

118 Mr. & Mrs. N. B. Higbie
122 Mrs. C. D. McGrew & dr.
124 Mr. & Mrs. J. P. Hubbell
302 Mr. & Mrs. Otis W. Gay
304 Mr. & Mrs. C. B. Harger
308 Mr. & Mrs. M. E. Capelle
366 Mr. & Mrs. A. T. Newhall
368 Mr. & Mrs. Chas. E. Johnson
368 Charles E. Mabie
368 Miss Litta Mabie
452 Dr. & Mrs. J. T. Binkley jr.

249 Mr. & Mrs. G. O. Knapp
249 Mrs. N. E. Knapp
257 Mr. & Mrs. Stephen N. Hurd
317 Mr. & Mrs. S. S. Beman
321 Mr. & Mrs. John S. Jones
321 Miss May Halderman
695 Mr. & Mrs. Lewis Rothschild
697 Mr. & Mrs. Sidney C. Sladden
697 Mr. & Mrs. C. E. Bartley
 Receive 1st and 3d Fridays

697 Mr. & Mrs. L. Wessel jr.
697 Mr. & Mrs. J. H. Wheeler
699 Mr. & Mrs. J. J. Abt
705 Mr. & Mrs. F. J. Reed
705 Mrs. Elizabeth Lane
707 Mrs. K. Moran
707 Harry Moran
711 Mr. & Mrs. Louis Rubens & drs.
 Receiving day 4th Tuesday
711 Charles Rubens

GARFIELD BOULEVARD.

944 Mr. & Mrs. A. M. Compton
946 Mr. & Mrs. August C. Keebler
 Receiving day Thursday

1010 Mr. & Mrs. Jerome P. Bowes
1012 Harry H. Muggley

WEST GARFIELD BOULEVARD.

129 Mr. & Mrs. C. F. Kinnally
129 John Kinnally
139 Mrs. T. H. Headley & dr.
139 Howard Headley
143 Dr. & Mrs. Francis G. Arter
335 Mr. & Mrs. P. J. Doyle & drs.
401 Dr. & Mrs. C. J. Phillips
411 Mr. & Mrs. P. J. Flynn & dr.
417 Mr. & Mrs. Theodore L. Price
425 Mr. & Mrs. Don J. Barnes
609 Dr. & Mrs. John D. Parker
633 Dr. & Mrs. F. M. Richardson
737 Mr. and Mrs. Fred A. Hart
737 Roy O. West
847 Dr. Minnie L. Allison
943 Rev. D. F. McGuire
1013 Dr. & Mrs. J. F. O'Neal

130 Mr. & Mrs. Louis Merki & drs.
130 George Merki
138 Mr. & Mrs. L. W. Collins
142 Mrs. J. F. Nelson
142 Mrs. Edward Lee
148 Mr. & Mrs. L. Groh
824 Mr. & Mrs. J. W. Sweeney & dr.
824 Alexander Sweeney
824 James J. Sweeney
838 Mr. & Mrs. C. E. Brush
838 Mr. & Mrs. M. A. Marx
946 Dennis L. Harmon
946 Miss Mary Harmon
952 Mr. & Mrs. J. G. Moore
952 Mr. & Mrs. W. H. Gorman
1110 Mrs. Magdalene Junk & drs.
1556 Mr. & Mrs. John Griffin & drs.
1556 James W. Griffin

GRAND BOULEVARD.

3515 Dr. Joseph E. R. Hawley
3515 Mrs. Chas. A. Hawley
 Receiving day Thursday
3515 Samuel F. Hawley
3517 Mr. & Mrs. Harry H. Cooper
3523 Mr. & Mrs. R. S. Dement & dr.
3523 Mr. & Mrs. James D. Packard
3525 Mr. & Mrs. M. J. Sarsfield
3529 Mr. & Mrs. Fred A. Weil
 Receiving day Wednesday
3529 Mr. & Mrs. M. L. Oppenheimer
3529 Mortimer Oppenheimer
3537 Mr. & Mrs. J. Aron & dr.
3539 Mr. & Mrs. George E. Cole
3543 Mr. & Mrs. Charles Jouvenat & dr.

3544 Mr. & Mrs. Henry E. Lyons
 Receiving day Thursday
3544 Mr. & Mrs. W. J. Sutherland
3560 Mr. & Mrs. F. B. Brede
3560 Mrs. Jonas Goldenberg & dr.
3560 Max Goldenberg
3562 Mr. & Mrs. John F. Finerty
 Receiving day Wednesday
3564 Mr. & Mrs. James Simms
3568 John Whiting
3568 Robert Whiting
3604 Judge & Mrs. Gwynn Garnett
3604 Eugene Garnett
3604 Gwynn Garnett jr
3604 Robert Garnett
3612 Dr. & Mrs. Emil G. Hirsch
3614 Mr. & Mrs. John Tait & dr.

3545 Mr. & Mrs. W. F. Hall
3549 Mr. & Mrs. Morris Salinger
3549 Louis Salinger
3551 Mr. & Mrs. Joseph M. Hirsch
    & drs.
    Receiving day Wednesday
3551 Arthur Hirsch
3565 Mr. & Mrs. James O. Twichell
3611 Mr. & Mrs. William Lowe
3611 Mr. & Mrs. A. E. Gilbert
    Receiving day Wednesday
3611 A. J. Fish
3619 Mr. & Mrs. Horace C. McConnell
3619 Mrs. Joanna L. Ellis
3623 Mr. & Mrs. H. R. Whiteside & dr.
3625 Mr. & Mrs. Geo. P. Whitcomb & dr.
3627 Mr. & Mrs. Frank I. Pearce
3627 Mr. & Mrs. Louis Rosenfield
3629 Mr. & Mrs. Chas. H. ReQua
3633 Dr. F. E. Waxham
3633 Miss M. H. Works
3639 Mrs. Annie M. Burgie
3639 Miss Jennie A. Moore
3645 Mr. & Mrs. Isaac B. Snow
3647 Mr. & Mrs. Charles Edward Kremer & dr.
3651 Mr. & Mrs. Max Mendel
3651 Herbert M. Mendel
3653 Mrs. R. A. Barclay
3655 Mr. & Mrs. Wm. A. S. Graham
3735 Mr. & Mrs. S. Leonard Boyce & dr.
3735 James L. Boyce
3741 Mr. & Mrs. W. H. Moorhouse
    Receiving day Thursday
3741 Miss Sybil Moorhouse
3741 L. C. Merrick
3741 Miss Zella Merrick
3811 Mr. & Mrs. S. P. Parmly
3811 Samuel P. Parmly jr.
3811 Mrs. H. C. Parmly
3811 Mrs. R. B. Sumner
3915 Mr. & Mrs. Wm. H. Godair
3917 Mr. & Mrs. J. J. Johnson
3917 Laris J. Johnson
3917 H. Stull Johnson
3923 Mrs. Samuel B. Foster
3925 Mrs. Norris G. Dodge
3925 Harry A. Dodge
3931 Mr. & Mrs. F. A. Howe
3933 Mr. & Mrs. Wm. P. Carey
3933 Charles N. Carey
3933 Joseph G. Carey

3614 Martin Roche
3622 Mr. & Mrs. Adolph Loeb & drs.
    Receive 1st & 3d Friday evenings
3622 Sidney A. Loeb
3624 Mr. & Mrs. Siegfried H. Kirchberger
3626 Mr. & Mrs. Herman F. Hahn
3626 Edmund J. Hahn
3628 Mr. & Mrs. J. L. Gatzert & dr.
3630 Mr. & Mrs. Charles H. Nichols
3632 Mr. & Mrs. Wm. D. O'Brien & dr.
3636 Mr. & Mrs. W. B. Crane
3636 Omer F. Crane
3638 Mr. & Mrs. J. Vehon & dr.
    Receive 1st Monday
3638 Morris Vehon
3642 Mr. & Mrs. Moses Adams
    Receive Wednesday
3644 Mr. & Mrs. Moses Stern & dr.
3646 Mr. & Mrs. Louis B. Lehman
    Receive Thursday
3648 Mr. & Mrs. Tobias Oberfelder & dr.
3648 Joseph Oberfelder
3650 Mr. & Mrs. J. S. Kimmelstiel & dr.
3650 A. A. Ballenberg
3656 Mr. & Mrs. Robert L. Henry
    Receiving day Tuesday
3710 Mr. & Mrs. J. C. Lamm
3712 Mrs. S. C. Lamm & dr.
3712 Louis Mandell
3714 Mr. & Mrs. E. Goldman
3714 Morris Epstein
3714 Max Epstein
3714 Hugo Epstein
3716 Mr. & Mrs. Albert Stein
3716 Ernest Stein
3716 Samuel Stein
3716 Siegmund Stein
3718 Mr. & Mrs. Louis Lepman
3720 Mr. & Mrs. L. J. Lamson
    Receiving day Tuesday
3736 Mr. & Mrs. Charles Corper
3740 Mr. & Mrs. B. Israel & dr.
    Receive 1st & 3d Tuesdays
3742 Mr. & Mrs. John W. Smith
    Receiving day Thursday
3744 Mr. & Mrs. L. H. Salomon & drs.
3750 Mr. & Mrs. Sylvester D. Foss & dr. *Receiving day Tuesday*
3750 Willis J. Foss
3924 Mr. & Mrs. H. Grossman

3933 Daniel J. Young
4001 Mr. & Mrs. W. A. McLean
4001 Mr. & Mrs. Harley C. Gage
4043 Dr. & Mrs. Weller VanHook
4045 Dr. & Mrs. J. G. Sinclair
4045 Mr. & Mrs. Geo. H. Johnson
4059 Mr. & Mrs. Fred Danks
4059 W. Sarsfield York
4059 Miss Lila York
4059 Mr. & Mrs. Edward C. Bates
4105 Mr. & Mrs. D. M. Pfaelzer
 Receive 4th Thursday
4105 Aaron Daube
4107 Mrs. S. B. Collins
 Receiving day Wednesday
4107 Miss Helen A. Bearup
4107 Miss Mariam A. Bearup
4109 Howard Henderson
4109 Miss Helen Henderson
4111 Mr. & Mrs. Louis Benjamin
 Receive 1st and 3d Fridays
4113 Mr. & Mrs. Herman Elson
 Receive 1st & 3d Wednesdays
4117 Mr. & Mrs. Solomon Hirsh & drs.
 Receive 2d and 4th Fridays
4117 Morris G. Hirsh
4119 Mr. & Mrs. Henry C. Jacobs & dr.
4119 Mr. & Mrs. Frank M. Staples
4119 Mr. & Mrs. Joseph Wright
4201 Mr. & Mrs. John W. Conley
4201 Mrs. Sarah A. Gilbert
4203 Mr. & Mrs. J. M. Sloss
4203 Henry Regensburg
4203 O. H. Regensburg
4203 James H. Regensburg
4205 Mr. & Mrs. James F. Meagher
4217 Mr. & Mrs. Albert C. Terry & dr.
4219 Mr. & Mrs. Felix Kahn
 Receive 1st and 3d Wednesday
4219 Mr. & Mrs. Lewis Kaufman
4223 Mr. & Mrs. F. A. Hibbard
 Receiving day Thursday
4223 Mrs. John Hibbard
4235 Mr. & Mrs. Dan S. Stern
4237 Mr.& Mrs.Thomas Miller&drs.
4239 Mr. & Mrs. Julius Rosenwald
4241 Mr. & Mrs. George P. Lee & r.
4243 Mr. & Mrs. Morris Cassard
4245 Mr.& Mrs. N.P.Richman & drs.
4257 Dr. & Mrs. Emmet L. Smith
4257 Mrs. B. F. Quimby
4257 Dr. & Mrs. Henry P. Woley

3926 Mr. & Mrs. Max Ederheimer
 Receiving day Monday
3928 Mr. & Mrs. Jacob R. Custer
3928 Esther R. Custer
3930 Mr. & Mrs. Edward C. Huling
3930 Mrs. Louisa Griggs
3932 Mr. & Mrs. Charles R. Cave
3936 Mr. & Mrs. Louis Becker
 Receive 1st and 3d Wednesday evgs.
3938 Mr. & Mrs. Max Steele & drs.
3938 Leo Steele
3942 Mr. & Mrs. John Farren
3942 Mrs. Sarah Lipe
4006 Mr. & Mrs. Harry Weil
4006 Maurice Wendell
4008 Mr. & Mrs. Albert H. Loeb
4008 Dr. & Mrs. Isaac A. Abt
4008 Mr. & Mrs. John N. Reynolds
4008 Mrs. M. E. Pasco
4018 Mr. & Mrs. James F. O'Brien
4018 Frank O'Brien
4020 Mr. & Mrs.Solms Marcus & dr.
 Receive last Friday
4020 Edward S. Marcus
4022 Dr. & Mrs. P. I. Mulvane & dr.
4022 Miss Elizabeth J. Mulvane
4024 Mrs. James Sullivan
4026 Mr. & Mrs. William Strawbridge & dr.
4026 Mr. & Mrs. John Nuveen
4028 Mr. & Mrs. B. M. Davies
4028 Mr. & Mrs. J. M. LeRoy
4050 Mr. & Mrs. James Lane Allen
 Receiving day Tuesday
4052 Mr. & Mrs. Richard W. Barger
4054 Mr. & Mrs. James A. Hill
4054 Fred Morgan Hill
4054 Berton Cutter Hill
4056 Mr. & Mrs. Edward H. Elwell
4058 Mr. & Mrs. Isa Monheimer
4108 Mr. & Mrs. E. B. Felsenthal
 Receiving day Wednesday
4112 Mr. & Mrs. Orr Sang
4112 Miss Georgia Post
4114 Mr. & Mrs. A. Florsheim & dr.
 Receive 1st and 3d Thursday
4114 Wilbur I. Florsheim
4114 Edson S. Florsheim
4118 Mr. & Mrs. Jas. W. Stevens
 Receiving day Wednesday
4118 Raymond W. Stevens
4120 Mr. & Mrs. Charles Smith
4122 Mr. & Mrs. Ralph E. Pratt
4122 Mrs. Margaret A. Young
4124 Mr. & Mrs. Milton J. Palmer

4257 Mr. & Mrs. Frank Weeks
    Receiving day Thursday
4257 Mrs. Carrie E. Martin
4257 Mrs. J. R. Wolfe
4257 Mr. & Mrs. Chas. F. Simonson
    Receive Tuesday
4259 Mr. & Mrs. Carroll H. Sudler
    Receiving day Thursday
4259 Mr. & Mrs. R. W. Peckham
4259 Mr. & Mrs. Carl D. Bradley
    Receive Tuesday
4259 Mr. & Mrs. F. W. Flint
    Receive Tuesday
4259 Mr. & Mrs. Kenesaw M. Landis
4259 Mr. & Mrs. George E. Wright
4259 Judge & Mrs. Peter S. Grosscup
4259 Frank R. Baker
4337 Mr. & Mrs. Frank J. Barnes
4337 Mrs. Mary A. Gaylord
4339 Mr. & Mrs. Siegmund Guth-
    mann
4341 Mr. & Mrs. F. MacKenzie
4341 Mrs. Joel Ellis
4341 Mrs. L. Pinney
4343 Mr. & Mrs. Henry Schwabacher
    jr.   *Receive Friday*
4345 Mr. & Mrs. Joseph Pajeau
4345 Chas. H. Pajeau
4347 Mr. & Mrs. Sol. Hamburger
    Receive 2d and 4th Wednesday
4349 Mr. & Mrs. Winfield N. Sattley
4427 Mr. & Mrs. Jacob Heissler
    Receive Thursday
4427 M. Louise Heissler
4427 Jacob F. Heissler
4427 Ed. R. Heissler
4445 Judge & Mrs. H. M. Shepard
4445 Stuart Gore Shepard
4445 Miss Helen E. Shepard
4445 Mrs. Charles B. Stuart
4455 Mr. & Mrs. Frank Sayre Os-
    borne & drs.
4455 Henry S. Osborne
4509 Mr. & Mrs. G. A. Kantrowitz
4511 Mr. & Mrs. Charles Hart
    Receive 1st Wednesday
4545 Dr. & Mrs. Charles W. Leem-
    ing
4547 Mr. & Mrs. M. A. Donohue &
    dr.
4547 Michael A. Donohue jr.
4547 William F. Donohue
4547 Edward T. Donohue
4619 Mr. & Mrs. Elliott H. Phelps
4635 Mr. & Mrs. W. C. Foley
4709 Mr. & Mrs. W. S. Booth

4124 Mrs. Wm. H. Atwood
4130 Mr. & Mrs. G. W. Shannon
4130 Mrs. Lucy Getty
4140 Mr. & Mrs. Frank Nixon
4140 Mrs. Maud Sobel
4140 Mr. & Mrs. Richard J. Murphy
4142 Mr. & Mrs. Geo. F. Stitch
    Receiving day Thursday
4142 George F. Stitch jr.
4142 Kirby Nicholas
4142 Mrs. Y. Ballenberg
4142 Jules Ballenberg
4144 L. J. Unna
4144 Mrs. G. B. Lesh
4144 L. B. Lesh
4144 Mr. & Mrs. H. A. Perry
4144 Mr. & Mrs. O. H. Matthews &
    dr.
4144 Miss Estella Patterson
4144 Miss Florence Patterson
4144 Mr. & Mrs. A. M. Harbaugh
4144 Mrs. Ida B. Kizer & dr.
4148 Mr. & Mrs. Morris Newman
    Receive last Wednesday
4148 Edward B. Grossman
4148 Dr. & Mrs. Martin M. Ritter
    Receiving day Monday
4148 Mr. & Mrs. W. C. B. Palmer
4148 Mr. & Mrs. R. S. Whitcomb
4218 Mr. & Mrs. W. J. Carney
4220 Mr. & Mrs. Andrew M. Lynch
    & drs.
    Receiving day Thursday
4222 Mr. & Mrs. Adolph Grossman
    & dr. *Receiving day Monday*
4222 George Grossman
4222 Mrs. Geo. Michaelsohn
4224 Mr. & Mrs. Milton L. Thacka-
    berry   *Receive Tuesday*
4224 Mrs. Mary A. Stinson
4228 Mr. & Mrs. Alfred Taylor
4228 Miss Ella Taylor
4228 Mr. & Mrs. Frank H. Roberts
4228 Mr. & Mrs. W. C. Schaefer
4230 Mr. & Mrs. William J. Hoag
4232 Mr. & Mrs. William Mida &
    dr.
4232 Lee Mida
4232 Walter Mida
4232 Mr. & Mrs. Henry Greenebaum
4330 Mr. & Mrs. Herman Oberndorf
4334 Mr. & Mrs. Bernhard Rosenberg
4336 Mr. & Mrs. M. C. Isaacs & dr.
4340 Judge & Mrs. Philip Stein & dr.
    Receive 1st and 2d Fridays
4342 Mr. & Mrs. Gustave D. Glaser

4717 Mr. & Mrs. George T. Smith
4725 Mr. & Mrs. Fred W. Smith
4731 T. P. Smith
4753 Dr. Ephraim Ingals & drs.
4757 Dr. & Mrs. E. Fletcher Ingals
4807 Mr. & Mrs. Oscar Rosenberg
4809 Mr. & Mrs. Joseph Cahn & drs.
   Receiving day Tuesday
4835 Mr. & Mrs. Thos. H. Wickes
4843 Mr. & Mrs. H. J. Powers
   Receive Thursday
4845 Mr. & Mrs. Geo. A. Gill
4847 Mr. & Mrs. George W. Pierce
4901 Mr. & Mrs. George S. Bigelow & dr.
   Receive Thursday
4901 Harry Towers Bigelow
4903 Mr. & Mrs. Wellington Leavitt
   Receive Wednesday
4907 Mr. & Mrs. Sidney B. Cahn
4909 Mrs. Viola Stern
4913 Mr. & Mrs. Simon Florsheim & drs.
   Receive 2d and 4th Wednesday
4913 Sidney E. Florsheim
4913 Norman S. Florsheim
4913 Isaac S. Florsheim
4915 Mr. & Mrs. Bernard Mayer

4736 Mr. & Mrs. Edward Mendel
   Receive 2d and 3d Wednesdays
4736 Miss Alice Voigt
4738 Mr. & Mrs. W. H. Cowles
4740 Mr. & Mrs. W. J. Davis
4742 Mrs. James L. Woodward & dr.
4742 Mr. & Mrs. Arthur H. Woodward
4750 Mr. & Mrs. Joseph Fish
   Receive Thursday
4756 Mr. & Mrs. J. L. Kesner
   Receive 1st and 3d Wednesday
4758 Mr. & Mrs. W. A. Lydon
4800 Mr. & Mrs. Carl A. Stonehill
4814 Mr. & Mrs. Albert P. Green
   Receive Wednesday
4814 Mrs. Margaret Peacock
4814 Miss Alice Peacock
4840 Patrick McManus & drs.

4344 Mr. & Mrs. Max Eichberg
   Receive Friday
4344 William N. Eichberg
4346 Mr. & Mrs. Max L. Falk
   Receiving day Friday
4346 Mrs. Louis Leopold
4346 Maurice Leopold
4348 Mr. & Mrs. William H. West
4348 Charles F. Hippach
4350 Mr. & Mrs. D. A. Hyman
   Receiving day 1st & 3d Friday
4350 Miss Clara Hyman
4352 Mr. & Mrs. Norris Cochran & dr
4354 Mr. & Mrs. Edward Baggot
4354 Miss Mary Rowena Harvey
4400 Frederick R. Barnheisel
4400 Charles H. Barnheisel
4400 Mrs. Henrietta Barnheisel & dr.
4404 Mr. & Mrs. Leo A. Loeb
4406 Dr. & Mrs. A. J. Baxter
   Receiving day Friday
4406 Mr. & Mrs. F. O. Bartlett
   Receiving day Tuesday
4426 Mr. & Mrs. John Trayner
   Receiving day Monday
4426 Miss Nettie G. Trayner
4426 Owen R. Trayner
4426 C. J. Trayner
4428 Mr. & Mrs. M. M. Hirsh
   Receive 1st and 2d Thursday
4428 William A. Hirsh
4434 Mrs. Emeline C. Thurston
4434 Frank W. Thurston
4442 Mr. & Mrs. John Morris & dr.
4442 Henry C. Morris
4508 Mr. & Mrs. J. E. Greenebaum
4510 Mr. & Mrs. Elias Greenebaum
4510 Mr. & Mrs. N. S. Gutman
4630 F. W. Hunerberg
4630 Dr. Charles F. Freiberg
4700 Dr. Robert W. Carrall
4700 Albert M. Hewes
4700 Mr. & Mrs. Lewis H. Falley
   Receive Thursday
4700 Dr. G. Mortimer Hill
4730 Mr. & Mrs. I. N. W. Sherman
   Receive Thursdays
4730 Mr. & Mrs. Charles K. Sherman
4734 Mr. & Mrs. M. M. Levison & dr.

GREENWOOD AVENUE.

4327 Dr. & Mrs. W. P. MacCracken
4327 Miss Cornelia B. Ward
4333 Mrs. Jerome K. Barton & dr.
4333 Mr. & Mrs. H. H. Strohm

cor. 42d The Arizona
  A3 Mrs. A. S. Moffett & dr.
  A3 E. J. Belden
  A3 T. J. Lynn

4333 Mr. & Mrs. P. S. Barton
4365 Mr. & Mrs. A. M. Smith
4403 Mr. & Mrs. G. R. Meitzler
4403 Mr. & Mrs. Council Greeley
& dr.
4405 Mr. & Mrs. F. H. Nichols
4407 Mr. & Mrs. M. F. Thometz
4407 Mrs. Jennie Rubel
4409 Mrs. Mary C. Palmer
4409 Mrs. Rowland Howland
4409 Mr. & Mrs. Charles Messer
4409 Mr. & Mrs. I. E. Barr
4409 C. S. Morehouse
4419 Mr. & Mrs. Chas. F. Hills
4421 Mr. & Mrs. O. A. Barnhart &
dr.
4425 Mr. & Mrs. C. Eugene Stokes
4425 Mr. & Mrs. Louis P. Hoyt
4427 Mr. & Mrs. Martin Hogan
4429 Mr. & Mrs. Charles Morris
Receiving day Thursday
4429 Miss Warde
4433 Mr. & Mrs. James H. Moore
4433 John James Moore
4433 Mrs. A. H. Tuthill
4439 Mr. & Mrs. Jacob O. Curry
4439 Mr. & Mrs. James Blair
4447 Mr. & Mrs. Edwin F. Daniels
4455 Mr. & Mrs. Henry Curtiss
4515 Lewis S. Perry
4519 Mr. & Mrs. Wm. H. Aldrich
4519 William H. Aldrich jr.
4519 W. F. Aldrich
4523 Mr. & Mrs. Mark Morton
4527 Mr. & Mrs. Oliver K. Johnson
4529 Mr. & Mrs. Henry M. Sherwood & dr.
4531 Mr. & Mrs. M. Swenson
4533 Mr. & Mrs. H. F. Vories
4537 Mr. & Mrs. Frederick C. Tyler
4541 Mr. & Mrs. D. A. Cohn
4543 Mr. & Mrs. Charles L. Dering
4545 Mrs. C. Follansbee
Receiving day Wednesday
4545 Mrs. J. A. Van O'Linda
4547 Mr. & Mrs. Charles A. Piercy
Receiving day Tuesday
4549 Mr. & Mrs. Chas. W. Hinckley
4621 Mr. & Mrs. Myron A. Pearce
4621 S. M. Fassett
4623 Mr. & Mrs. W. E. Higley & dr.
4623 A. M. Higley
4625 Dr. & Mrs. Milton R. Barker
4627 Mr. & Mrs. C. L. Hammond
4633 Mr. & Mrs. F. W. Barker
4637 Mr. & Mrs. Burton Hanson

cor 42d The Arizona (continued.)
A4 Mr. & Mrs. J. A. Brett
A5 Mr. & Mrs. W. H. Holway
A6 Mr. & Mrs. Sidney Lovell
A7 Mr. & Mrs. M. D. Hayes
A8 Mrs. S. Sharp & dr.
B1 Mr. & Mrs. G. S. Newsome
B3 Mr. & Mrs. J. M. Wood & dr.
B4 Mr. & Mrs. Alex. J. Frank-
land
B5 Mr. & Mrs. Robert E. M.
Cowie
B6 Mr. & Mrs. I. N. VanPelt
B7 Mr. & Mrs. R. D. Johnson
B8 Dr. & Mrs. Lee K. Stewart
C2 A. H. Carr
C2 Mrs. G. G. Frazer
C3 Mrs. M. Jameson
C4 Mr.&Mrs.H.S. Schneewind
C5 Mr. & Mrs. J. C. Groendyke
C8 Mr. & Mrs. J. H. Patrick
D2 Mrs. M. M. Norton
D2 Harry White
D3 Mr. &Mrs.Wm.P.Williams
D4 Mr. & Mrs. G.V.Dickinson
D6 Mr. & Mrs. G. M. Seward
D6 Mrs. H. H. Hazlett & dr.
D6 Mr. & Mrs. J. F. Wares
D8 Mr. & Mrs. F. N. Williams
E1 Miss F. D. Price
E1 Miss E. V. Miller
E1 E. W. Jewell
E2 Mr.&Mrs.R.Caswell Head
E3 Mr. & Mrs. T. F. Bowes
E4 Mr. & Mrs. B. F. Stewart
E5 Mr. & Mrs. C. H. Rhoades
E6 Mr. & Mrs. A. E. Atherton
E7 Mr. & Mrs. F. H. Tibbits
E8 Mr. and Mrs. H. O. Barden
F2 Mr. & Mrs. G. B. Brigham
F4 Mr. & Mrs. Chas. Burton
Darling
F5 Mr. & Mrs. S. G. Chard
F6 Mr.& Mrs.Bertram F.Clark
F7 M. & Mrs. G. G. Gibson
F8 Miss E. B. Townsend
F8 Mrs. A. C. Hasdell
F8 Miss F. E. Hasdell
G1 Mr. & Mrs. F. A. Bridge
G2 Mr. & Mrs. H. S. Ford
G3 Mr. & Mrs. John O'Keefe
G4 Mr. & Mrs. F. G. Wall
G5 Mr. & Mrs. A. E. Newsome
G6 Miss M. McElvaine
G6 Mr. & Mrs. A. A. Morton
G7 Mr. & Mrs. James Neal

4637 Mrs. Cornelius K. Martin
4727 Mr. & Mrs. H. S. Smith
4727 Frank W. Smith
4729 Mr. & Mrs. James W. Janney
4741 Mrs. Annie Hitchcock
4803 Mr. & Mrs. James P. Gardner
4807 Mr. & Mrs. J. J. Dau
4819 Mr. & Mrs. H. B. Bogue & dr.
4819 Hamilton B. Bogue jr.
4819 Arthur H. Bogue
4819 Wayne C. Bogue
4835 Mr. & Mrs. Franklin Ames
4835 James C. Ames
4841 Mr. & Mrs. Jas. P. Soper
4849 Mr. & Mrs. W. B. Kniskern
4857 Mr. & Mrs. John B. Lord & dr.
Receiving day Monday
4911 Mrs. T. G. McLaury
4911 Miss N. W. Herrick
4917 Mr. & Mrs. Chas. E. Gill & dr.
4917 Mrs. Mary Mitchell
4917 Preston Gill
4923 Mr. & Mrs. L. A. Carton
4929 Mr. & Mrs. John C. Neely
4929 John C. Neely jr.
4929 Miss Carrie B. Neely
4935 Mr. & Mrs. A. W. Green & dr.
Receiving day Thursday
4949 Mr. & Mrs. Edward F. Swift
Receiving day Wednesday
5035 Mr. & Mrs. Charles Counselman & dr.
5329 Mr. & Mrs. Chas. W. Gore & drs.
5331 Mrs. F. Lazelle & dr.
5345 Mr. & Mrs. J. L. Burke
Receiving day Thursday
5411 Mr. & Mrs. Edward E. Hill
5413 Mr. & Mrs. A. W. Cole
5413 Mrs. M. E. W. Cole
6323 Mr. & Mrs. F. A. Gregory jr.
6325 Dr. & Mrs. Andrew McDiarmid
6327 Mrs. Margaret Butts
6327 DeWitt C. Butts
6329 Mr. & Mrs. Walter Hendricks
6335 Mr. & Mrs. L. R. Schermerhorn
6345 Mr. & Mrs. Walter L. French
6351 Mr. & Mrs. Edgar M. Miller
6369 Miss A. E. Lane
6369 Mrs. M. E. Brooks
6369 Mr. & Mrs. Julius Brunton
6371 Mr. & Mrs. Douglas Bird
6411 Mr. & Mrs. S. G. Casad
6411 Mrs. Flora Carson
6419 Mr. & Mrs. J. A. Kearney
6429 Mr. & Mrs. W. B. Davies

4300 Dr. Robert C. Wilson
4306 Mr. & Mrs. R. Gosling
4306 Mrs. Floyd H. Culver
4310 Mrs. M. J. Maxwell
4312 Mr. & Mrs. Wm. J. Field
Receiving day Thursday
4314 Mr. & Mrs. J. S. Jacobus
4316 Dr. & Mrs. W. K. Jaques
Receiving day Thursday
4318 Mr. & Mrs. Frederick L. Merrick
4320 Mr. & Mrs. Oscar F. Schmidt
4322 Mr. & Mrs. E. E. Adams
4324 Mr. & Mrs. James L. Archer
4324 Mr. & Mrs. J. F. Kelly
4326 Mr. & Mrs. Charles L. Thayer
4326 Dr. & Mrs. Chas. P. Pruyn & dr.
Receiving day Wednesday
4326 Mrs. R. E. Morey
4326 Chas. S. Blackman
4326 Fred O. Blackman
4326 Harry L. Blackman
4330 Mr. & Mrs. E. P. Barry & dr.
4330 Fred Barry
4332 Mr. & Mrs. George F. Fisher & dr.
4334 J. R. Walls
4334 Mrs. M. L. Walls
4334 Miss Mae P. Walls
4334 Mrs. Emma Hoge
4342 Mr. & Mrs. Isaac N. Isham
4342 Mrs. C. M. Warren
4348 Mr. & Mrs. T. C. Harbers
Receiving day Wednesday
4348 Mrs. Mary Blanding
4352 Mr. & Mrs. Thomas F. Vaughn & dr.
Receiving day Thursday
4352 Mr. & Mrs. T. A. Ryan
4354 Mr. & Mrs. F. E. Hayne
4356 Dr. & Mrs. H. H. Deming
4400 Mrs. W. F. Vermilion
4400 J. H. Day
4400 J. R. Day
4400 Mr. & Mrs. John Marshall jr.
4400 James Marshall
4400 Mr. & Mrs. Wm. Williamson
4402 Mr. & Mrs. Fred. W. Moore
4402 Mr. & Mrs. Frank A. Fowler
4402 Mr. & Mrs. J. J. McClellan
4402 Mr. & Mrs. E. W. McClellan
4414 Dr. & Mrs. A. W. Harlan & dr.
4414 P. H. Harlan
4420 Mr. & Mrs. Geo. W. Chamberlin
4420 Mr. & Mrs. Willis M. Brown
4434 Mr. & Mrs. J. W. Fernald
4438 Mr. & Mrs. L. C. Lawton

6431 Mr. & Mrs. Fred K. Higbie
Receiving day Wednesday
6433 Mr. & Mrs. F. S. Crowell
6435 Mr. & Mrs. Eliodoro de Campi & dr.
Receiving day Thursday
6439 Mr. & Mrs. George W. Leighton
6441 Mr. & Mrs. O. L. McMurray
6527 Mr. & Mrs. John Chislett & drs.
6527 H. G. Chislett
6529 Mr. & Mrs. D. B. Fairman
6529 Mr. & Mrs. C. Fairman
6541 Mr. & Mrs. John E. Shea
6551 Mr. & Mrs. Julius Schneider
6553 Mr. & Mrs. W. H. Maynard & drs.
6555 Mr. & Mrs. W. S. Hendricks
6555 W. Lee Hendricks

5016 Mr. & Mrs. Charles H. Hawkins
5022 Mr. & Mrs. Geo. A. Tripp
5026 Mr. & Mrs. William O. Goodman *Receiving day Tuesday*
5316 Mrs. Elizabeth Underhill
5318 Mrs. U. S. Harper & dr.
5330 Dr. & Mrs. J. T. Lave
Receiving day Thursday
5338 Mr. & Mrs. Charles Antoine
Receiving day Wednesday
5338 Mrs. Belle Currie & dr.
5338 M. V. Kannally
5340 Mr. & Mrs. F. M. Blanchard
5342 Mr. & Mrs. C. F. Drozeski
5344 Mr. & Mrs. Wm. J. Leis
5344 Mr. & Mrs. B. F. Clifford
5344 Mr. & Mrs. Orlando Metcalf jr.
Receiving day Thursday
5344 Mrs. Victoria M. Logan & dr.
Receiving day Thursday
5344 J. C. Logan
5400 Mr. & Mrs. G. E. Cave
Receiving day Thursday
5426 Mr. & Mrs. Ernst M. Markwald
5450 Mr. & Mrs. Charles Eaton & drs.
Receiving day Friday
5478 Mr. & Mrs. Moritz Rosenthal
Receiving day Thursday
5482 Mr. & Mrs. Joseph W. Moses
Receiving day Thursday
5482 Mrs. Frank Muhr
Receiving day Thursday
6212 Mr. & Mrs. J. W. Ebersol
6218 Mr. & Mrs. W. O. Bacon
6220 Mr. & Mrs. Orvis A. Page
6224 Prof. & Mrs. James D. Bruner

4438 Mrs. R. Lawton
4444 Mr. & Mrs. Munson P. Buel
4444 Forrest L. Buel
4446 Mr. & Mrs. James Mullen & drs.
4500 Mr. & Mrs. Benj. F. DeMuth & dr.
4504 Mr. & Mrs. Edward D. Stevens
4504 Ralph C. Stevens.
4504 Edgar A. Stevens
4510 Mr. & Mrs. Alfred L. Fitch
4510 Mrs. Caroline S. Fitch
4510 Mr. & Mrs. Alfred B. Willcox
4516 Mr. & Mrs. D. W. Williams
Receiving day Wednesday
4516 Dr. & Mrs. Louis M. Williams
4522 Mr. & Mrs. Charles Squires
4522 H. B. Squires
4522 Mrs. H. P. Bradshaw
4526 Mr. & Mrs. J. B. Nellegar
4534 Mr. & Mrs. William Jones
4540 Mr. & Mrs. Frank Matthiessen
Receiving day Wednesday
4544 Mr. & Mrs. C. H. Thorne
4612 Mr. & Mrs. A. H. Hanson
4620 Dr. & Mrs. Alfred W. Hoyt
4620 Miss Caywood Hoyt
4624 Mr. & Mrs. E. A. Schoyer
4624 Mrs. O. H. Waldo
4630 Dr. & Mrs. H. V. Halbert
4634 Mr. & Mrs. Edwin F. Bayley
4700 Mr. & Mrs. William Lathrop Moss
4700 Miss Edith Helen Moss
4714 Mr. & Mrs. James R. Crocker
4726 Mr. & Mrs. Robert Strahorn
4728 Mr. & Mrs. Charles Loughridge
4734 Mr. & Mrs. Dexter G. Brown
4734 Miss Fannie Schaffenberg
4734 Mrs. Mary T. Libbey & dr.
4754 Mr. & Mrs. C. B. Vankirk
4754 Mrs. S. A. Vankirk
4804 Mr. & Mrs. Charles H. Morse & dr. *Receiving day Monday*
4804 Charles H. Morse jr.
4820 Mr. & Mrs. E. T. Cushing
4826 Mr. & Mrs. Abbott L. Mills
4830 Mr. & Mrs. Wm. R. Perrin
4850 Mr. & Mrs. E. K. Butler
4924 Dr. & Mrs. A. T. Arbuckle
4940 Mr. & Mrs. Frank E. Spooner
4940 Frank V. Spooner
4940 Miss Mae P. Spooner
4950 Mr. & Mrs. John C. Welling
5000 Mr. & Mrs. J. N. Barker
5000 Mrs. W. N. Hibbard
5008 Mrs. G. T. Williamson

6234 Mr. & Mrs. Arthur C. Jackman
6326 Mr. & Mrs. Herbert White
6326 Mrs. Ida M. Nettleton
6328 Mr. & Mrs. Chas. G. Burton
6334 Mr. & Mrs. Joseph Cormack
6336 Mr. & Mrs. W. H. Fleming
6340 Mr. & Mrs. W. H. Ford
6342 Mr. & Mrs. Hale G. Parker
6346 Mr. & Mrs. J. Singer
6348 Mr. & Mrs. Edwin L. Ward
6350 Mr. & Mrs. G. F. Rummel
6350 Mr. & Mrs. Leon E. Stanhope
6352 Mr. & Mrs. T. P. Lloyd
6354 Mr. & Mrs. J. J. Edgeworth
6412 Mr. & Mrs. Clinton Mott
6414 Mr. & Mrs. Cyril A. Hurssell
6418 Mr. & Mrs. H. C. Stevens
6420 Mr. & Mrs. W. W. Borders
6422 Mr. & Mrs. Thomas Plunkett
6428 Mr. & Mrs. B. F. Harris
6428 Dr. Harriet H. Davis

6430 Mr. & Mrs. W. A. Fulton
6430 Miss L. M. Doll
6432 Mr. & Mrs. H. W. Bennett
6436 Mr. & Mrs. S. H. Macomber
6438 Mr. & Mrs. W. R. Howett
6440 Mr. & Mrs. J. E. Wells
6440 Mr. & Mrs. Moses Jones
6442 Mrs. Mary Vogt
6444 Mr. & Mrs. E. W. Sims
6446 Mr. & Mrs. Albert E. Cagwin
6448 Mr. & Mrs. F. H. Hall
6454 Mr. & Mrs. James S. Murphy
6500 Mrs. Louise Clunn
6500 Mrs. E. M. Corbin
6534 Mr. & Mrs. W. H. Matthews
6534 Mr. & Mrs. Joseph Nelson
6552 Mr. & Mrs. James H. Christian
6556 Mr. & Mrs. Clarke Varnum
7610 Dr. & Mrs. Geo. H. Chapman
7530 Dr. & Mrs. Hiram L. Pease
Receiving day Thursday

GROVELAND AVENUE.

2907 Mr. & Mrs. F. K. Morrill
2909 Dr. Wm. E. Morgan
2915 Mr. & Mrs. James J. Egan
2917 Mr. & Mrs. H. W. Coolidge & drs.
2919 Mr. & Mrs. Geo. P. Benton
2921 George H. Taylor
2923 Mr. & Mrs. Orville Brewer
2925 Mr. & Mrs. P. H. Schifflin
2927 Mr. & Mrs. D. S. Vilas
2929 Geo. B. Cruickshank
2929 Miss Blanche Cruickshank
2931A Mr. & Mrs. Chas. Matthews
2935 George Zuber
2937 Mr. & Mrs. D. E. Gillingham
2945 Dr. & Mrs. Geo. W. Cox
2947 Mr. & Mrs. James Bowlan
Receiving day Tuesday
2947 Mr. & Mrs. James Bowlan
2951 Mrs. A. Toussaint
2959 Mr. & Mrs. Morris Kohn & dr.
2959 Milton Kohn
2959 Simon Kohn
2959 Henry M. Kohn
2967 Mr. & Mrs. Harrison Kelley
2969 Mr. & Mrs. Henry Sheffield
2973 Mr. & Mrs. Adolph Clasen & dr.
Receive 3d Friday
2973 Edward Clasen
2973 William R. C. Clasen
3001 Mr. & Mrs. Joseph Pfirshing
3015 Mrs. M. E. Board

2900 Mr. & Mrs. Frederick Grant & dr.
Receiving day Wednesday
2902 Mr. & Mrs. P. P. Wippell
2908 Mr. & Mrs. J. H. Brown & dr.
2908 Walter F. Brown
2910 Mrs. Cora Wilson & drs.
2912 Mr. & Mrs. H. P. Colberg
2914 Mr. & Mrs. A. W. Rood
2916 Mr. & Mrs. S. D. Hinman & dr.
2922½ Mr. & Mrs. C. H. Gillespie
2924 Mrs. C. Maynard & dr.
2926 Mr. & Mrs. B. D. Marks
Receive Monday
2926 Arthur M. Marks
2928 Mr. & Mrs. W. A. Knapp
2928 Miss Lillie Rosenblatt
2928 Miss Estelle Rose
2938 Mr. & Mrs. Thos. J. Holmes
2942 Mr. & Mrs. John A. McCormick
2948 Mr. & Mrs. Samuel Friend
2952 Mr. & Mrs. James W. Cooper
2952 Robert B. Cooper
2956 Mr. & Mrs. E. L. Barber
2956 S. M. Parish
2956 Mr. & Mrs. Clifford C. Chickering
2956 Frank E. Durfee
2960 Mr. & Mrs. J. F. Geary
2962 J. Westenberger
2962 Mrs. Serena Mendelsohn

3029 Mr. & Mrs. James H. Krebs
    Receiving day Tuesday
3039 Mr. & Mrs. N. N. Cronholm
3043 Judge & Mrs. Jonas Hutchinson
3047 Mr. & Mrs. M. McFarlin & dr.
3047 W. W. McFarlin
3101 F. S. Hendrickson
3103 Mr. & Mrs. A. J. Howard
3103 E. D. Howard
3109 Mr. & Mrs. James A. Sibley & dr.
3109 George M. Sibley
3109 Edward A. Sibley
3109 Mrs. H. H. Cooley
3111 Mr. & Mrs. I. H. Fry
3145 Mr. & Mrs. Franklin Lester & dr.
3157 Mr. & Mrs. John Campbell
3161 Mr. & Mrs. W. Scott Thurber
3161 Mr. & Mrs. Robert Sloan Wessels
3167 Mr. & Mrs. L. R. Hall
3169 Mrs. Alice B. Young
3213 Mr. & Mrs. A. C. Farnsworth
3213 Albert J. Farnsworth
3213 Mr. & Mrs. Harrison M. Wild
3217 Miss Julia C. Baldwin
3219 Mr. & Mrs. Harlan D. Cook
    Receiving day Thursday
3223 Mr. & Mrs. Matson Hill
    Receiving day Friday
3223 Miss Jean P. Hill
3225 Mr. & Mrs. Louis Regenstein & dr.
3227 Mr. & Mrs. Edward Marrenner
3227 Mr. & Mrs. Edw. S. Marrenner
    Receiving day Tuesday
3229 Mr. & Mrs. David Yondorf
    Receiving day Wednesday
3235 Mr. & Mrs. John M. Peeples
3235 Mr. & Mrs. D. F. Dorsett
3237 Mr. & Mrs. Owen W. Brewer
3241 Walter L. Johnson
3241 Mrs. Ellen M. Johnson
3243 Mr. & Mrs. F. G. Hoyne
3243 Miss Gertrude E. Ashton
3245 Mr. & Mrs. A. Blum
3247 Mr. & Mrs. J. M. Hopkins
3249 Mrs. H. R. Vynne
3249 W. B. Cunningham
3249 Miss Katherine Cunningham
3255 Mr. & Mrs. C. R. Hopkins
3257 Mr. & Mrs. Andrew J. Farley
    Receiving day Thursday

2964 Mr. & Mrs. Isaac Meyer & dr.
    Receive 1st & 2d Friday
2964 Abraham W. Meyer
2970 Mrs. Harriet C. Brainard
2970 Mrs. Martha Foote Crow
3000 Dr. & Mrs. L. L. Hertel
3006 Mr. & Mrs. Robert Lee Grant
3018 Mr. & Mrs. David Neumann & dr.
3018 Alexander Neumann
3018 Louis Neumann
3020 Mrs. Chas. Duffield & drs.
3020 A. Howard Duffield
3030 Frank Crozier
3034 Mr. & Mrs. M. M. Day
3038 Mr. & Mrs. W. K. Reed
3042 Mr. & Mrs. W. H. Schott
3042 Mr. & Mrs. Theodore F. Reese
3100-3106 The Groveland
    Col. J. Bliss
    Mrs. H. I. Burlingame
    Ben Cohen
    John DeFort
    R. Faxon & dr.
    J. W. Fitzgerald
    Miss Nellie Foley
    Dr. E. C. Gage
    M. K. Gandell
    Wm. Hirschbach
    F. L. Holmes
    Mrs. B. F. Howard
    William Israel
    Samuel W. Jackson
    I. C. Kahn
    Dr. Helen R. Kellogg
    Mr. & Mrs. J. E. Kennedy
    Isaac A. Loeb
    Martin G. Magill
    Dr. N. W. Marsh
    Dr. A. F. Martin
    Mr. & Mrs. James Morgan
    Mr. & Mrs. W. J. Oliphant
    William Palmer
    Mr. & Mrs. B. E. Tilden
    John B. Wallace
    Lincoln W. Walter
    J. W. Welsh
    R. W. Williams
    Mr. & Mrs. E. A. Woodward
3118 Mrs. E. F. DeMaine
3120 Mme. C. N. Rounseville
3128 Mr. & Mrs. Chas. L. Glass
    Receiving day Thursday
3128 Mr. & Mrs. J. D. Isaacs
    Receiving day Friday
3130 Mr. & Mrs. Charles A. Miller

3257 Mr. & Mrs. Samuel W. Kempster
3257 Mrs. M. J. Smith
3259 Mr. & Mrs. Edward A. James
3261 Mr. & Mrs. S. J. Cooke
3263 Mr. & Mrs. J. S. Buhrer
3269 Mrs. A. Vincent
3269 Mrs. C. F. Brown

————

3232 Mr. & Mrs. Charles F. Coffin
3232 Mr. & Mrs. Percival B. Coffin
3234 Mr. & Mrs. Albert F. Dexter
3238 Mr. & Mrs. J. W. Robertson
3238 Walter N. Wyville
3240 Rev. & Mrs. E. E. Chivers
3242 Mr. & Mrs. Alanson Henry Reed
Receiving day Wednesday
3244 Mr. & Mrs. George V. Harvey
3244 Mrs. Isabel C. Buckingham
3248 Mr. & Mrs. J. H. Milne & dr.
3252 Mr. & Mrs. M. C. Mayer
3258 Mr. & Mrs. Wm. H. Sherwood
Receiving day Thursday
3260 Mr. & Mrs. James T. Plumsted
3260 Mrs. Mary E. Blackwell
3262 Mr. & Mrs. F. G. Frank ·
3264 Mr. & Mrs. W. S. Forrest

3142 Mr. & Mrs. Julius N. Brown
Receiving day Thursday
3142 Mr. & Mrs. Thomas Semon
3146 Mr. & Mrs. W. Davidson
3148 Mr. &. Mrs. Amasa Orelup
3150 Mr. & Mrs. E. C. Darley
3152 Charles Alling jr.
3162 Mr. & Mrs. Frank B. Reed
3164 Mr. & Mrs. Chas. D. Hoard
3164 Mrs. Mary E. Woodruff & dr.
3166 Dr. & Mrs. Joseph Matteson
3166 Mr.&Mrs. Charles C. Matteson
3168 Mr. & Mrs. L. B. Cox & dr.
3170 Leopold Mayer
3170 Mr. & Mrs. James Witkowsky
Receive Friday eve.
3216 Mr. & Mrs. E. H. Goodrich
3216 Miss Edna L. Goodrich
3218 Mr. & Mrs. A. P. Upham
3218 William A. Upham.
3222 Mr. & Mrs. Thomas J. Dixon
Receiving day Friday
3226 Mrs. Nellie Carpenter
3226 Miss Flora Carpenter
3226 Mrs. Flora Fraser
3228 Mr. & Mrs. James Johnston
3230 Judge&Mrs.John BartonPayne
Receiving day Wednesday
3230 Mrs. D. A. Bunker
Receiving day Wednesday

GROVELAND PARK.

1 Mr. & Mrs. J. Dixon Avery
5 Mrs. Robert Warren & drs.·
7 Mr. & Mrs.·F. H. Wachsmuth
7 H. F. Wachsmuth
7 L. C. Wachsmuth
11 Mr. & Mrs. Moses Rittenhouse
15 Mr. & Mrs. Joy Morton
19 Mr. & Mrs. Frank Wells

————

34 Mr. & Mrs. Wm. ·H. Clark
34 Mrs. Chester M. Clark
36 Mr. & Mrs. John B. Mallers
40 Mr. & Mrs. Arba N. Waterman
48 Dr. & Mrs. John S. Marshall
Receiving day Thursday

2 Elias Colbert
8 Mr. & Mrs. Hiram A. Hanson & dr.
10 Mrs. Electa L. Thayer
·*Receiving day Friday*
10 Miss Florence A. Redway
12 Mr. & Mrs. H. Borden & dr.
16 Mr. & Mrs. John W.·Carrington & dr.
20 Mr. & Mrs. Geo. D. Haworth
26 Mr. & Mrs. Albert T. Dow
28 Mr. & Mrs. F. M. Sproehnle
30 Mr. & Mrs. O. L. Evans
Receiving day Friday
32 Mr. & Mrs. Wm. C. Powell
Receiving day Wednesday

HARVARD AVENUE.

6353 Mr. & Mrs. Fred Malkow & dr.
6421 Mr. & Mrs. W. C. Collins
6431 Mr. & Mrs. L. K. Scotford
6437 Mr. & Mrs. G. L. Carman & dr.

6314 Dr. & Mrs. E. E. Holman.
6328 Mr.&Mrs. Jesse Sherwood&dr.
6336 Dr. & Mrs. Henry R. Boettcher
6346 Mr. & Mrs. Samuel Thompson

6501 Mr. & Mrs. J. F. Olmsted
6505 Mr. & Mrs. Hans F. Rohde
6509 Mr. & Mrs. Allen Howes
6509 Allen C. Howes
6509 Frank W. Howes
6515 Mr. & Mrs. O. T. Bright
6521 Mr. & Mrs. G. L. Purinton
       Receiving day Friday
6521 Mr. & Mrs. W. H. Daniel
6521 Miss Clara Squire
6525 Mr. & Mrs. James A. Stoddard
6525 Mrs. Adelaide M. Daniels
6531 Mr. & Mrs. Frank J. Luken
6537 Mr. & Mrs. E. M. Condit
6537 James A. Bell
6565 Mr. & Mrs. Albert B. Southard
       Receiving 1st & 3d Wednesday
6565 Dan B. Southard
6601 Mr. & Mrs. C. H. Caldwell
6605 Mr. & Mrs. W. W. Ramsey
6613 Mr. & Mrs. H. B. Thearle
       Receiving day Thursday
6613 Mr. & Mrs. Ishi Smith
6617 Mr. & Mrs. C. H. Knights
6621 Mr. & Mrs. Edwin J. Noble
6627 Mr. & Mrs. F. M. Buck
6629 Dr. & Mrs. A. B. Spach
6629 Mrs. M. A. Brown
6631 Mr. & Mrs. Jesse R. Embree
6643 Mr. & Mrs. Wm. Law jr.
6647 Mr. & Mrs. Albert S. Race
       Receive Thursday
7101 Mr. & Mrs. Julius L. Obertop
7101 Mrs. R. H. Huston
7105 Mr. & Mrs. John M. Haley
7127 Mr. & Mrs. Geo. Wheeler
7143 Mr. & Mrs. Millard E. Mogg
7241 Mr. & Mrs. J. M. Pennington

7310 Mr. & Mrs. Howard McEl-
       downey
7524 Mr. & Mrs. George Jackson &
       drs.
7534 Mr. & Mrs. F. T. Haynes & dr.
7534 George M. Haynes
7534 Joseph R. Haynes

6350 Mr. & Mrs. Chas. A. Warren &
       drs.
6400 Mr. & Mrs. Fred Davis
6414 Mr. & Mrs. C.H.Vehmeyer&dr.
6432 Mr. & Mrs. W. H. Whiteside
6438 Mr. & Mrs. Bohn C. Hicks
6446 Mr. & Mrs. Wm. A. Carroll
6448 Mr. & Mrs. Frank P. Barkey
6448 Mr. & Mrs. John A. Hall
6500 Mr. & Mrs. A. D. Rich
6500 Ben C. Rich
6516 Mr. & Mrs. H. W. K. Cutter &
       dr.
6522 Mr. & Mrs. Daniel J. Hubbard
6536 Mr. & Mrs. H. L. Kent & drs.
6536 Mrs. Helen M. Kent
6536 Mr. & Mrs. Fred I. Kent
6544 Mr. & Mrs. Andrew M. Kistler
6550 Mr. & Mrs. W. O. Budd
6560 Mr. & Mrs. Lee Fargo
6560 Mr. & Mrs. Alexander McIn-
       tosh
6560 Alexander McIntosh jr.
6564 Mr. & Mrs. G. W. Kelly
6610 Mr. & Mrs. J. J. Nichols
6616 Mr. & Mrs. Wm. H. Little
6620 Mr. & Mrs. W. T. Eaton
6626 Mr. & Mrs. P. E. Lane &
       drs.   *Receive Wednesday*
6630 Mrs. Harriet J. Ledward & dr.
6636 Mr. & Mrs. James B. Gascoigne
6642 Mr. & Mrs. John M. Young
6648 Mr. & Mrs. T. B. Galbraith
6652 Mr. & Mrs. Frank J. Kitchell
7120 Mr. & Mrs. John Cunnea
7126 Mr. & Mrs. Geo. E. McCaughan
7130 Mr. & Mrs. F. H. Preston
7138 Mr. & Mrs. George B. Carter
7156 Mr. & Mrs. Joseph Badenoch
       & drs.
7156 R. N. Badenoch
7156 George Badenoch
7156 Charles H. Badenoch
7156 F. C. Hill
7216 Mr. & Mrs. M. A. Garrett
7216 Dr. Carlton M. Garrett

HAWTHORNE AVENUE.

7752 Mr. & Mrs. William W. Munsell
7762 Dr. & Mrs. S. A. Waterman
7772 Mr. & Mrs. G. F. McKnight
7772 S. C. McKnight
7834 Dr. & Mrs. Hiram F. Smiley

7834 Mr. & Mrs. Marvin Dighton
       Smiley
7842 Mr. & Mrs. George E. McFad-
       den
7844 Mr. & Mrs. W. A. Newell

HIBBARD AVENUE.

5101 C. H. Hunt
5101 Mrs. H. W. Hunt & dr.
Receiving day Wednesday
5103 Mr. & Mrs. A. G. Farr
5103 Mrs. William B. Snow
5111 Mr. & Mrs. George Catlin & dr.
5117 Mr. & Mrs. Wm. Seymour
5127 Mrs. William C. Ritchie
5127 Thomas W. Ritchie
5127 Robert H. Ritchie
5131 Mr. & Mrs. John B. Daniels
Receiving day Monday
5131 Alexander M. Daniels
5135 Mr. & Mrs. John H. Cameron
5141 Mr. & Mrs. Harvey L. Goodall
5201 Mr. & Mrs. F. G. Ranney & drs.
5203 Rev. & Mrs. A. W. Patten
5205 Mr. & Mrs. W. W. Curtis
5207 Mr. & Mrs. Clinton R. Taylor
5207 Mr. & Mrs. R. P. Decker & dr.
5209 Mr. & Mrs. R. E. Barrett
5211 Mrs. Thos. B. James
5211 Mrs. W. S. Gee
5211 Miss Hannah B. Clark
5213 Mr. & Mrs. Daniel H. Champlin
5215 Mr. & Mrs. A. E. Campbell & drs.

—

5218 Mr. & Mrs. Henry Rolfe
5218 Mr. & Mrs. Charles E. Pope
5222 Mr. & Mrs. W. Irving Beman
5228 Mr. & Mrs. S. M. Cantrovitz

5100-5104 The Oneida
Mrs. Ida McWhinney
Curtis A. McWhinney
Mr. & Mrs. H. G. Thompson
Mr. & Mrs. S. W. French
Receive Monday
Mr. & Mrs. R. LeBarre Goodwin & dr.
Clarence M. Goodwin
Mr. & Mrs. John J. Hackney
Mrs. Anna W. Knight
John W. Knight
Mr. & Mrs. Gideon E. Newman
5106 Mr. & Mrs. Frederick H. Trude
5108 Mr. & Mrs. George W. Stahl
5110 Mr. & Mrs. Ira M. Cobe
5112 Mr. & Mrs. Thomas J. Hudson
5112 Thomas J. Hudson jr.
5114 Mr. & Mrs. William D. McKey
5116 Mr. & Mrs. Edward B. McKey
5116 Miss Elsie M. Gross
5120 Mr. & Mrs. George L. Warner
5120 Dr. Caroline Smith
5130 Mr. & Mrs. T. G. McCulloh
5130 Thomas G. McCulloh, jr.
5130 J. W. McCulloh
5136 Dr. & Mrs. C. A. Williams & drs.
5140 Mr. & Mrs. William Chalmers
5206 Mr. & Mrs. John C. Craft
5210 Mr. & Mrs. Geo. W. Hoyt
5210 Mr. & Mrs. Spencer R. Udell
5214 Mr. & Mrs. Charles H. Ball & dr.

INDIANA AVENUE.

1609 Henry Sayers
1619 Dr. & Mrs. E. C. Dudley
1619 John H. Dudley
1623 Mr. & Mrs. Murry Nelson & dr.
1641 Mrs. C. R. Cummings
1641 Mrs. H. T. Robinson
1703 Mr. & Mrs. E. M. Phelps
1703 George E. P. Dodge
1713 Mr. & Mrs. C. D. Peacock & drs.
1713 Mr. & Mrs. Edgar Deyo-Smith
1809 Mr. & Mrs. E. A. Bell
1813 Dr. & Mrs. E. Russell Ogden
1813 Mr. & Mrs. P. Anderson McEwan
1813 J. M. Wright
1813 MacNaughton Wright
1813 Dr. Thomas A. Woodruff

1602 Mr. & Mrs. C. F. Gunther
1602 Burnell Gunther
1602 Whitman Gunther
1610 Mrs. William C. Grant
1610 Mrs. Ira P. Nudd
1610 Miss C. A. Baker
1612 Mr. & Mrs. H. M. Curtis & drs.
1612 Mrs. A. Murison
1612 George W. Murison
1618 Mr. & Mrs. Henry N. Hart & drs. *Receive 1st & 3d Thursday*
1618 Herbert L. Hart
1624 Mrs. Marie Lehmann
1624 Alfred A. Lehmann
1624 Edmund Lehmann
1628 Dr. H. S. Perkins
1628 Mr. & Mrs. A. E. Dorian

11

1815 Mrs. A. C. McHenry
1815 Mrs. C. W. Dunkley & dr.
1819 Mr. & Mrs. Isaac G. Lombard
1819 Mr. & Mrs. Herman E. Haass
1821 Mr. & Mrs. John C. Schubert
1821 Miss Kittie Brennan
1825 Mr.&Mrs. Frederick M. Talbot
1825 Miss Mary B. Dodson
1829 Mr. & Mrs. B. Loewenthal
    Receive 2d and 4th Saturday and
                      Tuesday eve.
1829 Julius W. Loewenthal
1833 Dr. & Mrs. T. S. Hoyne
1901 Edgar A. Lord & drs.
1901 James F. Lord
1915 Mr. & Mrs. Charles Silverman
1915 Albert Silverman
1915 David S. Simon
1915 Dr. Joseph P. Grabfield
1917 Rev. & Mrs. J. Wm.Van Ingen
1921 Mr. & Mrs. Robert M. Critchell
              Receive Saturday eve.
1923 Mr. & Mrs. S. Gillespie & drs.
1923 Mr. & Mrs. H. E. Brown
1933 Mr. & Mrs. F. A. Delano
2001 Mr. & Mrs. A. Courtney Camp-
    bell
2003 Mr. & Mrs. S. S. Whitehead
2007 Mr. & Mrs. Walter B. Mitchell
2013 Pliny B. Smith
2017 Thomas J. Rodman
2023 Mrs. H. G. Sutherland & dr.
2023 Henry W. McClellan
2023 Fuller McClellan
2107 Mr. & Mrs. C.F. Blakeslee & dr.
2107 John W. Gary
2115 Mr. & Mrs. Alfred L. Holman
    Receiving day Wednesday
2115 Miss Frances S. Dickerman
2115 Mrs. Ella P. Cole
2115 Miss Ernestine Emery
2117 Mrs. Jirah D. Cole
2311 Mr. & Mrs. J. B. Rayner
2327 Mr. & Mrs. F. E. Buddington
2401 Mr. & Mrs. A. J. Benson & dr.
2413 Mrs. Anne L. Bates
2421 Mr. & Mrs. J. R. Barker & drs.
    Receiving day Wednesday
2421 Mrs. E. H. Mott
2427 Mrs. O. B. Phelps
2427 Miss Hattie B. Snyder
2427 William B. Reddon
2437 Mr. & Mrs. A. Winklebleck &
    dr.
2437 Mr. & Mrs. H. C. Winklebleck
2437 Mr. & Mrs. F. S. Gaudreaux

1628 O. Fox
1628 R. Bishop Doane
1628 William B. Rinehart
1640 Mrs. Charles B. Sawyer
1640 Mr. & Mrs. Charles A. Sawyer
1706 Mr. & Mrs. Henry K. Elkins
1710 Mrs. Benj. E. Gallup
1710 Mr. & Mrs. Stephen Laskey
1718 Mrs. F. S. Smith & drs.
1718 Miss S. E. Sedgwick
1718 Mr. & Mrs. H. M. Russell
1718 Miss May Allport
1718 Miss Edith L. Cooley
1822 Mrs. M. Mannheimer & drs.
1822 Miss M. Norton
1826 Mr. & Mrs. C. Price & dr.
1826 Mr. & Mrs. James S. Price
1826 Samuel C. Price
1826 M. Wallace Price
1826 Miss Delia Price
1826 O. W. Stoughton
1826 Miss Abbie Benson
1838 Mr. & Mrs. Wm. H. Swift
1838 David Campbell
1840 Mr. & Mrs. George Lomax
              Receiving day Friday
1840 George Lomax jr.
1840 J. Alfred Lomax
1842 Mr. & Mrs. B. W. Thomas &
    drs.
1842 Lloyd Washington
1842 Wilberforce Veitch
1904 Mr. & Mrs. Herman Nathan
1904 Louis M. Cohen
1906 Mr. & Mrs. Charles Shaffner
1918 Mr. & Mrs. Seth F. Crews & dr.
1918 Seth F. Crews jr.
1918 Ralph Crews
1918 Mrs. C. S. Slocumb
1922 Dr. & Mrs. George W. Webster
1926 Mr. & Mrs. George P. Gore
2000 Mr. & Mrs. C. D. Peacock jr.
2000 Mr. & Mrs. Arthur F. McArthur
              Receiving day Tuesday
2000 Mr. & Mrs. Geo. H. Leatherbee
2002 Mr. & Mrs. Chas. C. Buell
              Receiving day Friday
2002 Mrs. A. C. Dew
2012 Baron & Baroness Curt E. W.
    von Biedenfeld
2012 Mr. & Mrs. J. Erb
2012 George B. Erb
2014 Mr. & Mrs. Geo. A. Gibbs
2014 Mr. & Mrs. Louis Weis
              Receive 2d & 4th Tuesday
2020 Mr. & Mrs. F. M. Thomas

2449 Mr. & Mrs. Howard E. Laing
2449 F. P. Kellogg
2453 Mr. & Mrs. Nelson Morris & dr.
2509 Mr. & Mrs. Eli M. Straus
    Receive 1st & 3d Friday
2511 Mrs. Michael Walsh
2511 Mrs. Ann Riley
2513 Dr. Walter W. Stafford
2519 Rev. & Mrs. Frank Crane
    Receiving day Wednesday
2529 Dr. & Mrs. A. V. Park
    Receiving day Wednesday
2539 Mr. & Mrs. Cyrus Dupee & dr.
2545 Mrs. James Couch
    Receiving day Friday
2547 Mr. & Mrs. Chas. Yondorf
    Receive 1st & 3d Monday in mo.
2613 Mr. & Mrs. H. W. Dudley & drs.
2613 Dr. Lewis W. Dudley
2613 Arthur H. Dudley
2613 Mrs. Mary A. Darrow
2613 Raymond C. Dudley
2615 Judge & Mrs. O. H. Horton & dr. *Receiving day Monday*
2615 Miss Lou Chamberlain
2615 Miss Jennie Johnson
2619 Mr. & Mrs. Jedediah R. Davis
2619 Mr. & Mrs. Walter L. Davis
2633 Dr. James H. Stowell
2633 Mrs. E. Stowell
2633 Miss Marian P. Stowell
2633 Miss Ida M. Stowell
2705 Mrs. Elizabeth S. Farwell
2705 Francis W. Farwell
2705 Mr. & Mrs. James R. Chapman
2705 Miss Florence Brigham
2709 Mr. & Mrs. M. W. Powell
2711 Wm. Ford Johnson
2711 Edward Ford Johnson
2711 Arthur L. Leeds
2711 J. Fleming Dutch
2813 Maj. & Mrs. J. H. McArthur
2817 Mr. & Mrs. W. E. Pardridge
    Receiving day Tuesday
2819 Mr. & Mrs. Edward Hillman
    Receive 1st Tuesday in mo.
2819 Miss Ruth E. Hillman
2825 Rev. Dr. & Mrs. Clinton Locke
    Receive Tuesday afternoon
2825 Mrs. A. Douthitt
2825 Mrs. Robert D. Locke
2829 Dr. & Mrs. Peter S. MacDonald
    Receiving day Wednesday
2829 James M. MacDonald

2022 Miss S. J. Clarke
2024 Mrs. Edward Forman
2024 Mrs. Robert G. Clarke
2024 D. Gage Clarke
2024 Mr. & Mrs. Jas. B. Heth
2024 Henry S. Heth
2024 Mr. & Mrs. Jos. C. Wilson
2024 Miss S. M. Wilcox
2028 C. Tillinghast
2030 Capt. & Mrs. P. S. Bomas
2036 Mr. & Mrs. J. G. M. Glessner
2126 Mrs. Alice Peterson
2126 Soren Mathison
    Rec. day Wednesday 3 to 5 p.m.
2126 Dr. L. A. Kierulff
2300 Dr. & Mrs. Wm. T. Gilman
    Receiving day Wednesday
2306 Dr. T. T. Oliver
2306 Dr. & Mrs. P. S. Replogle
2320 Mr. & Mrs. W. D. Preston
2326 Mr. & Mrs. Edward W. Jones
2326 Miss Frances C. Jones
2326 Miss Maria W. Jones
2326 Miss Mary R. Hays
2326 Mrs. Jefferson Van Horne
2330 Dr. & Mrs. E. O. F. Roler
2330 Dr. A. H. Roler
2334 Mr. & Mrs. Jas. A. Bovett jr.
2342 Mr. & Mrs. G. A. Follansbee & dr.
2342 M. D. Follansbee
2342 Mrs. M. M. Davis
2344-2358 The Concord Flats
    106 Mrs. S. L. Lockhart
    107 Miss Sarah E. Pierce
    111 Mr. & Mrs. William C. Fyfe
    201 Mrs. Nettie M. White
    202 Mr. & Mrs. George Evans Lewis
        Receiving day Tuesday
    203 Mr. & Mrs. Tony Faifer & dr.
    204 Mr. & Mrs. Wm. L. Campbell
    204 Dr. J. F. Campbell
    205 Rev. & Mrs. W. H. Parsons
    206 Mr. & Mrs. D. Irving Calhoun & dr.
    207 Mr. & Mrs. Louis Busch
        Receiving day Thursday
    209 Mrs. Ella Robinson
    212 Mr. & Mrs. P. J. May
    301 Mrs. J. C. Maslin
    302 Mrs. A. O. Holmes
    302 Mr. & Mrs. Orville van Thompson

2829 Ráymond J. MacDonald
2915 Mrs. Isabelle A. Gillette
2915 Mrs. T. J. Stilwell
2915 Miss Mary L. Colburn
2915 Theodore F. Colburn
2919 Mrs. Sarah Wilder Pratt
    Receiving day Thursday
2921 Mr. & Mrs. C. J. Jones
2921 Mr. & Mrs. Robt. McCune
    Stuart jr.
2925 Mr. & Mrs. George L. Brown
2925 Mr. & Mrs. A. W. Beidler
2927 Mr. & Mrs. S. S. Buckley
2927 Mr. & Mrs. W. H. Morrow
2927 Miss Jeanette Buckley
2931 Dr. & Mrs. C. E. Paddock
2935 Dr. & Mrs. Frank Cary
2935 Mrs. Ellen Cary
2937 Mr. & Mrs. J. B. Woodruff
2937 Albert H. Buck
2937 Miss Grace P. Buck
2941 Mr. & Mrs. E. C. Wentworth
2957 Mr. & Mrs. Dwight S. Bryant
2957 Miss Abbie Pond
2969 Dr. & Mrs. H. B. Fellows
2971 Mr. & Mrs. Edgar A. Clark
3027 Jacob Bloch
3027 Dr. Rosa Engelmann *
3031 Dr. & Mrs. Geo. M. Chamberlin
3031 Mr. & Mrs. Henry M. Sexton
3121 Mr. & Mrs. Thos W. Saunders
3121 Mrs. Lucinda Babcock
3129 Dr. & Mrs. Wm. Stirling Maxwell
3131-3133 The Atlanta Flats
  1 Mr. & Mrs. Edward J. Napier
  2 Mrs. E. A. Terry & dr.
  3 Mr. & Mrs. L. Rubovits
  3 Miss Dora Koethe
  4 Dr. & Mrs. Harry I. van Tuyl
  4 Mrs. J. E. van Tuyl
  5 Mr. & Mrs. Wm. Goodkind
  6 Mr. & Mrs. Ernest B. Lombard
  8 Tyrus L. Burger
  8 Jerman F. Burger
  8 Mrs. S. M. Perry
  8 Miss Laura Carr
3135 Mr. & Mrs. Dwight C. Haven
3143 Mr. & Mrs. C. J. Manvel & drs.
3143 Dr. R. W. Hardon
3145 Mrs. John Hutchinson
3145 Miss Florence C. Hutchinson
3147 Dr. & Mrs. D. B. Eaton

2344-2358 The Concord Flats (con.)
  304 Mr. & Mrs. Wm. M. Jackson
  305 Mary Towle Davis
  309 Mr. & Mrs. J. Warren Harrison
  312 Mr. & Mrs. J. G. Prebbin
  401 Mr. & Mrs. R. B. Whitsett
  402 Mr. & Mrs. Graham Davis
  402 Mrs. Mary Baldwin
  402 A. D. Baldwin
  404 Marie S. Russell
  407 Mr. & Mrs. C. B. Wells
  408 Mr. & Mrs. Geo. P. Beardsley
  409 Mr. & Mrs. Thos. M. Fish
  412 Mr. & Mrs. H. E. Gilmore
  503 Mr. & Mrs. Logan F. Lisle
    Receiving day Thursday
  504 Mr. & Mrs. A. F. Williams & dr.
  506 Mrs. A. M. Borngesser
  506 Dr. C. F. Smith
  508 Mr. & Mrs. V. H. Dumbeck
  510 Mr. & Mrs. Josiah Burnham & dr.
  511 Mr. & Mrs. A. E. H. Thompson
  601 Mr. & Mrs. Chas. F. Murphy
  604 Mrs. Marion Silva
  603 Mr. & Mrs. E. J. Hill
  604 Dr. P. B. Saur
  606 Mr. & Mrs. E. L. Merrill
  607 Mr. & Mrs. H. G. Longhurst
  608 Rev. & Mrs. John Rusk & dr.
    Receiving day Thursday
  609 Mr. & Mrs. J. Sherman Dudley
    Receiving day Thursday
  611 Mrs. M. Bucklin
  705 Mr. & Mrs. Wm. M. Wheatley
  705 Miss Kate Bucklin
  706 Mr. & Mrs. L. A. Thomas
  709 Mr. & Mrs. L. B. Langworthy
  710 Dr. & Mrs. Geo. A. Baynes
  711 John Mayo Palmer
  711 Robertson Palmer
  711 John T. Palmer
  712 Mr. & Mrs. Wellington Walker
2400 Dr. & Mrs. Daniel T. Nelson
2400 Francis C. Nelson
2424 Mr. & Mrs. Samuel Powell

3147 Miss Anna Abel
3147 Mrs. Bertha Kuhns
3159 Mrs. Jane L. Fitch
3159 Mr. & Mrs. H. M. Ayres
3159 Mr. & Mrs. Jas. H. Draper
3207 Dr. & Mrs. F. B. Ullery
3237 Dr. & Mrs. Charles Caldwell
3239 Dr. & Mrs. Elmer E. Babcock
3241 Mrs. A. S. Cook
3241 Horatio J. Jacoby
3245 Mrs. K. H. Spaids
3245 Miss Susan E. Spaids
3245 Miss K. L. Spaids
3251 Mr. & Mrs. Ira J. Mix
Receiving day Wednesday
3253 Mr. & Mrs. L. Ottenheimer
Receive 2d & 4th Friday in mo.
3253 Henry L. Ottenheimer
3253 Mrs. Herman Becker
3257 Mr. & Mrs. P. S. Howell
3257 Dr. James A. S. Howell
3257 Dr. J. W. Howell
3257 Dr. William Howell
3259 John E. Dean & drs.
3259 Mrs. John E. Wood
3259 M. R. Dean
3325 Mr. & Mrs. Elmer E. Baldwin
3327 Mr. & Mrs. B. D. Slocum
3329 Dr. Frederick E. Wadhams
3333 Mr. & Mrs. C. W. Van Ben-
schoten
3335 Mr. & Mrs. Isaac J. Lewis
3339 Mr. & Mrs. Albert E. Snow
3343 Mr. & Mrs. H. H. Roberts
3345 Mr. & Mrs. Thos. H. Brown &
dr.
3351 Mr. & Mrs. F. E. Halle
3359 Mrs. Daniel Goodman & dr.
3365 Mr. & Mrs. Alexander Allison
Receiving day Thursday
3403 Mr. & Mrs. George W. Watson
3407 Marie Birode Marion
3421 Dr. & Mrs. Kingston Hanna
3423 Dr. & Mrs. Wilson H. Davis
3427 Mr. & Mrs. Lumley Ingledew
& drs.
3427 Lumley Ingledew jr.
3429 Mr. & Mrs. Geo. W. Getchell
Receiving day Wednesday
3505 F. E. Olinger
3505 Mr. & Mrs. John P. Olinger
3505 Jean Prosper Olinger
3519 Dr. & Mrs. Jonas S. Newburgh
3519 Mr. & Mrs. Clarence H. Potter
Receiving day Tuesday

2426 Mr. & Mrs. J. W. Richards
2428 Mr. & Mrs. Thomas Ambrose
Receiving day Thursday
2428 Mr. & Mrs. James Ambrose
2428 Mr. & Mrs. A. P. Riker
2450 Dr. & Mrs. Chas. W. Leake
2450 Mr. & Mrs. Frank D. Tobey
Receiving day Wednesday
2450 Mr. & Mrs. J. W. Smithson
2454 Mr. & Mrs. Wm. S. Smithson
2454 Mr. & Mrs. Charles Busby
2458 Dr. Edmund J. Doering
2458 Dr. & Mrs. J. H. Low
2502 Mrs. M. Ettlinger
2502 Carl Wolfsohn
2506 Mrs. Irene B. Roney & dr.
2506 Henry B. Roney
2506 Charles J. Roney
2508 Dr. & Mrs. C. F. Hartt
2510 Dr. & Mrs. Milton Jay
2510 Dr. Frank W. Jay
2512 E. Bruce Chandler
2512 George M. Chandler
2512 Miss Alice Chandler
2516 Mrs. Annette Verniaud
2516 Mr. & Mrs. Thomas Whitney
2516 Mr. & Mrs. T. Birmingham
2516 Mr. & Mrs. C. J. Crowe
2516 Mr. & Mrs. S. P. Herron
2516 Mrs. Elizabeth Johnson
2516 Mr. & Mrs. Henry Hudson
2520 H. N. Wheeler
2520 Misses Wheeler
2528 Mr. & Mrs. J. H. Strong
2532 Mr. & Mrs. Geo. W. Mathews
& drs.
2532 Miss Clara Wardwell
2536 Miss Beatrice Harding
2542 Dr. & Mrs. S. Chas. DeVeny &
drs.
2614 Mr. & Mrs. Albert W. Kohn
Receiving day Thursday
2616 William Fitzgerald
2616 W. H. Fitzgerald
2616 Miss Mary A. Corbett
2616 Mr. & Mrs. W. P. Lawton
2640 Mr. & Mrs. M. A. Allen
2644 Mr. & Mrs. Geo. L. Gray
2712 Mr. & Mrs. Jacob Reinach
2712 Gustave S. Ullman
2714 Mr. & Mrs. Isaac Rubel
2714 Mrs. Bertha Pollak
2818 Rev. & Mrs. Arthur Edwards
& drs.
2818 Dr. Arthur R. Edwards
2826 Mr. & Mrs. Hugh Heron & dr.

3535 Mr. & Mrs. Thos. L. Maitland
3537 Mr. & Mrs. L. E. McPherson
3541 Dr. & Mrs. John Leeming
3541 Dr. Wm. B. Whitaker
3543 Mr. & Mrs. W. P. Nelson
3543 Miss Mary Nelson
3545 Mr. & Mrs. Sidney M. Spiegel
3547 Mr. & Mrs. Isaac F. Rubel
Receive 2d & 4th Thursday in mo.
3549 Mr. & Mrs. Samuel R. Wells
3551 Miss E. B. Shumway
3551 C. H. Bradley
3551 L. A. Fisk
3625 Dr. & Mrs. T. J. Watkins
3657 Mr. & Mrs. John H. Wood & dr.
3657 John E. Wood
3739 Mr. & Mrs. Walton Perkins
Receiving day Tuesday
3739 Mrs. S. L. Grosscup
3739 Mr. & Mrs. Chas. E. Fizette
3739 Mr. & Mrs. P. A. Auer
3745 Mr. & Mrs. G. B. Corey
3745 Mr. & Mrs. F. W. Bedee
3745 Mr. & Mrs. F. E. Beecher
Receiving day Thursday
3747 Mrs. J. M. Eyster & dr.
3749 Prof. & Mrs. William F. Black
3749 Mr. & Mrs. Horace W. Black
Receiving day Tuesday
3749 Fred W. Black
3749 Mr. & Mrs. Julius Abel
Receive 1st Friday in mo.
3751 J. W. Champion
3753 Adolph Dernburg
3755 Dr. & Mrs. W. C. Loar
Receiving day Tuesday
3755 Mrs. Addie Adams Hull
3929 Mr. & Mrs. Col. D. H. Perkins
3929 Mrs. M. H. Perkins
4013 Mr. & Mrs. F. P. Puterbaugh
4017 Mrs. Everett Richey
4017 Eugene Richey
4019 Mr. & Mrs. R. B. Organ
4023 Mr. & Mrs. Wm. J. Fleming
Receiving day Friday
4023 George A. Fleming
4025 Mr. & Mrs. M. P. Metcalf
4035 Mr. & Mrs. A. P. Brainard
4037 Mr. & Mrs. H. S. Tobey
4037 Miss Carrie B. Watkins
4039 Benjamin Auerbach
4053 Mr. & Mrs. John C. Lee
4109 Mr. & Mrs. Walter Scates & dr.
4237 Dr. & Mrs. Wm. H. Hipp

2832 Mr. & Mrs. Ira W. Buell
2836 Mr. & Mrs. Chas. A. McLean
2836 C. F. McLean
2838 Mr. & Mrs. A. H. Downs
2838 Mr. & Mrs. Theodore Emery
2840 Mr. & Mrs. Tracy C. Drake
2916 Mrs. Amos Grannis
2916 Albert A. Grannis
2916 Frank L. Grannis
2916 Mrs. Mary A. Taylor
2920 Dr. & Mrs D. A. K. Steele
2920 Joseph S. Tomlinson
2926 Mr. & Mrs. E. W. Pardridge
2926 Mr. & Mrs. C. S. Hutchins
2926 Mr. & Mrs. M. A. Hogan
2928 Mr. & Mrs. Ward C. Favorite
2928 Mr. & Mrs. Owen H. Fay
2928 Mr. & Mrs. Wm. Shippen Jenks
Receive Tuesday afternoons
2930 Mr. & Mrs. Wm. Henry Thompson
Receive Tuesday afternoon
2930 Mrs. Louise E. Hackett
Receiving day Tuesday
2930 Mrs. Sibyl T. Holbrook
2930 Dr. Marie J. Mergler
Receiving day 1st Monday in mo.
2932 Mr. & Mrs. James Viles jr.
2932 Mrs. P. L. Underwood & drs.
2932 Mr. & Mrs. Morris S. Rosenfield
2934 Mr. & Mrs. E. F. Robbins
2934 Mrs. P. L. Underwood & drs.
2938 Dr. & Mrs. Carl D. Stone
Receiving day Tuesday
2940 Mrs. Henry D. Warner & drs.
2942 Mr. & Mrs. W. W. Sherman
2942 Francis J. Hill
2944 Col. & Mrs. D. J. Hynes
2944 Mrs. Grace King Haviland
2952 Mr. & Mrs. M. B. Lydon
2952 Harry C. Lydon
2952 Miss Mollie Lydon
2956 Mrs. E. S. Reilly & drs.
2962 Mrs. Bernard Callaghan & dr.
2962 Mr. & Mrs. J. E. Callahan
2966 Miss M. J. O'Brien
2966 Miss M. V. O'Brien
2968 Mandred A. Morton
2968 Mrs. F. B. Morton
2974 Mrs. W. Marvin
3000 The Norwood Flats
  1 Dr. & Mrs. H. C. Dale
  Receiving day Thursday
  2 Dr. J. A. H. Wilson
  5 John W. Bate & dr.

4247 Dr. & Mrs. H. E. Almes
    Receiving day Tuesday
4327 Mr. & Mrs. Arthur Abraham
4327 Mr. & Mrs. Chas. P. Hulbert
4341 Mr. & Mrs. Charles Pulham
    Receiving day Thursday
4341 Mr. & Mrs. John A. Bender
4341 Mr. & Mrs. Sylvester Marshall
4401 Mrs. Caroline Rosenthal
    Receive 1st & last Fridays
4401 Lubin L. Rosenthal
4401 Mr. & Mrs. L. B. Shaw
4401 Mr. & Mrs. Chas. M. Updike
4401 William M. Updike
4401 Dr. & Mrs. Fred'k C. Test
4401 Jacob R. Wineman
4403 Dr. & Mrs. H. C. Waack
4403 Mr. & Mrs. F. E. Patterson
4403 Jacob Tallert
4405 Mr. & Mrs. Wm. H. White
4405 Mr. & Mrs. James J. Graham
    Receiving day Tuesday
4407 Mr. & Mrs. J. A. Jackson
4417 Dr. & Mrs. Edwin Klebs
4417 Henry Klebs
4501 Mr. & Mrs. P. Nacey & drs.
4503 Mr. & Mrs. Chas. Treichlinger
4505 Mr. & Mrs. L. H. Meyer
4511 Dr. & Mrs. Abraham L. Freund
4513 Dr. & Mrs. Julius Wise
4519 Mr. & Mrs. Wm. Conroy
4533 Mr. & Mrs. H. M. Nixon
4535 Mr. & Mrs. John W. Thomas
4535 Mr. & Mrs. Max Glaser
4535 Miss Blanche Glaser
4619 Dr. & Mrs. Albert H. Keats
    Receive Wednesday
4713 Dr. Theo. J. Knudson & dr.
4713 S. O. Knudson
4721 Mr. & Mrs. Jas. H. Campbell
4727 Mr. & Mrs. E. G. Stewart
4727 Mr. & Mrs. R. J. Middleton
    Receiving day Thursday
4727 William G. Middleton
4727 Mr. & Mrs. Guy B. Holmes
4729 Mr. & Mrs. Geo. S. Williams
4729 Mr. & Mrs. H. Magnus Jones
4731 Mr. & Mrs. J. Kinsey Hol-
    lingshead *Receive Friday*
4731 Mr. & Mrs. W. E. Richardson
4809 Mr. & Mrs. John Hickey
5229 Mr. & Mrs. H. J. Messing
5609 Dr. & Mrs. C. F. P. Korssell
5721 Mr. & Mrs. Joseph B. Bettles
5735 Elmer E. Kilmer
5735 Dr. Anna Kilmer

3000 The Norwood Flats (cont'd.)
  7 Prof. & Mrs. Willard I.
    Tinus
  10 Mr. & Mrs. Daniel Stone
    Receiving day Wednesday
  19 Dr. & Mrs. Myron E. Lane
3012 Gilbert W. Barnard & dr.
3018 Dr. & Mrs. E. H. Thurston
3020 Miss Nancy D. Mitchell
3020 Lucien C. Mitchell
3020 Mrs. Maria E. Smith
3026 Mr. & Mrs. L. H. Freiberger
3026 M. L. Freiberger
3036 Dr. Charles C. Singley
3120 Dr. & Mrs. H. I. Davis
3128 Mr. & Mrs. Michael Espert
3130 Dr. & Mrs. G. F. Shears
    Receiving day Thursday
3130 Dr. W. P. McGibbon
3136 Dr. & Mrs. Chas. Howard Lodor
    Receiving day Tuesday
3148 Dr. & Mrs. J. L. Hancock
3154 Dr. & Mrs. J. R. Kippax
3156 Dr. & Mrs. E. J. Burch
3160 Dr. & Mrs. William E. Quine
3200 Dr. & Mrs. Arthur E. Thomas
3230 Mr. & Mrs. J. T. Healy &. drs.
3244 Mr. & Mrs. James M. Reddy &
    drs.
3300 Dr. & Mrs. Horace M. Starkey
3300 Mrs. S. H. Clark
3300 Miss M. Ella Starkey
3302 Dr. & Mrs. Charles H. Thayer
    & dr.
3306 Mr. & Mrs. M. E. Swart
3306 Mr. & Mrs. Jas. Otis. Hinkley
3306 Mr. & Mrs. Harry A. Hubbard
3312 Mr. & Mrs. Henry Hefter & dr.
3312 C. H. Hefter
3320 Mr. & Mrs. E. P. Broughton
3320 Miss Lennie O. Carr
3322 Mr. & Mrs. Arnold Cohn
3322 Mr. & Mrs. Godfrey Harris
3328 Mr. & Mrs. John Tyrrell
3328 Mrs. Bronson Peck
3336 Mr. & Mrs. Chas. B. Eggleston
    Receiving day Thursday
3350 Mr. & Mrs. C. Edward Baker
3352 Mrs. Leander Stone & drs.
3428 Mr. & Mrs. Henry Dewitz
3438 Dr. & Mrs. M. J. Moth
    Receiving day Wednesday
3444 Dr. & Mrs. C. Harrison Craw-
    ford
3444 Miss Ada Douglas Rankin
3444 Miss Lillian Rankin

5737 Mr. & Mrs. A. C. Clark
5813 Mr. & Mrs. N. C. Thayer
5855 Mr. & Mrs. N. A. Lauer
5927 Mr. & Mrs. Wm. M. Hughes
5937 Mrs. Ella C. Reed
5939 Mr. & Mrs. H. H. Mansfield
 Receive Wednesday
5939 Mr. & Mrs. Wm. E. Larned
5941 Mr. & Mrs. J. G. Gondon
6001 Mr. & Mrs. H. H. Gross
6015 Mr. & Mrs. H. R. Stebbings &
 drs. *Receiving day Thursday*
6015 Walter L. Stebbings
6033 Dr.& Mrs.Horace P. Stebbings
6033 Mr. & Mrs. Charles E. Fowler
6125 Mr. & Mrs. A. C. Mann & dr.
 Receiving day Thursday

4552 Miss Emma C. Gregory
4562 Mr. & Mrs. Henry Sander
4564 Mr. & Mrs. L. J. Hanchett
4618 Mr. & Mrs. Robt. T. Hoyt
4620 Mr. & Mrs. Allen L. Howard
4620 Mr. & Mrs. Amos C. Dean
4620 Mr. & Mrs. D. C. Mallory
4624 Mr. & Mrs. J. W. Mackenzie
 & dr.
4624 Kenneth Mackenzie
4624 Chester H. Martin
4626 Mr. & Mrs. Martin C. Bell
4634 Mr. & Mrs. Nathaniel Bacon
4638 Mr. & Mrs. O. A. Mathison
4642 Dr. & Mrs. Zenas H. Going
4656 Mrs. Agnes E. Foss & dr.
 Receiving day Tuesday
4724 Mr. & Mrs. Wm. Hansbrough
4810 Mr. & Mrs. Edmund J. Mc-
 Quaid
4812 Mr. & Mrs. David Dudley Livingston
 Receiving day Thursday
4812 Mr.& Mrs. James Lawton & dr.
5024 Mrs. Helen M. Woods & dr.
 Receiving day Thursday
5610 Mr. & Mrs. O. S. Baylies
5644 Mr. & Mrs. John F. Reid
5738 Mr. & Mrs. W. W. Brissenden
5738 Frederick C. Brissenden
5738 Walter B. Hillmer
5830 Mr. & Mrs. Henry Thorne &dr.
5910 Mrs. A. B. Huson
5910 Mrs. Ollie A. McDowell
5946 Mr. & Mrs. W. R. Burcky
6000 Christian Burcky
6000 Mrs. Elise Burcky & drs.
6012 Mr. & Mrs. Henry B. Lewis

3514 Mr. & Mrs. J. E. Hansen
3646 Frank L. Honore
3666 Mr. & Mrs. I. Neumann
3666 Ignatz Hasterlik
3666 Henry Hasterlik
3756 Louis Morris & dr.
3756 Henry Morris
3760 Miss Clara J. Vierling
3760 Robert Vierling
3760 Louis Vierling
3764 Mr. & Mrs. J. Jos. Hoffman
 Receiving day Friday
3764 Mrs. P. Landman
3764 Fred C. Bryan
3800 Mr. & Mrs. Charles G. Livingston
3804 Mr. & Mrs. A. W. Becker
3804 Isaac J. Becker
3808 Dr. & Mrs. F. H. Honberger
4022 Mr. & Mrs. William A. Purcell
4044 Edward Slattery
4052 Mrs. H. R. Skinner & dr.
4052 Dr. Edward P. Skinner
4052 Dr. Frank H. Skinner
4054 Dr. & Mrs. Russell C. Kelsey
 Receive Wednesday & Friday
4104 Mr. & Mrs. Ransom Richards
 & drs.
4104 Charles R. Richards
4110 Mr. & Mrs. H. A. Bogardus
4114 Mr. & Mrs. T. A. Stevens
4144 Mr. & Mrs. E. K. Herrick
4212 Mr. & Mrs. W. B. Schwartz
4226 Dr. & Mrs. N. C. Kemp
4230 Harry Rothschild
4240 Mr.& Mrs.James T.Young &dr.
4310 Mr. & Mrs. John W. Paxson
4322 Mr. & Mrs. James Galvin
4338 Mrs. Wm. L. Wyness
4400 Mr. & Mrs. John H. Martin
4412 Mr. & Mrs. Roswell Z. Herrick
4412 Miss Gertrude T. Herrick
4412 Miss Marion Thurston
4412 Mrs. N. B. Thurston
4424 Dr. & Mrs. Abraham L.
 Thomas
4438 Mrs. Louis Neumann
4448 Mr. & Mrs. Horace C. Gardner
4506 Mr. & Mrs. H. A. Burnett
4506 Mr. & Mrs. C. E. Frankenthal
4508 Mr. & Mrs. Harlan E. Cook
4508 Mr. & Mrs. John C. Bosworth
 Receive Wednesday
4508 Mr. & Mrs. F. M. Hayden
4512 Mr. & Mrs. Austin A. Canavan
4516 Mr. & Mrs. T. G. McElligott

6012 Mr. & Mrs. Will W. Carter
6020 Mr. & Mrs. C. T. Manter & drs.
6020 F. H. Manter

6034 Mr. & Mrs. C. J. Rîley
6124 Mrs. A. L. Perkins
6128 Mr. & Mrs. C. D. W. Clapp

INGLESIDE AVENUE.

5309 Mr. & Mrs. John N. Bour
5309 John R. Bour
5309 Mrs. Louise C. Abbott
6323 Dr. & Mrs. C. W. Morrow
6413 Mr. & Mrs. George L. Franklin
6413 J. Clarke Dean ·
6421 Mrs. Ida Hammond & dr.
6557 Mr. & Mrs. Homer D. Russell
6557 R. Maxwell Cowing

6410 Mr. & Mrs. Henry Munzer
6436 Mr. & Mrs. Selwyn J. Barclay
6504 Mr. & Mrs. Taylor E. Brown
        Receiving day Wednesday
6518 Mr. & Mrs. David Chambers
6518 John E. Chambers
6522 Mr. & Mrs. Henry Lesch
————
6557 Mr. & Mrs. F. J. Hathaway

JACKSON AVENUE.

5823 Max Noel
6321 Mr. & Mrs. W. B. Gillette
6357 Mr. & Mrs. L. C. Wagner

5312 Mr. & Mrs. Allan F. Gordon ·
5632 Mr. & Mrs. S. D. Witkowsky & dr.
5704 Prof. & Mrs. Alonzo A. Stagg
5800 Prof. Frederick Starr

JACKSON PARK TERRACE.

223 Mr. & Mrs. I. W. Brown
233 Mr. & Mrs. P. J. Power

235 Andrew W. Kinnear
237 Hugh Crabbe

JEFFERSON AVENUE.

5029 Mr. & Mrs. T. W. Garland
        Receiving day Tuesday
5029 Dr. & Mrs. Geo. T. Bauzet
5031 Mr. & Mrs. Francis J. Schulte
5039 Mr. & Mrs. Everett T. Schuler
        Receiving day Tuesday
5117 Mr. & Mrs. E. H. Noyes
5117 William H. Noyes
5117 Albert Hamilton Noyes
5119 Mr. & Mrs. J. T. Harahan
5119 Mr. & Mrs. James B. Shirley
5125 Mr. & Mrs. R. J. O. Hunter
5125 Mrs. Robert Hunter
5129 Mrs. J. H. Miles & dr.
5129 Thomas D. Miles
5131 Mr. & Mrs. Albert S. Tyler & dr.
5135 Mr. & Mrs. Alfred R. Porter
5221 Mr . Rowland Longmire & dr.
5221 Stanley W. Longmire
5225 Mrs. T. S. E. Dixon
5229 Mr. & Mrs. James Taylor & dr.
5237 William B. Main
5321 Mr. & Mrs. Edward E. Powers
5321 Mr. & Mrs. Louis W. Wilson
5335 Mr. & Mrs. J. M. Marshall

5012 Mr. & Mrs. A. B. Carson
5014 Mr. & Mrs. Geo. B. Grosvenor
5016 Mr. & Mrs. E. A. S. Clarke
5036 T. G. Butlin
5036 Mrs. Minerva Butlin
5036 Mrs. L. R. Leonard
5046 Mrs. Noah Barnes
5104 Mr. & Mrs. Elisha C. Ware
5110 Mr. & Mrs. R. G. Clarke
5112 Mrs. Mary J. Bristol
5112 Mrs. Agnes J. Scott
5114 Mr. & Mrs. Warren F. Goodwin
5114 William G. Goodwin
5114 James Goodwin
5120 Mr. & Mrs. Walter C. Nelson
5124 Mr. & Mrs. Byron W. French
        & dr.
5146 Mr. & Mrs. W. C. Ott & drs.
5146 William H. Ott
5200 Mr. & Mrs. G. A. Webster
5206 Mr. & Mrs. Charles J. Dorrance
5208 Mr. & Mrs. Frederick W. Clark
5210 Mrs. Mary E. McChesney ·
5210 Mr. & Mrs. Martin K. Northam
5216 Mr. & Mrs. J. D. Stone
5216 Mrs. H. E. Parsons & dr.

5335 Mr. & Mrs. Albert M.Marshall
     Receive Tuesday
5401 Mrs. M. J. Ramsdell
5407 Mr. & Mrs. J. H. Stevison
     Receiving day Thursday
5407 Arthur Jameson
5409 Mr. & Mrs. C. A. Reed & drs.
5409 C. S. Reed
5415 Mr. & Mrs. DeWitt Brown
5417 Mr. & Mrs. E. B. Mower
5423 Mr. & Mrs. E. E. Abrams
5427 Mr. & Mrs. Wm. Lewis
5427 Frederick C. Lewis
5467 Mr. & Mrs. W. R. Head & drs.
5467 Paul D. Head
5467 James M. Head
6011 Mr. & Mrs. A. M. Woolfolk
6011 Clinton S. Woolfolk
6039 Mr. & Mrs. Edward E. Smith
6055 Mr. & Mrs. H. G. Kyle
6059 Mr. & Mrs. S. W. McMunn
6059 Mrs. M. S. Northrop
6065 Mr. & Mrs. J. H. Keating
6067 Mr. & Mrs. H. W. Foote

5488 George W. Haskins
5516 Dr.& Mrs.Charles BerrienHall
5516 Mr. & Mrs. Edward C. Brown
5516 Mrs. Amos T. Hall
5516 Mrs. R. T. Bacon
5532 Mr. & Mrs. Geo B. Parkins
5634 Mr. & Mrs. Otto Peltzer
6010 Mr. & Mrs. H. H. Cooke
6030 Mr. & Mrs. Hiram H. Cody
     Receiving day Tuesday
6030 Arthur B. Cody
6034 Mr.& Mrs.Wm. J. Button & drs.
6046 Mr. & Mrs. James Rosenthal
6048 Mr. & Mrs. J. C. Vaughan
6048 Roger Vaughan
6406 Mr. & Mrs. J. B. Meredith

5218 Mr. & Mrs. Thos. C. Clark
5218 Mr. & Mrs. Wm. Morgan
5218 Miss Harriet Morgan
5220 Dr. & Mrs. L. T. Dayan
5224 Mr. & Mrs. Geo. C. Bailey
5228 Mr. & Mrs. Wm. J. Carter
5238 Mr. & Mrs. Brian Philpot
5238 Mr. & Mrs. A. D. Philpot
5238 W. H. V. Rosing
5238 Miss Kate Rosing
5318 Dr. & Mrs. J. EugeneTremaine
5318 Mr. & Mrs. M. J. Tremaine
5320 Dr. & Mrs. J. Ramsay Flood &
     dr.
5320 Samuel D. Flood
5320 Robert D. Flood
5324 Mr. & Mrs. W. H. Richardson
     & dr.
5324 Mrs. R. H. Barnard
5330 Mr. & Mrs. W. Fay Tuttle
5344 Mrs. T. M. Fulton
5400 Mr. & Mrs. John A. Knapp
5406 Mrs. C. Robinson
5406 Mr. & Mrs. Argyle E.Robinson
5410 Dr. & Mrs. C. M. Oughton
5416 Mr. & Mrs. O. M. Powers
5426 Mr. & Mrs. Albert G. Mason
5426 William H. Mason
5426 Fred H. Mason
5432 Mr. & Mrs. S. H. Stevens & drs.
5432 S. H. Stevens jr.
5436 Mr. & Mrs. F. W. Wood
5436 Thomas R. Wood
5436 George S. Wood
5440 Mr. & Mrs. H. E. R. Wood
5458 Mr. & Mrs. George W. Dexter
5464 Mr. & Mrs. M. L. Beers
5464 Herbert P. Beers
5470 Mr. & Mrs. Henry A. Porter
5470 F. D. Porter
5488 H. Wolcott Haskins

KENWOOD AVENUE.

4717 Mr. & Mrs. John Nichol
4719 Mr. & Mrs. L. P. Morehouse
     & dr.
4719 Frederick B. Morehouse
4725 Dr. Rachel H. Carr
4733 Mr. & Mrs. J. M. Neuburger &
     dr.
4733 John M. Neuburger
4737 Charles T. Lawton
4739 Mr. & Mrs. W. B. Phister
4741 Mrs. Jean W. Carter
4741 Mrs. Katherine B. Rich

4714 Mr. & Mrs. Francis Etheridge
4716 Mr. & Mrs. C. J. Northup
4718 Mr. & Mrs. Geo. H. Cook
4720 Dr. & Mrs. Wm. H. Rumpf
4722 Mr. & Mrs. M. D. Downs
4724 Mr. & Mrs. J. H. Ives
4726 Mr. & Mrs. David I. Lillard &
     dr. *Receiving day Tuesday*
4726 Mr. & Mrs. George E. Arndt
4730 Robert B. De L'Armitage
4730 Mme. Arabella Root De L'Ar-
     mitage

4743 Mrs. Walter S. Dole
4801 Mr. & Mrs. Chas. Henry Cutler
4801 William H. Cutler
4815 Mr. & Mrs. J. R. Putnam & drs.
4827 Mr. & Mrs. Horace K. Tenney
4831 Mrs. E. M. Ludington
4831 Mr. & Mrs. C. H. M. Tobey
4831 Frank H. Tobey
4837 Mr. & Mrs. C. Harry Tobey
4839 Miss E. M. Tobey
4839 Miss F. E. Baker

4828 Mr. & Mrs. Edward D. Kim-
      ball *Receiving day Tuesday*
4828 Mrs. O. S. Hough & dr.
4830 Mr. & Mrs. Almer Coe
4852 Mr. & Mrs. Warren McArthur
4852 Mrs. Olive E. Weston
4858 Mr. & Mrs. Geo. W. Blossom

4732 Mr. & Mrs. J. C. Shand
4744 Mr. & Mrs. Frank Fairman
4744 Frank S. Fairman
4744 Mrs. E. F. Noble
4746 Mr. & Mrs. Chas. B. Whipple
4748 Mr. & Mrs. Frederick M. Rey-
      nolds
4750 Mr. & Mrs. L. J. Wolf
4754 Mr. & Mrs. Edw. D. McDougal
4754 Robert McDougal
4754 Alfred McDougal
4756 Mr. & Mrs. William H. Low
4756 Dr. Julia R. Low
4756 Arthur Wray Street
4800 Mr. & Mrs. Dillwyn V. Pur-
      ington
4810 Mr. & Mrs. John S. Miller
4822 Mr. & Mrs. E. H. Sargent
4822 Mr. & Mrs. Thos. P. Smith jr.

KIMBARK AVENUE.

4711 Mr. & Mrs. Frederick W. Jackson
4713 Mrs. S. R. Fuller & dr.
4717 Mr. & Mrs. Charles P. Parish
4721 Mr. & Mrs. Samuel C. Tobin
4721 Charles P. Tobin
4721 Robert P. Tobin
4721 Arthur C. Tobin
4721 Mrs. Rosamond P. Parish
4725 Mr. & Mrs. Chas. L. Currier
4725 Miss Evelyn B. Currier
4729 Mr. & Mrs. Wm. A. Bissell
4735 Mr. & Mrs. James H. Long
4735 Miss Clara E. Johnson
4737 Henry A. Osborn
4737 Mrs. S. M. Osborn
4737 Miss Blanche Swingley
4747 Mr. & Mrs. W. R. Page
4747 Miss Ethel F. Page
4747 Ralph H. Page
4747 William T. Page
4801 Mr. & Mrs. Joseph H. Howard
4805 Mr. & Mrs. J. Finley Barrell
4811 Mr. & Mrs. Willard R. Wiley
4819 Mr. & Mrs. Chas. S. Downs
4823 Mr. & Mrs. Maurice A. Mead
4823 Miss Lillian E. Mead
4829 Mrs. L. O. Downs
4829 A. O. Downs
4833 Mr. & Mrs. Edw. C. Hale
4837 Mr. & Mrs. Nathaniel L. Bar-
      more
4847 Mr. & Mrs. Will Hartwell
      Lyford
      Receiving day Tuesday

4700 Mr. & Mrs. A. Montgomery
      Ward
4714 Mr. & Mrs. Calvin DeWolf
4714 Mr. & Mrs. Wallace L. DeWolf
4714 Mrs. Julia R. Rea
4726 Mrs. Geo. R. T. Ward
4726 Mr. & Mrs. Eugene H. Pear-
      son & dr.
4730 Mr. & Mrs. H. G. Willard
4734 Mr. & Mrs. Reynolds Fisher
4740 Mrs. James H. Swan
4740 Miss Anna L. Morrison
4744 Mr. & Mrs. Robert B. Boak
4744 Robert Boak jr.
4752 Mr. & Mrs. W. G. Coolidge & dr.
4752 Winthrop Coolidge
4800 Mr. & Mrs. Edward N. Wiley
4800 Silas M. Moore
4808 Mr. & Mrs. Nathan Manasse
4812 Mr. & Mrs. Robert Mather
4812 Mrs. E. C. Kerby
4820 Mr. & Mrs. Platt P. Gibbs
4824 Mr. & Mrs. J. J. Lindman
4826 Mr. & Mrs. H. H. Field
4828 Mr. & Mrs. W. F. Parish
4828 W. F. Parish jr.
4828 Harry F. Parish
4830 Mr. & Mrs. Ernest H. Hicks
4840 Mr. & Mrs. Thomas S. Norton
4846 Mr. & Mrs. Theo. W. Letton
4846 Harold W. Letton
4850 Mr. & Mrs. John A. DeVore
4860 Mr. & Mrs. Norman Carroll
4860 Mrs. Samuel Ward

4847 Duke McComas
4847 Rufus F. McComas jr.
4853 Robert McMurdy
4853 Stuart H. Brown

4857 Mr. & Mrs. C. E. Woodruff
4857 Louis C. Woodruff
5101 Mr. & Mrs. Robert G. Smith
5101 Mr. & Mrs. Walter L. Githens
5101 Mr. & Mrs. John A. McLeod
 Receiving day Wednesday
5101 Mrs. Ward Stone
5101 Carl W. Hertel
5109 K. V. R. Lansingh & dr.
5109 Mrs. A. L. Tichenor
5121 Mr. & Mrs. Geo. C. Fry & dr.
5125 I. K. Boyesen
5125 Harold Boyesen
5125 Miss Austa Boyesen
5137 Mr. & Mrs. Wm. H. Sterling
5137 Mrs. Jessie D. Cushing
5141 Mr. & Mrs. Francis W. Walker
 Receiving day Tuesday
5201 Mr. & Mrs. H. W. Caldwell &
 drs.
5207 Mr. & Mrs. A. S. Hopkins
5207 Miss Valeria M. Hopkins
5209 Mr. & Mrs. A. A. Morrill
5211 Mr. & Mrs. G. C. Ball & dr.
5211 Woodruff Ball
5213 Dr. & Mrs. A. E. Garceau
 Receiving day Thursday
5213 Dr. Paul Gilford
5217 Mr. & Mrs. Emil Rudert
5217 Mr. & Mrs. Willis E. Thorne
5225 Mr. & Mrs. Frederick H. Dow
5227 Mr. & Mrs. Joseph F. Fulton
 Receiving day Thursday
5227 Fred F. Fulton
5227 Clair W. Fulton
5231 Mr. & Mrs. Harry F. Louns-
 bery
 Receiving day Thursday
5231 Frank X. Combs
5233 Mr. & Mrs. Chas. Grant Marquardt
5235 Mr. & Mrs. Amory E. Taylor
5733 Mr. & Mrs. F. A. Lorenz
5747 Mr. & Mrs. H. W. Hardy
5825 Mr. & Mrs. Thomas W. Allinson
5825 Miss Louise E. Volk
5825 Mr. & Mrs. Jas. R. Angell
5825 Mrs. Anne L. Danforth & drs.
5825 Mr. & Mrs. Chas. T. Parsons

5112 Mr. & Mrs. William Kent
5116 Mrs. Julius S. Grinnell
5116 Robert Grinnell
5120 Mr. & Mrs. C. S. Dennis
5126 Mr. & Mrs. E. B. Myers & dr.
 Receiving day Thursday
5126 Mr. & Mrs. Willis V. Myers
5132 Mr. & Mrs. James A. Bingham
5132 Miss Edyth V. Bingham
5136 Mrs. Henry McKey
5136 Mrs. W. S. Parkhurst
5200 Mr. & Mrs. Wilton B. Martin
5202 Mr. & Mrs. C. W. Crankshaw
5206 Mr. & Mrs. Geo. A. Soden
 Receiving day Wednesday
5208 Mrs. Fletcher S. Bassett
5208 Wilbur W. Bassett
5224 Dr. & Mrs. J. E. Hinkins
5226 Mr. & Mrs. E. H. Cornelius
5470 Rev. John J. Carroll
5630 Rev. & Mrs. Thos. W. Goodspeed
5630 Edgar J. Goodspeed
5630 Chas. T. Goodspeed
5630 Stephen Goodspeed
5630 Mrs. Jane Ten Broeke
5644 Mr. & Mrs. J. S. Washburn
5700 Dr. & Mrs. Geo. M. Emrick
5700 Harris Hancock
5718 Mr. & Mrs. George M. Naylor
5734 Mr. & Mrs. V. L. Cunningham
5748 Mr. & Mrs. David Baker
5756 Mr. & Mrs. Wm. A. Pridmore
6014 Mr. & Mrs. Minor Wamsley
6014 Mr. & Mrs. F. A. Jackson
6016 Dr. & Mrs. S. A. Wilson
6016 J. L. Barnum
6018 Mr. & Mrs. James F. Pershing
6022 Mr. & Mrs. H. H. Bell
6028 Mrs. C. Schoenman & drs.
6028 C. S. Schoenman
6028 B. J. Schoenman
6028 E. L. Schoenman
6030 Mr. & Mrs. Adelbert DeLand
6030 Mrs. John C. Heitbahn
6032 Mr. & Mrs. Geo. Middendorf
 Receiving day Thursday
6042 Miss Ina L. Robertson
 Receiving day Thursday
6042 Miss Phoebe J. Clements
 Receiving day Thursday
6046 Mr. & Mrs. Edwin M. Ashcraft
 Receiving day Wednesday
6046 Raymond M. Ashcraft
6052 Mr. & Mrs. John E. Zeublin
 Receive 4th Sunday

5825 Mr. & Mrs. Harrv M. Bates
5825 Mr. & Mrs. J. S. Mayon
5825 Mr. & Mrs. Theodore L. Neff
5827 Mr. & Mrs. Addison W. Moore
    Receiving day Wednesday
5835 Mr. & Mrs. B. H. Beckett & dr.
6115 Mr. & Mrs. Ed. A. Paterson
    Receiving day ·Tuesday
6119 Mr. & Mrs. James S. Paterson
6119 Miss Margaret·J. Paterson
6123 Mr. & Mrs. Geo. L. Andrew
6123 Mr. & Mrs. Victor Heinze
6127 Mr. & Mrs. Jason R. Cadwell
6127 Mrs. R. B. Pierpont
6127 George J. Cadwell
6131 Mr. & Mrs. Wm. H. Sterrett
6147 Dr. & Mrs. FrederickF.Chaffee
6149 Mr. & Mrs. E. Ramsdell
6153 Mr. & Mrs. Fred P. Cutting
6219 Dr. & Mrs. W. B. Carroll
6227 Mr. & Mrs. John Darby & dr.
6227 Benjamin L. Darby
6229 Mr. & Mrs. Frank W. Holder
6229 Mrs. M. L. Holder.
6319 Mrs. Grace Mayer
6321 Mr. & Mrs. Willet Rose
6325 Mr. & Mrs. Benjamin F. Rey-
    ·nolds
6325 Mrs. Elizabeth Dorr
6335 Mr. & Mrs. Isaac Anderson
6345 Mr. & Mrs. Orson W. Ray
6407 Dr. & Mrs. A. W. McCandless
6413 Dr. & Mrs. R. M. Barrows
6417 Mr. & Mrs. William A. Fowler
6427 Mr. & Mrs. John M. Levis & dr.
6431 Mrs. L. C. Strawbridge & drs.
6431 C. Heber Strawbridge
6431 Edgar J. Strawbridge
6431 Albert N. Strawbridge
6431 Mrs. M. S. Allen
6431 Joshua Nye
6435 Mr. & Mrs. Frank H. Wolcott
6435 John Manington
6441 Mr. & Mrs. G. W. McMillin
    Receiving day Thursday
6445 Mr. & Mrs. John M. Meyer
6451 Mr. & Mrs. Charles E. Bragdon
6451 J. A. Gammans
6463 Mr. & Mrs. Robert Johns
6463 Mrs. Anna W. Patten
6501 Mr. & Mrs. Hudson L. Henson
6501 Mr. & Mrs. Edward A.Wanner
6501 Mr. & Mrs. D. L. Sterling
6501 Mr. & Mrs.Chas. Hetherington
    & dr.
6501 Mr. & Mrs. Ernest J. Thiele

6052 Prof. & Mrs. Charles Zueblin
6054 Mr. & Mrs. A. J. Hirschl & dr.
    Receiving day Tuesday
6054 Harry B. Hurd
6056 Mr. & Mrs. A. F. Streich
6110 Mr. & Mrs. Charles E. Johnston
6112 Mr. & Mrs. J. C. Beifeld
6112 Mrs. Kate C. Jaggar
6116 Mr. & Mrs. Edmond G. Otton
6120 Mr. & Mrs. L. H. Ainsworth
6126 Mrs. J. H. Slater
6134 Mr. & Mrs. B. F. Tilden
6144 Mrs. W. S. Sparrow & dr.
6148 Mr. & Mrs. Chas. M. French
6154 Mr. & Mrs. W. G. Press
6154 Mrs. Mary A. Haskell
6200 Col. & Mrs. W. B. Keeler
    Receiving day Wednesday
6200 Capt. & Mrs. G. M. Farnham
6204 Mr. & Mrs. Jasper G. Gilkison
6210 Joseph Jellyman
6210 Richard Jellyman
6210 Miss M. Jellyman
6220 Mr. & Mrs. C. B. VerNooy
6224 Mr. & Mrs. A. D. Joslin
6230 Mr. & Mrs. Charles B. Helfen-
    stein
    Receiving day Tuesday
6234 Mr. & Mrs. S. N. Pierson
6244 Mr. & Mrs. John R. Towle &dr.
6412 Rév. & Mrs. Edward H. Curtis
6420 Mr. & Mrs. S. J. Stewart
6426 Mr. & Mrs. Benjamin Wol-
    haupter
6434 Mr. & Mrs. Albert E. Steven-
    son
6446 Mr. & Mrs. E. A. Young
6446 Mrs. Lucy C. Swinerton
6450 Mr. & Mrs. James W. Johnston
6510 Mrs. M. B. Stiles
6510 Mr. & Mrs. N. C. Wheeler
6514 Mr. & Mrs. John L. Fuelling
    Receiving day Thursday
6514 Miss Sophia Fuelling
6516 Mr. & Mrs. Herman Sturs-
    berg·jr.
6516 Miss Louise Bodine
6520 Mr. & Mrs. F. E. Crawford
    Receiving day Thursday
6520 Mrs. Althea L. Hall
6538 Mr. & Mrs. Elliott Flower
6542 Mr. & Mrs. A. F. Chamberlain
6542 Mr. & Mrs. M. H. McChesney
6620 Mr. & Mrs. O. E. Harden & dr.
6626 Mr. & Mrs. Owen W. Jones
6626 Ira Jones

6501 Mr. & Mrs. John Glossinger
6521 Mr. & Mrs. Geo. B. Haines
6521 Mr. & Mrs. S. N. Howard
6523 Dr. & Mrs. E. Vigneron
6537 Mr. & Mrs. J. W. Harrison
6541 Mr. & Mrs. John M. Daly
6543 Mr. & Mrs. Harvey S. Sheldon
    & dr.
6557 Mr. & Mrs. Herman J. Trum-
    bull
6557 Mrs. H. R. Foster
6641 Mr. & Mrs. James Inglis

6642 Mrs. A. J. Maher
6914 Mrs. Mary Gaulter & dr.
6914 Fred E. Gaulter
6914 Frank J. Gaulter
6940 Mr. & Mrs. Geo. P. Thwaite
7426 Mr. & Mrs. William Everett
7450 Mr. & Mrs. John C. Rhea & dr.
7520 Mr. & Mrs. Arthur J. Bassett
_____
7437 Mr. & Mrs. Corneilus Curtis &
    dr.
7437 John B. Curtis

LAFAYETTE AVENUE.

6511 Mrs. SaphroniaHarnette &drs.
6511 Frank B. Harnette
6531 Mr. & Mrs. William F. Axt-
    man
6543 Mr. & Mrs. C. F. Baum
6547 Dr. & Mrs. Edward Mc-
    Laughlin
6551 Mr. & Mrs. Marvin Judd & drs.
6601 Mr. & Mrs. James R. Mulroy
6633 Mr. & Mrs. C. A. Winship & dr.
6637 Mr. & Mrs. Julian Kune
6639 Mr. & Mrs. W. S. Anderson
    & drs.
6643 Mr. & Mrs. Thos. H. Winters
6703 Mr. & Mrs. Charles A. Wood-
    ruff
6709 Mr. & Mrs. W. S. Bielfeldt
6717 Mr. & Mrs. A. J. Sittig
6731 Mr. & Mrs. Edw. J. McGowen
6735 Mr. & Mrs. C. D. Armstrong
6753 Mr. & Mrs. Max Stein
_____
7112 Mr. & Mrs. F. L. Salisbury

6500 Mr. & Mrs. F. C. Vehmeyer
6506 Mr. & Mrs. F. B. Badt
6506 Miss Eleanor O'Donnell
6510 Mr. & Mrs. Charles D. Organ
6510 Robert A. Organ
6514 Mr. & Mrs. L. A. Hamlin
6522 Mr. & Mrs. F. S. Thompson
6522 Mrs. D. S. Thompson
6530 Rev. & Mrs. Willard H. Rob-
    inson
6534 Mr. & Mrs. Geo. H. Weaver
6544 Mr. & Mrs. Thomas J. Ross
6556 Mr. & Mrs. E. H. Jackson
6556 Miss Carrie Howell
6600 Mr. & Mrs. Geo. E. Marshall
6602 Mr. & Mrs. F. J. Martin
6618 Mr. & Mrs. T. F. Indermille
6618 W. M. Chase
6620 Mr. & Mrs. W. J. Black
6642 Mr. & Mrs. R. B. Jones
6752 Mr. & Mrs. A. G. Scott & dr.
6806 Mr. & Mrs. James C. Edwards
6820 Mr. & Mrs. John Lawrie

LAKE AVENUE.

3543 Judge & MrsFrank Baker&dr.
    Receiving day Saturday
3601 Mr. & Mrs. Adolph Sutter &
    dr.
3601 Edwin A. Sutter
3601 L. L. Sutter
3603 Mr. & Mrs. Jacob Sutter
3603 Raymond C. Sutter
3603 Clarence B. Sutter
3603 Walter C. Sutter
3615 Mr. & Mrs. Edward C. Cleaver
3615 Mr. & Mrs. Fred'k C. Cleaver
3615 James M. Cleaver
3727 Mrs. A. L. Scott
3727 George Cullins

3506 Dr. & Mrs. John Pischczak
3506 Wm. Pischczak jr.
3506 Mrs. C. P. Morgan
3510 Mr. & Mrs. E. S. Eldredge
3510 Mr. & Mrs. Chas. J. Eldredge
3512 J. W. Williams & drs.
3516 Mr. & Mrs.PhilanderPickering
3516 Linnaeus E. Overman
3520 Mr. & Mrs.Fowell B. Hill & drs
3534 Mr. & Mrs. L. Morrison
3536 Mr.& Mrs.William W.Watkins
3538 Mrs. E. E. Spence
3538 J. F. Brookes
3538 Miss Mary J. Brookes
3602 Mrs. Florence M. Donahue

3745 Mrs. Catherine Valentine
3745 William G. Valentine
3745 Louis L. Valentine
3747 Mr. & Mrs. Latham Carr
3751 Mr. & Mrs. Edward E. Roehl
3751 Mr. & Mrs. Frank D. Abbott & dr.
3755 Mr. & Mrs. J. C. Tucker
3769 Mr. & Mrs. Charles W. Rhodes
3801 Dr. & Mrs. Albert S. Gray
Receiving day Thursday
3801 Mr. & Mrs. H. Ferdinand Hoffmeyer
3815 Mr. & Mrs. T. H. McCoy & drs.
3815 M. Max McCoy
3831 Mrs. M. Pollard & dr.
Receiving day Tuesday
3831 William R. Henry
3835 Mr. &.Mrs. Alexander Cook & drs.
3835 Archibald Cook
3849 Mr. & Mrs. Oscar Schleiter
3859 Mr. & Mrs. Robert P. Brown
3861 Mr. & Mrs. C. W. Lobdell
3861 Mr. & Mrs. W. J. Bradford
3865 Mr. & Mrs. E. P. Baker & dr.
3903 Mr. & Mrs. Chas. A. Goodyear & drs.
3903 A. S. Goodyear
3905 Mr. & Mrs. George Carr & dr.
3935 Mr. & Mrs. Chas. H. Prindiville
3935 Mr. & Mrs. Chas. T. Trego & dr.
3935 Mr. & Mrs. Wm. T. Trégo
3945 Mr. & Mrs. J. G. McWilliams
Receiving day Thursday
3945 Roy McWilliams
3945 Charles R. Lee
3945 Mrs. Mary Lee Pardridge
3949 John Borden & dr.
3961 Mr. & Mrs. L. McWilliams & dr.
3961 Thomas G. McWilliams
3965 Mr. & Mrs. Julius Kessler
3967 Mr. & Mrs. Charles Howe
3967 Arthur C. Howe
4009 Mr. & Mrs. Robert Dunlap
4009 Mr. & Mrs. Nathan R. Salsbury
4009 Mr. & Mrs. Franklin W. Cornwall
4009 George W. Cornwall
4009 Mr. & Mrs. Frederick H. Hall
4015 Mr. & Mrs. Richard F. Peyton jr.
4015 Richard F. Peyton
4015 Mr. & Mrs. Dexter E. Kenyon

3602 Mr. & Mrs. H. R. Gillette
3602 Mrs. Mary E. Hilton
3608 Mr. & Mrs. Samuel C. Comstock & dr.
Receiving day Tuesday
3608 Francis T. Bacon
3612 Mr. & Mrs. Wallace D. Kimball
3614 Dr. E. R. Hawley
3614 Mr. & Mrs. Theodore B. Spiering
3616 Jacob C. Camburn
3618 Mr. & Mrs. John W. Clover
3618 Mrs. Wm. Boalch
3626 Mrs. Isabella Blacker
3636 Mr. & Mrs. Samuel E. Bliss
3636 Frank E. Bliss
3640 Mr. & Mrs. Frank E. Johnson
3700 Mr. & Mrs. Daniel E. Root
3700 Dr. A. P. Gilmore
3702 Wm. R. Ruffner
3702 Mr. & Mrs. Herbert W. Weld
3706 Mr. & Mrs. Henry D. Gilbert
3706 Mrs. M. L. Ewing
3706 Mr. & Mrs. Alfred E. Ranney
3706 Joseph Lathrop
3708 Mrs. C. H. Blakely
3708 Miss Alice J. Leland
3708 Mr. & Mrs. H. F. Dousman
3716 Mr. & Mrs. Robert N. Goldie
3716 Mr. & Mrs. William Goldie. jr.
3716 Mrs. Esther E. Free & dr.
3716 William C. Free
3716 Mr. & Mrs. Eli S. Hart & drs.
3716 H. Stilson Hart
3716 Mr. & Mrs. D. B. Stedman
3716 Capt. E. M. Stedman & dr.
3716 Josiah Stedman
3716 E. M. Stedman jr.
3716 Mrs. L. C. Farwell
3716 Mr. & Mrs. A. B. Sloan
3716 Mr. & Mrs. H. Edward Cobb
3716 Edward Mackey
3716 Mr. & Mrs. Robert P. Walker
3722 Richard T. Sylvester
3728 Mr. & Mrs. Wm. F. Cook
Receiving day Thursday
3730 Mr. & Mrs. Geo. E. Cook
3732 Mr. & Mrs. A. B. Cook
3736 Mr. & Mrs. Geo. H. Hess & drs.
3752 Mr. & Mrs. Maurice Watkins
3756 A. B. Jenks
3756 Miss Hattie Lyons
Receiving day Friday
3764 Mr. & Mrs. F. S. Bagg

4017 Mr. & Mrs. Chester C. Broomell
4017 Mr. & Mrs. A. M. Thomson
4017 Mr. and Mrs. Louis E. Burr
Receiving day Tuesday
4035 Mr. & Mrs. Charles Sumner
Harmon
4035 Joseph W. Harmon
4039 Mr. & Mrs. G.W. Thomas & dr.
4043 Mr. & Mrs. Washington Porter
Receiving day Thursday
4049 Mrs. E. C. Sumner
4049 Miss M. L. Hawkins
4059 O. P. Curran
4059 Mr. & Mrs. D. B. Curran
4059 Samuel H. Curran
4147 Dr. N. H. Henderson
4155 Mr. & Mrs. A. A. Dewey & drs.
4155 Allen A. Dewey
4201 Mr. & Mrs. Wm. H. DeLisle
4201 Mr. and Mrs. John J. Sinzich
& dr.
4203 Mr. & Mrs. T. E. King
4211 Mr. & Mrs. Jas. McDevitt
4219 Mr. & Mrs. Benj. Schneewind
4221 Mr. & Mrs. Oliver S. Ross
4223 Mr. & Mrs. E. G. Simms & dr.
4231 Mr. & Mrs. George H. Martin
4321 Dr. Edgar J. George
4323 Mr. & Mrs. Rudolph G. Giesler
4323 Mr. & Mrs. James Johnston &
drs.
4323 Mr. & Mrs. E. F. Lapham
4325 Mrs. Esther Brown
4327 Mr. & Mrs. J. P. Haire
4327 Mr. and Mrs. S. O. Levinson
4329 Mrs. Edwin H. Dorland
4331 Mr. & Mrs. Charles Pfaff
4343 Mr. & Mrs. E. H. Tharp
4345 Mr. & Mrs. William S. Adams
4349 Mr. & Mrs. Thomas Knapp
4349 J. F. A. Halbach
4351 Mr. & Mrs. John Havron
4353 Mr. & Mrs. George L. Hastings
4353 Otto W. Mitchel
4359 Mr. & Mrs. Jas. S. McConnell
4359 Mr. & Mrs. E. P. McConnell
4363 Mrs. E. L. Browne & dr.
4367 Mr. & Mrs. Joseph B. Keen
4403 Mr. & Mrs. Lewis T. Moore
4405 Mr. & Mrs. Robert C. Moore &
dr.
4407 Mr. & Mrs. T. H. Smith
4411 Mr. & Mrs. Joseph Spies & dr.
4415 Mr. &Mrs.H.H.Chandler&drs.
Receiving day Wednesday

3766 Mr. & Mrs. Charles H. Engel
Receiving day Thursday.
3802 Strickland Hotel
Dr. & Mrs. A. L. Hulett.
Mr. & Mrs. C. P. Luce & dr.
3820 Mr. & Mrs. Charles C. Ruggles
3830 Mr. & Mrs. Henry J. Thayer
3834 Miss Anna Morgan
3834 Mrs. Addison J. Trunkey
3838 Mr.& Mrs.JonathanC. Mitchell
3842 Mr. & Mrs. Gustav Hiller
Receiving day Friday
3844 Mr. & Mrs. L. Hiller
Receiving day Friday
3844 Martin Frank
3846 Mrs. Sarah B. Packard
3848 Mrs. James McArthur & dr.
3850 Mr. & Mrs. George A. Spicer
3850 Miss Edith Davis
3852 Mr. & Mrs. John A. Baldwin
3852 Harry H. Baldwin
3854 Mr. & Mrs. John W. Green
3856 John T. Shayne
3860 Mr. & Mrs. Chas. B. Shedd
3860 Edward A. Shedd
3866 Mr. & Mrs. Jacob Mayer
3870 Mr. & Mrs. H. M. Wilcox & dr.
Receiving day Wednesday
3870 E. O. Wilcox
3900 Mr. & Mrs. J. L. McKeever
3900 Buell McKeever
3906 Mr. & Mrs. O. C. Cleave
3906 Mr. & Mrs. Geo. W. Hunt
3906 Mr. and Mrs. Geo. E. West
3910 Mr. & Mrs. Walter R. Robbins
3912 Dr. and Mrs. Edmund Andrews
3912 Harry H. Carr.
3912 Mr. and Mrs. Joseph M. Burrows and dr.
3916 J. P. Hoit & dr.
3918 Mrs. M. E. Crook
3920 Mrs. Harriet A. Wilson & dr.
3920 Edward B. Kelley
3922 Mr. & Mrs. F. H. Warren&drs.
3924 Mr. and Mrs. M.B. McLenehan
3926 Mr. and Mrs. Jacob Rice
3926 Mr. & Mrs. Frank Strausser
3928 R. R. Street
3930 Mr. & Mrs. Wm. W. Bell & dr.
3930 Miss Lillian Bell
3930 Gen. & Mrs. W. H. Lessig
3932 Mr. & Mrs. Samuel Gans
3936 Mr. & Mrs. Simon Steiniger
3938 Mr. & Mrs. W. S. Rothschild
3940 Mrs. J. H. Conrad

4415 Edwin W. Chandler
4417 Samuel G. Hair
4417 Miss Miriam T. Hair
4417 Mrs. E. S. Hair
4417 Mrs. Margaret McHatton
4427 Mr. & Mrs. W. W. Dudley
4429 Mr. & Mrs. E. P. Fassett
4435 Mr. and Mrs. Harry N. Anderson
4439 Mr.& Mrs. W. Edward Ritchie
4449 Mr. and Mrs. Henry Young
4449 W. K. Young
4449 Miss Young
4463 Mr. & Mrs. J. W. Morse & dr.
4463 Mr. and Mrs. Arthur W. Jerrems.
4465 Mr. & Mrs. W. W. Young
4465 Thomas Clements
4467 Dr. & Mrs. H. G. Wildman
  Receiving day Thursday
4471 Mr. & Mrs. C. F. Love
4507 Dr.& Mrs. E. DeWitt Converse
4507 Mr. & Mrs. G. A. Masters
4509 A. B. Pease
4521 Mr. & Mrs. A. H. Cadwallader.
4523 Mr. & Mrs. Chas. W. Blackman
4533 Mrs. Margaret Herrick
4533 Dr. Martha J. Creighton
4535 Mr. & Mrs. Samuel M. Parker & dr.
4539 Mr. & Mrs. E. Solomon & dr.
  Receiving day 1st & 3d Fridays
4541 Mr. & Mrs. W. B. Biddle
4547 Mr. & Mrs. J. M. McGill
4555 Mrs. S. G. Thayer
  Receiving day Tuesday
4555 Clarence H. Thayer
4557 Mr. & Mrs. H. A. Callan
4559 Mr. & Mrs. M. J. Friedman
4561 Bernard Fowler & drs.
4563 Mr. & Mrs. D. W. Buchanan
4567 Mr. & Mrs. T. P. Bailey
4569 Mrs. Henry B. Rogers
4569 LeRoy T. Vernon
4571 Dr. & Mrs. Edward F. Wells
4571 Michael B. Wells
4575 Mr. & Mrs. Albert W. Sullivan
  Receiving day Thursday
4577 Dr. Kate E. MacRae
4577 Mr. & Mrs. Norman MacRae
4577 Miss Bessie F. Platt
4619 Mrs. H. W. Harmon
4619 Hubert P. Harmon
4619 John H. Harmon
4619 Donald M. Carter
4621 Mr. & Mrs. Chas. L. McMahan

12

3940 Charles H. Conrad
3946 Mr. & Mrs. Cyrus A. Barker
3978 Mrs. Henry Provost
3978 Mr. & Mrs. J. W. Maxwell
3980 Mr. & Mrs. E. E. Maxwell
3982 Mr. & Mrs. Calvin S. Smith
3984 Mr.&Mrs.W.A.Merigold & drs.
4000 Mr. & Mrs. Marion F. Barger
4000 Mr. and Mrs. George I. Reed
4000 Mr. & Mrs. R. D. Buckingham
4002 Mr. and Mrs. Orlando C. Gay
4002 Mr. & Mrs. Wm. E. Butterfield
4002 Mr. & Mrs. James A. Davis
4008 Mr. & Mrs. Harvey S. Hayden
4016 Mrs. George Trumbull
4016 Mr. & Mrs. J. P. Underwood
4026 Mr. & Mrs. J. H. Trumbull
4028 Mr. & Mrs. Godfrey H. Ball
4030 Mr. & Mrs. John Clay jr.
  Receive Friday
4056 Mr. & Mrs. John McAnrow & drs.
4056 John A. McAnrow
4058 Mr. & Mrs. W. J. Lavery
  Receiving day Tuesday
4060 Mr. and Mrs. Herman Frank
4066 Mr. & Mrs. A. Silberman
4068 Mr. & Mrs. James P. Barrett
4072 Mr. & Mrs. Thos. C. Goodman
4074 Mr. & Mrs. H. Lamberton
4076 Mr. and Mrs. Harry H. Lobdell
4078 Mr. and Mrs. B. F. M. Lutz
4100 Mrs. Peter Wallace
4108 Mrs. S. J. Wardner
4120 Mr. & Mrs. J. C. Ellis
4120 William Ellis
4120 Dr. Kate W. Ellis
4130 Mr. & Mrs. Wm. H. Reed
4130 Chester B. Reed
4134 Mr.& Mrs. S. J.Rosenthal &drs.
4136 Mrs. Alice B. Smith
4142 Mr. & Mrs. H. E. Dick
4150 Mr. & Mrs. F. W. Bull
4150 W. M. Cook
4156 Mr. & Mrs. A. J. Wampler
4160 Mr. & Mrs. C. H. Brittan
4162 Mr. & Mrs. L. M. French
4164 Mrs. F. R. Stevens & dr.
4304 Dr. S. C. Plummer
4306 Mr. & Mrs. Frank H. Brown
4328 Mr. & Mrs. F. B. VanNostrand
4330 Mr. & Mrs. G. W. Hancock
  Receiving day Tuesday
4400 Mr. & Mrs. W. R. Omohundro
4400 Louis M. Hopkins

4625 Miss Harriet E. Thomas
4625 Mr. & Mrs. James Linden
4627 Mr. & Mrs. G. P. Titus
       Receiving day Thursday
4627 Mrs. M. J. Miller & dr.
4627 Mrs. M. W. Brooks
4643 Dr.& Mrs.Almon Brooks & drs.
       Receiving day Monday
4643 Mrs. Oliver Brooks
4665 Dr. & Mrs. S. Leavitt
4665 Dr. & Mrs. C. F. Leavitt
4669 Dr. & Mrs. J. C. Hoag
4723 Mrs. Nelson Shaul & dr.
4727 Mr. & Mrs. Edward Rosing
4727 Mr. & Mrs. John C. Compton
4729 Mr. & Mrs. Austin B. Carpen-
       ter
4729 Mr. & Mrs. John H. Whiting
4729 Mr. & Mrs. H. Butler
4735 Mr. & Mrs. H. C. Fisher
4737 Mr. & Mrs. J. J. Parker & dr.
4737 J. J. Parker jr.
4747 Mr. & Mrs. Charles P. Packer
4747 Mrs. Julia M. Mack
4801 Mrs. Mary H. Ford
4805 Mr. & Mrs. J. G. Parkinson
4811 Warren G. Purdy & drs.
4811 Miss Sarah E. Purdy
4811 W. Fred Purdy
4815 Mr. & Mrs. O. W. Norton
4815 Ralph H. Norton
4815 Miss Lane
4815 Miss Norton
4815 Elliott S. Norton
4827 Mrs. E. Remmer & dr.
4827 C. G. Jones
4827 Alan C. McIlvaine
4827 James S. Merrill
4827 J. H. Jamar
4827 Paul Willis
4833 Mr.& Mrs. Howard V. Shaw
4835 Mr. & Mrs. Chas. T. Atkinson
4853 Mr. & Mrs. B. R. Wells
4853 Miss Lois Wells
4861 Mr. & Mrs. C. W. Clingman
4907 Mr. & Mrs. E. C. Long & dr.
4919 J. E. L. Frasher
4919 Mr. & Mrs. Wm. R. Gwinn
4923 Mr. & Mrs. Geo. W. Little
4923 Edward F. Little
4939 Mr. & Mrs. Wm. Irvine
4939 Mr. & Mrs. D. S. Wagner
4945 Mr.& Mrs. F.W. Norwood & dr.
4945 Mrs. Vina N. Jones
4965 Mr. & Mrs. Jas. L. VanUxem

4406 Mr. & Mrs. Walter G. Twitty
       & dr.
4412 Mr. & Mrs. S. P. Douthart
       Receiving day Tuesday
4424 F. W. Douglas
4426 Dr. & Mrs. Henry F. Lewis
4432 Mrs. T. S. Wright & dr.
4432 Mr. & Mrs. W. H. Merritt
4434 Mr. & Mrs. A. J. Toolen
       Receiving day Wednesday
4434 Fred C. Toolen
4504 Mrs. A. Otis & dr.
4508 Mr. & Mrs. T. G. Otis & dr.
4508 Irving Otis
4514 Mrs. A. Kleiminger & drs.
4514 Frank Kleiminger
4514 Mr. & Mrs. M. E. Kleiminger
4516 Mr. & Mrs. A. B. Farwell
4520 Mr. & Mrs. James N. Steele &
       drs.
4524 Rev. & Mrs. Henry G.Jackson
4528 Mr. & Mrs. F. W. Mehlhop
4528 Mr. & Mrs. George H. Bliss
4530 Mr. & Mrs. F. H. Foote
4532 Mr. & Mrs. Thomas W. Moore-
       head
4534 Mr. & Mrs. James B. Fraley &
       dr.
4534 Gassner F. Fraley
4536 Mr. & Mrs. S. J. Sherer
4542 Dr. & Mrs. C. Gurnee Fellows
       Receiving day Thursday
4544 Mr. & Mrs. I. V. Mettler
       Receiving day Tuesday
4544 Dr. L. Harrison Mettler
4544 Frederick S. Fales
4546 Mr. & Mrs. Luther C. Marley
4548 Mrs. A. L. Brandt
4548 Mr. & Mrs. Henry E. Lowe &
       dr.
4550 Mr. & Mrs. J. H. Kaufman
4552 Mr. & Mrs. John D. Sherman
4554 Mr. & Mrs. George C. Corning
4556 Mr. & Mrs. A. R. Vermilyea
4558 Mr. & Mrs. R. H. Field
4558 J. B. Rose
4558 G. W. Brandt
4608 Mrs. Hester B. Saxton
4614 Mr.&Mrs.Henry Martyn Bacon
4634 Mr. & Mrs. Penoyer L. Sher-
       man
4634 Samuel S. Sherman
4634 Roger Sherman
4736 Mr. & Mrs. Wm. E. Spencer
       & dr.
4736 Edward A. Packard

4969 Mr. & Mrs. John J. Silberhorn
  Receiving day Thursday
5025 Mr. & Mrs. W. H. H. Peirce & drs.
5027 Mr. & Mrs. C. N. Holmes
5029 Mr. & Mrs. George G. Standart & dr.
5031 Mr. & Mrs. J. W. Hibbard
5031 Miss Helen Jessamine
5031 Charles A. Jessamine
5033 Mr. & Mrs. Edmund H. Jones
5037 Mr. & Mrs. I. N. Neeld
5037 James T. Edwards
5039 Mr. & Mrs. Frank Douglas
5039 Mr. & Mrs. A. J. Smith
5067 Mrs. Edward F. Carry
5069 Mr. & Mrs. J. R. Hoagland

5000 Mrs. E. H. McDermitt
5000 Miss Jane H. McDermitt
5000 W. Starr Whiton

4740 Mr. & Mrs. Joseph W. Hiner
4740 Mr. & Mrs. Eldon J. Cassoday
4742 Mr. & Mrs. J. Morris Gwinn & dr.
4750 Mrs. Mary H. Hull
4756 Mr. & Mrs. J. T. Robison
4758 Mr. & Mrs. E. H. Reed
4762 Mr. & Mrs. Geo. M. Hord & dr.
4800 Mr. & Mrs. J. E. Davis
4800 Mrs. Fannie S. Rowe
4804 Mrs. Julia A. Fales
4804 Mr. & Mrs. E. R. Hibbard
  Receiving day Wednesday
4812 Mr. & Mrs. S. H. Wright
4818 Mr. & Mrs. Julius Steele
4822 W. H. Drake & drs.
4822 Charles F. Drake
4822 George H. Drake
4824 Mr.&Mrs.Tappen Halsey& dr.
4824 Mrs. W. H. King & dr.
4926 Rev. & Mrs. David W. Howard

LAKE PARK AVENUE.

2934 Dr. & Mrs. G. S. Thomas
2934 Dr. Mary W. Thomas
2940 Mr. & Mrs. Charles Kinsman
2968 Mr. & Mrs. O. S. Lyford
2968 Miss Laura A. Thyng
3000 J. S. Turner & drs.
3000 Lloyd C. Turner
3000 E. K. Grant
3002 Mr. & Mrs. Geo. G. Felton
3008 Mr. & Mrs. A. W. Fellows & dr.
3010 Mrs. F. W. S. Brawley
3010 Mr. & Mrs. P. Fred Harting
3024 Mr. & Mrs. J. R. Kester
3026 Mr. & Mrs.August M. Schilling
3028 Mrs. C. D. Otis
3028 Henry B. Otis
3030 Mrs. Wm. Dubois
3032 Mr. & Mrs. J. C. Kelley & drs.
3036 Mr. & Mrs. Joseph Ruff & dr.
3036 Joseph B. Ruff
3042 Mr. & Mrs. Gilbert Simonds
3136 Mrs. J. V. D. Wright
3136 F. K. Dunn
3138 Dr. & Mrs. Gilbert White
  Receiving day Tuesday
3142 Arthur T. Timewell & drs.
3142 Mr. & Mrs. ArthurW.Timewell
  Receiving day Tuesday
3142 Mr. & Mrs. Philip E. Durst
  Receiving day Tuesday
3146 Mrs. J. O'Brien

3146 Mrs. M. W. Ketcham
  Receiving day Friday
3150 Mr. & Mrs. Alfred Ennis & drs.
  Receiving day Wednesday
3154 Mr. & Mrs. F. G. Whiting
3160 Mr. & Mrs. J. M. Martin
3162 Mrs. Ellen Quinlan
3162 Mr. & Mrs. Louis F. Wickman
3166 Mr. & Mrs. Lyman B. Glover & dr.
3200 Mr. & Mrs. C. A. Beck
3200 Burt A. Beck
3210 Dr. & Mrs. Franklin H. Martin
3212 Mr. & Mrs. John D. Gates
3216 Mr.& Mrs.J.Frederick Wallach
3220 Dr. & Mrs. Thos. L. Gilmer
3222 Mrs. Geo. B. Carpenter
3222 Miss Marian Carpenter
  Receive 2d Thursday
3222 Mr. & Mrs. L. K. Cushing
3224 Mr. & Mrs. C. B. Evans
3228 Mr. & Mrs. Robert B. Miller
3230 Mr. & Mrs. John C. Cantner
3232 Mr. & Mrs.J.W. D. Kelley & dr.
3232 W. D. Kelley
3234 Mr. & Mrs. John D. Tobey
3242 Mr. & Mrs. Chas. R. Murray
3242 Miss Gertrude Eldredge
3244 Mr. & Mrs. J. C. Pennoyer
3246 Mr. & Mrs. Julius Schnering
3246 Miss Julia Curtis
3256 Dr. & Mrs. Joseph Zeisler
3266 Mr. & Mrs. C. P. Dewey

LANGLEY AVENUE.

3717 Mr. & Mrs. C. L. Miller
3725 Mr. & Mrs. D. Levi
3727 Mrs. David Robinson & drs.
3743 Mr. & Mrs. Geo. Green
3743 Miss Ruth M. Hallock
3745 Mr. & Mrs. Albert Felsenthal
3803 Mr. & Mrs. John E. Hall & dr.
3803 Mr. & Mrs. Ralph H. Thatcher
3805 Mrs. W. T. Burgess
3809 Mr.&Mrs. Henry C. Noyes&dr.
3811 Mr. & Mrs. Isaac Degen & dr.
3815 Mr. & Mrs. Raymond Gregg
3821 Mr. & Mrs. Dillon B. Hutchinson
3821 Miss Emily S. Hutchinson
3821 Mrs. E. E. Sprague
3829 Mr. & Mrs. R. Metcalf
3843 Mr. & Mrs. Ed. T. Lloyd & dr.
3921 Mr. & Mrs. B. R. Nickerson
3939 Rev.& Mrs. Jenkin Lloyd Jones
         & dr.
3639 Richard Lloyd Jones
3943 Dr. Robert Dodds
3943 Dr. Jessie B. Dodds
3943 Mr. &Mrs. Harry Benedict
4139 Mr. & Mrs. A. J. Vaughan
4139 C. L. Boon
4153 Mr. & Mrs. F. B. Lawson
4157 Mr. & Mrs. A. Pardridge
4215 Mr. & Mrs. Chas. E. Gregory
4223 Mrs. Amy B. Sheldon & dr.
         Receiving day Thursday
4313 Mrs. Charlotte Trude
4313 Dr. Mark W. Trude
4315 Mr. & Mrs. C. S. Allen
4325 Mrs. Catherine Keeler & dr.
4325 Harry Keeler
4333 George W. Becker
4333 Mrs. M. A. Becker
4333 Mrs. Kate C. Buddendorff
4335 Mr.&Mrs.Jacob Richman&drs.
4721 Mr. & Mrs. Maxwell M. Jones
4729 Mr. & Mrs. J. P. Ferre
4729 Dr. & Mrs. Albert C. Brown
4759 Mr. & Mrs. A. W. Kitchin
4805 Dr. & Mrs. F. C. Hageman
4815 Mr. & Mrs. Thomas Laughlin
4815 Mr. & Mrs. Charles B. Thompson
4815 William A. Thompson
4831 Mr. & Mrs. B. C. Payne
4835 Mr. & Mrs. A. E. Frost
4835 Mrs. S. E. Hand
4835 Oliver H. Hand

3708 Mr. & Mrs. Charles B. Simons
3716 Mr. & Mrs. Otis P. Swift
3716 Harry A. Swift
3722 Dr. & Mrs. James H. Allen
3730 Mrs. M. Livingston & dr.
3730 Samuel Livingston
3730 Emanuel Livingston
3730 Milton Livingston
3730 G. Livingston
3732 Mr. & Mrs. A. Moses
3736 Mrs. John Wade & dr.
3738 Mrs. E. M. Bourne & drs.
3748 Dr. & Mrs. Edgar M. Reading
3750 Mrs. Edgar Reading
3750 Miss H. E. Coolidge
3810 Mr. & Mrs. Walter H. Lum
3810 Mrs. Mary H. Lum
3822 Dr. & Mrs. A. E. Matteson
3822 Dr. Murray G. Matteson
3824 Mrs. E. S. Shardiche
3834 Mr. & Mrs. P. F. Wolff
3840 Charles E. Starr
3840 Mrs. Mary Starr & dr.
3842 Mrs. J. L. Hewitt
3842 Mr. & Mrs. Frank L. Miner
3844 Mrs. P. R. Chandler
3848 Mr. & Mrs. Samuel T. Alexander
3848 Walter W. Alexander
3910 Frederick W. Hill
3910 Mrs. James M. Hill & drs.
3964 Miss Ellen A. Martin
3966 Mr. & Mrs. G. E. Rood & dr.
4224 Mr. & Mrs. Lyman M. Paine
4314 Mr. & Mrs. Aug. Ruffner
4316 Mr. & Mrs. D. B. Woodbury
4328 John M. Stahl
4414 Mr. & Mrs. M. Foster & drs.
4416 Mr. & Mrs. S. Wolfe
4418 Mr. & Mrs. E. V. Wendell
4420 Mr. & Mrs. Peter B. White
4450 Mr. & Mrs. Moses Cohn
4640 Mr. & Mrs. Charles T. McKenney
4714 Mr. & Mrs. A. E. D'Ancona
4720 Mr. & Mrs. John M. Dodd
4726 Mrs. R. Watts
4726 George C. Watts
4728 Mr. & Mrs. E. C. Murphy
4734 Mr.&Mrs. Horace N. Saunders
4736 Mr. & Mrs. A. H. Lund
4740 Mr. & Mrs. H. R. Ford
4740 Mrs. Stewart D. Howe
4752 Mr. & Mrs. A. H. Hart & dr.

4849 Mr. & Mrs. Geo. W. Varney
6331 Mr. & Mrs. Arthur W. O'Neill

4834 Mr. & Mrs. L. Connart & dr.
4840 Mrs. S. J. Wiggins
4840 Mrs. A. W. Fitch
4842 Mr. & Mrs. J. Hafner
6030 Dr. & Mrs. C. H. Beard
6040 Mr.& Mrs.Geo.W.McKee & dr.
6040 D. Clay McKee

4754 Mr. & Mrs. E. C. Powell
        Receiving day Tuesday
4808 Mr. & Mrs. Henry Bonn & dr.
        Receiving day Friday
4820 Dr. & Mrs. John A.McGaughey
4822 Mr. & Mrs. A. L. Weil
4826 Mr. & Mrs. Israel Altman
4830 Mr. & Mrs. T. C. Mosely & dr.
4830 Geo. H. Mosely
4830 Mrs. Charles B. Bacon

LEXINGTON AVENUE.

5127 Mr. & Mrs. M. W. Nichols
5127 Miss Christine Hubbard.
5137 Mr. & Mrs. W. B. Lewis
5139 Mr.& Mrs.William B. Allbright
5217 Mr. & Mrs. A. Stamford White
5247 Jacob B. Smith jr.
5247 Lon K. Smith
5247 Miss Emma G. Smith
5247 Miss Lizzie M. Smith
5307 Mr. & Mrs. Geo. P. Barton
5471 Mr. & Mrs. H. R. Phillips
5479 Dr. & Mrs. Julius Stieglitz
5535 Mr. & Mrs. Geo. B. Foster
        Receiving day Thursday
5551 Rev. & Mrs. John R. Effinger
5551 H. Gerard Effinger
5607 Rev. & Mrs. J. L. Jackson
5629 Mr. & Mrs.Wm. D. McClintock
5635 Rev. & Mrs. N. I. Rubinkam
5743 Mr. & Mrs. Geo. E. Vincent
5747 Mr. & Mrs. J. Lawrence Laughlin
5757 Mr. & Mrs. W. G. Hale
        Receiving day Thursday
6025 Mr. & Mrs. Arthur W. Masters
6031 Mr. & Mrs. Byron E. Veatch
6039 Mr. & Mrs. Alex. Hillock
6151 Charles E. Patrick
6153 Mr. & Mrs.Walter E. Hoag
6221 Mr. & Mrs. Wm. F. Hobbs
6317 Mr. & Mrs. James Wadsworth
        & dr.
6317 Mrs. Caroline Bowman & dr.
6317 Miss Phoebe I. Fort
6335 Mr. & Mrs. A. R. Warner
6361 Mr. & Mrs. Wm. B. Hennersheets
6401 Mr. & Mrs. R. E. Farnham

5130 Mr. & Mrs. E. E. Chandler
5142 Mr. & Mrs. J. C. Robinson
5212 Mr. & Mrs. Pliny F.Munger
5222 Jacob P. Smith
5228 Mr. & Mrs. Edward S. Hunter
5244 Mr. & Mrs. J. A. Edwards
5300 Mr. & Mrs. D. F. Burke
5300 William Buckley
5316 Mr. & Mrs. Granville M. Holt
5326 Mr. & Mrs. James Casey
5428 Mr. & Mrs. Butler Lowry
5430 Mr. & Mrs. John Hosbury &
        dr.
5430 Mr. & Mrs. Max Young & dr.
5430 Mr. & Mrs. S. A. Park
5430 Mr. & Mrs. Wm. G. Stevens
6138 Rev. & Mrs. Frank S. VanEps
6156 Henry L. Barnet
6156 Mr. & Mrs. Henry L. Barnet jr.
6246 Mrs. M. J. Whitney & dr.
6354 Mr. & Mrs. Wm. H. Leonard
        & drs.
6422 Mr. & Mrs. J. M. Coburn
6422 Mrs. Martha S. Coman
6444 Mr. & Mrs. Henry S. Jaffray
6444 Frederick A. Burton
6446 Mr. & Mrs. M. A. Miner
6454 Mr. & Mr. Thos. H. Mitchell
6506 Mr. & Mrs. Charles J. Bour
6510 Mr.& Mrs.Geo.J.M. Porter&dr.
6520 Mr. & Mrs. Locke Perfitt
6530 Mr. & Mrs. Melville J. Wendell
        & dr.
6600 Mr. & Mrs. George S. English

6421 Mr. & Mrs. Ernest J. Spierling
6527 Mr. & Mrs. Howard L. Smith

LOWE AVENUE.

7703 Mr. & Mrs. Charles E. Harding
    Receiving day Wednesday
7721 William H. Matthews
7737 Mr. & Mrs. S. M. Weatherly
7737 Mr. & Mrs. C. A. Jay
7741 Charles H. Palmer
7745 Mr. & Mrs. J. F. Earl
7745 Fred C. Earl
7745 Mr. & Mrs. C. W. Challis
7757 Mr. & Mrs. J. L. Francis
7801 Mr. & Mrs. Charles Leyen-
    berger & dr.
7819 Mr. & Mrs. L. G. Gerrish & dr.
7819 Mrs. M. C. Gleason

6714 Mr. & Mrs. O. C. Harrower
6736 Mrs. Abbie F. Heywood
6746 Mr. & Mrs. Stephen Tucke
6752 Mr. & Mrs. O. R. Thompson
6800 Mr. & Mrs. Geo. Thompson
6800 Mr. & Mrs. Garret V. Weart
6814 Mr. & Mrs. Alfred Grossmith
7640 Mr. & Mrs. Joshua A. Stevens
7646 Mr. & Mrs. J. M. Bixby
7738 Samuel Penepacker
7748 Dr. & Mrs. G. H. Carder
    Receiving day Wednesday
7748 Mrs. M. J. Roberts
7754 Mr. & Mrs. C. E. Ferreira
7810 Mr. & Mrs. Chas. W. Smith & dr.
7812 Mr. & Mrs. J. B. Herron

MADISON AVENUE.

4759 Mr. & Mrs. Thomas Smith
    Receiving day Thursday
4759 C. J. Mauran
4759 Charles S. Mauran
4801 Mr. & Mrs. Edward J. Goit
4805 Mr. & Mrs. Benjamin C. Allin
4807 Mr. & Mrs. Leon C. Welch
4807 Albert G. Welch
4809 Judge & Mrs. Walter Olds
4809 Lee M. Olds
4813 Mr. & Mrs. Ralph T. Hoagland
4819 Mrs. H. M. Wright & dr.
4821 Mr. & Mrs. J. A. D. Vickers
4827 Dr. & Mrs. L. Blake Baldwin
4831 Mr. & Mrs. Edward Woodruff
4833 Mr. & Mrs. John Norcott
4835 Mr. & Mrs. Wm. A. Tilden
4839 Mr. & Mrs. C. H. Deethmann
4845 Mr. & Mrs. G. Hardie & dr.
4849 Mr. & Mrs. Edward J. Blossom
4857 Edwin C. Day
4859 Mr. & Mrs. R. R. Buchanan
4859 Mr. & Mrs. I. Lawrence Spen-
    cer
4859 Mr. & Mrs. Frank I. Furber
4901 Mr. & Mrs. M. J. Dunne & drs.
    Receiving day Wednesday
4913 Mr. & Mrs. William A. Amory
    & dr.
4919 Mr. & Mrs. Horatio L. Wait
4919 Henry H. Wait
4921 Mr. & Mrs. F. M. Atwood
4927 Mr. & Mrs. F. I. Moulton
4937 Mr. & Mrs. Rodney B. Swift
4937 W. C. Swift

4710 Dr. & Mrs. J. G. Reid
4712 N. Sherwood
4718 Mr. & Mrs. Jerome G. Steever
4740 Mrs. W. P. Halliday & dr.
4740 Dr. & Mrs. Elbert Wing
4740 G. A. Edward Kohler
4740 Frank W. Kohler
4740 Mr. & Mrs. J. L. Stack
4740 Mr. & Mrs. Henry L. Shute
4744 Mr. & Mrs. W. O. Swett
4744 Miss Mary Chase Swett
4744 Mr. & Mrs. F. J. V. Skiff
4746 Mr. & Mrs. John C. Neemes &
    dr.
4802 Mrs. Marie A. Kennicott
4802 Mrs. M. K. Reid
4830 Judge & Mrs. Lorin C. Collins.
    jr. *Receiving day Tuesday*
4830 Rev. Lorin C. Collins
4830 Lorin C. Collins, 3d
4832 Mr. & Mrs. W. G. Robbins
4832 Mr. & Mrs. F. R. Robbins
4858 Dr. & Mrs. Archibald Church
4956 Mr. & Mrs. M. C. Markham
4958 Mr. & Mrs. Wiley B. Ecton &
    dr.
5000 Mr. & Mrs. A. P. Callahan
5100 Mrs. William G. Lewis
    Receiving day Thursday
5100 Cornelius H. Shaver
5110 Mr. & Mrs. Chas. B. Keeler
5112 Mr. & Mrs. Chapin A. Day
5112 Mrs. M. J. Chamberlain
5114 Mr. & Mrs. Williston Fish
5118 Mr. & Mrs. Wm. A. Young

5003 Mr. & Mrs. Thos. S. Cruttenden
5003 Edmund S. Cruttenden
5003 Walter W. Cruttenden
5015 Mr. & Mrs. W. W. King
5029 Mr. & Mrs. Henry H. Courtright
5031 Mr. & Mrs. Frank H. Clark &
 drs.
5033 Mr. & Mrs. C.C. Greenley & drs.
5035 Mr. & Mrs. Wm. M. Derby jr.
 Receive Friday
5037 Col. David Quigg
5037 Miss Ethel Quigg
5041 Prof. & Mrs. T. C. Chamberlin
5047 Mr. & Mrs. A. M. Warrell
5119 Mr. & Mrs. Garson Myers
5123 Mr. & Mrs. E. Raymond Bliss
5139 Mrs. Mary E. Slocum
5139 J. E. Slocum
5139 Mrs. Anna L. Stouffer
5201 Mr. & Mrs. Geo. T. Nosler
5203 Mr. & Mrs. Hale L. Flint
5207 Mr. & Mrs. Ludlow S. Sherwood
5209 Mr. & Mrs. John A. Murphy
5217 Mrs. L. E. Loveday
5217 Mrs. A. R. Cockrill
5223 Mr. & Mrs. G. E. Harris
 Receive Tuesday
5241 Mr. & Mrs. Samuel Delamater
 & dr. *Receiving day Friday*
5311 Dr. & Mrs. Willis O. Nance
5325 Mr. & Mrs. Harry M. Boon
5327 Rev. & Mrs. Stephen D. Peet
 & drs.
5327 Charles E. Peet
5331 Frank A. Vanderlip
5337 Dr. & Mrs. Frank C. Hoyt
5337 Mr. & Mrs. Wm. F. Cameron
5337 George Lockhart
5337 Miss Margaret H. Lockhart
 Receiving day Thursday
5339 Mr. & Mrs. T. F. Andrews
5339 Emory C. Andrews
5401 Dr. & Mrs. C. B. Rockwell
5403 Mr. & Mrs. Elwood H. Tolman
5405 Peter J. Cairns
5405 Charles A. Cairns
5405 Miss Mary C. Cairns
5405 Miss Jennie Cairns
5413 Mr. & Mrs. James L. Ford
5429 Dr. & Mrs. Edwin H. Smith
5437 Miss Adele Ross
5495 Dr. & Mrs. H. N. Day
5517 Mr. & Mrs. A. L. Goldsmith
5517 Mr. & Mrs. F. P. Wheeler

5126 Dr. E. W. Hunter
5126 John O. K. Smith
5140 Mr. & Mrs. Wm. H. Alsip
5142 Mr. & Mrs. J. S. Hair
5206 Mr. & Mrs. Robert Stuart
5316 Mr. & Mrs. C. P. VanInwegen
5324 Mr. & Mrs. J. W. McKinnon
5328 Mr. & Mrs. George F. Wessels
5328 Mr. & Mrs. Frederick J. Wessels
5330 Mr. & Mrs. S. S. Page
5330 Cecil Page
5334 Mr. & Mrs. Arthur C. Bigelow
5336 Mr. & Mrs. H. C. Speer & dr.
5336 William W. Speer
5338 Mrs. Chas. D. Ballard & dr.
 Receiving day Thursday
5340 Mr. & Mrs. T. C. Ballard
5342 Mr. & Mrs. C. A. Johnson
5344 Mr. & Mrs. Thomas McCall
5406 Mr. & Mrs. Frank L. Davis
5410 Mr. & Mrs. Robert Gordon
5410 George A. Macdonald
5412 Mr. & Mrs. D. E. Evans
5414 Mr. & Mrs. E. L. Jayne
5414 Sam. R. Jenkins
5428 Mr. & Mrs. T. A. Lemmon
5428 Mrs. M. A. Ball
5428 Chandler F. Lemmon
5528 M. L. Willard
5528 G. G. Willard
5528 Mrs. P. H. Willard
5528 Mr. & Mrs. W. A. Pope
5536 Prof. & Mrs. George H. Mead
5542 Mr. & Mrs. Samuel A. Hyers
5542 Mr. & Mrs. R. Augustus Hevenor
5546 Mr. & Mrs. Charles E. Field
5604 Dr. & Mrs. E. V. MacDonald
5610 Mr. & Mrs. Thomas A. Banning
5610 Miss M. V. Gilchrist
5614 Mr. & Mrs. N A. Partridge
5614 Mrs. M. Hammond
5622 Horace P. Taylor
5642 Mrs. W. A. Olmsted & drs.
5704 Mr. & Mrs. C. G. Sholes & dr.
5704 Mr. & Mrs. W. P. Campbell
5704 Maj. & Mrs. Tenodor Ten
 Eyck & dr.
5708 Mr. & Mrs. M. D. Wilber
5708 Mrs. Mary E. Drake
5710 Mr. & Mrs. J. D. Wilber
5714 Mr. & Mrs. John C. Parsons
5720 Dr. & Mrs. L. D. Gorgas
5720 Mrs. E. F. Stewart & dr.
5722 William G. Witherell
5726 Mrs. J. O. Osborne & dr.

5517 Miss Anna E. Trimingham
5533 Mr. & Mrs. H. R. Lloyd
5535 Mr. & Mrs. Herbert E. Slaught
5541 Mr. & Mrs. Edmund A. Allen
5543 Mr. & Mrs. John C. Ware
5545 Mr. & Mrs. Chas. L. Nelson
5603 Mr. & Mrs. Robt. Foresman
5605 Mr. & Mrs. Leslie Lewis & drs.
5607 Mr. & Mrs. F. G. Davis
5617 Mr. & Mrs. T. W. Gilson
5619 Ferd Schumacher
5619 Mr. & Mrs. Franz Adolph Schumacher
      Receiving day Tuesday
5619 Miss Emma Schumacher
5635 Mr. & Mrs. C. L. Norton
5643 Mr. & Mrs. S. T. Mather
5711 Mr. & Mrs. L. L. Boyle
5717 Glenn M. Hobbs
5717 Samuel W. Stratton
5727 Dr. & Mrs. Chas. P. Small
5729 Mr. & Mrs. E. R. Woodle
5735 Prof. George W. Northrup
5735 Mr. & Mrs. Geo.W.Northrup jr.
5737 Dr. C. J. Deitz
5737 Miss Emma G. Stewart
5743 Miss M. M. Parkhurst
5743 Nelson D. Parkhurst
5745 Mr. & Mrs. J. B. McDonald
5747 Mr. & Mrs. James Peabody & drs.
5747 Earl W. Peabody
5751 Mr. & Mrs. George C. Bates
      Receiving day Thursday
5751 Fred G. Bates
5753 Mr. & Mrs. Alexander Stewart
5753 Charles C. Stewart
5753 Miss Elizabeth Ferguson

5726 Mrs. Elizabeth Ahern
5746 Prof. & Mrs. C. D. Buck
5748 Dr. & Mrs. C. F. Millspaugh
      Receive Thursday
5750 Mr. & Mrs. Justin J. Wetmore
5752 E. Hoyt & dr.
5752 Mrs. C. J. Ferguson
5752 A. W. Stratton
5756 Mr. & Mrs. John C. Hessler
6110 Dr. & Mrs. A. T. Buchanan
6120 Mr. & Mrs. Ralph F. Bogle
6126 Dr. & Mrs. William M. Cate
      Receiving day Thursday
6340 Mr. & Mrs. Edwin J. Wilber jr.
5759 Mr. & Mrs. Joseph Twyman & dr.
5761 Mr. & Mrs. Edmund J. James
      Receiving day Saturday
5761 Dr. George E. Shambaugh
5763 Felix Lengfeld
5815 Mr. & Mrs. L. M. Platt
5821 Mr. & Mrs. Walter Carroll Anderson
5823 Mr. & Mrs. Wm. B. Owen
5831 Mr. & Mrs. Charles Hughes
5833 Mr. & Mrs. Thomas Hancock
      Receiving day Tuesday
5841 Mr. & Mrs. Robert Kirkland
5845 Mr. & Mrs. H. S. Hawley
6043 Mr. & Mrs. Frank Vickers
6043 Charles Vickers
6047 Mr. & Mrs. Jul deHorvath
6049 Dr. & Mrs. Louis M. Turbin & dr.   *Receive Thursday*
6051 Mr. & Mrs. Isaac S. Dement
6055 Mr. & Mrs. George Wright
6107 Dr. Melancthon Stout
6305 Dr. Hugh A. Cuthbertson

MADISON PARK.

1 Mr. & Mrs. O. S. Favor & dr.
5 Mr. & Mrs. C. B. Wisner
7 Mr. & Mrs. Howard O. Sprogle
17 Mr. & Mrs. R. Bell & dr.
29 Mr. & Mrs. Roderick Nevers
31 Mr. & Mrs. J. M. Maris
41 Mr. & Mrs. George K. Kinney
      Receiving day Friday
41 Miss Anna G. Lippincott
41 Miss Harriet B. Denmead
41 Miss Blanche Denmead
53 Mr. & Mrs. Anthony F. Merrill
      & dr. *Receiving day Tuesday*
53 Miss Ella Smith

2 Mr. & Mrs. Fred C. Swett
16 Mr. & Mrs. Rufus P. Jennings
22 Mr. & Mrs. G. W. DeSmet
24 Mr. & Mrs. N. B. Cook
24 Mrs. L. B. Turrill
24 John F. Turrill
28 Mr. & Mrs. W. H. Henkle
34 Mr. & Mrs. Wm. R. Wilson
36 Mr. & Mrs. Edward M. Adams
36 E. M. Adams jr.
38 Mr. & Mrs. Howard G. Northrop
40 Mr. & Mrs. Asa F. Shiverick
44 Mr. & Mrs. Edward L. Brown
44 Miss Margaret S. Brown

55 Mr. & Mrs. Wm. L. Moyer
67 Mr. & Mrs. John H. Hartog
99 Mr. & Mrs. Walter J. Knight

———

70 Mr. & Mrs. Chas. Leonard Peirce
   & drs.
70 Edward H. Bingham

44 William C. Brown
44 Francis C. Brown
46 Mr. & Mrs. David Welling & dr.
50 Mr. & Mrs. Arthur G. Jones
52 Mr. & Mrs. John D. Hibbard
68 Mr. & Mrs. Julius R. Meyers
70 Frank Birkin
70 Ralph Sumner Peirce

MICHIGAN AVENUE.

cor. Adams street, Pullman bldg.
700 A C. J. Solomon
702 B. Calef
704 Charles A. Hanna
705 G. W. Montgomery
706 R. R. Bradley
707 E. L. Becker
708 W. S. Keith
709 D. M. Halbert
710 W. W. Main
712 A. Hyllested
713 E. E. Osgood
714 E. W. Eldridge
716 P. E. Zinkeisen
716 O. T. Zinkeisen
717 W. H. Bucher
719 J. B. Griffin
720 A. B. Pond
720 I. K. Pond
724 Morris Willner
801 F. A. Marsh
802 Preston C. Maynard
803 Fred A. Wann
806 Louis Eckstein
807 Adolph Kaufman
808 C. MacRitchie
809 Lieut.-Col. O. M. Smith
812 V. W. Burnside
815 Charles Field
820 R. E. Lidgerwood
821 H. P. Smith
822 J. Berr.
907 Alex. Euston
914 Otto Schaefer
916 G. A. Grant-Schaefer
917 H. M. Bruns
917 W. T. Chollar
919 R. C. Warde
225 E. Greble Killen
228 Mr. & Mrs. George C. Walker
228 George Keen
228 E. M. DeVol
229 Mrs. Stiles Burton
229 Mrs. Ira Holmes
229 E. Burton Holmes

229 Ira G. Holmes
229 Mrs. H. A. Sherman
230 Mr. & Mrs. William Blair
232 Dr. D. D. Richardson
232 De Del
233 Mrs. J. H. Dunham & dr.
235 Mrs. Washington Hesing
235 Douglass Hoyt
235 Mr. & Mrs. A. G. Pettibone
   Receiving day Tuesday
235 Charles Scates
235 Mrs. Susan G. Cook
235 Miss Alice G. Cook
235 E. P. Edwards
235 Henry W. Hill
235 R. P. Marks
235 Edgar Holt
235 Miss Carrie G. Adams
235 John G. Bronson
235 Mrs. Walter Q. Gresham
235 Otto Gresham
235 Mr. & Mrs. A. M. Barber
235 Mrs. H. L. Myer
235 Mrs. F. E. Perley
235 Mrs. E. H. Powers
235 Mrs. James T. Matthews
235 Peter Lapp
235 Mrs. Martha J. Boardman
241 Mrs. Jerome Beecher
252 Mr. & Mrs. Timothy B. Blackstone
258 Mrs. James McKindley
   Receives Tuesday 3 to 6 p. m.
258 Chas. M. Beall
259 Elmer E. Rogers
262 Mr. & Mrs. John B. Lyon
   Receiving day Tuesday
262 Mrs. William P. Conger
262 William C. Lyon
262 Mr. & Mrs. R. W. Hamill
265 Mr. & Mrs. H. E. Bucklen
265 Col. Cuthbert W. Laing
265 David R. Laing
265 David R. Carrier
267 Mr. & Mrs. H. L. Andrews

270 Mr. & Mrs. William B. Pettit
276 D. A. Clippinger
276 Mr. & Mrs. William J. Knight
276 Mr. & Mrs. Albert E. Ebert
276 Benj. F. Stauffer
276 Charles T. Barnes
276 Mr. & Mrs. E. R. Walsh &
    dr.
291 Mr. & Mrs. H. Milo Erkins
291 Mrs. Mildred F. Pemberton
291 Dr. & Mrs. E. M. DeSellen &
    dr.
306 Mrs. E. L. Gillette
306 Edwin F. Gillette
313 Mrs. Marcus C. Stearns
313 Mr. & Mrs. Richard I. Stearns
321 Mr. & Mrs. A. Tracy Lay & drs.

1217 Mr. & Mrs. Frederick Freiberg
1217 Mr. & Mrs. Julius Freiberg
1311 Mr. & Mrs. Herbert T. Clark
1311 Mrs. E. E. Sexton & drs.
1311 Mr. & Mrs. E. J. Hopson
1311 Mr. & Mrs. G. W. Leihy
1311 George W. Leihy jr.
1315 George H. Glover
1315 Miss F. M. Glover
1341 Isaac Lowenberg
1341 Mr. & Mrs. Carl Dernburg
1409 Mrs. M. Hanlon & dr.
1409 William J. Hanlon
1419 Mr. & Mrs. Alfred Cox
1459 John M. L. Sexton
1503 Mr. & Mrs. J. Parker Smith
1521 Mr. & Mrs. J. G. Weeks
1547 Mr. & Mrs. Charles B. Kirt-
    land
1547 Mrs. India U. Kirtland
1601 Mr. & Mrs. Augustus N. Eddy
1705 Mrs. Henry Horner
     Receives 1st and 3d Friday
1705 Mrs. D. Levy
1705 Albert Horner
1705 Isaac Horner
1705 Angel Horner
1705 Charles Horner
1705 Harry Horner
1717 Mr. & Mrs. Morris Selz
     Receive 2nd and 4th Thursdays
1717 Emanuel F. Selz
1717 Miss Theresa Kohn
1729 Mrs. M. J. Clifford & drs.
1729 Judge Richard W. Clifford
1729 James M. Clifford
1801 N. K. Fairbank & drs.
1801 Kellogg Fairbank

321 Mr. & Mrs. R. Floyd Clinch
322 W. H. King
325 Mr. & Mrs. Seth Gage
329 Mr. & Mrs. W. A. Jenkins
329 Mr. & Mrs. Arthur L. Clarke
339 Hotel Normandie
     James Brennan
     Ed C. Cooper
     Ed Davis
     H. H. Ingham
     Mr. & Mrs. L. C. Jackson
     D. L. Markle
     Mr. & Mrs. L. L. Sharpe
     Mr. & Mrs. John Y. Smith
     Mr. & Mrs. W. H. Worth
343-344 Glencoe Flats
     1 Charles H. Cougle
     4 Dr. & Mrs. A. W. Baer

1246 Mr. & Mrs. James A. Bovett
1254 Michigan Avenue Hotel
     Mr. & Mrs. J. M. Bishop
     Mr. & Mrs. E. A. Burbank
     D. L. Clinch
     Mrs. D. Greenidge
     Mrs. C. A. Kirkpatrick
     Mr. & Mrs. Geo. Mantellani
     Mr. & Mrs. L. H. Shelley
     C. J. Stack
     Edward Stone
     Miss Beatrice Tonneson
1340 Mr. & Mrs. P. J. Sexton
     Receive Wednesday afternoon
1420 Mr. & Mrs. John Ford
1426 James J. Healy
1428 Judge J. B. Bradwell
1428 Mr. & Mrs. Frank A. Helmer
1432-1434 The Baltimore
     Mrs. M. S. Bean
     Capt. & Mrs. Wm. Dollard
     Mr. & Mrs. A. E. G. Good-
     ridge
     Mr. & Mrs. Edward Good-
     ridge
1454 Rev. C. N. Murphey
1456 Mr. & Mrs. A. V. Lane
1458 Mr. & Mrs. Lewis H. Davis
1468 Mr. & Mrs. Charles F. Keeler
1474 Mrs. A. E. Goodrich
1474 Mr. & Mrs. A. W. Goodrich
1506 Mr. & Mrs. B. L. Newman
1506 Mr. & Mrs. W. H. Hosmer
1508 Mrs. Wm. J. Morden
1528 Mrs. Henry Merckle
1614 Mr. & Mrs. George H. Laflin
1614 Arthur K. Laflin

1801 Wallace Fairbank
1801 Miss Elizabeth Schmitt
1805 Alfred Cowles
1815 Mr. & Mrs. Benj. Allen
1815 Benjamin C. Allen
1819 Mr. & Mrs. Lewis L. Coburn
1819 Mrs. Olivia S. Swan
1823 Dr. & Mrs. R. Ludlam
1825 T. S. Dobbins
1825 Miss Annie Dobbins
1827 Mr. & Mrs. Charles D. See-
     berger
1837 Hotel Yorkshire
     A. B. Benard
     Mrs. M. J. Codd
     Judge & Mrs. Sam'l Ehrlich
     Mr. & Mrs. Thos. Horn ·
1839 Mr. & Mrs. Joseph Horner& dr.
1907 Mr. & Mrs. E. L. Eaton
     Receiving day Tuesday
1907 Mr. & Mrs. Geo. A. Hayes
1911 Dr. & Mrs. J. O. Ely
1911 Dr. and Mrs. E. A. Junkin
1911 Stuart B. Andrews
1913 Mrs. George W. Henry
1915 Mr. & Mrs. J. Forsyth & drs.
1915 Oliver O. Forsyth
1915 George W. Forsyth
1915 John J. Forsyth
1919 Mr. & Mrs. Edward T. Jeffery
     Receiving day Thursday
2001 The Pickwick   ·
     A Ole Owen
     B Dr. Mrs. Richard C. Fischer
     C Mrs. Wm. Bross
     D Mrs. J. A. House
        Receiving day Thursday
     D Mrs. F. E. Wilson
        Receiving day Thursday
     E Mrs. P. Floyd
     F Mrs. Elizabeth B. Beeman
        Receiving day Thursday
     F Mrs. Maud B. Lane & dr.
     F Henry W. Beauclerc
     F William A. Gaudette
     F Chas. A. Ridgley
     F George C. Ames
     F Miss Nannette Keim Bee-
       man
2007 Mr. & Mrs. CharlesH.Ferguson
     jr. *Receiving day Monday*
2007 Charles H. Ferguson
2013 Mrs. J. L. Corthell
2017 Mr. & Mrs. A.F. Seeberger &dr.
2019 John F. Wilson
2019 Mrs. J. D. Gardiner

1620 J. Rosenberg
1620 Mr. & Mrs. Maurice Rosenfeld
1634 Dr. & Mrs. J. H. Etheridge
     & dr.
1636 Dr. & Mrs. E. J. Ogden & dr.
1638 A. Booth
1638 Mr. & Mrs. Willard S. Gaylord
1704 Mr. & Mrs. Caryl Young & dr.
1704 Mr. & Mrs. Caryl B. Young
1706 Dr. & Mrs.M.H.McKillip & dr.
1710 H. J. Macfarland & dr.
1722 Mr. & Mrs. Philo A. Otis
1728 Ives L. Lake
1732 Mr. & Mrs. C. T. Boal & dr.
1806 Dr. & Mrs. J. E. Owens
     Receiving day Tuesday
1806 Miss Marie G. Owens
1810 C. H. Killough
1814 Patrick McTerney & drs.
1814 Mrs. W. W. Palmer & dr.
1826 Mr. & Mrs. Ferdinand W. Peck
1826 Ferdinand W. Peck jr.
1826 Miss Arline Peck
1838 Mr. & Mrs. Ralph Modjeski
1842 Mrs. J. H. McVicker
1902 Mr. & Mrs. James R. Owen
1906 Mrs. X. L. Otis & dr.
1912 Mr. & Mrs. Hugh T. Birch
1918 Mr. & Mrs. Edwin L. Brand
1918 Miss Belle Brand
1918 Edwin L. Brand jr.
2000 Mr. & Mrs. George Schneider
2010 Mr. & Mrs. Albert Keep
2010 Albert Keep jr.
2014 Mr. & Mrs. Geo. L. Otis & dr.
2018 Mrs. Albert J. Averell
2018 Prof. & Mrs. John C. Grant
2022 Frederick B. Tuttle
2026 Mrs. E. M. McKee
2028 Mrs. Josephine P. Alexander
2030 Mr. & Mrs. O. F. Fischer
2108 Mr.& Mrs. J.Russell Jones & dr.
2116 Mr. & Mrs. Eben Lane
2116 Miss F. G. Lane
2124 The Edinburgh
     H. C. E. Boynton
     Mrs. S. A. Boynton
     Mr. & Mrs. C. C. Chamberlain
     Mr. & Mrs. W. D. Crossman
     Mr. & Mrs. A. E. Davis
     Mr. & Mrs. Theo. O. Fraenkel
     Walter E. Gillespie
     Mr. & Mrs. Edward Goodman
     Rev. G. Heathcote Hills
     Mrs. G. M. Hills & dr.
     Reginald Hills

2023 Mr. & Mrs. Seymour Coleman
2027 Mrs. W. C. D. Grannis
2027 Uri B. Grannis
2027 Mr. & Mrs. H. L. Hollis
2103 Mr. & Mrs. Henry H. Honoré
2103 Adrian C. Honoré
2103 Lockwood Honoré
2103 N. Kingston Honoré
2119 Mrs. Irene Graham
2211 Dr. Georgia S. Ruggles
2215 Mrs. J. R. Winterbotham
2239 Dr.& Mrs. H. P. Merriman
2239 Mrs. P. A. Avery
2241 Mr. & Mrs. Thomas P. Phillips
2241 William E. Phillips
2243 Mr. & Mrs. H. Arms
2243 William A. Yager
2247 Mr. & Mrs. Charles Fargo & dr.
2247 Mrs. I. F. Andrews ·
2247 Livingston W. Fargo
2247 Miss Florence B. Fargo
2255 Mr. & Mrs. Wm. T. Baker & dr.
       Receiving day Friday
2255 Henry D. Baker
2317 Mr. & Mrs. J. A. Norris
2323 J. Firmenich & dr.
2323 George F. Firmenich.
2325 Josiah Stiles & dr.
2325 George N. Stiles
2325 Miss Emily Nichols
2327 Dr. & Mrs. E. F. Rush
       Receiving day Thursday
2327 Mrs. F. N. Pease
2333 Mr. & Mrs. W. Moseback & dr.
2335 Mr. & Mrs. A. S. Laflin
2337 Mr. & Mrs. W. H. Gleason
2339 Rev. & Mrs. Johnston Myers
2343 Mrs. Clara Mayer & dr.
2343 Jacob Mayer
2359 Mr. & Mrs. Charles H. Bogue &
       drs.
2359 Mrs. W. H. Stoddard & dr.
2409 Dr. & Mrs. James Nevins Hyde
       Receiving day Monday
2409 Charles Cheney Hyde
2409 Rt.Rev.& Mrs.Charles Edward
       Cheney *Receiving day Mon.*
2415 Mrs. J. N. Banks
2415 Mr. & Mrs. John Benham
2415 Mrs. Sidney Fairlee & dr.
2415 Sidney R. Fairlee
2417 Mrs. Jane W. Wiswell
2419 Arthur Woodcock
2419 Mr. & Mrs. F. P. Fisher
2419 Charles H. Goodykoontz
2419 Isaac H. Pedrick

2124 The Edinburgh (continued.)
       C. L. Hine
       Mr. & Mrs. Geo. H. Knebel
       Philip Kussel
       Chas. F. Miller
       Mr. & Mrs. L. C. Mowry
       Mr. & Mrs. W. F. Orcutt
       Mr. & Mrs. R. W. Petty
       Mr. & Mrs. Frank K. Reilley
       Mrs. S. Ricketts
       Mr. & Mrs. S. C. Rosenberg
       Mrs. David Runyon
       Mr. & Mrs. Chas. H. Sergel
       A. R. Sheriff
       Mr. & Mrs. Geo. B. Walker
       Mr. & Mrs. R. A. Wells
       E. Wendnagel
       Wm. Wendnagel
       Lieut. & Mrs. U. G. Wornlow
2204 Dr. Daniel Weston Rogers
2204 Dr. J. B. Devlin
2218 Mr. & Mrs. C. W. Butterfield
2242 Mr. & Mrs. Freeman F. Gross
2248 Mrs. M. A. Field
2248 John S. Field
2248 George D. Field
2250 William H. Sard
2250 Mrs. Anne Sard Simpson
2250 Howard Sard Simpson
2254 Mr. & Mrs. Clarence I. Peck
2254 Mrs. P. F. W. Peck
2428 Mr. & Mrs. Jacob Strader
2430 Mrs. William McLain & dr.
2430 Andrew J. McLain
2436 Dr. & Mrs. Frank H. Gardiner
2438 Mr. & Mrs. Thos. N. James
2440 Mr. & Mrs. J. W. Gates
2440 C. G. Gates
2446 Mr. & Mrs. Telford Burnham
2446 Mr. & Mrs. John H. Brown
2446 Mr. & Mrs. John M. Young
2446 Miss Anne Maibelle
2446 Miss Justice Maibelle
2446 Brode B. Davis
2446 Edward Ferguson
2446 John Vennema
2454 Mr. & Mrs. Charles W. ReQua
2458 Mr. & Mrs. Lucius B. Otis
2458 Mrs. Carrie O. Meacham
2504 Ernest V. Johnson
2506 Mr. & Mrs. John A. Farwell
2506 John A. Farwell jr.
2508 Mrs. A. F. Chambers
2512 Mr.& Mrs. I. Greensfelder &
       dr.
       Rec. days 1st & 3d Wednesday

2421 Mr. & Mrs. Martin Emerich
2421 Mr. & Mrs. B. Hallenstein
2429 Mr. & Mrs. G. F. Baldwin
2451 Mr. & Mrs. A. A. Spear
2451 Clarence M. Converse
2459 Dr. & Mrs. R. Ludlam jr.
2501 Mr. & Mrs. A. G. Leonard
 Receiving day Thursday
2505 The Berkshire
 4 Mr. & Mrs. D. I. Lufkin
 5 Mr. & Mrs. A. M. Adams
 8 Mr. & Mrs. W. I. Allen & dr.
 Receiving day Wednesday
 9 Mr. & Mrs. George Bass
 10 Mr. & Mrs. F. F. Ainsworth
2537 Mr. & Mrs. William A. Giles & drs.
2537 William F. Giles
2537 Mrs. Cyrus F. Hill
2541 Mr. & Mrs. Richard T. Crane
2541 Richard T. Crane jr.
2541 Mr. & Mrs. Edmund A. Russell
2559 Mr. & Mrs. Chas. R. Crane
2619 Mr. & Mrs. E. Sondheimer & drs.
 Receive 1st & 3d Wednesdays
2619 Edward A. Sondheimer
2619 Henry Sondheimer
2621 Mr. & Mrs. Geo. A. Sanderson
2623 Wilbur F. Henderson
2623 Mr.&Mrs.Wilbur S.Henderson
 & dr. *Receiving day Tuesday*
2631 Mrs. W. Scott Linn
2633 Mrs. J. A. Rothschild & drs.
 Receiving day Monday
2633 Benjamin Rothschild
2633 Leo J. Rothschild
2633 Mrs. Aaron Rosenblatt
2637 John Robson
2643 Mr. & Mrs. V. A. Watkins
 Receiving day Wednesday
2701 Mr. & Mrs. Chas. F. Babcock
2709 Mr. & Mrs. William R. Linn
2709 Mrs. M. L. Andrews
2715 Mr. & Mrs. Geo. W. Cass & dr.
 Receiving day Wednesday
2733 Col. & Mrs. J. S. Cooper
2735 Mr. & Mrs. Aaron Stern & dr.
2801 Mr. & Mrs. Jonas Kuppenheimer & dr.
2805 Mr. & Mrs. L. Schlesinger
2807 Mr. & Mrs. C. M. Favorite
2815 Mr. & Mrs. Michael Burke
2819 Mr. & Mrs. Geo. A. Seaverns
2819 Mrs. R. H. Mabbatt
2825 Cyrus A. Hardy

2512 Adolph Greensfelder
2512 Julius Greensfelder
2512 Nathan Greensfelder
2518 Mrs. S. G. Spaulding
2518 Mrs. Mabel H. Foxwell
2518 Mrs. Nellie S. Cooke
2522 Joseph G. Snydacker
2522 Arthur G. Snydacker
2522 Miss Elsie Snydacker
2522 Dr. & Mrs. M. L. Goodkind
 Receiving day Saturday
2550 Mr. & Mrs. M. D. Wells
2600 Mrs. S. K. Martin & dr.
2612 Mr. & Mrs. Edwin Walker
2612 Miss Alma Kimball
2612 Miss Louise Kimball
2622 Mr. & Mrs. J. Franklin Keeney
 Receiving day Tuesday
2626 Mr. & Mrs. T. J. Lefens
2702 Mr. & Mrs. H. H. Honore jr.
2704 Mrs. M. L. Satterlee
2704 George A. Satterlee
2706 Mr. & Mrs. Wm. A. Magie
2714 Rev. & Mrs. W. C. Richardson
 Receive Wednesdays
2724 Mr. & Mrs. Joseph Shepard
2724 J. J. Morsman
2802 Mrs. S. E. Muir & dr.
2802 Mr. & Mrs. M. W. Shanahan
2808 Mrs. M. S. Davis & dr.
2808 Allan H. Daugharty
2810 Robert T. Martin
2810 Miss Anne H. Martin
2816 Mr. & Mrs. C. W. Brega & dr.
2816 Miss Margaret Enders
2822 Mr. & Mrs. George Adams & dr.
2826 Mr. & Mrs. C. E. Kohl
2838 Mr. & Mrs. H. N. Higinbotham
2838 Harry M. Higinbotham
2838 Miss Florence Higinbotham
2900 Mr. & Mrs. J. H. S. Quick
2900 George A. Quick
2900 Harry J. Quick
2902 Mrs. J. F. Heyworth
2902 James O. Heyworth
2902 Mr.& Mrs.Lawrence Heyworth
2908 Mrs. J. F. Gillette
2908 Howard F. Gillette
2918 Mr. & Mrs. James Barrell
2918 Albert M. Barrell
2922 Mr. & Mrs. William H. Moore
 Receive Thursday
2934 Mr. & Mrs. D. E. Corneau
2934 Perry B. Corneau
2938 Mr. & Mrs. J. P. Dalton

2827 Mr. & Mrs. H. S. Fitch & dr.
2829 Mrs. Henry S. Stebbins
2835 Mrs. Charles B. Pope
2837 Mr. & Mrs. H. Botsford & dr.
2841 J. H. Witbeck
2841 Mr. & Mrs. J. F. L. Curtis
2841 Mrs. M. E. Guernsey
2901 Mr. & Mrs. N. F. Leopold
2901 Mr. & Mrs. A. C. Schwab
2909 Mr. & Mrs. A. Byram & dr.
2909 Charles F. Byram
2913 Mr. & Mrs. C. G. King
2913 William A. Fuller
2923 Mr. & Mrs. R. B. Crouch
2923 Miss Helen Johnston
2929 Mr. & Mrs. D. G. Hamilton
        Receiving day Wednesday
2929 Bruce P. Hamilton
2937 Mr. & Mrs. Cyrus D. Roys
        Receiving day Thursday
2937 Mr. & Mrs. J. Bertley Arnold
        Receiving day Thursday
2939 Mr. & Mrs. Frank L. Stevens
2939 Morehouse Stevens
2941 Mr. & Mrs. N. T. Wright & dr.
2951 Mr. & Mrs. Thomas Orton
2953 Mr. & Mrs. James F. Hervey
2953 Mr. & Mrs. W. C. Duell
2957 Mr. & Mrs. Chas. H. Hoops
2957 David H. Hoops
2957 Mrs. H. O. Hoops
2959 Mr. & Mrs. Roswell Miller
        Receiving day Tuesday
2961 Mr. & Mrs. Frank D. Lewis
        Receiving day Tuesday
2969 Mr. & Mrs. E. B. Sackett
2971 Miss Maria Holman
2971 Miss Harriet Holman
2971 Sam Brown & dr. .
2971 Mrs. Henry E. Phillips
2975 Elmer W. Hart
3017 Dr. & Mrs. C. N. Thompson
3027 Mrs. F. Surdam Stelle
        Receiving day Thursday
3121 Clarence Marks
3123 Mr. & Mrs. John F. Clare
3125 Dr. & Mrs. D. N. Eisendrath
        Receiving day Monday
3127 Mr. & Mrs. S. Minchrod & dr.
        Receiving day Thursday
3127 Clinton Rhodes
3129 Mrs. Julia R. Austrian & drs.
        Receive 1st Saturday
3129 Harvey S. Austrian
3129 Alfred S. Austrian
3131 Mr. & Mrs. Arthur Dixon&drs.

2944 Mr. & Mrs. S. A. Kent
2954 Mr.& Mrs.Joseph Austrian&dr.
        Receiving day Wednesday
2960 Dr. & Mrs. J. P. Morison & dr.
2962 Mrs. Hiram Wheeler   .
        Receiving day Wednesday
2962 Mr. & Mrs. Eugene Wheeler
2962 Arthur Wheeler
2968 Mr. & Mrs. Hiram B. Peabody
2976 Mr. & Mrs. John S. Cooke
        Receiving day Thursday
2976 John R. Cooke
2976 Dr. & Mrs. P. H. Welch
3000 to 3012 The Potomac
        Mr. & Mrs. I. B. Cougle
        Receiving day Thursday
        Mr. & Mrs. James I. Shea
        Dr. & Mrs. Frank Wieland
        Dr. William E. Morgan
        Dr. & Mrs. W. S. Barnes
        Dr. Chas. E. Hamilton
3112 Rev. George W. Browne
3116 Judge & Mrs. Elbridge Hanecy
        & dr.
3122 Mr. & Mrs. A. J. Earling & dr.
3122 Mrs. M. S. Peebles
3122 George Earling
3124 Mr. & Mrs. S. B. Chapin
        Receiving day Tuesday
3138 Mr. & Mrs. Michael Cudahy
        & drs.
3138 John P. Cudahy
3142 Mr. & Mrs. Wm. P. Cowan
        Receiving day Tuesday
3148 Mr. & Mrs. James E. Monroe
3150 Mrs. Maria Cole
3150 Mrs. M. S. Garland
3150 Mrs. R. H. Baker
3150 Miss Sara Hopkins
3150 John J. Dwyer
3152 Dr. & Mrs. John B. Murphy
3154 Mr. & Mrs. J. Brandt Walker
3154 Miss Pearl Gilson
3154 Mr. & Mrs. Archibald McNeill
3200 Mr. & Mrs. C. W. Pardridge &
        dr.
3200 Mrs. Evelyn P. Clayton
3200 Mrs. Thos. Gannon
3206 Mr.& Mrs.Simon Mandel&drs.
        Receiving day Friday
3206 Frank S. Mandel
3206 Leonard Jas. Mandel
3212 Mr. & Mrs. Philip Lichtenstadt
        & dr.
        Receiving day Saturday
3212 Harry Lichtenstadt

3131 Arthur A. Dixon
3131 George W. Dixon
3133 Mr. & Mrs. Julius Schwabacher
3133 Mr. & Mrs. M. L. Horner
3139 Mr. & Mrs. George K. Barrett
3139 Mrs. John B. Carson
3139 Mr. & Mrs. P. B. Shaffner
3141 Abraham Kuh
3141 Julius S. Kuh
3141 Mr. & Mrs. Emanuel Buxbaum
3143 Mrs. Henrietta Florsheim&dr.
 Receive 2d and 4th Fridays
3143 Felix Florsheim
3143 Mr. & Mrs. Alexander Beifeld
3155 Mr. & Mrs. Albert Hayden
 Receiving day Tuesday
3159 Mr. & Mrs. David Kelley
3159 Addison D. Kelley
3159 Paul D. Kelley
3201 Mr. & Mrs. Charles T. Yerkes
3207 Mr. & Mrs. G. C. Benton
3213 Mr. & Mrs. John Angus
3219 Mrs. Louise E. Frank
3219 Miss Adelaide L. Friend
3223 Mr. & Mrs. E. J. Kohn
 Receiving day Wednesday
3223 Bernard Cahn
3223 James B. Cahn
3223 Edgar B. Cahn
3229 Mrs. Louis Wampold & drs.
 Receiving day Friday
3229 Leo Wampold
3229 Frederick C. Cahn
3233 Mr. & Mrs. C. M. Fegenbush &dr.
 Receiving day Wednesday
3237 Mrs. J. J. Fox & drs.
3237 Thomas J. Fox
3253 Mrs. C. A. Kerfoot
3257 Mr. & Mrs. L. B. Doud
3301 Mr. & Mrs. Chas. H. Schwab
3301 Henry C. Schwab
3301 Jerome C. Schwab
3301 Levi Monheimer
3305 Isaac Woolf
3311 Mr. & Mrs. Morris Rosenbaum
 & dr. *Receiving day Wed.*
3317 Dr. Anna Dwyer
3319 Mrs. H. H. Hayden & dr.
3319 H. H. Hayden jr;
3319 Charles E. Hayden
3329 Mr. & Mrs. J. Harry Selz
 Receive 1st Friday
3333 Mr. & Mrs. Oscar Rosenthal
3335 Mr. & Mrs. S. Kaiser & dr
 Receiving day Monday

3212 Willie Lichtenstadt
3214 Mr. & Mrs. George L. Bradbury
3218 Mr. & Mrs. J. P. Primley
3222 Mr. & Mrs. J. P. Marsh
3222 Mr. & Mrs. John J. Abbott
3230 Mr. & Mrs. I. K. Hamilton
3232 W. Henry McDoel
3232 Mr. & Mrs. H. A. Hickman
 Receiving day Tuesday
3236 Dr. Lester Frankenthal
3236 Mr. & Mrs. E. Frankenthal & dr.
3240 Mr. & Mrs. Bernard Kuppenheimer
3240 Albert B. Kuppenheimer
3240 Louis B. Kuppenheimer
3254 Mr. & Mrs. John Cudahy
3254 Misses Bessie & Julia Cudahy
3300 Mrs. Conrad Seipp & dr.
 Receiving day Tuesday
3300 Mr. & Mrs. H. Bartholomay
3322 Mr. & Mrs. Levi Z. Leiter & drs.
3322 Joseph Leiter
3328 Dr. & Mrs. O. L. Schmidt
3334 Mr. & Mrs. E. W. Gillett & dr.
 Receiving day Tuesday
3334 Charles W. Gillett
3336 Mr. & Mrs. Wm. W. Miller
 Receiving day Wednesday
3340 Mr. & Mrs. David A. Kohn
 Receiving day Thursday
3340 Mr. & Mrs. Alfred D. Kohn
3340 Mr. & Mrs. Irving S. Bernheimer
3344 Miss Alice Chapin
 Receiving day Monday
3344 Miss Josephine Chapin
3358 Mr. & Mrs. George F. Jennings
3400 Mr. & Mrs. Emanuel Mandel
 & dr. *Receiving day Tuesday*
3400 Frank Mandel
3400 Edward Mandel
3408 Mr. & Mrs. Edward B. Butler
3416 F. T. Wheeler
3416 Mrs. Lovina M. Atwood & dr.
3420 Mr. & Mrs. Alfred H. Sellers
3420 Frank H. Sellers
3426 Mr. & Mrs. C. L. Shattuck
3426 Mr. & Mrs. John Brown
3428 Mr. & Mrs. Geo. Howard
3430 Mr. & Mrs. Jacob Hirsh
 Receiving day Thursday
3430 Solomon J. Hirsh
3430 Harry J. Hirsh
3432 Mr. & Mrs. R. Rubel & dr.

3337 Mr. & Mrs. H. E. Greenebaum
 Receiving day Friday
3339 Mr. & Mrs. S. F. Leopold &
 dr.
 Receiving day Friday
3339 Alfred F. Leopold
3341 Mr. & Mrs. George F. Kimball
 Receiving day Tuesday
3347 Mr. & Mrs. J. H. Shepard
3347 Henri Shepard
3357 Mr. & Mrs. Wm. F. Burrows
3401 Mr. & Mrs. Horace G. Chase
3401 Samuel M. Chase
3409 Mr. & Mrs. Leon Mandel
 Receive 1st & 3d Wednesdays
3409 Fred L. Mandel
3409 Robert Mandel
3415 Mr. & Mrs. O. G. Foreman
3423 Mr. & Mrs. Frank E. Vogel
3427 Mr. & Mrs. Solomon Hirsh &
 dr. *Receiving day Monday*
3427 Harry S. Hirsh
3427 Dwight S. Hirsh.
3429 Mrs. H. M. Loomis
3431 Mr. & Mrs. O. H. Manning
3433 Mr. & Mrs. Moses Born
3435 Mr. & Mrs. S. Gregsten & drs.
 Receiving day Tuesday
3435 Mrs. C. W. Nicholes
3439 Mrs. Caroline Clayburgh
3439 Miss Blanche Mayers
3439 Joseph Clayburgh
3439 Morris Clayburgh
3439 Harry Clayburgh :
3439 Albert Clayburgh
3441 Mr. & Mrs. L. W. Dennis
3537 Mr. & Mrs. H. C. Hackney
3537 Mr. & Mrs. F. H. Dukesmith
3537 Mr. & Mrs. Arthur T. Evans
3539 Mr. & Mrs. R. Pennington &
 drs.
3543 Mr. & Mrs. T. A. Webb
3545 Mr. & Mrs. Cady M. Jordan
3545 Mr. & Mrs. Thos. S. Deeves
3601 Mr. & Mrs. Thomas A. Wright
3639 Mr.& Mrs. Moses Waixel
 Receiving day Tuesday
3639 M. Sol. Waixel
3639 Mr. & Mrs. Fred Hirsch
 Receiving day Tuesday
3647 Mr. & Mrs. G. W. Wiggs &
 dr.
3647 Mrs. Luelle White & dr.
3651 Mr. & Mrs. Jacob Levi
3653 Samuel Nast
3653 Alexander D. Nast

3432 Milton Rubel
3432 David Rubel
3434 Mr. & Mrs. H. M. Marks
 Receive 1st and 3d Tuesdays
3440 Mrs. F. W. Straus & dr.
 Receiving day Thursday
3440 Samuel J. T. Straus
3440 Mr. & Mrs. Sam H.Regensburg
3456 Dr. & Mrs. S. A. McWilliams
3456 Miss Mary Scheibel
3522 Mr. & Mrs. H. O. Stone
3524 Mr. & Mrs. Vernon Shaw Kennedy
3600 Mr. & Mrs. J. Ellsworth Gross
 Receiving day Tuesday
3608 Mr. & Mrs. Joseph Donnersberger & drs.
3608 Geo. Donnersberger
3612 Dr. & Mrs. John McKinlock
3612 Mr. & Mrs. Geo.W.Mathews jr.
3612 Mr. & Mrs. Stewart E. Barrell
 Receiving day Tuesday
3614 Mr. & Mrs. Charles A. Paltzer
3614 Mrs. Alice D. Smith
3614 Mr. & Mrs. Julian W. Mack
3618 Mr. & Mrs. William C. Camp
3618 Mrs. Adah F. Burton
3618 Mr. & Mrs. Wm. G. Henry
3620 Mr. & Mrs. Weston G. Kimball
3620 Mr. & Mrs. Oren B. Taft
3620 Miss Ina Taft
3620 Harry L. Taft
3622 Mr. & Mrs. George J. Hamlin
3634 Mr. & Mrs. Heman G. Allen
 & dr.
3634 Mr. & Mrs. Fred W. Lipe
3634 Mr. & Mrs. E. H. Miller
3636 Mr. & Mrs. C. S. Williams
3642 Mr. & Mrs. Ferd Siegel
3646 Mrs. Sarah Gimbel
3646 Mr. & Mrs. Horace Gimbel
3646 Mr. & Mrs. Sylvan Cook
3650 Mr. & Mrs. A. Hart
3650 Harry R. Hart
3650 Milton R. Hart
3652 Mr.& Mrs. Edward E.Moberly
3656 Mr. & Mrs. Madison Barker
 Kennedy
3656 Miss Edith C. Kennedy
3658 Marcus Marx & dr.
3660 Mr. & Mrs. W. O. Hoffman
3660 Mrs. William McKindley
3662 Dr. & Mrs. Eugene O. Christoph
3668 Mr. & Mrs. H. M. McIntosh

3653 Mrs. E. J. Gutmann
3657 Mr. & Mrs. C. H. Chappell
  Receiving day Tuesday
3657 J. Dixon Chappell
3659 Mr. & Mrs. C. L. Willey
  Receiving day Tuesday
3659 Miss Katherine B. Sterritt
3661 Mr. & Mrs. S. Karger & dr.
  Receive 1st Saturday
3661 Mr. & Mrs. Jacob W. Gimbel
3661 Samuel I. Karger
3663 Mr. & Mrs. Lipman Glick
3667 J. F. Parker
3667 William C. Parker
3725 Mr. & Mrs. A. M. Rothschild
  Receiving day Wednesday
3817 Mr. & Mrs. M. R. M. Wallace
  & drs.
3819 Mr. & Mrs. J. L. Curtis
3827 Mr. & Mrs. E. T. Glennon
  Receiving day Friday
3827 Mrs. J. H. Slavin
3829 Mr. & Mrs. M. B. Madden
3831 Mr. & Mrs. George A. Seaverns jr.
3831 Charles H. Currier
3847 Mr. & Mrs. Chás. D. Ettinger
  & dr.
3849 Mrs. A. F. Baldwin
3849 Willis M. Baldwin
3907 Dr. & Mrs. F. R. Webb
3953 The Van Dyke
  B Mrs. S. E. Colver
  C Mr. & Mrs. Linn H. Young
  D Dr. & Mrs. John D. Parish
  D Mr. & Mrs. Will C. Thorbus
  E John Berry
  F Mr. & Mrs. John P. Edwards
  200 Dr. & Mrs. J. H. Prothero
  204 Mr. & Mrs. C. F. Dynes
  206 Mr. & Mrs. J. W. McIlroy
  208 Mr. & Mrs. J. M. Parker
  214 Miss Jennie Ladd
  304 Mr. & Mrs. Will R. Morse
  308 Mr. & Mrs. R. F. So Relle
  414 William E. Patten
  414 John B. Patten
4231 Mr. & Mrs. W. B. Judson
4235 Simon Rosenfeld
4235 Henry M. Gerstley
4237 Mr. & Mrs. J. N. Eisendrath
4239 Mr. & Mrs. H. C. Ingwersen
4415 Mr. & Mrs. Daniel E. Brush
4415 H. J. Brush
4417 Mr. & Mrs. Albert Pick, jr.
4425 Dr. & Mrs. C. P. Caldwell

13

3672 Mr. & Mrs. Leopold Bloom
  Receive 1st & 3d Thursdays
3672 Miss Cora B. Bloom
3672 Mrs. Aaron Wolf
3700 Mr. & Mrs. Philip D. Armour.
  jr. *Receiving day Tuesday*
3724 Mr. & Mrs. J. Ogden Armour
3736 Mr. & Mrs. A. J. Lichtstern
3740 Mrs. B. Lichtstern
3744 Mr. & Mrs. Benj. Arnheim
  Receive 2d and 4th Thursdays
3750 Mr. & Mrs. E. G. Foreman
  Receive 1st & 3d Tuesdays
3754 Mr. & Mrs. Julius L. Rosenberg
3800 Mr. & Mrs. Robt. M. Wells
3806 Mr. & Mrs. John Griffiths &
  drs.
3812 Mr. & Mrs. John W. Kiser
3816 Mr. & Mrs. Wm. M. Crilly
3816 Miss Lena Crilly
3820 Mr. & Mrs. Daniel F. Crilly
  & dr.
3820 Edgar Crilly
3924 Mr. & Mrs. S. E. Wood & dr.
3924 Kay Wood
3934 Mr. & Mrs. Lincoln M. Coy
3934 Harry I. Coy
4016 Mr. & Mrs. James A. Wood
4016 Dr. George A. Wood
4016 Charles A. Wood
4042 Mr. & Mrs. W. T. Keenan & dr.
  Receiving day Thursday
4042 Robert Keenan
4114 Mr. & Mrs Thomas English
4114 Philip English
4136 Mrs. Jane I. Tamblyn & dr.
4200 Mr. & Mrs. H. H. Motley
4202 Mr. & Mrs. H. C. Eddy
4202 Mr. & Mrs. C. C. Harris
4206 Mr. & Mrs. J. W. Merriam
4206 Mr. & Mrs. C. S. Bush
4206 Alex Bateson
4316 Mr. & Mrs. L. W. Stone
  Receiving day Tuesday
4346 Mr. & Mrs. H. C. Walker & dr.
4346 Clarence M. Walker
4400 Mr. & Mrs. John P. Barrett
4400 John P. Barrett, jr.
4402 Mr. & Mrs. Henry Best
4404 Mr. & Mrs. S. L. Sulzberger
4406 Mr. & Mrs. Henry Solomon
4406 Joseph Solomon
4406 Mrs. Fannie Peyser
4440 Mrs. John R. Hoxie
4440 J. Randolph Hoxie, jr.
4440 Gilbert H. Hoxie

4543 Mr. & Mrs. J. W. Donohue
   Receive last Thursday in mo.
4563 James McKenna
4631 Henry Hafer & drs.
4633 Mr. & Mrs. C. C. Harder& drs.
   Receive 1st Friday.
4709 Dr. & Mrs. T. J. Sullivan
4841 Mr. & Mrs. Alfred V. Booth
4841 Mr. & Mrs. M. M. Houseman
   Receiving day Monday
4841 Mr. & Mrs. F. W. Teegarden
4859 Mr. & Mrs. M. Clarkson
4927 Joseph Osher & dr.
5045 Mr. & Mrs. J. J. Dunn .
   Receiving day Friday
5045 Frank Dunn
5113 Mr. & Mrs. F. W. Connelly
5121 Mr. & Mrs. J. C. Griffin
5137 Mr. & Mrs. John E. Norton&dr.
5139 Mr. & Mrs. A. H. Uphof
5141 Mr. & Mrs. L. J. Eastland & dr.
5147 Mr. & Mrs. J. S. Rydell & drs.
5147 Oscar F. Rydell
5203 Mr. & Mrs. E. J. McArdle
5203 P. L. McArdle
5327 Mr. & Mrs. Austin H. Lord
5327 Mr. & Mrs. Henry Leopold
5349 Mr. & Mrs. Robert Muehleisen
5349 Emile M. Gross
5621 Mr. & Mrs. Allen McCullough

5608 Mr. & Mrs. J. D. Porter
5608 Mrs. Lucretia Hamm
5608 Solomon W. Hamm
5622 Mr. & Mrs. Louis Sloman
5622 Mr. & Mrs. W. E. Van de Venter
5640 Mrs. Sarah Hanrahan
5640 Mr. & Mrs. Wm. G. Maul
5642 Mr. & Mrs. James Webster
5642 Mr. & Mrs. F. S. Lenert
5646 Mr. & Mrs. C. B. A. Jerome
5648 Mr. & Mrs. Ulick Bourke
5648 Edward L. Bourke
5648 Robert E. Bourke
5648 Ulick Bourke, jr.
5808 Mr. & Mrs. G. M. Russell
5812 Mr. & Mrs. Walter S. Maher
   Receiving day Thursday
5812 Lester E. Maher
5812 Mr. & Mrs. Spencer E. Turner
6018 Mr. & Mrs. P. M. Ottman
6018 Mr. & Mrs. J. T. Webber
6106 Hugh Harding
6106 Dr. & Mrs. F. D. Rogers
6218 Mr. & Mrs. Harry J. Strong

4500 Mr. & Mrs. Edward Morris
   Receive 2d & 4th Wednesdays
4540 Mr. & Mrs. A. Junge & dr.
   Receive 1st Wednesday
4544 Dr. & Mrs. C. C. Beery
4556 Mrs. Sarah D. Noe
   Receives Thursday
4800 Mr. & Mrs. Simon Hasterlik
   Receiving day Tuesday
4800 Miss Bertha Hasterlik
4800 Miss Ray Hasterlik
4800 Mr. & Mrs. David Brede
4834 Mr. & Mrs. H. M. Mitchell
4834 Mr. & Mrs. D. Fish
   Receiving day Friday
4834 Isaac Fish
4836 Mr. & Mrs. Sigel Hess & drs.
   Receive Friday
4836 Leo Hess
4838 Mr. & Mrs. J. A. Robbins
4838 Mr. & Mrs. Louis C. Ehle
4910 Mr. & Mrs. R. G. Hayes & drs.
4910 Mr. & Mrs. G. M. Gunderson
4912 Mr. & Mrs. Edward G. Elcock
   Receive 1st Wednesday
4914 Mr. & Mrs. Thos. Gahan
4924 Mr. & Mrs L. Windmuller
5006 Mr. & Mrs. S. M. Rosenthal
5006 Mrs. William Young
5006 William Young jr.
5006 Mr. & Mrs. Andrew Hoffman
5010 Mr. & Mrs. Henry Appel
5128 Mr. & Mrs. W. H. Ebbert & drs.
5156 W. Elliott Hayes
5156 Mr. & Mrs. W. P. Hayes
5168 Mr. & Mrs. Seymour S. Borden & dr.
5168 Mrs. S. A. Andrews
5234 Mr. & Mrs. James J. Wade
   Receiving day Monday
5234 Thomas P. Wade
5238 Mr. & Mrs. David Coey
5238 Samuel B. Coey
5540 Mr. & Mrs. Jos. Stein & dr.
5540 Mr. & Mrs. William Hunter
5540 Mr. & Mrs. L. C. Monin
5542 Mr. & Mrs. E. G. Ahern
5542 Mr. & Mrs. F. O. Weeks
5606 Mr. & Mrs. L. H. Mahnke
5623 Mrs. George Beldam & drs.
5623 George C. Beldam
5627 Mrs. Sarah T. Slayton
5627 Mr. & Mrs. F. P. Kennedy
5606 Mr. & Mrs. W. G. Limbocker
5606 Mr. & Mrs. C. L. Porter

MICHIGAN TERRACE.

4024 Mrs. Sarah M. Weed
4024 Wm. F. Weed
4024 John R. Morgan

4060 Dr. Albert J. Roe
4064 Mrs. S. M. Fraser & dr.

MINERVA AVENUE.

6417 Mr. & Mrs. B. F. Langworthy
6423 Mr. & Mrs. John W. Kirk
6433 Mr. & Mrs. J. G. Hamilton
     Browne
6439 Mr. & Mrs. William C. Post
6439 Mr. & Mrs. D. W. Pomeroy
6445 Mrs. Emma E. Bowen & dr.
6453 Mr. & Mrs. Charles Erickson
6533 Mr. & Mrs. T. Stanley Davies
6533 Foster H. Bradley

6504 Mr. & Mrs. J. M. F. Erwin
6506 Mr.& Mrs. Herbert F. Seymour
6506 Mr. & Mrs. Edgar P. Albright
6506 Mrs. William Maxwell
6508 Mrs. Elizabeth C. Reiter
6508 Miss Maud Reiter
6508 Winfield S. Reiter
6532 Mr. & Mrs. Rufus J. Haight
6540 Rev. & Mrs. W. J. Petrie

6358 Mr. & Mrs. Howard G. Loomis
6358 Mr. & Mrs. John A. Butterly jr.
6358 Miss Cora Wood
6358 Miss Mae Wood
6360 Mr. & Mrs. Emerson Hough
6362 Mr. & Mrs. James H. Atwood
6362 Miss Kate G. Roche
6402 Mrs. Archie C. Cracraft
6418 Mr. & Mrs. M. L. Campbell &
     dr.
6422 Mr.&Mrs.George W. Coolidge
6422 Dr. Chas. E. Austin
6428 Mr. & Mrs. Harry V. King.
     Receiving day Thursday
6428 Jesse G. King
6432 Mrs.Elizabeth M. Pollock & dr.
6432 Charles A. Pollock
6440 Mr. & Mrs. J. W. Forsinger
6442 Mr. & Mrs. Herbert L. Hooker
6500 Mr. & Mrs. Edward W. Nason
6500 Albert H. Kinkaid

MONROE AVENUE.

5455 Mr. & Mrs. C. E. Crandall
5501 Dr. and Mrs. Wm. L. Wilson
5531 Miss Hannah M. Hart
5531 Mr. & Mrs. S. H. Jennings
5535 Mr. & Mrs. James S. Rogers
     Receiving day Thursday
5535 Prof. & Mrs. B. S. Terry
5539 Mr. & Mrs. R. M. McKey
5539 Mrs. W. B. Clancy
5539 Mr. & Mrs. L. B. Mason
5543 Mr. & Mrs. J. B. McCann & drs.
5543 George S. McCann
5543 Frank McCann
5545 Mr. & Mrs. Frank N. Hayden
5545 Mr. & Mrs. Robert H. Wiles
5551 Miss Ethel Tanner
5551 Mrs. I. S. Mahan
5553 Mr. & Mrs. Fred. S. Kenfield
5555 Mrs. Ellen M. Buchanan
5555 Miss S. M. Paine
5555 T. G. Day
5557 Mr. & Mrs. Frank B. Felt
5617 Mr. & Mrs. E. A. McGuire
5617 Miss Julia B. McGuire

5420 Mr. & Mrs. W. H. Woodward
5422 Mr. & Mrs. Joseph G. Pratt
5422 M. Elizabeth Pratt
5428 Dr. & Mrs. G. W. Whitfield
5428 Albert Whitfield
5428 Miss Carrie Carlisle
5436 Mr. & Mrs. H. C. Stacey
5438 Mr. & Mrs. D. C. Dunlap
5458 Henry F. Eggers
5458 Miss Louisa D. Eggers
5466 Mr. & Mrs. R. L. Hults
5468 J. Hagenbuck
5490 Mr. & Mrs. F. G. Brown
5490 Mr. & Mrs. G. F. Brown
5514 Mr. & Mrs. R. C. Garrabrant &
     dr.
5514 Robert Taft Garrabrant
5520 Mr. & Mrs. Albert C. Hawes
5524 Prof. & Mrs. Ernest D. Burton
5524 Miss Margaret Townson
5528 Dr. Anna Doyen
5532 Mrs. Ruth De Hand
     Receiving day Friday
5538 Kenneth S. Walbank

5621 Mr. & Mrs. W. Morava
5621 E. R. Keeler .
5625 Mr. & Mrs. Carlton White
5627 Mr. & Mrs. Frank B. Stone
  Receiving day Tuesday
5627 Mrs. Lucy E. Stone
5703 Mr. & Mrs. W. Clyde Jones
5707 Mrs. Joseph B. Doggett
5707 Miss Eunice S. Doggett
5715 Mrs. L. B. McKnight & drs.
5715 Mrs. M. B. McKnight
5717 Mr. & Mrs. E. R. Burley
5717 Mrs. John W. Moncrief
5723 Mr. & Mrs. S. A. Low & dr.
5723 Miss Mamie Andrews
5725 Mr. & Mrs. Charles E. Casey
5727 Mr. & Mrs. H. W. Chappell
5731 Mrs. A. H. Ray
5731 Miss Mary B. Herrick
5731 Mr. & Mrs. C. W. Moore
5731 Mrs. Katherine Lee
5733 Prof. & Mrs. C. R. Barnes
5733 Mrs. R. P. Davidson
5741 Mr. & Mrs. Edwin E. Sparks
5811 Dr. W. H. Wilder
5817 Mr. & Mrs. F. A. Johnson
5817 Quintard Johnson
5831 Rev. & Mrs. Wm. Goodfellow
5831 Mrs. Geo. H. Ballou
5833 Walter A. Payne
5833 Clarence A. Torrey
6017 Dr. & Mrs. T. Melville Hardie
6017 Mr. & Mrs. Lloyd D. Townsley
6017 Joseph F. Nickerson
6017 Mr. & Mrs. H. Rowland Curtis
  Receiving day Monday
6017 Mrs. Judson Morris Curtis
6019 Mrs. E. J. Walbank
6019 Dr. & Mrs. E. D. Chapman
6019 Alfred E. Stinson
6021 Mr. & Mrs. Clair E. Moore
6033 Mr. & Mrs. C. D. Beale
6037 Mr. & Mrs. John Roper
6037 Mr. & Mrs. C. J. Barr
6045 Mr. & Mrs. W. H. Potter & dr.
  Receiving day Thursday
6049 Mr. & Mrs. Lutellus Smith
6109 Dr. Thomas Winston
6109 Lieut. Thomas W. Winston
6109 Chas. S. Winston
6109 Miss Alice Winston
6109 Edward M. Winston
6109 Ambrose P. Winston
6109 Miss Eugenia Winston
6109 Miss Addie A. Mumford

5540 Mr. & Mrs. George S. Terry
5544 Mr. & Mrs. W. S. Whiteside
5548 Mr. & Mrs. W. O. Johnson
5552 Mr. & Mrs. E. W. Syer
  Receiving day Wednesday
5554 Mrs. Helen O. Brine
5556 Mrs. L. P. Miller
5600 Mr. & Mrs. W. H. Burton
5600 Mrs. Zella Allen Dixson
  Receiving day 4th Monday
5600 Mrs. Robert E. Smith & dr.
5612 Mr. & Mrs. Jeremiah Slocum
5612 Dr. J. K. Smith
5616 Mrs. F. G. Cobb
5620 Mr. & Mrs. Samuel Lyon
5624 Mr. & Mrs. James Dalzell
5624 Walter Dalzell
5624 Mr. & Mrs. C. R. Dickerson
5628 Mr.& Mrs. Chas. B. Allen & dr.
5628 J. F. MacKenzie
5642 J. L. Hotchkin
5642 Miss Harriet I. Hotchkin
5646 Mr. & Mrs. P. O. Kern
  Receive Monday
5652 Mr. & Mrs. Charles H. Rice
5654 Mr. & Mrs. F. Upman
5700 Ferdinand Schwill
5708 Dr. & Mrs. E. B. Hutchinson
  Receiving day Wednesday
5712 Mr. & Mrs. Alpheus W. Smith
5712 Webster T. Smith
5712 Mrs. Maria W. Smith
5726 Mr. & Mrs. J. B. Jackson
5730 Mr. & Mrs. W. R. Patterson
5732 Mr.& Mrs. Nicholas Hunt & dr.
5744 Mr. & Mrs. Albert G. Lester
5748 Miss Carrie B. Worrall
5748 I. E. Roll
5752 Mr. & Mrs. Herbert F. Kent
5754 Mr. & Mrs. T. Valentine
5810 Mrs. J. Young Scammon
  Receiving day Thursday
6032 Capt. & Mrs. James V. S. Paddock
6032 Mr. & Mrs. D. L. Hilson
6034 Mr.& Mrs. Frederick R. Powell
6036 Mr. & Mrs. Reuben L. Barker
  Receive Tuesday
6038 Wm. J. English
6038 Mrs. John English
6038 Mr. & Mrs. Wm. Hipp   i
  Receive Wednesday
6044 Mr. & Mrs. A. X. Schmitt
  Receiving day Wednesday
6050 Mr. & Mrs. C. W. Leffingwell
  Receiving day Wednesday

6117 Mr. & Mrs. William Reid
    Receiving day Thursday
6117 Mr. & Mrs. W. D. Clingman
6117 Mr. & Mrs. William Clingman
6117 Mr. & Mrs. E. C. Taylor
6119 Mr. & Mrs. Joseph Denison
6121 Mr. & Mrs. C. H. Southard
6123 Mr. & Mrs. John Eaton
6123 Walter Ingersoll
6123 Mr. & Mrs. J. H. Farwell
6123 John C. Farwell
6125 Mr. & Mrs. Archibald Cattell
6127 Mr. & Mrs. B.A.E. Landergren
6129 Mr. & Mrs. Benj. Hoskins
6133 Mr. & Mrs. W. K. Higley
6135 Mr. & Mrs. W. S. Gibson
6137 Miss M. A. Trainer
6137 Mr. & Mrs. W. H. Miner
6143 Dr. & Mrs. Chas. H. Crain
6147 Mrs. Margaret E. Burnside
6147 Mrs. D. L. Fletcher
6149 Mr. & Mrs. W. M. Mills
6149 Miss Myrtle Plant
6149 Miss Bessie Plant
6149 Mrs. I. F. Ingersoll
6235 Mr. & Mrs. C. H. Wilson & drs.
6237 Mr. & Mrs. R. C. Holmes
6237 Mr. & Mrs. Henry W. Nichols
    Receiving day Tuesday
6237 Robert A. Millikan
6239 Mrs. R. C. M. Locke
6239 Mr. & Mrs. Wm. R. Miner
6239 Miss Numa L. Miner
6241 Mr. & Mrs. H. D. Bogardus
6241 Mrs. E. Mead-Lane
    Receiving day Wednesday
6241 Miss Emily Mead
6241 Miss Linn A. Mead
6243 Dr. Florence Goff-Hall
6245 Mr. & Mrs. Henry Goodman
6247 Mr. & Mrs. Frank M. Morris
6249 Mr. & Mrs. James W. Boyd
6249 Dr. & Mrs. L. A. Shultz
6321 Frederick G. Atwood
6321 George C. Atwood
6321 Mrs. Martha M. Atwood
6321 Mr. & Mrs. Albert J. Mills
6325 Mr. & Mrs. Robt. Kercheval
6325 Mrs. Henry Murphy
6325 Miss Mary L. Southworth
6325 Mr. & Mrs. J. W. Burson
6325 Mr. & Mrs. Ossian Guthrie
6341 Mr. & Mrs. M. E. Dayton & dr.
6341 Charles Dayton
6403 Mr. & Mrs. S. W. Straub
6405 Miss Mary A. Beebe

6052 Frederick W. Courtright
6056 Prof. & Mrs. W. M. Lawrence
    & dr.
6056 Mr. & Mrs. Stephen S. Hubbard
6116 Mr. & Mrs. Wm. F. Wilson
6118 Mr. & Mrs. G. E. Scranton
6118 Mr. & Mrs. Elbert D. Weyburn
6118 Ned C. Weyburn
6134 Mr. & Mrs. W. F. Harvell
6134 Gaylord E. Harvell
6136 Mr. & Mrs. Joseph E. Francis
6138 Mr. & Mrs. C. W. Meeker
6146 Mr. & Mrs. C. H. Hillman
6150 Mr. & Mrs. Geo. W. Spencer &
    dr.
6212 Mr. & Mrs. W. B. Davidson &
    dr.
6214 Mr. & Mrs. Edwin W. Cobb
6214 H. C. W. Cowdery & dr.
6216 Mr. & Mrs. Geo. H. Kelland
6220 Mr. & Mrs. Silas T. Hawthorne
6222 Mrs. J. Baird & dr.
6222 James Baird
6242 Mrs. J. H. Dunn
6242 Mr. & Mrs. Wm. W. Russ
6312 Dr. Harry W. Cheney
6312 Mrs. I. M. McNama
6320 Mr. & Mrs. Frank Pearson
6334 Mr. & Mrs. D. V. Keedy
6334 Mrs. Madeline Sheldon
6334 J. Sheldon Riley
6336 Mr. & Mrs. E. A. Beeks
6344 Mr. & Mrs. James Wilson
    Receive Wednesday
6352 Dr. Helen M. Buchanan
6352 Mrs. N. D. Arnold
6352 Mr. & Mrs. Mahlon Barron &
    dr.   *Receive Thursday*
6352 Edward H. Barron
6352 Edward B. Springer
6356 Mrs. Daniel B. Hubbard
6356 Lyman G. Hubbard
6400 George W. Rodgers
6400 John L. Rodgers
6404 Mr. & Mrs. Harry Dolling & dr.
6410 Mr. & Mrs. F. A. Braymer
6410 Ernest S. Braymer
6410 Mrs. H. Story
6420 Mr. & Mrs. Hugh Irvine
6424 Augustus J. Burbank
6424 Miss Susan Rand
6436 Mr. & Mrs. George C. Fairman
6436 F. W. Disbrow
6438 Mr. & Mrs. Frank J. Smith
6442 Mr. & Mrs. Fred M. Farwell
6456 Mr. & Mrs. H. L. Miller

6405 Mr. & Mrs. T. J. Holton
6417 Mr. & Mrs. Robert W. Hall
6417 William Hall
6425 Mrs. L. Coffin Morris & dr.
6433 Mr. & Mrs. Charles Scholle
6435 Mr. & Mrs. Edgar L. Young
6435 Mr. & Mrs. A. L. Clifton
6435 Mr. & Mrs. Raymond T. Vent
6437 Mrs. Margaret R. Schultz &
     drs.
6445 Dr. S. O. Knapp
6447 Mr. & Mrs. Nolin Hathaway
6451 Mrs. E. S. Holmes & dr.
6451 George V. Holmes
6455 Mr. & Mrs. J. G. Hale
6463 John H. Keast
6501 Mrs. W. H. Adams
6501 Mr. & Mrs. W. Irving Midler
6505 Mr. & Mrs. Paul Henson
6519 Mr. & Mrs. W. E. Bond
6519 Mrs. Robert Fawcett

6462 Mr. & Mrs. M. W. Hill
6502 Mr. & Mrs. John Quinn
6506 Mr. & Mrs. A. E. Buisseret
6510 Mr. & Mrs. J. Claude Hill
6530 Mr. & Mrs. G. W. Ford
6530 Miss Cherry Ford
6534 Mr. & Mrs. John P. Mackenzie
6616 Mr. & Mrs. Adolph Keitel
     Receiving day Tuesday
6620 Mr. & Mrs.Wm.Winfield Cobb
     Receiving day Monday
6632 Mr. & Mrs. E. A. Erickson
7420 Mr. & Mrs. John W. Tinsley
7420 John H. Tinsley
7530 Mr. & Mrs. E. W. Hutchinson

6541 Mr. & Mrs. T. A. Lockwood
6547 Mr. & Mrs. Fred L. Fake jr.
6547 Mr. & Mrs. C. M. Poague
     Receiving day Thursday

NORTH NORMAL PARKWAY.

412 Mr. & Mrs. James L. Gates
416 Mr. & Mrs. J. D. Dymond & drs.
436 Mr. & Mrs. Herbert A Stoddard
440 Mr. & Mrs. Marshall F. Holmes
448 Mr. & Mrs. John J. McDonald
    Receiving day Wednesday
452 Mr. & Mrs. Darlington P.Jones
512 Rev. & Mrs. B. F. Matrau
    Receive Thursday

520 Mr. & Mrs. John W. Ellis
520 Mr. & Mrs. Thos. N. Ellis
528 Mr. & Mrs. E. H. Ericson
528 Felix H. Ericson
532 Mr. & Mrs. A. F. Walther
542 Mr. & Mrs. Julian C. Jones
550 Mr. & Mrs. H. A. Rubidge

SOUTH NORMAL PARKWAY.

437 Dr. & Mrs. A. R. Lyles
441 Mr. & Mrs. H. K. Burgess
533 Mrs. L. Mae Willms
533 Mr. & Mrs. A. Fox

535 Mr. & Mrs. Will A. Fox
539 Mr. & Mrs. J. J. Mogg
539 Clayton W. Mogg

OAKENWALD AVENUE.

4201 Mr. & Mrs. A. M. McKinney
     & dr.
4227 Dr. & Mrs. Edward R. Kellogg
4229 Mr. & Mrs. Alfred Kirk
4303 Mr. & Mrs. M. Shannon
4305 Mr. & Mrs. A. P. Spencer
4305 Mr. & Mrs. Sumner C. Palmer
4307 Mrs. Marie A. Youngs
4311 Mr. & Mrs. John S. Murray
4323 Philip P. Rudhart
4327 Mr. & Mrs. Edward P. Sills
4327 Mrs. E. J. Lamplugh
4329 Mr. & Mrs. A. W. Becker

4200 Mr. & Mrs. D. B. Sweet
     Receiving day Tuesday
4204 Mr. & Mrs. Chas. E. Adams
4206 Mr. & Mrs. George Watkins
4208 Mr. & Mrs. Mark R. Sherman
4212 Mr. & Mrs. J. F. Beals
     Receiving day Wednesday
4212 A. R. Thomas
4216 Mr. & Mrs. N. B. Koontz
4218 Mr. & Mrs. Jacob C. Dietz
     Receiving day Friday
4224 Mr. & Mrs. M. H. McCarthy
4306 Mr. & Mrs. W. H. A. Brown

4329 Mrs. S. T. Hoglen
4335 Mrs. B. C. Poitras
4335 Ernest J. Wagner
4339 Misses Chandler
4339 Walter T. Chandler
4339 L. Hamilton Chandler
4339 Norborne E. Chandler
4341 Mr. & Mrs. James T. Hall &drs.
4343 Wm. J. Gillingham
4347 Mr. &. Mrs. Walter C. Gillett
4347 Mr. & Mrs. H. Lockwood
4347 Mr. & Mrs. Wm. H. Little
4349 Mr. & Mrs. Geo. W. Little jr.
4351 Robert J. Gunning
4351 Mrs. Mary Silversparre
4351 Mr. & Mrs. H. S. Wilson
4353 Mr. & Mrs. H. T. Sidway
4353 L. B. Sidway
4353 Mrs. D. E. Milner
4355 Mrs. S. Strelitz & dr.
Receiving day Friday
4355 David I. Strelitz
4355 Victor B. Strelitz
4367 Mr. & Mrs. G. W. Traer
4371 Mr. & Mrs. Chas. A. Jones
4401 Mr. & Mrs. Porter Deardoff & dr.
4403 Mr.&Mrs.Edward W.Andrews
4413 Mr. & Mrs. R. A. Burton
4415 Mr. & Mrs. Wm. D. Alexander
4455 Mr. & Mrs. A. D. Gillis
4457 Mrs. Emily E. Calder & dr.
4459 Mrs. D. Norton
4459 Mr. & Mrs. A. A. Rolf
4465 Mr. & Mrs. W. B. Forsyth
4465 Mrs. F. I. Benson & dr.
4467 Mr. & Mrs. Barclay H. Dorland & dr.
4467 Mr. & Mrs. E. G. Carlisle
4467 Mr. & Mrs. G. A. Lepper
Receiving day Thursday
4467 Mrs. Louisa Hatten
4519 Mr. & Mrs. J. B. Wilson
4539 Mrs. Barbara Stein & dr.
4545 James P. Hankey
4547 Mr. & Mrs. A. Pam & dr.
4547 Max Pam
4553 Rev. & Mrs. I. S. Moses
4553 Mr. & Mrs. Watson J. Ferry
4557 Mr. & Mrs. Edward O'Bryan
4567 Mr. & Mrs. C. S. Hartley & dr.
4575 Mr. & Mrs. Frederick W. Job
4577 Mrs. Robt.W. McMahan & drs.
4581 Mr. & Mrs. Harvey M. Harper
4583 Mr. & Mrs. A. H. Pickering
4583 Miss Mary Lee Bufkin

4310 Mr. & Mrs. C. D. Warren
4310 Frederick Nicholas
4310 Mrs. Marcia Parker
4314 Mr. & Mrs. George T. Houston
4314 Mrs. Eleanor M. King
4318 Mr. & Mrs. John M. Fiske
4328 Mr. & Mrs. D. Albin Kistler
4330 Miss S. A. Pierce
4330 Mr. & Mrs. A. A. Turner
4340 Mr. & Mrs. Wm. F. White & dr.
4344 Mr. & Mrs. Henry Mills
4344 Mr. & Mrs. M. E. Mills
4346 Mr. & Mrs. C. L. Bingham
4354 John J. Grey
4356 Mr. & Mrs. George D. Milligan
4360 Mr. & Mrs. E. R. Lynch
4362 Mr. & Mrs. W. D. Wyman
4364 Mr. & Mrs. C. G. Armstrong
4366 Mr. & Mrs. Stuart F. Marchant
4366 Mrs. F. E. Frye
4368 Mr. & Mrs. Wm. J. Reynolds
4406 Mr. & Mrs. Charles O. Robinson
4410 Mr. & Mrs. Robert Nicholas
4412 Mr. & Mrs. Hugh T. Reed
4414 Mr. & Mrs. J. Morton & dr.
4416 Mr. & Mrs. W. J. Bligh
4418 Mr. & Mrs. J. Grafton Parker
4418 Mr. & Mrs. James J. Parker
4418 Miss E. Louise Parker
4420 Dwight B. Cheever
4422 Mr. & Mrs. Geo. H. Curtiss & dr.
4450 Mr. & Mrs. George A. Coe
4454 Mr. & Mrs. H. H. Cutler
Receiving day Thursday
4454 Mrs. H. C. Smith & drs.
4454 Mr. & Mrs. Charles G. James
4458 Mr. & Mrs. E. E. Overpeck
4460 Mr. & Mrs. Edwin R. Baker
4460 Mr. & Mrs. Wm. N. Thornburgh
4460 Mr. & Mrs. Edward G. Chase
4466 Mr. & Mrs. George F. Bartlett
4466 George F. Bartlett jr.
4470 Mr. & Mrs. George B. Bartlett
4514 Mr. & Mrs. August Pollak
4518 Mr. & Mrs. W. H. Gore
4528 W. S. Oppenheim
4528 William T. Alden
4528 Stephen A. Foster
4528 F. W. Harnwell
4530 Dr.&Mrs.Wm.CarverWilliams
4530 Day Williams
4532 Mr. & Mrs. Wm. McLain
4538 Mr. & Mrs. L. E. Steinman

4583 Dr. & Mrs. M. B. Pine
4585 Mr. & Mrs. Isaac F. Dickson
4585 Mrs. H. M. Gilbert
4589 Dr. & Mrs. Frank T. Andrews
4591 Mr. & Mrs. A. A. Paddon
4595 Mr. & Mrs. W. H. Wheeler
4597 Mr. & Mrs. J. S. Meyer
4597 Mrs. J. Weil
4599 Mr. & Mrs. J. D. Williams

4568 Miss Kate B. Martin
4568 Miss Annà M. Snively
4576 Mr. & Mrs. W. D. Oliver
4578 Mr. & Mrs. A. W. Hutchins
        Receive Thursday
4580 Mr. & Mrs. Edw. P. Buchanan
4584 Mr. & Mrs. C. L. Wilson & dr.
4596 Mr. & Mrs. C. H. Chadwick
4596 Frank L. Linden
4596 John Muir
4598 Mr. & Mrs. J. C. Sampson
4598 Mr. & Mrs. Lucius B. Sherman

4540 Mr. & Mrs. W. H. Welch
4540 Miss Tillie King
4542 Mr. & Mrs. Geo. A. Wrisley
4542 Rev. & Mrs. W. F. Irwin
4542 Ed Irwin
4544 Mr. & Mrs. Malcolm McNeill
4546 Mrs. Martha W. Millard
4546 C. C. Paddleford
4548 Mrs. H. B. Benjamin & drs.
4552 Mrs. J. V. McNeil & dr.
4552 Mr. & Mrs.HalmerE.McNeil jr.
4554 Mr. & Mrs. Ralph M. Shank-
        land
4558 James M. Gwin
4558 Misses Gwin
4558 J. P. Mentzer
4560 Mr. & Mrs. Geo. H. Heafford
4560 Mr. & Mrs. F. T. West
4560 Mr. & Mrs.Rudolph R.Magnus
4560 Isaac Colburn
4560 Mrs. P. A. Reynolds
4564 Mrs. J. C. Knowles & drs.
4564 Mrs. Louise Favard & dr.

OAKLAND CRESCENT.

2 Mrs. A. Meyer
2 Victor Barothy
2 Bela DeRimanoczy

8 Mr. & Mrs. Frank M. Parks
8 Guy Cramer

OAKWOOD AVENUE.

21 Mr. & Mrs. William Hoagland
23 Mr. & Mrs. E. W. Bailey
nw. cor. Ellis av. The Winamac
    Dr. & Mrs. C. F. Barker
    Mr. & Mrs. S. H. Black
    Mr. & Mrs. E. R. Dillingham
    Mr. & Mrs. W. J. Hynes
    Mrs. E. D. Moffett
    Mr. & Mrs. William Mueller jr.
    Mr. & Mrs. H. J. O'Neill
    Mr. & Mrs. Leroy Payne
    Mr. & Mrs. B. E. Pike
    Mr. & Mrs. F. A. Price
    Mr. & Mrs. J. L. Sexton
    Mr. & Mrs. E. Tosetti & drs.
    Otto L. Tosetti
    Mr. & Mrs. Harry M. Turner
93 Mr. & Mrs. Herman H. Mund
95 Mr. & Mrs. C. M. Hardy & dr.

50 Mr. & Mrs. A. L. McLauchlin
50 James E. Barnard
52 Mr. & Mrs. Sidney W Rice
        Receiving day Wednesday
52 Mrs. Jane Bruce & drs.
98 Mr. & Mrs. Samuel Faulkner &
        drs.

95 William Hardy
95 Guy Hardy
95 Mr. & Mrs. Chas. A. Burr
95 Mr.& Mrs. Chas. R. Penington
95 Mrs. Frank Supplee
95 Mr. & Mrs. Irving A. Lesher
95 Mr. & Mrs. Wm. Best jr.
97 William N. Cottrell
105 Dr. & Mrs. Wm. H. Schrader
105 Mr. & Mrs. Hubert M. Skinner

OAKWOOD BOULEVARD.

143 and 145 The Allen
   1 Dr. & Mrs.Bertram W. Sippy
   2 Mr. & Mrs. Geo. N. Bruner

164 Dr. & Mrs. G. F. Wetherell
166 Mr. & Mrs. Wm. Mavor & drs.
168 Mr. & Mrs. Wm. H. Vogell

143 and 145 The Allen (continued.)
5 Mr. & Mrs. J. D. Brown
6 Mrs. S. B. Pease
6 Mr. & Mrs. Jno. B. Viets
9 Mr. & Mrs. C. W. Allen
10 Mr. & Mrs. W. E. Rothermel
12 J. R. Brooks
13 Mrs. John W. Foster
14 Mr. & Mrs. W. H. Shaffer
15 Mrs. Hetty Lacey
17 Dr. M. A. Stevens
19 Bernard G. Brennan
21 Mrs. Lewis Fuess & drs.
22 Theo. G. Wehmer
22 Miss Minnie C. Wehmer
   Receiving day Wednesday
23 E. J. Sherwin
26 Mr. & Mrs. F. J. Berry
26 Mr. & Mrs. Thomas Hoops
   Receiving day Tuesday
27 Mr. & Mrs. E. A. Jewett
28 Mr. & Mrs. Geo. C. Jerome
29 Mr. & Mrs. Thomas Carr
   Receiving day Tuesday
30 Mr. & Mrs. Ermete Venni
30 Miss Fannie G. Kahn
31 Mr. & Mrs. John T. White
153 Dr. & Mrs. Geo. F. Parsons
157 Mr. & Mrs. Wm. Wirt Smith & dr.
157 Mr. & Mrs. Wm. R. Webb
167 Dr. & Mrs. L. B. Hayman
169 Mr. & Mrs. Melvin L. Wade
171 F. L. Trout
185 Mr. & Mrs. G. S. Bush
185 John Olney
187 Mr. & Mrs. E. J. Milligan
189 Mr. & Mrs. J. McDowell
189 R. P. McDowell
191 Mrs. L. A. Munger
191 A. Page Munger
191 Frank S. Munger
191 Mr. & Mrs. Arthur E. Hull
193 Mr. & Mrs. B. F. Troxell
195 Mr. & Mrs. Homer S. Wetherell
195 L. J. Hotchkiss
197 Mr. & Mrs. L. S. Leversedge
221 Dr. Flora M. Watson
231 Mr. & Mrs. T. C. Smith & dr.
   Receiving day Thursday
239 Mr. & Mrs. Cummings Cherry
245 Mr. & Mrs. Samuel Barnum
245 E. S. Barnum
245 Mr. & Mrs. W. W. Thacher
245 Mrs. Jennie B. Williams
251 Mr. & Mrs. Peter K. Lyon

168 Miss Clara A. Jones
168 Alfred L. Jones
170 Dr. & Mrs. R. B. Miller
170 Mrs. Fannie M. Jones
172 Mr. & Mrs. L. M. Smith
172 Mr. & Mrs C. B. McKibbin
172 Wm. C. McKibbin
172 Mr. & Mrs. Benjamin Ives
174 Mr. & Mrs. S. B. Davis & dr.
174 Mr. & Mrs. M. J. Scrafford
194 Mr. & Mrs. D. H. Hunt
194 Ralph H. Hunt
194 Harry W. Hunt
196 Mr. & Mrs. F. B. Griffing
196 Mr. & Mrs. Geo. A. Neatus
200 O. W. Ellis & dr.
200 Mr.& Mrs. E. W. Tillotson & dr
200 Dr. David H. Galloway
200 Mrs. W. A. Dunshee
202 Mr. & Mrs. Edwin E. Brown
202 Mrs. William H. Berger
206 H. H. Bowen
206 Mrs. L. C. Bowen & drs.
226 Mr. & Mrs. J. D. James
228 Mr. & Mrs. I. N. Conroy & dr.
228 Mr. & Mrs. Frank W. Somers
234 Mrs. J. M. Beverley
234 Mr. & Mrs. L. Manasse jr.
238 Mr. & Mrs. Julian C. Burdick
238 Wm. S. Burdick
238 Mr. & Mrs. George E. Rice
240 Mr. & Mrs. Jerome Jones & drs.
242 Dr. J. D. McGowan
244 Mr. & Mrs. C. M. Clark & dr.
244 Robert E. Clark
246 Mr. & Mrs. Charles Oliver Goss
248 John E. Munger
248 Mrs. Harriet E. Munger
248 H. B. Munger
248 Mrs. L. Munger Jones
250 Mr. & Mrs. Chas. S. Burkholder
314 Mrs. J. W. Houston & dr.
314 Frank B. Houston
314 James S. Houston
316 Mr. & Mrs. G. O. Garnsey
320 Mr. & Mrs. A. N. Warner
320 Mr. & Mrs. C. H. Brand
322 Mr. & Mrs. Frank Shepard
326 Mr. & Mrs. Allen F. Murray
330 W. D. S. Anderson
330 Mrs. V. D. Perkins
332 Mrs. C. M. Stokes
332 C. F. Stokes
332 Edwin M. Stokes
332 William B. Stokes
334 Mr. & Mrs. James R. Mann

255 Dr. & Mrs. John A. Hemsteger
    Receiving day Thursday
257 Mr. & Mrs. Charles J. C. Will .
265 Mr. & Mrs. George H. Sidwell
265 George T. Sidwell
265 Mr. & Mrs. F. E. King
271 Mrs. J. W. Boardman
271 Mr. & Mrs. Adelbert E. Brown
271 Mr. & Mrs. M. L. C. Funk-
    houser
271 Mr. & Mrs. W. A. Stanton
271 Harrison C. Lewis
271 Mr. & Mrs. Willis G. Wood
273 Mr. & Mrs. Jesse E. Hall
273 Orlando M. Cone
273 Dr. & Mrs. Adelbert E. Brown
    & dr.
273 Dr. L. Read Brown
323 Miss Emily J. Smith
337 Mr. & Mrs. Robert Excell
341 Mr. & Mrs. S. Daniels & drs.
    Receiving day Friday
343 Mr. & Mrs. Louis Newgass
343 Mrs. Mary Heineman & dr.
347 Mr. & Mrs. Edwin W. Wile
347 Mrs. Jennie Falk
353 Mrs. B. Powell
353 Henry Hirsch
353 I. Hirsch
353 M. Hirsch

336 Mr. & Mrs. Martin C. Kehoe
338 Mr. & Mrs. R. C. Morrison & dr.
338 R. V. Morrison
340 Mr. & Mrs. Hope R. Cody
344 Mr. & Mrs. D. P. Perry
346 Dr. & Mrs. Samuel C. Taylor & dr.
346 Mr. & Mrs. Arthur A. Taylor
348 Mr. & Mrs. J. Schoenfeld
348 H. W. Schoenfeld
348 L. M. Levy
378 Mrs. David Mayer & drs.
378 Tobey Mayer
382 Mr. & Mrs. N. Morganroth
384 Mr. & Mrs. Samuel Coffman &
    dr.
386 Mr. & Mrs. E. D. Murray jr. &
    dr.
386 E. B. Murray
    ————
355 Mr. & Mrs. George Woodland
    & dr.
355 Mr. & Mrs. Fred B. Woodland
361 Mr. & Mrs. James H. Ashby
365 Mr. & Mrs. Thomas Kelly
365 Charles Kelly
367 Mr. & Mrs. Morris Barbe
373 Mr. & Mrs. Arthur W. Allyn
377 Mr. & Mrs. J. W. Byers & drs.
385 Mr. & Mrs. H. C. Buhoup
387 Mr. & Mrs. W. M. Morrill

PARNELL AVENUE

6315 Mr. & Mrs. Joseph Buker
6317 Mr. & Mrs. George B. Denman
6331 Mrs. J. S. Barnes
6351 Dr. & Mrs. J. A. Meek
6411 Mr. & Mrs. Chas. Pugh
6441 Mr. & Mrs. S. H. Campbell
6511 Mr. & Mrs. Selden Thayer
6635 Mr. & Mrs. J. C. McFarland
6635 Mr. & Mrs. T. W. McFarland ·
6639 Mr. & Mrs. John Tredwell
6643 Mr. & Mrs. W. G. Gurnett
6711 Mrs. C. W. Culliton
6717 Mr. & Mrs. F. A. Griffith
6759 Dr. & Mrs. Wm. J. Arnold
6759 Mr. & Mrs. C. L. Stone
6927 Mr. & Mrs. J. R. Trenton
7047 Mr. & Mrs. W. W. Janery
    ————
7058 Dr. Martha T. Pearce
7058 Dr. Mary E. Stanford
7402 Mr. & Mrs. W. H. Dietz

5926 Mr. & Mrs. F. B. Howland
5932 Mr. & Mrs. M. B. Derrick
5932 Mrs. H. N. Nourse
5938 Mr. & Mrs. W. B. Kennedy
6328 Mr. & Mrs. Henry Ocorr
6346 Mrs. A. G. Hayden
6404 Mr. & Mrs. A. H. Waggener
6404 John N. Driver
6424 Mr. & Mrs. R. S. Iles
6434 Mr. & Mrs. H. D. Safford & dr.
6434 W. H. Safford
6454 Mr. & Mrs. Chas. F. Jordan
6504 Rev. & Mrs. J. A. Duff
6512 Mr. & Mrs. J. C. Church
6634 Dr. & Mrs. George W. Miller
6634 William H. Hopper
6636 Mr. & Mrs. J. M. Smith
6640 Mr. & Mrs. F. W. Parker
6738 Mr. & Mrs. F. W. Werneburg &
    drs.
6956 Mr. & Mrs. Charles H. Emery

PERRY AVENUE.

6539 Mr. & Mrs. Geo. F. England
6545 Mr. & Mrs. Thos. M. Meldrum
6545 Mrs. A. E. Sinclair & dr.
6549 William H. Sinclair
6549 Mr. & Mrs. M. H. Wagar
6549 Duane H. Wagar
6557 Wm. S. Baker
6557 Mr. & Mrs. F. Salter & dr.
6557 Albert C. Salter
6557 Wilbur G. Salter
6633 Mr. & Mrs. W. M. Alexander & dr.
6647 Mr. & Mrs. Julius Aagaard&dr.
6659 Mr. & Mrs. W. H. Sharp
6711 Capt. & Mrs. P. M. Boehm
6719 Dr. & Mrs. Alfred Guthrie
6731 Mr. & Mrs. John A. Bartlett
6735 Mr. & Mrs. Chas. A. Bartlett
6749 Mr. & Mrs. F. W. Croft & dr.
6801 S. H. Moore & dr.
6805 Mrs. Carrie C. Ely & drs.
6817 Mr. & Mrs. E. C. Tucker
6825 Mr. & Mrs. F. C. Silberhorn
6825 Rev. & Mrs. Theodore Clifton
6837 Mr. & Mrs. H. Vanderploeg
6837 Miss Flora Vanderploeg
6853 Mr. & Mrs. John Reynolds
6911 Mr. & Mrs. Thos. A. Soper
6921 Thomas Dwyer
6927 Mr. & Mrs. J. W. Roberts
6939 Mr. & Mrs. Calvin Carr

6532 Mr. & Mrs. Charles D. Dunann
6606 Mr. & Mrs. H. C. Draper
6628 Mr. & Mrs. P. R. Hilton
6628 Fred L. Hilton
6636 Mr. & Mrs. Myron H. Tichenor
6640 Mr. & Mrs. J. K. Hooper
6744 Thomas Day & dr.
6744 Mr. & Mrs. Fred L. Croft
6748 Mr. & Mrs. John Monroe
6756 Mr. & Mrs. Wm. L. Sharp
6800 Rev. & Mrs. Rufus A. White
6816 Dr. & Mrs. H. W. Hemingway & dr.
6826 Mr. & Mrs. Chas. Salmon & drs.
6836 Mr. & Mrs. Geo G. Custer & dr.
6916 Mr. & Mrs. Wilbur S. Jackman
6930 Mr. & Mrs. Wm. J. Edwards
6950 Mr. & Mrs. Willis Smith
7046 Mr. & Mrs. George D. Chason
7046 Mrs. Mary J. Chason
7056 Mr. & Mrs. August Tidholm

6943 Roy B. Tabor
6943 Mr. & Mrs. Rufus K. Tabor
6955 Dr. May Cushman Rice
6959 Mr. & Mrs. Joseph Keene
7013 Mr. & Mrs. Wm. J. Porter & dr.
7013 Miss Frances L. Goodwin
7013 Mr. & Mrs. Hiram P. Hoyt

PLAISANCE COURT.

3 Mr. & Mrs. E. R. Peck
15 Mr. & Mrs. E. A. Armstrong

2 Mr. & Mrs. P. F. Stone
4 Mr. & Mrs. John Stirlen

PRAIRIE AVENUE.

1601 Wm. Morton Payne
1601 Mr. & Mrs. Bernard H. Trumbull
1601 Chas. S. Thompson
1619 Mr. & Mrs. Howard E. Perry
1621 Mr. & Mrs. John H. Hamline
1621 George A. Mead
1625 Mr. & Mrs. Hugh J. McBirney
    Receiving day Tuesday
1635 Mr. & Mrs. Warren Springer
1637 Mr.& Mrs. Jesse Spalding & dr.
1701 Mr. & Mrs. William G. Hibbard
1701 William G. Hibbard jr.
1701 Mrs. O. Van Schaack Ward
1709 Mrs. Jessie D. Crane
    Receiving day Tuesday

1600 John G. Shortall
1604 Mr. & Mrs. John L. Shortall
1608 Mr. & Mrs. Henry L. Frank
1616 Mr. & Mrs. William R. Stirling
1620 Dr. & Mrs. Lyman Ware
1620 Robert H. Law
1626 Mr. & Mrs. Abraham Longini & dr.
    Receive. Thursday afternoon
1628 Mr. & Mrs. Morris Einstein & dr.
1628 Benjamin Einstein
1634 Erastus Foote jr.
1634 Mr. & Mrs. T. H. Bellas & drs.
1636 Mr. & Mrs. H. Morris Johnston

1709 Mrs. E. M. Doolittle
        Receiving day Tuesday
1729 Mrs. Geo. M. Pullman
        Receiving day Tuesday
1801 Mr. & Mrs. W. W. Kimball
        Receiving day Tuesday
1801 Mrs. M. M. Cone
1811 Mr. & Mrs. David Mayer
1815 Mr. & Mrs. Levy Mayer
1823 Mr. & Mrs. Thomas Dent
1827 Mr. & Mrs. J. W. Doane
1901 Mr. & Mrs. Norman B. Ream
        &drs. *Receiving day Tuesday*
1905 Marshall Field
1919 Mr. & Mrs. Leroy W. Fuller
1923 Mrs. C. P. Kellogg
1923 Mr. & Mrs. Pierrepont Isham
1945 Mrs. Henry Corwith
1945 Charles R. Corwith
1945 John W. Corwith
1945 Mrs. C. B. McGenniss
2001 Mr. & Mrs. J. L. Lombard
2009 Mrs. M. A. Meyer
2009 E. F. Meyer
2009 Albert Meyer
2009 Carl Meyer
2009 Abraham Meyer
2011 Augustus D. Lamb
2011 Benjamin B. Lamb
2013 Mr. & Mrs. William H. Reid
2017 Mr. & Mrs. A. J. McBean
2017 George B. McBean
2017 Mr. & Mrs. A. J. F. McBean
        Receiving day Tuesday
2021 Mrs. James L. High & dr.
2021 Shirley T. High
2027 Mr. & Mrs. Wm. Bentley Walker
2027 Charles Cobb Walker
2027 Silas B. Cobb
2031 Mr. & Mrs. Samuel A. Tolman
2033 Mr. & Mrs. F. R. Otis & dr.
2033 Charles T. Otis
2033 Lucius J. Otis
2035 Mrs. H. O. Stone
        Receiving day Tuesday
2101 Mrs. Helen Rockwell
2101 Mr. & Mrs. Eugene S. Pike
    Receive Tuesday afternoon 3 to 6
2101 Charles B. Pike
2101 William Wallace Pike
2109 Mr. & Mrs. Robert W. Roloson
        Receive Tuesday 2 to 5 p. m.
2109 Mrs. Judith L. Marshall
2115 Mr. & Mrs. Philip D. Armour
        . *Receive Tuesday afternoon*
2115 Mrs. Alice A. Sloan

1636 H. McB. Johnston
1636 Morris L. Johnston
1638 Mr. & Mrs. Robert B. Gregory
1638 Mrs. Elizabeth Gregory
1712 Mr. & Mrs. Geo. A. McKinlock
1720 Mrs. James M. Walker
        Receives Tuesday afternoon
1720 Mr. & Mrs. Wirt D. Walker
1726 Mr. & Mrs. James R. Walker
        Receiving day Tuesday
1730 Mr. & Mrs. Joseph E. Otis
1730 Ralph C. Otis
1730 Mr. & Mrs. John E. Jenkins
1736 Mr. & Mrs. Hugh McBirney
1800 Mr. & Mrs. John J. Glessner
        Receive Tuesday
1808 Mr. & Mrs. O. R. Keith
1808 Mrs. Henry W. Hoyt
1812 George Henry Wheeler
1812 Dr. Henry L. Wheeler
1812 Mr. & Mrs. Lawrence A. Young
1816 Mrs. Charles M. Henderson &
        dr.
        Receiving day Tuesday
1816 Mr. & Mrs. W. H. Merrill jr.
1824 Mr. & Mrs. Secor Cunningham
1828 Mr. & Mrs. Daniel B. Shipman
1834 Mr. & Mrs. Fernando Jones
1834 Mr. & Mrs. Graham Jones
1900 Mr. & Mrs. Elbridge G. Keith
        & dr.
1900 Carl Keith
1900 Clarence B. Hall
1904 Mr. & Mrs. Walter W. Keith
1906 Mrs. Edson Keith
1936 Mr. & Mrs. S. W. Allerton
1936 Robert H. Allerton
2000 Mr. & Mrs. John M. Clark &
        dr. *Receiving day Tuesday*
2000 Bruce Clark
2010 Mr. & Mrs. W. L. Grey & drs.
2010 Walter Grey
2018 E. Walter Herrick
2018 Mrs. L. A. Herrick
2018 Miss Louise Herrick
2018 Mrs. Nicolas de Teresa
2026 Mr. & Mrs. D. Stettauer & dr.
2026 Mr. & Mrs. Charles S. Stettauer
2036 E. Buckingham & drs.
2036 Clarence Buckingham
2100 Mr. & Mrs. John B. Sherman
2108 Mr. & Mrs. Alex. H. Seelye
2108 Mrs. Miner T. Ames
2108 Miss Eleonora Cowen
2110 Mr. & Mrs. Edson Keith jr.
        Receive Tuesday 3 to 5 p. m.

2123 Thomas M. Avery
2123 Mr. & Mrs. Frank M. Avery
2123 Mrs. Ella S. Clark
2125 Mr. & Mrs. C. H. Wheeler
2201 Mr. & Mrs. Eugene Rockwell
    Pike *Receiving day Tuesday*
2207 Mr. & Mrs. Frank M. Murphy
2209 Mr. & Mrs. Jas. Morrison Al-
    lan & drs.
2209 Mrs. A. G. Story
2209 C. G. Story
2213 Mr. & Mrs. Henry Warner
    Farnum.
2219 Mr. & Mrs. Abner Price & dr.
2221 Mr. & Mrs. John J. Herrick
2223 Mrs. Hosmer A. Johnson
2223 Miss M. F. Seward
2227 Mr. and Mrs. Fred'k P. Bagley
2227 Mrs. Almeda Hodges
2231 Dr. & Mrs. John N. Crouse
2231 D. Howard Crouse
2231 Miss Elizabeth Harrison
2233 Mr. & Mrs. Wilton C. Roosevelt
2233 Mrs. Chas. W. Blend
2411 Mr. & Mrs. D. F. Garland
2411 Mr. & Mrs. Arthur J. Singer
2443 Mr. & Mrs. O. D. Orvis & dr.
    Receiving day Wednesday
2447 Dr. & Mrs. James F. Todd & dr.
2447 Harry Todd
2449 Mrs. Joel Bigelow
2449 Mr. & Mrs. Chas. W. Peterson
2453 Thomas S. Robinson
2453 Mrs. E. L. Whitaker
2457 J. W. Waughop & dr.
2459 Mr. and Mrs. Wm. E. Sayer
2459 Frank E. Sayer
2521 Dr. & Mrs. Frank S. Johnson
2535 Mrs. Stella Dyer Loring & drs.
    Receive Tuesday afternoon
    and 2d & 4th Friday even-
    ings October to May
2535 Miss Mary Jean Miller
2601 Mr. & Mrs. D. W. Keith & dr.
2603 Mr. & Mrs. Charles A. Coolidge
2607 Mrs. George C. Campbell
2607 Miss Jeannette Campbell.
2607 Otis R. Glover
2607 Henry T. Glover
2623 Dr. & Mrs. E. Wyllys Andrews
    Receive Monday afternoon
2625 Mr. and Mrs. Chas. H. Stark-
    weather
2631 Mr. & Mrs. Albert B. Dewey.
    Receiving day Tuesday
2631 Miss Alma H. Shufelt

2112 Mrs. M. M. Rothschild
2112 Miss Mamie F. Rothschild
2112 Monroe R. Rothschild
2112 Jesse Rothschild
2120 Mr. & Mrs. Frank S. Gorton
2126 Mr. & Mrs. Chas. D. Hamill
    Receiving day Tuesday
2126 Charles H. Hamill
2126 Philip W. Hamill
2126 Laurence Hamill
2126 Miss Alice W. Page
2126 Miss Eleanor Page
2130 Thomas Murdoch
2130 Miss Jane Murdoch
2140 Mr. & Mrs. Byron L. Smith
2200 Dr. & Mrs. Edwin M. Hale
2200 Mrs. Fanny Hale Gardiner
2200 Miss Evelyn Gardiner
2204 Mr. & Mrs. Cyrus Henry Clarke
2204 Paul Symonds
2204 Mrs. Margaret McKay
2206 Mr. & Mrs. John M. Cutter
2208 Mrs. James T. Hoyne
2208 T. H. Willis
2210 Mr. & Mrs. Malcolm D. Owen
2212 Mr. & Mrs. J. Arthur Lane
    Receiving day Tuesday
2212 Miss Charlotte Kendall Hull
2212 Miss Edna L. Dow
2216 Mrs. Nathaniel Goold
2216 Mr. & Mrs. John E. Goold
2216 Mrs. Edward F. Dyke
2400 Dr. J. C. McPherson
2400 Mrs. George A. Hall
2400 Mrs. Lodema Sherman
2406 Dr. & Mrs. J. S. Perekhan
    Receiving day Wednesday
2410 Mr. & Mrs. R. A. Kettle.
2412 Mrs. M. Anderson
2414 Mr. & Mrs. Chas. Edward Brown
    Receiving day Tuesday
2414 George F. Brown
2414 George Francis Brown jr.
2430 Mr. & Mrs. Fred'k Migely & dr.
    Receiving day Wednesday
2430 Rudolph E. Migely
2430 Fred A. Migely
2432 Mrs. E. C. Place
2432 Mrs. Belle Butterfield
2432 F J Mulcahy
2432 Joseph F. Rock
2456 H. D. Penfield & dr.
2458 Mr. & Mrs. John O'Hara & drs.
    Receiving day Tuesday
2458 John O'Hara jr.
2458 Mrs. Chas. O'Hara & dr.

2637 Mr. & Mrs. Ernest A. Hamill
2641 Mr. & Mrs. Alfred Landon
     Baker
2701 Mr. & Mrs. Noble B. Judah
2703 Mr. & Mrs. E. A. Lancaster
2703 Mrs. B. P. Hutchinson
2709 Mr. & Mrs. C. L. Hutchinson
          Receiving day Tuesday
2713 Mrs. Louisa B. Stephens
          Receiving day Tuesday
2713 R. Edmond D. Stephens
2719 Mr.&Mrs. L. O. Goddard & dr.
2719 Sterling Goddard
2723 Mr. and Mrs. A. F. Gartz
2725 Mr. & Mrs. Lewis W. Pitcher
          *Receive 2d & 4th Wednes-
          days.*
2725 Winfield T. Haines
2729 Mrs. J. C. Walter
2729 Alfred M. Walter
2729 Miss Sarah Sherman
2735 Mr. & Mrs. Henry A. Blair
2801 Mr. & Mrs. Geo. Ellery Wood
2801 Miss Maud M. Kelley
2807 Mr. & Mrs. F. D. Gray & dr.
2811 Mrs. Thos. H. Sheppard & dr.
2811 Mr. and Mrs. S. G. Clarke
2811 Mrs. M.·H. Clarke
2815 Mr. & Mrs. M.·J. Smiley
2821 Mr. & Mrs. Geo. H. Webster
          Receive Tuesday afternoon
2821 H. A. Webster
2821 Dr. Stuart Webster
2821 Miss M. L. Webster
2825 Mr. & Mrs. Chauncey Keep
2825 Mrs. Lyman Blair
2829 Thomas F. Keeley
2829 E. M. Keeley
2829 Miss Catharine A. Keeley
2831 Mrs. Geo. W. Fuller
2831 Henry B. Fuller
2831 Mr. and Mrs. Joseph A. Kelsey
2909 Charles H. Blair & dr.
2909 Mr. & Mrs. L. D. Warren
2911 Mr.& Mrs. Wm. T. Underwood
2915 Mr. & Mrs. Henry Stern & dr.
          Receive 1st and 3d Tuesday
2917 Mr.&Mrs.John H.Wrenn & drs.
2917 Harold B. Wrenn
2919 Mr. & Mrs. Frank G. Logan
2925 Mrs. Charlotte A. Hutchinson
2925 Miss Jessie Hutchinson
2925 George A. Hutchinson
2925 Mr. & Mrs. Robert D. Ward-
     well
2941 Mr. & Mrs. N. W. Campbell

2458 Charles O'Hara
2458 Frank O'Hara
2458 George O'Hara
2500 Mr. & Mrs. C. J. Tanner
2500 Mrs. A. Raymond
2500 Miss May Ford Chase
2510 Mr. & Mrs. J. S. Bousquet
2512 Mr. & Mrs. Jas. C. Martin
2512 Stephen D. May
2512 Miss Anna E. Kirk
2518 Mrs. William W. Phelps
2518 Mrs. Lucina C. Zelie
2518 Brayton Saltonstall
2522 Mr. & Mrs. William Alton
2522 Davis C. Alton
2522 William Alton jr.
2532 Mr. & Mrs. Walter H. Wilson
2536 Mr. & Mrs. Eugene Cary
2540 Dr. & Mrs. F. W. Mercer
          Receive Thursday 3 to 5 p. m.
2548 ·Mr.& Mrs.Myron L.Pearce&dr.
2552 Mr. & Mrs. A. G. Clark
2552 Paul H. Clark
2606 Dr. & Mrs. Joel R. Gore
2606 Mr. & Mrs. George R. Day
2606 Mr. & Mrs. H. P. Caldwell
2606 George I. Elmers
2618 Rev. & Mrs. Frank W. Gun-
     saulus
2618 Joseph L. Gunsaulus
2618 Miss Martha W. Gunsaulus
2618 Miss Beatrice Gunsaulus
2618 Miss Mary Gunsaulus
2618 Miss Helen Gunsaulus
2620 Mrs. L. B. Doggett & drs.
2620 Mrs. Geo. Newell Doggett
2620 O. J. Doggett
2620 William L. Doggett
2620 H. E. L. Doggett
2620 Arthur M. Doggett
2622 Dr. & Mrs. Chas. Gilbert Davis
2622 Carl B. Davis
2622 George G. Davis
2626 Mr. & Mrs. Edwin L. Gaylord
2628 Bruce B. Barney
2628 Mr. & Mrs. Edwin F. Getchell
2628 Mrs. B. B. Barney
2632 Mr. and Mrs. Ralph M. Shaw
2636 Dr. & Mrs. F. S. Coolidge
2638 Mr. & Mrs. B. W. Kendall
2640 Mr. & Mrs. William J. Watson
2700 Mr. & Mrs. H. C. Lytton
2700 Howard George Lytton
2700 Mr. & Mrs. August Benziger
2710 Mr. & Mrs. A. A. Sprague
2710 Miss C. A. Sprague

2943 Dr. & Mrs. Noble M. Eberhart
     Receiving day Thursday
2947 John C. Everett
2947 Mrs. William S. Everett & dr.
2947 Coleman S. Everett
2947 Edward W. Everett
2953 Mr. & Mrs. P. F. Gillespie
2953 John P. Gillespie
2955 Mr. & Mrs. Leo. Straus
     Receive 2d & 4th Fridays
2963 Mr. & Mrs. Samuel Stern
     Receive 1st & 3d Tuesdays
2963 Milton R. Stern
2965 Mrs. Helen P. Wilbur
2969 Mrs. L. Handt
2971 Mrs. William G. Mead & dr.
2973 Mr. & Mrs. H. W. Bryant
2975 Mr. & Mrs. B. R. DeYoung & dr.
2979 Mr. & Mrs. J. Cameron Pancoast
2979 Mrs. Anna V. Lynne
3011 Mrs. Charles Hutchinson
3011 J. William Hutchinson
3015 Mr. & Mrs. William Hill
3025 Mrs. E. P. Hall.
3025 Miss Mollie Hahn
3025 Mr. & Mrs. A. G. Newell
3025 Herbert E. Newell
3025 Mr. & Mrs. Frank A. Crandall & dr.
3025 Mrs. Caroline Cromwell & dr.
3025 Charles Cromwell
3031 Mr. & Mrs. H. A. Walker
3031 Mr. & Mrs. J. C. Bley
3031 Mr. & Mrs. Charles W. Newton
3113 Mr. & Mrs. E. C. Hayde & drs.
3117 Mr. & Mrs. T. R. Melody & dr.
3117 Mrs. M. Synon
3141 Mr. & Mrs. Joseph S. Smith
3143 Mrs. I. Lockey & dr.
3145 Mr. & Mrs. M. H. Moss
3149 Mr. & Mrs. Thos. E. Sullivan
3151 Mr. & Mrs. C. H. Simmons
3151 Dr. & Mrs. F. J. Staehle
3151 Mrs. H. G. Knapp
3153 Mr. & Mrs. Martin Barbe & drs.
3153 S. L. Strauss
3153 S. W. Rosenfield
3211 Mr. & Mrs. C. H. Allen & dr,
3211 Mr. & Mrs. C. S. Peacock
3221 Mr. & Mrs. T. D. Hurley
3229 Mr. & Mrs. A. H. Pratt & dr.
3229 Frank F. Pratt
3229 Fred R. Pratt
3229 Roy B. Pratt

2716 Mrs. Hiram Kelly
2720 Mr. & Mrs. A. C. Bartlett
2720 Frank D. Bartlett
2720 Miss Florence D. Bartlett
2730 Mrs. E. F. Dore & drs.
2730 Walter J. Dore
2732 Mr. & Mrs. Wm. R. Busenbark & dr.
2734 Mrs. A. M. H. Ellis
     Receiving day Monday
2734 Arthur L. Moore
2734 Miss Helen A. Moore
2734 George E. Moore
2802 Mr. & Mrs. Conrad Witkowsky & drs.
2804 Rev. & Mrs. S. J. McPherson
2808 Mrs. Edwin Pardridge
2808 Miss Florence Pardridge
2808 Mrs. Elizabeth Bailey
2808 Mrs. Melissa Roberts
2822 Mr. & Mrs. Geo. B. Phelps jr.
2824 Mr. & Mrs. Frederick T. Haskell
2824 Ralph B. Thomas
2828 Mr. & Mrs. Marvin Hughitt
2828 Marvin Hughitt jr.
2832 Mr. & Mrs. Joseph E. Otis jr.
2834 Rev. and Mrs. Wm. J. Chichester   *Receiving day Tuesday*
2834 Gemmill Chichester
2842 Mrs. Michael Corrigan
2900 Mr. & Mrs. Isaac N. Perry
     Receiving day Tuesday
2902 Mr. & Mrs. Edmund Adcock
2902 Mrs. A. M. Nicholes
2904 Mr. & Mrs. Milton R. Wood
2904 Miss Ida M. Wood
2912 Mr. & Mrs. Ferdinand Kramer & dr.
2912 Adolph Kramer
2914 Mr. & Mrs. Simon Straus & dr.
2914 Joseph Straus
2918 Mr. & Mrs. B. Loewenthal
2922 Mr. & Mrs. Marshall J. Wilson
2922 Henry K. Wilson
2936 Mr. & Mrs. W. Dempster & dr.
2942 Dr. E. H. Pratt
2942 Dr. & Mrs. T. E. Costain
2942 Miss E. M. Myers
2942 Miss Lavinia Hingston
2946 Morris Bauland & drs.
2946 Mr. & Mrs. Ernst Hofheimer
2954 Mrs. J. Sidney Mitchell
2954 Miss Annie B. Mitchell
2954 Leeds Mitchell
2954 Sidney Mitchell

3241 Mr. & Mrs. Jerry Sullivan
3255 Mr. & Mrs. Le Roy Brown
3255 Mrs. James Irvin
3337 Mr. & Mrs. B. Schram
3339 Mr. & Mrs. Daniel Krause&dr.
3343 Mrs. M. Wilmersdorf
3343 Alex Schoenberg
3343 Joel Schoenberg
3345 Mr. & Mrs. John Lyons
3347 Mr. & Mrs. Amson Stern & dr.
3347 Harry Stern
3401 Mr. & Mrs. E. Sternberg
3401 Mr. & Mrs. S. Hexter
3405 Mr. & Mrs. P. Ringer & dr.
3405 Charles Oosten
3407 Mr. & Mrs. H. Shaffner
3409 Mr. & Mrs. B. Herrick
3409 Chas. S. Herrick
3409 Joseph W. Herrick
3409 Milton Herrick
3411 Mr. & Mrs. Sol Loewenstein
3411½ Mrs. Tilla Henshaw
3413 Mr. & Mrs. Julius Guettel & dr.
3413 Mr. & Mrs. Alfred J. Cohen
3415 Mr. & Mrs. I. Levinson
3417 Mr.& Mrs.HenryForeman&dr.
3417 Mr. & Mrs. David H. Foreman
3419 Mr. & Mrs. A. L. Stone
3419 L. D. Hirsheimer
3421 Mr. & Mrs. Samuel Spitz
3443 Mr. & Mrs. John McCoy & dr.
3445 Mr. & Mrs. Eugene S. Weil
3447 Mr. & Mrs. S. Rosenthal
    Receive 1st Thursday
3447 Mr. & Mrs. L. Singer
3449 Mrs. E. S. Mandel & drs.
3449 Mrs. F. R. Anderson & dr.
3449 Martin L. Smith
3455 Mr. & Mrs. R. E. Moss
3455 Miss Adella Farquharson
3455 Miss Emma Farquharson
3539 Lewis M. Hammond
3541 Dr. & Mrs. Horatio Keeler &
    dr.
3541 George W. Keeler
3545 Mr. & Mrs. Chas. Genung
3545 Mrs. Mary J. Genung & drs.
3549 Mr. & Mrs. P. J. Van Vranken
3553 Dr. & Mrs. Edwin B. Tuteur
    Receiving day Wednesday
3553 Mrs. I. Tuteur
    Receiving day Thursday
3561 Mr. & Mrs. Bernhard Wolf
3561 Wm. B. Wolf
3561 Mr. & Mrs. Numa Lachman
3563 Mr. & Mrs. Henry Mayer & drs.

2960 Mr. & Mrs. Simon Yondorf
    Receive 1st and 3d Wedues-
    days.
2962 Daniel Ullmann & dr.
2964 M. W. Murphy & drs.
2964 Miss Anna W. Synon
2968 Mrs. Archibald Shaw
2968 John Shaw
2978 Mr. & Mrs. George Miller
2978 Mr. & Mrs. C. B. Phillips
    Receiving day Tuesday
2978 Harry J. Kendig
2978 Mr. & Mrs. T. Morris
3000 Mrs. Marion M. Inness
3000 Mr. & Mrs. James G. Rowe
3000 Rev. and Mrs. J. J. Lewis
3000 Mr. & Mrs. Thos. Eustace & dr.
3000 Mr. & Mrs. Edward P. Phelps
3000 Albert B. Bullard
3000 Miss Margaret Cloyd
3000 Miss Elizabeth Goodman
3000 Mrs. George Bennett
3002 Rev. & Mrs. A. J. Canfield
    Receiving day Monday
3002 John B. Canfield
3002 Mr. & Mrs. Martin L. Chase
3004 Mr. & Mrs. C. W. Bryant
3004 Miss Mae Musgrave
3004 Mr. & Mrs. H. G. Robinson
3004 Mr. & Mrs. Fred'k J. Schroter
3004 Mr. & Mrs. Geo. South Martin
3004 Mrs. B. W. Underwood
3006 Mr. & Mrs. Schuyler Haughey
3006 Louis C. Haughey
3006 Delmon W. Norton
3006 James R. Kehlor
3006 Henry M. Young
3006 Joshua H. Douglas
3006 Mr. & Mrs. L. A. Goddard
    Receiving day Thursday
3006 Mr.& Mrs. H. Temple Bellamy
3010 Dr. & Mrs. R. D'Unger & drs.
3010 Mr. & Mrs. Claude V. D'Unger
3010 Mr. & Mrs. Paul H. D'Unger
3010 Mrs. John T. Chumasero
3010 Kenneth P. Chumasero
3012 Mrs. Allen McDonald
3012 Mr. & Mrs. N. H. White
3016 Mrs. E. C. Ryder
3016 Dr. & Mrs. W. C. Dyer
3016 J. D. Cory
3018 Mrs. A. A. Gaylord & drs.
3018 Robert Gaylord
3020 Mr. & Mrs. Howard F. Chap-
    pell
3122 Mr. & Mrs. W. Middelschulte

3565 Mr. & Mrs. S. Lipski
3601 Mr. & Mrs. Chas. M. Leopold
3603 Mr. & Mrs. Henry Myer
3605 Mr. & Mrs. Geo. B. Moore
3607 Dr. & Mrs. G. C. Somers & dr.
3611 Mr. & Mrs. I. F. Brown
3613 Mr. & Mrs. Simon L. Marks
3615 Mr. & Mrs. Thos. C. Nash
3617 Mr.& Mrs.Chas. M. Barnes&dr.
3617 Mr. & Mrs. Chas. Ward
3617 George Weber
3617 Mr. & Mrs. Chas. Gilkinson
3627 Mr. & Mrs. M. Rubovits & dr.
3627 Isidor Rubovits
3629 Mr. & Mrs. D. C. DeWolf
3631 Mr. & Mrs. Ernest Cuthbert
3633 Mr. & Mrs. Edward A. Jacobs
3633 John Goldman
3633 Mrs. Sara Goldman
3635 Mr. & Mrs. Chas. Fass
Receiving day Friday
3637 Mr. & Mrs. Austin W. Wright
3637 Willard H. Wright
3639 Dr. & Mrs. John C. Lindsay
3639 Miss Mary E. Frantz
3641½ Mr. & Mrs. B. Herman
3643 Mr. & Mrs. E. T. Hitchcock
3645 D. E. McCurdy
3645 Miss N. M. Parker
3647 Mr. & Mrs. George L.McCurdy
3649 Mr. & Mrs. William Lilienfeld
3651 Mr. & Mrs. James l. Bradburn
3651 Mrs. James Ryan
3651 Miss Jennie May
3727 Mr. & Mrs. Samuel Despres & dr.
3727 Arthur Despres
3727 Sidney Despres
3729 Mrs. P. O'Neill
3729 John Gilcreest
3733 Mr. & Mrs. J. H. Bowers
3735 Mr. & Mrs. S. Witkowsky & dr.
3735 Jacob Witkowsky
3735 Leon Witkowsky
3737 Mr. & Mrs. Elias Katz & dr.
3739 Mr. & Mrs. C. W. Weatherson
3739 Mr. & Mrs. John Weatherson
3745 Charles W.Gindele
3747 Mr. & Mrs. Fred Honkamp
3753 Mr. & Mrs. J.W. Merriman&dr.
3757 Mr. & Mrs. C. Francis Davies
3801 Mrs. R. Guthmann
3801 Miss Ida Seligman
3805 Mr. & Mrs. M. Jacob Daube
3809 Mrs. J. O. Smith
3809 E. J. Smith

3124 Mr. & Mrs. A. E. Dore & dr.
3124 Mr. & Mrs. Edward F. Moore
3130 Mr. & Mrs. Jacob Williams
3130 James D. Williams
3130 Mr. & Mrs. Geo. E. Lincoln
3136 Mr. & Mrs. I. A. Heath
3148 Mr. & Mrs. M. L. Kaiser
3148 Mrs. H. Auerbach & dr.
3150 Mr. & Mrs. Aaron Boehm
3152 Mr. & Mrs. J. A. Thain
3152 Mr. & Mrs. R. N. Clarke
3154 Mr. & Mrs. DeWitt C. Clapp
3156 Mr. & Mrs. G. H. Fox
3212 Mr. & Mrs. R. Warner Hare & dr.
3224 Mr. & Mrs. Isaac Hess & dr.
3226 Mr. & Mrs. S. Mossler
3226 Mr. & Mrs. Leonard S. Prince
3228 Mr. & Mrs. Weston Green
3326 Mr. & Mrs. George H. Bowen
3346 Mr. & Mrs. Wm. Lehman
Receive 2d & 3d Fridays
3346 Miss Stella Bing
3348 Mr. & Mrs. L. E. Lebolt
Receive 1st and 3d Friday
3348 M. H. Lebolt
3348 J. Y. Lebolt
3348 George W. Lebolt
3348 Sidney Lebolt
3348 Nathan Lebolt
3350 Mr. & Mrs. Eugene Harbeck
3350 Jervis R. Harbeck
3360 Mr. & Mrs. Fred Myer
3360 Mr. & Mrs. Moses Myer
3364 James W. Duncan & dr.
3400 Dr. &. Mrs. L. D. McMichael
3400 Mr. & Mrs. Sam'l Hobart Lockett
3402 Dr. George B. Warne
3402 Dr. Emma N. Warne
3408 Dr. & Mrs. J. B. McFatrich
3416 Daniel T. McGraw
3416 Mr. & Mrs. Michael McGraw
3418 Mr. & Mrs. Denis O'Connell
3418 Herbert O'Connell
3418 Harry O'Connell
3422 Mr. & Mrs. Spencer Johnson
3422 August Gatzert
3422 Miss Ola B. Fickes
3422 Edward Flonacher
3424 Mr. & Mrs. Gilbert Garraghan
3424 Edward F. Garraghan
3436 Mr. & Mrs.George A.Holloway & dr.
3436 Harry C. Holloway
3446 Mr. & Mrs. Chas. R. Anderson

14

3809 Mr. & Mrs. Edw. L. Turner
3809 Mrs. M. C. Whittal
3813 Mr. & Mrs. D. Heinsheimer jr.
3813 Mr. & Mrs. H. Wertheimer
    Receive 1st and last Wednesdays
3819 Mr.&Mrs. G. A. Springer&drs.
    Receiving day Tuesday
3819 Edward L. Springer
3819 Paul Springer
3819 Mr. & Mrs. S. Loudenback
3913 Harry L. Carpenter
3919 C. A. Mondschein
3929 Dr. & Mrs. Alex Loew
3931 Mr. & Mrs. Joseph C. Braden
3933 Mr. & Mrs. Geo. W. Stone & dr.
3933 Miss Helen H. Harrison
3945 Mr. & Mrs. W. J. McMullen &
    drs.
3947 Mrs. B. Waixel & drs.
4011 Mr. & Mrs. Chas. W. Pierce
4031 Mr. & Mrs. Wm. J. Urquhart
4051 Mr. & Mrs. Wm. J. Kelly
4051 Mr. & Mrs. Wm. Heller
4051 Mr. & Mrs. Alonzo Shaw
4053 Mrs. L. W. Childs & dr.
4053 F. W. Cook
4053 Mr. & Mrs. Florence E. Sullivan
4055 Mr. & Mrs. D. W. Russell
4055 Mr. & Mrs. Geo. Sinclair & dr.
4055 Mr. & Mrs. J. T. Burnham jr.
4057 Mr. & Mrs. E. B. Anderson
4057 Mr. & Mrs. E. T. Mygatt
4057 Rev. & Mrs. G. A. Pflug
4057 Mr. & Mrs. C. Crozet Lake
4059 Mr. & Mrs. W. B. Mack
4059 Mr. & Mrs. Geo. Sumner
4203 Mr. & Mrs. Elbridge B. Keith
4233 Mr. & Mrs. I. O. Morris
4235 Mr. & Mrs. A. L. Kesner
    Receiving day Wednesday
4237 Mr. & Mrs. Joseph Hyman
4239 Mr. & Mrs. R. D. Peacock
4241 Mrs. A. Rothschild
4241 Joseph Rothschild
4241 Emil Rothschild
4321 Mr. & Mrs. Jacob Auerbach
4323 Dr. & Mrs. W. E. Schroeder
    Receiving day Wednesday
4325 Mr.&Mrs.M.Leopold Wormser
    Receiving day Sunday
4329 Mrs. C. W. Dameier & drs.
4329 Wm. C. Dameier
4329 Gustave A. Dameier
4329 Charles W. Dameier
4329 Robert Dameier

3548 Mr. & Mrs. Henry Kaufman
3550 Mr. & Mrs. S. Friedman
    Receive 2d Thursday
3558 Mr. & Mrs. Isaac Katzauer &
    dr.
3558 Sol Katzauer
3564 Mr. & Mrs. A. Wertheimer
3566 Mr. & Mrs. Abraham Louis
3600 Mr. & Mrs. Henry Barnet
3600 J. W. Barnet
3602 Mr. & Mrs. Max Leopold
3604 Mr. & Mrs. Solomon Freehling
    & dr.
3604 Ike Freehling
3604 Julius Freehling
3606 Mr. & Mrs. B. Rosenberg
3606 Mr. & Mrs. Harry Lazarus
3608 Mr. & Mrs. Charles Sax
3608 Mr. & Mrs. E. E. Levy
3614 Mr. & Mrs. Louis Frank
3614 Marcus Frank
3616 Mr.& Mrs. Nathan Hoffheimer
3616 Mrs. Ada Wolf
3626 Mr. & Mrs. S. G. Livingston
3626 Mr. & Mrs. Charles Kaufman
3626 Aaron Kaufman
3628 Mr. & Mrs. Geo. L. Sauter
3628 Mrs. B. Fernberg & dr.
3628 Wm. P. Fernberg
3632 Mr. & Mrs. Chas. Bachrach
3634 Mrs. M DeLee & drs.
3634 Dr. Joseph B. DeLee
3634 Solomon T. DeLee
3636 Mr. & Mrs. E. B. Martin
3640 Mrs. Duncan S. McBean
3640 Miss Jeanette Kittredge
3640 Miss Josephine Kittredge
3640 Mrs. Harriet Anderson & dr.
3642 Mr. & Mrs. Orville W. Ballard
3642 George S. Ballard
3644 Mr. & Mrs. Wm. Blair
3654½ Mr. & Mrs. H. Wachenheimer
3658 Mr. & Mrs. Julius Starrett
3808 Rev. & Mrs. Jas. M. Green
3832 Mr. & Mrs. Jos. Heilbron
3834 Mr. & Mrs. Harry D. Irwin
3842 Mr. & Mrs. Benjamin Myer
3844 Mr. & Mrs. John P. Vidvard &
    drs.
3844 Walter Vidvard
3910 Mr. & Mrs. Louis Keefer & dr.
3910 E. F. Keefer
3914 Mr. & Mrs. Samuel Nathan
3914 Sidney S. Nathan
3914 Arthur S. Nathan

4331 Mr. & Mrs. A. M. Cobb
4333 Mr. & Mrs. Samuel Osterman
4337 Mr. & Mrs. Frank E. Hill
4337 Mr. & Mrs. I. H. Murray
4339 Mr. & Mrs. Jesse Boydell
4339 Mrs. Mary P. Bloom
4339 Mr. & Mrs. E. C. Kerdolff
4341 Mr. & Mrs. Aaron L. New
4357 Mr. & Mrs. Geo. J. Kendall
4357 Mrs. L. M. Bennett
4357 Mr. & Mrs. J. M. Hussey
4359 Mr. & Mrs. W. C. Snell
4359 Mr. & Mrs. Wm. H. Kane
4359 Mrs. Louise Mitchell & dr.
4401 Mr. & Mrs. J. K. Comstock
4401 Mr. & Mrs. R. W. Hayner
4403 Mr. & Mrs. John E. Kernott
4405 Mr.&Mrs. D.W.Babcock & drs.
4407 Mr. & Mrs. E. W. Westlake
4409 Mr. & Mrs. Ernest Heg
4411 Prof. & Mrs. Lewis H. Anderson
4423 Mr. & Mrs. Frank A. Brainard
Receiving day Wednesday
4423 Mr. & Mrs. Simon Bodenheimer
4423 Mr. & Mrs. Harry D. Piatt
4423 Mrs. S. M. Downie
4427 Mr. & Mrs. C. F. Tritschler
4439 Mr. & Mrs. G. B. VanNorman
4441 Mr. & Mrs. R. H. Lee
4507 Mr. & Mrs. M. Sondheimer
4509 Mr. & Mrs. Benj. F. Campbell
4509 Mrs. Nannie Hess
4509 M. W. Hess
4509 Mr. & Mrs. Chas. W. Turner
4509 Mr. & Mrs. Edgar Sawyer&drs.
4509 Mr. & Mrs. W. H. Hagerty
4515 Mrs. Catherine O'Connor & dr.
4515 Mrs. E. Gephart
4515 Mr. & Mrs. Wm. J. Slattery
4517 Mr. & Mr. Justin Keith
4517 Miss Lillian Willis
4517 Miss Hattie Willis
4517 Mr. & Mrs. A. Feltenstein & dr.
Receiving day Thursday
4517 Mr. & Mrs. H. W. Helm
4517 F. G. Parsons
4523 Mr. & Mrs. John O'Brien & drs.
4523 John O'Brien jr.
4523 Robert O'Brien
4713 Dr. & Mrs. Jas. T. Gilmour
4713 Robert McWhirter
4713 Mr. & Mrs. Byron Kingsbury & dr.
4715 D. C. Roberton

3918 Mr. & Mrs. B. Mergentheim
Receive 1st and 3d Fridays
3920 Mr. & Mrs. Julius Loeb
3922 Mr. & Mrs. A. Kleinert & dr.
3924 Mrs. Johanna M. Loeb
3924 Sidney Loeb
3926 Mr. & Mrs. H. Scarborough
3926 Mrs. E. E. Scarborough
3928 Mr. & Mrs. David Moog
3930 Mr. & Mrs. George T. Ward
3944 Mr. & Mrs. Austin E. Young
3950 Mr. & Mrs. John W. Morrison
3950 Clyde A. Morrison
4010 Mr. & Mrs. Herman Hart & dr.
4010 Leo H. Hart
4020 Mr. & Mrs. Thos. Sollitt & drs.
4020 Mr. & Mrs. Oliver Sollitt
4024 Mr. & Mrs. L. B. Kent & drs.
4030 Mr. & Mrs. Charles N. Gillett
4030 Mr. & Mrs. T. S. Gillett
4032 Mr. & Mrs. Henry G. Young
4036 Mr. & Mrs. R. Frank Quick
4112 Mr. & Mrs. Wm. B. Quinn
4120 Mr. & Mrs. T. H. Ingwersen
4128 Mr. & Mrs. Bion J. Arnold
4128 W. L. Arnold
4128 R. G. Arnold
4136 Mr. & Mrs. Wm. Maurer
Receive Thursday
4136 Raymond B. Swigart
4144 Mr. & Mrs. E. H. Ingwersen
4156 Mr. & Mrs. Charles S. Jones
4208 Mrs. Anna Peake
4208 Miss Margaret Wilson
4208 David Wilson
4210 Mrs. Florence C. Dodson
4210 James McElroy
4214 Mr. & Mrs. C. E. Bartell
Receiving day Thursday
4216 H. E. Updike & dr.
4216 P. B. Updike
4218 Mr. & Mrs. Simon Richter & dr.
4234 Mr. & Mrs. Robert T. Lunham
4316 Mr. & Mrs. Samuel Ayers
4318 Dr. & Mrs. B. Rel VanDoozer
4324 Mrs. L. Smith
4324 Mr. & Mrs. Chauncy W. Foster
4326 Mr. & Mrs. Arthur G. Baker
4416 Mr. & Mrs. Sol Zork
Receiving day Friday
4416 Mr. & Mrs. Wm. J. Mullen
4416 Mr. & Mrs. Wm. Phillips
4420 Mr. & Mrs. Horace M. Keenan
4420 Mrs. C. E. Plato
4422 Mr. & Mrs. Robt. E. Sackett
4430 Mr.& Mrs. T. H. Wickes jr.

4715 John Roberton
4715 Miss Helen Roberton
4715 Mr. & Mrs. Wm. Warner Abbott *Receiving day Friday*
4715 Edwin B. Frank
4715 Chas. D. Springer
4715 George B. Springer
4715 Miss Mary M. Springer
4715 Miss Gertrude Springer
4723 Mr. & Mrs. Henry E. Pierpont
4723 Mrs. H. S. Pierpont & dr.
4723 Mr. & Mrs. C. D. Shepherd .
4725 Mr. & Mrs. S. P. McKelvey
4725 L. C. Young & dr.
4725 Mr. & Mrs. Francis T. von Albade
4725 Mrs. Ella W. Felt
4725 Winchester W. Felt
4725 Mr. & Mrs. A. M. Gibson & dr.
4725 William A. Gibson
4731 Mr. & Mrs. John F. Norman
4731 Mrs. Caroline Clarke & dr.
4733 Mr. & Mrs.Wm. Murphy & drs.
4733 Mr. & Mrs. Wm. Apmadoc & dr.
4733 Dr. M. P. Apmadoc
4733 W. T. Apmadoc
4805 Mr. & Mrs. D. 'M. Kohner
4805 Mr. & Mrs. I. L. Maas
4807 Miss Lena Kline
4807 Miss Emma Kline
4811 Mrs. H. Danziger & dr.
4811 A. L. Danziger   .
4811 Oscar Danziger
4811 Emanuel Danziger
4813 Mr. & Mrs. Geo. E. Nichols
4813 Mrs. Clara F. Miller & dr.
4813 E. T. Means
4817 Mr. & Mrs. Louis E. Herrick
4819 Mr. & Mrs. Wm. Leckie
4839 Mr. & Mrs. L. J. Odell
4947 Mr. & Mrs. A. A. Reeve
4949 Mr. & Mrs. J. K. Blatchford
4949 Mr. & Mrs. Harry L. Holland
4957 Mr. & Mrs. M. D. Coffeen
4959 Mr. & Mrs. D. W. Caswell
4959 Mr. & Mrs. J. W. Hunter
4959 Mrs. Dora H. Somes
5149 Mr. & Mrs. S. Rubel
5153 Mr. & Mrs. Alex Whyte
5153 Alexander J. Whyte
5153 J. Allen Whyte
5153 Mrs. Geo. E. Sanderson
5155 Mr. & Mrs. Charles B. Ott
5335 Mr. & Mrs. Joseph C. Chapeck
    Receiving day Tuesday

4430 Mr. & Mrs. Geo. Morganroth
4430 Mr. & Mrs. Joseph S. Wheeler
4432 Mr. & Mrs. Henry Rosenfield
4432 Mr. & Mrs. J. H. Schoen
4438 Mr. & Mrs. A. G. Zulfer
4438 P. M. Zulfer
4450 Dr. & Mrs. Chas. Krusemarck
4506 Mr. & Mrs. Allan C. Story
4506 Mr. & Mrs. Fred W. Story
4512 Mr. & Mrs. John G. Willden
4520 Mr. & Mrs. Henry P. Sieh
4526 Mr. & Mrs. L. A. Barry
4526 Mr. & Mrs. R. W. Weber
4526 Mr. & Mrs. J. A. Thomas
4528 Mr. & Mrs. John J. Cashin
4528 Mr. & Mrs. Thos. Wainwright
4528 Mr. & Mrs. Louis Kronthal
4528 Benj. Kronthal
4528 Leo Kronthal
4530 Mrs. Wm. Brown & drs.
4530 Dr. Wm. H. D. Brown
4530 Fred A. Brown
4536 Mr. & Mrs. Frederick Geist
4540 Mr. & Mrs. George Wood
4540 Mr. & Mrs. M. B. Mackey
4600 Mr. & Mrs. J. Claude Bunch
4600 Mrs. Frederick F. Daggett
4600 Mr. & Mrs. C. E. Wickham
4602 Mr. & Mrs. Payson E. Crissey
4602 Mr. & Mrs. R. Harry Rouse
4616 Mr. & Mrs. Edward A. Bern
4626 Mr. & Mrs. J. P. Molloy
4628 Mrs. Albert W. Landon
4628 Mrs. Cora Knight
4628 Mrs. Ruth McDwire
4630 Mr. & Mrs. Leopold Newhouse
4630 Henry L. Newhouse
4630 Mr. & Mrs. Jacob M. Loeb
4632 Mr. & Mrs. Henry Liberman
4634 Mr. & Mrs. Ernest C. Cole
4636 Dr. & Mrs. S. Wesley Jacobs
4636 Rex J. Burlingame
4638 Mr. & Mrs. Judson A. Tolman
4638 Judson Allen Tolman jr.
4640 Mr. & Mrs. Arthur G. Lamm
4720 Mr. & Mrs. Richard Fitzgerald
4724 Mr. & Mrs. Isaac Jesselson
4728 Mr. & Mrs. C. A. Garvey
4728 Mr. & Mrs. Julius J. Cohen
4728 Mr. & Mrs. Harry Pagin
4732 Mr. & Mrs. Timothy Sullivan
4734 Mr. & Mrs. James O. Fisher
4734 Mr. & Mrs. Ned C. Smith
4736 Mr. & Mrs. Walter C. Huling
    Receiving day Thursday
4736 Mr. & Mrs. Sol Bloom

5903 Mr. & Mrs. Thomas C. Mould-
     ing
6031 Mr. & Mrs. J. L. Geist

4820 Lemuel J. Swift
4842 Mr. & Mrs. Benj. Deacon
4842 Mrs. Annie McConville & drs.
5484 Mr. & Mrs. F. W. Furry
5486 Mr. & Mrs. E. H. Raymond
4856 Mr. & Mrs. O. D. Irwin
4858 Dr. & Mrs. A. P. Sawyer
4950 Mr. & Mrs. Geo. G. McRoy
5234 Mr. & Mrs. W. R. Toppan
5248 Dr. & Mrs. Howard Crutcher
5250 Mrs. L. P. Harvey
5250 Mrs. L. B. Taylor
5250 Mrs. Hall Taylor
5250 Dr. David Bokhof
5956 Mr. & Mrs. J. H. Wilkerson

4740 Mr. & Mrs. Wm. Lederer
4740 Julius Oppenheimer
4740 Mr. & Mrs. W. B. Jerome
4740 Mr. & Mrs. A. D. Mergentheim
4748 Mr. & Mrs. Luis Jackson
4748 Mme. H. S. Peixotto
      Receiving day Thursday
4748 G. D. Maduro Peixotto
4748 The Misses Peixotto
4748 Mr. & Mrs. A. B. D'Ancona
4752 Mr. & Mrs. Leon A. Strauss
4752 Mr. & Mrs. Max M. Wolfarth
4752 Mr. & Mrs. Andrew C. Dallas
4756 Mr. & Mrs. N. E. Ives
4800 Dr. & Mrs. J. M. Lang
4800 Mr. & Mrs. E. Percy Warner
4800 Percy R. Stephens
4808 Dr. & Mrs. F. M. Celley
4808 Mr. & Mrs. J. D. Clark
4820 Mr. & Mrs. John A. Nourse

PRINCETON AVENUE.

6949 Mr. & Mrs. J. M. Towers
7047 Dr. & Mrs. J. S. Beaudry
7051 Mr. & Mrs. Julian A. Wentz &
     dr.
7105 Mr. & Mrs. Thomas J. Eulette
7105 Mrs. E. Heath
7131 Mr. & Mrs. D. R. Patterson
7141 Mr. & Mrs. Fred A. Jones & dr.
7141 Mrs. Maggie W. Hyde
7153 Mr. & Mrs. W. Forman Collins
      Receiving day Wednesday
7157 Mr. & Mrs. Chas. W. Baker
7207 Mr. & Mrs. J. E. G. Scott
7207 Mrs. Barclay Felch
7351 Mr. & Mrs. S. J. Stebbins

7100 Mr. & Mrs. Robert Rae jr.
7100 Miss L. J. Wolff
7106 Mr. & Mrs. E. C. Leach
7106 Harry L. Leach
7110 Mr. & Mrs. Geo. G. Spencer
7116 Mr. & Mrs. Charles R. Harsh-
     berger & dr.
7116 Adam Harshberger
7130 Mr.& Mrs. Frank F. Dickinson
7148 Mr. & Mrs. J. Hodgkins
7148 William Hodgkins
7214 Mr. & Mrs. L. A. Walton
7214 W. S. Woodworth
7220 Mr. & Mrs. H. C. Staver
      Receiving day Thursday
7316 Mr. & Mrs. Lincoln Bartlett

RHODES AVENUE.

3143 Mr. & Mrs. Wm. E. Crossette
3145 Mr. & Mrs. William W. Clay
3149 Carl H. Weil
3151 Mr. & Mrs. George McFadden
     & dr.
3155 Mr. & Mrs. Abner C. Harding
3201 Mr. & Mrs. J. A. Knisely
3205 Mr. & Mrs. Ben Steinfeld
3213 Mr. & Mrs. M. H. Berg
3215 Mr. & Mrs. Nathan Friedman
     & dr.
      Receiving day Wednesday
3215 Abraham B. Friedman
3217 Mr. & Mrs. A. M. Einstein
3219 Mr. & Mrs. J. Simonson

3126 Mr. & Mrs. Uzziel P. Smith
      Receiving day Friday
3146 Mr. & Mrs. Marcus I. Sloman
3200 Mrs. Elizabeth Porter
3200 J. T. Geltmacher
3218 Mr. & Mrs. Charles B. Orr
3222 Mrs. Frank VanVoorhis
3222 Apollos D. Foote
3224 Mr. & Mrs. Myron H. Beach
3224 Harry L. Beach
3226 Mr. & Mrs. A. J. Deniston
3238 Dr. F. M. Scott
3238 Dr. Lucy F. Scott
3240 Mr. & Mrs. E. M. Bowman
      Receive 3d Mondays

3223 Mr. & Mrs. Thomas Davies
    Receiving day Wednesday
3225 Mr. & Mrs. James Angus
3231 Mr. & Mrs. E. G. Ewart
3233 Mr.&Mrs. Abraham A. DeVore
3233 Miss Carrie Long
3235 Mr. & Mrs. Harry F. Conly
3235 Charles C. Belknap
3235 William S. Kenny
3239 Mr. & Mrs. Edw. J. Wiggin
3241 Mr. & Mrs. L. M. Wurzburger
3243 Mr. & Mrs. Harry Barnard
3245 Mr. & Mrs. S. M. Rothschild &
    drs.
3245 I. D. Rothschild
3245 Wm. L. Rothschild
3247 Mrs. M. Levie & dr.
3247 Charles M. Levie
3247 Jerome M. Levie
3247 Oliver M. Levie
3249 Mr. & Mrs. Frank Lewald
3307 Mrs. Alice E. Silke & dr.
3307 Mr. & Mrs. Edwin A. Munger
3309 Rev. & Mrs. Bernhard Felsen-
    thal & drs.
3309 Edwin I. Felsenthal
3311 Mr. & Mrs. Charles Matthias
3339 Bonham M. Fox
3339 Harvey Fox
3339 Dr. Harriet Magee Fox
3569 E. L. Morse
3839 Loyal W. Murphy
3839 William E. Williams
6559 Dr. & Mrs. Geo. W. Winslow
    Receiving day Wednesday

3242 Mr. & Mrs. D. VanNess Person
3248 Mr. & Mrs. L. W. Reiss & dr.
3248 William Reiss
3254 Mrs. B. Levison & dr.
    Receive Thursday
3256 Mr. & Mrs. Willard A. Smith
3312 Mr. & Mrs. Edgar D. Packard
3314 Justin E. Loomis & dr.
3334 Mr. and Mrs. Chas. H. Mac-
    Donald
3334 Mr. & Mrs. Geo. H. Camp-
    bell
3336 Mr. & Mrs. S. C. Knight
3342 Mr. & Mrs. Chas. E. Whit-
    more
3342 Mrs. W. W. Everts
3342 Miss Grace T. Smith
3344 Mr. & Mrs. John H. Leslie
3348 Mr. & Mrs. H. G. McCartney
3348 Mrs. A. Miller
3350 Mr. & Mrs. A. W. Merrill
3352 Dr. & Mrs. Willis H. Gale
3356 Mr. & Mrs. J. W. Prindiville
    Receiving day Thursday
3424 Mrs. David Moore
3430 Dr. & Mrs. John H. Hollister
3432 Mr. & Mrs. J. T. Richards
3434 Mr. & Mrs. Charles M. Gates
3438 Mr. & Mrs. Geo. Pitkin & dr.
3534 Mr. & Mrs. E. Edward Van
    Dalson
3756 Mr. & Mrs. Emanuel Weil
    Receive 1st Thursday in mo.
6738 Mr. & Mrs. Louis A. McDonald

RIDGEWOOD COURT.

5405 Mr. & Mrs. Henry Bosch
5413 Mr. & Mrs. C. S. Wheeler
    Receiving day Thursday
5423 Mr. & Mrs. A. F. McMillan
5463 Mr. & Mrs. B. W. Wight
5475 Mr. & Mrs. S. C. Goss
    Receiving day Friday

5468 Prof. & Mrs. Clarence F. Castle
5470 Mr. & Mrs. George R. English

5422 Mr. & Mrs. George W. James
5430 Mr. & Mrs. E. S. Hawley & drs.
5430 F. R. Hawley
5440 Mr. & Mrs. E. Joseph Ryan
    Receiving day Wednesday
5442 Prof. & Mrs. C. Riborg Mann
5450 Mr. & Mrs. A. S. Bradley & drs.
5450 A. S. Bradley jr.
5460 Mr. & Mrs. James Person

ROSALIE COURT.

5729 Mr. & Mrs. Hamilton Fraser
5729 Charles E. Slayback
5735 Mr. & Mrs. S. H. Richardson
5751 Mr. & Mrs. Chas. H. McCul-
    lough jr.

5708 Dr. & Mrs. John C. Cook
    Receiving day Tuesday
5712 Mr. & Mrs. Elliott Durand &
    dr.
5732 Mr. & Mrs. William B. Ottman

5755 Rev. James H. Bourns
5755 Mr. & Mrs. Geo. W. Gehlbach
5807 Mr. & Mrs. Wm. P. Ogden
5809 Mrs. F. W. Cleverdon
    Receives Friday p. m.

5816 Mr. & Mrs. J. H. Pratt
5824 Maj. & Mrs. Fred A. Smith
5838 Mr. & Mrs. Warner Smeenk
5838 Mr. & Mrs. Cassius M. Lewis
5850 Mr. & Mrs. Charles Ffrench
5854 Mr. & Mrs. Marc M. Reynolds
5854 Mr. & Mrs. N. Anderson
5854 Mrs. Hart Rawson

5736 Mr. & Mrs. Wm. F. Fox & dr.
5740 Henry T. Chace & dr.
5740 Henry T. Chace jr.
5744 Mr. & Mrs. Ernest W. Heath
5744 J. H. Hamilton
5752 Mr. & Mrs. Charles Bonner
5758 Mr. & Mrs. Chas. F. Adams
5760 Mr. & Mrs. C. M. Smalley
5804 Mr. & Mrs. A. H. Caryl & dr.
5806 Mr. & Mrs. John H. Wood
5810 Mr. & Mrs. William Waterman
5810 Mr. & Mrs. John Jay Magee
5812 Mr. & Mrs. Worth E. Caylor

ROSS AVENUE.

6518 Mr. & Mrs. G. T. Tompson
6554 Mr. & Mrs. Fred L. Chase
6558 Mrs. Harriet Brown & drs

6558 Lewis J. Brown
6558 Wm. T. Brown

SAINT LAWRENCE AVENUE.

4209 Mr. & Mrs. Moses B. Harrell
4227 Mrs. S. J. Neeson
4231 Mr. & Mrs. H. M. Jenner & drs.
    Receiving day Thursday
4233 Mrs. Martha J. Boomer & dr.
4321 Mr. & Mrs. Robert E. Dickey
4337 Mr. & Mrs. B. F. Horsting
4341 Mr. & Mrs. G. D. Barrett
4357 Mr. & Mrs. A. F. Brooks & dr.
4401 Mr. & Mrs. Arthur J. Stevens
4429 Mr. & Mrs. William G. Webber
4429 Mr. & Mrs. George S. Snider
4521 Mr. & Mrs. B. F. Hill
4523 Mr. & Mrs. Leslie J. Dodds
4523 Mr. & Mrs. S. M. Dille & dr.
4631 Mr. & Mrs. Joseph H. Lenehan
4637 Mr. & Mrs. K. F. Griffiths
4711 Mr. & Mrs. Robert N. Ward
4801 Mr. & Mrs. Edward A. Irwin
4821 Mr. & Mrs. G. D. Taylor
4821 Mr. & Mrs. Chas. A. VanAnden
4823 Mr. & Mrs. R. S. Hill
4823 Mr. & Mrs. Quimby W. Loverin
4837 Mr. & Mrs. Dennis R. Smith

4234 Mr. & Mrs. James M. Dibb
4236 Dr. & Mrs. Albert M. Markle
4238 Mr. & Mrs. W. S. Harpole
4252 Mr. & Mrs. S. A. DeBolt
4324 Mr. & Mrs. Jacob B. Hammond
4344 Mr. & Mrs. T. Lilienfeld
4344 Mr. & Mrs. S. P. Pollack
4346 Mr. & Mrs. Lee Rubens
    Receive 2d Wednesday
4416 Mr. & Mrs. W. H. Underwood
4422 Mr. & Mrs. William Groh
4424 Mr. & Mrs. J. N. Kirch
4424 W. B. Miller
4514 Mr. & Mrs. Wm. Austin
4530 Mr. & Mrs. E. L. Bishop
4544 Mr. & Mrs. R. Wolfner
4544 Mr. & Mrs. Charles L. Page
4800 Roy W. Irwin
4812 Mr. & Mrs. S. J. Chadwick
4812 Mr. & Mrs. Ordell H. Powers
4938 Mr. & Mrs. Maurice Reis

4839 Mr. & Mrs. Albert L. Swift

SOUTH SANGAMON STREET.

7748 Mr. & Mrs. J. H. Long

7754 Mr. & Mrs. T. M. Colwell
7804 Mr. & Mrs. G. A. Clark

SEVENTY-FIRST PLACE.

761 Dr. & Mrs. Chas. M. Pusey

780 Mr. & Mrs. G. H. Binkley
828 Mr. & Mrs. Alex. J. Jones
874 Mr. & Mrs. Henry W. Walton

SEVENTY-SECOND STREET.

1163 Col. & Mrs. Wm. V. Jacobs

874 Mr. & Mrs. H. H. Lyon
890 Mr. & Mrs. Edward J. Eames

SEVENTY-SECOND PLACE.

849 Mrs. John Penfield & dr.
943 Mr. & Mrs. J. W. Andrews
947 Mr. & Mrs. John Dempsey

858 Mr. & Mrs. Wm. P. Adams

SEVENTY-FIFTH STREET.

1437 Dr. Harry J. Lynn

WEST SEVENTY-EIGHTH STREET.

615 Mr. & Mrs. H. A. Smith

619 Mr.& Mrs. Jeremiah Watts & dr.
621 Mr. & Mrs. Clifford A. Lake

WEST SEVENTY-NINTH STREET.

507 Mr. & Mrs. J. J. Monahan

SIDNEY AVENUE.

4405 Dr. & Mrs. C. H. Briscoe
    Receiving day Tuesday
4407 Mr. & Mrs. Charles Northup
4433 Mr. & Mrs. Nelson H. Town
    Receiving day Thursday
4437 Mr. & Mrs. Otis H. Waldo
4441 Frank G. Gardner
4441 Harry Breese Signor
4443 Mr. & Mrs. Adolph Lund
4445 Mr. & Mrs. George B. Horr
4451 Mrs. John A. Grier
    Receiving day Tuesday
4451 Mrs. Russell H. Stevens
    ——
4456 Mr. & Mrs. John W. Skeele

4400 Mr. & Mrs. Clark D. Osborn
4404 Mr. & Mrs. A. M. Burns
4406 Mrs. Stella Tenney
4406 Miss Carrie M. Knowles
4408 Mr. & Mrs. S. Hallett Greeley
4432 Mr. & Mrs. Edward W. Williams
4438 Mr. & Mrs. Geo. B. Shattuck
4440 Mr. & Mrs. H. G. Dickenson
4442 Mr. & Mrs. W. O. Pringle
4442 Robert Pringle
4446 Mr. & Mrs. Henry D. Wetmore
4450 Mr. & Mrs. James T. Fulton
4452 Mr. & Mrs. I. A. Newman
4454 Mr. & Mrs. Charles M. Brooks

SIXTIETH STREET.

252 Mr. & Mrs. P. Henry Bettman
252 Mr. & Mrs. Arthur E. Lumsden
290 Mr. & Mrs. Geo. F. Greenleaf
322 Mrs. Isadore Van Hise & drs.

600 Mr. & Mrs. R. Chester Frost
910 Dr. & Mrs. Staley N. Chapin
910 Miss Mary E. Chapin

WEST SIXTIETH STREET.

341 Mr. & Mrs. J. J. Hayes
343 Mr. & Mrs. A. J. Schevers
539 Mr. & Mrs. F. D. Thomason
543 Mr. & Mrs. C. W. Carr
551 Mrs. B. T. Sample & dr.
611 Mr. & Mrs. Frank G. Brown &
     dr. *Receiving day Friday*
611 Oliver S. Brown
611 James S. Brown

520 Mr. & Mrs. O. A. Matthews
524 Dr. & Mrs. U. M. Richardson
524 Mr. & Mrs. C. J. Beattie
556 Mr. & Mrs. A. H. Ebersol
———
615 Mr. & Mrs. F. J. Johnson
619 Mr. & Mrs. Philip Allen
719 Mrs. Alice Demerse

WEST SIXTIETH PLACE.

317 Mrs. Cyrus F. Smith
327 Mr. & Mrs. Otto Kalteich
327 Emil A. Hoeppner
339 Mr. & Mrs. John Taylor
353 Mr. & Mrs. Homer Bevans
529 Mr. & Mrs. E. S. Swift

338 Mr. & Mrs. F. J. Bramhall
518 Mrs. Catherine Dietrich
518 Frank E. Dietrich
612 Mr. & Mrs. Ira W. Allen
612 Rev. Hamilton F. Allen

SIXTY-FIRST STREET.

215 Mr. & Mrs. Edward Browne
215 Dr. Marvin Chapin
221 Mr. & Mrs. D. S. Lasier
     Receiving day Tuesday
225 Mr. & Mrs. George W. Riggs
437 Prof. & Mrs. C. W. Votaw

222 Mr. & Mrs. William L. Shepard
     & dr.
240 Mr. & Mrs. John Shepherd
     Receiving day Thursday
240 Mr. & Mrs. John E. Shepherd
250 L. D. Wallace, jr.
260 Mr. & Mrs. F. C. Nicholas

WEST SIXTY-FIRST STREET.

321 Mr. & Mrs. Ralph E. Lidster
323 Mrs. E. W. True
325 Mr. & Mrs. Walter French
327 Mr. & Mrs. J. T. Peck
335 Mr. & Mrs. D. C. Stebbins
339 Edwin Brown
345 Mr. & Mrs. G. M. Stackpole
353 Mr. & Mrs. A. S. Green & drs.
623 Mr. & Mrs. C. Porter Johnson
627 Mr. & Mrs. A. L. Whitehall
———
620 Mr. & Mrs. Frank M. Hill
640 Mr. & Mrs. Ansel Hales
648 Dr. & Mrs. Lowell F. Ingersoll

318 James D. Marston
350 Dr. & Mrs. A. H. Champlin & dr.
418 Rev. & Mrs. Gilbert Frederick
418 Mrs. Emily Mann
418 Franklin Mann
514 Dr. & Mrs. A. F. Harris
528 Miss Edith Carpenter
528 Mr. & Mrs. Milton T. Zimmerman
     Receive Friday
528 Arthur P. Zimmerman
538 Mr. & Mrs. Jos. Couthoui
548 Mr. & Mrs. H. M. Henderson
548 Mrs. Martha Lyon
552 Mr. & Mrs. James D. Neilson
558 James E. Eaton

WEST SIXTY-FIRST PLACE.

317 Mr. & Mrs. Edward Larkin & dr.
325 Mr. & Mrs. I. LeGrand Lockwood
     Receiving day Thursday
335 Mrs. M. R. Kesler
335 Arthur E. Kesler
335 Mrs. S. C. Kesler
533 Mr. & Mrs. Samuel G. Goss

318 Mr. & Mrs. W. D. Nicholes & dr.
318 I. Ellsworth Nicholes
318 Mr. & Mrs. Chas. W. Braith-
     waite
340 Mr. & Mrs. F. A. Woodbury
356 Mr. & Mrs. P. W. George
356 Cyrus W. George

535 Rev. & Mrs. N. S. Haynes
603 Mr. & Mrs. W. W. Robinson
607 Mrs. C. E. Sloan & drs.
733 Mr. & Mrs. Charles W. Taylor

——

630 L. Bartholomew
732 Mr. & Mrs. Willard C. Smith

402 Mr. & Mrs. F. F. Porter
522 Mr. & Mrs. James Baynes
528 A. J. Cutler
532 Mr. & Mrs. C. S. Deneen
540 Mr. & Mrs. Robert J. Roulston
544 Mr. & Mrs. E. C. Field
608 Mr. & Mrs. E. T. Evans
608 B. C. Evans

SIXTY-SECOND STREET.

487 Mr. & Mrs. J. W. Bleasdale
487 James A. Fullenwider
515 Mr. & Mrs. A. A. Barnet
533 Mr. & Mrs. Munson T. Case

573 Mr. & Mrs. Archibald W. Taft
583 A. Norman Dempsey
647 R. S. Prindiville

WEST SIXTY-SECOND STREET.

505 Lee F. English
513 Rev. & Mrs. H. Francis Perry
515 Mr. & Mrs. Robert S. Padan
517 Dr. & Mrs. John Sumney & drs.
525 Mr. & Mrs. James C. Davis
529 Mr. & Mrs. J. E. Armstrong
533 Mr. & Mrs. David Ward Wood
539 Mr. & Mrs. W. W. Doolittle
545 Mr. & Mrs. J. C. Fleming
547 Mr. & Mrs. John H. Brown
551 Mr. & Mrs. L. H. Heinz
601 Mrs. F. G. Thearle & dr.
627 Mr. & Mrs. E. J. Chamberlin
633 Mr. & Mrs. Warren S. Palm

516 Mr. & Mrs. Fred G. Hill
516 Mr. & Mrs. Elbert M. Waterbury
524 Mr. & Mrs. James B. Kellogg
    Receiving day Thursday
528 Mr. & Mrs. W. G. Brimson
534 Mr. & Mrs. Wm. A. DuBreuil
548 Mr. & Mrs. John F. Pearce
558 Mr. & Mrs. J. C. Denison
612 Mr. & Mrs. C. S. VanDeursen
626 Mr. & Mrs. Webster Gould
630 Mr. & Mrs. N. C. Keeran
640 Mr. & Mrs. Roger W. Atwood &
    dr.

SIXTY-THIRD STREET.

455 Mrs. David Graham
455 Mr. & Mrs. G. D. Thompson

320 Fred T. Hamlin
510 Mr. & Mrs. A. S. Delaware
522 Mr. & Mrs. Samuel W. Dripps

WEST SIXTY-THIRD STREET.

603 Dr. William E. Duncan

603 Dr. Adelaide C. Duncan

WEST SIXTY-THIRD PLACE.

727 Mr. & Mrs. Manning Hunt

742 Mr. & Mrs. Charles Rose
756 Mr. & Mrs. Wm. Phelps

SIXTY-FOURTH STREET.

405 Mr. & Mrs. Wm. H. Bean
    Receiving day Monday
405 Mr. & Mrs. Victor T. Kissinger

358 Mrs. S. L. Bell & dr.
Hotel Hayes, Charles H. Fowler
514 Mr. & Mrs. Edmund T. Nicholas

WEST SIXTY-FOURTH STREET.

321 Mr. & Mrs. H. Worthington Judd
361 Mr. & Mrs. Frank F. Douglass
403 Mr. & Mrs. A. B. Hadden
403 Harry G. Hadden
403 Mr. & Mrs. Fred L. Fowle
439 Mr. & Mrs. Edw. C. Brainard
441 Mr. & Mrs. E. W. Maynard
441 Mr. & Mrs. Charles A. Mayo

410 Mr. & Mrs. William Jenkinson & dr.
    Receiving day Thursday
438 Mr. & Mrs. S. B. Maynard
438 Mr. & Mrs. W. W. Sweringen
438 Mr. & Mrs. Archibald Bouton
728 Mr. & Mrs. M. M. Martin
732 Mr. & Mrs. F. A. Wheeler
736 Mr. & Mrs. Newton F. Hart
736 Mr. & Mrs. A. E. Morley
746 Mr. & Mrs. Cyrus B. Boggs

SIXTY-FIFTH STREET.

485 Mr. & Mrs. J. D. Mendenhall & dr.

484 Mr. & Mrs. C. Van Alen Smith
608 Mr. & Mrs. Edwy L. Reeves

SIXTY-FIFTH PLACE.

219 Mr. & Mrs. W. E. Minshall
305 Mr. & Mrs. M. G. Siddall

230 Mr. & Mrs. Lyman A. White
230 Dr. Annie Hungerford White
230 Frank White
270 Harry G. Chase

WEST SIXTY-FIFTH STREET.

243 Dr. E. O. Gratton
249 Mr. & Mrs. J. A. Ahrens
249 Henry Ahrens
451 Mr. & Mrs. L. C. Noble
515 Dr. & Mrs. Alfred J. Oakey
537 Mr. & Mrs. I. L. Woods & dr.
553 Mr. & Mrs. W. M. Timberlake & dr.
553 Charles E. Timberlake
559 Dr. & Mrs. Lafayette Ringle
605 Mr. & Mrs. F. M. Timms

622 Mr. & Mrs. Hiram Colby

140 Mr. & Mrs. Geo. W. Hotaling
140 Mr. & Mrs. Chas. A. Hendricks
222 Mr. & Mrs. Geo. M. Sterne
230 Dr. & Mrs. W. W. Wentworth
230 Mrs. Catherine Monfort
402 Mr. & Mrs. L. Bruce Welker
438 Mr. & Mrs. A. B. St. John
438 Mr. & Mrs. J. L. Brewster & dr.
440 Mr. & Mrs. Carlos A. Miller
442 Mr. & Mrs. H. L. Blakeslee
444 Charles S. Stobie
444 Miss Isabella Stobie
450 Mr. & Mrs. Edward Maher
618 Wilbur M. Stine

SIXTY-SIXTH STREET.

253 Mr. & Mrs. Frank E. Bell
301 Mr. & Mrs. S. P. Adams
441 Mrs. Catherine C. Long
447 Mr. & Mrs. C. V. Barrington
449 Mr. & Mrs. Frank H. Connor

252 Mrs. Florence S. Reed
438 Mr. & Mrs. John D. Tash

521 E. L. Rinehart

WEST SIXTY-SIXTH STREET.

119 Mr. & Mrs. Alonzo J. Colt
    Receiving day Wednesday
441 Mr. & Mrs. C. W. Jackson
609 Mr. & Mrs. L. T. Regan

120 Mr. & Mrs. S. Pomeroy
614 Mr. & Mrs. C. M. Atterbury

747B Col. & Mrs. Michael J. Dunne

SIXTY-SIXTH PLACE.

266 Mr. & Mrs. A. L. Utz

267 Mr. & Mrs. Wm. A. Coleman

WEST SIXTY-SEVENTH STREET.

315 Dr. Viola H. Ludden
421 Mr. & Mrs. E. J. Noblett
423 Mr. & Mrs. James J. Kelly
515 Mr. & Mrs. Orson Potter & drs.
515 Mrs. Harriet P. Nourse
525 Mr. & Mrs. Albert Trebilcock
611 Mr. & Mrs. L. Ballinger
611 L. B. Ballinger

758 E. Norton White
762 Rev. & Mrs. S. M. Campbell

128 Dr. & Mrs. Horace G. Anderson
400 Mr. & Mrs. A. W. McCornack
   & dr.
516 Mr. & Mrs. Henry H. Nickerson
   & dr.
518 Mrs. M. V. B. VanArsdale&drs.
522 Mr. & Mrs. Michael J. Clark
534 David C. Smith
538 Mr. & Mrs. C. Lindsay Ricketts
602 Mr. & Mrs. R. E. Kehl
742 Mr. & Mrs. David Sloan

WEST SIXTY-EIGHTH STREET.

150 Mr. & Mrs. Francis W. Dewson

SIXTY-NINTH STREET.

712 Dr. & Mrs. Geo. G. Monroe

WEST SIXTY-NINTH STREET.

559 Mr. & Mrs. Albert G. Ferree

559 Harry C. Ferree

SOUTH PARK AVENUE.

2255 Mr. & Mrs. Stanley Waterloo
2403 Mr. & Mrs. H. Waldo Howe
   Receive Wednesday
2411 Mr. & Mrs. John Summerfield
2413 Mr. & Mrs. J. M. Lewey
2427 Mr. & Mrs. George P. Upton
2941 Dr.& Mrs.Herman Kirschstein
2973 Mr. & Mrs. George W. Underwood
2977 Mr. & Mrs. Jas. H. Fisk & drs.
   Receiving day Thursday
3017 Mr. & Mrs. G. T. Flershem
   Receiving day Wednesday
3017 Miss Annie L. Austen
3035 Dr. & Mrs. Wellman M. Burbank
3119 Mrs. Mary E. Holmes
   Receiving day Monday
3119 Mr. & Mrs. Chas. E. Barquist
   Receive Thursday
3137 Mr. & Mrs. Thomas Braun &
   dr.
3141 Dr. & Mrs. Albert G. Pickett
   & drs.

2300 Mr. & Mrs. W. N. Thompson
   & drs.
2400 Mr. & Mrs. Harmon Spruance
   & drs.
2400 L. J. C. Spruance
2448 Mr. & Mrs. George Dickinson
2976 Kenosha Flats
   Mrs. J. H. Schiller
3010 John R. Geary
3010 Thomas F. Geary
3010 W. T. Geary
3114 Mr. & Mrs. S. S. Riesenfeld
3116 Mr. & Mrs. W. E. Poulson
3116 Mrs. A. B. Pierce
3122 John Richardson
3130 Mrs. C. A. Josephi & dr.
3132 Mr. & Mrs. Joseph Basch
3134 Samuel Dreyer
3134 Mrs. D. Dreyer
3140 Mr. & Mrs. George T. Loker
3140 Harry A. Loker
3142 Mr. & Mrs. C. A. Whyland
3144 Mr. & Mrs. T. N. Donnelly
3152 Mr. & Mrs. E. Lederer

3141 Wm. A. Pickett
3141 Mrs. Alice S. Canty
3145 Mr. & Mrs. J. Spiegel
3147 Mr. & Mrs. J. P. Katz & dr.
3147 Aber L. Katz
3151 Mr. & Mrs. George Howison & dr.
3151 Mr. & Mrs. Hugh A. Howison
3151 George Howison jr.
3157 David Hoenisberger
3159 Mr. & Mrs. Charles F. Cooke
Receiving day Monday
3203 Dr. & Mrs. James E. Stubbs
3203 Mrs. E. E. Forester
3205 Mr. & Mrs. E. Seaman
3207 Mr. & Mrs. Jonas Brown
3209 Mr. & Mrs. Thomas Bradwell
3213 Mrs. B. Rosenthal & drs.
Receiving day Friday
3213 Kurt Rosenthal
3213 Joseph M. Schnadig
3215 Mr. & Mrs. D. Wormser
3217 Mr. & Mrs. F. M. Solomon
3217 Mrs. Emma Frank
3219 Mr. & Mrs. C. A. Raggio
3221 Mr. & Mrs. P. A. Hull
3223 Mr. & Mrs. Simon W. Straus
3229 Mr. & Mrs. Thos. R. Lombard & dr.
3229 Mrs. Conrad Steinmetz & drs.
3231 Dr. & Mrs. A. K. Crawford
3231 Mr. & Mrs. John A. Getty & dr.
3231 Harry A. Getty
3235 Mr. & Mrs. Cornelius P. Van Schaack
3237 Mr. & Mrs. L. Felsenthal
3239 Mr. & Mrs. M. Aaron
3241 Mr. & Mrs. Maurice Hillman
3243 Mr. & Mrs. M. L. Heller & drs.
3243 Dr. Charles L. Heller
3245 Mrs. M. Freeman
3245 Henry H. Freeman
3247 Mr. & Mrs. Henry F. Googins
3249 Rev.& Mrs. P. S. Henson
3249 Mr.& Mrs. Charles W. Henson
3249 Miss Mae Belle Henson
3249 W. Y. Henson
3249 Horace Henson
3251 Mrs. A. F. Risser
3315 Mrs. Marion J. Schmaltz
3315 Nathan J. Schmaltz
3323 Mrs. Nathan Cohen & drs.
3323 Reuben S. Cohen
3327 Mrs. Rose L. Newberger & dr.
3327 Miss Elizabeth Levy

3152 Louis Lederer
3156 Mr. & Mrs. D. S. Greenebaum & dr.
3158 Mr. & Mrs. Thomas Hoops jr.
3158 Mrs. W. L. French
3158 William Phelps
3158 H. G. Nye
3200 Mr. & Mrs. Louis Hutt
3216 Mr. & Mrs. Israel Cowen
3218 Mrs. Bertha Cowen & dr.
3218 Carlos Cowen
3226 Mrs. Horace W. Chase
3226 Mrs. Elizabeth M. Odlin
3228 Mr. & Mrs. Charles N. Perry
Receiving day Tuesday
3234 Mr. & Mrs. E. Leger
3234 Harry B. Leger
3236 Mr. & Mrs. W. L. Kerber
3238 Mr. & Mrs. Israel Stein
3238 Samuel Danziger
3238 Mrs. Sarah Danziger
3238 Mrs. Ernestine Heidelberger & drs.
3244 Mr. & Mrs. Jos. Rubenstein
3244 Mrs. C. Krueger
3250 Mrs. George W. Prickett & dr.
3250 Mr. & Mrs. G. W. Prickett jr.
3252 Mr. & Mrs. Francis A. Hayden & dr.
3254 Mr. & Mrs. M. Byron Rich
3256 Dr. & Mrs. J. Harvey Bates
3256 Harvey H. Bates
3314 Rev. & Mrs. Wm. A. Burch
3314 Mrs. Mary H. Bovee
3326 Mrs. N. C. Fay
3326 Mr. & Mrs. Albert R. Fay
3328 Mrs. H. S. Dimick & dr.
3330 Mr. & Mrs. I. Eisenstaedt & dr.
Receive 1st Wednesday
3330 A. Lincoln Eisenstaedt
3336 Mr. & Mrs. Morris Weil
3338 Mr. & Mrs. J. D. Robertson
3340 Mr. & Mrs. Jos. Lowenbach
3340 William L. Lowenbach
3342 Mr. & Mrs. Samuel Rosenwald
3342 Morris S. Rosenwald
3344 Mr. & Mrs. Joseph Spiegel
3346 Dr. & Mrs. Marcus P. Hatfield
3346 Harris A. Hatfield
3348 G. H. Cassard & drs.
3348 Vernon Cassard
3350 Mr. & Mrs. Charles F. Thompson jr.
3352 Mr. & Mrs. Samuel Herman & drs.
3354 Mr. & Mrs. D. A. Stein

3331 Mr. & Mrs. Charles Haas
    Receiving day Friday
3333 Mr. & Mrs. Sol Guthman
3335 Mr. & Mrs. George W. Ristine
3327 Mr. & Mrs. Louis Halle & drs.
3343 Mr. & Mrs. William A. Ranney
3347 Mr. & Mrs. M. L. Rothschild
3347 Mr. & Mrs. Philip Opper
3349 Mr. & Mrs. W. F. Behel & dr.
    Receiving day Thursday
3353 Mr. & Mrs. George E. Challa-
    combe
3355 Mrs. L. Liebenstein
3355 Mr. & Mrs. Leo Fox
3363 George G. Pope
3363 William G. E. Peirce
3363 Miss Mary M. Peirce
3363 Henry Peirce Pope
3365 Mr. & Mrs. J. G. Cella & drs.
3365 J. F. Cella
3365 Charles J. Cella
3365 Andrew Cella
3417 Mr. & Mrs. Rogers Porter
3419 Mrs. P. H. Linneen
3419 David F. Linneen
3419 William P. Linneen
3421 Mrs. David Frank & drs.
3421 Daniel Frank
3423 Mr. & Mrs. A. M. Hollstein
3423 Mr. & Mrs. Jacob W. Levy
3425 Mrs. J. Strauss
3425 Albert S. Strauss
3427 Mr. & Mrs. Morris Adler & dr.
3429 Mr. & Mrs. A. L. Simons & dr.
    Receiving day Friday
3429 Harry Simons
3431 Mr. & Mrs. F. H. Kochersper-
    ger   *Receive Wednesday*
3431 Mr.& Mrs.Chas. C. Jerome
    Receiving day Wednesday

3356 Mr. & Mrs. M. S. Florsheim
    Receive 1st & 3d Thursday p. m.
3358 Mr.& Mrs.Edward H.Foreman
3358 Isaac J. Bloom
3366 Mrs. M. M. Judson
3400 Mr. & Mrs. John Livingston
3402 Mr. & Mrs. Daly D. Davis
3408 Mr. & Mrs. A. Rheinstrom
3412 Mr. & Mrs. Henry Guth
3412 Mr. & Mrs. James R. Emery
3412 Charles Herbertz
3416 Mr. & Mrs.William C. Furman
    & dr.
3416 H. C. Baker
3424 Mrs. Sophia Sulzberger & drs.
3426 Mr. & Mrs. Moses Goodman
    & drs.
3426 Milton F. Goodman
3434 Mr. & Mrs. Louis A. Nathan
    Receive 1st and 3d Thursdays
3434 Mr. & Mrs. Fred LeRoy Jewett
3436 Mr. & Mrs. Frank M. Mont-
    gomery
3436 Mr. & Mrs. Western Starr
5134 Mr. & Mrs. James Hannan &
    dr.
5152 Mr. & Mrs. H. B. Leavitt
5154 Mr. & Mrs. T. M. Talcott
5154 Thaddeus M. Talcott jr.
5154 Mrs. A. C. Talcott
5154 Mr. & Mrs. Chas. M. Talcott
5228 Mr. & Mrs. Wm. Manson
5546 Mr. & Mrs. Alexander Squair
5546 Hugh Squair
5546 Francis Squair

3433 Mr. & Mrs. Arthur D. Dana
3361 Mr. & Mrs. Emanuel Hartman
    & drs.

STAR AVENUE.

6351 Mr. & Mrs. William H. Foulke
6401 Mr. & Mrs. Richard S. King

6405 Mr. & Mrs. D. B. Douglass
6441 Mr. & Mrs. J. H. Snyder

STEWART AVENUE.

6309 Rev. & Mrs. K. W. Benton
6329 Dr. John A. Messenger
6329 Mrs. Elizabeth Messenger
6329 Harry N. Messenger
6341 Mr. & Mrs. A. O. Kendall
6341 D. R. Kendall
6351 Dr. & Mrs. Wm. Minaker
6357 Mr. & Mrs. Albert Russell
    Receiving day Thursday

6122 Mr. & Mrs. William Graver &
    dr.
6122 James P. Graver
cor. W. 63d Julien Hotel
    F. A. Baux
    Mrs. M. E. Crissey
    M. H. Dey
    C. R. Hanna
    Leroy Hanna

6421 Mr. & Mrs. John T. Gascoigne
6421 William G. Holbrook
6429 Mr. & Mrs. E. S. Evarts
6435 Mr. & Mrs. H. Wangeman
6505 Mrs. F. M. Carsley
6511 Mr. & Mrs. E. H. Nichols
6533 Mr. & Mrs. T. Logan
6547 Mr. & Mrs. Charles H. Palmer
6601 Mr. & Mrs. J. A. Henry & dr.
6637 Mr. & Mrs. H. A. Lewis
6637 Mrs. John J. Fenn
6643 Mr. & Mrs. Fred R. Mitchell
6643 Mr. & Mrs. J. A. Ball
6643 John F. Howard
6649 Alfred P. Miller
6651 Mr. & Mrs. S. C. Mason
6655 James D. Pierce
6655 Miss Helen Pierce
6657 Eugene W. Whipple
6657 Warner E. Whipple
6701 Mr. & Mrs. Daniel R. Smart
6711 Mr. & Mrs. E. H. Thielens
6913 Judge & Mrs. H. T. Helm & dr.
6923 Dr. & Mrs. E. J. Parkison
6925 Mr. & Mrs. E. A. Dorrance
6947 Mr. & Mrs. E. A. Thearle
6951 Dr. C. H. L. Souder
6951 Dr. Ellen Starr Souder
7001 Mrs. Chas. D. Colson & dr.
7001 Mrs. E. F. Rowland
7523 Charles P. Wagner
7523 George A. Gary

7340 Mr. & Mrs. Oliver C. Kemp
7600 Mr. & Mrs. C. S. Thornton
7600 Mr. & Mrs. S. Thornton

cor. W. 63d Julien Hotel (cont'd.)
    A. J. Hawhe
    Dr. F. A. Larkin
    Frank Nunamaker
    Dr. F. A. Stanley
    Mr. & Mrs. B. Timmerman
    Mr. & Mrs. J. M. Warner
6316 Dr. & Mrs. D. Brix
6326 Mr. & Mrs. George W. Simpson
6348 Mr. & Mrs. George W. Wylie
6356 Mr. & Mrs. Howard S. Taylor & drs.
6356 Dr. Cora E. Taylor
6356 Dr. Rachel E. Hollingsworth
6410 Rev. & Mrs. P. H. Swift
6412 Dr. & Mrs. D. S. Hamilton
6418 Dr. & Mrs. E. T. Allen
6420 Mr. & Mrs. J. R. Harman
6450 Mr. & Mrs. William H. Frink
6450 Mrs. William T. Meech
6454 Mr. & Mrs. W. S. Hefferan
6508 Mr. & Mrs. J. C. Hallenbeck
6512 Mr. & Mrs. M. H. Collins & dr.
6512 Mr. & Mrs. George M. Collins
6534 Mr. & Mrs. R. T. Sayles
6538 Mr. & Mrs. S. C. Glover & dr.
6546 Mr. & Mrs. E. MacPhetridge & dr.
6558 Mr. & Mrs. Charles Howard
6562 Mr. & Mrs. C. T. Page
6632 Mr. & Mrs. Walter D. Rowles
6640 Mr. & Mrs. H. E. Daggett
6700 Dr. & Mrs. D. W. McNeal
6704 Mr. & Mrs. Fred A. Wells
6710 Mr. & Mrs. A. J. Miller
6924 Mr. & Mrs. Will B. Moak
7052 Mr. & Mrs. Walter N. Beecher

STONY ISLAND AVENUE.

6016 Mr. & Mrs. Walter C. McKinlock
6018 Prof. & Mrs. Adolph C. Miller
6008 Prof. & Mrs. John U. Nef
    Receiving day Monday

6028 Mr. & Mrs. Wm. Richardson & dr.
6028 Mr. & Mrs. Gerald Pierce
6030 Mr. & Mrs. Edward B. Blair
6030 Mrs. A. E. Best
7012 Mr. & Mrs. Evan Pusey
7036 Dr. & Mrs. Eugene A. Curtis

THIRTIETH STREET.

159 Mrs. Annie R. Gill & drs.
159 Joseph Gill
163 Miss E. McDonnell
    Receiving day Wednesday
163 Miss H. McDonnell
    Receiving day Wednesday
163 Thomas Brenan
197 Mr. & Mrs. D. D. Cougle
    Receiving day Wednesday

160 Mr. & Mrs. A. C. Anson
160 Miss Rose Fox
164 Miss Kate Carroll
    Receiving day Tuesday
164 George T. Carroll
306 Mrs. Susan C. Cummings

203 Mr. & Mrs. E. Von Hermann

THIRTY-FIRST STREET.

51 Dr. & Mrs. E. H. Sammons
255 Dr. & Mrs. L. A. Edwards
291 Dr. & Mrs. E. O. Sarber
214 Mr. & Mrs. I. E. Block
224 Dr. H. Henry Cook
284 Dr. & Mrs. George A. Sherwood

THIRTY-SECOND STREET.

53 Mr. & Mrs. M. Wolfe
83 Mr. & Mrs. Gabriel Wolf
95 Mrs. Louis Snydacker & dr.
95 Joseph L. Snydacker
95 Morris Snydacker
233 Simon Ettlinger

116 Mr. & Mrs. B. A. Blair & dr.
116 Frederick W. Lane
168 Mr. & Mrs. W. W. Dewees
212 Mr. & Mrs. Wm. Fairfax Wood
214 Mrs. Asa F. Leopold & dr.
    Receive 1st & 3d Tuesdays
284 Dr. & Mrs. C. J. Simons

THIRTY-THIRD STREET.

15 Mr. & Mrs. Peter Wolf & dr.
29 Mr. & Mrs. D. H. Keyes
37 Mr. & Mrs. E. S. Peaslee
39 Mr. & Mrs. Jas. M. Hubbard & dr.
41 Mrs. A. B. McCarty & drs.
55 The Rainier
   Mr. & Mrs. E. W. Arnold
   Mr. & Mrs. R. W. Caldwell
   DeWitt W. Chamberlin
   Mr. & Mrs. W. L. Judson
   A. W. Tobin
   George T. Mason
   Sam Netter
   Mr. & Mrs. B. F. Tobin
71 Mr. & Mrs. Geo. W. Davis
85 Mr. & Mrs. John P. Wolf & dr.
   Receiving day Wednesday
93 Stratford Flats—
   1 Miss Kittie Neather
   1 J. Pearce Neather
   3 Mr. & Mrs. Chas. L. Sullivan
   5 Mr. & Mrs. J. W. McBride
99 Avon Flats—
   B Mr. & Mrs. P. B. Osborn
   B Mr. & Mrs. Frank S. Hannah
   B Miss Jennie Osborn
   C Mr. & Mrs. Charles J. Wenderoth
   D Mr. & Mrs. George Ellison
147 Mr. & Mrs. Edward L. Glaser
155 Mr. & Mrs. Charles Reitler
399 Mrs. Mary Gunsaulus
399 Mrs. M. C. Moore

54 Mrs. Fannie Tuthill
    Receiving day Thursday
54 Mrs. Anna MacCanahan
54 Fred Rothschild
122 Mr. & Mrs. Levi Sprague
146 Mr. & Mrs. Nathan Eisendrath
148 Mr. & Mrs. Ben Hamburger
210 Miss Ellen C. Alexander
210 Mr. & Mrs. John N. Crawford
210 Miss Ellen C. Crawford
210 C. D. Crouch
212 Mr. & Mrs. Frederic A. Ward
    Receive Thursday
212 Mr. & Mrs. Clive N. Sherwood
212 Mrs. Anna Mueller
214 Dr. & Mrs. C. D. Lockwood
214 Mr. & Mrs. Eugene A. Bournique
216 Mr. & Mrs. William M. Baker
268 The Isabelle
    Mrs. Walter B. Hoag
    Mrs. Thomas E. Patterson
    Miss Annetta Murtha
    Mrs. Emma A. Woolley

401 Dr. & Mrs. C. G. Lumley
403 Mr. & Mrs. Everett C. Wiley
403 James A. Wiley
403 Paul Milner
405 Mr. & Mrs. William A. Gaw
407 Rev. & Mrs. D. C. Milner & drs.
407 Mr. & Mrs. E. C. Dodge

THIRTY-FOURTH STREET.

165 Bernard Schlesinger
331 Mr. & Mrs. Charles Marks & dr.
331 Moses M. Marks
331 Louis C. Marks
333 Mrs. A. W. Herr & drs.

132 Mr. & Mrs. E. Guthman
134 Mr. & Mrs. S. L. Eisendrath
162 Mr. & Mrs. Joseph Neuberger
428 Prof. Victor C. Alderson

THIRTY-FOURTH PLACE.

9 Mr. & Mrs. Ira L. Jones.
11½ Mr. & Mrs. John A. Richardson
25 Mr. & Mrs. J. B. Chandler
25 Miss Gertrude Roberts
35 Dr. Lester Curtis

41 Rev. & Mrs. C. F. Tolman & dr.
43 Mr. & Mrs. Noah C. Brower
43 Mr. & Mrs. Robert Ellis
53 Mr. & Mrs. Luther C. Humphrey
59 Mr. & Mrs. W. H. Thomas &drs.

THIRTY-FIFTH STREET.

21 Mrs. E. M. Tully & drs.
23 Mr. & Mrs. Dempster Ostrander
23 Jeanette W. Foye
25 Mr. & Mrs. D. Howard
29 Mrs. George Stearns & drs.
29 Mr. & Mrs. Walter A. Rapp

270 Dr. & Mrs. James M. Brydon

36 Mr. & Mrs. A. J. Warner
36 H. E. Warner
40 Dr. & Mrs. H. W. Vennell
44 Mr. & Mrs. O. M. Parsons
44 Miss Jennie Woodman
46 Mr. & Mrs. H. H. Blake
50 Dr. C. F. Matteson
52 Dr. & Mrs. James I. Tucker
190 James C. Burke
192 Mr. & Mrs. John C. Burke

THIRTY-SIXTH STREET.

55 Mr. & Mrs. F. L. Watson
55 George E. Gaddis
55 Mrs. M. W. Hoff
55 C. M. Wynekoop
151 Mr. & Mrs. Louis W. Haynes
173 Mr. & Mrs. Wm. J. Smith
175 Mr. & Mrs. Isaac Bond
    Receiving day Tuesday
175 Mr. & Mrs. Wm. H. Bond
175 Mrs. Lizzie T. Stone
179 Mr. & Mrs. George Brockway
179 Guy Brockway
185 Mr. & Mrs. Alexander S. Leib
    Receiving day Tuesday
185 Harry R. Leib
201 Mr. & Mrs. Chas. J. Merritt
203 Marks Lewy
207 Mr. & Mrs. Andrew Lenington
    & dr.
207 Hector C. Lenington

152 Mr. & Mrs. Luther N. Doty
162 Mr. & Mrs. R. Barnard
164 Mr. & Mrs. John F. Thacker
170 Mrs. Jane De Mary

ne. cor. Ellis av. The Lorraine
    Mr. & Mrs. James T. Brayton
    Mrs. Ella Shufeldt
    Mr. & Mrs. Chas. C. Sherman
    Mr. & Mrs. H. O. Brockway
    Mr. & Mrs. C. T. McWhinney
    Mr. & Mrs. B. F. Methven
    Mrs. M. J. Morton
    Mr. & Mrs. D. W. C. Merriam
    Receiving day Thursday
    Mr. & Mrs. Chas. W. Rice
ne. cor. Cottage Grove av. Ivanhoe
    Flats
    Dr. & Mrs. R. A. Letourneau
    Dr. & Mrs. E. F. Woodruff
104 Mr. & Mrs. H. H. Crocker
108 Mr. & Mrs. Henry J. Wanner
142 Mrs. C. M. Finch
146 Dr. and Mrs. Thos. Benton
    Swartz
    Receiving day Tuesday
152 W. A. Sansom
152 Mr. and Mrs. W. Odell Clark
152 Mr. & Mrs. J. B. Tuttle
152 Mr. & Mrs. J. A. Woodworth
152 Mr. & Mrs. M. M. Cohen

15

170 Mr. & Mrs.Donald M.Stevenson
184 Thomas F. Spooner
186 Miss Mary G. Chadwick
190 Mr. & Mrs. F. P. Leffingwell

194 Mr. & Mrs. W. K. Hilton
196 Mr. & Mrs. Alex Bauer
198 Mr. & Mrs. L. P. Herzog
198 Mrs. Mina Degen

THIRTY-SIXTH PLACE.

371 Mrs. S. Simon & dr.
     Receive 2d & 4th Wednesdays
407 Mr. & Mrs. Hoyt King

406 Mr. & Mrs. Arthur P. Burland
     Receiving day Friday

406 Mrs. E. F. Bigelow
406 Mr. & Mrs. L. K. Miller
406 Mr. & Mrs. Wm. R. Moorhouse
408 Mr. & Mrs. George J. Adams
416 Mr. & Mrs. Harold Sorby
416 Mrs. F. W. Boyle
416 Mrs. J. C. Wilkins

THIRTY-SEVENTH STREET.

29 Mr. & Mrs. L. J. Mason
33 Mr.& Mrs.William P.Penhallow
67 Dr. & Mrs. Frederick O. Pease
67 Mr. & Mrs. Archibald McLellan
91 Mrs. C. B. Gilbert
91 Mrs. S. A. Boyington
97 Mr. & Mrs. H. T. VanDenbergh
     & dr.
97 Mr. & Mrs. Edward H. Mc-
     Pherran
99 Dr. & Mrs. Thos. G. Roberts
103 Mr. & Mrs. Daniel V. Samuels
103 C. H. Crawford
107 Dr. & Mrs. Wm. W. Hester
107 Mr. & Mrs. Hill Beachey
107 R. Wilson More
107 Arthur R. Letts
107 Mr. & Mrs. John Wade
181 Mr. & Mrs. Charles L. Russ

16 Mr. & Mrs. A. C. Vanderburgh
148 Mrs. Margaret Dunlea
148 James Dunlea
176 Mr. & Mrs. E. P. Webster
194 Mr. & Mrs. T. H. Patterson & dr.
206 Mrs. Jacob Liberman & dr.
     Receive 1st Tuesday in mo.
208 Mr. & Mrs. Morris E. Nathan
     Receive last Thursday in mo.
210 Mrs. Wallace Warren & dr.
258 Dr. Rush E. Crissman
286 Mr. & Mrs. Wm. M. Tureman
318 Mrs. T. Stern
358 Nathan Friend

181 Mr. & Mrs. Alamando B. Russ
183 Lincoln A. Brown
183 Miss Ella W. Brown
447 Dr. J. W. Dostal

THIRTY-SEVENTH PLACE.

436 L. K. Hirsch

THIRTY-EIGHTH STREET.

140 Mr. & Mrs. F. A. Spink
438 Dr. & Mrs. C. E. Caldwell

450 Mr.& Mrs. Jacob Goodman &dr.

THIRTY-NINTH STREET.

17 Mr. & Mrs. A. Fletcher Brown
17 Mrs. Ellen B. Shepard

n.e. cor. Langley av. The Hampden
Mr. & Mrs. Nelson T. Barnard
Mr. & Mrs. A. W. Clancy
Miss Mary Douglas
Mrs. A. E. Edwards
Mrs. Hattie M. Ely
Mr. & Mrs. H. S. Gates
Mrs. Lois B. Hills

Mr. & Mrs. Odell E. Lansing
Roscoe U. Lansing
Mr. & Mrs. E. C. Moderwell
Dr. Wyllys Moore
Mrs. L. E. Quaw
Mr. & Mrs. Caleb F. Reynolds
Mr. & Mrs. Byron W. Roberts
Mrs. M. A. Rush & dr.
Mr. & Mrs. C. R. Stevens
Mr. & Mrs. H. G. Wilson & dr.
William W. Winton
Mr. & Mrs. John Zimmerman

TWENTIETH STREET.

53 Mr. & Mrs. Frank O. Lowden
57 Dr. & Mrs. Charles W. Purdy
57 George W. Hoffman
77 Mr. & Mrs. John K. Mackenzie
77 Mr. & Mrs. O. L. Fox
77 Louis F. Brown
79 Mr. & Mrs. Godfrey Macdonald
79 Mrs. Lucy Cook
79 Mrs. Laning Cook
83 V. H. Surghnor

TWENTY-FIRST STREET.

119 Mr. & Mrs. Madison H. Ferris
121 Mr. & Mrs. John V. Hess
90 Mr. & Mrs. Blewett Lee
90 Mr. & Mrs. C. E. Loss
92 Mr. & Mrs. Harris E. Hurlbut
92 Mr. & Mrs. John J. Simmons

TWENTY-SECOND STREET.

35 Dr. Frank Billings
35 Charles L. Billings
37 Mr. & Mrs. Peter VanSchaack
39 Mrs. L. C. Wheeler
39 David O. Arnold
43 Mr. & Mrs. G. Edwin Jones
45 Mr. & Mrs. Louis S. Owsley
47 Mrs. Emma C. Jenks
47 John G. Jenks
47 Mr.&Mrs. Geo. Miller Ferguson
47 Mr. & Mrs. Chas. F. Livermore
51 Mr. & Mrs. John B. Drake jr.
51 Dr. T. Frank Keys
51 Mr. & Mrs. Wm. O. King
51 Mr. & Mrs. Wm. P. Palmer
51 Mrs. B. M. Powell
51 Mrs. Nellie Bangs Skelton
55 Mr. & Mrs. M. J. Steffens
69 Dr. Albert B. Hale

TWENTY-THIRD STREET.

51 Mr. & Mrs. Augustus E. Bournique
51 Alvar L. Bournique
51 Lyman G. Bournique
64 Dr. & Mrs. Samuel M. French

51 Miss May E. Bournique

TWENTY-FOURTH STREET.

325 Mr. & Mrs. L. W. Framhein
52 Mrs. A. F. Vollmer
52 Thomas Brown
100 Mr. & Mrs. George E. Dawson

TWENTY-FIFTH STREET.

33 Mr. & Mrs. Robert Hervey
127 Mr. & Mrs. L. Deutsch
129 Mr. & Mrs. Louis Marks
161 Mr. & Mrs. Walter A. Barker
185 Mr. & Mrs. L. Polacheck
82 Mr. & Mrs. Andrew Hallen
152 Mr. & Mrs. James T. Mix
154 Mr. & Mrs. Joseph Hughes
156 Mr. & Mrs. Oscar M. Stern
164 Mr. & Mrs. A. T. Willett

TWENTY-SIXTH STREET.

78 W. A. Bruette
92 Mr. & Mrs. Watson S. Hinkley

TWENTY-EIGHTH STREET.

213 Rev. & Mrs. C. A. Lippincott
225 Mr. & Mrs. Robert H. Marston
229 Mr. & Mrs. J. P. Cadieux

TWENTY-NINTH STREET.

223 Mr. & Mrs. C. D. Newbury   231 Mr. & Mrs. Arthur G. Bigelow

TWENTY-NINTH PLACE.

49 Mr. & Mrs. D. Gordon Wells
49 George W. Packard
51 Mr. & Mrs. B. E. Uebele
53 Mr. & Mrs. Chas. B.English & dr.

38 Mr. & Mrs. Edwin L. Lobdell
40 Clarence S. Darrow
42 Mr. & Mrs. J. W. Nicholson
44 Prof. & Mrs. N. Gray Bartlett

UNION AVENUE.

5525 Mr. & Mrs. Edward Donker
6743 Dr. & Mrs. C. W. Piper
6801 Dr. & Mrs. E. C. Morton
6845 Mr. & Mrs. W. F. Madlung
7613 Rev. & Mrs. John Willard
7621 Mr. & Mrs. Seth A. Minard
7631 Mr. & Mrs. W. D. Pickels & dr.
        Receiving day Thursday
7631 Miss Mary E. Fielding
7631 Howard H. Fielding
7721 Mr. & Mrs. John W. Smith
7747 Mr. & Mrs. A. E. Walter

7746 Mr. & Mrs. H. H. Glidden
7754 Mr. & Mrs. Chas. A. Mallory
7754 Mrs. Harriet C. Mallory

4356 Mr. & Mrs. Harmon T. Clen-
        denning
6426 Mr. & Mrs. N. Michels
6850 J. Grant Teller
7200 Mr. & Mrs. Herbert E. Good-
        man
7248 Dr. Ellen C. Partridge
7534 Mr. & Mrs. George F. Jennings
7534 Mrs. George M. Jennings
7604 Wilfrid L. Smithies
7606 Mr. & Mrs. W. G. Deane
7606 Mr. & Mrs. Wm. Robinson
7608 Mr. & Mrs. John G. Thomas
7628 Mr. & Mrs. O. J. Buck
7630 Mr. & Mrs. Frank A. Burgess
7722 Mr. & Mrs. H. W. Magee

VERNON AVENUE.

2953 Mr. & Mrs. L. P. Boyle
2967 Mr. & Mrs. Thos. Middleton
        & drs.
2967 Mr. & Mrs. J. C. Ames
2967 Mr. & Mrs. Collins F. Hunt-
        ington
3005 Mr. & Mrs. C. F. Klunder &
        drs.
3005 Mr. & Mrs. H. E. Klunder
3021 Mr. & Mrs. R. H. Schell
3021 Miss J. M. Wheeler
3021 Miss Ethel C. Winter
3027 Willard S. Haynes
3027 Walter B. Day
3027 Henry A. Foster
3035 Mr. & Mrs. F. G. Pierson
3121 Mr. & Mrs. T. H. Flood & dr.
3121 Frank J. Flood
3123 Mr. & Mrs. J. H. Hogey
3125 Mr. & Mrs. D. B. Falter
3125 Benj. Franklin Falter
3135 Dr. S. G. Burkholder
3135 William Childs
3137 Mr. & Mrs. Samuel Goldsmith
3139 Mr. & Mrs. L. B. Meyer & dr.

2944 Mrs. A. E. Hall
2944 George Bohner
2970 Mr. & Mrs. D. J. Lyon
3000 Mr. & Mrs. Charles A. Crane
3010 Dr. & Mrs. Louis N. Barlow
3012 Mr. & Mrs. W. W. Wilcox
3012 Arthur Kent
3012 Miss Mary Kent
3024 Mr. & Mrs. Henry B. Mayer
3026 Mr. & Mrs. Arthur C. Hutch-
        inson
3130 Mr. & Mrs. O. L. American
3130 Miss Sadie American
3132 J. B. Staley
3132 Mrs. Mary E. Staley
3140 Mr. & Mrs. A. Batchelder
3144 Mr. & Mrs. Samuel B. Lingle
3146 Dr. & Mrs. W. W. Lazear
3146 Mrs. Anne Davies
3152 Mr. & Mrs. J. M. Mills & drs.
3156 Mr. & Mrs. Thomas R. Lynas-
        & dr.
3200 Dr. & Mrs. A. J. Park & dr.
3202 Mrs. C. Lazarus
3206 Mr. & Mrs. Sigmund Silberman

3139 Sigmund Meyer
3143 Mr. & Mrs. M. Keating
3145 Mr. & Mrs. A. Guthrie Curtis
Receiving day Wednesday
3145 Mr. & Mrs. D. J. Harris
3147 Mr. & Mrs. Eli Smith & dr.
3201 Mr. & Mrs. Theodore Wilken
3201 Miss Isabella Wilken
3211 Mr. & Mrs. D. C. Barringer & dr.
3211 Walter M. Barringer
3217 Mr. & Mrs. J. L. Chapman & dr.
3221 Mr. & Mrs. Gustav Freund & dr.
3223 Mr. & Mrs. Jos. Rosenthal
3225 Mr. & Mrs. L. Freiberger & drs.
3225 Edward Freiberger
3227 Mr. & Mrs. Martin Meyer
3233 Mr. & Mrs. N. H. Ernst
3235 Mr. & Mrs. Isaac Despres
3235 Isador Philipson
3239 Mr. & Mrs. Henry Heppner
3241 Mr. & Mrs. Alfred Kohn
3243 Mr. & Mrs. A. F. Slyder
Receiving day Friday
3249 Mr. & Mrs. Edward Hirsch
3253 Mr. & Mrs. M. A. Meyer
3255 Mr. & Mrs. Wm. J. Mohr
3257 Mr. & Mrs. P. D. Madigan
3261 Mr. & Mrs. M. Schwarz
3261 Albert Schwarz
3267 Mr. & Mrs. W. T. Hughes & dr.
3267 Edward J. Hughes
3301 Dr. & Mrs. D. C. Bartlett
3303 Mr. & Mrs. Edward Sincere
3305 Dr. & Mrs. S. Cole & dr.
Receiving day Tuesday
3307 Mr. & Mrs. S. Hartman
3307 Emanuel Hartman
3307 Edward Hartman
3321 Mr. & Mrs. George F. Harding jr.
3323 Mrs. Leon M. Friedlander & dr.
3323 Harry D. Friedlander
3325 Mr. & Mrs. Samuel Butler
3325 Samuel S. Butler
3329 Mr. & Mrs. M. Werkmeister
3329 Dr. Arthur M. Werkmeister
3331 Mr. & Mrs. W. H. Phelps
Receiving day Thursday
3333 Mr. & Mrs. J. M. Joseph
3335 Mr. & Mrs. Joseph Baer
3339 Mr. & Mrs. James Jay Smith
3339 Mrs. S. C. Avy

3210 Dr. Richard M. Genius
3210 Dr. Arthur E. Genius
3210 Rev. & Mrs. F. A. Genius & drs.
3212 Mr. & Mrs. Clement F. Street
3214 Mr. & Mrs. Joseph Berolzheim
3218 Mr. & Mrs. J. P. Ahrens
3218 Mrs. M. J. Hamblin & dr.
3220 Dr. & Mrs. F. B. Ives
3220 Mr. & Mrs. B. E. Tritt
3224 Mrs. Catherine Schwahn
3226 James D. Colt
3234 Mr. & Mrs. Chas. T. Whitgreave
3238 Mr. & Mrs. J. E. Levy
3242 Dr. & Mrs. Ed. Bert
3244 Mrs. M. L. Clancy
3244 William M. Clancy
3252 Mr. & Mrs. W. B. Wrenn
3258 Mr. & Mrs. M. Longini
Receive 2d Friday
3258 Leon J. Longini
3262 Mr. & Mrs. B. Whyland
3264 Mr. & Mrs. B. W. Eisendrath & dr.
3300 Mr. & Mrs. C. K. Nims
3300 O. L. Nims
3304 Mr. & Mrs. W. R. Raymond
3324 Judge & Mrs. Jesse Holdom
3326 Mr. & Mrs. James G. McBean
3326 George M. McBean
3332 Mr. & Mrs. N. J. Ullman
Receive 1st & 3d Friday
3334 Mr. & Mrs. Jonathan Abel
3334 Mr. & Mrs. Wesson Macomber
3340 Mrs. M. W. Sea
3340 Fred W. Sea
3344 Mr. & Mrs. T. Nicholson
3344 T. G. Nicholson
3344 J. S. Nicholson
3346 Mrs. Charles Kozminski
3348 Mrs. C. Sumerfield & dr.
3352 Mr. & Mrs. Henry Oberndorf
3352 Louis H. Oberndorf
3354 Mr. & Mrs. William Hirsch
3400 Mr. & Mrs. John K. Prindiville
3402 Mr. & Mrs. I. Blumenthal & dr.
3406 Mr. & Mrs. Samuel Hirschbein
3412 Mrs. Mary Foreman
3412 Milton J. Foreman
3414 Mr. & Mrs. Sol Rice
3416 Mr. & Mrs. Jacob Cohn
3418 Mr. & Mrs. S. H. Foreman
3420 Mrs. Rose Gottlieb & dr.
3422 Wm. Garnett & dr.
3422 John L. Garnett

3341 Mr. & Mrs. Israel Van Baalen & dr.
3343 Mr. & Mrs. Geo. J. Pope
3345 Mr. & Mrs. J. E. Gorman
3359 Mr. & Mrs. Emanuel Roth-schild
3401 Dr. & Mrs. J. Priestman & drs.
3407 Dr. & Mrs. H. Bak
3411 Mr. & Mrs. G. W. Stone
3411 Harry W. Stone
3413 Mr. & Mrs. R. S. Parker
3419 Mrs. Geo. Rumpf & dr.
       Receive 1st Wednesday
3421 Mr. & Mrs. Isaac Orschel
3423 Mrs. W. L. Schaub
3425 Mr. & Mrs. D. S. Pate
3425 Peter M. Lanehart
3427 Mr. & Mrs. Daniel J. Schuyler
3427 Daniel J. Schuyler jr.
3439 Mr. & Mrs. Andrew Wallace & dr.
3519 Mr. & Mrs. J. Musselwhite&dr.
3521 Mr. & Mrs. Geo. A. S. Wilson
3553 Mr. & Mrs. Fred Oberndorf
3553 Max F. Oberndorf
3557 Mr. & Mrs. D. Launder & dr.
3609 Mr. & Mrs. Bernhard Pfaelzer
3611 Mr. & Mrs. Leopold Pfaelzer
3625 Mr. & Mrs. B. J.McCleary & dr.
3627 Mrs. J. Truax
3627 Miss Nellie Chaffee
3639 Mr. & Mrs. Emil Guthmann & drs.
3639 Edward Guthmann
3643 Mr. & Mrs. William Spier
3645 Mrs. E. A. King
3645 Vere B. King
3745 Mr. & Mrs. Wm. Pickett & dr.
3745 Mrs. W. S. Pickett
3761 Mr. & Mrs. John W. Turner
3763 Mr. & Mrs. J. H. Kowalski
3815 Mr. & Mrs. Louis Kahn
3819 Mr. & Mrs. Benjamin F. Chase
       Receiving day Wednesday
3821 Mr. & Mrs. J. Emery Tate
3823 Mr. & Mrs. G. T. Bauer
3825 Mr. & Mrs. Edwin F. Master-son
3829 Mr. & Mrs. James M. Dawson
4311 Mr. & Mrs. H. W. Christian
4313 Dr. & Mrs. Charles F. Stewart
       Receiving day Wednesday
4321 Mr. & Mrs. F. T. Murphy

3424 Mr. & Mrs. Charles P. Mont-gomery
3426 Mr. & Mrs. James K. Burtis
3426 Mr. & Mrs. W. B. Ransom
3428 M. D. Aaron
3428 Bernard N. Aaron
3430 Mr. & Mrs. Emanuel Nusbaum & drs.
       Receive 1st & 3d Monday
3432 Mrs. F. W. Tourtellotte
3432 Mr. & Mrs. Frederick J. Tour-tellotte
3434 Mr. & Mrs. John K. Joyce
3436 Mr. & Mrs. Nathan Stone
3438 Mr. & Mrs. Al. A. Rosenbush
3440 Mr. & Mrs. Thomas D. O'Brien
3442 Mr. & Mrs. Geo. H. Rapp
3514 Mr. & Mrs. B. Davis & drs.
3514 David Davis
3516 Mr. & Mrs. R. K. Smith
3532 Mr. & Mrs. J. C. Schwartz
       Receive 1st Tuesday
3532 Mr. & Mrs. Olof G. Olson
3542 Mr. & Mrs. Patrick McMahon & drs.
3542 A. J. McMahon
3550 Dr. & Mrs. Wm. E. Hall
3552 Mr. & Mrs. Sidney T. Emerson
       Receiving day Thursday
3560 Mr. & Mrs. Jacob Mayer
       Receive 1st and 3d Friday
3564 Mr. & Mrs. Samuel Polkey
3604 Mr. & Mrs. James L. Ross
3604 James W. Ross
3620 W. A. Nye
3628 Mr. & Mrs. Burton W. Stadden
3630 Mr. & Mrs. Isaac Van Hagen
3632 Mrs. Thomas L. Dean
3634 Mr. & Mrs. Henry H. Heaford
3824 Mr. & Mrs. Louis Vehon
4314 Mr. & Mrs. Charles Hasterlik
4314 Samuel Hasterlik
4316 Simon H. Kohn
4316 Miss Dila Kohn
4316 Miss Clara Kohn
4320 Mr. & Mrs. Maurice Weill
4322 Mr. & Mrs. James E.Defebaugh
4326 Mr. & Mrs. Bernhard Engel & drs.
6912 Mr. & Mrs. David W. Mulloy
7132 Mr. & Mrs. Wm. J. Shedd
7224 Mr. & Mrs. F. H. Nonweiler
7232 Mr. & Mrs. R. G. Barrett
       Receiving day Wednesday

VINCENNES AVENUE.

3559 Mr. & Mrs. Charles B. Stanton
3559 Mr. & Mrs. Noah B. Dewey
3601 The Vincennes—
    J. H. Agnew
    Mrs. Jessie D. Altberger
    J. M. Anthony
    Benjamin Bartlett
    Mr. & Mrs. John W. Blaisdell
      Receiving day Wednesday
    Mrs. Margaret T. Clarke
    Herbert E. Cleaver
    Miss Helene Danken
    Mr. & Mrs. Meyer S. Emrich
      Receive 1st and 2d Thursday
    Mr. & Mrs. C. W. Fiske
    Mr. & Mrs. Emil Friend
    Mrs. R. Grossman & dr.
      Receive 3d and 4th Tuesday
    Mr. & Mrs. L. M. Herman
    Carl Levi
    Mr. & Mrs. Sanford McKeeby
    Mr. & Mrs. Wm. E. McQuiston
    Mr. & Mrs. L. F. Minzesheimer
      Receive 2d Thursday
    Mr. & Mrs. C. E. Phelps
    Mr. & Mrs. W. J. Root
    Fred L. Ryder
    Mr. & Mrs. A. F. Sauer
    Mr. & Mrs. M. Schlesinger
    Mrs. John Stett
    Mr. & Mrs. M. L. Strauss
    Mr. & Mrs. S. J. Woolner
    Mr. & Mrs. E. B. Wright
3917 Mr. & Mrs. Henry Gillett
3629 Mr. & Mrs. Edwin B. Durno
3629 Miss Jeannettie Durno
3637 Mrs. Jeanette Dessauer
3641 Mr. & Mrs. Henry G. Myers & dr.
3647 Mr. & Mrs. Thos. Cadwallader & dr.
3707 Mr. & Mrs. Hiram B. Johnson
3719 Mrs. Roxanna Millard
3719 George M. Millard
3725 Mr. & Mrs. C. L. Ely & dr.
3725 A. G. Ely
3731 Mr. & Mrs. Maurice Landsberg
3733 Mr. & Mrs. John F. Thompson & dr.
3741 Henry B. Ford
3743 Mr. & Mrs. Levi A. Fretts
3743 David A. Warley
3745 Mr. & Mrs. Jacob Batt
3751 Mr. & Mrs. C. L. Caswell & dr.

3634 Mrs. Mary Alison
3634 John M. Alison
3634 Rowland H. Alison
3648 William D. Cowles
3656 Dr. Alfred Lewy
3658 Maxwell Edgar
3812 Mr. & Mrs. W. A. Denny & dr.
      Receiving day Tuesday
3812 Mr. & Mrs. Fitzallen B. Williams & dr.
3812 Waldo A. Williams
3812 Frank B. Williams
3812 Mr. & Mrs. William F. Bode
3826 Christian Smith & dr.
3826 Henry W. Smith
3842 Isidore Rothstein
3848 Dr. & Mrs. Amos L. Lennard
3912 L. H. Bisbee & dr.
3912 Mrs. Helen E. Starrett
3976 Mr. & Mrs. Francisco Blair
3976 Dr. J. H. Blair
4002 Mr. & Mrs. Max Goldman
4016 Dr. & Mrs. Robert F. Zeit
4018 Mr. & Mrs. Matthew J. Brennan
4020 Thomas Conlin
4022 Mr. & Mrs. O. L. Etnier
4100 Mrs. Margaret E. Beals & dr.
4100 Mr. & Mrs. Hardin W. Beals
4104 Mr. & Mrs. George B. Kerr
4106 Mr. & Mrs. Charles E. Crone
      Receiving day Tuesday
4200 Mr. & Mrs. James C. Miller
4202 Mr. & Mrs. John Kelly
4208 Mr. & Mrs. Lawrence Honkamp & dr.
4214 Mr. & Mrs. Thos. F. Williamson & drs.
4226 Mr. & Mrs. Louis Rueckheim
4320 Mr. & Mrs. Louis Lindheim
4320 Mr. & Mrs. Michael Elkin
4322 Mr. & Mrs. R. A. Canterbury
4340 Mr. & Mrs. John P. Bowles
4346 Mr. & Mrs. Morris Alpiner & drs.
4348 Mr. & Mrs. C. W. Huggins
4350 Mr. & Mrs. Frank A. Coker
4430 Mrs. E. A. Wood & drs.
      Receive Wednesday
4440 Mr. & Mrs. Charles T. Farson
4442 D. A. Worley
4444 Mr. & Mrs. Gustave C. Strauss
4448 Mr. & Mrs. W. A. Foster
4450 Mr. & Mrs. Wm. Garnett
4452 Mr. & Mrs. E. A. Oliver

3751 C. L. Caswell jr.
3807 Mr. & Mrs. C. W. Fairrington
3807 Warren M. Fairrington
3807 Miss H. A. Manny
3815 Mr. & Mrs. M. D. Flavin
3817 Col. & Mrs. Geo. K. Brady
3819 Mr. & Mrs. J. R. Laing
   Receiving day Thursday
3819 William G. Laing
3825 Mr. & Mrs. Sidney Adler
   Receiving 1st & 3rd Thursdays
3827 Mrs. N. W. Swift
3835 Mr. & Mrs. David Lelewer
3835 Seward Lelewer
3857 Dr. O. H. E. Clarke
3857 Miss Yvonne Clarke
3905 Mr. & Mrs. John W. Moore
3915 Mr. & Mrs. C. H. Gillett
3917 Mr. & Mrs. Henry Gillett
3917 F. P. Gillett
3923 Mr. & Mrs. John H. Moberly
3927 Mr. & Mrs. James Plunkett
   Receiving day Friday
3927½ Mr. & Mrs. Nathan Frank
3929 Mr. & Mrs. John A. Waterman
3929 Miss Jessie H. Waterman
4001 Mrs. Florence Williams
4001 Mrs. Katherine Hibbard
4001 Mr. & Mrs. Wm. Guthridge
4001 Mrs. E. C. Howland
4001 Edward A. Howland
4007 John Hallett
4007 Harvey J. Hallett
4009 George A. Dunlap
4015 Mr.&Mrs.J.W.McDonald&drs.
   Receiving day Thursday
4015 Mrs. Anna Downing
4017 Mrs. George Wright
4017 George W. Wright
4019 Mrs. Mary C. Mevelle & drs.
4019 Chas. W. Mevelle
4021 Mr. & Mrs. James P. Lott
4021 Miss Nellie E. Kenyon
4023 E. M. Rosenthal
4031 Dr. & Mrs. H. S. Barnard
4033 Mr. & Mrs. Morris Haber
4033 Mrs. Babetta Newgass
4033 William Newgass
4103 Mr. & Mrs. James E. Baggot
4105 Mr. & Mrs. Henry P. Elliott &
   dr.
4107 Mr. & Mrs. Albert J. Elliott
4109 Mr. & Mrs. Frederick J. Rappal & drs.
   Receiving day Thursday
4109 Lawrence L. Rappal

4454 Dr. Charles M. Jacobs
4456 Mr. & Mrs. John A. Lomax
4456 Robert D. Lomax
4500 Mr. & Mrs. R. W. Playford jr.
4504 Mr. & Mrs. Thos. C. Roney
4504 Mr. & Mrs. P. L. Inglis
4504 Mrs. E. S. Harvey & drs.
   Receiving day Monday
4504 Mr. & Mrs. F. W. Zeddies
4512 Mr. & Mrs. David J. Pfaelzer
4532 Dr. & Mrs. Sidney E. Hulett
4538 Mr. & Mrs. A. B. Sherwood
4540 Dr. & Mrs. George E. Krieger
4542 Mr. & Mrs. Conrad Werner &
   dr.
4544 Mr. & Mrs. S. C. Fish
4546 Mrs. Henry A. Auer
4550 Mr. & Mrs. Leo Heller
   Receiving day 1st Saturday
4608 Mr. & Mrs. H. W. Mahan &
   dr.
4608 Mark C. Mahan
4632 Mr. & Mrs. Stephen Black
4634 Thomas J. Norton
4634 Mr. & Mrs. Joseph L. Daube
   Receive 2d Wednesday in mo.
4634 Mr. & Mrs. Isaac A. Michaels
4642 Dr. & Mrs. G. W. Hall
4646 Dr. Ross S. Vedder
4710 Judge & Mrs. Thos. A. Moran&
   drs. *Receiving day Tuesday*
4710 Thomas W. Moran
4804 Mr. & Mrs. H. Boore
4808 Mr. & Mrs. W. T. Nash
4812 Mr. & Mrs. James Mowatt
4824 Mr. & Mrs. F. J. Fitzwilliam
   Receiving day Tuesday
4824 Mrs. Susan H. Burr
4842 Mr. & Mrs. A. H. Veeder &
   dr.
4930 Mr. & Mrs. Daniel Gelder
4936 Mr. & Mrs. Myer M. Freeman
4938 Mr. & Mrs. M. Munzer & drs.
4938 Eugene I. Munzer
4940 Mr. & Mrs. Herman J. Millhauser
   Receiving day Wednesday
4942 David Witkowsky
4942 Leopold Witkowsky
4950 Mr. & Mrs. Robert E. Casey
4950 Mr. & Mrs. Abraham Harris
4952 Mr. & Mrs. Julius G. Goodrich
4952 Mr. & Mrs. Charles Turner
4952 Mr. & Mrs. C. E. Woolley
5010 Mr. & Mrs. Chauncey W. Martyn

4109 Symon P. Rappal
4109 John H. Rappal
4109 Frederick J. Rappal, jr.
4111 Mr. & Mrs. Timothy S. Casey
    & drs.
4119 Mr. & Mrs. Thomas A. Dean
4125 Mr. & Mrs. Joel M. Longeneck-
    er
4201 Mr. & Mrs. F. W. Rueckheim
4201 Miss Laura W. Rueckheim
4205 Mr. & Mrs. Paul Fernald
4211 Mrs. Mary K. Collins
4213 Mr. & Mrs. Isidor A. Rubel
4215 Mr. & Mrs. Ernest Jacoby
4217 Mrs. Jacob Thorne &drs.
4225 Mr. & Mrs. Blanford R. Pierce
4235 Mr. & Mrs. Charles L. Will
4239 Mr. & Mrs. David F. Haskell
4239 Reuben L. Haskell
4243 Mr. & Mrs. Robert S. Hill
4311 Mr. & Mrs. George D. Lord
4319 Mr. & Mrs. Edward Gudeman
4327 Mr. & Mrs. G. W. B. Hart &
    dr.
4327 Henry G. Hart
4329 Mr. & Mrs. Albert Hyman
4329 David Hyman
4343 Mr. & Mrs. Maurice Strauss
4351 Mr. & Mrs. Arnold Freshman
4353 Mr. & Mrs. Edward A. Stone-
    hill
4357 Mr. & Mrs. Robert Hart
4357 Edgar R. Hart
4421 Mr. & Mrs. Henry G. Eckstein
4423 Mrs. K. Murray & drs.
4425 Mr. & Mrs. Robert Russell
4425 Mr. & Mrs. Henry N. Poirier
4517 Dr. & Mrs. O. W. F. Snyder
    Receiving day Friday
4519 Mr. & Mrs. Arthur R. Jones
    Receive Thursdays
4521 Mr. & Mrs. G. Albert Mc-
    Collum
4525 Mr. & Mrs. Emanuel Loeb
4529 Mr. & Mrs. C. W. Cohen
4531 Mrs. R. Mossler & drs.
4531 Israel L. Mossler
4541 Mr. & Mrs. Henry T. Davis
4545 Mr. & Mrs. Abram S. Smith

4547 Mr. & Mrs. H. C. Wolf
4549 Mr. & Mrs. J. R. Davidson
    Receiving day Friday
4549 Siegfried W. Strauss
4551 Mr. & Mrs. Carl Joseph
4601 Mr. & Mrs. B. A. Branch
    Receiving day Thursday
4601 Mr. & Mrs. F. Bixby
4601 Dr. & Mrs. C. G. McCollough
4603 Mrs. Dewitt C. Leach
4603 Mrs. Duncan MacArthur
4611 Dr. & Mrs. W. W. Coker
4611 Miss Bertha A. Coker
4615 Mr. & Mrs. G. H. Casler
4617 William B. Snowhook
4617 Miss Belle L. Snowhook
4619 Mr. and Mrs. George Mehring
4619 Mr. & Mrs. P. A. Starck
    Receiving day Tuesday
4637 Mr. & Mrs. F. L. Harkness
4641 Mr. & Mrs. Jay G. Robinson
4641 Mr. & Mrs. Harry C. Adams
4647 Mr. & Mrs. W. B. Stevenson &
    drs.
4707 William H. Cunningham & dr.
4733 Mr. & Mrs. Thomas E. Wells
4825 Mr. & Mrs. Joseph M. Crennan
4827 Mr. & Mrs. J. S. Hummer & dr.
    Receiving day Wednesday
4829 Mr. & Mrs. Oliver W. Marble
    Receiving day Thursday
4831 Miss Minna Wies
4831 Charles A. Wies
4831 Mr. & Mrs. Frank E. Reed
4833 Mrs. Harriet Elliott & dr.
4833 Henry F. Elliott
4839 Mr. & Mrs. E. A. Still
    Receiving day Monday
4839 Mr. & Mrs. John Q. McAdams
4841 Mr. & Mrs. Henry Veeder
4901 Mr. & Mrs. A. W. Mitchell & dr.
4901 Mr. & Mrs. Donald A. Sage
4903 Mr. & Mrs. Abraham Weil
4907 Mr. & Mrs. Trusten B. Stafford
4919 Mr. & Mrs. William E. Brown
4947 Mr. & Mrs. Milo S. Bullock
4949 Mr. & Mrs. L. Oberndorf & dr.
4949 Max L. Oberndorf
4949 Dr. Abe L. Oberndorf

WABASH AVENUE.

2139 Dr. Philo L. Holland
    Receiving day Thursday
2251 Josiah H. Kellogg
2425 Mrs. A. Sweger

2450 Mrs. P. M. Cleary & drs.
    Receiving day Tuesday
2450 Edward E. Cleary
2512 Mrs. L. C. Dyer

2427 Mrs. W. H. Hafner
2427 W. H. Hafner jr.
2439 Mr. & Mrs. T. H. Miller
2439 Thomas H. Miller jr.
2441 Mr. & Mrs. W. W. Klore
    Receiving day Wednesday
2441 Dr. & Mrs. Russell H. Wheeler
2443 Mr. & Mrs. Charles Stein
2445 Mrs. M. Hayes & drs.
2501 Mrs. Elizabeth Marks
2501 Louis J. Marks
2501 Kossuth Marks
2501 Joseph E. P. Marks
2501 Edward C. Marks
2511 Mrs. H. Moses
2511 Charles Moses
2511 Eli Moses
2513 Mr. & Mrs. Kaufman Hexter &
    drs.
2513 Miss Rose Lebold
2521 George L. Hunter
2601 John R. Moore
2631 Dr. & Mrs. W. A. Stevens & dr.
2631 Wirt A. Stevens
2719 Mr. & Mrs. C. H. Wingate
2723 Mr. & Mrs. Anthony Lichten-
    heim
    Receiving day Wednesday
2725 Mrs. P. H. Sullivan
    Receiving day Thursday
2725 William J. Sullivan
2727 Mr. & Mrs. S. M. McConnell
2727 Mr. & Mrs. W. S. McConnell
2939 Mr. & Mrs. James W. Loomis
    & drs.
2941 Mr. & Mrs. Wm. A. Barton &
    dr.
2959 Mrs. A. Sanders & dr.
2959 John P. Sanders
2975 Mrs. H. Cowan & drs.
3115 Dr. & Mrs. J. R. Kewley
3125 Mr. & Mrs. J. S. Bassett
3125 J. Eugene H. Bassett
3125 George R. S. Bassett
3125 Mrs. Jane Beaver
3131 Mr. & Mrs. William Walsh & drs.
3137 Dr. & Mrs. Martin Matter
3139 Mr. & Mrs. Molesworth King
    & drs.
3139 Vincent M. King
3155 Mrs. Florence A. Camp
3155 A. Royce Camp
3211 Mrs. John Guerin & dr.
3211 Dr. John Guerin
3211 Thomas Edmund Guerin
3213 Mrs. Mary M. Morgan

2512 Randall H. White
2618 Mrs. M. L. Adams
2618 Mr. & Mrs. John A. Adams
2618 William T. Adams
2712 Mr. & Mrs. Simon Pfaelzer
2728 Mr. & Mrs. H. T. Pushman
2728 Mr. & Mrs. Chas. A. Russ
2728 Mr. & Mrs. J. S. McClelland
2956 Mr. & Mrs. A. B. Perrigo
2962 Mr. & Mrs. Nathan Davis
2974 Dr. & Mrs. E. Sincere
2974 Dr. M. B. Sincere
2978 Mr. & Mrs. A. Cummings
3126 Mr. & Mrs. Gustav L. Klein
3138 Mrs. Martin Crowe & dr.
3138 Mr. & Mrs. E. C. Smith
3156 Mrs. M. W. Wolf
3156 Henry F. Wolf
3156 Arthur C. Wolf
3232 Mr. & Mrs. I. G. Schwarz &
    drs.
3236 Mr. & Mrs. Isaac Pieser
3238 Mr. & Mrs. Chas. Liebenstein
    & dr.
3252 Mrs. L. Glaser
3252 Victor L. Glaser
3252 Mrs. L. Monheimer
3252 Milton Monheimer
3312 Mr. & Mrs. P. H. Rice
    Receiving day Tuesday
3326 Mr. & Mrs. Eugene Arnstein
    Receiving day Monday
3328 Mr. & Mrs. A. I. Radzinski
    Receiving day Friday
3336 Mr. & Mrs. T. F. DeVeney
3338 Mr. & Mrs. M. Dunne
3344 Mrs. S. A. Dowling
3344 R. A. Dowling
3350 Mr. & Mrs. A. H. Bliss
    Receiving day Thursday
3354 Jacob Franks
3354 Mr. & Mrs. Sol Rubin
3404 E. W. Peeke
3408 Mr. & Mrs. Reuben L. Sid-
    well
3410 Geo. Weise
3410 George B. Weise
3410 Frank A. Weise
3414 Mr. & Mrs. J. Dolese & drs.
3414 John Dolese jr.
3424 Mr. & Mrs. V. Falkenau
3438 Solva Brintnall
3438 Mrs. Mary L. Brintnall
3438 Arthur W. Brintnall
3438 Edward Shattuck
3440 Mr. & Mrs. J. C. Nickerson

3213 Miss Josie Sanders
3213 Miss Margaret Sanders
3219 Mr. & Mrs. B. J. Wertheimer
3221 Mrs. Lena Schuback & drs.
3223 Mr. & Mrs. C. D. Hancock
3225 Mr. & Mrs. M. E. Lindauer
3227 Mr. & Mrs. Jacob Kahn
  Receive 1st Thursday
3227 Harry Kahn
3229 Mrs. M. H. Mayer
  Receiving day Tuesday
3229 Leonard H. Mayer
3231 Mr. & Mrs. W. C. Ross
3241 Mr. & Mrs. Edward Rose & dr.
  Receiving day Thursday
3247 Mr.&Mrs.Julius Rosenthal&dr.
  Receiving day Friday
3247 Lessing Rosenthal
3251 Mr. & Mrs. Marvin S. Chase &
  dr. *Receiving day Thursday*
3255 Turner Hotel
  Mr. & Mrs. J. J. Epstein
  David Frank
  I. M. Frank
  James I. Loeb
  David Manheimer
  Mr. & Mrs. P. A. Turner
  Mr. & Mrs. Max Schlesinger
  Mrs. Eva Singer
3333 Mr. & Mrs. Jacob Newman
3333 Mrs. H. Goodman & dr.
  Receiving day Thursday
3333 Maurice Goodman
3333 Louis H. Goodman
3333 Harry Goodman
3333 Miss Hannah Miers
  Receiving day Thursday
3337 Mrs. A. Strauss &.dr.
  Receiving day Friday
3337 Henry X. Strauss
3337 Milton A. Strauss
3341 Mrs. Isaac Rubel
3341 Benjamin F. Rubel
3343 Mr. & Mrs. Levi G. Rubel
3343 Mrs. Therese Eliel
3347 Mr. & Mrs. C. C. Chandler
3347 Cornelius L. Chandler
3349 Mrs. Joseph Bee & dr.
  Receiving day Monday
3349 Harry Bee
3349 R. Addison Bee
3353 Mrs. Wallace C. Barker & dr.
3359 Mr. & Mrs. Geo. Fabyan
3401 J. C. McCord
3431 James Leahy & drs.
  Receiving day Wednesday

3442 Mr. & Mrs. Freeman Nickerson
3448 Mr. & Mrs. Albert Fishell
  Rec. days 2d & 4th Thursday in mo.
3448 Dr. E. W. Fishell
3518 Mr. & Mrs. J. P. McGrath
3524 Mr. & Mrs. Morris Mitchell &
  dr. *Receiving day Wednesday*
3528 Mr.& Mrs.Michael McDermott
3530 Mr. & Mrs. Charles Long & drs.
3530 Louis Long
3530 Lee Long
3530 Sidney Long
3532 Mr. & Mrs. Charles Pick
  Receiving day Wednesday
3532 Mr. & Mrs. Max Brede
  Receiving day Wednesday
3534 Mr. & Mrs. John T. Martin
  Receiving day Thursday
3534 Mrs. Sarah Martin
3534 Mrs. Lena P. Wagner
3542 Mr. & Mrs. Wm. H. Corbidge
3646 Mr. & Mrs. Samuel Beers
3662 Mr. & Mrs. Harry S. Thornton
3670 Mr. & Mrs. John Patterson
  & gr.
3672 Mr. & Mrs. Robert T. Keith
3706 Mr. & Mrs. Wm. E. Dee
3708 Rev. & Mrs. A. J. Messing
  Receiving day Friday
3708 Sigmund J. Messing
3716 Mr. & Mrs. John H. Ibsen
3720 Mr. & Mrs. Simon O'Donnell
3742 Mr. & Mrs. M. Klein & dr.
3752 Mr. & Mrs. Joseph Mayer
3812 Mr. & Mrs. H. R. Henry
3812 Mrs. Grace Osher
4136 Dr. & Mrs. A. L. Cory
  Receiving day Thursday
4136 V. P. Cory
4136 Dr. & Mrs. E. V. Cory
4156 Prof. & Mrs. Gabriel Bamberger
4156 Miss Alice Bamberger
4238 Mrs. J. F. Kelling
4240 Mr. & Mrs. Frank H. Bishop
4412 Mr. & Mrs. David Weber
  Receiving day Thursday
4550 R. J. Hercock
5112 Mrs. John Farren
5112 Dr. John A. Farren
5132 Mr. & Mrs. John MacMahon
5138 Mr. & Mrs. T. B. Skeeles
5138 Mr. & Mrs. Harry Skeeles
5142 Mrs. N. J. Wright
5142 Mr. & Mrs. B. F. Terhune

3433 Mr. & Mrs. W. F. Favorite
3435 Mr. & Mrs. W. C. Nixon
3435 Mr. & Mrs. H. B. Chichester
3437 Mr. & Mrs Henry Francis Loomis
      Receiving day Wednesday
3443 Mr. & Mrs. Max Weinberg
      Receive 1st & 3d Wednesdays
3443 David Berg
3519 Mr. & Mrs. Harry Byrne
3525 Mrs. W. Klinger & dr.
3525 William Klinger
3531 Caesar L. Hefter
3531 Miss Florence L. Hefter
3531 Miss Rebecca L. Hefter
3531 Mrs. Louis Harmon
3535 Mrs. Mary Wilson & niece
      Receiv'g day Tuesday
3603 Mr. & Mrs. C. Mulvey & dr.
3605 Mr. & Mrs. John T. Muir
3613 Mr. & Mrs. Jacob Ringer
      Receiving day Tuesday
3617 Mr. & Mrs. J. Frank Page
3667 Mr. & Mrs. Thos. H. Corbett
3669 Mrs. Patrick Farrell & dr.
3669 Thomas P. Farrell
3745 Mr. & Mrs. W. M. Cave
3805 Dr. & Mrs. M. G. Hart
3809 Mr. & Mrs. W. H. Krouskup
3809 Mr. & Mrs. Louis Diesel
3809 Otto Wiltz
3811 August Dosch
3817 Mr. & Mrs. James Ralston
3827 Mr. & Mrs. M. S. Rothschild
3829 Dr. & Mrs. G. H. Richardson
4207 Mr. & Mrs. E. W. Houser
4209 Mr. & Mrs. D. N. Howe
4217 Mrs. Caroline Katz

5160 Mr. & Mrs. Mathias Ross & dr.
5260 Mr. & Mrs. P. H. Keenan
5260 Dr. James Lawless & dr.
5654 Mr. & Mrs. Herman Schopflocher
5822 Mrs. H. L. Prentice
5900 Mr. & Mrs. John O'Neill
5924 Mr. & Mrs. C. H. Schlacks & dr.
      Receiving day Wednesday

4217 Mr. & Mrs. Henry Katz
4223 Thomas F. Delaney
4223 Mrs. Louisa Wiesler
4309 Mr. & Mrs. Wm. R. Everett
4807 Mr. & Mrs. J. J. McKenna
4915 Mr. & Mrs. George E. Lawson
5011 Mr. & Mrs. M. Coghlan & dr.
      Receiving day Thursday
5011 Henry D. Coghlan
5013 Mr. & Mrs. John Blum & dr.
5913 Edgar C. Blum
5013 Louis J. Blum
5017 Mr. & Mrs. H. E. Tingle
5119 Mr. & Mrs. H. W. Smith
5145 Mr. & Mrs. S. Wilks
5163 Mr. & Mrs. C. E. Pardridge
      Receiving day Thursday
5163 Mrs. J. R. Hull
5303 Mr. & Mrs. T. J. Prendergast
5405 Mrs. Edward Milan
5405 Edward Milan
5405 Mr. & Mrs. Edward F. White
5851 Edmund Wagner
5853 Dr. & Mrs. M. A. Colman
5855 Mr. & Mrs. Edward S. Fogg
5911 Mr. & Mrs. B. W. Bradley
5943 Mrs. J. P. Cordier

WALLACE STREET.

6956 Mr. & Mrs. E. S. Metcalf

6956 Guido C. S. Metcalf

WASHINGTON AVENUE.

4915 Mr. & Mrs. Lauren H. Turner
4915 L. Hamilton Turner
4917 Mr. & Mrs. Paul Morton
4917 Miss Caroline Norton
4919 Mr. & Mrs. J. R. Morron
4923 Mr. & Mrs. Morton Denison Hull
4925 Mr. & Mrs. C. D. Rogers
4947 Mr. & Mrs. Edward J. Stransky
5001 Mr. & Mrs. Wm. Stone
5011 Mr. & Mrs. Christian Eigenman
5011 Christian Eigenman jr.

4842 Mr. & Mrs. Charles H. Foote
4846 Mr. & Mrs. E. Williamson
4850 Mrs. Joseph P. Card
4850 Joseph B. Card
4850 Miss Grace B. Card
4850 Miss Mary P. Card
4852 Mr. & Mrs. E. L. Somers
4852 Mr. & Mrs. E. S. Sibley
4854 Mr. & Mrs. B. M. Chattell
4858 Mr. & Mrs. Ernest Robert Graham. *Receiving day Monday*

5011 Dr. John C. Eigenman
5021 Mrs. W. H. Benton & drs.
5021 W. H. Benton jr.
5037 Mr. & Mrs. O. A. Bogue
5037 Roswell C. Bogue
5037 Miss Agnes Belden
5037 Miss Grace Belden
5039 Mr. & Mrs. James A. Ostrom
5041 Mr. & Mrs. Thos. L. Parker
5043 Mr. & Mrs. Geo. H. Jenkins
5043 Mrs. H. B. Durfee & dr.
5121 Mr. & Mrs. G. E. Highley
5131 Mr. & Mrs. Thos. B. Brougham
    & dr.
5131 Seymour. Edgerton
5135 Judge & Mrs. M. F. Tuley
5139 Mr. & Mrs. A. I. Valentine
5211 Mr. & Mrs. W. C. Lawson & dr.
    Receiving day Thursday
5215 Mr. & Mrs. Joel B. Chapin
5227 Mr. & Mrs. Wm. H. Birkett
5311 Mr. & Mrs. John P. Roberson
5311 Mr. & Mrs. John E. Parke
5311 Mr. & Mrs. Amory W. Sawyer
5315 Mr. & Mrs. M. S. Bradley
5315 Mr. & Mrs. H. L. Ashton
5317 Mr. & Mrs. W. S. Caleb
5317 Mr. & Mrs. R. W. Kinahan
5319 Mr. & Mrs. Richard H. Kerr
5319 Mr. & Mrs. J. J. West
5321 Frank R. Ransford
5325 Mr. & Mrs. O. N. Caldwell
5325 Mr. & Mrs. G. H. Love
    Receiving day Thursday
5327 Mr. & Mrs. Charles L. Krum
5327 Mr. & Mrs. Walter F. Shattuck
5329 Mr. & Mrs. C. A. Tousey & dr.
    Receiving day Thursday
5337 Mr. & Mrs. C. D. Fullen
5343 Mr. & Mrs. Fred W. Stephens
5409 Mr. & Mrs. Martin J. Russell
5413 Eben Byron Smith
5413 Mr. & Mrs. Willis Byron Smith
5417 John King
5417 Mrs. Anna King
5417 Sam B. King
5423 Mr. & Mrs. Frederick H. Kilbourn
5425 Mr. & Mrs. A. H. Emmons
5425 Miss Alice Ayling
5427 Mrs. Laura J. Tisdale
5427 Mrs. Julia A. Darling
5427 James H. Miller
5451 Mr. & Mrs. W. Bodemann & dr.
5463 Dr. & Mrs. Ernest W. Keith
5465 Mr. & Mrs. David J. Lindsay

4860 Mr. & Mrs. Chas. B. Kelley
4860 Albert J. Morley
4862 Dr. & Mrs. James Burry
4900 Mr. & Mrs. Wilson K. Doty
4900 C. V. Marsh
4904 Mr. & Mrs. George M.Benedict
4904 Mr. & Mrs. H. J. Boyer
4904 Allen Boyer
4906 Mr. & Mrs. John A. Atkinson
4908 Mr. & Mrs. F. M. Dunbaugh
4916 Mr. & Mrs. W. F. Gorrell
4928 Mr. & Mrs. B. F. Ray
4940 Mrs. M. M. Noyes & dr.
4940 E. E. Noyes
4946 Mr. & Mrs. Chas. A. Birkle
4946 Mr. & Mrs. Julian P. Bliss
4948 Mr. & Mrs. J. Porter Joplin
4954 Mr. & Mrs. C. H. Holbrook
4956 Mr. & Mrs. E. E. Perley
4956 Wilson A. Glover
5000 Mr. & Mrs. James E. Hayes
5004 G. Harold Atkin
5006 Mr. & Mrs. H. B. Herr
5006 Percy B. Herr
5026 Mr. & Mrs. James F. Brown
5032 Dr. & Mrs. Edwin Pynchon
    Receiving day Wednesday
5034 Dr. & Mrs. Irwin Simpson
5036 Mr. & Mrs. Henry C. Smith
5036 Miss S. Gertrude Smith
5036 Miss Bessie C. Smith
5036 Miss Alice C. Smith
5038 Mr. & Mrs. Sydney Stein
5040 Mr. & Mrs. James Hewitt
5126 Mr. & Mrs. Richard O. Miller
5126 Mr. & Mrs. Frederic A. Stevenson
5128 Mr. & Mrs. S. G. Wilkins
5128 Lemuel L. Donnelly
5132 Mr. & Mrs. Will H.Moore & dr.
5136 Mr. & Mrs. Fletcher W. Rockwell
5136 Miss Nellie Rockwell
5136 Miss Charlotte Rockwell
5136 Fletcher W. Rockwell jr.
5142 Dr. & Mrs. Henry C. Allen &
    dr.
5142 Frank L. Allen
5200 Mr. & Mrs. A. V. Hartwell
5200 Mr. & Mrs. A. B. Emery
5210 Mr. & Mrs. Fred'k B. Perry,
5216 Mr. & Mrs. James Grassie
5226 Dr. & Mrs. Chas. S. Taylor
5314 Dr. & Mrs. Edward M. Bruce
    Receiving day Thursday
5326 Mrs. C. M. Hawley

5465 Miss Louisa A. Milner
5481 Mr. & Mrs. Charles C. Snyder
 Receiving day Tuesday
5487 Mr.& Mrs. Charles Peck & drs.
5517 Mr. & Mrs. Chas. A. Wear & dr.
5517 Mrs. Maria P. Hunter
5531 Mr. & Mrs. Henry H. Sessions
5533 Mr. & Mrs. F. D. Brown & dr.
5533 Berlyn B. Brown
5533 F. Junior Brown
5545 Mr. & Mrs. Herman J. Hall & dr.
5547 Mrs. M. R. Doty & dr.
5547 C. Edwin Doty
5547 Mrs. Norman T. Gassette
5601 Mr. & Mrs. Frank Harlow
5607 Mr. & Mrs. M. P. Barker
5609 Mrs. A. S. Kissell & drs.
5611 Mr. & Mrs. W. C. Brown & drs.
5617 Mr. & Mrs. F. W. Porter
5621 Mr. & Mrs. Wm. Zimmerman
5629 Mr. & Mrs. R. C. H. Catterall
5635 Mr. & Mrs. G. F. Bartholomew
5639 Mrs. Ella M. Burns
5639 Charles A. Marsh
5649 Mr. & Mrs. John H. Kintz
5657 Mr. & Mrs. W. C. Foresman
5663 Mr. & Mrs. Jas. T. Graves
5663 James A. Graves
5663 Robert E. Graves
5663 Dr. Kate I. Graves
5717 Prof. & Mrs. J. W. Thompson
5719 Mr. & Mrs. George F. Rush
5721 Mr. & Mrs. Alexander R. Beck & drs.
 Receiving days Tuesdays
5721 Alexander E. Beck
5723 Mr. & Mrs. Joseph G. Simpson
5723 Mrs. J. H. Eoff
5725 Mr. & Mrs. Fred. K. Root
5729 Mr. & Mrs. L. W. Messer
5731 Mr. & Mrs. Albion W. Small
 Receiving day Thursday
5739 Mr. & Mrs. Kenneth Barnhart
5743 Mr. & Mrs. Frank P. Leonard
5743 Mrs. Olive Shelton
5745 Mr. & Mrs. J. A. Sleeper
5761 Mr. & Mrs. S. H. Clark
5765 R. N. Baylies
5765 Mr. & Mrs. F. A. Poor
5801 Mr. & Mrs. John C. Carroll
5803 Mr. & Mrs. Robert Bines
5803 Miss Charlotte A. Farnham
5805 Mr. & Mrs. Lewis C. Straight
5807 Mr. & Mrs. Frank I. Bennett
5809 Mrs. Margaret M. Woods

5332 Dr. & Mrs.W. S. Johnson & drs
5332 Mrs. S. B. Reed
5332 Miss Mary L. Mason
5338 Mr. & Mrs. Arthur H. Rugg
5338 Mr. & Mrs. John C. Long
5338 Daniel A. Fraser
5338 Mr. & Mrs. Wilfred T. Caldwell
5338 Mr. & Mrs. George A. Dorsey
5342 Mr. & Mrs. Seymour Morris
5342 Mr. & Mrs. Joseph Morris
5344 Mrs. S. A. Dutton & drs.
5344 L. R. Le Furgy
5344 Frank T. Dickey
5400 Mrs. James M. Gilchrist & dr.
5400 Miss Harriet F. Gilchrist
5400 Mrs. G. S. Ingraham
5406 Mr. & Mrs. John F. Gilchrist
5408 Mrs. Anna A. Hinckley
5408 Abner T. Hinckley jr.
5408 Mrs. Sarah Ritchie
5410 Mrs. Charles H. Arms & dr.
5410 Herbert C. Arms
5418 Mr. & Mrs. A. W. Hayward
5420 Mr. & Mrs. Chas. F. Forster
5420 Miss Elizabeth Reid
5422 Mr. & Mrs. Nelson Fortin
5424 Mr. & Mrs. Geo. E. Harmon
5426 Mr. & Mrs. W. L. Bosworth
5426 Mr. & Mrs. F. F. Bosworth
5450 Mrs. A. G. Walter
5450 Philip M. Walter
5454 Mr. & Mrs. C. A. Wilson
5460 Mr. &Mrs.Charles Brewer &dr.
5460 Mrs. Julia Shaul
5464 Mr. & Mrs. D. A. Peirce & drs.
5468 Mr. & Mrs. Wm. Wm. S. Colwell
5468 Mr. & Mrs. C. V. Kellogg
5470 Mr. & Mrs. W. T. Beatty
5486 Mr. & Mrs. J. B. Whitney
5486 Mr. & Mrs. Fred H. Lord
5490 Dr. & Mrs. R. W. Conant
5490 Dr. & Mrs. W. E. Fraser
5510 Mr. & Mrs. Wilbur R. Davis
5510 Mrs. C. E. Bell
5520 Mr. & Mrs. Wm. M. Wright
5520 Warren Wright
5520 Miss Lucille Owen
5530 Mr. & Mrs. F. E. Parish & dr.
5532 Mr. & Mrs. Henry R. Williams
5534 Dr. & Mrs. John E. Harper
5536 Mr. & Mrs. B. Wightman
5538 Prof. & Mrs. E. H. Moore
5538 Ned A. Flood
5540 Mr. & Mrs. James P. Root

5809 Mr. & Mrs. F. B. Lines
5809 Mr. & Mrs. Lorado Taft
5813 Mr. & Mrs. W. H. Boice
  Receiving day Friday
5827 Mr. & Mrs. Fred Bode
5831 Mr.& Mrs. Wm. E.Webbe & dr.
5837 Mr. & Mrs. Frank Riedle
5859 Mr. & Mrs. Otis Jones
6117 Dr. & Mrs. Curtis T. Fenn
6617 Mr. & Mrs. E. D. Brown

5758 Mr. & Mrs. B. R. Kent
5804 Mrs. E. R. Crowell
5806 Mr. & Mrs. Giles N. Easton
5810 Mrs. M. A. Goodman
5810 Mr. & Mrs. A. L. Bell & dr.
5810 Royal W. Bell
5822 Mr. & Mrs. R. A. Shailer
5826 H. G. Gale
5826 Ralph W. Webster
5830 Prof. & Mrs. Frank Justus
  Miller
5830 Mrs. Emma F. Beardsley
5830 Mrs. Anna H. Olmsted
5830 Mr. & Mrs. Edwin D. Weary
5832 Mr. & Mrs. Edgar B. Tolman
6028 Dr. & Mrs. Albert O. Howe
6124 Mr. & Mrs. Chas. E. Shillaber

5540 Clarence J. Root
5540 Mr. & Mrs. J. H. Baldwin
5610 Mr. & Mrs. L. C. Kuhnert
5616 Mr. & Mrs. John S. Ford
5616 William A. Simpson
5620 Mr. & Mrs. H. M. Norton
5620 Mrs. T. C. Fanning
5642 Mr. & Mrs. E. O. Lanphere
5642 Mrs. J. E. Calkins
5656 M. E. Sanford
5656 Mrs. E. H. Griffith
5714 Mr. & Mrs. Thos. V. Connor
5714 Mr. & Mrs. R. E. Young
5716 Miss Gertrude P. Dingee
5720 Mr. & Mrs. D. W. Chapman
5722 Mr. & Mrs. H. F. Pennington
5722 Mr. & Mrs. H.F.Pennington jr.
5722 Mr. & Mrs. F. A. Pennington
5736 Prof.&Mrs.Chas.R.Henderson
5738 Mr. & Mrs. Henry H. Belfield
5738 Miss Ada Marshall Belfield
5738 A. Miller Belfield
5744 Mr. & Mrs. A. A. Adams
5748 Mr. & Mrs. P. F. Cameron
5752 Mr. & Mrs. Horace W. Nichols
  & dr. *Receiving day Friday*
5754 Mr. & Mrs. James Birney
  Johnston & dr.
  Receiving day Tuesday

WASHINGTON PARK COURT.

4935 Mr. & Mrs. Wm. K. Mitchell
4937 Mr. & Mrs. S. Percy Buchanan
4941 Mr.&Mrs.D. M. Lindauer & dr.
4941 Max Lindauer
4955 Mr. & Mrs. Arthur W. Draper
4959 Dr. & Mrs. J. J. Ahern

4902 Mr. & Mrs. C. H. Storm
4910 Mr. & Mrs. A. H Veeder, jr.

4957 Mr. & Mrs. F. B. King
  Receiving day Thursday

WELLINGTON COURT.

1 Mr. & Mrs. James A. Warren

WENTWORTH AVENUE.

6323 Mr. & Mrs. J. J. Horning
6545 Mr. & Mrs. Alvin L. Ringo
6615 Mr. & Mrs. Robert Craig
6629 Mr. & Mrs. Geo. L. Thompson
6635 Mr. & Mrs. J. C. Church
6717 Mr. & Mrs. J. E. Deakin
6719 Mr. & Mrs. W. C. Brown
6719 E. L. Brown
6719 A. S. Brown
6719 Dr. & Mrs. A. W. Rogers
6741 Dr. & Mrs. L. Hulbert Fuller
6757 Mr. & Mrs. A. R. Swift
6757 A. R. Swift jr.

5540 Mr. & Mrs. E. W. Adkinson
6058 Dr. & Mrs. C. H. Lovewell
6400 Mr. & Mrs. George P. Bay
6636 Mr. & Mrs. Bushrod E. Hoppin
6700 Mrs. Harry G. Brainard
6716 Mr. & Mrs. E. Kirk jr.
6726 Mr. & Mrs. L. M. Tracy & dr.
6732 Mr. & Mrs. D. W. Storrs
  Receiving day Thursday
6732 Miss Mary H. Storrs
6840 Mr. & Mrs. J. H. Earl
6842 Dr. & Mrs. Chas. L. Davis
  Receives Thursday

6805 Dr. & Mrs. E.H. Sparling & dr.
6817 Dr. & Mrs. M. W. Bacon & drs.
7117 Mr. & Mrs. James W. Porter &
    drs.
7117 Robert C. Porter
7121 Mr. & Mrs. A. W. Stuart & dr.
7127 Mrs. M. W. Farmer & drs.
7127 James F. Hill

6932 Mr. & Mrs. Edward Addy
6948 Mr. & Mrs. George P. Bent
7116 Mr. & Mrs. Emil Danne
7120 Mrs. Eliza Dorr & dr.
7120 Mr. & Mrs. Geo. W. Dorr
―――
7147 Mr. & Mrs. Chas. J. Fellows
    Receiving day Thursday

WINNECONNA AVENUE.

7805 Mr. & Mrs. C. G. Gibson
7811 Mr. & Mrs. Walter H. Merritt
7815 Mr. & Mrs. C. W. Gibson
7817 Mr. & Mrs. Martin V. Barney
7827 Dr. Sarah B. Duncan & dr.

7827 Miss Carrie O. Scobey
7831 Mr. & Mrs. Frank H. Mealiff
7843 Mr. & Mrs. Edw. S. Whittlesey
    & dr.

WOODLAND PARK.

9 Mr. & Mrs. W. E. Hughes
25 Dr. & Mrs. Z. E. Patrick & drs.
29 Mr. & Mrs. James A. Moffett
35 Mr. & Mrs. John W. Embree
39 M. A. O. Packard
47 Mr. & Mrs. A. Baldwin & dr.
―――
58 Mr. & Mrs. B. F. Nourse
58 John A. Nourse
58 Guy P. Nourse
60 Mr. & Mrs. Ambrose L. Thomas
    & dr.
62 Mr. & Mrs. Abner Crossman
    Receiving day Wednesday
62 Mr. & Mrs. Frank H. Thomas
    Receiving day Wednesday

14 Mr. & Mrs. William H. Flagg
14 Elmer T. Flagg
22 Mrs. M. H. Dunham & dr.
    Receiving day Wednesday
22 Arthur Dunham
30 Mr. & Mrs. Clarence Forsyth
    Receiving day Thursday
30 Mrs. Lucy H. Forsyth
32 Mrs. M. Baird & dr.
32 Mr. & Mrs. Wm. LeBaron
36 Mr. & Mrs. James G. Wright & dr.
36 J. Joseph Wright
42 Mr. & Mrs. Arthur J. Whipple
44 Mr. & Mrs. Robert L. Elliott
44 George C. Purdy
56 Mr. & Mrs. G. Herbert Jones

WOODLAWN AVENUE.

4513 Mr. & Mrs. Robert Thin
4515 Mr. & Mrs. Clift Wise
4517 M . & Mrs. E. C. Hatheway &
    drs.
4517 E. Morris Hatheway
4517 Charles Broughton
4517 Mrs. S. A. Murphy
4519 Mr. & Mrs. J. L. Hinckley
4519 Mrs. Martha L. Hubbard
4519 William W. Loomis
4521 Mr. & Mrs. M. J. Spain & dr.
4551 Mrs. W. M. Wilson
4559 Mr. & Mrs. Elmer Washburn
    & dr. *Receiving day Friday*
4559 Dr. & Mrs. C. Joseph Swan
4609 Mr. & Mrs. R. R. Donnelley & dr.
4609 T. E. Donnelley
4609 B. S. Donnelley
4613 Mr. & Mrs. Harlan W. Cooley

4436 Mr. & Mrs. Emil Gutwillig
    Receive Saturday
4436 Mr. & Mrs. Isaac Benjamin
4438 Prof. & Mrs. Chas. D'Almaine
4438 Mr. & Mrs. A. S. Berry & dr.
    Receive Wednesday
4440 Judge & Mrs. Henry B. Evans
4440 Charles D. Harless
4446 Mr. & Mrs. William H. Blase
4446 William P. Todd
4454 Mr. & Mrs. F. E. Walker & dr.
4500 Mr. & Mrs. Alfred E. Forrest
4504 Mr. & Mrs. Charles E. Maxwell
4504 Miss M. L. Cobb
4508 Mr. & Mrs. T. N. Jamieson
4510 Mr. & Mrs. S. B. Jamieson
4510 Stillman B. Jamieson
4520 Albert L. Deane
4520 Miss Lillie A. Deane

4613 Mrs. S. Sibley
4613 Mr. & Mrs. Wm. G. Bruen
4613 Mr. & Mrs. L. M. Crump
4615 Mr. & Mrs. Chas. H. Eldridge
4615 Miss Elizabeth Withington
4619 Mr. & Mrs. Louis C.Wiswell
4619 Mr. & Mrs. Orville M. Truman
4619 Ralph D. Small
4621 Mr. & Mrs. J. M. Denniston
4629 Mr. & Mrs. P. P. O'Donnell
4705 Mr. & Mrs. Wm. W. Michener
4709 Mr. & Mrs. Lyman A. Wiley
4711 Mr. & Mrs. Henry C. Champlin
& drs.
4711 Harry C. Champlin
4713 Mr. & Mrs. John Tweedy
Crocker
4713 Miss Crocker
4713 Miss Augusta Crocker
4723 Mr. & Mrs. A. E. Bingham
4729 Mr. & Mrs. H. M. S. Montgomery
4733 Mr. & Mrs. W. D. Washburn
4737 Mr. & Mrs. Marvin A. Farr
4737 J. G. Farr
4747 Mr.& Mrs. John W. Cloud & dr.
4747 Miss Lilean B. Weide
5127 Mr. & Mrs. Jacob Mansar
5227 Mr. & Mrs. Geo. Shaw Cook
5227 Mr. & Mrs. Fred W.Chickering
5227 Mr. & Mrs. James H. Davidson
5227 Mr. & Mrs. Francis M. Case
5357 Mr. & Mrs. Chas. L. Hunter
5419 Dr. & Mrs. Sydney Walker
5515 Mr. & Mrs. Geo. M. Eckels
5515 Mr. & Mrs. F. W. Shepardson
5515 Prof. & Mrs. Geo. L. Hendrickson
5515 Mr. & Mrs. Milton O. Higgins
5515 Dr. & Mrs. Hamilton Forline
5515 Frederick Johnstone
5533 Prof. & Mrs. F. I. Carpenter
5545 Mr. & Mrs. Hugo O. von Hof-
sten *Receiving day Friday*
5549 Dr. & Mrs. T. G. Allen
5549 Ralph S. Fralick
5555 Rev. & Mrs. Henry Willard
& drs.
5555 Dr. Rose Willard
5555 Norman P. Willard
5737 Mr. & Mrs. L. A. Walton
6019 Mr. & Mrs. Truman W. Crosby
6109 Mr. & Mrs. S. H. Stewart
6113 Mr. & Mrs. T. H. Carter
6127 Mr. & Mrs. W. S. Dawley
6129 Mr. & Mrs. Chas. G. L. Kelso
16

4520 Miss Margaret Deane
4526 Mr. & Mrs. A. M. Graves & dr.
4530 Mr. & Mrs. Wm. L. Clancy
4532 Mr. & Mrs. Jesse Titman
4532 Mr. & Mrs. George B. Titman
4534 Mr. & Mrs. C. R. E. Koch & dr.
4534 Mrs. A. B. Potts
4536 Mrs. W. R. King
4536 Mr. & Mrs. Wm. J. Bridgeman
4552 Mr.& Mrs. L. D. Condee & drs.
4552 Mrs. H. J. Johnson
4610 Mr. & Mrs. Robert S. Critchell
Receiving day Monday
4610 Mr. & Mrs. Hugh Henry Rimington
Receiving day Monday
4612 Mr. & Mrs. W. A. Green
4612 Mrs. M. E. Hanford
4614 Mr. & Mrs. M. L. Wheeler
Receiving day Tuesday
4614 Miss Emily F. Wheeler
4614 Charles F. White
4620 Mr. & Mrs. W. A. Thrall
4620 Mr. & Mrs. S. E. Thrall
4620 Mrs. Maria M. Boyce
4626 Mr. & Mrs. F. G. Kammerer
4706 Eugene S. Kimball
4706 Miss Helen E. Kimball
4722 Mr. & Mrs. J. S. Belden & dr.
4722 John S. Belden jr.
4722 Miss A. W. Pool
4726 Mr. & Mrs. E. E. Crepin
4726 Mrs. Delia Pierce
4738 J. B. Knight
4738 Mr. & Mrs. Fred H. Andrus
4738 Philip L. Marshall
4744 Mr. & Mrs. E. A. Sherburne
4750 Mr. & Mrs. John Marder &
dr.
4750 Mr. & Mrs. Walter S. Marder
4750 John W. Marder
4750 Clarence Marder
4812 Mr. & Mrs. Christopher B.
Bouton
4812 Miss Persis Bouton
4812 Dr. & Mrs. Raymond Custer
Turck
4824 Mr. & Mrs. H. M. Dupee & drs.
4824 Leroy C. Dupee
4850 Mr. & Mrs. John Davis
4912 Mr. & Mrs. J. W. Brooks jr.
4924 Mr. & Mrs. G. N. Caleb
4924 Mr. & Mrs. A. G. Spalding
4926 Keith Spalding
4948 Mrs. Van H. Higgins
4948 Mrs. W. E. Pinney

6203 Mr. & Mrs. Wm. J. Barnhart
6205 Dr. & Mrs. H. Barrie Milican
6207 Dr. & Mrs. Frank A. Barber
6207 Mr. & Mrs. Edward E. Hanna
6211 Mr. & Mrs. George Wagner
6217 Mrs. Isidore G. Smith
6217 J. Sewell Smith
6221 Mr. & Mrs. G. S. Hardenbrook
    & dr.
6221 Geo. P. Hardenbrook
6221 Burt C. Hardenbrook
6223 Mr. & Mrs. E. G. Hardenbrook
6243 Mr. & Mrs. John T. Sweetland
6243 Mr. & Mrs. Lucius P. Wilson
6311 Dr. W. D. Herriman
6311 Mrs. Stella Weller
    Receives Friday
6327 Dr. & Mrs. G. V. Hilton
6329 Mr. & Mrs. Timothy G. Hallinan
6329 Dr. Leo Loeb
6337 Dr. & Mrs. Wm. F. Dickson
6337 Mr. & Mrs. H. W. White
6427 Mr. & Mrs. Joseph W. Hill
6451 Rev. & Mrs. Arthur L. Williams
6451 Edward W. Griffith
6503 Mr. & Mrs. E. P. Marum
6503 Mrs. Julia Scanlon
6511 Mr. & Mrs. Seymour Walton
6513 Mr. & Mrs. R. A. Crandall
6513 Mrs. M. E. Ballard
6517 Mr. & Mrs. Robert Jones
6517 Frederick M. Jones
6519 Mr. & Mrs. C. Frank Jobson
6525 Mr. & Mrs. R. W. Cross
    Receiving day Tuesday
6627 Mr. & Mrs. Henry E. Scholle
6641 Mr. & Mrs. Robert F. Green
6641 Miss Alice Dickinson

6030 Mrs. E. M. Stryker & dr.
6030 James M. Stryker
6030 Louis H. Stryker
6106 Albert L. Spencer
6106 Mr. & Mrs. C. F. A. Spencer
6106 John M. Mott
6114 Mr. & Mrs. Chas. S. Partridge
    & dr.
6120 Mr. & Mrs. Geo. C. Wright
6122 Mr. & Mrs. R. R. Murdoch & dr.
6122 Miss Anna A. Bradley
6124 Mr. & Mrs. D. M. Hillis
6124 David S. Hillis
6128 Mr. & Mrs. W. H. Collins
6200 Mr. & Mrs. Frank A. Cotharin
6212 Mr. & Mrs. J. H. Lobdell

4948 Miss Kate Morse
4948 Miss Jessie Morse
5012 Mr. & Mrs. John J. Mitchell
5020 Mr. & Mrs. Edward A. Kimball
    & dr.
5046 Richard W. Rathborne & dr.
5046 Mr. & Mrs. W. H. Carruthers
5114 Carl B. Case
5114 Dr. & Mrs. C. S. Case & dr.
5116 Mr. & Mrs. George F. Hughson
    & dr.
5132 Mr. & Mrs. Isadore Heller
5134 Mr. & Mrs. M. Hamburger & dr.
    Receiving day Friday
5134 L. M. Hamburger
5134 Miss Elsie Wile
5140 Mr. & Mrs. George D. Cook &
    dr.
5210 Mr. & Mrs. John O'Connor
5214 Mr. & Mrs. Adelbert E. Coleman
5222 Mr. & Mrs. Frank H. Madden
    Receiving day Thursday
5234 Mr. & Mrs. H. T. Gilbert & drs.
5234 Alson Gilbert
5234 Mrs. M. B. Leland
5234 H. G. Andrews
5238 Prof. and Mrs. John Dewey
5300 Mr. & Mrs. L. B. Shattuck
5300 Miss Harriet K. Hill
5516 Prof. & Mrs. Paul Shorey
5520 Mr. & Mrs. D. L. Shorey
    Receive Tuesday
5548 Dr. & Mrs. F. H. Montgomery
5554 Mr. & Mrs. Theo. F. Rice & dr.
5630 Mr. & Mrs. D. Henry Sheldon
5630 Prof. & Mrs. W. C. Wilkinson
    & dr.
5720 Mr. & Mrs. Edwin O. Jordan
5730 Prof. Frank B. Tarbell
5730 Dr. Ernest Freund
5730 Prof. J. P. Iddings
5730 Prof. Rollin D. Salisbury
5736 Prof. & Mrs. Shailer Matthews
5740 Prof. & Mrs. H. H. Donaldson
5750 Mr. & Mrs. A. H. Tolman
5754 Prof. & Mrs. Jacques Loeb
5760 Judge & Mrs. Henry V. Freeman & drs.
    Receiving day Saturday
5810 Prof. & Mrs. H. Maschke
5810 Prof. Oscar Bolza
5828 Mr. & Mrs. Henry Pratt Judson
    Receiving day Thursday
5828 Miss Priscilla G. Gilbert
6030 Dr. & Mrs. Clifford Mitchell

6222 Hubert B. Clapp
6222 Dr. James L. Clapp
6222 Dr. Katherine B. Clapp
Receives Friday 3 to 5 & 8 to 10 p. m.
6222 Dr. & Mrs. E. Fred Brown
6222 Dr. E. Stillman Bailey
6230 Mr. & Mrs. Frank E. Brown & dr.
6230 Philip S. Brown

6246 Mr. & Mrs. J. J. Patchen
6320 Mr. & Mrs. David Sloan
6324 Dana W. Hall
6324 Mr. & Mrs. T. A. Evoy & dr.
6430 Mr. & Mrs. W. Y. Barnet
6450 Mr. & Mrs. Wm. L. Tarbet
6450 Mrs. S. J. Bishop & dr.
6554 Mr. & Mrs. S. N. Howard
6556 Mr. & Mrs. Kossuth H. Bell

YALE STREET.

6315 Dr. & Mrs. J. M. Foster
6319 Mr. & Mrs. James H. Brayton & dr.
6323 Mr. & Mrs. Robert Weir & dr.
6339 Mr. & Mrs. J. M. Warner
Receiving day Wednesday
6339 J. M. Warner, jr.
6343 Mr. & Mrs. Frank L. Robinson & dr.
6351 Mr. & Mrs. Frederick F. Judd
6353 Mr. & Mrs. F. H. McAdow
6359 Mr. & Mrs. Sidney W. Miller
6429 Mr. & Mrs. W. A. Haynes
6505 Mr. & Mrs. Charles H. Smith
6515 Mr. & Mrs. George B. Watson
6531 Mr. & Mrs. Eugene E. Loomis
6531 Frank E. Loomis
6531 Mrs. Laura Loomis
6539 Mr. & Mrs. J. E. Sanford
6545 Mr. & Mrs. Charles H. Race
6547 Mr. & Mrs. C. S. Newman
6549 Mr. & Mrs. W. T. Brownidge
6551 Mr. & Mrs. Samuel W. Allen
6565 "The Yale," ne. cor. 66th
C. W. Walters
1 Dr. R. E. Thexton
4 Mr. & Mrs. Barrett R. Hall
Receiving day Tuesday
7 Mr. & Mrs. Floyd T. Logan
21 Mr. & Mrs. C. B. Cooper
21 George W. Cooper
22 Mr. & Mrs. E. S. Brown
25 Mr. & Mrs. John P. Fowler
26 Mr. & Mrs. H. A. Morgan
27 Mr. & Mrs. J. F. Renfro
31 Mr. & Mrs. Harry Crawford
33 Mrs. Isaac Drake
35 Mr. & Mrs. J. B. Mansfield
37 Mr. & Mrs. R. D. Harvey
42 Mr. & Mrs. S. T. Rowley
44 Dr. Helen S. Williams
45 Dr. & Mrs. Albert S. Schneider
Receiving day Thursday

6320 Mrs. L. S. Bushnell & dr.
6320 H. Bushnell
6324 Mr. & Mrs. George A. Baker
6324 Miss Helen Wilkes
6334 Mr. & Mrs. John Whitley & dr.
6408 Dr. & Mrs. John J. Driscoll
6418 Mr. & Mrs. Charles F. Berg
6422 Mr. & Mrs. B. B. Redfield
Receiving day Thursday
6500 Mr. & Mrs. E. W. Sproul & dr.
6506 Mrs. Eliza A. Burton
6506 Mr. & Mrs. Geo. N. Sceets
6506 Mr. & Mrs. Harry B. Bogg
6510 Mr. & Mrs. John Moore & dr.
6514 Mr. & Mrs. Charles W. Jones
6514 Mr. & Mrs. Charles F. Jones
6524 Mr. & Mrs. A.H.Reeves & drs.
6524 A. Harry Reeves
6530 Mr. & Mrs. H. E. Briggs
6534 Mr. & Mrs. John W. Munday
6540 Mr. & Mrs. William J. Smith
6550 Miss Mary McCowen
6550 Miss Cornelia D. Bingham
6550 Mrs. C. M. Bryan
6558 Mr. & Mrs. C. J. Roberts
Receiving day Thursday
6560 Mr. & Mrs. Joseph Uhrig
6560 Mrs. Jane Young
6564 Mr. & Mrs. Frank Nowak
Receiving day Thursday
6564 Charles A. Nowak
6600 Mr. & Mrs. P. T. Barry
Receiving day Thursday
6600 Miss Katharine M. Barry
6600 Miss Margaret T. Barry
6606 Mr. & Mrs. J. M. Johnson
6606 Miss Ginevra Fisk
6610 Mr. & Mrs. Geo. T. French
6616 Mr. & Mrs. Charles A. Buell & dr.
6620 Mr. & Mrs. R. N. Woodworth & dr.
6626 Mr. & Mrs. Homer E. Tinsman
6636 Mr. & Mrs. Oscar Crandall
6640 Mr. & Mrs. Geo. C. Burton

6565 The "Yale" ne. cor. 66th (con.)
  52 Mr. & Mrs. G. W. Weippert
     Receiving day Friday
  53 Mr. & Mrs. Albert J. Fisher
  55 Mr. & Mrs. George S. Pingree
  57 Mr. & Mrs. H. F. Spencer
  62 Dr. & Mrs. G. Wilbert Watts
  66 Mr. & Mrs. Geo. W. Martin
6601 Mr. & Mrs. H. B. Diller & dr.
6601 Mr. & Mrs. Edwin S. Diller
6611 Mr. & Mrs. James G. Everest
6617 Mr. & Mrs. W. O. Mumford
     Receiving day Wednesday
6629 Mr. & Mrs. Franklin P. Simons
6633 Mr. & Mrs. Wm. Lichtner
6645 Mr. & Mrs. C. B. Woodruff
6647 Mr. & Mrs. Charles A. Chase
6915 Mr. & Mrs. Judson B. Thomas
6951 Mr. & Mrs. Frank L. Wean
6955 Mr. & Mrs. John Critchell & dr.
     Receiving day Thursday
6955 Geo. W. Critchell
6955 J. H. Critchell
6957 Rev. & Mrs. F. J. Walton
7023 Mr. & Mrs. S. M. Dowst
7023 Mrs. Annette Hosmer
7025 Mr. & Mrs. James M. Connell
7037 Mr. & Mrs. Henry Hathaway
     Receiving day Thursday
7111 Mr. & Mrs. Charles A. S. Mc-
    Cracken
7117 Mr. & Mrs. James T. Brink
7127 Mrs. A. C. Smith
7127 Mrs. William Lindley
7127 H. B. Walbridge

6826 Dr. Abbey J. Mace
6914 Mr. & Mrs. A. J. Hitt
6942 Mr. & Mrs. Walter H. Furlong
7024 Mr. & Mrs. Frank L. Porter
     Receiving day Wednesday
7040 Mr. & Mrs. Chas. H. Hubbell
7052 Mr. & Mrs. James A. Rankin
7100 Mr. & Mrs. R. E. Brownell
7106 Mrs. J. S. Kinkaid
7106 C. F. Kinkaid
7116 Mr. & Mrs. John S. Capper
     Receiving day Wednesday
7120 Mr. & Mrs. Bayard E. Hand
7124 Mr. & Mrs. G. T. Robie
     Receiving day Wednesday
7130 Mr. & Mrs. Ernest P. Crooker
7130 Mr. & Mrs. Robert L. McElroy
7140 Mr. & Mrs. J. M. Norris
7206 Mr. & Mrs. Geo. A. Erhart
7216 Mr. & Mrs. J. P. Mallette
     Receiving day Wednesday
7216 Sidney F. Mallette
7220 Mr. & Mrs. George H. Crosby
7226 Mr. & Mrs. C. D. Ellis
7236 Mr. & Mrs. W. D. Napheys
7236 Mrs. Cordelia G. Kisterbock
7330 Mr. & Mrs. George Young

7231 Mr. & Mrs. G. F. Wadsworth
     Receiving day Thursday
7241 Mr. & Mrs. DeWitt C. Prescott
7241 Mr. & Mrs. Edward L. Prescott
7301 Mr. & Mrs. W. J. Jackson
7311 Dr. & Mrs. A. M. Kinkaid
7315 Mr. & Mrs. Morris H. Adams

Corneau & Co.

WHOLESALE AND RETAIL

Fine Carriages.

545-547-549 WABASH AVE.

EXCLUSIVE SELLING AGENTS
FOR MANUFACTURERS OF

High Grade Vehicles

FOR CITY AND COUNTRY USE.

For the season of 1899 we will show over 100 styles, including

Runabout and Driving Wagons,

Station Wagons,   Golfers' Brakes,

Open and Top Cabriolets,

Stanhopes,   Spider Phaetons,

Traps, Surreys and Top Buggies.

Catalogue of Latest Styles Mailed Upon Request

INSPECTION SOLICITED

Owning our building, with low expenses, enables us to quote
lowest prices on the finest work obtainable.

PART SECOND.

NORTH DIVISION.

THE BLUE BOOK.

*ARRANGED ACCORDING TO STREETS AND NUMBERS,
NUMERICALLY, WITH OCCUPANTS' NAMES,
GIVING THE ODD NUMBERS IN
LEFT COLUMN, AND EVEN
IN THE RIGHT.*

NORTH DIVISION.

ADDISON STREET.

1446 Mr. & Mrs. Lawrence Nelson
1710 Mr. & Mrs. Augustus Newman
1740 Dr. & Mrs. Francis D. Holbrook
1740 Mrs. Francis W. Holbrook & drs.
1740 William G. Holbrook

ALDINE AVENUE.

1535 Mr. & Mrs. C. M. Netterstrom & dr.
Receiving day Thursday
1535 Walter Netterstrom
1535 Mr. & Mrs. John N. Lawson
1631 Mr. & Mrs. Benj. P. Van Court
1819 Mr. & Mrs. Cortlandt F. Ames
1819 Mr. & Mrs. Frank Penfield
1819 Mrs. Cheney Ames
1821 Mr. & Mrs. Frank B. Henderson
1823 Mr. & Mrs. Louis B. Flower
1823 Mr. & Mrs. Jesse M. Watkins

1508 Dr. & Mrs. L. W. Whitmer
1548 Mr. & Mrs. H. Behrens
1650 Mr. & Mrs. Carl Schneider
1650 Mr. & Mrs. J. W. Dietz
1650 Frederick Dietz
1842 Mrs. Caroline Stenbeck & dr.
1842 Dewitt C. Morrill
1850 Mrs. Robert L. North
1850 Robert L. North

1851 Mr. & Mrs. R. Hayes & dr.
Receiving day Thursday
1851 Dr. Harold H. Hayes

ARLINGTON PLACE.

1715 Mr. & Mrs. P. O. Fiedler
1717 Mrs. Peter Rinderer
1727 Mr. & Mrs. H. A. Kasten
1731 Mr. & Mrs. Henry Vocke
1739 Mr. & Mrs. Chas. V. Wohlhueter
1745 Mr. & Mrs. Herm. Unzicker
1751 Mr. & Mrs. William Schick
1805 Mr. & Mrs. Lawrence Hesselroth
1807 Mr. & Mrs. Sidney C. Eastman
1807 Mrs. Z. Eastman
1809 Mr. & Mrs. D. L. Morrill
1809 Mrs. Ellen V. Eaton
1815 Mrs. Henrietta Reinach
1817 Mr. & Mrs. John C. Windheim
1821 Mr. & Mrs. Chas. S. Gloeckler
1829 Mr. & Mrs. Herman Hartwig
Rec. day 3d Friday in mo.

1716 Mr. & Mrs. Fred Deecken
1744 Mr. & Mrs. H. C. Dovenmuehle
1744 Mr. & Mrs. Albert G. Meier
1760 Dr. & Mrs. C. W. Swank
1808 Mr. & Mrs. Frederick J. Tucker
1808 Mr. & Mrs. G. E. Keasel
1810 Samuel M. Richardson
1810 Fred Davis
1810 Mr. & Mrs. Henry J. Heister
1816 Louis Schroeder
1816 Mr. & Mrs. Oscar Schroeder
1818 Mr. & Mrs. E. A. Furst
1832 Mr. & Mrs. Ferdinand Schapper
1834 Dr. & Mrs. G. C. Paoli
1838 Mrs. Mary Starrett Newman
1838 Mr. & Mrs. Matthew P. Gilbert
1838 Clarence L. Runals
1838 Mr. & Mrs. Herbert M. Van Housen

1831 Emanuel D. Miller
1833 Mr. & Mrs. C. Lotz
1835 Mrs. Agnes Bromilow & dr.
1845 Mr. & Mrs. Albert C. Frost
1845 Mr. & Mrs. W. I. Way
1847 Mr. & Mrs. August Hausske
1847 Mr. & Mrs. Arthur T. Packard
1851 Mrs. Emma M. Elliott & drs.
1925 Mr.& Mrs. Wm. P. Powers &
     dr.
1925 Fred W. Powers
1927 Mr. & Mrs. Gustav Hessert jr.

1936 Mr. & Mrs S. A. Swanson
1938 Mr. & Mrs. S. Wilmer Cannel
1940 Mr. & Mrs. Arnold Tripp
1964 Ward W. Willits

1838 Mr. & Mrs. T. A. Henderson
1840 Carlos Dickson & drs.
1850 Mr. & Mrs. George W. Linn
1854 Mr. & Mrs. L. H. Semper
          Receiving day Thursday
1856 John V. Fox
1856 Mrs. James B. Fox & drs.
          Receiving day Friday
1856 Thomas E. Fox
1914 Mr. & Mrs. G. P. Allmendinger
          Receive 1st Wednesday in mo.
1914 Mrs. M. E. Koons
1918 Mr. & Mrs. F. L. Chapman
1922 Mr. & Mrs. Hans J. Lystad
1924 Dr. & Mrs. G. Wm. Reynolds
1928 Mr. & Mrs. W. V. O'Brien
1932 Mr. & Mrs. Axel Chytraus

NORTH ASHLAND AVENUE.

2271 Mr. & Mrs. Otto E. Pietsch
2301 Mrs. S. J. Dressler
2301 Mr. & Mrs. W. M. Dressler
2301 Miss M. E. McCormick
2469 Mr. & Mrs. Nicholas Kuhnen
2539 Mr. & Mrs. John A. G. Roberts
2555 Mr. & Mrs. L. C. Kiefer
2563 Mr. & Mrs. R. M. Simon
2569 Mr. & Mrs. August Ziesing
2595 Mr. & Mrs. T. Herbert Morgan
     & dr.
2607 Mr. & Mrs. Squire Dingee
2607 Squire Dingee jr.
2625 William C. McConnell
2627 Mr. & Mrs. Curran C. Weeks
2627 Mr. & Mrs. W. L. Cady
2637 Mr. & Mrs. August Hirschfield
2663 Mr. & Mrs. Charles W. Bassett
          Receiving day Wednesday
2687 Mr. & Mrs. Henry W. Fischer
2691 Mr. & Mrs. George L. Lerow
2703 Mr. & Mrs. Frank M. Button
2703 Mr. & Mrs. John Brison & drs.
2705 Rev. F. N. Perry
2753 Mr. & Mrs. J. E. Kavanagh
2757 Mr. & Mrs. Adam G. Bald
2843 Mr. & Mrs. E. Gast

2292 Mr. & Mrs. E. J. Ostling
2348 Mr. & Mrs. W. F. C. Mueller
2546 Mr. & Mrs. B. F. Weber
2556 Mr. & Mrs. James H. Norton
2566 Mr.& Mrs. Washington J. Irvin
2570 Mr. & Mrs. Wm. G. Stephens
2580 Charles B. Newell
2596 Mr. & Mrs. David Burr & dr.
2600 Mr. & Mrs. Freeman A. Mann
     & dr.
2622 Mr. & Mrs. Henry Schoeneck
2690 Mr. & Mrs. J. F. Brady
2826 Mr. & Mrs. Edward M. Mul-
     ford jr.
4132 Mr. & Mrs. Felix J. Weller
4260 Mr. & Mrs. Robert W. Vasey

4135 Mr. & Mrs. Geo. G. Bottum
4135 Geo. H. Bottum
4165 Mr. & Mrs. David J. Braun&dr.
4179 Mr. & Mrs. Thos. F. Easter
4197 Mr. & Mrs. Jacob A. Eiffert
4279 Mr. & Mrs. Henry Hiestand
4351 Mr. & Mrs. Elmer D. Brothers
4351 Miss Orrel Manley
4355 Mr. & Mrs. Allan T. Stearns
4399 Mr. & Mrs. Frank A. Turner

ASTOR STREET.

 7 Mrs. Horace F. Waite & dr.
 9 Mr. & Mrs. Harry L. Wilbur
11 Mr. & Mrs. H. J. Fitzgerald
13 Mr. & Mrs. Horace G. Waite
15 Mr. & Mrs. E. G. Holden & dr.

10 Mr. & Mrs. George Spencer
     Willits
          Receiving day Monday
10 1 Dr. & Mrs. F. S. Churchill
    2 Mr. & Mrs. J. St. John Nolan

23 Dr. & Mrs. John H. Chew
23 Mrs. Mary C. Meadowcroft
25 Mr. & Mrs. Edward G. Pauling
47 Mr. & Mrs. Fred L. Foltz
47 Miss Louise Foltz
47 Mrs. S. Corning Judd
49 Mrs. Helen S. Sturges
49 Miss A. Buck
53 Mr. & Mrs. Charles T. Wittstein
55 Mr. & Mrs. Wm. S. Monroe
55 Mr. & Mrs. George D. Holmes
85 Mrs. John F. Clements
85 Dr. Edwin J. Gardiner
87 Mr. & Mrs. R. S. Hotz
89 Mr. & Mrs. Chas. H. Hodges
99 Mr. & Mrs. James Charnley
99 Douglas Charnley
125 George W. Ellis
125 Mr. & Mrs. George Farnsworth
127 Mr. & Mrs. Wm. D. Kerfoot
127 Miss Ethel Kerfoot
127 Miss Reeda Kerfoot
131 Rensselaer W. Cox
131 William A. Angell
131 Mrs. Electra R. Cox
131 Miss Jennie E. Cox
133 Mr. & Mrs. Charles A. Street
133 Harry L. Street
133 Norman A. Street
135 Mr. & Mrs. Geo. Walker Meeker
135 Mr. & Mrs. W. K. Ackerman
141 Otto W. Meysenburg
141 R. C. Meysenberg
147 Mrs. Horatio N. May

52 Mr. & Mrs. S. Geo. D'Essauer
 *Receiving day 1st and 3d
 Wednesday*
52 Mrs. Eliza V. Harvey
56 Mr. & Mrs. Henry Jennings
 Smith
 Receiving day Thursday
56 Miss Mary Bush
58 Dr. & Mrs. Robt. Archibald
 MacArthur
 Receive 1st & 3d Fridays
62 Mr. & Mrs. David B. Jones
62 Thomas D. Jones
70 Mrs. Mary F. Magwire
70 Miss Grant Goodrich
72 Mr. & Mrs. Thomas R. Lyon
82 Mr.& Mrs. William H. Hubbard
82 Mr. & Mrs. Albert M. Day
84 Mr. & Mrs Conrad Furst
86 Mrs. Louise B. Clarke
88 Mr. & Mrs. George S. Payson

10 3 Mr. & Mrs. Harrison Musgrave
 4 Mr. & Mrs. Samuel P. Child
 5 Mr. & Mrs. E. R. Hutchins
 6 Mr. & Mrs. Frank R. Fuller
 7 Mrs. William B. Howard
 Receiving day Monday
 8 Mr. & Mrs. Charles W. Dempster
 9 Mr. & Mrs. Lewis D. Webster
10 Mrs. George M. High
11 Mr. & Mrs. Frank P. Blair
12 Mr. & Mrs. G. J. Farnsworth
13 Mr. & Mrs. Clarence M. Woolley
14 Leverett Thompson
14 Miss Susan Thompson
16 Maison du Nord—
 Mr. & Mrs. Geo. Bingham &
 drs.
 Mr. & Mrs. George P. Cary
 F. V. Dunham
 Miss Bertha E. Duppler
 Col. Frank A. Eastman
 Misses Susan & Florence Hayward
 Tracy Kirkman.
 Charles R. Lindsay
 N. R. Losch
 Miss Jessie May
 Donald Pierce
 Gabriel F. Slaughter
 Mr. & Mrs. Gregory Vigeant
20 Mr. & Mrs. Andrew Cuneo & dr.
22 Mr. & Mrs. Emil Liebling
22 Miss Florence M. Jones
26 Mr. & Mrs. John G. Garibaldi
30 Mrs. Eliphalet Cramer
30 Frank Cramer
32 Mr. & Mrs. Thos. Taylor jr.
34 Mr.& Mrs.David Frank'n Kenly
34 F. Corning Kenly
34 William K. Kenly
36 Mr. & Mrs. F. P. Schmitt & drs.
36 Charles S. Schmitt
38 Misses Alice M. and Lillian
 Smith *Receive Wednesday*
38 Reginald G. Smith
44 Mr. & Mrs. Charles D. Dana
44 Miss Mary Dana
44 C. Clayton Dana
46 Mr. & Mrs. Edward L. Brewster
 & dr. *Receiving day Monday*
46 Walter S. Brewster
50 Mr. & Mrs. Lewis B. Mitchell &
 dr.

96 Mr. & Mrs. G. W. Sheldon &
    dr.
106 Mrs. Agnes E. Platt
106 Mrs. L. Platt Hunt
110 Mr. & Mrs. Charles C. Curtiss
110 Dr. DeLaskie Miller
112 Mr. & Mrs. E. J. Martyn
112 Mr. & Mrs. Edward P. Bailey
118 Mr. & Mrs. Thomas Woodnutt
    Hinde
136 Mr. & Mrs. J. T. Bowen

138 Mr. & Mrs. B. E. Sunny
140 Mr. & Mrs. Wm. Warren Tracy
142 Mr. & Mrs. Harry B. Owsley
144 Mr. & Mrs. Geo. P. Fisher jr.
148 Mr. & Mrs. C. Vallette Kasson
    & drs.
150 Mr. & Mrs.Chas. M. Webber
154 Mr. & Mrs. Hempstead Wash-
    burne
    Receiving day Monday
166 Mr. & Mrs. Robert W. Patterson
    Receiving day Monday

BANKS STREET.

1 Mr. & Mrs. Edward E. Ayer
    Receiving day Monday 3 *to* 6 *p.m.*
27 Gen. & Mrs.Henry Strong & dr.
31 Mr. & Mrs. E. L. Ryerson
37 Mrs. Malcolm Caruthers
37 Miss Caruthers
43 Mrs. Perry H. Smith
    Receiving day Monday

2 Franklin H. Head & drs.
    Receiving day Tuesday
2 Miss Cara W. Durkee
32 Mr. & Mrs. S. C. Payson
40 Mr. & Mrs. William Waller
40 Miss Nannine Waller

43 Mrs. Francis A. Sawyer

BARRY AVENUE.

1649 Mr. & Mrs. Henry Wichert &
    dr.
1649 Hugo Franz
1673 Mr. & Mrs. C. O. Scudder
1675 Mr. & Mrs. Eugene A. Rang
1675 Mr. & Mrs. H. Kollmorgen
1675 Mr. & Mrs. T. P. Hallinan
1683 Mr. & Mrs. J. H. Frendenthal
1713 Mr. & Mrs. H. T. Sawford
1715 Charles W. Simon
1715 Mr. & Mrs. Henry B. Ferris
1801 Mr.& Mrs.Kendrick E.Morgan
1801 Mrs. R. A. Alden & dr.
1803 Dr. & Mrs. Charles Brockway
    Gibson
    Receive Friday 3 *to* 5 *p.m.*
1803 Mr. & Mrs. Wm. Castle
1805 Mr. & Mrs. J. P. Greene
1805 Mr. & Mrs. S. B. Brunaugh
1805 Miss Margaret Fullerton
1807 Mr. & Mrs. Henry V. Pierpont
1807 Mrs. C. B. Lawrence
1807 Mr. & Mrs. Eugene Dietzgen
1807 Mr. & Mrs. W. W. Hook
1817 Mrs. Harry Fox & dr.
1817 Fred H. Fox
1821 Mr.& Mrs.EdwardF.Comstock
1825 Mr. & Mrs. W. M. Knight
1843 Mr. & Mrs. John Stillwell &drs.
1843 James Stillwell

1626 Dr. & Mrs. C. V. Massey
1634 Mr. & Mrs. C. F. Weber & dr.
1642 Richard G. Schmid
1676 Mrs. C. A. Gerold
1684 Mr. & Mrs. Daniel Johnson
1686 Mr. & Mrs. George L.Douglass
1690 Mr. & Mrs. James McDonald
    & dr.
1708 Mr. & Mrs. Chas. J. Stratton &
    dr.
1714 Mr. & Mrs. Edward L. Cheet-
    ham
1714 Mrs. M. A. Smith & drs.
1716 Mr. & Mrs. Wm. N. Sturges
1716 Mr. & Mrs. Frank Price
1804 Mr. & Mrs. J. W. Kee & dr.
1812 Mr. & Mrs. John B. Meyer
1812 Christian B. Meyer
1828 Mr. & Mrs. Wm. L. Roseboom
1834 Mr. & Mrs. Adolph Heile & dr.
1834 Chas. Dyer Heile
1848 Mr. & Mrs. Wm. H. Redington
1856 Mr. & Mrs. Frank Yott
1864 Mr. & Mrs. Frank M. Luce
    Receiving day Thursday
1902 Mr. & Mrs. W. A. Purer & dr.
1912 Mr. & Mrs. Daniel O. Hill
1922 Mr. & Mrs. George Packard
1922 Henry J. Brandon
1922 Mrs. F. S. Howe

1849 Mr. & Mrs. Alex. M. Ross
1849 Arthur J. Ross
1851 Mr. & Mrs. Jos. Fleischmann
1851 Arthur J. Fleischmann
1853 Mr. & Mrs. Gustav Riebe
1855 Mr. & Mrs. C. R. Schniglau &
    dr. *Receiving day Wednesday*
1905 Mr.&Mrs.John C. Durgin & dr.

1926 Mr. & Mrs. Wm.Campbell&dr.
1928 Mr. & Mrs. J. Spencer Butter-
    field
1932 Mr. & Mrs. Albert Magnus
1942 Mr. & Mrs. E. A. Beauvais
1942 Joseph H. Bourassa
1950 Mr. & Mrs. Z. P. Brosseau

BEACON STREET.

3127 Mrs. Edward Carqueville
3127 Edgar H. Carqueville
3127 Alex. Carqueville
3149 Mr. & Mrs. Thos. J. Waters
3165 Mr. & Mrs. Frank J. Gallagher
    & dr.
3169 Mr. & Mrs. O. G. Ortman
3203 Mr. & Mrs. Samuel Brown jr.
3213 Mr. & Mrs. Wm. L. Abbott
3227 Mr. & Mrs. Wm. S. MacHarg
    Receiving day Friday
3247 Mr. & Mrs. Theodore Krueger
3247 Miss Johanna Rendtorff
3247 Leo Krueger
3267 Mr. & Mrs. Salvatore Tomaso
    Receiving day Thursday
3267 Miss Charlotte Petesch
3271 Dr. & Mrs. John Spirkel
    Receiving day Wednesday
3283 Mr. & Mrs. Herman Zitzewitz

3148 Mrs. D. Carroll & dr.
3158 Mr. & Mrs. Henry F. Streich
3166 Mr. & Mrs. Fred D. Stevers
3222 Mr. & Mrs. M. R. Kelly
    Receiving day Wednesday
3226 Mr. & Mrs. Jas. J. Bloomfield
    Receiving day Thursday
3232 Mr. & Mrs. Geo. Heicher
3260 Mr. & Mrs. John R. Leesley

3287 Mr. & Mrs. James A. Hart
    Receiving day Thursday
3297 Mrs. Catherina Haustetter &
    dr.
3297 Daniel W. Brenneman
3301 Mr. & Mrs. Oscar K. Kuehne
3311 Mr. & Mrs. John R. Stack
3311 Mr. & Mrs. Alvin G. Synnberg
3315 Mr. & Mrs. Robert H. Herring
    Receiving day Friday
3315 Alvin C. Thatcher

BEETHOVEN PLACE.

22 Mr. & Mrs. Julius Ehlers

36 Mr. & Mrs. W. B. Clifford & drs.

BELDEN AVENUE.

207 Mrs. Herman A. Kroeschell
207 Emil H. Frommann
209 Mr. & Mrs. C. Kroeschell & dr.
211 Mr.& Mrs.John Gertenrich & dr.
215 Mrs. Andrew Ortmayer
215 Mrs. Emma M. Pfister
217 Miss Annie J. Tahl
217½ Dr. & Mrs. Walter H. Fox
217½ Mrs. Sara A. Morse
219 Mr. & Mrs. E. W. Gilsdorff
251 Mrs. H. D. Ganse & dr.
253 Mrs. Cora K. Adams
253 Mrs. Catherine C. King
255 Mr. & Mrs. F. A. Doolittle &
    dr.
255 Oliver S. Doolittle
271 Mr. & Mrs. J. P. Boyle
283 Mr. & Mrs. J. G. Klais

224 Mr. & Mrs. J. W. McLean &
    drs.
232 Mr. & Mrs. Wm. H. Burke
272 Mr. & Mrs. Robt. Bluthardt
274 Chauncey M. Silliman & drs.
274 Frederick H. Silliman
276 Mrs. M. A. King & dr.
276 Charles W. King
280 Mr. & Mrs. Andrew Weber
280 Miss Lizzie Pinter
284 Dr. & Mrs. J. H. Hoelscher
286 Mr. & Mrs. Adolph Druiding
290 Mr. & Mrs. H. J. Thompson &
    drs. *Receiving day Friday*
292 Mr. & Mrs. Onward Bates
294 Mrs. H. W. Chipman
296 Mr. & Mrs. W. Cochran
298 Mrs. Emma Neubarth & dr.

285 Mr. & Mrs. HenryW.Haenichen
  Receiving day Saturday
295 and 297 The Belden Flats
 A Mr. & Mrs.William A. Kreidler *Receiving day Friday*
 B Mr. & Mrs. Wm. Brace
  Receiving day Wednesday
 D Mr. & Mrs. T. M. Luce
  Receiving day Wednesday
 Mrs. Adesta F. Shores & dr.
  Receiving day Thursday
 Mrs. Ellen S. Miller & drs.
 George L. Miller
301 Mrs. L. J. Halsey & dr.
301 Edward A. Halsey
305 Mr. & Mrs. Jas. P. Sherlock
307 Dr. & Mrs. E. J. Mellish
309 Mr. & Mrs. Louis Schlesinger
311 Mrs. S. B. Newell
311 Frederick O. Swannell
321 Mr. & Mrs. Robt. T. Howard
321 Mrs. Leonard Swett
321 Dr. & Mrs. E. E. Vaughan
323 Mr. & Mrs. G. Magee
  Receiving day Wednesday
325 Dr. & Mrs. Cyrenius A. David
325 Miss Rilla A. David
327 Mr. & Mrs. C. A. Smith & dr.
401 Mr. & Mrs. Frank L. Thorpe
409 Mr. & Mrs. J. Niemann
435 Mr. & Mrs. Chas. A. Nichols
  Receiving day Monday
435 Mr. & Mrs. Geo. J. Reed
437 Mr. & Mrs. John C. Bauer
437 Mr. & Mrs. John H. Johnson
437 Mr. & Mrs. J. H. Burgis
  Receiving day Friday
439 Mr. & Mrs. Fred G. Wessling
447 Mr. & Mrs. Edward Keir & dr.
447 Miss Mary Melody
449 Dr. & Mrs. J. W. Oswald
451 Mrs. Allen W. Peck
451 Mr. & Mrs. Wm. J. Donlin
  Receiving day Wednesday
453 Mr. & Mrs. J. D. C. Whitney
475 Dr. H. J. Haiselden
475 Mrs. H. Lilja
479 Mr. & Mrs. John R. Lilja &
 dr.
481 Mr. & Mrs. Charles Catlin
481 Mrs. Lottie A. Crane
481 A. B. Reynell & drs.
485 Mr. & Mrs. Oscar Mueller
489 Mr. & Mrs. S. L. Robinson &
 dr.
493 Adolph Nickelsen

302 Mr. & Mrs. Alfred Noble
304 Mrs. Emily P. Judd
304 Miss Anna E. Potwin
306 Mrs. C. E. Mussey
308 Miss Mary E. Squire
312 Mr. & Mrs. A. P. Bigelow
314 Mr. & Mrs. F. S. Hereth
316 Mr. & Mrs. Amos Pettibone
318 Mr. & Mrs. J. B. Moll
320 Rev.& Mrs.Benjamin L.Hobson
348 Mr. & Mrs. G. G. Congdon & dr.
348 Mr. & Mrs. W. A. Arms
348 Mr. & Mrs. Emil Gerber
352 Mr. & Mrs. James Hart
352 Mrs. M. L. Abernethy & drs.
396 Dr. & Mrs. H. M. Goodsmith
396 William Goodsmith
398 Mr. & Mrs. George Foster
402 Mr. & Mrs. Henry E. Shattock
404 Mr. &.Mrs. C. A. Morrill & dr.
406 Mrs. Hanca Ohm
406 Mr. & Mrs. Curt Ohm
  Receiving day Thursday
412 Mr. & Mrs. L. S. Hayes
  Receive Friday
418 Mr. & Mrs. Henry Turner
420 Mr. & Mrs. O. G. Wiley
422 Mr. and Mrs. Frederick A.
 Hoyer
422 Mr. & Mrs. M. Kahn & drs.
424 Dr. & Mrs. F. A. Sieber & drs.
430½ Mr. & Mrs. F. M. Mahan
434 Mrs. M. A. Farish
434 Mrs. J. H. Bethune
438 Harry B. Foley
440 Mr. & Mrs. Emil Hamilton
442 Mr. & Mrs. E. P. Upham & dr.
442 F. D. Upham
444 Mr. & Mrs. Chas. F. Gillmann
  Receiving day Wednesday
446 Mrs. Ida Gillmann & dr.
446 William Gillmann
446 Fred Gillmann
446 Mrs. M. E. Deacon & dr.
446 Fred A. Deacon
446 Mr. & Mrs. C. E. Sayler
450 Mrs. C. S. Gibbs & dr.
450 Mr. & Mrs. Robert B. Abbott
478 Mr. & Mrs. H. H. Hurlbut
480 Mr. & Mrs. W. L. Potter
488 Mr. & Mrs. Wm. H. Stockham
490 Mrs. Ann Halsted & dr.
490 Joseph Halsted
490 Henry P. Halsted
490 John Halsted
494 Mrs. Clara B. Curtis

493 Mrs. S. K. Trorlicht
  Receiving day Friday
519 Miss Louise Utley
521 Mr. & Mrs. Elwood McGrew
523 Mr. & Mrs. E. F. Thompson
529 Mr.& Mrs. Leonard H. Harland
  & dr.
531 Mr. & Mrs. Bicknell Young
531 Miss Late Young
531 Miss Jane Mackintosh
535 Mrs. Charles S. Carter
  Receiving day Thursday

502 Mrs. Edward W. Cobb & dr.
502 Mr. & Mrs. M. Henry Naber
508 Mr. & Mrs. H. A. Ressler
508 Mr. & Mrs. Chas. W. Davenport
  Receiving day Monday
508 Mr. & Mrs. M. R. Winchell
530 Mr. & Mrs. George E. Adams

———

537 Mr. & Mrs. T. A. Hagerty
537 Miss P. Himrod

BELLE PLAINE AVENUE.

955 Mr. & Mrs. Alex. Heatherington

908 Dr. & Mrs. F. A. Hess

BELLEVUE PLACE.

11 Mrs. D. Watterson
11 Mr. & Mrs. T. C. Hammond
11 Mrs. A. Hammond
15 Mr. & Mrs. F. B. Smith
17 Mrs. E. A. Chesbrough
17 Mr. & Mrs.Ellis S.Chesbrough jr.
19 Mr. & Mrs. Arthur D. Wheeler
19 George Hubbard Holt
21 Mr. & Mrs. Edward O'Brien
21 Mrs. Agnes D. Smith
23 Dr. & Mrs. Marvin E. Smith
23 Ross T. Parshall
23 Miss Elizabeth Osborne
23 Mrs. C. B. Thurber
27 Mr. & Mrs. Harry H. Jackson
29 Mr. & Mrs. J. S. Dunham
31 Mr. & Mrs. W. Vernon Booth
33 Mr. & Mrs. Theodore Sheldon
35 Mr. & Mrs. Joseph H. Chandler
  & dr.
39 Dr. Howard N. Lyon
39 Dr. Ellen Hancock Lyon
  Receiving day Monday
39 Mrs. Bradford Hancock
41 Mr. & Mrs. Orson Smith
43 Mr. & Mrs. Theodore Thomas
45 Mrs. Henry B. Stone
45 Miss Alice Stone
29 Robert J. Dunham
47 Mr. & Mrs. A. P. Richardson &
  dr.
  Receiving day Monday
49 Mr. & Mrs. F. C. Austin & dr.
  Receiving day Monday
53 Mr. & Mrs. George W. Hinman
57 Mr. & Mrs. Albert L. Coe
57 Albert Fletcher Smith

14 Mr. & Mrs. Herbert C. Wright
14 Ralph M. Fay
14 Mr. & Mrs. C. H. Kirkham & dr.
16 Miss Frances M. Pratt
16 Dr. & Mrs. R. S. Yarros
22 Mr. & Mrs. Alexander Marshall
22 J. B. White
22 Mr. & Mrs. Fred G. Stanley
  Receiving day Tuesday
36 Mr. & Mrs. Samuel B. Raymond
36 Lowry B. Raymond
36 William M. Raymond
36 Miss Helen Raymond
38 Mr. & Mrs. George B. Dunbar
38½ Mr. & Mrs. L. M. Greeley
40 Mrs. F. W. Christoph & drs.
  Receiving day Thursday
42 Mrs. Mary A. Curran & drs.
  Receiving day Monday
42 M. W. Diffley
42 T. Diffley Curran
44 Mr. & Mrs. J. W. Hosmer
44½ Dr. & Mrs. G. E. Richards
50 Mrs. Frank Clark
50 Frank K. Clark
50 Miss Mabel S. Vickery
50 Robert Thorburn
52 Mr. & Mrs. Frederick R. Fulton
52 James F. Hyde
54 Mrs. Horace Reed & dr.
56 Mr. & Mrs. F. Eberlein
58 Mrs. Junius J. Smith
66 Mr. & Mrs. Albert Antisdel
66 Mr. & Mrs. Henry W. Bishop
68 Mr. & Mrs. Johnston R. Bowman
70 Mr. & Mrs. Marshall Lapham
70 E. A. Biggs

59 Mr. & Mrs. Arthur Ryerson
61 Mr. & Mrs. George Manierre
63 Miss Scudder
  Receiving day Monday
69 Mr. & Mrs. Robert H. Parkinson *Receiving day Friday*
73 Mr. & Mrs. Chester M. Dawes
77 Mr. & Mrs. Bryan Lathrop
  Receiving day Monday
77 Owen F. Aldis

72 Mr. & Mrs. J. B. Wilbur & dr.
72 J. Benjamin Wilbur jr.
74 Mr. & Mrs. Angus S. Hibbard
76 I. S. Collins
76 Mr. & Mrs. Kreigh Collins
78 Mr. & Mrs. E. W. Cramer
88 Mr. & Mrs.Harold F.McCormick

77 Owen W. Aldis
89 Mr. & Mrs. William Borden

BELMONT AVENUE.

1631 Mr. & Mrs. H. Dittmann
1639 Mr. & Mrs. H. P. Victor
1639 Mrs. M. A. Sewell
1639 Edgar Sanders
1655 Mr. & Mrs.Otto Scheunemann
1705 Dr. & Mrs. E. N. Elliott
1725 Mr. & Mrs. Lawrence A.Spicer & dr.
  Receiving day Wednesday
1811 Mr. & Mrs. Ernst, Stock & dr.
1811 Mr. & Mrs. Isadore Dukes
1811 Mrs. David Kriegh & dr.
1817 Mrs. O. A. Ruthenberg & dr.
1817 Mr. & Mrs. Andrew Daigger
1817 Miss Ida Brehmer
1833 Mr. & Mrs. Wm. O. Tegtmeyer
1847 Mr. & Mrs. W. C. Pease & dr.
1849 Mr. & Mrs. James J. Hoch

1946 Miss Ruth G. Chase
1946 Miss E. S. L. Chase

1450 Mr. & Mrs. Oscar N. Blomgren
1530 Mr. & Mrs. Chas. Dahlane
1624 Mr. & Mrs. Kirk Himrod
1718 Mr. & Mrs.Jas. Thomson & dr.
1728 Mr. & Mrs. F.J. Lindsten & dr.
1812 Mr. & Mrs. Wm. H. Brown
1812 Allen A. Brown
1814 Mr. & Mrs. Wm. H. Chadwick
1824 Mr. & Mrs. Henry P. Klein
1824 T. Henry Klein
1832 Mr. & Mrs. S. E. Dale & drs.
1832 Walter Dale
1832 Fred Dale
1846 Mr. & Mrs. Thos. Whitworth
1922 Mr. & Mrs. David S. Wegg
1922 Mrs. John Wegg
1922 Donald R. Wegg
1928 Mr. & Mrs. Hugh McFarlane & drs.
  Receiving day Thursday
1928 Miss Helen McFarlane
  Receiving day Tuesday

BEST AVENUE,

21 Mr. & Mrs. Geo. M. Stevens

29 Mr. & Mrs. John M. Stevens

BIRCHWOOD AVENUE.

1137 Mr. & Mrs. Albert D. Langworthy

BISSELL STREET.

201 Mr. & Mrs. William J. Reed
277 Dr. & Mrs. W. C. Wermuth
353 Mr. & Mrs. John F. Walsh & dr.
375 Cornelius S. O'Leary
377 Mrs. Mary L. Rogerson

384 Charles G. Blake

240 Mr. & Mrs. Robert B. Palmer
240 Mr. & Mrs. C. H. Graves
  Receiving day Tuesday
278 Dr. James F. Graham
354 Mr. & Mrs. Albert Kroeschell
358 Mrs. B. Burns
358 Nicholas T. Burns

BITTERSWEET PLACE.

13 Mr. & Mrs. W. S. Hine
13 Ernest A. Collins
23 Mr. & Mrs. M. A. Seymour
35 Mr. & Mrs. R. M. Field

24 Mr. & Mrs. James Healy
60 W. L. B. Jenney
60 C. L. Marsh
60 Mr. & Mrs. Max Jenney

BOSWORTH AVENUE.

4111 Mr. & Mrs. Perley A. Russell
4125 Mrs. Frances King & dr.

4131 Mr. & Mrs. Carroll S. McMil-
    len

BRADLEY PLACE.

1519 Mr. & Mrs. Julius Gebhard

BRIAR PLACE.

1641 Mr. & Mrs. David S. Scoville
    & dr.
1653 Mr. & Mrs. H. M. Clarke
1657 Rev. Henry Chapin Granger
1741 Mr. & Mrs. Theodore C. Wuest
1741 Mr. & Mrs. C. F. Julin
1857 Mr. & Mrs. A. B. Cooke
1905 Mr. & Mrs. John G. Smyth
1905 Martin R. Smyth

1646 Henry Raske & dr.
1658 Mr. & Mrs. Henry C. Critten-
    den
1712 Mr. & Mrs. William H. Bennet
1726 Mr. & Mrs. Walter H. Smith
1726 Mr. & Mrs. Paul Beattie
1728 Mr. & Mrs. Frank N. Williams
1734 Mr. & Mrs. Edward Johnson
1738 Mrs. L. F. Gear
    Receiving day Friday

1844 Mr. & Mrs. S. L. Anable & drs.
1908 Mr. & Mrs. E. R. Bacon
1910 Mr. & Mrs. M. S. Bacon & drs
1920 Mr. & Mrs. Frederic H. Long

1824 David G. Brauckmann
1824 Mr. & Mrs. Geo. Brauckmann
    & drs.
    Receiving day Wednesday

BROMPTON AVENUE.

1629 Mr. & Mrs. Wm. Wernecke

1629 Richard L. Wernecke

BRYAN AVENUE.

804 Mr. & Mrs. Louis Dederick
804 Miss Frances A. Roles
1038 Mr. & Mrs. Louis H. Jennings

1120 Mrs. Amelia Erpelding
1120 George B. Erpelding
1120 John M. Erpelding

BRYN MAWR AVENUE.

1330 Mr. & Mrs. A. T. H. Brower

1350 Mr. & Mrs. F. C. Schoenthaler
    Receiving day Thursday

BUCKINGHAM PLACE.

1664 Mr. & Mrs. C. W. Seneco
1672 Mr. & Mrs. C. J. Warren
1674 Mr. & Mrs. Wm. E. Spangen-
    berg

1688 Mr. &. Mrs. F. H. Patten
1688 Mr. & Mrs. John G. Davies
1690 Mr. & Mrs. A. H. Vollintine
1734 Mr. & Mrs. A. W. Ring & dr.

BUENA AVENUE.

95 Mr. & Mrs. Robt. L. Greenlee &
   dr.   *Receiving day Tuesday*
95 William B. Greenlee
99 Mr. & Mrs. Earl L. Hambleton
103 Mr. & Mrs. James C. Page
119 Mr. & Mrs. Walter A. Daniels
165 Mr. & Mrs. Sanford Coe
169 Mr. & Mrs. W. J. Bryson

50 Mr. & Mrs. William E. Clow
50 Miss Martha M. Sarver
74 Mr. & Mrs. Joseph M. Rogers
74 John A. Rogers
74 Hopewell L. Rogers
80 Mr. & Mrs. Bernard F. Rogers
           Receiving day Thursday
106 Mr. & Mrs. O. S. Richardson
112 Mr. & Mrs. A. A. McCormick

BUENA TERRACE.

39 Mr. & Mrs. T. H. Chamberlin

————

40 Mrs. H. A. Tonnas

24 Mr. & Mrs. S. M. Hastings
32 Mr. & Mrs. Martin Howard
36 Mr. & Mrs. L. D. Eastman
40 Mr. & Mrs. R. G. Waggener

BURLING STREET.

333 Mrs. L. Wurzburger
333 Harry Wurzburger
333 Jonas Wurzburger
333 Lee Wurzburger
369 Mr. & Mrs. R. G. Uhlemann
369 Hugo P. Uhlemann
369 Louis H. Uhlemann
531½ Mrs. L. H. Weil
549 Mr. & Mrs. Julius Speyer
569 Mr. & Mrs. John Hanssen
577 Mr. & Mrs. H. E. Synwolt
581 Mr. & Mrs. Carl Mauch
589 Mr. & Mrs. Chas. E. Pain
591 Mr. & Mrs. Gustav G. Kaufmann
597 Mr. & Mrs. Eugene Weber
601 Mr. & Mrs. C. A. Hochschild
603 Mr. & Mrs. Walter E. Hecht
645 Mr. & Mrs. Adolf Haerle & dr.
687 Mr. & Mrs. Charles Hild

338 Mr. & Mrs. A. C. Kemper
344 Mr. & Mrs. A. Rauch & dr.
350 Mr. & Mrs. M. E. Morrison
352 Mr. & Mrs. Moritz Keil
522 Mr. & Mrs. J. A. Boland
526 Mr. & Mrs. Samuel E. Knecht
534 Dr. & Mrs. John W. VanWinkle
548 Mr. & Mrs. F. H. Ehlen
562 Mr. & Mrs. J. Manz & drs.
562 Paul H. Manz
576 Mrs. P. J. Hussander & dr.
592 Mr. & Mrs. George Kuehl
598 Mr. & Mrs. R. E. Breed
600 Mr. & Mrs. John C. Mackay.
604 Mr. & Mrs. William R. Schick
606 Albert H. Schick
608 Dr. & Mrs. G. G. Praetorius

————

695 Mr. & Mrs. Peter Anderson

BURTON PLACE.

14 Mr. & Mrs. Jabez Brewster

44 Mr. & Mrs. John A. Lynch

BYRON STREET.

522 Mr. & Mrs. Chas. R. Spalding

538 Mr. & Mrs. Abraham Mitchell

CARL STREET.

16 Mr. & Mrs. Charles Emmerich &
   dr.

CARMEN AVENUE.

1107 Mr. & Mrs. F. W. Abele

1076 Mr. & Mrs. August Abele
1080 Mr. & Mrs. Daniel Hesly

CASS STREET.

67 Mr. & Mrs. E. B. McCagg
67 Miss Caroline McCagg
83 Mr. & Mrs. A. A. Carpenter &dr.
87 Mr. & Mrs. James C. Brooks
87 Miss Edith Brooks
101 Joseph Medill
101 Mr. & Mrs.Robert S.McCormick
101 J. Medill McCormick
113 Mr. & Mrs. C. W. Davis
113 Mr. & Mrs. A. A. Mason
113 Mr. & Mrs. Edward H. Mason
113 Mr. & Mrs. Gurdon G. Moore
113 Mr. & Mrs. Frank Wright
113 Mr. & Mrs. E. R. Hurlbut
113 George Love
113 Mrs. Chas. L. Rutter
113 Dudley Rutter
113 Hibbard Porter
113 George P. Porter
113 Mr. & Mrs. W. E. McHenry
113 Mrs. F. L. Barrell
113 George Ade
113 Mr. & Mrs. E. A. Shepler
113 Miss Nellie Young
147 Mr. & Mrs. Edward Claussenius
157 Mr. & Mrs. Edward T. Blair
159 Mrs. Louisa C. Barnard
159 Mr. & Mrs. John B. Skinner
159 Edward W. Hodgkins
163 Mr. & Mrs. M. Sullivan
167 Mrs. Margaret Denison & dr.

94 Mr. & Mrs. Lambert Tree
 Receiving day Wednesday
108 Leslie Carter
108 Miss H. L. Carter
126 Mrs. John S. Reed
194 Mr. & Mrs. Vincent H. Perkins
194 Mr. & Mrs. James E. Isgrigg
194 Albert H. Scherzer
196 Mr. & Mrs. George Barnard
196 Mr. & Mrs. W. S. Corning
 · *Receiving day Thursday p.m*
196 John C. Patterson
202 Mr. & Mrs. John W. Mooney
204 Dr. H. A. Ware
216 Mr. & Mrs. H. J. Bonney
 Receiving day Friday
218 General & Mrs. Joseph B. Leake
220 Mr. & Mrs. Wm. Rapp & dr.
220 William J. Rapp
230 Miss Augusta Koch
230 George Koch
230 Leo Koch
230 Martin Koch

---

167 Andrew J. Denison
183 Mr. & Mrs. LeBaron Loring
 Austin
 Receiving day Tuesday
183 Mr.& Mrs. J.R.Lockwood & drs.
183 Dr. F. H. Lockwood
189 Dr. Hugo Oldenborg

CATALPA AVENUE.

1340 Mr. & Mrs. Frank F. Jaques
1340 Charles E. Jaques

1340 Willard W. Jaques

CEDAR STREET.

9 Dr. & Mrs. S. Cecil Stanton
35 Mr. & Mrs. C. M. Gottfried
37 Miss Katharine Colvin
37 Miss Jessie Colvin
 Receiving day Monday
39 Mr. & Mrs. R. Ortmann
41 Mr. & Mrs. E. M. Switzer
43 Mr. & Mrs. Don A. Moulton
43 Miss Jessie Scott
43 Miss Florence Scott
45 Mrs. Wm. H. Smith
45 Jay Herndon Smith
45 Miss Kate Weaver
17

32 Mr. & Mrs. Horace L. Brand
42 Mrs. Mary E. Ross
42 H. Russell Ross
42 Mrs. Thomas S. Robie
46 Col. & Mrs. Henry L. Turner
58 Mr. & Mrs. Warren M. Salisbury
62 Dr. & Mrs. Francis G. Bonynge
64 Mr. & Mrs. Edgar A. Bancroft
 Receiving day Monday
66 Mr. & Mrs. J. Whitcomb Cotton
 Receiving day Monday
68 Mr. & Mrs. Edward Ashley Ferguson

45 Mrs. Arthur T. Woods
47 Thomas Dougall
53 Mr. & Mrs. Rudolph Brand
53 Phil R. Brand
55 Mr. & Mrs. P. E. Stanley

57 Mr. & Mrs. J. Henry Norton
59 Mr. & Mrs. James S. Harlan
    Receiving day Monday
61 Mr. & Mrs. Ernest F. Smith
67 James Deering

CENTER STREET.

371 Dr. Elise Berwig
373 Mrs. Mary Cahill
373 Edward T. Cahill
417 Mrs. E. J. Maxwell
419 Mr. & Mrs. T. L. Forrest & dr.
423 Julius W. Dyrenforth
427 Dr. & Mrs. J. F. Williams
429 Mr. & Mrs. J. G. Moulton
429 Mrs. C. M. Bassett
431 Dr. Augusta Linderborg
433 Mr. & Mrs. Geo. C. Kober & drs.
    Receiving day Wednesday

200 Rev. & Mrs. Julius A. Mulfinger
202 Dr. & Mrs. Raymond C. Ulrich
334 Dr. & Mrs. James P. Lett
358 Mr. & Mrs. Chas. Scott Johnson
402 Dr. Frederick Everett
408 Dr. & Mrs. W. S. Christopher
412 Mrs. Patrick Joyce & drs.
412 Harry P. Joyce
420 Mrs. Ida Baines
420 Mrs. Alice Bellows
420 Mr. & Mrs. Angus C. Christie &
    drs.
422 Dr. Henry Dietrich
426 Dr. & Mrs. Chas. S. Bacon

CHALMERS PLACE.

1 Rev. & Mrs. David C. Marquis
3 Mr. & Mrs. William W. Collins
5 Mr. & Mrs. James L. Rowe
5 Miss Ella Rowe
7 Mr. & Mrs. F. O. Wyatt & dr.
13 Rev. & Mrs. Wm. S. P. Bryan
15 Mr. & Mrs. Ira J. Mason & dr.
15 Fred B. Mason
17 Mr. & Mrs. James S. Rossiter
19 Mr. & Mrs. Geo. F. Steele

2 Rev. & Mrs. Andrew C. Zenos
6 Mr. & Mrs. N. J. Goll
6 Mrs. S. R. Glenny
8 Rev. J. Ross Stevenson
12 Mr. & Mrs. Wm. D. Nelson
20 Mr. & Mrs. John Philbin
20 John J. Philbin

———

19 Dr. Geo. M. Steele

CHASE AVENUE.

719 Mr. & Mrs. Andrew F. Wan-
    ner
749 Mr. & Mrs. Robert M. Scholes
819 Mrs. Sarah G. Redfield
819 Mr. & Mrs. David W. Redfield
823 Mr. & Mrs. D. D. Bathrick
839 Mr. & Mrs. Harvey D. Orr
843 Mr. & Mrs. Albert F. Olgen &
    drs.
847 Mr. & Mrs. Milton R. Uhl
915 Dr. & Mrs. Ph. D. Paul
    Receiving day Monday
917 Mr. & Mrs. Z. C. Spencer & dr.

912 Mr. & Mrs. Chas. F. Barber
928 Mr. & Mrs. F. A. Lathrop
1040 Mr. & Mrs. David B. Mc-
    Mehan
1052 Mr. & Mrs. Edgar Whitehead
1058 Mr. & Mrs. Chas H. Thompson
1080 Mr. & Mrs. Edwin L. Waugh
1130 Mr. & Mrs. Edwin S. Bush

———

1065 Mr. & Mrs. Lyman L. Kellogg
1069 Mr. & Mrs. Stephen L. Walker
1125 Mr. & Mrs. John W. Kinney

CHESTNUT STREET.

267 Mr. & Mrs. D. W. Manchester
267 Milton C. Manchester
267 Percy J. Young

266 Mr. & Mrs. Frank Holme
266 George Bentham
268 Mrs. Florence H. Ives

333 Mr. & Mrs. Eric Bernstein
335 Mrs. Charles Harding
343 Charles C. Johnston
351 Mr. & Mrs. Joseph McDonald
351 Dr. & Mrs. Liston H. Montgomery
351 Edwin Brainard
351 Hubert Galt
377 Mrs. G. Sindlinger & dr.
379 Mrs. Geo. C. Kuhnen

446 Mr. & Mrs. Edward Shields Adams

306 Mr. & Mrs. C. B. Carpenter
306 Miss Carrie T. Kingman
308 Mr. & Mrs. P. B. Bradley
308 Philip H. Bradley
386 Mr. & Mrs. Henry R. Green jr.
386 Mrs. Josephine Bruning
402 Mr. & Mrs. Hudson H. Kellogg
408 James J. Moore
408 R. D. Walsh
444 Arthur Young
444 M. C. McEwan

CHICAGO AVENUE.

211 Dr. C. B. Saunders
211 Dr. Annetta Ayers-Saunders
349 Mr. & Mrs. Sylvester M. Tinthoff & dr.
349 Fred S. Tinthoff
351 Dr. & Mrs. James Montgomery
351 Mrs. M. M. Snoddy
369 Mr. & Mrs. John W. Dickinson
369 Mr. & Mrs. John Vance Cheney
369 Miss Janet Cheney
369 Miss Evelyn Hope Cheney
369 Mrs. J. A. Yale
369 Mr. & Mrs. M. S. Marsh
369 Mrs. L. F. Selfridge
369 Egbert S. Newberry

424 Samuel K. Colton
424 Simeon C. Colton

298 Mr. & Mrs. H. Schoellkopf
298 Henry Schoellkopf jr.
300 Mr. & Mrs. F. A. Waidner & dr.
302 Mr. & Mrs. H. F. Bartling
302 Eugene A. Grannis
346 Mrs. C. L. Epps
352 Mrs. J. W. Stearns & drs.
378 Mrs. Albert Varty
410 Mr. & Mrs. John L. Booth
412 Mr. & Mrs. Chas. H. Wilmerding
414 Mr. & Mrs. Clarence J. Porter
416 Mr. & Mrs. B. La Marche
418 Mrs. DeWitt C. Cregier
418 Mr. & Mrs. DeWitt C. Cregier jr.
420 Mrs. M. A. Fearing
420 Miss L. Blanche Fearing
424 Mrs. A. M. F. Colton
424 Miss S. S. Kirk

CLARENDON AVENUE.

2147 Mr. & Mrs. James Lugsdin
2151 Mr. & Mrs. Walter N. Evans
2155 Mr. & Mrs. Henry T. Brown
2159 Mr. & Mrs. Wm. H. Mather
2159 James Falley
2159 Wm. Falley
2159 Dr. & Mrs. W. Delano Eastlake
2339 Mrs. Eugene Field
2339 Miss Mary French Field

2110 Mr. & Mrs. J. Kellogg
2110 Mr. & Mrs. O. O. Agler
2118 Mr. & Mrs. G. M. Weeks
2354 Mr. & Mrs. B. Robbins

2339 Mrs. Ida C. Below
2339 W. C. Engler
2383 Mr. & Mrs. Henry T. Fry
2387 Mr. & Mrs. Thomas E. Fry

NORTH CLARK STREET.

307 The Walton
  2 Nathan Dickinson
  2 Albert Dickinson
  2 Miss M. Dickinson
  3 Mr. & Mrs. John P. Roberts
  5 Charles E. Deane

386 Mr. & Mrs. Armand F. Teefy
578 Mr. & Mrs. Henry Thorwart & dr.
se. cor. North av. The Plaza
  Frederick Merritt
  M. Paul Noyes
201 Dwight F. Cameron

307 The Walton (continued.)
  6 Robert Forsyth
  7 Mr. & Mrs. Howard O. Edmonds
  8 Mr. & Mrs. Newton Lull
  8 Miss Leila W. Lull
  9 Mr. & Mrs. Lyman Baird
  9 Max Baird
  9 Miss Elizabeth H. Baird
  10 Mr. & Mrs. Wm. H. Bush
307 Mr. & Mrs. Howard O. Edmonds
345 Mr. & Mrs. Alfred R. Edwards
375 Dr. & Mrs. Henry O. Redlich
375 Alexander E. Redlich
499 Mr. & Mrs. John Tempel & drs.
569 Mr. & Mrs. O. H. Kraft & dr.
569 Dr. Oscar H. Kraft
571 Mr. & Mrs. Julius Wegmann
571 Jules F. Wegmann
615 Mr. & Mrs. Frank H. Peak
699 Mr. & Mrs. Henry Eder
699 Charles H. Eder
741 Mr. & Mrs. Oliver W. Nixon
      Receiving day Friday
741 Mr. & Mrs. Charles E. Nixon
      Receiving day Friday
743 Mr.&Mrs.William Penn Nixon & drs.
743 Miss Elizabeth F. Risser
767 Mr. & Mrs. James W. Maxwell
767 Charles F. Maxwell
771 Mr.&Mrs. Julius Heineman
771 Mr. & Mrs. E. Kaeseberg
823 Dr. Emilie Siegmund
829 Mr. & Mrs. John Blocki & dr.
      Receiving day Wednesday
829 Frederick W. Blocki
835 Mr. & Mrs. G. Park Kinney
      Receiving day Wednesday
837 Dr. & Mrs. F. Wm. Ihne
837 Mr. & Mrs. Geo. R. Baker
919 Mr. & Mrs. Peter Seese
957 Mrs. Sarah Moulding
957 Dr. & Mrs. Wm. P. Goodsmith
1029 Mr. & Mrs. Louis Spiegel
1035 Mr. & Mrs. Olof Benson
1037 Harry S. Stevens
1049 Mr. & Mrs. Wm. R. Swinford
1059 Mr. & Mrs. Wm. C. Scupham
1065 Chas. L. Gamer
1065 Mr. & Mrs. George W. Gamer
1067 J. D. Spear
1071 Dr. & Mrs. T. W. Miller
1091 Dr. & Mrs. Allen T. Haight
1091 Mr. & Mrs. Edmund R. Krause

se. cor. North av. The Plaza (con.)
201 Miss Libbie F. Colvin
201 Miss Emma Preston
204 Miss Grace L. Stone
204 Miss Gertrude A. Stone
205 Mr. & Mrs. Robert T. Brewer
206 Mr. & Mrs. Fred D. Ludlow
206 Mrs. Cynthia A. Ludlow
210 Mr. & Mrs. Wilbur Haggers
212 Mr. & Mrs. Robert T. Brydon
214 Mr. & Mrs. James A. Phillips
216 Mrs. E. B. Preston
216 Miss Marguerite Preston
217 Dr. Emma B. Steyner
217 Miss Frances L. Marshall
219 Mr. & Mrs. F. G. Laird
220 Mr. & Mrs. Victor Robertson
301 Mr. & Mrs. Richard Polson
303 Mr. & Mrs. Wm. H. Klapp
304 Mrs. H. Cotton
305 Mrs. Susan H. Philleo
308 Mr. & Mrs. F. H. Tubbs
312 Cap. E. S. Chapin
313 F. P. Reynolds
315 John C. Wallis
316 Mr.&Mrs. Carlton Hudson
318 Mr. & Mrs. Thos. T. Morford
400 Mr. & Mrs. J. S. Brewer
403 Mr. & Mrs. A. W. Maltby
404 Mr. & Mrs. Wm. G. Wise
405 Mr. & Mrs. Daniel V. Gallery
      Reciving day Tuesday
405 Dr. Alfred C. Croftan
406 Mr. & Mrs. W. M. Lowrie
410 Mr.& Mrs.Wm.McC.Dodd
413 George H. Sager
413 Geo. W. Sager
414 Mr. & Mrs. Hepburn Johns
416 Mr. & Mrs. Joseph Wolf
417 Mr. & Mrs. Lawrence Proudfoot
419 Mr. & Mrs. W. G. Owens
421 Colin C. H. Fyffe
500 Karl Buenz
501 Mr.& Mrs.Jas.C. Halladay
502 Mrs. G. S. McCalmont
502 Mr. & Mrs. IsaacM.Sowers

1091 Dr. & Mrs. G. Frank Lydston
1103 Mr. & Mrs, Gebhardt W. Zeiger
1107 Mr. & Mrs. Edmund G. Fiedler
1115 Dr. & Mrs. E. M. Landis
1121 Daniel W. Maher
1121 Miss Tessie Maher
1127 Dr. & Mrs. Geo. J. Schaller
1143 Mr. & Mrs. Will I. Saunders
1147 Mr. & Mrs. George Oberne
1155 Mr. & Mrs. James Charlton & drs.
1161 Mr. & Mrs. Howard N. Wagg
1161 Mrs. Catherine B. Webb
1163 Mr. & Mrs. Frank Deppe & drs.
1171 Mr. & Mrs. John Fischback
1173 Mr. & Mrs. Patrick M. Hanney
1181 Mr. & Mrs. R. A. Meiswinkel
1265 Robert E. Buchanan
1457 Mrs. Mary A. J. Parker & dr.
4691 Mrs. Nettie D. Hanauer
Receiving day Wednesday
4691 Mr. & Mrs. Geo. E. Spoor
Receiving day Wednesday
4691 Miss Harriet I. Spoor
4691 Miss Maud L. Spoor
4773 Dr. & Mrs. A. D. Lowell
4915 Mrs. Della Benner & dr.

716 Mr. & Mrs. T. B. Wilcox
717 Mr. & Mrs. John Q. Adams
718 Miss Eunice Hooper
718 Miss Laura R. Copp
719 Mr. & Mrs. John M. Hagar
719 Edward M. Hagar
801 John K. Harmon & dr.
801 Fred H. Harmon
801 Albert C. Harmon
802 Mr. & Mrs. J. R. Chapman & dr.
802 Miss Gertrude A. Hagar
810 Mr. & Mrs. Charles E. Billin
813 Francis Vail
814 Mr. & Mrs. Frank S. Tenney
816 Mr. & Mrs. Jas. D. Springer & dr.
817 Mr. & Mrs. Chas. G. Ross
818 Dr. & Mrs. John Little Morris
Receiving day Thursday
819 Mr. & Mrs. Willis Counselman
821 Mr. & Mrs. C. Wirt Litchfield
822 Mrs. Chas. C. Chase

se. cor. North av. The Plaza (con.)
503 Mr. & Mrs. F. S. Peabody
503 Mrs. John H. McAvoy
504 Mr. & Mrs. Robt. B. Cotter
Receiving day Thursday
506 Mr. & Mrs. Alex. K. McRae
510 Henry S. Monroe & drs.
510 Miss Harriet Monroe
510 Miss Lucy Monroe
513 Mrs. Mary Magnus
514 Mrs. Lucy K. Platt
515 Horace S. Oakley
516 Mr. & Mrs. Frank P. Owings & dr.
518 Mr. & Mrs. Chas. W. Colehour
519 Lieut. Col. & Mrs. W. A. Elderkin
601 Miss Lydia A. Dimon
601 Mrs. Clinton W. Miller
603 Mr. & Mrs. John M. Locke
605 Mrs. Sarah McAvoy
608 Mr. & Mrs. Wm. B. Wicker
610 Mr. & Mrs. H. E. Rood
612 Mr. & Mrs. T. P. Shonts
Receiving day Friday
613 Miss Josephine Locke
615 Benjamin S. Cable
615 L. V. LeMoyne
616 Mrs. O. E. Babcock
616 Orville E. Babcock
616 Campbell E. Babcock
617 Mr. & Mrs. Edward M. Holloway
619 Mr. & Mrs. Hartley D. Harper
Receiving day Thursday
621 Mr. & Mrs. Wm. H. Finney
701 Henry Grassie
701 Arthur Booth
702 James C. Clow
702 Mr. & Mrs. Jas. B. Clow
702 Charles R. Clow
703 Mr. & Mrs. D. Gibson Drake
704 Mr. & Mrs. Henry L. Norton
705 Stewart Patterson
706 Mr. & Mrs. Jas. A. Farovid
706 Mr. & Mrs. Edward A. Lycett
710 Mr. & Mrs. Wm. D. McIlvaine
713 George H. Mead
714 Rev. Thaddeus A. Snively
715 Charles T. Haughey

1112 Mr. & Mrs. George C. Chapman & drs.
 Receiving day Wednesday
1112 Dr. George L. Chapman
1112 Chas. F. Chapman
1112 Paul R. Chapman
1186 Mr. & Mrs. John R. Magill
1186 Mr. & Mrs. Jacob K. Lesch
1186 Mr. & Mrs. Frank Parmelee jr.
1220 Mr. & Mrs. Henry Kleine
1234 Miss Catherine E. McNulty
1234 Miss May E. McNulty
1238 Mr. & Mrs. Chas. F. Perry
1238 Mrs. E. G. Titus & dr.
1238 Mrs. Newton Goodwin
1238 Mr. & Mrs. Adolph Karpen
1246 Dr. & Mrs. P. M. Woodworth

1246 Dr. John Teare
1314 Mr. & Mrs. M. J. Tillmann & dr.
1326 Mrs. E. J. Lehmann
1326 E. J. Lehmann jr.
1326 Miss Tillie Preasant
1326 Charles Preasant
1474 Mrs. Edmund Knauer
1474 Mr. & Mrs. R. J. Schwitzer
1474 Roy Knauer
1474 Adolph Hoffman
4298 Mr. & Mrs. Chas. Hitchcock
4298 Robbins S. Mott
5008 Mr. & Mrs. P. L. Touhy & drs.
5008 Stephen R. Touhy
5008 Joseph Touhy

CLEVELAND AVENUE.

411 Mr. & Mrs. N. M. Plotke
419 Mr. & Mrs. J. Back
427 Mr. & Mrs. Charles Werno
451 Mrs. M. G. Weick
451 Louis E. Weick
455 Mr. & Mrs. D. M. S. Cohen
455 Abraham L. Cohen
463 Mr. & Mrs. Nicholas Gerten
481 Mr. & Mrs. Charles Schumann
487 Mr.&Mrs. A. D. Wilmanns&drs.
487 Theodore O. Wilmanns
515 Mr. & Mrs. L. W. Campbell & dr. *Receiving day Thursday*
519 Dr. & Mrs. A. Goldspohn
519 Mr. & Mrs. Samuel Schneider
523 Mr. & Mrs. Joachim Saehn
525 Mr. & Mrs. W. R. Abbott
525 Mr. & Mrs. O. A. Blattner
533 Mr. & Mrs. Jacob Retterer
535 Mr. & Mrs. John McGillen
537 Mr. & Mrs. M. A. Delany & dr.
541 Mr. & Mrs. C. J. Sauter & drs.
541 L. E. Sauter
541 C. Frank Sauter
543 Mr. & Mrs. Julius Blum
545 Mr. & Mrs. John Booth & drs.
549 Mr. & Mrs. Wm. G. Wasmansdorff
549 Mrs. Otto Wasmansdorff
551 Mr. & Mrs. Louis Berlizheimer
553 Mr. & Mrs. M. Kaufman & dr.
555 Mr. & Mrs. John Schoen
555 George Schoen
555 Mr. & Mrs. J. P. Simon
565 Mrs. Elizabeth Engberg & dr.

530 Mr. & Mrs. Lee Fellows
 Receiving day Thursday
538 Mrs. W. Maxwell & dr.
538 D. G. Maxwell
540 Mr. & Mrs. John G. Roland
546 Mr. & Mrs. Samuel Friedlander
596 Mr. & Mrs. E. B. Bacon & drs.
596 Gordon E. Bacon
628 Mr. & Mrs. Robt. L. Thornton
640 Mr. & Mrs. Charles N. Strotz
646 Mr. & Mrs. A. V. Eilert
646 Mr. & Mrs. John Anderson
654 Mr. & Mrs. W. J. Fleming
654 Mrs. P. A. Reed

———

565 Martin J. Engberg
565 Miss Barbara Zimmerman
569 Rev. & Mrs. Philip Klein
575 Mr. & Mrs. R. H. Stewart & drs.
575 George R. Stewart
575 Mr. & Mrs. Nicolay Grevstad & dr.
587 Mr. & Mrs. A. Chaiser & drs.
591 Mr. & Mrs. Charles J. Schmidt
591 Charles F. Miller
597 Rev. & Mrs. J. M. Williams
603 Mr. & Mrs. J. Petersen
603 Nicholas Hand
609 Mr. & Mrs. C. R. Matson
615 Mrs. J. M. Watte
619 Mr. & Mrs. Arthur G. Jukes & dr.
619 Mr. & Mrs. C. W. Campbell
621 Mr. & Mrs. Hermann Mueller

625 Mr. & Mrs. Charles Heinemann
631 Mrs. Sarah L. Finney
631 Harry P. Finney
631 George M. Finney
649 Miss Emma Engleman

659-665 Cleveland Flats
  3 Miss Anna Clomes
 10 Mrs. Carl A. Servoss
 14 Mr. & Mrs. Nathaniel C. Wright
    Receiving day Thursday

CORNELIA AVENUE.

1721 Mr. & Mrs. S. M. Eisendrath

1438 Mr. & Mrs. Preston K. Lawrence
1628 Mr. & Mrs. J. Almon Austin

CRILLY COURT.

 1 William E. Lindsey
 1 Mrs. William L. Lindsey
 3 Mr. & Mrs. August Spielmann
 5 Mr. & Mrs. Geo. W. Claussenius
 7 Max N. Epstein
 9 Mr. & Mrs. David M. Kirton
19 Mr. & Mrs. John V. May

 2 Mr. & Mrs. Isaac Weil
 8 Mr. & Mrs. Albert Dooley
18 Mr. & Mrs. John H. Spangler
    Receiving day Wednesday

23 Mr. & Mrs. Edward A. Bennett

CUYLER AVENUE.

945 Charles West
955 Mr. & Mrs. Albert E. Fleig

424 Mr. & Mrs. Lewis B. Scott
980 Mr. & Mrs. Theo. Corten

DAKIN AVENUE.

1439 Mr. & Mrs. John B. Johnson
1529 Mr. & Mrs. Wm. Seiffe

1446 Dr. & Mrs. Wm. P. Richards
1448 Mr. & Mrs. Louis A. Heile
1518 Mr. & Mrs. Ira L. Gifford

DAYTON STREET.

351 Mr. & Mrs. A. H. Lockwood
365 Mr. & Mrs. Michael Brennan
435 Mr. & Mrs. Peter A. Selig
451 Mr. & Mrs. W. Glasser
457 Mr. & Mrs. W. L. Kroeschell
    Receive Wednesday eve.
459 Mr. & Mrs. C. G. Stowell

462 Mr. & Mrs. Frank A. Knipschield

294 Mr. & Mrs. E. W. Wander
    Receiving day Wednesday
294 Mrs. Pauline Wander
294 Miss Valesca W. Wander
380 Mr. & Mrs. E. R. Van Buren
392 Mr. & Mrs. Moses Meyer
450 Mr. & Mrs. Otto Kroeschell
452 Dr. & Mrs. Charles C. Bernard
460 Mr. & Mrs. J. P. Hettinger

DEARBORN AVENUE.

129 C. C. Crabb
131 Dr. & Mrs. C. D. Bradley & dr.
    Receiving day Monday
141 Mr. & Mrs. Frank S. Bash
169 Mr. & Mrs. A. A. Sample
181 Dr. Alice Barlow Brown
    Receiving day Monday
181 Miss Elizabeth H. Barlow

148 The Mentone
    Henry Cliff
    Capt. John Cliff
    Mr. & Mrs. P. S. Dickey
    Milton Marcuse
    Mr. & Mrs. S. T. Miles
    Mrs. Geo. P. Sexton
156 Mr. & Mrs. C. J. Wood

215 Dr. J. S. Christison
219 Edward A. Claypool
221 Jason W. Firestone
225-231 The Newberry
    O. H. Barnum
    Dr. Leila G. Bedell
    Miss Eve H. Brodlique
    Frank T. Brown
    F. F. Bullen
    C. S. Clark
    W. W. Cloon
    Mr. & Mrs. Wm. Fennimore
     . Cooper
    Mr. & Mrs. C. A. Daniels
    Thomas S. Denison
    Mr. & Mrs. Geo. S. Dixon
    O. G. Formhals
    Mr. & Mrs. F. A. Fulwiler
    Daniel J. Gallagher
    Mr. & Mrs. Henry E. Hamilton
    H. C. Henwood
    C. Herbst
    Miss Susan Hunting
    Miss Sadie Hurd
    Mr. & Mrs. Herbert Leroy Jones
    Dr. T. Y. Kayne
    Mr. & Mrs. Robert G. Kerr
    J. S. Lovejoy
    F. P. Luther
    John S. Luther
    A. J. McCausland
    Julius Moos
    E. W. Morrison
    Mrs. Wm. H. Morrison & dr.
    Miss Tillie Niehaus
    Frank C. O'Day
    Miss Sarah C. Purdy
    Mr. & Mrs. John Reid
    Charles H. Schub
    Mr. & Mrs. E. Scribner
    Miss M. Segnitz
    Mr. & Mrs. Chas. Shackleford
    Willard Smoot
    Mr. & Mrs. Harry D. Stevens
    Mr. & Mrs. Edwin C. Towslee
    C. E. Warden
    Miss T. Weil
    Thomas H. Wilcox
239 George E. Waldo
247 Mr. & Mrs. Albion Cate
    Receiving day Wednesday
247 Cyrus F. Cook
247 Clark W. Harrison
251 Mrs. Ella Burlingham
    Receiving day Monday
263 Dr. & Mrs. Robert N. Tooker & dr.

156 Mr. & Mrs. William C. Galla-
    way
156 Mr. & Mrs. Wm. T. Gallaway
156 Mrs. Susan Jacques
178 Mr. & Mrs. John Addison
178 Harold E. Addison
178 Mr. & Mrs. Edward N. Camp
228 Dr. & Mrs. A. Lagorio
234 Dr. & Mrs. A. H. Cooke
234 Dr. John M. Cooke
234 Alexander W. Cooke
236 Dr. & Mrs. S. Newton Schneider
236 Edward J. Hoyer
238 Jules Homery
242 Mr. & Mrs. R. H. Mead
242 Mr. & Mrs. Fred A. Hahn
244 Mr. & Mrs. A. J. Marble & dr.
250 Mr. & Mrs. Richard I. Field
250 George W. Field
250 Arthur C. Field
254 Mr. & Mrs. Augustus H. Burley
256 Mr. & Mrs. Thomas Lynch
332 Mr. & Mrs. M. W. Kerwin & dr.
336 Mrs. James W. Ferry
336 Mrs. M. A. H. Ferry
344 Livingston Griffin
346 Dr. & Mrs. N. J. Dorsey & dr.
356 Mrs. Edward Waller & dr.
    Receive Thursday afternoon
356 Edward Waller jr.
356 A. Rawson Waller
356 J. A. Waller
356 F. C. Waller
362 Dr. & Mrs. Fenton B. Turck
370 Mr. & Mrs. William M. Hoyt
    Receive Monday afternoon
370 Mr. & Mrs. N. Landon Hoyt
370 Miss H. J. Landon
374 Mr. & Mrs. H. P. Moyer
374 Mr. & Mrs. G. Sumner Evering-
    ham
374 Mr. & Mrs. W. N. Ball
374 Mr. & Mrs. Elliott T. Monett
374 Thomas C. Haynes & dr.
376 Mr. & Mrs. M. J. Hea
376 Mr. & Mrs. Theo. Springer
376 Fred W. Eldredge
386 Mr. & Mrs. Charles J. Moore
386 Timothy F. Mullen
386 William H. Mullen
400 Mrs. J. M. Adsit & drs.
400 Mrs. Ezra I. Wheeler
400 James M. Adsit jr.
402 Mrs. John DeKoven
408 Dr. & Mrs. Sven Windrow
408 Miss Sophia Windrow

263 Robert N. Tooker jr.
263 Dr. L. Sauveur & drs.
285 Mrs. J. H. Thompson
285 Watts C. Thompson
285 Payson Thompson
285 Benj. F. C. Thompson
289 Mr. & Mrs. John S. Hannah
293 Mr. & Mrs. George B. Carpenter
293 John Alden Carpenter
321 Dr. & Mrs. Ralph N. Isham
325 Mr. & Mrs. O. F. Fuller
325 Henry M. Fuller
337 Mr. & Mrs. James H. Dole & dr.
  Receive 2nd Tuesday in mo.
337 Miss Julia F. Dole
337 Mr. & Mrs. Henry W. Leman
337 George S. Dole
337 Charles E. Dole
345 Mr. & Mrs. C. W. Farr
  Receiving day Thursday
345 E. W. Hurst
347 Mrs. T. S. Phillips & drs.
349 Charles P. Willard
351 Mrs. G. S. Carmichael
359 Mr. & Mrs. William Ruxton
375 Mr. & Mrs. Edgar L. Webster
375 Mr. & Mrs. W. Edward Bell
385 Mrs. Louise M. Stockton & dr.
385 Algernon C. Stockton
387 William F. Keep
387 Frederick A. Keep
387 Miss Frances Keep
389 Mr. & Mrs. W. S. Potwin
399 Mr. & Mrs. E. C. Coulter
405 Mr. & Mrs. C. R. Larrabee & drs.
405 Rev. Edward A. Larrabee
405 Miss Eleanor P. Wood
409 Mr. & Mrs. P. L. Garrity & drs.
  Receiving day Thursday
409 Dr. Joseph Garrity
413 Mrs. M. L. Stern & drs.
413 Daniel Stern
413 Ralph F. Stern
415 Mrs. Juliet K. Woodward
415 Mr. & Mrs. Joseph S. Woodward
415 Mr. & Mrs. Herbert C. De-Camp
417 Mr. & Mrs. William Troost & dr.
433 George P. Gilman
433 Miss Mary Gilman
433 George P. Gilman jr.
435 Mr. & Mrs. Richard F. Redell
  Receiving day Thursday
437 Mr. & Mrs. W. H. Parsons

412 Mr. & Mrs. John N. Jewett
414 Dr. & Mrs. R. D. MacArthur
414 Dr. & Mrs. Ralph R. Campbell
426 Mr. & Mrs. F. B. Peabody
426 Augustus S. Peabody
440 Mr. & Mrs. Arthur C. Woodward
440 Mr. & Mrs. Chas. H. Felton
444 Mr. & Mrs. Wiley M. Egan
444 Miss Lizzie Egan
444 Mr. & Mrs. Lucian P. Cheney
446 Mr. & Mrs. Mahlon A. Vinnedge
448 Mr. & Mrs. C. A. Spring jr.
450 Peter Britten & dr.
450 Michael Britten
452 Mr. & Mrs. John G. Miller
460 Mr. & Mrs. George M. Clark
460 Mr. & Mrs. Harry Channon
460 Mr. &. Mrs. E. C. DeWitt
466 Dr. & Mrs. Robt. H. Babcock
476 Mr. & Mrs. Peter L. Yoe
476 Mr. & Mrs. L. G. Yoe & drs.
480 Mr. & Mrs. J. M. W. Jones
480 Edgcombe Lee Jones
480 Miss M. Katherine Jones
480 Miss Helen Snow Jones
486 Mr. & Mrs. Charles A. Dupee & dr.
486 Eugene H. Dupee
486 George W. Dupee
488 Mrs. Christian Lichtenberger
490 Mr. & Mrs. W. H. Gray
492 Mr. & Mrs. Henry Tifft
496 Mr. & Mrs. Albert Kuhlmey
502 Mr. & Mrs. C. O. Harz
  Receive 2d Thursday
508 Mr. & Mrs. Morris Griesheimer
512 Mr. & Mrs. A. F. Borcherdt
512 Herman Borcherdt
512 Miss Martha Starke
512 Albert Starke
514 Mr. & Mrs. F. O. Baumann
516 Mr. & Mrs. Frank Linsenbarth
518 Mr. & Mrs. W. Morgan Peters
522 August Magnus
522 Mr. & Mrs. H. F. Williams
524 Mr. & Mrs. Henry D. Estabrook
  Receiving day Tuesday
524 Miss Blanche D. Estabrook
524 R. C. Clowry
528 Mr. & Mrs. Adolph Loeb
528 Mr. & Mrs. Henry N. Greenebaum
532 Dr. & Mrs. Nicholas Senn
532 Dr. Emanuel J. Senn

441 Dr. L. D. Rogers.
441 Dr. Ida Wright Rogers
441 Dr. Paul Burmaster
443 Dr. Edward A. West
445 Mr.& Mrs.Edmund Loewenthal
445 Mr. & Mrs. Bernard Mandl
451 Mrs. J. Egan & drs.
   Receiving day Wednesday
453 Mr. & Mrs. M. Wolff & dr.
453 Samuel Wolff
453 Nathan Wolff
455 Mr. & Mrs. E. R. Schlick & drs.
   Receiving day Thursday
457 Mr. & Mrs. J. H. Batterman &
  dr.
459 Mr. & Mrs. R. Philip Gormully
   Receiving day Wednesday
459 Mrs. Ralph H. Hayes-Sadler
463 Mr. & Mrs. N. J. Sandberg
   Receiving day Thursday
463 Charles A. Sandberg
463 George N. Sandberg
465 Mr. & Mrs. Homer S. Chandler
465 Mr. & Mrs. Henry M. Wisler
465 Dr. H. G. Anthony
465 Mrs. Charles A. Church
   Receiving day Wednesday
465 Mr. & Mrs. A. W. Eschenburg
465 Thomas H. Creden
475 Dr. & Mrs. J. D. Kales
481 Miss Rebecca S. Rice
   Receiving day Monday
481 Miss Mary E. Beedy
481 Miss Caroline Morris Young
481 Mlle. Helene Bel-Fouche
481 Miss Mary D. Newcomb
483 Dr. & Mrs. Francis A. Henning
   Receiving day Friday
483 Mrs. Maria Anna Heyer
485 Mr. & Mrs. Edward G. Halle
  & dr.
485 Frank Halle jr.
485 Arthur Halle
487 Mr. & Mrs. Frederick Geo. Colley *Receiving day Thursday*
489 Mr. & Mrs. Fred'k A. Newton
489 Reuben W. Newton
489 Albert W. Newton
489 Mr. & Mrs. Geo. A. Hellman
489 George A. Hellman, jr.
489 Mr. & Mrs. Ulrich Duehr & dr.
491 Miss Helen Page Smith
491 Mr. & Mrs. Sabin Smith
491 Dr. Julia Holmes Smith
491 Dr. & Mrs. H. H. Brown
   Receiving day Tuesday

532 William N. Senn
538 Mr. & Mrs. D. H. Tolman
538 Miss Lucy Bull
540 Mr. & Mrs. J. P. Hand
   Receive 1st Thursday in mo.
550 Mr. & Mrs. A. T. Galt
550 Mason Bross
552 Mr. & Mrs. Philo R. King & dr.
552 William King
554 Mr. &. Mrs. F. McAuley
   Receiving day Wednesday
554 Miss Agnes McAuley
556 Mr. & Mrs. J. B. Lynch & drs.
556 Thomas G. Lynch
556 Andrew G. Lynch
558 Mr. & Mrs. Chalkley J. Hambleton
558 Miss Maude G. Hambleton
560 Mr. & Mrs. Wm. Edgar Baker
564 Mr. & Mrs. John P. Wilson
   Receiving day Monday
564 Miss Wilson
564 Miss Martha Wilson
568 J. C. Bullock
568 Mr. & Mrs. Carl C. Bullock
568 Miss Bertha Bullock
572 Mr. & Mrs. Geo. E. Rickcords
584 James D. Lynch
584 Mrs. Nelson H. Barnes & dr.
584 Mr. & Mrs. Murry Nelson jr.
584 Mrs. Edwin Blackman
586 Mr. & Mrs. Frank H. Starkweather
586 Mr. & Mrs. George T. Dyer
586 Mr. & Mrs. John T. Boddie
   Receiving day Monday
586 Mr. & Mrs. Wm. Wrigley jr
588 Mr. & Mrs. George C. Prussing
590 Dr. & Mrs. Robt. B. Preble
590 Mrs. H. Hosmer & dr.
592 Mr. & Mrs. Louis Stern
592 Mr. & Mrs. Charles A. Gimbel
594 Mr. & Mrs. Henry Elkan & dr.
594 Mr. & Mrs. Jos. Gutmann
596 Mrs. Anna E. Tripp
596 Arnold Tripp jr.
596 Edward A. Tripp
600 Mrs. A. H. Dainty
600 Mr. & Mrs. Henry C. Bellamy
600 J. Edwin Coursen
604 Dr. & Mrs. Harvey A. Tyler
606 Mr. & Mrs. M. J. Swatek & dr.
608 Mrs. J. S. Barnes & dr.
608 Mr. & Mrs. F. G. Barnes
610 Mr. & Mrs. Truman Penfield
610 Truman P. Gaylord

493 Mrs. Moses P. Handy & dr.
493 William Matthews Handy
493 Mr. & Mrs. Wm. Inglis & dr.
499 Mr. & Mrs. John G. Reber
499 Dr. & Mrs. B. M. Ross
503 Mr. & Mrs. Augustus Warner
505 Mr. & Mrs. John Irwin & drs.
507 Mr. & Mrs. J. C. Nyman
507 Mr. & Mrs. Fay Nyman
507 Fred Nyman
507 Mr. & Mrs. Louis Bliss
509 Mr. & Mrs. LeGrand W. Perce
    & drs.
509 H. Wallace Perce
513 A. H. Blackall & dr.
515 Mr. & Mrs. R. T. Whelpley
517 Mr. & Mrs. Herman Herbst
519 Mr.& Mrs.DeLancey H.Louder-
    back
521 Mr. & Mrs. D. E. Sasseen
    Receiving day Tuesday
521 E. J. Abel
521 Miss Minnie Abel
521 Mr. & Mrs Jas. Wallace Buell
521 Mr. & Mrs.Bradley Dixon Buell
531 Mr. & Mrs. L. W. McConnell
535 Mr. & Mrs. Thos. S. Wallin
537 Mr.& Mrs.William Sprague&dr.
537 Fred W. Sprague
541 Mr. & Mrs. Albert M. Gilbert
543 Mr. & Mrs. Emil Greifenhagen
543 Mr. & Mrs. Chas. D. Loper
545 Mr. & Mrs. August W. Rietz
545 Mr. & Mrs. Chas. W. Farr
547 Mr. & Mrs. W. C. Budd & drs.
    Receiving day Friday
547 Mr. & Mrs. W. B. Easton
547 Mr. & Mrs. C. T. A. McCormick
547 Mr. & Mrs. Samuel M. Fargo &
    dr.
547 Mr. & Mrs. John W. Hunter
547 Mr. & Mrs. Ward A. Stockton
547 Frank E. Scott
547 Mr. & Mrs. F. D. Freeman
549 Mr. & Mrs. F. D. Freeman
551 Dr. John J. Whaley
551 William Swannell
551 Mr. & Mrs. Frank B. Archibald
    Receiving day Tuesday
551 Mr. & Mrs. E. W. Copelin
551 Mr. & Mrs. Edward A. Bigelow

610 Miss Helen E. Starr
616 Mr. & Mrs. J. B. Grommes
616 Miss Frieda Grommes
620 Alexander Nuber
628 Charles W. Fullerton
628 Miss Mattie S. Hill
628 Mrs. J. H. Hill & dr.

———

551 Mr.& Mrs. Truman A. DeWeese
    Receiving day Monday
553 Henry Rea Hixson
555A Mr. & Mrs. Julius B. Fox
555A Mr. & Mrs. Frederick J.Squibb
    Receiving day Tuesday
555A Mr. & Mrs. David Eichberg
555 Mr. & Mrs. Richard O'Neill &
    drs.
557 Mr. & Mrs. Hugh L. Mason
559 James J. Rardon
559 Mr. & Mrs. F. D. Montgomery
561 Mr. & Mrs. Graham H. Harris
571 Mrs. Caroline E. Stanley & dr.
573 Mr. & Mrs. M. Shields
573 Mr. & Mrs. John B. Langan
575 Mr. & Mrs. Frank A. Rehm
579 Mr. & Mrs. Francis Lackner &
    drs.
585 Mrs. J. J. McGrath & dr.
585 Charles H. McGrath
587 Mr. & Mrs. E. E. Prussing
589 Mr. & Mrs. Jacob Rehm
589 William H. Rehm
595 Mr. & Mrs. Ransom J. Morse
595 B. Morse
595 W. D. Morse
597 Mr. & Mrs. C. R. Corbin
597 Lawrence Paul Corbin
597 C. Dana Corbin
599 Mr. & Mrs. Charles Lyon
599 Mr. & Mrs. E. G. Mabie
599 Mr. & Mrs. E. E. Foster
599 George D. Lyon
601 Mr. & Mrs. Hermann Petersen
601 Mr. & Mrs. August Kochs
603 Mr. & Mrs. H. V. Lester
619 Mr. & Mrs. Wm. C. Seipp
623 Mr. & Mrs. Wm. Stewart &
    drs.
627 Mr. & Mrs. John Kranz & dr.

DELAWARE PLACE.

17 Mrs. R. M. Hooley & dr.
17 Mr. & Mrs. George M. Pynchon
19 Mr. & Mrs. Charles W. Ware
29 Mr. & Mrs. Henry Burrall Mason
   Receive Wednesday afternoon
49 Mr. & Mrs. George A. Carpenter
49 Samuel Insull

24 Mr. & Mrs. Edward P. Russell
26 Mr. & Mrs. Robert Bruce Farson
   Receiving day Monday
28 Mrs. C. J. Richardson & dr.
32 Dr. & Mrs. O. J. Waters

51 Mr. & Mrs. A. Shreve Badger

DEMING PLACE.

1705 Mr. & Mrs. Henry Rieke & drs.
1705 Geo. W. Rieke
1705 H. Edward Rieke
1707 Mr. & Mrs. Oliver E. Pagin
1713 Mr. & Mrs. H. A. Haugan
1713 Oscar Haugan
1719 Mr. & Mrs. F. A. Powers
1719 George Powers
1723 Mr. & Mrs. J. W. Kindt & dr.
   Receiving day Thursday
1723 Arthur Kindt
1737 Mr. & Mrs. William Sieck
1745 Mr. & Mrs. John C. Schiess
1749 Mr. & Mrs. John B. Foley
   Receiving day Wednesday
1749 Mr. & Mrs. M. Johnson & dr.
1769 Mr. & Mrs. H. E. Bullock
1773 Mr. & Mrs. E. Gerstenberg &
   dr.
1907 Mr. & Mrs. J. M. Weeks
1909 Mr. & Mrs. Wm. L. Koehne
1911 Mr. & Mrs. O. F. Greifenhagen
1913 Mr. & Mrs. Peter Hand
1917 Mr. & Mrs. John Glenn Collins
   Receiving day Friday
1923 Mr. & Mrs. James B. Barnet
1925 Mr. & Mrs. Albert Breitung
1925 Miss Viola J. Dix
1927 Mr. & Mrs. Jas. H. Channon
1931 Mr. & Mrs. Douglas Dyrenforth
1931 Mr. & Mrs. J. G. S. Best
1939 Mr. & Mrs. Frank W. Pilsbry
   Receiving day Wednesday
1947 Mr. & Mrs. Edmond A. Fordyce
1947 Mr. & Mrs. Frank H. Pietsch
1949 Mr. & Mrs. Alex H. Levy
1949 Mr. & Mrs. A. Ruhstrat
1949 Mrs. Chas. L. Kelley
1953 Mrs. Jennie V. Scherenberg
1953 Henry A. Beneke

1944 Mrs. H. L. Kennon & drs.
1944 Mr. &. Mrs. J. H. McNulty

1710 Mr. & Mrs. James Hayde
1712 Mr. & Mrs. John T. Donaldson
1720 Mr. & Mrs. Adam Miller
1720 Mr. & Mrs. Fred Miller
1730 Mr. & Mrs. Jacob Gross & dr.
1730 William H. Gross
1730 Mr. & Mrs. William D. Falk
1732 Mr. & Mrs. A. J. Kasper & dr.
1734 Mrs. Geo. F. Blanke & dr.
   Receive 1st Saturday
1738 Mr. & Mrs. Wm. Schmidt
1744 Mr. & Mrs. Fred J. Lange
1744 Edward Lange
1754 Mr. & Mrs. C. E. Ernst & dr.
1754 Leo E. Ernst
1758 Mr. & Mrs. Fred'k M. Schmidt
1774 L. F. Nonnast
1778 Henry Ackhoff
1778 Miss L. Ackhoff
1788 Mr. & Mrs. Horace A. Goodrich
1912 Frank Roesch
1916 Mr. & Mrs. George J. Jaeger
1918 Mr. & Mrs. Wm. J. Rardon
1920 Mr. & Mrs. Everett Stillinger
1930 Arthur O. Probst
1920 Mr. & Mrs. Samuel D. Thompson
1930 Mr. & Mrs. Wm. D. Morris
1930 Mr. & Mrs. John V. Cowling jr.
   Receive Wednesday
1930 Mrs. Ida K. McLaughlin
1932 Mr. & Mrs. Florian P. Nelson
1932 Mr. & Mrs. M. H. Morris
1932 Miss Jennie Smith
1932 Chester T. Drake
1940 Mr. & Mrs. Benj. W. Welles &
   dr.
1940 Mr. & Mrs. Walter B. Pierce
   Receive 1st Monday
1940 Joseph T. Griffith jr.
1944 Mr. & Mrs. Homer W. Chandler
   Receiving day Monday
1944 H. B. Kennon

DEWEY PLACE.

1702 Mr. & Mrs. George J. Shepardson

DIVERSEY STREET.

1911 Mr. & Mrs. E. C. Berriman
1911 Thomas S. Simpson
1911 Charles A. Stroude
1911½ Mr. & Mrs. James R. Ward
1915 Mark A. Devine & dr.
1917 Mrs. A. W. Glaspell
 Receiving day Friday
1917 Mrs. E. E. L. Woodward
 Receiving day Friday

50 Mrs. Mary L. Brown
51 Mr. & Mrs. R. R. Lounabury
52 Mr. & Mrs. H. C. Burbank
53 Mr. & Mrs. K. E. Edwards
 Receiving day Wednesday
60 Mr. & Mrs. J. M. Jenks
 Receiving day Thursday
60 Miss Maxwell B. Jenks
62 Mr. & Mrs. W. A. Mays
 Receiving day Friday
63 Mr. & Mrs. James J. Casey
67 Todd Lunsford
71 Mr. & Mrs. R. S. Blome
73 Hon. & Mrs. John P. Altgeld
75 Mr. & Mrs. J. J. Rogers
77 Mr. & Mrs. William Collins
80 Mr. & Mrs. Eli A. Gage
80 Mrs. John Weare
81 Mr. & Mrs. W. I. Laird
85 Mr. & Mrs. O. H. Huszagh
 Receiving day Tuesday
85 Miss Agnes Peyton
86 Mr. & Mrs. W. J. Renicke

1302 Mr. & Mrs. Chas. J. Sterling
1534 Mr. & Mrs. R. W. Campion &
 drs. *Receiving day Thursday*
1610 Mr. & Mrs. Eugene Sugg
1610 George Sugg
1624 Mr. & Mrs. Alfred J. Cox
1624 Alexis J. Cox
1704 Mr. & Mrs. Gustaf Stieglitz &
 drs.
1712 Mrs. Catherine Kane
1726 Miss Ella Sullivan
1742 Dr. & Mrs. N. Ellis Oliver
1824 Mr. & Mrs. C. E. Affeld
1840 Thomas Boyle & dr.
 Receiving day Tuesday
1852 Mrs. P. J. Maginnis & dr.
1880 Mr. & Mrs. Thomas W. Wing
1882 Dr. & Mrs. J. H. Woolley.
1884 Mr. & Mrs. P. O'Malley
1886 and 1888—Lincoln Park Palace
 2 Mr. & Mrs. Wm. H. Walker
 20 Mrs. Mary C. C. Edwards
 22 Mr. & Mrs. L. D. Voak
 23 Mr. & Mrs. Frederick Daib
 32 Dr. John W. O'Neill
 33 Mr. & Mrs. F. L. Roach
 40 Mr. & Mrs. J. Crossgrove
 41 Mr. & Mrs. William B. Mann
 42 Mr. & Mrs. Henry S. Teal
 43 Mr. & Mrs. G. P. Richardson
  Receiving day Monday
 45 Mr. & Mrs. Conrad Hogenson
 46 Charles D. Gano
 47 Mr. & Mrs. F. J. Turnbull

DIVISION STREET.

305 Dr. A. H. Lane
305 Dr. E. M. Smith
451 Mr. & Mrs. Henry S. Kelsey
565 M. J. Keane
567 Mr. & Mrs. G. K. Shoenberger
 & dr.
571 Mr. & Mrs. Louis Adler & dr.
573 Mrs. Kate Phelizot
573 James A. Hemingway
577 Mr. & Mrs. John West & drs.
577 Albert L. West
607 Mr. & Mrs. George D. Rumsey

258 Mr. & Mrs. Levi Strauss
306 Dr. & Mrs. E. D. Smith
558 Dr. & Mrs. R. W. Holmes
558 Mr. & Mrs. Louis S. Taylor
560 Mrs. Ida Manchester & dr.
560 Mrs. C. J. Brackebush
560 Charles H. Brackebush
560 Frederick M. Brackebush
564 Mr. & Mrs. Joseph R. Wilkins
 & dr.
566 Mr. & Mrs. Charles S. McEntee
568 Mr. & Mrs. Sigmund Zeisler

609 Mr. & Mrs. A. S. Littlefield
613 Mr. & Mrs. Frederick T. West

602 Mr. & Mrs. Charles W. Comes
602 Mrs. Emma Bower & dr.
604 Charles D. Bickford & dr.
604 Mr. & Mrs. Wm. S. Crosby
604 Edward A. Crosby
604 Miss Helen Runnion
664 Nelson Runnion
604 Herman B. Wickersham
606 Mr. & Mrs. H. L. Matz
608 Mr. & Mrs. R. N. Dickman
608 Charles Fleetwood
610 Mr. & Mrs. Samuel G. Taylor
610 Mr. & Mrs. Samuel G. Taylor jr.
610 Francis W. Taylor
612 J. Devereux York
612 Mrs. E. J. T. Brooke
     Receiving day Monday
614 Mr. & Mrs. Robert W. Hunt
620 Mrs. L. A. Coonley-Ward
620 Miss Sarah Coonley

568 Miss Rosa Kanner
570 Mr. & Mrs. Charles L. Strobel
572 Mr. & Mrs. Harold A. Howard
576 Mr. & Mrs. Phelps B. Hoyt
578 Mrs. J. H. Trowbridge & dr.
578 James R. Trowbridge
578 Ray Clarke Rose
578 Mr. & Mrs. Henry M. Slaymaker
580 Mr. & Mrs. E. W. Beach
580 Dr. & Mrs. Thomas Gardner
     Corlett
580 Dr. Thomas G. Corlett
582 Mrs. W. Green & drs.
586 Mrs. Mary J. VanKeuren
     Receiving day Wednesday
588 Mr. & Mrs. H. M. Tibbetts
588½ Mr. & Mrs. Henry Kaufman
588½ Henry Mayer
590 Mr. & Mrs. Frank S. Weigley
594 Mr. & Mrs. William Dunn
594 Miss Alida Leavenworth
598 Mr. & Mrs. J. Edmund Strong
     & dr.

DOVER STREET.

3127 Dr. & Mrs. C. W. Leigh
3127 Dr. & Mrs. E. M. Fredericks
3127 Mrs. G. N. Esler
3129 Mr. & Mrs. Richard A. Car-
      queville
3129 Mr. & Mrs. E. K. Fleming
3129 Mr. & Mrs. C. H. Burton
3177 Mrs. Charlotte S. Saalfeld
3177 Mr. & Mrs. Herman Vorbeck
3207 Mrs. Catherine McIlhon
3211 Mrs. John A. E. Lindt
3211 Mr. & Mrs. Wm. McRoberts

3144 Mr. & Mrs. W. T. Buckley
3144 Mrs. Josephine H. Wrightson
3164 Mr. & Mrs. Levi C. Geahart
3174 Mr. & Mrs. Andrew P. Shogren
3180 Mr. & Mrs. F. B. Amend
3180 Mr. & Mrs. Edgar R. Steele
3180 William Mason
3186 Mr. & Mrs. Thomas Nolan
3212 Mr. & Mrs. James Pease
3242 Mr. & Mrs. Walter V. Hayt

3259 Mr. & Mrs. Christian Grawe

DUNNING STREET.

1131 Mr. & Mrs. W. H. Hackett
1335 Charles Lederer

1314 Mrs. M. A. Walsh & dr.

EARLY AVENUE.

1031 Mr. & Mrs. H. M. Scambler
1037 Mr. & Mrs. Robert J. Frank
     Receiving day Tuesday
1049 Mr. & Mrs. Chas. C. Russell
1049 Mrs. L. A. Havens
1101 Mr. & Mrs. W. H. Woollacott
1111 Mr. & Mrs. L. B. Bishop
1111 Paul Bishop
1115 Mr. & Mrs. A. D. Williston
1117 Dr. W. H. G. Logan

1018 Mr. & Mrs. J. F. Hecht
1074 Mr. & Mrs. Oscar Meyer
1084 Gen. & Mrs. Wm. B. Anderson
     Receiving day Thursday
1110 Mr. & Mrs. M. N. Simons

1117 Mrs. Anna Holt
1117 Rev. R. R. Stevens
1125 Mrs. Isabella W. Olin

EAST COURT.

se. cor. Belmont av. Mr. & Mrs. Wm.
    S. Granger

EASTWOOD AVENUE.

311 Mr. & Mrs. Joseph P. Tracy

EDGECOMB COURT.

1425 Lewis.E. Woodbury
1425 W. A. Woodbury
1463 Mr. & Mrs. Henry W. Wagner
1471 Mr. & Mrs. Pierre Funck

1444 Mr. & Mrs. Thomas Harrison
    & dr.
1444 C. Thomas Harrison
1454 Mr. & Mrs. George H. Wessling

ELAINE PLACE.

41 Mr. & Mrs. George E. Newlin
41 Dr. & Mrs. Ira B. Crissman

50 Mr. & Mrs. John Chiville

ELM STREET.

349 Herbert J. Davis
373 Dr. & Mrs. Charles F. Ely & dr.
379 Rev. & Mrs. James Grundy
383 Mrs. John Crampton & drs.
383 J. N. Crampton
383 George Mackay
383 David S. Mackay
407 Mrs. Edwards Corse
407 Redmond Prindiville
407 Thomas W. Prindiville
407 Miss Marguerite Prindiville
435 Mr. & Mrs. H. J. Porter
437 Mr. & Mrs. William S. Warren
441 Mr. & Mrs. Lloyd Milnor
443 Mr. & Mrs. John V. A. Weaver
445 Mr. & Mrs. Chas. M. Sherman
449 Mr. & Mrs. Chas. C. Gilbert
461 Mr. & Mrs Mau ice Prindiville
465 Mr. & Mrs. Moses J.Wentworth
467 Mr. & Mrs. John T. McAuley &
    dr.
471 Mr. & Mrs. Geo. D. McLaughlin
473 Mr. & Mrs. Arthur J. Magnus

474 Wilbur G. Bentley
474 Mrs. Belle Burnes
474 Mrs. Juliette Watters
474 Louis Carpenter
476 Mr. & Mrs. E. Y. Eltonhead
478 Mr. & Mrs. Charles H. Conover
    Receiving day Monday

408 Mr. & Mrs. John L. Hamilton
424 Mr. & Mrs. Hugh W. Montgomery
426 Mr. & Mrs. J. H. Curtis
428 Mrs. A. Lewandowska & drs.
    Receive Friday afternoon
430 Mr. & Mrs. Mason B. Starring
430 Mrs. A. M. Starring
432 Mr. & Mrs. WillisHowe
    Receiving day Monday
438 Mr. & Mrs. Albert F. Bullen
440 Mr. & Mrs. B. F. McConnell
442 Mr. & Mrs. Maurice Pincoffs
444 Dr. & Mrs. M. R. Brown
444 James Moreau Brown
446 Mr. & Mrs. Francis Keeling jr.
446 Mrs. Louisa Leonard
448 Mr. & Mrs. Oscar Charles
450 Mr. & Mrs. R. F. Keith
    Receiving day Thursday
452 Mr. & Mrs. William Fyffe
456 Mr. & Mrs. George S. Scott
456 David L. Gallup
456 Miss Agnes Gallup
462 Mr. & Mrs. P. J. Geraghty
466 Mr. & Mrs. Geo. Merryweather
    & dr.
466 A. M. Merryweather
470 Mr. & Mrs. James E. Eagle
472 Mr. & Mrs. F. A. Luce
472 Mrs. E. A. Prindle

ERIE STREET.

237 Dr. & Mrs. John Flood
267 Jonathan E. Woodbridge
311 Mr. & Mrs. H. H. Porter
311 Dr. & Mrs. Geo. S. Isham
317 Mr.& Mrs. Samuel M.Nickerson
 Receiving day Wednesday
317 Mr. & Mrs. Roland C. Nickerson
 Receiving day Wednesday
363 Henry I. Sheldon
363 Miss Sheldon
369 Mr. & Mrs. Louis E. Laflin
 Receives 1st and 3d.Thursday .
399 Gen. Walter C. Newberry
399 Miss M. L. Newberry
405 Mr. & Mrs. N. P. Bigelow
407 Mr. & Mrs. Tertius W. Wadsworth & drs.
 Receiving day Wednesday
409 Mr. & Mrs. A. A. Putnam
423 Dr. & Mrs. W. G. Cummins & drs.
429 Mr. & Mrs. Robert Hughes McCreary
 Receive Wednesday afternoon

———

406 Harry G. Sommers
406 Miss Lillian Sommers
408 Mr. & Mrs. Heaton Owsley

344 Mrs. Emmons Blaine
354 Mr. & Mrs. Frank W. Wentworth
354 Adam Thompson
360 Mr. & Mrs. Alphonso Bell Hudson
360 Miss Grace Hudson
360 Mr. & Mrs. Robert K. Reilly
360 James H. DeLany
360 Mr. & Mrs. Robert B. Peattie
360 Mrs. Elia W. Peattie
378 Mr. & Mrs. John T. Noyes & dr.
378 Ernest H. Noyes
380 Mrs. B. C. Davy & dr.
380 Harry Vincent
382 Mr. & Mrs. Thos. E. Copelin
384 Mr. & Mrs. William J. Quan
384 Henry W. Quan
384 James E. Quan
384 T. Albert Quan
386 Mr. & Mrs. Robert Mercer Parker & dr.
388 Mr. & Mrs. Robert T. Newberry
404 Mr. & Mrs. Victor Elting
404 P. L. F. Elting
404 Harrison G. Rhodes
406 Mr. & Mrs. Robt. Walker & dr.
 Receiving day Thursday
406 Herbert Walker

ESTES AVENUE.

505 Mr. & Mrs. George Q. Allen
763 Mr. & Mrs. Frank Hardcastle
767 Mr. & Mrs. James F. Pratt & dr.
767 Mrs. Emily M. Chaffin
767 George E. Pratt
817 Mr. & Mrs. Josiah T. Hair
817 Mrs. Amanda M. Ross

522 Mr. & Mrs. A. P. Clark Matson
550 Mr. & Mrs. H. G. Wright
620 Mr. & Mrs. Cassius E. Hillyer
902 Mr. & Mrs. John I. Marshall

———

821 Mr. & Mrs. Charles Adams

EUGENIE STREET.

157 Dr. & Mrs. Willard C. Sanford
159 Mr. & Mrs. Thomas A. Quinlan & drs.
 Receiving day Monday
159 Thomas A. Quinlan jr.
159 Daniel V. Casey
159½ Mr. & Mrs. Frank E. Nellis
 Receiving day Thursday

170 Mr. & Mrs. A. Holinger & drs.
174 Dr. Joseph Beck
174 Dr. Carl Beck

———

161 Mr. & Mrs. Thos. E. Gilpin
165 Dr. & Mrs. Henry Gradle
173 Mr. & Mrs. Samuel F. Boyd

EVANSTON AVENUE.

105 Mr. & Mrs. E. William Kalb
    Receiving day Friday.
107 Mr. & Mrs. Wm. A. Fuhring
    Receiving day Wednesday
109 Dr. & Mrs. Wesley M. Thomas
119 Mr. & Mrs. R. S. Elder
147 Mr. & Mrs. Otto Sommer & dr.
    Receive 1st & last Wednesday.
151 Mrs. A. B. Watkins
151 Frank A. Watkins
161 Mr. & Mrs. Adam Schneider
    Receiving day Tuesday
175 Mr. & Mrs. L. B. Hitchings
    Receiving day Thursday
175 C. L. Hitchings
175 Mrs. C. B. Allen
    Receiving day Thursday
179 Mr. & Mrs. Tabor P. Randall
179 Miss Grace Childs
179 Mrs. A. S. Randall
237 Mr. & Mrs. John Felbinger & dr.
283 Mr. & Mrs. F. F. Henning
385 Mrs. John Koch & drs.
385 Mr. & Mrs. John M. Bredt
395 Mr. & Mrs. J. C. Morper & dr.
    Receiving day Thursday
427 Mr. & Mrs. William S. Young
437 Mr. & Mrs. William Hudson
437 Frank W. Hudson
453 Mr. & Mrs. J. D. McIlvaine
457 Mr. & Mrs. S. W. McCaslin
    Receiving day Tuesday
457 Miss Eva Hubbard
    Receiving day Tuesday
543 Mr. & Mrs. Joseph E. Tilt & drs.
543 Arthur C. Tilt
575 Mr. & Mrs. Frederick T. Weigle
693 Mr. & Mrs. Oliver Colborne & drs.
907 Mrs. Eliza Mize
907 Mrs. Hattie A. Bischoff
917 Mr. & Mrs. James Nicol
917 Mrs. M. M. VanRensselaer
921 Mr. & Mrs. Jas. Stuart Templeton
921 James E. Templeton
sw. cor. Buena av. Mrs. James B.
    Waller & drs.
1031 Mr. & Mrs. Thos. H. Condell
    & drs.
1031 Dr. & Mrs. Frank Jenney
1035 Mr. & Mrs. John Bradley Carse

96 Mr. & Mrs. Granville Bates & drs.
158 Dr. & Mrs. Ethan A. Gray
158 Dr. E. L. Holmes
158 Miss Jennie R. Holmes
160 Mr. & Mrs. L. L. Schloss
296 Mr. & Mrs. Adolph Schoeninger
310 Mr. & Mrs. Herman H. Hoffmann
310 Benjamin S. Hoffmann
310 Harry H. Hoffmann
488 Mrs. T. Howard
514 Dr. & Mrs. Louis L. Gregory
534 Mr. & Mrs. James Payne
534 Mr. & Mrs. R. Preston Payne
534 Frank D. Payne
580 Mrs. H. F. Spread & dr.
    Receiving day Wednesday
614 Mrs. Ida Jordan
    Receiving day last Wednesday in mo.
614 Gustav Jordan
636 Mr. & Mrs. S. Frank Eagle
    Receiving day Tuesday
664 Mr. & Mrs. Karl Eitel
    Receiving day Tuesday
890 Dr. & Mrs. S. P. Hedges & dr.
890 William E. Hedges
912 Mr. & Mrs. J. Wyndham-Quinn Channer
1026 Mr. & Mrs. F. Geudtner
    Receiving day 1st Saturday in mo.
1026 Charles P. Geudtner
1050 Rev. & Mrs. Frank M. Carson
1078 Mr. & Mrs. Frank E. Habicht
1088 Mr. & Mrs. C. A. Spoehr
1792 Mr. & Mrs. H. H. Bloss
    Receiving day Friday
2664 Mr. & Mrs. John D. Hood
2678 Mrs. Harriet E. Cozzens
2678 Fred B. Cozzens
2682 Mr. & Mrs. Lewis F. Chapman
2704 Mr. & Mrs. T. J. Sellinger

———

1039 Mr. & Mrs. Hart Taylor
2653 Mr. & Mrs. Cyrus M. Avery
2653 Mrs. Isabella Sinn
    Receiving day Thursday
2659 Mr. & Mrs. Henry A. Ritter
2659 Mrs. S. A. Louderback

FARGO AVENUE.

811 Mr. & Mrs. Harry C. Edwards
811 Eugene Edwards
915 Mr. & Mrs. William I.McMaster

930 Mr.& Mrs. William E. Harman
936 Mr. & Mrs. Thomas W. Kava-
    nagh
1018 Mr.& Mrs.Wm. E.Vandervoort

FARWELL AVENUE.

467 Mr. & Mrs. Edward Lowy
501 Mr. & Mrs. A. H. Snyder
501 Mr. & Mrs. B. F. Snyder
501 Mr. & Mrs. Jacob Snyder & dr.
545 Mr. & Mrs. Merrick B. Dean
711 Mrs. M. A. Titus & dr.
729 Mr. & Mrs. Walter M. Sempill
811 Mr. & Mrs. William H. Titus
915 Mr. & Mrs. Gilbert C. Pryor
947 Mr. & Mrs. Chas. M. Bickford

464 Mr. & Mrs. H. C. Foster & dr.
464 Miss Florence S. Keeler
464 William H. Foster
812 M. S. Brady & dr.
904 Mr. & Mrs. Fred J. Holzapfel
1020 Mr. & Mrs. A. L. Evans

947 Mrs. Cornelia Ray
1005 Mr. & Mrs. Benj. Smith

FRÁNCIS STREET.

1032 Mr. & Mrs. T. C. Hardy
1070 Mr. & Mrs. L. S. Swanson

1074 Mr.&Mrs. Wm. M. Coulter&dr.
1074 E. F. Coulter

FREMONT STREET.

183 Rev. & Mrs. Karl Schmidt
195 Dr. & Mrs. Wilhelm Thies & dr.
        Receive Thursday
197 Mr. & Mrs. Harold Zimmerman
199 Miss Mamie Kettering
207 William Kreicker
209 Mr. & Mrs. Gustav Pick
209 Richard A. Pick
211 Mr. & Mrs. David Schnitzer
221 Mr. & Mrs. Judson F. Going
225 Mr. & Mrs. William Harms
259 Mr. & Mrs. John Bradford
265 Mr. & Mrs. Adolph Graeff
265 Alfred Graeff
259 Mr. & Mrs. W. N. Van Matre
261 Mr. & Mrs. W. H. Rattray
277 Mr. & Mrs. Jacob Lengacher

168 Henry W. Heuermann & drs.
202 Mr. & Mrs. C. D. Shoemaker
220 Mrs. Charlotte Cohen
226 Mr. & Mrs. Leopold Sonnen-
    schein
228A Mr. & Mrs. Adolph L. Kraus
228B Mrs. Jacob Danek
228B Miss Rosa Keller
260 Mr. & Mrs. H. H. Hirschfield
266 Mr. & Mrs. Charles Steinbeiss
268 Mr. & Mrs. Wm. C. Pfister
278 Mr. & Mrs. John Baur
        Receive Thursday
278 Henry Breidenstein

277 Oscar F. Lengacher

FULLERTON AVENUE.

465 Mrs. Charles H. Cowan
465 Harry R. Cowan
471 Prof. & Mrs. E. M. Booth & dr.
475 Mrs. V. Rolfe & dr.
479 Dr. Jessie G. Forrester
483 Mrs. F. B. Hosmer
485 Dr. & Mrs. Willis D. Storer
487 Mr. & Mrs. John C. Ambler
487 Miss Margaret Jarvis
491 Mr. & Mrs. Arthur Temple
495 Mrs. Annie Watson

274 Mr. & Mrs. Albert J. Ward
280 John McDonald
280 Harry J. McDonald
336 Mrs. C. O. Becker
342 Dr. & Mrs. J. Johnston Bell
        Receiving day Wednesday
342 Mrs. Hattie Myers & dr.
364 Mr. & Mrs. Michael Cahill& drs.
466 Mrs. Edward G. Garden
468 Mr. & Mrs. R. F. Maxwell
468 Dr. & Mrs. Wm. E. Pilcher

497 Mr. & Mrs. John S. Barrow
501 Mr. & Mrs. John Woodbridge
503 Mr. & Mrs. William M. Gregg
& dr.
503 Dr. Mary E. Gregg
509 Mr. & Mrs. R. S. Benham
Receiving day Thursday
509 Miss Florence A. Marrow
511 Mr. & Mrs. S. Mendelsohn
631 Mr. & Mrs. A. Schweitzer
631 Mr. & Mrs. Philip Dreesbach
637 Mrs. H. R. Medcalfe
637 Mr. & Mrs. Alfred R. Varian
637 Samuel W. Crawford
639 Mrs. Margaret Revell & dr.
639 J. T. Revell
639 D. J. Revell
639 Mrs. Mary Skelly
641 Mr. & Mrs. P. Peterson & dr.
643 Mr. & Mrs. Ernest Ammon
643 Frederick E. Ammon
645 Mr. & Mrs. Simon Blum
647 Mr. & Mrs. Louis Muench
649 Mr. & Mrs. Albert Miller
649 Mrs. Herman Kirchstein
651 Mr. & Mrs. Wicliff Peterson
657 Mr. & Mrs. Frederick Hauck
661 Mrs. Chas. H. Summers
661 Mr. & Mrs. L. L. Summers
669 J. Hamilton Farrar
679 Walter Lovegrove
681 Dr. & Mrs. J. J. Thompson
683 Mr. & Mrs. J. Henry Pank
685 Mr. & Mrs. Herman Vollmer
693 Mr.& Mrs. F. Herman Roessler
695 Mr. & Mrs. Henry Schaller
717 Mrs. John C. Barker
719 Mr.& Mrs.H.Hemmelgarn
719 Mr. & Mrs. A. von Glahn
725 Mr. & Mrs. G. G. Glaescher
725 Mr. & Mrs. Edward A. Parker
727 Miss Isabel McDougall
727 Mr. & Mrs. Arthur M. Morse
729 Mr. & Mrs. Frank M. Utt
729 Mr. & Mrs. Thos. C. Clark
729 Mr. & Mrs. W. S. Burling
Receiving day Thursday
731 Mr. & Mrs. Willis L. Goodwillie
789 Mrs. Julia F. Porter
789 James W. Porter
789 James F. Porter
789 Mrs. N. S. Foster

736 Mrs. E. E. Stelle
742 Miss Margaret Schultz

480 Mr. & Mrs. Bryan Y. Craig
484 Mr. & Mrs. Leander Sawyer
498 Mr. & Mrs. H. Howard Meriam
498 Mr. & Mrs. George Newkirk &
drs.
500 Mr. & Mrs. Edward Cheetham
508 Mr. & Mrs. W. R. Morrison
512 Dr. & Mrs. J. E. Hequembourg
Receiving day Thursday
518 Mr. & Mrs. H. C. Grosse & drs.
522 Mrs. W. W. Younglove & dr.
526 Mr. & Mrs.Wm. F.Zimmermann
568 Mrs. Mary Hassmer & dr.
568 Joseph A. Hassmer
570 Mrs. Lucy A. Lydston
572 Henry E. Ackerburg
574 Mr. & Mrs. Chas. H. Wallace
576 Dr. E. I. Kerlin
578 Mr. & Mrs. Justice Wilson
584 Dr. & Mrs. Albert H. Andrews
588 Mr. & Mrs. John W. Hasburg
590 Dr. & Mrs. Alex. C. Wiener
592 Mr. & Mrs. Max Tonk
624 Mr. & Mrs. Walter Butler
628 Mr. & Mrs. Zero Marx
638 Mr. & Mrs. C. A. Tinkham
638 Mrs. S. B. Titcomb & dr.
638 Arthur B. Titcomb
640 Mr. & Mrs. W. P. Dunn
Receiving day Thursday
640 Mrs. A. A. Pettengill
640 Miss Olive Holmes
642 Mr. & Mrs. Ernest Hecht
644 Mr. & Mrs. F. H. Guhl & dr.
Receiving day Wednesday
644 Walter F. Guhl
646 Dr. & Mrs. Clarendon Rutherford
650 Mr. & Mrs. L. O. Kohtz
654 Mr. & Mrs. Eugene Lipkau
656 Mr. & Mrs. L. Schaffner & drs.
656 Mr. & Mrs. Julius P. Meyer
674 Mrs. Daniel Jackson & dr.
674 Miss M. E. Philbrick
678 Mr. & Mrs. Anthony Freeman
690 Mr. & Mrs. J. D. Zernitz
690 Julius C. Zernitz
698 M. W. Robinson
698 Miss Ethel Robinson
700 Rev. &. Mrs. John H. Edwards
Receiving day Tuesday
712 Mr. & Mrs. C. M. Staiger
716 Dr. & Mrs. Gustav Futterer
720 Mr. & Mrs. J. Brucker
726 Mr. & Mrs. Edward A. Groetzinger

742 Miss Sallie Schultz
744 Mr. & Mrs. Charles B. Burt
746 Mr. & Mrs. Frank B. Bigelow
748 Mr. & Mrs. A. L. Balmer

748 Mr. & Mrs. Chas. E. Calm
748 Mr. & Mrs. Abraham Lamm
754 Dr. & Mrs. A. P. Hedges
754 Miss Carrie Pratt

GARFIELD AVENUE.

525 Mr. & Mrs. Olaf Vider
529 Mr. & Mrs. T. H. Lovejoy
531 Mr. & Mrs. J. Z. Vogelsang
531 Dr. & Mrs. A. S. Wais

536 Mrs. Jean Waldron
536 Mr. & Mrs. L. K. Waldron
566 Dr. & Mrs. Evan E. Gwynne

396 Mr. & Mrs. Sam. B. Chase & dr.
442 Mr. & Mrs. E. C. Jager & drs.
450 Dr. & Mrs. W. P. Verity
458 Mr.& Mrs. Solomon Mayer & dr.
458 Simon Mayer
486 Mr. & Mrs. Philip Apfel
524 Mrs. Anna Stearns
526 Mrs. Alice Houghton
528 Gerhard Huessen

GARY PLACE.

1718 Mr. & Mrs. Arthur Labes

GEORGE STREET.

1503 Mr. & Mrs. W. B. Getty

1258 Mr. & Mrs. Jos. Alexander
        Receiving day Thursday

1252 Mr. & Mrs. Hans Schloetzer
        Receiving day Saturday
1252 Mrs. E. T. Schloetzer
        Receiving day Wednesday
1332 Mr. & Mrs. Chas. E. Bateman

GOETHE STREET.

151 Mrs. E. Rhode
151 Rudolph E. Rhode
151 Otto Rhode
151 Mr. & Mrs. John Dillon
151 Mr. & Mrs. Adolph H. Hertz
153 Mr. & Mrs. Robert N. Stites
175 Mr. & Mrs. John Valentine
205 Mr. & Mrs. John Dorr Bradley
205 Mr. & Mrs. Arthur L. Farwell
205 Mr. & Mrs. Wilson LeRoy Mead
205 Solomon Sturges
205 Washington G. Sturges
205 Albert Sturges
205 Miss Mary D. Sturges
205 Mr. & Mrs. Frederick A. Smith
205 Miss Helen E. Snow
205 Mr. & Mrs. Russell Tyson
205 Mr. & Mrs. Chas. Dyer Norton
205 James H. Peirce
247 Mr.&Mrs.EdwinScottMatthews
249 Mr. & Mrs. W. Ewen & drs.
251 Henry B. Clarke

122 Mr. & Mrs. Andrew L. Williams
180 John George Graue
196 Mr. & Mrs. Fred A. Cary
198 Dr. & Mrs. Eugene S. Tarbot
200 Mr. & Mrs. Frederick T. Vaux
202 James H. Peirce
204 Mr. & Mrs. C. F. Spalding
        Receive Monday
206 Mr. & Mrs. Wm. H. Beebe &
        drs. *Receiving day Monday*
206 William H. Beebe jr.
208 Mr. & Mrs. J. V. Clarke
210 Mr. & Mrs. Emerson H. Brush
        Receive Wednesday afternoon
212 Mr. & Mrs. H. R. Durkee
214 Mr. & Mrs. Dwight W. Graves
214 W. H. Gallenkamp
240 Mrs. Wm. C. Goudy
240 Mr. & Mrs. Ira Jewett Geer

251 Louis B. Clarke
251 Miss M. L. Clarke

GORDON TERRACE.

7 Mr. & Mrs. Chas. S. Winslow
17 Mr. & Mrs. Geo. W. Keehn
17 Cyrus R. Shipman
17 Mrs. Harriet E. Fry
27 Mr. & Mrs. Wm. B. Mundie
41 Mr. & Mrs. Chas. A. Adams
47 Mr. & Mrs. G. E. Foss
Receiving day Friday
47 Mr. & Mrs. G. Edmund Foss

8 Mr. & Mrs. F. T. Simmons
8 Miss Mary K. Busch
18 Mr. & Mrs. Edward M. Murray
48 Mr. & Mrs. T. Deykes Whitney
Receiving day Thursday
48 George B. Whitney
———
57 Dr. & Mrs. Joseph Haven

GRACE STREET.

733 Dr. & Mrs. Walter H. Marble
1235 Mr. & Mrs. H. P. Schwennesen
1525 Fred W. Henning
1702 Mr. & Mrs. Fred'k Seeman & dr.

1525 Mr.& Mrs. Wm. Henning & dr.
Receiving day Thursday
1619 Mr. & Mrs. Henry Suder

GRACELAND AVENUE.

1478 Mr. & Mrs. David S. Anderson
Receiving day Wednesday
1478 Miss Theresa M. Anderson
———
cor. Lake Shore, Mr. & Mrs. Ralph Stebbins Greenlee
Mrs. Emily Brooks

ne. cor. Clarendon av., Mr. & Mrs. Luther Laflin Mills
Matthew Mills
1649 Mr. & Mrs. W. J. Bulger
cor. Lake Shore, Mr. & Mrs. James A. Lounsbury

GRANT PLACE.

57 Mr. & Mrs. George Kersten

73 Dr. & Mrs. William Doepp

GRANVILLE AVENUE.

1112 Mr. & Mrs. Geo. H. Lill
1118 Mr. & Mrs. Wm. Lill

1146 Mr. & Mrs. John B. Berryman
1150 Mr. & Mrs. W. J. Lukens

GREENLEAF AVENUE.

47 Mr. & Mrs. Alvah B. Mathews
203 Mr. & Mrs. Frank W. Loomis
517 Rev. & Mrs. Clarence Abel
523 Mr. & Mrs. Cephas H. Leach
531 Mr. & Mrs. Edmund Morier
539 Mr. & Mrs. Francis P. Sullivan
803 Charles F. Bunte
803 Mr. & Mrs. Ferdinand Bunte & dr.
835 M. Bates Iott & drs.
929 Mr. & Mrs. Charles Galloway
949 Dr. E. L. Kern
949 Dr. & Mrs. Frank L. Browne

832 Mr. & Mrs. C. H. Stoelting
928 Mr. & Mrs. Fred W. Gilbert
946 Mr. & Mrs. Francis DePfuhl
948 Mr. & Mrs. Llewellyn Dutton
1038 Mr. & Mrs. Jas. I. Ennis

504 Mr. & Mrs. Charles R. Adams
510 Mr. & Mrs. E. E. Johnson
510 Mr. & Mrs. Milton H. Johnson
532 Mr. & Mrs. J. R. Spicer
538 Mr. & Mrs. Albert O. Swift& dr.
538 Mrs. Mary Swift
538 Mrs. Sarah A. Smalley
602 Mr. & Mrs. Geo. R. Hinners
630 Mrs. Celia A. Nelson
630 Mrs. S. A. Leach
750 Dr. & Mrs. Edward L. Webb
762 Forest Hotel nw. cor. Forest av.
Mrs. S. C. Burdsal
Mr. & Mrs. D. L. Crawford
Mr. & Mrs. Geo. W. Flagg
Mr. & Mrs. C. Shackleford
Mr. & Mrs. Samuel D. Snow
Dr. Albert A. Sweet
810 Mr. & Mrs. Asahel Newton

NORTH HALSTED STREET.

701 Mr. & Mrs. Frank Diesel
1009 Rev. & Mrs. O. H. Cessna
1011 Mr. & Mrs. Rupert Coleman
1011 Mrs. Samuel Thorpe & dr.
1271 Dr. & Mrs. Alfred F. Sproesser
1375 Mr. & Mrs. William H. Peacock
1377 Mr. & Mrs. Francis W. Savage
    & dr.
1377 Mr. & Mrs. Edward P. Savage
1511 Andrew Bolter
1547 Mr. & Mrs. Robert R. Clarke
1547 Miss Blanche Bassett
1661 Mr. & Mrs. Arthur Schroeder

916 Mrs. Wm. Greiner & dr.
1022 Dr. & Mrs. W. A. Kimmet
1038 Mr. & Mrs. James M. Hills
1042 Dr. & Mrs. A. S. Carrier
1048 Rev. & Mrs. Willis G. Craig &
    dr.
1070 Rev. & Mrs. Herrick Johnson
1518 Mr. & Mrs. Carl Roehl & drs.
1594 Dr. & Mrs. F. D. Porter
1806 Dr. & Mrs. Frank M. Brewer
    ———
1681 Mr. & Mrs. Wm. Boldenweck
1799 Mr. & Mrs. Theo. Even

HAMILTON COURT.

869 Mr. & Mrs. A. V. Julin
871 Mr. & Mrs. Arthur Hawxhurst
899 Mrs. P. F. Eckstorm & drs.
899 Christian A. Eckstorm
    ———
916 Mr. & Mrs. Geo. N. Oberne

856 Mr. & Mrs. James F. Bate
862 Mrs. H. Gerstenberg & dr.
864 Mr. & Mrs. A. H. Apfel
910 Mr. & Mrs. E. P. McNaughten
    Receiving day Wednesday
912 Mr. & Mrs. E. F. Heinze
914 Mr. & Mrs. F. G. Heinze

HAMMOND STREET.

81 Mrs. Annie E. Buckie. & drs.

92 Mr. & Mrs. Martin A. Fiedler

HAMPDEN COURT.

219 Mr. & Mrs. Wm. W. Vernon
221 Mr. & Mrs. John S. Butler
221 Mr. & Mrs. Geo. W. Plummer
    Receiving day Friday
223 Mr. & Mrs. Frank P. Schmitt jr.
223 Mr. & Mrs. Wm. A. Sittig
227 Mr. & Mrs. Louis Bartling
227 William Bartling
227 Mr. & Mrs. Bruno M. Mai
231 Mrs. John Freeman
233 Mr. & Mrs. J. H. Frank & dr.
233 Mortimer Frank
239 Mr. & Mrs. F. A. Winslow
241 Dr. & Mrs. C. L. Clancy & dr.
241 Mr. & Mrs. Bernard J. Nockin
315 Mr. & Mrs. G. Douglas Potter
323 Mr. & Mrs. Frank J. Schaub
323 Peter A. Schaub
325 Mr. & Mrs. Gottlieb F. Schwarz
    & dr.
331 Mr. & Mrs. Alexander Fish
335 Mr. & Mrs. J. E. Martine
335 Mr. & Mrs. Edgar C. Smith
337 Mr. & Mrs. Robt. J. McLaughlin
345 Mr. & Mrs. Philip Maas

230 Mr. & Mrs. Wm. H. Howard
234 Mr. & Mrs. Chas. G. Y. King
240 Dr. & Mrs. Albert L. Farr & dr.
240 Mr. & Mrs. Wm. T. Scudder
242 Mr. & Mrs. E. D. Steen
242 Mr. & Mrs. James C. McMath
244 Mr. & Mrs. Adolph Uhrlaub
244 Mr. & Mrs. Adolph Stark
318 Mr. & Mrs. Reuben A. Denell
320 Mr. & Mrs. Hugh W. Dyar
326 Mr. & Mrs. Francis M. Taber
328 Mr. & Mrs. Arthur Leask
330 Mr. & Mrs. Wallace Wilson
332 Mr. & Mrs. Percival Steele
    Receiving day Tuesday
334 Mr. & Mrs. Hugh M. Wilson
334 Mr. & Mrs. Chas. F. Hamilton
334 Dr. & Mrs. John D. Andrews
340 Mrs. H. W. Jenney
    ———
345 Fred Maas
349 William C. Heinemann
349 Alfred R. Heinemann
349 Mr. & Mrs. William Heinemann
    & dr.

HAWTHORNE PLACE.

17 Mr. & Mrs. Azel F. Hatch
27 Mr. & Mrs. Philip C. Dyrenforth
27 Arthur Dyrenforth
37 Mr. & Mrs. H. H. Hettler
63 Mr. & Mrs. Rockwell A. King

10 Mr. & Mrs. Willis F. Johnson
10 Miss A. Blanche Johnson
30 Mr. & Mrs. George E. Marshall
30 Mrs A. J. Marshall
32 Mr. & Mrs. Geo. W. Low
60 Mr. & Mrs. John McConnell
60 Edward D. McConnell

HAZEL AVENUE.

41 Mr. & Mrs. W. F. Lubeke

NORTH HERMITAGE AVENUE.

2293 Mrs. Catherine Lang
2303 Mr. & Mrs. Julius N. Zeither
2339 Mrs. Eva Stewart Miller
2341 Mr. & Mrs. Fred'k C. Voss
2433 Mr. & Mrs. James S.McDonald jr.
2439 Mr. & Mrs. Charles A. Vail
2443 Mr. & Mrs. S. Frank Champlin
2449 Mr. & Mrs. Lloyd Canaday
2453 Mrs. H. Goodfellow & dr.
2475 Mr. & Mrs. John W. Salladay
2485 Mr. & Mrs. Charles A. Jennings
2487 Mr. & Mrs. Chas. A. Hollister
2509 Mr. & Mrs. Edwin M. Clark
2515 Mr. & Mrs. Frank P. Eyman
2541 Dr. & Mrs. Thomas A. Broadbent
2547 Miss Ellen Reedy •
Receiving day Tuesday
2567 Mr. & Mrs. Grant Newell
2585 Rev. & Mrs. William A. Lloyd
2585 Robert C. Lloyd
2603 Mrs. Sarah E. Watt
2607 Mr. & Mrs. Frank P. Collier
2609 Mr. & Mrs. Albert L. Stone
2613 Mr. & Mrs. Ferdinand Barnickol
2667 Mr. & Mrs.Charles W. Slauson
2671 Mr. & Mrs. George F. Koester
2675 Mr. & Mrs. Geo. W. Cope
2809 Mr.&Mrs. George R. Thomson
2835 Mr. & Mrs. S. Suton
2839 Mr. & Mrs. J. O. Wright

2846 Mr. & Mrs.Joseph E.Flanagan
Receiving day Thursday

2410 Mr. & Mrs. James S. McDonald & drs.
2412 Mr. & Mrs. Henry H. Roberts
2430 Miss May E. Gates
2430 Frank H. Frost
2434 Mr. & Mrs. H. P. Decker
2440 Mr. & Mrs. John E. Nelson
2444 Mr. & Mrs. A. S. Terrill
2478 Mr. & Mrs. Geo. Anderson
2478 H. A. Anderson
2486 Mr. & Mrs. Volney Chase
2490 Mr. & Mrs. Oscar J. Bersbach
2548 Mr. & Mrs. Samuel Powell
2558 Mr. & Mrs. L. F. Koehn jr.
2568 Mr. & Mrs. Alfred Bersbach
2574 Mr.& Mrs. William A.Gardner
2578 Mr. & Mrs. J. E. Martin
2588 Dr. & Mrs. Harry Parsons
2614 Mr. & Mrs. James W. Andrews
2614 Carlos S. Andrews
2614 J. Roy Andrews
2620 Albright Griffeth
2620 Abraham L. Griffeth
2624 Mr. & Mrs. George H. Bryant
2636 Mr. & Mrs. DeWitt Van Evera
2640 Dr. & Mrs. Peter H. Pursell
2666 Dr. & Mrs. Wallace C. Abbott
2680 Mr. & Mrs. T. D. Pickard
2684 Mr. & Mrs. Chas. P. Willems
2720 Dr. Stafford T. Mitchell
2742 Mrs. Anna M. Emrich & dr.
2742 William H. Emrich
2754 Mr. & Mrs. Charles G. Macklin
2764 Mr. & Mrs. J. B. Morrow
2832 Mr.& Mrs. Lewis P. Hammond
2840 Mr. & Mrs. William C. Biedenweg

HOLLYWOOD AVENUE.

1327 Mr. & Mrs. Thomas Balmer

1328 Mr. & Mrs. Jos. Lyman Silsbee

HOWE STREET.

61 Mr. & Mrs. Geo. J. Schmidt & drs.
163 Mr. & Mrs. A. C. Schmidt
   Receiving day Wednesday
165 Mr. & Mrs. J. M. Hitchcock

170 Mr. & Mrs. Charles N. Hale
173 Mr. & Mrs. A. J. Anderson
175 Dr. & Mrs. Chas. B. Prouty
175 James H. Prouty

HURON STREET.

271 Mr. & Mrs. C. A. Winship
289 Mr. & Mrs. W. M. Devine & drs.
   Receiving day Thursday
289 J. A. Devine
289 W. P. Devine
289 Arthur J. Devine
291 Dr. & Mrs. N. S. Davis
291 Dr. & Mrs. N. S. Davis jr.
295 Mr. & Mrs. David Rutter & dr.
   Receiving day Wednesday
295 Lynn R. Rutter
295 Max Rutter
299 Miss Eliza Allen Starr
   Receiving day Wednesday
299 Mrs. C. W. W. Wellington
   Receiving day Wednesday
301 Mr. & Mrs. Frederick W. Crosby
305 Mr. & Mrs. C. F. Pietsch
307 Mr. & Mrs. S. Harris Pomeroy
309 Mr. & Mrs. James C. Peasley
313 Mrs. J. S. Rumsey & drs.
313 J. M. Rumsey
321 Mr. & Mrs. Cyrus Hall McCormick
405 Judge & Mrs. Samuel P. McConnell & dr.
   Receiving day Wednesday
407 Mr. & Mrs. William H. French
407 Mrs. Caroline Bowen
407 Ira P. Bowen
409 Mrs. John Mountain & drs.
411 Mr. & Mrs. Arthur A. Maclean
411 Henry Memory & dr.

268 Mr. & Mrs. John H. Drury
270 Dr. & Mrs. F. A. Leusman
   Receiving day Thursday
272 Dr. & Mrs. Robert Laughlin Rea
   Receiving day Thursday
272 Gilbert Beebe Manlove
286 Lewis Edward Dickinson
288 Dr. Otto T. Freer
288 Mrs. Catherine Freer & dr.
330 Mrs. Anna Kilcoyne & drs.
332 Mr. & Mrs. M. F. Mallory
336 Mr. & Mrs. P. J. Quinn
   Receiving day Wednesday
354 Frank Hamlin
354 Robert F. Shanklin
354 William W. Rathborne
354 Mr. & Mrs. Harry L. Wilbur
422 Mr. & Mrs. Eugene H. Fishburn
422 Randolph E. Fishburn

413 Mr. & Mrs. O. Chanute & drs.
413 Mrs. A. E. Boyd
415 Mrs. Katherine P. Capps
415 Russell Colgate
415 J. M. Knapp
421 Mr. & Mrs. James H. Walker
421 James H. Walker jr.
423 Mr. & Mrs. Walter A. Cissna
   Receiving day Tuesday
423 Mrs. M. L. Kinney
425 Mr. & Mrs. Horace E. Stump
427 Mr. & Mrs. George F. Gail

INDIANA STREET.

297 Dr. & Mrs. L. H. Watson
305 Mrs. Alice P. Raymond
337 Rev. & Mrs. E. J. Alden & drs.

337 Carroll S. Alden
337 Emmons J. Alden
337 Dr. Ezekiel W. Clowes

JUNIOR TERRACE.

23 Mr. & Mrs. Charles Weber
39 Mr. & Mrs. Charles H. Bolster & dr.
39 Mr. & Mrs. J. Frank Smith

26 Mr. & Mrs. Edward Dickinson
44 Mr. & Mrs. A. W. Hester

·KEMPER PLACE.

15 Dr. & Mrs. W. W. Wetherla
17 Mr. & Mrs. Geo. F. Francis

19 Mrs. Sage G. Halla & dr.

KENESAW TERRACE.

131 Mr. & Mrs. W. W. Butterfield

8 Mr. & Mrs. John C. Scales
132 Mr. & Mrs. D. W. Campbell

KENMORE AVENUE.

1547 Mrs. George S. Smith
 Receiving day Tuesday
1549 Mr. & Mrs. T. W. Algeo
1551 Mr. & Mrs. F. J. Casterline
1573 Mr. & Mrs. Emery S. Walker
1573 Mrs. Betsey Walker
1577 Mr. & Mrs. David E. Platter
1593 Mr. & Mrs. G. M. Eddy
1599 Mr. & Mrs. Benj. T. VanAlen
 & dr.
1599 Walter T. Van Alen
1687 Mr. & Mrs. E. J. Nally
1691 Mr. & Mrs. Everett B. Deming
1693 Mrs. Elizabeth Copeland
1729 P. P. Pease
1729 P. P. Pease jr.
1737 Mr. & Mrs. I. J. Hodges
1737 Mrs. Eunice Thurston
1959 Mr. & Mrs. F. G. Ely
2089 Mr. & Mrs. J. C. Zipprich
2093 Mr. & Mrs. J. B. Wayman
2139 Mr. & Mrs. Henry Frankfurter
2145 Mr. & Mrs. T. C. Ketcham
2149 Mr. & Mrs. James P. Robertson
2155 Mr. & Mrs. J. W. Robertson
2169 Mr. & Mrs. A. F. Portman
2169 Miss May Faron
2193 Mr. & Mrs. L. G. Stiles
2197 Mr. & Mrs. M. Otis Hower
2207 Mr. & Mrs. John F. Lamberton
2207 Mr. & Mrs. B. W. Robbins
2227 Mr. & Mrs. T. C. Massey
2237 Rev. & Mrs. Frank D. Sheets
2241 Mr. & Mrs. Chas. V. Peckham
 Receiving day Thursday
2247 Mr. & Mrs. Wm. A. Vawter
2251 Mrs. Mary J. Dolph
2251 Mr. & Mrs. Edward Holden
2251 Miss Eva Adams
2337 Mr. & Mrs. Chas. H. King
2443 Mr. & Mrs. George J. Brine
2455 Mr. & Mrs. George I. Jones
2465 Judge & Mrs. Nathaniel Glinton Sears
2465 Mr. & Mrs. Amos G. Sears

1524 Mr. & Mrs. Philip Hahn
1524 Mr. & Mrs. Harry T. Aspern
1524 Mr. & Mrs. Edgar A. Bedford
1524 Mr. & Mrs. J. J. O'Donnell
1528 Mr. & Mrs. N. G. Harris
1528 Mrs. Catherine Miller
1528 George F. Miller
1540 Mr. & Mrs. C. W. Dingman
1544 Mr. & Mrs. Herman B. Seely
1546 Mr. & Mrs. Alfred A. Maynard
1558 Mr. & Mrs. James I. Hazard
1574 Mr. & Mrs. M. W. Phalen
 Receiving day Wednesday
1574 Frank J. Phalen
1600 Mr. & Mrs. Christian Koerner
 jr.
1600 Mr. & Mrs. Herbert Clark
1606 Edmund H. Taylor
1612 Mr. & Mrs. Richard H. Duryee
1630 Mr. & Mrs. J. B. Garner
1672 Mr. & Mrs. France Hempstead
1674 Edward L. Thornton
1674 Everett Thornton
1674 Miss Eva Thornton
1676 Mr. & Mrs. Geo. O. Fairbanks
1678 C. F. Loesch & dr.
1688 Mrs. Katharine J. Lobdell
1698 Mr. & Mrs. Chas. E. Lake
 Receiving day Wednesday
1698 Fred Irving Lake
1706 Mr. & Mrs. George Warrington
 Receiving day Wednesday
1706 Earl Chester
1718 Dr. & Mrs. G. F. Hawley
1718 Mr. & Mrs. H. A. Allen
1728 Mr. & Mrs. Henry F. Walliser
2056 Mr. & Mrs. Wm. McDonnell
 & dr.
2110 Mr. & Mrs. John C. Curtiss
2110 Mr. & Mrs. Alfred Lindell
2130 Mr. & Mrs. J. H. Dodson
2146 Mrs. C. A. Hoover
2146 Mr. & Mrs. E. L. Fitz Randolph
2170 Mr. & Mrs. Edward C. Portman
2194 Mr. & Mrs. J. H. Platt

2469 Mr. & Mrs. Jesse K. Farley
2479 Mr. & Mrs. A. A. Thomas
2487 Mr. & Mrs. Wm. R. Collins
2487 Harrie B. Collins
2505 Mr. & Mrs. Robert Clark
2505 Mr. & Mrs. Edwin H. Welch
2515 Mr.& Mrs. Francis E. Donohoe
2517 Mr. & Mrs. Chas. A. Birney
2517 Mrs. Laura B. French
2521 Dr. & Mrs. B. L. Hotchkin
2527 Mr. & Mrs. Jacob W. Skinkle
2527 George E. Skinkle
2537 Mr. & Mrs. E. J. Cusack
2545 Mr. & Mrs. Herbert F. Perkins
2585 Mrs. C. S. Brown
2585 Mrs. Caroline A. Spencer
2585 Mr. & Mrs. G. W. Powell
2591 Mr. & Mrs. Henry L. Angell
2601 Mrs. E. R. Wheeler
2659 Mrs. Edward Wright
2659 Perry Trumbull
2659 Miss Julia M. Trumbull
2679 Mr. & Mrs. M. H. Church
2679 Frank W. Church
2711 Mr. & Mrs. Edwin N. Lapham
2721 Mr. & Mrs. George P. Jones
  & dr.
2721 Graham P. Jones
2721 Mr. & Mrs. Belden D. Jones
2731 Mr. & Mrs. Fred S. Comstock
2731 Henry Comstock
2755 Mr. & Mrs. D. Franklin Flannery
2759 Mr. & Mrs. Wm. M. Bauer
2767 Mr. & Mrs. Jesse Lowe
2819 Mr. & Mrs. Ira A. Metcalf
2829 Mr. & Mrs. H. B. Slaughter
2849 Mr. & Mrs. Davis G. Mellor
2849 Mrs. John D. Boyd & dr.
2849 Miss Josephine D. Bullard
2853 Mr. & Mrs. Robt. M. Cherrie
2897 Mr. & Mrs. Edward Higgins
2907 Mr. & Mrs. B. C. Rogers
2921 Mr. & Mrs. Arden B. Lapham
2921 Arden B. Lapham, jr.
2937 Mr. & Mrs. C. E. Davis
2941 Dr. Emma Caswell Wood
2969 Mr. & Mrs. Fred S. Gardiner
2975 Mr. & Mrs. John M. Means
2975 Mrs. Anna L. Bruner
2977 Mr. & Mrs. M. J. Healy
2993 Mr. & Mrs. Henry C. Voute
3009 Mr. & Mrs. John C. F.Brockle-
  bank
3009 Miss Barbara H. Durell
3049 Mr. & Mrs. Charles D. Dunlop

2200 Mr. & Mrs. P. H. Early
2206 Mr. & Mrs. A. W. Pulver
2210 Mr. & Mrs. James Flanigan
2218 Mr. & Mrs. William N. Taylor
2224 Mrs. E. A. Ingalls & dr.
2226 Mr. & Mrs. N. C. Fisher
2238 Mr. & Mrs. L. T. M. Slocum
2242 Mr. & Mrs. Eli P. Chatfield
2268 Mr. & Mrs. William C. Dodge
2278 Mr. & Mrs. Nathaniel Moore
2278 Dr. Edward E. Moore
2350 Mr. & Mrs. Henry V. Conine
2444 Mr. & Mrs. D. B. Towner
2456 Mrs. Loraine J. Pitkin
2456 Mr..& Mrs. Howard J. Decker
2468 Mrs. Otillie R. Hatterman
2468 Chas. G. Ricklefs
2468 Mrs. Emma Ricklefs
2472 Mr. & Mrs. Howard N. Elmer
2488 Mr. & Mrs. H. W. Thornton
2532 Mr. & Mrs. Fritz Glogauer
2548 Mr. & Mrs. A. F. Sheldon
2584 Mr. & Mrs. Arthur T. Howe
2598 Mr.&Mrs. James P. Smith & dr.
2598 Feno E. Smith
2598 Rupert E. I. Smith
2660 Mr. & Mrs. Harrison J. Glaspell
2714 Dr. & Mrs. Lorenzo N. Grosvenor
2810 Mr. & Mrs. Peter P. Bilhorn
2820 Mr. & Mrs. Albert B. Hunt &
  drs.
2834 Mr. & Mrs. Walter S. Hull
2834 Mrs. Henrietta LaFayette
2850 Mr. & Mrs. J. F. Steward
2850 Mr. & Mrs. E. G. Davis
2886 Mr. & Mrs. J. G. Peters
2886 Mrs. Lois K. Peters
2900 Mr. & Mrs. Charles C. Wheeler
2918 Mr. & Mrs. D. H. Roe
2928 Mr. & Mrs. F. L. Bellows
2938 Mr. & Mrs. R. L. Duvall
2942 Mr. & Mrs. Edward A. Fisher
2974 Mr. & Mrs. Winfield S. Smyth
2974 Winfield S. Smyth jr.
2984 Mr. & Mrs. Wm. W. Rathbun
2984 John Rathbun
2998 Mrs. Amanda N. Sawyer
2998 Miss Martha E. Chamberlain
3010 Mr. & Mrs. A. D. Sheridan
3010 Fred L. Everitt
3040 Mr. & Mrs. Scott Jordan

————

3075 Mr. & Mrs. F. W. McKinney

LAKE SHORE DRIVE.

18 Mr. & Mrs. Charles Pope
18 Edward Pope
19 Mr. & Mrs. Alfred Henry Mulliken *Receiving day Monday*
21 Mr. & Mrs. Albert Blake Dick *Receiving day Monday*
48 Mr. & Mrs. S. E. Gross *Receiving day Monday*
55 Col. & Mrs. John Mason Loomis *Receiving day Monday*
57 Mr. & Mrs. Edward F. Lawrence *Receiving day Monday*
57 Dwight Lawrence
57 Richard Folsom
60 Mr. & Mrs. Robert T. Lincoln
63 Mr. & Mrs. Geo. Henry High *Receiving day Monday*
64 Mrs. J. Whitney Farlin *Receiving day Monday*
64 Myron Whitney Farlin
65 Mr. & Mrs. Carl C. Heisen, *Receiving day Monday*
65 Maj. George C. Waddill
67 Mr. & Mrs. Arthur Taylor Aldis *Receiving day Monday*

100 Mr. & Mrs. Potter Palmer
100 Honore Palmer
100 Potter Palmer jr.
100 Mr. & Mrs. B. L. Honore
103 Mr. & Mrs. Franklin MacVeagh *Receiving day Mon. 4 to 6 p.m.*
103 Eames MacVeagh
109 Mr. & Mrs. S. E. Barrett & dr. *Receiving day Monday*
109 Robert D. Barrett
111 Mrs. M. D. Ogden
112 Mr. & Mrs. V. C. Turner *Receiving day Monday*
112 Edward C. Green
117 Mr. & Mrs. Harry G. Selfridge *Receiving day Monday*
120 Mr. & Mrs. Herman H. Kohlsaat *Receiving day Monday*
125 Mr. & Mrs. Alex. C. McClurg *Receiving day Monday*
130 Mr. & Mrs. Orrin W. Potter *Receiving day Monday*
130 Miss Margaret Horton Potter

LAKE VIEW AVENUE.

5 Mr. & Mrs. Andrew E. Leicht *Receiving day Thursday*
5 Miss Stella Leicht
5 John Seba
11 Mr. & Mrs. Albert F. Madlener
17 Mrs. F. Madlener
17 Mr. & Mrs. Edward A. Leicht *Receiving day 1st Friday*
31 Mr. & Mrs. R. Lothholz
67 Mr. & Mrs. Joseph Theurer
71 Mr. & Mrs. Chas. T. Wilt jr.
71 Miss Anna H. Fairbairn
71 Miss Lila J. Fairbairn
73 Dr. & Mrs. F. H. Foster
73 Mrs. Eliza E. Dickinson

75 Mr. & Mrs. A. S. Maltman & drs. *Receiving day Wednesday*
77 Mr. & Mrs. J. S. Woolacott
207 Mr. & Mrs. M. A. Johnson
251 Mr. & Mrs. John Mackin
265 Mrs. R. Schloesser *Receiving day 1st. Tuesday*
265 Miss Frances Schloesser
265 Miss Jeanette Schloesser
285 Mr. & Mrs. Lem Whitney Flershem
285 Miss Albertine W. Flershem
285 Rudolph B. Flershem.
321 Mr. & Mrs. A. L. Sercomb

LAKEWOOD AVENUE.

2337 Mr. & Mrs. S. H. Farnham
2391 Mr. & Mrs. H. D. Tracy
2411 Mr. & Mrs. Henry Stolz
2427 Mr. & Mrs. Chas. A. Burton
2437 Mr. & Mrs. Wm. J. Cummings
2431 Mr. & Mrs. C. J. Blair
2439 Mrs. Lydia A. Beach
2439 Mr. & Mrs. John E. Wright *Receiving day Thursday*

2430 Mr. & Mrs. C. Berrall
2430 Mrs. F. E. Nash
2442 Mr. & Mrs. E. Isaiah Frankhouser
2442 Mr. & Mrs. Montgomery Gibbs
2564 Mr. & Mrs. M. A. Reynolds & dr.
2572 Mr. & Mrs. C. W. Beck

2465 Mr. & Mrs. Herman Rehtmeyer
2469 Mr. & Mrs. Maurice P. French
2477 Mr. & Mrs. I. J. Bryan
2481 Mrs. Susie Fisher
2483 Mr. & Mrs. Elzer C. Noe

2497 Mr. & Mrs. E. E. Bast
2505 Mr.&Mrs.H.P.Nicholson & drs.
Receiving day Wednesday
2573 Mrs. Ada M. Thul
Receiving day Wednesday

LANE COURT.

11 Mrs. C. L. Kaub
13 Mr. & Mrs. Adolph Sturm
17 Mr. & Mrs. Carlton H.Prindeville
25 Mr. & Mrs. Clayton F. Summy
29 Mr. & Mrs. Frederick Goetz

10 Mr. & Mrs. John P. Miller & dr.
16 Mr. & Mrs. W. C. Becker
24 Mr. & Mrs. L. B. Schaefer

49 Mr. & Mrs. Charles Ehman & dr.

LARRABEE STREET.

543 Mr. & Mrs. Henry W. Frische
543 Mr. & Mrs. C. Frische & dr.
545 Mr. & Mrs. M. Schmitz
769 Dr. & Mrs. Frederick Roesch
775 Mr. & Mrs. D. O. Gallear

774 Mrs. M. Bartelme & dr.
774 John H. Bartelme

775 Mr. & Mrs. Frank E. Butler

LA SALLE AVENUE.

223 Mr. & Mrs. E. C. Hamburgher
& dr.
Receiving days 1st & 3d Saturdays
245 George E. Purington & drs.
Receiving day Monday
269 Dr. & Mrs. Christian Fenger
271 John H. Johnson & dr.
273½ Mr. & Mrs. Henry G. Neeler
279 Mrs. P. A. Spurlock & dr.
Receiving day Tuesday
279 Henry B. Spurlock .
283 Mr. & Mrs. Joseph Rudolph
283 Charles Rudolph
283 Franklin Rudolph
303 Mr. & Mrs. D. Y. McMullen
Receiving day Tuesday
307 Mr. & Mrs. A. C. Brackebush
307 Carl A. Brackebush
317 Mr. & Mrs. Victor F. Lawson
339 Mr. & Mrs. Thomas J. Staley
& dr.
339 Thomas J. Staley, jr.
343 Mr.& Mrs. James B. Hobbs
Receiving days 2d & 3d Mon. p.m.
345 Mr. & Mrs. Ph. Jaeger & drs.
Receive last Friday in mo.
345 Philip Jaeger jr.
353 Dr. & Mrs. F. Henrotin
353 Mrs. Charles Prussing
359 George K. Dauchy & dr.
359 Samuel O. Dauchy
359 Mr. & Mrs. Otis B. Dauchy
359 G. Vivus Dauchy

172 Mr. & Mrs. J. Schmidt & dr.
172 E. C. Schmidt
260 D. J. Gallery & drs.
268 Dr. & Mrs. A. H. Gordon
268 Mrs. M. M. Ruggles
270 Mr. & Mrs. H. K. Macdonald
270½ Mr. & Mrs. John Sexton
Receiving day Wednesday
290 Mr. & Mrs. E. Bloch
Receiving day Wednesday
290 Mr. & Mrs. George B. Briggs
290 William T. Carrington
290 Mr. & Mrs. N. Gottlieb
Receiving day Wednesday
290 A. Gottlieb
290 Miss Anna Hill
290 Fred B. Jones
294 Mr. & Mrs. Wilfred Massey
294 Mr. & Mrs. Allen J. White
294 Mr. & Mrs. Harold O. Crane .
294 Harry P. Robinson
294 Mr. & Mrs. K. R. Owen
312 Dr. R. L. Leonard
316 Mrs. F. L. Atkins
320 Mr. & Mrs. C. J. Hurlbut & dr.
320 H. W. Rogers
320 Miss S. M. Rogers
320 Miss E. Rogers
322 Mr. & Mrs. Wm. A. Elmendorf
322 Willard Elmendorf
332 Mr. & Mrs. Charles J. Miller
334 Mr. & Mrs. Edward F. Koch &
dr. *Receive Thursdays*

363 Mr. & Mrs. Geo. H. Kettelle
 Receiving day Monday
367 Mr. & Mrs. N. H. Blatchford
375 Mr.& Mrs.E.W.Blatchford & dr.
 Receiving day Monday
375 Edward W. Blatchford
375 Charles H. Blatchford
381 Ralph Isham
387 Harry M. Hubbard
387 Mrs. Abijah Keith
387 Mrs. Max Hjortsberg
403 Mr. & Mrs. Oliver B. Green & dr.
403 Andrew Hugh Green
413 Dr. & Mrs. James P. Buck
415 Mrs. C. N. Davis
415 Mrs. Agnes Barker
415 Clyde Barker
425 Mrs. T. G. Springer
 Receiving day Thursday
425 Mrs. C. W. Doton
425 Mr. & Mrs. T. F. Gane & dr.
425 Mr. & Mrs. John R. Montgomery
425 Granville W. Browning
425 Rev. & Mrs. J. Q. A. Henry
 Receiving day Wednesday
425 Mr. & Mrs. Owen T. Wharton & dr.
 Receiving day Thursday
425 Joseph C. Wharton
425 George C. Wharton
425 Mrs. H. F. Kittredge
425 Miss A. A. Pollard
425 Mr. & Mrs. Robt. B. Hotchkin
 Receiving day Wednesday
425 Miss Charlotte M. Leland
425 Mr. & Mrs. E. F. Leland
425 Charles W. Leland
445 Judge & Mrs. Theodore Brentano
447 Mr. & Mrs. Otto Reiss
449 Mr. & Mrs. E. R. Weil
453 Dr. & Mrs. T. J. Bluthardt
453 Mr. & Mrs. Robert G. Calder
455 Mr. & Mrs. Sidney Mandl
457 Dr. & Mrs. F. W. Rohr
459 Mr. & Mrs. Gabriel Bloch
 Receiving day Monday
459 Dr. & Mrs. C. W. Barrett
461 Mr. & Mrs. Harry Hargis & dr.
461 Mr. & Mrs. John V. Kloeber
461 Mr. & Mrs. Fred Muench
463 Mr. & Mrs. August Fiedler & drs.
465 Dr. & Mrs. Hugh T. Patrick

334 Carl Koch
340 Mr.&Mrs.George H.Rozet & dr.
 Receiving day Wednesday
340 Mr. & Mrs. W. Prescott Hunt & dr.
 Receiving day Wednesday
342 Mr. & Mrs. Zack Hofheimer
342 Albert Ellinger
342 Morris Ellinger
346 Mr. & Mrs. Irving L. Gould
354 L. A. Torrens
356 Mr. & Mrs. Otto C. Schneider
360 Wm. D. Smith & dr.
362 Mr. & Mrs. J. F. Wollensak
366 Mr. & Mrs. A. L. Jepson
 Receiving day Tuesday
368 Dr. & Mrs. John Fisher
372 Mr. & Mrs. Hermann Benze & drs.
378 Col.& Mrs. A. F. Stevenson & dr.
380 Dr. Charles White & dr.
382 Miss E. Hosmer
382 R. W. Hosmer
384 Mr. & Mrs. Henry Bausher
386 Mr. & Mrs. J. H. Roseboom
388 Mrs. C. B. Blakemore & dr.
388 F. T. Blakemore
388 W. R. Blakemore
392 Mr. & Mrs. Charles M. Walker
394 Mr. & Mrs. Louis Stern
396 Mr. & Mrs. Peter Willems
402 C. C. Moeller
402 Mrs. Augustus Bauer & drs.
412 Wm. Loeb & drs.
412 Jacob W. Loeb
412 Dr. & Mrs. Alfred D. Kohn
414 Mrs. August Schrenk
420 Dr. & Mrs. John W. Niles
 Receiving day Monday
424 Mr. & Mrs. Joseph S. Phillips & drs. *Receiving day Saturday*
424 J. S. Phillips jr.
424 Abraham Phillips
428 Mrs. Katie Kohn & drs.
428½ Mr. & Mrs. Wm. C. Furst
430 Thos. Ritchie & drs.
432 Mr. & Mrs. H. L. Regensburg
434 Mr. & Mrs. William Hammermiller
436 Mr. & Mrs. H. A. Kirchhoff
 Receiving day 3d Saturday
436 Mrs. Emma Muench
438 Dr. & Mrs. H. P. Newman
440 Mrs. John McVoy & dr.
440 John A. McVoy
440 Eugene J. McVoy

467½ Mr. & Mrs. Louis Schott & dr.
    Receiving day Friday
467½ Mr. & Mrs. William Schott
471 Mr. & Mrs. Bernard Berlizheimer
    Receiving day Friday
471 Mrs. Johanna Kunreuther
483 Mr. & Mrs. E. E. Strauss
483½ Mr. & Mrs. Max Stern
    Receive 1st Saturday
485 Mr. & Mrs. Joseph M. Finn
495 Mr. & Mrs. Theodore Ascher
495 Martin Ascher
501 Mrs. Eliza DeClerque-Rabing
501 Mr. & Mrs. Henry DeClerque
501 Prof. R. Fischer
505 Dr. & Mrs. William F. Coy
507 Mrs. Joseph Deschauer
507 Dr. & Mrs. George A. Christ-
    mann
511 Mr. & Mrs. Christian Temple
513 Mrs. Emeline Dauchy
515 Mrs. Sebastian Anderson & dr.
    Receiving day Wednesday
515 W. G. Anderson
521 Rev. C. Koerner
521 Mr. & Mrs. Louis M. Melander
523 Dr. & Mrs. M. L. Harris
523 Charles D. Hoyt
525 Mr. & Mrs. Robert Stevenson
525 Charles Stevenson
525 James R. D. Stevenson
527 Mr. & Mrs. O. C. Foster & dr.
527 George B. Foster
529 Mr. & Mrs. Isador Bachrach
531 Dr. & Mrs. James E. Gross
531 Mrs. Mary Gross Canfield
533 Mr. & Mrs. E. Silverman
    Receive Friday evening
539 Mr. & Mrs. J. J. Kreer
541 Mr. & Mrs. Wm. Joy & drs.
561 Mr. & Mrs. James A. Sexton
    Receiving day Wednesday
563 Mr. & Mrs. Herman Wetterer
567 Gen. Joseph Stockton & dr.
567 Mr. & Mrs. August Yondorf
567 Mr. & Mrs. P. M. Schwarz
569 Mr. & Mrs. T. E. Miller
569 Mrs. Sarah Jones & dr.
571 Mr. & Mrs. Henry Channon
573 Mr. & Mrs. Louis Baer
    Receive 3d Saturday in mo.
573 Mr. & Mrs. Sol Baer
575 Mr. & Mrs. Abram Klee
577 Mr. & Mrs. Alex. H. Revell
577 Mr. & Mrs. George A. Bush
577½ Mr. & Mrs. Warren Barnhart

440 Joseph I. McVoy
448 Mr. & Mrs. Malcolm McNeil
452 Mr. & Mrs. H. A. Grannis
454 Mr. & Mrs. Nicholas Koch
456 Dr. H. Banga
456 Miss Emily Banga
462 Mr. & Mrs. Herman Weber &
    dr.
462 Harry F. Weber
462 Albert H. Weber
462 Edmund B. Weber
468 Mr. & Mrs. J. P. Reynolds
472 Mr. & Mrs. Victor D. Gowan
482 Mr. & Mrs. Jno. Wilkinson
482 John Wilkinson jr.
482 Arthur W. Wilkinson
486 Mr. & Mrs. Louis Specht
    Receive 3d Saturday
488 Mr. & Mrs. Paul Juergens & dr.
    Receiving day 2d Wed. in mo.
488 William F. Juergens
496 Dr. Thos. S. Middleton
504 Mr. & Mrs. Fred W. Wolf & dr.
506 Mr. & Mrs. Jacob Springer
512 Mr. & Mrs. John McEwen & dr.
512 Paul J. McEwen
512 John McEwen jr
512 Alfred McEwen
514 Mr. & Mrs. Morris Sellers & dr.
514 John M. Sellers
516 Mr. & Mrs. John F. Jelke
516 Ferdinand Jelke
520 Mr. & Mrs. Wm. Vocke
528 Mr. & Mrs. Joseph Wische-
    meyer
528 Mr. & Mrs. Wm. Grus & drs.
528 Wm. Grus jr.
528 Eugene Grus
530 Mr. & Mrs. Chas. Richards &
    dr.
532 Mrs. J. O'Connell & dr.
    Receiving day Wednesday
532 John J. O'Connell
538 Mr. & Mrs. F. Silberman & dr.
542 Miss Adelia Blauer
542 Fred J. Blauer
552 Dr. & Mrs. Charles E. Manierre
558 George C. Clark
576 Dr. & Mrs. Carl L. Barnes
    Receiving day Tuesday
576 Mr. & Mrs. L. C. Huck
576 Mr. & Mrs. Fred Greisheimer
576 Mr. & Mrs. James H. Caswell
578 Mr. & Mrs. W. H. Hoffbauer
580 Mr. & Mrs. A. C. Murdough
    Receiving day Tuesday

577½ Dr. & Mrs. W. W. Estabrooke
Receive 1st & 3d Monday
579 Mr. & Mrs. Francis F. Bruns
579 Louis W. Bruns
579 Frank W. Bruns
581 Mr. & Mrs. Rufus P. Spalding
Receiving day Monday
581 Bradbury Williams
581 Francis W. Adams
581 John M. Adams
587 Mr. & Mrs. Michael Ullrich
589 Mr. & Mrs. Philip Henne
611 Mrs. A. B. Fiedler
611 Anton B. Fiedler
611 Mr. & Mrs. Frank W. Hess
615 Mr. & Mrs. Philip Rinn & drs.
615 Walter J. Rinn
621 W. O. George
621 Mr. & Mrs. William E. George
621 Mrs. L. Troyer & dr.
625 Mrs. Chas. S. Waller & drs.
663 Dr. & Mrs. Theo. W. Heuchling
& drs. *Receiving day Friday*
669 Mrs. Emma E. Schumann
669 Mrs. Berta Eschenburg & dr.
669 H. A. Eschenburg
669 Franz Eschenburg

670 Miss Pattie Adele Cummings
Receiving day Monday
670 Morris C. Cummings
674 Mr. & Mrs. George P. Braun
674 Miss Mabel Braun
674 Miss Elizabeth Vail
678 Robert Lindblom
678 Miss Lenor Lindblom
678 Mrs. M. D. Lewis

580 Mr. & Mrs. Benj. J. Samuels
580 Mrs. Horace M. Kennedy
580 Mrs. Joseph Sieboth
Receive Thursday afternoon
586 Mr. & Mrs. S. Langbein
Receiving day Wednesday
592 Mr. & Mrs. Chas. Halla
602 Mr. & Mrs. Ernest Hess
602 Mr. & Mrs. Louis A. Hess
604 Mr. & Mrs. Charles E. Hess
606 Mr. & Mrs. S. Eichberg
606 Mrs. J. Florsheim
608 Mr. & Mrs. W. H. Flentye & drs.
620 Dr. & Mrs. Emil G. Beck
Receiving day Saturday
620 J. J. Holdsworth
622 Mr. & Mrs. Emil Eitel
624 Mr. & Mrs. M. F. Pardee & dr.
626 Dr. Paul R. Welcker
626 Dr. H. C. Welcker
632 Mr. & Mrs. Alfred B. Eaton
634 Mr. & Mrs. H. L. Dahl & drs.
640 Mrs. C. Jevne & drs.
640 Henry M. Jevne
646 Mr. & Mrs. Gottleib Merz & drs.
652 Mr. & Mrs. B. Gradle & dr.
654 Mr. & Mrs. Jacob Meyer & dr.
658 Mr. & Mrs. Ludwig Wolff
658 Mrs. Nicholas Strotz
666 Mr. & Mrs. W. H. Heegaard &
dr. *Receiving day 1st Monday*
666 Mr. & Mrs. R. W. Sprague
668 Mr. & Mrs. Ernst Wienhoeber
& dr.
670 Mr. & Mrs. Chas. C. Cummings
Receiving day Monday
670 Miss Eloise W. Cummings
Receiving day Monday

LAWRENCE AVENUE.

1418 George H. Kriete
1429 Mr. & Mrs. Henry D. Beam

1429 Mr. & Mrs. Wilson H. Cooke
1504 Mr. & Mrs. George D. Brown

LELAND AVENUE.

511 Mr. & Mrs. W. E. Wakefield

LILL AVENUE.

1527 Mr. & Mrs. Nathan Hyman &
dr.
1549 Mr. & Mrs. Thos. I. Lovdall &
drs.
1549 N. Harry Lovdall
1549 Thomas H. Lovdall
1549 Alex Lovdall
1571 Mr. & Mrs. C. J. Whitney

1560 Mr. & Mrs. Henry Hance
1560 Paul D. Hance
1570 Mr. & Mrs. Frank M. Power
1570 Mr. & Mrs. J. C. Dunbar & dr.
1578 Mrs. Harriet Jackson
1578 Mr. & Mrs. G. W. Barnett

1575 Mr. & Mrs. Henry Gundermann

LINCOLN AVENUE.

15 Dr. & Mrs. Rudolph Menn
17 Dr. & Mrs. Jacob Frank
25 Mr. & Mrs. Thos. Carney & drs.
51 Dr. & Mrs. J. N. Bartholomew
63 Mr. & Mrs. William Greiner jr.
71 Mr. & Mrs. James F. Bowers
77 D. J. Powers
79 Mr. & Mrs. Samuel Sternfeld
85 Mr. & Mrs. J. M. Armstrong
85 John J. Armstrong
91 Dr. & Mrs. E. G. Earle
97 Dr. & Mrs. G. E. Hawkins
133 Dr. Arthur G. Thome
133 Miss Hattie S. Thome
173 Mr. & Mrs. C. Roth & dr.
185 Dr. & Mrs. L. C. Grosvenor
269 Dr. Coresta T. Canfield
269 Mr. & Mrs. John F. Upham
271 Mr. & Mrs. Geo. W. Haines
281 Dr. D. C. Bacon
281 Dr. Marie Thompson-Bacon
303 Thos. Boland & dr.
315 Dr. Isadore L. Green
319 Mr. & Mrs. George E. Snell
321 Mr. & Mrs. Wm. H. Jennings
695 Dr. & Mrs. Grant J. Roberts
721 Dr. & Mrs. A. E. Palmer
    Receiving day Tuesday

14 Mr. & Mrs. N. Hosmer
20 Mrs. S. Goodman & dr.
20 Joseph Goodman
46 Mr. & Mrs. Louis Gathmann
48 Mr. & Mrs. Philip Henrici&dr.
50 Mr. & Mrs. Augustus I. Lewis
66 Mr. & Mrs. A. J. Press & dr.
66 Adam J. Press jr.
70 Mr.&Mrs. Christopher Pfeiffer
    & dr.
74 Dr. & Mrs. Carl Wagner
84 Dr. & Mrs. Emil Kunz
86 Dr. & Mrs. Alex Memelsdorf
90 Mr. & Mrs. H. F. Ender & dr.
94 Dr. May Hadley
140 Mr. & Mrs. Hiram Barber
142 Mrs. Helen L. Kadish
144 Mr. & Mrs. H. Levey & drs.
144 Mark Levey
170 Dr. & Mrs. Wm. F. Butterman
600 Dr. & Mrs. C. H. Ludwig

721 Miss Violet H. Palmer
cor. Peterson av. Mr. & Mrs. P. S.
    Peterson
cor. Peterson av. Mr. & Mrs. Wm.
    A. Peterson

LINCOLN PARK BOULEVARD.

51 Mr. & Mrs. Charles R. Barrett
55 Dr. & Mrs. C. E. Peck & dr.
55 David B. Peck
55 Mr. & Mrs. Robert Bowman
77 to 83 Newport Flats
    B Mrs. George W. Glover
    C Mrs. M. W. McReynolds
    D Mr. & Mrs. F. B. Newkirk
    E Mrs. Franklin H. Beckwith
    E S. H. Kerfoot jr.
    F Mr. & Mrs. R. W. Mutch-
        mor
    G Mr. & Mrs. Lewis J. Millet
    H Mr. & Mrs. Dudley A. Tyng
89 Mr. & Mrs. A. Poole & drs.
    Receiving day Monday
99 Mr. & Mrs. B. F. Ayer & dr.
    Receive Monday afternoon
99 Walter Ayer
99½ Mr. & Mrs. M. J. Power
101 Mrs. K. G. Forsyth & dr.
101 Miss Lucy Lee Hill

16 Mrs. J. P. Ferns & drs.
16 Mr. & Mrs. F. M. Cutter
90 Mr. & Mrs. Walter Kimbark
90 Mrs. S. J. Douglass & drs.
90 Leon F. Douglass
90 Mr. & Mrs. M. A. Kilvert
90 Mr. & Mrs. Nicholas J. Nelson
104 Mrs. I. N. Arnold & dr.
104 Miss Elizabeth Foote
106 Mrs. W. M. Scudder & dr.
106 J. Arnold Scudder
108 James D. Erskine
108 Mrs. Albert Erskine
108 Albert D. Erskine
108 Mr. & Mrs. James Cary Evans
112 Mr. & Mrs. H. Wilson Parker
118 Mr. & Mrs. James Fentress
    & dr.
118 Mr. & Mrs. James Fentress jr.
118 David Fentress
120 Mr. & Mrs. Sidney F. Andrews
    Receiving day Wednesday

103 Mr. & Mrs. George Weidig
105 Dr. & Mrs. Samuel J. Walker
107 Mrs. George Sturges & drs.
115 Mr. & Mrs. W. F. Dummer
135 Mr. & Mrs. Lynden Evans
135 Mr. & .Mrs. Albert Hall
135 Albert P. Hall
135 Mr. & Mrs. Wm. O. Chase
135 Mr. & Mrs. Morris St.P.Thomas
135 Mr. & Mrs. John R. Gott
Receiving day Monday
135 Sherwood J. Larned
135 Mr. & Mrs. Chas. E. Mosley
137 Mrs. J. S. Norton & dr.
Receiving day Monday
137 Mr. & Mrs. Chas. A. Hawks
137 Dr. & Mrs. Frank W. Reilly
137 Rodolphe R. Reilly
137 Mr. & Mrs. Edward S. Beck
137 Mr. & Mrs. Thos. B. Marston
137 Mr. & Mrs. Eugene V. Roddin
139 Mr. & Mrs. Paul Picard
Receiving day Friday
141 Mr. & Mrs. D. C. Deegan & dr.
Receiving day Wednesday
145 Mr. & Mrs. W. R. Odell
145 Mr. & Mrs. Bertram M. Winston
145 Mr. & Mrs. John Lawrence Mc-
Intyre
147 Mr. & Mrs. LeGrande Smith &
dr.
147 Mr. & Mrs. E. A. Meysenburg
147 Frank B. Stephenson
147 Mr. & Mrs. Herman Paepcke
149 Mr.& Mrs. Jonathan W. Jackson
149 Mr. & Mrs. Parmalee J. Mc-
Fadden
149 J. Edmund Holland
181 Mr. & Mrs. Graeme Stewart
Receiving day Monday
183 Mr. & Mrs. C. H. Ferry

122 Mr. & Mrs. Willis S. McCrea
Receiving day Monday
136 Mr. & Mrs. G. P. Everhart
138 Dr. & Mrs. Henry Baird Favill
144 to 150 Kinzie Flats
Mr. & Mrs. J. Leslie Gordon
Fred R. Hamlin
Harry L. Hamlin
Herbert W. Hamlin
Mr. & Mrs. Frank H. Cooper
Mr. & Mrs. Thomas L. Chadbourne, jr.
Dr. & Mrs. Jos. W. Wassall
Mrs. J. M. Love & dr.
James M. Love
Mrs. John E. Chapman & dr.
John Adams Chapman
Mr. & Mrs. Frank V. S. Hibbard
Mr. & Mrs. Henry D. Sturtevant
Mr. & Mrs. Everts Wrenn
184 Mr. & Mrs. S. D. Kimbark
184 Miss Marie Kimbark
184 Charles A. Kimbark
184 Mrs. Rebecca Church
220 John Dullaghan & drs.
220 Stephen M. Dullaghan
220 John P. Dullaghan
220 Edward P. Dullaghan
232 Dr. & Mrs. Geo. H. Bentley
232 Mrs. Thomas Corlett
236 John Miller & dr.
Receiving day Thursday
238 Mr. & Mrs. J. N. Anderson

183 Mansfield Ferry
185 Mr. & Mrs. D. Mark Cummings
Receiving day Monday p.m.
185 Mrs. Charles P. Dexter
185 Miss Edith Dexter
187 Mr. & Mrs. Wm. B. Bull

LINCOLN PLACE.

39 Mr. & Mrs. J. H. Verhalen

26 Mr. & Mrs. Joseph Staab
34 Mr. & Mrs. Alex. White
46 Mr. & Mrs. F. J. Loesch

12 Hugo W. Schmidt
12 Mr. & Mrs. F. W. Schmidt
12 Mr. & Mrs. F. C. Dammerau &
drs.
22 Mrs. Michael Bauer

NORTH LINCOLN STREET.

2667 Mr. & Mrs. Geo. E. Milligan
2671 Mr. & Mrs. Frederick White
2675 Mrs. George M. Grannis
19

2658 Mr. & Mrs. C. Rich
2666 Mr. & Mrs. Burr A. Kennedy
Receiving day Tuesday

2707 Mr. & Mrs. Chas. J. Chapin
2711 Mr. & Mrs. Wm. L. Wait
2723 Mr. & Mrs. Frank A. Brown
2723 Mr. & Mrs. David P. Brown
2725 Dr. & Mrs. Wm. S. Gates
2725 Mrs. Harriet Pillsbury
2731 Mr. & Mrs. Chas. A. Stewart
2735 Mr. & Mrs. Wm. G. Hovey
2753 Mr. & Mrs. Peter F. Kaehler
      & drs.
2765 Dr. & Mrs. G. W. Green
2777 Mr. & Mrs. Wm. B. Turner
2789 Mr. & Mrs. H. C. Preston
2795 Mr.&Mrs. H..Eschenburg& dr.

2672 Mr. & Mrs. Geo. J. Penfield
2720 Mr. & Mrs. Wm. Thompson
2724 Mr. & Mrs. B. J. Diefendorf
2738 Mr. & Mrs. John C. Hoof
2756 Mr. & Mrs. Wm. Dole
2766 Mr. & Mrs. D. R. Anderson
2790 Mr. & Mrs. H. F. Stone
2790 Mrs. Sadie M. Lane
2806 Mr. & Mrs. Chas. W. Chan-
      dler
———
2799 Mr. & Mrs. P. H. Eschen-
      burg
2799 Mrs. C. A. May & dr.

LINDEN COURT.

15 Mr. & Mrs. Wm. T. Egan
21 Mr. & Mrs. Carl M. Mohr
21 Mr. & Mrs. Howard E. Hitch-
    cock

26 Mr. & Mrs. Fred K. Maus
28 Mr. & Mrs. Thos. G. Milsted
30 Mr. & Mrs. E. R. Wetmore

LOCUST STREET.

149 Dr. & Mrs. Frederick Kohlha-
      mer
149 Mr. & Mrs. Eugene Caubert
159 Mrs. Helen M. Smith
161 Mr. & Mrs. T. E. Chandler

161 George D. Chandler
161 Henry T. Smith
161 Frank Young
161 John Knecht
165 Mr. & Mrs. Charles P. St. John

LUNT AVENUE.

521 Mr. & Mrs. Jas. Walmsley&dr.
541 Mrs. Paul Binner
541 Mr. & Mrs. Walter Binner
541 Herbert Binner
541 Mr. & Mrs. Harry S. Thomp-
      son
541 Miss Helen L. Hood
1121 Nathan Follett
1137 Mr. & Mrs. Emil Jung & dr.
1141 Mr. & Mrs. B. H. Babbitt
1147 Mr. & Mrs. W. S. Antes
1161 Mr. & Mrs. Robert Pigott &
      dr.
1161 Dr. A. H. Pigott
1167 Mr. & Mrs. Wilmer K. Roberts

522 Mrs. Eleanor A. Du Plaine
602 Mr. & Mrs. John S. Ziegler
620 Mr. & Mrs. John H. Hewitt
628 Mr. & Mrs. T. A. Lawson
646 Mr. & Mrs. Peter Phillip & dr.
770 Mr. & Mrs. Oscar F. Herren
920 Dr. & Mrs. W. De G. Clark
920 Miss Bertha Clark
930 Mr. & Mrs. Richard W. Leon-
      ard
930 Clifford C. Judson
1140 Mr. & Mrs. Elmer E. Beach
1140 Mr. & Mrs. Frank Edwards
1218 Mr. & Mrs. Clarence A. Powers

MAGNOLIA AVENUE.

1777 Mr. & Mrs. M. S. Sanders
1785 Mr. & Mrs. Robert Turney
1785 Robert E. Turney
1805 Mr. & Mrs. J. K. Stewart
      Receiving day Friday
1839 Mr. & Mrs. F. R. McDonald
1839 Mr. & Mrs. Geo. Hipple

1788 Rev.&Mrs.Elias Benzing &drs.
1794 Mr. & Mrs. L. P. Shriver
      Receiving day Wednesday
1794 Mrs. Hattie Plank
1800 Mr. & Mrs. C. L. Ibson
2420 Mr. & Mrs. Chas. A. Binz
      Receiving day Thursday

1847 Mr. & Mrs. Wm. G. Weigle
1895 Mr. & Mrs. B. C. Caldwell
2349 Mr. & Mrs. Fred Knauss
2395 Mr. & Mrs. W. R. Neel
2407 Mr. & Mrs. W. J. Stewart
2413 Mr. & Mrs. E. W. Jenks
2413 Edgar B. Isham
2429 Mr. & Mrs. M. W. Hanley
2469 Mr. & Mrs. Peter O'Connor
2475 Mr. & Mrs. Chas. C. Cobb
2501 Mr. & Mrs. J. E. Rastall
2531 Mr. & Mrs. Julius Huber
2531 Mr. & Mrs. E. W. Poinier
2545 Mr. & Mrs. John A. Bryant
2555 Mr. & Mrs. W. W. Blair
2647 Mr. & Mrs. A. Rosenbecker
2691 Mr. & Mrs. J. Byron Turck
2693 Mr. & Mrs. A. E. Mayer
2717 Mr. & Mrs. F. Voightman

2470 Mr. & Mrs. Charles W. Douglas
2478 Mr. & Mrs. August Heuer jr.
2478 Mr. & Mrs. Henry Heuer
2490 Mr. & Mrs. N. B. Lewis
2510 Mr. & Mrs. F. F. Cain
2556 Mr. & Mrs. J. M. Brown
2576 Mr. & Mrs. Max Henius
2632 Mrs. H. V. Tobey & drs.
2632 Mrs. A. J. McDonald
2644 Mr. & Mrs. A. Whiting Watriss
2644 Mrs. C. R. Sweetser
2646 Mr. & Mrs. F. Reusch
2652 Mr. & Mrs. F. H. Hathaway
2652 Mr. & Mrs. W. Herendeen
2668 Mr. & Mrs. George Rawll
2670 Mr. & Mrs. Henry L. Smith
2678 Mr. & Mrs. H. C. Hansen
2686 Mrs. M. A. Watson
2686 Mr. & Mrs. O. H. Watson
2690 Mr. & Mrs. John A. Downey

MALDEN STREET.

3133 Mr. & Mrs. Thos. B. Jeffery & dr.
3133 Chas. T. Jeffery
3159 Dr. & Mrs. Charles S. Terry
3159 Mrs. A. T. Harrington
3173 Mr. & Mrs. Robt. C. Berlin
    Receiving day Thursday
3179 Mr. & Mrs. Parker A. Jenks
3183 Mr. & Mrs. E. A. Morris
    Receiving day Thursday
3195 Mrs. Warren T. Clark
    Receiving day Wednesday
3195 Mrs. J. B. Halladay
3195 Galusha Emigh
3243 Mr. & Mrs. Augustus Berlin
3243 Dr. & Mrs. E. M. S. Fernandez

3128 Mr. & Mrs. William D. Hollis
3144 Mr. & Mrs. Chas. L. Wilder
3170 Mr. & Mrs. G. R. Murray
3170 H. W. Murray
3176 Mr. & Mrs. S. R. Bryan
3178 Mr. & Mrs. Theo. Gottman
3210 Mr. & Mrs. C. L. Carman
3210 Mr. & Mrs. E. D. Wilson

3225 Mr. & Mrs. H. D. Bowker
3225 Mr. & Mrs. H. A. Hulligan
3265 Mr. & Mrs. Louis W. Stayart
    Receive 3d Fridays
3287 Mr. & Mrs. Austin O. Sexton

MALVERN AVENUE.

cor. Birchwood av. Mr. & Mrs. William E. Hatterman

MAPLE STREET.

67 Mr. & Mrs. William P. Dickinson & dr.
67 H. T. Sudduth
71 Mrs. M. L. Meyer
73 Mr. & Mrs. Theodor Schrader & dr.
73 Edward Schrader
77 Mr. & Mrs. F. Campe

70 George Schmid
70 Mr. & Mrs. Godfrey Schmid
70 Louis Schmid
72 Mr. & Mrs. Wm. H. Johnson & dr.
72 Miss Edna L. Johnson
74 Harry A. Oberstella
76 Mrs. E. K. Branch
    Receiving day Wednesday
76 E. Norman Scott
82 Dr. & Mrs. Evert E. Tracy
    Receiving day Thursday

MARQUETTE TERRACE.

23 Mr. & Mrs. C. M. Walworth

—

22 H. C. Boone

14 Mr. & Mrs. William H. Coen & dr.

22 Mr. & Mrs. Tilbey D. Gray

MELROSE STREET.

1719 Mr. & Mrs. William Prentiss
    Receive 1st & 3d Thursdays
1719 Mr. & Mrs. Douglas C. Gregg
1825 Mr. & Mrs. R. H. Boericke
1847 Mr.&Mrs. Herrmann B.Washington
1849 Mrs. Alfred Swadkins
1855 Mr. & Mrs. S. P. Pugsley & dr.

—

1870 Mr. & Mrs. Albert Schonbeck
    Receiving day Thursday

1634 Mr. & Mrs. N. M. Tribou
1662 Mr. & Mrs. Edwin H. Popper
1812 Dr. Jean M. Cooke
1816 Frederic F. Norcross
1820 Mr. & Mrs. Theo. J. Amberg
1824 Mrs. Louis Schoeninger
1838 Mr. & Mrs. W. L. Butterfield
1860 Mr. & Mrs. W. H. Ross-Lewin
    & dr.
1860 H. F. Ross-Lewin
1866 Mr. & Mrs. Edward R. Jewett
1868 Dr. & Mrs. Frank Byrnes

MENOMONEE STREET.

8 Rev. & Mrs. William Nethercot
    & dr.

14 Dr. & Mrs. B. B. Maydwell

MILDRED AVENUE.

767 Mr. & Mrs. E. C. Pierce
779 Benj. Shurtleff

779 Harry L. Buker
779 Mr. & Mrs. Bruce M. Myers

MOHAWK STREET.

363 Mr. & Mrs. Edward Melchior
381 Rev. & Mrs. David Creighton
385 Mr. & Mrs. Fred Volger & dr.

222 Mr. & Mrs. Henry Schomer
354 Mr. & Mrs. F. W. Brenckle
370 Mr. & Mrs. H. B. Cady
372 Mr. & Mrs. Marcus Levy

MONTANA STREET.

1425 Mr. & Mrs. James Andrews &
    dr.
1425 James P. Andrews

1102 Mr. & Mrs. Edwin P. Goode
1116 Oswald von Lengerke

MONTROSE BOULEVARD.

1431 Mr. & Mrs. Ossian Simonds
1431 Mrs. Harriet N. Simonds
1507 Mr. & Mrs. Marshall M. Dutton
1507 Kirk Avery Dutton
1617 Mr. & Mrs. Charles G. Ludlow

1402 Mr. & Mrs. John N. Young
1416 Mr. & Mrs. Chas. M. White
1430 Mr. & Mrs. Geo. W. Davis

—

1617 Ebenezer Ludlow

MORSE AVENUE.

471 Mrs. Wm. A. Doolittle & dr.
471 William H. Doolittle
479 Mr. & Mrs. Arthur C. Doolittle
521 Mr. & Mrs. James H. Manny
533 Mr. & Mrs. Jedediah H. Smith
549 Mr. & Mrs. John Culver & dr.

462 Mr. & Mrs. Andrew T. Hodge
462 Miss Amy Hodge
462 Miss Ida Hodge
506 Mr.&Mrs.Albert E.Dickerman
548 Mr. & Mrs. William M. Welch
808 Dr. Bertha E. Bush

727 Dr. & Mrs. S. V. Romig & drs.
731 Rev. & Mrs. Augustus W. Wil-
        liams & dr.
811 Mr. & Mrs. F. D. Gifford
823 Mr. & Mrs. Robert Irvine & dr.
1345 Mr. & Mrs. Earl A. Pettibone

1222 Mr. & Mrs. James M. Taylor
1320 Charles H. Antes & drs.
1320 Miss Katherine M. Antes
1330 Mr. & Mrs. W. C. Seavey

808 Dr. Vida A. Latham
922 Mr.& Mrs. Joseph S. Brookman
928 Mr. & Mrs. William King
1020 Mr. & Mrs. George B. Simpson
1122 Mr. & Mrs. William T. Little
1142 Mr. & Mrs. William H. Lah-
        man
1204 Mr. & Mrs. Edward T. Keyes
1206 Mr. & Mrs. Harvey B. Keyes
1210 Mr. & Mrs. Merdo K. Williams
1210 Miss Clara M. Richardson

NEWGART AVENUE.

4105 Mr. & Mrs. Willard W. Low
4111 Mr. & Mrs. Henry C. Newgard
4117 Charles H. Prescott & dr.
4131 Mr. & Mrs. Morris Salmonson
4131 Axel H. Salmonson
4131 Edgar M. Salmonson

4102 Mr. & Mrs. Wm. O. Meisner
4118 Mr. & Mrs. S. W. Willard
4118 Mrs. Rebecca M. Forrest
4132 Mr. & Mrs. Madison Brower

4141 Mr. & Mrs. Chas. S. Norris

NEWPORT AVENUE.

617 Mr. & Mrs. George Hackell

NORTH AVENUE.

317 Mr. & Mrs. Henry F. Miller
445 Dr. & Mrs. Albert G. Seeglitz
453 Mr. & Mrs. George P. Rinn
453 Mr. & Mrs. A. Pattison

516 Francis F. McIver
516 Karl Demmler

454 Dr. & Mrs. Paul Kreye
514 Mr. & Mrs. David A. Noyes
514 Marshall P. Noyes
514 Thomas S. Noyes
514 Mr. & Mrs. Henry C. Wood
516 Mr. & Mrs. Thos. H. Devereaux
516 Mrs. James McIver
516 Mrs. A. McIver Brisbine

NORTH PARK AVENUE.

637 Hazen T. Miles
693 Mr. & Mrs. Wm. Hebel
693 Otto W. Hebel
693 Otto Meinshausen
697 Mr. & Mrs. C. Nigg
699 Mr. & Mrs. Jacob Henrich & dr.
699 Mr. & Mrs. Holger de Roode
709 Mr. & Mrs. Chas. A. Nau & drs.
709 Otto F. Nau
751 Robert A. Irving

Mrs. A. S. Kilbourn
Mr. & Mrs. H. B. King
Fred G. Morris
Paul Morrison
Mr. & Mrs. Allan A. Murray
Mr. & Mrs. B. L. Palmer
Mr. & Mrs. J. E. Ramar
George H. Riley
Mr. & Mrs. A. P. Schaack
Mr. & Mrs. F. W. Smith
H. G. Spensley

688 Mr. & Mrs. M. A. Smith,
704 Mr. & Mrs. Christoph Ramm
712 John H. Glade
712 Mrs. Louisa S. Glade
750 Mrs. John Macauley & dr.
750 Mr. & Mrs. Elmer Hill
780 Hotel Luzerne
    Charles A. Andrews
    Mr. & Mrs. A. J. Blakey
    Mr. & Mrs. E. D. Bosworth
    Mr. & Mrs. Frank Brausch
    Mr. & Mrs. R. H. Bulkley
    Mr. & Mrs. W. H. Burns
    F. D. Casanave
    Mr. & Mrs. W. J. Candlish
    Miss Helen Close
    Miss Abigail Cowley
    Mr. & Mrs. A. R. Edwards
    Mr. & Mrs. John R. Floyd & dr.
    Mr. & Mrs. T. J. Hughes
    Mrs. W. O. Jones
    Wm. E. Jones

780 Hotel Luzerne (continued.)
    Conrad Stoffregen ·
    Mrs. J. O. Stone
    Mr. & Mrs. Louis Stover
    Mrs. J. A. Straight
    Grant Underwood
    Meno Unzicker
    Otto Unzicker
    Mrs. L. N. Walton
    Mrs. C. G. Warren & dr.
    Miss M. A. Weiber

808 Mrs. R. A. Silcott
820 Mr. & Mrs. F. W. Stone
822 Mr. & Mrs. R. A. Bower
824 Mr. & Mrs. Andrew McNally
832 Mr. & Mrs. Alexander Belford
834 Mr. & Mrs. Harry B. Clow
836 Mr. & Mrs. Fred. G. McNally
852 Mr. & Mrs. Daniel McGuire
852 Simms McGuire

OAK STREET.

243 Thomas Cratty
265 Mrs. W. H. Bradley & dr.
293 C. H. Gentry
293 William H. H. Tyson
293 W. Stephenson Tyson
295 Mr. & Mrs. James C. Essick
381 Mr. & Mrs. H. M. Love
381 Mr. & Mrs. W. L. Beckwith
385 Mrs. C. Gallagher & dr.
387 Mr. & Mrs.. Wm. H. Thomson
387 Mr. & Mrs. B. M. Norton
389 Mrs. J. B. Johnson
399 Mr. & Mrs. David Hogg
399 Miss Lillian Canfield
401 Mrs. Thomas W. Grover
403 Mr. & Mrs. E. F. Heywood
403 Mr. & Mrs. M. M. Schultz
405 Miss Catherine Martindale
405 Mr. & Mrs. C. T. Cavanagh
407 Mr. & Mrs. F. W. Wickett
407 Mr. & Mrs. Frank S. Wheeler
409 Mr. & Mrs. Alexander D. Han-
    nah & drs.
    Receiving day Monday
409 A. W. Hannah
409 Miss Margaret Canfield
411 Mrs. J. V. Knapp
411 Kemper K. Knapp
421 Thomas H. Cannon

370 Mrs. K. C. Harrington
376 Mr. & Mrs. J. C. Burns
376 John S. Cooper
376 Mrs. H. W. Smith
376 Miss Grace Cooper
378 Mr. & Mrs. Alexander Sullivan
380 Mr. & Mrs. R.•A. Bowman
380 Miss Lillian Clow
384 Mr. & Mrs. George S. Essex
386 Mr. & Mrs. Geo. N. Beek & dr
386 William G. Beek
390 Mr. & Mrs. John Hitt
394 Mr. & Mrs. Charles Harpel
394 Mr. & Mrs. Charles J. Harpel
396 Mr. & Mrs. Thomas L. Dillon
410 Mr. & Mrs. Jacob Engel ·
410 Mrs. A. M. Payne
410 Mr. & Mrs. P. J. Doyle
410 Mr. & Mrs H. C. Ranney
412 Mr. & Mrs. Wm. S. Love
    Receiving day Friday
414 Mr. & Mrs. A. W. Browne
422 Mr. & Mrs. Francis Dana
    Receiving day Friday
424 Mr. & Mrs. John G. Frick
428 Mr. & Mrs. John H. Reardon

431 Mr. & Mrs. Otto H. Matz

OAKDALE AVENUE.

1511 Joseph Dietzgen
1515 Mr. & Mrs. David C. Bayha &
    drs.
1541 Mr. & Mrs. Frank R. Jackson
1547 Mr. & Mrs. Theo. W. Buhmann
1549 Mr. & Mrs. Harry S. Clough
Receive 1st and 3d Thursday in mo.
1763 Sidney W. Stevens   ·
1763 Mrs. G. W. Stevens
1763 Miss Helen M. Davol
1765 Mr. & Mrs. J. M. Hoffman

1512 Mr. & Mrs. August Semrad jr.
1532 Mr. & Mrs. Richard Michaelis
1532 Walter R. Michaelis
1534 Mr. & Mrs. Chas. M. Osborn jr.
1722 Mr. & Mrs. P. F. Groll
1748 Mr. & Mrs. Frank A. Rose
1758 Mrs. George Bedell
1758 William Bedell
1758 Miss N. Walsh
    Receiving day Tuesday
1810 Mr. & Mrs. Max W. Richter

1765 Mr. & Mrs. P. D. Stevens
1815 Mr. & Mrs. Edward J. Blake
1821 Mr. & Mrs.Carl G. Boldenweck
1821 J. W. Finkler
1831 Mr. & Mrs. James White
1851 Mr. & Mrs. Philip R. Smith
1853 Mr. & Mrs. Edward U. Roper ⸱
1937 Mr. & Mrs. Frank H. Scott
1937 Mr. & Mrs. Henry Drucker
1941 Mr. & Mrs. Joseph T. Quinn &
    dr.

   ———

1944 Mr.&Mrs.CharlesSeegers&drs.
      Receiving day Thursday
1944 George F. Seegers
1944 Melville H. Seegers

1812 Mr. & Mrs. Herman Rieser
      Receiving day Thursday
1812 Mrs. B. Moos
1814 Mr. & Mrs. J. B. Moos
      Receiving day Friday
1832 Mr. & Mrs. Geo. M. Clute & dr.
1832 James Clute
1842 Mr. & Mrs. John H. Behrens &
    drs.
1846 Mr. & Mrs. John Agar
1854 Mr. & Mrs. Lloyd James Smith
1854 Mr. & Mrs. John L. Flannery
1854 Miss Lulu Miles
1854 Mr. & Mrs. J. L. Flannery
1906 Rufus S. Simmons
1932 Mr. & Mrs. Chas. Schonlau

OHIO STREET.

245 Wm. T. Hill
245 Miss Kate L. Hill
245 Miss Mollie Hill
267 Dr. & Mrs. Wm. C. Rohu
ne. cor. N. State Studio Building
   1 James W. Pattison
   6 Miss Cora F. Freer
   9 Miss Pauline A. Dohn
  11 Miss Helen L. Bowman
  19 Miss Julia M. Bracken
  21 Mr. & Mrs. John F. Stacey
  26 Dr. Titus Piacentini
  34 Miss Marie Herndl
333 Dr. Fred H. Wallace
333 Mr. & Mrs. Wm. H. Wallace
333 Miss Ethel Lippitt
339 Mr. & Mrs. W. H. Barrett
345 Miss Ella Middleton
345 Miss Caroline Mears

   ———

   8 R. P. Williams
   9 Mr.&Mrs.Chauncey E.Bryant
  10 Mr. & Mrs. John H. Barnett
  11 Mr.&Mrs.Charles H. Baldwin
308 C. S. Engle
364 Mr. & Mrs. Patrick H. Shinners·

210 Mr. & Mrs. W. Levy & dr.
      Receiving day Tuesday
210 Morris F. Levy
210 Dr. V. F. Marshall
240 Leonard Gould
282 Mr. & Mrs. S. Swartchild & drs.
284 Mr. & Mrs. Henry Leeb
284 Mrs. Rosa Kraus
288 Mr. & Mrs. John McKechney
288 John McKechney jr.
288 Mrs. Caroline Hill
290 Mr. & Mrs. J. R. McKay
      Receiving day Wednesday
290 J. M. McKay
292 Mr. & Mrs.Jonathan Slade
292 Henry Slade
292 Arthur B. Slade
296 Jaeschke Flats
   1 Mrs. Adolph L. Jaeschke
   1 G. A. Jaeschke
   2 Mrs. Clara Street
   2 Wade L. Street
   4 Mr. & Mrs. W. S. Cotes
   4 Harry S. Gillette
   7 Mr. & Mrs. Fred Wilhelm
   8 Mrs. M. Williams & dr.

ONTARIO STREET.

227 J. B. Waldo
227 Mrs. M. A. Ayers
291 Dr. & Mrs. Oren O'Neal
301 Mrs. Sidney Sawyer
301 Mr. & Mrs. T. M. Garrett
359 Mrs. Mary B. Rogers
359 Miss S. C. Rogers ⸱
361 Mrs. Edna Foltz

 226 Dr. G. Beecher Malone
226 William H. Malone ⸱
252 Mr. & Mrs. S. P. Melander
256 Mr. & Mrs. Milo George
336 Mrs. H. K. Buel & dr.
336 Leonard Fiske
338 Mr. & Mrs. Leigh Reilly
348 Mrs. John Newell & dr.

361 Mrs. Mary Beckwith
361 John W. Blackledge
365 Mr.& Mrs.C.N.Hammond & drs.
369 Judge & Mrs. J. E. Gary
373 Edwin C. Harmon
373 Charles J. Harmon
373 Walter R. Harmon
375 Mr. & Mrs. Charles Higgins
381 Mrs. Samuel J. Walker & dr.
381 W. Ernst Walker
381 Mrs. O. H. Wallop
387 Mrs. G. P. A. Healy & dr.
387 George L. Healy
389 Walter W. Edsall
389 Mrs. H. A. Hurlbut
389 Miss S. E. Hurlbut
397 Mr. & Mrs. E. Vincent Gale
399 Mr. & Mrs. C. H. Besly
399 Mrs. Oliver Besly
401 Mr. & Mrs. W. W. Augur

350 Abbot L. Adams
350 Miss C. D. Adams
356 Mrs. J. S. McIlvaine & drs.
362 Mr. & Mrs. E. Earnshaw
362 Charles Earnshaw
364 Mr. & Mrs. Frederick Lathrop
366 Dr. & Mrs. J. H. Buffum
368 Mrs. Margaret Knight
370 Mr. & Mrs. Edward K. Rogers
     & drs.
376 Mrs. Frederick S. Eames
380 Mr. & Mrs. Charles Henry Cof-
     fin *Receiving day Thursday*
380 Miss Rhoda Howells Coffin
380 Chas. Howells Coffin
390 Mr. & Mrs. Charles W. Boynton
396 Mr. & Mrs. Lawrence Williams
     Receiving day Wednesday
398 Mr. & Mrs. S. A. Lynde
410 Mr. & Mrs. Geo. W. Haskell

ORCHARD STREET.

341 Mr. & Mrs. Hugo Schmoll
391 Mr. & Mrs. Philip Halla
399 Mr. & Mrs. Emil Mannhardt
407 Mrs. William Kuecken & dr.
407 Charles Kuecken
417 Mr. & Mrs. William E. Furness
     & dr.
423 Mr. & Mrs. Henry M. Elliott
425 Dr. & Mrs. Adolph Decker
473 Mr.& Mrs.William C. Dow
523 Mr. & Mrs. Chas. W. Newman
527 Mr. & Mrs. G. R. Newman
529 Mr. & Mrs. Otto Ernst
569 Mr. & Mrs. John S. Farrell & drs.
569 John E. Farrell
569 William J. Farrell
575 Mr. & Mrs.Edmund Furthmann
     Receiving day Wednesday
579 Mrs. Frederick Koehler & drs.

404 Mrs. Juliet M. Seavey
404 Mrs. Sibyl Seavey
414 Mr. & Mrs. Gilbert L. Grant
454 Mr. & Mrs. Adolph Ascher
456 Mr. & Mrs. Henry Goetz
460 Mr. & Mrs. Henry Baade
462 Mr. & Mrs. Gustav A. Hoffman
462 Fred F. Hoffman
526 Mr. & Mrs. C. H. Lathrop & dr
532 Mr. & Mrs. James Chisholm
536 Mr. & Mrs. A. M. Mothershead
     & dr.
536 Mr. & Mrs. H. B. Lusch

583 Dr. & Mrs. Karl Doepfner
587 Mr. & Mrs. Lorenz Mattern
591 Mr. & Mrs. Cornelius G. Boon
595 Mr. & Mrs. Felix A. Norden
701 Mr.& Mrs. Fred. W. Foehringer

OSGOOD STREET.

115 Mr. & Mrs. August Zander
151 Mr. & Mrs. John Weber
215 Mr. & Mrs. M. H. Hereley
225 Mr. & Mrs. Walter J. Gibbons
239 Mr. & Mrs. Alexander Klap-
     penbach

1436 Mr. & Mrs. L. M. Todd

245 Mr. & Mrs. Frank Amman &
     drs.
247 Mr. & Mrs. Wm. Sullivan

NORTH PAULINA STREET.

2293 Mr. &. Mrs. C. W. Galbraith
2337 Mr. & Mrs. H. Hochbaum
2371 Mr. & Mrs. E. R. Shnable
2397 Mr. & Mrs. Chas. Walton
2403 Mr. & Mrs. M. H. Vail
2421 Mr. & Mrs. John McLauchlan
2429 Dr. & Mrs. Alben Young
2429 Hale Knight
2433 Mr. & Mrs. John Trelease
2449 Mr. & Mrs. Robt. J. Bennett
2449 Mr. & Mrs. F. M. Taylor
2469 Mr. & Mrs. R. J. Bennett
2469 Mr. & Mrs. Arthur G. Bennett
2475 Mr. & Mrs. A. M. Johnson & dr.
2561 Mr. & Mrs. Daniel Naslund
2563 Mr. & Mrs. W. H. Bryan
2573 Mr. & Mrs. James W. McWilliams
2585 Joseph Handley & dr.
2601 Dr. Fredrica Baker
2601 Mr. & Mrs. Edward L. Hunter
2603 Mr. & Mrs. Ernest M. Chapin
2611 Mr. & Mrs. Wm. Finkler
2619 Mrs. James Wallace & dr.
2625 Mr. & Mrs. Geo. A. Dupuy
2641 Mr. & Mrs. Harry B. Field
2653 Mr. & Mrs. Thomas E. Barrett
2665 Hervey H. Anderson
2677 Rev. & Mrs. J. F. Berry
2681 Mr. & Mrs. John K. Livesey
2685 Mr. & Mrs. F. M. Sills
2697 Mr. & Mrs. A. M. McKay
2705 Mr. & Mrs. F. A. Tripp
2731 Mr. & Mrs. Chas. S. Eveland
2733 Mr. & Mrs. E. F. Angell
2755 Mr. & Mrs. E. R. Newman
2761 Mr. & Mrs. Henry E. Simon
2771 Mr. & Mrs. William L. Wood
2779 Mr. & Mrs. M. S. Holman
2843 Mr. & Mrs. C. I. Wolfinger
2851 Mr. & Mrs. Henry W. Meyer

2288 Mrs. Jane N. Sulzer
2288 Mrs. Charles M. Bowen
2298 Mr. & Mrs. Chas. W. Guhl
2298 Mr. & Mrs. Henry M. Cohen
2302 Mr. & Mrs. Geo. K. Rix & dr.
2302 Walter B. Rix
2312 Mr. & Mrs. J. A. Kreutzberg
2316 Mr. & Mrs. H. C. Burmester
2354 Mr. & Mrs. Edward H. Robinson
2362 Mr. & Mrs. Francis C. Bronson
2366 Mr. & Mrs. Fred C. Klein
2382 Mr. & Mrs. D. F. Kellogg
2382 Mr. & Mrs. E. V. Quimby
2384 Mr. & Mrs. P. J. Perry
2388 Mr. & Mrs. Chas. P. Knill
2430 Mr. & Mrs. Chas. N. Ettinger .
2440 Mr. &.Mrs. Frank D. Huth
2446 Mr. & Mrs. Richard I. McGinnis
2450 Mr. & Mrs. G. N. Ackley
2454 Mrs. W. K. McAllister.& dr.
2454 Mrs. Ellen Spencer
2478 Mr. & Mrs. Geo. B. Vance
2478 Mr. & Mrs. A. J. Gates
2486 Mr.&Mrs. Frederick T. Morris
2610 Mr. & Mrs. S. Bauer
2614 Mr. & Mrs. William F. Kienzle
2628 Mr. & Mrs D. Jones
2634 Mr. & Mrs. E. J. Chapin
2640 Mr. & Mrs. Peter Spain
2640 Stephen J. Spain
2642 Mrs. Elizabeth Schager & drs.
2642 Edward J. Schager
2654 Mr.& Mrs. Charles Truax& drs.
2666 Mr. & Mrs. Daniel J. Murphy
2682 Mr. & Mrs. D. H. McDaneld
Receiving day Tuesday
2684 Mr.&Mrs. James L. Batchelder
2820 Mrs. Josephine C. Moninger
2820 Mrs. Tracy Blair
2884 Mr. & Mrs. Thos. Thorkildsen

EAST PEARSON STREET.

35 Mrs. & Mrs. W. Irving Babcock
35 Mr. & Mrs. Frank H. Remien
35 Charles H. Remien
35 Mr. & Mrs. Joseph Garneau
39 Rev. & Mrs. Reuben A. Torrey
Receiving day Friday
57 Mr. & Mrs. Thomas Minchin
63 and 65 The Audubon
, Charles N. Fay

14 Mr. & Mrs. Martin Loescher
38 Mr. & Mrs. G. P. English
42 Mr. & Mrs. John R. Bisland&dr
42 William A. Bisland

John C. King
S. Franklin Remington
99 Mr. & Mrs. Charles B. Farwell
99 Mr. & Mrs. H. C. Chatfield-Taylor

99 Mrs. Dudley Winston
99 Walter Farwell
109 Mr. & Mrs. John V..Farwell

125 Mrs. Bertha S. Flesh
137 Mrs. J. M. Dowling

PERRY STREET.

1437 Mr. & Mrs. J. F. Kletzing
1475 Mr.&Mrs. Rudolph W.Gronow
1491 Charles E. Sinclair

———

4132 Mr. & Mrs. Charles E. Browne

1174 Mr. & Mrs. Adolph Traub
1256 Mr. & Mrs. D. G. Ramsey
1462 Mrs. A. Eugene Little
1534 Mr. & Mrs. C. H. Ripley
4108 Mr. & Mrs. Joseph B. Noelle
4118 Mr. & Mrs. J. L. Martini

PINE STREET.
(See Lincoln Park Boulevard.)

PINE GROVE AVENUE.

15 Mr. & Mrs. John R. True
17 Mr. & Mrs. C. Kollenberg & dr.
19 Mrs. Paula Seckel
19 Wm. Werner Fabian
29 Mr.&Mrs. Herman C. Buechner
33 Mr. & Mrs. Geo. N. Neise
49 Mr. & Mrs. E. Boettcher
107 Mr. & Mrs. William Grace
107 John W. Grace
109 Mr. & Mrs. B. C. Barnes
109 Mr. & Mrs. Andrew Crawford
    & dr. *Receiving day Thursday*
109 Andrew H. Crawford
147 Mr. & Mrs. Willard C. Coe
147 Mrs. L. W. Coe
149 Mr. & Mrs. Martin O'Brien & dr.
149 Joseph O'Brien
221 Mr. & Mrs. Herman Mueller
297 Mr. & Mrs. Chas. C. Wetherell
303 Mr. & Mrs. Chas. F. Rietz
307 Mr. & Mrs. Frederick Rietz
595 Mr. & Mrs. Geo. L. Peterson
599 Mr. & Mrs. H. M. Hansen&drs.
    Receiving day Wednesday
605 Mr. & Mrs. Wm. R. Dawson
607 Mr. & Mrs. Henry G. Dawson
    Receiving day Thursday
737 Mr. & Mrs. Otto E. Wolff & dr.
745 Mr. & Mrs. Leonard S. Mulford
751 Mr. & Mrs. Henry N. Mann
799 Mr. & Mrs. J. J. Mendelsohn
803 Mr. & Mrs. Gustav A. Mueller

16 Mrs. Henry Spiel
16 George Spiel
18 Mr. & Mrs. Victor J. Wuest
32 Mr. & Mrs. M. J. Stevenson
36 Mr. & Mrs. M. J. Faherty
38 Mrs. L. Jerome Baldwin & drs.
    Receiving day Wednesday
38 P. Paul Stamsen
40 Mr. & Mrs. J. C. Bartlett
42 Mr. & Mrs. James G. Martin
44 Mr. & Mrs. Frederick A. Lester
46 Mr.& Mrs. Archibald L. Brown
88 Mr. & Mrs. Sol Lande
90 Mr. & Mrs. John Fay
98 Mr. & Mrs. Henry Strassheim
98 Mr. & Mrs. Christopher Strass-
    heim
100 P. L. A. Schwarz
100 Miss Mahlie E. Weigle
100 Oscar Weigle
636 Mr. & Mrs. Geo. P. Hoover
636 Mr. & Mrs. J. W. Edminson
638 Mr. & Mrs. Chas. F. Morse
638 Mr. & Mrs. John M. Hardy
640 Mr. & Mrs. W. A. Patterson
640 Mr. & Mrs. Paul Kreismann
642 Mr. & Mrs. Edw. L. Barr
642 Mr. & Mrs. Arthur G. Morey
642 Mr. & Mrs. Geo. T. Odell
802 A. G. Wigeland
802 Mr. & Mrs. Albert W. Schroeder
804 Mr. & Mrs. Emil C. Bumiller

PRATT AVENUE.

431 Mr. & Mrs. H. J. Tweedie
857 Mr.& Mrs. Raymond W. Beach
857 Mrs. Helen S. Healy
901 Mr. & Mrs. Irvin E. Rockwell
923 Mr. & Mrs. Edward A. King

808 Dr. Harriet C. B. Alexander
808 Horace C. Alexander
930 Mr. & Mrs. Hiram Sweet
940 Mr. & Mrs. Lincoln E. Clark
    & dr.

1013 Mr. & Mrs. Oscar E. Binner
Receiving day Wednesday
1023 Mr. & Mrs. Christian L.Benson
& dr.
1045 Mr. & Mrs. Charles Evans
1051 Mr. & Mrs. H. T. Grund
1055 Mr. & Mrs. John M. Carlson
1107 Mr. & Mrs. B. F. George
1221 Mr. & Mrs. Max M. Schneider
1221 Miss Josephine Rust

940 Lincoln Clark
966 Mr. & Mrs. Charles V.Muehlke
1014 Mr. & Mrs. Geo. W. Higgins,jr.
1014 Mrs. E. M. Holmes
1048 Mr. & Mrs. Chas. F. Crane
1048 Mrs. Mary E. Crane

1231 Mr. & Mrs. Adolph Kreis
1231 Mr. & Mrs. John Kreis

RACINE AVENUE.

327 Mr. & Mrs. Thomas Goode
435 Mr. & Mrs. J. A. Seebaum
517 Mr. & Mrs. George M. Boyd
521 Dr. & Mrs. W. S. Walker

74 Mr. & Mrs. E. Riegert
260 Mr. & Mrs. Oscar A. Reum

525 Mr. & Mrs. A. E. Gamet & dr.

EAST RAVENSWOOD PARK.

1086 Mr. & Mrs. Thomas Jones & dr.
1462 Mr. & Mrs. Thomas B. Walton

1470 Mr. & Mrs. J. B. Washburne

WEST RAVENSWOOD PARK.

1209 Mr. & Mrs. John Fishleigh sr.
1219 Mrs. Cornelia Howard

1220 Mr. & Mrs. H. B. Tuttle

1241 Mr. & Mrs. Louis Semper

RETA STREET.

1837 Mr. & Mrs. Chas. Spangenberg
& drs.

1832 Mr. & Mrs. Louis Carson
1870 Mr. & Mrs. Albert D. Wentz

RIDGE AVENUE.

2736 Mr. & Mrs. Wm. J. Leacock
3824 Dr. & Mrs. Levi H. Thomas

3824 Mr. & Mrs. Edgar S. Foote

RITCHIE COURT.

5 Mr. & Mrs. John F. Harris
7 Mr. & Mrs. W. A. Scott
9 J. L. Yale
9 Mrs. Madeline G. Wynne
11 Mr.&Mrs.LloydWheaton Bowers
13 Rev.& Mrs.Newell Dwight Hillis
Receiving day Monday
15 Mr. & Mrs. E. A. Otis & dr.
15 William K. Otis

18 Mr. & Mrs. Joseph G. Coleman
& dr. *Receiving day Monday*
18 S. Cobb Coleman
20 Mr. & Mrs. Horace H. Martin
20 Mrs. J. G. Durkee
24 J. Harley Bradley
24 Miss Bradley
Receive 1st & 3d Monday
24 Miss Ella Bradley

2 Mr. & Mrs. Jas. B. Forgan
2 Miss Wilhelmina Forgan
2 Robert Donald Forgan
2 Mrs. Donald Murray
2 Miss Jane L. Murray
4 Judge & Mrs.William Alexander
Vincent
Receiving day Monday
6 Mr. & Mrs. Willis Hall Turner
6 T. G. Turner
8 Mr. & Mrs. Frederic W. Upham
10 Mr. & Mrs. Amos R. Smith & dr.
10 Mrs. C. A. Freeman
10 Lawrence W. Smith
10 Edward Page Smith
12 Mr. & Mrs. David C. Briggs
14 Mr. & Mrs. H. H. Forsyth
14 W. Holmes Forsyth
14 George H. Forsyth

NORTH ROBEY STREET.

.2597 Mr. & Mrs. J. C. Gardiner
2599 Mr. & Mrs. L. S. Carroll
2599 Mr. & Mrs. Otto Igel
2607 Mrs. Susan E. Davis & dr.
2607 W. Claude Davis
2607 Clarence S. Davis
2607 John T. Davis
2609 Mr. & Mrs. Henry M. Loughrin
2631 Rev. & Mrs. Joseph Adams
2641 Mr. & Mrs. L. R. Ermeling
2645 Mr. & Mrs. G. D. Dunham

2166 Mr. & Mrs. Charles E. Churchill

2675 Mr. & Mrs. David Frost jr.
2699 Mr. & Mrs. Joseph Norton
2699 Mr. & Mrs. Rollin H. Trumbull
2703 Mr. & Mrs. Joseph Patoille
2729 Mr. & Mrs. Thos. C. Thompson
2765 Mr. & Mrs. Wm. Gibson
2765 Mrs. F. R. Kimball
        Receiving day Tuesday
2773 Mr. & Mrs. E. W. Zander

ROKEBY STREET.

1257 Mr. & Mrs. Robt. C. Campbell

1222 Mr. & Mrs. Louis H. Schafer

ROSCOE STREET.

1619 Mr. & Mrs. Isaac R. Morris
1621 Mr. & Mrs. David M. Ross
1633 Dr. & Mrs. A. G. Haerther
1633 Fred W. Chittenden
1633 Geo. W. Chittenden
1633 Mrs. N. M. Chittenden
1723 Mr. & Mrs. L. Lorenzo Merriman
1733 Mr. & Mrs. Wm. I. Reedy
1735 Mr. & Mrs. Geo. E. Day
1737 Mr. & Mrs. Lafayette S. Berry

1414 Mr. & Mrs. John C. Paul & drs.
1744 Mr. & Mrs. Frederick Kaehler & dr.

1741 Mr. & Mrs. W. J. Haerther
1823 Mr. & Mrs. James H. Smith
1825 Rev. & Mrs. Samuel C. Edsall
        Receiving day Tuesday
1871 Mr. & Mrs. Louis H. Stafford
1893 Mr. & Mrs. Chas. H. Dennis

ROSLYN PLACE.

9 Mr. & Mrs. A. W. Barnard
11 Mr. & Mrs. Wm. J. Bartholf
15 Mrs. K. G. Huddlestone
15 Mr. & Mrs. Victor Garwood
15 Miss Sara Lacy
17 Mr. & Mrs. H. Vernon Seymour
25 Dr. & Mrs. Gustav Hessert
25 Dr. William Hessert
27 Mr. & Mrs. J. W. Sullivan
31 Mr. & Mrs. I. C. Ketcham
31 Mrs. J. C. Garretson
33 Mr. & Mrs. O. W. Ruggles
33 Miss A. Roberta Ruggles
33 Oliver E. Ruggles
33 Howard P. Ruggles
33 Edward M. Pomeroy
35 Mrs. J. W. Crawford
37 Mr. & Mrs. John W. Buehler
39 Mr. & Mrs. G. D. Searle
43 Mr. & Mrs. Roswell P. Fish & dr.
43 F. A. Fish
45 Prof. & Mrs. Carl Hause

20 Mr. & Mrs. David Goodwillie & drs.
34 Rev. J. A. Rondthaler & dr.
        Receive Friday
34 Wm. D. Rondthaler
36 Mr. & Mrs. Lorenzo Bull Roland
        Receiving day Friday
36 George N. Roland
38 Mr. & Mrs. George Weston
38 James C. Cox
38 Miss Mabel Payne
40 Mr. & Mrs. John P. Boughan
46 Mr. & Mrs. Brice A. Miller

47 Mr. & Mrs. Barton A. Ulrich
47 Miss Victoria U. Ulrich
47 Miss Gertrude U. Ulrich
47 Barton A. Ulrich jr.
47 A. Louis Ulrich
49 Mr. & Mrs. Ernest A. Shanklin
51 Mr. & Mrs. Perry H. Smith jr.

RUSH STREET.

85 Marquette Flats
   James H. May
   Mrs. Sarah May
   Alexander Nichols
   Howard B. Jackson
   Mr. & Mrs. Charles S. Weaver
   Miss Mabel Key
   Dr. & Mrs. W. H. Allport
87 Charlevoix Flats
   Mr. & Mrs. Wm. F. Pillsbury
   George C. Clarke
   Miss Florence E. Clarke
   Mr. & Mrs. Dwight W. Bowles
   Mrs. Elizabeth A. Ely
   Arthur B. Ely
   Mr. & Mrs. Geo. W. Evans
     Receive Monday
   Mrs. C. P. Abbott & dr.
   Sprague Abbott
   Mr. & Mrs. W. J. Head
     Receiving day Thursday
   Mr. & Mrs. Edgar W. Kirk ·
     Receiving day Wednesday
   Mr. & Mrs. Francis M. Lowry
     Receive Wednesday
97 Mr. & Mrs. W. F. McLaughlin
   & dr. *Receiving day Monday*
97 Frederic McLaughlin
101 Mr. & Mrs. L. Hamilton Mc-
   Cormick
     Receiving day Wednesday
135 Mrs. Cyrus H. McCormick
135 Stanley McCormick
151 Mrs. Henry W. King
155 Mr. & Mrs. Cyrus H. Adams
157 Mr. & Mrs. W. G. McCormick
   & dr.
159 Mr. & Mrs. A. B. Newell
159 Charles B. King
161 Mrs. Joseph Kirkland & drs.
     Receiving day Wednesday
163 Mr. & Mrs. Dudley P. Wilkinson
     Receiving day Monday 4 to 6
163 Dudley P. Wilkinson jr
163 Miss Laura Dallman
167 Mr. & Mrs. A. A. Carpenter jr.
169 Mrs. A. R. Heaton
169 Harold R. Heaton
169 Louie A. Hilliard
171 Col. & Mrs. B. J. D. Irwin
171 Mrs. David Leonard Barnes
173 Miss Fanny Chapin
179 Mr. & Mrs. E. H. Roche
181 Mr. & Mrs. W. N. D. Winnie

64 to 68 The Dubuque
   Mr. & Mrs. J. E. English
   Mrs. Sarah Gibson
   Mr. & Mrs. John H. Quinn
100 Miss E. Skinner
100 Miss F. Skinner
110 Mr. & Mrs. Henry J. Willing &
   dr.   *Receive Monday*
124 Mr. & Mrs. R. Hall McCormick
   & drs.
128 Rev. and Mrs. James S. Stone &
   dr.
   Receiving day Monday 3 to 10 p.m.
134 Mr. & Mrs. Arthur G. Bissell
134 Richard M. Bissell
134 Mrs. George F. Bissell
136 Mrs. S. H. Kerfoot & dr.
     Receiving day Monday
138 Mr. & Mrs. Walter F. Cobb
148 Mr. & Mrs. E. T. Watkins
156 Mr. & Mrs. W. K. Nixon
     Receiving day Monday
156 W. W. K. Nixon
158 Mr. & Mrs. Richard F. Howe
162 Mr. & Mrs. Charles Burrall Pike
164 Mr. & Mrs. W. F. Blair
182 Mr. & Mrs. Frank R. Chandler
     Receiving day Wednesday
182 Alphonse B. Chandler
224 Mr. & Mrs. Henry J. Bate
224 Miss Elsie Bate
290-292 Cambria Flats ·
   Mr. & Mrs. Robt. W. Gray
   John P. Agnew

———

183 Mrs. Robert D. McFadon
185 C. N. Lauman
185 George V. Lauman
185 Mrs. J. G. Lauman
187 Mr. & Mrs. P. L. Elder
     Receiving day Tuesday
187 P. L. Elder jr.
187 Samuel W. Elder
333 Mr. & Mrs. E. M. Watkins
333 Frederick A. Watkins
335 D. Frank Dearborn
335 Henry F. Brown
335 Mrs. B. H. Pope
335 Mr. & Mrs. Charles E. Rand
335 Otis King Hutchinson ·
337 Mr. & Mrs. Henry Newton
337 Mr. & Mrs. Wm. J. Louderback
     Receiving day Tuesday

339 Mrs. Richard S. Fay
341 Mrs. Rufus F. Chapin
341 Rufus F. Chapin
341 Elmer E. Wagner
341 Townsend V. Church
341 Dr. Sarah Hackett Stevenson
341 Charles H. Stevenson

341 Miss Alice E. Neale
345 Dr. & Mrs. John K. McKinnon
345 Mr. & Mrs. R. V. Wade
347 Mr. & Mrs. N. J. Gauer
347 Mr. & Mrs. A. H. Gauer
363 Mr. & Mrs. Joseph R. Richards

SCHILLER STREET.

191 Mr. & Mrs. Geo. H. Hartwell
193 Arthur J. Howe
215 Dr. John T. Manierre
217 Mr. & Mrs. George W. Gould
221 Mr. & Mrs. Harry N. Taylor
295 Hon. & Mrs. Carter H. Harrison
295 Wm. Preston Harrison
297 Mr. & Mrs. W. S. Chapman
297 Robert Clowry Chapman
297 W. S. Chapman jr.
299 Mr. & Mrs. A. C. Bodman
301 F. H. Armstrong
303 Mr. & Mrs. William A. Mason
305 Mr. & Mrs. G. H. Scribner
307 Miss Marie Richardson
307 Mr. & Mrs. Benjamin M. Shaff-
    ner   *Receiving day Thursday*
309 Mr. & Mrs. William Davis & drs.

302 Mr. & Mrs. Wm. D. C. Street
302 Mrs. Thomas F. Withrow
306 Mrs. George H. Kettelle
306 Mrs. Henry Stewart

214 Mr. & Mrs. Leo Canman
220 Mr. & Mrs. Julius Goldzier
224 Mr. & Mrs. S. G. Pitkin & dr.
224 Dr. John G. Message
244 Mr. & Mrs. Maier Rosenthal
246 Mrs. Hannah Rosenfield & dr.
246 Jacob A. Rosenfield
246 Mr. & Mrs. Leopold Stein
298 Mr. & Mrs. Franklin N. Corbin
300 Mrs. L. J. Tilton
300 Miss C. P. Tilton
300 Mr. & Mrs. Edward D. Hosmer
    & drs. *Receiving day Monday*
300 Mrs. C. M. Witherspoon & dr.
    Receiving day Monday
300 John M. Witherspoon
300 Leslie Witherspoon
300 Mrs. Katherine H. Bellows
    Receiving day Monday
300 Mr. & Mrs. Willliam Burry
    Receiving day Monday
300 Mr. & Mrs. J. McGregor Adams
    Receiving day Monday

SCOTT STREET.

5 Mrs. Robt. Mercer Sheridan
5 Madison Whiteside
5 Mrs. William H. Whiteside
7 Mrs. Mary E. Culver
7 Frank H. Culver
9 Mr. & Mrs. Hugh R. Ritchie
    Receiving day Tuesday
11 Mr. & Mrs. James McNally
15 Charles H. Briggs
15 Mrs. J. H. McMurray
17 Mr. & Mrs. S. H. Graves
17 Mr. & Mrs. F. E. Maitland
17 John G. Watson
19 Mr. & Mrs. William B. McKinley
19 Mrs. P. W. Frisbee
21 Mr. & Mrs. L. Mendelsohn & dr.
21 Jacob Mendelsohn
23 Gen. & Mrs. John C. Black
23 John D. Black

10 Miss Belle Davison
24 Mr. & Mrs. Charles Fuller
26 Mr. & Mrs. Richard Waterman
26 Richard Waterman jr.
40 Mrs. E. S. Adams & dr.
40 Samuel Adams
42 Dr. & Mrs. Omer C. Snyder
42 Mr. & Mrs. Allen T. Prentice
44 Miss Mary J. Holmes
48 Mr. & Mrs. Bernt Moe & dr.
50 Mr. & Mrs. Wm. M. LeMoyne
50 Francis J. LeMoyne

23 Rev. & Mrs. Frank Buffington
    Vrooman
    Receiving day Monday
25 Mr. & Mrs. John W. Ela
    Receiving day Monday
27 Mr. & Mrs. Ralph B. Corby

SEDGWICK STREET.

665 Dr. Jennie E. Smith
683 Mr. & Mrs. G. A. Zimmerman
687 Mr. & Mrs. S. R. Ireland
689 Mr. & Mrs. Bernard Herbst
697 Mr. & Mrs. L. G. Kunze
731½ Mr. & Mrs. James C. Mc-
  Naughton
731½ Guy McNaughton
731½ James N. McNaughton
735 Mr. & Mrs.CharlesWaldschmidt
735 August W. Waldschmidt
747 Mrs. Emilie Holland
755 Mrs. Fred G. Jungblut&dr.

636 Dr. Frederick A. Karst
642 Mr. & Mrs. Charles Barnes
648 F. X. Brandecker & dr.
648 F. X. Brandecker jr.
678 Mrs. C. M. Moritz
710 Dr. & Mrs. A. J. Ochsner
  Receiving day Saturday
730 Mr. & Mrs. Charles Sparre
738 Mr. & Mrs. A. H. Grunewald
740 Mr. & Mrs. F. Jager
744 Mr. & Mrs. George W. Kellner
756 K. G. Schmidt
756 Mr. & Mrs. George K. Schmidt
778 Mr. & Mrs. O. F. Mueller

SEMINARY AVENUE.

91 A. G. Brownlee
107 Mr. & Mrs. Fred Klein
107 Mr. & Mrs. R. E. Harrsch
135 Mr. & Mrs. John C. Parkes
135 John C. Parkes jr.
227 Mr. & Mrs. Thomas J. Coen
247 James Lyman
259 Fred L. Bryant
263 Mr. & Mrs. Jas. F. Bushnell
269 Mrs. Ellen Sage
277 Mr. & Mrs. Duncan Cameron
289 Mr. & Mrs. Peter Knauer
425 Mr. & Mrs. John Northen & drs.
437 Mrs. E. B. Charles & dr.
437 Robt. B. Charles
437 Mr. & Mrs. Harry C. Charles

100 Mr. & Mrs. John C. Ramcke
216 Mr. & Mrs. D. H. Carden
224 Mr. & Mrs. Geo. W. Williams
256 Mr. & Mrs. Fred H.Hildebrandt
256 Mr. & Mrs. Charles Eckstein
268 Mr. & Mrs. Edward J. Birk
278 Mr. & Mrs. Thomas Rankin
280 Rev. & Mrs. Robert D. Scott
406 Mr. & Mrs. Jacob Harth
448 Dr. & Mrs. E. R. Bennett

441 Mrs. E. L. Waterman & drs.
447 Mr. & Mrs. S. S. Jackman
  & dr.
555 Mr. & Mrs. M. Kaufman

SEMINARY PLACE.

1203 Dr. & Mrs. John G. Ames
1205 Mr. & Mrs. George Lill & dr.
1213 S. W. Mountz & drs.

1222 Mr. & Mrs. Herman Metzger

1213 Mrs. Jessie A. Fish

SHEFFIELD AVENUE.

399 Mr. & Mrs. Thomas P. Culloton
1311 Prof. & Mrs. R. F. Weidner
1357 Dr. & Mrs. Charles B. Reed
  Receiving day Tuesday
1357 Rev. & Mrs. Armstead H.
  Stephens
1357 Mr. & Mrs. Thos. W. Gilmore
  Receiving day Monday

1292 Dr. & Mrs. Wilbur Mackenzie
  Receiving day Wednesday

666 M. F. Madden
678 Rev. & Mrs.W.F. Walker &drs.
1180 Dr. & Mrs. James P. Houston
  Receiving day Friday
1190 Mr. & Mrs. A. O. Coddington
1202 Dr. & Mrs. E. A. Bergstrom
1210 Mrs. Ella M. Adams
  Receiving day Thursday
1210 Mrs. H. A. Fowler
1222 Ferdinand Goss
1282 Rev. & Mrs. Albert T. Clay

SHERIDAN ROAD.

1233 Mr. & Mrs. G. J. Prindiville
1233 Mr. & Mrs. L. A. Balthis
1235 Mr. & Mrs. B. A. Linderman
1235 Mr. & Mrs. E. L. Sharpneck & dr.
1239 Mr. & Mrs. M. J. Rompel
1239 Mr. & Mrs. Valentine Mueller
1353 Mr. & Mrs. Wm. H. O'Brien
1367 Mrs. Ida Hoskins
1563 Mr. & Mrs. Chas. A. MacDonald
1609 Mr. & Mrs. Duncan Mackay
1617 Mr. & Mrs. Wm. Treese Smith
1617 William C. Stone
1629 Mr. & Mrs. Henry O. Parker
1635 Mr. & Mrs. Arthur J. Eddy
1665 Mr. & Mrs. Robert A. Waller
1677 Mr. & Mrs. Henry A. Knott
1677 Mrs. Sarah Knott
1691 Mr. & Mrs. Wm. Dickinson
  Receiving day Wednesday
1701 Mr. & Mrs. Henry J. Peet
1711 Mr. & Mrs. James B. Waller
1727 Mr. & Mrs. John F. McGuire
1857 Mr. & Mrs. J. B. Scott
1943 Mr. & Mrs. P. D. Middlekauff
2065 Mr. & Mrs. John Krumm
2151 Mr. & Mrs. Joseph W. Slayton
2155 Mr. & Mrs. Wm. D. Owen
  Receiving day Thursday
2155 Mrs. H. M. Bradford
2175 Mr. & Mrs. A. F. Nightingale & drs.
  Receiving day Thursday
2175 Rev. C. H. Chase
2175 Harry Nightingale
2181 Mr. & Mrs. Wm. S. Warren
2211 Mr. & Mrs. Albert W. Rogers
2211 Mrs. Mary Bathrick
2219 Mr. & Mrs. Charles O. Barnes
2219 Wm. H. Barnes
2223 Mr. & Mrs. Edward S. Judd
2229 Mr. & Mrs. V. S. Woolley
2229 Mrs. Frances C. Woolley
2233 Mr. & Mrs. Frank Marshall
2237 Mr. & Mrs. B. B. Anderson

1244 Mr. & Mrs. Ernest H. Knoop
1332 Mr. & Mrs. G. W. Mathison
1342 Mr. & Mrs. J. A. Graham
1352 Mr. & Mrs. J. D. Bray
1352 Mr. & Mrs. John Sutcliffe
1356 Mr. & Mrs. M. Umbdenstock
1386 Mr. & Mrs. D. Sauer & drs.
1386 Dr. H. Edward Sauer
1408 Miss Ada Sweet
1408 Benjamin J. Sweet
1522 Mr. & Mrs. Robt. Griffith
1538 Mr. & Mrs. Augustus C. Barler
1680 Henry C. Eddy & dr.
1684 Mr. & Mrs. E. B. Mallory & drs.
  Receiving day Thursday
1754 Mr. & Mrs. Edward A. Renwick
1764 Mr. & Mrs. A. P. Brink & dr.
  Receiving day Friday
1764 Percy A. Brink
1960 Mr. & Mrs. H. S. Harris
1960 Dr. H. C. Will
1960 Mr. & Mrs. C. W. Phillips
3504 Mr. & Mrs. Wm. J. Mize
3660 Mr. & Mrs. Hervey E. Keeler
3714 Mr. & Mrs. Edwin F. Hill
3714 Mrs. Robert Hill

2887 Mr. & Mrs. Chas. A. Birney
2887 Mrs. Laura French
2915 Mr. & Mrs. Louis O'Neill
2915 Mr. & Mrs. B. F. Bush
3015 Mr. & Mrs. A. L. Dewar
3015 Harold Dewar
3075 Mr. & Mrs. A. W. Greene
  Receiving day Thursday
3229 Mr. & Mrs. John B. Fergus & dr.
3229 William L. Fergus
3701 Mrs. J. Sherman Hall & drs.
3701 Mr. & Mrs. Edward H. Alling
3701 Louis J. Hall
3707 Mr. & Mrs. George Straith
3707 Mrs. J. Higgins
3755 Mr. & Mrs. Lloyd G. Kirkland
3789 Mrs. J. Harry Coyne & dr.

SHERWIN AVENUE.

903 Mr. & Mrs. John F. Brueckner
1033 Mrs. F. S. Hine
1039 Mr. & Mrs. W. N. VandeWerker
1043 Mr. & Mrs. J. M. Glenn
1059 Mr. & Mrs. Frank Beebe

802 Mr. & Mrs. Ernest Bredow
822 Mr. & Mrs. Wm. H. Hess
822 Robert H. Given
832 Mr. & Mrs. Charles H. Johnson

1065 Mr. & Mrs. Chas. H. Reeves
1127 Mr. & Mrs. Walter H. Chamberlin

910 Mr. & Mrs. Calvin B. Cady
1062 Mr. & Mrs. Chas. E. Catlin

SOUTHPORT AVENUE.

2245 Mr. & Mrs. J. P. Bowman & dr.
2245 L. J. Bowman
3125 Mr. & Mrs. Henry Borsch
4035 Mr. & Mrs. John Friemann

4131 Mr. & Mrs. Geo. W. Shippey
4131 Mr. & Mrs. Geo. E. Shippey
4141 Mr. & Mrs. Hogan D. Cosby

ST. CLAIR STREET.

51 Rev. & Mrs. Elijah S. Fairchild
51 Meredith H. Fairchild

51 Arthur E. Fairchild
51 Emil L. Fairchild

ST. JAMES PLACE.

9 Mr. & Mrs. S. M. Custer
9 Mr. & Mrs. David Wylie
11 Samuel D. Stryker
25 Mr. & Mrs. C. H. Murray
25 Mrs. R. E. Cowdery
27 Mrs. J. H. Truman & dr.
29 Mr. & Mrs. Frank Peters
29 Frank M. Peters
37 Mr. & Mrs. Wm. W. Reid
43 Mr. & Mrs. E. W. Davy
49 Mr. & Mrs. William R. Barnes
49 Mr. & Mrs. Alexander Krauss
49 Marcel Krauss
55 Mrs. Augusta Erwin
55 Mrs. Ida Martin
57 Mrs. L. P. McDaid
57 Carl Haller

----

48 Mr. & Mrs. Fred K. Wells
50 Mr. & Mrs. S. Harnstrom
50 Mr. & Mrs. Lucian M. Williams

8 Mr. & Mrs. Miles S. Gregory
8 Mrs. Sarah Gregory & dr.
8 Dr. & Mrs. Carl Gramm
8 Dr. & Mrs. Wm. M. Thompson
10 Mr. & Mrs. Chas. A. Higgins
16 Mr. & Mrs. Richard McDaniel
16 Mr. & Mrs. R. N. Rogers
22 Mr. & Mrs. Theo. H. Purple
24 Mr. & Mrs. C. Daniels
    Receiving day Thursday
28 Mr. & Mrs. W. H. Gairnduff
28 Miss Netta Nixon
30 Mr. & Mrs. Chas. T. Wilt & dr.
    Receive Thursday
30 Elmer E. Wilt
30 Race N. Wilt
36 Mrs. Louisa Glanz & dr.
36 Louis D. Glanz
36 Alexander E. Glanz
38 Mr. & Mrs. Mathew W. Berriman
42 Mr. & Mrs. Paul Gerding
42 W. Meyer

NORTH STATE STREET.

205 Dr. & Mrs. Melvin A. Root
297 Mrs. D. W. Coakley & drs.
    Receiving day Tuesday
297 Dr. W. Byron Coakley
297 Mr. & Mrs. H. C. Muhlke
299 Mr. & Mrs. Joseph H. Muhlke
299 Dr. & Mrs. A. Belcham Keyes
307 Mr. & Mrs. J. H. Tiedemann & dr.
383 Andrew Scherer
385 Mrs. Kathryn E. Fallis
385 Mr. & Mrs. Geo. H. McCune & dr.
385 Dr. Philip Schuyler Doane

180 Dr. W. A. D. Montgomery
188 Mr. & Mrs. A. Hieronymus
190 Mr. & Mrs. Joseph S. Martin
    Receiving day Thursday
194 Mr. & Mrs. J. J. Gledhill
214 Dr. & Mrs. Richard A. Neale
    Receiving day Wednesday
226 Mr. & Mrs. Wm. Sharpe
    Receiving day Wednesday
296 Mr. & Mrs. W. W. Graves
302 Mr. & Mrs. A. A. Dwelle
304 Mr. & Mrs. Allen McIntyre
308 Miss Helen D. Wheeler
308 Mr. & Mrs. Alvin Carr McCord

20

387 Mr. & Mrs. Charles E. Hempstead
387 Dr. Geo. Paull Marquis
387 Dr. & Mrs. I. F. Upson
397 Frank Cunes
399 H. F. Jaeger
399 Mrs. Caroline Jaeger & drs.
399 Edward B. Burling
401 Mrs. Carrie Walker & dr.
401 William B. McCluer
401 Henry W. Brant
401 E. H. Stroud
401 John Maynard Harlan
401 Charles K. Foster
401 William C. Gamble
401 Francis C. Turner
401 George Valentine
401 Arthur T. Shattuck
401 Mrs. J. W. Kennicott
405 Mr. & Mrs. W. F. Childs
415 Mr. & Mrs. W. R. Sears & dr.
415 Miss A. M. Flanagan
415 Mr. & Mrs. Stanley Fleetwood
415 Mr. & Mrs. George S. Thurber
423 Mr. & Mrs. Chas. H. Hulburd & dr.
425 Mr. & Mrs. J. K. Cady
425 Mrs. Emma W. Case
427 Mr. & Mrs. Nelson Thomasson
427 Leonard Thomasson
429 Mr. & Mrs. R. D. Bokum
439 Mr. & Mrs. Robert Berger
449 Mr. & Mrs. Edw. H. Valentine
449 E. Archibald Valentine
461 Dr. & Mrs. Albert Harris Hoy
    Receiving day Monday
461 Miss Elizabeth Hoy
463 Mr. & Mrs. Walter L. Fisher
467 Mr. & Mrs. Samuel R. Jewett
469 Mr. & Mrs. C. H. Worcester
469 Mr. & Mrs. H. E. Southwell
483 Mr. & Mrs. Geo. T. Odell
485 Mr. & Mrs. Sherburn Sanborn & drs.
495 Mr. & Mrs. Stewart Spalding
495 George Burry
497 Mr. & Mrs. Edward M. Samuel
499 Mr. & Mrs. John E. Lloyd
499 Mr. & Mrs. Chas. P. Wurts
499 Mr. & Mrs. Chas. J. Lonergan
    Receive Tuesday
499 William Ives
499 Mr. & Mrs. H. N. Taylor
501 Mr. & Mrs. D. Milton Fisk
    Receiving day Monday

308 Mr. & Mrs. Elisha R. Nichols
314 Dr. & Mrs. C. J. E. Vermeren
314 Dr. & Mrs. B. H. Kershaw
388 Mr. & Mrs. John Prindiville & dr. *Receiving day Monday*
388 Redmond Prindiville
388 Thomas J. Prindiville
388 Miss A. Prendergast
396 Mr. & Mrs. Edward W. Bangs
398 Alfred H. Wittstein
398 August W. Wittstein
398 Miss Emma Wittstein
400 Mr. & Mrs. E. O. Brown
402 Dr. L. C. Pardee
402 Mrs. Agnes S. Pardee
402 Miss Agnes Pardee.
410 Mr. & Mrs. Henry C. Bannard
412 Mr. & Mrs. Charles F. Quincy
414 Mr. & Mrs. Henry S. Robbins
    Receiving day Monday
416 Mr. & Mrs. Geo. W. Reessing
418 Adolph Cudell
420 Dr. William J. Hawkes & dr.
422 Mr. & Mrs. Thos. D. Yates
424 Dr. & Mrs. Ernst Schmidt
424 Dr. Louis E. Schmidt
424 Miss Susan Hepp
426 Mrs. Eliza Talbot & dr.
426 Mrs. Porter P. Heywood
428 R. P. Bates
428 E. A. Bates
428 Miss J. H. Hiebler
430 Mr. & Mrs. Paul B. Warner
432 Mr. & Mrs. H. W. Henshaw
    Receiving day Monday
432 Charles W. Henshaw
434 Mr. & Mrs. John R. Wilson
434 Willis J. Ripley
440 Wm. C. Moulton
440 Rudolf Hasselgren
450 Leonard Schmidt
450 Leo F. Schmidt
450 Max Schmidt
450 Mr. & Mrs. Ferdinand Hotz
460 Mr. & Mrs. Edward Engle & dr.
460 Miss Amelia Vette
470 Mr. & Mrs. Geo. Castle
474 Mr. & Mrs. Horace E. Fisk
476 Mr. & Mrs. Charles A. Chapin & drs. *Receiving day Tuesday*
476 H. C. Chapin
480 Mr. & Mrs. John K. Stearns
482 Mr. & Mrs. Walter Morton Howland
502 Mr. & Mrs. W. B. McIlvaine

501 Mrs. Edward Craft Green
503 Mrs. W. H. Estey
503 Mr. & Mrs. E. B. Hawley
527 Mr. & Mrs. Ira Couch Wood
531 Mr. & Mrs. A. C. Mather
533 Mr. & Mrs. W. W. Gurley
533 Mrs. Kathryn T. Patterson
537 Mr. & Mrs. H. S. Durand & dr.
537 Mr. & Mrs. Samuel E. Hall
541 Dr. & Mrs. Henry Hooper & drs.
543 Mr. & Mrs. George B. Harris
545 Mr. & Mrs. S. S. Sherman & dr.
547 Mr. & Mrs. Fred S. Sherman
553 Mr. & Mrs. J. B. Inderrieden & drs.
553 John L. Inderrieden
553 Joseph S. Inderrieden
553 C. V. Inderrieden
555 Alexander Toll Felix
555 B. F. Felix
555 Mr. & Mrs. Ben Bates Felix
557 Mrs. C. S. Kirk
565 Mr. & Mrs. Frank W. Stanley
583 Mr. & Mrs. Charles A. Mair
Receiving day Monday
589 Mr. & Mrs. L. W. Bodman
591 Mr. & Mrs. John L. Cochran
593 Mr. & Mrs. J. S. Runnells & dr.
593 Clive Runnells
623 Most Rev. P. A. Feehan

608 Mr. & Mrs. Auguste Brosseau
Receiving day Monday
610 Mr. & Mrs. William Dickinson

504 Mr. & Mrs. Ruthven Deane
506 Mr. & Mrs. John Russell Adams
Receiving day Monday
506 John Hackett Adams
506 Miss Alice Montgomerie Adams
508 Mr. & Mrs. Arthur Brittan
508 Miss Caroline A. Brittan
510 Mrs. E. K. Beach & drs.
510 C. B. Beach
514 Mrs. George W. Smith
514 Kinney Smith
514 Miss Katherine Smith
518 Mr. & Mrs. C. T. Wheeler & dr.
528 Mr. & Mrs. Milton W. Kirk
528 Miss Emma Kirk
528 Walter T. Kirk
534 Mr. & Mrs. Thomas S. Chard
536 Mr. & Mrs. Chas. L. Allen
536 Miss Dora Allen
538 Gen. & Mrs. M. D. Hardin
540 Mr. & Mrs. George A. Weiss
544 Mr. & Mrs. C. K. Miller
550 Mr. & Mrs. A. M. Pence & drs.
552 Mr. & Mrs. Jacob A. Wolford
552 Thomas C. Dennehy
556 Mr. & Mrs. Augustus A. Engle
556 Walter J. Engle
560 Mr. & Mrs. A. Mackay
576 Mr. & Mrs. Fred'k Seymour Winston
596 Mr. & Mrs. John A. Spoor
Receiving day Monday
600 Dr. & Mrs. Arnold C. Klebs
606 Mr. & Mrs. William H. Bush
606 Miss Clara B. Bush

STRATFORD PLACE.

15 Mr. & Mrs. William Nash
15 Mrs. Christiana Schoen
27 Mrs. Louis H. Boldenweck
31 Mr. & Mrs. Frank P. Jackson
35 Mr. & Mrs. Edwin S. Hartwell & dr. *Receiving day Thursday*
35 Richard K. Hartwell
35 Joseph Lane
47 Dr. & Mrs. R. M. Paine
51 Mr. & Mrs. Abert B. Towers
65 Mr. & Mrs. S. S. Gregory

36 Mr. & Mrs. George M. Harvey
38 Mr. & Mrs. Egbert Jamieson
50 Mr. & Mrs. M. M. Jamieson
50 Malcolm M. Jamieson jr.
50 William D. Jamieson
68 Mr. & Mrs. Edward L. Canfield
68 George H. Jenney

77 Mr. & Mrs. Joseph B. Cavanaugh
Receiving day Tuesday
77 Mr. & Mrs. Bernard Cavanaugh

SUNNYSIDE AVENUE.

235 Mr. & Mrs. Joseph C. Brompton
737 Mr. & Mrs. Sherman H. Gillette
823 Mr. & Mrs. Wm. C. B. Richardson

496 C. L. Canda
496 Mr. & Mrs. Frank A. Nelles
538 Dr. & Mrs. T. A. Keeton

230 Mr. & Mrs. Oscar A. Beyer
236 Dr. & Mrs. Frank L. Peiro
310 Mr. & Mrs. F. Jaros
346 Mr. & Mrs. Geo. A. Upton
346 Dr. & Mrs. R. N. Morris
490 Rev. & Mrs. Henry C. Jennings
& drs.
496 Mr. & Mrs. Felix Canda & dr.

SUPERIOR STREET.

273 James E. Bourke
273 Mrs. D. Quirk
273 Mr. & Mrs. Nicholas J. Neary
277 Dr. J. J. Muldoon
313 Mr. & Mrs. E. B. Strong
315 Col. & Mrs. P. J. Hennessy
319 Mr. & Mrs. Chas. Henrotin
319 Edward C. Henrotin
319 Charles M. Henrotin
361 John A. Ryerson
361 Theodore R. Tyler
361 George K. Davol
361 W. H. Schmidt
361 John B. Dempster
361 Harold Eldridge
365 Mr. & Mrs. Alexander Fair
369 Mr. & Mrs. Frederick H. Winston
Receiving day Wednesday
369 Ralph T. Winston
371 Mr. & Mrs. Edgar H. Carmack
371 Mr. & Mrs. Walter K. Vrooman
& dr.
373 William E. Strong
373 Miss Carrie M. Strong
377-379 The McIntosh
Robert J. Cary
Mr. & Mrs. Samuel T. Chase
Mrs. W. H. Hearding & drs.
Mr. & Mrs. John Corse Howard
Mr. & Mrs. James Keeley
Mr. & Mrs. Edward MacGregor
Mr. & Mrs. Henry E. Mason
Mr. & Mrs. W. T. Morgan
Rev. Luther Pardee
Mr. & Mrs. Robert H. Carter
Potter
Mr. & Mrs. Fred A. Smith
381-383 The Garrard
Mr. & Mrs. J. H. Adams
Marvin E. Barnhart
Arthur F. Evans
Mr. & Mrs. Daniel Evans & dr.

296 William D. Beall
306 Mr. & Mrs. James Walsh & drs.
306 Walter Shankland
320 Miss Mary M. Anderson
320 Mrs. E. F. Anderson
320 Miss Josephine Large
322 John L. Lincoln
322 Colbert H. Greer
322 Jasper Whiting
322 William Hulin
324 Mr. & Mrs. T. H. Harney
326 Mr. & Mrs. Allan P. Millar
326 Earl B. Millar
326 Harry L. Arnold
326 Allan M. Arnold
328 Mr. & Mrs. Slason Thompson
396 Mr. & Mrs. E. W. Miller
400 Mr. & Mrs. James S. Gibbs
408 Miss M. Goggin
410 Mr. & Mrs. D. P. Phelps
420 Mr. & Mrs. Thomas Barry
424 Mrs. Hugh MacMillan & dr.
Receiving day Wednesday
424 Mrs. M. A. McMillan
426 Mr. & Mrs. N. Kniffen Goodrich

Mr. & Mrs. Chas. C. Finkler
Mr. & Mrs. Frederick H. Gade
George M. Lyon
Miss Elizabeth Lyon
Mr. & Mrs. Henry W. McKelvy
& dr.
Dr. & Mrs. Wm. A. Pusey
Mr. & Mrs. C. L. Stewart
Dr. & Mrs. Wm. H. Taggart
Mr. & Mrs. F. A. Thomas
397 Mr. & Mrs. J. T. Menefee & drs.
399 Mr. & Mrs. W. R. Manierre &
dr.
399 George Manierre. jr.
409 E. H. Haines
409 Norman Kellogg

409 W. B. McElevy
417 Mr. & Mrs. Thos. S. McClelland
   & drs.
417 Miss Ella M. McClelland
419 Mr. & Mrs. Thomas J. Shay &
   dr.

423 Mr. & Mrs. Henry Rogers
   Campbell & drs.
    Receiving day Thursday
425 Mr. & Mrs. Jewett E. Ricker
425 D. Swing Ricker

SURF STREET.

1815 Mr. & Mrs. J. S. Osgood
2007 Mr. & Mrs. John M. Roach

———

1904 Mr. & Mrs. Luther H. Peirce
1910 Mr. & Mrs. C. C. Merriman
    Receiving day Thursday
1920 Mr. & Mrs. Theodore Arnold

1824 Mr. & Mrs. Wm. Marshall
1828 Mr. & Mrs. R. Periolat & dr.
1828 Jacob Gross
1836 Mr. & Mrs. Theo. A. Kochs
1844 Mr. & Mrs. Nels Johnson
1848 Mr. & Mrs. C. H. Hanson
1852 Mr. & Mrs. Carl Binder
1860 Mr.&Mrs.CharlesG.Muller&dr

TOUHY AVENUE.

501 Mr. & Mrs. Geo. W. Adams
743 Mr. & Mrs. Harlow W. Phelps
   & drs.
765 Mr. & Mrs. Henry Daly
807 Mr. & Mrs. Henry P. Daly & dr.
817 Mr. & Mrs. Ashlin J. Beckler
839 Mr. & Mrs. Lyman H. Partridge

———

904 Mr. & Mrs. Wm. L. Crawford
904 Neil D. Crawford

532 Rev. & Mrs. Festus P. Cleveland
532 Mr. & Mrs. John D. Cleveland
618 Mr. & Mrs. Edward Fielding
760 Mr. & Mrs. Reuben E. Clark
764 Mr. & Mrs. James F. Ryan & dr.
776 Mr. & Mrs. Geo. S. Monroe & dr.
812 Mr. & Mrs. Wm. G. Diederich
828 Mr. & Mrs. Edward F. Webster
828 Mrs. Martha H. Webster
852 Mr. & Mrs. Franklin H. Doland
   & drs.

TOWER COURT.

1 Edward S. Isham
1 Edward S. Isham jr.
1 Miss A. E. Isham
1 Miss Frances Isham
1 Mr. & Mrs. Pierrepont Isham
    Receiving day Monday
3 Mr. & Mrs. Wm. R. Farquhar
3 Mrs. Harold S. Peck
3 Miss Annah M. Peck

6 Mr. & Mrs. Urban H. Broughton
    Receiving day Wednesday
10 Mr. & Mrs. Sartell Prentice
10 E. Parmalee Prentice
10 Miss Mary I. Prentice

———

3 Miss Haroldine Peck
5 Mr. & Mrs. Chas. H. Richardson

VICTOR STREET.

1089 Mr. & Mrs. Milton A. Daily

1089 Frank Daily

WALTON PLACE.

9 Mr. & Mrs. J. C. Black
15 Mr. & Mrs. Joseph Winterbotham
15 Joseph Winterbotham jr.
15 John H. Winterbotham
15 Miss Rue Winterbotham
19 Mr. & Mrs. C. M. Smith & drs.

16 Mr. & Mrs. Frank Gilbert
18 S. H. Hubbard
18 Lowrie McClurg
18 R. G. McGann
20 Mr. & Mrs. Fred W. Gookin
20 Miss Mary H. Gookin
22 Mrs. George F. Wright

19 Miss Mary Rozet Smith
19 Francis Drexel Smith
20 Mr.&Mrs.Chas.F.Mather Smith
59 Mr. & Mrs. G. D. Anthony
69 Mr. & Mrs. Joseph Paul & dr.
97 John F. Stafford
97 Miss Juniata Stafford
97 Miss Minnie Stafford
   Receives Monday afternoon
                —
K Mr. & Mrs. Chas. P. McAvoy
L Mr. & Mrs. Edwin P. Jaquith
M Mr. & Mrs. H. M. Schermer-
   horn
N Miss Grace T. Howe
O Dr. & Mrs. Arthur Burley
   Hosmer
R Mr. & Mrs. H. F. Carpenter
S Mr. & Mrs. Geo. Day Mc-
   Birney
T Mr. & Mrs. A. V. Abbott
V Mr.& Mrs. Geo.Mills Rogers
V Miss Grace J. Hayes
W Mrs. John G. Rogers
W Henry Rogers
X Mrs. Julia Ray
106 Mr. & Mrs. M. J. Naghten

24 Mr. & Mrs. Henry Sherman
   Boutell
24 Mrs. Charles Horatio Gates
26 Mr. & Mrs. Wm. S. North
28 Mr. & Mrs. John B. Lee
28 Mrs. John H. Avery
28 Mr. & Mrs. Jos. E. Dunton
28 John H. Hume
30 Dr. & Mrs. C. F. Noyes
30 Mrs. Sarah B. Moore
30 Mr. & Mrs. J. C. Ficklin
30 Mr. & Mrs. Frederick Swift
30 R. S. Emmet
30 W. H. Comstock
30 Andrew D. Lawrie
30 Alvah K. Lawrie
32 Dr. A. Melville Tully
32 Edward Inglis Frost
52 & 54 sw. cor. Rush, The
   Majestic
   Mr. & Mrs. Geo. F. Fischer
A Dr. & Mrs. W. F. Follansbee
B Mr. & Mrs. Harry Rubens
D Dr. & Mrs. W. K. Harrison
E Miss E. Frenz
F Mr. & Mrs. Wm. Borner
H Mr. & Mrs. E. A. Harriman
   Receiving day Wednesday
I Mrs. Ann E. Maclean & dr.

WARNER AVENUE.

945 Mr. & Mrs. Wm. Twick
965 Mr. & Mrs. Chas. E. Schick

930 William F. Gall
930 Mrs. Barbara Gall
930 Charles H. Gall
964 Mr. & Mrs. George E. Gall

WASHINGTON PLACE.

1 James R. Bryson
1 Miss May Bryson
5 Mrs. R. G. Bogue & dr.
7 Judge & Mrs. B. D. Magruder
7 Henry Latham Magruder
                —
8 Miss May W. Durfee

2 Mrs. Gordon Hall
2 Dr. & Mrs. Alfred M. Hall
2 Dr. John Chester Lyman
2 Mrs. Theodore Butler
8 Miss Charlotte S. Durfee
8 Edward H. Pease
8 George W. Brown

WAVELAND AVENUE.

1719 Mr. & Mrs. Henry Tewes

WEBSTER AVENUE.

233 Dr. & Mrs. J. F. Runnels
283 Mr. & Mrs. Jno. T. Long
289 Dr. C. J. Heylmann

286 Mr. & Mrs. Charles A. Dean
302 Mr. & Mrs. Henry F. Donovan
310 Louis G. Knight

289 Miss Angelica Heylmann
    Receive Thursday
289 Miss Minnie Heylmann
295 Mr. & Mrs. B. T. Kennedy & dr.
295 Mrs. Annie Wood
295 Mr. & Mrs. A. Wegener
305 Mr. & Mrs. Delavan S. Foote
305 W. C. Foote
305 D. C. Foote
307 Mr. & Mrs. Richard M. Hennessy
309 Mr. & Mrs. W. A. McGuire
309 Mrs. Margaret Crogan
311 Mr. & Mrs. Joseph Hodgson
    Receive Thursday
321 Mr. & Mrs. Otto Guenther
497 Mr. & Mrs. John A. Hand&drs.
511 Miss Josie S. Cary

320 Mr. & Mrs. Carl Huncke
398 Mr. & Mrs. J. H. Collins
398 George F. Collins
398 William M. Collins
488 Mr. & Mrs. A. B. Hill
488 H. P. Daw
508 Mr. & Mrs. John H. Stoddard
510 H. I. Howland
510 Mrs. James E. Howland
512 Mr. & Mrs. G. Dengler
514 Mr. & Mrs. M. Freehling

555 Mrs. C. Jeanneret
555 Harry G. Jeanneret
555 J. Sidney Browne
557 Mr. & Mrs. C. W. Jeanneret
563 Mr. & Mrs. E. Harland

WELLINGTON STREET.

1467 Mr. & Mrs. Robert M. Jaffray
    Receive 1st & 3d Wednesdays
1467 Mrs. R. T Reynolds
1469 Mr. & Mrs. E. A. Bolter
1503 Mr. & Mrs. W. T. Mason
1509 Mr. & Mrs. George Beaumont
1509 Mr. & Mrs. Fred Ascher
    Receive 3d Thursday in mo.
1693 Mr. & Mrs. H. C. Knoke
1705 Mr. & Mrs. W. M. Watson
1841 Mr. & Mrs. Chas. N. Holden & dr.
1843 Mr. & Mrs. M. D. Matteson
1847 Mr. & Mrs. Geo. Rounsavell
1901 Mr. & Mrs. Jacob Birk & drs.
1901 William A. Birk
1915 Mr. & Mrs. Wyllys W. Baird

1920 Mr. & Mrs. H. B. Butler
1924 Mr. & Mrs. Dunlap Smith
    Receiving day Wednesday
1928 Mr. & Mrs. Henry Rang
1928 Henry Rang jr.
1928 Louis A. Rang

1318 Mr. & Mrs. John O. Barber
    Receiving day Wednesday
1436 Mr. & Mrs. Frederick W. Spelz
1480 Mr. & Mrs. Justus Chancellor
    Receiving day Wednesday
1644 Mr. & Mrs. Geo. Messersmith
1668 Mr. & Mrs. Nicholas Watry
1698 Mr. & Mrs. Henry R. Platt
1698 Mr. & Mrs. E. C. Ritsher
1710 Mrs. Sarah A. Shutts
1710 Mr. & Mrs. Adelbert J. Shutts
1710 Mr. & Mrs. C. T. Messinger
1810 Mr. & Mrs. J. W. Buschwah
1820 Mr. & Mrs. David Williams
1826 Mr. & Mrs. Herman Arnold
1830 Mr. & Mrs. Arthur J. Kirkwood & dr.
1844 Mr. & Mrs. Frederick Baumann & drs.
1844 Edward S. Baumann
1854 Mr. & Mrs. John H. Law & dr.
    Receiving day Monday
1854 Mrs. Laura Law Meek
1900 Mr. & Mrs. John Clifford & dr.
    Receiving day Wednesday

NORTH WELLS STREET.

321 Mrs. Mary C. Hild
321 Frederick H. Hild
395 Dr. Edmund A. Boas
613 Mr. & Mrs. Charles E. Freund
617 Mr. & Mrs. John C. Hirt
617 Mr. & Mrs. Henry Piper & dr.
695 Mr. & Mrs. August Gross
721 Dr. & Mrs. A. H. Peck
721 Mr. & Mrs. Christian Kussel

460 Mr. & Mrs. Wm. Freund & dr.
460 Herman Freund
634 Mr. & Mrs. J. C. Ehlen
640 Mr. & Mrs. Moses M. Fletcher
696 Mr. & Mrs. Frank Tempel & dr.
700 Mr. & Mrs. Moritz Freytag
722 Mr. & Mrs. Thomas H. Dwyer

723 Mr. & Mrs. Hubert Press

WEST COURT.

301 Mr. & Mrs. Norbert Becker
301 Mr. & Mrs. Chas. W. Rogers
307 Mr. & Mrs. Wm. R. Dawes

304 Dr. & Mrs. Frank M. Johnson
304 Robert J. Hollister
306 Mr. & Mrs. John H. Free
308 Mr. & Mrs. Fred D. Shaver
308 Mr. & Mrs. W. J. Melick

WILSON AVENUE.

237 Mr. & Mrs. Carl Anderson
237 John G. Anderson
295 Mr. & Mrs. A. J. Schuler

———

1514 Mr. & Mrs. William H. Fisk ·
1514 Devotion C. Eddy
1514 Dr. & Mrs. Harry L. Williams

214 Mr. & Mrs. John A. Thompson
298 Mr. & Mrs. Edward F. Brown
704 Mr. & Mrs. Henry W. Hoyt
808 Dr. Abram J. Moore
822 Mr. & Mrs. Thos. McClay
822 John McClay
828 Mr. & Mrs. Wm. Lester Bodine
1436 Mr. & Mrs. Peter Schmidt

WILTON AVENUE.

1191 Mr. & Mrs. S. D. Herr
1195 Mr. & Mrs. Felix E. McHugh
1199 Mr. & Mrs. Wm. Mitchell
1297 Mr. & Mrs. Max P. Portman

1344 Mr. & Mrs. Chas. H. Pfeil & dr.

———

1323 Mr. & Mrs. Wm. H. Dorothy

NORTH WINCHESTER AVENUE.

2567 Mr. & Mrs. P. P. Porter
2567 Dr. P. B. Porter
2593 Mr. & Mrs. James E. Keith
          Receiving day Wednesday
2629 Mr. & Mrs. M. VanAllen & drs.
2665 Mr. & Mrs. E. E. Hutchins
2721 Mr. & Mrs. Edmund Q. Sewall
2725 Mr. & Mrs. G. J. Atkins
2763 Mr. & Mrs. P. W. Gray
2781 Mr. & Mrs. Irving I. Stone

———

2798 Mrs. Sarah E. Norton

2580 Mr. & Mrs. Hy. R. Sandes
2608 Mr. & Mrs. A. W. Mumford
2614 Rev. & Mrs. J. B. Lucas
2614 Chas. W. Lucas
2660 Mr. & Mrs. Martin C. Meader
2730 Mr. & Mrs. Robert W. Dunn
2736 Mrs. J. S. Seaverns
2758 Mrs. Charles R. Soule
2762 Mr. & Mrs. Edmund D. Brig-
          ham
2798 John F. Hack
2798 Edward Hack

WINDSOR AVENUE.

1531 Mr. & Mrs. John H. Johnson
1537 Mr. & Mrs. Edward P. Welles
1539 Mrs. S. Rinder

1542 Mr. & Mrs. W. C. Harrah
1544 Mr. & Mrs. David W. Miller

WINONA AVENUE.

1015 Miss G. C. Otterson
1015 Mrs. J. Otterson
1069 Mrs. John Shepherd & dr.
1069 Chester H. Freeman
1069 Miss Emma Blanche Freeman
1069 Edward C. Comfort

918 Mr. & Mrs. Albert L. Brown
1104 Mr. & Mrs. Myron D. Smith

1093 W. S. Pease
1093 Mrs. L. S. Pease
1099 Mr. & Mrs. D. F. Van Antwerp

WINTHROP AVENUE.

363 Mr. & Mrs. G. A. Pond
419 Rev. & Mrs. Gustav Zollmann & dr.
419 Mr. & Mrs. John Zollmann
585 Mr. & Mrs. Max Lau
609 Mr. & Mrs. Willis G.Stoughton
667 Mr. & Mrs. G. R. Peare
675 Mr. & Mrs. Frank A. B. Moore
869 Mr. & Mrs. Robert L. Morley
871 Mr. & Mrs. F. L. Macomber
875 Mr. & Mrs. W. J. Ammen
883 Mr. & Mrs. John C. Scovell
883 Mrs. Hamilton Spencer
891 Mr. & Mrs. S. H. Littlefield
921 Mr. & Mrs. Bernard Goldsmith & drs.
921 Howard F. Goldsmith.
1003 Mr. & Mrs. B. H. Pratt
1039 Mr. & Mrs. Clarence M. Stiles
1045 Mrs. Handley Mason
1049 Mr. & Mrs. E. L. Burrell
1069 Mr. & Mrs. John L. Tate
1117 Mr. & Mrs. E. F. Luce
1127 Mr. & Mrs. R. J. Zorge
1199 Mr. & Mrs. Albert M. Crane
1205 Mr. & Mrs. J. H. Gates
1211 Mr. & Mrs. C. De Peyster Berry
1219 Mr. & Mrs. B. D. Heeb
1229 Mr. & Mrs. Chas. B. Stearns
1255 Mr. & Mrs. E. J. Henry

1260 Mr. & Mrs. James A. Carey
1276 Mr. & Mrs. F. M. Smith & dr.
1076 Mr. & Mrs. Robert J. Morrow
1126 Mr. & Mrs. R. G. Tennant & dr.
1126 William G. Tennant
1132 Mr. & Mrs. Emil Goerke
1136 Mr. & Mrs. E. G. Heath

336 Mr. & Mrs. A. Collender
368 Mr. & Mrs. N. Lederer
412 Mr. & Mrs. Stewart Galbraith
416 Dr. & Mrs. Wm. W. Hartman
432 Mr. & Mrs. Daniel W. Wilson
436 Mr. & Mrs. Chas. A. McDonald
444 Mr. & Mrs. Robt. E. Ingal
502 Mr. & Mrs. Leo Karpen
684 Mr. & Mrs. Geo. F. Mills
684 Miss Jennie A. Drake
684 John A. Aitkins
688 Mr. & Mrs. Edwin S. Jackman
728 Mr. & Mrs. Henry Curtis
732 Mr. & Mrs. Edgar E. Rogers
732 Mr. & Mrs. A. N. Fitzsimmons
742 Mr. & Mrs. Martin Andrews
802 Mr. & Mrs. H. H. Osgood & drs.
812 Mr. & Mrs. John Hewitt
822 Mr. & Mrs. J. C. Gerstetter
822 Mrs. John Gerstetter
870 Mr. & Mrs. Edwin J. Bowes jr.
870 Mr. & Mrs. W. P. Ketcham
874 Mr. & Mrs. Henry L. Pitcher
874 Mrs. Caroline Cary & dr.
888 Mr. & Mrs. Thos. F. Sheridan
894 Mr. & Mrs. E. E. Dick
    Receiving day Thursday
1016 Mrs. Almira M. Gilbert & dr.
1016 Miss Mabel Shackleton
1030 Mr. & Mrs. Robert Wahl
1046 Mr. & Mrs. J. B. Thorsen
1066 Rev. & Mrs. J. M. D. Davidson
1066 Hilary E. Campbell
1210 Mr. & Mrs. S. W. Belknap & dr. *Receiving day Thursday*
1210 Mr. & Mrs. Benj. C. Hawkes
1220 Mr. & Mrs. Charles P. Whitney
1220 Mrs. Kate A. Whitney
1226 Mr. & Mrs. Geo. E. Watson

WISCONSIN STREET.

9 Mr. & Mrs. William McNeil
23 Mr. & Mrs. John Druecker
    Receiving day Thursday
25 Mr. & Mrs. A. I. Frank
27 Mrs. W. C. Andrus
27 Mr. & Mrs. William H. Andrus
    Receiving day Friday
29 Mr. & Mrs. R. Phillipson & dr.
35 Mrs. I. B. Hanna
57 Dr. & Mrs. Philip H. Matthei
    Receiving day last Wed. in mo.

22 Mr. & Mrs. Frank T. Bently
22 Mr. & Mrs. R. B. Chase & dr.
    Receiving day Thursday
22 Mr. & Mrs. Franklin L. Chase
46 Mr. & Mrs. Fritz Sontag
56 Mrs. David W. Rowlands
56 William D. Rowlands
60 and 62 Hotel De Lincoln
    Mr. & Mrs. R. R. Knapp

WÓLFRAM STREET.

1511 Mr. & Mrs. Fred Heinberg ·
1537 Fred C. Christy
1543 Mr. & Mrs. Chas. Harms & dr.

1506 Mr. & Mrs. Wm. H. Weckler
1510 Mr. & Mrs. Chas. Anwander
1528 Mr. & Mrs. Chas. J. Stromberg

WRIGHTWOOD AVENUE.

1225 Mr. & Mrs. F. J. Selden
1233 Mr. & Mrs.Rudolph C. Radtke
1239 Mr. & Mrs. N. J. Druecker
1239 Arthur J. Druecker
1239 Alexander Druecker
1243 Dr. & Mrs. Carl A. Weil
1245 John G. Tenney
1245 Mrs. Chas. Tenney
1247 Dr. & Mrs. Chas. F. Adams
1439 Ludwig Brown & dr.
1529 Mr. & Mrs. Lawrence J. Walsh
1725 George Liebman
1737 Mr. & Mrs. Edward Schultz
1741 Mr. & Mrs. Herman Meyer
1743 Mr. & Mrs. Arthur Dawson
1751 Mr. & Mrs. Augustus F. Nagle
Receiving day Monday
1761 Mr. & Mrs. Jay Lahmer
1765 Mr.&Mrs.Henry Schultz & drs.
1817 Mrs. Albertina Bosselman
1819 Mr. & Mrs. Adolph L. Singer
1839 Mr.& Mrs. Andrew G. Johnson
1843 Mr. & Mrs. August J. Dewes
1849 Mr. & Mrs. Francis J. Dewes
1849 Edwin P. Dewes
1901 Dr. & Mrs. Lucas R. Williams
1917 Mr. & Mrs. Chas. E. Bleyer
1919 Mr. & Mrs. Fielding L. Mercer
1921 Mr. & Mrs. George J. Williams
1921 Mr. & Mrs. Herbert W. Snow

1814 Mr. & Mrs. Philip B. Harley
1814 Mr. & Mrs. Chas. W. Fischer
1820 Mr. & Mrs. C. H. Gottig
1840 Mr. & Mrs. R. A. Greifenhagen
Receiving day 2d Tuesday
1850 Mr. & Mrs. W. D. Boyce
1938 Mr. & Mrs. Gustav Wilkie

1222 Mr. & Mrs. R. M. Hitchcock
1230 Mr. & Mrs. Geo. Kenyon Walton
Receiving day Thursday
1230 Mrs. Caroline W. Moe
1232 Mr. & Mrs. Edward C. Band
1254 Mr. & Mrs. Floyd V. Sessions
1256 Mr. & Mrs. C. Alfred Smith & dr.
1312 Mr. & Mrs. Reuben C. Mighell & dr.
1312 Mrs. Flora Moody ·
1450 Mr. & Mrs. Henry Best & dr.
1450 Mr. & Mrs. Richard Pick
1450 Gustave Mautner
1458 Mrs. Arthur Mackie & drs. ·
1512 Mrs. Jane Kinsella
1512 Joseph F. Kinsella
1512 Daniel P. Kinsella
1644 Dr. & Mrs. John A. Tomhagen
1728 Mr. & Mrs. F. A. Bischoff
1732 Robert White
1736 Mr. & Mrs. Solomon Karpen
1746 Mr. & Mrs. E. W. Bromilow
1746 Floyd Miller
1746 Dr. Chas. E. Meerhoff
1750 Mr. & Mrs. Wm. C. Titcomb
Receiving day Wednesday
1750 Mrs. Lewis O. Goodell
1754 Mr. & Mrs. Wm. M. Talcott
Receiving day Thursday
1760 Mr. & Mrs. Oscar F. Kosche
1760 Mr. & Mrs. Charles L. Loveland
1760 Mrs. Harriet Evens
1768 Mr. & Mrs. Elwyn B. Gould
1776 Mr. & Mrs. L. P. Hugel
1780 Mr. & Mrs. Frank D. Turner

YORK PLACE.

1741 Mr. & Mrs. Edward L. Humphrey

1758 Dr. & Mrs. John E. Beebe

1722 Mrs. Robert Morrow
1722 Louis R. Morrow
1724 Mr. & Mrs. Edward P. Flint
1732 Mr. & Mrs. H.O.Clausen & drs.
1752 Dr. & Mrs. Walter B. Metcalf

GARFIELD PARK

Oechslin Bros.
Props.

.....Tel. West-379

FLOWER CO.

GROWERS OF

Palms
Ferns and
Cut Flowers

Cut Roses

Party Orders, Funeral Designs, etc., Executed with Skill and Neatness on Short Notice.......

1688 W. MADISON ST.
Cor. St. Louis Ave.

PART THIRD.

WEST DIVISION.

THE BLUE BOOK

*ARRANGED ACCORDING TO STREETS AND NUMBERS,
NUMERICALLY, WITH OCCUPANTS' NAMES,
GIVING THE ODD NUMBERS IN
LEFT COLUMN, AND EVEN
IN THE RIGHT.*

WEST DIVISION.

ABERDEEN STREET.

59 Miss C. Addie Brown
59 Miss Helen Robinson

59 Edward C. Delano
95 Dr. & Mrs. R. G. Walker
171 Mr. & Mrs. Thomas H. Ling
Receiving day Tuesday

NORTH ADA STREET.

55 James W. Twohig

86 Mr. & Mrs. Fred K. Stone
86 Mrs. Calvin Stone

WEST ADAMS STREET.

267 Mr. & Mrs. James McCrea jr
267 Mr. & Mrs. M. C. Dean
267 Bradley Dean
269 Mr. & Mrs. James S. Harvey
275 Mr. & Mrs. S. T. Alling
281 Miss Virginia Sayre
285 Mr. & Mrs. W. H. Thayer
285 Mrs. Abbie D. Wilcox
285 Robert B. Wilcox
287 Mr. & Mrs. Peter Schuttler
 Receive 2d Friday in mo.
287 Peter Schuttler jr.
301 Mr. & Mrs. Christoph Hotz & dr.
339 Dr. Eugene S. Atwood
381 Jacob P. Debus
389 David Bradley
389 Mr. & Mrs. G. Cadogan Morgan
 & drs.
 Receiving day Monday
395 Mr. & Mrs. Charles H. Slack
399 Mr. & Mrs. J. B. Campbell
477 Mr. & Mrs. B. T. VanHousen
481 Mr. & Mrs. Francis Adams
483 Dr. & Mrs. W. S. Harvey
487 Mrs. Harriet A. Newton & dr.
491 Dr. & Mrs. A. C. Hewett
491 Miss Henrietta H. Waring
495 Mrs. Agnes Irons & drs.
 Receiving day Thursday

300 Mr. & Mrs. John M. Smyth & dr.
300 Thomas M. Smyth
372 Dr. & Mrs. P. J. Rowan & dr.
388 Mr. & Mrs. John F. Wright &
 dr.
392 Mr. & Mrs. E. S. Shepherd
392 Mrs. Fred Reed
398 Frank E. Donoghue
428 Dr. Sarah DeLoss
428 Dr. Sarah Kroll
430 Mr. & Mrs. Albert G. Lane
432 Mr. & Mrs. J. C. Kneale
434 Dr. H. N. Moyer
434 Mrs. Ellen Moyer
438 Philip N. Carter
438 Wallace Carter & dr.
440 Mrs. A. N. Carter
448 Mr. & Mrs. E. T. Mason & dr.
448 Frank B. Tobey
450 Dr. S. J. Beeson
454 Mrs. D. G. Sawyer
454 C. P. Sawyer
464 Mrs. L. H. Palmer & drs.
464 Dr. Andrew Stewart
464 Mr. & Mrs. George T. Link
464 Mr. & Mrs. E. A. West
464 Mrs. Elizabeth D. Jones & dr.
468 Mr. & Mrs. Geo. Blackburn
474 Mr. & Mrs. H. W. McKewin

499 Mr. & Mrs. Leverette H.Clarke
499 Mrs. John W. Hepburn .
501 Dr. & Mrs. F. Ziegfeld
501 William K. Ziegfeld
507 Mr. & Mrs. Wm. H. Morgan
507 Mr. & Mrs. Charles F. Ingalls
509 Mr. & Mrs. Wm. H. Smith
509 Jno. Zimmerman
509 Mr. & Mrs. C. C. Hilton
509 George Hilton
513 Mrs. Geo. Sherwood
517 Mr. & Mrs. W. O. Carpenter
519 Dr. David G. Rush
521 Mr. & Mrs. Wm. W. Dresden
531 Dr. Fred H. Blayney
539 Mrs. H. D. P. Bigelow
541 Mr. & Mrs. F. K. Bowes
541 Chas. Lane Bowes
541 Mrs. C. B. Lane
541 William H. Lane
543 A. C. Durborow jr.
543 Mr. & Mrs. C. E. Durborow
543 Conrad B. Durborow
575 Mr. & Mrs. George Birkhoff jr.
     & dr.
577 Mr. & Mrs. Geo. Birkhoff
581 Mr. & Mrs. S. B. Johnson & dr.
583 Mr. & Mrs. L. F. Daly
     Receiving day Wednesday
627 Mrs. Harriet D. Smibert & drs.
627 William H. Snow
629 Mrs. E. M. Little
645 Mr. & Mrs. J. D. McRae
647 Mr. & Mrs. W. S. Elliott & dr.
647 E. E. Elliott
651 Mr. & Mrs. S. B. Cochran & dr.
655 Mr. & Mrs. John C. Newcomb
655 Arthur Mercer
655 Mrs. F. R. Maher
677 Mr. & Mrs. H. S. Burkhardt &
     dr.
677 William Burkhardt
679 Dr. & Mrs. F. D. Marshall
679 George Duffy
683 Dr. & Mrs. G. M. Hammon
685 Mrs. Caroline Solbery
685 George B. Reid
687 Mr. & Mrs. G. G. Pierce
689 Mr. & Mrs. A. S. Devendorf &
     drs.
689 C. A. Devendorf
691 Mr. & Mrs. W. J. Rogan
691½ Mrs. Adelaide Lemon
691½ George S. Lemon
691½ Herbert L. Lemon
695 Mr. & Mrs. B. C. Prentiss & dr.

476 Robert Neely & drs.
476 Robert H. Neely
476 Joseph C. Neely
478 Mr. & Mrs. F. A. Bergman & dr.
484 Mr. & Mrs. E. M. Hough
484 Mrs. Eleanor M. Campbell
484 Mr. & Mrs. George Fishback &
     drs.
486 Mr. & Mrs. Edward Speakman
     Receive 4th Tuesday in mo.
486 Howland Speakman
492 Dr. & Mrs. Wm. A. Tichenor
500 Mr. & Mrs. R. S. Lyon
502 Mr. & Mrs. T. F. Mullaney
504 Mr. & Mrs. William C. Pull-
     man
506 Mr. & Mrs. G. N. Archibald &
     dr.
508 Mr. & Mrs. Peter S. Haywood
512 Mr. & Mrs. D. J. Avery & drs.
514 Rev. & Mrs J. Kittredge Wheel-
     er
516 Dr. Effa V. Davis
516 Mrs. Jennie P. Mullin & dr.
520 Rev. & Mrs. H. M. Scott
522 Mr. & Mrs. E. M. Teall
526 Mrs. Abbie J. Werst & drs.
532 Prof. & Mrs. Franklin W. Fisk
     Receiving day Saturday
538 Dr. & Mrs. O. J. Price
538 Dr. Arthur E. Price
538 Albert N. Marquis
540 Mr. & Mrs. Wm. Martin
578 Mr. & Mrs. John R. Trimmer
578 Mr. & Mrs. Chas. P. Abbey
580 M. B. Rutt
580 A. B. Rutt
582 Dr. & Mrs. A. G. Beebe
584 Dr. & Mrs. N. B. Rice
     Receive 3d Saturday in mo.
590 Dr. & Mrs. T. C. Duncan
590 Mrs. John Osborn
592 Mr. & Mrs. James Lynch & drs.
638 Mrs. Eugenia Dodd
642 Mr. & Mrs. William Ilett & dr.
644 Mr. & Mrs. J. B. Peabody & dr.
644 J. A. Peabody
656 Mr. & Mrs. C. A. Davies
660 Mrs. M. J. Forsyth & dr.
664 Mr. & Mrs. F. Hutchison & dr.
664 J. F. Hutchison
668 Mr. & Mrs. D. H. Henderson
668 Miss Ida Williams
672 Mrs. Catherine A. Sheldon &
     drs.
672 H. D. Sheldon

697 Mr. & Mrs. George D. Eddy & drs.
697 George A. Eddy
711 Mr. & Mrs. M. A. True
713 Mr. & Mrs. D. W. Baker
713 Robert R. Baker
715 Mr.& Mrs. John A. Cavanaugh
717 Mr. & Mrs. A. J. Mitchell
719 Dr. & Mrs. S. S. Bishop
719 Mrs. Peter Button
721 Col. & Mrs. J. H. Wood & dr.
729 Mr. & Mrs. F. R. McMullin
733 Mr. & Mrs. J. C. Magill & dr.
733 Geo. G. Magill
733 Charles S. Magill
735 Mr. & Mrs. N. A. Skinner
737 Mr. & Mrs. John Wain & dr.
737 Albert Wain
751 Mr. & Mrs. R. B. Arnold
757 Mr.& Mrs.W. S. S.Tucker & dr.
757 William R. Tucker
759 Judge & Mrs. E. W. Burke
759 William V. Webster
763 Mr. & Mrs. W. S. Elliott jr.
        Receiving day Thursday
763 Daniel M. Elliott
763 Lorenzo B. Elliott
821 Mr.& Mrs. James K. McGill jr.
841 Mr.& Mrs. Lothrop S. Hodges
841 Mrs. Henry Adams
843 Mr. & Mrs.W. H. Busbey& drs.
843 Mr. & Mrs. J. W. Hersey
873 Mr. & Mrs. S. E. Cleveland
875 Mr. & Mrs. A. Lewis Edgarton
877 Mr.& Mrs.Chas. T.Chandler jr.
899 Mr. & Mrs. J. B. Rogan
901 Mr. & Mrs. W. F. Rollo
903 Mr.&Mrs. Alvin Whitney & dr.
907 Dr. J. R. Corbus & drs.
907 B. Clark Corbus
913 Mr.&Mrs.Alexander C. Martin
927 Mr. & Mrs. James McGraw
927 Mr. & Mrs. I. W. Litchfield
939 Mrs. J. C. Grant
939 Duncan J. Grant
981 Mr. & Mrs. E. Erskine McMillan & drs.
983 Mr. & Mrs. James L. Board
999 Mr. & Mrs. W. J. Hemstreet & drs.
1135 John Williams
1153 Mr. & Mrs. John H. Harvey
1153 Osmond Dicker
1185 Mr.& Mrs. C. M. Holden & dr.
1189 Mr. & Mrs. J. H. Perkinson
1227 Mr. & Mrs. F. C. Morley

674 Mr. & Mrs. George Stoll
674 Mr. & Mrs. Robert H. Stoll
676 Mr. & Mrs. Frank W. Young & dr.
680 Mr. & Mrs. Emil Berger
680 Nathan Green
684 Mr. & Mrs. W. H. Iliff & dr.
688 Mr. & Mrs. Nathan De Lue
        Receiving day Friday
692 Dr. Sarah A. Conrad
692 Mr. & Mrs. Louis W. Conrad
692 Warren J. Anderson
696 Mrs. C. S. Butterfield & drs.
698 Mrs. J. C. Perrett
698 Galen J. Perrett
708 Dr. & Mrs. Martin H. Fash
710 Mr. & Mrs. A. Eddy & dr.
710 George S. Eddy
710 Thomas H. Eddy
712 Mr. & Mrs. L. Lloyd & drs.
714 Mr. & Mrs. T. A. Cantwell & dr.
        Receiving day Thursday
720 Miss Eunice A. Martin
726 Mr. & Mrs. Chas. F. Weinland
728 Mrs. Mary Vandenburgh & dr.
728 Wm. E. Vandenburgh
728 Mr. & Mrs. John D. Couffer
730 Prof. & Mrs. E. T. Harper
732 Mr. & Mrs. W. H. Gibson
734 Mrs. Elizabeth Street & dr.
736 Mr. & Mrs. Arthur B. Smith
738 Mr. & Mrs. Wm. H. Bartels
758 Dr. & Mrs. I. N. Danforth
760 Dr. & Mrs. D. Stearns White
766 Mr. & Mrs. Albert M. Osgood
766 Albert T. Osgood
766 Harry S. Osgood
766 George B. Osgood
794 Dr. & Mrs. Geo. F. Butler
800 Mrs. H. R. Josselyn
800 Dr. & Mrs. W. J. Martin
802 Mr. & Mrs. James L. Mallory
802 Mr. & Mrs. Chapman J. Root
802 Mr. & Mrs. Harvey S. Pyles
804 Mr. & Mrs. F. W. Cowlin
804 Mr. & Mrs. John H. Miller
816 Mr. & Mrs. T. C. MacMillan
816 Miss Margaret R. Goudie
820 Mr. & Mrs. Geo. W. Stoneman
822 Mr. & Mrs. Arthur Burnam
822 Mr. & Mrs. Robert Bowie
824 Mr. & Mrs. Clayton C. Pickett
828 Dr. & Mrs. A. E. Baldwin
836 Mr. & Mrs. B. F. Baker
        Receiving day Monday
836 William E. Baker

1231 Dr. & Mrs. William A. Barclay
1307 Mr. & Mrs. H. M. Pflager
1307 Mrs. Henry N. Barber
1309 Mr. & Mrs. S. W. Warner
1313 Mr. & Mrs. Frank D. Rogers
1519 Mr. & Mrs. W. M. Salter
1521 Mr. & Mrs. T. M. Humphreys
1521 William Humphreys
1537 Mr. & Mrs. Herman G. Pomy
1541 Mr. & Mrs. Chas. A. Goodwin
1541 Mr. & Mrs. Martin G. Good
1547 Mr. & Mrs. Forest Hopkins
1581 Mr. & Mrs. James Hay
1587 Dr. & Mrs. James A. Lydston
1593 Mr. & Mrs. Ernest T. Clarage
1601 Mr. & Mrs. Wm. J. Moore
1603 Mr. & Mrs. Geo. L. Ayres
1603 Mr. & Mrs. Chas. M. Roe
1605 Miss A. Thumser
1605 Miss E. Thumser
1607 Mr. & Mrs. Charles W. Gray
　　　Receive Tuesdays
1609 Mr. & Mrs. Nathan Herzog
1611 Mr. & Mrs. L. B. Shields
1611 William Lindsley
1621 Mr. & Mrs. Joseph B. Earl
　　　Receive Thursday
1629 Dr. & Mrs. J. Warren Walker
1631 Mr. & Mrs. Thos. A. Leach
1633 Mr. & Mrs. H. G. Steinson
1635 Mr. & Mrs. Sidney H. Warner
1639 Mr. & Mrs. Samuel Halls
　　　Receive Tuesday
1641 Mr. & Mrs. Calvin H. Hill
1643 Mr. & Mrs. Stephen B. Jones
　　　Receiving day Tuesday
1657 Mr. & Mrs. Frank McMartin
　　　Receiving day Thursday
1659 Mr. & Mrs. J. N. Hostetter
　　　Receiving day Thursday
1661 Mr. & Mrs. Samuel Sailor
1663 Mr. & Mrs. A. E. Barr
2281 Mr. & Mrs. William J. Maiden

———

1616 Mrs. Helen J. Stannard & dr.
1616 Harry W. Stannard
1616 Mrs. Jane P. Fittz
1622 Mr. & Mrs. Charles T. Barnes
1624 Mr. & Mrs. Adolph A. Kuhn
1640 Mr. & Mrs. Wm. J. Bristol
1642 Mr. & Mrs. Edw. S. Bristol
1644 Mr. & Mrs. Louis Nau
1644 Mr. & Mrs. W. F. Newbert
1656 Mrs. H. A. Williams

838 Mrs. Abram D. Skillman
838 Dr. Fred B. Skillman
840 Mr. & Mrs. John D. Clarke
840 J. N. Hunt
844 Dr. & Mrs. H. A. Phillips
844 James B. Muir
864 Mr. & Mrs. W. R. Cleveland
872 Mrs. A. Bielman
872 Mr. & Mrs. M. C. Paradise
874 Mr. & Mrs. Erwin H. Pifer
874 Mr. & Mrs. Wm. E. Wilcox
878 Dr. & Mrs. G. W. Newton
880 Mr. & Mrs. Albert Schwarz &
　　　dr.
880 Edward Schwarz
884 Mr. & Mrs. Job Webb
886 Mr. & Mrs. H. H. Scoville
　　　& dr.
886 Mrs. E. M. Scoville
888 Mr. & Mrs. F. E. Sagendorph
888½ Mr. & Mrs. I. Hoffert
890 Mr. & Mrs. George C. Wilce
896 Mrs. Kate A. Wise & dr.
904 Mr. & Mrs. W. Wheelock
904 William W. Wheelock
922 Mr. & Mrs. A. J. Perry
928 Mr. & Mrs. Chas. R. Williams
928 Mrs. E. A. Judson
932 Mr. & Mrs. Chas. H. Durphy
934 Mr. & Mrs. B. Subert & dr.
934 Max Subert
934 Charles Subert
936 Mr. & Mrs. B. C. Miller
938 Mr. & Mrs. S. M. Hall
942 Mr. & Mrs. David Straus
974 Mrs. Ida A. Mosher
974 E. W. Aldrich
982 Dr. & Mrs. J. H. Salisbury
982 Miss Laura Thomson
992 Dr. & Mrs. C. Todd Hood
1020 Edward J. Murphy
1020 Miss Anna M. Murphy
1022 Dr. & Mrs. M. H. McGrath
1200 Mr. & Mrs. Harvey C. Vernon
1200 Mr. & Mrs. N. DeCelle
1236 Mr. & Mrs. E. C. Chambers
1288 Dr. & Mrs. Wm. A. Barr
1302 Mr. & Mrs. E. L. McAdams
1310 Mr. & Mrs. Stephen Griffin
1312 Mr. & Mrs. Edward A. Davis
1334 Dr. & Mrs. E. L. Clifford
1524 Mr. & Mrs. S. T. Butler
1594 Mr. & Mrs. John A. Selleck
1606 Mr. & Mrs. Joseph A. Varty
1606 Mr. & Mrs. Frank E. Wagner
1616 Mr. & Mrs. J. H. Francis

SOUTH ALBANY AVENUE.

609 Mr. & Mrs. Wm. F. Stanton

ASHLAND BOULEVARD.

13 Mr. & Mrs. Allen B. Safford
17 William R. Griswold
19 Mr. & Mrs. Wm. A. Glasner
 Receiving day Tuesday
19 Col. L. O. Gilman
21 Dr. L. C. Fritts
31 Miss Helen Culver
 Receiving day Wednesday
31 Miss Martha E. French
31 Charles Hull Ewing
35 Mr. & Mrs. A. W. Brickwood
37 Mr. & Mrs. Abner M. Lewis &
 drs.
105 Rev. Walter H. Reynolds
131 Mr. & Mrs. Robert S. Grant
145 Mrs. J. P. Hart
147 Mr.& Mrs. Howard C. Pettibone
147 Rev. & Mrs. E. F. Williams
147 Frank P. Potter
147 Mr. & Mrs. E. B. Cobb
147 Charles R. Jacobs
147 Mr. & Mrs. E. Wiley Taylor
147 Mr. & Mrs. W. G. Jackson
149 Mr. & Mrs. Geo. W. Higgins
149 Henry Morton Brinckerhoff
149 Miss Mary Jones
153 Mr. & Mrs. Wm. P. Rend
 Receiving day Wednesday
153 Joseph P. Rend
161 Mr. & Mrs. Charles FitzSimons
 Receiving day Tuesday
179 Mr. & Mrs. Thomas Chalmers
179 Thomas Chalmers jr.
187 Mr. & Mrs. Bernard A. Eckhart
 Receive 1st Thursday
191 Mr. & Mrs. J. D. Hollingshead
199 Mr. & Mrs. Harvey T. Weeks
199 Miss Patti Weeks
201 Mr. & Mrs. Charles H. Case
 Receiving day Wednesday
209 Mr. & Mrs. John C. Polley & dr.
211 Mr. & Mrs. Thomas L. Haines
 & dr.
 Receiving day Tuesday
213 Mr. & Mrs. William Ridgway
215 Mr. & Mrs. Chas. H. Wright
217 Mr. & Mrs. Henry H. Aldrich
217 Clarence B. Hale
235 Dr. & Mrs. Alfred O. Hunt
235 Mrs. A. W. Wright

118 Mr. & Mrs. J. B. Overmeyer
120 Mrs. D. S. Place
122 Mr. & Mrs. J. M. Horton
124 Mr. & Mrs. W. W. Wait
124 Miss Helen M. Wait
130 Dr. & Mrs.Alfred W.Woodward
 Receiving day Wednesday
130 Miss Alexandra M. Shaw
132 Mr. & Mrs. J. W. Hedenberg
132 Mr. & Mrs. J. B. Tascott
140 Dr. & Mrs. Chas. L. Webster
140 Mr. & Mrs. Lucius Webster
144 Noble L. Biddle
144 George B. Whiting
146 Mr. & Mrs. Warren A. Wells
166 Mr. & Mrs. Geo. Bent & drs.
 Receive Wednesday
172 Mrs. Ward S. Minkler
172 Dr. & Mrs. Adam Miller
176 Dr. & Mrs. Truman W. Brophy
176 Miss Florence A. Brophy
176 Carlisle Mason
192 William J. Wilson
192 Miss Maggie V. Wilson
192 Mrs. Allen H. King
196 Wm. A. Pinkerton
196 Mr. & Mrs. Joseph O. Watkins
 Receiving day Friday
200 Dr. & Mrs. Henry M. Lyman
200 Miss Mary Lyman
204 Mr. & Mrs. Lewis Russ
204 Bertrand S. Russ
206 Mr. & Mrs. Henry H. Brown
206 Miss Orra S. Gibbs
210 Mr. & Mrs. E. A. Robinson & dr.
224 Mr. & Mrs. Ulric King & dr.
224 Miss M. G. Jenkins
226 Mr. & Mrs. S. A. Scribner
230 Mr. & Mrs. E. F. Gobel
230 Charles Grant Gobel
230 H. Elias Gobel
238 Mr. & Mrs. Charles F. Elmes &
 dr.
238 Carleton L. Elmes
238 C. Warren Elmes
242 Mr. & Mrs. John W. Midgley
248 Mr. & Mrs. B. M. Hair & dr.
254 Mr. & Mrs. George H. Taylor
258 Mr. & Mrs. George A. Cobb
258 Mr. & Mrs. D. S. Lovejoy

21

235 J. N. Wright
235 Mrs. R. K. Rollo
235 Chas. E. Rollo
235 Thomas E. Nelson
237 Mr. & Mrs. H. Lee Borden
237 Mr. & Mrs. Gerald M. Borden
237 Lewis L. Borden
239 Judge & Mrs. C. C. Kohlsaat & drs.
241 Mr. & Mrs. Albert L. Sweet
  Receive 2d and 4th Tuesdays
241 Charles Albert Sweet
243 Mr. & Mrs. Marshall D. Talcott & dr.
251 Mrs. Charles Brooks
251 Miss Maria M. Brooks
251 Miss F. E. Brooks
259 Mrs. Emma A. Goll & drs.
  Receiving day Wednesday
259 Bruno H. Goll
271 Mr. & Mrs. Oscar Burdick & drs.
271 Munson Burdick
273 Mr. & Mrs. Henry C. Hayt
275 Julius Petersen & drs.
277 Mrs. Ruth A. Featherstone
281 Mrs. E. B. Holmes
281 Harvey A. Holmes
281 Mr. & Mrs. A. M. Campbell
287 Mr. & Mrs. Solon D. Stanbro
  Receiving day Tuesday
289 Mr. & Mrs. Clayton Mark
  Receiving day Tuesday
291 Mr. & Mrs. James M. Pyott
291 James M. Pyott jr.
291 William C. Pyott
291 George W. Pyott
295 Mr. & Mrs. Wm. Wilhartz
297 Dr. & Mrs. John A. Robison
  Receive 1st Tuesday
299 Mr. & Mrs. Charles R. Ruggles
301 Mrs. Francis L. Rickcords
301 Frederick Rickcords
301 Rev. W. W. Diehl
303 Mr. & Mrs. Geo. A. Yuille
303 Thomas D. Miles
305 Mr. & Mrs. D. A. Allen
307 Mrs. Louise Waid
307 Miss Anna R. Walker
317 Mr. & Mrs. A. D. Plamondon
319 Mr. & Mrs. J. Edward Downs
319 Hubert C. Downs
325 Mr. & Mrs. Walter M. Pond
327 Mr. & Mrs. George R. Nichols
329 Mr. & Mrs. Chas. T. Nash
329 Mr. & Mrs. Hollis M. Thurston

258 D. L. Watkins
258 Miss Martha G. Watkins
260 Rev. & Mrs. Theo. N. Morrison
  Receiving day Thursday
260 Miss Louise Swazey
  Receiving day Thursday
272 Robert T. Weir
272 John M. Weir
272 Mrs. Anna Benson
274 Mr. & Mrs. Charles L. Rising
274 Frederick H. Rising
274 Philip A. Rising
276 Mr. & Mrs. John A. King
284 Mrs. Emma Fick & dr.
  Receiving day Thursday
284 B. W. Fick
286 Mr. & Mrs. Murdoch Campbell & dr. *Receiving day Thursday*
286 Mr. & Mrs. J. Albert Campbell
  Receiving day Thursday
288 Mr. & Mrs. J. H. Powell
292 Mr. & Mrs. Lewis L. Barth & dr.
  Receiving day Thursday
294 Mr. & Mrs. Chas. Stein
310 Mr. & Mrs. S. D. Chaney
314 Mr. & Mrs. Phillip L. Auten & dr.
322 Mr. & Mrs. F. G. Jordan
322 Mr. & Mrs. Augustine W. Wright
326 Thomas Templeton
326 Miss Mary Templeton
330 Mr. & Mrs. Edward G. Clark
330 Mr. & Mrs. Lemuel M. Bushnell
330 Charles E. Bushnell
342 Mr. & Mrs. Jefferson L. Fulton & dr.
342 Lester B. Fulton
346 Mr. Mrs. Burton F. Hales
348 Mr. & Mrs. E. L. Thompson
  Receiving day Thursday
348 Mrs. Eliza Reddish
352 Mr. & Mrs. R. H. Piratzky & dr
  Receive 2d Wednesday in mo.
356 Mr. & Mrs. George B. Kane
356 William D. Kane
360 Mr. & Mrs. Louis Woltersdorf & dr.
360 Arthur F. Woltersdorf
360 Mr. & Mrs. Frederick Blocki
364 Mr. & Mrs. Wm. B. Kennedy & dr.
368 Mrs. Meta Dore
  Receives 1st Tuesday in mo.
368 Gustave P. Matthei
368 Charles A. Matthei
368 William H. Matthei

333 Mr. & Mrs. John H. Bradshaw & drs.
339 Mr. & Mrs. John McLaren & drs.
339 J. Loomis McLaren
343 Mr. & Mrs. T. W. Sennott
Receiving day Monday
347 Mr. & Mrs. W. J. Mayer
351 Mr. & Mrs. Arthur Gray
353 Mr. & Mrs. Geo. L. Shuman
Receiving day Thursday
355 Mr. & Mrs. Gustav Friedlander
357 Mr. & Mrs. Jacob Schram & drs.
357 Harry S. Schram
357 Elmer E. Schram
359 Mr. & Mrs. Robert J.Smith
359 Miss Irma Lois Smith
359 R. Earl Smith
361 Mrs. Eva R. Wilce
Receiving day Tuesday
363 Mr. & Mrs. John C. Spry
Receiving day Thursday
365 Mr. & Mrs. Henry B. Maxwell
367 Mr. & Mrs. James Maxwell
Receiving day Thursday
369 Mr. & Mrs. Adolph Stein & dr.
Receive 1st Saturday in month
373 Mr. & Mrs. Oliver W. Holmes
375 Mr. & Mrs. Harry Woolf
Receive 1st Thursday, afternoon and evening
379 Mr. & Mrs. Charles K. Offield
Receiving day Thursday
385 Mr. & Mrs. Wm. W. Shaw
Receive 2d Thursday
385 Mr. & Mrs. Robert Shaw
389 Mr.& Mrs.John L. Haverkampf
389 J. L. Haverkampf jr.
391 Mr. & Mrs. M. R. Cobb
Receiving day Thursday
393 Mr. & Mrs. Ignatz Stein
393 Mrs. B. Baumgartl
399 Mr. & Mrs. J. F. Laubender
399 Mr. & Mrs. R. E. Cruzen
Receive Thursdays
399 Mr. & Mrs. B. S. Crocker
423 Mr. & Mrs.Adolph Goldschmidt & dr.
443 Mr. & Mrs. Henry Scherer &dr.
443 Louis H. Scherer
445 Mr. & Mrs. Chas. H. Alsip
445 Miss Maud Alsip
445 Miss Mildred Alsip
449 August Rietz
449 Mr. & Mrs. Alexander Reitz
449 Edward Hymers

386 Mr. & Mrs. Mark L. Crawford
386 Dr. & Mrs. E. F. Snydacker
388 Mr. & Mrs. Chas. N. Fessenden
Receiving day Thursday
394 Mr. & Mrs. F. V. Gindele & drs.
Receiving day 2d Wednesday
398 Mr. & Mrs. James Dunne
Receiving day Wednesday
398 Mr. & Mrs. Frank T. O'Connell
406 Mr. & Mrs. Gabriel Franchere & drs.
Receiving day Tuesday
408 Mr. & Mrs. Griffen H. Deeves
Receiving day Thursday
408 Miss Mary O'Brien
410 Mr. & Mrs.Jens L. Christensen
424 Mr. & Mrs. Louis Martens
426 Mr. & Mrs. I. Jonas
Receiving day Thursday
426 B. F. Greenbaum
428 Mr. & Mrs. John Goodwin
428 Miss Catherine Hart
430 Mr. & Mrs. A. Ragor
Receiving day Thursday
436 Mr. & Mrs. Max Eberhardt &dr.
Receiving day Thursday
440 Dr. John J. McDonnell
440 Miss Lizzie McDonnell
Receiving day Wednesday
442 James E. Baggot
444 Patrick H. Fleming
444 John T. Fleming
470 Dr. & Mrs. David O'Shea
472 Mr. & Mrs. John Rawle
474 Dr. & Mrs. E. L. Moorhead
480 Mr. & Mrs. John O. Batterman & dr.
482 Dr.& Mrs. Theo. S. Bidwell
502 Patrick Brennan & drs.
512 Dr. & Mrs. A. E. Bertling
514 Dr. & Mrs. G. A. Fischer & drs.
514 Oscar Fischer
516 Mr. & Mrs. John Tatge
538 Dr. & Mrs. F. W. E. Henkel

473 Mr. & Mrs. Joseph Turk & drs.
475 Mr. & Mrs. Frank Wenter
481 Mr. & Mrs. Leon Klein
483 Mr. & Mrs. S. Klein
489 Mr. & Mrs. T. C. Diener
495 Dr. & Mrs. J. C. Hoffman
Receiving day Tuesday
495 Miss Alma Marie Hoffman
495 Mr. & Mrs. Wm. J. Diener
495 Dr. & Mrs. Edmund Christie

503 William Ruehl
503 Harry A. Ruehl
503 Mr. & Mrs. Chas. W. Kopf
505 Mr. & Mrs. Henry Furst
 Receive last Thursday in mo.

505 Mr. & Mrs. Henry Furst jr.
 Receive last Thursday in mo.
527 Rev. & Mrs. H. L. Hoelter
527 Rev. Edward Hoelter
527 Rev. Jacob Seidel
623 Mr. & Mrs. John E. Fowler & dr.

SOUTH AVERS AVENUE.

979 Mr. & Mrs. John Kralovec

NORTH CALIFORNIA AVENUE.

710 Mr. & Mrs. Geo. A. Mugler
 Receiving day Friday

SOUTH CALIFORNIA AVENUE.

25 Mr. & Mrs. Wm. F. Albright

117 Dr. & Mrs. David Duncan

SOUTH CAMPBELL AVENUE.

377 Dr. & Mrs. Edward L. Stahl jr.
379 William H. Edwards

348 Dr. & Mrs. T. B. Mitchell
366 Mrs. Sarah E. Lightfoot

260 Mrs. M. J. Frawley & dr.
282 Mr. & Mrs. Francis T. Colby
308 Mr. & Mrs. A. A. Rawson
336 Mr. & Mrs. Wm. Hall
344 Dr. & Mrs. Isaac N. Albright

CAMPBELL PARK.

3 John M. Staples
29 Mr. & Mrs. Wm. H. Maple & dr.
39 Mr. & Mrs. George K. Hazlitt
39 Mr. & Mrs. George H. Hazlitt
45 Mr. & Mrs. A. Ransom
47 Mr. & Mrs. John W. Voorhees
49 Dr. & Mrs. J. Homer Coulter

2 Mr. & Mrs. Samuel Taylor
12 Mr. & Mrs. Thomas Wilson & dr.
30 Mr. & Mrs. H. H. Henshaw
52 Dr. Vira A. Brockway
52 Mr. & Mrs. Richard M. Peare jr.

CARROLL AVENUE.

1529 Mr. & Mrs. Samuel L. Mc-
 Leish & drs.

1529 Archibald McLeish

CENTRAL BOULEVARD.

1377 Mr. & Mrs. Wm. P. Black

SOUTH CENTRAL PARK AVENUE.

861 Mr. & Mrs. Thos. McEnerny
897 Mr. & Mrs. P. W. Snowhook
981 Mr. & Mrs. W. P. Hatfield
1085 Mr. & Mrs. John Wood
1101 Dr. & Mrs. Richard F. Worth
1189 Mr. & Mrs. David Hitchcock

1124 Warwick A. Shaw
1124 Dr. & Mrs. Sam'l W. Shaw &
 drs.

144 Mr. & Mrs. Geo. J. Holmes
 Receiving day Thursday
146 Mr. & Mrs. E. W. Kohlsaat
148 Mrs. George P. Holmes
170 Mr. & Mrs. Luther P. Friestedt
184 Mr. & Mrs. William H. Baker
960 Dr. & Mrs. David Rose
964 Mrs. E. E. Lanterman & dr.
1090 Frank W. Riley
1120 Mr. & Mrs. P. T. Platt

CENTRE AVENUE.

37 Mr. & Mrs. George C. Furst & drs.
·43 Mr. & Mrs. John York & dr.
43 John B. York
203 Dr. Clinton DeWitt Collins

88 Mr. & Mrs. I. H. Holden & dr.
90 Mrs. Elizabeth Keogh
326 Mrs. John Fitzpatrick

SOUTH CLAREMONT AVENUE.

273 Mrs. Emma Dickinson
273 Mr. & Mrs. R. F. W. Beardsley
287 Mrs. Thomas J. Marshall
293 W. D. Sager

446 Mr. & Mrs. Wm. J. Lloyd
————
301 Mr. & Mrs. Wm. L. Snell

COLUMBIA STREET.

45 Dr. & Mrs. Nels Nelson & dr.
59 Mr. & Mrs. Ole A. Thorp

46 Mr. & Mrs. Wm. F. Wiemers
Receive 1st Friday

WEST CONGRESS STREET.

349 Dr. Philip Sattler & dr.
365 Frank Crowe
365 Miss Genevieve Crowe
441 Mr. & Mrs. C.G.Lichtenberger
445 Mr. & Mrs. W. J. Moxley
447 Mrs. John Young & dr.
455 Mr. & Mrs. William F. Swissler
459 Mr. & Mrs. John Nicholls
461 Mr. & Mrs. Isadore Baumgartl
463 Mr. & Mrs. I. G. Loeber
481 Mr. & Mrs. John F. Alexander
491 Mr. & Mrs. Lewis R. Bain
493 Mr. & Mrs. John N. Dole
493 Andrew R. Dole
497 Mr. & Mrs. John C. King
497 William J. King
497 Miss Stella Marie King
499 Mr. & Mrs. J. B. Carter & dr.
503 Mr. & Mrs. J. W. Walsh
505 Mr.& Mrs.Wm. G. Outerbridge
517 Mr. & Mrs. Joseph Pomeroy
519 Mr. & Mrs. A. J. Murphy
525 Mrs. James C. O'Brien & dr.
567 Dr. & Mrs. W. T. Montgomery
569 Mr. & Mrs. Geo. E. Griswold
571 Mr. & Mrs. Joseph Barstow
571 Henry C. Fuller
575 Mr. & Mrs. Chas. H. Mitchell
581 Mr. & Mrs. F. H. Roeschlaub
583 Mr. & Mrs. G. W. Miley
607 Mr.& Mrs. Stephen D. Creedon
607 Mrs. Elizabeth A. Wright
607 William E. Wright

394 Mr. & Mrs. O. R. Erwin
446 A. D. Oyer & dr.
450 Mr. & Mrs. Wm. D. Kent
452 Mrs. Doris Butzow
452 Robert C. Butzow
468 Mrs. Charlotte Hartmann
470 Dr. & Mrs. F. G. Mason
470 Mr. & Mrs. Wm. H. Groat
472 Mr. & Mrs. F. L. Gerwig
·478 Mr. & Mrs. Albert M. Eddy
·*Receiving day Thursday*
482 Mrs. P. H. Fitzpatrick & dr.·
488 Mr. & Mrs. Anson Mark
506 Mr. & Mrs. S. T. Knowles
506 Henry Knowles
508 Mr. and Mrs. Horace F. Brown
508 Dr. Harry L. Brown
512 Mr. and Mrs. R. F. Stiller
514 Mr. & Mrs. J. M. Oliver
514 J. W. Showalter.
520 Mrs. J. F. Brabrook & dr.
522 Mr. & Mrs. S. S. Williams
524 Mr. & Mrs. J. F. McIntosh
524 Mr. & Mrs. Frank Gazzolo
568 Dr. & Mrs. F. S. Hartmann
570 Mr. & Mrs. J. S. Sosman
Receiving day Thursday
578 Mr. & Mrs. D. A. Starrett ·
586 Mr. & Mrs. N. B. Holden
594 Mr. & Mrs. Frank H. Hèbard
614 Mr. & Mrs. Joseph Brown
624 Mr. & Mrs. Fred A. Parker
636 Mr. & Mrs. Floyd E. Jennison

635 Dr. & Mrs. H. B. Stehman
657 Mr. & Mrs. Frederick Carlisle
657 Alfred W. Carlisle
707 Mr. & Mrs. James S. Hubbard
825 Mrs. A. B. Ingram
839 Mr. & Mrs. Robert Van Sands
839 Dr. Robert Van Sands jr.
1359 L. G. Squire

1176 Mr. & Mrs. Robert M. Kerr
  Receiving day Wednesday
1186 Mr. & Mrs. C. B. Stone
1414 Mr. and Mrs. H. M. Mills
1680 Mr. & Mrs. T. H. Gault

2069 Dr. James G. McCurdy

DE KALB STREET.

57 Mr. & Mrs. Louis I. Blackman
83 Mrs. T. E. Flower
99 Mr. & Mrs. A. E. Wells
107 Mr. & Mrs. I. P. Poinier

102 Mr. & Mrs. Stephen R. Wilson
106 Mr. & Mrs. S. D. Simpson
108 Mr. & Mrs. Frank R. Swift
142 Mr. & Mrs. A. H. Lord

EVERGREEN AVENUE.

599 Mr. & Mrs. Jas A. McCarthy

———

196 Mrs. Hedveg Johnson & drs.

42 Mrs. Anna C. Thompson
56 Mr. & Mrs. F. H. Paysen
128 Mrs. Annie Tollakson
140 Mr. & Mrs. P. O. Stensland

EWING PLACE.

5 Mr. & Mrs. John Buehler
17 Mr. & Mrs. Chas. S. Petrie
21 Mr. & Mrs. P. J. Benson
27 Mr.& Mrs.A. F.Weinberger &dr.
27 George A. Weinberger
27 Felix V. Weinberger
33 Mr. & Mrs. George Rahlfs & drs.
37 Mr. & Mrs. W. Spengler
79 Mr. & Mrs. H. D. Runge
79 William Demme
85 Mr. & Mrs. Kickham Scanlan
85 Mr. & Mrs. M. W. Conway
89 Mr. & Mrs. John C. Horn
89 Mr. & Mrs. Wm. Legner

20 Dr. & Mrs. James B. Williams
24 Mr. & Mrs. John P. Hanson&drs.
34 Mr. & Mrs. Edward G. Uihlein
 & drs.
70 Mr. & Mrs. Fred C. Mueller &
 drs.
76 Mr. & Mrs. H. Weinhardt & drs.
82 Mr. & Mrs. Theodore D. Juergens & dr.

———

89 Miss Katie Legner
93 Mr. & Mrs. August Lenke
93 August Lenke jr.

FLOURNOY STREET.

45 Mr. & Mrs. H. L. Swissler
69 Mr. & Mrs. W. T. Cushing
315 Mr. & Mrs. Frederick Peake
465 Mr. & Mrs. Walter Brown
543 Mr. & Mrs. Frank W. Hoyt

114 Mr. & Mrs. C. V. Osborn
116 Mr. & Mrs. Thos. H. Webster
574 Dr. & Mrs. Konrad Schaefer
758 Mr. & Mrs. Jos. O. Linebarger
840 Mr. & Mrs. Eugene Baker
840 Miss Ada Robilliard

FOWLER STREET.

93 Dr. &-Mrs. Arthur J. Behrendt
95 Mr. & Mrs. Fred Grimsell
101 Mrs. Adeline Dresselhaus

———

86 Mr. & Mrs. Ernst A. Erickson
92 Mr. & Mrs. C. E. Erickson & dr.
98 Mr. & Mrs. Hans L. Anderson

8 Mr. & Mrs. Charles E. Meyer
42 Mr. & Mrs. Harris Cohn
52 Dr. & Mrs. N. T. Quales & dr.
 Receive 1st Thursday in mo.
52 Iver L. Quales
60 Dr. & Mrs. B. I. Meyer
62 Mr. & Mrs. Halvor Michelson
84 Mr. & Mrs. Charles F. Elsner

FULTON STREET.

481 Mr. & Mrs. John B. Rogers&dr.
625 Mr. & Mrs. James Frake
667 Mr. & Mrs. J. J. Swenie
717 Miss May E. Halsted
1335 Mr. & Mrs. Wm. H. Arthur
1357 Mr. & Mrs. Edgar A. Hall
1447 Mr. & Mrs. T. W. Eaton & drs.
1455 Mr. & Mrs. O. S. Ward
1493 Mr. & Mrs. William League
1533 Mrs. F. A. Funk & drs.
1543 Mr. & Mrs. Samuel S. Parks
1543 Mr. & Mrs. Birch F. Rhodus
1551 Mr. & Mrs. David Tilt
1623 Mr. & Mrs. Joseph L. Locke
1623 Mrs. Nancy J. Mitchell
1623 Charles C. Bartlett
1629 Mr. & Mrs. E. T. Sederholm

1544 G. C. Otis
1564 Mr. & Mrs. George W. Trout

424 Mr. & Mrs. C. C. Bonney & dr.
430 Mr. & Mrs. L. Pfaelzer & dr.
430 David Pfaelzer
458 Mr. & Mrs. F. W. Munson
460 Mr. & Mrs. Thomas Goodman & dr.
460 Mr. & Mrs. W. A. Goodman
500 Mr. & Mrs. J. H. Tallmadge
518 Dr. & Mrs. Robt. H. Lowry
528 Miss Sara D. Michaels
662 Mr. & Mrs. John H. Whipple
1386 Mr. & Mrs. John C. Satterlee
1404 Mr. & Mrs. A. W. Smith
1404 Mr. & Mrs. John Cordes
1454 Mr. & Mrs. David Edward Russell
1484 G. P. Bartelme
1484 Miss Adeline T. Bartelme
1484 Miss May M. Bartelme
1542 Mr. & Mrs. A. H. Foskett

GILPIN PLACE.

12 Mr. & Mrs. M. C. Miniter

16 Mr. & Mrs. Joseph P. Magee&dr.

SOUTH HAMILTON AVENUE.

13 Mr. & Mrs. Samuel G. Artingstall
& dr. *Receiving day Tuesday*

23 Mr. & Mrs. Frank W. Swett

WEST HARRISON STREET.

387 Mr. & Mrs. W. M. Sherman
649 Mr. & Mrs. J. H. Synon
691 Dr. & Mrs. A. M. Corwin
717 Mr. & Mrs. Jesse Cox
717 Arthur M. Cox
743 Rev.& Mrs. J.C.Armstrong&dr.
875 Mr. & Mrs. Cesaire Gareau
949 James S. Gadsden
951 Dr. & Mrs. G. H. Cleveland

662 Mr. & Mrs. J. L. Howe
708 Mrs. Thomas Wilce
      Receiving day Tuesday
708 Thomas E. Wilce
708 E. Harvey Wilce
708 George C. Wilce
762 James H. Harper
946 Mr. & Mrs. John Rick

SOUTH HERMITAGE AVENUE.

219 Joseph Smart & drs.
363 Mr. & Mrs. Alexander Rodgers

322 A. T. Turnbull

SOUTH HOMAN AVENUE.

271 Prof. & Mrs. Henry M. Soper
763 Mr. & Mrs. J. G. Lobstein jr.

282 Mr. & Mrs. Conrad Kahler
282 John J. Kahler

HONORE STREET.

157 John W. Hedenberg
157 Miss Cecilia Hedenberg
157 Mrs. C. Hedenberg-Wells
161 Mr. & Mrs. J. L. Barry & dr.
195 Mr. & Mrs. Chas. F. Nagl

158 Mr. & Mrs. Freling C. Foster
200 Mr. & Mrs. S. Rush Harris
238 Mr. & Mrs. Fillmore Weigley
———
233 Rev. & Mrs. Adam C. Dodds

NORTH HOYNE AVENUE.

437 Ernest Gill
613 Mr. & Mrs. Henry Schroeder
619 Mr. & Mrs. S. D. Thorson
625 Mr. & Mrs. John Heinsen
631 Mr. & Mrs. Hermann Kirchhoff
637 Mr. & Mrs. Morris Schlesinger
    & dr.
637 T. R. Schlesinger
643 Dr. & Mrs. D. G. Moore
667 Mr. & Mrs. Wm. H. Thompson
697 Mr. & Mrs. Henry Grusendorf
697 Edward Grusendorf
703 Dr. & Mrs. D. C. Stillians
721 Dr. & Mrs. H. J. Burwash
    Receiving day Thursday
727 Mr. & Mrs. George C. Mages
731 Mr. & Mrs. C. H. Plautz
735 Mr. & Mrs. Phil Rosenberg

464 Mr. & Mrs. J. E. Maass
492 Mr. & Mrs. Harry Levy
498 Rev. & Mrs. H. J. G. Bartholo-
    mew *Receiving day Thursday*
498 Dr. & Mrs. J. K. Bartholomew
622 Dr. & Mrs. K. F. M. Sandberg
628 Mr. & Mrs. Henry L. Hertz
    Receiving day Wednesday
632 Mr. & Mrs. Henry Rieper & dr.
666 Mr. & Mrs. Wm. O. Johnson
    & drs.
672 Mr. & Mrs. Nels Arneson
700 Mr. & Mrs. Adolph Borgmeier
    & dr.
724 F. P. Schreiber
746 Mr. & Mrs. Charles Bodach
746 Frank Bodach

SOUTH HOYNE AVENUE.

143 Mr. & Mrs. Fred A. Bangs
163 Mr. & Mrs. Henry Cordes
163 Lewis Cordes
181 Mr. & Mrs. Chas. Deming & dr.
181 William B. Deming
183 Mr. & Mrs. Wm. Francis
183 Mr. & Mrs. James Buchanan
195 Rev. & Mrs. G. C. Knobel & dr.
    Receiving day Wednesday

195 John E. Knobel
197 Mr. & Mrs. James T. Dickson
215 Mr. & Mrs. Thos. E. Archibald
219 Mr. & Mrs. John Roberts
219 Mrs. Belle Keuthan & drs.
237 Dr. & Mrs. J. M. Patton
295 Mr. & Mrs. Philipp Benzp
339 Mr. & Mrs. Michael W. Connery
377 Mr. & Mrs. Josiah Swartz

HUMBOLDT PARK BOULEVARD.

27 Dr. & Mrs. Henry Harms

1831 Mr. & Mrs. Samuel O. Olin

SOUTH IRVING AVENUE.

219 Mr. & Mrs. David Blair & drs.
223 Mr. & Mrs. M. H. Buzzell
225 Mr. & Mrs. S. E. Blaisdell
227 Mr. & Mrs. P. A. Niebergall &
    dr.
233 Mr. & Mrs. O. W. Snyder
235 Mr. & Mrs. E. P. Benz
271 Mr. & Mrs. Chas. Van Sickel
271 Mrs. Catharine Watson

220 Mr. & Mrs. A. H. Arnold
    Receiving day Tuesday
222 Mr. & Mrs. J. M. Wait
228 Mr. & Mrs. C. W. Gilmore
228 Mr. & Mrs. Walter S. Bogle
230 Mr. & Mrs. O. H. Jewell & dr.
    Receiving day Tuesday
230 Ira H. Jewell
266 Mrs. Waldo Abeel & drs.

271 A. D. Watson
273 Mr. & Mrs. Edward Rueb
 Receiving day Thursday
275 Mr. & Mrs. Charles D. Bull
283 Mr. & Mrs. L. C. Jaquish
285 Mrs. Anna Harbridge
285 Chester Harbridge
287 Mr. & Mrs. J. F. Ahles
 Receiving day Wednesday
295 Mr. & Mrs. E. W. Fowler & dr.
295 George J. Fowler
295 Samuel W. Fowler
299 Mr.& Mrs. F. D. Hennessy
303 Mrs. Eliza T. Paige

272 Mr. & Mrs. John D. Osgood&dr.
278 Mr. & Mrs. Chas. B. Kinley
278 Mr. & Mrs. Wm. W. Marcy
298 Mr. & Mrs. Chas. P. Whetston
300 Mrs. Lottie J. Groshon
300 Dr. & Mrs. A. D. Groshon

303 John N. Clarke
305 Mrs. Mary A. Newton
307 Mr. & Mrs. Frederick R. Baldwin
463 Mr. & Mrs. A. O. Whitcomb
463 Mrs. C. P. Tuttle

WEST JACKSON BOULEVARD.

365 Dr. & Mrs. M. W. Borland
365 Mr. & Mrs. C. H. MacDowell
369 Mr. & Mrs. Hugh Mason
391 Mrs. Herman Raster
393 Mrs. Malcolm McDonald
403 Mr. & Mrs. Malcolm McDonald
 jr.
403 Dr. & Mrs. J. G. Wolfe
405 Mr. & Mrs. A. H. Loomis & dr.
 Receiving day Thursday
405 Philip A. Loomis
459 Mr. & Mrs.George F.Wetherell
467 Mr. & Mrs. Frank S. Wright &
 drs.
483 Mrs. Sarah C. King
483 Mr. & Mrs. Frank B. Alsip
485 Mr. & Mrs. J. R. Graves
489 Mr. & Mrs. R. J. Mason
491 Mrs. Sarah M. Tomblin & dr.
493 Mr. & Mrs. F. C. Taylor & drs.
493 John S. Taylor
493 W. C. Hale
493 Geo. L. Armour
495 Mr. & Mrs. F. H. Lamb
497 Mr. & Mrs. Charles A. Lamb
497 Miss Mabelle Howard Lamb
501 Mr. & Mrs. George G. Parker
503 Mr. & Mrs. Edward Hines
 Receive Friday
505 Mr. & Mrs. A. E. Barnhart &dr.
505 Mrs. Harriet N. French
509 Mr. & Mrs. J. H. Pearson
509 Arthur L. Pearson
511 Mr. & Mrs. Obadiah Sands & dr.
511 Obadiah Sands jr.
513 Rev. & Mrs. W. M. Lawrence
 & dr.
515 Mrs. John Sollitt
515 Walter R. Sollitt

316A Mr. & Mrs. Minor H. Williamson
412 Mr. & Mrs. E. D. Ellis
414 Mr. & Mrs. John F. Ellis
418 Mr. & Mrs. A. W. Martin
418 E. H. S. Martin
424 Dr. & Mrs. John J. Alderson
426 Mr. & Mrs. J. S. Conger
426 Mr. & Mrs. E. L. Stewart
444 Dr. George L. Beach
450 John Murray & drs.
452 Dr. & Mrs. J. O. Hobbs
452 Dr. Charles Hobbs
456 Dr. & Mrs. O. T. Shenick
496 Mr. & Mrs. A. N. Eastman
496 Henry A. Eastman
498 Mr. & Mrs. J. L. Pattison
498 William L. Pattison
500 Mr. & Mrs. James A. McMahon
502 Mr. & Mrs. William Hinchliff
508 Mr. & Mrs. P. J. Healy
510 Mr. & Mrs. G. V. Drake & drs.
510 Louis S. Drake
510 Mrs. S. Sheppard
512 Mr. & Mrs. F. A. Riddle
514 Dr. & Mrs. G. Horace Somers
516 Mr. & Mrs. C. W. Storey
 Receiving day Wednesday
516 Mrs. E. W. Westfall
 Receiving day Wednesday
518 Mrs. E. Walker & dr.
518 Mr. & Mrs. A. R. Gibson
518 William E. Walker
522 Capt. & Mrs. J. G. Keith & dr.
524 Mr. & Mrs. C. F. Wiehe
526 Mr. & Mrs. John Fortune
526 William J. Fortune
526 Thomas F. Fortune
532 Judge & Mrs. R. S. Tuthill & dr.

519 Mr. & Mrs. Walter Shoemaker
519 Chas. W. Shoemaker
519 Miss May E. Shull
521 Mr. & Mrs. W. T. Bussey
523 Mr. & Mrs. James L. Clark
525 Mrs. J. D. Marshall
525 Charles G. Marshall
527 Mr. & Mrs. George J. Titùs
527 Mrs. J. B. Hewitt
529 Mrs. D. M. Goodwillie
 Receive Wednesday afternoon
529 Douglas Goodwillie
529 Perley Goodwillie
533 Mr. & Mrs. A. F. Doremus
533 Mrs. Addie Moulton
535 Mr. & Mrs. R. E. Shimmin
537 Mr.& Mrs. Alonzo Wygant & dr.
537 Mrs. Laura D. Ayres
537 Mr. & Mrs. Wm. Barber
539 Mr. & Mrs. George Ross
539 Robert H. Ross
541 M. N. Moyer
541 H. Clayton Moyer
543 Mr. & Mrs. W. P. Henneberry
545 Mr. & Mrs. F. K. Tracy
547 Mr. & Mrs. B. A. Railton
551½ Rev. &. Mrs. F. DeWitt Talmage
 Receiving day Thursday
551½ Miss L. E. Burgess
553 Dr. & Mrs. R. N. Foster & drs.
553 Mrs. Geo. F. Washburne
589 Dr. & Mrs. E. P. Noel
593 Mr. & Mrs. Stalham L.Williams
597 Dr. & Mrs. Daniel Roberts Brower
597 Daniel Roberts Brower jr.
597 Miss Eunice Anne Brower
599 Mr. & Mrs. H. Fall
601 Mr. & Mrs. Charles E. Hyde & dr.
601 Chas. Albert Hyde
601 Walter W. Hyde
603 Mrs. C. H. Jordan
603 Mrs. J. A. Griffith
617 Mr. & Mrs. Adam Schaaf
617 John Schaaf
617 Harry Schaaf
627 Mr. & Mrs. E. C. Ward
635 Mr. & Mrs. Chas. W. Grassly
637 Millard P. Gray
637 Mr. & Mrs. B. B. Wilcox
639 Mr. & Mrs. Frank A. Hecht
677 Dr. & Mrs. Alfred C. Cotton
705 Mr. & Mrs. Chas A. Patterson
705 Dr. & Mrs. T. J. Shaw

534 Judge R. Prendergast
536 Mr. & Mrs. F. L. Welles
538 Mr. & Mrs. J. J. Townsend
538 Miss M. A. Townsend
538 Miss S. M. Townsend
540 Mrs. Margaret Hastie
540 Miss Martha Gemmell
540 Mr. & Mrs. Frank T. Cutler
542 Mrs. H. C. Morey
544 DeForrest W. Heath
544 Mrs. A. C. Cox
544 Mrs. S. Collier
546 Mrs. Luella Barnes Thatcher
548 Mr. & Mrs. W. D. Messinger
550 Dr. & Mrs. W. S. Downey
552 Mrs. C. C. Fisher
552 Justus P. Fisher
552 Mrs. Flora M. Chisholm
554 Mr. & Mrs. Charles M. Foskett
560 Dr. & Mrs. B. Dorr Colby
610 Prof. & Mrs. Geo. N. Carman
 Receiving day Tuesday
610 Mrs. Clara Kerr Rice
610 Mrs. Mary V. Haines & dr.
610 Fred H. Haines
610 Mrs. Matilda B. Carse
 Receiving day Saturday .
610 David Bradley Carse
612 Wm. G. Forrest
612 Mrs. Mary Gates Forrest
 Receiving day Wednesday
612 Prof. & Mrs. Edwin H. Lewis
 Receive Tuesday
612 Dr. &Mrs. Nelson D. Edmonds
612 Rev. A. K. Parker
622 Patrick Finn
622 Nicholas R. Finn
624 Mr. & Mrs. David Pyott
626 Mr. & Mrs. E. G. Stearns
628 Mr. & Mrs. P. D. Rathbone
630 Dr. H. N. Small
658 Rev. Thomas F. Cashman
658 Rev. Michael Cotter
658 Rev. T. E. Cox
658 Miss Helena Cashman
708 Mr. & Mrs. Frank S. Butler
768 Mr. & Mrs. W. H. Hawes
768 Miss Martha Warner
774 Mr. & Mrs. John A. Duncan
818 Mr. & Mrs. E. R. Bullard
820 Dr. & Mrs. J. C. Webster & drs.
876 Mr. & Mrs. Rollin A. Abel
 Receive Friday afternoon
880 Mr.& Mrs. Francis E.Halligan
924 Mr. & Mrs. David T. Lyon
928 Mr. & Mrs. F. A. Barnes & dr.

707 Dr. & Mrs. D. Lee Shaw
707 Charles E. Cook
709 Dr. & Mrs. C. A. Wade
713 Mr. & Mrs. J. W. Enright & drs.
761 Mr. & Mrs. T. K. Edwards
761 Mrs. E. K. Edwards
761 Harry E. Edwards
767 Mr. & Mrs. S. Salomon
767 Moses Salomon
767 Joseph Salomon
767 William Salomon
767 Leo Salomon
769 Mr. & Mrs. Harry Berger
769 Mrs. H. Goodkind
821 Mr. & Mrs. Walter H. Munroe
823 Mr. & Mrs. R. C. Demarest
823 Joseph H. Brandimore
823 James F. Brandimore
859 Mrs. Elizabeth Loehr & drs.
859 Leon Loehr
859 Karl C. Loehr
865 Dr. Samuel Willard & drs.
877 Mr. & Mrs. Daniel G. Trench
879 Mr. & Mrs. Chas. B. Morrow
901 Dr. & Mrs. S. S. Baker
907 Mr. & Mrs. William Smillie
907 Thomas B. Smillie
909 Mr. & Mrs. Wm. L. Newman
   & drs.
913 Mrs. O. H. Allen
   Receiving day Thursday
913 Mr. & Mrs. H. W. Allen
   Receiving day Tuesday
923 Mr. & Mrs. Charles Kaestner
   Receive 3d Friday in mo.
923 Mr. & Mrs. C. Cutting
925 Mr. & Mrs. Thos. H. McNeill
927 Mr. & Mrs. H. M. Lemon
   Receiving day Monday
929 Mr. & Mrs. George Rockwood
933 Mr. & Mrs. T. N. McCauley
937 Mr. & Mrs. Thos. F. Dunton &
   dr.
945 Mr. & Mrs. Samuel Harris
951 Mr. & Mrs. Robert B. Williamson
951 W. G. Williamson
951 John C. Williamson
953 Mr. & Mrs. Jas. A. Davidson
955 Dr. & Mrs. Charles Davison
955 Mrs. Martha Davison
965 Mr. & Mrs. Thomas McCann
967 Mr. & Mrs. Elias C. Greenlee
981 Mr. & Mrs. C. N. Ford
983 Mr.&Mrs.B.Frank Howard& dr.
987 Dr. & Mrs. T. A. Davis

936 Dr. & Mrs. J. L. Mulfinger
936 Mrs. J. S. M. Gils
936 G. H. Gils
942 Mr. & Mrs. J. W. Slosson
946 Mr. & Mrs. Henry Simon
948 Mr. & Mrs. E. W. Thompson
950 Dr. & Mrs. E. Perry Rice
   Receiving day Wednesday
952 Mr. & Mrs. L. C. Rollo
   Receiving day Thursday
956 Mr. & Mrs. Isaac R. Haskett
956 Mr. & Mrs. Geo. B. Whitman
   & drs.
956 Mr. & Mrs. Wm. J. Jewell
960 Dr. Louise Acres
960 Dr. Carrie M. Hayward
964 Mr. & Mrs. Wm. F. Grower
   Receiving day Wednesday
966 Mr. & Mrs. Frank Jerome
   Receiving day Thursday
968 Mr. & Mrs. M. R. Harris
970 Mayer H. Eichengreen
972 Dr. Mary A. Dearlove
972 Miss Mabel H. Dearlove
972 George M. Dearlove
972 George Dearlove
972 Richard T. Dearlove
1034 Mr. & Mrs. Jas. L. Morris
1036 Mr. & Mrs. H. L. Wayne
1036 Mr. & Mrs. E. F. Judkins &
   dr.
1036 Rickard Judkins
1038 Dr. Thomas A. Olney
1038 Mr. & Mrs. Louis Bloch
1040 Daniel Donahoe
1048 Dr. & Mrs. Wm. B. Marcusson
   Receiving day Tuesday
1362 Mr. & Mrs. E. Greenburg
1380 Mr. & Mrs. E. R. Ozias
   Receiving day Tuesday
1380 Mr. & Mrs. F. R. Donahue
   Receiving day Tuesday
1398 Dr. & Mrs. F. C. Linden
1400 Mr. & Mrs. U. G. Peters
1644 Mr. & Mrs. Andrew J. Ryan
1646 Mr. & Mrs. John B. Scully
1656 Mr. & Mrs. Ben T. Hosking
1656 Ernest B. Hosking
1664 Mr.& Mrs.Chauncey M. Stokes
1664 Mr. & Mrs. Albert J. Street
1674 Mr. & Mrs. Edward Allyn
   Featherstone
1678 Mr. & Mrs. John J. Hart
1680 Mr. & Mrs. Joseph Downey
2008 Mr. & Mrs. E. S. Richards
2008 Mrs. M. E. Lumsden

989 Mr. & Mrs. Charles P. Kidd
989 Albert Kidd
1005 Mr. & Mrs. J. B. Stafford
1007 Mr. & Mrs. Homer W. Howe
1009 Mr. & Mrs. W. B. Howe
1021 Mr. & Mrs. John Knox
1217 Dr. & Mrs. Richard H. Brown
1301 Mr. & Mrs. John H. Huyck
1301 John H. Huyck jr.
1301 Miss Lyda M. Huyck

1359 Dr. & Mrs. P. B. Hayes
1369 Mr. & Mrs. Joshua Reeves
Receiving day Thursday
1441 H. J. Stegemann
1449 Dr. & Mrs. Homer S. Warren
Receiving day Friday
1449 William L. Warren
1463 Mr. & Mrs. Geo. A. Rose
1491 Mrs. R. L. Harris
1491 George J. Harris

NORTH KEDZIE AVENUE.

94 Dr. & Mrs. Thomas Faith

98 Mr. & Mrs. O. S. Hinds

SOUTH KEDZIE AVENUE.

865 Mr. & Mrs. A. W. Miller

890 Mr. & Mrs. Wm. H. Wood
894 Mr. & Mrs. Charles G. Wink
898 Mr. & Mrs. William M. Gunton
904 Mr. & Mrs. D. A. Arnold & dr.

134 Dr. & Mrs. C. Bruce Walls
192 Mr. & Mrs. W. C. Bishop
758 Mr. & Mrs. N. Atchison
758 John D. Atchison
758 Dr. James A. Atchison
890 Mr. & Mrs. James A. Calbick

KIMBALL AVENUE.

1527 Mr. & Mrs. Spencer S. Kimbell

1551 Mr. & Mrs. Henry W. Matthews

LAFLIN STREET.

37 Mr. & Mrs. John Raber
39½ Mr. & Mrs. Victor Jacobs
57 Mr. & Mrs. Elbridge F. Russell
61 Mr. & Mrs. Frank W. Putnam

63 Mr. & Mrs. G. A. Marshall
65 Mr. & Mrs. C. S. Blackman
69 Mr. & Mrs. Henry Saunders & dr.

WEST LAKE STREET.

504 Mrs. A. M. Billings

SOUTH LAWNDALE AVENUE.

1043 Mr. & Mrs. O. A. Riggle
1045 Mr. & Mrs. Charles F. Riggle
1153 Rev. Norman A. Millerd & dr.
1195 Mr. & Mrs. C. F. Shepard & dr.

610 Mrs. Hollis M. Chase
988 Mr. & Mrs. J. H. McNamara
1102 Mr. & Mrs. T. Oliver Stokes
1112 Mr. & Mrs. Wm. P. Northcott

NORTH LEAVITT STREET.

803 Mr. & Mrs. M. J. Seifert
Receiving day Thursday

SOUTH LEAVITT STREET.

111 Mr. & Mrs. C. A. Dibble
159 Mr. & Mrs. Wm. Scott & dr.
205 Mr. & Mrs. John Graham & drs.
207 Mr. & Mrs. Adam Short & drs.
209 Mr. & Mrs. T. D. Wayne & dr.
209 Albert Wayne
209 Mrs. M. P. Lyon
213 Mr. & Mrs. John H. Williams

110 Mr. & Mrs. P. F. Young
112 Rev. & Mrs. J. P. Brushingham
116 Mr. & Mrs. C. B. Wilson
158 W. S. McLean
234 Mr. & Mrs. Thos. Sutton
234 Mrs. F. Scales & dr.
282 Mr. & Mrs. John Gillespie & dr.
412 Dr. & Mrs. James P. Prestley
418 Mr. & Mrs. O. A. Smith

217 Mr. & Mrs. H. J. Luders
    Receiving day Thursday
217 Harry C. Luders
223 Mr. & Mrs. Walter S. Kaestner
233 Rev. & Mrs. Geo. R. Merrill
    & dr.
233 George P. Merrill
237 Mr. & Mrs. C. A. Vosburgh
237 Aylward H. Vosburgh
243 Dr. & Mrs. C. M. Ballard
    Receiving day Thursday

245 Mr. & Mrs. James M. Banks & dr
267 Mr. & Mrs. Chas. H. Smith
283 Dr. & Mrs. Guy B. Dickson
287 Mr. & Mrs. A. P. Redfield
    Receiving day Friday
291 Mr. & Mrs. J. R. Coulter
293 Mr. & Mrs. N. E. Dillie
295 Mr. & Mrs. H. D. Hatch
295 Mr. & Mrs. Andrew J. Keefe
395 Mr. & Mrs. A. Coulter & dr.
435 Mr. & Mrs. A. G. Dayton

LE MOYNE STREET.

21 Mr. & Mrs. Charles H. Fleischer

SOUTH LINCOLN STREET.

227 Mr. & Mrs. James Crighton
229 Mr. & Mrs. E. C. Barnard
229 Albert E. Barnard
269 Mr. & Mrs. Arthur B. Elford

114 Mr. & Mrs. Z. T. Griffen
188 Mr. & Mrs. Jos. Fieldhouse
228 Mr. & Mrs. Abraham Brokaw
244 Mr. & Mrs. Thomas F. Judge

LOOMIS STREET.

15 Mr. & Mrs. Wm. W. Foss & dr.
    Receiving day Wednesday
45 Mr. & Mrs. Frank L. Strong & dr.
89 Mr. & Mrs. C. J. Shields & dr.
91 Mr. & Mrs. James H. Ward
103 Mr. & Mrs. Sanford D. Reeve
105 Mr. & Mrs. Frederick L. East-
    man
109 Dr. & Mrs. A. H. Brumback
131 Dr. & Mrs. D. W. Young.
241 Mr. & Mrs. John T. Donlan
241 Joseph H. Donlan

126 Dr. John B. Ewing
140 Mrs. M. E. Crane & dr.
222 Mr. & Mrs. Alexis Desjardins
    & dr.
    Receiving day Wednesday
222 Arthur Desjardins
232 Dr. & Mrs. Jos Z. Bergeron
240 Mr. & Mrs. D. F. Bremner & dr.
256 Dr. & Mrs. O. G. Wernicke
276 Mr. & Mrs. Thomas Connelly
318 Mr. & Mrs. M. McNellis

14 Dr. & Mrs. R. H. Bartlett
40 Mr. & Mrs. J. R. Francis
40 Wilfred R. Morgan
40 V. F. Mashek
46 Mrs. J. W. Tuohy & dr.
    Receiving day Tuesday
46 Miss Kate Cavanaugh
46 Dr. W. S. Haines
48 Mr. & Mrs. William M. Dandy
50 Mrs. Robert Owens & drs.
50 Frederick Owens
52 Mr. & Mrs. Geo. B. Swift & drs.
52 Dr. Brown F. Swift
52 Geo. L. Switt
52 Herbert B. Swift
54 Mr. & Mrs. Mathias Benner
86 Mr. & Mrs. D. S. Munger
88 Mr. & Mrs. Harvey Pickrell
96 Mrs. Geo. Robins & drs.
96 Geo. W. B. Robins
98 Dr. Byron Robinson
98 Dr. Lucy Waite
104 Mrs. Caroline M. Fellows
108 Dr. & Mrs. Wm. W. Sheppard
120 Mr. & Mrs. J. C. Harper

LYTLE STREET.

56 Dr. & Mrs. C. P. Harrigan
56 Mr. & Mrs. John T. McEnery

60 Mrs. Mary A. Garvy & dr.
    Receiving day Thursday
60 William J. Garvy

MACALISTER PLACE.

19 Mrs. E. C. Ragor
29 Mr. & Mrs. John Brenock & dr.
29 William Brenock
41 Mr. & Mrs. John Coughlan
41 T. E. Coughlan
47 Mr. & Mrs. Wm. J. Onahan
53 Mr. & Mrs. Edward Powell & drs.
53 Edward L. Powell
53 George J. Powell
59 Mr. & Mrs. M. Considine & dr.
59 John P. Considine

63 Mr. & Mrs. T. E. Ryan
85 Mrs. Susan O'Connell & dr.
Receiving day Tuesday
85 Andrew J. O'Connell
85 Theo. W. O'Connell
93 Mrs. Emma Amberg
97 Mr. & Mrs. M. J. Corboy
99 Mrs. Helena Stamm & drs
Receiving day Tuesday
99 Dr. J. Carl Stamm

WEST MADISON STREET.

Gault house R. J. Hendricks
   Sidney G. Many
577 Dr. Wm. A. Pitt
969 Mr. & Mrs. Julius Rothenberg
1037 Dr. & Mrs. C. R. Warren
1251 Dr. M. O. Heckard
1377 Dr. G. H. Edgerton
1453 Robert T. Davis

———

664 Mr. & Mrs. Lemuel Baldwin
774 Mrs. E. W. Prentiss

220 Winfield S. Coy
480 Mr. & Mrs. Richard Morgan
548 Dr. C. B. Plattenburg
548 C. S. A. Plattenburg
580 Chicago View Hotel
   Dr. A. B. Bausman
   Frank J. Fanning
   Florez Genaro
   Charles H. George
   Frank J. Kilcrane
   Mr. & Mrs. W. C. Reid
   Edward C. Williams

SOUTH MARSHFIELD AVENUE.

219 Mr. & Mrs. Stalham L. Williams
   jr.   *Receiving day Monday*
219 Mr. & Mrs. F. A. Arnold
223 Mr. & Mrs. F. D. Meacham
223 Mr. & Mrs. George S. Sloan
223 George B. Sloan
223 Mrs. Mary Whitford
235 Mr. & Mrs. Hill C. Smyth
   Receiving day Tuesday
237 Mr. & Mrs. Francis B. Lane
365 Mr. & Mrs. Frank J. Hanchett
   Receiving day Friday
367 Mrs. A. C. Curtis & drs.
367 Dr. J. H. Curtis
367 Eugene B. Curtis
401 Dr. & Mrs. Alfred Schirmer
415 H. G. Underwood & dr.
415 H. M. Underwood
417 Mr. & Mrs. Joseph Hirsch
427 Mr. & Mrs. S. Kraus

———

446 Mr. & Mrs. B. F. King
458 Dr, & Mrs, S. L. McCreight

230 Mr. & Mrs. Geo. J. Harrison
234 Dr. & Mrs. S. M. Strohecker
276 Mrs. E. Weldon & dr.
278 Dr. & Mrs. H. O. Bates
278 Dr. C. D. Bates
288 Mr. & Mrs. Murdock MacLeod
292 Chas. E. Higbee
296 Mr. & Mrs. A. E. Pyott
   Receiving day Thursday
300 Mrs. George V. DeForest
300 Fred B. DeForest
312 Mr. & Mrs. Walter T. Clark
316 Mr. & Mrs. V. W. Dashiell
316 C. Russ Dashiell
318 Mr. & Mrs. Wm. F. Monroe
320 Albert W. True
320 Charles J. True
320 Miss M. Elizabeth True
322 Mr. & Mrs. Wm. B. McChesney
326 Mr. & Mrs. Thos. Clark
344 Mr. & Mrs. Edward F. Price
408 Dr. & Mrs. David Birkhoff
446 Rev. & Mrs. P. Moerdyke

MILLARD AVENUE.

975 Dr. & Mrs. H. W. Scaife
989 Ray Loveridge
1007 James Kerby
1085 Mr. & Mrs. Chas. H. Smith
1105 Mr. & Mrs. Dana Slade
1127 Mr. & Mrs. George Martin
1139 Mr. & Mrs. Edmund A. Curtis
1145 Mrs. George E. Bliss
1145 Arthur I. Bliss
1161 Mr. & Mrs. G. S. Needham
1221 Mr. & Mrs. Chas. H. Beckler

976 Mr. & Mrs. Wm. M. Koblens
1062 Mr. & Mrs. Samuel A. Cooper
1092 Mr. & Mrs. T. P. Rogers & dr.
1102 Mr. & Mrs. Edwin J. Decker
    & dr.
1108 Mr. & Mrs. J. C. Sieh & drs.
1186 Mr. & Mrs. H. L. Billings & dr.
1326 Mr. & Mrs. Herbert H. Hart
1358 Mrs. Chas. A. Pardee
1406 Mr. & Mrs. James E. Cross

WEST MONROE STREET.

313 Mr. & Mrs. M. A. Wells
345 Mr. & Mrs. E. Kirchberg
397 Rev. & Mrs. Augustine C. Hirst
    & drs.
399 Mr. & Mrs. R. M. Outhet
399 John C. Outhet
411 Mr. & Mrs. John H. Amberg
413 Mr. & Mrs. Chas. A. Plamondon
    Receiving day Tuesday
413 George Plamondon
447 Mr. & Mrs. John P. Foss
447 Fred D. Foss
461 Mr. & Mrs. C. E. Hambleton
    Receiving day Tuesday
463 Mr. & Mrs. M. A. Bartlett
475 Mrs. Eliza Foss
475 Horace B. Foss
475 Miss Harriet E. Trevett
481 Mrs. John Spry & dr.
    Receiving day Wednesday
481 Walter P. Spry
487 William J. Pope
487 Mr. & Mrs. August C. Magnus
489 Jerome Root
489 Dr. Eliza H. Root
489 Mr. & Mrs. J. Sherman Root
501 Mr. & Mrs. Melville Clark
503 Mrs. Henrietta W. Cornell
    Receiving day Wednesday
503 William B. Cornell
507 Mr. & Mrs. T. Newton Bond
507 Edwin Wynn
509 Rt. Rev. & Mrs. Stephen M.
    Merrill
511 Mr. & Mrs. Charles Mackie
    Receiving day Thursday
511 George Mason
519 Mr. & Mrs. Joseph Hogan
    Receiving day Thursday
519 Miss Esther G. Lonergan

494 Mr. & Mrs. Romaine M. Conger
494 Richard Fennimore
496 Mr. & Mrs. George D. Broomell
    Receiving day Saturday
496 George D. Broomell jr.
496 Francis E. Broomell
496 Mrs. Maria W. Babcock
498 Mr. & Mrs. Henry R. Shaffer
    Receiving day 1st & 3d Tuesdays
498 Mr. & Mrs. Frank M. Gray
500 Mr. & Mrs. William H. Holden
500 William M. Holden
504 Mr. & Mrs. John McArthur & dr.
504 John McArthur jr.
510 Mr. & Mrs. E. A. Blodgett & drs.
512 Mr. & Mrs. Lester L. Bond
518 Gen. & Mrs. R. N. Pearson &
    dr.
518 Mr. & Mrs. Haynie R. Pearson
518 Miss Mary Logan Pearson
520 Mr. & Mrs. Robert Smale & dr.
    Receiving day Thursday
520 W. R. Smale
522 Mr. & Mrs. David W. Bergey
528 Henry Towne
530 Mr. & Mrs. J. B. Sherwood & dr.
530 Miss Mary Holabird
532 Mrs. Jane K. Strong & dr.
534 Mrs. W. W. Farwell
534 J. W. Farwell
632 Mr. & Mrs. John E. Decker
    Receiving day Friday
640 Mr. & Mrs. J. B. Myers
640 Mrs. M. L. Andrews
640 Dr. Edward A. Platt
644 Mrs. Esther E. Rennels & dr.
644 Loy L. Rennels
648 Mr. & Mrs. I. R. Krum
648 Mrs. Jennie L. Brett
650 Mr. & Mrs. A. M. Forbes & drs.

521 Mrs. David Boyle
521 Mr. & Mrs. Charles R. Smith
Receiving day Thursday
525 Mr. & Mrs. Ralph L Wyman
Receive Thursday
525 Miss Elizabeth M. Russell
531 Rev. & Mrs. J. Vila Blake & drs.
531 Clinton F. Blake
533 Dr. Albert B. Strong
533 Mr. & Mrs. Theron G. Carroll
535 Dr. & Mrs. Homer M. Thomas & dr.
Receiving day Thursday
535 Rev. Hiram W. Thomas
539 Dr. Leonard St. John
539 Frederick St. John
539 Mrs. J. St. John Booth
545 Mr. & Mrs. J. P. Wathier
547 John W. Vokoun
547 Frank F. Story
547 Mrs. Marion L. Story
549 Mrs. Mary Dunn
549 Mr. & Mrs. Isaac W. Nichols
549 Dr. Emilie C. Ransch
551 Mr. & Mrs. Simeon F. Leonard
613 Dr. & Mrs. E. C. Sweet
619 Dr. Rose C. McFall
631 William Jauncey
631 Mrs. M. W. Chase
645 Dr. & Mrs. C. M. Fitch
645 Dr. & Mrs. Walter M. Fitch
647 Mr. & Mrs. Alonzo P. Read & dr.
647 Louis H. Read
649 Mr. & Mrs. R. E. Haskett
649 Miss M. D. Wingate
649 Miss Rebecca Kerr
655 Mr. & Mrs. Wm. E. Best
655 William H. Best
661 Mr. & Mrs. J. W. Benham & dr.
665 Mr. & Mrs. John Dadie
671 Mr. & Mrs. Albert Willey & dr.
681 Mrs. C. N. Holden
683 Mr. & Mrs. N. L. Lenham
683 Mr. & Mrs. L. S. Lenham
683 Mr. & Mrs. G. M. Whitney
Receiving day Thursday
695 Mr. & Mrs. D. C. Jones
695 Fred H. Jones
699 Mrs. Ellen J. Baker
703 Mr. & Mrs. Martin E. Cole & dr.
703 Mr. & Mrs. Daniel K. Boughton
709 Mrs. Mary G. Bowen & dr.
711 Mr. & Mrs. George Daniels
715 Mr. & Mrs. Benj. F. McNeill
719 M. Mullaney & drs.

650 Fred A. Forbes
652 Mr. & Mrs. H. A. Wheeler
652 Mrs. L. A. Small
654 Mr. & Mrs. George W. Warvelle
Receiving day Wednesday
656 Mrs. S. E. W. Martin
656 Mr. & Mrs. Albert H. Tyrrell
660 Daniel Gregory
660 Walter D. Gregory
660 Mr. & Mrs. William Rodiger
672 Dr. & Mrs. D. W. Graham
672 Mrs. S. A. Pratt
676 Mrs. C. E. Benson
Receiving day Tuesday
676 Chas. E. Benson
678 Mr. & Mrs. H. T. Lyon & dr.
680 Mr. & Mrs. Geo. S. Mackenzie
Receiving day Thursday
686 Mr. & Mrs. Henry Hebard
688 Mr. & Mrs. L. K. Tucker
690 Dr. & Mrs. John H. Byrne & dr.
Receiving day Thursday
692 Mrs. William McGregor
694 Mrs. E. A. Bell & dr.
694 Leonard F. Bell
694 Mr. & Mrs. Albert F. Solbery
698 Mrs. Simon Wolf & dr.
698 Alphonso S. Wolf
698 Benjamin Wolf
700 Dr. & Mrs. Eugene Marguerat & dr.
700 Dr. Eugene Marguerat jr.
700 George Marguerat
700 Henri Marguerat
700 John Marguerat
712 Mrs. E. L. Martin
Receiving day Monday
714 Dr. & Mrs. John M. Auld & dr.
714 Ralph Auld
716 Mr. & Mrs. John W. Eckhart
Receive Thursday
720 Mr. & Mrs. Wm. C. Dunwell
720 Mrs. Alma J. Peck
722 Mr. & Mrs. D. Munro
Receive 1st Wednesday
728 Mrs. Orissa C. Carpenter
728 Albert J. Carpenter
728 Aldert Smedes
728 T. Lyell Smedes
732 Mr. & Mrs. Wm. J. Hack
738 Mr. & Mrs. Marcus C. Stearns
740 Mr. & Mrs. Thos. Shaughnessy & drs.
740 Richard D. Shaughnessy
742 Dr. & Mrs. Amos. J. Nichols
744 Henry Hofman

725 Mr. & Mrs. T. J. Gilmore
727 Mr. & Mrs. Horace H. Stod-
    dard
727 Horace A. Stoddard
729 Mr. & Mrs. H. B. Galpin
729 Mr. & Mrs. Homer K. Galpin
733 Mr. & Mrs. D. F. Holman & drs.
735 Mr. & Mrs. George I. Hicks
735 Mr. & Mrs. David F. Hicks
743 Mr. & Mrs. W. T. Litson
745 Mr. & Mrs. F. H. Hill
747 Dr. & Mrs. Chas. C. O'Byrne
        Receive Tuesdays
749 Mr. & Mrs. R. J. Rundell
749 Mr. & Mrs. C. L. Rundell
751 Mr. & Mrs. A. W. Johnston
751 Alfred B. Johnston
779 Dr. & Mrs. A. H. Foster
779 Chas. S. Foster
781 Mr. & Mrs. G. W. Stanford
785 Mrs. O. W. Barrett
787 Mrs. Sarah Agnes Hitchcock
        Receive Tuesday
787 Edward J. Hitchcock
791 Mr. & Mrs. Edward D. Wills
        Receive Friday
793 Dr. & Mrs. R. B. Tuller
        Receiving day Thursday
793 Mrs. Emma S. Pribyl
797 Mr. & Mrs. Chas. F. Unrath
799 Mr. & Mrs. Thos. E. D. Bradley
        Receiving day Thursday
799 Mr. & Mrs. Alois Podrasnik
        Receive 3d Tuesday
799 Joseph N. Podrasnik
805 Dr. & Mrs. Mark M. Thompson
        & dr.
831 Mr. & Mrs. C. J. Wolff
833 Mr. & Mrs. David Vernon & drs.
839 Mr. & Mrs. Harry Fox
847 Mr. & Mrs. Louis H. Sass & dr.
849 Mr. & Mrs. David Oliver
849 Roy O. Oliver
849 David Oliver jr.
851 Mr. & Mrs. W. S. Maple
855 Mr. & Mrs. J. M. Carroll
857 Mr. & Mrs. W. J. Aiken
859 Mrs. S. C. Schultz & drs.
859 James M. Schultz
859 Alex J. Schultz
867 H. C. Odell & drs.
        Receive Friday
869 Mr. & Mrs. Charles A. Allen
869 Albert J. Allen
871 Mr. & Mrs. T.-S. Albright
871 Miss Belle Stein

744 Mr. & Mrs. Samuel Hofman
746 Mr. & Mrs. James H. Hildreth
        Receiving day Wednesday
750 Mr. & Mrs. John Wingrave
750 Miss Sarah Wingrave
750 John W. Van Valkenburgh
752 Dr. & Mrs. Edward C. Kaye
754 Mr. & Mrs. Robert Barlow
770 Mrs. R. F. Parshall
770 Mr. & Mrs. W. W. Beaty
772 Mrs. Ella Graham
772 Mrs. Ena B. Scarritt
772 Miss May Oliver
780 Dr. & Mrs. W. A. Knox
780 Miss Belle Danolds
790 Mr. & Mrs. I. W. McCasky & drs.
792 Mr. & Mrs. J. G. Aldridge
794 Mrs. Catherine Russell & drs.
796 Mrs. Lucy Haywood & drs.
798 Mr. & Mrs. J. K. Allen
800 Mr. & Mrs. Howard Watson
800 Joseph Dell
802 Mrs. Elizabeth Holden
802 Mr. & Mrs. Andrew J. Wood
804 Mr. & Mrs. Silas L. Wood
812 Mr. & Mrs. Chas. F. Judd
        Receiving day Friday
824 Mr. & Mrs. W. H. Price
824 Mrs. Alice Rutherford
830 Mr. & Mrs. N. R. Wakefield & dr.
834 Dr. & Mrs. A. V. Hutchins & dr.
834 Edwin S. Hutchins
840 Mr. & Mrs. J. C. Wintermeyer
        Receiving day Friday
848 Mr. & Mrs. Wm. H. Vehon
850 Dr. & Mrs. George J. Tobias
852 Mr. & Mrs. Geo. C. Farnum
854 Mr. & Mrs. E. E. R. Tratman
854 Mrs. Annie M. Radcliffe
856 Dr. & Mrs. C. J. Adams
856 Elmer K. Adams
862 J. A. Ewing & dr.
864 Mr. & Mrs. C. D. Weinland &
        drs.
866 Dr. & Mrs. W. L. Copeland
878 Mr. & Mrs. C. S. Gurney
882 Mr. & Mrs. L. L. Troy
882 Mr. & Mrs. Ernest G. Troy
882 Harry L. Troy
882 C. L. Miles
902 Mrs. J. M. Campbell
902 Thomas M. Campbell
908 Mr. & Mrs. W. H. Tyler
910 Dr. & Mrs. Joseph Rogers & dr.
912 Mr. & Mrs. Thomas Collins &
        drs.   *Receive Wednesday*

22

881 Mrs. Susan W. Beardsley
883 Dr. & Mrs. F. C. Wells
895 Mr. & Mrs. A. E. Havens
 Receive Wednesday
897 Mr. & Mrs. W. C. Hickox
903 Dr. & Mrs. Frank B. Earle
905 Mr. & Mrs. John A. McCully
905 Fred McCully
905 Wm. H. McMillan
907 Mr. & Mrs. James A. Mason
907 Mrs. J. H. Cleveland
907 Mr. & Mrs. C. H. Bennett
917 Mr. & Mrs. James M. Wanzer
 & drs.
921 Mr. & Mrs. J. S. Fifield & dr.
 Receiving day Friday
921 F. W. Brainerd
921 E. T. Brainerd
923 Mr. & Mrs. Jos. W. Swafford
923 Mrs. F. M. Loveday & dr.
923 Thomas E. Loveday
923 Mrs. Helen M. Stayman
927 Dr. & Mrs. Chas. P. Donelson
929 Mr. & Mrs. Walter K. Fifield
933 Mr. & Mrs. A. L. Gardner
935 Mr. & Mrs. D. A. Hill & drs.
937 Mr. & Mrs. Ithiel P. Farnum
 & dr.
943 E. B. Friedman
943 Mr. & Mrs. Joseph B. David
943 Mrs. Rosa David
943 Miss Blanche Mayer
945 Dr. William W. Simpson
961 Dr. & Mrs. Frank Branen
 Receiving day Thursday
963 Dr. & Mrs. H. P. Skiles
967 Rt. Rev. & Mrs. Sam'l Fallows
 Receiving day Monday
969 Mr. & Mrs. Eben A. Delano
969 Harry M. Delano
969 Mrs. Caroline N. Underwood
1023 Mrs. Louise Dilley
1077 Mr. & Mrs. J. W. Ostrander
1077 John G. Ostrander
1331 Judge & Mrs. Orrin N. Carter
1387 Mr. & Mrs. Chas. C. P. Holden
1393 Mr. & Mrs. T. J. Nicholl
1393 Mrs. J. A. Webster
1453 Mr. & Mrs. Richard I. Marr
1471 Mr. & Mrs. J. H. Whiteside
1473 William A. Bowers
1473 Mrs. Nancy Bowers
1475 Mr. & Mrs. John H. Chapman
1481 Dr. & Mrs. Adelbert H. Tagert
1481 Dr. & Mrs. A. E. Kay
1487 Mr. & Mrs. Noble C. Shumway

916 Mr. & Mrs. Daniel Kusworm
918 Mr. & Mrs. A. Levine
922 Mr. & Mrs. Robt. E. Cantwell
926 Dr. & Mrs. E. L. Hayford
930 Charles F. Bowey
930 Miss Elizabeth Bowey
930 Miss Alice Bowey
932 Mr. & Mrs. C. H. Rollins
934 Mr. & Mrs. Frank S. Smith
938 Mr. & Mrs. G. W. VanZandt
938 O. C. Van Zandt
940 Mr. & Mrs. A. J. Miksch
946 Mr. & Mrs. E. C. Thomas
950 Mr. & Mrs. W. H. Austin
950 Mr. & Mrs. G. W. Griffin
952 Mr. & Mrs. J. C. Huteson
956 Mr. & Mrs. M. S. P. Bond
958 Mr. & Mrs. T. W. Draper
962 Mrs. M. A. Kavanagh
962 Mr. & Mrs. Charles J. Kavanagh
968 Dr. & Mrs. Lawley York
1028 Dr. & Mrs. S. K. Falls
1044 Mr. & Mrs. A. H. Darrow &drs.~
1044 Robert Darrow
1390 Mr. & Mrs. Anton C. Berg
1390 Chas. O. Berg
1424 Mr. & Mrs. George Oliver
1436 Mrs. Mary C. Sturgiss
1440 Dr. & Mrs. H. H. Merrell
1440 Mrs. W. M. Merrell
1440 Mr. & Mrs. J. H. Logue
1444 Mr. & Mrs. E. R. Pritchard
1472 Mr. & Mrs. Frank Richardson
1498 Mr. & Mrs. Levi L. Leach
1514 Mr. & Mrs. Frank H. Chase
1514 Mr. & Mrs. F. L. Goulding
1514 Mr. & Mrs. H. J. M. Schroeter
1518 Mr. & Mrs. John F. Vette
1520 Mr. & Mrs. William Meredith
 Receive Thursday
1520 Mr. & Mrs. J. P. Litsey
1520 James N. Litsey
1530 Mr. & Mrs. Wm. T. R. Collette
1530 Miss Anna B. Collette
1530 Miss Louise N. Collette
1532 Mr. & Mrs. John A. Fulton
1538 Mr. & Mrs. John Sherman jr.
1548 Mr. & Mrs. Geo. P. Longwell
1552 Mr. & Mrs. G. R. Bocher
1564 Mr. & Mrs. L. G. Blessing
1566 Mr. & Mrs. John F. Higgins
1566 Mr. & Mrs. T. W. Edwards
1574 Mr. & Mrs. B. F. Ayers
1592 Mr. & Mrs. G. E. W. DeClercq
1592 Dr. & Mrs. C. L. Enslee
1624 Mr. & Mrs. Charles J. Magee

1487 Mrs. Mary E. Shumway
1489 Mr. & Mrs. S. H. Harris
1489 Mrs. Cecil O'Neill
1491 Mr. & Mrs. Wm. E. Couffer
1491 Mr. & Mrs. Frank W. Watts
1493 Mr.&Mrs. Eugene J. Macheret
1495 Mr. & Mrs.John A.Montgomery
  Receiving day Thursday
1495 Mr. & Mrs. Charles Lane
1503 Mr. & Mrs. E. T. Williams
1525 Mr. & Mrs. Hugh Watt & drs.
1525 Archibald M. Watt
1525 John Hatch
1525 Mr. & Mrs. Silas H. Brand
1527 Mr. & Mrs. W. J. Ellis
1529 Mr. & Mrs. W. E. Babcock
1529 Mrs. Eliza O. Harvey
1539 Mr. & Mrs. L. H. Whittemore
1543 Mr. & Mrs. W. G. Oliver
1543 Mr. & Mrs. Charles Baltz
1543 Mr. & Mrs. Wm. Gardner
1551 Mr. & Mrs. P. H. McLaughlin
1551 John J. McLaughlin
1555 Mrs. Sophia Meinel
1555 Frank A. Meinel
1555 William Meinel
1559 Mr. & Mrs. W. A. Barron
1561 Mr. & Mrs. G. F. Hutchinson
1563 Mr. & Mrs. E. A. Puster
1563 Dr. Eldridge Wyncoop
1565 Mr. & Mrs. W. H. Mortimer
1575 Mr. & Mrs. F. J. McCain
1585 Mr. & Mrs. Geo. A. Strong
1611 Mr. & Mrs. Michael R. Leyden
1615 Mr. & Mrs. Louis Schram
1619 Mr. & Mrs. Carey D. Wykel
1621 Mr. & Mrs. F. M. Nichols
1651 Mr. & Mrs. N. A. Williams

1664 Mr. & Mrs. Fred E. Groth & dr.
1664 Fred J. Groth
1668 Mr. & Mrs. E. J. Monahan
  Receiving day Tuesday
1670 Mr. & Mrs. F. O. Griffin
1680 Mr. & Mrs. J. F. Wolff
  Receive 1st Friday
1684 Mr. & Mrs. Chas. A. Roberts
1686 Mr. & Mrs. Chas. C. Reed
1688 Mr. & Mrs. Robt. J. Puster
1690 Mr. & Mrs. A. Hosking
1692 Mr. & Mrs. Fred'k C. Traver
1694 Mr. & Mrs. T. C. H. Wegeforth
2106 Dr. & Mrs. George Moe
2116 Mr. & Mrs. Ezra G. Herr

1651 Mr. & Mrs. M. D. Williams
1657 Mr.& Mrs.Geo.F.Featherstone
  Receiving day Tuesday
1659 Mr. & Mrs. John Naghten
  Receive Friday
1659 James J. Naghten
1659 Frank A. Naghten
1661 Mr. & Mrs. Philip H. Mallen
  Receiving day Friday
1663 Mr. & Mrs. Willis Young
1663 Mr. & Mrs. F. W. Yeager
1665 Mr. & Mrs. Chas. E. Matthews
  Receiving day Wednesday
1669 Mr.&Mrs. John Memhard & dr.
  Receiving day Tuesday
1669 Dr.&Mrs. John Edwin Rhodes
  Receiving day Thursday
1673 Mr. & Mrs. John T. Clark
1673 Mr. & Mrs. W. S. Canright
1673 Mr. & Mrs. Will M. Harriman
1675 Mr. & Mrs. James Hogan
1681 Mr. & Mrs. H. L. Bushnell

SOUTH MORGAN STREET.

248 James U. Borden

NORTH OAKLEY AVENUE.

79 Rev. Henry G. Perry

20 Mr. & Mrs. Dow F. Williams

SOUTH OAKLEY AVENUE.

109 Mr. & Mrs. Henry Potwin
109 Homer Potwin
109 Miss May S. Potwin
153 Mrs. Charles H. Brower & dr.
157 Mr. & Mrs. George G. Robinson
185 Mr. & Mrs. Frank Young
227 Mr. & Mrs. John A. McKay
287 Dr. & Mrs. E. W. Olcott

54 Mr. & Mrs. Alma J. O'Neill
110 Dr. & Mrs. D. A. Payne
118 Rev. & Mrs. Franklin C. Southworth
120 Mrs. Emily Corby & drs.
222 Mr. & Mrs. John H. Durham
222 Howard F. Durham
222 Roy L. Durham

289 Mr. & Mrs. Aaron Williams
289 Miss Annie E. Williams - ;
305 Mr. & Mrs. Joseph Trienens
353 Dr. & Mrs. Edward E. Reininger
353 Mrs. C. S. Traver
355 Mr. & Mrs. J. H. McCormick
355 Frank P. McCormick
357 Mr. & Mrs. G. M. Lovelock
 Receiving day Thursday
359 Mr. & Mrs. O. E. Whitcomb
361 Mr. & Mrs. George W. Hicks &
 dr.
361 Wm. H. Engelman
361 Mr. & Mrs. Henry E. Marble
363 Rev. & Mrs. Wm. G. Clarke
365 Mr. & Mrs. Thomas Greig &
 dr.
365 Thomas Greig jr.
371 Mr. & Mrs. E. D. Powell
373 Mr. & Mrs. S. H. Case & dr.
373 Guy H. Case
411 Mr. & Mrs. James A. S. Reed
411 Mr. & Mrs. O. W. Fay
411 Mr. & Mrs. J. Oliver Smillie
431 Mr. & Mrs. P. R. McLeod & dr.
 Receiving day Wednesday
451 Mrs. Louise W. Percy

224 Mr. & Mrs. Chas. E. Bonnell
234 Mr. & Mrs. Geo. A. Turnbull
234 George L. Turnbull
234 Percy G. Turnbull
236 Mr. & Mrs. A. M. Searles
236 Miss Marie L. Mosser
268 Mr. & Mrs. A. H. Halleman
302 Dr. Frank J. Dewey
390 Mr. & Mrs. J. F. Moore & drs.
390 Frank J. Moore
394 J. V. McAdam
394 Charles V. McAdam
394 Miss Anna J. McAdam
394 Miss May Rose McAdam
414 Mrs. J. A. Winter & drs.
 Receiving day Wednesday
434 Mrs. S. H. Cady
434 George W. Cady
434 Orvan L. Cady
454 Mr. & Mrs. Frederick Watson
456 Mr. & Mrs. Wm. H. Dunn & dr.
464 Mr. & Mrs. J. William Allen
514 Dr. Henry J. Way
514 Miss Lillian Way
514 Dr. & Mrs. J. E. Reynolds

513 Mrs. Bertha Y. Hollenbec

OGDEN AVENUE.

685 Dr. L. C. Borland
1417 Mr. & Mrs. C. F. Schultz
1441 Mr. & Mrs. Z. R. Carter

34 Mrs. Franklin Finch
34 James T. Milner
78 Mr. & Mrs. Benton Warder

OREGON AVENUE.

26 Mr. & Mrs. P. Hines
26 Mr. & Mrs. D. S. Sattler & dr.

34 Mr. & Mrs. Joseph Chalifoux

PARK AVENUE.

1 Mrs. L. M. Dunn
19 Henry Meiselbar
21 Mr. & Mrs. Thomas Walls & dr.
23 Dr. & Mrs. Orrison B. Damon
33½ Mr. & Mrs. E. F. Bosley
35 Dr. & Mrs. John R. McCullough
69 Mr. & Mrs. E. B. Bennett
71 Mr. & Mrs. P. C. Sears & dr.
71 Mr. & Mrs. J. E. Young & dr.
75 Mr. & Mrs. Franklin Sawyer
75 Robert F. Sawyer
99 Mr. & Mrs. Chas. Hayward & dr.
103 Mrs. M. C. Thomason & drs.
105 Mr. & Mrs. John P. Lydiard
117 Mr. & Mrs. Louis Sievers
117 Alexander C. Sievers
123 Mr. & Mrs. F. Cortez Wilson &
 dr.

18 Mr. & Mrs. J. M. Sherman
48 Edward T. Singer
48 Mrs. H. A. Singer
72 Mr. & Mrs. Robert Tarrant
84 Dr. & Mrs. Edw. P. Koch
106 Mr. & Mrs. G. B. Fritts
114 Mr. & Mrs. Thomas Charles
132 Mr. & Mrs. John S. Zimmerman
 & drs.
138 Mr. & Mrs. W. W. Wheeler
144 W. H. Bunge
148 Mr. & Mrs. J. Edwards Fay & dr.
150 Dr. & Mrs. J. R. Buchan
150 Mr. & Mrs. R. C. Bassett
160 Mr. & Mrs. J. A. Ruth & dr.
180 Mr. & Mrs. M. T. Cole
182 Dr. & Mrs. J. W. Meek
186 Mr. & Mrs. S. M. Meek

123 Henry Warren Wilson
127 Mr. & Mrs. Henry Warrington
127 James N. Warrington
127 William H. Warrington
131 Mr. & Mrs. B. Wygant & dr.
      Receiving day Thursday
135 Mr. & Mrs. G. T. Gould
175 Mr. & Mrs. P. F. Bryce & dr.
175 Robert M. Bryce
179 Mr. & Mrs. B. W. Veirs
197 William Johnston
201 Mr. & Mrs. J. F. Balkwill
203 Mr. & Mrs. James A. Hitchcock
213 Mr. & Mrs. Charles E. Newton
233 Mr. & Mrs. D. H. Fritts
235 Mrs. Fannie B. Ruth
249 Dr. & Mrs. A. K. Smith
267 Mr. & Mrs. C. H. Baldwin
277 Mr. & Mrs. Rufus King
287 Mr. & Mrs. W. C. C. Lartz
293 Mr. & Mrs. DeWitt C. Palmeter
299 Mr. & Mrs. A. A. Burnham
301 Mr. & Mrs. W. A. Hutchings
      Receiving day Wednesday
311 Mr. & Mrs. John O. Dunn
315 Mr. & Mrs. J. A. Sperry
317 Mrs. A. Sterling Cornell
319 Mrs. M. E. Ward & drs.
321 Mr. & Mrs. J. W. Wolfenstetter
      Receiving day Thursday
339 Mr. & Mrs. George W. Strell
341 Mr. & Mrs. G. W. Wilson
341 Mr. & Mrs. A. F. Gebhart
343 Mr. & Mrs. W. Cummings & dr.
345 Mr. & Mrs. J. H. White & dr.
353½ Miss Estelle Wentworth
353½ George O. Wentworth
357 Mr. & Mrs. M. M. Warner
361 Mr. & Mrs. F. G. Bradley
367 Mr. & Mrs. S. B. Mills
647 Mr. & Mrs. Frank M. S. Brazelton
671 Mr. & Mrs. C. E. Cruikshank
925 Mr. & Mrs. Alexander D. Kennedy

194 Mr. & Mrs. Alvin Hulbert & drs.
      Receiving day Thursday
198 Mr. & Mrs. C. S. O'Meara
      Receiving day Tuesday
210 Mr. & Mrs. Theodore H. Elmer
210 Mr. & Mrs. H. E. Ball
214 Dr. Elmer E. Prescott
216 Mr. & Mrs. Daniel Reily & dr.
218 John J. Mayberry
238 Dr. & Mrs. J. Brown Loring
258 Peter Fortune & dr.
262 Mrs. A. M. Cook & dr.
262 Miss E. J. McMillan
282 Mr. & Mrs. J. G. McCarthy
284 Mr. & Mrs. Will C. Rood & dr.
290 Dr. & Mrs. James Beckett
298 Mr. & Mrs. Edwin D. Wilder
312 Mr. & Mrs. Walter Lister & dr.
      Receiving day Monday
318 Dr. & Mrs. E. Honsinger
338 Dr. & Mrs. Alex R. McDonald
350 Mr. & Mrs. Frank B. Davidson
364 Mr. & Mrs. T. H. Pease
364 Albert A. Pease
408 Frank W. Thomas
670 Mr. & Mrs. David C. Dewey
678 Mrs. M. E. Barstow & dr.
682 Mrs. M. H. Ogden
944 Mrs. Elizabeth Jones & dr.
944 David Price Jones
968 Dr. & Mrs. J. Warren Van Derslice
1018 Mr. & Mrs. Alfred Rohn
1028 Mr. & Mrs. J. H. Sayle

———

955 Mr. & Mrs. H. C. Latus
959 Mr. & Mrs. W. H. Wright
967 Mr. & Mrs. M. P. Brady
971 Mr. & Mrs. E. A. Grimm
971 Mr. & Mrs. James H. Wilson
1005 Mrs. F. C. Neagle & drs.
1007 Mr. & Mrs. J. J. Hyland
1009 Mr. & Mrs. M. W. Hyland
1025 Mr. & Mrs. Thos. O. Perry
1613 Dr. & Mrs. John T. Milnamow

SOUTH PAULINA STREET.

149 Rev. & Mrs. W. T. Meloy
149 Dr. Wm. W. Meloy
149 Robert B. Meloy
149 Harry B. Meloy
233 Mr. & Mrs. A. S. Ross
233 Mr. & Mrs. J. E. Ingram
405 Mr. & Mrs. J. H. Simon
425 Dr. & Mrs. E. F. Buecking
      Receiving day Friday

144 Mrs. Ella C. Lewis
150 Mr. & Mrs. Louis B. Krum
340 Mr. & Mrs. J. M. Vernon & dr.
344 Mrs. Mary Dorr
344 Mrs. Rodney L. Taylor
396 Mr. & Mrs. Edward B. Gallup
402 Dr. & Mrs. Chas. N. Ballard
406 Mr. & Mrs. C. C. Carnahan

WEST POLK STREET.

831 Charles I. Goodhart
935 Mr. & Mrs. Robert D. Smith
937 Mr. & Mrs. E. S. Pratt & dr.

586 Mr. & Mrs. Fred H. Lutwyche
974 Dr. Espy L. Smith
1072 Mr. & Mrs. Geo. W. Bailey

WEST RANDOLPH STREET.

391 Mr. & Mrs. John J. Badenoch   350 Mr. & Mrs. G. L. Robertson

SOUTH RIDGEWAY AVENUE.

1119 Mr. & Mrs. Robert R. Fox

NORTH ROBEY STREET.

413 Mr. & Mrs. Joseph Hermann
499 Dr. & Mrs. J. W. Dal
547 Dr. Samuel L. Weber
639 Mr. & Mrs. M. D. Stecher
647 Mr. & Mrs. F. W. Belz
667 Mr. & Mrs. R. Gottlieb
667 Mr. & Mrs. John Grosse
667 Mr. & Mrs. J. J. Meldahl
675 Mr. & Mrs. Fred. Herhold &
    drs
685 Dr.& Mrs.Merritt W.Thompson

630 Rev. & Mrs. Wm. B. Leach
632 Mr. & Mrs. Erik L. Vognild
720 Mr. & Mrs. M. Schulz & drs.
720 Otto L. Schulz

689 Dr. Ralph S. Michel
695 Mr. & Mrs. Andrew P. Johnson
697 Dr. & Mrs. Theo. Wild & dr.
707 John Mohr
707 Joseph Mohr
717 Mr.& Mrs.Frank Patzack & drs.

SOUTH ROBEY STREET.

145 Dr. & Mrs. E. B. Loomis
161 James K. Lake & dr.
163 Mr. & Mrs. Lewis H. Mitchell
163 Robert C. Mitchell
165 Mrs. A. J. Spicer
235 Robert L. Benson

194 Mr. & Mrs. F. M. Blount
198 J. M. Deane
198 Mrs. Eloise A. Deane & dr.
380 Dr. F. A. Phillips

241 Mr. & Mrs. George E. Newcomb

NORTH SACRAMENTO AVENUE.

30 Thomas S. Hogan   36 Mr. & Mrs. J. George Smith

SOUTH SACRAMENTO AVENUE.

109 Mr. & Mrs. James Abbott
169 Dr. Henry N. Pitt

12 Chester C. Dodge
12 M. Eugene Dodge

SOUTH SANGAMON STREET.

167 Mrs. Jacob Beidler   167 George Beidler

SOUTH SAWYER AVENUE.

805 Edward J. McCarthy
817 Dr. & Mrs. A. V. Bergeron
859 Mr. & Mrs. James Cairns & dr.
871 Dr. George R. Bassett
871 George H. Bassett

864 Mr. & Mrs. Pleasant Amick
866 Mr. & Mrs. S. M. Randolph
870 Mr. & Mrs. N. K. Sheibley
872 Mr. & Mrs. John J. Coburn
966 Mr. & Mrs. Henry B. Eastman

877 Rev. & Mrs. F. T. Lee
   Receiving day Tuesday
879 Mr. & Mrs. Cuthbert McArthur
907 Mr. & Mrs. Wm. Harlev
915 Mr. & Mrs. Henry S. Tibbits
921 Mr. & Mrs. E. P. Peacock & dr.
   Receiving day Wednesday

921 Mr. & Mrs. Lee V. Tucker
923 Mrs. J. Jukes & drs.
   Receiving day Thursday
931 Mr. & Mrs. F. E. Peacock
933 Mr. & Mrs. Chas. A. Rusco
943 Mrs. Margaret Malahy & drs.
949 Mrs. H. Huebner & drs.

SOUTH SEELEY AVENUE.

15 Mrs. Perry A. Moxley
41 Mr. & Mrs. H. V. Reed & dr.
43 Mr. & Mrs. G. M. Vanzwoll
45 Mr. & Mrs. A. C. Selleck & dr.
47 Mr. & Mrs. H. J. Whitcomb
47 Mr. & Mrs. J. C. Whitcomb
71 Mr. & Mrs. W. H. Rose
73 Mrs. Eliza J. White
73 Mrs. Peter Sinclair
85 Mr. & Mrs. E. E. Hooper·
85 Wyly E. Hooper

42 Dr. & Mrs. L. L. Skelton
82 Mrs. Elizabeth Penny
82 Frank H. Penny
84 Mrs. Clara V. Hurley
108 Mr. & Mrs. Rudolph Rohn
108 Robert F. Rohn
124 Mr. & Mrs. Franklin Emery
——
93 Mr. & Mrs. Chas. M. Smith & dr.
93 James G. Smith

NORTH SHELDON STREET.

39 Frank E. Hayner

62 Mr. & Mrs. Wm. A. Amberg & drs. *Receive Wednesday.*
62 J. Ward Amberg

SIBLEY STREET.

61 Mr. & Mrs. Samuel H. Smith
63 Mr. & Mrs. Robert A. Smith
65 Gen. & Mrs. J. C. Smith & dr.
   Receiving day Friday

18 Frederic J. Bourgeau

SOUTH SPAULDING AVENUE.

907 Mr. & Mrs. Charles W. Clark
913 Mr. & Mrs. John H. Triggs & dr.
913 Charles W. Triggs

933 Mr. & Mrs. E. M. Craig
949 Mr. & Mrs. Herman Spitz
953 Mr. & Mrs. John T. Hanna

ST. JOHN'S COURT.

21 Blackman N. Foster
23 Mr. & Mrs. B. Burr & dr.
23 W. C. C. Gillespie

20 Mr. & Mrs. L. Sonnenschein
——
27 Mr. & Mrs. R. T. Sill & drs.

SOUTH ST. LOUIS AVENUE.

865 Mr. & Mrs. F. M. Kluge
871 Mr. & Mrs. Wm. Kluge

1023 Mrs. Elizabeth B. Lanterman

WEST TAYLOR STREET.

399 Mr. & Mrs. John P. Barron.
439 Dr. George S. Gfroerer
625 Dr. & Mrs. Gustav Schirmer
675 Dr. & Mrs. F. J. Patera

452 Mr. & Mrs. Thomas Coughlan
——
1079 Mr. & Mrs. E. J. H. Wright

THROOP STREET.

36 Mrs. Celia Plamondon
40 Mr. & Mrs. M. W. Ryan
44 Mr. & Mrs. George Duddleston
   & dr.
52 Mr. & Mrs. R. C. Gannon
58 Mrs. O. W. Goit & dr.

62 Mr. & Mrs. Wm. Thompson
78 Mr. & Mrs. A. H. Arnold
80 William W. Nutting
160 Mr. & Mrs. Franz Amberg
160 John F. Amberg
176 Mr. & Mrs. William Phillips

SOUTH TROY STREET.

347 Mr. & Mrs. Wm. W. Norris

TURNER AVENUE.

950 Mrs. Elizabeth Gorton & dr.
950 Miss Belle L. Gorton

954 Mr. & Mrs. Lawrence M. Ennis
Receive Friday

WEST TWENTY-SECOND STREET.

1853 Mr. & Mrs. James F. Lee
———
1820 Clarence W. Albro

1804 Mr. & Mrs. Jno. S. Stiles & dr.
1820 Mrs. Martha J. Albro & drs.

WEST VAN BUREN STREET.

455 Mr. & Mrs. A. H. Van de Water
605 Dr. & Mrs. H. P. Nelson
719 Mr. & Mrs. Robert L. Martin
735 William M. McRae

596 Mr. & Mrs. Alfred Russell
934 Mrs. Alice Plantz
———
735 Mrs. William McRae

VERNON PARK PLACE.

(Now Oregon Avenue.)

WALNUT STREET.

183 Mr. & Mrs. H. P. Stimson
183 Fred. D. Stimson
293 Mr.& Mrs.William R. Mumford
345 Rev. Thomas P. Hodnett
593 Mr. & Mrs. R. J. Tugwell
635 Mrs. Laleah B. Osgood
655 W. S. Felton
697 Mr. & Mrs. T. P. Hicks
713 George H. Mason
713 William G. Jackson
715 Mr. & Mrs. Abbott Baldwin
   Receiving day Wednesday
737 Mr. & Mrs.Eugene J.McCarthy
739 Mr. & Mrs. E. P. Burroughs
749 O. M. Brady
899 Mr. & Mrs. Henry E. Fisk
899 Mr. & Mrs. C. E. Reed
905 Mr. & Mrs. Joseph A. Painter
917 Mrs. J. H. Mellinger
923 Mr. & Mrs. F. D. Tracy
1011 Mr. & Mrs. Charles Carleton

162 Mr.& Mrs. Thos.M.Wignall&dr.
314 Mr. & Mrs. W. C. Lyman & drs.
314 Benj. K. Lyman
314 Wilfred C. Lyman jr.
652 Mr. & Mrs. John W. Tindall
658 Dr. & Mrs. W. M. W. Davison
694 Mr. & Mrs. J. M. Coughlin
698 Mr. & Mrs. Harry McKee
762 Dr. H. P. Pratt
764 Mrs. Jennie H. Wilkin & dr.
780 Dr. & Mrs. S. J. Avery
816 Dr. W. M. Brown
816 John S. Brown
818 Mr. & Mrs. A. W. Ovitt & dr.
   Receiving day Thursday
820 Mr. & Mrs. E. E. Palmer
   Receiving day Thursday
832 Mrs. J. A. Adams & dr.
834 Mr. & Mrs. Geo. C. Sanborn
836 Mr. & Mrs. George E. M. Pratt
842 Mr. & Mrs. Roger C. Sullivan

854 Mr. & Mrs. E. C. Brown
856 Mr. & Mrs. C. E. Cable
874 Mr. & Mrs. F. T. Kinnare
874 Mr. & Mrs. Ed. S. Cummings
904 Mr. & Mrs. Chas. J. Luck

906 Dr. & Mrs. Don. M. Gallie
912 Mrs. Nellie B. Smith
934 Dr. Jennie E. Hayner
934 Mr. & Mrs. H. C. Ambler
942 Dr. & Mrs. Jas. D. Higgins

WARREN AVENUE.

53 Anna M. Parker, M. D.
53 Helen M. Parker, M. D.
55 Dr. Charles S. Wood.
61 Mr. & Mrs. William K. Thomas
   & drs.
     Receiving day Thursday
61 George H. Thomas
67 Dr. & Mrs. L. J. Davis
71 Mrs. Elizabeth W. Krayeill
77 Mr. & Mrs. Dwight K. Tripp
79 Mr. & Mrs. A. Wallie Patterson
     Receiving day Thursday
81 Mr. & Mrs. Fergus Campbell
83 Mr. & Mrs. C. Hamlin Smith
95 Mr. & Mrs. H. S. Newton
155 Mr. & Mrs. F. Pettibone
155 Miss Alice Hulbert
155 Col. Ira W. Pettibone
159 Mr. & Mrs. P. F. Pettibone
159 Miss Alice Woodbury
171 Mr. & Mrs. W. Gray Brown &
   drs.
171 Mr. & Mrs. Wm. F. Peterson
175 Mrs. L. A. Bushnell & dr.
177 Mr. & Mrs. Francis B. Little
     Receiving day Wednesday
183 Col. M. D. Birge
207 Mr. & Mrs. Wm. Baldwin
207 Dr. Nora S. Davenport
215 Mr. & Mrs. John H. Cowper
225 Dr. Alfonse L. De Camp
231 Mr. & Mrs. George T. Clark
233 Mr. & Mrs. Jonathan Clark
263 Rev. & Mrs. Thomas D. Wallace
263 W. R. White & dr.
265 Dr. Franklin Patterson
265 Mrs. S. A. Patterson
269 Mr. & Mrs. S. V. Shipman & dr.
     Receiving day Thursday
271 Mrs. S. N. Brooks
271 Mrs. Jean Brooks Somers
273 H. B. Vanzwoll
273 Mrs. Maie W. Vanzwoll
275 Mr. & Mrs. Thos. L. Hanson
275 John P. Hanson
279 Dr. & Mrs. A. J. Harris & dr.
281 Dr. Helga Ruud

14 Mr. & Mrs. John Milloy
64 Sanford B. French
66 Mr. & Mrs. Ervin Hopkins jr.
88 John Berry
100 Mr. & Mrs. Lloyd G. Spencer &
   dr.
134 Miss M. Elizabeth Farson
134 Mrs. Harriet C. Farson
150 Mr. & Mrs. James Van Inwagen
150 James Van Inwagen jr.
164 Mr. & Mrs. Horace W. Beek
164 Stephen Thorne
188 Dr. & Mrs. Allen C. Cowperthwaite & dr.
190 Mrs. S. S. Gardner & dr.
190 George A. Gardner
220 Lawrence Oster
222 Mr. & Mrs. Sidney Bear
226 Alexander M. Stewart
230 Dr. & Mrs. L. Swartz
236 G. W. Newcomb & dr.
236 William H. Newcomb
236 Francis H. Newcomb
252 Mr. & Mrs. Robt. A. Williams
254 Mr. & Mrs. W. G. Miller
256 Mr. & Mrs. F. A. Oswald & drs.
256 Arthur Oswald
256 Hugo Oswald
256 Edwin Oswald
260 Mr. & Mrs. T. E. Dougherty
262 Mr. & Mrs. C. V. L. Peters & dr.
272 Mrs. Charles A. Taylor & dr.
272 Mr. & Mrs. Tracy J. Taylor
276 Mrs. L. M. Jones & dr.
306 Mr. & Mrs. Wm. K. Sullivan
322 Mrs. Thomas B. Rice
322 Mr & Mrs. Waldo F. Miller
330 Mr. & Mrs. T. J. Sammons
332 Mr. & Mrs. Horace T. Currier &
   dr. *Receiving day Wednesday*
332 Mrs. M. E. Fuller
336 Mr. & Mrs. Isaac Borg
338 Mr. & Mrs. Theodore G. Case
338 William S. Case
340 J. A. Reichelt & dr.
350 Mrs. S. A. Scully
352 Mr. & Mrs. C. W. Austin
352 Mr. & Mrs. W. R. Marshall

293 Mrs. Mary Baird & drs.
293 Mr. & Mrs. Frank E. Baird
297 Mrs. Mary E. Studley
297 Miss Hattie B. Studley
301 Mr. & Mrs. H. L. Brown
301 Miss Ada Hicks
303 Mr. & Mrs. Frank Binne & dr.
327 Mrs. E. L. Young
327 Mr. & Mrs. A. W. Adcock
327 Albert Y. Adcock
327 Earl E. Adcock
331 Mr. & Mrs. A. F. Burnett & dr.
333 Mr. & Mrs. Arthur E. Wilcox
335 Mr. & Mrs. N. A. Phillips
 Receiving day Wednesday
339 Dr. & Mrs. R. N. Hall
339 Louis E. Hart
349 Dr. & Mrs. William S. White
363 Louis J. Block
375 Mr. & Mrs. Jas. A. Gaynor&drs.
 Receiving day Tuesday
377 Mr. & Mrs. Frank S. Waters
381 Mr. & Mrs. John A. Sweet
381 John A. Sweet jr.
385 Mr. & Mrs. T. C. Baldwin & dr.
387 Mr. & Mrs. F. A. Winkelman
391 Mr. & Mrs. J. H. Beers
393 Mr. & Mrs. Frank L. Morse
395 Mr. & Mrs. Theo. D. Eagle
395 W. H. Eagle
395 Miss M. Eagle
397 Mr. & Mrs. W. B. Coit
401 Dr. & Mrs. Stephen G. West
403 Mr. & Mrs. Burns L. Newman
403 Lewis E. Newman
405 Mr. & Mrs. Henry S. Rich
405 Herbert G. Rich
405 Frank E. Rich
409 W. R. Kellogg & dr.
413 Mr. & Mrs. J. Henry Deakin
413 Earl Deakin
427 Mr. & Mrs. N. C. Safford
 Receiving day Thursday
427 Mr. & Mrs. W. W. Brunson &
 dr. *Receiving day Thursday*
431 Mr. & Mrs. M. Unger & dr.
437 Mr. & Mrs. Jas. Parker
451 Mr. & Mrs. W. F. Merle & dr.
461 Mr. & Mrs. John Young
461 Mr. & Mrs. Albert Mathews
569 Mr. & Mrs. Wm. B. Bangs
569 R. E. Smith
569 Dr. O. R. Bluthardt
747 Mrs. A. K. Ingersoll
747 Miss Elizabeth Ryan
749 Mr. & Mrs. George H. Clark

370 Mr. & Mrs. Charles H. Fuller
370 Luther C. Fuller
376 Mr. & Mrs. J. Eugene Smith &
 drs.
376 Mr. & Mrs. Benjamin M. Smith
376 Mrs. Adele Bascom
376 Henry Wolcott
378 Mrs. Ira Blanchard
378 Theodore F. Blanchard
384 Austin L. Patterson
384 Mr. & Mrs. Sheldon P. Patterson
390 Mr. & Mrs. R. M. Birdsall & dr.
394 Mr. & Mrs. M. R. Brainard
394 Mrs. Lenna B. Green
414 Mr. & Mrs. Joseph Rogerson
416 Edwin C. Swiney & dr.
418 Mr. & Mrs. George T. Giles
418 Mr. & Mrs. L. R. Kimberly
420 Mr. & Mrs. John C. Bennett
 Receiving day Tuesday
426 Mr. & Mrs. Fred M. Gale
426 Fred Gale
434 Mr. & Mrs. J. Bernhard
434 Mrs. E. Woolf
434 B. Woolf
436 Mr. & Mrs. W. B. Smith
 Receiving day Thursday
440 Mrs. A. Douglas
 Receiving day Wednesday
440 Dr. Percy E. Douglas
440 Clyde Douglas
442 Mrs. H. W. Dobson & dr.
442 Robert Dobson
452 Mr. & Mrs. Silas Palmer
452 Mrs. W. H. Money
452 William H. Palmer
704 Mrs. W. B. Laparle
704 Mrs. C. A. Cotter
716 Mr. & Mrs. H. L. Childs
716 M. E. Ames
718 Louis J. Holtzman & dr.
742 Mr. & Mrs. George P. Blair
742 Mrs. L. E. Johnson & dr.
766 Mr. & Mrs. Theodore I. Wilson
766 Mr. & Mrs. Walpole Wood
768 Col. & Mrs. Barent Van Buren
 Receiving day Tuesday
770 Mr. & Mrs. J. C. Holenshade
770 Dr. & Mrs. H. E. Santee
782 Mr. & Mrs. William D. Fischer
802 Mr. & Mrs. Thos. W. Cole
802 Wilford B. Cole
804 Dr. & Mrs. Albert E. Halstead
810 Dr. & Mrs. Samuel P. McKinney
812 Mr. & Mrs. Aaron F. Walcott
812 Dr. Edwin Hamill

751 Dr. & Mrs. James B. Herrick
   Receiving day Thursday
751 Mr. & Mrs. J. G. Evenden
761 Mr. & Mrs. John R. Schofield
765 Mr. & Mrs. Frank Holmes
767 Mr. & Mrs. Lawrence J. Reed
   Receiving day Friday
769 Mr. & Mrs. F. H. Fogarty
771 Mr. & Mrs. Harry A. Wilkie
771 Mrs. W. B. Mason & dr.
771 Mrs. E. C. Marshall
773 Mr. & Mrs. Ira Stover
791 Mr. & Mrs. Edgar French
791 Mrs. H. M. Herbert
795 Mr. & Mrs. F. E. Coyne
797 Mrs. Florence A. Graves
797 Mrs. Mabel Ely
801 Mr. & Mrs. Edwin S. Rooks
801 Franklin G. Robbins
815 Mr. & Mrs. J. Thompson Gill
   Receiving day Friday
815 Henry R. Paul
821 Dr. Annette S. Richards
825 Mr. & Mrs. Marc Sherwood
825 Mr. & Mrs. Benj. F. Johnston
833 Dr. & Mrs. James C. Gill
839 Mr. & Mrs. J. C. Benedict
841 Mr. & Mrs. D. W. Wells & drs.
843 Mr. & Mrs. B. Giroux
843 George W. Giroux
845 Mr. & Mrs. H. W. Stroker
845 Mr. & Mrs. R. Fairclough
847 Mr. & Mrs. J. Neal Blake & dr.
847 Arnold M. Bigelow
849 Mrs. M. Carpenter
849 Walter C. Newhall
849 Mr. & Mrs. L. Ernest Rodgers
853 Dr. & Mrs. Eli Wight
853 Mrs. Sarah M. Eddy
875 Mr. & Mrs. V. Hofmann
879 William A. Taylor
887 Mr. & Mrs. F. W. Bryan & dr.
891 Mr. & Mrs. Wm. J. Walker
891 Geo. L. Walker
905 Mr. & Mrs. J. Hainsworth
909 Mr. & Mrs. Alfred J. Youngdahl
   Receiving day Wednesday
919 Dennis S. Daly & drs.
925 Dr. & Mrs. F. C. Zapfe
947 Mr. & Mrs. C. W. Striger
949 Mr. & Mrs. R. C. Haskins
949 Mrs. Mary A. Haskins
973 Mr. & Mrs. H. B. Eaver
   Receiving day Friday
975 Mrs. A. Swenson & drs.
975 Dr. & Mrs. Wm. Rittenhouse

812 Dr. John C. Hamill
812 Harry Hamill
826 Mr. & Mrs. F. M. Sisson
826 Dr. & Mrs. G. W. Wolgamott & dr.
826 Mr. & Mrs. Samuel H. Bloom
828 Mrs. Elizabeth Kendall & dr.
828 Mrs. Martha Perkins
834 Mr. & Mrs. J. S. Jackson
848 Mr. & Mrs. C. K. Munson & dr.
868 Dr. & Mrs. Levi E. Miley
868 Mr. & Mrs. Wm. E. Elliott
870 Dr. J. Mills Mayhew
870 Mrs. James E. Mills & dr.
886 Thomas F. Crosby
892 Mr. & Mrs. Albert C. Perrill
   Receiving day Thursday
898 Rev. & Mrs. J. K. Arnold
   Receive 1st Sunday
906 Mr. & Mrs. Geo. H. Benedict
908 Mr. & Mrs. E. A. Dicker & dr.
918 Mr. & Mrs. G. B. Fern
   Receiving day Wednesday
918 Miss Clara Louise Fern
918 C. A. Fern
920 Mr. & Mrs. Frank E. Clark
956 Mr. & Mrs. David W. Clark
966 Dr. & Mrs. Lisle C. Waters
974 Mr. & Mrs. Andrew Stark & drs.
1006 Joseph Berg & drs.
1016 Mr. & Mrs. Frank E. Locke
1058 Mr. & Mrs. Harry W. Pardey
1060 Mr. & Mrs. F. W. Hedgeland
1060 Mrs. I. Lamb
1066 Rev. & Mrs. E. Corwin & dr.
1066 Mr. & Mrs. L. L. Taylor
1074 Dr. & Mrs. Peter Fahrney & dr.
1074 W. H. Fahrney
1074 Homer E. Fahrney
1074 J. H. Fahrney

983 George S. Hunt
983 Mr. & Mrs. Charles R. Barrett
987 Mr. & Mrs. Charles A. L. Kramer
1003 Dr. & Mrs. Philon C. Whidden & dr.
1009 Mr. & Mrs. Thomas Davis & dr.
1015 Mr. & Mrs. Frederick F. Bullen
1023 Mr. & Mrs. Henry Rice
1025 Dr. Elizabeth H. Trout & dr.
1025 Edgar W. Trout
1029 Mr. & Mrs. P. Bird Price
1033 Mr. & Mrs. Warren F. Holden & drs.
1035 Dr. & Mrs. J. E. Hetherington
   Receiving day Thursday

1037 Mrs. Emma Pratt
1065 Mr. & Mrs. H. W. Thorp
1065 Mrs. Sarah Granger·
1065 Mrs. Mary Tryon
1067 Mr. & Mrs. John L. Hoffmann
1067 Mrs. John Hoffmann
1069 Mr. & Mrs. A. D. MacGill

1071 Mr. & Mrs. Merritt S. Conner
1071 Mr. & Mrs. J. H. Livesey &
      drs.
1089 Frank H. Schaefer
1089 Louis H. Schaefer
1089 Emil C. Schaefer
1089 Miss Emma Schaefer

WASHINGTON BOULEVARD.

323 Elijah C. Cole
335 Dr. & Mrs. G. W. Reynolds
341 Dr. & Mrs. J. S. Young
      Receive 2nd Friday in mo.
341 Miss Edith G. Young
341 Leon W. Young
369 Dr. & Mrs. G. Van Zandt
381 Mr. & Mrs. George E. White
409 Mr. & Mrs. D. H. Curtis & dr.
413 Miss F. Groesbeck
      Receiving day Wednesday
413 Mr. & Mrs. Augustus VanBuren
425 Mrs. A. J. Snell
427 Mr. & Mrs. C. E. Rollins
429 Harry S. Lewis
429 Dr. William L. Noble
429 Chas. E. Rollins jr.
429 Edward C. F. Dolle
429 Clark B. Samson
431 Mr. & Mrs. A. J. Stone
445 Mr. & Mrs. Fred L. Fuller
445 Mr. & Mrs. I. R. Rowland
      Receiving day Wednesday
445 B. F. Martin
449 Willard P. Alward
451 Mr. & Mrs. Wm. W. Green
451 Mrs. Mary Hopkinson
451 Mr. & Mrs. Wm. S. Johnson
453 Mr. & Mrs. William W. Strong
455 Dr. & Mrs. W. B. Hanna·
      Receiving day Wednesday
457 Mrs. C. C. Wheeler
457 C. M. Wheeler
457 Miss Josephine E. Orvis
459 Mr. & Mrs. Geo. W. Pitkin & dr.
459 Harry E. Pitkin
463 Mr. & Mrs. W. E. Rollo & drs.
465 Mrs. M. G. Merrill
465 Fred G. Merrill
469 Judge & Mrs. C. D. F. Smith&dr.
471 Mrs. Mary Barnhart
471 Dr. & Mrs. John A. McDonell
477 Miss Minnie Peterson
485 Mrs. M. J. Richards
505 Mrs. A. Farrar & drs.
513 Rev. & Mrs. W. F. McMillen

304 Dr. & Mrs. Z. P. Hanson
316 Mr. & Mrs. Ezra A. Cook & drs.
316 Ezra A. Cook jr.
316 Prof. W. W. Leffingwell
346 H. D. Hunter
346 G. A. Williams
354 Mrs. C. C. Newell
354 Rev. & Mrs. E. P. Goodwin
354 Albert P. Goodwin
376 Mrs. Dot Thompson
398 Edward T. Noonan
398 Mrs. Mary H. Noonan
400 Mr. & Mrs. Thos. Carbine
410 Dr. & Mrs. J. E. Low
420 Mrs. A. Roberts
422 Dr. & Mrs. J. H. Plecker & dr.
428 Mrs. Joseph P. Ross & drs.
      Receiving day Wednesday
428 Robert E. Ross
428 William H. Ross
432 Mr. & Mrs. Daniel J. Haynes
434 Mrs. Emma Rosenfeld
434 Sidney Rosenfeld
436 Mr. & Mrs. W. W. Cheney
436 W. W. Cheney jr.
444 Mrs. A. R. Briggs & dr.
444 Miss Mary R. Whitley
468 C. H. Ruddock
468 Miss Harriet M. Farnsworth
470 Mr. & Mrs. C. K. G. Billings
502 Mr. & Mrs. B. W. Ellis & dr.
512 Prof. & Mrs. G. B. Willcox & drs.
516 Mr.& Mrs. J. H. Ohlerking & drs.
524 Mr. & Mrs. David Thresher
524 William D. Thresher
528 Mr. & Mrs. E. C. Thurber & dr.
532 Rev. & Mrs. F. A. Noble
      Receiving day Friday
532 Frederic P. Noble·
534 Prof. & Mrs. Geo. H. Gilbert
536 Mr. & Mrs. W. Wallace Clark
538 D. W. Bosley
538 Mr. & Mrs. Joseph S. Wells
      Receiving day Thursday
540 Dr. & Mrs. R. J. Piper
      Receiving day Thursday

521 Mr. & Mrs. J. E. Haskell & dr.
535 Mrs. C. W. Earle
535 Miss Carolyn Earle
535 Dr. George H. Weaver
549 Mrs. Catherine Ford
557 Mr. & Mrs. J. W. C. Haskell
569 Mr.& Mrs. H. M. Hooker & drs.
571 Mr. & Mrs. C. E. Waters
585 Mrs. John A. Tyrrell
585 Charles T. Tyrrell
585 Mr. & Mrs. Fred S. Tyrrell
587 Mr. & Mrs. Willey B. Waters
591 Oran Ott
591 John N. Ott
591 Mrs. Katherine Ott
593 Mrs. Nony R. Williams & drs.
595 Mr. & Mrs. J. D. Wallace & dr.
599 Mr. & Mrs. Perley Lowe
601 Dr. & Mrs. E. P. Murdock
603 Mr. & Mrs. T. F. Farrell
609 Mr. & Mrs. J. A. Guilford & dr.
611 Dr. & Mrs. W. H. Woodbury
611 Miss Carrie E. Hill
619 Mr. & Mrs. J. B. Keeler
621 Mrs. P. B. Merwin
621 Jos. B. Redfield & dr.
625 Dr. & Mrs. S. J. Boyd
631 Mrs. F. L. Fitch
631 Mrs. Annie H. Williams
631 Mrs. Mary C. Vary
633 Mr. & Mrs. L. Friedman
    Receiving day 1st and last
    Tuesday in mo.
633 William Friedman
633 Miss Jennie Friedman
633 Burnett Friedman
635 Mr. & Mrs. Chester Warner
639 Mr. & Mrs. M. D. Temple
647 Mr. & Mrs. John E. Wright &
    dr.
647 Frank P. Wright
647 Dr. Clarence H. Wright
649 Mr. & Mrs. G. D. Pease & dr.
649 Mrs. S. J. Osgood
651 Mr. & Mrs. D. H. Dickinson
651 Mr. & Mrs. Harry J. Farnham
651½ Mr. & Mrs. J. E. Loomis & dr.
657 Mr. & Mrs. L. J. Blades & drs.
663 Mr. & Mrs. Chas. Perkins & dr.
663 Mr. & Mrs. C. H. Robinson
681 Mrs. J. D. Skeer & drs.
681 Charles H. Skeer
681 Geo. M. Skeer
683 Dr. & Mrs. A. E. Hoadley
683½ Mr. & Mrs. E. Wisdom
683½ Harry E. Wisdom

544 Dr. & Mrs. Wm. G. Willard
    Receiving day Tuesday
544 Mrs. Ellen W. Carpenter
558 Mrs. Harriet M. Blake
560 Alexander H. Peters & drs.
562 Mr. & Mrs. William W. Evans
564 Mr. & Mrs. L. H. Evans
566 Mr. & Mrs. E. T. Marshall & dr.
566 Randall E. Marshall
568 Dr. & Mrs. John Milton Dodson
570 Mr. & Mrs. J. F. Talbot & dr.
570 Miss Jessica H. Talbot
570 Frederic S. Hebard
576 Mr. & Mrs. O. C. DeSouchet
576 Mr. & Mrs. John A. Gunn
576A Mr.& Mrs. Milton C. Smucker
582 Dr. & Mrs. F. C. Schaefer
604 Mr. & Mrs. E. T. Harris
606 Mr. & Mrs. J. S. Meckling & dr.
608 Mr. & Mrs. H. L. Marshall &drs.
610 Mr.&Mrs. George A. Head&drs.
612 Mrs. L. W. Foley
    Receiving day Thursday
612 Mr. & Mrs. Wm. C. Heinroth
614 Mr. & Mrs. L. D. Collins
614 James R. Lane
618 Mr. & Mrs.W.H.Anderson & dr.
622 Mrs. Catherine Clinton & dr.
622 Mrs. Julia C. Howe
622 Miss Mary Clinton Howe
622 George F. Barker
622 Charles E. Barker
628 Rev. & Mrs. G. S. F. Savage
632 Mr. & Mrs. Aaron B. Mead
632 Miss Agnes R. Mead
632 Mrs. J. B. Packard
632 Miss Lizzie McDonald
634 Mr. & Mrs. J. C. Borcherdt
636½ Dr. & Mrs. P. Adolphus
640 Mr. & Mrs. Alfred F. Scott
642 Mrs. H. A. Winter
    Receiving day Friday
642 Miss Grace L. Winter
642 Frank F. Winter
642 Will C. Hayhurst
644 Mr.&Mrs.C.M. Linington & dr.
644½ Mr. & Mrs. Charles R. Clark
646 Mr. & Mrs. G. T. Burroughs
646 Edward R. Burroughs
646 Mrs. E. J. Hight
650 Mr. & Mrs. L. R. Harsha
650 Mrs. J. L. Burns
654 Miss Harriet A. Farrand
654 Mrs. J. C. French
658 Mr. & Mrs. T. J. Cochrane
660 Mr. & Mrs. N. H. Curtis

685 Mr. & Mrs. E. Banning
   Receiving day Tuesday
687 Mr. & Mrs. W. H. Salisbury
689 Mr. & Mrs. Robert L. Tatham
   & drs.
691 Dr. & Mrs. T. D. Palmer
691½ Mr. & Mrs. Henry O. Shepard
   Receiving day Tuesday
695 Mr. & Mrs. Frank T. Fowler
695 Mrs. C. D. Hill
697 Mr. & Mrs. C. A. Weare
697 John Weare
699 Dr. & Mrs. Clarence M. Rankine
   Receive Wednesday afternoon
701 Mr.& Mrs.Thomas Hood & drs.
709 Mr. & Mrs. O. W. Wallis & drs.
709 Frank E. Wallis
711 Mr. & Mrs. Fred G. Brooks
711 Mrs. Julia A. Brooks
721 Dr. & Mrs. E. A. Royce
723 Mr. & Mrs. J. W. Corlies & dr.
725 Mr. & Mrs. James E. Joyce
725 Miss Clara L. Joyce
725 James F. Joyce
727 Mr. & Mrs. J. T. Rawleigh
727 Miss Ava F. Rawleigh
727 Mrs. Mary R. Warner
731 Mr. & Mrs. J. Harry Rawleigh
733 Rev. & Mrs. W. C. DeWitt
739 Mr. & Mrs. Thos. Sharp
745 Mrs. W. D. Gibson & dr.
745 Miss Belle Gibson
751 Mrs. F. L. Garrott & drs.
751 Mrs. D. P. Lee
757 Mr. & Mrs. H. A. Christy
757 Dr. & Mrs. Sanger Brown
767 Mrs. Ida M. Featherstone & dr.
767 Miss Jane A. Washburn
769 Mr. & Mrs. Chas. S. MacCarty
   Receiving day Wednesday
769 Miss Mae Blessing
777 Miss Mollie E. Moody
777 Miss Lillian R. Moody
777 Frank A. Moody
783 Mr. & Mrs. Wm. Ripley
783 Mr. & Mrs. B. W. Ripley
793 Mrs. Mary M. Webster
793 Miss Mabel T. Webster
793 Mrs. C. D. Otis
811 Maurice H. Scully
813 Mr. & Mrs. Chas. W. Richards
815 Dr. & Mrs. Wells Andrews
815 Jay A. Andrews
817 Mr. & Mrs. Sydney S. Date
   Receiving day Monday

678 Alexander Vaughan
678 Mr. & Mrs. S. S. Vaughan
678 Mr. & Mrs. Frank S. Atherton
682 Mr. & Mrs. Edward Nevers
686 Mr. & Mrs. W. A. Golder & dr.
686½ Mr. & Mrs. C. H. Weaver
686½ Arthur C. Weaver
690 Mr. & Mrs. J. K. Stevens
690 Mrs. Jacob S. Cater
692 Mr. & Mrs. Geo.R.Davis &drs.
692 Benjamin Davis
696 Mr. & Mrs. Chas. A. Brown
698½ Mr. & Mrs.Robert C.Newton
   Receiving day Thursday
710 Mr. & Mrs. Calvin F. Taylor
712 Mr. & Mrs. J. F. Mendsen
724 Mr. & Mrs. E. G. W. Rietz
730 Mr. & Mrs. A. H. McClurg
734 Rev. & Mrs. R. A. Jernberg
734 Mrs. Prudence E. Libby
740 Mr. & Mrs. Andrew Scott
742 Mr. & Mrs. H. King Smith
742 Mrs. R. G. Clark
744 Mr. & Mrs. James F. Griffin
748 Mr. & Mrs. James F. Criswell
754 Mr. & Mrs. F. P. Stone
756 Lucius A. Steveley
756 Mrs. John F. Steveley
756 Mr.& Mrs. Geo. W.Hutchinson
760 Mr. & Mrs. J. K. Barry
762 Mr. & Mrs. Alex. J. Hodge
768 Millard F. Bingham
768 Misses Bingham
   Receiving day Thursday
786 Henry Cohn & drs.
788 Mr. & Mrs. A. Longstreet
792 Mr. & Mrs. D. A. Price
794 Miss Emma S. Brett
794 Theodore F. Brett
804 Mrs. W. W. Wilcox & dr.
806 Mr. & Mrs. Alexander White
806 Mr. & Mrs. Alonzo D. Smith
836 Mr. & Mrs. B. A. Corcoran
   Receiving day Tuesday
840 Mr. & Mrs. Otto Heper
844 Mr. & Mrs Charles Noyes
850 Mr. & Mrs. Edward Harzfeld
850 Mr. & Mrs. Jacob W. Strauss
858 Mr. & Mrs. William P. Frailey
858 Mr. & Mrs. J. S. Watson
868 Mr. & Mrs. Jas. J. Sullivan
878 Mr. & Mrs. Wm. F. MacLachlan *Receiving day Thursday*
880 Mr. & Mrs. W. R. Clark
882 Mrs. Edith S. Weaver
890 Miss Nellie F. McAndrews

817 Miss Marcia Moffatt
821 Mr. & Mrs. Alonzo Weston
821 Mr. & Mrs. Reuben Hatch
823 Mr. & Mrs. J. W. Gehrig
831 Mr. & Mrs. Frank Hayes
833 Dr. John A. Benson
833 Dr. & Mrs. Chauncey F. Chapman
877 Mrs. Simeon Cobb
881 Mr. & Mrs. D. T. Helm
887 Dr. & Mrs. E. E. Holroyd
1069 Mr. & Mrs. Geo. H. Bishop
1079 Mr. & Mrs. John C. Bryan
 Receiving day Thursday
1093 Mr. & Mrs. F. W. Morgan
1103 Mr. & Mrs. R. Wright
1103 Mrs. L. M. Hadley
1113 Rev. William Jason Gold &drs.
1113 Mrs. S. E. E. Chamberlin
1135 Mr. & Mrs. T. J. Rice
1139 Mrs. A. B. Rundell & drs.
1139 Miller H. Rundell
1149 Mr. & Mrs. Fred O. Streich
1151 Mr. & Mrs. Wm. Herrick
1159 Mr. & Mrs. J. T. Matthews
1159 Mr. & Mrs. W. D. Bradshaw
1159 Mrs. P. Hickcox
1159 Mr. & Mrs. Charles E. Hill & drs.
1173 Mr. & Mrs. Uri Weaver
1177 Mr. & Mrs. J. E. Keating
1179 Mr. & Mrs. Frank R. Grout
1179 Charles R. Grout
1179 Mr. & Mrs. H. F. Chandler
1181 Mr. & Mrs. George R. Allen
1183 Mrs. Nettie E. Gunlock & dr.
1183 Philip L. Gunlock
1187 Mr. & Mrs. M. C. Bullock & dr.
1195 Mrs. M. M. McCourtie
1195 Mrs. M. E. Bell
1197 Mr.& Mrs.A.B.McCourtie & dr.
 Receiving day Thursday
1205 Mr. & Mrs. M. D. Lamoreaux
1225 Mr. & Mrs. J. B. Allan
1229 Mr. & Mrs. F. J. Dennis
 Receiving day Tuesday
1231 Mr. & Mrs. Henry B. Utley
1237 Mr. & Mrs. E. A. Hill & dr.
1237 Charles B. Hill
1239 Mr. & Mrs. S. T. Gunderson
 Receiving day Wednesday
1239 Mr. & Mrs. G. O. Gunderson
1241 Mr. & Mrs. N. D. Fraser
1241 Miss M. M. Sterling
1257 Mr. & Mrs. Wm. Sollitt
1261 Mr. & Mrs. W. E. Mortimer

890 James McAndrews jr.
890 Joseph R. McAndrews
1010 Mr. & Mrs. L. K. Stevens
 Receiving day Wednesday
1010 Robert W. Stevens
1050 Mrs. C. H. Clancy
1050 Mr. & Mrs. Edwin M. Clancy
1050 Mr. & Mrs. A. C. Leebrick
1056 Dr. & Mrs. C. St.Clair Drake
 Receiving day Tuesday
1056 Mr. & Mrs. Edward Atkinson
1056 Edward Atkinson jr.
1060 Mr. & Mrs. A. W. Neff
1076 Dr. & Mrs. Wm. J. Stewart
1076 George W. Stewart
1100 Mr. & Mrs. R. M. McKinney
1100 Mr. & Mrs. Albert Cole Dodge
1102 Mr. & Mrs. Chas. W. Bard &
1102 Mrs. Charity E. Sanders
1110 Mr. & Mrs. H. C. Stewart
1116 Mr. & Mrs. A. E. Nickerson & dr.
1118 Mrs. Julia G. Colson
1118 Harry G. Colson
1118 Mrs. J. W. Hart
1120 Mrs. H. E. Patrick
1122 Mrs. R. A. Drummond
1122 Mr. & Mrs. D. M. Reynolds
1124 Mr. & Mrs. Henry R. Baldwin
1128 James Quirk
1128 Dr. James P. Quirk
1130 Mrs. Emily Ahles
1130 William Ahles
1136 Mr. & Mrs. J. L. Kneisly
1142 Mr. & Mrs. J. C. Henderson & dr.
1170 Rev. & Mrs. Wm. E. Holyoke
1174 Mr. & Mrs. John Gilbert
1176 Mr. & Mrs. George Fyfe & dr.
1176 Arthur Fulton
1178 Dr. & Mrs. A. I. Bouffleur
1180 Mrs. Mary Kenny & drs.
1180 Mr. & Mrs. J. F. McBride
1188 Mr. & Mrs. Hiram Parshall Thompson
1192 Mr. & Mrs. Wm. E. Ottie
1194 Mr. & Mrs. F. W. Hoffman
1212 Mrs. M. A. Richardson
1212 M. Arthur Richardson
1220 John Mullin
1220 John J. Naghten
1234 Mr. & Mrs. R. F. Conway & drs.
1234 Mrs. Mary A. Reed
1236 Mr. & Mrs. Wallace Casler

1263 Mr. & Mrs. Louis Karcher
 Receiving day Thursday
1269 Mrs. Wm. G. Metzger
1271 Mr. & Mrs. Henry J. Evans
 Receiving day Wednesday
1271 Mr. & Mrs. Chas. J. Mortimer
1285 Mr. & Mrs. J. G. Harlow
1287 Mr. & Mrs. F. I. Wilson
1287 Dr. A. Bromley Allen
1289 Mr. & Mrs. Chas. H. Solomon
 Receiving day Thursday
1295 Mr. & Mrs. F. F. Whitman
1295 Miss Hattie E. Whitman
1295 John M. Whitman
1319 Mr. & Mrs. L. Wolff
1319 Herman M. Hoelscher
1319 Edward C. Hoelscher
1323 Mr. & Mrs. Samuel Kerr
1371 Mr.& Mrs. Richard W. Knisely
1373 Dr. & Mrs. J. Leggett
 Receiving day Thursday
1373 Mrs. Kate Leggett
1373 George J. Ryan
1375 Mr. & Mrs. K. S. McLennan &
 dr. *Receiving day Friday*
1375 Miss Katheryn Dee
1375 Wm. H. Lusk
1375 Miss S. E. Lusk
1379 Mr. & Mrs. Daniel Forbes
1383 Mr. & Mrs. B. Quirk & dr.
1389 Mr. & Mrs. John McMahon
1399 Miss Mary J. Fish
 Receiving day Friday
1399 Miss Sarah C. Fish
1411 Mr. & Mrs. A. J. Graham
1417 Mr. & Mrs. Wm. A. Doyle
1423 Mr. & Mrs. Arnold Heap
 Receiving day Thursday
1427 Mr. & Mrs. Carl Moll
1427 Mrs. J. C. Witte & dr.
1469 Mr. & Mrs. M. M. Brown
1477 Mr. & Mrs. Duke M. Farson
1487 Mr. & Mrs. John Eiszner
1487 Frank J. Eiszner
1491 Mr. & Mrs. A. H. Sanders
1497 Mr. & Mrs. Elisha W. Case
1497 Mr. & Mrs. P. M. Vermaas
2199 Mr. & Mrs. Joseph W. Brown
 Receiving day Tuesday
2227 Mr. & Mrs. Wilson G. Barker

1520 Miss Florence M. Spofford
1520 H. Arthur Rice
2140 Mr. & Mrs. John J. A. Dahmke

1240 Mr. & Mrs. W. Fred Main
1242 Mr. & Mrs. Harvey L. Thompson
1248 Mr. & Mrs. C. A. Hallam
1268 Mr. & Mrs. James A. Sackley
 Receiving day Wednesday
1270 Mr. & Mrs. R. D. Huszagh
 Receiving day Wednesday
1272 Mrs. Abigail Harris & drs.
 Receiving day Wednesday
1276 Mrs. Chas. Munson & dr.
 Receiving day Thursday
1276 Charles W. Munson
1276 Mrs. Elizabeth Kelly & dr.
1278 Mr. & Mrs. F. Marion Woods
1286 Mr. & Mrs. Albert J. Danz
1286 Mr. & Mrs. Charles A. Danz
1286 Mrs. Margaret Danz
1288 Mr. & Mrs. Michael Hayes
1290 Mr. & Mrs. W. H. Genung
1292 Mr. & Mrs. Charles Dickinson
1292 Mr. & Mrs. B. F. Richolson
1294 Mr. & Mrs. C. M. Kelsey
1304 Mr. & Mrs. Francis M. Barrett
1304 Miss Nora Buckley
1316 Mr. & Mrs. Thos. S. Keirnan
1330 Mrs. Annie E. Leekley & dr.
1330 Harlow A. Leekley
1332 Mrs. Emilie Backus
1336 Mr.& Mrs. Henry B. Mathews jr
1336 Mr. & Mrs. D. R. Fraser
1338 Mr. & Mrs. G. M. Richardson
1338 E. Perrin Richardson
1338 M. L. Richardson
1344 Mr. & Mrs. Frank R. Millard
 Receiving day Tuesday
1344 Albert F. Musgrave
1356 Mr. & Mrs. W. George Morris
1364 Mrs. Henry Van Buren
1388 Mr. & Mrs. Chas. S. Bartholf
1410 Dr. & Mrs. A. W. Gray
1410 Louis A. I. Gray
1426 Mrs. John Oliver
1428 Mr. & Mrs. John W. Kilmore
1436 Mr. & Mrs. Wm. B. Ives
 Receiving day Tuesday
1436 Miss L. Buckley
1482 Mrs. Eliza J. Crane
1482 Mr. & Mrs. Frank R. Crane
 Receiving day Wednesday
1492 Mr. & Mrs. C. H. Chamberlain
1492 Miss Nellie Nicholas
1494 Mr. & Mrs. Edward Horan
1510 Mr. & Mrs. Daniel W. Mills
1520 Mr. & Mrs. George W. Spofford

WAVERLY COURT.

19 Mr. & Mrs. A. E. Rawson
23 Robert A. Baker
25 Mr. & Mrs. Henry L. Slayton

16 Dr. & Mrs. J. B. Armstrong
24 Mr. & Mrs. R. J. Taylor

SOUTH WESTERN AVENUE.

1145 Mr. & Mrs. Florence McCarthy

WILCOX AVENUE.

1045 Mr. & Mrs. T. Addison Busbey
1045 Mrs. Mary M. Coggeshall
1175 Mr. & Mrs. John W. Lyke
1223 Mr. & Mrs. M. W. Gleason
1239 Mrs. E. A. Chapman

1300 Mr. & Mrs. F. A. Barnard
1310 Mr. & Mrs. Joseph Short
2146 Dr. & Mrs. William E. Dunn

1036 Mr. & Mrs. B. F. Davison
1174 Mr. & Mrs. John Russell
1226 Mr. & Mrs. F. B. Stevenson
1232 Mrs. Emma Riford
1232 Ira B. Riford
1260 Dr. & Mrs. W. F. Haley
1262 Mr. & Mrs. Joseph R. Payson
1294 Rev. & Mrs. D. F. Fox
1298 Mr. & Mrs. M. D. Madigan

SOUTH WINCHESTER AVENUE.

105 Mr. & Mrs. H. E. Hunt
105 Mr. & Mrs. W. H. Cuyler & dr.
151 Mr. & Mrs. Alex. Meyer
213 Mr. & Mrs. Wm. F. O'Hearne
  Receiving day Thursday
215 Mr. & Mrs. Theodore B. Wells
267 Mrs. H. T. Wynkoop
  Receiving day Thursday
299 Mrs. Elizabeth Butler & drs.
301 Rev. & Mrs. R. W. French
367 Mr. & Mrs. Jacob J. Goodhart
445 Mr. & Mrs. Wm. G. Ruehl

232 Rt. Rev. & Mrs. T. Bowman
  Receiving day Thursday
234 Mr. & Mrs. E. B. Esher
  Receiving day Wednesday
276 Mr. & Mrs. Victor Behrens
  Receiving day Thursday.
276 William A. Reed & dr.
342 Mr. & Mrs. Nath'l Cameron & dr.

501 Mr. & Mrs. John Geringer
507 Mr. & Mrs. Charles J. Vopicka

WINTHROP COURT.

23 Mr. & Mrs. M. J. Breen

31 Mr. & Mrs. Jos. A. Koenig & dr.

SOUTH WOOD STREET.

117 Mr. & Mrs. A. E. Shader
203 Mr. & Mrs. Jas. M. Doyle & dr.
203 Austin J. Doyle jr.

36 Mr. & Mrs. S. Bailey Martin
36 Miss Harriett H. Sheets
416 Mr. & Mrs. John McGovern & dr.

23

PART FOURTH.

THE HOTELS.

THE BLUE BOOK.

*CONTAINING LISTS OF THE PERMANENT BOARDERS
OF THE PROMINENT HOTELS*

THE HOTELS.

AUDITORIUM HOTEL.

Michigan Avenue nw. cor. Congress.

Mr. & Mrs. Milward Adams
Mrs. Mary Stuart Armstong
Webster Batcheller
Mr. & Mrs. Oscar F. Bane
E. R. Brainerd
Harry N. Butterfield
Mr. & Mrs. Henry C. Clement
Mr. & Mrs. J. W. Cofran
Allen Conkling
W. H. Cronkhite
Walter Cullerton
Albert Dallemand
J. L. Day
Mr. & Mrs. Nathaniel C. Dean
Thaddeus Dean
Mrs. R. E. Dickinson
Mr. & Mrs. W. H. Durant
Miss Carrie Durant
James P. Edof

Dr. A. R. Elliott
B. L. Ferguson
William Fleming
Miss Marcella Friedel
Mr. & Mrs. William R. Kerr
Miss Lulu Kerr
L. Laflin
Mr. & Mrs. B. F. Norris
F. A. Palmer
J. B. Shafer
W. S. Shafer
Mr. & Mrs. Richard H. Southgate
Thomas J. Storr
George W. Tewksbury
C. E. Tripp
Joseph F. Tucker
Mrs. C. W. Wallace
Dr. Wm. J. Younger

AUDITORIUM ANNEX.

Michigan Avenue sw. cor. Congress.

Walter C. Arnold
Mr. & Mrs. C. J. Barnes
Nelson L. Barnes
Sam. Block
Mr. & Mrs. W. H. Bowman
J. E. Bromley
George B. Christie
Clinton C. Clark
Mr. & Mrs. William C. Com-
  stock
Maurice Coster
Roscoe Crary
Mr. & Mrs. J. J. Driscoll
A. Featherstone
W. A. Halbert
Mr. & Mrs. D. Harry Hammer
  & dr.

Dr. Jabez D. Hammond
William B. Keep
Huntington W. Jackson
Mr. & Mrs. J. Frank Lawrence
Wm. Orville Lindley
Gol. & Mrs. Marshall I. Luding-
  ton
Mrs. Nelson Ludington
Mr. & Mrs. Thomas W. Magill
William Munro
J. A. Murphy
Dr. & Mrs. B. Newton
Miss Newton
Alex. Nicol
J. F. O'Shaughnessy
M. J. O'Shaughnessy
Dr. Josephine D. Pfeifer

349

Mr. & Mrs. H. S. Pickands
Frank H. Ray
Mr. & Mrs. P. E. Reilly
Mr. & Mrs. P. J. Ryan
Mrs. Martin Ryerson
G. A. Schwartz
W. F. Studebaker
Mr. & Mrs. Abner Taylor

Mr. & Mrs. Wm. S. Walker
William Watson jr.
Mr. & Mrs. C. W. Wheeler
Mrs. H. M. Wilmarth
M. B. Wilson
Mme. M. Yale
Mr. &. Mrs. George W. Young

CHICAGO BEACH HOTEL.

Fifty-First Street and the Lake.

Mrs. William Aldridge
Mr. & Mrs. W. M. Alister
Mr. & Mrs. C. W. Allen
Mr. & Mrs. Wm. H. Alley
Mr. & Mrs. J. G. Arnold
H. M. Auning
Mr. & Mrs. C. M. Baker & dr.
Frank Barbour
Mr. & Mrs. C. W. Barnes
Miss F. B. Barnhart
A. M. Barnhart
Col. & Mrs. Thos. F. Barr
Dr. William L. Baum
William A. Beckler
Mrs. A. Bishop   -
W. H. Bishop
Mr. & Mrs. W. T. Blaine
Ross Bookwalter
Mr. & Mrs. W. L. Breyfogle
Dr. & Mrs. W. C. Brinkerhoff
J. F. Brower
John B. Brown
Mrs. J. Austin Brown
Gordon Buchanan
Mr. & Mrs. M. D. Buchanan &
    drs.
Mr. & Mrs. Milton J. Budlong
E. R. Burdick
Mr. & Mrs. Clifford Cabell
Col. & Mrs. A. B. Carey & dr.
Mr. & Mrs. H. C. Clark   •
Harry A. Cole
Wm. D. Cooper
William Corlies
E. C. Crane
Harry C. Cranz
W. P. Crenshaw
J. W. Crocker
G. M. Cutter
Mr. & Mrs. H. A. D'Acheul
Albert E. Dacy
Mrs. L. T. Darling & drs.

Mr. & Mrs. Hamilton Dewar
Dr. Edward T. Dickerman
J. A. Dickson
Arthur H. Dodge
Hamilton B. Dox
Mr. & Mrs. P. R. Earling
Prof. Daniel G. Elliot
Mr. & Mrs. Otto L. Erdt
P. D. Fenn
C. A. Funk
Philip H. Gaspard
Frederic Gaylord
George G. Getz
Mr. & Mrs. Wells Goodhue
J. R. Goodman
Mr. & Mrs. Paul Gores
Edward E. Gray
C. W. Hammill
Mrs. L. K. Hammill
Mrs. R. C. Hammill
Mr. & Mrs. Joseph Harris
G. W. Hatch
Mr. & Mrs. John C. Hately&drs.
Mr. & Mrs. John F. Hazen & drs.
Walter Helmsley
Mr. & Mrs. Edwin Henning
Miss Bertha Hintz
Charles R. Holden
Mr. & Mrs. George H. Hovey
C. H. Hubbert
H. R. Hunt
E. J. Irwin
Dr. Ira D. Isham
W. J. Kennedy
Mrs. Charles Kern
Henry W. Kern
Mr. & Mrs. M. A. Knapp
Rev. & Mrs. M. G. Knight & dr.
Mr. & Mrs. A. E. Lane & dr.
Mrs. J. B. Lapham
Mrs. F. T. Lee & dr.
Mr. & Mrs. J. L. Loose

Mr. & Mrs. W. H. Loper.
Mr. & Mrs. Jesse P. Lyman
Mrs. E. M. Lynch
I. G. McColl
J. D. McDonald
Mrs. J. E. McElroy
William H. McKinlock
Mr. & Mrs. A. C. McNeill
Charles J. Miller
Maynard Miller
J. M. Morehead
Mr. & Mrs. C. H. Mulliken
M. C. Myers
Mr. & Mrs. C. M. Nichols
Mr. & Mrs. Jas. W. Nye & dr.
Mrs. H. E. Owsley
Mr. & Mrs. J. F. Palmer
J. H. Palmer
Mr. & Mrs. J. M. Patterson
Clyde D. Peck
Mr. & Mrs. O. D. Peck
Theodore D. Peck
James Pettit
Mr. & Mrs. O. D. Pillsbury
Chas. P. Pinckard
Nathan E. Platt
Mr. & Mrs. E. A. Potter
Geo. C. Power
Mrs. M. A. Pricture
Jerome Probst
Mr. & Mrs. John R. Pruyn
Mr. & Mrs. H. M. Ralston
Mr. & Mrs. A. N. Reece & dr.
J. K. Ridgley

Mr. & Mrs. C. S. Roberts
Alexander Robertson
D. W. Ross
Mr. & Mrs. Geo. B. Ross
G. E. Sanborn
Miss Emma P. Scott
Jefferson D. Shatford
Mr. & Mrs. G. B. Shaw
Mr. & Mrs. W. N. Shirley
Mr. & Mrs. A. B. Shubert
Mr. & Mrs. E. S. Skillen
Mr. & Mrs. C. E. Stafford
Warren S. Stilwell
Wm. A. Swaby
Dr. L. S. Tenney
Mr. & Mrs. George Thomas
Mrs. W. T. Tibbetts
Mr. & Mrs. W. D. Tilden
Mr. & Mrs. J. Jackson Todd
Mr. & Mrs. George H. Tousey
James Tullock
Mrs. J. R. Valentine
P. A. Valentine
Wm. E. Ward
Harry C. Waters
John E. Waters
Mr. & Mrs. George L. Webb
Miss S. C. Winstanley
T. F. Woodman
William J. Woods
Mr. & Mrs. T. R. Woodward & dr.
J. H. Wyeth jr.

CLIFTON HOUSE.

Monroe nw. cor. Wabash Avenue.

Arthur T. Begley
Dr. Robert D. Boyd
Ellis Brooks
Thomas Buckley
DeWitt W. Campbell
Mrs. C. C. Collins
James A. Doane
Mr. & Mrs. J. A. Gates
Mr. & Mrs. H. Gunderling
E. M. Hopkins
James Keenan
R. Bruce Kennedy
R. J. Killick
J. F. Kirkendall
George D. Knab
John T. Lake
Morris Livingston

Samuel Livingston
W. Morrison
W. D. Munhall
D. W. Nickerson
R. M. Patterson
W. H. Porter
George A. Riddle
G. A. Rollins
Mr. & Mrs. D. J. Smith
Silas C. Stevens
Charles J. Stocking
E. Spencer Sturges
R. M. VanWycke
C. G. Warren
Abraham Washer
Dr. Frank Whetzel
George W. Youst

GRANADA HOTEL.

70 to 76 Rush.

Mr. & Mrs. H. W. Baker
Mrs. F. M. Clark
Mr. & Mrs. R. H. Clark
Mr. & Mrs. A. G. Cox & drs.
A. E. Davidson
Capt. Wm. L. DeRemer
Mr. & Mrs. T. S. Flournoy
G. Goward
Mr. & Mrs. W. B. Herrick
Mr. & Mrs. C. M. Howell
Albert E. Jessurun
Mrs. A. T. Jones
Edward S. Keeley
Miss Adelaide Kettler
John R. Key

Mr. & Mrs. S. H. Larrabee
Mr. & Mrs. C. W. Morris
Mr. & Mrs. LaVerne W. Noyes
Mr. & Mrs. Robert B. Peck
        Receiving day Thursday
Mr. & Mrs. F. S. Pixley
W. W. Post
Mr. & Mrs. W. H. Proctor
Mr. & Mrs. Siegfried W. Rinds-
    kopf *Receive 2d & 4th Tues.*
Mr. & Mrs. W. E. Rollins
Harry B. Shantz
Frederick E. Smith
C. S. Spottswood
C. A. Wilcox

GRAND PACIFIC HOTEL.

Clark nw. cor. Jackson Boulevard.

Albert E. Glennie

Dr. & Mrs. C. P. Stringfield

GREAT NORTHERN HOTEL.

Dearborn ne. cor. Jackson.

Daniel R. Cameron
Alexander M. Davidson
Mr. & Mrs. W. S. Eden
Willard Gentleman

L. B. Jackson
H. D. Laughlin
Dr. Duncan R. MacMartin
Chas. K. Parmelee

HOTEL DEL-PRADO.

59th Street cor. Washington av.

Mr. & Mrs. Howard Ames
Mrs. F. C. Anderson
Dr. & Mrs. J. W. Baker
Mr. & Mrs. Albert G. Beaunisne
W. H. Bennett
Mrs. H. L. Bickford
Mr. & Mrs. J. L. Bigelow
Mr. & Mrs. A. H. Blum
Mr. & Mrs. C. A. Bowers
Mr. & Mrs. A. R. Bradley
Mr. & Mrs. S. R. Brocken-
    brough & dr.
E. M. Brown
Mrs. S. M. Brown
Rev. & Mrs. J. G. Brownwell
Mrs. Martha Burke

Col. B. M. Callender
Miss Mary Campbell
Mr. & Mrs. H. S. Canfield
Robert E. Charlton
Mr. & Mrs. H. W. Chevalier
Miss C. E. Chitteck
Mr. & Mrs. E. C. Churchill & dr.
Mr. & Mrs. R. L. Clark
W. H. Clarke
Mr. & Mrs. J. F. Conover
Mr. & Mrs. C. S. Corning
Mrs. Minnie Crandall
Mr. & Mrs. R. B. Daggett
Mr. & Mrs. James H. Delaney
Mr. & Mrs. H. Duval
Mr. & Mrs. E. Ferguson

James H. Ferguson
Col. A. T. Fleet
Mr. & Mrs. Samuel Franklin
Mr. & Mrs. J. H. Freedman
Mrs. J. H. Friedman
Mr. & Mrs. L. J. Friedman
Mr. & Mrs. J. P. Gallagher
Dr. & Mrs. Percival Gerson
A. C. Gilmour
Mr. & Mrs. A. R. Gray
Mr. & Mrs. Otis O. Hall
Mr. & Mrs. Horace Hans
Mr. & Mrs. Edward C. Hart
Mr. & Mrs. O. H. Hicks
Miss E. M. Hill
Mr. & Mrs. Louis Hornthal
Mr. & Mrs. J. Horwitz
Mr. & Mrs. D. T. Hunt
Miss H. Hutchins
Mr. & Mrs. W. S. Hyland
Dr. C. B. Jacobs
Mr. & Mrs. C. E. Jarvis
Mrs. E. D. Johnson
Mr. & Mrs. Jacob Kellar
Mrs. L. K. Kuh & dr.
Mr. & Mrs. C. W. Lee
Mr. & Mrs. D. Lilienfeld
Mr. & Mrs. E. M. Love
Mr. & Mrs. A. Lozier
Mr. & Mrs. A. S. Lyons
Mrs. J. P. Martin
Mr. & Mrs. Nathan Mayer
Mr. & Mrs. S. E. McDowell
Miss Jennie McIntosh
J. M. McIntosh

Miss Mary McIntosh
Mrs. A. B. Miller & drs.
C. M. Moore
Mr. & Mrs. J. H. Moore
Mr. & Mrs. S. F. B. Morse
Capt. J. S. Munson & dr.
Miss Ida Murphy
Miss Ida Pahlman
Mrs. E. A. Peirce
Mr. & Mrs. Merritt W. Pinckney
Mr. & Mrs. J. Allen Preisch
Miss W. P. Quackenbos
Mrs. E. Quegoor
Mr. & Mrs. Julian Roe
Mr. & Mrs. J. B. Rohrer
Mr. & Mrs. J. D. Rose
Mr. & Mrs. Benj. J. Rosenthal
Mr. & Mrs. Mark A. Ross
Mr. & Mrs. M. Salinger
Mark Schloss
Mr. & Mrs. H. H. Schwabacher
Mr. & Mrs. M. Schwabacher
Mr. & Mrs. B. F. Smith
Mr. & Mrs. E. Soper
Miss Edith Staples
Mr. & Mrs. J. A. Strobhart
W. T. Strong
A. R. Stumer
Louis M. Stumer
Mr. & Mrs. C. S. Tomlinson
Mr. & Mrs. J. S. Toppan & dr.
Mr. & Mrs. F. R. Warner
William A. Wegener
Mr. & Mrs. G. S. Woodford
Lieut. F. W. Wooster

HOTEL METROPOLE.

Michigan Avenue sw. cor. 23d.

Alfredo B. Adams
A. G. Allen
A. W. Allen
Mr. & Mrs. Frank Allport
Miss V. T. Artz
Mr. & Mrs. W. C. Bailey
J. A. Baker
Mrs. S. B. Barker
Thomas Beard
C. B. Beardsley
Mr. & Mrs. H. F. Billings
Leopold Black
P. D. Block
Mr. & Mrs. W. T. Black
H. K. Bolton

James Bolton
Loraine F. Bowyer
Mr. & Mrs. J. H. Brown
Mr. & Mrs. Cholett Cady
Miss G. A. Carpenter
J. R. Case
Mrs. J. D. Chapman
E. V. Church
Mr. & Mrs. A. E. Clark
M. T. Clark
Miss Fannie Daggett
Mrs. William Derby
Gail Dray
Mrs. Walter S. Dray
Walter H. Dupee

Mr. & Mrs. John Dupee
Mr. & Mrs. J. M. Durand
Dr. E. J. Farnum.
Mr. & Mrs. S. G. Field
W. G. Field
Capt. Chas. W. Forrester
Mr. & Mrs. Jos. Frank
Stephen F. Gale
Mr. & Mrs. B. P. Gates
Dr. & Mrs. J. E. Gilman
Mr. & Mrs. J. Guckenheimer
E. S. Heaton
Mr. & Mrs. C. E. Hill
Mr. & Mrs. E. H. Hipple
Mr. & Mrs. E. D. Hulbert
Mr. & Mrs. James Hunnell
F. N. Huschart
M. M. Joseph
Mr. & Mrs. E. D. Kenna
Mr. & Mrs. F. J. Kennett & dr.
J. Durand Kennett
Luther Kennett
G. E. Kline
Mr. & Mrs. M. W. Kozminski
Mr. & Mrs. A. K. Lee
G. Lehmer
Charles H. Lester
Mr. & Mrs. A. W. Longley
A. S. Louer
Edward A. Magee
J. E. Mann
E. A. Matthiessen & dr.
J. C. McKeon
Mr. & Mrs. James Hobart Moore
N. S. Munn
Mr. & Mrs. G. G. Newbury
Mr. & Mrs. A. E. Nussbaum
W. E. O'Neill
Bernard Oppenheimer
E. P. Palmer
C. R. Paul
Mr. & Mrs. Fred C. Pardridge
Mr. & Mrs. Wm. N. Pelouze
E. O. Perry
Charles Pickler
Mr. & Mrs. H. L. Pinney

Mr. & Mrs. C. H. Platt
Mr. & Mrs. L. Powell
Miss M. Powell
Mrs. M. B. Pulsifer
Mr. & Mrs. J. B. Reeme & dr.
Mr. & Mrs. Daniel G. Reid
Mr. & Mrs. W. B. ReQua
Mr. & Mrs. I. M. Rice
Roderick Richardson
Mr. & Mrs. R. J. Richardson
John R. Rigby
Walter L. Roloson
Mrs. F. J. Rucavado
W. D. Sargent
Mr. & Mrs. Hugo Schumacher
Mrs. C. M. Sebree
Mr. & Mrs. J. H. Shepard
Joseph Siegel
Franklin P. Smith
Miss J. F. Smith
Judge & Mrs. Sidney Smith
Sidney W. Smith
Theo. W. Smith
Mrs. William J. Smith
Mr. & Mrs. F. P. Snyder
Mr. & Mrs. James Stettauer
Rev. & Mrs. E. M. Stires
Mrs. J. B. Storey
Joseph T. Talbert
Mrs. Lydia Tewkesbury
William J. Tewkesbury
Gail Thompson
Percival Thompson
Wm. Hale Thompson
Mrs. Wm. Hale Thompson
E. J. Travis.
Mr. & Mrs. Louis Ullman
Mr. & Mrs. Geo. Frederic West-
    over *Receiving day Tuesday*
Mr. & Mrs. Chas. B. White
Mrs. Abraham Williams
J. M. Wineman
M. R. Wineman
Mr. & Mrs. E. W. Woodcock
Andrew S. Work
Mr. & Mrs. C. C. Yoe

HOTEL WINDERMERE.

56th nw. cor. Cornell av.

Mrs. I. S. Agnew
Mr. & Mrs. B. N. Austin
Mr. & Mrs. A. K. Baldwin
A. N. Benn
A. Blauvelt
Miss E. S. Blood
Mr. & Mrs. C. L. Bonney
Mr. & Mrs. John S. Bowen
C. LeRoy Brown
Mr. & Mrs. C. F. Bullen
W. J. Dee
Mr. & Mrs. Joseph H. Defrees
Miss Louise E. Dew
Mr. & Mrs. J. D. Dezendorf
Mr. & Mrs. W. F. Donovan
Mr. & Mrs. C. F. Esbaugh
Mr. & Mrs. C. E. Fargo
Mr. & Mrs. John B. Fay
Mr. & Mrs. Richard Foster
Miss Carrie C. Gibbins
Miss Florence Guilbert
O. H. Guilbert
Mr. & Mrs. James I. Gulick
Mr. & Mrs. L. D. Hammond &
. dr.
Luther S. Hammond
Mr. & Mrs. R. C. Hayden
S. J. Holland
James W. Hyde
Mr. & Mrs. W. J. Kelly
Col. & Mrs. J. G. C. Lee
Mr. & Mrs. W. J. L'Engle
Mr. & Mrs. I. G. Lewis
W. H. Lewis & dr.
Mr. & Mrs. J. M. Low
Dr. H. C. Macy
Robert Manners
Mr. & Mrs. L. D. Mayhew
G. J. McBride

Rev. Percival McIntire
Mrs. P. E. McNaughton
Mr. & Mrs. Herbert C. Metcalf
Thomas Metcalf
Prof. Albert A. Michelson
Mr. & Mrs. A. J. Minard
Prof. & Mrs. R. G. Moulton
Mr. & Mrs. J. M. Olcott
Robert M. Orr
Mr. & Mrs. W. L. Parrotte
R. L. Parsons
John F. Phillips
Romaine Pierson
W. F. Rawson
C. H. Robbins
Mr. & Mrs. John C. Roth
Miss M. A. Sawyer
Mr. & Mrs. W. W. Schultz
Walter Scott
Miss Ethel Marie Featherstone-
Haugh Scull
Receiving day Thursday
Mr. & Mrs. Harry Scull
Receiving day Thursday
W. A. Shaw
Mr. & Mrs. S. S. Shields
Mr. & Mrs. H. E. Skinner
Mr. & Mrs. F. W. Snow
Mr. & Mrs. T. W. Sprague
Mr. & Mrs. C. F. Stickney
Louis H. Sullivan
Mr. & Mrs. S. A. Treat
Receiving day Friday
J. R. Vansant
Col. & Mrs. P. D. Vroom
Mr. & Mrs. R. W. Watson
Mr. & Mrs. J. N. Witherill
H. H. Wood
Mr. & Mrs. Ira S. Younglove

HOTEL WOODRUFF.

Wabash av. se. cor. 21st.

Mr. & Mrs. H. V. Bemis
P. Bernard
Mrs. F. Bloom
C. W. Daniels
Prof. Denvivier
C. A. Hough
Mr. & Mrs. D. McKee
Mr. & Mrs. E. V. Price
W. E. Price

Mr. & Mrs. Ulrich Rosenheim
Mr. & Mrs. J. W. Scott
Mrs. S. Stern
Mr. & Mrs. F. E. Stubbs
F. E. Toynton
W. Y. Winthrope
Mr. & Mrs. David Wise
J. W. Woodworth

HYDE PARK HOTEL.
Fifty-first sw. cor. Lake Avenue.

Mrs. E. M. Andrews
Mr. & Mrs. C. W. Badger
Mr. & Mrs. A. M. Bates
C. H. Birdsall
G. W. Brayton
Mrs. J. Breed
John E. Burke
Mr. & Mrs. L. R. Carswell & dr.
Mr. & Mrs. James Corby
J. M. Corneau
Mr. & Mrs. Geo. K. Cornell
Miss Helen Cornell
Paul Cornell
Paul Cornell jr.
Mr. & Mrs. John E. Cornell
Mrs. E. E. Crampton
C. W. Crawford & dr.
Dr. & Mrs. W. H. Dade
Mr. & Mrs. W. E. Davis
Mrs. L. S. Diller & dr.
W. R. Donnelly
Mr. & Mrs. E. P. Dunning
Oscar P. Erskine
Mr. & Mrs. W. H. Gale
E. E. Greathead
Mr. & Mrs. Frank Hall
Mr. & Mrs. Thos. F. Harvey
Mr. & Mrs. Charles Himrod
I. W. Holman
Mr. & Mrs. M. A. Isaacs
Miss Anna Johnson
Mrs. J. S. B. Knox
Mr. & Mrs. F. B. Leonard
Mr. & Mrs. F. S. Leonard

Mr. & Mrs. A. Liebenstein
E. M. Lund
Mr. & Mrs. J. A. McDonald
A. H. McLaughlin
Mr. & Mrs. Wm. A. Merriman
Miss C. J. Miller
Mr. & Mrs. E. W. Mitchell & drs.
M. J. Morehouse
Mr. & Mrs. H. A. Newkirk
Mr. & Mrs. A. H. Pike
Mr. & Mrs. L. E. Pollock
Dr. & Mrs. R. H. Porter
Mr. & Mrs. Chas. N. Post
Receiving day Monday
Charles E. Post
Junius S. Post
Mr. & Mrs. N. B. Rappleye & dr.
Ridgley Rea
Mr. & Mrs. L. E. Reed & dr.
Charles Riddell
Mr. & Mrs. B. F. Rhodehamel
Mr. & Mrs. B. C. Rowell
W. N. Sharp
Mr. & Mrs. J. P. Sidwell
Mr. & Mrs. S. T. Smith
Miss L. E. Smythe
J. F. Stanton
Miss R. L. Stanton
Benton Sturges
Edwin Swobe
Mr. & Mrs. Milford J. Thompson
Mr. & Mrs. Howard T. Willson
W. E. C. Windsor

THE KENWOOD.
Kenwood av. sw. cor. 47th

Mr. & Mrs. C. M. Armstrong
Mrs. Florence Blackman
Mr. & Mrs. E. A. Bryan
Mr. & Mrs. Fred L. Champlin
Mrs. Wm. R. Champlin
Dr. George Cook
Dr. J. C. Cook
Mr. & Mrs. W. N. Craine
Mr. & Mrs. Levi R. Doty
Mr. & Mrs. John A. Drake
Mr. & Mrs. C. F. Eiker
Mr. & Mrs. J. S. Frasher
Mr. & Mrs. C. C. Germain
Mr. & Mrs. H. C. Gray
Mr. & Mrs. Barret Hall
Mr. & Mrs. Fred H. Hancock

Mr. & Mrs. W. C. Hately
Mr. & Mrs. J. H. Hiland
Oscar L. Hunter
Mr. & Mrs. W. W. Hunter
Mr. & Mrs. W. T. Joyce
Mr. & Mrs. T. K. Long
Mr. & Mrs. W. H. Mallory
Mr. & Mrs. Geo. E. Marcy
Mr. & Mrs. Fred K. Pulsifer
Col. & Mrs. Robert Rae
Mr. & Mrs. J. G. Shedd
Dr. Orrin L. Smith
Mr. & Mrs. H. B. Speed
Mr. & Mrs. A. W. Walburn
Mr. & Mrs. C. O. Webster
Mr. & Mrs. H. R. Wilson

LAKOTA HOTEL.

Michigan av. se. cor. 30th

Mr. & Mrs. Joseph Adams
Miles Almy
J A Armour
Mr. & Mrs. J. M. Arnold
R. H. Austin
Ohio C. Barber
Mr. & Mrs. W. L. Barnum
Dr. & Mrs. A. G. Bevan
Clinton Briggs & drs.
Geo. S. Bullock
Frank W. Buskirk
Mr. & Mrs. F. J. Carlisle
H. H. Clark
Mr. & Mrs. J. D. Clark
Dr. George J. Dennis
M. F. Driscoll
Mrs. H. F. Eames
Mr. & Mrs. Geo. C. Eldredge
Mrs. G. V. Evans
Walter E. Faithorn
Mr. & Mrs. J. M. Faithorn & dr.
  Receiving day Thursday
Louis Falkenau
Mr. & Mrs. A. A. Fisher & dr.
Budd Fisher
G. M. Fisher
Mr. & Mrs. H. G. Foreman
Emanuel J. Frank
Mrs. Joseph Frank
Mr. & Mrs. H. J. Furber
Henry J. Furber jr.
D. B. Gerrett
Mr. & Mrs. W. M. Graves
Mr. & Mrs. M. E. Greenebaum
Col. Roy B. Harper
W. H. Harper & drs.
Paul Healy
Mrs. C. Hill & dr.
Mr. & Mrs. Edward Hoffman
  Receiving day Friday
Mrs. E. Holton & dr.
Mr. & Mrs. E. S. Hyman

W. P. Irwin
Mr. & Mrs. Geo. F. Jennings
Mr. & Mrs. I. Kein
Mrs. Mark Kimball
Mr. & Mrs. S. J. Kline
Miss E. Long
J. B. Long
Mr. & Mrs. M. A. Loring
H. W. Magill
Mrs. Geo. L. Matthews
Mrs. L. D. Mayer & dr.
Mrs. Mary McClure
J. D. McCune
E. F. McLaughlin
Miss M. McNarney
Mrs. H. H. Nash
Mr. & Mrs. Herman J. Reiling
Dr. Arthur R. Reynolds
R. R. Reynolds
Mr. & Mrs. Geo. L. Rhodes
Mr. & Mrs. J. Foster Rhodes
Mr. & Mrs. J. K. Robinson &drs.
J. K. Robinson jr.
Mr. & Mrs. W. H. Rockwood
Mrs. A. L. Ruth
Mr. & Mrs. C. B. Scoville
Mr. & Mrs. Max Sello
James Shirrill
George S. Steere
Mrs. H. N. Stephens
L. F. Swift
Mrs. Trippe
Mr. & Mrs. J. W. Ulm
B. Walker
W. H. Walker
Mr. & Mrs. H. H. Walker
Mrs. W. J. Walker
W. R. Walker
Morris E. Ward
Mrs. C. G. Wheeler
Mr. & Mrs. B. C. White
Mr. & Mrs. F. S. White

LELAND HOTEL.

Michigan Avenue sw. cor. Jackson Street.

G. W. Boynton
Miss Louise Burns
C. W. Clark
John S. Cowan
Mr. & Mrs. C. W. Dabb
Mr. & Mrs. W. R. Dabb

Robert W. Francis
Mr. & Mrs. W. J. Hill
Mrs. Florence Huntley
George H. Lally
Maurice T. Moloney
Jacob Morris

Mr. & Mrs. G. V. Penwell
Mr. & Mrs. J. M. Phillips
John Ready
Mr. & Mrs. J. L. Rynearson

Mr. & Mrs. F. A. Smith
H. P. Snyder
Mrs. Sarah Steenburg
R. A. Young

LEXINGTON HOTEL.

Michigan Avenue ne. cor. Twenty-second.

Dr. & Mrs. J. S. Appleman
Mr. & Mrs. E. A. Bacheldor
Mr. & Mrs. Hugh R. Belnap.
Miss M. Buckingham
Frank E. Burley
Miss J. B. Chappel
W. H. Chappel
Mr. & Mrs. E. A. Clark
Mrs. Nathan Corwith & dr.
Mr. & Mrs. R. S. Cox
George H. Curtis
Uri B. Curtis
Mr. & Mrs. A. R. Delmont
Max Dembufsky
Mr. & Mrs. O. P. Dickinson
Miss M. L. Dion
George J. Dowling
Joseph Fels
H. W. Fenton
Mrs. J. L. Fenton
Mr. & Mrs. W. B. Fisk jr.
Henry C. Flonacher
Mrs. C. H. Gibbs
Frederick C. Gibbs
W. B. Gibbs
Mr. & Mrs. Robert C. Givens
Mr. & Mrs. Chas. U. Gordon
Clarence J. Gray
Mr. & Mrs. H. N. Greene
D. Russell Greene
Mr. & Mrs. C. H. Gurney
Mrs. G. M. Haller
W. T. Hansen
Mr. & Mrs. L. Hartman
Milton L. Hartman
Wilbur Higgins
R. A. Hitchcock
Dr. Florence W. Hunt
Leopold Kahn
Fred Kauffman
Col. M. Kavanagh
Mrs. John A. J. Kendig
Charles Klatz
Mr. & Mrs. D. S. Komiss
Miss A. B. Lawrence
Mrs. A. S. Lawrence
Denison J. Leahy

Mrs. Urquhart Lee
Mr. & Mrs. W. B. Leeds
Mr. & Mrs. E. C. Lott
Mr. & Mrs. Louis Manheimer & dr.
Mrs. W. G. Mann
John McCarthy
Dr. F. M. McKenzie
D. McNetton
James C. McShane
Mrs. M. A. Mesick & dr.
Mr. & Mrs. J. H. Michener
F. A. Miller
Bernard Neu
Mr. & Mrs. G. P. Noyes
A. Duncan Pacaud
John McAuley Palmer
Mr. & Mrs. A. A. Parker & drs.
Mr. & Mrs. S. W. Parker
John W. Parmelee
Mrs. M. A. Patrick & dr.
Mr. & Mrs. Walter L. Peck
Miss N. A. Peniston
Mr. & Mrs. H. E. Pitkin
J. S. Qualey
P. W. Raber
C. Ward Rapp
Mr. & Mrs. F. Willis Rice
G. A. Rose
H. H. Rose
Mrs. Landon C. Rose
L. C. Rose
A. C. Rous
Gen. H. E. Sargent
J. R. W. Sargent
Mr. & Mrs. H. B. Schuler
Charles H. Scott
Louis Seligman
Israel Shrimski
Mr. & Mrs. E. E. Silver
Mr. & Mrs. Chas. G. Singer
H. J. Slater
Burton Smith
Edward L. Smith
Mr. & Mrs. G. W. Smith
Mr. & Mrs. O. C. Smith
Mrs. W. A. Sneed

Alfred M. Snydacker
Mr. & Mrs. G. N. Spencer
Mr. & Mrs. N. L. Spencer
Mrs. M. A. Steele & drs.
Sol H. Stix
Albert L. Strauss
A. H. Strauss
Mrs. C. L. Strauss
Louis L. Strauss
Mrs. George Straut

Samuel B. Thomas
Mrs. D. Thornton
Dr. & Mrs. R. T. VanPelt
Mr. & Mrs. E. C. Walker
Frank Wenderoth
William M. Whitehead
Mrs. F. S. Wilmarth
Sigmund A. Winkler
Dr. & Mrs. Casey A. Wood
Maj. & Mrs. J. L. Woods

NEW HOTEL HOLLAND.

Lake Avenue nw. cor. Fifty-third.

Mr. & Mrs. B. D. Adsit
H. E. Bailey
Mr. & Mrs. A. E. Ballou
J. F. Bour
James Bradley
Mr. & Mrs. H. K. Brooks
Mr. & Mrs. W. A. Burch
Dr. & Mrs. F. A. Carter
Mr. & Mrs. H. W. Carter
T. F. Conway
Miss Ida Cross
J. W. Cruth
Mr. & Mrs. J. L. Dorsett
T. Draper
Miss F. Forbes
Mr. & Mrs. H. G. Fordyce
Mr. & Mrs. T. H. Gibson
Edward S. Glickauf
Miss Mildred Glickauf
Miss A. M. Guillett
Dr. & Mrs. C. W. Hanford
Mr. & Mrs. W. E. Hanson

Mr. & Mrs. J. H. James
Thomas Kennedy
Mr. & Mrs. W. J. Leadbeater
J. L. Lenfesty
Mr. & Mrs. D. S. Levy
Mr. & Mrs. E. Y. Loomis
Mr. & Mrs. Forbes Munson
Burton Powell
Mr. & Mrs. J. Powell
A. D. Reid
Mr. & Mrs. W. J. Richardson
Mr. & Mrs. I. S. Richter
J. E. Shaw
Mr. & Mrs. Geo. F. Shutt
S. C. Simms
Mr. & Mrs. L. K. Torbet
Miss Jane Waters
Mrs. W. E. Webster
Mr. & Mrs. C. H. Wessels
Mr. & Mrs. H. O. Wilkinson
Mr. & Mrs. F. C. Willis

NORTH SHORE HOTEL.

Lake View av. sw. cor. Deming pl.

Miss E. M. Bailey
Miss Fannie Barber
Mr. & Mrs. G. M. Barber
A. H. Bishop
Miss Grace Brantingham
Mr. & Mrs. G. W. Calder
J. L. Clark
Mr. & Mrs. H. S. Decker
Miss Bertha Dougherty
Miss H. Dupuy
Mr. & Mrs. W. O. Field
Mr. & Mrs. H. A. Frank
Miss C. M. Grashoff
Dr. & Mrs. J. G. Harris

Mr. & Mrs. W. P. Healy
Miss Flora Helm
H. M. Hosick
H. N. Hosick
Miss L. Kinkade
John K. Kirkland
Miss Bertha Knobe
Mr. & Mrs. F. H. Marks
Mr. & Mrs. G. C. Morgan jr.
Mrs. J. M. Mott & dr.
Mr. & Mrs. J. B. Pinkham
J. L. Pinkstaff
Mr. & Mrs. B. D. Southard
James Taylor

Mrs. C. Theurer
Mr. & Mrs. C. L. Tomlinson
Mrs. L. M. Tuttle

Mr. & Mrs. J. W. Wilcox
Miss Ethel Wilkinson
Mr. & Mrs. F. F. Wood

THE ONTARIO.

118 North State.

Miss Margaret Boyde
Mr. & Mrs. E. R. Bradley
Benjamin H. Campbell
Mrs. J. L. Clark & drs.
Mr. & Mrs. J. E. Colby
George B. Havercamp
F. J. Hefling
G. C. Hempstead
F. Horton

J. C. Jackson
E. C. Morris
Mrs. W. J. Scott
Mr. & Mrs. B. F. Smith
David Spangler
Mrs. J. E. Spangler
Mr. & Mrs. Henry M. Sperry
H. P. Wall
Simeon B. Williams & drs.

PALMER HOUSE.

State se. cor. Monroe.

Mr. & Mrs. W. B. Andrews
Frank M. Burroughs
Martin Dawson
Dr. & Mrs. C. S. Eldredge
Dr. A. E. Evans
Mr. & Mrs. J. M. Hodge
Mr. & Mrs. Gurdon S. Hubbard
  jr.
Chauncey Kelsey

E. G. Lésynsky
Dr. Wm. Martin
Mr. & Mrs. J. I. Metcalf
Miss Florence Olmstead
Mr. & Mrs. Frank Parmelee
R. C. Rounseville
Mr. & Mrs. H. L. Seixas
Mr. & Mrs. Wm. H. Turner &
  dr.

REVERE HOUSE.

N. Clark se. cor. Michigan st.

E. F. Bunn
T. L. Case
James Fitzpatrick
W. L. French
E. J. Friel
Oscar A. Friend
W. F. Gay
P. H. Goodhart
E. T. Green
J. D. Hall
Martin E. Hanley
William H. Harrell
George Johnson
Charles A. Kerr
A. N. King
Richard Kruger
F. S. Langrall
H. W. Loveday

Eric R. Mackay
William D. Miller
John H. Musgrave
Mr. & Mrs. E. A. Potter
Capt. A. B. Price
Charles V. Price
H. W. Prouty
Geo. T. Rounsaville
Mr. & Mrs. H. T. Russell
Albert Snoots
C. E. Thurston
Charles Waller
J. D. Warren
Frederick Weise
Henry E. Wheeler
Mr. & Mrs. Trumbull White
Mr. & Mrs. C. M. Wilson
James Wingfield

SHERMAN HOUSE.

Clark nw. cor. Randolph.

C. C. Barrett
W. H. Blackler
Duncan B. Campbell
H. S. Cantrovitz
S. Cantrovitz
Mr. & Mrs. M. Conrad
E. W. Denahy
Frank Hart
James C. King
William E. Parsons

Mr.& Mrs. John Irving Pearce jr
Mr. & Mrs. J. Irving Pearce
Myron Pearce
William C. Pearce
Mr. & Mrs. James E. Purnell
Judge S. P. Shope
Clarence W. Shope
Joseph B. Wertheim
Frank M. Witmark

TREMONT HOUSE.

Dearborn se. cor. Lake.

Charles P. Bartleson
C. H. Bayard
Charles D. Cook
Alfred C. Danser
N. D. Laughlin

E. B. Mantz
Mrs. M. S. McGue
Charles F. Rapp
Frank Tillotson

VICTORIA HOTEL.

Michigan Avenue nw. cor. Vanburen

James C. Curtis
E. A. Drummond.
Samuel Eckstein jr.
Axel Ekstrom
Charles F. Milligan

Mr. & Mrs. F. S. Mordaunt
C. H. Neely
J. L. Nelson
Edwin P. Smith
Mr. & Mrs. Frank Upman

THE VIRGINIA HOTEL.

Rush and Ohio.

Guests' Receiving day, Wednesday. *Guest Evening*, Thursday.

Mr. & Mrs. Chas. C. Adsit
C. W. Andrews
Dr. & Mrs. E. Benj. Andrews
F. R. Babcock
Frank T. Baird
Mr. & Mrs. Charles L. Bartlett
Mr. & Mrs. L. C. Bonney
Ransom R. Cable
Mrs. P. Cavanagh & dr.
Mr. & Mrs. Wm. J. Chalmers
Mr. & Mrs. S. S. Chisholm
Mrs. George C. Clark
Mr. & Mrs. Samuel Colgate
W. G. Collins
John Crerar
A. D. Currier
C. J. Dewes

Mr. &·Mrs. F. C. Donald
Mr. & Mrs. W. W. Douglas
F. P. Dunn
Mr. & Mrs. R. P. H. Durkee
Mrs. C. H. Dyer
Mr.&Mrs. James Herron Eckles
Mr. & Mrs. J. M. Flower
George B. French
Mr. & Mrs. Frederick P. Good-
hart
Mr. & Mrs. A. H. Goodwin
Frank C. Greene
John P. Grier
Mr. & Mrs. Thos. A. Griffin
Mr. & Mrs. John A. Hamlin&dr.
Mr. & Mrs. Chas. H. Hapgood
Mr. & Mrs. Chas. M. Hewitt

24

Mr. & Mrs. C. W. Hillard
J. C. King
Mr. & Mrs. R. D. Kirby
Miss Amy Leslie
Mr. & Mrs. Sidney C. Love
Mrs. E. E. Lowe
H. W. Marsh
Mr. & Mrs. Wm. P. Martin
Mr. & Mrs. Leander J. McCormick
Mr. & Mrs. George S. McReynolds
Mr. & Mrs. James F. Peavey
George R. Peck & drs.
Dr. & Mrs. Norval H. Pierce
Mr. & Mrs. S. G. Puterbaugh

Mr. & Mrs. Harry Raymond
Mr. & Mrs. C. E. Rector
Mr. & Mrs. C. E. Rumsey
Baron Schlippenbach
Mrs. J. W. Scott
Mr. & Mrs. W. H. Truesdale & dr.
Mr. & Mrs. C. H. Wacker
Mr. & Mrs. James P. Whedon
Henry J. Whigham
Mr. & Mrs. Sydney Williams
Mr. & Mrs. George Z. Work
Mrs. John Worthy
Sidney Worthy
Willis Worthy
W. F. Zeller

THE WELLINGTON.

Wabash Avenue ne. cor. Jackson.

Mr. & Mrs. M. J. Buxbaum
Charles C. Carhart
Mr. & Mrs. C. E. Cass
Mrs. C. B. Crocker
Mr. & Mrs. Albert S. Gage
Miss Mary McMahon

William A. Prime
W. H. Schimpferman
L. L. Smith
Mr. & Mrs. W. R. Stewart
Mrs. D. S. Williams

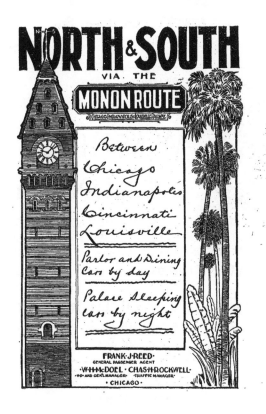

NORTH & SOUTH

VIA THE

MONON ROUTE

CHICAGO, INDIANAPOLIS & LOUISVILLE RAILWAY

Between

Chicago

Indianapolis

Cincinnati

Louisville

Parlor and Dining
Cars by day

Palace Sleeping
Cars by night

FRANK·J·REED·
GENERAL PASSENGER AGENT
·W·H·McDOEL· CHAS·H·ROCKWELL·
·V·P· AND GENL·MANAGER· ·TRAFFIC MANAGER·
· CHICAGO ·

PART FIFTH.

CLUBS AND SOCIETIES.

THE BLUE BOOK.

*OFFICERS, DIRECTORS, AND ACTIVE MEMBERS OF
THE PROMINENT CLUBS AND SOCIETIES.
OF CHICAGO AND SUBURBS*

CLUBS.

AMATEUR MUSICAL CLUB.

OFFICERS.

Mrs. William S. Warren, - - - President.
Mrs. George V. Harvey, - - - Vice-President.
Miss Katharine D. Kriegh, - - - Secretary.
Mrs. C. F. Ely, - - - - - - - Treasurer.

EXECUTIVE COMMITTEE.

Mrs. Robert G. Clarke   Mrs. P. B. Bradley   Mrs. Proctor Smith
Mrs. N. K. Bigelow   Miss Frances D. Gould

MEMBERS.

Addison Mrs. J.
Adler Miss Lois S.
Allen Miss Helen M.
Allinson Mrs. T. W.
Allport Miss May
Alshuler Miss Laura
Andersen Miss Dagmar
Anderson Mrs. Geo. W.
Austrian Miss Estelle
Ayer Mrs. E. E
Bacon Miss
Bagg Mrs. F. S.
Balfour Mrs. J.
Bangs Mrs. Fred. A.
Barbour Mrs. Edward
Barnum Miss Edna
Barrett Miss M. F.
Bartlett Mrs. J. C.
Barton Miss Katherine
Bates Miss Harriet
Baxter Miss E. C.
Beardslee Miss
Beaumont Mrs. C.
Beidler Mrs. A. W.
Benedict Mrs. Geo. M.
Bigelow Mrs. E. A.
Bigelow Mrs. N. K.
Bingham Mrs. A. E.
Birch Mrs. Hugh T.
Borman Miss Alma
Bradley Mrs. Philip B.
Bragg Miss A. P.
Branckman Miss M.
Brentano Mrs. Theo.
Brown Mrs. L. F.
Brush Mrs. E. H.
Bryant Mrs. Anna G.
Buck Miss Grace
Burnet Miss Anna L.

Burr Mrs. L. E.
Butterfield Mrs. W. E.
Cable Mrs. H. D.
Calkins Mrs. Ida B.
Cameron Miss Margaret
Campbell Mrs. Courtney
Campbell Mrs. D. W.
Canfield Miss N. C.
Carpenter Mrs. Geo. B.
Carpenter Miss
Chappell Mrs. H.
Clark Mrs. J. M.
Clarke Mrs. Melville
Clarke Miss C. N.
Clarke Mrs. Robert G.
Cleave Mrs. Oliver
Coburn Mrs. L. L.
Cole Mrs. Geo. S.
Cones Mrs. N.
Coolbaugh Miss W.
Coonley Mrs. John Stuart
Cornell Mrs. John C.
Cripe Miss Mabel
Crow Miss F. G.
Custer Mrs. J. R.
Day Miss Annie T.
Denison Miss Madge
DeWolf Mrs. Wallace L.
Dunn Miss Jessie
Durno Miss Jeanette
Easter Miss Marguerite
Ebeling Mrs. Regina
  Zeisler
Eddy Miss F. M.
Eisendrath Mrs. J. N.
Ely Mrs. C. F.
Englemann Dr. Rosa
Evans Miss Edith
Everett Mrs. Chas. F.

Farr Mrs. M. A.
Farwell Mrs J. A.
Foster Miss Harriet
Frank Mrs. Henry L.
Frasher Mrs. Edw. S.
Frasher Mrs. J. Stuart
French Miss Natalie
Funk Mrs. K. M.
Gane Miss Gertrude
Germain Mrs. Chas. C.
Gilpin Mrs. T. E.
Goldsmith Mrs. E. W.
Goodrich Miss Helen
Gorton Mrs. E. F.
Gorton Mrs. Frank
Gould Miss F. D.
Groves Mrs. G. M.
Haass Mrs. H. E.
Haight Miss Irma
Haines Miss T. M.
Hale Miss
Hall Miss Adelaide
Hanson Mrs. Burton
Harbers Mrs. E.
Harding Miss A.
Harvey Mrs G. V.
Hastreiter Mrs. G.
Hickox Mrs. C. V.
Hilton Miss Gertrude
Hiner Mrs. J. W.
Hinckley Mrs. J. O.
Hinman Miss
Hoag Mrs. Junius
Hoagland Miss J.
Howells Miss Una
Hoyt Mrs. A. W.
Hubbard Miss Daisy
Hubbard Mrs. W. H.
Hudson Mrs. Charles

Hunkins Miss Virginia
Hunt Mrs. James A.
Hypes Mrs. W. F.
Jenks Mrs. W. S.
Jennings Miss Maude
Johnson Miss Harriet
Johnson Mrs. O. K.
Jones Mrs. Nettie R.
Kelley Miss A. S.
King Mrs. C. H.
King Mrs. Francis
King Miss Fanny
Knickerbocker Mrs. H.
Knickerbocker Miss
Kriegh MissKatharine D.
Krum Mrs. C. L.
Lancaster Mrs. R. M.
Lapham Mrs. Edwin
Large Miss J.
Larrabee Miss C.
Lawson Mrs. W. C.
Leidigh Miss C.
Leonard Mrs. Mark T.
Little Mrs. W. H.
Lynde Mrs. S. A.
MacDonald Mrs. M. C.
Mace Miss Gertrude W.
Magnus Mrs. Folrence R.
Martin Miss Marion
Mason Mrs. A. O.
Mathews Miss Clara L.
Matz Mrs. Rudolph
McIlvaine Mrs. W. D.
McLaughlin Mrs. R.
Menefee Miss Jamie
Merrick Miss Gertrude
Metcalf Miss Mabel
Metz Mrs. F. W.
Miles Miss Edith M.
Miner Miss H. H.
Mitchell Miss Winifred
Moore Mrs. James H.
Moore Mrs. James S.
Morrill Miss Nellie
Morse Miss May
Moses Mrs J. W.
Moss Miss F. W.
Murphy Miss Veronica

Newton Mrs. H. S.
Nixon Miss Bertha
Officer Miss
Olcott Miss Grace
Palmer Miss Helen
Palmer Mrs. M. S.
Parsons Mrs. Emily
Payson Mrs. Clifford
Peck Miss Maude
Phillips Miss Bertha
Phillips Miss Daisy
Pincoffs Mrs. Maurice
Powers Miss Mary L.
Prickett Mrs. G. Willis
Purdy Mrs. Chas. W.
Ramus Miss Sylba
Reitz Mrs. Alexander
Remmer Mrs. Oscar B.
Rexford Miss L. B.
Richards Miss K. P.
Richards Miss May L.
Richardson Mrs. R. E.
Rockener Miss Olga
Roelle Miss Emma
Roemheld Miss
Rommeiss Miss Pauline
Root Miss Jessie F.
Russell Mrs. Wm. Seward
Rust Miss Mary
Scheib Miss Eleanor
Scott Mrs. Daisy F.
Sears Miss Helen A.
Selfridge Mrs. H. G.
Shaw Mrs. Francis S.
Sheffield Mrs. Henry
Sherman Miss Bessie W.
Sherman Miss Blanch
Smith Mrs. Alton L.
Smith Mrs. Frank M.
Smith Miss Gertrude
Smith Miss Helen P.
Smith Mrs. Proctor
Sparling Miss Juna B.
Spencer Mrs. A. P.
Starr Mrs. Chandler
Starr Miss Flora
Stearns Mrs. R. I.
Steel Mrs. Sanger

Steever Mrs. J. G.
St. John Miss Esther D.
Stires Mrs. Ernest
Stone Miss Helena
Storrs Miss M.
Strauss Mrs. B. A.
Strong Miss Blanche E.
Strong Miss Marion
Sturkow Miss T.
Summy Mrs. C. F.
Swabacher Mrs. I.
Swarts Mrs. H. L.
Taylor Miss K. W.
Temple Miss Grace
Thacker Mrs. J. Frank
Thomas Mrs. Theodore
Thomson Miss Marion
Trego Mrs. C. H.
Trimble Mrs. C. G.
Troost Miss Louise
Tuthill Miss Zoe G.
Tyng Mrs. Dudley
Ullmann Mrs. Frederic
Ullmann Miss
Underwood Mrs. A. W.
Warren Mrs. Aubrey
Warren Mrs. Wm. S.
Way Miss Lillian M.
Webber Miss Mildred
Wheeler Miss Helen D.
Wheeler Mrs. J. Harry
Whiting Miss Olive F.
Wicker Mrs. Charles
Wild Mrs. Harrison M.
Wile Mrs. D. J.
Wilkes Mrs. C. M.
Williams Miss Ada
Williams Mrs. Clifford
Williams Mrs. Harry
Wood Miss S. Ella
Wood Mrs. W. F.
Woolley Mrs. Clarence M.
Wright Mrs. S. H.
Yoe Miss C. W.
Zarbell Miss Meda
Zeisler Mrs. Joseph
Zimmerman Mrs. O.

ARCHÉ CLUB.

ROSALIE HALL, FIFTY-SEVENTH STREET AND ROSALIE COURT.

OFFICERS AND DIRECTORS.

MRS. WALTER OLDS, ... President.
MRS. CHARLES F. MILLSPAUGH, . First Vice-President.
MRS. HARRISON D. BOGARDUS, Second Vice-President.
MRS. JOHN C. HESSLER, . . Recording Secretary.
MRS. EDWARD L. MURFEY, Corresponding Secretary.
MRS. CHARLES R. DICKERSON, . . . Treasurer.

DIRECTORS.

Mrs. Walter Olds
Mrs. Chas. F. Millspaugh
Mrs. Harrison D. Bogardus
Mrs. John C. Hessler

Mrs. Edward L. Murfey
Mrs. Chas. R. Dickerson
Mrs. Walter C. Nelson
Mrs. C. F. Adams

Mrs. Frank Harlow
Mrs. N. A. Partridge
Mrs. E. E. Abrams
Mrs. Mary K. Schumacher

MEMBERS.

Abel Mrs. Jonathan
Abrams Mrs. E. E.
Abrams Miss Louise C.
Adams Mrs. Chas. F.
Adams Miss Helen F.
Ahern Mrs. Elizabeth M.
Ahrens Mrs. J. P.
Allee Mrs. F.
Allen Mrs. C. W.
Allen Mrs. Edmund
Allen Miss Haidee
Anderson Mrs. N.
Anderson Mrs. Walter C.
Ayleshire Mrs. Jas. B.
Ayling Miss Alice
Ballard Mrs. Thos. C.
Ballou Mrs. Geo. H.
Banning Mrs. Thos. A.
Banzet Mrs. Geo. T.
Barker Mrs. M. P.
Barnhart Mrs. Kenneth
Bash Mrs. Frank S.
Bassett Mrs. Roger M.
Bates Mrs. Anne L.
Beckett Mrs. B. H.
Beeman Miss Eugenie
Behel Mrs. Julia
Bennett Mrs. F. I.
Benson Mrs. Andrew J.
Best Mrs. Wm.
Blackwood Mrs. Alex. L.
Blair Mrs. Sidney O.
Bogardus Mrs. H. A.
Bogardus Mrs. H. D.
Bogle Mrs. Daniel
Bonner Mrs. Charles
Boon Mrs. Harry M.
Bowes Mrs. F. K.
Boyd Mrs. E. K.
Boyle Mrs. Mary F.
Boynton Mrs. C. W.
Brown Mrs. Dewitt
Brown Mrs. J. D.
Browne Mrs. Edward
Buchanan Mrs. J. N.
Buckley Dr. Sara
Bunnell Mrs. John A.
Burdick Mrs. Julian C.
Burke Mrs. Daniel F.
Burr Mrs. Louis Edwin
Burton Mrs. Charles H.
Burton Mrs. Wm. H.
Button Mrs. W. J.
Caldwell Mrs. Charles E.
Carter Mrs. Lincoln J.
Caryl Mrs. A. H.
Chamberlin Mrs. T. C.
Chapman Mrs. James L.
Clampet Mrs. A. B.
Clapp Mrs. Henry
Clark Mrs. Edgar A.
Clark Mrs. George W.
Clark Mrs. Henry C.
Clark Mrs. J. Truman

Clark Mrs. Margaret V., M.D.
Clement Mrs. N. L.
Conkey Mrs. W. B.
Conley Mrs. Harry
Cook Mrs. Henry L.
Core Mrs. Albert S.
Cornelius Mrs. E. H.
Cozzens Mrs. Samuel
Crosby Mrs. Arthur A.
Crosier Mrs. W. C.
Curtis Mrs. Cornelius
Dana Mrs. A. P.
Davies Mrs. B. M.
Day Mrs. C. A.
Dean Mrs. Amos C.
Dean Mrs. Thomas L.
DeVore Mrs. Abraham A.
Dezendorf Mrs. James D.
Dickerson Mrs. Charles R.
Dickson Mrs. Isaac F.
Dorsey Mrs. George A.
Doty Miss Lois
Douglass Mrs. Darwin B.
Dow Mrs. Frederick H.
Drake Mrs. Lauren J.
Dunn Mrs. J. Austin
Earling Mrs. P. R.
Eastman Mrs. Frank L.
Elliott Mrs. W. S., jr.
Elwell Mrs. Albert
Elwell Mrs. Edward H.
Epps Mrs. Frank P.
Evans Mrs. Charles H.
Farrington Mrs. Oliver C.
Fay Mrs. J. B.
Fegenbush Mrs. Chas. M.
Fegenbush Miss J. M.
Ferry Mrs. Watson J.
Field Mrs. Charles E.
Fiske Mrs. Horace
Forbes Mrs. Alexander
Ford Mrs. J. Sawtelle
Fordham Mrs. Arthur J.
Fordyce Mrs. Homer G.
Foresman Mrs. H. A.
Foresman Mrs. Robert
Foresman Mrs. W. C.
Forrest Mrs. A. E.
Forster Mrs. Chas. F.
Foster Mrs. Samuel B.
Gallagher Mrs. J. P.
Gardner Mrs. H. Chase
Garrigue Mrs. R. H.
Gilchrist Miss M. V.
Gillett Mrs. Henry
Gilman Mrs. J. E.
Gilson Mrs. T. W.
Goodman Mrs. Thomas C.
Goodnow Mrs. Frank A.
Goodwin Mrs. John S.
Googins Mrs. H. F.
Grier Miss Margaret G.

Hall Miss Anna E.
Hall Mrs. Herman J.
Hall Mrs. Lemuel R.
Hammett Mrs. John C.
Hanauer Mrs. J. C.
Hardie Miss Nellie M.
Hardy Mrs. Henry W.
Harlow Mrs. Frank
Harsha Mrs. Wm. M.
Hartwell Mrs. Edwin D.
Hasbrouck Mrs. Chas. A
Haskins Mrs. Geo. W.
Hawley Mrs. Henry S.
Heaford Mrs. Henry H.
Heath Mrs. A. M.
Heatherington Mrs. Chas.
Hendrickson Mrs. J. S.
Herrick Mrs. R. Z.
Hessler Mrs. John C.
Hill Mrs. Edward E.
Hilton Mrs. Wm. K.
Hobbs Mrs. Joshua N.
Hoops Mrs. Thomas
Houser Mrs. E. W.
Howe Mrs. Frederick A.
Hoxie Mrs. J n R.
Hoyt Miss Hattie C.
Hoyt Mrs. Lucius
Huling Mrs. Walter C.
Hunt Mrs. D. Hopkins
Hunt Mrs. Geo. W.
Innis Miss Katharine C.
Irvin Miss Marie
Iverson Mrs. Edward
Johnson Mrs. Edward L.
Johnson Mrs. Joseph J.
Johnstone Mrs. Quintin
Jones Mrs. A. R.
Jones Mrs. Charles S.
Kenfield Mrs. Fred. S.
Kent Mrs. B. R.
Kimball Mrs. Charles F.
Kimball Mrs. J.
King Mrs. Robert
Kissinger Mrs. Victor T.
Laing Mrs. John R.
Landis Mrs. Kenesaw M.
Lapham Mrs. Arden B.
La Victoire Mrs. S. R.
La Zelle Miss Stella
Lee Miss Anna W.
Leeds Mrs. W. B.
Leiter Mrs. T. B.
Leonard Mrs. Frank P.
Lepper Mrs. George A
LeRoy Mrs. Joseph
Lloyd Mrs. Henry R.
Long Mrs. John B.
Lord Miss Nellie M.
Lorenz Mrs. Frederick A.
Lynne Mrs. Anna V.
Lyon Mrs. H. H.
Lyons Miss Hattie
Magee Miss E. J.

Mallory Mrs. D. C.
Manning Mrs. Wm. J.
Marchant Mrs. Stuart F.
Marie Mme. Eugène
Marshall Mrs. John S.
Martin Mrs. Carrie E.
Martin Mrs. George H.
Mather Mrs. Stephen T.
Matthews Mrs. Henry M.
Mayou Mrs. Joseph S.
McCall Mrs. Thomas
McDougall Mrs. Esther
McFarland Mrs. J. H.
McLauchlin Mrs. A. L.
McMillan Mrs. Alex. F.
McNair Mrs. Harry M.
McVeagh Mrs. C. F.
Millspaugh Mrs. Chas. F.
Mitchell Mrs. Charles F.
Moore Mrs. W. J.
Morgan Mrs. John N.
Morrill Mrs. Wm. M.
Morris Mrs. Seymour
Morrison Mrs. Charles E.
Moseley Mrs. Bryant
Mulvane Mrs. Phineas I.
Murfey Mrs. Edward L.
Neal Mrs. Charles A.
Nelson Mrs. Walter C.
Nichols Mrs. Henry W.
Norton Mrs. Henry M.
O'Donnell Mrs. Patrick P.
Olds Mrs. Walter
Olmsted Miss Anna H.
Orr Mrs. Charles B.
Oughton Mrs. Chas. M.
Parker Mrs. William R.
Parsons Miss H. L.
Partridge Mrs. Newton A.
Pate Mrs. D. S.
Patterson Mrs. Wm. R.
Pearce Mrs. Chas. F.
Penington Mrs. Chas. R.
Perry Mrs. Charles N.
Phillips Mrs. H. R.
Phillips Mrs. Richard W.
Pinney Mrs. Henry L.
Platt Miss Mabel
Porter Mrs. Frank W.
Potter Miss Mazie
Potter Mrs. W.
Pratt Mrs. Ralph E.
Pulsifer Mrs. C. A.
Race Mrs. Albert S.

Radford Mrs. Isaac H.
Ramsey Mrs. Laura
Randle Mrs. Chas. H.
Rankin Mrs. Wm. T.
Rawson Mrs. Nannie W.
Reppert Miss Florence
Rice Mrs. C. H.
Rice Mrs. E. S.
Rice Mrs. George E.
Richards Mrs. I. D.
Richardson Mrs. S. H.
Ricker Mrs. William L.
Robinson Mrs. A. M.
Rogers Mrs. Charles D.
Rogers Mrs. James S.
Root Mrs. Frederick K.
Ross Miss Adele
Ruffner Mrs. Augustus
Rush Mrs. Frederick
Russell Mrs. W. H.
Sanders Mrs. J. F.
Saxton Mrs. H. B.
Schaberg Mrs. Charles W.
Schell Mrs. R. H.
Schumacher Mrs. F. A.
Scull Miss Ethyl
Scull Mrs. Harry
Sears Mrs. Charles
Senour Mrs. William F.
Shearer Mrs. W. W.
Shedd Mrs. Ezra T.
Shelton Mrs. Olive
Shepherd Mrs. John
Sidwell Mrs. George H.
Sieg Mrs. Charles H
Silkworth Mrs. Chas.
Skene Mrs. Edward P.
Sleeper Mrs. J.
Slimmer Mrs. Jacob
Smalley Mrs. Chas. M.
Smith Mrs. Alpheus W.
Smith Mrs. Fred A.
Smith Mrs. Homer A.
Smith Mrs. James M.
Smith Mrs. James R.
Smith Mrs. Robert E.
Snyder Mrs. Franklin P.
Soper Mrs. Horace W.
Steck Mrs. E. M.
Stevens Mrs. Chas. A.
Stewart Mrs. Alexander
Stone Mrs. Frank B.
Stone Mrs. L. E.

Storm Mrs. C. H.
Sullivan Mrs. David
Sweeney Mrs. George W.
Swift Mrs. E. F.
Swinerton Miss Carrie P.
Syer Mrs. Edmund W.
Thacker Mrs. Albert H.
Thomas Mrs. John A.
Thompson Mrs. Mary W.
Todd Mrs. Frank M.
Tolman Mrs. Elwood H.
Tompkins Mrs. S. L.
Troutman Mrs. J. H.
Trude Miss Algenia
Trude Mrs. A. S.
Updike Mrs. M.
Volk Miss Louise E.
Walker Miss Emma L.
Wallwork Mrs. Edward L.
Walter Mrs. A. G.
Watkins Mrs. Maurice
Weary Mrs. Edwin D.
Webb Mrs. William R.
Webster Mrs. C. O.
Welker Mrs. L. Bruce
Wells Mrs. Willis J.
West Mrs. Wm. H.
Wetherell Mrs. Homer S.
Wheeler Miss J. M.
White Mrs. J. S.
Whyland Mrs. C. A.
Wiggin Mrs. Twing B.
Wilber Mrs. Marshall D.
Wilken Miss Isabella
Wilken Mrs. Theodore
Willard Mrs. J. W.
Williams Mrs. Ben
Williams Mrs. John P.
Wilson Mrs. Charles L.
Wilson Mrs. Emily L.
Wilson Mrs. Horatio R.
Wilson Mrs. Samuel A.
Wilson Mrs. Wm. M.
Wingate Mrs. Charles H.
Winter Miss Ethel C.
Wise Mrs. Clift
Woodbury Mrs. DeW. B.
Woodward Mrs. G. M.
Wright Mrs. Frank G.
Wright Mrs. George E.
Wright Miss Lora
Young Mrs. R. E.
Zimmerman Mrs. Wm.

THE ARGONAUTS.

The Argo, Randolph Street Viaduct.

OFFICERS.

FRANKLIN H. WATRISS, - - - - - - Skipper.
J. HENRY NORTON, - - - - - - First Mate.
FRANK H. RAY, - - - - - Jack o' the Dust.
JOSEPH LEITER, - - - - - - - - Mate.

MEMBERS.

Beale William G.
Burnham Dan'l H.
Deering Charles
Fish Stuyvesant
Forsyth Robert

Insull Samuel
Leiter Joseph
Macdonald Chas.B.
Norton J. Henry

Ray Frank H.
Raymond Sam'l B.
Ryerson EdwardL.
Tracy William W.

WatrissFranklinH.
Wheeler George H.
Wheeler H, A.

ASHLAND CLUB.

575 WASHINGTON BOULEVARD.

OFFICERS.

WALTER S. HOLDEN, - - - - -	President.
CHARLES T. CHANDLER, JR., -	First Vice-President.
A. T. OSGOOD, - - - -	Second Vice-President.
GEORGE F. WISSHACK, - - - -	Treasurer.
FREDERICK T. HOYT, - - - - -	Secretary.

DIRECTORS.

Charles T. Tyrrell
Charles H. Kilpatrick

R. F. W. Beardsley
Louis C. De Proft

Don M. Gallie
Geo. W. Hutchinson

MEMBERS.

Adams Wm. M.
Adkins F. A.
Agnew R. G.
Alden Wm. T.
Alexander W. R.
Almquist J. F.
Ambler Eugene
Ambler H. C.
Ambler H. E.
Archibald Thos. E.
Ault Geo. S.
Austin C. W.
Austin M. B.
Bailey R. R.
Baker D. W. jr.
Baker Frank J.
Baker Dr. S. S.
Balis Walker J.
Bangs Fred A.
Bangs Wm. B.
Barber H. A. jr.
Barker Alfred
Barker Geo. F.
Baughman Chas.O.
Baxter Wm. G.
Beardsley R. F. W.
Bell Frank H.
Bell Herbert E.
Bennett Allen N.
Benson Charles E.
Benson Robert L.
Biddle Noble L.
Birkland N. S.
Bobb P. M.
Bonnell Charles E.
Borcherdt Fred H.
Bosley E. F.
Boughton Danl. K.
Bowes Chas. L.
Bowyer L. F.
Boyd W. J.

Boyles Chas. D.
Bridges J. S. Dr.
Briggs R. C.
Brinsley H. G.
Brooks Fred G.
Brower Dr. D. R.
Brown Dr. E. M.
Brown Thomas R.
Brown Walter
Browne Wm. A.
Bunge Albert J.
Bushnell C. E.
Buss William
Butzow Robert C.
Campbell A. D.
Campbell A. M.
Campbell Fergus
Campbell John A.
Carpenter E. A.
Carpenter W.W. S.
Chamberlin Jos. H.
Chandler C. T. jr.
Chandler Ed. W.
Chase A. W.
Chase Orrin P.
Chrystal W. L.
Clarke E. L.
Cleveland W. R.
Coates J. H.
Cobb Elliot
Cobb Thomas A.
Collins J. D.
Cone Charles B.
Corcoran B. A.
Cox George
Criswell James F.
Crosby D. K.
Cunningham Hugh
Cunningham Percy
Curran A. W.
Curtis Dr. J. H.

Danz Albert J.
Danz Chas. A.
Dare John R.
Davis Will H.
Day V. R.
Dennis Fred J.
DeProft Louis C.
Disinger W. P.
Dodge Orrin D.
Dodson Dr. J. M.
Donahue F. R.
Donlan John T.
Dougherty T. E.
Downs Herbert C.
Drake C. St. Clair
Driggs Arthur W.
Duffy Frederick
Duffy Geo.
Duffy Harry C.
Dunn Thomas, jr.
Dunwell Wm. C.
DurborowConradB
Durborow C. E.
Durham Howard
Dyer R. M.
Eaton Jo. W. jr.
Eddy Charles M.
Edwards F. W.
Eilers P. C.
Ellicott Ed. B.
Elliott Albert J.
Evans Louis H.
Fick Bruno W.
Flook William C.
Fogarty F. H.
Forbes Fred A.
Ford Silas M.
Foreman Grant
Frost F. S.
Gale Fred
Gallie Don M.

Galpin Homer K.
Gardner G. A.
Ghislin Henry
Gillispie S. T.
Golden J. H.
Goll B. H. jr.
Goodman Alf. L.
Goodman Fred M.
Gray Charles W.
Gunderson Geo. O.
Gunderson S. M.
Gutchus H. B.
Gutchus John H.
Hafner W. F.
Hammon V. O.
Hanna Dr. E. A.
Harlow J. G.
Hart Louis E.
Hatch Henry D.
HaverkampfJ.L.jr.
Hawkins Ralph
Hayner Frank E.
Heath D. W.
Heckard Dr. M. O.
Heinemann H. C.
Henriques A. G.
Heron Lester G.
Heron Presley M.
Hickey A. C.
Hicks George I.
Hill Charles B.
Hill Walter O.
Hitch E. L.
Hoerber W. F.
Holden Joseph F.
Holden W. S.
Holenshade J. C.
Holmes George I.
Hooper Wyly E.
Hosking Ernest B.
Hoyt Fred. T.

Huff Thomas D.	McFarland F. W.	Robbins S. L.	Stubbs Edwin J.
Humphrey A. O.	McGee Wm. A.	Robertson A. Y.	Stubbs James A.
Humphreys W. A.	McNally W. J.	Rogan R. K.	Swartz Alva R.
Hunt Edward B.	McRae W. M.	Rogers Edward S.	Sweitzer R. M.
Hutchinson Geo. W.	McVicker Charles D	Rogerson Edw. J.	Tarrant Robert
Ickes J. Roy	Meade Thomas	Rollins Chas. E. jr.	Taylor C. T.
Ingersoll Walter E.	Meckling W. C.	Root C. J.	Taylor H. C.
Innes Alexander J.	Meinel Frank A.	Rose Alfred T.	Thatcher R. K.
Jack Harry T.	Mendenhall W. J.	Roth J. D.	Thomas Edward C.
Jacobs C. R.	Merrill F. S.	Rounds Charles H.	Thomas Frank W.
Johnston Benj. F.	Merrill James S.	Rounds Fred C.	Thompson Thomas
Johnston John A.	Midgely Stanley W.	Russ Bertrand S.	Thornburgh H. L.
Johnston William S.	Millard Frank R.	Rutt A. B.	Tracy E. A.
Jones Ford	Miller A. E.	St. Cyr E. D.	Traver F. C.
Jones Frank L.	Moody Frank A.	Safford Allen B.	Trout George W.
Jones Fred H.	Moore George W.	Sager W. D.	True Albert W.
Jones Oscar E.	Moore R. Wilson	Salisbury D. B.	True Charles J.
Jones Thomas A.	Morley J. H.	Sands Mark	Tucker William R.
Jones W. A.	Muldoon John A.	Sattler D. S.	Tyrrell A. H.
Judkins Putnam R.	Mullen James D.	Sawyer Carlos P.	Tyrrell Charles T.
Kastler John W.	Munroe Walter H.	Schaaf Fred A.	Updike J. C.
Kellett Fred'k H.	Murphy Jos. L.	Schmid Richard G.	Vanderwicken E.P.
Kilgallin M. H.	Murphy L. W.	Schroder H. F.	Vanzwoll H. B.
Kilmore John W.	Musgrave A. F.	Schub C. H.	Vette E. P.
Kilpatrick Chas. H.	Nelson Frank G.	Schultz Alex. J.	Vette John F.
Kimbark E. H.	Neu Peter W.	Schultz Jas. M.	Vokoun J. W.
Kimberly E. E.	Newcomb Wm. H.	Scott Frank G.	Waddle James
King Charles H.	Newman B. L.	Scully Morris H.	Walker Geo. L.
Klink A. Foster	Nichols Dr. A. J.	Shackelton W. C.	Walker Wm. J.
Koch Edward P.	Nickerson J. F.	Shaw Dr. D. Lee	Walkup W. A.
Kolar Frank J.	Noble Dr. W. L.	Shaw Warwick A.	Waters Beverly L.
Kormack Harry	Norton Joel H.	Sheldon H. D.	Watson James S.
Krupka Charles	Nye Wm. J.	Sherman Roger	Weaver Charles A.
Lamkey Arthur E.	O'Neill J. P.	Shipman S. V.	Webb Harry S.
Lampert Chas. N.	Oefinger J. L.	Shuman Geo. L.	Wenter Frank, jr.
Landon Ellsworth	Oliver David, jr.	Skillman F. B.	West E. A.
Lange Leonard A.	Oliver Royston	Slack W. H.	Wheelock E. U.
Leekley Harlow A.	Osgood A. T.	Sloan George B.	Whipple John H.
LeGros Emil A.	Outhet John C.	Smedes Albert	White Ernest E.
Le Messurier John	Overlock F. F.	Smedes T. L.	White Fred G.
Lewis E. J.	Passow Henry E.	Smith E. Nesbitt	White Dr. Wm. S.
Lewis H. S.	Patera Frank J.	Smith Fred E.	Whiting Geo. B.
Lloyd Arthur H.	Pigall Jos. S. Dr.	Smith Howard H.	Wight J. R.
Lobstein John G. jr.	Pitt W. A.	Smith J. E.	Wilcox Rob't B.
Loomis Philip A.	Platter E. C.	Smith J. G.	Wilkinson C. D.
Luke E. B.	Powell Geo. H.	Smith Richard E.	Williams W. E.
Lyon Charles R.	Quirk John J.	Smith Robert J.	Williamson Geo. M.
MacLeod M.	Rapp Lee S.	Smyth John M.	Wilson A. B.
Magill Charles S.	Rathbone Edw. B.	Soderstrom F. O.	Wilson Frank D.
Marquis A. N.	Rathbun A. W.	Sperbeck E. M.	Wilson R. T.
Martin Robt. L.	Rawleigh J. H.	Stafford Chas. W.	Wisshack Geo. F.
Marshall Dr. F. D.	Redington F. B.	Stannard Harry W.	Witbeck Richard T.
Marshall W. R.	Reed L. J.	Stege George R.	Worth W. P.
Mason E. T.	Reid George B.	Steveley L. A.	Wygant Bernard
Mason Dr. Frank G.	Richards C. W.	Stewart Edward L.	Young Abner T.
Mason George H.	Richards Guy A.	Stoll Robert H.	Young Leon W.
Mayberry J. J.	Ridgway Grant	Story F. F.	Young Peter F.
Mayhew Dr. John M.	Rising Fred H.	Street Charles R.	Zollar Walter G.
McDowell C. H.	Rising P. A.	Streich Fred O.	

BANKERS' CLUB.

OFFICERS.

JOHN McLAREN,	- - - - - - -	President.
W. F. DUMMER,	- - - - - -	Vice-President.
W. D. C. STREET,	- - -	Secretary and Treasurer.

EXECUTIVE COMMITTEE.

John McLaren. • W. F. Dummer John C. Neely •
W. D. C. Street Seymour Coman

MEMBERS.

Becker A. G.	Forgan James B.	Lindgren John R.	Ryther Gates A.
Billings H. F.	Gary John W.	Lobdell E. L.	Seipp Wm. C.
Black John C.	Gibbs James S.	Lombard I. G.	Shaw G. B.
Black Elmer E.	Gilbert James H.	Lord George S.	Slaughter A. O.
Blair C. J.	Goddard L. A.	Lynch John A.	Smith Byron L.
Blount Fred M.	Hall E. R.	MacVeagh Frank-	Smith Orson
Blum Aug.	Hamill Ernest A.	lin	Stensland Paul O.
Boulton George D.	Hankey F. L.	Mayer N. A.	Stone Melville E.
Bowen Ira P.	Harris N. W.	McKeon John C.	Street R. J.
Brintnall Wm. H.	Haskell Fred T.	McLaren John	Street W. D. C.
Brown Frank E.	Haugan H. A.	Mitchell John J.	Stuart Robert
Bryant Edw. F.	Henrotin Chas.	Morton Joy	Taft O. B.
Buehler John W.	Herrick R. Z.	Moulton D. A.	Talbert Joseph T.
Cameron John H.	Hinckley C. W.	Neely John C.	Tilden Edward
Castle Charles S.	Hoge Holmes	O'Grady J. W. deL.	Tilden Wm. A.
Coman Seymour	Hoover Geo. P.	Orchard J. G.	VanVlissingen A.
Craft John C.	Hulbert E. D.	Orr R. M.	Wacker C. H.
Crosby F. W.	Hutchinson C. L.	Palmer Percy W.	Walsh John R.
Dewar A. L.	Jackson T. M.	Pearsons Henry A.	Walton Lyman A.
Dickinson Edw.	Johnson Edwin T.	Perry Isaac N.	Walworth Chas. M.
Doud Levi B.	Judson F. P.	Phelps Erskine M.	Ware H. A.
Dummer W. F.	Keith E. G.	Pike Eugene S.	Watson R. W.
Eckels J. H.	Kelley David	Rawson Fred H.	Watson William J.
Embree J. R.	Kent H. R.	Rawson S. W.	Wilbur James B.
Farson John	King John A.	Reed Charles C.	Wilder F. N.
Farwell Granger	Lacey Edward S.	Reynolds Geo. M.	Wilson G. M.
Fenton Wm. T.	Lake Richard C.	Rickards W. T.	Witbeck J. H.
Foreman Edwin G.	Lathrop E. B.	Robertson Alex.	Woodland George
Foreman Oscar G.	Lawrence E. F.	Rothschild A. M.	
Forgan David R.			

NON-RESIDENT MEMBERS.

Coffin W. K., Eau Claire, Wis.	Reed L. E., St. Paul, Minn.
Doe Wilson H., Elgin, Ill.	Robertson Wm. T., Rockford, Ill.
Drake Luther, Omaha, Neb.	Talcott C. H., Joliet, Ill.
Lindsey C. T., South Bend, Ind.	Tracy W. W., Springfield, Ill.
Malott V. T., Indianapolis, Ind.	Waldron E. D., Elgin, Ill.
Northrop B. B., Racine, Wis.	Wendell Emory, Detroit, Mich.
Ostrom James A. Hammond, Ind.	Woodruff W. F. Rockford, Ill.

HONORARY MEMBERS.

Gage Hon. L. J., Washington, D. C. Sturges James D., Chicago

BRYN MAWR CLUB.

7149 JEFFERY AVENUE.

OFFICERS.

MARTIN H. BENNETT, - - - - - President.
TIMOTHY J. SCOFIELD - - - - Vice-President.
FRED K. RICKER, - - = Secretary and Treasurer.

DIRECTORS.

Luther N. Flagg Dr. Thomas H. Rockwell Martin H. Bennett
Henry H. Horr F. K. Ricker T. J. Scofield

MEMBERS.

Bennett C. M.	Blymyer Benj. F.	Clark A. C.	Delbridge J. B.
Bennett Martin H.	Bour George C.	Clingman Geo. F.	Flagg Luther N.
Bennett M. H.	Bulkley A. W.	Clingman Wm.	Frothingham J. Rev

Griswold H. S.   Hurlbut F.   Pusey Chas M. Dr.   Siddall Jos. J. jr.
Hagenbuck E. L.   Jones John H.   Pusey Evan   Siddall Michael G.
Harvey George S.   Kent H. R.   Remmer Oscar   Smith Percy H.
Harvey John H.   Lundie John   Ricker F. K.   Stone J. R.
Heidenreich E. Lee   Lutz T. C.   Rockwell Thos. H.   Stone Oren B.
Horr Henry H.   Otis George A.   Sayler H. L.   Swan Dr. C. F.
Howell C. H.   Peckham Chas. L.   Scofield Chas.   Webster Geo. T.
Hume S. W.   Price Henry W.   Scofield T. J.

THE BUILDERS' CLUB.
OF CHICAGO.

OFFICERS.

D. V. PURINGTON,	President.
EDW. KIRK, JR.,	Vice-President.
ALEX. MCLACHLAN,	2d Vice-President.
CHARLES W. GINDELE,	Treasurer.
EDWD. E. SCRIBNER,	Secretary.

BOARD OF MANAGERS.

S. S. Kimbell   W. D. Gates   M. Dencer
A. Lanquist   Wm. Grace   Geo. H. Fox
L. L. Leach   J. R. Hansell   H. E. Horton
M. B. Madden   Wm. Mavor   John Rawle
J. C. McFarland   Frank S. Wright   Chas. B. Sears

MEMBERS.

Alsip Wm. H.   Gardner Geo. C.   Lanquist A.   Prosser H. B.
Appel Henry   Gartz A. F.   Lay A. Tracy   Purington D. V.
Baggot E.   Gates Wm. D.   Leach Levi L.   Rawle Juo.
Bagley F. P.   Gindele Chas. W.   Leach Thomas A.   Reynolds W. J.
Beidler A. W.   Goldie Wm.   Ledgerwood A.J.C.   Richards I. D.
Bodwell Geo. F.   Grace Wm.   Madden M. B.   Robinson Jno. C.
Boice Hugh M.   Griffith Jno.   Manson Wm.   Rodatz Jacob
Brainerd E. R.   Haldeman R. S.   Mavor Wm.   Scoullar Chas. C,
Brownell Ralph E.   Halls Samuel   McCarthy E. J.   Sears C. B.
Butterfield W. W.   Hammett Jno. A.   McCarthy J. G.   Sheeler Harvey
Cabell Clifford   Hansell Jos. R.   McConnell Edwd.   Shefler C. B.
Campbell Murdock   Harper Robt. C.   D.   Slavton J. W.
Clark Geo. T.   Harris Henry S.   McFarland J. C.   Sollitt Oliver
Clark Walter T.   Hay James   McLachlan Alex.   Sproul E. W.
Clark W. Irving   Hayes D. H.   McLachlan Jno.   Tapper Geo.
Corboy M. J.   Heldmaier Ernst   Meacham F. D.   Thomas E. A.
Crilly Dan'l F.   Herzog Nathan   Messersmith Geo.   Vanderkloot A.
Crilly W. M.   Hogan James A.   Miller James A.   Van Woert Geo. E.
Crow Louis W.   Holmes O. W.   Montgomery Fr'nk   Verity Geo. W.
Davis Frank L.   Horton Horace E.   M.   Vierling Robert
Dencer Mathias   Hyde F. D.   Morava W.   Voss Frederick
Downey Joseph   Illsley W. A.   Mortimer W. H.   Wade James J,
Dungan Thomas A.   Johnson Ernest V.   Moses Chas. A.   Wagner Fritz
Earnshaw Charles   Johnson Frank J.   Nacey P.   Weckler Adam J.
Earnshaw Emanuel   Jones J. L.   Nelson F. P.   Wells Addison E.
Evans Chas. R.   Kent Wm. D.   Nelson W. P.   Whitney T. D.
Flavin M. D.   Kimbell Spencer S.   O'Connell Jno. C.   Wilce E. Harvey
Fox Geo. H.   Kirk Edward, jr.   Pierce E. F.   Wright Frank S.
Fuller Geo. A.   Knisely Harry C.   Powell M. W.

HONORARY.

Prussing Geo. C.   Sayward Wm. H.   Stevens Jno. S.   Wright S. M.

CALUMET CLUB.

MICHIGAN AVENUE, CORNER TWENTIETH STREET.

OFFICERS.

E. M. PHELPS, - - - - - - - President.
C. F. KIMBALL, - - - - First Vice-President.
CHAS. D. SEEBERGER, - - - Second Vice-President.
E. WALTER HERRICK, - - - - - - Secretary.
J. W. GARY, - - - - - - - Treasurer.

DIRECTORS.

G. M. Alexander   B. B. Davis   P. A. Otis
Otto Young   Wm. P. Palmer   Chas. A. Ridgely
S. R. Wells   John H. Witbeck   L. Heyworth

MEMBERS.

Adam A. B.	Chandler E. B.	Gardiner Frank H.	Judah Noble B.
Adsit Jas. M. jr.	Chapin Simeon B.	Gary J. W.	Keck Geo. S.
Alexander G. M.	Chappel C. H.	Gates C. G.	Keep Albert
Allen Benj.	Christie Geo. B.	Gates John W.	Keith Walter W.
Allerton Rob't H.	Chumasero K. P.	Gaylord W. S.	Kelley A. D.
Allerton Sam'l W.	Clark A. E.	Getty H. H.	Kelley C. B.
Andrews Jos. H.	Clark John M.	Gibbs F. C.	Kelley Wm. E.
Armour J. O.	Cobb Silas B.	Gibbs W. B.	Kennedy M. B.
Armour P. D.	Coburn Lewis L.	Giles Wm. A.	Kent S. A.
Armour P. D. jr.	Coffeen William	Gillette E. W.	Kettle R. A.
Austin F. C.	Collier Clinton	Goodman J. B.	Kimball Chas. F.
Avery Frank M.	Cooper John S.	Goodman Robt. F.	Kimball W. W.
Avery T. M.	Corwith C. R.	Goodrich A. W.	Knickerbocker J. J.
Badger A. S.	Cowles Alfred	Gorton Frank S.	Laflin A. K.
Baker A. L.	Crandall Arthur	Graves W. M.	Laflin A. S.
Baker Wm. T.	Crane Chas. R.	Gray Edward E.	Laflin Geo. H.
Baker W. V.	Cromwell Chas.	Gray Franklin D.	Laflin Jno. P.
Baldwin Geo. F.	Crouse John N.	Greene F. C. Dr.	Landis K. M.
Ballard D. P.	Cummings D. M.	Gresham Otto	Lane Ebenezer
Barber O. C.	Cummings M. C.	Grey William L.	Leeds W. B.
Barker J. H.	Currier Chas. H.	Gurney C. H.	Leiter Joseph
Barnes Chas. J.	Custer J. R.	Hackney H. C.	Leiter Levi Z.
Barrett Chas. C.	Cutter John M.	Hamline John H.	Linebarger P. W.
Barrett O. W.	Davis Brode B.	Henderson E. F.	Lombard J. L.
Bartlett A. C.	Davis Wilson H.	Herrick E. Walter	Longley A. W.
Batcheldor E. A.	Dewar Hamilton	Heyworth J. O.	Loomis J. M.
Baxter T. M.	Dexter A. F.	Heyworth L.	Lord Edgar A.
Billings C. K. G.	Dickason L. T.	Hibbard Wm. G.	Lowden Frank O.
Billings C. L.	Dillman L. M.	Higinbotham H.M.	Ludlam R.
Billings F. Dr.	Dixon Arthur	Hill J. T.	Lyon Thomas R.
Blackstone T. B.	Doane J. W.	Hill Lysander	Macfarland H. J.
Boal Chas. T.	Dodge G. E. P.	Hills Chas. F.	Mackey Frank J.
Booth A. A.	Drew Chas. W.	Hoffman Geo. W.	Magie Wm. A.
Booth E. A.	Eddy Aug. M.	Hughitt Marvin jr.	Markley John A.
Borden J. U.	Ely J. O. Dr.	Hulbert E. D.	Matz Rudolph
Bowyer L. F.	Fairbank N. K.	Hurlbut H. E.	Mayo John B.
Bradbury Geo. L.	Fargo Chas.	Hutchinson C. L.	McDoel W. H.
Brand Edwin L.	Farnum A. H.	Insull Samuel	McKechney Jno. jr.
Breese J. B.	Fenton H. W.	Isham E. S.	McKeon John C.
Brewster E. L.	Fenton W. T.	Jackson A. S.	McKinlock W. H.
Bryan Fred'k C.	Ferguson Chas. H.	Jackson H. W.	McMahon J. B.
Burley Frank E.	Ferguson Geo. M.	Jamieson M. M.	Midlen Thos. Y.
Burns R. M.	Field John S.	Janes J. J.	Miller E. H.
Byram C. F.	Field Marshall	Jay Milton	Mitchell M. G.
Camp W. C.	Fleetwood Chas.	Jeffery E. T.	Mitchell W. B.
Cass George W.	Fleming Robt. H.	Jenkins J. E.	Mixer C. H. S.
Cassidy J. A.	Fuller Leroy W.	Jenkins T. R.	Montgomery G. W.
Caton Arthur J.	Gage Albert S.	Jones G. Edwin	Moore J. H.

Moore Wm. H.
Moorhouse Wm. R.
Murdoch Thos.
Murison Geo. W.
Murphy F. M.
Mygatt Wm. R.
Newbury Geo. G.
Nickerson R. C.
Olmstead E.
O'Neill Wm. E.
Otis Chas. T.
Otis Geo. L.
Otis Joseph E.
Otis Philo A.
Overman L. E.
Owen M. D.
Owen Ole
Owens John E.
Palmer W. P.
Pardridge W. E.
Parker Sam'l W.
Patterson C. C.
Peacock C. D.
Peats Alfred
Peck C. I.
Peck Ferd W.
Peck Ferd W. jr.
Peck Walter L.
Peirce A. H.

Perkins F. W.
Perry I. N.
Perry L. S.
Phelps E. M.
Phelps W. H.
Phillips C. H.
Phillips T. P.
Phillip Wm. E.
Pitkin H. E.
Powell Samuel
Price James S.
Pullman Geo. M. jr.
Pullman W. S.
Pulsifer Fred. K.
Purdy Chas. W.
Raber P. W.
Rawson Fred H.
Ream N. B.
Reid D. G.
Rice F. Willis
Richberg John C.
Ridgely Chas. A.
Robbins Edward F.
Robinson J. K.
Roloson R. W.
Rous A. C.
Rutter David
Sanderson Geo. A.
Sard Wm. H.

Schimpferman W.H
Schmitt A.
Schuyler Dan'l J,jr.
Seeberger A. F.
Seeberger C. D.
Sharpe H. McV.
Shayne John T.
Shedd E. A.
Shipman D.B.
Shirk E. W.
Singer A. J.
Smith Byron L.
Smith Franklin P.
Smith G. T.
Sollitt Oliver
Starkweather C. H.
Stevens Frank L.
Stiles George N.
Stiles Josiah
Stone Carl Downer
Stone H. O.
Streeter John W.Dr.
Strong J. H.
Surghnor V. H.
Talbert Jos. T.
Taylor Ge. H.
Thomas Benj.
Tillinghast Craw-
ford

Tuttle Frederick B.
Uhl Edwin F.
Vilas C. H. Dr.
Wachsmuth L. C.
Wagner W. L.
Walker Edwin
Walker Edwin C
Walker Geo. C.
Walker W. B.
Walsh John R.
Warner E. Percy
Washburn Jas. M.
Watson J. V.
Wells M. D.
Wells S. R.
Wentworth M. J.
Wheeler A.
Wheeler F. T.
Wheeler G. H.
Whitney J. C.
Williams Norman
Witbeck John H.
Wood Geo. E.
Work A. S.
Worthington E. E.
Wrenn John H.
Wyatt S. W.
Young Caryl
Young Otto

THE CASINO AT EDGEWATER.

OFFICERS.

W. A. VAWTER, - - - - - - - President.
CHARLES A. BINZ, - - - - - - Vice-President.
D. F. FLANNERY, - - - - - - - Secretary.
J. K. FARLEY, - - - - - - - - Treasurer.
CHARLES P, WHITNEY, - - - - - - Director.

MEMBERS.

Balmer Thomas
Bast Elmer E.
Beck Charles W.
Berrall Charles jr.
Berry C. D.
Binz Charles A.
Blair Charles J.
Brine Geo. J.
Brockelbank J. C.
Bryan I. J.
Bryant J. A.
Burrell E. L.
Burton C. A.
Chatfield E. P.
Cochran J. L.
Coe Albert J.
Cummings W. J.
Davidson J. M. D.
Rev.
Decker H. J.
Dick E. E.
Dunlop C. D.
Dunoon George
Early P. H.
Farley J. K.
Flannery D. F.

Frankhauser E. I.
French M. P.
Gardner Fred S.
Graves Albert H.
Grosvenor L. N.Dr.
Harris Henry S.
Haven Joseph Dr.
Henius Max
Henry E. J.
Heuer August jr.
Heuer Henry F.
Hewitt J.
Hodge J. M.
Hotchkin B. L.
Howe A. T.
Hunt A. B.
Ingal R. E.
Jaques F. F.
Jenks E. W.
Jones George P.
Judd E. S.
Ketcham T. C.
King Charles H.
Kriete George H.
Lamberton J. F.

Lapham A. B.
Lapham E. N.
Leacock W. J.
Lewis N. B.
Logan W. H. G.
Lukens W. J.
McDonnell W.
McDonald C. A.
Macomber F. L.
Massey T. C.
Mellor D. G.
Meyer J. P.
Mills George F.
Moore E. E. Dr.
Moore Frank A. B.
Morley Robert L.
Nightengale A. F.
Noe E. C.
Owen W. D.
Peckham Chas. V.
Peters Jos. G.
Powell George W.
Powell M. H.
Pulver A. W.
Randolph R. J.

Robertson James P.
Rogers B. C.
Rosenbecker
Adolph
Russell C. C.
Schoenthaler F. C.
Scovel John C.
Sears N. C.
Silsbee J. L.
Skinkle J. W.
Slaughter H. B.
Slayton J. W.
Smyth W. S.
Steward John F.
Stiles C. M.
Stiles L. G.
Stoughton W. G.
Taylor W. N.
Thul Frank F.
Thornton H. W.
Thorsen James B.
Vawter W. A.
Watson George E.
Whitney Chas. P.
Woolley V. S.

THE CHICAGO CLUB.

MICHIGAN AV. SW. COR. VANBUREN.

OFFICERS.

ARTHUR J. CATON, - - - - - President.
ROCKWOOD W. HOSMER, - - - Vice-President.
ELIPHALET W. CRAMER, - Secretary and Treasurer.

EXECUTIVE COMMITTEE.

Kellogg Fairbank   Chas. A. Mair   Melville E. Stone
John T. Noyes   F. Willis Rice   Granger Farwell
Charles L. Billings   Rockwood W. Hosmer   Eliphalet W. Cramer

MEMBERS.

Ackerman Wm. K.
Adam AlexanderB.
Adams Edward S.
Adams George E.
Adams J.McGregor
Adams John R.
Adams Joseph
Adams Milward
Adsit Charles C.
Adsit James M. jr.
Aldis Arthur T.
Aldis Owen F.
AlexanderStuartR.
Alexander Wm. A.
Allen Benjamin
Allen Charles L.
Allerton Robert H.
Ames John C.
Andrews Walter S.
Antisdel Albert
Armour Allison V.
Armour George A.
Armour J. Ogden
Armour Philip D.
Armour PhilipD.jr.
Austin FrederickC.
Avery Frank M.
Ayer Benjamin F.
Ayer Edward E.
Babcock W. Irving
Baker Alfred L.
Baker Frank E.
Baker William T.
Baker William V.
Ball George C.
Bangs Edward W.
Bannard Henry C.
Barber Ohio C.
Barnes Charles J.
Barnes Nelson L.
Barnum Wm. H.
Barrell James
Barrett Sam'l E.
Bartlett A. C.
Bartlett Wm. H.
Barton Enos M.
Bausher Henry
Beale William G.
Beman Solon S.

Bigelow Nelson P.
Billings Chas. L.
Billings C. K. G.
Billings Frank
Billings Harry F.
Birch Hugh T.
Bishop Henry W.
Black H. S.
Black John C.
Blackstone T. B.
Blair Chauncey J.
Blair Edward T.
Blair Henry A.
Blair Watson F.
Blatchford E. W.
Boal Charles T.
Bokum Richard D.
Booth W. Vernon
Borden William
Botsford Henry
Boutell Henry S.
Bowen Joseph T.
Bowers Lloyd W.
Boyce S. Leonard
Boyesen Ingolf K.
Bradbury Geo. L.
Bradley Edw.
Bradley J. Harley
Breese Jacob B.
Brega Chas. W.
BrewsterEdwardL.
Brosseau August
BrosseauZenophile
P.
Broughton UrbanH
Brown FrancisU.
Brown William L.
Buckingham Clarence
Buffum Joseph H.
Bull Wm. B.
Bullen Chas. F.
Burley Frank E.
Burnet William H.
Burnham DanielH.
Burrows Daniel W.
Burry William
Busenbark Wm. R.
Butler Edward B.

Butterfield C. W.
Cable Ransom R.
Campbell Wm. N.
Carpenter Aug. A.
Carpenter A. A. jr.
Carpenter Benj.
Carpenter Myron J.
Carrington Wm. T.
Carter Leslie
Cary Eugene
Caton Arthur J.
Cavaroc Chas.
ChadbourneT.L.jr.
Chalmers Wm. J.
Chandler JosephH.
Chapin Simeon B.
Chatfield - Taylor
H. C.
Chisholm Sam'l S.
Church Townsend
V.
Clark Alson E.
Clark John M.
Clarke EdwardA.S.
Clay John jr.
Clowry Robert C.
Cobb Walter F.
Coffeen M. Lester
Coffeen William
Collins Lorin C. jr.
Comstock Wm. C.
Conley John W.
Connell Charles J.
Conover Chas. H.
Coolidge Chas. A.
Coolidge Frederic
S.
Corwith Chas. R.
Counselman Chas.
Cox Rensselaer W.
Cramer E. W.
Crane Albert M.
Crane Chas. R.
Crane Richard T.
CrosbyChaunceyH.
Crosby Fredk. W.
Cummings D. M.
Cunningham Secor
Curran Orville P.

Cutter John M.
Dau J. J.
Davis George R.
Davis Lewis H.
Dawes Chas. G.
Day Albert M.
Deering Charles
Deering James
Dewar A. L.
Dibblee Henry
Doane John W.
Dodge George E.P.
Donnelley Reuben
H.
Donovan Wm. F.
Douglas John M. jr.
Dows David jr.
Drake John B. jr.
Drake Tracy C.
Driver Edward A.
Dummer Wm. F.
Dunn Frank K.
Dupee John
Durand John M.
Durkee R. P. H.
Earling Albert J.
Eckels James H.
Eddy Arthur J.
Eddy Augustus N.
Edwards Eugene P.
Eldredge Geo. C.
Elkins William L.
Ellsworth JamesW.
Ely Arthur C.
Fabyan George
Fair Joseph B.
Fair Robert M.
Fairbank Kellogg
Fairbank N. K.
Faithorn John N.
Fargo Charles
Fargo Livingston
W.
Farwell Charles B.
Farwell Granger
Farwell John V. jr.
Farwell Walter
Fay Charles N.
Fentress James

Ferry Chas. H.
Ferry Watson J.
Field Marshall
Field Marshall jr.
Field Stanley
Fiske George F.
Fitch Henry S.
FitzHughCarter H.
Fleming John C.
Fleming Robert H.
FletcherWilliamM.
Flower James M.
Floyd Frank
Forsyth Robert
French George B.
Fuller Leroy W.
Fuller William A.
Fullerton Chas. W.
Gage Albert S.
Gage Eliphalet B.
Garneau Jos.
Garrett T. Mauro
Gary Eugene H.
Gary John W.
Gates Charles G.
Gates John W.
Geddes Alexander
Gibbs James S.
Gilbert Albert M.
Gilkison Jasper G.
Glessner John G.M.
Glessner John J.
Glover Otis R.
Goddard Lester O.
Goodheart Fred. E.
Goodman James B.
Goodrich Adams A.
Goodrich AlbertW.
Gorton Frank S.
Graves S.Haughton
Green AdolphusW.
Green Andrew H.
Grepe J. Stanley
Gresham Otto
Grier John P.
Griffin Thomas A.
Griswold Fitz-Edward
Gross Samuel E.
Gurney Charles H.
Hamill Charles D.
Hamill Ernest A.
Hamilton David G.
Hamline John H.
Hammond Jabez D.
Hannah John S.
Hapgood Chas. H.
Harahan James T.
HarbeckEugene,jr.
Harlan John M.
Harper Wm. R.
Harris George B.
Harris John F.
Harvey Joel D.
Haskell Fred. T.
Hately Walter C.

Havemeyer Wm.A.
Hayden Albert
Head Franklin H.
Hellyer Frederick
Henderson W. S.
Henrotin Charles
Herrick E. Walter
Herrick John J.
Hewitt Charles M.
HeyworthLawr'nce
Hibbard Wm. G.
High Geo. H.
Higinbotham H. D.
Higinbotham H. N.
Hillard Chas. W.
Hofstra William S.
Holmes E. Burton
Holt Charles S.
Holt George H.
Honore Nathaniel K.
Hosmer R. W.
Hotz Christoph
Howard Harold A.
Howe James T.
Howe Richard F.
Howland WilliamI.
Hughitt Marvin
Hulburd Chas. H.
Hunt Jarvis
Hunt Robert W.
Hutchinson C. L.
Insull Samuel
Isham Edward S.
Isham Pierrepont
Jackson H. W.
Jacobson Augustus
James Frederick S.
JamiesonMalcomM
Janes John J.
Jeffery Edward T.
Jenks William S.
Johnston John
Jones Judson M.W.
Jones Samuel J.
Jones Samuel M.
Keep Albert
Keep Chauncey
Keep Frederic A.
Keep William P.
Keith Edson jr.
Keith Walter W.
Keith W. Scott
Kelley William E.
Kenna Edward D.
Kennedy V. Shaw
Kent Sidney A.
Kerfoot WilliamD.
Key John R.
Keyes Rollin A.
Kimball Chas. F.
Kimball Wm. W.
Kimbark Seneca D.
King Charles G.
King Francis
King John C.

King Rockwell
Kirk John B.
Kirk Milton W.
KirkmanM'sh'll M.
Kirkwood William
Kitchen John B.
Knapp George O.
Kohlsaat H. H.
Laflin Albert S.
Laflin George H.
Lamb Benjamin B.
Larned Walter C.
Lathrop Bryan
Lawrence Dwight
Lawrence E. F.
Lawson Victor F.
Leask Arthur
LeBaron William
Lee Blewett
Leeds William B.
Leiter Joseph
Leiter Levi Z.
Leland Edward F.
Leman Henry W.
Lester FrederickA.
Lewis David R.
Lincoln Robert T.
Linn William R.
Lloyd Henry D.
Logan John A.
Loomis John M.
Loose Jacob L.
Lord John B.
Louderback Wm.J.
Lowden Frank O.
Lyford Will H.
Lyman David B,
Lyon George M.
Lyon John B.
Lyon Thomas R.
Lyon William C.
Madonald Chas. A.
Macdonald Chas.B.
Macfarland H. J.
Mackay Alexander
MacVeagh Franklin
Mair Charles A.
Manierre George
Maris John M.
Marsh Frank A.
Martin Thomas J.
Maynard PrestonC.
McAuley John T.
McCagg Ezra B.
McClurg Alex. C.
McCormick C.H.
McCormick Harold F.
M c C o r m i c k L. Hamilton
McCormickRobt.S.
McCormick R. Hall
McCormickStanley R.
McCormick Wm.G.

McCrea W. S.
McCullough Chas. H. jr.
McEwanMatthewC
McKay James R.
McKeon John C.
McLaughlin Geo.D
McMahon J. B.
McNulta John
McReynolds Geo.S.
McWilliams J. G.
Meagher James F.
Meeker Arthur
Merryweather Geo.
MeysenburgOttoW
Miller John S.
Miller Roswell
Milnor Lloyd
Mitchell John J.
MitchellMalcolmC.
Montgomery G. W.
Moore James H.
Moore William H.
Moran Thos. A.
Morse Charles H.
Morse Jay C.
Morton Joy
Morton Mark
Morton Paul
Moss Jesse L.
MudgeD.Archibald
Mulliken A. Henry
Mulliken Chas. H.
Mundy Norris W.
Munro William
Murdoch Thomas
Musgrave Harrison
Mygatt William R.
Nelson Murry
Niblack William C.
Nickerson R. C.
Nickerson Sam'l M.
Noble Alfred
Northcote AmyasS.
Norton J. Henry
Noyes John T.
Odell John J. P.
O'Grady John Waller de Courcy
Oliver John M.
Orr Arthur
Ortmann Rudolph
Otis George L.
Pacaud A. Lincoln
Palmer Potter
Palmer Wm. P.
Parker Samuel W.
Parkinson Rob't H.
Parmelee Chas. K.
Parmelee John W.
Patterson R. W.
Payson George S.
Peabody Francis B.
Peasley James C.
Peck Clarence I.
Peck Ferd W.

Peck George R.
Peters Roswell A.
Pettibone Asa G.
Phelps Elliott H.
Phelps Erskine M.
Pickands Henry S.
Pike Eugene S.
Pope Charles
Pope William J.
Porter Henry H.
Porter William D.
Potter Orrin W.
PrenticeEParmelee
Prime William A.
Prussing EugeneE.
Pullman Wm. C.
Pulsifer Fred'k K.
Quincy Chas. F.
Ray Frank H.
Raymond Chas. L.
Raymond Sam'l B.
Ream Norman B.
Reed Earl H.
Reid Alan L.
Reid Daniel G.
Rhodes J. Foster
Rice F. Willis
Richardson Aug. P.
Ripley Edward P.
Robbins Henry S.
Robertson Alex.
Robinson Chas. O.
Robinson Harry P.
Robinson John K.
Roloson Robt. W.
Roloson Walter L.
Rood James jr.
Runnells John S.
Russell Edward P.
Ryan Thomas J.
Ryerson Arthur
Ryerson Edward L.
Ryerson Martin A.
Salisbury W. M.

Sanderson Geo. A.
Sard William H.
Schimpferman WH
Schwartz G. A.
Sears Joseph
Seaverns Geo. A.
Seaverns Geo.A. jr.
Seeberger Chas. D.
Selfridge Harry G.
Sellers Frank H.
Shedd John G.
Shirk E. W.
Shortall John G.
Singer Charles J.
Skiff Fred'k J. V.
Slaughter ArthurO.
Smith Byron L.
Smith Dunlap
Smith Ernest F.
Smith George T.
Smith Orson
Smith Robert J.
Somers Edgar L.
Southgate R. H.
Spalding Jesse
Spencer Earl W.
Spoor John A.
Sprague Albert A.
Stauffer Benj. F.
Stewart Graeme
Stirling William R.
Stone Herbert S.
Stone Melville E.
Strobel Chas. L.
Stuart Chas. U.
Stuart Robert
Sturges Solomon
Sullivan Louis H.
Sunny Bernard E.
Swift George B.
Switzer Edward M.
Talbert Joseph T.
Templeton Thomas

Thomas Benjamin
Thomas Theodore
ThompsonLeverett
Tracy Wm. W.
Traer Glenn W.
Tree Arthur M.
Tree Lambert
Trumbull Perry
Tufts Eugene L.
Tuttle Emerson B.
Tuttle Frederick B.
Tuttle Henry N.
Ullrich Michael
ValentineAlastairI.
Valentine P. A.
Van Inwagen Jas.
Vilas Charles H.
Vilas Royal C.
Viles James jr.
Vincent Wm. A.
Walker Charles C.
Walker Edwin
Walker Edwin C.
Walker Frank W.
Walker George C.
Walker Henry H.
Walker Herbert B.
Walker James H.
Walker James R.
Walker William B.
Walker William R.
Walker Wm. S.
Walker Wirt D.
Waller James B.
Waller Robert A.
Walling Willough-
    by
Walsh John R.
Ware Henry A.
Ware John H.
Warner Ezra J.
Washburne Hemp-
    stead

Watson John G.
Watson Robert W.
Wean Frank L.
Weare Portus B.
Webster Lewis D.
Welling John C.
Wells Moses D.
Wells Thomas E.
Wheeler Arthur
Wheeler Arthur D.
Wheeler Chas. W.
Wheeler Eugene
Wheeler Geo. H.
Wheeler Harris A.
Wheeler SamuelH.
White A. Stamford
Whitehouse F. M.
Whiting John H.
Wickes Thomas H.
Widener PeterA.B.
Wilbur James B.
Williams Lawrence
Williams Norman
Williams Norman,
    jr.
Willing Henry J.
Wilson Benj. M.
Wilson Walter H.
Winston Fred'k H.
Winston Fred'k S.
Wooster ClarenceK
Wrenn John H.
Wright Joseph
Wright Julian V.
Wright Thomas A.
Yale Julian L.
Yoe Charles C.
Young Arthur
Young George W.
Young LawrenceA.
Younger Wm. J.
Zeller William F.

CHICAGO ATHLETIC ASSOCIATION.

125 MICHIGAN AVE.

OFFICERS:

D. M. LORD,	President.
WM. HALE THOMPSON,	Vice-President.
FRANK W. WENTWORTH,	Secretary.
E. D. HULBERT,	Treasurer.

DIRECTORS.

J. K. Armsby
Frank W. Wentworth
Geo. D. Kirkham
George E. Watson
Frank J. Howell
J. A. Post
G. A. Thomas
Geo. Ebeling
John H. Jones
Chas. S. Downs

Elliott Durand
Geo. W. Davis
E. R. Woodle
H. A. Kasten
Wm.Hale Thompson
E. A. Russell
Henry F. Frink
E. D. Hulbert
Wm. Kent
Walter J. Feron

C. K. Wooster
H. E. Raymond
Fred. B. Jones
Geo. J. Williams
Chas. H. Hoops
Geo. H. Jenney
H. M. Higinbotham
Chas. M. Faye
R. M. Critchell
W. F. Fowler

Abbott A. H.
Abbott R. B.
Ackerman F. S.
Ackert C. H.
Ackhoff Henry W.
Adam George J.
Adams Abbot L.
Adams Albert A.
Adams Cyrus H.
Adams George E.
Adams H C.
Adolphus Wolfe
Adsit J. M. jr.
Agler Oliver O.
Akin Henry F.
Aldis Owen F.
Aldis Owen W.
Allen Chas. W.
Allen C. B.
Allen Herbert W.
Allen H. A.
Alling John jr.
Almy Miles
Amberg J. Ward
Ames W. V. B.
Anderson A. E.
Anderson W. C.
Anderson W. G.
Andrews E. W.
Andrews S. F.
Armour Allison V
Arnd Charles
Arnold Fred'k A.
Ash L. H.
Ashton H. L.
Atkin G. Harold
Atkins G. J.
Atkinson J. A.
Austin F. C.
Auten G. W.
Avery Frank M.
Babcock Fred. R.
Bailey Theo. P.
Baker Alfred L.
Baker Jas. R.
Baldwin A. K.
Baldwin Geo. F.
Baldwin Henry R.
Baldwin Willis M.
Bane Oscar F.
Banks A. F.
Bardwell O. H.
Barge W. D.
Barnard Jas. H.
Barrell J. F.
Barrell S. E.
Barrett E. E.
Barrington C. V.
Bartholomay H. jr.
Bartlett E. B.
Bartlett Geo. F. jr.
Bassett O. P.
Batchelder A.
Bates Lindon W.

Beach C. B.
Beach Elmer E.
Beale Wm. G.
Beardsley C. B.
Beatty W. R.
Beers L. G.
Beidler Francis
Beidler George
Belfield Wm. T. Dr.
Belford Alex
Belknap C. C.
Bell K. H.
Bellamy H. C.
Bellows Frank L.
Benedict Geo. H.
Beneke Henry
Benner Adolph L.
Bennett A. F.
Bennett A. G.
Bennett E. B.
Bennett Jas. E.
Bennett Thomas
Bensinger M.
Bentley Harry G.
Besly C. H.
Bevan A. D.
Beverley W. W.
Biddle W. B.
Bigelow Arthur C.
Billings Frank
Binner Oscar E.
Birch Hugh T.
Bishop Chas. Nelson
Black Harry St. F.
Black John D.
Blackman C. W.
Blaine W. T.
Blair Chauncey J.
Blair Henry A.
Blair Watson F.
Blanchard Wm.
Blatchford T. W.
Bleyer C. E.
Bliss Chas. L.
Bliss E. Raymond
Blood Jas. A.
Blount T. M.
Bode Fred'k.
Bodman A. C.
Bodman L. W.
Boericke R. H.
Booth Chas. E.
Booth Ralph H.
Booth W. E.
Borden Jas. U.
Borner Wm.
Bosch Henry
Bourassa Jos. H.
Bourke Jas. E.
Bournique Alvar L.
Bournique Augustus E.
Bowen A. P.

Boyce W. D.
Boynton Chas. T.
Brainard Edwin
Brand E. L.
Braun Geo. P.
Brennan Jas. J.
Brewer O. W.
Briggs Charles H.
Briggs Geo. B.
Brocklebank J. C.
Brooks Almon
Brooks C. M.
Brooks Jas. C.
Brooks J. W.
Brophy Dr. T. W.
Bross Mason
Brower Jule F.
Brown Archibald L.
Brown Chas. E.
Brown D. G.
Brown Everett C.
Brown Geo. F. jr.
Brown James M.
Brown Lincoln A.
Brown O. G.
Brown Taylor E.
Brown W. C.
Brownlee A. G.
Bruette W. A.
Bryan Ben B.
Bryant Edw. F.
Bryson Wm. J.
Buchanan Gordon
Bucher W. H.
Budlong M. J.
Buehler Edward H.
Bullen A. F.
Bullen Fred F.
Bullock C. C.
Bullock F. W.
Burdett Samuel M.
Burgesser Geo. E.
Burkhardt Henry S.
Burley Frank E.
Burnam Frank
Burns Robt. M.
Burr Louis E.
Burrows W. F.
Burry Geo.
Butler H. B.
Buttolph A. C.
Byford Dr. H. T.
Byrne Harry
Byrne John P.
Cadow Sam'l B.
Callahan Jas. E.
Callan Henry A.
Camburn J. C.
Cameron D. R.
Camp Edward N.
Campbell Chas. W.
Campbell D. W.
Campbell L. W.
Campbell Robt. C.

Campbell Wm.
Canary D. J.
Cannell S. Wilmer
Capelle M. Eugene
Capron F. E.
Card Wm. D.
Carey James A.
Carmack E. H.
Carpenter E. F.
Carqueville E. H.
Carr R. F.
Carrington Wm. T.
Carroll W. A.
Carse David B.
Carse Jno. Bradley
Carson Samuel
Carter James S.
Cary Frank
Cary George P.
Case J. E.
Casey Charles E.
Casey Edwin A.
Cass Geo. W.
Cassady H. J.
Cassard Morris
Cassard Vernon
Cassidy H. C.
Catlin George
Caton Arthur J.
Chadbourne Thos. jr.
Chalmers Wm. J.
Chamberlin G. M.
Champlin D. H.
Chandler H. W.
Channer J. W.
Channon Harry
Channon Henry
Channon Jas. H.
Chapin S. B.
Charles G. M.
Charlton Geo. J.
Chase Horace G.
Chase Wm. O.
Chattell B. M.
Cheney C. C.
Chipley Gardiner
Christian H. W.
Christie Geo. B.
Christie H. A.
Church Edmund V
Churchill Chas. E.
Clark Alfred C.
Clark George T.
Clark John M.
Clark Dr. W. C.
Clark Walter T.
Clarke George
Clarke W. E.
Clement Henry C.
Clements Thos.
Clifton Chas. E.
Clow Chas. R.
Clow Harry B.

Cody Arthur B.
Cody Hope Reed
Coe Almer
Coen W. H.
Coghlan H. D.
Colburn Isaac
Colburn J. E.
Cole W. H. -
Collins John G.
Collins W. G.
Colton Samuel K.
Conkey W. B.
Conkling Allen
Conkling B. H.
Conley John W.
Conover Chas. H.
Conrad Chas. H.
Conway Edwin S.
Cook H. B.
Cooke H. H.
Cooley Norman P
Cooper E. C.
Cooper Frank H.
Cooper Wm. D.
Cooper W. F.
Copeland F. K.
Copelin E. W.
Corbin F. N.
Corby R. B.
Cordo F. I.
Corneau D. E.
Counselman Chas.
Cowles Alfred
Cox A. G.
Cox Chas. D.
Cox R. W.
Crabb C. C.
Crane Albert M.
Crane C. R.
Crane H. P.
Crane R. T.
Crane R. T. jr.
Cranz H. C.
Crary Roscoe
Crilly Geo. S.
Critchell John
Critchell R. M.
Croft Fred W.
Cromwell Chas.
Crowell H. P.
CrumpLawrenceM.
Cruttenden Thos.S.
Cudahy John
Cummings C. C.
Cummings MorrisC
Cummings N P.
Cummins B. F.
Cummins Wm. G.
Curtis Jas. C.
Curtis F. L.
Curtis J. H.
Curtis Uri B.
Dabney John P.
Dacy Albert E.
Dadie John
Daggett H. E.

Daily Chas. T.
Danforth Frank L.
Daniels E. F.
Darlington Herbert
Darrow C. S.
Darvill Fred'k
DaughartyAllan H.
Davies Colby
Davis Geo. W.
Davis Simon S.
Davis Will J.
Davis W. E.
Davis W. J. Nixon
Dawson Martin
Dayan L. F.
Deane Chas E.
DeCamp A. L. Dr.
DeLoss H. H.
Deming E. B.
Demmler Karl
DeMuth B. F.
Denell Reuben A.
Dennehy Thos. C.
Dering J. Kemper
Dewar Hamilton
DeWees W. W.
Dewes Charles J.
Dewes Francis J.
DeWitt Elden C.
Dick A. B.
Dickason L. T.
Dickerson C. W.
Dickinson Charles
Dickson H. M.
Dillingham E. R.
jr.
Dillman L. M.
Dixon Geo. W.
Dixon Thomas J.
Doggett W. L.
Donker Edward
Donnelley Reuben
H.
Donnelley Thos. E.
Donohue John W.
Dore Walter J.
Dorrance E. A.
Doty L. R.
Dougherty T. E.
Douglas Frank W.
Douglas F. L.
Dovenmuehle H.E.
Downe Geo. C.
Downs J. Edward
Drake Francis E.
Drake John A.
Driscoll M. F.
Dryer H. W.
Duddleston George
Duffy George
Dumont C. W.
Dunn A. E.
Dunn Frank K.
Durborow A. C. jr.
Durgin John C.
Dwight J. H.

Dyrenforth Doug-
las
Dyrenforth Julius
W.
Eagle J. E.
Eames John H.
Eastland L. J.
Ebeling Geo.
Eckel John C.
Eckstorm C. A.
Eddy A. D.
Edgar Wm. H.
Edwards E. P.
Edwards J. A.
Eiker Chas. F.
Eitel Karl
Elliott Edw. S.
Ellis Jno. C.
Ellsworth E. S.
Elmendorf Willard
Elmes Charles W.
Elmes C. L.
Elting P. L. F.
Ennis R. Berry
Erwin Chas. R.
Esson John H.
Eustis Percy S.
Eustis Truman W.
Evans Dr. A. E.
Evans R. O.
Ewart W. D.
Ewen J. M.
Fairbank Kellogg
Faithorn Jno. N.
Farlin M. W.
Farnum A. H.
Farson John
Farwell Chas. B.
Farwell John A. jr.
Farwell John W.
Farwell Walter
Fauber Wm. H.
Fay A. R.
Faye Charles M.
Fellows Dr. C. G.
Felton Chas. E.
Ferguson C. H.
Ferguson E. A.
Feron Walter J.
Ferris Henry B.
Ferry Charles H.
Field Chas. E.
Field John S.
Field Marshall
Finkler I. W.
Finney W. H.
Fischer O. F.
Fish S. C.
Fishburn Randolph
E.
Fisher C. E.
Fisher Francis P.
Fisher Hart C.
Fisk Franklin P.
Flagg W. H.
Flannery J. L.

Flershem L. W.
Foley John B.
Foreman Milton J.
Foresman W. C.
Forrest Wm. H.
Forsinger J. W.
Fortin Nelson
Foster Dr. F. H.
Foster Henry A.
Fowler W. F.
Fox John V.
Frasher J. S.
Free W. C.
French Geo. B.
Freshman Arnold
Frink Henry F.
Frost Walter A.
Frothingham H. H
Fuller Chas. H.
Fuller George A.
Funk Chas. A.
Funkhouser M. L.
C.
Furry Frank W.
Furst Edw. A.
Fyffe Wm. J.
Gage A. S.
Gallup Howard H.
Gardner Frank G.
Gardner Fred.
Gardner F. W.
Gardner Geo. C.
Gardner Jas. P.
Gartside John M.
Gartz Adolph F.
Gary E. H.
Gaspard P. H.
Gates Chas G.
Gates J. W.
Gates W. D.
Gaylord A. P.
Gaylord W. S.
Gentry C. H.
Gerwig F. L.
Gibbons Wm. M.
Gibbs F. B.
Gibbs Fred'k C.
Gilbert Hiram T.
Gilbert H. K.
Gilkison J. G.
Gill Charles E.
Gill Ernest
Gillespie Chas. H.
Gillette Edwin F.
Gilmore Dr. A. P.
Gilmore Thos. W.
Glennon E. T.
Gobel H. Elias
Goldie Wm. jr.
Goodman Wm. O.
Goodrich AdamsA.
Goodrich A. W.
Goodrich Edson H.
Goodridge A. E. G.
Gordon Thos. S.
Gores Paul

Gormully R. Philip
Gorton F. S.
Gottfried Carl M.
Grace William
Graham Beeckman
Graham W. A. S.
Grassie Henry
Graue John Geo.
Gray A. W.
Gray Louis A.
Greene D. R.
Greene F. C.
Greene J. P.
Gregory S. S.
Gregory W. D.
Grey John J.
Grey Walter C.
Grier J. P.
Groetzinger Ed. A.
Gross S. E.
Grower Wm. F.
Gunning Robert J.
Gunther Whitman
Gurney Chas. H.
Hackell Geo. E.
Hagenbuck E. L.
Haines E. H.
Haines Geo. B.
Hale Albert B.
Hall Rich'd C.
Hall W. F.
Halsey Tappan
Hamilton J. H.
Hamlin F. R.
Hamlin Geo. A.
Hamlin Geo. J.
Hammond Thos. C.
Hanecy Elbridge
Hanes J. K.
Hankey F. L.
Hankey James P.
Hanney P. M.
Hanson A. H.
Hapgood Wm. P.
Hardie T. Melville
Hardin John H.
Harding Geo. F.
Harding Geo. F. jr.
Hardy Cyrus A.
Hardy Francis A.
Harlan Dr. A. W.
Harlow Frank
Harmon Edw. C.
Harmon Geo. E.
Harper H. D.
Harrington S. H.
Harris Geo. B.
Harris Jno. F.
Harrison Wm. Preston
Hart Howard S.
Hartog John H.
Hartwell D. E.
Hartwell E. S.
Hartz Irving T.
Harvey Geo. M.

Harvey Dr. W. S.
Hasbrouck L.
Haskell Geo. W.
Haskell Jno. W. C.
Haughey L. C.
Havron John
Hawxhurst J. M.
Healy George L.
Heath Arthur M.
Hebard Fred'k S.
Heegaard Wm. H.
Hellyer Fred'k
Henderson T. A.
Hennig Wm. R.
Henrotin Dr. Fernand
Henry E. J.
Herrick E. Walter
Herrick Wm.
Hessert Gustav jr.
Hewitt Chas. M.
Hewitt H. H.
Heyworth Lawrence
Hibbard Frank V.S
Hibbard Wm. G.
Hibbard Wm. G. jr.
Higinbotham H. D.
Higinbotham H. M.
Hild F. H.
Hill James Tracy
Hill R. D.
Hill W. T.
Hillock Alex
Hitchcock R. A.
Hoard Charles D.
Hodges W. E.
Hoefer Thos. J.
Hoffman Geo. W.
Hoffman J. Jos.
Hoffmann John L.
Holland J. Edmund
Holman Dr. E. E.
Holmes Geo. J.
Holt Geo. H.
Hook W. W.
Hoops C. H.
Hopkins John P.
Hopkins Marcellus
Horr H. H.
Hosmer Dr. A. B.
Hotchkiss C. W.
Howard John H.
Howe Arthur J.
Howe Thad H.
Howell Frank J.
Hoyne Frank G.
Hudson A. B.
Hulbert Edmund D.
Hulbert Thos. H.
Hulbert Wm. M.
Hulin William
Huling Walter C.
Humiston S. A.
Hunt Chas. H.
Hunt Geo. W.

Hunt Ralph H.
Hunter William C.
Hurd Jas. D.
Hurlbut Harris E.
Hurlbut Horace E.
Hutchinson Geo. A.
Hyde James Nevins
Hyman R. W. jr.
Hynes Wm. J.
Ingalls F. A.
Irvine Hugh
Irving Robert A.
Ismond Robert E.
Jackman Edwin S.
Jackson Arthur S.
Jackson Howard B.
Jaquith E. P.
Jenkins Geo. R.
Jeuks John G.
Jenks Wm. S.
Jenney Geo. H.
Jennings Chas. A.
Jennings Rufus P.
Jennings Wm. H.
Jerrems A. W.
Jevne Henry M.
Jewell Ira H.
Jewett Fred L.
Johnson Alex. J.
Johnson C. Porter
Johnson E. V.
Johnson F. E.
Johnson Wm. H.
Johnson Wm. O.
Jones Ed. L.
Jones Fred. B.
Jones G. Herbert
Jones Harry J.
Jones John H.
Jordan Cady M.
Jordan Scott
Juergens W. F.
Kammerer Frank G.
Karpen Adolph
Kavanagh Chas. J.
Keating J. H.
Kee James W.
Keeley Edw. S.
Keeley Eugene M.
Keeley Thomas F.
Keen Edwin H.
Keep Chauncey
Keep F. A.
Keep Wm. B.
Keith H. A.
Kelley Addison D.
Kelley Edward B.
Kelley Wm. E.
Kellogg Norman
Kelly D. F.
Kelsey Chauncey
Kelsey H. N.
Kelsey J. A.
Kennedy W. B.
Kennedy W. J.

Kennett J. Durand
Kenny Wm. S.
Kenyon D. E.
Keogh James B.
Keogh John W.
Kessler Julius
Kilbourne L. Bernard
Kilgallen M. H.
Killen E. G.
Kimball Charles F.
Kimball Geo. F.
Kimbark Chas. A.
Kimbark Walter
Kinnear A. W.
Kirk John B.
Kirkham Geo. D.
Kiser J. W.
Kistler Andrew M.
Kitchell Frank J.
Klebs A. C. Dr.
Knapp Thomas
Knight Clarence A.
Knisely John A.
Kraus Adolph
Kreissl F.
Kremer Charles E.
Kretzinger Geo W.
Kuhnert Louis C.
Kussner Albert J.
Laflin A. S.
Laflin Geo. H.
Laflin Louis E.
Laflin Lycurgus
Lake I. L.
Lake Wm. H.
Lalor W. A.
Lamb Chas. A.
Lamb Frank H.
Lambert John
Lane Ebenezer
Lane Henry M.
Lapp Peter
Lartz W. C. C.
Lathrop Bryan
Law Wm. jr.
Lawrence James A.
Laws F. B.
Lawson Victor F.
Lawton L. C.
Leach F. W.
Leach L. L.
Leach Thomas A.
Leahy Thos. F.
Leask Arthur
Lee Charles W.
Lee Harry G.
Leeds W. B.
Leeming Chas. W.
Lehmann Edmund
Lehmann Edw. J.
Leicht Edward A.
Leigh E. B.
Leiter Joseph
Leiter T. Benton
Lenehan J. H.

Leonard Harry B.
Lesher J. H.
Lester C. H.
Lester F. A.
Lester H. V.
Levis John M.
Levy Alex H.
Lewis Dr. Denslow
Lewis H. C.
Lewis Isaac J.
Lidgerwood J. M.
Lincoln Robt T.
Linebarger J. O.
Lipkau Eugene
Livermore C. F.
Lloyd A. H.
Lobdell H. H.
Loker Geo. T.
Lomax George
Long J. B.
Longley Albert W.
Loose J. L.
Lord Daniel M.
Lord James F.
Love S. C.
Lovejoy Geo. M.
Luken William
Lusch Harry B.
Lydston G. Frank
Lyford W. H.
Lyman J. P.
Lynch Jas. D.
Lynch John A.
MacDonald Chas.
Macdonald C. A.
Macdonnell J. A.
Mackenzie John F.
MacMartin Dr. D. R.
MacVeagh Eames
Madden Frank H.
Madden M. F.
Madlener Albert F.
Magill H. W.
Magnus Arthur J.
Magnus A. C.
Mahin J. Lee
Mahoney Jos. P.
Marcy Geo. E.
Marks L. J.
Marks R. P.
Marrenner E.
Marshall Geo. E.
Marshall Philip L.
Martin Elmer B.
Martin Fred'k S.
Martin Geo. H.
Martin Wm. A.
Massey Wilfred
Masters A. W.
Matthews Edwin S.
Matthews Geo. W. jr
Matthews Wm. H.
Maxwell Chas. E.
Maxwell Edw. E.
May H. N.

McArthur A. F.
McArthur Dr. L. L.
McArthur Warren
McCarthy E. J.
McCartney H. G.
McClean Samuel A. jr.
McClellan E. W.
McConnell Chas.
McConnell John
McConnell W. S.
McCormick A. A.
McCormick Harold
McCormick F.
McCormick L. H.
McCormick R. H.
McCormick Stanley R.
McCullough H. R.
McDonald J. J.
McEwen John jr.
McEwen Paul
McFatrich Jas. B.
McGann L. E.
McGuire Daniel
McGuire Edward A.
McHie Geo. E.
McIntosh H M.
McKay A. A.
McKeon John C.
McKnight H. P.
McMahon J. B.
McMurray Geo. N.
McNally Fred G.
McNeill Alex. C.
McNeill Archibald
McNulty James H.
McVoy John A.
McWilliams J. G.
Mead W. Leroy
Meeker Chas. W.
Mehring George
Meier Albert G.
Memory Henry
Merigold W. A.
Merrick Fred'k L.
Merrill B. W.
Michels Nicholas
Michener W. W.
Midlen Thos. Y.
Millard G. M.
Miller Frank E.
Miller Jas. H.
Miller Joseph J.
Miller Robert B.
Milligan G. E.
Milner Jas. T.
Milnor Lloyd
Miner H. H.
Moberly E. E.
Moffett J. A.
Mohr Joseph
Montgomery F. D.
Montgomery Geo. W.
Montgomery H. W.

Moore Geo. B.
Moore Jas. H.
Moore Jas. J.
Moorehead T. W.
Moran T. A. jr.
Morava John
Morford T. T.
Morgan A. C.
Morgan Fred W.
Morgan K. E.
Morgan O. H.
Morrill Allan A.
Morrill C. A.
Morrill Donald L.
Morrill Fred K.
Morris F. M.
Morrison A. M.
Morrison Chas. E.
Morrisson Jas. W.
Morron J. R.
Morsman J. J.
Moulton Geo. M.
Moxley Wm. J.
Mueller Wm. jr.
Muir John
Munger P. F.
Munn Noel S.
Murison C. E.
Murphy D. J.
Murphy John B.
Murray Charles R.
Myers E. B.
Myers Sam'l
Neafus Geo. A.
Neeler H. G.
Neely John C.
Neely W. I.
Neilson J. H.
Nellegar J. B.
Nelson C. L.
Nelson John L.
Nelson Murry, jr.
Nelson W. P.
Nicol Alex
Norris C. S.
Norton Edwin
Norton J. Henry
Norton Thos. S.
Noyes David A.
Noyes L. W.
O'Brien Edward
O'Brien Thomas D.
O'Bryan Edw.
O'Connor T. G.
O'Neill W. E.
Oakley Horace S.
Odell F. S.
Oliver Frederick S.
Olmsted O. A.
Orr Edw. K.
Orr G. H.
Ortmann Rudolph
Orvis Orland D.
Ostrom J. A.
Otis Chas. T.
Otis Philip A.

Owen K. R.
Pacaud A. Lincoln
Pacaud Duncan
Paden Willard S.
Page J. C.
Palmer J. F.
Pardey H. W.
Pardridge C. W.
Pardridge F. C.
Pardridge F. R.
Parker Lewis W.
Parmelee Ed. D.
Patrick B. F. jr.
Patrick Chas. E.
Patrick Joseph H.
Patten H. J.
Patterson A. W.
Patterson John C.
Patterson R. W.
Paul C. R.
Pauling E. G.
Peabody F. S.
Peacock C. D.
Peacock C. D. jr.
Pearson W. H.
Pease Edw. H.
Pease James
Peats Alfred
Peck Clarence I.
Peck C. D.
Peck Ferd. W.
Peck Walter L.
Peirce Arthur H.
Pelouze Wm. N.
Penhallow Wm. P.
Pennington M. P.
Pennoyer Geo. M.
Perkins Dwight H.
Perkins Fred'k W.
Perry Thos. O.
Person D. VanNess
Peters Homer H.
Pettibone A. G.
Phelps C. E.
Phelps E. H.
Phillips W. E.
Pinckney M. W.
Pine M. B.
Pinkerton W. A.
Plamondon A. D.
Plamondon Geo.
Plumb Theo. W.
Plummer D. C.
Polson Richard
Pomy Herman G.
Poor J. Harper
Porter Washington
Post John A.
Post Wm. W.
Potter Edwin A.
Poucher Barent G.
Powers L. D.
Pratt B. H.
Preasent C. W.
Prentice Leon H.
Preston Ernest J.

Price F. A.
Primley J. P.
Pringle Robert
Probst Jerome
Pullman Geo. M. jr.
Pullman W. C.
Pulsifer Fred. K.
Purcell Chas. A.
Purinton H. G.
Putnam A. A.
Putnam F. W.
Quan Henry W.
Quincy C. F.
Rand Chas. E.
Rappal F. J. jr.
Ratcliffe F. A.
Rathborne Wm. W.
Rawson A. E.
Rawson Fred H.
Ray Allen S.
Raymond Chas. E.
Raymond H. E.
Raymond H. S.
Raymond Lowry B.
Reddon W. B.
Redington W. H.
Reed Frank F.
Reed I. N.
Rehm W. H.
Reid Arthur S.
Reid Daniel G.
Reid George B.
Revell Alexander H.
Revell David
Revell John T.
Rew George C.
Rew Irwin
Reynolds C. H.
Reynolds Marc M.
Rhodes John E.
Rhodes J. Foster
Rice Elliott S.
Rich Elmer A.
Richards G. E.
Richardson Danl. E
Richardson Harry B
Richardson L. G.
Richter Paul K.
Riggs George W.
Rinn George P.
Ripley B. W.
Robb Thomas P.
Roberts C. A.
Roberts C. S.
Robertson F. C. N.
Robertson Jas. P.
Robertson John B.
Robertson J. W.
Robie Geo. T.
Robinson Elisha A.
Rockwell Chas. H.
Rockwell Irvin E.
Rockwood Sprague S.
Rodiger Wm.
Rogers Charles D.

Rogers R. M. jr.
Rollo L. C.
Rosing W. H. V.
Ross George B.
Ross G. F.
Ross Wm. K.
Rounds Chas. H.
Rubens Harry
Ruddock C. H.
Rudhart Philip P.
Rudolph Franklin
Ruffner W. R.
Ruggles Chas. R.
Ruh F. E.
Rumpf W. H.
Rumsey Julian M.
Rush J. W.
Russell E. A.
Ruxton Wm.
Ryan J. F.
Rycroft H. E.
Rydell John S.
Ryerson Edw. L.
Ryerson Martin A.
Sanborn Geo. C.
Sanders Jacob F.
Sargent Wm. D.
Sattley W. N.
Sayler C. E.
Scates Charles
Schaub F. J.
Schaub Peter A.
Scherzer Albert H.
Schilling Geo. F.
Schmidt Fred. M.
Schmidt Leonard
Schmidt Leonard F.
Schmidt Dr. O. L.
Schmitt Anthony
Schmitt Chas. S.
Schmitt E. J.
Schneider O. C.
Schnur Jacob
Schroeder Geo.
Schub C. H.
Schultz M. M.
Schuttler Peter jr.
Schwab A. C.
Schwarz Herbert E.
Scott Walter A.
Scull Harry
Scully A. B.
Seaverns Geo. A. jr
Seipp W. C.
Selden F. J.
Sellers F. H.
Sellers John M.
Senn Emanuel J.
Senn N. Dr.
Senour W. F.
Seymour Herbert V.
Sharp Wm. N.
Shaw Edward R.
Shaw Howard V. D.
Shaw T. A. jr.
Shayne John T.

Shedd Edward A.
Sheldon Geo. W.
Sheldon Theodore
Shepard Harry E.
Shepard W. L.
Shepherd Edward S.
Sheridan A. D.
Sheridan Thos. F.
Sherlock Chas. L.
Sherman L. B.
Sherwood Marc
Shonts T. P.
Shortall John L.
Shourds C. B.
Shubert A. B.
Sidway H. T.
Sills Edward P.
Sills W. H.
Sittig W. A.
Skillen E. S.
Skinner J. Richard
Slade C. B.
Slaughter Harry B.
Smith Chas. F. M.
Smith Dunlap
Smith Edgar C.
Smith E. E.
Smith Frank M.
Smith Franklin P.
Smith Fred M.
Smith F. Stewart
Smith Gilbert A.
Smith Granger
Smith James P.
Smith Jay H.
Smith J. Frank
Smith Lloyd J.
Smith Loyal L.
Smith Lewis M.
Smith Marvin E.
Smith Orson
Smith R. K.
Smith W. S. jr.
Snow Albert E.
Soden G. A.
Sollitt Oliver
Sommers H. G.
Spalding Chas. F.
Spalding Chas. R.
Spink F. A.
Spoor John A.
Stack J. L.
Stanley Frank W.
Stanley P. E.
Stanton W. A.
Starkweather Fk. H.
Stearns Edgar G.
Stedman Josiah
Steele Julius
Sterling W. H.
Stevens Chas. R.
Stevens Frank C.
Stevens Harry D.
Stevens S. H. j.
Stevenson H. M.

Stewart A. A.
Stiles L. G.
Stone C. L.
Stone Frank B.
Stone Geo. N.
Street Richard J.
Streeter Allen R.
Streeter D. L.
Streeter J. H.
Streeter W. C.
Strong H. G.
Strotz Charles N.
Stuart Chas. U.
Studebaker W. F.
Sturges Benton
Sturges Lee
Sullivan James H.
Sullivan Jeremiah
Sullivan Louis H.
Sullivan T. E.
Surghnor V. H.
Sutter E. A.
Swanson S. A.
Swenson Magnus
Swift Edward F.
Swift L. F.
Syer E. W.
Sylvester R. T.
Talbot J. F.
Taylor Abner
Taylor Arthur A.
Taylor Geo. H.
Taylor H. N.
Taylor Thomas jr.
Taylor Wm. N.
Thayer Chas. L.
Theurer Joseph
Thomas A. L.
Thomas Frank H.
Thomas Frank W.
Thomas F. M.
Thomas G. A.
Thompson Percival
Thompson S. B.
Thompson Wm. Henry
Thorkildsen Thos.
Thorne Chas. H.
Thorne James W.
Thorsen J. B.
Thurber Geo. S.
Thurston F. W.
Tietgens Paul
Tilden Edward
Tilt J. E.
Tinthoff Fred S.
Titcomb W. C.
Todd James A.
Tossetti Otto L.
Tousey Chester A.
Towers A. B.
Townsend J. J.
Toynton F. E.
Tripp F. A.
Trumbull John H.
Turner A. A.

Tuttle Wm. P.
Twichell J. O.
Twitty Walter G.
Tyng Dudley A.
Ubsdell J. Arnold
Ullmann Frederic
Ullrich Michael
Underwood J. P.
Unzicker Otto
Upman Frank
Utz A. L.
Vail H. S.
VanHamm F. R.
VanSicklen N. H.
VanVlissingen J.H.
VanVlissingen P.
Veatch B. E.
Veeder Albert H.
Veeder Henry
Veitch Wilberforce
Vent R. T.
Vermilyea A. R.
VonGlahn August
Voorhees John W.
Vories H. F.
WachsmuthFr'dH.
Wacker Chas. H.
Wadhams F. E Dr.
Wagner Emil W.
Wagner F. J.
Wagner George
Wagner Wm. L.
WalbankKennethS

Walburn A. W.
Waldschmidt Aug.
Walker Francis W.
Walker George B.
Walker Geo. C.
Walker J. Brandt
Walker W. B.
Waller Wm.
Walsh R. D.
Walter Alfred M.
Walter Lincoln W.
Ward Chas. A.
Wares J. F.
Warrell A. M.
Warren Ogle T.
Waters F. S.
Watson Geo. E.
Watson Thos. T.
Watt Jas. B.
Webber Chas. M.
Weber George A.
Webster George W.
Webster G. A.
Weeks Gilbert M.
Weeks Harvey T.
Weeks J. G.
Wegener Wm. A.
Weidig Geo.
Weiss George A.
Weiss John H.
Wellington C. L.
Wells Brenton R.
Wells Orson C.

Wells Willis J.
Wentz A. D.
West Geo. E.
Weston George
Weston John W.
Whedon James P.
White Aug. J.
White Carleton
White Harry
White Sam T.
Whitehead E. P.
Whitehead Sidney S.
Whitehead William M.
Whitehouse S. S.
Whiting Chas. H.
Whiting F. G.
Wightman C. J.
Wilder T. Edward
Wiley Edward N.
Wiley Lyman A.
Wiley Sterling P.
Wilkins S. S.
Willard F. E.
Williams Chas. S.
WilliamsEdwardC.
Williams Edw. W.
Williams H. F.
Williams John
Williams L. M.
Williamson Wm.
Williamson W. G.

Willits Ward W.
Wilson H. R.
Wilson H. S.
Wilson Monmouth B.
Wilson Samuel C.
Winston F. S.
Winterbotham Jos.
Wolf Henry M.
Wolford Jacob A.
Wood John H
Woodbury S. H.
Woodle Edwd. R.
Woods Wm. J.
Woodward M. S.
Work A. S.
Work Geo. Z.
Wrenn Wm. B.
Wright Geo. C.
Wright Rufus
Wright Thos. A.
Wright Warren
Wrigley Wm. jr.
Wygant A.
Wylde Edward
Yager W. A.
Yerkes Chas. T.
Young Henry M.
Young Otto
Young W. W.
Younglove Ira S.
Zeiss H. C. F.
Ziesing August

LIFE MEMBERS.

Adams Joseph
Andrus Fred H.
Armour J. Ogden
Armour P. D.
Armour P. D. jr.
Armsby J. K.
Barbour Frank
Barler A. C.
Barnhart A. M.
Barrett John F.
Bennet Wm. H.
Billings C. K. G.
Blair Lyman
Bogert W. B.
Boland John
Bonney C. L.
Bonney L. C.
Booth A.
Booth Wm. M.
Booth W. S.
Booth W. Vernon
Bowers L. W.
Bradley James D.
Broadbent T. A.
Brown Charles E.
Brown Edwin
Brown Moreau R.
Brown William T.
Buchanan Milford D.

Carlisle E. G.
Cavanagh Chas. T.
Champlin Chas. P.
Champlin Fred L.
Chatfield-TaylorH. C.
Cobb Henry Ives
Coffeen Wm.
Collins Harrie B.
Conrad J. H.
Corbin C. D.
Cummings D. M.
Dennis C. S.
Dennis E. W.
Derby W. M. jr.
Devin D. T.
DeWolf Wallace L.
Dickinson Albert
Diffley M. W.
Donohue Wm. F.
Downs Charles S.
Drake Juo. B. jr.
Drake Tracy C.
Dupee John
Dupee Walter H.
Durand Elliott
Fisher L. G.
Fiske Geo. F.
Flanders J. J.
Franche D. C.

Fraser Norman D.
Fullerton C. W.
Gaylord Edw. L.
Gerould Frank W.
Gifford I. C.
Gillett W. C.
Gilman J. E.
Gormley J. H.
Green H. L.
Griffin T. A.
Hamburger L. M.
Harlan Jno. Maynard
Hart James A.
Hartwell F. G.
Heath E. W.
Hecht Ernest
Henneberry W. P.
Hettler H. H.
Hildreth L. E.
Hodge A. T.
Hotz Robert S.
Houston Geo. T.
Hunt Samuel H.
Hutchinson Chas.L
Ingals E. Fletcher
Isham Ralph
Jones G. Edwin
Jones William J.
Kasten Herman A

Kellogg Milo G.
Kent William
Kern Jacob J.
Kimball Eugene S.
Kirby R. D.
Kirk Milton W.
Kirkman M. M.
Knapp Geo. O.
Lamson S. Warren
Leake Joseph B.
Leland E. F.
Linn W. R.
Loftis S. T. A.
Mackey F. J.
Mansure E. L.
Marks Kossuth
Martin Joseph S.
Matile Herman O.
May F. E.
Mayer David
Mayo John B.
McCarthy M. H.
McCormick C. H.
McCrea W. S.
McElligott Thos.G
McHugh P.
McNally A.
Means J. Mac
Miller B. C.
Miller E. W.

Mitchel O. W.
Monroe W. F.
Nickerson R. C.
Parson John B.
Patterson Stewart
Paulsen W. A.
Peasley J. C.
Pike Charles B.
Pike Eugene R.
Pike Wm. W.
Porter H. H.
Porter James W.
Porter Rogers
Pratt R. E.
Prussing E. E.
Prussing Geo. C.
Ray Frank H.
Ream Norman B.
Reed Isaac N.
Reiling Herman J.
Rew Henry C.

Richardson A. P.
Rintoul Robert
Robinson Chas. O.
Schmitt Arthur G.
Scudder J. A.
Simmons Chas. H.
Smith Byron L.
Smith Calvin S.
Smith J. Parker
Spalding A. G.
Spry S. A.
Stearns R. I.
Steele H. B.
Steever J. G.
Stephens W. C.
Stewart A. M.
Strobel C. L.
Sutherland W. J.
Taylor Henry A.
Teeple F. W.
Thompson Gale

Thompson Wm
Hale
Thomson H. C. M.
Thorne George A.
Thorne George R.
Thorne W. C.
Thrall Sam E.
Thrall W. A.
Trude A. S.
Turrill J. F.
Tuttle FrederickB.
Ullman H. J.
Upham Fred'k W.
VanKirk CharlesB.
Vawter Wm. A.
Vierling Louis
Viles James, jr.
Wachsmuth L. C.
Wallach J. F.
Wampler A. J.

Ward A. Montgomery
Ware H. A.
Ware J. H.
Waters W. B.
Weary E. D.
Wentworth F. W.
Wheeler A. L.
Wheeler A. W.
White George E.
Whitehead PercyD
Whitney Chas. P.
Wilbur J. B.
Williams George J.
Williams L. R.
Williamson John
Willing Henry J.
Willoughby C. L.
Wilson John R.
Wooster C. K.

NON-RESIDENT MEMBERS.

Abbot Willis J.
Alden I. C.
Alexander Alex.
Allen Nathan
Ansley Robert
Armstrong W. F.
Bacon D. H.
Baker H. C.
Balke Julius
Bardeen George E.
Batterton J. M.
Baumann Gustav
Birchard Frank H.
Birchett F. W.
Blodgett Jno. W.
Booth G. G.
Bowers L. H.
Bowes Frank B.
Braine L. F.
Bristol Thos. J.
Broenniman E. G.
Brown J. Mabbett
Browning Jas. M.
Buck Ira D.
Bull F. K.
Burnett W. H. C.
Burnham Robt. D.
Calcott Frank H.
Callahan A. F.
Campbell J. W.
Carlisle C. A.
Carney Fred jr.
Carroll James F.
Cate S. E.
Catlin Charles
Catterson Geo. N.
Cavanah James
Church S. M.
Clifton Frank
Coan C. C.
Cochran J. E.
Coleman R. L.

Comstock J. H.
Conley James
ConnollyAndrewC.
Corbin L. P.
Cotton Joseph B.
Cunningham L. S.
CunninghameAlex.
Curry George A.
Davidson J. O.
Davis Warren J.
DeMott Howard
DeVay Wm. P.
Dixon DanielMcD.
Dommick Carleton
Dreier Carl
Ellis M. E.
Ellwood I. L.
Engle Wm. J.
Fairbank Wallace
Fay Louis E.
Felton H. E.
Fish Frederick S.
Fleming John A.
Flershem R.Byford
Fort Robert B.
Fowler G. A.
Fraser Robert G.
Fuller Edward M.
Fuller E. Chubb
Fuller E. C.
Furlong James
Gambrill Richard
Gardner F. A.
Garrison O. L.
Gilbert W. M.
Gill Thomas H.
Gray Willis E.
Greene Edw. H.R.
Griffiths G. R.
Groetzinger W. C.
Hackney W. S.
Hamilton Andrew

Hancock Frank A.
Harris W. J.
Harvey J. R.
Hastings F. S.
Haswell H.
Hayes R. P.
Hennessy Steve
HequembourgC.E.
Herrick Wm. B.
Hicks W. T.
Hogan Daniel
Hogue Eugene
Holland Frank P.
Huber Otto
Hughes C. C.
Huiskamp H. J.
Hulbert S. S.
Johnson Ernest C.
Johnson Fred I.
Jones Harry F.
Joyce W. T.
Kent Carrol C.
Kessler Walter
Ketcham Frank D.
Kibbey W. B.
Kimberly J. A.
Kirkpatrick J. C.
Kissam George
Kitchen A. M.
Kramer H. L.
Laflin A. King
Laflin J. P.
Lamprecht Theo.H
LanahanCharlesM.
Law Charles D.
Leask Frank
Lederle Geo. A.
Lemoine E. S.
Libbey Frank H.
Liebhart Frank C.
Lindsley F. B.
Lingle H. D.

Loring Abbott
Lusk Wm. H.
Marsh Henry W.
Martin A. D.
Martin A. Watson
May Charles H.
Mayer E. J.
McBride George J.
McCanna C. B.
McCaskellJasperA.
McChesney T. D.
McCoy Thos. J.
McCrea Samuel H.
McIntosh C. L.
McKinnon R. W.
McMiller Jno. W.
McPherran S. H.
McRoy John T.
Merritt Wesley
Miles B. F.
Miller James W.
Mills A. J.
Mills M. B.
Mollenhauer F. D.
Montrose J. E.
Morgan Henry M.
Morris Howard
Murphy F. M.
Murphy Wm. J.
Myers W. B.
Nebeker S. A.
Nevin W. G.
O'Bannon John W.
O'Neill V. T.
Offerman C. C.
Orendorf U. G.
Peck Theo. D.
Phinney T. W.
Puff Frederick
Pulver C. C.
Raisbeck Geo. A.
Remer Clarence E.

Roirdan D. M.
Ross C. G.
Rust R. E.
Ruttan W. E.
Sanger Frank M.
Scoville C. B.
Searles C. S.
Seifert Edward
Shackleford T. W.
Sharp Edw. F.
Shearman Chas. W.
Sheldon C. E.
Sherwin W. W.
SherwoodLudlowS.
Shipman Chas. G.
Simmons Z. G. jr.

Sladden Sidney C.
Smith E. C.
Smith N. M. jr.
Speare E. R.
Speare Lewis R.
Stanton F. McM.
Starrett Theo.
Stephenson Fred
M.
StephensonIsaac jr.
Stocking C. J.
Stokes Chas. F.
Stone Foster
Stone J. F.
Studebacker Clem
jr.

Studebacker Geo.
M.
Tenney H. Morton
Tewksbury George
W.
Thompson Delos
Townsend H. C.
Tracey F. M.
Trimble A.J.
Trube G. A.
Upton King
Ustick W. J.
VanNortwick John
Walker Lyman T.
Walker Wm. B.

Walton Charles
Wardlow John
Wardrop W. jr.
Wardwell R. D.
Washburne E. B.
Wells W. H. jr.
West Edward A.
Whitely B. H.
Williams Walter
Wills H. R.
Wilson C. E.
Woodward E. A.
Wright Charles H
Young W. J. jr.
Yule George A.

CHICAGO CULTURE CLUB.

ILLINOIS HALL, W. MADISON STREET NW. COR. OGDEN AVENUE.

OFFICERS.

MRS. JANE ST. JOHN BOOTH, - - - President.
MRS. N. M. SIMONDS, - - First Vice-President.
MRS. ERASMUS GARROTT, - Second Vice-President.
MRS. EDWARD F. PRICE, - - Recording Secretary.
MRS. ARNOLD B. MCCOURTIE, Corresponding Secretary.
MRS. HORACE T. CURRIER, - - - - Treasurer.

DIRECTORS.

Catharine R. Judd
Annie W. Crawford
Katharine H. Powell

Ella M. Stanford
Alice M. Wells
Alinda C. Elliott

Florence E. Clark
Margaret V. Wilson

MEMBERS.

Adcock Mrs. A. W.
Aiken Mrs. Wm. J.
Alsip Mrs. Charles H.
Alsip Mrs. W. H.
Avery Mrs. D. J.
Bachelle Mrs. Otto
Bain Mrs. Lewis R.
Baker Mrs. B. F.
Baldwin Mrs. Theron C.
Ballard Mrs. Charles N.
Banning Mrs. E.
Barr Mrs. A. E.
Barrett Mrs. Charles R.
Barry Mrs. J. L.
Beardsley Mrs. Susan W.
Beek Mrs. Horace W.
Bogle Mrs. W. S.
Booth Mrs. J. St. John
Boughton Mrs. D. K.
Bowes Mrs. F. K.
Brett Miss Emma S.
Brown Mrs. Joseph W.
Brown Mrs. W. G.
Bryan Mrs. Fred'k W.
Burkhart Mrs. H. S.
Casey Mrs. James J.
ChamberlainMrs.Chas:H.
Clark Mrs. George H.
Clark Mrs. L. H.

Clark Mrs. Walter S.
Cochrane Mrs. Thos. J.
Cole Mrs. T. W.
Collins Mrs. Thomas
Conger Mrs. Romaine
Corcoran Mrs. B. A.
Cornell Mrs. A. Sterling
Cowper Mrs. J. H.
Crane Mrs. Frank R.
Crawford Mrs. Mark L.
Currier Mrs. Horace T.
Dadie Mrs. John
De Celle Mrs. N.
Dennis Mrs. Fred. J.
Derickson Mrs. J. L.
DeSouchet Mrs. Albert
Dexter Mrs. C. F.
Dibble Mrs. Charles A.
Dickinson Mrs. L. L.
Dickson Mrs. James S.
Donelson Mrs. C. P.
Downey Mrs. W. S.
Drake Mrs. Geo. M.
Duncan Mrs. John H.
Durborow Mrs. C. E.
Dwyer Mrs. E. J.
Eckhart Mrs. John W.
Ehler Mrs. J. C.
Elliott Mrs. W. S. jr.

Everett Mrs. Joseph D.
Fairman Mrs. Geo. C.
Falvey Mrs. P. J.
Featherstone Mrs.JohnM.
Fifield Mrs. Walter K.
Finch Mrs. Franklin C.
Fisher Mrs. W. A.
Fitch Mrs. F. L.
Fowler Mrs. Frank T.
Frailey Mrs. W. P.
Fuller Mrs. Charles H.
Galpin Mrs. Homer B.
Galpin Mrs. Homer K.
Gardner Mrs. Addison L.
Garrott Mrs. Erasmus
Gilbert Mrs. Wm. J.
Gray Mrs. F. M.
Griffin Mrs. James F.
Griffith Mrs. J. A.
Gurney Mrs. Chester S.
Hanna Mrs. Edward
Harris Mrs. A. J.
Hartwig Mrs. Charles F.
Harvey Mrs. W. S.
Haskett Mrs. I. R.
Hecht Mrs. F. A.
Heper Mrs. Otto
Hill Mrs. E. A.
Holden Mrs. N. B.

Holman Mrs. D. F.
Hood Mrs. C. Todd
Hooper Mrs. Edwin E.
Hosking Mrs. Anthony
Hosking Mrs. Ben. T.
Hostetter Mrs. John N.
Howe Mrs. J. L.
Johnson Mrs. J. D.
Jones Mrs. DeWitt C.
Jordan Mrs. C. H.
Jordan Mrs. Scott
Judd Mrs. C. F.
Karcher Mrs. Louis
King Mrs. A. H.
Knapp Mrs. William M.
Knox Mrs. John
Lane Mrs. C. B.
Laubender Mrs. J. F.
Lawrence Miss Garda
Lowe Mrs. Perley
MacCarty Mrs. C. S.
Mackie Mrs. Charles
Magill Mrs. J. C.
Marshall Mrs. F. D.
Marshall Mrs. H. L.
Marshall Mrs. J. D.
Martin Miss Eunice A.
Martin Mrs. S. Baily
Maxwell Mrs. James
McBride Mrs. John F.
McChesney Mrs. W. B.
McClelland Mrs. J. S.
McCourtie Mrs. A. B.
McDonell Mrs. J. A.
McGregor Mrs. Wm.
McLennan Mrs. Kenneth
McNeill Mrs. Benjamin F.
McNeill Mrs. Thomas
Metzger Mrs. William
Miller Mrs. J. A.
Mills Mrs. D. W.
Mitchell Mrs. A. J.
Morey Mrs. H. C.
Moulton Mrs. Addie
Moxley Mrs. W. J.

Murphy Mrs. Anthony
Nair Mrs. J. H.
Nichols Mrs. F. M.
Nichols Mrs. Geo. R.
Nickerson Mrs. A. E.
Oliver Mrs. J. M.
Parker Mrs. Geo. G.
Patterson Mrs. A. W.
Peak Mrs. Frank H.
Perry Mrs. A. J.
Peterson Mrs. W. F.
Phillips Mrs. H. A.
Piper Mrs. R. J.
Piratzky Mrs. R. H.
Podrasnik Mrs. Alois
Powell Mrs. J. H.
Pratt Mrs. Emma
Pratt Mrs. G. E. M.
Price Mrs. E. F.
Pyles Mrs. Harvey S.
Rathbone Mrs. P. D.
Reid Mrs. W. C.
Reininger Mrs. Edward E.
Rend Mrs. William P.
Richards Mrs. Edward S.
Richolson Mrs. B. F.
Robinson Mrs. E. A.
Rollins Mrs. C. E.
Root Mrs. F. A.
Ross Mrs. W. H.
Ruggles Mrs. Charles R.
Rutherford Mrs. Alice
Schriver Mrs. P. A.
Scully Mrs. D. B.
Sennott Mrs. T. H.
Sharp Mrs. Thomas H.
Sherman Mrs. W. M.
Shoemaker Mrs. Walter
Simonds Mrs. N. M.
Sinclair Mrs. Peter
Skillman Mrs. H.
Smith Mrs. B. M.
Smith Mrs. Charles H.
Smith Mrs. Frank S.

Smith Mrs Robert D.
Stanford Mrs. Geo. W.
Stearns Mrs. E. G.
Stearns Mrs. M. C.
Steinson Miss Gertrude M.
Steinson Mrs. H. L.
Stevens Mrs. J. K.
Stiller Mrs. Richard F.
Strong Miss E. G.
Sullivan Mrs. Wm. K.
Sutton Mrs. Thomas
Sweet Mrs. John Allen
Swissler Mrs. Henry L.
Swissler Mrs. W. F.
Talcott Mrs. M. D.
Tapper Mrs. Geo.
Tatham Mrs. R. L.
Thompson Mrs. W. A.
Traver Mrs. C. S.
Utley Mrs. H. B.
Vary Mrs. Mary C.
Walton Mrs. T. B.
Ward Mrs. E. C.
Waters Mrs. C. E.
Watson Mrs. J. S.
Weidner Mrs. R. F.
Welles Mrs. Arthur T.
Welles Mrs. Fred'k L.
Wells Mrs. Addison E.
Wells Mrs. W. A.
Werst Mrs. J. Z.
White Mrs. Eliza J.
Wiehe Mrs. Christian F.
Wilcox Mrs. John S.
Wilcox Mrs. W. W.
Williams Mrs. A.
Williams Mrs. Martin
Wilson Miss M. V.
Wintermeyer Mrs. J. C.
Woltersdorf Mrs. Louis
Wood Mrs. Walpole
Woods Mrs. Francis M.
Woodward Mrs. A. W.
Young Mrs. Willis

CHICAGO GOLF CLUB.
Wheaton.

OFFICERS.

Arthur J. Caton,	President.
S. H. Graves,	Captain.
Wm. Prescott Hunt,	Treasurer.
Charles L. Strobel,	Secretary

DIRECTORS.

Arthur J. Caton
Edward L. Ryerson
S. H. Graves

Wm. Prescott Hunt
Charles P. McAvoy
F. A. Keep

Edwar I. Frost
Joseph Leiter
Charles L. Strobel

MEMBERS.

Abbott Sprague
Adam Elizabeth B.
Miss
Aldis Owen F,

Alexander Stuart
R.
Armour Allison V.
Armour George A.

Armour J. Ogden
Armour Philip D.
jr.
Avery Frank M.

Baker Wm. Vincent
Bangs E. W.
Barnes Charles J.
Beale William G,

Bentley Cyrus
Blair Watson F.
Booth W. Vernon
Borden William
Bowles Dwight W.
Bradley John D.
Breese Jacob
Briggs David C.
Broughton Urban H.
Buel Mary Miss
Bull William B.
Bullen Charles F.
Burrows Daniel W.
Butler Herman B.
Cable R. R.
Carrington W. T.
Caton Arthur J.
Chatfield-TaylorH.
C.
Chisholm S. S.
Church Townsend V.
Clark John M.
Clarke E. A. S.
Clarke Florence E. Miss
Cobb W. F.
Cochran J. Lewis
Coleman Joseph G.
Coolidge CharlesA.
Corwith Charles R.
Cotton J. Whitcomb
Cramer E. W.
Cramer Frank
Crerar John
Cummings D. M.
Dawes Chester M.
Deering Charles
Deering Chas.W.C.
Deering James
Dick A. B.
Dudley Peter
Dunn F. K.
Dunne Finley P.
Eckels James H.
Eddy Arthur J.
Ellsworth JamesW.
Ely Arthur C.
Emmett R. S.
Farquhar William R.
Farwell John V. jr.
Favill Henry B. Dr.
Fay C. Norman
Ferguson Edward A.
Fleming, R. H.
Forgan James B.
Forrest E. W.

Frazier F. P.
French George B.
Frost Edward I.
Fullerton C. W.
Gary E. H.
Gibbs James S.
Goodrich A. W.
Gorton F. S.
Gott John R.
Graves S. H.
Grier J. P.
Griffin T. A.
Hamlin Fred R.
Hamlin George
Hamlin Harry L.
Harlan John Maynard
Henrotin Charles
Horton Frederic
Hosmer Arthur B. Dr.
Howard H. A.
Howe R. F.
Howland W. I.
Hulbert E. D.
Hunt Jarvis
Hunt L. Platt Mrs.
Hunt Wm.Prescott
Hynes William J.
Insull Samuel
Isham E. S. jr.
Isham Pierrepont
Jacques Eustace
Johnstone Hugo R.
Jones Helen S. Miss
Keck George S.
Keep F. A.
Keep W. F.
Kenna E. D.
Kennedy V. Shaw
Kimball W. W.
King Francis
King John C.
Kirk Wallace F.
Kittredge Jeanette Miss
Laflin Albert S.
Lamport F. W.
Lathrop Bryan
Lawrence Dwight
Leiter Joseph
LeRoy Stuyvesant
Lincoln John L.
Lincoln Robert T.
Logan John A.
Lowden Frank O.
Macdonald C. A.
Macdonald C. B.
MacdonaldGodfrey
MacVeagh Eames

MacVeagh Franklin
Mair Charles A.
Maitland F. E.
Marsh F. A.
Martin William P.
Matile Herman O.
McAvoy Charles P.
McCormick J. Medill
McCormick L. Hamilton
McCormick R. S.
McDoel W. H.Gen.
McEwan Matthew C.
McKay James R
Medill Joseph
Meeker Arthur
Meeker George W.
Moore J. Hobart
Moore William H.
Morris Howard
Morse Jay C.
Munro William
Neale Alice E. Miss
Northcote A. S.
Norton J. Henry
Pacaud A. L.
Palmer William P.
Parker J. H.
Patterson J. M.
Patterson Rob.
Payson George S.
Payson S. Clifford
Pike Charles B.
Pike Eugene Rockwell
Pike W. W.
Pillsbury Wm. F.
Poor James Harper
Pope R. D.
Pratt E. H. Dr.
Pullman Geo. M.
Quan James E.
Ray Frank H.
Reid Alan LeRoy
Robinson Harry P.
Robinson J. K.
Rockwood F. M. Miss
Rumsey Julian M.
Ryerson Arthur
Ryerson Edward L.
Salisbury W. M.
Schlippenbach Baron Von
Schwartz G. A.
Scudder Arnold
Scull Henry

Seaverns Geo. A.jr.
Shearson Edward.
Shearson H. H.
Sheldon Theodore
ShermanCharlesM.
Shirk E. W.
Smith Byron L.
Smith C. F. Mather
Smith Delavan
Smith Ernest F.
Smith Francis D.
Smith Le Grand
Smith Solomon A.
Smith Walter B.
Spoor John A.
Stephenson Frank B.
Stone Herbert S.
Stone M. E.
Strobel C. L.
Stuart C. U.
Tracy W. W.
Tuttle Emerson B.
Tyson Russell
Valentine E. A.
Valentine John
Valentine P. A.
Van Nortwick John
Vincent W. A.
Wadsworth Helen C. Miss
Waite H. G.
Walker Charles M.
Walker George C.
Walker H. H.
Walker James R.
Walker Samuel Dr.
Walker William B.
Waller Edward C.
Waller James B.
Waller R. A.
Waller Wm.
Warren Paul
Watson John G.
Webster Lewis D.
Wells Frederick L
Wheeler George H
Whigham H. J.
Whitehouse F Meredith
Wilkins Joseph R.
Willits George S.
Wilmerding C. H.
Wilson B. M.
Winston F. H.
Woolley C. M.
Wright Julian V.
Yale Julian L.
Young Arthur
Young W. J. jr.

CHICAGO LITERARY CLUB.
116 AND 118 DEARBORN STREET.

OFFICERS.

HENRY V. FREEMAN, - - - - - - President.
HUNTINGTON W. JACKSON, ⎫
HORACE S. OAKLEY, ⎬ - - Vice-Presidents.
EDWARD P. BAILEY, ⎭
CHARLES F. BRADLEY, - - Corresponding Secretary.
FREDERICK W. GOOKIN, - - Recording Sec. and Treas.
The above officers constitute the Board of Directors.

MEMBERS.

Adams Geo. E.
Adams Joseph
Aldis Owen F.
Allen Chas. L.
Anderson Galusha
  Rev.
Andrews Clement
  W.
Andrews Frank T.
Ayer Benj. F.
Bacon Henry M.
Bailey Edward P.
Bancroft Edgar A.
Barnum Wm. H.
Barrows John H.
Bartlett A. C.
Bates Henry M.
Belfield Henry H.
Belfield Wm. T.
Billings Frank
Bissell Richard M.
Blatchford E. W.
Block Louis J.
Blodgett H. W.
Boutell Henry S.
Boutell Lewis H.
Boyesen Ingolf K.
Bradley Charles F.
Bross Mason
Brown Edward O.
Brown Geo. W.
Burley Clarence A.
Burnham Daniel H.
Canfield Andrew J.
Carman George N.
Case William W.
Cass George W.
Cheney Chas. E.
Churchill Frank S.
Cole John A.
Curtiss Chas. C.
Dauchy Geo. K.
Davis Charles W.
Davis N. S. jr.
Dawson George E.
Delano Frederic A.
Denison Franklin
Dent Thomas
Dudley Emilius C.
Dupee Chas. A.

Eckels James H.
Elliot Frank M.
Fairbank N. K.
Fales David
Farr Marvin A.
Farwell J. V. jr.
Favill Henry B.
Fay Chas. Norman
Fenn Wm. W.
Fisher Walter L.
Fiske Geo. F.
Follansbee George
  A.
Freeman Henry V.
French W. M. R.
Fuller Chas. G.
Fullerton Chas. W.
Furber Henry J., jr.
Furness Wm. Eliot
Gardiner Edwin J.
Glessner John J.
Gookin Fred'k W.
Grant John C.
Greeley Fred'k
Greeley S. S.
Green Oliver B.
Hamill Chas. D.
Hamline John H.
Hardin Martin D.
Harmon Chas. S.
Harper William R.
Harriman Edward A.
Hatch Azel F.
Head Franklin H.
Hebard Frederick S.
Herrick John J.
Hild Fred'k H.
Hirsch Emil G.
Holt Chas. S.
Holt Geo. H.
Horton Oliver H.
Howland George C.
Howland W. M.
Hubbard Joseph D.
Hubbard Wm. H.
Hulburd Chas. H.
Hunter George L.
Hutchinson C. L.
Hyde James Nevins
Isham Edward S.

Jackson H. W.
James Edmund J.
Johnson Frank S.
Jones David B.
Jones Thos. D.
Kales John D.
Keith Edson jr.
Keith Elbridge G.
Larned Walter C.
Lathrop Bryan
Leake Joseph B.
Lee Blewett
Lewis Leslie
Lincoln Robert T.
Lippincott Chas. A.
Little Charles J.
Lloyd Henry D.
Locke Clinton
Long James H.
Lowden Frank O.
Lyman David B.
Lynde Samuel A.
Mack Julian W.
MacVeagh Fr'nklin
Marston Thos. B.
Martin Horace H.
Mason E. G.
Mason Henry B.
Matz Herman L.
Matz Rudolph
McClure J. G. K.
McClurg Alex. C.
McCordie Alfred E.
McCormick Alex. A.
McCormick C. H.
McFadden Parma-
  lee J.
McPherson S. J.
  Rev.
Merriman Henry P.
Messer Loring W.
Miller James A.
Miller John S.
Morse Charles J.
Musgrave Harrison
Nelson Murry
Nelson Murry, jr.
Nixon W. W. K.
Oakley Horace S.
Oppenheim Wm. S.

Otis Ephraim A.
Packard Geo.
Paddock Geo. L.
Paige Alonzo W.
Parkinson Rob't H.
Partridge Newton A
Patrick Hugh T.
Payne Wm. Morton
Peabody Selim H.
Peck George R.
Peirce James H.
Pence Abram M.
Perkins Herbert F.
Petrie Wm. J.
Pond Allen B.
Pond Irving K.
Poole Charles C.
Prentice Sartell
Ridlon John
Rogers Joseph M.
Root Frederic W.
Rosenthal Julius
Rosenthal Lessing
Runnels John S.
Ryerson Martin A.
Salter William M.
Schneider George
Schobinger J. J.
Scott Frank H.
Sheldon Theodore
Sheppard Robt. D.
Shorey Daniel L.
Shorey Paul
Shortall John G.
Shortall John L.
Sidley William P.
Smith Edwin B.
Smith Fred'k B.
Smith Pliny B.
Sprague Albert A.
Starr Merritt
Steele Fred'k M.
Stirling Wm. R.
Stone George F.
Stone James S.
Sullivan Louis H.
Taft Lorado
Taylor Thomas, jr.
Thomas Alfred A.
Thompson Lever'tt

Thompson Slason	Ware Henry A.	Williams Edward	Wolhaupter Benj.
Ullmann Frederic	Waterman Arba N.	F.	Wright Samuel H.
Wait Henry H.	Wegg David S.	Williams Norman	Young A. V. E.
Wait Horatio L..	Wells Arthur B.	Wilson John P.	Zeisler Joseph
Wait James J.	Wheeler Arthur D.	Winslow Wm. H.	Zeisler Sigmund
Walker Wirt D.	Wilkinson John		

THE CHICAGO SOUTH SIDE CLUB.

FIFTIETH STREET NE. COR. MADISON AVENUE.

OFFICERS.

LUCY D. HALL FAKE,	President.
ANNIE ALICE BOND,	First Vice-President.
MARTHA M. NEWKIRK,	Second Vice-President.
FLORA O. CHAPIN,	Recording Secretary.
MARY RYALL LAING,	Corresponding Secretary.
MINNIE A. WATKINS,	Treasurer.

DIRECTORS.

Annie D. Swenson	Josephine M. Smith
Maria F. George	Anna M. Dillman
Florence B. Case	Lucy Sackett Adams

MEMBERS.

Abbott Miss Sara	Byllesby Miss Mary L.	Dudley Mrs. Walter W.
Abbott Mrs. Wm. W.	Caldwell Mrs. Wilfred T.	Earling Mrs. P. R.
Abel Mrs. Jonathan	Carlisle Mrs. Edwin G.	Ecton Mrs. W. B.
Adams Mrs. Chas. E.	Carr Mrs. Latham	Errant Mrs. Jos. W.
Alexander Mrs. John T.	Carter Mrs. L. J.	Fairweather Mrs. Wm.
Alexander Mrs. J. F.	Case Mrs. C. S.	Fake Mrs. Frederick L.
Ambrose Mrs. James	Casey Mrs. Edwin A.	Fake Mrs. F. L. jr.
Anderson Mrs. Joseph	Cassoday Mrs. Eldon J.	Farr Mrs. Albert G.
Arnold Mrs. B. J.	Cate Mrs. Albion	Felt Mrs. F. B.
Baker Mrs. Frank H.	Chandler Mrs. H. H.	Felton Mrs. George G.
Bangs Mrs. John Dean	Chapin Mrs. Joel D.	Field Mrs. Heman H.
Barnes Mrs. A. C.	Chase Mrs. E. S.	Fisher Mrs. A. F.
Bartlett Mrs. George B.	Church Mrs. Bert S.	Fisher Mrs. H. C.
Barton Mrs. Geo. P.	Clark Mrs. Edgar A.	Flersheim Mrs. John P.
Barton Mrs. Jerome K.	Clendenning Mrs. H. T.	Follansbee Mrs. Chas. E.
Becker Mrs. A. W.	Coe Mrs. George A.	Forester Mrs. Geo. L.
Bellows Mrs. F. L.	Coleman Mrs. J. A.	Frazer Mrs. Sara M.
Benedict Mrs. Harry	Conant Mrs. Robert N.	Fuller Mrs. S. R.
Best Mrs. George	Conkling Mrs. B. H.	Gardner Mrs. J. P.
Bettman Mrs. P. H.	Corby Mrs. James	Garty Mrs. M. J.
Biddle Mrs. W. B.	Cox Mrs. Leroy B.	Gauger Mrs. John A.
Black Mrs. Elmer E.	Crandall Mrs. Chester D.	Gaylord Mrs. Henry
Blossom Mrs. Edw. J.	Crary Mrs. Charles W.	George Mrs. Marshall W.
Blossom Mrs. Geo. W.	Curtiss Mrs. Henry	Gibbs Mrs. Platt P.
Bobo Mrs. J. L.	Dana Mrs. Annette P.	Gifford Mrs. Chas.
Bogardus Mrs. H. D.	Day Mrs. Chapin A.	Gifford Mrs. Chas. E.
Bond Mrs. J. H.	Defebaugh Mrs. J. E.	Gillette Mrs. Walter C.
Brachvogel Mrs. Chas. H	Delamater Miss Etta M.	Gordon Mrs. Frank L.
Brintnall Mrs. W. H.	Deming Mrs. H. H.	Gould Mrs. Webster
Brooks Mrs. Almon	Denig Miss Eleanor	Graham Mrs. Beechman
Brooks Mrs. C. M.	Derby Mrs. James D.	Greeley Mrs. S. H.
Brooks Mrs. Oliver	Devitt Mrs. Martin A.	Green Mrs. F. B.
Brown Mrs. Edward C.	Dewar Mrs. Hamilton H.	Grey Mrs. Mary Felton
Browne Miss Lyra	Dickason Mrs. Livingston	Grier Mrs. John A.
Buchanan Mrs. E. P.	Dillman Mrs. Louis M.	Hageman Mrs. Anthony J.
Buel Mrs. Munson P.	Dole Mrs. Walter S.	Hall Mrs. Charles B.
Bunker Mrs. C. H.	Donald Mrs. Francis	Hall Mrs. J. T.
Burke Mrs. Daniel F.	Donnelley Mrs. R. R.	Halsey Mrs. Tappen
Butler Mrs. Frank O.	Dorland Mrs. Edwin H.	Hammond Mrs. Chas. L.
Butler Mrs. J. W.	Downs Mrs. Myron D.	Hammond Mrs. Herbert
Butts Miss Annice E.	Drake Mrs. Lanser J.	Harding Mrs. Chas. F.

Harlan Mrs. A. W.
Harper Mrs. Hartley D.
Harris Mrs. N. W.
Harwood Mrs. H. W.
Hayes Mrs. F. W. C.
Helmer Mrs. F. D.
Hill Miss E. Webster
Hill Mrs. James A.
Hills Mrs. Charles F
Hine Mrs. Lucius A.
Hiner Mrs. Joseph W.
Hoag Mrs. Junius C.
Holt Mrs. Granville M.
Hord Mrs. Geo. M.
Horr Mrs. George B.
Horton Mrs. O. H.
Howe Mrs. F. A.
Howe Mrs. Silas
Hoyt Mrs. Alfred W.
Hull Mrs. Mary H.
Hull Mrs. Perry A.
Hunter Mrs. R. J.-O.
Ingals Miss Elizabeth F.
Ingals Mrs. E. Fletcher
Ingals Miss Mary E.
Irwin Mrs. Harry L.
Isham Mrs. I. N.
James Mrs. James H.
Jaques Mrs. W. K.
Jayne Mrs. Edgar L.
Jennison Mrs. Edward S.
Jones Mrs. Chas A.
Kaufman Mrs. J. H.
Keeler Mrs. C. B.
Keepers Mrs. William E.
Kelley Mrs. Charles B.
Kellogg Mrs. M. G.
Kerr Mrs. Richard H.
Kerr Mrs. W. R.
Keyes Mrs. David H.
King Mrs. Frank B.
Kistler Mrs. D. A.
Knight Mrs. Anna W.
Laing Mrs. John R.
Lathrop Mrs. Edward B.
Lawrence Mrs. George W.
Letton Mrs. Theodore
LeVally Mrs. J. R.
Lewis Mrs. E. H.
Lewis Mrs. W. G.
Lindsay Mrs. David J.
Livermore Mrs. Chas.
　　Field
Lockwood Mrs. Henry
Lord Mrs. Daniel M.
Lord Mrs. John B.
Love Mrs. Charles G.
Lytton Mrs. Henry C.
MacCracken Mrs. W. P.
Mansure Mrs. Edmund L.
Marshall Mrs. Wm.
Martin Mrs. Daniel
Mather Mrs. Robert
McArthur Mrs. Warren
McChesney Mrs. Jas. B.
McConnell Mrs. Chas. H.

McConnell Miss Cora
Meads Mrs. Albert H.
Middendorf Mrs. George
Millard Mrs. Martha W.
Milligan Mrs. George D.
Mills Mrs. Morris E.
Milner Miss Louise A.
Mitchell Mrs. Margaret A.
Monroe Mrs. Nelson
Morris Mrs. Charles
Morse Mrs. Alice Scofield
Morse Mrs. C. H.
Nellegar Mrs. J. B.
Nelson Mrs. Walter C.
Newberry Mrs. Walter F.
Newkirk Mrs. Garrett
Newman Mrs. G. E.
Nicholas Mrs. Robert
Norton Mrs. Oliver
Olds Mrs. Walter
Orr Mrs. Frank B.
Otis Mrs. Frank C.
Otis Mrs. T. G.
Palmer Mrs. P. B.
Parker Mrs. J. Grafton
Parker Mrs. J. J.
Parmly Mrs. S. P.
Parrotte Mrs. Walter L.
Payne Mrs. John Barton
Pearson Mrs. Eugene H.
Perkins Mrs. V. D.
Perry Mrs. D. P.
Phillips Mrs. Chas.
Pickering Mrs. A. H.
Pope Mrs. Henry A.
Pratt Mrs. Ralph E.
Purcell Mrs. Wm. A.
Purdy Miss Sallie E.
Purdy Mrs. William A.
Reed Mrs. Alanson Henry
Reed Mrs. F. S.
Reed Mrs. Hugh T.
Reed Miss Winifred
Reynolds Mrs. William J.
Rhodes Mrs. James H.
Richards Mrs. L. C.
Richter Mrs. Paul K.
Ricker Mrs. Frederick K.
Riggs Mrs. George W.
Rimington Mrs. Hugh H.
Ristine Mrs. Geo. W.
Robinson Mrs. Chas. O.
Robinson Mrs. John C.
Rockwell Mrs. Chas. H.
Rogers Mrs. Clara T.
Rogers Mrs. John J.
Rothermel Mrs. W. E.
Schmidt Mrs. Oscar F.
Schuhmann Mrs. Henry H.
Schuhmann Mrs. Herman
Scribner Mrs. Chas. E.
Sedgwick Mrs. Edwin H.
Shattuck Mrs. Geo. B.
Shattuck Mrs. L. Brace
Shepard Mrs. Helen F.
Sherman Mrs. Mark R.

Sherman Mrs. Penoyer L.
Shourds Mrs. C. B.
Sidway Mrs. Henry T.
Sills Mrs. E. P.
Sills Mrs. Wm. H.
Simpson Mrs. Irwin
Skinner Mrs. E. L.
Smith Mrs. Howard L.
Smith Mrs. Jacob S.
Smith Mrs. Lewis M.
Somers Mrs. Edgar L.
Spencer Mrs. Aaron Page
Spencer Mrs. Wm. E.
Sprogle Mrs. Howard O.
Stevens Mrs. Wm. G.
Stewart Mrs. B. F.
Sumner Mrs. Henry A.
Swain Mrs. Edgar D.
Swenson Mrs. Magnus
Teller Mrs. James H.
Terhune Mrs B. F.
Thayer Mrs. Henry J.
Thomas Mrs. Benjamin
Thomas Mrs. George
Thomas Miss Harriet E.
Thomas Mrs. Leslie D.
Thompson Mrs. Mary W.
Titus Mrs Gardner P.
Turner Mrs. Edward A.
Valentine Mrs. Gordon
VanUxem Mrs. James L.
VanWoert Mrs. G. E.
Viets Mrs. John B.
Walden Mrs. Hugh P.
Wallace Mrs. John F.
Wallace Mrs. Peter
Ware Mrs. Elisha
Warner Mrs. James M.
Warren Mrs. Chas. M.
Warren Mrs. C. D.
Warwick Mrs. George W.
Watkins Mrs. George
Webster Mrs. C. O.
Welch Mrs. Leon C.
Wells Mrs. Edward F.
Wells Mrs. Willis J.
Wheeler Mrs. W. H.
Whipple Mrs. Chas. B.
White Mrs. Jere S.
White Mrs. W. F.
Whiteman Mrs. Sarah C.
Williams Mrs. Dyke
Williamson Mrs. Wm.
Wilson Mrs. Chas. L.
Wilson Mrs. E. Crane
Wilson Mrs. W. M.
Winchester Mrs. Chas. J
Wolseley Mrs. Henry W.
Woodruff Mrs. Edward
Woods Mrs. Helen M.
Worley Mrs. Brice
Wright Mrs. Mary E.
Young Mrs. Frank
Young Mrs. Wm. A.
Yount Mrs. Silas T.

CHICAGO WOMAN'S CLUB.

203-207 MICHIGAN AVENUE.

OFFICERS.

LOUISE DICKINSON SHERMAN, - - - President.
CLARA M. J. FARSON, - - First Vice-President.
LUCY F. FURNESS, - - - - Second Vice-President.
NANNIE W. RAWSON, - - Corresponding Secretary.
M. J. R. TYLER, - - - - Recording Secretary.
MARY F. VAN VOORHIS, - - - - - Treasurer.

DIRECTORS.

Edith C. Hancock
Nellie Robb Collins
Cecelia Hedenberg
Caroline L. Hamilton
Frances Whidden
Harriett A. Fox
Clara Wilson Kretzinger

Jessie Willard Bolte
Emily J. Keith
Ella M. Blatchford
Marian Burton Upton
Isabel McDougall
Mary E. Bundy

Adele F. Adams
Emily L. Alling
Zella Allen Dixson
Caroline S. Twyman
Florence Potter Seaton

MEMBERS.

Abbott Mrs. A. C.
Abbott Mrs. A. R.
Abbott Mrs. Wm. Warner
Ackert Mrs. C. H.
Adam Mrs. Alexander B.
Adams Mrs. Chas. A.
Adams Mrs. Egerton
Adams Mrs. Elvira H.
Adams Mrs. E. S.
Adams Mrs. Geo. E.
Adams Mrs. John R.
Addams Miss Jane
Adkinson Mrs. Elmer W.
Affeld Mrs. Charles E.
Aldis Mrs. Arthur T.
Alexander Miss Ellen C.
Alexander Dr. H. C. B.
Allerton Mrs. Samuel
Alling Mrs. Edward H.
Altgeld Mrs. John P.
American Miss Sadie
Andrews Mrs. Fargo
Andrews Mrs. James
Andrews Miss Katherine
Angell Dr. Katharine
Annis Mrs. Frank M.
Arnold Mrs. Charles C
Atkins Mrs. F. L.
Ayer Mrs. Edward
Babcock Miss Ethel
Babcock Mrs. Henry H.
Babcock Miss Mabel K.
Bacon Miss Georgia
Bacon Mrs. Moses S.
Badger Mrs. Horace H.
Bagg Mrs. Frank S.
Bagley Mrs. Frederick P.
Baird Mrs. Wyllys W.
Baker Mrs. Alfred L.
Baker Mrs. Charles S.
Baker Mrs. Frank H.
Baker Mrs. Wilson G.
Ball Mrs. Farlin Q.

Bangs Mrs. John D.
Barbour Mrs. Lyman L.
Barker Mrs. Cyrus A.
Barnes Miss Minnie W.
Barnes Mrs. Nelson H.
Barnum Mrs. Wm. L.
Bartelme Miss Mary M.
Bartlett Mrs. Geo. F.
Bass Mrs. George
Bassett Mrs. Fletcher S.
Bates Mrs. H. M.
Bates Mrs. Lindon W.
Bayley Mrs. Edwin F.
Becker Mrs. Frederick W.
Bedell Leila G., M.D.
Beebe Mrs. Emma A.
Beedy Miss Mary E.
Beers Mrs. J. H.
Belden Mrs. J. S.
Belfield Miss Ada Marshall
Belfield Mrs. H. H.
Bell Miss Lilian
Bellamy Mrs. Henry C.
Bennet Mrs. Will H.
Bettman Mrs. Boerne
Bigelow Mrs. Edward A.
Bigelow Mrs. James L.
Billings Mrs. C. K. G.
Billings Mrs. Henry F.
Blackman Mrs. Carlos H.
Blackman Mrs. Edwin
Blackwelder Mrs. I. S.
Blatchford Mrs. N. H.
Blodgett Miss Carrie A.
Blood Miss Emma S.
Bloomingston Mrs. J. S.
Bodman Mrs. Albert C.
Bolté Mrs. Charles Guy
Booth Miss Rachel M.
Borland Mrs. John J.
Bower Mrs. R. A.
Boyesen Mrs. Janie S.

Bradwell Mrs. Thomas
Brainard Mrs. Harriet C.
Brewer Mrs. John S.
Brine Mrs. George J.
Brodlique Miss Eve H.
Brooks Mrs. James C.
Broomell Mrs. Geo. D.
Brown Mrs. E. O.
Brown Mrs. Wm. T.
Brown Mrs. W. L.
Bruce Mrs. E. M.
Bryan Miss Anna E.
Bryant Mrs. John J.
Brydon Mrs. Robt. T.
Buckingham Mrs. John
Buckingham Mrs. Jno. H.
Bundy Mrs. John C.
Burnett Anna Louise
Burnham Mrs. Telford
Burt Miss Mary E.
Bush Mrs. Wm. H.
Butler Mrs. A. O.
Butlin Mrs. M.
Butterfield Mrs. Wm. W.
Butts Miss Annice E. Bradford
Calder Mrs. L. A.
Campbell Miss Mary R.
Campbell Mrs. Wm. J.
Carman Mrs. George N.
Carpenter Mrs. A. A.
Carpenter Mrs. Frederic I.
Carpenter Mrs. Geo. B.
Carpenter Miss Marian L.
Carpenter Mrs. Wm. O.
Carse Mrs. Matilda B.
Carton Mrs. Laurence A.
Cary Mrs. Frank
Chadwick Miss Mary G.
Chalmers Mrs. W. J.
Chapin Mrs. A. B.
Chapman Mrs. Jas. R.
Chapman Mrs. W. S.

Chappell Mrs. Henry W.
Cheney Mrs. John Vance
Chisholm Mrs. James
Chittenden Mrs. Nellie M
Churchill Mrs. Frank S.
Clapp Mrs. George
Clapp Miss Anna C.
Clark Mrs. Alson E.
Clark Mrs. Andrew G.
Clark Mrs. Edgar A.
Clark Mrs. George M.
Clark Miss Hannah B.
Clark Dr. Margaret V.
Clarkson Mrs. Phillip
Clinton Mrs. George O.
Cloud Mrs. John W.
Clow Mrs. Wm. E.
Coburn Mrs. L. L.
Coddington Mrs. A. O.
Coffin Mrs. Arthur S.
Coffin Mrs. Charles F.
Coffin Mrs. Charles H.
Coleman Mrs. J. A.
Coleman Mrs. W. Franklin
Collins Mrs. Lorin C. jr.
Colvin Miss Katharine
Coman Mrs. Martha S.
Conant Mrs. Luther
Conger Mrs. Wm. Perry
Conover Mrs. Charles H.
Conrad Mrs. J. Henry
Cooke Mrs. A. B.
Cooke Mrs. A. H.
Cooley Mrs. Harlan W.
Coolidge Mrs. F. S.
Coonley Miss Sarah
Cooper Mrs. Harry H.
Corby Mrs. Emily
Corey Mrs. G. J.
Corneau Mrs. D. E.
Coulter Miss Hortense
Cox Mrs. Charles E.
Cox Mrs. LeRoy B.
Coy Mrs. Reuben D.
Crane Mrs. Charles R.
Crane Mrs. Herbert P.
Crane Mrs. R. T.
Crane Mrs. Simeon H.
Crepin Mrs. Ernest E.
Cronise Miss Caroline C.
Cropp Mrs. Carl
Crouse Mrs. J. N.
Crow Mrs. Martha F.
Cummings Mrs. C. C.
Currier Miss Evelyn B.
Curtis Mrs. J. Harvey
Curtis Mrs. J. LaFayette
Cushing Mrs. Frederic W.
Cutler Mrs. Charles H.
Dainty Mrs. Albert H.
Davidson Mrs. Ada D.
Davidson Mrs. S. Frank
Davis Mrs. Charles G.
Davis Mrs. Charles W.
Delano Mrs. F. A.
Dempster Miss Nellie A.

Dennis Mrs. Charles S.
deWindt Mrs. H. A.
DeWolf Mrs. Wallace R.
Dickey Mrs. E. M.
Dickinson Dr. Frances
Dickinson Mrs. Frederick
Dietz Mrs. Jacob C.
Dillman Mrs. Louis M.
Dingee Miss Gertrude P.
Dixon Miss Clara L.
Dixon Mrs. L. B.
Dixson Mrs. Zella A.
Donald Mrs. Francis C.
Donnelley Mrs. R. H.
Doud Mrs. L. B.
Dow Mrs. Wm. Carey
Dreier Mrs. Carl
Dresden Mrs. W. Wallace
Driver Mrs. Edward A.
Duncanson Mrs. H. W.
Dunn Mrs. John O.
Dupee Mrs. E. W.
Durand Miss Frances E.
Durgin Mrs. John C.
Eagle Mrs. James E.
Eastman Mrs. S. C.
Edwards Miss Alice
Edwards Mrs. Arthur
Edwards Miss Grace
Edwards Mrs. J. A.
Effinger Mrs. John R.
Ela Mrs. John W.
Elmes Mrs. Chas. F.
Emery Mrs. Theodore
Engleman Miss Emma
Englemann Dr. Rosa
Ernst Mrs. Edward F.
Estabrook Mrs. Henry D.
Evald Mrs. Emmy C.
Evans Mrs. Lynden
Fairbanks Mrs. Geo. Otis
Fake Mrs. Frederick L.
Farnham Mrs. R. E.
Farnsworth Mrs. Geo. J.
Farr Mrs. Marvin A.
Farson Mrs. R. B.
Farwell Mrs. J. A.
Fay Mrs. J. B.
Fearing Miss L. Blanche
Ferguson Mrs. W. G.
Ferry Mrs. James W.
Fessenden Mrs. Benj. A.
Finch Mrs. Hunter W.
Fischer Mrs. A. C.
Fiske Mrs. George F.
Fitch Mrs. Henry S.
Fitz Simons Mrs. Chas.
Flemming Miss Martha
Flood Miss Nellie J.
Flower Mrs. James M.
Follansbee Mrs. Geo. A.
Ford Mrs. Mary H.
Forsyth Mrs. Wm.
Fox Miss Harriott A.
Fox Dr. Bonham M.
Foye Mrs. Jeanette W.

Frake Mrs. James
Frank Mrs. Henry L.
Frank Mrs. Louis
Freeman Mrs. Henry V.
Fry Mrs. Henry T.
Fry Mrs. Thomas E.
Fulton Mrs. J. L.
Furber Mrs. H. J.
Furness Mrs. Wm. Eliot
Furness Miss Elizabeth M.
Fyffe Dr. Edith A. H.
Gane Miss Gertrude
Gane Mrs. Thomas F.
Garnett Mrs. Gwynn
Gartz Mrs. A. F.
Gilbert Mrs. Frank
Gilbert Mrs. James H.
Gilman Mrs. J. E.
Girling Mrs. Winthrop
Givins Mrs. Robert C.
Glaspell Mrs. Albert
Goff Mrs. Guy D.
Gorton Miss Belle L.
Granger Mrs. Wm. S.
Graves Mrs. Dwight W.
Graves Mrs. James T.
Graves Mrs. John M.
Graves Miss Martha L.
Graves Miss Sarah L.
Greele Miss Louisa M.
Greeley Mrs. Louis M.
Green Mrs. Augustus W.
Green Miss Mary P.
Greenleaf Mrs. Walter G.
Gregory Mrs. George D.
Gridley Mrs. Nelson C.
Griffith Mrs. Herbert E.
Griggs Miss Alice L.
Gross Mrs. J. Ellsworth
Gross Mrs. Samuel E.
Gunther Mrs. Chas. F.
Hageman Mrs. Anthony J.
Hagerty Mrs. Thomas A.
Haire Miss Anna R.
Hale Mrs. Geo. W.
Hall Mrs. Frederick H.
Hall Mrs. Hermon J.
Hall Miss Matilda C.
Hallberg Mrs. L. G.
Haller Mrs. G. Morris
Halsted Miss N.
Hamilton Mrs. Henry E.
Hammer Mrs. D. Harry
Hammond Mrs. L. D.
Hancock Mrs. Bradford
Handy Mrs. Henry H.
Harding Mrs. Addie C.
Harding Mrs. Charles F.
Harding Mrs. George F.
Harris Mrs. Rachel A.
Harrison Miss Elizabeth
Harvey Mrs. George V.
Harvey Mrs. J. D.
Harvey Mrs. Wm. P.
Harwood Mrs. Henry W.

Haskell Mrs. Geo. W.
Hastings Mrs. T. D.
Haworth Mrs. Geo. D.
Hayt Mrs. Henry C.
Head Miss Elizabeth
Head Miss Katherine
Heard Mrs. Dwight B.
Hedenberg Miss Cecilia
Heile Mrs. Adolf
Heisen Mrs. C. C.
Helmer Mrs. F. A.
Henderson Mrs. C. R.
Henrotin Mrs. Charles
Hequembourg Mrs. J. E.
Herrick Mrs. James B.
Hervey Mrs. James
Heywood Mrs. F. S.
Heywood Mrs. P. P.
Hibbard Mrs. W. N.
Hickman Mrs. Henry A.
Hicks Mrs. Oliver H.
Hiestand Mrs. Henry
Higgins Mrs. Milton O.
Higginson Mrs.CharlesM.
Hill Mrs. J. M.
Himrod Mrs. Charles
Himrod Miss Phebe
Hinckley Mrs. Chas. W.
Hinckley Mrs. James O.
Hitchcock Mrs. Charles
Hobart Mrs. Horace R.
Hobbs Mrs. James B.
Hodges Mrs. Walter E.
Holbrook Mrs. Amelia W.
Holden Mrs. T. N.
Holmes Mrs. Bayard
Holmes Mrs. Mary E.
Holt Mrs. Granville M.
Holton Mrs. E.
Hoppin Mrs. Bush E.
Horton Mrs. Henry B.
Hosmer Miss Eliza
Hosmer Mrs. Frank B.
Hosmer Mrs. J. W.
Hotchkiss Dr. Isabella S
Howard Mrs. Thomas
Howe Mrs. F. S.
Howe Mrs. Willis
Howell Mrs. S. R.
Hoyt Mrs. Henry W.
Hoyt Mrs. Wm.
Huddlestone Mrs. K. G.
Hughes Mrs. John B.
Hunt Dr. Florence W.
Hutchins Mrs. E. R.
Hutchinson Miss F. C.
Ingals Mrs. E. Fletcher
Jackman Mrs.Wilbur S.
Jay Mrs. Milton
Jenney Mrs. H. W.
Jewell Mrs. C. VanSiclen
Johnson Miss A. Blanche
Johnson Mrs. Edw. S.
Johnson Mrs. Frank A.
Johnson Mrs. Frank S.
Johnson Mrs. Willis F.

Johnston Mrs. Jas. B.
Jones Mrs. George H.
Jones Mrs. Jenkins L.
Jones Miss Katherine A.
Judah Mrs. Noble B.
Judd Miss Susan Alice
Judson Mrs. W. B.
Kales Mrs. John D.
Keeling Mrs. Francis, jr.
Keen Mrs. Edwin H.
Keen Mrs. W. B. jr.
Keepers Mrs. Wm. E.
Kelth Mrs. Elbridge
Keith Mrs. James E.
Kelley Mrs. Florence
Kendall Mrs. Benj. W.
Kendig Mrs. J. A. J.
Kennedy Mrs. Horace M.
Kent Mrs. William
Kett Mrs. H. F.
Keyes Mrs. Rollin A.
King Mrs. Philo R.
Kingman Mrs. Chas. H.
Kinnear Miss Margaret
Kirkland Miss Cordelia
Kirkwood Mrs. A. J.
Knapp Mrs. John A.
Knight Mrs. Wm. M.
Kohlsaat Mrs. HermanH.
Kretschmar Mrs. H. S.
Kretzinger Mrs. Geo. W.
Krout Miss Mary H.
Kuh Mrs. Edwin J.
Kuh Mrs. Henry
Lacy Miss Sara
Laing Mrs. John R.
Lane Mrs. Albert G.
Lane Miss Ida M.
Lasher Mrs. C. W.
Latham Mrs. Carlton R.
Lathrop Miss Julia C.
Leavens Miss Julia P.
LeBaron Mrs. William
LeBaron Miss Frances
Lee Mrs. Frederick W.
Lee Mrs. J. O.
Leman Mrs. Henry W.
Leopold Mrs. Max
Lewis Mrs. Leslie
Lewis Miss Marian M.
Libby Mrs. C. P.
Linn Mrs. Wm. R.
Lloyd Mrs. Henry D.
Lobdell Mrs. Edwin L.
Lobdell Mrs. Harry H.
Logan Mrs. Frank G.
Lombard Mrs. Isaac G.
Lombard Mrs. Josiah
Long Mrs. James H.
Loomis Mrs. M. B.
Loose Mrs. Jacob L.
Loring Mrs. Malek A.
Love Miss Ella L.
Loveday Mrs. Fannie M.
Low Dr. Julia Ross
Luce Mrs. Franklin

Lumm Miss Emma G.
Lyford Mrs. Will Hartw'l
Lyon Dr. Ellen H.
Lyon Mrs. George W.
MacArthur Mrs. Archibald
MacArthur Mrs. A. F.
MacArthur Miss F. B.
Magee Mrs. Henry W.
Mandel Mrs. Emanuel
Mang Mrs. Albert G.
Mann Mrs. James R.
Manierre Mrs. Wm. R.
Marguerat Mrs. Eugene
Marsh Mrs. James P.
Marsh Mrs. Wm. D.
Marshall Mrs. Geo. E.
Martin Miss Ellen A.
Martin Mrs. Franklin H.
Martin Mrs J. Motte
Martin Mrs. S. K.
Marvin Mrs. William
Mason Mrs. Wm. A.
Mather Mrs. Alonzo C.
Matson Mrs. Canute R.
Matz Mrs. Otto H.
Maxwell Mrs. E. E.
Mayer Mrs. Levy
McBean Mrs. A. J.
McConnell Mrs.LutherW.
McCrea Mrs. James
McCrea Mrs. Willis S.
McCulloch Mrs. C. W.
McDougall Miss Isabel
McDowell Miss Mary E.
McEntee Mrs. Chas. S.
McGraw Mrs. Jeremiah W.
McLeish Mrs. Andrew
McMahan Mrs. R. W.
McMahan Miss Una
Mergler Dr. Marie J.
Merrill Mrs. Anthony F.
Metcalf Mrs. Herbert C.
Michaels Miss Sara D.
Middendorf Mrs. Geo.
Millard Mrs. S. M.
Miller Mrs. A. C.
Miller Mrs. Charles P.
Millington Mrs. L. B.
Milner Miss Louisa A.
Milsted Mrs. Thos. G.
Mitchell Mrs. J. Sidney
Mitchell Mrs. L. B.
Mixer Dr. Mary A.
Montgomery Mrs. Frank H.
Montgomery Mrs.Wm. A.
Moore Mrs. James H.
Moore Mrs. James S.
Moore Mrs. John W.
Moore Mrs William H.
Morford Mrs. T. T.
Morgan Miss Anna
Morris Mrs. Thomas G.
Murray Mrs. L. W.

Nagle Mrs. Aug. F.
Neale Miss Alice E.
Nelson Miss Josephine
Nelson Mrs. Murry Jr.
Nelson Mrs. Walter C.
Nevers Mrs. Edward
Newman Mrs. Jacob
Nixon Mrs. Wm. Penn
Nolan Mrs. John H.
North Mrs. C. A.
North Mrs. R. L.
Norton Mrs. Edwin
Norton Mrs. Henry M.
Norton Mrs. O. W.
Noyes Mrs. LaVerne W.
O'Connor Mrs. John
Odell Mrs. J. J. P.
Olson Mrs. N. F.
Ostrander Mrs. D.
Packard Mrs. George
Page Mrs. C. L.
Pajeau Mrs. Joseph
Palmer Mrs. Potter
Pancoast Mrs. J. Cameron
Parker Mrs. Francis W.
Parker Mrs. J. J.
Parker Mrs. Lewis W.
Patrick Mrs. Hugh T.
Payne Miss Bertha
Peabody Mrs. S. H.
Peattie Mrs. Robert B.
Peck Mrs. Clarence I.
Peck Mrs. Ferdinand W.
Peck Mrs. Walter L.
Peckham Mrs. Orville
Peirce Mrs. Arthur H.
Peirce Mrs. L. H.
Penfield Mrs. Truman
Perce Mrs. L. W.
Perkins Mrs. Dwight
Perkins Mrs. V. D.
Perry Mrs. Frederick B.
Peters Mrs. W. Morgan
Pettibone Mrs. A. G.
Pettibone Mrs. Howard
Pettibone Mrs. Philo F.
Phelps Mrs. Erskjne M.
Phelps Mrs. O. B.
Pierce Mrs. Chas F.
Pittman Mrs. Clement K.
Plummer Mrs. G. W.
Plummer Mrs. J. W.
Pope Mrs. Charles B.
Porter Mrs. Edward C.
Porter Mrs. James F.
Potter Mrs. Edwin A.
Potter Mrs. O. W.
Potter Mrs. W. L.
Potwin Mrs. William S.
Pratt Mrs. Ralph E.
Pratt Mrs. Sarah W.
Preble Mrs. Robert H.
Preston Mrs. E. B.
Price Mrs. Frank
Prindle Mrs. Jason R.
Pryor Mrs. Gilbert

Purdy Miss Sara C.
Putnam Mrs. Joseph R.
Rand Mrs. John C.
Rawson Mrs. Hart
Raymond Mrs. Chas. L.
Raynolds Mrs. James D.
Reed Mrs. Charles B.
Reed Mrs. Earl H.
Reed Mrs. Frank F.
Reed Mrs. George J.
Reed Mrs. H. V.
Reid Mrs. Wm. H.
Remick Mrs. Marie C.
Rice Miss Rebecca S.
Richardson Mrs. A. P.
Richardson Mrs. Chas. J.
Richardson Mrs. D. E.
Rickcords Mrs. Geo. E.
Ripley Mrs. Edward P.
Robbins Mrs. Walter R.
Robinson Mrs. John K.
Rogers Mrs. James C.
Rogers Mrs. John G.
Rohde Mrs. H. F.
Roler Mrs. E. O. F.
Roper Mrs. Edward U.
Rowe Mrs. Chas. H.
Rowe Miss Elizabeth L.
Rowe Mrs. James L.
Russell Mrs. Edmund A.
Ryerson Mrs. Martin A.
Salter Mrs. Wm. M.
Sands Mrs. O.
Sawyer Mrs. C. B.
Sawyer Mrs. Francis A.
Saxton Mrs. Hester B.
Schoyer Mrs. Ernest A.
Scott Mrs. Frank H.
Scott Mrs. James W.
Scribner Mrs. Charles E.
Sears Mrs. Nathaniel C.
Seaton Mrs. Chauncey E.
Seaverns Mrs. Geo. A.
Seaverns Mrs. Geo. A. jr.
Seavey Mrs. D. H.
Seckel Mrs. Albert
Seeberger Mrs. Louis A.
Selz Mrs. J. Harry
Shackleford Mrs. Charles
Shackleton Mrs. A.
Shaffer Mrs. J. C.
Shattuck Mrs. L. B.
Shaw Mrs. Gilbert B.
Shears Mrs. G. F., M.D.
Shepard Mrs. Frank
Sheppard Mrs. Thos. H.
Sheridan Mrs. W. A.
Sherman Mrs. E. B.
Sherman Mrs. John jr.
Sherman Mrs. John D.
Sherman Mrs. Penoyer L.
Sherwood Mrs. E. L.
Sherwood Mrs. Jo n B.
Sherwood Mrs. Mark
Shoemaker Mrs. Walter
Shorey Mrs. D. L.

Shorey Mrs. Paul
Shortall Mrs. John L.
Sill Mrs. Robert T.
Simmons Mrs. F. T.
Smith Mrs. Byron L.
Smith Mrs. Calvin S.
Smith Miss Clara A.
Smith Mrs. Clara R.
Smith Mrs. Frederick A.
Smith Mrs. Fred. Mather
Smith Mrs. George W.
Smith Miss Helen Page
Smith Mrs. Henry J.
Smith Mrs. Horace S.
Smith Dr. Julia Holmes
Smith Mrs. Lewis M.
Smith Miss Mary Rozet
Smith Mrs. Perry H.
Smith Mrs. Procter
Smoot Mrs. Kenneth R.
Smyth Mrs. John G.
Snively Miss Anna M.
Solger Mrs. P. K.
Solomon Mrs. Henry
Somerville Mrs. Robert
Soper Mrs. James
Southwell Mrs. Henry E.
Spear Mrs. A. A.
Spicer Mrs. George A.
Spicer Mrs. V. K.
Sprague Mrs. A. A.
Springer Miss Ada E.
Spry Mrs. John C.
Squire Miss Mary E.
Stafford Miss Juniata
Stanley Mrs. Caroline E.
Stanton Mrs. Edgar
Stanton Mrs. S. Cecil
Starkey Mrs. Horace M.
Starkweather Mrs. Frank H.
Starin Mrs. Wm. A.
Starr Miss Ellen Gates
Starr Miss Helen
Starr Mrs. Merritt
Starrett Mrs. Helen E.
Steele Mrs. D. A. K.
Steiniger Mrs. S.
Stephens Mrs. Louise B.
Sterling Mrs. Chas. J.
Stettler Dr. Cornelia S.
Stevenson Mrs. Alex. F.
Stevenson Dr. Sarah H.
Stiles Miss Lucy Goddard
Stirling Mrs. Wm. R.
Stone Mrs. Henry B.
Stone Mrs. Melville E.
Straight Mrs. Lewis C.
Straus Mrs. Michael
Streeter Mrs John W.
Strong Mrs. E. B.
Studebaker Mrs. Jacob H.
Sturges Mrs. George
Sturges Miss Marion D.
Summers Miss Maud
Swan Mrs. O. S.

Sweet Miss Ada C.
Talbot Mrs. Eugene S.
Taylor Mrs. Homer S.
Taylor Mrs. S. G.
Temple Miss Alice
Temple Miss Grace E.
Tenney Miss Mary S.
Thatcher Mrs. Solomon
Thayer Mrs. Nathaniel C.
Thomas Mrs. Benjamin
Thomas Mrs. Charles G.
Thomas Mrs. Herbert A.
Thomas Mrs. John W.
Thompson Mrs.Wm.Hale
Thorne Mrs. George R.
Thurber Mrs. George S.
Tilt Miss Maud M.
Tilton Miss Catherine P.
Tilton Mrs. Lucian
Tisdale Mrs. Laura J.
Trippe Mrs. Martha G.W.
Tucker Mrs. Luther K.
Tuley Mrs. M. F.
Turner Mrs. W. D.
Twyman Mrs. Joseph
Tyler Mrs. Harvey A.
Tyler Mrs. Wm. H.
Ullmann Mrs. Frederick
Underhill Mrs. Elizabeth
Upton Mrs. Edward L.
Upton Mrs. George P.
VanBenschoten Mrs.M.C.
VanNortwick Mrs. Wm.
Van Voorhis Mrs. Frank
Vaughan Mrs. J. C.
Vaughan Miss Mary E.

Viles Mrs. James
Vollmer Mrs. A. F.
Wagg Mrs. Howard N.
Wait Mrs. Horatio L.
Waite Dr. Lucy
Wakeman Mrs. A. V. H.
Waldo Mrs. Otis H.
Waldron Mrs. Louis K.
Wallace Mrs. James
Wallace Mrs. M. R. M.
Walsh Mrs. John R.
Walter Mrs. J. C.
Wanzer Mrs. James M.
Ward Mrs. Carlos J.
Ward Mrs. L. A. Coonley
Ware Mrs. Henry A.
Warner Mrs. William C.
Washburn Miss Emily L.
Washburn Mrs. Wm. D.
Washburne Mrs. Geo. F.
Watson Mrs. I. A.
Wegg Mrs. David S.
Weidner Mrs. R F.
Welch Mrs. Wm. M.
Welling Mrs. John C.
Wells Mrs. Frank
Wells Mrs. Robert M.
West Mrs. James J.
Weston Mrs. Olive E.
Wetherell Mrs. Oscar D.
Whedon Mrs. James P.
Wheeler Mrs. C. G.
Wheeler Mrs. Sarah E.
Whidden Mrs. Geo. F.
Whitcomb Miss Adele

White Mrs. Katharine F.
White Miss Wilomene T.
Whiteford Mrs. David
Whitney Mrs. Charles P.
Whitney Mrs. John B.
Wiggin Mrs. Edward J.
Wiles Mrs. Robert H.
Wiley Mrs. Edward N.
Wilder Mrs. Charles L.
Wilkinson Mrs. John
Willard Mrs. Charles E.
Willard Miss Mary F.
Willard Mrs. P. H.
Willard Dr. Rose
Williams Mrs. Fannie B.
Williams Mrs. Stalham L.
Wilmarth Mrs. H. M.
Wilson Mrs. E. Crane
Wilson Mrs. John P.
Wilson Mrs. John R.
Winslow Mrs. W. H.
Withrow Mrs. Thomas F.
Wood Mrs. Casey A.
Wood Dr. Emma Caswell
Wood Mrs. Milton R.
Woodward Miss FannieP.
Woodward Mrs. Geo. W.
Woodward Mrs. James L.
Woodyatt Mrs. W. H.
Woolley Mrs. J. H.
Worthy Mrs. John
Wygant Mrs. Alonzo
Young Mrs. Ella F.
Young Mrs. H. P.
Zeisler Mrs. Fannie B.

COLUMBUS CLUB.

43 AND 45 MONROE STREET.

OFFICERS.

D. F. BREMNER, - - - - - - President.
MICHAEL W. PHALEN, - - - - First Vice-President.
JOHN C. SCHUBERT, - - - - Second Vice-President.
H. V. HAYES, - - - - - - - Secretary.
HENRY R. EAGLE - - - - - - Treasurer.

DIRECTORS.

M. W. Murphy   Joseph Donnersberger   J. Ward Amberg
J. J. Egan   P. T. Barry   E. O. Brown

MEMBERS.

Agnew John P.
Amberg John H.
Amberg J. Ward
Amberg Theo. J.
Amberg W. A.
Barry P. T.
Bauerle Michael
Beauvais Elzear A.
Bransfield M. J.
Bremner D. F.
Bremner D. F. jr.
Brenan Thos.
Brennan J. J.

Brenock John
Bryant Moses
Brosseau Aug.
Brosseau Z. P.
Brown Edward O.
Brueckner J. F.
Buerlbach Rev.
Francis
Bush H. W.
Byrne J. P.
Cashman Rev. T.F.
Clifford R. W.
Conley Dr. P. H.

Conley Dr. T. J.
Corboy M. J.
Creedon A. L.
Cremin Jno. F.
Cudahy John
Cudahy Michael
Cunningham W. H.
Dalton Jno. E.
Delaney Daniel
Donnersberger Jos.
Donohue M. A.
Driscoll Dr. J. J.
Duddleston Geo.

Duffy Jno. M.
Dunne Edward F.
Dunne Rev. R.
Eagle Harry R.
Egan J. J.
Egan M. F.
Faherty Michael J.
Green A. W.
Guerin Thomas E.
Hayes David
Hayes H. V.
Hayes John
Healy P. J.

Heissler Jacob	McBride D. H.	Murphy M. W.	Ryan M. W.
HeldmannRev.GD.	McDougald A. W.	Murray Rev. B. P.	Schubert John C.
Henneberry W. P.	McGuire Wm. A.	Nally E. J.	Sexton John
Hinsdale W. R.	McKindley D. M.	O'Brien Wm. H.	Shanahan M. W.
Hodnett Rev. T. P	McLaughlin Geo.D	Ohlhesier J. T.	Smith J. Charles
Hyland J. S.	McShane James	O'Neill Richard	Smith Dr. W. H.
Hynes W. J.	Melody Rev. J. W.	O'Neill Wm. E.	Sullivan J. G.
Judge T.F.	Moran J. P.	Phalen M. W.	Swenie Dennis J.
Keefe Dr. Jas. E.	Moran Thomas A.	Rend Wm. P.	Thomas M. St. P.
Kelly Jas. J.	Morrison R. W.	Rice Patrick H.	Walsh James
Long Edward	Mulcahy F. J.	Riordan Rev. D. J.	Ward Albert J.
Mair Chas. A.	Murphy Dr.J. B.	Russell M. J.	Winslow C. S.
Malone Rev. T. H.	Murphy J. H.	Ryan John J.	Winslow E. D.

THE COMMERCIAL CLUB.

OFFICERS.

EUGENE CARY, - - - - - - President.
CYRUS H. McCORMICK, - - - Vice-President.
JOHN J. JANES, - - - - - - Secretary.
HENRY J. MACFARLAND, - - - - Treasurer.

EXECUTIVE COMMITTEE.

William A. Fuller   John M. Clark   R. C. Clowry

MEMBERS.

Armour P. D.	Fairbank N. K.	Hutchinson C. L.	Peabody F. B.
Ayer Edward E.	Fargo Charles	Janes John J.	Phelps E. M.
Baker Wm. T.	Farwell C. B.	Jones David B.	Porter H. H.
Bartlett A. C.	Farwell John V. jr.	Keith E. G.	Potter O. W.
Blatchford E. W.	Field Marshall	Kimball C. F.	Ream Norman B.
Bradley J. Harley	Fuller W. A.	Kohlsaat H. H.	Ripley Edward P.
Butler Edward B.	Gage L. J.	Lefens Thies J.	Ryerson Martin A.
Carpenter A. A.	Glessner J. J.	Lincoln.Robert T.	Smith Byron L.
Cary Eugene	Head Franklin H.	MacFarland H. J.	Sprague A. A.
Chalmers Wm. J.	Hibbard W. G.	MacVeagh F.	Stone Melville E.
Clark John M.	Higinbotham H. N.	McClurg A. C.	Walker George C
Clowry R. C.	Hotz Christoph	McCormick C. H.	Walker J. H.
Crane R. T.	Houghteling J. L.	Munro William	Waller Robert A.
Doane J. W.	Hughitt Marvin	Murdock Thomas	Watkins E. T.

THE COUNTRY CLUB OF EVANSTON.

OFFICERS.

MARSHALL M. KIRKMAN, - - - - President.
FREDERICK ARND, - - - First Vice-President.
BENJAMIN F. ADAMS, - - Second Vice-President.
J. H. KEDZIE, JR., - - - - - Secretary.
NICHOLAS G. IGLEHART, - - - - Treasurer.

DIRECTORS.

Marshall M. Kirkman	Benjamin F. Adams	T. S. Creighton
Frederick Arnd	John W. Scott	Francis A. Hardy
Charles T. Boynton	J. H. Kedzie jr.	William Holabird
W. B. Bogert	Nicholas G. Iglehart	

MEMBERS—GENTLEMEN.

Adams Benj. F.	Anthony W. M.	Arnd Frederick	Bartlett Wm. H.
Adams Dr. Chas.	Armsby E. R.	Baird Edward P.	Bartlett W. H., jr.
Aldrich Charles H.	Armsby Gordon	Ball E. H.	Bates Thomas
Allen John M.	Armsby Jas. K.	Barry Chas. H.	Battle J. A.
Ames K. L.	Arnd Charles	Bartlett NormanW.	Bayless James E.

Beecher LeonardT.
Belknap Edwin C.
Blackledge JohnW.
Blanchard Wm.
Blandy Gray
Blunt John E., jr.
Bogert W. B.
Boice H. M.
Boynton Charles T.
Bragdon Dr. M. C.
Brooks Noah W.
Brown Edwin F.
Brown W. L.
Buckingham H. W.
Buckley Chas. W.
Buckner ThomasA.
Buehler E. H.
Buell A. C.
Burnet W. H.
Burnham DanielH.
Burt Wm. Griswold
Cable Herman D.
Caldwell B. D.
Campbell Colin
Candee W. S.
Carlisle John A.
Carr Clyde M.
Chandler C. H.
Chapin Fred S.
Childs John A.
Clark Marshall
Clark Robert S.
Clark Stewart
Clayton Dr. A..B.
Cobb George D.
Coffeen M. Lester
Comstock Louis K.
Condict W. R. jr.
Connell Chas. J.
Connell Chas. M.
Cook David S.
Cook J. O.
CrawfordEdwardC.
Creighton T. S.
Currier Albert D.
Dakin Frank C.D1.
Dakin H. W.
Dalgleish Chas. H.
Damsel W. H.
Daniels Francis B.
Dawes Charles G.
Dawes R. C.
Dean W. M.
Deering Chas. W.
Deering Chas. W. jr.
DeGolyerDonaldL.
DeGolyer L. N.
DeGolyer Nelson
DeGolyer Robert
Dempster J. B.
Dickinson Clarence
Dithmer Frank R.
Donelson D. P.
Dwight Walter T.
Earle John D.

Echlin Henry M.
Elliot Frank M.
Eldridge Harold
Englehard G. P.
Evans Wm. C.
Eversz Ernest H.
Ewen John M.
Ewen Malcolm F.
Fabian Wm. J.
Fair J. B.
Farwell H. S.
Ferguson L. A.
Follett N.
Forgan D. R.
Foster Adelbert M.
Foster Albert V.
Foster Volney W.
Fowle E. H.
Fowler T. Melvin
Frazier F. P.
French C. P.
French Fred. E.
French S. Tenney
Fuller Charles
Fuller Charles G.
Fuller F. R.
Garaghty J. H.
Gardner Burt M.
Gates William W.
Gerould F. W.
Gifford Archer
Gifford Frank W.
Gilbert A. M.
Gilbert Chas. J.
Gilbert H. K.
Gilbert Miles S.
Gilbert Wm. C.
Givins R. S.
Gray Howard P.
Grepe J. Stanley
Grey Charles F.
Gridley Martin M.
Gridley Nelson C.
Griffith Geo. F.
GriswoldEdwardL.
Griswold E. P.
Griswold F. E.
Griswold Harold T.
Gross A. H.
Hall Edward R.
Hall Louis J.
Hallberg L. G.
Hamilton W. A.
Harbert A. B.
Harding Dwight S.
Harding John C.
Harding Lucien E.
Hardy F. A.
Harper William H.
Harris W. M.
Hart C. S.
Harvey George L.
Haskin Chas. G.
Hawks Thomas H.
Hayden Ralph N.
Hazlehurst Andrew

Hebert Dr. A. W.
Hertle Louis
Hinman B. P.
Hitchens R. K.
Hoag Wm. G.
Hofstra W. S.
Hoge Holmes
Holabird R. G.
Holabird Wm.
Hoskins M. G.
Howard O. McG.
Hubbard Will
Hurlbut Dr. Chas. H.
Hurlbut E. R.
Hutchinson Thos.
Hutchinson W. B.
Ide Charles B.
IglehartNicholasG.
Insull Martin J.
Jackson W. A.
Jacobsen Rud'phC.
James C. W.
James Louis N.
James Whitney P.
Jenkins Geo. R.
Kedzie J. H. jr.
Keen Herbert I.
Kennedy M. B.
Kerr H. H.
Keyes Rollin A.
Kimball Dorr A.
Kimbark Frank M.
Kirk John B.
Kirk Joseph G.
Kirk Milton W.
KirkmanMarshall J
Kirkman Marshall M.
Kirkman W. Bruce
Knight Newell C.
Lacey E. S.
Lake R. C.
Lane Maurice T.
Lawrence Chas. H.
Lewis Chas. G.
Lewis D. R.
Lewis Thos. H.
Lindgren John R.
Littlejohn W. J.
Lord BenjaminW.
Lord Frank E.
Lord Geo. S.
Lord Thos.
Lothrop Fred'k L.
Lott Uriah
Ludlow James B.
Lynch Richard W.
Manson W. F.
Marsh Wm. D.
Martin F. S.
Mayo E. A.
McCarrell A. F.
McConnell W. J.
McCormick W. A.
McDowell Hanson

McIver F. F.
McLaughlin Fred'k
McMullen F. B.
McMullen H. Y.
McMullen R. B.
Mears Charles H..
Merrit Frederick
Metcalf John S.
Miller F. C.
Miller Geo. H.
Moore B. J.
Moore Thos. C.
Moseley Geo. V. H.
Mudge D. A.
Northup Joseph C.
Noyes Thomas S.
Onderdonk Dudley
Orchard James G.
Orr Arthur
Osborn E. E.
Osborn L. J.
Osborne W. I.
Paterson J. H.
Patterson Stewart
Peabody F. F.
Pearsons Henry A.
Pearsons H. P.
Phillips Dr. W. A.
Poage J. H.
Poole William F.
Porter C. H.
Poucher B. G.
Powers Wm. S.
Price Lester
Quan James E.
Raeder Henry
Rawson H. D.
Raymond James H.
Read Gardner
Remy Curtis H.
ReQua S. F.
Rice Calvin F.
Richmond F. S.
Rickards Wm. T.
Ridlon Dr. John
Robinson H. H.
Rodgers J. W.
Ross Walter W.
Russell F. H.
Sargent George H.
Sargent Geo. M.
Sawe Harry L.
Sawyer Ward B.
Schmidt W. H.
Schwender John
Scott Charles F.
Scott Frederick N.
Scott John Wm.
Scott Robert L.
Sears Barry
Shaffer J. C.
Shaw Alfred D.
Sheldon F. P.
Sherman Edwin
Sholes Zalmon G.
Shumway P. R.

Sickel William G.
Simmons Parke E.
Slaughter G. F.
Smith Edward J.
Smith Herbert S.
Smith J. Condit
Smith J. Eugene
Spaulding Bates
Spencer C. J.
Spencer Earl W.
Spining Chas. P.
Stanford Arthur L.
Stearns D. F.
Stockton John T.
Stockton Wm. E.
Stubbs Joseph D.

Tallmadge L. C.
Tallmadge T. E.
Thoman Leroy D.
Thorne G. A.
Tiernan John
Tilghman Wm.
Towne Arthur F,
Towne Charles E.
Tyson Will S.
Underwood A. W.
VanArsdale Wm.T.
Vance W. L.
Vandercook R. O.
Vandoozer J. P.
Vilas R. C.
Vilas R. C., jr.

Walker Harry W.
Walker R. W.
Ward Chas. A.
Ward J. F.
Warren Wm. H.
Weaver Chas. S.
Webster Chas. R.
WebsterDr.Edw.H
Webster W. A.
Wells Wm. L.
Wentworth Wm.G.
Wheeler Chas. P.
WhiteheadFrankC.
Whitehead Harry
Whitfield Geo. W.
Dr.

Wickes Roscoe L.
Wilder John E.
Williams Chris. L.
Williams E. J.
Williams Geo.
Williams H. D.
Wilson H. R.
Wilson M. H.
Wilson O. T.
Winne Frank N.
Wright Herbert C.
Wyman RichardH.
Zang Edw. F.
Zang William
Zimmerman Chas.
H.

MEMBERS—LADIES.

Adams Mrs. Benjamin F.
Adams Mrs. Chas.
Aishton Miss Elizabeth
Aldrich Mrs. Charles H.
Ames Mrs. K. L.
Anderson Miss Maria
Anthony Mrs. W. M.
Armsby Mrs. Jas. K. jr.
Armsby Mrs. Lena B.
Armstrong Miss Helen
Arnd Miss Carlena
Arnd Mrs. Frederick
Ayars Mrs. Charles G.
Ayars Mrs. Lucy M.
Baird Mrs. Edward P.
Ball Mrs. E. H.
Barry Mrs. Chas. H.
Bartlett Miss Mary W.
Bartlett Mrs. W. H.
Bates Mrs. Thomas
Bates Miss Rosa C.
Battle Mrs. J. A.
Bayless Miss Wilhelmina
Beach Mrs. Franklin G.
Belknap Mrs. Edwin C.
Blanchard Mrs. Wm.
Blandy Mrs. Gray
Bliss Miss Helen E.
Bliss Miss Jessie :
Blunt Miss Margaret E.
Bogert Mrs. W. B.
Boice Mrs. H. W.
Boyde Miss Lottie
Boynton Mrs. Chas. T.
Bragdon Miss Elizabeth
Bragdon Mrs. M. C.
Brayton Dr. Sarah H.
Brisbine Mrs. A. McIver
Brooks Mrs. Noah W.
Brown Mrs. Edwin F.
Brown Mrs. Wm. L.
Buckingham Mrs. H. W.
Buckley Mrs. Chas. W.
Buckner Mrs. Thomas A.
BuehlerMissKatharineB.
Buehler Mrs. E. H.
Buell Mrs. A. C.
Burdsal Mrs. C. S.

Burdsal Miss Gertrude
Burnet Miss Bessie O.
Burnet Mrs. W. H.
Burnett Mrs. Anna Louise
Burnham Mrs. Daniel H.
Burnham Miss Ethel
Cable Mrs. Herman D.
Caldwell Mrs. B. D.
Candee Miss Mary A.
Candee Mrs. W. S.
Carr Mrs. Clyde M.
Chandler Mrs. C. H.
Chapin Miss Betsy C.
Chapin Mrs. Jennie
Chapin Miss Marietta P.
Chapman Mrs. Belle B
Childs Mrs. John A.
Clark Mrs. Albert B.
Clark Miss Katharine H.
Clark Mrs. Robt. S.
Clark Mrs. Stewart
Clayton Mrs. A. B.
Cobb Mrs. Geo. D.
Coffeen Miss Mae
Coffeen Mrs. M. Lester
Comstock Miss Alice J.
Connell Mrs. Chas. J.
Cook Mrs. David S.
Cook Miss Helen
Cox Miss Sallie I.
Creighton Mrs. T. S.
Dakin Mrs. Frank C.
Dakin Mrs. H. W.
Dale Miss Alice M.
Damsel Miss Jessamine
Damsel Mrs. W. H.
Daniels Miss Caroline S.
Daniels Mrs. Francis B.
Daniels Miss Lucy B.
Dawes Mrs. Chas. G.
Dawes Mrs. R. C.
Deering Mrs. Charles W.
DeGolyer Mrs. Nelson
Dietrich Miss Grace B.
Donelson Mrs. D. P.
Dwight Mrs. Mary B.
Dwight Mrs. Walter T.
Earle Mrs. E. C.

Elliot Mrs. Frank M.
Ely Miss Lou S.
Englehard Mrs. G. P.
Eversz Miss Jessie E.
Ewen Mrs. John M.
Fabian Mrs. Wm. J.
Farwell Mrs. Harry S.
Ferguson Mrs. L. A.
Forgan Mrs. D. R.
Foster Mrs. Adelbert M.
Foster Miss Eva C.
Frazier Mrs. F. P.
French Mrs. C. P.
French Mrs. Frederick E.
French Miss Josephine
French Mrs. S. Tenney
Fuller Mrs. Charles
Fuller Mrs. Charles G.
Gallup Miss Stella Hunt
Garaghty Mrs. J. H.
Gardner Mrs. Burt M.
Gardner Miss Jeanne L.
Garghill Miss Isabel
Gates Mrs. A. H. •
Gates Miss Pearlev
Gerould Mrs. F. W.
Gifford Mrs. Archer
Gilbert Mrs. A. M.
Gilbert Mrs. Chas. J.
Gilbert Mrs. H. K.
Gould Miss Ruth
Gray Miss Alice C.
Gray Mrs. Howard P.
Gray Miss Ida C.
Green Miss Mary I.
Grepe Mrs. J. Stanley
Grey Mrs. Charles F.
Grey Miss Ethel
Gridley Mrs. Martin M.
Gridley Mrs. Nelson C.
Griffith Miss Elsie V.
Griffith Mrs. Geo. F.
Griswold Miss Clara C.
Griswold Mrs. E. P.
Griswold Miss Grace
Griswold Miss Maud M.
Gross Mrs. A. H.
Hall Mrs. Edward R.

Hammond Mrs. Wm. A.
Hanford Miss Alice E.
Harbert Miss Corinne B.
Harbert Miss ElizabethB.
Harding Mrs. Lucien E.
Hardy Mrs. F. A.
Harper Mrs. Wm. H.
Hartshorn Miss Grace E.
Harvey Mrs. Geo. L.
Haskin Mrs. Chas. G.
Haskin Miss Helen
Hawks Mrs. Thomas H.
Hazlehurst Mrs. Andrew
Hertle Mrs. Louis
Hess Miss Grace E.
Hess Mrs. Minnie S.
Hill Mrs. E. N.
HitchensMissElizabethB.
Hitchens Mrs. R. K.
Hofstra Mrs. W. S.
Hoge Mrs. Holmes
Hoge Miss Jane H.
Hoge Miss Louise
Holabird Miss CorneliaB.
Holabird Mrs. Wm.
Hollberg Mrs. L. G.
Howell Mrs. J. W.
Hughes Miss Blanche
Hurlbut Mrs. E. R.
Insull Mrs. Martin J.
Ives Mrs. Blanche D.
Jackson Mrs. W. A.
Jenkins Miss Anna E.
Jenkins Mrs. George R.
Jones Mrs. Wm. Victor
Kedzie Mrs. John H.
Kedzie Miss Margaret F.
Keen Mrs. Herbert Ide
Kennedy Mrs. Madison B.
Kerr Mrs. H. H.
Keyes Miss Frances
Keyes Mrs. Rollin A.
Kidder Mrs. Henry M.
Kirk Miss Emma
Kirk Mrs. John B.
Kirk Mrs. Milton W.
Kirkman Mrs. M. M.
Kirkman Miss Minnie S.
Kirkman Mrs.Wm. Bruce
Knight Mrs. Newell C.
Lacey Miss Edith M.
Lacey Mrs. E. S.
Lacey Miss J. P.
Lake Miss Amy
Lake Miss Jessie
Lane Miss Ella
Lane Miss Irene
Lane Mrs. Maurice T.
Lewis Mrs. D. R.
Lewis Mrs. Mary
Littlejohn Mrs. W. J.
Lord Miss Annie W.
Lord Mrs. Benj. W.
Lord Miss Cornelia F.
Lord Mrs. Geo. S.
Lord Miss Katherine M.

Lord Miss Mary W.
Lothrop Miss Clara L.
Lott Mrs. Uriah
Ludlow Mrs. Jas. B.
Lunt Miss Cornelia G.
Lynch Mrs. Richard W.
Marsh Miss Josie E.
Marsh Mrs. William D.
Martin Mrs. F. S.
MattesonMiss Jean McN.
Mayo Mrs. E. A.
McCabe Miss Alice
McCabe Miss Carrie
McCarrell Mrs. A. F.
McConnell Mrs. W. J.
McMullen Mrs. R. B.
Mears Mrs. Chas. H.
Metcalf Mrs. John S.
Metcalf Miss Terresa
Miller Miss Alta D.
Miller Miss Grace E.
Miller Miss Josephine
Moore Mrs. B. J.
Moore Miss Ella F.
Moore Miss Louise D.
Moore Miss Miriam P.
Morse Miss Leila
Mudge Mrs. Daniel A.
Norton Miss Charlotte E.
Noyes Mrs. E. E.
Noyes Mrs. George E.
Orr Mrs. Arthur
Osborn Mrs. E. E.
Osborne Mrs. W. I.
Parkhurst Mrs. J. J.
Paterson Mrs. J. H.
Peabody Mrs. F. F.
Pearsons Mrs. Henry A.
Phillips Mrs. W. A.
Pitner Miss Ina K.
Porter Mrs. C. H.
Poucher Mrs. B. G.
Powers Mrs. Wm. S.
Pratt Miss Elizabeth A.
Price Mrs. Lester
Quan Miss Mary A.
Raeder Mrs. Henry
Raftery Mrs. Edmond
Raymond Mrs. James H.
Reese Mrs. Theodore F.
Reimers Miss Anna C.
Remy Mrs. Curtis H.
Re Qua Mrs. S. F.
Revell Miss Elizabeth
Rice Mrs. Calvin F.
Rice Miss Lillian
Rice Miss Lois A.
Rice Miss Louise
Rice Miss May Louise
Rickards Mrs. Wm. T.
Ridlon Miss Hester
Ridlon Mrs. John
Robinson Mrs. H. H.
Rogers Miss Nettie
Rogers Mrs. Sarah K.
Ross Mrs. Walter W.

Rowe Mrs. Lucy J.
Sargent Mrs. Geo. M.
Sawyer Miss Ida E.
Sawyer Miss Jessie S.
Scott Miss Lida G.
Sears Miss Helen D.
Shaffner Mrs. J. C.
Sheldon Mrs. F. P.
Sherman Mrs. Edwin
Sherman Mrs. M. E.
Sholes Mrs. Zalmon G.
Shumway Mrs. Mary R.
Sickel Mrs. Wm. G.
Simmons Mrs. Parke E.
Simpson Mrs. Andrew
Smith Mrs. Edward J.
Smith Miss Florence L.
Smith Miss Floy M.
Smith Mrs. Herbert S.
Smith Mrs. J. Eugene
Smith Miss Mabel P.
Smith Miss Mary A.
Spencer Mrs. C. J.
Spencer Mrs. Earl W.
Spining Mrs. Chas. P.
Stanford Miss Mary E.
Stearns Mrs. D. F.
Stockton Mrs. John T.
Stockton Miss Martha C.
Stockton Mrs. William E.
Tallmadge Miss Abby L.
Tallmadge Mrs. L. C.
Thoman Mrs. Leroy D.
Thompson Miss Ella
Thorne Mrs. G. A.
Tiernan Miss Bessie
Tillson Miss Nina A.
Tinsman Mrs. Homer E.
Towle Miss Mae E.
Towne Mrs. Arthur F.
Underwood Mrs. A. W.
Van Arsdale Mrs. Wm.
Vance Mrs. W. L.
Vandercook Mrs. R. O.
Vilas Miss Elsie
Vilas Mrs. Royal
Walker Mrs. R. W.
Ward Miss Anabel M.
Ward Mrs. Chas. A.
Ward Miss Estelle F.
Ward Mrs. J. F.
Ward Miss Rosella
Ward Miss Sadie G.
Ware Miss Lillian
Warren Mrs. W. H.
Watson Mrs. Julia M.
Watson Miss Margaret S.
Weaver Mrs. Chas. S.
Webster Mrs. Chas. R.
Webster Mrs. Edward H.
Webster Mrs. W. A.
Wells Mrs. W. L.
Wentworth Mrs. Wm. G.
Wheeler Mrs. Chas. P.
White Miss Elizabeth
White Mrs.Rose Lindsley

Whitely Mrs. C. J.
Whitely Miss Elizabeth
Whitfield Mrs. Geo. W.
Wilcox Miss Anna J.

Wilder Mrs. John E.
Williams Mrs. C. L.
Williams Miss Madeline
Wilson Mrs. H. R.

Wilson Miss Mary T.
Winne Mrs. Frank N.
Wyman Mrs. Richard H.

DAUGHTERS OF THE AMERICAN REVOLUTION.

MRS. HENRY M. SHEPARD, 4445 Grand Boul., State Regent.

CHICAGO CHAPTER.

ASSEMBLY HALL, FINE ARTS BUILDING.

OFFICERS.

MRS. FREDERICK DICKINSON, 26 Bryant av. - - - Regent.
MRS. FREDERICK A. SMITH, - - - - - - - Vice-Regent.
MRS. MADISON B. KENNEDY, - - - Recording Secretary.
MRS. J. ELLSWORTH GROSS, 3600 Michigan av. Corresponding Sec'y.
MRS. CHARLES H. CONOVER, - - - - - - - Treasurer.
MRS. RICHARD H. KERR, - - - - - - - - Registrar.
MRS. JOHN C. BUNDY, - - - - - - - - Historian.

DIRECTORS.

Mrs. Franklin H. Beckwith
Mrs. John R. Wilson
Mrs. Robert B. Farson
Mrs. Benjamin F. Ayer
Mrs. Walter C. Nelson

MEMBERS.

Adams Mrs. Cyrus H.
Adams Mrs. Geo. W.
Adolphus Mrs. Wolfe
Allen Mrs. Arthur W.
Allyn Mrs. W. H.
Anderson Mrs. Mary S.L.
Andrews Mrs. Irene F.
Anthony Mrs. Chas. E.
Arnold Mrs. Chas. C.
Atkinson Mrs. Frank
Ayer Mrs. Benjamin F.
Babcock Mrs. Charles F.
Bailey Mrs. Samuel G.
Bailey Miss Charlotte O.
Baker Miss Ethel
Baldwin Mrs. Robert R.
Ball Mrs. George C.
Bane Mrs. George W.
Bannard Mrs. Henry C.
Barber Mrs. J. O.
Barbour Mrs. Lyman L.
Barker Mrs. Frank W.
Barker Mrs. Joseph N.
Barnes Mrs. Charles J.
Barry Mrs. George
Bartlett Mrs. A. C.
Bartlett Mrs. Geo. F.
Bassett Mrs. Roger M.
Beach Mrs. Myron H.
Becker Mrs. Frederick W.
Beckwith Mrs. F. H.
Beebe Mrs. Wm. H.
Belden Mrs. John S.
Benedict Mrs. Robt. P.
Bentley Mrs. Cyrus
Benzinger Mrs. August
Blair Mrs. Henry A.

Blatchford Mrs. E. W.
Block Mrs. Willard T.
Bloomingston Mrs.JohnS.
Blye Mrs. Emlen S.
Bodman Mrs. L. W.
Bogardus Mrs. Henry A.
Bogue Mrs. Charles B.
Bolté Mrs. Anson T.
Bonney Mrs. Charles L.
Booth Miss Mary E.
Borland Mrs. John J.
Boughton Mrs. Daniel K.
Bouton Mrs. Sherman H.
Bowden Miss Addie E.
Bowie Mrs. Robert R.
Boyeson Mrs. Janie G. S.
Boyle Mrs. Lawrence P.
Boyle Mrs. Loren L.
Bradford Mrs. David G.
Bradley Miss Frances C.
Bradley Mrs. M. S.
Bradley Mrs. Philip B.
Braun Mrs. George P.
Brooks Mrs. Almon
Brooks Mrs. James C.
Brooks Mrs. J. W.
Brown Mrs. Charles F.
Brown Mrs. John H.
Brown Miss Leila C.
Brown Mrs. Wm. Thayer
Brush Mrs. Emerson H.
Bryan Mrs. Benjamin B.
Bryan Miss Jennie Byrd
Bryant Mrs. Henry W.
Bull Mrs. E. F.
Bundy Mrs. John C.
Burchard Mrs. M. Nelson

Burleigh Mrs. Wm. R.
Burnham Mrs. Arthur
Burt Mrs. Sarah
Buschwah Mrs. Nicholas
Bush Mrs. Clara B.
Bush Miss Emma C.
Bushnell Miss Sylvia
Campbell Miss Fannie
Capwell Mrs. Charles A.
Card Miss Grace Barton
Caryl Mrs. Alex. H.
Caryl Miss Christine
Chamberlain Mrs.Chas.C.
Chamberlain Mrs. Geo.M.
Chamberlain Mrs. Philo
Chamberlin Mrs. Eugene G.
Chapin Mrs. Simeon
Chapman Miss Bertha S.
Chapman Mrs. Charles A.
Chard Mrs. Thomas S.
Chatfield Mrs. Ida P.
Cheney Mrs. Chas. E.
Chester Mrs. Harry W.
Churchill Mrs. H. P.
Claflin Mrs. A. St. M.
Clark Mrs. Alson E.
Clark Mrs. Andrew G.
Clark Miss Caroline F.
Clark Miss Emma E.
Clark Mrs. Frances F.
Clinch Mrs.RichardFloyd
Coe Mrs. A. L.
Cole Mrs. Ella P.
Cole Miss Lillie E.
Cole Mrs. Thomas W.
Coleman Mrs. J. A.

Coleman Miss Martha E
Collins Mrs. Wm. A.
Collins Mrs. Wm. R.
Colvin Mrs. Wm. H.
Cone Mrs. Albert G.
Conover Mrs. Charles H.
Cook Miss Marjorie H.
Cook Mrs. Orrin S.
Corbin Mrs. C. R.
Corey Mrs. G. J.
Corthell Miss Alice E.
Couch Mrs. James
Coulter Mrs. Anna B.
Counselman Miss Edith
Counselman Mrs. Willis
Couthoui Mrs. Joseph
Craig Mrs. Ida S.
Cramer Mrs. E. W.
Crane Miss Marie P.
Crane Mrs. Simeon H.
Crawford Miss Marion T.
Crawford Mrs. Mark L.
Critchell Miss Nellie M.
Crossman Mrs. Abner
Currier Mrs. Horace T.
Curtis Mrs. J. LaFayette
Cutter Miss Helen B.
Dada Mrs. Geo. S.
Dainty Mrs. A. H.
Dana Mrs. John A.
Dana Miss Mary
Daniels Mrs. John B.
Daniels Miss Mary E.
Darling Mrs. Julia A.
Davidson Mrs. J., M.D.
Davis Mrs. John S.
Day Mrs. Albert Morgan
Dean Mrs. M. A.
Dewey Mrs. Chas. P.
Dewey Mrs. Harriet B.
Dickerman Miss Frances S
Dickinson Mrs. Frederick
Dickinson Miss Louise M.
Dickinson Mrs. Oliver P.
Dickinson Mrs. Wm.
Dickson Miss Mabel C.
Dillman Mrs. Louis M.
Doty Mrs. Levi R.
Doud Mrs. Levi B.
Dow Mrs. Jonathan
Downs Mrs. Myron D.
Duell Mrs. Wm. Comstock
Dunham Mrs. Phoebe S.
Dunning Mrs. S. M.
Durand Mrs. Elliott
Durgin Mrs. John Cooper
Dutton Mrs. Everell F.
Duval Mrs. Louis A.
Eames Mrs. Emily
Earle Mrs. Samuel W.
Egan Mrs. Charles W.
Elliott Mrs. Lizzie N. McL.
Ellwood Mrs. Isaac L.
Elmer Mrs. Howard N.
Ely Mrs. Oliver C.
Emery Miss Ernestine

English Mrs. Gustavus P.
Everett Mrs. Charlotte S.
Everhart Miss Mella D.
Ewell Mrs. Juliana H.
Ewing Mrs. Adlai T.
Fargo Miss Florence B.
Farr Mrs. Marvin A.
Farson Mrs. R. B.
Faville Mrs. Amos S.
Featherstone Mrs. Edw.
  A.
Fegenbush Mrs. Chas. M.
Fegenbush Miss J. M.
Fellows Mrs. G. E.
Felt Mrs. Frank B.
Fernald Mrs. C. K.
Ferry Mrs. Abby Farwell
Field Mrs. Richard I.
Fisher Miss Caroline E.
Fisher Miss Flora A.
Fisher Mrs. George
Fisher Mrs. Lucius G.
Fitzsimons Mrs. Chas.
Fitzsimons Mrs. E. M.
Foley Mrs. John B.
Forbes Mrs. Caroline E. B.
Foster Mrs. Frederick N.
Fowler Miss Harriet
Fox Miss Frances M.
Fox Miss Harriott A.
Francis Mrs. Geo. H.
Frank Mrs. Monroe
Freeman Mrs. Henry V.
Frink Mrs. W. H.
Fry Mrs. Wm. E.
Fuller Mrs. Charles
Fuller Mrs. Frank R.
Fuller Mrs. Lucius E.
Fullerton Mrs. Thos. C.
Furst Mrs. Wm. C.
Gale Mrs. Fred'k G.
Galt Mrs. A. T.
Gardner Mrs. Anna R.
Gee Mrs. Frances J. D.
Ghislin Mrs. Henry
Gibson Mrs. Martha H.
Gilbert Miss Helen R.
Gilbert Miss Rose E.
Gillett Mrs. Egbert W.
Gillett Miss Lillian M.
Gillette Mrs. E. L.
Glaspell Mrs. Albert
Glessner Mrs. John J.
Goodhart Mrs. F. E.
Goodrich Miss Mary W.
Goodrich Miss Nellie
Goodspeed Mrs. E. J.
Goodwin Mrs. Daniel
Gordon Mrs. Frank L.
Goss Mrs. Chas. O.
Graves Mrs. Dwight W.
Green Mrs. Horatio N.
Gridley Mrs. Nora
Grier Miss Margaret G.
Griffith Mrs. John J.
Gross Mrs. J. Ellsworth

Guthrie Mrs. Ossian
Guthrie Mrs. Seymour
Guthrie Mrs. Wardell
Gwinn Mrs. John Morris
Hall Mrs. Herman J.
Hamill Mrs. Charles D.
Hamill Mrs. Ernest A.
Hamill Mrs. Fannie E.
Hamilton Mrs. H. H.
Hammond Mrs. Lyman D.
Hancock Mrs. Bradford
Hardy Mrs. Charles M.
Harris Mrs. Graham H.
Harris Mrs. Norman W.
Hart Mrs. J. P.
Harwood Mrs. Henry W.
Haskell Mrs. George W.
Haworth Mrs. Geo. D.
Haynes Mrs. Leander
Heath Mrs. William
Heegaard Mrs. Wm. H.
Helmer Mrs. Frank A.
Hendricks Miss Anna P.
Hequembourg Mrs. J. E.
Hervey Mrs. James Fred'k
Hesing Mrs. Washington
Hewlings Mrs. Andrew J.
Hill Mrs. William K.
Hoag Mrs. J. C.
Hobler Mrs. Edwin G.
Holcomb Mrs. W. B.
Holman Mrs. Alfred L.
Holmes Miss Jennie R.
Hooper Mrs. James K.
Hoops Mrs. Thomas
Hoover Mrs. George P.
Hopkins Mrs. A. W.
Hopkins Mrs. Mary C.
Hosmer Miss Eliza
Howe Mrs. F. S.
Howland Mrs. Walter M.
Hoy Mrs. Albert H.
Hoy Miss Mary E.
Huguenin Miss Edith
Hull Mrs. Genevieve
Humiston Mrs. Samuel H.
Hunt Mrs. William P., jr.
Hurlbut Mrs. H. A.
Hurlbut Miss Sarah E.
Husted Mrs. William H.
Hutchinson Mrs. Jonas
Hutchinson Miss Mary D.
Hutchison Miss Matilda
  D.
Hyde Mrs. James N.
Hynes Mrs. Wm. J.
Isam Mrs. Wm. H.
Ives Mrs. John H.
Jameson Miss Alice W.
Jameson Mrs. John Alex.
Jameson Miss Mary
Jayne Mrs. Edgar L.
Jelke Mrs. John F.
Jenkins Mrs. Robert E.
Jenks Mrs. Wm. S.
Jenney Mrs. Harvey W.

Jewell Miss Jennie E.
Jewett Mrs. John N.
Jewett Mrs. Samuel R.
Johnson Mrs. William W.
Johnstone Mrs. John, jr.
Jones Mrs. Cassius Clay
Jones Mrs. Vina N.
Jordan Mrs. Scott,
Judd Mrs. Edward James
Judd Mrs. Norman B.
Judson Mrs. Mary M.
Karner Mrs. Wm. J.
Kaufman Mrs. Jacob H.
Kavanagh Mrs. Morgan R.
Keep Mrs. Chauncey
Kennedy Mrs. Madison B.
Kent Mrs. Wm.
Kerfoot Mrs. Samuel H.
Kerr Mrs. Richard H.
Kimball Miss Alma L.
Kimball Miss Louise E.
Knight Miss Alice A.
Knight Mrs. Walter J.
Knight Mrs. Wm. M.
Koch Mrs. C. R. E.
Kohlsaat Mrs. Herman H.
Krout Miss Mary H.
Lacey Miss Ruth S.
Lay Mrs. Catharine R.
Lay Miss Margaret S.
Lee Mrs. Allen
Lee Mrs. Frank F.
Lee Mrs. Fred'k W.
Leonard Mrs. E. M.
Lewis Mrs. Edward H.
Lewis Mrs. E. R.
Lewis Mrs. James
Lewis Mrs. J. H.
Libbey Miss Gertrude B.
Lockwood Mrs. Henry
Long Mrs. John C.
Loomis Mrs. John H.
Loose Mrs. Jacob L.
Lord Miss Clara S.
Loverin Mrs. Quinby W.
Luce Mrs. Franklin A.
Lull Mrs. Newton
Lyman Miss Elizabeth L.
Lyman Mrs. Jesse P.
Lyman Miss Mary E.
Lytton Mrs. Henry C.
MacArthur Mrs. Archib'd
MacArthur Miss Florence
   B.
MacArthur Miss Marion E.
MacCalla Miss Helen W.
MacCarthy Mrs. Joseph P.
MacGrew Mrs. Elwood
MacPherran Mrs. Jas. E.
MacVeagh Mrs. Franklin
Manning Mrs. Walter H.
Marguerat Mrs. Eugene
Marsh Mrs. George S.
Marsh Mrs. John W.
Marsh Mrs. Rufus J.
Marsh Mrs. Wm. D.

Marshall Mrs. Geo. E.
Marshall Mrs. James A.
Martin Miss Ellen A.
Martin Mrs. Elmer B.
Marvin Mrs. Fanny C.
Mason Mrs. Henry B.
Mason Mrs. N. A.
Mather Mrs. A. C.
Matthews Mrs. Edwin S.
Mayo Mrs. Edward L.
McClaughry Mrs. C. C.
McClelland Mrs. Thos. S.
McCord Mrs. Alvin C.
McCormick Miss Eliza-
   beth D.
McCormick Miss Henri-
   etta H.
McCormick Mrs. Leander
McCormick Mrs. Robert
McCreery Mrs. R. M.
McCurdy Mrs. George L.
McDonald Mrs. John B.
McEntee Mrs. Charles S.
McKinley Mrs. William B.
McLain Mrs. L. A.
McMullin Mrs. Frank R.
Meachum Mrs. F. D.
Means Miss Elizabeth S.
Meeker Miss Margaret B.
Merriam Miss Bertha S.
Messinger Mrs. Wm. D.
Metcalf Mrs. Ralph
Miller Miss Mary A.
Mills Mrs. James M.
Milner Mrs. James W.
Miner Mrs Edna B.
Moderwell Miss Mary W.
Moore Mrs. Jas. M.
Moore Mrs. J. Hobart
Moore Mrs. William H.
Morris Mrs. Joseph
Morris Mrs. Seymour
Morse Mrs. Edwin D.
Moss Mrs. Wm. Lathrop
Moyer Mrs. Waldenstein
Murphey Mrs. Henry C.
Myers Mrs. Fanny B.
Mygatt Mrs. William R.
Nelson Mrs. Walter C.
Neltnor Miss Cornelia E.
Newcomb Mrs. Geo. E.
Nicholls Mrs. William H.
Norton Mrs. James H.
Norwood Mrs. Frederick
Norwood Miss Winifred A.
Noyes Mrs. LaVerne W.
Noyes Mrs. Oliver J.
Ogden Mrs. Mahlon D.
Okeson Miss Jane B.
Okeson Miss Margaret
Ormsbee Mrs. Wm. W., jr.
Orr Mrs. Frank B.
Osgood Mrs. Henry D.
Otis Mrs. Ephraim A.
Owens Miss Maria Gervia
Packard Mrs. Arthur T.

Page Miss Florence Ethel
Pajeau Mrs. Joseph
Parker Mrs. Wm. R.
Partridge Mrs. N. A.
Peck Mrs. Walter L.
Peirce Mrs. Daniel N.
Perry Mrs. Fred'k B.
Perry Mrs. Harriet D. S.
Pettibone Mrs. A. G.
Pettibone Mrs. Philo F.
Phelps Mrs. Delos P.
Phillips Miss Harriet G.
Pierce Mrs. Charles W.
Pitkin Miss Gertrude
Pitkin Mrs. Roger S.
Pomeroy Mrs. S. Harris
Pool Miss Anna W.
Pope Mrs. Charles B.
Porter Mrs. Frank W.
Porter Mrs. Mary H.
Potts Mrs. A. B.
Potwin Mrs. W. S.
Pratt Mrs. B. S.
Preston Miss Carl W.
Preston Mrs. Ernest B.
Preston Mrs. Ernest J.
Prindeville Mrs. Charles H.
Pullman Mrs. George M.
Putman Miss Alice
Putman Miss Judith
Pynchon Mrs. Daniel
Quincy Mrs. Charles F.
Quine Mrs. William E.
Ramage Mrs. George W.
Rand Mrs. William H.
Rappleye Miss Maud M.
Ray Mrs. B. F.
Reed Miss Julia Lyle
Reid Mrs. Wm. H.
Remick Mrs. M. C.
ReQua Mrs. Chas. Howard
Rice Mrs. Fletcher C.
Rice Mrs. Mark W.
Riker Mrs. Alpheus P.
Rippey Miss Sara C.
Robbins Mrs. Walter R.
Robertson Mrs. Charlotte
   C.
Robinson Miss Martha A.
Rock Mrs. Frank D.
Ross Miss Elizabeth G.
Ross Mrs. J. P.
Rozet Mrs. George H.
Rozet Miss Marie J.
Ruger Mrs. Lillian B.
Rupp Mrs. Jessie R.
Salmon Mrs. Charles
Sampson Mrs. Osborne
Sanger Mrs. F. W.
Sanger Mrs. Mary C.
Sargent Mrs. John S.
Satterlee Mrs. M. L.
Sawyer Mrs. Francis A.
Scammon Mrs. J. Young
Schaffenberg Miss Lydia
   F.

Scott Mrs. George S.
Scribner Mrs. C. E.
Scribner Mrs. Sanford A.
Sears Mrs. Nathaniel C.
Selby Mrs. Paul
Shaw Miss Helen L.
Shefler Mrs. C. B.
Shepard Miss Harriet W.
Shepard Mrs. Henry M.
Sherman Mrs. Penoyer L.
Sherman Mrs. William W.
Sherwood Mrs. Nehemiah
Shippey Mrs. Chas. W.
Shumway Miss Emma B.
Shumway Miss Mary
Shumway Mrs. Noble C.
Simmons Mrs. F. T.
Sims Mrs. Josephine C.
Sims Mrs. William E.
Sinclair Mrs. Albert C.
Sinclair Miss Judith P.
Sinclair Miss Mattie M.
Skinner Mrs. Emory F.
Slack Mrs. Charles H.
Smith Mrs. Edward E.
Smith Mrs. Edwin K.
Smith Mrs. Ernest N.
Smith Mrs. Frances S.
Smith Mrs. Frank M.
Smith Mrs. Frederick A.
Smith Mrs. Jesse W. J.
Smith Mrs. Lloyd J.
Smith Mrs. Monroe A.
Smith Mrs. Marvin E.
Smith Mrs. Perry H.
Smith Mrs. R. J.
Smith Miss Sarah G.
Smith Miss Valentine
Smith Mrs. Wm. W.
Smith Mrs. Wyllys K.
Snow Mrs. Albert E.
Somerville Mrs. Robert
Soper Mrs. Horace W.
Spaids Miss Susie E.
Spalding Miss Jessie

Sparks Mrs. Edwin E.
Springer Mrs. Geo. A.
Squires Mrs. Collins S.
Starkweather Mrs. Frank H.
Starr Mrs. Western
Stedman Mrs. Asa W.
Steele Mrs. Fred'k M.
Stevenson Mrs. Alex F.
Stewart Mrs. Charles B.
Stewart Mrs. Henry
Stockton Miss Alice L.
Stockton Miss Josephine
Stone Mrs. Leander
Stone Miss Maud H.
Stone Mrs. Melville E.
Stone Mrs. Newton R.
Stone Mrs. W. S.
Strobel Mrs. Charles L.
Sweet Miss Mary E.
Swift Mrs. Louis F.
Teller Mrs. James H.
TenEyck Mrs. Tenedor
Theile Mrs. E. J.
Thomas Miss Darley
Tibbitts Mrs. Elisha
Tisdale Mrs. Laura J.
Tobey Miss Mary E.
Tobin Mrs. Samuel C.
Tracy Mrs. F. K.
Trego Miss Alleen
Trego Mrs. Charles T.
Trippe Mrs. Martha G.W.
Trumbull Mrs. Lyman
Tuck Mrs. George H.
Tucker Miss Martha E.
Turner Mrs. Volentine C.
Tuthill Mrs. George M.
Ullery Mrs. Frank B.
Underwood Mrs. J. Platt
Vail Miss Delphi E.
Valentine Mrs. John
Vaughan Mrs. Edward J.
Vaux Mrs. Frederick T.

Veirs Mrs. B. W.
Wait Mrs. Horatio L.
Wakeman Mrs. Albert C.
Waldo Mrs. Otis H.
Walker Miss Annie C.
Walker Mrs. James H.
Walker Mrs. James M.
Walker Mrs. S. T.
Ward Mrs. Chas. A.
Ward Mrs. Henry B.
Wardner Mrs. Sylvia J.
Washburn Mrs. R. H.
Watson Mrs. James S.
Watson Mrs. John
Webster Miss Floi E.
Welch Mrs. E. G.
Welch Mrs. Leon C.
Welles Mrs. Benj. W.
Welles Miss Isabella W.
Welling Mrs. John C.
Wellington Mrs. Chas. L.
Wells Mrs. Frank
Wells Mrs. Willis J.
West Mrs. Frederick T.
Weston Miss Lillian R.
Wheaton Mrs. Loyd
White Miss Emma G.
Whiton Miss Louise
Wiles Mrs. Robert H.
Williams Mrs. Frank.
Wilson Miss Belle
Wilson Mrs. John P.
Wilson Mrs. John R.
Wilson Miss Margaret J.
Winslow Mrs. John H.
Wood Mrs. Helen M.
Wood Mrs. John H.
Woodruff Mrs. Chas. E.
Woodward Mrs. Geo. W.
Wright Mrs. Edward
Wright Miss Fannie C.
Wright Miss Fannie L.
Wright Mrs. Parry L.
Yoe Mrs. Charles C.

DOUGLAS CLUB.

3518 ELLIS AVENUE.

OFFICERS.

C. C. SWINBORNE,	- - - - - - President.
C. E. SEATON,	- - - - - First Vice-President.
A. H. BARBER,	- - - - Second Vice-President.
S. A. HARVEY,	- - - Third Vice-President.
A. L. BAILHACHE,	- - - - - - Secretary.
W. P. PENHALLOW,	- - - - - Treasurer.

DIRECTORS.

C. M. Nichols   C. A. W. Platt   W. W. Watkins
Samuel Parliament   T. E. Milchrist   E. S. Eldredge

MEMBERS.

Ackers T. B.
Aykroyd Geo. M.
Bailhache A. L.

Baker Frank
Baldwin Abraham
Baldwin Dr. L. B.

Barber A. H.
Bartley C. E.
Bell Geo. H.

Bertrand F. M.
Best George W.
Best Wm.

Bishopp W. D.
Blaisdell J. W.
Blake H. H.
Bliss F. E.
Bliss S. E.
Bloomingston J. S.
Booth Wm. M.
Brown Wm. F.
Buchanan E. P.
Bulkley Almon W.
Burnham S. W.
Casey E. A.
Caswell C. L. jr.
Clover John W.
Collom E. E.
Collom H. E.
Cooke M. E.
Cowles W. D.
Curtis W. G.
Day'.Walter B.
Deitz C. J. Dr.
Dick William.F.

Edwards J. Frank
Eldredge C. J.
Eldredge E. S.
Fink E. S.
Fisher George F.
Flagg W. H.
Forrest A. E.
Fox B. M.
Fox Harvey
Frost W. A.
Fry G. C.
Gassette W. K.
Gaddis Geo. E.
Gayle A. C.
Giesler R. G.
Goddard L. O.
Gordon Allan F.
Gorham W. H.
Harvey S. A.
Hoag W. E.
Jones W. S.

Keyes D. H.
King Hoyt
Launder D.
LeBaron Wm.
Lightner C. F.
Matheson R. S
Matteson A. E.
Milchrist T. E.
Milchrist W. A.
Moore J. R.
Nichols C. M.
Palmer E. P.
Parliament Samuel
Parsons O. M.
Paulsen W. A.
Penhallow W. P.
Platt C. A. W.
Plumsted J. T.
Purcell W. A.
Rumsey J. Frank
Russ C. A.

Ryder Fred L.
Selleck W. E.
Sheldon T. C.
Slade Sam.
Stevens E. D.
Stone G. W.
Stone Harry
Sutter A.
Sutter J.
Swinborne C. C.
VanDalson Edward
Vierbuchen Wm.C
Vincent J. R.
Wade Jno.
Warden T. G.
Watson F. L.
Watkins W. W.
Welch A. S.
White Dr. J. W.
Young A. S.
Young Max

EVANSTON CLUB.

GROVE AND CHICAGO AV., EVANSTON.

OFFICERS.

N. C. GRIDLEY - - - - - - - President.
WM. HOLABIRD - - - - - First Vice-President.
F. A. HARDY - - - - Second Vice-President.
WILLIAM T. RICKARDS - - - - - Secretary.
GEORGE R. JENKINS - - - - - Treasurer.

DIRECTORS.

E. S. Lacey
Nicholas G. Iglehart
Nelson C. Gridley
William Holabird

Marshall M. Kirkman
Francis A. Hardy
William H. Bartlett

H. S. Stevens
George R. Jenkins
George M. Sargent
C. T. Boynton

MEMBERS.

Adams Benj. F.
Allen John M.
Anthony C. E.
Armour M. C.
Arnd Charles
Arnd Frederick
Ayars C. G.
Baker George S.
Ballenger Wm. L.
Barnes A. R.
Barry Charles H.
Bartlett Chas. L.
Bartlett William H.
Battle J. A.
Bayless Benj.
Bigelow N. K.
Bird A. C.
Blanchard William
Boice Hugh M.
BoltwoodProf.H.L.
Boynton C. T.
Bradley David E.
Bragdon Dr. M. C.
Brooks Noah W.
Brown William L.

Buell Augustine C.
Cable H. D.
Carpenter O. F.
Carr Clyde M.
Carter Edward C.
Chaffee Theodore W.
Charles Joseph J.
Childs John A.
Clapp E. P.
Clark Stewart
Cleveland Chas. B.
Cobb W. L.
Coe David A.
Connell C. J.
Cook David S.
Creighton Thos. S.
Cutler William H.
Dakin Richard L.
Damsell W. H.
Dawes Chas. G.
Dawes Rufus C.
DeGolyer Nelson
Dodd Oscar
Donelson D. P.

Donnell·Jas. W.
Doran George H.
Dunn A. E.
Dyche William A.
Eddy Augustus
Elliot Frank M.
Elphicke Chas. W.
Eyer C. B.
Fabian William J.
Farwell Simeon
Forgan David R.
Forrey F. M.
Foster A. M.
Foster Volney W.
Frazier F. P.
French S. Tenney
Fuller Dr. Chas. G.
Fyffe John L.
Gates P. W.
Gerould F. W.
Gilleland D. J.
Gooch George E.
Graves C. E.
Gridley Martin M.
Gridley Nelson C.

Grier J. P.
Griffin Joseph A.
Griswold F. E.
Grover Frank R.
Hall Ed. R.
Hamilton W. A.
Handy Frank W.
Harbert Charles H.
Harding Amos J.
Harding L. E.
Hardy Francis A.
Harpham E. L.
Hawks T. H.
Hazlehurst A.
Hitchins R. K.
Hoge Holmes
Holabird William
Holbrook Fred A.
Hubbard Will
Hurd Harvey B.
IglehartNicholasG.
Jenkins George R.
Jernegan Charles
Johnston Wm. J.
Jones William H.

Judson Frank P.
Kappes Charles R.
Keyes Rollin A.
Kimball Dorr A.
Kimball R. H.
Kimbark E. U.
Kirk John B.
Kirkman M. M.
Knight Newell C.
Lacey Edw. S.
Lake Richard C.
Lawrence Jas. A.
Lewis Charles G.
Littlejohn W. J.
Llewellyn S. J.
Lord Alonzo B.
Lord Frank E.
Lowrey Wm. K.
Lyons Jesse R.
Manson W. F.
Marsh George S.
Marsh Wm. D.
Martin F. S.

McFarland Chas. H.
McMullen Roger B.
Mears Charles H.
Merrick Geo. P.
Millard Addison
Miller H. H. C.
Moore G. H.
Morris Joseph O.
Mudge Daniel A.
Murray James S.
Neeley Charles G.
O'Kane W. E.
Orchard J. G.
Orr Arthur
Osborne Charles M.
Osborné E. E.
Osborne W. Irving
Paden Joseph E.
Paden Willard S.
Parker Lewis W.
Parkes William R.
Parkhurst Josiah J.
Patten James A.

Peabody F. F.
Pearsons Henry A.
Phillips W. B.
Pittman C. K.
Porter Charles H.
Raeder Henry
Raymond Jas. H.
Reed Edward H.
Rice Louis S.
Rickards Wm. T.
Rodgers John W.
Rogers R. M.
Ross Orrington
Sargent George M.
Schwender John
Sherman Edwin
Shumway Philip R.
Shutterly Eugene E.
Smith Gilbert A.
Spencer Earl W.
Sproule A. L.
Stearns Deshler F.

Stevens Harry S.
Stockton John T.
Stockton Wm. E.
Towne A. F.
Towne Charles E.
Turner John C.
VanVlissingen J. H.
Walker R. W.
Ward Charles A.
Ward Joseph F.
Webster C. R.
Wheeler Chas. P.
Wicks Roscoe L.
Wightman Chas. A.
Williams C. L.
Williams N. P.
Wilson Hugh R.
Wilson Milton H.
Woodbridge J. R.
Woodford P. R.
Yates Ernest G.
Young Aaron N.

THE FELLOWSHIP CLUB.

OFFICERS.

M. E. STONE, - - - - - - - President.
R. A. WALLER, - - - - - - Vice-President.
F. WILLIS RICE, - - - - - - Secretary.
H. G. SELFRIDGE, - - - - - - Treasurer.

MEMBERS.

Adams Milward
Baumann Gustav
Beale William G.
Burnham Daniel H.
Butler E. B.
Caton Arthur J.
Chalmers William J
Chatfield - Taylor H. C.
Corwith C. R.
Counselman Chas.
Cowles Alfred
Davis George R.
Davis Will J.

Deering James
Field Roswell M.
Fish Stuyvesant
Foster Volney W.
Head Franklin H.
Higinbotham H. N.
Hoard W. D.
Insull Samuel
Jacobson Augustus
Keyes Rollin A.
Kimball C. Fred
Kirk Milton W.
Kirkman M. M.

Kohlsaat H. H.
Lawson Victor F.
Lederer Charles
MacFarland H. J.
MacDonald Chas.
Nye James W.
Peck Ferd W.
Peck George R.
Pettibone P. F.
Ray Frank H.
Raymond S. B.
Revell Alex. H.

Rice F. Willis
Runnels John S.
Selfridge Harry G
Skiff F. J. V.
Smith Dunlap
Stone Melville E.
Switzer Edward M.
Wacker Charles H.
Waller R. A.
Washburne Hempstead
Wheeler Harris A.
Winston F. S.

THE FORTNIGHTLY OF CHICAGO.

203 MICHIGAN AVENUE.

OFFICERS.

MRS. EMMA WINNER ROGERS, - - - President.
MRS. LUCY L. FLOWER, - - - Vice-President.
MRS. ANNA T. DUDLEY, - - - Vice-President.
MRS. EVA R. WEGG, - - Corresponding Secretary.
MRS. ABBY FARWELL FERRY, - Recording Secretary.
MRS. HENRIETTE G. FRANK, - - - Treasurer.

DIRECTORS.

Mrs. Mary H. Wilmarth
Mrs. Emily E. MacVeagh

Mrs. Mary L. Matz
Mrs. Addie H. Gregory

Mrs. Julia D. Herrick
Mrs. Harriet S. Hale

Abbott Mrs. A. R.
Adams Mrs Milward
Alling Mrs. John
Allport Mrs. Frank
Allport Miss May
Armour Mrs. Geo. A.
Ayer Mrs. B. F.
Babcock Mrs. Henry H.
Baldwin Mrs. Abraham
Barrett Mrs. Samuel E.
Bartlett Mrs. Geo. F.
Bates Mrs. Lindon W.
Becker Mrs. Fred'k W.
Bellóws Mrs. Catherine H.
Bentley Mrs. Cyrus jr.
Blackstone Mrs. T. B.
Blair Mrs. Henry A.
Blair Mrs. William
Blatchford Mrs. E. M.
Bodman Mrs. L. W.
Brainard Mrs. Harriet C.
Brayton Dr. Sarah H.
Brown Mrs. Wm. Thayer
Buffum Mrs. Joseph H.
Butler Mrs. William P.
Campbell Mrs. N. W.
Carmichael Mrs. Geo. S.
Carpenter Mrs. Geo. B.
Cheney Mrs. Chas. Edw.
Coleman Mrs. W. Franklin
Coolidge Mrs. Chas. A.
Coolidge Mrs. E. S.
Crow Mrs. M. F.
Day Mrs. Albert M.
Donaldson Mrs. H. H.
Dudley Mrs. E. C.
Eames Mrs. Henry F.
Eames Mrs. Fred.
Ela Mrs. John W.
Ellis Mrs. Sumner
Emerson Mrs. Ralph
Emerson Mrs. Joseph
Evans Mrs Lynden
Ewen Mrs. John M.
Farwell Mrs. C. B.
Ferry Mrs. Abbie Farwell
Fessenden Mrs. B.A.
Flower Mrs. James M.
Frank Mrs. Henry L.
Fuller Mrs. Chas. G.
Galt Mrs. A. T.
Gane Mrs. Thomas F.
Gardiner Mrs. Frances H.
Gilbert Mrs. Frank
Glessner Mrs. John J.
Goodwin Mrs. Daniel
Gregory Mrs. Robert B.
Griggs Mrs. S. C.
Hale Mrs. Wm. G.
Halsted Miss Nellie
Hamill Mrs. Charles D.
Hannah Mrs. John
Hanson Mrs. Burton

Harding Mrs. George F.
Harper Mrs. Wm. R.
Hays Miss Mary
Healy Miss Edith
Henderson Mrs. Chas. M.
Henrotin Mrs. Charles
Herrick Mrs. John J.
Hitchcock Mrs. Annie
Howe Miss Grace T.
Hubbard Mrs. James M.
Hutchinson Mrs. Chas.L.
Hyde Mrs. James Nevins
Isham Mrs. Ralph N.
Jackson Mrs. A. Reeves
Jewett Mrs. John N.
Johnson Mrs. Herrick
Johnson Mrs. H. A.
Judson Mrs. H. P.
Keith Miss Julia L.
Kendig Mrs. J. A. J.
Kennedy Mrs. Horace M.
Kerfoot Miss Alice
Kimball Mrs. Edward A.
Kimball Mrs. W. W.
Kirkland Mrs. Joseph
Kirtland Mrs. Chas. B.
Kretzinger Mrs. Geo. W.
Larned Mrs. W. C.
Lathrop Mrs. Bryan
Lawrence Mrs. C. B.
Lawrence Mrs. Mary D.
Lay Miss Margaret S.
Leake Mrs. Joseph B.
Lloyd Mrs. Henry D.
Locke Mrs. Clinton
Lockwood Mrs. Walter
Loomis Mrs. John M.
Lord Mrs. George
Loring Mrs. Stella Dyer
Lunt Miss Nina Grey
Lyman Mrs. M. E.
MacVeagh Mrs. Franklin
Mackenzie Mrs. John K.
Magruder Mrs. B. D.
Martin Miss Kate B.
Mason Mrs. Henry B.
Mason Mrs. Alverin A.
Matz Mrs. Otto H.
Matz Mrs. Rudolph
Matz Miss Evelyn
McCagg Mrs. Ezra B.
McClurg Mrs. A. C.
McCormick Mrs. Robert
McCormick Mrs. R. Hall
McCormick Mrs. Wm. G.
McMurray Mrs. E. W.
Merrill Mrs. A. F.
Miller Mrs. Emily H.
Miller Mrs. J. A.
Mitchell Mrs. J. B.
Mitchell Mrs. J. S.
Monroe Miss Harriet S.

Mooie Mrs. Gurdon G.
Moore Mrs. William H.
Mott Mrs. John Grenville
Mulliken Mrs. Chas. H.
Nixon Mrs. Wm. Penn
Norton Mrs. J. Henry
Owen Mrs. James R.
Palmer Mrs. Potter
Parker Mrs. Frank W.
Peattie Mrs. Elia W.
Peck Mrs. Clarence
Peirce Mrs. L. H.
Perkins Miss Janet R.
Phelps Mrs. Erskine M.
Porter Mrs. William D.
Potter Mrs. O. W.
Ray Mrs. Julia A.
Rice Miss Rebecca S.
Rich Mrs. M. Byron
Rockwell Mrs. Helen
Rogers Mrs. Henry W.
Root Mrs. John W.
Scammon Mrs. J. Y.
Scott Mrs. James W.
Sheldon Mrs. Theodore
Shepard Mrs. Henry M.
Sherman Mrs. Penoyer L.
Shorey Mrs. Daniel L.
Silsbee Mrs. J. L.
Smith Mrs. Fred A.
Smith Mrs. Sabin
Starr Miss Eliza E.
Starrett Mrs. Helen E
Stevenson Mrs. A. F.
Stevenson Dr. Sarah H.
Stone Miss Eliza A.
Stone Mrs. H. O.
Stone Mrs. Henry B.
Swan Mrs. James H.
Talbot Miss Marion
Thomas Mrs. R. F.
Thompson Mrs. Slason
Tilton Mrs. Lucretia J.
Trimingham Miss A. E.
Ullman Mrs Frederick
Underhill Mrs. Elizabeth
Walker Mrs. J. M.
Walker Mrs. Wm. B.
Waller Mrs. Edward.
Ward Mrs. L. A. Coonley
Ward Mrs. O Van Schaack
Watson Mrs. L. H.
Wegg Mrs. D. S.
Wilkinson Mrs. Dudley
Williams Mrs. Stalham
Willing Mrs. Henry J.
Willits Mrs. Geo. S.
Wilmarth Mrs. H. M.
Winterbotham Mrs. Jos.
Withrow Mrs. Thomas F.
Wright Mrs. Edward
Wynne Mrs. Madeline Yale

THE FORTY CLUB.

OFFICERS.

W. T. HALL, - - - - - - President.
EDWARD FREIBERGER, - - - Vice-President.
GEORGE W. HANCOCK, - - - - - Secretary.
GEORGE H. JENNEY, - - - - - - Treasurer.

MEMBERS OF EXECUTIVE COMMITTEE.

George J. Hamlin   Albert S. Laflin   Rev. E. M. Stires

MEMBERS.

Akin H. F.	Ewing Judge W. G.	Hart James A.	Powers Harry J.
Allen James Lane	Freiberger Edward	Horton Judge O. H.	Powers L. D.
Channon J. H.	Glenn J. M.	Hunt Charles H.	Pullman W. C.
Charlton Geo. J.	Graham W. A. S.	Jenney George H.	Root Frederick W.
Chatfield - Taylor	Hale Edward C.	Kayzer Samuel	Smith Frederick A.
H. C.	Hall W. T.	Kohlsaat E. W.	Sommers Harry G.
Clark Frank K.	Hamlin George J.	Laflin Albert S.	Stires Rev. Ernest
Clayton C. B.	Hancock GeorgeW.	Moore W. H.	M.
Cone G. W.	Hanecy Elbridge	Morris Frank M.	Swift H. B.
Curtis W. W.	Judge	Pierce Norval Dr.	Wachsmuth L. C.
Eldredge GeorgeC.			

NON-RESIDENT MEMBERS.

Barron Elwyn A., London, Eng.	MacIntosh Burr, New York
Crawford S. A., Denver, Colo.	Murray Frank, New York
Gardiner Cornelius, Washington	Reade Capt. Philip H., U. S. A.
Gibbs Montgomery B., Akron, Ohio	Richardson Leander, New York
Hayman Alf, New York	Salsbury Nate, New York
King Gen. Charles, Milwaukee	Unitt E. G., New York
Kuhns E. Louis, South Bend, Ind.	Wallace Laurie, Omaha
LaShelle Kirke, New York	Williams Walter, New York

HONORARY MEMBERS.

Barnabee Henry C.	Holland Edmund	Morris Felix	Russell Edmund
Barrymore Maurice	M.	Morris Ramsay	Skinner Otis
Boniface Geo. C.jr.	Karl Tom	O'Neill James	Smith F. Hopkin-
Clay Cecil	Kennan George	O'Rell Max	son
Dixey Henry E.	Lackaye Wilton	Page Thomas N.	Sweatnam Willis
Goodwin.Nat C.	MacDonald W. H.	Paulding Frederick	Willard Edward S
Hoff Edwin W.	McWade John E.	Reed Roland	Wilson Francis

THE FRIDAY CLUB.

OFFICERS.

MRS. HORACE H. MARTIN, - .- - - President.
MISS ELIZABETH HEAD, - - First Vice-President.
MRS. SLASON THOMPSON, - - Second Vice-President.
MRS. S. A. LYNDE, - - - Corresponding Secretary.
MRS. WM. S. JENKS, - - - Recording Secretary.
MRS. GEORGE S. PAYSON, - - - - Treasurer.

EXECUTIVE COMMITTEE.

Miss Edith Healy	Miss Jennie E. Cox	Mrs. Francis A. Sawyer
Miss Lucy Monroe	Mrs. Hugh J. McBirney	Mrs. Arthur J. Eddy
Miss Dora Seeberger		Mrs. Charles T. Atkinson

MEMBERS.

Aldis Mrs. Arthur T.	Bell Miss Lillian	Blatchford Mrs. Paul
Atkinson Mrs. Chas.	Bentley Mrs. Cyrus jr.	Bradley Mrs. J. D.
Augur Mrs Wheaton	Besly Mrs. C. H.	Bryan Miss Jennie B.
Baldwin Mrs. Charles H.	Blaine Mrs. Emmons	Burke Mrs. Edmund
Barnes Miss Minnie W.	Blatchford Miss F. M.	Burry Mrs. William

Butler Mrs. Hermon B.
Carpenter Mrs. G. A.
Carpenter Miss Nellie
Case Mrs. John R.
Chappell Mrs. Howard F.
Chatfield-Taylor Mrs.H.C
Churchill Mrs. Frank S.
Cochran Mrs. J. Lewis
Coolidge Mrs. Frederic S.
Cox Miss Jennie E.
Cramer Mrs. Ambrose
Curtiss Mrs. C. C.
Davis Mrs. N. S. jr.
Davis Mrs. R. L.
Dawes Mrs. C. M.
Deane Mrs. Ruthven
Delano Mrs. F. A.
Durkee Miss Cara W.
Eddy Mrs. A. J.
Enders Miss Margaret
Evans Mrs. Lynden
Ewen Mrs. J. M.
Farwell Mrs. Arthur L.
Farwell Mrs. F. C.
Farwell Mrs. J. V. jr.
Ferry Mrs. Abby F.
Ferry Mrs. Charles H.
Fisher Mrs. George P. jr.
Fuller Mrs. F. R.
Garrett Mrs. T. Mauro
Gott Mrs. John R.
Goudy Mrs. Wm. J.
Gray Miss I. C.
Hale Miss Mary B.
Harriman Mrs. E. A.
Head Miss Elizabeth
Head Miss Katharine
Healy Miss Edith.
Herrick Miss Louise
Herrick Mrs. Robert
Hill Miss M. S.
Hodges Mrs.
Hooper Mrs. Henry
Houghteling Mrs. J. L.
Hubbard Mrs. William H.

Hunt Mrs. L. Platt
Isham Miss A. E.
Isham Mrs. George S.
Jenks Mrs. Wm. S.
Jewett Mrs. Edward
Jewett Mrs. Samuel R.
Jones Miss M. K.
Kales Mrs. John D.
Keep Miss Frances
Kelley Miss Maud M.
Kellogg Miss Emma C.
King Mrs. Francis
King Mrs. Rockwell
Kirkland Miss Caroline
Knott Mrs. H. A.
Laflin Mrs. Louis E.
Landon Miss H. J.
Lynde Mrs. S. A.
Marston Mrs. Thomas B.
Martin Mrs. Horace H.
Martyn Mrs. E. Jenner
McBirney Mrs. H. J.
McCagg Mrs. E. B.
McCormick Mrs. Cyrus H.
McCormick Mrs.Hamilton
McGenniss Mrs. Charles
Meeker Mrs. George W.
Meysenburg Mrs. E. A.
Monroe Miss Lucy
Moore Mrs. E. W.
Nelson Mrs. Murry, jr.
Nixon Miss Mary S.
Northcote Mrs. Amyas S.
Otis Mrs. William A.
Packard Mrs. George
Payson Mrs. George S.
Peabody Mrs. F. S.
Phillips Mrs. W. A.
Pomeroy Mrs. S. H.
Risser Miss Elizabeth F.
Rowe Miss Elizabeth L.
Runnells Miss Lucy
Ryerson Mrs. E. L.
Sawyer Mrs. Frances A.
Scott Mrs. James W.

Seeberger Miss Dora
Shufeldt Mrs. W. B. E.
Skeele Mrs. H. B.
Skinner Miss Elizabeth
Skinner Miss Frederika
Smith Mrs. Dunlap
Smith Mrs. Ernest F.
Smith Miss Mary Rozet
Snow Miss Helen E.
Spicer Mrs. V. K.
Stone Miss Eliza A.
Street Mrs. Charles A.
Sturges Mrs. Helen S.
Sturges Miss Mary D.
Thompson Mrs. Slason
Towner Miss E. W.
Troost Miss Louise S.
Trowbridge Miss Cornelia R.
Tuttle Mrs. Henry N.
Tyson Mrs. Russell
Wadsworth Miss Helen
Waite Miss Ella R.
Walker Mrs. Charles M.
Waller Mrs. James B. jr
Waller Mrs. Robert A.
Waller Mrs. William
Wallop Mrs. O. H.
Webster Mrs. Lewis D.
Wells Miss Luda
Wentworth Mrs. Moses J
West Mrs. Frederic T.
Wheeler Mrs. Arthur D.
Wheeler Mrs. Frank S.
Whitman Mrs. Russell
Williams Miss Annie
Williams Miss Cora B.
Williams Mrs. Lawrence
Willing Mrs. Heury J.
de Windt Mrs. H. A.
Winston Mrs. Dudley
Winston Mrs. F. S.
Witherspoon Miss Grace
Wood Mrs. Ira C.

NON-RESIDENT MEMBERS.

Alward Mrs. Herbert
Bates Mrs. Lindon W.
Bowen Mrs. Clarence W.
Dabney Miss Frances S.

Fay Mrs. Charles
Martin Miss Maud
Newell Mrs. John E.
Norton Mrs. Charles D.

Preston Miss Emma C.
Ryerson Miss Eleanor
Stewart Mrs. P. B.

HONORARY MEMBERS.

Adams Mrs. Milward
Chetlain Mrs A. L.

French Miss Hannah K.
Henrotin Mrs. Charles

Monroe Miss Harriet
Palmer Mrs. Potter

GERMANIA MÆNNERCHOR.
NORTHWEST CORNER CLARK STREET AND GERMANIA PLACE.

OFFICERS.

OTTO C. SCHNEIDER,	President.
GUSTAV WITTMEYER,	Vice-President.
GODFREY SCHMID,	Secretary.
AD. UHRLAUB,	Treasurer.

Mayer Oscar F.
McCrea W. S.
Meagher J. F.
Meerhoff Dr. C. E.
Meinshausen O.
Menn Dr. Rudolph
Meyenschein F. A.
MeyerFerdinandC.
Meyer Fred
Meyer George
Meyer Jacob
Meyer Magnus
Meyer Martin
Michaelis W. R.
Michalowski H.von
Miller B.
Milling William
Moeller C. C.
Morrill Donald L.
Mueller Herman
Mueller Valentin
Muench Fred.
Muench Louis
Neymann A. M.
Nickelsen A.
Nockin Bernhard jr
Ogilby Chas.
Olsen A. G.
Orb John A.
Paepcke H.
Pank J. Henry
Patterson Robt. W.
Pauling E. G.
Peabody F. S.
Peak F. H.
Peters F.
Peters F. M.
Petersen George L.
Petersen Hermann
Petersen Hugo T.
Petersen Victor J.
Peterson P. S.
Petrie M.
Pfister Mrs. Emma
Piper Henry
Plautz C. H.
Pomy H.

Puckner Wm. A.
Ramm C.
Rapp William, jr.
Raster Edwin
Rehm Jacob
Rehm William H.
Revell Alex. H.
Revell David
Revell Alex. H.
Rhode J. C. W.
Rhode Rud. E.
Rice John C.
Richberg J. C.
Richter Arthur C.
Richter Aug. F.
Richter Robert H.
Rinn Phil
Rintelman A. H.
Roehling Geo.
Roesch Frank
Rohr Dr. F.
Roland L. B.
Roth Charles
Rothbarth Paul
Rothe Aug.
Rubens Harry
Rudolph Emil
Rudolph Frank
Ruehl Dr. L. A.
Ruh Frank E.
Ruhstrat Ad.
Saurenhaus Dr. E.
Schaller Henry
Schaub F. J.
Scherzer Alb. H.
Schlachter J. W.
Schlick E. R.
Schlogl Edw. H.
Schlogl Joseph
Schlotthauer G. H.
Schmid Godfrey
Schmid Rich G.
Schmidgall F. L.
Schmidt Leo
Schmidt L. F.
Schmidt Wm.
Schneider George
Schneider Otto C.

Schoenefeld Henry
Schoepflin A.
Scholbe M. A.
Schonlau Charles
Schrader Theo.
Schultz Martin M.
Seidel Ludwig A.
Seidel Walter F.
Seipp W. C.
Sheldon George W.
Shields Michael
Simon Chas. W.
Sittig Eugene A.
Sittig Wm. A.
Smith C. A.
Sontag Fritz
Spalding C. F.
Spicker Dr. M.
Spielmann Alfred
Spielmann Arthur
Steffens A. B.
Stein Carl
Stern Max
Stevenson Alex. F.
Stroever Carl
Thaler A. J.
Theurer Joseph
Thielemann Chas.
Thielen Jacob
Thielmann Franz
Thome M.
Thorwart H.
Tosetti Ernst
Trude A. S.
True John R.
Uhlendorf L.
Uhrlaub Ad.
Uihlein Ed. G.
Ullrich Michael
Unzicker Herman
Unzicker M.
Unzicker Otto
Upham Fred W.
VanVlissingen P.
Vocke Wm.
Voelcker John J.
Vogel Carl A.

Vogler Hermann
Volger Fred.
Vollmer Herman
Wacker Chas. H.
Wagner Dr. Carl
Wagner Dr. Chas.
 B.
Wagner E. W.
Wagner Fritz
Wahl Robert
Walsh John R.
Wassmandorff
 Wm. G.
Weaver Chas. S.
Weber P. J.
Wegmann Jules F.
Wegmann Julius
Weinsheimer W. J.
Weiss George A.
Weiss John H.
Welcker Dr. P. R.
Werner Otto B.
Wertheim Edw.
Wetterer Dr. Her-
 mann
Wichert Henry
Wilke Gustav
Winston F. S.
Winter Philipp
Witte Conrad
Wittmeyer Gustav
Wittstein A. H.
Woelfel George
Wohlhuetter C. V.
Wollensak J. F.
WoltersdorfArthur
Woltersdorf Louis
Woltz J.
Yerkes Chas. T.
Zander Aug.
Zeiger Geb. W.
Zeisler Dr. Jos.
Zeisler Sigmund
Zimmermann Alb.
ZimmermanDrG.A
Zschuppe C. jr.

GLEN VIEW GOLF AND POLO CLUB.

EVANSTON.

OFFICERS.

WILLIAM H. BARTLETT, - - - - President.
HUGH R. WILSON, - - - - - Vice-President.
W. J. LITTLEJOHN, - - - - - Treasurer.
GEORGE P. MERRICK, - - - - - Secretary.

DIRECTORS.

William H. Bartlett
Hugh R. Wilson
William Holabird
John M. Allen

Marshall M. Kirkman
Frank P. Frazier
Fred S. James
J. C. Peasley

John W. Scott
George P. Merrick
W. J. Littlejohn

MEMBERS.

Ackert C. A.
Adams B. F.
Allen Benjamin
Allen J. M.
Anthony W. M.
Armour M.Cochran
Armsby Mrs. Cor-
nelia B.
Arnd Charles
Arnd Frederick
Ash L. H.
Banks A. F.
Barclay S. J.
Barnhart A. M.
Barrell J. Finley
Barry Charles H.
Bartlett N o r m a n
W.
Bartlett Wm. H.
Bartlett Wm. H. jr.
Beard Thomas
Beidler H. A.
Biddle Wm. B. ~
Billings H. F.
Bogart W. B.
Borden G. M.
Borden Louis L.
Boynton Charles T.
Britten Louis
Brooks James C.
Brown George D.
Brown William L.
Buckley Charles W.
Buell A. C.
Burnet W. H.
Burnham D. H.
Burnham Hugh L.
Butler J. Fred
Cable H. D.
Cadow S. B.
Caldwell B. D.
Campbell W. N.
Carr Clyde M.
Carson Samuel
Chapin Betsey Miss
Chapin F. S.
Church E. V.
Clarke John V.
Clarke Mrs. L. B.
Clarkson Ralph
Cleveland Chas. B.
Coman Seymour
Comstock Wm. C.
Congdon C. B.
Connell C. J.
Crane A. M.

Crawford Henry jr.
Creighton Thos. S.
Dakin Frank C.
Dale H. S.
Damsel W. H.
Deering Chas.W.C.
DeGolyer L. N.
Donelson D. P.
Donnell James W.
Drake F. E.
Drake John B. jr.
Dray Gail
Dwight Walter T.
Dyche William A.
Elliott Frank M.
Elphicke C. W.
Evans A. F.
Ewen John M.
Fair J. B.
Farnum A. H.
Farnum H. W.
Farson John
Farwell H. S.
Farwell Simeon
Foster Volney W.
Frazier Frank D.
Frazier F. P.
Fuller Charles G.
Garaghty J. H.
Gerould F. W.
Gilbert A. M.
Gilbert H. K.
Givens R. C.
Grant Louis M.
Grepe J. S.
Grey Charles F.
Gridley Martin M.
Gridley Nelson C.
Harding J. C.
Hardy F. A.
Harris J. F.
Harvey George L.
Henrotin Fernand
Dr.
Henry Eugene J.
Hibbard Angus S.
Hoag William G.
Hofstra William S
Holabird William
Horton O. H.Judge
Hoyt Phelps B.
Hubbard William
Irwin D. M.
James Fred S.
Jamieson M. M.
Jenkins George R.

Jerrems A. N.
Kedzie John H. jr.
Keyes Rollin A.
Kirk James M.
Kirk John B.
Kirk Milton W.
Kirk Walter T.
Kirkman Marshall
M.
Lacey Edward S.
Lake Richard C.
Lake William H.
Larned S. J.
Lawrence J. A.
Leland E. F.
Lewis Charles G.
Lewis D. R.
Lindsay W. W.
Little Charles G.
Littlejohn Wiley J.
Lord George S.
Lynch Richard W.
Macdonald C. A.
Martin F. S.
McBirney Day
McCullough H. R.
Mears C. H.
Merrick George P.
Miller Frederick C.
Miller H. H. C.
Mudge D. A.
Munn Noel S.
Nash Wm.
Nickerson R. C.
Nicol James
Noyes David A.
Orr Arthur
Osborne W. Irving
Page J. C.
Parker H. O.
Patten George W.
Patten James
Peabody F. F.
Pearsons Harry P.
Pearsons H. A.
Peters Homer H.
Pirie John T. jr.
Poucher B. G.
Quan James E.
Quincy Charles F.
Read Gardner
Remy Curtis H.
Reynolds Dr. A. R.
Richards Dr. G. E.
Robinson Harry P.
Robinson J. K.

Rodgers Florence
Miss
Rogers Mrs. S.
Katherine
Rowe Mrs. C. H.
Rycroft Herbert E.
Salisbury W. M.
Sargent George H.
Sargent George M.
Sargent W. D.
Schwender John
Scott John W.
Sears J. B.
Shaffer J. C.
Shumway Philip
R.
Silsbee J. L.
Simonds O. C.
Slade Charles B.
Smith E. J.
Smith Henry T.
Smith H. Sanborn
Spalding Charles F.
Stockton Wm. E.
Sweet John W.
Thoman Leroy D.
Thorne George A.
Tietgens Paul
Thorne Wm. C.
Towne Charles E.
Tweedy Herbert J.
Upham Frederic W.
Vance W. L.
Van Vlissingen
James H.
Ward C. A.
Ward Miss Estelle F
Watson J. V.
Webster Edward H.
Webster William A.
Weeks Gilbert M.
Wheeler Charles P.
Wickes Roscoe L.
Williams C. L.
Williams Norman
Wilson E. C.
Wilson Hugh R.
Wilson H. S.
Wilson J. Eldredge
Wilson Milton H.
Wilson Oliver T.
Winne Wm. N. D.
Worcester Chas.H.
Work George Z.
Young A. N.
Young William S.

HAMILTON CLUB.
114 MADISON STREET.

MEMBERS.

Adams Wm. Porter
Adkinson Elmer W.
Aldrich J. Frank
Allen John K.
Allerton Samuel W.
Alling Charles jr.
Alling Edward H.
Ames John C.
Anderson B. N.
Andrews James D.
Anthony Charles E.
Anthony George D.
Apmadoc W. Tudor
Ashcraft E. M.
Babcock Alfred J.
Bacon Henry M.
Baer A. W.
Baker Frank E.
Baldwin Henry R.
Baldwin J. A.
Ball Farlin H.
Bancroft E. A.
Bangs Fred A.
Barbee William S.
Barber E. L.
Barbour James J.
Barker G. F.
Barker John T.
Barnes Albert C.
Barr Edward
Barry Edw. P.
Bassett O. P.
Bassett R. C.
Batten John H
Bauman H.
Beachey Hill
Beardsley George
Beaumont John F.
Becker Abraham G.
Becker A. W.
Behan Louis J.
Beitler H. C.
Belknap Hugh R.
Benedict Geo. H.
Bennett J. L.
Bennett Wm. H.
Benton George P.

Berry F. J.
Bersbach Alfred
Best Henry
Billings Charles L.
Bingham F. A.
Bither W. A.
Bliss E. R.
Blocki W. Gale
Blume George P.
Boland James F.
Bowyer Lorraine F.
Boyd Thoma C.
Brace William
Bradburn James
Braden Jos. C.
Bradley C. H.
Brainerd Edw. R.
Brand Chas. H.
Brand E. L.
Branuhold Louis F.
Brintnall Wm. H.
Brown Adelbert E.
Brown Edwin S.
Browne Edward
Buck O. J.
Burlingham F. W.
Burnan Arthur
Burres J. R.
Burton Robert A.
Busse Fred A.
Butler Rust C.
Calkins Charles R.
Campbell D. A.
Card Wilfred H.
Carpenter Harry H.
Carter Donald M.
Carter George B.
Carter O. N.
Castle P. V.
Caswell C. L.
Catlin Donald C.
Chapin Ora E.
Cheever Dwight B.
Clancy A. W.
Clark Charles M.
Clarke Henry T. jr.
Clemence D. D.

Cody Arthur B.
Cody Hope Reed
Cody Sherman P.
Coffin Percy B.
Cohen Samuel
Colburn W. E.
Coleman Wm. A.
Collins Charles E.
Collins Lorin C. Jr.
Colt A. J.
Condee L. D.
Converse C. M.
Cook O. S.
Cook R. S.
Cooley Harlan W.
Cooper A. O.
Coussens P. W.
Cox F. M.
Coyne F. E.
Crawford C. H.
Crilly D. F.
Crilly Edward
Crilly W. M.
Crowley Albert E.
Crozier Frank
Cruikshank C. E.
Curry J. Seymour
Curtis Henry M.
Curtis Walter W.
Cutter W. F.
Cutting C. S.
Danziger Louis
Davies Thomas
Davis Milton R.
Davidson Chas.
Dayton Melville E.
Defrees Joseph H..
Delaware A. S.
Dempsey Edward
Deneen Charles S.
Denney Milton
Dennis Albert E.
Dicker E. A.
Dixon Arthur
Dixon Arthur A.
Dixon George Wm.
Dixon Thomas J.

Dorsett J. T.
Dow Lorenzo E.
Draper A. W.
Draper Frank B.
Dundas Joseph H.
Dutton Charles N.
Eastman E. P.
Eddy Alfred D.
Eidmann Henry F.
Egan John G.
Elliott W. S. jr.
Ely James O.
Eppstein J. M.
Everett Coleman S.
Everett Edw. Warren
Everett John C.
Everett Wm. R.
Fairbanks N. H.
Farovid John R.
Fellows Charles
Fish A. C.
Fisher Harry H.
Fitch John H.
Fletcher Wm. M.
Flood R. D.
Foell Charles M.
Foreman Milton J.
Foss George E.
Foster D. J.
Foster W. A.
Frank Isaac M.
Frederickson Wm.
Freeman H. V.
Freeman John L.
Friedman Monroe J.
Fullenwider J. A.
Fuller L. H.
Gansberger F. H.
Gauger John A.
Geer David S.
Gemmill W. N.
Gibbons John
Giertsen Waldemar
Gilbert Allan A.
Gilbert James H.
Gilbert M. P.

Gleason H. W.	Holmes Thos. J.	Lewis H. C.	Mulford Leonard S.
Glennie Albert E.	Holway Wesley H.	Linden James	Mund Herman H.
Glennon E. T.	Hooper Edwin E.	Lindley E. C.	Munger Edwin A.
Glick Ulysses S.	Hopkins F. A.	Lindsay D. J.	Munger H. B.
Goff Fred L.	Horr George B.	Loeb Adolph	Murray C. A.
Goodman Herbt.E.	Horton O. H.	Long T. K.	Murray C. R.
Goodnow Chas. N.	Houston W. T.	Longenecker Joel	Nance Willis O.
Goodspeed F. C.	Howard D.	M.	Nelson John L.
Goodwin Leonard	Howison Geo. jr.	Louer A.	Newman Gideon E.
Goodyear C. A.	Hughes Chas.	Lowell W. A.	Newman Jacob
Goodykoontz C. H.	Hull.Perry A.	Luken Frank J.	Nichols C. M.
Gordon Charles W.	Hunt W. B.	Lund Adolph	Nichols Edward C.
Goss Charles O.	Hyde Edwin N.	Lutz T. C.	Nichols Franklin
Gould Frank	Iles Robert S.	Mabie C. E.	Nisbet L. K.
Graves Albert H.	Irwin Alexander	MacDonald R. J.	Nickerson D. W.
Green Maxwell S.	Irwin Harry L.	Madden M. B.	Noble W. S.
Greenebaum Henry	Irwin James C.	Magee John J.	Norton Charles L.
Greenebaum M. E.	Jackson H. B.	Magerstadt E. J.	Norton Willard D.
Greenfield Chas.W.	Jackson Samuel W.	Mann James R.	Nourse B. F.
Gregory W. C.	Jackson.T. H.	Marchand G. L.	Noyes William S.
Grier G. W.	Jacobs S. W.	Marnott A. R.	Olds Lee H.
Gross Howard H.	Jacobsen J. A.	Martyn Chauncey	Olds Walter
Gunderson Geo. O.	Jamieson Stillman	W.	Oliver Frederick S.
Gundlach C. J.	B.	Martyn R. Delos	Olson Edw. H.
Gunning Robt. J.	Jayne Edward L.	Marx M. A.	Olson Henry
Hall Wm. T.	Jenkins Geo. R.	Mason William C.	Orr E. K.
Hamburg L. E.	Johnston H. B.	Massey Wilford	Orr Louis T.
Hamill T. W.	Jones S. J.	Mathews Albert	Orr William T.
Hamline John H.	Jones W. Clyde	Mathews Geo. W.	Osborne Frank S.
Hanberg John	Judah Noble B.	Mayou J. S.	Othmer Henry
Hanecy Elbridge	Judd Edward J.	McArdle E. J.	Parish John D.
Harmon Chas. S.	Judd Frederick F.	McCandless A. W.	Parish S. M.
Harper C. L.	Jukes A. G.	McCarthy M. H.	Parker Francis W.
Harper Wm. H.	Juul Niels	McCloud Sidney	Partridge N. A.
Harpham Edwin L.	Kavanagh Marcus	McCollum G.Albert	Patterson C. Earl
Harrold James P.	Keating Arthur J.	McConahey J. M.	Patterson James C.
Hart Elmer W.	Kehlor J. M.	McCortney J. H.	Patterson W. C.
Hart Harry	Kemper A. L.	McCoy Chas. S.	Peale Charles M.
Harvey John H.	Kimball C. F.	McDermid JulianM	Pearse J. D.
Hastings G. L.	Kimball Granville	McDonaldWalterH	Pease Frank B.
Hatch G. Walter	King Edward A.	McElroy John H.	Pedrick Isaac H.
Hayes F. W. C.	King Fred W.	McGuire J. Fred	Penington T. C.
Haynes D. J.	King Hoyt	McLaren Wm.	Pennoyer Jas. C.
Headburg A. L.	Kinney George K.	McMurdy Robt.	Pentecost William
Healy James J.	Kinney James A.	McNulta John	Perkins L. W.
Hebel Oscar	Kirk Charles W.	McSurley W. H.	Perkins Walton
Heckman Wallace	Kline Samuel J.	Mercer Lewis P.	Perley E. E.
Henderson Wm.	Kneisley John L.	Merchant Walter	Perry George B.
Henry John A.	Knox R. H.	Metcalf Ralph	Perry Isaac N.
Helmer Frank A.	Koch Charles R. E.	Meyer Oscar	Petit A. J.
Herr Percy B.	Kohn Louis H.	Milchrist Thos. E.	Phillips W. E.
Herrick William B.	Kozminski M. W.	Miller Chas. P.	Pick Albert
Hertz Henry L.	Kramer Adolph F.	Miller Charles S.	Pierce D. A.
Hewitt James	Lafnbert John	Miller Geo. W.	Plumsted J. F.
Hibbard J. W.	Lampert Nelson	Miller John S.	Porter Breske D.
Hickman Charles	Lane T. S.	Miller W. C.	Porter George P.
Hills W. E.	Lauth J.	Mills D. W.	Porter John B.
Hiner Joseph W.	Lawson William C.	Mix James T.	Powell Isaac N.
Hirsch James H.	Lee A. V.	Monroe C. A.	Price Henry W.
Hirschl A. J.	Lee Charles T.	Moore G. C.	Pringle F. W.
Hitchens K. K.	Lee Harry F.	More R. Wilson	Purington D. V.
Hodgkins Jefferson	Leeds C. S.	Morgan G. C. jr.	Randall C. E.
Hogan D. J.	Leopold Alfred F.	Morris Ira	Randall Milo B.
Holden H. P.	Leopold Nathan F.	Moses Hamilton	Rathbone H. R.
Holdom Jesse	Levinson S. O.	Moulton F. I.	Raymond Samuel B
Holman W. A.	Levis John M.	Moulton William C.	Redick G. C.

Reed F. Raymond
Remington H. W.
Revell Alexander H
Richards J. T.
Richards L.
Richardson F. G.
Richardson John
Richardson J. A.
Rigby William C.
Riggs George W.
Ringer Jacob
Roberts E. L.
Roberts William B.
Robertson Wm. A.
Robinson Wm. F.
Roblin David H.
Rose Frank A.
Rosenthal A b r a -
 ham L.
Rosenthal James
Ross C. A.
Ross F. R.
Rountree Harrison
 H.
Royer J. C. F.
Rummler Wm. R.
Rush G. Fred
Ruth V. B.
Sackett R. E.
Scanlan Thomas
Schlecht Charles
Schryver H. A.
Schuyler D. J.
Schuyler D. J. jr.
Sears C. B.
Sears N. C.
Severson O. F.
Shaeter Wm. C.

Shaw Warwick A.
Shedd E. T.
Shepherd Frank L.
Sheriff Andrew R.
Sherman Mark R.
Sherman Roger
Sherman Ward B.
SherwoodLudlowS.
Sherwood N.
Shipman Geo. E.
Shipnes Wilford C.
Sibley James W.
Sieg Charles H.
Simon Robert M.
SimontonHarveyP.
Singer Charles G.
Sinclair Jas. G.
Skinner F. M.
Small Ralph D.
Smith Abner
Smith Benjamin M.
Smith Frederick A.
Smith H.-S.
Smith Oscar M.
Smyth John M.
Sollitt Oliver
Sollitt Ralph
Sollitt Sumner
Southard A. B.
Spalding Chas. D.
Spofford Geo. W.
Spooner F. E.
Sprogle Howard O.
Standish Chas.A.V.
Steele Henry B.
Steiglitz N.
Stern Julius
Stevens Lester W.

Stevens L. G.
Stewart Charles C.
Stillman H. W.
Stowell Harry A.
Straus Simon W.
Strickler Harvey
Stringfield C. P.
Sullivan W. K.
Swett W. H.
Taylor A. A.
Taylor Clayton R.
Taylor Edward H.
Thatcher Ralph H.
Thomas Abram L.
Thomas B.
Thomas J. P.
Thurston F. W.
Tiball Z. L.
Tisdale Clark J.
Tobin Arthur W.
Torrison Oscar M.
Towle Henry S.
Towler E. T.
Towne W. M.
Turner John C.
Turner Thomas M.
UnderwoodGeo.W.
Upham Fred W.
Vail Charles W.
Vierling Robert
VonAlbade Francis
 T.
Waidner L. H.
Walker George R.
Walker Herman L.
Walter William A.
Ware Orlando C.
Warner A. J.

Warner F.Harrison
Warren Chas. D.
Warren Clinton J.
Warren F. A.
Washburn Wm. D.
Wathier Chas. A.
Wayne H. L.
Weber W. H.
Weil Theodore
Wells Frank
Welch Arthur S.
Wenban A. C.
West Roy O.
Westwood E. C.
Wheeler M. L.
Wheeler Newton C.
Wheelock W. W.
Whirl John J.
Whitesell J. H.
Whiton W. Starr
Whittemore M. W.
Wiemers Wm. F.
Wight Samuel A.
Wiles Robert H.
Wilkerson Jas. H.
Williams F. M.
Williston Alfred D.
Wisler Henry M.
Wood L. C.
Wood Walpole
Woods F. M.
Woodward W. E.
Wooley J. H.
Wringer S. B.
Wygant Alonzo
Young Linn H.
Youngberg John E.

HIGHLAND PARK CLUB.
HIGHLAND PARK.

OFFICERS.

R. W. PATTON, - - - - - - President.
F. D. EVERETT, - - - - First Vice-President.
K. R. SMOOT, - - - - Second Vice-President.
DANIEL COBB, - - - - - - - Secretary.
A. C. MORGAN, - - - - - - Treasurer.

DIRECTORS.

K. R. Smoot   F. D. Everett   F. P. Hall
Daniel Cobb   A. C. Morgan   T. Barbour Brown
R. W. Patton   F. P. Boynton   R. D. Hill

MEMBERS.

Adams J. McG.
Alexander W. A.
Basye A. A.
Boulton G. D.
Boulton K.
Boynton Edgar
Boynton F. P.
Brown F. C.

Brown T. B.
Chandler H. H.
Chandler R. G.
Chapman C. A.
Cobb Daniel
Coe S. M.
Cregier W. R.
Cushing F. W.

Egan W. C.
Everett C. F.
Everett F. D.
Fischer Fred
Fullerton Chas. W.
Gray Elisha
Green C. M.
Gump B. F.

Hall F. P.
Hawkins F. P.
Hill R. D.
Hodson M. E.
James Mrs. W. A.
Kirk Chas. W.
Knox S. F.
Lasher W. S.

Lightner T.	Newman Dr. H. P.	Smith Mrs. C. R.	Vail H. S.
Mason G. A.	Patton R. W.	Smoot K. R.	VanSchaick H.
Mersereau J. D.	Phillips C. G.	Snow E. M.	Wakem J. W.
Millard S. M.	Prall J. S.	Street H. C.	Winchester F. C.
Montgomery P. A.	Rice Chas. B.	Street R. J.	Wolcott Rev. P. C.
Morgan A. C.	Schumacher B. W.	Stubbs W. C.	Yoe C. C.
Morgan O. H.	Shields J. H.	Thorn Francis	Yoe L. G.
Moseley Carlton	Small Mrs. E. A.	Troxel T. G.	

THE HINSDALE CLUB.
HINSDALE.

OFFICERS.

JAMES A. BLOOD, - - - - - - President.
F. S. CABLE, - - - - - - Vice-President.
H. R. THAYER, - - - Secretary and Treasurer.

DIRECTORS.

James A. Blood	A. B. Freeman	W. W. Waite
F. S. Cable	M. A. Myers	T. C. Tallman
	H. R. Thayer	

MEMBERS.

Allen C. A.	Danforth Jerome J.	Jackson W. W.	Pape T. C.
Allen F. G.	Davidson W.	Jefferson N.	Payne W. C.
Ayers F. E.	Davis E. F.	Johnson Wm. A.	Perry W. D.
Bassett O. P.	Dean Harvey	Johnston W. S.	Pollock Geo. L.
Bebb Wm Dr.	Dean R. L.	Joseph J. F.	Preston D. H.
Beidler A. F.	Dennison C. G.	Kimbell C. B.	Raftree M. L.
Bird C. D.	Duncan Wm.	Kimbell S. T.	Raymond C. E.
Blackman W. L.	Earle J. E.	Kittle E. B.	Redfern J. N.
Blood J. A.	Eustis T. W.	Kline George	Reed J. W.
Bogue Geo. M.	Fairchild E. J.	Knight W. H.	Richie Bruce E.
Bohlander J. jr.	Fayerweather E.E.	Knisely H. C.	Robbins George B
Boyd Robert	Freeman A. B.	Krohn W. F.	Robinson A. R.
Bradley J. C. F.	Freeman W. H.	Landis J. W.	Ross J. C.
Bradley J. H.	Froscher Adolph	Lemmon T. A.	Ruth L. C.
Bradley R. R.	Fulton H. A.	Lewis George F.	Schuyler F. J.
Briggs L.	Gardner Geo. C.	Linsley Charles	Scotford F. E.
Buffington W. J.	Gardner H. A.	Linsley T. H.	Scotford H. A.
Burton John H.	Gear F. O.	McClintock B. R.	Shaw Edward E.
Burton O. M.	Gordon Wm. G.	McClintock Jas.	Sherry M. R. M.
Butler Frank O.	Hawtin F. W.	McCredie William	Smith Donald
Cable F. S.	Heaphy A. T.	McCurdy Geo. L.	Smith F. C.
Carleton W. B.	Heineman S.	McDonald James	Smith George E
Cary G. P.	Hench J. B.	McGee W. E.	Tallman L. C.
Childs R. A.	Hess Charles H.	Marsh W. P.	Thayer C. H.
Coffeen W.	Higgins C. W.	Mason John	Thayer H. R.
Colburn H.	Hildebrand L. K.	Maydwell H. F.	Wadington John
Colburn W. R.	Hinds C. E.	Merrill J. C. F.	Waite W. W.
Conover L. P.	Hinds E. P.	Merritt C. T.	Walker A. E.
Cooke H. H.	Hinds E. P. jr.	Middaugh H. C.	Washburn C. L.
Cortis W. P.	Hines A. G.	Morrow A. W.	Weiss H. W.
Courter D. A.	Holverscheid H.	Muller L. jr.	Williams Geo. H.
Crossette C. D.	Hudson Charles	Myers M. A.	Wilson S. C.
Crossette C. H.	Irvine F. R.	Newell L. C.	Wylde E.
Dana H. C.	Jackson Horace	Pape E. T.	Wylie H. D.

HYDE PARK CLUB.

WASHINGTON AVENUE N.W. COR. FIFTY-FIRST.

OFFICERS.

WILL H. MOORE, - - - - - - - President.
THOMAS S. CRUTTENDEN, - - - - - Vice-President.
F. H. TRUDE, - - - - Second Vice-President.
DAVID W. ROSS, - - - - - - - - Secretary.
EDWARD E. SMITH, - - - - - - Treasurer.

DIRECTORS.

Elliott Durand	George C. Bailey	Edward E. Smith
E. C. Day	George Catlin	J. H. Hiland
J. W. Crocker	C. V. Banta, jr.	D. E. Evans
Will H. Moore	F. H. Trude	W. C. Lawson
Thomas S. Cruttenden	David W. Ross	

MEMBERS.

Allbright Wm. B.	Crocker John T.	Gage Ed M.	Kohler G. A. E.
Allen Thomas	Crocker J. W.	Garceau A. E. Dr.	Lansingh K. V. R.
Andrews E. W.	Crozier Frank	Garland T. W.	Lawson Wm. C.
Armstrong C. G.	Cruttenden T. S.	Garrigue R. H.	LeFurgy L. R.
Bailey G. C.	Cummings R. F.	Germain C. C.	Leonard G. Russell
Banta C. V. jr.	Curtis Cornelius	Gilbert H. T.	Lewis Denslow Dr.
Banzet G. T.	Cuthbertson Wm.	Githens J. N.	Livingston G. W.
Barnes Albert C.	Cutter G. M.	Glover Wilson A.	Loomis Edwin C.
Becker G. W.	Dacy A. E.	Goodall H. L.	Lynch E. R.
Berkeley R. C. jr.	Dade W. H. Dr.	Goodykoontz	Mabie C. E.
Biden E. C.	Danforth Frank L.	Chas. H.	MacLachlan J. W.
Bigelow George S.	Danks I.	Grosvenor Geo. B.	Dr.
Bigelow H. T.	Davis F. G.	Grubb J. E.	Madden F. H.
Bigelow Thos. M.	Davis George W.	Hacker N. W.	Markham M. C.
Birkle Charles A.	Davis John	Hall E. A.	Marlow Chas. F.
Bliss E. R.	Davis W. J. N.	Hall H. J.	Marquardt C. G.
Boland John	Day E. C.	Harahan J. T.	Martin H. J.
Bradley M. S.	Day H. N.	Hartigan J. G.	Mason F. H.
Bradley R. R.	DeMuth B. F.	Hartwell A. V.	McClean S. A. jr.
Brinkerhoff W. C.	Dickason L. T.	Harvey T. F.	McKey E. B.
Dr.	Dickey Frank T.	Hatch G. W.	McKey W. D.
Brower J. F.	Donnelley Reuben	Hawley E. S.	Milligan George D.
Burke John E.	H.	Heath A. M.	Montgomery G. W.
Caleb G. N.	Douglas B. M.	Herr H. B.	Moore Will H.
Campbell A. E.	Dow F. H.	Hertel C. W.	Moore Wm. J.
Campbell J. A.	Draper F. S.	Hickman Chas.	Morehouse M. J.
Carpenter E. R.	Dunlop Alexander	Hiland J. H.	Morgan F. W.
Carter D. M.	Dunne M. J.	Hinkins Dr. J. E.	Morrill C. E.
Case C. B.	Dupee H. M.	Hoyt G. W.	Morron J. R.
Case C. S. Dr.	Durand Elliott	Hudson T. J.	Mower E. B.
Case M. T.	Durst P. E.	Hughson Geo. F.	Moyer W. L.
Catlin George	Dyer Charles E.	Hunt Charles H.	Munger P. F.
Chalmers William	Eames E J.	Hunter R. J. O.	Myers E. B.
Champlin D. H.	Eldridge C. H.	Hutchinson E. W.	Newman Gideon E.
Chattell B. M.	Emery A. B.	Hyman R. W.	Nicholas Fred C.
Chesrown M. M.	Evans C. H.	Jocelyn F. C.	Nichols H. W. jr.
Clarke R. G.	Evans D. E.	Johnson C. Porter	Nosler Geo. F.
Colby C. C.	Everett John C.	Jones A. G.	Nye H. G.
Coleman Edward r	Farr A. G.	Joyce W. T.	Parker Thos. L.
Collins Lorin C. j	Favor Otis S.	Keepers William E.	Perley E. E.
Colt J. D.	Fenn P. D.	Kenyon D. E.	Peters Homer H.
Conkey W. B.	Ferguson Chas. H.	Kerr George B.	Phillips R. W.
Connor T. V.	Feron Walter J.	Kerr William R.	Platt Nathan E.
Corning C. S.	Flint H. L.	Kilbourn F. H.	Porter R. H.
Cowie R. E. M.	Friend E.	King Samuel B.	Price W. B.
Crawford C. H.	Fullen C. D.	Kohler Frank W.	Prouty H. W.

Purdy George C.	Shatford J. D.	Stone William	Warner Geo. L.
Ramsey E. P.	Shaw Ed. R.	Stuart Robert	Warner J. G.
Randle C. H.	Shields Henry B.	Sutherland W. J.	Warrell A. M.
Ratsch F. J.	Shirley James B.	Swett F. C.	Waters J. E.
Reid Dr. J. G.	Sidway H. T.	Thayer C. H.	Weed W. F.
Reynolds F. M.	Signor H. B.	Thomas Benj.	Wheeler A. W.
Reynolds W. J.	Smith Arthur J.	Thompson M. J.	Wheelock W. G.
Rhodehamel B. F.	Smith Edward E.	Timewell A. T.	Whitehead S. S.
Richardson W. H.	Smith H. C.	Tompkins S. L.	Whitfield Albert
Richt C. C.	Smith Jacob S.	Tousey C. A.	Wight B. W.
Robinson J. C.	Smith J. O. K.	Trude F. H.	Wilkins S. G.
Robinson W. L.	Smith J. P.	Tuley M. F. Judge	Willard N. P.
Rogers C. D.	Smith Lon K.	Tulloch James	Wilson L. P.
Ross D. W.	Smith R. G.	Twichell J. O.	Windsor W. E. C.
Russell Martin J.	Spear H. E.	Udell S. R.	Woodman T. F.
Sackett R. E.	Sprogle H. O.	Underwood S. L.	Woodward T. R.
Sanders J. F.	Stafford Chas. B.	Updike M.	Wright W. M.
SchimpfermanW.H	Stegemann H. J.	Walbank K. S.	Wyeth J. H. jr.
Scull Harry	Stevens C. N.	Wallace H. R.	Zimmerman Wm.
Sewell Barton	Stilwell Warren S.	Wallace J. F.	

IDEAL CLUB.

300 LASALLE AV.

OFFICERS.

Jos. WEINREB,	- - - - - -	President.
F. SILBERMAN,	- - - - - -	Vice-President.
A. MARKS,	- - - - - - -	Secretary.
J. BLUM,	- - - - - - -	Treasurer.

DIRECTORS.

M. Griesheimer	J. Goodman	B. Engelhard
M. Rosenthal	L. Birkenstein	B. Sinsheimer
L. Spiesberger		

MEMBERS.

Adams J.McGregor	Fish Ike	Klee Simon jr.	Schiff S.
Alschuer Arthur	Frank Anton	Langbein S.	Schneider S.
Altschul O.	Frank George	Leeser E.	Seligman H.
Bach A. Julius	Frank Dr. J.	Leiser D.	Sidder A. J.
Baer Louis	Frank J. H.	Leiser Jos.	Silberman F.
Baer S.	Fridkyn P. B.	Levi M.	Sinsheimer B.
Beck Dr. J. C.	Friedlander S.	Levy M.	Sinsheimer S.
Becker B. V.	Friedman W.	Levy S.	Sommers C.
Berlizheimer A. D.	Gallinger M.	Lindenthal S. C.	Sonnensheim L.
Birkenstein David	Goetz D. L.	Loebman Gus	Spiesberger L.
Birkenstein Louis	Goodman Jos.	Maas M.	Spiesberger N. L.
Blum J.	Goodman Lee	Mahler Jac	Stern L.
Blum S. S.	Gradle B.	Mandl S.	Stern L.
Collat M.	Griesheimer F.	Marks Abe	Strauss Ed. E.
Eichberg F.	Griesheimer M.	Mayer S.	Strauss L.
Eichberg L.	Hamburgher E. C.	Morrison P.	Waldbott E. S.
Eisendrath H. J.	Haslacher E.	Mossler I. A.	Wangersheim D.
Eisendrath S. J.	Hecht A. S.	Nachman I.	Wangersheim Wm.
Eisner E. R.	Henry L.	Norden Dr. A.	Weil V.
Elkan H.	Herbst B.	Oesterreicher L.	Weinreb Jos.
Elkan L.	Hirshberg Rev. A.	Possner M.	Wolf A. D.
Englehard B. M.	Hofheimer Z.	Regensburg H. L.	Wurzburger H.
Epstein M. N.	Kingsbacker Sam	Rohrheimer B. M.	Wurzburger J.
Felsenthal A.	Kingsbacker Sol	Rosenthal M.	Wurzburger Lee
Finn Joseph	Klee A.	Schallman Sam'l	Yondorf A.

THE ILLINOIS CLUB.
154 ASHLAND BOULEVARD.

OFFICERS.

EDGAR A. HILL,	- - - - - - -	President.
J. F. TALBOT,	- - - - - -	Vice-President.
WILLIAM RODIGER,	- - - - - -	Secretary.
JOHN McLAREN,	- - - - - -	Treasurer.

TRUSTEES.

Edgar A. Hill	William Rodiger	A. F. Solbery.
John McLaren	E. B. Cobb	James L. Clark
W. H. Alsip	A. B. McCourtrie	Anthony Hosking
R. Earle Smith	J. F. Talbot	F. P. Potter
C. B. Samson		

MEMBERS.

Adams Hon Francis	Bullard Elihu R.	Doremus A. F.	Gormley James H·
Adcock A. W.	Burdick Oscar	Dougherty T. E.	Graham Andrew J·
Aiken W. J.	Burgett J. M. H.	Downey Joseph	Graham Dr. D. W·
Aldrich H. H.	Burke Edmund W.	Downey Dr. W.	Grant E. K.
Alsip Wm. H.	Burkhardt Henry S.	Stewart	Grant Robert S.
Arnold A. H.	Burkhardt Wm.	Drake John A.	Grassie Jas.
Artingstall S. G.	Burroughs Geo. T.	Duncanson H. W.	Graves James R.
Auten P. L.	Bushnell L. M.	Durborow A. C. jr.	Gray Frank M.
Avery Daniel J.	Bussey W. T.	Durgin John C.	Gregory Walter D.
Avery Frank M.	Carpenter W. O.	Early Frank B. Dr.	Griffin Thomas A.
Badenoch John J.	Carson Samuel	Eckhardt Wm. N.	Griswold Geo. E.
Baker William H.	Chalmers Thos., jr.	Eckhart B. A	Gunderson G. M.
Baldwin L.	Chalmers W. J.	Eckhart J. W.	Hair Benj. M.
Banning Ephraim	Champlin F. L.	Eddy Albert M.	Hales Burton F.
Barr A. E.	Chandler H. H.	Eddy George D.	Hall Geo. W.
Barrett Charles R.	Chapman Dr.	Edmonds N. D. Dr.	Hall L. R.
Barrett M. L.	Chauncey F.	Egan W. M.	Hambleton C. E.
Bartels William H.	Clark A. E.	Elliott W. S. jr.	Handy H. H.
Bausman Dr. A. B.	Clark E. G.	Ellis Edward D.	Hardy Cyrus A.
Beek Horace W.	Clark Jas. L.	Elmer T. H.	Harlan Dr. A. W.
Beidler A. W.	Clark Walter T.	Elmes Chas. F.	Harris George J.
Beidler Francis	Cobb Emmons B.	Emigh G.	Harris Squire R.
Bennett E. B.	Cobb Martin R.	Evans W. W.	Harsha Leslie R.
Bennett J. W.	Cole Thomas W.	Farrell Thos. F.	Hartwell A. V.
Benson Dr. John A.	Conger R. M.	Farson John	Harvey W. S. Dr.
Bidwell Theo. S. Dr.	Conkey W. B.	Farwell John W.	Hawes William H.
Billings C. K. G.	Cowperthwaite Dr	Fisk Franklin P.	Hay James
Bingham M. F.	A. C.	Fitz Simons Chas.	Hayes Frank
Birkhoff George jr.	Cox E. R.	Flannery D. F.	Hayt Henry C.
Bishop Chas. N.	Crane R. T.	Forbes A. M.	Healy P. J.
Blackman C. S.	Crane S. H.	Forbes Fred. A.	Helm D. T.
Blodgett Edward A.	Crawford Mark L.	Foskett Chas. M.	Henneberry W. P.
Blount F. M.	Crocker Benjamin S	Foster Dr. R. N.	Hill Calvin H.
Blount Harry D.	Crossman F. M.	Fowler Frank T.	Hill Chas. Erwin
Bodman W. C.	Dalton John E.	Frake James	Hill Edgar A.
Bogle W. S.	Danforth I. N. Dr.	Fraser David R.	Hinkley Chas. W.
Bond L. L.	Darrow A. H.	Fraser Norman D.	Holden N. B.
Bond Thomas N.	Date Sydney S.	French Edgar	Holden Wm. H.
Booth Hervey W.	Davis C. G. Dr.	French W. H.	Hooker Henry M.
Borland L. C. Dr.	Davis George R.	Fuller Fred L.	Hosking Anthony
Bosley Daniel W.	Dean Thad	Fulton J. L.	Hosking Ben. T.
Bremner D. F.	Deane John M.	Gadsden Jas. S.	Hotz Chris
Brinckerhoff H. M.	Dickinson Albert	Gallagher D. J.	Hulin William
Brophy Dr. T. W.	Dickinson Chas.	Gates P. W.	Hunt Alfred O.
Brower Dr. D. R.	Dickson James T.	George Charles H.	Hyde Charles E.
Brown M. O.	Dodson John M. Dr.	Gillett E. W.	Jackson Willis G.
Brown W. Gray	Dole Andrew R.	Gobel E. F.	James Fred S.
Bryan F. W.	Dole John N.	Golder W. A.	Johnston Wm.

Jones J. H.
Kane Thomas
Keith John G.
Kennedy W. B.
Kent W. D.
Ketcham Wm.P.
King John A.
King Ulric
Kohlsaat C. C.
Kohlsaat ErnestW.
Kralovec John
Kremer Charles E.
Krum Iretus R.
Lane Francis B.
Lane James R.
Lane Wm. H.
Lansing Mark S.
Lasier D. S.
Lawrence J. Frank
Ledgerwood A.J.C.
Leonard Simeon F.
Leszynsky E. G.
Linington C. M.
Loomis Dr. E. B.
Lydiard John P.
Lyon Richard S.
MacCarty Chas. S.
MacKenzie Geo. S.
MacLeod M.
MacMillan Thos. C
Magnus August C.
Magill Jacob C.
Many Sidney G.
Marder John
Mark Anson
Mark Clayton
Marshall Chas. G.
Marshall George A.
Marshall H. L.
Martin A. W.
Martin E. B.
Martin Robt. L.
Mason Carlile
Mason George
Maxwell Henry B.
Maxwell James
McCarthy Florence
McCarthy J. G.
McCourtie A. B.
McCrea W. S.
McDonald J. B.
McKeeby Sanford
    M.
McLaren John

McMahon James A.
McMullin F. R.
Meacham F. D.
Meek S. M.
Mercer Arthur
Merriman Wm A.
Mills D. W.
Mitchell Arthur J.
Montgomery Wm.
    T. Dr.
Mortimer W. H.
Moxley W. J.
Murphy Dr. J. B.
Murray John
Nash Charles T.
Newcomb John C.
Newton Geo.W.Dr.
Newton Henry S.
Nichols Frank M.
Norris W. W.
Noyes LaVerne W.
NuttingWilliamW.
Offield C. K.
Oliver J. Milton
Outhet R. M.
Overmeyer John B.
Palmer W. C. B.
Parker Geo. G.
Patten James A.
Patterson ArthurW
Peters Chas. V. L.
Peters Joseph G.
PettiboneHowardC
Pettibone P. F.
Pitkin Frank H.
Pitkin Geo. W.
Pond Walter M.
Pope Wm. J.
Post Charles N.
Potter F. P.
Price Dr. O. J.
Price P. Bird
Pyott Albert E.
Rawle John
Rawleigh Jas. T.
Reed C. C.
Reeve S. D.
Rend William P.
Richolson Benj. F.
Riddle Francis A.
Ripley BradfordW.
Rising C. L.
Robison Dr.JohnA.
Rodgers John L.

Rodiger William
Roeschlaub F. H.
Rogerson E. J.
Rollins Charles E.
Rollo C. E.
Ross George
Royce Dr. E. A.
Ruddock Chas. H.
Sagendorph F. E.
Salisbury W. H.
Samson C. B.
Sands Obadiah
Sattler Dr. Philip
Scanlan Kickham
Schaaf Harry
Schuttler Peter
Scully D. B.
Sennott Thos. W.
Shackleford Chas.
Shaffer Henry R.
Shaw W. A.
Shepard Henry O.
Sherwood Marc
Shoemaker C. W.
Shoemaker Walter
Showalter J. W.
Skinkle J. W.
Slack Chas. H.
Sloan Geo. S.
Smith Charles H.
Smith R. Earle
Smith R. J.
Smyth Hill C.
Smyth John M.
Solbery A. F.
Soper James P.
Spry Geo. E.
Spry John C.
Spry S. A.
St. John Fred.
St.JohnDr.Leon'rd
Stanford Geo. W.
Stearns Edgar G.
Stehman Dr. H. B.
Stevens J. K.
StewartArchibaldA
Stewart A. M.
Stewart Graeme
Stone A. J.
Stone Frank P.
Street R. R.
Strong George A.
Swift George B.
Talbot J. F.

Tapper George
Tatham R. L.
Taylor E. Wiley
Taylor F. C.
Taylor Geo. H.
Teall E. M.
Thomas Dr. H. M.
Thomas John W.
Thompson Harvey
    L.
Thorp Ole A.
Thresher Wm. E.
Thurston H. M.
Tichenor Wm. A.
    Dr.
Titus Virgil E.
Tobey Frank B.
Tuthill R. S.
Tuttle W. P.
Utley Henry B.
Valentine E. H.
VanderklootAdrian
Vanzwoll G. M.
Vernon John M.
Vopicka Charles J.
Wallace Jas. D.
Wallis O. W.
Warvelle Geo. W.
Waters Wiley B.
Watkins J. O.
Weaver C. H.
Weeks Harvey T.
Weinland Chas. F.
Wells A. E.
Wells M. A.
Wells W. A.
West E. A.
Wheeler H. A.
Wiehe C. F.
Wilce E. Harvey
Willard M. L.
Williams J. D.
Williamson John
Wilson F. Cortez
Wilson Wm. J.
Wood Joseph H.
Woodward T. R.
Work A. S.
Wright Aug. W.
Wright Frank S.
Wright Rufus
Wygant Alonzo
Yuille George A.
Ziegfeld F. Dr.

ILLINOIS SOCIETY SONS OF THE AMERICAN REVOLUTION.

HEADQUARTERS, ROOM 1514 MASONIC TEMPLE.

OFFICERS.

LT.-COL. GEORGE VIELE LAUMAN, - - President.
I. S. BLACKWELDER, - - - First Vice-President.
FRANCIS T. SIMMONS, - - Second Vice-President.
JOHN D. VANDERCOOK, - - - - Secretary.
FLETCHER B. GIBBS, - - - - - Treasurer.
ALBERT JUDSON FISHER, - - - - - Historian.
WILLIS J. RIPLEY, - - - - - - Registrar.
REV. THADDEUS A. SNIVELY, - - - Chaplain.
HENRY B. FERRIS, - - - - Sergeant-at-Arms.

MEMBERS.

Abbott Edwin F.
Adams Edward M.
Adams George W.
Adams William P.
Allen William D.
Allin Richard F.
Ally Charles Q.
Alvord John W.
Ambrose Thomas
Andrew George L.
Angell William T.
Arnold Fred'k A.
Atkinson Chas. T.
Austin C. G.
Babcock Charles F.
Babcock Courtland
Babcock Robert H.
Bailey August
Bailey Martin B.
Baker Frank
Balch Frank W.
Bald D. M.
Baldwin Robt. R.
Bancroft Horace H.
Barbour Frank
Barbour W. Ernest
Bardwell Harry J.
Barnes Erastus A.
Barry George
Bartholf Charles S.
Bartholf W. J.
Bartram Wheeler
Bass Alonzo
Baxter Thomas M.
Beardsley C. B.
Beaver W. H.
Beck Edward S.
Beckwith Warren
  L.
Bennett Asahel F.
Bennett John W.
Bensley John R.
Bent Charles
Birch Hugh T.
Black Charles N.
Blackwelder I. S.
Blair Frank P.
Bliss Samuel E.

Block Willard T.
Blodgett Phineas
Bond Wililam A.
Boone Harry C.
Booth William M.
Boutell Henry S.
Boutell Lewis H.
Brackett WilliamS.
Bradish Walter C.
Bradish Walter H.
B r a d l e y P r o f.
  Charles F.
Bradley David E.
Bradley John E.
Bradley Philip B.
Brennan George A.
Bridge Dr. N.
Brocklebank John
  F. C.
Brooks Andrew M.
Brooks Kennedy
Brown H. D.
Brown William T.
Brown W. C.
Buford Charles
Burchard Mortimer
  N.
BurleighWilliamB.
Burns Randall
Butters George
Butterworth Wm.
Buttolph Wm. W.
Bryan CharlesPage
Bryant John J.
Camp Edward N.
Canfield Andrew J.
Canfield John B.
Capen C. L.
Case L. W. Dr.
Cass George W.
Castle Arthur H.
Catlin Charles
Catlin George
Chamberlain Geo.
  M.
C h a t f i e ld-Taylor
  Hobart C.
Cheney August J.

Cheney Rt. Rev.
  Charles E.
Clark A. B.
Clark Frederick
Clark Joseph H
Clark William D.
Clark William O.
Cleveland Homer
Coe Schuyler M
Cole Festus B.
Coleman Steph. R.
Collins Frank
Colton Samuel K.
Connelly B. D.
Connelly H. C.
Cook Joshua O.
Cooley Harlan W.
Cornell George H.
Corthell Elmer L.
Cowan William K.
Cox Leroy B.
Cragg George L.
Crandon Frank P.
Crawford Charles
Crouch Franklin T.
Currier Horace T.
Cushing Francis J.
Custer Jacob R.
Dana Charles D.
Dana Henry C.
Danforth Isaac N.
Darling Charles B.
Davis George W.
Dering Henry Ray
Dickinson Oliver P.
Disbrow F. W.
Drummond JohnN.
Drury Edwin
Drury Horace G.
Dudley Dr.Emilius
  C.
Duffy Frederick
Dumont Chas. W.
Dunlap William P.
Dunning Willis E.
Durand Elliot
Earley Robert G.
Edgerton Seymour

Elkins Henry K.
Elwell Edward H.
Emery John E.
Emmons FrancisA.
Erskine Oscar P.
Everett Coleman S.
Everett Edward W.
Everett William R.
Everhart George P.
Farr Marvin A.
Farrington C. L.
Farwell H. S.
Favorite George C
Favorite Ward C.
Fellows Dr. C. G.
Ferris Henry B.
Ferris Hiram B.
Ferris J. C.
Fessenden Benj. A.
Fessenden Chas.N.
Finch Francis M.
Fisher Albert J.
Fisher Francis P.
Fitzgerald PorterB.
Flower James M.
Foster Albert V.
Foster F. H.
Foster Volney W.
Foster W. E.
Friese Christopher
Fuller Henry C.
Fuller T. W.
Funkhouser Metal-
  lus L. C.
Furness WilliamE.
Gardner AddisonL
Gary John H.
Gerold Frank W.
Gibbs Fletcher B.
Gilbert James H.
Gillette Edwin F.
Gore Joel R.
Green Robert L.
Green William A.
Greenough Edw. P.
Gridley Martin M.
Gridley Nelson C.
Gross Samuel E.

Spoor John A.
Standish CharlesD.
Starkweather F. H.
Starkweather Dr.
  Ralph E.
Starring Mason B.
Steele Frederick M.
Stevens Harry D.
Strong Dr. A. B.
Stubblefield G. W.
Stubblefield John
Stubbefield R W.
Surghnor Valentine
  H.
Talcott Harvey H.
Talmadge Lewis C.
Teall Edward M.
Tenny H. K.
Terry Albert S.
Thayer Stephen A.
Thomas E. D.
Thomas William
Thomasson Nelson

Thorpe James W.
Tiffany Luther S.
Tobey Frank B.
Tolman Edgar B.
Towne Henry
Tracy Edward A.
Tree Lambert
Trego Charles H.
Trego Frank H.
Trumbull John H.
Tucker Edgar P.
Tucker Gilbert R.
Tucker William R.
Tucker William S.
Turner Henry L.
Turnley Parmenas
Tyler John
Upham Fred'k W.
Vail Henry S.
Vance Joseph W.
Vandercook J. D.
Vastine Sedgwick
  S.

Vernon William W.
Wadsworth C. F.
Waite Horace L.
Wakefield Dr.
  Homer
Waldron E. D.
Walker George R.
Walker Robert P.
Wallingford Henry
Walter William A.
Ward Joseph F.
Ware Dr. John D.
Warren Benjamin
Warren Nathan
Washburne Hemp-
  stead
Wa ers F. R.
Weld Herbert W.
Wentworth W. G.
Weston Henry C.
Wetherell O. D.
Wheeler George H.
White George E.

Whitehall Alex N.
Whitney CharlesP.
Wicker Albert B.
Wilcox Albert B.
Wilder John E.
Wilder Thomas E.
Williams Lawrence
Williams R. E. jr.
W i l l o u g h b y
  Charles L.
Wilson Huntington
Winn James H.
Winston Fred'k H.
Wood G. S.
Wood Joseph
Woodbridge John
Woodford Phil R.
Woodward Theron
  R.
Worthington Rob-
  ert S.
Young Joseph W.

ILLINOIS WOMAN'S PRESS ASSOCIATION.

OFFICERS.

MRS. H. EFFA WEBSTER, - - - - - - President.
MRS. JULIA HOLMES SMITH, - - - - - First Vice-President.
JULIA K. BARNES, - - - - -. Second Vice-President.
MRS. ELIZABETH A. REED, - - - - Third Vice-President.
MRS. MARY B. POWELL, - - - - - Recording Secretary.
MISS MARY H. STEWART, - - - Asst. Recording Secretary.
A. SHACKLEFORD SULLIVAN, - - - Corresponding Secretary.
MRS. ALICE ROSSETER WILLARD, - Asst. Corresponding Secretary.
MRS. FRANCES E. OWENS, - - - - - - - Treasurer.
MRS. IDA A. NICHOLS, - - - - - - - Historian.
FANNY M. HARLEY, - - - - - - - Librarian.

MEMBERS.

Abbott Mrs. E. Jeannette
Ahrens Mrs. Mary A.
Ames Mrs. Bertha E.
Ashton Mrs. Mary J.
Ballard Miss Anna
Barnes Mrs. Julia K.
Bash Mrs. Daniel U.
Bell Mrs. Esther Crane
Blinn Odelia, M. D.
Bogg Mrs. Ada B.
Bowman Miss Eliza W.
Boylan Mrs. Grace Duffie
Brinkman Mrs. A. P.
Burt Miss Mary E.
Campbell Mrs. Theo. C.
Chandler Mrs. L. B.
Clark Ada R. E.
Colson Miss Ethel Maude
Conant Mrs. Frances A.
Conger Dr. Rosamond C.
DeGraff Mrs. Ellen E.
DeLuce Mrs. Arvilla C.
D'Unger Miss Giselle
Dye Mrs. Mary Irene

Edholm Mrs Charlton
Emmons Mrs. Rose A.
Fowler Miss Almira M.
Gordon Miss Anna A.
Grannis Mrs.Elizabeth B.
Grinnell Mrs. G. G.
Harley Mrs. Fanny M.
Hart Mrs. Elize Houk
Harvey Lucia M.
Hazlett Mrs. Genie F.
Heath Mrs. Louisa M.
Heegaard Mrs. B. Louise
Hooker Miss Jennie E.
Huling Miss Caroline A.
Jenks Mrs. Anna Burt
Johnson Mrs. C. Ashton
Judson Mrs. Mary M.
Kells Mrs. Harriet S.
Kline Mrs. John
Lane Mrs. E. Mead
LeFavre Mrs. Carrica
Light Mrs. Ellen M.
Madden Mrs. Edgar
McGinnis Mrs. Grace C.

McKinney Mrs. J. A.
McKinnie Mrs. Celestia
  Gray
Mead Mrs. Ransom H.
Metcalf Mrs. Ada P.
Moses Mrs. Sallie M.
Nichols Mrs. Ida A.
Nourse Mrs. Harriet P.
Ogilvie Mrs. Carolyn M.
Orwig Mrs. Maria S.
Owens Mrs. Frances E.
Palmer Mrs. Mate
Pashley Mrs. Alfred F.
Perry Miss Carlotta
Pierce Mrs. Elizabeth C.
Powell Mrs. Lewis B.
Pratt Miss Candace A.
Pratt Mrs. Sarah Wilder
Rae Mrs. Mary E. M.
Reed Mrs. Elizabeth A.
Reed Miss Myrtle
Roberts Miss Jessie
Robertson Mrs. Char-
  lotte C.

Romney Mrs. Caroline
  Westcott
Sawyer Mrs. C. B.
Schramm Miss Emma I.
Sergel Mrs. Annie Myers
Smith Mrs. Eva Munson
SmithMissJenny Fairman
Smith Julia Holmes,M.D.
Somerset Lady Henry
Stewart Miss Mary H.
Stockham Dr. Alice B.
Stockham Miss Cora L.

Sullivan Mrs. Amelia S.
Swalm Miss Maude A.
Swarthout Mrs. M. F.
Taylor Mrs. Everett
Taylor Mrs. Florence
  Montgomery
Thayer Miss Julia H.
VanBenschoten Mrs.M.C.
Vincent Mrs. Martha Car-
  penter
Wallace Mrs. M. R. M.
Wardner Mrs. Louise R.

Webster Miss Alice
Webster Mrs. H. Effa
Weeks Mrs. Anna R.
Wheeler Mrs. Sarah J.
White Dr. A. Hungerford
Will Miss Kate
Willard Mrs. A. R.
Wood Mrs. J. A.
Woodward Mrs. George
  W.
Yarnall Mrs. Jane W.

IROQUOIS CLUB.

110 MONROE STREET.

OFFICERS.

ARTHUR J. EDDY, - - - - - - President.
HORACE S. OAKLEY,
SIGMUND ZEISLER,
RIVERS MCNEILL,
J. W. ECKHART,
CHARLES F. GUNTHER, } - - - Vice-Presidents.
AUGUST BLUM,
GEORGE E. DAWSON,
W. J. ONAHAN,
WILLIAM O. COLEMAN,
L. W. WINCHESTER, - - Recording Secretary.
FRANK H. MCCULLOCH. - - Corresponding Secretary.
HERBERT DARLINGTON, - - - - - - Treasurer.

MEMBERS.

Ackers Thos. B.
Addison John
Babcock C. F.
Baker H. W.
Baker William T.
Barnhart A. M.
Bartlett Benj.
Barton George P.
Bauer A.
Black Henry S.
Blackman Frank P.
Blum August
Bolte Anson L.
Boyle Lawrence P.
Brandt Geo. W.
Breyfogle W. L.
Brosseau Zen P.
Brown Edward O.
Brown Charles A.
Browning G. W.
Buell C. C.
Bulger W. J.
Burry William
Callaghan James E.
Camp Edward N.
Cass George W.
Chandler W. T.
Clark T. C.
Clark W. Irving
Clifford R. W.
Coleman Wm. O.

Conover C. H.
Cooper John S.
Couch Ira J.
Cowan W. P.
Cowen Israel
Crane Chas. R.
D'Ancona Edw. N.
Darlington H.
Darrow C. S.
Dawson George E.
Defebaugh Jas. E.
Delano F. A.
Devine Wm. M.
de Windt H. A.
Dimery Joseph H.
Doane John W.
Doggett Herb E. L.
Doggett Wm. L.
Eckels James H.
Eckhart John W.
Eddy Arthur J.
Edgar Maxwell
Edwards W. H.
Elliott S. C.
EngelmannChas.P.
Evans O. L.
Ewing Adlai T.
Ewing Wm. G.
Fellows Byron M.
Florez Genaro
Ford Henry B.

Foreman Oscar G.
Forrest Wm. S.
Franche D. C.
Franks Jacob
Furber H. J. jr.
Gilbert Hiram T.
Gilman T. L. Dr.
Gray Edward E.
Green W. M.
Gregory F. A. jr.
Gregory Stephen S.
Gunther Charles F.
Hacker N. W.
Harris George J.
Haskell Geo. W.
Hemsley Walter
Henry E. J.
Henry R. L.
Heth Henry S.
Hexter Kaufman
Holland John F.
Hollis H. L.
Hotaling G. W.
Howland G. C.
Hoyne Frank G.
HoyneTempleS.Dr
Hoyne Thos. M.
Hurlbut Horace E.
Hutchinson Jonas
Jones David B.
Keeley Thos. F.

King John A.
Kraus Adolph
Lasier D. S.
Leaming Jeremiah
Leiter Levi Z.
Lorenz F. A.
Loss C. E.
Lowrey W. K.
Lynch John A.
Mack Julian W.
MacVeagh Frank-
  lin
Mandel Emanuel
Mayer I. H.
Mayer Oscar F.
McCauley T. N.
McConnell S. P.
McCormick C. H.
McCulloch F. H.
McGann Lawr. E.
McHugh P.
McLaughlin A. H.
McLellan A.
McLester Geo. W.
McNeill Rivers
McNeill Thos. H.
McShane James C.
Miles Hazen T.
Miller Thos.
Miner James A.
Moffett James A.

Moran Thos. A.
Morford Thos. T.
Morton Joy
Moses Adolph
Mueller G. A.
Newberry W. C.
Niblack William C.
Noonan Edward T.
Oakley Horace S.
O'Brien T. D.
Odell John J. P.
Oehne Theo.
Onahan Wm. J.
Oppenheim Wm.S.
Page Samuel S.
Palmer Potter
Peabody F. B.
Peabody F. S.
Phelps D. P.
Phelps E. M.
Phelps G. B. jr.
Prindiville John K.
Prouty Henry W.

Raymond J. H.
Richberg John C.
Robbins H. S.
Roberts Jesse E.
Robson John
Rogers George M.
Rogers Henry W.
Rogers James C.
Rollins Charles E.
Rolston H. M.
Rosenthal Edw. A.
Samuels D. V.
Sanborn Joseph B.
Sang Orr
Schwab Chas. H.
Scott Frank H.
Seixas Hyman L.
Sherwood Jesse
Shipman D. B.
Smith Alonzo D.
Smith Edwin B.
Smith Frank J.
Smith Fred M.

Smith Howard L.
Smith Robt J.
Somerville Robert
Squire L. G.
Steever J. G.
Stein Philip
Stein Sydney
Strawn Silas H.
Street R. R.
Strong J. H.
Stryker S. D.
Taylor Wm. A.
Thoman L. D.
Thornton Chas. S.
Tolman E. B.
Tree Lambert
Tuley Murray F.
Uhl Edwin F.
Veitch Wilberforce
Vopicka C. J.
Wacker Chas. H.
Walker Geo. C.
Waller E. C.

Waller Henry jr.
Waller J. B.
Waller Robt. A.
Walsh John R.
Walsh W. C.
Walton Seymour
Washington Lloyd
Watkins W.
Wells W. J.
WhitehouseSilas S.
Wilkinson Harry
Williams C. A.
Willden John G.
Wilt Charles T.
Wilt Charles T. jr.
Winchell M. R.
Winchester L. W.
Windes Thos. G.
Wolf Joseph
Wood C. B.
Woodle E. R.
Zeisler Joseph
Zeisler Sigmund

IRVING PARK CLUB,
2460 N. FORTY-SECOND AVENUE,

OFFICERS.

BENSON LANDON, - - - - - - President.
W. M. McEWEN, - - - - - - Vice-President.
J. FINLEY HOLLIS, - - - - - - Secretary.
C. C. SHERMAN, - - - - - Treasurer.
W. H. CALHOUN, - - - - Financial Secretary.

DIRECTORS.

A. Johnson
Benson Landon
J. J. Wallace

C. F. Bennett
L. D. Garratt
W. M. McEwen

W. N. Julien
C. E. Mee
H. H. Wilson

MEMBERS.

Allison J. A.
Armstrong J. D.
Baker Isaac
Barber W. L.
Barrett A. A.
Barrett Henry
Barstow C. F.
Bender G. E.
Bennett C. F.
Bennett W. B.
Berz O. H.
Binyon L. D.
Blair D. W.
Brown F. I.
Brown J. C.
Brown W. H.
Bullock H. S.
Bunch Roy C.
Butler H. W.
Calhoun Mrs. M. R.
Calhoun W. H.
Calkins N. D.
Clauss A. F.
Collins Samuel
Crego F. A.
Curtis W. H.
Davis Sam

Dixon L. S.
Drissbach C. E.
Dunlop S. A.
Elliott L. L.
Fatzinger J. R.
Fischer Arthur
Garratt L. D.
Geise J. A.
Gray W. A.
Gray W. H.
Hammitt A. C.
Hearn John
Hill A. H.
Hollis J. Finley
Holton Mrs. F. E.
Hotchkiss E. S.
Houston John
Johnson A. Arthur
Johnson A. L.
Jordan W. C.
Julien W. N.
Kalberlah F. W.
Kane J. A.
Kellogg W. R.
Kendrick W. J.
Kimbell S. S.
Landon Benson

Lang L. A.
Livesey H. B.
Mamerow Geo. T.J.
Marshall W. C.
Mates Frank
Mates Fred
McClintock A. C.
McEwen W. M.
Mee D. D.
Mee Ed.
Mitchell C. R.
Mitchell Wm. E.
Parnham John
Pentecost W. H.
Race Miss Ednah
Reynolds E. W.
Richardson F. M.
Richey A. D.
Ropp Solomon
Savage L. P.
Sayler W.
Schmidt H. F.
Sethness C. O.
Seydel Louis V.
Sherman C. C.
Sherman G. W.

Sloan B. R.
Smith Archie C.
Smith Dr. D. A.
Smith K. H.
Smyser J. H.
Stark M. W.
Stephenson P. K.
Swartz John
Tallman Chas.
Tallman J. B.
Tanner E. J.
Turner H. E.
VanHorn Geo.
Wallace J. J.
Wallis Thomas
Wallis W. H.
Walmsley A. H.
Walter G. E.
Wernle A. E.
Whitelaw Miss M.
Williams J. W.
Wilson F. J.
Wilson H. H.
Wilson S. R.
Wolfinger C. I.
Zander H. G.

KENWOOD CLUB.

FORTY-SEVENTH STREET AND LAKE AVENUE.

OFFICERS.

WARREN G. PURDY,	President.
WARREN B. KNISKERN,	Vice-President.
CHARLES R. STRONG,	Secretary.
EDWIN S. SIBLEY	Treasurer.

DIRECTORS.

William E. Ritchie	Edward T. Cushing	Edward A. Turner
Hamilton Dewar	Henry M. Lane	Lyman A. Wiley
Willard R. Wiley	Warren McArthur	Paul Willis

MEMBERS.

Adolphus W.
Alden William T.
Allen Franklin L.
Andrus F. H.
Armstrong C. M.
Ash L. H.
Atkinson J. A.
Atwood M. W.
Bacon Henry M.
Baldwin Dr. L. B.
Barbour Frank
Barker F. W.
Barker J. N.
Barker Dr. M. R.
Barrell James F.
Barrett James W.
Bayley E. F.
Baylies Ripley N.
Belden J. S.
Belden John S. jr.
Bennett F. I.
Biddle Wm. B.
Bingham A. E.
Bingham Chas. L.
Bingham Edw. H.
Bishop W. C.
Black Elmer E.
Blackman Mrs. Carlos H.
Blair Chauncey J.
Blauvelt Albert
Bliss Julian P.
Blossom Geo. W.
Boak Robert B.
Boak Robert jr.
Bogue Hamilton B.
Bogue Hamilton B. jr.
Bond John H.R.Dr.
Bouton Archibald
Bouton C. B.
Bouton N. S.
Bouton Sherman H.
Bridge R. W.
Brooks Dr. A.
Brooks C. M.
Brooks E. W.
Brooks J. W. jr.
Buchanan D. W.

Bunker Charles H.
Butler E. K.
Buttolph A. C.
Cameron Gorden
Canby Caleb H.
Capelle Marcus Eugene
Card Joseph B.
Carroll Norman
Carry Edward F. jr.
Carton L. A.
Champlin Henry C.
Chase Edward G.
Clingman Chas. W.
Cloud John W.
Cole H. A.
Coleman Julius A.
Collom G. Alvord
Condee L. D.
Conkling Benj. H.
Coolidge W. G.
Counselman Chas.
Cowles J. E.
Crary Dr. C. W.
Critchell R. S.
Crocker James R.
Cruttenden Edmund S.
Cruttenden T. S.
Cunningham W.H.
Curtiss George H.
Cushing E. T.
Daniels E. F.
Dau J. J.
Davis John
Day Chapin A.
Dering Charles L.
Dewar Hamilton
DeWolf Calvin
DeWolf W. L.
Dickson Isaac F.
Donnelley R. H.
Donnelley R. R.
Doty Levi R.
Doty Wilson K.
Douglas Frank
Downs Chas. S.
Downs M. D.
Drake Charles F.

Drake George H.
Drake W. H.
Dray Gail
Dudley Walter W.
Dupee H. M.
Dupee Leroy C.
Durand Elliott
Edwards J. A.
Eiker Chas. F.
Elliott Edward S.
Etheridge Francis
Fairman F.
Fales Fred'k S.
Farr M. A.
Fellows Dr. C. Gurnee
Fenton W. T.
Field Heman H.
Fisher Hart C.
Fiske Juo. M.
Flood Samuel D.
Follansbee C. E.
Foote Chas. H.
Fowler Bernard
Fraley James B.
Frasher John S.
Frothingham Dr. H. H.
Fry George C.
Fuller Alonzo M.
Fuller Mrs. Samuel R.
Furber Frank I.
Gates Charles G.
Gifford C. E. jr.
Gifford J. C.
Gilbert Chas. B.
Gill Chas. E.
Girling Winthrop Dr.
Givin Miss Anna D.
Graves A. M.
Gray Henry C.
Green A. W.
Gregory Jacob H.
Guion George M.
Gwin Miss Anna D.
Gwin Cornelius V.
Gwinn J. Morris

Gwinn W. R.
Hale Edward C.
Hall James T.
Halsey Tappen
Hammond C. L.
Hammond L. S.
Hammond Lyman D.
Hanson A. H.
Hanson David N.
Harding Chas. F.
Harkness Edson J.
Harlan Alison W. Dr.
Harper Harvey M.
Harris Norman W.
Hartz Irving T.
Hattstaedt John J.
Hawkins Chas. H.
Heckman Wallace
Henning Edwin
Hibbard John D.
Hicks Ernest H.
Higbie Nathan B.
Higgie James L.
Higley W. E.
Hoagland John R.
Hoagland Ralph T.
Holdom Jesse
Howard J. H.
Hoyt Alfred W.Dr.
Hudson Thomas J. jr.
Hughson Geo. F.
Hunt George W.
Hunt Samuel H.
Hunter Oscar L.
Hunter R. J. O.
Hunter W. W.
Hutchins J. C.
Ives John H.
Jackson F. W.
Jenkins George R.
Johnson William F.
Jones C. G.
Jones G. Edwin
Jones John Sutphin
Jones John H.
Jones Wm.

Jones Wm. M.
Judd Curtis J.
Keen E. H.
Kelley W. V.
Kellogg Leroy D.
Kellogg M. G.
Kimball E. S.
Kirkland Robt.
Knapp George O.
Knight J. B.
KniskernCharlesA.
KniskernWarrenB
Lane Henry M.
Lawton Lyndon C
Letton Theo. W.
Le Vally J. R.
Lewis Dr. D.
Lewis H. F. Dr.
Lewis I. G.
Linden Frank L.
Lindman John J.
Lindman O. F.
Little Edward F.
Little George W.jr.
Little W. H.
Lockwood Henry
Long J. H.
Loose J. L.
Lord D. M.
Lord J. B.
Loughridge Chas.
Lumsden ArthurE.
Lyman William
MacCracken Wm.
   P. Dr.
Mallory Chas. A.
Mansure Edmund
   L.
Marcy George E.
Marder Clarence C.
Marder John
Markwald ErnestM
Marsh C. V.
Marshall Benj. H.
Marshall Caleb H.
Marshall Philip L.
McArthur Warren
McDougal Robt.
McKey Edward B.
McMurray Geo. N.
Meads Albert H.
Mehlhop Frederick
   W.
Mehring George
Mettler L.Harrison
   Dr.
Miller John S.

Mills A. L.
Mitchell Geo. R.
Mitchell John J.
Moore S. M.
Moorehead Thom-
   as W.
Morehouse L. P.
Morgan James
Morris Seymour
Morse C. H.
Morse C. H. jr.
Morton Mark
Morton Paul
Moss W. L.
Nash W. T.
Neely John C.
Nellegar J. B.
Nelson W. C.
Newhall Arthur T
Niblack W. C.
Nichols C. M.
NimmonsGeorgeC.
Norton C. L.
Norton Oliver W.
Norwood F. W.
Oppenheim Wm. S.
Osborn Clark D.
Otis Thos. G.
Packer C. P.
Page W. R.
Palmer Geo. R.
Palmer Percival L
Parker Francis W.
Pearson Eugene H.
Peters Homer H.
Phelps Elliott H.
Phillips C. H.
Phister Walter B.
Plummer Sam'l C.
   Dr.
Porter Frank W.
Porter John L.
Potter E. A.
Potter E. C.
Pratt Lorenzo
Preston E. J.
Proby J. W.
Purdy Warren F.
Purdy Warren G.
Putnam Joseph R.
Reece Alonzo N.
RenshawWilliam F
Rhodes James H.
Riggs George W.
Ritchie Robert H.
Ritchie ThomasW.

Ritchie William E.
Roberts Chas. S.
Robinson Chas. O.
Roche John A.
Root Frederick W.
Rosing Edward
Rush George F.
Schmitt Anthony
Schoyer E. A.
Scribner Charles E.
SeavernsWilliam S.
Sedgwick EdwinH.
Seymour Horatio
   W.
Shankland Ralph
   M.
Shattuck George B.
Shattuck Walter F.
Shedd John G.
Sherman John D.
Sherman Lucius B.
Sherman P. L.
Sherwood N.
Shourds Clayton B.
Shumway E. G.
Sibley E. S.
Skeele John W.
Smith Edwin M.
Smith Frank W.
Smith Horace S.
Soden George A.
Soper James P.
SpencerI.Lawrence
Spooner Frank E.
Spooner Frank V.
Springer Miss G.
Squires Chas.
Squires H. B.
Steele Julius
Steever J. G.
Stein Otto J. Dr.
Sterling WilliamH.
Stinson James
Strong Charles R.
Strong David O.
Swan Charles J.Dr.
Swett F. C.
Swift Charles H.
Swift Edward F.
Swift Gustavus F.
Tenney H. K.
Thacker John F.
Thomas Benj.
Thompson R. S.
Thorne C. H.
Thorne Geo. R.

Thorne William C.
Thrall S. E.
Thrall W. A.
Tobey C. Harry
Tobey C. H. M.
Tobey Frank H.
Tripp Geo. A.
Trude Frederick H.
Turner A. A.
Turner E. A.
Turrill John F.
Ullmann Frederic
Valentine A. I.
VanKirk C. B.
VanUxem J. L.
Veeder AlbertH.jr.
Veeder Henry
Vierling Louis
Vierling Robert
Viets John B.
Vories H. F.
Wagner Ernest J.
Walburn AlbertW.
Wales AlbertH.Dr.
Walker A. E. Mrs.
Wallace John F.
Walter Philip M.
Walton Samuel B.
Ward A. M.
Warren Allyn D.
Warren Charles D.
Waters Harry C.
Watkins George
Weed William F.
Welch A. G.
Welling John C.
Wells B. R.
Wells Edward F.
White William F.
Wiley Edward N.
Wiley Lyman A.
Wiley Williard R.
Willard Henry G.
Williamson Mrs.G.
   T.
Willis Paul
Wilson Charles L.
Wilson E. Crane
Wolseley HenryW
Woodruff Chas. E
Woods Wm. J.
Woodward T. R.
Worley Brice
Wright S. H.
Wrisley A. B.
Young William A.

KLIO ASSOCIATION.

COMMANDERY HALL, 17TH FLOOR MASONIC TEMPLE.

OFFICERS.

EMILY O. GROWER, - - - - - - President.
MAY K. HOLMES, - - - - First Vice-President.
EVA H. EASTMAN, - - - Second Vice-President.
HELEN HOYT HILL, - - - - - - Treasurer.
STELLA C. McCOURTIE, - - Corresponding Secretary.
EMMA L. JAQUISH, - - - - Recording Secretary.

DIRECTORS.

Fannie A. Blount   May K. Holmes   Stella C. McCourtie
Eva H. Eastman   Emily L. Jaquish   Charlotte P. Milchrist
Emily S. Grower   Marie Lenheer   Euphemia C. Strell
Helen H. Hill   Mary R. Mann

MEMBERS.

Abbott Mrs. James   Hawley Mrs. E. H.   Perry Mrs. Hermon
Atkin Mrs. Ferdinand   Hill Miss Helen Hoyt   Pierson Mrs. Charles
Baer Mrs. Almerin   Holmes Mrs. A. W.   Pitcher Mrs. L. W.
Baker Mrs. Hiram   Howard Mrs. Joseph B. jr. Rathbone Mrs. P. D.
Barnes Mrs. Julia K.   Huszagh Mrs. R. D.   Rich Mrs. F. A.
Bassett Mrs. R. C.   Hynes Mrs. D. J.   Roberts Mrs. Clarke
Bender Mrs. G. E.   Jackson Mrs. C. A.   Ross Mrs. M. R.
Biddison Mrs. S. M   Jaquish Mrs. Louis C.   Rowland Mrs. William
Bigelow Mrs. E. A.   Jennison Mrs. Floyd E.   Royston Mrs. J. M.
Blount Mrs. S. P.   Johnston Mrs. James   Severinghaus Miss Vista
Bowen Mrs. F. W.   Johnstone Mrs. Stuart   Seymour Mrs. Harriett
Brown Mrs. Benjamin   Keeney Mrs. N. M.   Sherwood Mrs. J. B.
Campbell Mrs. J. L.   Kellogg Dr. Helen R.   Slosson Mrs. A. H.
Chadwick Mrs. R. R.   Kinley Mrs. C. Byron   Smith Mrs. Chas. R.
Chase Mrs. Rodney G.   Kloeber Mrs. J. S.   Smith Mrs. Fred A.
Clark Mrs. L. H.   Leenheer Mrs. B.   Smith Mrs. Fred M.
Corkery Mrs. Daniel   Loomis Mrs. J. H.   Smith Mrs. J. Hubert
Dean Mrs. Mary   Mann Mrs. C. W.   Smith Mrs. M. R.
Demmon Mrs. E. A.   Mathews Mrs. J. T.   Snider Miss Harriett
Dent Mrs. T. Ashley   Marcy Mrs. William W.   Springer Mrs. Elmina
Dwyer Mrs. Anna   McClelland Mrs. F.   Stanwood Mrs. E. W.
Eastman Mrs. J. C.   McCourtie Mrs. M. M.   Stoddard Mrs. H. H.
Ebert Mrs. Albert E.   McCourtie Mrs. A. B.   Strell Mrs. Geo. W.
Eilers Mrs. Paul C.   Mead Mrs. R. H.   Strong J. F.
Fay Mrs. J. B.   Milchrist Mrs. Thos. E. Talcott Mrs. Elva
Ford Mrs. Chas. N.   Montgomery Mrs. J. A.   Temple Mrs. T. S.
Ford Mrs. Wilbur H.   Morgan Mrs. Harry A.   Thayer Mrs. Geo. H
Golding Mrs. John F.   Morse Mrs. F. L.   Tilt Mrs. David
Gray Mrs. F. M.   Murdock Mrs. E. P.   Todd Mrs. T.
Greene Mrs. F. H.   Nourse Mrs. Harriet   Vanzwoll Mrs. G. W.
Grower Mrs. Wm. F.   Palmer Mrs. T. D.   Watt Miss M. H.
Haskett Mrs. I. R.   Parks Mrs. Samuel S.   Westfall Mrs. K. S.
Haas Mrs. Charles   Perkins Mrs. V. H.   Winchester Mrs. Alonzo H.
Hanna Mrs. E. B.

LA GRANGE CLUB.

LAGRANGE.

OFFICERS.

S. B. MOODY, - - - - - - - President.
C. C. CAMPBELL, - - - - First Vice-President.
F. D. COSSITT, jr., - - - Second Vice-President.
O. E. HAMAN, - - - - - - Treasurer.
HARLEY C. McDONALD, - - - - Secretary.

DIRECTORS.

H. E. Patterson
C. L. Stiles

John A. Dillon
S. S. Gorham

O. B. Marsh
A. S. Rothwell

MEMBERS.

Allén A. C.
Allen Chas. A. jr.
Allen F. H.
Allison John T.
Babbitt C. M.
Bain Foree
Baker M. M.
Barr S. E.
Bearse Hiram
Beatty W. R.
Berry Robert H.
Blount S. P.
Boisot E. K.
Borwell F. L.
Bradley J. C.
Briggs N. E.
Broffett C. F.
Brown L. C.
Brydon J. A.
Bunker W. I.
Burkholder H. P.
Cadle W. L.
Cadwallader B.
Campbell C. C.
Campbell John D.
Carey Warren Dr.
Carpenter M. J.
Cartlidge Chas. H.
Clark Jason E.
Collins W. A.
Cooley E. G.

Cooper H. N.
Cossitt F. D. jr.
Coulter Edward
Crane F. A.
Darlington H.
Davidson S. F.
Davis W. Crosbie
Detweiler E. S. Dr.
Dickey Robert L.
Dillon John A.
Dixon Geo. E. jr.
Edwards Chas.
Esson John H.
Ewing W. B.
Farley J. W.
Fisher Frank F.
Ford F. D.
Fox C. M.
Freer L. H.
Fulton H. L.
Gilbert J. R.
Gillett C. F.
Goodwin H. E.
Gorham Sidney S.
Haman O. E.
Hall Ferd.
Hapeman Edw.
Harter H. P.
Hawley C. W.
Hoskins Wm.
Isham Forrest

Kellogg M. L.
Kidston James
Kidston Wm.
Kimball Thomas
Lautz W. A.
Lyman D. B.
Marsh O. B.
Marshall J. A.
McDonald HarleyC
McGregor P. D.
McGrew J. H.
Mertz J. H.
Meyers D. L.
Moffitt C. T.
Moody S. B.
Moore C. B.
Morgan Geo. W.
Moses Chas. A.
Munn D. W.
Munn Fred O.
Neely E. R.
Newcomb E. R.
Newman J. B.
Packer J. F.
Pagin L. A.
Parker H. B.
Patterson H. E.
Pratt George E.
Rich E. A.
Roberts Dwight J.

Roberts Jesse E.
Rothwell H. L.
Rothwell R. E.
Scoville C. M.
Shergold W. L.
Slocum L. W.
Smith E. P.
Smith Jesse E.
Stiles C. L.
Stiles L. C.
Strasser J. M.
Trask F. M. Dr.
Turner J. W.
Upton C. M.
Walker Dudley
Walker Hayward
Walker J. R.
Walker M. B.
Walker R. D.
Wallace G. W. R.
Webb A. W.
Werno Henry
Williams C. B.
Witherell A. W.
Wolcott J. G.
Wright Wm.
Rockwood H. T.
Rogerson E. J.
Rollo A. G.
Rothwell A. S.

LAKE VIEW WOMAN'S CLUB.

BELMONT HALL, 1682 AND 1684 N. CLARK.

OFFICERS.

MRS. ALICE J. HESTER, - - - - - - - President.
MRS. ELIZABETH F. HEQUEMBOURG, - - First Vice-President.
MRS. CORNELIA D. HEILE, - - - Second Vice-President.
MRS. PAULA HOLMES GRAY, - - - Recording Secretary.
MRS. MINNIE E. G. VOLLINTINE, - Corresponding Secretary.
MRS. IDA M. PAINE, - - - - - - - Treasurer.

DIRECTORS.

Mrs. Alice Dickinson Foster
Mrs. Ellen E. L. Woodward
Dr. Alice Barlow Brown

Mrs. Martha J. L. Roper
Mrs. Fanny A. Barber
Mrs. Ann E. Smyth

MEMBERS.

Affeld Mrs. Charles E.
Affeld Miss Helen M.
Anable Miss Sara Alma
Andrews Miss Flora B.
Arend Mrs. Frank A.
Atwood Miss Lenna G.
Bacon Miss Ellen L.
Baird Mrs. Wyllys W.

Barber Miss Fanny A.
Barber Mrs. George M.
Barstow Dr. Rhoda Pike
Barthel Mrs. Fred W.
Bartholomew Mrs. James
Bass Mrs. Perkins B.
Becker Mrs. A. H.
Beebe Mrs. John E.

Bennet Mrs. Will H.
Bishop Mrs. J. H.
Bloomfield Mrs. W. E.
Bowyer Mrs. R. A.
Boyce Mrs. W. D.
Brackett Mrs. E. R.
Brauckmann Miss Minnie
Brecher Mrs. Oscar W.

Brosseau Mrs. Z. P.
Brown Dr. Alice Barlow
Bryant Mrs. F. L.
Butterfield Mrs. J. S.
Butterfield Mrs. Wm. W.
Cannell Mrs. S. Wilmer
Cannon Miss Theresa A.
Catlin Mrs. Charles
Chamberlin Mrs. T. H.
Chandler Mrs. F. E.
Chase Miss Ruth G.
Clark Miss Maria
Clift Mrs. A. F.
Cobb Mrs. Oscar
Comstock Mrs. Edward F.
Cooke Dr. Jean Mottram
Cram Mrs. John
Crane Mrs. A. M.
Crawford Mrs. Andrew
Crittenden Mrs. F. F.
Curtis Miss Emma L.
Dale Mrs. S. E.
Dawson Mrs. W. R.
Dennis Mrs. Charles H.
Dunn Mrs. Winfield P.
Durgin Mrs. John C.
Dyrenforth Mrs. Phillip C.
Eastman Mrs. Sidney C.
Eastman Mrs. Z.
Eaton Mrs. Ellen V.
Elliott Mrs. E. N.
Finch Mrs. J. C.
Fisk Mrs. Elizabeth E.
Fitch Mrs. Margaret S.
Flannery Mrs. John L.
Foley Mrs. John Burton
Foote Mrs. Delavan S.
Foote Miss Katharine
Foster Mrs. F. H.
Foster Mrs. John W.
Foster Mrs. Orrington C.
Fox Miss Harriott A.
Freer Mrs. Frederick W.
Gardiner Mrs. Warren C.
Glaspell Mrs. Albert
Glenn Mrs. John M.
Goodrich Mrs. Horace A.
Granger Mrs. Wm. Sterling
Gray Mrs. Ethan A.
Gray Miss Mary R.
Green Dr. Isadore
Greenlee Mrs. Robert L.
Gregg Dr. Mary E.
Gregory Mrs. L. L.
Hagerty Mrs. Thomas A.
Hanna Mrs. E. B.

Harland Mrs. Edward
Hedges Mrs. A. P.
Heegaard Mrs. Wm. H.
Heile Mrs. Adolf
Henshaw Mrs. D. C.
Hequembourg Mrs. Julien E.
Hester Mrs. Albert W.
Heuermann Miss Minna S.
Higgins Mrs. Charles H.
Hill Mrs. D. O.
Hills Mrs. James
Himrod Mrs. Kirk
Hitchcock Mrs. Howard E.
Holden Mrs. Charles W. jr.
Holmes Miss R. Brickell
Houston Mrs. James P.
Howard Mrs. Thomas
Johnson Mrs. Wm. H.
Jones Mrs. W. H.
Kasten Mrs. Herman A.
Keith Mrs. James E.
Kellogg Mrs. James L.
Ketcham Mrs. Ira C.
Knight Mrs. Wm. M.
Lamberton Mrs. John F.
Lawdis Mrs. E. M.
Larrabee Miss Jane
Larrison Miss Eleanor R.
Laubender Mrs. John F.
Loudon Mrs. Clarissa
Lull Mrs. Walter
Lydston Mrs. G. Frank
MacGrew Mrs. Elwood
Madson Mrs. Martin
Marx Mrs. Zero
Matteson Mrs. M. D.
McConnell Mrs. John
Mead Mrs. Edwin Ruthven
Merriman Mrs. C. C.
Meyer Mrs. John B.
Miller Mrs. Brice A.
Miller Mrs. R. T.
Milsted Mrs. T. G.
Mohr Mrs. Carl Martin
Morgan Miss Esther
Morrill Mrs. Donald L.
Mott Mrs. John M.
Murray Mrs. Edward
Nash Mrs. L. C.
Nelson Miss Edith R.
Nicol Mrs. James
Osgood Miss Alice F.
Paine Mrs. Romeyn M.

Palmer Mrs. A. E.
Parker Miss Keta Bell
Pease Mrs. Waldstein C.
Peats Miss Anna E.
Peirce Miss Clara M.
Peirce Mrs. Luther H.
Peters Miss Clara J.
Pettibone Mrs. Amos
Phillips Miss Angela
Quinn Miss Rose C.
Rainburg Miss Mary A.
Randall Mrs. A. S.
Randall Mrs. Tabor P.
Randall Mrs. Wm. B.
Redington Mrs. Wm. H.
Reed Mrs. George J.
Reid Mrs. John
Rogers Mrs. P. Conway
Roper Mrs. Edward U.
Ruthenberg Miss Blanca L.
Ruthenberg Mrs. Olga A.
Ruthenberg Mrs. Otto A.
Seligman Mrs. Julius
Smith Mrs. Lloyd J.
Smyth Mrs. John G.
Spread Mrs. Henry F.
Stillwell Miss Elizabeth F.
Sturges Mrs. W. N.
Swadkins Mrs. Alfred
Telling Mrs. John
Tifft Mrs. Henry
Tilt Mrs. Joseph E.
Troendle Miss Lina E.
True Mrs. John R.
Turner Mrs. Henry
Vollintine Mrs. A. Hale
Wagg Mrs. Howard A.
Waite Miss Ida M.
Warner Mrs. Augustus
Warren Mrs. Minnie A.
Warrington Mrs. George
Watkins Miss Evelyn M.
Wayman Mrs. James B.
Weidner Mrs. R. F.
White Mrs. Charles M.
Widdicombe Mrs. Robt.
Wigeland Mrs. Andrew G.
Wiley Mrs. Benjamin
Williams Mrs. D.
Wilt Mrs. Charles T.
Woodward Mrs. Ellen E. L.
Wrisley Mrs. A. W.
Younglove Mrs. May A.
Younglove Miss Mary G.

LAKESIDE CLUB.

FORTY-SECOND SW. COR. GRAND BOUL.

OFFICERS.

E. L. WEDELES, - - - - - - - President.
H. M. SPIEGEL, - - - - - - Vice-President.
I. KEIM, - - - - - - - Treasurer.
ARTHUR POLLAK, - - - - Recording Secretary.
L. WITKOWSKY, - - - - Financial Secretary.

DIRECTORS.

M. L. Freiberger	M.'J. Oppenheimer	D. R. Levy
M. Haber	Aaron H. Wolf	L. Wessel jr.
H. Spiegel	L. Witkowsky	B. J. Rosenthal
L. Rothschild	I. H. Keim	Arthur Pollak
E. Newman		I. A. Loeb

MEMBERS.

Aaron Max	Eppstein Sam.	Harris Samuel H.	Kiper Charles
Aaron M. B.	Epstein Jacob J.	Hart Joseph	Klein Charles
Adler Morris	Epstein Max	Hart Leo H.	Klein G. L.
Ash M. L.	Epstein Morris	Hart Robert	Klein Leon
Auerbach Ben.	Falk M. L.	Hartman Abraham	Klein Nathan
Auerbach J. C.	Falter D. B.	Hartman H. S.	Klein Sam
Bachmann Sig.	Felsenthal Henry	Hartman Louis	Klein Sidney
Barbe Martin	Fernbach Louis	Hartmann Jos. S.	Kohn Henry M.
Barnet Jesse Weil	Finn Joseph M.	Hasterlik Adolph	Kohn Milton M.
Baum Herman	Fischer S. M.	Hasterlik Charles	Kohn Simon M.
Becker A. E.	Fish Isaac	Hasterlik Ignatz	Kohner J. B.
Benjamin Louis	Fisher L. K.	Hasterlik Sam.	Kramer J. A.
Bensinger A. W.	Fleishman M. S.	Hasterlik Simon	Kraus Adolf
Berolzheim Joseph	Floersheim J.	Hefter Charles	Kraus Harry
Bert Ed Dr.	Frank David	Hefter L. B.	Kuh Julius S.
Bloch Simon	Frank I. M.	Hefter Moses	Kunstadter A.
Block Isaac	Franklin Samuel	Heinsheimer D. jr.	Lachman Numa
Blum E. C.	Franks Jacob	Heller Gustav	Lazarus H.
Blum Louis J.	Freehling Ike	Heller Leo	Lebolt Jos. Y.
Brown Isidor F.	Freehling S.	Herbst William	Lederer Isaac S.
Buxbaum E. L.	Freeman H. H.	Herman L. M.	Lederer Louis
Caspary O. S.	Freeman M. M.	Herman S. J.	Lederer Simeon
Childs William	Freiberger M. L.	Herz Joseph	Lehman Herman
Cohen A. L.	Frensdorf E.	Hess Leo R.	Lepman Louis
Cornhauser M.	Frensdorf Samuel	Hess Segel	Levi Carl
Cowen Carlo; K.	Freshman Arnold	Hexter K.	Levy D. R.
Cowen Israel	Friedberg R. T.	Heyman E. S.	Levy Ed. E.
Daniels Sam.	Friedman L. J.	Hirsch Adolph	Levy L. M.
Danziger A. L.	Friend Charles	Hirsch Henry	Levy Morris F.
Danziger Emanuel	Friend Henry	Hirsch Oscar	Lewis Eugene
Daube Abe	Friend Nathan	Hirsch William	Lichtstern Isaac
Daube Leop.	Friend Oscar A.	Hirschhorn Clarence	Lilienfeld Wm.
Daube Louis	Friend Sam.		Lindauer Max
Davis David D.	Frohmann Fred.	Hirsh Sol.	Lindheim Louis
Degginger Sidney	Gans Leopold	Hochstadter Gust.	Lindheimer Jacob
DeLee Sol. T.	Gans Samuel	Hoenigsberger David	Livingston Chas.G.
Dembufsky Max	Goldenberg Max		Livingston Morris
Dernburg A.	Goldman Carl	Horner Harry	Livingston S. G.
Despres Alex.	Goldman Eugene	Hornthal Louis	Loeb Isaac A.
Despres Emile M.	Goldman Max	Hyman Joseph	Loeb Moses
Despres Isaac	Goldschmidt A.	Isaacs M. C.	Mandelbaum M. H.
Despres Sam.	Goldschmidt Moses	Israel Bernard	Mandl Bernard
Deutsch Louis	Goldsmith Albert	Jacobs Leon	Marcus Ed. S.
Dreyer Samuel	Goldsmith Moses	Jacoby Ernest	Marcus Solms
Eichberg Max	Goldsmith M. L.	Joseph H. L.	May Henry
Eichberg Wm. H.	Goldsmith Simon	Kahn Louis	Mayer Leopold
Eiseman Max	Goodhart Chas. I.	Karger Sam. I.	Mayer L. H.
Eisendrath S. B.	Goodhart P. H.	Karger Simon	Mayer Max
Eisenstaedt Leo	Greenewald M. E.	Katzauer I.	Mayer Morris
Eisenstaedt Rud.	Greenhoot Salomon	Kauffman Fred	Mayer N. A.
Eisenstaedt Sol. H.	Grossman E. B.	Kaufman Aaron	Mayer Tobias
Ellbogen M.	Grossman Herman	Kaufman Ad.	Mendel Herbert M.
Engel Bernhard	Guthmann Sieg.	Keim Isaac H.	Mendelsohn B. E.
Engel Nathan	Haber Morris	Kempner Ad.	Mendelsohn J. S.
Eppenstein M. C.	Hallenstein B.	Kesner A. L.	Meyer Leo H.
Eppenstein S. C.	Harris Joseph	Kesner J. L.	Meyer Martin

Meyer Sieg.
Michaels Isaac
Minzesheimer L.F.
Monash Chas. P.
Moog David
Morris Jacob
Morris Louis
Moses Adolph
Moses I. S. Rev.
Moss Leopold
Moss M. H.
Moyses E. M.
Munzer E. I.
Munzer Henry
Nast A. D.
Nast Sam
Nathan L. A.
Netter Sam
Neuberger Albert
Neumann Ignatz
Neumann Louis
New Aaron L.
Newburger Wm. S.
Newgass Louis M.
Newgass Wm.
Newman E.
Newman Jacob jr.
Newman Morris
Newman M.
Nye Wm. A.
Oberndorf Fred.
Oberndorf H'rm'nn
Oppenheim M. J.
Oppenheimer Juli's
Perlberg S. E.
Pfaelzer David
Pfaelzer Eli
Pfaelzer Simon
Philipsborn M.
Philipson Isidor
Phillips Wm.
Pick Albert
Pieser Isaac
Plotke N. M.
Polacheck Leo

Pollak Arthur
Powell Leopold
Price L.
Radzinski A. I.
Regensburg Henry
Regenstein Louis
Reinach J.
Reiss William
Reitler Charles
Rhodes Clinton
Rice Jacob
Rice Sol.
Ritterband M. M.
Rosenbaum M.
Rosenberg Ben.
Rosenberger Otto J.
Rosenfeld Simon
Rosenheim M. B.
Rosenthal Benj. J.
Rosenthal Edw. A.
Rosenthal Sam.
Rothschild Harry
Rothschild Lew
Rothschild Mau-
rice F.
Rothstein Isidore
Rubel Isaac
Ruben Charles
Rubens Charles
Rubin Sol.
Salomon L. H.
Salomon Moses
Samuel Albert E.
Schaffner Abe
Schaffner A. J.
Schamberg Lewis
Schindler Alfred
Schlesinger B.
Schlesinger Max
Schlesinger P.
Schneewind Ben
Schoenberg Alex.
Schoenberg Joel
Schoenfeld Frank
Schoenfeld H. W.

Schopflocher Her-
man
Schram H. S.
Schroder Milton
Schwabacher H. jr.
Schwabacker J.
Schwarz Moses
Seaman Leop.
Seligman L.
Sello Max
Shakman H. A.
Shrimski Israel
Silverman Lazarus
Sincere Ed.
Singer E. A.
Sittig Charles
Sloman Marcus l.
Sloss Jacob
Solomon F. M.
Sondheimer Ed.
Son S. J.
Spiegel Hamlin
Spiegel Jonas
Spitz Henry
Stein Albert
Stein Ernest
Stein Philip
Stein Sam
Stein Sydney
Steiner Jacob
Steinfeld Ben.
Stern Daniel
Stern Max
Stettauer James
Stransky E. J.
Straus Ben. F.
Straus Irving J. Dr.
Straus Simeon
Strauss Gus.
Strauss Henry
Strauss J. N.
Strauss Maurice
Strauss Sig.
Strausser Frank
Strouss Emile

Stumer A. R.
Stumer Louis
Tallert Jacob
Taussig Wm.
Theobald J. H.
Treichlinger Chas.
Tuteur E. B. Dr.
Vallens Eugene
Vehon Morris
Wasserman David
Wedeles E. L.
Wedeles Sig.
Weil Harry
Weil Morris
Weil Theo.
Weill Maurice
Wertheim Jos. B.
Wertheimer Max
Wertheimer Nath S.
Wessel L. jr.
Wheeler Leo. W.
Wheeler Meyer
Winkler S. A.
Wise David
Witkowsky Conrad
Witkowsky David
Witkowsky David
Witkowsky Leo-
pold
Witkowsky Moses
D.
Witkowsky Sam. D.
Wolf A. H.
Wolf Ben.
Wolf Sol.
Wolf Wm. B.
Wolff H. D. Dr.
Wolff Leopold
Wolff William
Wolff William
Wurzburger Harris
Wurzburger Jonas
Wygant Alonzo
Yondorf David

LINCOLN CLUB OF CHICAGO.

COR. ASHLAND AND JACKSON BOULEVARD.

OFFICERS.

WINFIELD S. COY, - - - - - -	President.
E. A. ROBINSON, - - - -	First Vice-President.
R. H. LIDDELL, - - - -	Second Vice-President.
C. C. CARNAHAN, - - - - - -	Secretary.
MURDOCH CAMPBELL, - - - - -	Treasurer.

DIRECTORS.

Elisha Robinson
Joseph E. Bidwell
Winfield S. Coy
C. C. Carnahan

George H. Greene
S. T. Gunderson
Murdoch Campbell
W. H. Alsip

M. R. Harris
R. H. Liddell
Alfred Russell
W. S. Kaufman

MEMBERS.

Abbey C. P.
Abbott E. O.
Aiken Thomas
Albreht G. A.
Albright T. S.
Allen Howard
Almquist J. F.
Alsip W. H.
Anderson Geo.
Anderson J. B.
Arthur M. H.
Avery Daniel
Babcock A. C.
Badenoch J. J.
Baird F. S.
Ball Farlin Q.
Baltz Chas.
Bannerman Wm.
Banning Ephraim
Barnes P. R.
Barr Alfred E.
Barrett E. E.
Barth L. L.
Bee Joseph
Beebe Curtis M.Dr.
Bell John A.
Bell W. S.
Benson J. H.
Berz George
Betts George
Bidwell Joseph E.
Binnie W. A.
Bishop Elmer
Blodgett E. A.
Blount Fred. M.
Borland M. W.
Boughton Dr. C. H.
Bowen E. K.
Bowyer Dr. L. F.
Bradbury E. L.
Bregstone B.
Bregstone H. H.
Brickwood Albert
Brown E. K.
Brown HenryA.Dr.
Brown W. E.
Bryan M. J.
Buechel Charles C.
Buehler Eugene
Bunnell Chas. H.
Burke E. W.
Burkhart Frank L.
Burnett H. L.
Burnham Josiah
Burrows A. W.
Bushspies Dr. F.
Bussey W. T.
Cameron N.
Campbell DanielA.
Campbell J. B.
Campbell J. L.
Campbell M.
Campbell R. A.
Carnahan Chas.

Carnahan H. H.
Carpenter Grant
Carrington A. R.
Carter O. N.
Carter Zina R.
Case S. H.
Casmer Max L.
Caws P. J.
Challman G. A.
Chapin F. E.
Chapin S. P.
Chase Hollis M.
Chott Q. J.
Cigrand B. J.
Clark D. W.
Clark R. Porter
Clark W. W.
Cline Geo. S.
Coan F. A.
Coda D.
Coda John B.
Cole D. B.
Cole M. E.
Coleman James
Collier P.
Colson Robert K.
Commons J. R.
Commons Robert
Conger W. M.
Conors H. S.
Cooper A. O.
Conrick Frank
Corwin Dr. John
Cotton Dr. A. C.
Cox Dr. S. J.
Coy Winfield S.
Coyne Fred E.
Craig E. M.
Craine W. P.
Crawford A. M.
Crowe Wm.
Curtis Geo. P.
Curtis D. H.
Cusack J. I.
Dana W. H.
Darrow A. H.
Davis C. A.
Davy John
Dawson B. D.
Day Edward S.
DeCelle N.
Deming Gail E.
Dempster Thomas
DeWitt E. C.
Dexter Allen S.
Dickson S. M.
Dietz W. P.
Dodds A. C.
Doremus A. F.
Downey Joseph
Drake C. T.
Drum J. E.
Dryer E. J.
Dudley Oscar

Duncan Dr. T. C.
Dunkleberg J. J.
Dunn O. T.
Dunne R. O.
Dusenberry W. P.
Dwyer Edward J.
Earle Dr. F. B.
Eastman A. N.
EastmanEdwardR.
Eastman R. A.
Eberhardt Max
Eckhart B. A.
Edwards Joseph B.
Edwards T. K.
Eicke Adolph Dr.
Eiderberg S. W.
Eilers P. C.
Elliott C. P.
Elliott D. M.
Elliott L. B.
Elliott W. S. jr.
Ellis A. W.
Ellithorpe L. A.
Engle G. W.
Evans W. H.
Ferguson C. E.
Ferguson Frank
Fiedler Julius
Fisk David E.
Fitzgerald A. F.
Fitzgerald William
Fogarty G. F.
Forbes A. M.
Formaneck F. Dr.
Fortner Dr. E. C.
Fox O.
Frake James
Franklin S.
Friedel Dr. M. J.
Fucik Frank
Fullenwider J. A.
Fuller L. B.
Gainty John F.
Gard Charles H.
Gareau C.
George C. H.
Gerwig Frank H.
Geyse J. H.
Giles Henry F.
Gillis James E.
Gindele George W
Gobel E. F.
Gobel E. H.
Godfrey Walter G.
Goldsberry C. A.
Graham D. W. Dr.
Green G. H.
Greenlee E. C.
Gross John N.
Gunderson S. T.
Haines T. L.
Halbe Charles F.
Hale Clarence B.
Hambleton C. E.

Hamilton W. O.
Happel Chas. A.
Harbridge C. C.
Harris M. R.
Harris S. R.
Hart John J.
Harts E. B.
Harvey Dr.Andrew
Haskins Frank E.
Hawes W. H.
Hay William S.
Hecht F. A.
Held Charles H.
Henderson William
Hendricks Chas L.
Hendricks John C.
Henkle E. G.
Heper Charles
Hertz H. L.
Higgie Noble K.
Holden Walter S.
Hopkins W. M.
Hopple C. J.
Hull Chas L.
Hulvey Willis G.
Hunter J. H.
Hupp J. M.
Ingram J. E.
Insley Edward
Ives Morse
Izard C. F.
Joadwine Wallace
Jackson E. W.
Jackson J. S.
Jarvis Philip A.
Johnson E. T.
Johnson R. M.
Jones D. C.
Kahler Conrad
Karcher Louis
Kasmer Max L.
Kaufman W. S.
Keeler M. J.
Kelly L. P.
Kelsey Frank C.
Kemper C. A.
Kent W. D.
Kessler Chas. H.
Kessler Christ J.
Kester Dr. P. J.
King Simeon
Koch Edward P.
Kohler Conrad
Konig Bernard
Krohmer W. F.
Krueger Chas.
Landon E.
Lange M. H.
Lauth Adam
Lauth J.
Lee E. E.
Lee W. H.
Leonard J. G.
Levin M.

Lewellyn E. H.
Lewis Henry
Liddell R. H.
Light Judd B.
Lincoln Willis L.
Little A. H.
Loeber T. A.
Lomas E. A.
Lombard W. C.
LongeneckerJoelM.
Loop C. B.
Lorimer William
Loveless C. L.
Luken W. M.
Lyon Richard F.
McAdam J. V.
McCartney James
McCarty C. S.
McCullough John R.
McClintock S. H.
McCorkle Andrew
McCormack H.
McCullen Dr. J. L.
McDevett Bernard, jr.
McElroy J. L.
McEvoy John A.
McGovern John
McGrath J. J.
McGregor George L.
McKenzie George
McMillan E. E.
McNichols Thos. J.
McNulty T. F.
McWhorter P. A.
Mackie Chas.
MacMillanThos.C.
Magill J. C.
MamerChristopher
Mandelbaum W. R.
Martin A. W.
Marchesseault J. B. A.
Maskell John W.
Mason Dr.FrankG.
Mason George
Mason Hugh
Mason William E.
Matlock T. C.
Mattern C. C.
Maulsby R. S.
Maxwell James
Maxwell M. H. B.
Meacham F. D.

Melins Richard
Midgeley F.
Miller A. W.
Miller J. L.
Mills D. W.
Mincer A.
Minkler W. S.
Mitchell A. J.
Monroe W. T.
More Clark E.
Morrison John J.
Munro Daniel
Murdock E. P.
Murphy John D.
Newcomb Geo. W.
Nicholas H. E.
Nichols H. D.
Noel E. P.
Nohren John E.
Nolan Gabriel J.
Norden G. J.
Norman S.
Norvick Anton
Nye F. E.
O'Donnell Chas.
O'Donnell John F
O'Donnell P. H.
O'Hara W. S.
Oliphant J. M.
Oliver William
Osgood H. S.
Parker John R.
Parks A. G.
Parry Samuel
Patterson A. C.
Patterson R. M.
Patterson W. C.
Peck M. D.
Pendarvis R. E.
Perkins S. H.
Peters C. H.
Pierce J. W. D.
Pierce Dr. O. F.
Pilgrim E. J.
Piper Charles E.
Plummer Geo. W.
Powers F. H.
Preis Wm.
Preston Robert
Prosser Henry B.
Puffer R. A.
Pyott J. M. jr.
Quitman Dr. E. L.
Randolph S. M.
Rawlins W. D.

Raymer Walter J.
Reeves Joshua
Reilly Geo.
Rennacker E. F.
Rhodes Joseph
Richards N. B.
Richolson B. F.
Riley Wm. W.
RobertsClarenceV.
Roberts F. E.
Robinson E. A.
Rogers John A.
Rood Dudley H.
Roy M. A.
Ross Alexander
Rowe Peter A.
Rowland O. H.
Russell Alfred
Salt M. H.
Sanborn John H.
Sanditz Joseph
Sawtelle C. A.
Schack Joseph
Scharlau CharlesE.
Scherer Henry
Schriener H. B.
Schuen Fred. C.
Sennott Thos. W.
Sharp Edward J.
Shaw Arthur J.
Shenick Dr. O. T.
Simmons C. H.
Sitts Lewis D.
Slade Robert
Slavik Frank jr.
Slayton H. L.
Sloan Geo. S.
Sloan W. H.
Smart W. F.
SmedbergJosephD.
Smith Horace
Smith T. J.
Smith W. R.
Smyth John M.
Smulski J. F.
Snow George
Snow Taylor A.
Snow W. H.
Soule Chas. B.
Sparks Walter E.
Spaulding R. E.
Spinning Roy
Stansbaugh G. F.
StansfieldJamesH.
Stark A. M.

Stein Bernard
Stender C. F. G.
Stepina John F.
Stevens Loren G.
Stevens J. K.
Stewart E. L.
Stoll R. H.
Stone A. J.
Stone E. B.
Sullivan W. K.
Swartz Seymour
Sweet John A.
Swift Geo. B.
Taylor M. H.
Theiss A. P.
Thompson H. P.
Tice A. R.
Tomblins Edwin J.
Tone A. R.
Tracy F. K.
Traver R. C.
Tredick B. A.
Turner Geo. D.
Tuthill R. S.
Utitz A. S.
VanBuren Aug'stus
VanHousen H. L.
Vanpell Wm. R.
Viers B. W.
Wade C. A.
Wahl Albert
Watson A. H.
Weaver Charles M.
Weeks J. S.
Wells Romanta
Wells Warren A.
Wetherell G. F.
Wheeler H. A. Gen.
Whigam Wm. H.
White George E.
Whitney F. A.
Wilcox Geo. N. Dr.
Wiley H. L.
Wilk Fred L.
Williams Geo. W.
Williamson John
Wilson F. H.
Wilson W. J.
Wolf Samuel
Wolfinger Wm. H.
Woods F. H.
Wright J. F.
Wyman R. L.
Wyman V. W.
Ziegfeld F.

MARQUETTE CLUB.

CORNER DEARBORN AVENUE AND MAPLE STREET.

OFFICERS.

EDWARD G. PAULING, - - - - - President.
WILLIAM DICKINSON, - - - First Vice-President.
HOMER A. DRAKE, - - Second Vice-President.
FENO E. SMITH, - - - - - - - Secretary.
JOHN W. KENNEDY, - - - - - - Treasurer.
EDWIN F. HEYWOOD, - - Chairman House Committee.

DIRECTORS.

William F. Zibell   F. J. Lange   Edwin S. Hartwell
Edwin F. Heywood   George H. Jenney   J. B. Foley

MEMBERS.

Adams George E.	Blake F. K.	Comstock L. K.	Fathauer Theo.
Adams H. C.	Bliler H. E.	Cook Cyrus F.	Fellows Lee
Agler O. O.	Bodman A. C.	Cook Jas. A.	Field R. I.
Ahern John H.	Boutell H. S.	Cook J. L.	Fishburn E. H.
Aldrich Chas. H.	Bowe John T.	Cooke Arthur J.	Fisher John
Allen R. A.	Boyd S. F.	Copeland Wm. M.	Flannery D. F.
Allerton Samuel W	Brace Wm.	Corbin C. R.	Foell Chas. M.
Alling Edward H.	Bradley Philip B.	Corbin C. Dana	Foley Jno. B.
Anderson A. E.	Braunhold Louis F.	Corlett Dr.Thos.G.	Foltz Fritz
Anderson C. K.	Bredt John M.	Coyne F. E.	Forbes Frank G.
Archer R. E.	Brentano Theo.	Crafts M. B.	Forch John L.
Armstrong J. M. jr.	Breuer Adam	Cratty Thomas	Ford S. B.
Arney John J.	Bristol F. M.	Crawford F. H.	Forrest Thomas L.
Arntzen B. E.	Brocklebank J. C.	Crissman Dr.Ira B.	Foss Geo. E.
Ascher Martin	Brown Dr. H. H.	Cross M. J.	Foster Sam
Babcock C. E.	Brundage E. J.	Crow Louis W.	Frankenstein W.B.
Bacon D. C.	Burns P. C.	Curtis John H.	Frankhauser E. J.
Baker Frank E.	Bush W. L.	Davenny W. I.	Frisbee Geo. L.
Baker Geo. R.	Busse Fred A.	Davis Herbert J.	Fritze F. A.
Baldwin R. R.	Cairnduff W. H.	Davis M. R.	Frost A. C.
Ball Wm. T.	Cameron Alex. S.	Dawes Chas. G.	Fry John A.
Bancroft E. A.	Campbell R. C.	Dellano E. F.	Fuchs Albert
Barber Hiram	Campbell R. L.	Denney Dr. J. A.	Fuller H. M.
Barbour J. J.	Canfield E. L.	DeWeese T. A.	Furst Edward A.
Barnes Carl L.	Carpenter L. T.	DeWitt Elden C.	Gardiner H. M.
Barrett E. E.	Carroll Dr. J. M.	Dick A. B.	Garity G. C.
Bassett Charles W.	Carter H. M.	Dickinson Edward	Geer I. J.
Baum Dr. W. L.	Catlin Charles	Dickinson John W.	Gelderman W. M.
Baur Jacob	Chancellor Justus	Dickinson Wm.	Gentry Chas. H.
Beckerman W. H.	Channon Harry	Dickson Samuel M.	Getchell Louis F.
Beebe John E.	Channon J. H.	Dolan John J.	Gilbert Charles C.
Beitler H. C.	Chapin O. E.	Doolittle O. S.	Gilbert J. Thornton
Belfield Dr.Wm.T.	Charles A. N.	Dorrance Chas. J.	Giles William A.
Bennett E. R.	Chatfield E. P.	Dorrance F. K.	Going Judson F.
Benson C. L.	Chetlain A. H.	Douglas George L.	Good Robert
Bent E. M.	Child Gerald R.	Drake Dr. H. A.	Goodman Joseph
Bentley W. G.	Chott Q. J.	Draper L. V.	Goodwin Leonard
Bentz Richard R.	Chytraus Axel	Dunham J. S.	Gordon C. U.
Berriman M. W.	Clark Geo. M.	Durand H. Z.	Gordon John L.
Berry C. S.	Clarke Dr. W. G.	Eastman S. C.	Gormully R. P.
Bevington E. L.	Cockley W. A.	Elliott W. S.	Gould Elwyn B.
Bigelow E. A.	Coddington A. O.	Ely Dr. C. F.	Gould I. L.
Biggs E. A.	Cody Hope Reed	Englehard G. P.	Gray W. H.
Bingham R. W.	Collins Chas. H.	Eschenburg H. A	Gross Jacob
Bishop S. H.	Collins John G.	Essick J. C.	Gross S. E.
Black J. R.	Colton S. C.	Estabrook H. D.	Gross W. H.
Black M. C.	Colton S. K.	Fairbanks Geo. O.	Hadley H. H.

Hagerty Thos. A.	Knauss John A.	Morgan G. C.	Riley C. W.
Hall, Dr. A. M.	Kober Geo. C.	Morgan Otho H.	Rinn G. P.
Hall H. F.	Kohlsaat H. H.	Morrill C. A.	Ripley Chas. H.
Hall L. T.	Krause E. R.	Morris Dr. John L.	Ritchie J. W.
Halle E. G.	Lamson Wm. A.	Morris William G.	Ritter H. A.
Hambleton C. J.	Lange Fred J.	Morse B. B.	Roberts Wm. B.
Hamburgher E. C.	Lapham D. A.	Morton Oliver T.	Roche John E.
Hamilton R. A.	Lapham M.	Moulton D. A.	Rockwell Irvin E.
Hamlin Frank	Lauman Geo. V.	Muhlke Henry C.	Rondthaler Rev. J.
Hamlin H. J.	Leake Jos. B.	Muhlke Jos.	A.
Harbeck Eugene	Leavens C. A.	Munzer Hugo	Rood H. H.
Harlan J. M.	Leffingwell W. B.	Munzer Rudolf	Rose F. A.
Harpel Chas. J.	Leman Henry W.	Neeley Chas. G.	Rotsted William
Hartwell Edwin S.	Leonard Geo. E.	Nelson W. D.	Royce J. L.
Hasberg John W.	Levis John M.	Newberry R. T.	Rummler W. R.
Haynes T. C.	Lewis O. A.	Nisbet L. K.	Runnells J. S.
Hebel Oscar	Lindsay S. W.	Nixon Wm. Penn	Ryan J. E. G.
Hecht Ernst	Linebarger PaulW.	Noble Orlando	Sackett R. E.
Heegaard W. H.	Loeb Adolph	Nolan Arthur	Sandberg Geo. N.
Henry J. M.	Loeb Jacob W.	Norcross F. F.	Saylor H. G.
Herring Robt. H.	Loesch Frank J.	Noyes L. W.	Schaeffer A. J.
Hewen Frederick	Lovejoy Geo. T.	O'Brien Edward	Schaller Henry
Heyman Alex. H.	Lowden Frank O.	Olendorf C. W.	Sharkey John L.
Heywood E. F.	Luce Franklin A.	Olson Harry	SchedlerWilliam C.
Heywood J. P.	Lunceford C. D.	Olson Nils F.	Scherzer Albert H.
Hilton W. B.	Lundahl J.	Olson O. C. S.	Schloss Lee L.
Hirchl Andrew	McCormick A. A.	Osburn M. R.	Schmidt Wm.
Hirsch James H.	McNally Jas.	Osgood Geo. W.	Schmitt Charles S.
Hoffbauer William	McNally T. G.	Oswald Julius W.	Schmitt Frank P.
Hogland Chas. H.	McNaughton J.	Oviatt F. F.	Schmitt Frank P.jr.
Holdom Jesse	McNulta Genl John	Pain Charles	Schneider Otto C.
Holstad S. H.	C.	Parkins Horace D.	Schneider Dr. S. N.
Horn Adie B.	Maas Philip	Parkinson R. H.	Schrader Otto
Horton O. H.	Mabie C. E.	Pauling E. G.	Schroeder Oscar
Howard Robert T.	MacMillan T. C.	Pease E. H.	Schweitzer R. J.
Hume J. H.	Mahler Jacob H.	Peck G. R.	Sears N. C.
Humphrey Arthur	Mandeville Samuel	Pence A. M.	Seeman Emil H.
Humphrey Wirt E.	Marks Henry E.	Pettit F. W.	Sercomb A. L.
Hunter Percival	Marshall Alex.	Phillips Abe	Sexton James A.
Huntinghouser R.	Marshall Frank C.	Phillips J. S.	Shepler E. A.
G.	Martin Dr. Ross N.	Phillips Samuel	Sherlock James P.
Hush A. B.	Marx Dr. Zero	Pierce W. H.	Sherwood W. W.
Hynson Cromie	Mason Hugh L.	Plotke N. M.	Shnable E. R.
Jacobs J. Frank	Mason W. A.	Porter C. J.	Shoenthaler F. C.
Jaffray R. M.	Massey Wilfred	Porter H. J.	Simpson T. S.
Jaques C. E.	Mather A. C.	Pratt Benj. H.	Slocum L. T. M.
Jaques Frank F.	Mather R. H.	Preston E. W.	Smith Albert F.
Jaques William W.	Matson C. R.	Propach C.	Smith Ben M.
Jenney G. H.	May Albert	Pulver A. W.	Smith Frederick A.
Johnson C S.	Mayer Simon	Putnam A. A.	Smith F. A.
Johnson John	Mayer Sol.	Quinlan Dr. W. W.	Smith F. E.
Johnson John H.	Merrill B. W.	Ransom Allan	Smith H. T.
Johnson Wm. H.	Miles George R.	Rathbone Henry R.	Smith Lloyd J.
Johnson W. H.	Miller Brice A.	Ray Beecher B.	Smith M. E.
Johnson W. F.	Miller Frederick	Raymond G. W.	Smith Philetus
Jones C. A.	Miller G. H.	Raymond S. B.	Snyder H. P.
Jukes A. G.	Miller James H.	Reed N. A.	Spahn Louis
Kavanaugh M.	Miller John A.	Reeves Irving W.	Sperling Dr. I. D.
Kendall E. B.	Miller T. E.	Remick A. E.	Spruhan H. J.
Kennedy John W.	Mohr Louis	Rennacker W. R.	Spry Geo. E.
Kepler J. W.	Moloney James	Revell A. H.	Stacy C. P.
Kerr Robert G.	Monett E. T.	Revell David	Staubery H. jr.
Kettering F. O.	Montgomery H. W.	Rhode John C. W.	Stanford G. W.
Kimball C. V.	Moore Arthur L.	Rhodes Wm. M.	Stearns W. E.
Kimbark S. D.	Moore James S.	Rickcords Geo. E.	Steele Percival
Knapp Kemper K.	Morey A. G.	Riggles M. F.	Steven James A.

Stevens P. D.	Torgerson LloydR.	Vollner Herman	White A. L.
Stevenson A. F.	Tostevin C. W.	Wader S. F.	Whitesell J. H.
Steward LeRoy T.	Tracy W. W.	Wagg Howard N.	Whitman John L.
Stewart Graeme	Traub Adolph	Waide W. Arthur	Wicker W. B.
Stillwell James	Truax Charles	Waite Geo. A.	Wickersham H. B
Stoelker W. H.	Tucker F. J.	Waldron L. K.	Wilbur R. M.
Stolz E. H.	Turner J. W.	Wallace Fred H.	Wilk F. L.
Strasburg J. M.	Ulrich A. L.	Wallen C. E.	Willis L. M.
Strong A. W.	Ulrich B. A.	Walters A.	Willits Geo. S.
Strong E. B.	Ulrich B. A. jr	Washburn Wm. D.	Wincher Wm. P.
Stump H. E.	Umdenstock W. M.	Watt Frank	Wing H. L.
Sundell Chas. F.	Upham Fred W.	Weaver John V. A.	Wirth Henry
Swannell Wm.	Upham R. A.	Webster E. L.	Wisler Bond
Taylor L. D.	VanBuren E. R.	Weigley F. S.	Wisler Henry M.
Taylor S. G.	Van Gilder W. C.	Weil Walker G.	Wissler Geo. E.
Terrill A. S.	Van Hofften Alex.	Weimers W. F.	Wittstein A. H.
Thomas F. A.	Vaughn Harry C.	Welch C. B.	Wolff Oscar
Thompson M. V.	Vaux F. T.	Wells Chas. D.	Wood N. E.
Thompson Wm. M.	Vawter Wm. A.	Wells James L.	Woods G. H.
Thornton E. L.	Vernon Wm. W.	Wendell John H.	Wynne J. Edward
Thurber G. S.	Vinnedge A. R.	West E. G.	Yates T. D.
Tisdel Clark J.	Vinnedge M. A.	Whalley J. J.	Zibell Wm. F.
Tomaso S.	Vogelsang John Z.	Whedon Jas. P.	

MENOKEN CLUB.
1196 Washington Boul.

OFFICERS.

LUDWIG WOLFF,	President.
ALOIS PODRASNIK,	First Vice-President.
SAMUEL KERR,	Second Vice-President.
H. G. COLSON,	Secretary.
JOHN F. EISZNER,	Treasurer.

TRUSTEES.

Alois Podrasnik	H. S. Brackett	Samuel Kerr
John F. Eiszner	W. H. Dymond	H. G. Colson
Fred E. Clark	H. M. Hoelscher	G. W. Spofford
S. T. Gunderson	Ludwig Wolff	Thomas P. Hicks
H. J. Evans		

MEMBERS.

Albright W. F.	Bingham Dr. M. F.	Bryan Dr. John C.	Cleveland S. E.
Allen John K.	Bingle John H.	Bullen Fred F.	Cleveland W. R.
Amerson W. H. Dr.	Blair George P.	Bunge Wm. H.	Clifford Dr. E. L.
Argo H. E.	Blouke Dr. M. B.	Burton F. J.	Cochrane H.
Atchinson John D.	Blount F. M.	Cable C. E.	Cody S. P.
Austin Robert	Blueler C. W.	Callan F. D.	Coffin G. B.
Ayers Geo. L.	Bocher Geo. R.	Calley J. S.	Coffin Percy B.
Babcock Wm. E.	Bouffleur A. I. Dr.	Canright W. S.	Cole C. D.
Bachus Anson	Bowey Chas. F.	Capouch Edward	Collins John
Bahntge Chas. F.	Boyd H. J.	Carrell H. E.	Colson H. G.
Bailey John R.	Boyd S. J. Dr.	Carrier R. J.	Conan Eugene
Baird F. S.	Boyd Wm. T.	Carter Judge O. N.	Connable A. W.
Baldwin A. L.	Brackett M. S.	Case Elmer G.	Connon Wm. L.
Barker Alfred	Brady Rufus T.	Case S. H.	Conway R. F.
Barr A. E.	Brand S. H.	Casler Wallace	Cook W. H.
Bartelme Geo. P.	Brewster J. H.	Chamberlain C. H.	Cooper A. O.
Bartholf Chas. S.	Brown C. H.	Christensen F. O.	Cowan W. H.
Bearcroft J. H.	Brown M. B.	Christy R. C.	Coyne F. E.
Beckwith James A.	Brown T. J.	Clark D. W.	Crane F. R.
Benedict Geo. H.	Brown W. E.	Clark Fred E.	Crary Arthur V.
Berman Wm. F.	Brunck A. F.	Clark George T.	Crocker B. S.
Bigelow James K.	Bryan F. W.	Clark Louis A.	Cruikshank C. E.

Cummings E. S.
Date Sidney S.
Davenport H. W. Dr.
Davidson F. B.
Davis D. W.
Davison Chas. Dr.
Dawson J. H.
DeClercq G. E. W.
Decker Myron A.
Denman H. M.
Dicker E. A.
Dickinson Chas.
Dieter J. P.
Dodge C. C.
Downey Joseph
Doyle W. A.
Dozais L. A.
Dunham A. H.
Dunton T. F.
Dymond W. H.
Dynes O. W.
Eastman E. P.
Eaton T. W.
Edgerton G. H. Dr.
Eiszner Henry G.
Eiszner John
Eiszner John F.
Elliott W. S. jr.
Evans H. J.
Everett J. Edgar Dr.
Felton W. S.
Fern Charles A.
Fern G. B.
Fischer Wm. D.
Formanek F. Dr.
Foskett A. H.
Foster J. W.
Fowler S. W.
Francis Chas. R.
French Edgar
Friestedt L. P.
Fuller E. L.
Fulton A. W.
Galvin J. C.
Gardner D. B.
Gaynor James
Gill Dr. J. C.
Gillespie John
Gillespie R. H.
Giroux Geo. W.
Gray Charles W.
Grimm E. A.
Grussing E.
Gunderson S. T.
Hall Edgar A.
Harvey A. M. Dr.
Hayes S. C.
Heap Arnold
Helm Daniel T.
Hemstreet W. J.
Herrick J. B. Dr.
Hetherington J. E.
Hewett John

Hicks T. P.
Higbee J. W. H.
Higgins G. W.
Higgins James D.
Hoelscher E. C.
Hoelscher H. M.
Holland J. E.
Holmes Frank F.
Holroyd Dr. E. E.
Hood C. T. Dr.
Hopkins R. N.
Hostetter J. N.
Hostler S. P.
Howe H. W.
Howe Warren B.
Howland A. M.
Huszagh R. D.
Huyck J. H. jr.
Jackman W. G.
Jackson James S.
Jackson W. B.
Jones W. Gifford
Karcher Louis
Keating Arthur J.
Keirman T. S.
Kendall Geo. W.
Keneagy H. G.
Kenning R. H. Dr.
Kerr Ellis K.
Kerr Samuel
Kersten G. F.
Kessler Geo. D.
Kneisly John L.
Knight Jerome
Kovi Peter
Kuhns Adolph A.
Kuhns Frank C.
Lamoreaux M. D.
LeFevre J. J.
Lemay W. G.
Letz Frederick C.
Lightcapp S. P.
Locke J. L.
Loomis J. E.
Loomis T. T. jr.
Lyndon Geo. W.
Lyon James A
MacCarty C. S.
Main W. F.
Mallen H. Z.
Mallen P. H.
Many S. G.
Mapledoram Eug'e
Martin R. L.
Mason Wm. E.
Matthes John F.
Matthews Albert
Matthews Hugh W.
McBride J. F.
McCarthy E. J.
McCarthy John J.
McCauley T. W.
McClurg A. H.
McCourtie A. B.
McDonald Edward

McFarlane Richard D.
McKinney Dr. S. P.
McLelland H. B.
McNeill T. H.
Memhard Fred H.
Meredith William
Millard F. R.
Miller B. C.
Miller Chas. E.
Mills D. W.
Milner Geo. R.
Moll Carl
Mortimer A. E.
Mortimer C. J.
Mortimer Wm. E.
Murdock Wm. A.
Musgrave Albert
Newton Chas. E.
Nichols I. W.
Nickerson A. E.
Noble Thomas G.
Norton L. A.
Oliver A. J.
Oliver John jr.
Oliver Wm. G.
Owens R. W.
Ozias E. R.
Pagels Wm. T.
Painter Joseph A.
Palmer Silas
Pank C. Walter
Parks Sam Shaw
Patterson J. C.
Pendergast Jos. Dr.
Penfield L. R.
Perrill A. C.
Perry Thomas O.
Pflager C. W.
Pflager H. M.
Pitt H. M.
Podrasnik Alois
Pratt Wm. H.
Prendergast M. J. Dr.
Price D. A.
Price Wm. H.
Ray Wm. E.
Reed Charles E.
Reed L. J.
Rice E. P. Dr.
Rice H. A.
Rice T. J.
Rich H. S.
Richards C. D.
Richardson Frank
Richardson G. M.
Rinder Geo. L.
Ripley William
Rittenhouse L. P.
Robertson H. E.
Robinson W. J.
Robison Jno. A. Dr.
Rogers Frank D.
Rohn Alfred

Rojahn F. C.
Ross C. S.
Rundell M. H.
Runyan E. F. jr.
Russell D. E.
Sackley James A.
Sailor Samuel
Sanborn Geo. C.
Sanders A. H.
Sandes R. H.
Sands A. J.
Sargent F. R.
Satterlee John C.
Sawyer C. S. Dr.
Schlueter H. W.
Schofield John R.
Scully John B.
Sears George F.
Sharp Thomas
Shepard Frank L.
Shepard Geo. P.
Sherwood Marc
Sholes Edward
Shumway N. C.
Sipperly Erastus
Smith E. L. Dr.
Smith G. W.
Smith J. George
Smith Morton G.
Smith Sherman W.
Smith Waldo E.
Sollitt Wm.
Spofford G. W.
Spring F. C.
Stanwood E. W.
Steinson H.
Steinson H. G.
Steker Frank J.
Stevens L. G.
Stokes C. M.
Storey J. R.
Stover Ira
Street Charles R.
Stroker H. W.
Sullivan W. K.
Tate H. F.
Thayer Charles A.
Thompson C. L.
Thompson Hiram P.
Thompson H. L.
Thompson R. S.
Thorp H. W.
Tillotson W. S.
Tilt David
Traquair Wm. M.
Tuller R. B. Dr.
VanAuken C. E.
VanMatre W. N.
VanZandt Geo.
Varty J. A.
Varty Lester A.
Waite A. C.
Walduck C. W.
Walsh R. J.

Warner S. W.   Whitman F. F.   Wilson Frank I.   Wolff Ludwig
Washburn W. O.   Whitman J. M.   Wolff C. J.   Wood Walpole
Wengler M.   Wilcox Wm. E.   Wolff John F.   Woods F. M.
Wheelock W. W.   Williams Martin D.   Wolff Louis jr.   Young Willis
Whiteside John H.

MIDLOTHIAN COUNTRY CLUB.

OFFICERS.

GEORGE R. THORNE, - - - - - - - - - President.
H. N. HIGINBOTHAM, - - - - - - - Vice-President.
EDWIN A. POTTER, 132 Lasalle Street, - - - - Treasurer.
JOHN G. SHEDD, 200 Adams Street, - - - - - Secretary.

DIRECTORS.

George R. Thorne   Walter H. Wilson   E. C. Potter
A. C. Bartlett   Marvin A. Farr   W. O. Goodman
Chas. L. Raymond   H. N. Higinbotham   Wallace L. DeWolf
Edwin A. Potter   E. C. Wilson   John Clay, jr.
John Barton Payne   W. G. Purdy   John G. Shedd

MEMBERS.

Allen James Lane   Doty L. R.   Kent William   Sebastian John
Archer James L.   Doud Levi B.   Kimball Eugene S.   Shaw G. B.
Atkinson Chas. T.   Drake John A.   Kitchell Frank J.   Shedd John G.
Bailey E. P.   Durand Elliott   Lane Eben   Small Ralph D.
Baker William T.   Edwards J. A.   Lindman O. F.   Smith Calvin S.
Baldwin Willis M.   Fair Charles M.   Loftis S. T. A.   Smith Geo. T.
Barnhart Kenneth   Fair R. M.   Lord J. B.   Spalding A. G.
Barrell J. Finley   Farr Marvin A.   Marshall Dr. Juo.S.   Steever Jerome G.
Bartlett A. C.   Ferguson C. H. jr.   Martin Franklin H.   Stone J. D.
Binkley Dr. J.T. jr. Fisher L. G.   Mather Robert   Swift Edward F.
Bingham A. E.   Fitzgerald R.   Mathews Geo.W.jr.   Swift G. F.
Blair Chauncey J.   Foster Henry A.   May F. E.   Swift Louis F.
Blair Henry A.   Foster Stephen A.   Merigold W. A.   Taft Harry L.
Botsford Henry   Gaylord Edward L.   Merrill T. B.   Taft Oren B.
Brown Dr. Sanger   Gillett E. W.   Messer Paul   Taylor Dr. H. S.
Bryant Henry W.   Gilson Tillotson W. Mitchell John J.   Thomas Benjamin
Buel.M. P.   Goddard L. O.   MontgomeryH.M.S   Thompson R. S.
Bunnell John A.   Goodman W. O.   Moran T. A.   Thorne Chas. H.
Butler Edward B.   Halliwell Ashleigh   Morron John R.   Thorne Geo. R.
Butler Eugene K.   Hamlin L B.   Morse C. H.   Thorne Robert J.
Canby C. H.   Hammond L. D.   Morton Paul   Thorne W. C.
Chapman Jas. R.   Hanson David N.   Nolan John H.   Thrall W. A.
Clark M. T.   Harper W. R.   Norton Thos. S.   Trumbull John H.
Clay John jr.   Harris N. W.   Noyes LaVerne W.   Turner E. A.
Cloud John W.   Hartwell D. E.   Page S. S.   Ullman Frederick
Connor Frank H.   Harvey Geo. V.   Palmer Percival B.   Underwood J. Platt
Counselman Chas.   Hately John Craig   Palmer Wm. P.   VanKirk Chas. B.
Crawford Charles   Hately Walter C.   Payne John Barton   Wachsmuth L. C.
Critchell R. M.   Heath Ernest W.   Phelps E. H.   Walburn Albert W.
Critchell R. S.   Helmer F. A.   Porter F. W.   Ward A. Montg'y
Cudahy John   Higinbotham H.M.   Potter Edwin A.   Ware J. H.
Cunningham W.H.   Higinbotham H. N.   Potter E. C.   Warfield E. A.
Daniels E. F.   Hinkley James O.   Pulsifer F. K.   Webster Geo. H.
Day Chapin A.   Holdom Jesse   Purdy Warren G.   Wells M. D.
DeFrees James H.   Hollis Henry L.   Raymond Chas. L.   Wells S. J.
Devlin Frank A.   Holmes Thos. J.   Ream Norman B.   Wells T. E.
Dewar H.   Hoyne Frank G.   ReQua Chas. H.   Whitehouse S. S.
DeWolf Wallace L.   Hull Morton D.   Revell Alexand'rH.   Wilcox J. Fred
Dickason L. T.   Hunt Chas. H.   Robinson Chas. O.   Wiley E. N.
Donnelley Reuben   Ingalls F. A.   Robinson J. K.   Wilson E. Crane
  H.   Jones G. Edwin   Russell E. A.   Wilson Luke I.
Donnelley R. R.   Jones John H.   Schmitt A.   Wilson Walter H.
Donnelley Thos. E.   Keep Chauncey   Schmitt A. G.   Wooster C. K.

JUNIOR MEMBERS.

Cloud Frederick W.
Counselman Charles jr.
Goodman Kenneth S.

Harris Hayden Bartlett
Potter Orin W. jr.

Wilson J. Eldirdge
Wilson Milton D.

JUNIOR SUBSCRIPTION MEMBERS.

Grannis Uri B.

Potter Edwin

SUBSCRIPTION MEMBERS.

Hoxie Mrs. John R.

Oakley Mrs. Janè M.

MORTON PARK CLUB.
MORTON PARK.

OFFICERS.

WM. W. WEARE, - - - - - - - President.
F. W. RILEY, - - - - - - - Vice-President.
W. D. HYSLOP, - - - - - - - Secretary.
O. M. SCHAUTZ, - - - - - - - Treasurer.

DIRECTORS.

Wm. W. Weare
F. W. Riley

O. M. Schautz
Ralph S. Hawkins

W. D. Hyslop
H. E. Blowney

MEMBERS.

Baldwin C. M.
Bennett Guy
Bennett N. J.
Blowney H. E.
Bridges W. E.
Brown Lot
Corris H.
Cox A. W.
Danskowski J. S.
Edgerly D. G.
Edwards George
Flagler S. A.
Flagler W. B.
Flucke E. T.

Fluke C. E.
Fox R. R.
Gardin J. E.
Gilbert A. L.
Hall W. B.
Hancock Albert L.
Hawkins R. S.
Hawks F. M.
Higgs E. B.
Hyslop Wm. D.
Linden C. J.
Loveridge Ray
MacNeal A. Dr.
McClintock F.

Meany E. J.
Moore G. E.
Moore W. A. jr.
Morley John H.
Morrison F. W.
Pardee E. A.
Pardee W. E.
Payne W. B.
Purvis Miller
Rickards H. R.
Rhelden F. N.
Riley Frank W.
Riley H. S.
Rubins C. C.

Rubins H. W.
Rubins W. F.
Salbe P.
Schants O. M.
Shelden W. T.
Smith A. S.
Starling C. H.
Tibbets S. E.
Walter Chas. A.
Weare P. B.
Weare Wm. W.
Wolfe O. F.
Wright C. B.

THE NAKAMA.
MASONIC HALL, OAK PARK.

OFFICERS.

MRS. JAMES ADAMS, - - - - - President.
MRS. STANLEY CARLETON, - - Vice-President.
MISS LAURA R. RICHARDS, - - - - Secretary.
MRS. A. F. JAMES, - - - - - Treasurer.

MEMBERS.

Abbey Miss Jennie B.
Ackert Mrs. C. H.
Adams Mrs. James
Angel Mrs. H. A.
Austin Mrs. C. W.
Banks Mrs. A. F.
Bishop Mrs. Kathryn A.
Brown Miss E. Irene
Bryant Mrs. A. W.
Burton Mrs. E. F.
Carleton Mrs. Stanley

Castle Mrs. C. W.
Cleary Miss Kathleen
Cleveland Miss Eva M.
Coleman Mrs. John
Coleman Mrs. W. O.
Crockett Miss Gertrude
Duncombe Mrs. H. S.
Dunlop Mrs. Joseph K.
Eckart Mrs. H. S.
Evans Miss Anna
Gale Mrs. Walter H.

Gerts Mrs. G. E.
Gerts Miss Kate
Gerts Miss Mary C.
Giles Miss Florence M.
Giles Miss Mabel S.
Godee Mrs. Carl
Grimes Mrs. Charles B.
Hall Mrs. G. Roy
Harris Miss Nellie
Hatcher Miss N. C.
Hayden Mrs. Geo. W.

Hayden Miss Helen M.
Hayden Mrs. J. T. jr.
Hendy Dr. Clara A.
Ingram Miss Mary Belle
Ingram Miss Susie
James Mrs. A. F.
Johnson Mrs. E. T.
Jones Miss M. D.
Kiel Mrs. Julius H.
Knott Miss Lottie E.
Lawson Miss Florence
Lee Mrs. F. W.
Luff Dr. Emily M.
Many Mrs. Robert
Melville Mrs. Belle W.

Melvin Mrs. A. S.
Miller Mrs. S. C.
Morris Miss Ida M.
Moser Mrs. Geo. W.
Niles Mrs. S. S.
Nye Mrs. Wm. J.
Owen Miss Susie D.
Owen Mrs. Wm. R.
Parsons Mrs. E. D.
Quick Mrs. Wm. F.
Ray Mrs. A. S.
Reynolds Miss Stella J.
Richards Miss E. Harriet
Richards Miss Laura R.

Rigby Mrs. E. K.
Rogers Miss E. D.
Rogers Miss S. A.
Schuyer Miss M. H.
Seaman Mrs. J. A.
Southward Mrs. W. J.
Swirles Mrs. T. S.
Thomson Mrs. James W
Underwood Mrs. Pierce
Wallis Mrs. H. H.
Wells Mrs. C. H.
Willard Mrs. C. F.
Willard Miss Kate S.
Winslow Mrs. S. D.

THE OAK PARK CLUB.

115 PARK PLACE, OAK PARK.

OFFICERS.

FLETCHER B. GIBBS,	President.
MELANCTHON SMITH,	First Vice-President.
JULIAN T. BUTLER,	Second Vice-President.
H. W. AUSTIN,	Treasurer.
HENRY R. HAMILTON,	Secretary.

DIRECTORS.

Fletcher B. Gibbs
Melancthon Smith
Julian T. Butler
Henry R. Hamilton

H. W. Austin
Allen S. Ray
Charles A. Schroyer
H. S. Duncombe

J. E. Nyman
C. H. Wells
Theo. F. Bliss

MEMBERS.

Abbott A. H.
Ackert Chas. H.
Adams Albert H.
Adams E. L.
Ainslie Samuel R.
Ames C. L.
Armbruster F. P.
Austin H. W.
Austin M. B.
Ball Farlin H.
Ball Farlin Q.
Banks A. F.
Barfield W. G.
Barnard F. G.
Barnard W. F.
Bartlett Earle B.
Bassett H. W.
Bentley Harry G.
Bickford R. K.
Blanchard W. A.
Blatchford Paul
Blinn E. B.
Bliss Charles L.
Bliss Theo. F.
Bolles C. E.
Brown Paul G.
Bryant A. W.
Burgett J. M. H.
Burton E. F.
Butler A. O.

Butler A. O. jr.
Butler F. M.
Butler Julian T.
Butler J. Fred
Carleton Stanley
Carr Walter S.
Castle C. W.
Chase G. M.
Cheney Augustus J.
Claflin William
Conant W. C.
Conyne C. B. S.
Cooke W. J.
Coolidge P. B.
Coombs Hiram
Cotter William H.
Crampton R. L.
Cribben W. H.
Crosby D. K.
Day Elias V.
Dorsey R. E.
Duncombe H. S.
Dunlop Jos. K.
Elliott Frank A.
Ellsworth F. O.
Everett J. D.
Farson John
Faxon J. Warren
Fitch A. L.
Freer Nathan M.

French W. H.
Furbeck Geo. W.
Furbeck R. J.
Furbeck Warren F.
Gale Abram
Gale E. Vincent
Gale Thos. H.
Gale Walter H.
Gates S. M.
Gerts Geo. E.
Gerts Walter S.
Gibbs F. B.
Gilbert J. T.
Godee Carl
Gormley J. H.
Gustorf Arthur
Hall Fred E.
Hall George E.
Hall Wm. D.
Halloway Geo. F.
Hamilton Henry R.
Hammond Oliver
Harvey James
Harvey S. B.
Hascall Milo S.
Hatch Wm. H.
Hawley Chas. W.
Hayden Geo. W.
Hayden James T.
Heald James H.

Heurtley Arthur
Hoggins John
Hopkins H. H.
Horton Ben. P.
Howard H. Benton
Hull Delos
Hunter W. C.
Hutchinson W. A.
Ingalls Emerson
Ingalls John G.
Ingersoll Geo. W.
Ingram Jos. S.
Jackson Dwight
Jackson Leigh H.
Jackson Thomas M.
Jacoby W. L.
Jaicks Andrew
James Austin F.
Johnson Edwin T.
Johnson F. S.
Jones John I.
Jones W. Clyde
Keeney Newton M.
Kettlestrings W.
King C. H.
Knight C. Y.
Leach F. W.
Lee George
Leonard S. F.
Lewis Geo. R.

Lieb H. jr.
Lovett L. M.
Lunsford Todd
MacDonald W. J.
Malone E. T.
Many Robert
Marseilles W. P.
Martin E. P.
Mathews Allan A.
Maynard R. K.
McCary C. J.
McClary N. A.
McConnell W. A.
McCready E. W.
McDonald Silas E.
McDonald William
Melville A. B.
Melville Geo. W.
Miller Charles P.
Miller J. J.
Morris Thos. G.
Morris T. Gardner
Morse W. E.
Moser Geo. W.
Newell Frank B.
Nickerson J. F.
Nye W. J.

Nyman J. E.
Owen W. R.
Page Charles G.
Patch Geo. M.
Pattison Arthur
Pebbles A. W.
Pebbles H. R.
Peck V. H.
Pellet Clarence S.
Pickard C. E.
Pierce H. D.
Potwin H. A.
Pfall Wm. G.
Pringle F. W.
Putnam A. C.
Quick Wm. F.
Ratcliff E. W.
Ray Allen S.
Reineck E. F.
Reynolds W. J.
Richards Lincoln
Riddell Charles
Roberts C. E.
Roberts T. E.
Robertson Wm. A.
Rogers James C.
Rosenberry A. J.

Roser Elwin A.
Ross John D.
Rothermel S. A.
Salter Richard H.
Schroyer Chas. A.
Scott Lee C.
Seabury C. W.
Seaman John A.
Sears R. W.
Sharpe Caswell A.
Sherman F. B.
Shuey William H.
Sinden Henry P.
Skeen J. C.
Skillin E. J.
Skillin Thomas J.
Smith Melancthon
Smith W. S.
Steines C. W.
Storke A. F.
Sutphen G. C.
Suydam J. D.
Swartwout L. G.
Sweet C. S.
Swirles T. S.
Taylor H. A.
Thatcher David A.

Thatcher Geo. L.
Thompson W. W.
Tomlinson E. S.
Tope J. W.
Towle H. S.
Tristram Jas. E.
Underwood Pierce
Updike F. D.
Van Vliet Leonard S.
Von Platen Maurice
Walker Chas. F.
Waller Edward C.
Wallis H. H.
Ward Jas. L.
Waterman H. B.
Watts E. S.
Weaver A. L.
Wells C. H.
Wells F. L.
Wells J. H.
White Charles R.
Wilkie John E.
Wilson Geo. Landis
Wood Wm. H.
Woodbury Geo. W.
Worthington Harry
C.

OAKLAND CLUB.

OAKWOOD AVENUE N.E. COR. ELLIS AVENUE.

OFFICERS.

H. L. KOCHERSPERGER, - - - - President.
SIMEON STRAUS, - - - First Vice-President.
H. S. WETHERELL, - - - Second Vice-President.
C. E. BRADEN, - - - - - - - Secretary.
L. A. FRETTS, - - - - - - - Treasurer.

DIRECTORS.

B. E. Pike
Dr. T. J. Watkins
Geo. Howison, jr.

F. K. Lyon
C. J. Dunlap
A. J. Morrison

Thomas Hoops
E. W. Bailey

MEMBERS.

Bailey E. W.
Bailey W. E.
Barnard J. E.
Beeman C. W.
Bender J. A.
Bensley John R.
Berry F. J.
Beverly J. M. Mrs.
Biggs E. A.
Blackmar Paul
Blackmarr F. H. Dr.
Bliss Frank T.
Blume G. P.
Bowen T. C.
Braden C. E.
Brayton J. T.
Brewster G. O.
Bull F. W.

Carpenter H. L.
Cheever Dwight B.
Child G. B.
Clancy A. W. Maj.
Conroy I. N.
Cook W. M.
Cornell W. F.
Cosby W. C.
Crawford Hon. C. H.
Crawford C. F.
Crissman R. E. Dr.
Dunlap C. J.
Dunlap W. P.
Ennis L. J.
Flagg W. F.
Foley H. B.
Ford H. B.
Forsythe B.

Fountain M. A.
Franklin G. L.
Fretts G. W
Fretts L. A.
Geer David S.
Gillett F. P.
Green J. M. Rev.
Green O. C.
Hamm S. W.
Hamm T. P.
Harbers T. C.
Hayes W. E.
Hayhurst W. C.
Haynes L. W.
Heckard M. O.
Henry W. R.
Hill F. W.
Hilton W. K.

Hoerlein H. A.
Holway W. H.
Hoops Thomas
Hotchkiss L. J.
Houston F. B.
Houston J. S.
Howe C. A.
Howison George jr.
Howland E. A.
Hume Frank L.
Hynes W. J.
Jerome G. C.
Johnson F. R.
Jones Alfred L.
Jones E. L.
Jones Jenkin Lloyd
Rev.
Jordan R. M.

Keitel Adolph
Kimball Charles F.
Kingman Mrs. Ella
KocherspergerD.H
KocherspergerH.L
Lamb A. D.
Letts A. R.
Leversedge L. S.
Lovett T. J.
Lyon F. K.
Mann James R.
Masters G. A.
Mavor Wm.
McCartney J. A.
McFarland J. H.
McLain A. O.
Moderwell E. C.
Mondschein C. A.
Moon B. F.
Moore Wyllys Dr.
Moore W. C.

Morrison Arthur J.
Morse E. L.
Moss M. T.
Moulton W. A.
Naylor J. W.
Noyes H. C.
O'Neill H. J.
Paddock B. S.
Parish J. H.
Parks W. R.
Pearson Andrew
Pease A. B.
Pike B. E.
Poston T. J.
Price F. A.
Randall P. L.
Randolph J. F.
Reynolds J. N.
Rice S. W.
Ruffner W. R.
Schmidt C. J.

Schmidt W. D.
Shaw John
Sherman J'dgeE.B.
Shirk George M.
Shissler Louis
Sidwell Geo. T.
Skinner E. P. Dr.
Skinner H. M.
Smith A. W.
Somers F. W.
Speer W. W.
Stevenson A. L.
Stone C. H.
Straus Simeon
Strickland H. E.
Thacker Robert
Thomas G. A. Dr.
Thomas J. C.
Thorbus W. C.
Tillotson E. W.
Trout F. L.

Trude M. W. Dr.
Valentine L. L.
Valentine W. G.
Vaughan A. J.
Walker George R.
Watkins T. J. Dr.
Webster E. P.
Wells J. L.
West W. H. Dr.
Wetherell H. S.
White W. M.
Wiggins A. D.
Williams W. E.
Wilson H. G.
Wilson L. M. Mrs.
·WilsonWm.W.Rev
Wood F. W.
Wood S. E.
Worley D. A.
Young A. E.

THE OAKS CLUB.
AUSTIN.

OFFICERS.

F. C. BEESON, - - - - - - - President.
J. E. THORNDIKE, - - - - First Vice-President.
G. A. KREIS, - - - - Second Vice-President.
S. J. WHITTOCK, - - - - - - - Secretary.
E. D. ROBINSON, - - - - - - Treasurer.

DIRECTORS.

F. R. Schock   J. J. Walser   F. A. Hill
A. A. Strom   J. A. Martin   A. G. Bagley
G. M. Davis   W. H. Bennett

MEMBERS.

Alden F. A.
Andrew Edward
Andrew Lester
Andrew W. D.
Austin H. W.
Bagley A. G.
Baker E. O.
Barker Alfred
Beeson F. C.
Bennett W. H.
Benson A. T.
Biggs B. P.
Blair J. E.
Bonney C. F.
Bowes John R.
Buck B. F.
Castle Chas. S.
Castle Percy V.
Cornell W. D.
Crafts Clayton E.
Crafts Miles B.
Crafts Sigel J.
Crafts Stanley C.
Crafts Will
Crafts Z. B.
Cummings H. D.
Cutting C. S.
Davis George C.

Davis Geo. M.
Davis W. G.
Denniston Geo. R.
Denniston U. R.
Dickinson S. B.
Dorland W. S.
Duryee J. M.
Emerson H. A.
Emerson H. H.
Falk Louis
Frink H. F.
Frost Z. J.
Gardner H. M.
Garner J. P.
Giles W. A.
Hall L. E.
Hart F. E.
Hatch T. W.
Hathaway J. N.
Hecox J. F.
Hill Fred. A.
Hood Thomas C.
Howland W. B.
Hulbert W. M.
Hunsinger E. C.
Hunter Thos. M.
Huston Phil W.
Jampolis Robert R.

Johnson A. A.
Kampp J. B.
Kemp R. A.
Knowlton E. R.
Kreis G. A.
Kurtz G. E.
Lloyd A. J.
Lloyd W. G.
Lyon M. T.
McCarthy J. J.
McFarland W. W.
McFarlandW.W. jr
Malum A. A.
Marlow H. E.
Martin Jas. A.
Miller J. J.
Milnamow J. T.
Mitchell W. A.
Modine Edw.
Moore W. H.
Moore E. B.
Murray F. G.
Murray Geo. R.
Nelson Eric J.
Norton L. A.
Oliphant David
Oliphant J. B.
Park Geo. H.

Pither A. H.
Powell F. M.
Price J. L.
Ray W. F.
Rearden H. H.
Robinson E. D.
Rooklidge H. E.
Rounds C. H.
Schlecht C. F.
Schlecht O. G.
Schock Fred'k. R
Snow A. T.
Snow J. C.
Sperry A. N.
Stanfield C. W
Strickler Harvey
Strom A. A.
Thorndike J. E.
Torbert A. C.
Traill R. H.
Wakefield J. G.
Walser J. J.
Whitlock S. J.
Wilcoxon H. T.
Williams A. B.
Woodbury S. H.
Wright W. H.
Yager L. E.

THE ONWENTSIA CLUB.

CLUB HOUSE, LAKE FOREST, ILLINOIS.

OFFICERS.

H. C. CHATFIELD-TAYLOR, - - - - - -	President.
CHARLES R. CORWITH, - - - - -	First Vice-President.
ARTHUR T. ALDIS, - - - - - -	Second Vice-President.
HUGH J. McBIRNEY, - - - - - - - -	Secretary.
T. S. FAUNTLEROY, - - - - - - - -	Treasurer.

EXECUTIVE COMMITTEE.

H. C. Chatfield-Taylor   Delavan Smith
Hugh J. McBirney   T. S. Fauntleroy   Frank Hamlin

GOVERNORS.

Term expires Nov. 14, 1899.

Albert M. Day   David B. Jones
Alfred Cowles   T. S. Fauntleroy   Hugh J. McBirney

Term expires Nov. 14, 1900.

Edward S. Adams   Ambrose Cramer
. Frank Hamlin   John S. Hannah   Delavan Smith

Term expires Nov. 14, 1901.

Arthur T. Aldis   Charles R. Corwith
H. C. Chatfield-Taylor   Henry Ives Cobb   Henry N. Tuttle

MEMBERS.

Adams Cyrus H.	Brewster Walter	Cutter John M.
Adams Edward S.	Broughton Urban H.	Davis Dr. N. S.
Adams George E.	Brown C. E.	Day Albert M.
Adams J. McGregor	Brown George F.	Deering Chas. W.
Adsit Charles C.	Browning Granville W.	Deering James E.
Aldis Arthur T.	Buckingham Clarence	Dempster Chas. W.
Aldis Owen F.	Burke Edmund	Dick A. B.
Aldrich Frederick C.	Burrows D. W.	Drake Tracy C.
Alexander W. A.	Butler Herman B.	Dunn Finley P. Calvin
Allen Charles L.	Cable Ransom R.	Durand Charles E.
Andrews Clement W.	Campbell Treat	Durand Henry Z.
Andrews Walter S.	Carpenter A. A. jr.	Durand Scott S.
Armour Allison V.	Carpenter George A.	Dwight John H.
Augur W. W.	Carrington W. T.	Eddy Arthur J.
Baker Alfred L.	Carter Leslie	Elting Victor
Baker Frank E.	Caruthers Mrs. Malcolm	Evans J. C.
Bartlett Charles E.	Cassard Herbert	Fabyan George
Beale William G.	Casselberry Dr. Wm. E.	Fales David
Beauclerc H. W.	Caton Arthur J.	Fargo Livingston W.
Beckwith Warren L.	Chapin E. F.	Farwell Arthur L.
Beebe Wm. H.	Chase S. T.	Farwell Charles B.
Bentley Cyrus	Charnley Douglas	Farwell Francis C.
Bigelow Nelson P.	Chatfield-Taylor H. C.	Farwell Granger
Bissell Arthur G.	Clarke George C.	Farwell Henry S.
Bissell Richard M.	Clarke Louis B.	Farwell John V.
Blaine Mrs. Emmons	Cobb George W.	Farwell John V. jr.
Blair Henry A.	Cobb Henry Ives	Farwell Walter
Blair Watson F.	Cochran John L.	Fauntleroy Thomas S.
Boal Charles T.	Coolidge Frederick S.	Favill Dr. Henry B.
Bodman L. W.	Corwith Charles R.	Ferry Charles H.
Booth W. Vernon	Counselman Chas.	Field Stanley
Bowen Joseph T.	Cowles Alfred	Fiske Dr. George F.
Boyce S. Leonard	Cox R. W.	Fitz-Hugh Carter H.
Bradley J. D.	Cramer Ambrose	Forgan David R.
Bradley J. Harley	Crosby Frederick W.	French George F.
Brega C. W.	Crowell Henry P.	Frost C. S.

Fuller William A.
Fullerton C. W.
Gade F. H.
Gardiner Dr. E. J.
Gaylord Willard S.
Gilbert Henry K.
Giles C. K.
Gillette Howard F.
Glover Otis R.
Goodhart Fred'k P.
Gorton Edward F.
Gould John
Green Edward C.
Grier John P.
Hall Clifford P.
Hall F. G.
Hamill Ernest A.
Hamlin Frank
Hamline John H.
Hannah John S.
Harlan James S.
Harlan John M.
Harvey John R.
Haven Dr. A. C.
Heyworth J. O.
Hinde Thomas W.
Hodges Charles H.
Holt Charles S.
Holt George H.
Hooper Dr. Henry
Houghteling James L.
Hubbard Harry M.
Hubbard J. D.
Hubbard Wm. H.
Hughitt Marvin
Hughitt Marvin, jr.
Hulburd Charles H.
Hunt Mrs. L. Platt
Hutchinson Charles L.
Hyde Dr. James Nevins
Inglis John
Insull Samuel
Isham Edward S.
Isham Dr. George S.
Isham Pierrepont
Isham Ralph
Jebb William T.
Johnson L. M.
Jones David B.
Jones Lee
Jones Thomas D.
Kales Dr. J. D.
Keep Chauncey
Keep Frederick A.
Keith Edson, jr.
Keith Elbridge G.
Keith Walter Woodruff
Kelley Wm. E.
King C. Garfield
King John C.
Kirby Richard D.
Kirkman A. T.
Kirkman M. J.
Kirkman M. M.
Kirkman Wm. Bruce
Knott Henry A.

Kohlsaat H. H.
Laflin Arthur K.
Laflin Louis E.
Lamb B. B.
Larned Walter C.
Lathrop Bryan
Lawrence Dwight
Lawrie Alvah K.
Lawrie Andrew D.
Lawson Victor F.
Learned E. J.
Leeds William B.
LeMoyne Louis V.
LeMoyne Wm. M.
Linn William R.
Loomis John Mason
Lowe J. W.
Lynde Samuel A.
Lyon Thomas R.
Macdonald Chas. B.
Mackey Frank J.
MacVeagh Franklin
Magill Henry W.
Manierre W. R.
Marsh Frank A.
Mather-Smith C. F.
McBirney Geo. D.
McBirney Hugh J.
McCagg E. B.
McClurg A. C. Gen.
McCormick A. A.
McCormick Cyrus H.
McCormick Harold F.
McCormick L. Hamilton
McCormick Leander J.
McCormick R. Hall
McCormick Stanley R.
McCullough H. R.
McDonald Charles A.
McEwen M. C.
McGenniss Mrs. Isabel
McIlvaine William B.
McIntosh Henry M.
McIntyre J. Lawrence
McKinlock Geo. A.
McNeill Malcolm
McReynolds George S.
Mead Wilson L.
Meeker Arthur
Meeker George W.
Merryweather George
Miller James A.
Mills Matthew
Mitchell John J.
Moss Jesse L.
Newell A. B.
Nixon Miles B.
Owens John E. Dr.
Parkinson Robt. H.
Patterson Stewart
Payson George S.
Peabody F. S.
Peck Mrs. Harold
Phillips Mrs. Thomas
Pike Charles B.
Pike Eugene S.

Pillsbury W. F.
Poole Abraham
Pope C. Edward
Prentice E. Parmelee
Rathborne William W.
Raymond Chas. L.
Reid Arthur S.
Rhea Forster A.
Rhodes Harrison G.
Richardson Charles H.
Robbins Henry S.
Rumsey Geo D.
Rumsey J. Frank
Runnels John S.
Rutter Dudley
Ryerson Edward L.
Scott George A. H.
Scudder W. M.
Seaverns George A. jr.
Shaw Howard Van D.
Shaw Theodore A. jr.
Shields James H.
Slaughter G. F.
Smith Byron L.
Smith Delavan
Smith Dunlap
Smith Francis D.
Smith Solomon A.
Smith Prof. Walter
Smith Walter B.
Sprague Albert A.
Sprague Frederick W.
Stewart Graeme
Stirling W. R.
Stone Herbert Stuart
Stone Melville E.
Stone Melville E. jr.
Swift L. F.
Taber Sidney R.
Taylor Thomas jr.
Thompson Leverett
Thompson Slason
Tracy Howard
Truesdale W. H.
Tuttle Emerson B.
Tuttle Henry N.
Tyson Russell
Valentine John
Viles James jr.
Walker Bertrand
Walker H. H.
Walker James R.
Walker Dr. Samuel J.
Walker Wirt D.
Waller James B.
Waller Robert A.
Waller William
Warner Ezra J.
Warner Ezra J. jr.
Washburne Hempstead
Watson John G.
Watson R. G.
Weaver C. S.
Webster Lewis D.
Welch Albert G.
Wentworth Moses J.

West Frederick T.	Wilson John P.	Yaggy T. A.
Whigham H. J.	Wilson Walter H.	Yoe Charles C.
Wilbur James B.	Winston F. S.	Yoe Lucien G.
Williams John C.	Woolley Clarence R.	Young Arthur
Williams Sydney	Wrenn Everts	Young Kimball
Willing Henry J.	Wrenn John H.	Zellar William F.

PRESS CLUB.

108 MADISON STREET.

OFFICERS.

WILLIAM KNOX,	President.
C. M. FAYE,	First Vice-President.
W. H. FREEMAN,	Second Vice-President.
J. M. LOUGHBOROUGH,	Third Vice-President.
E. J. BAKER,	Secretary and Treasurer.
FRED B. STEVENSON,	Recording Secretary.
JOHN T. BRAMHALL,	Librarian.

DIRECTORS.

A. H. Yount	F. J. Schulte	W. M. Freeman
R. H. Little		R. R. Jones

MEMBERS.

Almy C. D.	Bryan I. J.	Davis Augustine	Flinn John J.
Anderson John	Bunting Harry S.	Davis H. O.	Forman Allan
Andrews Byron	Burdette R. J.	Day Joseph R.	Fox O. L.
Andrews O. F.	Burdette Sam M.	Defebaugh Jas. E.	Francis P. D.
Andrews R. F. M.	Burlingame H. J.	Denison T. S.	Freeman W. H.
Armstrong Geo. B.	Burrelle F. A.	Denslow W. W.	Friend E.
Atwell Benj. H.	Busby W. H.	Depew Chauncey	Frizelle Charles E.
Babbitt Geo. A.	Butler George F.	M.	Fuller J. J.
Bailey W. W.	Calkins E. A.	Dickson M. E.	Fuller L. E.
Baker E. J.	Canfield H. S.	Dillabaugh Jos.	Gaither Charles
Baker Fred W.	Carr H. J.	Dillingham E. R.	Gardiner C.
Baldwin G. P.	Cartwright C. M.	Donaldson HenryF	Gay H. Lord
Ball Slocum	Carus Dr. Paul	Donnon D. D.	Gesswein A. J.
Banks C. E.	Chaiser A.	Downey C. J.	Gibbons John
Barrett Elmer E.	Chapin W. E.	Downey J. R.	Glenn W. M.
Barron E. A.	Chivington Thos.M	Dowst Chas.	Glessner A. W.
Barry P. T.	Clark Afred C.	Dowst Sam M.	Grevstad N.
Baum L. Frank	Clarke A. L.	Duffy S. R.	Griffith Geo. H.
Bemis H. V.	Clements Geo. H.	Duncan Thomas	Gruenstein S. E.
Benham P. D.	Cline W. O.	Dunlop Joseph R.	Gunn M. Dr.
Bennett F. O.	Clissold H. R.	Durand Elliott	Haight R. J.
Bennett Rawson	Clover Sam T.	Dustin W. G.	Hall Wm. T.
Benzinger Fred	Cobb B. F.	Dyer Charles M.	Hamilton John B.,
Bertault Paul L.	Collier C.	Easley Ralph M.	M. D.
Bicknell E. P.	Conkey W. B.	Eastman Barrett	Hamilton R. A.
Bird Harry L.	Coulter John	Ehlert John	Hammond P. H.
Blakely Charles F.	Coxey W. D.	Emerson Willis G.	Handy W. M.
Bloomingston J. S.	Crawford Jack Capt.	Etten W. J.	Harper W. H.
Bloss Harry H.	Crawford John M.	Ewing E. A.	Harris Kennett F.
Boen Haldor E.	Crawford O. W.	Fairchild E. W.	Harrison William P.
Bohn H. J.	Creedon S. D.	Faraday W.	Hart Herbert L.
Bowen Wm. A.	Cross Wm. R.	Fargo H. D.	Hartwell Geo. H.
Boyd James	Crowell C. H.	Fay H. W.	Harvey Thos. F.
Bradwell J. B.	Crutcher Howard	Fay John	Hatch A. F.
Bramhall John T.	Curtis Wm. E.	Faye C. M.	Hatton Joseph
Brower A. T. H.	Daley J. R.	Finerty John F.	Hayner Fred H.
Browne F. G.	Darley Samuel E.	Finn Joseph	Heinemann A. H.
Brucker Joseph	Darrow C. S.	Flanders A. R.	Heinemann H.E.O.
Bruner Alfred W.	Davidson S. F.	Fleming I. A.	Henderson David

Henderson J. F.
Henius Dr. Max
Henley W. S.
Herbert B. B.
Hild F. H.
Hinman Geo. W.
Hitchcock C. I.
Holmes Fred L.
Hough E.
Housman L. M.
Howse Paul D.
Hughes Wm.
Hull Paul
Hunt H. M.
Hunter W. B.
Huston Frank M.
Hutchin Geo. L.
Hyde W. T. C.
Ickes H. L.
Igleheart Wm.
Insley Edward
Jackson Jefferson
Jacobsen R. C.
Jameson John
Jeffery J. B.
Johnson B. A.
Johnson Charles C.
Johnson F. E.
Johnston H.
Jones Geo. W.
Jones Herbert L.
Jones R. R.
Keiselbach Otto
Kellogg J. H.
Kimball E. R.
Kimball M. D.
Knapp Thomas
Knight H. W.
Knox W. M.
Kochersperger H.L
Kochersperger D. H.
Kohlsaat H. H.
Kraus Adolf
Lahiff Edw. M.
Lancaster F. H.
Lane J. J.
Lane Marcus Rev.
Langland James
Lawson Victor F.
Layton Harry B.
Leckie A. S.
Lederer Chas.
LeRoy Fred
Link D. M.
Little Richard
Lloyd B. F.

Lockwood A. H.
Logan F. A.
Long Chas. C. Col.
Loughborough J.M.
Lower Elton
Lowrie H. A.
Lubeck E. M.
Lucas J. B.
Lush Chas·K.
MacGowan D. B.
MacRae W. G.
Malkoff M.
Mann C. A.
Manning Harry
Mansfield J. B.
Marble Earl
Marchette Blanche R.
Matthias Chas.
Maughan C. B.
McAuliff C.
McEldowney J. H.
McGaffey Ernest
McGovern John
McKay Wm. K.
McKee C. T.
McKenzie Fred'k
McKinnie P. L.
McNally James
McNeil Angus
McQuilkin A. H.
Medill Joseph
Meredith W. M.
Michaels C. D.
Mills Luther Laflin
Mindie P. K.
Montgomery P.
Moore Willis L.
Morris Ira M.
Mullaney B. J.
Murphy R. J.
Nicholas W. G.
Nixon Wm. Penn
Northrup G. T.
Norton S. F.
O'Neill Thomas J.
O'Ryan P. S.
Odell W. M.
Oviatt F. C.
Packard A. T.
Paddock James
Palmer Thos. W.
Patterson Raymo'd
Payne Frank
Payne J. E.
Peattie Robt. B.
Peck F. W.

Penton John A.
Perkins Walton
Persinger H. R.
Persons D. Van Ness
Pickard E. W.
Pierce Gerald
Polachek Victor H.
Pollard J. Percival
Pomeroy P. P.
Powell Henry B.
Priest J. L.
Pritchard E. R.
Putnam Frank
Radford W. A.
Rae F. G.
Rand John C.
Read Opie
Reed N. A. jr.
Reeder David H.
Reiwitch Herman L.
Remey O. E.
Rend J. E.
Rhodes Charles L.
Rice F. W.
Riley J.Whitcombe
Ritchie John
Roberts W. C.
Robinson H. P.
Rollins C. E.
Russell James
Sarka Charles
Sasseen D. E.
Sayler H. L.
Schneider Geo.
Schulte F. J.
Scovel H. M.
Sergel Chas. H.
Shanks W. J.
Shehan J. M.
Shepard H. O.
Sheridan Ed.
Siler George
Smith Abbie, jr.
Smith C. L.
Smith H. J.
Smith W. V.
Smulski John F.
Smythe Hill C.
Snyder Harry W.
Stanton S. C.
Steele S. V.
Steiger Chas. H.
Stevenson Fred B.
Stiver P. O.
Stone Melville E.

Strong W. H.
Stroome P. O.
Sullivan W. K.
Sutherland Geo.
Taylor E. H.
Taylor Horace
Taylor W. A.
Thompson T. O.
Thrift M. B.
Tillotson Leonard
Todd F. M.
Tracy F. K.
Turner H. O.
Underwood H.·G.
Upton George P.
Vanderlip F. A.
Vermont Edgar deV.
Visscher William Lightfoot
Waldo J. B.
Walker W. S.
Wallace W. L.
Walsh John R.
Walsh M. F.
Walton L. R.
Warren Geo. C.
Waterloo Stanley
Waterman Nixon
Watterson Henri
Weddell Thos. R.
Weippiert G. W.
Welch F. B.
Westlake E. G.
Weston John W.
Wharton Geo. C.
Whitmarsh C. F.
Wiese Theodore
Wilcox W. W.
Wilkie John E.
Williams Chauncey L.
Williams Hugh Blake
Wilmarth J. C.
Windsor H. H.
Wood George S.
Woodruff Henry
Woodward T. R.
Wright John E.
Wright Nat C.
Wright W. C.
Wyatt Frank T.
Yarras Victor S.
Youatt J. R.
Young J. R.
Yount A. H.

THE QUADRANGLE CLUB.

LEXINGTON AVENUE AND FIFTY-EIGHTH STREET.

OFFICERS.

ROBERT FRANCIS HARPER,	President.
GEORGE E. VINCENT,	Vice-President.
EDWARD CAPPS,	Secretary.
JOHN PAXSON IDDINGS,	Treasurer.

HOUSE COMMITTEE.

J. J. Glessner   Shailer Matthews   Frank W. Shepardson

MEMBERS.

Abbott Frank Frost
Angell James R.
Baldwin Charles F.
Barnes A. R.
Bartlett A. C.
Beaunisne A. G.
Belfield H. H.
Billings Dr. Frank
Blair Chauncey
Blair H. A.
Bolza Oskar
Bond Joseph
Boyd James Harrington
Boyesen I. K.
Breasted J. H.
Brown Joseph
Buck Carl Darling
Burton Ernest D.
Capps Edward
Capps J. A. Dr.
Carpenter Frederick Ives
Cary Dr. Frank
Castle Clarence F.
Catterall Ralph C. H.
Chamberlin Thomas C.
Clark S. H.
Cole John A.
Cook Dr. J. C.
Coulter John M.
Crandall Rev. L. A.
Crane C. R.
Damon L. T.
Davies Bradley M.
Delamater Dr. N. B.
Derby William M.
Dewey John
Dillman L. M.
Donaldson Henry H.
Donnelley R. R.
Donnelley Thomas E.
Echlin H. M.
Eckels George M.
Farrington O. C.
Favill H. B. Dr.
Fellows George E.
Fenn Rev. W. W.
Ferguson Dr. A. H.
Flood N. A.
Foreman A. J.
Foreman M. J.

Forrest Wm. S.
Foster George B.
Frankenthal Dr. L. E.
Freeman Henry V.
Freund Ernst
Fütterer Dr. Gustav
Gale H. G.
Gentles Dr. H. Wernicke
Glessner George
Glessner J. J.
Good J. Paul
Goodkind Dr. M. L.
Goodspeed George S.
Goodspeed Thomas W.
Hale William Gardner
Hall D. W.
Hamill C. D.
Hamilton D. G.
Hancock Harris
Harper James H.
Harper Robert Francis
Harper William Rainey
Head Franklin H.
Henderson C. R.
Hendrickson George L.
Herrick John J.
Herrick Robert H.
Hicks Oliver H.
Hirsch Emil G.
Hobbs Glenn M.
Horn Alfred A.
Howerth Ira W.
Howland George C.
Huston Charles
Hutchinson Charles L.
Hutchinson Dr. E. B
Iddings Joseph Paxson
Ingalls Dr. E. Fletcher
Isham E. S.
Jackson Rev. J. L.
James Edmund J.
James George F.
Jordan Edwin O.
Judson Henry Pratt
Kent William
Knapp George O.
Kohlsaat H. H.
Kuh Dr. Sydney
Laughlin J. L.
Lengfeld Felix

Lewis Dr. Denslow
Lewis Leslie
Linn W. R.
Loeb Jacques
Loeb Leo
Lorenz F. A.
Lovett Robert M.
Manly John M.
Mann C. Riborg
Manning W. J.
Marsh C. A.
Marshall Dr. J. S.
Maschke Heinrich
Mathews Shailer
Matthews S. A. Dr.
McArthur Dr. L. L.
McClintock W. D.
McMurry Charles A.
Mead George H.
Merrill A. F.
Michelson A. A.
Miller Adolph C.
Miller Frank Justus
Millikan R. A.
Montgomery Dr. F. H.
Moore A. W.
Moore E. Hastings
Moulton Richard Green
Naylor George M.
Nef J. U.
Northrup George W. jr.
O'Connor John
Owen W. B.
Palmer John
Parker Rev. A. K.
Parson John C.
Payne Walter A.
Peck F. W.
Penrose R. A. jr.
Raycroft Joseph E.
Rice T. F.
Rubinkam Rev. N. I.
Ruddick R. L.
Rust Henry A.
Ryerson Martin A.
Salisbury Rollin D.
Schmidt-Wartenberg H.
Schobinger J. J.
Schwill Ferdinand
Scott E. H.

Shambaugh Dr. Geo. E.
Shepardson Frank W.
Shorey Daniel L.
Shorey Paul
Small A. W.
Small Dr. C. P.
Smith Alexander
Smith B. L.
Smith E. Burritt
Smith F. A.
Smith Willard A.
Sparks E. E.
Spiering Theodore
Sprague A. A.
Stagg A. A.
Starr Frederick

Stieglitz Julius
Stratton A. W.
Stratton S. W.
Tarbell Frank Bigelow
Terry Benjamin S.
Thatcher Oliver J.
Thomas W. I.
Thompson Jas. Westfall
Tolman A. H.
Tolman E. B.
Torrey C. A.
Triggs O. L.
Troop J. G. C.
Twyman Joseph
Vincent George E.
VonKlenze Camillo

Walker George C.
Walker W. B.
Walling Wm. E.
Watasé Sho
Webster Ralph W.
Wheeler W. M.
Wilder W. H. Dr.
Wiles R. H.
Willard N. P.
Willett H. L.
Williams Norman
Williams Wardner
Woodle E. R.
Wrenn John H.
Zueblin Charles

NON-RESIDENT MEMBERS.

Baillot Edwin P.
Baldwin Jessie A.
Bridge Norman Dr.
Brobeck Dr. J. G.
Burnham D. H.
Caldwell E. L.
Callender J. E.
Chase W. J.
Clark H. T.
Cooley E. J.
Davis N. K.
Denman Stephen
Dougherty N. C.
Ely Frederick

Fuller Dr. C. G.
Goodyear William H.
Goss David K.
Hale George E.
Hardy G. Dr.
Hilton H. H.
Hulbert Eri B.
Hill G. F.
Hussey George B.
Johnston Harold H.
Lovett Edgar Odell
Manly W. G.
McKee William P.

McLeish Andrew
Miller Newman
Moses Bernard
Nichols Fred D.
Pringle W. J.
Runyon W. A.
Sisson E. O.
Talbot Eugene Dr.
Thurber Charles H.
Tunell George
Turner F. J.
Walsh Arthur T.
Wightman A. R.

SHERIDAN CLUB.

4100 MICHIGAN AVENUE.

OFFICERS.

MICHAEL CUDAHY,	President.
E. BAGGOT,	Vice-President.
ZACHARY T. DAVIS,	Secretary.
JAMES PLUNKETT,	Treasurer.

DIRECTORS.

D. J. Leahy
P. H. Monks

Thomas F. Keeley
Dr. J. J. Ahern

J. F. Doerr

MEMBERS.

Ahern J. J. Dr.
Alexander S.T.
Alexander W.H.
Alexander W. W.
BaggotE.
Baggot James E.
Ball William
Barrett J. P. Prof.
Barry L. A.
Birmingham J. H.
Boland James F.
Bowles J. P.
Boyle J. P.
Bradburn James
Braden J. C.
Bransfield M. J.

Breen J. W.
Brennan B. G.
Burke A.
Byrne Chas. T.
Byrne Harry
Caffrey P. F.
Caldwell Dr. C. P.
Callahan E. J.
Camp E. M.
Canavan A. A.
Carey C. N.
Carey Jos. T.
Carey W. P.
Carney Thos.
Carpenter P. E.
Carroll D. J.

Carroll W. F.
Casey T. S.
Cella A. S.
Cella J. F.
Clare James
Clare John F.
Cleary J. J.
Clifford John
Clinnen J. G.
Clowry James
Clowry W. J.
Collins Thomas A.
Conlan James jr.
Connolly F. W.
Conway S. S.
Cook John F.

Cooke Chas F.
Cooke Geo. J.
Cooke John R.
Cooke J. S.
Cooper John S.
Corboy M. J.
Corigan R. E.
Cox Thos.
Cragin M. J.
Crennan J. M.
Crilly D. F.
Crilly Wm. M.
CroarkinFrancisE.
Cronin A. J.
Crowe F.
Cudahy John

Cudahy Michael	Gray James J.	Maher Joseph P.	O'Connell John C
Cummings A.	Griffin James	Maher Phillip	O'Connell T. W.
Cummings W. A.	Griffiths John	Mahoney James	O'Donnell James L.
Curran Richard	Griffiths K. F.	Maloney M. T.	O'Donnell J. S.
Davis Z. T.	Guerin T. E.	Martin James C.	O'Hare T. J.
Dean Thomas A.	Gunning R. C.	Masterson E. F.	O'Malley John
Dee Wm. E.	Hanrihan S. J.	McArdle E. J.	O'Meara Jos. E.
Detmar M. J.	Hardin D.	McArdle P. L.	O'Toole D.
Detmer J. F.	Hardin P. K.	McCarthy John	Olinger F. E.
DeVeney T. F.	Hart W. B.	McCarthy P. F.	Olinger J. P. jr.
Dimery J. H.	Heeney J. P.	McCormick J. A.	Ortseifen Adam
Dixon Arthur	Henneberry W. P.	McDermott M.	Perkins H. A.
Doerr J. F.	Hennessy P. J.	McDonald J. W.	Perrigo A. P.
Donlin J. F.	Hennessy W. B.	McElherne D. J.	Plamondon A. D.
Donnelly T. N.	Hickey C. M.	McFadden Martin B	Plunkett James
Donnersberger Geo	Hickey J. V.	McGoorty J. P.	Powell W. H.
Donohue M. A. jr.	Higbie Fred K.	McGrath J. P.	Quinlan D. B.
Donohue J. W.	Hipp Dr. W. H.	McGraw D. T.	Quinlan W. A.
Donohue M. A.	Hoffman Andrew	McGuire W. A.	Reddy James M.
Donohue W. F.	Honan M. W.	McHugh J.	Reilly John J.
Dowling R. A.	Hopkins J. P.	McHugh O. J.	Rice P. H.
Downey J. F.	Hudson E.	McKenna W. J.	Roach Martin
Downey N. J.	Hudson E. jr.	McLaughlin J. T.	Roemheld J. E.
Doyle A. J.	Hughes Joseph	McManus J. B.	Rourke M. A.
Doyle Edward	Hunt N. J.	McShane James	Sanders E.
Driscoll M. F.	Hyland M.	McVoy Eugene J.	Sanders E. S.
Duffy John J.	Jenkins J. B.	McVoy John A.	Sanders J. P.
Duggan P. H.	Kane C. D.	Mealiff F. H.	Schneider J. J.
Duffin Dan'l	Keeley E. M.	Merle W. F.	Sharp W. B.
Dunn J. J.	Keeley T. F.	Mix Ira J.	Shields J. E.
Egan Edward	Keenan P. H.	Monks P. H.	Shortall J. P.
Ebbert W. H.	Kelley James J.	Moody F. A.	Slattery Edward
English R. R.	Kelly John J. M.	Moore James	Slattery W. J.
Ennesy Frank	Kelly Joseph I.	Moran T. A.	Smith E. C.
Espert Michael	Kelly Thomas F.	Morgan J. L.	Smyth John M.
Fitzgerald H. J.	Kenney J. J.	Morrison R. W.	Solon D. A.
Fitzpatrick Dr. A. H	Keys John W.	Morrison Wm. M.	Stringfield C. P.
Flavin M. D.	Kinsella F. D.	Moxley W. J. jr.	Sullivan Alex.
Fleming James D.	Kinsella J. E.	Mullay T. H.	Sullivan J.
Flood Frank J.	Kinsella J. J.	Mullen James J.	Swenie J. J.
Flood L. J.	Knisely John	Murphy E. J.	Tait John
Foley Daniel	Lane G. M.	Murphy F. T.	Tomlinson H. S.
Foley W. C.	Lawler P. J.	Murphy James D.	Toner H. J.
Fortune W. J.	Leahy D. J.	Murphy James S.	Toolen A. J.
Foster George P.	Leahy R. P.	Murphy John E.	Trainor J. W.
Gahan Thomas	Leonard P.	Murphy Dr. J. B.	Turner B. S.
Gallagher Daniel	Lord W. B.	Murphy J. G.	Uebele B. E.
Gallagher Jos. P.	Ludden J. H.	Murphy M. W.	Wade Thomas P.
Gallery J. J.	Lydon H. C.	Murphy P. M.	Weadly J. L.
Galvin James	Lydon W. A.	Nacey P.	Welch Dr. P. H.
Gavin W.	Lynch James C.	Naghten Frank	Whelan P. H.
Geary John R.	Macdonell J. A.	Nelson J. L.	Whitney H. E.
Geary T. F.	MacMahon John	Nelson N. J.	Wild H. C.
Geary W. T.	Madden M. B.	Nelson W. P.	Wright George A
Gibbons John	Madden M. F.	Nolan T. J.	Wright G. K.
Gillespie G. H.	Madden M. S.	O'Brien John	Young D. J.
Gorman A. F.	Madigan P. D.	O'Brien M. G.	Young Jas. T.
Graham F. H.			

THE SOCIAL ECONOMICS CLUB.

OFFICERS.

Mrs. Emma R. Pratt, - - - - - - - - - President.
Dr. Rachelle S. Yarros, - - - - - - First Vice-President.
Mrs. Jessie T. Galpin, - - - - - - Second Vice-President.
Mrs. Laura V. Tabb, - - - - - - Third Vice-President.
Mrs. May E. Turney, - - - - Corresponding Secretary.
Mrs. Millie R. Trumbull, - - - - Recording Secretary.
Mrs. Fanny B. Stone, - - - - - - - - Treasurer.
Mrs. Caroline F. Ober, - - - - - Honorary President.

MEMBERS.

Aldrich Mrs.
Biddison Mrs.
Bleasdale Mrs. John W.
Bowes Mrs. Frederick
Branch Mrs. Edina K.
Brown Mrs. Frank
Collins Mrs. Thomas
Dickinson Dr. Frances
Ford Mrs. Elizabeth
Frake Mrs. James.
Galpin Mrs. Jessie T.
Helfenstein Mrs. C. B.
Herron Mrs. J. B.
Holt Mrs. G. M.

Hoxie Mrs. J. R.
Krebs Mrs. J. H.
Mitchell Mrs. Chas. F.
Morgan Mrs. W. J.
Munro Mrs. Daniel
Ober Mrs. C. F.
Orr Dr. Julia M.
Osgood Miss Nellie
Patten Mrs. Fred H.
Powers Mrs. C. A.
Pratt Mrs. George
Russell Miss ElizabethM
Russell Mrs. E. F.
Sands Mrs. Alacia

Shippen Mrs. E. W.
Squires Mrs. Havilah
Stafford Miss Juanita
Stevens Mrs. A. P.
Stone Mrs. Percy F.
Tabb Mrs. Laura V.
Trotman Mrs. T. R
Trumbull Mrs.B. H.
Turney Mrs. May E.
Werst Mrs. J.
Wyman Mrs. Charlotte
Yarros Dr. Rachelle S.
Young Mrs. Emma L.

SOCIETY OF COLONIAL WARS.

OFFICERS.

Edward McKinstry Teall, ... Governor.
Frank Eugene Spooner . . . . Deputy-Governor.
Charles Ridgely, ... Lieutenant-Governor.
Wyllys King Smith, ... Secretary.
Landon Cabell Rose, ... Deputy-Secretary.
Charles Thomson Atkinson, - . . . . Treasurer.
Oliver Partridge Dickinson, ... Registrar.
Ebenezer Lane, ... Historian.
Judge Frank Baker, ... Chancellor.
Rev. Dr. Frank Wakely Gunsaulus, . . . Chaplain.

GENTLEMEN OF THE COUNCIL.

John Smith Sargent
Marvin Andrus Farr
Edward Payson Bailey
Edward McKinstry Teall
Charles Thomson Atkinson

Frank Eugene Spooner
Charles Ridgely
Oliver Partridge Dickinson
Ebenezer Lane
Wyllys King Smith

MEMBERS.

Adams Edward Milton
Alderson Victor Clifton
Atkinson Charles Thomson
Bailey Edward Payson
Baker Frank Judge
Bardwell Harry Jenkins
Bassett Roger M.
Beckwith Warren Lippitt
Bennett Asahel Frank
Bogert William B.
Boutell Henry Sherman

Brocklebank John C. F.
Burt Andrew Sheridan Col. U.S.A.
Butters George
Case Edward Beecher
Castle Alfred Henry
Chatfield-Taylor Hobart C.
Cromwell Charles
Daggett Daniel Charles
Dana Charles Durkee
Dickinson Frederick
Dickinson Oliver Partridge

Eaton Alfred Beers
Farr Marvin Andrus
Fessenden Charles Newton
Fisher Albert Judson
Fisher Francis Porter
Fiske Dr. George Foster
Flint Wyman Kneeland
Flower James Monroe
Foster Volney William
Fuller Henry Clay
Gilbert James Harris
Gillette Edwin Fraser
Goddard Lester Orestes
Graves Albert Mattoon
Gridley Nelson Cowles
Gross Samuel Eberly
Gunsaulus Frank Wakely Rev.
Hall Lemuel Ruggles
Hammond Lyman Dresser
Hardy Cyrus Austin
Harrison Carter H.
Hill John Whipple
Hulbert Edmund D.
Hyde Dr. James Nevins
Ives Marvin Allen
Janes Edmund J.
Jordan Scott
Kittridge Abbott Eliot Rev.
Lane Ebenezer
Lathrop Joseph
Lincoln John Larkin jr.
Lombard Josiah Lewis
Lyon George Mulhollan
MacVeagh Eames
Marsh George Samuel
Meacham Franklin Adams Dr.
Merrick Frederick Laforrest
Messinger William Dorrance
Mill Charles David
Miller Charles Kingsbury
Moore George Henry
Moore William John .
Morris Seymour
Moulton George Mayhew
Newcomb George Whitfield

Osborn Henry Austin
Otis Joseph Edward, jr.
Otis Philo Adams
Pell Rodman Corse
Pettibone Asa G.
Pfoutz Gilbert Benj. Dr.
Pierce Frederick Clinton
Poole Charles Clarence
Powers Heman Rogers
Preston Deming Haven
Quincy Charles Frederick
Reade Philip Capt. U. S. A.
ReQua Charles Howard
Ridgely Charles
Rose Hiram Holbrook
Rose Landon Cabell
Sargent John Smith
Sedgwick Edwin Henry
Slosson Frank
Smith Wyllys King
Spooner Frank Eugene
Spoor John Alden
Strong William Wolcott
Teall Edward McKinstry
Tenney Horace Kent
Tobey Frank Bassett
Tucker William Ruggles
Turner Henry Lathrop
Upham Frederic William
Vail Henry Sherman
Wait Horatio Loomis
Waite Horace Garfield
Washburne Hempstead
Wells Samuel Rogers
Wentworth Moses John
Wentworth Wm. Grafton
Wheelock Wm. Barker
Whitney Eugene Wolcott Dr.
Whitney Jasper
Wight William Ward
Winston Frederick Hampden
Woodbridge Jonathan Edwards
Wright Harry Linn
Wyman Walter Channing

SOCIETY OF MAYFLOWER DESCENDANTS IN THE STATE OF ILLINOIS.

OFFICERS.

WALTER MORTON HOWLAND, - - - Governor.
J. McGREGOR ADAMS, - - - Deputy Governor.
RT. REV. CHARLES EDWARD CHENEY, - - Elder.
MRS. SEYMOUR MORRIS, - - - - - Secretary.
FREDERICK MORGAN STEELE, - - - Treasurer.
JOHN SMITH SARGENT, - - - - - Captain.
PROF. VICTOR CLIFTON ALDERSON, - - Historian.
DR. HENRY CUSHMAN WORTHINGTON, - - Surgeon.

BOARD OF ASSISTANTS.

George Whitfield Newcomb
Mrs. John R. Wilson

Mrs. Edward Nevers
Rollin Arthur Keyes
Josiah Lewis Lombard

Lester Orestes Goddard
Mrs. Dwight W. Graves

Adams Edward Milton
Adams J. McGregor
Alderson Prof. Victor Clifton
Babcock Mrs.Mary Keyes
Barbour William Ernest
Butters George
CheneyRev.Chas.Edward
Doud Mrs. Levi B.
Downs Hubert Cowles
Farwell Miss Emma Jane
Farwell Jesse H.
Foster Miss Eva C.
Foster Volney W.
Freeman Judge Henry V.
Gade Frederick H.
Goddard Lester Orestes
Graves Mrs. Dwight W.

Gridley Martin Medbury
Gridley Mrs. Nelson Cowles
Hartwell Mrs. Fred G.
Howland Walter Morton
Howland Mrs. Walter M.
Hyde Dr. James Nevins
Jordan Scott
Keyes Miss Frances
Keyes Rollin Arthur
Lombard Josiah Lewis
McDill Mrs. Geo. Edward
Merrick Mrs. Frederick L.
Morris Mrs. Seymour
Nevers Mrs. Edward
Newcomb George Whitfield
Orr Arthur

Preston Mrs. Carl Weber
Purmort Mrs. Henry C.
Quincy Chas. Frederick
Ridgely Charles
Sargent John Smith
Sargent Mrs. John S.
Schaffenberg Miss Lydia Frances
Smith Wyllys King
Spoor John Alden
Standish Charles Dana
Steele Frederick Morgan
Waldo Mrs. Otis H.
Wiles Mrs. Robert H.
Wilson Mrs. John R.
Worthington Dr. Henry Cushman

STANDARD CLUB.

CORNER TWENTY-FOURTH STREET AND MICHIGAN AVENUE.

OFFICERS.

DAVID WORMSER - - - - - - -	President.
ALFRED S. AUSTRIAN, - - - -	Vice-President.
SIMON A. KOHN, - - - - - -	Secretary.
JOSEPH G. SNYDACKER, - - - - -	Treasurer.

DIRECTORS.

Levi A. Eliel
Joseph C. Lamm
Louis Falkenau
Isaac Horner
Norman S. Florsheim

Solomon T. DeLee
Jacob Friedman
Alfred M. Snydacker
Louis Eckstein
Morris S Rosenwald

Julius W. Loewenthal
Alfred S. Austrian
Joseph G. Snydacker
Simon A. Kohn

MEMBERS.

Abt H. H.
Abt J. J.
Abt Sol L.
Adams Moses
Adler Dankmar
Adler Henry
Adler Sidney
Arnheim Benj.
Arnold Walter C.
Arnstein Eugene
Austrian A.S.
Austrian Joseph
Bach Emanuel
Ballenberg A. A.
Ballenberg Jules
Ballin Joseph
Barth Alex.
Basch Joseph
Bauer G. T.
Becker A. G.
Becker Louis
Beiersdorf A. J.
Beifeld Alexander
Beifeld Joseph
Benjamin Louis
Bensinger Ben. E.

Bensinger Moses
Berg Morris H.
Bernheimer I. S.
Block Isaac
Block Leopold
Block P. D.
Bloom Isaac J.
Bloom Leopold
Born Moses
Buxbaum Emanuel
Cahn Ben. R.
Cahn Bernard
Cahn Fred C.
Cahn Joseph
Cahn Sidney B.
Cohn Dan A.
D'Ancona Alf. E.
D'Ancona E. N.
Daube M. Jacob
DeLee S. T.
Dernburg Carl
Eckstein L. E.
Ederheimer Max
Eichberg Max
Eichberg W. N.
Einstein Arthur

Einstein B. M.
Einstein Morris
Eisendrath Jos. N.
Eisendrath L.
Eisendrath Sig. L.
Eisendrath Wm. N.
Eliel Levi A.
Elkan Henry
Elson Herman
Emerich Martin
Ettlinger Simon
Falk M. L.
Falkenau Louis
Fechheimer E. S.
Feibelman D. L.
Felsenthal Eli B.
Fischer S. M.
Fish Joseph
Fish Sol T.
Flonacher H. C.
Florsheim Felix
Florsheim MiltonS.
Florsheim Norman
Florsheim Simon
Foreman Edw'd H.
Foreman Edwin G.

Foreman Henry G.
Foreman Isaac H.
Foreman Milton J.
Foreman Oscar G.
Foreman S. H.
Fox Leo
Frank D. L.
Frank Emanuel J.
Frank Fred. G.
Frank Joseph
Frank Louis
Frank Max
Frankenthal C. E.
Frankenthal E.
FrankenthalDrLE.
Freudenthal Jos.
Freund Gustav
Friedman A. B.
FriedmanJosephN.
Friedman J.
FriedmanMonroeJ.
Friedman Oscar J.
Friend Ed.
Gatzert August
Gatzert J. L.
Gimbel Charles A.

Schoenbrun Irving
Schoenbrun Sampson
Schoenman C. S.
Schuhmann H. H.
Schwab Alfred C.
Schwab Chas. H.
Schwab Henry C.
Schwabacher H. H.
Schwabacher Julius
Schwabacher M.
Selz E. F.
Selz J. Harry
Selz M.
Shaffner Charles
Sholem Sam
Shrimski I.
Siegel Ferdinand
Siegel Joseph
Siegel Sylvan
Silberman A.
Silberman Sigmund
Silverman Chas.
Simon Carl S.
Simon David S.

Simonson Jul
Smith Samuel H.
Snydacker Alf. M.
Snydacker J. G.
Snydacker Jos. L.
Sondheimer Em'l
Spiegel Modie J.
Spiegel Sidney M.
Spitz Samuel
Steele H. B.
Steele Maurice B.
Steele S. B.
Stein Artnur
Stein D. A.
Stein Sydney
Steiniger Simon
Stellauer Chas.
Stern Aaron
Stern D. S.
Stern Henry
Stern Herman
Stern Louis
Stern Oscar M.
Stern Sam
Stettauer David

Stix S. H.
Stonehill Edw. A.
Straus Eli M.
Straus Leo
Straus Simon W.
Strauss Albert L.
Strauss Aaron
Strauss Henry X.
Strauss Jacob N.
Strauss Julius
Strauss Louis L.
Strauss Milton A.
Strauss Milton L.
Strauss Sam J. T.
Strouss Emil
Stumer Louis M.
Sulzberger Sol. L.
Sutton Wm. H.
Swabacker Isa
Uhlmann Fred
Ullman Gus
Ullman Louis
Ullman Nathan J.
Ullman Percy G.
Vogel Frank E.

Waïxel M. S.
Wampold Leo
Wedeles Edward L.
Weil Carl H.
Weil Julius E.
Weil Morris
Weil Theodore
Wendell M.
Wertheimer A.
Willner L. J.
Wineman J. R.
Wineman Milton R.
Wise Maurice
Witkowsky Conrad
Witkowsky James
Wolbach J. S.
Wolf A. H.
Wolf Henry M.
Wolf L. J.
Woolf Benjamin
Woolf Isaac
Wormser David
Wormser Louis
Yondorf Chas.
Yondorf S.

THE TWENTIETH CENTURY CLUB.

OFFICERS.

H. N. HIGINBOTHAM, - - - - - - President.
L. C. COLLINS, JR. }
MRS. FERNANDO JONES, } - Vice-Presidents.
WILLIAM MORTON PAYNE, - Secretary and Treasurer.
1601 Prairie Avenue.

GENERAL COMMITTEE.

Hugh T. Birch
Mrs. Fredk. W. Becker
L. C. Collins jr.
Peter S. Grosscup
LeGrand Burton
Thomas Dent
H. N. Higinbotham
William R. Harper

William Morton Payne
Ernest M. Stires
Mrs. L. L. Coburn
Mrs. John Wilkinson
Martin A. Ryerson
John S. Runnells
Mrs. James McKindley

Mrs. O. H. Matz
Mrs. Fernando Jones
Mrs. C. L. Raymond
Mrs. N. B. Ream
Mrs. Heaton Owsley
Mrs. H. M. Wilmarth
Mrs. Harriet C. Brainard

MEMBERS.

* after a name signifies Mr. & Mrs.

Addams Miss Jane
Allerton S. W. *
Austin Frederick C. *
Babcock Courtlandt
Bailey Edward P. *
Baker Alfred L. *
Baker F. H. *
Baldwin Miss Annie
Bartlett A. C. *
Bass George *
Bassett Roger M. *
Bates Lindon W. *
Becker Frederick W. *
Bell Miss Lillian
Billings Henry F. *

Birch Hugh T.
Blair Chauncey J. *
Block Louis J.
Brainard Mrs. Harriet C.
Bross Mason
Brush Emerson H. *
Burton LeGrand *
Carlisle Chas. A. *
Carmichael Mrs. George S.
Carton Lawrence A. *
Case Mrs. Emma W.
Cass George W. *
Chalmers William J. *
Church Edmund V.
Clark Clinton C.

Clowry Col. R. C.
Coburn Lewis L. *
Collins Judge L. C. jr. *
Colvin Wm. H. jr. *
Cooley Harlan W. *
Crofton Alfred C. Dr.
Crouch R. B. *
Crow Mrs. Martha Foote
Cummings Eloise W. Miss
Davis Col. Chas. W. *
Dent Thomas *
Dewey Albert B. *
Dickinson O. P. *
Doud L. B. *
Doud Miss Marion E.

Dunham Miss M. V.
Ellis Mrs. A. M. H.
Estabrook Henry D. *
Ewen John Meiggs *
Field Marshall
Fiske Dr. Geo. F. *
Fitch Henry S. *
Fitch Miss Julia
Fitch Winchester
Fletcher Wm. Meade *
Fullerton Charles W.
Galt Mrs. A. T.
Gane Thomas F. *
Gillett E. W. *
Gilmore Thomas W. *
Goodman James B.
Green Augustus W. *
Greene H. N. *
Greene Mrs. Mosher T.
Gross S. E. *
Grosscup Judge Peter S. *
Hammer D. Harry *
Harper Pres. Wm. R. *
Harris N. W. *
Harrison Carter H. *
Hart Elmer W.
Hawes Judge Kirk *
Helmer Frank *
Hervey James F. *
Higinbotham Miss F.
Higinbotham H. N. *
Hoyne Mrs. Frank G.
Huddleston Mrs. K. G.
Hughitt Marvin *
Hutchinson Charles L. *
Hutchinson Miss Florence
Jackson Mrs. A. Reeves
Jenkins R. E. *

Jones Ferriando *
Keep Chauncey*
Keith Elbridge G. *
Kennedy Madison B. *
Laflin Louis E. *
Leighton George W. *
Lewis H. L.
Lobdell Edwin L. *
Lombard Josiah L. *
Loose J. L. *
Lyon Thomas R. *
Magnus August C. *
Manners Robert R.
Mather A. C. *
Matz Mrs. O. H.
Matz Rudolph *
McCrea Mrs. Wiley S. H.
McKindley Mrs. James
Morgan Miss Anna
Norton J. Henry *
Owsley Heaton *
Paige Alonzo W.
Pardridge Mrs. Mary Lee
Payne William Morton
Pease Arthur B.
Peck Clarence I. *
Peck Ferd. W. *
Pettibone A. G. *
Potter Edwin A. *
Primley Jonathan P. *
Purdy Charles W. *
Raymond Charles L. *
Ream Norman B. *
Reed Earl H. *
Robinson John K. *
Ross Miss Bessie Gates
Ross Mrs. Joseph P.

Runnels John S. *
Ryan Thomas J.
Ryerson Martin A. *
Scott Mrs. James W.
Sheldon Mrs. George W.
Sherman E. B. *
Smith Byron L. *
Stevens Frank L. *
Stewart Graeme *
Stewart Mrs. Henry
Stires Rev. Ernest M. *
Summers Leland
Summers Miss Maud
Thompson James W. *
Tower Mrs. Lyman H.
Towle Miss Helen M.
Towle Henry S. *
Tracy W. W. *
Trippe Mrs. M. G. W.
Tuttle F. B.
Wacker Charles H. *
Wakeman Mrs. A. V. H.
Walker Edwin *
Walker H. H.
Walker James R. *
Ware Henry A. *
Webster Lewis D. *
White B. C. *
Wilkinson John *
Willing Henry J. *
Wilmarth Mrs. H. M.
Wilson E. C. *
Wilson Milton H. *
Wolfsohn Carl
Wood Miss S. Ella
York John Devereux
Young W. J., jr.

UNION CLUB.

WASHINGTON PLACE AND DEARBORN AVENUE.

OFFICERS.

WILLIAM G. BEALE, - - - - - President.
W. VERNON BOOTH, - - - - - Vice-President.
RICHARD S. EMMET, - - - - - Treasurer.
JAMES M. MACKAY, - - - - - Secretary.

DIRECTORS.

Charles M. Walker
Charles H. Wilmerding
William J. Louderback,

Milton W. Kirk
Jasper Whiting
S. Clifford Payson

Julian L. Yale
Wilson L. Mead
William Sprague

MEMBERS.

Adams George E.
Adams J. McGregor
Adsit James M.
Allen Chas. L.
Andrews C. W.
Antes C. H.
Auten Philip L.
Babcock C. E.
Babcock Fred'k R.

Babcock O. E.
Bartlett C. L.
Beach C. B.
Beale William G.
Beall William Dent
Beebe W. H.
Billings C. K. G.
Billings H. F.
Bishop Henry W.

Black J. C.
Bokum R. D.
Bonynge Dr. F. G.
Booth W. Vernon
Borden William
Brackebush C. H.
Brainard Edwin
Brandon Henry J.
Brewster E. L.

Briggs D. C.
Brooks James C.
Brown Geo. W.
Bullen A. F.
Burley Aug. H.
Burley Clarence A.
Burrows D. W.
Burry Geo.
Burry Wm.

Campbell Benj. H.
Carrington W. T.
Carter Leslie
Chandler J. H.
Chanute O.
Church Townsend V.
Clarke Geo. C.
Cobb A. W.
Coffin Charles H.
Coleman J. G.
Comstock W. H.
Conover Chas. H.
CookeAlex'nderW.
Corwith C. R.
Cotton J. W.
Cramer E. W.
Cramer Frank
Crane E. C.
Creden Thomas H.
Crerar John
Crosby Fred W.
Davol Geo. K.
Dawes Chester M.
Deane Chas. E.
Deane Ruthven
Deering James E.
Dempster C. W.
Dick Albert B.
Dox Hamilton B.
Dudley J. G.
Dunlap G. L.
Dunton J. E.
Durgin John C.
Eaton A. B.
Edwards Thos. C.
Emmet R. S.
English G. P.
Evans James Carey
Farnsworth Geo.
Farnsworth Geo. J.
Favill Dr. H. B.
Fay Ralph M.
Ferguson E. A.
Ferguson Geo. M.
Ferry Chas. H.
Fessenden Chas.N.
Field Marshall
Fishburn E. H.
Forsyth Robt.
Frost E. I.
Fuller Geo. A.
Fullerton Chas. W.
Galt Hubert
Garrett T. Mauro
Gibbs J. S.
Gormully R. Philip
Green E. C.
Greer C. H.
Griffin T. A.
Gross Sam'l E.
Gurley W. W.

Hale G. W.
Hamlin Frank
Hammill Caleb W.
Hammond T. C.
Hannah John S.
Hannah W. H.
Hardin M. D. Gen.
Harlan John M.
Harris Geo. B.
Hartwell E. S.
Havron John
Heisen C. C.
Hempstead G. C.
Henrotin Chas.
Henrotin Fernand
Hettler H. H.
Hill Lysander
Hinde T. W.
Hodgkins E. W.
Honore A. C.
Honore N. K.
Hosmer R. W.
Howard H. A.
Howard J. C.
Howe R. F.
Hubbard S. H.
Hudson A. B.
Hull L. L.
Hume J. H.
Hunt Jarvis
Hunt Robert W.
Hurlbut Horace E.
Ingersoll D. W.
Insull Samuel
Isham E. S.
Isham G. S.
Isham Pierrepont
Jacobson Aug. Col.
Jamieson M. M.
JohnsonWilliam H.
Johnston C. P.
Jones E. Lee
Kenly D. F.
Kennon H. B.
King J. C.
King Rockwell
Kirk J. B.
Kirk M. W.
Kitchen J. B.
Laflin A. K.
Laflin A. S.
Lamport F. W.
Larned S. J.
Lathrop Bryan
Lawrie A. D.
Lawson V.F.
Leiter Joseph
Leiter Levi Z.
Lincoln J. L. jr.
Lincoln R. T.
Littlefield A. S.
Loomis J. Mason

Louderback W. J.
Love Sidney C.
Lowe John W.
Lycett Edward A.
MacArthur R. D.
MacKay James M.
Maltby A. W.
Marsh H. W.
Martin E. P.
Martin W. P.
McAuley J. T.
McClurg Lowrie
McCormick C.H.
McGann R. G.
McIntyre J. L.
McKay James R.
McLaughlin G. D.
Mead Wilson L.
Millar Allan P.
Miller Truman W.
Mix James T.
Montgomery Geo. W.
Moore Gurdon G.
Moulton D. A.
Nash Wm.
Newberry R. T.
Nickerson R. C.
Nickerson Sam'lM.
Norton J. Henry
Noyes David A.
Noyes J. T.
Nuber A.
O'Brien Edward
Odell W. R.
Ortmann R.
Osborn Chas. M.
Parker R. M.
Parmelee John W.
Parsons J. B.
Payson S. C.
Pease E. H.
Peck George R.
Perkins Fred'k W.
Pierce J. H.
Pierce N. H.
Pope Charles
Porter Henry H.
Prentice Sartell
Pynchon G. M.
Quincy C. F.
Rathborne W. W.
Raymond Sam'l B.
Remington Franklin
Rhea Foster A.
Richardson A. P.
Richardson Chas. H.
Roach John M.
Robbins Henry S.
Robinson H. P.

Rozet George H.
Runnells J. S.
Russell Edward P.
Rutter David
Rutter L. R.
Ryerson Edward L.
Salisbury W. M.
Schlippenbach Albert A.
Schmitt Frank P.
Scott E. N.
Scudder J. A.
Selfridge H. G.
Sellers J. M.
Sherman Chas. M.
Sherman Fred'k S.
Smith C. F. Mather
Smith Ernest F.
Smith Frederick B.
Smith LeGrand
Smith Orson
Spoor J. A.
Sprague Wm.
Stanley F. W.
Stephenson F. B.
Stewart Graeme
Swift Fred'k
Tracy William W.
Truesdale W. H.
Tully A. Melville
Ullrich M.
Wakem J. Wallace
Walker Chas. M.
Walker H. H.
Walker W. E.
Waller A. R.
Waller R. A.
Walsh James
Wassall Jos. W.
Watkins Elias M.
Watriss F. H.
Webster Lewis D.
Wheeler Frank S.
Wheeler G. Henry
Wheeler Sam'l H.
Whiting Jasper
Whitman G. A.
Wickersham H. B
Wilbur Harry L.
Wilkins Jos. R.
Wilkinson D. P.
Willard Chas. P.
Willing Henry J.
Wilmerding C. H.
Winston B. M.
Winston Fredk. S.
Winston F. H.
Woodbridge J. E.
Woolley C. M.
Yale J. L.
Yoe Chas. C.

UNION LEAGUE CLUB.

CORNER JACKSON BOULEVARD AND CUSTOM HOUSE COURT.

OFFICERS.

ALEXANDER H. REVELL,	President.
GEORGE A. FOLLANSBEE,	First Vice-President.
HIRAM R. McCULLOUGH,	Second Vice-President.
WILL H. CLARK,	Secretary.
JOHN C. NEELY,	Treasurer.

DIRECTORS.

William W. Gurley	J. S. Belden	Josiah L. Lombard
John C. Hately	Charles M. Hewitt	Frank H. Scott
J. L. Archer	Frank G. Logan	Frederic W. Upham

MEMBERS.

Ackert C. H.	Barker James	Block Williard T.	Buckingham E.
Ackhoff H. W.	Barnes Albert R.	Blodgett E. A.	Buell Ira W.
Adams Cyrus H.	Barnhart A. M.	Blossom Geo. W.	Bullock Geo. S.
Adams George E.	Barnum Wm. H.	Blount F. M.	Bullock Milan C.
Adams J. McG.	Barnum Wm. L.	Bode Frederick	Burchard M. N.
Adams W. P.	Barrett Elmer E.	Bodman Luther W.	Burhans Jas. A.
Adler Dankmar	Barrett Marcus L.	Bogert W. B.	Burkhardt H. S.
Affeld Chas. E.	Barrett Samuel E.	Bond Joseph	Burley Clarence A.
Agee J. A.	Barry Charles H.	Bond Lester L.	Burley Frank E.
Aldrich Chas. H.	Bartle J. S.	Bond Wm. A.	Burnham D. H.
Aldrich J. Frank	Bartlett Alvin C.	Bonney C. L.	Burrows W. F.
Alexander Wm. A.	Bartlett William H.	Bonney Lawton C.	Burt H. G.
Allen Benjamin	Barton E. M.	Boorn W. C.	Busenbark W. R.
Allen Charles L.	Barton George P.	Borden Hamilton	Butler Edward B.
Allen W. D.	Bass George	Botsford Henry	Butler Edward K.
Allerton S. W.	Bayley Edwin F.	Boutell Henry S.	Butler J. Fred
Alling John	Beach Myron H.	Bowen M. K.	Butler J. W.
Allport Dr. F. K.	Beale William G.	Bower Robt. A.	Cable Herman D.
Ames Franklin	Beardsley C. B.	Boyce W. D.	Cairnduff W. H.
Angell Wm. A.	Beaunisne Albert G.	Boyesen I. K.	Cameron D. F.
Angus John	Beidler Francis	Boyles Chas. D.	Camp Wm. Carpen-
Archer James L.	Belden John S.	Boynton C. T.	ter
Armour Philip D.	Bell J. H.	Bradley F. B.	Campbell John G.
Armstrong F. H.	Beman S. S.	Bradley J. Harley	Campbell Robt. B
Arnold B. J.	Benham John	Bradley P. B.	Carpenter Geo. B.
Avery Daniel J.	Bennett Frank I.	Bradwell Jas. B.	Carr H. H.
Babcock Fred R.	Bensley John R.	Brainerd Ed. R.	Cary Eugene
Bacheldor E. A.	Bentley Wilber G.	Brooks C. M.	Cary W. P.
Bacon Henry M.	Besly Chas. H.	Brooks E. W.	Case Chas. H.
Badenoch J. J.	Bettman Boerne	Brooks J. W.	Case E. B.
Badt Francis B.	Bigelow Alfred P.	Brophy Dr. Tru-	Cavanaugh J. B.
Bagley Frederick P.	Bigelow E. A.	man W.	Chadwick Wm. H.
Bailey Edward P.	Billings C. K. G.	Brown Chas. A.	Chalmers Wm. J.
Baird Lyman	Bingham Arthur E.	Brown Geo. F.	Chamberlain Dr.
Baird Wyllys W.	Bingham J. A.	Brown Paul	G. M.
Baker Alfred L.	Bird A. C.	Brown Sanger M.D.	Chamberlin W. H.
Baker Frank H.	Birkhoff George jr.	Brown Wm. H.	Chandler Frank R.
Baker Samuel	Bissell R. M.	Brown Wm. L.	Chandler R. G.
Baldwin Jesse A.	Black E. E.	Brown W. C.	Chandler Walter T.
Baldwin Willis M.	Blackstone T. B.	Brucker Joseph	Chapin Simeon B.
Ballard Thomas P.	Blackwelder I. S.	Brush Emerson H.	Chappell C. H.
Bancroft Edgar A.	Blair Chauncey J.	Bryan Ben B.	Chard Thos. S.
Bane Oscar F.	Blair Henry A.	Bryan Thos. B.	Charnley James
Banks A. F.	Blair William	Bryant H. W.	Chase Benjamin F.
Banning Ephraim	Blatchford N. H.	Bryant John J.	Cheney Clarence C.
Banning Thos. A.	Bleyer C. E.	Buck F. M.	Chytraus Axel
Barker David N.	Bliss E. R.	Buckingham C.	Clancy A. W.

Clapp O. W.
Clark F. W.
Clark Geo. M.
Clark John M.
Clark Jonathan
Clark Will H.
Cleveland Chas. B.
Cloud John W.
Clowry Robert C.
Coburn Lewis L.
Coe Albert L.
Coffin Charles F.
Coffin Charles H.
Cofran J. W. G.
Colby John A.
Cole Geo. E.
Collier Clinton
Collins W. G.
Colvin W. H. jr.
Coman Seymour
Cone Albert G.
Congdon CharlesB.
Conkey W. B.
Conover Charles H.
Conway E. E.
Conway E. S.
Cook George D.
Cook Wm. H.
Coolidge Walter G.
Cooper Wm. D.
Corbin C. R.
Corneau D. E.
Cottrell William N.
Counselman Chas.
Cox Charles D.
Cox R. W.
Craft J. C.
Cragin Edward F.
Crandall ChesterD.
Crane Rev. Frank
Crane H. P.
Crane Richard T.
Crane Simeon H.
Cratty Thomas
Craver Charles F.
Crawford Andrew
Crilly Daniel F.
Critchell Robert S.
Cross Clarence L.
Crowell H. P.
Cruttenden T. S.
Cudahy John
Cudahy Michael
Cummings Andrew
Cummings E. A.
Cummins B. F.
Cunningham W.H.
Cushing E. T.
Custer Jacob R.
Dale John T.
Damsel W. H.
Dana Charles D.
Daniels E. F.
Dauchy Geo. K.
Davies B. M.
Davies C. F.

Davis Geo. R.
Davis Herbert J.
Davis John
Davis Lewis H.
Davis William J.
Dawes Chas. G.
Dawes Rufus C.
Dayton M. E.
Dean A. F.
Defebaugh J. E.
Defrees Joseph H.
Demmon Stephen D.
DeMuth B. F.
Deneen Charles S.
Dent Thomas
Devitt M. A.
Devore John A.
Dewar A. L.
Dewes F. J.
Dewey Albert B.
DeWitt Elden C.
DeWolf Wallace L.
DeYoung Benj. R.
Dickason L. T.
Dickerson J. S.
Dickinson Albert
Dickinson Charles
Dickinson Wm.
Dixon Arthur
Dixon Geo. Wm.
Dixon Thos. J.
Dodge Edmond F.
Donald F. C.
Donnelley R. H.
Donnelley R. R.
Dorrance Chas. J.
Doud Levi B.
Douglas Frank L.
Douglass Wm. A.
Downey Joseph
Downs J. Edward
Drake L. J.
Drake Tracy C.
Drew Chas. W.
Driscoll M. F.
Drucker Henry
DuBois Charles G.
Dudley W. W.
Dummer Wm. F.
Dunlop C. D.
Dunn F. K.
Dupee Chas. A.
Durand Calvin
Duvall R. L.
Dwight John H.
Eames John H.
Eastman Sidney C.
Eaton William T.
Eckels James H.
Eckhart BernardA.
Eddy H. C.
Edmonds H. O.
Edwards J. A.
Ellicott Edw. B.
Elliott John G.

Ellsworth Jas. W.
Engelhard Geo. P.
Estabrook Henry D.
Etheridge Dr. Jas. H.
Ettinger Chas. D.
Eustis Truman W.
Evans Clinton B.
Evans C. H.
Everett John C.
Ewart Wm. D.
Ewen John M.
Fairbank N. K.
Falkenau Victor
Fargo Chas. E.
Farr Albert G.
Farr Marvin A.
Farson John
Farson Robert B.
Farwell Chas. B.
Farwell John A.
Farwell John V.
Fauntleroy T. S.
Fay Ralph M.
Felsenthal Eli B.
Ferguson Chas. H.
Ferguson Elbert C.
Ferry Chas. H.
Fessenden Benj. A.
Field John S.
Field Marshall
FishburnRandolph
Fisher Geo. M.
Fisher L. G.
Fisher Walter L.
Fiske Dr. GeorgeF.
Fitch Henry S.
Fitz Simons Chas.
Fleming John C.
Flower James M.
Follansbee Chas E.
Follansbee Geo. A.
Foote Erastus
Forbes Allen B.
Foreman Henry G.
Foreman Oscar G.
Forgan James B.
Foss Geo. E.
Foster Volney W.
FosterWm.Elmore
Fowler E. M.
Fraser Norman D
Frazier Frank F.
French W. M. R.
Frost Albert C.
Frost Chas. S.
Fry George C.
Fuller Charles H.
Fuller George A.
Fuller G. Edward
Fuller Henry C.
Fuller Wm. A.
Fulton J. L.
FunkhouserM.L.C.

Furbeck W. F.
Gardner Wm. A.
Garnett William,jr.
Gartside J. M.
Gartz A. F.
Gary Elbert H.
Gates J. W.
Getchell Edwin F.
Gilbert Allan A.
Gilbert C. B.
Gilbert James H.
Gilchrist John F.
Giles Wm. A.
Gillett E. W.
Glessner John J.
Glidden H. H.
Gobel E. F.
Goddard L. A.
Goddard L. O.
Goodman Wm. O.
GoodwinWarren F.
Goodyear Charles A.
Gordon Charles U.
Gormully R. P.
Gould Chas. H.
Gould John
Grace Wm.
Graves A. M.
Gray Elisha
Gray W. H.
Green A. W.
Green E. H. R.
Green John W.
Greene Frank R.
Greenlee R. L.
Greenlee R. S.
Gregory Robert B.
Grey Chas. F.
Grey William L.
Gridley Martin M.
Griffin Chas. F.
Griffin Livingston
Griffiths John
Griswold E. P
Griswold F. E.
GroetzingerEdw.A.
Gross S. E.
GunsaulusRev.FW
Gunther Chas. F.
Gurley Wm. W.
HackerNicholasW
Hagar John M.
Halbach J. F. A.
Hale Geo. W.
Hall Augustus O.
Hall Frank G.
Hall Jesse E.
Hall Samuel E.
Halle E. G.
Hambleton Earl L.
Hamill Ernest A.
Hamilton D. G.
Hamilton Dr. John B.
Hamlin John A.

Hamline John H.
Hammer D. Harry
Hammond L. D.
Handy Henry H.
Hanecy Elbridge
Hanna Charles A.
Hannah Wm. H.
Harbeck Eugene
Harding Abner C.
Harding Amos J.
Harding Geo. F.
Harding Lucien E.
Hare R. W.
Harkness E. J.
Harmon John K.
Harper Wm. H.
Harper Dr. Wm. R.
Harris Albert W.
Harris N. W.
Harrison Clark W.
Harvey Geo. V.
Haskell Fred. T.
Hatch Azel F.
Hately John C.
Hately Walter C.
Haugan H. A.
Hawes Kirk
Hayt Henry C.
Head Franklin H.
Healy P. J.
Heath Ernest W.
Hebard Frederic S.
Hecht Frank A.
Heckman Wallace
Henning Dr. F. A.
Henion W. B.
Henkle William H.
Henry Robert L.
Hertle Louis
Hewitt C. M.
Hewitt H. H.
Heyworth Jas. O.
Hibbard Angus S.
Higbee Wm. E.
High Geo. Henry
Highley G. E.
Higinbotham H.D.
Higinbotham H.M.
Higinbotham H. N.
Hiland J. H.
Hill Edgar A.
Hill Lysander
Hillis David M.
Hillis N. D. Rev.
Hills Chas. F.
Himrod Charles
Hinkley Charles W.
Hinkley Watson S.
Hinman George W.
Hirsch EmilG.Rev.
Hitt John
Hixon Henry Rea
Hobbs J. B.
Hobbs P. J.
Hodgkins J.
Hoelscher H. M.

Holabird William
Holden J. E.
Holdom Jesse
Hollett R. P.
Hollis H. L.
Holt Chas. S.
Holt Geo. H.
Horton Horace E.
Horton Oliver H.
Hosmer Jos. W.
Howard J. H.
Howell C. D. B.
Hubbell Charles W.
Huck Louis C.
Hughes John B.
Hughitt Marvin
Hughitt Marvin, jr.
Hulburd Chas. H.
Hunter W. W.
Hurd Harvey B.
Hutchins E. R.
Hutchins Jas. C.
Hutchinson C. L.
Hyman Robt. W.jr
Illsley William A.
Irwin C. D.
Jackson Wm. A.
Janney James W.
Jelke John F.
Jenkins George H.
Jenkins J hn E.
Jenkins Robt. E.
Jenkins T. R.
Jenney Wm. L. B.
Jerrems Wm. G.
Jerrems Wm. G. jr.
Jocelyn F. C.
Johnson C. Porter
Johnson Ernest V.
Johnson J. M.
Jones Frank H.
Jones George P.
Jones J. S.
Jones Otis
Jones William H.
Joyce W. T.
Judd Curtis J.
Judson Wm. B.
Kane Thomas
Kavanagh M. R.
Keeler Chas.Butler
Keep Chauncey
Keith Elbridge G.
Kelley David
Kelley Wm. E.
Kellogg Milo G.
Kelsey J. A.
Kendall Benj. W.
Kennedy David J.
Kennedy Henry H.
Kent Sidney A.
Kent William
Kent William D.
Kerfoot Wm. D.
Kerr Wm. R.
Keyes Rollin A.

Kimball George F.
Kimbark Chas. A.
Kimbell Spencer S.
King John A.
Kirk John B.
Kirk M. W.
Kline George E.
Knight Clarence A.
Knight John B.
Knight Newell C.
Kniskern W. B.
Knott Henry A.
Kochersperger D. H.
Kochs Theodore A.
Kohlsaat C. C.
Kohlsaat H. H.
Kreidler W. A.
Kultchar M. R.
Lacey Edward S.
Lackner Francis
Lake Richard C.
Lane Eben
Lathrop E. B.
Laubender John F.
Lavery Geo. L.
Law Geo. W.
Law John H.
Lawrence E. F.
Lawrence W. E.
Lawson Victor F.
Lay A. Tracy
Lay Chas. C.
Leach Levi L.
Leach Thomas A.
Leake Joseph B.
Lefens Thies J.
Leffingwell F. P.
Leigh E. B.
Leiter Levi Z.
Lermit G. H.
Letton T. W.
Lewis W. B.
Lindblom Robt.
Lindgren John R.
Linn Wm. R.
Littlefield A. S.
Littlejohn W. J.
Lloyd W. J.
Lobdell E. L.
Locke John M.
Lockett Oswald
Loesch Frank J.
Logan Frank G.
Lombard Isaac G.
Lombard Josiah L.
Long James H.
Long Theodore K.
Longenecker JoelM
Loose J. L.
Lord Frank E.
Lord Geo. S.
Lord John B.
Louderback D. H.
Lounsbury Jas. A.
Lowden Frank O.

Lundie John
Lyman D. B.
Lyman Edson W.
Lynas Thomas R.
Lynch Richard W.
Lyon Richard S.
Lyon Thomas R.
Mackenzie G. S.
Mallette J. P.
Mann Henry N.
Mann James R.
Manning Wm. J.
Mark Clayton
Marsh Chas. Allen
Marsh Wm. D.
Marshall Chas. H.
Marshall Geo. E.
Marshall Dr. JohnS.
Mason Fred B.
Mason Ira J.
Mather Alonzo C.
Mather Robert
Mathews Geo. W.
Matthiessen C. H.
Matthiessen E. A.
Mayberry J. J.
Mayer David
Mayer Isaac H.
Mayer Levy
McArthur Arthur F.
McBerty Frank R.
McConnell L. W.
McCord Alvin C.
McCormick A. A.
McCrea Willey S.
McCullough H. R.
McCurdy Geo. L.
McDoel W. Henry
McDonald J. J.
McEwen Willard M.
McGregor P. D.
McIlvaine William D.
McKay A. A.
McKay Geo. A.
McKinlock G. A.
McLaren John
McLeish Andrew
McLennan J. A.
McNally Andrew
McNally F. G.
McNulta John
McVoy John A.
McWilliams L.
Mead Aaron B.
Mecum C. H.
Medill Joseph
Mehring George
Merigold W. A.
Metcalf H. C.
Millard S. M.
Miller Chas. K.
Miller H. H. C.
Miller James A.
Miller John G.

Swift Louis F.
Swift M. Lewis
Swift Wm..H.
Taft O. B.
Templeton Thos.
Tenney Horace Kent
Thoman Leroy D.
Thomas Benjamin
Thomas Herbert A.
Thomasson Nelson
Thompson R. S.
Thorn Frank
Thorne George R.
Tobey Frank B.
Towle Henry S.
Tracy Joseph P.
Treat Samuel A.
Trego Chas. T.
Tripp Chas. E.
Troutman J. Hamilton
Truax Charles
Trumbull John H.
Turner E. A.
Turner Wm. H.
Ullmann Frederic
Underwood J. Platt
Underwood Wm.T.
Upham Fred W.

Upton Geo.-P.
Valentine E. H.
Vanderkloot A.
VanKirk Chas. B.
Van Vlissingen J.H.
Van Woert G. E.
Vaux Frederick T.
Vierling Louis
Vierling Robert
Vocke Wm.
Wachsmuth L. C.
Wacker Charles H.
Wait J. J.
Walker Francis W.
Walker H. H.
Walker James R.
Walker John H.
Walker Robt. P.
Wallace John F.
Wallach John F.
Waller E. C.
Waller Robt. A.
Wallin Thomas S.
Walsh John R.
Ware Henry A.
Warner Geo. L.
Warren Charles D.
Warren Wm. S.
Washburn Wm. D.
Watkins Wm. W.

Watson Wm. J.
Watson Wm. jr.
Weare Portus B.
Weare William W.
Weary E. D.
Weaver Henry E.
Webster Thos. H.
Webster T. K.
Wegg D. S.
Weinsheimer A. S.
Welling J. C.
Wells Addison E.
Wells Frank
Wells Robert. M.
Werner P. E.
West Roy O.
Weston Chas.Howard
Wetherell O. D.
Wheeler H. A.
Whelpley R. T.
Whitehead W. M.
Whitehouse S. S.
Whittemore C. L.
Wilbur J. B.
Wilcox J. Fred
Wilkinson Harry
Wilkinson John
Willard George
Williams Geo.T.

Williams Wm. P.
Willing Henry J.
Willits Ward W.
Wilson Albert B.
Wilson E. Crane
Wilson Hugh R.
Wilson John P.
Wilson John R.
Wilson M. J.
Wilson Milton H.
Wilson Walter H.
Winslow FrancisA.
Winslow W. H.
Wise Clift
Witbeck John H.
Wolff John F.
Wolseley HenryW.
Wood Casey A.
Wood George E.
Wood Ira C.
Wood Wm. F.
Woodward Arthur H.
Woodward M. S.
Wyman W. D.
Yaggy L. W.
Yerkes C. T.jr.
Young Otto
Zeiss Henry C. F.
Zimmerman W.

UNITY CLUB.

3140 INDIANA AVENUE.

OFFICERS.

D. GUTHMAN, - - - - - - President.
H. J. ELIEL, - - - - - Financial-Secretary.
J. E. WOLFF, - - - - - - Secretary.
MAX L. WOLFF, - - - - - - Treasurer.

DIRECTORS.

David Davis
H. J. Eliel
I. R. Gardner

L. Guthman
Abe Kahnweiller
Benj. Lowenmeyer

Louis H. Oberndorf
I. Rosenthal

MEMBERS.

Aaron Louis
Baer Isaac
Bauman E.
Baumberger J. R.
Baumgart Leon
Bing Jacob Dr.
Davis David
Eliel H. J.
Ettlinger B.
Ettlinger Max
Fass Charles
Fass Jacob
Freshman A.
Frey Joseph M.
Gardner I. R.
Getz Dan

Getz Meier
Guthman Dan
Guthman L.
Heldman Julius L.
Hirsch Rev. E. G.
Kahn M.
Kahnweiller Abe
Klein G. L.
Landauer Fred
Lanz George
Lazarus Harry
Lichtenstadt Philip
Lindauer Frank
Loeb A. S.
Lowenmeyer Benj.
Lubliner S.

Madden M. B.
Marks L. C.
Mayer Benjamin F.
Meyer A. M.
Miller Milton
Moses Rev. I. S.
Myers Ed.
Nathan Isadore M.
Neuman A.
Oberndorf LouisH.
Oluff Max
Reiss Otto
Rice I. M.
Rosenthal Isaac
Rosenthal S. E.
Rothschild J.

Rothschild William
Spiegel J.
Spiegel Leon
Stein Amos
Stolz Joseph
Straus David
Strauss J. G.
Strouss Levi
Wachenheimer David
Werthan Sidney
Wolfe A. R.
Wolfe Samuel R.
Wolff J. E.
Wolff Max L.

UNIVERSITY CLUB.

118 DEARBORN STREET.

OFFICERS.

HENRY S. BOUTELL, - - - - - - - President.
JAMES S. HARLAN, - - - - - - Vice-President.
WILLIAM C. BOYDEN, - - - - - - Secretary.
GEORGE W. MEEKER, - - - - - - Treasurer.

DIRECTORS.

Benjamin Carpenter   Alfred Cowles   Henry E. Mason
J. Lewis Cochran   Walter L. Fisher   Edwin B. Smith
                        Hermon B. Butler

MEMBERS.

Ackerman Fred S.	Boyden Wm. C.	Durkee Henry R.	Halsey Edward A.
Adams Edward S.	Bradley David E.	Edgerton Seymour	Hamlin Frank
Adams George E.	Bradley John D.	Edsall Sam'lC.Rev.	Hamlin Fred R.
Adams Samuel	Bradley J. Harley	Elliot Frank M.	Hamlin HerbertW.
Alden Wm. T.	Bross Mason	Elting Victor	Hamlin H. L.
Alderson Victor C.	Brown Frank T.	Ethridge Dr. J. H.	Hamline John H.
Aldis Arthur T.	Brown George W.	Evans Lynden	Harding Chas. F.
Aldis Owen F.	Browning G. W.	Ewen John M.	Harlan James S.
Aldrich F. C.	Burley Clarence A.	Fales David	Harnwell F. W.
Allen Charles L.	Burling E. B.	Fargo L. W.	Harper R. F. Prof.
Allport Dr. Walter H.	Burlingham F. W.	Farnum H. W.	HarperWm.R.Prof
	Burry George	Farwell Arthur L.	Harriman E. A.
Alton William jr.	Burry William	Farwell F. C.	Harris Graham H.
Andrews Clement W.	Butler Hermon B.	Farwell Granger	Harris N. W.
	Butz Otto C.	Farwell John V. jr.	Harrison Carter H.
Andrews Dr. E. W.	Cable B. S.	Favill Dr. H. B.	Harvey George L.
Andrews Dr. Frank T.	Cady Jeremiah K.	Fenn Wm. W.	Harvey, Dr. R. H.
	Carpenter A. A. jr.	Ferguson E. A.	Hatch Azel F.
Andrews J. H.	Carpenter Benj.	Ferry C. H.	Head Franklin H.
Armour Allison V.	Carpenter F.I.Prof.	Field Marshall jr.	Helmer Frank A.
Armour George A.	Carpenter Geo. A.	Fisher Walter L.	Henderson W. F.
Augur Walter W.	Cary Robert J.	Fiske Dr. Geo. F.	Herrick John J.
Babcock O. E.	Cass George W.	Flower Louis B.	Heyworth James O.
Babcock Dr. Robt. H.	Casselberry Dr. W. E.	Follansbee M. D.	Hibbard Angus S.
		Forsyth G. H.	Hibbard Wm. G. jr.
Baird Max	Chase Samuel T.	Forsyth W. H.	Higginson Geo. jr.
Baker Alfred L.	Chatfield-TaylorH. C.	Foster Stephen A.	Hodges C. H.
Baker H. D.		Freeman Henry V.	Holabird William
BartholomayHenry jr.	Clark John M.	French S. T.	Holland John F.
	Clarke G. C.	Freund Ernest	Holt C. S.
Bartlett C. L.	Clarke J. V.	Fullerton Chas. W	Honore Adrian C.
Bartlett Wm. H.	Cochran John L.	Furness Wm. E.	Honore Lockwood
BeckwithWarrenL.	Colgate Russell	Gade F. H.	Houghteling J. L.
Bentley Cyrus	Coolidge Dr. F. S.	Galloway Jas. B.	Howland Geo. C.
Bigelow Nelson P.	Corwith Charles R.	Gamble W. C.	Howland WalterM.
Billings Dr. Frank	Cowles Alfred	Gardiner Dr. Edwin J.	Hoyt Phelps B.
Birch Hugh T.	Cramer Ambrose		Hubbard H. M.
Bissell Richard M.	Crane R. T. jr.	Gardner Henry A.	Hubbard Joseph D.
Blair Frank P.	Daniels Francis B.	Gardner James P.	Hubbard Wm. H.
BlatchfordEdw.W.	Dauchy Samuel	Giles Wm. F.	Hulbert E. D.
Blatchford E. W.	Davis Dr. N. S. jr.	Gillette Edwin F.	Hull Morton D.
Blatchford Paul	Dawes Chester M.	Glessner J. G. M.	Hunter Geo. L.
Boddie John T.	Delano Frederic A.	Gookin F. W.	Hutchins E. R.
Borden G. M.	De Windt H. A.	Granger Alfred H.	Hutchinson C. L.
Boutell Henry S.	Donnelley T. E.	Gray J. H.	Hutchinson Geo. A.
Bowen Joseph T.	Dudley Dr. Emilius C.	Hadduck B. F.	Hyde James N. Dr.
Bowers Lloyd W.		Halbert Walter A.	Isham Dr. Geo. S.
Boyce S. Leo	Durand Scott S.	Hall Ford P.	Isham Ralph

Isham Dr. RalphN.
Jackson H. W.
James Edmund J.
James G. F. Prof.
Jerrems A. N.
Johnston John jr.
Johnston, M. L.
Jones David B.
Jones E. H.
Jones Thomas D.
Kales Dr. John D.
Kedzie J. H. jr.
Keith Edson jr.
Kent William
Kerfoot Wm. D.
Kilvert M. A.
King Charles G.
King Francis
King Rockwell
Kirk Walter T.
Knapp J. M.
Knapp K. K.
Knott Henry A.
Lackner Francis
Laflin Arthur K.
Laflin L. E.
Lamb Benj. B.
Larned Walter C.
Lathrop Bryan
Lawrence Dwight
Lawson Victor F.
Lee Blewett
LeMoyne Louis V.
LeMoyne Wm. M.
Lewis Charles G.
Lewis David R.
Lincoln John L. jr.
Lord Frank E.
Lowden Frank O.
Lowe John W.
Lyman David B.
Lynde Samuel A.
Magill Henry W.
Magruder H. L.
Maitland F. E.
Marsh C. L.
Marsh Henry W.
Marston Thos. B.
Martin F. S.
Martin Horace H.
Mashek V. F.
Mason Edward G.
Mason Henry B.
Mason Henry E.

Matz Herman L.
Matz Rudolph
McArthur Arthur F
McBirney H. J.
McCagg Ezra B.
McCluer Wm. B.
McClurg Alex. C.
McClurg Lowrie
McCordic Alfred E.
McCormick A. A.
McCormick Cyrus H.
McCormick Harold F.
McCormickStanley R.
McFadden P. J.
McIlvaine Wm. B.
Meeker Geo. W.
Merrick Geo. P.
Merrill Wm. H. jr.
Miller Adolph C.
Miller Amos C.
MontgomeryJohnR
Moody John A.
Morse Clarence T.
Musgrave H.
Newell A. B.
Newman Dr. H. P.
Nolan J. St. John
Norcross Fred k F.
Norton C. D.
Norton James H.
Noyes E. H.
Oakley Horace S.
Olmsted Oliver A.
Osborn Chas. M.jr.
Osborn E. E.
Otis Chas. T.
Otis Ephraim A.
Otis J. E. jr.
Otis Philo Adams
Otis Wm. A.
Owsley Heaton
Paddock George L.
Page Wm. R.
Parsons John C.
Payson Geo. S.
Peabody A. S.
Peck George R.
Peet Henry J.
Peirce James H.
Phelps George B.
Pike Charles B.

Pike Eugene R.
Pike W. W.
PillsburyWilliam F
Pond Irving Kane
Porter A. B.
Porter James F.
Prentice Ezra P.
Prentice Sartell
Raeder Henry
Reynolds W. H.
Rev.
Ridlon John Dr.
Ritsher Edward C.
Ritter Henry A.
Rodman Thos. J.
Rogers Geo. Mills
Rogers John A.
Rogers Joseph M.
Rose Hiram H.
Rumsey Geo. D.
Rush George F.
Rutter David
Ryerson Arthur
Ryerson John A.
SalisburyR.D.Prof.
Sargent J. R. W.
Sargent W. D.
Scott Frank H.
Selfridge H. G.
Sellers Frank H.
Shankland E. C.
Shanklin Robt. F.
Sheldon Henry I.
Sheldon Theodore
Shumway Philip R.
Silsbee Joseph L.
Simmons P. E.
Simmons Rufus S.
Smith Byron L.
Smith Delevan
Smith Dunlap
Smith Ed. Burritt
Smith Kinney
Snively Thaddeus
A. Rev.
Sprague Albert A.
Sprague Fred'k W.
Starkweather Dr.
R. E.
Stephens R. D.
Stevens Harry S.
Stires E. M. Rev.
Stone Herbert S.
Sturgis Chas. I.

Taylor Thos. jr.
Thatcher O. J.
Thomas M. St.P.
ThompsonLeverett
Thompson Percival
Thompson Slason
Thornton Chas. S.
Thurber Chas. H.
Rev.
Tilton John Neal
Todd J. Jackson
Tracy W. W.
Triggs O. L.
Truesdale W. H.
Tuttle Emerson B.
Tuttle Henry N.
Tyson Russell
Vocke William
Waite H. G.
Waldo Otis H.
Walker Bertrand
Walker J. R.
Walker Dr. Sam'l J.
Walker Wirt D.
Waller Edward
Waller James B.
Waller Robert A.
Waller William
Warrington J. N.
Washburne Hempstead
Wassall J. W.
Wentworth F. W.
Wentworth M. J.
Wertheimer Benj.J
West Fredric T.
Wheeler Arthur D.
Wheeler C. P.
Whitman Russell
Wilkes C. M.
Willard G. G.
Willard M. L.
Willard Norman P.
Williams John R.
Williams Lawrence
Williams Norman
Williams Norman jr.
Wilson John P.
Wolf Albert H.
Wolf Henry M.
Wood Kay
Wrenn Everts
Yeomans Geo. G.

NON-RESIDENT MEMBERS.

Abbott Edward H.
Avery H. E.
Barber Joel Allen
Bosworth H. I.
Boutell Lewis H.
Bradley Wm.H. jr.
Bryan Chas. Page
Caldwell Brown jr.
Clarke Fred'k W.

CollinsHoldridge O
Copley Ira C.
Corwith James W.
Cowles Wm. H.
Doane John E.
Eddy Spencer
Fisher Lucius G. jr.
Goltra E. F.
Gresham Otto

Hall Thos. C. Rev.
HedstromArthurE.
Isham Edward jr.
Keene F. B.
Kernan J. F.
Ketcham F. D.
Lathrop Barbour
Lord Nathaniel
MacKinlayThos.E.

McLaren W. A.
Merriam R. H.
Merrill Wm. F.
Morris Howard
Newell John E.
Nixon Miles G.
Osborne Thos. M.
Palmer E. C.
Patton Wm. L.

Penfield E. W.
Ridgely Wm. B.
Rogers Henry
Wade Prof.
Rogers James G.
ScaddingChas.Rev.

Scott Henry B.
Sheppard Robt. D.
Sherwin W. W.
Smith H. F.
Starrow James J.
Stephenson F. M.

Strong F. M.
Strong Henry
Stuart C. B.
Stuart Wm. V.
Stuart W. Z.

Warren Lansing
Wheeler S. H.
Whitney George B.
Williams J. C.
Young Kimball

WASHINGTON PARK CLUB.

SIXTY-FIRST STREET AND SOUTH PARK AVENUE.

OFFICERS.

GEORGE HENRY WHEELER, - - President.

SAMUEL W. ALLERTON,
GEO. E. P. DODGE,
HENRY J. MACFARLAND, } - - Vice-Presidents.
CHARLES D. HAMILL,

JOHN R. WALSH, - - - - - Treasurer
JAMES HOWARD, - - - - - Secretary

BOARD OF DIRECTORS.

Until December, 1898.	Until December, 1899.	Until December, 1900.
N. K. Fairbank	George Henry Wheeler	Gustavus A Schwartz
Samuel W. Allerton	N. B. Ream	Charles A. Mair
D. M. Cummings	James W. Ellsworth	George E. P. Dodge
John R. Walsh	Charles J. Barnes	F. J. Kennett
Albert S. Gage	J. Henry Norton	Charles D. Hamill
Henry J. Macfarland	Robert H. Fleming	Robert W. Roloson
Arthur O. Slaughter	Charles J, Singer	Frank S. Gorton
John Dupee	E. L. Brewster	Thomas Cratty

EXECUTIVE COMMITTEE.

The President
The Vice-Presidents } Ex officio
The Treasurer

Frank S. Gorton   Robert W. Roloson
G. A. Schwartz   D. M. Cummings
J. Henry Norton   John Dupee
             Albert S. Gage

MEMBERS.

Ackerman Fred S.
Adams George J.
Adams Joseph
Adsit James M.
Alexander Gerard M.
Allerton Robert H.
Allerton Samuel W.
Andrews William B.
Armour Allison V.
Armour George A.
Armour J. Ogden
Armour Phil D. jr.
Arms Harrison.
Ashby James H.
Austin Frederick C.
Avery Frank M.
Babcock Frederick R.
Bacheldor E. A.
Baker William T.
Baker W. V.
Baldwin Dr. L. B.
Baldwin Willis M.
Bane Oscar F.

Barber O. C.
Barker John H.
Barnes Charles J.
Barrell James
Barrell J. Finley
Barrell Stewart E.
Barrett John F.
Bartlett F. O.
Bartlett Lincoln
Baumann Gustav
Bayley Edwin F.
Beale William G
Beard Thomas
Beardsley C. B.
Beidler Francis
Bennett Thomas
Bevan Arthur D.
Billings C. K. G.
Billings Dr. Frank
Black H. S.
Blair Chauncey J.
Blair Henry A.
Blair Lyman

Blair Watson F.
Bloom Leopold
Boal Charles T.
Booth William S.
Borden William
Botsford Henry
Bournique A. E.
Bowyer Lorraine F.
Bradbury George L.
Bradley Edward.
Brand Edwin L.
Breese Jacob B.
Brega Charles W.
Brewer John S.
Brewer Owen W.
Brewster Edward L.
Brewster Walter S.
Bromley Joseph E.
Brosseau August
Brosseau Z. P.
Broughton Urban H.
Brown George D.
Bullen George

Bunker Hiram S.
Burke Michael
Burkhardt H. S.
Burrows D. W.
Butler E. B.
Byers Jacob E.
Caleb Gideon N.
Camp Wm. Carpenter
Canby C. H.
Carpenter A. A. jr.
Cary Eugene
Cassard Herbert
Cassidy James A.
Caton Arthur J.
Chalmers William J.
Chamberlin George M.
Champlin Chas. Pope
Champlin Fred L.
Chapin S. B.
Charlton George J.
Christie George B.
Church Edmund V.
Clark E. A.
Clark John M.
Clark M. Lewis
Clarke Henry B.
Clay John jr.
Cleave O. C.
Cloud John W.
Coffeen William
Collier Clinton
Collins Lorin C. jr.
Collins Lorin C. 3d
Colvin Wm. H.
Conkey W. B.
Conkling Allen
Conkling B. H.
Conley John W.
Connor Thomas V.
Cooper John S.
Counselman Charles
Counselman Willis
Cowan William P.
Cowles Alfred
Cox R. W.
Craine William N.
Crane Edward C.
Cratty Thomas
Crawford Andrew
Crawford Henry jr
Crerar John
Cromwell Charles
Cronkhite William H.
Crouch R. B.
Cudahy John
Cudahy John P.
Cudahy Michael
Cummings D. Mark
Cummings Morris C.
Cunningham Secor
Currier Charles H.
Curtis W. W.
Cutter John M.
Davis George R.
Davis H. J.
Davis John

Davis William J.
Day Joseph L.
Deering James
DeMuth B. F.
Dennehy Thomas C.
Dewar Hamilton
Devlin Frank A.
DeWolf Wallace L.
Dick Albert B.
Dickason L. T.
Dickerman Edward T.
Dillman Louis M.
Doane J. W.
Dodge George E. P.
Doering E. J.
Donnelley Reuben H.
Dore Walter J.
Douglas W. W.
Downs A. Ogden
Drake John A.
Drake John B. jr.
Drew Charles W.
Dunlap Robt.
Dunn Frank K.
Dupee John
Dupee Walter H.
Durand John M.
Eddy Augustus N.
Edwards Eugene P.
Edwards James A.
Edwards Thomas C.
Edwards W. S.
Elkins Henry K.
Ellsworth James W.
Ellwood Isaac L.
Ettinger Charles D.
Fabyan George
Fairbank N. K.
Fargo Charles
Fargo Livingston W.
Farwell John A.
Fay Ralph Morse
Featherstone Alfred
Felton Charles E.
Fenton Hamilton W.
Ferguson Charles H.
Ferguson Geo. Miller
Field Marshall
Fish Stuyvesant
Fisher Lucius G.
Fitzgerald Richard
Flagg William H.
Fleet Geo. Stanley
Fleming Robert H.
Flershem Lem W.
Fletcher Wm. Meade
Floyd Frank
Foreman Henry G.
Forrest William H.
Forsyth J. J.
Forsyth Robert
Fort Robert B.
Frankenthal E.
Fuller Frank H.
Fuller George A.
Fuller Leroy W.

Fullerton Charles W.
Gage Albert S.
Gage E. B.
Garneau Joseph
Gary John W.
Gates Charles G.
Gates John W.
Gaylord A. P.
Gaylord Willard S.
Geddes Alexander
Getty Henry H.
Gibbs Frederick C.
Gilbert James H.
Gillett Charles W.
Gillett E. W.
Glover Otis R.
Goodman James B.
Goodman Wm. O.
Goodrich Albert W.
Goodwin Warren F.
Gore George P.
Gorton Frank S.
Greene Frank C.
Gregory Walter D.
Grey John J.
Grey William L.
Griffin Thomas A.
Gross Samuel E.
Gurney Charles H.
Hall William F.
Hamburger Louis M.
Hamill Charles D.
Hamilton D. G.
Hamlin Fred R.
Hamlin George J.
Hamlin Harry L.
Hamlin John A.
Hammond J. Dean
Handy H. H.
Hanecy Elbridge
Harding George F.
Harper William H.
Harriman Edward A.
Harris George B.
Harris John F.
Hartog John H.
Hartwell E. S.
Harvey W. S.
Haskell Fred'k T.
Hayden Albert
Head William J.
Heath Ernest W.
Henderson W. S.
Herrick E. Walter
Hettler Herman H.
Heyworth James O.
Heyworth Lawrence
Hibbard William G.
Hibbard William G. jr.
Hill James T.
Hinde Thomas W.
Hogg David
Hughes Joseph
Hughitt Marvin jr.
Hull Leverett L.
Hunt George W.

Rynearson James L.
St. John Leonard
Salsbury Nate R.
Sanderson Geo. A.
Sard William H.
Sargent William Durham
Sattley W. N.
Schimpferman Wm. H.
Schmitt Eugene J.
Schwartz G. A.
Scull Henry
Seaverns Geo. A.
Seaverns George A. jr.
Seipp William C.
Sexton Patrick J.
Shattuck Charles L.
Shaw Ralph Martin
Shaw Robert
Shaw Wiliam A.
Shayne John T.
Shepherd Edward S.
Shipman D. B.
Shirk E. W.
Shubert A. B.
Singer Charles J.
Slaughter Arthur O.
Smith Burton
Smith Byron L.
Smith Edward E.
Smith Ernest F.
Smith Frank M.
Smith Franklin P.
Smith George T.
Smith Jacob P.
Smith Lon K.
Smith Orlando C.
Smith Orson
Smith Thomas
Southgate R. H.
Spalding Jesse
Spoor John A.
Spry Samuel A.
Stanley P. E.
Stauffer Benjamin F.
Stearns Richard I.
Stephens Redmond D.

Sterling William H.
Stevens Charles A.
Stiles George N.
Stinson James
Stone Horatio O.
Strahorn Robert
Strong Henry
Strong J. H.
Stuart C. U.
Stuart Robert
Studebaker W. F.
Sturges Solomon
Sturtevant H. D.
Swift Edward F.
Swift Louis F.
Taylor George H.
Taylor George H.
Taylor Thomas jr.
Tewksbury George W.
Theurer Joseph
Thompson Gale
Thompson Percival
Thompson William Hale
Thorne George A.
Thorne George R.
Thorne Robert J.
Thorne William C.
Townsend James J.
Travis E. J.
Trego C. T.
Tufts Eugene L.
Tyng Dudley A.
Udell S. R.
Valentine Alistair I.
Valentine P. A.
Vogel Frank E.
Wachsmuth Louis C.
Wainwright Ellis
Walker E. C.
Walker Edwin
Walker Henry H.
Walker Henry W.
Walker J. Brandt
Walker James R.
Walker Wirt D.
Waller William

Walsh John R.
Ward A. Montgomery
Ware J. Herbert
Warner A. R.
Wassall Joseph W. Dr.
Weaver Henry E.
Wells Moses D.
Wells Orson C.
Wells Samuel R.
Wells Warren A.
Wentworth Frank W.
Wheeler Arthur
Wheeler Charles W.
Wheeler Eugene
Wheeler Francis T.
Wheeler George Henry
Wheeler H. A.
Wheeler Henry L.
White Augustus J.
White A. Stamford
White Charles E.
Whitehouse S. S.
Whitman George A.
Whitney Joel C.
Wickes Thomas H.
Willey C. L.
Wilson Horatio R.
Wilson W. J.
Winston Fred S.
Wolford Jacob A.
Wood Samuel E.
Woodbury Sidney H.
Work Andrew S.
Wright Julian V.
Wright Thomas A.
Wright Warren
Wright William M.
Yager William A.
Yale Julian L.
Yerkes Charles T.
Young Caryl
Young Lawrence A.
Young Otto
Young William J. jr.
Zeiss Henry

WEST END WOMAN'S CLUB.

542 WEST MONROE STREET.

OFFICERS.

MRS. H. M. SCOTT, - - - - - - President.
MRS. GEORGE D. BROOMELL, - - First Vice-President.
MRS. MARY A. BULLOCK, - - Second Vice-President.
MRS. WILLIMINA PRICE, - - - Recording Secretary.
MRS. KETURAH G. BEERS, - - Corresponding Secretary.
MRS. MARY E. SANDS, - - - - - Treasurer.

DIRECTORS.

Bella Christes Brown
Mary H. Busby
Mary M. Clark
Mary A. Downs

Flora J. Jackson
Mary C. Kohlsaat
Mary B. Little
Rose A. Sears

Jennie W. Spry
Clara E. Taylor
Mary A. Wells
Caroline S. Wygant

Adcock Mrs. A. W.
Aldrich Mrs. H. H.
Allen Mrs. J. K.
Alsip Mrs. Wm.
Arnold Mrs. Alvan H.
Arnold Mrs. R. B.
Auten Mrs. P. L.
Ayres Mrs. L. D.
Barbour Mrs. Lyman L.
Barnhart Mrs. A. E.
Bartholf Mrs. C. S.
Bartlett Mrs. Murray A.
Beebe Mrs. A. G.
Beek Mrs. H. W.
Beers Mrs. J. Hobart
Benham Mrs. Jas. W.
Benson Mrs. C. E.
Bidwell Mrs. T. S.
Bigelow Mrs. H. D. P.
Billings Mrs. C. K. G.
Birkhoff Mrs. George jr.
Blackman Mrs. Chester
Blades Mrs. L. J.
Bley Mrs. J. C.
Blodgett Mrs. Edw. A.
Bogle Mrs. W. T.
Bond Mrs. L. L.
Booth Mrs. J. St. J.
Borland Mrs. M. W.
Broomell Mrs. Geo.
Brophy Mrs. Truman W.
Brower Mrs. D. R.
Brown Mrs. C. A.
Brown Mrs. Sanger
Bullock Mrs. M. C.
Burdick Mrs. Oscar
Burkhardt Mrs. H. S.
Burt Miss Mary E.
Busbey Mrs. Wm. H.
Bussey Mrs. W. T.
Campbell Mrs. Fergus
Carpenter Mrs. Ellen W.
Carpenter Mrs. W. O.
Chalmers Mrs. W. J.
Chandler Mrs. H. H.
Chapman Mrs. J. M.
Chappell Mrs. C. H.
Cheney Mrs. W. W.
Christy Mrs. H. A.
Clark Mrs. A. E.
Clark Mrs. C. R.
Clark Mrs. E. G.
Clark Mrs. Jas. L.
Clark Mrs. Walter T.
Clarke Mrs. Leverett H.
Clement Mrs. Austin
Cobb Mrs. E. B.
Cobb Mrs. H. E.
Cobb Mrs. M. R.
Coggeshall Mrs. Mary M.
Cole Mrs. M. E.
Cole Mrs. T. W.
Collins Mrs. L. D.
Conger Mrs. J. S.
Conger Mrs. Romaine
Cornell A. S.

Cornell Mrs. H. W.
Cox Mrs. Agnes C.
Crane Mrs. E. J.
Crane Mrs. Frank R.
Cusack Mrs. James I.
Cushing Mrs. W. T.
Dandy Mrs. William M.
Danforth Mrs. I. N.
Dashiell Mrs. V. W.
Date Mrs. Sydney S.
Davis Mrs. G. R.
Dean Mrs M. C.
Dennis Mrs. Fred J.
Dole Mrs. John N.
Dougherty Mrs. T. E.
Downs Mrs. J. E.
Drake Mrs. Geo. V.
Dresden Mrs. Wm. W.
Dunn Mrs. Jno. O.
Earle Mrs. C. W.
Earle Mrs. Frank B.
Eckhart Mrs. B. A.
Eckhart Mrs. J. W.
Eddy Mrs. Azariah
Elmes Mrs. Chas. F.
Evans Mrs. W. W.
Farson Miss M. E.
FitzSimons Mrs. Chas.
Flannery Mrs. D. F.
Forbes Mrs. A. M.
Foster Mrs. R. N.
Frake Mrs. Jas.
Fulton Mrs. J. L.
Gardner Miss Jessie S.
Gibson Miss Belle
Golder Miss Lena
Golder Mrs. W. A.
Graham Mrs. D. W.
Gray Mrs. Arthur
Gray Mrs. A. W.
Greenlee Mrs. E. C.
Greenlee Mrs. Ralph S.
Greenlee Mrs. Robert L.
Hair Mrs. B. M.
Hall Mrs. L. R.
Hall Mrs. R. N.
Hanson Mrs. Z. P.
Harlow Mrs. Jefferson G.
Harris Mrs. A. J.
Harsha Mrs. L. R.
Hart Mrs. J. P.
Hartwell Mrs. F. G.
Haskell Mrs. J. W. C.
Haven Mrs. Jos.
Hawes Mrs. W. Harrison
Hayt Mrs. Henry C.
Healy Mrs. P. J.
Heinroth Mrs. W. C.
Henneberry Mrs. Wm. P.
Hewett Mrs. A. C.
Higgins Mrs. G. W.
Hill Mrs. C. D.
Hill Mrs. Edgar A.
Hodges Mrs. Lothrop S.
Hogan Mrs. Joseph
Holden Mrs. Jane

Holden Mrs. W. H.
Holmes Mrs. G. P.
Holmes Mrs. Oliver W.
Hooker Mrs. H. M.
Hostetter Mrs. J. N.
Hough Mrs. Edward M.
Hutchinson Mrs. G. C.
Ingals Mrs. E. F.
Ingram Mrs. A. B.
Jackson Mrs. W. G.
Judd Mrs. C. F.
Kane Mrs. Geo. B.
Kane Mrs. Thomas
Keeler Mrs. J. B.
Kilmore Mrs. J. W.
King Mrs. John A.
King Mrs. Ulric
Kohlsaat Miss Anna M.
Kohlsaat Miss Bertha F.
Kohlsaat Mrs. C. C.
Kohlsaat Mrs. Ernest W
Krum Mrs. I. R.
Lamb Mrs. Chas.
Lamb Mrs. Frank
Lane Mrs. Albert G.
Lansing Mrs. Mark S.
Lawrence Mrs. W. M.
Leonard Mrs. S. F.
Linington Mrs. C. M.
Little Mrs. F. B.
Loomis Mrs. A. H.
Loomis Mrs. M. B.
Loring Mrs. J. Brown
Lyon Mrs. R. S.
Mackenzie Mrs. G. S.
Mackenzie Mrs. W. Douglas
Martin Mrs. A. W.
Mason Mrs. James A.
Maxwell Mrs. Henry B.
Maxwell Mrs. Jas.
McBride Mrs. John F.
McCasky Mrs. I. W.
McLaren Mrs. John
McNeill Mrs. T. H.
Mead Mrs. A. B.
Mergler Dr. Marie J.
Midgley Mrs. John W.
Miller Mrs. Waldo F.
Minkler Mrs. Ward S.
Montgomery Mrs. W. T.
Moore Mrs. W. J.
Morey Mrs. H. C.
Moyer Mrs. W.
Mulfinger Mrs. J. Leonard
Munger Mrs. D. S.
Munson Mrs. Charles
Nevers Mrs. Edward
Newton Mrs. Ashael
Newton Mrs. H. A.
Newton Mrs. R. C.
Nichols Mrs. G. R.
Norris Mrs. W. W.
Ott Mrs. Katharine
Pearson Mrs. J. H.
Perry Mrs. T. O.

Peters Mrs. Joseph G.
Pettibone Mrs. P. F.
Phillips Mrs. N. A.
Pitkin Mrs. G. W.
Plamondon Mrs. C. A.
Polley Mrs. J. C.
Pond Mrs. Walter M.
Port Mrs. E. V.
Price Mrs. O. J.
Price Mrs. W. H.
Pullman Mrs. W. C.
Rawleigh Mrs. Jas. T.
Reece Mrs. A. W.
Rend Mrs. W. P.
Richolson Mrs. Benj. F.
Ripley Mrs. Bradford W.
Ripley Mrs. William
Rising Mrs. C. L.
Rockwood Mrs. G. H.
Roe Mrs. D. Herbert
Roeschlaub Mrs.Frank H.
Rogan Mrs. J. B.
Rollins Mrs. Chas. E.
Rollins Mrs. Chas. H.
Rollo Mrs. William
Root Mrs. J. Sherman
Ross Mrs. Geo.
Royce Mrs. E. A.
Ruggles Mrs. C. R.
Russ Mrs. Lewis
Russell Mrs. D. E.
Salisbury Mrs. W. H.

Sands Mrs. O.
Sawyer Mrs. Daniel G.
Sayre Miss Virginia
Scott Mrs. H. M.
Scribner Mrs. S. A.
Schriver Mrs. P. A.
Sears Mrs. P. C.
Shepherd Mrs. Edward S.
Sherwood Mrs. Geo.
Sherwood Mrs. Jno. B.
Sherwood Mrs. Marc
Shoemaker Mrs. Walter
Simonds Mrs. N. M.
Skelton Mrs. Nellie Bangs
Sloan Mrs. G. S.
Small Mrs. L. A.
Smith Mrs. R. J.
Solomon Mrs. Charles H.
Sosman Mrs. Jos. S.
Spry Mrs. J. C.
Spry Mrs. S. A.
Stanford Mrs. George W.
Stearns Mrs. Edgar G.
Stehman Mrs. H. B.
Stevens Mrs. J. K.
Stewart Mrs. E. L.
Stone Mrs. A. J.
Storey Mrs. C. W.
Storey Mrs. J. B.
Strong Mrs. Jane K.
Studley Mrs.Mary Button
Swift Mrs. George B.

Talbot Mrs. J. F.
Talcott Mrs. Marshall
Tatham Mrs. Robt. L.
Taylor Mrs. Chas. A.
Taylor Mrs. F. C.
Taylor Mrs. G. H.
Thatcher Mrs. A. T.
Thatcher Mrs.Solomon jr
Tilton Mrs. G. W.
Tower Mrs. C. O.
Tracy Mrs. F. K.
Trout Mrs. Geo. W.
True Miss Mary E.
Tucker Mrs. M. E.
Vaughan Mrs. J. C.
Wakefield Mrs. N. R.
Wallace Mrs. T. D.
Warner Mrs. Chester
Warner Mrs. Mary R.
Weeks Mrs. H. T.
Wells Mrs. Addison E.
Wells Mrs. T. B.
Wilcox Mrs. W. W.
Williams Mrs. N. A.
Williams Mrs. Robt. A.
Wilson Mrs. F. C.
Winchell Miss H. N.
Wolff Mrs. Christian J.
Woods Mrs. F. M.
Woodbury Mrs. W. H.
Wygant Mrs. Alonzo

WESTWARD HO GOLF CLUB.

CLUB HOUSE, OAK PARK.

OFFICERS.

CHAUNCEY L. WILLIAMS, - - - - - - - President.
A. F. BANKS, - - - - - - - - - Vice-President.
ROWLAND S. LUDINGTON, - - - - - - Treasurer.
A. HADDOW SMITH, - - - - - Captain and Secretary.

MEMBERS.

*After a name signifies Mr. and Mrs.

Ackert C. H. *
Ackert Fred
Ainslie Miss Genevieve
Ainslie Nellie V.
Ainslie S. R. *
Ames Charles L.
Austin Henry W.
Austin M. B. *
Banks A. F. *
Barker Katherine
Bassett H. W. Dr.
Bentley H. G.
Bingham Horace W.
Blatchford Paul *
Browne W. A.
Butler J. Fred
Caldwell Frank C.
Caldwell W. G.

Carpenter Miss Johnnie
   Anna
Carpenter Miss Mary F.
Chase Guy M.
Cleveland A. F.
Cleveland J. F.
Crenshaw W. Percy *
Darrow Clarence S.
Dodge H. A.
Douglass William A.
Duncombe Herbert S.
Edwards John T.
Elliot Frank
Farson John
Farson John, jr.
Fullerton Thomas
Furbeck George W. * .
Furbeck Philip J.

Furbeck W. F.
Gale Thomas H.
Gates Herbert W.
Hatch William H.
Heurtley Arthur
Higgins H. H.
Hilton J. A.
Hopkins Marguerite
Huff Thomas D.
Jones F. B.
Jones W. Clyde
Kennedy D. J.
Kittle E. B.
Lancaster F.
Ludington Rowland S.
Lyman Miss Ednia
Lyman E. W.
Mackenzie G. W. Rev.

McCary Clyde J.
McClary Nelson A.
McCready E. W.
Moore N. G.*
Moser George W.*
Niver D. R.
Noyes William S.
Pebbles H. R.
Pierce R. H.*
Pitkin E. H.
Prall William G.
Quayle Robert
Rattle Thomas S.
Richards L.*

Ripley J. T.
Rockwell Harold H.
Rogers Ellen D.
Rogers James C.
Rogers Lydia
Rogers Susan A.
Roser E. A.
Rountree H. H.
Sharp Louis H.
Smith A. Haddow
Smith Irene
Straight Bertha K.
Strong Sidney Rev.
Taylor H. H.

Toomey John J.
Towle H. S.
Towle Miss Helen M.
Treadway Ralph B.
Tweedie Herbert J.
Walker George
Waller Miss Lillian
Walters A. E.
Wilce Miss Edwena
Wilce Mrs. E. P. .
Willard C. F.*
Williams Chauncey L.
Williams Mrs. Helen W.
Worthington H. C. Dr.

WOODLAWN MATINEE MUSICALE.

WOODLAWN PARK CLUB, WOODLAWN AV. COR. 64TH.

OFFICERS.

MRS. R. L. BARKER, - - - - - - - - - President.
MRS. H. B. DEWEY, - - - - - - - Vice-President.
MRS. PERRY J. POWER, 233 Jackson Park Terrace, Secy. and Treas.

MEMBERS.

Atwood Mrs. Harry A.
Barker Mrs. R. L.
Barton-Strohm Olivia
Bell Miss Cora
Chamberlain Mrs. A. F.
Coulter Mrs. Edward
Crawford Mrs. J. S.
Cropper Mrs. M. D.
Curtis Mrs. Edw.
Dewey Mrs. H. B.
Foster Mrs. Thomas
Fowler Mrs. Wm. A.

Frothingham Miss Frances
Goldbeck Mrs. Robt.
Goodwin Miss Mabel E.
Hall Mrs. Thos.
Jones Mrs. M. M.
Kurtz Mrs. J. H.
Lester Mrs. F. M.
Loomis Miss Florence
Peabody Mrs. Arthur
Power Mrs. Perry J.

Rathbun Miss Bessie
Roberts Miss Agnes
Roelle Miss Emma
Simms Mrs. Edw.
Stern Mrs. Julius
Streich Mrs. A. F.
Trumbull Miss Florence
Wilber Mrs. Isadora
Wilber Mrs. Edward
Wilson Miss Mary J.
Wolcott Mrs. Frank

WOODLAWN PARK CLUB.

WOODLAWN AVENUE COR. 64TH STREET.

OFFICERS.

G. J. M. PORTER, - - - - - - - President.
GEORGE WAGNER - - - - - - Vice-President.
E. A. ERICKSON, - - - - - - - Secretary.
BURT C. HARDENBROOK, - - - Assistant Secretary.
HARRY V. KING, - - - - - - Treasurer.

DIRECTORS.

W. A. Coleman,
M. E. Rose

J. W. Hill
A. S. Delaware

Charles H. Scholle
Geo. E. Harrison

MEMBERS.

Andrews H. C.
Ashcraft Edwin M.
Atwood Fred G.
Austin C. E. Dr.
Bacon W. O.
Baird James
Barnhart W. J.
Beard C. N.

Bennett Frank I.
Boller C. V.
Bour Charles J.
Bragdon Chas. E.
Brown P. S.
Catlin T. B.
Chaffee F. F. Dr.
Chamberlain A. F.

Clark G. W.
Coleman Wm. A.
Cuthbertson Hugh
A. Dr.
Delaware Ambrose
S.
Dewey H. B. Mrs.
Dorn Gay Dr.

Douglass D. B.
Dripps Samuel W.
Dunning W. D.
Erickson Edw. A.
Evoy Thomas A.
Fairman Clarence
Fairman Dan'l B.
Farwell John C.

Ford George W.
Forsinger J. W.
Fowler Wm. A.
Gammans J. A.
Gaulter Frank J.
Gerrish G. G.
Gilkison Jasper G.
Gillmore Robt. T.
Geltz William
Graver Wm. F.
Green Fred. W.
Green R. F.
Greene Carl D.
Guerin M. H.
Hall Robert W.
Hamm T. P.
Hardenbrook Burt C.
Hardenbrook Edwin G.
Hardenbrook G. S.
Harrison Geo. E.
Harrison Jas. W.
Herriman W. D., M. D.
Hill Joseph W.
Hirschl A. J.
Holbrook F. S.
Holton Thos. J.
Hopkins Francis A.
Hoxey E. F.
Humphrey A.
Hunt W. R.
Hunter E. L. Dr.

Hurd H. G.
Irvine Hugh
Irwin John
Irwin J. C.
James W. S. Dr.
Jellyman Joseph
Jobson C. Frank
Joslin Alex D.
Keast John H.
Keeler Wm. B.
Kelland Geo. H.
Kerr W. W.
Kimball Ralph R.
King Harry V.
King Jesse G.
Knight O. B.
LaClair A. P.
Lafferty Chas. C.
Lafferty Wm. J.
Langford E. G.
Leon A. T.
Leonard W. H.
Levis John M.
Lockwood Thos. A.
MacKellerO.W.Dr.
Malley W. C.
Manington John
McCandless A. W.
McGoorty John P.
Miller E. M.
More C. E.
Nicholas Edmd. T.
Niles H. G. jr.
Nowak C. A.

O'Neill John
Olin Frank E.
Organ C. D.
Paddleford Fred A.
Painter J. V.
Pashley Alfred F.
Peck Edgar W.
Pershing J. F.
Porter Geo. J. M.
Press Whiting G.
Reed Florence S. Mrs.
Rose M. E.
Rose Willett
Ross George H.
Sachen Harry
Saxton H. I.
Schoenman Chas.S.
Scholle Charles H,
Schroeder A. F.
Seymour E. K.
Seymour J. P.
Sheffield G. S.
Sims Edwin W.
Sims R. Harry
Smith E. N.
Smith Howard L.
Snow W. I.
Southworth Mary L. Miss
Spencer Chas. H.
Stern Julius
Stevenson A. E.
Storrow J. McK.

Strawbridge C. H.
Strawbridge E. J.
Streich Albert F.
Stursberg Herman, jr.
Sweetland John T.
Tarbox C. S.
ThompsonGlennD.
Thompson J. L.
Titzell F. C. Dr.
Torrance J. R.
Towle John R.
Utz A. L.
Vent Raymond T.
Wagner Edmund
Wagner George
Walker Edwin K.
Wanner E. A.
Warner Addison R.
Warren F. A.
Week's J. G.
Werntz Carl N.
Wheeler Martin L.
Wheeler Newton C.
White Chas. F.
White Henry W.
White Lyman A.
Wilson James
Wilson S. K.
Wolford Frank H.
Woodworth David B.
Young Edgar L.

PART SIXTH.

ALPHABETICAL LIST.

THE BLUE BOOK.

CONTAINING THE NAMES OF PROMINENT HOUSE-
HOLDERS OF CHICAGO AND SUBURBS, AR-
RANGED IN ALPHABETICAL ORDER
ACCORDING TO NAMES,
GIVING ALSO THE SUMMER RESIDENCE.

ALPHABETICAL LIST.

The italics after the names in this list indicate the principal down-town clubs of which such individuals are members. The following abbreviations have been used:

Cal. Calumet.   *Ill.* Illinois.   *Un.* Union.
Chi. Chicago.   *Irq.* Iroquois.   *U.L.* Union League.
C.A. Chicago Athletic Association.   *Lksd.* Lakeside.   *Univ.* University.
   Stan. Standard.   *W.P.* Washington Park.

A AGAARD JULIUS, 6647 Perry av.
Aaron Bernard N. 3428 Vernon av.
Aaron M. 3239 South Park av. *Lksd.*
Aaron M. D. 3428 Vernon av. *Lksd.*
Abbey Charles P. 578 W. Adams
Abbott A. A. Mrs. Morgan Park
Abbott A. H. 50 Madison, *C.A.*
Abbott A. R. Mrs. 353, 41st
Abbott A. V. 52 Walton pl.
Abbott A. W. Evanston
Abbott C. P. Mrs. 87 Rush
Abbott Edwin F. Austin
Abbott Frank D. 3751 Lake av.
Abbott Frank E. LaGrange
Abbott Frank F. Prof. 137, 56th
Abbott James, 109 S. Sacramento av.
Abbott John Jay, 3222 Michigan av.
Abbott Lizzie Miss, Oak Park
Abbott Louise C. Mrs. 5309 Ingleside av.
Abbott L. Berwyn
Abbott Orvil S. Mrs. 3344 Calumet av.
Abbott Robert B. 450 Belden av. *C.A.*
Abbott Sprague, 87 Rush
Abbott William L. 3213 Beacon
Abbott William Warner, 4715 Prairie av.
Abbott Wilson N. 7436 Eggleston av.
Abbott W. C. Dr. 2666 N. Hermiage av.
Abbott W. R. 525 Cleveland av.
Abeel Waldo Mrs. 266 S. Irving av.
Abel Anna Miss, 3147 Indiana av.
Abel Clarence Rev. 517 Greenleaf av.
Abel C. C. 876 W. Jackson boul.
Abel E. J. 521 Dearborn av.
bel Jonathan, 3334 Vernon av.
Abel Julius, 3749 Indiana av.
Abel Minnie Miss, 521 Dearborn av.
Abel Rollin A. 876 W. Jackson boul.
Abele August, 1076 Carmen av.
Abele Frederick W. 1107 Carmen av.
Abenathy C. B. Mrs. Evanston
Abercrombie J. J. The Renfost
Abernethy M. L. Mrs. 352 Belden av.
Abernethy Samuel H. Austin
Abraham Arthur, 4327 Indiana av.

Abrams Edwin E. 5423 Jefferson av.
Abt Herman H. 4452 Ellis av. *Stan.*
Abt Isaac A. Dr. 4008 Grand boul.
Abt Jacob J. 699, 49th. *Stan.*
Abt Levi, 4452 Ellis av.
Abt Sol L. 466, 44th, *Stan.*
Aby S. F. Dr. Norwood Park
Ackerburg Henry E. 572 Fullerton av.
Ackerman Fred S. 5490 East End av. *C.A., Univ., W.P.*
Ackerman William K. 135 Astor, *Chi.*
Ackers Thomas B. 68 Bryant av. *Irq.*
Ackert Charles H. Oak Park, *CA., U.L.*
Ackhoff Henry W. 1778 Deming pl. *C.A., U.L.*
Ackhoff Louisa Miss, 1778 Deming pl.
Ackley G. Newton, 2450 N. Paulina
Acres Louise Dr. 960 W. Jackson boul.
Adair Addison A. Oak Park
Adair Charles M. Oak Park
Adair George W. Maj. Fort Sheridan
Adam A. B. 2249 Calumet av. *Cal., Chi.*
Adam George J. Chicago Athletic assn. *C.A.*
Adams Abbot L. 350 Ontario. *C.A.*
Adams A. Albert 5744 Washington av. *C.A.*
Adams Albert H. Oak Park
Adams Albert M. 2505 Michigan av.
Adams Alfredo B. Hotel Metropole
Adams Alice Montgomerie Miss, 506 N. State
Adams Benjamin F. Evanston
Adams Caroline D. Miss, 350 Ontario
Adams Carlos J. Dr. 856 W. Monroe
Adams Carrie G. Miss, 235 Michigan av.
Adams Charles, 821 Estes av.
Adams Charles Dr. Kenilworth
Adams Charles A. 41 Gordon Terrace
Adams Charles E. 4204 Oakenwald av.
Adams Charles F. 5758 Rosalie ct.
Adams Charles F. Dr. 1247 Wrightwood av.
Adams Charles R. 504 Greenleaf av.

473

Adams Cora K. Mrs. 253 Belden av.
Adams Cyrus H. 155 Rush. *C.A.*, *U.L.*
Adams Edward A. Austin
Adams Edward L. Austin
Adams Edward M. 36 Madison Park
Adams Edward M. jr 36 Madison Park
Adams Edward Shields, 446 Chestnut, *Chi.*, *Univ.*
Adams Ella M. Mrs. 1210 Sheffield av.
Adams Elmer K. 856 W. Monroe
Adams Eugene E. 4322 Greenwood av.
Adams Eva Miss. 2251 Kenmore av.
Adams E. S. Mrs. 40 Scott
Adams Francis, 481 W. Adams, *Ill.*
Adams Francis W 581 Lasalle av.
Adams George, 2822 Michigan av.
Adams George Davis Rev. Riverside
Adams George E. 530 Belden av. *C i.*, *C.A.*, *Un.*, *U.L.*, *Univ.*
Adams George J. 408, 36th pl. *W.P.*
Adams George W. 501 Touhy av.
Adams George W. Mrs. 2716 Calumet av.
Adams Harry C. 4641 Vincennes av. *C.A.*
Adams Harry W. 207, 41st
Adams Hattie Mrs. 3135 Forest av,
Adams Henry Mrs. 841 W. Adams
Adams Henry E. Irving Park
Adams James, Oak Park
Adams James H. 381 Superior
Adams Joanna A. Mrs. 832 Walnut
Adams John A. 2618 Wabash av.
Adams John B. 19 Bryant av.
Adams John Hachett, 506 N. State
Adams John M. 581 Lasalle av.
Adams John Q. 717 The Plaza
Adams John Russell, 506 N. State, *Chi.*
Sum. res. "The Grange," Beloit, Wis.
Adams Joseph, Lakota hotel, *Chi.*, *C.A.*, *W.P.*
Adams Joseph Rev. 2631 N. Rboey
Adams J. E. River Forest
Adams J. McGregor, 300 Schiller, *Chi.*, *Un.*, *U.L.*
Sum. res. "Yarrow," Highland Park
Adams J. Porter, Maywood
Adams Louisa H. Mrs. 335, 53d
Adams Milward, Auditorium hotel, *Chi.*
Adams Morris H. 7315 Yale
Adams Moses, 3642 Grand boul. *Stan.*
Adams M. L. Mrs. 2618 Wabash av.
Adams Nellie M. Miss, 19 Bryant av.
Adams Samuel, 40 Scott, *Univ.*
Adams Samuel P. 301, 66th
Adams William C. 682, 48th
Adams William G. Oak Park
Adams William P. 858, 72d pl.
Adams William P. Wheaton, *U.L.*
Adams William S. 4335 Lake av.
Adams William T. 2618 Wabash av.
Adams W. H. Mrs. 6501 Monroe av.
Adcock Albert W. 327 Warren av. *Ill.*
Adcock Albert Young, 327 Warren av.
Adcock Earl Edward, 327 Warren av.
Adcock Edmund, 2902 Prairie av.
Addams Jane Miss, 335 S. Halsted
Addison Harold E. 178 Dearborn av.

Addison John, 178 Dearborn av. *Irq.*
Addy Edward, 6932 Wentworth av.
Ade George, 113 Cass
Adkinson Elmer W. 5540 Wentworth av.
Adler A. K. 3543 Ellis av.
Adler Dankmar, 3543 Ellis av. *Stan.*, *U.L.*
Adler Henry, 2625 Calumet av. *Stan.*
Adler Louis, 571 Division
Adler Louis, 599, 46th
Adler Morris, 3427 South Park av. *Lksd.*
Adler Sidney, 3825 Vincennesav. *Stan.*
Adler Sidney J. 3543 Ellis av.
Adolph Charles H. 613 Englewood av.
Adolphus Philip Dr. 636½ Washington boul.
Adolphus Wolfe, 250, 47th *C.A.*
Adsit Byron D. New Hotel Holland
Adsit Charles C. Virginia hotel. *Chi.*
Adsit James M. Mrs. 400 Dearborn av.
Adsit James M. jr. 400 Dearborn av. *C .l.*, *C.A.*, *Chi.*, *Un.*, *W.P.*
Aeppli Oscar D. Edgebrook
Affeld Charles E. 1824 Diversey. *U.L.*
Agar John, 1846 Oakdale av.
Agee Joseph A. 475, 42d, *U.L.*
Agler Oliver O. 2110 Clarendon av. *C.A.*
Agnass Jean E. C. Norwood Park
Agnew I. S. Mrs. Hotel Windermere
Agnew John P. 292 Rush
Agnew J. H. 3601 Vincennes av.
Ahern David P. 776, 44th
Sum. res. Minneapolis, Minn.
Ahern Elizabeth Mrs. 5726 Madison av.
Ahern Elliott G. 5542 Michigan av.
Ahern J. J. Dr. 4959 Washington Part ct.
Ahlenfeld O. J. Mrs. 573, 43d
Ahles Emily Mrs. 1130 Washington boul.
Ahles Julius F. 287 S. Irving av.
Ahles William, 1130 Washington boul.
Ahrens C. H. L. Washington Heights
Ahrens Henry, 249 W. 65th
Ahrens Herman, 306 Ogden av.
Ahrens John A. 249 W. 65th
Ahrens John H. 54 Campbell av.
Ahrens J. P. 3218 Vernon av.
Ahrensfeld John C. Park Ridge
Aiken Jennie Hall Mrs. 2616 Calumet av.
Aiken Joseph F. 2616 Calumet av.
Aiken Mayhew P. Evanston
Aiken Rose T. Miss, Evanston
Aiken William J. 857 W. Monroe. *Ill.*
Aiken Charles W. Evanston
Ainslie Samuel R. Oak Park
Ainsworth Franklin F. 2505 Michigan av.
Ainsworth L. H. 6120 Kimbark av.
Aishton Richard H. Evanston
Aitkins John A. 684 Winthrop av.
Akin Abel Mrs. Maywood
Akin Henry F. Maywood. *C.A.*
Albee P. Mrs. Lombard
Alber Max, 4928 Forrestville av.
Albert Christopher J. Prof. Elmhurst
Albertson Joseph R. Maywood
Albright E. P. 6506 Minerva av.
Albright Isaac N. Dr. 344 S. Campbell av

Albright T. S. 871 W. Monroe
Albright William F. 25 S. California av.
Albro Clarence W. 1820 W. 22d
Albro Clark B. Oak Park
Albro Martha J. Mrs. 1820 W. 22d
Alcock·William H. 581, 45th pl.
Alden Carroll S. 337 Indiana
Alden Emmons J. 337 Indiana
Alden E. Judson Rev. 337 Indiana
Alden Frederick H. Austin
Alden R. A. Mrs. 1801 Barry av.
Alden William T. 4528 Oakenwald av.
   Univ.
Alderson John J. Dr. 424 W.Jackson boul.
Alderson Victor C. Prof. 428, 34th. Univ.
Aldis Arthur Taylor, 67 Lake Shore drive
   Chi., Univ.
      Sum. res. York Harbor, Me.
Aldis Owen F. 77 Bellevue pl. Chi., C.A.,
   Univ.
Aldis Owen W. 77 Bellevue pl. C.A.
Aldrich Charles H. Evanston. U.L.
Aldrich E. W. 974 W. Adams
Aldrich F. C. Lake Forest. Univ.
Aldrich Henry H. 217 Ashland boul. Ill.
Aldrich William H. 4519 Greenwood av.
Aldrich W. F. 4519 Greenwood av.
Aldrich W. H. jr. 4519 Greenwood av.
Aldridge John G. 792 W. Monroe
Aldridge William Mrs. Chicago Beach
   hotel
Aleshire James B. Capt. 666, 48th pl.
Alex F. W. Lake Forest
Alexander A. W. Highland Park
Alexander Charles A. Austin
Alexander Ellen C. Miss, 210, 33d
Alexander G. M. Calumet club. W.P.
Alexander Harriet C. B. Dr. 808 Pratt av.
Alexander Henry M. Austin
Alexander Henry O. 13 Aldine sq.
Alexander Horace C. 808 Pratt av.
Alexander John F. 481 W. Congress
Alexander John T. 221, 46th
Alexander Joseph, 1258 George
Alexander J. P. Mrs. 2028 Michigan av.
Alexander Mary Mrs. Evanston
Alexander Samuel T. 3848 Langley av.
Alexander Stuart R. Wheaton. Chi.
Alexander Walter W. 3848 Langley av.
Alexander William D. 4415 Oakenwald
   av.
Alexander William H. Mrs.13 Aldine sq.
Alexander William M. 6633 Perry av.
Alexander W. A. Highland Park. Chi.,
   U.L.
Algeo Thomas W. 1549 Kenmore av.
Alison John M. 3634 Vincennes av.
Alison Mary Mrs. 3634 Vincennes av.
Alison Rowland H. 3634 Vincennes av.
Alister William M. Chicago Beach Hotel
Allan James Morrison, 2209 Prairie av.
Allan John B. 1225 Washington boul.
Allbright William B. 5139 Lexington av.
Allebone Joseph A. Evanston
Allen Abel L. Evanston
Allen Albert J. 869 W. Monroe

Allen Alexander C. LaGrange
Allen Anna M. Mrs. Highland Park
Allen Arthur G. 339, 53d
Allen Arthur G. Hotel Metropole
Allen Arthur W. Hotel Metropole
Allen A. Bromley Dr. 1287 Washington
   boul.
Allen Benjamin, 1815 Michigan av. Cal.,
   Chi., U.L.
Allen Benjamin C. 1815 Michigan av.
Allen Charles A. 869 W. Monroe
Allen Charles A. jr. LaGrange
Allen Charles B. 5628 Monroe av. C.A.
Allen Charles B. Mrs. 175 Evanston av.
Allen Charles E. Riverside
Allen Charles L. 536 N. State. Chi., Un ,
   U.L., Univ.
Allen Charles W. 143 Oakwood boul. C.
   A.
Allen Charles W. 611, 46th
Allen C. A. Hinsdale
Allen C. H. 3211 Prairie av.
Allen C. S. 4315 Langley av.
Allen C. W. Chicago Beach hotel
Allen Daniel A. 305 Ashland boul.
Allen Dora Miss, 536 N. State
Allen Edmund A. 5541 Madison av.
Allen Edmund T., Dr.6418 Stewart av.
Allen Edward A. 339, 53d
Allen Frances Dr. 333, 41st
Allen Frank E. Evanston
Allen Frank L. 5142 Washington av.
Allen F. G. Hinsdale
Allen George Q. 505 Estes av.
Allen George R. 1181 Washington boul.
Allen Hamilto: F. Rev. 612 W. 60th pl.
Allen Harry K. Riverside
Allen Heman G. 3634 Michigan av.
Allen Henry C. Dr. 5142 Washington av.
Allen Herbert W. 913 W. Jackson boul.
Allen H. A. 1718 Kenmore av. C.A.
Allen Ira W. 612 W. 60th pl.
Allen James H. Dr. 3722 Langley av.
Allen James Lane, 4050 Grand boul.
Allen John, Evanston
Allen John K. 798 W. Monroe
Allen John M. Evanston
Allen J. William, 464 S. Oakley av.
Allen Mary Mrs. Evanston
Allen M. A. 2640 Indiana av.
Allen M. A. Mrs. 339, 53d
Allen M. S. Mrs. 6431 Kimbark av.
Allen Omar H. Mrs. 913 W. Jackson boul.
Allen Oscar D. Oak Park
Allen Philip, 619 W. 60th
Allen Phoebe E. Mrs. Evanston
Allen Samuel W. 6551 Yale
Allen Sarah C. Mrs. Riverside
Allen Thomas, 166, 51st
Allen T. G. Prof. 5549 Woodlawn av.
Allen William D. Evanston. U.L.
Allen William I. 2505 Michigan av.
      Sum. res. Manitou, Col.
Allenberg Lewis W. 4734 Champlain av.
Allerton Robert H. 1936 Prairie av. Cal.,
   Chi., W.P.

Allerton Samuel W.1936 Prairie av. *Cal.*,
   U.L., *W.P.*
Alles John jr. Winnetka
Alles John Mrs. Winnetka
Alley William H. Chicago Beach Hotel
Allin B. C. 4805 Madison av.
Alling.Charles jr. 3150 Groveland av.
Alling Edward H. 3701 Sheridan rd.
Alling John, 2131 Calumet av. *U.L.*
Alling John jr. 2131 Calumet av. *C.A.*
Alling Joseph H. Rev. Evanston
Alling Samuel T. 275 W. Adams
Allinson Thomas W. 5825 Kimbark av.
Allison Alexander, 3365 Indiana av.
Allison A. E. Miss, 5402 Cornell av.
Allison C. W. Glencoe.
Allison George E. Oak Park
Allison John T. jr. LaGrange
Allison Minnie L.Dr.847W.Garfield boul.
Allmendinger George P. 1914 Arlington
   pl. Sum. res. Paw Paw Lake, Mich.
Allport Frank, Hotel Metropole *U.L.*
Allport May Miss, 1718 Indiana av.
Allport Walter H. Dr. 85 Rush *Univ.*
Allyn Arthur W. 373 Oakwood boul.
Allyn Charles T. The Tudor
   Sum res. Delavan Lake, Wis.
Allyn O. F. Mrs. 173, 51st
Almes Herman E. Dr. 4247 Indiana av.
Almy Miles, Lakota Hotel. *C.A.*
Alpiner Morris, 4346 Vincennes av.
Alshuler S. Mrs. 3979 Drexel boul.
Alsip Charles H. 445 Ashland boul.
Alsip Frank B. 483 W. Jackson boul.
Alsip Maud Miss, 445 Ashland boul.
Alsip Mildred Miss, 445 Ashland boul.
Alsip William H. 5140 Madison av. *Ill.*
Altberger Jessie D. Mrs. 3601 Vincennes
   av.
Altgeld John P. Hon. 1886 Diversey
Altman Israel, 4826 Langley av.
Alton Davis C. 2522 Prairie av.
Alton William, 2522 Prairie av.
Alton William jr. 2522 Prairie av. *Univ.*
Alvord M. M. Mrs. 271, 53d
Alward Willard P. 449 Washington boul.
Amberg Emma Mrs. 93 Macalister pl.
Amberg Franz, 160 Throop
Amberg John F. 160 Throop
Amberg John H. 411 W. Monroe
Amberg J. Ward, 62 N. Sheldon. *C.A.*
Amberg Theodore J. 1820 Melrose
Amberg William A. 62 N. Sheldon
   Sum. res. Mackinac Island
Ambler F. W. LaGrange
Ambler H. C. 934 Walnut
Ambler John C. 487 Fullerton av.
Ambrose George W. 79 Bowen av.
Ambrose James, 2428 Indiana av.
Ambrose Thomas, 2428 Indiana av.
Amend F. B. 3180 Dover
American Oscar L. 3130 Vernon av.
American Sadie Miss, 3130 Vernon av.
Amerson George C. Austin
Amerson Harvey S. Austin
Amerson William, Austin

Ames A. F. Riverside
Ames Charles L. Oak Park
   Sum. res. Mackinac Island, Mich.
Ames Cheney Mrs. 1819 Aldine av.
Ames Cortlandt F. 1819 Aldine av.
Ames Franklin, 4835 Greenwood av. *U.L.*
Ames George C. 2001 Michigan av.
Ames Howard, Hotel Del Prado
Ames James C. 4835 Greenwood av.
Ames John G. Dr. 1203 Seminary pl.
Ames J. C. 2967 Vernon av. *Chi.*
Ames Knowlton, Evanston
Ames Miner T. Mrs. 2108 Prairie av.
Ames M. E. 716 Warren av.
Ames W. V. B. Dr. 47, 46th. *C.A.*
Amick Pleasant, 864 S. Sawyer av.
Amman Frank, 245 Osgood
Ammen William J. 875 Winthrop av.
Ammon Ernest, 643 Fullerton av.
Ammon Frederick E. 643 Fullerton av.
Amory William A. 4913 Madison av.
Anable Samuel L. 1844 Briar pl.
Anderson Andrew J. 173 Howe
Anderson A. E. 83 Alice ct. *C.A.*
Anderson Benjamin B. 2237 Sheridan rd.
Anderson Benjamin L. Norwood Park
Anderson Carl, 237 Wilson av.
Anderson Charles P. Rev. Oak Park
Anderson Charles R. 3446 Prairie av.
Anderson David, 4311 Ellis av.
Anderson David R. 2766 N. Lincoln
Anderson David S. 1478 Graceland av.
Anderson Eugene D. 3806 Forest av.
Anderson E. B. 4057 Prairie av.
Anderson E. F. Mrs. 320 Superior
Anderson F. C. Mrs. Hotel Del-Prado
Anderson F. R. Mrs. 3449 Prairie av.
Anderson Galusha Prof. Morgan Park
Anderson George, 2478 N. Hermitage av
Anderson George H. Berwyn
Anderson George W. 3540 Calumet av.
Anderson Hans L. 98 Fowler
Anderson Harriet Mrs. 3640 Prairie av.
Anderson Harry N. 4435 Lake av.
Anderson Hervey H. 2665 N. Paulina
Anderson Horace G. Dr. 128 W. 67th
Anderson H. A. 2478 N. Hermitage av.
Anderson Isaac, 6335 Kimbark av.
Anderson John, 646 Cleveland av.
Anderson John G. 237 Wilson av.
Anderson John N. 238 Lincoln Park boul.
Anderson Joseph, Morgan Park
Anderson Lewis H. Prof. 4411 Prairie av.
Anderson Maria Miss, Evanston
Anderson Mary M. Miss, 320 Superior
Anderson M. Mrs. 2412 Prairie av.
Anderson Nils, 5854 Rosalie ct.
Anderson Peter, 695 Burling
Anderson Sarah B. Miss, Morgan Park
Anderson Sarah C. Mrs. 4748 Evans av.
Anderson Sebastian Mrs. 515 Lasalle av.
Anderson Theresa M. Miss, 1478 Grace-
   land av.
Anderson Walter Carroll, 5821 Madison
   av. *C.A.*
Anderson Warren J. 692 W. Adams

Anderson William B. Gen. 1084 Early av.
Anderson William G.515 Lasalle av. *C.A.*
Anderson Wm. H. 618 Washington boul.
Anderson William S. 6639 Lafayette av.
Anderson W. D. S. 330 Oakwood boul.
Anderson W. S. L. Lake Forest
Andrew Ed. Mrs. Austin
Andrew Edward, Austin
Andrew F. A. Glencoe
Andrew George L. 6123 Kimbark av.
Andrew George W. Evanston
Andrew Lester, Austin
Andrew William D. Austin
Andrews Albert H. Dr. 584 Fullerton av.
Andrews Alfred H. Lombard
Andrews Carlos S. 2614 N. Hermitage av.
Andrews Charles A. 780 North Park av.
Andrews C.W.Virginia hotel. *Un.,Univ.*
Andrews Edmund Dr. 3912 Lake av.
Andrews Edward, Berwyn
Andrews Edward W. 4403 Oakenwald av.
  C.A.
Andrews Emory C. 5339 Madison av.
Andrews E. Benj. Dr. Virginia hotel
Andrews E. M. Mrs. Hyde Park hotel
Andrews E. Wyllys Dr. 2623 Prairie av.
  Univ.
Andrews FrankT.Dr. 4589 Oakenwald av,
  Univ.
Andrews Herbert L. 267 Michigan av.
Andrews H. G. 5234 Woodlawn av.
Andrews Irene F. Mrs. 2247 Michigan av.
Andrews James, 1425 Montana
Andrews James P. 1425 Montana
Andrews James S. Riverside
Andrews James W. 2614 N.Hermitage av.
Andrews Jay A. 815 Washington bcul.
Andrews John D. Dr. 334 Hampden ct.
Andrews John W. 943. 72d pl.
Andrews J. D. Oak Park
Andrews J. H. Calumet club. *Univ.*
Andrews J. Roy, 2614 N. Hermitage av.
Andrews Mamie Miss. 5723 Monroe av.
Andrews Margaret L. Mrs. 2709 Michigan
  av.
Andrews Martin, 742 Winthrop av.
Andrews Mary L. Mrs. 640 W. Monroe
Andrews Sarah A. Mrs. 5168 Michigan av.
Andrews Sarah R. Mrs. Hinsdale
Andrews Sarah W. Dr. 319 Bowen av
Andrews Sidney F. 120 Lincoln Park boul.
Andrews Stuart B. 1911 Michigan av.
Andrews Theodore F. 5339 Madison av.
Andrews Walter S. Chicago club
Andrews Wells Dr. 815 Washington boul,
Andrews Wilber J. Berwyn
Andrews W. B. Palmer House. *W.P.*
Androvette George E. Greenwood Inn,
  Evanston
Andrus Frank B. Capt. Fort Sheridan
Andrus Fred H. 4738 Woodlawn av. *C.A.*
Andrus William H. 27 Wisconsin
Andrus W. C. Mrs. 27 Wisconsin
Anerson Eli, Oak Park
Angel Harry A. Oak Park
Angell Edward F. 2733 N. Paulina

Angell Henry L. 2591 Kenmore av.
Angell James R. 5825 Kimbark av.
Angell Katharine Dr. 3745 Indiana av.
Angell William A. 131 Astor. *U.L.*
Angsten Philip, 672, 48th
Anguish Benjamin D. Evanston
Angus James, 3225 Rhodes av.
Angus John, 3213 Michigan av. *U.L.*
  Sum. res. Hartland, Wis.
Anson Adrian C. 160, 30th
Antes Charles H. 1320 Morse av. *Un.*
Antes Katherine M. Miss, 1320 Morse av.
Antes William S. 1147 Lunt av.
Anthony Alfred W. Berwyn
Anthony C. E. Evanston
Anthony George D. 59 Walton pl.
  Winter res. Pasadena, Cal.
Anthony Henry G. Dr. 465 Dearborn av.
Anthony J. M. 3601 Vincennes av.
Anthony Walter M. Evanston
Antisdel Albert, 66 Bellevue pl. *Chi.*
Antoine Charles, 5338 Greenwood av.
Anwander Charles, 1510 Wolfram
Apfel Arthur H. 864 Hamilton ct.
Apfel Philip, 486 Garfield av.
Aplin Frank A. Evanston
Apmadoc Maurice P. Dr. 4733 Prairie av.
Apmadoc William, 4733 Prairie av.
Apmadoc W. T. 4733 Prairie av.
Appel Henry, 5010 Michigan av.
Appleman J. S. Dr. Lexington hotel
Appleton Ernest, Berwyn
Appleton John G. M. Berwyn
Arbuckle Alphonso T. Dr. 4924 Green-
  wood av.
Archer I. J. Dr. Berwyn
Archer James L. 4324 Greenwood av. *U.
  L.*
Archibald Frank B. 553 Dearborn av.
Archibald George N. 506 W. Adams
Archibald Thos. E. 215 S. Hoyne av.
Armbruster Ferdinand P. Oak Park
Armour George L. 493 W. Jackson boul.
Armour James A. Lakota hotel
Armour J.Ogden, 3724 Michigan av. *Cal.,
  Chi.,C.A.,W.P.*
  Sum. res. Oconomowoc, Wis.
Armour M. Cochrane, Evanston
Armour Philip D. 2115 Prairie av. *Cal.,
  Chi,.C.A.,U.L.*
Armour Philip D. jr. 3700 Michigan av.
  Cal.,Chi.,C.A.,W.P.
  Sum. res. Oconomowoc, Wis.
Armour William S. 4926 Champlain av.
ArmsCharlesH.Mrs. 5410Washington av.
Arms Frank D. 41 Aldine sq.
Arms Harrison, 2243 Michigan av. *W.P.*
Arms Herbert C. 5410 Washington av.
Arms May W. Mrs. 41 Aldine sq.
Arms William A. 348 Belden av.
Armsby E. R. Evanston
Armsby George N. Evanston
Armsby Gordon, Evanston
Armsby James K. Mrs. Evanston
Armsby James K. jr. Evanston. *C.A.*
Armstrong Charles G. 4364 Oakenwald av.

Armstrong Charles M. The Kenwood
Armstrong Clyde D. 6735 Lafayette av.
Armstrong Edwin A. 15 Plaisance ct.
Armstrong Edwin R. T. Evanston
Armstrong F. H. 301 Schiller. *U.L.*
Armstrong H. A. Maywood
Armstrong James E. 529 W. 62d
Armstrong John B. Dr. 16 Waverly ct.
Armstrong John J. 85 Lincoln av.
Armstrong John M. 85 Lincoln av.
Armstrong J. C. Rev. 743 W. Harrison
Armstrong Mary Stuart, Auditorium
  . ~ hotel
Arnd Charles, Evanston. *C.A.*
Arnd Frederick, Evanston
Arnd Louise Miss, Evanston
Arndt George E. 4726 Kenwood av.
Arndt John, Wilmette
Arneson Nels, 672 N. Hoyne av.
Arnheim Benjamin, 3744 Michigan av.
  Stan.
Arnold Allan M. 326 Superior
Arnold Alvan H. 78 Throop. *Ill.*
Arnold Andrew H. 220 S. Irving av.
Arnold Bion J. 4128 Prairie av. *U.L.*
Arnold Charles C. Winnetka
Arnold Daniel A. 904 S. Kedzie av.
Arnold David O. 39, 22d
Arnold E. W. 55, 33d
Arnold Frederick A. 219 S. Marshfield av.
  C.A.,U.L.
Arnold Harry L. 326 Superior
Arnold Herman, 1826 Wellington
Arnold I   c N. Mrs. 104 Lincoln Park
  boul.saa
Arnold James M. Lakota hotel
Arnold John Bertley 2937 Michigan av.
Arnold Joseph K. Rev. 898 Warren av.
Arnold J. G. Chicago Beach hotel
Arnold Llewellyn W. LaGrange
Arnold N. D. Mrs. 6352 Monroe av.
Arnold R. B. 751 W. Adams
Arnold R. G. 4128 Prairie av.
Arnold Theodore, 1920 Surf
Arnold Walter C. Auditorium annex.
  Stan.
Arnold William J. Dr. 6759 Parnell av.
Arnold W. L. 4128 Prairie av.
Arnstein Eugene, 3326 Wabash av. *Stan.*
Aron Jacob, 3537 Grand boul.
Arter Francis G. Dr. 143 W. Garfield boul.
Arth H. W. Rev. Lakeside
Arthur James A. Wilmette
Arthur William H. 1335 Fulton
Artingstall Samuel G. 13 S. Hamilton av.
  Ill.
Artz V. T. Miss, Hotel Metropole
Asay William C. 85, 47th
Ascher Adolph, 454 Orchard
Ascher Fred, 1509 Wellington
Ascher Martin, 495 Lasalle av.
Ascher Theodore, 495 Lasalle av.
Ash I. N. Mrs. 221, 47th
Ash Levi H. 148, 46th. *C.A.*
Ash Maurice L. 399 Bowen av. *Lksd.*
Ash Michael, 399 Bowen av.

Ashby G. W. Berwyn
Ashby James H. 361 Oakwood boul. *W.P.*
Ashcraft Edwin M. 6046 Kimbark av.
Ashcraft Raymond S. M. 6046 Kimbark
  av.
Ashleman John, Oak Park
Ashleman Laura Mrs. Oak Park
Ashleman Paul, Oak Park.
Ashley Albert B. LaGrange
Ashton Gertrude E. Miss, 3243 Grove-
  land av.
Ashton Harry L. 5315 Washington av. *C.A.*
Aspden T. Fred, LaGrange
Aspden William, LaGrange
Aspenwall Prudence Mrs. Austin
Aspern Harry T. 1524 Kenmore av.
Aspinwall M. H. Dr. Oak Park
Atchinson Hugh Rev. Wilmette
Atchison James A. Dr. 758 S. Kedzie av.
Atchison John D. 758 S. Kedzie av.
Atchison Nathaniel, 758 S. Kedzie av.
Atherton A. E. The Arizona
Atherton Frank S. 678 Washington
  boul.
Atkin Ferdinand S. Edgebrook
Atkin Godfrey Harold, 5004 Washington
  av. *C.A.*
Atkins F. L. Mrs. 316 Lasalle av.
Atkins George J. 2725 N. Winchester av.
  C.A.
Atkinson Arthur R. Evanston
Atkinson Charles T. 4835 Lake av.
Atkinson Edward, 1056 Washington boul.
Atkinson Edward jr. 1056 Washington
  boul.
Atkinson Frank H. 5488 East End av.
Atkinson Frank H. jr. 5488 East End av.
Atkinson George W. P. Evanston
Atkinson G. Clarence, Evanston
Atkinson John A. 4906 Washington av.
  C.A.
Atkinson Reginald, Evanston
Atterbury Charles M. 614 W. 66th
Atterbury George S. The Renfost
Attley James M. Austin
Attridge James W. Oak Park
Attridge Samuel D. Oak Park
Atwater A. J. Morgan Park
Atwater Walter H. 3957 Ellis av.
Atwell Charles B. Prof. Evanston
Atwood Eugene S. Dr. 339 W. Adams
Atwood Frederick G. 6321 Monroe av.
Atwood F. M. 4921 Madison av.
Atwood George C. 6321 Monroe av.
Atwood James H. 6362 Minerva av.
Atwood Lovina M. Mrs. 3416 Michigan av.
Atwood Martha M. Mrs. 6321 Monroe av.
Atwood Myron W. 4324 Ellis av.
Atwood Roger W. 640 W. 62d
Atwood William H, Mrs. 4124 Grand
  boul.
Auer Henry A. Mrs. 4546 Vincennes av.
Auer Philip A. 3739 Indiana av.
Auerbach Benjamin, 4039 Indiana av.
  Lksd.
Auerbach H. Mrs. 3148 Prairie av.

Auerbach Jacob C. 4321 Prairie av. *Lksd.*
Augur Walter W. 401 Ontario. *Univ.*
Augustus Albert A. Edgebrook
Auld John M. Dr. 714 W. Monroe
Auld Ralph, 714 W. Monroe
Auning H. M. Chicago Beach hotel
Austen Annie L. Miss, 3017 South Park
av.
Austermell Lewis W. 420, 42d
Austin Alexander, Oak Park
Austin B. N. Hotel Windermere
Austin Charles E. Dr. 6422 Minerva av.
Austin C. W. 352 Warren av.
Austin Frederick C. 49 Bellevue pl. *Cal.
Chi., C.A., W.P.*
Austin Harry W. Oak Park
Austin J. Almon, 1628 Cornelia av.
Austin LeBaron L. 183 Cass
Sum. res. Plymouth, Mass
Austin M. B. Oak Park
Austin R. H. Lakota hotel
Austin William, 4514 St. Lawrence av.
Austin William H. 950 W. Monroe
Austrian Alfred S.3129 Michigan av.*Stan.*
Austrian Harvey S. 3129 Michigan av.
Austrian Joseph, 2954 Michigan av.*Stan.*
Austrian Julia R. Mrs. 3129 Michigan av.
Auten Aaron O. Evanston
Auten Gustavus W. 677, 48th pl. *C.A.*
Auten Phillip L. 314 Ashland boul. *Ill.,
Un.*
Averell Albert J. Mrs. 2018 Michigan av.
Avers Franklin G. 4538 Forestville av.
Avers Herbert M. Riverside
Avery Cyrus M. 2653 Evanston av.
Avery Daniel J. 512 W. Adams. *Ill., U.L.*
Avery Frank M. 2123 Prairie av. *Cal.,
Chi., C.A., Ill., W.P.*
Avery John H. Mrs. 28 Walton pl.
Avery J. Dixon, 1 Groveland Park
Avery Phoebe A. Mrs. 2239 Michigan av.
Avery Samuel J. Dr. 780 Walnut
Avery Thomas M. 2123 Prairie av. *Cal.*
Avy Sara C. Mrs. 3339 Vernon av.
Axtell J. L. Miss, Lake Forest
Axtman William F. 6531 Lafayette av.
Ayars Charles G. Avenue house, Evans-
ton
Ayars Charles R. Evanston
Ayars Harry M. Wilmette
Ayer Benjamin F. 99 Lincoln Park boul.
Chi.
Ayer Edward E. 1 Banks. *Chi.*
Sum. res. "The Oaks" Lake Geneva,
Wis.
Ayer Walter, 99 Lincoln Park boul.
Ayers B. F. 1574 W. Monroe
Ayers Charles B. Oak Park
Ayers Frank D. 3916 Calumet av.
Ayers Mary A. Mrs. 227 Ontario
Ayers Samuel, 4316 Prairie av,
Ayers Seymour W. 3916 Calumet av.
Aykroyd George M. 3523 Ellis av.
Ayling Alice Miss, 5425 Washington av.
Ayres Anson, Mrs. Hinsdale
Ayres Edgar, Morgan Park

Ayres Frank E. Hinsdale
Ayres George L. 1603 W. Adams
Ayres Harry Melville 3159 Indiana av.
Ayres Laura D. Mrs. 537 W.Jackson boul

BAADE HENRY, 460 Orchard
Babbitt Benton H. 1141 Lunt av.
Babbitt Clarence M. LaGrange
Babbitt Lewis, Evanston
Babcock Campbell E. 616 The Plaza. *Un.*
Babcock Charles F.2701 Michigan av. *Irq.*
Babcock C. M. LaGrange
Babcock D. W. 4405 Prairie av.
Babcock Elmer E.,M.D. 3239 Indiana av.
Babcock Fred R. Virginia hotel. *C.A.,
Un.,U.L., W.P.*
Babcock Henry H. Kenilworth
Babcock John N. Mrs. Morgan Park
Babcock Lucinda Mrs. 3121 Indiana av.
Babcock Maria W. Mrs. 496 W. Monroe
Babcock Mary Keyes Mrs. Kenilworth
Babcock Orville E. 616 The Plaza. *Un.,
Univ.*
Babcock O. E. Mrs. 616 The Plaza.
Babcock R. H., M.D. 466 Dearborn av.
Univ.
·Babcock W. E. 1529 W. Monroe
Sum. res. Edgerton, Wis.
Babcock W. I. 35 E. Pearson. *Chi.*
Bach Emanuel, 3545 Ellis av. *Stan.*
Bacheldor E. A. Lexington hotel. *Cal.
.U.L., W.P.*
Bachmann Sigmund, 4341 Calumet av.
Lksd.
Bachrach Charles, 3632 Prairie av.
Bachrach Isidor, 529 Lasalle av.
Back Joseph, 419 Cleveland av.
Backman W. Wallace, 634 Englewood av.
Backus EmilieMrs.1332Washington boul.
Bacon Bayard T. 5326 Cornell av.
Bacon Charles B. Mrs. 4830 Langley av.
Bacon Charles S. Dr. 426 Center
Bacon DeWitt C., D.D.S. 281 Lincoln av.
Bacon Edward R. 1908 Briar pl.
Bacon E. B. 596 Cleveland av.
Bacon Francis T. 3608 Lake av.
Bacon Gordon E. 596 Cleveland av.
Bacon Henry Martyn, 4614 Lake av. *U.L.*
Bacon Joseph B. Dr. 4125 Drexel boul.
Bacon Marie Thompson, D. D. S. 281
Lincoln av.
Bacon Martin W. Dr. 6817 Wentworth av.
Bacon Moses S. 1910 Briar pl.
Bacon Nathaniel, 4634 Indiana av.
Bacon R. T. Mrs. 5516 Jefferson av.
Bacon W. O. 6218 Greenwood av.
Badenoch Charles H. 7156 Harvard av.
Badenoch George, 7156 Harvard av.
Badenoch John J. 391 W.Randolph . *Ill.,
U.L.*
Badenoch Joseph, 7156 Harvard av.
Badenoch R. N. 7156 Harvard av.
Bader Charles A. Berwyn
Badger Ada C. Miss, 2106 Calumet av.
Badger Alpheus C. 2106 Calumet av.
Badger A. Shreve, 51 Delaware pl. *Cal.*

Badger Carlton S. Riverside
Badger C. W. Hyde Park hotel
Badger Edward, Riverside
Badger Harry A. Riverside
Badger Horace H. Riverside
Badger Sheridan S, 2106 Calumet av.
Badt Francis B. 6506 Lafayette av. *U.L.*
Baer A. W. Dr. 343 Michigan av.
Baer Camille Miss, 579, 45th pl.
Baer Joseph, 3335 Vernon av.
Baer Louis, 573 LaSalle av.
Baer Sol, 573 LaSalle av.
Bagg F. S. 3764 Lake av.
Baggot Edward, 4354 Grand boul.
Baggot James E. 442 Ashland boul.
Baggot James E. 4103 Vincennes av.
Bagley Albert G. Austin
    Sum. res. Old Orchard Beach, Maine.
Bagley Frederick P. 2227 Prairie av. *U.L.*
Bagley John, 354, 41st
Bailey Brunot, River Forest
Bailey Edward P. 112 Astor. *U.L.*
Bailey Edward W. 23 Oakwood av.
Bailey Elizabeth Mrs. 2808 Prairie av.
Bailey E. M. Miss, North Shore Hotel
Bailey E. Stillman Dr. 6222 Woodlawn av.
Bailey George C. 5224 Jefferson av.
Bailey George W. 1072 W. Polk
Bailey H. E. New Hotel Holland
Bailey J. G. LaGrange
Bailey L. E. Oak Park
Bailey O. L. Oak Park
Bailey Samuel G. Dr. 83 Bryant av.
Bailey Sarah Mrs. Evanston
Bailey Sterling L. 569, 51st
Bailey Theodore P. 4567 Lake av. *C.A.*
Bailey William C. Hotel Metropole
Bailey W. E. 3806 Ellis av.
Bailhache A. L. 3523 Ellis av.
Bain Foree, LaGrange
Bain Lewis R. 491 W. Congress
Bainbridge August H. Lieut. Col. Fort
    Sheridan
Baines Ida Mrs. 420 Center
Baird C. A. Norwood Park
Baird Edward P. Evanston
Baird Elizabeth H. Miss, 307 N. Clark
Baird Frank E. 293 Warren av.
Baird Frank T. Virginia hotel
    Sum. res. Aurora, Ill.
Baird James, 6222 Monroe av.
Baird J. Mrs. 6222 Monroe av.
Baird Lyman, 307 N. Clark. *U.L.*
Baird Mary Mrs. 293 Warren av.
Baird Max, 307 N. Clark. *Univ.*
Baird M. Mrs. 32 Woodland Park
Baird Robert Prof. Evanston
    Sum. res. Spring Lake. Mich.
Baird Wyllys W. 1915 Wellington. *U.L.*
Bak H., M.D. 3407 Vernon av.
Baker Alfred Landon, 2641 Prairie av.
    Cal., Chi., C.A., U.L., Univ.
    Sum. res. Lake Forest
Baker Arthur G. 4326 Prairie av.
Baker Benjamin F. 836 W. Adams
Baker Caroline J. Mrs. 7334 Bond av.

Baker Charles jr. 7737 Emerald av.
Baker Charles E. 7737 Emerald av.
Baker Charles H. Highland Park
Baker Charles W. 7157 Princeton av.
Baker C. A. Miss, 1610 Indiana av.
Baker C. Edward, 3350 Indiana av.
Baker C. M. Chicago Beach hotel
Baker David, 5748 Kimbark av.
Baker David J. Judge, 5517 Cornell av.
Baker Digory W. 713 W. Adams
Baker Edward F. Dr. Evanston
Baker Edwin R. 4460 Oakenwald av.
Baker Ellen J. Mrs. 699 W. Monroe
Baker Eugene, 840 Flournoy
Baker E. Darwin, Hinsdale
Baker E. O. Austin
Baker E. P. 3865 Lake av.
Baker Frank Judge, 3543 Lake av.
Baker Frank E. Chicago Club
    Sum. res. Lake Forest
Baker Frank H. 206, 46th. *U.L.*
Baker Frank R. 4259 Grand boul.
Baker Fredrica Dr. 2601 N. Paulina
Baker F. E. Miss 4839 Kenwood av.
Baker George, Winnetka
Baker George A. 6324 Yale
Baker George R. 837 N. Clark
Baker George S. Evanston
Baker Griffin, Ravinia
Baker Henry, LaGrange
Baker Henry D. 2255 Michigan av. *Univ*
Baker Horace, 4433 Berkeley av.
Baker H. C. 3416 South Park av.
Baker H. D. Evanston
Baker H. M. Park Ridge
Baker H. W. Granada hotel. *Irq.*
Baker James E. 205, 53d
Baker James R. 3995 Ellis av. *C.A.*
Baker John M. Oak Park
Baker John W. 5517 Cornell av.
Baker J. A. Hotel Metropole
Baker J. W. Dr. Hotel DelPrado
Baker Leander H. Dr. Oak Park
Baker Milton H. jr. Highland Park
Baker Moses, 4410 Ellis av.
Baker M. H. Mrs. Highland Park
Baker Robert A. 23 Waverly ct.
Baker Robert R. 713 W. Adams
Baker R. H. Mrs. 3150 Michigan av.
Baker Samuel, 3995 Ellis av. *U.L.*
Baker Samuel E. River Forest
Baker Stephen Maj. Fort Sheridan
Baker S. S. Dr. 901 W. Jackson boul.
Baker William Edgar, 560 Dearborn av.
Baker William E. 836 W. Adams
Baker William H. 184 S. Central Park av.
    Ill.
Baker William M. 216, 33d
Baker William M. Mrs. 3518 Calumet av.
Baker William S. 6557 Perry av.
Baker William T. 2255 Michigan av. *Cal..
    Ch'. Irq., W.P.*
Baker Wilson G. 2227 Washington boul.
Baker W. Vincent, 2125 Calumet av. *Cal.
    Ch'., W.P.*
Bald Adam G. 2757 N. Ashland av.

Baldwin Abbott, 715 Walnut
Baldwin Abraham, 47 Woodland Park
Baldwin A. D. 2358 Indiana av.
Baldwin A. E. Dr. 828 W. Adams
Baldwin A. F. Mrs. 3849 Michigan av.
Baldwin A. K. Hotel Windermere. *C.A.*
Baldwin Benson D. Evanston
Baldwin Charles F. 205, 46th
Baldwin Charles Handy, 298 Ohio
            Sum. res. Elmhurst
Baldwin C. C. Berwyn
Baldwin C. H. 267 Park av.
Baldwin David S. Oak Park
Baldwin Elbert D. 4049 Ellis av.
Baldwin Elmer E. 3325 Indiana av.
Baldwin Frederick R. 3078 Irving av.
Baldwin F. H. Mrs. 4049 Ellis av.
Baldwin George F, 2429 Michigan av.
   Cal., C.A.
Baldwin Harry H. 3852 Lake av.
Baldwin Henry R. 1124 Washington boul.
   C.A.
Baldwin James A. 4101 Calumet av.
Baldwin Jesse A. Oak Park. *U.L.*
Baldwin John A. 3852 Lake av.
         Sum. res. Pine Lake, Ind.
Baldwin Julia C. Miss, 3217 Groveland av.
Baldwin J. H. 5540 Washington av.
Baldwin Lauris Blake Dr. 4827 Madison
   av. *W.P.*
Baldwin Lemuel, 664 W. Madison. *Ill.*
Baldwin L. Jerome Mrs. 38 Pine Grove av.
Baldwin Mary Mrs. 2358 Indiana av.
Baldwin Merchant Lieut. 4049 Ellis av.
Baldwin T. C. 385 Warren av.
Baldwin Walter H. 64 Bryant av.
Baldwin William, 207 Warren av.
Baldwin Willis M. 3849 Michigan av.
   C.A., U.L., W.P.
Balfour Alexander, Evanston
Balfour Harry, Riverside
Balfour John, Riverside
Balfour Walter E. Riverside
Balhatchett T. J. Dr. 260, 53d
Balkwill J. F. 201 Park av.
Ball Charles H. 5214 Hibbard av.
Ball David M. Norwood Park
Ball Edward H. Evanston
Ball Farlin H. Oak Park
Ball Farlin O. Judge, Oak Park
Ball Fred, Edison Park
Ball George C. 5211 Kimbark av. *Chi.*
Ball Godfrey H. 4028 Lake av.
Ball Hobart E. 210 Park av.
Ball James M. 4628 Ellis av.
Ball John A. 6643 Stewart av.
Ball Joseph L. Highland Park
Ball L. Curtis, 4717 Champlain av.
Ball M. A. Mrs. 5428 Madison av.
Ball Woodruff. 5211 Kimbark av.
Ball W. N. 374 Dearborn av.
Ballagh James H. The Renfost
Ballagh Lillian Mrs. The Renfost
Ballard Addison, 241, 53d
Ballard Charles D. Mrs 5338 Madison av.
Ballard Charles K. Oak Park.

Ballard Charles M. Dr. 243 S. Leavitt
Ballard Charles N. Dr. 402 S. Paulina
Ballard DeWitt P. 4550 Ellis av. *Cal.*
Ballard Frank E. Oak Park
Ballard George S. 3642 Prairie av.
Ballard M. E. Mrs. 6513 Woodlawn av.
Ballard Orville W. 3642 Prairie av.
Ballard Thomas P. Evanston. *U.L.*
Ballard T. C. 5340 Madison av.
Ballard W. P. Maywood
Ballenberg Abraham A. 3650 Grand boul.
   Stan.
Ballenberg Jules, 4142 Grand boul. *Stan.*
Ballenberg Yette Mrs. 4142 Grand boul.
Ballenger William L. Dr. Evanston
Ballin Joseph, 4512 Drexel boul. *Stan.*
Ballinger Leon D. 611 W. 67th
Ballinger Libanus, 611 W. 67th
Ballou A. E. New Hotel Holland
Ballou George H. Mrs. 5831 Monroe av.
Balmer A. L. 748 Fullerton av.
Balmer Thomas, 1327 Hollywood av.
Balthis L. A. 1233 Sheridan rd.
Baltz Charles, 1543 W. Monroe
Bamant W. N. LaGrange
Bamberger Alice Miss, 4156 Wabash av.
Bamberger Gabriel Prof. 4156 Wabash av.
Bancroft Edgar A. 64 Cedar. *U.L.*
Bancroft George, Evanston
Band Edward C. 1232 Wrightwood av.
Bane Levi B. 3147 Calumet av.
Bane Oscar F. Auditorium hotel. *C.A.,*
   U.L., W.P.
Banga Emily Miss, 456 Lasalle av.
Banga H., M.D. 456 Lasalle av.
Bangs Dean Mrs. 386 Ellis av.
Bangs Edward W. 396 N. State. *Chi.*
Bangs Fred A. 143 S. Hoyne av.
Bangs Harrie L. 3861 Ellis av.
Bangs John D. 3861 Ellis av.
Bangs William B. 569 Warren av.
Banker Edward H. 3409 Forest av.
Banks A. F. Oak Park. *C.A., U.L.*
Banks C. E. Mrs. 286, 42d
Banks Grace Miss, Evanston
Banks James M. 245 S. Leavitt
Banks J. C. LaGrange
Banks J. N. Dr. 2415 Michigan av.
Bannard Henry C. 410 N. State. *Chi.*
Banning Ephraim, 685 Washington boul.
   Ill., U.L.
Banning Thomas A. 5610 Madison av.
   U.L.
Bannister Henry M. Dr. Evanston
Banta Cornelius V. jr. 4407 Ellis av.
Banzet George T. Dr. 5029 Jefferson av.
Barbe Martin, 3153 Prairie av. *Lksd.*
Barbe Morris, 367 Oakwood boul.
Barbeau James T. Oak Park
Barber Albert H. 22 Bryant av.
         Sum. res. Macatawa Park, Mich.
Barber A. M. 235 Michigan av.
Barber Charles F. 912 Chase av.
Barber E. L. 2956 Groveland av.
Barber Fannie Miss, North Shore hotel
Barber F. A., M.D. 6207 Woodlawn av.

Barber G. M. North Shore hotel
Barber Henry N. Mrs. 1307 W. Adams
Barber Hiram, 140 Lincoln-av.
Barber John O. 1318 Wellington
Barber Louis M. 184, 41st
Barber Ohio C. Lakota hotel. *Cal.*, *Chi.*,
  W.P.
Barber William, 537 W. Jackson boul.
Barbour Frank, Chicago Beach hotel. *C.A.*
Barbour Lyman L. Mrs. 126, 50th.
Barbour William T. River Forest
Barclay R. A. Mrs. 3653 Grand boul.
Barclay Selwyn J. 6436 Ingleside av.
Barclay William A. Dr. 1231 W. Adams
Bard Charles W. 1102 Washington boul.
Bard David J. 12 Bryant av.
Barden H. O. The Arizona
Bardill Florence B. Miss, Oak Park
Bardwell Orsamus H. 4733 Champlain av.
  C.A.
Barfield W. G. Oak Park
Barge Albert, Berwyn
Barger Marion F. 4000 Lake av.
Barger Richard W. 4052 Grand boul.
Barhydt Frank, Evanston
Barker Agnes Mrs. 415 Lasalle av.
Barker Alfred, Austin
Barker Charles A. 7149 Euclid av.
Barker Charles E. 622 Washington boul.
Barker Clyde, 415 Lasalle av.
Barker Cyrus A. 3946 Lake av.
Barker C. F. Dr. The Winamac
Barker David E. Mrs. Evanston
Barker David N. Evanston. *U.L.*
Barker Frank W. 4633 Greenwood av.
Barker Geo. F. 622 Washington boul.
Barker John C. Mrs. 717 Fullerton av.
Barker John R. 2421 Indiana av.
Barker John S. Evanston
Barker John T. Evanston
Barker Joseph N. 5000 Greenwood av.
Barker Maurice P. 5607 Washington av.
Barker Milton R. Dr. 4625 Greenwood av.
Barker Olcott B. Oak Park
Barker Reuben Ludlam, 6036 Monroe av.
Barker R. Alice Miss, Evanston
Barker S. B. Mrs. Hotel Metropole
Barker Wallace C. Mrs. 3353 Wabash av
Barker Walter A. 161, 25th
Barkey Frank P. 6448 Harvard av.
Barler Augustus C. 1538 Sheridan rd. *C.A.*
Barlow Catherine N. Mrs. Evanston
Barlow Elizabeth H. Miss, 181 Dearborn
  av.
Barlow L. N. Dr. 3010 Vernon av.
Barlow Napoleon B. Evanston
Barlow Robert, 754 W. Monroe
Barmore Nathaniel L. 4837 Kimbark av.
Barnard Albert E. 229 S. Lincoln
Barnard Alice L. Miss, Tracy
Barnard A. Wayne, 9 Roslyn pl.
Barnard Charles J. River Forest
Barnard Cornelius R. Evanston
Barnard Daniel, Tracy
Barnard Daniel E. Tracy
Barnard Elizabeth Miss, Tracy

Barnard Erastus A. Tracy
Barnard Eugene E. Evanston
Barnard E. C. 229 S. Lincoln
Barnard Frank A. 1300 Wilcox av.
Barnard Frank E. 3982 Ellis av.
Barnard F. G. Oak Park
Barnard George, 196 Cass
Barnard Gilbert W, 3012 Indiana av.
Barnard Harry, 3243 Rhodes av.
Barnard Hayden S. Dr. 4031 Vincennes av
Barnard James E. 50 Oakwood av.
Barnard James H. Chicago Athletic assn.
Barnard Louisa C. Mrs. 159 Cass
Barnard Nelson T. The Hampden
Barnard Richard, 162, 36th
Barnard R. H. Mrs. 5324 Jefferson av.
Barnard Will F. Oak Park
Barnes Albert C. 198, 50th
Barnes Albert R, Evanston. *U.L.*
Barnes Burdette C. 109 Pine Grove av
Barnes Carl L. Dr. 576 Lasalle av.
Barnes Charles, 642 Sedgwick
Barnes Charles J. Auditorium Annex.
  Cal., *Chi.*, *W.P.*
Barnes Charles M. 3617 Prairie av.
Barnes Charles O. 2219 Sheridan rd.
Barnes Charles R. Prof. 5733 Monroe av.
  Sum. res. Madison, Wis.
Barnes Charles T. Dr. 276 Michigan av.
Barnes Charles T. 1622 W. Adams
Barnes C. W. Chicago Beach hotel
Barnes David Leonard Mrs. 171 Rush
Barnes Don J. 425 W. Garfield boul.
Barnes Francis A. 928 W. Jackson boul.
Barnes Francis W. Wilmette
Barnes Frank J. 4337 Grand boul.
Barnes Frederick M. 7554 Bond av.
Barnes F. G. 608 Dearborn av.
Barnes James M. Evanston
Barnes John D. Morgan Park
Barnes J. S. Mrs. 608 Dearborn av.
Barnes J. S. Mrs. 6331 Parnell av.
Barnes Minnie W. Miss. 584 Dearborn av.
Barnes Nelson H. Mrs. 584 Dearborn av.
Barnes Nelson L. Auditorium Annex
  Chi.
Barnes Noah Mrs. 5046 Jefferson av.
Barnes Walter S. Dr. 3000 Michigan av.
Barnes William H. 2219 Sheridan rd.
Barnes William R. 49 St. James pl.
Barnet A. A. 515, 62d
Barnet Henry, 3600 Prairie av.
Barnet Henry L. 6156 Lexington av.
Barnet Henry L. jr. 6156 Lexington av.
Barnet James B. 1923 Deming ct.
Barnet Jesse Weil, 3600 Prairie av. *Lksd.*
Barnet W. Y. 6430 Woodlawn av.
Barnett George W. 1578 Lill av.
Barnett John H. 296 Ohio
Barnett Joseph H. Austin
Barnett Otto, Glencoe
Barney Bruce B. 2628 Prairie av.
Barney B. B. Mrs. 2628 Prairie av.
Barney Martin V. 7817 Winneconne av.
Barnhart Arthur M. Chicago Beach hotel.
  C.A., *Irq.*, *U.L.*

Barnhart A. E. 505 W. Jackson boul.
Barnhart F. B. Miss, Chicago Beach hotel
Barnhart Kenneth, 5739 Washington av.
Barnhart Marvin E. 381 Superior
Barnhart Mary Mrs. 471 Washington boul.
Barnhart O. A. 4421 Greenwood av.
Barnhart Warren, 577½ Lasalle av.
Barnhart Wm. J. 6203 Woodlawn av.
Barnheisel Charles H. 4400 Grand boul.
Barnheisel Frederick R. 4400 Grand boul.
Barnheisel Henrietta Mrs. 4400 Grand boul.
Barnickol Ferdinand, 2613 N. Hermitage av.
Barnum Albert W. Riverside
Barnum E. S. 245 Oakwood boul.
Barnum J. L. 6016 Kimbark av.
Barnum O. H. 225 Dearborn av.
Barnum Samuel, 245 Oakwood boul.
Barnum W. H. Riverside. Chi., U.L.
Barnum W. L. Lakota hotel. U.L.
Barothy Victor, 2 Oakland crescent
Barquist Charles E. 3119 South Park av.
Barr Alfred E. 1663 W. Adams
Barr C. J. 6037 Monroe av.
Barr Edward L. 642 Pine Grove av.
Barr I. E. 4409 Greenwood av.
Barr Oliver M. River Forest
Barr Thos. F. Col. Chicago Beach hotel
Barr William A. Dr. 1288 W. Adams
Barr William T. Hinsdale
Barratt Edgar G. Kenilworth
Barrell Albert M. 2918 Michigan av.
Barrell F. L. Mrs. 113 Cass
Barrell James, 2918 Michigan av. Chi., W.P.
Barrell J. Finley, 4805 Kimbark av. C.A., W.P.
Barrell Stewart Evans, 3612 Michigan av. C.A., W.P.
Barrett Anthony J. River Forest
Barrett Channing W. Dr. 459 Lasalle av.
Barrett Charles C. Sherman House. Cal.
Barrett Charles R. 51 Lincoln Park boul.
Barrett Charles R. 983 Warren av. Ill.
Barrett Elmer E. Western Springs C.A., U.L.
Barrett Francis M. 1304 Washington boul.
Barrett George D. 4341 St. Lawrence av.
Barrett George K. 3139 Michigan av.
Barrett James P. 4068 Lake av.
Barrett James W. 180, 51st
Barrett John F. River Forest, C.A., W.P.
Barrett John P. Prof. 4400 Michigan av.
Barrett John P. jr. 4400 Michigan av.
Barrett John R. 3230 Calumet av.
Barrett June, 186, 41st
Barrett Marcus L. 4238 Drexel boul. Ill., U.L.
Barrett Oliver S. 2233 Calumet av.
Barrett O. W. 2233 Calumet av. Cal.
Barrett O. W. Mrs. 785 W. Monroe
Barrett Robert D. 109 Lake shore drive

Barrett Robert G. 7232 Vernon av.
Barrett R. Evans, 5209 Hibbard av.
Barrett Saxton S. 3230 Calumet av.
Barrett S. E. 109 Lake Shore drive Chi U.L.
Barrett Thomas E. 2653 N. Paulina
Barrett William H. 339 Ohio
Barrie Mary L. Miss, Evanston
Barringer D. C. 3211 Vernon av.
Barringer Walter M. 3211 Vernon av.
Barrington C. V. 447, 66th, C.A.
Barron Edward H. 6352 Monroe av.
Barron John P. 399 W. Taylor
Barron Mahlon, 6352 Monroe av.
Barron William A. 1559 W. Monroe
Barrow John S. 497 Fullerton av.
Barrows George A. Oak Park
Barrows George G. 7339 Bond av.
Barrows John Henry Rev. 5519 Cornell av. Sum. res. Mackinac Island, Mich.
Barrows R. M., M.D. 6413 Kimbark av.
Barry Charles H. Evanston, U.L.
Barry Edward P. 4330 Greenwood av.
Barry Fred. 4330 Greenwood av.
Barry George, Wilmette
Barry George F. Wilmette
Barry James L. 161 Honore
Barry John, 429 Huron
Barry Joseph K. 760 Washington boul.
Barry Katharine M. Miss, 6600 Yale
Barry L. A. 4526 Prairie av.
Barry Margaret T. Miss, 6600 Yale
Barry P. T. 6600 Yale Summer res. Lake Geneva
Barry Thomas, 420 Superior
Barstow C. F. Dr. Irving Park
Barstow H. D. Irving Park
Barstow Joseph, 571 W. Congress
Barstow M. E. Mrs. 678 Park av.
Bartell C. E. 4214 Prairie av.
Bartelme Adeline T. Miss, 1484 Fulton
Bartelme Alfred E. Austin
Bartelme Ferdinand E. Austin
Bartelme Ferdinand M. Austin
Bartelme George P. 1484 Fulton
Bartelme John H. 774 Larrabee
Bartelme May M. Miss, 1484 Fulton
Bartelme M. Mrs. 774 Larrabee
Bartels Harry A. Evanston
Bartels William H. 738 W. Adams, Ill.
Barth Alexander, 3309 Calumet av. Stan
Barth Lewis L, 292 Ashland boul.
Bartholf Charles S. 1388 Washington boul. Sum. res. Plainfield, Ill.
Bartholf William J. 11 Roslyn pl.
Bartholomay Henry jr. 3300 Michigan av. C.A., Univ.
Bartholomew George F. 5635 Washington av.
Bartholomew Henry J. G. Rev. 498 N. Hoyne av.
Bartholomew James K. Dr. 498 N. Hoyne av.
Bartholomew J. N. Dr. 51 Lincoln av.
Bartholomew Lemuel, 630 W. 61st pl.
Bartleson Charles P. Tremont house

Bartlett A. C. 2720 Prairie av. *Cal.*,*Chi.*,
  U.L. Sum. res. "Floranon," Ashe-
  ville, N. C.
Bartlett Benjamin, 3601 Vincennes av.
  Irq.
Bartlett Charles A. 6735 Perry av.
Bartlett Charles C. 1623 Fulton
Bartlett Charles H. Evanston
Bartlett Charles L. Evanston
Bartlett Charles L. Virginia hotel. *Un.*,
  Univ.
Bartlett Charles T. Evanston
Bartlett Daniel C. Dr. 3301 Vernon av.
Bartlett Earl B. Oak Park. *C.A.*
Bartlett Emily S. Mrs. Evanston
Bartlett Florence D.Miss,2720Prairie av.
Bartlett Florian O. 4406 Grand boul. *W.P.*
Bartlett Frank D. 2720 Prairie av.
Bartlett George B. 4470 Oakenwald av.
Bartlett George F. 4466 Oakenwald av.
Bartlett George F. jr. 4466 Oakenwald av.
  C.A.
Bartlett John A. 6731 Perry av.
Bartlett Joseph F. Rev. Austin
Bartlett Josiah C. 40 Pine Grove av.
Bartlett Lincoln, 7316 Princeton av. *W.P.*
Bartlett Murray A. 463 W. Monroe
Bartlett Norman W. Evanston
Bartlett N. Gray, Prof. 44, 29th pl.
Bartlett Rufus H. Dr. 14 Loomis
Bartlett William H. Evanston. *Chi.*
  U.L., *Univ.*
Bartlett William H. jr. Evanston.
Bartley C. E. 699, 49th
Bartling Henry F. 302 Chicago av.
Bartling Louis, 227 Hampden ct.
Bartling William, 227 Hampden ct.
Barton Enos M. 143, 47th. *Chi.*, *U.L.*
Barton George P. 5307 Lexington av. *Irq.*
  U.L.
Barton Jesse B. Hinsdale
Barton J. K. Mrs. 4333 Greenwood av.
Barton Philip S. 4333 Greenwood av.
Barton William A. 2941 Wabash av.
Basch Joseph, 3132 South Park av. *Stan.*
Bascom Adele Mrs. 376 Warren av.
Bascom Fred. 3612 Ellis av.
Bascom William R. 3612 Ellis av.
Bash Frank S. 141 Dearborn av.
Bass Ann E. Mrs. Evanston
Bass George, 2505 Michigan av. *U.L.*
Bass J e K. Evanston
Bass Perkins B. Evanston
Bassett Arthur J. 7520 Kimbark av.
Bassett Asahel O. Evanston
Bassett Blanche Miss, 1547 N. Halsted
Bassett Charles, Austin
Bassett Charles F. Dr. 20 Aldine sq.
Bassett Charles W. 2663 N. Ashland av.
Bassett C. M. Mrs. 429 Center
Bassett Fletcher S. Mrs. 5208 Kimbark
  av.
Bassett George H. 871 S. Sawyer av.
Bassett George R. Dr. 871 S. Sawyer av.
Bassett George R. S. 3125 Wabash av.
Bassett Howard W. Dr. Oak Park

Bassett James S. 3125 Wabash av.
Bassett Jared, Evanston
Bassett J. Eugene H. 3125 Wabash av.
Bassett Laura B. Mrs. 4425 Ellis av.
Bassett Nelson M. Austin
Bassett Orlando P. Hinsdale. *C.A.*
Bassett Robert J. Evanston
Bassett R. C. 150 Park av.
Bassett Wilbur W. 5208 Kimbark av.
Bassett William D. Evanston
Bast E. E. 2497 Lakewood av.
Basye A. A. Highland Park
Basye H. C. Highland Park
Batchelder Adelbert, 3140 Vernon av.
  C.A.
Batchelder James L. 2684 N. Paulina
Batchelder John H. Winnetka
Batcheller Webster, Auditorium hotel
Bate Elsie Miss, 224 Rush
Bate Henry J. 224 Rush
Bate John W. Dr. 3000 Indiana av.
Bate James F. 856 Hamilton ct.
Bateman Charles E. 1332 George
Bates Anne L. Mrs. 2413 Indiana av.
Bates A. M. Hyde Park hotel
Bates Charles W. Elmhurst
Bates C. D. Dr 278 S. Marshfield av.
Bates Edward C. 4059 Grand boul.
Bates E. A. 428 N. State
Bates Fred. G. 5751 Madison av.
Bates Frederick H. Dr. Elmhurst
Bates George C. 5751 Madison av.
Bates Granville, 96 Evanston av.
Bates Harry M. 5825 Kimbark av.
Bates Harvey H. 3256 South Park av.
Bates Homer O. Dr. 278 S. Marshfield av.
Bates James P. Berwyn
Bates J. Harvey Dr. 3256 South Park av.
Bates Onward, 292 Belden av.
Bates Rosa C. Miss, Evanston
Bates R. P. 428 N. State
Bates Theron M. 148, 50th
Bates Thomas, Evanston
Bates Walter N. Riverside
Bates William S. 18 Bryant av.
Bateson Alexander, 4206 Michigan av.
Bathrick D. D. 823 Chase av.
Bathrick Mary Mrs. 2211 Sheridan rd.
Batt Jacob, 3745 Vincennes av.
Battams Walter J. Evanston
Battams Walter J. jr. Evanston
Batterman John H. 457 Dearborn av.
Batterman John O. 480 Ashland boul.
Battle Joseph A. Evanston
Bauer Alex. 196, 36th. *Irq.*
Bauer Augustus Mrs. 402 Lasalle av.
Bauer Charles Prof. Elmhurst
Bauer Gustave T. 3823 Vernon av. *Stan.*
Bauer John C. 437 Belden av.
Bauer Julius Mrs. 4412 Ellis av.
Bauer Michael Mrs. 22 Lincoln pl.
Bauer Richard, 4412 Ellis av.
Bauer S. 2610 N. Paulina
Bauer William M. 2759 Kenmore av.
Bauland Morris, 2946 Prairie av.
Bauland Pauline Miss, 3615 Ellis av.

Baum C. F. 6543 Lafayette av.
Baum Herman, 4843 Calumet av. *Lksd.*
Baum William L. Dr. Chicago Beach hotel
Baumann Edward S. 1844 Wellington
Baumann Frederick, 1844 Wellington
Baumann F. O. 514 Dearborn av.
Baumgartl B. Mrs. 393 Ashland boul.
Baumgartl Isadore, 461 W. Congress
Baur George Prof. 357, 58th
Baur John, 278 Fremont
Bausher Henry, 384 Lasalle av. *Chi.*
Bausman A. B. Dr. 576 W. Madison. *Ill.*
Baux F. A. Julien hotel
Baxter Andrew J., M.D. 4406 Grand boul.
Baxter Thomas M. Evanston. *Cal.*
Bay George P. 6400 Wentworth av.
Bayard Charles H. Tremont house
Bayha David C. 1515 Oakdale av.
Bayless Benjamin,' Greenwood Inn, Evanston
Bayless George W. Greenwood Inn, Evanston
Bayless V. L. Greenwood Inn, Evanston
Bayley Edwin F. 4634 Greenwood av. *U.L., W.P.*
Baylies Oscar S. 5610 Indiana av.
Baylies R. N. 5765 Washington av.
Bayliss James E. Evanston
Bayliss J. H. Mrs. Evanston
Baynes George A. Dr. 2358 Indiana av.
Baynes James, 522 W. 61st pl.
Beach Chandler B. Riverside. *C.A.*
Beach Clinton S. 57 Bryant av.
Beach C. B. 510 N. State. *Un.*
Beach Edwin W. 580 Division
Beach Elli A. 57 Bryant av.
Beach Elmer E. 1140 Lunt av. *C.A.*
Beach E. K. Mrs. 510 N. State
Beach Franklin G. Mrs. Avenue house, Evanston
Beach George, Hinsdale
Beach George L. Dr. 444 W. Jackson boul.
Beach Harry L. 3224 Rhodes av.
Beach Henry L. 57 Bryant av.
Beach Lydia A. Mrs. 2439 Lakewood av.
Beach Myron H. 3224 Rhodes av. *U.L.*
Beach Raymond W. 857 Pratt av.
Beachey Hill, 107, 37th
Beal T. W. Mrs. 3842 Ellis av.
Beale Christopher D. 6033 Monroe av.
Beale Wm. G. Union club. *Chi., C.A., Un., U.L., W.P.*
Beall Charles M. 258 Michigan av.
Beall William D. 296 Superior. *Un.*
Beals Hardin W. 4100 Vincennes av.
Beals John F. 4212 Oakenwald av.
Beals M. Eliza Mrs. 4100 Vincennes av.
Beam Henry D. 1429 Lawrence av.
Beamer William, Berwyn
Bean Edward E. Evanston
Bean M. S. Mrs. 1432 Michigan av.
Bean William H. 405, 64th
Bear Sidney, 222 Warren av.
Beard C. H. Dr. 6030 Langley av.

Beard Frank T. 3525 Calumet av.
   Sum. res. Chautauqua, N. Y.
Beard Richard, Oak Park
Beard Thomas, Hotel Metropole. *W.P.*
Beardsley Clarence B. Hotel Metropole. *C.A., U.L.*
Beardsley Emma F. Mrs. 5830 Washington av.
Beardsley George P. 2358 Indiana av.
Beardsley R. F. W. 273 S. Claremont av.
Beardsley Susan W. Mrs. 881 W. Monroe
Bearse Hiram, LaGrange
Bearup Helen A. Miss, 4107 Grand boul.
Bearup Mariam A. Miss, 4107 Grand boul.
Beason Olive Mrs. Evanston
Beattie Chas. J. 524 W. 60th
Beattie Paul, 1726 Briar pl.
Beatty James T. LaGrange
Beatty William Mrs. 546, 44th
Beatty William R. La Grange, *C.A.*
Beatty William T. 5470 Washington av.
Beaty William W. 770 W. Monroe
Beauclerc Henry W. 2001 Michigan av.
Beaudry John S., M. D. 7047 Princeton av.
Beaumont George, 1509 Wellington
Beaunisne Albert G. Hotel Del Prado. *U.L.*
Beauvais Elezear A. 1942 Barry av.
Beaver Jane Mrs. 3125 Wabash av.
Beazley John G. Evanston
Bebb Edwin, Tracy
Bebb Robert, Tracy
Bebb William Dr. Hinsdale
Beck Alexander E. 5721 Washington av.
Beck Alexander R. 5721 Washington av.
Beck Anthony, 414, 42d
Beck Burt A. 3200 Lake Park av.
Beck Carl A. Dr. 174 Eugenie
Beck Charles A. 3200 Lake Park av.
Beck C. W. 2572 Lakewood av.
Beck Edward S. 137 Lincoln Park boul.
Beck Emil G. Dr. 620 Lasalle av.
Beck Joseph Dr. 174 Eugenie
Beck Milton I. 7116 Euclid av.
Becker Abraham G. 5132 East End av. *Stan.*
Becker A. E. Oakland Hotel. *Lksd.*
Becker A. W. 4329 Oakenwald av.
Becker A. W. 3804 Indiana av.
Becker Benjamin F. 4924 Ellis av.
Becker C. O. Mrs. 336 Fullerton av.
Becker E. L. 707 Pullman bldg.
Becker Frederick W. 4169 Berkeley av.
Becker George W. 4333 Langley av.
Becker Herman Mrs. 3253 Indiana av.
Becker Isaac J. 3804 Indiana av.
Becker Louis, 3938 Grand boul. *Stan.*
Becker Mary A. Mrs. 4333 Langley av.
Becker Norbert, 301 West ct.
Becker S. Mrs. 4924 Ellis av.
Becker S. Max, 411, 41st
Becker William C. 16 Lane ct.
Beckett B. H. 5835 Kimbark av.
Beckett James Dr. 290 Park av.
Beckler Ashlin J. 817 Touhy av.
Beckler Charles H. 1221 Millard av.

Beckler William A. Chicago Beach hotel
Beckley Major H. E. Riverside
Beckwith Franklin H. Mrs. 77 Lincoln
Park boul.
Beckwith Mary Mrs. 361. Ontario
Beckwith Warren L. 381 Oak. *Univ.*
Bedee Frank W. 3745 Indiana av.
Bedell George Mrs. 1758 Oakdale av.
Bedell Leila G., M.D. 225 Dearborn av.
Bedell S. E. Mrs. Evanston
Bedell William, 1758 Oakdale av.
Bedford Edgar A. 1524 Kenmore av.
Bee Harry, 3349 Wabash av.
Bee Joseph Mrs. 3349 Wabash av.
  Sum. res. Glenwood Springs, Lake
  Geneva
Bee R. Addison, 3349 Wabash av.
Beebe Albert G., M.D. 582 W. Adams
Beebe Archibald A. Evanston
Beebe Frank, 1059 Sherwin av.
Beebe M. S. LaGrange
Beebe Ralph E. Evanston
Beebe Thomas H. Evanston
Beebe William H. 206 Gothe. *Un.*
Beebe William H. jr. 206 Gothe
Beecher F. E. 3745 Indiana av.
Beecher Jerome Mrs. 241 Michigan av.
Beecher Leonard T. Evanston
Beecher Walter N. 7052 Stewart av.
Beecroft Felix W. La Grange
Beedy Mary E. Miss, 481 Dearborn av.
Beegle H. B. Dr. Washington Heights
Beek George N. 386 Oak
Beek Horace W. 164 Warren av. *Ill.*
  Sum. res. Winnetka
Beek William G 386 Oak
Beeks Edward A. 6336 Monroe av.
Beeman Charles H. 4018 Ellis av.
Beeman Charles W. 4018 Ellis av.
Beeman Elizabeth B. Mrs. 2001 Michigan
av.
Beeman Nannette Keim Miss 2001 Michi-
gan av.
Beers Herbert Page, 5464 Jefferson av.
Beers John Mrs. 3616 Ellis av.
Beers John H. 391 Warren av.
Beers Lila Dr. Morgan Park
Beers Minard L. 5464 Jefferson av.
Beers Samuel, 3646 Wabash av.
Beery C. C. Dr. 4544 Michigan av.
  Sum. res. Lake Maxinkuckee, Ind.
Beeson Frederick C. Austin
Beeson S. J. Dr. 450 W. Adams
Beggs S. W. Rev. Evanston
Begley Arthur T. Clifton house
Behel Wilbur F. 3349 South Park av.
Behr Arno Dr. 5501 Cornell av.
Behrendt Arthur J. Dr. 93 Fowler
Behrens Hartwig 1548 Aldine av.
Behrens John H. 1842 Oakdale av.
Behrens Victor, 276 S. Winchester av.
Beidler A. F. Hinsdale
Beidler A. W. 2925 Indiana av. *Ill.*
Beidler Francis, 4736 Drexel boul. *C.A.,
Ill., U.L.. W.P.*
Beidler George, 167 S. Sangamon. *C.A.*

Beidler Herbert A. Evanston
Beidler Jacob Mrs. 167 S. Sangamon
Beiersdorf Arthur J. 4547 Ellis av. *Stan*
Beiersdorf Jacob, 4547 Ellis av.
Beifeld Alexander, 3143 Michigan av
  Stan.
Beifeld Jacob C. 6112 Kimbark av.
Beifeld Joseph, 3304 Calumet av. *Stan.*
Beisel George W. Riverside
Beldam George Mrs. 5623 Michigan av.
Beldam George C. 5623 Michigan av.
Belden Agnes Miss, 5037 Washington av.
Belden Grace Miss, 5037 Washington av.
Belden John S. 4722 Woodlawn av. *U.L.*
Belden John S. jr. 4722 Woodlawn av.
Belfield Ada M. Miss, 5738 Washington av.
Belfield A. Miller, 5738 Washington av.
Belfield Henry H. 5738 Washington av
Belfield Wm. T. Dr. Chicago Athletic
  Assn.
Belford Alexander, 832 North Park av.
  C.A., Un.
Bel-Fouche Hélène M'lle, 481 Dearborn
  av.
Belknap Augustus L Evanston
Belknap Charles C. 3235 Rhodes av. *C.A.*
Belknap Edwin C. Evanston
Belknap Hugh R. Lexington hotel
Belknap Stephen W. 1210 Winthrop av.
Bell A. L. 5810 Washington av.
Bell E. C. Mrs. 5510 Washington av.
Bell Dillwyn M. 36 Aldine sq.
Bell Eliza A. Mrs. 694 W. Monroe
Bell E. A. 1809 Indiana av.
Bell Frank E. 253, 66th
Bell George H. 4753 Calumet av.
Bell Harry H. 6022 Kimbark av.
Bell James A. 6537 Harvard av.
Bell J. H. 4037 Drexel boul. *U.L.*
Bell J. Johnston, M.D. 342 Fullerton av.
Bell J. Lee, 3846 Ellis av.
  Sum. res. Atlantic City, N. J
Bell K. H. 6556 Woodlawn av. *C.A.*
Bell Leon A. 185, 51st
Bell Leonard F. 694 W. Monroe
Bell Lillian Miss, 3930 Lake av.
Bell Martin C. 2625 Indiana av.
Bell Mifflin E. 36 Aldine sq.
Bell M. E. Mrs. 1195 Washington boul.
Bell Robert, 17 Madison Park
Bell Robert, Lake Forest
Bell Royal W. 5810 Washington av.
Bell S. L. Mrs. 358, 64th
Bell Thomas W. Evanston
Bell William H. 4345 Ellis av.
Bell William W. 3930 Lake av.
Bell W. Edward, 375 Dearborn av.
Bellamy Henry C. 600 Dearborn av. *C.A*
Bellamy H. Temple, 3006 Prairie av.
Bellas Thomas H. 1634 Prairie av.
Bellows Alice Mrs. 420 Center
Bellows Frank L. 2928 Kenmore av. *C.A*
Bellows John A. Evanston
Bellows Katharine H. Mrs. 300 Schiller
Below Ida C. Mrs. 2339 Clarendon av.
Belz Frederick W. 647 N. Robey

Beman S. S. 317, 49th, *Chi.*, *U.L.*
Beman W. Irving, 5222 Hibbard av.
Bemis Henry V. Hotel Woodruff
Benard A. B. 1837 Michigan av.
Bender John A. 4341 Indiana av.
Benedict George H. 906 Warren av. *C.A.*
    Sum. res. Oconomoc, Wis.
Benedict George M. 4904 Washington
    av.
Benedict Harry, 3943 Langley av.
Benedict James C. 839 Warren av.
Beneke Henry A. 1953 Deming pl. *C.A.*
Benham James W. 661 W. Monroe
Benham John, 2415 Michigan av. *U.L.*
Benham R. S. 509 Fullerton av.
Benjamin H. B. Mrs. 4548 Oakenwald av.
Benjamin Isaac, 4436 Woodlawn av.
Benjamin Louis, 4111 Grand boul. *Lksd.*,
    Stan.
Benn A. L. Hotel Windermere
Benner Adolph L. 7032 S.Elizabeth. *C.A.*
Benner Mathias, 54 Loomis
Bennet William H. 1712 Briar pl. *C.A.*
Bennett Arthur G. 2469 N. Paulina. *C.A.*
Bennett Asahel F. Oak Park
Bennett Clark H. 907 W. Monroe
Bennett Edward A. 23 Crilly ct.
Bennett E. B. 69 Park av. *C.A.*, *Ill.*
Bennett E. R. Dr. 448 Seminary av.
Bennett E. W. Longwood
Bennett Frank I. 5807 Washington av.
    U.L.
Bennett George Mrs. 3000 Prairie av.
Bennett George A. Evanston
Bennett George R. 7109 Euclid av.
Bennett H. W. 6432 Greenwood av.
Bennett James E. Hinsdale, *C.A.*
Bennett John C. 420 Warren av.
Bennett John W. Austin. *Ill.*
Bennett L. M. Mrs. 4357 Prairie av.
Bennett Martin H. 7240 Jeffery av.
Bennett Mary E. Dr. Norwood Park
Bennett Robert J. 2449 N. Paulina
Bennett R. E. 2469 N. Paulina
Bennett Thomas, Hinsdale, *C.A.*, *W.P.*
    Sum. res. Sand Lake, Mich.
Bennett William L. 7109 Euclid av.
Bennett Willis H. Austin
Bennett W. H. Hotel Del Prado
Bensinger Alfred W. 535 47th. *Lksd.*
Bensinger B. E. 2217 Calumet av. *Stan.*
Bensinger M. 2217 Calumet av. *C.A.*,
    Stan.
Bensley John R. 3929 Ellis av. *U.L.*
Bensley John R. jr. 3929 Ellis av.
Bensley Kate W. Miss, 3929 Ellis av.
Benson Abbie Miss, 1826 Indiana av.
Benson Alvarado T. Austin
Benson Andrew J. 2401 Indiana av.
Benson Anna Mrs. 272 Ashland boul.
Benson Charles E. 676 W. Monroe
Benson C. E. Mrs. 676 W. Monroe
Benson Christian L. 1023 Pratt av.
Benson F. J. Mrs. 4465 Oakenwald av.
Benson John A. Dr. 833 Washington boul.
    Ill.

Benson Olof, 1035 N. Clark
Benson Paul, Evanston
Benson Paul J. 21 Ewing pl.
Benson Robert L. 235 S. Robey
Bent George, 166 Ashland boul.
Bent Geo. P. 6948 Wentworth av.
Bentham George, 266 Chestnut
Bentley Cyrus, Elmhurst. *Univ.*
Bentley C. S. Gen. 4453 Ellis av.
Bentley Frank T. 22 Wisconsin
Bentley George H. Dr. 232 Lincoln Park
    boul.   Sum. res, Fox Lake, Wis.
Bentley Harry G. Oak Park. *C.A.*
Bentley O. F. Ravinia
Bentley Walter G. Oak Park
Bentley Wilbur G. 474 Elm. *U.L.*
Benton E. L. Hinsdale
Benton George C. 3207 Michigan av.
Benton George P. 2919 Groveland av.
Benton Kendrick W.Rev. 6309 Stewart av.
Benton William H. Mrs. 5021 Washing-
    ton av
Benton W. H. 5021 Washington av.
Benz E. P. 235 S. Irving av.
Benz Philipp, 295 S. Hoyne av.
Benze Herman, 372 Lasalle av.
Benziger August, 2700 Prairie av.
Benzing Elias Rev. 1788 Magnolia av.
Berens August Rev. Elmhurst
Berg Anton C. 1390 W. Monroe
Berg Charles F. 6418 Yale
Berg Charles O. 1390 W. Monroe
Berg David, 3443 Wabash av.
Berg John V. 185, 51st
Berg Joseph, 1006 Warren av.
Berg Morris H. 3213 Rhodes av. *Stan.*
Bergen George B. Evanston
Bergen Lloyd M. Dr. Highland Park
Bergen Theodore L. LaGrange
Berger Emil, 680 W. Adams
Berger Harry, 769 W. Jackson boul.
Berger Robert, 439 N. State
Berger William H. Mrs. 202 Oakwood
    boul.
Bergeron A. V. Dr. 817 S. Sawyer av.
Bergeron Jos. Z. Dr. 232 Loomis
Bergersen Louis, 378 Bowen av.
Bergey David W. 522 W. Monroe
Bergman Frank A, 478 W. Adams
Bergstrom E. Algot Dr. 1202 Sheffield av.
Berkeley J. F. Berwyn
Berlin Augustus, 3243 Malden
Berlin Robert C. 3173 Malden   Sum.
    res. Glenwood Springs, Lake Geneva
Berlizheimer Bernard, 471 Lasalle av.
Berlizheimer Louis, 551 Cleveland av.
Bermann Moritz, 4726 Evans av.
Bern Edward A. 4616 Prairie av.
Bernard Charles C. Dr. 452 Dayton
Bernard P. Hotel, Woodruff
Bernhard Joseph 434 Warren av.
Bernheimer Irving S. 3340 Michigan av.
    Stan.
Bernhisel L. M. Evanston
Bernstein Eric, 333 Chestnut
Berolzheim Joseph, 3214 Vernon av. *Lksd.*

Berr J. 822 Pullman bldg.
Berrall Charles, 2430 Lakewood av.
Berriman Edward C. 1911 Diversey
Berriman Mathew W. 38 St. James pl.
Berriozabal Felipe, 4009 Drexel boul.
Berry Alvah S. 4438 Woodlawn av.
Berry A. V. Irving Park
Berry Charles H. Dr. 24 Wisconsin
Berry C. DePeyster, 1211 Winthrop av.
Berry Frank, Wilmette
Berry F. J. 143 Oakwood boul.
Berry John, 88 Warren av.
Berry John, 3953 Michigan av.
Berry Joseph J. Evanston
Berry J. F. Rev. 2677 N. Paulina
Berry J. G. Dr. 249, 43d
Berry Lafayette S. 1737 Roscoe
Berryman John B. 1146 Granville av.
Bersbach Alfred, 2568 N. Hermitage av.
Bersbach Oscar J. 2490 N. Hermitage av.
Bert E., M. D. 3242 Vernon av. *Lksd.*
Bertling A. E. Dr. 512 Ashland boul.
Bertrand Frank M. 3555 Ellis av.
Berwig Elise Dr. 371 Center
Besler John D. 4425 Ellis av.
Besly Charles H. 399 Ontario. *C.A., U.L.*
Besly Oliver Mrs. 399 Ontario
Best A. E. Mrs. 6030 Stony Island av.
Best E. E. Dr. Park Ridge
Best George, 7126 Euclid av.
Best George W. 3610 Ellis av.
Best Henry, 1450 Wrightwood av.
Best Henry, 4402 Michigan av.
Best James G. S. 1931 Deming pl.
Best William, 4331 Drexel boul.
Best William jr. 95 Oakwood av.
Best William E. 655 W. Monroe
Best William H. 655 W. Monroe
Best William T. Oak Park
Bethell Thomas T. Oak Park
Bethune J. H. Mrs. 434 Belden av.
Bettles Joseph B. 5721 Indiana av.
Bettman P. Henry, 252, 60th
Betts Norman C. Oak Park
Bevan A. D. Dr. Lakota hotel. *C.A., W.P.*
Bevans Homer, 353 W. 60th pl.
Beveridge Frank L. 607, 46th
Beverly J. M. Mrs. 234 Oakwood boul.
Bevington Benton L. Oak Park
Beye William Mrs. Oak Park
Beyer Oscar A. 230 Sunnyside av.
Beyerlein John, 707, 47th
Bickford Charles D. 604 Division
Bickford Charles M. 947 Farwell av.
Bickford H. L. Mrs. Hotel Del Prado
Bickford Russell K. Oak Park
Bicknell Edwin D. Oak Park
Bicknell Franklin W. Oak Park
Bicknell Orlando L. Oak Park
Bicknell William W. Oak Park
Biddle Noble L. 144 Ashland boul.
Biddle William B. 4541 Lake av. *C.A.*
Biden Edmund C. 4160 Ellis av.
Bidwell Theo. S., M.D. 482 Ashland boul. *Ill.*

Biedenweg Wm. C. 2840 N. Hermitage av.
Bielfeldt William S. 6709 Lafayette av.
Bielman A. Mrs. 872 W. Adams
Bigelow Alfred P. 312 Belden av. *U.L.*
Bigelow Arnold M. 847 Warren av.
Bigelow Arthur C. 5334 Madison av. *C.A.*
Bigelow Arthur G. 231, 29th
Bigelow Clarissa Dr. 4645 Evans av.
Bigelow Edna Calvin Miss, 3845 Ellis av.
Bigelow Edward A. 551 Dearborn av. *U.L.*
Bigelow E. F. Mrs. 406, 36th pl.
Bigelow Frank Burr, 746 Fullerton av.
Bigelow Frederick E. Dr. 3638 Cottage Grove av.
Bigelow George S. 4901 Grand boul.
Bigelow Harry Towers, 4901 Grand boul.
Bigelow H. D. P. Mrs. 539 W. Adams
Bigelow Joel, Mrs. 2449 Prairie av.
Bigelow J. L. Hotel Del Prado
Bigelow Nathan Kellogg, Evanston
Bigelow Nelson Calvin, 3845 Ellis av.
Bigelow Nelson P. 405 Erie. *Cht., Univ.*
Biggs A. K. Mrs. Evanston
Biggs Bert P. Austin
Biggs E. A. 70 Bellevue pl.
Biggs Foster H. Evanston
Biggs Paul G. Austin
Biggs Vernon A. Austin
Bilhorn Peter P. 2810 Kenmore av.
Billin Charles E. 810 The Plaza
Billings A. M. Mrs. 504 W. Lake
Billings Charles L. 35, 22d. *Cal., Chi.*
Billings Cornelius K. G. 470 Washington boul. *Cal., Chi., C.A., Ill., Un., U.L., W.P.*
        Sum. res. Lake Geneva, Wis.
Billings Frank Dr. 35, 22d. *Cal., Chi., C.A., Univ., W.P.*
Billings Henry F. Hotel Metropole, *Chi., Un.*
Billings Henry L. 1186 Millard av.
Billingslea Albert, Evanston
Billingslea Albert jr. Evanston
Billingslea Claud, Evanston
Billingslea Edward, Evanston
Billow Elmer E. Evanston
Billow Susan Mrs. Evanston
Binder Carl, 1852 Surf
Bines Robert, 5803 Washington av.
Binford George W. 48, 53d
Bing Stella Miss, 3346 Prairie av.
Bingham Arthur L. 4723 Woodlawn av. *U.L.*
Bingham Cornelia D. Miss, 6550 Yale
Bingham C. L. 4346 Oakenwald av.
Bingham Edyth V. Miss 5132 Kimbark av.
Bingham Edward H. 70 Madison Park
Bingham Frank A. 91 Bowen av.
Bingham George, 16 Astor
Bingham Horace W. Oak Park
Bingham James A. 5132 Kimbark av. *U.L.*
Bingham Millard F. 768 Washington boul. *Ill.*
        Sum. res. Pittsfield, Mass.

Bingham Misses, 768 Washington boul.
Bingham S. H. LaGrange
Binkley George H. 780, 71st pl.
Binkley J. T. jr. M.D. 452, 49th
Binne Frank, 303 Warren av.
Binner Herbert, 541 Lunt av.
Binner Oscar E. 1013 Pratt av. *C.A.*
Binner Paul Mrs. 541 Lunt av.
Binner Walter, 541 Lunt av.
Binswanger Alvin, 3315 Calumet av.
Binswanger August, 3315 Calumet av.
Binz Charles A. 2420 Magnolia av.
Birch Hugh T. 1912 Michigan av. *Chi.,*
   C.A.,Univ. Sum.res. Highland Park
Bird A. C. Evanston. *U.L.*
Bird Curtis D. Hinsdale
Bird Douglas, 6371 Greenwood av.
Bird O. O. LaGrange
Birdsall C. H. Hyde Park Hotel
Birdsall Richard M. 390 Warren av.
Birge M.D. Col. 183 Warren av.
Birk Edward J. 268 Seminary av.
Birk Jacob, 1901 Wellington
Birk William A. 1901 Wellington
Birkett William H. 5227 Washington av.
Birkhoff David Dr. 408 S. Marshfield av.
Birkhoff George, 577 W. Adams
Birkhoff George jr. 575 W. Adams. *Ill.,*
   U.L.
Birkin Frank, 70 Madison Park
Birkle Charles A. 4946 Washington av.
Birmingham H. P. Capt. Fort Sheridan
Birmingham James H. 500, 42d pl.
Birmingham Thomas, 2516 Indiana av.
Birney Charles A. 2887 Sheridan rd.
Bisbee Jesse D. 3366 Calumet av.
   Sum. res. Chautauqua, N. Y.
Bisbee Lewis H. Mrs. 3912 Vincennes av.
Bischoff Fred. A. 1728 Wrightwood av.
Bischoff Hattie A. Mrs. 907 Evanston av.
Bishop A. Mrs. Chicago Beach hotel
Bishop A. H. North Shore hotel
Bishop Charles Mrs. Evanston
Bishop Charles Nelson, Oak Park. *C.A.,*
   Ill.
Bishop Edward L. 4530 St. Lawrence av.
Bishop Edwin R. Mrs. La Grange
Bishop Frank H. 4240 Wabash av.
Bishop George H. 1069 Washington boul.
Bishop Henry W. 66 Bellevue pl. *Chi.,*
   Un.
Bishop H. N. Mrs. Oak Park
Bishop J. A. 15, 40th
Bishop J. M. 1254 Michigan av.
Bishop L. Brackett, 1111 Early av.
Bishop Paul J. 1111 Early av.
Bishop Rufus W. Dr. 484, 42d
Bishop Seth Scott Dr. 7½9 ½ Adams
   Sum. res. Fond du Lac, Wis.
Bishop S. J. Mrs. 6450 Woodlawn av.
Bishop Thomas R. 7624 Emerald av.
Bishop W. C. 192 S. Kedzie av.
Bishop W. H. Chicago Beach hotel
Bishopp Weller D. 3652 Calumet av.
Bisland John R. 42 E. Pearson
Bisland William A. 42 E. Pearson
32

Bissell Arthur G. 134 Rush
   Sum. res. Lake Forest
Bissell Florence E. Miss, Oak Park
Bissell Frank R. Evanston
Bissell George F. Mrs. 134 Rush
   Sum. res. Lake Forest
Bissell Richard M. 134 Rush,*U.L.,Univ.*
   Sum. res. Lake Forest
Bissell William A. 4729 Kimbark av.
Bither William A. 4206 Ellis av.
Bitner Harry, Berwyn
Bixby Charles H. Rev. 76, 50th
Bixby Frank, 4601 Vincennes av.
Bixby John M. 7646 Lowe av.
Black Arthur D. 174, 42d pl.
Black Elmer E. 256, 51 t. *U.L.*
Black Fred W. 3749 Indiana av.
Black George M. Oak Park
Black Harry St. Francis, 4353 Drexel
   boul. *Chi., C.A., Irq., W.P.*
Black Horace W. 3749 Indiana av.
Black James P. 28 Aldine sq.
Black John C. 9 Walton pl.
Black John C. Gen. 23 Scott. *Chi., Un.*
Black John D, 23 Scott. *C.A.*
Black Stephen, 4632 Vincennes av.
Black S. H. The Winamac
Black William F. Prof. 3749 Indiana av.
Black William J. 6620 Lafayette av.
Black William P. 1377 Central boul.
Blackall Alfred H. 513 Dearborn av.
Blackburn George, 468 W. Adams
Blacker Isabella Mrs. 3626 Lake av.
Blackledge John W. 361 Ontario
Blackler Samuel, Lake Forest
Blackler William H. Sherman house
Blackman Charles S. 4326 Greenwood
   av.
Blackman Charles W. 4523 Lake av. *C.A*
Blackman Chester S. 65 Laflin. *Ill.*
Blackman Edwin Mrs. 584 Dearborn av.
Blackman Florence Mrs. The Kenwood
Blackman Frank P. 3756 Ellis av. *Irq.*
Blackman Fred O. 4326 Greenwood av.
Blackman Harry L. 4326 Greenwood av.
Blackman Louis I. 57 Dekalb
Blackman Willis L. Hinsdale
Blackmarr F. H. Dr. 4058 Ellis av.
Blackstone Andrew P. Oak Park
Blackstone T. B. 252 Michigan av. *Cal.,*
   Chi., U.L.
Blackstone William E. Oak Park
Blackwelder I. S. Morgan Park *U.L.*
Blackwell Mary E. Mrs. 3260 Groveland
   av.
Blackwood Alex. L. Dr. 9128 Erie av.
Blades Leonard J. 657 Washington boul.
Blaine Emmons Mrs. 344 Erie
Blaine W. T. Chicago Beach hotel, *C.A.*
Blair B. A. 116, 32d
Blair Charles H. 2909 Prairie av.
Blair Chauncey J. 4830 Drexel boul. *Chi.,*
   C.A., U.L., W.P.
Blair C. J. 2431 Lakewood av.
Blair David, 219 S. Irving av.
Blair David W. Irving Park

Blair Edward T. 157 Cass. *Chi.*
Blair E. B. 6030 Stony Island av.
Blair Francisco, 3976 Vincennes av.
Blair Frank P. 10 Astor. *Univ.*
Blair Gardiner C. Irving Park
Blair George P. 742 Warren av.
Blair Henry A. 2735 Prairie av. *Chi.,*
  C.A., U.L., W.P.
Blair James, 4439 Greenwood av.
Blair James E. Austin
Blair J. H. Dr. 3976 Vincennes av.
Blair Lyman Mrs. 2825 Prairie av.
Blair S. O. 4319 Drexel boul.
Blair Thomas S. jr. Evanston
Blair Tracy Mrs. 2820 N. Paulina
Blair Watson F. 164 Rush. *Chi., C.A.,*
  W.P.
Blair William, 230 Michigan av. *U.L.*
Blair William, 3644 Prairie av.
Blair William S. Evanston
Blair William W. 2555 Magnolia av.
Blaisdell Hiram, Evanston
Blaisdell John W. 3601 Vincennes av.
Blaisdell S. E. 225 S. Irving
Blake Charles G. 384 Bissellav
Blake Clinton F. 531 W. Monroe
Blake Edward J. 1815 Oakdale av.
Blake Harriet M. Mrs. 558 Washington
  boul.
Blake Henry H. 3845 Ellis av.
Blake Henry H. 46, 35th
Blake James Vila Rev. 531 W. Monroe
Blake J. Neal, 847 Warren av.
Blake Wallace H. Evanston
Blake Walter, 3845 Ellis av.
Blake William H. Evanston
Blakelidge George W. LaGrange
Blakely Cyrene H. Mrs. 3708 Lake av.
Blakemore C. B. Mrs. 388 Lasalle av.
Blakemore F. T. 388 Lasalle av.
Blakemore W. R. 388 Lasalle av.
Blakeslee C. F. 2107 Indiana av.
Blakeslee George S. 3240 Calumet av.
Blakeslee Homer L. 442 W. 65th
Blakeslee Levi, LaGrange
Blakey A. J. 780 North Park av.
Blanchard Arthur S. Oak Park
Blanchard Clinton R. Oak Park
Blanchard Edward R. Oak Park
Blanchard F. M. 5340 Greenwood av.
Blanchard Ira Mrs. 378 Warren av.
Blanchard Julius M. Austin
Blanchard Marvin, Austin
Blanchard Theodore F. 378 Warren av.
Blanchard William, Evanston. *C.A.*
Blanchard William A. Oak Park
Blanden Charles G. Berwyn
Blanding Mary Mrs. 4348 Greenwood av.
Blandy Gray, Evanston
Blank Jessie B. River Forest
Blanke George F. Mrs. 1734 Deming pl.
Blasé William H. 4446 Woodlawn av.
Blatchford Charles H. 375 Lasalle av.
Blatchford Edward W. 375 Lasalle av.
Blatchford Eliphalet W. 375 Lasalle av.
  Chi.,Univ.

Blatchford Frances M. Miss, 375 Lasalle
  av.
Blatchford John K. 4949 Prairie av.
  Sum. res. Paw Paw Lake, Mich.
Blatchford N. H. 367 Lasalle av. *U.L.*
Blatchford Paul, Oak Park. *Univ.*
Blatchford Thomas W. 79, 44th. *C.A.*
Blatherwick Charles W. Austin
Blattner O. A. 525 Cleveland av.
Blauer Adelia Miss, 542 Lasalle av.
Blauer Fred J. 542 Lasalle av.
Blaurock Charles A. Oak Park
Blauvelt A. Hotel Windermere
Blayney Arthur C. 398, 40th
Blayney Fred H. Dr. 531 W. Adams
Blayney Louise Mrs. Riverside
Blayney Thomas C. Riverside
Bleasdale John W. 487, 62d
Blend Charles W. Mrs. 2233 Prairie av.
Blessing Lewis G. 1564 W. Monroe
Blessing Mae Miss, 769 Washington
  boul.
Bley J. C. 3031 Prairie av.
Bleyer Charles E. 1917 Wrightwood av.
  C.A., U.L.
Bligh William J. 4416 Oakenwald av.
Bliler H. E. Dr. Marquette club
Blinn Edmund B. Oak Park
Bliss Abel, 49, 46th
Bliss Arthur I. 1145 Millard av.
Bliss A. H. 3350 Wabash av.
Bliss Charles L. Berwyn, *C.A.*
Bliss Edgar B. Riverside
Bliss E. Raymond, 5123 Madison av.*C.A.,*
  U.L.
Bliss E. S. Mrs. Evanston
Bliss Frank E. 3636 Lake av.
Bliss Frank T. 3839 Ellis av.
Bliss George E. Mrs. 1145 Millard av.
Bliss George H. 4528 Lake av.
Bliss George J. Oak Park
Bliss J. Col. 3100 Groveland av.
Bliss Julian P. 4946 Washington av.
Bliss Louis 507 Dearborn av.
Bliss N. W. Longwood
Bliss Samuel E. 3636 Lake av.
Bliss Theodore F. Oak Park
Bliss Theodore F. jr. Oak Park
Bliven Charles E. Mrs. 2 Aldine sq.
Bliven Edward, 3848 Ellis av.
Bliven Howard, 2 Aldine sq.
Bliven Waite, 2 Aldine sq.
Bloch Charles E. 3500 Ellis av.
Bloch E. 290 Lasalle av.
  Sum. res. Atlantic City, N. J.
Bloch Gabriel, 459 Lasalle av.
  Sum. res. Waukesha, Wis.
Bloch Jacob, 3027 Indiana av.
Bloch Louis, 1038 W. Jackson boul.
Bloch Louis E. 4717 Champlain av.
Bloch Simon, 4252 Drexel boul. *Lksd.*
Block Isaac, 4521 Ellis av. *Lksd., Stan.*
Block I. E. 214, 31st
Block John Rev. Jefferson Park
Block Leopold, Hotel Metropole, *Stan.*
Block Louis J. 363 Warren av.

Block P. D. Hotel Metropole. *Stan.*
Block Sam, Auditorium Annex
Block Williard T. Hotel Metropole. *U.L.*
Blocki Frederick, 360 Ashland boul.
Blocki Frederick W. 829 N. Clark
Blocki John, 829 N. Clark
Blodgett Edward A. 510 W. Monroe, *Ill.*, *U.L.*
Blodgett H. W. Judge, Waukegan
Blome Rudolph S. 1886 Diversey
Blomgren Oscar N. 1450 Belmont av.
Blood Emma S. Miss, Hotel Windermere
Blood James A. Hinsdale. *C.A.*
Blood Mary A. Miss, 3258 Forest av.
Bloom Cora B. Miss. 3672 Michigan av.
Bloom F. Mrs. Hotel Woodruff
Bloom Isaac J. 3358 South Park av. *Stan.*
Bloom Leopold, 3672 Michigan av. *Stan.*, *W.P.*
Bloom Mary P. Mrs. 4339 Prairie av.
Bloom Moses, 3423 Forest av.
Bloom Samuel, 3423 Forest av.
Bloom Samuel H. 826 Warren av.
Bloom Sol. 4736 Prairie av.
Bloomfield James J. 3226 Beacon
Bloomingston John A. 3728 Ellis av.
Bloomingston John S. 3728 Ellis av.
Bloss Harry H. 1792 Evanston av.
Blossom Alonzo, 35 Aldine sq.
Blossom Edward J. 4849 Madison av.
Blossom George W. 4858 Kenwood av. *U.L.*
Blount Frederick M. 194 S. Robey, *C.A.*, *Ill.*, *U.L.*
Blum August, 3245 Groveland av. *Irq.*
Blum A. H. Hotel Del Prado
Blum Edgar C. 5013 Wabash av. *Lksd.*
Blum John, 5013 Wabash av.
Blum Julius, 543 Cleveland av.
Blum Louis J. 5013 Wabash av. *Lksd.*
Blum Simon, 645 Fullerton av.
Blume George A. 561, 45th pl.
Blume G. P. 359, 44th
Blumenthal I. 3402 Vernon av.
        Sum. res. Battle Creek, Mich.
Blunt Frank T. Evanston
Blunt John E. Evanston
Blunt John E. jr. Evanston
Blunt Margaret E. Miss, Evanston
Bluthardt O. R. Dr. 569 Warren av.
Bluthardt Robert S. 272 Belden av.
Bluthardt T. J. Dr. 453 Lasalle av.
Blymyer Benjamin F. 7216 Euclid av.
Boak Robert jr. 4744 Kimbark av.
Boak Robert B. 4744 Kimbark av.
Boal C. T. 1732 Michigan av. *Cal.*, *Chi.*, *W.P.*
Boalch William Mrs. 3618 Lake av.
Board Ellsworth M. Evanston
Board James L. 983 W. Adams
Board M. E. Mrs. 3015 Groveland av.
Boardman C. Y. 402, 40th
Boardman J. W. Mrs, 271 Oakwood boul.
Boardman Martha J. Mrs. 235 Michigan av.
Boas Edmund A. Dr. 395 N. Wells

Bobb Samuel A. Irving Park
Bobo J. L. 4246 Drexel boul.
Bocher George R. 1552 W. Monroe
Bockius Eisen, M.D. Mayfair
Bockius Joseph A. Wilmette
Bodach Charles, 746 N. Hoyne av.
Bodach Frank, 746 N. Hoyne av.
Boddie John T. 586 Dearborn av. *Univ.*
Bode Fred, 5827 Washington av. *C.A.*, *U.L.*
Bode William F. 3812 Vincennes av.
Bodemann W. 5451 Washington av.
Bodenheimer Simon, 4423 Prairie av.
Bodenschatz Gustav A. Oak Park
Bodenschatz John G. 4444 Ellis av.
Bodine Jacob, Evanston
Bodine Jacob jr. Evanston
Bodine Louise Miss, 6516 Kimbark av.
Bodine William Lester, 828 Wilson av.
        Sum. res. Oconomowoc, Wis.
Bodinghouse Richard, Wilmette
Bodman Albert C. 299 Schiller, *C.A.*
Bodman Luther W. 589 N. State. *C.A.*, *U.L.*
Bodwell George F. 3311 Forest av.
Boeber Frederick W. Dr. Elmhurst
Boehm Aaron, 3150 Prairie av.
Boehm Peter M. Capt. 6711 Perry av.
Boericke Richard H. 1825 Melrose, *C.A*
Boerlin Albert E. La Grange
Boerlin August J. La Grange
Boerlin Henry T. La Grange
Boerner W. R. Ravinia
Boess John G. 485 Bowen av.
Boettcher E. 49 Pine Grove av.
Boettcher Henry R. Dr. 6336 Harvard av.
Bogardus Harry A. 4110 Indiana av.
Bogardus H. D. 6241 Monroe av.
Bogert William B. Evanston. *C.A.*, *U.L.*
Bogg Harry B. 6506 Yale
Boggs Albert W. 4451 Ellis av.
Boggs Annie M. Miss, 4451 Ellis av.
Boggs A. Emmet, 4451 Ellis av.
Boggs Cyrus B. 746 W. 64th
Bogle Ralph F. 6120 Madison av.
Bogle Walter Scott, 228 S. Irving av. *Ill.*
Bogue Arthur H. 4819 Greenwood av.
Bogue Charles H. 2359 Michigan av.
Bogue Elias, Hinsdale
Bogue George M. Hinsdale
Bogue Hamilton B. 4819 Greenwood av.
Bogue Hamilton B. jr. 4819 Greenwood av.
Bogue John H. 96, 42d pl.
Bogue O. A. 5037 Washington av.
Bogue Roswell C. 5037 Washington av.
Bogue R. G. Mrs. 5 Washington pl.
Bogue Wayne C. 4819 Greenwood av.
Bohart William H., M.D. 4436 Emerald av.
Bohlander John jr. Hinsdale
Bohlander J. Maywood
Bohn Henry J. Morgan Park
Bohner George, 2944 Vernon av.
Boice Hugh M. Evanston
Boice William H. 5813 Washington av
Boisot Emile K. LaGrange
Bokhof David Dr. 5250 Prairie av.

Bokum R. D. 429 N. State. *Chi.*, *Un.*
Boland John A. 522 Burling
Boland Thomas, 303 Lincoln av.
Boldenweck Carl G. 1821 Oakdale av.
Boldenweck Louis H. Mrs. 27 Stratford pl.
Boldenweck William, 1681 N. Halsted
Bolles Charles E. Oak Park
Bolster Charles H. 39 Junior terrace
Bolte Anson L. 3757 Ellis av. *Irq.*
Bolte Charles Guy, Winnetka
Bolter Andrew, 1511 N. Halsted
Bolter Edward A. 1469 Wellington
Bolton H. K. Hotel Metropole
Bolton James, Hotel Metropole
Bolton S. Henry, Austin
Boltwood H. L. Evanston
Bolza Oscar Prof. 5810 Woodlawn av.
Bomas P. S. Capt. 2030 Indiana av.
Bonbright Daniel, Evanston
Bond Isaac, 175, 36th
Bond James M. Evanston
Bond John H. R. Dr. 123, 51st
Bond Joseph, 3332 Calumet av. *U.L.*
Bond Laurence Colton, 4025 Drexel boul.
Bond Lester L. 512 W. Monroe, *Ill.*, *U.L.*
Bond Marshall S. P. 956 W. Monroe
Bond Thomas S. Mrs. Evanston
Bond T. Newton, 507 W.Monroe,*Ill.*
Bond William A. 4025 Drexel boul. *U.L.*
Bond William E. 6519 Monroe av.
Bond William H. 175, 36th
Bond William Scott, 4025 Drexel boul.
Bond W. S. Mrs. 4148 Drexel boul.
Bonn Henry, 4808 Langley av.
Bonnell Charles E. 224 S. Oakley av.
Bonnell David, Evanston
Bonner Charles, 5752 Rosalie ct.
Bonney Charles C. 424 Fulton
Bonney Charles F. Austin
Bonney C. L. Hotel Windermere. *C.A.*, *U.L.*
Bonney E. A. Mrs. Austin
Bonney H. J. 216 Cass
Bonney Lawton C. Virginia hotel, *C.A.*, *U.L.*
Bonynge Francis G. Dr. 62 Cedar. *Un.*
Bookwalter Ross, Chicago Beach hotel
Boomer George A. 353, 46th
Boomer John, 353, 46th
Boomer John B. 353, 46th
Boomer Martha J. Mrs. 4233 St. Lawrence av.
Boon Cornelius G. 591 Orchard
Boon C. L. 4139 Langley av.
Boon Harry M. 5325 Madison av.
Boone Harry C. 22 Marquette terrace
Boore Henry, 4804 Vincennes av.
Boorman James M. Evanston
Boorman James N. Evanston
Boorn Charles P. 4130 Berkeley av.
Boorn William C. 4060 Ellis av. *U.L.*
Booth Alfred, 1638 Michigan av. *Cal.*.*CA.*
Booth Alfred Vernon, 4841 Michigan av.
Sum. res. Neenah, Wis.
Booth Arthur, 701 The Plaza

Booth Edward M. Prof. 471 Fullerton av.
Booth Edwin A. 44, 53d. *Cal.*
Booth Hervey W. Oak Park. *Ill.*
Booth John, 545 Cleveland av.
Booth John L. 410 Chicago av.
Booth J. St. John Mrs. 539 W. Monroe
Booth Ralph H. Chicago Athletic assn.
Booth Sarah W. Mrs. 4315 Champlain av.
Booth Thomas G. Evanston
Booth William Morris, 3605 Ellis av. *C.A.*
Booth William S. 4709 Grand boul. *C.A.*, *W.P.*
Booth W. Vernon, 31 Bellevue pl. *Chi.*, *C.A.*, *Un.*
Borcherdt Albert F. 512 Dearborn av.
Borcherdt Herman, 512 Dearborn av.
Borcherdt Julius C. 634 Washington boul.
BordenGerald M.237Ashland boul. *Univ.*
Borden Hamilton, 12 Groveland Park. *U.L.*
Borden Henry Lee, 237 Ashland boul.
Sum. res. St. Clair, Mich.
Borden James U. 248 S. Morgan. *Cal.*, *C.A.*
Borden John, 3949 Lake av.
Borden Lewis L. 237 Ashland boul.
Borden Seymour S. 5168 Michigan av.
Borden William, 89 Bellevue pl. *Chi.*, *Un.*, *W.P.*
Borg Isaac, 336 Warren av.
Borgmeier Adolph, 700 N. Hoyne av.
Boring Charles O. Evanston
Borland J. J. Morgan Park
Borland L. C. Dr. 685 Ogden av. *Ill.*
Borland Matthew W., M.D. 365 W. Jackson boul.
Born Moses, 3433 Michigan av. *Stan.*
Borner William. 52 Walton pl. *C.A.*
Borngesser A. M. Mrs. 2358 Indiana av.
Borroughs Walter, 476, 72d
Borsch Henry, 3125 Southport av.
Borton Frank L. Evanston
Bortree Herbert W. Austin
Borwell Frank, Oak Park
Borwell Frank L. LaGrange
Borwell I. M. Mrs. Oak Park
Bosch Henry, 5405 Ridgewood ct. *C.A.*
Bosley Daniel W. 538 Washington boul. *Ill.*
Bosley Edward F. 33½ Park av.
Bosselman Albertina Mrs. 1817 Wrightwood av.
Bostedo Alfred L. Oak Park
Bostedo Louis G. River Forest
Bosworth E. D. Hotel Luzerne
Bosworth F. F. 5426 Washington av.
Bosworth John C. 4508 Indiana av.
Bosworth W. L. 5426 Washington av.
Botsford B. B. Mrs 2100 Calumet av.
Botsford Henry, 2837 Michigan av. *Chi.*, *U.L.*, *W.P.*
Botsford H. L. Mrs. 3500 Ellis av.
Bottum George G. 4135 N. Ashland av.
Bottum George H. 4135 N. Ashland av.
Bouffleur Albert I., M.D. 1178 Washington boul.

Boughan John P. 40 Roslyn pl.
Boughton Daniel K. 703 W. Monroe
Boughton Fred N. Mrs. 4321 Forrestville av.
Boulton George D. Highland Park
Boulton Kenneth B. Highland Park
Bour Charles J. 6506 Lexington av.
Bour George C. 440 Kenwood terrace
Bour John N. 5309 Ingleside av.
Bour John R. 5309 Ingleside av.
Bour J. F. New Hotel Holland
Bourassa Joseph H. 1942 Barry av. C.A.
Bourgeau Frederic J. 18 Sibley av.
Bourgeois Oscar T. LaGrange
Bourke Edward L. 5648 Michigan av.
Bourke James E. 273 Superior. C.A.
Bourke Robert E. 5648 Michigan av.
Bourke Ulick, 5648 Michigan av.
Bourke Ulick jr. 5648 Michigan av.
Bourne Emma M. Mrs. 3738 Langley av.
Bournique Alvar L. 51, 23d. C.A.
Bournique Augustus E. 51, 23d. C.A., W.P.
Bournique Eugene A. 214, 33d
Bournique Lyman G. 51, 23d
Bournique May E. Miss, 51. 23d
Bourns James H. Rev. 5751 Rosalie ct.
Bousquet J. S. 2510 Prairie av.
Boutell Henry Sherman, 24 Walton pl. Chi., U.L., Univ.
Boutelle Joshua P. Evanston
Boutelle Lewis H. Evanston
Bouton Archibald, 438 W. 64th
Bouton Christoper B. 4812 Woodlawn av.
Bouton Nathaniel S. 191, 47th
Bouton Persis Miss, 4812 Woodlawn av.
Bouton Sherman H. 6051 Ellis av.
Bovee Mary H. Mrs. 3314 South Park av.
Bovett James A. 1246 Michigan av.
Bovett James A. jr. 2334 Indiana av.
Bowden Thomas A. 4309 Ellis av.
Bowen Arthur P. Riverside. C.A.
Bowen Caroline Mrs. 407 Huron
Bowen Charles M. Mrs. 2288 N. Paulina
Bowen Emma E. Mrs. 6445 Minerva av.
Bowen George H. 3326 Prairie av.
Bowen Handy H. 206 Oakwood boul.
Bowen Ira P. 407 Huron
Bowen John S. Hotel Windermere
Bowen Joseph T. 136 Astor. Chi., Univ. Sum. res. Bar Harbor. Me.
Bowen L. C. Mrs. 206 Oakwood boul.
Bowen Mary G. Mrs. 709 W. Monroe
Bowen Menard K. 4908 Ellis av. U.L.
Bowen Thomas C. 3913 Cottage Grove av.
Bower Emma Mrs. 602 Division,
Bower Robert A. 822 North Park av. U.L.
Bowers C. A. Hotel Del Prado
Bowers James F. 71 Lincoln av.
Bowers J. H. 3733 Prairie av.
Bowers Lloyd W. 11 Ritchie ct. Chi., C.A., Univ.
Bowers Nancy Mrs. 1473 W. Monroe
Bowers Wallace W. 6420 Greenwood av.
Bowers William A. 1473 W. Monroe

Bowes Chas. Lane, 541 W. Adams
Bowes Edwin J. jr. 870 Winthrop av.
Bowes F. K. 541 W. Adams
Bowes Jerome P. 1010 Garfield boul.
Bowes John R. Austin
Bowes T. F. The Arizona
Bowey Alice Miss, 930 W. Monroe
Bowey Charles F. 930 W. Monroe
Bowey Elizabeth Miss, 930 W. Monroe
Bowie Robert R. 822 W. Adams
Bowker Hugh D. 3225 Malden
Bowlan James, 294 Groveland av.
Bowles Dwight W. 87 Rush
Bowles Frederick A. 252, 53d
Bowles John P. 4340 Vincennes av.
Bowman Caroline Mrs. 6317 Lexington av.
Bowman Ernest M. 3240 Rhodes av.
Bowman Helen M. Miss, Ohio, cor. N. State
Bowman John R. Evanston
Bowman Johnston R. 64 Bellevue pl.
Bowman J. P. 2245 Southport av.
Bowman L. J. 2245 Southport av.
Bowman M. A. Mrs. 171, 51st
Bowman Robert, 55 Lincoln Park boul.
Bowman R. A. 380 Oak
Bowman Thomas Rt. Rev. 232 S. Winchester av.
Bowman William H. Auditorium Annex
Bowne Geo. W. Rev. 3112 Michigan av.
Bowyer Loraine F. Hotel Metropole, Cal., W.P.
Boyce James L. 3737 Grand boul.
Boyce Maria M. Mrs. 4620 Woodlawn av.
Boyce S. Leonard, 3735 Grand boul. Chi., Univ.
Boyce William D. 1850 Wrightwood av. C.A., U.L.
Boyd Alexander, Hinsdale
Boyd Alice E. Mrs. 413 Huron
Boyd E. K. Evanston
Boyd George M. 517 Racine av.
Boyd Hattie Mrs. 3107 Forest av.
Boyd James Harrington Dr. 363, 58th
Boyd James W. 6249 Monroe av.
Boyd John, Elmhurst
Boyd John jr. Glen Ellyn
Boyd John D. Mrs 2849 Kenmore av.
Boyd John H. Dr. Evanston
Boyd Joseph N. Rev. River Forest
Boyd Robert, Hinsdale
Boyd Robert D. Dr. Clifton house
Boyd R. G. Glen Ellyn
Boyd R. L. Oak Park
Boyd Samuel F. 173 Eugenie
Boyd S. J. Dr. 625 Washington boul.
Boyd William S. Hinsdale
Boyd W. P. Hinsdale
Boyde Margaret Miss, The Ontario
Boydell Jesse, 4339 Prairie av.
Boyden William C. 3005 Calumet av. Univ
Boyer Allen, 4904 Washington av.
Boyer Henry J. 4904 Washington av.
Boyesen Austa Miss, 5125 Kimbark av.
Boyesen Harold, 5125 Kimbark av.

Boyesen Ingolf K. 5125 Kimbark av. *Chi.,*
   U.L.
Boyington Arthur M. Highland Park
Boyington George B. Highland Park
Boyington S. A. Mrs. 91, 37th
Boyington W. W. Mrs. Highland Park
Boyle Daniel, 4610. Champlain av.
Boyle David Mrs. 521 W. Monroe
Boyle F. W. Mrs. 46, 36th pl.
Boyle John P. 271 Belden av.
Boyle Lawrence P. 2953 Vernon av. *Irq.*
Boyle Loren L. 5711 Madison. av.
Boyle Thomas, 1840 Diversey
Boyles Charles C. Riverside
Boyles Charles D. Riverside. *U.L.*
Boyles Thomas D. Riverside
Boynton Charles T. Evanston *C.A.,U.L.*
Boynton Charles W. 390 Ontario
Boynton C. E. Dr. 2124 Michigan av.
Boynton Edgar S. Highland Park
Boynton Frances Miss, Evanston
Boynton Frederick P. Highland Park
Boynton G. W. Leland hotel
Boynton Isabell Miss, Evanston
Boynton S. A. Mrs. 2124 Michigan av.
Brabrook J. F. Mrs. 520 W. Congress
Brabrook W. Fred jr. LaGrange
Brace William, 297 Belden av.
   Sum. res. Lake Bluff
Brachvogel Charles H. 7626 Saginaw av.
Brackebush A. C. 307 Lasalle av
Brackebush Carl A. 307 Lasalle av.
Brackebush Charles H. 560 Division, *Un.*
Brackebush C. J. Mrs. 560 Division
Brackebush Frederick M. 560 Division
Bracken Julia M. Miss, Ohio ne.cor.State
Bradburn James I. 3651 Prairie av.
Bradbury George L. 3214 Michigan av.
   Cal., Chi., W.P.
Braden C. E. 3935 Ellis av.
Braden Joseph C. 3931 Prairie av.
Bradford Anna E. Mrs. Austin
Bradford C. Rev. Longwood
Bradford Edwin R. Evanston
Bradford H. M. Mrs. 2155 Sheridan rd..
   Sum. res. Lauderdale Lake, Wis.
Bradford John, 259 Fremont
Bradford W. J. 3861 Lake av.
Bradley Alexander S. 5450 Ridgewood ct.
Bradley Alexander S. jr. 5450 Ridgewood
   ct.
Bradley Anna A. Miss,6122 Woodlawn av.
Bradley A. R. Hotel Del Prado
Bradley B. W. 5911 Wabash av.
Bradley Carl D. 4259 Grand boul.
Bradley Charles D. Dr. 131 Dearborn av.
Bradley Charles Frederick, Evanston
   Sum. res. Annisquam, Mass.
Bradley Charles H. 3551 Indiana av.
Bradley Charles M. 3812 Calumet av.
Bradley Chauncey B. Evanston
Bradley C. H. 213, 40th
Bradley David, 389 W. Adams
Bradley David E. Avenue house, Evanston. *Univ.*
Bradley Edward, Evanston

Bradley Elizabeth W. Mrs. Evanston
Bradley Ella Miss, 24 Ritchie ct.
Bradley E. L. Mrs. Hinsdale
Bradley E. R. The Ontario
Bradley Foster H. 6533 Minerva av.
Bradley Francis Mrs. Evanston
Bradley Frank A. Mrs. Evanston
   Sum. res. Lake Mills. Wis.
Bradley Frank B. 3814 Forest av. *U.L.*
Bradley Frank W. Evanston
Bradley Fred O. Evanston
Bradley F. G. 361 Park av.
Bradley James, New Hotel Holand
Bradley James D. 4203 Drexel boul. *C.A.*
Bradley James P. 3734 Calumet av.
Bradley John Dorr, 205 Goethe. *Univ.*
Bradley John H. Hinsdale
Bradley J. C. F. Hinsdale
Bradley J. Harley, 24 Ritchie ct. *Chi.,*
   U.L., Univ.
Bradley Kate Miss, Oak Park
Bradley Loring Mrs. 213, 40th
Bradley Matthew S. 5315 Washington av.
Bradley Miss, 24 Ritchie ct.
Bradley Philip H. 308 Chestnut
Bradley P. B. 308 Chestnut. *U.L.*
Bradley Ralph R. Hinsdale
Bradley R. R. 706 Pullman bldg.
Bradley Seth E. Wilmette
Bradley Street, Riverside
Bradley Thomas E. D. 799 W. Monroe
   Sum. res. Waynesville, Ill.
Bradley W. H. Mrs. 265 Oak
Bradshaw H. P. Mrs. 4522 Greenwood
   av.
Bradshaw John H. 333 Ashland boul.
Bradshaw William D. 1159 Washington
   boul.
Bradstreet J. Edwin, Winnetka
Bradwell J. B. Judge, 1428 Michigan av.
   U.L.
Bradwell Thomas, 3209 South Park av.
Brady George K. Col. 3817 Vincennes av.
Brady George P. Dr. 5524 Drexel av.
Brady Hugo, 4355 Calumet av.
Brady John B. 3744 Ellis av.
Brady J. F. 2690 N. Ashland av.
Brady Mack S. 812 Farwell av.
Brady M. P. 967 Park av.
Brady Oscar M. 749 Walnut
Braffette C. F. LaGrange
Bragdon Charles E. 6451 Kimbark av.
Bragdon C. P. Mrs. Evanston
Bragdon M. C. Dr. Evanston
Brainard A. P. 4035 Indiana av.
Brainard Edward C. 439 W. 64th
Brainard Edwin, 351 Chestnut. *C.A.,Un.*
Brainard Frank A. 4423 Prairie av.
Brainard Harriet C. Mrs. 2970 Groveland
   av.
Brainard Harry G. Mrs. 6700 Wentworth
   av.
Brainard H. F. LaGrange
Brainard Marvin R. 394 Warren av.
Brainard W. N. Mrs. Evanston
Brainerd Ed. R. Auditorium hotel, *U.L.*

Brainerd Edward T. 921 W. Monroe
Brainerd Frank W. 921 W. Monroe
Braithwaite Charles W. 318 W. 61st pl.
Bramhall Frank J. 338 W. 60th pl.
Brammer Frederick H. Evanston
Branch Albert E. Oak Park
Branch Burton A. 4601 Vincennes av.
Branch E. K. Mrs. 76 Maple
Branch E. P. Mrs. Evanston
Branch John W. Evanston
Brand Belle Miss, 1918 Michigan av.
Brand Charles H. 320 Oakwood boul.
Brand Edwin L. 1918 Michigan av. *Cal.
C.A., W.P.
Brand Edwin L. jr. 1918 Michigan av.
Brand Horace L. 32 Cedar
Brand Jacob J. Highland Park
Brand Phil K. 53 Cedar
Brand Rudolph, 53 Cedar
Brand Silas H. 1525 W. Monroe
Brand William E. Highland Park
Brandecker Frank X. 648 Sedgwick
Brandecker Frank X. jr. 648 Sedgwick
Brandimore James F. 823 W. Jackson
    boul.
Brandimore Joseph H. 823 W. Jackson
    boul.
Brandon Henry J. 1922 Barry av. *Un.
Brandt A. L. Mrs. 4548 Lake av.
Brandt George W. 4558 Lake av. *Irq.
Branen Frank Dr. 961 W. Monroe
Branston William F., Austin .
Brant Henry W. 401 N. State
Brantingham Grace J. Miss, North Shore
    hotel
Brashears James B. Evanston
Brauckmann David G. 1824 Briar pl.
Brauckmann George, 1824 Briar pl.
Braun David J. 4165 N. Ashland av.
Braun George P. 674 Lasalle av. *C.A.
    Sum. res. Lake Geneva, Wis.
Braun Mabel Miss, 674 Lasalle av.
Braun Thomas, 3137 South Park av.
Brausch Frank, Hotel Luzerne
Brawley Francis.W. S. Mrs. 3010 Lake
    Park av.
Bray Joseph D. 1352 Sheridan rd.
Braymer Ernest S. 6410 Monroe av. .
Braymer Frederick A. 6410 Monroe av.
    Sum. res. Delavan Lake, Wis.
Brayton G. W. Hyde Park hotel
Brayton James H. 6319 Yale
Brayton James T. 36th ne. cor. Ellis av.
Brayton Laura T. Miss, 338, 57th
Brayton Sarah H. Dr. Evanston
Brazelton Frank M. S. 647 Park av.
Brearley Annie E. Miss, Lake Forest
Breasted James H. Prof. 301, 56th
Breckenridge J.Howard, 4351 Calumet av.
Breckinridge Stephen L. Dr. Riverside
Breckinridge W. L. Mrs. Evanston
Brede David, 4800 Michigan av.
Brede F. B. 3560 Grand boul.
Brede Max, 3532 Wabash av.
Bredon Ernest, 802 Sherwin av.
Bredt John M. 385 Evanston av.

Breed Charles L. La Grange
Breed J. Mrs. Hyde Park hotel
Breed Richard E. 598 Burling
Breen J. C. Wilmette
Breen Martin J. 23 Winthrop ct.
Breese Charlotte Mrs. 2624 Calumet av.
Breese J. B. Calumet club. *Chi., W.P.
Breese Leland, Wilmette
Brega Charles W. 2816 Michigan av. *Chi.,
    W.P.
Brehmer Ida Miss, 1817 Belmont av.
Breidenstein Henry, 278 Fremont
Breitling John P. Oak Park
Breitung Albert, 1925 Deming ct.
Bremer Albert R. 4938 Ellis av. .
Bremner B. Mrs. 4442 Ellis av.
Bremner D. F. 240 Loomis. *Ill.
Bremner Edward A. 4442 Ellis av.
Bremond Marian Miss, Evanston
Brenan Thomas, 163, 30th
Brenckle F. W. 354 Mohawk
Brennan Bernard G. 143 Oakwood boul.
Brennan James J. Hotel Normandie.*C.A.
Brennan Kittie Miss, 1821 Indiana av.
Brennan Matthew J. 4018 Vincennes av.
Brennan Michael, 365 Dayton
Brennan Patrick, 502 Ashland boul.
Brenneman Daniel W. 3297 Beacon
Brenock John, 29 Macalister pl.
Brenock William, 29 Macalister pl.·
Brentano Theodore Judge, 445 Lasalle av.
Brethold Charles H. Wilmette
Brett Emma S.Miss,794 Washington boul.
Brett Jennie L. Mrs. 648 W. Monroe
    Sum. res. Charlevoix, Mich.
Brett J. A. The Arizona
Brett Theodore F. 794 Washington boul.
Brewer Charles, 5460 Washington av.
Brewer C. S. Evanston
Brewer Frank B., M.D. Evanston .
Brewer Frank M. Dr. 1806 N. Halsted
Brewer John S. 400 The Plaza. *W.P.
Brewer Orville, 2923 Groveland av.
Brewer Owen W. 3237 Groveland av. *C.A.,
    W.P.
Brewer Robert T. 205 The Plaza
Brewster Edward L. 46 Astor. *Cal., Chi..
    Un., W.P.
Brewster G. O. 573, 51st
Brewster Jabez, 14 Burton pl.
Brewster James P. Glencoe
Brewster J. L. 438 W. 65th
Brewster Walter S. 46 Astor. *W.P. l
Brewster William S. 569, 51st
Breyfogle W. L. Chicago Beach hotel.*Irq.
Breytspraak John, Evanston
Bricker Aura Mrs. Oak Park
Brickwood A. W. 35 Ashland boul.
Bridge F. A. The Arizona
Bridge R. W. 5402 Cornell av.
Bridgeman William J. 4536 Woodlawn av.
Bridges J. Soloman, 234, 47th
Bridgman Walter R. Prof. Lake Forest
Briggs Ann R. Mrs. 444 Washington
    boul. a
Briggs Charles H. 15 Scott *C.A.

Briggs Clinton, Lakota hotel
Briggs David C. 12 Ritchie ct. *Un.*
Briggs George B. 290 LaSalle av. *C.A.*
Briggs George M. La Grange
Briggs H. Elwin, 6530 Yale .
Briggs Lafayette, Hinsdale
Briggs Nathan E. La Grange
Briggs S. W. Oak Park
Brigham Edmund D. 2762 N. Winchester av.
Brigham Florence Miss, 2705 Indiana av.
Brigham G. B. The Arizona
Brigham R. B. Morgan Park
Bright Orville T. 6515 Harvard av.
Brimson W. Geo. 528 W. 62d
Brinckerhoff Henry Morton, 149 Ashland boul. *Ill.*
Brinckerhoff Lesley, Kenilworth
Brine George J. 2443 Kenmore av.
Brine Helen Q. Mrs. 5554 Monroe av.
Brink Arthur P. 1764 Sheridan rd.
Brink D. E. Oak Park
Brink James T. 7117 Yale
Brink Percy A. 1764 Sheridan rd.
Brinkerhoff Wm. C., M.D. Chicago Beach hotel
Brinkman William M. 3351 Calumet av.
        Sum. res. Fox Lake, Ill.
Brintnall Arthur W. 3438 Wabash av.
Brintnall Mary L. Mrs. 3438 Wabash av.
Brintnall Solva, 3438 Wabash av.
Brintnall Wm. H. 4621 Ellis av.
Brisbine A. McIver Mrs. 516 North av.
Briscoe C. H. Dr. 4405 Sidney av.
Brislen A. J. Dr. 614, 46th
Brislen E. Mrs. 614, 46th
Brison John, 2703 N. Ashland av.
Brissenden Frederick C. 5738 Indiana av.
Brissenden Walter W. 5738 Indiana av.
Bristol Edward S. 1642 W. Adams
Bristol Lucien D. 6808 Butler
Bristol Mary J. Mrs. 5112 Jefferson av.
Bristol William J. 1640 W. Adams
Brittan Arthur, 508 N. State
        Sum. res. Beloit, Wis.
Brittan Caroline A. Miss, 508 N. State
Brittan Charles H. 4160 Lake av.
Britten Michael, 450 Dearborn av.
Britten Peter, 450 Dearborn. av.
Brix Dominicus Dr. 6316 Stewart av.
Broadbent Thomas A. Dr. 2541 N. Hermitage av. *C.A.*
Broberg Gustavus, 1407 N. Maplewood av.
Brochon Louis M. Oak Park
Brock Lizzie Miss, Winnetka
Brockenbrough S. R. Hotel Del Prado
Brocklebank John C. F. 3009 Kenmore av. *C.A.*
Brockway George, 179, 36th
Brockway Guy, 179, 36th
Brockway H. O. 36th, ne. cor. Ellis av.
Brockway Vira A. Dr. 52 Campbell Park
        Sum. res. St. Joseph, Mich.
Brodhead Frederick A. 3627 Ellis av.
Brodlique Eve H. Miss, 225 Dearborn av.
Brodt Herman, Prof. Elmhurst

Brokaw Abraham, 228 S. Lincoln
Bromilow Agnes Mrs. 1835 Arlington pl.
Bromilow Ernest W. 1746 Wrightwood av.
Bromley Joseph E. Auditorium-annex. *W.P.*
Brompton Joseph C. 235 Sunnyside av.
Bronson Ethel V. Mrs. Oak Park
Bronson Francis C. 2362 N. Paulina
Bronson John G. 235 Michigan av.
Bronson Solon C. Prof. Evanston
Brook Ida Bell Miss, Evanston
Brooke E. J. T. Mrs. 612 Division
Brooke Orson H. Evanston
Brooke William Lieut. Fort Sheridan
Brookes Frederick A. Morgan Park
Brookes Frederick W. Morgan Park
Brookes John F. 3538 Lake av.
Brookes Mary J. Mrs. 3538 Lake av.
Brookman Joseph S. 922 Morse av.
Brooks Almon Dr. 4643 Lake av. *C.A.*
Brooks A. F. 4356 St. Lawrence av.
Brooks Charles Mrs. 251 Ashland boul.
Brooks Charles M. 4454 Sidney av. *C.A.*, *U.L.*
Brooks Edith Miss, 87 Cass
Brooks Ellis, Clifton house
Brooks Emily Mrs. 1692 Graceland av.
Brooks Everett W. 4623 Drexel boul. *U.L.*
Brooks Fred G. 711 Washington boul.
Brooks F. E. Miss. 251 Ashland boul.
Brooks H. K. New Hotel Holland
Brooks James C. 87 Cass. *C.A.*, *Un.*
Brooks Jesse W. Rev. Irving Park
Brooks Julia A. Mrs.711 Washington boul.
Brooks . R. 143 Oakwood boul.
Brooks J. W. jr. 4912 Woodlawn av. *C.A.*, *U.L.*
Brooks Maria M. Miss, 251 Ashland boul.
Brooks M. E. Mrs. 6369 Greenwood av.
Brooks M. W. Mrs. 4627 Lake av.
Brooks Noah W. Evanston
Brooks Oliver Mrs. 4643 Lake av.
Brooks S. A. Mrs. 569, 51st
Brooks S. N. Mrs. 271 Warren av.
Brooks Virginia Miss, 4643 Lake av.
Brooks William C. Greenwood Inn, Evanston
Broomell Chester C. 4017 Lake av.
Broomell Francis E. 496 W. Monroe
Broomell George D. 496 W. Monroe
Broomell George D. jr. 496 W. Monroe
Brophy Florence A. Miss, 176 Ashland boul.
Brophy Truman W. Dr. 176 Ashland boul. *C.A.*, *Ill.*, *U.L.*
        Sum. res. Fox Lake, Ill.
Bross Mason, 550 Dearborn av. *C.A.*, *Univ.*
Bross William Mrs. 2001 Michigan av.
Brosseau Auguste, 608 N. State. *Chi.*, *W.P.*
Brosseau Zenophile P. 1950 Barry av. *Chi* , *Irq.*, *W.P.*
Brothers Elmer D. 4351 N. Ashland av.
Brothers William E. Evanston
Brougham Thos. B. 5131 Washington av.

Broughton Charles, 4517 Woodlawn av.
Broughton E. P. 3320 Indiana av.
Broughton John W. River Forest
Broughton Urban H. 6 Tower ct. *Chi.,*
  W.P.
Brower A. T. H. 1330 Bryn Mawr av.
Brower Charles H. Mrs. 153 S. Oakley av.
Brower Daniel Roberts Dr. 597 W. Jackson boul. *Ill.*
Brower Daniel Roberts jr. 597 W. Jackson boul.
Brower Eunice Anne Miss, 597 W. Jackson boul.
Brower J. F. Chicago Beach hotel. *C.A.*
Brower Madison, 4132 Newgart av.
Brower Noah C. 43, 34th pl.
Brown Adelbert E. Dr. 273 Oakwood boul.
Brown Albert C. Dr. 4729 Langley av.
Brown Albert L. 918 Winona av.
Brown Albert Sidney, 6719 Wentworth av.
Brown Alice Barlow Dr. 181 Dearborn av.
Brown Allen A. 1812 Belmont av.
Brown Andrew J. Evanston
Brown Annie Miss, Lake Forest
Brown Archibald L. 46 Pine Grove av. *C.A.*
Brown Austin H. Lieut. Fort Sheridan
Brown A. Fletcher, 17, 39th
Brown A. S. Rev. Evanston
Brown Berlyn B. 5533 Washington av.
Brown Charles A. 696 Washington boul. *Irq., U.L.*
Brown Charles B. 3157 Calumet av.
Brown Charles E. 2414 Prairie av. *C.A.*
  Sum. res. Lake Forest
Brown Clara J. Miss, Lake Forest
Brown C. Addie Miss, 59 Aberdeen
Brown C. F. Mrs. 3269 Groveland av.
Brown C. Leroy, Hotel Windermere
Brown C. S. Mrs. 2585 Kenmore av.
Brown David, Austin
Brown David P. 2723 N. Lincoln
Brown DeWitt, 5415 Jefferson av.
Brown Dexter G. 4734 Greenwood av. *C.A.*
Brown Edmund Lee, 6719 Wentworth av.
Brown Edward C. 5516 Jefferson av.
Brown Edward D. 6617 Washington av.
Brown Edward F. 298 Wilson av.
Brown Edward Houghton, Highland Park
Brown Edward L. 44 Madison Park
Brown Edward O. 400 N. State. *Irq.*
Brown Edwin, 339 W. 61st. *C.A.*
Brown Edwin E. 202 Oakwood boul.
Brown Edwin F. Evanston
  Sum. res. Lake Geneva, Wis.
Brown Edwin S. 6565 Yale
Brown Elias H. 854 Walnut
Brown Emma E. Miss, Irving Park
Brown Esther Mrs. 4325 Lake av.
Brown Everett C. 3 Aldine sq. *C.A.*
Brown E. Fred. Dr. 6222 Woodlawn av.
Brown E. Herrick, Oak Park
Brown E. M. Hotel Del Prado
Brown Finley D. 5533 Washington av.
Brown Florence Miss, 171 Warren av.
Brown Francis C. Highland Park. *Chi.*

Brown Francis C. 44 Madison Park
Brown Frank A. 2723 N. Lincoln
Brown Frank E. 6230 Woodlawn av.
Brown Frank G. 611 W. 60th
  Sum. res. Lake Minnetonka, Minn
Brown Frank G. 5490 Monroe av.
Brown Frank H. 4306 Lake av.
Brown Frank T. 225 Dearborn av. *Univ.*
Brown Fred A. 4530 Prairie av.
Brown Frederick I. Dr. Irving Park
Brown F. H. Oak Park
Brown F. Junior, 5533 Washington av.
Brown F. S. Evanston
Brown F. W. Evanston
Brown George D. 1504 Lawrence av. *W.P.*
Brown George F. 2414 Prairie av. *U.L.*
Brown George F. 5490 Monroe av.
Brown George F. jr. 2414 Prairie av. *C.A.*
Brown George H. Austin
Brown George L. 2925 Indiana av..
Brown George R. Evanston
Brown George Wesley, 4531 Forrestville av.
  Sum. res. Spring Lake, Mich.
Brown George W. 8 Washington pl. *Un., Univ.*
Brown Grace Miss, Evanston
Brown Harriet Mrs. 6558 Ross av.
Brown Harry L., M. D. 508 W. Congress
Brown Henry E. 1923 Indiana av.
Brown Henry F. 335 Rush
Brown Henry H. 206 Ashland boul.
Brown Henry T. 2155 Clarendon av.
Brown Horace F. 508 W. Congress
Brown H. F. 3363 Forest av.
Brown H. H. Dr. 491 Dearborn av.
Brown H. L. 301 Warren av.
Brown H. W. Rev. Morgan Park
Brown Isaac E. Oak Park
Brown Isaac W. 223 Jackson Park Terrace
Brown Isabelle Miss, Glencoe
Brown Isidore F. 3611 Prairie av. *Lksd.*
Brown James F. 5026 Woodlawn av.
Brown James Moreau, 444 Elm. *C.A.*
Brown James S. 611 W. 60th
Brown John, 3426 Michigan av.
Brown John B. Chicago Beach hotel
Brown John G. Evanston
Brown John H. 2446 Michigan av.
Brown John H. 2908 Groveland av.
Brown John H. 547 W. 62d
Brown John M. Evanston
Brown John S. 816 Walnut
Brown John W. Evanston
Brown Jonas, 3207 South Park av.
Brown Joseph, 614 W. Congress
Brown Joseph W. 2199 Washiugton boul.
Brown Julius N. 3142 Groveland av.
Brown J. Austin Mrs. Chicago Beach hotel
Brown J. D. 143 Oakwood boul.
Brown J. H. Hotel Metropole
Brown J. M. 2556 Magnolia av.
Brown J. Rice, Oak Park
Brown LeRoy, 3255 Prairie av.

Brown Lewis J. 6558 Ross av.
Brown Lincoln A. 183, 37th. *C.A.*
Brown Lot, Morton Park
Brown Louis F. 77, 20th
Brown Ludwig, 1439 Wrightwood av.
Brown L. Cass, LaGrange
Brown L. L. Morgan Park
Brown L. Read Dr. 273 Oakwood boul.
Brown Margaret S. Miss, 44 Madison Park
Brown Mary L. Mrs. 1886 Diversey
Brown Minnie M. Mrs. 4421 Ellis av.
Brown Moreau R. Dr. 444 Elm. *C.A.*
Brown Murray M. 1469 Washington boul.
Brown M. A. Mrs. 6629 Harvard av.
Brown Oliver S. 611 W. 60th
Brown O. G. 872, 50th. *C.A.*
Brown Paul, 3330 Calumet av. *U.L.*
Brown Philip S. 6230 Woodlawn av.
Brown Richard, Evanston
Brown Richard H. Dr. 1217 W. Jackson boul.
Brown Robert C. River Forest
Brown Robert K. Evanston
Brown Robert P. 3859 Lake av.
Brown Sam, 2971 Michigan av.
Brown Samuel jr. 3203 Beacon
Brown Sanger Dr. 757 Washington boul. *U.L.*
Brown Spencer A. 53, 53d
    Sum. res. Lake Geneva, Wis.
Brown Spencer M. 53, 53d
Brown Stuart H. 4853 Kimbark av.
Brown S. M. Hotel DelPrado
Brown Taylor E. 6504 Ingleside av. *C.A.*
Brown Thomas, 52, 24th
Brown Thomas jr. 3 Aldine sq.
Brown Thomas H. 3345 Indiana av.
Brown T. Barbour, Highland Park
Brown Walter, 465 Flournoy
Brown Walter Frazer, 2908 Groveland av.
Brown Walter Lee, Evanston
Brown William Mrs. 4530 Prairie av.
Brown William C. 44 Madison Park
Brown William C. 5611 Washington av. *U.L.*
Brown William C. 6719 Wentworth av.
Brown William C. Evanston. *C.A.*
Brown William C. Oak Park
Brown William E. 4919 Vincennes av.
Brown William H. 1812 Belmont av. *U.L.*
Brown William H. D. Dr. 4530 Prairie av.
Brown William Liston, Evanston. *Chi.*, *U.L.*
Brown William M. Dr. 816 Walnut
Brown William T. 6558 Ross av.
Brown W. Gray, 171 Warren av. *Ill.*
Brown W. H. A. 4306 Oakenwald av.
Brown W. Morton, 4420 Greenwood av.
Browne A. W. 414 Oak
Browne Charles E. 4132 Perry
Browne Edward, 215 61st
Browne Edward H. Capt. Fort Sheridan
Browne E. L. Mrs. 4363 Lake av.
Browne Frank L. Dr. 949 Greenleaf av.

Browne Josiah Mrs. LaGrange
Browne J. Sidney, 555 Webster av.
Browne Lizzie R. Miss, 4021 Vincennes av.
Browne Malcolm J. LaGrange
Browne Willis W. LaGrange
Brownell Albert S. Elmhurst
Brownell Ralph E. 7100 Yale
Browning Granville W. 425 Lasalle av. *Irq.*, *Univ.*
Brownlee A. G. 91 Seminary av. *C.A.*
Brownridge William T. 6549 Yale
Brownwell J. G. Rev. Hotel Del Prado
Bruce Charles, Morton Park
Bruce Edward M. Dr. 5314 Washington av.
Bruce Jane Mrs. 52 Oakwood av.
Bruce Josephine Lester Mrs. 3515 Calumet av.
Brucker Joseph, 720 Fullerton av. *U.L.*
Brueckner John F. 903 Sherwin av.
Bruen William G. 4613 Woodlawn av.
Bruette W. A. 78, 26th. *C.A.*
Brumback Arthur H. Dr. 109 Loomis
Brunaugh Samuel B. 1805 Barry av.
Bruner Anna L. Mrs. 2975 Kenmore av.
Bruner George N. 143 Oakwood av.
Bruner James D. Prof. 6224 Greenwood av.
Bruning Josephine Mrs. 386 Chestnut
Bruns Francis F. 579 Lasalle av.
Bruns Frank W. 579 Lasalle av.
Bruns H. M. 917 Pullman bldg.
Bruns Louis Wilkens, 579 Lasalle av.
Brunson F. M. Morgan Park
Brunson W. W. 427 Warren av.
Brunton Julius, 6369 Greenwood av.
Brush Charles E. 838 W. Garfield boul.
Brush Daniel E. 4415 Michigan av.
Brush Emerson H. 210 Goethe. Sum. res. Elmhurst. *U.L.*
Brush Homer J. 4415 Michigan av.
Brush William Mrs. 7657 Butler
Brushingham J. P. Rev. 112 S. Leavitt
Brust Frank, 6127 Ellis av.
Bryan Alfred C. Hinsdale
Bryan Anna E. Miss, 2943 Calumet av.
Bryan Benjamin B. 5124 Cornell av. *C.A.*, *U.L.*
Bryan C. M. Mrs. 6550 Yale
Bryan E. A. The Kenwood
Bryan E. H. Mrs. Austin
Bryan E. S. Maywood
Bryan Fred C. 3764 Indiana av. *Cal.*
Bryan Frederick W. 887 Warren av. *Ill.* Sum. res. Fox Lake, Ill.
Bryan Isaac J. 2477 Lakewood av.
Bryan John C. 1079 Washington boul.
Bryan Symon R. 3176 Malden
Bryan Thomas B. Elmhurst. *U.L.*
Bryan William S. P. Rev. 13 Chalmers pl.
Bryan W. H. 2563 N. Paulina
Bryant Arthur W. Oak Park
Bryant Chauncey E. 296 Ohio
Bryant Clifford W. 3004 Prairie av. Sum. res. Lexington, Mass.
Bryant Dwight S. 2957 Indiana av.

Bryant Edward F. Pullman. *C.A.*
Bryant Fred L. 259 Seminary av.
Bryant George H. 2624-N. Hermitage av.
Bryant Henry W. 2973 Prairie av. *U.L.*
Bryant John A. 2545 Magnolia av.
Bryant John J. Riverside. *U.L.*
Bryant John J. jr. Riverside
Bryant Nellie A. Mrs. 447 Englewood av.
Bryce P. F. 175 Park av.
Bryce Robert M. 175 Park av.
Brydon James M. Dr. 270. 35th
Brydon J. A. LaGrange
Brydon Robert T. 212 The Plaza
Bryson James R. 1 Washington pl.
Bryson Mary Miss, 1 Washington pl.
Bryson Wm. J. 169 Buena av. *C.A.*
Bubb John W. Maj. Fort Sheridan
Buchan J. R. Dr. 150 Park av.
Buchanan A. T. Dr. 6110 Madison av.
Buchanan Charles H. Dr. 193, 41st
Buchanan D. W. 4563 Lake av.
Buchanan Edward P. 4580 Oakenwald av.
Buchanan Ellen M. Mrs. 5555 Monroe
　　av.
Buchanan Gordon, Chicago Beach hotel.
　　C.A.
Buchanan Helen M. Dr. 6352 Monroe av.
Buchanan James, 183 S. Hoyne av.
Buchanan J. N. 3635 Ellis av.
Buchanan Milford D. Chicago Beach
　　hotel. *C.A.*
Buchanan Robert E. 1265 N. Clark
Buchanan Robert R. 4859 Madison av.
Buchanan S. Percy, 4937 Washington Park
　　ct.
Bucher W. H. 717 Pullman bldg. *C.A.*
Buck Albert H. 2937 Indiana av.
Buck A. Miss, 49 Astor
Buck C. D. Prof. 5746 Madison av.
　　　　Sum. res. Bucksport, Me.
Buck Francis M. 6627 Harvard av. *U.L.*
Buck Grace P. Miss, 2937 Indiana av.
Buck Harry R. Austin
Buck James P., M.D. 413 Lasalle av.
Buck Orlando J. 7628 Union av.
Buckbee Julian E. Col. Winnetka
Buckbee Julian E. jr. Winnetka
Buckie Annie E. Mrs. 81 Hammond
Buckingham Clarence, 2036 Prairie av.
　　Chi, *U.L.*
Buckingham E. 2036 Prairie av. *U.L.*
Buckingham Henry W. Evanston
Buckingham Isabel C. Mrs. 3244 Grove-
　　land av.
Buckingham John, 1832 Calumet av.
Buckingham M. Miss, Lexington hotel
Buckingham Reuben D. 4000 Lake av.
Buckingham Roswell H. Evanston
Bucklen Herbert E. 265 Michigan av.
Buckley Charles W. Evanston
Buckley Elizabeth M. Miss 3131 Forest av.
Buckley Frank S. Dr. Oak Park
Buckley Jeanette Miss, 2927 Indiana av.
Buckley L. Miss, 1436 Washington boul.
Buckley Nora Miss, 1304 Washington boul.
Buckley Sara C. Dr. 301, 56th

Buckley S. S. 2927 Indiana av.
Buckley Thomas, Clifton House
Buckley William, 5300 Lexington av.
Buckley W. T. 3144 Dover
Bucklin Kate Miss, 2358 Indiana av.
Bucklin M. Mrs. 2358 Indiana av.
Budach P. H. Rev. Washington Heights
Budd William O. 6550 Harvard av.
Budd W. C. 547 Dearborn av.
Budde Albert, Oak Park
Buddington F. E. 2327 Indiana av.
Buderbach William, Elmhurst
Budlong Milton J. Chicago Beach hotel.
　　C.A.
Buechner Herman C. 29 Pine Grove av.
Buecking Edward F., M.D. 425 S. Paulina
Buehler Edward H. Evanston. *C.A.*
Buehler John, 5 Ewing pl.
Buehler John W. 37 Roslyn pl.
Buehler Katharine B. Miss, Evanston
Buehler William, Evanston
Buel Forrest L. 4444 Greenwood av.
Buel Henry K. Mrs. 336 Ontario
Buel Munson P. 4444 Greenwood av.
Buell Augustine C. Evanston.
Buell Bradley Dixon, 521 Dearborn av.
Buell Charles A. 6616 Yale
Buell Charles C. 2002 Indiana av. *Irq.*
Buell Ira W. 2832 Indiana av. *U.L.*
Buell James Wallace, 521 Dearborn av.
Buenz Karl, 500 The Plaza
Buffington Eugene J. Evanston
Buffington Walter J. Hinsdale
Buffum A. P. Mrs. Evanston
Buffum Joseph H. Dr. 366 Ontario. *Chi.*
Bufkin Mary Lee Miss, 4583 Oakenwald
　　av.
Buhmann Theodore W. 1547 Oakdale av.
Buhoup H. C. 385 Oakwood boul.
Buhrer John S. 3263 Groveland av.
Builder John, Oak Park
Buisseret Armand E. 6506 Monroe av.
Buker Harry L. 779 Mildred av.
Buker Joseph, 6315 Parnell av.
Bulckens Isabel Miss, Austin
Bulckens Louise Miss, Austin
Bulger William J. 1649 Graceland av.
　　Irq.
Bulkley Almon W. 7154 Euclid av.
Bulkley Julia E. Miss, University of
　　Chicago.
Bulkley R. H. 780 North Park av.
Bull Charles D. 275 S. Irving av.
Bull Follett W. 4150 Lake av.
Bull Lucy Miss, 538 Dearborn av.
Bull William B. 187 Lincoln Park boul.
　　Chi.
Bullard Albert B. 3000 Prairie av.
Bullard Charles W. Maywood
Bullard Elihu R. 818 W. Jackson boul.
Bullard Josephine D. Miss, 2849 Kenmore
　　av.
Bullen Albert F. 438 Elm. *C.A.*, *Un.*
Bullen C. F. Hotel Windermere. *Chi.*
Bullen Frederick F. 1015 Warren av. *C.A.*
Bullen F. F. 225 Dearborn av.

Bullen George, Oconomowoc, Wis. *W.P.*
Bullen John T. Oak Park
Bullock Bertha Miss, 568 Dearborn va.
Bullock Carl C. 568 Dearborn av. *C.A.*
Bullock F. W. 4432 Berkeley av. *C.A.*
Bullock George S. Lakota hotel. *U.L.*
Bullock Henry E. 1769 Deming pl.
Bullock J. C. 568 Dearborn av.
Bullock Milan C. 1187 Washington boul. *U.L.*
Bullock Milo S. 4947 Vincennes av. *Stan.*
Bumiller Emil C. 804 Pine Grove av.
Bunch F. M. La Grange
Bunch J. Claude, 4600 Prairie av.
Bunch R. H. La Grange
Bunday George F. 3358 Calumet av.
Bundy John C. Mrs. Evanston
Bunge W. H. 144 Park av.
Bunker Charles H. 484, 42d
Bunker D. A. Mrs. 3230 Groveland av.
Bunker Hiram S. 756 W. 44th. *W.P.*
Bunker William I. LaGrange
Bunn Ernest F. Revere house
Bunnell John A. 5140 Cornell av.
Bunte Charles F. 803 Greenleaf av.
Bunte Ferdinand, 803 Greenleaf av.
Burbank Augustus J. 6424 Monroe av.
Burbank Edward A. 2632 Calumet av.
    Sum. res. Suffield, Conn.
Burbank E. A. 1254 Michigan av
Burbank E. M. Mrs. Austin
Burbank Henry C. 1886 Diversey
Burbank Wellman M. Dr. 3035 South Park av.
Burbank W. B. Mrs. 2632 Calumet av.
Burch E. J. Dr. 3156 Indiana av.
Burch William A. Rev. 3314 South Park av.
Burch Wirt, Berwyn
Burch W. A. New Hotel Holland
Burchard Ernest F. Evanston
Burchard George W. Evanston
Burchard Mortimer N. Kenilworth, *U.L.*
Burchmore John H., M.D. Evanston
Burcky Christian, 6000 Indiana av.
Burcky Elise Mrs. 6000 Indiana av.
Burcky William R. 5946 Indiana av.
Burden William E. Evanston
Burdick A. S. Dr. Hinsdale
Burdick E. R. Chicago Beach hotel
Burdick Julian C. 238 Oakwood boul.
Burdick Munson, 271 Ashland boul.
Burdick Oscar, 271 Ashland boul. *Ill.*
Burdick William S. 238 Oakwood boul.
Burdsal George B. Evanston
Burdsal John W. Evanston
Burdsal S. C. Mrs. 762 Greenleaf av.
Burdsall Marion C. Miss, 3526 Forest av.
Burdsall Mary J. Miss, 3526 Forest av.
Burdsall Wm. J. 3526 Forest av.
Burge Edward A. Wilmette
Burger Jerman F. 3131 Indiana av.
Burger Tyrus L. 3131 Indiana av.
Burgess Albert, Oak Park
Burgess A. C. Mrs. 3621 Ellis Park
Burgess Frank A. Evanston

Burgess Frank A. 7630 Union av.
Burgess Harry K. 441 S. Normal Parkway
Burgess I. S. Morgan Park
Burgess Lilly E. Miss, 551½ W. Jackson bou .
Burgess Warren E. Austin
Burgess W. T. Mrs. 3805 Langley av.
Burget Mark, LaGrange
Burgett John M. H. Oak Park. *Ill.*
Burgie Annie M. Mrs. 3639 Grand boul.
Burgis Joseph H. 437 Belden av.
Burhans James A. Evanston. *U.L.*
Burke Daniel F. 5300 Lexington av.
Burke Edmund, Waukegan
Burke E. W. Judge, 759 W. Adams. *Ill.*
Burke George W. Capt. Highland Park
Burke James C. 190, 35th
Burke John C. 192, 35th
Burke John E. Hyde Park hotel
Burke John L. 5345 Greenwood av.
Burke Martha Mrs. Hotel Del Prado
Burke Michael, 2815 Michigan av. *W.P.*
Burke Richard Mrs. Austin
Burke Richard H. Rev. Austin
Burke Thomas M. Rev. Evanston
Burke William H. 232 Belden av.
Burkhardt H. S. 677 W. Adams. *C.A. Ill., U.L., W.P.*
Burkhardt William, 677 W. Adams. *Ill.*
Burkholder Charles S. 250 Oakwood boul.
Burkholder Henry, LaGrange
Burkholder Henry P. La Grange
Burkholder R. Cortland, Evanston
Burkholder S. G. Dr. 3135 Vernon av.
Burkitt Charles H. Evanston
Burland Arthur P. 406, 36th pl.
Burleigh William R. La Grange
Burleson Harriet H. Mrs. 4319 Ellis av.
Burley Augustus H. 254 Dearborn av. *Un.*
Burley Clarence A. Union club, *U.L., Univ*
Burley Elbridge R. 5717 Monroe av.
Burley Frank E. Lexington hotel. *Cal., Chi., C.A., U.L.*
Burley F. C. Edison Park
Burling Edward B. 399 N. State. *Univ.*
Burling William S. 729 Fullerton av.
Burlingame Calvin G. Oak Park
Burlingame H. I. Mrs. 3100 Groveland av.
Burlingame Rex J. 4636 Prairie av.
Burlingham Ella Mrs. 251 Dearborn av.
Burlingham E. P. Mrs. 3005 Calumet av
Burlingham Frederick W. 3005 Calumet av. *Univ.*
Burmaster Paul Dr. 441 Dearborn av.
Burmester F. C. 2316 N. Paulina
Burnam Arthur, 822 W. Adams
Burnam Frank, 2611 Calumet av. *C.A.*
Burnap Margaretta E. Mrs. 4212 Ellis av.
Burnes Belle Mrs 474 Elm
Burnet William H. Evanston. *Chi.*
Burnett Andrew F. 331 Warren av.
Burnett H. A. 4506 Indiana av.
Burnham A. A. 299 Park av.
Burnham A. J. 95, 51st

Burnham Daniel H. Evanston. *Chi.,*
   U.L.. Univ.
Burnham Edward, 389, 50th
Burnham Ellen W. Miss, Evanston.
Burnham Ethel Miss, Evanston
Burnham E. Mrs. 2729 Calumet av.
Burnham Hugh L. Glenview
Burnham John, Evanston
Burnham Josiah, 2358 Indiana av.
Burnham J. T. jr. 4055 Prairie av.
Burnham R. W. 95, 51st
Burnham Sherburne W. 95, 51st
Burnham Telford, 2446 Michigan av.
Burns Allen M. 4404 Sidney av.
Burns Bridget Mrs. 358 Bissell
Burns Ella M. Mrs. 5639 Washington av.
Burns Jonas J. 678, 48th
Burns Joseph Harry, Evanston
Burns J. C. 376 Oak
Burns J. L. Mrs. 650 Washington boul.
Burns Louise Miss, Leland hotel
Burns Nicholas T. 358 Bissell
Burns Warren E. 678, 48th
Burns W. H. 780 North Park av.
Burns W. W. Park Ridge
Burnside Margaret E. Mrs. 6147 Monroe
   av.
Burnside V. W. 812 Pullman bldg.
Burr Albert H. Dr. 3504 Ellis av.
Burr Bradley, 23 St. John's ct.
Burr Charles A. 95 Oakwood av.
Burr Chauncy S., M.D. Longwood
Burr David, 2596 N. Ashland av.
Burr Louis E. 4017 Lake av. *C.A.*
Burr Susan H. Mrs. 4824 Vincennes av.
Burrell E. L. 1049 Winthrop av.
Burroughs Edward R. 646 Washington
   boul.
Burroughs E. P. 739 Walnut
Burroughs Frank M. Palmer house
Burroughs Geo. T. 646 Washington boul.
   Ill.
Burrows Daniel W. Union Club. *Chi.,*
   W.P.
Burrows Joseph M. 3912 Lake av.
Burrows William A. 225, 52d
Burrows William F. 3357 Michigan av.
   C.A., U.L.
Burry George, 495 N. State, *C.A., Un.,*
   Univ.
Burry James, M.D. 4862 Washington av.
Burry Wm. 300 Schiller, *Chi., Irq., Un.,*
   Univ.
Burson J. W. 6325 Monroe av.
Burt Charles B. 744 Fullerton av.
Burt James D. Evanston
Burt Nellie Mrs. 7112 Eggleston av.
Burt William, Evanston
Burt Wm. Griswold, Evanston
Burtis James K. 3426 Vernon av.
Burton Adah F. Mrs. 3618 Michigan av.
Burton Charles A. 2427 Lakewood av.
Burton Charles G. 6328 Greenwood av.
Burton Charles H. 440, 57th
Burton Charles S. Oak Park
Burton C. H. 3129 Dover

Burton Edmund F. Oak Park
Burton Eliza A. Mrs. 6506 Yale
Burton Ernest D. Prof. 5524 Monroe av.
Burton Frederick A. 6444 Lexington av.
Burton George C. 6440 Yale
Burton John, Hinsdale
Burton O. W. Hinsdale
Burton Robert A. 4413 Oakenwald av.
Burton Stiles Mrs. 229 Michigan av.
Burton William H. 5600 Monroe av.
Burwash Henry J. Dr. 721 N. Hoyne av.
Busbey T. Addison, 1045 Wilcox av.
Busbey William H. 843 W. Adams
Busby Charles, 2454 Indiana av.
Busch Louis, 2358 Indiana av.
Busch Mary K. Miss, 8 Gordon Terrace
Buschwah Jacob W. 1810 Wellington
Busenbark William R. 2732 Prairie av.
   Chi., U.L.
Bush Benjamin F. 2915 Sheridan rd.
Bush Bertha E. Dr. 808 Morse av.
Bush Clara B. Miss, 606 N. State
Bush C. S. 4206 Michigan av.
Bush Edwin S. 1130 Chase av.
Bush George A. 577 Lasalle av.
Bush George S. 185 Oakwood boul.
Bush I. S. Hinsdale
Bush Lorenzo Dr. LaGrange
Bush Mary Miss, 56 Astor
Bush William H. 606 N. State
Bush William H. 307 N. Clark
Bush William L. Marquette club
Bushnell Charles E. 330 Ashland boul.
Bushnell Edmund B. LaGrange
Bushnell Edna Miss, 4830 Forrestville av.
Bushnell George W. Morton Park
Bushnell Herbert L. 1681 W. Monroe
Bushnell H. 6320 Yale
Bushnell H. A. Rev. LaGrange
Bushnell James F. 263 Seminary av.
Bushnell Lemuel M. 330 Ashland boul.
   Ill.
Bushnell Lewis H. Evanston
Bushnell L. A. Mrs. 175 Warren av.
Bushnell L. S. Mrs. 6320 Yale
Buskirk Frank W. Lakota hotel
Buss Edward W. Norwood Park
Buss Frederick B. 49, 46th
Bussey W. T. 521 W. Jackson boul. *Ill.*
Butler Albert E. Evanston
Butler Andrew O. Oak Park
Butler Andrew O. jr. Oak Park
Butler Edward B. 3408 Michigan av. *Chi.,*
   U.L.. W.P.
Butler Elizabeth Mrs. 299 S. Winchester
   av.
Butler E. K. 4850 Greenwood av. *U.L.*
Butler Frances Mrs. Austin
Butler Frank D. River Forest
Butler Frank E. 775 Larrabee
Butler Frank H. Evanston
   Sum. res. Indian River, Mich.
Butler Frank M. Oak Park
Butler Frank O. Hinsdale
Butler Fred H. LaGrange
Butler F. S. 708 W. Jackson boul.

Butler George F. Dr. 794 W. Adams
Butler Herbert L. Austin
Butler Hermon B. 1920 Wellington, *C.A.*,
    Univ.
Butler Hubert W. Jefferson Park
Butler H. 4729 Lake av.
Butler John S. 221 Hampden ct.
Butler Julian T. Oak Park
Butler J. Fred, Oak Park. *U.L.*
Butler J. H. Park Ridge
Butler J. W. Hinsdale, *U.L.*
Butler Morton, Evanston
Butler Samuel, 3325 Vernon av.
Butler Samuel S. 3325 Vernon av.
Butler Sarsfield T. 1524 W. Adams
Butler Theodore Mrs. 2 Washington pl.
Butler Thomas G. Oak Park
Butler Thomas H. Oak Park
Butler Walter, 624 Fullerton av.
Butler Walter H. Evanston
Butler Walter L Austin
Butler William P. 76, 50th
Butlin Minerva Mrs. 5036 Jefferson av.
Butlin Thomas G. 5036 Jefferson av.
Butterfield Belle Mrs. 2432 Prairie av.
Butterfield Charles W. 2218 Michigan av
    Chi.
Butterfield C. S. Mrs. 696 W. Adams
Butterfield Harry N. Auditorium hotel
Butterfield J. Spencer, 1928 Barry av.
Butterfield William E. 4002 Lake av.
Butterfield William L, 1838 Melrose
Butterfield Wm. W. 131 Kenesaw terrace
Butterly John A. jr. 6358 Minerva av.
Butterman William F. Dr. 170 Lincoln av.
Butters George, Oak Park
Buttolph A. C. 4822 Ellis av. *C.A.*
Buttolph William A. 4332 Forrestville
    av.
Button Frank M. 2703 N. Ashland av.
Button Peter Mrs. 719 W. Adams
Button William J. 6034 Jefferson av.
Butts Annice E. Miss, 40, 47th
Butts DeWitt C. 6327 Greenwood av.
Butts Emily W. Mrs. 40, 47th
Butts Kathryn B. Miss, 40, 47th
Butts Margaret Mrs. 6327 Greenwood av.
Butts M. A. Miss. 40, 47th
Butz Otto C. Winnetka, *Univ.*
Butzow Doris Mrs. 452 W. Congress
Butzow Robert C. 452 W. Congress
Buxbaum Emanuel, 3141 Michigan av.
    Stan.
Buxbaum Emanuel L. Oakland Hotel,
    Lksd.
Buxbaum Leopold, Oakland Hotel
Buxbaum M. J. The Wellington
Buzzell Delos L. Irving Park
Buzzell E. A. 6136 Ellis av.
    Sum. res. Delavan Lake, Wis.
Buzzell Marcus H. 223 S. Irving av.
Byam John W. Evanston
Byers J. W. 377 Oakwood boul.
Byford H. T. Dr. 3021 Calumet av. *C.A.*
Byllesby Mary L. Miss, 5473 Cornell av.
Byram Augustus, 2909 Michigan av.

Byram Charles F. 2909 Michigan av. *Cal.*,
    W.P.
Byrne Harry, 3519 Wabash av. *C.A.*
Byrne John H. Dr. 690 W. Monroe
Byrne John P. 4202 Ellis av. *C.A.*
Byrnes Frank Dr. 1868 Melrose

CABELL CLIFFORD, Chicago Beach
    hotel
Cable Annie S. Miss,Hinsdale
Cable Benjamin S. 615 The Plaza. *Univ.*
Cable Charles E. 856 Walnut
Cable Fayette S. Hinsdale
Cable Herman D. Evanston, *U.L.*
Cable Hobart M. 3848 Ellis av.
Cable Jerome B. Edgebrook
Cable Ransom R. Virginia Hotel
Cade Robert, Park Ridge
Cadieux J. P. 229, 28th
Cadle William L. La Grange
Cadow Samuel B. Kenilworth, *C.A.*
Cadwallader Arthur H. 4521 Lake av.
Cadwallader Bassett, LaGrange
Cadwallader Thomas, 3647 Vincennes av.
Cadwell Edward S. Mrs. LaGrange
Cadwell George J. 6127 Kimbark av.
Cadwell Jason R. 6127 Kimbark av.
Cady Calvin Brainerd, 910 Sherwin av.
Cady Cholett, Oak Park
    Winter res. Hotel Metropole
Cady George W. 434 S. Oakley av.
Cady H. B. 370 Mohawk
Cady Jeremiah K. 425 N. State, *Univ.*
Cady Orvan L. 434 S. Oakley av.
Cady S. H. Mrs. 434 S. Oakley av.
Cady W. L. 2627 N. Ashland av.
Cagwin Albert E. 6446 Greenwood av.
Cahill Edward T. 373 Center
Cahill Mary Mrs. 373 Center
Cahill Michael, 364 Fullerton av.
Cahn A. Mrs. 4135 Drexel boul
Cahn Benjamin R. 3550 Ellis av. *Stan.*
Cahn Bernard, 3223 Michigan av. *Stan.*
Cahn Edgar B. 3223 Michigan av.
Cahn Fanny Mrs. 3521 Ellis av.
Cahn Frederick C.3229 Michigan av.*Stan.*
Cahn James B. 3223 Michigan av.
Cahn Joseph, 4809 Grand boul. *Stan.*
Cahn Sidney B. 4907 Grand boul. *Stan.*
Caine F. F. 2510 Magnolia av.
Cairnduff William H. 28 St. James pl.
    U.L.
Cairns Charles A. 5405 Madison av.
Cairns James, 859 S. Sawyer av.
Cairns Jennie Miss, 5405 Madison av.
Cairns Mary C. Miss, 5405 Madison av.
Cairns Peter J. 5405 Madison av.
Calahan John Y. Kenilworth
Calamara Emilio, 3156 Forest av.
Calbick James A. 890 S. Kedzie av.
Calder Emily E. Mrs. 4457 Oakenwald av.
Calder G. W. North Shore Hotel
Calder L. A. Mrs Evanston
Calder Robert G. 453 Lasalle av.
Caldwell B. C. 1895 Magnolia av.
Caldwell B. D. Evanston

Caldwell Charles, M.D. 3237 Indiana av.
Caldwell Charles E., M.D. 438, 38th
Caldwell Charles H. 6601 Harvard av.
Caldwell Charles P., M.D. 4425 Michigan av.
Caldwell Ernest L. Morgan Park
Caldwell Henry P. 2606 Prairie av.
Caldwell Henry W. 5201 Kimbark av.
Caldwell John D. 460, 44th
Caldwell J. D. Oak Park
Caldwell Oliver N. 5325 Washington av.
Caldwell R. W. 55, 33d
Caldwell Warren D. Evanston
Caldwell Wilfred T. 5338 Washington av.
Caldwell William, Evanston
Caleb Gideon N. 4924 Woodlawn av. W.P.
Caleb Walter S. 5317 Washington av.
Calef B. 702 Pullman bldg.
Calhoun D. Irving, 2358 Indiana av.
Calhoun Francis C. S. Oak Park
Calhoun George Mrs. Irving Park
Calkins Elias A. 4359 Berkeley av.
Calkins Gary G. Evanston
Calkins George A. Evanston
Calkins George S. 417, 41st
Calkins J. E. Mrs. 5642 Washington av.
Callaghan Bernard Mrs. 2962 Indiana av.
Callaghan Simon, Austin
Callahan Andrew P. 5000 Madison av.
Callahan James E. 2962 Indiana av, C.A.,
   Irq.
Callan H. A. 4557 Lake av. C.A.
Callendar B. M. Col. Hotel Del Prado
Calligan John B. Evanston
Calm Charles E. 748 Fullerton av.
Calrow Harriet E. Mrs. Winnetka
Calrow J. G. Winnetka
Calvert Edgar S. Lake Forest
Calvert Frank, Lake Forest
Camburn Jacob C. 3616 Lake av. C.A.
Cameron Daniel R. Great Northern hotel
   C.A.
Cameron Duncan, 277 Seminary av.
Cameron Dwight F. 201 The Plaza. U.L.
Cameron Gordon, 1015, 59th
Cameron John H. 5135 Hibbard av.
Cameron John M. Riverside
Cameron Mary Mrs. 1015, 59th
Cameron Nathaniel, 342 S. Winchester
   av.
Cameron P. F. 5748 Washington av.
Cameron William F. 5337 Madison av.
Camp A. Royce, 3155 Wabash av.
Camp Charles D. Dr. 7020 Butler
Camp Charles E. Oak Park
Camp Edward N. 178 Dearborn av. C.A.,
   Irq.
Camp Florence A. Mrs. 3155 Wabash av.
Camp William C. 3618 Michigan av. Cal.,
   U.L., W.P.
Campbell Archibald M. 28i Ashland boul.
Campbell A. Courtney, 2001 Indiana av.
Campbell A. E. 5215 Hibbard av.
Campbell Benjamin F. 4509 Prairie av.
Campbell Benjamin H. The Ontario, Un.
Campbell Charles P. Longwood

Campbell Charles W. 619 Cleveland av.
   C.A.
Campbell Colin C. La Grange
Campbell Corinne Miss, 248, 51st
Campbell Daniel W. 132 Kenwood Terrace
Campbell David, 1838 Indiana av.
Campbell DeWitt W. Clifton house. C.A.
Campbell Duncan B. Sherman house
Campbell D. C. Longwood
Campbell Eleanor M. Mrs. 484 W. Adams
Campbell E. Mrs. LaGrange
Campbell Fanny F. Miss, 299, 47th
Campbell Fergus, 81 Warren av.
Campbell Frank W. 3538 Calumet av.
Campbell George C. Mrs. 2607 Prairie av.
   Sum. res. Forest Lodge, Cable, Wis.
Campbell George H. 3334 Rhodes av.
Campbell Harry O. Austin
Campbell Henry R. 423 Superior
Campbell Hilary E. 1066 Winthrop av.
Campbell .1. S. Miss, Riverside
Campbell James, 186 Bowen av.
Campbell James B. 399 W. Adams
Campbell James H. 4721 Indiana av.
Campbell James M. Lombard
Campbell Jeannette Miss, 2607 Prairie av.
Campbell John, 3157 Groveland av.
Campbell John Allyn, 248, 51st
Campbell John D. La Grange
Campbell John G. 186 Bowen av. U.L.
Campbell John P. Mrs. Norwood Park
Campbell John R. 4503 Ellis av.
   Sum. res. Waterford, Mich.
Campbell J. Albert, 286 Ashland boul.
Campbell J. F. Dr. 2358 Indiana av.
Campbell J. M. Mrs. 902 W. Monroe
Campbell Leonard W. 515 Cleveland av.
   C.A.
Campbell Louis A. Rev. Austin
Campbell Martin L. 6418 Minerva av.
Campbell Mary Miss, Hotel Del Prado
Campbell Murdoch, 286 Ashland boul.
Campbell Nathan W. 2941 Prairie av.
Campbell Ralph R. Dr. 414 Dearborn av.
Campbell Robert C. 1257 Rokeby. C.A.
Campbell Samuel H. 6441 Parnell av.
Campbell S. M. Rev. 762 W. 67th
Campbell Thomas M. 902 W. Monroe
Campbell Thomas T. Evanston
Campbell William, 1926 Barry av. C.A.
Campbell William A. Dr. 4645 Evans av.
Campbell William J. Mrs. Riverside
Campbell William L. 2358 Indiana av.
Campbell William N. Union club. Chi.
Campbell W. P. 5704 Madison av.
Campe Frank, 77 Maple
Campion R. W. 1534 Diversey
Canaday Lloyd, 2449 N. Hermitage av.
Canary D. J. Chicago Athletic assn.
Canavan Austin A. 4512 Indiana av.
Canby C. Harlan, 4821 Ellis av. W.P.
Canda C. L. 496 Sunnyside av.
Canda Felix, 496 Sunnyside av.
Candee Fred J. Hinsdale
Candee Henry W. Hinsdale

Candee William B. 3703 Ellis av.
Candee William S. Evanston
Candlish William J. Hotel Luzerne
Canfield Andrew J. Rev. 3002 Prairie av.
　　　Sum. res. Warren, Mass.
Canfield Charles A., M.D. Highland Park
Canfield Coresta T. Dr. 269 Lincoln av.
Canfield Edward L. 68 Stratford pl.
Canfield Horace J. Elmhurst
Canfield Horace J. jr. Elmhurst
Canfield H. S. Hotel Del Prado
Canfield John B. 3002 Prairie av.
Canfield Lillian Miss, 399 Oak
Canfield Margaret Miss, 409 Oak
Canfield Mary Gross Mrs. 531 Lasalle av.
Canfield William J. Mrs. Evanston
Canman Leo, 214 Schiller
Cannell S. Wilmer, 1938 Arlington pl. C.
　A.
Cannon Thomas H. 421 Oak
Canright William S. 1673 W. Monroe
Canterbury Richard A. 4322 Vinecnnes
　av.
Cantlie George, Wilmette
Cantner John C. 3230 Lake Park av.
Cantrovitz H. S. Sherman house
Cantrovitz S. Sherman house
Cantrovitz S. M. 5228 Hibbard av.
Cantwell Robert E. 922 W. Monroe
Cantwell Thomas A. 714 W. Adams
Canty Alice S. 3141 South Park av.
Capelle Marcus Eugene, 308, 49th. C.A.
Capper Charles W. Longwood
Capper John S. 7116 Yale
Capps Katherine P. Mrs. 415 Huron
Capps Joseph A. Dr. 228, 53d
Capron A. B. Winnetka
Capron Fred S. Evanston
Carbine Thomas, 400 Washington boul
Card Grace B. Miss, 4850 Washington av.
Card Joseph B. 4850 Washington av.
Card Joseph P. Mrs. 4850 Washington av.
　　　Sum. res. Nashotah, Wis.
Card Mary P. Miss, 4850 Washington av.
Card William D. Chicago Athletic assn.
Carden D. H. 216 Seminary av.
Carder George H. Dr. 7748 Lowe av.
Carey A. B. Col. Chicago Beach hotel
Carey Charles N. 3933 Grand boul.
Carey James A. 1260 Winthrop av. C.A.
Carey Joseph G. 3933 Grand boul.
Carey Warren Dr. LaGrange
Carey William P. 3933 Grand boul. U.L.
Cargill Charles S. Austin
Carhart Charles C. The Wellington
Carleton Charles, 1011 Walnut
Carleton Stanley, Oak Park
Carleton Welby B. Hinsdale
Carlisle Addison Alexander, Evanston
Carlisle Alfred W. 657 W. Congress
Carlisle Carrie Miss, 5428 Monroe av.
Carlisle E. G. 4467 Oakenwald av. C.A.
Carlisle Frederick, 657 W. Congress
Carlisle F. J. Lakota hotel
Carlisle Jo, n Andrew, Evanston
Carlisle Meade Woodson, Evanston

Carlisle William G., 232, 52d
Carlisle William W. Evanston.
Carlson Axel, Evanston
Carlson John M. 1055 Pratt av.
Carmack Edgar H. 371 Superior. C.A.
Carman Alexander R. Evanston
Carman George L. 6437 Harvard av.
Carman George N. Prof. 610 W. Jackson
　boul.
Carman Kathlen Miss, Evanston
Carman Rufus Mrs. Evanston
Carmichael G. S. Mrs. 351 Dearborn av.
Carnahan Charles C. 406 S. Paulina
Carne E. W. Oak Park
Carnegie Barbara Mrs. The Tudor
Carnegie John F. The Tudor
Carney Thomas, 25 Lincoln av.
Carney William J. 4218 Grand boul
Carpenter Albert J. 728 W. Monroe
Carpenter Austin B. 4729 Lake av.
Carpenter A. A. 83 Cass. Chi.
　　　Sum. res. Menominee, Mich.
Carpenter A. A. jr. 167 Rush. Chi.,
　Univ., W.P.
Carpenter Benjamin, Winnetka. Chi.,
　Univ.
Carpenter Benjamin J. LaGrange
Carpenter Clinton B. 306 Chestnut
Carpenter Edith Miss, 528 W. 61st
Carpenter Ellen W. Mrs. 544 Washing-
　ton boul.
　　　Sum. res. Honey Creek, Wis.
Carpenter Elliott R. Dr. 4128 Berke-
　ley av.
Carpenter E. F. Evanston. C.A.
Carpenter Flora Miss, 3226 Groveland
　av.
Carpenter F. I. Prof. 5533 Woodlawn av.
　Univ.
Carpenter George A. 49 Delaware pl.
　Univ.　　　Sum. res. Lake Geneva
Carpenter George B. 293 Dearborn av.
　U.L.　　　Sum. res. Park Ridge
Carpenter George B. Mrs. 3222 Lake
　Park av.
Carpenter Grant, 230, 56th
Carpenter G. A. Miss, Hotel Metropole
Carpenter Harry E. Pullman
Carpenter Harry H. 512 Englewood av.
Carpenter Hubbard F. 52 Walton pl.
Carpenter H. L. 3913 Prairie av.
Carpenter John Alden, 293 Dearborn av.
Carpenter John S. 5125 Cornell av.
Carpenter Lewis B. Oak Park
Carpenter Louis, 474 Elm
Carpenter Marian Miss, 3222 Lake Park
　av.
Carpenter Myron J. LaGrange, Chi.
Carpenter M. Mrs. 849 Warren av.
Carpenter Nellie Mrs. 3226 Groveland av.
Carpenter Newton H. LaGrange
Carpenter N. E. Mrs. Oak Park
Carpenter Orissa C. Mrs. 728 W. Monroe
Carpenter Orrin F. Evanston
Carpenter William O. 517 W. Adams. Ill.
　　　Sum. res. Menominee, Mich.

Carqueville Alexander, 3127 Beacon
Carqueville Edgar H. 3127 Beacon. *C.A.*
Carqueville Edward Mrs. 3127 Beacon
Carqueville Richard A. 3127 Beacon
Carr Adaline Miss, 4004 Drexel boul.
Carr A. H. The Arizona
Carr Calvin, 6939 Perry av.
Carr Charles C. Oak Park
Carr Charles W. 543 W. 60th
Carr Clyde M. Evanston
Carr Courtland P. Mrs. Evanston
Carr E. A. Mrs. Oak Park
Carr George, 3905 Lake av.
Carr Henry H. 3912 Lake av. *U.L.*
Carr Latham, 3747 Lake av.
Carr Laura Miss, 3131 Indiana av.
Carr Lennie O. Miss, 3320 Indiana av.
Carr Rachel H., M.D. 4725 Kenwood av.
Carr Richard B. Evanston
Carr Robert F. Oak Park. *C.A.*
Carr Sylvester L. Austin
Carr Thomas, 143 Oakwood boul.
Carr Walter S. Oak Park
Carrall Robert W. Dr. 4700 Grand boul.
Carrier Augustus S. Dr. 1042 N. Halsted
Carrier David R. 265 Michigan av.
Carrigan Mary J. Miss, 2616 Calumet av.
Carrington John W. 16 Groveland Park
Carrington William T. 290 Lasalle av.
    Chi., C.A., Un.
Carroll D. Mrs. 3148 Beacon
Carroll George T. 164. 30th
Carroll John C. 5801 Washington av.
Carroll John J. Rev. 5470 Kimbark av.
Carroll John M. 855 W. Monroe
Carroll Kate Miss, 164, 30th
Carroll Lester Scott, 2599 N. Robey
Carroll Margaret Miss, Evanston
Carroll Norman, 4860 Kimbark av.
Carroll Theron G. 533 W. Monroe
Carroll William A. 6446 Harvard av. *C.A.*
Carroll William W. Wilmette
Carroll W. B. Dr. 6219 Kimbark av.
Carruthers James, Austin
Carruthers Robert, Austin
Carruthers W. H. 5046 Woodlawn av.
Carry Edward F. jr. 191, 54th
Carry Edward F. Mrs. 5067 Lake av.
Carse David Bradley 610 W. Jackson boul.
    C.A.
Carse John Bradley, 1035 Evanston av.
    C.A.
    Sum. res. Briewood Lake, Geneva, Wis.
Carse Matilda B. Mrs. 610 W. Jackson boul.
Carsley F. M. Mrs. 65c5 Stewart av.
Carson Adolphus B. 5012 Jefferson av.
Carson Flora Mrs. 6411 Greenwood av.
Carson Frank M. Rev. 1050 Evanston av.
Carson Harry F. The Tudor
Carson John B. Mrs. 3139 Michigan av.
Carson Louis, 1832 Reta
Carson Oliver, Austin
Carson Oliver M. Evanston
Carson Samuel, Evanston. *C.A., Ill.*
Carstens A. J. Park Ridge
Carswell L. R. Hyde Park hotel
33

Carter A. N. Mrs. 440 W. Adams
Carter Bettie L. Miss, Cornell av.
Carter Byron B. Hinsdale
Carter Charles S. Mrs. 535 Belden av.
Carter Donald M. 4619 Lake av.
Carter Edward C. Evanston
Carter Fred B. Evanston
Carter F. A. Dr. New Hotel Holland
Carter George B. 7138 Harvard av.
Carter H. L. Miss, 108 Cass
Carter H. W. New Hotel Holland
Carter James B. 499 W. Congress
Carter James S. 121, 51st. *C.A.*
Carter Jean W. Mrs. 4741 Kenwood av.
Carter John S. 5415 Cottage Grove av.
Carter J. N. LaGrange
Carter Leslie, 108 Cass. *Chi., Un.*
Carter Lincoln J. 4401 Ellis av.
Carter Merritt T. Wilmette
Carter Orrin N. Judge, 1331 W. Monroe
Carter Philip N. 438 W. Adams
Carter Thomas H. 6113 Woodlawn av.
Carter Wallace, 438 W. Adams
Carter Will W. 6012 Indiana av.
Carter William J. 5228 Jefferson av.
Carter Zina R. 1441 Ogden av.
Carton Laurence A. 4923 Greenwood av.
    Sum. res. Lake Geneva, Wis.
Caruthers Elizabeth Miss, 37 Banks
Caruthers Malcolm Mrs. 37 Banks
Carver Fred R. Evanston
Carver Henry C. Mrs. Highland Park
Cary Caroline Mrs. 874 Winthrop av.
Cary Ellen Mrs. 2935 Indiana av.
Cary Eugene, 2536 Prairie av. *Chi., U.L., W.P.*
Cary Frank, M.D. 2935 Indiana av. *C.A.*
    Sum. res. Greenbush, Wis.
Cary Fred A. 196 Goethe
Cary George P. 16 Astor. *C.A.*
Cary John W. Mrs. Hinsdale
Cary Josie S. Miss, 511 Webster ay.
Cary Paul V. Hinsdale
Cary Robert J. 379 Superior. *Univ.*
Caryl Alexander H. 5804 Rosalie ct.
Casad S. G. 6411 Greenwood av.
Casanave F. D. Hotel Luzerne
Case Calvin S. Dr. 5114 Woodlawn av.
Case Carl B. 5114 Woodlawn av.
Case Charles H. 201 Ashland boul. *U.L.*
Case Edward B. Evanston. *U.L.*
Case Elisha W. 1497 Washington boul.
    Sum. res. Block Island, R. I.
Case Emma W. Mrs. 425 N. State
Case E. G. Oak Park
Case Francis M. 5227 Woodlawn av.
Case George J. Glencoe
Case Guy H. 373 S. Oakley av.
Case John R. Elmhurst
Case J. R. Hotel Metropole
Case M. T. 533, 62d
Case Selon H. 373 S. Oakley av.
Case Theodore G. 338 Warren av.
Case T. L. Revere house
Case William S. 338 Warren av.
Case Wm. Warren, Winnetka

Casey Charles E. 5725 Monroe av. *C.A.*
Casey Daniel V. 159 Eugenle
Casey Edwin A. 3960 Ellis av. *C.A.*
Casey James, 5326 Lexington av.
Casey James J. 1886 Diversey
Casey John W. Washington Heights
Casey Robert E. 4950 Vincennes av.
Casey Timothy S. 4111 Vincennes av.
Cashin John J. 4528 Prairie av.
Cashman Helena Miss, 658 W. Jackson boul.
Cashman Thomas F. Rev. 658 W.Jackson boul.
Casler George H. 4615 Vincennes av.
Casler Wallace, 1236 Washingten boul.
Caspary O. S. 3362 Calumet av. *Lksd.*
Casper Adolph M. Dr. 4828 Evans av.
Casper Orley, Kenilworth
Cass C. E. The Wellington
Cass George W. 2715 Michigan av. *Cal. C.A., Irq., Univ.,*
Cassady H. J. 7137 Euclid av. *C.A.*
Cassard Gilbert H. 3348 South Park av.
Cassard Margaret Mrs. Evanston
Cassard Morris, 4243 Grand boul. *C.A.*
Cassard Vernon, 3348 South Park av. *C.A.*
Casselberry Wilham Evans Dr. 1830 Calumet av. *Univ.*
Cassell Ella Miss, 4207 Ellis av.
Cassidy Harry C. 2205 Calumet av. *C.A.*
Cassidy J. A. 2205 Calumet av. *Cal., W.P.*
Cassoday Eldon J. 4740 Lake av.
Caster Herbert E. 419, 41st
Casterline Fred J. 1551 Kenmore av.
Castle Charles S. Austin
Castle Charles W. Oak Park
Castle Clarence F. Prof. 5468 Ridgewood ct.
Castle George, 470 N. State
Castle Harry B. Oak Park.
Castle L. Frank, 5482 East End av.
Castle L. B. Mrs. Oak Park
Castle Percy V. Austin
Castle Perley D. Austin
Castle William, 1803 Barry av.
Caswell Charles L. 3751 Vincennes av.
Caswell Charles L. jr. 3751 Vincennes av.
Caswell D. W. 4959 Prairie av.
Caswell James H. 576 Lasalle av.
Cate Albion, 247 Dearborn av.
Cate Stephen E. Oak Park
Cate William M. Dr. 6126 Madison av. Sum. res. Kilbourn, Wis.
Cater Jacob S. Mrs. 690 Washington boul.
Catherwood William L. Mrs. 162, 51st
Cathrae J. H. LaGrange
Catlin Charles, 481 Belden av.
Catlin Charles E. 1062 Sherwin av.
Catlin Donald C. The Tudor
Catlin George, 5111 Hibbard av. *C.A.* Sum. res. Fox Lake, Ill.
Catlin W. E. Glen Ellyn

Caton Arthur J. 1910 Calumet av. *Cal., Chi., C.A., W.P.*
Cattell Archibald, 6125 Monroe av.
Catterall Ralph C..H. 5629 Washington av.
Caubert Eugene, 149 Locust
Cavanagh Charles T. 405 Oak. *C.A.*
Cavanagh Patrick Mrs. Virginia hotel
Cavanaugh Beinard, 77 Stratford pl.
Cavanaugh John A. 715 W. Adams
Cavanaugh Joseph B. 77 Stratford pl. *U.L.*
Cavanaugh Kate Miss, 46 Loomis
Cavaroc Charles, Chicago club
Cave Charles R. 3932 Grand boul.
Cave G. E. 5400 Greenwood av.
Cave W. M. 3745 Wabash av.
Caven George, 354, 51st
Cavey Thomas J. Austin
Caylor Worth E. 5812 Rosalie ct.
Cayzer Alfred L. Evanston
Cella Andrew D. 3365 South Park av.
Cella Charles J. 3365 South Park av.
Cella John G. 3365 South Park av.
Cella J. F. 3365 South Park av.
Celley F. M. Dr. 4808 Prairie av.
Cessna O. H. Rev. 1009 N. Halsted
Chace Emory B. Austin
Chace Henry T. 5740 Rosalie ct.
Chace Henry T. jr. 5740 Rosalie ct.
Chadbourne Thomas L. jr. 150 Lincoln Park boul. *Chi., C.A.*
Chadwick Charles H. 4596 Oakenwald av.
Chadwick Mary G. Miss, 186, 36th
Chadwick Seneca J. 4812 St. Lawrence av.
Chadwick William H. 1814 Belmont av. *U.L.*
Chaffee Frederick F. Dr. 6147 Kimbark av.
Chaffee Nellie Miss, 3627 Vernon av.
Chaffee Theodore W. Evanston
Chaffin Emily M. Mrs. 767 Estes av.
Chainey George, 22 Aldine sq.
Chaiser Andrew, 587 Cleveland av.
Chalfant Edward J. Wilmette
Chalitoux Joseph, 34 Oregon av.
Challacombe Geo. E. 3353 South Park av.
Challis Charles W. 7745 Lowe av.
Challoner Robert Dr. Oakland hotel
Chalmers Thomas, 179 Ashland boul.
Chalmers Thomas jr. 179 Ashland boul. *Ill.*
Chalmers William, 5140 Hibbard av.
Chalmers William J. Virginia hotel *Chi., C.A., Ill. U.L., W.P.* Sum. res. Dronley Cottage, Lake Geneva, Wis.
Chamberlain Arthur F. 6542 Kimbark av.
Chamberlain Bayard L. Maywood
Chamberlain Charles H.1492 Washington boul.
Chamberlain C. C. 2124 Michigan av.
Chamberlain Lou Miss, 2615 Indiana av.
Chamberlain Martha E. Mrs. 2998 Kenmore

Chamberlain M. J. Mrs. 5112 Madison av.
    Sum. res. Lake Hesse, Mich.
Chamberlain William B. Prof. Oak Park
Chamberlin DeWitt W. 55, 33d
Chamberlin Elmer J. 627 W. 62d
Chamberlin George B. 492, 42d pl.
Chamberlin George M., Dr. 3031 Indiana av. C.A., U.L., W.P.
Chamberlin George W. 4420 Greenwood av.   Sum. res, Lake Beulah, Wis.
Chamberlin Sarah E. E. Mrs. 1113 Washington boul.
    Sum. res. Wentworth, N. H.
Chamberlin Thomas H. 39 Buena Terrace.
Chamberlin T. C. Prof. 5041 Madison av.
Chamberlin Walter H. 1127 Sherwin av. U.L.
Chambers A. F. Mrs. 2508 Michigan av.
Chambers Benjamin C. Evanston
Chambers David, 6518 Ingleside av.
Chambers Edward C. 1236 W. Adams
Chambers John E. 6518 Ingleside av.
Chambers William E. Evanston
Chamblin Stella Miss, Evanston
Champion J. W. 3751 Indiana av.
Champlin Alfred H. Dr. 350 W. 61st
Champlin Charles P. 4342 Drexel boul. C.A., W.P.
Champlin Daniel H. 5213 Hibbard av. C.A.   Sum. res. Westerly, R. I.
Champlin Fred L. The Kenwood, C.A., Ill., W.P.
Champlin George W. 4342 Drexel boul.
Champlin Harry C. 4711 Woodlawn av.
Champlin Henry C. 4711 Woodlawn av.
Champlin S. Frank, 2443 N. Hermitage av.
Champlin William R. Mrs. The Kenwood
Chance J. L. 4400 Ellis av.
Chancellor Justus, 1480 Wellington
Chandler Alice Miss, 2512 Indiana av.
Chandler Charles H. Evanston
Chandler Charles T. jr. 877 W. Adams
Chandler Charles W. 2806 N. Lincoln
Chandler Cornelius L. 3347 Wabash av.
Chandler C. C. 3347 Wabash av.
Chandler C. W. C. Oak Park
Chandler Edwin W. 4415 Lake av.
Chandler E. Bruce, 2512 Indiana av. Cal.
Chandler E. E. 5130 Lexington av.
Chandler Frank R. 182 Rush, U.L.
    Sum. res. Lake Geneva, Wis.
Chandler George D. 161 Locust
Chandler George M. 2512 Indiana av.
Chandler Gertrude Miss, 4339 Oakenwald av.
Chandler G. W. 4451 Champlain av.
Chandler Henry E. Evanston
Chandler Homer S. 465 Dearborn av.
Chandler Homer W. 1944 Deming pl. C.A.
Chandler H. F. 1179 Washington boul.
Chandler H. H. 4415 Lake av. Ill.
    Sum. res. Highland Park. Ill.

Chandler Joseph B. 25, 34th pl.
Chandler Joseph H. 35 Bellevue pl. Chi. Un.
Chandler Lucy Miss, 4339 Oakenwald av.
Chandler L. Hamilton, 4339 Oakenwald av.
Chandler Norborne E. 4339 Oakenwald av.
Chandler N. E. Mrs. Oak Park
Chandler Peyton R. Mrs. 3844 Langley av.
Chandler R. G. Highland Park, U.L.
Chandler T. E. 161 Locust
Chandler Walter T. 4339 Oakenwald av. Irq., U.L.
Chaney Samuel D. 310 Ashland boul.
Channer J. Wyndham-Quinn, 912 Evanston av. C.A.
Channon Harry, 460 Dearborn av. C.A.
Channon Henry, 571 Lasalle av. C.A.
Channon James H. 1927 Deming pl. C.A.
Chanute Octave, 413 Huron. Un.
Chapeck Joseph C. 5335 Prairie av.
Chapin Alice Miss, 3344 Michigan av.
Chapin Charles A. 476 N. State
Chapin Charles J. 2707 N. Lincoln
Chapin Charles O. Lombard
Chapin Edward F. Lake Forest
Chapin Ernest M. 2603 N. Paulina
Chapin E. J. 2634 N. Paulina
Chapin E. S. Capt. 312 The Plaza
Chapin Fanny Miss, 173 Rush
Chapin Frederick S. Evanston
Chapin H. C. 476 N. State
Chapin Josephine Miss, 3344 Michigan av.
Chapin J. B. 5215 Washington av.
    Sum. res. South Haven, Mich.
Chapin Marvin Dr. 215, 61st
Chapin Mary E. Miss, 910, 60th
Chapin Rufus F. 341 Rush
Chapin Rufus F. Mrs. 341 Rush
Chapin Simeon B. 3124 Michigan av. Cal., Chi., C.A., U.L., W.P.
Chapin Staley N. Dr. 910, 60th
Chapin W. M. Mrs. Evanston
Chapman Belle B. Mrs. Evanston
Chapman Charles A. Highland Park
Chapman Charles F. 1112 N. Clark
Chapman Chauncey F. Dr. 833 Washington boul. Ill.
Chapman Clarence C. Highland Park.
Chapman Denison W. 5720 Washington av.
Chapman Edward D. Dr. 6019 Monroe av.
Chapman Emelie A. Mrs. 1239 Wilcox av.
Chapman Frederick L. 1918 Arlington pl.
Chapman George C. 1112 N. Clark
Chapman Geo. H., M.D. 7510 Greenwood av.
Chapman George L. Dr. 1112 N. Clark
Chapman James L. 3217 Vernon av.
Chapman James R. 802 The Plaza
Chapman James R. 2705 Indiana av.
Chapman John Adams, 150 Lincoln Park boul.

Chapman John E. Mrs. 150 Lincoln Park boul.
Chapman John H. 1475 W. Monroe
Chapman J. D. Mrs. Hotel Metropole
Chapman Lewis F. 2682 Evanston av.
Chapman Paul R. 1112 N. Clark
Chapman Robert Clowry, 297 Schiller
Chapman Theodore, 3020 Groveland av.
Chapman Walter A. Highland Park
Chapman Wilson S. 297 Schiller
Chapman W. S. jr. 297 Schiller
Chappel J. B. Miss, Lexington hotel
Chappel W. H. Lexington hotel
Chappell C. H. 3657 Michigan av. *Cal.*, *U.L.*
Chappell Henry W. 5727 Monroe av.
Chappell Howard F. 3020 Prairie av.
Chappell J. Dixon, 3657 Michigan av.
Chappell Richard W. Wilmette
Chappelle Grace B. Miss, 7 Aldine sq.
Chard S. G. The Arizona
Chard Thomas S. 534 N. State. *U.L.*
Charles E. B. Mrs. 437 Seminary av.
Charles Frederick L. Austin
Charles George B. Dr. Austin
Charles G. M. Chicago Athletic assn.
Charles Harry C. 437 Seminary av.
Charles Joseph J. Evanston
Charles Oscar, 448 Elm
Charles Robert B. 437 Seminary av.
Charles Thomas, 114 Park av.
Charlton George J. Oak Park. *C.A.*, *W.P.* Sum. res. Charlevoix, Mich.
Charlton James, 1155 N. Clark
Charlton Robert E. Hotel Del Prado
Charnley Douglas, 99 Astor
Charnley James, 99 Astor. *U.L.*
Charter James A. 3607 Ellis av.
Chase Benjamin F. 3819 Vernon av. *U.L.*
Chase Benjamin F. 3353 Forest av.
Chase Benjamin F. jr. 3353 Forest av.
Chase Charles A. 6647 Yale
Chase Charles C. Mrs. 822 The Plaza
Chase Charles H. Rev. 2175 Sheridan rd.
Chase Edward G. 4460 Oakenwald av.
Chase E. S. Mrs. The Tudor
Chase E. S. L. Miss, 1946 Belmont av.
Chase Frank H. 1514 W. Monroe
Chase Franklin L. 22 Wisconsin
Chase Fred. L. 6554 Ross av.
Chase Guy M. Oak Park
Chase Harry G. 270, 65th pl. *C.A.*
Chase Henry T. 5740 Rosalie ct.
Chase Henry T. jr. 5740 Rosalie ct.
Chase Horace G. 3401 Michigan av. *C.A.* Sum. res. Hopkinton, N. H.
Chase Horace W. Mrs. 3226 South Park av.
Chase Lillian Mrs. 610 S. Lawndale av.
Chase Martin L. 3002 Prairie av.
Chase Marvin S. 3251 Wabash av.
Chase May Ford Miss, 2500 Prairie av.
Chase M. W. Mrs. 631 W. Monroe
Chase Robert S. The Tudor
Chase Ruth G. Miss, 1946 Belmont av.
Chase R. B. 22 Wisconsin
    Sum. res. Deerfield, Ill.

Chase Sam B. 396 Garfield av.
Chase Samuel M. 3401 Michigan av.
Chase Samuel Thompson, 377 Superior, *Univ.*
Chase Volney, 2486 N. Hermitage av.
Chase Wayland J. Prof. Morgan Park
Chase William M. 6618 Lafayette av.
Chase William O. 135 Lincoln Park boul. *C.A.*
Chason George D. 7046 Perry av.
Chason Mary J. Mrs. 7046 Perry av.
Chatfield Eli P. 2242 Kenmore av.
Chatfield-Taylor Hobart Chatfield, 99 E. Pearson. *Chi.*, *C.A.*, *Univ.* Sum. res. Lake Forest
Chattell Bertram M. 4854 Washington av. *C.A.*
Cheeseman Frank E. Dr. 4043 Ellis av.
Cheeseman Harry, 4856 Evans av.
Cheeseman W.O. Dr. 4856 Evans av.
Cheetham Edward, 500 Fullerton av.
Cheetham Edward L. 1714 Barry av.
Cheever Dwight B. 4420 Oakenwald av.
Cheney Augustus J. Oak Park
Cheney Charles Edward, Rt. Rev. 2409 Michigan av.
    . Sum. res. Prouts Neck, Me.
Cheney Clarence C. Kenilworth. *C.A.*, *U.L.*
Cheney Edwin H. Oak Park
Cheney Evelyn Hope Miss, 369 Chicago av.
Cheney Harry W. Dr. 6312 Monroe av.
Cheney Janet Miss, 369 Chicago av.
Cheney John Vance, 369 Chicago av.
    Sum. res. "The Hemlocks," Vermont
Cheney Lucian P. 444 Dearborn av.
Cheney William W. 436 Washington boul.
    Sum. res. Lake Geneva, Wis.
Cheney W. W. jr. 436 Washington boul.
Chenoweth Charles L. Oak Park
Chenoweth W. H. River Forest
Chenoweth W. H. jr. River Forest
Cherrie Robert M. 2853 Kenmore av.
Cherry Cummings, 239 Oakwood boul.
Chesbrough Ellis S. jr. 17 Bellevue pl.
Chesbrough E. A. Mrs. 17 Bellevue pl.
Chesrown M. M. 7206 Euclid av.
Chester Earl, 1706 Kenmore av.
Chester Harry G. Riverside
Chetlain Arthur H. Judge, Marquette club Sum. res. Galena
Chevalier H. W. Hotel Del Prado
Chew John H., M.D. 23 Astor
Chichester Gemmill, 2834 Prairie av.
Chichester Henry B. 3435 Wabash av.
Chichester William J. Rev. 2834 Prairie av.
Chickering Clifford C. 2956 Groveland av.
Chickering Fred W. 5227 Woodlawn av.
Child George F. 6510 Butler
Child Guy B. 42, 53d
Child Samuel Penny, 10 Astor
Childs Albert C. Oak Park
Childs Albert H. Evanston
Childs A. S. Dr. Wilmette

Childs Frank A. Evanston
Childs Frank Hall, 2241 Calumet av.
Childs Grace Miss, 179 Evanston av.
Childs Henry L. 716 Warren av.
Childs John A. Evanston
Childs L. W. Mrs. 4053 Prairie av.
Childs Mary A. Mrs. Evanston
Childs Ralph, Wilmette
Childs Robert A. Hinsdale
Childs William, 3135 Vernon av. *Lksd.*
Childs William F. 405 N. State.
Chipley Gardiner, 4548 Champlain av. *C.A.*
Chipman H. W. Mrs. 294 Belden av.
Chisholm Flora M. Mrs. 552 W. Jackson boul.
Chisholm James, 532 Orchard
Chisholm Samuel S. Virginia hotel. *Chi.*
Chislett H. G. 6527 Greenwood av.
Chislett John, 6527 Greenwood av.
Chittenden Fred W. 1633 Roscoe
Chittenden George W. 1633 Roscoe
Chittenden Nellie M. Mrs. 1633 Roscoe
Chittendon George C. Park Ridge
Chittendon W. S. Park Ridge
Chittick C. E. Miss Hotel Del Prado
Chivers E. Rev. 3240 Groveland av.
Chiville John, 50 Elaine pl.
Chollar W. T. 917 Pullman bldg.
Christensen Jens L. 410 Ashland boul.
Christensen Sophia A. Mrs. Irving Park
Christensen S. J. Irving Park
Christenson August, Austin
Christian Henry. W. 4311 Vernon av. *C.A.*
Christian James H. 6552 Greenwood av.
Christie Angus C. 420 Center
Christie Edmund, M. D., 495 Ashland boul
Christie George B. Auditorium annex. *Cal., C.A., W.P.*
Christison J. S. Dr. 215 Dearborn av.
Christman John C. Evanston
Christmann George A. Dr. 507 Lasalle av.
Christoph Eugene O. Dr. 3662 Michigan av.
Christoph F. W. Mrs. 40 Bellevue pl.
Christopher J. Irving, LaGrange
Christopher Theodore D. LaGrange
Christopher WalterShieldsDr.408 Center
Christy Fred C. 1537 Wolfram
Christy Harry A. Elmhurst
Christy Henry A. 757 Washington boul. *C.A.*
Chumasero John T. Mrs. 3010 Prairie av.
Chumasero Kenneth Page, 3010 Prairie av. *Cal.*
Church Archibald Dr. 4858 Madison av.
Church Charles A. Mrs. 465 Dearborn av.
Church Edmund V. Hotel Metropole. *C.A., W.P.*
Church Edward, Austin
Church Frank W. 2679 Kenmore av.
Church Freeman S. Longwood
Church Jared C. 6512 Parnell av.
Church J. C. 6635 Wentworth av.

Church Lloyd, Evanston
Church Myron H. 2679 Kenmore av.
Church Rebacca Mrs. 184 Lincoln Park av.
Church Rollin, Evanston
Church Thomas Mrs. 184 Lincoln Park boul.
Church Townsend V. 341 Rush. *Chi., Un.*
Church William E. Evanston
Church William L. Mrs. Evanston
Church William T. Longwood
Churchill Charles E. 2166 N. Robey. *C.A.*
Churchill E. C. Hotel Del Prado
Churchill Frank H. LaGrange
Churchill Frank Spooner Dr. 10 Astor
Chytraus Axel, 1932 Arlington pl. *U.L.*
Cissna Walter A. 423 Huron
Claflin Isaac Mrs. Lombard
Claflin M. A. Oak Park
Claflin S. Mrs. Oak Park
Claflin William, Lombard
Claflin William T. Lombard
Clancy A. W. The Hampden. *U.L.*
Clancy Caroline H. Mrs. 1050 Washington boul.
Clancy C. L. Dr. 241 Hampden ct.
Clancy Edwin M. 1050 Washington boul.
Clancy Merrill C. Evanston
Clancy M. B. 4400 Ellis av.
Clancy M. L. Mrs. 3244 Vernon av.
Clancy William B. Mrs. 5539 Monroe av.
Clancy William L. 4530 Woodlawn av.
Clancy William M. 3244 Vernon av.
Clapp A. E. Mrs. Evanston
Clapp Caleb, 4160 Ellis av.
Clapp Charles DeWitt, 6128 Indiana av.
Clapp Clement L. 4043 Ellis av.
Clapp DeWitt C. 3154 Prairie av.
Clapp Eben P. Dr. Evanston
Clapp Edwin Mrs. 4160 Ellis av.
Clapp George, Oak Park
Clapp Henry, 4515 Emerald av.
Clapp Hubert B. 6222 Woodlawn av.
Clapp Irvine E. Evanston
Clapp James L. Dr. 6222 Woodlawn av.
Clapp Katherine B. Dr. 6222 Woodlawn av.
Clapp O. W. Union League club
Clarage Ernest T, 1593 W. Adams
Clare John F. 3123 Michigan av.
Clark Albert B. Dr. Evanston
Clark Albert C. 7248 Euclid av.
Clark Alexander, Evanston
Clark Alfred C. 5737 Indiana av. *C.A.*
Clark Alson E. Hotel Metropole. *Cal., Chi., Ill.*
Clark Andrew G. 2552 Prairie av.
Clark Arthur R. 4330 Ellis av.
Clark Bertha Miss, 920 Lunt av.
Clark Bertram F. The Arizona
Clark Bruce, 2000 Prairie av.
Clark Charles M. 244 Oakwood boul.
Clark Charles R. 644½ Washington boul.
Clark Charles W. 907 S. Spaulding av.
Clark Chester M. Mrs. 34 Groveland Park
Clark Clinton C. Auditorium Annex

Clark C. M. Longwood
Clark C. S. Newberry hotel
Clark C. S. Wilmette
Clark C. W. Leland hotel
Clark David W. 956 Warren av.
Clark Edgar A. 2971 Indiana av.
Clark Edward G. 330 Ashland boul. *Ill.*
Clark Edwin M. 2509 N. Hermitage av.
Clark Egbert B. LaGrange
Clark Elizabeth Mrs. Maywood
Clark Ella S. Mrs. 2123 Prairie av.
Clark Ernest L. Evanston
Clark E. Miss, Evanston
Clark E. A. Lexington hotel. *W.P.*
Clark E. E. Mrs. 401, 40th
Clark E. R. 401, 40th
Clark Frank Mrs. 50 Bellevue pl.
Clark Frank E. 920 Warren av.
Clark Frank H. 3821 Ellis av.
Clark Frank H. 5031 Madison av.
Clark Frank K. 50 Bellevue pl.
Clark Frederic, 234, 47th
Clark Frederick W. 5208 Jefferson av. *U.L.*
Clark F. M. Mrs. Granada hotel
Clark George A. 7804 S. Sangamon
Clark George C. 558 Lasalle av.
Clark George C. Mrs. Virginia hotel
Clark George H. 749 Warren av.
Clark George M. 460 Dearborn av. *U. L.*
Clark George T. 231 Warren av. *C. A.*
Clark George W. River Forest
Clark G. E. Park Ridge
Clark Hannah B. Miss, 5211 Hibbard av.
Clark Henry C. Chicago Beach hotel
Clark Herbert, 1600 Kenmore av.
Clark Herbert T. 1311 Michigan av.
Clark H. H. Lakota hotel
Clark James L. 523 W. Jackson boul. *Ill.*
Clark James L. Tracy
Clark Jason E. LaGrange
Clark John C. Oak Park
Clark John J. Mrs. 247, 53d
Clark John M. 2000 Prairie av. *Cal., Chi. C. A., U. L., Univ., W. P.*
Clark Jonathan, 233 Warren av. *U. L.*
Clark J. D. 4808 Prairie av.
Clark J. D. Lakota hotel
Clark J. H. Churchill, 232, 47th
Clark J. L. North Shore hotel
Clark J. L. Mrs. The Ontario
Clark J. Scott, Prof. Evanston
Clark J. Truman Dr. 338, 57th
Clark Katharine H. Miss, Evanston
Clark Lincoln, 940 Pratt av.
Clark Lincoln E. 940 Pratt av.
Clark Louise D. Miss, Evanston
Clark Lucius, 5144 East End av.
Clark Marshall, Evanston
Clark Mary A. Mrs. 4330 Ellis av.
Clark Mary J. Miss, Austin
Clark Melville, 501 W. Monroe
Clark Michael J. 522 W. 67th
Clark M. T. Hotel Metropole
Clark Paul H. 2552 Prairie av.
Clark Reuben E. 760 Touhy av.

Clark Richard F. 142, 50th
Clark Robert, 2505 Kenmore av.
Clark Robert E. 244 Oakwood boul.
Clark Robert S. Evanston
Clark Russell S. 5438 Cornell av.
Clark R. E. Dr. 3408 Calumet av.
Clark R. H. Mrs. 742 Washington boul.
Clark R. H. Granada hotel
Clark R. L. Hotel Del Prado
Clark Solomon H. 5761 Washington av.
    Sum. res. Chautauqua Lake, N.Y.
Clark Stewart, Evanston
Clark S. H. Mrs. 3300 Indiana av.
Clark Theodore M. Highland Park
Clark Thomas, 326 S. Marshfield av.
Clark Thomas Collier, 5218 Jefferson av. *Irq.*
Clark Thomas C. 729 Fullerton av.
Clark Urilla Mrs. 3821 Ellis av.
Clark Wallace G. 4520 Forrestville av.
Clark Walter T. 312 S. Marshfield av. *C.A., Ill.*
Clark Warren T. Mrs. 3195 Malden
Clark William D. 196, 40th
Clark William H. 34 Groveland Park. *U.L.*
Clark William R. 880 Washington boul.
Clark William R. Austin
Clark W. DeG. Dr. 920 Lunt av.
Clark W. Irving 803, 44th. *Irq.*
Clark W. Odell, 152, 36th
Clark W. Wallace, 536 Washington boul.
Clarke Arthur L. 329 Michigan av.
Clarke Caroline Mrs. 4731 Prairie av.
Clarke Cyrus Henry, 2204 Prairie av.
    Sum. res. Oakland Cottage, St. Clair Springs, Mich.
Clarke D. Gage, 2024 Indiana av.
Clarke E. A. S. 5016 Jefferson av. *Chi.*
Clarke Florence Miss, 87 Rush
Clarke Francis B., M.D. Oak Park
Clarke Frank H. Oak Park
Clarke George C. 87 Rush. *Un., Univ.*
Clarke George R. Mrs. Morgan Park
Clarke Harry M. 1653 Briar pl.
Clarke Henry, 3338 Calumet av.
Clarke Henry B. 251 Goethe. *W. P.*
Clarke Henry L. 3338 Calumet av.
Clarke John C. Glencoe
Clarke John D. 842 W. Adams
Clarke John N. 303 S. Irving av.
Clarke John W. Prof. Washington Heights
Clarke J. B. Washington Heights
Clarke J. V. 208 Goethe. *Univ.*
Clarke Louis B. 251 Goethe
Clarke Louise B. Mrs. 86 Astor
Clarke L. H. 499 W. Adams
Clarke Margaret T. Mrs. 3601 Vincennes av.
Clarke M. H. Mrs. 2811 Prairie av.
Clarke M. L. Miss, 251 Goethe
Clarke O. H. E. Dr. 3857 Vincennes av.
Clarke Robert G. 5110 Jefferson av.
Clarke Robert G. Mrs. 2024 Indiana av.
Clarke Robert R. 1547 N. Halsted
Clarke Robert W. Mrs. Hinsdale

Clarke R. N. 3152 Prairie av.
Clarke S. G. 2811 Prairie av.
Clarke S. J. Miss, 2022 Indiana av.
Clarke William E. Mrs. River Forest
Clarke William G. Rev. 363 S. Oakley av.
Clarke W. H. Hotel Del Prado
Clarke Yvonne Miss, 3857 Vincennes av.
Clarkson M. 4859 Michigan av.
Clarkson Ralph, Evanston
Clarkson William H. Morton Park
Clasen Adolph, 2973 Groveland av.
Clasen Edward, 2973 Groveland av.
Clasen William R. C. 2973 Groveland av.
Clason George B. 50 Bryant av.
Clatworthy Fred Dr. Evanston
Clausen Hans O. 1732 York pl.
Claussenius Edward, 147 Cass
Claussenius George W. 5 Crilly ct.
Claussenius G. A. 6320 Ellis av.
Clausson J. F. Washington Heights
Clay Albert T. Rev. 1282 Sheffield av.
Clay John jr. 4030 Lake av. *Chi. W. P.*
Clay John B. Wilmette
Clay William W. 3145 Rhodes av.
Clayberg George M. Oak Park
Clayburgh Albert, 3439 Michigan av.
Clayburgh Caroline Mrs. 3439 Michigan av.
Clayburgh Harry, 3439 Michigan av.
Clayburgh Joseph, 3439 Michigan av.
Clayburgh Morris, 3439 Michigan av.
Clayton Allen B. Dr. Evanston
Clayton Evelyn P. Mrs. 3200 Michigan av.
Cleary Edward E. 2450 Wabash av.
Cleary John J. Oak Park
            Sum. res. South Haven, Mich.
Cleary P. M. Mrs. 2450 Wabash av.
Cleave O. C. 3906 Lake av. *W. P.*
Cleaveland Frederick B. Norwood Park
Cleaveland F. A. Norwood Park
Cleaver Arthur W. 4400 Champlain av.
Cleaver Edward C. 3615 Lake av.
Cleaver Frederick C. 3615 Lake av.
Cleaver Herbert E. 3601 Vincennes av.
Cleaver James M. 3615 Lake av.
Clement Allan M. 3946 Ellis av.
Clement F. M. Dr. Longwood
Clement Henry B. Longwood
Clement Henry C. Auditorium hotel *C.A*
Clement Nathan Lamb, 3500 Ellis av.
Clements John F. Mrs. 85 Astor
Clements Phoebe J. Miss, 6042 Kimbark av.
Clements Thomas, 4465 Lake av. *C. A.*
Clemmons Mary A. Mrs. 3233 Forest av.
Clendenen Irving Dr. Maywood
Clendenen Irving B. Dr. Maywood
Clendenning Harmon T. 4356 Union av.
Cleveland Augustus F. Oak Park
Cleveland C. B. Evanston *U. L.*
Cleveland Festus P. Rev. 532 Touhy av.
Cleveland Festus W. Evanston
Cleveland G. H., M.D. 951 W. Harrison
Cleveland John D. 532 Touhy av.
Cleveland . F. Oak Park
Cleveland J. H. Mrs. 907 W. Monroe

Cleveland Paul, Evanston
Cleveland S. E. 873 W. Adams
Cleveland Willard R. 864 W. Adams
Clevenger S. V. Dr. 5415 Cottage Grove. av.
Cleverdon F. W. Mrs. 5809 Rosalie ct.
Cleverdon Joseph S. Austin
Cliff Henry, 148 Dearborn av.
Cliff John Capt. 148 Dearborn av.
Clifford B. F. 5344 Greenwood av.
Clifford Eugene L. Dr. 1334 W. Adams
Clifford James M. 1729 Michigan av.
Clifford John, 1900 Wellington
            Sum. res. Williams Bay
Clifford Martin J. Mrs. 1729 Michigan av.
Clifford Richard W. Judge, 1729 Michigan av. *Irq.*
Clifford William B. 36 Beethoven pl.
Clifford Winchester E. Mrs. Evanston
Clifton Arthur L. 6435 Monroe av.
Clifton Charles E. Chicago Athletic Assn.
Clifton E. F. Winnetka
Clifton Theodore Rev. 6825 Perry av.
Clinch D. L. 1254 Michigan av.
Clinch R. Floyd, 321 Michigan av.
            Sum. res. Highland Park
Clingman Charles W. 4861 Lake av.
            Sum. res. Channel Lake, Ill.
Clingman George F. 7210 Euclid av.
Clingman William, 6118 Monroe av.
Clingman W. D. 6117 Monroe av.
Clinton Catherine Mrs. 622 Washington boul.
Clippinger D. A. 276 Michigan av.
Clissold H. R. Morgan Park
Clizbe Wesley J. 878, 50th
Clomes Anna Miss, 659 Cleveland av.
Cloon W. W. 225 Dearborn av.
Close Helen Miss, 780 North Park av.
Cloud John W. 4747 Woodlawn av. *U. L., W.P.*
Clough Harry Sumner, 1549 Oakdale av.
Clover John W. 3618 Lake av.
Clow Catharine S. Mrs. Evanston
Clow Charles R. 702 The Plaza. *C. A.*
Clow Harry B. 834 North Park av. *C. A.*
Clow James B. 702 The Plaza
Clow James C. 702 The Plaza
Clow Lillian Miss, 380 Oak
Clow William E. 50 Buena av.
Clowes Ezekiel W. Dr. 337 Indiana
Clowry James, 4200 Ellis av.
Clowry Robert C. 524 Dearborn av. *Chi., U. L.*
Cloyd Margaret Miss, 3000 Prairie av.
Clunn Louise Mrs. 6500 Greenwood av.
Clute George M. 1832 Oakdale av.
Clute James, 1832 Oakdale av.
Coakley D. W. Mrs. 297 N. State
Coakley W. Byron Dr. 297 N. State
Coates Philip M. LaGrange
Coates Thomas R. Austin
Cobb A. M. 4331 Prairie av.
Cobb A. W. Lake Forest *Un.*
Cobb Charles C. 2475 Magnolia av.
Cobb Daniel, Highland Park

Cobb Edmund P. 254, 47th
Cobb Edward W. Mrs. 502 Belden av.
Cobb Edwin W. 6214 Monroe av.
Cobb Ella F. Miss, 3745 Ellis av.
Cobb Emmons B. 147 Ashland boul. *Ill.*
Cobb F. G. Mrs. 5616 Monroe av.
Cobb George A. 258 Ashland boul.
      Sum. res. Lake Geneva
Cobb George D. Evanston
Cobb George W. Lake Forest
Cobb H. Edward, 3716 Lake av.
Cobb Joseph P. Dr. 254, 47th
Cobb M. L. Miss, 4504 Woodlawn av.
Cobb M. R. 391 Ashland boul. *Ill.*
Cobb Silas B. 2027 Prairie av. *Cal.*
Cobb Simeon Mrs. 877 Washington boul.
Cobb Thomas A. River Forest
Cobb Walter F. 138 Rush. *Chi.*, *Un.*
Cobb Willard L. Evanston
Cobb William Winfield, 6620 Monroe av.
Cobe Ira M. 5110 Hibbard av.
Cobham James M. 326, 41st
Coble N. Arthur, Evanston
Coble Robert K. Evanston
Coburn John J. 872 S. Sawyer av.
Coburn John M. 6422 Lexington av.
Coburn Lewis Larned, 1819 Michigan av.
    Cal., *U.L.*
Cochran A. W. Park Ridge
Cochran John Lewis, 591 N. State. *Univ.*
Cochran Norris, 4352 Grand boul.
Cochran Samuel, Park Ridge
Cochran S. B. 651 W. Adams
Cochran William 296 Belden av.
Cochrane David M. 3530 Ellis av.
Cochrane D. K. 3530 Ellis av.
Cochrane Thomas J. 658 Washington boul.
Cockrill A. R. Mrs. 5217 Madison av.
Codd M. J. Mrs. 1837 Michigan av.
Coddington Archibald O. 1190 Sheffield av.
Cody Arthur B. 6030 Jefferson av. *C.A.*
Cody Hiram H. 6030 Jefferson av.
    Sum. res. Charlevoix, Mich.
Cody Hope R. 340 Oakwood boul. *C.A.*
Coe Albert G. Evanston
Coe Albert L. 57 Bellevue pl. *U.L.*
Coe Almer, 4830 Kenwood av. *C.A.*
Coe D. A. Evanston
Coe George A. 4450 Oakenwald av.
Coe George A. Prof. Evanston
Coe John C. Ravinia
Coe L. W. Mrs. 147 Pine Grove av.
Coe Milton F. Mrs. 4024 Drexel boul.
Coe Sanford, 165 Buena av.
Coe Wilbur E. Evanston
Coe Willard C. 147 Pine Grove av.
Coen Thomas J. 227 Seminary av.
Coen William H. 14 Marquette Terrace
    C.A.
Coey David, 5238 Michigan av.
Coey Samuel B. 5238 Michigan av.
Coffeen M. D. 4957 Prairie av.
Coffeen M. Lester, Kenilworth. *Chi.*
Coffeen William, Hinsdale. *Cal.*, *Chi.*
    C.A., *W.P.*
Coffey John S. Oak Park

Coffin Arthur S. Winnetka
Coffin Charles F. 3232 Groveland av. *U.L.*
Coffin Charles Henry. 380 Ontario. *Un.*,
    U.L.
    Win. res. Roseheart, Pass Christian,
    Miss.
Coffin Charles Howells, 380 Ontario
Coffin Charles P. Evanston
Coffin Gorham B. Austin
Coffin Percival Brooks, 3232 Groveland
    av.
Coffin Percy B. Austin
Coffin Rhoda Howells Miss, 380 Ontario
Coffman Samuel, 384 Oakwood boul.
Cofran J. W. G. Auditorium hotel. *U.L.*
Cogdal George B. Austin
Coggeshall Charles P. Irving Park
Coggeshall Mary M. Mrs. 1045 Wilcox av.
Coghlan Henry D. 5011 Wabash av. *C.A.*
Coghlan Michael, 5011 Wabash av.
    Sum. res. "Fairoaks Farm" Hobart, Ind.
Cohen Abraham L. 455 Cleveland av.
    Lksd.
Cohen Alfred J. 3413 Prairie av.
Cohen Benjamin, 3100 Groveland av.
Cohen Charlotte Mrs. 220 Fremont
Cohen David M. 3335 Calumet av.
Cohen David M. S. 455 Cleveland av.
Cohen Henry M. 2298 N. Paulina
Cohen Joseph J. 3335 Calumet av.
Cohen Julius J. 4728 Prairie av.
Cohen Louis M. 1904 Indiana av.
Cohen Melvin M. 152, 36th
Cohen Mendel A. Dr. 3335 Calumet av.
Cohen Morris I. 4160 Ellis av.
Cohen M. 3404 Forest av.
Cohen Nathan Mrs. 3323 South Park av.
Cohen Reuben S. 3323 South Park av.
Cohen Samuel A. Dr. 3335 Calumet av.
Cohn Arnold, 3322 Indiana av.
Cohn Daniel A. 4541 Greenwood av.
    Stan.
Cohn Harris, 42 Fowler
Cohn Henry, 786 Washington boul.
Cohn Henry, Prof. Evanston
Cohn Jacob, 3416 Vernon av.
Cohn L. H. LaGrange
Cohn Morris, 3321 Calumet av.
Cohn Moses, 4450 Langley av.
Coit W. B. 397 Warren av.
Coker Bertha A. Mrs. 4611 Vincennes av.
Coker Frank A. 4350 Vincennes av.
Coker W. W. Dr. 4611 Vincennes av.
Colberg Henry P. 2912 Groveland av.
Colbert Elias, 2 Groveland Park
Colborne Oliver, 693 Evanston av.
Colburn Harry, Hinsdale
Colburn Isaac, 4560 Oakenwald av. *C.A.*
Colburn Josiah E. Glencoe
Colburn J. Elliott Dr. Highland Park.
    C.A.
Colburn Mary L. Miss, 2915 Indiana av.
Colburn S. A. Mrs. Hinsdale
Colburn Theodore F. 2915 Indiana av.
Colburn William, Hinsdale
Colby B. Dorr Dr. 560 W. Jackson boul.

Colby Charles C. 5238 Calumet av.
Colby Francis T. 282 S. Campbell av.
Colby Henry C. Evanston
    Sum. res. Delavan, Wis.
Colby Hiram, 622 W. 65th
Colby John A. 43, 73d. *U.L.*
    Sum. res. Sag Bridge, Ill.
Colby J. E. The Ontario
Coldwell George G. Morgan Park
Cole Annette Miss, 3724 Ellis av.
Cole Arthur W. 5413 Greenwood av.
Cole Charles W. Winnetka
Cole C. C. Mrs. 4423 Ellis av.
Cole Edward S. 271, 53d
Cole Elijah C. 323 Washington boul.
Cole Ella P. Mrs. 2115 Indiana av.
Cole Ernest C. 4634 Prairie av.
Cole E. R. Prof. La Grange
Cole Festus B. 3824 Ellis av.
Cole George E. 3539 Grand boul. *U.L.*
Cole George H. 3139 Forest av.
Cole George S. Highland Park
Cole G. W. I. 432 Englewood av.
Cole Harry A. Chicago Beach hotel.
Cole Jirah D. sr. Mrs. 2117 Indiana av.
Cole Jirah D. Winnetka
Cole John A. 271, 53d
    Sum. res. Bay View, Mich.
Cole Julius, 7121 Eggleston av.
Cole Maria Mrs. 3150 Michigan av.
Cole Martin E. 703 W. Monroe
Cole Moses T. 180 Park av.
Cole M. E. W. Mrs. 5413 Greenwood av.
Cole M. T. Oak Park
Cole Phoebe Mrs. 3724 Ellis av.
Cole S., M.D. 3305 Vernon av.
Cole Thomas W. 802 Warren av. *Ill.*
Cole Thomas W. 439, 41st
Cole Wilford B. 802 Warren av.
Colegrove H. P. 2600 Calumet av.
Colehour C. W. 518 The Plaza
Coleman A. E. 5214 Woodland av.
Coleman Edward, 130, 47th
Coleman John, River Forest
Coleman Julius A. 19, 46th
Coleman J. G. 18 Ritchie ct. *Un.*
Coleman J. Pearson, 47 Bryant av.
Coleman Rupert, 1011 N. Halsted
Coleman Seymour, 2023 Michigan av.
    W.P.
Coleman S. Cobb, 18 Ritchie ct.
Coleman William A. 267, 66th pl.
Coleman William O. River Forest. *Irq.*
Coleman W. Franklin Dr.5118 Cornell av.
Colgate Russell, 415 Huron. *Univ.*
Colgate Samuel, Virginia hotel
Collender A. 336 Winthrop av.
Collette Anna B. Miss, 1530 W. Momroe
Collette Louise N. Miss, 1530 W. Monroe
Collette Wm. T. R. 1530 W. Monroe
Colley Frederick George, 487 Dearborn
    av.   Sum. res. Spring Lake, Mich.
Collier Clinton, Calumet club. *U.L.,*
    W.P.
Collier Frank P. 2607 N. Hermitage av.
Collier Sarah Mrs. 544 W. Jackson boul.

Colling George, Evanston
Collings W. P. 4060 Ellis av.
Collins Clinton DeWitt Dr.203 Centre av.
Collins C. C. River Forest
Collins C. C. Mrs. Clifton house
Collins Ernest A. 13 Bittersweet pl.
Collins George F. 398 Webster av.
Collins George M. 6512 Stewart av.
Collins Harrie B. 2487 Kenmore av. *C.A.*
Collins I. S. 76 Bellevue pl.
Collins James H. 398 Webster av.
Collins John Glenn, 1917 Deming pl.
    C.A.
Collins Kreigh, 76 Bellevue pl.
Collins Levi D. 614 Washington boul.
Collins Lorin C. Rev. 4830 Madison av.
Collins Lorin C. jr. Judge, 4830 Madison
    av. *Chi., W.P.*
Collins Lorin C. 3d, 4830 Madison av.
    W.P.
Collins Martin H. 6512 Stewart av.
Collins Mary K. Mrs. 4211 Vincennes av.
Collins Saide B. Mrs. 4107 Grand boul.
Collins S. T. Hinsdale
Collins Thomas, 912 W. Monroe
Collins T. L. Berwyn
Collins William, 1886 Diversey
Collins William M. 398 Webster av.
Collins William R. 2487 Kenmore av.
Collins William W. 3 Chalmers pl.
Collins W. C. 6421 Harvard av.
Collins W. Forman, 7153 Princeton av.
Collins W. G. Virginia hotel. *C.A.,U.L.*
Collins W. H. 6128 Woodlawn av.
Colman Martin A. Dr. 5853 Wabash av.
Colson Charles D. Mrs. 7001 Stewart av.
Colson Harry G. 1118 Washington boul.
Colson Julia G. Mrs. 1118 Washington
    boul.
Colt Alonzo J. 119 W. 66th
Colt James D. 3226 Vernon av.
Colton A. M. F. Mrs. 424 Chicago av.
Colton George A. Wilmette
Colton Samuel K. 424 Chicago av. *C.A.*
Colton Simeon C. 424 Chicago av.
Colver S. E. Mrs. 3953 Michigan av.
Colvin Jessie Miss, 37 Cedar
Colvin Katharine Miss, 37 Cedar
Colvin Libbie F. Miss, 201 The Plaza
Colvin William A. 7751 Emerald av.
Colvin William H. 113, 47th. *U.L.*
    W.P.
Colvin W. H. Dr. Mayfair
Colwell Clyde B. 3040 Calumet av.
Colwell J. M. Mrs. 3040 Calumet av.
Colwell Ray M. 3040 Calumet av.
Colwell Thomas M. 7754 S. Sangamon
Colwell William S. 5468 Washington av.
Coman Martha S.Mrs.6422 Lexington av.
Coman Seymour, Union League club
Combs Frank X. 5231 Kimbark av.
Combs Helen Dr. 4709 Evans av.
Combs Thomas W. 4709 Evans av.
Combs Will Augustus, 195, 44th
Comes Charles W. 602 Division
Comfort Edward C. 1069 Winona av.

Comley Fred, Oak Park
Compton Alfred M. 944 Garfield boul.
Compton John C. 4727 Lake av.
Comstock Alice J. Miss. Evanston
Comstock Alphonso S. Evanston
Comstock Charles Mrs. Evanston
Comstock Edward F. 1821 Barry av.
Comstock Fred S. 2731 Kenmore av.
Comstock Henry, 2731 Kenmore av.
Comstock John A. Evanston
Comstock J. A. Mrs. Evanston
Comstock J. K. 4401 Prairie av.
Comstock Levi M. Ravinia
Comstock Samuel C. 3608 Lake av.
Comstock William H. 30 Walton pl. Un.
Comstock W. C. Auditorium annex. Chi.
Conant Luther, Oak Park
Conant Robert W. Dr. 5490 Washington
    av.
Conant William C. Oak Park
Condee L. D. 4552 Woodlawn av.
Condell Thomas H. 1031 Evanston av.
Condict W. R. Evanston
Condict Wallace R. jr. Evanston
Condit Edgar M. 6537 Harvard av.
Condon James G. 5941 Indiana av.
Cone A. G. 4148 Drexel boul. U.L.
Cone George W. Austin
Cone Julius, 3649 Forest av.
Cone M. M. Mrs. 1801 Prairie av.
Cone Orlando M. 273 Oakwood boul.
Congdon Anna M. Mrs. University of
    Chicago
Congdon B. Mrs. Oak Park
Congdon C. B. Evanston. U.L.
Congdon G. G. 348 Belden av.
Congdon J. Lyman, M.D. Riverside
Conger Charles T. 99, 47th
Conger John S. 426 W. Jackson boul.
Conger Romaine M. 494 W. Monroe. Ill.
Conger Theodore H. Dr. Highland Park
Conger William P. Mrs. 262 Michigan av.
Conine Henry V. 2350 Kenmore av.
Conkey Lucius W. Evanston
Conkey W. B. 5518 East End av. C.A.,
    Ill., U.L., W.P.
Conkling Allen, Auditorium hotel. C.A.,
    W.P.
Conkling B. H. 168, 45th. C.A., W.P.
Conley John W. 4201 Grand boul. Chi.,
    C.A., W.P.
Conley J. Stafford, Evanston
Conley J. W. Rev. Oak Park
Conlin Thomas, 4020 Vincennes av.
Conly Harry F. 3235 Rhodes av.
Conly John A. 36, 42d pl.
Connard Isaac N. Oak Park
Connart Louis, 4834 Langley av.
Connell Charles J. Evanston. Chi.
Connell Charles M. Evanston
Connell James M. 7025 Yale
Connell Joseph A. LaGrange
Connelly Francis W. 5113 Michigan av.
Connelly Thomas, 276 Loomis
Conner Frank F. 376, 40th
Conner Merritt S. 1071 Warren av.

Connery Michael W. 339 S. Hoyne av.
Connor Frank H. 449, 66th
Connor John L. Evanston
Connor J. C. Mrs. Evanston
Connor Thomas E. Evanston
Connor Thomas V. 5714 Washington av.
    W.P.
Conover Charles H. 478 Elm. Chi., C.A.,
    Irq., Un., U.L.
Conover George W. 4743 Champlain av.
Conover J. F. Hotel Del Prado
Conover Lawrence P. Hinsdale
Conpropst Thomas M. Riverside
Conrad Charles H. 3940 Lake av. C.A.
Conrad Frederick T. 4949 Champlain av.
Conrad J. Henry, 3940 Lake av. C.A.
Conrad Louis W. 692 W. Adams
Conrad Martin, Sherman house
Conrad Sarah A. Dr. 692 W. Adams
Conroy I. Newton, 228 Oakwood boul.
Conroy William, 4519 Indiana av.
Considine John C. 469 Bowen av.
Considine John P. 59 Macalister pl.
Considine M. 59 Macalister pl.
Converse Clarence M. 2451 Michigan av.
Converse E. DeWitt Dr. 4507 Lake av.
Converse E. T. River Forest
Converse James W. Irving Park
Convis Alonzo P. Mrs. Wilmette
Convis A. A. Mrs. Hinsdale
Convis James E. Hinsdale
Conway Edwin S. Oak Park. C.A., U.L.
Conway E. E. Oak Park. U.L.
Conway Michael W. 85 Ewing pl.
Conway Richard F. 1234 Washington boul.
Conway T. F. New Hotel Holland
Conyne Charles B. S. Oak Park
Conyne Wallace K. Oak Park
Cook Alexander, 3835 Lake av.
Cook Alice G. Miss, 235 Michigan av.
Cook Archibald, 3835 Lake av.
Cook A. B. 3732 Lake av.
Cook A. M. Mrs. 262 Park av.
Cook A. S. Mrs. 3241 Indiana av.
Cook Charles A. Irving Park
Cook Charles D. Tremont house
Cook Charles E. 707 W. Jackson boul.
Cook Cyrus F. 247 Dearborn av.
Cook David S. Evanston
Cook Edward, Oak Park
Cook Ezra A. 316 Washington boul.
    Sum. res. Wheaton
Cook Ezra A. jr. 316 Washington boul.
Cook Frank L. Irving Park
Cook F. King, Kenilworth
Cook F. W. Oak Park
Cook George Dr. The Kenwood
Cook George D. 5140 Woodlawn av. U.L.
Cook George E. 3730 Lake av.
Cook George F. Oak Park
Cook George H. 4718 Kenwood av.
Cook George M. 207, 41st
Cook George Shaw, 5225 Woodlawn av.
Cook Harlan D. 3219 Groveland av.
Cook Harlan E. 4508 Indiana av.
Cook Harry B. Kenilworth. C.A.

Cook Henry L. 552, 46th pl.
Cook Henry W. 4101 Drexel boul.
Cook H. Henry Dr. 224, 31st
Cook John C., M.D. 5708 Rosalie ct.
Cook John H. 4214 Ellis av.
Cook Joshua O. Evanston
Cook J. C. Dr. The Kenwood
Cook Laning Mrs. 79, 20th
Cook Louis, Oak Park
Cook Lucy Mrs. 79, 20th
Cook N. B. 24 Madison Park
Cook Orrin S. 74 Bryant av.
Cook Owen D. Hinsdale
Cook Robert S. 74 Bryant av.
Cook Susan G. Mrs. 235 Michigan av.
Cook Sylvan, 3646 Michigan av.
Cook Wallace K. Evanston
Cook William F. 3728 Lake av.
Cook William H. DesPlaines. *U.L.*
Cook W. M. 4150 Lake av.
Cook W. W. Dr. Irving Park
Cooke Alexander W. 234 Dearborn av. *Un.*
Cooke A. B. 1857 Briar pl.
Cooke A. H., M.D. 234 Dearborn av.
Cooke Charles F. 3159 South Park av.
    Sum. res. Lake Geneva, Wis.
Cooke E. M. Mrs. 198, 44th
Cooke George J. 3305 Calumet av.
Cooke Harry H. 6010 Jefferson av. *C.A.*
Cooke Henry C. Oak Park
Cooke Jean M. Dr. 1812 Melrose
Cooke John M., M.D. 234 Dearborn av.
Cooke John R. 2976 Michigan av.
Cooke John S. 2976 Michigan av. Sum. res.
    Ara Glen Cottage Lake Geneva, Wis.
Cooke Joseph H. 214, 51st
Cooke Marcus E. 3547 Ellis av.
Cooke Nellie S. Mrs. 2518 Michigan av.
Cooke S. J. 3261 Groveland av.
Cooke William J. Oak Park
Cooke Wilson H. 1429 Lawrence av.
Cookingham Theron W. Irving Park
Coolbaugh W. F. Mrs. 2252 Calumet av.
    Sum. res. Newburgh N. Y.
Cooley L. Edith Miss, 1718 Indiana av.
Cooley Edwin G. La Grange
Cooley Harlan W. 4613 Woodlawn av.
Cooley H. H. Mrs. 3109 Groveland av.
Cooley John B. Oak Park
Cooley Norman P. 5490 East· End av.
    C.A.
Cooley William, Evanston
Cooley William H. Evanston
Coolidge Dr. Lakeside
Coolidge Charles A. 2603 Prairie av. *Chi.*
    Sum. res. Marion, Mass.
Coolidge Frederic S. Dr. 2636 Prairie av.
    Chi., Univ.
Coolidge George W. 6422 Minerva av.
Coolidge Henry W. 2917 Groveland av.
Coolidge H. E. Miss, 3750 Langley av.
Coolidge Porter B. Oak Park
Coolidge Walter G. 4752 Kimbark av.
    U.L.
Coolidge Winthrop, 4752 Kimbark av.
Coombs Hiram, Oak Park

Coon Emma Martin Mrs. 3132 Calumet
    av.
Coon Marietta Miss, Irving Park
Coonley John S. 5537 Cornell av.
Coonley Sarah Miss, 620 Division
Cooper Arthur W. Dr. Evanstor
Cooper A. J. Mrs. Evanston
Cooper Charles, B. 6565 Yale
Cooper Ed. C. Hotel Normandie. *C.A.*
Cooper Frank H. 150 Lincoln Park boul.
    C.A.
Cooper George W. 6565 Yale
Cooper Grace Miss, 376 Oak
Cooper Harry H. 3517 Grand boul.
Cooper Henry N. LaGrange
Cooper Horace L. 4740 Champlain av.
Cooper H. C. Evanston
Cooper James W. 2952 Groveland av.
Cooper John S. Col. 2733 Michigan av.
    Cal., W.P.
Cooper John S. 376 Oak. *Irq.*
Cooper Joseph I. Oak Park
Cooper L. C. Glen Ellyn
Cooper Robert B. 2952 Groveland av.
Cooper Samuel A. 1062 Millard av.
Cooper William D. Chicago Beach hotel.
    C.A., U.L.
Cooper Wm. Fenimore, 225 Dearborn av.
    C.A.
Cope George W. 2675 N. Hermitage av.
Copeland Elizabeth Mrs. 1693 Kenmore
    av.
Copeland Frederick K. Winnetka. *C.A.*
Copeland Lowell, Winnetka
Copeland William L. Dr. 866 W. Monroe
Copelin A. J. W. 3633 Ellis av.
Copelin Bertram, 3633 Ellis av.
Copelin Eudolphus W. 551 Dearborn av.
    C.A.
Copelin Thomas, Winnetka
Copelin Thomas E. 382 Erie
Copp Laura R. Miss, 718 The Plaza
Corbet James C. 4548 Forrestville av.
Corbett Mary A. Miss, 2616 Indiana av.
Corbett Thomas H. 3667 Wabash av.
Corbidge William H. 3542 Wabash av.
Corbin Calvin R. 597 Dearborn av. *U.L.*
Corbin C. Dana, 597 Dearborn av. *C.A.*
Corbin E. M. 6500 Greenwood av.
Corbin Franklin N. 298 Schiller.· *C.A.*
Corbin Lawrence Paul, 597 Dearborn
    av.
Corboy Michael J. 97 Macalister pl.
Corbus B. Clark, 907 W. Adams
Corbus J. R., M.D. 907 W. Adams
Corby Emily Mrs. 120 S. Oakley av.
Corby James, Hyde Park hotel
Corby Ralph B. 27 Scott. *C.A.*
Corcoran Bernard A. 836 Washington
    boul.
Cordes Henry, 163 S. Hoyne av.
Cordes John, 1404 Fulton
Cordes Lewis, 163 S. Hoyne av.
Cordier J. P. Mrs. 5943 Wabash av.
Cordo Frank I. 4508 Forrestville av. *C.A.*
Core A. S. 4601 Champlain av.

Corey G. B. 3745 Indiana av.
Corlett T   Mrs. 232 Lincoln Park
   boul..homas
Corlett Thomas Gardner Dr. 580 Division
Corlett Walter R. Oak Park
Corlies John W. 723 Washington boul
Corlies William, Chicago Beach hotel
Corliss George D. 252, 53d
Cormack Joseph, 6334 Greenwood av.
Corneau D. Ellis, 2934 Michigan av. *C.A.*,
   U.L.
Corneau Edwin G. Oak Paik
Corneau Edwin N. Oak Park
Corneau J. M. Hyde Park hotel
Corneau Perry B. 2934 Michigan av.
Cornelius Edward H. 5226 Kimbark av. *Lksd.*
Cornelius Max Dr. 4725 Calumet av.
Cornell Addie S. Mrs. 14 Bryant av.
Cornell Alice Sterling Mrs. 317 Park av.
Cornell George K. Hyde Park hotel
Cornell G. H. Park Ridge
Cornell Helen Miss, Hyde Park hotel
Cornell Henrietta W. Mrs. 503 W. Monroe
Cornell H. C. Austin
Cornell John E. Hyde Park hotel
Cornell Paul, Hyde Park hotel
Cornell Paul jr. Hyde Park hotel
Cornell William B. 503 W. Monroe
Cornell W. D. Austin
Cornell W. D. LaGrange
Cornell W. F. 4109 Drexel boul.
Cornhauser Maurice, 149, 42d pl. *Lksd.*
Corning Charles S. Hotel Del Prado
Corning George C. 4554 Lake av.
Corning Winfield S. 196 Cass
Cornwall Franklin W. 4009 Lake av.
Cornwall George W. 4011 Lake av.
Corper Charles, 3736 Grand boul.
Corrigan Michael Mrs. 2842 Prairie av.
Corse C. J. Longwood
Corse Edwards Mrs. 407 Elm
Corten Theodore, 980 Cuyler av.
Corthell J. L. Mrs. 2013 Michigan av.
Cortis W. P. Hinsdale
Corwin Arthur M. Dr. 691 W. Harrison
Corwin Eli Rev. 1066 Warren av.
Corwith Charles R. 1945 Prairie av. *Cal.* .
   Chi., Un., Univ.
Corwith Henry Mrs. 1945 Prairie av.
Corwith John W. 1945 Prairie av.
Corwith Nathan, Highland Park
Corwith Nathan Mrs. Lexington hotel
Cory Alfonzo L. Dr. 4136 Wabash av.
Cory E. V. Dr. 4136 Wabash av.
Cory J. D. 3016 Prairie av.
Cory V. P. 4136 Wabash av.
Coryell George R. Evanston
Coryell M. E. Mrs. Evanston
Cosby Hogan D. 4141 Southport av.
Cosgrove H. J. Kenilworth
Cosgrove Sarah Mrs. Evanston
Cossar Thomas, 7111 Eggleston av.
Cossitt Franklin D. LaGrange
Cossitt Franklin D. jr. LaGrange
Cost Jacob A. River Forest
Costain T. E. Dr. 2942 Prairie av.

Costello Margaret Mrs. 4511 Forrestville
   av.
Coster Maurice Auditorium annex
Cotes Warren S. 296 Ohio
Cotharin Frank A. 6200 Woodland av.
Cotter C. A. Mrs. 704 Warren av.
Cotter Michael Rev. 658 W. Jackson boul.
Cotter Robert B. 504 The Plaza
Cotter William H. Oak Park
Cotton Alfred C. Dr. 677 W. Jackson boul.
Cotton Caroline H. Mrs. 69 Bryant av.
Cotton Charles H. 69 Bryant av.
Cotton H. Mrs. 304 The Plaza
Cotton J. Whitcomb, 38 Bellevue av. *Un.*
Cottrell Harry W. Morton Park
Cottrell William N. 97 Oakwood av. *U.L.*
Couch Ira Mrs. 4419 Ellis av.
Couch Ira J. 4419 Ellis av. *Irq.*
Couch James Mrs. 2545 Indiana av.
Couffer John D. 728 W. Adams
Couffer William E. 1491 W. Monroe
Coughlan John, 41 Macalister pl.
Coughlan Thomas, 452 W. Taylor
Coughlan T. E. 41 Macalister pl.
Coughlin James M. 694 Walnut
Cougle Charles H. 343 Michigan av.
Cougle Daniel Depue, 197, 30th
Cougle Irvin B. 3012 Michigan av.
Coulter Adrian, 395 S. Leavitt
Coulter Edward, LaGrange
Coulter Eugene C. 399 Dearborn av.
Coulter E. F. 1074 Francis
Coulter John, 4756 Champlain av.
Coulter John M. 362, 57th
Coulter John R. 291 S. Leavitt
Coulter J. Homer Dr. 49 Campbell Park
Coulter William M. 1074 Francis
Counselman Charles, 5035 Greenwood av.
   Chi., C.A., U.L., W.P.
Counselman Willis, 819 The Plaza. *W.P.*
Countiss Frederick D. 3222 Calumet av.
Countiss Robert H. 3222 Calumet av.
Coursen J. Edwin, 600 Dearborn av.
Courter David A. Hinsdale
Courtright Frederick W. 6052 Monroe av.
Courtright Henry H. 5029 Madison av.
Couthoui Joseph, 538 W. 61st
Covell Marias C. LaGrange
Covert M. Mrs. Oak Park
Cowan Charles H. Mrs. 465 Fullerton av.
Cowan E. LaGrange
Cowan Harry R. 465 Fullerton av.
Cowan H. Mrs. 2975 Wabash av.
Cowan John S. Leland hotel
Cowan William P. 3142 Michigan av.
   Irq., W.P.
Cowdery H. C. W. 6214 Monroe av.
Cowdery R. E. Mrs. 27 St. James pl.
Cowen Bertha Mrs. 3218 South Park av.
Cowen Carlos K. 3218 South Park av.
   Lksd.
Cowen Eleonora Miss, 2108 Prairie av.
Cowen Israel, 3216 South Park av. *Irq.*,
   Lksd.
Cowie Robert E. M. The Arizona
Cowing R. Maxwell, 6557 Ingleside av.

Cowles Alfred, 1805 Michigan av. *Cal.,*
   C.A., Univ., W.P.
Cowles Frederick S. 3605 Ellis Park
Cowles John E. 174, 47th
   Sum. res. St. Joseph, Mich.
Cowles John T. 174, 47th
Cowles John T. Morgan Park
Cowles William H. 4738 Grand boul.
Cowles W. D. 3648 Vincennes av.
Cowley Abigail Miss, Hotel Luzerne
Cowlin Frederick W. 804 W. Adams
Cowling John V. jr. 1930 Deming pl.
Cowper Charles H. Evanston
Cowper John H. 215 Warren av.
Cowperthwaite A. C. Dr. 188 Warren av.
   Ill.
Cox Alexis J. 1624 Diversey
Cox Alfred, 1419 Michigan av.
Cox Alfred J. 1624 Diversey
Cox Arthur M. 717 W. Harrison
Cox A. C. Mrs. 544 W. Jackson boul.
Cox A. G. Granada hotel. *C.A.*
Cox Charles C. Evanston
Cox Charles D. 4432 Ellis av. *C.A., U.L.*
Cox Charles E. 3544 Ellis av.
Cox Cornelius, Tracy
Cox Electra R. Mrs. 131 Astor
Cox Eugene R. 3544 Ellis av. *Ill.*
Cox George W. Dr. 2945 Groveland av.
Cox James C. 38 Roslyn pl.
Cox Jennie E. Miss, 131 Astor
Cox Jesse, 717 W. Harrison
Cox LeRoy B. 3168 Groveland av.
Cox Rensselaer W. 131 Astor. *Chi., C.A.,*
   U.L., W.P.
Cox R. S. Lexington hotel
Cox Sallie I. Miss, Evanston
Cox T. E. Rev. 658 W. Jackson boul.
Coy Harry I. 3934 Michigan av.
Coy Lincoln M. 3934 Michigan av.
Coy R. D. Glencoe
Coy William F. Dr. 505 Lasalle av.
Coy Winfield S. 220 W. Madison
Coyne F. E. 795 Warren av.
Coyne J. Harry Mrs. 3789 Sheridan rd.
Cozard George J. 378 Bowen av.
Cozzens Fred B. 2678 Evanston av.
Cozzens Harriet E. Mrs. 2678 Evanston
   av.
Cozzens James G. 3608 Ellis Park
Cozzens Samuel, 4515 Emerald av.
Crabb C. C. 129 Dearborn av. *C.A.*
Crabbe Hugh, 237 Jackson Park terrace
Cracraft Archie C. Mrs. 6402 Minerva av
Craft John C. 5206 Hibbard av. *U.L.*
Crafts Clayton E. Austin
Crafts Miles B. Austin
Crafts Sigel J. Austin
Crafts Stanley C. Austin
Crafts William C. Austin
Crafts Z. B. Austin
Cragin Edward F. Evanston. *U.L.*
Cragin Henry B. Evanston
Craig A. Dewes, Riverside
Craig Bryan Y. 480 Fullerton av.
Craig E. M. 933 S. Spaulding av.

Craig John, 242, 45th
Craig Robert, 6615 Wentworth av.
Craig Willis G. Rev. 1048 N. Halsted
Crain Charles H. Dr. 6143 Monroe av.
Crain Osro A. Mrs. Evanston
Crain Sarah Mrs. Evanston
Crain William, Evanston
Craine W. N. The Kenwood. *W.P.*
Cram George F. 4166 Drexel boul.
Cramer Ambrose, Lake Forest. *Univ.*
Cramer C. D. Wilmette
Cramer Eliphalet Mrs. 30 Astor
Cramer E. W. 78 Bellevue pl. *Chi., Un.*
Cramer Frank, 30 Astor. *Un.*
Cramer Guy, 8 Oakland Crescent
Crampton E. E. Mrs. Hyde Park hotel
Crampton John Mrs. 383 Elm
Crampton John N. 383 Elm
Crampton Richard L. Oak Park
Crandal Frederick E. 4136 Ellis av.
Crandal Loretta M. Mrs. 4136 Ellis av.
Crandall Bruce V. 3844 Ellis av.
Crandall Chester D. 4558 Ellis av. *U.L.*
Crandall C. E. 5455 Monroe av.
Crandall Frank A. 3025 Prairie av.
Crandall Latham A. Rev. 3844 Ellis av.
Crandall Miles, Oak Park
Crandall Minnie Mrs. Hotel Del Prado
Crandall Oscar, 6636 Yale
Crandall Roland A. 6513 Woodlawn av.
Crandon Frank P. Evanston
Crane Albert M. 1199 Winthrop av. *Chi.,*
   C.A.
Crane Charles A. 3000 Vernon av.
Crane Charles F. 1048 Pratt av.
Crane Charles R. 2559 Michigan av. *Cal.,*
   Chi., C.A., Irq.
   Sum. res. Lake Geneva, Wis.
Crane Edward C. Chicago Beach hotel.
   Un., W.P.
Crane Eliza J. Mrs. 1482 Washington boul.
Crane Frank Rev. 2519 Indiana av. *U.L.*
Crane Frank P. 504 Englewood av.
Crane Frank R. 1482 Washington boul.
   Sum. res. Escanaba, Mich
Crane Frederick A. LaGrange
Crane Harold O. 294 Lasalle av.
Crane Henry A. Wilmette
Crane Jessie D. Mrs. 1709 Prairie av.
   Sum. res. Lake Geneva, Wis.
Crane Laura B. Mrs. Austin
Crane Lottie A. Mrs. 481 Belden av.
Crane Mary E. Mrs. 1048 Pratt av.
Crane M. E. Mrs. 140 Loomis
Crane Omer F. 3636 Grand boul.
Crane Richard T. 2541 Michigan av. *Chi.,*
   C.A., Ill., U.L.
   Sum. res. Lake Geneva, Wis.
Crane Richard T. jr. 2541 Michigan av.
   C.A., Univ.
Crane Simeon H. 4238 Drexel boul. *Ill.,*
   U.L.
Crane William B. 3636 Grand boul.
Crane Willis E. Wilmette
Crankshaw Charles W. 5202 Kimbark
   av.

Cranz Harry C. Chicago Beach hotel. *C.A.*
Crary Charles W. Dr. 83, 47th
Crary Roscoe, Auditorium annex. *C.A*
Cratty Josiah, Oak Park
Cratty Thomas, 243 Oak. *U.L.*, *W.P.*
Craven Henry, Evanston
Craven Thomas Rev. Evanston
Craver Charles F. Harvey. *U.L.*
Crawford Andrew, 109 Pine Grove av.
  Sum res. Royalton Heights, St. Joseph, Mich. *U.L.*, *W.P.*
Crawford Andrew H. 109 Pine Grove av.
Crawford A. K. Dr. 3231 South Park av.
Crawford Charles H. 103, 37th
Crawford C. Harrison, M.D. 3444 Indiana av. Sum. res. Bar Harbor, Me.
Crawford C. W. Hyde Park hotel
Crawford D. L. 762 Greenleaf av.
Crawford Edwin C. Evanston
Crawford Ellen C. Miss, 210, 33d
Crawford Frederick E. 6520 Kimbark av.
Crawford Harry, 6565 Yale
Crawford Henry, 2000 Calumet av.
Crawford Henry jr. 2329 Calumet av. *W.P.*
Crawford John N. 210, 33d
Crawford J. W. Mrs. 35 Roslyn pl.
Crawford Mark L. 386 Ashland boul. *Ill.*
Crawford Neil D. 904 Touhy av.
Crawford Samuel W. 637 Fullerton av.
Crawford William Mrs. 424, 41st
Crawford William H. Mrs. Evanston
Crawford William L. 904 Touhy av.
Crawford William Randall, 1840 Calumet av.
Creden ThomasH. 465 Dearborn av. *Un.*
Creedon Stephen D. 607 W. Congress
  Sum. res: Spring Haven, Lake Geneva
Cregier DeWitt C. Mrs. 418 Chicago av.
  Sum. res. St. Charles, Ill.
Cregier DeWitt C. jr. 418 Chicago av.
Cregier Washington R. Highland Park
  Sum. res. "Valley View," St.Charles,Ill.
Crego Frank A. Irving Park
Creighton David Rev. 381 Mohawk
Creighton Martha J. Dr. 4533 Lake av.
Creighton Thomas S. Evanston
Cremin John F. Austin
Crennan Joseph M. 4825 Vincennes av.
Crenshaw William Percy, River Forest
  Sum. res. Post Lake, Wis.
Creote Clara Miss, Austin
Crepin E. E. 4726 Woodlawn av.
Crerar John, Virginia hotel. *Un.*, *W.P.*
Crew Henry, Prof. Evanston
Crews Ralph, 1918 Indiana av.
Crews Seth F. 1918 Indiana av.
Crews Seth F. jr. 1918 Indiana av.
Cribben Henry, Oak Park
Cribben W. H. Oak Park
Crighton James, 227 S. Lincoln
Crilly Daniel F. 3820 Michigan av. *U.L*
Crilly Edgar, 3820 Michigan av.
Crilly George S. 3808 Calumet av. *C.A.*
Crilly Lena Miss, 3816 Michigan av.

Crilly Wm. M. 3816 Michigan av.
Crippen Claude, Lake Forest
Crissey M. E. Mrs. Julien hotel
Crissey Payson E. 4602 Prairie av.
Crissman Ira B. Dr. 41 Elaine pl.
Crissman Rush E. Dr. 258, 37th
Criswell James F. 748 Washington boul.
Critchell George W. 6955 Yale
Critchell John, 6955 Yale. *C.A.*
Critchell J. H. 6955 Yale
Critchell Robert M. 1921 Indiana av. *C.A.*
Critchell Robert S. 4610 Woodlawn av. *U.L.*
Crittenden Henry C. 1658 Briar pl.
Crocker Augusta Miss, 4713 Woodlawn av.
Crocker Benjamin S. 399 Ashland boul. *Ill.*
Crocker Charles W. Wilmette
Crocker C. B. Mrs. The Wellington
Crocker Harry H. 104, 36th
Crocker James R. 4714 Greenwood av.
Crocker John Tweedy, 4713 Woodlawn av.
Crocker J. W. Chicago Beach hotel
Crocker Miss, 4713 Woodlawn av.
Crocker Percy O. Wilmette
Crocker W. H. Mrs. Hinsdale
Crockett George H. Evanston
Crockett R. L. Oak Park
Croft Fred L. 6744 Perry av.
Croft Fred. W. 6749 Perry av. *C.A.*
Crofton Alfred C. Dr. The Plaza
Crogan Margaret Mrs. 309 Webster av.
Cromelien D. 4749 Calumet av.
Cromwell Caroline Mrs. 3025 Prairie av.
Cromwell Charles, 3025 Prairie av. *Cal.*, *C.A.*, *W.P.*
Crone Charles E. 4106 Vincennes av.
Cronholm N. N. 3039 Groveland av.
Cronise Caroline C. Miss, 530, 47th
Cronkhite W. H. Auditorium hotel. *W.P.*
Crook M. E. Mrs. 3918 Lake av.
Crooke William D. Mrs. Hinsdale
Crooker Ernest P. 7130 Yale
Crooker William W. 3131 Forest av.
Cropp Carl, Western Springs
Crosby Amanda Mrs. Riverside
Crosby Arthur A. 307, 53d
Crosby Benjamin F. Oak Park
Crosby Bessie E. Miss, Oak Park
Crosby Chauncey H. Riverside. *Chi.*
Crosby David K. Oak Park
Crosby Edward A. 604 Division
Crosby Eugene C. Hinsdale
Crosby E. C. Mrs. 213, 42d
Crosby Frederick W. 301 Huron. *Chi.*, *Un.* Sum. res. Lake Forest
Crosby George H. 7220 Yale
Crosby N. D. Oak Park
Crosby Samuella Miss, 213, 42d
Crosby Thomas F. 886 Warren av.
Crosby Truman W. 6019 Woodlawn av.
Crosby William S. 604 Division
Crosier Winfield C. 4506 Forrestville av.
Cross Albert E. La Grange
Cross Albert M. Mayfair

Cross Clarence L. Riverside. *U.L.*
Cross George W. Evanston
Cross Ida Miss, New Hotel Holland
Cross James E. 1406 Millard av.
Cross Jesse M. Rev. Mayfair
Cross R. W. 6525 Woodlawn av.
Cross W. R. Rev. Hinsdale
Crossette Charles D. Hinsdale
Crossette Charles H. Hinsdale
Crossette William E. 3143 Rhodes av.
Crossgrove J. 1886 Diversey
Crossman Abner, 62 Woodland Park
Crossman F. M. Arlington Heights. *Ill.*
Crossman Henry, Morgan Park
Crossman W. D. 2124 Michigan av.
Crouch Albert W. 15, 46th
Crouch C. D. 210, 33d
Crouch Herbert E. 7740 Butler
Crouch Robert B. 2923 Michigan av. *W.P.*
Crouch Thomas, 15, 46th
Crounse Silas H. Oak Park
Crouse D. Howard 2231 Prairie av.
Crouse John N. 2231 Prairie av. *Cal.*
. Crow Martha Foote Mrs. 2970 Groveland av.
Crowe C. J. 2516 Indiana av.
Crowe Frank, 365 W. Congress
Crowe Genevieve Miss, 365 W. Congress
Crowe Martin Mrs. 3138 Wabash av.
Crowell Edward R. Mrs. 5804 Washington av.
Crowell F. S. 6433 Greenwood av.
Crowley Albert E. 359, 41st
Croy Simeon W. The Tudor
Crozier Frank, 3030 Groveland av.
Cruickshank Blanche Miss, 2929 Groveland av.
Cruickshank Geo. B. 2929 Groveland av.
Cruikshank C. E. 671 Park av.
Crumbaugh Frederick, 3323 Forest av.
Crump Lawrence M. 4613 Woodlawn av. *C.A.*
Crutcher Howard Dr. 5248 Prairie av.
Cruth J. W. New Hotel Holland
Cruttenden Edmund S. 5003 Madison av.
Cruttenden Thomas S. 5003 Madison av. *C.A., U.L.*
Cruttenden Walter W. 5003 Madison av.
Cruver Austin, Oak Park
Cruzen Ralph E. 399 Ashland boul.
Cudahy Bessie Miss, 3254 Michigan av.
Cudahy John, 3254 Michigan av. *C.A., U.L., W.P.* Sum. res. "The Pines," Mackinac Island
Cudahy John P. 3138 Michigan av. *W.P.*
Cudahy Julia Miss, 3254 Michigan av.
Cudahy Michael, 3138 Michigan av. *U.L., W.P.* Sum. res. Mackinac Island
Cudell Adolph, 418 N. State
Culbertson James A. Kenilworth
Cullerton Walter, Auditorium hotel
Cullins George, 3727 Lake av.
Culliton Charles W. Mrs. 6711 Parnell av.
Culloton Thomas P. 399 Sheffield av.
Culver Alvin H. Glencoe

Culver Floyd H. Mrs. 4306 Greenwood av.
Culver Frank H. 7 Scott
Culver Helen Miss, 31 Ashland boul.
Culver John, 549 Morse av.
Culver Mary E. Mrs. 7 Scott
Culver Morton, Glencoe
Culver Morton T. Glencoe
Cummings Andrew, 2978 Wabash av. *U.L.*
Cummings Charles C. 670 Lasalle av. *C.A.*
Cummings C. R. Mrs. 1641 Indiana av.
Cummings D. Mark, 185 Lincoln Park boul. *Cal., Chi., C.A., W.P.*
Cummings Edmund A. Oak Park, *U.L.*
Cummings Edward S. 874 Walnut
Cummings Eloise W. Miss, 670 Lasalle av.
Cummings E. Mrs. Oak Park
Cummings Geo. B. Highland Park
Cummings Harry D. Austin
Cummings Joseph Mrs. Evanston
Cummings Morris C. 670 Lasalle av. *Cal., C.A., W.P.*
Cummings Norman P. 4958 Forrestville av. *C.A.*
Cummings Pattie Adele Miss, 670 Lasalle av.
Cummings Samuel, Park Ridge
Cummings Susan C. Mrs. 306, 30th
Cummings William J. 2437 Lakewood av.
Cummings W. 343 Park av.
Cummins Benjamin F. 166, 51st. *C.A., U.L.*
Cummins James S. 5473 Cornell av.
Cummins William G. Dr. 423 Erie, *C.A.*
Cumnock R. L. Prof. Evanston
Cuneo Andrew, 20 Astor
Cuneo Frank, 397 N. State
Cunnea John, 7120 Harvard av.
Cunningham John A. Winnetka
Cunningham J. A. jr. Lakeside
Cunningham Katherine Miss, 3249 Groveland av.
Cunningham Secor, 1824 Prairie av. *Chi., W.P.* Sum. res. Highland Park
Cunningham V. L. 5734 Kimbark av.
Cunningham William B. 3249 Groveland av.
Cunningham William H. 4707 Vincennes av. *U.L.*
Curran D. B. 4059 Lake av.
Curran John M. Evanston
Curran Mary A. Mrs. 42 Bellevue pl.
Curran O. P. 4059 Lake av. *Chi.*
Curran Samuel H. 4059 Lake av.
Curran T. Diffley, 42 Bellevue pl.
Currey Arthur L. Evanston
Currey J. Seymour, Evanston
Currie Belle Mrs. 5338 Greenwood av.
Currier Albert D. Evanston
Currier A. D. Virginia hotel
Currier Charles H. 3831 Michigan av. *W.P.*
Currier Charles L. 4725 Kimbark av.
Currier Evelyn B. Miss, 4725 Kimbark av.

Currier Horace T. 332 Warren av.
Currier Jonathan T. Evanston
Curry Jacob O. 4439 Greenwood av.
Cursham Charles L. 2340 Calumet av.
Curtis Augusta C. Mrs. 367 S. Marshfield av,
Curtis A. Guthrie, 3145 Vernon av.
Curtis Clara B. Mrs. 494 Belden av.
Curtis Cornelius, 7437 Kimbark av.
Curtis D. H. 409 Washington boul.
Curtis Edmund A. 1139 Millard av.
Curtis Edward H. Rev. 6412 Kimbark av.
Curtis Eugene A. Dr. 7036 Stony Island av.
Curtis Eugene B. 367 S. Marshfield av.
Curtis George H. Lexington hotel
Curtis Henry, 728 Winthrop av.   .
Curtis Henry M. 1612 Indiana av.
Curtis H. Rowland, 6017 Monroe av.
    Sum. res. Spring Lake,Mich.
Curtis James C. Victoria hotel, C.A.
Curtis John B. 7437 Kimbark av.
Curtis John F. L. 2841 Michigan av. C.A.
    Sum. res. Delavan, Wis.
Curtis John H. 426 Elm, C.A.
Curtis Judson Morris Mrs. 6017 Monroe av.
Curtis Julia Miss, 3246 Lake Park av.
Curtis J. H. Dr. 367 S. Marshfield av.
Curtis J. Lafayette, 3819 Michigan av.
Curtis Lester Dr. 35, 34th pl.
Curtis Nelson H. 660 Washington boul.
Curtis Uri B..Lexington hotel. C.A..
Curtis Walter W. 5205 Hibbard av. W.P.
Curtis William G. 146, 42d pl.
Curtis William W. Dr. 78, 50th
Curtis W. C. Oak Park
Curtiss Charles C. 110 Astor
Curtiss George H. 4422 Oakenwald av.
Curtiss Henry, 4455 Greenwood av.
Curtiss John C. 2110 Kenmore av.
Cusack Edward J. 2537 Kenmore av.
Cushing Charles H. Hinsdale
Cushing Edward T. 4820 Greenwood av. U.L.
Cushing Frederick W. Highland Park
Cushing F. J. Irving Park
Cushing George W. Evanston
Cushing Jessie D. Mrs. 5137 Kimbark av.
Cushing Lemuel K. 3222 Lake Park av.
Cushing N. S. Mrs. Lombard
Cushing Otis, Hinsdale
Cushing William T. 69 Flournoy
Cushman J. C. Highland Park
Cushman Lillian S. Miss, Lake Forest
Cushman Thomas W. Irving Park
Custard Morris B. 4722 Evans av.
Custer George G. 6836 Perry av.
Custer Hugh C. Austin
Custer Jacob R. 3928 Grand boul. Cal., U.L.   Sum. res. Highland Park
Custer Samuel M. 9 St. James pl.
Cuthbert Ernest, 3631 Prairie av.
Cuthbertson Hugh A. Dr. 6305 Madison av.
Cuthbertson Wm. Dr. 189, 41st

Cutler Alonzo J. 528 W. 61st pl.
Cutler Carroll Mrs. 438, 57th
Cutler Charles W. Evanston   .
Cutler Frank T. 540 W. Jackson boul.
Cutler C. Henry, 4801 Kenwood av.
Cutler Harry H. 4454 Oakenwald av.
Cutler William H. 4801 Kenwood av.
Cutler William H. Evanston
Cutter Frederick M. 16 Lincoln Park boul.
Cutter George, Kenilworth
Cutter G. M. Chicago Beach hotel
Cutter Henry W. K. 6516 Harvard av.
Cutter John M. 2206 Prairie av. Cal., Chi., W.P.
Cutting Charles, 923 W. Jackson boul.
Cutting Charles S. Austin
Cutting Fred P. 6153 Kimbark av.
Cutts D. A. Mrs. Evanston
Cuyler William H. 105 S. Winchester av.

DABB CHARLES W. Leland hotel
    Dabb W. R. Leland hotel
Dabney John P. Lakeside. C.A.
D'Acheul H. A. Chicago Beach hotel
Dacy Albert E. Chicago Beach hotel. C.A.   -
Dade W. H. Dr. Hyde Park hotel
Dadie John, 665 W. Monroe, C.A.
Daggett Fannie Miss, Hotel Metropole
Daggett Frederick F. Mrs. 4600 Prairie av.
Daggett Harry E. 6640 Stewart av. C.A.
Daggett J. F. LaGrange
Daggett R. B. Hotel Del Prado
Daggitt Joseph, Glencoe
Dahl Henry L. 634 Lasalle av.
Dahlane Charles, 1530 Belmont av.
Dahlberg Alfred Dr. 4546 Evans av.
Dahmke John J. A. 2140 Washington boul.
Dahms Edward J. Evanston
Daib Frederick, 1886 Diversey
Daigger Andrew, 1817 Belmont av.
Daily Charles T. 4117 Berkeley av.
Daily Frank, 1089 Victor
Daily Milton, 1089 Victor
Dainty A. H. Mrs. 600 Dearborn av.
Dakin Frank C. Dr. Evanston
Dakin Harry W. Evanston
Dakin Richard L. Evanston
Dal John W. Dr. 499 N. Robey
Dale Fred, 1832 Belmont av.
Dale Henry C. Dr. 3000 Indiana av.
Dale Hervey S. 33, 46th
Dale Jane E. Miss, Winnetka
Dale John T. Winnetka, U.L.
Dale Mary W. Mrs. Evanston
Dale Samuel E. 1832 Belmont av.
Dale Walter, 1832 Belmont av.
Dallas Andrew C. 4752 Prairie av.
Dallemand Albert, Auditorium hotel
Dallman Laura Miss, 163 Rush
D'Almaine Charles Prof. 4438 Woodlawn av.
Dalton James P. 2938 Michigan av.
Daly Dennis S. 919 Warren av.
Daly F. J. LaGrange

Daly Henry, 765 Touhy av.
Daly Henry P. 807 Touhy av.
Daly John M. 6541 Kimbark av.
Daly Luke F. 583 W. Adams
Dalzell James, 5624 Monroe av.
Dalzell Walter, 5624 Monroe av.
Dameier Charles W. 4329 Prairie av.
Dameier C. W. Mrs. 4329 Prairie av.
Dameier Gustave A. 4329 Prairie av.
Dameier Robert, 4329 Prairie av.
Dameier Wm. C. 4329 Prairie av.
Dammerau Frank C. 12 Lincoln pl.
Damon Lindsay T. 228, 53d
Damon Orrison B., M.D. 23 Park av.
Damsel Ethel B. Miss, Evanston
Damsel Jessamine Miss, Evanston
Damsel William H. Evanston, U.L.
        Sum. res. Prior Lake, Minn.
Dana Arthur D. 3433 South Park av.
Dana A. P. Mrs. 4960 Drexel boul.
Dana Charles D. 44 Astor, U.L.
Dana C. Clayton, 44 Astor
Dana Francis, 422 Oak
Dana Harry C. Hinsdale
Dana Mary Miss, 44 Astor
Dana Paul, 18 Aldine sq.
D'Ancona Alfred E. 4714 Langley av.
    Stan.
D'Ancona August B. 4748 Prairie av.
D'Ancona Edward N. 458, 44th. Irq.,
    Stan.
Dandliker R. A. Morgan Park
Dandy William M. 48 Loomis
Dane S. E. Mrs. Riverside
Danek Jacob Mrs. 228B Fremont
Danforth Anne L. Mrs. 5825 Kimbark av.
Danforth Frank L. 4462 Berkeley av. C.A.
Danforth Isaac N., M.D. 758 W. Adams,
    Ill.   Sum. res. Lake Bluff
Danforth Jerome J. Hinsdale
Danforth Martin G. Hinsdale
Daniel A. M. Mrs. Oak Park
Daniel William H. 6521 Harvard av.
Daniels Adelaide N. Mrs. 6525 Harvard av.
    Sum. res. Lake Beulah, Wis.
Daniels Alexander M. 5131 Hibbard av.
Daniels Alfred, 194 Bowen av.
Daniels Charles, 24 St. James pl.
Daniels C. A. 225 Dearborn av.
Daniels C. W. Hotel Woodruff
Daniels Edwin F. 4447 Greenwood av.
    C.A., U.L.
Daniels F. B. Evanston. Univ.
Daniels George, 711 W. Monroe
Daniels John B. 5131 Hibbard av.
Daniels Julius, 4716 Champlain av.
Daniels Samuel, 341 Oakwood boul. Lksd.
Daniels Walter A. 119 Buena av.
Danken Helene Miss, 3601 Vincennes
    av.
Dankert William E. Norwood Park
Danks Fred F. 4059 Grand boul.
Danks Isaiah, 162, 42d pl.
Danne Emil, 7116 Wentworth av.
Danolds Belle Miss, 780 W. Monroe
Danser A. C. Tremont house
34

Danz Albert J. 1286 Washington boul.
Danz Charles A. 1286 Washington boul.
Danz Margaret Mrs. 1286 Washington
    boul.
Danziger A. L. 4811 Prairie av. Lksd.
Danziger Emanuel, 4811 Prairie av. Lksd.
Danziger Hannah Mrs. 4811 Prairie av.
Danziger Oscar, 4811 Prairie av.
Danziger Samuel S. 3238 South Park av.
Danziger Sarah Mrs. 3238 South Park av.
Darby Benj. L. 6227 Kimbark av.
Darby John, 6227 Kimbark av.
Darby J. F. Prof. LaGrange
Darley E. C. 3150 Groveland av.
Darling Chas. Burton, The Arizona
Darling Harry W. 7346 Bond av.
Darling James G. Evanston
Darling Julia A. Mrs. 5427 Washington av.
Darling L. F. Mrs. Chicago Beach hotel
Darlington Henry P. 4650 Drexel boul.
Darlington Herbert, LaGrange. C.A.,
    Irq.
Darrow Alexander H. 1044 W. Monroe
    Ill.   Sum. res. Minocqua, Wis.
Darrow Clarence S. 40, 29th pl. C.A.,
    Irq.
Darrow E. N. Park Ridge
Darrow Mary A. Mrs. 2613 Indiana av.
Darrow Noble C. Park Ridge
Darrow Robert, 1044 W. Monroe
Dart Guy J. Evanston
Dart Louise Miss, 5126 East End av.
Darvill Fred'k, Evanston. C.A.
Dashiel C. Morgan Park
Dashiell C. Russ, 316 S. Marshfield av.
Dashiell Virgil W. 316 S. Marshfield av.
Date Henry, Austin
Date Sydney S. 817 Washington boul. Ill.
Dater E. R. Miss, 4319 Ellis av.
Dau J. J. 4807 Greenwood av. Chi.
Daube Aaron, 4105 Grand boul.
Daube Joseph L 4634 Vincennes av.
Daube Leopold, 4227 Calumet av. Lksd
Daube Louis, 637, 46th pl. Lksd.
Daube M. Jacob, 3805 Prairie av. Stan,
Dauchy Emeline Mrs. 513 Lasalle av.
Dauchy George K. 359 Lasalle av. U.L.
Dauchy G. Vivus, 359 Lasalle av.
Dauchy Otis B. 359 Lasalle av.
Dauchy Samuel O. 359 Lasalle av. Univ.
Daugharty Allan H. 2808 Michigan av.
    C.A.
Daul Frank X. Austin
Davenport Charles W. 508 Belden av.
Davenport Elizabeth Mrs. Wilmette
Davenport N. Soule Dr. 207 Warren av.
David Cyrenius A. Dr. 325 Belden av.
David Joseph B. 943 W. Monroe
David Rilla A. Miss, 325 Belden av.
David Rosa Mrs. 943 W. Monroe
Davidson Alexander M. Great Northern
    hotel
Davidson Alice S. Miss, Highland Park
Davidson A. E. Granada hotel
Davidson Frank B. 350 Park av.
Davidson George M. Oak Park

Davidson Harlan P. Col. Highland Park
Davidson James A. 953 W. Jackson boul.
Davidson James H. 5227 Woodlawn av.
Davidson John A. 2128 Calumet av.
Davidson J. M. D. Rev. 1066 Winthrop av.
Davidson J. R. 4549 Vincennes av.
Davidson Royal P. Maj. Highland Park
Davidson R. P. Mrs. 5733 Monroe av.
Davidson S. Frank, LaGrange
Davidson Walter, Hinsdale
Davidson William B. 6212 Monroe av.
Davidson W. 3146 Groveland av.
Davies Anne Mrs. 3146 Vernon av.
Davies B. M. 4028 Grand boul. *U.L.*
Davies Charles Francis, 3757 Prairie av
    U.L.
Davies Colby, Evanston. *C.A.*
Davies C. A. 656 W. Adams
Davies Edwin C. K. Maywood
Davies E. L. Lake Forest
Davies John G. 1688 Buckingham pl.
Davies Thomas, 3223 Rhodes av.
Davies T. Stanley, 6533 Minerva av.
Davies W. B. 6429 Greenwood av.
David Alfred B. LaGrange
Davis Alvin F. Austin
Davis Andrew, Lakeside
Davis Annie M. Mrs. Evanston
Davis A. E., 2124 Michigan av.
Davis Benjamin, 692 Washington boul.
Davis Bernard, 3514 Vernon av.
Davis Brode B. 2446 Michigan av. *Cal.*
Davis Carl B. 2622 Prairie av.
Davis Charles, River Forest
Davis Charles E. 2937 Kenmore av.
Davis Charles G. Dr. 2622 Prairie av. *Ill.*
    Sum. res. Waunita, Hot Springs, Colo.
Davis Charles L. Dr. 6842 Wentworth av.
Davis Charles W. Evanston
Davis Charles W. 113 Cass
Davis Clarence S. 2607 N. Robey
Davis C. N. Mrs. 415 Lasalle av.
Davis Daly D. 3402 South Park av. *Lksd.*
Davis David, 3514 Vernon av.
Davis Ed. Hotel Normandie
Davis Edgar F. Hinsdale
Davis Edith Miss, 3850 Lake av.
Davis Edward G. 2850 Kenmore av.
Davis Effa V. Dr. 516 W. Adams
Davis Elisha T. Park Ridge
Davis Frank B. 330. 40th
Davis Frank B. LaGrange
Davis Frank L. 5406 Madison av.
Davis Frank S. Evanston
Davis Fred, 1810 Arlington pl.
Davis Fred, 6400 Harvard av.
Davis F. G. 5607 Madison av.
Davis F. H. Dr. Berwyn
Davis George C. Austin
Davis George C. LaGrange
Davis George G. 2622 Prairie av.
Davis George M. Austin
Davis George R. 692 Washington boul.
    Chi., Ill., U.L., W.P.
        Sum. res. Fox Lake, Wis.
Davis George W. 71, 33d *C.A.*

Davis George W. 1430 Montrose boul.
Davis Graham, 2358 Indiana av.
Davis G. N. Norwood Park
Davis Harriet H. Dr. 6428 Greenwood av.
Davis Harry-G. 4227 Champlain av.
Davis Henry H. 7024 Eggleston av.
Davis Henry T. 4541 Vincennes av.
Davis Herbert J. 349 Elm. *U.L., W.P.*
Davis Howard, 4215 Ellis av.
Davis H. I. Dr. 3120 Indiana av.
Davis I. E. Mrs. 4406 Ellis av.
Davis James A. 4002 Lake av.
Davis James C. 525 W. 62d
Davis Jedediah R. 2619 Indiana av.
Davis Jerome E. Oak Park
Davis John, 4850 Woodlawn av. *U.L.,*
    W.P.
Davis John T. 2607 N. Robey
Davis Juliette Mrs. Oak Park
Davis J. E. 4800 Lake av.
Davis Lewis H. 1458 Michigan av. *Chi.,*
    U.L.
Davis Lewis L. 2340 Calumet av.
Davis L. J. Dr. 67 Warren av.
Davis Martin S. Mrs. 2808 Michigan av.
Davis Mary Towle, 2358 Indiana av.
Davis M. M. Mrs. 2342 Indiana av.
Davis Nathan, 2962 Wabash av.
Davis Nathan S. Dr. 291 Huron
Davis Nathan S. jr. Dr. 291 Huron. *Univ.*
Davis P. I. Irving Park
Davis Robert T. 1453 W. Madison
Davis Samuel B. 174 Oakwood boul.
Davis Simon S. Evanston. *C.A.*
Davis Susan E. Mrs. 2607 N. Robey
Davis S. E. 3623 Ellis Park
Davis S. L. Park Ridge
Davis Thomas, 1009 Warren av.
Davis T. A. Dr. 987 W. Jackson boul.
Davis W te E. Chicago Athletic Assn.
    *C.A.*al r
Davis Walter L. 2619 Indiana av.
Davis Wilbur Rude,5510 Washington av.
Davis William, 309 Schiller
Davis Wilson H., M.D. 3423 Indiana av.
    Cal
Davis W. Claude, 2607 N. Robey
Davis W. Crosbie Dr. La Grange
Davis W. E. Hyde Park hotel
Davis W. F. 7024 Eggleston av.
Davis W. J. 4740 Grand boul. *C.A.,*
    U.L., W.P.
Davis W. J. Nixon Dr. 123, 51st. *C.A.*
Davis Zachariah W. Hinsdale
Davison Belle Miss, 10 Scott
Davison Benjamin F. 1036 Wilcox av.
Davison Charles, M.D. 955 W. Jackson
    boul
Davison Martha Mrs.955 W.Jackson boul.
Davison Robert A. Evanston
Davison Wm. M. W., M.D. 658 Walnut
Davol George K. 361 Superior. *Un.*
Davol Helen M. Miss, 1763 Oakdale av.
Davy B. C. Mrs. 380 Erie
Davy Edward W. 43 St. James pl.
Daw H. P. 488 Webster av.

Dawes Chester Mitchell, 73 Bellevue pl. *Un.; Univ.*
Dawes Rufus C. Evanston, *U.L.*
Dawes William R. 307 West ct.
Dawley William S. 6127 Woodlawn av.
Dawson Arthur, 1743 Wrightwood av.
Dawson Arthur C. Prof. Lake Forest
Dawson Edwin A. Evanston
Dawson George E. 100, 24th. *Irq.*
Dawson Henry G. 607 Pine Grove av.
Dawson James M. 3829 Vernon av.
Dawson Martin, Palmer house. *C.A.*
Dawson William R. 605 Pine Grove av.
Day Albert M, 82 Astor *Chi.*
    Sum. res. Lake Forest
Day Arthur H. Glencoe
Day Chapin A. 5112 Madison av.
    Sum. res. Hesse Lake, Mich.
Day Charles L. Glencoe
Day Edwin C. 4857 Madison av.
Day Elias V. River Forest
Day Fred F. 3413 Calumet av.
Day George B. Rev. River Forest
Day George E. 1735 Roscoe
Day George R. 2606 Prairie av.
Day Harry N. Dr. 5495 Madison av.
Day Hiram Rev. Glencoe
Day John E. 4726 Champlain av.
Day John L. Glencoe
Day Joseph L. Auditorium hotel. *W.P,*
Day . H. 4400 Greenwood av.
Day J. R. 4400 Greenwood av.
Day May Mrs. Morton Park
Day M. M. 3034 Groveland av.
Day Thomas, 6744 Perry av.
Day T. G. 5555 Monroe av.
Day Walter B. 3027 Vernon av.
Dayan Louis F. Dr. 5220 Jefferson av. *C.A.*
Dayton Arthur G. 435 S. Leavitt
Dayton Charles, 6341 Monroe av.
Dayton Melville E. 6341 Monroe av. *U.L*
Deacon Benjamin, 4842 Prairie av.
Deacon Frederick A. 446 Belden av.
Deacon M. E. Mrs. 446 Belden av.
Deakin Earl, 413 Warren av.
Deakin J. Edward, 6717 Wentworth av.
Deakin J. Henry, 413 Warren av.
Dean Albert F. Evanston. *U. L.*
Dean Amos C. 4620 Indiana av.
Dean Arthur A. Austin
Dean Bradley 267 W. Adams
Dean Charles A. 286 Webster av.
Dean Edward B. Rev. Wilmette
Dean Harvey, Hinsdale
Dean John E. 3259 Indiana av.
Dean J. Clarke, 6413 Ingleside av.
Dean Marvin A. Evanston
Dean Merrick B. 545 Farwell av.
Dean Messer C. 267 W. Adams
Dean M. R. 3259 Indiana av.
Dean Nathaniel C. Auditorium hotel
Dean Robert L. Hinsdale
Dean Robert M. Hinsdale
Dean Thaddeus, Auditorium hotel, *Ill.*
Dean Thomas A. 4119 Vincennes av.

Dean Thomas L. Mrs. 3632 Vernon av.
Dean Walter M. Evanston
Dean William O. Evanston
Deane Albert L. 4520 Woodlawn av.
Deane Charles E. 307 N. Clark, *C.A., Un.*
Deane Eloise A. Mrs. 198 S. Robey
Deane John M. 198 S. Robey. *Ill.*
Deane Lillie A. Miss, 4520 Woodlawn av.
Deane Margaret Miss. 4520 Woodlawn av.
Deane Ruthven, 504 N. State, *Un.*
Deane William G, 7606 Union av.
Dearborn Asa, Riverside
Dearborn D. Frank, 335 Rush
Deardoff Porter, 4401 Oakenwald av.
Dearlove George, 972 W. Jackson boul.
Dearlove George M. 972 W. Jackson boul.
Dearlove Mabel H. Miss, 972 W. Jackson boul.
Dearlove Mary A., M.D. 972 W. Jackson boul.
Dearlove Richard T. 972 W. Jackson boul.
DeArmond William W. Oak Park
DeBerard Charles J. Norwood Park
DeBolt Samuel A, 4252 St. Lawrence av.
Debus Jacob P. 381 W. Adams
DeCamp Alfonse L. Dr. 225 Warren av. *C.A.*
DeCamp Herbert C. 415 Dearborn av.
DeCamp H. E. LaGrange
DeCampi Eliodoro, 6435 Greenwood av.
DeCelle Napoleon, 1200 W. Adams
Decker Adolph Dr. 425 Orchard
Decker Edwin J. 1102 Millard av.
Decker Howard J. 2456 Kenmore av.
Decker H. P. 2434 N. Hermitage av.
Decker H. S. North Shore hotel
Decker Jacob E. Austin
Decker Jay, Austin
Decker John E. 632 W. Monroe
    Sum. res. Mellette, South Dakota
Decker Richard P. 5207 Hubbard av.
DeClercq George E. W. 1592 W. Monroe
DeClerque Henry, 501 Lasalle av.
De Clerque-Rabing Eliza Mrs. 501 La-salle av.
DeCosta P. Darlington, 4650 Drexel boul.
De Coudres Addison M. Evanston
Dederick Louis, 804 Bryan av.
Dee Katheryn Miss, 1375 Washington boul.
Dee William E. 3706 Wabash av.
Dee William H. Mrs. Evanston
Dee William M. Mrs. 4047 Calumet av.
Dee W. J. Hotel Windermere
Deecken Frederick, 1716 Arlington pl.
Deegan Daniel C. 141 Lincoln Park boul.
Deering Charles, Evanston
Deering Charles W. Evanston
Deeing Charles W. C. Avenue house, Evanston. *Chi.*
Deering James, 67 Cedar, *Chi., Un., W.P.*
Deering William, Evanston
Deethmann C. H. 4839 Madison av.
Deeves Griffen H. 408 Ashland boul.

Deeves Thomas S. 3545 Michigan av.
Defebaugh J e E. 4322 Vernon av. *Irq., U.L.*am s
DeForest Frederick B. 300 S. Marshfield av.
DeForest George V.Mrs.300 S. Marshfield av.
DeFort John, 3100 Groveland av.
Defrees Joseph H. Hotel Windermere, *U.L.*
DeGan Emma Miss, River Forest
Degen Isaac, 3811 Langley av.
Degen Mina Mrs. 198, 36th
Degginger F. Mrs. 4445 Berkeley av.
Degginger Sidney, 4445 Berkeley av. *Lksd.*
DeGolyer C. F. Mrs. Evanston
DeGolyer Donald L. Evanston
DeGolyer L. N. Evanston
DeGolyer Nelson, Evanston
DeGolyer Robert S. Evanston
DeGolyer Watts, Riverside
DeGraff A. Mrs. 2222 Calumet av.
　　　　Sum. res. Bay Ridge, N. Y.
DeHand Ruth Mrs. 5532 Monroe av.
DeHaye John, Wilmette
DeHorvath Jul. 6047 Madison av.
Deimel Joseph, 3141 Calumet av.
Deimel Rudolph, 3141 Calumet av.
Deitsch R. Mrs. 3529 Calumet av.
Deitz C. J. Dr. 5737 Madison av.
DeKoven John Mrs. 402 Dearborn av.
Del De, 232 Michigan av.
Delafield Herbert, 4333 Ellis av.
Delafield Selwyn, 4333 Ellis av.
Delafield Walter Rev. 4333 Ellis av.
　　　　Sum. res. Delafield, Wis.
Delamater Etta M. Miss, 5241 Madison av.
Delamater N. B. Dr. 55, 53d
Delamater Samuel, 5241 Madison av.
DeLand Adelbert, 6030 Kimbark av.
DeLand Elliott, Washington Heights
DeLand Walter, Washington Heights
DeLand W. P. J. 4128 Berkeley av.
Delaney James H. Hotel Del Prado
Delaney Thomas F. 4223 Wabash av.
DeLang F. C. Glencoe
Delano Eben A. 969 W. Monroe
Delano Edward C. 59 Aberdeen
Delano Frederic A. 1933 Indiana av. *Irq., Univ.*
Delano Harry M. 969 W. Monroe
Delano Samuel M. Oak Park
DeLany James H. 360 Erie
Delany Martin A. 537 Cleveland av.
DeL'Armitage Arabella Root Mme. 4730 Kenwood av.
DeL'Armitage Robert B. 4730 Kenwood av.
Delaware Ambrose S. 510, 63d
Delbridge John B. 7122 Euclid av.
DeLee Joseph B. Dr. 3634 Prairie av.
DeLee Morris, 3634 Prairie av.
DeLee Solomon T. 3634 Prairie av. *Lksd. Stan.*

DeLisle William H. 4201 Lake av.
Dell Joseph, 800 W. Monroe
Delmont A. R. Lexington Hotel
DeLoss Henry H. Evanston. *C.A.*
De Loss Sarah Dr. 428 W. Adams
DeLue Nathan, 688 W. Adams
DeMaine E. F. Mrs. 3118 Groveland av.
DeMar Willis C. 3712 Ellis av.
Demarest Raymond C. 823 W. Jackson boul.
DeMarion Marie Biro, 3407 Indiana av.
DeMary Jane Mrs. 170, 36th
Dembufsky Max, Lexington hotel. *Lksd.*
Dement Isaac S. 6051 Madison av.
Dement R. S. 3523 Grand boul.
Demerse Alice Mrs. 719 W. 60th
Deming Charles, 181 S. Hoyne av.
Deming Everett B. 1691 Kenmore av. *C.A.*
Deming Henry H., M.D. 4356 Greenwood av.
Deming William B. 181 S. Hoyne av.
Demme William, 79 Ewing pl.
Demmler Karl, 516 North av. *C.A.*
Demmon Stephen D. Union League Club
　　　　Sum. res. Lake Geneva, Wis.
Dempsey A. Norman, 583, 62d
Dempsey John, 947, 72d pl.
Dempster Charles W. 10 Astor *Un.*
Dempster John B. 361 Superior
　　　　Sum. res. Evanston
Dempster Wesley, 2936 Prairie av.
DeMuth Benjamin F. 4500 Greenwood av. *C.A., U.L., W.P.*
Denahy Edward W. Sherman house
Deneen Chas. S. 532 W. 61st pl. *U.L.*
Denell Reuben A. 318 Hampden ct. *C.A.*
Dengler Gottlob, 512 Webster av.
Denham Charles, 72, 48th
Denig Lewis A. Elmhurst
Denison Andrew J. 167 Cass
Denison Franklin, 5316 Cornell av.
Denison Joseph, 6119 Monroe av.
Denison J. Curtis, 558 W. 62d
Denison Margaret Mrs. 167 Cass
Denison Thomas S. 225 Dearborn av.
Deniston Albert J. 3226 Rhodes av.
Denman George B. 6317 Parnell av.
Denmark G. Ravinia
Denmead Blanche Miss, 41 Madison Park
Denmead Harriet B. Miss, 41 Madison Park
Dennehy Thomas C. 552 N. State. *C.A., W.P.*
Dennis Charles H. 1893 Roscoe
Dennis Charles S. 5120 Kimbark av. *C.A.*
Dennis Edward W. 5477 Cornell av. *C.A.*
Dennis Frederick J. 1229 Washington boul.
Dennis George, 4554 Emerald av.
Dennis George J. Dr. Lakota hotel
Dennis James F. Glencoe
Dennis James J. Mrs. Glencoe
Dennis Leander W. 3441 Michigan av.

Dennis William, Berwyn
Dennison Charles G. Hinsdale
Denniston James M. 4621 Woodlawn av.
Denniston S. S. Oak Park
Denniston Uriah R. Austin
Denny W. A. 3812 Vincennes av.
Densmore A. E. Mrs. 4928 Ellis av.
Densmore James B. Winnetka
Dent Thomas, 1823 Prairie av. *U.L.*
Dent Timothy A. Longwood
Denvivier Prof. Hotel Woodruff
DePfuhl Francis, 946 Greenleaf av.
Deppe Frank, 1163 N. Clark.
Derby James D. 4406 Ellis av.
Derby William Mrs. Hotel Metropole
Derby William M. jr. 5035 Madison av.
    C.A. Sum. res. Les Cheneaux Club,
    Les Cheneaux Islands, Mackinac Co.,
    Mich.
Derbyshire W. G. Oak Park
De Remer W. L. Capt. Granada hotel
Derickson Emma C. Mrs. Kenilworth
DeRimanoczy Bela, 2 Oakland crescent
Dering Charles L. 4543 Greenwood av.
Dering Henry Ray, 124, 47th
Dering J. Kemper, 196, 44th
Dernburg Adolph, 3753 Indiana av. *Lksd.*
Dernburg Carl, 1341 Michigan av. *Stan.*
deRoode Holger, 699 North Park av.
Derrick Morris B. 5932 Parnell av.
Deschauer Joseph Mrs. 507 Lasalle av.
De Sellen E. M. Dr. 291 Michigan av.
Desjardins Alexis, 222 Loomis
Desjardins Arthur, 222 Loomis
DeSmet G. W. 22 Madison Park
DeSouchet Osman C. 576 Washington
    boul.
Despres Albert, 4133 Calumet av.
Despres Alexander, 3218 Calumet av.
    Lksd.
Despres Alfred, 3218 Calumet av.
Despres Anaise Miss, 3218 Calumet av.
Despres Arthur, 3727 Prairie av.
Despres Emile, 3218 Calumet av. *Lksd.*
Despres Isaac, 3235 Vernon av. *Lksd.*
Despres Samuel, 3218 Calumet av.
Despres Samuel, 3727 Prairie av. *Lksd.*
Despres Sidney, 3727 Prairie av.
Dessauer Jeanette Mrs. 3637 Vincennes
    av.
Dessauer S. George, 52 Astor
deTeresa Nicolas Mrs. 2018 Prairie av.
Detrick James M. 5514 Ellis av.
Detweiler E. S. Dr. LaGrange
Deutsch David M. 99, 77th
Deutsch Frederick, 7816 Bond av.
Deutsch Louis, 127, 25th, *Lksd.*
Devendorf A. S. 689 W. Adams
Devendorf Charles A. 689 W. Adams
DeVeney T. F. 3336 Wabash av.
DeVeny S. Charles, M.D. 2542 Indiana av.
Devereux Sarah A. Mrs. Oak Park
Devine Arthur J. 289 Huron
Devine James A. 289 Huron
Devine Mark A. 1915 Diversey
Devine William M. 289 Huron, *Irq.*

Devine William P. 289 Huron
Devitt Martin Allen, 269, 46th, *U. L.*
Devlin Edward I. Evanston
Devlin Frank A. 4044 Ellis av. *W. P.*
Devlin J. B. Dr. 2204 Michigan av.
DeVol E. M. 228 Michigan av.
Devore Abraham A. 3233 Rhodes av.
Devore Annie Carnegie Mrs. The Tudor
Devore John A. 4850 Kimbark av. *U.L.*
DeVos John, Irving Park
DeVries F. P. Dr. Morgan Park
Dew A. C. Mrs. 2002 Indiana av.
Dew Louise E. Miss, Hotel Windermere
Dewar Alexander L. 3015 Sheridan rd.
    Chi., U.L.
Dewar Hamilton, Chicago Beach hotel.
    Cal., C.A., W.P.
Dewar Harold, 3015 Sheridan rd.
DeWees R. Adelbert, 4334 Ellis av.
DeWees William W. 168, 32d. *C.A.*
DeWeese Truman A. 551 Dearborn av.
Dewes August J. 1843 Wrightwood av.
Dewes C. J. Virginia hotel. *C.A.*
Dewes Edwin T. 1849 Wrightwood av.
Dewes Francis J. 1849 Wrightwood av.
    C.A., U.L.
Dewey Albert B. 2631 Prairie av. *U.L.*
Dewey Allen A. 4155 Lake av.
Dewey Amariah A. 4155 Lake av.
Dewey Charles P. 3266 Lake Park av.
Dewey David B. Mrs. Evanston
Dewey David C. 670 Park av.
Dewey Fred M. LaGrange
Dewey F. J. Dr. 302 S. Oakley av.
Dewey Herbert C. LaGrange
Dewey James, Lake Forest
Dewey John Prof. 5238 Woodlawn av.
Dewey Noah B. 3559 Vincennes av.
Dewey O. J. LaGrange
Dewey William E. 171, 51st
DeWindt Heyliger A. Winnetka. *Irq.,*
    Univ.
DeWitt Elden C. 460 Dearborn av. *C.A.'*
    U.L.
DeWitt F. L. LaGrange
DeWitt William C. Rev. 733 Washing-
    ton boul.
Dewitz Henry, 3428 Indiana av.
DeWolf Calvin, 4714 Kimbark av.
DeWolf D. C. 3629 Prairie av.
    Sum. res. The Elms, Chester Hill,
    Mass.
DeWolf Wallace L. 4714 Kimbark av.
    C.A., U.L., W.P.
    Sum. res. Midlothian, Blue Island
DeWolfe Eda Miss, 621 W. 59th
DeWolfe Freeman, 621 W. 59th
Dewson Francis W. 150 W. 68th
Dexter Albert A. 193, 54th
Dexter Albert F. 3234 Groveland av. *Cal.*
Dexter C   e P. Mrs. 185 Lincoln Park
    boul. harl s
Dexter Ed t   Miss, 185 Lincoln Park
    boul. i h
Dexter Geo. W. 5458 Jefferson av.
Dexter Ransom Mrs. 2920 Calumet av.

Dey M. H. Julien hotel
DeYoung Benjamin R. 2975 Prairie av.
　U.L.
Dezendorf J. Douglas, Hotel Windermere
DeZeng Caroline Mrs. Wilmette
Dial Morris R. 4453 Ellis av.
Dibb James M. 4234 St. Lawrence av.
Dibble Charles A. 111 S. Leavitt
Dibble Harvey M. Wilmette
Dibblee Henry, 1922 Calumet av. *Chi.*
Dick Albert Blake, 21 Lake Shore Drive,
　C.A., Un., W.P.
Dick Elmer E. 894 Winthrop av.
Dick H. E. 4142 Lake av.
Dick J. C. F. LaGrange
Dickason Livingston T. 4940 Ellis av.
　Cal., C.A., U.L., W.P.
Dickenson Carleton, Edison Park
Dickenson Henry G. 4440 Sidney av.
Dicker Edward A. 908 Warren av.
Dicker Osmond 1153 W. Adams
Dickerman Albert E. 506 Morse av.
Dickerman Edward T. Dr. Chicago
　Beach hotel, *W.P.*
Dickerman Fletcher W. 3971 Drexel boul.
Dickerman Frances S. Miss, 2115 Indiana
　av.
Dickerson Charles R. 5624 Monroe av.
Dickerson J. Spencer, Evanston, *U.L.*
Dickey Frank H. 3626 Ellis av.
　Sum. res. Burlington, Wis.
Dickey Frank T. 5344 Washington av.
Dickey Philip S. 148 Dearborn av.
Dickey Robert E. 4321 St. Lawrence av.
Dickey Robert L. LaGrange
Dickie F. L. Mrs. 4403 Ellis av.
Dickinson Albert, 307 N. Clark, *C.A.,*
　Ill., U.L.
Dickinson Alice Miss, 6641 Woodlawn av.
Dickinson Baxter A. 445 Englewood av.
Dickinson Belle Miss, Highland Park
Dickinson Charles, 1292 Washington
　boul. *C.A., Ill., U.L.*
Dickinson Clarence, Evanston
Dickinson David H. 651 Washington
　boul.
Dickinson Edward, 26 Junior terrace
Dickinson Eliza E. Mrs. 73 Lake View av.
Dickinson Emma Mrs. 273 S. Claremont
　av.
Dickinson Frank F. 7130 Princeton av.
Dickinson Frederick, 26 Bryant av.
Dickinson Geo. 2448 South Park av.
Dickinson G. V. The Arizona
Dickinson H.F. Greenwood Inn, Evanston
Dickinson Henry G. Highland Park
Dickinson John, Evanston
Dickinson John R. 26 Bryant av.
Dickinson John W. 369 Chicago av.
Dickinson Lewis Edward, 286 Huron
Dickinson M. Miss, 307 N. Clark
Dickinson Nathan, 307 N. Clark
　Sum. res. Lake Geneva, Wis.
Dickinson Oliver P. Lexington hotel
Dickinson R. E. Mrs. Auditorium hotel
Dickinson Stanley B. Dr. Austin

Dickinson Wm. 610 N. State, *U.L.*
Dickinson William, 1691 Sheridan rd.
　Sum. res. St. Joseph, Mich.
Dickinson William C. Rev. Evanston
Dickinson William P. 67 Maple
Dickman R. N. 608 Division
Dickson Carlos, 1840 Arlington pl.
Dickson Guy B. Dr. 283 S. Leavitt
Dickson H. M. 3122 Forest av. *C.A.*
Dickson Isaac F. 4585 Oakenwald av.
Dickson James T. 197 S. Hoyne av. *Ill.*
Dickson J. A. Chicago Beach hotel
Dickson William F. Dr. 6337 Woodlawn
　av.
Diederich William G. 812 Touhy av.
Diefendorf B. J. 2724 N. Lincoln
Diehl W. W. Rev. 301 Ashland boul.
Diener Traugott C. 489 Ashland boul.
Diener William J. 495 Ashland boul.
Diesel Frank, 701 N. Halsted
Diesel Louis, 3809 Wabash av.
Dietrich Catherine Mrs. 518 W. 60th pl.
Dietrich Frank E. 518 W. 60th pl.
Dietrich Harry S. Evanston
Dietrich Henry Dr. 422 Center
Dietz Albert B. Wilmette
Dietz Frederick, 1650 Aldine av.
Dietz Jacob C. 4218 Oakenwald av.
Dietz John G. Wilmette
Dietz John W. 1650 Aldine av.
Dietz Joseph E. Irving Park
Dietz Joseph M. Irving Park
Dietz William H. 7402 Parnell av.
Dietzgen Eugene, 1807 Barry av.
Dietzgen Joseph, 1511 Oakdale av.
Diffley M. W. 42 Bellevue pl. *C.A.*
Dille Sam M. 4523 St. Lawrence av.
Diller Edwin S. 6601 Yale
Diller Henry B. 6601 Yale
Diller L. S. Mrs. Hyde Park hotel
Dilley Louise Mrs. 1023 W. Monroe
Dilley William, Berwyn
Dillie Nathaniel E. 293 S. Leavitt
Dillingham Edwin R. The Winamac.
　C.A.
Dillman Louis C. 4508 Ellis av.
Dillman Louis M. 4508 Ellis av. *Cal.,*
　C.A., W.P.
Dillon I. F. Mrs. 7526 Eggleston av.
Dillon John, 151 Goethe
Dillon John A. LaGrange
Dillon Thomas L. 396 Oak
Dimery Joseph H. 3001 Calumet av. *Irq.*
Dimick H. S. Mrs. 3328 South Park av.
Dimick M. D. LaGrange
Dimon Lydia A. Miss, 601 The Plaza
Dingee Gertrude P. Miss, 5716 Washing-
　ton av.
Dingee Mae Miss, Evanston
Dingee Samuel M. Wilmette
Dingee Samuel S. Wilmette
Dingee Squire, 2607 N. Ashland av.
Dingee Squire jr. 2607 N Ashland av.
Dingley Blanche Miss, 3500 Ellis av.
Dingman Charles W. 1540 Kenmore av.
Dings John, Ravinia

Dinwoody J.A.Dr. 3300 Cottage Grove av.
Dion M. L. Miss, Lexington hotel
Dirks Chris. LaGrange
Disbrow D. F. River Forest
Disbrow Frank W. 6436 Monroe av.
Dithmer Frank R. Evanston
Dittman A. S. Mrs. Tracy
Dittmann Henry, 1631 Belmont av.
Ditzler Eli H. Hinsdale
Dix F. A. Evanston
Dix Viola J. Miss, 1925 Deming pl.
Dixon Arthur, 3131 Michigan av. *Cal.,*
U.L.
Dixon Arthur A. 3131 Michigan av.
Dixon George E. LaGrange
Dixon George S. 225 Dearborn av.
Dixon George W. 3131 Michigan av.
C.A., U.L.
Dixon Laban Beecher, 3212 Calumet av.
Dixon Lawrence Belmont, 3212 Calumet
av.
Dixon Thomas J. 3222 Groveland av.
C.A., U.L.
Sum. res. Oconomowoc, Wis.
Dixon T. S. E. Mrs. 5225 Jefferson av.
Dixson Zella Allen Mrs. 5600 Monroe av.
Sum. res. Wisteria Cottage, Gran-
ville, Ohio
Doane James A. Clifton House
Doane John B. Dr. Hinsdale
Sum. res. Thompson, Conn.
Doane John W. 1827 Prairie av. *Cal.,Chi.,*
Irq., W.P.
Sum. res. Thompson, Conn.
Doane Philip S. Dr. 385 N. State
Doane R. Bishop, 1628 Indiana av.
Doane Thomas H. Oak Park
Dobbins Annie Miss, 1825 Michigan av.
Dobbins C. E. Maywood
Dobbins Thomas S. 1825 Michigan av.
Dobie Arthur L. Oak Park
Dobson H. W. Mrs. 442 Warren av.
Dobson Robert, 442 Warren av.
Doctor Jacob J. 497, 42d pl.
Dodd A. F. Norwood Park
Dodd Eugenia Mrs. 638 W. Adams
Dodd John M. 4720 Langley av.
Dodd J. L. Washington Heights
Dodd Oscar Dr. Evanston
Dodd William McC. 410 The Plaza
Dodds Adam C. Rev. 233 Honore
Dodds Jessie B., M.D. 3943 Langley av.
Dodds Leslie J. 4523 St. Lawrence av.
Dodds Robert, M.D. 3943 Langley av.
Dodge Albert Cole, 1100 Washington
boul.
Dodge Arthur H.Chicago Beach hotel
Dodge Benoni L. Oak Park
Dodge Charles H. Austin
Dodge Chester C. 12 S. Sacramento av.
Sum. res. Bolton, Ill.
Dodge Edmond F. 4827 Forrestville av.
U.L.
Dodge E. C. 407, 33d
Dodge George E. P. 1703 Indiana av.
Cal., Chi., W.P.

Dodge Harry A. 3925 Grand boul.
Dodge Herbert A. Oak Park
Dodge M. Eugene, 12 S. Sacramento av.
Sum. res. Bolton, Ill.
Dodge Norris G. Mrs. 3925 Grand boul.
Dodge O. D. Glen Ellyn
Dodge Philo G. Mrs. 3117 Forest av.
Dodge S. S. Norwood Park
Dodge William C. 2268 Kenmore av.
Dodgshun Charles J. 4441 Berkeley av.
Dodson Florence C. Mrs. 4210 Prairie
av.
Dodson John Milton Dr. 568 Washington
boul. *Ill.*
Dodson Joseph H. 2130 Kenmore av.
Dodson Mary B. Miss, 1825 Indiana av.
Doe Ivar M. Mayfair
Doepfner Karl Dr. 583 Orchard
Doepp William Dr. 73 Grant pl.
Doering Edmund J. Dr. 2458 Indiana av.
W.P.
Doerr Jacob F. 4920 Champlain av.
Doerr John P. 4924 Champlain av.
Doerr William P. 4924 Champlain av.
Doggett Arthur M. 2620 Prairie av.
Doggett Eunice S. Miss, 5707 Monroe av.
Doggett Geo. Newell Mrs. 2620 Prairie av.
Doggett Harry Harlan 4911 Forrestville
av.
Doggett Herbert E. L. 2620 Prairie av.
Irq.
Doggett Joseph B. Mrs. 5707 Monroe av.
Doggett L. B. Mrs. 2620 Prairie av.
Doggett MaryE.Mrs.4911 Forrestville av.
Doggett Osce J. 2620 Prairie av.
Doggett William Francis 4911 Forrest-
ville av.
Doggett William L. 2620Prairie av. *C.A.,*
Irq.
Doherty John A. 4158 Calumet av.
Dohn Paulina A. Miss, Ohio ne. cor. N.
State
Dolan Frank, 7822 Bond av.
Doland Franklin H. 852 Touhy av.
Dole Andrew R. 493 W. Congress. *Ill.*
Dole Charles E. 357 Dearborn av.
Dole George S. 337 Dearborn av.
Dole James H. 337 Dearborn av.
Dole John N. 493 W. Congress. *Ill.*
Dole Julia F. Miss, 337 Dearborn av.
Dole Walter S. Mrs. 4743 Kenwood av.
Dole William P. 2756 N. Lincoln
Dolese John 3414 Wabash av.
Dolese John jr. 3414 Wabash av.
Doll L. M. Miss, 6430 Greenwood av.
Dollard William Capt. 1432 Michigan
av.
Dolle Edward C. F. 429 Washington boul.
Dolling Harry, 6404 Monroe av.
Dolph Mary J. Mrs. 2251 Kenmore av.
Donahoe Daniel, 1040 W. Jackson boul.
Donahoe Florence M. Mrs. 3602 Lake av.
Donahue Frank R. 1380 W. Jackson boul.
Donald F. C. Virginia hotel. *U.L.*
Donaldson Frank L. Evanston
Donaldson Harry V. Wilmette

Donaldson H. H. Prof. 5740 Woodlawn av.
Donaldson John T. 1712 Deming pl.
Donaldson Robert P. 41, 53d
Sum. res. Maywood
Donaldson Samuel H. Maywood
Donelson Charles P. Dr. 927 W. Monroe
Donelson Dexter P. Evanston
Donker Edward, 5525 Union av. *C.A.*
Donlan John T. 241 Loomis
Donlan Joseph H. 241 Loomis
Donlin William J. 451 Belden av.
Donnell James W. Evanston
Donnelley B. S. 4609 Woodlawn av.
Donnelley Reuben H. 90, 47th. *Chi.*, *C.A.,U.L.,W.P.*
Donnelley R. R. 4609 Woodlawn av. *U.L.*
Donnelley T. E. 4609 Woodlawn av. *C.A., Univ.*
Donnelly Lemuel L. 5128 Washington av.
Donnelly Thomas N. 3144 South Park av.
Donnelly W. R. Hyde Park hotel
Donnersberger Geo. 3608 Michigan av.
Donnersberger Joseph, 3608 Michigan av.
Donoghue Frank E. 398 W. Adams
Donohoe Francis E. 2515 Kenmore av.
Donohue Edward T. 4547 Grand boul.
Donohue John W. 4543 Michigan av. *C.A.*
Sum. res. Dixon, Ill.
Donohue Michael A. 4547 Grand boul.
Donohue Michael A. jr. 4547 Grand boul.
Donohue Wm. F. 4547 Grand boul. *C.A.*
Donovan Henry F. 302 Webster av.
Donovan W. F. Hotel Windermere. *Chi.*
Dooley Albert, 8 Crilly ct.
Dooling Annie Miss, 3359 Calumet av.
Dooling Ellen Miss, 3359 Calumet av.
Doolittle Arthur C. 479 Morse av.
Doolittle Edgar M. Mrs. 1709 Prairie av.
Sum. res. Lake Geneva, Wis.
Doolittle F. A. 255 Belden av.
Doolittle Oliver S. 255 Belden av.
Doolittle William A. Mrs. 471 Morse av.
Doolittle William H. 471 Morse av.
Doolittle William W. 539 W. 62d
Doran George H. Evanston
Dore Alfred E. 3124 Prairie av.
Dore Elizabeth Mrs. 6325 Kimbark av.
Dore E. F. Mrs. 2730 Prarie av.
Dore Meta Mrs. 368 Ashland boul.
Dore Walter J. 2730 Prairie av. *C.A., W.P.*
Doremus A. F. 533 W. Jackson boul. *Ill*
Dorey Halsted Lieut. Fort Sheridan
Dorian A. E. 1628 Indiana av.
Dorland Barclay H. 4467 Oakenwald av.
Dorland Edwin H. Mrs. 4329 Lake av.
Dorland Willet S. Austin
Dorn Peter W. Tracy
Doron Eugene V. 586, 45th pl.
Dorothy William H. 1323 Wilton av.
Dorr C. J. LaGrange
Dorr Eliza Mrs. 7120 Wentworth av.
Dorr George W. 7120 Wentworth av.

Dorr Mary Mrs. 344 S. Paulina
Dorr Nellie E. Mrs. Morton Park
Dorrance Charles J. 5206 Jefferson av. *U.L.*
Dorrance E. A. 6925 Stewart av. *C.A.*
Dorsett D. F. 3235 Groveland av.
Dorsett J. L. New Hotel Holland
Dorsey George A. 5338 Washington av.
Dorsey Nicholas J. Dr. 346 Dearborn av.
Dorsey Robert E. Oak Park
Dosch August, 3811 Wabash av.
Dostal Joseph W. Dr. 447, 37th
Doton C. W. Mrs. 425 Lasalle av.
Doty C. Edwin, 5547 Washington av.
Doty Flora M. Mrs. Austin
Doty Henry H. 4156 Ellis av.
Doty Leman D. 3050 Calumet av.
Doty Levi R. The Kenwood. *C.A.*
Doty Luther N. 152, 36th
Doty Marshall L. Oak Park
Doty Mary J. Mrs. 290, 48th
Doty Maurice F. Dr. Austin
Doty Melville R. 5547 Washington av.
Doty N. Mrs. LaGrange
Doty Wilson K. 4900 Washington av.
Doty W. H. 3500 Ellis av.
Doud Levi B, 3257 Michigan av. *U.L.*
Dougall Thomas, 47 Cedar
Dougherty Bertha Miss, North Shore hotel
Dougherty Charles, 4402 Berkeley av.
Dougherty T. E. 260 Warren av. *C.A.,Ill.*
Doughty Martha G. Mrs. Evanston
Douglas A. Mrs. 440 Warren av.
Douglas Bernard M. 4406 Berkeley av.
Douglas Charles W. 2470 Magnolia av.
Douglas Clyde, 440 Warren av.
Douglas Frank, 5039 Lake av.
Doug s Frank L. 5461 Cornell av. *C.A., U.L.*
Douglas Frank W. 4424 Lake av. *C.A.*
Douglas John M. jr. Chicago Club
Douglas Joshua H. 3006 Prairie av.
Douglas Percy E. Dr. 440 Warren av.
Douglas W. W. Virginia hotel. *W.P.*
Douglass D. B. 6405 Star av.
Douglass Frank F. 361 W. 64th
Douglass Gayton A. 4216 Berkeley av.
Douglass George L. 1686 Barry av.
Douglass Leon F. 90 Lincoln Park boul.
Douglass Leonard B. 4216 Berkeley av.
Douglass Mary Miss, The Hampden
Douglass Roger L. Evanston
Douglass S. J. Mrs. 90 Lincoln Park boul.
Douglass William A. Oak Park. *U.L.*
Dousman H. F. 3708 Lake av.
Dousman Robert S. Edgebrook
Douthart S. P. 4412 Lake av.
Douthitt A. Mrs. 2825 Indiana av.
Dovenmuehle Henry C. 1744 Arlington pl. *C.A.*
Dow Albert T. 26 Groveland Park
Dow Arthur, 4440 Ellis av.
Dow Edna L. Miss, 221 Prairie av.
Dow Frederick H. 5225 Kimbark av.
Dow Lorenzo E. 4505 Ellis av.

Dow Mary G. Mrs. 5422 Cornell av.
Dow Samuel K. 10 Aldine sq.
Dow William C. 473 Orchard
Dowd Edward R. 4821 Vincennes av.
Dowd Quincy L. Rev. Winnetka
Dowling George J. Lexington Hotel
Dowling John M. Mrs. 137 E. Pearson
Dowling R. A. 3344 Wabash av.
Dowling S. A. Mrs. 3344 Wabash av.
Downe G. E. 4322 Ellis av. *C.A.*
Downer Abner P. 5474 Cornell av.
Downey John Mrs. River Forest
Downey John A. 2690 Magnolia av.
Downey Joseph, 1680 W. Jackson boul. *Ill., U.L.*
Downey W. Stewart; Dr. 550 W. Jackson boul. *Ill.*
Downie S. M. Mrs. 4423 Prairie av.
Downing Anna Mrs. 4015 Vincennes av.
Downs A. H. 2838 Indiana av.
Downs A. Ogden 4829 Kimbark av. *W.P*
Downs Charles S. 4819 Kimbark av. *C.A.*
Downs Ebenezer A. Evanston
Downs Hubert C. 319 Ashland boul.
Downs J. Edward, 319 Ashland boul. *C.A., U.L.*
Downs Lewis C. Evanston
Downs Lucy Ogden Mrs. 4829 Kimbark av.
Downs M. D. 4722 Kenwood av.
Dowst Charles, Evanston
Dowst Samuel M. 7023 Yale
Dox Hamilton B. Chicago Beach hotel. *Un.*
Doyen Anna Dr. 5528 Monroe av.
Doyle Austin J. jr. 203 S. Wood
Doyle Edward T. 91, 44th
Doyle Jas. M. 203 S. Wood
Doyle P. J. 410 Oak
Doyle P. J. 335 W. Garfield boul.
Doyle William A. 1417 Washington boul.
Drain Charles L. Evanston
Drain Julia A. Mrs. Evanston
Drake Charles F. 4822 Lake av.
Drake Chester T. 1932 Deming pl.
Drake C. St. Clair Dr. 1056 Washington boul.
Drake D. Gibson, 703 The Plaza
Drake Francis E. 2114 Calumet av. *C.A.*
Drake George Mrs. Park Ridge
Drake George H. 4822 Lake av.
Drake George V. 510 W. Jackson boul.
Drake Isaac, 6565 Yale
Drake Jennie A. Miss, 684 Winthrop av.
Drake John A. The Kenwood. *C.A., Ill., W.P.*
Drake John B. Mrs. 2114 Calumet av.
Drake John B. jr. 51, 22d. *Chi., C.A., W.P.*
Drake Lauren J. 4950 Ellis av. *U.L.*
Drake Louis S. 510 W. Jackson boul.
Drake Mary E. Mrs. 5708 Madison av.
Drake Tracy Corey, 2840 Indiana av. *Chi., C.A., U.L.*
Drake William H. 4822 Lake av.
Drake W. A. Riverside

Draper Arthur W. 4955 Washington Park ct.
Draper A. M. Mrs. Oak Park
Draper Grace Miss, Oak Park
Draper Herbert L. Oak Park
Draper H. C. 6606 Perry av.
Draper James H. 3159 Indiana av.
Draper John S. Oak Park
Draper Thomas W. 958 W. Monroe
Draper T. New Hotel Holland
Dray Gail, Hotel Metropole
Dray Walter S. Mrs. Hotel Metropole
Dreesbach Philip, 631 Fullerton av.
Drennan John G. 5434 Cornell av.
Dresden William W. 521 W. Adams
Dresselhaus Adeline Mrs. 101 Fowler
Dressler Sarah J. Mrs. 2301 N. Ashland av.
Dressler William M. 2301 N. Ashland av.
Drew Charles W. 2230 Calumet av. *Cal., U.L., W.P.*
Drew Edward P. Rev. Elmhurst
Drew Edward W. 614 Englewood av.
Drew G. H. Morgan Park
Drew Henry H. 4322 Berkeley av.
Drew William C. 4324 Berkeley av.
Dreyer D. Mrs. 3134 South Park av.
Dreyer Samuel, 3134 South Park av. *Lksd.*
Dreyfus Jacob, 4454 Ellis av.
Driggs George Mrs. 5461 Cornell av.
Driggs Herbert, 5461 Cornell av.
Dripps Samuel W. 522, 63d
Driscoll Jeremiah J. Auditorium Annex
Driscoll John J. Dr. 6408 Yale
Driscoll M. F. Lakota hotel. *C.A., U.L.*
Driver Edward A. Riverside. *Chi.*
Driver E. Raymond, Riverside
Driver John N. 6404 Parnell av.
Driver John S. Riverside
Drom Lee 4918 Calumet av.
Drozeski Charles F. 5342 Greenwood av.
Drucker Henry, 1937 Oakdale av. *U.L.*
Druecker Alexander, 1239 Wrightwood av.
Druecker Arthur J. 1239 Wrightwood av.
Druecker John, 23 Wisconsin
Druecker Nicholas, J. 1239 Wrightwood av.
Druiding Adolph, 286 Belden av.
Druliner David L. 93 Bowen av.
Drummond E. A. Victoria hotel
Drummond R. A. Mrs. 1122 Washington boul.
Drury Edwin, Wilmette
Drury Frank, Wilmette
Drury Horace G. Wilmette
Drury John H. 268 Huron
Drury Myron M. Evanston
Dryer Herschel W. 1129 N. Western av. *C. A.*
DuBois Charles G. 38, 46th. *U. L.*
Dubois William Mrs. 3030 Lake Park av.
DuBreuil William A. 534 W. 62d
Duddleston George, 44 Throop. *C.A.*
Dudgeon William H. 5918 Butler
Dudley Arthur H. 2613 Indiana av.
Dudley Charles E. Evanston

Dudley E. C., M.D., 1619 Indiana av. *Univ.* Sum. res. Huron Mountain ciub, Marquette, Mich.
Dudley Henry W. 2613 Indiana av.
Dudley James G. Union club
Dudley John H. 1619 Indiana av.
Dudley J. Sherman, 2358 Indiana av.
Dudley Lewis W. Dr. 2613 Indiana av.
Dudley L.F. Kenilworth
Dudley Mary Mrs. Evanston
Dudley Peter, Union club
Dudley Raymond C. 2613 Indiana av.
Dudley Robert N. Evanston
Dudley Walter W. 4427 Lake av. *U.L.*
Dudley W. Frank, Evanston
Duehr Ulrich, 489 Dearborn av.
Duell William C. 2953 Michigan av.
Duensing Edwin H. River Forest
Duff John A. Rev. 6504 Parnell av.
Duffield A. Howard, 3020 Groveland av.
Duffield Charles Mrs. 3020 Groveland av.
Duffield William H. 4132 Berkeley av.
Duffy George, 679 W. Adams. *C.A.*
Duffy J. Mason, Austin
Dugan George M. 3942 Ellis av.
Dukes Isadore, 1811 Belmont av.
Dukesmith Frank H. 3537 Michigan av.
Dullaghan Edward P. 220 Lincoln Park boul.
Dullaghan John, 220 Lincoln Park boul.
Dullaghan John P. 220 Lincoln Park boul.
Dullaghan Stephen M. 220 Lincoln Park boul.
Dumbeck Victor H. 2358 Indiana av.
Dummer William F. 115 Lincoln Park boul. *Chi., U.L.* Sum. res. Lake Geneva, Wis.
Dunann Charles D. 6532 Perry av.
Dunbar George B. 38 Bellevue pl.
Dunbar James C. 1570 Lill av.
Dunbaugh F. M. 4908 Washington av.
Duncan Adelaide C. Dr. 603 W. 63d
Duncan Alexander C. Wilmette
Duncan David Dr. 117 S. California av.
Duncan George B. Capt. Fort Sheridan
Duncan James W. 3364 Prairie av.
Duncan John A. 774 W. Jackson boul.
Duncan Sarah B.Dr.7827Winneconna av.
Duncan Thomas C. Dr. 590 W. Adams
Duncan William, Hinsdale
Duncan William E. Dr. 603 W. 63d
Duncanson Herbert W. 1976 Fillmore. *Ill.*
Duncombe H. S. Oak Park
Dunfee Jonathan, Austin
D'Unger Claude V. 3010 Prairie av.
D'Unger Paul H. 3010 Prairie av.
D'Unger Robert Dr. 3010 Prairie av.
Dunham Arthur, 22 Woodlawn Park.
Dunham F. V. 16 Astor
Dunham George B. Mrs. Evanston
Dunham George S. Evanston
Dunham German D. 2645 N. Robey
Dunham James S. 29 Bellevue pl. Sum. res. Lake Geneva

Dunham John H. Mrs. 233 Michigan av
Dunham M. H. Mrs. 22 Woodland Park
Dunham Robert J. 29 Bellevue pl.
Dunklee Belle Miss, 4553 Ellis av.
Dunkley C. W. Mrs. 1815 Indiana av.
Dunlap Charles C. 5488 East End av.
Dunlap Clement J. 4356 Forrestville av.
Dunlap DeClermont C. 5438 Monroe av.
Dunlap Emma M. Miss, 3500 Ellis av.
Dunlap George A. 4009 Vincennes av.
Dunlap Robert, 4009 Lake av. *W.P.*
Dunlap S. P. Rev. Maywood
Dunlap William B. 5438 Cornell av.
Dunlap William P. 4356 Forrestville av.
Dunlea James 148, 37th
Dunlea Margaret, 148, 37th
Dunlop Alexander, 4037 Ellis av.
Dunlop Charles D. 3049 Kenmore av. *U.L.*
Dunlop Joseph K. Oak Park
Dunlop Simpson, Oak Park
Dunn Adam E. Evanston. *C.A.*
Dunn Frank, 5045 Michigan av.
Dunn Frank K. 3136 Lake Park av. *Chi., C.A. U.L. W.P.*
Dunn F. P. Virginia hotel
Dunn John J. 5045 Michigan av.
Dunn John O. 311 Park av.
Dunn J. Austin Dr. 198, 44th
Dunn J. E. Berwyn
Dunn J. H. Mrs. 6242 Monroe av.
Dunn L. M. Mrs. 1 Park av.
Dunn Mary Mrs. 549 W. Monroe
Dunn Robert W. 2730 N. Winchester av.
Dunn William, 594 Division Sum. res. Tacoma, Wash.
Dunn William E. Dr. 2146 Wilcox av.
Dunn William H. 456 S. Oakley av.
Dunn Winfield P. 640 Fullerton av.
Dunne Edward F. River Forest
Dunne G. R. LaGrange
Dunne James, 398 Ashland boul. Sum. res. Delavan, Wis.
Dunne Julia Miss, Austin
Dunne Mary Miss, Austin
Dunne Michael J. Col. 747 W. 66th
Dunne M. 3338 Wabash av.
Dunne M. J. 4901 Madison av.
Dunne Richard, Austin
Dunne Thomas Mrs. 4105 Drexel boul.
Dunning David S. Jefferson Park
Dunning E. P. Hyde Park hotel
Dunning Louise M. Miss, 411 Bowen av.
Dunoon David, Evanston
Dunoon George, Evanston
Dunshee W. A. Mrs. 200 Oakwood boul.
Dunton Joseph E. 28 Walton pl. *Un.*
Dunton Mary P. Mrs. Austin
Dunton Thomas F. 937 W. Jackson boul.
Dunwell William C. 720 W. Monroe
Dunwiddie I. F. Park Ridge
Dupee Charles A. 486 Dearborn av. *U.L.* Sum. res. Oconomowoc, Wis.
Dupee Cyrus, 2539 Indiana av.
Dupee C. F. Glencoe
Dupee Emeline W. Mrs. Glencoe

Dupee Eugene H. 486 Dearborn av.
Dupee George W. 486 Dearborn av.
Dupee H. M. 4824 Woodlawn av.
Dupee John, Hotel Metropole. *Chi., C A., W.P.*
Dupee Leroy C. 4824 Woodlawn av.
Dupee Walter H. Hotel Metropole. *C.A., W.P*
DuPlaine Eleanor A. Mrs. 522 Lunt av.
Duppler Bertha E. Miss, 16 Astor
Dupre Chris, Evanston
Dupuy George A. 2625 N. Paulina
Dupuy H. Miss, North Shore hotel
Durand Calvin, Lake Forest. *U.L.*
Durand Charles E. Lake Forest
Durand Charles E. Mrs. Lake Forest
Durand Elliott, 5712 Rosalie ct. *C.A.* Sum. res. Lake Wauwasee, Ind.
Durand Henry Calvin, Evanston
Durand Henry C. Lake Forest
Durand Henry Z. Lake Forest
Durand H. S. 537 N. State
Durand Joseph B. Lake Forest
Durand J. M. Hotel Metropole. *Chi. W.P.*
Durand Scott S. Lake Forest. *Univ.*
Durant Carrie Miss, Auditorium hotel
Durant Thankful Mrs. 576, 43d
Durant W. H. Auditorium hotel
Durborow Allan C. jr. 543 W. Adams. *C.A., Ill.*
Durborow Clarence E. 543 W. Adams
Durborow Conrad B. 543 W. Adams
Durell Barbara H. Miss, 3009 Kenmore av.
Duren Harry L. Evanston
Durfee Charlotte S. Miss, 8 Washington pl.
Durfee Frank E. 2956 Groveland av.
Durfee H. B. Mrs. 5043 Washington av.
Durfee Mary W. Miss, 8 Washington pl.
Durgin John C. 1905 Barry av. *C.A., Ill., Un.*
Durham Albert, Evanston
Durham Emily Mrs. Evanston
Durham Howard F. 222 S. Oakley av.
Durham John H. 222 S. Oakley av.
Durham Roy L. 222 S. Oakley av.
Durham Theron, Oak Park
Durkee Cara W. Miss, 2 Banks
Durkee Henry R. 212 Goethe. *Univ.*
Durkee J. G. Mrs. 20 Ritchie ct.
Durkee R. P. H. Virginia hotel. *Chi.*
Durno Edwin B. 3629 Vincennes av.
Durno Jeannette Miss, 3629 Vincennes av.
Durphy Charles H. 932 W. Adams
Durrie Frank, Oak Park
Durst Philip E. 3142 Lake Park av.
Duryea John M. Austin
Duryee Richard H. 1612 Kenmore av.
Dutch J. Flemming, 2711 Indiana av.
Dutton Buell B. Morton Park
Dutton Kirk Avery, 1507 Montrose boul.
Dutton Llewellyn, 948 Greenleaf av.
Dutton M. M. 1507 Montrose boul.
Dutton S. A. Mrs. 5344 Washington av.
Duval H. Hotel Del Prado

Duvall Richard L. 2938 Kenmore av. *U.L.*
Dwelle A. A. 302 N. State
Dwen Robert G. 3736 Ellis av. Sum. res. Fox Lake
Dwight Henry E. Evanston
Dwight John H. Lake Forest. *C.A., U.L.*
Dwight Timothy, Evanston
Dwight Walter T. Evanston
Dwyer Anna Dr. 3317 Michigan av.
Dwyer John J. 3150 Michigan av.
Dwyer Thomas, 6921 Perry av.
Dwyer Thomas H. 722 N. Wells
Dyar Hugh W. 320 Hampden ct.
Dyche David R. Mrs. Evanston
Dyche Frank B. Evanston
Dyche George B. Dr. Evanston
Dyche H. B. Mrs. Evanston
Dyche William A. Evanston
Dye C. Nathan Mrs. Longwood
Dyer Arthur E. 5458 Cornell av.
Dyer Mrs. Virginia hotel
Dyer Edwin Mrs. Highland Park
Dyer George Turnley, 586 Dearborn av.
Dyer L. C. Mrs. 2512 Wabash av.
Dyer W. C. Dr. 3016 Prairie av.
Dyke Edward F. Mrs. 2216 Prairie av.
Dymond Edwin, Jefferson Park
Dymond Jas. D. 416 N. Normal Parkway
Dymond John H. Jefferson Park
Dynes Charles F. 3953 Michigan av.
Dyrenforth Arthur, 27 Hawthorne pl.
Dyrenforth Douglas, 1931 Deming pl. *C.A.*
Dyrenforth Julius W. 423 Center. *C.A.*
Dyrenforth Lewis F. Riverside
Dyrenforth Philip C. 27 Hawthorne pl.
Dyrenforth Wm. H. Elmhurst
Dyson Lewis E. Evanston
Dyson William H. Evanston

EAGLE JAMES E. 470 Elm. *C.A.*
Eagle M. Miss, 395 Warren av.
Eagle S. Frank, 636 Evanston av.
Eagle Theodore D. 395 Warren av.
Eagle William H. 395 Warren av.
Ealy Elijah R. 7730 Eggleston av.
Eames Edward J. 890, 72d
Eames E. O. Berwyn
Eames Frederick S. Mrs. 376 Ontario
Eames Henry F. Mrs. Lakota hotel
Earhart William I. Evanston
Earl Fred C. 7745 Lowe av.
Earl James F. 7745 Lowe av.
Earl John H. 6840 Wentworth av.
Earl Joseph B. 1621 W. Adams
Earle Carolyn Miss 535 Washington boul.
Earle Charles Warrington Mrs. 535 Washington boul.
Earle Edwin G. Dr. 91 Lincoln av.
Earle E. C. Mrs. Evanston
Earle Frank B. Dr. 903 W. Monroe. *Ill.*
Earle John D. Evanston
Earle John E. Hinsdale
Earle M. J. Mrs. Oak Park
Earle Samuel W. 7648 Eggleston av.

Earling Albert J. 3122 Michigan av. *Chi.*
Sum. res. Oconomowoc, Wis.
Earling George, 3122 Michigan av.
Earling Peter R. Chicago Beach hotel
Early P. H. 2200 Kenmore av.
Earnshaw Charles, 362 Ontario
Earnshaw Emanuel, 362 Ontario
Easley Ralph M. Berwyn
Eastburn Job H. 4319 Champlain av.
Eastburn Lincoln S. 4337 Evans av.
Easter Thomas F. 4179 N. Ashland av.
Eastlake Lewis S. Dr. 4754 Champlain av.
Eastlake W. Delano Dr. 2159 Clarendon av.
Eastland Leonard J. 5141 Michigan av. *C.A,*
Eastman Albert N. 496 W. Jackson boul.
Eastman Charles, Winnetka
Eastman Frank A. Col. 16 Astor ·
Eastman Frank L. 5534 Cornell av.
Eastman Frederick L. 105 Loomis
Eastman George L. Oak Park
Eastman Henry A. 496 W. Jackson boul
Eastman Henry B. 966 S. Sawyer av. ·
Eastman Lorenzo D. 36 Buena Terrace
Eastman L. C. Mrs. 205, 47th
Eastman Osgood T. Evanston
Eastman Sidney C. 1807 Arlington pl. *U.L.*
Eastman Z. Mrs. 1807 Arlington pl.
Easton Giles N. 5806 Washington av.
Easton William P. 547 Dearborn av.
Eaton Alfred B. 632 Lasalle av. *Un.*
Eaton Arthur J. Austin .
Eaton Charles, 5450 Greenwood av.
Eaton David B. Dr. 3147 Indiana av.
Eaton Edric L. 1907 Michigan av.
·Eaton Ellen V. Mrs. 1809 Arlington pl.
Eaton Harry Mrs. Highland Park
Eaton Ira T. 140, 42d pl.
Eaton Isaac I. Austin
Eaton James E. 558 W. 61st
Eaton John, 6123 Monroe av.
Eaton T. W. 1447 Fulton
Eaton W.Thomas,6620 Harvard av. *U.L.*
Eaver Henry B. 973 Warren av.
Sum. res. Madison, Wis.
Ebbert William H. 5128 Michigan av.
Ebbert W. A. 7732 Butler
Ebel Henry C. jr. Washington Heights
Ebeling George, Evanston, *C.A.*
Eberhardt Max, 436 Ashland boul.
Eberhart Frank S. 4203 Ellis av.
Eberhart Noble M. Dr. 2943 Prairie av.
Eberlein F. 56 Bellevue pl.
Ebersol Albert H. 556 W. 60th
Ebersol J. W. 6212 Greenwood av.
Ebert Albert E. 276 Michigan av.
Ebert George F. 4826 Evans av.
Echlin Henry M. Quadrangle club
Eckart George, Oak Park
Eckart Harry S. Oak Park
Eckel John C. Chicago Athletic assn.
Eckels George M. 5515 Woodlawn av.
Eckels James Herron, Virginia hotel.
Chi., Irq., U.L.

Eckhardt William N. 149 S. Western av. *Ill.*
Eckhart Bernard A. 187 Ashland boul. *Ill., U.L.*
Eckhart John W. 716 W. Monroe, *Ill Irq.*
Eckhoff George J. Mrs. Norwood Park
Eckstein Charles, 256 Seminary av.
Eckstein Henry A. 4421 Vincennes av.
Eckstein Louis, 806 Pullman bldg. *Stan.*
Eckstein Samuel jr. Victoria hotel
Eckstorm Christian A. 899 Hamilton ct. ⁻ *C.A.*
Eckstorm P. F. Mrs. 899 Hamilton ct.
Ecton Wiley B. 4958 Madison av.
Edbrooke W. J. Mrs. 3965 Drexel boul.
Eddie E. H. Oak Park
Eddy Albert M. 478 W. Congress. *Ill.*
Eddy Alfred D. 3836 Ellis av. *C.A.,*
Eddy Arthur J. 1635 Sheridan rd. *Chi., Irq.*
Eddy Augustus N. 1601 Michigan av. *Cal., Chi., W.P.*
Eddy Azariah, 710 W. Adams
Eddy Devotion C. 1514 Wilson av.
Eddy Frances M. Miss, 4036 Ellis av.
Eddy Frederick, Austin
Eddy George A. 697 W. Adams
Eddy George D. 697 W. Adams. *Ill.*
Eddy George M. 1593 Kenmore av.
Eddy George S. 710 W. Adams
Eddy Henry C. 1680 Sheridan rd. *U.L., W.P.*
Eddy Henry C. 4202 Michigan av.
Eddy Sarah M. Mrs. 853 Warren av.
Eddy Thomas H. 710 W. Adams
Eden William S. Great Northern hotel
Eder Charles H. 699 N. Clark
Eder Henry, 699 N. Clark
Ederheimer Max, 3926 Grand boul. *Stan.*
Edes Warren S. LaGrange
Edgar Maxwell, 3658 Vincennes av. *Irq.*
Edgar Thomas, Irving Park
Edgar William H. 4240 Champlain av. *C.A.*
Edgar W. H. Mrs. 4240 Champlain av.
Edgarton A. Lewis, 875 W. Adams
Edgerly Daniel G. Morton Park
Edgerly Risley, Morton Park
Edgerton B. G. Hinsdale
Edgerton George H. Dr. 1377 W. Madison
Edgerton Seymour, 5131 Washington av. *Univ.*
Edgeworth James J. 6354 Greenwood av.
Edgren August Rev. Evanston
Edler Fred C. LaGrange
Edminson John W. 638 Pine Grove av.
Edmonds Howard O. 307 N. Clark. *U.L.*
Edmonds Nelson D. Dr. 612 W. Jackson boul. *Ill.*
Edmonds Timothy W. Evanston
Edmunds Abraham, Oak Park
Edof James P. Auditorium hotel
Edsall Samuel C. Rev. 1825 Roscoe. *Univ.*
Edsall Walter W. 389 Ontario

Edson Julius T. Riverside .
Edwards Alfred R. 345 N. Clark
Edwards Anna G. Mrs. Highland Park
Edwards Arthur, Rev. 2818 Indiana av.
Edwards Arthur R. Dr. 2818 Indiana av.
Edwards A. E. Mrs. The Hampden
Edwards A. R. 780 North Park av.
Edwards Charles, LaGrange
Edwards Eugene, 811 Fargo av.
Edwards E. K. Mrs. 761 W. Jackson boul
Edwards E. P. 235 Michigan av. *Chi.
   C.A., W.P.*
Edwards Frank, 1140 Lunt av.
Edwards Harry C. 811 Fargo av.
Edwards Harry E. 761 W. Jackson boul.
Edwards Harry L. Evanston
Edwards Harry L. Hinsdale
Edwards James A. 5244 Lexington av.
   C.A., U.L., W.P.
Edwards James C. 6806 Lafayette av.
Edwards James T. 5037 Lake av.
Edwards John H. Rev. 700 Fullerton av.
Edwards John P. 3953 Michigan av.
Edwards J. Frank, 4203 Ellis av.
           Sum. res. Manitou, Colo.
Edwards Knut E. 1886 Diversey
Edwards K. D. Mrs. Evanston
Edwards L. A. Dr. 255, 31st
Edwards Mary C. C. Mrs. 1886 Diversey
Edwards Thomas C. Union club. *W.P.*
Edwards Thomas K. 761 W. Jackson boul.
Edwards Thomas W. 1566 W. Monroe
Edwards Willard H. Hinsdale
Edwards Wm. H. 379 S. Campbell av. *Irq.*
Edwards William J. 6930 Perry av.
Edwards Wm. S. 3010 Calumet av. *W.P.*
Effinger H. Gerard, 5551 Lexington av.
Effinger John R. Rev. 5551 Lexington av.
Egan James J. 2915 Groveland av.
Egan J. Mrs. 451 Dearborn av.
Egan Lizzie Miss, 444 Dearborn av.
Egan Wiley M. 444 Dearborn av. *Ill.*
Egan William C., Egandale, Highland
   Park
Egan William T. 15 Linden ct.
Egan W. M. Wilmette
Eggers Henry F. 5458 Monroe av.
Eggers Louisa D. Miss, 5458 Monroe av.
Eggleston Charles B. 3336 Indiana av.
Ehle Louis C. 4838 Michigan av.
Ehlen Frank H. 548 Burling
Ehlen J. C. 634 N. Wells
Ehlers Julius, 22 Beethoven pl.
Ehman Charles, 49 Lane ct.
Ehrhart J. T. Oak Park
Ehrlich Samuel Judge, 1837 Michigan av.
Eichberg David, 555A Dearborn av.
Eichberg Max, 4344 Grand boul. *Lksd.
   Stan.*
Eichberg S. 606 Lasalle av.
Eichberg Wm. N. 3644 Grand boul. *Lksd.,
   Stan.*
Eichengreen Mayer H. 970 W. Jackson
   boul.
Eiffert Jacob A., 4197 N. Ashland av.
Eigenman Christian, 5011 Washington av.

Eigenman Christian jr. 5011 Washington
   av.
Eigeman John C. Dr. 5011 Washington av.
Eiker Charles F. The Kenwood. *C.A.*
Eilers Paul C. Austin
Eilert Arthur V. 646 Cleveland av.
Einfeldt August, Oak Park
Einstein Arthur M. 3217 Rhodes av.
   Stan.
Einstein Benjamin M. 1628 Prairie av.
   Stan.
Einstein Morris, 1628 Prairie av. *Stan.*
Eiseman Max, 3722 Forest av. *Lksd.*
Eiseman Moses, 3569 Forest av.
Eisenberg Morris, 477, 42d pl.
Eisendrath B. W. 3264 Vernon av.
Eisendrath Daniel N. Dr. 3125 Michigan
   av.
Eisendrath Helen Mrs. 3949 Ellis av.
Eisendrath J. N. 4237 Michigan av. *Stan.*
Eisendrath Louis, 3402 Calumet av.
   Stan.
Eisendrath Nathan, 146, 33d
Eisendrath Oscar, 3500 Ellis av.
Eisendrath Sam B. 3500 Ellis av.
Eisendrath Sigmund L. 134, 34th. *Stan.*
Eisendrath Sigmund M. 1721 Cornelia av.
Eisendrath Simeon B. 3500 Ellis av.
   Lksd.
Eisendrath Wm. N. 3949 Ellis av. *Stan*
Eisenhart William A. Rev. Morgan Park
Eisenstaedt A. Lincoln, 3330 South Park
   av.
Eisenstaedt Isadore, 3330 South Park av.
Eisenstaedt Leopold, 3210 Calumet av.
   Lksd.
Eisenstaedt Solomon H. 3740 Forest av.
   Lksd.
Eisenstedt Rudolph, 674, 48th. *Lksd.*
Eiszner Frank J. 1487 Washington boul.
Eiszner John, 1487 Washington boul.
Eitel Emil, 622 Lasalle av.
Eitel Karl, 664 Evanston av. *C.A.*
Ela John W. 25 Scott. *Irq.*
Ela S. J. Mrs. 3331 Calumet av.
Elcock Edward G. 4912 Michigan av.
Elder P. L. 187 Rush
Elder P. L. jr. 187 Rush
Elder Robert S. 119 Evanston av.
Elder Samuel W. 187 Rush
Elderkin W. A. Lieut.-Col. 519 The Plaza
Eldred C. H. Dr. Wilmette
Eldred Fred E. Jefferson park
Eldredge Chas. J. 3510 Lake av.
Eldredge Cornelius S. Dr. Palmer house
Eldredge Elnathan S. 3510 Lake av.
Eldredge Fred W. 376 Dearborn av.
Eldredge George C. Lakota hotel. *Chi.*
Eldredge Gertrude Miss, 3242 Lake Park
   av
Eldridge Byron H. LaGrange
Eldridge Charles H. 4615 Woodlawn av
Eldridge E. W. 714 Pullman bldg.
Eldridge Harold, 361 Superior
Eldridge John H. LaGrange
Elford Arthur B. 269 S. Lincoln

Eliel Alexander B. 4443 Ellis av.
Eliel Eugene D. 4443 Ellis av.
Eliel Levi A. 3538 Ellis av. *Stan.*
Eliel M. Mrs. 4443 Ellis av.
Eliel Roy A. 4443 Ellis av.
Eliel Therese Mrs. 3343 Wabash av.
Eliel Walter R. 4443 Ellis av.
Elkan Henry, 594 Dearborn av. *Stan.*
Elkin Michael, 4320 Vincennes av.
Elkins Henry K. 1706 Indiana av. *W.P.*
Ellbogen Max, 3700 Forest av. *Lksd.*
Ellett Edwin H. 3767 Ellis av.
Ellett Harry L. 3767 Ellis av.
Ellicott Edward B. 190, 45th. *U.L.*
Ellinger Albert, 342 Lasalle av.
Ellinger Morris, 342 Lasalle av.
Ellingwood Finley, Dr. Evanston
Elliot Daniel E. Prof. Chicago Beach
    hotel
Elliot Frank M. Evanston. *Univ.*
Elliott Albert J. 4107 Vincennes av.
Elliott A. R. Dr. Auditorium hotel
Elliott C. F. Rev. Hinsdale
Elliot Daniel M. 763 W. Adams
Elliott Edward E. 647 W. Adams
Elliott Edward S. 5461 Cornell av.
Elliott Elihu N. Dr. 1705 Belmont av.
Elliott Emma M. Mrs. 1851 Arlington pl.
Elliott Frank A. Oak Park
Elliott Harriet Mrs. 4833 Vincennes av.
Elliott Henry F. 4833 Vincennes av.
Elliott Henry M. 423 Orchard
Elliott Henry P. 4105 Vincennes av.
Elliott John G. 46, 50th. *U.L.*
Elliott Lorenzo B. 763 W. Adams
Elliott Margaret Miss, Riverside
Elliott Margaret A. Mrs. Oak Park
Elliott Robert L. 44 Woodlawn Park
Elliott Sheldon C. Austin. *Irq.*
Elliott William E. 868 Warren av.
Elliott W. P. 4206 Ellis av.
Elliott W. S. 647 W. Adams
Elliott W. S. jr. 763 W. Adams. *Ill.*
Ellis A. M. H. Mrs. 2734 Prairie av.
Ellis Benjamin W. 502 Washington boul
Ellis Clifford J. Evanston
Ellis Clinton D. 7226 Yale
Ellis Edgar, Wilmette
Ellis Edward D. 412 W. Jackson boul.
    Ill.
Ellis George H. Evanston
Ellis George W. 125 Astor
Ellis Jerome A. Riverside
Ellis Joanna L. Mrs. 3619 Grand boul.
Ellis Joel Mrs. 4341 Grand boul.
Ellis John C. 4120 Lake av. *C.A.*
Ellis John F. 414 W. Jackson boul.
Ellis John W. 520 N. Normal Parkway
Ellis Kate W. Mrs. 4120 Lake
Ellis M. A. Mrs. Austin
Ellis O. W. 200 Oakwood boul.
Ellis Robert, 43, 34th pl.
Ellis Thomas N. 520 N. Normal Parkway
Ellis William J. 1527 W. Monroe
Ellis William S. 4120 Lake av.
Ellis W. S. LaGrange

Ellison George, 99, 33d
Ellsworth F. O. Everett
Ellsworth John J. 4337 Ellis av.
Elmendorf Willard, 322 Lasalle av. *C.A.*
Elmendorf William A. 322 Lasalle av.
Elmer Howard N. 2472 Kenmore av.
Elmer Theodore H. 210 Park av. *Ill.*
Elmers George I. 2606 Prairie av.
Elmes Carleton L. 238 Ashland boul. *C.A.*
Elmes Charles F. 238 Ashland boul. *Ill*
Elmes C. Warren,238 Ashland boul. *C.A.*
Elmstedt John, Washington Heights
Elphicke Charles W. Evanston
Elsdon James G. 6401 Butler
Elsner Charles F. 84 Fowler
Elson Herman, 4113 Grand boul. *Stan.*
    Sum. res. Mackinac Island
Elting P. L. F. 404 Erie. *C.A.*
Elting Victor, 404 Erie. *Univ.*
    Sum. res. Lake Forest
Eltonhead Edward Y. 476 Elm
Elwell Albert, 558, 45th pl.
Elwell Edward H. 4056 Grand boul.
Ely Adin G. 3725 Vincennes av.
Ely Arthur B. 87 Rush
Ely Arthur C. Wheaton. *Chi.*,
Ely Calvin L. 3725 Vincennes av.
Ely Carrie C. Mrs. 6805 Perry av.
Ely Charles F. Dr. 373 Elm
Ely Clare A. Mrs. Evanston
Ely Edward S. La Grange
Ely Elizabeth A. Mrs. 87 Rush
Ely Frank G. 1959 Kenmore av.
Ely Hattie M. Mrs. The Hampden
Ely H. B. LaGrange
Ely James O. Dr. 1911 Michigan av. *Cal.*
Ely Mabel Mrs. 797 Warren av.
Embree Jesse R. 6631 Harvard av.
Embree John W. 35 Woodland Park
Emerich Martin, 2421 Michigan av. *Stan.*
Emerson Ella Mrs. Evanston
Emerson Frank, Austin
Emerson Herbert A. Austin
Emerson Horace H. Austin
Emerson Ozias P. Austin
Emerson Sidney T. 3552 Vernon av.
Emery Albert F. Elmhurst
Emery Alfred B. 5200 Washington av.
Emery Chas. H. 6956 Parnell av.
Emery Ernestine Miss, 2115 Indiana av.
Emery Franklin, 124 S. Seeley av.
Emery James, Elmhurst
Emery James R. 3412 South Park av.
Emery Theodore, 2838 Indiana av.
Emery William H. Elmhurst
Emigh Galusha, 3195 Malden. *Ill.*
Emmerich Charles, 16 Carl
Emmet Richard S. 30 Walton place. *Un.*
Emmons Abram H. 5425 Washington av.
Emmons F. A. Dr. 4129 Drexel boul.
Emmons F. S. Mrs. 4211 Ellis av.
Emory Stephen, 3609 Ellis av.
Emory Theodosia Mrs. Evanston
Emrich Anna M. Mrs. 2742 N. Hermit-
    age av.
Emrich Myer S. 3601 Vincennes av.

Emrich William H. 2742 N. Hermitage av.
Emrick Geo. M. Dr. 5700 Kimbark av.
Ender Henry F. 90 Lincoln av.
Enders Margaret Miss, 2816 Michigan av.
Endicott Edward M. 3757 Ellis av.
Engberg Elizabeth Mrs. 565 Cleveland av.
Engberg Martin J. 565 Cleveland av.
Engel Bernhard, 4326 Vernon av. *Lksd.*
Engel Charles H. 3766 Lake av.
Engel Jacob, 410 Oak
Engel Nathan, 3940 Calumet av. *Lksd.*
Engelhard George P. Evanston. *U.L.*
Engelman Emelie Mrs. Oak Park
Engelman William H. 361 S. Oakley av.
Engelman William T. Oak Park
Engelmann C. P. Evanston, *Irq.*
Engelmann Rosa Dr. 3027 Indiana av.
England George F. 6539 Perry av.
Engle Augustus A. 556 N. State
Engle C. S. 308 Ohio
Engle Edward 460 N. State
Engle George B. jr. 6042 Ellis av.
Engle Walter J. 556 N. State
Engleman Emma Miss, 649 Cleveland av.
Engler William C. 2339 Clarendon av.
English Charles B. 53, 29th pl.
English George R. 5470 Ridgewood ct.
English George S. 6600 Lexington av.
English Gustavus P. 38 E. Pearson, *Un.*
English John Mrs. 6038 Monroe av.
English J. E. 66 Rush
English Lee F. 505 N. 62d
English Leland G. 5252 Calumet av.
English Philip, 4114 Michigan av.
English Thomas, 4114 Michigan av.
English William J. 6038 Monroe av.
Ennis Alfred, 3150 Lake Park av.
Ennis James I. 1038 Greenleaf av.
Ennis Lawrence M. 954 Turner av.
Ennis Lullus J. 25 Aldine sq.
Ennis R. Berry, Chicago Athletic assn.
Enright J. W. 713 W. Jackson boul.
Ensign Frank G. Oak Park
Ensign Frederick G. Oak Park
Enslee Charles L. Dr. Oak Park
Ensley E. S. Mrs. The Arizona
Ensminger William H. Dr. 4801 Champlain av.
Eoff J. H. Mrs. 5723 Washington av.
Epps Charles L. Mrs. 346 Chicago av.
Epps Frank Parker, 583, 45th pl.
          Sum. res. Milford, N. H.
Eppstein Samuel, 4323 Calumet av. *Lksd.*
Epstein Hugo, 3714 Grand boul.
Epstein Jacob J. 3255 Wabash av. *Lksd.*
Epstein Max, 3714 Grand boul. *Lksd.*
Epstein Max N. 7 Crilly ct.
Epstein Morris, 3714 Grand boul. *Lksd.*
Erb George B. 2012 Indiana av.
Erb Jacob, 2012 Indiana av.
Erdt Otto L. Chicago Beach hotel
Erfert Fred J. Austin
Erhart George A. 7206 Yale
Erickson Charles, 6453 Minerva av.
Erickson Christian E. 92 Fowler
Erickson Ernst A. 86 Fowler

Erickson E. A. 6632 Monroe av.
Ericson Albert F. Prof. Evanston
Ericson Edward H. 528 N. Normal Parkway
Ericson Felix H. 528 N. Normal Parkway
Ericson Otto C. Evanston
Erkins H. Milo, 291 Michigan av.
Erler Robert G. 4515 Forrestville av.
Ermeling Lewis R. 2641 N. Robey
Ernst Charles E. 1754 Deming pl.
Ernst Edward F. Wilmette
Ernst Leo, Highland Park
Ernst Leo E. 1754 Deming pl.
Ernst Nathan H. 3233 Vernon av.
Ernst Otto, 529 Orchard
Erpelding Amelia Mrs. 1120 Bryan av.
Erpelding George B. 1120 Bryan av.
Erpelding John N. 1120 Bryan av.
Errant Joseph W. 346, 54th
Erskine Albert Mrs. 108 Lincoln Park boul.
Erskine Albert D. 108 Lincoln Park boul.
Erskine David M. jr. Highland Park
Erskine Emily L. Miss, Highland Park
Erskine James D. 108 Lincoln Park boul.
Erskine Oscar P. Hyde Park hotel
Erskine Robt. Oak Park
Ervine L. W. Oak Park
Erwin Augusta Mrs. 55 St. James pl.
Erwin Charles R. Oak Park, *C.A.*
Erwin J. M. F. 6504 Minerva av.
Erwin Orlando R. 394 W. Congress
Esbaugh C. F. Hotel Windermere
Eschenburg Arnold W. 465 Dearborn av.
Eschenburg Berta Mrs. 669 Lasalle av.
Eschenburg Franz, 669 Lasalle av.
Eschenburg Herman, 2795 N. Lincoln
Eschenburg H. A. 669 Lasalle av.
Eschenburg Peter H. 2799 N. Lincoln
Esdohr Henry, Jefferson Park
Esdohr Herman H. Jefferson Park
Esher Edward B. 234 S. Winchester av.
Esler G. N. Mrs. 3127 Dover
Espert Frederick jr. 2419 Calumet av.
Espert Frederick Mrs. 2419 Calumet av.
Espert Michael, 3128 Indiana av.
Essex George S. 384 Oak
Essick James C. 295 Oak
Esson John H. LaGrange. *C.A.*
Estabrook Blanche D. Miss, 524 Dearborn av.
Estabrook Henry D. 524 Dearborn av. *U.L.*
Estabrooke W. W. Dr. 577½ Lasalle av.
Estes Mabel Clara Miss, LaGrange
Estes St. Louis A. LaGrange
Estey W. H. Mrs. 503 N. State
Etheridge Charles L. 44, 50th
Etheridge Francis, 4714 Kenwood av.
Etheridge J. H. Dr. 1634 Michigan av. *U.L., Un.*
Etnier O. L. 4022 Vincennes av.
Ettinger Charles D. 3847 Michigan av. *U.L., W.P.*
Ettinger Charles N. 2430 N. Paulina
Ettinger J. M. Edison Park

Ettlinger M. Mrs. 2502 Indiana av.
Ettlinger Simon. 233, 32d. *Stan.*
Eulette Charles H. 595, 46th
Eulette Ira F. 6550 Butler
Eulette Thomas J. 7105 Princeton av.
Eustace Thomas, 3000 Prairie av.
Eustis Percy S. LaGrange, *C.A.*
Eustis Truman W. Hinsdale, *C.A., U.L.*
Euston Alexander, 907 Pullman bldg.
Evans Albert E. Dr. Palmer house, *C.A.*
　　　Sum. res. Cape May
Evans Arthur F. 381 Superior
Evans Augustus L. 1020 Farwell av.
Evans A. T. 3537 Michigan av.
Evans Boulden C. 608 W. 61st pl.
Evans Charles, 1045 Pratt av.
Evans Charles H. 300, 53d *U.L.*
Evans Clinton B. 3224 Lake Park av. *U.L.*
Evans Daniel, 381 Superior
Evans Daniel E. 5412 Madison av.
Evans Evan T. 608 W. 61st pl.
Evans Fannie M. Miss, Oak Park
Evans Filmore, Highland Park
Evans George H. Norwood Park
Evans George W. 87 Rush
Evans G. V. Mrs. Lakota hotel
Evans Henry B. Judge, 4440 Woodlawn
　　　av.
Evans Henry J. 1271 Washington boul.
　　　Sum. res. Lake Geneva, Wis.
Evans James Cary, 108 Lincoln Park boul.
　　　Un.
Evans Jesse M. Oak Park
Evans John, Evanston
Evans Louis H. 564 Washington boul.
Evans Lynden, 135 Lincoln Park boul.
　　　Univ.
Evans Maurice, Oak Park
Evans Orrin Lee, 30 Groveland Park. *Irq.*
Evans Raymond O. 7413 Butler. *C.A.*
Evans Richard Morgan, 497, 42d pl.
Evans Robert G. Highland Park
Evans Walter N. 2151 Clarendon av.
Evans William C. Evanston
Evans William W. 562 Washington boul.
　　　Ill.
Evarts Edward S. 6429 Stewart av.
Eveland Charles S. 2731 N. Paulina
Eveleth S. H. Austin
Even Theodore, 1799 N. Halsted
Evenden John G. 751 Warren av.
Evens Harriett Mrs. 1760 Wrightwood av.
Everest James G. 6611 Yale
Everett Charles F. Highland Park
Everett Coleman S. 2947 Prairie av.
Everett Edward W. 2947 Prairie av.
Everett Frank D. Highland Park
Everett Frederick Dr. 402 Center
Everett John C. 2947 Prairie av. *U.L.*
Everett William, 7426 Kimbark av.
Everett William R. 10 Bryant av.
Everett William S. Mrs. 2947 Prairie av.
　　　Sum. res. Macatawa, Mich.
Everhart George P. 136 Lincoln Park
　　　boul.
Everingham Edward L. 5503 Cornell av.

Everingham G. Sumner, 374 Dearborn av.
　　　Sum. res. Highland Park
Everingham H. Dickson, 5503 Cornell av.
Everingham Lyman, 5503 Cornell av.
　　　Sum. res. Traverse City, Mich.
Everitt Fred L. 3010 Kenmore av.
Evernden William, Hinsdale
Eversz Ernest H. Evanston
Eversz Moritz E. Rev. Evanston
Everts W. W. Mrs. 3342 Rhodes av.
Evoy Thomas A. 6324 Woodlawn av.
Ewart Edward G. 3231 Rhodes av.
Ewell Marshall D. Judge, Evanston
Ewen Harriet Miss, Evanston
Ewen John Meiggs, Evanston, *C.A.,*
　　　U.L., Univ.
Ewen Lilian Miss, Evanston
Ewen Malcolm F. Evanston
Ewen Warren, 249 Goethe
Ewen Warren Mrs. Evanston
Ewing Adlai T. 3747 Ellis av. *Irq.*
Ewing Charles Hull, 31 Ashland boul.
Ewing John B. Dr. 126 Loomis
Ewing J. A. 862 W. Monroe
Ewing M. L. Mrs. 3706 Lake av.
Ewing William B. 4136 Ellis av.
　　　Sum. res. LaGrange
Ewing William G. Judge, 3743 Ellis av.
　　　Irq.
Excell Edwin O. 4349 Ellis av.
Excell Robert, 337 Oakwood boul,
Excell Wm. Alonzo, 4349 Ellis av.
Eyer Claredon B. Evanston
Eyman Frank P. 2515 N. Hermitage av.
Eyre Clarence Preston, 4806 Champlain
　　　av.
Eyster J. M. Miss. 3747 Indiana av.

FABIAN WILLIAM J. Evanston
　　Fabian Wm. Werner, 19 Pine Grove
　　　av.
Fabyan George, 3359 Wabash av. *Chi.,*
　　　W.P.
Faherty Michael J. 36 Pine Grove av.
Fahrney Homer E. 1074 Warren av.
Fahrney J. H. 1074 Warren av.
Fahrney Peter Dr. 1074 Warren av.
　　　Sum. res. Mapleville, Md.
Fahrney William H. 1074 Warren av.
Faifer Tony, 2358 Indiana av.
Fair Alexander, 365 Superior
Fair A. M. Miss, 2222 Calumet av.
　　　Sum. res. Bay Ridge, N.Y.
Fair Charles M. 2222 Calumet av.
Fair Joseph B. 2222 Calumet av. *Chi.*
　　　Sum. res. Bay Ridge, N.Y.
Fair Robert M. 2222 Calumet av. *Chi.*
　　　Sum. res. Bay Ridge, N.Y.
Fairbairn Anna H. Miss. 71 Lake View av.
Fairbairn Lila J. Miss, 71 Lake View av.
Fairbank Kellogg, 1801 Michigan av.
　　　Chi., C.A.
Fairbank N. K. 1801 Michigan av. *Cal.,*
　　　Chi., U.L., W.P.
　　　Sum. res. Lake Geneva, Wis
Fairbank Wallace, 1801 Michigan av.

Fairbanks Geo. O. 1676 Kenmore av.
Fairbanks Newton H. 4623 Champlain av.
Fairchild Arthur E. 51 St. Clair
Fairchild Edward J. Hinsdale
Fairchild Elijah S. Rev. 51 St. Clair
Fairchild Emil L. 51 St. Clair
Fairchild Meredich H. 51 St. Clair
Fairclough Richard, 845 Warren av,
Fairfield Albert B. Tracy
Fairfield Albert B. jr, Tracy
Fairfield Frank M. Tracy
Fairlee Sidney Mrs. 2415 Michigan av.
Fairlee Sidney R. 2415 Michigan av.
Fairman Clarence, 6529 Greenwood av.
Fairman Daniel B. 6529 Greenwood av.
Fairman Frank, 4744 Kenwood av.
Fairman Frank S. 4744 Kenwood av.
Fairman George C. 6436 Monroe av.
Fairrington Chas. W. 3807 Vincennes av.
Fairrington Warren M.3807 Vincennes av.
Faith Thomas Dr. 94 N. Kedzie av.
Faithorn John M. Lakota hotel. *Chi.,*
    C.A.
Faithorn Walter E. Lakota hotel.
Fake Frederick L. 250, 66th
Fake Frederick L. jr. 6547 Monroe av.
Falcy Blanche C. Miss, Austin
Fales Catherine Miss, Lake Forest
Fales David, Lake Forest *Univ.*
Fales David jr. Lake Forest
Fales Frederick S. 4544 Lake av.
Fales Julia A. Mrs. 4804 Lake av.
Falk Jennie Mrs. 347 Oakwood boul.
Falk Louis, Austin
Falk Max I.. 4346 Grand boul. *Lksd.,*
    Stan.
Falk William D. 1730 Deming pl.
Falkenau Harry, 565 Kenwood pl.
Falkenau Louis, Lakota hotel. *Stan.*
Falkenau Victor, 3424 Wabash av. *U.L.*
Falker Henry, 4433 Drexel boul.
Fall Humphrey, 599 W. Jackson boul.
Falley James, 2159 Clarendon av.
Falley Katharine Mrs. Evanston
Falley Lewis H. 4700 Grand boul.
Falley William, 2159 Clarendon av.
Fallis Kathryn E. Mrs. 385 N. State
Fallows Samuel Rt. Rev. 967 W. Monroe
Falls S. K., M.D. 1028 W. Monroe
Falter B. Franklin, 3125 Vernon av.
Falter David B. 3125 Vernon av. *Lksd.*
Fanning Arthur L. Evanston
Fanning Frank J. 580 W. Madison
Fanning John, Glencoe
Fanning T. C. Mrs. 5620 Washington av.
Fansler Thomas, Evanston
Faraday Walter, Wilmette
Fargo Charles, 2247 Michigan av. *Cal.,*
    Chi., W.P.
        Sum. res. Loon Lake, N. Y.
Fargo C. E. Hotel Windermere. *U.L.*
Fargo Edward A. 2310 Calumet av.
Fargo Florence B. Miss, 2247 Michigan
    av.
Fargo F. C. Evanston
Fargo James L. Oak Park
35

Fargo Lee, 6560 Harvard av.
Fargo Livingston W. 2247 Michigan av.
    Chi., Univ. W. P.
Fargo Samuel M. 547 Dearborn
Fargo William H. Evanston
Farish Mary A. Mrs. 434 Belden av.
Farley Andrew J. 3257 Groveland av.
Farley C. M. Mrs. LaGrange
Farley Jesse K. 2469 Kenmore av.
Farley John W. LaGrange
Farlin J. Whitney Mrs. 64 Lake Shore
    Drive
Farlin Myron Whitney, 64 Lake Shore
    Drive. *C.A.*
Farling Georgia A. Mrs. 3344 Calumet av.
Farmer M. W. Mrs. 7127 Wentworth av.
Farnham Charlotte A. Miss, 5803 Wash-
    ington av.
Farnham G. M. Capt. 6200 Kimbark av.
Farnham Harry J. 651 Washington boul.
Farnham Louise M. Miss,3351 Forest av.
Farnham Neal, Oak Park
Farnham Roscoe E. 6401 Lexington av.
Farnham S. H. 2337 Lakewood av.
Farnsworth Albert J. 3213 Groveland av.
Farnsworth Andrew C. 3213 Groveland av.
Farnsworth Ann Miss, Wilmette
Farnsworth Charles E. Jefferson Park
Farnsworth Ernest L. Mayfair
Farnsworth George, 125 Astor. *Un.*
Farnsworth George J. 10 Astor. *Un.*
Farnsworth Granville H. Evanston
Farnsworth Harriet M. Miss, 468 Wash-
    ington boul.
Farnsworth J. B. Mayfair
Farnum Albert H. 2209 Calumet av. *Cal.,*
    C.A.
Farnum E. J., M.D. Hotel Metropole
Farnum George C. 852 W. Monroe
Farnum Henry Warner, 2213 Prairie av.
    Univ.
Farnum H. A. Norwood Park
Farnum Ithiel P. 937 W. Monroe
Faron May Miss, 2169 Kenmore av.
Farovid James A. 706, The Plaza
Farquhar Charles, 4444 Evans av.
Farquhar William R. 3 Tower pl.
Farquharson Adella Miss, 3455 Prairie av.
Farquharson Emma Miss, 3455 Prairie av.
Farr A. G. 5103 Hibbard av. *U.L.*
Farr A. L. Dr. 240 Hampden ct.
Farr Charles W. 545 Dearborn av.
        Sum. res. Mackinac Island
Farr C. W. Irving Park
Farr J. George, 4737 Woodlawn av.
Farr Marvin A. 4737 Woodlawn av. *U.L.*
Farrand Harriet A. Miss, 654 Washington
    boul.
Farrar Arthur,Mrs. 505 Washington boul.
Farrar Charles S. Prof., Evanston
Farrar J. Hamilton, 669 Fullerton av.
Farrell James E. 541 Englewood av.
Farrell John E. 569 Orchard
Farrell John S. 569 Orchard
Farrell Patrick Mrs. 3669 Wabash av.
Farrell Thomas P. 3669 Wabash av.

Farrell T. F. 603 Washington boul. *Ill*
Farrell William J. 569 Orchard
Farrelly James J. 4418 Champlain av.
Farren John, 3942 Grand boul.
Farren John Mrs. 5112 Wabash av.
Farren John A. Dr. 5112 Wabash av.
Fatrington O. C. Prof. 338. 57th
Farson Charles T. 4440 Vincénnes av.
Farson Duke M. 1477 Washington boul.
Farson Harriet C. Mrs. 134 Warren av.
Farson John, Oak Park. *C.A., Ill., U.L.*
Farson M. Elizabeth Miss, 134 Warren av.
Farson Robert Bruce, 26 .Delaware pl.
    U.L.   Sum. res. St. Charles, Ill.
Farwell Arthur L. 205 Goethe. *Univ.*
Farwell A. B. 4516 Lake av.
Farwell Charles B. Hon. 99 E. Pearson
    Chi., C.A., U.L.
                Sum. res. Lake Forest
Farwell Elizabeth S. Mrs. 2705 Indiana av.
Farwell Frank C. Lake Forest. *Univ.*
Farwell Francis W. 2705 Indiana av.
Farwell Fred M. 6442 Monroe av.
FarwellGranger,LakeForest. *Chi.,Univ.*
Farwell H. S. Chicago Athletic Assn.
Farwell John A. 2506 Michigan av. *U.L.,*
    W.P.
Farwell John A. jr. 2506 Michigan av.
    C.A., W.P.
Farwell John C. 6123 Monroe av.
Farwell John H. 6123 Monroe av.
Farwell John V. 109 E. Pearson. *U.L.*
                Sum. res. Lake Forest, Ill.
Farwell John V. jr. Lake Forest. *Chi.,*
    Univ.
Farwell J. W. 534 W. Monroe. *C.A., Ill.*
Farwell L. C. Mrs. 3716 Lake av.
Farwell Simeon, Evanston
Farwell Walter, 99 E. Pearson. *Chi.,*
    C.A.
Farwell W. W. Mrs. 534 W. Monroe
Fash Martin H. Dr. 708 W. Adams
Fass Charles, 3635 Prairie av.
Fass Jacob, 485, 42d pl.
Fassett E. P. 4429 Lake av.
Fassett S. M. 4621 Greenwood av.
Fatch Edward P. Wilmette
Fate John L. 1069 Winthrop av.
Fauber William H. Chicago Athletic
    Assn.
Faulkner John, Austin
Faulkner Samuel, 98 Oakwood av.
Faulkner Thomas H. 428, 42d pl.
Faulknor Lillian Miss, Oak Park
Fauntleroy Thos. S. Lake Forest. *U.L.*
Faurot Henry, 603, 46th
Favard Louise Mrs. 4564 Oakenwald av.
Favill Henry B   d Dr. 138 Lincoln Park
    boul. *Un., Univ.*
Favor Otis S. 1 Madison Park
Favorite Calvin M. 2807 Michigan av.
Favorite Ward C. 2928 Indiana av.
Favorite Wm. Foster, 3433 Wabash av.
Fawcett Robert Mrs. 6519 Monroe av.
Fawcett William Rev. River Forest

Faxon J. Warren, Oak Park
Faxon R. 3100 Groveland av.
Fay Albert R. 3326 South Park av. *C.A.*
Fay Charles M. 4332 Ellis av.
Fay Charles Norman, 63 E. Pearson.
    Chi.   Sum. res. Newport, R.I.
Fay E. J. 30, 44th pl.
Fay John, 90 Pine Grove av.
Fay John B. Hotel Windermere
Fay J. Edwards, 148 Park av.
Fay N. C. Mrs. 3326 South Park av.
Fay Osmar W. 411 S. Oakley av.
Fay Owen H. 2928 Indiana av.
Fay Ralph M. 14 Bellevue pl. *Un.,U.L.,*
    W.P.
Fay Richard S. Mrs. 339 Rush
Faye Charles M. 89 Bowen av. *C.A.*
Fayerweather Edward E. Hinsdale
Fearing Harry L. Oak Park
Fearing L. Blanche Miss, 420 Chicago av.
Fearing Mary S. Mrs. Oak Park
Fearing M. A. Mrs. 420 Chicago av.
Fearing Roy M. Oak Park
Featherstone A. Auditorium hotel. *W.P.*
Featherstone Edward Allyn, 1674 W.
    Jackson boul.
Featherstone George F. 1657 W.Monroe
                Sum. res. Brown's Lake, Wis.
Featherstone Ida M. Mrs. 767 Washing-
    ton boul.
Featherstone K. J. W. 515, 45th
Featherstone Ruth A. Mrs. 277 Ashland
    boul.
Fechheimer Edwin S. Winnetka. *Stan.*
Feehan P. A. Most Rev. 623 N. State
Fegenbush Charles M. 3233 Michigan av-
Feibelman David L. 4234 Calumet av.
    Stan.
Feibelman R. Mrs. 4529 Ellis av.
Feiler William, Evanston
Felbinger John, 237 Evanston av.
Felch Barclay Mrs. 7207 Princeton av.
Felix Alexander Toll, 555 N. State
Felix Ben Bates, 555 N. State
                Sum. res. Lake Villa, Ill.
Felix Benjamin F. 555 N. State
                Sum. res. Lake Villa, Ill.
Fellingham George, Evanston
Fellingham Robert J. Evanston
Fellows Alfred W. 3008 Lake Park av.
Fellows Antoinette K. Dr. 134, 50th
Fellows Byron M. 4555 Forrestville av.
    Irq.
Fellows Caroline M. Mrs. 104 Loomis
Fellows Charles J. 7147 Wentworth av.
Fellows C. Gurnee Dr. 4542 Lake av.
    C.A.
Fellows George E. Prof. Quadrangle club
Fellows Henry B., M.D. 2969 Indiana av.
Fellows John B. 134, 50th.
Fellows Lee, 530 Cleveland av.
Fellows R. L. LaGrange
Fellows William K. 134, 50th
Fels Joseph, Lexington hotel
Felsenthal Albert, 3745 Langley av.
Felsenthal Bernhard Rev. 3309 Rhodes av.

Felsenthal Edwin I. 3309 Rhodes av.
Felsenthal Eli B. 4108 Grand boul. *Stan.*,
    U.L.
Felsenthal Gabriel, 4518 Champlain av.
Felsenthal Henry, 275, 46th, *Lksd.*
Felsenthal Herbert, 4510 Ellis av.
Felsenthal Herman, 4510 Ellis av.
Felsenthal Julius L. 275, 46th.
Felsenthal L. 3237 South Park av.
Felt Ella W. Mrs. 4725 Prairie av.
Felt Frank B. 5557 Monroe av.
Felt Winchester W. 4725 Prairie av.
Feltenstein Aaron, 4517 Prairie av.
Felton Charles E. 3153 Calumet av. *C.A.*,
    W.P.
Felton Charles H. 440 Dearborn av.
Felton George G. 3002 Lake Park av.
Felton Walter S. 655 Walnut
Fenger Christian Dr. 269 Lasalle av.
Fenn Curtis T. Dr. 6117 Washington av.
Fenn John J. Mrs. 6637 Stewart av.
Fenn P. D. Chicago Beach hotel
Fennimore Richard, 494 W. Monroe
Fenton Howard Withrow, 4619 Ellis av.
Fenton H.W.Lexington hotel,*Cal.*,*W.P.*
Fenton J. L. Mrs. Lexington hotel
Fenton W. T. 4619 Ellis av. *Cal.*
Fentress David, 118 Lincoln Park boul.
Fentress James, 118 Lincoln Park boul.
    Chi.
Fentress James jr. 118 Lincoln Park boul.
Fergus John B. 3229 Sheridan rd.
Fergus William L. 3229 Sheridan rd.
Ferguson A. H., M.D. 548, 51st
Ferguson B. L. Auditorium hotel
Ferguson Chas. H. 2007 Michigan av.
    Cal., *C.A.*, *U.L.*, *W.P.* Sum. res.
    Norwood, Mich.
Ferguson Charles H, jr. 3912 Lake av.
            Sum. res. Norwood, Mich.
Ferguson C. J. Mrs. 5752 Madison av.
Ferguson Edward, 2446 Michigan av.
Ferguson Edward Ashley, 68 Cedar,
    C.A., *Un.*, *Univ.*
Ferguson Elbert C. 4551 Ellis av. *U.L.*
Ferguson ElizabethMiss,5753Madison av.
Ferguson E. Hotel Del Prado
Ferguson George M. 47, 22d, *Cal.*, *Un.*,
    W. P.
Ferguson Henry A. 7720 Eggleston av.
Ferguson James H. Hotel Del Prado
Ferguson James L. Kenilworth
Ferguson Louis A. Evanston
Ferguson William G. 4551 Ellis av.
Ferguson W. G. Morgan Park
Fern Clara Louise Miss, 918 Warren av.
Fern C. A. 918 Warren av.
Fern G. B. 918 Warren av.
Fernald George E. Wilmette
Fernald James W. 4434 Greenwood av.
Fernald Paul, 4205 Vincennes av.
Fernandez E. M. S. Dr. 3243 Malden.
Fernbach Louis, 482, 42d pl. *Lksd.*
Fernberg B. Mrs. 3628 Prairie av.
Fernberg William P. 3628 Prairie av.
Ferns John P. Mrs. 16 Lincoln Park boul.

Feron Walter J. 5326 Cornell av. *C.A.*
Ferre John P. 4729 Langley av.
Ferree Albert G. 559 W. 69th
Ferree Harry C. 559 W. 69th
Ferreira Chas. E. 7754 Lowe av.
Ferris Henry B. 1715 Barry av. *C.A.*
Ferris L. Vernon, Maywood
Ferris Madison H. 119, 21st
Ferris Seymour, Oak Park.
Ferris Uriah B., M.D. 7554 Bond av.
Ferry Abbie F. Mrs. Lake Forest
Ferry Albert D. Evanston
Ferry Charles H. 183 Lincoln Park boul.
    Chi., *C.A.*, *Un.*, *U.L. Univ.*
Ferry James W. Mrs. 336 Dearborn av.
Ferry Mansfield, 183 Lincoln Park boul.
Ferry M. A. H. Mrs. 336 Dearborn av.
Ferry Watson J. 4553 Oakenwald av. *Chi.*
Fessenden Benjamin A. Highland Park
    U.L.
Fessenden Charles Newton, 388 Ashland
    boul. *Un.*
    Sum. res. "Ellinore" Cascade, Col.
Fessler Ada G. Miss, Evanston
Ffrench Charles, 5850 Rosalie ct.
Fick Bruno W. 284 Ashland boul.
Fick Emma Mrs. 284 Ashland boul.
Fickes Ola B. Miss, 3422 Prairie av.
Ficklin Joseph C. 30 Walton pl.
Ficklin Leonard, Tracy
Fiedler Anton B. 611 Lasalle av.
Fiedler August 463 Lasalle av.
Fiedler A. B. Mrs. 611 Lasalle av.
Fiedler Edmund G. 1107 N. Clark
Fiedler Martin A. 92 Hammond
Fiedler Paul O. 1715 Arlington pl.
Field Arthur C. 250 Dearborn av.
Field Charles, 815 Pullman bldg.
Field Charles E. 5546 Madison av. *C.A.*
Field Charles H. LaGrange
Field Elisha C. 544 W. 61st pl.
Field Eugene Mrs. 2339 Clarendon av.
Field George D. 2248 Michigan av.
Field George W. 250 Dearborn av.
Field Harry B. 2641 N. Paulina
Field Heman H. 4826 Kimbark av.
Field Howard, Evanston
Field John S. 2248 Michigan av. *Cal.*,
    C.A., *U.L.*
Field Marshall, 1905 Prairie av. *Cal.*,
    Chi., *C.A.*, *Un.*, *U.L.*, *W.P.*
Field Martha A. Mrs. 2248 Michigan av.
Field Mary French Miss, 2339 Clarendon
    av
Field Richard I. 250 Dearborn av.
Field Roswell M. 35 Bittersweet pl.
Field R. H. 4558 Lake av.
Field Samuel G. Hotel Metropole
Field Stanley, 1922 Calumet av. *Chi.*
Field Wentworth G. Hotel Metropole
Field William J. 4312 Greenwood av.
Field W. O. North Shore hotel
Fielding Edward, 618 Touhy av.
Fielding Howard H. 7631 Union av.
Fielding Mary E. Miss, 7631 Union av.
Fifield John S. 921 W. Monroe

Fifield Walter K. 929 W. Monroe
File William F. 88 Bryant av.
Filer Alanson, Evanston
Finch C. M. Mrs. 142, 36th
Finch Franklin Mrs. 34 Ogden av.
Finch Hunter W. 275, 52d
Finden Frederick, Norwood Park
Finerty John F. 3562 Grand boul.
Finkler Charles C. 381 Superior
Finkler John W. 1821 Oakdale av. C.A.
Finkler William, 2611 N. Paulina
Finley George, Lake Forest
Finn Joseph M. 485 Lasalle av. Lksd.
Finn Nicholas R. 622 W. Jackson boul.
Finn Patrick, 622 W. Jackson boul. -
Finney George M. 631 Cleveland av.
Finney Harry P. 631 Cleveland av.
Finney John, Highland Park
Finney Sarah L. Mrs. 631 Cleveland av.
Finney William H. 621 The Plaza, C.A.
Firestone Jason W. 221 Dearborn av.
Firman B. W. Oak Park
Firmenich George F. 2323 Michigan av.
Firmenich Joseph, 2323 Michigan av.
Fischback John, 1171 N. Clark
Fischer Charles W. 1814 Wrightwood av.
Fischer Frederick, Highland Park
Fischer Gustave A. Dr. 514 Ashland boul.
Fischer G. F. 52 Walton pl.
Fischer Henry W. 2687 N. Ashland av.
Fischer Oscar, 514 Ashland boul.
Fischer Oscar F. 2030 Michigan av. C.A.
Fischer Reinhold-Prof. 501 Lasalle av.
Fischer Siegfried M. 5012 Drexel boul.
    Lksd., Stan.
Fischer William D., 782 Warren av.
Fish Abner C. 4138 Ellis av.
Fish Alexander, 331 Hampden ct.
Fish Arthur C. 4138 Ellis av.
Fish A. J. 3611 Grand boul.
Fish David, 4834 Michigan av.
Fish Edwin S. 4138 Ellis av.
Fish E. F. Rev. Evanston
Fish Frank F. 4138 Ellis av.
Fish F. A. 43 Roslyn pl.
Fish Isaac, 4834 Michigan av. Lksd.
Fish Jessie A. Mrs. 1213 Seminary pl.
Fish Joseph, 4750 Grand boul. Stan.
Fish Mary J.Miss, 1399 Washington boul.
Fish Roswell P. 43 Roslyn pl.
Fish Sarah C.Miss,1399 Washington boul
Fish Selden, 3226 Calumet av.
Fish Sigmund C. 4544 Vincennes av. C.A.
Fish S. T. 4508 Drexel boul. Stan., U.L.
Fish Thomas M. 2358 Indiana av.
Fish Williston, 5114 Madison av.
Fishback George, 484 W. Adams
Fishburn Eugene H. 422 Huron, Un.
Fishburn Randolph E. 422 Huron, C.A.,
    U.L.
Fishell Albert, 3448 Wabash av.
Fishell E. W. Dr. 3448 Wabash av.
Fisher Albert J. 6565 Yale
Fisher Arthur N. 3810 Forest av.
Fisher A. A. Lakota hotel
Fisher Budd, Lakota hotel

Fisher B. R. Mrs. 171, 51st
Fisher Charles E. Oak Park, C.A.
Fisher Charles E. Dr. 4016 Drexel boul.
Fisher C. C. Mrs. 552 W. Jackson boul.
Fisher Edward A. 2942 Kenmore av.
Fisher Eugene C. Oak Park
Fisher Francis P. 2419 Michigan av.
    C.A.
Fisher Frank F. LaGrange
Fisher Frederick J. T. Dr. Elmhurst
Fisher George F. 4332 Greenwood av.
    Sum. res. Lake Beulah, Wis.
Fisher George F. jr. 164, 42d pl.
    Sum. res. Lake Beulah, Wis.
Fisher George M. Lakota hotel. U.L.
Fisher George P. jr. 144 Astor
    Sum. res. Highland Park
Fisher Harry H. 2716 Calumet av.
Fisher Hart C. 4735 Lake av. C.A.
Fisher James O. 4734 Prairie av.
Fisher John Dr. 368 Lasalle av.
Fisher Justus P. 552 W. Jackson boul.
Fisher Louis K. 4400 Berkeley av. Lksd.
Fisher Lucius G. 4036 Ellis av. C.A.,
    U.L., W.P. Sum. Res. Mackinac Isl-
    and
Fisher Napoleon C. 2226 Kenmore av.
Fisher Reynolds, 4734 Kimbark av.
Fisher R. C. Dr. 2001 Michigan av.
Fisher Susie Mrs. 2481 Lakewood av.
Fisher Walter L. 463 N. State, Univ.,
    U.L.   Sum. res. Lakeside, Ill.
Fisher William E. Norwood Park
Fisher W. A. Dr. 4161 Berkeley av.
Fishleigh John, sr. 1209 W. Ravenswood
    Park
Fisk D. B. Mrs. 2100 Calumet av.
Fisk D. Milton, 501 N. State
Fisk Franklin P. Chicago Athletic Assn.
    Ill.
Fisk Franklin W. Prof. 532 W. Adams
    .   Sum. res. Lake Geneva, Wis.
Fisk Ginevra Miss, 6606 Yale
Fisk Henry E. 899 Walnut
Fisk Henry E. 2100 Calumet av.
Fisk Herbert F. Prof. Evanston
Fisk Horace E. 474 N. State
Fisk James H. 2977 South Park av.
Fisk Jane M. Mrs. Evanston ·
Fisk Louis A. 3551 Indiana av.
Fisk William H. 1514 Wilson av.
Fisk W. B. jr. Lexington hotel
Fiske C. W. 3601 Vincennes av.
Fiske Geo.F.Dr. Lake Forest Chi.,C.A.,
    U.L., Univ.
Fiske Horace S. 344, 57th
Fiske John M. 4318 Oakenwald av.
Fiske Leonard, 336 Ontario
Fitch Alfred L. 4510 Greenwood av.
Fitch Amza L. Oak Park
Fitch Anna W. Mrs. 4840 Langley av.
Fitch Caroline S.Mrs. 4510 Greenwood av.
Fitch Calvin M. Dr. 645 W. Monroe
    Sum. res. Twin Lakes, Wis.
Fitch Ellis B. Austin
Fitch F. L. Mrs. 631 Washington boul.

Fitch Harriet H. Miss, Evanston
Fitch Henry S. 2827 Michigan av. *Chi.*,
　U.L.
Fitch Jane L. Mrs. 3159 Indiana av.
Fitch John W. 610 Englewood av.
Fitch Julian R. Capt. Evanston
Fitch Walter M. Dr. 645 W. Monroe
Fittz Jane P. Mrs. 1616 W. Adams
Fitzgerald Henry J. 11 Astor
Fitzgerald J. W. 3100 Groveland av.
Fitzgerald Richard, 4720 Prairie av. *W.P.*
Fitzgerald William, 2616 Indiana av.
Fitzgerald William H. 2616 Indiana av.
FitzHugh Carter H. Lake Forest. *Chi.*
Fitzpatrick James, Revere house
Fitzpatrick John Mrs. 326 Centre av.
Fitzpatrick P. H. Mrs. 482 W. Congress
FitzRandolph Emerson L. 2146 Kenmore
　av.
Fitzsimmons Arthur N. 732 Winthrop av.
FitzSimons Chas. 161 Ashland boul. *Ill.*,
　U.L.
Fitzwilliam F. J. 4824 Vincennes av.
Fizette Charles E. 3739 Indiana av.
Flagg Elmer T. 14 Woodland Park
Flagg George W. 762 Greenleaf av.
Flagg Luther N. 7216 Jeffery av
Flagg William H. 14 Woodland Park
　C.A., W.P.
Flagg W. F. 4626 Champlain av.
Flagler Samuel A. Morton Park
Flagler William B. Morton Park
Flanagan A. M. Miss, 415 N. State
Flanagan Joseph E. 2846 N. Hermitage
　av.
Flanders John J. Glencoe. *C.A.*
Flanigan James, 2210 Kenmore av.
Flannery D. Franklin 2755 Kenmore av.
　Ill.
Flannery John L. 1854 Oakdale av. *C.A.*
Flavin Michael D. 3815 Vincennes av.
Fleet A. T. Col. Hotel Del Prado
Fleet Geo. Stanley, 1927 Calumet av.
　W.P.
Fleetwood Charles, 608 Division. *Cal.*
Fleetwood Stanley, 415 N. State
Fleig Albert E. 955 Cuyler av.
Fleischer Charles H. 21 LeMoyne
Fleischmann Arthur J. 1851 Barry av.
Fleischmann Joseph, 1851 Barry av.
Fleishman M. S. 4753 Champlain av.
　Lksd.
Fleishman S. M. Mrs. 3207 Calumet av.
Fleming E. K. 3129 Dover
Fleming George A. 4023 Indiana av.
Fleming Isaac A. 225, 74th
Fleming James D. 3851 Ellis av.
Fleming John C. 5505 Cornell av. *Chi.*,
　U.L.
Fleming John T. 444 Ashland boul.
Fleming Josiah C. 545 W. 62d
Fleming Patrick H. 444 Ashland boul.
Fleming Robert Mrs. 4003 Drexel boul.
Fleming Robert H. Calumet club. *Cal.*,
　Chi., W.P.
Fleming William, Auditorium hotel

Fleming Wm. J. 654 Cleveland av.
Fleming William J. 4023 Indiana av.
Fleming W. H. 6336 Greenwood av.
Flemming Alice Mrs. Austin
Flemming Jeffry Dr. Austin
Flentye William H. 608 Lasalle av.
Flershem Albertine W. Miss, 285 Lake
　View av.
Flershem G. T. 3017 South Park av.
　　　Sum. res. Highwood, Ill.
Flershem LemWhitney,285 LakeView av.
　C.A., W.P.
Flershem Rudolph B. 285 Lake View av.
Flesh Bertha S. Mrs. 125 E. Pearson
Flesheim Edna Miss, Evanston
Fletcher Archibald W. Highland Park
Fletcher D. L. Mrs. 6147 Monroe av.
Fletcher F. A. Avenue house, Evanston
Fletcher Moses M. 640 N. Wells
Fletcher Robert C. Evanston
Fletcher R. S. Elmhurst
Fletcher Wm. Meade, 130, 50th. *Chi.*,
　W.P.
Flinn Charles B. Oak Park
Flinn Wm. W. Highland Park
Flint Edward P. 1724 York pl.
Flint Franklin F. Mrs. Highland Park
Flint F. W. 4259 Grand boul.
Flint Hale L. 5203 Madison av.
Floersheim Jacob, 4336 Forrestville av.
　Lksd.
Flonacher Edward, 3422 Prairie av.
Flonacher Henry C. Lexington hotel.
　Stan.
Flood Frank J. 3121 Vernon av.
Flood J. Ramsay Dr. 5320 Jefferson av.
Flood Ned A. 5538 Washington av.
Flood Robert D. 5320 Jefferson av.
Flood Samuel D. 5320 Jefferson av.
Flood Thomas H. 3121 Vernon av.
Florance William Mrs. Irving Park
Florey Genaro, 580 W. Madison. *Irq.*
Florsheim Augustus, 4114 Grand boul.
Florsheim Edson S. 4114 Grand boul.
Florsheim Felix, 3143 Michigan av. *Stan.*
Florsheim Henrietta Mrs. 3143 Michigan
　av.
Florsheim Isaac S. 4913 Grand boul.
Florsheim J. Mrs. 606 Lasalle av.
Florsheim M. S. 3356 SouthPark av. *Stan.*
Florsheim Norman S. 4913 Grand boul.
　Stan.
Florsheim Sidney E. 4913 Grand boul.
Florsheim Simon, 4913 Grand boul. *Stan.*
Florsheim Wilbur I. 4114 Grand boul.
Flournoy T. S. Granada hotel
Flower Elliott, 6538 Kimbark av. *Chi.*,
　U.L.
Flower James M. Virginia hotel. *Chi.*,
　U.L.
Flower Louis B. 1823 Aldine av. *Univ.*
Flower Samuel, 3647 Forest av.
Flower T. E. Mrs. 83 DeKalb
Floyd Frank,4650 Drexel boul. *Chi., W.P*
Floyd Helen C. Mrs. Highland Park.
Floyd John Dr. 237 Erie
Floyd John R. 780 North Park av.

Floyd P. Mrs. 2001 Michigan av.
Flynn Patrick J. 411 W. Garfield boul.
Foehringer Frederick W. 701 Orchard
Fogarty F. H. 769 Warren av.
Fogg Edward S. 5855 Wabash av.
Fogg Simon F. 236, 53d
F ley Harry B. 438 Belden av.
Foley John B. 1749 Deming pl. *C.A.*
      Sum. res. Cedar Lake, Wis.
Foley Louisa W. Mrs. 612 Washington
    boul.
Foley Michael, Evanston
Foley Nellie Miss, 3100 Groveland av.
Foley Walter, LaGrange
Foley William C. 4635 Grand boul.
Follansbee Charles Mrs. 4545 Greenwood
    av.
Follansbee Charles E. 4515 Ellis av. *U.L.*
Follansbee Frank H. 2301 Calumet av.
Follansbee George A. 2342 Indiana av.
    U.L.
Follansbee M. D. 2342 Indiana av. *Univ.*
Follansbee W. F. Dr. 52 Walton pl.
Follett Nathan, 1121 Lunt av.
Follette W. A. LaGrange
Folsom O. W. Mrs. 606, 44th
Folsom Richard, 57 Lake Shore drive
Foltz Edna Mrs. 361 Ontario
Foltz Fred L. 47 Astor
Foltz Louise Miss, 47 Astor
Fonda David B. Dr. Jefferson Park
Foote Apollos D. 3222 Rhodes av.
Foote Charles H. 4842 Washington av.
Foote Delevan S. 305 Webster av.
Foote D. C. 305 Webster av.
Foote Edgar S. 3824 Ridge av.
Foote Elizabeth Miss, 104 Lincoln Park
    boul.
Foote Erastus jr. 1634 Prairie av. *U.L.*
Foote F. H. 4530 Lake av.
Foote Howard W. 6067 Jefferson av.
Foote John B. Norwood Park
Foote Mark, Irving Park
Foote W. C. 305 Webster av.
Forbes Alexander, 197, 47th
Forbes Allen B. 197, 47th. *U.L.*
Forbes A. M. 650 W. Monroe. *Ill.*
Forbes Daniel, 1379 Washington boul.
Forbes Fred A. 650 W. Monroe. *Ill.*
Forbes F. Miss, New Hotel Holland
Forbes George S. 197, 47th
Forbes John A. 197, 47th
Forbes Robert R. 197. 47th
Forbush William, Oak Park
Ford Catherine Mrs. 549 Washington
    boul.
Ford Charles N. 981 W. Jackson boul.
Ford Cherry Miss, 6530 Monroe av.
Ford Frederick D. LaGrange
Ford George W. 6530 Monroe av.
Ford Henry B. 3741 Vincennes av. *Irq.*
Ford H. R. 4740 Langley av.
Ford H. S. The Arizona
Ford James L. 5413 Madison av.
Ford John, 1420 Michigan av.
Ford John S. 5616 Washington av.

Ford Mary H. Mrs. 4801 Lake av.
Ford Robert Floyd, 213, 42d
Ford Thomas P. Austin
Ford William J. Austin
Ford W. H. 6340 Greenwood av.
Fordham Arthur John Sidney, Evanston
Fordham Guy Hampdon, Evanston
Fordyce Edmond A. 1947 Deming pl.
Fordyce Homer G. New Hotel Holland
    Sum. res. Spring Lake, Mich.
Foreman David H. 3417 Prairie av.
Foreman Edward H. 3358 South Park av.
    Stan.
Foreman Edwin G. 3750 Michigan av.
    Stan.
Foreman Henry, 3417 Prairie av.
Foreman Henry G. Lakota hotel. *Stan.*,
    U.L., W.P.
Foreman Isaac H. 547, 44th. *Stan.*
Foreman Mary Mrs. 3412 Vernon av.
Foreman Milton J. 3412 Vernon av. *C.A.*,
    Stan.
Foreman Oscar G. 3415 Michigan av. *Irq.*,
    Stan., U.L.
Foreman Samuel H. 3418 Vernon av. *Stan.*
Foresman H. A. 166, 51st
Foresman Robert, 5603 Madison av.
Foresman W. Coates, 5657 Washington
    av. *C.A.*
Forester E. E. Mrs. 3203 South Park av.
Forester George L. 229, 54th
Forgan David R. Evanston
Forgan James B. 2 Ritchie ct. *U.L.*
Forgan Robert D. 2 Ritchie ct.
Forgan Wilhelmina Miss, 2 Ritchie ct.
Forline Hamilton Dr. 5515 Woodlawn av.
Forman Edward Mrs. 2024 Indiana av.
Forman John Mrs. Evanston
Formhals O. G. 225 Dearborn av.
Forrest Alfred E. 4500 Woodlawn av.
Forrest Frank J. 146, 42d pl.
Forrest George D. La Grange
Forrest Mary Gates Mrs. 612 W. Jackson
    boul.
Forrest Rebecca M. Mrs. 4118 Newgart
    av.
Forrest Thomas L. 419 Center
Forrest William G. 612 W. Jackson boul.
Forrest William S. 3264 Groveland av.
Forrester Charles W. Capt. Hotel Metro-
    pole
Forrester Jessie G. Dr. 479 Fullerton av.
Forrester Rose Mrs. 3623 Ellis Park
Forrey Frank M. Evanston
Forsinger John W. 6440 Minerva av. *C.A.*
Forsman Susan T. Mrs. 45, 46th
Forster Charles F 5420 Washington av.
Forsyth Clarence, 40 Woodland Park
Forsyth George H. 14 Ritchie ct. *Univ.*
Forsyth George W. 1915 Michigan av.
Forsyth H. H. 14 Ritchie ct.
Forsyth Jacob, 1915 Michigan av.
Forsyth James, Riverside
Forsyth John J. 1915 Michigan av. *W.P.*
Forsyth Joseph F. Glencoe
Forsyth J. E. 3763 Ellis av.

Forsyth Kitty G. Mrs. 101 Lincoln Park boul.
Forsyth Lucy H. Mrs. 30 Woodland Park
Forsyth Mark J. Mrs. 660 W. Adams
Forsyth Oliver O. 1915 Michigan av.
Forsyth Robert, 307 N. Clark. *Chi.*, *Un.*, *W.P.*
Forsyth Wellington B. 4465 Oakenwald av.
Forsyth W. Holmes, 14 Ritchie ct. *Univ.*
Forsyth W. K. 3113 Forest av.
Fort Gerrit, 4060 Ellis av.
Fort Hiram P. 4060 Ellis av.
Fort James G. 4060 Ellis av.
Fort Phoebe I. Miss, 6317 Lexington av.
Fortin George, 408, 41st
Fortin Nelson, 5422 Washington av. *C.A.*
Fortune John, 526 W. Jackson boul.
Fortune Peter. 258 Park av.
Fortune Thomas F. 526 W. Jackson boul.
Fortune William J. 526 W. Jackson boul.
Foskett Andrew H. 1542 Fulton
Foskett Charles M. 554 W. Jackson boul *Ill.*
Fosner W. H. LaGrange
Foss Agnes E. Mrs. 4656 Indiana av.
Foss Eliza Mrs. 475 W. Monroe
Foss Fred. D. 447 W. Monroe
Foss George E. 47 Gordon Terrace. *U.L.*
Foss George Edmund, 47 Gordon Terrace
Foss Horace B. 475 W. Monroe
Foss John P. 447 W. Monroe
Foss Sylvester D. 3750 Grand boul.
Foss William W. 15 Loomis
Foss Willis J. 3750 Grand boul.
Foster Adelbert M. Evanston
Foster Albert Volney, Evanston
Foster A. H. Dr. 779 W. Monroe
Foster Blackman N. 21 St. John's ct.
Foster Charles K. 401 N. State
Foster Charles S. 779 W. Monroe
Foster Chauncy W. 4324 Prairie av.
Foster Eva C. Miss, Evanston
Foster E. E. 599 Dearborn av.
Foster Freliug C. 158 Honore
Foster F. H. Dr. 73 Lake View av. *C.A.*
Foster George, 398 Belden av.
Foster George A. Evanston.
Foster George B. 527 Lasalle av.
Foster George B. 5535 Lexington av.
Foster George H. Mrs. Evanston
Foster G. F. Evanston
Foster Hannah R. Mrs. 6557 Kimbark av.
Foster Henry A. 3027 Vernon av. *C.A.*
Foster Henry C. 464 Farwell av.
Foster Jacob T. Col. 231, 42d
Foster John W. Mrs. 143 Oakwood boul.
Foster J. M. Dr. 6315 Yale
Foster M. 4414 Langley av.
Foster N. S. Mrs. 789 Fullerton av.
Foster Orrington C. 527 Lasalle av.
Foster Richard, Hotel Windermere
Foster Richard N. Dr. 553 W. Jackson boul. *Ill.* Sum. res. Lake Geneva, Wis.
Foster Seaward, Austin

Foster Stephen A. 4528 Oakenwald av. *Univ.*
Foster S. B. Mrs. 3923 Grand boul.
Foster Thomas, 459 Bowen av.
Foster Volney W. Evanston. *U.L.*
Foster William A. 4448 Vincennes av.
Foster William A. Mrs. 829, 50th
Foster William Elmore, 829, 50th, *U.L.*
Foster William H. 464 Farwell av.
Foulke Mary S. Mrs. 4210 Berkeley av.
Foulke William H. 6351 Star av.
Fountain Martin Alford, 3547 Ellis av.
Fowle E. H. Mrs. Evanston
Fowle Fred L. 403 W. 64th
Fowler Bernard, 4561 Lake av.
Fowler Charles E. 6033 Indiana av.
Fowler Charles H. Hotel Hayes
Fowler Ernest S. Oak Park
Fowler E. W. 295 S. Irving av.
Fowler Frank A. 4402 Greenwood av.
Fowler Frank T. 695 Washington boul. *Ill.*
Fowler George J. 295 S. Irving av.
Fowler G. A. Chicago Athletic Assn.
Fowler Harriet A. Mrs. 1210 Sheffield av.
Fowler John E. 623 Ashland av.
Fowler John P. 6565 Yale
Fowler Samuel W. 295 S. Irving av.
Fowler William A. 6417 Kimbark av.
Fowler William F. Dr. 2346 Calumet av. *C.A.*
Fox Alpheus, 533 S. Normal Parkway
Fox Bonham M. 3339 Rhodes av.
Fox Charles Mrs. Hinsdale
Fox Clarence E. Oak Park
Fox D. F. Rev. 1294 Wilcox av.
Fox Frank W. Norwood Park
Fox Fred H. 1817 Barry av.
Fox G. H. 3156 Prairie av.
Fox G. M. Dr. LaGrange
Fox Harriet Magee Dr. 3339 Rhodes av.
Fox Harry, 839 W. Monroe
Fox Harry Mrs. 1817 Barry av.
Fox Harvey, 3339 Rhodes av.
Fox Heman, Hinsdale
Fox James B. Mrs. 1856 Arlington pl.
Fox John V. 1856 Arlington pl. *C.A.*
Fox Julius B. 555 Dearborn av.
Fox J. J. Mrs. 3237 Michigan av.
Fox Leo, 3355 South Park av. *Stan.*
Fox O. 1628 Indiana av.
Fox O. L. 77, 20th
Fox Robert R. 1119 S. Ridgeway av.
Fox Rose Miss, 160, 30th
Fox Thomas E. 1856 Arlington pl.
Fox Thomas J. 3237 Michigan av.
Fox Walter H. Dr. 217½ Belden av.
Fox Will A. 535 S. Normal Parkway
Fox William F. 5736 Rosalie ct.
Fox William O. Hinsdale
Foxwell Mabel H. Mrs. 2518 Michigan av.
Foye Jeanette W. 23, 35th
Fraenkel Theo. O. 2124 Michigan av.
Frailey William P. 858 Washington boul.
Frake James, 625 Fulton. *Ill.*
Fraley Gassner F. 4534 Lake av.

Fraley James B. 4534 Lake av.
Fralick Raiph S. 5549 Woodlawn av.
Framhein Louis W. 325, 24th
France R. E. Mrs. Evanston
Franche Darius C. Longwood, *C.A.*, *Irq.*
Franchere Gabriel, 406 Ashland boul.
Francis Edward, Austin
Francis Edward C. 594, 46th
Francis George F. 17 Kemper pl.
Francis James L. 7757 Lowe av.
Francis Joseph E. 6136 Monroe av.
Francis Joseph H. 1616 W. Adams
Francis J. R. 40 Loomis
Francis Robert W. Leland hotel
Francis William, 183 S. Hoyne av.
Frank Abraham I. 25 Wisconsin
Frank Daniel, 3421 South Park av.
Frank David Mrs. 3421 South Park av.
Frank David, 3255 Wabash av. *Lksd.*
Frank David L. 547, 44th. *Stan.*
Frank Edwin B. 4715 Prairie av.
Frank Emanuel J. Lakota hotel, *Stan.*
Frank Emma Mrs. 3217 South Park av.
Frank Frederick G. 3262 Groveland av.
　Stan.
Frank Henry L. 1608 Prairie av.
Frank Herman, 4060 Lake av.
Frank H. A. North Shore hotel
Frank I. M. 3255 Wabash av. *Lksd.*
Frank Jacob Dr. 17 Lincoln av.
Frank Joseph, Hotel Metropole. *Stan.*
Frank Joseph Mrs. Lakota hotel
Frank Joseph H. 233 Hampden ct.
Frank Louis, 3614 Prairie av. *Stan.*
Frank Louise E. Mrs. 3219 Michigan av.
Frank Marcus, 3614 Prairie av.
Frank Martin, 3844 Lake av.
Frank Max, 4516 Drexel boul. *Stan.*
Frank Mortimer, 233 Hampden ct.
Frank Nathan, 3927½ Vincennes av.
Frank Robert J. 1037 Early av.
Frankenthal Charles E. 4506 Indiana av.
　Stan.
Frankenthal Emanuel, 3236 Michigan av.
　Stan., W.P.
Frankenthal Lester Dr. 3236 Michigan av.
　Stan.
Frankfurter Heury, 2139 Kenmore av.
Frankhauser E. Isaiah, 2442 Lakewood
　av.
Frankland Alexander J. The Arizona
Frankland A. E. Mrs. 4718 Champlain av.
Frankland E. The Arizona
Frankland Morris J. 4718 Champlain av.
Franklin Charles P. 4516 Ellis av.
Franklin George L. 6413 Ingleside av.
Franklin Percy R. Mrs. 4516 Ellis av.
Franklin Samuel, Hotel del Prado, *Lksd.*
Franks Jacob, 3354 Wabash av. *Irq., Lksd.*
Frantz Mary E. Miss, 3639 Prairie av.
Franz Hugo, 1649 Barry av.
Fraser Daniel A. 5338 Washington av.
Fraser David R. 1336 Washington boul.
　Ill.
Fraser Flora Mrs. 3226 Groveland av.
Fraser Hamilton, 5729 Rosalie ct.

Fraser Norman D. 1241 Washington boul
　C.A., Ill., U.L.
Fraser William E. Dr. 5490 Washington
　av.
Frasher Edward S. 5100 Lake av.
Frasher John E. L. 4919 Lake av.
Frasher John S. The Kenwood. *C.A.*
Frater William, Evanston
Frawley M. J. Mrs. 260 S. Campbell av.
Frazer G. G. Mrs. The Arizona
Frazer S. M. Mrs. 4064 Michigan Terrace
Frazier Charles E. Austin
Frazier Frank D. Evanston
Frazier Frank P. Evanston, *U.L.*
Frazier George E. Morgan Park
Fredenhagen F. P. LaGrange
Frederick Emma D. Mrs. 3001 Calumet
　av.
Frederick Gilbert Rev. 418 W. 61st
Fredericks Enoch M. Dr. 2127 Dover
Fredericks Frank, Riverside
Fredericks Frank jr. Riverside
Free Esther E. Mrs. 3716 Lake av.
Free John H. 306 West ct
Free William C. 3716 Lake av. *C.A.*
Freedman J. H. Hotel Del Prado
Freehling Isaac, 3604 Prairie av. *Lksd.*
Freehling Julius, 3604 Prairie av.
Freehling Moses 514 Webster av.
Freehling Solomon, 3604 Prairie av.
　Lksd.
Freeman Anthony, 678 Fullerton av.
Freeman A. B. Dr. Hinsdale
Freeman A. W. Mrs. 9 Aldine sq.
Freeman Chester H. 1069 Winona av.
Freeman C. A. Mrs. 10 Ritchie ct.
Freeman D. B. Dr. 4000 Drexel boul.
Freeman Emma Blanche Miss, 1069 Win-
　ona av.
Freeman F. D. 549 Dearborn av.
Freeman Henry A. Dr. Evanston
Freeman Henry H. 3245 South Park av.
　Lksd.
Freeman Henry V. Judge 5760 Woodlawn
　av. *Univ.*
Freeman Howard 9 Aldine sq.
Freeman I. A. Dr. 4438 Berkeley av.
Freeman James C. Evanston
Freeman Jay C. Austin
Freeman John Mrs. 231 Hampden ct.
Freeman John L. Oak Park
Freeman Lemuel H. 9 Aldine sq.
Freeman Meyer M. 4936 Vincennes av.
　Lksd.
Freeman M. Mrs. 3245 South Park av.
Freeman N. O. Rev. Morgan Park
Freeman William H. Hinsdale
Freeman William S. 356, 51st
Freeman Windsor P. Austin
Freer Catherine Mrs. 288 Huron
Freer Cora F. Miss, Ohio ne. cor. N. State
Freer L. H. LaGrange
Freer Nathan M. Oak Park
Freer Otto T., M.D. 288 Huron
Freiberg Charles F. Dr. 4630 Grand boul
Freiberg Frederick, 1217 Michigan av.

Freiberg Julius, 1217 Michigan av.
Freiberger Edward, 3225 Vernon av.
Freiberger Leon H. 3026 Indiana av.
Freiberger Leopold, 3225 Vernon av.
Freiberger M. L. 3026 Indiana av. *Lksd.*
French Byron W. 5124 Jefferson av.
French Charles M. 6148 Kimbark av.
French Clinton K. Evanston
French Edgar, 791 Warren av. *Ill.*
French Frederick E. Greenwood Inn,
  Evanston
French Garrie S. 7443 Bond av.
French George B. Virginia hotel. *Chi.*
  C.A. · ··
French George E. Lieut. Fort Sheridan
French George G. Dr. Lake Forest
French George H. Mrs. 5422 Cornell av.
French George R. 622, 46th pl.
French George T. 6610 Yale
French G. M. Tracy
French H   et N. Mrs. 505 W. Jackson
  boul.· arri
French Henry C. Evanston
French John W. LaGrange
French J. C. Mrs. 654 Washington boul.
French Laura Mrs. 2887 Sheridan rd.
French Laura Birney Mrs. 2517 Kenmore
  av.
French L. M. 4162 Lake av.
French Martha E. Miss. 31 Ashland boul.
French Maurice P. 2469 Lakewood av.
French Orvis, Greenwood Inn, Evanston
French O. Clinton, Evanston
French Rensellaer W. Rev. 301 S. Win-
  chester av.
French Samuel A, 7443 Bond av.
French Samuel M. Dr. 64, 23d
French Sanford B. 64 Warren av.
French Stuart W. 5100 Hibbard av.
French S. T. Evanston. *Univ.*
French Walter, 725 W. 61st
French Walter L. 6345 Greenwood av.
French William H. 407 Huron
French W. H. Oak Park, *Ill.*
French W. L. Revere house
French W. L. Mrs. 3158 South Park av.
French W. M. R. Longwood. *U.L.*
Frendenthal J. H. 1683 Barry av.
Frensdorf Edward, 3145 Forest av. *Lksd.*
Frensdorf Samuel, 3145 Forest av. *Lksd.*
Frenz E. Miss, 52 Walton pl.
Freschl William, Oakland hotel
Freshman Arnold, 4351 Vincennes av.
  C.A., *Lksd.*
Fretts George W. 677, 48th
Fretts Levi A. 3743 Vincennes av.
Freudenthal Joseph, 3403 Forest av. *Stan.*
Freund Abraham L., M. D. 4511 Indiana
  av.
Freund Charles E. 613 N. Wells
Freund Ernest Dr. 5730 Woodlawn av.
  Univ.
Freund Gustav, 3221 Vernon av. *Stan.*
Freund Herman, 460 N. Wells
Freund William, 460 N. Wells
Frey Emma B. Mrs. Evanston

Freymuth William C. River Forest
Freytag Moritz, 700 N. Wells
Frick John G. 424 Oak
Fricke G. H. Dr. Park Ridge
Fricke William G. Oak Park
Friedel Marcella Miss, Auditorium Hote.
Friedenthal Hulda Miss, Oakland hotel
Friedlander Edward D. 4814 Forrestville
  av,
Friedlander Gustav, 355 Ashland boul.
Friedlander Harry D. 3323 Vernon av.
Friedlander Jacob, 515, 44th pl.
Friedlander Leon Mrs. 3323 Vernon av.
Friedlander Max, 4752 Champlain av.
Friedlander Samuel, 546 Cleveland av.
Friedman Abraham B. 3215 Rhodes av.
  Stan.
Friedman Burnett, 633 Washington boul.
Friedman Emanuel B. 943 W. Monroe
Friedman Isaac K. 5132 East End av.
Friedman Jacob, 4446 Berkeley av. *Stan.*
Friedman Jennie Miss, 633 Washington
  boul.
Friedman Joseph N. 542, 44th. *Stan.*
Friedman J. H. Mrs. Hotel Del Prado ·
Friedman Leopold,633 Washington boul.
Friedman Louis J. Hotel Del Prado.
  · *Lksd.*
Friedman Monroe J. 4559 Lake av. *Stan.*
Friedman Nathan, 3215 Rhodes av.
Friedman Oscar J. 5132 East End av.
  Stan.
Friedman S. 3550 Prairie av. ·
Friedman S. Mrs. 4446 Berkeley av.
Friedman William, 633 Washington boul.
Friel E. J. Revere house
Friemann John, 4035 Southport av.
Friend Adelaide L. Miss, 3219 Michigan
  av.
Friend Charles, 4445 Calumet av. *Lksd.*
Friend Edward, 2623 Calumet av. *Stan.*
Friend Emil, 3601 Vincennes av.
Friend Henry, 3419 Forest av. *Lksd.*
Friend Nathan, 358, 37th. *Lksd.*
Friend Oscar A. Revere house. *Lksd.*
Friend Samuel, 2948 Groveland av. *Lksd*
Friend William Mrs. 2623 Calumet av.
Friendly Rosa Mrs. 2623 Calumet av.
Friestedt L. P. 170 S. Central Park av.
Frink George M. Austin
Frink Henry F. Austin. *C.A.*
Frink William H. 6450 Stewart av.
Frisbee P. W. Mrs. 19 Scott
Frische Christopher, 543 Larrabee
Frische Henry W. 543 Larrabee
Fritts D. H. 233 Park av.
Fritts G. B. 106 Park av.
Fritts Louis C. Dr. 21 Ashland boul.
Fritz Harry A. 4714 Evans av.
Frohman Fred. 3530 Forest av. *Lksd.*
Frohman Sarah Mrs. 3530 Forest av.
Frommann Emil H. 207 Belden av.
Froscher Adolph, Hinsdale
Frost Abel H. Oak Park
Frost Albert C. 1845 Arlington pl. *U.L.* ·
Frost Albert E. 4835 Langley av.

Frost Charles S. Lake Forest. *U.L*
Frost David jr. 2675 N. Robey
Frost Edward Inglis, 32 Walton pl. *Un.*
        Sum. res. Wheaton
Frost Frank H. 2430 N. Hermitage av.
Frost J. M. Hinsdale
Frost R. Chester; 600, 60th
Frost Walter A. 3360 Calumet av. *C.A.*
Frost Z. J. Austin
Frothingham H. H. Dr. 5200 East End av. *C.A.*
Frothingham James Rev. 527 Kenwood terrace
Frothingham M. F. D. Miss, 527 Kenwood terrace
Frowe Jennie Mrs. Evanston
Fry George C. 5121 Kimbark av. *U.L.*
Fry Harriet E. Mrs. 17 Gordon Terrace
Fry Henry T. 2383 Clarendon av.
Fry I. H. 3111 Groveland av.
Fry Thomas E. 2387 Clarendon av.
Frye F. E. Mrs. 4366 Oakenwald av.
Fuelling John L. 6514 Kimbark av.
Fuelling Sophia Miss. 6514 Kimbark av.
Fuess Lewis Mrs. 143 Oakwood boul.
Fuhring William A. 107 Evanston av.
Fulghum William, 367 Bowen av.
Fullagar Mary Miss, Evanston
Fullen Charles D. 5337 Washington av.
Fullenwider James A. 487, 62d
Fuller Alonzo M. 4832 Ellis av.
Fuller Charles, 24 Scott
Fuller Charles G. Dr. Evanston
Fuller Charles H. 370 Warren av. *C.A., U.L.*
Fuller Frank Hoyt, 4832 Ellis av. *W.P.*
Fuller Frank R. 10 Astor
Fuller Fred L. 445 Washington boul. *Ill.*
Fuller George A. 4353 Drexel boul. *C.A., Un., U.L., W.P.*
Fuller George E. Hinsdale
Fuller George W. Mrs. 2831 Prairie av.
Fuller Grace Miss, Glencoe
Fuller G. Edward, Union League Club
Fuller Henry B. 2831 Prairie av.
Fuller Henry C. 571 W. Congress. *U.L.*
Fuller Henry M. 325 Dearborn av.
Fuller Judson M. Oak Park
Fuller LeRoy W. 1919 Prairie av. *Cal., Chi., W.P.*
Fuller Luther C. 370 Warren av.
Fuller L. Hulbert Dr. 6741 Wentworth av.
Fuller M. E. Mrs. 32 Warren av.
Fuller Oliver F. 329 Dearborn av.
Fuller S. R. Mrs. 4713 Kimbark av.
Fuller William Dr. 4707 Calumet av.
Fuller William A. 2913 Michigan av. *Chi., U.L.*
Fullerton Charles W. 628 Dearborn av. *C.A., Chi., Un., Univ., W.P.*
        Sum. res. Highland Park
Fullerton Margaret Miss. 1805 Barry av.
Fulton Arthur. 1176 Washington boul.
Fulton Clair W. 5227 Kimbark av.
Fulton Fred F. 5227 Kimbark av.
Fulton Frederick R. 52 Bellevue pl.

Fulton Henry A. Hinsdale
Fulton H. L. LaGrange
Fulton James T. 4450 Sidney av.
Fulton Jefferson L 342 Ashland boul. *Ill., U.L.*
Fulton John A. 1532 W. Monroe
Fulton Joseph F. 5227 Kimbark av.
Fulton Lester B. 342 Ashland boul.
Fulton T. M. Mrs. 5344 Jefferson av.
Fulton W. A. 6430 Greenwood av.
Fulwiler F. A. 225 Dearborn av.
Funck Pierre, 1471 Edgecomb ct.
Funk C. A. Chicago Beach hotel, *C.A.*
Funk F. A. Mrs. 1533 Fulton
Funkhouser M. L. C. 271 Oakwood boul. *C.A., U.L.*
Furbeck George Warren, Oak Park
Furbeck J. Philip, Oak Park
Furbeck R. J. Oak Park
        Sum. res. Lake Geneva, Wis.
Furbeck Warren Fuller, Oak Park, *U.L.*
Furber Frank I. 4859 Madison av.
Furber Henry J. Lakota hotel
Furber Henry J. jr. Lakota hotel, *Irq.*
Furlong John, Evanston
Furlong John, Oak Park
Furlong Moses Dr. 228, 47th
Furlong Walter H. 6942 Yale
Furman Jeanie Miss, Wilmette
Furman Nettie Miss, Wilmette
Furman William C. 3416 South Park av.
Furness William Eliot 417 Orchard, *Univ.*
Furry Frank W. 4854 Prairie av. *C.A.*
Furst Charles J. 3352 Calumet av.
Furst Conrad, 84 Astor
Furst Edward A. 1818 Arlington pl. *C.A.*
Furst George C. 37 Centre av.
Furst Henry, 505 Ashland boul.
Furst Henry jr. 505 Ashland boul.
Furst William C. 482½ Lasalle av.
Furthmann Edmund, 575 Orchard
Futterer Gustav Dr. 716 Fullerton av.
Fyfe George, 1176 Washington boul.
Fyfe William C. 2358 Indiana av.
Fyffe Colin H. 421 The Plaza
Fyffe John L. Evanston
Fyffe William J. 452 Elm, *C.A.*

GABRIEL C. H. 3625 Ellis av.
   Gaddis George E. 55, 36th
Gade Frederick H. 381 Superior. *Univ.*
Gadsden James S. 949 W. Harrison. *Ill.*
Gage Albert S. The Wellington, *Cal., Chi. C.A., W.P.*
Gage August N. Wilmette
Gage Edward B. Wilmette, *W.P.*
Gage Edward M. 166, 51st
Gage Eli A. 1886 Diversey
Gage Eliphalet B. The Arizona. *Chi.*
Gage E. C. Dr. 3100 Groveland av.
Gage Frank N. 4028 Ellis av.
Gage Harley C. 4001 Grand boul.
Gage Helen S. Mrs. Wilmette
Gage Henry H. Evanston
Gage Henry H. Wilmette

Gage John S. Wilmette
Gage Mary T. Mrs. Morgan Park
Gage Seth, 325 Michigan av.
Gahan Thomas, 4914 Michigan av.
Gail George F. 427 Huron
Gaines Egbert S. Evanston
Gaither Otho S. 4455 Champlain av.
Galbraith Charles W. 2293 N. Paulina
Galbraith Stewart, 412 Winthrop av.
Galbraith T. B. 6648 Harvard av.
Gale D. W. Mrs. 3845 Ellis av.
Gale E. Vincent, 397 Ontario
Gale Fred, 426 Warren av.
Gale Fred M. 426 Warren av.
Gale H. G. 5826 Washington av.
Gale Stephen F. Hotel Metropole
Gale Thomas H. Oak Park
Gale Walter H. Oak Park
Gale William M. Evanston
Gale Willis H. Dr. 3352 Rhodes av.
Gale W. H. Hyde Park hotel
Gall Barbara Mrs. 930 Warner av.
Gall Charles H. 930 Warner av.
Gall George E. 964 Warner av.
Gall William F. 930 Warner av.
Gallagher C. Mrs. 385 Oak
Gallagher Daniel J. 225 Dearborn av. *Ill.*
Gallagher Frank J. 3165 Beacon
Gallagher J. P. Hotel Del Prado
Gallaway William C. 156 Dearborn av.
Gallaway William T. 156 Dearborn av.
Gallear David O. 775 Larrabee
Gallenkamp W. H. 214 Goethe
Gallery Daniel J. 260 Lasalle av.
Gallery Daniel V. 405 The Plaza
Gallie Don M. Dr. 906 Walnut
Galloway A. J. 7600 Emerald av.
Galloway Charles, 929 Greenleaf av.
Galloway David H. Dr. 200 Oakwood
  boul.
Galloway James B. 7600 Emerald av. *Univ.*
Gallup Agnes Miss, 456 Elm
Gallup Benjamin E. Mrs. 1710 Indiana av.
Gallup David L. 456 Elm
Gallup Edward B. 396 S. Paulina
Gallup O. D. S. Park Ridge
Galpin Homer K. 729 W. Monroe
Galpin H. B. 729 W. Monroe
Galt A. T. 550 Dearborn av.
Galt Hubert, 351 Chestnut. *Un.*
Galvin James, 4322 Indiana av.
Galvin John C. Monoken Club
Gamble Edwin H. Evanston
Gamble William C. 401 N. State. *Univ.*
Gamer George W. 1065 N. Clark
Gamet A. E. 525 Racine av.
Gammans J. A. 6451 Kimbark av.
Gammon Charles D. Austin
Gandell M. K. 3100 Groveland av.
Gane Thomas F. 425 Lasalle av.
Gann David B. 5342 Cornell av.
Gannon Richard C. 52 Throop
Gannon Thomas Mrs. 3200 Michigan av.
Gano Charles D. 1886 Diversey
Gans Leopold, 3945 Ellis av. *Lksd.*
Gans Samuel, 3932 Lake av. *Lksd.*

Ganse H. D. Mrs. 251 Belden av.
Gantt I. W. Morgan Park
Garceau Alexander E. Dr. 5213 Kimbark
  av.   Sum. res. San Mateo, Cal.
Garcelon C. A. 3730 Forest av.
Garcelon Duncan D. Oak Park
Garden Edward G. Mrs. 466 Fullerton av.
Gardin John E. Morton Park
Gardiner Edwin J. Dr. 85 Astor. *Univ.*
Gardiner Evelyn Miss, 2200 Prairie av.
Gardiner Fanny Hale Mrs. 2200 Prairie
  av.
Gardiner Frank H. Dr. 2436 Michigan av.
  Cal.
Gardiner Fred S. 2969 Kenmore av.
Gardiner James, Austin
Gardiner John C. 2597 N. Robey
Gardiner John D. Mrs. 2019 Michigan av
Gardner Addison L. 933 W. Monroe.
Gardner A. S. Mrs. Austin
Gardner Burt M. Evanston
Gardner David B. Avenue house, Evanston
Gardner Florence I. Mrs. 554, 45th
Gardner Frank G. 441 Sidney av.
Gardner Frank J. 228, 47th
Gardner Frederic W. 671, 48th pl. *C.A.*
Gardner Frederick, 4130 Ellis av. *C.A.*
Gardner George A. 190 Warren av.
Gardner George Cadogan, Hinsdale, *C.A.*
Gardner Harold M. Austin
Gardner Henry A. Hinsdale, *Univ.*
Gardner Horace C. 4448 Indiana av.
Gardner James C. Mrs. Evanston
Gardner James P. 4803 Greenwood av.
  C.A., Univ.
Gardner James W. Evanston
Gardner Katharine Miss, Lake Forest
Gardner Laura Mrs. Evanston
Gardner Peter G. LaGrange
Gardner S. P. Mrs. Hinsdale
Gardner S. S. Mrs. 190 Warren av.
Gardner Walter W. Austin
Gardner William, 1543 W. Monroe
Gardner William A. 2574 N. Hermitage
  av. *U.L.*
Gareau Cesaire, 875 W. Harrison
Garibaldi John G. 26 Astor
Garland D. F. 2411 Prairie av.
Garland Maria J. Mrs. Evanston
Garland M. A. Mrs. 2119 Calumet av.
Garland M. S. Mrs. 3150 Michigan av.
Garland Theodore W. 5029 Jefferson av.
Garneau Joseph, 35 E. Pearson. *Chi., W.P.*
Garner James B. 1630 Kenmore av.
Garner John P. Austin
Garnett Eugene, 3604 Grand boul.
Garnett Gwynn Judge, 3604 Grand boul.
Garnett Gwynn, jr. 3604 Grand boul.
Garnett John L. 3422 Vernon av.
Garnett Robert, 3604 Grand boul.
Garnett William, 3422 Vernon av.
Garnett William, 4450 Vincennes av. *U.L.*
Garnsey George O. 316 Oakwood boul.
Garrabrant Robert C. 5514 Monroe av.
Garrabrant Robert Tait, 5514 Monroe av.

Garraghan Edward F. 3424 Prairie av.
Garraghan Gilbert, 3424 Prairie av.
Garretson J. C. Mrs. 31 Roslyn pl.
Garrett Carlton M. 7216 Harvard av.
Garrett Myers A. 7216 Harvard av.
Garrett T. M. 301 Ontario, *Chi.*, *Un.*
Garrigue Rudolph H. 263, 53d
Garrison Marie Harrold Mrs. 3629 Ellis
    Park
Garrison Marshall, Evanston
Garrity Joseph Dr. 409 Dearborn av.
Garrity Patrick L. 409 Dearborn av.
Garrott F. L. Mrs. 751 Washington boul.
Gartside J. M. 4329 Drexel boul. *C.A.*,
    U.L.
Gartside William C. 6151 Ellis av.
Garty M. J. 3546 Ellis av.
Gartz Adolph F. 2723 Prairie av. *C.A.*,
    U.L.
Garvey Christopher A. 4728 Prairie av.
Garvy Mary A. Mrs. 60 Lytle
Garvy William J. 60 Lytle
Garwood Victor, 15 Roslyn pl.
Gary Elbert H. Wheaton, *C.A.*, *U.L.*
Gary George A. 7523 Stewart av.
Gary John W. 2107 Indiana av. *Cal.*, *Chi.*,
    W.P.
Gary Joseph E. Judge, 369 Ontario
Gasche Ferd G. 7212 Merrill av. .
Gascoigne James B. 6636 Harvard av.
Gascoigne John T. 6421 Stewart av.
Gascoigne L. M. Mrs. Evanston
Gascoigne William T. Evanston
Gaspard Philip H. Chicago Beach hotel,
    C.A.
Gasparo Jane Mrs. Austin
Gassette Norman T. Mrs. 5547 Washing-
    ton av.
Gast Engelbert, 2843 N. Ashland av.
Gately William, 5931 Eggleston av.
Gates Albert H. Avenue house, Evanston
Gates Albert R. 3847 Langley av.
Gates A. J. 2478 N. Paulina
Gates Charles G. 2440 Michigan av. *Cal.*,
    Chi., *C.A.*, *W.P.*
Gates Charles Horatio Mrs. 24 Walton
    p l.
Gates Charles M. 3434 Rhodes av.
Gates Elizabeth Mrs. Edgebrook
Gates Henry B. Wilmette
Gates H. S. The Hampden
Gates James L. 412 N. Normal Parkway
    Sum. res. East Gloucester, Mass.
Gates John D. 3212 Lake Park av.
Gates John W. 2440 Michigan av. *Cal.*,
    Chi., *C.A.*, *U.L.*, *W.P.*
Gates J. A. Clifton house
Gates J. H. 1205 Winthrop av.
Gates May E. Miss, 2430 N. Hermitage
    av.
Gates P. B. Hotel Metropole   -
Gates P. W. Evanston. *Ill.*
Gates Ralph, 4457 Ellis av.
Gates Ryerson D. Oak Park
Gates Walter S. Evanston
Gates William D. Hinsdale. *C.A.*

Gates William S. Dr. 2725 N. Lincoln
Gates William W. Evanston
Gathmann Louis, 46 Lincoln av.
Gattman Henry, 4760 Champlain av.
Gattman R. Mrs. 4760 Champlain av.
Gatzert August, 3422 Prairie av. *Stan.*
Gatzert Joseph L. 3628 Grand boul. *Stan.*
Gaudette William A. 2001 Michigan av.
Gaudreaux F. L. 2437 Indiana av.
Gauer August H. 347 Rush
Gauer Nicholas J. 347 Rush
Gauger John A. 4241 Drexel boul.
Gault T. H. 1680 W. Congress
Gaulter Frank J. 6914 Kimbark av.
Gaulter Fred E. 6914 Kimbark av.
Gaulter Mary Mrs. 6914 Kimbark av.
Gaunt Thomas, Evanston
Gaw William A. 405, 33d
Gay Orlando C. 4002 Lake av.
Gay Otis W. 302, 49th
Gay W. F. Revere house
Gaylord Albin P. 688, 48th. *C.A.*, *W.P.*
Gaylord A. A. Mrs. 3018 Prairie av.
Gaylord Edwin L. 2626 Prairie av. *C.A.*
Gaylord Frederic, Chicago Beach hotel
Gaylord Henry Mrs. 4942 Ellis av.
Gaylord Mary A. Mrs. 4337 Grand boul.
Gaylord Robert, 3018 Prairie av.
Gaylord Truman P. 610 Dearborn av.
Gaylord Willard S. 1638 Michigan av.
    Cal., *C.A.*, *W.P.*
Gaynor James A. 375 Warren av.
Gaynor Jessie L. Mrs. 3500 Ellis av.
Gazzolo Frank F. 524 W. Congress
Gear F. O. Hinsdale
Gear L. F. Mrs. 1738 Briar pl.
Gearing L. A. Wilmette
Geary Helen Miss, 4455 Drexel boul.
Geary John R. 3010 South Park av.
Geary J. F. 2960 Groveland av.
Geary Thomas F. 3010 South Park av.
Geary William T. 3010 South Park av.
Geary William V. 4221 Ellis av.
Gebhard Julius, 1519 Bradley pl.
Gebhart A. F. 341 Park av.
Gee W. S. Mrs. 5211 Hibbard av.
Geer David S. 178, 41st
Geer Ira Jewett, 240 Goethe
Gehlbach George W. 5755 Rosalie ct.
Gehr Arthur C. Riverside
Gehr Herbert B. Riverside
Gehr Phebe B. Mrs. Riverside
Gehr S. Whipple, Riverside
Gehrig Joseph W. 823 Washington boul.
Gehrity Peter, Ravinia
Gehrmann Adolph, M.D. 3816 Ellis av.
Gehrmann Felix, 3816 Ellis av.
Gehrmann Theodore A. 3816 Ellis av.
Geist Frederick, 4536 Prairie av.
Geist George F. 4422 Champlain av.
Geist John W. 3746 Wabash av.
Geist J. L. 6031 Prairie av.
Gelder Daniel, 4930 Vincennes av.
Geltmacher J. T. 3200 Rhodes av.
Gemmell Martha Miss, 540 W. Jackson
    boul.

Genius Arthur E. Dr. 3210 Vernon av.
Genius Frederick A. Rev. 3210 Vernon av.
Genius Richard M. Dr. 3210 Vernon av.
Gentleman Willard, Great Northern hotel
Gentles H. Wernicke Dr. 210, 51st
Gentry C. H. 293 Oak. *C.A.*
Genung Charles 3545 Prairie av.
Genung Mary. J. Mrs. 3545 Prairie av.
Genung W. H. 1290 Washington boul.
George Benjamin F. 1107 Pratt av.
George Charles H. 578 W. Madison, *Ill.*
George Cyrus W. 356 W. 61st pl.
George Edgar J. Dr. 4321 Lake av.
George Marshall W. 4516 Ellis av.
George Milo, 256 Ontario
George P. W. 356 W. 61st pl.
George William E. 621 Lasalle av.
George William O. 621 Lasalle av.
Gephart E. Mrs. 4515 Prairie av.
Geraghty Joseph H. Evanston
Geraghty Patrick J. 462 Elm
Gerber Emil, 348 Belden av.
Gerding Paul, 42 St. James pl.
Geringer John, 501 S. Winchester av.
German W. H., M.D. Morgan Park
Gerold Charles A. Mrs. 1676 Barry av.
Gerould Frank W. Evanston, *C.A.*
Gerrett D. B. Lakota hotel
Gerrish Lory G. 7819 Lowe av.
Gerson Percival Dr. Hotel Del Prado
Gerstenberg Erich, 1773 Deming pl.
Gerstenberg H. Mrs. 862 Hamilton ct.
Gerstetter John Mrs. 822 Winthrop av.
Gerstetter John C. 822 Winthrop av.
Gerstley Henry M. 4235 Michigan av.
Gerten Nicholas, 463 Cleveland av.
Gertenrich John, 211 Belden av.
Gerts George E. Oak Park
Gerts Walter S. Oak Park
Gerwig Frank L. 472 W. Congress. *C.A.*
Geselbracht Henry H. Austin
Getchell Edwin F., 2628 Prairie av. *U.L.*
Getchell George W. 3429 Indiana av.
Gettier Nellie Mrs. Riverside
Getty Harry A. 3231 South Park av.
Getty Henry H. Calumet Club. *W.P.*
Getty John A. 3231 South Park av.
Getty Lucy Mrs. 4130 Grand boul.
Getty Walter B. 1503 George
Getz George G. Chicago Beach hotel
Geudtner Charles P. 1026 Evanston av.
Geudtner Francis, 1026 Evanston av.
Gfroerer George S., M.D. 439 W. Taylor
Gibbins Carrie C. Miss, Hotel Windermere
Gibbons Walter J. 225 Osgood
Gibbons William M. Briggs house. *C.A.*
Gibbs Catherine S. Mrs. 450 Belden av.
Gibbs C. H. Mrs. Lexington hotel
Gibbs Fletcher B. Oak Park. *C.A.*
Gibbs Frederick C. Lexington hotel. *Cal., C.A., W.P.*
Gibbs George A. 2014 Indiana av.
Gibbs H. M. Mrs. Hinsdale
Gibbs James S. 400 Superior. *Chi., Un.*

Gibbs Montgomery 2442 Lakewood av.
Gibbs Orlando F. Evanston
Gibbs Orva S. Miss, 206 Ashland boul.
Gibbs Platt P. 4820 Kimbark av.
Gibbs William B. Lexington hotel. *Cal*
Gibson Allan R. 518 W. Jackson boul.
Gibson A. M. 4725 Prairie av.
Gibson Belle Miss, 745 Washington boul.
Gibson Charles B. Dr. 1803 Barry av.
Gibson Charles H. 5149 Cornell av.
Gibson Charles J. Austin
Gibson C. G. 7805 Winneconna av.
Gibson C. W. 7815 Winneconna av.
Gibson Douglas Mrs. 5149 Cornell av.
Gibson Guy G. The Arizona
Gibson Lilian W. Miss, 5149 Cornell av.
Gibson Mary J. Mrs. 6136 Ellis av.
Gibson Sarah Mrs. 66 Rush
Gibson Thomas, 3613 Ellis av.
Gibson T. H. New Hotel Holland
Gibson Walter S. 6135 Monroe av.
Gibson Watts C. 5149 Cornell av.
Gibson William, 2765 N. Robey
Gibson William A. 4725 Prairie av.
Gibson William H. 732 W. Adams
Gibson William T. 5149 Cornell av.
Gibson W. D. Mrs. 745 Washington boul.
Giddings Edward E. Oak Park
Giesler Rudolph G. 4323 Lake av.   -
Gifford Archer, Evanston
Gifford Chas. E. 4637 Drexel boul.
Gifford Chas. E. jr. 56, 47th
Gifford Frank W. Evanston
Gifford Frederic D. 811 Morse av.
Gifford Ira L. 1518 Dakin av.
Gifford I. Cushman, 4637 Drexel boul. *C.A.*
Gifford Robert L. 4623 Drexel boul.
Gifford William L. Maywood
Gilbert Albert M. 541 Dearborn av. *Chi.*
Gilbert Almira M. Mrs. 1016 Winthrop av.
Gilbert Alson, 5234 Woodlawn av.
Gilbert Ashley L. Morton Park
Gilbert Augustus E. 3611 Grand boul.
Gilbert Charles B. 3959 Ellis av. *U.L.*
Gilbert Charles C. 449 Elm
Gilbert Charles J. Evanston
Gilbert Charles T. Morgan Park
Gilbert C. B. Mrs. 91, 37th
Gilbert Frank, 16 Walton pl.
Gilbert Fred W. 928 Greenleaf av.
Gilbert George A. 3356 Calumet av.
Gilbert Geo ge H. Prof. 534 Washington boul.   r
Gilbert Henry D. 3706 Lake av.
Gilbert Henry K. Evanston. *C.A.*
Gilbert H. M. Mrs. 4585 Oakenwald av.
Gilbert H. T. 5234 Woodlawn av. *C.A., Irq.*
Gilbert James H. 3336 Calumet av. *U.L., W.P.*
Gilbert James R. LaGrange   '
Gilbert John, 1174 Washington boul.
Gilbert J. Thornton, Oak Park
Gilbert Matthew P. 1838 Arlington pl.

Gilbert Miles S. Evanston
Gilbert Morton V. Evanston
Gilbert Newell D. Austin
Gilbert Priscilla G. Miss, 5823 Woodlawn av.
Gilbert Roy O. Austin
Gilbert Sarah A. Mrs. 4201 Grand boul.
Gilbert Wallace B. Austin
Gilbert William C. Evanston
Gilchrist Harriet F. Miss, 5400 Washington av.
Gilchrist James M. Mrs. 5400 Washington av.
Gilchrist John F. 5406 Washington av. U.L.
Gilchrist M. V. Miss, 5610 Madison av.
Gilcreest John, 3729 Prairie av.
Giles Albert W. Oak Park
Giles Alice Miss, 2537 Michigan av.
Giles Anne Miss, 2537 Michigan av.
Giles Charles K. Lake Forest
Giles George T. 418 Warren av.
Giles Walter M. Oak Park
Giles William A. 2537 Michigan av. Cal., U.L.
Giles William F. 2537 Michigan av. Univ.
Gilford Paul Dr. 5213 Kimbark av.
Gilkinson Charles, 3617 Prairie av.
Gilkison Jasper G. 6204 Kimbark av. Chi., C.A.
Gill Annie R. Mrs. 159, 30th
Gill Charles E. 4917 Greenwood av. C.A.
Gill Ernest, 437 N. Hoyne av. C.A.
Gill George A. 4845 Grand boul.
Gill Hannah Mrs. Oak Park
Gill James Prof. Kenilworth
Gill James C. Dr. 833 Warren av.
Gill Joseph, 159, 30th
Gill J. Thompson, 815 Warren av.
              Sum. res. Delavan, Wis.
Gill Preston, 4917 Greenwood av.
Gill Winn Winship, 5252 Calumet av.
Gilleland Delos J. Evanston
Gillespie Charles H. 2922½ Groveland av. C.A.
Gillespie John, 282 S. Leavitt
Gillespie John P. 2953 Prairie av.
Gillespie Mary Miss, Evanston
Gillespie Patrick F. 2953 Prairie av.
Gillespie Samuel, 1923 Indiana av.
Gillespie Walter E. 2124 Michigan av.
Gillespie W. C. C. 23 St. Johns ct.
Gillespie W. C. D. River Forest
Gillett Charles H. 3915 Vincennes av.
Gillett Charles N. 4030 Prairie av.
Gillett Charles W. 3334 Michigan av. W.P.
Gillett C. F. LaGrange
Gillett Egbert W. 3334 Michigan av. Cal., Ill., U.L., W.P.
Gillett F. P. 3917 Vincennes av.
Gillett Henry, 3917 Vincennes av
Gillett Truman S. 4030 Prairie av.
Gillett Walter C. 4347 Oakenwald av. C.A.
Gillette Edwin F. 306 Michigan av. C.A., Univ. Sum. res. Lake Beulah, Wis.

Gillette E. L. Mrs. 306 Michigan av.
              Sum. res. Lake Beulah, Wis.
Gillette Harry S. 296 Ohio
Gillette Henry R. 3602 Lake av.
Gillette Howard F. 2908 Michigan av.
Gillette Isabelle A. Mrs. 2915 Indiana av.
Gillette James F. Mrs. 2908 Michigan av.
Gillette Robert, Highland Park
Gillette Sherman H. 737 Sunnyside av.
Gillette Wilmarth B. 6321 Jackson av.
Gillies William, 7810 Bond av.
Gillingham D. E. 2937 Groveland av.
Gillingham William J. 4343 Oakenwald av.
Gillis Alexander D. 4455 Oakenwald av.
Gillmann Charles F. 444 Belden av.
Gillmann Fred, 446 Belden av.
Gillmann Ida Mrs. 446 Belden av.
Gillmann William, 446 Belden av.
Gillmore Thomas J. 725 W. Monroe
Gillson Louis K. Evanston
Gilman George P. 433 Dearborn av.
Gilman George P. jr. 433 Dearborn av.
Gilman John E. Dr. Hotel Metropole. C.A.
Gilman L. O. Col. 19 Ashland boul.
Gilman Mary Miss, 433 Dearborn av.
Gilman William T. Dr. 2300 Indiana av.
Gilmer Thomas L. Dr. 3220 Lake Park av. Irq.
Gilmore A. P. Dr. 3700 Lake av. C.A.
Gilmore Charles W. 228 S. Irving av.
Gilmore H. E. 2358 Indiana av.
Gilmore John E. LaGrange
Gilmore Thomas W. 1357 Sheffield av. C.A.
Gilmour A. C. Hotel Del Prado
Gilmour James T. Dr. 4713 Prairie av.
Gilpin Thomas E. 161 Eugenie
Gilroy Bernard J. Lake Forest
Gils G. Henry, 936 W. Jackson boul.
Gils J. S. M. Mrs. 936 W. Jackson boul.
Gilsdorff Edward W. 219 Belden av.
Gilson Pearl Miss, 3154 Michigan av.
Gilson T. W. 5617 Madison av.
Gimbel Charles A. 592 Dearborn av. Stan.
Gimbel Horace. 3646 Michigan av. Stan.
Gimbel Jacob W. 3661 Michigan av. Stan.
Gimbel Sarah Mrs. 3646 Michigan av.
Gindele Charles W. 3745 Prairie av.
Gindele Ferdinand V. 394 Ashland boul.
Gindele George A. 6710 Butler
Ginty James, Ravinia
Girardin Jules, 5431 Cottage Grove av.
Girling Winthrop Dr. 264, 51st
Giroux Benjamin, 843 Warren av.
Giroux George W. 843 Warren av.
Githens Walter L. 5101 Kimbark av.
Gitterman Stephen, Riverside
Given Robert H. 822 Sherwin av.
Givens Robert C. Lexington hotel
Givins Robert S. Evanston
Glade John H. 712 North Park av.
Glade Louisa S. Mrs. 712 North Park av.
Glaescher Gustavus G. 725 Fullerton av.
Glaess Herman, River Forest
Glanz Alexander E. 36 St. James pl.

Glanz Louis D. 36 St. James pl.
Glanz Louisa Mrs. 36 St. James pl.
Glaser Blanche Miss, 5435 Indiana av.
Glaser B. Z. 566, 45th. *Stan.*
Glaser Edward L. 147, 33d. *Stan.*
Glaser Gustave D. 4342 Grand boul. *Stan.*
Glaser J. Mrs. 566, 45th
Glaser L. Mrs. 3252 Wabash av.
Glaser Max, 4535 Indiana av.
Glaser Victor L. 3252 Wabash av.
Glasner William A. 19 Ashland boul.
Glaspell A. W. Mrs. 1917 Diversey
Glaspell Harrison J. 2660 Kenmore av.
Glass Charles Lockwood, 3128 Groveland
    av.
Glasser Wendell, 451 Dayton
Gleason Charles, Evanston
Gleason C. O. Mrs. Evanston
Gleason Horace W. 4219 Ellis av.
Gleason Melissa C. Mrs. 7819 Lowe av.
Gleason Michael W. 1223 Wilcox av.
Gleason William H. 2337 Michigan av.
Gledhill John J. 194 N. State
Glenn John M. 1043 Sherwin av.
Glennie Albert E. Grand Pacific hotel
Glennon Edward T. 3827 Michigan av.
    C.A.
Glenny Sarah R. Mrs. 6 Chalmers pl.
Glessner John J. 1800 Prairie av. *Chi.,
    U.L.*
    Sum. res. The Rocks, Littleton, N. H.
Glessner J. G. M. 2036 Indiana av. *Chi.,
    Univ.*
Glick Lipman, 3663 Michigan av. *Stan.*
Glickauf Edward S. New Hotel Holland
Glickauf Mildred Miss, New Hotel Hol-
    land
Glickauf Simon. 3618 Ellis av.
Glidden Henry H. 7746 Union av. *U.L.*
Gloeckler Charles S. 1821 Arlington pl.
Glogauer Fritz, 2532 Kenmore av.
Glos Henry L. Elmhurst
Glos Jacob, Elmhurst
Glossinger John, 6501 Kimbark av.
Glover Erwin C. Oak Park
Glover Fannie M. Miss, 1315 Michigan av.
Glover George H. 1315 Michigan av.
Glover George W. Mrs. 77 Lincoln Park
    boul.
Glover Henry T. 2607 Prairie av.
Glover Lyman B. 3166 Lake Park av.
Glover Otis R. 2607 Prairie av. *Chi., W.P.*
Glover Samuel N. C. 6538 Stewart av.
Glover Wilson A. 4956 Washington av.
Gobel Charles Grant, 230 Ashland boul.
Gobel Elias F. 230 Ashland boul. *Ill.,
    U.L.*
Gobel H. Elias, 230 Ashland boul. *C.A.*
Goble George G. Evanston
Godair William H. 3915 Grand boul.
Goddard Leroy A. 3006 Prairie av. *U.L.*
Goddard Lester O. 2719 Prairie av. *Chi.,
    U.L.*
Goddard Sterling, 2719 Prairie av.
Godee Charles, Oak Park
Godwin T. W. Hinsdale

Goerke Emil, 1132 Winthrop av.
Goes Charles B. Tracy
Goetz Frederick, 29 Lane ct.
Goetz Henry, 456 Orchard
Goffe Louis K. Evanston
Goggin Mary Miss, 408 Superior
Going Judson F. 221 Fremont
    Sum. res. Lake Geneva.
Going Zenas H. Dr. 4642 Indiana av.
Goit Edward J. 4801 Madison av.
Goit O. W. Mrs. 58 Throop
Gold Wm. Jason Rev. 1113 Washington
    boul.   Sum. res. Lima, Ind.
Goldenberg Jonas Mrs. 3560 Grand boul.
Goldenberg Max, 3560 Grand boul. *Lksd.*
Golder W. Arthur, 686 Washington boul.
    Ill.   Winter res. Daytona, Fla.
Goldie Robert N. 3716 Lake av.
Goldie William jr. 3716 Lake av. *C.A.*
Goldman Carl, 365, 42d.   *Lksd.*
Goldman Eugene, 3714 Grand boul. *Lksd.*
Goldman John, 3633 Prairie av.
Goldman Max, 4002 Vincennes av. *Lksd.*
Goldman Sara Mrs. 3633 Prairie av.
Goldschmidt Adolph, 423 Ashland boul.
    Lksd.
Goldschmidt Marion Mrs. 3341 Calumet
    av.
Goldschmidt Moses, 3341 Calumet av.
    Lksd.
Goldsmith Alfred L. 5517 Madison av.
Goldsmith Bernard, 921 Winthrop av.
Goldsmith Howard F. 921 Winthrop av.
Goldsmith Morris L. 563, 45th pl. *Lksd.*
Goldsmith Moses, 4517 Forrestville av.
    Lksd.
Goldsmith Samuel, 3137 Vernon av. *Stan.*
Goldsmith Simon, 4551 Forrestville av.
    Lksd.
Goldspohn Albert Dr. 519 Cleveland av.
Goldzier Julius, 220 Schiller
Goll Bruno H. 259 Ashland boul.
Goll Emma A. Mrs. 259 Ashland boul.
Goll Nicholas J. 6 Chalmers pl.
Gooch George E. Evanston
Gooch Hiram A. 4045 Drexel boul.
Good Martin G. 1541 W. Adams
Goodall Harvey L. 5141 Hibbard av.
Goode Edwin P. 1102 Montana
Goode J. Paul, Quadrangle club
Goode Thomas, 327 Racine av.
Goodell Lewis O. Mrs. 1750 Wrightwood
    av.
Goodfellow H. Mrs. 2453 N. Hermitage av.
Goodfellow William Rev. 5831 Monroe av.
Goodhart Charles I. 831 W. Polk. *Lksd.*
Goodhart Frederick P. Virginia hotel
Goodhart Jacob J. 367 S. Winchester av.
Goodhart P. H. Revere house. *Lksd.*
Goodhue A. Homer, 54 Bryant av.
Goodhue Wayland S. 54 Bryant av.
Goodhue Wells, Chicago Beach hotel
Gooding C. F. Irving Park
Gooding Gertrude E. Miss, Evanston
Gooding I. A. Mrs. Wilmette
Gooding S. Edgar, Wilmette

Gooding William S. Wilmette
Goodkind H. Mrs. 769 W. Jackson boul.
Goodkind M. L., M.D. 2522 Michigan av.
Goodkind William, 3131 Indiana av.
Goodman Alexander, 3529 Calumet av.
Goodman Daniel Mrs. 3359 Indiana av.
Goodman Edward, 2124 Michigan av.
Goodman Elizabeth Miss, 3000 Prairie av.
Goodman Harry, 3333 Wabash av.
Goodman Henry, 6245 Monroe av.
Goodman Herbert E. 7200 Union av.
Goodman H. Mrs. 3333 Wabash av.
Goodman Jacob, 450, 38th
Goodman James B. Calumet club. *Chi.,*
    W.P.
Goodman James E. 3810 Forest av.
Goodman James S. River Forest
Goodman Joseph, 20 Lincoln av.
Goodman J. R. Chicago Beach hotel
Goodman Louis H. 3333 Wabash av.
Goodman Magnus, 4533 Ellis av.
Goodman Maurice, 3305 Forest av.
Goodman Maurice, 3333 Wabash av.
Goodman Milton F. 3426 South Park av.
    Stan.
Goodman Moses, 3426 South Park av.
Goodman M. A. Mrs. 5810 Washington
    av.
Goodman Robert F. Calumet club
Goodman S. Mrs. 20 Lincoln av.
Goodman Thomas, 460 Fulton
Goodman Thomas C. 4072 Lake av.
Goodman William A. 460 Fulton
Goodman William O. 5026 Greenwood av.
    C.A., U.L., W.P.
Goodnow Carl A. Evanston
Goodnow Frank A. 679, 48th
Goodrich Adams A. Judge, 4508 Forrest-
    ville av. *Chi., C.A.*
Goodrich Albert W. 1474 Michigan av.
    Cal., Chi., C.A., W.P.
Goodrich A. E. Mrs. 1474 Michigan av.
Goodrich C. Harry, 4239 Drexel boul.
Goodrich Edna L. Miss, 3216 Groveland
    av.
Goodrich Edson H. 3216 Groveland av.
    C.A.
Goodrich Grant Mrs· 70 Astor
Goodrich Hattie S. Mrs. 7436 Bond av.
Goodrich Horace A. 1788 Deming pl.
Goodrich Julius G. 4952 Vincennes av.
Goodrich J. G. 4239 Drexel boul.
Goodrich N. Kniffen, 426 Superior
Goodridge A. E. G. 1432 Michigan av.
    C.A.
Goodridge A. G. Irving Park
Goodridge Edward, 1432 Michigan av.
Goodsmith H. M. Dr. 396 Belden av.
Goodsmith William, 396 Belden av.
Goodsmith William P., M.D. 957 N.Clark
Goodspeed Chas. T. 5630 Kimbark av.
Goodspeed Edgar J. 5630 Kimbark av.
Goodspeed George S. Prof. 363, 58th
Goodspeed Stephen, 5630 Kimbark av.
Goodspeed Thos. W. Rev. 5630 Kimbark
    av.

Goodwillie David, 20 Roslyn pl.
Goodwillie Douglas,529 W. Jackson boul.
Goodwillie D. L. Oak Park
Goodwillie D. M. Mrs. 529 W. Jackson
    boul.
Goodwillie Edgar N. Oak Park
    Sum. res. Little Cedar Lake, Wis.
Goodwillie Perley, 529 W. Jackson boul.
Goodwillie Willis L. 731 Fullerton av.
Goodwin Albert P. 354 Washington boul.
Goodwin A. H. Virginia hotel
Goodwin Carrie Mrs. 604, 46th
Goodwin Charles A. 1541 W. Adams
Goodwin Clarence M. 5100 Hibbard av.
Goodwin E. P. Rev. 354 Washington boul.
Goodwin Frances L. Miss, 7013 Perry av.
Goodwin Harry, 267 Bowen av.
Goodwin Hollister E. LaGrange
Goodwin James, 5114 Jefferson av.
Goodwin John, 428 Ashland boul.
Goodwin John S. 5540 Cornell av.
Goodwin Karl H. 604, 46th
Goodwin Lucia Miss, Lake Forest
Goodwin Mabel E. Miss, 604, 46th
Goodwin Margaret Mrs. Irving Park
Goodwin Newton Mrs. 1238 N. Clark
Goodwin R. LeBarre, 5100 Hibbard av.
Goodwin Warren F. 5114 Jefferson av.
    U.L., W. P.
Goodwin William, 5114 Jefferson av.
Goodwin William G. 5114 Jefferson av.
Goodyear A. S. 3903 Lake av.
Goodyear Charles A. 3903 Lake av. *U.L.*
    Sum. res. Tomah, Wis
GoodykoontzCharles H.2419Michigan av
Googins David S. 4337 Drexel boul.
Googins Henry F. 3247 South Park av.
Gookin Frederick W. 20 Walton pl.*Univ.*
Gookin Mary H. Miss, 20 Walton pl.
Goold John E. 2216 Prairie av.
Goold Nathaniel Mrs. 2216 Prairie av.
Goold Allan F. 5312 Jackson av.
Gordon Arthur H. Dr. 268 Lasalle av.
Gordon A. E. Miss, The Tudor
Gordon Charles U. Lexington hotel.*U.L.*
Gordon Edward K. Hinsdale
Gordon Frank L. 153, 51st
Gordon George O. 4742 Champlain av.
Gordon John Leslie, 150 Lincoln Park
    boul.
Gordon J. W. Mrs. Hinsdale
Gordon Newton F. Glen Ellyn
Gordon Robert, 5410 Madison av.
Gordon Thomas S. Kenilworth *C.A.*
Gordon William G. Hinsdale
Gore Charles W. 5329 Greenwood av.
Gore George P. 1926 Indiana av. *W.P.*
    Sum. res. Lake Beulah, Wis.
Gore Joel R. Dr. 2606 Prairie av.
Gore Truman D. 4724 Champlain av.
Gore Willis K. 670, 48th
Gore W. H. 4518 Oakenwald av.
Gores Paul, Chicago Beach hotel. *C.A.*
Gorgas Lawrence D. Dr. 5720 Madison av.
Gorham Sidney S. LaGrange
Gorique Albert, Riverside

Gorman J. E. 3345 Vernon av.
Gorman Robert, Morton Park
Gorman William H. 952 W. Garfield boul.
Gormley James H. Oak Park. *C.A., Ill*
Gormully Michael Mrs. Glencoe
Gormully R. Philip, 459 Dearborn av. *C.A., Un., U.L.*
Gorrell William F. 4916 Washington av.
Gorton Belle L. Miss, 950 Turner av.
Gorton C. H. Tracy
Gorton Edward F. Lake Forest
Gorton Elizabeth Mrs. 950 Turner av.
Gorton Frank S. 2120 Prairie av. *Cal., Chi., C.A., W.P.*
Gosling R. 4306 Greenwood av.
Goss Charles Oliver, 246 Oakwood boul. Sum. res. Winnetka
Goss Ferdinand, 1222 Sheffield av.
Goss Frederick L. Oak Park
Goss Samuel G. 533 W. 61st pl.
Goss Stephen C. 5475 Ridgewood ct.
Goss William T. Austin
Gott John R. 135 Lincoln Park boul.
Gottfried Carl M. 35 Cedar. *C.A.*
Gottfried Matthew 4559 Ellis av.
Gottig Curd H. 1820 Wrightwood av.
Gottlieb A. 290 Lasalle av.
Gottlieb Nober, 290 Lasalle av.
Gottlieb Rose Mrs. 3420 Vernon av.
Gottlieb Rudolph, 667 N. Robey
Gottman Theodore. 3178 Malden
Goudie Margaret R. Miss, 816 W. Adams
Goudy William C. Mrs. 240 Goethe
Gould Charles H. Riverside. *U.L.*
Gould C. W. Dr. Irving Park
Gould Elwyn B. 1768 Wrightwood av.
Gould Frank, Evanston
Gould George W. 217 Schiller
Gould G. T. 135 Park av.
Gould Irving L. 346 Lasalle av.
Gould John, Lake Forest. *U.L.*
Gould John S. 2310 Calumet av.
Gould Leonard, 240 Ohio
Gould S. P. Mrs. Lake Forest
Gould Webster, 626 W. 62d
Goulding Frank L. 1514 W. Monroe
Gove Alice Mrs. Evanston
Gowan Victor D. 472 Lasalle av.
Goward G. Granada hotel
Grabfield Jacob, 605, 46th. *Stan.*
Grabfield Joseph P. Dr. 1915 Indiana av.
Grace John W. 107 Pine Grove av.
Grace William, 107 Pine Grove av., *C.A., U.L.*
Gradle B. 652 Lasalle av.
Gradle Henry Dr. 165 Eugenie
Grady Edward Mrs. Tracy
Grady Robert L. 4834 Champlain av.
Graeff Adolph, 265 Fremont
Graeff Alfred, 265 Fremont
Graham Andrew J. 1411 Washington boul *Ill.* Sum. res. Lake Geneva, Wis.
Graham Beeckman, 228, 47th. *C.A.*
Graham David Mrs. 455, 63d
Graham David W. Dr. 672 W. Monroe. *Ill.*
36

Graham Dennis Mrs. 21 Bryant av.
Graham Dennis C. 21 Bryant av.
Graham Ella Mrs. 772 W. Monroe
Graham Ernest Robert, 4858 Washington av.
Graham F. H. 5229 Michigan av.
Graham Irene Mrs. 2119 Michigan av.
Graham James F. Dr. 278 Bissell
Graham James J. 4405 Indiana av.
Graham John, 205 S. Leavitt
Graham John A. 1342 Sheridan rd.
Graham John I. Austin
Graham M. L. Mrs. 4724 Evans av.
Graham William A. S. 3655 Grand boul. *C.A.*
Grainger John, Morgan Park
Gramm Carl Dr. 8 St. James pl.
Granger Alfred H. Lake Forest. *Univ.*
Granger Henry Chapin Rev. 1657 Briar pl.
Granger Sarah Mrs. 1065 Warren av.
Granger William S. East ct. se. cor. Belmont av.
Granick Joseph, 4907 Calumet av.
Grannis Albert A. 2916 Indiana av.
Grannis Amos Mrs. 2916 Indiana av.
Grannis Eugene A. 302 Chicago av.
Grannis Frank L. 2916 Indiana av.
Grannis George M. Mrs. 2675 N. Lincoln
Grannis Harry A. 452 Lasalle av.
Grannis Uri B. 2027 Michigan av.
Grannis W. C. D. Mrs. 2027 Michigan av.
Grant Allen P. River Forest
Grant Duncan J. 939 W. Adams
Grant E. K. 3000 Lake Park av. *Ill.*
Grant Frank L. LaGrange
Grant Frederick, 2900 Groveland av.
Grant Gilbert L. 414 Orchard
Grant John C. Prof. 2018 Michigan av.
Grant J. C. Mrs. 939 W. Adams
Grant Robert Lee, 3006 Groveland av.
Grant Robert S. 131 Ashland boul. *Ill.*
Grant Schaefer G. A. 916 Pullman bldg.
Grant William C. Mrs. 1610 Indiana av.
Grashoff C. M. Miss, North Shore hotel
Grassie Henry, 701 The Plaza. *C.A.*
Grassie James, 5216 Washington av. *Ill.*
Grassly Charles W. 635 W. Jackson boul.
Gratton Emory O. Dr. 243 W. 65th
Graue John George, 180 Goethe. *C.A.*
Graue William, Elmhurst
Graver James P. 6122 Stewart av.
Graver William, 6122 Stewart av.
Graves Albert M. 4526 Woodlawn av. *U.L.*
Graves A. H. 2712 Magnolia av.
Graves Charles, Winnetka
Graves Charles E. Evanston
Graves Charles H. 240 Bissell
Graves Dwight W. 214 Goethe
Graves Florence A. Mrs. 797 Warren av.
Graves Henry E. River Forest
Graves James A. 5663 Washington av.
Graves James R. 485 W. Jackson boul. *Ill.*
Graves James T. 5663 Washington av.
Graves John M. 3236 Calumet av.
Graves Justin R. Evanston

Graves Kate I. Dr. 5663 Washington av.
Graves Neil S. Austin
Graves Paul S. Evanston
Graves Riley M. Winnetka
Graves Robert E. 5663 Washington av.
Graves S. H. 17 Scott. *Chi.*
Graves Wm. W. 296 N. State
Graves W. M. Lakota hotel. *Cal.*
Grawe Christian, 3259 Dover
Gray Albert S. Dr. 3801 Lake av.
Gray Arthur, 351 Ashland boul.
Gray Arthur W. 3524 Forest av. *C.A.*
Gray A. R. Hotel Del Prado
Gray A. W. Dr. 1410 Washington boul.
Gray Charles W. 1607 W. Adams
Gray Clarence J. Lexington hotel
Gray Edward E. Chicago Beach hotel. *Cal., Irq.*
Gray Edwin W. Evanston
Gray Elisha Prof. Highland Park. *U.L*
Gray Ethan A., Dr. 158 Evanston av.
Gray F. D. 2807 Prairie av. *Cal.*
Gray F. M. 498 W. Monroe. *Ill.*
Gray George L. 2644 Indiana av.
Gray George W. Rev. Evanston
Gray Howard A. Evanston
Gray Howard P. Evanston
Gray H. C. The Kenwood
Gray Ida Cornelia Miss, Evanston
Gray James R. Morgan Park
Gray John H. Prof. Evanston. *Univ.*
Gray Louis A. I. 1410 Washington boul. *C.A.*
Gray Mary B. Mrs. Evanston
Gray Millard P. 637 W. Jackson boul.
Gray P. W. 2763 N. Winchester av.
Gray Robert W. 292 Rush
Gray Tilbey D. 22 Marquette terrace
Gray William P. Jefferson Park
Gray W. C. Dr. Oak Park
Gray W. H. 490 Dearborn av. *U.L.*
Gray W. H. Irving Park
Greathead E. E. Hyde Park hotel
Greaves J. E. Mrs. Evanston
Greeley Council, 4403 Greenwood av.
Greeley Frederick, Winnetka
Greeley L. M. 38½ Bellevue pl.
Greeley Minerva M. Miss, 4403 Greenwood av.
Greeley Morris L. Winnetka
Greeley M. R. Mrs. 4504 Ellis av.
Greeley Samuel S. Winnetka
Greeley S. Hallett, 4408 Sidney av.
Green Adolphus W. 4935 Greenwood av. *Chi.*
Green Albert P. 4814 Grand boul.
Green Albert S. 353 W. 61st
Green Andrew Hugh, 403 Lasalle av. *Chi.*
Green Ann Mrs. 416 Bowen av.
Green Augustus W. 2306 Calumet av. *U.L.* Sum res. Sodus, N.Y.
Green Benjamin A. Rev. Evanston
Green Catherine Miss, Evanston
Green Charles M. Highland Park
Green Charles W. Evanston

Green Edward Craft, 112 Lake Shore drive. *Un.*
Green Edward Craft Mrs. 501 N. State
Green E. T. Revere house
Green Frank B. Highland Park
Green George, 3743 Langley av.
Green George W. Dr. 2765 N. Lincoln
Green Helen R. Miss, Glencoe
Green Henry L. 4320 Ellis av. *C.A.*
Green Henry R. jr. 386 Chestnut
Green Henry R. Mrs. Riverside
Green H. R. Mrs. Highland Park
Green Irwin, 2306 Calumet av.
Green Isadore L. Dr. 315 Lincoln av.
Green James M. Rev. 3808 Prairie av.
Green John W. 3854 Lake av. *U. L.*
Green Kenyon Mrs. 414 Bowen av.
Green Lenna B. Mrs. 394 Warren av.
Green Mary T. Miss, Evanston
Green Nathan, 680 W. Adams
Green Oliver B. 403 Lasalle av.
Green Robert F. 6641 Woodlawn av.
Green Walter H. Glencoe
Green Weston, 3228 Prairie av.
Green William W. 451 Washington boul.
Green W. Mrs. 582 Division
Green W. A. 4612 Woodlawn av.
Green W. M. Evanston. *Irq.*
Greenacre I. T. Washington Heights
Greenbaum B. F. 426 Ashland boul
Greenbaum Selig, 4617 Ellis av. *Stan.*
Greenburg E. 1362 W. Jackson boul.
Greene Albert W. 3075 Sheridan rd.
Greene Cyrenius M. Highland Park
Greene D. Russell, Lexington hotel. *C.A.*
Greene Frank C. Dr. Virginia hotel. *Cal., C.A., W.P.*
Greene Frank R. 3818 Calumet av. *U.L.*
Greene H. N. Lexington hotel
Greene James P. 1805 Barry av. *C.A.*
Greene Jesse T. 3633 Ellis Park
Greenebaum D. S. 3156 South Park av. *Stan.*
Greenebaum Elias, 4510 Grand boul.
Greenebaum Henry 4232 Grand boul.
Greenebaum Henry E. 3337 Michigan av. *Stan.*
Greenebaum Henry N. 528 Dearborn av.
Greenebaum James E. 4508 Grand boul. *Stan.*
Greenebaum Moses E. Lakota hotel. *Stan.*
Greenebaum Moses S. 2243 Calumet av.
Greenewald Moses E. 4734 Champlain av. *Lksd.*
Greenfield Charles W. 728, 50th
       Sum. res. Lake Mills, Wis.
Greenhoot Bertha Mrs. 4411 Ellis av.
Greenidge D. Mrs. 1254 Michigan av.
Greenleaf George F. 290, 60th
Greenleaf Walter G. Riverside
Greenlee Elias C. 967 W. Jackson boul.
Greenlee Ralph Stebbins, Graceland av. and Lake Shore. *U.L.*
Greenlee Robert L. 95 Buena av. *U.L.*
Greenlee William B. 95 Buena av.

Greenley C. C. Mrs. 5033 Madison av.
Greenough Edward P. Evanston
Greensfelder Adolph, 2512 Michigan av.
Greensfelder Isaac, 2512 Michigan av. *Stan.*
GreensfelderJulius, 2512 Michigan av.
Greensfelder Nathan, 2512 Michigan av. *Stan.*
Greer Colbert H. 322 Superior. *Un.*
Gregg Charles O. Riverside
Gregg Douglas C. 1719 Melrose
Gregg Joseph, 205, 47th
Gregg Mary E. Dr. 503 Fullerton av.
Gregg William N. 503 Fullerton av.
Gregory Charles E. 4215 Langley av.
Gregory Daniel, 660 W. Monroe
Gregory Elizabeth Mrs. 1638 Prairie av.
Gregory Emma C. Miss, 4552 Indiana av.
Gregory F. A. 6323 Greenwood av.
Gregory F. A. jr. 6323 Greenwood av. *Irq.*
Gregory Jacob H. 4121 Drexel boul. *C.A.*
Gregory Louis L. Dr. 514 Evanston av.
Gregory Miles S. 8 St. James pl.
Gregory Robert B. 1638 Prairie av. *U.L*
Gregory Sarah Mrs. 8 St. James pl.
Gregory Stephen S. 65 Stratford pl. *C.A., Irq.*
Gregory Walter D. 660 W. Monroe *C.A., Ill., W.P.*
Gregson William L. Morgan Park
Gregsten Samuel, 3435 Michigan av.
Greifenhagen Emil, 543 Dearborn av.
Greifenhagen O. F. 1911 Deming pl.
Greifenhagen Richard A. 1840 Wrightwood av.
Greig P. C. Berwyn
Greig Thomas, 365 S. Oakley av.
Greig Thomas jr. 365 S. Oakley av.
Greiner Wm. Mrs. 916 N. Halsted
Greiner William, 63 Lincoln av.
Grenell Howard, Oak Park
Grepe J. Stanley, Evanston. *Chi.*
Gresham Otto, 235 Michigan av. *Cal.,Chi.*
Gresham Walter Q. Mrs. 235 Michigan av.
Grevstad Nicolay, 575 Cleveland av.
Grey Charles F. Evanston *U.L.*
Grey John J. 4354 Oakenwald av. *C.A., W.P.*
Grey Mary Felton Mrs. 3153 Calumet av.
Grey Walter, 2010 Prairie av. *C.A.*
Grey William L. 2010 Prairie av. *Cal., U.L., W.P.* ·
   Sum. res. York Harbor, Me.
Gridley G. N. Morton Park
Gridley Martin M. Evanston. *U.L.*
Gridley Nelson C. Evanston
Grier James P. Evanston
Grier John A. 224, 53d
Grier John A. Mrs. 4451 Sidney av.
Grier John P. Virginia hotel. *Chi., C.A.*
Grier Robert J. Evanston
Grier R. M. Mrs. Evanston
Griesheimer Fred, 576 Lasalle av.
Griesheimer Morris, 508 Dearborn av. *Stan.*
Griffen Felix J. River Forest

Griffen Z. T. 114 S. Lincoln
Griffeth Abraham L. 2620 N. Hermitage av.
Griffeth Albright, 2620 N. Hermitage av.
Griffin Charles F. Hammond, Ind. *U.L.*
Griffin Francis O. 1670 W. Monroe
Griffin George W. 950 W. Monroe
Griffin George W. Elmhurst
Griffin H. 424, 41st
Griffin James F. 744 Washington boul.
Griffin Jas.W., 1556 W. Garfield boul.
Griffin John, 1556 W. Garfield boul.
Griffin John C. 5121 Michigan av.
Griffin Joseph A. Evanston
Griffin J. B. 719 Pullman bldg.
Griffin Livingston, 344 Dearborn av.*U.L.*
Griffin Stephen, 1310 W. Adams
Griffin Thomas A. Virginia hotel. *Chi., C.A., Ill., Un., W.P.*
Griffing Frank B. 196 Oakwood boul.
Griffing Josephine C. Miss, 5461 Cornell av.
Griffith Edward W. 6451 Woodlawn av.
Griffith E. H. Mrs. 5656 Washington av.
Griffith Frank A. 6717 Parnell av.
Griffith George D. Oak Park
Griffith George F. Evanston
Griffith Joseph T. jr. 1940 Deming pl.
Griffith J. A. Mrs. 603 W. Jackson boul.
Griffith J. Clarkson, Oak Park
Griffiths John, 3806 Michigan av. *U.L.*
Griffiths Kenneth F. 4637 St. Lawrence av.
Griffitts John R. LaGrange
Griffitts William F. LaGrange
Griggs Alida M. Mrs. Evanston
Griggs John, Evanston
Griggs Louisa Mrs. 3930 Grand boul.
Grimes Charles B. Maywood
Grimm E. A. 971 Park av.
Grimsell Fred, 95 Fowler
Grinnell Julius S. Mrs. 5116 Kimbark av.
Grinnell K. V. Mrs. Mayfair
Grinnell Robert, 5116 Kimbark av.
Griswold Edward B. Evanston
Griswold Edward L. Evanston
Griswold Edward P. Evanston. *U.L.*
Griswold Fitz-Edward Evanston. *Chi., U.L.*
Griswold George E. 569 W. Congress *Ill.*
Griswold Harold T. Evanston
Griswold Harry S. 7209 Merrill av.
Griswold J. M. Mrs. Tracy
Griswold Watson P. 5125 Cornell av.
Griswold William R. 17 Ashland boul.
Gritman Charles, Austin
Groat William H. 470 W. Congress
Groendyke J. C. The Arizona
Groesbeck F. Miss, 413 Washington boul.
Groetzinger Edward A. 726 Fullerton av. *C.A., U.L.*
Groff Carl, Hinsdale
Groh Louis, 148 W. Garfield boul.
Groh William, 4422 St. Lawrence av.
Groll Philip F. 1722 Oakdale av.
Grommes Frieda Miss, 616 Dearborn av.

Grommes J. B. 616 Dearborn av. '
Gronow Rudolph W. 1475 Perry
Groover W. G. Wilmette
Groshon A. D. Dr. 300 S. Irving av.
Groshon Lottie J. Mrs. 300 S. Irving av.
Gross Alfred H. Evanston
Gross August, 695 N. Wells
Gross Charles, 559, 45th pl.
Gross D. W. Prof. Ravinia
Gross Elsie M. Miss, 5116 Hibbard av.
Gross Emile M. 5349 Michigan av.
Gross Freeman F. 2242 Michigan av. .
Gross Howard H. 6001 Indiana av.
Gross Jacob, 1730 Deming pl.
Gross Jacob, 1828 Surf
Gross James E. Dr. 531 Lasalle av.
Gross J. Ellsworth, 3600 Michigan av.
Gross Samuel E. 48 Lake Shore Drive.
    Chi., C.A,, Un., U.L., W.P.
Gross William H. 1730 Deming pl.
Grosscup Peter S. Judge, 4259 Grand boul.
Grosscup S. L. Mrs. 3729 Indiana av.
    Sum. res. Charlevoix, Mich.
Grosse Henry C. 518 Fullerton av.
Grosse John, 667 N. Robey
Grossenheider Julius, 3201 Calumet av.
Grossman Adolph, 4222 Grand boul. *Stan.*
Grossman Edward B. 4148 Grand boul.
    Lksd., Stan.
Grossman George, 4222 Grand boul. *Stan.*
Grossman Herman, 3924 Grand boul.
    Lksd., Stan.
Grossman R. Mrs, 3601 Vincennes av.
Grossmith Alfred, 6814 Lowe av.
Grosvenor George B. 5014 Jefferson av.
Grosvenor Lemuel C., M. D. 185 Lincoln
    av.
Grosvenor Lorenzo N. Dr. 2714 Kenmore
    av.
Groth Fred E. 1664 W. Monroe
    Sum. res. Loon Lake, Ill.
Groth Fred J. 1664 W. Monroe
    Sum. res. Loon Lake, Ill.
Grout Charles R. 1179 Washington boul.
Grout Frank R. 1179 Washington boul.
Grove Joseph, Berwyn
Grover Frank R. Evanston
Grover Louise Miss, Evanston
Grover Marguerite P. Miss, Evanston
Grover Thomas W. Mrs. 401 Oak
Groves Dennison F. 3946 Ellis av.
Groves Geo. M. 174, 47th
Grower William F. 964 W. Jackson boul.
    C.A.
Grubb Emma F. Miss, 475, 42d
Grubb Joseph E. 461, 73d
Grund Harry T. 1051 Pratt av.
Grundy James Rev. 379 Elm
Grunewald Augustus H. 738 Sedgwick
Grus Eugene, 528 Lasalle av.
Grus Wm. 528 Lasalle av.
Grus Wm. jr. 528 Lasalle av.
Grusendorf Edward, 697 N. Hoyne av.
Grusendorf Henry, 697 N. Hoyne av.
Gruss Albert, 4059 Grand boul.
Gscheidlen Emily Miss, Hinsdale

Guckenheimer Joseph, Hotel Metropole.
    Stan.
Gudeman Edward, 4319 Vincennes av.
Guenther Otto, 321 Webster av.
Guerin John Dr. 3211 Wabash av.
Guerin John Mrs. 3211 Wabash av.
Guernsey M. E. Mrs. 2841 Michigan av.
    Sum. res. Delavan, Wis.
Guettel Julius, 3413 Prairie av.
Guhl Charles W. 2298 N. Paulina
Guhl Frederick H. 644 Fullerton av.
Guhl Walter F. 644 Fullerton av.
Guilbert Florence Miss, Hotel Winder-
    mere
Guilbert James, Norwood Park
Guilbert O. H. Hotel Windermere
Guilford J. A. 609 Washington boul.
Guilford Samuel, Ravinia
Guillett A. M. Miss, New Hotel Holland
Guilliams John, Evanston
Guion George Murray Gen. 111, 47th
Guion Leroy P. 111, 47th
Gulick James I. Hotel Windermere
Gumbiner Charles, 510, 44th pl.
Gump B. F. Highland Park
Gunderling H. Clifton house
Gundermann Henry, 1575 Lill av.
Gunderson Geo.O. 1239 Washington boul.
Gunderson G. M. 4910 Michigan av. *Ill.*
Gunderson H. Prof. Morgan Park
Gunderson Matilda Miss, Evanston
Gunderson S. T. 1239 Washington boul.
Gundrum Ferdinand, 4944 Ellis av.
Gunlock Nettie E. Mrs. 1183 Washington
    boul.
Gunlock Philip L. 1183 Washington boul.
Gunn A. H. Mrs. Evanston
Gunn Janet, M.D. 5127 Cornell av.
Gunn John A. 576 Washington boul.
Gunn Malcolm Dr. 2101 Calumet av.
Gunn Moses Mrs. 2101 Calumet av.
Gunn Walter C. 2101 Calumet av.
Gunning Robert J. 4351 Oakenwald av.
    C.A.
Gunsaulus Beatrice Miss, 2618 Prairie av.
Gunsaulus Frank W.Rev. 2618 Prairie av.
    U.L.
Gunsaulus Helen Miss, 2618 Prairie av.
Gunsaulus Joseph L. 2618 Prairie av.
Gunsaulus Martha W. Miss, 2618 Prairie
    av.
Gunsaulus Mary Miss, 2618 Prairie av.
Gunsaulus Mary Mrs. 399, 33d
Gunther Burnell, 1602 Indiana av.
Gunther C. F. 1602 Indiana av. *Irq., U.L.*
Gunther Whitman, 1602 Indiana av. *C.A*
Gunthorp Walter J. Austin
Gunthorp W. Percy, Austin
Gunton William M. 898 S. Kedzie av.
Gurley Ida B. Miss, Oak Park
Gurley Wm. W. 533 N. State. *Un., U.L.*
Gurnett William G. 6643 Parnell av.
Gurney Charles H. Lexington hotel. *Cal.,*
    Chi., C.A., W.P.
Gurney Chester S. 878 W. Monroe
Gustorf Arthur, Oak Park

Gustorf Fred, Oak Park
Gute Herman J. 780 North Park av.
Guth Henry, 3412 South Park av.
Guthman Daniel, 4456 Berkeley av.
Guthman Edward, 132, 34th
Guthman Sol. 3333 South Park av. *Stan.*
Guthmann Edward, 3639 Vernon av.
Guthmann Emil, 3639 Vernon av.
Guthmann R. Mrs. 3801 Prairie av.
Guthmann Siegmund, 4339 Grand boul. *Lksd., Stan.*
Guthridge Wm. 4001 Vincennes av.
Guthrie Alfred Dr. 6719 Perry av.
Guthrie Ossian, 6325 Monroe av.
Guthrie Seymour, Riverside
Gutman Nathan S. 4510 Grand boul. *Stan.*
Gutmann E. J. Mrs. 3653 Michigan av.
Gutmann Joseph, 594 Dearborn av.
Gutwillig Emil, 4436 Woodlawn av.
Gwin Alice Miss, 4558 Oakenwald av.
Gwin Anna Davis Miss, 4558 Oakenwald av.
Gwin James M. 4558 Oakenwald av.
Gwinn J. Morris, 4742 Lake av.
Gwinn William R. 4919 Lake av.
Gwynn J. K. 3500 Ellis av.
Gwynne Evan E. Dr. 566 Garfield av.

HAAGEN LOUISE J. MISS. 4453 Berkeley av.
Haagsma Ysbrand B. Evanston
Haas Charles, 3331 South Park av. *Stan.*
Haase Emil R. Oak Park
Haass Herman E. 1819 Indiana av. Sum. res. Magnolia and Cape Cod, Mass.
Haber Morris, 4033 Vincennes av. *Lksd.*
Haberer J. G. Mayfair
Habicht Frank E. 1078 Evanston av.
Hack Edward, 2798 N. Winchester av.
Hack John F. 2798 N. Winchester av.
Hack William J. 732 W. Monroe
Hackell George E. 617 Newport av. *C.A.*
Hacker Nicholas W. 99, 49th. *Irq., U.L.*
Hacker Robert C. Evanston
Hackett Louise E. Mrs. 2930 Indiana av.
Hackett W. H. 1131 Dunning
Hackney George, 3963 Drexel boul.
Hackney H. C. 3537 Michigan av. *Cal.*
Hackney John J. 5100 Hibbard av. Sum. res. Bay View, Mich.
Hadden Alexander B. 403 W. 64th
Hadden Harry G. 403 W. 64th
Hadfield G. A. Dr. 440, 57th
Hadley Edwin M. 4214 Ellis av.
Hadley James M. 4214 Ellis av.
Hadley L. M. Mrs. 1103 Washington boul.
Hadley May Dr. 94 Lincoln av.
Hadley Robert, Kenilworth
Haenichen Henry W. 285 Belden av.
Haerle Adolf, 645 Burling
Haerther Augustus G. Dr. 1633 Roscoe
Haerther William J. 1741 Roscoe
Hafer Henry, 4631 Michigan av.
Hafner C. F. Oak Park
Hafner J. 4842 Langley av.

Hafner Mary Mrs. Oak Park
Hafner William H. Mrs. 2427 Wabash av.
Hafner W. H. 2427 Wabash av.
Hagan James M. Rev. LaGrange
Hagan Thomas F. 5332 Ellis av.
Hagan Thomas F. jr. 5332 Ellis av.
Hagans L. A. Mrs. Elmhurst
Hagans Samuel E. Elmhurst
Hagans Wilber E. Elmhurst
Hagans William L 3120 Calumet av.
Hagar Edward M. 719 The Plaza
Hagar Gertrude A. Miss, 802 The Plaza
Hagar John M. 719 The Plaza. *U.L.*
Hageman Frederick C. Dr. 4805 Langley av.
Hagenbuck Ellis L. 7251 Jeffery av. *C.A.*
Hagenbuck Joseph, 5468 Monroe av.
Hagerty T. A. 537 Belden av.
Hagerty W. H. 4509 Prairie av.
Haggard John D. Austin
Haggard Samuel B. Austin
Haggers Wilbur, 201 The Plaza
Hahn Edmund J. 3626 Grand boul.
Hahn Fred A. 242 Dearborn av.
Hahn Harry W. 2018 Calumet av. *Stan.*
Hahn Herman F. 3626 Grand boul. *Stan.*
Hahn Max, Evanston
Hahn Mollie Miss, 3025 Prairie av.
Hahn Philip, 1524 Kenmore av.
Haigh William, Evanston
Haight Allen T. Dr. 1091 N. Clark
Haight Rufus J. 6532 Minerva av.
Haines E. H. 409 Superior. *C.A.*
Haines Fred H. 610 W. Jackson boul.
Haines George B. 6521 Kimbark av. *C.A.*
Haines George W. 271 Lincoln av.
Haines Mary V. Mrs. 610 Jackson boul.
Haines Thomas L. 211 Ashland boul.
Haines Winfield T. 2725 Prairie av.
Haines W. S. Dr. 46 Loomis
Hainsworth Joseph, 905 Warren av.
Hair Benjamin M. 248 Ashland boul. *Ill*
Hair Josiah T. 817 Estes av.
Hair J. S. 5142 Madison av.
Hair Miriam T. Miss, 4417 Lake av.
Hair Samuel G. 4417 Lake av.
Haire J. P. 4327 Lake av.
Haiselden H. J. Dr. 475 Belden av.
Hakes M. W. River Forest
Hakes Webster, River Forest
Halbach J. F. A. 4349 Lake av. *U.L.*
Halbert D. M. 709 Pullman bldg.
Halbert Homer V. Dr. 4630 Greenwood av
Halbert Walter A. University club
Halderman May Miss, 321, 49th
Hale Albert B. Dr. 69, 22d. *C.A.*
Hale Charles N. 170 Howe
Hale Clarence B. 217 Ashland boul.
Hale Edward C. 4833 Kimbark av.
Hale Edwin M. Dr. 2200 Prairie av.
Hale George D. Oak Park
Hale George W. 908, 169 Jackson boul. *Un.*
Hale George W. 4545 Drexel boul. *U.L.*
Hale John G. 6455 Monroe av.
Hale William B. 4545 Drexel boul.

Hale William E. Mrs. 4545 Drexel boul.
Hale William Gardner Prof. 5757 Lexington av.
    Sum. res. Moosehead Lake,Minn.
Hale W. C. 493 W. Jackson boul.
Hales Ansel, 640 W. 61st.
Hales Burton F. 346 Ashland boul. *Ill.*
Haley John M. 7105 Harvard av.
Haley William F. Dr. 1260 Wilcox av.
Hall Albert, 135 Lincoln Park boul.
    Sum. res. Long Pond,Plymouth,Mass.
Hall Albert P. 135 Lincoln Park boul
Hall Alfred M. Dr. 2 Washington pl.
Hall Althea L. Mrs. 6523 Kimbark av.
Hall Amos T. Mrs. 5516 Jefferson av.
Hall Augustus O. 32 Aldine sq. *U.L.*
Hall A. E. Mrs. 2944 Vernon av.
Hall A. H. Evanston
Hall Barrett R. The Kenwood
Hall Charles B. Dr. 5516 Jefferson av.
Hall Charles H. Evanston .
    Winter res. Lake Maitland, Fla.
Hall Christopher W. 81, 47th
Hall Clarence B. 1900 Prairie av.
Hall Clifford P. Lake Forest
Hall Dana W. 6324 Woodlawn av.
Hall Daniel L. Oak Park
Hall Edgar A. 1357 Fulton
Hall Edward R. Evanston
Hall Ernest, Oak Park
Hall Eugene J. Oak Park
Hall E. P. Mrs. 3025 Prairie av.
Hall Ferd, LaGrange
Hall Florence Goff Dr. 6243 Monroe av.
Hall Ford P. Highland Park. *Univ.*
Hall Frank, 2616 Calumet av.
Hall Frank, Morton Park
Hall Frank E. Oak Park
Hall Frank G. Lake Forest. *U.L.*
Hall Fred. E. Oak Park
Hall Frederick H. 4009 Lake av.
Hall F. D. Mrs. Glencoe
Hall F. H. 6448 Greenwood av.
Hall George A. Mrs. 2400 Prairie av.
Hall George E. Oak Park
Hall George W. Hinsdale. *Ill.*
Hall George W. Dr. 4642 Vincennes av.
Hall Gordon Mrs. 2 Washington pl.
Hall G. D. Glencoe
Hall Henry A. Kenilworth
Hall Herman J. 5545 Washington av.
Hall H. M. Morton Park
Hall Irving, LaGrange
Hall James T. 4341 Oakenwald av.
Hall Jesse E. 273 Oakwood boul. *U.L.*
Hall John A. 6448 Harvard av.
Hall John B. 4207 Calumet av.
Hall John E. 3803 Langley av.
Hall Joseph H. Mrs. 26 Aldine sq.
Hall J. D. Revere house
Hall J. D. Morton Park
Hall J. Sherman Mrs. 3701 Sheridan rd.
Hall Leicester C. Oak Park
Hall Lemuel R. 5498 East End av. *Ill.*
Hall Lorenzo E. Austin
Hall Louis J. 3701 Sheridan rd.

Hall L. R. 3167 Groveland av.
Hall Miller, Oak Park
Hall Newman G. 32 Aldine sq.
Hall Otis O. Hotel Del Prado
Hall Richard C. Evanston. *C.A.*
Hall Rider, Oak Park
Hall Robert W. 6417 Monroe av.
Hall Ross C. Oak Park
Hall Russell, Austin
Hall R. N. Dr. 339 Warren av.
Hall Samuel E. 537 N. State. *U.L.*
Hall S. M. 938 W. Adams
Hall William, 336 S. Campbell av.
Hall William, 6417 Monroe av.
Hall William E. Dr. 3550 Vernon av.
Hall William F. 3545 Grand boul. *C.A.*, *W.P.*
Hall William T. 3519 Calumet av.
Hall W. D. Oak Park
Hall W. S. Dr. Berwyn
Halla Charles, 592 Lasalle av.
Halla Philip, 391 Orchard ‹
Halla Sage G. Mrs. 19 Kemper pl.
Halladay James C. 501 The Plaza
Halladay J. B. Mrs. 3195 Malden
Hallam Charles A. 1248 Washington boul.
Hallberg Lawrence G. Evanston
Halle Arthur, 485 Dearborn av.
Halle Edward G. 485 Dearborn av. *U.L.*
Halle Frank jr. 485 Dearborn av.
Halle F. E. 3351 Indiana av.
Halle Louis, 3337 South Park av.
Halleman Andrew H. 236 S. Oakley av.
Hallen Andrew, 82, 25th
Hallenbeck John C. 6508 Stewart av.
Hallenstein Bennett, 2421 Michigan av. *Lksd.*
Haller Carl, 57 St. James pl.
Haller G. M. Mrs. Lexington hotel
Haller Mary E. Mrs. Oak Park
Hallett Harvey J. 4007 Vincennes av.
Hallett John, 4007 Vincennes av.
Halley Belton, 72, 44th
Halliday John W. Riverside
Halliday W. P. Mrs. 4740 Madison av.
    Sum. res. Osterville, Mass.
Halligan Francis E. 880 W.Jackson boul.
Hallinan John, Austin
Hallinan Thomas P. 1675 Barry av.
Hallinan Timothy G. 6329 Woodlawn av.
Halliwell A. C. Tracy
Hallock L. Elmhurst
Hallock Ruth M. Miss. 3743 Langley av.
Halls Samuel, 1639 W. Adams
Halsey Edward A. 301 Belden av. *Univ.*
Halsey George E. 3621 Ellis av.
Halsey John G. 367, 44th
Halsey J. J. Prof. Lake Forest
Halsey L. J. Mrs. 301 Belden av.
Halsey Tappen, 4824 Lake av. *C.A.*
Halstead Albert E. Dr. 804 Warren av.
Halstead Frank Lieut. Fort Sheridan
Halstead Ann Mrs. 490 Belden av.
Halstead Henry P. 490 Belden av
Halsted John, 490 Belden av.

Halsted Joseph, 490 Belden av.
Halsted May E. Miss, 717 Fulton
Haman Otto E. LaGrange
Hambleton Chalkley J. 558 Dearborn av.
Hambleton Charles E. 461 W. Monroe. *Ill.*
Hambleton Earl L. 99 Buena av. *U.L.*
Hambleton Maud G. Miss, 558 Dearborn av.
Hamblin M. J. Mrs. 3218 Vernon av.
Hamblin William B. Riverside
Hamburger Ben. 148, 33d
Hamburger Louis M. 5134 Woodlawn av. *C.A., W.P.*
Hamburger Max, 5134 Woodlawn av.
Hamburger Sol, 4347 Grand boul. *Stan.*
Hamburgher E. C. 223 Lasalle av.
Hamill Charles D. 2126 Prairie av. *Chi., W.P.*
Hamill Charles H. 2126 Prairie av.
Hamill Edwin, M.D. 812 Warren av.
Hamill Ernest A. 2637 Prairie av. *Chi., U.L.*
Hamill Ernest S. 315, 58th
Hamill Harry, 812 Warren av.
Hamill John C. Dr. 812 Warren av.
Hamill Laurence, 2126 Prairie av.
Hamill Philip W. 2126 Prairie av.
Hamill R. W. 262 Michigan av.
Hamill S. B. Hinsdale
Hamill Theophilus W. 315, 58th
Hamilton Adelbert, Evanston
Hamilton Bruce P. 2929 Michigan av.
Hamilton B. E. Evanston
Hamilton Catherine Mrs. Evanston
Hamilton Charles E. Dr. 3000 Michigan av.
Hamilton Charles F. 334 Hampden ct.
Hamilton David G. 2929 Michigan av. *Chi., U.L., W.P.*
Hamilton Delmah S. Dr. 6412 Stewart av.
Hamilton Emil, 440 Belden av.
Hamilton F. W. Evanston
Hamilton Henry E. 225 Dearborn av.
Hamilton Henry R. Oak Park. Sum. res. "Glen Carrie," Twin Lakes, Wis.
Hamilton I. K. 3230 Michigan av.
Hamilton I. K. jr. 231, 45th
Hamilton John B. Dr. 100 State. *U.L.* Sum. res. Elgin, Ill.
Hamilton John L. 408 Elm
Hamilton J. H. 5744 Rosalie ct. *C.A.*
Hamilton William J. Evanston
Hamilton W. A. Evanston
Hamlin Edward E. 3400 Calumet av.
Hamlin Frank, 354 Huron. *Un., Univ.*
Hamlin Fred R. 150 Lincoln Park boul. *C.A., Univ., W.P.*
Hamlin Fred T. 320, 63d
Hamlin George A. 3400 Calumet av. *C.A.*
Hamlin George J. 3622 Michigan av. *C.A., W.P.*
Hamlin Harry L. 150 Lincoln Park boul. *Univ., W.P.*
Hamlin Herbert W. 150 Lincoln Park boul. *Univ.*

Hamlin John A. Virginia hotel. *U.L., W.P.*
Hamlin Lorenzo A. 6514 Lafayette av.
Hamline John H. 1621 Prairie av. *Cal., Chi., U.L., Univ.*
Hamline L. P., Mrs. Evanston
Hamm Lucretia Mrs. 5608 Michigan av.
Hamm Solomon W. 5608 Michigan av.
Hamm Thomas P. 3850 Ellis av.
Hammell F. F. Mrs. 299, 47th.
Hammer D. Harry Judge, Auditorium annex. *U.L.* Sum. res. Hinsdale
Hammermiller Wm. 434 Lasalle av.
Hammett A. C. Dr. Irving Park
Hammett John A. Austin
Hammill Caleb W. Chicago Beach hotel. *Un.*
Hammill L. K. Mrs. Chicago Beach hotel
Hammill R. C. Mrs. Chicago Beach hotel
Hammon Charles N. Evanston
Hammon Glenn M. Dr. 683 W. Adams
Hammond A. Mrs. 11 Bellevue pl.
Hammond C. G. Mrs. Highland Park
Hammond C. L. 4627 Greenwood av.
Hammond C. N. 365 Ontario
Hammond Herbert, The Tudor
Hammond Ida Mrs. 6421 Ingleside av.
Hammond Jacob B. 4324 St. Lawrence av.
Hammond J. D.,M.D. Auditorium annex *Chi., W.P.*
Hammond J. E. Oak Park
Hammond Lewis P. 2832 N. Hermitage av.
Hammond Luther S. Hotel Windermere
Hammond L. D. Hotel Windermere. *U.L.*
Hammond L. M. 3539 Prairie av.
Hammond M. Mrs. 5614 Madison av.
Hammond Oliver, Oak Park
Hammond T. C. 11 Bellevue pl.. *C.A., Un.*
Hammond W. A. Mrs. Evanston
Hanauer Nettie D. Mrs. 4691 N. Clark
Hance Henry, 1560 Lill av.
Hance Paul D. 1560 Lill av.
Hanchett Frank J. 365 S. Marshfield av.
Hanchett Louis J. 4564 Indiana av.
Hancock Bradford Mrs. 39 Bellevue pl.
Hancock C. D. 3223 Wabash av.
Hancock Fred H. The Kenwood
Hancock George W. 4330 Lake av.
Hancock Harris, 5700 Kimbark av.
Hancock J. L. Dr. 3148 Indiana av.
Hancock Thomas, 5833 Madison av.
Hancock William S. 555 Englewood av.
Hand Bayard E. 7120 Yale
Hand F. L. Irving Park
Hand John A. 497 Webster av.
Hand J. P. 540 Dearborn av. Sum. res. Pine Lake
Hand Nicholas, 603 Cleveland av.
Hand Oliver H. 4835 Langley av.
Hand Peter, 1913 Deming pl.
Hand S. E. Mrs. 4835 Langley av.
Handford John, Evanston
Handley Joseph, 2585 N. Paulina

Handt L. Mrs. 2969 Prairie av.
Handy Frank W. Evanston
Handy H. H. 4423 Ellis av. *Ill.*, *U.L.*, *W.P.*
Handy Moses P.Mrs. 493 Dearborn av.
    Sum. res. Berlin, Md.
Handy William Matthews, 493 Dearborn av.
Hanecy ElbridgeJudge,3116 Michigan av. *C.A.*, *U.L.*, *W.P.*
Hanecy Olive Miss, 3116 Michigan av.
Hanford C. W. Dr. New Hotel Holland
Hanford Hopkins J. Evanston
  Sum. res. Eagle Lake, Kansasville,Wis.
Hanford M. E. Mrs. 4612 Woodlawn av.
Hanford P. C. Mrs. 2008 Calumet av.
Hanford Scott, Evanston
Hankey F. L. Glencoe. *C.A.*
Hankey James P. 4545 Oakenwald av. *C.A.*
Hanley Martin E. Revere house
Hanley M. W. 2429 Magnolia av.
Hanlon M. Mrs. 1409 Michigan av.
Hanlon William J. 1409 Michigan av.
Hanna Charles A. 704 Pullman bldg. *U.L.*
Hanna Clarence R. Julien hotel
Hanna Edward E. 6207 Woodlawn av.
Hanna I. B. Mrs. 35 Wisconsin
Hanna John T. 953 S. Spaulding av.
Hanna Kingston Dr. 3421 Indiana av.
Hanna Leroy. Julien hotel
Hanna Wm. B. Dr. 455 Washington boul.
Hannah Alexander D. 409 Oak
    Sum. res. Mackinac Island
Hannah A. W. 409 Oak
Hannah Frank S. 99, 33d
Hannah John S. 289 Dearborn av. *Chi.*, *Un.*
Hannah Thomas C. Riverside
Hannah William H. Union League club. *Un.*
Hannan Charles S. Evanston
Hannan James, 5134 South Park av.
Hanney Patrick M., 1173 N. Clark. *C.A.*
Hano Horace, Hotel Del Prado
Hanrahan Sarah Mrs. 5640 Michigan av.
Hansbrough William, 4724 Indiana av.
Hanscom P. L. Oak Park
Hansel Agnes M. Miss, Oak Park
    Sum. res. Lake Geneva, Wis.
Hansel John W. jr. Oak Park
Hansell J. R. 5444 Ellis av.
Hansen E. Mrs. Evanston
Hansen Harold M. 599 Pine Grove av.
    Sum. res. Lake Geneva, Wis.
Hansen H. C. 2678 Magnolia av.
Hansen J. E. 3514 Indiana av.
Hansen Waldemar T. Lexington hotel
Hanson A. H. 4612 Greenwood av. *C.A*
Hanson Burton, 4637 Greenwood av.
Hanson Christian H. 1848 Surf
Hanson David N. 4737 Ellis av.
Hanson F. S. 4455 Drexel boul.
Hanson Hiram A. 8 Groveland Park
Hanson John P. 24 Ewing pl.
Hanson John P. 275 Warren av.

Hanson Thomas L. 275 Warren av.
Hanson W. E. New Hotel Holland
Hanson Zenas P. Dr. 304 Washington boul. Sum. res. Old Orchard, Me.
Hanssen John, 569 Burling
Hapeman Edgar, LaGrange
Hapgood C. H. Virginia hotel. *Chi.*
Hapgood H. M. Mrs. 116, 43d
Hapgood William P. 5115 Cornell av. *C.A.*
Harahan J. T. 5119 Jefferson av. *Chi.*
Harbaugh A. M. 4144 Grand boul.
Harbeck Eugene, 3350 Prairie av. *Chi.*, *U.L.*
Harbeck Jervis R. 3350 Prairie av.
Harbers Theodore C. 4348 Greenwood av.
Harbert Arthur B. Evanston
Harbert A. A. Mrs. Evanston
Harbert Charles H. Evanston
Harbert William S. Evanston
    Sum. res. Lake Geneva, Wis.
Harbridge Anna Mrs. 285 S. Irving av.
Harbridge Chester, 285 S. Irving av.
Hardcastle Frank, 763 Estes av.
Harden O. E. 6620 Kimbark av.
Hardenbrook Burt C. 6221 Woodlawn av.
Hardenbrook E. G. 6223 Woodlawn av.
Hardenbrook George P. 6221 Woodlawn av.
Hardenbrook G. S. 6221 Woodlawn av.
Harder Charles C. 4633 Michigan av.
Hardie George, 4845 Madison av.
Hardie George F. Evanston
Hardie T. Melville Dr. 6017 Monroe av. *C.A.*
Hardie William T. Evanston
Hardin F. A. Rev. 6414 Butler
Hardin I. N. Evanston
Hardin John H. Evanston. *C.A.*
Hardin M. D. Gen. 538 N. State. *Un.*
Hardin Raymond A. Rev. 6414 Butler
Harding Abner C. 3155 Rhodes av. *U.L.*
Harding Amos J. Evanston. *U.L.*
Harding Beatrice Miss, 2536 Indiana av.
Harding Charles Mrs. 335 Chestnut
Harding Charles Edward, 7703 Lowe av.
Harding Charles F. 235, 45th. *Univ.*
Harding Dwight S. Evanston
Harding George F. Union League club. *C.A.*, *W.P.*
Harding George F. jr. 3321 Vernon av. *C.A.*
Harding George F. Mrs. 3230 Forest av.
Harding Hugh, 6106 Michigan av.
Harding Jo n C. Evanston. *Univ.*
Harding Lucien E. Evanston. *U.L.*
Harding P. D. Dr. Evanston
Harding Victor M. 3230 Forest av.
Hardman F. W. Evanston
Hardon R. W. Dr. 3143 Indiana av.
Hardy Charles M. 95 Oakwood av.
Hardy Cyrus A. 2825 Michigan av. *C.A.*, *Ill.*
Hardy Francis A. Evanston. *C.A.*
Hardy Guy, 95 Oakwood av.
Hardy Hannah H. Mrs. Evanston

Hardy Henry W. 5747 Kimbark av.
Hardy John M. 638 Pine Grove av.
Hardy T. C. 1032 Francis
Hardy William, 95 Oakwood av.
Hare D. Arthur Dr. Austin
Hare R. Warner, 3212 Prairie av. *U.L.*
Harger Charles B. 304, 49th
Hargis Harry, 461 Lasalle av.
Hargreaves George, Riverside
Haring L. W. Berwyn
Harkness Edson J. 291, 48th. *U.L.*
Harkness Fred L. 4637 Vincennes av.
Harlan A. W. Dr. 4414 Greenwood av.
  C.A., Ill.
  Sum. res. Calumet Heights
Harlan James S. 59 Cedar. *Univ.*
  Sum. res. Essex, Essex Co. N.Y.
Harlan John Maynard, 401 N. State. *Chi.,*
  C.A., Un.
Harlan P. H. 4414 Greenwood av.
Harland Edward, 563 Webster av.
Harland Leonard H. 529 Belden av.
Harless Charles D. 4440 Woodlawn av.
Harley William, 907 S. Sawyer av.
Harley Philip B. 1814 Wrightwood av.
Harlow Frank, 5601 Washington av.
  C.A.
Harlow Jefferson G. 1285 Washington
  boul. Sum. res. Lake Geneva, Wis.
Harman J. Robert, 6420 Stewart av.
Harman William E. 930 Fargo av.
Harman W. M. Oak Park
Harmon Albert C. 801 The Plaza
Harmon Charles J. 373 Ontario
Harmon Charles Sumner, 4035 Lake av.
Harmon Dennis L. 946 W. Garfield boul.
Harmon Edwin C. 373 Ontario. *C.A.*
Harmon Fred H. 801 The Plaza
Harmon George E. 5424 Washington av.
  C.A.
Harmon Henry I. 3820 Ellis av.
Harmon Hubert P. 4619 Lake av.
Harmon H. W. Mrs. 4619 Lake av.
Harmon I. N. Miss, 3975 Ellis av.
Harmon John C. 4058 Ellis av.
Harmon John H. 4619 Lake av.
Harmon John K. 801 The Plaza. *U.L.*
Harmon Joseph W. 4035 Lake av.
Harmon Louis Mrs. 3531 Wabash av.
Harmon Mary Miss, 946 W. Garfield
  boul.
Harmon Walter R. 373 Ontario
Harms Charles, 1543 Wolfram
Harms William, 225 Fremont
Harned Henry P. Oak Park
Harnette Frank B. 6511 Lafayette av.
Harnette Saphronia Mrs. 6511 Lafayette
  av.
Harney Thomas H. 324 Superior
Harnstrom Sandfrid, 50 St. James pl.
Harnwell F. W. 4528 Oakenwald av.
  Univ.
Harpel Charles, 394 Oak
Harpel Charles J. 394 Oak
Harper E. T. Prof. 730 W. Adams
Harper Harry E. 585, 45th pl.

Harper Hartley D. 619 The Plaza. *C.A.*
Harper Harvey M. 4581 Oakenwald av.
Harper James H. 762 W. Harrison
Harper James M. 3240 Forest av.
Harper John E. Dr. 5534 Washington av.
Harper J. C. 120 Loomis
Harper Mable Miss, 5318 Greenwood av.
Harper Robert Francis Prof. Quadrille
  club. *Univ.*
Harper Roy B. Col. Lakota hotel
Harper U. S. Mrs. 5318 Greenwood av.
Harper William Hudson, Evanston
Harper William H. Lakota hotel,
  U.L., W.P.
  Sum. res. Williams Bay, Wis.
Harper William R. 59th ne. cor. Lexing-
  ton av. *Chi., U.L., Univ.*
Harpham Edwin L. Evanston
Harpole Enoch, 390 Bowen av.
Harpole Winfield S. 4238 St. Lawrence av.
Harrah William C. 1542 Windsor av.
Harrell Moses B. 4209 St. Lawrence av.
Harrell William H. Revere house
Harries D. C. Berwyn
Harries H. H. Park Ridge
Harries Ira, Park Ridge
Harrigan C. P. Dr. 56 Lytle
Harriman Edward A. 52 Walton pl. *Univ.,*
  W.P.
Harriman Will M. 1673 W. Monroe
Harrington A. T. Mrs. 3159 Malden
Harrington Emma Mrs. Oak Park
Harrington George K. 3832 Calumet av.
Harrington K. C. Mrs. 3730 Oak
Harrington L. B. LaGrange
Harrington Stephen H. Riverside. *C.A.*
Harris Ab g Mrs. 1272 Washington
  boul. i ail
Harris Abraham, 4950 Vincennes av.
Harris Albert W. 4530 Ellis av. *U.L.*
Harris A. Fuller Dr. 514 W. 61st
Harris A. J. Dr. 279 Warren av.
Harris B. F. 6428 Greenwood av,
Harris Cornelius C. 4202 Michigan av.
Harris Dora A. Mrs. 569, 51st
Harris D. J. 3145 Vernon av.
Harris Elijah T. 604 Washington boul.
Harris George B. 543 N. State. *Chi.,*
  C.A., Un., W.P.
Harris George J. 1491 W. Jackson boul.
  Ill., Irq.
Harris Godfrey, 3322 Indiana av.
Harris Graham H. 561 Dearborn av.
  Univ.
Harris G. E. 5223 Madison av.
Harris Henry 3714 Forest av.
Harris Henry S. 1960 Sheridan rd.
Harris Isaac, Oakland hotel
Harris James H. 402, 40th
Harris John F. 5 Ritchie ct. *Chi., C.A.,*
  W.P.
Harris Joseph, Chicago Beach hotel.
  Lksd.
Harris J. G. Dr. North Shore hotel
Harris J. L. 688, 48th pl.
Harris Madison R. 968 W. Jackson boul.

Harris Malcolm L. Dr. 523 Lasalle av.
Harris Moses, 4804 Champlain av.
Harris Nelson G. 1528 Kenmore av.
Harris. Norman W. 4520 Drexel boul.
  U.L., Univ.
Harris N. Dwight, 4520 Drexel boul.
Harris R. L. Mrs. 1491 W. Jackson boul.
Harris Samuel, 945 W. Jackson boul.
Harris Samuel H. 231, 45th. *Lksd.*
Harris Saul G. 4920 Forrestville av.
Harris Squire Rush, 200 Honore. *Ill.*
Harris S. H. 1489 W. Monroe
Harris W. L. Mrs. Evanston
Harris W. M. Evanston
Harrison Carter H. Hon. 295 Schiller.
  Univ.
Harrison Clark W. 247 Dearborn av. *U.L.*
Harrison C. Thomas, 1444 Edgecomb ct.
Harrison Elizabeth Miss, 2231 Prairie av.
Harrison E. J. Berwyn
Harrison E. M. Dr. Morgan Park
Harrison George J. 230 S. Marshfield av.
Harrison Helen H. Miss, 3933 Prairie av.
Harrison Henry S. Mrs. LaGrange
Harrison J. Warren, 2358 Indiana av.
Harrison J. W. 6537 Kimbark av.
Harrison Thomas, 1444 Edgecomb ct.
Harrison William Preston, 295 Schiller.
  C.A.
Harrison W. K. Dr. 52 Walton pl.
Harrower Oscar C. 6714 Lowe av.
Harrsch R. E. 107 Seminary av.
Harsha Leslie R. 650 Washington boul.
  Ill.
Harsha W. M. Dr. 479 Bowen av.
Harshberger Adam, 7116 Princeton av.
Harshberger Charles R.7116 Princeton av.
Hart Abraham 3650 Michigan av. *Stan.*
Hart Alexander H. 4752 Langley av.
Hart Catherine Miss, 428 Ashland boul.
Hart Charles, 4511 Grand boul. *Stan.*
  Sum. res. Hart's Ease, Cal.
Hart Charles S. Evanston
Hart Edgar R. 4357 Vincennes av.
Hart Edward C. Hotel Del Prado
Hart Eli S. 3716 Lake av.
Hart Elmer W. 2975 Michigan av.
Hart Emil, 541, 44th. *Stan.*
Hart Frank, Sherman house
Hart Fred A. 737 W. Garfield boul.
Hart Frederick E. Austin
Hart G. W. B. 4327 Vincennes av.
Hart Hannah M. Miss, 5531 Monroe av.
Hart Harry, 4639 Drexel boul.
Hart Harry R. 3650 Michigan av. *Stan.*
Hart Hattie E. Mrs. Oak Park
Hart Henry G. 4327 Vincennes av.
Hart Henry N. 1618 Indiana av. *Stan.*
Hart Henry W. 4221 Ellis av.
Hart Herbert H. 1346 Millard av.
Hart Herbert L. 1618.Indiana av. *Stan.*
Hart Herman, 4010 Prairie av.
Hart Howard S. 5504 Cornell av. *C.A.*
Hart H. Stilson, 3716 Lake av.
Hart Jacob, 4915 Forrestville av.
Hart James, 352 Belden av.

Hart James A. 3287 Beacon. *C.A.*
Hart Jesse, Riverside
Hart John J. 1678 W. Jackson boul.
Hart John W. Mrs. 1118 Washington boul.
Hart Joseph, 4327 Calumet·av. *Lksd.*
Hart J. M. LaGrange
Hart J. P. Mrs: 145 Ashland boul.
Hart Leo H. 4010 Prairie av. *Lksd.*
Hart Louis E. 339 Warren av.
Hart Max 4643 Drexel boul. *Stan.*
Hart Milton R. 3650 Michigan av. *Stan.*
Hart M. G., M.D. 3805 Wabash av.
Hart Newton F. 736, W. 64th
Hart Robert, 4357 Vincennes av. *Lksd.,*
  Stan.
Harth Jacob, 406 Seminary av.
Hartigan J. G. 4429 Berkeley av.
Harting P. Fred. 3010 Lake Park av.
Hartley Calvin S. 4567 Oakenwald av.
Hartman A. 4440 Berkeley av. *Lksd.*
Hartman Edward, 3307 Vernon av.
Hartman Emanuel, 3307 Vernon av.
Hartman Emanuel, 3361 South Park av.
  Sum. res. Twin Lakes, Wis.
Hartman Leon, Lexington hotel. *Stan.*
Hartman Louis, 4335 Forrestville av.
  Lksd.
Hartman Milton L.Lexington hotel. *Stan.*
Hartman Simon, 3307 Vernon av.
Hartman Wm. W. Dr. 416 Winthrop av.
Hartman Wilton, Berwyn
Hartmann Charlotte Mrs.468W.Congress
Hartmann Frederick S. Dr. 568 W. Con-
  gress
Hartmann Henry S. 403 Bowen·av. *Lksd.*
Hartmann Joseph S. 403 Bowen av. *Lksd.*
Hartmann Samuel, 403 Bowen av.
Hartog Jn . H. 67 Madison Park. *C.A.,*
  W.P. o
Hartray James, Evanston
Hartray William C. Evanston
Harts Edwin B. 4455 Drexel boul.
Hartshorn J. Willard, Evanston
Hartt C. F. Dr. 2508 Indiana av.
Hartwell A. V. 5200 Washington av. *Ill.*
Hartwell D. E. 4624 Emerald av. *C.A.*
Hartwell Edwin S. 35 Stratford pl. *C.A..*
  Un., W.P.
Hartwell E. A. Oak Park
Hartwell F. G. 124, 50th. *C.A.*
Hartwell George ·H. 191 Schiller
  Sum. res. Lake Noquebay, Wis.
Hartwell Richard K. 35 Stratford pl.
Hartwig Herman, 1829 Arlington pl.
Hartz Irving T. 29, 46th. *C.A.*
Harvell Gaylord E. 6134 Monroe av.
Harvell William F. 6134 Monroe av.
Harvey Eliza O. Mrs. 1529 W. Monroe
Harvey Eliza V. Mrs. 52 Astor
Harvey E. S. Mrs. 4504 Vincennes av.
  Sum. res. Macatawa Park hotel
Harvey George L. Evanston. *Univ.*
Harvey George M. 36 Stratford pl. *C.A.*
Harvey George S. 7242 Euclid av.
Harvey George V. 3244 Groveland av.
  U.L.

Harvey James, Oak Park
Harvey James S. 269 W. Adams
Harvey Joel D. Geneva. *Chi.*
Harvey John, 351, 44th
Harvey John, Morgan Park
Harvey John H. 7242 Euclid av.
Harvey John H. 1153 W. Adams
Harvey L. P. Mrs. 5250 Prairie av.
Harvey Mary Rowena Miss, 4354 Grand boul,
Harvey Robert H. Dr. 58, 43d. *Univ.*
Harvey R. D. 6565 Yale
Harvey Sebastian A. 4203 Ellis av.
Harvey Sydney B. Oak Park
Harvey Thomas F. Hyde Park hotel
Harvey William R. Oak Park
Harvey Winnifred Mrs. 7641 Saginaw av.
Harvey W. S. Dr. 483 W. Adams. *C.A. Ill., W.P.*
Harwood Henry W. 5012 Ellis av.
Harz Cæsar O. 502 Dearborn av.
Harzfeld Edward, 850 Washington boul.
Hasbrouck Charles A. 234, 47th
Hasbrouck Louis, 196 Bowen av. *C.A.,*
Hasburg John W. 588 Fullerton av.
Hascall Milo S. Gen. Oak Park
Hasdell A. C. Mrs. The Arizona
Hasdell F. E. Miss, The Arizona
Haseltine H. B. Dr. Evanston
Haskell David F. 4239 Vincennes av.
Haskell Frederick T. 2824 Prairie av. *Chi., U.L., W.P.*
Haskell George W. 410 Ontario. *C.A., Irq.*
Haskell J. W. C. 557 Washington boul. *C.A.*
Haskell Joseph E. 521 Washington boul.
Haskell Loomis P. Dr. Hinsdale
Haskell Mary A. Mrs. 6154 Kimbark av.
Haskell Reuben L. 4239 Vincennes av.
Haskett Isaac R. 956 W. Jackson boul.
Haskett Robert E. 649 W. Monroe
Haskin Charles G. Evanston
Haskin Geo. W. Dr. Wilmette
Haskin Henry L. Dr. Highland Park
Haskins George W. 5488 Jefferson av.
Haskins H. Wolcott, 5488 Jefferson av.
Haskins Mary A. Mrs. 949 Warren av.
Haskins Robert C. 949 Warren av.
Haslett John M. Mrs. 4449 Champlain av.
Hass Walter K. 4211 Ellis av.
Hasselgren Rudolf, 440 N. State
Hassmer Joseph A. 568 Fullerton av.
Hassmer Mary Mrs. 568 Fullerton av.
Hasterlik Adolph, 4345 Forrestville av. *Lksd.*
Hasterlik Bertha Miss, 4800 Michigan av.
Hasterlik Charles, 4314 Vernon av. *Lksd.*
Hasterlik Henry, 3666 Indiana av.
Hasterlik Ignatz, 3666 Indiana av. *Lksd.*
Hasterlik Ray Miss, 4800 Michigan av.
Hasterlik Samuel, 4314 Vernon av. *Lksd.*
Hasterlik Simon, 4800 Michigan av. *Lksd.*
Hastie Margaret Mrs. 540 W. Jackson boul.
Hastings George L. 4353 Lake av.
Hastings Samuel M. 24 Buena terrace

Hatch Allen, Maywood
Hatch Azel F. 17 Hawthorne pl. *U.L., Univ.*
Hatch B. S. Evanston
Hatch Charles W. Austin
Hatch Edward P. LaGrange
Hatch Edwin H. 25 Aldine sq.
Hatch George, Maywood
Hatch G. W. Chicago Beach Hotel
Hatch Henry D. 295 S. Leavitt
Hatch James M. Austin
Hatch John, 1525 W. Monroe
Hatch John C. 25 Aldine sq.
Hatch Luther, Oak Park
Hatch Reuben, 821 Washington boul.
Hatch Thomas W. Austin
Hatch William H. Oak Park
Hatch William H. River Forest
Hatcher I. G. Oak Park
Hately John C. Chicago Beach hotel, *U.L.*
Hately Walter C. The Kenwood. *Chi. U.L.*
Hatfield Harris A. 3346 South Park av.
Hatfield James Taft, Evanston
Hatfield Marcus P. Dr. 3346 South Park av.
Hatfield R. M. Mrs. Evanston
Hatfield Wm. P. 981 S. Central Park av.
Hathaway Carrie B. Mrs. 324 Park av.
Hathaway Charles H. Evanston
Hathaway Elizabeth Mrs. Evanston
Hathaway Elizabeth A. Mrs. Evanston
Hathaway Frank J. 6557 Ingleside av.
Hathaway F. H. 2652 Magnolia av.
Hathaway Henry, 7037 Yale
Hathaway James N. Dr. Austin
Hathaway Nolin, 6447 Monroe av.
Hatheway Elias C. 4517 Woodlawn av.
Hatheway E. Morris, 4517 Woodlawn av.
Hatten Louisa Mrs. 4467 Oakenwald av.
Hatter George W. 6328 Ellis av.
Hatterman Ottilie R. Mrs. 2468 Kenmore av.
Hatterman William E. Malvern av. cor. Birchwood av.
Hattstaedt John J. 212, 51st
Hauck Frederick, 657 Fullerton av.
Haugan H. A. 1713 Deming pl. *U.L.*
Haugan Oscar, 1713 Deming pl.
Haughey Charles T. 715 The Plaza
Haughey Louis, 3006 Prairie av.
Haughey L. C. 3004 Prairie av. *C.A.*
Haughey Schuyler, 3006 Prairie av.
Haupt Edward, Evanston
House Carl Prof. 45 Roslyn pl.
Hausske August, 1847 Arlington pl.
Haustetter Catherina Mrs. 3297 Beacon
Havard Charles H. Irving Park
Havemeyer William A. Riverside. *Chi.*
Havemeyer W. A. jr. Riverside
Haven Alfred C., M.D. Lake Forest
Haven Dwight C. 3135 Indiana av.
Haven Joseph Dr. 57 Gordon terrace
Havens Arthur E. 895 W. Monroe
Havens L. A. Mrs. 1049 Early av.
Havercamp George B. The Ontario

Haverkampf John L. 389 Ashland boul.
Haverkampf John L. jr. 389 Ashland
  boul.
Haviland Grace King Mrs. 2944 Indiana
  av.
Haviland R. C. LaGrange
Havron John, 4351 Lake av. C.A., Un.
Hawes Albert C. 5520 Monroe av.
Hawes Kirk Judge, 2235 Calumet av. U.L.
Hawes William H. 768 W. Jackson boul.
  Ill.
Hawhe Arthur J. Julien hotel
Hawk M. C. Dr. Morgan Park
Hawkes Benjamin C. 1210 Winthrop av.
Hawkes Thomas Mrs. Winnetka
Hawkes William J. Dr. 420 N. State
Hawkins Charles H. 5016 Greenwood av.
Hawkins Frank P. Highland Park
Hawkins George E., D.D.S. 97 Lincoln
  av.
Hawkins M. L. Miss, 4049 Lake av.
Hawkins Richard W. Highland Park
Hawks Charles A. 137 Lincoln Park boul.
Hawks Rebecca Mrs. Evanston
Hawks Thomas H. Evanston
Hawley Charles A. Mrs. 3515 Grand boul.
Hawley Clark W. Dr. La Grange
Hawley C. M. Mrs. 5326 Washington av.
Hawley C. W. Oak Park
Hawley Edgar R. Dr. 3614 Lake av.
Hawley Elmer B. 503 N. State
Hawley E. S. 5430 Ridgewood ct.
Hawley Frank R. 5430 Ridgewood ct.
Hawley George F., M.D. 1718 Kenmore
  av.
Hawley Henry S. 5845 Madison av.
Hawley Joseph E.R.Dr. 3515 Grand boul.
Hawley Samuel F. 3515 Grand boul.
Haworth George D. 20 Groveland Park
Hawson Thomas B. 3725 Ellis av.
Hawson Thomas W. 3725 Ellis av.
Hawthorne Silas T. 6220 Monroe av.
Hawtin F. Walter, Hinsdale
Hawxhurst Arthur, 871 Hamilton ct.
Hawxhurst J. M. Evanston. C.A.
Hay James, 1581 W. Adams. Ill.
Hayde Edmond C. 3113 Prairie av.
Hayde James, 1710 Deming pl.
Hayden Albert, 3155 Michigan av. Chi.,
  W.P.
Hayden A. G. Mrs. 6346 Parnell av.
Hayden Charles E. 3319 Michigan av.
Hayden Francis A. 3252 South Park av.
Hayden Frank N. 5545 Monroe av.
Hayden Frederick M. 4508 Indiana av.
Hayden George R. 7529 Eggleston av.
Hayden George W. Oak Park
Hayden Harvey S. 4008 Lake av.
Hayden H. H.Mrs.3319 Michigan av
Hayden H. H. jr. 3319 Michigan av.
Hayden James T. Oak Park
Hayden Ralph, Evanston
Hayden R. C. Hotel Windermere
Hayden Wm. Evanston
Hayes D. A. Prof. Evanston
Hayes Frank, 831 Washington boul. Ill.

Hayes F. W. C. Mrs. 4334 Ellis av.
Hayes F. A. S. LaGrange
Hayes George A. 1907 Michigan av.
Hayes Grace J. Miss, 52 Walton pl.
Hayes Harold H. Dr. 1851 Aldine av.
Hayes James E. 5000 Washington av.
Hayes James J. 341 W. 60th
Hayes Louis S. 412 Belden av.
Hayes Michael, 1288 Washington boul.
Hayes M. Mis. 2445 Wabash av.
Hayes M. E. Mrs. 6440 Ellis av.
Hayes P. B. Dr. 1359 W. Jackson boul.
Hayes Richard G. 4910 Michigan av.
Hayes Robert H. 1851 Aldine av.
Hayes William F. Oak Park
Hayes W. Elliott, 5156 Michigan av.
Hayes W. P. 5156 Michigan av.
Hayes-Sadler Ralph H. Mrs. 459 Dear-
  born av.
Hayford Ernest L. Dr. 926 W. Monroe
Hayhurst Will C. 642 Washington boul.
Hayman L. B. Dr. 167 Oakwood boul.
Hayne Frederick E. 4354 Greenwood av.
Hayner Clark, 341, 41st
Hayner Frank E. 39 N. Sheldon
Hayner Jennie E. Dr. 454 Walnut
Hayner R. W. 4401 Prairie av.
Haynes Daniel J. 432 Washington boul.
Haynes Everett L. 4943 Champlain av.
Haynes Frank T. 7534 Harvard av.
Haynes George M. 7534 Harvard av.
Haynes John P. 7716 Eggleston av.
Haynes Joseph R. 7534 Harvard av.
Haynes Louis W. 151, 36th
Haynes N. S. Rev. 535 W. 61st pl.
Haynes Thomas C. 374 Dearborn av.
Haynes Willard S. 3027 Vernon av.
Haynes William A. 6429 Yale
Haynes W. Knox, 4243 Champlain av.
Hays Allan M. 279, 53d
  Sum. res. East Kensington, N. H.
Hays Mary R. Miss, 2326 Indiana av.
Hays M. D. The Arizona
Hayt Henry C. 273 Ashland boul. U.L. Ill.
Hayt Walter V. 3242 Dover
Hayward Arthur W. 5418 Washington
  av.
Hayward Carrie M. Dr. 960 W. Jackson
  boul.
Hayward Charles, 99 Park av.
Hayward Florence Miss, 16 Astor
Hayward F. Sydney, 4757 Champlain av.
Hayward Susan, Miss, 16 Astor
Haywood Lucy Mrs. 796 W. Monroe
Haywood Peter S. 508 W. Adams
Hazard James I. 1558 Kenmore av.
Hazen Henry C. Mrs. Oak Park
Hazen John F. Chicago Beach hotel
Hazen W. Lee, 3801 Ellis av.
Hazlehurst Andrew, Evanston
Hazlehurst Samuel, Winnetka
Hazlett H. H. Mrs. The Arizona
Hazlitt George H. 39 Campbell Park
Hazlitt George K. 39 Campbell Park
Hea M. J. 376 Dearborn av.
Head Benjamin F. 4128 Drexel boul.

Head Franklin H. 2 Banks. *Chi.*, *U.L.*, *Univ.*
Head George A. 610 Washington boul.
Head Gustavus P. Dr. Austin
Head Harry C. 4128 Drexel boul.
Head James M. 5467 Jefferson av.
Head Paul D. 5467 Jefferson av.
Head R. Caswell, 4200 Lake av.
Head William J. 87 Rush. *W.P.*
Head W. R: 5467 Jefferson av.
Headley Howard, 139 W. Garfield boul.
Headley Thomas H. Mrs. 139 W. Garfield boul.
Heafford Geo. H. 4560 Oakenwald av.
Heaford Henry H. 3634 Vernon av.
Heald James H. Oak Park
Heald James H. jr. Oak Park
Healy Edith Miss, 387 Ontario
Healy Edward B. 680, 48th pl.
Healy George L. 387 Ontario. *C.A.*
Healy G. P. A. Mrs. 387 Ontario
Healy Helen S. Mrs. 857 Pratt av.
Healy James, 24 Bittersweet pl.
Healy James J. 1426 Michigan av.
Healy James T. 3230 Indiana av.
Healy J. J. 222, 42d pl.
Healy M. J. 2977 Kenmore av.
Healy Paul, Lakota hotel
Healy P. J. 508 W. Jackson boul. *Ill.*, *U.L.* Sum res. Williams Bay, Wis.
Healy Stephen, 3247 Calumet av.
Healy W. P. North Shore hotel
Heap Arnold, 1423 Washington boul.
      Sum. res. Portsmouth, N. H.
Heaphy A. T. Hinsdale
Hearding W. H. Mrs. 377 Superior
Heath Arthur M. 164, 51st. *C.A.*.
Heath Charles A. 471, 42d
Heath De Forrest W. 544 W. Jackson boul.
Heath Edward G. 1136 Winthrop av.
Heath Ernest W. 5744 Rosalie ct. *C.A.*, *U.L.*, *W.P.*
Heath E. Mrs. 7105 Princeton av.
Heath I. A. 3136 Prairie av.
Heath J. S. Irving Park
Heatherington Alex: 955 Belle Plaine av.
Heaton A. R. Mrs. 169 Rush
Heaton E. S. Hotel Metropole
Heaton Harold R. 169 Rush
Hebard Frank H. 594 W. Congress
Hebard Frederic S. 570 Washington boul. *C.A.*, *U.L.*.
Hebard Henry, 686 W. Monroe
Hebard J. E. Mrs. 3348 Calumet av.
Hebel Otto W. 693 North Park av.
Hebel William, 693 North Park av.
Hebert Alfred W. Dr. Evanston
Hebert Letitia Miss, Evanston
Hecht Ernest, 642 Fullerton av. *C.A.*
Hecht Frank A. 639 W. Jackson boul. *U.L.*
Hecht J. F. 1018 Early av.
Hecht Morris, 3436 Calumet av.
Hecht Walter E. 603 Burling
Heckard Martin O. Dr. 1251 W. Madison

Heckman Wallace, 4505 Ellis av. *U.L.* Sum. res. "Ganymede," Oregon, Ill.
Hecox Daisy Miss, Austin
Hecox John F. Austin
Hecox Marion Miss, Austin
Hecox Mattie D. Miss, Austin
Hedenberg Cecilia Miss, 157 Honore
Hedenberg James W. 132 Ashland boul.
Hedenberg John W. 157 Honore
Hedenberg-Wells C. Mrs. 157 Honore
Hedgeland Frederick W. 1060 Warren av.
      Sum. res. South Haven, Mich.
Hedges Albert P. Dr. 754 Fullerton av.
Hedges Samuel P. Dr. 890 Evanston av.
Hedges William E. 890 Evanston av.
Hedglin James A. 3558 Forest av.
Heeb Benjamin D. 1219 Winthrop av.
Heegaard B. Louise M.D. 666 Lasalle av.
      Sum. res. Lake Geneva, Wis.
Heegaard W. H. 666 Lasalle av. *C.A.*
      Sum. res. Lake Geneva, Wis.
Heermans T. W. Evanston
Hefferan William S. 6454 Stewart av.
Heffron A. D. Washington Heights
Heffron D. S. Rev. Washington Heights
Hefling F. J. The Ontario
Hefter Cæsar L. 3531 Wabash av.
Hefter Charles, 490, 42d pl. *Lksd.*
Hefter C. H. 3312 Indiana av.
Hefter Florence L. Miss, 3531 Wabash av.
Hefter Henry, 3312 Indiana av.
Hefter Herman, 350, 42d
Hefter Louis B. 632, 46th pl. *Lksd.*
Hefter Moses L. 3641 Forest av. *Lksd.*
Hefter Rebecca L. Miss, 3531 Wabash av.
Heg Ernest, 4409 Prairie av.
Heicher George, 3232 Beacon
Heidelberger Ernestine Mrs. 3238 South Park av.
Heideman George F. Dr. Elmhurst
Heidenreich E. Lee, 524 Kenwood terrace
Heilbron Joseph, 3832 Prairie av.
Heile Adolph, 1834 Barry av.
Heile Charles Dyer, 1834 Barry av.
Heile Louis A. 1448 Dakin av.
Heilprin Louis, 4409 Berkeley av. *Stan.*
Heim Eugene, Maywood
Heimerdinger Henry H. 3405 Forest av.
Heinberg Fred, 1511 Wolfram
Heineman Julius, 771 N. Clark
Heineman Mary Mrs. 343 Oakwood boul.
Heineman Oscar, 250, 47th
Heineman Samuel, Hinsdale
Heinemann Alfred R. 349 Hampden ct.
Heinemann Charles, 625 Cleveland av.
Heinemann William, 349 Hampden ct.
Heinemann William C. 349 Hampden ct.
Heinig Frank, Lakeside
Heinroth William C. 612 Washington boul.
Heinsen John, 625 N. Hoyne av.
Heinsheimer D. 3813 Prairie av.
Heinsheimer D. jr. 3813 Prairie av. *Lksd*
Heinz Lorenz H. 551 W. 62d
Heinze E. F. 912 Hamilton ct.
Heinze F. G. 914 Hamilton ct.

Hemze Victor, 6123 Kimbark av.
Heisen Carl C. 65 Lake Shore drive. *Un.*
Heissler Ed R. 4427 Grand boul.
Heissler Jacob, 4427 Grand boul.
Heissler Jacob F. 4427 Grand boul.
Heissler M. Louise Miss, 4427 Grand boul.
Heister Henry J. 1810 Arlington pl.
Heitbahn John C. Mrs. 6030 Kimbark av.
Heldmann Charles C. The Tudor
          Sum. res. Govanston, Md.
Helfenstein Charles B. 6230 Kimbark av.
          Sum. res. Fox Lake
Heller Charles L. Dr 3243 South Park av.
Heller Gustav, 584, 45th. *Lksd.*
Heller Isadore, 5132 Woodlawn av.
Heller Leo, 4550 Vincennes av. *Lksd.*
Heller M. L. 3243 South Park av.
Heller William, 4051 Prairie av.
Hellman George A. 489 Dearborn av.
Hellman George A. jr. 489 Dearborn av.
Hellyer Frederick, Riverside. *Chi., C.A.*
Helm Daniel T. 881 Washington boul. *Ill.*
Helm Flora Miss, North Shore hotel
Helm Henry T. Judge, 6913 Stewart av.
Helm H. W. 4517 Prairie av.
Helm John W. Evanston
Helmer Edward E. Riverside
Helmer Frank A. 1428 Michigan av. *Univ.*
Helmer Harry, 34 Aldine sq.
Helmer Joseph W. 34 Aldine sq.
Hemenover W. Elmer, 7107 Eggleston av.
Hemenway Henry B. Dr. Evanston
Hemingway Anson T. Oak Park
Hemingway Clarence E. Dr. Oak Park
Hemingway George R. Oak Park
          Sum. res. Mt. Pleasant, O.
Hemingway H. W. Dr. 6816 Perry av.
Hemingway James A. 573 Division
Hemingway Willoughby A. Oak Park
Hemmelgarn Henry, 719 Fullerton av.
Hempstead Charles E. 387 N. State
Hempstead Edward Mrs. Evanston
Hempstead France, 1672 Kenmore av.
Hempstead G. C. The Ontario. *Un.*
Hempstead William G. Evanston
Hemsley Walter, Chicago Beach hotel. *Irq.*
Hemsteger John A. Dr. 255 Oakwood boul.
Hemstreet W. J. 999 W. Adams
Hench John B. Dr. Hinsdale
Henderson Charles M. Mrs. 1816 Prairie av.
Henderson Chas. R. Prof. 5736 Washington av.
Henderson David H. 668 W. Adams
Henderson Edgar F. Calumet club
Henderson Edward G. Evanston
Henderson Edwin J. 6443 Drexel av.
Henderson E. G. Mrs. Evanston
Henderson Frank B. 1821 Aldine av.
Henderson Helen Miss, 4109 Grand boul.
Henderson Howard, 4109 Grand boul.
Henderson H. M. 548 W. 61st
Henderson John C. 1142 Washington boul.

Henderson L. D. Dr. Evanston
Henderson N. H. Dr. 4147 Lake av.
Henderson T. A. 1838 Arlington pl. *C.A.*
Henderson Wilbur F. 2623 Michigan av. *Univ.*
Henderson Wilbur S. 2623 Michigan av. *Chi., W.P.*
Hendricks Charles A. 140 W. 65th
Hendricks R. J. Gault house
Hendricks Walter, 6329 Greenwood av.
Hendricks W. Lee, 6555 Greenwood av.
Hendricks W. S. 6555 Greenwood av.
Hendrickson Ernest, 5510 Cornell av.
Hendrickson F. S. 3101 Groveland av.
Hendrickson George L. Prof. 5515 Woodlawn av.
Hendy A. Mrs. Oak Park
Hendy Clara A. Dr. Oak Park
Henion W. B. 35, 46th. *U.L.*
Henius Max, 2576 Magnolia av.
Henkel Fred. W. E. Dr. 538 Ashland boul.
Henkle Wm. H. 28 Madison Park. *U.L.*
Henne Phillip, 589 Lasalle av.
Henneberry William P. 543 W. Jackson boul. *C.A., Ill.* Sum. res. Wheaton
Hennegen Richard H. Oak Park
Hennersheets William B. 6361 Lexington av.
Hennessy C. M. Miss, 4123 Drexel boul.
Hennessy Frank D. 299 S. Irving av.
Hennessy Peter J. Col. 315 Superior
Hennessy Richard M. 307 Webster av.
Hennessy W. B. 4123 Drexel boul.
Hennessy W. E. Mrs. 4123 Drexel boul.
Hennick Charles, Austin
Henning Edwin, Chicago Beach hotel.
Henning Francis Alexander, M.D. 483 Dearborn av. *U.L.*
          Sum. res. Delavan, Wis.
Henning Frank F. 283 Evanston av.
Henning Frederick W. 1525 Grace
Henning William, 1525 Grace
Henrich Jacob, 699 North Park av.
Henrici Philip, 48 Lincoln av.
Henricks Edward W. Pullman
Henrotin Charles, 319 Superior, *Chi., Un.*
Henrotin Charles Martin, 319 Superior
Henrotin Edward Clement, 319 Superior
Henrotin Fernand, M. D. 353 Lasalle av. *C.A., Un.*
Henry Eugene J. 1255 Winthrop av. *C.A., Irq.*
Henry George W. Mrs. 1913 Michigan av. Sum. res. "The Woods," Goodenow, Ill.
Henry Harvey R. 3812 Wabash av.
Henry John A. 6601 Stewart av.
Henry J. Q. A. Rev. 425 Lasalle av.
Henry Robert L. 3656 Grand boul. *Irq., U.L.*
Henry William G. 3618 Michigan av.
Henry William R. 3831 Lake av.
Henshaw Charles W. 432 N. State
Henshaw Henry H. 30 Campbell Park
Henshaw Horace W. 432 N. State
          Sum. res. Wiesbaden, Germany.
Henshaw Tilla Mrs. 3411½ Prairie av.

Henson Charles W. 3249 South Park av.
Henson Horace, 3249 South Park av.
Henson Hudson L. 6501 Kimbark av.
Henson Mae Belle Miss, 3249 South Park av.
Henson Paul, 6505 Monroe av.
Henson P. S. Rev. 3249 South Park av.
Henson Wilmer Y. 3249 South Park av.
Henwood H. C. 225 Dearborn av.
Henzell William, Morton Park
Hepburn John W. Mrs. 499 W. Adams
Heper Otto, 840 Washington boul.
Hepp Susan Miss, 424 N. State
Heppner Henry, 3239 Vernon av. *Stan.*
Hequembourg Julian E. Dr. 512 Fullerton av.
Herbert H. M. Mrs. 791 Warren av.
Herbertz Charles, 3412 South Park av.
Herbst Bernard, 689 Sedgwick
Herbst C. 225 Dearborn av.
Herbst Herman, 517 Dearborn av.
Herbst William, 4211 Calumet av. *Lksd*
Hercock Robert J. 4550 Wabash av.
Herdman F. E. Winnetka
Hereley Michael H. 215 Osgood
Herendeen W. 2652 Magnolia av.
Hereth Frank S. 314 Belden av.
Herhold Fred, 675 N. Robey
Herman Benjamin, 3641½ Prairie av.
Herman Leonard M. 3601 Vincennes av. *Lksd., Stan.*
Herman Samuel J. 3352 South Park av. *Lksd.*
Hermann Joseph, 413 N. Robey
Hermann J. Oakland hotel
Herndl Marie Miss, Ohio ne. cor. State
Heron Hugh, 2826 Indiana av.
Herr A. W. Mrs. 333, 34th
Herr Ezra G. 2116 W. Monroe
Herr Hiero B. 5006 Washington av.
Herr Percy B. 5006 Washington av.
Herr Stephen D. 1191 Wilton av.
Herren Oscar F. 770 Lunt av.
Herrick Bernard, 3409 Prairie av.
Herrick Charles S. 3409 Prairie av.
Herrick Dwight C. Oak Park
Herrick Eugene E. 4144 Indiana av.
Herrick E. Walter, 2018 Prairie av. *Cal., Chi., C.A., W.P.*
Herrick Gertrude T. Miss, 4412 Indiana av.
Herrick Harry, Oak Park
Herrick James B., M.D. 751 Warren av.
Herrick John J. 2221 Prairie av. *Chi., Univ.* Sum. res. Camden, Me.
Herrick Joseph W. 3409 Prairie av.
Herrick Louis E. 4817 Prairie av.
Herrick Louise Miss, 2018 Prairie av.
Herrick L. A. Mrs. 2018 Prairie av.
Herrick Margaret Mrs. 4533 Lake av.
Herrick Mary B. Miss, 5731 Monroe av.
Herrick Milton, 3409 Prairie av.
Herrick N. W. 4911 Greenwood av.
Herrick O. W. Oak Park
Herrick Robert, 5488 East End av.
Herrick Roswell Z. 4412 Indiana av.

Herrick William, 1151 Washington boul. *C.A.*
Herrick W. B. Granada hotel
Herrick W. S. Oak Park
Herriman Morris M. River Forest
Herriman Wilfred D., M. D. 6311 Woodlawn av.
Herriman William N. River Forest
Herring Robert H. 3315 Beacon
Herron James B. 7812 Lowe av.
Herron Samuel P. 2516 Indiana av.
Hersey J. W. 843 W. Adams
Hertel Carl W. 5101 Kimbark av.
Hertel L. L. Dr. 3000 Groveland av.
Hertle Louis, Evanston, *U.L.*
Hertz Adolph H. 151 Goethe
Hertz Henry L. 628 N. Hoyne av.
Hervey James F. 2953 Michigan av.
Hervey Robert, 33, 25th
Herz Arthur, 4720 Evans av.
Herz Joseph, 4720 Evans av. *Lksd.*
Herzog Louis P. 198, 36th
Herzog Nathan, 1609 W. Adams
Hesing Washington Mrs. 235 Michigan av.
Hesly Daniel, 1080 Carmen av.
Hess A. M. Mrs. 219, 48th
Hess Chas. E. 604 Lasalle av.
Hess Charles H. Hinsdale
Hess Christopher J. 4431 Ellis av.
Hess Daniel W. Evanston
Hess Ernest, 602 Lasalle av. Sum. res. Lake Villa, Ill.
Hess Frank W. 611 Lasalle av.
Hess Franklin, 6950 Butler
Hess Frederick A., Dr., 908 Belle Plaine av.
Hess George H. 3736 Lake av.
Hess George W. Wilmette
Hess Howard A. 4431 Ellis av.
Hess Isaac, 3224 Prairie av.
Hess John V. 121, 21st
Hess Leo, 4836 Michigan av. *Lksd.*
Hess Louis A. 602 Lasalle av.
Hess M. W. 4509 Prairie av.
Hess Nannie Mrs. 4509 Prairie av.
Hess Siegel, 4836 Michigan av. *Lksd.*
Hess William H. 822 Sherwin av.
Hess Winter D. Evanston
Hesse Emma Miss, 7120 Eggleston av.
Hesse Marie Miss, 7120 Eggleston av.
Hesse Philip, 7120 Eggleston av.
Hesselroth Lawrence, 1805 Arlington pl.
Hessert Gustav Dr. 25 Roslyn pl.
Hessert Gustav jr. 1927 Arlington pl. *C.A.*
Hessert William Dr. 25 Roslyn pl.
Hessler John C. 5756 Madison av.
Hester Albert W. 44 Junior terrace
Hester William W. Dr. 107, 37th
Heth Henry S. 2024 Indiana av. *Irq., W.P.*
Heth James B. 2024 Indiana av.
Hetherington Charles, 6501 Kimbark av.
Hetherington Henry J. 7300 Bond av.
Hetherington John F. 250, 51st
Hetherington John T. 7306 Bond av.

Hetherington Judson E. Dr. 1035 Warren av.
Hettich Harry L. 4056 Calumet av.
Hettinger John P. 460 Dayton
Hettler Herman H. 37 Hawthorne pl. *Cai., C.A., Un., W.P.*
Hetzler Herbert G. Hinsdale ·
Heuchling Theodore W., M.D. 663 La-salle av.
Heuer August, jr. 2478 Magnolia av.
Heuer Henry, 2478 Magnolia av.
Heuermann Henry W. 168 Fremont
Heurtley Arthur, Oak Park
    Sum. res. LesCheneaux Islands, Mich.
Heusner John A. 4655 Calumet av.
Heusner Louis D. 675, 48th pl.
Hevenor R. Augustus, 5542 Madison av.
Hewes Albert M. 4700 Grand boul.
Hewes Herbert H. Oak Park
Hewett A. C. Dr. 491 W. Adams
Hewitt Carlton C. Pullman
Hewitt Charles A. 487, 42d pl.
Hewitt Charles M. Virginia hotel. *Chi., C.A., U.L.*
Hewitt Ephraim, 347, 56th
Hewitt F. H. Mrs. Lake Forest
Hewitt James, 5040 Washington av.
Hewitt Jerome, 4318 Forrestville av.·
Hewitt John, 812 Winthrop av.
Hewitt John H. 620 Lunt av.
Hewitt J. B. Mrs. 527 W. Jackson boul.
Hewitt J. L. Mrs. 3842 Langley av.
Hexter Kaufman, 2513 Wabash av. *Irq., Lksd.*
Hexter S. 3401 Prairie av.
Heyer Christian F. Hinsdale
Heyer Maria Anna Mrs. 483 Dearborn av.
Heylmann Angelica Miss, 289 Webster av.
Heylmann C. J. Dr. 289 Webster av.
Heylmann Minnie Miss, 289 Webster av.
Heyman Emanuel S. 4529 Ellis av. *Lksd., Stan.*
Heyman Samuel, 3363 Calumet av.
Heywood Abbie F. Mrs. 6736 Lowe av.
Heywood Edwin F. 403 Oak
Heywood Joseph T. Berwyn
Heywood Porter P. Mrs. 426 N. State
Heyworth James O. 2902 Michigan av. *Cal., U.L., Univ., W.P.*
Heyworth J. F. Mrs. 2902 Michigan av.
Heyworth Lawrence, 2902 Michigan av. *Cal., Chi., C.A., W.P.*
Hiatt A. H., M.D. 4024 Drexel boul.
Hibbard Angus S. 74 Bellevue pl. *U.L., Univ.*
Hibbard Edward R. 4804 Lake av.
    Sum. res. Chautauqua, N. Y.
Hibbard Frank V. S. 150 Lincoln Park boul. *C.A.*
Hibbard Frederick A. 4223 Grand boul.
Hibbard John Mrs. 4223 Grand boul.
Hibbard John D. 52 Madison Park
Hibbard J. W. 5031 Lake av.
Hibbard Katherine Mrs. 4001 Vincennes av.

Hibbard Lewis B. Highland Park
Hibbard M. L. Mrs. Evanston
Hibbard William G. 1701 Prairie av. *Cal., Chi., C.A., W.P.*
Hibbard William G. jr. 1701 Prairie av. *C.A., Univ., W.P.*
Hibbard W. N. Mrs. 5000 Greenwood av.
Hibben Helen H. Mrs. 426, 41st
Hibben Heron K. 426, 41st
Hibben James, Evanston
Hibben Samuel E. 426, 41st
Hibler John J. 6618 Ellis av.
Hick George C. Evanston
Hickcox P. Mrs. 1159 Washington boul.
Hickey Charles M. 2712 Calumet av.
Hickey John, 4809 Indiana av.
Hickey Joseph V. 2712 Calumet av.
Hickey Michael C. 2712 Calumet av.
Hickman Charles, Wyoming hotel
Hickman Henry A. 3232 Michigan av.
Hickox William C. 897 W. Monroe
Hicks Ada Miss, 301 Warren av.
Hicks Bohn C. 6438 Harvard av.
Hicks David F. 735 W. Monroe
Hicks Ernest H. 4830 Kimbark av.
Hicks E. L. LaGrange
Hicks George I. 735 W. Monroe
Hicks George W. 361 S. Oakley av.
Hicks Hervey B. 3763 Ellis av.
Hicks James A. LaGrange
Hicks O. H. Hotel Del Prado
Hicks Thomas·P. 697 Walnut
Hiebler J. H. Miss, 428 N. State
Hield George C. Irving Park
Hieronymus Adolph, 188 N. State
Hiestand Henry, 4279 N. Ashland av.
Hiester Alvin C. Dr. 1062 Millard av.
Higbee Charles E. 292 S. Marshfield av.
Higbee Jennie Mrs. 4045 Ellis av.
Higbee William E. 4045 Ellis av. *U.L.*
Higbie Fred K. 6431 Greenwood av.
    Sum. res. Green Lake, Wis.
Higbie Nathan B. 118, 49th
Higgie Archibald A. 4933 Ellis av.
Higgie Arthur M. 4933 Ellis av.
Higgie George W. 4933 Ellis av.
Higgie James L. 4933 Ellis av.
Higgie M. L. Miss, 4933 Ellis av.
Higgie Noble K. 4933 Ellis av.
Higgins A. E. Dr. LaGrange
Higgins Charles, 375 Ontario
Higgins Charles A. 10 St. James pl.
Higgins C. W. Hinsdale
Higgins Edward, 4297 Kenmore av.
Higgins George W. 149 Ashland boul.
Higgins George W. jr. 1014 Pratt av.
Higgins Harvey A. Oak Park
Higgins James D. Dr. 942 Walnut
Higgins John F. 1566 W. Monroe
Higgins J. Mrs 3707 Sheridan rd.
Higgins Milton O. 5515 Woodlawn av.
Higgins Van H. Mrs. 4948 Woodlawn av.
Higgins Wilbur, Lexington hotel
Higginson Charles M. Riverside
Higginson Dudley T. Elmhurst
Higginson George jr. Winnetka. *Univ.*

Higgs Edward B. Morton Park
High George Henry, 63 Lake Shore drive, *Chi., U.L.*
High George Meeker Mrs. 10 Astor
High James L. Lakeside
High James L. Mrs. 2021 Prairie av.
High Shirley T. 2021 Prairie av.
Highley G. E. 5121 Washington av. *U.L.*
Hight E. J. Mrs. 646 Washington boul.
Higinbotham Florence Miss, 2838 Michigan av.
Higinbotham Harlow D. Joliet *Chi., C.A., U.L.*
Higinbotham Harry M. 2838 Michigan av. *Cal., C.A., U.L.*
Higinbotham H. N. 2838 Michigan av. *Chi., U.L.*
  Sum. res. New Lennox, Ill.
Higley A. M. 4623 Greenwood av.
Higley Wm. K. Prof. 6133 Monroe av.
Higley W. E. 4623 Greenwood av.
Hiland James H. The Kenwood, *U.I.*
Hild Charles, 687 Burling
Hild Frederick H. 321 N. Wells. *C.A.*
Hild John G. Rev. Elmhurst
Hild Mary C. Mrs. 321 N. Wells
Hildebrand Lewis K. Hinsdale
Hildebrandt Frederick H. 256 Seminary av.
Hildreth Charles H. 7 Aldine sq.
Hildreth James H. 746 W. Monroe
Hildreth Leslie E. Evanston. *C.A.*
Hiles Theron L. Mayfair
Hilgard Marie Mrs. 5431 Cottage Grove av.
Hill Albert B. 488 Webster av.
Hill Albert E. 7100 Eggleston av.
Hill Alonzo H. Irving Park
Hill Anna Miss, 290 Lasalle av.
Hill Benjamin F. 4521 St. Lawrence av.
Hill Berton Cutter, 4054 Grand boul.
Hill Calvin H. 1641 W. Adams *C.A.*
Hill Caroline Mrs. 288 Ohio
Hill Caroline D. Mrs. 695 Washington boul.
Hill Carrie E. Miss, 611 Washington boul.
Hill Charles B. 1237 Washington boul.
Hill Charles Erwin, 1159 Washington boul. *Ill.*
Hill Charles S. Highland Park
Hill Cyrus F. Mrs. 2537 Michigan av.
Hill C. Mrs. Lakota hotel
Hill C. E. Hotel Metropole
Hill Daniel A. 935 W. Monroe
Hill Daniel O. 1912 Barry av.
Hill David K. Evanston
Hill Edgar A. 1237 Washington boul. *Ill., U.L.*
Hill Edward E. 5411 Greenwood av.
Hill Edward Niles, 4519 Forrestville av.
Hill Edwin F. 3714 Sheridan rd.
Hill Elizabeth P. Mrs. 4201 Ellis av.
Hill Elmer, 750 North Park av.
Hill Ezra N. Mrs. Evanston
Hill E. J. 2358 Indiana av.
Hill E. J. 7100 Eggleston av.
Hill E. M. Miss, Hotel Del Prado
37

Hill Fowell B. 3520 Lake av.
Hill Francis H. 745 W. Monroe
Hill Francis J. 2942 Indiana av.
Hill Frank E. 4337 Prairie av.
Hill Frank M. 620 W. 61st
Hill Fred A. Austin
Hill Fred G. 516 W. 62d
Hill Fred Morgan, 4054 Grand boul.
Hill Fred W. 7100 Eggleston av.
Hill Frederick W. 3910 Langley av.
Hill Fremont, LaGrange
Hill F. C. 7156 Harvard av.
Hill George, Lombard
Hill Grace Miss, 628 Dearborn av.
Hill G. Mortimer Dr. 4700 Grand boul.
Hill Harlan B. Evanston
Hill Harriet K. Miss, 5300 Woodlawn av.
Hill Helen Miss, 4201 Ellis av.
Hill Henry L. Mrs. 2316 Calumet av.
Hill Henry W. 235 Michigan av.
Hill James A. 4054 Grand boul.
Hill James F. 7127 Wentworth av.
Hill James M. Mrs. 3910 Langley av.
Hill Jean P. Miss, 3223 Groveland av.
Hill John jr. Tracy
Hill John H. 4156 Berkeley av.
Hill Joseph W. 6427 Woodlawn av.
Hill J. Claude, 6510 Monroe av.
Hill J. H. Mrs. 628 Dearborn av.
Hill Kate L. Miss, 245 Ohio
Hill Louis E. Lieut. Fort Sheridan
Hill Lucy Lee Miss, 101 Lincoln Park boul.
Hill Lysander Judge, Highland Park. *Cal., Un., U.L.*
Hill Mabel Miss, Highland Park
Hill Mary M. Mrs. 4156 Berkeley av.
Hill Matson, 3223 Groveland av.
Hill Mattie S. Miss, 628 Dearborn av.
Hill Mollie Miss, 245 Ohio
Hill M. W. 6462 Monroe av.
Hill Richard S. 4823 St. Lawrence av.
Hill Robert Mrs. 3714 Sheridan rd.
Hill Robert J. 4608 Champlain av.
Hill Robert S. 4243 Vincennes av.
Hill Russell D. Highland Park, *C.A.*
Hill Thomas E. Glen Ellyn
Hill Walter O. Oak Park
Hill William Prof. 338, 57th
Hill William, 3015 Prairie av.
Hill William J. Leland hotel
Hill William T. 245 Ohio, *C.A.*
Hillard Charles W. Virginia hotel. *Chi*
Hiller Gustav, 3842 Lake av.
Hiller Louis, 3844 Lake av.
Hilliard Louie A. 169 Rush
Hilliard Wm. P. Longwood
Hillis David M. 6124 Woodlawn av. *U.L.*
Hillis David S. 6124 Woodlawn av.
Hillis Newell Dwight Rev. 13 Ritchie ct. *U.L.*
Hillman Charles H. 6146 Monroe av
Hillman C. W. Evanston
Hillman Edward, 2819 Indiana av. *Stan.*
Hillman Maurice, 3241 South Park av.
Hillman Ruth E. Miss, 2819 Indiana av.

Hillmer Frank H. River Forest
Hillmer Walter B. 5738 Indiana av.
Hillock Alexander S. 6039 Lexington av. *C.A.*
Hills Charles F. 4419 Greenwood av. *Cal.*, *U.L.*
Hills E. O. Mrs. Evanston
Hills Frederick D. 213, 53d
Hills G. Heathcote Rev. 2124 Michigan av.
Hills G. M. Mrs. 2124 Michigan av.
Hills James M. 1038 N. Halsted
Hills Lois B. Mrs. The Hampden
Hills Reginald, 2124 Michigan av.
Hills William E. Evanston
Hillyer Cassius E. 620 Estes av.
Hilson D. L. 6032 Monroe av.
Hilton Charles C. 509 W. Adams
Hilton Edward, Oak Park
Hilton Fred L. 6628 Perry av.
Hilton George 509 W. Adams
Hilton G. V. Dr. 6327 Woodlawn av.
Hilton J. B. Mrs. Evanston
Hilton Mary E. Mrs. 3602 Lake av.
Hilton P. R. 6628 Perry av.
Hilton William K. 194, 36th
Himrod Charles, Hyde Park hotel. *U.L.*
Himrod Kirk, 1624 Belmont av.
Himrod Phoebe Miss, 537 Belden av.
Hinchliff William, 502 W. Jackson boul.
Hinchman E. D. Mrs. Evanston
Hinckley Abner T. jr. 5408 Washington av.
Hinckley Anna A. Mrs. 5408 Washington av.
Hinckley Bessie Otis Miss, Oak Park
Hinckley Charles W. 4549 Greenwood av. *Ill.*, *U.L.*
Hinckley George W. Hinsdale
Hinckley John L. 4519 Woodlawn av.
Hinckley Otis Ward, Evanston
Hinckley William B. Hinsdale
Hinckley William S. Hinsdale
Hinde Thomas Woodnutt, 118 Astor. *Un.*, *W.P.*
            Sum. res. Elkhorn, Ky.
Hinds Charles E. Hinsdale
Hinds E. P. Hinsdale
Hinds E. P. jr. Hinsdale
Hinds O. S. 98 N. Kedzie av.
Hine C. L. 2124 Michigan av.
Hine Frank S. Mrs. 1033 Sherwin av.
Hine Lucius Alvin, 140, 50th
Hine M. F. Mrs. 3407 Forest av.
Hine William S. 13 Bittersweet pl.
Hiner Joseph W. 4740 Lake av.
Hines A. G. Hinsdale
Hines Edward, 503 W. Jackson boul.
Hines Nannie Miss, Evanston
Hines Peter, 26 Oregon av.
Hingston Lavinia Miss, 2942 Prairie av.
Hinkins J. E. Dr. 5224 Kimbark av.
Hinkle Abbie A. Dr. Evanston
Hinkle Elizabeth T. Mrs. Evanston
Hinkle Maria R. Miss, Evanston
Hinkley James Otis, 3306 Indiana av.
Hinkley Jared H. 229, 42d

Hinkley Watson S. 92, 26th. *U.L.*
Hinman Benjamin P. jr. Kenilworth
Hinman George Wheeler, 53 Bellevue pl. *U.L.*
Hinman S. D. 2916 Groveland av.
Hinners George R. 602 Greenleaf av.
Hinsdale Benjamin S. Evanston
Hinsdale Henry K. Evanston
Hinsdale Henry W. Evanston
Hinson James A. 606 Englewood av.
Hintermeister Julia Miss, Evanston
Hintz Bertha Miss, Chicago Beach hotel
Hipp William, 6038 Monroe av.
Hipp W. Harrison Dr. 4237 Indiana av.
Hippach Charles F. 4348 Grand boul.
Hipple E. H. Hotel Metropole
Hipple George, 1839 Magnolia av.
Hipwell W. O. Highland Park
Hirsch Arthur, 3551 Grand boul.
Hirsch A. 4531 Ellis av. *Lksd.*, *Stan.*
Hirsch Edward, 3249 Vernon av.
Hirsch Emil G. Dr. 3612 Grand boul. *U.L.*
Hirsch Fred, 3639 Michigan av. *Stan.*
Hirsch Henry, 353 Oakwood boul. *Lksd*
Hirsch Isaac, 353 Oakwood boul. *Stan.*
Hirsch Joseph, 417 S. Marshfield av.
Hirsch Joseph M. 3551 Grand boul.
Hirsch L. K. 436, 37th pl. *Stan.*
Hirsch Morris, 3304 Calumet av. *Stan.*
Hirsch M. 353 Oakwood boul. *Stan.*
Hirsch Oscar, 4531 Ellis av. *Lksd.*
Hirsch Ralph J. River Forest
Hirsch William, 3354 Vernon av. *Lksd.*
Hirschbach William, 3100 Groveland av.
Hirschbein Samuel, 3406 Vernon av.
Hirschfield Herman H. 260 Fremont
Hirschfield August, 2663 N. Ashland av.
Hirschhorn Clarence, 4417 Berkeley av. *Lksd.*
Hirschl Andrew J. 6054 Kimbark av.
            Sum. res. Colon, Iowa
Hirsh Dwight S. 3427 Michigan av. *Stan.*
Hirsh Harry J. 3430 Michigan av. *Stan.*
Hirsh Harry S. 3427 Michigan av. *Stan.*
Hirsh Jacob, 3430 Michigan av. *Stan.*
Hirsh Morris G. 4117 Grand boul. *Stan.*
Hirsh Morris M. 4428 Grand boul. *Stan.*
Hirsh Solomon, 3427 Michigan av. *Stan.*
            Sum. res. Mackinac Island, Mich.
Hirsh Solomon, 4117 Grand boul. *Lksd.*
Hirsh Solomon J. 3430 Michigan av. *Stan.*
Hirsh William A. 4428 Grand boul. *Stan.*
Hirsheimer L. D. 3419 Prairie av.
Hirst Augustine C. Rev. 397 W. Monroe
Hirt John C. 617 N. Wells
Hitchcock Alvirus N. Rev. Oak Park
Hitchcock Annie Mrs. 4741 Greenwood av.
Hitchcock Charles A. Mrs. Austin
Hitchcock Charles A. jr. Austin
Hitchcock David, 1189 S. Central Park av.
Hitchcock Edward J. 787 W. Monroe
Hitchcock E. T. 3643 Prairie av.
Hitchcock Frank A. Riverside
Hitchcock Howard E. 21 Linden ct.

Hitchcock H. H. Wilmette
Hitchcock James A. 203 Park av.
Hitchcock John M. 165 Howe
Hitchcock Luke Dr. 4613 Drexel boul.
Hitchcock Mary E. Mrs.4356 Berkeley av.
Hitchcock M. M. Berwyn
Hitchcock Roderick M. 1222 Wright-
    wood av.
Hitchcock R. A. Lexington hotel. C.A.
Hitchcock Sarah A. Mrs. 787 W. Monroe
Hitchens Roy K. jr. Evanston
Hitchens R. K. Evanston
Hitchings Cebert L. 175 Evanston av.
Hitchings Louis B. 175 Evanston av.
Hitt Andrew J. 6914 Yale
Hitt A. W. Dr. 95, 51st
Hitt John, 390 Oak. U.L.
Hitt W. I. Tracy
Hixson Henry Rea, 553 Dearborn av.
    U.L.
Hjortsberg Max Mrs. 387 Lasalle av.
Hoadley Albert E. Dr. 683 Washington
    boul.
Hoadley J. M. 608, 44th
Hoag Charles A. Dr. 4808 Evans av.
Hoag Junius C. Dr. 4669 Lake av.
Hoag Walter B. Mrs. 268, 33d
Hoag Walter E. 6153 Lexington av.
Hoag William G. Avenue house, Evans-
    ton
Hoag William J. 4230 Grand boul.
Hoagland John R. 5069 Lake av.
Hoagland Ralph Townley, 4813 Madison
    av.
Hoagland William, 21 Oakwood av.
Hoard Charles D. 3164 Groveland av.C.A.
Hoar Edward, Hinsdale
Hoard Elijah W. Oak Park
Hobart H. M. Mrs. Evanston
Hobart H. R. 5110 East End av.
Hobart Ralph Hastings, 5110 East End
    av.
Hobbs Charles Dr. 452 W. Jackson boul.
Hobbs Glenn M. 5717 Madison av.
Hobbs James B. 343 Lasalle av. U.L.
    Sum. res. Lake Bluff
Hobbs Joshua N. 4455 Berkeley av.
Hobbs J. O. Dr. 452 W. Jackson boul.
Hobbs Perry J. Union League club
Hobbs William F. 6221 Lexington av.
Hobson Benjamin L. Rev. 320 Belden av.
Hoch James J. 1849 Belmont av.
Hochbaum Henry, 2337 N. Paulina
Hochschild Christian A. 601 Burling
Hochstadter Gustav, 4352 Forrestville av.
    Lksd.
Hodge A e nde J. 762 Washington
    boul. l xa   r
Hodge Amy Miss, 462 Morse av.
Hodge Andrew T. 462 Morse av. C.A.
Hodge C. W. 4918 Ellis av.
Hodge Ida Miss. 462 Morse av.
Hodge John M. Palmer House
Hodges Almeda Mrs. 2227 Prairie av.
Hodges Charles H. 89 Astor. Univ.
Hodges Irving J. 1737 Kenmore av.

Hodges Lothrop S. 841 W. Adams
Hodges Lucy H. Mrs. 426, 41st
Hodges Walter E. Riverside, C.A.
Hodgkins Edward W. 159 Cass. Un.
Hodgkins J. 7148 Princeton av. U.L.
Hodgkins William, 7148 Princeton av.
Hodgson Joseph, 311 Webster av.
Hodgson Joseph T. River Forest
Hodnett Thos. P. Rev. 345 Walnut
Hodson John G. Maywood
Hodson M. E. Highland Park
Hoelscher Edward C. 1319 Wash'n boul.
Hoelscher Herman M. 1319 Washington
    boul. U.L.
Hoelscher Julius H. Dr. 284 Belden av.
Hoelter Edward Rev. 527 Ashland boul.
Hoelter H. L. Rev. 527 Ashland boul.
Hoeningsberger David, 3157 South Park
    av. Lksd.
Hoeppner Emil A. 327 W. 60th pl.
Hoerlein Henry A. 369, 44th
Hoes James H. Austin
Hoff Herman J. Evanston
Hoff M. W. Mrs. 55, 36th
Hoffbauer William H. 578 Lasalle av.
Hoffert Isaac, 888½ W. Adams
Hoffheimer Harry W. 4343 Calumet av.
Hoffheimer Nathan, 3616 Prairie av.
Hofflund Alexander, Evanston
Hoffman Adolph, 1474 N. Clark
Hoffman Alma Marie Miss, 495 Ashland
    boul.
Hoffman Andrew, 5006 Michigan av.
Hoffman Charles A. Evanston
Hoffman Edward, Lakota hotel. Stan.
Hoffman Emil, Norwood Park
Hoffman Francis A. jr. Elmhurst
Hoffman Fred F. 462 Orchard
Hoffman F. W. 1194 Washington boul.
Hoffman George W. 57, 20th. Cal., C.A.
Hoffman Gustav A. 462 Orchard
Hoffman Henry A. Evanston
Hoffman Herbert, Morton Park
Hoffman John M. 1765 Oakdale av.
Hoffman John W. Mrs. Evanston
Hoffman Julius, Norwood Park
Hoffman J. C. Dr. 495 Ashland boul.
Hoffman J. Jos. 3764 Indiana av. C.A.
Hoffman Otto E. H. Norwood Park
Hoffman William O. 3660 Michigan av.
Hoffmann Benjamin S. 310 Evanston av
Hoffmann Harry H. 310 Evanston av.
Hoffmann Herman H. 310 Evanston av.
Hoffmann John Mrs. 1067 Warren av.
Hoffmann John L. 1067 Warren av. C.A.
Hoffmeyer H. Ferdinand, 3801 Lake av.
Hofheimer Ernst, 2946 Prairie av.
Hofheimer Zach. 342 Lasalle av.
Hofman Henry, 744 W. Monroe
Hofman Samuel, 744 W. Monroe
Hofmann Valentine, 875 Warren av.
Hofstra William S. Evanston, Chi.
Hogan James, 1675 W. Monroe
Hogan Joseph, 519 W. Monroe
Hogan Martin, 4427 Greenwood av.
Hogan M. A. 2926 Indiana av.

Hogan Thomas, Elmhurst
Hogan Thomas S. 30 N. Sacramento av.
Hoge Emma Mrs. 4324 Greenwood av. .
Hoge George C. Winnetka
Hoge Holmes, Evanston
Hogensen Conrad, 1886 Diversey
Hogey Julius H. 3123 Vernon av.
Hogg David, 399 Oak. *W.P.*
Hoggins John, Oak Park
Hogle William W. Evanston
Hoglen S. T. Mrs. 4329 Oakenwald av.
Hohmann John, Oak Park
Hoit Jeremiah P. 3916 Lake av.
Holabird Mary Miss, 530 W. Monroe
Holabird Robert G. Evanston
Holabird William, Evanston. *U.L., Univ*
Holbrook A. P. Oak Park
Holbrook Charles H. 4954 Washington av.
Holbrook Florence Miss, 4441 Champlain av.
Holbrook Francis D. Dr. 1740 Addison
Holbrook Francis W. Mrs. 1740 Addison
Holbrook F. A. Evanston
Holbrook Graves, Oak Park
Holbrook Maud Miss, 4441 Champlain av.
Holbrook O. J. LaGrange
Holbrook Sibyl T. Mrs. 2930 Indiana av.
Holbrook William G. 1740 Addison
Holbrook William G. 6421 Stewart av.
Holcomb Byron T. Evanston
Holcomb Herbert W. Hinsdale
Holcomb William H. Hinsdale
Holcomb William H. jr. Hinsdale
Holden Charles C. P. 1387 W. Monroe
Holden Charles N. 1841 Wellington
Holden Charles R. Chicago Beach hotel
Holden C. M. 1185 W. Adams
Holden C. N. Mrs. 681 W. Monroe
Holden Edward, 2251 Kenmore av.
Holden Edward G. 15 Astor
Holden Elizabeth Mrs. 802 W. Monroe
Holden Frank H. 363 Bowen av.
Holden Harry R. Evanston
Holden Henry R. Greenwood Inn, Evanston
Holden Hollis D. Evanston
Holden Isaac H. 88 Centre av.
Holden James E. 5401 Cornell av. *U.L.*
Holden Jane Mrs. Greenwood Inn, Evanston
Holden Joseph S. LaGrange
Holden Mary E. Mrs. 5401 Cornell av.
Holden N. B. 586 W. Congress. *Ill.*
Holden Walter S. Oak Park
Holden Warren F. 1033 Warren av.
Holden William H. 500 W. Monroe. *Ill.*
Holden William M. 500 W. Monroe
Holder Frank W. 6229 Kimbark av.
Holder M. L. Mrs. 6229 Kimbark av.
Holdom Jesse, Judge 3324 Vernon av. *U.L.*
Holdrege Charles B. Oak Park
Holdsworth J. J. 620 Lasalle av.
Holenshade J. C. 770 Warren av.
Holgate Thomas F. Prof. Evanston
Holinger Arnold, 170 Eugenie
Holland Emilie Mrs. 747 Sedgwick

Holland Harry L. 4949 Prairie av.
Holland John F. 4928 Ellis av. *Irq., Univ.*
Holland J. Edmund, 149 Lincoln Park boul. *C.A.*
Holland Philo L. Dr. 2139 Wabash av.
Holland S. J. Hotel Windermere
Hollenbec Bertha Y. Mrs. 513 S. Oakley av.
Hollett R. P. Evanston. *U.L.*
Holley Dwight E. Lieut. Fort Sheridan
Holley Lyman G. Oak Park
Holley Sarah A. Mrs. Oak Park
Hollingshead J. D. 191 Ashland boul.
Hollingshead J. Kinsey, 4731 Indiana av.
Hollingshead Thomas C. Evanston
Hollingsworth Rachel E. Dr. 6356 Stewart av.
Hollis Henry L. 2027 Michigan av. *Irq., U.L.*
Hollis William D. 3128 Malden
Hollister Bertram K. 344, 57th
Hollister Charles A. 2481 N. Hermitage av.
Hollister E. F. Mrs. 398, 40th
Hollister Harry D. 4313 Cottage Grove av.
Hollister Henry M. Oak Park
Hollister John H., M.D. 3430 Rhodes av.
Hollister Robert J. 304 West ct.
Holloday J. Avenue house. Evanston
Holloway Edward M. 617 The Plaza
Holloway George A. 3436 Prairie av.
    Sum. res. Lake Marie Antioch, Ill.
Holloway George F. Oak Park
Holloway Harry C. 3436 Prairie av.
Holloway Horace G. 457 Bowen av.
Hollstein Albert M. 3423 South Park av. *Stan.*
Holman Alfred L. 2115 Indiana av.
Holman Daniel F. 733 W. Monroe
    Sum. res. Lake Geneva
Holman Edward E. Dr. 6314 Harvard av. *C.A* Sum. res, Oregou, Ill.
Holman Harriet Miss, 2971 Michigan av.
Holman Isaac W. Hyde Park hotel
Holman Maria H. Miss, 2971 Michigan av.
Holman M. S. 2779 N. Paulina
Holman O. Q. La Grange
Holman Theo. 4514 Ellis av.
Holmberg Ch. Washington Heights
Holmboe Leonard, 7535 Saginaw av.
Holme Frank, 266 Chestnut
Holmes Albert W. Jefferson Park
Holmes A. O. Mrs. 2355 Indiana av.
Holmes Bayard, M.D. 104, 40th
Holmes C. N. 5027 Lake av.
Holmes David, Highland Park
Holmes Delavan A. Evanston
Holmes Edward B. Mrs. 281 Ashland boul.
Holmes Edward L., M.D. 158 Evanston av.
Holmes E. Burton, 229 Michigan av. *Chi.*
Holmes E. M. Mrs. 1014 Pratt av.
Holmes E. S. Mrs. 6451 Monroe av.
Holmes Francis R. Evanston
Holmes Frank F. 765 Warren av. ·
Holmes F. L. 3100 Groveland av.

Holmes George D. 55 Astor
Holmes George J. 144 S. Central Park av. *C.A.*
Holmes George P. Mrs. 148 S. Central Park av.
Holmes George V. 6451 Monroe av.
Holmes Guy B. 4727 Indiana av.
Holmes Harriet Mrs. 4160 Ellis av.
Holmes Harvey A. 281 Ashland boul.
Holmes Ira Mrs. 229 Michigan av.
Holmes Ira G. 229 Michigan av.
Holmes Jennie R. Miss, 158 Evanston av.
Holmes Julia A. Mrs. Evanston
Holmes Louis H. LaGrange
Holmes Marshall F. 440 N. Normal Parkway
Holmes Mary E. Mrs. 3119 South Park av.
Holmes Mary J. Miss, 44 Scott
Holmes Olive Miss, 640 Fullerton av.
Holmes Oliver W. 373 Ashland boul.
Holmes Ralph H. LaGrange
Holmes Robert, Evanston
Holmes Robert C. 6237 Monroe av.
Holmes Roy C. Evanston
Holmes Rudolph W. Dr. 558 Division
Holmes Thomas J. 2938 Groveland av.
Holroyd E. E. Dr. 887 Washington boul.
Holt Alfred E. 7209 Jeffrey av.
Holt Anna Mrs. 1117 Early av.
Holt Charles Sumner, 1931 Calumet av. *Chi., U.L., Univ.*
Holt D. R. Lake Forest
Holt Edgar, 235 Michigan av.
Holt George Hubbard, 19 Bellevue pl. *Chi., C.A., U.L.*
Holt Granville M. 5316 Lexington av.
Holt Mary E. Mrs. 3716 Forest av.
Holton E. Mrs. Lakota hotel
Holton Frank G. Riverside
Holton George D. 4345 Drexel boul.
Sum. res. Charlestown, N. H.
Holton Thomas J. 6405 Monroe av.
Holtz Henry, Evanston
Holtzman Louis J. 718 Warren av.
Holverscheid Caroline Mrs. Hinsdale
Holverscheid Henry, Hinsdale
Holway W. H. The Arizona
Holyoke William E. Rev. 1170 Washington boul.
Holzapfel Fred J. 904 Farwell av.
Holzheimer Eda Mrs. 3538 Ellis av.
Holzner Clara Mrs. 413 Bowen av.
Homer Benjamin F. Evanston
Homer Frank B. Evanston
Homer Fred M. River Forest
Homer George W. River Forest
Homery Jules, 238 Dearborn av.
Honberger F. H. Dr. 3808 Indiana av.
Honkamp Fred, 3747 Prairie av.
Honkamp Lawrence, 4208 Vincennes av.
Honore Adrian C. 2103 Michigan av. *Un., Univ.*
Honore B. L. 100 Lake Shore drive
Honore Frank L. 3646 Indiana av.
Honore Henry H. 2103 Michigan av.
Honore H. H. jr. 2702 Michigan av.

Honore Lockwood, 2103 Michigan av. *Univ.*
Honore N. Kingston, 2103 Michigan av. *Chi., Un.*
Honsinger Emanuel Dr. 318 Park av.
Hood C. H. La Grange
Hood C. Todd Dr. 992 W. Adams
Hood Helen L. Miss, 541 Lunt av.
Hood John D. 2664 Evanston av.
Sum. res. Lake Bluff, Ill.
Hood Thomas, 701 Washington boul.
Hood Thomas C. Austin
Hoof John C. 2738 N. Lincoln
Hook William W. 1807 Barry av. *C.A.*
Hooker Henry M. 569 Washington boul. *Ill.*
Hooker Herbert L. 6442 Minerva av.
Hooper Edwin E. 85 S. Seeley av.
Hooper Eunice Miss, 718 The Plaza
Hooper Henry, M.D. 541 N. State.
Sum. res. Huron Mountain club, Marquette, Mich.
Hooper James K. 6640 Perry av.
Hooper Wyly E. 85 S. Seeley av.
Hoops Charles H. 2957 Michigan av. *C.A.*
Hoops David H. 2957 Michigan av.
Hoops Hannah O. Mrs. 2957 Michigan av.
Hoops P. C. 4112 Drexel boul.
Hoops Thomas, 143 Oakwood boul
Hoops Thomas jr. 3158 South Park av.
Hoops William H. 4105 Drexel boul.
Hoover Charles W. Evanston
Hoover C. A. Mrs. 2146 Kenmore av.
Hoover George K. Rev. Evanston
Hoover George Percy, 636 Pine Grove av.
Hoover Olin G. Evanston
Hoover Thomas W. LaGrange
Hopkins Anson S. 5207 Kimbark av.
Hopkins Charles R. 3255 Groveland av.
Hopkins Ervin jr. 66 Warren av.
Hopkins E. M. Clifton house
Hopkins Forest, 1547 W. Adams
Hopkins Francis A. 7206 Euclid av.
Hopkins Frederick P. 4438 Champlain av.
Hopkins George E. Evanston
Hopkins George L. Evanston
Hopkins H. G. 3935 Ellis av.
Hopkins H. H. Oak Park
Hopkins James M. 3247 Groveland av.
Hopkins John P. Pullman. *C.A.*
Hopkins Louis M. 4400 Lake av.
Hopkins Marcellus, 3728 Forest av. *C.A.*
Hopkins M. F. Mrs. 2813 Calumet av.
Hopkins Sara Miss, 3150 Michigan av.
Hopkins Sumner, 4045 Ellis av.
Hopkins Valeria M. 5207 Kimbark av.
Hopkins William, Hinsdale
Hopkins William H. 4814 Champlain av.
Hopkins William P. Evanston
Hopkinson Mary Mrs. 451 Washington boul.
Hopper William H. 6634 Parnell av.
Hoppin Bushrod E. 6636 Wentworth av.
Hopson E. Joseph, 1311 Michigan av.
Horan Edward, 1494 Washington boul
Hord George M. 4762 Lake av.

Horn John C. 89 Ewing pl.
Horn O. C. Mayfair
Horn Thomas, 1837 Michigan av.
Hornbaker William R. Berwyn
Horner Albert, 1705 Michigan av. *Stan.*
Horner Angel, 1705 Michigan av. *Stan.*
Horner Charles, 1705 Michigan av. *Stan*
Horner Harry, 1705 Michigan av. *Lksd.*
Horner Henry Mrs. 1705 Michigan av.
Horner Isaac, 1705 Michigan av. *Stan.*
Horner Joseph, 1839 Michigan av. *Stan.*
Horner MauriceL.3133 Michigan av. *Stan*
Horning J. J. 6323 Wentworth av.
Hornstein Leon, 6839 Calumet av.
Hornthal Louis, Hotel Del Prado. *Lksd.*
Horr George B. 4445 Sidney av.
Horr Henry H. 7205 Jeffery av. *C.A.*
Horsting B. F. 4337 St. Lawrence av.
Horswell Charles Prof. Evanston
Horton Ben P. Oak Park
Horton F. The Ontario
Horton George T. Tracy
Horton Henry, Lake Forest
Horton Henry B. Oak Park
Horton H. E. Tracy. *U.L.*
Horton J. M. 122 Ashland boul.
Horton O. H. Judge, 2615 Indiana av.
   U.L.   Sum. res. Evanston
Horton Richard, LaGrange
Horton Sarah M. Miss, 2 Aldine sq.
Horwitz J. Hotel Del Prado
Hosbury John, 5430 Lexington av.
Hosick Henry M. North Shore hotel
Hosick H. N. North Shore hotel
Hosking A. 1690 W. Monroe. *Ill.*
Hosking Ben. T. 1656 W. Jackson boul.
   Ill.
Hosking Ernest B. 1656 W. Jackson boul.
Hoskins Benjamin, 6129 Monroe av.
Hoskins Ida Mrs. 1367 Sheridan rd.
Hoskins John, LaGrange
Hoskins Murray G. Evanston
Hoskins William, LaGrange
Hosmer Annette Mrs. 7023 Yale
Hosmer Arthur B. Dr. 52 Walton pl. *C.A.*
Hosmer Edward D. 300 Schiller
Hosmer E. Miss, 382 Lasalle av.
Hosmer F. B. Mrs. 483 Fullerton av.
Hosmer H. Mrs. 590 Dearborn av.
Hosmer J. W. 44 Bellevue pl. *U.L.*
Hosmer Nelson, 14 Lincoln av.
Hosmer R. W. 382 Lasalle av. *Chi., Un.*
Hosmer William H. 1506 Michigan av.
Hosmer William J. Wilmette
Hossack I. Barbara Miss, Evanston
Hossack John Mrs. Evanston
Hostetter J. N. 1659 W. Adams
Hotaling George W. 140 W. 65th. *Irq.*
Hotchkin Benjamin L. Dr. 2521 Kenmore
   av.
Hotchkin C. Marion Mrs. Evanston
Hotchkin Harriet I. Miss,5642 Monroe
   av.
Hotchkin John L. 5642 Monroe av.
Hotchkin Paul M. Evanston
Hotchkin Robert B. 425 Lasalle av.

Hotchkiss C. W. 293, 53d. *C.A.*
Hotchkiss Everett S. Mayfair
Hotchkiss Freelon. Riverside
Hotchkiss George W. Evanston
Hotchkiss Hariette Miss, Riverside
Hotchkiss Isabella S., M.D. Riverside
Hotchkiss L. J. 195 Oakwood boul.
Hotton Eliza A. Mrs. River Forest
Hotton J. Sidney, River Forest
   Sum. res. Lake Geneva, Wis.
Hotz Christoph, 301 W.Adams. *Chi., Ill.*
Hotz Ferdinand 450 N. State
Hotz Robert S. 87 Astor. *C.A.*
Hough C. A. Hotel Woodruff
Hough Edward M. 484 W. Adams
Hough Emerson, 6360 Minerva av.
Hough George J. Evanston
Hough George W. Prof. Evanston
Hough O. S. Mrs. 4828 Kenwood av.
Hough William, Evanston
Houghteling James L. Winnetka. *Univ.*
Houghton Alice Mrs. 526 Garfield av.
House J. A. Mrs. 2001 Michigan av.
Houseman Morris M. 4841 Michigan av.
   Sum. res. Ottawa Beach, Mich.
Houser E. W. 4207 Wabash av.
Houston Alexander S. 573, 46th pl.
Houston Elizabeth E. Mrs. Evanston
Houston E. A. Mrs. 3552 Ellis av.
Houston Frank B. 314 Oakwood boul.
Houston George T. 4314 Oakenwald av.
   C.A.
Houston James P. Dr. 1180 Sheffield av.
Houston James S. 314 Oakwood boul.
Houston John, Mayfair
Houston J. W. Mrs. 314 Oakwood boul.
Houston William T. 3552 Ellis av.
Hovey A. H. Morgan Park
Hovey George H. Chicago Beach hotel
Hovey William G. 2735 N. Lincoln
Hovey W. A. Glencoe
Howard Allen L. 4620 Indiana av.
Howard A. J. 3103 Groveland av.
Howard B. Frank, 983 W. Jackson boul.
Howard B. F. Mrs. 3100 Groveland av.
Howard Charles, 6558 Stewart av.
Howard Charles, Austin
Howard Cornelia Mrs. 1219 W. Ravens-
   wood Park
Howard C. H. Gen. Glencoe
Howard Daniel 25, 35th
Howard David W. Rev. 4926 Lake av.
Howard Edward L. Evanston
Howard E. D. 3103 Groveland av.
Howard Frank L. Dr. Oak Park
Howard George, 3428 Michigan av.
Howard George Mrs. LaGrange
Howard Harold A.572 Division. *Chi., Un.*
   Sum. res. Bar Harbor, Me.
Howard Harry E. Evanston
Howard H. Benton, Oak Park
Howard John Corse, 377 Superior. *Un.*
Howard John F. 6643 Stewart av.
Howard John H. Oak Park. *C.A.*
Howard John J. 32, 42d pl.
Howard Joseph H. 4801 Kimbark av. *U.L.*

Howard Margaret D. Mrs. 4227 Champlain av.
Howard Martin, 32 Buena Terrace
Howard Mary Mrs. Evanston
Howard O. McG. Glencoe
Howard Robert T. 321 Belden av.
Howard Sylvester N. 6554 Woodlawn av.
Howard Thomas Mrs. 488 Evanston av.
Howard William, Evanston
Howard William B. Mrs. 10 Astor.
    Sum. res. Bar Harbor, Me.
Howard William H. 230 Hampden ct.
Howe Abbie L. Miss, 363 Bowen av.
Howe Albert O. Dr. 6028 Washington av.
Howe Arthur C. 3967 Lake av.
Howe Arthur J. 193 Schiller. C.A.
Howe Arthur T. 2584 Kenmore av.
Howe Charles, 3967 Lake av.
Howe Charles M. Evanston
Howe C. A. 3975 Drexel boul.
Howe Dwight N. 4209 Wabash av.
Howe Frederick A. 3931 Grand boul.
Howe F. S. Mrs. 1922 Barry av.
Howe Grace T Miss, 52 Walton pl.
Howe Homer W. 1007 W. Jackson boul.
Howe H. Waldo, 2403 South Park av.
    Sum. res. Sherborn, Mass.
Howe James T. Chicago club
Howe Julia C. Mrs. 622 Washington boul.
Howe J. L. 662 W. Harrison
Howe Mary Clinton Miss, 622 Washington boul.
Howe Noble Hill, 7221 44th
Howe Richard F. 158 Rush. Chi., Un.
Howe Samuel J. 4948 Forrestville av.
Howe Silas, 4459 Ellis av.
Howe Stewart D. Mrs. 4740 Langley av.
Howe Thaddeus H. 4208½ Berkeley av. C.A.
Howe William A. 407, 41st
Howe Willis, 432 Elm
Howe W. B. 1009 W. Jackson boul.
Howell Carrie Miss, 6556 Lafayette av.
Howell Cornelius DuB. Evanston. U.L.
Howell Cyrus H. 7400 Bond av.
Howell C. M. Grenada hotel
Howell Frederick G. Glencoe
Howell James Arthur Sullivan Dr. 3257 Indiana av.
Howell John C. LaGrange
Howell John H. B. Evanston
Howell J. Wilson, Evanston
Howell J. W. Dr. 3257 Indiana av.
Howell P. S. 3257 Indiana av.
Howell S. R. 3258 Forest av.
Howell Thomas S. 4528 Forrestville av.
Howell William Dr. 3257 Indiana av.
Howell W. Lieut. Fort Sheridan
Hower M. Otis, 2197 Kenmore av.
    Sum. res. Akron, O.
Howerth Ira W. 226, 53d
Howes Adelaid E. Mrs. Oak Park
Howes Allen, 6509 Harvard av.
Howes Allen C. 6509 Harvard av.
Howes Frank W. 6509 Harvard av.
Howett W. R. 6438 Greenwood av.

Howison George, 3151 South Park av.
Howison George jr. 3151 South Park av.
Howison Hugh A. 3131 South Park av.
Howland Edward A. 4001 Vincennes av.
Howland E. C. Mrs. 4001 Vincennes av.
Howland Fred B. 5926 Parnell av.
Howland George Carter, Prof. 4605 Drexel boul. Irq., Univ.
Howland Hiram I. 510 Webster av.
Howland Howard N. Austin
Howland James E. Mrs. 510 Webster av.
Howland John E. Austin
Howland Lucius A. Riverside
Howland Rowland Mrs. 4409 Greenwood av.
Howland Walter Morton, 482 N. State. Univ.
Howland Ward B. Austin
Howland William I. Evanston. Chi.
Howser George T. River Forest
Hoxey Edward F. 560, 42d
Hoxie Gilbert H. 4440 Michigan av.
Hoxie John R. Mrs. 4440 Michigan av.
    Sum. res. Thornton, Ill.
Hoxie J. Randolph jr. 4440 Michigan av.
Hoy Albert Harris, M.D., 461 N. State
Hoy Elizabeth Miss, 461 N. State
Hoyer Edward J. 236 Dearborn av.
Hoyer Frederick A. 422 Belden av.
Hoyne Frank G. 3243 Groveland av. C.A., Irq.
Hoyne James T. Mrs. 2208 Prairie av.
Hoyne Maclay, 2201 Calumet av.
Hoyne Temple S., M.D. 1833 Indiana av. Irq.
Hoyne Thomas M. 3369 Calumet av. Irq.
    Sum. res. Waukegan
Hoyne Thomas Temple, 3369 Calumet av.
Hoyt Alfred W. Dr. 4620 Greenwood av.
Hoyt Charles D. 523 Lasalle av.
Hoyt Charles S. Rev. Oak Park
Hoyt Douglass, 235 Michigan av.
Hoyt Ephraim, 5752 Madison av.
Hoyt Frank C. Dr. 5337 Madison av.
Hoyt Frank W. 543 Flournoy
Hoyt Frederick J. 95 Evanston av
Hoyt George W. 5210 Hibbard av.
Hoyt Henry W. 704 Wilson av.
Hoyt Henry W. Mrs. 1808 Prairie av.
Hoyt Hiram P. 7013 Perry av.
Hoyt Louis P. 4425 Greenwood av.
Hoyt N. Landon, 370 Dearborn av.
    Sum. res. Winnetka
Hoyt Phelps B. 576 Division. Univ.
    Sum. res. Winnetka
Hoyt Robert T. 4618 Indiana av.
Hoyt S. C. Mrs. Oak Park
Hoyt William M. 370 Dearborn av.
Hoyt-Caywood Miss, 4620 Greenwood av.
Hubbard A. E. Mrs. Evanston
Hubbard Christine Miss, 5127 Lexington av.
Hubbard Daniel B. Mrs. 6356 Monroe av.
Hubbard Daniel J. 6522 Harvard av.
Hubbard DeWitt P. Winnetka
Hubbard Eva Miss, 457 Evanston av.

Hubbard Gurdon S. jr. Palmer House
Hubbard Gurdon S. jr. Mrs. Riverside
Hubbard Harry A. 3306 Indiana av.
Hubbard Harry E. 5476 Cornell av.
Hubbard Harry M. 387 Lasalle av. *Univ.*
Hubbard Harvey W. Evanston
Hubbard Henry H. 3727 Ellis av.
Hubbard Horace S. 3048 Calumet av.
Hubbard James M. 39, 33d
Hubbard James S. 707 W. Congress
Hubbard John M. 7145 Euclid av.
Hubbard John N. Mrs. Evanston
Hubbard Joseph Derwin, Evanston. *Univ.*
Hubbard Laura M. Miss, 3157 Forest av.
Hubbard Lyman G. 6356 Monroe av.
Hubbard Martha L. Mrs. 4519 Woodlawn av.
Hubbard Mary Mrs. 3727 Ellis av.
Hubbard Stephen S. 6056 Monroe av.
Hubbard S. H. 18 Walton pl. *Un.*
Hubbard T. M. Evanston
Hubbard Will. Avenue house, Evanston
Hubbard William H. 82 Astor. *Univ.*
      Sum. res. Lake Forest
Hubbell Charles H. 7040 Yale
Hubbell Charles W. 213, 48th. *U.L.*
Hubbell J. P. 124, 49th
Hubbell Orin, Berwyn
Hubbell Sarah Mrs. Maywood
Hubbert C. H. Chicago Beach hotel
Huber Julius H. 2531 Magnolia av.
Huck L. C. 576 Lasalle av. *U.L.*
Huddlestone K. G. Mrs. 15 Roslyn pl.
Hudson Alphonso Bell, 360 Erie. *C. A. Un.*
Hudson Carlton, 316 The Plaza
Hudson Charles, Hinsdale
Hudson E. J. Mrs. Evanston
Hudson Frank W. 437 Evanston av.
Hudson Grace Miss, 360 Erie
Hudson Henry, 2516 Indiana av.
Hudson Mary Miss, 4121 Drexel boul.
Hudson Peter S. 6618 Butler
Hudson Thomas, Highland Park
Hudson Thomas J. 5112 Hibbard av.
Hudson Thomas J. jr. 5112 Hibbard av.
Hudson William, 437 Evanston av.
Huebner H. Mrs. 949 S. Sawyer av.
Huessen Gerhard, 528 Garfield av.
Huestis Isaac N. Jefferson Park
Huet C. F. Mrs. 207, 41st
Huff H. M. LaGrange
Huffaker T. S. Dr. 245, 43d
Hugel Louis P. 1776 Wrightwood av.
Huggins Charles W. 4348 Vincennes av.
Hughes Charles, 5831 Madison av.
Hughes Edward J. 3267 Vernon av.
Hughes E. H. Evanston
Hughes E. T. Maywood
Hughes Frank, Hinsdale
Hughes Joseph, 154, 25th. *W.P.*
Hughes J. B. Union League Club
Hughes J. H. Lieut. Fort Sheridan
Hughes J. O. Dr. Norwood Park
Hughes T. J. Hotel Luzerne

Hughes William M. 5927 Indiana av.
Hughes William T. 3267 Vernon av.
Hughes W. E. 9 Woodland Park
Hughes W. E. Oak Park
Hughitt Marvin, 2828 Prairie av. *Chi.,*
      U.L. Sum. res. Lake Forest
Hughitt Marvin jr. 2828 Prairie av. *Cal.,*
      U.L., W.P.
Hughson George F. 5116 Woodlawn av.
Hulbert Alice Miss, 155 Warren av.
Hulbert Alvin, 194 Park av.
      Sum. res. Coldwater, Mich.
Hulbert Charles P. 4327 Indiana av.
Hulbert E. D. Hotel Metropole. *Cal.,*
      C.A., Univ.
Hulbert Palmer S. Mrs. Oak Park
Hulbert Thomas H. Chicago Athletic assn.
Hulbert William M. Maywood. *C.A.*
Hulburd Charles H. 423 N. State. *Chi.,*
      U.L.
Hulburd Joel H. Maywood
Hulett A. L. Dr. 3802 Lake av.
Hulett Sidney E. Dr. 4532 Vincennes av.
Hulin William, 322 Superior
Huling Edward Bentley, 543, 44th
Huling Edward C. 3930 Grand boul.
Huling Walter C. 4736 Prairie av. *C.A.*
Hull Addie Adams Mrs. 3755 Indiana av.
Hull Andress B. Evanston
Hull Arthur E. 191 Oakwood boul.
Hull A. J. Mrs. 46, 53d
Hull Charlotte Kendall Miss, 2212 Prairie av.
Hull David J. Riverside
Hull DeLos, Oak Park
Hull J. R. Mrs. 5163 Wabash av.
Hull Leverett L. Evanston. *Un., W.P.*
Hull Mary H. Mrs. 4750 Lake av.
Hull Morton D. 4923 Washington av. *Univ.*
Hull P. A. 3221 South Park av.
Hull Susie H. Miss, Lake Forest
Hull Tracy D. Highland Park
Hull Walter Scott, 2834 Kenmore av.
Hulligan H. A. 3225 Malden
Hults R. L. 5466 Monroe av.
Humble L. C. Irving Park
Hume Frank L. 4213 Ellis av.
Hume John H. 28 Walton pl. *Un.*
Hume Sumner W. 7250 Jeffery av.
Humiston Samuel A. 4202 Drexel boul.
      C.A. Sum. res. Swampscott, Mass.
Hummer John S. 4827 Vincennes av.
      Sum. res. St. Clair Springs, Mich.
Humphrey A. H. LaGrange
Humphrey A. O. LaGrange
Humphrey Edward L. 1741 York pl.
Humphrey John, River Forest
Humphrey Luther C. 53, 34th pl.
Humphrey T. M. Mrs. 155, 42d pl.
Humphreys T. M. 1521 W. Adams
Humphreys William, 1521 W. Adams
Huncke Carl, 320 Webster av.
Hunerberg Frederick W. 4630 Grand boul.
Hunn A. M. Mrs. 213, 53d

Hunnell James, Hotel Metropole
Hunnemann Nellie E. Mrs. 273, 52d
Hunsinger Charles C. Austin
Hunsinger Edward C. Austin
Hunt Albert B. 2820 Kenmore av.
Hunt A. Lucas, 2241 Calumet av.
Hunt A. O. Dr. 235 Ashland boul. *Ill.*
Hunt Clara Miss, 2241 Calumet av.
Hunt Clement M. 2241 Calumet av.
Hunt C. H. 5101 Hibbard av. *C.A.*
Hunt Daniel H. 194 Oakwood boul.
Hunt D. T. Hotel Del Prado
Hunt Edward S. Evanston
Hunt Eugene, Austin
Hunt E Hamilton, Evanston
Hunt E. H. Park Ridge
Hunt Florence W. Dr. Lexington hotel
Hunt Frederick R. Dr. Austin
Hunt George, Riverside
Hunt George E. Rev. Tracy
Hunt George S. 983 Warren av.
Hunt George W. 3906 Lake av. *C.A.,*
    W.P.
Hunt Haines E. 105 S. Winchester av.
Hunt Harry W. 194 Oakwood boul.
Hunt Homer C. Evanston
Hunt H. H. Mrs. Oak Park
Hunt H. R. Chicago Beach hotel
Hunt H. W. Mrs. 5101 Hibbard av.
Hunt Jarvis, Wheaton. *Chi., Un.*
Hunt John E. Oak Park
Hunt John R. Austin
Hunt John S. Dr. 440 Englewood av.
Hunt J. N. 840 W. Adams
Hunt L. Platt Mrs. 106 Astor
Hunt Manning, 727 W. 63d pl.
Hunt Marie Louise Dr. 462 Bowen av.
Hunt Mary H. Mrs. Edgebrook
Hunt Myron, Evanston
Hunt Nancy D. Mrs. Evanston
Hunt Nicholas, 5732 Monroe av.
Hunt Ralph H. 194 Oakwood boul. *C.A.*
Hunt Robert W. 614 Division. *Chi., Un.*
Hunt Rodney Dr. Oak Park
Hunt Samuel H. 4243 Drexel boul. *C.A.,*
    W.P.
Hunt S. Wade, Evanston
Hunt William B. Dr. 41, 42d pl.
Hunt William F. 5126 East End av.
Hunt William Prescott, 340 Lasalle
Hunt W. Prescott, 340 Lasalle av.
Hunter Charles L. 5357 Woodlawn av.
    W.P.
Hunter David W. Oak Park
Hunter Edward L. 2601 N. Paulina
Hunter Edward S. 5228 Lexington av.
    W.P.
Hunter E. W. Dr. 5126 Madison av.
Hunter George L. 2521 Wabash av. *Univ.*
Hunter Hugh D. 346 Washington boul.
Hurter John W. 547 Dearborn av.
Hunter J. W. 4959 Prairie av.
Hunter Maria P. Mrs. 5517 Washington av.
Hunter Oscar L. The Kenwood
Hunter Robert Mrs. 5125 Jefferson av.
Hunter R. J. O. 5125 Jefferson av.

Hunter Thomas B. 3846 Ellis av.
Hunter Thomas M. Austin
Hunter William, 5540 Michigan av.
Hunter William C. Oak Park. *C.A.*
Hunter William W. The Kenwood. *U.L.*
Hunter W. C. LaGrange
Hunting Charles F. Irving Park
Hunting C. Fred, Mayfair
Hunting Susan Miss, 225 Dearborn av.
Huntington Collins F. 2967 Vernon av.
Huntley Florence Mrs. Leland hotel
Huntley Silas, 3336 Calumet av.
Hurd Abner, LaGrange
Hurd A. Haynes, LaGrange
Hurd Harry B. 6054 Kimbark av.
Hurd Harvey B. Evanston. *U.L.*
Hurd Sadie Miss, 225 Dearborn av.
Hurd Stephen N. 257, 49th
Hurford S. R. Glencoe
Hurlbut Charles H. Dr. Evanston
Hurlbut C. J. 320 Lasalle av.
Hurlbut E. R. 113 Cass
Hurlbut Frank, 7248 Euclid av.
Hurlbut Harris E. 92, 21st. *Cal., C.A.,*
    W.P.
Hurlbut Hiram H. 478 Belden av.
Hurlbut Horace A. Mrs. 389 Ontario
Hurlbut Horace E. Kenilworth. *C.A.,*
    Irq., Un.
Hurlbut J. H. Evanston
Hurlbut Samuel E. Evanston
Hurlbut Sarah E. Miss, 389 Ontario
Hurley Clara V. Mrs. 84 S. Seeley av.
Hurley Frank J. Austin
Hurley T. D. 3221 Prairie av.
Hurssell Cyril A. 641 Greenwood av.
Hurst E. W. 545 Dearborn av.
Huschart F. N. Hotel Metropole
Husche Charles, Evanston
Huse Frank J. Evanston
Huse James B. Evanston
Huson A. B. Mrs. 5910 Indiana av.
Hussander Peter J. Mrs. 576 Burling
Hussey Augustus, 6340 Drexel av.
Hussey J. M. 4357 Prairie av.
Husted F. T. Morgan Park
Huston George, 7659 Butler
Huston Phil W. Evanston
Huston R. H. Mrs. 7101 Howard av.
Huszagh O. H. 1886 Diversey
Huszagh Rudolph D. 1270 Washington
    boul. Sum. res. Paw Paw Lake, Mich.
Hutchens George W. Evanston
Hutchens Oscar B. Evanston
Hutches Benjamin F. jr. 3500 Ellis av.
    Sum. res. Grafton, Mass.
Hutchings William A. 301 Park av.
Hutchins Albert W. 4578 Oakenwald av.
Hutchins Asa V. Dr. 834 W. Monroe
Hutchins Carleton S. 2926 Indiana av.
Hutchins Edwin S. 834 W. Monroe
Hutchins Eugene R. 10 Astor. *U.L.,*
    Univ.
Hutchins E. E. 2665 N. Winchester av.
Hutchins H. Miss, Hotel Del Prado
Hutchins James C. 4810 Ellis av. *U.L.*

Hutchinson Arthur C. 3026 Vernon
Hutchinson B. P. Mrs. 2703 Prairie av.
Hutchinson Charles Mrs. 3011 Prairie av.
Hutchinson ·Charles L. 2709 Prairie av.
  Cal., Chi., C.A., U.L., Univ.
Hutchinson Charlotte A. Mrs. 2925
  Prairie av.
Hutchinson Dillon B. 3821 Langley av.
Hutchinson Edward B. Dr. 5708 Monroe
  av.
Hutchinson Edward W. 7530 Monroe av.
Hutchinson Emily S. Miss, 3821 Langley
  av.
Hutchinson Florence C. Miss, 3145
  Indiana av.
Hutchinson George A. 2925 Prairie av.
  C.A ,. Univ.
Hutchinson George F. 1561 W. Monroe
Hutchinson George W. 756 Washington
  boul.
Hutchinson Jessie Miss, 2925 Prairie av.
Hutchinson John Mrs. 3145 Indiana av.
Hutchinson Jonas Judge, 3043 Groveland
  av. Irq.
Hutchinson Joshua, Oakland hotel
Hutchinson J. William, 3011 Prairie av.
Hutchinson Otis King, 335 Rush
Hutchinson Thomas, Evanston
Hutchinson William A. Oak Park
Hutchinson W. B. Evanston
Hutchinson W. W. Mrs. Riverside
Hutchison Francis, 664 W. Adams
Hutchison James F. 664 W. Adams
Hutchison John N. Rev. Norwood Park
Huteson James C. 952 W. Monroe
Huth Frank D. 2440 N. Paulina
Hutt Louis, 3200 South Park av.
Huwald John E. Austin
Huyck John H. 1301 W. Jackson boul.
Huyck John H., jr.1301 W. Jackson boul.
Huyck Lyda M. Miss, 1301 W. Jackson
  boul.
Hyde Chas. Albert, 601 W.Jackson boul.
Hyde Charles Cheney, 2409 Michigan
  a
Hyde Charles E. 601 W. Jackson boul. Ill.
         Sum. res. Fox Lake, Ill.
Hyde James F. 52 Bellevue pl.
Hyde James Nevins Dr. 2409 Michigan av.
  C.A., Univ.
         Sum. res. Prouts Neck, Me
Hyde James W. Hotel Windermere
Hyde J. D. 7125 Euclid av.
Hyde Maggie W. Mrs. 7141 Princeton av.
Hyde Walter W. 601 W. Jackson boul.
Hyers George, 4201 Ellis av.
Hyers Samuel A. 5542 Madison av.
Hyland J. J. 1007 Park av.
Hyland M. W. 1009 Park av.
Hyland W. S. Hotel Del Prado
Hyllested A. 712 Pullman bldg.
Hyman Albert, 4329 Vincennes av.
Hyman Clara Miss, 4350 Grand boul.
Hyman David, 4329 Vincennes av.
Hyman David A. 4350 Grand boul.
Hyman Edward S. Lakota hotel, Stan.

Hyman Harry S. 4830 Forrestville av.
Hyman Joseph, 4237 Prairie av. Lksd.
Hyman Nathan, 1527 Lill av.
Hyman Robert W. jr. 5495 Cornell av.
  C.A., U.L..
Hyman Thomas J. Oak Park
Hymers Edward, 449 Ashland boul.
Hyne Laura M. Miss, Oak Park
Hynes D. J. Col. 2944 Indiana av.
Hynes W. J. The Winamac. C.A.
Hypes W. Finley, Evanston
Hyslop William D. Morton Park

IBSEN JOHN H. 3716 Wabash av.
  Isbon C. L. 1800 Magnolia av.
Iddings J. P. Prof. 5730 Woodlawn av.
Ide Charles B. Evanston
Ide Helen M. Mrs. Evanston
Ide William K. Evanston
Igel Otto, 2599 N. Robey
Iglehart Charles A. Morgan Park
Iglehart Elizabeth Mrs. Morgan Park
Iglehart Nicholas G. Evanston
Ihne F. William Dr. 837 N. Clark
Iles Robert S. 6424 Parnell av.
Ilett William, 642 W. Adams
Iliff John W. 4166 Drexel boul.
Iliff William H. 684 W. Adams
Illsley William A. Evanston. U.L.
Ilse John C. 689, 48th pl.
Indermille Thomas F. 6618 Lafayette av.
Inderrieden C. V. 553 N. State
Inderrieden John B. 553 N. State
Inderrieden John L. 553 N. State
Inderrieden Joseph S. 553 N. State
Ingal Robert E. 444 Winthrop av.
Ingalls Charles F. 507 W. Adams
Ingalls Eliza A. Mrs. 2224 Kenmore av.
Ingalls Frank M. Dr. Highland Park
Ingalls Frederick A. 32, 42d pl.
Ingalls F. A. 219, 48th. C.A.
Ingalls Grant, Oak Park
Ingalls John G. Oak Park
Ingals Ephraim Dr. 4753 Grand boul.
Ingals E. Fletcher Dr. 4757 Grand boul.
  C.A.
Ingersoll A. K. Mrs. 747 Warren av.
Ingersoll George W. Oak Park
Ingersoll I. F. Mrs. 6149 Monroe av.
Ingersoll Lowell F. Dr. 648 W. 61st
Ingersoll Walter, 6123 Monroe av.
Ingham H. H. Hotel Normandie
Ingledew Lumley, 3427 Indiana av.
Ingledew Lumley jr. 3427 Indiana av.
Inglis J   es, 6641 Kimbark av.
Inglis Parh. 4504 Vincennes av.
Inglis William, 493 Dearborn av.
  Sum. res.Crab Apple Island, Fox Lake
Ingman Lucius S. Dr. Oak Park
Ingraham F. E. Mrs. Oak Park
Ingraham G. Foster, Oak Park
Ingraham G. S. Mrs. 5400 Washington av.
Ingraham Sidney C. Evanston
Ingraham William B. 7929 Muskegon av.
Ingram A. B. Mrs. 825 W. Congress
Ingram Joseph E. 233 S. Paulina

Ingram J. S. Oak Park
Ingram Robert J. Austin
Ingwersen Charles H. 3748 Forest av.
Ingwersen E. H. 4144 Prairie av.
Ingwersen H. C. 4239 Michigan av.
Ingwersen Julius H. 3844 Calumet av.
Ingwersen Marvin, 3748 Forest av.
Ingwersen T. H. 4120 Prairie av.
Ingwersen William B. 4918 Forrestville
    av.
Inman David Mrs. Highland Park
Inness Marion M. Mrs. 3000 Prairie av.
Innis Katharine C. Miss, 4 Aldine sq.
Inskeep Charles C. 6518 Ingleside av.
Insull Martin J. Evanston
Insull Samuel. 49 Delaware pl. *Cal.,
    Chi., Un., W.P.*
Iott George H. Evanston
Iott M. Bates, 835 Greenleaf av.
Ireland Sidney R. 687 Sedgwick
Irion Daniel Prof. Elmhurst
Irish H. C. Mrs. Hinsdale
Irons Agnes Mrs. 495 W. Adams
Irvin James Mrs. 3255 Prairie av.
Irvin Washington J. 2566 N. Ashland av.
Irvine Frank R. Hinsdale
Irvine Hugh, 6420 Monroe av. *C.A.*
Irvine Robert, 823 Morse av.
Irvine William, 4939 Lake av.
Irving Robert A. 751 North Park av. *C.A.*
Irwin B. J. D. Col. 171 Rush
    Sum. res. Cobourg, Canada
Irwin Charles D. Evanston. *U.L.*
Irwin Ed. 4542 Oakenwald av.
Irwin Edward A. 4801 St. Lawrence av.
Irwin E. J. Chicago Beach hotel
Irwin Harry D. 3834 Prairie av.
Irwin Harry L. 733, 50th
Irwin John, 505 Dearborn av.
Irwin O. D. 4856 Prairie av.
Irwin Roy W. 4800 St. Lawrence av.
Irwin W. Francis Rev. 4542 Oakenwald
    av.
Irwin W. P. Lakota hotel
Isaacs J. D. 3128 Groveland av.
Isaacs Martin J. 4446 Calumet av.
Isaacs M. A. Hyde Park hotel
Isaacs M. C. 4336 Grand boul. *Lksd.*
Isbester John H. Evanston
Isbester Tunis, Evanston
Isgrig Margaret I. Miss, Austin
Isgrigg James E. 194 Cass
Isham Anne E. Miss, 1 Tower ct.
Isham Edgar B. 2413 Magnolia av.
Isham Edward S. 1 Tower ct. *Cal., Chi.,
    Un., W.P.*
    Sum. res. Ormsby Hill, Manchester, Vt.
Isham Edward S. jr. 1 Tower ct.
Isham Frances Miss, 1 Tower ct.
Isham F. D. LaGrange
Isham George S., M.D. 311 Erie. *Un.,
    Univ.*
Isham Ira D. Dr. Chicago Beach hotel
Isham Isaac N. 4342 Greenwood av.
Isham Pierrepont, 1 Tower ct. *Chi., Un.,
    W.P.*

Isham Ralph, 381 Lasalle av. *C.A., Univ*
Isham Ralph N., Dr. 321 Dearborn av.
    Univ. Sum. res. Lake Geneva, Wis.
Ismond R. E. 343 Bowen av. *C.A.*
Isom W. H. Kenilworth
Israel Bernhard, 3740 Grand boul. *Lksd.,
    Stan.*
Israel William, 3100 Groveland av.
Israel W. R. Berwyn
Iverson Chester L. LaGrange
Iverson Edward, 4630 Drexel boul.
Iverson Ralph W. LaGrange
Ives Benjamin, 172 Oakwood boul,
Ives Blanche D. Mrs. Evanston
Ives Florence H. Mrs. 268 Chestnut
Ives F. B. D. 3220 Vernon av.
Ives J. H. 472 Kenwood av.
Ives Norman E. 4756 Prairie av.
Ives Rebecca Mrs. 561, 45th pl.
Ives William, 499 N. State
Ives William B. 1436 Washington boul.
    Sum. res. Lake Geneva, Wis.

JACKMAN ARTHUR C. 264, 51st
    Jackman Edwin S. 688 Winthrop av.
    C.A.
Jackman Jennie E. Mrs. 184, 51st
Jackman Solon S. 447 Seminary av.
Jackman Wilbur S. 6916 Perry av.
Jackson Abram, Oak Park
Jackson Arthur S. 3846 Ellis av. *Cal.*
Jackson A. Reeves Mrs. 569, 51st
Jackson Charles W. 441 W. 66th
Jackson Daniel Mrs. 674 Fullerton av.
Jackson Dwight, Oak Park
Jackson Emily Mrs. Evanston
Jackson Erskine H. 6556 Lafayette av.
Jackson Frank P. 31 Stratford pl.
Jackson Frank R. 1541 Oakdale av.
Jackson Frederick D. Evanston
Jackson Frederick W. 4711 Kimbark av.
Jackson F. A. 6014 Kimbark av.
Jackson George, 7524 Harvard av.
Jackson Harriet Mrs. 1578 Lill av.
Jackson Harry H. 27 Bellevue pl.
    Sum. res. Lake Geneva
Jackson Henry G. Rev. 4524 Lake av.
Jackson Horace, Hinsdale
Jackson Howard B. 85 Rush, *C.A.*
Jackson Huntington W. Auditorium an-
    nex. *Cal., Chi., Univ.*
Jackson H. B. Mrs. 182, 45th
Jackson James S. 834 Warren av.
Jackson John A. 4407 Indiana av.
Jackson John B. 5726 Monroe av.
Jackson John L. River Forest
Jackson John L. Rev. 5607 Lexington
Jackson Jonathan W. 149 Lincoln Park
    boul.
Jackson J. C. The Ontario
Jackson Leigh H. Oak Park
Jackson Leonard C. Hotel Normandie
Jackson Luis, 4748 Prairie av.
Jackson L. B. Great Northern hotel
Jackson Mary L. Mrs. Evanston
Jackson Oliver, 4430 Ellis av.

Jackson Oliver A. 4430 Ellis av.
Jackson Paul, 4430 Ellis av.
Jackson Ray Miss, 2633 Calumet av.
Jackson Samuel, 2633 Calumet av.
Jackson Samuel W. 3100 Groveland av.
Jackson Sarah E. Mrs. Riverside
Jackson Thomas M. River Forest
Jackson William A. Evanston. U.L.
Jackson William C. 37 Aldine sq.
Jackson William G. 713 Walnut
Jackson William J. 7301 Yale av.
Jackson William M. 2358 Indiana av.
Jackson William S. 37 Aldine sq.
          Sum. res. Lake Geneva, Wis.
Jackson Willis G. 147 Asland boul. Ill.
Jackson W. W. Hinsdale
Jacobs B. F. 2201 Calumet av.
Jacobs Charles M. Dr. 4454 Vincennes av.
Jacobs Charles R. 147 Ashland boul.
Jacobs C. B. Dr. Hotel Del Prado
Jacobs Edward A. 3633 Prairie av.
Jacobs Henry C. 4119 Grand boul.
Jacobs John, 531, 44th
Jacobs Leon, 459 Bowen av. Lksd.
Jacobs Montefiore M. 4720 Champlain av.
Jacobs S. Wesley Dr. 4636 Prairie av.
Jacobs Victor, 39½ Laflin
Jacobs William B. 65 Bryant av.
Jacobs William V. Col. 1163, 72d. W.P.
Jacobsen R. C. Greenwood Inn, Evanston
Jacobson Augustus Col. Union Club. Chi.
Jacobson D. 4461 Ellis av.
Jacobus Judson S. 4314 Greenwood av.
Jacoby Ernest, 4215 Vincennes av. Lksd.
Jacoby Horatio J. 3241 Indiana av.
Jacoby Jacob, 4445 Calumet av.
Jacques Susan Mrs. 156 Dearborn av.
Jaeger Caroline Mrs. 399 N. State
Jaeger George J. 1916 Deming pl.
Jaeger Herman F. 399 N. State
Jaeger Julius, Austin
Jaeger Louise Mrs. Austin
Jaeger Philip, 345 Lasalle av.
Jaeger Philip jr. 345 Lasalle av.
Jaeschke Adolph L. Mrs. 296 Ohio
Jaeschke G. A. 296 Ohio
Jaffray Henry S. 6444 Lexington av.
Jaffray Robert M. 1467 Wellington
Jager E. C. 442 Garfield av.
Jager Frank, 740 Sedgwick
Jaggar Kate C. Mrs. 6112 Kimbark av.
Jagoe James H. Evanston
Jaicks Andrew, River Forest
Jakway Isabel Miss, Evanston
Jakway William H. Evanston
Jamar J. H. R. 4827 Lake av.
James Austin F. Dr. Oak Park
James Charles G. 4454 Oakenwald av.
James Charles W. Dr Evanston
James Edmund J. 5761 Madison av. Univ.
James Edward A. 3259 Groveland av. C.A.
James Fred S. Evanston. Chi., Ill.
James George F. Prof. 301, 56th, Univ.
James George W. 5422 Ridgewood ct.
James James A. Prof. Evanston
James John D. 226 Oakwood boul.

James John M. Evanston
James J. H. New Hotel Holland
James Louis N. Evanston
James Thomas B. Mrs. 5211 Hibbard
     av.
James Thomas N. 2438 Michigan av.
James Whitney P. Evanston
James W. A. Mrs. Highland Park
Jameson Arthur, 5407 Jefferson av.
Jameson Eliza D. Mrs. 5316 Cornell av.
Jameson John A. 5316 Cornell av.
Jameson M. Mrs. The Arizona
Jamieson Egbert, 38 Stratford pl.
Jamieson Malcolm M. 50 Stratford pl. Cal.,
     Chi., Un.
Jamieson Malcolm M. jr. 50 Stratford
     pl.
Jamieson Thomas N. 4508 Woodlawn av.
Jamieson William D. 50 Stratford pl.
Jampolis Robert R. Austin
Janery Walter W. 7047 Parnell av.
Janes John J. Calumet club. Chi.
Janney James W. 4729 Greenwood av.
     U.L.
Jannotta Alfredo A. Sig. Oak Park
Jaques Charles E. 1340 Catalpa av.
Jaques Frank F. 1340 Catalpa av.
Jaques Willard W. 1340 Catalpa av.
Jaques W. K. Dr. 4316 Greenwood av.
Jaquish Louis C. 283 S. Irving av.
Jaquith Edwin P. 52 Walton pl. C.A.
          Sum. res. Rockport, Me.
Jaros Ferdinand, 310 Sunnyside av.
Jarrett John R. Hinsdale
Jarvis C. E. Hotel Del Prado
Jarvis George R. 714 Englewood av.
Jarvis Margaret Miss, 487 Fullerton av.
Jauncey William, 631 W. Monroe
Jay Charles A. 7737 Lowe av.
Jay Frank W. Dr. 2510 Indiana av.
Jay Milton Dr. 2510 Indiana av. Cal.
Jayne E. L. 5414 Madison av.
Jeanneret Charles Mrs. 555 Webster av.
Jeanneret Charles W. 557 Webster av.
Jeanneret Harry G. 555 Webster av.
Jefferson Benjamin H. 3614 Calumet av.
Jefferson N. Hinsdale
Jefferson Ralph, 3616 Calumet av.
Jeffery Charles T. 3133 Malden
Jeffery Edward T. 1919 Michigan av. Cal.,
     Chi.
Jeffery Thomas B. 3133 Malden
Jelke Ferdinand, 516 Lasalle av.
Jelke John F. 516 Lasalle av. U.L.
Jellyman Joseph, 6210 Kimbark av.
Jellyman M. Miss, 6210 Kimbark av.
Jellyman Richard. 6210 Kimbark av.
Jenison Edward Spencer 4356 Ellis av.
Jenison Edward S. jr. 4356 Ellis av.
Jenkins Bella D. Miss, Oak Park
Jenkins Charles E. Oak Park
Jenkins George H. 5043 Washington av.
     U.L.
Jenkins George R. 4200 Drexel boul.
Jenkins George R. Evanston. C.A.
Jenkins John E. 1730 Prairie av. Cal., U.L.

Jenkins Margaret G. Miss, 224 Ashland boul.
Jenkins Robert E. 4200 Drexel boul. *U.L.*
Jenkins Samuel R. 5414 Madison av.
Jenkins Thomas R. Union League club. *Cal., W.P.*
Jenkins William P. Austin
Jenkins Wilton A. 329 Michigan av.
Jenkinson Wm. 410 W. 64th
Jenks A. B. 3756 Lake av. *W.P.*
Jenks Emma C. Mrs. 47, 22d
Jenks E. W. 2413 Magnolia av.
Jenks James M. 1886 Diversey
Jenks John G. 47, 22d. *C.A.*
Jenks Maxwell B. 1886 Diversey
Jenks Parker A. 3179 Malden
Jenks Wm. Shippen, 2928 Indiana av. *Chi., C.A.*
  Sum. res. Narasaki, Lake Beulah, Wis.
Jenner H. M. Mrs. 4231 St. Lawrence av.
Jenness Hattie Miss, Oak Park
Jenney Frank Dr. 1033 Evanston av.
Jenney George H. 68 Stratford pl. *C.A.*
Jenney H. W. Mrs. 340 Hampden ct.
Jenney Max, 60 Bittersweet pl.
Jenney William L. B. 60 Bittersweet pl. *U.L.*
Jennings Charles A. 2485 N. Hermitage av. *C.A.*
Jennings Charles P. 304, 54th
Jennings George, Evanston
Jennings George F. 3358 Michigan av.
Jennings George F. 7534 Union av.
Jennings George F. Lakota hotel
Jennings George M. Mrs. 7534 Union av.
Jennings Henry C. Rev. 490 Sunnyside av.
Jennings John H. Highland Park
Jennings John T. W Evanston
Jennings Joseph Mrs. Maywood
Jennings Louis H. 1038 Bryan av.
Jennings Mary E. Mrs. Highland Park
Jennings Rufus P. 16 Madison Park. *C.A.*
Jennings S. H. 5531 Monroe av.
  Sum. res. Trout Lake, Wis.
Jennings William H. 321 Lincoln av. *C.A.*
Jennison Floyd E. 636 W. Congress
Jennison N. Edward, LaGrange
Jepson A. Lincoln, 366 Lasalle. av.
Jernberg Reinert A. Rev. 734 Washington boul.
Jernegan Charles, Elmhurst
Jerome Charles C. 3431 South Park av.
Jerome C. B. A. 5646 Michigan av.
Jerome Frank, 966 W. Jackson boul.
Jerome George C. 143 Oakwood boul.
Jerome W. B. 4740 Prairie av.
Jerrems Alex. N. 38 Aldine sq. *Univ.*
Jerrems Arthur W. 4463 Lake av. *C.A.*
Jerrems William G. 38 Aldine sq. *U.L.*
Jerrems William G. jr. 3021 Calumet av. *U.L.*
Jessamine Charles A. 5031 Lake av.
Jessamine Helen Miss, 5031 Lake av.
Jesselson Isaac, 4724 Prairie av.
Jessurun Albert E. Granada hotel
Jevne Christian Mrs. 640 Lasalle av.

Jevne Henry M. 640 Lasalle av. *C.A.*
Jewell Albert G. 4319 Forrestville av.
Jewell Edwin S. 4319 Forrestville av.
Jewell E. W. The Arizona
Jewell Ira H. 230 S. Irving av. *C.A.*
Jewell Omar H. 230 S. Irving av.
Jewell William J. 956 W. Jackson boul.
Jewett Allen R. 4150 Ellis av.
Jewett Edward A. 143 Oakwood boul.
Jewett Edward R. 1866 Melrose
Jewett Fred LeRoy, 3434 South Park av. *C.A.*
Jewett George A. 4317 Champlain av.
Jewett John N. 412 Dearborn av.
Jewett Samuel R. 467 N. State. *W.P.*
Job Frederick W. 4575 Oakenwald av.
Job Samuel, Morgan Park
Jobson C. Frank, 6519 Woodlawn av.
Jocelyn Franklin C. 4415 Drexel boul. *U.L.*
Jocelyn Robert McC. 4415 Drexel boul.
Joel E. D. Mrs. 4229 Calumet av.
Johns Hepburn, 414 The Plaza
Johns Robert, 6463 Kimbark av.
Johnson Adolph M: 2475 N. Paulina
Johnson Alex. J. Glen Ellyn. *C.A.*
Johnson Alfred B. Austin
Johnson Allen A. Austin
Johnson Andrew G. 1839 Wrightwood av.
Johnson Andrew P. 695 N. Robey
Johnson Anna Miss, Hyde Park hotel
Johnson A. Blanche Miss, 10 Hawthorne pl.
Johnson Catherine Mrs. Evanston
Johnson Charles E. 368, 49th
Johnson Charles H. 832 Sherwin av.
Johnson Charles J. 7620 Bond av.
Johnson Charles Scott, 358 Center
Johnson Clara E. Miss, 4735 Kimbark av.
Johnson Cornelia Mrs. Evanston
Johnson C. A. 5342 Madison av.
Johnson C. Porter, 623 W. 61st. *C.A., U.L.*
Johnson Daniel, 1684 Barry av.
Johnson D. S. Rev. Hinsdale
Johnson Edna L. Miss, 72 Maple
Johnson Edward, 1734 Briar pl.
Johnson Edward E. 510 Greenleaf av.
Johnson Edward Ford, 2711 Indiana av.
Johnson Edward P. Evanston
Johnson Edwin T. Oak Park
Johnson Elizabeth Mrs. 2516 Indiana av.
Johnson Ellen M. Mrs. 3241 Groveland av.
Johnson Enos H. LaGrange
Johnson Ernest V. 2504 Michigan av. *C.A., U.L.*
Johnson E. D. Mrs. Hotel Del Prado
Johnson E. L. 4630 Drexel boul.
Johnson Frank A. 5817 Monroe av.
Johnson Frank E. 3640 Lake av. *C.A.*
Johnson Frank J. 615 W. 60th
Johnson Frank M. Dr. 304 West ct.
Johnson Frank S. Dr. 2521 Prairie av.
  Sum. res. Lake Geneva, Wis.
Johnson Franklin Rev. 222, 53d
Johnson George E. Revere house

Johnson George H. 4045 Grand boul.
Johnson G. D. Mrs. Evanston
Johnson Hedveg Mrs. 196 Evergreen av.
Johnson Henry C. 215, 42d
Johnson Herrick Rev. 1070 N. Halsted
Johnson Hiram B. 3797 Vincennes av.
Johnson Hosmer A. Mrs. 2223 Prairie av.
Johnson H. J. Dr. 171, 51st
Johnson H. J. Mrs. 4552 Woodlawn av.
Johnson H. Stull, 3917 Grand boul.
Johnson Jennie Miss, 2615 Indiana av.
Johnson John Alfred, 3500 Ellis av.
Johnson John B. 1439 Dakin av.
Johnson John H. 271 Lasalle av.
Johnson John H. 437 Belden av.
Johnson John H. 1531 Windsor av.
Johnson John M. 6606 Yale. U.L.
Johnson J. B. Mrs. 389 Oak
Johnson J. E. Berwyn
Johnson J. J. 3917 Grand boul.
Johnson J. M. Wilmette
Johnson Laris J. 3917 Grand boul.
Johnson L. E, Mrs. 742 Warren av.
Johnson L. W. Edgebrook
Johnson Martin, 1749 Deming pl.
Johnson McMillan A. 207 Lake View av.
Johnson Milton H. 510 Greenleaf av.
Johnson M. Dwight, Oak Park
Johnson Nels, 1844 Surf
Johnson Oliver K. 4527 Greenwood av.
Johnson Peter C. Hinsdale
Johnson Quintard, 5817 Monroe av.
Johnson Rezen P. Dr. Oak Park
Johnson R. D. The Arizona
Johnson Sidney B. 581 W. Adams
Johnson Spencer, 3422 Prairie av.
Johnson Walter L. 3241 Groveland av.
Johnson Wm. Ford, 2711 Indiana av.
Johnson Wm. H. 72 Maple. C.A., Un.
   Sum. res. Lake Geneva, Wis.
Johnson William O. 5548 Monroe av. C.A.
Johnson William O. 666 N. Hoyne av.
Johnson William P. 4433 Ellis av.
Johnson William S. 451 Washington boul.
Johnson Willis F. 10 Hawthorne pl.
Johnson W. A. Hinsdale
Johnson W. H. Glencoe
Johnson W. S. Dr. 5332 Washington av.
Johnston Alexander C. Evanston
Johnston Alfred B. 751 W. Monroe
Johnston Alfred W. 751 W. Monroe
Johnston Archibald, Riverside
Johnston A. S. Hinsdale
Johnston Benjamin F. 825 Warren av.
Johnston Charles C. 343 Chestnut. Un.
Johnston Charles E. 6110 Kimbark av.
Johnston C. P. Union club
Johnston Daniel, 5484 East End av.
Johnston Helen Miss, 2923 Michigan av.
Johnston Howard Agnew Rev. 489 Bowen
 av.
Johnston H. McB. 1636 Prairie av.
Johnston H. Morris, 1636 Prairie av.
Johnston James, 3228 Groveland av.
Johnston James, 4323 Lake av.
Johnston James W. 6450 Kimbark av.

Johnston John jr. Lake Geneva, Wis
 Chi., Univ.
Johnston John W. Oak Park
Johnston J. Birney, 5754 Washington av
Johnston J. Milton, Irving Park
Johnston Morris L. 1636 Prairie av. Univ.
Johnston S. T. Riverside
Johnston Thomas T. Evanston
Johnston William, 197 Park av. Ill.
Johnston William, Hinsdale
Johnston William J. Evanston
Johnstone A. Ralph Dr. 4454 Cottage
 Grove av.
Johnstone Frederick, 5515 Woodlawn av.
Johnstone Quintin Mrs. 7557 Seipp av.
Johnstone Stuart Dr. 550, 51st
Johonnot Rodley F. Rev. Oak Park
Joly J. W. Mrs. Evanston
Jonas I. 426 Ashland boul.
   Sum. res. St. Cruz Co., Cal.
Jones Alexander J. 828, 71st pl.
Jones Alfred L. 168 Oakwood boul.
Jones Arthur B. Evanston
Jones Arthur B. Winnetka
Jones Arthur G. 50 Madison Park
Jones Arthur Russell 4519 Vincennes av.
Jones A. T. Mrs. Granada hotel
Jones Belden D. 2721 Kenmore av.
Jones Ben. C. Mrs. Highland Park
Jones Charles A. 4371 Oakenwald av.
Jones Charles E. Dr. Austin
Jones Charles F. 6514 Yale
Jones Charles J. 117, 49th
Jones Charles S. 4156 Prairie av.
Jones Charles W. 6514 Yale
Jones Clara A. Miss, 168 Oakwood boul.
Jones Cyrus M. Riverside
Jones C. G. 4827 Lake av.
Jones C. J. 2921 Indiana av.
Jones C. T. Mrs. Oak Park
Jones Daniel A. Mrs. 2140 Calumet av.
Jones Darlington P. 452 N. Normal Park-
 way
Jones David B. 62 Astor. Irq.,Univ.
   Sum. res. Lake Forest
Jones David Price, 944 Park av.
Jones De Quincey, 2628 N. Paulina
Jones DeWitt C. 695 W. Monroe
Jones Dorothy Miss, 531, 44th
Jones Ed. L. 3825 Forest av. C.A.
Jones Edgcombe Lee, 480 Dearborn av.
 C.A.,Un.
Jones Edmund H. 5033 Lake av. Univ.
Jones Edward W. 2326 Indiana av.
Jones Elizabeth Mrs. 944 Park av.
Jones Elizabeth D. Mrs. 464 W. Adams
Jones Elliott C. Wilmette
Jones E. Lee, 480 Dearborn av.
Jones Fannie M. Mrs. 170 Oakwood boul.
Jones Fernando, 1834 Prairie av.
Jones Florence M. Miss, 22 Astor
Jones Frances C. Miss, 2326 Indiana av.
Jones Frank H. Union League club
Jones Fred A. 7141 Princeton av.
Jones Fred B. 290 Lasalle av. C.A.,W.P.
Jones Fred H. 695 W. Monroe

Jones Frederick M. 6517 Woodlawn av.
Jones George I. 2455 Kenmore av.
Jones George P. 2721 Kenmore av. *U.L.*
Jones Graham, 1834 Prairie av.
Jones Graham P. 2721 Kenmore av.
Jones G. Edwin, 43, 22d. *C.A., Cal., W.P.*
Jones G. Herbert, 56 Woodland Park. *C.A.*
Jones Helen Snow Miss, 480 Dearborn av.
Jones Henry D. 132, 53d
Jones Henry F. 4045 Ellis av.
Jones Herbert Leroy, 225 Dearborn av.
Jones H. Magnus, 4729 Indiana av.
Jones Ira, 6626 Kimbark av.
Jones Ira L. 9, 34th pl.
Jones Jenkin Lloyd Rev. 3939 Langley av.
Jones Jerome, 240 Oakwood boul.
Jones John H. 3825 Forest av.
Jones John H. 4422 Ellis av. *C.A., W.P.*
Jones John H. 7636 Bond av.
Jones John I. Oak Park
Jones John L. 46 Bryant av.
Jones John M. Austin
Jones John Sutphin, 321,49th. *U.L., W.P.*
Jones Julian C. 542 N. Normal Parkway
Jones J. Howard, Oak Park. *Ill.*
Jones J. J. Irving Park
Jones J. M. W. 480 Dearborn av. *Chi.*
    Sum. res. Sunnycroft, Lake Geneva, Wis.
Jones J. Russell, 2108 Michigan av.
Jones Lewis D. Oak Park
Jones L. Munger Mrs. 248 Oakwood boul.
Jones L. M. Mrs. 276 Warren av.
Jones Maria W. Miss, 2326 Indiana av.
Jones Mary Miss, 149 Ashland boul.
Jones Mattie M. Mrs. Oak Park
Jones Maxwell M. 4721 Langley av.
Jones Moses, 6440 Greenwood av.
Jones M. Augusta Mrs. Evanston
Jones M. J. Dr. 5417 Cottage Grove av.
Jones M. Katherine Miss, 480 Dearborn av.
Jones Nathaniel M. Oak Park
Jones Otis, 5859 Washington av. *U.L.*
Jones Owen W. 6626 Kimbark av.
Jones Richard B. 6642 Lafayette av.
Jones Richard Lloyd, 3939 Langley av.
Jones Robert, 6517 Woodlawn av.
Jones Robert Mrs. Hinsdale
Jones Samuel J. Dr. 387, 54th *Chi.*
Jones Samuel M. Chicago club
Jones Sarah Mrs. 569 Lasalle av.
    Sum. res. Burlington, Wis.
Jones Stephen B. 1643 W. Adams
Jones Thomas, 1086 East. Ravenswood Park
Jones Thomas D. 62 Astor. *Univ.*
Jones Vina N. Mrs. 4945 Lake av.
Jones Walter B. Evanston
Jones Walter S. 4356 Berkley av.
Jones William, 4534 Greenwood av.
Jones William B. 7452 Bond av.
Jones William E. 780 North Park av.
Jones William H. Evanston. *U.L.*

Jones William M. 117, 49th
Jones William O. Evanston
Jones W. Clyde, 5703 Monroe av.
Jones W. Morris, 117, 49th
Jones W. O. Mrs. 780 North Park av.
Jones W. S. 267 Bowen av.
Joplin J. Porter, 4948 Washington av.
Jordan Cady M. 3545 Michigan av. *C.A.*
    Sum. res. Green Lake, Wis.
Jordan Charles F. 6454 Parnell av.
Jordan Collins H. Mrs. 603 W. Jackson boul.
Jordan Edwin O. 5720 Woodlawn av.
Jordan Frederick G. 322 Ashland boul.
Jordan Gustav, 614 Evanston av.
Jordan Helen Lester Mrs. 3515 Calumet av.
Jordan Helles, Riverside
Jordan Ida Mrs. 614 Evanston av.
Jordan Scott, 3040 Kenmore av. *C.A.*
    Sum. res. Lake Geneva, Wis.
Jordan Thomas, Hinsdale
Jordan W. C. Irving Park
Jorgesson F. C. Park Ridge
Joseph Carl, 4551 Vincennes av.
Joseph Henry, Oakland hotel
Joseph Herbert L. Oakland hotel. *Lksd.*
Joseph H. Mrs. Oakland hotel
Joseph Jacob M. 3333 Vernon av.
Joseph James F. Hinsdale
Joseph M. 481 Bowen av.
Joseph M. N. Hotel Metropole
Joseph Samuel L. 3746 Ellis av. *Stan.*
Josephi C. A. Mrs. 3130 South Park av.
Joslin A. D. 6224 Kimbark av.
Joslin Charles T. Mrs. 490 Lasalle av.
Josselyn Henry M. Mrs. 800 W. Adams
Jouvenat Charles, 3543 Grand boul.
Joy Frank L. Wilmette
Joy William, 541 Lasalle av.
Joyce Clara L. Miss, 725 Washington boul.
Joyce George A. LaGrange
Joyce Harry P. 412 Center
Joyce James E. 725 Washington boul.
Joyce James F. 725 Washington boul.
Joyce John K. 3434 Vernon av.
Joyce Patrick Mrs. 412 Center
Joyce William T. The Kenwood. *U.L.*
    Sum. res. Joyceville, Conn.
Judah Noble B. 2701 Prairie av. *Cal., W.P.*
Judd Charles F. 812 W. Monroe
Judd Edward J. 3522 Calumet av.
Judd Edward S. 2223 Sheridan rd.
Judd Emily P. Mrs. 304 Belden av.
Judd Frederick F. 6351 Yale
Judd Henry S. 615 Englewood av.
Judd H. Worthington, 321 W. 64th
Judd Marvin, 6551 Lafayette av.
Judd N. B. Mrs. 3522 Calumet av.
Judd S. Alice Miss, Mayfair
Judd S. Corning Mrs. 47 Astor
Judge Thomas F. 244 S. Lincoln
Judkins Edward F. 1036 W. Jackson boul.
Judkins Richard, 1036 W. Jackson boul.
Judson Clifford C. 930 Lunt av.
Judson E. A. Mrs. 928 W. Adams

Judson Frank P. Evanston
Judson George P. Evanston
Judson Harry B: Evanston
Judson Harry Pratt Prof. 5828 Wood-
lawn av.
Judson Mary M. Mrs. 3366 South Park
av.
Judson William B. 4231 Michigan av.
    U.L. Sum. res. Harbor Point, Mich.
Judson William H. Evanston
Judson W. L. 55, 33d
Juergens Charles, River Forest
Juergens Frederick, River Forest
Juergens Paul, 488 Lasalle av.
Juergens Theodore D. 82 Ewing pl.
Juergens Wilhelmine Mrs. Oak Park
Juergens William F. 488 Lasalle av. *C.A.*
Jukes Arthur G. 619 Cleveland av.
Jukes J. Mrs. 923 S. Sawyer av.
Julin A. V. 869 Hamilton ct.
Julin Charles F. 1741 Briar pl.
June Frank H. Oak Park
June Jennie A. Mrs. Oak Park
June Jesse D. Oak Park
June Paul S. Oak Park
Jung Emil, 1137 Lunt av.
Jungblut Fred G. Mrs. 755 Sedgwick
Junge August, 4540 Michigan av.
Junk Magdalene Mrs. 1110 W. Garfield
boul.
Junkin E. A. Dr. 1911 Michigan av.

KADISH HELEN L. Mrs. 142 Lincoln
av.
Kaehler Frederick, 1744 Roscoe
Kaehler Peter F. 2753 N. Lincoln
Kaeseberg Ehrgott, 771 N. Clark
Kaestner Charles, 923 W. Jackson boul.
Kaestner Walter S. 223 S. Leavitt
Kahler Conrad, 282 S. Homan av.
Kahler John J. 282 S. Homan av.
Kahn Aaron, 3145 Forest av.
Kahn Fannie G. Miss, 143 Oakwood boul.
Kahn Felix, 4219 Grand boul. *Stan.*
Kahn Harry, 3227 Wabash av. *Stan.*
Kahn Henry, 3633 Forest av. *Stan.*
Kahn J. C. 3100 Groveland av.
Kahn Jacob, 220, 42d pl.
Kahn Jacob, 3227 Wabash av. *Stan.*
Kahn Leopold, Lexington hotel
Kahn Louis, 3815 Vernon av. *Lksd.*
Kahn Meyer, 422 Belden av.
Kahn S. H. Mrs. 4431 Berkeley av.
Kaiser Henry R. 200, 44th
Kaiser M. L. 3148 Prairie av.
Kaiser Solomon, 3335 Michigan av. *Stan.*
Kalb E. William, 105 Evanston av.
Kales J. D. Dr. 475 Dearborn av. *Univ.*
Kalteich Otto, 327 W. 60th pl.
Kammerer F.G. 4626 Woodlawn av. *C.A.*
Kammerer W. S. Riverside
Kane Catherine Mrs. 1712 Diversey
Kane George B. 356 Ashland boul.
Kane Joseph A. Irving Park
Kane Thomas, Evanston. *Ill., U.L.*
Kane William D. 356 Ashland boul.

Kane William H. 4359 Prairie av.
Kannally M. V. 5338 Greenwood av.
Kannenberg Baldwin H. Oak Park
Kannenberg Charles F. Oak Park
Kanner Rosa Miss, 568 Division
Kantrowitz G. A. 4509 Grand boul. *Stan.*
Kappes Chas. R. Evanston
Karcher Louis, 1263 Washington boul.
Karger Samuel I. 3661 Michigan av.
    Lksd., Stan.
Karger Simon, 3661 Michigan av. *Lksd.*
Karnes Geo. 3708 Ellis av.
Karnes Wm. 3708 Ellis av.
Karpen Adolph, 1238 N. Clark. *C.A.*
Karpen Leo, 502 Winthrop av.
Karpen Solomon, 1736 Wrightwood av.
Karst Frederick A. Dr. 636 Sedgwick
Kasper Adam J. 1732 Deming pl.
Kasper Peter J. Evanston
Kasson C. Valette, 148 Astor
Kasson Henry R. 3525 Ellis av.
Kasten Herman A. 1727 Arlington pl.
    C.A.
Katz Aber L. 3147 South Park av.
Katz Caroline Mrs. 4217 Wabash av.
Katz Elias, 3737 Prairie av.
Katz Henry, 2247 Calumet av.
Katz Henry, 4217 Wabash av.
Katz J. P. 3147 South Park av.
Katz Samuel B. 2247 Calumet av.
Katzauer Isaac, 3558 Prairie av. *Lksd.*
Katzauer Sol. 3558 Prairie av.
Kaub Charles L. Mrs. 11 Lane ct.
Kauffman Fred, Lexington hotel. *Lksd*
    Stan.
Kaufman Aaron, 3626 Prairie av. *Lksd.*
Kaufman Adolph, 807 Pullman bldg.
    Lksd.
Kaufman Charles, 3626 Prairie av.
Kaufman Henry, 588½ Division
Kaufman Henry, 3548 Prairie av.
Kaufman J. H. 4550 Lake av.
Kaufman Moritz, 555 Seminary av.
Kaufman Moses, 553 Cleveland av.
Kaufmann Gustav G. 591 Burling
Kaufmann Gustav W. Dr. Evanston
Kavanagh Charles J. 962 W. Monroe.
    C.A.
Kavanagh John E. 2753 N. Ashland av.
Kavanagh Marcus Col. Lexington hotel
Kavanagh Mary A. Mrs. 962 W. Monroe
Kavanagh M. R. LaGrange. *U.L.*
Kavanagh Thomas W. 936 Fargo av.
Kay A. E. Dr. 1481 W. Monroe
Kaye Edward C. Dr. 752 W. Monroe
Kaye J. R. Rev. Berwyn
Kayne T. Y. Dr. 225 Dearborn av.
Kaynor A. Wilmette
Kean S. A. Mrs. Evanston
Keane Michael J. 565 Division
Kearney Anastatia M.Mrs. 4846 Evans av.
Kearney James A. 6419 Greenwood av.
Kearney Margaret Miss, Wilmette
Kearsley Mary J. Dr. Austin
Keasel George E. 1808 Arlington pl.
Keast John H. 6463 Monroe av.

Keating James E. 1177 Washington boul.
Keating J. H. 6065 Jefferson av. *C.A.*
Keating Michael, 3143 Vernon av.
Keats Albert H. Dr. 4619 Indiana av.
Keck William S. 5135 Cornell av.
Kedzie John H. Evanston
Kedzie John H. jr. Evanston. *Univ.*
Kee James W. 1804 Barry av. *C.A.*
Keebler August C. 946 Garfield boul.
Keebler Edward F. 3833 Forest av.
    Sum. res. Pine Lake, Ind.
Keedy Dyke V. 6334 Monroe av.
Keefe Andrew J. 295 S. Leavitt
Keefe James E. Dr. Oak Park
Keefer E. F. 3910 Prairie av.
Keefer Frank H. Oak Park
Keefer George D. Oak Park
Keefer Harry H. Oak Park
Keefer Louis, 3910 Prairie av. *Stan.*
Keehn George W. 17 Gordon Terrace
Keeler Catharine Mrs. 4325 Langley av.
Keeler Charles B. 5110 Madison av. *U.L.*
Keeler Charles F. 1468 Michigan av.
Keeler E. R. 5621 Monroe av.
Keeler Florence S. Miss, 464 Farwell av.
Keeler George W. 3541 Prairie av.
Keeler Harry, 4325 Langley av.
Keeler Hervey E. 3660 Sheridan rd.
Keeler Homer D. LaGrange
Keeler Horatio Dr. 3541 Prairie av.
Keeler J. B. 619 Washington boul.
Keeler William B. Col. 6200 Kimbark av.
Keeley Catherine A. Miss, 2829 Prairie
  av.
Keeley Edward S. Granada hotel. *C.A.*
Keeley E. M. 2829 Prairie av. *C.A.*
Keeley James, 377 Superior
Keeley Thomas F. 2829 Prairie av. *C.A.*,
  Irq.
Keeling Francis jr. 446 Elm
Keelyn James E. Evanston
Keen Edwin H. 4555 Ellis av. *C.A.*
Keen George, 228 Michigan av.
Keen Herbert I. Evanston
Keen Joseph B. 4367 Lake av.
Keenan Horace M. 4420 Prairie av.
Keenan James, Clifton house
Keenan Patrick H. 5238 Calumet av.
Keenan Robert, 4042 Michigan av.
Keenan Wilson T. 4042 Michigan av.
    Sum. res. Fox Lake
Keene Joseph, 6959 Perry av.
Keeney J. Franklin, 2622 Michigan av.
  W.P.
Keeney Newton M. Oak Park
Keep Albert, 2010 Michigan av. *Cal., Chi.*
    Sum. res. Lake Geneva, Wis.
Keep Albert jr. 2010 Michigan av.
Keep Chauncey, 2825 Prairie av. *Chi.,*
  C.A., U.L.
Keep Frances Miss, 387 Dearborn av.
Keep Frederick A. 387 Dearborn av. *Chi.,*
  C.A., W.P.
Keep William B. Auditorium annex. *C.A.*
Keep William F. 387 Dearborn av. *Chi.*
  W.P.
  38

Keepers Wm. E. 185, 51st
Keeran Norris C. 630 W. 62d
Keeton Theodore A., M.D. 538 Sunnyside
  av.
Kehl Charles H. Austin
Kehl Robert E. 602 W. 67th
Kehlor James R. 3006 Prairie av.
Kehoe Martin C. 336 Oakwood boul.
Kehoe Rossiter Mrs. 4200 Ellis av.
Kehr Cyrus, Lakeside
Keighin David, Oak Park
Keil Moritz, 352 Burling
Keim Isaac, Lakota hotel. *Lksd.*
Keim Jacob, 3146 Calumet av.
Keir Edward, 447 Belden av.
Keirnan Thomas S. 1316 Washington
  boul.
Keitel Adolph, 6616 Monroe av.
Keith Abijah Mrs. 387 Lasalle av.
Keith A. E. Hinsdale
Keith Carl, 1900 Prairie av.
Keith D. W. 2601 Prairie av.
Keith Edson Mrs. 1906 Prairie av.
Keith Edson jr. 2110 Prairie av. *Chi.*
  Univ., W.P.
    Sum. res. Charlevoix, Mich.
Keith Elbridge B. 4203 Prairie av.
Keith Elbridge G. 1900 Prairie av. *U.L.*
    Sum. res. Charlevoix, Mich.
Keith Ernest W. Dr. 5463 Washing-
  ton av.
Keith Henry A. Evanston. *C.A.*
Keith James E. 2593 N. Winchester av.
Keith John G. Capt. 522 W. Jackson boul.
  Ill.
Keith Justin, 4517 Prairie av.
Keith O. R. 1808 Prairie av.
Keith Robert F. 450 Elm
Keith Robert T. 3672 Wabash av.
Keith Walter W. 1904 Prairie av. *Cal.,*
  Chi., W.P.
Keith W. Scott, 708 Pullman bldg. *Chi.*
Kellam John H. Evanston
Kelland George H. 6216 Monroe av.
Kellar Jacob, Hotel Del Prado
Kellar J. S. Berwyn
Keller Rosa Miss, 228B Fremont
Keller Theodore C. 220, 46th
Kelley Addison D. 3159 Michigan av.
  Cal., C.A., W.P.
Kelley Asa P. Mrs. 2244 Calumet av.
Kelley Charles B. 4860 Washington av.
  Cal., W.P.
Kelley Charles L. Mrs. 1949 Deming pl.
Kelley David, 3159 Michigan av. *U.L.*
Kelley D. F. 3828 Calumet av. *C.A.*
Kelley Edward B. 3920 Lake av. *C.A.*
Kelley Florence Mrs. 335 S. Halsted
Kelley George H. Evanston
Kelley Harrison, 2967 Groveland av.
Kelley Irving M. 6501 Drexel av.
Kelley James W. D. 3232 Lake Park av.
Kelley Joseph C. 3032 Lake Park av.
Kelley Maud M. Miss, 2801 Prairie av.
Kelley Paul D. 3159 Michigan av.
Kelley Pearce C. 623 Englewood av.

Kelley Samuel H. Dr. Austin
Kelley William E. 2129 Calumet av. *Cal.,*
 Chi., C.A., U.L., W.P.
  Summer res. Oconomowoc, Wis.
Kelley William R. 2129 Calumet av.
Kelley W. D. 3232 Lake Park av.
Kelley W. V. 5320 Cornell av.
Kelling J. F. Mrs. 4238 Wabash av.
Kellner George W. 744 Sedgwick
Kellogg Clarence V. 5468 Washington av.
Kellogg C. P. Mrs. 1923 Prairie av.
Kellogg D. F. 2382 N. Paulina
Kellogg Edgar H. 42, 53d
Kellogg Edward R. Dr. 4227 Oakenwald
 av.
Kellogg E. B. 42, 53d
Kellogg Frank P. 2449 Indiana av.
Kellogg Helen R. Dr. 3100 Groveland av.
Kellogg Henry H. Evanston
Kellogg Hudson H. 402 Chestnut
Kellogg James B. 524 W. 62d
Kellogg James L. 2110 Clarendon av.
Kellogg Josiah H. 2251 Wabash av.
Kellogg Julius F. Mrs. Evanston
Kellogg Leroy D. 135, 47th
Kellogg Lyman L. 1065 Chase av.
Kellogg Milo G. 135, 47th. *C.A., U.L.*
Kellogg Myron L. LaGrange
Kellogg Norman W. 409 Superior. *C.A.*
Kellogg O. G. Ravinia
Kellogg Roy, 135, 47th
Kellogg William R. Irving Park
Kellogg W. R. 409 Warren av.
Kelly Alexander, Lake Forest
Kelly Charles, 365 Oakwood boul.
Kelly Edward J. Oak Park
Kelly Elizabeth Mrs. 1276 Washington
 boul.
Kelly George T. Greenwood Inn, Evans-
 ton
Kelly George W. 6564 Harvard av.
Kelly Hiram Mrs. 2716 Prairie av.
Kelly James J. 423 W. 67th
Kelly John, 4202 Vincennes av.
Kelly John A. 80, 74th
Kelly J. F. 4324 Greenwood av.
Kelly J. William, Evanston
Kelly M. R. 3222 Beacon
Kelly R. H. Mrs. 9 Aldine sq.
Kelly Thomas, 365 Oakwood boul.
Kelly Walter J. River Forest
Kelly William J. 4051 Prairie av.
Kelly W. J. Hotel Windermere
Kelsey Aleyn C. River Forest
Kelsey Chauncey, Palmer house. *C.A.*
Kelsey Clarence M. 1294 Washington boul.
Kelsey Henry S. 451 Division
Kelsey Horatio Nelson, Evanston. *C.A.*
Kelsey Joseph A. 2831 Prairie av. *C.A.,*
 U.L.
Kelsey Russell C. Dr. 4054 Indiana av.
 Sum. res. Lake Minnetonka, Minn.
Kelso Charles G. L. 6129 Woodlawn av.
Kelso Hugh A. jr. 222, 53d
Kemeys Edward, 7209 Euclid av.
Kemp N. C. Dr. 4226 Indiana av.

Kemp Oliver C. 7340 Stewart av.
Kemp Richard A. Austin
Kemper Alfred C. 338 Burling
Kempner Adolph, 4218 Calumet av
 Lksd.
Kempster Samuel W. 3257 Groveland av.
Kendall Albert O. 6341 Stewart av.
Kendall Benjamin W. 2638 Prairie av
 U.L.
Kendall D. Roy, 6341 Stewart av.
Kendall Elizabeth Mrs. 828 Warren av.
Kendall George J. 4357 Prairie av.
Kendig Harry J. 2978 Prairie av.
Kendig John A. J. Mrs. Lexington hotel
Kenfield E. D. Morgan Park
Kenfield Fred Standish, 5553 Monroe av.
Kenfield Joel W. 7206 Euclid av.
Kenly David Franklin, 34 Astor. *Un.*
Kenly F. Corning, 34 Astor
Kenly William K. 34 Astor
Kenna E. D. Hotel Metropole. *Chi.*
Kenna John J. 3815 Forest av.
Kennard W. P. Pullman
Kennedy Alexander D. 925 Park av.
Kennedy Burr A. 2666 N. Lincoln
Kennedy B. T. 295 Webster av.
Kennedy David J. Oak Park. *U.L.*
Kennedy Edith C. Miss, 3656 Michigan av.
Kennedy F. P. 5627 Michigan av
Kennedy Henry H. 4840 Ellis av. *U.L.*
Kennedy Horace M. Mrs. 580 Lasalle av.
 Sum. res. 53 Rutger st. Utica, N.Y.
Kennedy H. Howell, 69, 48th
Kennedy J. Edward, 3100 Groveland av.
Kennedy Madison Barker, 3656 Michigan
 av. *Cal., W.P.*
 Sum. res. "Bitter Sweet," Saratoga
 Co., N. Y.
Kennedy R. Bruce, Clifton house
Kennedy Thomas, New Hotel Holland
Kennedy Vernon Shaw, 3524 Michigan av.
 W.P.
Kennedy William B. 364 Ashland boul.
 C.A. Ill.
Kennedy William B. 5938 Parnell av.
Kennedy W.J. Chicago Beach hotel. *C.A.*
Kennett Francis J. Hotel Metropole
 Chi., W.P.
Kennett J. Durand, Hotel Metropole. *C.A.*
Kennett Luther, Hotel Metropole
Kennicott Cass L. 4050 Ellis av.
Kennicott Donald, 4050 Ellis av.
Kennicott J. W. Mrs. 401 N. State
Kennicott Lynn S. 4050 Ellis av.
Kennicott Marie A. Mrs. 4802 Madison av
Kennicott Ransom, 4050 Ellis av.
Kennon H. B. 1944 Deming pl. *Un.*
Kennon H. L. Mrs. 1944 Deming pl.
Kenny Mary Mrs. 1180 Washington boul.
Kenny William R. Highland Park
Kenny William S. 3235 Rhodes av. *C.A.*
Kent Arthur, 3012 Vernon av.
Kent B. R. 5758 Washington av.
Kent E. L. Miss, 2000 Calumet av.
Kent Fred I. 6536 Harvard av.
Kent Helen M. Mrs. 6536 Harvard av.

Kent Henry L. 6536 Harvard av.
Kent Henry R. 7130 Euclid av.
Kent Herbert F. 5752 Monroe av.
    Sum. res. Madison, Wis.
Kent Luman B. 4024 Prairie av.
Kent Mary Miss, 3012 Vernon av.
Kent Sidney A. 2944 Michigan av. *Cal*,,
   Chi., U.L., W.P.
    Sum. res. Suffield, Conn.
Kent Thomas, 3203 Calumet av.
Kent William, 5112 Kimbark av. *C.A.,*
   U.L., Univ. Sum. res. San Rafael,
   Cal.
Kent William D. 450 W. Congress. *Ill.,*
   U.L.
Kenyon Dexter E. 4015 Lake av. *C.A.,*
   W.P.
Kenyon F. C. 4335 Ellis av.
Kenyon Nellie E. Miss, 4021 Vincennes
   av.
Keogh Chester H. 4346 Drexel boul.
Keogh Elizabeth Mrs. 90 Centre av.
Keogh James B. 4346 Drexel boul. *C.A.*
Keogh John Blanchfield, 4200 Ellis av.
Keogh John W. 4346 Drexel boul. *C.A.,*
   W.P.
Keogh William H. 4346 Drexel boul.
Keough W. C. H. Maywood
Kerber Henry Mrs. 3253 Calumet av.
Kerber William L. 3236 South Park av.
Kerby E.-C. Mrs 4812 Kimbark av.
Kerby James, 1007 Millard av.
Kercheval Robert, 6325 Monroe av.
Kerdolff Edward C. 4339 Prairie av.
Kerfoot C. A. Mrs. 3253 Michigan av.
Kerfoot Ethel Miss, 127 Astor
Kerfoot Reeda Miss, 127 Astor
Kerfoot Samuel H. Mrs. 136 Rush
   Sum.res. Dawn near Kilbourn City,Wis.
Kerfoot Samuel H. jr. 77 Lincoln Park
   boul.
Kerfoot William D. 127 Astor. *Chi.,*
   U.L.,Univ.
Kerlin Elijah I., M.D. 576 Fullerton av.
Kern E. L. Dr. 949 Greenleaf av.
Kern Charles Mrs. Chicago Beach hotel
Kern Henry W. Chicago Beach hotel.
   W.P.
Kern Paul O. 5646 Monroe av.
Kernott John E. 4403 Prairie av.
Kerns Benjamin F. Dr. 106, 43d
Kerr Charles A. Revere house
Kerr George B. 4104 Vincennes av.
Kerr Henry H. Evanston
Kerr Lulu Miss, Auditorium hotel
Kerr Rebecca Miss, 649 W. Monroe
Kerr Richard M. 5319 Washington av.
Kerr Robert G. 225 Dearborn av.
Kerr Robert J. Oak Park
Kerr Robert M. 1176 W. Congress
Kerr Samuel, 1323 Washington boul.
Kerr William R. Auditorium hotel. *U.L.*
Kershaw Bert H. Dr. 314 N. State
Kersten George, 57 Grant pl.
Kerwin Michael W. 332 Dearborn av.
Kesler Arthur E. 335 W. 61st pl.

Kesler M. R. Mrs. 335 W. 61st pl.
Kesler S. C. Mrs. 335 W. 61st pl.
Kesner Abraham L. 4235 Prairie av.
   Lksd.
Kesner Jacob L. 4756 Grand boul. *Lksd.*
   Stan.
Kesner Louis, 3918 Calumet av.
Kessler George T. 7329 Bond av.
Kessler Julius, 3965 Lake av. *C.A.*
Kester John R. 3024 Lake Park av.
Ketcham I. C. 31 Roslyn pl.
Ketcham M. W. Mrs. 3146 Lake Park av.
Ketcham Thomas C. 2145 Kenmore av.
Ketcham William P. 870 Winthrop av.
   Ill.
Ketcham W. N. Irving Park
Ketchum William N. Oak Park
Ketchum W. D. Wilmette
Kettelle George H. 363 Lasalle av.
Kettelle George H. Mrs. 306 Schiller
Kettering Mamie Miss, 199 Fremont
Kettle Rupert A. 2410 Prairie av. *Cal.*
   W.P.
Kettler Adelaide Miss, Granada hotel
Kettlestrings Fred W. Dr. Oak Park
Kettlestrings Joseph, Oak Park
Kettlestrings J. W. Mrs. Oak Park
Kettlestrings Orrin R. Oak Park
Kettlestrings Walter N. Oak Park
Kettlestrings Wilbur, Oak Park
Keuthan Belle Mrs. 219 S. Hoyne av.
Kewley J. R. Dr. 3115 Wabash av
Key John R. Granada hotel. *Chi.*
Key Mabel Miss, 85 Rush
Keyes A. Belcham Dr. 299 N. State
Keyes D. H. 29, 33d
Keyes Edward T. 1204 Morse av.
Keyes Harvey B. 1206 Morse av.
Keyes Rollin A. Kenilworth. *Chi., U.L*
Keys T. Frank Dr. 51, 22d
Keyser William H. 4414 Ellis av.
Kidd Albert, 989 W. Jackson boul.
Kidd Charles P. 989 W. Jackson boul.
Kidd William E. Dr. Oak Park
Kidder Albert F. Elmhurst
Kidder Harriette S. Mrs. Evanston
Kidder Henry M. Col. Evanston
Kidston James, LaGrange
Kidston W. H. LaGrange
Kiefer Louis C. 2555 N. Ashland av.
Kiel J. H. Oak Park
Kienzle William F. 2614 N. Paulina
Kierulff L. A. Dr. 2126 Indiana av.
Kilbourn A. S. Mrs. 780 North Park av.
Kilbourn Frederick H. 5423 Washington
   av.
Kilbourne F. A. Mrs. 4020 Ellis av.
Kilbourne L. Bernard, 4020 Ellis av. *C.A.*
Kilcoyne Anna Mrs. 330 Huron
   Sum. res. Mackinac Island
Kilcrane Frank J. 578 W. Madison
Kile Asa B. 534 Englewood av.
Kilgallen Martin H. Mayfair. *C.A.*
Kilgore John C. 533 Englewood av.
Killen E. Greble, 225 Michigan av. *C.A.*
Killick R. J. Clifton house

Killough Charles H. 1810 Michigan av.
Kilmer Anna Dr. 5735 Indiana av.
Kilmer Elmer E. 5735 Indiana av.
Kilmore John W. 1428 Washington boul.
Kilvert Maxwell A. 90 Lincoln Park boul.
    Univ.
Kimball Alma Miss, 2612 Michigan av.
Kimball Alonzo W. Evanston
Kimball Curtis N. 5436 Cornell av.
Kimball C. Frederick, Calumet club.
    Chi., C.A., U.L., W.P.
Kimball Dorr A. Evanston
Kimball Edward A. 5020 Woodlawn av.
Kimball Edward D. 4828 Kenwood av .
Kimball Ernest M. 138, 73d
Kimball Eugene S. 4706 Woodlawn av.
    C.A.   Sum. res. Waynesville. N.C.
Kimball F. R. Mrs. 2765 N. Robey
Kimball George F. 3341 Michigan av.
    C.A., W.P.
        Sum. res. Narragansett Pier, R. I.
Kimball Granville, 449, 41st
Kimball Helen E. Miss, 4706 Woodlawn
    av.
Kimball Louise Miss, 2612 Michigan av.
Kimball L. T. Mrs. 4543 Ellis av.
Kimball Mark Mrs. Lakota hotel
Kimball R. H. Dr. Evanston
Kimball Thomas, La Grange   .
Kimball Wallace D. 3612 Lake av.
Kimball Weston G. 3620 Michigan av.
Kimball W. W. 1801 Prairie av. *Cat.,*
    Chi., W.P.
Kimbark Charles A. 184 Lincoln Park
    boul. *C.A., U.L.*   .
Kimbark D. Avery, Evanston
Kimbark Edward H. Evanston
Kimbark Eliza U. Mrs. Evanston
Kimbark Eugene U. Evanston
Kimbark Frank M. Evanston.
Kimbark George Chandlin, Riverside
Kimbark Marie Miss, 184 Lincoln Park
    boul.
Kimbark Seneca D. 184 Lincoln Park
    boul. *Chi.*
        Sum. res. Bear Lake, Mich
Kimbark Walter, 90 Lincoln Park boul.
    C.A.
Kimbell C. B. Hinsdale
Kimbell H. M. Hinsdale
Kimbell Spencer S. 1527 Kimball av.
    U.L.
Kimbell S. T. Hinsdale
Kimberly L. R. 418 Warren av.
Kimmelstiel Jacob S. 3650 Grand boul.
    Stan.
Kimmet William A. Dr. 1022 N. Halsted
Kimmey Fred L. Morgan Park
Kinahan Robert W. 5317 Washington av.
Kindt Arthur, 1723 Deming pl.
Kindt J. W. 1723 Deming pl.
King Allan H. Mrs. 192 Ashland boul.
King Anna Mrs. 5417 Washington av.
King A. N. Revere house
King Benjamin F. 446 S. Marshfield av.
King Catherine C. Mrs. 253 Belden av.

King Charles B. 159 Rush
        Sum. res. Elmhurst
King Charles C. 42, 42d pl.
King Charles G. 2913 Michigan av. *Chi.,*
    Univ.
King Charles G. Y. 234 Hampden ct.
King Charles H. 2337 Kenmore av.
King Charles H. Oak Park
King Charles W. 276 Belden av.
King Edward, Oak Park
King Edward A. 923 Pratt av.
King Eleanor M. Mrs. 4314 Oakenwald av
King E. A. Mrs. 3645 Vernon av.
King Frances Mrs. 4125 Bosworth av.
King Francis, 5 Tower ct. *Chi., C.A.,*
    Univ.   Sum. res. Elmhurst
King Frank B. 4957 Washington Park ct.
King Frederick E. 265 Oakwood boul.
King Geo. E. 4445 Ellis av.
King Grace F. Miss, Evanston
King G. H. Prof. Glencoe
King Harry V. 6428 Minerva av.
King Henry W. Mrs. 151 Rush
        Sum. res. Elmhurst
King H. B. 780 North Park av.
King Hoyt, 407, 36th pl.
King James, Elmhurst
King James C. Sherman house
King Jesse G. 6428 Minerva av.
King John, 5417 Washington av.
King John A. 276 Ashland boul. *Ill., Irq.,*
    U.L.
King John C. 63 E. Pearson, *Chi., Un.*
King John C. 497 W. Congress
King J. C. Virginia hotel
King John F. Evanston
King Mary J. Mrs. Evanston
King Molesworth, 3139 Wabash av.
King M. A. Mrs. 276 Belden av.
King M. H. Morgan Park   .
King Philo R. 552 Dearborn av.
King Richard S. 6401 Star av.
King Rockwell, 63 Hawthorne pl. *Chi.,*
    Un., Univ.
King Rufus, 277 Park av.
King Sarah C. Mrs. 483 W. Jackson boul.
King Stella Marie Miss, 497 W. Congress
King S. B. 5417 Washington av.
King Thomas C. Glencoe
King Tillie Miss, 4540 Oakenwald av.
King T. E. 4203 Lake av.
King Ulric, 224 Ashland boul. *Ill.*
King Vere B. 3645 Vernon av.
King Vincent M. 3139 Wabash av.
King William, 552 Dearborn av.
King William, 928 Morse av.
King William H. 322 Michigan av.
King William H. Winnetka
King William J. 497 W. Congress
King William O. 51, 22d
King W. G. Wilmette
King W. H. Mrs. 4824 Lake av.
King W. R. Mrs. 4536 Woodlawn av.
King W. W. 5015 Madison av.
Kingman Abbie M. Mrs. Oak Park
Kingman Barry, 2253 Calumet av.

Kingman Carrie J. Miss, 306 Chestnut
Kingman Charles H. 2253 Calumet av.
Kingman Jane Mrs. Evanston
Kingsbury Byron, 4713 Prairie av.
Kingsley C. L. Mayfair
Kingsley Frank W. Mayfair
Kingsley Homer H. Prof. Evanston
Kinkade L. Miss, North Shore hotel
Kinkaid Albert H. 6500 Minerva av.
Kinkaid Alexander M. Dr. 7311 Yale
Kinkaid Charles F. 7106 Yale
Kinkaid J. S. Mrs. 7106 Yale
Kinley Charles B. 278 S. Irving av.
Kinnally Cornelius F. 129 W. Garfield
boul.
Kinnally John, 129 W. Garfield boul.
Kinnare F. T. 874 Walnut
Kinnear Andrew W. 235 Jackson Park
Terrace. C.A.
Kinnear Margaret Miss, 5118 Cornell
av.
Kinney Clark, Evanston
Kinney Corydon B. 7620 Eggleston av.
Kinney George K. 41 Madison Park
Kinney G. Park, 835 N. Clark
Kinney John W. 1125 Chase av.
Kinney J. Fred, Evanston
Kinney M. L. Mrs. 423 Huron
Kinney W. H. Wilmette
Kinsella Daniel P. 1512 Wrightwood av.
Kinsella Jane Mrs. 1512 Wrightwood av.
Kinsella Joseph F. 1512 Wrightwood av.
Kinsman Charles, 2940 Lake Park av.
Kintz John H. 5649 Washington av.
Kinzie Arthur M. Riverside
Kiper Charles, 683, 48th pl. Lksd.
Kiper Julius, 561, 45th
Kiper Louis, 4845 Calumet av.
Kipp Frank S. Oak Park
Kipp Mary E. Mrs. Oak Park
Kippax John R. Dr. 3154 Indiana av.
Kirby R. D. Virginia hotel C.A., W.P.
Kirch John N. 4424 St. Lawrence av.
Kirchberg Edward, 345 W. Monroe
Kirchberger Siegfried H. 3624 Gran
boul. Stan.
Kirchhoff Hermann, 631 N. Hoyne av.
Kirchhoff H. August, 436 Lasalle av.
Kirchstein Herman Mrs. 640 Fullerton av.
Kirk Alfred, 4229 Oakenwald av
Kirk Anna E. Miss, 2512 Prairie av.
Kirk Charles S. Mrs. 557 N State
Kirk Charles Wright Highland Park
Kirk Edgar W. 87 Rush
Kirk Emma Miss, 528 N. State
Kirk E. jr. 6716 Wentworth av.
Kirk James J. Evanston
Kirk James M. Evanston
Kirk James S. Mrs. Evanston
Kirk John B. Evanston. Chi., C.A.,
U.L., W.P.
Kirk John W. 6423 Minerva av.
Kirk Milton W. 528 N. State. Chi., C.A.,
U.L.
Kirk S. S. Miss, 424 Chicago av.
Kirk Wallace F. Wheaton

Kirk Walter T. 528 N. State. Univ.
Kirkendall J. F. Clifton house
Kirkham C. H. 14 Bellevue pl.
Kirkham George D. Chicago Athletic
Assn.
Kirkhoff William H. Oak Park
Kirkland John K. North Shore hotel
Kirkland Joseph Mrs. 161 Rush
Kirkland Lloyd G. 3755 Sheridan rd.
Kirkland Robert, 5841 Madison av.
Kirkland W. T. Evanston
Kirkman A. T. Evanston
Kirkman Marshall J. Evanston
Kirkman Marshall M. Evanston. Chi.
C.A.
Kirkman Tracy, 16 Astor
Kirkman William Bruce, Evanston
Kirkpatrick C. A. Mrs. 1254 Michigan av.
Kirkpatrick F. A., Greenwood Inn, Evanston
Kirkpatrick John, Oak Park
Kirkpatrick John A. Dr. 396, 43d
Kirkwood Arthur J. 1830 Wellington
Kirschstein Herman Dr. 2941 South Park
av.
Kirschten Nicholas, Evanston
Kirtland Charles B. 1547 Michigan av.
Kirtland India U. Mrs. 1547 Michigan av.
Kirtland Sanford C. 5474 Cornell av.
Kirton David M. 9 Crilly ct.
Kiser John W. 3812 Michigan av. C.A.,
W.P.
Kissack William, Austin
Kissell A. S. Mrs. 5609 Washington av
Kissinger Victor T. 405, 64th
Kisterbock Codelia G. Mrs. 7236 Yale
Kistler Andrew M. 6544 Harvard av. C.A.
Kistler D. Albin, 4328 Oakenwald av.
Kistner John H. Washington Heights
Kitchell Frank J. 6652 Harvard av. C.A
Kitchell Helen M. Miss, Evanston
Kitchell Jane E. Miss, Evanston
Kitchell Laura Miss, Evanston
Kitchen John B. Union club. Chi.
Kitchin A. W. 4759 Langley av. W.P.
Kittle E. B. Hinsdale
Kittredge George A. Evanston
Kittredge H. F. Mrs. 425 Lasalle av.
Kittredge Jeanette Miss, 3640 Prairie av
Kittredge Josephine Miss, 3640 Prairie
av.
Kizer Ida B. Mrs. 4144 Grand boul.
Klais J. G. 283 Belden av.
Klapp William H. 303 The Plaza
Klappenbach Alexander, 239 Osgood
Klatz Charles, Lexington hotel
Klebs Arnold C. Dr. 600 N. State. C.A.
Klebs Edwin Dr. 4417 Indiana av.
Klebs Henry, 4417 Indiana av.
Klee Abram, 575 Lasalle av.
Kleiminger A. Mrs. 4514 Lake av.
Kleiminger Frank, 4514 Lake av.
Kleiminger M. E. 4514 Lake av.
Klein Adolph, 61 Bryant av.
Klein Charles, 4724 State. Lksd.
Klein Frances Mrs. 182 Bowen av.
Klein Fred, 107 Seminary av.

Klein Fied C. 2366 N. Paulina
Klem Gottlieb, Washington Heights
Klein Gustav L. 3126 Wabash av. *Lksd.*
Klein Henry P. 1824 Belmont av.
Klein Leon, 481 Ashland boul. *Stan.*
Klein Leon, 3151 Forest av. *Lksd.*
Klein Mayer, 3742 Wabash av.
Klein Moses, 4341 Calumet av.
Klein Nathan, 3151 Forest av. *Lksd.*
Klein Philip Rev. 569 Cleveland av.
Klein Samuel, 3151 Forest av. *Lksd.*
Klein Samuel W. 3722 Forest av.
Klein Samuel W. 4229 Calumet av.
Klein Sidney, 4341 Calumet av. *Lksd.*
Klein Simon, 483 Ashland boul. *Stan*
Klein Simon, 4315 Drexel boul.
Klein T. Henry, 1824 Belmont av.
Kleine Henry, 1220 N. Clark
Kleinert Adolph, 3922 Prairie av.
Kletzing J. F. 1437 Perry
Kline Aaron V. The Tudor
Kline Emma Miss, 4807 Prairie av.
Kline George, Hinsdale
Kline George R. Evanston
Kline G. E. Hotel Metropole. *U.L.*
Kline Lena Miss, 4807 Prairie av.
Kline Rolland R. Evanston
Kline Samuel J. Lakota hotel. *Stan.*
Kline Sigmund, 3940 Calumet av.
Klinger William, 3525 Wabash av.
Klinger W. Mrs. 3525 Wabash av.
Klock Frank B. River Forest
Kloeber John V. 461 Lasalle av.
Klopfer Henry, 3407 Calumet av. *Stan.*
Klore W. W. 2441 Wabash av.
Kluge Frank M. 865 S. St. Louis av.
Kluge William, 871 S. St. Louis av.
Klunder C. F. 3005 Vernon av.
Klunder Henry E. 3005 Vernon av.
Knab George D. Clifton house
Knabenshue F. G. Lieut. Fort Sheridan
Knaggs George B. Evanston
Knaggs Robert C. Evanston
Knapp Charles H. LaGrange
Knapp George Owen 249, 49th. *Chi.,C.A.*
            Sum. res. Lake George, N. Y.
Knapp George S. LaGrange
Knapp Henry S. Evanston
Knapp H. G. Mrs. 3151 Prairie av.
Knapp John A. 5400 Jefferson av.
Knapp J. M. 415 Huron. *Univ.*
Knapp J. V. Mrs. 411 Oak
Knapp Kemper K. 411 Oak. *Univ.*
Knapp M. A. Chicago Beach hotel
Knapp N. E. Mrs. 249, 49th
            Sum. res. Lake George, N. Y.
Knapp Randolph R. 62 Wisconsin
Knapp S. O. Dr. 6445 Monroe av.
Knapp Thomas, 4349 Lake av. *C.A.*
            Sum. res. Channel Lake
Knapp William M. 3816 Calumet av.
Knapp W. A. 2928 Groveland av.
Knauer Edmund Mrs. 1474 N. Clark
Knauer Peter, 289 Seminary av.
Knauer Roy, 1474 N. Clark
Knauss Fred, 2349 Magnolia av.

Kneale J. C. 432 W. Adams
Knebel George H. 2124 Michigan av.
Knecht John, 161 Locust
Knecht Samuel E. 526 Burling
Kneisly John L. 1136 Washington boul.
Kneller G. St. John, 597, 46th. *W.P.*
Knickerbocker Charles K. 4045 Ellis
Knickerbocker Henry M. Mrs. 4045 Ellis
   av.
Kniffen LeGrand, Austin
Knight Anna W. Mrs. 5100 Hibbard av
Knight Charles Y. Oak Park
Knight Clarence A. 3322 Calumet av.
   C.A., U.L.
Knight Cora Mrs. 4628 Prairie av.
Knight Edgar F. 634, 46th pl.
Knight Eugene C. Dr. Evanston
Knight Hale, 2429 N. Paulina
Knight John B. 4738 Woodlawn av. *U.L.*
Knight John B. 634, 46th pl.
Knight John W. 5100 Hibbard av.
Knight J. F. 634, 46th pl.
Knight Louis G. 310 Webster av.
Knight Margaret Mrs. 368 Ontario
Knight M. G. Rev. Chicago Beach hotel
Knight Newell C. Evanston. *U.L.*
Knight Stephen C. 3336 Rhodes av.
Knight Walter J. 99 Madison Park
Knight William H. Hinsdale
Knight William J. 276 Michigan av.
Knight William M. 1825 Barry av.
Knights Charles H. 6617 Harvard av.
Knill Charles P. 2388 N. Paulina
Knipschield Frank A. 462 Dayton
Knisely Harry C. Hinsdale
Knisely John A. 3201 Rhodes av. *C.A.*
Knisely Richard W. 1371 Washington
   boul.
Kniskern Charles A. 49, 64th
Kniskern Warren B. 4849 Greenwood av.
   U.L.
Knobe Bertha Miss, North Shore hotel
Knobel G. C. Rev. 195 S. Hoyne av.
            Sum. res. Linwood Park, Ohio
Knobel John Esher, 195 S. Hoyne av.
Knoblock Henry P. Austin
Knoke Herman C. 1693 Wellington
Knoop Ernest H. 1244 Sheridan rd.
Knott Frederick J. Oak Park
Knott Henry A. 1677 Sheridan rd. *U.L.,
   Univ.*
Knott Sarah Mrs. 1677 Sheridan rd.
Knowles Carrie M. Miss, 4406 Sidney av.
Knowles Henry, 506 W. Congress
Knowles Jerry, 3123 Forest av.
Knowles J. C. Mrs. 4564 Oakenwald av.
Knowles Solomon F. 506 W. Congress
Knowlton Aimee Miss, 3989 Drexel boul.
Knowlton Edward R. Austin
Knox Charles M. Evanston
Knox George G. Wilmette
Knox John, 1021 W. Jackson boul.
Knox J. S. B. Mrs. Hyde Park hotel
Knox Reuben, Evanston
Knox S. Fred. Highland Park

Knox Thomas M. Wilmette
Knox Wesley L. Evanston
Knox William A. Dr. 780 W. Monroe
Knudson Mary A.K.Miss,4713 Indiana av.
Knudson Samuel O. 4713 Indiana av.
Knudson Theo. J. Dr. 4713 Indiana av.
Kober George C. 433 Center
Koblens William M. 976 Millard av.
Koch Augusta Miss, 230 Cass.
Koch Carl, 334 Lasalle av.
Koch C. R. E. Dr. 4534 Woodlawn av.
Koch Edward F. 334 Lasalle av.
Koch Edward P. Dr. 84 Park av.
Koch Frederick Mrs. Elmhurst
Koch George, 230 Cass
Koch John Mrs. 385 Evanston av.
Koch Leo, 230 Cass
Koch Martin, 230 Cass
Koch Nicholas, 454 Lasalle av.
Kochersperger Daniel H.3987Drexel boul.
U L.
Kochersperger Frank H.3431 So. Park av.
Kochersperger Harding L. 3989 Drexel
boul.
Kochs August, 601 Dearborn av.
Kochs Theodore A. 1836 Surf. U.L.
Koehler Frederick Mrs. 579 Orchard
Koehn Louis F. jr. 2558 N. Hermitage av.
Koehne William L. 1909 Deming pl.
Koelling Carl Prof. 3523 Calumet av.
Koelling John, 3523 Calumet av.
Koenig Joseph A. 31 Winthrop ct.
Koerner Christian jr. 1600 Kenmore av.
Koerner C. Rev. 521 Lasalle av.
Koester George F. 2671 N. Hermitage av.
Koethe Dora Miss, 3131 Indiana av.
Kohl Charles E. 2826 Michigan av.
Sum. res. Oconomowoc, Wis.
Kohler Frank W. 4740 Madison av.
Kohler G. A. Edward, 4740 Madison av.
Kohlhamer Frederick Dr. 149 Locust
Kohlsaat C. C. Judge, 239 Ashland boul.
Ill., U.L.
Sum. res. Lake Geneva, Wis.
Kohlsaat Ernest W. 146 S. Central Park
av. Ill.
Kohlsaat H. H. 120 Lake Shore drive.
Chi., U.L.
Sum. res. Oconomowoc, Wis.
Kohn Albert W. 2614 Indiana av. Stan.
Kohn Alfred, 3241 Vernon av. Stan.
Kohn Alfred D. 3340 Michigan av. Stan.
Kohn Alfred D. Dr. 412 Lasalle av.
Kohn A. H. 2240 Calumet av. Stan.
Kohn Clara Miss, 4316 Vernon av.
Kohn David A. 3340 Michigan av. Stan.
Kohn Dila Miss, 4316 Vernon av.
Kohn Emanuel J. 3223 Michigan av.
Stan. Sum. res. Lake Geneva, Wis.
Kohn Henrietta Miss, 3541 Ellis av.
Kohn Henry M. 2959 Groveland av. Lksd.
Kohn Isaac A. 3541 Ellis av. Stan.
Kohn John, Oak Park
Kohn Joseph A. 2018 Calumet av.
Kohn Katie Mrs. 428 Lasalle av.
Kohn Louis A. 3541 Ellis av. Stan.

Kohn Louis H. 4639 Drexel boul. Stan.
Kohn Milton H. 2240 Calumet av.
Kohn Milton M.2959 Groveland av.Lksd.
Kohn Morris, 2959 Groveland av.
Kohn Simon, 2959 Groveland av. Lksd.
Kohn Simon A. 3541 Ellis av. Stan.
Kohn Simon H. 4316 Vernon av. Stan.
Kohn Theresa Miss, 1717 Michigan av.
Kohner D. M. 4805 Prairie av.
Kohner J. B. 471 Bowen av. Lksd.
Kohner P. Mrs. 471 Bowen av.
Kohnhurst O. Glen Ellyn
Kohtz Louis O. 650 Fullerton av.
Kollar Charles, Ravinia
Kollenberg C. 17 Pine Grove av.
Kollman Ida H. Miss, 5524 Drexel av.
Kollmorgen Herman, 1675 Barry av.
Komiss D. S. Lexington hotel
Koob Anna Miss, Evanston
Koob Michael L. Evanston
Koons M. E. Mrs. 1914 Arlington pl.
Koontz N. B. 4216 Oakenwald av.
Kopf Charles W. 503 Ashland boul.
Korssell C. F.P. Dr. 5609 Indiana av.
Kosche Oscar F. 1760 Wrightwood av.
Kowalski Joseph H. 3763 Vernon av.
Kozminski Charles Mrs. 3346 Vernon av.
Kozminski Maurice W. Hotel Metropole.
Stan.
Kraft Oscar H. 569 N. Clark
Kraft Oscar H. jr. Dr. 569 N. Clark
Kralovec John, 979 S. Avers av. Ill.
Kramer Adolph, 2912 Prairie av. Stan.
Kramer Charles A. L. 987 Warren av.
Kramer Ferdinand, 2912 Prairie av.
Kramer Joseph A. 3744 Forest av. Lksd.
Kranz John, 627 Dearborn av.
Kranz Nicholas F. Evanston
Kraus Adolph, 4518 Drexel boul. C.A.,
Irq., Lksd., Stan.
Kraus Adolph L. 228A Fremont
Kraus Harry, 4816 Forrestville av. Lksd.
Kraus Rosa Mrs. 284 Ohio
Kraus Simon, 427 S. Marshfield av.
Krause Daniel, 3339 Prairie av.
Krause Edmund R. 1091 N. Clark
Krauss Alexander, 49 St. James pl.
Krauss Marcel, 49 St. James pl.
Krayeill Elizabeth W. Mrs. 71 Warren av.
Krebs Conrad F. 4408 Berkeley av.
Krebs James H. 3029 Groveland av.
Kreer John J. 539 Lasalle av.
Kreicker William, 207 Fremont
Kreidler William A. 295 Belden av. U.L.
Kreis Adolph, 1231 Pratt av.
Kreis Gus A. Austin
Kreis John, 1231 Pratt av.
Kreismann Paul, 640 Pine Grove av.
Kreissl Filip Dr. 177, 51st. C.A.
Krémer Charles Edward, 3647 Grand
boul. C.A., Ill.
Kretzinger George W. Austin. C.A.
Kretzinger George W. jr. Austin
Kretzinger Joseph, Austin
Kreutzberg J. A. 2312 N. Paulina
Krieger George E. Dr. 4540 Vincennes av.

Kriegh David Mrs: 1811 Belmont av.
Kriete George H. 1418 Lawrence av.
Kroeschell Albert, 354 Bissell
Kroeschell Charles, 209 Belden av.
Kroeschell Herman A. Mrs.207 Belden av.
Kroeschell Otto, 450 Dayton
Kroeschell William L. 457 Dayton
Kroeshall William, Evanston
Krohn Frank, Hinsdale
Kroll Sarah Dr. 428 W. Adams
Kronthal Benjamin, 4528 Prairie av.
Kronthal Leo, 4528 Prairie av.
Kronthal Louis, 4528 Prairie av.
Krouskup Walter·H. 3809 Wabash av.
Krueger C. Mrs. 3244 South Park av.
Krueger Leo, 3247 Beacon
Krueger Theodore, 3247 Beacon
Kruger Richard, Revere house
Krum Charles L. 5327 Washington av.
Krum Iretus R. 648 W. Monroe. *Ill.*
    Sum. res. Charlevoix, Mich.
Krum Louis B. 150 S. Paulina
Krumm John, 2065 Sheridan rd.
Kruse George, Kenilworth
Krusemarck Charles, M.D. 4450 Prairie
    av.   Sum. res. Marseilles, Ill.
Kuecken Charles, 407 Orchard
Kuecken William Mrs. 407 Orchard
Kuehl George, 592 Burling
Kuehne Oscar K. 3301 Beacon
Kuh Abraham, 3141 Michigan av. *Stan.*
Kuh Edwin J. Dr. 4330 Drexel boul.
Kuh Henry, 4502 Ellis av.
Kuh Isaac, 4413 Ellis av.
Kuh Julius S. 3141 Michigan av. *Lksd.,*
   Stan.
Kuh L. K. Mrs. Hotel Del Prado
Kuh Sydney Dr. 4413 Ellis av.
Kuhlmey Albert, 496 Dearborn av.
Kuhn Adolph A. 1624 W. Adams
Kuhnen George C. Mrs. 379 Chestnut
Kuhnen Nicholas, 2469 N. Ashland av.
Kuhnert L. C. 5610 Washington av. *C.A.*
Kuhns Bertha Mrs. 3147 Indiana av.
Kultchar M. Richard, Winnetka. *U.L.*
Kune Julian, 6637 Lafayette av.
Kunreuther Johanna Mrs. 471 Lasalle av.
Kunstadter Albert, 4218 Champlain av.
   Lksd.
Kunz Emil Dr. 84 Lincoln av.
Kunz Frank, Wilmette
Kunze Louis G. 697 Sedgwick
Kuppenheimer Albert B. 3240 Michigan
   av. *Stan.*
Kuppenheimer Bernard, 3240 Michigan
   av. *Stan.*
Kuppenheimer Jonas, 2801 Michigan av.
   Stan.
Kuppenheimer Louis B. 3240 Michigan
   av. *Stan., W.P.*
Kurts George E. Austin
Kurtz Carl E. Dr. 4460 Berkeley av.
Kurz Adolph, 3414 Calumet av. *Stan.*
Kurz Benne Mrs. 3414 Calumet av.
Kussel Christian, 721 N. Wells
Kussel Philip, 2124 Michigan av.

Küssner Albert J. 3813 Forest.av. *C.A.*
Küssner Lorenz, 3813 Forest av.
Küssner Louise C. Miss, 3813 Forest av.
Kusworm Daniel, 916 W. Monroe
Kyle H. G. 6055 Jefferson av.

L ABARTHE ALBERT, 6520 Cham-
  plain av.
Labes Arthur, 1718 Gary pl.
Lacey Edward S. Evanston. *U.L.*
Lacey Hetty Mrs. 143 Oakwood boul.
Lachman Numa, 3561 Prairie av. *Lksd.*
Lackey Walter E. Berwyn
Lackner Ernest Dr. 3201 Calumet av.
Lackner Francis, 579 Dearborn av. *U.L.,*
  Univ.
LaCroix Joseph, Greenwood Inn, Evans-
  ton
Lacy Sara Miss, 15 Roslyn pl.
Ladd Jennie Miss, 3953 Michigan av.
LaFayette Henrietta W. Mrs. 2834 Ken-
  more av.
Laflin Albert S. 2335 Michigan av. *Cal.,*
  Chi., C.A., Un., W.P.
Laflin Arthur K. 1614 Michigan av. *Cal.,*
  Un., Univ., W.P.
Laflin George H. 1614 Michigan av. *Cal.,*
  Chi., C.A., W.P. Sum.res. Pittsfield,
  Mass.
Laflin John P. 2305 Calumet av. *Cal.*
  Sum. res. Belle Haven, Conn.
Laflin Louis E. 369 Erie. *C.A., Univ.*
Laflin Lycurgus, Auditorium hotel *C.A.*
Lagergren C. G. Prof. Morgan Park
Lagorio A. Dr. 228 Dearborn av.
Lahman William H. 1142 Morse av.
Lahmer Jay, 1761 Wrightwood av.
Laing Cuthbert W. Col. 265 Michigan av.
Laing David R. 265 Michigan av.
Laing Howard E. 2449 Indiana av.
Laing John R. 3819 Vincennes av.
Laing William G. 3819 Vincennes av.
Laird Frederick G. 219 The Plaza
Laird Orlando P. Tracy
Laird W. I. 1886 Diversey
Lake Charles E. 1698 Kenmore av
Lake Clifford A. 621 W. 78th
Lake C. Crozet, 4057 Prairie av.
Lake Fred Irving, 1698 Kenmore av.
Lake Ives L. 1728 Michigan av. *C.A.*
Lake James K. 161 S. Robey
Lake John T. Clifton house
Lake Richard C. Evanston. *U.L.*
Lake William H. 4438 Ellis av. *C.A.*
Lakey Amos, 487, 42d
Lalk Edward L. Riverside
Lally George H. Leland hotel
Lalor Willard A. LaGrange. *C.A.*
LaMarche B. 416 Chicago av.
Lamb Augustus D. 2011 Prairie av.
Lamb Benjamin B. 2011 Prairie av. *Chi.,*
  Univ.
Lamb Charles Allison, 497 W. Jackson
  boul. *C.A.*
Lamb Frank H. 495 W. Jackson boul.
  C.A.

Lamb Frederick R. 5326 Cornell av.
Lamb I. Mrs. 1060 Warren av.
Lamb Mabelle Howard Miss, 497 W. Jackson boul.
Lamb Sophia C. Mrs. Evanston
Lamberson D. Harvey, Evanston
Lamberson Frank, Evanston
Lamberson Josie M. Miss, Evanston
Lambert John A. Maywood
Lamberton Hull, 4074 Lake av.
Lamberton John F. 2207 Kenmore av.
Lamm Abraham, 748 Fullerton av. *Stan.*
Lamm Arthur G. 4640 Prairie av. *Stan.*
Lamm Joseph C. 3710 Grand boul. *Stan.*
Lamm S. C. Mrs. 3712 Grand boul.
Lammert Charles F. 4845 Forrestville av.
Lamont Robert P. 217, 52d
LaMonte Madison, Evanston
Lamoreaux Manning D. 1205 Washington boul. Sum. res. North Fairfield, O.
Lamplugh E. J. Mrs. 4327 Oakenwald av.
Lamport F. W. Union club
Lamson J. V. Evanston
Lamson Lorenzo J. 3720 Grand boul.
Lamson S. Warren, 3991 Ellis av. *C.A.*
Lancaster Eugene A. 2703 Prairie av.
Lancaster Frederick P. Maywood
Lancaster R. Mrs. 4129 Drexel boul.
Landauer Herman, 3735 Ellis av. *Stan.*
Lande Solomon, 88 Pine Grove av.
Landergren B. A. E. 6127 Monroe av.
Landis Edmund M. Dr. 1115 N. Clark
Landis John W. Hinsdale
Landis Kenesaw M. 4259 Grand boul. *Cal.*
Landis Perry, Evanston
Landis Roland R. Hinsdale
Landis William, Hinsdale
Landman P. Mrs. 3764 Indiana av.
Landon Albert W. Mrs. 4628 Prairie av.
Landon Benson, Irving Park
Landon H. J. Miss, 370 Dearborn av.
Landsberg Maurice, 3731 Vincennes av.
Landt Charles C. 4204 Drexel boul.
Lane Albert G. 430 W. Adams
Lane Arthur M. Irving Park
Lane A. E. Chicago Beach hotel
Lane A. E. Miss, 6369 Greenwood av.
Lane A. H., Dr. 305 Division
Lane A. V. 1456 Michigan av.
Lane Charles, 1495 W. Monroe
Lane Chas. E. 307, 56th
Lane C. B. Mrs. 541 W. Adams
Lane Eben, 2116 Michigan av. *Cal., C.A., U.L.*
Lane Elizabeth Mrs. 705, 49th
Lane E. Mead Mrs. 6241 Monroe av.
Lane Francis B. 237 S. Marshfield av. *Ill.*
Lane Frederick W. 116, 32d
Lane F. G. Miss, 2116 Michigan av.
Lane Henry M. 286, 48th. *C.A.*
Lane Ida M. Miss, 4815 Lake av.
Lane James R. 614 Washington boul. *Ill.*
Lane Joseph, 35 Strattord pl.
Lane Joseph G. 3528 Ellis av.
Lane J. Arthur, 2212 Prairie av.

Lane Maud B. Mrs. 2001 Michigan av.
Lane Maurice T. Evanston
Lane Myron E. Dr. 3000 Indiana av.
Lane Philander E. 6626 Harvard av.
Lane Sadie M. Mrs. 2790 N. Lincoln
Lane Wm. H. 541 W. Adams. *Ill.*
Lanehart Ada Mrs. Evanston
Lanehart Peter M. 3425 Vernon av.
Lang Alexander, Ravinia
Lang Catherine Mrs. 2293 N. Hermitage av.
Lang J. M. Dr. 4800 Prairie av.
Langan John B. 573 Dearborn av.
Langbein Ferdinand, 4226 Calumet av.
Langbein S. 586 Lasalle av.
Langdon C. F. 676, 48th pl.
Langdon Richard B. 3528 Ellis av.
Lange Charles, Riverside
Lange Edward, 1744 Deming pl.
Lange Fred J. 1744 Deming pl.
Langford Thomas, Austin
Langhenry Bertha Miss, Evanston
Langlois Ellen E. Mrs. Evanston
Langrall F. S. Revere house
Langston John W. Oak Park
Langwill A. M. LaGrange
Langworthy Albert D. 1137 Birchwood av.
Langworthy Benjamin F. 6417 Minerva av.
Langworthy L. B. 2358 Indiana av.
Lanphere Edwin O. 5642 Washington av.
Lansing Mark S. Elmhurst. *Ill.*
Lansing Odell E. The Hampden
Lansing Roscoe U. The Hampden
Lansingh Killian V. R. 5100 Kimbark av.
Lanterman Elizabeth B. Mrs. 1023 S. St. Louis av.
Lanterman Etta E. Mrs. 964 S. Central Park av.
Lantz W. A. LaGrange.
Laparle Wm. B. Mrs. 704 Warren av.
Lapham Arden B. jr. 2921 Kenmore av.
Lapham A. B. 2921 Kenmore av.
Lapham C. W. 4013 Ellis av.
Lapham E. F. 4323 Lake av.
Lapham E. N. 2711 Kenmore av.
Lapham Joseph B. Mrs. Chicago Beach hotel
Lapham Marshall, 70 Bellevue pl.
Lapp Henry, 4840 Champlain av.
Lapp Peter, 235 Michigan av. *C.A., W.P.*
Large Josephine Miss, 320 Superior
Larimer Fannie L. Mrs. Evanston
Larkin Edward, 317 W. 61st pl.
Larkin F. A. Dr. Julien hotel
Larkins B. H. Maywood
Larned Frances Greene Miss, Lake Forest
Larned Sherwood J. 135 Lincoln Park boul. *Un.*
Larned Walter C. Lake Forest. *Chi., Univ.*
Larned William E. 5939 Indiana av.
Larrabee Charles R. 405 Dearborn av.
Larrabee C. D. Mrs. 5106 Cornell av.

Larrabee Edw. A. Rev. 405 Dearborn av.
Larrabee S. H. Granada hotel
Larson F. E. Irving Park
Lartz William C. C. 287 Park av. *C.A.*
LaShelle C. M. LaGrange
Lasher Charles W. Evanston
Lasher Wm. S. Highland Park
Lasier David S. 221, 61st. *Ill., Irq.*
Laskey Stephen, 1710 Indiana av.
Latham Carl R. Wilmette
Latham Ellis C. Wilmette
Latham Harry H. Wilmette
Latham Hattie Miss, Wilmette
Latham Hubbard, Wilmette
Latham Vida A. Dr. 808 Morse av.
Lathrop Bryan, 77 Bellevue pl. *Chi*,
 C.A., Un., Univ., W.P.
     Sum. res. York Harbor, Maine
Lathrop Clarence H. 526 Orchard
Lathrop Ebenezer Dr. 7526 Eggleston av.
Lathrop Edward B. 4436 Ellis av. *U.L.*
Lathrop Frederick, 364 Ontario
Lathrop Frederick A. 928 Chase av.
Lathrop Joseph, 3706 Lake av.
Lathrop May Miss, Austin
Latimer Charles E. Lake Forest
Latshaw H. C. Berwyn
Latus H. C. 955 Park av.
Lau Max, 585 Winthrop av.
Laubender John F. 399 Ashland boul.
 U.L.
Laubenstein George H. LaGrange
Lauer N. A. 5855 Indiana av.
Laughlin H. D. Great Northern hotel
Laughlin J. Lawrence, 5747 Lexington av.
Laughlin Nicholas D. Tremont house
Laughlin Thomas, 4815 Langley av.
Lauman Charles N. 185 Rush
Lauman George V. 185 Rush
Lauman J. G. Mrs. 185 Rush
Launder D. 3557 Vernon av.
Laurine Robert, Mayfair
Lave J. T. Dr. 5400 Greenwood av.
Lavery George L. The Tudor. *U.L.*
     Sum. res. Antioch, Ill
Lavery W. J. 4058 Lake av.
LaVictoire M. K. Mrs. 3603 Ellis av.
Lavigne Theodore Mrs. Evanston
Law Anna E. Miss, Wilmette
Law Francis B. Wilmette
Law George W. 32 Hawthorne pl. *U.L.*
Law Ida I. Miss, Wilmette
Law John H. 1854 Wellington. *U.L.*
Law Robert H. 1620 Prairie av.
Law William, Ravinia
Law William, Tracy
Law William jr. 6643 Harvard av. *C.A.*
Lawless James Dr. 5260 Wabash av.
Lawrence A. B. Miss, Lexington hotel
Lawrence A. S. Mrs. Lexington hotel
Lawrence Charles H. Evanston
Lawrence C. B. Mrs. 1807 Barry av.
Lawrence Dwight, 57 Lake Shore drive.
 Chi., Univ.
Lawrence Edward F. 57 Lake Shore drive.
 Chi., U.L.

Lawrence George W. 404c Ellis av.
Lawrence Henry C. Evanston
Lawrence James A. Evanston. *C.A.*
Lawrence J. Frank, Auditorium annex.
 Ill.
Lawrence Marie D. Mrs. 4000 Ellis av.
Lawrence Pliny I. Oak Park
Lawrence Preston K. 1438 Cornelia av.
Lawrence William E. Riverside. *U.L.*
Lawrence William M. Prof. 6056 Monroe
 av.
Lawrence Wm. M. Rev. 513 W. Jackson
 boul.
Lawrie Alvah K. 30 Walton pl.
Lawrie Andrew D. 30 Walton pl. *Un.*
Lawrie Henry, 4140 Berkeley av.
Lawrie John, 6820 Lafayette av.
Lawrie William, 4140 Berkeley av.
Laws F. B. Chicago Athletic assn.
Lawson George E. 4915 Wabash av.
Lawson John N. 1535 Aldine av.
Lawson Lawrence O. Capt. Evanston
Lawson Thomas A. 628 Lunt av.
Lawson Victor F. 317 Lasalle av. *Chi.,*
 C.A., U.L., Un., Univ.
Lawson William C. 5211 Washington av.
     Sum. res. Delafield, Wis.
Lawton Charles T. 4737 Kenwood av.
Lawton James, 4812 Indiana av.
Lawton Lyndon C. 4438 Greenwood av.
 C.A.
Lawton R. Mrs. 4438 Greenwood av.
Lawton Thomas Dr. Hinsdale
Lawton W. P. 2616 Indiana av.
Lay A. Tracy, 321 Michigan av. *U.L.*
     Sum. res. Highland Park
Lay Charles C. 3963 Ellis av. *U.L.*
Lay Frederick C. 3963 Ellis av.
Lay Robert D. 3963 Ellis av.
Lay Robert H. Oak Park
Layton M. F. Mrs. Evanston
Layton R. P. Tracy
Lazarus Celestine Mrs. 3202 Vernon av.
Lazarus Harry, 3606 Prairie av. *Lksd.*
Lazarus Maurice, Oakland hotel
Lazear George C. 19 Aldine sq.
Lazear Wm. W. Dr. 3146 Vernon av.
Lazelle F. Mrs. 5331 Greenwood av.
Leach Cephas H. 523 Greenleaf av.
Leach Dewitt C. Mrs. 4603 Vincennes
 av.
Leach Egbert C. 7106 Princeton av.
Leach Ferry W. Oak Park. *C.A.*
Leach Harry L. 7106 Princeton av.
Leach Levi L. 1498 W. Monroe. *C.A.,*
 U.L.
Leach S. A. Mrs. 630 Greenleaf av.
Leach Thomas A. 1631 W. Adams. *C.A.,*
 U.L.
Leach Thomas F. 2613 Shields av. *C.A.*
Leach William B. Rev. 630 N. Robey
Leacock William J. 2736 Ridge av.
Leadbeater W. J. New Hotel Holland
League William, 1493 Fulton
Leahy Denison J. Lexington hotel
Leahy James, 3431 Wabash av.

Leake Charles W. Dr. 2450 Indiana av.
Leake Joseph B. Gen. 218 Cass. *C.A.,*
    U.L.
Leaming Jeremiah, 3869 Ellis av. *Irq.*
Leaming Joseph F. Highland Park. *Irq.*
Learned Edwin J. Lake Forest
Learned Samuel J. Mrs. Lake Forest
Leask Arthur, 328 Hampden ct. *Chi.,*
    C.A., W.P.
Leatherbee George H. 2000 Indiana av.
Leavenworth Alida Miss, 594 Division
Leavitt C. Franklin Dr. 4665 Lake av.
Leavitt Herbert B. 5152 South Park av.
Leavitt Sheldon Dr. 4665 Lake av.
Leavitt Wellington, 4903 Grand boul.
LeBaron Wm. 32 Woodland Park. *Chi.*
Lebold Rose Miss, 2513 Wabash av.
Lebolt George W. 3348 Prairie av.
Lebolt J. Y. 3348 Prairie av. *Lksd.*
Lebolt Levy, 563. 45th pl.
Lebolt L. E. 3348 Prairie av.
Lebolt M. H. 3348 Prairie av. *Stan.*
Lebolt Nathan, 3348 Prairie av.
Lebolt Sidney, 3348 Prairie av.
Leckie Archibald S. LaGrange
Leckie Evelyn Mrs. 4306 Calumet av.
Leckie William, 4819 Prairie av.
Le Croart Edouard Prof. 3613 Ellis av.
Lederer Charles, 1335 Dunning
Lederer Emanuel, 3152 South Park av.
Lederer Isaac S. 4444 Champlain av.
    Lksd.
Lederer Louis, 3152 South Park av. *Lksd.*
Lederer Nathan, 368 Winthrop av.
Lederer Simeon, 4800 Forrestville av.
    Lksd.
Lederer William, 4740 Prairie av.
Ledgerwood A. J. C. Austin. *Ill.*
Ledward Harriet J. Mrs. 6630 Harvard av.
Lee A. Miss, Oak Park
Lee A. K. Hotel Metropole
Lee Blewett, 90, 21st. *Chi., Univ.*
Lee Charles R. 3945 Lake av.
Lee Charles W. Hotel Del Prado. *C.A.,*
    W.P.
Lee D. P. Mrs. 751 Washington boul.
Lee Edward Mrs. 142 W. Garfield boul.
Lee Frank T. Rev. 877 S. Sawyer av.
Lee Frederick W. 3737 Forest av.
Lee F. T. Chicago Beach hotel
Lee George, Oak Park
Lee George F. 3804 Calumet av.
Lee George P. 4241 Grand boul.
Lee Harry G. 226, 56th. *C.A.*
    Sum. res. LaPorte, Ind.
Lee James F. 1853 W. 22d
Lee John B. 28 Walton pl.
Lee John C. 4053 Indiana av.
Lee Joseph L. Evanston
Lee J. G. C. Col. Hotel Windermere
Lee J. Lewis, Riverside
Lee J. W. Rev. Mayfair
Lee Katherine Mrs. 5731 Monroe av.
Lee Philip P. Evanston
Lee R. H. 4441 Prairie av.
Lee Urquhart Mrs. Lexington hotel

Lee Walter A. Evanston
Lee Wm. H. Evanston
Lee William L. Evanston
Leeb Henry, 284 Ohio
Leebrick Arthur C. 1050 Washington
    boul.
Leech Charles E. Morgan Park
Leech Charles H. Hinsdale
Leech T. F. Dr. Hinsdale
Leeds Arthur L. 2711 Indiana av.
Leeds W. B. Lexington hotel. *Cal.,Chi.,*
    C.A., W.P.
Leekley Annie E. Mrs. 1330 Washington
    boul.
Leekley Harlow A. 1330 Washington
    boul.
Leeming Chas. W. Dr. 4545 Grand boul.
    C.A.
Leeming John, M.D. 3541 Indiana av.
    Sum. res. Harbor Point, Mich.
Leesley John R. 3260 Beacon
Lefens Thies J. 2626 Michigan av. *U.L.,*
    W.P.
Leffingwell C. W. 6050 Monroe av.
Leffingwell Frank P. 190, 36th. *U.L.*
Leffingwell Robert, Evanston
Leffingwell W. W. Prof. 316 Washington
    boul.
Leffler P. W. LaGrange
Le Furgy L. R. 5344 Washington av.
Leger Edward, 3234 South Park av.
Leger. Harry B. 3234 South Park av.
Leggett John Dr. 1373 Washington boul.
Leggett Kate Mrs.1373 Washington boul.
Legler George A. Berwyn
Legner Katie Miss, 89 Ewing pl.
Legner William, 89 Ewing pl.
Lehman Herman, 4327 Calumet av. *Lksd.*
Lehman Louis B. 3646 Grand boul. *Stan.*
Lehman William, 3346 Prairie av. *Stan.*
Lehmann Alfred A. 1624 Indiana av.
Lehmann Edmund, 1624 Indiana av. *C.A.*
Lehmann E. J. Mrs. 1326 N. Clark
Lehmann E. J. jr. 1326 N. Clark. *C.A.*
Lehmann Marie Mrs. 1624 Indiana av.
Lehmer Gilbert, Hotel Metropole
Leib Alexander S. 185, 36th
Leib Harry R. 185, 36th
Leicht Andrew E. 5 Lake View av.
Leicht Edward A. 17 Lake View av. *C.A.*
Leicht Stella Miss, 5 Lake View av.
Leigh C. W. Dr. 3127 Dover
Leigh Edward B. 3838 Calumet av. *C.A.,*
    U.L.
Leighton George W. 6439 Greenwood av.
Leihy George W. 1311 Michigan av.
Leihy George W. jr. 1311 Michigan av.
Leis William J. 5344 Greenwood av.
Leison Charles G. Riverside
Leiter Joseph, 3322 Michigan av. *Cal.,*
    Chi., C.A., Un., W.P.
    Sum. res. Lake Geneva
Leiter Levi Z. 3322 Michigan av. *Cal.,*
    Chi.,Irq., Un., U.L., W.P.
    Sum. res. Lake Geneva
Leland Alice J. Miss, 3708 Lake av.

Leland Charles W. 425 Lasalle av.
Leland Charlotte M. Miss, 425 Lasalle av.
Leland E. F. 425 Lasalle av. *Chi.*, *C.A.*
Leland M.·B. Mrs. 5234 Woodlawn av.
Leland Warren F. 4651 Drexel boul.
Lelewer David, 3835 Vincennes av.
Lelewer Seward, 3835 Vincennes av.
Leman Henry W. 337 Dearborn av. *Chi.*
Le Messurrier John, Glen Ellyn
Lemmon Chandler F. 5428 Madison av.
Lemmon T. A. 5428 Madison av.
Lemoine Edwin S. Chicago Athletic assn.
Lemon Adelaide Mrs. 691½ W. Adams
Lemon George S. 691½ W. Adams
Lemon Henry M. 927 W. Jackson boul.
Lemon Herbert L. 691½ W. Adams
LeMoyne Francis J. 50 Scott
LeMoyne Louis V. 615 The Plaza. *Univ.*
LeMoyne William M. 50 Scott. *Univ.*
Lenehan Joseph H. 4631 St. Lawrence av. *C.A.*
Lenert Frank S. 5642 Michigan av.
Lenfesty J. L. New Hotel Holland
Lengacher Jacob, 277 Fremont
Lengacher Oscar F. 277 Fremont
Lengfeld Felix, 5763 Madison av.
L'Engle William J. Hotel Windermere
Lenham Louis S. 683 W. Monroe
Lenham Nathan L. 683 W. Monroe
Lenington Andrew, 207, 36th
Lenington Hector C. 207' 36th
Lenke August, 93 Ewing pl.
Lenke August jr. 93 Ewing pl.
Lennard Amos L. Dr. 3848 Vincennes av.
Lenox John P. Oak Park
Lenox Mary A. Mrs. Oak Park
Leonard Alice S. Miss, Lake Forest
Leonard Arthur G. 2501 Michigan av.
Leonard Charles C. 399, 46th
Leonard Egbert W. 171, 51st
        Sum. res. Mackinac Island
Leonard Frank P. 5743 Washington av.
Leonard F. B. Hyde Park hotel
Leonard F. S. Hyde Park hotel
Leonard G. Russell, 76, 50th
Leonard Louisa Mrs. 446 Elm
Leonard L. R. Mrs. 5036 Jefferson av.
Leonard M. 6600 Ellis av.
Leonard Ophelia A. Mrs. Oak Park
Leonard Richard W. 930 Lunt av.
Leonard R. L. Dr. 312 Lasalle av.
Leonard Simeon F. Oak Park. *Ill.*
Leonard William H. 6354 Lexington av.
Leopold Alfred F. 3339 Michigan av. *Stan.*
Leopold Asa F. Mrs. 214, 32d
Leopold Charles M. 3601 Prairie av. *Stan.*
Leopold Henry, 5327 Michigan av. *Stan.*
Leopold Henry jr. 4330 Forrestville av. *Stan.*
Leopold Henry F. 4346 Berkeley av.
Leopold Louis Mrs. 4346 Grand boul.
Leopold Maurice, 4346 Grand boul. *Stan.*
Leopold Max, 3602 Prairie av. *Stan.*
Leopold Nathan F. 2901 Michigan av. *Stan.*

Leopold Ralph M. 4213 Calumet av.
Leopold Samuel F. 3339 Michigan av.
Lepman David, 4556 Ellis av.
Lepman Horace, 4556 Ellis av.
Lepman Louis, 3718 Grand boul. *Lksd.*
Leppel S. 4231 Calumet av.
Lepper George A. 4467 Oakenwald av.
Lermit Gerald H. 3409 Calumet av. *U.L.*
Lerow George L. 2691 N. Ashland av.
LeRoy Joseph M. 4028 Grand boul.
LeRoy William G. Dr. Lombard
Lesch Henry, 6522 Ingleside av.
Lesch Jacob K. 1186 N. Clark
Lesh G. B. Mrs. 4144 Grand boul.
Lesh L. B. 4144 Grand boul.
Lesher Irving A. 95 Oakwood av.
Lesher J. H. Chicago Athletic assn.
Leslie Amy Miss, Virginia hotel
Leslie Arthur M. Evanston
Leslie George H. Winnetka
Leslie Jane Mrs. Oak Park
Leslie John H. 3344 Rhodes av.
Leslie Walter, Hinsdale
Lessig William H. Gen. 3930 Lake av.
Lester Albert G. 5744 Monroe av.
Lester Charles H. Hotel Metropole. *C.A.* *W.P.*
Lester Franklin, 3145 Groveland av.
Lester F. A. 44 Pine Grove av. *Chi.,* *C.A.*
Lester Henry V. 603 Dearborn av. *C.A.*
Lester Mary S. Mrs. 3515 Calumet av.
Leszynsky E. G. Palmer house. *Ill.*
Letourneau Robert A. Dr. 36th ne. cor. Cottage Grove av.
Letton Harold W. 4846 Kimbark av.
Letton Theo W. 4846 Kimbark av. *U.L.* Sum. res. Highland Park
Letts Arthur R. 107, 37th
Letts James P. Dr. 334 Center
Leusman Frederick A. Dr. 270 Huron
LeVally John R. 4424 Ellis av.
Leversedge L. S. 197 Oakwood boul.
Levey Henry, 144 Lincoln av.
Levey Mark, 144 Lincoln av.
Levi Carl, 3601 Vincennes av. *Lksd.,Stan.*
Levi David, 3725 Langley av.
Levi Jacob, 3651 Michigan av. *Stan.*
Levi Joel H. 4404 Berkeley av.
Levie Charles M. 3247 Rhodes av.
Levie Jerome M. 3247 Rhodes av. *Stan.*
Levie M. Mrs. 3247 Rhodes av.
Levie Oliver M. 3247 Rhodes av.
Levine A. 918 W. Monroe
Levinson I. 3415 Prairie av.
Levinson S. O. 4327 Lake av.
Levis John M. 6427 Kimbark av. *C.A.*
Levison B. Mrs. 3254 Rhodes av.
Levison Michael M. 4734 Grand boul.
Levy Alexander H. 1949 Deming ct. *C.A*
Levy David R. 4234 Calumet av. *Lksd.*
Levy Dila Mrs. 1705 Michigan av.
Levy D. S. New Hotel Holland
Levy Elizabeth Miss, 3327 South Park av.
Levy E. E. 3608 Prairie av. *Lksd.*
Levy Harry, 492 N. Hoyne av.

Levy I. G. 5477 Ellis av.
Levy Jacob W. 3423 South Park av.
Levy J. E. 3238 Vernon av.
Levy L. M. 348 Oakwood boul. *Lksd.*
Levy Marcus, 372 Mohawk
Levy Morris F. 210 Ohio. *Lksd.*
Levy Wolf, 210 Ohio
Levy Zadig, 4234 Calumet av.
Lewald Frank, 3249 Rhodes av. *Stan.*
Lewald William B. Evanston
Lewandowska A. Mrs. 428 Elm
Lewey J. M. 2413 South Park av.
Lewin Solomon Dr. 6400 Eggleston av.
Lewis Abner M. 37 Ashland boul.
Lewis Arthur B. Mayfair
Lewis Augustus I. 50 Lincoln av.
Lewis Cassius M. 5838 Rosalie ct.
Lewis Charles Ray, 4140 Ellis av.
Lewis C. George, Evanston. *Univ*
Lewis David R. Evanston. *Chi., Univ.*
Lewis Denslow, M.D. 217, 53d. *C.A.*
Lewis Edward H. 21' 46th
Lewis Edwin H. Prof. 612 W. Jackson boul.
Lewis Ella C. Mrs. 144 S. Paulina
Lewis Eugene, 587, 45th pl. *Lksd.*
Lewis E. W, Mayfair
Lewis Frank C. Evanston
Lewis Frank D. 2961 Michigan av.
Lewis Frank F. Evanston
Lewis Frederick C. 5427 Jefferson av.
Lewis F. H. Evanston
Lewis F. J. 409 Bowen av.
Lewis George Evans, 2358 Indiana av.
Sum. res. Toronto, Ont.
Lewis George F. Hinsdale
Lewis George R. Oak Park
Lewis Harry G. 3500 Ellis av.
Lewis Harry S. 429 Washington boul.
Lewis Henry B. 6012 Indiana av.
Lewis Henry F., M.D. 4426 Lake av.
Lewis H. Albert, 6637 Stewart av.
Lewis H. C. 271 Oakwood boul. *C.A.*
Lewis Isaac J. 3335 Indiana av. *C.A., W.P.*
Lewis I. Giles, Hotel Windermere
Lewis James A. Oak Park
Lewis James S. Evanston
Lewis John, Oak Park
Lewis John C. 4140 Ellis av.
Lewis Joseph B. Mrs. 56, 47th
Lewis Joseph K. Evanston
Lewis Joshua H. 446, 55th
Lewis J. J. Rev. 3000 Prairie av.
Lewis Leslie, 6605 Madison av.
Lewis Martin, Evanston
Lewis Martin O. Evanston
Lewis M. D. Mrs. 678 Lasalle av.
Lewis N. B. 2490 Magnolia av.
Lewis Samuel T. 537 Englewood av.
Lewis Thomas H. Evanston
Lewis Walter Fay, Evanston
Lewis William, 5427 Jefferson av.
Lewis William B. 5137 Lexington av. *U.L.*
Lewis William G. Mrs. 5100 Madison av.

Lewis William H. Hotel Windermere
Lewis W. R. Dr. Oak Park
Lewy Alfred Dr. 3656 Vincennes av.
Lewy Marks, 203, 36th
Leyden Michael R. 1611 W. Monroe
Leyenberger Chas. 7801 Lowe av. *W.P.*
Libbey Mary T. Mrs. 4734 Greenwood av.
Libby Prudence E. Mrs. 734 Washington boul.
Liberman Henry, 4632 Prairie av.
Liberman Jacob Mrs. 206, 37th
Lichtenberger C. Mrs. 488 Dearborn av.
Lichtenberger C. G. 441 W. Congress
Lichtenheim Anthony, 2723 Wabash av.
Lichtenstadt Harry, 3212 Michigan av.
Lichtenstadt Philip, 3212 Michigan av.
Lichtenstadt Wille, 3212 Michigan av.
Lichtenstein R. Miss, 4556 Ellis av.
Lichtner William, 6633 Yale av.
Lichtstern Adolph J. 3736 Michigan av.
Stan. Sum. res. Oconomowoc, Wis.
Lichtstern Bernard Mrs.3740Michigan av.
Lichtstern Isaac, 3346 Forest av. *Lksd.*
Lidgerwood J. M. Chicago Athletic assn.
Lidgerwood R. E. 820 Pullman bldg.
Lidster Ralph E. 321 W. 61st
Lieb Hermann, jr. Oak Park
Liebensberger L. 4447 Ellis av.
Liebenstein A. Hyde Park hotel
Liebenstein A. Mrs. 3150 Calumet av.
Liebenstein A. M. 3150 Calumet av. *Stan.*
Liebenstein Charles, 3238 Wabash av. *Stan.*
Liebenstein L. Mrs. 3355 South Park av.
Liebling Emil, 22 Astor
Liebman George, 1725 Wrightwood av.
Ligare Ashbel G. Glencoe
Ligare George G. Glencoe
Lightfoot Sarah E. Mrs. 366 S. Campbell av.
Lightner Turnley, Highland Park
Lilienfeld David, Hotel Del Prado
Lilienfeld Theodore, 4344 St. Lawrence av.
Lilienfeld William, 3649 Prairie av. *Lksd. Stan.*
Lilienthal Albert L. 3500 Ellis av.
Lilienthal Charles J. 451, 41st
Lilja Hilda Mrs. 475 Belden av.
Lilja John R. 479 Belden av.
Liljencrantz G. A. M. 3808 Elmwood ct.
Lill George, 1205 Seminary pl.
Lill George H. 1112 Granville av.
Lill James, Evanston
Lill William, 1118 Granville av.
Lillard David I. 4726 Kenwood av.
Limbocker Walter G. 5606 Michigan av.
Lincoln Augustus A. Hinsdale
Lincoln Charles, Evanston
Lincoln George E. 3130 Prairie av.
Lincoln John Larkin, 322 Superior. *Un., Univ.*
Lincoln M. C. Mrs. Irving Park
Lincoln Robert T. 60 Lake Shore drive.
Chi., C.A., Un., W.P.
Lind Sylvester Mrs. Lake Forest

Lindauer Benjamin, 3312 Calumet av.
 Stan.
Lindauer David M. 4941 Washington
 Park ct.
Lindauer Julius B. 3312 Calumet av.
Lindauer Max, 4941 Washington Park ct.
 Lksd.
Lindauer Meyer E. 3225 Wabash av.
Lindblom Lenor Miss, 678 Lasalle av.
Lindblom Robert, 678 Lasalle av. U.L.
Lindell Alfred, 2110 Kenmore av.
Linden Frank L. 4596 Oakenwald av.
Linden F. C. Dr. 1398 Jackson boul.
Linden James, 4625 Lake av.
Linderborg Augusta Dr. 431 Center
Linderman B. A. 1235 Sheridan rd.
Lindgren John R. Evanston. U.L.
Lindheim Louis, 4320 Vincennes av.
 Lksd.
Lindheimer Jacob, 3518 Forest av. Lksd.
Lindley William Mrs. 7127 Yale
Lindley William Orville, Auditorium an-
 nex
Lindman John J. 4824 Kimbark av.
Lindman O. F. 4731 Ellis av.
Lindop Frank R. Oak Park
Lindquist Joseph, 3563 Forest av.
Lindsay Charles R. 16 Astor
Lindsay David J. 5465 Washington av.
Lindsay John C. Dr. 3639 Prairie av.
Lindsey Andrew, Austin
Lindsey William E. 1 Crilly ct.
Lindsey William L. Mrs. 1 Crilly ct.
Lindsley William, 1611 W. Adams
Lindsten Frank J. 1728 Belmont av.
Lindt John A. E. Mrs. 3211 Dover
Linebarger J eph O. 758 Flournoy. C.A.
Linebarger Raul W. Calumet club
Lines Frank B. 5809 Washington av.
Ling John, Wilmette
Ling Thomas H. 171 Aberdeen
Lingle Samuel B. 3144 Vernon av.
Linington Chas. M. 644 Washington boul.
 Ill.
Link George T. 464 W. Adams
Linn George W. 1850 Arlington pl.
Linn Ida Miss, 8952 Houston av.
Linn William A. Edgebrook
Linn William R. 2709 Michigan av. Chi.,
 C.A., U.L., W.P.
Linn W. Scott Mrs. 2631 Michigan av.
Linneen David F. 3419 South Park av.
Linneen P. H. Mrs. 3419 South Park av.
Linneen William P. 3419 South Park av.
Linnell Angeline M. Mrs. Evanston
Linsenbarth Frank, 516 Dearborn av.
Linsley Charles, Hinsdale
Linsley F. Mrs. Hinsdale
Linsley Theron H. Hinsdale
Linsley Thomas H. Evanston
Lipe Fred W. 3634 Michigan av.
Lipe Sarah Mrs. 3942 Grand boul.
Lipkau Eugene, 654 Fullerton av. C.A.
Lippincott Anna G. Miss, 41 Madison
 Park
Lippincott Charles A. Rev. 213, 28th

Lippincott Henry Maj. Ft. Sheridan
Lippitt Ethel Miss, 333 Ohio
Lipsey Andrew G. Riverside
Lipsey James H. Riverside
Lipski S. 3565 Prairie av.
Lipson Isaac B. 3311 Calumet av.
Lisle Logan F. 2358 Indiana av.
 Sum. res. Whitby, Ont.
Lister Walter, 312 Park av.
Litchfield C. Wirt, 821 The Plaza
Litchfield I. W. 927 W. Adams
Litchfield Wm. H. Elmhurst
Litsey James N. 1520 W. Monroe
Litsey John P. 1520 W. Monroe
Litson William T. 743 W. Monroe
Littell M. Raum Mrs. 569, 51st
Little Arthur Y. Dr. Evanston
Little A. Eugene Mrs. 1462 Perry
Little Charles G. Evanston
Little Charles J. Rev. LL.D. Evanston
Little Edward F. 4923 Lake av.
Little E. M. Mrs. 629 W. Adams
Little Francis B. 177 Warren av.
Little Frank, River Forest
Little George W. 4923 Lake av.
Little George W. jr. 4349 Oakenwald av.
Little William H. 4347 Oakenwald av.
Little William H. 6616 Harvard av.
Little William T. 1122 Morse av.
Littlefield Andrew S. 609 Division. Un.,
 U.L.
Littlefield O. B. Mrs. Evanston
Littlefield S. H. 891 Winthrop av.
Littlejohn Wiley J. Evanston. U.L.
Lively Frank L. Irving Park
Livermore Charles F. 47, 22d. C.A.
Livesey Anna Mrs. Irving Park
Livesey John K. 2681 N. Paulina
Livesey Joseph H. 1071 Warren av.
 Sum. res. Riverdale, N. H.
Livingston Albert E. Oak Park
Livingston Charles G. 3800 Indiana av.
 Lksd.
Livingston David Dudley, 4812 Indiana
 av. Sum. res. Spring Lake, Mich.
Livingston Emanuel, 3730 Langley av.
Livingston Gustav, 3730 Langley av.
Livingston Howard W. 3835 Calumet
 av.
Livingston John, 3400 South Park av.
Livingston Kittie Miss, Evanston
Livingston Milton, 3730 Langley av.
Livingston Morris, Clifton house. Lksd.
Livingston M. Mrs. 3730 Langley av.
Livingston M. L. Mrs. 3835 Calumet av.
Livingston Sam. 3730 Langley av.
Livingston Samuel Clifton house
Livingston Sigmund, 3708 Wabash av.
Livingston S. G. 3626 Prairie av. Lksd.
Livingston Thomas, 3835 Calumet av.
Livingston Van R. 7200 Merrill av.
Livingston William R. Dr. Maywood
Livingstone Archie T. 358, 40th
Livingstone Thomas B. 358, 40th
Llewellyn Henry S. Dr. LaGrange
Llewellyn Joseph C. LaGrange

Llewellyn Silas J. Evanston
Lloyd Edwin T. 3843 Langley av.
Lloyd Evan, 4458 Cottage Grove av.
Lloyd E. Starr, 3319 Calumet av.
Lloyd George, 87, 44th
Lloyd Henry D. Winnetka. *Chi.*
Lloyd H. R. 5533 Madison av.
Lloyd John E. 499 N. State
Lloyd Llewellyn H. Glencoe
Lloyd Louis, 712 W. Adams
Lloyd Robert C. 2585 N. Hermitage av.
Lloyd T. P. 6352 Greenwood av.
Lloyd William A. Rev. 2585 N. Hermitage av.
Lloyd William G. Austin
Lloyd William J. 446 S. Claremont av. *U.L.*
Loar W. C. Dr. 3755 Indiana av.
Loba Jean F. Rev. Evanston
Lobdell C. W. 3861 Lake av.
Lobdell Edwin L. 38, 29th pl. *U.L.*
Lobdell Harry H. 4076 Lake av. *C.A.*
Lobdell J. H. 6212 Woodlawn av.
Lobdell Katharine J. Mrs. 1688 Kenmore av.
Lobstein John G. jr. 763 S. Homan av.
Locke Clinton Rev. Dr. 2825 Indiana av.
    Sum. res. "Lockehaven" Wequetonsing, Mich.
Locke Frank E. 1016 Warren av.
Locke John M. 603 The Plaza. *U.L.*
Locke Joseph L. 1623 Fulton
Locke Josephine Miss, 613 The Plaza
Locke Robert D. Mrs. 2825 Indiana av.
Locke R. C. M. Mrs. 6239 Monroe av.
Lockett Oswald, 44, 50th. *U.L.*
Lockett Samuel Hobart, 3400 Prairie av.
Lockey Isaac Mrs. 3143 Prairie av.
Lockhart George, 5337 Madison av.
Lockhart Margaret H. Miss, 5337 Madison av.
Lockhart S. L. Mrs. 2358 Indiana av.
Lockwood Albert H. 351 Dayton
Lockwood Charles D. Dr. 214, 33d
Lockwood Frederick H. Dr. 183 Cass
Lockwood Henry, 4347 Oakenwald av.
Lockwood Henry C. Hinsdale
Lockwood I. LeGrand, 325 W. 61st pl.
Lockwood James R. 183 Cass
Lockwood Thomas A. 6541 Monroe av.
Lockyer Benjamin, Oak Park
Locy William A. Prof. Evanston
Lodor Charles Howard, M.D. 3136 Indiana av.
Loeb Adolph, 528 Dearborn av. *Stan.*
Loeb Adolph, 3622 Grand boul. *Stan.*
Loeb Albert H. 4008 Grand boul. *Stan.*
Loeb Albert S. 148, 42d pl.
Loeb Emanuel, 4525 Vincennes av.
Loeb Hugo D. Oakland hotel
Loeb Isaac A. 3100 Groveland av. *Lksd.*
Loeb Jacob M. 4630 Prairie av.
Loeb Jacob W. 412 Lasalle av.
Loeb Jacques Prof. 5754 Woodlawn av.
Loeb James I. Turner hotel. *Stan.*
Loeb Johanna M. Mrs. 3924 Prairie av.

Loeb Julius, 3920 Prairie av. *Stan.*
Loeb Leo A. 4404 Grand boul. *Stan.*
Loeb Leo Dr. 6329 Woodlawn av.
Loeb Moses, 3521 Ellis av. *Lksd.*
Loeb Sidney, 3924 Prairie av. *Stan.*
Loeb Sidney A. 3622 Grand boul.
Loeb William, 412 Lasalle av. *Stan.*
Loeber Isaac G. 463 W. Congress
Loehr Elizabeth Mrs. 859 W. Jackson boul. •
Loehr Karl C. 859 W. Jackson boul.
Loehr Leon, 859 W. Jackson boul.
Loesch Charles F. 1678 Kenmore av.
Loesch Emma Miss, 1678 Kenmore av.
Loesch Frank J. 46 Lincoln pl. *U.L.*
Loescher Martin, 14 Pearson
Loew Alex. Dr. 3929 Prairie av.
Loewenstein Emanuel L. 3316 Calumet av. *Stan.*
Loewenstein L. Mrs. 3316 Calumet av.
Loewenstein Sidney, 3316 Calumet av. *Stan.*
Loewenstein Solomon, 3411 Prairie av.
Loewenthal B. 1829 Indiana av. *Stan.*
Loewenthal B. 2918 Prairie av. *Stan.*
Loewenthal Edmund, 445 Dearborn av.
Loewenthal Julius, 52 Bryant av.
Loewenthal Julius W. 1829 Indiana av. *Stan.*
Loewenthal Milton, 52 Bryant av.
Loewy Arthur Dr. Oak Park •
Loewy Louis, Austin
Loftis S. T. A. Chicago Athletic assn. •
Logan C. C. Mrs. 14 Aldine sq.
Logan Floyd T. 6565 Yale
Logan Frank G. 2919 Prairie av. *U.L.*
Logan John A. Chicago Club
Logan J. C. 5344 Greenwood av.
Logan Theron, 6533 Stewart av.
Logan V. M. Mrs. 5344 Greenwood av.
Logan W. H. G. Dr. 1117 Early av.
Logue Joseph H. 1440 W. Monroe •
Loker George T. 3140 South Park av. *C.A.*
Loker Harry A. 3140 South Park av.
Lomax George, 1840 Indiana av. *C.A.*
    Sum. res. Fox Lake, Ill.
Lomax George jr. 1840 Indiana av.
Lomax John A. 4456 Vincennes av.
    Sum. res. Lomax, Ind.
Lomax J. Alfred, 1840 Indiana av.
Lomax Robert D. 4456 Vincennes av.
Lombard Benjamin F. Mrs. Evanston
Lombard Ernest B. 3131 Indiana av.
Lombard Isaac G. 1819 Indiana av. *U.L.*
    Sum. res. Magnolia and Cape Cod, Mass.
Lombard Josiah L. 2001 Prairie av. *Cal.*, *U.L.*
Lombard Thomas R. 3229 South Park av.
Lonas Frank, Maywood
Lonergan Charles J. 499 N. State.
    Sum. res. Amboy, Ill.
Lonergan Esther G. Miss, 519 W. Monroe
Long Albert D. 349, 44th
Long Albert W. 3404 Calumet av.

Long Carrie Miss, 3233 Rhodes av.
Long Catherine C. Mrs. 441, 66th
Long Charles, 3530 Wabash av.
Long Eugene C. 4907 Lake av.
Long E. Miss, Lakota hotel
Long Frederic H. 1920 Briar pl.
Long H. Mrs. 6710 Butler
Long James H. 4735 Kimbark av. *U.L.*
Long John Conant, 5338 Washington av.
Long John H. 7748 S. Sangamon
Long John T. 283 Webster av.
Long J. B. Lakota hotel. *C.A., W.P.*
Long Lee, 3530 Wabash av. *Stan.*
Long Louis, 3530 Wabash av.
Long R. H. Mrs. 204, 74th
Long Sidney, 3530 Wabash av. *Stan.*
Long T. K. The Kenwood. *U.L.*
Longenecker Joel M. 4125 Vincennes av. *U.L.*
Longhurst Henry G. 2358 Indiana av.
Longini Abraham, 1626 Prairie av. *Stan.*
Longini Leon J. 3258 Vernon av.
Longini Moyis, 3258 Vernon av.
Longley Albert W. Hotel Metropole. *C.A., Cal., W.P.*
Longmire Rowland Mrs. 5221 Jefferson av.
Longmire Stanley W. 5221 Jefferson av.
Longstreet Aaron, 788 Washington boul.
Longwell George P. 1548 W. Monroe
Loomis Augustus H. 405 W. Jackson boul.
Loomis Edwin C. 171, 51st
Loomis Eugene E. 6531 Yale
Loomis E. Beach Dr. 145 S. Robey. *Ill.*
Loomis E. Y. New Hotel Holland
Loomis Frank E. 6531 Yale
Loomis Frank W. 203 Greenleaf av.
Loomis Henry Francis, 3437 Wabash av.
Loomis Henry S. Hinsdale
Loomis Howard G. 6358 Minerva av.
Loomis H. M. Mrs. 3429 Michigan av.
Loomis James W. 2939 Wabash av.
Loomis John E. 651½ Washington boul.
Loomis John M. Col. 55 Lake Shore drive. *Cal., Chi., Un., W.P.*
Loomis Justin E. 3314 Rhodes av.
Loomis Laura Mrs. 6531 Yale
Loomis Mason B. Evanston
Loomis Philip A. 405 W. Jackson boul.
Loomis William W. 4519 Woodlawn av.
Loose J. L. Chicago Beach hotel. *Chi., C.A., U.L., W.P.*
Loper Charles D. 543 Dearborn av.
Loper W. Harvey, Chicago Beach hotel
Loranger J. A. 4429 Calumet av.
     Sum. res. Colorado Springs, Col.
Lord Alonzo B. Evanston
Lord Andrew H. 142 DeKalb
Lord Arthur D. 5450 Cornell av.
Lord Austin H. 5327 Michigan av.
Lord Benjamin Willis, Evanston
Lord Clara S. Miss, 4857 Greenwood av.
Lord D. M. 5450 Cornell av. *C.A.*
Lord Edgar A. 1901 Indiana av. *Cal., W.P.*
Lord Edward A. Evanston

Lord Frank E. Evanston. *U.L., Univ.*
Lord Fred H. 5486 Washington av.
Lord Fred. W. River Forest
Lord George D. 4311 Vincennes av.
Lord George S. Evanston. *U.L.*
Lord Herbert J. River Forest
Lord James F. 1901 Indiana av. *C.A.*
Lord John B. 4857 Greenwood av. *Chi., U.L.*
Lord Lucinda S. Mrs. River Forest
Lord Mary Miss 4857 Greenwood av.
Lord Parley A. LaGrange
Lord Priscilla R. Mrs. Oak Park
Lord Thomas, Evanston
Lord William S. Evanston
Lorenz Frederick A. 5733 Kimbark av. *Irq.*
Loring J. Brown Dr. 238 Park av.
Loring M. A. Lakota hotel
Loring Stella Dyer Mrs. 2535 Prairie av.
Losch N. R. 16 Astor
Loss C. E. 90, 21st. *Irq.*
Lothholz Richard, 31 Lake View av.
Lothrop Frederick L. 518 Larchmont av.
Lott E. C. Lexington hotel
Lott James P. 4021 Vincennes av.
Lotz Carl, 1833 Arlington pl.
Loucks Charles N. Irving Park
Loudenback Simeon, 3819 Prairie av.
Louderback DeLancey H. 519 Dearborn av. *U.L.*
Louderback Sarah A. Mrs. 2659 Evanston av.
Louderback William J. 337 Rush. *Chi., Un.*
Louer Albert S. Hotel Metropole. *Stan*
Loughridge Charles, 4728 Greenwood av.
Loughrin Henry M. 2609 N. Robey
Louis Abraham, 3566 Prairie av.
Lounsbury James Allen, Graceland av. and Lake Shore. *U.L.*
Lounsbury R. R. 1886 Diversey
Lovdall Alexander, 1549 Lill av.
Lovdall N. Harry, 1549 Lill av.
Lovdall Thomas H. 1549 Lill av.
Lovdall Thomas I. 1549 Lill av.
Love Charles F. 4471 Lake av.
Love E. M. Hotel Del Prado
Love George, 113 Cass
Love George H. 5325 Washington av.
Love Henry M. 381 Oak
Love James M. 150 Lincoln Park boul.
Love J. M. Mrs. 150 Lincoln Park boul.
Love Sidney C. Virginia hotel. *C.A., Un.*
Love William S. 412 Oak
Loveday F. M. Mrs. 923 W. Monroe
     Sum. res. Twin Lakes, Wis.
Loveday H. E. LaGrange
Loveday H. W. Revere house
Loveday Julia Miss 923 W. Monroe
Loveday L. E. Mrs. 5217 Madison av.
Loveday Thomas E. 923 W. Monroe
     Sum. res. Twin Lakes, Wis.
Lovegrove Walter, 679 Fullerton av.
Lovejoy D. S. 258 Ashland boul.
     Sum. res. Lake Geneva, Wis.

Lovejoy George M. 613, 46th pl. *C.A.*
Lovejoy J. S. 225 Dearborn av.
Lovejoy Thomas H. 529 Garfield av.
Loveland Chas. L. 1760 Wrightwood av.
Loveland W. L. Evanston
Lovell Sidney, The Arizona
Lovelock George M. 357 S. Oakley av.
Loveridge Ray, 989 Millard av.
Loverin QuimbyW. 4823 St. Lawrence av.
Lovering Leonard A. Capt. Fort Sheridan
Lovett Lamotte M. Oak Park
Lovett Mary Mrs. Oak Park
Lovett Robert M. 5501 Cornell av.
Lovett Thomas J. 4001 Drexel boul.
Lovewell Charles H. Dr. 6058 Wentworth av.
Low Anson, 112, 45th
Low Charles H. 86 Bryant av.
Low James E. Dr. 410 Washington boul.
Low James E. Evanston
Low John M. Hotel Windermere
Low John W. Evanston
Low Joseph H. Dr. 2458 Indiana av.
Low Julia R. Dr. 4756 Kenwood av.
Low Samuel A. 5723 Monroe av.
Low Willard W. 4105 Newgart av.
Low William H. 4756 Kenwood av.
Lowden Alex H. Evanston
Lowden Frank O. 53, 20th. *Cal., Chi., U.L., Univ., W.P.*
Lowe E. E. Mrs. Virginia hotel
Lowe Henry E. 4548 Lake av.
Lowe Jesse, 2767 Kenmore av.
Lowe John W. Union club, *Univ.*
Lowe Perley, 599 Washington boul.
Lowe William, 3611 Grand boul.
Lowell Lucerne D. Jefferson Park
Lowell Wallace A. 351, 41st
Lowenbach Joseph, 3340 South Park av.
Lowenbach William L. 3340 South Park av. *Stan.*
Lowenberg Isaac, 1341 Michigan av. *Stan.*
Lowenthal Adolph S. 3412 Calumet av.
Lowenthal LouisDr.Washington Heights
Lowery Francis M. 87 Rush
Lowman C. O. Park Ridge
Lowrey William K. Evanston. *Irq.*
Lowrie Wesley M. 406 The Plaza
Lowry Butler, 5428 Lexington av.
Lowry Edward, 467 Farwell av.
Lowry Robert H. Dr. 518 Fulton
Lozier A. Hotel Del Prado
Lubeke William F. 41 Hazel av.
Lucas Charles W. 2614 N. Winchester av.
Lucas J. B. Rev. 2614 N. Winchester av.
Lucas Samuel P. Ravinia
Luce C. P. 3802 Lake av.
Luce Edward M. 146, 50th
Luce E. F. 1117 Winthrop av.
        Sum. res. Marion, Mass.
Luce Frank M. 1864.Barry av.
Luce Franklin A. 472 Elm
Luce Theodore M. 295 Belden
Luck Charles J. 904·Walnut av.
39

Ludden Viola H. Dr. 315 W. 67th
Luders Harry C. 217 S. Leavitt
Luders Henry J. 217 S. Leavitt
Ludington E. M. Mrs. 4831 Kenwood av.
Ludington Marshall I. Col. Auditorium annex
Ludington M. K. Mrs. Oak Park
Ludington Nelson Mrs. Auditorium annex
Ludington Rowland S. Oak Park
Ludlam Edward M. P. Dr. Evanston
Ludlam Florence Miss, Evanston
Ludlam Jacob W. Evanston
Ludlam Mary Miss, Evanston
Ludlam Reuben Dr. 2459 Michigan av. *Cal.*
Ludlam Reuben jr. Dr. 2459 Michigan av.
Ludlow Charles G. 1617 Montrose boul.
Ludlow Cynthia A. Mrs. 206 The Plaza
Ludlow Ebenezer, 1617 Montrose boul.
Ludlow Fred D. 206 The Plaza
Ludlow James B. Evanston
Ludlow James R. Evanston
Ludwig C. H. Dr. 600 Lincoln av.
Ludwig Roscoe F. Dr. LaGrange
Lueder Arthur, Elmhurst
Lueder John Prof. Elmhurst
Luff Edmund Capt. Oak Park
Luff Emily M. Dr. Oak Park
Luff Henry E. Oak Park
Lufkin Daniel I. 2505 Michigan av.
Lug d n James, 2147 Clarendon av.
Lukeni Frank J. 6531 Harvard av.
Luken William, 587 W. North av. *C.A.*
Lukens W. J. 1150 Granville av.
Lukey J. Ernest, Evanston
Lukey William, Evanston
Lull Leila W. Miss, 307 N. Clark
Lull Newton, 307 N. Clark
Lum Mary H. Mrs. 3810 Langley av.
Lum Walter H. 3810 Langley av.
Lumbard Frank H. Oak Park
Lumbard Henry, Oak Park
Lumbard S. J. Lombard
Lumley C. G. Dr. 401, 33d
Lumsden Arthur E. 252, 60th
Lumsden M. E. Mrs. 2008 W. Jackson boul.
Lund Adolph, 4443.Sidney av.
Lund Arthur H. 4736 Langley av.
Lund Charles E. 4404 Champlain av.
Lund E. M, Hyde Park hotel
Lundie John, 7126 Euclid av. *U.L.*
Lundy Ayres D. LaGrange
Lunham Robert T. 4234 Prairie av.
Lunsford Todd, 1888 Diversey
Lunt E. Sidney Mrs. 4245 Drexel boul.
Lunt Orrington Mrs. Evanston
Lusch Harry B. 536 Orchard, *C.A.*
Lusche Fred, Austin
Luse James P. River Forest
Lusk S. E. Miss, 1375 Washington boul.
Lusk William H. 1375 Washington boul.
Lussky Arthur, 156, 50th
Lussky Edward A. 156, 50th·
Lussky G. Hermann, 156, 50th

Lusted Warren, Wilmette
Luther F. P. Newberry hotel
Luther George H. Austin
Luther John S. Newberry hotel
Lutkin Peter·C. Evanston
Lutrell W. A. Morgan Park
Lutwyche Fred H. 586 W. Polk
Lutz B. F. M. 4078 Lake av.
Lutz Caroline H. Mrs. 4227 Champlain av.
Lutz Theodore C. 7734 Bond av.
Lycett Edward A. 708 The Plaza. *Un.*
Lydiard John P. 105 Park av. *Ill.*
Lydon Harry C. 2952 Indiana av.
Lydon Mollie Miss, 2952 Indiana av.
Lydon M. B. 2952 Indiana av.
Lydon William A. 4758 Grand boul.
Lydston G. Frank.Dr. 1091 N.Clark.*C.A.*
Lydston James A. Dr. 1587 W. Adams
Lydston Lucy A. Mrs. 570 Fullerton av.
Lyford Oliver S. 2968 Lake Park av.
Lyford Will Hartwell, 4847 Kimbark av.
    Chi., C.A.
    Sum. res. Fox Lake, Lake Villa, Ill.
Lyke John W. 1175 Wilcox av.
Lyle George W. Evanston
Lyles A. R. Dr. 437 S. Normal Parkway
Lyman Benjamin K. 314 Walnut
Lyman David, LaGrange
Lyman David B. LaGrange. *Chi., U.L.,*
    Univ.
Lyman Edson W. Oak Park. *U.L.*
    Sum. res. Mackinac Island, Mich.
Lyman Eugene W. 3228 Calumet av.
Lyman Francis O. Winnetka
Lyman Henry M. Dr. 200 Ashland boul.
Lyman James, 247 Seminary av.
Lyman JesseP.Chicago Beach hotel.*C.A.*
Lyman John Chester Dr. 2 Washing-
    ton pl.
Lyman Mary Miss, 200 Ashland boul.
Lyman M. J., M.D. Austin
Lyman Nathan W. 3228 Calumet av.
Lyman Otis S. LaGrange
Lyman Wilfred C. 314 Walnut
Lyman Wilfred C. jr. 314 Walnut
Lyman William, 144, 50th
Lynas Thomas R. 3156 Vernon av. *U.L.*
Lynch Andrew G. 556 Dearborn av.
Lynch Andrew M. 4220 Grand boul.
Lynch E. M. Mrs. Chicago Beach hotel
Lynch E. R. 4360 Oakenwald av.
Lynch Helen M. Dr. Highland Park
Lynch James, 592 W. Adams
Lynch James D. 584 Dearborn av. *C.A.*
Lynch John W. Mrs. Highland Park
Lynch John A. 44 Burton pl. *C.A., Irq.*
Lynch J. B. 556 Dearborn av.
Lynch Thomas, 256 Dearborn av.
Lynch Thomas, Elmhurst
Lynch Thomas G. 556 Dearborn av.
Lynde S. A. 398 Ontario. *Univ.*
Lynn Charles F. Mrs. 7432 Bond av.
Lynn Harry J. Dr. 1437, 75th
Lynne Anna V. Mrs. 2979 Prairie av.
Lyon Albert J. Wilmette
Lyon Charles, 599 Dearborn av.

Lyon C. B. LaGrange
Lyon David J. 2970 Vernon av.
Lyon David T. 924 W. Jackson boul.
    Sum. res. Brown's Lake, Wis.
Lyon Elizabeth Miss, 381 Superior
Lyon Ellen Hancock Dr. 39 Bellevue
    pl. ·
Lyon F. K. 201, 44th
Lyon George D. 599 Dearborn av.
Lyon George M. 381 Superior. *Chi., W.P.*
Lyon Henry T. 678 W. Monroe
Lyon Howard N., M.D. 39 Bellevue pl.
Lyon H. H. 874, 72d
Lyon John B. 262 Michigan av. *Chi.,*
    W.P.
Lyon John L. Oak Park ·
Lyon Joseph M. LaGrange
Lyon Mark T. Austin
Lyon Martha Mrs. 548 W. 61st
Lyon Mary P. Mrs. 209 S. Leavitt
Lyon Peter K. 251 Oakwood boul.
Lyon Richard S. 500 W. Adams. *Ill.,*
    U.L.
Lyon Samuel, 5620 Monroe av.
Lyon Thomas R. 72 Astor. *Cal., Chi.,*
    U.L., W.P.
    Sum. res. Ludington, Mich.
Lyon William C. 262 Michigan av. *Chi.*
Lyons Andrew G. 7115 Eggleston av.
Lyons A. S. Hotel Del Prado
Lyons Hattie Miss, 3756 Lake av.
Lyons Henry E. 3544 Grand boul.
Lyons Jesse R. Evanston
Lyons John, 3345 Prairie av.
Lyons J. Harvey Dr. 4229 Calumet av.
Lystad Hans J. 1922 Arlington pl.
Lytle Ann G. Mrs. Austin
Lytton Henry Charles, 2700 Prairie av.
    W.P.
Lytton Howard George, 2700 Prairie av.
    W.P.

MAAS FRED, 345 Hampden ct.
    Maas Isaac L. 4805 Prairie av.
Maas Phillip, 345 Hampden ct.
Maass J. E. 464 N. Hoyne av.
Mabbatt R. H. Mrs. 2819 Michigan av.
Mabie Charles E. 368, 49th
Mabie E. G. 599 Dearborn av.
Mabie Litta Miss, 368, 49th
MacAdams Edward J. River Forest
Macafee William Rev. Evanston
MacArthur Archibald, 635 W. 56th pl.
MacArthur Arthur Duncan Mrs.4603 Vin-
    cennes av.
MacArthur Robert Archibald Dr. 58As-
    tor
MacArthur R. D. Dr. 414 Dearborn av.
    Un.
Macauley John, 750 North Park-av.
MacBurney J. A. Irving Park
MacCanahan Anna Mrs. 54, 33d
MacCarty Chas. S. 769 Washington boul.
    Ill.
MacCracken W. P Dr. 4327 Greenwood
    av. Sum. res. Cayuga Lake, N. Y.

MacDonald Charles, Chicago Athletic assn.
Macdonald Chas. A. 1563 Sheridan rd. *Chi., C.A.*
MacDonald Charles Blair, Wheaton. *Chi., W.P.*
MacDonald Chas. H. 3334 Rhodes av.
MacDonald David W. Riverside
MacDonald Edward V. Dr. 5604 Madison av.
MacDonald George A. 5410 Madison av.
Macdonald Godfrey, 79, 20th
Macdonald H. K. 270 Lasalle av.
Macdonald James, Evanston
MacDonald James M. 2829 Indiana av..
MacDonald Peter S. Dr. 2829 Indiana av.
MacDonald Raymond J. 2829 Indiana av.
MacDonald William J. Oak Park
Macdonnell Joseph A. 228, 47th. *C.A.*
MacDowell Charles H. 365 W. Jackson boul.
Mace Abbie J. Dr. 6826 Yale
Mace Alfred C. 4336 Berkeley av.
Mace Harry W. 7318 Bond av.
MacEdward James, LaGrange
Macfall Margaretta Mrs. 4551 Evans av.
Macfarland Henry J. 1710 Michigan av. *Cal., Chi., W. P.*
MacGill Alex D. 1069 Warren av.
MacGregor Edward, 377 Superior
MacHarg William S. 3227 Beacon
Macheret Eugene J. 1493 W. Monroe
Mack Julia M. Mrs. 4747 Lake av
Mack Julian W. 3614 Michigan av. *Irq.*
Mack W. B. 4059 Prairie av.
Mackay Alexander, 560 N. State. *Chi.*
Mackay David S. 383 Elm
Mackay Eric R. Revere house
Mackay George, 383 Elm
Mackay John C. 600 Burling
MacKay Joseph Evan, 232, 47th
MacKenzie Frederick, 4341 Grand boul.
Mackenzie George S. 680 W. Monroe. *Ill., U. L.*
Mackenzie John K. 77, 20th
Mackenzie John P. 6534 Monroe av.
Mackenzie John W. 4624 Indiana av.
MacKenzie J. F. 5628 Monroe av. *C.A.*
Mackenzie Kenneth, 4624 Indiana av.
Mackenzie Wilbur Dr. 1292 Sheffield av.
Mackenzie W. D. Oak Park.
Mackey Duncan, 1609 Sheridan rd.
Mackey Edward, 3716 Lake av.
Mackey M. B. 4540 Prairie av.
Mackie Arthur Mrs. 1458 Wrightwood av.
Mackie Charles, 511 W. Monroe
    Sum. res. Fox Lake, Ill.
Mackin John, 251 Lake av.
Mackin Margaret Miss, Austin
Mackintosh Jane Miss, 531 Belden av.
Macklem Wm. Tracy
Macklin Charles G. 2754 N. Hermitage av.
MacLachlan Wm. F. 878 Washington boul. Sum. res. "The Pines," Lake Co. Ill.

MacLean Alexander W. Wilmette
Maclean Ann E. Mrs. 52 Walton pl.
Maclean Arthur A. 411 Huron
Maclean George A. Riverside
Maclean John D. Austin
MacLeod Murdock, 288 S. Marshfield av. *Ill.*
MacMahon John, 5132 Wabash av.
MacMartin Duncan R. Dr. Great Northern hotel. *C. A.*
Macmillan Everett, 230, 47th
MacMillan Hugh Mrs. 424 Superior
Macmillan J. H. 230, 47th
MacMillan M. A. Mrs. 424 Superior
MacMillan Thomas C. 816 W. Adams
MacMurphy Letitia Mrs. 164, 47th
MacNab Malcolm D. Dr. 6749 Emerald av.
MacNaughtan David, Austin
MaeNeal Arthur Dr. Berwyn
Macomber Frank L. 871 Winthrop av.
Macomber S. H. 6436 Greenwood av.
Macomber Wesson, 3334 Vernon av.
Macomber William W. Oak Park
MacPhetridge Euclid, 6546 Stewart av.
MacRae Kate E. Dr. 4577 Lake av.
MacRae Norman, 4577 Lake av.
MacRae Norman A. 4557 Evans av.
MacRitchie C. 808 Pullman bldg.
MacVeagh Eames, 103 Lake Shore drive *C. A.*
MacVeagh Franklin, 103 Lake Shore drive *Chi., Irq., W. P.*
Macy H. C. Dr. Hotel Windermere
Madden Frank H. 5222 Woodlawn av. *C.A.*
Madden Martin B. 3829 Michigan av.
Madden M. F. 666 Sheffield av. *C.A.*
Madeira C. W. Mrs. Morgan Park
Madigan John H. Washington Heights
Madigan M. D. 1298 Wilcox av.
Madigan P. D. 3257 Vernon av.
Madison John R. Mrs. Irving Park
Madison J. T. Irving Park
Madlener Albert F. 11 Lake View av. *C. A.*
Madlener F. Mrs. 17 Lake View av.
Madlung William F. 6845 Union av.
Magee Charles J. 1624 W. Monroe
Magee Edward A. Hotel Metropole
Magee Ethel J. Miss, 289, 53d
Magee George, 4319 Berkeley av.
Magee Guy, 323 Belden av.
Magee Henry W. 7722 Union av.
Magee John J. 5810 Rosalie ct.
Magee Joseph P. 16 Gilpin pl.
Magee M. E. Mrs. 4319 Berkeley av.
Mages George C. 727 N. Hoyne av.
Magie Frank Ogden, 2324 Calumet av.
Magie William A. 2706 Michigan av. *Cal.*
Magill Charles S. 733 W. Adams
Magill George G. 733 W. Adams
Magill G. L. 3024 Calumet av.
Magill H. W. Lakota hotel. *C. A., Univ.*
Magill Jacob C. 733 W. Adams. *Ill.*

Magill John R. 1186 N. Clark
Magill Martin G. 3100 Groveland av.
Magill Matthew E. 3813 Forest av.
Magill T o W. Auditorium annex
  W.Ph mas
Magill William C. Evanston
Magin Francis J. Evanston
Maginnis P. J. Mrs. 1852 Diversey
Magnus Albert, 1932 Barry av.
Magnus Arthur J. 473 Elm. *C. A.*
Magnus August, 522 Dearborn av.
Magnus August C. 487 W. Monroe. *C. A. Ill.*
Magnus Mary Mrs. 513 The Plaza
Magnus Rudolph R. 4560 Oakenwald av.
Magruder B. D. Judge, 7 Washington pl.
Magruder Henry Latham, 7 Washington pl. *Univ.*
Maguire M. Miss, 4838 Forrestville av.
Magwire Mary F. Mrs. 70 Astor
Mahan Frank M. 430½ Belden av.
Mahan H. W. 4608 Vincennes av.
Mahan I. S. Mrs. 5551 Monroe av.
Mahan Mark C. 4608 Vincennes av.
Maher A. J. Mrs. 6642 Kimbark av.
Maher Daniel W. 1121 N. Clark
Maher Edward, 450 W. 65th
Maher Frances R. Mrs. 655 W. Adams
Maher George W. Kenilworth
Maher Lester E. 5812 Michigan av.
Maher Tessie Miss, 1121 N. Clark
Maher Theophile, Wilmette
Maher Walter S. Wilmette
Maher Walter S. 5812 Michigan av.
Mahin John Lee, 204, 44th. *C.A.*
Mahnke Louis H. 5606 Michigan av.
Mahoney Joseph P. 297 W. 14th pl. *C.A.*
Mai Bruno M. 227 Hampden ct.
Maibelle Anne Miss, 2446 Michigan av.
Maibelle Justice Miss, 2446 Michigan av.
Maiden William J. 2281 W. Adams
Main William B. 5237 Jefferson av.
Main W. Fred, 1240 Washington boul.
Main W. W. 710 Pullman bldg.
Mair Charles A. 583 N. State. *Chi., W.P.*
Maitland F. E. 17 Scott. *Univ.*
Maitland Thomas L. 3535 Indiana av.
Malahy Margaret Mrs. 943 S. Sawyer av.
Malkow Fred. 6353 Harvard av.
Mallen Herman, Austin
Mallen Philip H. 1661 W. Monroe
Mallers John B. 36 Groveland Park
Mallette James P. 7216 Yale. *U.L.*
  Sum. res. Waupaca, Wis.
Mallette Sidney F. 7216 Yale
Mallin John A. Oak Park
Mallory Charles A. 7754 Union av.
Mallory D. C. 4620 Indiana av.
Mallory E. Blakeslee, 1684 Sheridan rd.
Mallory Harriet C. Mrs. 7754 Union av.
Mallory H. C. Kenilworth
Mallory James L. 802 W. Adams
Mallory Michael F. 332 Huron
Mallory William H. The Kenwood
Malnofske Augusta Miss, Austin
Malone Edwin T. Oak Park

Malone G. Beecher Dr. 226 Ontario
Malone William H. 226 Ontario
Maltby Adolphus W. 403 The Plaza. *Un.*
Maltman Alexander S. 75 Lake View av.
Malum Andrew A. Austin
Mamerow George, Irving Park.
Manasse L. jr. 234 Oakwood boul.
Manasse Nathan, 4808 Kimbark av.
Manchester Daniel W. 267 Chestnut
Manchester Ida Mrs. 560 Division
Manchester Milton C. 267 Chestnut
Mandel Edward, 3400 Michigan av.
Mandel Emanuel, 3400 Michigan av. *Irq.,* *Stan.*
Mandel E. S. Mrs. 3449 Prairie av.
Mandel Frank, 3400 Michigan av. *Stan.*
Mandel Frank S. 3206 Michigan av. *Stan.*
Mandel Fred L. 3409 Michigan av. *Stan.*
Mandel Leon, 3409 Michigan av. *Stan.*
  Sum. res. Long Branch, N. J.
Mandel Leonard J. 3206 Michigan av. *Stan.*
Mandel Robert, 3409 Michigan av. *Stan.*
Mandel Simon, 3206 Michigan av. *Stan.*
Mandelbaum Clara Mrs. 3726 Forest av.
Mandelbaum Morris H. 3726 Forest av. *Lksd., Stan.*
Mandell Fred, LaGrange
Mandell Louis, 3712 Grand boul.
Mandl Bernard, 445 Dearborn av. *Lksd.*
Mandl Sidney, 455 Lasalle av.
Maney Robert, Oak Park
Mang Albert G. 229, 42d
Manheimer David, 3255 Wabash av.
Manheimer Joseph C. 3405 Calumet av.
Manheimer Louis, Lexington hotel. *Stan.*
Manheimer William S. 3405 Calumet av. *Stan.*
Manierre A. H. Mrs. 1928 Calumet av.
  Sum. res. Saranac Lake, Adirondack Mountains
Manierre Benjamin, 1928 Calumet av.
Manierre Charles E. Dr. 552 Lasalle av.
Manierre Edward, 1928 Calumet av.
Manierre George, 61 Bellevue pl. *Chi.*
Manierre George jr. 399 Superior
Manierre John T. Dr. 215 Schiller
Manierre William R. 399 Superior.
Manington John, 6435 Kimbark av.
Manley Orrel Miss, 4351 N. Ashland av.
Manlove Gilbert Beebe, 272 Huron
  Sum. res. Forest Home Farms, Ind.
Manly John M. 5488 East End av.
Mann A. C. 6125 Indiana av.
Mann C. Riborg Prof. 5442 Ridgewood ct.
Mann Earl Mac N. 3500 Ellis av.
Mann Emily Mrs. 418 W. 61st
Mann Franklin, 418 W. 61st
Mann Freeman A. 2600 N. Ashland av.
Mann Henry N. 751 Pine Grove av. *U.L.*
Mann H. V. Winnetka
Mann James R. 334 Oakwood boul. *U.L.*
Mann Joseph B. 7735 Butler. *Irq.*
Mann J. E. Hotel Metropole
Mann William B. 1886 Diversey
Mann William Bell Dr. Evanston

Mann W. A. Dr. 13, 43d
Mann W. G. Lexington hotel
Manners Robert R. Hotel Windermere
Mannhardt Emil, 399 Orchard
Mannheimer M. Mrs. 1822 Indiana av.
Manning O. H. 3431 Michigan av.
Manning Ralph C. 3242 Calumet av.
Manning Randolph, Riverside
Manning William J. 3242 Calumet av
    U.L.
Manny H. A. Miss, 3807 Vincennes av.
Manny James H. 521 Monroe av.
Mansar Jacob, 5127 Woodlawn av.
Mansfield Harold H. 5939 Indiana av.
Mansfield John, Morgan Park
Mansfield John B. 6565 Yale
Mansfield R. Ivan, Morgan Park
Manson William, 5228 South Park av.
Manson William F. Evanston
Mansure Edmund L. 45, 46th. C.A
    W.P.
Mantellani George, 1254 Michigan av.
Manter C. T. 6020 Indiana av.   •
Manter F. H. 6020 Indiana av.
Mantz Edward B. Tremont House
Manvel C. J. 3143 Indiana av.
Many Robert, Oak Park
Many Sidney G. Gault house. Ill.
Manz Jacob, 562 Burling
Manz Paul H. 562 Burling
Mapes Dorchester, Austin
Maple William H. 29 Campbell Park
Maple W. Sherman, 851 W. Monroe
Marble Andrew J. 244 Dearborn av.
Marble Charles E. River Forest
Marble Edward M. Austin
Marble Henry E. 361 S. Oakley av.
Marble Oliver W. 4829 Vincennes av.
Marble Walter H. Dr. 733 Grace
Marchant Stuart F. 4366 Oakenwald av.
Marcus Edward S. 4020 Grand boul.
    Lksd.
Marcus Solms, 4020 Grand boul. Lksd.
Marcuse Milton, 148 Dearborn av.
Marcusson H. H. LaGrange
Marcusson J. W. Rev. LaGrange
Marcusson William B. Dr. 1048 W. Jackson boul.
Marcy George E. The Kenwood. C.A.,
    W.P.
Marcy Oliver Dr. Evanston
Marcy William W. 278 S. Irving av.
Marder Clarence C. 4750 Woodlawn av.
Marder John, 4750 Woodlawn av. Ill.
Marder John W. 4750 Woodlawn av.
Marder Walter S. 4750 Woodlawn av.
Marguerat Eugene Dr. 700 W. Monroe
Marguerat Eugene jr. Dr. 700 W. Monroe
Marguerat George, 700 W. Monroe
Marguerat Henri D. 700 W. Monroe
Marguerat John, 700 W. Monroe
Marhoefer Charles J. Elmhurst
Marie Eugene, 409, 46th
Mariner William E. Evanston
Maris John M. 31 Madison Park. Chi.
Mark Anson, 488 W. Congress. Ill.

Mark Clayton 289 Ashland boul. Ill., U.L
Markham Frank H. 3403 Calumet av.
Markham M. C. 4956 Madison av.
Markham Robert, 3403 Calumet av.
Markheim Joseph, 3527 Calumet av.
Markheim M. D. 3527 Calumet av.
Markle Albert M. 4236 St. Lawrence av.
Markle D. L. Hotel Normandie
Markley John A. 2125 Calumet av. Cal.
Marks Arthur M. 2926 Groveland av.
Marks B. D. 2926 Groveland av.
Marks Charles, 331, 34th
Marks Clarence W. 3121 Michigan av.
    W.P.
Marks Edward C. 2501 Wabash av.
Marks Elizabeth Mrs. 2501 Wabash av.
Marks F. H. North Shore hotel
Marks Harry M. 3434 Michigan av. Stan
Marks Isaac N. jr. 3942 Ellis av.
Marks Joseph E. P. 2501 Wabash av.
Marks Kossuth, 2501 Wabash av. C.A.
Marks Louis, 129, 25th
Marks Louis C. 331, 34th
Marks Louis J. 2501 Wabash av. C.A.
Marks Mary W. Miss, Oak Park
Marks Moses M. 331, 34th
Marks R. P. 235 Michigan av. C.A.
Marks Simon L. 3613 Prairie av. Stan.
Marks William J. 21 Bryant av.
Markwald Ernst M. 5426 Greenwood av.
    W.P.
Marley Luther C. 4546 Lake av.
Marlow Charles F. 24, 44th pl.
Marlow H. E. Austin
Marquardt C. Grant, 5233 Kimbark av.
Marquardt George W. jr. Evanston
Marquis Albert N. 538 W. Adams
Marquis David C. Rev. 1 Chalmers pl.
Marquis Geo. P. Dr. 387 N. State
Marr Richard I. 1453 W. Monroe
Marrenner Edward, 3227 Groveland av.
    C.A.
Marrenner Edward S. 3227 Groveland
    av.
Marriott Abraham R. Austin
Marrow Florence A. Miss, 509 Fullerton
    av.
Mars Robert R. Evanston
Marseilles W. P. Oak Park
Marsh Alfred H. Tracy
Marsh Charles A. 5639 Washington av.
    U.L.
Marsh Charles G. Oak Park
Marsh Charles H. Park Ridge
Marsh Charles L. 60 Bittersweet pl.
    Univ.
Marsh Clyde Ellsworth, Oak Park
Marsh C. V. 4900 Washington av.
Marsh Edward P. Oak Park
Marsh E. P. Tracy
Marsh F. A. 801 Pullman bldg. Chi., W.P.
Marsh George S. Evanston
Marsh Henry W. Virginia hotel. Un.,
    Univ.
Marsh Hiram C. LaGrange
Marsh James P. 3222 Michigan av.

Marsh John P. 12 Aldine sq.
Marsh John W. Mrs. 12 Aldine sq.
Marsh Marshall S. 369 Chicago av.
Marsh N. W. Dr. 3100 Groveland av.
Marsh Ossian B. LaGrange
Marsh Philo, Evanston
Marsh William Dixon, Evanston. *U.L.*
Marsh W. P. Evanston
Marshall Albert M. 5335 Jefferson av.
Marshall Alexander, 22 Bellevue pl.
Marshall A. J. Mrs. 30 Hawthorne pl.
Marshall Benjamin H. 4730 Drexel boul.
Marshall Caleb H. 4730 Drexel boul.
Marshall Charles G. 525 W. Jackson boul.
    Ill.
Marshall Charles H. Oak Park. *U.L.*
Marshall Edward T. 566 Washington boul.
Marshall E. C. Mrs. 771 Warren av.
Marshall Frances L. Miss, 217 The Plaza
Marshall Frank, 2233 Sheridan rd.
Marshall Fred D., M.D., 679 W. Adams
Marshall Geo. A. 63 Laflin. *Ill.*
Marshall George E. 30 Hawthorne pl.
    C.A., U.L.
Marshall George E. 6600 Lafayette av.
Marshall Harry L. 608 Washington boul.
    Ill.   Sum. res. Fox Lake, Ill.
Marshall James, 4400 Greenwood av.
Marshall James D. Mrs. 525 W. Jackson
    boul.
Marshall John Jr. 4400 Greenwood av.
Marshall John I. 902 Estes av.
Marshall John S. Dr. 48 Groveland Park.
    U.L.
Marshall Joseph A. Capt. LaGrange
Marshall Judith L. Mrs. 2109 Prairie av.
Marshall J. M. 5335 Jefferson av.
Marshall Medora Estes Mrs. LaGrange
Marshall Nicholas R. Dr. Evanston
Marshall Philip L. 4738 Woodlawn av.
    C.A.
Marshall Randall E. 566 Washington
    boul.
Marshall Sarah Mrs. 62 Bryant av.
Marshall Sylvester, 4341 Indiana av.
Marshall Thomas J. Mrs. 287 S. Clare-
    mont av.
Marshall V. F. Dr. 210 Ohio
Marshall William, 1824 Surf
Marshall William R. 352 Warren av.
Marshall Wm. L. Major U.S.A. 171, 51st
Marston Harry Col. 24, 44th pl.
Marston James D. 318 W. 61st
Marston Robert H. 225, 28th
Marston Thomas B. 137 Lincoln Park
    boul. *Univ.*
Martens Louis, 424 Ashland boul.
Marthens Chester M. LaGrange
Martin Alexander C. 913 W. Adams
Martin Alfred V. Kenilworth
Martin Anne H. Miss, 2810 Michigan av.
Martin A. F. 3100 Groveland av.
Martin A. W. 418 W. Jackson boul. *Ill.*
Martin Benjamin F. 445 Washington boul.
Martin Carrie E. Mrs. 4257 Grand boul.
Martin Charles E. Irving Park

Martin Chester H. 4624 Indiana av.
Martin Cornelius K. Mrs. 4637 Greenwood
    av.
Martin Daniel, 400 Bowen av.
Martin Daniel R. Pullman
Martin E. P. Oak Park. *Un.*
Martin Ellen A. Miss, 3964 Langley av.
Martin Ellen A. Miss, Lombard
Martin Emma L. Mrs. 712 W. Monroe
Martin Eunice A. Miss, 720 W. Adams
Martin E. B. 3636 Prairie av. *C.A., Ill.*
Martin E. H. S. 418 W. Jackson boul.
Martin Franklin H. Dr. 3210 Lake Park
    av.
Martin Fred J. 6602 Lafayette av.
Martin Frederick S. Evanston. *C.A., Univ.*
Martin George, 1127 Millard av.
Martin George H. 4231 Lake av. *C.A.*
Martin George H. 4340 Ellis av.
Martin George South, 3004 Prairie av.
Martin George W. 6565 Yale
Martin Henry J. 11949 Eggleston av.
Martin Henry Scoville, LaGrange
Martin Horace H. 20 Ritchie ct. *Univ.*
Martin Ida Mrs. 55 St. James pl.
Martin James C. 2512 Prairie av.
Martin James G. 42 Pine Grove av.
Martin John H. 4400 Indiana av.
Martin John T. 3534 Wabash av.
Martin Joseph S. 190 N. State. *C.A.*
Martin J. Earl, 2578 N. Hermitage av.
Martin J. Motte, 3160 Lake Park av.
Martin J. P. Mrs. Hotel Del Prado
Martin Kate B. Miss, 4568 Oakenwald av
Martin Matthew M. 728 W. 64th
Martin Nicholas, 3246 Forest av.
Martin Robert G. 3132 Calumet av.
Martin Robert L. 719 W. Vanburen. *Ill.*
Martin Robert T. 2810 Michigan av.
Martin Samuel K. Mrs. 2600 Michigan av.
Martin Sarah Mrs. 3534 Wabash av.
Martin S. Bailey, 36 S. Wood
Martin S. E. W. Mrs. 656 W. Monroe
Martin Thomas J. Kenilworth. *Chi.*
Martin William, 540 W. Adams. *C.A.*
Martin William Dr. Palmer House
Martin William P. Virginia hotel. *Un.*
    Sum. res. Wheaton
Martin Wilton B. 5200 Kimbark av.
Martin W. H. Park Ridge
Martin W. H. Winnetka
Martin W. J. Dr. 800 W. Adams
Martindale Catherine Miss, 405 Oak
Martine James E. 335 Hampden ct.
Martini John L. 4118 Perry
Martyn Chauncey W. 5010 Vincennes av
Martyn Edward J. 112 Astor
Martyn R. Delos, 4450 Berkeley av.
Marum Edmund P. 6503 Woodlawn av.
Marvin William Mrs. 2974 Indiana av.
Marx Marcus, 3658 Michigan av. *Stan.*
Marx Mathew A. 838 W. Garfield boul.
Marx Zero, 628 Fullerton av.
Maschke H. Prof. 5810 Woodlawn av.
Mashek V. F. 40 Loomis. *Univ.*
Maslin J. C. Mrs. 2358 Indiana av.

Mason Albert G. 5426 Jefferson av.
Mason A. A. 113 Cass
Mason Carlisle, 176 Ashland boul. *Ill.*
Mason Carrie Mrs. Evanston
Mason Charles W. Capt. Ft. Sheridan
Mason Edward G. 4623 Ellis av. *Univ.*
Mason Edward H. 113 Cass
Mason Edward T. 448 W. Adams
Mason Frank G. Dr. 470 W. Congress
Mason Fred B. 15 Chalmers pl. *U.L.*
Mason Fred H. 5426 Jefferson av.
Mason George, 511 W. Monroe. *Ill.*
        Sum. res. Fox Lake
Mason George H. 713 Walnut
Mason G. A. Highland Park
Mason Handley Mrs. 1045 Winthrop av.
Mason Henry Burrall, 29 Delaware pl.
   Univ.
Mason Henry E. 377 Superior. *Univ.*
Mason Hugh, 369 W. Jackson boul.
Mason Hugh L. 557 Dearborn av.
Mason Ira J. 15 Chalmers pl. *U.L.*
Mason James Mrs. Austin
Mason James A. 907 W. Monroe
Mason John, Hinsdale
Mason Julian S. 4623 Ellis av.
Mason Leonard B. 5539 Monroe av.
Mason Lewis J. 29, 37th
Mason Lucy Miss, Evanston
Mason Mary L. Miss, 5332 Washington
   av.
Mason Roswell B. 4623 Ellis av.
Mason R. J. 489 W. Jackson boul.
Mason Stephen C. 6651 Stewart av.
Mason William, 3180 Dover
Mason William A. 303 Schiller
Mason William H. 5426 Jefferson av.
Mason William Smith, Evanston
Mason William T. 1503 Wellington
Mason W. B. Mrs. 771 Warren av.
Massey Columbus V. Dr. 1626 Barry av.
Massey Thomas C. 2227 Kenmore av.
Massey Wilfred, 294 Lasalle av. *C.A.*
Massman John Dr. Austin
Masters Arthur W. 6025 Lexington av.
   C.A.
Masters Edgar Lee, 4200 Drexel boul.
Masters G. A. 4507 Lake av.
Masterson Edwin F. 3825 Vernon av.
Mather Alonzo C. 531 N. State. *U.L.*
Mather Charles S. 6802 Butler
Mather C. A. LaGrange
Mather Henry H. Dr. 7847 Butler
Mather Robert, 4812 Kimbark av. *U.L.*
Mather S. T. 5643 Madison av.
Mather William H. 2159 Clarendon av.
Matheson R. S. 3742½ Forest av.
Mathews Albert, 461 Warren av.
Mathews Allan A. Dr. Oak Park
Mathews Alvah B. 47 Greenleaf av.
Mathews Anna M. Miss. Oak Park
Mathews George W. 2532 Indiana av. *U.L.*
Mathews George Wm. jr. 3612 Michigan
   av. *C.A., W.P.*
Mathews Henry B. jr. 1336 Washington
   boul.

Mathews Jessie Miss, Oak Park
Mathews Shailer Prof. 5736 Woodlawn av.
Mathews W. S. B. 3436 Calumet av.
Mathison George W. 1332 Sheridan rd.
Mathison O. A. 4638 Indiana av.
Mathison Soren, 2126 Indiana av.
Matile Herman O. Wheaton. *C.A.*
Matlack Vernon E. Evanston
Matrau Benjamin F. Rev. 512 N. Norma
   Parkway
Matson A. P. Clark, 522 Estes av.
Matson Canute R. 609 Cleveland av.
Matson N. Mrs. Lombard
Matter Martin Dr. 3137 Wabash av.
Mattern Lorenz, 587 Orchard
Matteson Arthur E., D.D.S. 3822 Lang-
   ley ay.
Matteson Charles C. 3166 Groveland av.
Matteson C. F. Dr. 50, 35th
Matteson Joseph Dr. 3166 Groveland av.
Matteson Milo D. 1843 Wellington
        Sum. res. Chautauqua, N. Y.
Matteson Murray G., D.D.S. 3822 Langley
   av.
Matteson William P. Evanston
Matthei Charles A. 368 Ashland boul.
Matthei Gustave P. 368 Ashland boul.
Matthei Philip H. Dr. 57 Wisconsin
Matthei William H. 368 Ashland boul.
Matthews Charles, 2931A Groveland av.
Matthews Charles E. 1665 W. Monroe
Matthews Edwin Scott, 247 Goethe. *C.A.*
Matthews Frank W. The Tudor
Matthews Geo. L. Mrs. Lakota hotel
Matthews Henry M. 1551 Kimball av.
Matthews James T. Mrs. 235 Michigan av.
Matthews John T. 1159 Washington boul.
Matthews Oscar A. 520 W. 60th
Matthews O. H. 4144 Grand boul.
        Sum. res. Warsaw, Ind.
Matthews Pascal P. Hinsdale
Matthews Samuel C. 569, 46th pl,
Matthews Walter C. Austin
Matthews William H. 7721 Lowe av. *C.A.*
Matthews W. H. 6534 Greenwood av.
Matthias Charles, 3311 Rhodes av.
Matthiessen C. H. 4917 Drexel boul. *U.L.,
   W.P.*
Matthiessen E. A. Hotel Metropole. *U.L.*
        Sum. res. Cornwall on Hudson, N.Y.
Matthiessen Frank, 4540 Greenwood av.
Matthius John D. Rev. Evanston
Mattison Olin F. Rev. Evanston
Matz Herman L. 606 Division. *Univ.*
Matz Otto H. 431 Oak
Matz Rudolph, 2300 Calumet av. *Cal.,
   Univ.*
Mauch Carl, 581 Burling
Maul William G. 5640 Michigan av.
Mauran Charles J. 4759 Madison av.
Mauran Charles S. 4759 Madison av.
Maurer William, 4136 Prairie av.
Maus Frederick K. 26 Linden ct.
Mauntner Gustave, 1450 Wrightwood av.
Mavor John, LaGrange
Mavor William, 166 Oakwood boul.

Maxham Hiram S. Mrs. Pullman
Maxwell Charles E. 4504 Woodlawn av.
   C.A.,U.L.
Maxwell Charles F. 767 N. Clark
Maxwell D. G. 538 Cleveland av.
Maxwell E. E. 3980 Lake av. *C.A.*
Maxwell E. J. Mrs. 417 Center
Maxwell Fannie Belle Miss, Lake Forest
Maxwell Henry B. 365 Ashland boul. *Ill.*
Maxwell James, 367 Ashland boul. *Ill.*
Maxwell James W. 767 N. Clark
Maxwell John E. A. LaGrange
Maxwell J. W. 3978 Lake av.
Maxwell M. J. Mrs. 4310 Greenwood av.
Maxwell Robert F. 468 Fullerton av.
Maxwell William Mrs. 6506 Minerva av.
Maxwell Wm. Stirling Dr. 3129 Indiana
   av.
Maxwell W. Mrs. 538 Cleveland av.
May Benjamin W. 518, 53d
May B. A. Winnetka
May Charles A. Mrs. 2799 N. Lincoln
May Frank E. 69, 48th. *C.A.*
May Henry, 4327 Berkeley av. *Lksd.*
May Horatio N. Mrs. 147 Astor.
May Jacob Mrs. 3207 Calumet av.
May James F. 252, 51st
May James H. 85 Rush
May Jennie Miss, 3651 Prairie av.
May Jessie Miss, 16 Astor
May John V. 19 Crilly ct.
May P. J. 2358 Indiana av.
May Sarah Mrs. 85 Rush
May Stephen D. 2512 Prairie av.
Mayberry John J. 218 Park av. *U.L.*
Maydwell B. B. Dr. 14 Menomonee
Maydwell Harry F. Hinsdale
Mayer Adolph E. 2693 Magnolia av.
Mayer.Bernard, 4915 Grand boul. *Stan.*
Mayer Blanche Miss, 943 W. Monroe
Mayer Clara Mrs. 2343 Michigan av.
Mayer David, 1811 Prairie av. *C.A.,*
   Stan., U.L., W.P.
Mayer David Mrs. 378 Oakwood boul.
Mayer Grace Mrs. 6319 Kimbark av.
Mayer Harry L. 3428 Calumet av. *Stan.*
Mayer Henry, 588½ Division
Mayer Henry, 3563 Prairie av.
Mayer Henry B. 3024 Vernon av.
Mayer Isaac H. 3548 Ellis av. *Irq., Stan.,*
   U.L.
Mayer Isaac M. 4527 Ellis av.
Mayer Jacob, 2343 Michigan av. *Stan.*
Mayer Jacob, 3560 Vernon av.
Mayer Jacob, 3866 Lake av.
Mayer Jo. 3428 Calumet av. *Stan.*
Mayer Joseph, 3752 Wabash av.
Mayer Lee, 3428 Calumet av.
Mayer Leonard H. 3229 Wabash av. *Lksd.*
Mayer Leopold, 3170 Groveland av. *Lksd.*
Mayer Levy, 1815 Prairie av. *U.L.*
Mayer L. D. Mrs. Lakota hotel
Mayer Max, 417, 45th. *Lksd.*
Mayer Morris, 461, 42d. *Lksd.*
Mayer Murray C. 3252 Groveland av.
   Stan.

Mayer M. H. Mrs. 3229 Wabash av.
Mayer Nat. A. 4250 Drexel boul. *Lksd.,*
   Stan.
Mayer Nathan, Hotel Prado *Stan.*
Mayer O. W. Park Ridge
Mayer R. Mrs. 4527 Ellis av.
Mayer Simon, 458 Garfield av.
Mayer Solomon, 458 Garfield av.
Mayer Toby, 378 Oakwood boul. *Lksd.*
Mayer William J. 347 Ashland boul.
Mayers Blanche Miss, 3439 Michigan av.
Mayhew John Mills Dr. 870 Warren av.
Mayhew L. D. Hotel Windermere
Maynard Alfred A. 1546 Kenmore av.
Maynard Alfred C. Winnetka
Maynard Charles W. Maywood
Maynard C. Mrs. 2924 Groveland av.
Maynard Edwin, Winnetka
Maynard Everett W. 441 W. 64th
Maynard E. Percy, Winnetka
Maynard Joseph S. The Tudor
Maynard Preston C. 802 Pullman bldg.
   Chi., W.P.
Maynard Raymond K. Oak Park
Maynard Stephen B. 438 W. 64th
Maynard W. H. 6553 Greenwood av.
Mayo Charles A. 441 W. 64th
Mayo Ernest A. Evanston
Mayo John Browne, 2312 Calumet av.
   Cal., C.A., W.P.
           Sum. res. Pittsfield, Mass.
Mayo Lewis B. River Forest
Mayou J. S. 5825 Kimbark av.
Mays Walter A. 1886 Diversey
McAdam Anna J. Miss, 394 S. Oakley
   av.
McAdam Charles V. 394 S. Oakley av.
McAdam John V. 394 S. Oakley av.
McAdam May Rose Miss, 394 Oakley
   av.
McAdams Andrew, 316, 53d
McAdams Edwin L. 1302 W. Adams
McAdams John Q. 4839 Vincennes av.
McAdow Finley H. 6353 Yale
McAfee James L. Kenilworth
McAlister Katherine Mrs. Oak Park
McAllaster Howard, Winnetka
McAllister W. K. Mrs. 2454 N. Paulina
McAndrews Jas. jr. 890 Washington boul.
McAndrews Joseph R. 890 Washington
   boul.
McAndrews Nellie F. Miss, 890 Wash-
   ington boul.
McAnrow John, 4056 Lake av.
McAnrow John A. 4056 Lake av.
McArdle Edward J. 5203 Michigan av.
McArdle Peter L. 5203 Michigan av.
McArthur Archibald, Riverside
McArthur Arthur F. 2000 Indiana av.
   C.A., U.L., Univ.
McArthur Cuthbert, 879 S. Sawyer av.
McArthur Florence B. Miss, Riverside
McArthur James Mrs. 3848 Lake av.
McArthur John, 504 W. Monroe
McArthur John jr. 504 W. Monroe
McArthur J. H. Maj. 2813 Indiana av.

McArthur Lewis L. Dr. 4247 Drexel boul. *C.A., W.P.*
 Sum. res. Mackinac Island, Mich.
McArthur Warren, 4852 Kenwood av. *C.A.*
McAuley Agnes Miss, 554 Dearborn av.
McAuley Daniel R. Austin
McAuley Frank, 554 Dearborn av.
McAuley John T. 467 Elm
McAuley John T. 467 Elm. *Chi., Un.*
McAuliff Cornelius, 619, 46th
McAvoy Charles P. 52 Walton pl.
 Sum. res. Wheaton
McAvoy John H. Mrs. 503 The Plaza
McAvoy Sarah Mrs. 605 The Plaza
McBean Archibald J. F. 2017 Prairie av.
McBean Archie J. 2017 Prairie av.
McBean Duncan S. Mrs. 3640 Prairie av.
McBean George B. 2017 Prairie av.
McBean George M. 3326 Vernon av.
McBean James G. 3326 Vernon av.
McBean LeRoy H. 673' 48th
McBerty Frank R. Evanston. *U.L.*
McBirney Day, 52 Walton pl.
McBirney Hugh, 1736 Prairie av.
McBirney Hugh J. 1625 Prairie av. *Univ.*
McBride George J. Hotel Windermere
McBride John F. 1180 Washington boul.
McBride J. W. 93, 33d
McCabe Robert R. Evanston
McCagg Caroline Miss, 67 Cass
McCagg Ezra B. 67 Cass. *Chi., Univ.*
McCain Frank J. 1575 W. Monroe
McCall Thomas, 5344 Madison av.
McCall Warner B. Austin
McCallum Alpheus, Austin
McCallum Joseph, Evanston
McCallum Joseph N. Evanston
McCally Emma Mrs. 4818 Evans av.
McCalmont G. S. Mrs. 502 The Plaza
McCandless A. W. Dr. 6407 Kimbark av.
McCann Daniel, Evanston
McCann Frank, 5543 Monroe av.
McCann George S. 5543 Monroe av.
McCann John B. 5543 Monroe av.
McCann Thomas, 965 W. Jackson boul.
McCarrell Albert F. Evanston
McCarthy Daniel E. Capt. Ft. Sheridan
McCarthy Edward J. 805 S. Sawyer av.
McCarthy Eugene J. 737 Walnut. *C.A.*
McCarthy Florence, 1145 S. Western av. *Ill.*
McCarthy James A. 599 Evergreen av.
McCarthy James J. Austin
McCarthy John, Lexington hotel
McCarthy J. G. 282 Park av. *Ill.*
McCarthy M. H. 4224 Oakenwald av. *C.A.*
McCartney F. J. Evanston
McCartney Harry G. 3348 Rhodes av. *C.A.*
McCartney James, Berwyn
McCartney Joseph A. 4014 Drexel boul.
McCarty A. B. Mrs. 41, 33d
McCarty W. W. Mrs. Oakland Hotel
McCary Clyde J. Oak Park

McCasky Isaac W. 790 W. Monroe
McCaslin Samuel W. 457 Evanston av.
McCaughan Geo. E. 7126 Harvard av.
McCauley James J. Evanston
McCauley Thomas N. 933 W. Jackson boul. *Irq.*
McCaull George M. Austin
McCausland A. J. Newberry hotel
McChesney James B. Dr. 5484 Cornell av.
McChesney Martin H. 6542 Kimbark av.
McChesney Mary E. Mrs. 5210 Jefferson av.
McChesney W. B. Dr. 322 S. Marshfield
McClain William C. 4436 Evans av.
McClanahan E. B. Mrs. Lake Forest
McClary Nelson A. Oak Park
McClay John, 822 Wilson av.
McClay Thomas, 822 Wilson av.
McClean Samuel A. jr. 4554 Ellis av. *C.A., W.P.*
McCleary B. J. 3625 Vernon av.
McClellan Edward W. 4402 Greenwood av. *C.A.*
McClellan Fuller, 2023 Indiana av.
 Sum. res. Tower Hill, Mich.
McClellan George A. Kenilworth
McClellan Geo. H. 4412 Berkeley av.
McClellan Henry W. 2023 Indiana av.
 Sum. res. Tower Hill, Mich.
McClellan J. J. 4402 Greenwood av. *U.L.*
McClelland Ella M. Miss, 417 Superior
McClelland J. S. 2728 Wabash av.
McClelland Thomas S. 417 Superior
McClintock B. R. Hinsdale
McClintock H. J. Mrs. Riverside
McClintock James, Hinsdale
McClintock William D. Prof. 5629 Lexington av.
McClintock William H. LaGrange
McCloud E. C. Mrs. Riverside
McCloud Roy M. Riverside
McCluer Lora Mrs. 33 Aldine sq.
McCluer Wm. B. 401 N. State. *Univ*
McClure Frank M. Tracy
McClure James G. K. Rev. Lake Forest
McClure Mary Mrs. Lakota hotel
McClure T. H. Dr. 4043 Ellis av
McClurg Aaron H. 730 Washington boul.
McClurg Alex. C. 125 Lake Shore Drive. *Chi., Univ.*
 Sum. res. Sharon, Conn.
McClurg Lowrie, 18 Walton pl. *Un., Univ.*
McColl I. G. Chicago Beach hotel
McCollough Calvin G. Dr. 4601 Vincennes av.
McCollum G. Albert, 4521 Vincennes av.
McComas Duke, 4847 Kimbark av.
McComas Rufus F. jr. 4847 Kimbark av.
McConn Richard W. 5155 Cornell av.
McConnel George M. Winnetka
McConnel Robert B. Winnetka
McConnell Alexander, Evanston
McConnell B. F. 440 Elm
McConnell Chas. H. 4417 Ellis av. *C.A.*

McConnell Edward D. 60 Hawthorne pl.
McConnell Edward P. 4359 Lake av.
McConnell E. C. Mrs. Evanston
McConnell Horace C. 3619 Grand boul.
McConnell Howard, Evanston
McConnell James H. Evanston
McConnell James S. 4359 Lake av.
McConnell John, 60 Hawthorne pl. *C.A.*
McConnell Luther W. 531 Dearborn av.
  U.L.
McConnell Samuel P. Judge, 405 Huron.
  Irq. Sum. res. Forest Lodge, Long
  Lake, Mich.
McConnell S. M. 2727 Wabash av.
          Sum. res. Whitehall, Mich.
McConnell Washington A. Oak Park
McConnell William C. 2625 N. Ashland ·
  av.
McConnell William J. Evanston
McConnell W. S. 2727 Wabash av. *C.A.*
McConville Annie Mrs. 4842 Prairie av.
McCord Alvin Carr, 308 N. State. *U.L.*
McCord J. C. 3401 Wabash av.
McCordic Alfred E. Winnetka. *Univ.*
McCormick ·Alexander Agnew, 112
  Buena av. *C.A., Univ., U.L.*
McCormick Andrew J. Evanston
McCormick Charles T. A. 547 Dearborn
  av.
McCormick Cyrus Hall, 321 Huron *C.A.,*
  Chi., Irq., Un., Univ. ·
McCormick Cyrus H. Mrs. 135 Rush
McCormick Frank P. 355 S. Oakley av.
McCormick Harold F. 88 Bellevue pl.
  Chi., C.A., Univ.
McCormick John A. 2942 Groveland av.
McCormick John H. 355 S. Oakley av.
McCormick J. Medill, 101 Cass
McCormick Leander J. Virginia hotel ·
          Sum. res. Lake Forest
McCormick L. Hamilton, 101 Rush. *Chi.,*
  C.A.   Sum. res. Lake Forest
McCormick Martha E. Miss, 2301 N.
  Ashland av.
McCormick Robert S. 101 Cass. *Chi.,*
  W.P. ··
McCormick R.Hall ,124 Rush. *Chi., C.A.,*
  W.P. Sum. res. Lake Forest, Ill. and
  Bar Harbor, Maine ·
McCormick Stanley R. 135 Rush. *Chi.,*
  C.A., Univ.
McCormick William A. Evanston
McCormick William G. 157 Rush. *Chi.,*
  W.P.
McCornack A. W. 400 W. 67th
McCourtie Arnold B. 1197 Washington
  boul. *Ill.*
McCourtie Martha M. Mrs. 1195 Wash-
  ington boul.
McCowen Mary Miss, 6550 Yale
McCoy Daniel C. Rev. Hinsdale
McCoy George, LaGrange
McCoy John, 3443 Prairie av.
McCoy M. Max, 3815 Lake av.
McCoy T. H. 3815 Lake av.
McCracken Charles A. S. 7111 Yale

McCrea James jr. 267 W. Adams
McCrea Willis S. 122 Lincoln Park boul.
  C.A., Chi., Ill., U.L., W.P.
          Sum. res. Lake Geneva, Wis.
McCready E. W. Oak Park
McCready John S. Oak Park
McCreary Robert Hughes, 429 Erie
McCredie William, Hinsdale
McCreight S. L. Dr. 458 S. Marshfield av.
McCrillis Mary F. Dr. Evanston
McCullach Robert, Austin
McCulloch Catharine Waugh Mrs. Evan-
  ston
McCulloch Frank H. Evanston. *Irq.*
McCulloh J. W. 5130 Hibbard av,
McCulloh Thomas G. 5130 Hibbard av.
McCulloh Thomas G. jr. 5130 Hibbard
  av.
McCullough Allen, 5621 Michigan av.
McCullough Charles H. 5751 Rosalie ct.
  Chi.
McCullough C. Mrs. Evanston
McCullough H. R. Lake Forest. *C.A.,*
  U.L.
McCullough John R. Dr. 35 Park av.
McCully Fred, 905 W. Monroe
McCully John A. 905 W. Monroe
McCune George H. 385 N. State
McCune J. D. Lakota hotel
McCurdy D. E. 3645 Prairie av.
McCurdy George L. 3647 Prairie av. ·*U.L.*
McCurdy James G. Dr. 2069 W. Congress
McDaid L. P. Mrs. 57 St. James pl.
McDaneld Daniel H. 2682 N. Paulina
McDaniel Alexander, Wilmette
McDaniel Charles W. Oak Park.
McDaniel D. L. Oak Park
McDaniel Richard, 16 St. James pl.
McDermid Ferdinand, 4032 Ellis av.
McDermid John J. Mrs. 4032 Ellis av.
McDermid John J. jr. 4032 Ellis av.
McDermid Julian M. 4032 Ellis av.
McDermid Ralph, 4032 Ellis av.
McDermitt E. H. Mrs. 5000. Lake av.
McDermitt Jane Hoge Miss, 5000 Lake
  av.
McDermott Michael, 3528 Wabash av.
McDermut Wilson E. 7408 Bond av.
McDevitt James, 4211 Lake av.
McDiarmid Andrew Dr. 6325 Greenwood
  av.
McDoel W. Henry, 3232 Michigan av.
  Cal., U.L., W.P.
McDonagh Patrick J. 7465 Bond av.
McDonald Alexander Dr. 338 Park av.
McDonald Allen Mrs. 3012 Prairie av.
McDonald A. J. Mrs. 2632 Magnolia av.
McDonald Charles A. 436 Winthrop av.
McDonald F. R. 1839 Magnolia av.
McDonald George H. LaGrange
McDonald Harley C. LaGrange ·
McDonald Harry J. 280 Fullerton av.
McDonald James, 1690 Barry av.
McDonald James, 2433 N. Hermitage av.
McDonald James, Highland Park
McDonald James, Hinsdale

McDonald James Stuart, 2410 N. Hermitage av.
McDonald James W. 4015 Vincennes av.
McDonald John, 280 Fullerton av.
McDonald John C. Oak Park
McDonald John J. 448 N. Normal Parkway. *C.A., U.L.*
McDonald Joseph, 351 Chestnut
McDonald J. A. Hyde Park hotel
McDonald J. B. 5745 Madison av. *Ill.*
McDonald J. D. Chicago Beach hotel
McDonald Lizzie Miss, 632 Washington boul.
McDonald Louis A. 6738 Rhodes av.
McDonald Malcolm Mrs. 393 W. Jackson boul.
McDonald Malcolm jr. 403 W. Jackson boul.
McDonald Silas E. Oak Park
McDonald Walter, LaGrange
McDonald William, Oak Park
McDonell John A. Dr. 471 Washington boul.
McDonnell E. Miss, 163, 30th
McDonnell Harriet Miss, 163, 30th
McDonnell John J. Dr. 440 Ashland boul.
McDonnell Lizzie Miss,440 Ashland boul.
McDonnell Martin W. Evanston
McDonnell William, 2056 Kenmore av.
McDougal Alfred, 4754 Kenwood av.
McDougal Anna Wood Mrs. Riverside
McDougal Edward D. 4754 Kenwood av.
McDougal Robert, 4754 Kenwood av.
McDougall Esther A. Mrs. 4156 Ellis av.
McDougall Isabel Miss, 727 Fullerton av.
McDougall William, 4156 Ellis av.
McDowell Hanson, Evanston
McDowell Irvin, Evanston
McDowell Jacob, 189 Oakwood boul.
McDowell Malcolm, Evanston
McDowell Ollie A. Mrs. 5910 Indiana av.
McDowell R. P. 189 Oakwood boul.
McDowell S. E. Hotel Del Prado
McDuffee Henry H. 4347 Ellis av.
McDwire Ruth Mrs. 4628 Prairie av.
McEldowney Howard, 7310 Harvard av.
McElevey W. B. 409 Superior
McElligott Thomas G. 4516 Indiana av. *C.A.*
McElroy James, 4210 Prairie av.
McElroy J. E. Mrs. Chicago Beach hotel
McElroy Robert L. 7130 Yale
McElwain Frank, Evanston
McElwain Ruth Mrs. Evanston
McEnerny Thomas, 861 S. Central Park av.
McEnery John T. 56 Lytle
McEntee Charles S. 566 Division
McEvoy Stephen, Maywood
McEwan Matthew C. 444 Chestnut. *Chi.*
McEwan P. Anderson, 1813 Indiana av.
McEwen Alfred, 512 Lasalle av.
McEwen John, 512 Lasalle av.
McEwen John jr. 512 Lasalle av. *C.A.*
McEwen Paul J. 512 Lasalle av. *C.A.*
McEwen W. M. Irving Park. *U.L.*

McFadden George, 3151 Rhodes av.
McFadden George E. 7842 Hawthorne av.
McFadden Parmalee J. 149 Lincoln Park boul.
McFadon Robert D. Mrs. 183 Rush
McFall Rose C. Dr. 196 W. Monroe
McFarland Charles H. Evanston
McFarland John C. 6635 Parnell av.
McFarland John H. 4001 Drexel boul.
McFarland Thomas W. 6635 Parnell av.
McFarland William W. Austin
McFarland William W. jr. Austin
McFarlane Helen Miss, 1928 Belmont av.
McFarlane Hugh, 1928 Belmont av.
McFarlane Hugh F. Mrs. Hinsdale
McFarlin John Mrs. Winnetka
McFarlin M. 3047 Groveland av.
McFarlin W. W. 3047 Groveland av.
McFatrich J. B. Dr. 3408 Prairie av. *C.A.*
McGann Lawrence E. 3620, 5th av. *C.A., Ill., Irq.*
McGann Robert Greaves, 18 Walton pl. *Un.*
McGaughey John A. Dr. 4820 Langley av.
McGee Harry L. 636, 56th
McGee Willford J. 636, 56th
McGee William E. Hinsdale
McGenniss C. B. Mrs. 1945 Prairie av.
McGibbon W. P. Dr. 3130 Indiana av.
McGill David B. LaGrange
McGill George F. LaGrange
McGill James K. 821 W. Adams
McGill James P., M.D. 4553 Forrestville av.
McGill Judith W. Mrs. Evanston
McGill J. A. Dr. 4938 Drexel boul.
McGill J. M. 4547 Lake av.
McGill Virginia H. Mrs. 7226 Euclid av.
McGill Wm. 7226 Euclid av.
McGillen John, 535 Cleveland av.
McGinn Julian B. Evanston
McGinnis Richard I. 2446 N. Paulina
McGinnis W. G. Edison Park
McGovern John, 416 S. Wood
McGowan J. D. 242 Oakwood boul.
McGowan Edward J. 6731 Lafayette av.
McGrath Charles H. 585 Dearborn av.
McGrath George B. 7138 Euclid av.
McGrath John J. Mrs. 585 Dearborn av.
McGrath John P. 3518 Wabash av.
McGrath Maurice J. 7138 Euclid av.
McGrath Michael H. Dr. 1022 W. Adams
McGraw Daniel T. 3416 Prairie av.
McGraw James, 927 W. Adams
McGraw Jeremiah, 5701 Drexel av.
McGraw Michael, 3416 Prairie av.
McGregor Gardner Mrs. 4434 Ellis av.
McGregor James R. Oak Park
McGregor John B. 3835 Ellis av.
McGregor P. D. LaGrange. *U.L.*
McGregor William Mrs. 692 W. Monroe
McGrew C. D. Mrs. 122, 49th
McGrew Elwood, 521 Belden av.
McGrew J. H. LaGrange
McGue M. S. Mrs. Tremont house

McGuire Daniel, 852 North Park av.
    C. A. Sum res. South Haven, Mich.
McGuire Daniel F. Rev. 943 W. Garfield
    boul.
McGuire Edward A. 5617 Monroe av.
    . C.A.
McGuire John F. 1727 Sheridan rd.
McGuire Julia B. Miss, 5617 Monroe av.
McGuire Sims, 852 North Park av.
McGuire William A. 309 Webster av.
McHatton Margaret Mrs. 4417 Lake av.
McHenry A. C. Mrs. 1815 Indiana av.
McHenry W. E. 113 Cass
McHie George E. 3912 Calumet av. C.A.
McHugh C. R. Oak Park
McHugh Felix E. 1195 Wilton av.
McHugh Patrick, Chicago Athletic assn.
    C.A., Irq.
McIlhon Catherine Mrs. 3207 Dover
McIlroy Joseph W. 3953 Michigan av.
McIlvaine Allan C. 4827 Lake av.
McIlvaine John D. 453 Evanston av.
McIlvaine John S. Mrs. 356 Ontario
McIlvaine William B. 502 N. State. Univ.
McIlvaine William D. 710 The Plaza.
    U.L.
McIntire Percival Rev. Hotel Winder-
    mere
McIntosh Alexander, 6560 Harvard av.
McIntosh Alexander jr. 6560 Harvard av.
McIntosh Harry M. 3668 Michigan av.
    C.A., W.P.
McIntosh Jennie Miss, Hotel Del Prado
McIntosh John F. 524 W. Congress
McIntosh J. M. Hotel Del Prado
McIntosh Mary Miss, Hotel Del Prado
McIntyre Allan, 304 N. State
McIntyre John, 4114 Ellis av.
McIntyre John Lawrence, 145 Lincoln
    Park boul. Un.
McIntyre P. J. 3815 Forest av.
McIntyre Robert Rev. 4611 Ellis av.
McIver Francis F. 516 North av.
McIver James Mrs. 516 North av.
McKallor H. L. Mrs. River Forest
McKay Aaron M. 2697 N. Paulina
McKay Alexander A. Union League club,
    C.A.
McKay Charles R. Lombard
McKay Eugene, Evanston
McKay George A. Union League club
McKay George H. LaGrange
McKay James M. 290 Ohio. Un.
McKay James R. 290 Ohio. Chi., Un.
McKay John A. 227 S. Oakley av.
McKay Margaret Mrs. 2204 Prairie av.
McKay M. Mrs. LaGrange
McKechney John, 288 Ohio
McKechney John, jr. 288 Ohio. Cal.
McKee D. Hotel Woodruff
McKee D. Clay, 6040 Langley av.
McKee E. M. Mrs. 2026 Michigan av.
McKee George W. 6040 Langley av.
McKee Harry, 698 Walnut
McKee Joseph W. 3147 Calumet av.
McKeeby Sanford, 3601 Vincennes av. Ill.

McKeever Buell, 3900 Lake av.
McKeever John A. Tracy
McKeever J. L. 3900 Lake av.
McKelvey Samuel P. 4725 Prairie av.
    Irq.
McKelvy Henry W. 381 Superior
McKenna James, 4563 Michigan av.
McKenna John J. 4807 Wabash av.
McKenney Charles T. 4640 Langley av.
McKenzie F. M. Dr. Lexington hotel
McKenzie William C. Ravinia
McKenzie William L. Ravinia
McKeon John C. Hotel Metropole. Chi.,
    Cal., C.A.
McKewin Hugh W. 474 W. Adams
McKey Edward B. 5116 Hibbard av.
McKey Henry Mrs. 5136 Kimbark av.
McKey R. M. 5539 Monroe av.
McKey William D. 5114 Hibbard av.
McKibbin C. B. 172 Oakwood boul.
McKibbin Wm. C. 172 Oakwood boul.
McKillip M. H. Dr. 1706 Michigan av.
McKindley James Mrs. 258 Michigan av.
McKindley Wm. Mrs. 3660 Michigan av.
McKinley Wm. Brown, 19 Scott
McKinlock George A. 1712 Prairie av.
    U.L., W.P.
McKinlock John Dr. 3612 Michigan av.
McKinlock Walter C. 6016 Stony Island
    av.
McKinlock William H. Chicago Beach
    hotel. Cal.
McKinney A. M. 4201 Oakenwald av.
McKinney Fred W. 3075 Kenmore av.
McKinney George, Winnetka
McKinney R. M. 1100 Washington boul.
McKinney Samuel P. Dr. 810 Warren av.
McKinnie Emily Miss, Hinsdale
McKinnie Leonard G. Evanston
McKinnie P. Leon Dr. Evanston
McKinnie Ralph R. Evanston
McKinnon D. C. Morgan Park
McKinnon John K. Dr. 345 Rush
McKinnon John W. 5324 Madison av.
McKittrick Joseph L. Wilmette
McKnight George F. 7772 Hawthorne av.
McKnight H. P. Chicago Athletic assn.
McKnight Louisa B. Mrs. 5715 Monroe av.
McKnight M. B. Mrs. 5715 Monroe av.
McKnight Sanford C. 7772 Hawthorne av.
McLain Albert O. 413, 45th
        Sum res. Watervliet, Mich.
McLain Andrew J. 2430 Michigan av.
McLain Charles R. 4524 Forrestville av.
McLain William Mrs. 2430 Michigan av.
    Sum. res. Mackinaw Straits, Mich.
McLain William, 4532 Oakenwald av.
McLane Josephine Miss, 3540 Calumet
    av.
McLaren John, 339 Ashland boul. Ill.,
    U.L.
McLaren J. Loomis, 339 Ashland boul.
McLaren Wm. E. Rt. Rev. Highland
    Park.
        Sum. res. Point Pleasant, N. J.
McLaren W. A. Highland Park

McLaroth Kenneth, Austin
McLauchlan John, 2421 N. Paulina
McLauchlin Alexander L. 50 Oakwood
  boul.
McLaughlin Albert, LaGrange
McLaughlin A. H. Hyde Park hotel
McLaughlin Edward Dr. 6547 Lafayette
  av.
McLaughlin E. F. Lakota hotel
McLaughlin Frederic, 97 Rush
McLaughlin George A. Rev. Evanston
McLaughlin George D. 471 Elm. *Chi.,*
  Un., W.P.
McLaughlin Ida K. Mrs. 1930 Deming pl.
McLaughlin James B. Riverside
McLaughlin John J. 1551 W. Monroe
McLaughlin Patrick H. 1551 W. Monroe
McLaughlin Robert J. 337 Hampden ct.
McLaughlin William F. 97 Rush
McLaury T. G. Mrs. 4911 Greenwood av.
McLean Charles A. 2836 Indiana av.
McLean Charles F. 2836 Indiana av.
McLean John Dr. Pullman
McLean J. W. 224 Belden av.
McLean William S. 158 S. Leavitt
McLean W. A. 4001 Grand boul.
McLeish Andrew, Glencoe. *U.L.*
McLeish Archibald, 1529 Carroll av.
McLeish Samuel L. 1529 Carroll av.
McLellan A. 67, 37th. *Irq.*
McLenehan M. B. 3924 Lake av.
McLennan Christopher, 3822 Ellis av.
McLennan J. A. 3105 Calumet av. *U.L.*
McLennan K. S. 1375 Washington boul.
McLennan Wm. E. Rev. Berwyn
McLeod Gordon, 4337 Ellis av.
McLeod John A. 5101 Kimbark av.
McLeod Peter R. 431 S. Oakley av.
McLester George W. Iroquois club
McLoraine F. B. La Grange
McMahan Charles L. 4621 Lake av.
McMahan Robert W. Mrs. 4577 Oaken-
  wald av.
McMahon Andrew J. 3542 Vernon av.
McMahon James A. 500 W. Jackson boul.
  Ill.
McMahon John, 1389 Washington boul.
McMahon J. B. Calumet club. *Chi.,*
  C.A., W.P.
McMahon Mary Miss, The Wellington
McMahon Patrick, 3542 Vernon av.
McMahon S. P. LaGrange
McManus Patrick, 4840 Grand boul.
McMartin Christy Miss, Evanston
McMartin Frank, 1657 W. Adams.
McMaster William I. 915 Fargo av.
McMath James C. 242 Hampden ct.
McMehan David B. 1040 Chase av.
McMichael James G. 569, 51st
McMichael L. D., M. D. 3400 Prairie av.
McMillan Alexander F. 5423 Ridgewood
  ct.
McMillan Anna Miss, 4403 Berkeley av.
McMillan E. J. Miss, 262 Park av.
McMillan E. Erskine, 981 W. Adams
McMillan James, 7721 Emerald av.

McMillan Neil, 464 Bowen av.
McMillan T. W. Mrs. La Grange
McMillan William H. 905 W. Monroe.
McMillan William M. 4403 Berkeley av.
McMillen Carroll S. 4131 Bosworth av.
McMillen William F. Rev. 513 Washington
  boul.
McMillin George W. 6441 Kimbark av.
McMullen David S. Evanston
McMullen D. Y. 303 Lasalle av.
McMullen Frederick B. Evanston
McMullen H. Y. Evanston
McMullen Roger B. Evanston
McMullen William J. 3945 Prairie av.
McMullin Frank R. 729 W. Adams. *Ill.*
McMunn Samuel W. 6059 Jefferson av.
McMurdy Robert, 4853 Kimbark av.
McMurray Albert M. 244, 53d
McMurray George N. 244, 53d. *C. A.*
McMurray G. T. Mrs. 244, 53d
McMurray J. H. Mrs. 15 Scott
McMurray Oscar L. 6441 Greenwood av.
McNab John, Evanston
McNab John, Glen Ellyn
McNab Joseph L. Evanston
McNair Harry M. 4541 Emerald av.
McNally Andrew, 824 North Park av.
  C.A., U.L.
McNally Fred G. 836 North Park av. *C.A.,*
  U.L., W. P.
McNally James, 11 Scott
McNama I. M. Mrs. 6312 Monroe av.
McNamara James H. 988 S. Lawndale av.
McNarney M. Miss, Lakota hotel
McNaughten E. P. 910 Hamilton ct.
McNaughton Guy, 731½ Sedgwick
McNaughton James C. 731½ Sedgwick
McNaughton James N. 731½ Sedgwick
McNaughton P. E. Mrs. Hotel Windermere
McNeal D. W. Dr. 6700 Stewart av.
McNeal Frank, Austin
McNeil Halmer E. jr. 4552 Oakenwald av.
McNeil Justine V. Mrs. 4552 Oakenwald av.
McNeil Malcolm, 448 Lasalle av.
McNeil William, 9 Wisconsin
McNeill Archibald, 3154 Michigan av.
  C. A.
McNeill A. C. Chicago Beach hotel. *C.A.*
McNeill Benjamin F. 715 W. Monroe
McNeill Malcolm Prof. Lake Forest
McNeill Malcom. 4544 Oakenwald av.
McNeill Rivers, Evanston. *Iroq.*
McNeill Thomas H. 925 W. Jackson boul.
  Irq.
McNellis M. 318 Loomis
McNett C. S. Irving Park
McNetton D. Victoria hotel
McNulta John, 5112 East End av. *Chi.*
  U.L.
McNulty Catherine E. Miss, 1234 N.
  Clark
McNulty James H. 1944 Deming ct. *C.A.*
McNulty May E. Miss, 1234 N. Clark
McPherran Edward H. 97, 37th
McPherson J. C. Dr. 2400 Prairie av.
McPherson L. E. 3537 Indiana av.

McPherson S. J. Rev. 2804 Prairie av.
McQuaid Edmund J. 4810 Indiana av.
McQueen Thomas, Elmhurst
McQuiston William E. 3601 Vincennes
  av.
McRae J. D. 645 W. Adams
McRae William Mrs. 735 W. Vanburen
McRae William M. 735 W. Vanburen
McReynolds Geo. S.Virginia hotel. *Chi.*,
  W.P.   Sum. res. Lake Forest, Ill.
·McReynolds M. W. Mrs. 77 Lincoln Park
  boul.
McRoberts William, 3211 Dover
McRoy George G. 4950 Prairie av.
McSchooler E. Berwyn
McShane James C. Lexington hotel. *Irq.*
McTerney Patrick, 1814 Michigan av.
McVeagh Charles F. 575, 46th pl.
McVicker James H. Mrs.1842 Michigan av.
McVoy Eugene J. 440 Lasalle av.
McVoy John Mrs. 440 Lasalle av.
McVoy John A. 440 Lasalle av. *C.A.,U.L.*
McVoy Joseph I. 440 Lasalle av.·
McWhinney Curtis A. 5100 Hibbard av.
McWhinney C. T. 36th ne. cor. Ellis av.
McWhinney Ida Mrs. 5100 Hibbard av.
McWhirter David A. Austin
McWhirter Robert, 4713 Prairie av.
McWilliams Eliza J. Miss, Lake Forest
McWilliams James W. 2573 N. Paulina
McWilliams J. G. 3945 Lake av. *Chi.*,
  C.A.
McWilliams Lafayette,3961Lake av. *U.L.*
McWilliams Mary Miss, 3961 Lake av. ·
McWilliams Roy, 3945 Lake av.
McWilliams S. A. Dr. 3456 Michigan av.
McWilliams Thomas G. 3961 Lake av.
Meacham Carrie O. Mrs. 2458 Michigan
  av.
Meacham F. D. 223 S. Marshfield av. *Ill.*
Meacham George, Glen Ellyn
Meacham G. W. Glen Ellyn
Mead Aaron B. 632 Washington boul.
  U.L.   Sum. res. Charlevoix, Mich.
Mead AgnesR.Miss,632Washington boul.
Mead Clayton B. Berwyn
Mead Emily Miss, 6241 Monroe av.
Mead George A. 1621 Prairie av.
Mead Geo. H. 713 The Plaza
  Sum. res. White Bear, Minn.
Mead Geo. H. Prof. 5536 Madison av.
Mead John G. 3849 Ellis av.
Mead Lillian E. Miss, 4823 Kimbark av.
Mead Linn A. Miss, 6241 Monroe av.
Mead Lydia Miss, Oak Park
Mead Maurice A. 4823 Kimbark av.
Mead Ransom H. 242 Dearborn av.
Mead William G. Mrs. 2971 Prairie av.
Mead Wilson Leroy, 205 Goethe. *C.A,.*
  Un.   Sum. res. Grand Haven, Mich.
Meader John R. 6439 Minerva av.
Meader I. F. Tracy
Meader Martin C. 2660 N. Winchester av.
Meadowcroft Mary C. Mrs. 23 Astor
Meadows Frederick W. Austin
Meads Albert H. 4444 Berkeley av.

Meagher James F. 4205 Grand boul. *Chi.*,
  W.P.
Mealiff Frank H. 7831 Winneconna av.
Meany E. J. Morton Park
Means E. T. 4813 Prairie av.
Means G. R. Mrs. Oak Park
Means John M. 2975 Kenmore av.
Mears Caroline Miss, 345 Ohio
Mears Charles H. Evanston
Mears L. Byron, LaGrange
Mecartney Harry S. Evanston
Mecartney James C. Evanston
Meckling Jonas S. 606 Washington boul.
Mecum Charles H. Evanston. *U.L.*
Medcalfe H. R. Mrs. 637 Fullerton av.
Medill Joseph, 101 Cass. *U.L.*
Meech George A. Morgan Park
Meech William T. Mrs. 6450 Stewart av.
Meek Joseph A. Dr. 6351 Parnell av.
Meek J. W. Dr. 182 Park av.
Meek Laura Law Mrs. 1854 Wellington
Meek S. Mason, 186 Park av. *Ill.*
Meeker Arthur, 2016 Calumet av. *Chi.*,
  W.P.
Meeker Arthur, Hinsdale
Meeker Arthur B. 2107 Calumet av.
Meeker Charles W. 6138 Monroe av. *C.A.*
Meeker George Walker, 135 Astor *Univ.*
Meeker R. D. Mrs. 6950 Butler
Meerhoff Charles E. Dr. 1746 Wright-
  wood av.
Mehlhop F. W. 4528 Lake av.
Mehring Frederick, Evanston
Mehring George,4619 Vincennes av. *C.A.,*
  U.L.
Meier Albert G. 1744 Arlington pl.
Meier John W. Oak Park
Meinel Frank A. 1555 W. Monroe
Meinel Sophia Mrs. 1555 W. Monroe.
Meinel William, 1555 W. Monroe
Meinshausen Otto, 693 North Park av.
Meiselbar Henry, 19 Park av.
Meisner William O. 4102 Newgart av.
Meiswinkel Richard A. 1181 N. Clark
Meitzler G. R. 4403 Greenwood av.
Melander Louis M. 521 Lasalle av.
Melander Silas P. 252 Ontario
Melcher Charles W. LaGrange
Melchior Edward, 363 Mohawk
Meldahl J. Jelsmark, 667 N. Robey
Meldrum Thomas M. 6545 Perry av.
Meleney Geo. B. 4 Aldine sq.
Meleney Henry E. Mrs. 4 Aldine sq.
Melick Walter J. 308 West ct.
Melin O. P. Mrs. Oak Park
Mellinger J. H. Mrs. 917 Walnut
Mellish Ernest J. Dr. 307 Belden av.
Mellor Davis G. 2849 Kenmore av.
Mellor Vivia E. Miss, Riverside
Melody Mary Miss, 447 Belden av.
Melody T. R. 3117 Prairie av.
Meloy Edward S. 4427 Champlain av.
Meloy Harry B. 149 S. Paulina
Meloy Robert B. 149 S. Paulina
Meloy William T. Rev. 149 S. Paulina
Meloy William W. Dr. 149 S. Paulina

Melville Alansing B. Oak Park
Melville Geo. W. Oak Park
Melvin A. S. jr. Dr. Oak Park
Memelsdorf Alex. Dr. 86 Lincoln av.
Memhard John, 1669 W. Monroe
Memory Henry, 411 Huron. *C.A.*
Mendel Edward, 4736 Grand boul.
Mendel Herbert M. 3651 Grand boul.
    Lksd.
Mendal Max, 3651 Grand boul.
Mendelsohn Abram, 21 Scott
Mendelsohn Benjamin E. 4202 Calumet
    av. *Lksd.*
Mendelsohn Jacob, 21 Scott
Mendelsohn Jacob S. 4202 Calumet av.
    Irq., Lksd.
Mendelsohn Joseph J. 799 Pine Grove av.
Mendelsohn Louis, 21 Scott
Mendelsohn Serena Mrs. 2962 Groveland
    av.
Mendelsohn Sigmond, 4202 Calumet av.
Mendelsohn Simon S. 4202 Calumet av.
Mendelsohn Solomon, 511 Fullerton av.
Mendenhall James D. 485, 65th
Mendsen Charles F. Evanston
Mendsen Edward, Evanston
Mendsen John F. 712 Washington boul.
Menefee James T. 397 Superior
Menge Frederick Dr. 154, 42d pl.
Menge Frederick A. 154, 42d pl.
Menn Rudolph Dr. 15 Lincoln av.
Mentzer J. P. 4558 Oakenwald av.
Mercer Arthur, 655 W. Adams. *Ill.*
Mercer Byron, Norwood Park
Mercer Fielding L. 1919 Wrightwood av.
Mercer F. W. Dr. 2540 Prairie av.
Mercer Louis P. Rev. 4539 Ellis av.
Mercer Louis P. jr. 4539 Ellis av.
Merchant John F. Irving Park
Merckle Henry Mrs. 1528 Michigan av.
Meredith James B. 6406 Jefferson av.
Meredith William, 1520 W. Monroe
Meredith William M. Austin
Mergentheim Aaron D. 4740 Prairie av.
    Stan.
Mergentheim B. 3918 Prairie av. *Stan.*
Mergler Marie J. Dr. 2930 Indiana av.
Meriam H. Howard, 498 Fullerton av.
Merigold Wm. A. 3984 Lake av. *C.A.,*
    U.L.
Merimee Edward J. 32 Bryant av.
Merki George, 130 W. Garfield boul.
Merki Louis, 130 W. Garfield boul.
Merle William F. 451 Warren av.
Merrell Henry H. Dr. 1440 W. Monroe
Merrell Wm. M. Mrs. 1440 W. Monroe
Merriam Charles W. 3975 Ellis av.
Merriam D. W. C. 36th ne. cor. Ellis av.
Merriam Joseph W. 4206 Michigan av.
Merriam Mary A. Mrs. Evanston
Merriam T. H. LaGrange
Merriam W. J. Wilmette
Merrick Frederick L. 4318 Greenwood av
    C.A.
Merrick George P. Evanston. *Irq., Univ*
Merrick Levi C. 3741 Grand boul. *W.P.*

Merrick Zella Miss, 3741 Grand boul.
Merrilies C. W. Winnetka
Merrilies John, Lakeside
Merrill Alba W. 3350 Rhodes av.
Merrill Anthony F. 53 Madison Park
Merrill A. B. Mrs. Evanston
Merrill E. L. 2358 Indiana av.
Merrill Fred G. 465 Washington boul.
Merrill George P. 233 S. Leavitt
Merrill George R. Rev. 233 S. Leavitt
Merrill Harry W. Dr. Maywood
Merrill Hattie Miss, Hinsdale
Merrill James S. 4827 Lake av.
Merrill J. C. F. Hinsdale
Merrill M. G. Mrs. 465 Washington boul.
Merrill Stephen M. Rt. Rev. 509 W.
    Monroe
Merrill T. B. Morgan Park
Merrill W. H. jr. 1816 Prairie av. *Univ.,*
    W.P.
Merriman Andrews T. Mrs. Evanston
Merriman Andrews T. jr. Evanston
Merriman C. C. 1910 Surf
Merriman Henry P. Dr. 2239 Michigan av.
Merriman John W. 3753 Prairie av.
Merriman L. Lorenzo, 1723 Roscoe
Merriman William A. Hyde Park hotel.
    Ill.
Merritt Charles J. 201, 36th
Merritt Charles T. Hinsdale
Merritt Eugene L. 4335 Ellis av.
Merritt Frederick, The Plaza
Merritt Walter H. 7811 Winneconna av.
Merritt W. H. 4432 Lake av.
Merryweather A. M. 466 Elm
Merryweather George, 466 Elm. *Chi.*
Mersereau J. D. Highland Park
Mertens Robert J. 7626 Saginaw av.
Merwin P. B. Mrs. 621 Washington boul.
Merwin Samuel, Evanston
Merwin Samuel jr. Evanston
Merz Gottlieb, 646 Lasalle av.
Mesick M. A. Mrs. Lexington hotel
Message John G. Dr. 224 Schiller
Messenger Elizabeth Mrs. 6329 Stewart
    av.
Messenger Harry N. 6329 Stewart av.
Messenger John A. Dr. 6329 Stewart av.
Messenger W. D. Highland Park
Messer Charles, 4409 Greenwood av.
Messer Lucy W. Mrs. 4040 Ellis av.
Messer L. W. 5729 Washington av.
Messer Paul, 4040 Ellis av.
Messersmith George, 1644 Wellington av.
Messick Frederick, 4344 Forrestville av.
Messing Aaron J.Rev.Dr.3708Wabash av.
Messing Henry J. 5229 Indiana av.
Messing Sigmund J. 3708 Wabash av.
Messinger Charles T. 1710 Wellington
Messinger W. D. 548 W. Jackson boul.
Metcalf Edwin S. 6956 Wallace
Metcalf Guido C. S. 6956 Wallace
Metcalf Herbert C. Hotel Windermere.
    U.L.
Metcalf Ira A. 2819 Kenmore av.
Metcalf James I. Palmer house

Metcalf John S. Evanston
Metcalf Merton P. 4025 Indiana av.
Metcalf M. A. Mrs. 4032 Ellis av.
Metcalf Orlando jr. 5344 Greenwood av.
Metcalf Ralph, 3829 Langley av.
Metcalf Thomas, Hotel Windermere
Metcalf Walter B. Dr. 1752 York pl.
Metcalfe Arthur R. Oak Park
Methven Benjamin F. 36th ne. cor. Ellis av.
Mettler I. V. 4544 Lake av.
Mettler John K. LaGrange
Mettler L. Harrison Dr. 4544 Lake av.
Metz H. J. Mrs. 3408 Forest av.
Metzgar George A. Oak Park
Metzger Herman, 1222 Seminary pl.
Metzger William G. Mrs.1269 Washington boul.
Mevelle Charles W. 4019 Vincennes av.
Mevelle Mary C. Mrs. 4019 Vincennes av.
Meyer Abraham, 2009 Prairie av.
Meyer Abraham W. 2964 Groveland av. Stan.
Meyer Albert, 2009 Prairie av. Stan.
Meyer Alexander, 151 S. Winchester av.
Meyer Alice Mrs. 2 Oakland crescent
Meyer Amelia Mrs. 3709 Ellis av.
Meyer Balthasar I. Dr. 60 Fowler
Meyer Carl, 2009 Prairie av.
Meyer Charles E. 8 Fowler
Meyer Charles H. Evanston
Meyer Christian B. 1812 Barry av.
Meyer E. F. 2009 Prairie av. Stan.
Meyer Frederick, 3837 Ellis av.
Meyer Henry W. 2851 N. Paulina
Meyer Herman, 1741 Wrightwood av.
Meyer Herman P. 202 Belden av.
Meyer Isaac, 2964 Groveland av. Stan.
Meyer Jacob, 654 Lasalle av.
Meyer John B. 1812 Barry av.
Meyer John M. 6445 Kimbark av.
Meyer Julius P. 656 Fullerton av.
Meyer J. S. 4597 Oakenwald av.
Meyer Leopold H. 4505 Indiana av. Lksd.
Meyer Louis B. 3139 Vernon av.
Meyer Martin, 3227 Vernon av. Lksd.
Meyer Mary L. Mrs. 71 Maple
Meyer Moses, 392 Dayton
Meyer Moses A. 3253 Vernon av.
Meyer M. A. Mrs. 2009 Prairie av.
Meyer Oscar, 1074 Early av.
Meyer Sigmund, 3139 Vernon av. Lksd.
Meyer William 42 St. James pl.
Meyers Julius R. 68 Madison Park
Meysenburg Edward A. 147 Lincoln Park boul.
Meysenburg Otto W. 141 Astor. Chi. Sum. res. White Oaks, Walworth Co., Wis.
Meysenburg R. C. 141 Astor
Michaelis Richard, 1532 Oakdale av.
Michaelis Walter R. 1532 Oakdale av.
Michaels Isaac A. 4634 Vincennes av.
Michaels Sara D. Miss, 528 Fulton
Michaelsohn George Mrs. 4222 Grand boul.

Michel Ralph S. Dr. 689 N. Robey
Michelet Charles J. Wilmette
Michelet W. E. Dr. Wilmette
Michels Nicholas, 6426 Union av. C.A.
Michelson Albert A. Prof. Hotel Windermere
Michelson Halvor, 62 Fowler
Michener Jas. Hart, Lexington hotel
Michener Wm. W. 4705 Woodlawn av. C.A.
Mida Lee. 4232 Grand boul.
Mida Walter, 4232 Grand boul.
Mida William, 4232 Grand boul.
Middagh Asher F. 7646 Bond av.
Middaugh Henry C. Hinsdale
Middelschulte W. 3122 Prairie av.
Middendorf George, 6032 Kimbark av.
Middlekauff Peter D. 1943 Sheridan rd.
Middleton Ella Miss, 345 Ohio
Middleton James W. Oak Park
Middleton John, Highland Park
Middleton Robert J. 4727 Indiana av.
Middleton Thomas, 2967 Vernon av.
Middleton Thomas S. Dr. 496 Lasalle av.
Middleton William G. 4727 Indiana av.
Midgley John W. 242 Ashland boul.
Midlen Thomas Y. Calumet club. C.A., W.P.
Midler W. Irving, 6501 Monroe av.
Miers Hannah Miss, 3333 Wabash av.
Mies John, 332 W. 59th pl.
Mifflin Charles H. 240, 53d
Migely Fred A. 2430 Prairie av.
Migely Frederick, 2430 Prairie av.
Migely Rudolph E. 2430 Prairie av.
Mighell Ina M. Dr. LaGrange
Mighell Reuben C. 1312 Wrightwood av.
Mihills Merrick A. Highland Park
Miksch Aaron J. 940 W. Monroe
Milan Edward, 5405 Wabash av.
Milan Edward Mrs. 5405 Wabash av.
Milchrist Thomas E. 6 Aldine sq.
Miles Charles L. 882 W. Monroe
Miles F. B. Mrs. 3231 Forest av.
Miles Hazen T. 637 North Park av. Irq.
Miles Hollon F. 228, 53d
Miles J. H. Mrs. 5129 Jefferson av.
Miles Lulu Miss, 1854 Oakdale av.
Miles Samuel T. 148 Dearborn av.
Miles Thomas D. 303 Ashland boul.
Miles Thomas D. 5129 Jefferson av.
Miley George W. 583 W. Congress
Miley Levi E. Dr. 868 Warren av.
Milhening Frank, Evanston
Milhening Joseph, Evanston
Millar Allan P. 326 Superior. Un.
Millar Earl B. 326 Superior
Millard Addison, Evanston
Millard Everett Lee, Highland Park
Millard E. Mrs. Park Ridge
Millard Frank R. 1344 Washington boul.
Millard George M. 3719 Vincennes av. C.A.
Millard Martha W. Mrs. 4546 Oakenwald av.

Millard Roxanna Mrs. 3719 Vincennes av.
Millard S. M. Highland Park. *U.L.*
Millard William, Highland Park
Millard W. K. Irving Park
Miller Abner J. 6710 Stewart av.
Miller Adam Dr. 172 Ashland boul.
Miller Adam, 1720 Deming pl.
Miller Adolph C. Prof. 6018 Stony Island av. *Univ.*
Miller Albert, 649 Fullerton av.
Miller Albert, 892, 60th
Miller Alfred P. 6649 Stewart av.
Miller Amos C. Riverside. *Univ.*
Miller August W. 865 S. Kedzie av.
Miller A. Mrs. 3348 Rhodes av.
Miller A. B. Mrs. Hotel Del Prado
Miller A. R. Mrs. Evanston
Miller Benjamin L. Evanston
Miller Brice A. 46 Roslyn pl.
Miller B. C. 936 W. Adams. *C.A.*
Miller Catherine Mrs. 1528 Kenmore av.
Miller Carlos, 440 W. 65th
Miller Charles Allen, 3130 Groveland av.
Miller Charles B. 3122 Calumet av.
Miller Charles F. 591 Cleveland av.
Miller Charles F. 2124 Michigan av.
Miller Charles J. 332 Lasalle av.
Miller Charles J. Chicago Beach hotel
Miller Charles K. 544 N. State. *U.L.*
Miller Charles L. 3717 Langley av. *Stan.*
Miller Charles P. Oak Park
Miller Charles P. 2941 Calumet av.
Miller Christopher, Oak Park
Miller Clara F. Mrs. 4813 Prairie av.
Miller Clinton W. Mrs. 601 The Plaza
Miller C. J. Miss, Hyde Park hotel
Miller David W. 1544 Windsor av.
Miller De Laskie Dr. 110 Astor
Miller Edgar M. 6351 Greenwood av.
Miller Edward W. 396 Superior. *C.A.*
Miller Ellen S. Mrs. 295 Belden av.
Miller Emanuel D. 1831 Arlington pl.
Miller Emily Huntington Mrs. Evanston
Miller Eva Stewart Mrs. 2339 N. Hermitage av.
Miller E. B. Mrs. Oak Park
Miller E. H. 3634 Michigan av. *Cal.*, *W.P.*
Miller E. V. Miss, The Arizona
Miller Floyd, 1746 Wrightwood av.
Miller Frank E. Evanston. *C.A.*
Miller Frank Justus Prof. 5830 Washington av.
Miller Fred, 1720 Deming pl.
Miller Fred C. Evanston
Miller F. A. Lexington hotel
Miller George, 2978 Prairie av.
Miller George F. 1528 Kenmore av.
Miller George H. Evanston
Miller George L. 295 Belden av.
Miller George W. Dr. 6634 Parnell av.
Miller Grace E. Miss, Evanston
Miller Harry L. 6456 Monroe av.
Miller Henry F. Elmhurst
Miller Hiram•G. Dr. Evanston
Miller Hubert F. 4749 Calumet av.
40

Miller Humphreys H. C. Evanston. *U.L.*
Miller Isaac H. 4547 Ellis av.
Miller James A. Lake Forest. *U.L.*
Miller James C. 4200 Vincennes av.
Miller James E. Mrs. 3122 Calumet av.
Miller James H. 5427 Washington av. *C.A.*
Miller John, 236 Lincoln Park boul.
Miller John B. River Forest
Miller John C. Oak Park
Miller John G. 452 Dearborn av. *U.L.*, *W.P.*
Miller John H. 804 W. Adams.
Miller John J. Austin
Miller John P. 10 Lane ct.
Miller John S. 4810 Kenwood av. *Chi.*, *U.L.*
Miller Joseph J. Oak Park. *C.A.*
Miller J. D. Oak Park
Miller Lanson D. Austin
Miller Lizette Mrs. 3146 Calumet av.
Miller Louis K. 406, 36th pl. *Stan.*
Miller Lula Miss, Riverside
Miller L. P. Mrs. 5556 Monroe av.
Miller Mary Jean Miss, 2535 Prairie av.
Miller Maynard, Chicago Beach hotel. *Un.*
Miller Milton B. 3122 Calumet av.
Miller M. J. Mrs. 4627 Lake av.
Miller Philip C. 453 Englewood av.
Miller Ralph, Glencoe
Miller Richard O. 5126 Washington av.
Miller Robert B. 3228 Lake Park av. *C.A.*
Miller Roswell, 2959 Michigan av. *Chi.*
Miller R. B. Dr. 170 Oakwood boul.
Miller Sidney W. 6359 Yale
Miller S. C. Oak Park
Miller Thomas, 4237 Grand boul.
Miller Thomas, Riverside. *Irq.*
Miller Thomas E. 569 Lasalle av.
Miller Thomas H. 2439 Wabash av.
Miller Thomas H. jr. 2439 Wabash av.
Miller Thomas L. Austin
Miller Thomas S. Rev. Oak Park
Miller Truman W. Dr. 1071 N. Clark. *Un.*
Miller T. F. Highland Park
Miller Waldo F. 322 Warren av.
Miller Walter E. 17, 40th
Miller Walter H. 551 Englewood av.
Miller William D. Revere house
Miller William G. 254 Warren av.
Miller William G. Evanston
Miller William H. Highland Park
Miller William W. 3336 Michigan av. Sum. res. Phillips, Wis.
Miller W. B. 4424 St. Lawrence av.
Millerd Norman A. Rev. 1153 S. Lawndale av.
Millet Lewis J. 77 Lincoln Park boul.
Millhauser Herman J. 4940 Vincennes av.
Millican H. Barrie Dr. 6205 Woodlawn av.
Milligan Charles F. Victoria hotel
Milligan E. J. 187 Oakwood boul.
Milligan George D. 4356 Oakenwald av.
Milligan George E. 2667 N. Lincoln. *C.A.*
Millikan Allan F. River Forest

Millikan Robert A. 6237 Monroe av.
Milliken H. T. Mrs. Edgebrook
Millis Henry L. Oak Park
Milloy John, 14 Warren av.
Mills Abbott L. 4826 Greenwood av. *U.L.*
Mills Albert J. 6321 Monroe av.
Mills Daniel W. 1510 Washington boul. *Ill.*
Mills George F. 684 Winthrop av.
Mills George P. Evanston
Mills Harry, 134, 47th
Mills Harry I. Wilmette
Mills Henry, 4344 Oakenwald av.
Mills Herbert S. Austin
Mills H. M. 1414 W. Congress
Mills James E. Mrs. 870 Warren av.
Mills John R. Evanston
Mills J. M. 3152 Vernon av.
Mills Luther Laflin, Graceland av. ne. cor. Clarendon av.
Mills Mary J. Mrs. Wilmette
Mills Matthew, Graceland av. ne. cor. Clarendon av.
Mills M. E. 4344 Oakenwald av.
Mills S. B. 367 Park av.
Mills W. M. 6149 Monroe av.
Millspaugh C. F. Dr. 5748 Madison av.
Milnamow John T. Dr. 1613 Park av.
Milne James H. 3248 Groveland av.
Milner Duncan C. Rev. 407, 33d
Milner D. E. Mrs. 4353 Oakenwald av.
Milner James T. 34 Ogden av. *C.A.*, *W.P.*
Milner Louisa A. Miss, 5465 Washington av.
Milner Paul, 403, 33d
Milnor Lloyd, 441 Elm. *Chi.*, *C.A.*, *W.P.*
Milsted Thomas G. 28 Linden ct.
Minaker Wilham Dr. 6351 Stewart av.
Minard A. J. Hotel Windermere
Minard Seth A. 7621 Union av.
Minchin Thomas, 57 E. Pearson
Minchrod S. 3127 Michigan av.
Miner Frank L. 3842 Langley av.
Miner Fred M. 4421 Ellis av.
Miner George B. Riverside
Miner H. H. Chicago Athletic assn.
Miner Imogene S. Mrs. 922 W. Jackson boul.
Miner James A. 4421 Ellis av. *Irq.*
Miner Maurice A. 6446 Lexington av.
Miner Noyes B. Riverside
Miner Numa L. Miss, 6239 Monroe av.
Miner William H. 6137 Monroe av.
Miner William R. 6239 Monroe av.
Miniter Michael C. 12 Gilpin pl.
Minkler Warden S. Mrs. 172 Ashland boul.
Minor Anderson, LaGrange
Minor A. C. Mrs. Evanston
Minshall W. E. Tower hotel
Minzesheimer L. F. 3601 Vincennes av. *Lksd.*
Mitchel Otto W. 4353 Lake av. *C.A.*
Mitchell Abraham, 538 Byron
Mitchell Abram, 5340 Cornell av.
Mitchell Andrew W. 4901 Vincennes av.
Mitchell Anna Belle Miss, Hinsdale

Mitchell Annie B. Miss. 2954 Prairie av.
Mitchell Arthur J. 717 W. Adams. *Ill.*
Mitchell A. Ravinia
Mitchell Charles F. 609, 46th
Mitchell Charles H. 575 W. Congress
Mitchell Charles R. Irving Park
Mitchell Clifford Dr. 6030 Woodlawn av.
Mitchell D. J. Hinsdale
Mitchell Edward G. Hinsdale
Mitchell Edward J. 3736 Forest av.
Mitchell E. W. Hyde Park hotel
Mitchell Frederick R. 6643 Stewart av.
Mitchell F. E. Evanston
Mitchell F. H. LaGrange
Mitchell George H. Hinsdale
Mitchell George R. 5155 Cornell av.
Mitchell Grant, Hinsdale
Mitchell G. W. LaGrange
Mitchell Harley B. LaGrange
Mitchell Herbert S. LaGrange
Mitchell H. M. 4834 Michigan av.
Mitchell Jenny Mrs. 4427 Champlain av.
Mitchell John J. 5012 Woodlawn av. *Chi.*, *U.L.* Sum. res. Lake Geneva, Wis.
Mitchell Jonathan C. 3838 Lake av.
Mitchell J. Sidney Mrs. 2954 Prairie av. Sum. res. Nantucket, Mass.
Mitchell Leeds, 2954 Prairie av.
Mitchell Lewis B. 50 Astor. *U.L.*
Mitchell Lewis H. 163 S. Robey
Mitchell Louise Mrs. 4359 Prairie av.
Mitchell Lucien C. 3020 Indiana av.
Mitchell Malcom C. 3157 Calumet av. *Cal.*, *Chi.*
Mitchell Mary Mrs. 4917 Greenwood av.
Mitchell Morris, 3524 Wabash av. Sum. res. Spring Lake, Mich.
Mitchell Nancy D. Miss, 3020 Indiana av.
Mitchell Nancy J. Mrs. 1623 Fulton
Mitchell N. Adelaide Miss, Hinsdale
Mitchell Robert C. 163 S. Robey
Mitchell Sidney, 2954 Prairie av.
Mitchell Stafford T. Dr. 2720 N. Hermitage av.
Mitchell Thomas B. Dr. 348 S. Campbell av.
Mitchell Thomas H. 6454 Lexington av.
Mitchell Walter B. 2007 Indiana av. *Cal.*, *U.L.*
Mitchell Will A. Austin
Mitchell William, 1199 Wilton av.
Mitchell William H. 2004 Calumet av. *W.P.*
Mitchell Wm. K. 4935 Washington Park ct.
Mix Ira J. 3251 Indiana av.
Mix James T. 152, 25th. *Un.*, *U.L.*
Mix Mary Mrs. Hinsdale
Mize Eliza Mrs. 907 Evanston av.
Mize William J. 3504 Sheridan rd.
Moak Will B. 6924 Stewart av.
Moberly E. E. 3650 Michigan av. *C.A.*
Moberly John H. 3923 Vincennes av.
Moderwell Erastus C. The Hampden
Modine Edward, Austin
Modjeski Ralph, 1838 Michigan av. *U.L.*

Moe Bernt, 48 Scott
Moe Caroline W. Mrs. 1230 Wrightwood av.
Moe George Dr. 2106 W. Monroe
Moeller Carl C. 402 Lasalle av.
Moeller E. C. River Forest
Moerdyke Peter Rev. 446 S. Marshfield av.
Moffat F. S. Morgan Park
Moffatt Marcia Miss, 817 Washington boul.
Moffett A. S. Mrs. The Arizona
Moffett E. D. Mrs. The Winamac
Moffett James A. 29 Woodland Park. C.A., Irq.
Mogg Clayton W. 539 S. Normal Parkway
Mogg J. J. 539 S. Normal Parkway
Mogg Marion F. 4358 Berkeley av.
Mogg Millard E. 7143 Harvard av.
Mohor J. C. Hinsdale
Mohr Albert, 7305 Bond av.
Mohr Carl M. 21 Hampden ct.
Mohr John, 707 N. Robey
Mohr Joseph, 707 N. Robey. C.A.
Mohr William J. 3255 Vernon av.
Moll Carl, 1427 Washington boul. U.L.
Moll J. B. 318 Belden av.
Molloy J. P. 4626 Prairie av.
Monahan Edward J. 1668 W. Monroe
Monahan John J. 507 W. 79th
Monash Charles P. 4418 Berkeley av. Lksd.
Moncrief John W. Mrs. 5717 Monroe av.
Mondschein C. A. 3919 Prairie av.
Monett Elliot T. 374 Dearborn av.
Money W. H. Mrs. 452 Warren av.
Monfort Catherine Mrs. 230 W. 65th
Monheimer Isa, 4058 Grand boul. Stan., W.P.
Monheimer Levi, 3301 Michigan av. Stan.
Monheimer L. Mrs. 3252 Wabash av.
Monheimer Milton, 3252 Wabash av.
Monin Louis C. 5540 Michigan av.
Moninger Josephine C. Mrs. 2820 N. Paulina
Monk John S. Irving Park
Monnett Fletcher, Evanston
Monrad J. H. Winnetka
Monroe George G. Dr. 712, 69th
Monroe George S. 776 Touhy av.
Monroe Harriet Miss, The Plaza
Monroe Henry S. 510 The Plaza
Monroe Jo n, 6748 Perry av.
Monroe Lucy Miss, The Plaza
Monroe Nelson, 4313 Ellis av.
Monroe William F. 318 S. Marshfield av. C.A.
Monroe William S. 55 Astor
Montague Gilbert Mrs. 4553 Ellis av.
Montgomery Charles P. 3424 Vernon av.
Montgomery Edward M. 4114 Ellis av.
Montgomery Frank H. Dr. 5748 Woodlawn av.
Montgomery Frederick D. 559 Dearborn av. C.A. Sum. res. Delavan, Wis.
Montgomery F. M. 3436 South Park av.
Montgomery George F. 5413 Calumet av.

Montgomery George W. 705 Pullman bldg. Cal., Chi., C.A., Un., W.P.
Montgomery Hugh W. 424 Elm. C.A.
Montgomery H. M. S. 4729 Woodlawn av.
Montgomery James Dr. 351 Chicago av.
Montgomery John A. 1495 W. Monroe
Montgomery John R. 425 Lasalle av. Univ.
Montgomery J. A. Rev. LaGrange
Montgomery Liston H. Dr. 351 Chestnut
Montgomery Palmer A. Highland Park. U.L.
Montgomery W. A. D. Dr. 180 N. State
Montgomery W. T. Dr. 567 W. Congress. Ill.
Mooar J. C. Mrs. River Forest
Moody Flora Mrs. 1312 Wrightwood av.
Moody Frank A. 777 Washington boul.
Moody John A. 4404 Champlain av. Univ.
Moody L n R. Miss, 777 Washington boul. illia
Moody Mollie E. Miss, 777 Washington boul.
Moody Samuel B. LaGrange
Moody William V. 5488 East End av.
Moog David, 3928 Prairie av. Lksd.
Moon B. Frederick, 4168 Drexel boul.
Moon Sampson W. 5409 Calumet av.
Mooney Frank A. 3540 Ellis av.
Mooney John W. 202 Cass
Mooney William H. 3540 Ellis av.
Mooney William R. 286, 42d
Moore Abram J. Dr. 808 Wilson av.
Moore Addison W. 5827 Kimbark av.
Moore Alexander P. 8 Aldine sq.
Moore Arthur L. 2734 Prairie av.
Moore Birney J. Evanston U.L.
Moore Carlton Wood, Evanston
Moore Charles J. 386 Dearborn av.
Moore Clarence E. 8 Aldine sq.
Moore Clarence W. 5731 Monroe av.
Moore C. M. Hotel Del Prado
Moore Daniel G. Dr. 643 N. Hoyne av.
Moore David Mrs. 3424 Rhodes av.
Moore Edward E. Dr. 2278 Kenmore av.
Moore Edward F. 3124 Prairie av.
Moore Edwin White, Winnetka
Moore Eliakim H. Prof. 5538 Washington av.
Moore Emory B. Austin
Moore Francis S. 8 Aldine sq.
Moore Frank A. B. 675 Winthrop av.
Moore Frank J. 390 S. Oakley av.
Moore Frederick W. 4402 Greenwood av.
Moore George Albert, Evanston
Moore George B. 3605 Prairie av. C.A.
Moore George E, 2734 Prairie av.
Moore George E. Morton Park
Moore George H. Evanston. U.L.
Moore Gurdon G. 113 Cass. Un.
Moore Helen A. Miss, 2734 Prairie av.
Moore Henry E. Wilmette
Moore James, Evanston
Moore James B. Winnetka
Moore James Hobart, Hotel Metropole. Cal., Chi., C.A., W.P.
Moore James H. 4433 Greenwood av. U.L.

Moore James J. 408 Chestnut. *C.A.*
Moore James S. Riverside
Moore Jennie A. Miss, 3639 Grand boul.
Moore Jesse C. Evanston
Moore John, 6510 Yale
Moore John F. 390 S. Oakley av.
Moore John G. 952 W. Garfield boul.
Moore John James, 4433 Greenwood av.
Moore John R. 2601 Wabash av.
Moore John W. 3905 Vincennes av.
Moore Joseph L. Morton Park
Moore Josiah Mrs. Lake Forest
Moore Julian C. Oak Park
Moore J. H. Highland Park
Moore J. H. Hotel Del Prado
Moore J. J. 4433 Greenwood av.
Moore Leonard E. River Forest
Moore Lewis T. 4403 Lake av.
Moore L. C. 4118 Ellis av.
Moore Malcomb T. Dr. Jefferson Park
Moore M. C. Mrs. 399, 33d
Moore M. H. Mrs. 5400 Ellis av.
Moore Nathaniel, 2278 Kenmore av.
Moore N. G. Oak Park. *U.L.*
Moore Orin Mrs. Evanston
Moore Robert C. 4405 Lake av.
Moore Rose A. Miss, Evanston
Moore Samuel R. 6556 Butler
Moore Sarah B. Mrs. 30 Walton pl.
Moore Silas M. 4800 Kimbark av.
Moore Stewart H. 6801 Perry av.
Moore S. M. 4800 Kimbark av. *U.L.*
Moore S. M. Dr. Avenue house, Evanston
Moore Thomas C. Evanston
Moore Thornton L. 6501 Kimbark av.
Moore T. Mrs. Evanston
Moore Walter H. Austin
Moore Will H. 5132Washington av. *U.L.*, *W.P.*
Moore William A. Morton Park
Moore William C. 4333 Evans av.
Moore William H. 95 Evanston av.
Moore William H.2922 Michigan av. *Cal.*, *Chi.*, *W.P.*
Moore William H. 4419 Champlain av.
Moore William J. 1601 W. Adams
Moore William J. 5400 Ellis av.
Moore Wyllys Dr. The Hampden
Moorehead Thomas W. 4532 Lake av. *C.A.*
Moorhead E. L. Dr. 474 Ashland boul.
Moorhouse Sybil Miss, 3741 Grand boul.
Moorhouse William H. 3741 Grand boul.
Moorhouse William R. 406, 36th pl. *Cal.*, *W.P.*
Moos B. Mrs. 1812 Oakdale av.
Moos Joseph B. 1814 Oakdale av.
Moos Julius, 225 Dearborn av.
Mora A. R. Park Ridge
Moran Harry, 707, 49th
Moran K. Mrs. 707, 49th
Moran Thomas A. Judge, 4710 Vincennes av. *Chi.*, *Irq.*
Moran Thomas W. 4710 Vincennes av. *C.A.*

Morava John, LaGrange. *C.A.*
Morava Wensel, 5621 Monroe av.
    Sum. res. Lake Geneva, Wis.
Mordaunt Frank S. Victoria hotel
Morden William J. Mrs. 1508 Michigan av.
More Clair E. 6021 Monroe av.
More R. Wilson, 107, 37th
Morehead J. M. Chicago Beach hotel
Morehouse C. S. 4409 Greenwood av.
Morehouse Frederick B. 4719 Kenwood av.
Morehouse Louis P. 4710 Kenwood av.
Morehouse M. J. Hyde Park hotel
Morey Albert E. Oak Park
Morey Anna M. Mrs. Oak Park
Morey Arthur G. 642 Pine Grove av.
Morey F. E. LaGrange
Morey Henry C. Mrs. 542W.Jackson boul.
Morey R. E. Mrs. 4326 Greenwood av.
Morford Thomas T. Riverside. *C.A.*,*Irq.*, *U.L.*
Morgan Ada B. Dr. Tracy
Morgan Anna Miss, 3834 Lake av.
Morgan Arthur M. Evanston
Morgan A. C. Highland Park. *C.A.*
Morgan Charles Dr. 3500 Ellis av.
Morgan C. P. Mrs. 3506 Lake av.
Morgan Elisha, Highland Park
Morgan F. W. 1093 Washington boul. *C.A.*
Morgan George W. LaGrange
Morgan G. Cadogan, 389 W. Adams
Morgan G. C. jr. North Shore hotel
Morgan Harriet Miss, 5218 Jefferson av.
Morgan H. A. 6565 Yale
Morgan James, 3100 Groveland av.
Morgan James Mrs. 5200 East End av.
Morgan James F. Austin
Morgan John A. 636 Englewood av.
Morgan John R. 4024 Michigan Terrace
Morgan Kendrick E. 1801 Barry av. *C.A.*
Morgan Mary M. Mrs. 3213 Wabash av.
Morgan Otho H. Capt. Highland Park. *C.A.*, *U.L.*
Morgan Platt M. Evanston
Morgan Richard, 480 W. Madison
Morgan Sidney S. Evanston
Morgan T. Herbert, 2595 N. Ashland av.
Morgan Wilfred R. 40 Loomis
Morgan William, 5218 Jefferson av.
Morgan William A. Lake Forest
Morgan William E., M.D. 2909 Groveland av.
Morgan William H. 507 W. Adams
Morgan William R. Berwyn
Morgan William T. 379 Superior
Morgan W. C. Greenwood Inn, Evanston
Morgan W. J. 6500 Ellis av.
Morganroth George, 4430 Prairie av.
Morganroth Jos. H. 4331 Forrestville av.
Morganroth N. 382 Oakwood boul.
Morgenthau George Dr. 3327 Calumet av.
Morgenthau Lewis, 3327 Calumet av.
Morgenthau Milton, 3327 Calumet av.
Morgenthau Selma Miss, 3327 Calumet av.

Morgenthau Sidney, 3327 Calumet av.
Morier Edmund, 531 Greenleaf av.
Morison J. P. Dr. 2960 Michigan av.
Moritz C. M. Mrs. 678 Sedgwick
Morley Alverson E. 736 W. 64th
Morley Albert J. 4860 Washington av.
Morley F. C. 1227 W. Adams
Morley John H. Morton Park
Morley Robert L. 869 Winthrop av.
Morley William R. Wilmette
Morper John C. 395 Evanston av.
Morrell Edward E. Oak Park
Morrill Allan A. 5209 Kimbark av. C.A.
    S m. res. Twin Hills, East Kingston,
    NuH.
Morrill Charles A. 404 Belden av. C.A.
Morrill Charles E. 275, 53d. U.L., W.P.
Morrill De Witt C. 1842 Aldine av.
Morrill Donald L. 1807 Arlington pl. C.A.
Morrill Frederick K. 2907 Groveland av.
    C.A.
Morrill John B. Avenue house, Evanston
Morrill John W. LaGrange
Morrill William M. 387 Oakwood boul.
Morris Charles, 4429 Greenwood av.
Morris Charles E. Evanston
Morris C. W. Berwyn
Morris C. W. Granada hotel
Morris Edward, 4500 Michigan av. Stan.
    Sum. res. "Grey Rock," Dartford, Wis.
Morris Ernest A. 3183 Malden
Morris E. C. The Ontario
Morris E. E. Evanston
Morris Frank M. 6247 Monroe av. C.A.
Morris Fred. G. 780 N. Park av.
Morris Frederick T. 2486 N. Paulina
Morris Gardner, Oak Park
Morris Henry, 3104 Calumet av.
Morris Henry, 3756 Indiana av.
Morris Henry C. 4442 Grand boul.
Morris Horace S. Edgebrook
Morris H. I. Highland Park
Morris Ira N. 4425 Drexel boul.
Morris Isaac R. 1619 Roscoe
Morris I. O. 4233 Prairie av.
Morris Jacob, Leland hotel. Lksd.
Morris James L. 1034 W. Jackson boul.
Morris John, 4442 Grand boul.
Morris John, Evanston
Morris John Little Dr. 818 The Plaza
Morris Joseph, 5342 Washington av.
Morris Joseph O. Evanston
Morris Louis, 3104 Calumet av. Lksd.
Morris Louis, 3756 Indiana av.
Morris L. Coffin Mrs. 6425 Monroe av.
Morris Miles H. 1932 Deming pl.
Morris Nelson, 2453 Indiana av. Stan.
Morris R. N. Dr. 346 Sunnyside av.
Morris Seymour, 5342 Washington av.
Morris Thomas G. Oak Park
Morris T. 2978 Prairie av.
Morris William D. 1930 Deming pl.
Morris W.George, 1356 Washington boul.
Morrison Anna L. Miss, 4740 Kimbark
    av.
Morrison Arthur J. 3987 Drexel boul.

Morrison Charles E. 4024 Ellis av. C.A.
Morrison Clyde A, 3950 Prairie av.
Morrison David, Highland Park
Morrison E. W. 225 Dearborn av.
Morrison Franc C. Miss, 472, 42d
Morrison F. W. Berwyn
Morrison G. H. Mrs. Winnetka
Morrison James H. Oak Park
Morrison John C. 299, 53d
Morrison John W. 3950 Prairie av.
Morrison Lorenzo, 3534 Lake av.
Morrison M. Eugene, 350 Burling
Morrison Paul, Hotel Luzerne
Morrison Richard W. 3551 Ellis av.
Morrison R. C. 338 Oakwood boul.
Morrison R. V. 338 Oakwood boul.
Morrison Theo.N. Rev. 260 Ashland boul.
Morrison William H. Mrs. 225 Dearborn
    av.
Morrison Wm. M. 3704 Elmwood ct.
Morrison W. Clifton house
Morrison W. R. 508 Fullerton av.
Morrisson James W. 3957 Ellis av. C.A.
Morrisson Robert Mrs. 3957 Ellis av.
Morron John R. 4919 Washington av.
    C.A.
Morrow Arthur W. Dr. Hinsdale
Morrow Charles B. 879 W. Jackson boul.
Morrow Charles W. Dr. 6323 Ingleside av.
Morrow J. B. 2764 N. Hermitage av.
Morrow Louis R. 1722 York pl.
Morrow Robert Mrs. 1722 York pl.
Morrow Robert J. 1076 Winthrop av.
Morrow William H. 2927 Indiana av.
Morse Abbie C. Miss, Evanston
Morse Albert A. Evanston
Morse Arthur M. 727 Fullerton av.
Morse A. S. Mrs. 25, 46th
Morse Bert, 595 Dearborn av.
Morse Charles F. 638 Pine Grove av.
Morse Charles H. Mrs. Evanston
Morse Charles H. 4804 Greenwood av.
    Chi., U.L.
Morse Charles H. jr. 4804 Greenwood av.
Morse Charles J. Evanston
Morse Clarence T. Kenilworth. Univ.
Morse Edward B. Oak Park
Morse Edward L. 3569 Rhodes av.
Morse Eliza R. Dr. 4337 Berkeley av.
Morse Ella F. Mrs. Evanston
Morse Elmira Miss, Evanston
Morse Eugene S. Mrs. Longwood
Morse Frank L. 393 Warren av.
Morse Harold Rev. 2340 Calumet av.
Morse Jay C. Wheaton. Chi.
Morse Jessie Miss, 4948 Woodlawn av.
Morse John W. 4463 Lake av.
Morse Joseph L. Evanston
Morse Kate Miss, 4948 Woodlawn av.
Morse Ransom J. 595 Dearborn av.
Morse Sara A. Mrs. 217½ Belden av.
Morse S. F. B. Hotel Del Prado
Morse Will R. 3953 Michigan av.
Morse W. D. 595 Dearborn av.
Morse W. E. Oak Park
Morsman J. J. 2724 Michigan av. C.A.

Mortenson Jacob, Oak Park
Mortimer Chas. J. 1271 Washington boul.
Mortimer William E. 1271 Washington boul.
Mortimer William H.1565 W. Monroe. *Ill.*
Morton Caroline Miss, 4917 Washington av.
Morton Charles M. Oak Park
Morton Edward C. Dr..6801 Union av.
Morton Evan J. Mayfair
Morton F. B. Mrs. 2968 Indiana av.
Morton George, Riverside
Morton Jay, 4414 Oakenwald av.
Morton Joy, 15 Groveland Park. *Chi., Irq*
Morton Mandred, 3139 Michigan av.
Morton-Mandred A. 2968 Indiana av.
Morton Mark, 4523 Greenwood av. *Chi.*
Morton M. J. Mrs. 36th ne. cor. Ellis av.
Morton Paul, 4917 Washington av. *Chi.*
Moseback William, 2333 Michigan av. *U.L.*
Moseley A. B. Mrs. Evanston
Moseley Carleton, Highland Park
Moseley George D. Avenue house, Evanston.
Mosely George H. 4830 Langley av.
Mosely Thomas C. 4830 Langley av.
Moser George W. Oak Park
Moses Adolph, 4139 Drexel boul. *Irq., Lksd., Stan.*
Moses Albert, 3732 Langley av.
Moses Charles, 2511 Wabash av.
Moses Charles A. LaGrange
Moses Eli, 2511 Wabash av..
Moses H. Mrs. 2511 Wabash av.
Moses Isaac S. Rabbi, 4553 Oakenwald av. *Lksd.*
Moses Joseph W. 5482 Greenwood av.
Mosher Ida A. Mrs. 974 W. Adams
Mosley Charles E. 135 Lincoln Park boul.
Moss Edith Helen Miss, 4700 Greenwood av.
Moss Jesse L. Lake Forest, *Chi.*
Moss Julia L. Miss, Lake Forest
Moss Leopold, Oakland hotel. *Lksd.*
Moss Meyer H. 3145 Prairie av. *Lksd.*
Moss Monroe T. 277, 43d.
Moss R. E. 3455 Prairie av.
Moss Sol C. 3104 Calumet av.
Moss Wm. Lathrop, 4700 Greenwood av.
Mosser Marie L. Miss, 236 S. Oakley av.
Mossler Israel L. 4531 Vincennes av.
Mossler R. Mrs. 4531 Vincennes av.
Mossler S. 3226 Prairie av.
Moth M. J., M. D. 3438 Indiana av.
Moth Richard S. Winnetka
Mothershead Alvin M. 536 Orchard
Motley Holcombe H. 4200 Michigan av.
Motlong Effie Miss, Austin
Mott Clinton, 6412 Greenwood av.
Mott Edgar W. Berwyn
Mott E. H. Mrs. 2421 Indiana av.
Mott John M. 6106 Woodlawn av.
Mott J. M. Mrs. North Shore hotel
Mott Robins S. 4298 N. Clark

Moulding Sarah Mrs. 957 N. Clark.
Moulding Thomas C. 5903 Prairie av.
Moulton Addie Mrs. 533 W. Jackson boul.
Moulton C. L. Glen Ellyn
Moulton Don A. 43 Cedar. *Un., U.L.*
Moulton Frank I. 4927 Madison av. *U.L.*
Moulton Garland, 2119 Calumet av.
Moulton George M. 2119 Calumet av. *C.A., U.L.*
Moulton James G. 429 Center
Moulton Richard G. Prof. Hotel Windermere
Moulton Thomas O. Evanston
Moulton William A. 5 Aldine sq.
Moulton William B. The Tudor
Moulton William C. 440 N. State
Mountain John Mrs. 409 Huron
Mountz Silas W. 1213 Seminary pl.
Moury L. C. 2124 Michigan av.
Mowat A. Mrs. Oak Park
Mowatt James, 4812 Vincennes av.
Mower E. B. 5417 Jefferson av.
Moxley Perry A. Mrs. 15 S. Seeley av.
Moxley William J. 445 W. Congress. *C.A., Ill.*
Moyer Ellen Mrs. 434 W. Adams
Moyer H. Clayton, 541 W. Jackson boul.
Moyer H. N. Dr. 434 W. Adams
Moyer H. P. 374 Dearborn av.
Moyer Levi N. Wilmette
Moyer M. N. 541 W. Jackson boul.
Moyer George A. L. 55 Madison Park. *U.L.*
Moyer W. Mrs. 434 W. Adams
Moyses Emanuel, 501, 42d pl. *Lksd.*
Mudd Frank X. Austin
Mudge Daniel Archibald, Avenue house, Evanston. *Chi.*
Muehleisen Robert, 5349 Michigan av.
Muehlke Charles V. 966 Pratt av.
Mueller Anna Mrs. 212, 33d
Mueller A. O. 4412 Ellis av.
Mueller-Fred C. 70 Ewing pl.
Mueller Gustav A. 803 Pine Grove av.
Mueller Herman, 221 Pine Grove av.
Mueller Hermann, 621 Cleveland av.
Mueller Oscar, 485 Belden av.
Mueller Oscar F. 778 Sedgwick
Mueller Valentine, 1239 Sheridan rd.
Mueller William, 3118 Calumet av.
Mueller William jr. The Winamac. *C.A., W.P.*
Mueller William F. C. 2348 N. Ashland av.
Muench Emma Mrs. 436 Lasalle av.
Muench Fred, 461 Lasalle av.
Muench Louis, 647 Fullerton av.
Muggley Harry H. 1012 W. Garfield boul.
Mugler George A. 710 N. California av.
Muhlke H. C. 297 N. State
Muhlke Joseph H. 299 N. State
Muhr Frank Mrs. 5482 Greenwood av.
Muir James B. 844 W. Adams
Muir John, 4596 Oakenwald av. *C.A.*
Muir John T. 3605 Wabash av.
Muir S. E. Mrs. 2802 Michigan av.
Mulcahey James McD. Mrs. 84 Bryant av.

Mulcahy F. J. 2432 Prairie av.
Muldoon John J. Dr. 277 Superior
Mulfinger Julius A. Rev. 200 Center
Mulfinger J. Leonard Dr. 963 W. Jackson
  boul.
Mulford Anna R. Mrs. 30 Aldine sq.
Mulford A. H. 166, 51st
Mulford Edward M. jr. 2826 N. Ashland
  av.
Mulford Leonard S. 745 Pine Grove av.
Mulford Mary L. Mrs. Evanston
Mulford M. A. Mrs. 166, 51st
Mullaney Martin, 719 W. Monroe
Mullaney T. F. 502 W. Adams
Mullen James, 4446 Greenwood av.
Mullen James J. 3320 Calumet av.
Mullen Patrick L. Lake Forest
Mullen Timothy F. 386 Dearborn av.
Mullen William H. 386 Dearborn av.
Mullen William J. 4416 Prairie av.
Muller Charles G. 1860 Surf
Muller Louis, Hinsdale
Mulliken Alfred Henry, 19 Lake Shore
  Drive. *Chi.*, *W.P.*
Mulliken Charles H. Chicago Beach hotel.
  Chi.,
Mullin Ambrose P. Austin
Mullin Jennie P. Mrs. 516 W. Adams
Mullin John, 1220 Washington boul.
Mullmann Frank, Evanston
Mullmann Paul, Evanston
Mulloy David W. 6912 Vernon av.
Mulroy James R. 6601 Lafayette av.
Mulvane Elizabeth Miss, 4022 Grand boul.
Mulvane Phineas I. Dr. 4022 Grand boul.
Mulvey Arthur B. 5130 Cornell av.
Mulvey C. 3603 Wabash av.
Mulvey Julia F. Miss, 5130 Cornell av.
Mulvey Richard J. 5130 Cornell av.
Mumford Addie A. Miss, 6109 Monroe av.
Mumford Alvin W. 2608 N. Winchester
  av.
Mumford Wm. R. 293 Walnut
Mumford W. O. 6617 Yale
Mund Herman H. 93 Oakwood av.
Munday John W. 6534 Yale
Mundie William B. 27 Gordon terrace.
  U.L.
Mundy Norris H. Riverside
Mundy Norris W. Riverside. *Chi.*
Munger A. Page, 191 Oakwood boul.
Munger David S. 88 Loomis
Munger Edwin A. 3307 Rhodes av.
Munger Frank S. 191 Oakwood boul.
Munger Harriet E. Mrs. 248 Oakwood
  boul.
Munger Henry H. 2818 Calumet av.
Munger H. B. 248 Oakwood boul.
Munger John E. 248 Oakwood boul.
Munger Laura M. Miss, 546, 51st
Munger L. A. Mrs. 191 Oakwood boul.
Munger Mary E. Mrs. 4213 Ellis av.
Munger Orett L. 546, 51st.
Munger Pliny F. 5212 Lexington av. *C.A.*
Munhall W. D. Clifton house
Munn Daniel W. LaGrange

Munn Fred O. LaGrange
Munn Noel S. Hotel Metropole. *C.A.*,
  W.P.]
Munns William H. A. 55, 53d
Munro Daniel, 722 W. Monroe
Munro William, Auditorium annex. *Chi.*,
Munroe Frank L. River Forest
Munroe James E. 3148 Michigan av.
Munroe Walter H. 821 W. Jackson boul.
Munsell William W. 7752 Hawthorne av.
Munson Charles Mrs. 1276 Washington
  boul.
Munson Charles W. 1276 Washington
  boul.
Munson Cyrus K. 848 Warren av.
Munson Forbes, New Hotel Holland
Munson Francis, 107, 75ht
Munson Frank W. 107, 5th
Munson Frederick W. 458 Fulton
Munson G. W. Hinsdale
Munson J. F. Capt. Hotel Del Prado
Munton James, Maywood
Munzer Eugene I. 4938 Vincennes av.
  Lksd.
Munzer Henry, 6410 Ingleside av. *Lksd.*
Munzer M. 4938 Vincennes av.
Murch Charlotte S. Miss, 14 Bryant av.
Murchie George L. LaGrange
Murchie George L. jr. LaGrange
Murdoch Jane Miss, 2130 Prairie av.
Murdoch R. R. 6122 Woodlawn av.
Murdoch Thomas, 2130 Prairie av. *Cal.*,
  Chi., *W.P.*
Murdock E. P. Dr. 601 Washington boul.
Murdock William D. Evanston
Murdock William H. Evanston
Murdough Andrew C. 580 Lasalle av.
Murdow Edward, Glencoe
Murison A. Mrs. 1612 Indiana av.
Murison Charles E. 188, 50th. *C.A.*
Murison George W. 1612 Indiana av. *Cal.*,
  W.P.
Murphey C. M. Rev. 1454 Michigan av.
Murphy Andrew C. Evanston
Murphy Anna M. Miss, 1020 W. Adams
Murphy Anthony J. 519 W. Congress
Murphy Charles F. 2358 Indiana av.
Murphy Daniel J. 2666 N. Paulina. *C.A.*,
  W.P.
Murphy Edward J. 1020 W. Adams
Murphy E. C. 4728 Langley av.
Murphy Francis T. 4321 Vernon av.
Murphy Frank M. 2207 Prairie av. *Cal.*,
  W.P.
Murphy Henry Mrs. 6325 Monroe av.
Murphy Ida Miss, Hotel Del Prado
Murphy James S. 6454 Greenwood av.
Murphy John A. 5209 Madison av.
Murphy John A. jr. LaGrange
Murphy John B. M.D. 3152 Michigan av.
  Ill., *U.L.*, *W.P.*
Murphy John B. 4800 Champlain av.
  C.A., *U.L.*
Murphy John C. Evanston
Murphy John E. 535, 44th
Murphy John H. 2119 Calumet av.

Murphy J. A. Auditorium annex
Murphy Loyal W. 3839 Rhodes av.
Murphy Michael W. 2964 Prairie av.
Murphy M. W. Hinsdale
Murphy Richard J. 4140 Grand boul.
Murphy S. A. Mrs. 4517 Woodlawn av.
Murphy William, 4733 Prairie av.
Murphy William J. Berwyn
Murray Allan A. Hotel Luzerne
Murray Allen F. 326 Oakwood boul.
Murray Charles, 3242 Lake Park av.
Murray Charles C. Austin
Murray Charles R. 3242 Lake Park av. C.A.
Murray C. H. 25 St. James pl.
Murray Donald, LaGrange
Murray Donald Mrs. 2 Ritchie ct.
Murray Edward M. 18 Gordon terrace
Murray E. B. 386 Oakwood boul.
Murray E. D. jr. 386 Oakwood boul.
Murray Fanny Mrs. Oak Park
Murray Frank G. Austin
Murray George R. 3170 Malden
Murray George R. Austin
Murray George W. Tracy
Murray Harold G. Austin
Murray Harry W. 3170 Malden
Murray Hugh A. Oak Park
Murray I. H. 4337 Prairie av.
Murray James, Hinsdale
Murray James S. Evanston
Murray Jane L. Miss, 2 Ritchie ct.
Murray John, 450 W. Jackson boul. Ill.
Murray John J. Morton Park
Murray John S. 4311 Oakenwald av.
Murray J. Miss. 2 Ritchie ct.
Murray K. Mrs. 4423 Vincennes av.
Murray Leverett W. Mrs. Riverside
Murray M. Frank, Austin
Murray O. E. Rev. 7657 Butler
Murray Thomas P. 40 Bryant av.
Murray Thomas W. B. Hinsdale
Murray W. H. Evanston
Murtha Annetta Miss, 268, 33d
Musgrave Albert F. 1344 Washington boul.
Musgrave Harrison, 10 Astor. Chi.,Univ.
Musgrave John H. Revere house
Musgrave Mae Miss, 3004 Prairie av.
Musselwhite Jay, 3519 Vernon av.
    Sum. res. Coldwater, Mich.
Mussey Charles E. Mrs. 306 Belden av.
Musson Charles S. Wilmette
Mutchmor Ralph W. 77 Lincoln Park boul.
Muther Lawrence, Oak Park
Myer Benjamin, 3842 Prairie av.
Myer Emanuel, 405 Bowen av.
Myer Fred, 3360 Prairie av.
Myer Henry, 3693 Prairie av.
Myer H. L. Mrs. 235 Michigan av.
Myer Moses, 3360 Prairie av.
Myers Bruce M. 779 Mildred av.
Myers Eugene B. 5126 Kimbark av. C.A.
Myers E. B. 5041 Calumet av.
Myers E. M. Miss, 2942 Prairie av.

Myers Garson, 5119 Madison av.
Myers Hattie Mrs. 342 Fullerton av.
Myers Henry G. 3641 Vincennes av.
Myers James B. 640 W. Monroe
Myers Jenny G. Mrs. 4349 Forrestville av.
Myers Johnston Rev. 2339 Michigan av.
Myers Myron A. Hinsdale. U.L.
Myers M. C. Chicago Beach hotel
Myers Samuel M. Highland Park. C.A.
Myers Willis V. 5126 Kimbark av.
Mygatt Edward T. 4057 Prairie av.
Mygatt William R. 46, 53d. Cal., Chi., W.P.
Myrick Frederick W. 7125 Eggleston av.

NABER M. HENRY, 502 Belden av.
    Nacey Patrick, 4501 Indiana av.
Nafis Abraham T. Evanston
Nafis Louis F. Evanston
Naghten Frank A. 1659 W. Monroe
Naghten James J. 1659 W. Monroe
Naghten John, 1659 W. Monroe
Naghten John J. 1220 Washington boul.
Naghten M. J. 106 Walton pl.
Nagl Charles F. 195 Honore
Nagle Augustus F. 1751 Wrightwood av.
Nair John H. Mrs. 5325 Cornell av.
Nally Edward J. 1687 Kenmore av. U.L.
Nance Willis O. Dr. 5311 Madison av.
Nangle W. J. Avenue house, Evanston
Napheys William D. 7236 Yale
Napier Edward J. 3131 Indiana av.
Nash Charles T. 329 Ashland boul. Ill.
Nash Chester C. Evanston
Nash Daniel B. 569, 51st
Nash Edwin N. Oak Park
Nash Elizabeth Mrs. 4427 Champlain av.
Nash F. E. Mrs. 2430 Lakewood av.
Nash H. H. Mrs. Lakota hotel
Nash Orrin W. Oak Park
Nash Richard, 211, 48th
Nash Samuel S. 4437 Champlain av.
Nash Thomas C. 3615 Prairie av.
Nash William, 15 Stratford pl. Un.
Nash William R. Lake Forest
Nash Wilmar H. Oak Park
Nash W. T. 4808 Vincennes av.
Naslund Daniel, 2561 N. Paulina
Nason Edward W. 6500 Minerva av.
Nassauer H. Mrs. 4400 Berkeley av.
Nast Alexander D. 3653 Michigan av. Lksd., Stan.
Nast Samuel, 3653 Michigan av. Lksd.
Nathan Adolph, 5016 Drexel boul. Stan., U.L.
Nathan Arthur S. 3914 Prairie av.
Nathan Herman, 1904 Indiana av. Stan.
Nathan Louis A. 3434 South Park av. Lksd.
Nathan Miss, 5016 Drexelboul.
Nathan Morris E. 208, 37th
Nathan Samuel, 3914 Prairie av. Stan.
Nathan Sidney S. 3914 Prairie av. Stan.
Nathanson Laura Mrs. 4740 Evans av.
Nau Charles A. 709 North Park av.
Nau Louis, 1644 W. Adams

Nau Otto F. 709 North Park av.
Naugle Edward E. LaGrange
Naylor George M. 5718 Kimbark av.
Naylor James E. Morton Park
Neafus George A. 196 Oakwood boul. *C.A.*
Neagle F. C. Mrs. 1005 Park av.
Neahr George H. 3155 Calumet av.
Neahr Melvin J. 3155 Calumet av.
Neal Charles A. 612, 46th
Neal E. 409, 41st
Neal James, The Arizona
Neal S. S. Mrs. Evanston
Neale Alice E. Miss, 341 Rush
Neale Richard A. Dr. 214 N. State
    Sum. res. W. Baden, Ind.
Neary Nicholas J. 273 Superior
Neather J. Pearce, 93, 33d
Neather Kittie Miss, 93, 33d
Needham Erwin B. Hinsdale
Needham Gerrit S. 1161 Millard av.
Neel W. R. 2395 Magnolia av.
Neeld Isaac N. 5037 Lake av.
Neeler Henry G. 273½ Lasalle av. *C.A.*
Neely Carrie B. Miss, 4929 Greenwood
    av.
Neely Charles G. Judge, Evanston
Neely Charles H. Victoria hotel
Neely Edwin R. LaGrange
Neely Isaac M. Dr. Evanston
Neely John C. 4929 Greenwood av. *C.A.*,
    U.L.
Neely John C. jr. 4929 Greenwood av.
Neely Joseph C. 476 W. Adams
Neely Robert, 476 W. Adams
Neely Robert H. 476 W. Adams
Neely William I. 3122 Forest av. *C.A.*
Neemes John C. 4746 Madison av.
Neeson S. J. Mrs. 4227 St. Lawrence av.
Nef John Ulric, 6018 Stony Island av.
Neff Aaron W. 1060 Washington boul.
Neff A. C. Mayfair
Neff Theodore L. 5825 Kimbark av.
Neill Charles W. 2731 Calumet av.
Neilson James D. 552 W. 61st
Neilson James H. 3845 Ellis av. *C.A.*
Neise George N. 33 Pine Grove av.
Neist Julius, Ravinia
Nell B. F. 44 Bryant av.
Nellegar John B. 4526 Greenwood av. *C.A.*
Nelles Frank A. 496 Sunnyside av.
Nellis Aaron, 4212 Ellis av.
Nellis C. S. Mrs. Longwood
Nellis Frank E. 159½ Eugenie
Nellis James, 360, 44th
Nelson Celia A. Mrs. 630 Greenleaf av.
Nelson Charles L. 5545 Madison av. *C.A.*
Nelson Daniel T., M.D. 2400 Indiana av.
Nelson Eric J. Austin
Nelson E. Case, Evanston
Nelson Florian P. 1932 Deming pl.
Nelson Francis C. 2400 Indiana av.
Nelson H. P. Dr. 605 W. Vanburen
Nelson Isaac O. Evanston
Nelson Jay O. Dr. 244, 57th.
    Sum. res. Twinsburg, Ohio

Nelson John E. 2440 N. Hermitage av.
    C.A. Sum. res. Macatawa Park,
    Mich.
Nelson John, Oak Park
Nelson John L. Victoria hotel. *C.A.*
Nelson Joseph, 6534 Greenwood av.
Nelson J. F. Mrs. 142 W. Garfield boul.
Nelson Lawrence, 1446 Addison
Nelson Mary Miss, 3543 Indiana av.
Nelson Murry, 1623 Indiana av. *Chi.*
Nelson Murry jr. 584 Dearborn av. *C.A.*
Nelson Nels Dr. 45 Columbia
Nelson Nicholas J. 90 Lincoln Park boul.
Nelson Theodore, 4559 Forrestville av.
Nelson Thomas E. 235 Ashland boul.
Nelson Walter C. 5120 Jefferson av. *U.L.*
Nelson William D. 12 Chalmers pl.
Nelson William P. 3543 Indiana av. *C.A.*,
    W.P.
Nessler Samuel C. 3420 Calumet av.
Netcher Charles, 4427 Drexel boul.
Nethercot William Rev. 8 Menomonee
Nethercott George, Winnetka
Netter Sam, The Rainier. *Lksd.*
Netterstrom Charles M. 1535 Aldine av.
Netterstrom Walter, 1535 Aldine av.
Nettleton E. Frank, Oak Park
Nettleton Ida M. Mrs. 6326 Greenwood
    av.
Neu Bernard, Lexington hotel. *Stan.*
Neubarth Emma Mrs. 298 Belden av.
Neuberger Albert, 4851 Forrestville av.
    Lksd.
Neuberger C. Mrs. 4327 Berkeley av.
Neuberger Edward, 4851 Forrestville av.
Neuberger Henry, 4851 Forrestville av.
Neuberger Joseph, 162, 34th.
Neuburger Jacob M. 4733 Kenwood av.
Neuburger John M. 4733 Kenwood av.
    U.L.
Neuman Mark, 66 Bryant av.
Neumann Alexander, 3018 Groveland av.
Neumann David, 3018 Groveland av.
Neumann Ferdinand W. 3500 Ellis av.
Neumann Ignatz, 3666 Indiana av. *Lksd.*
Neumann I. D. 3206 Forest av.
Neumann Josephine Miss, 3206 Forest av.
Neumann Julius Prof. 3206 Forest av.
Neumann Louis Mrs. 4438 Indiana av.
    Lksd.
Neumann Maier, 674, 48th pl. *Stan.*
Nevers Edward, 682 Washington boul.
Nevers Roderick, 29 Madison Park
New Aaron L. 4341 Prairie av. *Lksd.*
Newberger Rose L. Mrs. 3327 South
    Park av.
Newberry Egbert S. 369 Chicago av.
Newberry Mary L. Miss, 399 Erie
Newberry Robert T. 388 Erie. *Un.*
Newberry Walter C. Gen. 399 Erie. *Irq.*
Newberry W. F. 4415 Ellis av.
Newbert W. F. 1644 W. Adams.
Newbre Carlton H. 437, 60th
Newburger E. Newton, 3706 Ellis av.
    Stan.
Newburger Frank D. 3706 Ellis av.

Newburger G. Mrs. 3706 Ellis av.
Newburger James M. 3706 Ellis av.
Newburger William S. 3706 Ellis av. *Lksd.*
Newburgh Jonas S. Dr. 3519 Indiana av.
Newbury Charles D. 223, 29th
Newbury George G. Hotel Metropole. *Cal., W.P.*
Newbury William G. Oak Park
Newby Aaron J. 569, 51st
Newcomb Charles A. Maywood
Newcomb Edward R. LaGrange
Newcomb Francis H. 236 Warren av.
Newcomb George E. 241 S. Robey
Newcomb George W. 236 Warren av.
Newcomb John C. 655 W. Adams. *Ill.*
Newcomb Mary D. Miss, 481 Dearborn av.
Newcomb William H. 236 Warren av.
Newell Allen G. 3025 Prairie av.
Newell A. B. 159 Rush. *Univ.*
Newell Charles B. 2580 N. Ashland av.
Newell Charlotte C. Mrs. 354 Washington boul.
Newell E. K. Mrs. 4020 Ellis av.
Newell Frank B. Oak Park
Newell Grant, 2567 N. Hermitage av.
Newell Herbert E. 3025 Prairie av.
Newell Hulda H. Miss, Evanston
Newell John Mrs. 348 Ontario
Newell Lester C. Hinsdale
Newell Robert C., M.D. Austin
Newell S. B. Mrs. 311 Belden av.
Newell W. A. 7844 Hawthorne av.
Newyard Henry C. 4111 Newgart av.
Newgass Babetta Mrs. 4033 Vincennes av.
Newgass Louis, 343 Oakwood boul. *Lksd.*
Newgass William, 4033 Vincennes av. *Lksd.*
Newhall Arthur T. 366, 49th
Newhall Benjamin, Glencoe
Newhall Franklin, Glencoe
Newhall Hiram H. 4736 Champlain av.
Newhall S. F. Glencoe
Newhall Walter C. 849 Warren av.
Newhaus August, 3000 Cottage Grove av.
Newhouse Henry L. 4630 Prairie av.
Newhouse Leopold, 4630 Prairie av.
Newkirk F. B. 77 Lincoln Park boul.
Newkirk Garrett Dr. 205, 44th
Newkirk George, 498 Fullerton av.
Newkirk H. A. Hyde Park hotel
Newlin George E. 41 Elaine pl.
Newman Abraham Mrs. 3305 Forest av.
Newman Augustus, 1710 Addison
Newman Burns L. 403 Warren av.
Newman B. L. 1506 Michigan av.
Newman Charles S. 6547 Yale
Newman Charles W. 523 Orchard
Newman Elias R. 2755 N. Paulina
Newman E. 3436 Calumet av. *Lksd.*
Newman Gideon E. 5102 Hibbard av.
Newman Gustav R. 527 Orchard
Newman Harry B. 3615 Ellis av.
Newman H. P. Dr. 438 Lasalle av. *Univ*
    Sum. res. Highland Park

Newman Ira A. 4452 Sidney av.
Newman Jacob, 3333 Wabash av. *Stan., U.L.*
Newman Jacob jr. 3615 Ellis av. *Lksd.*
Newman Lewis E. 403 Warren av.
Newman Mary Starrett Mrs. 1838 Arlington pl.
Newman Morris, 4148 Grand boul. *Lksd.*
Newman William L. 909 W. Jackson boul.
Newton Albert W. 489 Dearborn av.
Newton Asahel, 810 Greenleaf av.
Newton B. Dr. Auditorium Annex
Newton Charles E. 213 Park av.
Newton Charles W. 3031 Prairie av.
Newton Frederick A. 489 Dearborn av.
Newton G. W. Dr. 878 W. Adams. *Ill.*
Newton Harriet A. Mrs. 487 W. Adams
Newton Henry, 337 Rush
Newton H. S. 95 Warren av. *Ill.*
Newton L. Q. Glen Ellyn
Newton Mary A. Mrs. 305 S. Irving av.
Newton Miss, Auditorium Annex
Newton Reuben W. 489 Dearborn av.
Newton Robert C. 698½ Washington boul.
Newton William, Glen Ellyn
Niblack William C. 125, 47th. *Chi., Irq.*
Niblock Charles B. 421, 48th
Nichelson Duke, Oak Park
Nichol John, 4717 Kenwood av.
Nicholas Edmund T. 514, 64th
Nicholas Fred C. 260, 61st
Nicholas Frederick, 4310 Oakenwald av.
Nicholas Kirby, 4142 Grand boul.
Nicholas Nellie Miss, 1492 Washington boul.
Nicholas Robert, 4410 Oakenwald av.
Nicholes A. M. Mrs. 2902 Prairie av.
Nicholes C. W. Mrs. 3435 Michigan av.
Nicholes I. Elsworth, 318 W. 61st pl.
Nicholes Willard D. 318 W. 61st pl.
Nicholl Thomas J. 1393 W. Monroe
Nicholls John, 459 W. Congress
Nichols Aaron S. 3853 Ellis av.
Nichols Alexander, 85 Rush
Nichols Amos J. Dr. 728 W. Monroe
Nichols Charles A. 435 Belden av.
Nichols Charles H. 3630 Grand boul.
Nichols C. M. Chicago Beach hotel. *U.L.*
Nichols David B. Morgan Park
Nichols Edgar H. 6511 Stewart av.
Nichols Edward C. Maywood. *U.L.*
Nichols Emily Miss, 2325 Michigan av.
Nichols E. R. 308 N. State
Nichols Frank M. 1621 W. Monroe. *Ill.*
Nichols Franklin, 2342 Calumet av.
Nichols Fred D. Morgan Park
Nichols Frederick W. Evanston
Nichols F. H. 4405 Greenwood av.
Nichols George, 7565 Bond av.
Nichols George E. 4813 Prairie av.
Nichols George P. Riverside
Nichols George R. 327 Ashland boul.
Nichols Harrison P. Maywood
Nichols Harry H. Maywood

Nichols Henry W. 6237 Monroe av.
    Sum res. Cohasset, Mass.
Nichols Horace W. 5752 Washington av.
Nichols Isaac W. 547 W. Monroe
Nichols Jean O. 7565 Bond av.
Nichols John J. 6610 Harvard av.
Nichols Lewis B. 3500 Ellis av.
Nichols Melville S. 3800 Forest av.
Nichols Myron W. 5127 Lexington av.
Nichols Sidney H. Oak Park
Nichols Washington A. Lake Forest
Nicholson Henry P. 2505 Lakewood av.
    Sum. res. Muskegon, Mich.
Nicholson James S. 3344 Vernon av.
Nicholson John W. 42, 29th pl.
Nicholson Thomas, 3344 Vernon av.
Nicholson Thomas G. 3344 Vernon av.
Nickelsen Adolph, 493 Belden av.
Nickerson A. E. 1116 Washington boul.
Nickerson Benjamin R. 3921 Langley
    av.
Nickerson Dexter W. Clifton house
Nickerson Freeman, 3442 Wabash av.
Nickerson Henry H. 516 W. 67th
Nickerson Joseph F. 6017 Monroe av.
Nickerson J. C. 3440 Wabash av.
Nickerson Roland C. 317 Erie. *Cal.*,
    Chi., *C.A.*, *Un.*, *W.P.*
    Sum. res. East Brewster, Mass.
Nickerson Samuel M. 317 Erie. *Chi.*, *Un.*
    Sum. res. East Brewster, Mass.
Nicodemus Edwin, 3020 Calumet av.
Nicol Alex. Auditorium annex. *C.A.*
Nicol James, 917 Evanston av.
Niebergall P. A. 227 S. Irving av.
Niehaus Tillie Miss, 225 Dearborn av.
Niemann Joseph, 409 Belden av.
Nigg C. 697 North Park av.
Nightingale Augustus F. 2175 Sheridan
    rd.   Sum. res. Lake Geneva, Wis.
Nightingale Harry, 2175 Sheridan rd.
Nihlean Swan J. 3342 Forest av.
Niies John Whiting Dr. 420 Lasalle av.
    Sum. res. Lake Harbor, Mich.
Niles Mary L. Mrs. Oak Park
Niles M. C. Oak Park
Niles S. S. Oak Park
Nimmons George C. 76, 50th
Nims C. K. 3300 Vernon av.
Nims O. L. 3300 Vernon av.
Nitchie J. H. Evanston
Niver D. R. Oak Park
Nixon Charles E. 741 N. Clark
Nixon Frank, 4140 Grand boul.
Nixon Harry M. 4533 Indiana av.
Nixon Miles G. Waukegan
Nixon Netta Miss, 28 St. James pl.
Nixon Oliver W. 741 N. Clark
Nixon William Penn, 743 N. Clark. *U.L*
Nixon W. C. 3435 Wabash av.
Nixon W. K. 156 Rush
Nixon W. W. K. 156 Rush
Noake William H. Oak Park
Noble Alfred, 302 Belden av. *Chi.*
Noble Edwin J. 6621 Harvard av.
Noble E. F. Mrs. 4744 Kenwood av.

Noble Frederic Perry 532 Washington
    boul.
Noble Frederick A. Rev. 532 Washington
    boul.
Noble George W. Hinsdale
Noble L. Clarence, 451 W. 65th
Noble William L. Dr. 429 Washington
    boul.
Noblett Edward J. 421 W. 67th
Nockin Bernhard J. 241 Hampden ct.
Nockin Joseph M. Oak Park
Noe Elzer C. 2483 Lakewood av.
Noe Sarah D. Mrs. 4556 Michigan av.
Noel Elijah P. Dr. 589 W. Jackson boul.
Noel Joseph R. Oak Park
Noel Max, 5823 Jackson av.
Noelle Joseph B. 4108 Perry
Nolan John H. 4941 Drexel boul. *U.L.*
Nolan Julian St. John, 10 Astor. *Un.*
    Univ.
Nolan J. E. Evanston
Nolan Thomas, 3186 Dover
Nonnast Louis F. 1774 Deming pl.
Nonweiler Francis H. 7224 Vernon av.
Noonan Edward T. 398 Washington boul.
    Irq.
Noonan Mary H. Mrs. 398 Washington
    boul.
Noonan P. 4730 Champlain av.
Norcott John, 4833 Madison av.
Norcross Frederic F. 1816 Melrose. *Univ.*
Norden Felix A. 595 Orchard
Nordenholt George, Oak Park
Nordling Ernest A. Lake Forest
Norman Frederick, Wilmette •
Norman John F. 4731 Prairie av.
Normoyle Patrick B. 4921 Champlain av.
Norris Benjamin F. Auditorium hotel
Norris Charles S. 4141 Newgart av. *C.A.*
Norris C. P. Mrs. 136, 50th
Norris Frank Y. Evanston
Norris Joseph M. 7140 Yale
Norris J. A. 2317 Michigan av.
Norris Mary Harriet Miss, Evanston
Norris Robert A. Dr. 136, 50th
Norris William W. 347 S. Troy. *Ill.*
Norten Leland, 4011 Drexel boul.
North Robert L. Mrs. 1850 Aldine av.
North Robert L. 1850 Aldine av.
North William S. 26 Walton pl.
Northam Martin K. 5210 Jefferson av.
Northcott William P. 1112 S. Lawndale
    av.
Northen John, 425 Seminary av.
Northrop Howard G. 38 Madison Park
Northrop John Willard, 3132 Calumet av.
    Sum. res. Lake Beulah, Wis.
Northrop M. S. Mrs. 6059 Jefferson av.
Northrup George W. Prof. 5735 Madison
    av.
Northrup George W. jr. 5735 Madison
    av.
Northup Charles, 4407 Sidney av.
Northup C. J. 4716 Kenwood av.
Northup C. W. Mrs. Evanston
Northup George T. Evanston

Northup James H. 3742 Forest av.
Northup Joseph C. Evanston
Northup J. E. Elmhurst
Northup Willet, 4543 Ellis av. *U.L., W.P.*
Norton Arthur L. Evanston
Norton B. M. 387 Oak
Norton Charles Dyer, 205 Goethe. *Univ.*
Norton Charles L. 5635 Madison av.
Norton C. D. 205 Goethe
Norton Delmon W. 3006 Prairie av.
Norton D. Mrs. 4459 Oakenwald av.
Norton Edmund, Highland Park. *Un.*
Norton Edwin, Maywood. *C.A., U.L.*
Norton Elliott S. 4815 Lake av.
Norton Henry L. 704 The Plaza
Norton H. M. 5620 Washington av.
Norton H. N. Oak Park
Norton James H. 2556 N. Ashland av. *Un., Univ.*
Norton James S. Mrs. 137 Lincoln Park boul.
Norton John E. 5137 Michigan av.
Norton Joseph, 2699 N. Robey
Norton J. Henry, 57 Cedar. *Chi., C.A., Un., W.P.*
Norton Lawrence A. Austin
Norton Lemuel D. Evanston
Norton Mary Miss. 1822 Indiana av.
Norton Miss, 4815 Lake av.
Norton M. M. Mrs. The Arizona
Norton Oliver W. 4815 Lake av.
Norton Ralph H. 4815 Lake av.
Norton Sarah E. Mrs. 2798 N. Winchester av.
Norton Thomas, 4352 Calumet av.
Norton Thomas J. 4634 Vincennes av.
Norton Thomas S. 4840 Kimbark av. *C.A.*
Norwood F. W. 4945 Lake av.
Nosler George T. 5201 Madison av.
Nossé T. G. Hon. 169, 51st
Nott Henry A. 6353 Ellis av.
Nourse B. F. 58 Woodland Park
Nourse Guy F. 58 Woodland Park
Nourse Harriet P. Mrs. 515 W. 67th
Nourse H. N. Mrs. 5932 Parnell av.
Nourse John A. 4820 Prairie av.
Nourse John A. 58 Woodland Park
Nowak Charles A. 6564 Yale
Nowak Frank, 6564 Yale
Nowlen Addison J. Irving Park
Noyes Albert Hamilton, 5117 Jefferson av.
Noyes Charles, 844 Washington boul.
Noyes Charles F. Dr. 30 Walton pl.
Noyes David A. The Plaza. *C.A., Un.*
Noyes Edmund Dr. Evanston
Noyes Edward H. 5117 Jefferson av.
Noyes Edward S. Evanston
Noyes Ernest H. 378 Erie. *U.L. Univ.*
Noyes Everett E. 4940 Washington av.
Noyes Frederick B. Dr. 625, 41st
Noyes Gideon P. Lexington hotel
Noyes Harry B. Oak Park
Noyes Henry C. 3809 Langley av.
Noyes John T. 378 Erie. *Chi., Un.*

Noyes LaVerne W. Granada hotel. *C.A., Ill., U.L.*
Noyes M. C. 3819 Ellis av.
Noyes M. M. Mrs. 4940 Washington av.
Noyes M. Paul, The Plaza
Noyes Thomas S. 514 North av.
Noyes William H. 5117 Jefferson av.
Nuber Alexander, 620 Dearborn av. *Un.*
Nuckols John W. River Forest
Nudd Ira P. Mrs. 1610 Indiana av.
Nunamaker Frank, Julien hotel
Nusbaum Aaron E. Hotel Metropole. *Stan.*
Nusbaum Emanuel, 3430 Vernon av.
Nussbaum A. E. Hotel Metropole
Nutt John Dr. Glencoe
Nutting William W. 80 Throop. *Ill.*
Nuveen John, 4026 Grand boul.
Nuveen Margaret Mrs. Irving Park
Nye H. G. 3158 South Park av.
Nye James W. Chicago Beach hotel
Nye Joshua, 6431 Kimbark av.
Nye William J. Oak Park
Nye W. A. 3620 Vernon av. *Lksd.*
Nyman Fay, 507 Dearborn av.
Nyman Fred, 507 Dearborn av.
Nyman John C. 507 Dearborn av.
Nyman John E. Dr. Oak Park

O'BRIEN BELLE MISS, Highland Park
O'Brien D. D. Mrs. River Forest
O'Brien Edward, 21 Bellevue pl. *C.A., Un.*
O'Brien Frank, 4018 Grand boul.
O'Brien James C. Mrs. 525 W. Congress
O'Brien James F. 4018 Grand boul.
O'Brien John, 4523 Prairie av.
O'Brien John jr. 4523 Prairie av.
O'Brien John E. 427, 41st
O'Brien Joseph, 149 Pine Grove av.
O'Brien J. Mrs. 3146 Lake Park av.
O'Brien J. Gregg, Highland Park
O'Brien Margaret V. Miss, 2966 Indiana av.
O'Brien Martin, 149 Pine Grove av.
O'Brien Mary Miss, 408 Ashland boul.
O'Brien Mary H. Miss, Evanston
O'Brien Mary J. Miss, 2966 Indiana av.
O'Brien Robert, 4523 Prairie av.
O'Brien Thomas D. 3440 Vernon av. *C.A., Irq., W.P.*
O'Brien William D. 3632 Grand boul.
O'Brien William H. 1353 Sheridan rd.
O'Brien William V. 1928 Arlington pl.
O'Bryan Edward, 4557 Oakenwald av. *C.A.*
O'Byrne Charles C. Dr. 747 W. Monroe
O'Connell Andrew J. 85 Macalister pl.
O'Connell Denis, 3418 Prairie av.
O'Connell Frank T. 398 Ashland boul.
O'Connell Harry, 3418 Prairie av.
O'Connell Herbert, 3418 Prairie av.
O'Connell John Mrs. 532 Lasalle av.
O'Connell John J. 532 Lasalle av.
O'Connell Susan Mrs. 85 Macalister pl.

O'Connell Theo. W. 85 Macalister pl.
O'Connell W. H. 4111 Drexel boul.
O'Connor Catherine Mrs. 4515 Prairie av.
O'Connor John, 5210 Woodlawn av.
O'Connor Peter, 2469 Magnolia av.
O'Day Frank C. 225 Dearborn av.
O'Donnell Eleanor Miss, 6506 Lafayette av.
O'Donnell J. J. 1524 Kenmore av.
O'Donnell Patrick P. 4629 Woodlawn av.
O'Donnell Simon, 3720 Wabash av.
O'Grady J. W. de Courcy, Kenilworth. *Chi.*
O'Hara Charles, 2458 Prairie av.
O'Hara Charles Mrs. 2458 Prairie av.
O'Hara Frank. 2458 Prairie av.
O'Hara George, 2458 Prairie av.
O'Hara John, 2458 Prairie av.
O'Hara John jr. 2458 Prairie av.
O'Hearne William F. 213 S. Winchester av.
O'Kane William Eaton, Evanston
O'Keefe John, The Arizona
O'Leary Arthur J. 4013 Drexel boul.
O'Leary Cornelius S. 375 Bissell
O'Leary David P. Evanston
O'Leary John Mrs. Evanston
O'Malley Patrick 1884 Diversey
O'Meara Cornelius S. 198 Park av.
O'Neal Joseph F. Dr. 1013 W. Garfield boul.
O'Neal Oren Dr. 291 Ontario
O'Neil Joseph, Lake Forest
O'Neill Alma J. 54 S. Oakley av.
O'Neill Arthur W. 6331 Langley av.
O'Neill Cecil Mrs. 1489 W. Monroe
O'Neill H. J. The Winamac
O'Neill John, 5900 Wabash av.
O'Neill John W. Dr. 1886 Diversey
O'Neill Louis, 2915 Sheridan rd.
O'Neill P. Mrs. 3729 Prairie av.
O'Neill Richard, 555 Dearborn av.
O'Neill William E. Hotel Metropole. *Cal., C.A., W.P.*
O'Shaughnessy J. F. Auditorium annex. *W.P.*
O'Shaughnessy M. J. Auditorium annex
O'Shea David Dr. 470 Ashland boul.
Oakey Alfred J. Dr. 515 W. 65th
Oakley Annie Miss, 4700 Drexel boul.
Oakley Bertha Miss, 4700 Drexel boul.
Oakley Horace S. 515 The Plaza *C.A., Irq., Univ., W.P.*
Oakley James W. Mrs. 4700 Drexel boul.
Oaks J. F. Dr. 347, 62d
Oaks K. Oak Park
Oaks W. W. Oak Park
Oates James F. Evanston
Oberfelder Joseph, 3648 Grand boul.
Oberfelder Tobias, 3648 Grand boul. *Stan.*
Oberndorf Abe L. Dr. 4949 Vincennes av.
Oberndorf Fred, 3553 Vernon av. *Lksd.*
Oberndorf Henry, 3352 Vernon av.
Oberndorf Herman, 4330 Grand boul. *Lksd.*
Oberndorf Lewis, 4949 Vincennes av.

Oberndorf Louis H. 3352 Vernon av.
Oberndorf Max F. 3553 Vernon av.
Oberndorf Max L. 4949 Vincennes av. *Stan.*
Oberne George, 1147 N. Clark
Oberne George N. 916 Hamilton ct.
Oberstella Harry A. 74 Maple
Obertop Julius L. 7101 Harvard av.
Ochsner Albert J. Dr. 710 Sedgwick
Ocorr Henry, 6328 Parnell av.
Odelius Julius E. 3825 Elmwood ct.
Odell F. S. Chicago Athletic Assn.
Odell George T. 642 Pine Grove av.
Odell Henry C. 867 W. Monroe
Odell J. J. P. 483 N. State. *Chi., Irq.*
Odell L. J. 4839 Prairie av.
Odell Mary A. Mrs. River Forest
Odell R. S. River Forest
Odell W. R. 145 Lincoln Park boul. *Un.*
Odlin Elizabeth M. Mrs. 3226 South Park av.
Oehne Theodore, 5401 Ellis av. *Irq.*
Officer Alexander, Kenilworth
Offield Charles K. 379 Ashland boul. *Ill., U.L.*
Ogden E. J. Dr. 1636 Michigan av.
Ogden E. Russell, M. D. 1813 Indiana av.
Ogden Howard N. 6352 Drexel av.
Ogden Mahlon D. Mrs. 111 Lake Shore Drive   Sum. res. Pittsfield, Mass.
Ogden M. H. Mrs. 682 Park av.
Ogden William P. 5807 Rosalie ct.
Ohlerking John H. 516 Washington boul.
Ohm Charles Mrs. 406 Belden av.
Ohm Curt, 406 Belden av.
Ohm Hanca, 406 Belden av.
Olbrich Stephen J. Austin
Olcese Louis, Oak Park
Olcott Edwin W. Dr. 287 S. Oakley av.
Olcott J. M. Hotel Windermere
Oldenborg Hugo Dr. 189 Cass
Oldfather George W. Winnetka
Olds Lee Merritt, 4809 Madison av.
Olds S. J. Mrs. 7620 Bond av.
Olds Walter Judge, 4809 Madison av. *U.L.*
Oleson Charles W. Dr. Lombard
Oleson Richard B. Lombard
Olgen Albert F. 843 Chase av.
Olin Isabelle W. Mrs. 1125 Early av.
Olin Samuel O. 1831 Humboldt Park boul.
Olinger Fred E. 3505 Indiana av.
Olinger Jean Prosper, 3505 Indiana av.
Olinger John P. 3505 Indiana av.
Oliphant David, Austin
Oliphant James B. Austin
Oliphant W. J. 3100 Groveland av.
Oliver David, 849 W. Monroe
Oliver David jr. 849 W. Monroe
Oliver Ernest A. 4452 Vincennes av.
Oliver Francis S. Evanston
Oliver Frederick S. Evanston. *C.A.*
Oliver George, 1424 W. Monroe
Oliver John Mrs. 1426 Washington boul.
Oliver John M. 514 W. Congress. *Chi., Ill., U.L.*

Oliver May Miss, 772 W. Monroe
Oliver N. Ellis Dr. 1742 Diversey
Oliver Roy O. 849 W. Monroe
Oliver T. T., M.D. 2306 Indiana av.
Oliver William G. 1543 W. Monroe
Oliver William G. Evanston
Oliver W. D. 4576 Oakenwald av.
Olmstead Clare J. 582 45th pl.
Olmstead Edmund, 444 Bowen av. *Cal.*
Olmstead Florence Miss, Palmer house
Olmsted Anna H. Mrs. 5830 Washington av.
Olmsted George, Evanston
Olmsted James F. 6501 Harvard av.
Olmsted Oliver A. 5538 Cornell av. *C.A., Univ.*
Olmsted William A. Mrs.5642 Madison av.
　　　　Sum. res. Turin, N. Y.
Olmsted William B. Evanston
Olney Eva Miss, Hinsdale
Olney John, 185 Oakwood boul.
Olney Thomas A. Dr. 1038 W. Jackson boul.
Olson Nils F. 166 Locust
Olson Olof G. 3532 Vernon av.
Olwin Jacob B. Evanston
Olwin John M. Evanston
Omohundro William R. 4400 Lake av.
Onahan William J. 47 Macalister pl. *Irq.*
Onderdonk Dudley, Evanston
Onderdonk Forman, Evanston
Onderdonk William Holmes, Evanston
Onderdonk W. H. Mrs. Evanston
Oosten Charles, 3405 Prairie av.
Oppenheim M. J. 4818 Forestville av. *Lksd.*
Oppenheim W. S. 4528 Oakenwald av. *Irq., U.L.*
Oppenheimer Bernhard, Hotel Metropole. *Stan.*
Oppenheimer Julius, 4740 Prairie av. *Lksd.*
Oppenheimer Mortimer, 3529 Grand boul.
Oppenheimer M. L. 3529 Grand boul.
Opper Philip, 3347 South Park av.
Oram James C. Austin
Orb John A.3211 Calumet av. *W.P.*
Orchard James G. S. Evanston
Orchard John G. Evanston
Orcutt W. F. 2124 Michigan av.
Orde George F. Glencoe
Orde Markham B. Glencoe
Orelup Amasa, 3148 Groveland av.
Organ Charles D. 6510 Lafayette av.
Organ Robert A. 6510 Lafayette av.
Organ Rollin B. 4019 Indiana av.
Oriel Frank H. Oak Park
Orr Arthur, Evanston. *Chi., U.L.*
Orr A. C. Park Ridge
Orr Charles B. 3218 Rhodes av.
Orr C. Frederick, Evanston
Orr Edward K. 317 41st. *C.A.*
Orr Frank B. 4450 Ellis av. *U.L.*
Orr G. H. Oak Park. *C.A.*
Orr Harvey D. 893 Chase av.
Orr John F. Dr. 4433 Champlain av.

Orr J. G. Park Ridge
Orr Mary W. Miss, Evanston
Orr Orton G. 4420 Champlain av.
Orr Robert M. Hotel Windermere. *U.L.*
Orr Samuel C. Lake Forest
Orr Thornton M. 4317 Ellis av.
Orschel Isaac, 3421 Vernon av.
Ortman O. G. 3169 Beacon
Ortmann Rudolph, 39 Cedar. *Chi., C.A., Un., W.P.*
Ortmayer Andrew Mrs. 215 Belden av.
Ortmayer Carl G. Mrs. 4557 Ellis av.
Orton Esther M. Mrs. Oak Park
Orton Thomas, 2951 Michigan av.
Orvis John S. Evanston
Orvis Josephine E. Miss, 457 Washington boul.
Orvis Margaret E. Mrs. Evanston
Orvis Orland D. 2443 Prairie av. *C.A.*
　　　　Sum. res. Vassar, Mich.
Orvis Purdy W. Evanston
Orwig Harry I. Winnetka
Osborn Anna T. Miss, Evanston
Osborn A. C. Irving Park
Osborn Charles M. Evanston. *Un.*
Osborn Charles M. jr. 1534 Oakdale av. *Univ.*
Osborn Chauncey V. 114 Flournoy
Osborn Clark D. 400 Sidney av.
Osborn Eugene E. Evanston. *Univ.*
Osborn Hartwell, Evanston
Osborn Henry A. 4737 Kimbark av.
Osborn Jenny Miss, 99, 33d
Osborn John Mrs. 590 W. Adams
Osborn Kate Miss, Evanston
Osborn L. J. Evanston
Osborn P. B. 99, 33d
Osborn S. M. Mrs. 4737 Kimbark av.
Osborne Elizabeth Miss, 23 Bellevue pl.
Osborne Frank Sayre, 4455 Grand boul.
Osborne Henry S. 4455 Grand boul.
Osborne J. C. LaGrange
Osborne J. O. Mrs. 5726 Madison av.
Osborne S. S. 2233 Calumet av.
Osborne W. Irving, Evanston
Osgood Albert M. 766 W. Adams
Osgood Albert T. 766 W. Adams
Osgood Edwin, Oak Park
Osgood Edwin S. Austin
Osgood Everett W. Winnetka
Osgood E. E. 713 Pullman bldg.
Osgood Frederic S. Austin
Osgood George B. 766 W. Adams
Osgood Harry S. 766 W. Adams
Osgood Henry H. 802 Winthrop av.
Osgood James S. 1815 Surf
Osgood John D. 272 S. Irving av.
Osgood Laleah B. Mrs. 635 Walnut
Osgood Sarah J. Mrs. 649 Washington boul.
Osgood Stacy W. Winnetka
Osgoodby R. H. Hinsdale
Osher Grace Miss, 3812 Wabash av.
Osher Joseph, 4927 Michigan av.
Osmun Daniel C.17 Aldine sq. *U.L.*
Oster Lawrence, 220 Warren av.

Osterman Samuel, 4333 Prairie av.
Ostling E. J. 2292 N. Ashland av.
Ostrander B. Mrs. Winnetka
Ostrander Dempster, 23, 35th
Ostrander John G. 1077 W. Monroe
Ostrander J. W. 1077 W. Monroe
Ostrander Ralph L. Austin
Ostrom Alfred Rev. LaGrange
Ostrom James A. 5039 Washington av. C.A.
Oswald Arthur, 256 Warren av.
Oswald Edwin, 256 Warren av.
Oswald F. A. 256 Warren av.
　　　　Sum. res. Johnsburg, Ill.
Oswald Hugo, 256 Warren av.
Oswald J. W. Dr. 449 Belden av.
Otis A. Mrs. 4504 Lake av.
Otis Charles D. 3028 Lake Park av.
Otis Charles T. 2033 Prairie av. Cal., C.A., Univ.
Otis C. D. Mrs. 793 Washington boul.
Otis Ephraim A. 15 Ritchie ct. Univ.
Otis Frank C. Mrs. 4168 Drexel boul.
Otis F. R. 2033 Prairie av.
Otis George A. 7156 Euclid av.
Otis George C. 1544 Fulton
Otis George L. 2014 Michigan av. Cal., Chi.
Otis Henry A. LaGrange
Otis Henry B. 3028 Lake Park av.
Otis Irving, 4508 Lake av.
Otis Joseph E. 1730 Prairie av. Cal.
Otis Joseph E. jr. 2832 Prairie av. Univ.
Otis Lucius B. 2458 Michigan av.
Otis Lucius J. 2033 Prairie av.
Otis Philip A. Chicago Athletic assn.
Otis Philo A. 1722 Michigan av. Cal., Univ., W.P.
Otis Ralph C. 1730 Prairie av.
Otis Thomas G. 4508 Lake av.
Otis William A. Winnetka. Univ.
Otis William K. 15 Ritchie ct.
Otis X. L. Mrs. 1906 Michigan av.
Ott Charles B. 5155 Prairie av.
Ott John N. 591 Washington boul.
Ott J. W. Oak Park
Ott Katherine Mrs. 591 Washington boul.
Ott Oran, 591 Washington boul.
Ott William C. 5146 Jefferson av.
Ott William H. 5146 Jefferson av.
Ottenheimer David M. 4231 Calumet av.
Ottenheimer Henry L. 3253 Indiana av.
Ottenheimer Leopold, 3253 Indiana av.
Otterson G. C. Miss, 1015 Winona av.
Otterson J. Mrs. 1015 Winona av.
Ottie William E. 1192 Washington boul.
Ottman P. M. 6018 Michigan av.
Ottman William B. 5732 Rosalie ct.
　　　　Sum. res. Silver Lake, Wis.
Otto Arthur L. 4347 Ellis av.
Otto Emil Prof. Elmhurst
Otton Edmond G. 6116 Kimbark av.
Oughton Charles M. Dr. 5410 Jefferson av.
Outerbridge William G. 505 W. Congress
Outhet John C. 399 W. Monroe
Outhet Reuble M. 399 W. Monroe. Ill.

Overbagh Franklin, Evanston
Overman Linnæus E. 3516 Lake av. Cal.
Overmeyer John B. 118 Ashland boul. Ill.
Overpeck Elmer E. 4458 Oakenwald av.
Ovitt A. W. 818 Walnut
Owen Edwin G. Oak Park
Owen Ernest Dale, 3710 Ellis av.
　　　　Sum. res. Marquette, Mich.
Owen George H. Oak Park
Owen Ira J. Oak Park
Owen James R. 1902 Michigan av. U.L.
Owen K. R. 294 Lasalle av. C.A.
Owen Lucille Miss, 5520 Washington av.
Owen Malcolm D. 2210 Prairie av. Cal., W.P.
Owen Ole, 2001 Michigan av. Cal.
Owen Richard, Glen Ellyn
Owen R. W. Glen Ellyn
Owen William D. 2155 Sheridan rd.
　　　　Sum. res. Lauderdale Lake, Wis.
Owen William R. Oak Park
Owen Willis P. Oak Park
Owen W. B. 5823 Madison av.
Owens Frederick, 50 Loomis
Owens F. M. Mrs. Austin
Owens J. E. Dr. 1806 Michigan av. Cal.
Owens Marie G. Miss, 1806 Michigan av.
Owens Robert Mrs. 50 Loomis
Owens W. G. 419 The Plaza
Owings Frank P. 516 The Plaza
Owsley Harry B. 142 Astor
Owsley Heaton, 408 Erie. Univ.
　　　　Sum. res. Glencoe
Owsley H. E. Mrs. Chicago Beach hotel
Owsley Louis S. 45, 22d. W.P.
Oxnam William B. 435 Englewood av.
Oyer A. D. 446 W. Congress
Ozias Eli R. 1380 W. Jackson boul.

PACAUD A. D. Lexington hotel. C.A.
　　Pacaud A. Lincoln, Chicago club. C.A., W.P.
Pack William Morris Dr. 3850 Ellis av.
Packard Arthur T. 1847 Arlington pl.
Packard Edgar D. 3312 Rhodes av.
Packard Edward A. 4736 Lake av. U.L.
Packard George, 1922 Barry av.
Packard George W. 49, 29th pl.
Packard James B. Mrs. 632 Washington boul.
Packard James D. 3523 Grand boul.
Packard Marcus A. O. 39 Woodland Park
Packard Samuel W. Oak Park
Packard Sarah B. Mrs. 3846 Lake av.
Packer Charles Mrs. 3361 Calumet av.
Packer Charles P. 4747 Lake av. U.L.
Packer John F. LaGrange
Padan Robert S. 515 W. 62d
Paddleford C. C. 4546 Oakenwald av.
Paddock Benjamin S. 4618 Evans av.
Paddock C. E. Dr. 2931 Indiana av.
Paddock George L. 5451 Cornell av. Univ.
Paddock James V. S. Prof. 6032 Monroe av.
Paddock Martin L. LaGrange
Paddock Wilburn E. 3532 Ellis av.

Paddock William E. Evanston
Paddock William G. Mrs. Evanston
Paddon A. A. 4591 Oakenwald av.
Padelford George W. Oak Park
　　　　Sum. res. South Haven, Mich.
Paden Joseph E. Evanston. *U.L.*
Paden Willard S. Evanston *C.A.*
Paepcke Herman, 147 Lincoln Park boul.
　　　　Sum. res. Glencoe
Page Alice W. Miss, 2126 Prairie av.
Page Cecil, 5330 Madison av.
Page Charles, Evanston
Page Charles G. Oak Park
Page Charles L. 4544 St. Lawrence av.
Page Charles T. 6562 Stewart av.
Page Eleanor Miss, 2126 Prairie av.
Page Ethel F. Miss, 4747 Kimbark av.
Page F. P. LaGrange
Page Harvey L. Oak Park
Page H. E. River Forest
Page James C. 103 Buena av. *C.A.*
Page J. Frank, 3617 Wabash av.
Page Minnie Mrs. 4551 Champlain av.
Page Orvis A. 6220 Greenwood av.
Page Ralph Hugh, 4747 Kimbark av.
Page Samuel S. 5330 Madison av. *Irq.*,
　　U.L.
Page William R. 4747 Kimbark av. *U.L.*,
　　Univ.
Page William T. 4747 Kimbark av.
Pagin Harry, 4728 Prairie av.
Pagin L. A. LaGrange
Pagin Oliver E. 1707 Deming pl.
Pahlman Ida Miss, Hotel Del Prado
Paige Eliza T. Mrs. 303 S. Irving av.
Paige F. W. Irving Park
Pain Charles E. 589 Burling
Paine Albert G. Dr. 3964 Drexel boul.
Paine Cornelius D. Oak Park
Paine Lyman M. 4224 Langley av.
Paine Romeyn M. Dr. 47 Stratford pl.
Paine S. M. Miss, 5555 Monroe av.
Painter Charles S. 117, 49th
Painter Joseph A. 905 Walnut
Pajeau Charles H. 4345 Grand boul.
Pajeau Joseph, 4345 Grand boul.
Pallett Frank S. Wilmette
Palm Warren S. 633 W. 62d
Palmer Albert E. Dr. 721 Lincoln av.
Palmer B. L. Hotel Luzerne
Palmer Charles H. 6547 Stewart av.
Palmer Charles H. 7741 Lowe av.
Palmer Charles M. 496, 42d
Palmer Edwin B. Highland Park
Palmer Ernest E. 820 Walnut
Palmer Eugene P. Hotel Metropole
Palmer F. A. Auditorium hotel
Palmer George R. 5002 Ellis av.
Palmer Honore, 100 Lake Shore drive
Palmer John F. Riverside. *C.A.*
Palmer John Mayo, 2358 Indiana av.
Palmer John McCauley, Lexington hotel
Palmer John T. 2358 Indiana av.
Palmer John W. Oak Park. *U.L.*
Palmer J. F. Chicago Beach hotel
Palmer J. H. Chicago Beach hotel

Palmer J. P. Dr. Riverside
Palmer Louisa H. Mrs. 464 W. Adams
Palmer L. A. Mrs. 496, 42d
Palmer Mary C. Mrs. 4409 Greenwood av.
Palmer Milton J. 4124 Grand boul.
Palmer Percival B. 5006 Ellis av. *U.L.*
Palmer Percy W. Evanston. *U.L.*
Palmer Potter, 100 Lake Shore drive.
　　Chi., Irq., W.P.
Palmer Potter jr. 100 Lake Shore drive
Palmer Robert B. 240 Bissell
Palmer Robertson, 2358 Indiana av.
Palmer Silas, 452 Warren av.
Palmer Sumner C. 4305 Oakenwald av.
Palmer Thomas D. Dr. 691 Washington
　　boul.
Palmer Truman G. Irving Park
Palmer Violet H. Miss, 721 Lincoln av.
Palmer William, 3100 Groveland av.
Palmer Wm. H. 295, 53d
Palmer William H. 452 Warren av.
Palmer William P. 51, 52d. *Cal., Chi.,*
　　W.P.
Palmer W. C. B. 4148 Grand boul. *Ill.*
Palmer W. W. Mrs. 1814 Michigan av.
Palmeter DeWitt C. 293 Park av.
Palmiter Alta Mae Miss, 4432 Ellis av.
Palmiter M. Mrs. 4432 Ellis av.
Paltzer Charles A. 3614 Michigan av
Pam Alexander, 4547 Oakenwald av.
Pam Max, 4547 Oakenwald av. *Stan.*
Pancoast J. Cameron, 2979 Prairie av.
Pank J. Henry, 683 Fullerton av.
Panter J. C. Dr. Oak Park
Panushka John W. Wilmette
Panushka William, Wilmette
Paoli Gerhard C. Dr. 1834 Arlington pl.
Pape E. T. Hinsdale
Pape T. C. Hinsdale
Paradise M. C. 872 W. Adams
Parcells Frank, Lake Forest
Pardee Agnes Miss, 402 N. State
Pardee Agnes S. Mrs. 402 N. State
Pardee Charles A. Mrs. 1358 Millard av.
Pardee Luther Rev. Austin
Pardee L. C. Dr. 402 N. State
Pardee M. F. 624 Lasalle av.
Pardey Harry W. 1058 Warren av. *C.A,*
Pardridge Anson, 4157 Langley av.
Pardridge C. E. 5163 Wabash av.
Pardridge C. W. 3200 Michigan av. *C.A.,*
　　W.P.
Pardridge Edward W. 2926 Indiana av.
Pardridge Edwin Mrs. 2808 Prairie av.
Pardridge Florence Miss, 2808 Prairie av.
Pardridge Frank R. 4403 Ellis av. *C.A.*
Pardridge Fred C. Hotel Metropole. *C.A.,*
　　W.P.
Pardridge M. L. Mrs. 3945 Lake av.
Pardridge W. E. 2817 Indiana av. *Cal.*
Parent Arthur M. Pullman
Parish Charles P. 4717 Kimbark av.
Parish F. E. 5530 Washington av.
Parish Harry F. 4828 Kimbark av.
Parish John D. Dr. 3953 Michigan av.
Parish Lucius W. Irving Park

Parish Rosamond P. Mrs. 4721 Kimbark av.
Parish S. M. 2956 Groveland av.
Parish William F. 4828 Kimbark av.
Parish William F. jr. 4828 Kimbark av.
Park Augustus V. Dr. 2529 Indiana av.
       Sum. res. Bluff Lake, Ill.
Park A. J., M.D. 3200 Vernon av.
Park George H. Austin
Park Stephen A. 5430 Lexington av.
Parke John E. 5311 Washington av.
Parker Albert O. 248, 53d
Parker Anna M., M.D. 53 Warren av.
Parker Austin H. 248, 53d
Parker A. A. Lexington hotel
Parker A. H., M.D. Evanston
Parker A. K. Rev. 612 W. Jackson boul.
Parker Brainerd M. 248, 53d
Parker Charles H. Dr. 4707 St. Lawrence av.
Parker Charles W. Evanston
Parker Edward A. 725 Fullerton av.
Parker E. Harry, Evanston
Parker E. H. Evanston
Parker E. Louise Miss, 4418 Oakenwald av.
Parker Francis W. Union League club
Parker Frank W. 6640 Parnell av.
Parker Frederick A. 624 W. Congress
Parker George G. 501 W. Jackson boul. *Ill.*
Parker G. H. Mrs. Evanston
Parker Hale G. 6342 Greenwood av.
Parker Harry E. River Forest
Parker Harry M. Evanston
Parker Helen M., M.D. 53 Warren av.
Parker Henry O. 1629 Sheridan rd.
Parker Hilon A. Tracy. *U.L.*
Parker Horace B. LaGrange
Parker H.Wilson, 112 Lincoln Park boul.
Parker James H. Evanston
Parker James J. 4418 Oakenwald av.
Parker James K. Winnetka
Parker James O. Winnetka
Parker John D. 31 Aldine sq.
Parker John D. Dr. 609 W. Garfield boul.
Parker John F. 3667 Michigan av.
Parker J. Grafton, 4418 Oakenwald av. *U.L.*
Parker J. Grafton jr. 5425 Cottage Grove av.
Parker J. J. 4737 Lake av.
Parker J. J. jr. 4737 Lake av.
Parker J. M. 3953 Michigan av.
Parker Lamont E. 4128 Ellis av.
Parker Leander D. Evanston
Parker Lewis W. Evanston. *C.A.*
Parker Marcia Mrs. 4310 Oakenwald av.
Parker Mary A. J. Mrs. 1457 N. Clark
Parker M. L. River Forest
Parker N. M. Miss, 3645 Prairie av.
Parker Robert Mercer, 386 Erie. *Un.*
Parker Robert P. Oak Park
Parker R. S. 3413 Vernon av.
Parker Samuel M. 4535 Lake av.
41

Parker Samuel W. Lexington hotel. *Cal. Chi., W.P.*
Parker Sidney, Tracy
Parker Thomas L. 5041 Washington av.
       Sum. res. Oconomowoc, Wis.
Parker William C. 3667 Michigan av.
Parker William R. 491, 42d pl.
Parker William W. Dr. Irving Park
Parkes Isabella Mrs. Evanston
Parkes John C. 135 Seminary av.
Parkes John C. jr. 135 Seminary av.
Parkes William B. Evanston
Parkes William R. Dr. Evanston
Parkhurst Alton, Evanston
Parkhurst Emogene Dr. Evanston
Parkhurst George L. Evanston
Parkhurst H. W. 47, 77th
Parkhurst Josiah J. Evanston. *U.L.*
Parkhurst M. M. Miss, 5743 Madison av.
Parkhurst Nelson D. 5743 Madison av.
Parkhurst W. S. Mrs. 5136 Kimbark av.
Parkins Geo. B. 5532 Jefferson av.
Parkins Horace G. 4736 Champlain av.
Parkinson Joseph G. 4805 Lake av.
Parkinson Robert H. 69 Bellevue pl. *Chi. U.L.*
Parkison Edwin J. Dr. 6923 Stewart av.
Parks Frank M. 8 Oakland crescent
Parks Samuel S. 1543 Fulton
Parks William R. 379, 44th
Parliament S. 3331 Calumet av.
Parmelee Charles K. Great Northern hotel. *Chi., W.P.*
Parmelee Edward D. Kenilworth. *C.A.*
Parmelee Frank, Palmer house. *W.P.*
Parmelee Frank jr. 1186 N. Clark
Parmelee John W. Lexington hotel. *Chi., Un., W.P.*
Parmenter Dr. Lake Forest
Parmly H. C. Mrs. 3811 Grand boul.
Parmly Samuel P. 3811 Grand boul.
Parmly Samuel P. jr. 3811 Grand boul.
Parr Alexander Mrs. Wilmette
Parr Edward S. Wilmette
Parr George R. Wilmette
Parrotte Walter Lee, Hotel Windermere. *U.L.*
Parry John C. Glencoe
Parshall Ross T. 23 Bellevue pl.
Parshall R. F. Mrs. 770 W. Monroe
Parsons Charles T. 5825 Kimbark av.
Parsons F. G. 4517 Prairie av.
Parsons George F. Dr. 153 Oakwood boul.
Parsons Harry Dr. 2588 N. Hermitage av.
Parsons H. E. Mrs. 5216 Jefferson av.
Parsons John C. 5714 Madison av. *Univ.*
Parsons J. B. Union club
Parsons O. M. 44, 35th
Parsons R. L. Hotel Windermere
Parsons William E. Sherman house
Parsons William H. 437 Dearborn av.
Parsons William R. Dr. 4506 Emerald av.
Parsons W. H. Rev. 2358 Indiana av.
Parsons W. R. Irving Park
Partridge Charles S. 6114 Woodlawn av.

Partridge Ellen C. Dr. 7248 Union av.
Partridge Lyman H. 839 Touhy av.
Partridge Newton A. 5614 Madison av. U.L.
Pasco M. E. Mrs. 4008 Grand boul.
Pashley Alfred F. Palos Park. U.L.
Patch George M. Oak Park
Patchen J. J. 6246 Woodlawn av.
Patchen Sarah A. Miss, Highland Park
Pate Davey S. 3425 Vernon av.
Patera F. J., M. D. 675 W. Taylor
Paterson E. A. 6115 Kimbark av.
Paterson James H. Avenue house, Evanston
Paterson James S. 6119 Kimbark av.
Paterson Margaret J. Miss, 6119 Kimbark av.
Patoille Joseph, 2703 N. Robey
Paton Jessie Miss, LaGrange
Patrick Benjamin F. jr. 4412 Berkeley av. C.A.
Patrick Charles B. Austin
Patrick Charles E. 6159 Lexington av. C.A.
Patrick Henry E. Oak Park. U.L.
Patrick Hugh T. Dr. 465 Lasalle av.
Patrick H. E. Mrs. 1120 Washington boul.
Patrick Joseph H. The Arizona. C.A.
Patrick M. A. Mrs. Lexington hotel
Patrick M. L. Mrs. Austin
Patrick Ralph W. Oak Park
Patrick Zorah E. Dr. 25 Woodland Park
Patten Agnes Mrs. Evanston
Patten Anna W. Mrs. 6463 Kimbark av.
Patten A. W. Rev. 5203 Hibbard av.
Patten Frederick H. 1688 Buckingham pl.
Patten George W. Evanston
Patten Harry J. Evanston. C.A.
Patten James A. Evanston. Ill.
Patten John B. 3953 Michigan av.
Patten William E. 3953 Michigan av.
Patterson Anna Miss, Evanston
Patterson Austin L. 384 Warren av.
Patterson A. Wallie, 79 Warren av. C.A., Ill.
Patterson Charles A. 705 W. Jackson boul.
Patterson Don R. 7131 Princeton av.
Patterson Estella Miss, 4144 Grand boul.
Patterson Florence Miss, 4144 Grand boul.
Patterson Frank E. 4403 Indiana av.
Patterson Franklin Dr. 265 Warren av.
Patterson Fred W. 166, 51st
Patterson George M. Evanston
Patterson Howard E. LaGrange
Patterson John, 3670 Wabash av.
Patterson John C. 196 Cass. C.A.
Patterson John H. Lombard
Patterson J. M., Chicago Beach hotel
Patterson Kathryn T. Mrs. 533 N. State
Patterson Robert W. Mrs. Evanston
          Winter res. Washington, D. C.
Patterson Robert W. 166 Astor. Chi., C.A. W.P.

Patterson R. M. Clifton house
Patterson Stewart, 705 The Plaza. C.A.
Patterson S. A. Mrs. 265 Warren av.
Patterson S. P. 384 Warren av.
Patterson Theodore H. 194, 37th
Patterson Thomas E. Mrs. 268, 33d
Patterson William A. 640 Pine Grove av.
Patterson W. R. 5730 Monroe av.
Patterson W. R. River Forest
Pattison Arthur, 453 North av.
Pattison James L. 498 W. Jackson boul.
Pattison James W. Ohio ne. cor. N. State
Pattison Thomas, Oak Park
Pattison William L. 498 W. Jackson boul.
Patton E. K. Mrs. 3753 Ellis av.
Patton J. M. Dr. 237 S. Hoyne av.
Patton Norman S. Oak Park. U.L.
Patton Robert W. Highland Park. U.L
Patzack Frank, 717 N. Robey
Paul C. R. Hotel Metropole. C.A.
Paul Edgar T. Wilmette
Paul Frank M. Wilmette
Paul Henry R. 815 Warren av.
Paul John C. 1414 Roscoe
Paul Joseph, 69 Walton pl.
Paul Ph. D., Dr. 915 Chase av.
Paulin Fred C. Morgan Park
Pauling Edward G. 25 Astor. C.A., U.L.
Paullin George W. Evanston
Paulsen William A. 3529 Ellis av. C.A.
Paxson John W. 4310 Indiana av.
Payen Cecile E. Miss, 4043 Ellis av.
Payen C. Mrs. 4043 Ellis av.
Payen Juliette Miss, 4043 Ellis av.
Payn R. E. Mrs. Oak Park
Payne Alfred Mrs. Hinsdale
Payne Annie Miss, Hinsdale
Payne A. M. Mrs. 410 Oak
Payne Bertha Miss, 335 S. Halsted
Payne Bruce C. 4831 Langley av.
Payne D. A. Dr. 110 S. Oakley av.
Payne Frank D. 534 Evanston av.
Payne Henry, Hinsdale
Payne James, 534 Evanston av.
Payne John Barton Judge, 3230 Groveland av. U.L.
Payne Leroy, The Winamac
          Sum. res. Chebanse, Ill.
Payne Mabel Miss, 38 Roslyn pl.
Payne Robert Preston, 534 Evanston av.
Payne Walter A. 5833 Monroe av.
Payne Wm. C. Hinsdale
Payne William Morton, 1601 Prairie av.
Paynter Henry M. 4045 Calumet av.
Paysen Frederick H. 56 Evergreen av.
Payson Edward, Oak Park
Payson George S. 88 Astor. Chi., Univ.
          Sum. res. Hyannis Port, Mass.
Payson Joseph R. 1262 Wilcox av.
Payson Joseph R. jr. Oak Park
Payson S. C. 32 Banks. Un.
Peabody Augustus S. 426 Dearborn av. Univ.
Peabody Earl W. 5747 Madison av.
Peabody F. B. 426 Dearborn av. Chi., Irq.

Peabody Frederick F. Evanston. *U.L.*
Peabody F. Stuyvesant, 503 The Plaza. *C.A.,Irq.* Winter res. Thomasville, Ga.
Peabody Hiram B. 2968 Michigan av.
Peabody James, 5747 Madison av.
Peabody James B. 644 W. Adams
Peabody J. A. 644 W. Adams
Peabody Selim H. 7424 Butler
Peacock Alice Miss, 4814 Grand boul.
Peacock Charles S. 3211 Prairie av.
Peacock C.D.1713 Indiana av. *Cal., C.A., W.P.* Sum. res. Green Lake, Wis.
Peacock C. D. jr. 2000 Indiana av. *C.A.*
Peacock Elijah P. 921 S. Sawyer av.
Peacock Frederick E. 931 S. Sawyer av.
Peacock Margaret A. Mrs. 4814 Grand boul.
Peacock Russell D. 4239 Prairie av.
Peacock William H. 1375 N. Halsted
Peak Frank Harris, 615 N. Clark
Peake Anna Mrs. 4208 Prairie av.
Peake Frederick, 315 Flournoy
Pearce Charles F. 5815 Drexel av.
Pearce Frank I. 3627 Grand boul.
Sum. res. "The Island," Fox Lake, Ill.
Pearce John F. 548 W. 62d
Pearce John Irving, Sherman house
Pearce John Irving jr. Sherman house
Pearce Martha T. Dr. 7058 Parnell av.
Pearce Mary Miss, Evanston
Pearce Myron, Sherman house
Pearce Myron A. 4621 Greenwood av.
Pearce Myron L. 2548 Prairie av.
Pearce William C. Sherman house
Peare George R. 667 Winthrop av.
Peare Richard M. jr. 52 Campbell Park
Pearsall Albert L. Hinsdale
Pearson Andrew, 4058 Ellis av.
Pearson Arthur L. 509 W. Jackson boul.
Pearson Charles W. Prof. Evanston
Pearson Eugene H. 4726 Kimbark av. *Ill., U.L.*
Pearson Frank, 6320 Monroe av.
Pearson Haynie R. 518 W. Monroe
Pearson James H. 509 W. Jackson boul.
Pearson John L. Oak Park
Pearson Margaret J. Miss, Evanston
Pearson Mary Logan Miss, 518 W. Monroe
Pearson Mowbray F. Evanston
Pearson P. M. Prof. Evanston
Pearson R. N. Gen. 518 W. Monroe
Pearson William H. Chicago Athletic assn.
Pearsons D. K. Hinsdale
Pearsons Harry P. Evanston
Pearsons Henry A. Evanston. *U.L.*
Pearsons John A. Evanston
Pease Albert A. 364 Park av.
Pease Arthur B. 4509 Lake av.
Pease Edward H. 8 Washington pl. *C.A., Un.*
Pease Frank B. Berwyn
Pease F. N. Mrs. 2327 Michigan av.
Pease Frederick O. Dr. 67, 37th

Pease George D. 649 Washington boul.
Pease Hiram L., M. D. 7530 Greenwood av.
Pease James, 3212 Dover. *C.A.*
Pease J. W. Kenilworth
Pease Laura S. Mrs. 1093 Winona av.
Pease Philander P. 1729 Kenmore av.
Pease Philander P. jr. 1729 Kenmore av.
Pease Sarah B. Mrs. 143 Oakwood boul.
Pease Thomas H. 364 Park av.
Pease Walstein C. 1847 Belmont av.
Pease Wendell S. 1093 Winona av.
Peaslee E. S. 37, 33d
Peasley James C. 309 Huron. *Chi., C.A.*
Peattie Elia W. Mrs. 360 Erie
Peattie Robert B. 360 Erie
Peavey James F. Virginia hotel
Pebbles A. W. Oak Park
Pebbles Frank M. Oak Park
Pebbles Frank M. jr. Oak Park
Pebbles Henry R. Oak Park
Peck Allen S. LaGrange
Peck Allen W. Mrs. 451 Belden av.
Peck Alma J. Mrs. 720 W. Monroe
Peck Annah M. Miss, 3 Tower pl.
Peck Arline Miss, 1826 Michigan av.
Peck A. H. Dr. 721 N. Wells
Peck Bronson Mrs. 3328 Indiana av.
Peck Charles, 5487 Washington av.
Peck Clarence I. 2254 Michigan av. *Cal., Chi., C.A., U.L.*
Peck Clyde D. Chicago Beach hotel. *C.A.*
Peck Comfort E. Dr. 55 Lincoln Park boul.
Peck Daniel P. The Tudor
Peck David B. 55 Lincoln Park boul.
Peck Edwin R. 3 Plaisance ct.
Peck Ferdinand W. 1826 Michigan av. *Cal., Chi., C.A., U.L.* Sum. res. Oconomowoc, Wis.
Peck Ferdinand W. jr. 1826 Michigan av. *Cal., W.P.*
Peck Frank L. LaGrange
Peck George R. Virginia hotel. *Chi.,Un., U.L., Univ.*
Peck Harold S. Mrs. 3 Tower ct.
Sum. res. Oconomowoc, Wis.
Peck Haroldine Mrs. 3 Tower pl.
Peck Henry, Lombard
Peck Jerome T. 327 W. 61st
Peck Katherine G. 55 Pine
Peck O. D. Chicago Beach hotel. *U.L.*
Peck P. F. W. Mrs. 2254 Michigan av.
Sum. res. Oconomowoc, Wis.
Peck Robert Bowman, Granada hotel
Peck Staunton B. 415, 48th
Peck Theodore D. Chicago Beach hotel
Peck V. H. Lombard
Peck Walter L. Lexington hotel. *Cal., C.A., U.L.* Sum. res. Oconomowoc, Wis.
Peckham Charles L. 7150 Euclid av.
Peckham Charles V. 2241 Kenmore av.
Peckham R. W. Mrs. 4259 Grand boul.
Pedrick Isaac H. 2419 Michigan av.
Peebles Arthur S. 5126 East End av.

Peebles Milicent S. Mrs. 3122 Michigan av.
Peebles William S. 5126 East End av.
Peeke E. W. 3404 Wabash av.
Peeke William H. jr. 2728 Calumet av.
Peeples John M. 3235 Groveland av.
Peet Charles E. 5327 Madison av.
Peet Henry J. 1701 Sheridan rd. *Univ.*
Peet Stephen D. Rev. 5327 Madison av.
Peirce Albert E. Evanston
Peirce Arthur H. Calumet club. *C.A.,* *W.P.*
Peirce Charles Leonard, 70 Madison Park
Peirce Daniel A. 5464 Washington av.
Peire E. A. Mrs. Hotel Del-Prado
Peirce James H. 202 Goethe. *Un.;* *Univ.*
Peirce Luther H. 1904 Surf
Peirce Mary M. Miss, 3363 South Park av.
Peirce Ralph Sumner, 70 Madison Park
Peirce William G. E. 3363 South Park av.
Peirce W. H. H. 5025 Lake av.
Peiro Frank L. Dr. 236 Sunnyside av.
Peiser J. Mrs. 3408 Forest av.
Peiser Samuel C. 3348 Forest av.
Peixotto Beatrix Madura Miss, 4748 Prairie av.
Peixotto G. D. Maduro, 4748 Prairie av.
Peixotto H. S. Mme. 4748 Prairie av.
Peixotto Victoria Maud Miss, 4748 Prairie av.
Pellet Clarence S. Oak Park
Pelouze Wm.NelsonCol.HotelMetropole. *C.A.*
Peltzer Otto, 5634 Jackson av.
Pemberton Mildred F. Mrs. 291 Michigan av.
Pence A. M. 550 N. State. *U.L.*
Pendleton Edmund, 3338 Calumet av.
Penepacker Samuel, 7738 Lowe av.
Penfield Frank, 1819 Alden av.
Penfield George J. 2672 N. Lincoln
Penfield H. D. 2456 Prairie av.
Penfield John Mrs. 849, 72d pl.
Penfield Truman, 610 Dearborn av.
Penhallow William P. 33, 37th. *C.A.*
Penington Charles R. 95 Oakwoods av.
Penington Thomas C. 4012 Drexel boul.
Penington Walter V. 4012 Drexel boul.·
Peniston N. A. Miss, Lexington hotel
Penniman F. C. Wilmette
Pennington Fred A. 5722 Washington av.·
Pennington Henry F. 5722Washington av.
Pennington Henry F. jr. 5722 Washington av.
Pennington J. M. 7241 Harvard av.
Pennington M. P. 7137 Eggleston av.*C.A.*
Pennington R. 3539 Michigan av.
Pennoyer George M. 4037 Ellis av. *C.A.*
                Sum. res. Kenosha, Wis.
Pennoyer G. M. Mrs. 4037 Ellis av.
Pennoyer James C. 3244 Lake Park av.
Penny A. W. Park Ridge. *U.L.*
Penny Elizabeth Mrs. 82 S. Seeley av.
Penny Frank H. 82 S. Seeley av.
Pentecost W. H. Irving Park
Penwell G. V. Leland hotel

Perce H. Wallace, 509 Dearborn av.
Perce-LeGrand W. 509 Dearborn av. *U.L.*
Percy Louise W. Mrs. 451 S. Oakley av.
Perekhan J. S. Dr. 2406 Prairie av.
Perfitt Locke, 6520 Lexington av.
Periam Jonathan, 526 Englewood av.
Perine Josiah W. 2818 Calumet av.
Perine Margaret S. Mrs. 2818 Calumet av.
Periolat R. 1828 Surf
Perkins Alonzo D. 3258 Cottage Grove av.
Perkins A. L. Mrs. 6124 Indiana av.
Perkins B. Chapman, LaGrange
Perkins B. W. LaGrange
Perkins Charles, 663 Washington boul.
Perkins Dwight H. 3920 Indiana av. *C.A.*
Perkins Frederick W. Union club. *Cal.,* *C.A., W.P.*
Perkins Henry S. Dr. 1628 Indiana av.
Perkins Herbert F. 2545 Kenmore av.
Perkins Martha Mrs. 828 Warren av.
Perkins M. H. Mrs. 3929 Indiana av.
Perkins Robert, Berwyn
Perkins Vincent H. 194 Cass
Perkins V. D. Mrs. 330 Oakwood boul.
Perkins Walton, 3739 Indiana av.
                Sum. res. Charlevoix, Mich.
Perkinson J. H. 1189 W. Adams
Perlbach C. Adolphus, 4160 Ellis av.
Perley E. E. 4956 Washington av.
Perley F. E. Mrs. 235 Michigan av.
Perrett Galen J. 698 W. Adams
Perrett J. C. Mrs. 698 W. Adams
Perrigo A. B. 2956 Wabash av.
Perrill Albert C. 892 Warren av.
Perrin William R. 4830 Greenwood av.
Perry Alvah Mrs. 319 Bowen av.
Perry Arthur J. 922 W. Adams
Perry Charles F. 1238 N. Clark
Perry Charles N. 3228 South Park av.
Perry Crooker, 343, 53d
Perry David P. 344 Oakwood boul.
Perry E. O. Hotel Metropole
Perry Francis N. Rev. 2705 N. Ashland av.
Perry Frederick B. 5210 Washington av.
Perry Henry G. Rev. priest Epis. ch. 79 N. Oakley av. nr. Fulton
Perry Howard E. 1619 Prairie av. *U.L.*
Perry H. A. 4144 Grand boul.
Perry H. Francis Rev. 513 W. 62d
Perry Isaac N. 2900 Prairie av. *Cal.,U.L.*
Perry Lewis S. 4515 Greenwood av. *Cal., W.P.*
Perry P. J. 2384 N. Paulina
Perry S. M. Mrs. 5131 Indiana av.
Perry S. Q. 343, 53d
Perry Thomas O. 1025 Park av. *C.A.*
Perry W. D. Hinsdale
Pershing James F. 6018 Kimbark av.
Person David Van Ness, 3242 Rhodes av. *C.A.*
Person James, 5460 Ridgewood ct.
Peters Alexander H. 560 Washington boul.
Peters C. V. L. 262 Warren av. *Ill.*
Peters Frank, 29 St. James pl.

Peters Frank M. 29 St. James pl.
Peters Harry V. Mayfair
Peters Homer H. 5528 East End av. *C.A.*
Peters Joseph G. 2886 Kenmore av. *Ill.*
Peters Lois K. Mrs. 2886 Kenmore av.
Peters Roswell A. Chicago club
Peters Ulric G. 1400W.Jackson boul.*C.A.*
Peters W. Morgan, 518 Dearborn av.
Petersen Hermann, 601 Dearborn av.
Petersen James, 603 Cleveland av.
Petersen Julius, 275 Ashland boul.
Peterson Alice Mrs. 2126 Indiana av.
Peterson Andrew, Union League club
Peterson Charles W. 2449 Prairie av.
Peterson George L. 595 Pine Grove av.
Peterson James A. Irving Park
Peterson Kate B. Dr. Irving Park
Peterson Minnie Miss, 477 Washington boul.
Peterson Peter 641 Fullerton av.
Peterson P. S. Rose Hill. *U.L.*
Peterson Wickliff, 651 Fullerton av.
Peterson William A. Rose Hill. *U.L.*
Peterson William F. 171 Warren av.
Petesch Charlotte Miss, 3267 Beacon
Petrie Charles S. 17 Ewing pl.
Petrie William J. Rev. 6540 Minerva av.
Pettengill A. A. Mrs. 640 Fullerton av.
Pettibone Amos, 316 Belden av.
Pettibone Asa G. 235 Michigan av. *Chi.*,
    C.A., U.L., W.P. Sum. res. Evergreen Lawn, New YorkMills, N. Y.
Pettibone Earl A. 1345 Morse av.
Pettibone Frank B. Oak Park
Pettibone Frederick, 155 Warren av.
Pettibone Howard C. 147 Ashland boul. *Ill.*
Pettibone Ira W. Col. 155 Warren av.
Pettibone Philo Foster, 159 Warren av. *Ill., U.L.*
Pettibone R. S. Austin
Pettis Catherine A. Miss, Evanston
Pettis William, 7330 Bond av.
Pettit James, Chicago Beach hotel
Pettit William, B. 270 Michigan av.
Petty R. W. 2124 Michigan av.
Peyser F. Mrs. 4406 Michigan av.
Peyton Agnes Miss, 1886 Diversey
Peyton Richard F. 4015 Lake av.
Peyton Richard F. jr. 4015 Lake av.
Pfaelzer Bernhard, 3609 Vernon av.
Pfaelzer David, 430 Fulton. *Lksd.*
Pfaelzer David J. 4512 Vincennes av.
Pfaelzer David M. 4105 Grand boul. *Stan.*
    Sum. res. Winnetka, Ill.
Pfaelzer Eli, 4614 Champlain av. *Lksd.*
Pfaelzer Leopold, 3611 Vernon av.
Pfaelzer Louis, 430 Fulton. *Stan.*
Pfaelzer Simon, 2712 Wabash av. *Lksd.*
Pfaff Charles B. 4331 Lake av.
Pfanstiehl A. A. Rev. Highland Park
Pfeifer Josephine D. Dr. Auditorium Annex
Pfeiffer Christian R. 486 Bowen av.
Pfeiffer Christopher, 70 Lincoln av.
Pfeil Charles H. 1344 Wilton av.

Pfirshing Joseph, 3001 Groveland av.
Pfister Emma M. Mrs. 215 Belden av.
Pfister William C. 268 Fremont
Pflager Harry M. 1307 W. Adams
Pflaum Abram, 3311 Calumet av.
Pflaum Harry, 3311 Calumet av. *Stan.*
Pflaum Morris, 3311 Calumet av.
Pflug G. A. Rev. 4057 Prairie av.
Pfuderer W. F. Berwyn
Pfuhl George A. Morgan Park
Phalen Frank J. 1574 Kenmore av.
Phalen Michael W. 1574 Kenmore av.
Phelizot Kate Mrs. 573 Division
Phelps Charles E. 3601 Vincennes av. *C. A.*
Phelps D. P. 410 Superior. *Irq.*
Phelps Edward J. 5115 Cornell av.
Phelps Edward P. 3000 Prairie av.
Phelps Elliott H. 4619 Grand boul. *Chi., C.A., U.L., W.P.*
Phelps Erskine M. 1703 Indiana av. *Cal., Chi., Irq., W. P.*
Phelps Foster C. 267, 47th
Phelps George B. jr. 2822 Prairie av. *Irq., U.L., Univ.*
Phelps Harlow W. 743 Touhy av.
Phelps Irene Miss, 5320 Cornell av.
Phelps Joseph A. Park Ridge
Phelps Minnie A. Miss, Evanston
Phelps O. B. Mrs. 2427 Indiana av.
Phelps S. F. 55, 53d
Phelps Wm. 756 W. 63d pl.
Phelps William 3158 South Park av.
Phelps William J. Elmwood
Phelps William W. Mrs. 2518 Prairie av.
Phelps W. H. 3331 Vernon av. *Cal.*
Philbin John, 20 Chalmers pl.
Philbin John J. 20 Chalmers pl.
Philbrick George A. Austin
Philbrick M. E. Miss, 674 Fullerton av.
Philipsborn Max, 4760 Champlain av. *Lksd.*
Philipson Isador, 3235 Vernon av. *Lksd.*
Philleo Susan H. Mrs. 305 The Plaza
Phillip Peter, 646 Lunt av.
Phillips Abraham, 424 Lasalle av.
Phillips Arthur E. 426, 41st
Phillips Carrie L. Miss, 4730 Drexel boul.
Phillips Charles H. 175, 47th. *Cal.*
Phillips Charles W. 1960 Sheridan rd.
Phillips Clesson B. 2978 Prairie av.
Phillips Cornelius J. Dr. 401 W. Garfield boul.
Phillips C. G. Highland Park
Phillips Edmund R. 4730 Drexel boul.
Phillips Francis V. LaGrange
Phillips Frank A. Dr. 380 S. Robey
Phillips Fred L. Austin
Phillips Henry, 5511 Cornell av.
Phillips Henry A. Dr. 844 W. Adams
Phillips Henry E. Mrs.2971 Michigan av.
Phillips H. R. 5471 Lexington av.
Phillips James A. 214 The Plaza
Phillips John F. Hotel Windermere
Phillips John F. Longwood
Phillips Joseph S. 424 Lasalle av.

Phillips J. M. Leland hôtel
Phillips J. S. jr. 424 Lasalle av.
Phillips Nathaniel A. 335 Warren av.
      Sum. res. Sans Souci, Mich.
Phillips Richard W. 5508 Cornell av.
Phillips Thomas P. 2241 Michigan av.
   Cal.
Phillips T. S. Mrs. 347 Dearborn av.
Phillips William, 176 Throop. Lksd.
Phillips William, 4416 Prairie av.
Phillips William A., M.D. Evanston
Phillips William B. Evanston
Phillips William E. 2241 Michigan av.
   Cal., C.A.
Phillipson Ralph, 29 Wisconsin
Philo E. B. Mrs. LaGrange
Philpot Albert D. 5238 Jefferson av.
Philpot Brian, 5238 Jefferson av.
Phipps Park, Evanston
Phister Walter B. 4739 Kenwood
Phoenix Charles R. Austin
Piacentini Titus Dr. Ohio, ne. cor. N.
   State
Piatt Abner, 4356 Calumet av.
Piatt Harry D. 4423 Prairie av.
Picard Paul, 139 Lincoln Park boul.
Pick Albert jr. 4417 Michigan av. Lksd.
Pick Charles, 3532 Wabash av.
Pick Gustav, 209 Fremont
Pick Richard, 1450 Wrightwood av.
Pick Richard A. 209 Fremont
Pickands Henry S. Auditorium annex.
   Chi.
Pickard Charles E. Maywood. U.L.
Pickard T. D. 2680 N. Hermitage av.
Pickels William D. 7631 Union av.
Pickering A. H. 4583 Oakenwald av.
Pickering Philander, 3516 Lake av. W.P.
      Sum. res. Mukwonago, Wis.
Pickett Albert G. Dr. 3141 South Park av.
Pickett Clayton C. 824 W. Adams
Pickett John D. River Forest
Pickett Joseph D. River Forest
Pickett William, 3745 Vernon av.
Pickett William A. 3141 South Park av.
Pickett W. S. Mrs. 3745 Vernon av.
Pickler Charles, Hotel Metropole
Pickrell Harvey, 88 Loomis
Pierce Addison S. 4209 Calumet av.
Pierce A. B. Mrs. 3116 South Park av.
Pierce Blanford R. 4225 Vincennes av.
Pierce Charles W. 4011 Prairie av.
Pierce Delia Mrs. 4726 Woodlawn av.
Pierce Donald, 16 Astor
Pierce Elmer E. Oak Park
Pierce Eva M. Mrs. Morgan Park
Pierce E. C. 767 Mildred av.
Pierce Frank H. Austin
Pierce Gerald, 6028 Stony Island av.
Pierce George W. 4847 Grand boul.
Pierce Grenville G. 687 W. Adams
Pierce Helen Miss, 6655 Stewart av.
Pierce Henry D. Oak Park
Pierce Herbert A. 4209 Calumet av.
Pierce James D. 6655 Stewart av.
Pierce Mary A. Mrs Austin

Pierce Nathan F. 689, 57th
Pierce Norval H. Dr. Virginia hotel
Pierce Osborn J. Oak Park
Pierce Sarah E. Miss 2358 Indiana av.
Pierce S. A. Miss, 4330 Oakenwald av.
Pierce Walter Bryant, 1940 Deming pl.
      Sum. res. " Ayrlie," Shepherdstown,
      W. Va.
Piercy Charles A. 4547 Greenwood av.
Pierpont Henry E. 4723 Prairie av.
Pierpont Henry V. 1807 Barry av.
Pierpont H. S. Mrs. 4723 Prairie av.
Pierpont R. B. Mrs. 6127 Kimbark av.
Pierson Frederick G. 3035 Vernon av,
Pierson John C. Wilmette
Pierson Louis J. Wilmette
Pierson Romaine, Hotel Windermere
Pierson Stephen N. 6234 Kimbark av.
Pierson T. E. Highland Park
Pieser Isaac, 3236 Wabash av. Lksd.
      Sum. res. Spring Lake, Mich.
Pietsch Charles F. 305 Huron
Pietsch Frank H. 1947 Deming pl.
Pietsch Otto E. 2271 N. Ashland av.
Pifer Erwin H. 874 W. Adams
Pigott A. H. Dr. 1161 Lunt av.
Pigott Robert, 1161 Lunt av.
Pike Albert H. Hyde Park hotel
Pike B. E. The Winamac
Pike Charles Burrall, 162 Rush
Pike Charles B. 2101 Prairie av. C.A.,
      Univ., W.P.
Pike Charles S. 3908 Ellis av.
Pike Eugene Rockwell, 2201 Prairie av.
      C. A., Univ., W.P.
Pike Eugene S. 2101 Prairie av. Chi., W.P.
Pike Samuel, 3908 Ellis av.
Pike William Wallace, 2101 Prairie av.
      C.A., Univ., W.P.
Pilcher William E. Dr. 468 Fullerton av.
Pillinger William A. Austin
Pillsbury Harriet Mrs. 2725 N. Lincoln
Pillsbury Ossian D. Chicago Beach hotel
Pillsbury William F. 87 Rush. Univ.
Pilsbry Frank W. 1939 Deming pl. U.L.
Pinckard Charles P. Chicago Beach hotel
Pinckney Merritt W. Hotel Del Prado.
      C. A.
Pincoffs Maurice, 442 Elm
Pindell W. M. Greenwood Inn, Evans-
   ton
Pine M. B. Dr. 4583 Oakenwald av. C.A
Pingree George S. 6565 Yale
Pinkerton William A. 196 Ashland boul.
      C. A.
Pinkham . B. North Shore hotel
Pinkstaff J. L. North Shore hotel
Pinney Henry L. Hotel Metropole
Pinney Lorenzo S. Austin
Pinney L. Mrs. 4341 Grand boul.
Pinney W. E. Mrs. 4948 Woodlawn av.
Pinter Lizzie Miss, 280 Belden av.
Piper Charles W., M.D., 6743 Union av.
Piper C. E. Berwyn
Piper Henry, 617 N. Wells
Piper Otis, Berwyn

Piper Richard J. Dr. 540 Washington boul.
Piratzky Robert H. 352 Ashland boul.
Pirie John T. jr. Evanston
Pischczak John Dr. 3506 Lake av.
Pischczak Wm. jr. 3506 Lake av.
Pitcher E. D. Irving Park
Pitcher Henry L. 874 Winthrop av.
Pitcher Lewis W. 2725 Prairie av.
Pither John B. Austin
Pitkin Edward H. Oak Park. *U. L.*
   Sum. res. Mackinac Island, Mich.
Pitkin Frank L. Oak Park
Pitkin Frank H. 4004 Ellis av. *Ill.*
Pitkin George, 3438 Rhodes av.
Pitkin George W. 459 Washington boul.
  Ill.
Pitkin Harry E. 459 Washington boul.
Pitkin Harvey E. Lexington hotel, *Cal.*
Pitkin Lorraine J. Mrs. 2456 Kenmore av.
Pitkin Roger S. Evanston
Pitkin Stephen G. 224 Schiller
Pitner Ina K. Miss, Evanston
Pitner Levi C. Evanston
Pitt Henry N. Dr. 169 S. Sacramento av.
Pitt William A. Dr. 577 W. Madison
Pittman Clement K. Evanston
Pitts C. M. LaGrange
Pitts M. B. Mrs. 4401 Berkeley av.
Pixley Frank S. Granada hotel
Place D. S. Mrs. 120 Ashland boul.
Place E. C. Mrs. 2432 Prairie av.
Place G. G. 55, 53d
Plamondon Alfred D. 317 Ashland boul.
  C.A.
Plamondon Celia Mrs. 36 Throop
Plamondon Charles A. 413 W. Monroe.
  W.P.
Plamondon George A. 413 W. Monroe
  C.A.
Plank Hattie Mrs. 1794 Magnolia av.
Plant Bessie Miss, 6149 Monroe av.
Plant Myrtle Miss, 6149 Monroe av.
Plantz Alice Mrs. 934 W. Vanburen
Plato C. E. Mrs. 4420 Prairie av.
Platt Agnes E. Mrs. 106 Astor
Platt Bessie F. Miss, 4577 Lake av.
Platt Carlos A. W. 4453 Berkeley av.
Platt C. H. Hotel Metropole
Platt Edward A. Dr. 640 W. Monroe
Platt Henry Russell, 1698 Wellington
Platt Jarvis H. 2194 Kenmore av.
Platt Lucius C. Lake Forest
Platt Lucy K. Mrs. 514 The Plaza
Platt L. M. 5815 Madison av.
Platt Nathan E. Chicago Beach hotel
Platt Philander T. 1120 S.Central Park av.
Plattenburg C. B. Dr. 548 W. Madison
Plattenburg C. S. A. 548 W. Madison
Platter David E. 1577 Kenmore av.
Plautz C. Herman, 731 N. Hoyne av.
Playford Robert W. jr. 4500 Vincennes av.
Plecker James H. Dr. 422 Wash'ton boul.
Plew James E. 542 W. 59th
Plotke Nathan M. 411 Cleveland av. *Lksd.*
Plum Henry W. Lombard
Plum William R. Lombard

Plumb Glenn E. River Forest
Plumb Isabel Mrs. River Forest
Plumbe George, Austin
Plummer A. W. Glencoe
Plummer D. C. 180, 45th. *C.A.*
Plummer George W. 221 Hampden ct.
   Sum. res. Tyrone, Pa.
Plummer Jonathan W. Glencoe
Plummer Joseph P. Glencoe
Plummer S. C. Dr. 4304 Lake av.
Plumsted James T. 3260 Groveland av.
Plunkett James, 3927 Vincennes av.
Plunkett Thomas. 6422 Greenwood av.
Poage James H. Greenwood Inn, Evanston
Poague Charles M. 6547 Monroe av.
Poarch Catherine C. Mrs. Evanston
Poarch M. L. Miss, Evanston
Pode J. S. Mrs. Riverside
Podrasnik Alois, 799 W. Monroe
  Sum. res. Little Cedar Lake, West
  Bend, Wis.
Podrasnik Joseph N. 799 W. Monroe
Pogue George N. 4206½ Berkeley av.
Poinier Edward W. 2531 Magnolia av.
Poinier Isaac P. 107 DeKalb
Poirier Henry N. 4425 Vincennes av.
Poitras B. C. Mrs. 4335 Oakenwald av.
Polacheck Leo, 185, 25th. *Lksd.*
Pole Robert G. Austin
Polkey Samuel, 3564 Vernon av.
Pollak Arthur, 4212 Calumet av. *Lksd.*
Pollak August, 4514 Oakenwald av.
Pollak Bertha Mrs. 2714 Indiana av.
Poilak H. J. 413 Bowen av.
Pollak Sidney B. 4344 St. Lawrence av.
Pollard A. A. Miss, 425 Lasalle av.
Pollard Jerome B. 4464 Berkeley av.
Pollard M. Mrs. 3831 Lake av.
Polley John C. 209 Ashland boul.
Pollock Charles A. 6432 Minerva av.
Pollock E. M. Mrs. 6432 Minerva av.
Pollock George L. Hinsdale
Pollock Louis E. Hyde Park hotel
Pollock W. J. Hinsdale
Polson Richard, 301 The Plaza, *C.A.*
Pomeroy D. W. 6439 Minerva av.
Pomeroy Edward M. 33 Roslyn pl.
Pomeroy Francis W. Evanston
Pomeroy F. A. 7204 Merrill av.
Pomeroy Joseph, 517 W. Congress
Pomeroy Sterling, 120 W. 66th
Pomeroy S. Harris, 307 Huron
Pomy Herman G. 1537 W. Adams. *C.A.*
Pond Abbie Miss, 2957 Indiana av.
Pond A. B. 720 Pullman bldg. *U.L.*
Pond Gilbert A. 363 Winthrop av.
Pond H. S. Mrs. 569, 51st
Pond I. K. 720 Pullman bldg. *Univ.*
Pond Walter M. 325 Ashland boul. *Ill.*
Pontious W. H. Dr. Park Ridge
Pool A. W. Miss, 4722 Woodlawn av.
Poole Abram, 89 Lincoln Park boul.
  U.L.   Sum. res. Lake Forest
Poole C. Clarence, Evanston
Poole George A. 5522 East End av.

Poole George A. jr. 5522 East End av.
Poole Isaac Dr. Evanston
Poole O. E. Lakeside
Poole William F. Evanston
Poole W. F. Mrs. Evanston
Poole W. H. Morgan Park
Pooler Frederick S. Evanston
Pooler Lemuel F. Evanston
Poor Fred Arthur, 5765 Washington av.
Poor John E. Evanston
Pope B. H. Mrs. 335 Rush
Pope Charles, 18 Lake Shore drive. *Chi.,*
  Un.   Sum. res. Geneva, Ill.
Pope Charles B. Mrs. 2835 Michigan av.
Pope Charles E. 5218 Hibbard av.
Pope Edgar, 4551 Champlain av.
Pope Edward, 18 Lake Shore drive
Pope George G. 3363 South Park av.
Pope George J. 3343 Vernon av.
Pope Henry A. 4317 Berkeley av.
Pope Henry Peirce, 3363 South Park
  av.
Pope Isabella H. Miss, Evanston
Pope J. T. Edison Park
Pope Mary Miss, Evanston
Pope Paulina Miss, 3998 Ellis av.
Pope Richard D. Wheaton
Pope William J. 487 W. Monroe. *Chi.,*
  Ill., W.P.
Pope W. A. 5528 Madison av.
Poppenhusen Conrad H. Evanston
Poppenhusen P. Albert, Evanston
Popper Edwin H. 1662 Melrose
Port Elizabeth V. Mrs. Oak Park
Porter Albert B. Evanston. *Univ.*
Porter Alfred R. 5135 Jefferson av.
Porter Charles H. Evanston
Porter Charles L. 5606 Michigan av.
Porter Clarence J. 414 Chicago av.
Porter Duff, 4203 Ellis av.
Porter Edward C. Oak Park
Porter Elizabeth Mrs. 3200 Rhodes av.
Porter Flora D. Mrs. 6336 Drexel boul.
Porter Frank L. 7024 Yale
Porter Frank W. Evanston
Porter Frederick D. 5470 Jefferson av.
Porter F. D., M.D. 1594 N. Halsted
Porter F. F. 402 W. 61st pl.
Porter F. W. 5617 Washington av.
Porter George J. M. 6510 Lexington av.
Porter George P. 113 Cass
Porter George Rupert, 6336 Drexel av.
Porter Gilbert E. Elmhurst
Porter Henry A. 5470 Jefferson av.
Porter Henry H. 311 Erie, *Chi. C.A., Un.*
Porter Herbert J. 435 Elm
Porter Hibbard, 113 Cass
Porter James F. 789 Fullerton av. *Univ.*
Porter James W. 789 Fullerton av. *C.A.,*
  U.L.
Porter James W. 7117 Wentworth av.
Porter John Albert, 4203 Ellis av.
Porter John L. Dr. 25, 47th
Porter Joseph D. 5608 Michigan av.
Porter Julia F. Mrs. 789 Fullerton av.
Porter Lucy G. Mrs. Riverside

Porter M. N. 567, 45th pl.
Porter Parker C. River Forest
Porter Placidus P. 2567 N. Winchester
  av.
Porter P. B. Dr. 2567 N. Winchester av.
Porter Robert C. 7117 Wentworth av.
Porter Robert H. Dr. Hyde Park hotel
Porter R ge , 3417 South Park av. *C.A.,*
  U.L.o rs
Porter Washington, 4043 Lake av. *C.A.,*
  W.P.
Porter William B. Morton Park
Porter William J. 7013 Perry av.
Porter W. H. Clifton house
Portman August F. 2169 Kenmore av.
Portman Edward C. 2170 Kenmore av.
Portman Max P. 1297 Wilton av.
Post Charles E. Hyde Park hotel
Post Charles N. Hyde Park hotel. *Ill.*
  Sum. res. Lake Geneva
Post Georgia Miss, 4112 Grand boul.
Post John A. Riverside. *C.A.*
Post Junius S. Hyde Park Hotel
Post Minnie E. Miss, Austin
Post William C. 6439 Minerva av.
Post W. W. Granada hotel. *C.A.*
Postlewait S. C. Oak Park
Poston Thomas J. 177, 40th
Potter Augustus E. 4421 Champlain av.
Potter Augustus L. 4421 Champlain av.
Potter Bessie O. Miss, 135, 56th
Potter Clarence Henry, 3519 Indiana av.
Potter Delonas W. 4620 Drexel boul.
Potter Edwin A. Chicago Beach hotel,
  C.A., U.L., W.P.
Potter E. A. Revere house
Potter E. C. 4800 Ellis av. *U.L.*
Potter Frank P. 147 Ashland boul. *Ill.*
Potter G. Douglas, 315 Hampden ct.
Potter Margaret Horton Miss, 130 Lake
  Shore drive
Potter Mary E. Mrs. 135, 56th
Potter Orrin W. 130 Lake Shore drive.
  Chi., U.L. Sum. res. Lake Geneva
Potter Orson, 515 W. 67th
Potter Robert H. McCarter, 377 Superior
Potter W. H. 6045 Monroe av.
Potter W. L. 480 Belden av.
Pottle E. L. 4317 Forrestville av.
Potts A. B. Mrs. 4534 Woodlawn av.
Potwin Annie E. Miss, 304 Belden av.
Potwin Harry A. Oak Park
Potwin Henry, 109 S. Oakley av.
Potwin Homer, 109 S. Oakley av.
Potwin May S. Miss, 109 S. Oakley av.
Potwin William S. 389 Dearborn av.
Poucher Barent G. Evanston. *C.A.*
Poulson William E. 3116 South Park av.
Poultney Franklin, Berwyn
Pound William, 3841 Elmwood ct.
Powell Burton, New Hotel Holland
Powell B. Mrs. 353 Oakwood boul.
Powell B. M. Mrs. 51, 22d
Powell Charles B. Winnetka
Powell C. B. Lakeside
Powell Edward, 53 Macalister pl.

Powell Edward L. 53 Macalister pl.
Powell Edwin C. 4754 Langley av.
Powell Elias D. 371 S. Oakley av.
Powell Francis M. Austin
Powell Frank D. Austin
Powell Frederick R. 6034 Monroe av,
Powell Geo. J. 53 Macalister pl.
Powell George W. 2585 Kenmore av.
Powell John H. 288 Ashland boul.
Powell J. New Hotel Holland
Powell Leopold, Hotel Metropole. *Lksd.*
Powell Medford, Evanston
Powell M. Miss, Hotel Metropole
Powell M. W. 2709 Indiana av.
Powell Regina Mrs. Oakland hotel
Powell Samuel, 2424 Indiana av. *Cal.*
Powell Samuel, 2548 N. Hermitage av.
Powell William C. 32 Groveland Park
Powell W. M. Mrs. River Forest
Power Frank M. 1570 Lill av.
Power George C. Chicago Beach hotel
Power Mortimer, Wilmette
Power M. J. 99½ Lincoln Park boul.
Power Perry J. 233 Jackson Park terrace
Powers Clarence A. 1218 Lunt av.
Powers D. J. 77 Lincoln av.
Powers Edward E. 5321 Jefferson av.
Powers E. H. Mrs. 235 Michigan av.
Powers Frank A. 1719 Deming pl.
Powers Fred W. 1925 Arlington pl.
Powers George, 1719 Deming pl.
Powers Harry J. 4843 Grand boul. *U.L.*
    W.P.
Powers L. D. 4815 Forrestville av. *C.A.*
Powers Ordell H. 4812 St. Lawrence av.
Powers Orville M. 5416 Jefferson av.
Powers U. S. Dr. Berwyn
Powers William P. 1925 Arlington pl.
Powers William S. Evanston
Praetorius G. G. Dr. 608 Burling
Prall Johnson S. Highland Park
Prall Wm. George, Oak Park
Pratt Albert H. 3229 Prairie av.
Pratt Benjamin H. 1003 Winthrop av.
    C.A.
Pratt Carrie Mrs. 754 Fullerton av.
Pratt Clinton B. 4111 Drexel boul.
Pratt Edwin H. Dr. 2942 Prairie av.
Pratt Elbert S. 937 W. Polk
    Sum. res. Nantasket, Mass.
Pratt Elizabeth A. Miss, Evanston
Pratt Emma Mrs. 1037 Warren av.
Pratt Frances M. Miss, 16 Bellevue pl.
Pratt Francis N. Lake Forest
Pratt Frank F. 3229 Prairie av.
Pratt Fred R. 3229 Prairie av.
Pratt George E. 767 Estes av.
Pratt George E. M. 836 Walnut
Pratt George L. 4115 Drexel boul.
Pratt George N. jr. 420 N. State
Pratt George O. LaGrange
Pratt Harry P., M.D. 762 Walnut
Pratt Jacob C. LaGrange
Pratt James F. 767 Estes av.
Pratt Jerome H. 5816 Rosalie ct.
Pratt Joseph G. 5422 Monroe av,

Pratt J. D. Austin
Pratt Lorenzo, 267, 47th
Pratt Mary R. Mrs. Evanston
Pratt M. B. A. Mrs. Highland Park
Pratt M. Elizabeth, 5422 Monroe av.
Pratt M. E. Mrs. Kenilworth
Pratt Nelson D. Lake Forest. *U.L.*
Pratt Ralph E. 4122 Grand boul. *C.A.*
Pratt Rodney K. 267, 47th
Pratt Roxana Mrs. 3815 Ellis av.
Pratt Roy B. 3229 Prairie av.
Pratt Sarah A. Mrs. 672 W. Monroe
Pratt Sarah Wilder Mrs. 2919 Indiana av.
Pratt William E. Lake Forest
Pray Francis E. Austin
Preasant Charles, 1326 N. Clark. *C.A.*
Preasant Tillie Miss, 1326 N. Clark
Prebbin J. G. 2358 Indiana av.
Preble R. B., M.D. 590 Dearborn av.
Preisch J. Allen, Hotel Del Prado
Prendergast A. Miss, 388 N. State
Prendergast R. Judge, 534 W. Jackson
    boul.
Prendergast Thomas J. 5303 Wabash av.
Prentice Allen T. 42 Scott
Prentice E. Parmalee, 10 Tower ct. *Chi.,*
    Univ.
Prentice H. L. Mrs. 5822 Wabash av.
Prentice Leon H. Waukegan. *C.A.,U.L.*
Prentice Mary I. Miss, 10 Tower ct.
Prentice Sartell, 10 Tower ct. *Un., Univ.*
Prentiss B. C. 695 W. Adams
Prentiss George D. Morgan Park
Prentiss Lewis M. Mrs. Evanston
Prentiss Norman A. Rev. Evanston
Prentiss William, 1719 Melrose
Prénzlauer Herman, 34 Bryant av. *Stan.*
Prescott Charles H. 4117 Newgart av.
Prescott Dewitt C. 7241 Yale
Prescott Edward L. 7241 Yale
Prescott Elmer E. Dr. 214 Park av.
Press Adam J. jr. 66 Lincoln av.
Press A. J. 66 Lincoln av.
Press Hubert, 723 N. Wells
Press W. G. 6154 Kimbark av.
Prestley James P. Dr. 412 S. Leavitt
Preston Annie E. Mrs. Oak Park
Preston Daniel H. Hinsdale
Preston Emma Miss, 201 The Plaza
Preston Ernest J. 4520 Ellis av. *C.A.*
Preston E. B. Mrs. The Plaza
Preston Frank H. 7130 Harvard av.
Preston Franklin W. 4435 Berkeley av.
Preston Harrison C. 2789 N. Lincoln
Preston Marguerite Miss, The Plaza
Preston M. N. Rev. Hinsdale
Preston Thomas C. Oak Park
Preston Wm. N. Oak Park
Preston W. D. 2320 Indiana av.
Prettyman C. W. Dr. 573, 43d
Pribyl Emma S. Mrs. 793 W. Monroe
    Sum. res. Twin Lakes, Wis.
Price Abner, 2219 Prairie av.
Price Arthur E. Dr. 538 W. Adams
Price A. B. Capt. Revere house
Price Butler D. Capt. Ft. Sheridan

Price Charles V. Revere house
Price Cornelius, 1826 Indiana av.
Price David A. 792 Washington boul.
Price Delia Miss, 1826 Indiana av.
Price Edward F. 344 S. Marshfield av.
Price E. V. Hotel Woodruff
Price Frank, 1716 Barry av.
Price Fred A. The Winamac. *C.A.*
Price F. D. Miss, The Arizona
Price Henry W. 7217 Merrill av.
Price Ira M. Prof. Morgan Park
Price James S. 1826 Indiana av. *Cal.*
Price John F. Morgan Park
Price John P. Austin
Price J. L. Austin
Price Leopold, 4339 Forrestville av. *Lksd., Stan.*
Price Lester, Evanston
Price M. Wallace, 1826 Indiana av. *Lksd., Stan.*
Price Oscar J. Dr. 538 W. Adams. *Ill.*
Price P. Bird, 1029 Warren av. *Ill.*
Price Robert P. Austin
Price Samuel C. 1826 Indiana av.
Price Theodore L. 417 Garfield boul.
Price Vincent C. Waukegan. *W.P.*
Price William Bates, 137, 56th
          Sum. res. Hendersonville
Price W. D. Jefferson Park
Price W. E. Hotel Woodruff
Price W. H. 824 W. Monroe
Prickett Edward P. Evanston
Prickett George W. Mrs. 3250 South Park av.
Prickett George W. jr. 3250 South Park av.
Pricture M. A. Mrs. Chicago Beach hotel
Pride Joseph F. Evanston
Pridham Daniel J. Oak Park
Pridham Edwin, LaGrange
Pridmore Wm. A. 5756 Kimbark av.
Priestman John, M.D. 3401 Vernon av.
Prime William A. The Wellington. *Chi.*
Primley J. P. 3218 Michigan av. *C.A., U.L.*
Prince Leonard S. 3226 Prairie av.
Prindeville Carlton H. 17 Lane ct.
Prindiville Charles H. 3935 Lake av.
Prindiville George J. 1233 Sheridan rd.
Prindiville James W. 3356 Rhodes av.
Prindiville John, 388 N. State
Prindiville John K. 3400 Vernon av. *Irq.*
Prindiville Marguerite Miss, 407 Elm
Prindiville Maurice, 461 Elm
Prindiville Redmond, 388 N. State
Prindiville Redmond, 407 Elm
Prindiville R. Spencer, 647, 62d
Prindiville Thomas J. 388 N. State
Prindiville Thomas W. 407 Elm
Prindle C. E. Evanston
Prindle E. A. Mrs. 472 Elm
Prindle Frank Mrs. Oak Park
Prindle Jason R. Evanston
Pringle Frederick W. Oak Park
Pringle Robert, 4442 Sidney av. *C.A., W.P.*

Pringle W. Ogilvie, 4442 Sidney av.
Prins R. J. 3636 Calumet av.
Prinz William H. Austin
Prior W. A. 6440 Ellis av.
Pritchard Edward R. 1444 W. Monroe
Probst Arthur O. 1930 Deming pl.
Probst Jerome, Chicago Beach hotel. *C.A.*
Proctor W. H. Granada hotel
Prothero James H., M.D., 3953 Michigan av.
Proudfoot Lawrence, 417 The Plaza
Prouty Carlton, Winnetka
Prouty Charles B. Dr. 175 Howe
Prouty H. W. Revere house. *Irq.*
Prouty James H. 175 Howe
Prouty M. F. Winnetka
Prouty M. W. Mrs. River Forest
Provost Henry Mrs. 3978 Lake av.
Prussing Charles Mrs. 353 Lasalle av.
Prussing Eugene E. 587 Dearborn av. *Chi., C.A., U.L.*
Prussing George C. 588 Dearborn av. *C.A., U.L.*
Pruyn Charles E. Oak Park
Pruyn Charles P. Dr. 4326 Greenwood av.
Pruyn Edythe May Miss, 4326 Greenwood av.
Pruyn John R. Chicago Beach hotel
Pruyn Samuel R. 231, 42d
Pruyn Samuel S. Oak Park
Pruyn William H. jr. 231, 42d
Pruyn W. H. 231, 42d
Pryor Gilbert C. 915 Farwell av.
Puffer Edwin R. Riverside
Pugh Charles, 6411 Parnell av.
Pugh James A. Winnetka
Pugsley S. P. 1855 Melrose
Pulham Charles, 4341 Indiana av.
          Sum. res. Brown's Lake, Wis.
Pullen William, Evanston
Pullman George M. Mrs. 1729 Prairie av.
          Sum. res. Alexandria Bay, Thousand Is.
Pullman William C. 504 W. Adams. *Chi., W.P.*
Pulsifer Fred K. The Kenwood. *Cal., C.A., W.P.*
Pulsifer Frederick C. Calumet club
Pulsifer M. B. Mrs. Hotel Metropole
Pulver Arthur W. 2206 Kenmore av.
Pulver C. Gertrude Miss, Hinsdale
Pulver Frances L. Mrs. Hinsdale
Purcell Charles A. Oak Park. *C.A.*
Purcell William A. 4022 Indiana av.
Purdy Charles S. 27 Aldine sq.
Purdy Charles W. Dr. 57, 20th. *Cal., W.P.*
Purdy Fred A. 7820 Bond av.
Purdy George C. 44 Woodland Park
Purdy John H. 27 Aldine sq.
Purdy Sarah C. Miss, Newberry hotel
Purdy Sarah E. Miss, 4811 Lake av.
Purdy Warren G. 4811 Lake av. *U.L.*
Purdy W. Fred, 4811 Lake av.
Purer William A. 1902 Barry av.

Purington Dillwyn V. 4800 Kenwood av. *U.L.*
Purington George E. 245 Lasalle av.
Purinton G. L. 6521 Harvard av.
Purnell James E. Sherman House
Purple Theo H. 22 St. James pl.
Pursell Peter H. Dr. 2640 N. Hermitage av
Purves Thomas C. LaGrange
Purvis John, Austin
Purvis Miller. Morton Park
Pusey Charles M. Dr. 761, 71st pl.
Pusey Evan, 7012 Stony Island av.
Pusey William A. Dr. 381 Superior
Pushman Hohannes T. 2728 Wabash av.
Puster Edward A. 1563 W. Monroe
Puster Robert J. 1688 W. Monroe
Puterbaugh Franklin P. 4013 Indiana av.
Puterbaugh Samuel G. Virginia hotel
Putnam Albert C. Oak Park
Putnam A. A. 409 Erie. *C.A.*
Putnam Frank H. Oak Park
Putnam Frank W. 61 Laflin. *C.A.*
　　　　　Sum. res. Brattleboro, Vt.
Putnam Frederick H. Austin
Putnam H. E. Mrs. 4503 Forrestville av.
Putnam J. R. 4815 Kenwood av.
Putnam Mary E. Mrs. Oak Park
Pyles Harvey S. 802 W. Adams
Pynchon Edwin Dr. 5032 Washington av.
Pynchon George M. 17 Delaware pl. *Un.*
Pyott Albert E. 296 S. Marshfield av. *Ill.*
Pyott David, 624 W. Jackson boul.
Pyott George W. 291 Ashland boul.
Pyott James M. 291 Ashland boul.
Pyott James M. jr. 291 Ashland boul.
Pyott William C. 291 Ashland boul.

QUACKENBOS HUGH M. 364, 41st
　　Quackenbos W. P. Miss, Hotel Del Prado
Quales Iver L. 52 Fowler
Quales Niles T. Dr. 52 Fowler
Qualey J. S. Lexington hotel
Quan Henry W. 384 Erie. *C.A.*
Quan James E. 384 Erie. *Un.*
Quan T. Albert, 384 Erie
Quan William J. 384 Erie
Quaw L. E. Mrs. The Hampden
Quayle Robert, Oak Park
Quayle Thomas, Oak Park
Queeny Edward J. 4228 Calumet av.
Quegoor E. Mrs. Hotel Del Prado
Quick George A. 2900 Michigan av.
Quick Harry J. 2900 Michigan av.
Quick John H. S. 2900 Michigan av.
　　　　Sum. res. Holderness, N. H.
Quick R. Frank, 4036 Prairie av.
Quick William F. River Forest
Quigg David Col. 5037 Madison av.
Quigg Ethel Miss, 5037 Madison av.
Quigg Nellie Miss, 5422 Cornell av.
Quigley Annie Miss, 5326 Cornell av.
Quimby E. V. 2382 N. Paulina
Quincey Thomas S. 472, 42d

Quincy Charles F. 412 N. State. *Chi.*, *C.A., Un., W.P.*
Quine William E., M. D. 3160 Indiana av.
Quinlan Charles E. Avenue house, Evanston
Quinlan Charles S. Evanston
Quinlan C. H. Mrs. Evanston
Quinlan Daniel B. 3015 Calumet av.
Quinlan Edward B. Evanston
Quinlan Ellen Mrs. 3162 Lake Park av.
Quinlan George H. Evanston
Quinlan Kate C. Miss, Evanston
Quinlan Thomas A. 159 Eugenie
　　　　Winter res. Los Angeles, Cal.
Quinlan Thomas A. jr. 159 Eugenie
Quinn John, 6502 Monroe av.
Quinn John H. 66 Rush
Quinn Joseph T. 1941 Oakdale av.
Quinn Patrick J. 336 Huron
Quinn William B. 4112 Prairie av.
Quirk Bartholomew, 1383 Washington boul.
Quirk D. Mrs. 273 Superior
Quirk James, 1128 Washington boul.
Quirk James P. Dr. 1128 Washington boul.

RABER JOHN, 37 Laflin
　　Raber P. W. Lexington hotel. *Cal.*, *Un., U.L., W.P.*
Race Albert S. 6647 Harvard av.
Race Ambrosia Miss, Irving Park
Race Charles H. 6545 Yale
Race Jane M. Miss, Irving Park
Race Luther E. Austin
Race R. T. Irving Park
Racey Harry J. Riverside
Radcliffe Annie M. Mrs. 854 W. Monroe
Raddin Charles S. Evanston
Raddin H. Augusta Mrs. Evanston
Radeker H. Elwood, The Tudor
Rader Estella Mrs. 3552 Ellis av.
Radford Isaac H. 5526 Cornell av.
Radford J. W. Morton Park
Radford William, Riverside
Radtke Rudolph C. 1233 Wrightwood av.
Radzinski A. I. 3328 Wabash av. *Lksd.*
　　　　Sum. res. Libertyville, Ill.
Rae Frank B. 362, 57th
Rae Robert Col. The Kenwood. *W.P.*
Rae Robert jr. 7100 Princeton av.
Raeder Henry, Evanston. *Univ.*
Raftree Michael L. Hinsdale
Raggio C. A. 3219 South Park av.
Ragor Andrew, 430 Ashland boul.
Ragor E. C. Mrs. 19 Macalister pl.
Rahlfs George, 33 Ewing pl.
Railton B. A. 547 W. Jackson boul.
Ralston H. M. Chicago Beach hotel
Ralston James, 3817 Wabash av.
Ramar J. E. 780 North Park av.
Ramcke John C. 100 Seminary av.
Ramm Christoph, 704 North Park av.
Ramsay Daniel G. 1256 Perry
Ramsay Elijah P. 5540 Cornell av.
Ramsdell E. 6149 Kimbark av.

Ramsdell J. Park Ridge
Ramsdell M. J. Mrs. 5401 Jefferson av.
Ramsey James A. Pullman
Ramsey William W. 6605 Harvard av.
Rand Charles E. 335 Rush. C.A.
Rand H. S. Lombard
Rand H. V. Mrs. Lombard
Rand Lory O. 7133 Eggleston av.
Rand L. G. 939 W. Adams
Rand Susan Miss, 6424 Monroe av.
Randall A. S. Mrs. 179 Evanston av.
Randall Benjamin G. 4625 Ellis av.
Randall Charles H. 2624 Calumet av.U.L.
Randall C. E. 4747 Champlain av.
Randall Milo B. 4625 Ellis av.
Randall Tabor P. 179 Evanston av.
Randall Thomas D. 2624 Calumet av.
  W.P.
Randell Hattie Mrs. Oak Park
Randle Charles H. 4339 Drexel boul.
Randlev Peter, Evanston
Randolph Isham, Riverside
Randolph Jackson F. 410 Bowen av.
Randolph P. C. Miss, Riverside
Randolph Ruth F. Miss, 410 Bowen av.
Randolph Smith M. 866 S. Sawyer av.
Rang Eugene A. 1675 Barry av.
Rang Henry, 1928 Wellington
Rang Henry jr. 1928 Wellington
Rang Louis A. 1928 Wellington
Ranier Paul, Norwood Park
Rankin Ada Douglas Miss, 3444 Indiana
  av.
Rankin George, Oak Park
Rankin James A. 7052 Yale. W.P.
Rankin John, Oak Park
Rankin Lillian Miss, 3444 Indiana av.
Rankin Thomas, 278 Seminary av.
Rankin William T. 4917 Forrestville av.
Rankine Clarence M. Dr. 699 Washington boul.
Ranney Alfred E. 3706 Lake av.
Ranney F. G. 5201 Hibbard av.
Ranney Henry C. 410 Oak
Ranney William A. 3343 South Park av.
Ransch Emilie C. Dr. 549 W. Monroe
Ransford Frank R. 5321 Washington av.
Ransom Albert, 45 Campbell Park
Ransom William B. 3426 Vernon av.
Ransome William S. 3834 Ellis av.
Raper Mary M. Mrs. 97, 51st
Raphael Ph. L. 4214 Calumet av.
Rapp August, Pullman
Rapp Charles F. Tremont house
Rapp C. Ward. Lexington hotel. U.L.
Rapp George H. 3442 Vernon av.
Rapp Walter A. 29, 35th
Rapp William, 220 Cass
Rapp Wm. J. 220 Cass
Rappal Frederick . 4109 Vincennes av.
Rappal Frederick J. jr.4109 Vincennes av.
  C.A.
Rappal John H. 4109 Vincennes av.
Rappal Lawrence L. 4109 Vincennes av.
Rappal Symon P. 4109 Vincennes av.
Rappleye N. B. Hyde Park hotel

Rardon James J. 559 Dearborn av.
Rardon Wm. J. 1918 Deming pl.
Raske Henry, 1646 Briar pl.
Rasmussen H. Edison Park
Rastall J. E. 2501 Magnolia av.
Raster Herman Mrs. 391 W.Jackson boul.
Ratcliff E. Wood, Oak Park
Ratcliffe F. A. 524 Cleveland av. C.A.
Ratcliffe William A. Evanston
Rathbone Peter D. 628 W. Jackson boul.
Rathborne Richard W. 5046 Woodlawn
  av.
Rathborne William W. 354 Huron. C.A.,
  Un.
Rathbun A. W. Glen Ellyn
Rathbun John, 2984 Kenmore av.
Rathbun William W. 2984 Kenmore av.
Rathje Louis, 754 Englewood av.
Ratledge Charles Mrs. Longwood
Ratsch Fred J. 4124 Ellis av.
Rattle Orrin J. Oak Park
Rattle Thomas S. Oak Park
Rattray William H. 261 Fremont
Raubold John G. Oak Park
Rauch Albert, 344 Burling
Raum Green B. Gen. 569, 51st
Rawle John, 472 Ashland boul. Ill.
Rawleigh Ava F. Miss, 727 Washington
  boul.
Rawleigh J. Harry, 731 Washington boul.
Rawleigh J. T. 727 Washington boul. Ill.
  Sum. res. Lake Geneva, Wis.
Rawlings J. N. Riverside
Rawll George, 2668 Magnolia av.
Rawson Adrian A. 308 S. Campbell av.
Rawson Albert E. 19 Waverly ct. C.A.
Rawson C. A. Mrs. Hinsdale
Rawson F. H. 4945 Ellis av. Cal., C.A.
Rawson Hart Mrs. 5854 Rosalie ct.
Rawson S. W. 4945 Ellis av.
Rawson W. F. Hotel Windermere
Ray A. H. Mrs. 5731 Monroe av.
Ray A. S. Oak Park. C.A.
Ray B. F. 4928 Washington av.
Ray Cornelia Mrs. 947 Farwell av.
Ray Edward C. Rev. Evanston
Ray Frank H. Auditorium annex. Chi.,
  C.A., W.P.
Ray Julia Mrs. 52 Walton pl.
Ray Orson W. 6345 Kimbark av.
Ray Phila A. Mrs. Oak Park
Ray William F. Austin
Raycroft Joseph E. University of Chicago
Raymond Addie M. Miss, Hinsdale
Raymond Alice P. Mrs. 305 Indiana
Raymond A. Mrs. 2500 Prairie av.
Raymond Charles, Evanston
Raymond Chas. E. Hinsdale. C.A.,U.L.
Raymond Charles L. 2239 Calumet av.
  Chi., U.L., W.P.
Raymond Edward F. Evanston
Raymond Edward H. 4856 Prairie av.
Raymond Frederick D. Evanston
Raymond Harry, Virginia hotel. W.P.
Raymond Harry S. 3802 Forest av. C.A.
Raymond Helen Miss, 36 Bellevue pl.

Raymond James H. Evanston. *Irq.,U.L.*
Raymond James N. 4902 Drexel boul. *U.L.*
Raymond Lowry B. 36 Bellevue pl. *C.A.*
Raymond Ruth Miss, 32, 42d pl.
Raymond Samuel B. 36 Bellevue pl. *Chi., Un., W.P.*
Raymond William M. 36 Bellevue pl.
Raymond W. R. 3304 Vernon av.
Rayner J. B. 2311 Indiana av.
   Sum. res. Saratoga Springs, N. Y.
Raynolds James D. Riverside
Rea I. H. Dr. 4348 Ellis av.
Rea Julia R. Mrs. 4714 Kimbark av.
Rea Ridgley, Hyde Park hotel
Rea Robert Laughlin Dr. 272 Huron
   Sum. res. Forest Home Farms, Ind.
Read Alonzo P. 647 W. Monroe
Read Gardner, Evanston
Read Louis H. 647 W. Monroe
Read Nathaniel T. 4033 Drexel boul.
Reade J. T. Lombard
Reading Edgar Mrs. 3750 Langley av.
Reading Edgar M. Dr. 3748 Langley av.
Ready John, Leland hotel
Reagan Nannie Mrs. Winnetka
Ream Norman B. 1901 Prairie av. *Cal., Chi., C.A., U.L., W.P.*
   Sum. res. Thompson, Ct.
Rearden Henry H. Austin
Reardon John H. 428 Oak
Reber John G. 499 Dearborn av.
Reber John Q. A. Lombard
Record Milton L. Evanston
Rector Charles E. Virginia hotel
Rector Edward, 4411 Berkeley av.
Reddick G. W. Prof. Highland Park
Reddish Eliza Mrs. 348 Ashland boul.
Reddon William B. 2427 Indiana av. *C.A., W.P.*
Reddy James M. 3244 Indiana av.
Redell Richard F. 435 Dearborn av.
Redfern Joseph N. Hinsdale
Redfield Anson P. 287 S. Leavitt
Redfield B. B. 6422 Yale
Redfield Chandler S. Evanston
Redfield David W. 819 Chase av.
Redfield Joseph B. 621 Washington boul.
Redfield Sarah G. Mrs. 819 Chase av.
Redington Edward D. Evanston
Redington William H. 1848 Barry av. *C.A., U.L.*
Redlich Alexander E. 375 N. Clark
Redlich Henry O. Dr. 375 N. Clark
Redmond A. J. Oak Park
Redway Florence A. Miss, 10 Groveland Park
Reece Alonzo N. Chicago Beach hotel
Reed Alanson Henry, 3242 Groveland av.
Reed Albert M. Oak Park
Reed A. C. Oak Park
Reed Charles A. 5409 Jefferson av.
Reed Charles B. Dr. 1357 Sheffield av.
Reed Charles C. 1686 W. Monroe. *Ill.*
Reed Charles S. 5409 Jefferson av.
Reed Chester B. 4130 Lake av,

Reed C. E. 899 Walnut
Reed Earl H. 4758 Lake av. *Chi.*
Reed Edwin H. Evanston
Reed Ella C. Mrs. 5937 Indiana av.
Reed Florence S. Mrs. 252, 66th
Reed Frank, 4434 Berkeley av.
Reed Frank B. 3162 Groveland av.
Reed Frank E. 4831 Vincennes av.
Reed Frank F. Riverside. *C.A.*
Reed Frank J. 705, 49th
Reed Fred Mrs. 392 W. Adams
Reed George I. 4000 Lake av.
Reed George J. 435 Belden av.
Reed Horace Mrs. 54 Bellevue pl.
Reed Hugh T. 4412 Oakenwald av.
Reed H. V. 41 S. Seeley av.
Reed Isaac N. Chicago Athletic assn.
Reed James A. S. 411 S. Oakley av.
Reed James H. Evanston
Reed John S. Mrs. 126 Cass
Reed J. Warner, Hinsdale
Reed Lawrence J. 767 Warren av.
Reed L. E. Hyde Park hotel
Reed Mary Miss, Riverside
Reed Mary A. Mrs. 1234 Washington boul.
Reed Morey L. Dr. 320 Bowen av.
Reed M. D. Mrs. Riverside
Reed N. R. Miss, 276 S. Winchester av.
Reed P. A. Mrs. 654 Cleveland av.
Reed Sarah Mrs. Evanston
Reed S. B. Mrs. 5332 Washington av.
Reed William A. 276 S. Winchester av.
Reed William H. 4130 Lake av.
Reed William J. 201 Bissell
Reed William Kelsey, 3038 Groveland av.
Reedy Ellen Miss, 2547 N. Hermitage av.
Reedy William H. River Forest
Reedy William I. 1733 Roscoe
Reeme Josiah B. Hotel Metropole
Reese Harvey H. Evanston
Reese Theodore, Evanston
Reese Theodore F. 3042 Groveland av.
Reessing George W. 416 N. State
Reeve Albert A. 4947 Prairie av.
Reeve Sanford D. 103 Loomis. *Ill.*
Reeves Andrew H. 6524 Yale
Reeves A. Harry, 6524 Yale
Reeves Charles H. 1065 Sherwin av.
Reeves Edwy L. 608, 65th
Reeves Joshua, 1369 W. Jackson boul.
Regan Clement M. Morgan Park
Regan L. T. 609 W. 66th
Regensburg Henry, 4203 Grand boul. *Lksd.*
Regensburg Henry L. 432 Lasalle av.
Regensburg James H. 4203 Grand boul.
Regensburg O. H. 4203 Grand boul.
Regensburg Samuel H. 3440 Michigan av. *Stan.*
Regenstein Louis, 3225 Groveland av. *Lksd.*
Regensteiner Theodore, 4435 Ellis av.
Rehm Frank A. 575 Dearborn av.
Rehm Jacob, 589 Dearborn av.
Rehm William H. 589 Dearborn av. *C.A.*
Rehtmeyer Herman, 2465 Lakewood av.

Rehwoldt Ernest H. Irving Park
Reichelt John A. 340 Warren av.
    Sum. res. Crystal Lake, Ill.
Reichmann F. J. River Forest
Reid Alan LeRoy, Wheaton. *Chi.*
Reid Arthur S. Lake Forest. *C.A.*
Reid A. D. New Hotel Holland
Reid Daniel G. Hotel Metropole. *Cal.,*
    Chi., C.A., U.L., W.P.
Reid Elizabeth Miss, 5420 Washington av
Reid George B. 685 W. Adams. *C.A.*
Reid John, 225 Dearborn av.
Reid John F. 5644 Indiana av.
Reid J. G. Dr. 4710 Madison av.
Reid Mary M. Miss, Evanston
Reid M. K. Mrs. 4802 Madison av.
Reid Simon S. Mrs. Lake Forest
Reid William, 6117 Monroe av.
    Sum. res. Wellesley, Canada
Reid William H. 2013 Prairie av.
Reid William W. 37 St. James pl.
Reid W. Clinton, 582 W. Madison
Reifschneider Charles L. Austin
Reifsnider Charles, Oak Park
Reiling Herman J. Lakota hotel. *C.A.*
Reilley Frank K. 2124 Michigan av.
Reilly E. S. Mrs. 2956 Indiana av.
Reilly Frank W. Dr. 137 Lincoln Park
    boul.
Reilly Leigh, 338 Ontario
Reilly Peter E. Auditorium annex
Reilly Robert Kennicott, 360 Erie
Reilly Rudolphe Ransom, 137 Lincoln
    Park boul.
Reily Daniel, 216 Park av.
Reiman M. 4325 Drexel boul.
Reimers J. J. Evanston
Reinach Henrietta Mrs.1815 Arlington pl.
Reinach Jacob, 2712 Indiana av. *Lksd.*
Reininger Edward E. Dr. 353 S. Oakley
    av.
Reis Maurice, 4938 St. Lawrence av.
Reiss Jacob L. 4350 Forrestville av.
Reiss L. W. 3248 Rhodes av.
Reiss Otto, 447 Lasalle av.
Reiss William, 3248 Rhodes av. *Lksd.*
Reissig Charles Mrs. Riverside
Reiter Elizabeth C. Mrs. 6508 Minerva av.
Reiter Maud Miss, 6508 Minerva av.
Reiter Winfield S. 6508 Minerva av.
Reitler Charles, 155, 33d. *Lksd.*
Remien Charles F. 35 E. Pearson
Remien Frank H. 35 E. Pearson
Remington Franklin, 63 E. Pearson. *Un.*
Remmer E. Mrs. 4827 Lake av.
Remmer Oscar, 422 Kenwood terrace
Remmers G. W. Evanston
Remy Curtis H. Evanston. *U.L.*
Rend Joseph P. 153 Ashland boul.
Rend William P. 153 Ashland boul. *Ill.,*
    U.L.
Rendtorff Johanna Miss, 3247 Beacon
Renfro James F. 6565 Yale
Renicke W. J. 1886 Diversey
Rennels Esther E. Mrs. 644 W. Monroe
Rennels Loy L. 644 W. Monroe

Renshaw William, 4439 Ellis av.
Renwick Edward A. 1754 Sheridan rd.
Repka August, Riverside
Replogle L. E. 3806 Ellis av.
Replogle P. S. Dr. 2306 Indiana av.
Reppert George L. 293, 53d
ReQua Charles H. 3629 Grand boul.
ReQua Charles W. 2454 Michigan av.
ReQua Frederick N. Evanston
ReQua Harry L. Highland Park
ReQua S. Frederick, Evanston
ReQua William B. Hotel Metropole
Ressler Henry A. 508 Belden av.
Retterer Jacob, 533 Cleveland av.
Reum Oscar A. 260 Racine av.
Reusch Ferdinand, 2646 Magnolia av.
Revell Alex. H. 577 Lasalle av. *C.A.,*
    U.L., W.P.
Revell David. Chicago Athletic Assn.
Revell David J. 639 Fullerton av. *C.A.*
Revell Fleming H. Evanston
Revell John T. 639 Fullerton av. *U.L.,*
    C.A.
Revell Margaret Mrs. 639 Fullerton av.
Rew George C. Kenilworth. *C.A.*
Rew Henry C. Evanston. *C.A., U.L.,*
    W.P.
Rew Irwin, Evanston. *C.A.*
Rew Mary Mrs. Kenilworth
Reynell Arthur B. 481 Belden av.
Reynolds Arthur R. Dr. Lakota hotel
Reynolds Benjamin, Riverside
Reynolds Benjamin F. 6325 Kimbark av.
Reynolds Caleb F. The Hampden
Reynolds Charles Rev. 334 W. 59th pl.
Reynolds Daniel M. 1122 Washington
    boul.
Reynolds Elizabeth Miss, The Renfost
Reynolds Francis D. Evanston.
Reynolds Francis M. Dr. Oak Park
Reynolds Frank P. 213 The Plaza
Reynolds Frederick M. 4748 Kenwood av.
Reynolds George B. Evanston
Reynolds George W. Berwyn
Reynolds George W. Dr. 335 Washington
    boul
Reynolds G. M. 3961 Drexel boul.
Reynolds G. William Dr. 1924 Arlington
    pl.
Reynolds James E. Dr. 514 S. Oakley av.
Reynolds Jennie E. Mrs. 582, 45th pl.
Reynolds John, 6853 Perry av.
Reynolds John N. 4008 Grand boul.
Reynolds John P. 468 Lasalle av.
Reynolds Marc M. 5854 Rosalie ct. *C.A.*
Reynolds Montgomery A. 2564 Lake-
    wood av.
Reynolds Myra Miss, University of Chi-
    cago
Reynolds P. A. Mrs. 4560 Oakenwald av.
Reynolds R. R. Lakota hotel
Reynolds R. T. Mrs. 1467 Wellington
Reynolds T. J. Edison Park
Reynolds Walter H. Rev. 105 Ashland
    boul. *Univ.*
Reynolds William J. 4368 Oakenwald av.

Reynolds William J. Oak Park
Rhea Foster A. Lake Forest. *Un.*
Rhea John C. 7450 Kimbark av.
Rheinstrom A. 3408 South Park av.
Rhoades C. H. The Arizona
Rhode E. Mrs. 151 Goethe
Rhode Otto, 151 Goethe
Rhode Rudolph E. 151 Goethe
Rhodehamel B. F. Hyde Park hotel
Rhodes Charles W.3769 Lake av.
Rhodes Clinton. 3127 Michigan av. *Lksd.*
Rhodes George, Evanston
Rhodes George L. Lakota hotel
Rhodes Harrison G. 404 Erie
Rhodes James H. 41, 46th
Rhodes John Edwin Dr. 1669 W. Monroe. *C.A.*
Rhodes J. Foster, Lakota hotel. *Chi., C.A.*
Rhodes J. Wolcott, Evanston
Rhodus Birch F. 1543 Fulton
Rice Bernard A. Evanston
Rice Calvin F. Evanston
Rice Charles E. Highland Park
Rice Charles H. 5652 Monroe av.
Rice Charles W. 36th ne. cor. Ellis av.
Rice Clara Kerr Mrs. 610 W. Jackson boul.
Rice Elliott S. 5530 East End av. *C.A.*
Rice Emma L. S. Mrs. Evanston
Rice E. G. Berwyn
Rice E. Perry Dr. 950 W. Jackson boul.
Rice Fordyce B. Evanston
Rice F. Willis, Lexington hotel. *Cal., Chi.*
Rice George E. 238 Oakwood boul.
Rice Henry, 1023 Warren av.
Rice H. Arthur, 1520 Washington boul.
Rice Isaac M. 3521 Ellis av.
Rice I. M. Hotel Metropole
Rice Jacob, 3926 Lake av. *Lksd.*
Rice Louis S. Evanston
Rice Maria Mrs. 5533 Cornell av.
Rice May Cushman Dr. 6955 Perry av.
Rice May Louise, Evanston
Rice Myron B. Riverside
Rice N. B. Dr. 584 W. Adams
Rice P. H. 3312 Wabash av.
Sum. res. Elmhurst
Rice Rebecca S. Miss, 481 Dearborn av.
Rice Sidney W. 52 Oakwood av.
Rice Sol, 3414 Vernon av. *Lksd.*
Rice Susie W. Miss, Oak Park
Rice Theo. F. 5554 Woodlawn av. *U.L.*
Rice Thomas B. Mrs. 322 Warren av.
Rice Thomas J. 1135 Washington boul.
Rice William, Evanston
Rice William A. Oak Park
Rice W. S. 3848 Ellis av.
Rich Albert D. Riverside
Rich Arthur D. 6500 Harvard av.
Rich Ben. C. 6500 Harvard av.
Rich Christopher, 2658 N. Lincoln
Rich Elmer A. LaGrange. *C.A.*
Rich Frank E. 405 Warren av.
Rich Fred A. Norwood Park

Rich Frederick W. Riverside
Rich Henry S. 405 Warren av. *U.L.*
Rich Herbert G. 405 Warren av.
Rich Katharine B. Mrs. 4741 Kenwood av.
Rich M. Byron, 3254 South Park av.
Richards Annette S. Dr. 821 Warren av.
Richards Charles, 530 Lasalle av.
Richards Charles D. Oak Park
Richards Charles R. 4104 Indiana av.
Richards Charles W.813Washington boul
RichardsEdward S. 2008 W.Jackson boul.
Richards Frederick D. Evanston
Richards George A. Evanston
Richards G. E., M. D. 44½ Bellevue pl. *C.A.*
Richards Herbert V. 77 Bryant av.
Richards Hugh, Morton Park
Richards Isaac D. 4132 Calumet av.
Richards Jacob W. 2426 Indiana av. *Irq.*
Richards John T. 135, 51st
Richards John T. 3432 Rhodes av.
Richards Joseph R. 363 Rush. *W.P.*
Richards Lincoln, Oak Park
Richards Maurice G. Evanston
Richards Moses J. Mrs. 485 Washington boul
Richards O. K. 3147 Calumet av.
Richards P. C. Berwyn
Richards Ransom, 4104 Indiana av.
Richards Seaman P. Riverside
Richards William P. Dr. 1446 Dakin av.
Richardson A. P. 47 Bellevue pl. *Cal., Chi., C.A., Un.*
Richardson Charles H. 5 Tower ct. *Un.*
Richardson Clara M. Miss, 1210 Morse av.
Richardson C. J. Mrs. 28 Delaware pl.
Richardson Daniel E. Riverside. *C.A.*
Richardson Donald, Oak Park
Richardson D. D. Dr. 232 Michigan av.
Richardson Edwin C. 3841 Calumet av.
Sum. res. Antioch, Ill., Channel Lake
Richardson E. Perrin, 1338 Washington boul.
Richardson Francis M.,M.D. 633 W. Garfield boul.
Richardson Frank, 1472 W. Monroe
Richardson George P. 1886 Diversey. *U.L.*
Richardson Gordon M. 1338 Washington boul.
Richardson G. H. Dr. 3829 Wabash av.
Richardson Harry B. Oak Park. *C.A.*
Richardson John, 3122 South Park av.
Richardson John A. 11½, 34th pl.
Richardson John B. Oak Park
Richardson John R., M..D. 479, 42d pl.
Richardson Louis G. 5322 Cornell av. *C.A.*
Richardson L. B. Morton Park
Richardson Mary Miss, 307 Schiller
Richardson M. A. Mrs. 1212 Washington boul.
Richardson M. Arthur, 1212 Washington boul.
Richardson M. L. 1338 Washington boul.
Richardson Omar S. 106 Buena av. *Irq.*

Richardson Orlo W. 3910 Calumet av.
　Sum. res. Channel Lake, Antioch, Ill.
Richardson Rebecca A. Miss, Elmhurst
Richardson Robert E. 3910 Calumet av.
Richardson Roderick, Hotel Metropole
Richardson R. J. Hotel Metropole. *U.L.*
Richardson Samuel H. 5735 Rosalie ct.
Richardson Samuel M. 1810 Arlington pl.
Richardson Ulysses M. Dr. 524 W. 60th
Richardson William C. B. 823 Sunnyside
　av.
Richardson William E. 4731 Indiana av.
Richardson W. C. Rev. 2714 Michigan av.
Richardson W. H. 5324 Jefferson av.
Richardson W. J. New Hotel Holland
Richberg Donald R. 2227 Calumet av.
Richberg John C. 2227 Calumet av. *Cal.,*
　Irq. Sum. res. Woodstock, Vt.
Richey A. D. Irving Park
Richey Eugene, 4017 Indiana av.
Richey Everett Mrs. 4017 Indiana av.
Richey F. L. Irving Park
Richie Bruce E. Hinsdale
Richman Jacob, 4335 Langley av.
Richman Nathaniel P. 4245 Grand boul.
Richmond C. D. LaGrange
Richmond C. W. Mrs. LaGrange
Richmond W. C. Glencoe
Richolson Benjamin F. 1292 Washington
　boul. *Ill.*
Richt Christian C. 570, 50th pl.
Richter I. S. New Hotel Holland
Richter Max W. 1810 Oakdale av.
Richter Paul K. 3729 Ellis av. *C.A.*
Richter Simon 4218 Prairie av.
Rick John, 946 W. Harrison
Rickards William T. Evanston. *U.L.*
Rickcords Frances L. Mrs. 301 Ashland
　boul.
Rickcords Frederick, 301 Ashland boul.
Rickcords George E. 572 Dearborn av.
　U.L.
Ricker D. Swing, 425 Superior
Ricker Fred, 7222 Euclid av.
Ricker Jewett E. 425 Superior
Ricketts C. Lindsay, 538 W. 69th
Ricketts S. Mrs. 2124 Michigan av.
Ricklefs Charles G. 2468 Kenmore av.
Ricklefs Emma Mrs. 2468 Kenmore av.
Riddell Charles, Hyde Park hotel
　Sum. res. Evanston
Riddle A. E. Glen Ellyn
Riddle Francis A. 512 W. Jackson boul.
　Ill., U.L.
Riddle George A. Clifton house
Rider M. Mrs. 3624 Ellis av.
Rider William H. 3624 Ellis av.
Ridgaway Henry B. Mrs. Evanston
Ridgley Charles A. 2001 Michigan av.
　Cal.
Ridgley J. K. Chicago Beach hotel
Ridgway James V. Hinsdale
Ridgway Margaret L. Mrs. Evanston
Ridgway William, 213 Ashland boul.
Ridlon John Dr. Evanston. *Univ.*
Riebe Gustav, 1853 Barry av.

Riedle Frank, 5837 Washington av.
Riegert E. 74 Racine av.
Rieke George W. 1705 Deming pl.
Rieke Henry, 1705 Deming pl.
Rieke H. Edward, 1705 Deming pl.
Rieper Henry, 632 N. Hoyne av.
Riesenfeld S. S. 3114 South Park av.
Rieser Herman O. 1812 Oakdale av.
Rietz Alexander, 449 Ashland boul.
　Sum. res. Powers Lake, Wis.
Rietz August, 449 Ashland boul.
Rietz August W. 545 Dearborn av.
Rietz Charles F. 303 Pine Grove av.
Rietz Edward G. W. 724 Washington
　boul.
Rietz Frederick, 307 Pine Grove av.
Riford Ira B. 1232 Wilcox av.
Riford Emma Mrs. 1232 Wilcox av.
Rigby John R. Hotel Metropole
Rigby William C. Berwyn
Riggle Charles F. 1045 S. Lawndale av.
Riggle Ozias A. 1043 S. Lawndale av.
Riggs George W. 225, 61st. *C.A.*
Riggs L. E. Riverside
Riggs W. E. Riverside
Riker A. P. 2428 Indiana av.
Riley Ann Mrs. 2511 Indiana av.
Riley Charles J. 6034 Indiana av.
Riley Frank W. 1090 S. Central Park av.
Riley George H. 780 North Park av.
Riley Ida Morey Mrs. 3258 Forest av.
Riley J. Sheldon, 6334 Monroe av.
Rimes Mervin B. Dr. 432 Englewood av.
Rimington Hugh H. 4610 Woodlawn av.
Rinder Sophia Mrs. 1539 Windsor av.
Rinderer Peter Mrs. 1717 Arlington pl.
Rindskopf Siegfried W. Granada hotel
　Sum. res. Saranac Lake, N. Y.
Rinehart E. L. 521, 66th
　Sum. res. Grand Haven, Mich.
Rinehart William B. 1628 Indiana av.
Ring August W. 1734 Buckingham pl.
Ringer Jacob, 3613 Wabash av.
Ringer Philip, 3405 Prairie av.
Ringle Lafayette Dr. 559 W. 65th
Ringo Alvin L. 6545 Wentworth av.
Rinn George P. 453 North av. *C.A.*
Rinn Jacob, Evanston
Rinn Philip, 615 Lasalle av.
Rinn Walter J. 615 Lasalle av.
Ripley Bradford W. 783 Washington boul.
　C.A., Ill. Sum. res. Lake Geneva,
　Wis.
Ripley Carrie Miss, Lake Forest
Ripley Charles H. 1534 Perry
Ripley Edward P. Riverside. *Chi.*
Ripley Edwin S. Hinsdale
Ripley John A. Hinsdale
Ripley Joseph T. Oak Park
Ripley William, 783 Washington boul.
Ripley Willis J. 434 N. State
Risch John P. Evanston
Risch Peter, Evanston
Risdon Ambrose, 3307 Forest av.
Rising Charles L. 274 Ashland boul. *Ill.*
Rising Frederick H. 274 Ashland boul.

Rising Philip A. 274 Ashland boul.
Risser A. F. Mrs. 3251 South Park av.
Risser Elizabeth F. Miss, 743 N. Clark
Ristine George W. 3335 South Park av.
Ritchie Frank, Evanston
Ritchie Hugh R. 9 Scott
Ritchie Mary L. Miss, Oak Park
Ritchie Robert H. 5127 Hibbard av.
Ritchie Sarah Mrs. 5408 Washington av.
Ritchie Thomas, 430 Lasalle av.
Ritchie Thomas W. 5127 Hibbard av.
Ritchie William, Oak Park
Ritchie William C. Mrs. 5127 Hibbard av.
Ritchie W. Edward, 4439 Lake av.
Ritsher Edward C. 1698 Wellington. *Univ.*
Rittenhouse Moses, 11 Groveland Park
Rittenhouse T. A. 203, 46th
Rittenhouse Wm. Dr. 975 Warren av.
Ritter Henry A. 2659 Evanston av. *Univ.*
Ritter Martin M. Dr. 4148 Grand boul.
Ritterband Moses M. 419, 48th. *Lksd.*
Rivenburgh Eugene L. Dr. Mayfair
Rix George K. 2302 N. Paulina
Rix Walter B. 2302 N. Paulina
Roach Fred L. 1886 Diversey
Roach John M. 2007 Surf. *Un.*
Robb Thomas P. Chicago Athletic assn.
Robb Wilson J. Maywood
Robbins Burnett W. 2207 Kenmore av.
Robbins Burr, 2354 Clarendon av.
Robbins C. H. Hotel Windermere
Robbins David B. 4201 Ellis av.
Robbins E. F. 2932 Indiana av. *Cal.,
W.P.*
Robbins Franklin G. 801 Warren av.
Robbins F. R. 4832 Madison av.
Robbins George B. Hinsdale
Robbins Henry S. 414 N. State. *Chi., Irq.,
Un.*
Robbins James A. 4838 Michigan av.
Robbins Walter R. 3910 Lake av.
Robbins W. G. 4832 Madison av.
Roberson John P. 5311 Washington av.
Roberton D. C. 4715 Prairie av.
Roberton Helen Miss, 4715 Prairie av.
Roberton John, 4715 Prairie av.
Roberts Alonzo Mrs. 420 Washington
boul.
Roberts A. J. Dr. La Grange
Roberts Byron W. The Hampden
Roberts B. T. Morgan Park
Roberts Charles A. 1684 W. Monroe. *C.A.*
Roberts Charles E. Oak Park
Roberts Clark, Jefferson Park
Roberts C. J. 6558 Yale
Roberts C. N. Jefferson Park
Roberts C. S. Chicago Beach hotel. *C.A.*
Roberts Dwight J., M.D. LaGrange
Roberts Elias J. Austin
Roberts E. L. Tracy
Roberts Frank E. Maywood
Roberts Frank H. 4228 Grand boul.
Roberts Gertrude Miss, 25, 34th pl.
Roberts Grant J. Dr. 695 Lincoln av.
Roberts G. W. Highland Park
Roberts Henry H. 2412 N. Hermitage av.
42

Roberts H. H. 3343 Indiana av.
Roberts Jesse E. LaGrange. *Irq.*
Roberts John, 219 S. Hoyne av.
Roberts John A. G. 2539 N. Ashland av.
Roberts John E. Evanston
Roberts John P. 307 N. Clark
Roberts John W. 6927 Perry av.
Roberts Lydia Mrs. Maywood
Roberts Mary J. Mrs. 7748 Lowe av.
Roberts Melissa Mrs. 2808 Prairie av.
Roberts Roscoe L. Jefferson Park
Roberts Thomas E. Dr. Oak Park
Roberts Thomas G. Dr. 99, 37th
Roberts Walter C. Mrs. Maywood
Roberts Willard A. 4748 Champlain av.
Roberts William G. Edgebrook
Roberts William H. Tracy
Roberts Wilmer K. 1167 Lunt av.
Robertson Alexander, 185, 51st. *Chi.,
W.P.*
Robertson F. C. N. 107, 49th. *C.A.*
Robertson George L. 350 W. Randolph
Robertson Ina L. Miss, 6042 Kimbark av.
Robertson James Dr. 334, 44th
Robertson James D. 3338 South Park av.
Robertson James G. Evanston
Robertson James P. 2149 Kenmore av.
C.A.
Robertson John Blair, 4212 Drexel boul.
C.A.
Robertson John W. 2155 Kenmore av.
Robertson J. W. 3238 Groveland av. *C.A.*
Robertson Victor, 220 The Plaza
Robertson William A. Oak Park
Robertson William H. Evanston
Robeson T. Jay, M.D. 2600 Calumet av.
Robie George T. 7124 Yale.
Robie Thomas S. Mrs. 42 Cedar
Robilliard Ada Miss, 840 Flournoy
Robins George Mrs. 96 Loomis
Robins George W. B. 96 Loomis
Robinson Albert R. Hinsdale
Robinson Argyle E. 5406 Jefferson av.
Robinson Benjamin G. 40 Aldine sq.
Robinson-Byron Dr. 98 Loomis
Robinson Charles O. 4406 Oakenwald av.
Chi., C.A., W.P.
Robinson Clarence R. Prof. Evanston
Robinson Clayton H. 663 Washington
boul.
Robinson C. 5406 Jefferson av.
Robinson Daniel Capt. Highland Park
Robinson David Mrs. 3727 Langley av.
Robinson Edward H. 2354 N. Paulina
Robinson Elisha A. 210 Ashland boul.
C.A.
Robinson Ella Mrs. 2358 Indiana av.
Robinson Elmer D. Austin
Robinson Ethel Miss, 698 Fullerton av.
Robinson E. P. Mrs. Evanston
Robinson Frank B. 40 Aldine sq.
Robinson Frank L. 6343 Yale
Robinson George G. 157 S. Oakley av.
Robinson Harry H. Evanston
Robinson Helen Miss, 59 Aberdeen
Robinson Henry E. Capt. Fort Sheridan

Robinson H. G. 3004 Prairie av.
Robinson H. P. 294 Lasalle av. *Chi., Un.*
Robinson H. T. Mrs. 1641 Indiana av.
Robinson Ithamer A. Austin
Robinson Jay G. 4641 Vincennes av.
Robinson John C. 5142 Lexington av.
Robinson J. K. Lakota hotel. *Cal., Chi., W.P.*
Robinson J. K. jr. Lakota hotel
Robinson M. W. 698 Fullerton av.
Robinson Robert, Oak Park
Robinson Robert C. Oak Park
Robinson Samuel, Evanston
Robinson Stephen L. 489 Belden av.
Robinson S. W. Park Ridge
Robinson Thomas S. 2453 Prairie av.
Robinson Willard H. Rev. 6530 Lafayette av.
Robinson William, 7606 Union av.
Robinson William, Kenilworth
Robinson William Colin, 188, 54th
Robinson William F. Kenilworth
Robinson William H. Oak Park
Robinson William W. 603 W. 61st pl.
Robinson W. L. 5214 Cornell av.
Robison C. H. Mrs. Maywood
Robison John A., M.D. 297 Ashland boul. *Ill.*
Robison J. T. 4756 Lake av.
Robson John, 2637 Michigan av. *Irq.*
Roche Edmund H. 179 Rush
Roche John A. 4605 Drexel boul. *U.L.*
Roche Kate G. Miss. 6362 Minerva av.
Roche Martin, 3614 Grand boul.
Roche P. J. 2342 Calumet av.
Rock Joseph F. 2432 Prairie av.
Rockfeller George R. 3732 Calumet av.
Rockwell Charles H. 111, 49th. *C.A.*
Rockwell Charlotte Miss, 5136 Washington av.
Rockwell C. B. Dr. 5401 Madison av.
Rockwell Fletcher W 5136 Washington av. *U.L.*
Rockwell Fletcher W. jr. 5136 Washington av.
Rockwell Helen Mrs. 2101 Prairie av.
Rockwell Irvin E. 901 Pratt av. *C.A.*
Rockwell Nellie Miss, 5136 Washington av.
Rockwell Thos. H., M.D. 480, 72d
Rockwood Charles D. Evanston
Rockwood Frank B. Elmhurst. *U.L.*
Rockwood Frederick S. Elmhurst
Rockwood George, 929 W. Jackson boul.
Rockwood Harvey, Elmhurst
Rockwood Sprague S. Elmhurst. *C.A.*
Rockwood W. H. Lakota hotel
Roddin Eugene Vincent, 137 Lincoln Park boul.
Rodgers Alexander, 363 S. Hermitage av.
Rodgers F. Miss, Evanston
Rodgers George W. 6400 Monroe av.
Rodgers John L. 6400 Monroe av. *Ill.*
Rodgers John W. Evanston
Rodgers Julia Mrs. Evanston
Rodgers L. Eruest, 849 Warren av.

Rodiger William, 660 W. Monroe *C.A., Ill.*
Rodman Thomas J. 2017 Indiana av. *Univ.*
Roe Albert J. Dr. 4060 Michigan Terrace
Roe Charles E. Oak Park
Roe Charles M. 1603 W. Adams
Roe D. Herbert, 2918 Kenmore av.
Roe E. T. Edison Park
Roe Julian, Hotel Del Prado
Roecker H. Leon, 481, 42d pl.
Roecker M. Mrs. 481, 42d pl.
Roecker Oscar E. 481, 42d pl.
Roehl Carl, 1518 N. Halsted
Roehl Edward E. 3751 Lake av.
Roesch Frank, 1912 Deming pl.
Roesch Frederick, M.D. 769 Larrabee
Roeschlaub F. H. 581 W. Congress. *Ill.*
Roessler F. Herman, 693 Fullerton av.
Rogan J. B. 899 W. Adams. *U.L.*
Rogan W. J. 691 W. Adams
Rogers Albert W. 2211 Sheridan rd.
Rogers Andrew W. Dr. 6719 Wentworth av.
Rogers Bennajah C. 2907 Kenmore av.
Rogers Bernard F. 80 Buena av. *U.L.*
Rogers Charles M. Evanston
Rogers Charles W. 301 West ct.
Rogers C. A. Evanston
Rogers C. D. 4925 Washington av. *C.A., W.P.*
Rogers Daniel Weston Dr. 2204 Michigan av.
Rogers Edgar E. 732 Winthrop av.
Rogers Edward K. 370 Ontario
Rogers Elmer E. 259 Michigan av.
Rogers Ernest J. Evanston
Rogers E. Miss, 320 Lasalle av.
Rogers Frank D. 1313 W. Adams
Rogers F. D. Dr. 6106 Michigan av.
Rogers George H. Lombard
Rogers Geo. Mills, 52 Walton pl. *Irq., Univ.*
  Sum. res. Forest Lodge, Traverse City, Mich.
Rogers George W. Wilmette
Rogers Henrietta L. Miss, Evanston
Rogers Henry, 52 Walton pl.
Rogers Henry B. Mrs. 4569 Lake av.
Rogers Henry Wade, Pres. L.L. D. Evanston. *U.L.*
Rogers Hopewell L. 74 Buena av.
Rogers H. M. Berwyn
Rogers H. W. 320 Lasalle av. *Irq.*
Rogers Ida Wright, M.D. 441 Dearborn av.
Rogers James C. Evanston
Rogers James C. Oak Park. *Irq.*
  Winter res. Azusa, Cal.
Rogers James S. 5535 Monroe av.
  Sum. res. Cape Ann
Rogers John A. 74 Buena av. *Univ.*
Rogers John B. 481 Fulton
Rogers John G. Mrs. 52 Walton pl.
  Sum. res. Forest Lodge, Traverse City, Mich.
Rogers John J. 4750 Champlain av.

Rogers Joseph Dr. 910 W. Monroe
Rogers Joseph M. 74 Buena av. *Univ.*
Rogers J. J. 1886 Diversey
Rogers J. W. R. LaGrange
Rogers L. D., M.D. 441 Dearborn av.
Rogers Mary B. Mrs. 359 Ontario
Rogers Nellie M. Mrs. 569, 51st
Rogers Robert M. Llewellyn Park
Rogers R. C. Oak Park
Rogers R. N. 16 St. James pl.
Rogers Sampson, Oak Park
Rogers Samuel S. Oak Park
Rogers Sarah K. Mrs. Evanston
Rogers Sarah N. Mrs. Evanston
Rogers S. C. Miss, 359 Ontario
Rogers S. M. Miss, 320 Lasalle av.
Rogers Thomas P. 1092 Millard av.
Rogers W. H. Oak Park
Rogerson A. Berwyn
Rogerson Edward J. LaGrange. *Ill.*
Rogerson Joseph, 414 Warren av.
Rogerson M y L. Mrs. 377 Bissell
Rohde HansaF. 6505 Harvard av.
Rohn Alfred, 1018 Park av.
Rohn Robert F. 108 S. Seeley av.
Rohn Rudolph, 168 S. Seeley av.
Rohr F. W., M.D. 457 Lasalle av.
Rohrer J. B. Hotel Del Prado
Rohu William C. Dr. 267 Ohio
Roland George N. 36 Roslyn pl.
Roland John G. 540 Cleveland av.
Roland Lorenzo Bull, 36 Roslyn pl.
Roler A. H. Dr. 2330 Indiana av.
Roler E. O. F., M.D. 2330 Indiana av.
Roles Frances A. Miss, 804 Bryan av.
Rolf Abraham A. 4459 Oakenwald av.
Rolf Frank S. Elmhurst
Rolfe Henry, 5218 Hibbard av.
Rolfe V. Mrs. 475 Fullerton av.
Roll Isaac E. 5748 Monroe av.
Rollins Charles H. 932 W. Monroe
Rollins C. E. 427 Washington boul. *Ill. Irq.*
Rollins C. E. jr. 429 Washington boul.
Rollins G. A. Clifton house
Rollins W. E. Granada hotel
Rollo A. G. LaGrange
Rollo Charles E. 235 Ashland boul. *Ill.*
Rollo Frank C. LaGrange
Rollo Louis E. LaGrange
Rollo L. Chester, 952 W. Jackson boul. *C.A., W.P.*
Rollo R. R. Mrs. 235 Ashland boul.
Rollo William E. 463 Washington boul.
Rollo W. F. 901 W. Adams
Roloson Robert W. 2109 Prairie av. *Cal., Chi., W.P.*
Roloson Walter L. Hotel Metropole *Chi., W.P.*
Rolston H. M. 11446 Indiana av. *Irq.*
Romig Samuel V. Dr. 727 Morse av.
Rommeiss Geo. R. 4018 Ellis av.
Rompel M. Joseph, 1239 Sheridan rd.
Rondthaler J. A. Rev. 34 Roslyn pl.
Rondthaler William D. 34 Roslyn pl.
Roney Charles J. 2506 Indiana av.

Roney Henry B. 2506 Indiana av.
Roney Irene B. Mrs. 2506 Indiana av.
Roney Thomas C. 4504 Vincennes av.
Rood A. W. 2914 Groveland av.
Rood George L. 3535 Calumet av.
Rood Golden E. 3966 Langley av.
Rood Horace E. 610 The Plaza
Rood James, Evanston
Rood James jr. Evanston. *Chi.*
Rood John H. 4334 Ellis av.
Rood Will C. 284 Park av.
Rooks Edwin S. 801 Warren av.
Roosevelt Wilton C. 2233 Prairie av.
Root Benjamin W. Mrs. 3236 Calumet av.
Root Chapman J. 802 W. Adams
Root Clara Mrs. Evanston
Root Clarence J. 5540 Washington av.
Root Daniel E. 3700 Lake av.
Root Eliza H. Dr. 489 W. Monroe
Root E. T. Mrs. 5200 Cornell av.
Root Fanny A. Miss, 5200 Cornell av.
Root Fred K. 5725 Washington av.
Root Frederick W. 5333 Cornell av.
Root F. K. Kenilworth
Root George F. 5200 Cornell av.
Root James P. 5540 Washington av.
Root Jerome, 489 W. Monroe
Root Judson A. 196, 40th
Root J. Sherman, 489 W. Monroe
Root L. B. Mrs. 3712 Ellis av.
Root Melvin A. Dr. 205 N. State
Root Sally G. Mrs. River Forest
Root Walter R. Kenilworth
Root William A. 5200 Cornell av.
Root William J. 3601 Vincennes av.
Root Z. D. Park Ridge
Roovaart William, 5933 Butler
Roper Edward U. 1853 Oakdale av.
Roper John, 4021 Ellis av.
Roper John, 6037 Monroe av.
Ropp Silas, Irving Park
Rosche George F. Prof. Elmhurst
Rose Charles, 742 W. 63d pl.
Rose David Dr. 960 S. Central Park av.
Rose Edward, 3241 Wabash av. *Stan.*
Rose Estelle Miss, 2928 Groveland av.
Rose Frank A. 1748 Oakdale av.
Rose George A. 1463 W. Jackson boul.
Rose G. A. Lexington hotel
Rose H. H. Lexington hotel. *Univ.*
Rose J. B. 4558 Lake av.
Rose J. D. Hotel Del Prado
Rose L. C. Lexington hotel
Rose L. C. Mrs. Lexington hotel
Rose Ray Clarke, 578 Division
Rose Willet, 6321 Kimbark av.
Rose W. H. 71 S. Seeley av.
Roseboom J. H. 386 Lasalle av.
Roseboom William L. 1828 Barry av.
Rosekrans Edward M. Austin
Rosenbaum Blanche B. Miss, 2229 Calumet av.
Rosenbaum Emanuel F. 2231 Calumet av.
Rosenbaum Joseph, 2229 Calumet av. *Stan.*

Rosenbaum Morris, 3311 Michigan av. *Lksd., Stan.*
Rosenbaum William, 3423 Forest av.
Rosenbecker Adolph, 2647 Magnolia av.
Rosenberg Benjamin, 3606 Prairie av. *Lksd., Stan.*
Rosenberg Bernhard, 4334 Grand boul,
Roseuberg Charles, Evanston
Rosenberg Jacob, 1620 Michigan av. *Stan.*
Roseuberg Julius L. 3754 Michigan av. *Stan.*
Roseuberg Oscar, 4807 Grand boul. *Stan.*
Rosenberg Philip, 735 N. Hoyne av.
Rosenberg S. C. 2124 Michigan av.
Rosenberger Julius, 3744 Forest av.
Rosenberger Otto J. 3744 Forest av. *Lksd.*
Rosenberry A. J. Dr. Oak Park
Rosenblatt Aaron Mrs. 2633 Michigan av.
Rosenblatt Lillie Miss, 2928 Groveland av.
Rosenbush A. A. 3438 Vernon av.
Rosenfeld Emma Mrs. 434 Washington boul.
Rosenfeld Maurice, 1620 Michigan av. *Stan., W.P.*
Rosenfeld Sidney, 434 Washington boul.
Rosenfeld Simon, 4235 Michigan av. *Lksd.*
Rosenfield Hannah Mrs. 246 Schiller
Rosenfield Henry, 4432 Prairie av.
Rosenfield Isaac, 3404 Calumet av. *Stan.*
Rosenfield Jacob A. 246 Schiller
Rosenfield Joseph S. 3306 Calumet av. *Stan.*
Rosenfield Louis, 3627 Grand boul. *Stan.*
Rosenfield Morris S. 2932 Indiana av. *Stan.*
Rosenfield S. W. 3153 Prairie av.
Rosenheim Bernard, 3342 Calumet av.
Rosenheim Morris B. 637, 46th pl. *Lksd.*
Rosenheim Simon, 3750 Elmwood ct.
Rosenheim Ulrich, Hotel Woodruff
Rosenthal Benjamin J. Hotel Del Prado. *Lksd., Stan.*
Rosenthal B. Mrs. 3213 South Park av.
Rosenthal Caroline Mrs. 4401 Indiana av.
Rosenthal Emil R. 4120 Ellis av.
Rosenthal E. A. 4343 Calumet av. *Irq., Lksd.*
Rosenthal E. M. 4023 Vincennes av. *Stan.*
Rosenthal James, 6046 Jefferson av.
Rosenthal Joseph, 3223 Vernon av.
Rosenthal Julius, 3247 Wabash av. *Stan. U.L.*
Rosenthal Kurt, 3213 South Park av.
Rosenthal Lessing, 3247 Wabash av. *Stan.*
Rosenthal Lubin L. 4401 Indiana av. *Stan.*
Rosenthal Maier, 244 Schiller
Rosenthal Moritz, 5478 Greenwood av.
Rosenthal Oscar, 3333 Michigan av. *Stan.*
Rosenthal Rose E. Miss, 3410 Calumet av.
Rosenthal Samuel, 3447 Prairie av. *Lksd.*
Rosenthal Samuel H. 3410 Calumet av.
Rosenthal Samuel J. 4134 Lake av.
Rosenthal Sigmund M. 5006 Michigan av.

Rosenwald Julius, 4239 Grand boul. *Stan.*
Rosenwald Morris S. 3342 South Park av. *Stan.*
Rosenwald Samuel, 3342 South Park av.
Roser Elwin A. Oak Park
Rosing Edward, 4727 Lake av.
Rosing Kate Miss, 5238 Jefferson av.
Rosing W. H. V. 5238 Jefferson av. *C.A.*
Ross Adele Miss, 5437 Madison av.
Ross Alex M. 1849 Barry av.
Ross Amanda M. Mrs. 817 Estes av.
Ross Arthur J. 1849 Barry av.
Ross A. S. 233 S. Paulina
Ross Bernard M., M.D. 499 Dearborn av.
Ross Charles G. 817 The Plaza
Ross David M. 1621 Roscoe
Ross D. W. Chicago Beach hotel
Ross Ellison H. River Forest
Ross George, 539 W. Jackson boul. *Ill.*
Ross George B. Chicago Beach Hotel. *C.A.*
Ross George W. 690, 48th
Ross Hugh R. Evanston
Ross H. Russell, 42 Cedar
Ross James L. 3604 Vernon av.
Ross James W. 3604 Vernon av.
Ross John C. Hinsdale
Ross John D. Oak Park
Ross John F. Oak Park
Ross Joseph P. Mrs. 428 Washington boul.
Ross J. S. Mrs. Riverside
Ross Mark A. Hotel Del Prado
Ross Mary E. Mrs. 42 Cedar
Ross Mathias, 5160 Wabash av.
Ross M. Mrs. 3500 Ellis av.
Ross N. J. Evanston
Ross Oliver S. 4221 Lake av.
Ross Ovington, Evanston
Ross Robert E. 428 Washington boul.
Ross Robert H. 539 W. Jackson boul.
Ross Thomas J. 6544 Lafayette av.
Ross Walter W. Evanston
Ross William H. 428 Washington boul.
Ross William K. Chicago Athletic assn
Ross W. C. 3231 Wabash av.
Rossbach Victor A. Evanston
Rossiter E. M. Mrs. Austin
Rossiter Gilbert, Lake Forest
Rossiter Harold, Austin
Rossiter James S. 17 Chalmers pl.
Rossiter William Austin
Ross-Lewin Harry F. 1860 Melrose
Ross-Lewin William H. 1860 Melrose
Rossman Ceylon Dr. LaGrange
Roth Charles, 173 Lincoln av.
Roth John C. Hotel Windermere
Roth Marshall L. Hinsdale
Rothenberg Julius, 967 W. Madison
Rothermel Samuel A. Oak Park
Rothermel William E. 143 Oakwood boul.
Rothermel William H. 4338 Berkeley av.
Rothschild Abram M. 3725 Michigan av. *Stan.*
Rothschild A. Mrs. 4241 Prairie av.
Rothschild Benjamin, 2633 Michigan av. *Stan.*

Rothschild Charles E. 3416 Calumet av. *Stan.*
Rothschild Emanuel, 3359 Vernon av. *Stan.*
Rothschild Emil, 4241 Prairie av. .
Rothschild Emil, 4500 Forrestville av.
Rothschild Fred, 54, 33d. *Stan.*
Rothschild F. 3411 Forest av. *Stan.*
Rothschild Harry, 4230 Indiana av. *Lksd.*
Rothschild Isaac D. 3245 Rhodes av. *Stan.*
Rothschild Jesse A. 2112 Prairie av.
Rothschild Joseph, 4241 Prairie av.
Rothschild J. A. Mrs. 2633 Michigan av.
Rothschild Leo J. 2633 Michigan av. *Stan.*
Rothschild Lewis, 695, 49th. *Lksd.*
Rothschild Mamie F. Miss, 2112 Prairie av.
Rothschild Maurice T. 4751 Champlain av. *Lksd.*
Rothschild Monroe R. 2112 Prairie av.
Rothschild M. L. 3347 South Park av. *Stan.*
Rothschild M. M. Mrs. 2112 Prairie av.
Rothschild M. S. 3827 Wabash av.
Rothschild S. M. 3245 Rhodes av.
Rothschild William L. 3245 Rhodes av. *Stan.*
Rothschild W. S. 3938 Lake av. *Stan.*
Rothstein Isidore, 3842 Vincennes av. *Lksd.*
Rothwell Arnold S. LaGrange
Rothwell Harry L. LaGrange
Rothwell Harry R. LaGrange
Rothwell R. E. LaGrange
Roulet William, 7728 Eggleston av.
Roulston Robert J. 540 W. 61st pl.
Rounds Charles H. Austin. *C.A.*
Rounds Fred C. Austin
Rounds T. C. Mrs. Oak Park
Rounds William H. Mrs. Austin
Rounsavell George 1847 Wellington
Rounsaville George T. Revere house
Rounseville C. N. Mme, 3120 Groveland av.
Rounseville Richard C. Palmer house
Rountree Harrison H. Kenilworth
Rous A. C. Lexington hotel. *Cal.*
Rouse R. Harry, 4602 Prairie av.
Routledge John F. Oak Park
Rowan P. J. Dr. 372 W. Adams
Rowe Charles H. Mrs. Evanston
Rowe Ella Miss, 5 Chalmers pl.
Rowe Fannie S. 4800 Lake av.
Rowe James A. Evanston
Rowe James G. 3000 Prairie av.
Rowe James L. 5 Chalmers pl. *U.L.*
Rowe Samuel M. 87, 74th
Rowe Samuel M. Evanston
Rowell B. C. Hyde Park hotel
Rowland E. F. Mrs. 7001 Stewart av.
Rowland Harriett A. Mrs. Evanston
Rowland Ivan R. 445 Washington boul.
Rowlands David W. Mrs. 56 Wisconsin
Rowlands William D. 56 Wisconsin
Rowles E. W. A. 7131 Eggleston av.
Rowles Walter D. 6632 Stewart av.

Rowley Fanny M. Dr. Oak Park
Rowley Frank, Oak Park
Rowley Samuel T. 6565 Yale
Roy Joseph E. Rev. Oak Park
Royal George, Oak Park
Royal George Mrs. Oak Park
Royce E. A. Dr. 721 Washington boul, *Ill.*
Roys Cyrus D. 2937 Michigan av.
  Sum. res. Morehouse Place, Elkhart, Ind,
Rozet George H. 340 Lasalle av. *Un.*
Rozwadowski Anthony Count, The Tudor
Ruan Jennie Miss, Oak Park
Ruan Walter, Oak Park
Rubel Benj. F. 3341 Wabash av. *Stan.*
Rubel Charles D. 3424 Calumet av. *Stan.*
Rubel David, 3432 Michigan av.
Rubel Hannah Mrs. 492, 42d pl.
Rubel Isaac Mrs. 3341 Wabash av.
Rubel Isaac, 2714 Indiana av. *Lksd.*
Rubel Isaac F. 3547 Indiana av. *Stan.*
Rubel Isidor A. 4213 Vincennes av. *Stan.*
Rubel Jennie Mrs. 4407 Greenwood av.
Rubel Levi G. 3343 Wabash av. *Stan.*
Rubel Milton, 3432 Michigan av. *Stan.*
Rubel Reuben, 3432 Michigan av.
Rubel Simon, 5149 Prairie av.
Ruben Charles, 4236 Calumet av. *Lksd.*
Rubens Charles, 711, 49th. *Lksd., Stan.*
Rubens Harry, 52 Walton pl. *C.A., U.L.*
Rubens Lee, 4346 St. Lawrence av.
Rubens Louis, 711, 49th
Rubenstein Joseph, 3244 South Park av.
Rubidge H. A. 550 N. Normal Parkway
Rubinkam Nathaniel I. Rev. 5635 Lexington av.
Rubin Sol, 3354 Wabash av. *Lksd.*
Rubins Barbara E. Mrs. Morton Park
Rubins Chas. C. Morton Park
Rubins Harry W. Morton Park
Rubins Willis F. Morton Park
Rubovits Isidor, 3627 Prairie av.
Rubovits Louis, 3131 Indiana av.
Rubovits Morris, 3627 Prairie av.
Rucavado F. J. Mrs. Hotel Metropole
Rucker B. C. Mrs. Austin
Rucker Hamline P. 4300 Ellis av.
Rud Anthony Dr. Austin
Ruddecham C. W. Berwyn
Ruddock Charles H. 468 Washington boul. *C.A., Ill.*
Rudert Emil, 5217 Kimbark av.
Rudhart Philip P. 4323 Oakenwald av. *C.A.*
Rudolph Charles, 283 Lasalle av.
Rudolph Emil, Highland Park
Rudolph Franklin, 283 Lasalle av. *C.A*
Rudolph Joseph, 283 Lasalle av.
Rueb Edward, 273 S. Irving av.
Rueckheim F. W. 4201 Vincennes av.
Rueckheim Laura W. Miss 4201 Vincennes av.
Rueckheim Louis, 4226 Vincennes av.
Ruedy Byron G. Evanston
Ruehl Harry A. 503 Ashland boul.

Ruehl William, 503 Ashland boul.
Ruehl William G. 445 S. Winchester av.
Ruel George H. Winnetka
Ruff Joseph, 3036 Lake Park av.
Ruff Joseph B. 3036 Lake Park av.
Ruffner Augustus, 4314 Langley av.
Ruffner Will R. 3702 Lake av. *C.A.*
Rugg Arthur H. 5338 Washington av.
Ruggles A. Roberta Miss, 33 Roslyn pl.
Ruggles Charles C. 3820 Lake av.
Ruggles Charles R. 299 Ashland boul.
  C.A.
Ruggles Georgia S. Dr. 2211 Michigan
  av.
Ruggles Howard P. 33 Roslyn pl.
Ruggles M. M. Mrs. 268 Lasalle av.
Ruggles Oliver E. 33 Roslyn pl.
Ruggles O. W. 33 Roslyn pl.
Ruh Frank E. Franklin Park. *C.A.*
Ruhstrat A. 1949 Deming pl.
Rumpf George Mrs. 3419 Vernon av.
Rumpf W. H. Dr. 4720 Kenwood av. *C.A.*
Rumsey Cornelius E. Virginia hotel.
  U.L.
Rumsey George D. 607 Division. *Un.,*
  Univ.
Rumsey Israel P. Lake Forest. *U.L.*
Rumsey Julian M. 313 Huron. *C.A.*
Rumsey Julian S. Mrs. 313 Huron
Rumsey J. Franck, Lake Forest. *U.L.*
Rumsey S. Edward, Washington Heights
Runals Clarence L. 1838 Arlington pl.
Rundell A. B. Mrs. 1139 Washington boul.
Rundell Charles L. 749 W. Monroe
Rundell Miller H. 1139 Washington boul.
Rundell Richard J. 749 W. Monroe
Runge H. Detlef, 79 Ewing pl.
Runnells Clive, 593 N. State
Runnells John S. 593 N. State. *Chi., Un.,*
  U.L. Sum. res. Chocorua, N. H.
Runnels John F. Dr. 233 Webster av.
Runnion Helen Miss, 604 Division
Runnion Nelson, 604 Division
Runyon David Mrs. 2124 Michigan av.
Rusco Charles A. 933 S. Sawyer av.
Rush David G. Dr. 519 W. Adams
Rush Edwin F., M.D., 2327 Michigan av.
Rush George F. 5719 Washington av.
  Univ.
Rush J. W. 3608 Ellis av. *C.A.*
Rush M. A. Mrs. The Hampden
Rushton Alfred, Morgan Park
Rushton Joseph Rev. Evanston
Rushton Joseph A. Evanston
Rusk John Rev. 2358 Indiana av.
Russ Alamando B. 181, 37th
Russ Bert S. 204 Ashland boul.
Russ Carrie Miss, 3989 Drexel boul.
Russ Charles Mrs. Oak Park
Russ Charles A. 2728 Wabash av.
Russ Charles L. 181, 37th
Russ Lewis, 204 Ashland boul.
Russ William W. 6242 Monroe av.
Russell Albert, 6357 Stewart av.
Russell Alfred, 596 W. VanBuren
Russell Catherine Mrs. 794 W. Monroe

Russell C. C. 1049 Early av.
Russell David Edward, 1454 Fulton
  Sum. res. Swan Lake, Wis.
Russell D. W. 4055 Prairie av.
Russell Edmund A. 2541 Michigan av.
  C.A., U.L.
  Sum. res. Lake Geneva, Wis.
Russell Edward P. 28 Delaware pl. *Chi.,*
  Un.
Russell Edward W. Evanston
Russell Elbridge F. 57 Laflin
Russell Elizabeth M. Miss, 525 W. Monroe
Russell Frank H. Evanston
Russell George M. 5808 Michigan av.
Russell Harris, 4214 Ellis av.
Russell H. Clay, Morgan Park
Russell H. D. 6557 Ingleside av.
Russell H. M. 1718 Indiana av.
Russell H. T. Revere house
Russell Isaac Mrs. Ravinia
Russell John, 1174 Wilcox av.
Russell Lena L. Miss, Wilmette
Russell L. M. Morton Park
Russell Marie S. 2358 Indiana av.
Russell Martin J. 5409 Washington av.
Russell Mary D. Miss, Morgan Park
Russell M. J. Mrs. Oak Park
Russell Perley A. 4111 Bosworth av.
Russell Robert, 4425 Vincennes av.
Russell Samuel W. 14 Aldine sq.
Russell William H. 3126 Calumet av.
Russell William H. Highland Park
Rust Henry A. Quadrangle club
Rust Josephine Miss, 1221 Pratt av.
Ruth A. L. Mrs. Lakota hotel
Ruth Fannie B. Mrs. 235 Park av,
Ruth John A. 160 Park av.
Ruth Linus C. Hinsdale
Ruth VanBuren, 3852 Ellis av.
Ruthenberg Otto A. 1817 Belmont av.
Rutherford Alice Mrs. 824 W. Monroe
Rutherford C., M.D. 646 Fullerton av.
Rutherford James L. 216, 42d pl.
Rutt A. B. 580 W. Adams
Rutt M. B. 580 W. Adams
Rutter Charles L. Mrs. 113 Cass
Rutter David, 295 Huron. *Cal., Un., Univ.*
  Sum. res. Mackinac Island
Rutter Dudley, 113 Cass
Rutter Lynn R. 295 Huron. *Un.*
Rutter Max, 295 Huron
Ruud Helga Dr. 281 Warren av.
Ruxton William, 359 Dearborn av. *C.A.*
Ryan Andrew J. 1644 W. Jackson boul.
Ryan Elizabeth Miss, 747 Warren av.
Ryan E. Joseph, 5440 Ridgewood ct.
Ryan George J. 1373 Washington boul
Ryan James Mrs. 3651 Prairie av.
Ryan James F. 764 Touhy av. *C.A.*
Ryan John J. River Forest
Ryan J. Longwood
Ryan M. W. 40 Throop
Ryan P. J. Auditorium annex
Ryan Thomas J. Chicago club
Ryan Timothy E. 63 Macalister pl.
Ryan T. A. 4352 Greenwood av.

Rycroft Herbert E. 4511 Forrestville av. *C.A.*
Rydell J. S. 5147 Michigan av. *C.A.*
     Sum. res. Pistaqua Bay, Ill.
Rydell Oscar F. 5147 Michigan av.
Ryder Chauncey F. Hinsdale
Ryder E. C. Mrs. 3016 Prairie av.
Ryder Fred L. 3601 Vincennes av.
Ryerson Arthur, 59 Bellevue pl. *Chi., Univ.*
Ryerson Edward L. 31 Banks. *Chi., C.A., Un.* Sum. res. Edgewood, Conn.
Ryerson John A. 361 Superior. *Univ.*
Ryerson Martin Mrs. Auditorium annex
Ryerson Martin A. 4851 Drexel boul. *Chi., C.A., U.L., W.P.*
Rynearson James L. Leland hotel. *W.P.*
Ryther Gates A. 6638 Butler

ST. CLAIR SAMUEL M. Irving Park
   St. John Alpheus B. 438 W. 65th
St. John Charles P. 165 Locust
St. John Frederick, 539 W. Monroe. *Ill.*
St. John Leonard Dr. 539 W. Monroe. *Ill., W.P.*
Saalfeld Charlotte S. Mrs. 3177 Dover
Sabin Albert, Hinsdale
Sabin Albert R. Irving Park
Sackett Charles L. LaGrange
Sackett Edward B. 2969 Michigan av.
Sackett Frank V. La Grange
Sackett Grove, 7138 Eggleston av. *U.L.*
Sackett Henry R. Dr. Austin
Sackett Robert E. 4422 Prairie av.
Sackley James A. 1268 Washington boul.
Saehrn Joachim, 523 Cleveland av.
Safford Allen B. 13 Ashland boul.
Safford Henry D. 6434 Parnell av.
Safford N. C. 427 Warren av.
Safford William H. 6434 Parnell av.
Sage C. Frank, 17, 40th
Sage Donald A. 4901 Vincennes av.
Sage Ellen Mrs. 269 Seminary av.
Sage G. Kenneth, 17, 40th
Sage William G. 126, 47th
Sage William M. Mrs. 17, 40th
Sagendorph Frank E. 888 W. Adams. *Ill.*
Sager George H. 413 The Plaza
Sager George W. 413 The Plaza
Sager H. N. Hinsdale
Sager W. D. 293 S. Claremont av.
Sailor Samuel, 1661 W. Adams
Sale W. B. LaGrange
Salinger David H. 4845 Calumet av.
Salinger Louis, 3549 Grand boul.
Salinger Morris, 3549 Grand boul.
Salinger M. Hotel Del Prado
Salisbury F. L. 7112 Lafayette av.
Salisbury Jerome H. Dr. 982 W. Adams
Salisbury J. C. Mrs. 4202 Drexel boul.
Salisbury Rollin D. Prof. 5730 Woodlawn av. *Univ.*
Salisbury Warren M. 58 Cedar. *Chi., Un.*
Salisbury William H. 687 Washington boul. *Ill.*
     Sum. res. North Andover, Mass.

Salisbury W. D. Evanston
Salladay John W. 2475 N. Hermitage av.
Salmon Chas. 6826 Perry av.
Salmonson Axel H. 4131 Newgart av.
Salmonson Edgar M. 4131 Newgart av.
Salmonson Morris, 4131 Newgart av.
Salomon Godfrey S. Dr. 4106 Ellis av. *Stan.*
Salomon Joseph, 767 W. Jackson boul.
Salomon Leo, 767 W. Jackson boul.
Salomon Louis H. 3744 Grand boul. *Lksd.*
Salomon Moses, 767 W. Jackson boul. *Lksd.*
Salomon S. 767 W. Jackson boul.
Salomon William, 767 W. Jackson boul.
Salsbury Nathan R. 4009 Lake av. *W.P.*
Salter Albert C. 6557 Perry av.
Salter Frank, 6557 Perry av.
Salter George B. Dr. 166, 42d pl.
Salter Richard H. Oak Park
Salter Wilbur G. 6557 Perry av.
Salter William M. 1519 W. Adams.
Saltonstall Brayton, 2518 Prairie av.
Sammons E. Hudson Dr. 51, 31st
Sammons T. J. 330 Warren av.
Sample Alexander A. 169 Dearborn av.
Sample B. T. Mrs. 551 W. 60th
Sampsell M. E. The Tudor
Sampson Henry C. Highland Park
Sampson J. C. 4598 Oakenwald av.
Sampson Nels, Norwood Park
Samson Clark B. 429 Washington boul. *Ill.*
Samuel Albert E. 4322 Calumet av. *Lksd.*
Samuel Edward M. 497 N. State, *U.L.*
Samuels Benjamin J, 580 Lasalle av.
Samuels Daniel V. 103, 37th, *Irq.*
Sanborn Benjamin S. Evanston
Sanborn George C. 834 Walnut, *C.A.*
Sanborn George Edwin, Chicago Beach hotel, *U.L.*
Sanborn Joseph B. Winnetka. *Irq.*
Sanborn Kate Mrs. Riverside
Sanborn Sherburn, 485 N. State
Sanborn Victor C. LaGrange
Sandberg Charles A. 463 Dearborn av.
Sandberg George N. 463 Dearborn av.
Sandberg Karl F. M. Dr. 622 N. Hoyne av.
Sandberg N. J. 463 Dearborn av.
Sander Henry, 4562 Indiana av.
Sanders Albert D. Evanston
Sanders Alvin H. 1491 Washington boul.
Sanders A. Mrs. 2959 Wabash av.
Sanders Charity E. Mrs. 1102 Washington boul.
Sanders Edgar, 1639 Belmont av.
Sanders H. B. Dr. 3245 Forest av.
Sanders John P. 2959 Wabash av.
Sanders Josie Miss, 3213 Wabash av.
Sanders J. F. 289, 53d, *C.A.*
Sanders Margaret Miss, 3213 Wabash av.
Sanders Milton S. 1777 Magnolia av.
Sanders W. H. Mrs. 3245 Forest av.
Sanderson George A. 2621 Michigan av. *Cal., Chi., W.P.*

Sanderson George E. Mrs. 5153 Prairie
· av.
Sandes Henry R. 2580 N. Winchester av.
Sands Lizzie A. Miss, Evanston
Sands Obadiah, 511 W. Jackson boul. *Ill.*
Sands Obadiah jr. 511 W. Jackson boul.
Sandy Alfred C. Austin·
Sanford Frank E. LaGrange
Sanford J. Eugene, 6531 Yale
Sanford Merritt E. 5656 Washington av.·
Sanford Nelson, Evanston
Sanford Willard C. Dr. 157 Eugenie
Sang Orr, 4112 Grand boul. *Irq.*
Sanger Henry A. Pullman
Sansom W. A. 152, 36th
Santee Harris E. Dr. 770 Warren av.
Sarber E. O. Dr. 291, 31st
Sard William H. 2250 Michigan av. *Cal.*,
Chi., *W. P.*
Sargeant Elicia F. Mrs. 84 Bryant av.
Sargent Celia Miss, Avenue house,
Evanston
Sargent E. H. 4822 Kenwood av.
Sargent George H. Evanston
Sargent George M. Evanston. *U. L.*
Sargent H.E.Gen. Lexington hotel. *U.L.*
Sargent John, Oak Park
Sargent J. R. W. Lexington hotel. *Univ.*
Sargent Sabra L. Miss, Lake Forest
Sargent William Durham, Evanston
Sargent William D. Hotel Metropole.
C.A.,*Univ.*,*U.L.*,*W. P.*
Sarsfield J. M. 3525 Grand boul.·
Sarver Martha M. Miss, 50 Buena av.
Sass Louis, 847 W. Monroe
Sasseen D. E. 521 Dearborn av.
Satterlee Daniel S. Dr. 4633 Evans av.
Satterlee Frank W. Dr. LaGrange
Satterlee George A. 2704 Michigan av.
Satterlee John C. 1386 Fulton
Satterlee M. L. Mrs. 2704 Michigan av.
Sattler Dennis S. 26 Oregon av.
Sattler Philip Dr. 349 W. Congress, *Ill.*
Sattley Winfield N. 4349 Grand boul.
C. A.,*W.P.* Sum. res. Green Lake,
Wis.
Sauer Albert F. 3601 Vincennes av.
Sauer Dittmar, 1386 Sheridan rd.
Sauer H. Edward Dr. 1386 Sheridan rd.
Sauer J. Casper, 106, 40th
Saunders Annetta-Ayers Dr. 211 Chicago
, av.
Saunders Charles B. Dr. 211 Chicago av.
Saunders Henry, 69 Laflin
Saunders Horace N. 4734 Langley av.
Saunders Thomas W. 3121 Indiana av.
Saunders Will I. 1143 N. Clark
Saur P. B., M.D. 2358 Indiana av.
Sauter C. Frank, 541 Cleveland av.
Sauter C. J. 541 Cleveland av.
Sauter George L. 3628 Prairie av.
Sauter L. E. 541 Cleveland av.
Sauveur L. Dr. 263 Dearborn av.
Savage Edward P. 1377 N. Halsted
Savage Francis W. 1377 N. Halsted
Savage Geo. W. Mayfair

Savage G. S. F. Rev. Dr. 628 Washington
boul.
Savage Henry G. Wheaton. *U. L.*
Savage James C. Wilmette
Savage James K. Evanston
Sawe Harry L. Evanston
Sawe Henry J. Evanston.
Sawford H. F. 1713 Barry av.
Sawin D. W. Mrs. 2954 Calumet av.
Sawin George, Elmhurst
Sawyer Amanda N. Mrs. 2998 Kenmore
av. .
Sawyer Amory W. 5311 Washington av.
Sawyer A. P. Dr. 4858 Prairie av.·
Sawyer Carlos P. 454 W. Adams
Sawyer Charles A. 1640 Indiana av.
Sum. res. Chatham, Mass.
Sawyer Charles B. Mrs. 1640 Indiana av.
Winter res. Pasadena, Cal.
Sawyer D. G. 454 W. Adams
Sawyer Edgar, 4509 Prairie av.
Sawyer Francis A. Mrs. 43 Banks
Sawyer Franklin, 75 Park av.
Sawyer Jo n E. Dr. 4643 Evans av.
Sawyer Leander, 484 Fullerton av.
Sawyer Lewis M. Evanston
Sawyer M. A. Miss, Hotel Windermere
Sawyer Robert F. 75 Park av.
Sawyer Sidney Mrs. 301 Ontario
Sawyer Ward B. Evanston
Sax Charles, 3608 Prairie av.
Saxton Henry I. Morgan Park
Saxton Hester B. Mrs. 4608 Lake av.
Saxton I. A. Lieut. Fort Sheridan
Sayer Frank E. 2459 Prairie av.
Sayer James P. Berwyn
Sayer Wm. E. 2459 Prairie av.
Sayers Henry, 1609 Indiana av.
Sayle J. H. 1028 Park av.
Sayler Carl E. 446 Belden av. *C. A.*
Sayler Harry L. 7134 Euclid av.
Sayler Walter, Irving Park
Sayles Harold F. Oak Park
Sayles Russell T. 6534 Stewart av.
Saylor Herman G. 616, 46th
Sayre Virginia Miss, 281 W. Adams
Scadding Charles Rev. LaGrange
Scaife Henry W. Dr. 975 Millard av. .
Scales Caroline C. Mrs. Evanston
Scales Frank Mrs. 234 S. Leavitt
Scales John C. 8 Kenesaw terrace
Scambler H. M. 1031 Early av.
Scammon J. Young Mrs. 5810 Monroe av.
Scanlan Kickham, 85 Ewing pl. *Ill.*
Scanlon Julia Mrs. 6503 Woodlawn av.
Scannell Belle Miss, Austin
Scarborough E. E. Mrs. 3926 Prairie av.
Scarborough Harry, 3926 Prairie av.
Scarritt Ena B. Mrs. 772 W. Monroe
Scates Charles, 235 Michigan av. *C. A.*
Scates Walter, 4109 Indiana av.
Sceets George N. 6506 Yale
Schaack A. P. 780 North Park av.
Schaaf Adam, 617 W. Jackson boul.
Schaaf Harry, 617 W. Jackson boul. *Ill.*
Schaaf John, 617 W. Jackson boul.

Schackford Samuel, Winnetka
Schaefer Emil C. 1089 Warren av.
Schaefer Emma Miss, 1089 Warren av.
Schaefer Frank H. 1089 Warren av.
Schaefer Frederick C. Dr. 582 Washington boul.
Schaefer Konrad Dr. 574 Flournoy
Schaefer Louis B. 24 Lane ct.
Schaefer Louis H. 1089 Warren av.
Schaefer Otto, 914 Pullman bldg.
Schaefer W. C. 4228 Grand boul.
Schafer Louis H. 1222 Rokeby
Schaffenberg Fannie Miss, 4734 Greenwood av.
Schaffner Abe, 559, 45th. Lksd.
Schaffner Abraham J. 559, 45th, Lksd.
Schaffner Fannie Mrs. 559, 45th
Schaffner Joseph, 4742 Drexel boul. Stan.
Schaffner Louis, 656 Fullerton av.
Schaffner Rachel Miss, 4742 Drexel boul.
Schager Edward J. 2642 N. Paulina
Schager Elizabeth Mrs. 2642 N. Paulina
Schaller George J. Dr. 1127 N. Clark
Schaller Henry, 695 Fullerton av.
Schamberg Louis, 4427 Ellis av. Lksd.
Schantz O. M. Morton Park
Schapper Ferdinand, 1832 Arlington pl.
Schatz William W. 627 Englewood av.
Schaub Frank J. 323 Hampden ct. C.A.
Schaub Peter A. 323 Hampden ct. C.A.
Schaub William L. Mrs. 3423 Vernon av.
Schauffler Charles E. Highland Park
Schauffler Robert Haven, Evanston
Scheibel Mary Miss, 3456 Michigan av.
Schell Edwin Dr. Berwyn
Schell Robert H. 3021 Vernon av.
Schell T. Mrs. 5401 Ellis av.
Scherenberg Jennie V. Mrs. 1953 Deming pl.
Scherer Andrew, 383 N. State
Scherer Henry, 443 Ashland boul.
Scherer Louis H. 443 Ashland boul.
Schermerhorn A. M. V. Evanston
Schermerhorn Flora Mrs. 2903 Groveland av.
Schermerhorn H. M. 52 Walton pl.
Schermerhorn Lucas R. 6335 Greenwood av.
Scherzer Albert H. 194 Cass. C.A.
Scheunemann Otto, 1655 Belmont av.
Schevers Arnold J. 343 W. 60th
Schick Albert H. 606 Burling
Schick Charles E. 965 Warner av.
Schick William, 1751 Arlington pl.
Schick William R. 604 Burling
Schiess John C. 1745 Deming pl.
Schiff Felix, 614, 46th
Schifflin Philip H. 2925 Groveland av.
Schiller Arthur, 4331 Berkeley av.
Schiller J. H. Mrs. 2976 South Park av.
Schilling August M. 3026 Lake Park av.
Schilling George F. 4436 Berkeley av. C.A.
Schimpferman W. H. The Wellington Cal., Chi.; W.P.
Schirmer Alfred Dr. 401 S. Marshfield av.

Schirmer Gustav, M.D. 625 W. Taylor
Schlacks Charles H. 5924 Wabash av.
Schlacks Henry J. 639, 46th pl.
Schlecht Catherine Mrs. Austin
Schlecht Charles F. Austin
Schlecht Oscar G. Austin
Schlegel Frank, 4858 Evans av.
Schleiter Oscar, 3849 Lake av.
Schlesinger Benjamin F. Wilmette
Schlesinger Bernard, 165, 34th. Lksd.
Schlesinger Leopold, 2805 Michigan av. Stan., U.L.
Schlesinger Louis, 309 Belden av.
Schlesinger Max, 3255 Wabash av. Lksd.
Schlesinger Morris, 3601 Vincennes av.
Schlesinger Morris, 637 N. Hoyne av.
Schlesinger Theodore R. 637 N. Hoyne av.
Schlick E. R. 455 Dearborn av.
Schlippenbach Albert A. Baron, Virginia hotel, Un.
Schloesser Frances Miss, 265 Lake View av.
Schloesser Jeanette Miss, 265 Lake View av.
Schloesser Rudolph Mrs. 265 Lake View av.
Schloetzer Eliza Mrs. 1252 George
Schloetzer Hans. 1252 George
Schloss Lee L. 160 Evanston av.
Schloss Mark, Hotel Del Prado
Schlossman Joseph B. 3652 Calumet av.
Schmaltz Joseph H. 681, 48th pl. Stan.
Schmaltz Marion J. Mrs. 3315 South Park av.
Schmaltz Nathan J. 3315 South Park av. Stan.
Schmid George, 70 Maple
Schmid Godfrey, 70 Maple
Schmid Louis, 70 Maple
Schmid Richard G. 1642 Barry av.
Schmidt A. C. 163 Howe
Schmidt Charles J. 369, 44th
Schmidt Charles J. 591 Cleveland av.
Schmidt Ernst, M.D. 424 N. State
Schmidt E. C. 172 Lasalle av.
Schmidt Frederick M. 1758 Deming pl. C.A.
Schmidt F. W. 12 Lincoln pl.
Schmidt George, Elmhurst
Schmidt Geo. J. 61 Howe
Schmidt George K. 756 Sedgwick
Schmidt Hugo W. 12 Lincoln pl.
Schmidt John, 172 LaSalle av.
Schmidt Karl Rev. 183 Fremont
Schmidt Kaspar G. 756 Sedgwick
Schmidt Leo F. 450 N. State. C.A.
Schmidt Leonard, 450 N. State. C.A.
Schmidt Louis E. Dr. 424 N. State
Schmidt Max, 450 N. State
Schmidt Oscar F. 4320 Greenwood av.
Schmidt Otto L. Dr. 3328 Michigan av. C.A.
Schmidt Peter, 1436 Wilson av.
Schmidt William, 1738 Deming pl.
Schmidt William D. 369, 44th
Schmidt William F. Edgebrook

Schmidt W. H. 361 Superior
Schmitt Andrew X. 6044 Monroe av.
Schmitt Anthony, 4537 Drexel boul.
　Cal., *C.A.*, *U,L.*
Schmitt Arthur G. 4537 Drexel boul. *C.A.*
Schmitt Charles S. 36 Astor. *C.A.*
Schmitt Dora Miss, 4537 Drexel boul.
Schmitt Elizabeth Miss, 1801 Michigan av.
Schmitt Eugene J. 4537 Drexel boul.
　C.A., *W.P.*
Schmitt Frank P. 36 Astor. *Un.*
　Sum. res. Willow Farm, Madison, N. H.
Schmitt Frank P. jr. 225 Hampden ct.
Schmitt Henry W. Austin
Schmitt Herman, Morgan Park
Schmitt William A. 392 Bowen av.
Schmitz Michael, 7839 Bond av.
Schmitz M. 545 Larrabee
Schmoll Hugo, 341 Orchard
Schnadig Jacob, 214, 42d. *Stan.*
Schnadig Joseph M. 3213 South Park av. *Stan.*
Schneewind Ben, 4219 Lake av. *Lksd.*
Schneider Adam, 161 Evanston av.
Schneider Albert S. Dr. 6565 Yale
Schneider Carl, 1650 Aldine av.
Schneider George, 2000 Michigan av. *U.L.*
Schneider Henry, 5944 Eggleston av.
Schneider Joseph H. 5944 Eggleston av.
Schneider Julius, 6551 Greenwood av.
Schneider Mary Mrs. Austin
Schneider Max M. 1221 Pratt av.
Schneider Otto C. 356 Lasalle av. *C.A.*, *U.L.*
Schneider Samuel, 519 Cleveland av.
Schneider S. Newton, M.D. 236 Dearborn av.
Schnering Julius, 3246 Lake Park av.
Schniglau Charles R. 1855 Barry av.
Schnitzer David, 211 Fremont
Schnur Jacob, Glencoe. *C.A.*
Schobinger J. J. Prof. 125, 51st
Schock Frederick R. Austin
Schock Louise M. Miss, Austin
Schoellkopf Henry, 298 Chicago av.
Schoellkopf Henry jr. 298 Chicago av.
Schoen Christiana Mrs. 15 Stratford pl.
Schoen George, 555 Cleveland av.
Schoen J. Henry, 4432 Prairie av.
Schoen John 555 Cleveland av.
Schoenberg Alex, 3343 Prairie av. *Lksd.*, *Stan.*
Schoenberg Joel, 3343 Prairie av. *Lksd.*, *Stan.*
Schoenbrun Irving, 3500 Ellis av. *Stan.*
Schoenbrun Sampson, 3500 Ellis av. *Stan.*
Schoeneck Henry, 2622 N. Ashland av,
Schoenfeld Frank, 502, 42d pl. *Lksd.*
Schoenfeld H. W. 348 Oakwood boul. *Lksd.*
Schoenfeld J. 348 Oakwood boul.
Schoening C. J. River Forest
Schoeninger Adolph, 296 Evanston av.

Schoeninger Louis Mrs. 1824 Melrose
Schoenman Byron J. 6028 Kimbark av.
Schoenman Charles S. 6028 Kimbark av. *Stan.*
Schoenman C. Mrs. 6028 Kimbark av.
Schoenman E. L. 6028 Kimbark av.
Schoenthaler Frank C. 1350 Bryn Mawr av.
Schofield John R. 761 Warren av.
Scholes Robert M. 749 Chase av.
Scholle Charles, 6433 Monroe av.
Scholle Henry E. 6627 Woodlawn av.
Schomer Henry, 222 Mohawk
Schonbeck Albert, 1870 Melrose
Schonlau Charles, 1932 Oakdale av.
Schopflocher Herman, 5654 Wabash av. *Lksd.*
Schott Louis, 467½ Lasalle av.
Schott William, 467½ Lasalle av.
Schott William H. 3042 Groveland av.
Schoyer Ernest A. 4624 Greenwood av.
Schrader Edward, 73 Maple
Schrader Theodor, 73 Maple
Schrader William H. Dr. 105 Oakwood av.
Schram Bernhard, 3337 Prairie av.
Schram Elmer E. 357 Ashland boul.
Schram Harry S. 357 Ashland boul. *Lksd.*
Schram Jacob, 357 Ashland boul.
Schram Louis, 1615 W. Monroe
Schramm Frederick, Kenilworth
Schreiber Frank P. 724 N. Hoyne av.
Schrenk August Mrs. 414 Lasalle av.
Schroder Albert, 2718 Calumet av.
Schroder Jacob, 2718 Calumet av.
Schroder Milton, 2718 Calumet av. *Lksd.*
Schroeder Albert W. 802 Pine Grove av.
Schroeder Arthur, 1661 N. Halsted
Schroeder Carl S. Wilmette
Schroeder Fritz, Evanston
Schroeder George, 663 W. Superior. *C.A.*
Schroeder Henry, 613 N. Hoyne av.
Schroeder Louis, 1816 Arlington pl.
Schroeder Oscar, 1816 Arlington pl.
Schroeder W. E. Dr. 4323 Prairie av.
Schroeter Herman J. M. 1514 W. Monroe
Schroter Frederick J. 3004 Prairie av.
Schroyer Charles A. Oak Park
Schub Charles H. 225 Dearborn av. *C.A.*
Schuback Lena Mrs. 3221 Wabash av.
Schubert John C. 1821 Indiana av.
Schuhmann Herman, 539, 44th
Schuhmann H. H. Dr. 539, 44th. *Stan.*
Schulein Arthur E. 4404 Ellis av.
Schuler Abram J. 295 Wilson av.
Schuler Everett T. 5039 Jefferson av.
Schuler H. B. Lexington hotel
Schulte Francis J. 5031 Jefferson av.
Schultz Alexander A. 859 W. Monroe
Schultz C. F. 1417 Ogden av.
Schultz Edward, 1737 Wrightwood av.
Schultz George W. 3848 Ellis av.
Schultz Henry, 1765 Wrightwood av.
Schultz Ja e M. 859 W. Monroe
Schultz Margaret Miss, 742 Fullerton av.
Schultz Margaret R. Mrs. 6437 Monroe av.

Schultz Martin M. 403 Oak. *C.A.*
Schultz Sallie Miss, 742 Fullerton av.
Schultz Sarah C. Mrs. 859 W. Monroe
Schultz W. W. Hotel Windermere
Schulz Matthias, 720 N. Robey
Schulz Otto L. 720 N. Roby
Schumacher Abraham, 579, 45th pl.
Schumacher Bowen W. Highland Park
Schumacher Ferd, 5619 Madison av.
Schumacher Fred, Highland Park
Schumacher F. Adolph, 5619 Madison av.
Schumacher Hugo, Hotel Metropole
Schumann Charles, 481 Cleveland av.
Schumann Emma E. Mrs. 669 Lasalle av.
Schuttler Peter, 287 W. Adams. *Ill.*
Schuttler Peter jr. 287 W. Adams. *C.A.*
Schuyler Daniel J. 3427 Vernon av.
Schuyler Daniel J. jr. 3427 Vernon av. *Cal.*
Schuyler Frederick J. Hinsdale.
Schwab Alfred C. 2901 Michigan av. *C.A.*, *Stan.*
Schwab Charles H. 3301 Michigan av. *Irq.*, *Stan.*, *U.L.*
Schwab Henry C. 3301 Michigan av. *Stan.*
Schwab Jerome C. 3301 Michigan av.
Schwab Leslie W. Dr. 449, 41st
Schwabacher Henry jr. 4343 Grand boul. *Lksd.*
Schwabacher H. H. Hotel Del Prado. *Stan.*
Schwabacher Julius, 3133 Michigan av. *Lksd.*, *Stan.*
Schwabacher Morris, Hotel Del Prado. *Stan.*
Schwaegermann William, Austin
Schwahn Catherine Mrs. 3224 Vernon av.
Schwartz Fannie Miss, 77 Bowen av.
Schwartz Gustavus A. Auditorium annex. *Chi.*, *W.P.*
Schwartz J. C. 3532 Vernon av.
Schwartz W. B. 4212 Indiana av.
Schwarz Albert, 880 W. Adams
Schwarz Albert, 3261 Vernon av.
Schwarz Edward, 880 W. Adams
Schwarz Gottlieb F. 325 Hampden ct.
Schwarz Hannah Mrs. 4510 Ellis av.
Schwarz Herbert E. Highland Park. *C.A.*
Schwarz I. G. 3232 Wabash av.
Schwarz Moses, 3261 Vernon av. *Lksd.*
Schwarz Peter M. 567 Lasalle av.
Schwarz P. L. August, 100 Pine Grove av.
Schwarz Theodore, Highland Park
Schweitzer Abraham, 631 Fullerton av.
Schweitzer Richard J. 1474 N. Clark
Schwender John, Avenue house, Evanston
Schwennesen Hans P. 1235 Grace
Schwill Ferdinand, 5700 Monroe av.
Schycker Moritz Dr. 4625 Evans av.
Scobey Carrie O. Miss, 7827 Winneconna av.
Scobey M. C. 371 Bowen av.
Scobey Zephania D. Mrs. 7868 Eggleston av.
Scofield Charles, 7221 Jeffery av.
Scofield J. W. 3232 Forest av.

Scofield Lewis K. 25, 46th
Scofield Timothy J. 7221 Jeffery av.
Scotford F. E. Hinsdale
Scotford H. A. Hinsdale
Scotford Louis K. 6431 Harvard av.
Scott Adolphus G. 6752 Lafayette av.
Scott Agnes J. Mrs. 5112 Jefferson av.
Scott Alfred F. 640 Washington boul.
Scott Andrew, 740 Washington boul.
Scott A. L. Mrs. 3727 Lake av
Scott Charles F. Evanston
Scott Charles H. Lexington hotel
Scott C. B. 3126 Calumet av.
Scott Edwin Dow, 4449 Ellis av.
Scott Elmer L. Evanston
Scott Emma P. Miss, Chicago Beach hotel
Scott Erastus H. 4216 Ellis av.
Scott E. Norman, 76 Maple. *Un.*
Scott Florence Miss, 43 Cedar
Scott Frank E. 547 Dearborn av.
Scott Frank H. 1937 Oakdale av. *Irq.* *U.L.*, *Univ.*
Scott Frederick H. Evanston
Scott F. M. Dr. 3238 Rhodes av.
Scott George, Lakeside
Scott George M. Riverside
Scott George S. 456 Elm
Scott George W. Pullman
Scott Hugh M. Rev. 520 W. Adams
Scott Jessie Miss, 43 Cedar
Scott John A. Evanston
Scott John B. 1857 Sheridan rd.
Scott John E. Evanston
Scott John William, Evanston
Scott J. E. G. 7207 Princeton av.
Scott J. W. Hotel Woodruff
Scott J. W. Mrs. Virginia hotel
Scott Lee C. Oak Park
Scott Lewis B. 424 Cuyler av.
Scott Lucy F. Dr. 3238 Rhodes av.
Scott L. Oak Park
Scott Martha Miss, Lakeside
Scott Mary Mrs. Riverside
Scott M. B. Mrs. 4449 Ellis av.
Scott O. C. Prof. Berwyn
Scott Robert D. Rev. 280 Seminary av.
Scott Robert L. Evanston
Scott Robert S. Lakeside. *U.L.*
Scott Walter, Hotel Windermere
Scott Walter A. 7 Ritchie ct. *C.A.*, *U.L.*
Scott William, 159 S. Leavitt
Scott William C. Oak Park
Scott William H. 4449 Ellis av.
Scott William M. Evanston
Scott W. A. LaGrange
Scott W. J. Mrs. The Ontario.
　　　　Sum. res. Evanston
Scovel Robert A. 3745 Ellis av.
Scovell John C. 883 Winthrop av.
Scovil M. M. Mrs. Evanston
Scoville Amasa U. Riverside
Scoville C. B. Lakota hotel
Scoville David S. 1641 Briar pl.
Scoville Eugene M. Mrs. 886 W. Adams
Scoville Hiram H. 886 W. Adams

Scoville John S. 4424 Ellis av.
Scrafford M. J. 174 Oakwood boul.
Scranton George E. 6118 Monroe av.
Scranton Mary E. Mrs. Evanston
Scribner Charles E. 172, 45th. *U.L.*
    Sum. res. North Williston, Vt.
Scribner E. 225 Dearborn av.
Scribner G. H. 305 Schiller
Scribner Sanford A. 226 Ashland boul.
Scruggs Finley, 4851 Forrestville av.
Scudder A. V. Chicago Athletic assn.
Scudder Clarence O. 1673 Barry av.
Scudder J. Arnold, 106 Lincoln Park
    boul. *C.A., Un.*
Scudder Miss, 63 Bellevue pl.
Scudder William M. Mrs. 106 Lincoln
    Park boul.
Scudder William T. 240 Hampden ct.
Scull Ethel Marie Featherstone-Haugh
    Miss, Hotel Windermere
Scull Harry, Hotel Windermere. *C.A.*
  W.P.   Sum. res. Wheaton
Scullin Frederic W. The Tudor.
    Sum. res. Lake Champlain
Scully Alexander B. Chicago Athletic
    assn
Scully D. B. Waukegan, *Ill.*
Scully John B. 1646 W. Jackson boul.
Scully Maurice H. 811 Washington boul.
Scully S. A. Mrs. 350 Warren av.
Scupham William C. 1059 N. Clark
Sea Fred W. 3340 Vernon av.
Sea M. W. Mrs. 3340 Vernon av.
Seabury C. W. Oak Park
Seaman E. 3205 South Park av.
Seaman John A. Oak Park
Seaman Leopold, 3317 Calumet av. *Lksd.*
Searle G. D. 39 Roslyn pl.
Searles Aaron M. 236 S. Oakley av.
Sears Amos G. 2465 Kenmore av.
    Sum. res. Lake Geneva, Wis.
Sears Charles B. 4338 Ellis av.
Sears John B. Kenilworth
Sears Joseph, Kenilworth. *Chi.*
Sears J ep M. Kenilworth
Sears Nathaniel Clinton Judge, 2465 Ken-
    more av.
    Sum. res. Lake Geneva, Wis.
Sears Peter C. 71 Park av.
Sears Richard W. Oak Park
Sears William R. 415 N. State
Seaton Chauncey E. 3360 Calumet av.
Seaton E. D. 7526 Eggleston av.
Seaton Samuel G. LaGrange
Seaverns Anna F. Miss Evanston
Seaverns Edwin I. Evanston
Seaverns E. M. Mrs. Evanston
Seaverns George A. 2819 Michigan av.
  Chi., W.P.
    Sum. res. Oconomowoc, Wis.
Seaverns George A. jr. 3831 Michigan av.
  Chi., C.A., W.P.
Seaverns J. S. Mrs. 2736 N. Winchester
    av.
Seaverns William S. 148, 46th
Seavey Daniel H. Mrs. Evanston

Seavey Juliet M. Mrs. 404 Orchard
Seavey Sibyl Mrs. 404 Orchard
Seavey William C. 1330 Morse av.
Seba John, 5 Lake View av.
Sebastian Don B. 4409 Ellis av.
Sebastian John, 4409 Ellis av.
Sebree C. M. Mrs. Hotel Metropole
Seckel Albert, Riverside. *U.L.*
Seckel Elise Mrs. Riverside
Seckel Paula Mrs. 19 Pine Grove av.
Secord Frank G. Pullman
Sederholm Edward T. 1629 Fulton
Sedgwick Edwin H. 4524 Ellis av.
Sedgwick Fred, Mayfair
Sedgwick Louise M. Mrs. Austin
Sedgwick S. E. Miss, 1718 Indiana av.
Seebaum Joseph A. 435 Racine av.
Seeberger Anthony F. 2017 Michigan av.
  Cal.   Sum. res. Mount Vernon, O.
Seeberger Charles D. 1827 Michigan av.
  Cal., Chi.
Seeberger Louis A. Riverside
Seegers Charles, 1944 Oakdale av.
Seegers George F. 1944 Oakdale av.
Seegers Melville H. 1944 Oakdale av.
Seely Herman B. 1544 Kenmore av.
Seelye Alex H. 2108 Prairie av.
Seelye Frank R. Evanston
Seelye Henry E. Evanston
Seelye Isaac H. Evanston
Seeman Frederick, 1702 Grace
Seese Peter, 919 N. Clark
Segnitz M. Miss, 225 Dearborn av.
Segsworth John Dr. Wilmette
Seidel Jacob Rev. 527 Ashland boul.
Seifert Matthias J. 803 N. Leavitt
Seiffe William, 1529 Dakin av.
Seipp Conrad Mrs. 3300 Michigan av.
    Sum. res. Lake Geneva, Wis.
Seipp William C. 619 Dearborn av. *C.A.,*
  U.L., W.P.
Seixas Hyman L. Palmer house. *Irq.*
Selden F. J. 1225 Wrightwood av. *C.A.*
Selfridge Harry Gordon. 117 Lake Shore
    drive. *Chi., Un., U.L., Univ.*
    Sum. res. Lake Geneva, Wis.
Selfridge L. F. Mrs. 369 Chicago av.
Selig Peter A. 435 Dayton
Seligman Ida Miss, 3801 Prairie av.
Seligman Louis, Lexington hotel. *Lksd.*
Selleck Arthur, Austin
Selleck A. C. 45 S. Sangamon
Selleck John A. 1594 W. Adams
Selleck Wm. E. Union League Club
Sellers Alfred H. 3420 Michigan av. *U.L.*
Sellers Frank H. 3420 Michigan av. *Chi.,*
  C.A., Univ.
Sellers John M. 514 Lasalle av. *C.A., Un.*
Sellers Morris, 514 Lasalle av.
Sellinger Thomas J. 2704 Evanston av.
Sello Max, Lakota hotel. *Lksd.*
Selz Emanuel F. 1717 Michigan av. *Stan.*
Selz J. Harry, 3329 Michigan av. *Stan.*
    Sum. res. Crystal Lake
Selz Morris, 1717 Michigan av. *Stan.,U.L.*
Semon Thomas, 3142 Groveland av,

Semper Louis, 1241 W.Ravenswood Park
Semper L. H. 1854 Arlington pl.
Sempill Walter M. 729 Farwell av.
Semrad August jr 1512 Oakdale av.
Seneco Charles W. 1664 Buckingham pl.
Senn Emanuel J., M. D. 532 Dearborn av. *C.A.*
Senn Nicholas, M.D., 532 Dearborn av. *C.A.*
Senn Thomas C. Washington Heights
Senn William N. 532 Dearborn av.
Sennott Thomas W. 343 Ashland boul. *Ill.*
Senour William F. 3034 Calumet av. *C.A.*
Sercomb Albert L. 321 Lake View av. *U.L.*
Sergel Charles H. 2124 Michigan av.
Servoss Carl A. Mrs. 665 Cleveland av.
Sessions Floyd V. 1254 Wrightwood av.
Sessions Frank M. 228, 54th pl.
Sessions Henry Howard, 5531 Washington av.
Sethness Charles O. Irving Park
Seton Henry Capt. Fort Sheridan
Sewall Edmund Q. 2721 N. Winchester av.
Seward G. M. The Arizona
Seward M. F. Miss, 2223 Prairie av.
Sewell Barton, 129, 51st.
Sewell M. A. Mrs. 1639 Belmont av.
Sexauer Samuel C. Wilmette
Sexton Austin O. 3287 Malden
Sexton Edith E. Mrs. 1311 Michigan av.
Sexton George P. Mrs. 148 Dearborn av.
Sexton Henry M. 3031 Indiana av.
Sexton James A. 561 Lasalle av.
Sexton John, 270½ Lasalle av.
Sexton John M. L. 1459 Michigan av.
Sexton J. L. The Winamac
Sexton Patrick J. 1340 Michigan av. *W.P.*
Sum. res. Waukegan
Seymour Frank C. 315 Bowen av.
Seymour Herbert F. 6506 Minerva av.
Seymour H. Vernon, 17 Roslyn pl. *C.A.*
Seymour H. W. 4615 Ellis av.
Seymour Lynden A. Norwood Park
Seymour Mayhew A. 23 Bittersweet pl.
Seymour T. H. Norwood Park
Seymour William, 5117 Hibbard av.
Shackelton Alfred, 5618 Drexel av.
Shackleford Charles, 225 Dearborn av. *Ill.*
Shackleford C. 762 Greenleaf av.
Shackleford William C. 2108 Washington boul.
Shackleton Mabel Miss, 1016 Winthrop av.
Shader A. E. 117 S. Wood
Shafer J. B. Auditorium hotel
Shafer W. S. Auditorium hotel
Shaffer Henry R. 498 W. Monroe *Ill.*
Shaffer John Charles Evanston. *U.L.*
Shaffer William H. 143 Oakwood boul.
Shaffner Benjamin M. 307 Schiller
Sum. res. "The Pines," Lakota, Wis.
Shaffner Charles, 1906 Indiana av. *Stan.*
Shaffner H. 3407 Prairie av.
Shaffner Philip B. 3139 Michigan av.

Shailer Robert A. 5822 Washington av. *U.L.*
Shakman Adolph, 467 Bowen av.
Shakman Henry A. 467 Bowen av. *Lksd.*
Shambaugh George E. Dr. 5761 Madison av.
Shanahan M. W. 2802 Michigan av.
Shand J. C. 4732 Kenwood av.
Shankland Edward C. 4808 Champlain av. *Univ.*
Shankland Ralph M. 4554 Oakenwald av.
Shankland Walter, 306 Superior
Shanklin Ernest A. 49 Roslyn pl.
Shanklin Robert F. 354 Huron. *Univ.*
Shannon G. W. 4130 Grand boul.
Shannon J. S. Hinsdale
Shannon Michael, 4303 Oakenwald av.
Shannon Osbourne J. 3716 Forest av.
Shannon Oscar M. Riverside
Shantz Harry B. Granada hotel
Shantz Jane Mrs. Wilmette
Sharp George, Oak Park
Sharp George P. Oak Park
Sharp John A. Lombard
Sharp Joseph P. Oak Park
Sharp Louis H. Oak Park
Sharp S. Mrs. The Arizona
Sharp Thomas, 739 Washington boul.
Sharp William L. 6756 Perry av.
Sharp William N. Hyde Park hotel. *C.A.*
Sharp W. H. 6659 Perry av.
Sharpe Caswell A. Oak Park.
Sharpe L. L. Hotel Normandie
Sharpe William, 226 N. State
Sharpneck E. L. 1235 Sheridan rd.
Shatford Jefferson D. Chicago Beach hotel
Shattock Henry E. 402 Belden av.
Shattuck Arthur T. 401 N. State
Shattuck Charles L. 3426 Michigan av. *W.P.*
Shattuck Edward, 3438 Wabash av.
Shattuck Geo. B. 4438 Sidney av.
Shattuck L. Brace, 5300 Woodlawn av.
Shattuck Walter F. 5327 Washington av.
Shaughnessy Richard D. 740 W. Monroe
Shaughnessy Thomas, 740 W. Monroe
Shaul Julia Mrs. 5460 Washington av.
Shaul Nelson, Mrs. 4723 Lake av.
Shaver Cornelius H. 5100 Madison av. *U.L.*
Shaver Fred D. 308 West ct.
Shaw Alexandra M. Miss, 130 Ashland boul.
Shaw Alfred D. Evanston
Shaw Alonzo, 4051 Prairie av.
Shaw Archibald Mrs. 2968 Prairie av.
Shaw Archibald D. Austin
Shaw D. Lee M.D. 707 W. Jackson boul.
Shaw D. P. 4744 Champlain av.
Shaw Edward E. Hinsdale
Shaw Edward R. 130, 47th. *C.A.*
Shaw Edward W. Edgebrook
Shaw E. M. Miss, Hinsdale
Shaw Fred D. Evanston
Shaw G. B. Chicago Beach hotel. *U.L.*

Shaw Howard VanDoren, 4833 Lake av. C.A.
Shaw James W. Hinsdale
Shaw John; 2968 Prairie av.
Shaw John W. Hinsdale
Shaw Joseph, Austin
Shaw Joseph S. 81 Bryant av.
Shaw J. E. New Hotel Holland
Shaw Louis B. 4401 Indiana av.
Shaw Ralph Martin,2632 Prairie av. U.L., W.P.
Shaw Robert, 385 Ashland boul. W.P.
Shaw Samuel W., M.D. 1124 S. Central Park av.
Shaw Sarah J. Mrs. Evanston
Shaw Theodore A. 2124 Calumet av. Sum. res. Lake Forest, Ill.
Shaw Theodore A. jr. 2124 Calumet av. C.A.
Shaw Thomas J., M.D. 705 W. Jackson boul.
Shaw Warwick A. 1124 S. Central Park av.
Shaw William A. Hotel Windermere. W.P.
Shaw William S. 130, 47th
Shaw William W. 385 Ashland boul.
Shawcross Mary J. Mrs. Oak Park
Shay Thomas J. 419 Superior
Shayne John T. 3856 Lake av. Cal., C.A., U.L., W.P.
Shea James I. 3000 Michigan av.
Shea John E. 6541 Greenwood av.
Sheahan James D. 3238 Calumet av.
Shearer William W. 4601 Emerald av.
Shearman O. R. Park Ridge
Shears G. F., M.D., 3130 Indiana av.
Shearson H. H. Wheaton
Shedd A. F. Greenwood Inn, Evanston
Shedd Charles B. 3860 Lake av. U.L.
Shedd Edward A. 3860 Lake av. Cal., C.A., U.L.
Shedd E. T. 3233 Forest av.
Shedd Henry S. Evanston
Shedd John G. The Kenwood. Chi., U.L.
Shedd William J. 7132 Vernon av.
Sheets Frank D. Rev. 2237 Kenmore av.
Sheets Harriett H. Miss, 36 S. Wood
Sheffield Henry, 2969 Groveland av..
Shefler Connell B. 4420 Ellis av.
Sheibley Nathaniel K. 879 S. Sawyer av.
Sheldon Amy B. Mrs. 4223 Langley av.
Sheldon A. F. 2548 Kenmore av.
Sheldon Catherine A. Mrs. 672 W. Adams
Sheldon D. Henry, 5630 Woodlawn av.
Sheldon Frank N. Riverside
Sheldon Frank P. Evanston
Sheldon George W. 96 Astor. C.A., U.L.
Sheldon Harvey S. 6543 Kimbark av.
Sheldon Henry I. 363 Erie. Univ.
Sheldon Herbert D. 672 W. Adams
Sheldon H. E. Dr. Morgan Park
Sheldon Madeline Mrs. 6334 Monroe av.
Sheldon Miss, 363 Erie
Sheldon Theodore, 33 Bellevue pl. C.A., Univ. Sum. res. Lake Geneva, Wis.

Sheldon Thomas Carlton, 3737 Ellis av.
Sheldon William T. Riverside
Shelley L. H. 1254 Michigan av.
Shellito A. M. Evanston
Shelton Olive Mrs. 5743 Washington av.
Shenick Q. T. Dr. 456 W. Jackson boul.
Shepard Amos, Austin
Shepard Charles C. 101, 51st
Shepard Charles F. 1195 S. Lawndale av.
Shepard C. J. 190 Bowen av.
Shepard Ellen B. Mrs. 17, 39th
Shepard Frank, 322 Oakwood boul.
Shepard Helen E. Mrs. 4445 Grand boul.
Shepard Henri E. 3347 Michigan av. C.A.
Shepard Henry M. Judge;4445 Grand boul.
Shepard Henry O. 691½ Washington boul. Ill.
Shepard H. V. Irving Park
Shepard Jason H. 3347 Michigan av.
Shepard Joseph, 2724 Michigan av.
Shepard J. H. Hotel Metropole
Shepard J. Robert, Austin
Shepard Stuart Gore, 4445 Grand boul.
Shepard William L. 222, 61st. C.A.
Shepardson Francis W. 5515 Woodlawn av.
Shepardson George J. 1702 Dewey pl.
Shepherd Clinton D. 4723 Prairie av.
Shepherd Edward S. 392 W. Adams. C.A., U.L., W.P.
Shepherd John, 240, 61st
Shepherd John Mrs. 1069 Winona av.
Shepherd John E. 240, 61st
Shepler E. A. 113 Cass
Sheppard Robert D.Prof.LL.D.Evanston
Sheppard S. Mrs. 510 W. Jackson boul.
Sheppard Thomas H. Mrs. 2811 Prairie av.
Sheppard William W. Dr. 108 Loomis,
Sherburne E. A. 4744 Woodlawn av.
Sherer John C. 569, 51st
Sherer Samuel J. 4536 Lake av.
Shergold W. L. LaGrange
Sheridan Albert D. 3010 Kenmore av. C.A.
Sheridan Millard J. 4351 Calumet av.
Sheridan Robert Mercer Mrs. 5 Scott
Sheridan Thomas F. 888 Winthrop av. C.A.
Sheridan William A. Oak Park
Sheridan William G. 24, 44th pl.
Sheriff A. R. 2124 Michigan av.
Sherlock Charles L. 89, 18th. C.A.
Sherlock George W. Riverside
Sherlock James P. 305 Belden av.
Sherlock Joseph, Winnetka
Sherman Bessie W. Mrs. Riverside
Sherman B. W. 3985 Drexel boul.
Sherman Charles C. 36th ne. cor. Ellis av.
Sherman Charles D. Riverside
Sherman Charles K. 4730 Grand boul.
Sherman Charles M. 435 Elm. Un.
Sherman C. C. Irving Park
Sherman Edwin, Evanston
Sherman E. B. Judge, 3985 Drexel boul. U.L.

Sherman Frank, Evanston
Sherman Frank C. Rev. 3724 Ellis av.
Sherman Fred J. Irving Park
Sherman Fred S. 547 N. State. *Un.*
Sherman F. B. Oak Park
Sherman F. C. Winnetka
Sherman H. A. Mrs. 229 Michigan av.
Sherman I. N. W. 4730 Grand boul.
Sherman James M. 18 Park av. *U.L.*
Sherman John jr. 1538 W. Monroe
Sherman John B. 2100 Prairie av.
Sherman John D. 4552 Lake av.
Sherman Lodema Mrs. 2400 Prairie av.
Sherman Lucius B. 4598 Oakenwald av.
    C.A.
Sherman Mark R. 4208 Oakenwald av.
Sherman Martha E. Mrs. Evanston
Sherman Penoyer L. 4634 Lake av.
Sherman Roger, 4634 Lake av.
Sherman Rollin, Evanston
Sherman Samuel S. 4634 Lake av.
Sherman Sarah Miss, 2729 Prairie av.
Sherman S. Stirling, 545 N. State
Sherman Walter B. 564. 46th pl.
Sherman Ward B. 3724 Ellis av.
Sherman William Wallace, 2942 Indiana
    av.
Sherman W. M. 387 W. Harrison
Shermer Elizabeth Mrs. 3607 Ellis Park
Sherry Mark R. M. Hinsdale
Sherwin E. J. 143 Oakwood boul.
Sherwood Alexander B. 4538 Vincennes
    av.
Sherwood Clive N. 212, 33d
Sherwood Evangeline Miss,530W.Monroe
Sherwood E. N. Mrs. Glencoe
Sherwood F. B. Morgan Park
Sherwood George Mrs. 513 W. Adams
Sherwood George A. Dr. 284, 31st
Sherwood Grace Miss, 4529 Greenwood av.
Sherwood Henry M. 4529 Greenwood av.
    U.L.
Sherwood Jesse, 6328 Harvard av. *Irq.*
Sherwood John B. 530 W. Monroe
    Sum. res. Westport, Conn.
Sherwood Ludlow S. 5207 Madison av.
Sherwood Marc, 825 Warren av. *C.A., Ill.*
Sherwood Nehemiah, 4712 Madison av.
Sherwood P. N. Mrs. Glencoe
Sherwood William H. 3258 Groveland av.
    Sum. res. Chautauqua, N. Y.
Shewell Susan C. Mrs. Hinsdale
Shibley Elizabeth O. Miss, Winnetka
Shields Charles J. 89 Loomis
Shields James H. Highland Park.
Shields John E. 4857 Forrestville av.
Shields Louis B. 1611 W. Adams
Shields Michael, 573 Dearborn av.
Shields S. S. Hotel Windermere
Shields William S. Evanston
Shillaber Chas. E. 6124 Washington av.
Shimmin Robert E. 535 W. Jackson boul.
Shinners Patrick H. 364 Ohio
Shipman Cyrus R. 17 Gordon terrace
Shipman Daniel B. 1828 Prairie av. *Cal.,
    Irq., W.P.*

Shipman Stephen V. 269 Warren av.
Shippen E. W. Mrs. Winnetka
Shippey George E. 4131 Southport av.
Shippey George W. 4131 Southport av.
Shirk Elbert W. Calumet club. *Chi.,
    W.P.*
Shirley Ja e B. 5119 Jefferson av.
Shirley WmNs Chicago Beach hotel
Shirra Jane Mrs. 171, 51st
Shirrill James, Lakota hotel
Shiverick Asa Frank, 40 Madison Park
Shnable Emile R. 2371 N. Paulina
Shoemaker Charles W. 519 W. Jackson
    boul. *Ill.*
Shoemaker Clarence D. 202 Fremont
Shoemaker F. A. 3937 Ellis av.
Shoemaker Walter, 519 W. Jackson boul.
    Ill.
Shoemaker Westley C. Riverside
Shoenberger G. K. 567 Division
Shogren Andrew P. 3174 Dover
Sholem Samuel, 4514 Forrestville av.
    Stan.
Sholes C. G. 5704 Madison av.
Sholes Zalmon G. Evanston
Shoninger B. 575, 45th pl.
Shoninger Sol H. 4216 Calumet av.
Shonts Theodore P. 612 The Plaza. *C.A.*
Shope Clarence W. Sherman house
Shope Simeon P. Judge, Sherman house.
    U.L.
Shordiche E. S. Mrs. 3824 Langley av.
Shore Rose Mrs. 4730 Evans av.
Shores Adesta F. Mrs. 295 Belden av.
Shorey Daniel L. 5520 Woodlawn av.
Shorey Paul Prof. 5516 Woodlawn av.
Short Adam, 207 S. Leavitt
Short E. G. Morgan Park
Short Freeman J. Morgan Park
Short Joseph, 1310 Wilcox av.
Shortall John G. 1600 Prairie av. *Chi.*
Shortall John L. 1604 Prairie av. *C.A.*
    Sum res. Lake Geneva, Wis.
Shortle J. S. Greenwood Inn, Evanston
Shotwell Ida J. Mrs. Evanston
Shourds Clayton B. 108, 45th. *C.A.*
Shourds James L. 108, 45th
Showalter John W. 514 W. Congress. *Ill.*
Shrimski Israel, Lexington hotel. *Lksd.,
    Stan.*
Shriver L. P. 1794 Magnolia av.
Shubart Aaron, 467 Bowen av.
Shubert A. B. Chicago Beach hotel. *C.A.,
    W.P.*
Shuey William H. Oak Park
Shufeldt Ella Mrs. 36th ne. cor. Ellis av.
Shufeldt George A. Mrs. Oak Park
Shufeldt W. B. E. 2244 Calumet av.
    Sum. res. Oconomowoc, Wis.
Shufelt Alma H. Miss, 2631 Prairie av.
Shull May E. Miss, 519 W. Jackson boul.
Shultz Louis A. Dr. 6249 Monroe av.
Shuman Edwin L. Evanston
Shuman George L. 353 Ashland boul.
Shuman Percy L. Evanston
Shuman R. Roy, Evanston

Shumway Edward G. 4549 Ellis av.
Shumway E. B. Miss, 3551 Indiana av.
Shumway Mary E. Mrs. 1487 W. Monroe
Shumway Mary R. Mrs. Evanston
Shumway Noble C. 1487 W. Monroe
Shumway Philip R. Evanston. *Univ.*, *U.L.*
Shurtleff Benjamin, 779 Mildred av.
Shurtleff B. M. Austin
Shurtleff Wilford C. Wilmette
Shute G. H. Edison Park
Shute Henry L. 4740 Madison av.
Shutt George F. New Hotel Holland
Shutterly Eugene E. Dr. Evanston
Shutterly John J. Evanston
Shutterly John J. jr. Evanston
Shutts Adelbert J. 1710 Wellington
Shutts Sarah A. Mrs. 1710 Wellington
Siberts Paul R. Evanston
Siberts Samuel W. Rev. Evanston
Sibley Edward A. 3109 Groveland av.
Sibley Edwin S. 4852 Washington av.
Sibley George M. 3109 Groveland av.
Sibley Ira G. Austin
Sibley James A. 3109 Groveland av.
Sibley Sylvester Mrs. 4613 Woodlawn av.
Sickel John Trust, Evanston. *U.L.*
Sickel William G. Evanston
Sickles William A. Evanston
Siddall Joseph J. jr. 7212 Jeffery av.
Siddall Michael G. 305, 65th pl.
Sidley Frank C. 3823 Ellis av.
Sidley Fred K. 3823 Ellis av.
Sidley William K. 3823 Ellis av.
Sidley William P. 3823 Ellis av:
Sidway H. T. 4353 Oakenwald av. *C.A.*
Sidway L. B. 4353 Oakenwald av. *U.L.*
Sidwell George H. 265 Oakwood boul.
Sidwell George T. 265 Oakwood boul.
Sidwell J. P. Hyde Park hotel
Sidwell Reuben L. 3408 Wabash av.
Sieber Francis A. Dr. 424 Belden av.
Sieboth Joseph Mrs. 580 Lasalle av.
Sieck William, 1737 Deming pl.
Siegel Ferdinand, 3642 Michigan av. *Stan.*
Siegel Joseph, Hotel Metropole. *Stan.*
Siegmund Emilie Dr. 823 N. Clark
Sieh Henry P. 4520 Prairie av.
Sieh John C. 1108 Millard av.
Sievers Alexander C. 117 Park av.
Sievers Louis, 117 Park av.
Signor Harry B. 4441 Sidney av.
Sigshee L. P. Oak Park
Silberhorn Frederick C. 6825 Perry av.
Silberhorn John J. 4969 Lake av.
Silberman Adolph, 4066 Lake av. *Stan.*
Silberman Ferdinand, 538 Lasalle av.
Silberman Sigmund, 3206 Vernon av. *Stan.*
Silcott R. A. Mrs. 808 North Park av.
Silke Alice E. Mrs. 3307 Rhodes av.
Sill Robert T. 27 St. John's ct.
Silliman Chauncy M. 274 Belden av.
Silliman Frederick H. 274 Belden av.
Sills Edward P. 4327 Oakenwald av. *C.A.*
Sills F. M. 2685 N. Paulina

Sills Mary A. Mrs. 4416 Berkeley av.
Sills William H. 4416 Berkeley av. *C.A.*
Silsbee Joseph Lyman, 1328 Hollywood av. *Univ.*
Silsby E. W. LaGrange
Silva Charles P. Morgan Park
Silva Frank P. Morgan Park
Silva Marion Mrs. 2358 Indiana av.
Silver E. E. Lexington hotel
Silverman Albert, 1915 Indiana av.
Silverman Charles, 1915 Indiana av. *Stan.*
Silverman Emanuel, 533 Lasalle av.
Silverman Lazarus, 2213 Calumet av. *Lksd.*
Silverman Simon N. Oakland hotel
Silversparre Mary Mrs. 4351 Oakenwald av.
Silverthorne David, 603, 46th
Silvey Edward, 3836 Ellis av.
Simmons C. H. 3151 Prairie av. *C.A.*
Simmons Francis T. 8 Gordon terrace, *U.L.*
Simmons Herbert DeVere, Evanston
Simmons H. P. 5415 Cottage Grove av.
Simmons John J. 92, 21st
Simmons J. W. 4227 Berkeley av.
Simmons Parke E. Evanston. *Univ.*
Simmons Rufus S. 1906 Oakdale av. *Univ.*
Simms E. G. 4223 Lake av.
Simms James, 3564 Grand boul.
Simms S. C. New Hotel Holland
Simon Benjamin F. 2243 Calumet av.
Simon Carl S. 419, 43d. *Stan.*
Simon Charles W. 1715 Barry av.
Simon David S. 1915 Indiana av. *Stan.*
Simon Henry, 946 W. Jackson boul.
Simon Henry E. 2761 N. Paulina
Simon J. E. 3569 Forest av.
Simon J. H. 405 S. Paulina
Simon J. P. 555 Cleveland av.
Simon Leopold Mrs. 2243 Calumet av.
Simon Robert M. 2563 N. Ashland av.
Simon S. Mrs. 371, 36th pl.
Simonds Edwin F. 220, 48th. *U.L.*
Simonds Gilbert, 3042 Lake Park av.
Simonds Harriet N. Mrs. 1431 Montrose boul.
Simonds Ossian, 1431 Montrose boul.
Simons Abraham L. 3429 South Park av.
Simons Charles B. 3708 Langley av.
Simons C. J., M.D. 284, 32d
Simons Franklin P. 6629 Yale
Simons Harry, 3429 South Park av.
Simons H. 3639 Forest av.
Simons Irving N. 3733 Ellis av.
Simons Leonard, 3733 Ellis av.
Simons Louis E. 3733 Ellis av.
Simons Munro N. 1110 Early av.
Simons Robert I. 3733 Ellis av.
Simonsen N. E. Evanston
Simonson Charles F. 4257 Grand boul.
Simonson Julius, 3219 Rhodes av. *Stan.*
Simpson Alexander J. 7433 Bond av.
Simpson Andrew, Evanston
Simpson Anna Sard Mrs. 2250 Michigan av.
Simpson Clarence, 128, 47th

Simpson George B. 1020 Morse av.
Simpson George E. Edgebrook
Simpson George W. 4422 Ellis av.
Simpson George W. 6326 Stewart av.
Simpson Howard Sard, 2250 Michigan av.
Simpson Irwin Dr. 5034 Washington av.
Simpson Jerome W. Riverside
Simpson Joseph G. 5723 Washington av.
Simpson Joseph T. 6413 Drexel av.
Simpson J. W. LaGrange
Simpson Marcus D. L. Gen. Riverside
Simpson P. L. 6413 Drexel av.
Simpson P. L. jr. 6413 Drexel av.
Simpson Samuel D. 106 DeKalb
Simpson Thomas S. 1911 Diversey.
Simpson T. J. C. LaGrange
Simpson William, 6413 Drexel av.
Simpson Wm. A. 5616 Washington av.
Simpson William W. Dr. 945 W. Monroe
Sims E. W. 6444 Greenwood av.
Sincere Edward, 3303 Vernon av. *Lksd.*
Sincere E., M.D. 2974 Wabash av.
Sincere M. B. Dr. 2974 Wabash av.
Sinclair A. E. Mrs. 6545 Perry av.
Sinclair Charles E. 1491 Perry
Sinclair George, 4055 Prairie av.
Sinclair Janet Mrs. Oak Park
Sinclair J. C. Park Ridge
Sinclair J. G. Dr. 4045 Grand boul.
Sinclair M. A. Mrs. Oak Park
Sinclair Peter Mrs. 73 S. Seeley av.
Sinclair William H. 6549 Perry av.
Sinden George, Oak Park
Sindlinger Godfrey, 377 Chestnut
Sine Charles J. Highland Park
Singer Adolph L. 1819 Wrightwood av. *U.L.*
Singer Arthur J. 2411 Prairie av. *Cal.*
Singer Charles G. Lexington hotel
Singer Charles J. Chicago club. *W.P.*
Singer Edward T. 48 Park av. *U.L.*
Singer Eva Mrs. 3255 Wabash av.
Singer H. A. Mrs. 48 Park av.
Singer J. 6346 Greenwood av.
Singer L. 3447 Prairie av.
Singer M. D. 3650 Forest av.
Singler Henry R. Morgan Park
Singler Joseph A. Washington Heights
Singler N. Mrs. Morgan Park
Singley C. C. Dr. 3036 Indiana av.
Sinn Isabella Mrs. 2653 Evanston av.
Sinzich John J. 4201 Lake av.
Sippy Bertram W. Dr. 143 Oakwood boul.
Sisson Frederick M. 826 Warren av.
Sites George L. Highland Park
Sittig Arthur J. 6717 Lafayette av.
Sittig Charles, 4417 Berkeley av. *Lksd.*
Sittig William A. 223 Hampden ct. *C.A*
Sizer Annie K. Miss, Lake Forest
Sizer Wells B. Oak Park
Skeele Henry B. Chicago Heights
Skeele John W. 4456 Sidney av.
Skeeles Harry, 5138 Wabash av.
Skeeles T. B. 5138 Wabash av.
Skeen Joseph C. Oak Park
Skeer Charles H. 681 Washington boul.

Skeer George M. 681 Washington boul.
Skeer J. D. Mrs. 681 Washington boul.
Skelly Mary Mrs. 639 Fullerton av.
Skelton L. L. Dr. 42 S. Seeley av.
Skelton Nellie Bangs Mrs. 51, 22d
Skene Edward P. 7750 Bond av.
Skiff F. J. V. 4744 Madison av. *Chi.*
Skiles Hugh P. Dr. 963 W. Monroe
Skillen E. S. Chicago Beach hotel. *C.A.*
Skillin E. J. Oak Park
Skillin Thomas J. Oak Park
Skillman Abram D. Mrs. 838 W. Adams
Skillman Fred B. Dr. 838 W. Adams
Skinkle George E. 2527 Kenmore av.
Skinkle Jacob W. 2527 Kenmore av. *Ill.*
Skinner Edward P. Dr. 4052 Indiana av.
Skinner Edwin S. Lake Forest
Skinner Elizabeth Miss, 100 Rush
　　　　Sum. res. Manchester, Vt.
Skinner E. L. Mrs. 197, 44th
Skinner Frank H. Dr. 4052 Indiana av.
Skinner Fredericka Miss, 100 Rush
　　　　Sum. res. Manchester, Vt.
Skinner George R. 678, 48th pl.
Skinner H. E. Hotel Windermere
Skinner H. M. 105 Oakwood av.
Skinner H. R. Mrs. 4052 Indiana av.
Skinner John B. 159 Cass
Skinner J. R. Chicago Athletic assn.
Skinner Nathan A. 735 W. Adams
Slack Charles H. 395 W. Adams. *Ill.*
Sladden Sidney C. 697, 49th
Slade Arthur B. 292 Ohio
Slade Charles B. 4401 Champlain av. *C.A.*
Slade Dana, 1105 Millard av.
Slade Dana jr. Hinsdale
Slade Henry, 292 Ohio
Slade Jonathan, 292 Ohio
Slade Samuel, 3603 Ellis av.
Slafter J. G. 3135 Forest av.
Slagle Edward R. 4219 Ellis av.
Slater H. J. Lexington hotel
Slater J. H. Mrs. 6126 Kimbark av.
Slattery Edward, 4044 Indiana av.
Slattery William J. 4515 Prairie av.
Slaught Herbert E. 5535 Madison av.
Slaughter Arthur O. 4548 Drexel boul. *Chi., W.P.*
Slaughter Arthur O. jr. 4548 Drexel boul.
Slaughter Gabriel F. 16 Astor
Slaughter Henry B. 2829 Kenmore av. *C.A.*
Slauson Charles W. 2667 N. Hermitage av.
Slavin J. H. Mrs. 3827 Michigan av.
Slayback Charles E. 5729 Rosalie ct.
Slaymaker Henry M. 578 Division
Slaymaker Henry S. Evanston
Slaymaker Letitia Miss, Evanston
Slayton Henry L. 25 Waverly ct.
Slayton Joseph W. 2151 Sheridan rd.
Slayton Sarah T. Mrs. 5627 Michigan av.
Sleeper Joseph A. 5745 Washington av.
Sloan Alice A. Mrs. 2115 Prairie av.
Sloan Ambrose B. 3716 Lake av.
Sloan C. E. Mrs. 607 W. 61st pl.
Sloan David, 6320 Woodlawn av.

Sloan George B. 223 S. Marshfield av.
Sloan George S. 223 S. Marshfield av. *Ill.*
Sloat George W. Greenwood Inn, Evanston
Sloate C. J. Mrs. Winnetka
Slocum Benjamin D. 3327 Indiana av.
Slocum Jeremiah, 5612 Monroe av.
Slocum J. E. 5139 Madison av.
Slocum Louis T. M. 2238 Kenmore av.
Slocum L. W. LaGrange
Slocum Mary E. Mrs. 5139 Madison av.
Slocumb C. S. Mrs. 1918 Indiana av.
Sloman Louis, 5622 Michigan av.
Sloman Marcus I. 3146 Rhodes av. *Lksd.*
Slonaker J. W. Dr. Wilmette
Sloss Jacob M. 4203 Grand boul. *Lksd.*
Slosson J. W. 942 W. Jackson boul.
Slyder Albert F. 3243 Vernon av.
Smale Robert, 520 W. Monroe
Smale William R. 520 W. Monroe
Small Albion W. 5731 Washington av. ‑
Small Charles P. Dr. 5727 Madison av.
Small Edward A. Highland Park
Small Henry N. Dr. 630 W. Jackson boul.
Small Henry W. Maywood
Small Lydia A. Mrs. 652 W. Monroe
    Sum. res. Charlevoix, Mich.
Small Ralph D. 4619 Woodlawn av.
Smalley Charles M. 5760 Rosalie ct.
Smalley Sarah A. Miss, 538 Greenleaf av.
Smart Alexander, Evanston
Smart Daniel R. 6701 Stewart av.
Smart James R. Evanston
Smart Joseph, 219 S. Hermitage av.
Smart M. A. Mrs. Evanston
Smedes Aldert, 728 W. Monroe
Smedes T. Lyell, 728 W. Monroe
Smeenk Warner, 5838 Rosalie ct.
Smibert Harriet D. Mrs. 627 W. Adams
Smiley Hiram F. Dr. 7834 Hawthorne av.
Smiley Marvin Dighton, 7834 Hawthorne a .
Smiley M. J. 2815 Prairie av.
Smillie J. Oliver, 411 S. Oakley av.
Smillie Thomas B. 907 W. Jackson boul.
Smillie William, 907 W. Jackson boul.
Smith Abner, 15 Aldine sq. *U.L.*
Smith Abram S. 4545 Vincennes av.
Smith Adelbert W. 1404 Fulton
Smith Agnes D. Mrs. 21 Bellevue pl.
Smith Albert Fletcher, 57 Bellevue pl.
Smith Alexander Prof. Quadrangle club
Smith Alfred K. Dr. 249 Park av.
Smith Alice Miss, Evanston
Smith Alice B. Mrs. 4136 Lake av.
Smith Alice C. Miss, 5036 Washington av.
Smith Alice D. Mrs. 3614 Michigan av.
Smith Alice M. Miss, 38 Astor
Smith Alonzo D. 806 Washington boul. *Irq.*
Smith Alpheus M. 4365 Greenwood av.
Smith Alpheus W. 5712 Monroe av.
Smith Amos R. 10 Ritchie ct.
    Sum. res. Harbor Point, Mich.
Smith Arthur B. 736 W. Adams
Smith Arthur J. 5039 Lake av.

Smith A. C. Mrs. 7127 Yale
Smith A. P. Mrs. Highland Park
Smith Benjamin M. 1005 Farwell av.
Smith Benjamin M. 376 Warren av.
    Sum. res. Spring Lake, Mich.
Smith Bessie C. Miss, 5036 Washington av.
Smith Burton, Lexington hotel. *W.P.*
Smith Byron L. 2140 Prairie av. *Cal.,*
    Chi., C.A., U.L., Univ., W.P.
    Sum res. Lake Forest
Smith B. F. Hotel Del Prado
Smith B. F. The Ontario
Smith Calvin S. 3982 Lake av. *C.A., U.L.*
Smith Caroline Dr. 5120 Hibbard av.
Smith Charles, 4120 Grand boul.   ‚
Smith Charles A. 327 Belden av.
Smith Charles D. F. Judge, 469 Washington boul.
Smith Charles E. Evanston
Smith Charles Frederic Mather, 21 Walton pl. *C.A., Un.*
Smith Charles H. 267 S. Leavitt
Smith Charles H. 1085 Millard av. *Ill.*
Smith Charles H. 4328 Berkeley av.
Smith Charles H. 6505 Yale
Smith Charles M. 93 S. Seeley av.
Smith Charles R. 521 W. Monroe
Smith Charles R. Oak Park
Smith Charles S. Dr. Kenilworth
Smith Charles W. 5496 East End av.
Smith Charles W. 7810 Lowe av.
Smith Christian, 3826 Vincennes av.
Smith Clara Mrs. 3532 Calumet av.
Smith Clara R. Mrs. Highland Park
Smith Clarence L. The Tudor
Smith Cyrus F. Mrs. 317 W. 60th pl.
Smith C. Alfred, 1256 Wrightwood av.
Smith C. D. Oak Park
Smith C. F. Mrs. Irving Park
Smith C. F. Dr. 2358 Indiana av.
Smith C. Hamlin, 83 Warren av.
Smith C. M. 19 Walton pl. *U.L.*
Smith C. R. Mrs. Highland Park
Smith C. VanAlen, 484, 65th
Smith David C. 534 W. 67th
Smith David J. Clifton house
Smith David R. jr. LaGrange
Smith Delavan, Lake Forest. *Univ.*
Smith Dennis R. 4837 St. Lawrence av.
Smith Dexter A., M.D. Irving Park
Smith Donald, Hinsdale
Smith Dunlap, 1924 Wellington. *Chi.,*
    C.A.. Univ.
Smith D. B. Evanston
Smith Eben Byron, 5413 Washington av.
Smith Edgar C. 335 Hampden ct. *C.A.*
Smith Edgar Deyo, 1713 Indiana av.
    Sum. res. Green Lake, Wis.
Smith Edgar D. Dr. 306 Division
Smith Edward E. 158, 51st. *C.A., W.P.*
Smith Edward E. 6039 Jefferson av.
Smith Edward L. Lexington hotel
Smith Edward M. Evanston
Smith Edward Page, 10 Ritchie ct.
Smith Edwin Burritt, 5530 Cornell av.
    Irq., Univ., U.L.

Smith Edwin H. Dr. 5429 Madison av.
Smith Edwin P. Victoria hotel
Smith Eli, 3147 Vernon av.
Smith Ella Miss, 53 Madison Park
Smith Emily J. Miss, 323 Oakwood boul.
Smith Emma G. Miss, 5247 Lexington av.
Smith Emmet L. Dr. 4257 Grand boul.
Smith Ernest Fitzgerald, 61 Cedar. *Chi., Un., W.P.*
Smith Espy L. Dr. 974 W. Polk
Smith E. B. 1837 Michigan av.
Smith E. C. 3138 Wabash av.
Smith E. E. Riverside
Smith E. . 3809 Prairie av.
Smith E. J. Evanston
Smith E. M. Dr. 305 Division
Smith Feño E. 2598 Kenmore av.
Smith Francis Drexel, 19 Walton pl.
Smith Frank J. 6438 Monroe av. *Irq.,U.L.*
Smith Frank M. 1274 Winthrop av.
Smith Frank M. 4620 Drexel boul. *C.A.. W.P.*
Smith Frank S. 934 W. Monroe.
Smith Frank W. 4727 Greenwood av.
Smith Frank W. 5539 Cornell av.
Smith Franklin P. Hotel Metropole. *Cal., C.A., W.P.*
Smith Fred A. Maj. 5824 Rosalie ct.
Smith Fred M. 4545 Ellis av. *C.A., Irq.*
Smith Fred T. Oakland hotel
Smith Fred W. 4725 Grand boul.
Sum. res. Pomfret, Conn.
Smith Frederick A. 377 Superior
Smith Frederick A. 205 Goethe. *U.L.*
Smith Frederick B. 15 Bellevue. pl. *Ṿn., U.L.*
Smith Frederick B. 4160 Ellis av.
Smith Frederick E. 76 Rush
Smith Frederick L. 3845 Ellis av.
Smith Frederick W. Evanston
Smith F. A. Leland hotel
Smith F. C. LaGrange
Smith F. Stewart, Chicago Athletic Assn.
Smith F. S. Mrs. 1718 Indiana av.
Smith F. W. 780 North Park av.
Smith George A. Evanston
Smith George A. Riverside
Smith George E. Hinsdale
Smith George H. Evanston
Smith George S. Mrs. Evanston
Smith George S. Mrs. 1547 Kenmore av
Smith George T. 4717 Grand boul. *Cal., Chi., W.P.*
Smith George W. Austin
Smith George W. Evanston
Smith George W. Mrs. 514 N. State
Smith George W. Oak Park
Smith Gilbert A. Evanston. *C.A.*
Smith Grace T. Miss, 3342 Rhodes av.
Smith Granger, Waukegan. *C.A., U.L.*
Smith G. W. Lexington hotel
Smith G. W. Mayfair
Smith Harold, The Tudor
Smith Harry D. 42 Aldine sq.
Smith Hayden K. Oak Park
Smith Helen M. Mrs. 159 Locust

Smith Helen Page Miss, 491 Dearborn av.
Smith Henry A. 615 W. 78th
Smith Henry C. 5036 Washington av.
Smith Henry D. 42 Aldine sq.
Smith Henry Jennings, 56 Astor
Smith Henry L. 2670 Magnolia av.
Smith Henry T. 161 Locust
Smith Henry W. 3826 Vincennes av.
Smith Herbert C. Evanston
Smith Herbert E. Riverside
Smith Herbert S. Evanston
Smith Horace S. 4727 Greenwood av. *U.L.*
Smith Howard L. 6527 Lexington av. *Irq.*
Smith H. C. Mrs. 4454 Oakenwald av.
Smith H. King, 742 Washington boul.
Smith H. P. 821 Pullman bldg.
Smith H. W. 5119 Wabash av.
Smith H. W. Mrs. 376 Oak
Smith Irma Lois, 359 Ashland boul.
Smith Isadore G. Mrs. 6217 Woodlawn av.
Smith Ishi, 6613 Harvard av.
Smith Jacob B. jr. 5247 Lexington av.
Smith Jacob P. 5222 Lexington av. *U.L., W.P.*
Smith Jacob S. 4500 Ellis av. *U.L.*
Sum. res. Mercer, Pa.
Smith James G. 93 S. Seeley av.
Smith James H. 1823 Roscoe
Smith James Jay, 3339 Vernon av.
Smith James M. 6636 Parnell av.
Smith James P. 2598 Kenmore av. *C.A.*
Smith James R. 162, 51st
Smith Jay Herndon, 45 Cedar. *C.A.*
Smith Jedediah H. 533 Morse av.
Smith Jennie Miss, 1932 Deming pl.
Smith Jennie E. Dr. 665 Sedgwick
Smith Jerome A. Evanston
Smith Jesse E. LaGrange
Smith John C. Austin
Smith John C. Gen. 65 Sibley
Smith John K. Dr. 5612 Monroe av.
Smith John O. K. 5126 Madison av.
Smith John W. 3742 Grand boul.
Smith John W. 7721 Union av.
Smith John Y. Hotel Normandie
Smith Jonathan, 230, 74th
Smith Joseph S. 3141 Prairie av.
Smith Julia Holmes, M. D. 491 Dearborn av.
Smith Junius J. Mrs. 58 Bellevue pl.
Smith J. Eugene, 376 Warren av.
Smith J. Frank, 39 Junior terrace. *C.A.*
Smith J. F. Miss, Hotel Metropole
Smith J. George, 36 N. Sacramento av.
Smith J. H. 306, 41st
Smith J. O. Winnetka
Smith . O. Mrs. 3809 Prairie av.
Smith J. Parker, 1503 Michigan av. *C.A.*
Sum. res. Lake Geneva, Wis.
Smith J. Sewell, 6217 Woodlawn av.
Smith J. W. Riverside
Smith Katherine Miss, 514 N. State
Smith Kinney, 514 N. State. *Univ.*
Smith Lawrence W. 10 Ritchie ct.
Smith LeGrand, 147 Lincoln Park boul. *Un.*

Smith Lewis M. 172 Oakwood boul. *C.A.*
Smith Lillian Miss, 38 Astor
Smith Lizzie M. Miss, 5247 Lexington av.
Smith Lloyd H. Austin
Smith Lloyd James, 1854 Oakdale av. *C.A.*
Smith Lon K. 5247 Lexington av. *W.P.*
Smith Loyal L. The Wellington. *C.A.*
Smith Lucy M. Miss, Lake Forest
Smith Lutellus, 6049 Monroe av.
Smith Luther L. Evanston
Smith L. Mrs. 4324 Prairie av.
Smith Maria E. Mrs. 3020 Indiana av.
Smith Maria W. Mrs. 5712 Monroe av.
Smith Martin L. 3449 Prairie av.
Smith Marvin E., M.D. 23 Bellevue pl. *C.A.*
Smith Mary Alice Miss, Evanston
Smith Mary Rozet Miss, 19 Walton pl.
Smith Melancthon, Oak Park
Smith Monroe A. 688 North Park av.
Smith Myron D. 1104 Winona av.
Smith M. A. Mrs. 1714 Barry av.
Smith M. J. Mrs. 3257 Groveland av.
Smith Ned C. 4734 Prairie av.
Smith Nellie B. Mrs. 912 Walnut
Smith Orange A. 418 S. Leavitt
Smith Orrin L. Dr. The Kenwood.
Smith Orson, 41 Bellevue pl. *Chi.*, *C.A. Un., W.P.*
Smith Osborn F. 5539 Cornell av.
Smith Oskaloosa M. Lieut.-Col. 809 Pullman bldg.
Smith O. C. Lexington hotel. *W.P.*
Smith Paul L. Evanston
Smith Percy H. 240, 76th
Smith Perry H. Mrs. 43 Banks
Smith Perry H. jr. 51 Roslyn pl.
Smith Philip R. 1851 Oakdale av.
Smith Pliny B. 2013 Indiana av. *U.L.*
Smith Proctor Mrs. 182, 45th
Smith Ralph, Evanston
Smith Ralph Soper, 116, 45th
Smith Reginald G. 38 Astor
Smith Richard K. 3516 Vernon av. *C.A.*
Smith Robert A. 63 Sibley
Smith Robert D. 935 W. Polk
Smith Robert E. Mrs. 5600 Monroe av.
Smith Robert G. 5101 Kimbark av.
Smith Robert J. 359 Ashland boul. *Chi., Ill., Irq., U.L.*
Smith Rupert E. I. 2598 Kenmore av.
Smith R. Earle, 359 Ashland boul. *Ill.*
Smith R. E. 569 Warren av.
Smith Sabin, 491 Dearborn av.
Smith Samuel H. 61 Sibley
Smith Samuel H. 3430 Calumet av. *Stan.*
Smith Shea, 3971 Ellis av. *U.L.*
Smith Sidney Judge, Hotel Metropole
Smith Sidney W. Hotel Metropole
Smith Solomon A. Lake Forest
Smith Spencer R. Austin
Smith Susan Mrs. Winnetka
Smith Sylvia L. Mrs. 3430 Calumet av.
Smith S. Gertrude Miss, 5036 Washington av.

Smith S. T. Hyde Park hotel
Smith Theo. W. Hotel Metropole
Smith Thomas, 4759 Madison av. *W.P.*
Smith Thomas B. 613, 50th pl.
Smith Thomas C. 231 Oakwood boul.
Smith Thomas H. 4407 Lake av. *U.L.*
Smith Thomas P. 4731 Grand boul.
Smith Thomas P. jr. 4822 Kenwood av.
Smith Uzziel P. 3126 Rhodes av.
Smith Walter Prof. Lake Forest
Smith Walter B. Evanston
Smith Walter H. 1726 Briar pl.
Smith Walter S. Oak Park
Smith Webster T. 5712 Monroe av.
Smith Willard A. 3256 Rhodes av. *U.L.*
Smith Willard C. 732 W. 61st pl.
Smith William A. Austin
Smith William D. 360 Lasalle av.
Smith William H. Mrs. 45 Cedar
    Sum. res. Harbor Point, Mich.
Smith William H. 509 W. Adams
Smith William H. 5496 East End av.
Smith William J. 173, 36th.
Smith William J. 6540 Yale
Smith William J. Mrs. Hotel Metropole
Smith William Moody, 4334 Forestville av.
Smith William Penn, 116, 45th
Smith William Sooy Gen. Maywood. *U.L.*
Smith William S. 3430 Calumet av.
Smith William T. 4328 Berkeley av.
Smith William Wirt, 157 Oakwood boul.
Smith Willis, 6950 Perry av.
Smith Willis Byron, 5413 Washington av.
Smith Wilton C. Oak Park. *U.L.*
Smith Winfield S. Evanston
Smith Wyllys K. Hinsdale
Smith W. Mrs. Winnetka
Smith W. Binnie, 436 Warren av.
Smith W. P. Mrs. Oak Park
Smith W. S. jr. Maywood. *C.A.*
Smith W. Treese, 1617 Sheridan rd. *U.L.*
Smithies Wilfrid L. 7604 Union av.
Smithson J. W. 2450 Indiana av.
Smithson William S. 2454 Indiana av.
Smoot Kenneth R. Highland Park
Smoot Willard, 225 Dearborn av.
Smucker Milton C. 576 Washington boul.
Smyth Hill C. 235 S. Marshfield av. *Ill.*
Smyth Hugh P. Rev. Evanston
Smyth John G. 1905 Briar pl.
Smyth John M. 300 W. Adams. *Ill., U.L.*
Smyth Martin K. 1905 Briar pl.
Smyth Thomas M. 300 W. Adams
Smyth Winfield S. 2974 Kenmore av.
Smyth Winfield S. jr. 2974 Kenmore av.
Smythe Lillian E. Miss, Hyde Park hotel
Sneed W. A. Mrs. Lexington hotel
Snell Amos J. Mrs. 425 Washington boul.
Snell George E. 319 Lincoln av.
Snell William L. 301 S. Claremont av.
Snell W. C. 4359 Prairie av.
Snider George S. 4429 St. Lawrence av.
Snider H. K. Evanston
Snively Anna M. Miss, 4568 Oakenwald av.
Snively Thaddeus A. Rev. 714 The Plaza *Univ.*

Snoddy M. M. Mrs. 351 Chicago av.
Snodgrass John M. Lake Forest
Snoots Albert, Revere house
Snow Albert E. 3339 Indiana av. *C.A.*
         Sum. res. Orleans, Mass.
Snow Edgar M. Highland Park
Snow F. W. Hotel Windermere
Snow Helen E. Miss, 205 Goethe
Snow Herbert W. 1921 Wrightwood av.
Snow Isaac B. 3645 Grand boul. *U.L.*
Snow J. C. Austin
Snow Leslie E. Mrs. Longwood
Snow Samuel D. 762 Greenleaf av.
Snow Taylor A. Austin
Snow William B. Mrs. 5103 Hibbard av.
Snow William H. 627 W. Adams
Snowhook Belle L. Miss, 4617 Vincennes
     av.
Snowhook Patrick W. 897 S. Central Park
     av.
Snowhook William B. 4617 Vincennes av.
Snydacker Alfred M. Lexington hotel.
     Stan.
Snydacker Arthur G. 2522 Michigan av.
Snydacker Elsie Miss, 2522 Michigan av.
Snydacker Emanuel F. Dr. 386 Ashland
     boul.
Snydacker Joseph G. 2522 Michigan av.
     Stan.
Snydacker Joseph L. 95, 32d. *Stan.*
Snydacker Louis Mrs. 95, 32d
Snydacker Morris, 95, 32d
Snyder Albert H. 501 Farwell av.
Snyder Benjamin F. 501 Farwell av.
Snyder Charles C. Rev. Riverside
Snyder Charles C. 5481 Washington av.
Snyder F. P. Hotel Metropole
Snyder Harvey A. 185, 51st
Snyder Hattie B. Miss, 2427 Indiana av.
Snyder H. P. Leland hotel
Snyder Jacob, 501 Farwell av.
Snyder James H. 6441 Star av.
Snyder John S. Evanston
Snyder John S. 3555 Ellis av.
Snyder Karl F. Riverside
Snyder Omer C. Dr. 42 Scott
Snyder Oscar W. 233 S. Irving av.
Snyder O. W. F. Dr. 4517 Vincennes av.
Soames Arthur F. 2804 Calumet av.
Soames John, 2804 Calumet av.
Sobel Maud Mrs. 4140 Grand boul.
Soden George A. 5206 Kimbark av. *C.A.*
Soden J. Stephen, 4220 Ellis av.
Solbery Albert F. 694 W. Monroe. *Ill.*
Solbery Caroline Mrs. 685 W. Adams
Solenberger A. R. Dr. 4236 Calumet av.
Solger Parry K. Riverside
Sollitt John Mrs. 515 W. Jackson boul.
Sollitt Oliver, 4020 Prairie av. *Cal.. C.A.,*
     U.L.
Sollitt Ralph T. 4545 Forrestville av.
Sollitt Sumner, 4922 Forrestville av.
Sollitt Thomas, 4020 Prairie av.
     Sum. res. "At Sunset" Cottage, Fox
     Lake
Sollitt Walter R. 515 W. Jackson boul.

Sollitt William, 1257 Washington boul.
Solomon CharlesH.1289Washington boul.
Solomon C. J. 700A Pullman bldg.
Solomon Ernest, 4539 Lake av.
Solomon Fred M. 3217 South Park av.
     Lksd
Solomon Henry, 4406 Michigan av.
Solomon Joseph, 4406 Michigan av.
Solomon Mark, 422, 41st
Solomon William T. 234, 47th
Somers Edgar L. 4852 Washington av.
     Chi.
Somers Frank W. 228 Oakwood boul.
Somers G. C. Dr. 3607 Prairie av.
Somers G. Horace Dr. 514 W. Jackson
     boul.
Somers Jean Brooks Mrs. 271 Warren av.
Somerville Robert, Riverside. *Irq.*
Somes Dora H. Mrs. 4959 Prairie av.
Sommer Otto, 147 Evanston av.
Sommers Harry G. 406 Erie. *C.A.*
Sommers Lillian E. Miss, 406 Erie
Sommerville Robert, Riverside
Son Sol J. 403, 41st. *Lksd.*
Sondheimer Edward A. 2619 Michigan av.
     Lksd.
Sondheimer Emanuel, 2619 Michigan av.
     Stan.
Sondheimer Henry, 2619 Michigan av.
Sondheimer Maxwell, 4507 Prairie av.
Sonnenschein Leopold, 226 Fremont
Sonnenschein L. 20 St. John's ct.
Sontag Fritz, 46 Wisconsin
Sontag Henry, Evanston
Soper Alexander C. 3998 Ellis av. *U.L.*
Soper Alexander C. jr. 3998 Ellis av.
Soper E. Hotel Del Prado
Soper Henry M. Prof. 271 S. Homan av.
Soper Horace W. Mrs. 4004 Drexel boul.
     Sum. res. Verona, N.Y.
Soper James Mrs. Riverside
Soper James P. 4841 Greenwood av. *Ill.,*
     U.L.
Soper Noble D. 207, 41st
Soper Thomas A. 6911 Perry av.
Sorby Harold, 416, 36th pl.
So Relle Rupert P. 3953 Michigan av.
Sorrick George A. Prof. Elmhurst
Sosman Joseph S. 570 W. Congress
Souder Charles H. L. Dr. 6951 Stewart av.
Souder Ellen Starr Dr. 6951 Stewart av.
Soule Charles R. Mrs. 2758 N. Winchester
     av.
Southard Albert B. 6565 Harvard av.
Southard B. D. North Shore hotel
Southard Charles H. 6121 Monroe av.
Southard Dan B. 6565 Harvard av.
Southgate Richard H. Auditorium hotel.
     Chi., W.P.
Southwell Henry E. 469 N. State
Southwood Edward, Riverside
Southworth Franklin C. Rev. 118 S. Oak-
     ley av.
Southworth Mary L. Miss, 6325 Monroe
     av.
Sowers Isaac M. 502 The Plaza

Spach Amuel B. Dr. 6629 Harvard av.
Spaids K. H. Mrs. 3245 Indiana av.
Spaids K. L. Miss, 3245 Indiana av.
Spaids Susan E. Miss, 3245 Indiana av.
Spain N. J. 4521 Woodlawn av.
Spain Peter, 2640 N. Paulina
Spain Stephen J. 2640 N. Paulina
Spalding A. G. 4924 Woodlawn av. *C.A.,*
    U.L.
Spalding Charles F. 204 Goethe. *C.A.*
Spalding Charles R. 522 Byron. *C.A.*
Spalding Jesse, 1637 Prairie av. *Chi.,*
    U.L., W.P.
Spalding Joel J. Mrs. Evanston
Spalding Rufus P. 581 Lasalle av.
Spalding Stewart, 495 N. State
Spangenberg Charles, 1837 Reta
Spangenberg W. E. 1674 Buckingham pl.
Spangler David, The Ontario
Spangler John H. 18 Crilly ct.
Spangler J. E. Mrs. The Ontario
Sparks.Edwin E. 5741 Monroe av.
Sparling Ellis H. Dr. 6805 Wentworth av.
Sparre Charles, 730 Sedgwick
Sparrow William S. Mrs. 6144 Kimbark
    av.
Spaulding Howard H. Kenilworth
Spaulding S. G. Mrs. 2518 Michigan av.
Speakman Edward, 486 W. Adams
Speakman Howland, 486 W. Adams
Spear Albert A. 2451 Michigan av.
Spear Charles E. Hinsdale
Spear Elbridge B. Evanston
Spear E. Raymond, Hinsdale
Spear Harry E. 97, 51st
Spear James D. 1067 N. Clark
Spear John J. Wilmette
Spear William H. 97, 51st
Spear William H. jr. 97, 51st
Specht Louis, 486 Lasalle av.
Speed H. B. The Kenwood. *U.L.*
Speer H. C. 5336 Madison av.
Speer William W. 5336 Madison av.
Speidel Laurence H. Lake Forest
Spelz Frederick W. 1436 Wellington
Spence Elizabeth E. Mrs. 3538 Lake av.
Spence Florence Miss, 7728 Eggleston
    av.
Spencer Albert L. 6106 Woodlawn av.
Spencer A. P. 4305 Oakenwald av.
Spencer Bennett W. Evanston
Spencer Caroline A. Mrs. 2585 Kenmore
    av.
Spencer Charles F. A. 6106Woodlawn av.
Spencer Clinton J. Highland Park
Spencer Earl W. Evanston. *Chi.*
Spencer Ellen Mrs. 2454 N. Paulina
Spencer George G. 7110 Princeton av.
Spencer George W. 6150 Monroe av.
Spencer G. N. Lexington hotel
Spencer Hamilton Mrs. 883 Winthrop av.
Spencer H. F. 6565 Yale
Spencer I. Lawrence, 4859 Madison av.
Spencer Lloyd G. 100 Warren av.
    Sum. res. Palos Park, Ill.
Spencer L. Mrs. Evanston

Spencer N. L. Lexington hotel
Spencer Thomas H. Highland Park
Spencer Waldo H. 7444 Jeffery av.
Spencer William E. 4736 Lake av.
Spencer William H. Evanston
Spencer Z. C. 917 Chase av.
Spengler Werner, 37 Ewing pl.
Spensley H. G. 780 North Park av.
Sperry Albert N. Austin
Sperry Fred A. Oak Park
Sperry Henry M. The Ontario
Sperry James A. 315 Park av.
Speyer Isaac, 4738 Champlain av.
Speyer Julius, 549 Burling
Spicer A. J. Mrs. 915 S. Robey
Spicer George A. 3850 Lake av. *U.L.*
Spicer James R. 532 Greenleaf av.
Spicer Lawrence A. 1725 Belmont av.
Spicer Mary C. Miss, Evanston
Spicer Vive K. Kenilworth
Spiegel Hamlin M. 4415 Berkeley av.
    Lksd.
Spiegel Jonas, 3145 South Park av. *Lksd.*
Spiegel Joseph, 3344 South Park av.
Spiegel Louis, 1029 N. Clark
Spiegel Modie J. 4537 Ellis av. *Stan.*
Spiegel Sidney M. 3545 Indiana av. *Stan.*
Spiel George, 16 Pine Grove av.
Spiel Henry Mrs. 16 Pine Grove av.
Spielmann August, 3 Crilly pl.
Spier William, 3643 Vernon av.
Spiering Theodore B. 3614 Lake av.
Spierling Ernest J. 6421 Lexington av.
Spies Joseph, 4411 Lake av.
Spining Charles P. Evanston
Spink Frank A. 140, 38th. *C.A.*
Spinney Ellery C. Mrs. 4007 Drexel boul.
Spirkel John Dr. 3271 Beacon
Spitz Henry, 3637 Forest av. *Lksd.*
Spitz Herman, 949 S. Spaulding av.
Spitz Samuel, 3421 Prairie av. *Stan.*
Spoehr Charles A. 1088 Evanston av.
Spofford Florence M. Miss, 1520 Wash-
    ington boul.
Spofford George W.1520Washington boul.
    Sum. res. Highland Place, West Chi-
    cago, Ill.
Spooner Frank E. 4940 Greenwood av.
    U.L.
Spooner Frank V. 4940 Greenwood av.
Spooner Harry S. Oak Park
Spooner Mae P. Miss, 4940 Greenwood av.
Spooner Thomas F. 184, 36th
Spooner William, Oak Park
Spoor George E. 4691 N. Clark
Spoor Harriet I. Miss, 4691 N. Clark
Spoor Maud L. Miss, 4691 N. Clark
Spoor John A. 596 N. State. *Chi., C.A.,*
    Un., W.P. Sum.res.Nonquitt,Mass.
Spottswood C. S. Granada hotel
Sprague Albert A. 2710 Prairie av. *Chi.,*
    Univ.
Sprague C. A. Miss, 2710 Prairie av.
Sprague E. E. Mrs. 3821 Langley av.
Sprague Frederick W. 537 Dearborn av.
    Univ.

Sprague Levi, 122, 33d
Sprague Ralph W. 666 Lasalle av.
Sprague S. A. Mrs. The Renfost
Sprague T. W. Hotel Windermere
Sprague William, 537 Dearborn av. *Un.*, *U.L.*
Spread Henry F. Mrs. 580 Evanston av.
Spring C. A. jr. 448 Dearborn av.
Springer Ada E. Miss, 3819 Prairie av.
Springer Adel G. Miss, 78, 44th
Springer Charles D. 4715 Prairie av.
Springer Charles E. 3833 Calumet av. *U.L.*
Springer Edward B. 6352 Monroe av.
Springer Edward L. 3819 Prairie av.
Springer Emily J. Miss, 78, 44th
Springer Frank G. 3814 Calumet av.
Springer George A. 3819 Prairie av.
Springer George B. 4715 Prairie av.
Springer George W. Wilmette
Springer Georgiana Miss, 78, 44th
Springer Gertrude Miss, 4715 Prairie av.
Springer Jacob, 506 Lasalle av.
Springer James D. 816 The Plaza
Springer Lewis B. Wilmette
Springer Mary M. Miss, 4715 Prairie av.
Springer Milton C. Mrs. Wilmette
Springer Paul, 3819 Prairie av.
Springer Theodore, 376 Dearborn av.
Springer T. G. Mrs. 425 Lasalle av.
Springer Warren, 1635 Prairie av.
Sproehnle A. W. 4343 Ellis av.
Sproehnle F. M. 28 Groveland Park.
Sproesser Alfred F. Dr. 1271 N. Halsted
Sprogle Howard O. 7 Madison Park
Sproul Elliott W. 6500 Yale
Sproule Alfred L. Evanston
Spruance Harmon, 2400 South Park av.
Spruance Lewis J. C. 2400 South Park av.
Spry George E. Wilmette. *Ill.*
Spry John Mrs. 481 W. Monroe
Spry John C. 363 Ashland boul. *Ill., U.L.*
Spry Samuel A. 4849 Ellis av. *C.A., Ill., W.P.*
Spry Walter P. 481 W. Monroe
Spurlock Henry B. 279 Lasalle av.
Spurlock P. A. Mrs. 279 Lasalle av.
    Sum. res. Lake Bluff
Squair Alexander, 5546 South Park av.
Squair Francis, 5546 South Park av.
Squair Hugh, 5546 South Park av.
Squibb Frederic J. 555A Dearborn av.
Squier Jennie Miss, 186, 53d
Squire Clara Miss, 6521 Harvard av.
Squire Harry W. Morton Park
Squire L. G. 1359 W. Congress. *Irq.*
Squire Mary E. Miss, 308 Belden av.
Squirer William, LaGrange
Squires Charles, 4522 Greenwood av.
Squires Herbert Bradshaw, 4522 Greenwood av.
Staab Joseph, 26 Lincoln pl.
Stacey Henry C. 5436 Monroe av.
Stacey John F. Ohio ne. cor. N. State
Stacey Thómas I. Evanston
Stacey William, Evanston

Stacey William A. Evanston
Stack C. J. 1254 Michigan av.
Stack James L. 4740 Madison av. *C.A.*
Stack John R. 3311 Beacon
Stackpole George M. 345 W. 61st
Stacy P. W. Glen Ellyn
Stadden Burton W. 3628 Vernon av.
Staehle F. J. Dr. 3151 Prairie av.
Stafford Charles B. 3822 Calumet av.
Stafford C. E. Chicago Beach hotel
Stafford John F. 97 Walton pl.
Stafford Juniata Miss, 97 Walton pl.
Stafford J. B. 1005 W. Jackson boul.
Stafford Louis H. 1871 Roscoe
Stafford Minnie Miss, 97 Walton pl.
Stafford Trusten B. 4907 Vincennes av.
Stafford W. H. Longwood
Stafford W. Walter Dr. 2513 Indiana av.
Stagg Alonzo A. Prof. 5704 Jackson av.
Stagg Robert, Park Ridge
Stahl Edward L. jr. Dr. 377 S. Campbell av.
Stahl George W. 5108 Hibbard av.
Stahl John M. 4328 Langley av.
Staiger C. M. 712 Fullerton av.
Staley Justin B. 3132 Vernon av.
Staley Mary E. Mrs. 3132 Vernon av.
Staley Maud Miss. 3132 Vernon av.
Staley Thos. J. 339 Lasalle av.
Staley Thomas J. jr. 339 Lasalle av.
Stallwood Harold G. Austin
Stamm Helena Mrs. 99 Macalister pl.
Stamm J. Carl Dr. 99 Macalister pl.
Stamsen P. Paul, 38 Pine Grove av.
Stanbery Edward, Evanston
Stanbro Solon D. 287 Ashland boul.
Standard George, Austin
Standart George G. 5029 Lake av.
Standiford Marcellus, Riverside
Standish Albert H. Oak Park
Stanford Arthur L. Evanston
Stanford E. Mrs. Evanston
Stanford George E. Evanston
Stanford George W. 781 W. Monroe. *Ill.*
Stanford Mary E. Dr. 7058 Parnell av.
Stange Otto H. Elmhurst
Stanger Christopher G. Rev. Elmhurst
Stanhope Leon E. 6350 Greenwood av.
Stanley Caroline E. Mrs. 571 Dearborn av.
Stanley Cornelia C. Mrs. Lake Forest
Stanley Frank W. 565 N. State. *C.A., Un.*
Stanley Fred G. 22 Bellevue pl.
Stanley F. A. Dr. Julien hotel
Stanley Hiram M. Lake Forest
Stanley P. E. 55 Cedar. *C.A., W.P.*
Stanley William O. 3731 Forest av.
Stannard Harry W. 1616 W. Adams
Stannard Helen J. Mrs. 1616 W. Adams
Stansbury Charles W. Park Ridge
Stanton A. E. Mrs. Oak Park
Stanton Charles B. 3559 Vincennes av.
Stanton Edgar, Evanston
    Sum. res. Lake Forest
Stanton Edna Miss, Evanston
Stanton Harry S. Longwood
Stanton Henry L. Longwood

Stanton J. F. Hyde Park hotel
Stanton L. O. Oak Park
Stanton R. L. Miss, Hyde Park hotel
Stanton R. T. LaGrange
Stanton S. Cecil, M.D. 9 Cedar
Stanton William A. 271 Oakwood boul. *C.A., U.L.*
Stanton William F. 609 S. Albany av.
Stanwood Thaddeus P. Evanston
Staples Edith Miss, Hotel Del Prado
Staples Frank M. 4119 Grand boul.
Staples John M. 3 Campbell Park
Starbuck W. H. 4101 Drexel boul.
Starck P. A. 4619 Vincennes av.
Stark Adolph, 244 Hampden ct.
Stark Adolph, Ravinia
Stark Andrew, 974 Warren av.
Starke Albert, 512 Dearborn av.
Starke Martha Miss, 512 Dearborn av.
Starkey Horace M., M.D. 3300 Indiana av.
Starkey M. Ella Miss, 3300 Indiana av.
Starkweather Charles H. 2625 Prairie av. *Cal.*
Starkweather Frank H. 586 Dearborn av. *C.A., U.L.*
Starr Charles E. 3840 Langley av.
Starr Eliza Allen Miss, 299 Huron
Starr Ellen Gates Miss, 355 S. Halsted
Starr Frederick Prof. 5800 Jackson av.
Starr Helen E. Miss, 610 Dearborn
Starr J. C. Mrs. Glencoe
Starr Mary Mrs. 3840 Langley av.
Starr Merritt, Winnetka. *U.L.*
Starr Western, 3436 South Park av.
Starrett David A. 578 W. Congress
Starrett Helen E. Mrs. 3912 Vincennes av.
Starrett Julius, 3658 Prairie av. *U.L.*
Starring A. M. Mrs. 430 Elm
Starring Mason B. 430 Elm
Staud Fernando H. The Renfost
Stauffer Benj. F. 276 Michigan av. *Chi.. W.P.*
Staver.Henry.C. 7220 Princeton av. *U.L.*
Stayart Louis W. 3265 Malden
Stayman Helen M. Mrs. 923 W. Monroe
Stearns Allan T. 4355 N. Ashland av.
Stearns Anna Mrs. 524 Garfield av.
Stearns Charles B. 1229 Winthrop av.
Stearns Deshler F. Evanston
Stearns Edward F. 3508 Ellis av.
Stearns E. G. 626 W. Jackson boul. *A C.,. Ill.*
Stearns George Mrs. 29, 35th
Stearns John K. 480 N. State. *U.L.*
Stearns J. W. Mrs. 352 Chicago av.
Stearns Marcus C. 738 W. Monroe
Stearns Marcus C. Mrs. 313 Michigan av.
Stearns Richard I. 313 Michigan av. *C.A., U.L.,W.P.*
Stearns William H. Oak Park
Stearns William M., M.D. Kenilworth
Stebbings C. E. Park Ridge
Stebbings Horace P., M.D. 6033 Indiana av.
Stebbings Horace R. 6015 Indiana av.

Stebbings Walter L. 6015 Indiana av.
Stebbins Don C. 335 W. 61st
Stebbins Henry S. Mrs. 2829 Michigan av.
Stebbins S. J. 7351 Princeton av.
Stecher Martin D. 639 N. Robey
Stedman D. B. 3716 Lake av.
Stedman E. M. Capt. 3716 Lake av.
Stedman E. M. jr. 3716 Lake av.
Stedman Josiah, 3716 Lake av. *C.A.*
Steele Bernard Mrs. 3123 Calumet av.
Steele D. A. K., M.D. 2920 Indiana av.
Steele Edgar R. 3180 Dover·
Steele Frederick M. 3815 Ellis av.
Steele George F. 19 Chalmers pl.
Steele George M. Dr. 19 Chalmers pl.
Steele Henry B. 3119 Calumet av. *C.A., Stan.*
Steele James, Evanston
Steele James N. 4520 Lake av.
Steele Julius, 4818 Lake av. *C.A.*
Steele Leo, 3938 Grand boul.
Steele Maurice B. 3123 Calumet av. *Stan.*
Steele Max, 3938 Grand boul.
Steele M. A. Mrs. Lexington hotel
Steele Percival, 332 Hampden ct. *U.L.*
Steele Samuel B. 3123 Calumet av. *Stan.*
Steele William L. Evanston
Steen Erasmus D. 242 Hampden ct.
Steenburg Sarah Mrs. Leland hotel
Steere George S. Lakota hotel. *U.L.*
Steers Jonas Mrs. Highland Park
Steever Jerome G. 4718 Madison av. *C.A., Irq., U.L.*
Steffens Charles M. 7657 Saginaw av.
Steffens M. J. 55, 22d
Stegemann H. J. 1441 W. Jackson boul.
Stehman Henry B. Dr. 635 W. Congress. *Ill.*
Stein Adolph, 369 Ashland boul.
Stein Albert, 3716 Grand boul. *Lksd.*
Stein Arthur, 4133 Drexel boul. *Stan.*
Stein Barbara Mrs. 4539 Oakenwald av.
Stein Belle Miss, 871 W. Monroe
Stein Charles, 294 Ashland boul.
Stein Charles, 2443 Wabash av.
Stein David A. 3345 South Park av. *Stan.*
Stein Ernest, 3716 Grand boul. *Lksd.*
Stein Fannie Miss, 4340 Grand boul.
Stein Ignatz, 393 Ashland boul.
Stein Israel, 3238 South Park av.
Stein Joseph, 5540 Michigan av.
Stein Lawrence, 153, 42d pl.
Stein Leopold, 246 Schiller
Stein Louis, 153, 42d pl.
Stein Max, 6753 Lafayette av.
Stein O. J. Dr. 25, 47th
Stein Phillip Judge, 4340 Grand boul. *Irq., Lksd.*
Stein Samuel, 3716 Grand boul, *Lksd.*
Stein Siegmund, 3716 Grand boul.
Stein Sigmund, 3362 Forest av.
Stein Sydney, 5038 Washington av. *Irq., Lksd., Stan.*
Stein S. Mrs. 4133 Drexel boul.
Stein William D. 4338 Forrestville av.
Steinbeiss Charles, 266 Fremont

Steiner Jacob, 493, 42d pl. *Lksd.*
Steines C. W. Maywood
Steinfeld Ben, 3205 Rhodes av. *Lksd.*
Steiniger Simon, 3936 Lake av. *Stan.*
Steinmann E. A. 4538 Oakenwald av.
Steinmann L. E. 4538 Oakenwald av.
Steinmetz Conrad Mrs. 3229 South Park av.
Steinson Henry G. 1633 W. Adams
Stelle E. E. Mrs. 736 Fullerton av.
Stelle F. Surdam Mrs. 3027 Michigan av.
　　　Sum. res. Lake George, N. Y.
Stenbeck Caroline Mrs. 1842 Aldine av.
Stennett William H., M.D. Oak Park
Stensland Paul O. 140 Evergreen av. *U.L.*
Stenson James Mrs. 2704 Calumet av.
Stephan Caroline Mrs. Austin
Stephan Emanuel L. Austin
Stephan Traugott F. Austin
Stephens Armstead H. Rev. 1357 Sheffield av.
Stephens Fred W. 5343 Washington av.
Stephens Helen B. Mrs. 7429 Bond av.
Stephens H. N. Mrs. Lakota hotel
Stephens James S. Maywood
Stephens Louisa B. Mrs. 2713 Prairie av.
　　　Sum. res. Lake Placid, N. Y.
Stephens Percy R. 4800 Prairie av.
Stephens R. D. 2713 Prairie av. *Univ.,*
　　W.P. Sum. res. Lake Placid, N. Y.
Stephens William C. Oak Park. *C.A.*
　　　Sum. res. Sea Gate, N. Y.
Stephens William G. 2570 N. Ashland av.
　　　Sum. res. Wheaton
Stephenson Frank B. 147 Lincoln Park boul. *Un.*
Sterl Alexander Dr. Riverside
Sterling Charles J. 1302 Diversey av.
Sterling D. L. 6501 Kimbark av.
Sterling M. M. Miss, 1241 Washington boul.
Sterling William H. 5137 Kimbark av. *C.A., W.P.*
Stern Aaron, 2735 Michigan av. *Stan.*
Stern Amson, 3347 Prairie av.
Stern Daniel, 413 Dearborn av. *Lksd.*
Stern Daniel S. 4235 Grand boul. *Stan.*
Stern Harry, 3347 Prairie av.
Stern Henry, 2915 Prairie av. *Stan.*
Stern Herman, 4512 Drexel boul. *Stan.*
Stern Louis, 394 Lasalle av.
Stern Louis, 592 Dearborn av. *Stan.*
Stern Max, 481 Bowen av. *Lksd.*
Stern Max, 483½ Lasalle av.
Stern Milton R. 2963 Prairie av.
Stern Morris L. Mrs. 413 Dearborn av.
Stern Moses, 3644 Grand boul.
Stern Oscar M. 156, 25th. *Stan.*
Stern Ralph F. 413 Dearborn av.
Stern Samuel, 2963 Prairie av. *Stan.*
Stern S. Mrs. Hotel Woodruff
Stern Tobias Mrs. 318, 37th
Stern Viola Mrs. 4909 Grand boul.
Sternberg E. 3401 Prairie av.
Sterne George M. 222 W. 65th
Sternfeld Samuel, 79 Lincoln av.

Sterrett Maurice G. 5533 Cornell av.
Sterrett William H. 6131 Kimbark av.
Sterritt Katherine B. Miss, 3659 Michigan av.
Stetson Wellington, Austin
Stett John Mrs. 3601 Vincennes av.
Stettauer Charles S. 2026 Prairie av. *Stan.*
Stettauer David, 2026 Prairie av. *Stan.*
Stettauer James, Hotel Metropole. *Lksd.*
Steveley John F. Mrs. 756 Washington boul.
Steveley Lucius A. 756 Washington boul.
Stevens Arthur J. 4401 St. Lawrence av.
Stevens A. B. Washington Heights
Stevens Charles A, 4003 Ellis av. *U.L., W.P.*
Stevens Charles N. 4715 Champlain av.
Stevens Charles P. Evanston
Stevens C. Nelson, Evanston
Stevens C. R. The Hampden, *C.A.*
Stevens Edgar A. 4504 Greenwood av.
Stevens Edmund H. 4715 Champlain av.
Stevens Edward D. 4504 Greenwood av. *U.L.*
Stevens Edwin F. 6756 Butler
Stevens Frank C. Chicago Athletic assn. *C.A.*
Stevens Frank E. 6848 Anthony av.
Stevens Frank K. Evanston
Stevens Frank L. 2939 Michigan av. *Cal.*
Stevens Fred H. LaGrange
Stevens F. R. Mrs. 4164 Lake av.
Stevens George L. Evanston
Stevens George M. 21 Best av.
Stevens George W. Mrs. 1763 Oakdale av.
Stevens Harry C. 6418 Greenwood av.
Stevens Harry D. 225 Dearborn av. *C.A.*
Stevens Harry S. 1037 N. Clark. *Univ.*
Stevens Harry S. Evanston
Stevens Jacob W. 4715 Champlain av.
Stevens James D. Mrs. 5480 Cornell av.
Stevens James W. 4118 Grand boul. *U.L.*
Stevens John K. 690 Washington boul. *Ill.*
Stevens John L. 629 Englewood av.
Stevens John M. 29 Best av.
Stevens Joshua S. 7640 Lowe av.
Stevens J. H. 682, 48th pl.
Stevens J. M. Rev. Morton Park
Stevens Lewis K. 1010 Washington boul.
Stevens Morehouse, 2939 Michigan av.
Stevens M. A. Dr. 143 Oakwood boul.
Stevens Percy D. 1765 Oakdale av.
Stevens Ralph C. 4504 Greenwood av.
Stevens Raymond W. 4118 Grand boul. *U.L.*
Stevens Robert W. 1010 Washington boul.
Stevens Rollo R. Rev. 1117 Early av.
Stevens Russell H. Mrs. 4451 Sidney av.
Stevens R. G. Mrs. 334, 44th
Stevens Sidney W. 1763 Oakdale av.
Stevens Silas C. Clifton house
Stevens Sylvanus H. 5432 Jefferson av.
Stevens S. H. jr. 5432 Jefferson av. *C.A.*
Stevens Thomas A. 4114 Indiana av.
Stevens William G. 5430 Lexington av.
Stevens Walter A. Dr. 2631 Wabash av.

Stevens Wirt A. 2631 Wabash av.
Stevenson Albert E. 6434 Kimbark av.
Stevenson Alexander F. Col. 378 Lasalle av.
Stevenson Charles, 525 Lasalle av.
Stevenson Charles H. 341 Rush
Stevenson Donald M. 170, 36th
Stevenson Frederic A. 5126 Washington av.
Stevenson Frederick B. 1226 Wilcox av.
Stevenson H. M. 670, 48th pl. CA.
Stevenson James R. D. 525 Lasalle av.
Stevenson J. Ross Rev. 8 Chalmers pl.
Stevenson Lucille Miss, 465 Bowen av.
Stevenson Morton J. 32 Pine Grove av.
Stevenson Robert, 525 Lasalle av.
        •   Sum. res. Lake Bluff
Stevenson Sarah Hackett, M.D. 341 Rush
Stevenson William, 458, 44th
Stevenson Wilham B. 4647 Vincennes av.
Stevers Fred D. 3166 Beacon
Stevers M. D. Mrs. Jefferson Park
Stevison J. H. 5407 Jefferson av.
Steward John F. 2850 Kenmore av.
Steward W. T. Hinsdale
Stewart Abbie H. Mrs. Hinsdale
Stewart Alexander, 5753 Madison av.
Stewart Alexander M. 226 Warren av. C.A., Ill.
Stewart Andrew Dr. 464 W. Adams
Stewart Archibald A. Oak Park. C.A. Ill.
Stewart B. F. The Arizona
Stewart Charles, 151, 42d pl·
Stewart Charles A. 2731 N. Lincoln
Stewart Charles C. 5753 Madison av.
Stewart Charles F. Dr. 4313 Vernon av.
Stewart Charles L. 381 Superior
Stewart Edmund G. 4727 Indiana av.
Stewart Edward L. 426 W. Jackson boul.
Stewart Elizabeth S. Miss, 171, 51st
Stewart Emma G. Miss, 5737 Madison av.
Stewart E. F. Mrs. 5720 Madison av.
Stewart Frank, Tracy
Stewart George A. Austin
Stewart George B. S. 121, 51st
Stewart George R. 575 Cleveland av.
Stewart George W. 1076 Washington boul.
Stewart Graeme, 181 Lincoln Park boul. Chi., Ill., Un. Sum. res. Winnetka
Stewart Henry Mrs. 306 Schiller
Stewart Henry C. 1116 Washington boul.
Stewart John F. Evanston
Stewart John K. 1805 Magnolia av.
Stewart Lee K. Dr. The Arizona
Stewart N. Mrs. Evanston
Stewart Ramsey H. 575 Cleveland av.
Stewart Samuel J. 6420 Kimbark av.
Stewart Sidney H. 6109 Woodlawn av.
Stewart William, 623 Dearborn av.
Stewart William J. Dr. 1076 Washington boul.
Stewart William J. 2407 Magnolia av.
Stewart William R. The Wellington
Stewart W. C. Evanston
Steyner Emma B. 217 The Plaza
Stickney Charles F. Hotel Windemere

Stickney W. Frank, Mayfair
Stieglitz Gustaf, 1704 Diversey
Stieglitz Julius Dr. 5479 Lexington av.
Stiles Clarence L. LaGrange
Stiles Clarence M. 1039 Winthrop av.
Stiles George N. 2325 Michigan av. Cal., U.L., W.P.
Stiles John S. 1804 W. 22d
Stiles Josiah, 2325 Michigan av. Cal.
Stiles Lawrence G. 2193 Kenmore av. C.A.
Stiles Lucy Goddard Miss, 2325 Michigan av.
Stiles Luther C. LaGrange
Stiles M. B. Mrs. 6510 Kimbark av.
Still Elisha A. 4839 Vincennes av. U.L.
Stiller Richard F. 512 W. Congress
Stillians Daniel C. Dr. 703 N. Hoyne av.
Stillinger Everett, 1920 Deming pl.
Stillman Herman W. 30 Bryant av.
Stillman Thomas W. 30 Bryant av.
Stillwell Homer A. 671 48th.
Stillwell James, 1843 Barry av.
Stillwell John, 1843 Barry av.
Stilwell T. J. Mrs. 2915 Indiana av.
Stillwell Warren S. Chicago Beach hotel
Stimpson James M. Maywood
Stimson Fred D. 183 Walnut
Stimson Harlan P. 183 Walnut
Stine Wilbur M. 618 W. 65th
Stinson Alfred E. 6019 Monroe av.
Stinson Cornelia Miss, 4436 Drexel boul.
Stinson Henry J. 4436 Drexel boul.
Stinson James, 4436 Drexel boul. W.P.
Stinson Mary A. Mrs. 4224 Grand boul.
Stires E. M. Rev. Hotel Metropole. Univ.
Stirlen John, 4 Plaisance ct.
Stirling William R. 1616 Prairie av. Chi. Sum. res. Lake Forest
Stitch George F. 4142 Grand boul. Sum. res. Asbury Park, N. J.
Stitch George F. jr. 4142 Grand boul.
Stites Robert N. 153 Goethe
Stix Sol H. Lexington hotel. Stan.
Stobie Charles S. 444 W. 65th
Stobie Isabella Miss, 444 W. 65th
Stock Ernst, 1811 Belmont av.
Stockdale R. F. Park Ridge
Stockham Alice B. Dr. Evanston
Stockham William H. 488 Belden av.
Stocking Charles J. Clifton house
Stockton Algernon C. 385 Dearborn av.
Stockton Diantha Mrs. 3767 Ellis av.
Stockton John L. Highland Park
Stockton John T. Evanston. U.L.
Stockton Joseph Gen. 567 Lasalle av. U.L.
Stockton Louise M. Mrs. 385 Dearborn av.
Stockton Ward, 547 Dearborn av.
Stockton Wm. E. Evanston
Stoddard Herbert A. 436 N. Normal Parkway
Stoddard Horace A. 727 W. Monroe
Stoddard Horace H. 727 W. Monroe
Stoddard James A. 6525 Harvard av. Sum. res. Lake Beulah, Wis.

Stoddard John H. 508 Webster av.
Stoddard W, H. Mrs. 2359 Michigan av.
Stoelting Christian H. 832 Greenleaf av.
Stoffregen Conrad, Hotel Luzerne
Stoker Eugene L. Evanston
Stokes Charles F. 332 Oakwood boul.
Stokes Charles J. Evanston
Stokes Chauncey M. 1664 W. Jackson boul.
Stokes C. Eugene, 4425 Greenwood av.
Stokes C. M. Mrs. 332 Oakwood boul.
Stokes Edwin M. 332 Oakwood boul.
Stokes Frederick C. Evanston
Stokes T. Oliver, 1102 S. Lawndale av.
Stokes William B. 332 Oakwood boul.
Stoll George, 674 W. Adams
Stoll Robert H. 674 W. Adams
Stolp Byron C., M. D. Wilmette
Stolp Rufus B. Dr. Kenilworth
Stoltz Joseph, 627 Englewood av.
Stolz Henry, 2411 Lakewood av.
Stolz Joseph Rabbi, 157, 42d pl.
Stone Abe L. 3419 Prairie av.
Stone Addison C. 3613 Ellis av.
Stone Albert L. 2609 N. Hermitage av.
Stone Alfred Bates, 4525 Ellis av.
Stone Alice Miss, 45 Bellevue pl.
Stone A. J. 431 Washington boul. *Ill.*
Stone Burke, 4525 Ellis av.
Stone Calvin Mrs. 86 N. Ada
Stone Carl D. Dr. 2938 Indiana av. *Cal.*
Stone Charles H. 52, 40th
Stone Charles J. Austin
Stone Curtis B. 1186 W. Congress
Stone C. L. 6749 Parnell av. *C.A.*
Stone Daniel, 3000 Indiana av.
Stone Edward, 1254 Michigan av.
Stone Frank B. 5627 Monroe av. *C.A.* *U.L.*
Stone Fred K. 86 N. Ada
Stone F. P. 754 Washington boul. *Ill.*
Stone F. W. 820 North Park av.
Stone George F. Evanston
Stone George N. Evanston. *C.A.*
Stone George W. 3933 Prairie av.
Stone Gertrude A. Miss, 200 The Plaza
Stone Grace L. Miss, 200 The Plaza
Stone G. W. 3411 Vernon av.
Stone Harold R. 7247 Jeffery av.
Stone Harry W. 3411 Vernon av.
Stone Henry B. Mrs. 45 Bellevue pl.
Stone Herbert S. Glencoe. *Chi., Univ.*
Stone Homer F. 2790 N. Lincoln
Stone Horatio O. 3522 Michigan av. *Cal., W.P.*
Stone H. G. 6019 Champlain av. *U.L.*
Stone H. O. Mrs. 2035 Prairie av.
Stone Irving I. 2781 N. Winchester av.
Stone James D. 5216 Jefferson av.
Stone James S. Rev. 128 Rush
Stone John R. 7141 Jeffery av.
Stone J. O. Mrs. Hotel Luzerne
Stone Leander Mrs. 3352 Indiana av.
Stone Lewis W. 4316 Michigan av.
Stone Lizzie T. Mrs. 175, 36th
Stone Lucy E. Mrs. 5627 Monroe av.

Stone Melville E. Glencoe. *Chi., U.L.*
Stone Melville E. jr. Glencoe
Stone M. M. Mrs. LaGrange
Stone Nathan, 3436 Vernon av.
Stone Oren B. 7141 Jeffery av.
Stone Percy F. 2 Plaisance ct.
Stone Ward Mrs. 5101 Kimbark av.
Stone Wellington B. 7650 Bond av.
Stone William, 5001 Washington av.
Stone William C. 1617 Sheridan rd.
Stone Willis C. Dr. 615 W. 56th pl.
Stonehill Carl A. 4800 Grand boul.
Stonehill Edward A. 4353 Vincennes av. *Stan.*
Stoneman George W. 820 W. Adams
Stookey Orren V. 4427½ Champlain av.
Storer John Dr. Oak Park
Storer Willis D. Dr. 485 Fullerton av.
Storey Charles W. 516 W. Jackson boul. Sum. res. Lake Geneva, Wis.
Storey J. B. Mrs. Hotel Metropole
Storke A. F. Dr. Oak Park
Storm C. H. 4902 Washington Park ct.
Storr Thomas J. Auditorium hotel
Storrs David W. 6732 Wentworth av. Sum. res. Lake Geneva, Wis.
Story Allan C. 4506 Prairie av.
Story A. G. Mrs. 2209 Prairie av.
Story C. G. 2209 Prairie av.
Story Edward H. Riverside
Story Frank F. 547 W. Monroe
Story Fred W. 4506 Prairie av.
Story H. Mrs. 6410 Monroe av.
Story Marion L. Mrs. 547 W. Monroe
Stouffer Anna L. Mrs. 5139 Madison av.
Stouffer C. Robert, Evanston
Stoughton O. W. 1826 Michigan av.
Stoughton Willis G. 609 Winthrop av.
Stout Benjamin F. Oak Park
Stout Melancthon Dr. 6107 Madison av.
Stover Frank C. Evanston
Stover Ira, 773 Warren av.
Stover Louis, Hotel Luzerne
Stow Jane R. Mrs. The Tudor
Stowell Corydon G. 459 Dayton
Stowell E. Mrs. 2633 Indiana av.
Stowell Ida M. Miss, 2633 Indiana av.
Stowell James H., M.D. 2633 Indiana av.
Stowell John D. 3351 Forest av.
Stowell Marion P. Miss, 2633 Indiana av.
Strackbein John W. Austin
Strader Jacob, 2428 Michigan av.
Strader Jacob E. 462 Bowen av.
Strahorn Harry C. 4168 Drexel boul.
Strahorn Robert, 4626 Greenwood av. *W.P.*
Straight Hiram J. Oak Park. *U.L.*
Straight J. A. Mrs. Hotel Luzerne
Straight Lewis C. 5805 Washington av.
Straith George, 3707 Sheridan rd.
Straiton Alexander M. LaGrange
Stransky Edward J. 4947 Washington Park ct. *Lksd.*
Strassheim Christopher, 98 Pine Grove av.
Strassheim Henry, 98 Pine Grove av.
Stratford Charles J. Austin

Stratford Henry K., M.D. Austin
Stratton Abram B. 4848 Evans av.
Stratton A. W. 5752 Madison av.
Stratton Charles J. 1708 Barry av.
Stratton Samuel W. 5717 Madison av.
Straub Solomon W. 6403 Monroe av.
Straus Aaron, 3434 Calumet av. *Stan.*
Straus Abraham S. 548, 44th
Straus B. F. 3914 Calumet av. *Lksd.*
Straus David, 942 W. Adams
Straus Eli M. 2509 Indiana av. *Stan.*
Straus Frederick W. Mrs. 3440 Michigan av.
Straus Irving J. Dr. 3638 Cottage Grove av. *Lksd.*
Straus Joseph, 2914 Prairie av.
Straus Joseph G. 3725 Forest av.
Straus Leo, 2955 Prairie av.
Straus Samuel J. T. 3440 Michigan av. *Stan.*
Straus Sarah L. Mrs. 3914 Calumet av.
Straus Simeon, 3943 Ellis av. *Lksd.*
Straus Simon, 2914 Prairie av.
Straus Simon W. 3223 South Park av. *Stan.*
Straus S. Mrs. 3725 Forest av.
Strauss Albert L. Lexington hotel. *Stan.*
Strauss Albert S. 3425 South Park av.
Strauss A. Mrs. 3337 Wabash av.
Strauss A. H. Lexington hotel
Strauss C. L. Mrs. Lexington hotel
Strauss Edward E. 483 Lasalle av.
Strauss Frank R. 4442 Berkeley av.
Strauss Gustave C. 4444 Vincennes av. *Lksd.*
Strauss Henry, 365, 42d. *Lksd.*
Strauss Henry X. 3337 Wabash av. *Stan.*
Strauss Jacob Mrs. 3425 South Park av.
Strauss Jacob N. 545, 44th. *Lksd., Stan.*
Strauss Jacob W. 850 Washington boul.
Strauss Julius, 2240 Calumet av. *Stan.*
Strauss Leon A. 4752 Prairie av.
Strauss Levi, 258 Division
Strauss Louis L. Lexington hotel. *Stan.*
Strauss Maurice, 4343 Vincennes av. *Lksd.*
Strauss Milton A. 3337 Wabash av. *Stan.*
Strauss M. Glen Ellyn
Strauss M. L. 3601 Vincennes av. *Stan.*
Strauss S egf ed W. 4549 Vincennes av. *Lksd* i ri
Strauss Sigmund L. 3153 Prairie av.
Strausser Frank, 3926 Lake av. *Lksd.*
Straut George Mrs. Lexington hotel
Strawbridge Albert N. 6431 Kimbark av.
Strawbridge C. H. 6431 Kimbark av.
Strawbridge Edgar J. 6431 Kimbark av.
Strawbridge L. C. Mrs. 6431 Kimbark av.
Strawbridge William, 4026 Grand boul.
Strawn Silas H. 267, 46th. *Irq., U.L.*
Street Albert J. 1664 W. Jackson boul.
Street Arthur Wray, 4756 Kenwood av.
Street Charles A. 133 Astor
Street Clara Mrs. 296 Ohio
Street Clement F. 3212 Vernon av.
Street C. A. LaGrange

Street Elizabeth Mrs. 734 W. Adams
Street Harry L. 133 Astor
Street Henry C. Highland Park
Street Ida Maria Miss, Lake Forest
Street J. H. Miss, Highland Park
Street Norman A. 133 Astor
Street Richard H. Highland Park
Street Richard J. Highland Park. *C.A.*
Street Richard P. Highland Park
Street R. R. 3928 Lake av. *Ill., Irq.*
Street Wade L. 296 Ohio
Street William D. C. 302 Schiller
Streeter Allen R. Chicago Athletic assn.
Streeter Edward Clark, 2646 Calumet av.
Streeter Herbert A. Evanston
Streeter Herbert C. Evanston
Streeter John W. Dr. 2646 Calumet av. *Cal.*
Streeter J. H. 2621 Calumet av. *C.A.*
Streeter Marjorie Miss, 2646 Calumet av.
Streeter Washington C. Chicago Athletic assn.
Strehl Benedict C. 397, 50th
Streich Albert F. 6056 Kimbark av.
Streich Fred O. 1149 Washington boul.
Streich Henry F. 3158 Beacon
Strelitz David I. 4355 Oakenwald av.
Strelitz S. Mrs. 4355 Oakenwald av.
Strelitz Victor B. 4355 Oakenwald av.
Strell George W. 339 Park av.
Strickler Harvey, Austin
Striger Charles W. 947 Warren av.
Stringfield C. Pruyn Dr. Grand Pacific hotel
Strobel Charles L. 570 Division. *Chi., C.A.,*
Strobhart J. A. Hotel Del Prado
Strohecker Samuel M. Dr. 234 S. Marshfield av.
Strohm Henry H. 4333 Greenwood av.
Stroker Herman W. 845 Warren av.
Strom Axel, Austin
Stromberg Charles J. 1528 Wolfram
Strong A. B. Dr. 533 W. Monroe
Strong Calvin A. Wilmette
Strong Carrie M. Miss, 373 Superior
Strong Charles R. 290, 48th
Strong D. O. 290, 48th
Strong Edward B. 313 Superior
Strong Eliza B. Mrs. Evanston
Strong E. G. Miss, 532 W. Monroe
Strong Frank L. 45 Loomis
Strong George A. 1585 W. Monroe. *Ill.*
Strong Harry J. 6218 Michigan av.
Strong Henry Gen. 27 Banks. *W.P.*
Strong Jane K. Mrs. 532 W. Monroe
Strong Joseph H. 2528 Indiana av. *Cal., Irq., U.L., W.P.*
Strong J. Edmund, 598 Division
Strong Mary M. Mrs. Mayfair
Strong Sydney Rev. Oak Park
Strong Ullman, Kenilworth
Strong William E. 373 Superior
Strong William W. 453 Washington boul.
Strong W. T. Hotel Del Prado
Strotz Charles N. 640 Cleveland av. *C.A.*

Sturges William N. 1716 Barry av.
Sum..res. Kenilworth
Sturgis Charles I. Kenilworth. *Univ.*
Sturgiss Mary C. Mrs. 1436 W. Monroe
Sturm Adolph, 13 Lane ct.
Stursberg Herman jr. 6516 Kimbark av.
Sturtevant Chester D. Oak Park
Sturtevant Edwin Mrs. 2950 Calumet av.
Sturtevant F. H. Mrs. Oak Park
Sturtevant George W. jr. 2510 Prairie av.
Sturtevant Henry D. 150 Lincoln Park
boul. *W.P.*
Stype Joseph, Ravinia
Stype Sebastian, Ravinia
Subert Bermann, 934 W. Adams
Subert Charles, 934 W. Adams
Subert Max, 934 W. Adams
Sudduth H. T. 67 Maple
Suder Henry, 1619 Grace
Sudler Carrol H. 4259 Grand boul.
Sugg Eugene, 1610 Diversey
Sugg George, 1610 Diversey
Sullivan Albert W. 4575 Lake av.
Sullivan Alexander, 378 Oak
Sullivan Arthur N. Oak Park
Sullivan Charles L. 93, 33d
Sullivan Cornelius, Riverside
Sullivan David, 680, 48th pl.
Sullivan Ella Miss, 1726 Diversey
Sullivan Florence E. 4053 Prairie av.
Sullivan Francis P. 539 Greenleaf av.
Sullivan James Mrs. 4024 Grand boul.
Sullivan James J. 868 Washington boul.
Sullivan Jerry, 3241 Prairie av. *C.A.*
Sullivan John E. Riverside
Sullivan Joseph H. The Tudor
Sullivan Joseph W. 27 Roslyn pl.
Sullivan Louis H. Hotel Windermere.
Chi., C.A., U.L.
Winter res. Ocean Springs, Miss.
Sullivan Michael, 163 Cass
Sullivan P. H. Mrs. 2725 Wabash av.
Sullivan Retta Miss, 3344 Calumet av.
Sullivan Roger C. 842 Walnut
Sullivan Thomas E. 3149 Prairie av. *C. A.*
Sullivan Thomas J. Dr. 4709 Michigan av.
Sum. res. Fox River
Sullivan Timothy, 4732 Prairie av.
Sullivan Timothy J. Austin
Sullivan William, 247 Osgood
Sullivan William J. 2725 Wabash av.
Sullivan Wm. K. 306 Warren av.
Sulzberger Sol. L. 4404 Michigan av.
Stan.
Sulzberger Sophia Mrs. 3424 South Park
av.
Sulzer Jane N. Mrs. 2288 N. Paulina
Sumerfield C. Mrs. 3348 Vernon av.
Summerfield John, 2411 South Park av.
Summers Charles H. Mrs. 661 Fullerton
av.
Summers Leland L. 661 Fullerton av.
Summy Clayton F. 25 Lane ct.
Sumner E. C. Mrs. 4049 Lake av.
Sumner George, 4059 Prairie av.
Sumner Henry A. 486, 44th pl.

Sumner Richard B. Mrs. 3811 Grand boul.
Sumney John Dr. 517 W. 62d
Sunderland George Mrs. 3732 Forest av.
Sunny B. E. 138 Astor. *Chi., U. L.*
Supplee Frank Mrs. 95 Oakwood av.
Surghnor V. H. 83, 20th. *Cal., C. A.*
Sutcliffe John, 1352 Sheridan rd.
Sutherland D. W. Tracy
Sutherland H. G. Mrs. 2023 Indiana av.
Sutherland John E. 6040 Ellis av.
Sutherland Stephen M. 500 Englewood av.
Sutherland Thomas J. 59 Bryant av.
Sutherland William J. 3544 Grand boul. *C. A.*
Sutphen George C. Oak Park
Sutter Adolph, 3601 Lake av.
Sutter Clarence B. 3603 Lake av.
Sutter Edward A. 185, 51st
Sutter Edwin A. 3601 Lake av. *C.A.*
Sutter Jacob, 3603 Lake av.
Sutter L. L. 3601 Lake av.
Sutter Raymond C. 3603 Lake av.
Sutter Victor U. Oakwood hotel
Sutter Walter C. 3603 Lake av.
Sutton Frederic W. 3840 Ellis av.
Sutton Isaac T. 7301 Bond av.
Sutton Samuel, 2835 N. Hermitage av.
Sutton Thomas, 234 S. Leavitt
Sutton William H. 4812 Forrestville av. *Stan.*
Sutton William W. Wilmette
Suydam John D. Oak Park
Swabacker Isa, 3306 Calumet av. *Stan.*
Swaby William A. Chicago Beach hotel
Swadkins Alfred Mrs. 1849 Melrose
Swafford Joseph W. 923 W. Monroe
Swain Edgar D., M.D. 105, 45th
Swain Oliver D. Dr. Glencoe
Swan Charles F. Dr. 7251 Jeffery av,
Swan Clare Miss, Austin
Swan C. Joseph Dr. 4559 Woodlawn av.
Swan James H. Mrs. 4740 Kimbark av.
Swan Olivia Shailer Mrs. 1819 Michigan av.
Swan Oscar, Glen Ellyn
Swan S. N. 3415 Calumet av.
Swank C. W., M. D. 1760 Arlington pl.
Swannell Frederick O. 311 Belden av.
Swannell William, 551 Dearborn av.
Swanson Andrew A. Evanston
Swanson L. F. 1070 Francis
Swanson S. A. 1936 Arlington pl. *G. A.*
Swanzey H. Alfred, 508 Englewood av.
Swart M. E. 3306 Indiana av.
Swartchild Samuel, 282 Ohio
Swartout Charles R. Wilmette
Swarts Harry L. 464, 44th
Swartwout Geo. A. Oak Park
Swartwout Leslie G. Oak Park
Swartz Josiah, 377 S. Hoyne av.
Swartz L. Dr. 230 Warren av.
Swartz Thomas Benton, M.D. 146, 36th
Swatek Matthew J. 606 Dearborn av.
Swazey Arthur Mrs. 4324 Ellis av.
Swazey Louise Miss, 260 Ashland boul.
Swearingen Francis M. The Tudor
Swearingen W. H. 6448 Greenwood av.

Sweeney Alexander, 824 W. Garfield boul.
Sweeney Alexander J. Austin
Sweeney James J. 824 W. Garfield boul.
Sweeney John W. 824 W. Garfield boul.
Sweet Ada C. Miss, 1408 Sheridan rd.
Sweet Albert A. Dr. 762 Greenleaf av.
Sweet Albert L. 241 Ashland boul.
          Sum. res. Lake Geneva, Wis
Sweet Benjamin Jeffrey, 1408 Sheridan rd.
Sweet Charles Albert, 241 Ashland boul.
Sweet Charles S. Oak Park
Sweet Dexter B. 4200 Oakenwald av.
Sweet Ellen Miss, 3726 Ellis av.
Sweet E. C. Dr. 613 W. Monroe
Sweet E. D. L. Oak Park
Sweet Hiram, 930 Pratt av.
Sweet John A. 381 Warren av.
Sweet John A. jr. 381 Warren av.
Sweet John W. Evanston. *U.L.*
Sweet Julia J. Miss, 3726 Ellis av.
Sweet Leonard Mrs. 321 Belden av.
Sweet Samuel H. Mrs. 4537 Ellis av.
          Sum. res. Delavan, Wis.
Sweetland Dale W. Highland Park
Sweetland John T. 6243 Woodland av.
Sweetland Warren M. Dr. Highland Park
Sweetman William G. Wilmette
Sweetser Clara R. Mrs. 2644 Magnolia av.
Sweger A. Mrs. 2425 Wabash av.
Swenie J. J. 667 Fulton
Swenson A. Mrs. 975 Warren av.
Swenson Magnus, 4531 Greenwood av. *C.A.*
Sweringen William W. 438 W. 64th
Swett Frank W. 23 S. Hamilton av.
Swett Frederick C. 2 Madison Park
Swett Mary Chase Miss, 4744 Madison av.
Swett Wm. O. 4744 Madison av.
Swezey Otto H. Prof. Evanston
Swift Albert L. 4839 St. Lawrence av.
Swift Albert O. 538 Greenleaf av.
Swift Asa R. 6757 Wentworth av.
Swift Asa R. jr. 6757 Wentworth av.
Swift Brown F. Dr. 52 Loomis
Swift Charles H. 4824 Forrestville av.
Swift Edward F. 4949 Greenwood av. *C.A., W.P.*
Swift Edward S. 529 W. 60th pl.
Swift Frank R. 108 Dekalb
Swift Frederick, 30 Walton pl.
Swift Frederick, Union Club
Swift George B. 52 Loomis. *Chi., Ill., U.L.*
          Sum. res. Fox Lake, Ill.
Swift George L. 52 Loomis
Swift Gustavus F. 4900 Ellis av.
Swift Harry A. 3716 Langley av.
Swift Herbert B. 52 Loomis
Swift Lemuel J. 4820 Prairie av.
Swift L. F. Lake Forest. *C. A., W.P.*
Swift L. F. Lakota hotel. *U.L.*
Swift Mary Mrs. 538 Greenleaf av
Swift M. Lewis, 4458 Ellis av. *U. L.*
Swift N. W. Mrs. 3827 Vincennes av.
Swift Otis P. 3716 Langley av.
Swift Palemus H. Rev. 6410 Stewart av.
Swift Rodney B. 4937 Madison av.

Talcott William M. 1754 Wrightwood av.
Tallert Jacob, 4403 Indiana av. *Lksd.*
Tallmadge Harriet Mrs. 4731 Ellis av.
Tallmadge John H. 500 Fulton
Tallmadge Lewis C. Greenwood Inn, Evanston
Tallmadge T. E. Greenwood Inn, Evanston
Tallman J. B. Irving Park
Tallman L. C. Hinsdale
Talmage Frank DeWitt Rev. 551½ W. Jackson boul.
Tamblyn Jane I. Mrs. 4136 Michigan av.
Tanner C. J. 2500 Prairie av.
Tanner Ely J., M.D. Irving Park
Tanner Ethel Miss, 5551 Monroe av.
Tansey Elmer E. Dr. 263, 79th
Tapper George E. Riverside. *Ill.*
Tarbell Frank B. Prof. 5730 Woodlawn av.
Tarbell Paul, 229, 42d
Tarbet Wm. L. 6450 Woodlawn av.
Tarnow Charles, Riverside
Tarrant Robert, 72 Park av.
Tascott James B. 132 Ashland boul.
Tash John D. 438, 66th
Tate J. Emery, 3821 Vernon av.
Tatge Gustavus J. 750 Englewood av.
Tatge John, 516 Ashland boul.
Tatge Sophia Mrs. 752 Englewood av.
Tatham Robert L. 689 Washington boul. *Ill.*
Taussig William, 4337 Forrestville av. *Lksd.*
Taylor Abner, Auditorium annex. *C.A.*
Taylor Albert H. Wilmette
Taylor Alfred, 4228 Grand boul.
Taylor Amory E. 5235 Kimbark av.
Taylor Arthur A. 346 Oakwood boul. *C.A.*
Taylor Calvin C. 35, 53d
Taylor Calvin F. 710 Washington boul.
Taylor Channing, Oak Park
Taylor Charles A. Mrs. 272 Warren av.
Taylor Charles S. Dr. 5226 Washington av.
Taylor Charles W. 733 W. 61st pl.
Taylor Clinton R 5207 Hibbard av.
Taylor Cora E. Dr. 6356 Stewart av.
Taylor Cortland C. Wilmette
Taylor Edmund H. 1606 Kenmore av.
Taylor Edward H. 2954 Calumet av.
Taylor Edward S. Evanston
Taylor Ella Miss, 4228 Grand boul.
Taylor Ethan, LaGrange
Taylor E. C. 6117 Monroe av.
Taylor E. Wiley, 147 Ashland boul. *Ill.*
Taylor Francis W. 610 Division
Taylor Frank C. 493 W. Jackson boul. *Ill.*
Taylor Fred O. 4000 Ellis av.
Taylor Frederick M. 2449 N. Paulina
Taylor George, Evanston
Taylor George D. 4821 St. Lawrence av.
Taylor George H. 254 Ashland boul. *C.A., Ill., W.P.*
    Sum. res. Lake Geneva, Wis.
Taylor George H. 2921 Groveland av.
Taylor George H. Calumet club. *W.P.*

Taylor George O. Dr. 4206 Drexel boul.
Taylor Gerry H. Evanston
Taylor Hall Mrs. 5250 Prairie av.
Taylor Harry N. 221 Schiller. *C.A.*
Taylor Hart, 1039 Evanston av.
Taylor Henry, Kenilworth
Taylor Henry A. Oak Park. *C.A.*
Taylor Homer S. Kenilworth
Taylor Horace P. 5622 Madison av.
Taylor Howard S. 6356 Stewart av.
Taylor H. N. 499 N. State. *C.A.*
Taylor James, North Shore hotel
Taylor James E. 2954 Calumet av.
Taylor James M. 1222 Morse av.
Taylor James M. 5229 Jefferson av.
Taylor John, 339 W. 60th pl.
Taylor John S. 493 W. Jackson boul.
Taylor John W. Oak Park
Taylor . Howard, 4001 Drexel boul.
Taylor J. Mitchell Dr. 4001 Drexel boul.
  | Sum. res. Paw Paw Lake, Mich.
Taylor J. S. Mrs. Riverside
Taylor J. V. Greenwood Inn, Evanston
Taylor Louis D. Oak Park
Taylor Louis S. 558 Division
Taylor Louis S. Riverside
Taylor Louise M. Mrs. Lake Forest
Taylor L. B. Mrs. 5250 Prairie av.
Taylor L. L. 1066 Warren av.
Taylor Mary A. Mrs. 2916 Indiana av.
Taylor Mary C. Mrs. 339 Bowen av.
Taylor Mary E. Miss, Lake Forest
Taylor M. J. Mrs. 4000 Ellis av.
Taylor Peter, Evanston
Taylor Robert J. 24 Waverley ct.
Taylor Rodney L. Mrs. 344 S. Paulina
Taylor Samuel, 2 Campbell Park
Taylor Samuel C. Dr. 346 Oakwood boul.
Taylor Samuel G. 610 Division
Taylor Samuel G. jr. 610 Division
Taylor Thomas jr. 32 Astor. *C.A.*, *Univ.*,
  W.P.
Taylor Tracy J. 272 Warren av.
Taylor William A. 879 Warren av. *Irq.*
Taylor William J. Kenilworth
Taylor William N. 2218 Kenmore av.
  C.A.
Teagle E. W. Austin
Teal Henry S. 1886 Diversey
Teall Edward M. 522 W. Adams. *Ill.*
Teare John, M.D. 1246 N. Clark
Teefy Armand F. 386 N. Clark
Teegarden Frank W. 4841 Michigan av.
Teel George W. 228, 42d pl.
Teele Horace G. Austin
Teeple Frank W. Chicago Athletic assn.
Tegtmeyer William O. 1833 Belmont av.
Teller James H. 4315 Berkeley av.
Teller J. Grant, 6850 Union av.
Tempel Frank, 696 N. Wells
Tempel John, 499 N. Clark
Temple Arthur, 491 Fullerton av.
Temple Christian, 511 Lasalle av.
Temple John F. Mrs. 2943 Calumet av.
Temple Morris D. 639 Washington boul.
Temple Thomas S. 3705 Ellis av.

Templeton Herbert, Oak Park
  Sum. res. South Haven, Mich.
Templeton James E. 921 Evanston av.
Templeton James Stuart, 921 Evanston av,
Templeton Mary Miss, 326 Ashland boul.
Templeton Thomas, 326 Ashland boul.
  Chi., U.L.
TenBroeke Charles O. Morgan Park
TenBroeke Jane Mrs. 5630 Kimbark av.
Ten Eyck Tenodor Maj. 5704 Madison av.
Tennant Robert G. 1126 Winthrop av.
Tennant William G. 1126 Winthrop av.
Tenney Charles Mrs. 1245 Wrightwood av.
Tenney Frank S. 814 The Plaza
Tenney Horace K. 4827 Kenwood av. *U.L.*
Tenney John G. 1245 Wrightwood av.
Tenney J. Frank, 3402 Forest av.
Tenney L. S. Dr. Chicago Beach hotel
Tenney Stella Mrs. 4406 Sidney av.
Terhune B. Fred. 5142 Wabash av.
Terras John D. Evanston
Terrill A. S. 2444 N. Hermitage av.
Terry Albert C. 4217 Grand boul.
Terry Benjamin S. Prof. 5535 Monroe av.
Terry Charles Stone Dr. 3159 Malden
  Sum. res. Rose Hill, Kan.
Terry E. A. Mrs. 3131 Indiana av.
Terry George S. 5540 Monroe av.
Terry Milton S. Prof. Evanston
Test Frederick C. Dr. 4401 Indiana av.
Teter George H. Oak Park
Tewes Henry, 1719 Waveland av.
Tewkesbury Lydia Mrs. Hotel Metropole
Tewkesbury Wm. J. Hotel Metropole
Tewksbury George W. Auditorium hotel.
  W.P.
Thacher Chester I. Dr. LaGrange
Thacher William W. 245 Oakwood boul.
Thackaberry Milton L. 4224 Grand boul.
Thacker Albert H. 4109 Drexel boul.
Thacker C. Edward, 4111 Drexel boul.
Thacker Jennes R. 4111 Drexel boul.
Thacker John F. 164, 36th
Thacker J. Robert, 4111 Drexel boul.
Thackray Henry, 3852 Ellis av.
Thain J. A. 3152 Prairie av.
Thain Richard S. Oak Park
Tharp E. H. 4343 Lake av.
Thatcher David A. River Forest
Thatcher David W. River Forest
Thatcher Frederic S. River Forest
Thatcher George L. River Forest
Thatcher Luella Barnes Mrs. 546 W. Jack-
  son boul.
Thatcher Oliver J. Prof. Univ. of Chicago,
  Univ.
Thatcher Ralph H. 3803 Langley av.
Thatcher Solomon, Mrs. River Forest
Thayer A. Judson, Evanston
Thayer Carl H. Hinsdale
Thayer Charles H. Dr. 3302 Indiana av.
Thayer Charles L. 4326 Greenwood av.
  C.A.
Thayer Clarence H. 4555 Lake av.
Thayer Electa L. Mrs. 10 Groveland Park
Thayer George H. Norwood Park

Thayer Gilbert Mrs. Morgan Park
Thayer Harry W. Morgan Park
Thayer Henry J. 3830 Lake av.
Thayer Herbert, Hinsdale
Thayer H. A. Edison Park
Thayer H. E. Mrs. Morgan Park
Thayer H. R. Hinsdale
Thayer Myrtle W. Mrs. 41 Aldine sq.
Thayer Nathaniel C. 5813 Indiana av.
Thayer Selden, 6511 Parnell av.
Thayer S. G. Mrs. 4555 Lake av.
Thayer William, Hinsdale
Thayer Williard H. 285 W. Adams
Thearle Ernest A. 6947 Stewart av.
Thearle Fred G. jr. 457 Englewood av.
Thearle Fred G. Mrs. 601 W. 62d
Thearle Harry B. 6613 Harvard av.
     Sum. res. Lake Geneva, Wis.
Theobald J. Harry, 3411 Forest av. *Lksd.*
Theurer C. Mrs. North Shore hotel
Theurer Joseph, 67 Lake View av. *C.A.,*
     W.P.
Thexton Richard E. Dr. 6565 Yale ·
Thiele Ernest J. 6501 Kimbark av.
Thielens Edward H. 6711 Stewart av.
Thies Wilhelm Dr. 195 Fremont
Thin Robert, 4513 Woodlawn av.
Thoman LeRoy D. Evanston. *Irg.,U.L.*
Thomas Abraham L. Dr. 4424 Indiana av.
Thomas Addison C. 140, 47th
Thomas Albert R. 4212 Oakenwald av.
Thomas Alfred A. 2479 Kenmore av.
Thomas Ambrose L. 60 Woodland Park.
     C.A.
Thomas Arthur E., M.D. 3200 Indiana av.
Thomas Benjamin, 4942 Ellis av. *Chi.,*
     U.L.
Thomas Benjamin W. 1842 Indiana av.
Thomas C. G. 434, 45th
Thomas Edward C. 946 W. Monroe
Thomas Edward S. 4204 Ellis av.
Thomas Frank H. 62 Woodland Park.
     C.A.
Thomas Frank W. 408 Park av. *C.A.*
Thomas Fred, Evanston
Thomas Fréderic M. 2020 Indiana av.
     C.A. Sum. res. Lake Beulah, Wis.
Thomas F. A. 381 Superior
Thomas George, Chicago Beach hotel
Thomas George A. 9, 47th pl. *C.A.*
Thomas George H. 61 Warren av.
Thomas George O. Evanston
Thomas George W. 4039 Lake av.
Thomas George W. Irving Park
Thomas GranvilleS. Dr. 2934 LakePark av.
Thomas Harriet E. Miss, 4625 Lake av.
Thomas Herbert A. Evanston. *U.L.*
Thomas Hiram W. Rev. 535 W. Monroe
Thomas Homer M. Dr. 535 W. Monroe
     Ill.   Sum. res. Kirkland, Wis,
Thomas Horatio, Irving Park
Thomas Jessie Mrs. Lombard
Thomas John G. 7608 Union av.
Thomas John M. Evanston
Thomas John W. 4535 Indiana av. *Ill.*
Thomas Judson B. 6915 Yale
44

Thomas J. A. 4526 Prairie av.
Thomas J. C. 3981 Drexel boul.
Thomas J. H. Evanston
Thomas Leonidas, Irving Park
Thomas Levi H., M.D. 3824 Ridge av.
Thomas L. A. 2358 Indiana av.
Thomas Mary W. Dr. 2934 Lake Park av.
Thomas Melville J. 140, 47th
Thomas Milton, Riverside
Thomas Morris St. P. 135 Lincoln Park
     · boul. *Univ.*
Thomas M. Bross Prof. Lake Forest
Thomas M. P. Mrs. Austin
Thomas Ralph B. 2824 Prairie av.
Thomas Samuel B. Lexington hotel
Thomas Theodore, 43 Bellevue pl. *Chi.*
     Sum. res. Sunset, Fairhaven, Mass.
Thomas Wesley M. Dr. 109 Evanston av
Thomas William H. 59, 34th pl. ·
Thomas William K. 61 Warren av.
Thomas William S. 4204 Ellis av.
Thomason Frank D. 539 W. 60th
Thomason M. C. Mrs. 103 Park av.
Thomasson Leonard, 427 N. State
Thomasson Nelson, 427 N. State. *U.L.*
Thome Arthur G. Dr. 133 Lincoln av.
Thome A. M. Rev. Jefferson Park
Thome Hattie S. Miss, 133 Lincoln av.
Thometz M. F. 4407 Greenwood av.
Thompson Adam, 354 Erie
Thompson Anna C. Mrs. 42 Evergreen
     av.
Thompson Arthur J. Evanston
Thompson A. E. H. 2358 Indiana av.
Thompson Benjamin F. C. 285 Dearborn
     av.
Thompson Charles B. 4815 Langley av.
Thompson Charles F. 4305 Ellis av.
Thompson Charles F. jr. 3350 South Park
     av.
Thompson Charles H. 1058 Chase av.
Thompson Charles N. Dr. 3017 Michigan
     av.
Thompson Charles S. 1601 Prairie av.
Thompson David D. Evanston
Thompson Dot Mrs. 376 Washington
     boul.
Thompson D. S. Mrs. 6522 Lafayette av.
Thompson Edward. W. 948 W. Jackson
     boul.
Thompson E. F. 523 Belden av.
Thompson E. L. 348 Ashland boul.
     Sum. res. Mackinac Island
Thompson Frank D. River Forest
Thompson Fred S. 6522 Lafayette av.
Thompson Gale, Hotel Metropole.. *C.A.,*
     W.P.
Thompson George, 6800 Lowe av.
Thompson George L. 6629 Wentworth av.
Thompson George R. 2809 N. Hermitage
     av.
Thompson Glenn D. 455, 63d
Thompson Harry G. 5248 Calumet av.
Thompson Harry S. 541 Lunt av.
Thompson Harvey L. 1242 Washington
     boul. *Ill.*

Thompson Henry G. 5100 Hibbard av.
Thompson Hiram J. 290 Belden av.
Thompson Hiram Parshall, 1188 Washington boul.
Thompson H. S. LaGrange
Thompson James W. Prof. 5717 Washington av.
Thompson Jay J. Dr. 681 Fullerton av.
Thompson John, Austin
Thompson John A. 214 Wilson av.
Thompson John F. 3733 Vincennes av.
Thompson John H. Mrs. 285 Dearborn av.
Thompson John W. Evanston
Thompson Leverett, 10 Astor. *Chi.*, *Univ.*
Thompson Mark M. Dr. 805 W. Monroe
Thompson Merritt W. Dr. 685 N. Robey
Thompson Milford J. Hyde Park hotel
Thompson M. L. Mrs. Evanston
Thompson N. S. Mrs. Evanston .
Thompson Ogle R. 6752 Lowe av.
Thompson Payson, 285 Dearborn av.
Thompson Percival, Hotel Metropole. *C.A.*, *Univ.*, *W.P.*
Thompson Richard S. Col. 5406 East End av. *U.L.*
Thompson Robert S. 232, 47th
Thompson R. D. LaGrange
Thompson Samuel, 6346 Harvard av.
Thompson Samuel D. 1930 Deming pl.
Thompson Slason, 328 Superior. *Univ.*
Thompson Susan Miss, 10 Astor
Thompson S. C. LaGrange
Thompson Thomas C. 2729 N. Robey
Thompson Watts C. 285 Dearborn av.
Thompson William, 62 Throop
Thompson William, 2720 N. Lincoln
Thompson William A. 4815 Langley av.
Thompson William A. Riverside
Thompson William Hale, Hotel Metropole. *C.A.*, *W.P.*
Thompson William Hale Mrs. Hotel Metropole
Thompson William Henry, 2930 Indiana av. *C.A.*
Thompson William H. Oak Park
Thompson William H. 667 N. Hoyne av.
Thompson William H. jr. 4457 Emerald av.
Thompson William M. Dr. 8 St. James pl.
Thompson William W. Austin
Thompson W. N. 2300 South Park av.
Thoms Harriet Miss, Evanston
Thomsen Peter F. Jefferson Park
Thomson Alexander M. 4017 Lake av.
Thomson Henry C. M. 5533 East End av. *C.A.*
Thomson James, 1718 Belmont av.
Thomson John, 569, 45th pl.
Thomson Laura Miss, 982 W. Adams
Thomson Robert B. Morgan Park
Thomson William H. 387 Oak
Thorburn Robert, 50 Bellevue pl.
Thorbus Will C. 3953 Michigan av.
Thorkildsen Thomas, 2884 N. Paulina. *C.A.*

Thorn Francis, Highland Park. *U.L.*
Thornburgh Wm. N. 4460 Oakenwald av.
Thorndyke J. Edward, Austin
Thorne A. P. Berwyn
Thorne Charles H. 4544 Greenwood av. *C.A.*
Thorne Charles S. Winnetka
Thorne George Arthur, Evanston. *C.A.*, *W.P.*
Thorne George R. 90, 47th. *C.A.*, *U.L.*, *W.P.*
Thorne Henry, 5830 Indiana av.
Thorne Jacob Mrs. 4217 Vincennes av.
Thorne James Ward, 90, 47th. *C.A.*
Thorne Robert J. 90, 47th. *W.P.*
Thorne Stephen, 164 Warren av.
         Sum. res. Winnetka
Thorne Wm. C. 164, 47th. *C.A.*, *W.P.*
Thorne Willis E. 5217 Kimbark av.
Thornton Charles S. 7600 Stewart av. *Irq.*, *Univ.*
Thornton D. Mrs. Lexington hotel
Thornton Edward C. LaGrange
Thornton Edward L. 1674 Kenmore av.
Thornton Eva Miss, 1674 Kenmore av.
Thornton Everett A. 1674 Kenmore av.
Thornton Harry S. 3662 Wabash av.
Thornton H. W. 2488 Kenmore av.
Thornton Robert L. 628 Cleveland av.
Thornton Solon, 7600 Stewart av.
Thornton W. P. Park Ridge
Thorp David L. Evanston
Thorp Frank H. LaGrange
Thorp Harry W. 1065 Warren av.
Thorp Ole A. 59 Columbia. *Ill.*
Thorpe Frank L. 401 Belden av.
Thorpe Samuel Mrs. 1011 N. Halsted
Thorsen James B. 1046 Winthrop av. *C.A.*
Thorson Soren D. 619 N. Hoyne av.
Thorwart Henry, 578 N. Clark
Thrall Sam E. 4620 Woodlawn av. *C.A.*
Thrall W. A. 4620 Woodlawn av. *C.A.*
Thresher David, 524 Washington boul.
Thresher. William E. 524 Washington boul. *Ill.*
Thul Ada M. Mrs. 2573 Lakewood av.
Thumser A. Miss, 1605 W. Adams
Thumser E. Miss, 1605 W. Adams
Thurber C. B. Mrs. 23 Bellevue pl.
Thurber C. H. Rev. Morgan Park. *Univ.*
Thurber Elias C. 528 Washington boul.
Thurber George S. 415 N. State. *C.A.*
Thurber Seymour J. 4306 Calumet av.
Thurber Wm. E. Austin
Thurber W. Scott, 3161 Groveland av.
Thurston C. E. Revere house
Thurston Emeline C. Mrs. 4434 Grand boul.
Thurston Eunice Mrs. 1737 Kenmore av.
Thurston E. H., M.D. 3018 Indiana av.
Thurston Frank W. 4434 Grand boul. *C.A.* *Ill.*
Thurston Hollis M. 329 Ashland boul. *Ill.*
Thurston Marion Miss, 4412 Indiana av.
Thurston N. B. Mrs. 4412 Indiana av.
Thurston Stephen R. Lombard

Thwaite George P. 6940 Kimbark av.
Thyng Laura A. Miss, 2968 Lake Park av.
Tibbetts H. M. 588 Division
Tibbetts W. T. Mrs. Chicago Beach hotel
Tibbils M. A. Mrs. Evanston
Tibbits Frank H. The Arizona
Tibbitts Henry S. 915 S. Sawyer av.
Tice James W. 3555 Ellis av.
Tichenor A. L. Mrs. 5109 Kimbark av.
Tichenor Myron H. 6636 Perry av.
Tichenor William A. Dr. 492 W. Adams. *Ill.*
Tidholm August, 7056 Perry av.
Tidmarsh James D. 7721 Emerald av.
Tiedemann Jacob H. 307 N. State
Tiernan John, Evanston
Tiernan Michael, Evanston
Tietgens Ernest, Evanston
Tietgens Paul, Evanston, *C.A.*
Tiffany Henry S. 3742 Ellis av.
Tiffany H. C. Mrs. 3742 Ellis av.
Tifft Henry, 492 Dearborn av.
Tilden B. E. 3100 Groveland av.
Tilden B. F. 6134 Kimbark av.
Tilden Edward, 4612 Emerald av. *C.A.*
Tilden J. B. Mrs. 4548 Drexel boul.
Tilden William A. 4835 Madison av.
Tilden W. D. Chicago Beach hotel
Tilghman William, Evanston
Tilghman William J. Evanston
Tillinghast Clark, Evanston
Tillinghast Crawford, 2028 Indiana av. *Cal.*
Tillinghast E. R. Berwyn
Tillinghast Henry C. Evanston
Tillmann Mathias J. 1314 N. Clark
Tillotson E. W. 200 Oakwood boul.
Tillotson Frank, Tremont house
Tilt Arthur C. 543 Evanston av.
Tilt David, 1551 Fulton
Tilt Joseph E. 543 Evanston av. *C.A.*
Tilton C. P. Miss, 300 Schiller
Tilton J. Neal. LaGrange. *Univ.*
Tilton L. J. Mrs. 300 Schiller
Timberlake Charles E. 553 W. 65th
Timberlake Margaret Mrs. LaGrange
Timberlake Thomas M. LaGrange
Timberlake William M. 553 W. 65th
Timerman George, Evanston
Timewell Arthur T. 3142 Lake Park av.
Timewell Arthur W. 3142 Lake Park av.
Timmerman Bernard, Julien hotel
Timms Frank M. 605 W. 65th
Tindall John W. 652 Walnut
Tingle H. E. 5017 Wabash av.
Tinkham Charles A. 638 Fullerton av.
Tinsley John H. 7420 Monroe av.
Tinsley John W. 7420 Monroe av.
Tinsman Homer E. 6626 Yale
Tinthoff Fred S. 349 Chicago av. *C.A.*
Tinthoff Sylvester M. 349 Chicago av.
Tinus Willard I. Prof. 3000 Indiana av.
Tisdale Laura J. Mrs. 5427 Washington av.
Tisdel Clark J. Evanston

Titcomb Arthur B. 638 Fullerton av.
Titcomb E. P. Mrs. 4128 Ellis av.
Titcomb S. B. Mrs. 638 Fullerton av.
Titcomb William C. 1750 Wrightwood av. *C.A.*
Titman George B. 4532 Woodlawn av.
Titman Jesse, 4532 Woodlawn av.
Titus Elizabeth G. Mrs. 1238 N. Clark
Titus George J. 527 W. Jackson boul.
Titus G. P. 4627 Lake av.
Titus Joseph F. 4211 Ellis av.
Titus Mary A. Mrs. 711 Farwell av.
Titus S. M. Miss, 4211 Ellis av.
Titus Virgil E. Oak Park. *Ill.*
Titus William H. 811 Farwell av.
Tobey C. Harry, 4837 Kenwood av.
Tobey C. H. M. 4831 Kenwood av.
Tobey Edgar H. Evanston
Tobey E. M. Miss, 4839 Kenwood av.
Tobey Frank B. 448 W. Adams. *Ill., U.L.*
Tobey Frank D. 2450 Indiana av.
Tobey Frank H. 4831 Kenwood av.
Tobey Henry S. 4037 Indiana av.
Tobey H. V. Mrs. 2632 Magnolia av.
Tobey John D. 3234 Lake Park av.
Tobias Arthur W. Longwood
Tobias Clayton H. 128, 50th
Tobias George J. Dr. 850 W. Monroe
Tobias John J. 128, 50th
Tobin Arthur C. 4721 Kimbark av.
Tobin Charles P. 4721 Kimbark av.
Tobin Robert P. 4721 Kimbark av.
Tobin Samuel C. 4721 Kimbark av.
Toby Thomas, 3614 Ellis av.
Tod Walter, Lombard
Todd Charles Dr. 3305 Cottage Grove av.
Todd Charles C. Oak Park
Todd Harry, 2447 Prairie av.
Todd Henry C. Oak Park
Todd James, 692, 48th
Todd James A. LaGrange. *C.A.*
Todd James F. Dr. 2447 Prairie av.
Todd J. Jackson, Chicago Beach hotel. *Univ.*
Todd Laura Miss, 3819 Ellis av.
Todd Libanus M. 1436 Osgood
Todd Walter W. 3819 Ellis av.
Todd William P. 4446 Woodlawn av.
Toles William A. Austin
Tollakson Annie Mrs. 128 Evergreen av.
Tolman Albert H. Prof. 5750 Woodlawn av.
Tolman Cyrus F. Rev. 41, 34th pl.
Tolman D. H. 538 Dearborn av.
Tolman Edgar B. 5832 Washington av. *Irq.* Sum. res. Turin, N. Y.
Tolman Elwood H. 5403 Madison av. Sum. res. Rockland, Me.
Tolman H. L. Evanston
Tolman John A. 4727 Ellis av.
Tolman Judson A. 4638 Prairie av.
Tolman Judson Allen jr. 4638 Prairie av.
Tolman Samuel A. 2031 Prairie av.
Tomaso Salvatore, 3267 Beacon
Tomblin Sarah M. Mrs. 491 W. Jackson boul.

Tomhagen John A. Dr. 1644 Wrightwood av.
Tomlins Wm. L. Evanston
Tomlinson Clinton S. Hotel Del Prado
Tomlinson C. L. North Shore hotel
Tomlinson Edward Dr. 404, 43d
Tomlinson Everett·S. Oak Park
Tomlinson Joseph S. 2920 Indiana av.
Tomlinson William M. Dr. Wilmette
Tompkins James Rev. Oak Park
Tompkins Mary W. Mrs. Oak Park
Tompkins S. L. 301, 53d
Tompkins William C. Oak Park
Tompson George T. 6518 Ross av.
Tonk Max, 592 Fullerton av.
Tonnas H. A. Mrs. 40 Buena terrace
Tonnesen Beatrice Miss, 1254 Michigan av.
Toogood Ernest, Evanston
Tooker Robert N., M.D. 263 Dearborn av.
    Sum. res. Newburyport, Mass.
Tooker Robert N. jr. 263 Dearborn av.
Toolen Andrew J. 4434 Lake av.
Toolen Fred C. 4434 Lake av.
Tope George B. Dr. Glen Ellyn
Tope John W. Dr. Oak Park
Topliff Samuel, Evanston
Topliff William B. Evanston
Toppan James S. Hotel Del Prado
    Sum. res. Newburyport, Mass.
Toppan William R. 5234 Prairie av.
Topping A. M. Mrs. 4453 Berkeley av.
Topping Helen M. Miss, 4453 Berkeley av.
Torbet L. K. new Hotel Holland
Torrens L. A. 354 Lasalle av.
Torrey Clarence A. 5833 Monroe av.
Torrey Reuben A. Rev. 39 E. Pearson
    Sum. res. Claremont, E. Northfield, Mass.
Tosetti E. The Winamac
Tosetti Otto L. The Winamac. C.A.
Tostiven Clarence W. Winnetka
Totten Harry, Winnetka
Totten Harry B. Glencoe
Totten Susan Mrs. Winnetka
Touhy Patrick L. 5008 N. Clark
Touhy Stephen R. 5008 N. Clark
Tourtellotte Frederick J. 3432 Vernon av
Tourtellotte F. W. Mrs. 3432 Vernon av.
Tousey C. A. 5329 Washington av. C.A.
Tousey George H. Chicago Beach hotel
Toussaint A. Mrs. 2951 Groveland av.
Tower Anne W. Mrs. Evanston
Tower Arthur, Evanston
Tower J. B. La Grange.
Towers Albert B. 51 Stratford pl. C.A.
Towers Josiah M. 6949 Princeton av.
Towle Eliza J. Mrs. Evanston
Towle Helen M. Miss, Oak Park
Towle Henry S. Oak Park. U.L.
Towle John R. 6244 Kimbark av.
Town Nelson H. 4433 Sidney av.
Towne Arthur F. Evanston
Towne Carrie L. Mrs. Lombard
Towne Charles E. Evanston

Towne Henry, 528 W. Monroe
Towne Julia R. Mrs. Evanston
Towne Margaret Miss, Lombard
Towner Daniel B. 2444 Kenmore av.
Towner Henry A. Highland Park
Towner Henry A. jr. Highland Park
Townsend A. F. Evanston
Townsend Cornelia Miss, 2340 Calumet av.
Townsend E. B. Miss, The Arizona
Townsend George, 2340 Calumet av.
Townsend G. H. Dr. Highland Park
Townsend Jame J. 538 W. Jackson boul. C.A., W.P.s
Townsend M. A. Miss, 538 W. Jackson boul.
Townsend Perry S. Hinsdale
Townsend S. M. Miss, 538 W. Jackson boul.
Townsend William R. Oak Park
Townsley Lloyd D. 6017 Monroe av.
Townson Margaret Miss, 5524 Monroe av.
Towslee Edwin C. 225 Dearborn av.
Toynton F. E. Hotel Woodruff. C.A.
Tracy Edward, River Forest
Tracy Edward C. Kenilworth
Tracy Evert E Dr. 82 Maple
Tracy Frank D. 923 Walnut
Tracy F. K. 545 W. Jackson boul.
Tracy Howard, Evanston
Tracy H. D. 2391 Lakewood av.
Tracy Joseph P. 311 Eastwood av. U.L.
Tracy Luther M. 6726 Wentworth av.
Tracy L. R. Mrs. Evanston
Tracy William Warren, 140 Astor. Chi., C.A., Un., Univ.
Traer Glennwood W. 4367 Oakenwald av. Chi.
Traff Nicholas, Evanston.
Trail R. H. Austin
Trainer J. Milton, 4523 Forrestville av.
Trainer M. A. Miss, 6137 Monroe av.
Trask B. E. Capt. Highland Park
Trask F. M. Dr. LaGrange
Tratman E. E. Russell, 854 W. Monroe
Traub Adolph, 1174 Perry.
Traver C. S. Mrs. 353 S. Oakley av.
Traver Frederick C. 1692 W. Monroe
Travis Clarence C. Evanston
Travis E. J. Hotel Metropole. W.P.
Travis R. P. Riverside
Trayner Charles J. 4426 Grand boul.
Trayner John, 4426 Grand boul.
Trayner Nettie G. Miss, 4426 Grand boul.
Trayner Owen R. 4426 Grand boul.
Treat Blanche E. Miss, Lake Forest
Treat Robert, Hinsdale
Treat Samuel A. Hotel Windermere. U.L. Sum. res. Greenville, Me.
Trebilcock Albert, 525 W. 67th
Tredwell John, 6639 Parnell av.
Tree Lambert, 94 Cass. Chi., Irq.,
Trego Charles H. 4346 Berkeley av.
Trego Charles T. 3935 Lake av. U.L., W.P.
Trego William T. 3935 Lake av.

Treichlinger Charles, 4503 Indiana av *Lksd.*
Trelease John, 2433 N. Paulina
Treleaven Jane Mrs. Austin
Treleaven William T. Austin
Tremaine J. Eugene Dr. 5318 Jefferson av.
Tremaine Matthew O.4841 Forrestville av.
Tremaine Myron J. 5318 Jefferson av.
Trench Daniel G. 877 Jackson boul.
Trench Richard R. 455, 47th
Trenton Joseph R. 6927 Parnell av.
Trevett Harriet E. Miss, 475 W. Monroe
Tribou N. M. 1634 Melrose
Trienens Joseph, 305 S. Oakley av.
Triggs Charles W. 913 S. Spaulding av.
Triggs John H. 913 S. Spaulding av.
Triggs Oscar L. Univ. of Chicago. *Univ.*
Trimingham Anna E. Miss, 5517 Madison av.
Trimingham Ralph N. Oak Park
Trimmer John R. 578 W. Adams
Trine John G. Dr. 3621 Ellis Park
Tripp Annie E. Mrs. 596 Dearborn av.
Tripp Arnold, 1940 Arlington pl.
Tripp Arnold jr. 596 Dearborn av.
Tripp C. E. Auditorium hotel. *U.L.*
Tripp Dwight K. 77 Warren av.   •
Tripp Edward A. 596 Dearborn av.
Tripp F. A. 2705 N. Paulina. *C.A.*
Tripp George A. 5022 Greenwood av.
Trippe Martha G. W. Mrs. Lakota hotel
Trissal Frank M. 4744 Evans av.
Tristram James E. Oak Park
Tritschler C. F 4427 Prairie av.
Tritt B. E. 3220 Vernon av.
Troeger J. W. La Grange
Troendle Lena E. Miss, Evanston ·
Troendle Victor H. Evanston
Troop J. G. C. 358, 57th
Troost William, 417 Dearborn av.
Trorlicht S. K. Mrs. 493 Belden av.
Trout Edgar W. 1025 Warren av.
Trout Elizabeth H. Dr. 1025 Warren av.
Trout F. L. 171 Oakwood boul.
Trout George W. 1564 Fulton
Trowbridge James R. 578 Division
Trowbridge J. H. Mrs. 578 Division
Trowbridge William R. Kenilworth
Troxell B. F. 193 Oakwood boul.
Troxell Thomas G. Capt. Highland Park
Troy Ernest G. 882 W. Monroe
Troy Harry L. 882 W. Monroe
Troy Louis L. 882 W. Monroe
Troyer Louise Mrs. 621 Lasalle av.
Truax Charles, 2654 N. Paulina. *U. L.*
Truax Edith Miss, 2654 N. Paulina
Truax J. Mrs. 2654 N. Paulina
Truax Ruth Miss, 2654 N. Paulina
Trude Alfred Percy, 4960 Drexel boul.
Trude Algenia Miss, 4960 Drexel boul.
Trude A. S. 4960 Drexel boul. *C.A.*
        Sum. res. Arangee, Idaho
Trude Cecelia Miss, 4960 Drexel boul.
Trude Charlotte Mrs. 4313 Langley av.
Trude Daniel P. 4960 Drexel boul.

Trude Frederick H. 5106 Hibbard av.
        Sum. res. Manitou Island, Mich.
Trude George A. 4960 Drexel boul.
Trude Mark W. Dr. 4313 Langley av.
True Albert W. 320 S. Marshfield av.
True Charles J. 320 S. Marshfield av.
True Ella W. Mrs. 323 W. 61st
True John R. 15 Pine Grove av.
True M. A. 711 W. Adams
True M. Elizabeth Miss, 320 S. Marshfield av.
True William H. 334, 44th
Truesdale W. H. Virginia hotel. *Un.,*
        Univ.   Sum. res. Lake Forest
Truman J. H. Mrs. 27 St. James pl.
Truman Orville M. 4619 Woodlawn av.
Trumbull Bernard H. 1601 Prairie av.
Trumbull George Mrs. 4016 Lake av.
Trumbull Herman J. 6557 Kimbark av.
Trumbull Julia M. Miss, 2659 Kenmore av.
Trumbull J. H. 4026 Lake av. *C.A., U.L.*
Trumbull Perry, 2659 Kenmore av. *Chi.*
Trumbull Rollin H. 2699 N. Robey
Trunkey Addison J. Mrs. 3834 Lake av.
Trussell H. M. Berwyn
Tryon LeRoy C. Irving Park
Tryon Mary Mrs. 1065 Warren av.
Tubbs Frank W. 4605 Emerald av.
Tubbs Frederick H. 308 The Plaza ·
Tubman Margaret Mrs. Evanston
Tucker Edmund C. 6817 Perry av.
Tucker Fred W. 3517 Ellis av.
Tucker Frederick J. 1808 Arlington pl.
Tucker Horace, 3517 Ellis av.
Tucker H. S. Dr. 464, 42d
Tucker James D. Evanston
Tucker James I. Dr. 52, 35th
Tucker Jessie M. Mrs. 39 Bryant av.
Tucker John, Oak Park
Tucker Joseph F. Auditorium hotel
Tucker J. C. 3755 Lake av.
Tucker J. L. Oak Park
Tucker Lee V. 921 S. Sawyer av.
Tucker Luther K. 688 W. Monroe
        Sum. res. Paw Paw Lake, Mich. ·
Tucker Stephen, 6746 Lowe av.
Tucker William R. 757 W. Adams
Tucker W. S. S. 757 W. Adams
Tufts E. L. 3800 Forest av. *Chi., W.P.*
Tugwell Richard J. 593 Walnut
Tuley M. F. Judge, 5135 Washington av.
        Irq.   Sum. res. Pine Lake, Wis.
Tullar Grant Colfax, Tracy
Tuller Rollin B. Dr. 793 W. Monroe
        Sum. res. Twin Lakes, Wis. ·
Tullock James, Chicago Beach hotel
Tully A. Melville Dr. 32 Walton pl. *Un.*
Tully Eleanor M. Mrs. 21, 35th
Tuohy J. W. Mrs. 46 Loomis
Turbin Louis M. Dr. 6049 Madison av.
Turck Fenton B. Dr. 362 Dearborn av.
Turck J. Byron, 2691 Magnolia av.
Turck Raymond Custer Dr. 4812 Woodlawn av.
Tureman Wm. M. 286, 37th

Turk Joseph, 473 Ashland boul.
Turnbull A. T. 322 S. Hermitage av.
Turnbull Frank J. 1886 Diversey
Turnbull Geo. Lauder, · 234 S. Oakley av.
Turnbull G. A. 234 S. Oakley av.
Turnbull John T. Evanston
Turnbull Percy G. 234 S. Oakley av.
Turner A. A. 4330 Oakenwald av. C.A.
Turner Charles, 4952 Vincennes av.
Turner Charles C. Austin
Turner Charles W. 4509 Prairie av.
Turner Edward A. 227, 47th. U.L.
Turner Edward L. 3809 Prairie av.
Turner Edward S. Evanston
Turner Francis C. 401 N. State
Turner Frank A. 4399 N. Ashland av.
Turner Frank D. 1780 Wrightwood av.
Turner Harry M. Winamac flats
Turner Henry, 418 Belden av.
Turner Henry L. Col. 46 Cedar
Turner James W. La Grange
Turner John C. Evanston
Turner John W. 3761 Vernon av.
Turner J. D. Edison Park
Turner J. Lyle, 3601 Ellis Park
Turner J. S. 3000 Lake Park av.
Turner Lauren H. 4915 Washington av.
Turner Leighton Mrs. Evanston
Turner Lloyd C. 3000 Lake Park av.
Turner L. Hamilton, 4915 Washington av.
Turner P. A. 3255 Wabash av.
Turner Spencer E. 5812 Michigan av.
Turner Thomas M. 3601 Ellis Park
Turner Thomas M. jr. 3601 Ellis Park
Turner T. G. 6 Ritchie ct.
Turner V. C. 112 Lake Shore drive.
Turner Walter I. Evanston
Turner William B. 2777 N. Lincoln
Turner William H. Palmer house. U.L.
Turner William H. River Forest
Turner William M. Evanston
Turner Willis Hall, 6 Ritchie ct.
Turney John E. Oak Park
Turney Leander Rev. Berwyn
Turney Robert, 1785 Magnolia av.
Turney Robert E. 1785 Magnolia av.
Turnley Parmenas T. Col. Highland Park
Turrill John F. 24 Madison Park. C.A.
Turrill L. B. Mrs. 24 Madison Park
Tuteur Edwin B., M.D. 3553 Prairie av. Lksd.
Tuteur I. Mrs. 3553 Prairie av.
Tuthill A. H. Mrs. 4433 Greenwood av.
Tuthill Fannie Mrs. 54, 3d
Tuthill Richard S. Judge, 532 W. Jackson boul. Ill.
Tuttle C. P. Mrs. 463 S. Irving av.
Tuttle D. H. S. 5201 Drexel av.
Tuttle Emerson B. Chicago club. Univ.
Tuttle Frank W. Evanston
Tuttle Frederick B. 2022 Michigan av. Cal., Chi., C.A.
Tuttle Henry B. 1223 W. Ravenswood Park.

Tuttle Henry N. Lake Forest. Chi., Univ.
Tuttle J. B. 152, 36th
Tuttle L. M. Mrs. North Shore hotel
Tuttle W. Fay, 5330 Jefferson av.
Tuttle W. H. Berwyn
Tuttle W. P. Chicago Athletic assn. Ill.
Tweedie Herbert J. 431 Pratt av.
Twichell James O. 3565 Grand boul. C.A.
Twick William, 945 Warner av.
Twitty Walter G. 4406 Lake av. C.A.
Twohig James W. 55 N. Ada
Twyman Joseph, 5759 Madison av.
Tyler Albert S. 5131 Jefferson av.
Tyler Frederick C. 4537 Greenwood av
Tyler Harvey A. Dr. 604 Dearborn av.
Tyler Orson K. 4201 Ellis av.
Tyler Theodore R. 361 Superior
Tyler William H. 908 W. Monroe
Tyng Dudley A. 77 Lincoln Park boul. C.A., W.P.
Tyrrell Albert H. 656 W. Monroe
Tyrrell Charles T. 585 Washington boul.
Tyrrell Frederick S. 585 Washington boul.
	Sum. res. Lake Geneva, Wis.
Tyrrell John, 3328 Indiana av.
Tyrrell John, Evanston
Tyrrell John A. Mrs. 585 Washington boul.
Tyrrell Patrick, Evanston
Tyson Howard N. Wilmette
Tyson Russell, 205 Goethe. Univ.
Tyson William H. H. 293 Oak
Tyson W. Stevenson, 293 Oak

UDELL SPENCER R. 5210 Hibbard av. W.P.
Uebele Berthold E. 51, 29th pl.
Ufer Emil, 6552 Ellis av.
Uhl Milton R. 847 Chase av.
Uhlemann Hugo P. 369 Burling
Uhlemann Louis H. 369 Burling
Uhlemann Richard G. 369 Burling
Uhlmann Fred, 4859 Forrestville av. Stan.
Uhrig Joseph, 6560 Yale
Uhrlaub Adolph, 244 Hampden ct.
Uhlein Edward G. 34 Ewing pl.
Ullery Frank B. Dr. 3207 Indiana av.
Ullery Joseph E. 4649 Forrestville av.
Ullman A. I. Elmhurst
Ullman Gustave S. 2712 Indiana av. Stan.
Ullman Louis, Hotel Metropole, Stan.
Ullman Nathan J. 3332 Vernon av. Stan.
Ullman Percy G. 4504 Ellis av. Stan.
Ullmann R. H. Mrs. Oak Park
Ullmann Daniel, 2962 Prairie av.
Ullmann Frederic, 282, 48th. C.A., U.L.
Ullmann Herbert J. Oak Park. C.A.
Ullrich Albert H. Evanston
Ullrich Michael, 587 Lasalle av. Chi., C.A., Un.
Ulm John W. Lakota hotel
Ulrich A. Louis, 47 Roslyn pl.
Ulrich Bartow A. 47 Roslyn pl.
Ulrich Bartow A. jr. 47 Roslyn pl.
Ulrich Bernard, 240 Roscoe boul.

Ulrich Gertrude U. Miss, 47 Roslyn pl.
Ulrich Raymond C. Dr. 202 Center
Ulrich Victoria U. Miss. 47 Roslyn pl.
Umbdenstock Michael, 1356 Sheridan rd.
Underhill Elizabeth Mrs. 5316 Greenwood av.
Underwood Arthur W. Evanston
Underwood B. W. Mrs. 3004 Prairie av.
Underwood Caroline N. Mrs. 969 W. Monroe
Underwood George W.2973South Park av.
Underwood Grant, Hotel Luzerne.
Underwood Harry M. 415 S.Marshfield av.
Underwood Henry G. 415 S.Marshfield av.
Underwood J. Platt, 4016 Lake av. C.A., U.L.
Underwood Pierce, Oak Park
Underwood P. L. Mrs. 2934 Indiana av.
Underwood Sidney F. 5327 Cornell av.
Underwood Sidney L. 5327 Cornell av.
Underwood William H. 4416 St. Lawrence av.
Underwood William T. 2911 Prairie av.
    U.L.   Sum. res. Fox Lake, Wis.
Unger M. 431 Warren av.
Unna L. J. 4144 Grand boul.
Unold George D. LaGrange
Unold lohn, LaGrange
Unrath Charles F. 797 W. Monroe
Unzicker Herman, 1745 Arlington pl.
Unzicker Meno, Hotel Luzerne
Unzicker Otto, Luzerne hotel, C.A.
Updike Charles M. 4401 Indiana av.
Updike F. D. Oak Park
Updike George W. La Grange
Updike H. E. 4216 Prairie av.
Updike M. 12024 Stewart av.
Updike P. B. 4216 Prairie av.
Updike William M. 4401 Indiana av.
Upham Abel Putnam, 3218 Groveland av.
Upham Ebenezer P. 442 Belden av.
Upham Frederic W. 8 Ritchie ct. C.A., U.L.
Upham F. D. 442 Belden av. •
Upham John F. 269 Lincoln av.
Upham William A. 3218 Groveland av.
Uphof Adolph H. 5139 Michigan av.
    Winter res. Santa Rosa Park, Fla.
Upman Frank, 5654 Monroe av. C.A.
Upman Frank, Victoria hotel
Upson Irwin F. Dr. 387 N. State
Upton Cassius M. LaGrange
Upton Edward L. Waukegan
Upton George A. 346 Sunnyside av.
Upton George P. 2427 South Park av. U.L.
Upton L. C. Mrs. 4130 Ellis av.
Urann Mary Miss. Evanston
Urion Alfred R. 106, 40th
Urquhart William J. 4031 Prairie av.
Utley Edward F. Mrs. 53, 53d
Utley Henry B. 1231 Washington boul. Ill.
Utley Hiram S. Austin
Utley Louise Miss, 519 Belden av.
Utley W. P. Oak Park

Utt Frank M. 729 Fullerton av.
Utz A. L. 266, 66th pl. C.A.

VAIL CHARLES A. 2439 N. Hermitage av.
Vail Elizabeth Miss, 674 Lasalle av.
Vail Ellen P. Mrs. 2129 Calumet av.
Vail Francis, 813 The Plaza
Vail Henry S. Highland Park. C.A.
Vail I. H. Morgan Park
Vail Morrison H. 2403 N. Paulina
Valentine Alistair I. 5139 Washington av. Chi., W.P.
Valentine Catherine Mrs. 3745 Lake av.
Valentine Edward H. 449 N. State. Ill.; U.L.
Valentine E. Archibald, 449 N. State
Valentine George, 401 N. State
Valentine Gordon, 4342 Ellis av.
Valentine John, 175 Goethe
Valentine J. R. Mrs. Chicago Beach hotel
Valentine Kimball E. The Renfost
Valentine P. Louis L. 3745 Lake av.
Valentine P. Anderson, Chicago Beach hotel. Chi., W.P.
Valentine Theodore, 5754 Monroe av.
Valentine William G. 3745 Lake av.
Vallens Eugene, 3617 Ellis av. Lksd.
Vallette Clair D. Oak Park
VanAlen Benjamin T. 1599 Kenmore av.
Van Alen Walter T. 1599 Kenmore av.
VanAllen Martin, 2629 N. Winchester av.
Van·Alstine M. A. Mrs. Evanston
VanAnda Carmi A. Rev. 7601 Eggleston av.
VanAndén Charles A. 4821 St. Lawrence av.
Van Antwerp Daniel F. 1099 Winona av.
Van Arsdale D. Mrs. 225, 42d pl.
Van Arsdale John R. Evanston
Van Arsdale J. R. Mrs. Evanston
VánArsdale Martin V.-B. Mrs. 518W.67th
VanArsdale Robert L. 4421 Berkeley av.
VanArsdale William T. Evanston
VanBaalen Israel, 3341 Vernon av.
VanBenschoten Charles W. Evanston
VanBenschoten Samuel, Evanston
VanBergen F. S. Mrs. Oak Park
VanBergen W. Fred, Oak Park
VanBuren Augustus, 413 Washington boul.
VanBuren Barent Col. 768 Warren av.
VanBuren Edgar R. 380 Dayton
VanBuren Henry Mrs. 1364 Washington boul.
Vance George B. 2478 N. Paulina
Vance Thomas H. Lombard
Vance William L. Evanston
VanCourt Benjamin P. 1631 Aldine av.
VanDalson Edward, 3534 Rhodes av.
VanDenbergh H. T. 97, 37th
Vandenburgh Mary Mrs. 728 W. Adams
Vandenburgh William E. 728 W. Adams
Vanderburgh Abraham C. 16, 37th
Vandercook Charles R. Austin
Vandercook Emma Mrs. Evanston

Vandercook Henry R. 4045 Ellis av.
Vandercook John D. Austin
Vandercook Robert O. Evanston
Vanderkloot A. Lake Bluff. *Ill., U.L.*
Vanderlip Frank A. 5331 Madison av.
Vanderploeg Flora Miss, 6837 Perry av.
Vanderploeg H. 6837 Perry av.
Vanderpoel John H. Longwood
VanDerlice J. Warren Dr. 968 Park av.
Vanderwood William E. 1018 Fargo av.
Vanderwicken Edwin P. Ashland club
VanDeursen Charles S. 612 W. 62d
VanDeusen Arthur S. Evanston
Van de Venter W. E. 5622 Michigan av.
Van de Water A. H. 455 W. Vanburen
Van de Werker William N. 1039 Sherwin av.
VanDoozer J. P. Evanston
VanDoozer B. R., M.D. 4318 Prairie av.
VanDorn A. Morton Park.
VanDuyn A. C. Dr. The Renfost
Vanduyn Emma Mrs. Ravinia
VanEps F. S. Rev. 6138 Lexington av.
VanEps George A. Mrs. Evanston
VanEvera DeWitt, 2636 N. Hermitage av.
VanEvery Joseph J. Evanston
VanHagen George E. 4206 Vernon av.
VanHagen Isaac, 3630 Vernon av.
VanHamm Francis R. 4306 Forrestville av. *C.A.*
VanHise Isadore Mrs. 322, 60th
VanHook Weller Dr. 4043 Grand boul.
VanHorneJefferson Mrs. 2326 Indiana av.
VanHoosen Bertha Dr. 489, 42d
VanHousen B. T. 477 W. Adams
VanHousen Herbert M. 1838 Arlington pl.
VanIngen J. Wm. Rev. 1917 Indiana av.
VanInwagen Fred, Hinsdale
VanInwagen James, 150 Warren av. *Chi.* Sum. res. Lake Geneva, Wis.
VanInwagen James jr. 150 Warren av.
VanInwegen Clarence P. 5316 Madison av.
VanKeuren Charles W. Oak Park
VanKeuren Edward, Oak Park
VanKeuren Mary J. Mrs. 586 Division
Van Keuren W. J. Oak Park
VanKirk Charles B. 4754 Greenwood av. *C.A., U.L.*
VanKirk Sarah A. Mrs. 4754 Greenwood av.
VanKirk Stephen, 329 Bowen av.
VanLiew Frederick Mrs. Hinsdale
VanLiew Lewis C. Hinsdale
Van Matre Willard N. 259 Fremont
VanNess Carrie Mrs. Irving Park
VanNess Frank C. Wilmette.
VanNess Lester T. Irving Park
VanNorman G. B. 4439 Prairie av.
VanNostrand John J. 4737 Champlain av.
VanO'Linda J. A. Mrs. 4545 Greenwood av.
VanOstrand Archibald E. Irving Park
VanPatten Andrew L. Dr. 408 Bowen av.
Van Pelt I. N. The Arizona
VanPelt Ryan T. Dr. Lexington hotel

VanRensselaer M. M. Mrs. 917 Evanston av.
VanRiper Louis O. Highland Park
VanSands Robert, 839 W. Congress
VanSands Robert jr. Dr. 839 W. Congress
VanSant J. R. Hotel Windermere
VanSchaack Cornelius P. 3235 South Park av.
VanSchaack Peter, 37, 22d
VanSchaack Robert H. Kenilworth
VanSchaick A. G. Mrs. Highland Park
VanSchaick H. Highland Park
VanSickel Charles, 271 S. Irving av.
VanSicklen N. H. 5138 Cornell av. *C.A.*
VanThompson Orville, 2358 Indiana av.
VanTuyl Edward A., M.D. Riverside
VanTuyl Harry I. Dr. 3131 Indiana av.
VanTuyl J. E. Mrs. 3131 Indiana av.
VanTuyl Margaret Miss, Riverside
VanUxem James L. 4965 Lake av.
VanValkenburg John L. Dr. 4201 Drexel boul.
VanValkenburgh John W. 750 W. Monroe
VanVliet Leonard S. Oak Park
VanVlissingen A. 10858 Michigan av.
VanVlissingen James H. Evanston. *C.A., U.L.*
VanVoorhis Charles E. Evanston
VanVoorhis Frank Mrs. 3222 Rhodes av.
VanVranken Peter J. 3549 Prairie av.
VanWinkle John W. Dr. 534 Burling
VanWoert G. E. 4465 Ellis av. *U.L.*
VanWycke R. M. Clitton house
VanZandt George W. 938 W. Monroe
VanZandt G. Dr. 369 Washington boul.
VanZandt Ossian C. 938 W. Monroe
Vanzwoll G. M. 43 S. Seeley av. *Ill.*
Vanzwoll Henry B. 273 Warren av.
Vanzwoll Maie W. Mrs. 273 Warren av.
Varian Alfred R. 637 Fullerton av.
Varney George W. 4849 Langley av.
Varney G. C. 41, 53d Sum. res. Maywood
Varnum Clarke, 6556 Greenwood av.
Varty Albert Mrs. 378 Chicago av.
Varty Joseph A. 1606 W. Adams
Vary Mary C. Mrs. 631 Washington boul.
Vasey Robert W. 4260 N. Ashland av.
Vaughan Alexander, 678 Wash'ton boul.
Vaughan Arthur J. 4139 Langley av. Sum. res. Lodie, Wis.
Vaughan Elmer E. Dr. 321 Belden av.
Vaughan J. C. 6048 Jefferson av.
Vaughan Roger, 6048 Jefferson av.
Vaughan Sanford S. 678 Washington boul.
Vaughn Thomas F. 4352 Greenwood av.
Vaux Frederick T. 200 Goethe. *U.L.*
Vawter William A. 2247 Kenmore av. *C.A.*
Vear William, Washington Heights
Veatch Byron E. 6031 Lexington av. *C.A.*
Vedder Ross S. 4646 Vincennes av.
Veeder Albert H. 4842 Vincennes av. *C.A.*

Veeder Albert H. jr. 4910 Washington Park ct..
Veeder Coles V. Kenilworth
Veeder Henry, 4841 Vincennes av. *C.A.*
Vehmeyer C. H. 6414 Harvard av.
Vehmeyer Frederick C. 6500 Lafayette av.
Vehmeyer Henry F. 4552 Forrestville av.
Vehon Joseph, 3638 Grand boul.
Vehon Louis, 3824 Vernon av.
Vehon Morris, 3638 Grand boul. *Lksd.*
Vehon William H. 848 W. Monroe
Veirs Bazel W. 179 Park av.
Veitch Wilberforce, 1842 Indiana av *C.A., Irq.*
Vennell H. W. Dr. 40, 35th
Vennema John, 2446 Michigan av.
Venni Ermete, 143 Oakwood boul.
Vent Charles F. 89, 44th
Vent Fred G. 89, 44th
Vent Raymond T. 6435 Monroe av. *C.A.*
Vent Thomas G. 89, 44th
Verdier T. T. Tracy
Verhalen Joseph H. 39 Lincoln pl.
Verity William P. Dr. 450 Garfield av.
Vermaas P. M. 1497 Washington boul.
Vernaud Annette Mrs. 2516 Indiana av.
Vermeren Cyrille J. E. Dr. 314 N. State
Vermilion W. F. Mrs. 4400 Greenwood av.
Vermilyea A. R. 4556 Lake av. *C.A.*
Vernon David, 833 W. Monroe
Vernon Harvey C. 1200 W. Adams
Vernon John M. 340 S. Paulina. *Ill.*
Vernon LeRoy Tudor, 4569 Lake av.
Vernon William W. 219 Hampden ct.
VerNooy Charles B. 6220 Kimbark av.
Vette Amelia Miss, 460 N. State
Vette John F. 1518 W. Monroe
Vial George M. LaGrange
Vial Joseph, LaGrange
Vial Samuel, LaGrange
Vickers Charles, 6043 Madison av.
Vickers Frank, 6043 Madison av.
Vickers John A. D. 4821 Madison av.
Vickery Mabel S. Miss, 428 N. State
Victor H. Peter, 1639 Belmont av.
Vidvard John P. 3844 Prairie av.
Vidvard Walter, 3844 Prairie av.
Vierbuchen William C. The Renfost
Vierling Clara J. Miss, 3760 Indiana av.
Vierling Louis, 3760 Indiana av. *C.A., U.L.*
Vierling Robert, 3760 Indiana av. *U.L.*
Viets John B. 143 Oakwood boul.
Vigeant Gregory, 16 Astor
Vigneron E. Dr. 6523 Kimbark av.
Viguers William, N. Evanston
Vilas Albert H. Oak Park
Vilas Charles H. Dr. Calumet club. *Chi.*
Vilas Dana S. 2927 Groveland av.
Vilas Henry C. Riverside
Vilas Royal Cooper, Evanston. *Chi.*
Vilas R. C. jr. Evanston
Viles James Jr. 2932 Indiana av. *Chi., C.A.*

Vilim Joseph Prof. Riverside
Vincent A. Mrs. 3269 Groveland av.
Vincent George E. 5743 Lexington av.
Vincent Hamilton E. Oak Park
Vincent Harry, 380 Erie
Vincent J. Russell, 4336 Ellis av.
Vincent William Alexander Judge, 4 Ritchie ct. *Chi.*
    Sum. res. Harbor Point, Mich.
Vinnedge Allen R. Evanston
Vinnedge Mahlon A. 446 Dearborn av.
Vinnedge Samuel J. Evanston
Virden Frederick B. 344 W. 59th pl.
Voak L. D. 1886 Diversey
Vocke Henry, 1731 Arlington pl.
Vocke Wm. 520 Lasalle av. *U.L., Univ.*
Vogel Frank E. 3423 Michigan av. *Stan., W.P.*
Vogell William H. 168 Oakwood boul.
Vogelsang John Z. Garfield av.
Vognild Erik L. 632 N. Robey
Vogt Mary Mrs. 6442 Greenwood av.
Voightman F. 2717 Magnolia av.
Voigt Alice Miss, 4736 Grand boul.
Voigts Henry, Evanston
Vokoun John W. 547 W. Monroe
Volger Frederick, 385 Mohawk
Volk Louise E. Miss, 5825 Kimbark av.
Vollintine A. Hale, 1690 Buckingham pl.
Vollmer A. F. Mrs. 52, 24th
Vollmer Herman, 685 Fullerton av.
Von Albade Francis T. 4725 Prairie av.
Von Biedenfeld Curt E. W. 2012 Indiana av.
VonDoeming Hugo, Park Ridge
VonGlahn August, 719 Fullerton av. *C.A.*
VonGlahn William, Wilmette
VonHermann E. 203, 30th
VonHofsten Hugo O.. 5545 Woodlawn av.
VonKlenze Camillo, Univ. of Chicago
VonLengerke Oswald, 1116 Montana
VonPlaten Maurice, Oak Park
VonWeisenfluh Frederick, 438, 41st
Voorhees John W. 47 Campbell Park. *C.A.*
Voorhees Martha Mrs. Norwood Park
Vopicka Charles J. 507 S. Winchester av. *Ill., Irq.*
Vorbeck Herman, 3177 Dover
Vories Harry F. 4533 Greenwood av. *C.A.*
Vosburgh Aylward H. 237 S. Leavitt
Vosburgh Cyrus A. 237 S. Leavitt
Vosburgh William R. Oak Park
Vose Frederick P. Evanston
Vose William M. R. Evanston
Voss Frederick C. 2341 N. Hermitage av.
Votaw Clyde W. Prof. 437, 61st
Voute Henry C. 2993 Kenmore av.
Vowell Stewart B. Evanston
Vroom P. D. Col. Hotel Windermere
Vrooman Frank Buffington Rev. 23 Scott
Vrooman Walter K. 371 Superior
Vynne H. R. Mrs. 3249 Groveland av.

WAACK H. C. Dr. 4403 Indiana av.
Wachenheimer H. 3654½ Prairie av.
Wachsmuth F. H. 7 Groveland-Park. *C.A.*
Wachsmuth H. F. 7 Groveland Park
Wachsmuth L. C. 7 Groveland Park. *Cal., C.A., U.L., W.P.*
Wachtmeister Carl A. University Club
Wacker Charles H. Virginia hotel. *C.A., Irq., U.L.*
Waddell E. S. Mrs. Evanston
Waddill George C. Major, 65 Lake Shore drive
Wade Carrie Miss, Elmhurst
Wade Charles, Elmhurst
Wade C. A. Dr. 709 W. Jackson boul.
Wade Henry J. Austin
Wade James J. 5234 Michigan av.
Wade John. 107, 37th
Wade John Mrs. 3736 Langley av.
Wade Melvin L. 169 Oakwood boul.
Wade Ralph V. 345 Rush
Wade Thomas P. 5234 Michigan av.
Wadhams Frederick E. Dr. 3329 Indiana av. *C.A.*
Wadhams John A. Irving Park
Wadington John, Hinsdale
Wadsworth Frank R. Oak Park
Wadsworth George F. 7231 Yale
Wadsworth James R. 6317 Lexington av.
Wadsworth S. F. Mrs. Oak Park
Wadsworth Tertius W. 407 Erie
Wagar Duane H. 6549 Perry av.
Wagar M. H. 6549 Perry av.
Wagg Howard N. 1161 N. Clark
Waggener Albert H. 6404 Parnell av.
Waggener Robert G. 40 Buena terrace
Wagner Carl Dr. 74 Lincoln av.
Wagner Charles P. 7523 Stewart av.
Wagner David C. Tracy
Wagner D. S. 4939 Lake av.
Wagner Edmund, 5851 Wabash av.
Wagner Edwin L. Berwyn
Wagner Elmer E. 341 Rush
Wagner Ernest J. 4335 Oakenwald av.
Wagner E. W. Chicago Athletic assn.
Wagner Frank E. 1606 W. Adams
Wagner Frederick J. 7456 Bond av. *C.A.*
Wagner F. M. Glen Ellyn
Wagner George, 6211 Woodlawn av. *C.A*
Wagner G. M. H. Glen Ellyn
Wagner Henry W. 1463 Edgecomb ct.
Wagner Jo n H. Elmhurst
Wagner Lena P. Mrs. 3534 Wabash av.
Wagner Louis C. 6357 Jackson av.
Wagner William L. Calumet club. *C.A., U.L.*
Wagner William R. Oak Park
Wagoner John J. 4458 Berkeley av.
Wagoner Stanley, 4458 Berkeley av.
Wahl Robert, 1030 Winthrop av.
Waid Louise Mrs. 307 Ashland boul.
Waidner Fred A. 300 Chicago av.
Wain Albert, 737 W. Adams
Wain John, 737 W. Adams
Wainwright Robert P. P. Capt. Fort Sheridan

Wainwright Thomas, 4528 Prairie av.
Wais A. S. Dr. 531 Garfield av.
Wait Helen M. Miss, 124 Ashland boul.
Wait Henry H. 4919 Madison av.
Wait Horatio L. 4919 Madison av.
Wait James J. 221, 48th. *U.L.*
Wait James M. 222 S. Irving av.
Wait Wayland W. 124 Ashland boul.
Wait Wilber, 4552 Ellis av.
Wait William L. 2711 N. Lincoln
Waite Horace F. Mrs. 7 Astor
Waite Horace G. 13 Astor. *Univ.*
Waite Lucy Dr. 98 Loomis
Waite M. W. Mrs. Evanston
Waite William W. Hinsdale
Waixel B. Mrs. 3947 Prairie av.
Waixel Henry, 4323 Berkeley av.
Waixel Ike H. 4323 Berkeley av.
Waixel Moses, 3639 Michigan av.
Waixel M. Sol. 3639 Michigan av. *Stan.*
Waixel Sol H. 4323 Berkeley av.
Wakefield J. G. Austin
Wakefield Nathan R. 830 W. Monroe
Wakefield William E. 511 Leland av.
Wakem J. Wallace, Highland Park. *Un.*
Walbank E. J. Mrs. 6019 Monroe av.
Walbank Kenneth S. 5538 Monroe av. *C.A.*
Walbridge H. B. 7127 Yale
Walbridge W. H. Mrs. LaGrange
Walbridge W. P. LaGrange
Walburn Albert W. The Kenwood. *C.A.*
Walcott Aaron F. 812 Warren av.
Walcott Chester P. Evanston
Walden Hugh P. 7316 Bond av.
Waldo George E. 239 Dearborn av.
Waldo John B. 227 Ontario
Waldo Otis H. 4437 Sidney av. *Univ.*
Waldo O. H. Mrs. 4624 Greenwood av.
Waldo William A. Rev. 7804 Butler
Waldron Jean Mrs. 536 Garfield av.
Waldron John J. Evanston
Waldron Louis K. 536 Garfield av.
Waldschmidt August W. 735 Sedgwick. *C.A.*
Waldschmidt Charles, 735 Sedgwick
Wales Albert H. Dr. The Tudor
Wales Frederick M. Dr. The Tudor
Wales Henry N. jr. The Tudor
Walker Alfred E. Hinsdale
Walker Anna R. Miss, 307 Ashland boul.
Walker Athalia A. Mrs. Hinsdale
Walker Augustus Evans Mrs. 47, 49th
Walker Betsey Mrs. 1573 Kenmore av.
Walker B. Lakota hotel. *Univ.*
Walker Carrie Mrs. 401 N. State
Walker Charles Cobb, 2027 Prairie av. *Chi.*
Walker Charles F. Oak Park
Walker Charles H. La Grange
Walker Charles M. 392 Lasalle av. *Un.*
Walker Charles N. La Grange
Walker Clarence M. 4346 Michigan av.
Walker C. A. Hinsdale
Walker C. Hayward, LaGrange
Walker C. M. L. Riverside

Walker Dudley, LaGrange
Walker Edwin, 2612 Michigan av. *Cal.*, *Chi.*, *W.P.*
Walker Edwin C. Lexington hotel. *Cal.*, *Chi.*, *W.P.*
Walker Edwin F. Evanston
Walker Emery S. 1573 Kenmore av.
Walker E. Mrs. 518 W. Jackson boul.
Walker Francis H. Evanston
Walker Francis W. 5141 Kimbark av. *Chi.*, *C.A.*, *U.L.*
Walker Frank A. 107, 44th
Walker F. E. 4454 Woodlawn av.
Walker George, Oak Park
Walker George B. 2124 Michigan av. *C.A.*
Walker George C. 228 Michigan av. *Cal.*, *Chi.*, *C.A.*, *Irq.*
Walker George L. 891 Warren av.
Walker George R. 10 Aldine sq.
Walker Georgiana Miss, 47, 49th
Walker G. Albert, Oak Park
Walker Harry W. Evanston
Walker Henry C. 4346 Michigan av.
Walker Henry H. Chicago club. *Un.* *U.L.*, *W.P.*
Walker Henry K. Hinsdale
Walker Henry M. Evanston
Walker Henry S. Evanston
Walker Herbert, 406 Erie
Walker Herbert B. Kenilworth. *Chi.*
Walker Hester E. Mrs. Evanston
Walker H. A. 3031 Prairie av.
Walker H. H. Lakota hotel
Walker James H. 421 Huron. *Chi.*
Walker James H. jr. 421 Huron
Walker James M. Mrs. 1720 Prairie av.
Walker James R. 1726 Prairie av. *Chi.*, *U.L.*, *Univ.*, *W.P.*
Walker James R. LaGrange
Walker John H. Union League club
Walker J. Brandt, 3154 Michigan av. *C.A.*, *W.P.*
Walker J. Warren Dr. 1629 W. Adams
Walker Lizzie M. Miss, Hinsdale
Walker Martha A. Mrs. 39 Bryant av.
Walker Mary A. Mrs. 4247 Drexel boul.
Walker Mathew H. LaGrange
Walker Mathias, 4102 Ellis av.
Walker Moses B. LaGrange
Walker Porter J. Morgan Park
Walker Robert, 406 Erie
Walker Robert G. Dr. 95 Aberdeen
Walker Robert P. 3716 Lake av. *U.L.*
Walker Russell W. Evanston
Walker Samuel J. Dr. 105 Lincoln Park boul. *Univ.*
Walker Samuel J. Mrs. 381 Ontario
Walker Stephen L. 1069 Chase av.
Walker Sydney Dr. 5419 Woodlawn av.
Walker S.,S. Mrs. Oak Park
Walker Wellington, 2358 Indiana av.
Walker William Bentley, 2027 Prairie av. *Cal.*, *Chi.*, *C.A.* Sum. res. Manchester-by-the-Sea, Mass.
Walker William Ernst, 381 Ontario. *Un.*

Walker William E. 518 W. Jackson boul.
Walker William F. Rev. 678 Sheffield av.
Walker William H. 1886 Diversey
Walker William J. 891 Warren av.
Walker William R. Lakota hotel. *Chi.*
Walker William S. Auditorium annex: *Chi.*
Walker Winfield S. Dr. 521 Racine av.
Walker Wirt Dexter, 1720 Prairie av.*Chi.*, *Univ.*, *W.P.*
　　　　Sum. res. Pittsfield, Mass.
Walker W. H. Lakota hotel
Walker W. J. Mrs. Lakota hotel
Walkup C. M. Mrs. Evanston
Wall F. G. The Arizona
Wall H. P. The Ontario
Wallace Andrew jr. 83, 74th
Wallace Andrew, 3439 Vernon av.
Wallace Charles H. 574 Fullerton av.
Wallace C. W. Mrs. Auditorium hotel
Wallace Elizabeth Miss, University of Chicago
Wallace Frank P. Austin
Wallace Fred H. Dr. 333 Ohio
Wallace George W. R. LaGrange
Wallace H. R. Dr. 116, 43d
Wallace James Mrs. 2619 N. Paulina
Wallace Jas. F. Mrs. 4240 Champlain av.
Wallace John B. 3100 Groveland av.
Wallace John F. 4317 Ellis av. *U.L.*
Wallace J. D. 595 Washington boul. *Ill.*
Wallace L. D. jr. 250, 61st
Wallace Martin R. M. 3817 Michigan av.
Wallace Michael G. Oak Park
Wallace Norman B. Austin
Wallace Peter Mrs. 4100 Lake av.
Wallace Thomas D. Rev. 263 Warren av.
Wallace William, Irving Park
Wallace William H. 333 Ohio
Wallace William J. Oak Park
Wallach J. Frederick, 3216 Lake Park av. *C.A.*, *U.L.*
Waller A. Rawson, 356 Dearborn av. *Un.*
Waller Charles, Revere house
Waller Chas. S. Mrs. 625 Lasalle av.
Waller Edward jr. 356 Dearborn av.*Univ.*
Waller Edward Mrs. 356 Dearborn av.
Waller Edward C. River Forest.*Irq.*,*U.L.*
Waller F. C. 356 Dearborn av.
Waller Henry, River Forest. *Irq.*
Waller James B. 1711 Sheridan rd. *Chi.*, *Irq.*, *Univ.*
Waller James B. Mrs. Evanston av. sw. cor. Buena av.
Waller John D. Dr. Oak Park
Waller J. A. 356 Dearborn av.
Waller Nannine Miss, 40 Banks
Waller Robert A. 1665 Sheridan rd. *Chi.* *Irq.*, *Un.*, *U.L.*, *Univ.*
Waller William, 40 Banks *C.A.*, *Univ.*, *W.P.*
Wallerstein Clara Miss, 3940 Calumet av.
Wallin Thomas S. 535 Dearborn av. *U.L.*
Walling William E. 4127 Drexel boul.

Walling Willoughby Dr. 4127 Drexel boul.
  Chi.
Wallingford Henry J. Evanston
Wallis Frank E. 709 Washington boul.
Wallis Henry H. Oak Park
Wallis John C. 315 The Plaza
Wallis Obed W. 709 Washington boul. *Ill.*
Walliser Henry F. 1728 Kenmore av.
Wallop O. H. Mrs. 381 Ontario
Walls C. Bruce Dr. 134 S. Kedzie av.
Walls Frank X. 4307 Ellis av.
Walls James R. 4334 Greenwood av.
Walls Mae P. Miss, 4334 Greenwood av.
Walls Mercy L. Mrs. 4334 Greenwood av.
Walls Thomas, 21 Park av.
Wallwork Edward L. 426, 42d pl.
Walmsley A. H. Irving Park
Walmsley James, 521 Lunt av.
Walmsley Wm. LaGrange
Walser Jacob J. Austin
Walsh Edward R. 276 Michigan av.
Walsh James, 306 Superior. *Un.*
  Sum. res. Mackinac Island, Mich.
Walsh James T. Norwood Park
Walsh John F. 353 Bissell
Walsh John R. 2133 Calumet av. *Cal.,*
  Chi., Irq., U.L., W.P.
Walsh John W. 503 W. Congress
  Sum. res. Fox Lake
Walsh John W. 4243 Calumet av.
Walsh Lawrence J. 1529 Wrightwood av.
Walsh Mary A. Mrs. 1314 Dunning
Walsh Michael Mrs. 2511 Indiana av.
Walsh N. Miss, 1758 Oakdale av.
Walsh Richard, 4441 Ellis av.
Walsh R. D. 408 Chestnut. *C.A.*
Walsh William, 3131 Wabash av.
Walsh William C. River Forest. *Irq.*
Walshe Robert J. 2339 Calumet av.
Walter Albert E. 7747 Union av.
Walter Alfred M. 2729 Prairie av. *C.A.*
Walter Anna K. Mrs. Oak Park
Walter A. G. Mrs. 5450 Washington av.
Walter Charles A. Riverside
Walter Grove E. Mayfair
Walter J. C. Mrs. 2729 Prairie av.
  Sum. res. Lynn, Mass
Walter Lincoln W. 3100 Groveland av.
Walter Philip M. 5450 Washington av.
Walter William Dr. Evanston
Walter William A. 3142 Calumet av.
Walters Alfred E. Oak Park
Walters C. W. 6565 Yale
Walters Horace E. Evanston
Walters Marie Mrs. Evanston
Walters M. E. Wilmette
Walters Will, Evanston
Walther August F. 532 N. Normal Park-
  way
Walton Charles, 2397 N. Paulina
Walton E. L. Miss, Hinsdale
Walton Frederick J. Rev. 6957 Yale
Walton George Kenyon, 1230 Wright-
  wood av.
Walton Hannah Mrs. 7659 Butler
Walton Henry H. 874, 71st pl.

Walton Lyman A. 5747 Woodlawn av.
Walton L. N. Mrs. 780 North Park av.
Walton Mabel Barnard Miss, 4740 Drexel
  boul.
Walton M. Elizabeth Miss, 4740 Drexel
  boul.
Walton R. French, LaGrange
Walton Samuel B. 4740 Drexel boul.
Walton Seymour, 6511 Woodlawn av. *Irq.*
Walton Thomas B. 1462 E. Ravenswood
  Park
Walworth Charles M. 23 Marquette Ter-
  race
Wampler A. J. 4156 Lake av. *C.A.*
Wampold Leo, 3229 Michigan av. *Stan.*
Wampold Louis, 3229 Michigan av.
Wamsley Minor, 6614 Kimbark av.
Wander Edward W. 294 Dayton
  Sum. res. Mishicott, Wis.
Wander Pauline Mrs. 294 Dayton
Wander Valesca W. Miss, 294 Dayton
Wangeman Hugo, 6435 Stewart av.
Wann Fred A. 803 Pullman bldg.
Wanner Andrew F. 719 Chase av.
Wanner Edward A. 6501 Kimbark av.
Wanner Henry J. 108, 36th
Wanzer Clarence H. Austin
Wanzer Elias Mrs. Austin
Wanzer James M. 917 W. Monroe
Ward Albert J. 274 Fullerton av.
Ward A. Montgomery, 4700 Kimbark av.
  C.A., W.P.
  Sum. res. Oconomowoc, Wis.
Ward Carlos J. Oak Park
Ward Charles, 3617 Prairie av.
Ward Charles A. Evanston. *C.A.*
Ward Cornelia B. Miss, 4327 Greenwood
  av.
Ward David A. Evanston
Ward Edmund C. 627 W. Jackson boul.
Ward Edwin Lindsay, 6348 Greenwood
  av.
Ward Edward P. Dr. Lake Forest
Ward Frederic A. 212, 33d
Ward George R. T. Mrs. 4726 Kimbark av.
Ward George T. 3930 Prairie av.
Ward Guy W. Evanston
Ward James H. 91 Loomis
Ward James R. 1911½ Diversey
Ward Joseph F. Evanston
Ward Julia Mrs. 189, 54th pl.
Ward J. L. Oak Park
Ward L. A. Coonley Mrs. 620 Division
Ward L. C. Mrs. Evanston
Ward Morris E. Lakota hotel
Ward M. E. Mrs. 319 Park av.
Ward O. S. 1455 Fulton
Ward O. VanSchaack Mrs. 1701 Prairie av
Ward Robert N. 4711 St. Lawrence av.
Ward Samuel Mrs. 4860 Kimbark av.
Ward S. D. 3536 Ellis av.
Ward William E. Chicago Beach hotel
Ward William H. Riverside
Ward W. Mrs. 4934 Forrestville av.
Warde Miss. 4429 Greenwood av.
Warde R. Cuttriss, 919 Pullman bldg.

Wardell Charles F. Riverside
Wardell Richard J. Riverside
Warden C. E. 225 Dearborn av.
Warden Theodore G. 3601 Ellis av.
Warder Benton, 78 Ogden av.
Wardner S. J. Mrs. 4108 Lake av.
Wardrop Walter, 146, 54th
Wardwell Clara Miss, 2532 Indiana av.
Ware Charles, Kenilworth
Ware Charles E. Evanston
Ware Charles W. 19 Delaware pl.
Ware Elisha C. 5104 Jefferson av.
Ware Frederic D. 5147 Cornell av.
Ware Harry A. Dr. 204 Cass. *Chi.*, *C.A.*, *U.L.*
Ware H. A. Winnetka
Ware John C. 5543 Madison av.
Ware J. Herbert, 5480 Cornell av. *Chi.*, *C.A. W.P.*
Ware Lyman Dr. 1620 Prairie av.
Ware Mary Lillian Miss, Evanston
Ware Robert M. Riverside
Ware Thornton, 4201 Ellis av.
Wares Jerome F. The Arizona. *C.A.*
Warfield Edwin A. Tracy
Warfield Edwin A. jr. Tracy
Warfield Robert, Tracy
Waring Henrietta H. Miss, 491 W. Adams
Warley David A. 3743 Vincennes av.
Warne Emma N. Dr. 3402 Prairie av.
Warne George B. Dr. 3402 Prairie av.
Warner Aaron N. 320 Oakwood boul.
Warner Addison R. 6335 Lexington av. *W.P.*
Warner Augustus, 503 Dearborn av.
Warner A. J. 36, 35th
Warner Chester, 635 Washington boul.
Warner Ezra J. Lake Forest. *Chi.*
Warner E. Percy, 4800 Prairie av. *Cal.*
Warner Frank A. Evanston
Warner F. R. Hotel Del Prado
Warner George L. 5120 Hibbard av. *U.L.*
Warner Henry D. Mrs. 2940 Indiana av.
Warner H. E. 36, 35th
Warner John M. 6339 Yale
Warner John M. jr. 6339 Yale
Warner J. G. 123, 51st
Warner J. M. Julien hotel
Warner Martha Miss, 768 W. Jackson boul.
Warner Mary R. Mrs. 727 Washington boul.
Warner M. M. 357 Park av.
Warner Paul B. 430 N. State.
Warner Samuel W. 1309 W. Adams
Warner Sidney H. 1635 W. Adams
Warner William C. Oak Park
Warrell Arthur M. 5047 Madison av. *C.A.*
Warren Allyn D. 44, 50th
Warren Aubrey Mrs. Oak Park
Warren Charles A. 6350 Harvard av.
Warren Charles C. Hinsdale
Warren Charles H. Highland Park
Warren Clark R. Dr. 1037 W. Madison
Warren Clinton J. 1672 Buckingham pl.
Warren C. D. 4310 Oakenwald av. *U.L.*

Warren C. G. Clifton house
Warren C. G. Mrs. 780 North Park av.
Warren C. M. Mrs. 4342 Greenwood av.
Warren C. T. Hinsdale
Warren Frank H. 3922 Lake av.
Warren Homer S. Dr. 1449 W. Jackson boul.
Warren James A. 1 Wellington ct.
Warren . D. Revere house
Warren J. Latham, Riverside
Warren Lansing, University club
Warren L. D. 2909 Prairie av.
Warren Robert Mrs. 5 Groveland Park
Warren Wallace Mrs. 210, 37th
Warren William H. Evanston
Warren William L. 1449 W. Jackson boul.
Warren William S. 437 Elm. *U.L.*
Warren William S. 2181 Sheridan rd.
Warrington George, 1706 Kenmore av.
Warrington Henry, 127 Park av.
Warrington James N. 127 Park av. *Univ.*
Warrington William H. 127 Park av.
Warvelle George W. 654 W. Monroe. *Ill.*
  Sum. res. Kenosha, Wis.
Warwick George W. 5155 Cornell av.
Washburn Charles L. Hinsdale
Washburn Elmer, 4559 Woodlawn av.
Washburn Hiram C. 438 Englewood av.
Washburn James M. Calumet club
Washburn Jane A. Miss, 767 Washington boul.
Washburn Joseph S. 5644 Kimbark av.
Washburn William D. 4733 Woodlawn av. *U.L.*
Washburn William W. Morgan Park
Washburne George F. Mrs. 553 W. Jackson boul.
Washburne Hempstead, 154 Astor. *Chi.*, *Univ* Sum. res. Marquette, Mich.
Washburne John B. 1470 E. Ravenswood Park
Washer Abraham, Clifton house
Washington Hermann B. 1847 Melrose
Washington Lloyd, 1842 Indiana av. *Irq.*
Wasmansdorff Otto Mrs. 549 Cleveland av.
Wasmansdorff Wm. G. 549 Cleveland av.
Wass Allen, Evanston
Wassall Joseph W. Dr. 150 Lincoln Park boul. *Un.*, *Univ.*, *W.P.*
Wasserman David, 4500 Forrestville av. *Lksd.*
Wasson Buren S. 4345 Ellis av.
Watase Sho, 6024 Ellis av.
Waterbury Elbert M. 516 W. 62d
Waterbury John C. Mrs. Evanston
Waterloo Stanley, 2255 South Park av.
Waterman Arba N. 40 Groveland Park.
Waterman Chauncey N. Evanston
Waterman E. L. Mrs. 441 Seminary av.
Waterman Jessie H. Miss, 3929 Vincennes av.
Waterman John A. 3929 Vincennes av.
Waterman Richard, 26 Scott
Waterman Richard jr. 26 Scott
Waterman Samuel A. Dr. 7762 Hawthorne av.

Waterman William, 5810 Rosalie ct.
Waters Charles E. 571 Washington boul.
Waters Edward D. 624, 46th pl.
Waters Frank S. 377 Warren av. *C.A.*
Waters Harry C. Chicago Beach hotel
Waters Jane Miss, New Hotel Holland
Waters John E. Chicago Beach hotel
Waters Lisle Cummins Dr.966Warren av.
Waters N. McGee Rev. Evanston
Waters O. J. Dr. 32 Delaware pl.
Waters Thomas J. 3149 Beacon
Waters Willey B. 587 Washington boul.
C.A., Ill.
Wathier Joseph P. 545 W. Monroe
Watkins A. B. Mrs. 151 Evanston av.
Watkins Carrie B. Miss, 4037 Indiana av.
Watkins D. L. 258 Ashland boul.
Watkins E. M. 333 Rush. *Un.*
Watkins E. T. 148 Rush
Watkins Frank A. 151 Evanston av.
Watkins Frederick A. 333 Rush
Watkins George, 4206 Oakenwald av.
Watkins Jesse M. 1823 Aldine av.
Watkins Joseph O. 196 Ashland boul. *Ill.*
Watkins Martha Grace Miss, 258 Ashland
boul.
Watkins Maurice, 3752 Lake av.
Watkins T. J. Dr. 3625 Indiana av.
Watkins Vine A. 2643 Michigan av.
Watkins William, 4329 Forrestville av.
Irq.
Watkins William W. 3536 Lake av. *U.L*
Watriss A. Whiting, 2644 Magnolia av.
Watriss Franklin H. Union club
Watry Nicholas, 1668 Wellington
Watson Alexander, Riverside
Watson Annie Mrs. 495 Fullerton av.
Watson Arthemus D. 271 S. Irving av.
Watson Catherine Mrs. 271·S. Irving av.
Watson Flora M. Dr. 221 Oakwood boul.
Watson Frederick, 454 S. Oakley av.
Watson F. L. 55, 36th
Watson George B. 6515 Yale
Watson George E.1226 Winthrop av. *C.A.*
Watson George W. 3403 Indiana av.
Watson Howard. 800 W. Monroe
Watson James, Wilmette
Watson James S. 858 Washington boul.
Watson John G. 17 Scott. *Chi.*
Watson Julia M. Mrs. Evanston
Watson Louis H., M.D., 297 Indiana
Watson Lyda E. Miss, Highland Park
Watson Margaret A. Mrs. 2686 Magnolia
av.
Watson Orson H. 2686 Magnolia av.
Watson Richard G. Lake Forest
Watson Robert W. Hotel Windermere.
Chi.
Watson Thomas, Wilmette
Watson Thomas H. Evanston
Watson Thomas W. Wilmette
Watson T. T. Highland Park. *C. A.*,
Watson William jr. Auditorium annex.
U.L.
Watson William J. 2640 Prairie av. *U.L.*
Watson William M. 1705 Wellington

Watson W. B. Mrs. Evanston
Watson W. J. Lakeside
Watt Archibald M. 1525 W. Monroe
Watt Hugh, 1525 W. Monroe
Watt James B. 678, 48th pl. *C.A.*
Watt Robert, Lakeside
Watt Sarah E. Mrs. 2603 N. Hermitage
av.
Watte Joseph M. Mrs. 615 Cleveland av.
Watterman Harry H. Morgan Park
Watters Juliette Mrs. 474 Elm
Watterson D. Mrs. 11 Bellevue pl.
Watts E. S. Oak Park
Watts Francis, 4347 Ellis av.
Watts Frank W. 1091 W. Monroe
Watts George C. 4726 Langley av.
Watts G. Wilbert Dr. 6565 Yale
Watts Jeremiah, 619 W. 78th
Watts Robert Mrs. 4726 Langley av.
Waugh Edwin L. 1080 Chase av.
Waughop Arthur B. 3804 Forest av.
Waughop James F. 4207 Ellis av.
Waughop J. W. 2457 Prairie av.
Waxham F. E. Dr. 3633 Grand boul.
Way Henry J. Dr. 514 S. Oakley av.
Way Lillian Miss, 514 S. Oakley av.
Way W. Irving, 1845 Arlington pl. ·
Wayman James B. 2093 Kenmore av.
Wayman John S. Austin
Wayne Albert, 209 S. Leavitt
Wayne H. L. 1036 W. Jackson boul.
Wayne Thomas D. 209 S. Leavitt
Wayt Edward, Austin
Wayte John Mrs. Morgan Park
Weage Charles A. Oak Park
Wean Frank L. 6951 Yale. *Chi.*
Sum. res. White Lake, Mich.
Wear Charles A. 5517 Washington av.
Weare Charles A. 697 Washington boul.
Weare John, 697 Washington boul.
Weare J n Mrs. 1886 Diversey
Weare Portus B. Morton Park. *Chi.*, *U.L.*
Weare William W. Morton Park. *U.L.*
Weart Garret V. 6800 Lowe av.
Weart James G. Winnetka
Weary Edwin D. 5830 Washington av.
U.L.
Weatherly Sidney M. 7737 Lowe av.
Weatherson C. W. 3739 Prairie av.
Weatherson John, 3739 Prairie av.
Weatherstone James P. LaGrange
Weatherstone William W. LaGrange
Weaver Albert L. Oak Park
Weaver Arthur C. 686½ Wash'ton boul.
Weaver Charles H. 686½ Wash'ton boul.
Ill.
Weaver Charles S. 85 Rush
Weaver EdithS.Mrs.882Washington boul.
Weaver George H. 6534 Lafayette av.
Weaver George H. Dr. 535 Washington
boul.
Weaver Henry E. 506, 53d. *U.L.*, *W.P.*
Weaver Homer W. Evanston
Weaver John V. A. 443 Elm
Weaver Joseph D. Evanston
Weaver Kate Miss, 45 Cedar

- Weaver Uri, 1173 Washington boul.
Weaver William A. Austin
Weaver William H. Austin
Webb Catherine B. Mrs. 1161 N. Clark
Webb Edward L. Dr. 750 Greenleaf av.
Webb Frank R., M.D. 3907 Michigan av.
Webb George D. Oak Park.
Webb George L. Chicago Beach hotel
Webb James B. Oak Park .
Webb Job, 884 W. Adams
Webb T. A. 3543 Michigan av.
Webb T. E. Mrs. 3149 Forest av.
Webb William R. 157 Oakwood boul.
Webbe William E. 5831 Washington av.
    Sum. res. Sister Lakes, Mich.
Webber Charles M. 150 Astor. C.A.
Webber Edward R. Wilmette
Webber Joseph T. 6018 Michigan av.
Webber William G. 4429 St. Lawrence av.
Weber Albert H. 462 Lasalle av.
Weber Andrew, 280 Belden av.   .
Weber Bernard F. 2546 N. Ashland av.
Weber Charles, 23 Junior terrace
Weber Charles F. 1634 Barry av.
Weber David, 4412 Wabash.av.
Weber Edmund B. 462 Lasalle av.
Weber Eugene, 597 Burling
Weber Ewald, Jefferson Park
Weber George, 3617 Prairie av.
Weber George. 7738 Butler. C.A.
Weber Harry F. 462 Lasalle av.
Weber Henry, 7738 Butler
Weber Herman, 462 Lasalle av.
Weber John, 151 Osgood
Weber Rudolph W. 4526 Prairie av.
Weber Samuel L. Dr. 547 N. Robey
Webster Catherine Mrs.4140 Berkeley av.
Webster Charles L. Dr. 140 Ashland boul.
Webster Chas. R. Evanston .
Webster Chevalier O. The Kenwood
Webster David V. Evanston
Webster Edgar L. 375 Dearborn av.
Webster Edna Miss, Hinsdale   ,
Webster Edward F. 828 Touhy av.;
Webster Edward H. Dr. Evanston·
Webster E. Carlton, 4738 Evans av.
Webster E. P. 176, 37th
Webster George A. 5200 Jefferson av.
    C.A.
Webster George H. 2821 Prairie av.
Webster George O. Capt. Fort Sheridan
Webster George T. 480 Kenwood terrace
Webster George W., M.D. 1922 Indiana
    av. C.A.
Webster Henry K. Evanston
Webster H. A. 2821 Prairie av.
Webster James, 5642 Michigan av.
Webster John C. Dr. 820W.Jackson boul.
Webster John P. Dr. 441 Englewood av.
Webster J. A. Mrs. 1393 W. Monroe
Webster J. W. Hinsdale
Webster Lewis D. 10 Astor. Chi., Un.
Webster Lucius, 140 Ashland boul.
Webster Mabel T. Miss, 793 Washington
    boul
Webster Martha H. Mrs. 828 Touhy av.

Webster Mary M. Mrs. 793 Washington
    boul.
Webster M. L. Miss, 2821 Prairie av.
Webster N. H. Hinsdale
Webster Ralph W. 5826 Washington av.
Webster Roy, Hinsdale
Webster Stuart Dr. 2821 Prairie av.
Webster S. L. Mrs. Evanston
Webster Thos. H. 116 Flournoy. U.L.
Webster Towner K. Evanston. U.L.
Webster Willett A. Evanston
Webster William H. Evanston
Webster Wm. V. 759 W. Adams
Webster W. E. Mrs. New Hotel Holland
Weckler William H. 1506 Wolfram
Wedeles Anna Mrs. 3216 Calumet av.
Wedeles Babetta Miss,·4920 Ellis av.
Wedeles Celia Mrs. 4920 Ellis av.
Wedeles Edward L. 3216 Calumet av.
    Lksd., Stan.
Wedeles Isaac, 3127 Calumet av.
Wedeles Sigmund, 3216 Calumet av.
    Lksd.
Wedeles Solomon, 4920 Ellis av.
Weed Sarah M. Mrs. 4024 Michigan ter-
    race
Weed William F. 4024 Michigan terrace
Weeden Elnathan S. Evanston
Weeden John V. Evanston
Weeks Benjamin F. Evanston
Weeks Charles D. 4828 Forrestville av.
Weeks Clinton, Longwood
Weeks Curran C. 2627 N. Ashland av.
Weeks E. A. 4828 Forrestville av.
Weeks Frank, 4257 Grand boul..   ·
Weeks Frank O. 5542 Michigan av.
Weeks Gilbert M. 2118 Clarendon av.C.A.
Weeks Harvey T. 199 Ashland boul. C.A.,
    Ill.
Weeks Horace S. Hinsdale
Weeks J. B. Irving Park   ·
Weeks J. G. 1521 Michigan av. C.A.
Weeks J. M. 1907 Deming pl.
Weeks Patti Miss. 199 Ashland boul.
Wegeforth Theodore C. H. 1694 W. Mon-
    roe
Wegener Arnold, 295 Webster av.
Wegener William A. Hotel Del Prado,.
    C.A. · Sum. res. Oconomowoc, Wis.
Wegg David Spencer 1922 Belmont av.
    U.L.
Wegg Donald R. 1922 Belmont av.
Wegg John Mrs. 1922 Belmont av.
Wegmann Jules F. 571 N. Clark
Wegmann Julius, 571 N. Clark
Wehmer Minnie C. Miss,143 Oakwood
    boul.
Wehmer Theo. G. 143 Oakwood boul.
Weiber M. A. Miss, 780 North Park av.
Weick Louis E. 451 Cleveland av.
Weick M. G. Mrs. 451 Cleveland av.
·Weide Lillian B. Miss, 4747 Woodlawn
    av.
Weidig Adolph, Hinsdale
Weidig George, 103 Lincoln Park boul.
    C.A.

Weidner Revere F. Prof. 1311 Sheffield v.
Weigle Fred T. 575 Evanston av.
Weigle Mahlie E. Miss, 100 Pine Grove av.
Weigle Oscar, 100 Pine Grove av.
Weigle William G. 1847 Magnolia av.
Weigley Fillmore, 238 Honore
Weigley Frank S. 590 Division
Weil Abraham, 4903 Vincennes av.
Weil A. L. 4822 Langley av.
Weil Carl A. Dr. 1243 Wrightwood av.
Weil Carl H. 3149 Rhodes av. *Stan.*
Weil Emanuel, 3756 Rhodes av.
Weil Emanual R. 449 Lasalle av.
Weil Eugene S. 3445 Prairie av.
Weil Fred A. 3529 Grand boul.
Weil Harry, 4006 Grand boul. *Lksd.*
Weil Henry, 4909 Forrestville av.
Weil Isaac, 2 Crilly ct.
Weil Julius E. 3 31 Ellis av. *Stan.*
Weil J. Mrs. 4587 Oakenwald av.
Weil L. H. Mrs. 531½ Burling
Weil Morris, 3336 South Park av. *Lksd., Stan.*
Weil N. J. 6448 Ellis av.
Weil Samuel, 4853 Forrestville av.
Weil Theodore, 4429 Ellis av. *Lksd.,Stan*
Weil T. Miss, 225 Dearborn av.
Weilhart C. E., M.D., 3709 Ellis av.
Weill Maurice, 4320 Vernon av. *Lksd.*
Weinberg Max, 3443 Wabash av.
Weinberger Albert F. 27 Ewing pl.
Weinberger Felix V. 27 Ewing pl.
Weinberger George A. 27 Ewing pl.
Weinhardt Herman, 76 Ewing pl.
Weinland Charles D. 864 W. Monroe
Weinland Charles F. 726 W. Adams. *Ill.*
Weinsheimer Alfred S. 3028 Calumet av *U.L.*
Weinsheimer Warren E. 3028 Calumet av
Weippert Gustave W. 6565 Yale
Weir John M. 272 Ashland boul.
Weir J. M. Riverside
Weir Robert, 6323 Yale
Weir Robert T. 272 Ashland boul.
Weir Silas, Riverside
Weis Louis, 2014 Indiana av.
Weise Frank A. 3410 Wabash av.
Weise Frederick, Revere house
Weise George, 3410 Wabash av.
Weise George B. 3410 Wabash av.
Weiss George A. 540 N. State. *C.A.*
Weiss Henry W. Hinsdale
Weiss John H. 4419 Drexel boul. *C.A.*
Welch Albert G. 4807 Madison av.
Welch Arthur S. 3827 Ellis av.
Welch Edwin H. 2505 Kenmore av.
Welch Eugene, 3827 Ellis av.
Welch Leon C. 4807 Madison av.
Welch P. H. Dr. 2976 Michigan av.
Welch William M. 548 Morse av.
Welch W. H. 4540 Oakenwald av.
Welcker H. C. Dr. 626 Lasalle av.
Welcker Paul R. Dr. 626 Lasalle av.
Weld Herbert W. 3702 Lake av.

Welden T. J. Edison Park
Weldon Elizabeth Mrs. 276 S. Marshfield av.
Welge Frederick, Austin
Welker L. Bruce, 402 W. 65th
Weller Felix J. 4132 N. Ashland av.
Weller Stella Mrs. 6311 Woodlawn av.
Welles Benjamin W. 1940 Deming pl.
Welles Edward P. 1537 Windsor av.
Welles Frederick L. 536 W. Jackson boul.
Welling David, 46 Madison Park
Welling Dwight G. Evanston
Welling John C. 4950 Greenwood av. *Chi., U.L.*
Wellington Charles L. 299, 47th. *C.A.*
Wellington Charles W. W. Mrs. 299 Huron
Wells Addison E. 99 DeKalb. *Ill., U.L.*
Wells Arthur B. LaGrange
Wells Brenton R. 4853 Lake av. *C.A.*
Wells Charles B. 2358 Indiana av.
Wells Charles E. Evanston
Wells Charles H. Oak Park
Wells D. Gordon, 49, 29th pl.
Wells D. W. 841 Warren av.
Wells Edgar L. 4724 Evans av.
Wells Edward F., M.D. 4571 Lake av.
Wells Edwin S. Lake Forest
Wells Frank, 19 Groveland Park. *U.L.*
Wells Franklin C. Dr. 883 W. Monroe
Wells Fred A. 6704 Stewart av.
Wells Fred K. 48 St. James pl.
Wells Frederick L. Wheaton
Wells George V. 4839 Forrestville av.
Wells G. S. Park Ridge
Wells H. G. Norwood Park
Wells James H. Oak Park
Wells Joseph S. 538 Washington boul.
Wells J. E. 6440 Greenwood av.
Wells J. G. Irving Park
Wells Lois Miss, 4853 Lake av.
Wells Mary Miss, 512, 53d
Wells Michael B. 4571 Lake av.
Wells Moses A. 313 W. Monroe. *Ill.*
Wells Moses D. 2550 Michigan av. *Cal., Chi., C.A., W.P.*
        Sum. res. Lakeville, Conn.
Wells O. C. Chicago Athletic assn. *C.A., W.P.*
Wells Raymond A. 2124 Michigan av.
Wells Rinnah A. 4724 Evans av.
Wells Robert M. 3800 Michigan av. *U.L.*
Wells Samuel, Tracy
Wells Samuel R. 3549 Indiana av. *Cal., W.P.*
Wells S. C. Mrs. Evanston
Wells Theodore B. 215 S. Winchester av.
Wells Thomas E. 4733 Vincennes av. *Chi.*
Wells Warren A. 146 Ashland boul. *Ill., W.P.*
Wells William L. Evanston
Wells Willis J. 3753 Ellis av. *C.A., Irq.*
Welsh J. W. 3100 Groveland av.
Wendell Edward E. 3107 Forest av.
Wendell Emanuel V. 4418 Langley av.
Wendell Maurice, 4006 Grand boul. *Stan.*

Wendell Melville J. 6530 Lexington av.
Wenderoth Charles J. 99, 33d
Wenderoth Frank, Lexington hotel
Wendnagel E. 2124 Michigan av.
Wendnagel William, 2124 Michigan av.
Wenter Frank, 475 Ashland boul.
Wentworth Edward C. 2941 Indiana av.
Wentworth Estelle Miss, 353½ Park av.
Wentworth Frank W. 354 Erie. *C.A.*,
　Univ., W.P.
Wentworth George O. 353½ Park av.
Wentworth Moses J. 465 Elm. *Cal., Univ.*
Wentworth William G. Evanston
Wentworth Wm. W. Dr. 230 W. 65th
Wentz Albert D. 1870 Reta. *C.A.*
Wentz Julian A. 7051 Princeton av.
Werkmeister Arthur M. Dr. 3329 Vernon
　av.
Werkmeister Martin, 3329 Vernon av.
Wermuth William C. Dr. 277 Bissell
Werneburg F. William, 6738 Parnell av.
Wernecke Richard L. 1629 Brompton av.
Wernecke William, 1629 Brompton av.
Werner Conrad, 4542 Vincennes av.
Wernicke Oscar G. Dr. 256 Loomis
Werno Charles, 427 Cleveland av.
Werno Henry, LaGrange.
Werst Abbie J. Mrs. 526 W. Adams
Wertheim Joseph B. Sherman house.
　Lksd.
Wertheimer Abraham, 3564 Prairie av.
　Stan.
Wertheimer B. J. 3219 Wabash av. *Univ.*
Wertheimer H. 3813 Prairie av.
Wertheimer Max, 440, 41st. *Lksd.*
Wertheimer N. S. 4339 Calumet av. *Lksd.*
Wesencraft Jane Mrs. Riverside
Wesencraft Lotta Mrs. Riverside
Wessel L. jr. 697, 49th. *Lksd.*
Wessels Charles H. New Hotel Holland
Wessels Frederick J. 5328 Madison av.
Wessels George F. 5328 Madison av.
Wessels Robert Sloan, 3161 Groveland av.
Wessling Fred G. 439 Belden av.
Wessling George H. 1454 Edgecomb ct.
West Albert L. 577 Division
West Charles, 945 Cuyler av.
West Edward A. Dr. 443 Dearborn av.
West E. A. 364 W. Adams. *Ill.*
West Francis T. 4560 Oakenwald av.
West Frederick T. 613 Division. *Univ.*
　Sum. res. Pittsfield, Mass.
West George E. 3906 Lake av. *C.A.*
West James J. 5319 Washington av.
　Sum. res. Spring Lake, Mich.
West James R. Lakeside
West John, 577 Division.
West Roy O. 737 W. Garfield boul. *U.L.*
West Stephen G. Dr. 401 Warren av.
　Sum. res. Lauderdale, Wis.
West William H. 4348 Grand boul.
Westcott Charles, Maywood
Westcott George T. Maywood
Westcott Oliver J. Maywood
Westenberger Joseph, 2962 Groveland av.
Westerfield Charles I. 7107 Eggleston av.
45

Westervelt W. D. Rev. Morgan Park
Westfall E. W. Mrs. 516 W. Jackson boul.
Westlake Emory W. 4407 Prairie av.
Westlake Isabella E. Miss, 3203 Calumet
　av.
Weston Alonzo, 821 Washington boul.
Weston George, 38 Roslyn pl. *C.A.*
Weston George A. Evanston
Weston John W. 5318 Calumet av. *C.A.*
Weston Olive E. Mrs. 4852 Kenwood av.
Westover Frank A. 230, 45th
Westover George Frederic. Hotel Metro-
　pole. Sum. res. Cottage Park, Win-
　throp, Mass.
Westwood E. C. Austin
Wetherell Charles C. 297 Pine Grove av.
Wetherell George F. 459 W. Jackson boul.
Wetherell George F., M. D. 164 Oakwood
　boul.
Wetherell Homer S. 195 Oakwood boul.
Wetherla William W. Dr. 15 Kemper pl.
Wetmore C. Orton, Oak Park
Wetmore Ethelbert R. 30 Linden ct.
Wetmore Henry D. 4446 Sidney av.
Wetmore Justin J. 5750 Madison av.
　Sum. res. Minocqua, Wis.
Wetterer Herman, 563 Lasalle av.
Wettstein J. R. 4315 Ellis av.
Weyburn Elbert D. 6118 Monroe av.
Weyburn Ned C. 6118 Monroe av.
Whaley John J. Dr. 551 Dearborn av.
Whaling Julia Cone Dr. Oakland hotel
Whaples Judson L. Oak Park
Wharton George C. 425 Lasalle av.
Wharton Joseph C. 425 Lasalle av.
Wharton Owen T. 425 Lasalle av.
Wheat C. L. LaGrange
Wheatley William M. 2358 Indiana av.
Wheaton A. C. Mrs. 7749 Muskegon av.
Wheaton Frederic S. Morgan Park
Whedon James P. Virginia hotel. *C.A.*
Wheeler Arthur, 2962 Michigan av. *Cal.,
　Chi., W.P.*
Wheeler Arthur Dana, 19 Bellevue pl.
　Chi., Univ. Sum. res. Lake Forest
Wheeler Augustus W. 44, 53d *C.A.*
Wheeler Calvin T. 518 N. State
Wheeler Charles C. 2900 Kenmore av.
Wheeler Charles H. 2125 Prairie av.
Wheeler Charles M. 457 Washington boul.
Wheeler Charles P. Evanston. *Univ.*
Wheeler Charles S. 5413 Ridgewood ct.
Wheeler C. C. Mrs. 457 Washington boul.
Wheeler C. Gilbert Mrs. Lakota hotel
Wheeler C. W. Auditorium annex. *Chi.,
　W.P.*
Wheeler Edwin S. Oak Park
Wheeler Emily F. Miss, 4614 Woodlawn
　av.
Wheeler Eugene, 2962 Michigan av. *Chi.,
　W.P.*
Wheeler Ezra I. Mrs. 400 Dearborn av.
Wheeler E. R. Mrs. 2601 Kenmore av.
Wheeler Felix A. 732 W. 64th
Wheeler Francis T. 3416 Michigan av.
　Cal., W.P.

Wheeler Frank S. 407 Oak. *Un.*
Wheeler Frederick S. Evanston
Wheeler F. P. 5517 Madison av.
Wheeler George, 7127 Harvard av.
Wheeler George Henry, 1812 Prairie av.
   Cal., Chi., Un., W.P.
Wheeler Harris A. Gen. 652 W. Monroe.
   Chi., Ill., U.L., W.P.
     Sum. res. Charlevoix, Mich.
Wheeler Harry A. 4613 Ellis av.
Wheeler Helen D. Miss, 308 N. State
Wheeler Henry E. Revere house
Wheeler Henry L. Dr. 1812 Prairie av.
   W.P.
Wheeler Henry N. 2520 Indiana av.
Wheeler Hiram Mrs. 2962 Michigan av.
Wheeler H. Mrs. 3613 Ellis av.
Wheeler John A. Dr. Irving Park
Wheeler Joseph H. 697, 49th
Wheeler Joseph S. 4430 Prairie av.
Wheeler . Kittredge Rev. 514 W. Adams
Wheeler J. M. Miss, 3021 Vernon av.
Wheeler Leo W. 3615 Ellis Park. *Lksd.*
Wheeler L. C. Mrs. 39, 22d
Wheeler Mark, Lieut. Fort Sheridan
Wheeler Martin L. 4614 Woodlawn av.
Wheeler Meyer, 3615 Ellis Park. *Lksd.*
Wheeler N. C. 6510 Kimbark av.
Wheeler Russell H. Dr. 2441 Wabash av.
Wheeler Sarah E. Mrs. Evanston
Wheeler William M. Prof. 357, 58th
Wheeler W. H. 4595 Oakenwald av.
Wheeler W. W. 138 Park av.
Wheelock Everett B. Wilmette
Wheelock Harry B. Evanston
Wheelock Seymour A. Wilmette
Wheelock Washington, 904 W. Adams
Wheelock William W. 904 W. Adams
Wheelwright T. Highland Park
Whelpley Richard T. 515 Dearborn av.
   U.L.
Wherry Elwood M. Rev. River Forest
Wherry William B. River Forest
Whetston Charles P. 298 S Irving av.
Whetzel Frank Dr. Clifton house
Whidden George F. Oak Park .
Whidden Philon C. Dr. 1003 Warren av.
Whigham Henry J. Virginia hotel
Whinnery William, 540 W. 59th
Whipple Arthur J. 42 Woodland Park
Whipple Charles B. 4739 Kenwood av.
   Sum. res. Chestnut-oaks, Algonquin,
   Ill.
Whipple Eugene W. 6657 Stewart av.
Whipple Henry, Evanston
Whipple H. E. Mrs. 4600 Ellis av.
Whipple John H. 662 Fulton
Whipple Warner E. 6657 Stewart av.
Whitaker Alton E. 343, 41st
Whitaker E. L. Mrs. 2453 Prairie av.
Whitaker William B. Dr. 3541 Indiana av.
Whitcomb Adele Miss, 3625 Grand boul.
Whitcomb A. J. Park Ridge
Whitcomb A. O. 463 S. Irving av.
Whitcomb F. L. Riverside
Whitcomb George P. 3625 Grand boul.

Whitcomb Henry S. 5131 Cornell av.
Whitcomb H. J. 47 S. Seeley av.
Whitcomb J. C. 47 S. Seeley av.
Whitcomb Oscar E. 359 S. Oakley av.
Whitcomb Rodney S. 4148 Grand boul.
Whitcomb W. C. Evanston
White Abel M. Rev. Austin
White Alexander, 34 Lincoln pl.
White Alexander, 806 Washington boul.
White Allen J. 294 Lasalle av.
White Andrew B. Austin
White Annie E. Miss, Austin
White Annie Hungerford Dr. 230, 65th pl.
White Augustus J. 3842 Elmwood ct.
   C.A., W.P.
White A. Stamford, 5217 Lexington av.
   Chi., W.P.
White Bruce C. Lakota hotel
White Burton F. Kenilworth
White Carlton, 5625 Monroe av. *C.A.*
White Catherine Mrs. 4047 Calumet av.
White Charles Dr. 380 Lasalle av.
White Charles B. Hotel Metropole
White Charles E. 180, 51st. *W.P.*
White Charles F. 4614 Woodlawn av. . .
White Charles M. 1416 Montrose boul. .
White Charles R. Oak Park
White Clifford N. 302, 41st
White D. Stearns Dr. 760 W. Adams
White Edward F. 5405 Wabash av.
White Eliza J. Mrs. 73 S. Seeley av.
White Elizabeth Miss, Evanston
White Elizabeth C. Mrs. 3126 Calumet av.
White E. G. Mrs. Evanston·
White E. Norton, 758 W. 67th
White Frank, 230, 65th pl.
White Frank, Tracy
White Frank B. Oak Park
White Frederick, 2671 N. Lincoln
White F. S. Lakota hotel
White George E. 381 Washington boul.
   C.A.
White Gilbert J. Dr. 3138 Lake Park av.
White G. H. Austin
White Harley C. 4402 Ellis av.
White Harry, The Arizona. *C.A.*
White Henry W. 6337 Woodlawn av.
White Herbert, 6326 Greenwood av.
White Hugh A. Mrs. Evanston
White H. S. Prof. Evanston
White H. T. 91, 43d
White James, 1831 Oakdale av.
White James W. Dr. 3931 Drexel boul.
White John H. 345 Park av.
White John M. 3842 Elmwood ct.
White John T. 143 Oakwood boul.
White J. B. 22 Bellevue pl.
White Luelle Mrs. 3647 Michigan av.
White Lyman A. 230, 65th pl.
White Maria A. Mrs. 5517 Cornell av.
White Marie L. Dr. 4645 Evans av.
White Nettie M. Mrs. 2358 Indiana av.
White N. H. 3012 Prairie av.
White Peter B. 4420 Langley av.
White Randall H. 2512 Wabash av..
White Robert, 1732 Wrightwood av.

White Rufus A. Rev. 6800 Perry av.
White Sam T. Continental hotel. *C.A.*
White Sarah A. Mrs. Austin
White Selden F. Evanston
White Trumbull, Revere House
White William F. 4340 Oakenwald av.
White William G. Mrs. Evanston
White William H. 4405 Indiana av.
White William J. Mrs. Evanston
White William M. 4402 Ellis av.
White William R. 263 Warren av.
White William S. Dr. 349 Warren av.
White Wilomene T. Miss, 263 Warren av.
White W. B. Highland Park
Whitefield George W. Dr. Evanston
Whitefield John Rev. Evanston
Whitehall Alexander L. 627 W. 61st
Whitehead Edgar, 1052 Chase av.
Whitehead Elisha P. 1932 Calumet av. *C.A.*
Whitehead Frank C. Evanston
Whitehead Harry, Evanston
Whitehead Herbert C. 2151, 48th
Whitehead S. S. 2003 Indiana av. *C.A.*
Whitehead William, Evanston
Whitehead William H. Evanston
Whitehead William M. Lexington hotel. *C.A., U.L.*
Whitehouse F. Meredith, Chicago club
Whitehouse S. S. 3965 Ellis av. *C.A., Irq:, U.L., W.P.*
Whitely C. J. Mrs. Evanston
Whitely Elizabeth Miss, Evanston
Whiteman Sarah C. Mrs. 4748 Champlain av.
Whiteside Henry R. 3623 Grand boul. Sum. res. Rockford, Ill.
Whiteside J. Henry 1471 W. Monroe
Whiteside Madison, 5 Scott
Whiteside Walton H. 6432 Harvard av.
Whiteside William H. Mrs. 5 Scott
Whiteside William S. 5544 Monroe av.
Whitfield Albert, 5428 Monroe av.
Whitfield George W. Dr. 5428 Monroe av. Sum. res. Pueblo, Col.
Whitfield Joseph H. Evanston
Whitfield William, Evanston
Whitford Mary Mrs. 223 S. Marshfield av.
Whitgreave Christopher T. 3234 Vernon av.
Whiting Frederick G. 3154 Lake Park av. *C.A.*
Whiting George B. 144 Ashland boul.
Whiting Jasper, 322 Superior. *Un.*
Whiting John, 3568 Grand boul.
Whiting John H. 4729 Lake av. *Chi.*
Whiting Robert, 3568 Grand boul.
Whitley C. Mrs. 464, 42d
Whitley John, 6334 Yale.
Whitley Mary R. Miss, 444 Washington boul.
Whitlock A. E. Park Ridge
Whitlock Charles, Park Ridge
Whitlock J. L. Evanston
Whitlock Silas J. Austin

Whitman Arthur T. 4353 Berkeley av.
Whitman Charles O. Prof. 223, 54th
Whitman Freeman F. 1295 Washington boul.
Whitman George B. 956 W. Jackson boul.
Whitman G. A. Union club. *W.P.*
Whitman Hattie E. Miss, 1295 Washington boul.
Whitman John H. 2950 Calumet av.
Whitman John M. 1295 Washington boul.
Whitman Russell, Kenilworth. *Univ.*
Whitmer Lawrence W. Dr. 1508 Aldine av.
Whitmore Charles C. Dr. 4834 Cottage Grove av.
Whitmore Charles E. 3342 Rhodes av.
Whitney Alvin, 903 W. Adams
Whitney Charles A. La Grange
Whitney Charles P. 1220 Winthrop av. *C.A.*
Whitney Clarence J. 1571 Lill av.
Whitney Frank, Lakeside
Whitney George B. 48 Gordon terrace
Whitney George M. 683 W. Monroe
Whitney James D. C. 453 Belden av.
Whitney John B. 5486 Washington av.
Whitney J. C. Calumet club. *W.P.*
Whitney Kate A. Mrs. 1220 Winthrop av.
Whitney M. J. Mrs. 6246 Lexington av.
Whitney Thomas, 2516 Indiana av.
Whitney T. Deykes, 48 Gordon terrace
Whiton W. Starr, 5000 Lake av.
Whitsett R. Bon, 2358 Indiana av.
Whittal M. C. Mrs. 3809 Prairie av.
Whittemore Charles L. Evanston. *U.L.*
Whittemore Luther H. 1539 W. Monroe
Whittlesey Edward S. 7843 Winneconna av.
Whittlesey L. F. Mrs. Oak Park
Whittlesey N. H. Oak Park
Whittlesey Walter H. Oak Park
Whitworth Thomas, 1846 Belmont av.
Whyland Bernard, 3262 Vernon av.
Whyland C. A. 3142 South Park av.
Whyte Alexander, 5153 Prairie av.
Whyte Alexander J. 5153 Prairie av.
Whyte J. Allen, 5153 Prairie av.
Wichert Henry, 1649 Barry av.
Wicker Charles G. Morgan Park
Wicker William B. 608 The Plaza
Wickersham D. Lemoyne Mrs. Irving Park
Wickersham Herman B. 604 Division. *Un.*
Wickersham Joseph R. Irving Park
Wickes Roscoe L. Evanston
Wickes Thomas H. 4835 Grand boul. *Chi., W.P.*
Wickes Thomas H. jr. 4430 Prairie av.
Wickett Frederick W. 407 Oak
Wickham C. E. 4600 Prairie av.
Wickham Wesley W. 615 Englewood av.
Wickman Louis F. 3162 Lake Park av.
Wicks Charles, Winnetka
Wicks George L. 3410 Calumet av.
Wiehe C. F. 524 W. Jackson boul. *Ill.*
Wieland Frank Dr. 3000 Michigan av.
Wiemers Wm. F. 46 Columbia

Wiener Alexander C.Dr.590 Fullerton av.
Wienhoeber Ernst, 668 Lasalle av.
      Sum. res. Waukegan
Wies Charles A. 4831 Vincennes av.
Wies Minna Miss, 4831 Vincennes av.
Wiesler Louisa Mrs. 4223 Wabash av.
Wigeland Andrew G. 802 Pine Grove av.
Wiggin Edward J. 3239 Rhodes av.
Wiggin Twing B. Dr. 690. 48th pl.
Wiggins Arthur D. 3823 Elmwood ct.
Wiggins John B. 3823 Elmwood ct.
Wiggins Sarah J. Mrs. 4840 Langley
    av.
Wigginton James, Evanston
Wiggs George W. 3647 Michigan av.
Wight B. W. 5463 Ridgewood ct.
Wight Eli Dr. 853 Warren av.
Wightman Benjamin, 5536 Washington
    av.
Wightman Charles A. Evanston
Wightman C. J. 5409 Calumet av. C.A.
Wigmore John Henry Prof. Evanston
      Sum. res. Cambridge, Mass.
Wignall Thomas M. 162 Walnut
Wikoff Benjamin D. Austin
Wilber Edwin J. jr. 6340 Madison av.
Wilber J. D. 5710 Madison av.
Wilber M. D. 5708 Madison av.
Wilbur George W. Oak Park
      Sum. res. Belvidere, Ill.
Wilbur Harry Lawrence, 9 Astor. Un.
Wilbur Helen P. Mrs. 2965 Prairie av.
Wilbur James B. jr. 72 Bellevue pl.
Wilbur Josephine M. Miss, Evanston
Wilbur J. B. 72 Bellevue pl. Chi., C.A.,
    U.L.
Wilbur J. Herick, Evanston
Wilbur Ralph, Evanston
Wilce Eva R. Mrs. 361 Ashland boul.
Wilce E. Harvey, 708 W. Harrison. Ill.
Wilce George C. 708 W. Harrison
Wilce George C. 890 W. Adams
Wilce Thomas Mrs. 708 W. Harrison
Wilce Thomas E. 708 W. Harrison
Wilcox Abbie D. Mrs.285 W. Adams
Wilcox Arthur E. 333 Warren av.
Wilcox Burton B. 637 W. Jackson boul.
Wilcox Charles H. 59, 77th
Wilcox Charles S. 4346 Forrestville av.
Wilcox C. A. Granada hotel
Wilcox C. E. Highland Park
Wilcox Edward O. 3870 Lake av.
Wilcox Frederick W. Oak Park
Wilcox Gaylord S. Evanston
Wilcox George G. Evanston.
Wilcox George H. Oak Park
Wilcox Henry M. 3870 Lake av.
Wilcox Henry S. 4759 Calumet av.
Wilcox J. Fred, Joliet. U.L.
Wilcox J. W. North Shore hotel
Wilcox Robert B. 285 W. Adams
Wilcox S. M. Miss, 2024 Indiana av.
Wilcox Theodore B. 716 The Plaza
Wilcox Thomas H. 225 Dearborn av.
Wilcox Wesley W. 3012 Vernon av.
Wilcox William D. Irving Park

Wilcox William E. 874 W. Adams
Wilcox William L. Mrs. Irving Park
Wilcox W. W. Mrs. 804 Washington boul.
      Sum. res. Surry, N.H.
Wilcoxon H. T. Austin
Wild Frederick, Pullman
Wild Harrison M. 3213 Groveland av.
Wild Theodore, M. D. 697 N. Robey
Wilder Charles L. 3144 Malden
Wilder Edwin D. 298 Park av.
Wilder Frank L. LaGrange
Wilder F. N. Morgan Park
Wilder George J. Dr. 443 Englewood av.
Wilder H. H. Washington Heights
Wilder John E. Evanston
Wilder T. Edward, Elmhurst. C.A.
Wilder Walter L. La Grange
Wilder William H. Dr. 5811 Monroe av.
Wildman H. G. Dr. 4467 Lake av.
Wile Edwin W. 347 Oakwood boul.
Wile Elsie Miss, 5134 Woodlawn av.
Wile Joseph M. 4525 Forrestville av.
Wiles Robert H. 5545 Monroe av.
      Sum. res. Freeport, Ill.
Wiley Benjamin S. 3023 Calumet av.
Wiley Edward N. 4800 Kimbark av. C.A.
      Sum. res. Charlevoix, Mich.
Wiley Everett C. 403, 33d
Wiley George W. 3023 Calumet av.
Wiley James A. 403, 33d
Wiley James R. 3023 Calumet av.
Wiley Lyman A. 4709 Woodlawn av. C.A.
Wiley Oscar G. 420 Belden av.
Wiley Sterling P. 4332 Berkeley av. C.A.
Wiley Willard R. 4811 Kimbark av.
Wilhartz William, 295 Ashland boul.
Wilhelm Fred, 296 Ohio
Wilken Isabella Miss, 3201 Vernon av.
Wilken Theodore, 3201 Vernon av.
Wilkerson James H. 5956 Prairie av.
Wilkes Charles M. 47, 46th. Univ.
Wilkes Helen Miss, 6324 Yale
Wilkie Gustav, 1938 Wrightwood av.
Wilkie Harry A. 771 Warren av.
Wilkin Jennie H. Mrs. 764 Walnut
Wilkins Charles H. 41 Aldine sq.
Wilkins Delos A. 4407 Calumet av.
Wilkins Edwin P. 41 Aldine sq.
Wilkins Joseph R. 564 Division. Un.
Wilkins J. C. Mrs. 416, 36th pl.
Wilkins Myrtilla W. Mrs. 41 Aldine sq.
Wilkins S. Grafton, 5128 Washington av.
    C. A.
Wilkinson Arthur W. 482 Lasalle av.
Wilkinson Dudley P. 163 Rush, Un.
Wilkinson Dudley P. jr. 163 Rush
Wilkinson Ethel Miss, North Shore hotel
Wilkinson Harry, 4413 Berkeley av. Irq.,
    U. L.
Wilkinson H. O. New Hotel Holland
Wilkinson John, 482 Lasalle av. U. L.
      Sum. res. Fox Lake
Wilkinson John jr. 482 Lasalle av.
Wilkinson William C. Prof. 5630 Wood-
    lawn av.
Wilks S. 5145 Wabash av.

Will Chas. J. C. 257 Oakwood boul.
Will Charles L. 4235 Vincennes av.
Will Harry C. Dr. 1960 Sheridan rd.
Willard Alonzo J. Winnetka.
Willard C. F. Oak Park
Willard C. P. 349 Dearborn av. *Un.*
Willard Edward O. Oak Park
Willard Frank E. 672, 48th pl, *C.A.*
Willard Gardner G. 5528 Madison av. *Univ.*
Willard George, 262, 53d. *U. L.*
        Sum. res. Asbury Park, N. J.
Willard George E. Dr. 470. 44th
Willard George R. 264, 53d
Willard Henry Rev. 5555 Woodlawn av.
Willard Henry G. 4730 Kimbark av.
Willard James M. Wilmette
Willard John Rev. 7613 Union av.
Willard John B. Oak Park
Willard Mary F. Miss, 865 W. Jackson boul.
Willard M. L. 5528 Madison av. *Ill., Univ.*
Willard. Norman P. 5555 Woodlawn av. *Univ.*
Willard P. H. Mrs. 5528 Madison av.
Willard Rose Dr. 5555 Woodlawn av.
Willard Samuel Dr. 865 W. Jackson boul.
        Sum. res. Harbor Springs, Mich.
Willard S. W. 4118 Newgart av.
Willard William G. Dr. 544 Washington boul. Sum. res. Honey Creek, Wis.
Willcox Alfred B. 4510 Greenwood av.
Willcox G. B. Prof. 512 Washington boul.
Willden John G. 4512 Prairie av. *Irq.*
Willems Charles P. 2684 N. Hermitage av.
Willems Peter, 396 Lasalle av.
Willett Alvin T. 164, 25th
Willett Herbert L. 429, 57th
Willey Albert, 671 W. Monroe
Willey Cameron L. 3659 Michigan av. *W. P.*
Williams Aaron, 289 S. Oakley av.
Williams Abraham Mrs. Hotel Metropole
Williams Alfred S. 5822 Drexel av.
Williams Andrew L. 122 Goethe
Williams Annie Miss, The Ontario
Williams Annie E. Miss, 289 S. Oakley av.
Williams Annie H. Mrs. 631 Washington boul.
Williams Arthur L. Rev. 6451 Woodlawn av.
Williams Augustus W. Rev. 731 Morse av.
Williams A. B. Austin
Williams A. F. 2358 Indiana av.
Williams Bradbury, 581 Lasalle av.
Williams Carrie E. Miss, 3532 Ellis av.
Williams Charles A. Dr. 5136 Hibbard av. *Irq.*
Williams Charles R. 928 W. Adams
Williams Charles S. 3636 Michigan av. *C.A.*
Williams Christopher L. Evanston
Williams Clifford, 3253 Forest av.
Williams Clifford Hoyne, 3253 Forest av.

Williams Cora B. The Ontario
Williams C. D. Rev. Mayfair
Williams C. L. River Forest
Williams Daniel H. Dr. 3301 Forest av.
Williams Daniel W. 4516 Greenwood av.
Williams David, 1820 Wellington
Williams David Irwin, Evanston
Williams Day, 4530 Oakenwald av.
Williams Don F. 20 N. Oakley av.
Williams Dyke, 219, 46th
Williams D. S. Mrs. The Wellington
Williams Edward C. 580 W. Madison, *C. A.*
Williams Edward F. Rev. 147 Ashland boul.
Williams Edward T. 1503 W. Monroe
Williams Edward W. 4432 Sidney av. *C.A.*
Williams Edwin C. Dr. 4405 Ellis av.
Williams E. J. Evanston
Williams E. T. 4600 Ellis av.
Williams Fitzallen B. 3812 Vincennes av.
Williams Florence Mrs. 4001 Vincennes av.
Williams Frank B. 3812 Vincennes av.
Williams Frank N. 1728 Briar pl.
Williams Frederick Newton, The Arizona Sum. res. Groton, Mass.
Williams Frederick W. Evanston
Williams F. M. Berwyn
Williams George, Evanston
Williams George A. 346 Washington boul.
Williams George H. Hinsdale
Williams George J. 1921 Wrightwood av. *C. A.*
Williams George P. Morgan Park
Williams George S. 4729 Indiana av.
Williams George S. 4724 Drexel boul.
Williams George T. 4724 Drexel boul. *U. L.*
Williams George W. 324 Seminary av.
Williams Grant, 4724 Drexel boul.
Williams Grant, Edgebrook
Williams Harney D. Evanston
Williams Harry L. Dr. 1514 Wilson av.
Williams Henry N. Evanston
Williams Henry R. 5532 Washington av.
Williams Helen S. Dr. 6565 Yale
Williams Homer A. Mrs. 1656 W. Adams
Williams H. Mrs. Edgebrook
Williams H. F. 522 Dearborn av. *C. A.*
Williams H. H. Mayfair
Williams Ida Miss, 668 W. Adams
Williams Jacob, 3130 Prairie av.
Williams James B. Dr. 20 Ewing pl.
Williams James D. 3130 Prairie av.
Williams James D. 4599 Oakenwald av. *Ill.*
Williams Jennie B. Mrs. 245 Oakwood boul.
Williams John, 1135 W. Adams. *C.A.*
Williams John C. Evanston
Williams John E. Evanston
Williams John F. Dr. 427 Center
Williams John H. 213 S. Leavitt
Williams John J. 7409 Eggleston av.

Williams John Milton Rev. 597 Cleveland av.
Williams John Oliver, 230, 47th
            Sum. res. Boston, Mass.
Williams John P. 686, 48th pl.
Williams John Q. Evanston
Williams John R. 4600 Ellis av.
Williams Joseph W. 3512 Lake av.
Williams J. Charles, Evanston
Williams J. H. S. Winnetka
Williams J. Oliver, 230, 47th
Williams J. W. Irving Park
Williams Lawrence, 396 Ontario. *Chi.,*
    Univ. Sum. res. Charlevoix, Mich.
Williams Louis M. Dr. 4516 Greenwood
    av.
Williams Lucas R. Dr. 1901 Wrightwood
    av. *C.A.*
Williams Lucian M. 50 St. James pl.
    C.A.
Williams Martin D. 1651 W. Monroe
Williams Mary E. Mrs. 3532 Ellis av.
Williams Merdo K. 1210 Morse av.
Williams M. Mrs. 296 Ohio
Williams Nathan W. Evanston
Williams Newton P. Evanston
Williams Nony R. Mrs. 593 Washington
    boul.
Williams Norman jr. 1836 Calumet av.
    Cal., Chi., Univ.
Williams Norman A. 1651 W. Monroe
Williams Robert A. 252 Warren av.
Williams R. P. 296 Ohio
Williams R. W. 3100 Groveland av.
Williams Sam H. jr. 4160 Ellis av.
Williams Seth S. 522 W. Congress
Williams Simeon B. The Ontario
Williams Stalham L. 593 W. Jackson boul.
            Sum. res. Rochester, N. Y.
Williams Stalham L. jr. 219 S. Marshfield av.
Williams Sydney, Virginia hotel
Williams Thomas D. LaGrange
Williams T. C. jr. 3831 Ellis av.
Williams Waldo A. 3812 Vincennes av.
Williams Wardner, 5822 Drexel av.
Williams Wm. Carver Dr. 4530 Oakenwald av.
Williams William E. 3839 Rhodes av.
Williams William L. Evanston
Williams William Porter, The Arizona.
    U.L. Sum. res. Lake Beulah, Wis.
Williamson E. 4846 Washington av.
Williamson George T. Mrs. 5008 Greenwood av.
Williamson Harry Dr. 3546 Ellis av.
Williamson John C. 951 W. Jackson boul.
            Sum. res. Lake Geneva, Wis.
Williamson Minor H. 316 W. Jackson
    boul.
Williamson Robert B. 951 W. Jackson
    boul.
Williamson Thos. F. 4214 Vincennes av.
Williamson Wm. Longwood
Williamson William, 4400 Greenwood av.
    C.A.

Williamson W. G. 951 W. Jackson boul.
    C.A.
Willing Henry J. 110 Rush. *Chi., C. A.,*
    Un., U. L.
Willis Edwin E. Evanston
Willis F. C. New Hotel Holland
Willis Hattie Miss, 4517 Prairie av.
Willis Lillian Miss, 4517 Prairie av.
Willis Paul, 4827 Lake av.
Willis T. H. 2208 Prairie av.
Williston A. D. 1115 Early av.
Willits George Spencer Mrs. 412 Chicago
    av.
Willits Ward W. 1964 Arlington pl. *C.A.,*
    U. L.
Willms L. Mae Mrs. 533 S. Normal Parkway
Willner Louis J. 673, 48th pl. *Stan.*
Willner Morris, 724 Pullman bldg.
Willner Moses, 3715 Ellis av.
Willoughby A. V. Mrs. Ravinia
Wills Edward D. 791 W. Monroe
Wills John, 31 Aldine sq.
Willson Howard T. Hyde Park hotel
Wilmanns Arnold D. 487 Cleveland av.
Wilmanns Theodore O. 487 Cleveland av.
Wilmarth F. S. Mrs. Lexington hotel
Wilmarth H. M. Mrs. Auditorium annex
Wilmarth Thomas W. 3733 Forest av.
Wilmerding Charles Henry, 412 Chicago
    av. *Un.* Sum. res. Wheaton
Wilmeroff Carl A. River Forest
Wilmersdorf Maurice Mrs. 3343 Prairie
    av.
Wilner Charles E. 184 Bowen av.
Wilson Adelaide Miss, 4613 Drexel boul.
Wilson Albert B. 3960 Drexel boul. *U.L.*
Wilson Albert E. 21 Aldine sq.
Wilson Anna E. Mrs. 55, 53d
Wilson Benjamin M. Wheaton. *Chi.*
Wilson Charles A. 5454 Washington av.
Wilson Charles B. 116 S. Leavitt
Wilson Charles H. 6235 Monroe av.
Wilson Charles L. 4584 Oakenwald av.
Wilson Cora Mrs. 2912 Groveland av.
Wilson C. M. Revere house
Wilson Daniel W. 432 Winthrop av.
Wilson David, 4208 Prairie av.
Wilson Elvira L. Mrs. Evanston
Wilson Emily L. Mrs. 331, 50th
Wilson E. Crane, 4613 Drexel boul. *U.L.*
Wilson E. D. 3210 Malden
Wilson Frank I. 1287 Washington boul.
            Sum. res. Lake Geneva, Wis.
Wilson Fred S. 55, 53d
Wilson F. Cortez, 123 Park av. *Ill.*
Wilson F. E. Mrs. 2001 Michigan av.
Wilson F. J. Irving Park
Wilson George A. S. 3521 Vernon av.
Wilson George Landis, Oak Park
Wilson George W. 341 Park av.
Wilson George W. Hinsdale
Wilson George W. Oak Park
Wilson Granville M. 331, 50th
Wilson Harriet A. Mrs. 3920 Lake av.
Wilson Helen M. Miss, Evanston

Wilson Harry S. 4351 Oakenwald av. *C.A.*
Wilson Henry G. The Hampden
Wilson Henry K. 2922 Prairie av.
Wilson Henry Warren, 123 Park av.
Wilson Horatio R. The Kenwood. *C.A.*, *W.P.*
Wilson Hugh M. 334 Hampden ct.
Wilson Hugh R. Evanston. *U.L.*
Wilson James, 6344 Monroe av.
Wilson James E. 3857 Ellis av.
Wilson James H. 726, 42d
Wilson James H. 971 Park av.
Wilson James W. Austin
Wilson John B. 4519 Oakenwald av.
Wilson John E. Mrs. 3307 Calumet av.
Wilson John F. 2019 Michigan av.
Wilson John H, 3942 Ellis av.
Wilson John P. 564 Dearborn av. *U.L.*, *Univ.* Sum. res. Charlevoix, Mich.
Wilson John R. 434 N. State *C.A.*, *U.L.* Sum. res. Lake Geneva, Wis.
Wilson Joseph C. 2024 Indiana av.
Wilson Justice, 578 Fullerton av.
Wilson J. A. H. Dr. 3000 Indiana av.
Wilson J. H. 4405 Calumet av.
Wilson Louis W. 21 Aldine sq.
Wilson Lucius P. 6243 Woodlawn av.
Wilson Luella M. Mrs. 4313 Drexel boul.
Wilson Luke E. 3307 Calumet av.
Wilson Luke I. 4613 Drexel boul.
Wilson Maggie V. Miss, 192 Ashland boul.
Wilson Margaret Miss, 4208 Prairie av.
Wilson Marshall J. 2922 Prairie av. *U.L.*
Wilson Martha Miss, 564 Dearborn av.
Wilson Mary Miss, Oakland hotel
Wilson Mary Mrs. 3535 Wabash av.
Wilson Mary A. Miss, Park Ridge
Wilson Milton H. Evanston. *U.L.*
Wilson Miss, 564 Dearborn av.
Wilson Monmouth B. Auditorium annex, *C.A.*
Wilson Oliver T. Evanston
Wilson Paul E. 3307 Calumet av.
Wilson Pe Adelaide Miss, 4613 Drexel boul. arl
Wilson Peter E. Oak Park
Wilson Robert C. Dr. 4300 Greenwood av.
Wilson R. C. LaGrange
Wilson Samuel A. 3805 Forest av.
Wilson Samuel C. Hinsdale. *C.A.*
Wilson Samuel R. Irving Park
Wilson Solon D. 4051 Ellis av.
Wilson Stephen R. 102 Dekalb
Wilson S. A. Dr. 6016 Kimbark av.
Wilson Theodore I. 766 Warren av.
Wilson Thomas, 12 Campbell Park
Wilson Thomas H. Austin
Wilson Wallace, 330 Hampden ct.
Wilson Walter H. 2532 Prairie av. *Chi.*, *U.L.* Sum. res. Westbrook, Conn.
Wilson William C. Evanston
Wilson William F. 6116 Monroe av.
Wilson William J. 192 Ashland boul. *Ill.*, *W.P.*
Wilson William L. Dr. 5501 Monroe av.

Wilson William M. Mrs. 4551 Woodlawn av.
Wilson William R. 34 Madison Park
Wilson William White Rev. 21 Aldine sq.
Wilson W. A. Prof. Highland Park
Wilt Charles T. 30 St. James pl. *Irq.*
Wilt Charles T. jr. 71 Lake View av. *Irq.*
Wilt Elmer E. 30 St. James pl.
Wilt Race N. 30 St. James pl.
Wiltz Otto, 3809 Wabash av.
Winans Frank E. Evanston
Winchell F. A. Norwood Park
Winchell M. R. 508 Belden av. *Irq.*
Winchell S. Robertson Prof. Evanston
Winchester C. J. Highland Park
Winchester F. C. Highland Park
Winchester Lucius W. Downer's Grove. *Irq.*
Wincote Charles E. 5335 Cornell av.
Windes Thomas G. Winnetka. *Irq.*
Windes Zell, Winnetka
Windett Vilette Miss, 4332 Berkeley av.
Windheim John C. 1817 Arlington pl.
Windmuller Levi, 4924 Michigan av.
Windrow Sophia Mrs. 408 Dearborn av.
Windrow Sven Dr. 408 Dearborn av.
Windsor Charles J. LaGrange
Windsor Herbert T. Riverside
Windsor Joseph L. LaGrange
Windsor J. E. LaGrange
Windsor J. H. Rev. LaGrange
Windsor W. E. C. Hyde Park hotel
Wineman Jacob R. 4401 Indiana av. *Stan.*
Wineman Joseph M. Hotel Metropole
Wineman Milton R. Hotel Metropole *Stan.*
Wing Daniel, Maywood
Wing Elbert Dr. 4740 Madison av.
Wing Frederick M. Evanston
Wing Henry, Maywood
Wing Luman R. Evanston
Wing Luman R. jr. Evanston
Wing Peter G. Austin
Wing Russell M. Judge, Evanston
Wing Thomas W. 1880 Diversey
Wingate Charles H. 2719 Wabash av.
Wingate Marcia D. Miss, 649 W. Monroe
Winger Elam B. 532 Kenwood terrace
Winger Oswald E. 532 Kenwood terrace
Wingert John, Edison Park
Wingfield James, Revere house
Wingrave John, 750 W. Monroe
Wingrave Sarah Miss, 750 W. Monroe
Wingren Eric Rev. Norwood Park
Wink Charles G. 894 S. Kedzie av.
Winkelman Frederick A. 387 Warren av.
Winklebleck Andrew, 2437 Indiana av.
Winklebleck Homer C. 2437 Indiana av.
Winkler Sigmund A. Lexington hotel. *Lksd.*
Winn Albert Dr. Glen Ellyn
Winn James H. 138 W. 59th
Winne Archibald, 3534 Ellis av.
Winne Frances Mrs. Evanston
Winne Frank N. Evanston

Winne John, 3534 Ellis av.
Winne William N. D. 181 Rush
Winship Charles A. 271 Huron
Winship Charles A. 6633 Lafayette av.
Winship Joseph C. Winnetka
Winslow Charles S. 7 Gordon terrace
Winslow F. A. 239 Hampden ct. *U.L.*
Winslow George W.Dr. 6559 Rhodes av.
Winslow J. H. Glencoe
Winslow William H. River Forest. *U.L.* Sum. res. Tower Hill, Wis.
Winslow William P. Oak Park
Winstanley S. C. Miss, Chicago Beach hotel
Winston Alice Miss, 6109 Monroe av.
Winston Ambrose P. 6109 Monroe av.
Winston Bertram M. 145 Lincoln Park boul. *Un.*
Winston Charles S. 6109 Monroe av.
Winston Dudley Mrs. 99 E. Pearson
Winston Edward M. 6109 Monroe av.
Winston Eugenia Miss, 6109 Monroe av.
Winston F.H. 369 Superior. *Chi., Un.*
Winston Frederick Seymour,576 N. State. *Chi., C.A., Un., W.P.*
Winston Ralph T. 369 Superior
Winston Thomas Dr. 6109 Monroe av.
Winston T. W. Lieut. 6109 Monroe av.
Winter Ethel C. Miss, 3021 Vernon av.
Winter Frank F. 642 Washington boul.
Winter Grace L. Miss, 642 Washington boul.
Winter H g A. Mrs. 642 Washington boul. u h
Winter J. A. Mrs. 414 S. Oakley av.
Winterbotham John H. 15 Walton pl.
Winterbotham Joseph,15 Walton pl. *C.A.*
Winterbotham Joseph jr. 15 Walton pl.
Winterbotham J.R.Mrs. 2215 Michigan av.
Winterbotham Rue Miss, 15 Walton pl.
Wintermeyer Julius C. 840 W. Monroe
Winters Thomas H. 6643 Lafayette av.
Winthrope W. Y. Hotel Woodruff
Winton William W. The Hampden
Wippell P. P. 2902 Groveland av.
Wire Nancy B. Mrs. Evanston
Wire William C. Evanston
Wischmeyer Joseph, 528 Lasalle av
Wisdom Edward, 683½ Washington boul.
Wisdom Harry E. 683½ Washington boul.
Wise Clift, 4515 Woodlawn av. *U.L.*
Wise David, Hotel Woodruff. *Lksd.*
Wise Julius Dr. 4513 Indiana av.
Wise Kate A. Mrs. 896 W. Adams
Wise Maurice, Evanston. *Stan.*
Wise William G. 404 The Plaza
Wiser Clinton B. 321, 49th. *U.L.*
Wisler Henry M. 465 Dearborn av.
Wisner Albert, 4825 Drexel boul.
Wisner Clarence B. 5 Madison Park
Wiswall A. Morgan Park
Wiswall Charles E. Evanston
Wiswall C. E. Hotel Monnett, Evanston
Wiswall George A. Evanston
Wiswall M. E. Mrs. Evanston
Wiswell Jane W. Mrs. 2417 Michigan av.

Wiswell Louis C. 4619 Woodlawn av.
Witbeck J. H. 2841 Michigan av. *Cal., U.L.* Sum. res. Guernsey terrace, Delavan, Wis.
Witherell William G. 5722 Madison av.
Witherill J. H. Hotel Windermere
Witherspoon C. M. Mrs. 300 Schiller
Witherspoon John M. 300 Schiller
Witherspoon Leslie, 300 Schiller
Withington Elizabeth Miss, 4615 Woodlawn av.
Withrow Thomas F. Mrs. 302 Schiller
Witkowsky Conrad,2802 Prairie av. *Lksd. Stan.*
Witkowsky David, 4714 Champlain av. *Lksd.*
Witkowsky David, 4942 Vincennes av. *Lksd.*
Witkowsky Ernestine Miss, 4342 Forrestville av.
Witkowsky Jacob, 3735 Prairie av.
Witkowsky James, 3170 Groveland av. *Stan.*
Witkowsky Leon, 3735 Prairie av.
Witkowsky Leopold, 4942 Vincennes av. *Lksd.*
Witkowsky M. D. 4342 Forrestville av. *Lksd.*
Witkowsky Sam D.5632 Jackson av. *Lksd.*
Witkowsky Samuel, 3735 Prairie av.
Witmark Frank M. Sherman house
Witmer Mary A. Miss, Lakeside
Witte Ernest, LaGrange
Witte Joachim C. 1427 Washington boul.
Wittstein Alfred H. 398 N. State
Wittstein August W. 398 N. State
Wittstein Charles T. 53 Astor
Wittstein Emma Miss, 398 N. State
Wixson Annie A. Mrs. Evanston
Wohlhueter Charles V. 1739 Arlington pl.
Wolbach J. S. 4329 Calumet av. *Stan.*
Wolcott Francis P. A. 4535 Ellis av.
Wolcott Frank H. 6435 Kimbark av.
Wolcott Henry, 376 Warren av.
Wolcott James G. LaGrange
Wolcott Maria C. Mrs. Evanston
Wolcott Peter C. Rev. Highland Park
Woley Henry P. Dr. 4257 Grand boul.
Wolf Aaron Mrs. 3672 Michigan av.
Wolf Ada Mrs. 3616 Prairie av.
Wolf Alphonso S. 698 W. Monroe
Wolf Arthur C. 3156 Wabash ay.
Wolf A. H. 3939 Ellis av. *Lksd., Stan Univ.*
Wolf Benjamin, 698 W. Monroe. *Lksd.*
Wolf Bernhard, 3561 Prairie av.
Wolf Fred W. 504 Lasalle av.
Wolf F. L. Wilmette
Wolf Gabriel, 83, 32d
Wolf Henry, 504, 42d pl.
Wolf Henry F. 3156 Wabash av.
Wolf H. C. 4547 Vincennes av.
Wolf H.M.3939 Ellis av.*C.A.,Stan., Univ*
Wolf John P. 85, 33d
Wolf Joseph, 416 The Plaza. *Irq.*
Wolf L. J. 4750 Kenwood av. *Stan.*

Wolf M. W. Mrs. 3156 Wabash av.
Wolf Paul A. Lieut. Fort Sheridan
Wolf Peter, 15, 33d
Wolf Silas A. Capt. Fort Sheridan
Wolf Simon Mrs. 698 W. Monroe
Wolf Sol, 4431 Berkeley av. *Lksd.*
Wolf Victorine Mrs. 4154 Ellis av.
Wolf William B. 3561 Prairie av. *Lksd.*
Wolfarth Max M. 4752 Prairie av.
Wolfe Ida M. Miss. Morton Park
Wolfe Joseph G.Dr. 403 W. Jackson boul.
Wolfe J. R. Mrs. 4257 Grand boul.
Wolfe Lottie Miss, Morton Park
Wolfe Mary Mrs. Morton Park
Wolfe Moses, 53, 32d
Wolfe Oswald F. Morton Park
Wolfe Solomon, 4416 Langley av.
Wolfenstetter J. W. 321 Park av.
Wolff C. J. 831 W. Monroe
    Sum. res. Channel Lake, Ill.
Wolff H. D.Dr.4333 Forrestville av. *Lksd.*
Wolff John F. 1680 W. Monroe. *U.L.*
    Sum. res. Channel Lake, Ill.
Wolff Leopold, 4463 Ellis av. *Lksd.*
Wolff Louis G. 3426 Calumet av.
Wolff Louise J. Miss, 7100 Princeton av.
Wolff Ludwig, 658 Lasalle av.
Wolff Ludwig, 1319 Washington boul.
Wolff Maurice B. 3426 Calumet av.
Wolff M. 453 Dearborn av.
Wolff Nathan, 453 Dearborn av.
Wolff Otto E. 737 Pine Grove av.
Wolff Peter F. 3834 Langley av.
Wolff Samuel, 453 Dearborn av.
Wolff William, 4333 Forrestville av.*Lksd.*
Wolfinger C. I. 2843 N. Paulina
Wolfner Rudolph, 4544 St. Lawrence av.
Wolford Frank H 6450 Ellis av.
Wolford J. A. 552 N. State. *C.A.,W. P.*
Wolfsohn Carl, 2502 Indiana av.
Wolgamott Geo. W. Dr. 826 Warren av.
Wolhaupter Benjamin, 6426 Kimbark av.
Wollensak J. F. 362 Lasalle av.
Wolseley Henry W. 4456 Ellis av. *U.L.*
Woltersdorf Arthur F. 360 Ashland boul.
Woltersdorf Ernest, Oak Park
Woltersdorf Louis, 360 Ashland boul.
Wood Andrew J. 802 W. Monroe
Wood Annie Mrs. 295 Webster av.
Wood C ey A. Dr. Lexington hotel.
    *U.L.*as
Wood Charles A. 4016 Michigan av.
Wood Charles B. 5420 East End av. *Irq.*
    Sum. res. Lake Zurich, Ill.
Wood Charles H. Oak Park
Wood Charles S. Dr. 55 Warren av.
Wood Clark C. Austin
Wood Cora Miss, 6358 Minerva av.
Wood Cyrus J. 156 Dearborn av.
Wood David Ward, 533 W. 62d
Wood Edmond A. 620 Englewood av.
Wood Eleanor P. Miss, 405 Dearborn av.
Wood Emily Mrs. Austin
Wood Emma Caswell Dr. 2941 Kenmore
Wood Eneas A. Mrs. 4430 Vincennes av.
    Sum. res. Lake Bluff

Wood Ernest G. Capt. Highland Park
Wood Frank C. Oak Park
Wood Frank M. 5313 Cornell av.
Wood Frank W. 188, 41st
Wood Frederick H. Oak Park
Wood Frederick W. 5436 Jefferson av.
Wood F. F. North Shore hotel
Wood George, 4540 Prairie av.
Wood George A. Dr. 4016 Michigan av.
Wood George Ellery,2801 Prairie av. *Cal.,*
    U.L. Sum. res. Lakeville, Conn.
Wood George S. 5436 Jefferson av.
Wood Harriet B. Miss, 5420 East End av.
Wood Horace E. R. 5440 Jefferson av.
Wood Horatio F. Dr. 248, 57th
Wood H. H. Hotel Windermere
Wood Ida M. Miss, 2904 Prairie av.
Wood Ira Couch, 527 N. State. *U.L.*
Wood James A. 4016 Michigan av.
Wood John, 1085 S. Central Park av.
Wood John E. 3657 Indiana av.
Wood John E. Mrs. 3259 Indiana av.
Wood John H. 3657 Indiana av.
Wood John H. 5806 Rosalie ct. *C.A.*
Wood Julia Miss, 5420 East End av.
Wood J. C. Park Ridge
Wood J. H. Col. 721 W. Adams. *Ill.*
Wood J. M. Mrs. The Arizona
Wood Kay, 3924 Michigan av. *Univ.*
Wood Mae Miss, 6358 Minerva av.
Wood Milton R. 2904 Prairie av.
Wood M. M. Berwyn
Wood O. F. Mrs. 248, 57th
Wood Silas L. 804 W. Monroe
Wood S E. Dr. 3924 Michigan av. *W.P*
Wood S. Ella Miss, 3924 Michigan av.
Wood Thomas R. 5436 Jefferson av.
Wood Walpole, 766 Warren av.
Wood Wm. Fairfax, 212, 32d. *U.L.*
Wood William H. 890 S. Kedzie av.
Wood William H. Oak Park
Wood William L. 2771 N. Paulina
Wood William W. Oak Park
Wood Willis G. 271 Oakwood boul.
Woodard Charles S. Oak Park
Woodbridge John, 501 Fullerton av.
Woodbridge John R. Evanston
Woodbridge Jonathan E. 267 Erie. *Un.*
Woodbury Alice Miss, 159 Warren av.
Woodbury De Wilton B. 4316 Langley av
Woodbury Fitz Allan, 340 W. 61st pl.
Woodbury George W. Oak Park
Woodbury Lewis E. 1425 Edgecomb ct.
Woodbury S. H. Austin. *C.A., W.P.*
Woodbury William A. 1425 Edgecomb ct.
Woodbury W.H.Dr.611 Washington boul.
Woodcock Arthur, 2419 Michigan av.
Woodcock E. W. Hotel Metropole
Woodcock Lindsay T. Oak Park
Woodcock Thomas J. Mrs. Hinsdale
Woodford G. S. Hotel Del Prado
Woodford Jerome A. Oak Park
Woodford Philip R. Evanston
Woodhead Howard, 5016 Ellis av.
Woodhead J. E. 5016 Ellis av.

Woodland Fred B. 355 Oakwood boul.
Woodland George, 355 Oakwood boul.
Woodle Edward R. 5729 Madison av.,C.A.,
 Irq. Sum. res. Syracuse, N. Y.
Woodley George, Evanston
Woodman Jennie Miss, 44, 35th
Woodman T. F. Chicago Beach hotel
Woodruff Charles A. 6703 Lafayette av.
Woodruff Charles A. Riverside
Woodruff Charles E. 4857 Kimbark av.
Woodruff C. B. 6645 Yale
Woodruff Edward, 4831 Madison av.
Woodruff E. F., M. D. 36th ne. cor. Cottage Grove av.
Woodruff Franklin R. 677, 48th pl.
Woodruff Joseph B. 2937 Indiana av.
Woodruff Louis C. 4857 Kimbark av.
Woodruff Mary E.Mrs. 3164 Groveland av.
Woodruff Samuel Mrs. Maywood
Woodruff Thomas A.Dr. 1813 Indiana av.
Woods Arthur T. Mrs. 45 Cedar
Woods Clinton E. 512, 53d
Woods F. Marion, 1278 Washington boul.
Woods Helen M. Mrs. 5024 Indiana av.
Woods Isaac L. 537 W. 65th
Woods J. L. Major, Lexington hotel
Woods M. M. Mrs. 5809 Washington av.
Woods William J. Chicago Beach hotel. C.A.
Woodside Nevin G. Oak Park
Woodson Emily A. Mrs. Evanston
Woodward Arthur C. 440 Dearborn av.
Woodward A. H. 4742 Grand boul. *U.L.*
Woodward A. W. Dr. 130 Ashland boul.
Woodward E. A. 3100 Groveland av.
Woodward E. A. Mrs. Evanston
Woodward E. E. L. Mrs. 1917 Diversey
Woodward George B. Oak Park
 Sum. res. De Funiak Springs, Fla.
Woodward G. M. 4516 Forrestville av.
Woodward James L.Mrs. 4742Grand boul.
Woodward Joseph Sarchet, 415 Dearborn av.
Woodward Juliet K. Mrs. 415 Dearborn av.
Woodward Morgan S. Evanston
Woodward Morgan S. Evanston. *C.A.,*
 U.L.
Woodward T.R. Chicago Beach hotel.*Ill.*
Woodward Walter H. 5420 Monroe av.
Woodward W. H. Berwyn
Woodworth George B. Evanston
Woodworth J. A. 152, 36th
Woodworth J. W. Hotel Woodruff
Woodworth Plumer M. Dr. 1246 N. Clark
Woodworth Rome H. 6620 Yale
Woodworth S. A. Dr. Park Ridge
Woodyatt Clara L. Mrs. Evanston
Woodyatt Ernest, Evanston
Woodyatt Rollin T. Evanston
Wooley Edwin, 5535 Cornell av.
Wooley John, 5535 Cornell av.
Woolf Benjamin 434 Warren av. *Stan.*
Woolf E. Mrs. 434 Warren av.
Woolf Harry, 375 Ashland boul.
Woolf Isaac, 3305 Michigan av. *Stan.*

Woolfolk Alexander M. 6011 Jefferson av.
Woolfolk Clinton S. 6011 Jefferson av.
Woollacott John S. 77 Lake View av.
Woolacott W. H. 1101 Early av.
Woolley Clarence M. 10 Astor. *Un.*
Woolley C. E. 4952 Vincennes av.
Woolley Emma A. Mrs. 268, 33d
Woolley Frances C. Mrs.2229 Sheridan rd.
Woolley Francis J. Oak Park
Woolley Jefferson H. Dr. 1882 Diversey
Woolley Vernon S. 2229 Sheridan rd.
Woolner Sig. J. 3601 Vincennes av.
Wooster Clarence K. 69, 48th. *Chi.,C.A.*
Wooster F. W. Lieut. Hotel Del Prado
Worcester C. H. 469 N. State
Work A. S. Hotel Metropole. *Cal., C.A.,*
 Ill., W.P.
Work George R. Evanston
Work George Z. Virginia hotel. *C.A.*
Work J. W. Evanston
Works M. H. Miss, 3633 Grand boul.
Worley Brice, 4419 Ellis av.
Worley David A. 4442 Vincennes av.
Worman William S. Winnetka
Wormser D. 3215 South Park av. *Stan.*
Wormser M. Leopold, 4325 Prairie av.
Wornlow U. G. Lieut. 2124 Michigan av.
Worrall Carrie B. Miss, 5748 Monroe av.
Worth R. F. Dr. 1101 S. Central Park av.
Worth William H. Hotel Normandie
Worthington E. E. 3952 Ellis av. *Cal.*
Worthington Harry C. Dr. Oak Park
Worthington James L. Oak Park
Worthington Martha Miss, Oak Park
Worthington Robert S. Oak Park
Worthy John Mrs. Virginia hotel
Worthy Sidney, Virginia hotel
Worthy Willis, Virginia hotel
Wray James T. Evanston
Wray Robert C. P. Austin
Wray Susan P. Mrs. Evanston
Wrenn Everts, 150 Lincoln Park boul.
 Univ.
Wrenn George L. Rev. Highland Park
Wrenn Harold B. 2917 Prairie av.
Wrenn John H. 2917 Prairie av. *Cal., Chi.*
Wrenn William B. 3252 Vernon av. *C.A.*
Wright Alfred J. The Tudor
Wright Anna L. Mrs. Oak Park
Wright A. W. 322 Ashland boul. *Ill.*
Wright A. J. Evanston
Wright A. M. Mrs. 235 Ashland boul.
Wright A. W. 3637 Prairie av.
Wright Charles A. Oak Park
Wright Charles H. 215 Ashland boul.
Wright C. H. Dr. 647 Washington boul.
Wright Cookson M. Oak Park
Wright C. Walter, LaGrange
Wright Edward Mrs. 2659 Kenmore av.
Wright E. A. Mrs. 607 W. Congress
Wright E. B. 3601 Vincennes av.
Wright E. J. H. 1079 W. Taylor
Wright Frances E. A. Miss, Hinsdale
Wright Frank, 113 Cass
Wright Frank G. 5538 Cornell av.
Wright Frank L. Oak Park

Wygant Alonzo, 537 W. Jackson boul. *C.A., Ill., Lksd.*
Wygant Bernard, 131 Park av.
Wykel Carey D. 1619 W. Monroe
Wykopf John, Highland Park
Wylde Edward, Hinsdale. *C.A.*
Wylie David, 9 St. James pl.
Wylie George W. 6348 Stewart av.
Wylie H. D. Hinsdale
Wylie Stephen W. Evanston
Wyllis Ruth Mrs. Evanston
Wyman Edward F. Evanston
Wyman Ralph L. 525 W. Monroe
Wyman Richard F. Mrs. Evanston
Wyman Richard H. Evanston
Wyman Walter C: Evanston
Wyman W. D. 4362 Oakenwald av. *U.L.*
Wynekoop C. M. 55, 36th
Wynekoop Eldridge Dr. 1563 W. Monroe
Wyness William L. Mrs. 4338 Indiana av.
Wynkoop H. T. Mrs. 267 S. Winchester av.
Wynn Edwin, 507 W. Monroe
Wynne Madeline G. Mrs. 9 Ritchie ct.
Wyper James, LaGrange
Wyville Walter N. 3238 Groveland av.

YAGER LOUIS E. Austin
    Yager William A. 2243 Michigan av. *C.A., W.P.*
Yaggy Levi W. Lake Forest. *U.L.*
Yaggy T. A. Lake Forest
Yakel John A. 4220 Ellis av.
Yalding H. W. River Forest
Yale Frank W. Austin
Yale John A. Mrs. 369 Chicago av.
Yale J. L. 9 Ritchie ct. *Chi., Un., W.P.*
Yale M. Mme. Auditorium annex
Yarnell John K. 4551 Evans av.
Yarros Rochelle S. Dr. 22 Bellevue pl.
Yates Ernest G. Evanston
Yates Thomas D. 422 N. State
Yeager Frederick W. 1663 W. Monroe
Yeager N. R. Dr. 110, 53d
Yeomans George G. 4167 Berkeley av. *Univ.*
Yerkes Charles S. Oak Park
Yerkes Charles T. 3201 Michigan av. *C.A., W.P.*
Yerkes·R. Archie, Oak Park
Yoe Charles C. Hotel Metropole. *Chi., Un.* Sum. res. Highland Park
Yoe Lucien G. 476 Dearborn av.
            Sum. res. Highland Park
Yoe Peter L. 476 Dearborn av.
Yondorf August, 567 Lasalle av.
Yondorf Charles, 2547 Indiana av: *Stan.*
Yondorf David, 3229 Groveland av. *Lksd.*
Yondorf Simon, 2960 Prairie av. *Stan.*
York John, 43 Centre av.
York John B. 43 Centre av.
York J. Devereux, 612 Division
York Lawley Dr. 968 W. Monroe
York Lila Miss, 4059 Grand boul.
York William Sarsfield, 4059 Grand boul.

Yorty John, Mayfair
Yott Frank, 1856 Barry av.
Young Alben Dr. 2429 N. Paulina
Young Alice B. Mrs. 3169 Groveland av.
Young Arthur, 444 Chestnut. *Chi.*
Young Austin E. 3944 Prairie av.
Young A. N. Evanston
Young A. V. E. Prof. Avenue house, Evanston
Young Bicknell, 531 Belden av.
Young Caroline M. Miss, 481 Dearborn av.
Young Caryl, 1704 Michigan av. *Cal., W.P.*
Young Caryl B. 1704 Michigan av.
Young Catherine O. Miss, 2032 Calumet av.
Young Daisy M. Miss, 2032 Calumet av.
Young Daniel J. 3933 Grand boul.
Young D. Webster Dr. 131 Loomis
Young Edgar L. 6435 Monroe av.
Young Edith G. Miss, 341 Washington boul.
Young Edward C. Longwood
Young Elbert S. 5406 Ellis av.
Young Ella F. Mrs. 338, 57th
Young Ernest W. Austin
Young E. A. 6444 Kimbark av.
Young E. L. Mrs. 327 Warren av.
Young Frank, 161 Locust
Young Frank, 185 S. Oakley av.
Young Frank W. 676 W. Adams
Young George, 7330 Yale
Young George W. Auditorium annex. *Chi.*
Young Harrison P. Oak Park
Young Henry, 4449 Lake av.
Young Henry G. 4032 Prairie av.
Young Henry M. 3006 Prairie av. *C.A.*
Young James M. Tracy
Young James T. 4240 Indiana av.
Young Jane Mrs. 6560 Yale
Young John Mrs. 447 W. Congress
Young John, 461 Warren av.
Young John M. 2446 Michigan av.
Young John M. 6642 Harvard av.
Young John N. 1402 Montrose boul.
Young Joseph S. Dr. 341 Washington boul.
Young J. E. 71 Park av.
Young Late Miss, 531 Belden av.
Young Leon W. 341 Washington boul.
Young Lewis W. 4058 Ellis av.
Young Linn H. 3953 Michigan av.
Young Luther C. 4725 Prairie av.
Young L. A: 1812 Prairie av. *Chi., W.P.*
Young Margaret A. Mrs. 4122 Grand boul.
Young Max, 5430 Lexington av.
Young Miss, 4449 Lake av.
Young Nellie Miss, 113 Cass
Young Otto, 2032 Calumet av. *Cal., C.A., U.L., W.P.*
    Sum. res. Lake Geneva, Wis.
Young Percy J. 267 Chestnut
Young Peter F. 110 S. Leavitt
Young Robert E. 5714 Washington av.
Young R. A. Leland hotel
Young Ulrich, 227, 52d
    Sum. res. Beulah Lake, Wis.

Young William, Evanston
Young William jr. 5006 Michigan av.
Young William Mrs. 5006 Michigan av.
Young William A. 5118 Madison av.
Young William S. 427 Evanston av.
Young William S. Evanston
Young Willis, 1663 W. Monroe
Young W. K. 4449 Lake av.
Young W. W. 4465 Lake av. *C.A.*
Youngdahl Alfred J. 909 Warren av.
    Sum. res. Lake Geneva, Wis.
Younger William J. Dr. Auditorium hotel *Chi.*
Younglove Ira S. Hotel Windermere. *C.A.*
Younglove T. G. 4518 Forrestville av.
Younglove W. W. Mrs. 522 Fullerton av.
Youngs Marie A. Mrs. 4307 Oakenwald av.
Youngs P. R. Glen Ellyn
Yount Silas T. Dr. 4168 Drexel boul.
Youst George W. Clifton house
Yuille George A. 303 Ashland boul. *Ill.*

ZAHRINGER CHARLES T. 4420 Champlain av.
Zander August, 115 Osgood
Zander E. W. 2773 N. Robey
    Sum. res. Ravinia
Zander H. G. 2335 N. 41st st
Zang Edward F. Evanston
Zang William, Evanston
Zapfe Fred. C. Dr. 925 Warren av.
Zarbell Iver C. 4132 Ellis av.
Zeddies Frederick W. 4504 Vincennes av.
Zeiger Gebhardt W. 1103 N. Clark
Zeisler Jos. Dr. 3256 Lake Park av. *Irq.*
Zeisler Sigmund, 568 Division. *Irq.*
Zeiss C. Morgan Park
Zeiss Henry C. F. 11 Aldine sq. *C.A., U.L., W.P.*
Zeit Robert F. Dr. 4016 Vincennes av.
Zeither Julius N. 2303 N. Hermitage av.
Zelie Lucina C. Mrs. 2518 Prairie av.
Zeller W. F. Virginia hotel. *Chi.,*
Zeltner John E. 3848 Ellis av.
Zenos Andrew C. Rev. 2 Chalmers pl.
Zernitz Julius C. 690 Fullerton av.
Zernitz J. D. 690 Fullerton av.
Zeublin John E. 6052 Kimbark av.
Ziegfeld Florence Dr. 501 W. Adams. *Ill.*
Ziegfeld William K. 501 W. Adams
Ziegler John S. 602 Lunt av.
Ziesing August, 2569 N. Ashland av. *C.A.*
Zilla John Rev. Elmhurst
Zimmerman Arthur P. 528 W. 61st
Zimmerman Barbara Miss, 565 Cleveland av.
Zimmerman Cecil E. Evanston
Zimmerman Charles, Austin
Zimmerman Charles H. Rev. Evanston
Zimmerman Gustav A. 683 Sedgwick
Zimmerman Harold, 197 Fremont
Zimmerman John, 509 W. Adams
Zimmerman John, The Hampden
Zimmerman John S. 132 Park av.

immerman Milton T. 528 W. 61st
immerman Wm. 5621 Washington av.
. U. L.
immermann Wm. F. 526 Fullerton av.
inkeisen O. T. 716 Pullman bldg.
inkeisen P. E. 716 Pullman bldg.
ipprich John C. 2089 Kenmore av.
itzewitz Herman, 3283 Beacon
oellin Horace, Maywood
ollmann Gustav Rev. 419 Winthrop av.

Zollmann John, 419 Winthrop av.
Zook David L. Highland Park
Zorge Robert J. 1127 Winthrop av.
Zork Sol. 4416 Prairie av.
Zuber George, 2935 Groveland av.
Zuckerman S. Mrs. 77 Bowen av.
Zueblin Charles Prof. 6052 Kimbark av.
Zuetell William, Edison Park
Zulfer Anton G. 4438 Prairie av.
Zulfer P. M. 4438 Prairie av.

PART SEVENTH.

SUBURBAN LIST.

THE BLUE BOOK.

CONTAINING THE NAMES OF THE PROMINENT
HOUSEHOLDERS OF THE SUBURBS OF
CHICAGO WITHIN A RADIUS OF
TWENTY-FIVE MILES.

SUBURBAN LIST.

AUSTIN.

AUSTIN BOULEVARD.

229 Dr. & Mrs. Wm. H. Weaver

BAIRD AVENUE.

121 Mr. & Mrs. Fred H. Putnam
133 Mr. & Mrs. Wm. Schwaeger-
    mann
223 Mr. & Mrs. John A. Hammett

---

210 Mr. & Mrs. A. J. C. Ledgerwood
218 Mr. & Mrs. Chas. Howard
236 Mr. & Mrs. Samuel H. Aber-
    nethy
302 Dr. & Mrs. H. R. Sackett & dr.
304 Mr. & Mrs. I. A. Robinson
304 Mr. & Mrs. J. D. Pratt
318 Mr. & Mrs. A. E. Bartelme

NORTH CENTRAL AVENUE.

211 Mr. & Mrs. W. A. Toles
213 Mr. & Mrs. H. C. Custer
215½ Mrs. Mary P. Dunton
221 Dr. & Mrs. R. C. Newell
225 Mr. & Mrs. N. B. Wallace & dr.
227 Mr. & Mrs. Chas. J. Gibson
229 Mr. & Mrs. H. A. Emerson
229 Horace H. Emerson
229 H. E. Marlow
303 Mr. & Mrs. Charles S. Castle
303 Mr. & Mrs. Edward Church
311 Mr. & Mrs. Andrew Lindsey
313 Mr. & Mrs. Clark C. Wood
313 Mrs. Emily Wood
317 Mr. & Mrs. Wm. P. Jenkins
319 Mr. & Mrs. Edward Francis
    Receiving day Tuesday
337 Mr. & Mrs. Francis E. Pray
339 Mr. & Mrs. Frank Emerson

405 Dr. & Mrs. Geo. B. Charles
    & dr.
    Receiving day 1st Wednesday
405 Fred L. Charles
435 Mr. & Mrs. Geo. W. Cone & drs.
529 Mr. & Mrs. Russell Hall & dr.

116 Mr. & Mrs. J. J. McCarthy & drs.
126 Mr. & Mrs. Edward A. Adams
    & dr.
126 Edward L. Adams
136 Dr. & Mrs. Anthony Rud
    Receiving day Friday
208 Dr. & Mrs. M. J. Lyman
238 Mr. & Mrs. E. O. Baker
310 Mrs. M. L. Patrick & dr.
310 Charles B. Patrick
316 Mr. & Mrs. Thos. Langford
324 Mr. & Mrs. A. T. Benson
    Receiving day Friday
408 Mr. & Mrs. Wm. Amerson & dr.
408 George C. Amerson
408 Harvey S. Amerson
408 Mr. & Mrs. Charles Zimmerman
534 Mr. & Mrs. A. N. Sperry
    Receiving day Thursday

SOUTH CENTRAL AVENUE.

117 Dr. & Mrs. G. P. Head
123 Mr. & Mrs. George M. Davis
123 George C. Davis
209 Mr. & Mrs. Charles H. Kehl
231 Mr. & Mrs. Charles S. Cargill
231 Mr. & Mrs. John P. Garner
301 Mr. & Mrs. Edward R. Knowl-
    ton
305 Mr. & Mrs. Z. J. Frost
317 Mr. & Mrs. C. F. Bonney
317 Mrs. E. A. Bonney
325 Mr. & Mrs. Geo. A. Philbrick

403 Mr. & Mrs. T. A. Snow
403 J. C. Snow

———

108 Mr. & Mrs. R. R. Jampolis
122 Mr. & Mrs. J. W. Bennett & drs.
136 Mr.& Mrs.M.Frank Murray& dr.
136 Mr. & Mrs. C. C. Murray
136 Frank G. Murray
136 George R. Murray
136 Harold G. Murray
230 Mr. & Mrs. Edward Andrew
   Receiving day Thursday
230 Mrs. E. Andrew & dr.
230 Lester Andrew
300 Mr. & Mrs. W. A. Mitchell
306 Mr. & Mrs. David Oliphant
306 James B. Oliphant
310 Mr. & Mrs. W. F. Branston
312 Mr. & Mrs. Jacob J. Walser
328 Mr. & Mrs. Harvey Strickler
400 Mr. & Mrs. Fred A. Hill
400 Mr. & Mrs. Eric J. Nelson
408 Mr. & Mrs. Stanley C. Crafts

CHICAGO AVENUE.

5437 Mr. & Mrs. Paul G. Biggs
5437 Vernon A. Biggs
5437 B. P. Biggs
5515 Mr.&Mrs.Chas.W.Blatherwick

CLARK AVENUE.

106 William R. Clark
106 Miss Mary J. Clark
125 Mr. & Mrs. W. E. Burgess
125 Mrs. S. A. White
127 Mr. & Mrs. S. C. Elliott & dr.
131 Dr. & Mrs. Edward M. Rosekrans

ERIE STREET.

5718 Mr. & Mrs. Wm. A. Andrew

FIFTY-THIRD AVENUE.

309 Mr. & Mrs. Willis H. Bennett

SOUTH FRANKLIN AVENUE.

315 Fred Eddy
319 Mr. & Mrs. Jos. H. Barnett
333 Mr. & Mrs. A. J. Eaton
333 Mr. & Mrs. Isaac I. Eaton
415 Joseph Shaw & drs.
415 A. D. Shaw

517 Mr. & Mrs. Charles C. Turner
   Receiving day Wednesday
517 Mrs. Anna E. Bradford
   Receiving day Wednesday
541 Mr. & Mrs. Frank X. Daul

308 Mr. & Mrs A. G. Bagley
   Receiving day Wednesday
320 Mr. & Mrs. G. W. Kretzinger
  & dr.
320 G. W. Kritzinger jr.
412 Mr. & Mrs. H. H. Geselbracht
416 Mr. & Mrs. Alfred B. Johnson
  & dr.

FRINK STREET.

5737 Mr. & Mrs. Frank P. Wallace

———

5815 Mr. & Mrs. J. G. Wakefield

SOUTH HOWARD AVENUE.

117 Mr. & Mrs. Gus A. Kreis
123 Mr. & Mrs. Willet S. Dorland
221 Mr. & Mrs. Wellington Stetson
225 Mr. & Mrs. H. C. Cornell
225 W. D. Cornell
303 Mr. & Mrs. Wm. H. Prinz
305 Mr. & Mrs. J. C. Smith & dr.
305 Harry O. Campbell
329 Mr. & Mrs. F. H. Alden
329 Dr. S. H. Kelley
421 Mr. & Mrs. W. T. Goss
421 Mrs. E. M. Burbank & dr.

136 Mr. & Mrs. Fred J. Erfert
214 Dr. & Mrs. Jas. N. Hathaway
326 Mrs. F. Butler
326 Walter L. Butler
540 Mr. & Mrs. H. L. Butler
540 Mr. & Mrs. Thomas P. Ford

INDIANA STREET.

5411 Mr. & Mrs. B. M. Shurtleff & dr.
   Receiving day Thursday
5411 Ira G. Sibley
5437 E. S. Osgood & dr.
5437 F. S. Osgood
5437 Mrs. E. H. Bryan
5437 Mrs. M. P. Thomas
5437 Miss Annie E. White

MADISON STREET.

5615 Miles B. Craft
5615 Z. B. Crafts

MIDWAY PARK.

5715 Mrs. E. M. Rossiter & dr.
5715 Harold Rossiter
5715 Mr. & Mrs. Wm. Rossiter
5735 Mr. & Mrs. E. J. Whitehead
5803 Mr. & Mrs. F. R. Schock
5811 Mr. & Mrs. F. C. Beeson
5911 Mr. & Mrs. Perley D. Castle
5911 Alvin F. Davis & dr.
5923 Mr. & Mrs. Wm. J. Ford
5927 Mrs. Wm. H. Rounds
5927 Charles H. Rounds
5927 Fred C. Rounds
5933 Mr. & Mrs. Thos. C. Hood
5933 Mr. & Mrs. Henry J. Wade
5939 Mr. & Mrs. Daniel R. McAuley
5939 Miss Belle Scannell
5943 Mr. & Mrs. A. J. Sweeney
5953 Mr. & Mrs. Elmer D. Robinson

5914 Mr. & Mrs. H. P. Knoblock & drs.
5918 Mr. & Mrs. C. C. Hunsinger

OHIO STREET.

5411 Mr. & Mrs. Thos. H. Wilson
5521 Mr. & Mrs. S. J. Crafts
5531 Mr. & Mrs. N. M. Bassett
5641 Dr. Mary J. Kearsley
5641 Miss Margaret I. Isgrig
5641 Mrs. Louise M. Sedgwick
5719 Mr. & Mrs. T. R. Coates
5723 Mr. & Mrs. O. P. Emerson
5723 Mrs. F. M. Owens & dr.
5727 Mr. & Mrs. R. C. S. Wray
5737 Mr. & Mrs. Geo. B. Cogdal
5739 Mr. & Mrs. Eugene Hunt
5803 Mrs. Catherine Schlecht & drs.
5803 Oscar G. Schlecht
5803 Chas. F. Schlecht
5809 Mr. & Mrs. Lawrence A. Norton
5809 Miss Isabel Bulckens
5809 Miss Louise Bulckens
5815 Mr. & Mrs. L. E. Hall
5901 Mr. & Mrs. Ernest W. Young
5905 Mr. & Mrs. Alpheus McCallum
5913 Mr. & Mrs. H. G. Stallwood
5933 Mr. & Mrs. Allen A. Johnson

5430 Mr. & Mrs. S. J. Whitlock
5700 Mr. & Mrs. L. E. Race
cor. Prairie av. Miss Louise M.
Schock
Miss Blanche C. Falcy

46

5810 Mr. & Mrs. F. W. Meadows
5812½ Mr. & Mrs. Dorchester Mapes
5902 Mr. & Mrs. Charles E. Frazier
5916 Mr. & Mrs. Charles R. Phoenix
5930 Mr. & Mrs. Benjamin D. Wikoff
5946 Mr. & Mrs. John Thompson & dr.
5946 W. W. Thompson
5950 Mr. & Mrs. A. P. Mullin
Receiving day Wednesday

ONTARIO STREET.

5703 Mr. & Mrs. Charles A. Hitchcock jr.
5729 Mr. & Mrs. L. S. Pinney & dr.
5729 Mr. & Mrs. Arthur Selleck
5735 H. T. Wilcoxon
5901 Mr. & Mrs. W. P. Freeman & dr.
5901 Mr. & Mrs. J. M. Duryee
5917 Mr. & Mrs. Axel Strom & dr.
5931 Mr. & Mrs. August Christenson
5941 Mr. & Mrs. Wm. A. Weaver & dr.
5955 Mr. & Mrs. Charles H. Dodge

5706 Mr. & Mrs. Percy V. Castle
5710 Mr. & Mrs. R. H. Trail
5710 Richard A. Kemp
5722 Mr. & Mrs. John R. Bowes
5726 Mr. & Mrs. H. W. Schmitt
5726 Mrs. Mary Schneider
5726 Miss Augusta Malnofske
5800 Dr. & Mrs. John Massman
5806 Mr. & Mrs. A. A. Dean
5812 Mr. & Mrs. J. E. Huwald
5818 Mr. & Mrs. E. C. Hunsinger
5820 Mr. & Mrs. Thomas L. Miller
5902 Mr. & Mrs. Herman Mallen
5914 Mr. & Mrs. Jas. M. Attley
5944 Mr. & Mrs. LeGrand Kniffen
5948 Mr. & Mrs. John Faulkner.

NORTH PARK AVENUE.

542 Mr. & Mrs. Andrew B. White

SOUTH PARK AVENUE.

113 Mr. & Mrs. N. S. Graves
113 Mr. & Mrs. S. L. Carr
Receive 1st & 3rd Wednesdays
119 Mr. & Mrs. E. B. Moore & dr.
119 Walter H. Moore
123 Mr. & Mrs. G. H. White
127 Emory B. Chace

127 Mr. & Mrs. W. C. Matthews
131 Mr. & Mrs. H. M. Alexander &
　　 drs.
131 Charles A. Alexander
135 Mr. & Mrs. George H. Park
205 Mr. & Mrs. George Plumbe & dr.
205 Miss Minnie E. Post
213 Mr. & Mrs. C. R. Vandercook
213 Mrs. Prudence Aspenwall
217 Mr. & Mrs. J. D. Vandercook
221 Mr. & Mrs. W. W. McFarland
　　 & dr.
221 Wm. W. McFarland jr.
227 Mr. & Mrs. Joseph Kretzinger
313 Mr. & Mrs. J. B. Pither
317 Mr. & Mrs. James Carruthers
317 Robert Carruthers
319 Mr. & Mrs. Spencer R. Smith
331 Mr. & Mrs. R. J. Ingram
413 Mr. & Mrs. F. X. Mudd
421 Mr. & Mrs. A. C. Sandy
425 Mrs. M. A. Ellis
425 Mr. & Mrs. H. H. Reardon
429 Mr. & Mrs. Jay C. Freeman
　　　 Receiving day Wednesday
435 Mr. & Mrs. Jonn Hallinan
527 Mr. & Mrs. John F. Cremin
531 Mr. & Mrs. Fred Lusche
535 Mr. & Mrs. J. Mason Duffy
553 Mr. & Mrs. Simon Callaghan

---

108 Dr. Stanley B. Dickinson
108 John F. Hecox
108 Miss Daisy Hecox
108 Miss Marion Hecox
108 Miss Mattie D. Hecox
108 Mrs. A. S. Gardner & drs.
108 Walter W. Gardner
108 Harold M. Gardner
108 Geo. S. Gardner
116 Mr. & Mrs. Wm. E. Thurber
116 E. W. Teagle
118 Mr. & Mrs. Wm. Kissack
118 A. B. Williams
124 Mr. & Mrs. Gorham B. Coffin
　　 & dr.
124 Percy B. Coffin
128 Mr. & Mrs. Geo. A. Stewart
138 Mr. & Mrs. R. P. Price
138 John P. Price
206 Mr. & Mrs. F. E. Bartelme & dr.
206 Ferdinand M. Bartelme
222 Mr. & Mrs. Mark T. Lyon
226 Mr. & Mrs. H. D. Cummings
232 Mr. & Mrs. Alfred Barker

NORTH PINE AVENUE.

315 Mrs. Mary A. Pierce
315 Frank H. Pierce
401 Mr. & Mrs. Warner B. McCall
409 Dr. & Mrs. Frederick R. Hunt
413 Mr. & Mrs. Newell D. Gilbert
421 Mr. & Mrs. J. S. Cleverdon
425 Rev. & Mrs. Abel M. White
441 Mr. & Mrs. Stephen J. Olbrich
　　　 Receiving day Thursday
519 Mr. & Mrs. Samuel H. Bolton
521 Mr. & Mrs. Ellis B. Fitch
523 Mr. & Mrs. John S. Wayman
537 Mr. & Mrs. Jonathan Dunfee

514 Rev. & Mrs. Joseph F. Bartlett
540 Mr. & Mrs. Peter G. Wing

SOUTH PINE AVENUE.

109 Mr. & Mrs. Louis Loewy
123 Mr. & Mrs. Amos Shepard
123 J. Robert Shepard
127 Samuel B. Haggard
127 Mrs. B. C. Rucker
127 Mr. & Mrs. E. M. Marble
205 Mr. & Mrs. James Gardiner
215 Mr. & Mrs. C. D. Gammon & dr.
221 Mr. & Mrs. Charles Hennick
227 Mrs. Jane Gasparo & dr.
309 Mr. & Mrs. J. D. Haggard
309 Mr. & Mrs. Frank W. Yale
311 Mr. & Mrs. Wm. M. Meredith &
　　 dr.
325 Mrs. Louis Jaeger & dr.
325 Julius Jaeger
337 Mr. & Mrs. Charles Bassett & dr.
341 Mr. & Mrs. Frederick E. Hart

116 Dr. M. F. Doty
116 Mrs. Flora M. Doty & drs.
118 Dr. & Mrs. C. E. Jones & dr.
330 Mr. & Mrs. J. D. MacLean & dr.

POPLAR AVENUE.

529 Mr. & Mrs. J. L. Price

NORTH PRAIRIE AVENUE.

113 Dr. & Mrs. Arthur Hare
　　　 Receiving day Tuesday

SOUTH PRAIRIE AVENUE.

119 Mrs. C. Stephan & drs.
119 Emanuel L. Stephan
119 Traugott F. Stephan

123 Mr.& Mrs.David MacNaughtan
123 Miss Effie Motlong
127 Mr. & Mrs. Kenneth McLaroth
209 Mrs. Richard Burke
209 Rev. & Mrs. R. H. Burke
209 Miss Margaret Mackin
215 Mrs. James Mason & dr.
217 Mr. & Mrs. R. S. Pettibone
225 Mr. & Mrs. Thomas M. Hunter
313 S. H. Eveleth
435 Mr. & Mrs. Andrew A. Malum
543 Mr. & Mrs. Wm. A. Smith & drs.
547 Richard Dunne
547 Miss Julia Dunne
547 Miss Mary Dunne
549 Mr. & Mrs. Geo. E. Kurts

124 Mr. & Mrs. W.P. Gunthorp
124 Walter J. Gunthorp
128 Mr. & Mrs. Robert McCullach & drs.
130 Mr. & Mrs. Geo. H. Luther
136 Mr. & Mrs. John Purvis & drs.
214 Mr. & Mrs. James C. Oram
234 Mr. & Mrs. John E. Howland & dr.
316 Mr. & Mrs. Julius M. Blanchard
316 Mr. & Mrs. Marvin Blanchard
Receiving day Thursday.
324 Mr. & Mrs. J. I. Graham
428 Mr. & Mrs. E. J. Roberts
558 Mr. & Mrs. Lanson D. Miller
Receiving day Thursday
558 Miss May Lathrop

RANDOLPH STREET.

5707 Mr. & Mrs. Ward B. Howland

ROBINSON AVENUE.

94 Mr. & Mrs. H. W. Bortree

SOUTH BOULEVARD.

5636 Mr. & Mrs. H. F. Frink
5636 Miss Clara Creote
5640 Mr. & Mrs. Geo. M. Frink
Receiving day Tuesday
5646 Mr. & Mrs. John J. Miller
5800 Mr. & Mrs. James H. Hoes
5804 Mr. & Mrs. H. S. Mills
Receiving day Tuesday
5816 Mr. & Mrs. Robert G. Pole
5820 Mr. & Mrs. Hiram S. Utley
5904 Mr. & Mrs. Charles Gritman

5920 Mr. & Mrs. Geo. W. Smith
5920 L. H. Smith
5920 Miss Clare Swan

SUPERIOR STREET.

5625 Mr. & Mrs. Jacob E. Decker & dr.
5625 Jay Decker
5803 Mr. & Mrs. Frank McNeal
5811 Mr. & Mrs. Chas. L. Reifschneider & dr.
5915 Mr. & Mrs. John M. Jones
5915 Mr. & Mrs. H. R. Buck
5929 Mr. & Mrs. F. L. Phillips

5900 Mrs. Elias Wanzer
5900 Clarence H. Wanzer

NORTH WALLER AVENUE.

212 Edward Modine

SOUTH WALLER AVENUE.

109 Mr. & Mrs. D. A. McWhirter
117 Mr. & Mrs. Wm. G. Lloyd
121 Mr. & Mrs. S. H. Woodbury
129 Mr. & Mrs. J. E. Thorndyke
205 Mr. & Mrs. Henry Date
207 Dr. & Mrs. Henry Stratford
207 Charles J. Stratford
207 Edward Wayt
207 Mr. & Mrs. Wm. F. Ray
211 Mr. & Mrs. Chas. W. Hatch
215 Mr. & Mrs. Geo. Standard
223 Mr. & Mrs. John R. Hunt
223 Miss May Hunt
227 Mrs. Jane Treleaven & drs.
227 W. T. Treleaven
273 Mr. & Mrs. R. L. Ostrander
315 Mr. & Mrs. John W. Strackbein
Receiving day Thursday
325 Mr. & Mrs. Seaward Foster
333 Mrs. L. B. Crane & dr.
335 Mr. & Mrs. A. R. Marriott
349 Mr. & Mrs. David Brown
349 George H. Brown
529 Mr. & Mrs. Oliver Carson

112 Mr. & Mrs. James E. Blair
116 Mr. & Mrs. Louis Falk
128 Mr. & Mrs. James M. Hatch
128 Mr. & Mrs. Geo. M. McCaull
128 Thomas W. Hatch
132 Mr. & Mrs. Chas. S. Cutting
132 Mrs. Ann G. Lytle

202 Mr. & Mrs. Louis E. Yager
206 Mr. & Mrs. Wm. A. Pillinger
328 Mr. & Mrs. T. J. Sullivan
424 Mr. & Mrs. H. N. Howland
426 Mrs. Alice Flemming
426 Jeffrey Flemming M. D.

WALNUT AVENUE.

113 E. C. Westwood
117 Mr. & Mrs. Thomas J. Cavey
137 Mr. & Mrs. Horace G. Teele
345 Mr. & Mrs. Uriah R. Denniston
345 Frank D. Powell
345 F. M. Powell

124 Mr. & Mrs. Fred Welge
cor. Vanburen Mr. & Mrs. Paul C.
    Eilers
    Receiving day Wednesday

WASHINGTON BOULEVARD.

5303 Mr. & Mrs. Charles J. Stone
5433 Mr. & Mrs. Clayton E. Crafts
5433 William C. Crafts
5915 Mr. & Mrs. Edwin F. Abbott

5410 Mr. & Mrs. Frank J. Hurley
5702 Rev. Louis A. Campbell

NORTH WILLOW AVENUE.

218 Mr. & Mrs. Wallace B. Gilbert
    & dr.
218 Roy O. Gilbert

229 Mr. & Mrs. Jas. W. Wilson
315 George E. Swinscoe

SOUTH WILLOW AVENUE.

208 Mr & Mrs. James F. Morgan

BERWYN.

Mr. & Mrs. L. Abbott
Mr. & Mrs. George H. Anderson
Edward Andrews
Mr. & Mrs. W. J. Andrews
Mr. & Mrs. A. W. Anthony
Mr. & Mrs. John G. M. Appleton
Mr. & Mrs. Ernest Appleton
Dr. & Mrs. I. J. Archer
Mr. & Mrs. G. W. Ashby
Mr. & Mrs. C. A. Bader
Mr. & Mrs. C. C. Baldwin
Mr. & Mrs. Albert Barge
James P. Bates
Mr. & Mrs. Wm. Beamer
Mr. & Mrs. J. F. Berkeley
Mr. & Mrs. Harry Bitner
Mr. & Mrs. Charles G. Blanden
Mr. & Mrs. C. L. Bliss
Mr. & Mrs. Wirt Burch
Mr. & Mrs. T. L. Collins
Dr. & Mrs. F. H. Davis
Mr. & Mrs. William Dennis
Mr. & Mrs. Wm. Dilley
Mr. & Mrs. J. E. Dunn
Mr. & Mrs. E. O. Eames
Mr. & Mrs. Ralph M. Easley
Mr. & Mrs. P. C. Greig
Joseph Grove
Dr. & Mrs. W. S. Hall
Mr. & Mrs. L. W. Haring
Mr. & Mrs. D. C. Harries
E. J. Harrison
Mr. & Mrs. Wilton Hartman

Mr. & Mrs. Joseph T. Heywood
Mr. & Mrs. M. M. Hitchcock
Mr. & Mrs. W. R. Hornbaker
Mr. & Mrs. Orin Hubbell
Mr. & Mrs. W. R. Israel
Mr. & Mrs. J. E. Johnson
Rev. & Mrs. J. R. Kaye
Mr. & Mrs. J. S. Kellar
Mr. & Mrs. Walter E. Lackey
Mr. & Mrs. H. C. Latshaw
Mr. & Mrs. George A. Legler
Dr. & Mrs. Arthur MacNeal
Mr. & Mrs. James McCartney
Rev. & Mrs. William E. McLennan
Mrs. E. McSchooler
Mr. & Mrs. Clayton B. Mead
Mr. & Mrs. William R. Morgan
Mr. & Mrs. C. W. Morris
Mr. & Mrs. F. W. Morrison
Mr. & Mrs. Edgar W. Mott
Mr. & Mrs. Wm. J. Murphy
Mr. & Mrs. Frank B. Pease
Mr. & Mrs. Robert Perkins
Mr. & Mrs. W. F. Pfuderer
Mr. & Mrs. C. E. Piper
Mr. & Mrs. Otis Piper & dr.
Mr. & Mrs. F. Poultney
Dr. V. S. Powers
Mr. & Mrs. George W. Reynolds &
    dr.
Mr. & Mrs. E. G. Rice
Mr. & Mrs. P. C. Richards
Mr. & Mrs. Wm. C. Rigby

Mr. & Mrs. H. M. Rogers
Mr. & Mrs. A. Rogerson
Mr. & Mrs. E. W. Rudderham
Mr. & Mrs. James P. Sayer
Dr. & Mrs. Edwin Schell
Prof. & Mrs. O. C. Scott
Mr. & Mrs. W. F. Struckmann
Mr. & Mrs. G. S. Thompson
Mr. & Mrs. A. P. Thorne

Mr. & Mrs. E. R. Tillinghast
Mr. & Mrs. H. M. Trussell
Rev. & Mrs. Leander Turney
Mr. & Mrs. W. H. Tuttle
Mr. & Mrs. Edwin L. Wagner
Mr. & Mrs. F. M. Williams
Mr. & Mrs. M. M. Wood
Mr. & Mrs. W. H. Woodward

BRYN MAWR.

EUCLID AVENUE.

7109 Mr. & Mrs. W. L. Bennett
7109 George R. Bennett
7125 Mr. & Mrs. J. D. Hyde & dr.
7137 Mr. & Mrs. H. J. Cassady
7145 Mr. & Mrs. John M. Hubbard
7149 Mr. & Mrs. Chas. A. Barker
7209 Mr. & Mrs. Edward Kemeys
    Receiving day Tuesday

7116 Mr. & Mrs. M. I. Beck
7122 Mr. & Mrs. John B. Delbridge
7126 Mr. & Mrs. George Best
    Receive Saturday evg.
7126 John Lundie
7130 Mr. & Mrs. H. R. Kent
    Receiving day Tuesday
7134 Mr. & Mrs. H. L. Sayler
    Receiving day Tuesday
7138 Mr. & Mrs. Maurice J. McGrath
7138 George B. McGrath
7150 Mr. & Mrs. Charles L. Peckham
7154 Almon W. Bulkley
7156 Mr. & Mrs. George A. Otis
    Receiving day Friday
7206 Mr. & Mrs. Joel W. Kenfield
7206 Mr. & Mrs. M. M. Chesrown
7206 Francis A. Hopkins
7210 Mr. & Mrs. Geo. F. Clingman
7216 Mr. & Mrs. Benj. F. Blymyer
7222 Mr. & Mrs. Fred. Ricker
7226 Mrs. Virginia H. McGill
    Receiving day Tuesday
7226 William McGill
7242 Mr. & Mrs. John H. Harvey
7242 George S. Harvey
7248 Mr. & Mrs. Albert C. Clark
7248 Frank Hurlbut

JEFFERY AVENUE.

7141 Mr. & Mrs. John R. Stone
    Receiving day Tuesday
7141 Oren B. Stone
7205 Mr. & Mrs. Henry H. Horr

7209 Mr. & Mrs. Alfred E. Holt
7221 Mr. & Mrs. Timothy J. Scofield
7221 Charles Scofield
7247 Mr. & Mrs. Harold R. Stone
7251 Dr. & Mrs. Chas. F. Swan
    Receiving day Thursday
7251 Ellis L. Hagenbuck

7212 Joseph J. Siddall jr.
7216 Mr. & Mrs. L. N. Flagg
7240 Mr. & Mrs. M. H. Bennett
7250 Mr. & Mrs. S. W. Hume
7444 Mr. & Mrs. Waldo H. Spencer

KENWOOD TERRACE.

527 Rev. & Mrs. J. Frothingham
527 Miss M. F. D. Frothingham
    Receives Tuesday & Saturday

422 Mr. & Mrs. Oscar Remmer
    Receiving day Friday
440 Mr. & Mrs. George C. Bour
    Receiving day Thursday
480 Mr. & Mrs. George T. Webster
524 Mr. & Mrs. E. Lee Heidenreich
532 Mr. & Mrs. E. B. Winger
532 O. E. Winger

MERRILL AVENUE.

7209 Mr. & Mrs. Harry S. Griswold
7217 Mr. & Mrs. Henry W. Price

7200 Mr. & Mrs. Van R. Livingston
7204 Mr. & Mrs. F. A. Pomeroy
7212 Mr. & Mrs. Ferd G. Gasche

SEIPP AVENUE.

7557 Mrs. Quintin Johnstone

SEVENTY-SECOND STREET.

476 Mr. & Mrs. Walter Borroughs
480 Dr. & Mrs. Thos. H. Rockwell

SEVENTY-THIRD STREET.

461 Mr. & Mrs. Joseph E. Grubb

CHELTENHAM.

BOND AVENUE.

7839 Mr. & Mrs. Michael Schmitz

7810 Mr. & Mrs. Wm. Gillies
Receiving day Friday
7816 Mr. & Mrs. Frederick Deutsch
7820 Mr. & Mrs. Fred A. Purdy
Receiving day Thursday

7822 Mr. & Mrs. Frank Dolan

MUSKEGON AVENUE.

7749 Mrs. A. C. Wheaton
7929 Mr. & Mrs. W. B. Ingraham

SEVENTY-NINTH STREET.

263 Dr. & Mrs. Elmer E. Tansey

EDGEBROOK.

Mr. & Mrs. Oscar D. Aeppli
Mr. & Mrs. Ferdinand S. Atkin
Mr. & Mrs. Albert A. Augustus
Mr. & Mrs. Jerome B. Cable
Mr. & Mrs. Robert S. Dousman
Mrs. Elizabeth Gates
Mrs. Mary H. Hunt
Mr. & Mrs. L. W. Johnson
Mr. & Mrs. William A. Linn

Mrs. H. T. Milliken & drs.
Mr. & Mrs. Horace S. Morris
Receiving day Thursday
Mr. & Mrs. William G. Roberts
Mr. & Mrs. William F. Schmidt
Mr. & Mrs. Edward W. Shaw
Mr. & Mrs. George E. Simpson & dr.
Mr. & Mrs. Grant Williams
Mrs. H. Williams & dr.

EDISON PARK.

Mr. & Mrs. Fred Ball
Mr. & Mrs. F. C. Burley
Mr. & Mrs. Carleton Dickenson
Mr. & Mrs. J. M. Ettinger
Mr. & Mrs. W. G. McGinnis
Mr. & Mrs. J. T. Pope
Mr. & Mrs. H. Rasmussen
Mr. & Mrs. T. J. Reynolds

Mr. & Mrs. E. T. Roe
Mr. & Mrs. G. H. Shute
Mr. & Mrs. H. A. Thayer
Mr. & Mrs. J. D. Turner
Mr. & Mrs. T. J. Welden
Mr. & Mrs. John Wingert
Mr. & Mrs. William Zuetell

ELMHURST.

Prof. & Mrs. C. J. Albert
Dr. & Mrs. F. H. Bates
Mr. & Mrs. Charles W. Bates
Prof. Chas. Bauer
Mr. & Mrs. Cyrus Bentley
Rev. & Mrs. August Berens
Dr. & Mrs. F. W. Boeber
Mr. & Mrs. John Boyd & dr.
Prof. & Mrs. HermanBrodt
Mr. & Mrs. A. S. Brownell
Thos. B. Bryan
Mr. & Mrs. William Buderbach
Mr. & Mrs. Horace J. Canfield
Horace J. Canfield jr.
Mr. & Mrs. John R. Case
Mr. & Mrs. H. A. Christy
Mr. & Mrs. L. A. Denig & drs.
Rev. & Mrs. Edward P. Drew
Mr. & Mrs. Wm. H. Dyrenforth

Mr. & Mrs. A. F. Emery
Mr. & Mrs. James Emery
Mr. & Mrs. W. H. Emery & dr.
Dr. & Mrs. F. J. T. Fisher
Mr. & Mrs. R. S. Fletcher
Mr. & Mrs. Henry L. Glos
Mr. & Mrs. Jacob Glos
Mr. & Mrs. William Graue
Mr. & Mrs. George W. Griffin
Mrs. L. A. Hagans
Mr. & Mrs. Samuel L. Hagans
Mr. & Mrs. Wilbur E. Hagans
Mr. & Mrs. I. Hallock
Dr. & Mrs. Geo. F. Heideman
Mr. & Mrs. D. T. Higginson
Rev. & Mrs. J. G. Hild
Mr. & Mrs. F. A. Hoffman, jr.
Mr. & Mrs. Thomas Hogan
Prof. & Mrs. Daniel Irion

Charles Jernegan
Mr. & Mrs. Francis King
Mr. & Mrs. James King
Mr. & Mrs. Albert F. Kidder
Mrs. Henry W. King
Mrs. F. Koch
Mr. & Mrs. Mark S. Lansing
Wm. H. Litchfield
Arthur Lueder
Prof. & Mrs. John Lueder
Mr. & Mrs. Thomas Lynch
Mr. & Mrs. Charles J. Marhoefer
Mr. & Mrs. Thomas McQueen
Mr. & Mrs. H. F. Miller
Mr. & Mrs. J. E. Northup
Prof. & Mrs. Emil Otto
Mr. & Mrs. G. E. Porter
Miss Rebecca A. Richardson
Mr. & Mrs. Frederick S. Rockwood
Mr. & Mrs. F. B. Rockwood & dr.

Harvey Rockwood
Sprague S. Rockwood
Mr. & Mrs. Frank S. Rolf
Prof. & Mrs. Geo. F. Rosche
Mr. & Mrs. George Sawin
Mr. & Mrs. George Schmidt
Prof. & Mrs. George A. Sorrick
Mr. & Mrs. O. H. Stange
Rev. C. G. Stanger
Mr. & Mrs. H. G. Struckmann
Mr. & Mrs. Emil Stuedle
Mr. & Mrs. Frank Sturges & drs.
Mr. & Mrs. Lee Sturges
Mr. & Mrs. A. I. Ullman
Charles Wade
Miss Carrie Wade
John H. Wagner
Mr. & Mrs. T. Edward Wilder
Rev. John Zilla

EVANSTON.

ASBURY AVENUE.

921 Mr. & Mrs. Charles Page
939 Mr.&Mrs. Patrick Tyrrell & dr.
939 John Tyrrell
1123 Mr. & Mrs. C. C. Travis
1145 Mr. & Mrs. Edw. B. Griswold
        Receiving day Wednesday
1231 Mr. & Mrs. Willard L. Cobb.
        Receiving day Wednesday
1231 Miss Julia Hintermeister
1251 Mr. & Mrs. Wm. I. Howland
1321 Mr. & Mrs. C. J. Ellis
1501 M. & Mrs. Chas. M. Osborn
1501 Chas. R. Kappes
1501 L. J. Osborn
1513 Charles E. Towne
1583 Mr. & Mrs. Walter T. Dwight
1713 Mr. & Mrs. H. K. Hinsdale & dr.
1719 Mr. & Mrs. H. W. Hinsdale
1719 B. S. Hinsdale
1719 Mrs. A. B. Moseley
1723 Mr. & Mrs. Colby Davies
1733 Mr. & Mrs. Chas. H. Chandler
        Receive Monday
1733 H. E. Chandler
1735 Mr. & Mrs. Thomas Gaunt
1745 Mr. & Mrs. Henry Raeder
1801 Mr. & Mrs. E. P. Prickett
1801 Mrs. Sarah E. Wheeler
1807 Mr. & Mrs. Frank S. Davis
1807 Mr. & Mrs. Madison LaMonte

1817 B. S. Hatch & drs.
1825 Mr. & Mrs. Charles J. Morse
1833 Mr. & Mrs. W. G. Hempstead
1847 Mr. & Mrs. F. C. Stover
1849 Mrs. Blanche D. Ives
1849 Mr. & Mrs. Chas. J. Gilbert

---

902 Mr. & Mrs. H. L. Edwards
902 Mrs. Laura Gardner
902 James W. Gardner
922 Mr. & Mrs. F. H. Lewis
928 Mr. & Mrs. W. A. Ratcliffe
936 Mr. & Mrs. Frank E. Allen
936 Mrs. Phoebe E. Allen
1124 Mr. & Mrs. Asahel O. Bassett
        & drs.
1204 Mrs. C. O. Gleason
1204 Mr. & Mrs. Charles Gleason
1232 Mr. & Mrs. C. K. Pittman
1302 Mr. & Mrs. W. J. Battams
1302 Walter J. Battams jr.
1308 Mr. & Mrs. Thomas S. Blair jr.
1308 Mr. & Mrs. James H. Parker
1314 Mr. & Mrs. E. A. Mayo
1314 Mr. & Mrs. Hartwell Osborn
1314 Miss Kate Osborn
1314 Miss Anna T. Osborn
1318 Mrs. C. H. Morse
1326 Mrs. Leighton Turner & drs.
1326 Walter I. Turner
1334 Mr. & Mrs. Milton L. Record

1404 Mr. & Mrs. Thomas H. Beebe & dr.
1404 Archibald A. Beebe
1410 Mr. & Mrs. Alanson Filer
1416 Mr. & Mrs. R. E. Beebe
1426 Mr. & Mrs. B. G. Poucher
1454 Mr. & Mrs. S. E. Hurlbut
1454 Chas. H. Hurlbut
1460 Mr. & Mrs. Charles W. Buckley
1512 Mrs. Edward Hempstead & dr.
1554 Mr. & Mrs. Henry Holtz
1554 Mr. & Mrs. W. D. Caldwell
1554 Mr. & Mrs. Wm. Kroeshall & drs.
1554 Mr. & Mrs. John T. Turnbull & dr.
1554 Mr. & Mrs. Thos. G. Booth
1560 Mr. & Mrs. John E. Blunt & dr.
1560 John E. Blunt jr.
1560 Frank T. Blunt
1570 Dr. & Mrs. Wm. Bell Mann
1570 Mr. & Mrs. Geo. H. Crockett
1570 Mrs. Sarah Bailey
1704 Mr. & Mrs. John Dickinson
1720 Mr. & Mrs. Thos. H. Hawks
1720 Mrs. Rebecca Hawks
1724 Mr. & Mrs. Peter C. Lutkin
1724 Mrs. Rufus Carman
1724 Alex. R. Carman
1724 Miss Kathleen Carman
1734 Mr. & Mrs. Birney J. Moore
1734 Mrs. Orin Moore
1742 Mr. & Mrs. Herman D. Cable
1800 Mr. & Mrs. C. M. Howe
1812 Mr. & Mrs. J. H. Raymond & drs.
1812 E. F. Raymond
1828 Mr. & Mrs. F. S. Brown
1832 Mr. & Mrs. F. W. Pomery
1840 Mr. & Mrs. C. J. Stokes & drs.
1840 Frederick C. Stokes

ASHLAND AVENUE.

1615 Mr. & Mrs. J. R. Lyons
1615 Ernest Tietgens
1625 Mr. & Mrs. Benj. W. Lord

1580 Mr. & Mrs. John T. Sickel
1580 Mr. & Mrs. Wm. G. Sickel
1600 Mr. & Mrs. Henry S. Shedd
1602 Mr. & Mrs. O. W. Hinckley
1602 Mrs. E. P. Branch
1610 Mr. & Mrs. R. Roy Shuman
1618 Mr. & Mrs. N. K. Bigelow
1628 Mr. & Mrs. H. H. DeLoss

AYARS PLACE.

1101 Mr. & Mrs. Clark J. Tisdel
1101 Miss Carrie Mason
1109 Rev. & Mrs. Geo. A. McLaughlin & dr.

1018 Mr. & Mrs. E. E. Bean
1018 Rev. & Mrs. S. W. Beggs
1100 Prof. & Mrs. P. M. Pearson
1104 Mr. & Mrs. J. N. Boorman & dr.
1104 James M. Boorman
1106 Mrs. Charles Bishop
1118 Mr. & Mrs. Geo. Fellingham & dr.
1118 R. J. Fellingham
1124 Mr. & Mrs. Winfield S. Smith

BENSON AVENUE.

909 Mr. & Mrs. H. DeVere Simmons
913 Mr. & Mrs. F. W. Brown
939 Mr. & Mrs. W. H. Robertson & dr.
939 James G. Robertson
943 Mr. & Mrs. E. Bradley
943 Mrs. Marie Walters
1001 Mr. & Mrs. J. C. Freeman
1015 Mr. & Mrs. Geo. W. Hotchkiss
1019 Mr. & Mrs. Wm. W. Hogle
1029 Mr. & Mrs. David D. Webster
1035 Mr. & Mrs. C. C. Nash
1145 Rev. & Mrs. B. A. Green & drs.
1203 Mr. & Mrs. G. H. Kelley
1205 Mr. & Mrs. O. B. Hutchens
1205 Mrs. Sarah Reed
1207 Mr. & Mrs. F. S. Pooler
1207 Lemuel F. Pooler
1207 Mrs. J. M. Fisk
1209 Mr. & Mrs. E. L. Howard
1215 Mr. & Mrs. W. M. Turner
1219 Mr. & Mrs. James J. McCauley
1223 Mr. & Mrs. Wilbur E. Coe
1227 Mr. & Mrs. A. D. Sanders
1305 Mr. & Mrs. Fritz Schroeder
1315 Rev. & Mrs. J. H. Alling & drs.
1317 Mr. & Mrs. William Haigh
1321 Mr. & Mrs. Robert Leffingwell
1325 Mr. & Mrs. H. B. Hill & dr.
1329 Mrs. J. B. Hilton & dr.
1335 Mr. & Mrs. R. C. Hacker
1401 Mr. & Mrs. J. G. Darling
1401 Mrs. M. J. Switzer
1403 Rev. & Mrs. Thos. Craven
1403 Henry Craven
1407 Mr. & Mrs. Chas. C. Cox & drs.

1407 Mr. & Mrs. E. P. Baird
1419 Mr. & Mrs. J. R. Graves & dr.
1419 Paul S. Graves

838 Mrs. Elizabeth A. Hathaway
928 Mr. & Mrs. T. Fansler
930 Mrs. J. W. Joly
930 Mrs. Theodore Lavigne
934 Mrs. M. F. Layton
938 Mr. & Mrs. James Hibben
1002 Mrs. A. J. Cooper & dr.
1002 Mr. & Mrs. William Cooley
1006 Mr. & Mrs. Geo. W. Hutchens
1010 Mrs. Ella F. Morse
1010 Miss Mary C. Spicer
1018 Mr. & Mrs. Geo. W. Cross
1028 Mr. & Mrs. W. L. Williams
1034 Mrs. W. H. Dee & dr.
1034 Mr. & Mrs. Harry A. Bartels
1040 Mr. & Mrs. James E. Low
1040 Mrs. D. E. Barker
1040 Miss R. A. Barker
1108 Mr. & Mrs. W. S. Shields
1112 Mr. & Mrs. Wm. D. Bassett
1124 Mr. & Mrs. Geo. B. Woodworth
1134 Mr. & Mrs. Henry Voigts
1146 Mr. & Mrs. C. H. Poppenhusen
1146 P. Albert Poppenhusen
1206 Mr. & Mrs. John McNab & drs.
1206 Joseph L. McNab
1212 Mr. & Mrs. Edwin H. Gamble
1218 Mr. & Mrs. H. L. Boltwood
1222 Mr. & Mrs. W. A. Webster
1226 Mr. & Mrs. Frank Barhydt
1230 Mr. & Mrs. Joseph D. Weaver
1238 Mrs. M. L. Thompson & dr.
1244 Mr. & Mrs. N. B. Barlow
1312 Mr. & Mrs. R. N. Dudley
1322 Mrs. E. S. Bliss & drs.
1322 Mrs. E. B. Strong
1326 Mr. & Mrs. George M. Patterson
1418 Mr. & Mrs. Wm. B. Lewald
1422 Mr. & Mrs. C. E. VanVoorhis
1430 Mrs. Hannah H. Hardy & drs.
1430 Mr. & Mrs. James Macdonald
1432 George Woodley
1432 Mrs. S. N. Rogers

CENTRAL STREET.

2121 Mr. & Mrs. John F. Stewart
2209 Dr. & Mrs. Finley Ellingwood & dr.
2403 Mr. & Mrs. John S. Orvis

2218 Mr. & Mrs. John W. Brown
2218 Richard Brown
2218 Mrs. R. E. France & dr.
2624 Mrs. Ella Emerson

CHICAGO AVENUE.

527 Mr. & Mrs. Jacob Rinn
815 Dr. & Mrs. G. W. Kaufmann
933 Rev. & Mrs. O. F. Mattison
941 Mr. & Mrs. O. F. Gibbs & dr.
1011 Mr. & Mrs. Myron M. Drury
1023 Mr. & Mrs. J. M. Brown
1023 Mr. & Mrs. Wm. S. Powers
1039 Mr. & Mrs. T. H. Watson & drs.
1201 Mrs. Thomas S. Bond & drs.
1201 John R. Mills
1209 Mrs. John O'Leary & dr.
1209 D. P. O'Leary
1211 Mr. & Mrs. Benj. L. Miller
1217 Mr. & Mrs. A. J. Thompson
1239 Miss Mary M. Reid
1239 Mrs. Alida M. Griggs
1239 Mrs. E. G. White
1243 Mr. & Mrs. G. C. Hick
1301 Dr. & Mrs. Fred Clatworthy
1303 Rev. & Mrs. W. C. Dickinson & dr.
1303 Clarence Dickinson
1307 Mr. & Mrs. Henry Whipple
1311 Mr. & Mrs. Geo. H. Smith & dr.
1311 Edward M. Smith
1311 Mrs. Sophia C. Lamb
1315 Mr. & Mrs. Park Phipps
1319 Mr. & Mrs. Lewis Babbitt
1323 Mr. & Mrs. R. B. Carr
1327 Mr. & Mrs. P. R. Woodford
1403 Mr. & Mrs. W. F. Dudley
1405 Mrs. N. S. Thompson & drs.
1405 Mr. & Mrs. F. W. Hamilton
1411 Mr. & Mrs. George Dunoon
1419 Mr. & Mrs. Samuel VanBenschoten
1423 Dr. & Mrs. E. E. Shutterly
1427 Mrs. H. M. Hobart
1505 Mr. & Mrs. J. H. Hurlbut
1509 Mr. & Mrs. J. J. Reimers & dr.
1515 Mr. & Mrs. W. C. Wilson
1619 Mrs. C. H. Quinlan & drs.
1619 Charles E. Quinlan
1619 George H. Quinlan
1619 Edward B. Quinlan

1633 Hotel Monnett
    Mr. & Mrs. B. D. Anguish
    Mr. & Mrs. C. W. Hillman
    Thomas C. Hollingshead
    Mr. & Mrs. Fletcher Monnett
    C. E. Prindle
    Mr. & Mrs. C. E. Wiswall
1703 Mrs. Annie M. Davis
1703 Dr. Oliver Marcy
1709 Dr. & Mrs. M. C. Bragdon &
    dr.
1717 Mr. & Mrs. Orson H. Brooke
1717 Mr. & Mrs. J. A. Burhans
1717 Mr. & Mrs. W. C. Whitcomb
1717 Miss Stella Chamblin
1717 Mrs. L. A. Calder
1723 Mr. & Mrs. Wm. Burt
1723 Wm. Griswold Burt
1729 Mr. & Mrs. Edward R. Hall
1735 Mr. & Mrs. Chas. H. Hall
1745 Mr. & Mrs. James A. Patten
1745 Mrs. Agnes Patten
1745 George W. Patten
1803 Mr. & Mrs. A. E. Dunn & dr.
1815 Mrs. R. M. Hatfield
1815 Mrs. S. A. Kean
1817 Mr. & Mrs. W. E. O'Kane
1817 Robert C. Fletcher
1831 Mr. & Mrs. Harry J. Patten

1138 Mr. & Mrs. Wm. E. Mariner
1144 Mr. & Mrs. C. P. Engelmann
1148 Mr. & Mrs. Andrew C. Murphy
1202 Prof. & Mrs. S. R. Winchell & dr.
    Receiving day Monday
1202 Guy J. Dart
1218 Mr. & Mrs. Francis J. Magin·
1220 J. J. Shutterly & drs.
1220 John J. Shutterly jr.
1228 Mr. & Mrs. Wallace K. Cook
1230 Mr. & Mrs. Y. B. Haagsma
1234 Clark Kinney
1234 Dr. & Mrs. Frank B. Brewer
1234 C. S. Brewer
1312 Mr. & Mrs. A. C. Bird & drs.
1318 Mr. & Mrs. Harry W. Dakin
1318 Dr. & Mrs. Frank C. Dakin
1318 Roscoe L. Wickes
1326 Mrs. C. C. Scales
1326 Mrs. Emily S. Bartlett & dr.
1332 Dr. & Mrs. Edw. H. Webster
    & dr.
1332 Mrs. Frances Winne
1402 Mr. & Mrs. Z. G. Sholes
    Receiving day Thursday

1406 Mr. & Mrs. Geo. A. Bennett
1410 Mr. & Mrs. Edw. Stanbery
1414 B. S. Sanborn & drs.
1420 Dr. E. P. Clapp
1420 Mrs. A. E. Clapp
1426 Mr. & Mrs. D. A. Kimball
1430 Dr. & Mrs. J. H. Boyd
1434 Mrs. E. M. Seaverns
1434 Edwin I. Seaverns
1434 Miss Anna F. Seaverns
1456 Mr. & Mrs. Geo. Taylor
1460 Mr. & Mrs. John C. Christman
    Receiving day Thursday
1468 Mr. & Mrs. M. S. Woodward
1512 Dr. & Mrs. A. B. Clayton
    Receiving day Wednesday
1614 Dr. & Mrs. P. D. Harding
1616 Dr. & Mrs. Oscar Dodd
1618 Mrs. W. E. Clifford ·
1618 Mr. & Mrs. Fred B. Carter
1628 Mr. & Mrs. Lucius W. Conkey
1632 Mrs. W. M. Chapin & drs.
1632 Frederick S. Chapin
1632 John Allen
1634 Mr. & Mrs. Alfred D. Shaw
1534 Dr. & Mrs. E. M. P. Ludlam
1634 Miss Florence Ludlam
1636 Prof. & Mrs. J. Scott Clark
1640 Mr. & Mrs. W. H. Judson & dr.
1640 Miles S. Gilbert
1640 William C. Gilbert
1640 George P. Judson
1640 Mr. & Mrs. Ralph Smith
1704 Mrs. E. P. Robinson
1704 Mr. & Mrs. F. W. Cleveland
1704 Paul Cleveland
1704 Miss Nannie Hines
1714 Mr. & Mrs. William Rice & dr.
1714 Mr. & Mrs. J. A. Pearsons
1718 Mr. & Mrs. H. A. Pearsons
1718 Harry P. Pearsons
1724 Capt. & Mrs. J. R. Fitch
1724 Mrs. C. P. Bragdon
1728 Mr. & Mrs. Alonzo Weston
    Kimball
1730 Mr. & Mrs. H. E. Walters
1730 Will Walters
1732 Mr. & Mrs. Frank H. Butler
1732 Walter H. Butler
1732 Albert E. Butler
1738 Mrs. E. G. Henderson
1738 Mr. & Mrs. Samuel Merwin
1738 Samuel Merwin jr.
1744 Dr. & Mrs. H. B. Hemenway
1802 Mr. & Mrs. C. A. Rogers
1802 Miss Henrietta L. Rogers

1808 Mr. & Mrs. Wm.H.Whitehead & dr.
1808 Harry Whitehead
1808 Frank C. Whitehead
1808 William Whitehead
1810 Mr. & Mrs. Chas.E. Smith & dr.
1812 Mr. & Mrs. Amos J. Harding
1812 John C. Harding
1812 Dwight S. Harding
1830 T. P. Ballard
1834 Mrs. K. D. Edwards
1838 Mrs. Joseph Cummings
1838 Mr. & Mrs. Daniel Bonbright

CHURCH STREET.

615 Mr. & Mrs. W. J. Tilghman
615 William Tilghman
707 Mr. & Mrs. Andrew Simpson
713 Mrs. Emma Vandercook
713 Mr. & Mrs. Robt. O. Vander-cook
715 Prof. & Mrs. Charles Horswell
1127 Fordyce B. Rice & drs.
1127 Bernard A. Rice
1217 Mr. & Mrs. J. K. Savage
1217 Miss Isabell Boynton
1217 Miss Frances Boynton
1315 Mr. & Mrs. G. E. Gooch
1319 Mrs. Ruth McElwain & dr.
1319 Mrs. Ada Lanehart
1319 Frank McElwain
1327 Mr. & Mrs. Delos J. Gilleland
1333 Mr. & Mrs. G. W. P. Atkinson
1333 G. Clarence Atkinson
1333 Arthur Randolph Atkinson
1333 Reginald Atkinson
1333 Miss Marguerite P. Grover
1333 Miss Mary Pearce

408 Mr. & Mrs. William Deering
518 Mrs. Mary S. Taggart & dr.
518 Calvin E. Taggart
608 Mr. & Mrs. J. H. B. Howell
612 Miss Isabella H. Pope
612 Miss Mary Pope
614 Mrs. W. L. Harris & dr.
1016 Mr. & Mrs. W. B. Olmsted
1104 Mr. & Mrs. N. P. Williams
1106 Mr. & Mrs. A. F. Dean
1106 Walter M. Dean
1114 Mr. & Mrs. A. J. McCormick
1114 W. A. McCormick
1120 Mr. & Mrs. Edwd.P.Greenough
1302 Mr. & Mrs.DavidD.Thompson & drs.

1312 Mr. & Mrs. T. I. Stacey
1318 Henry S. Slaymaker & dr.
1330 Mr. & Mrs. John T. Pirie jr.

CLARK STREET.

615 Mr. & Mrs. J. L. Morse & drs.
615 Albert A. Morse
615 Miss Abbie C. Morse

710 Mrs. E. H. Fowle
710 A. W. Abbott
710 Miss Edna Flesheim
710 Miss Mary W. Orr
710 J. Stafford Conley
710 Edward F. Zang
710 William Zang
710 J. P. Van Doozer
710 Mr. & Mrs. G. H. Farnsworth
710 Wm. J. Hamilton
710 M. G. Hoskins
710 Dr. Chas. W. James
710 Miss Alice Smith

DAVIS STREET.

305 Mr. & Mrs. E. S. Lacey & drs.
    Receive Tuesday
307 Mr. & Mrs. H. M. Boice
309 Mr. & Mrs. Fred'k Arnd
309 Charles Arnd
309 Miss Louise Arud
309 Miss Marion Bremond
315 Mr.& Mrs. Joseph H. Geraghty
325 Thos. C. Moore & drs.
331 Miss Kate C. Quinlan
331 Charles S. Quinlan
ne. cor. Chicago av. Avenue House
    Mr. & Mrs. Charles G. Ayars
    Mrs. Franklin G. Beach
    D. E. Bradley
    Mr. & Mrs. Horace C. Cooper
    Chas. W. C. Deering
    Mr. & Mrs. F. A. Fletcher & drs.
    Mr. & Mrs. D.B.Gardner & drs.
    Mr. & Mrs. Albert H. Gates & drs.
    W. A. Hamilton
    William G. Hoag
    Mr. & Mrs. J. Holloday & dr.
    Will Hubbard
    Dr. S. M. Moore
    John B. Morrill
    Mr. & Mrs. John Morris

ne. cor. Chicago av. Avenue House·
   (continued.)
   Mr. & Mrs. Geo. D. Moseley
   W. I. Nangle
   Mr. & Mrs. J. H. Paterson
   Charles E. Quinlan
   N. J. Ross
   Miss Celia Sargent
   John Schwender
   E. J. Williams
   Mr. & Mrs. H. D. Williams
   Prof. A. V. E. Young
815 Charles S. Hart
1105 Dr. & Mrs. Arthur Y. Little
1105 Mrs. Emma B. Frey & dr.
1127 Mr. & Mrs. J. J. Parkhurst
1221 Mr. & Mrs. H. E. Howard
1221 Mrs. Mary Howard
1221 Mrs. James C. Gardner
1309 Mrs. M. A. VanAlstine & dr.
1309 Mr. & Mrs. C. M. Carr
1309 Mrs. Elizabeth W. Bradley & dr.
1315 Mr. & Mrs. H. J. Wallingford
   & dr.
1425 Mr. & Mrs. Wm. S. Young

204 Mr. & Mrs. Joseph O. Morris
   Receiving day Tuesday
204 E. E. Morris
210 Mr. & Mrs. E. E. Willis
210 Miss Helen M. Kitchell
cor. Forest av. Mr. & Mrs. H. R.
   Wilson & dr.
   Oliver T. Wilson
404 Mr. & Mrs. L. H. Boutelle & dr.
410 Mr. & Mrs. James Rood & dr.
502 Mr. & Mrs. Charles H. Porter
520 Dr. & Mrs. Wm. Lincoln Ballenger
520 Mrs. Catharine C. Poarch
520 Miss Martha L. Poarch
526 Mr. & Mrs. Wm. Caldwell
   Receiving day Wednesday
522 H. Y. McMullen
522 Frederick B. McMullen
522 Mr. & Mrs. Paul L. Smith
526 Mr. & Mrs. John A. Childs
1106 Mr. & Mrs. L. C. Pitner
1106 Miss Ina K. Pitner
1300 Robert S. Givins
1300 Harry L. Sawe
1300 Henry J. Sawe
1300 Mr. & Mrs. P. W. Gates
1300 Mrs. Belle B. Chapman
1300 Dr. H. B. Haseltine
1300 J. O. Cook

1316 Mr. & Mrs. Chas. W. Elphicke
1502 Mr. & Mrs. Henry C. Durand

DEMPSTER STREET.

85 Miss Ethel Burnham
217 Mr. & Mrs. Wm. Liston Brown
217 Miss Mary Alice Smith
221 Mr. & Mrs. C. P. Wheeler
227 Mr. & Mrs. I. N. Hardin & drs.
227 John H. Hardin
231 Mrs. C. L. Woodyatt
231 Ernest Woodyatt
231 Rollin T. Woodyatt
415 Mr. & Mrs. Addison Millard
   & dr.
519 Mr. & Mrs. Phil W. Huston
523 Mr. & Mrs. Frank E. Miller
   Receiving day Wednesday
1013 Mr. & Mrs. W. M. Harris

cor. Forest av. Mr. & Mrs. Daniel
   H. Burnham & dr.
   John Burnham
   Miss Ellen W. Burnham
318 Mr. & Mrs. Norton V. Gilbert
418 Mrs. W. H. Onderdonk
418 Dudley Onderdonk
418 Forman Onderdonk
418 Wm. Holmes Onderdonk
910 Mr. & Mrs. Wm. O. Jones
1020 Mr. & Mrs. Henry N. Williams
1020 Mrs. A. P. Bluffum & dr.
1030 Frederick Darvill

EMERSON STREET.

711 Mr. & Mrs. Chas. D. Rockwood
717 Mr. & Mrs. Andrew Paterson
725 Mr. & Mrs. H. H. Gage
725 Robert Haven Schauffler
725 Miss Grace A. Miller
729 Mr. & Mrs. E. S. Weeden
729 John V. Weeden

718 Prof. & Mrs. D. A. Hayes
724 Mr. & Mrs. J. F. Oates
726 Rev. & Mrs. Chas. M. Stuart
726 Mrs. O. B. Littlefield
730 T. M. Hubbard & drs.
730 Mrs. A. E. Hubbard
732 Mr. & Mrs. Irvine E. Clapp

FOREST AVENUE.

653 Mr. & Mrs. Wm. Pullen & drs.
733 Mr. & Mrs. W. M. R. Vose
733 Frederick P. Vose

739 Mr. & Mrs. E. A. Downs.& dr.
739 Lewis C. Downs
741 Mr. & Mrs. F. S. Wheeler
817 Mrs. Elizabeth Hathaway&dr.
817 Charles H. Hathaway
829 Mrs. Katharine Falley & dr.
1005 Mr. & Mrs. W. L. Brown
1005 Mrs. Sarah Cosgrove
1011 Mr. & Mrs. James W. Donnell
1015 Mr. & Mrs. W. M. Green
1015 Mr. & Mrs. David Bonnell
1039 Mr. & Mrs. C. M. Rogers
1047 Mr. & Mrs. Chas. E. Graves
1127 Mr. & Mrs. E. F. Wyman
1127 Frederick W. Williams
1133 Mr. & Mrs. J. L. Fyffe & dr.
1139 Mr. & Mrs. A. L. Belknap & dr.
1143 Mr. & Mrs. Eugene J. Buffington
1305 Dr. & Mrs. Charles G. Fuller
1305 Miss Elizabeth White
1331 Mr. & Mrs. W. H. Bartlett & dr.
1331 Willium H. Bartlett jr.
1331 Norman W. Bartlett
1509 Mr. & Mrs. E. R. T. Armstrong & dr.
1513 Mr. & Mrs. W. L. Vance

---

534 Rev. & Mrs. Geo. K. Hoover
534 Charles W. Hoover
534 Olin G. Hoover
610 Mr. & Mrs. Sidney S. Morgan
    Receiving day Tuesday
630 Mr. & Mrs. H. S. Walker & dr.
726 Mrs. Catherine Johnson & dr.
726 Edward P. Johnson
730 Mr. & Mrs. W. C. Brown
736 Mr. & Mrs. Henry M. Walker
736 Miss Hulda H. Newell
740 Mr. & Mrs. Charles H. Cowper
746 Mr.&Mrs.O. F. Carpenter & dr.
806 Mr. & Mrs. R. H. Wyman
830 Mr. & Mrs. Merrill C. Clancy
926 Mr. & Mrs. C. E. Wells
932 Mr. & Mrs. John E. Poor
936 Mr. & Mrs. Jonathan T. Currier & dr.
1006 Mr.& Mrs. Geo. W. Andrew.
1010 Mr. & Mrs. John Breytspraak
1014 Mrs. Sarah J. Shaw
1014 Fred D. Shaw
1014 Hollis D. Holden
1020 Mr. & Mrs. Wm. G. Miller
1026 Mr. & Mrs. W. A. Sickles.

1048 Enfield Place
     Mr. &.Mrs. Wm. Dixon Marsh
     Receiving day Wednesday
1100 Milton H. Wilson
1228 Mr. & Mrs. W. H. Burnet & dr.
1230 Mr. & Mrs. Edward I. Devlin
1232 Mr. & Mrs. Albert B. Porter
1236 Mrs. Richard F. Wyman
1236 Walter C. Wyman
1244 Mr. & Mrs. Chas. R. Ayars
1244 Stewart B. Vowell
1246 Mr. & Mrs. Wm. Young & dr.
1304 Mr. & Mrs. Jared Bassett
1304 Robert J. Bassett
1304 Mr. & Mrs. Rollin Sherman
1314 Mr. & Mrs. J. R. Lindgren
1314 Mr. & Mrs. N. E. Simonsen
1318 Mr. & Mrs. D. P. Donelson
1324 Mr. & Mrs. W. T. Rickards
1332 Mr. & Mrs. Wm. S. Hofstra
1404 Mr. & Mrs. Frank P. Frazier
1404 Frank D. Frazier
1414 Mr. & Mrs. F. P. Crandon&drs.
1418 Mr. & Mrs. George Bancroft
1422 Mr. & Mrs. B. F. Weeks & dr.
1426 Mrs. E. E. Houston & drs.
1432 Mr. & Mrs. D. S. Cook & dr.
1508 Mr.& Mrs. Charles F. Grey&dr.

FOREST PLACE.

1608 Mr. & Mrs. Geo. A. Thorne
1622 Mr. & Mrs. Curtis H. Remy

FOSTER STREET.

617 Mr. & Mrs. Jas. Taft Hatfield
621 Prof. & Mrs. J. H. Gray
721 Mrs. T. Moore & drs.
733 Mr. & Mrs. D. A. Ward & dr.
733 Guy W. Ward

620 Mr. & Mrs. Robt. R. Mars & dr.
720 Prof. & Mrs. S.C. Bronson & dr.

GREENLEAF AVENUE.

827 Mr. & Mrs. Chas. T. Bartlett & dr.
827 Charles H. Bartlett

510 Mr. & Mrs. Henry E. Seelye
510 Mrs. M. E. Wiswall & dr.
510 Charles E. Wiswall
530 George A. Wiswall

1016 Mr. & Mrs. Peter Randlev
1020 Mr. & Mrs. Geo. L. Parkhurst

GREENWOOD BOULEVARD.

nw. cor. Sheridan rd. Prof. & Mrs.
   Robt. D. Sheppard
235 Mrs. W. A. Hammond & dr.
239 Mrs. Charles H. Rowe & dr.
239 Samuel D. Rowe
415 Mr. & Mrs. Chas. H. Harbert
419 Mr. & Mrs. Seldon F. White
421 Mrs. Wm. G. White & drs.
nw. cor. Hinman av. Greenwood Inn
   Geo. E. Androvette
   Benj. Bayless & dr.
   Geo. W. Bayless
   Mrs. V. L. Bayless
   Mr. & Mrs. W. C. Brooks
   Mr. & Mrs. George D. Cobb
   H. F. Dickinson
   Mr. & Mrs. Frederick E. French
   Mrs. Orvis French & dr.
   H. P. Holden
   Mrs. Jane Holden & dr.
   W. B. Hutchinson
   R. C. Jacobsen
   George T. Kelly
   F. A. Kirkpatrick
   Mr. & Mrs. Joseph LaCroix
   Julian B. McGinn
   W. C. Morgan
   W. M. Pindell
   James H. Poage
   A. F. Shedd
   J. S. Shortle
   Geo. W. Sloat
   Mr. & Mrs. Lewis C. Tallmadge
     & dr.
   T. E. Tallmadge
   Mr. & Mrs. J. V. Taylor
   Mr. & Mrs. M. Wise & dr.
1007 Mr. & Mrs. Thomas W. Bell
1007 Mr. & Mrs. Charles T. Boynton
1015 Mr. & Mrs. E. J. Smith
1015 Herbert C. Smith
1021 Mr. & Mrs. David K. Hill
1021 Mrs. L. A. Tracy
1027 Mr. & Mrs. D. A. Coe
1319 Mr. & Mrs. R.H. Aishton & drs.
1325 Mr. & Mrs. Archer Gifford
1325 Frank W. Gifford

---

202 Mr. & Mrs. Arthur Orr
214 Mr. & Mrs. Frederick F. Peabody

228 Mr. & Mrs. W. B. Phillips & dr.
320 Mr. & Mrs. James S. Murray
330 Mr. & Mrs. Cornelius DeB.
   Howell
330 Mr. & Mrs. Geo. R. Brown
404 Mr. & Mrs. C. L. Williams & dr.
404 George Williams
408 Mr. & Mrs. F. D. Raymond &
   drs.
412 Mr. & Mrs. Edward C.-Carter
416 Dr. & Mrs. H. A. Freeman
422 Mr. & Mrs. Edwin Sherman
518 Mr. & Mrs. E. C. Belknap
518 Mrs. W. N. Brainard
526 Mr. & Mrs. Frank N. Winne
528 Mr. & Mrs. George L. Stevens
1004 Mr. & Mrs. Gilbert A. Smith &
   drs.
1014 Mrs. Ezra N. Hill
1014 Volney W. Foster
1014 Albert Volney Foster
1014 Miss Eva C. Foster
1022 Mr. & Mrs. A. J. Wright
1022 Mr. & Mrs. C. H. Mears
1028 Mr. & Mrs. Fleming H. Revell
   & dr. *Receiving day Monday*
1104 Mr. & Mrs. W. O. Dean & dr.
1224 Mr. & Mrs. Wm. H. Cutler
1224 Charles W. Cutler
1228 Mr. & Mrs. J. L. Whitlock & dr.
1410 Rev. & Mrs. J. D. Matthius

GROVE STREET.

405 William K. Lowrey
405 Mrs. Martha G. Doughty
405 Mrs. Mary L. Jackson & dr.
411 Mr. & Mrs. H. K. Gilbert
913 Mr. & Mrs. David Dunoon
913 Miss Christy McMartin
1017 Mr. & Mrs. D. S. McMullen
1021 Mr. & Mrs. Roger B. McMullen
1027 Mrs. Ann E. Bass
1027 Mr. & Mrs. Perkins B. Bass
1027 James K. Bass
1029 Mr. & Mrs. Carl. A. Goodnow
1223 Mr. & Mrs. Tunis Isbester
1223 John H. Isbester

---

922 Mr. & Mrs. H. S. Mecartney
1016 Dr. & Mrs. Albert B. Clark
1016 Miss Katharine H. Clark
1020 Mr. & Mrs. W. Irving Osborne
1020 Miss Mary T. Green
1020 Miss Catherine Green
1022 Mrs. W. F. Poole & dr.

1022 William F. Poole
1024 Mr. & Mrs. Arthur F. Towne
1026 Mrs. C. McCullough
1028 Mr. & Mrs. W. J. McConnell
1030 Mr. & Mrs. James B. Ludlow
1030 Mr. & Mrs. Wm. N. Viguers
1420 Mr.&Mrs. H. C. Dithmer & drs.
1420 Frank R. Dithmer

HAMILTON STREET.

225 Mr. & Mrs. C. E. Anthony & drs.
323 Mr. & Mrs. Osgood T. Eastman

318 Mr. & Mrs. George Olmsted
428 Mr. & Mrs. William S. Lord
428 Miss Gertrude E. Gooding
428 Mrs. H. A. Rowland

HAMLIN STREET.

617 Prof. & Mrs. Thos. F. Holgate
627 Prof. & Mrs. Henry Crew

HARRISON STREET.

2101 Mr. & Mrs. John W. Branch
2101 Mrs. G. H. Parker
2115 Mr. & Mrs. Wm. M. Gale
2323 Mr. & Mrs. D. B. Smith
2407 Mr. & Mrs. Frank Y. Norris
2423 Mr. & Mrs. John Guilliams
2515 Mr. & Mrs. John Q. Williams
2519 Mr. & Mrs. Edward Billingslea
2519 Mr. & Mrs. Albert Billingslea
2711 Mr. & Mrs. Claude Billingslea
2711 Albert Billingslea jr.

2030 Mr. & Mrs.AndrewA.Swanson
2514 Mr. & Mrs. Edward J. Dahms
2514 Mrs. Mary Allen
2526 Mr. & Mrs. Fred'k D. Richards
2602 Mr. & Mrs. Geo. A. Richards
2602 Mr. & Mrs. M. G. Richards
2622 Mr. & Mrs. Frederick S.Oliver
2712 Mr. & Mrs. Edward S. Hunt ·

HARTZELL STREET.

2311 Mr. & Mrs. John G. Brown

2210 Mrs. M. E. Orvis & drs.
2210 Purdy W. Orvis
2220 Mr. & Mrs. John C. Williams
2414 Mr. & Mrs. Eugene McKay
2418 Mr. & Mrs. James H. Jagoe
2622 John S. Snyder

HINMAN AVENUE.

537 Mr. & Mrs. J. V. Lamson
649 Mr. & Mrs. E. H. Hughes & dr.
703 Mrs. W. B. Watson
703 Mrs. G. D. Johnson
707 Mr. & Mrs. John E. Williams & dr.
713 Mrs. C. A. Ely & dr.
713 Mr. & Mrs. James C. Rogers
715 Mr. & Mrs. J. H. Wilbur
715 Miss Josephine M. Wilbur
715 Ralph Wilbur
723 Mr. & Mrs. Frederick Mehring
743 Mr. & Mrs. John F. King
743 Miss Grace F. King
747 Judge & Mrs. M. D. Ewell
817 Mr. & Mrs. Hiram Blaisdell
817 Jacob B. Olwin
817 John M. Olwin
827 Mr. & Mrs. Chas. F. Mendsen
831 Mr. & Mrs. Wm. H. Dyson
831 Mr. & Mrs. Lewis E. Dyson
837 Mr. & Mrs. J. Milhening & dr.
837 Frank Milhening
911 Mr. & Mrs. Geo. F. Hardie
915 Mr. & Mrs. A. H. Hall
919 Mr. & Mrs. H. L. Tolman
919 Miss Mary H. O'Brien
927 Mr. & Mrs. Charles Dowst
1015 Mr. & Mrs. S. F. ReQua
Receiving day Thursday
1015 Frederick N. ReQua
1019 Mr. & Mrs. E. H. Ball
1033 Mr. & Mrs. J. E. Nolan
1033 Miss Louise Grover
1043 Mr. & Mrs. Roger S. Pitkin
1109-1111 "The Oaks"
  Mr. & Mrs. Henry B. Cragin
  Mr. & Mrs. R. P. Hollett
  Mrs. Benjamin Lombard
  Mr. & Mrs. A. C. Minor
  Mr. & Mrs. William G. Oliver
  Mr. & Mrs. Frank W. Porter
1123 Mr. & Mrs. H. R. Ross & dr.
1203 Mr. & Mrs. A. M. Shellito & dr.
1205 Mr. & Mrs. Wm. Hayden & dr.
1205 Ralph Hayden
1205 Mrs. E. A. Woodward
1211 Mr. & Mrs. Albert R. Barnes
1221 Mr. & Mrs. Thaddeus P. Stanwood
1225 Mr. & Mrs. Arthur B. Jones
1229 Mr. & Mrs. H. A. Keith
1235 Mr. & Mrs. Alonzo B. Lord ·
1241 Mr. & Mrs. Edw. H. Buehler

1241 William Buehler
1241 Miss Katharine B. Buehler
1247 Mr. & Mrs. A. D. Ferry
1247 Mr. & Mrs. Robt. K. Coble
1247 J. Fred. Kinney
1319 Mr. & Mrs. Wm. H. Lee & drs.
1319 Joseph L. Lee
1319 William L. Lee
1319 Walter A. Lee
1323 Mr. & Mrs. F. A. Holbrook & drs.
1323 Harry R. Holden
1327 Mr. & Mrs. Luman R. Wing
1327 Luman R. Wing, jr
1405 Mr. & Mrs. N. C. Gridley
1417 Mr. & Mrs. A. N. Young,
1427 Miss F. Rodgers
1427 Roger L. Douglass
1433 Mr. & Mrs. Simeon Farwell
1507 Mr. & Mrs. John E. Wilder
1513 Mr. &Mrs. W.E. Stockton & dr.
1521 Mr. & Mrs. G. P. Engelhard
1605 Mrs. Mary R. Shumway
1605 Miss Sarah H. Brayton, M. D.
1605 P. R. Shumway
1625 Mrs. S. K. Rogers
1625 Dr. A. W. Hebert
1625 Miss Letitia Hebert
1625 Mr. & Mrs. S. T. French
1625 Mrs. S. C. Wells
1625 Prof. & Mrs. J. H. Wigmore
1625 Mr. & Mrs. Ralph Clarkson
1625 Mr. & Mrs. Wm. D. Allen
1625 Mr. & Mrs. B. E. Hamilton
1625 Mr. & Mrs. Gray Blandy
1631 Mr. & Mrs. James Rood jr.
1639 Dr. & Mrs. A. H. Parker & dr.
1639 E. Harry Parker
1639 Charles W. Parker
1707 Mr. & Mrs. H. H. C. Miller & dr.
1707 George H. Miller
1711 Dr. & Mrs. W. A. Phillips
1719 Mr. & Mrs. A. F. Townsend & dr.
1725 Mr.&Mrs. Joseph F.Ward &dr.
1733 Gaylord S. Wilcox
1733 Mr. & Mrs. George G. Wilcox & dr.
1741 Mr. & Mrs. Thos. Kane
1745 Prof. & Mrs. C. F. Bradley
1805 Mr. & Mrs. F. E. Griswold & dr.
1805 Edward L. Griswold
1813 Mr. & Mrs. Chas. A. Ward
1815 Mrs. C. J. Whitely
1815 Miss Elizabeth Whitely

1819 Mr. & Mrs. Nelson DeGolyer
1819 Donald L. DeGolyer
1819 L. N. DeGolyer
1819 Robert S. DeGolyer
1823 Dr. & Mrs. John Ridlon & dr.
   Receiving day Saturday

652 Mrs. G. A. VanEps & dr.
700 A. M. V. Schermerhorn
706 Mr. & Mrs. Medford Powell
710 Mr.& Mrs. Francis D.Reynolds
716 Mr. & Mrs. J. T. W. Jennings
716 George Jennings
722 Mr. & Mrs. W. L. Tomlins &dr.
730 Mr. & Mrs. Timothy Dwight
730 Henry E. Dwight.
740 Mr. & Mrs. L. L. Smith
746 Mrs. A. H. Gunn
746 James D. Burt
804 Mr. & Mrs. W. L. Knox
832 Mr. & Mrs. J. H. Thomas &dr.
832 George O. Thomas
832 Fred Thomas
904 Mr. & Mrs. H. C. Lawrence
904 Charles H. Lawrence
906 Mr. & Mrs. I. O. Nelson
   Receive Tuesdays and Thursdays
914 Mr. & Mrs. W. H. Blake
914 W. Herbert Blake
922 Mr. & Mrs. Paul Benson & drs.
922 Mr. & Mrs. Vernon E. Matlack
926 Mr. & Mrs. C. H. McFarland
926 Mrs. Wm. L. Church
930 Mr. & Mrs. F. E. Mitchell
932 Mr. & Mrs. F. W. Nichols
936 Mrs. M. A. Smart & dr.
936 Alexander Smart
936 James R. Smart
1004 Mr.&Mrs.JohnW.Burdsal & dr.
1004 George B. Burdsal
1012 Mr. & Mrs. Benj. F. Homer & dr.
1012 Frank B. Homer
1014 Mr. & Mrs. Platt M. Morgan
1024 Mr. & Mrs. A. T. Nafis & dr.
1024 Louis F. Nafis
1040 Mr. & Mrs. Harry B. Wheelock
1042 Mr. & Mrs. Percy W. Palmer
1118 Mr. & Mrs. A. L. Cayzer
1120 Mr. & Mrs. F. A. Dix
1120 Prof. & Mrs. James A. James
1120 John M. James
1134 Mr. & Mrs. W.C.Stewart & dr.
1142 Mr. & Mrs. D. A. Holmes & dr.
1142 Mrs. Julia A. Holmes
1142 Roy C. Holmes

1142 Francis R. Holmes
1202 Mr. & Mrs. John T. Stockton
1206 Miss Mary Ludlam
1206 J. W. Ludlam
1216 Mr. & Mrs. J. Chas. Williams & drs.
1216 David Irwin Williams
1220 Mr. & Mrs. Adelbert M. Foster
1224 Mr. & Mrs. Philo Marsh
1224 Mr. & Mrs. W. P. Marsh
1228 Mr. & Mrs. M. A. Dean
1228 Mrs. Wm. J. Canfield
1232 Mr. & Mrs. David N. Barker
1236 Mr. & Mrs. Frank Ritchie
1240 Mr. & Mrs. Jas. A. Lawrence
1240 Mrs. Ruth Wyllis
1246 Mr. & Mrs. Herbert A.Streeter
1246 Mr. & Mrs. Herbert C. Streeter
1246 R. Cortland Burkholder
1302 Mr. & Mrs. George S. Marsh
1306 Mr. & Mrs. Ernest J. Rogers
1310 Mr. & Mrs. J. J. Charles
1310 Mrs. Martha E. Sherman
1314 Mr. & Mrs. E. F. Carpenter
1318 Mr. & Mrs. Wm. B. Topliff
1318 Samuel Topliff
1322 Rev. & Mrs. J. F. Loba
1328 E. A. Lord & dr.
1328 P. A. Lord
1328 Frank E. Lord
1328 Mrs. S. L. Webster
1332 Dr. & Mrs. R. H. Kimball
1332 W. D. Hess
1334 Mr. & Mrs. Russell W. Walker
Receiving day Wednesday
1334 Harry W. Walker
1334 Mrs. Jane Kingman
1408 Mr. & Mrs. J. H. Van-Vlissingen
1414 Mr. & Mrs. O. C. French
1414 Dr. & Mrs. L. D. Henderson
1414 Mrs. Alice Gove
1414 Miss Harriet Thoms
1414 Miss Mary Gillespie
1414 Mrs. A. R. Miller & dr.
1414 Mr. & Mrs. C. R. Stouffer
1422 Mr.& Mrs.AndressB.Hull&drs.
1422 Miss Grace Brown
1422 Miss Grace Banks
1426 Mrs. J. H. Bayliss & drs.
1426 James E. Bayliss
1502 Mr. & Mrs. G. M. Sargent
1502 Mrs. Emily Durham
1502 George H. Sargent
1502 Wm. Durham Sargent
1508 Mr. & Mrs. C. B.Cleveland&dr.

1518 Dr. & Mrs. G. W. Whitefield
1518 Rev. & Mrs. John Whitefield
1602 Mr. & Mrs. Daniel A. Mudge
1610 Dr. & Mrs. Wm. Walter
1614 Mr. & Mrs. Walter M. Anthony
1614 Gardner Read
1624 Mrs. Francis Bradley & dr.
1624 Luther D. Bradley
1632 Rev. & Mrs. Wm. Macafee
1714 Mrs. Henry B. Ridgaway
1714 Prof. A. V. E. Young
1726 Mrs. L. C. Ward & drs.
1746 Mr. & Mrs. P. E. Simmons.
1804 Prof. & Mrs. R. L. Cumnock
1810 Mr. & Mrs. Charles J. Connell
1810 Charles M. Connell
1812 Prof. & Mrs. M. S. Terry & dr.
1818 Mr. & Mrs. Addison M. De Coudres
1824 Mr. & Mrs. E. M. Board
1830 Mr. & Mrs.GeorgeF.Stone&dr.
1832 Mr. & Mrs. Wiley J. Littlejohn
1838 Mr. & Mrs. G. B. Reynolds

INGLESIDE PARK.

Mr. & Mrs. Wm. Blanchard
Mr. & Mrs. Joseph A. Allebone
Mr. & Mrs. H. K. Snider
Mr. & Mrs. J. Wilson Howell
Mr. & Mrs. Aaron O. Auten
Mr. & Mrs. Henry C. French

JUDSON AVENUE.

543 Mr. & Mrs. E. R. Bradford
543 Miss Helen M. Wilson
551 Mr. & Mrs. Edgar H. Tobey
745 Mr. & Mrs. John E. Roberts
807 Mr. & Mrs. John W. Byam
813 Mr. & Mrs. C. E. Dudley
813 Mrs. Mary Dudley
817 Mr. & Mrs.Chauncey N.Waterman
831 F. H. Brammer
925 Mr. & Mrs. Abel L. Allen
927 Mr. & Mrs. Horatio Nelson Kelsey *Receiving day Wednesday*
1007 Mr. & Mrs. C. N. Hammon
1013 Mr. & Mrs. C. Frederick Orr
1013 Mrs. E. D. Hinchman
1021 Mr. & Mrs. C. E. Ware
Receiving day Thursday
1021 Miss Mary Lillian Ware
1027 Mr. & Mrs. George Rhodes

47

1027 Mrs. Maria C. Wolcott
102/ J. Wolcott Rhodes
1031 Mr. & Mrs. W. H. Spencer
1031 Bennett W. Spencer
1031 Mrs. L. M. Spencer
1041 Mr. & Mrs. John W. Sweet
1045 Mrs. S. H. Sweet & dr.
1045 Mr. & Mrs. H. C. Colby
1119 Mr. & Mrs. EugeneU.Kimbark
1139 Mr. & Mrs. Richard C. Hall ·
1141 Mr. & Mrs. J. H. Burns
1143 Mrs. Margaret Cassard
1143 Mr. & Mrs. Ernest Toogood
1145 Mrs. W. J. White
1145 Mrs. John Forman
1205 Dr. & Mrs. Edmund Noyes &
dr.
1205 Ed S. Noyes
1207 Mr. & Mrs. Newell C. Knight
1207 Dr. Eugene C. Knight
1211 Mr. & Mrs. J. H. Nitchie
1213 Mr. & Mrs. Wm. G. Wentworth
1215 Mr. & Mrs. Arthur L. Norton
1217 Mrs. M. W. Waite
1221 Mr. & Mrs. John M. Thomas
1221 Samuel Robinson
1225 Mr. & Mrs. E. A. Dawson
1229 Prof. & Mrs. H. H. Kingsley
1229 Miss Harriet H. Fitch
1235 Mr. & Mrs. Perry Landis
Receiving day Wednesday
1235 Miss Ada G. Fessler
1237 Mr. & Mrs. Harvey H. Reese
1247 Mr. & Mrs. W. E. Burden
1301 Mrs. Susan P. Wray
1301 James T. Wray
1305 Mr. & Mrs. James Bradley
Brashears
Receiving day Saturday
1305 Mrs. Mary Alexander
1307 Mrs. C. F. De Golyer
1323 Mr. & Mrs. J. W. Helm
1325 Mr. & Mrs. H. D. Baker & dr.
1325 Mrs. Jennie Frowe & dr.
1327 Mrs. M. J. King & dr.
1405 Mr. & Mrs. John E. Scott
1405 John William Scott
1405 Robert L. Scott
1405 Frederick H. Scott
1405 Mrs. John Hossack
1405 Miss I. B. Hossack
1411 Mr. & Mrs. E. S. Turner
1415 Mr. & Mrs. Chas. Lincoln
Bartlett
1419 Mrs. Geo. B. Dunham
1419 George S. Dunham

1423 Mr. & Mrs. John S. Barker
1423 Mr. & Mrs. Nelson Sanford
1427 Mr. & Mrs. C. B. Congdon
1431 Mrs. Lewis M. Prentiss
1431 Miss Louise D. Clark
1431 Mr. & Mrs. Chas. W. Davis
1431 Mr. &. Mrs. Joseph F. Pride
1433 Mrs. Mary A. Merriam
1433 Dwight G. Welling
1433 Leonard T. Beecher
1615 Mrs. C. W. Northup
1615 George T. Northup
1615 Josiah C. Northup
1615 William G. Hoag
1621 Mr. and Mrs. Geo. A. Calkins
1625 Prof. & Mrs. H. F. Fisk & dr.
1629 Mrs. Warren Ewen
1629 Miss Harriet Ewen
1629 Miss Lilian Ewen
1629 Malcolm F. Ewen
1637 Mr. & Mrs. John Meiggs Ewen
1637 Mrs. R. W. Patterson
1637 Stewart Patterson

634 Mr. & Mrs. Lewis H. Bushnell
638 Mr. & Mrs. Geo. L. Hopkins
638 Mr. & Mrs. Geo. E. Hopkins
638 William P. Hopkins
712 Mr. & Mrs. G. W. Remmers
716 Mr. & Mrs. W. H. Fargo
724 Mr. & Mrs. F. R. Seelye
730 Mr. & Mrs. Isaac H. Seelye
828 Dr. & Mrs. Henry M. Bannister
840 Mr. & Mrs. B. C. Chambers
Receiving day Friday
846 Mr. & Mrs. Arthur J. S. Fordham
Receiving day Wednesday
846 Guy Hampdon Fordham
904 Mr. & Mrs. Wm. T. Hardie
906 Mr. & Mrs. G. W. Marquardt jr.
908 Mr. & Mrs. Albert E. Peirce
926 Mr. & Mrs. Alexander Clark
928 Mr. & Mrs. W. H. Murray &
drs. *Receiving day Monday*
932 Mr. & Mrs. A. H. Ullrich
Receiving day Tuesday
938 Mr. & Mrs. David L. Thorp &
dr.
1012 Mrs. M. Coryell & drs.
1012 George R. Coryell
1016 Mr. & Mrs. Walter B. Smith
1016 Mr. & Mrs. W. P. Matteson
1016 Mr. & Mrs. T. W. Edmonds
1028 Mr. & Mrs. B. D. Baldwin

1040 Mr. & Mrs. W. E. Church &
    drs.
1040 Rollin Church
1040 Lloyd Church
1102 Mrs. Eliza U. Kimbark
1102 Edward H. Kimbark
1102 D. Avery Kimbark
1102 Frank M. Kimbark
1114 Mr. & Mrs. Chester P. Walcott
1118 Mr. & Mrs. John Griggs &
    drs.
1122 Mr. & Mrs. M. W. Carlisle&dr.
1122 William W. Carlisle
1122 John Andrew Carlisle
1122 Addison Alexander Carlisle
1124 Mr. & Mrs. N. W. Williams
1126 Mr. & Mrs. Chas. L. Drain
    Receiving day Friday
1126 Mrs. Julia Drain
1130 Mr. & Mrs. E. W. Spencer
1134 Mr. & Mrs. H. W. Bucking-
    ham
1138 Mr. & Mrs. N. W. Brooks
1142 Mr. & Mrs. Frank Gould & dr.
1142 Mr. & Mrs. Geo. R. Work
1200 Mr. & Mrs. Frank W. Gerould
1208 Mrs. A. T. Merriman & dr.
1208 Andrews T. Merriman jr.
1208 Mr. & Mrs. Peter Taylor
1212 Mr. & Mrs. J. M. Hawxhurst
1212 Mrs. W. H. Crawford
1216 Mr. & Mrs. T. W. Heermans.
1226 Mr. & Mrs. Geo. F. Griffith &
    dr.
1228 Mr. & Mrs. Leslie E. Hildreth
1228 Miss Mary L. Barrie
1232 Mr. & Mrs. B. D. Caldwell
1236 Mr. & Mrs. Frank A. Warner &
    drs.
1242 Mr. & Mrs. George N. Stone
1246 Mr. & Mrs. A. M. Leslie
1304 James G. Kirk
1304 Mr. & Mrs. T. M. Baxter & dr.
1308 Mr. & Mrs. J. Seymour Currey
1310 Mr. & Mrs. Chas. H. Barry
1314 Mr. & Mrs. Edward Haupt
1314 Mrs. Annie A. Wixson
1318 Mrs. E. C. Earle
1318 John D. Earle
1322 Mr. & Mrs. E. H. Hunt & drs.
1326 Mr. & Mrs. S. J. Vinnedge
1412 Mr. & Mrs. W. S. Harbert &
    drs.
1412 Arthur B. Harbert
1412 Mrs. A. A. Harbert
1412 Miss E. Clark

1418 Mr. & Mrs. Robert A. Davison
1422 Mr. & Mrs. F. K. Stevens
1422 Miss Elmira Morse
1512 Mr. & Mrs. Wm. M. Scott &
    dr.
1512 Charles F. Scott
1574 Mrs. Nancy B. Wire
1574 Mr. & Mrs. William C. Wire
1704 Mr. & Mrs. John Charles Shaf-
    fer
1722 Mrs. L. P. Hamline
1722 Mr. & Mrs. Thos. S. Creighton
1742 Mrs. Orrington Lunt & dr.
1742 Miss Ida Cornelia Gray

KEDZIE AVENUE.

221 Mr. & Mrs. Edwin L. Shuman
223 Mr. & Mrs. Wm. Lukey
    Receiving day Wednesday
223 J. Ernest Lukey

LAKE STREET.

215 Mr. & Mrs. Michael Tiernan
    & dr.
215 John Tiernan
225 Mr. & Mrs. Frank M. Elliot
1015 Mr. & Mrs. S. J. Llewellyn
1115 Robert Holmes
1119 Mr. & Mrs. Samuel Carson
1121 Mr. & Mrs. R. K. Hitchens & dr.
1121 Roy K. Hitchens jr.
1323 Mr. & Mrs. Robt. J. Grier &
    drs.
1327 Mr. & Mrs. Alex. Hofflund
1415 Mr. & Mrs. Chris. Dupre

222 Mr. & Mrs. Stewart Clark
222 Marshall Clark
320 Mr. & Mrs. M. J. Insull
404 Mr. &. Mrs. M. V. Gilbert
408 Mr. & Mrs. B. F. Adams
412 Mr. & Mrs. George P. Mer-
    rick
416 Mr. & Mrs. Martin M. Gridley
502 Mr. & Mrs. H. P. Gray & dr.
502 Howard A. Gray
512 Mrs. J. R. Towne
512 Mr. & Mrs. E. D. Redington &
    dr.
610 Prof. & Mrs. Henry Cohn
910 Mr. & Mrs. P. P. Lee & drs.
1002 Mr. & Mrs. Lucien E. Hard
    ing
1010 Mr. & Mrs. Burt M. Gardner

1012 Mr. & Mrs. George S. Baker
1016 Mrs. R. M. Grier
1016 Mr. & Mrs. James P. Grier
1020 Mr. & Mrs. James C. Mecartney
1026 Rev. Hugh P. Smyth
1026 Rev. Thomas M. Burke

LAKE SHORE BOULEVARD.

1012 Mr. & Mrs. J. Stanley Grepe
1040 Mrs. Mary W. Dale

LEE STREET.

1017 Mr. & Mrs. G. A. Smith
1017 Mrs. Mary Urann
1017 Mrs. Mary R. Pratt
1021 Mrs. Geo. S. Smith
1021 Miss Lucy Mason
1021 Mr. & Mrs. V. A. Rossbach

LINCOLN STREET.

1705 Col. & Mrs. H. M. Kidder

LYONS STREET.

1320 Mr. & Mrs. John C. Turner

MAIN STREET.

809 Mr. & Mrs. J. C. Murphy
809 Miss Margaret Carroll
1129 Mr. & Mrs. James A. Rowe
1315 Mr. & Mrs. J. B. Calligan
1319 Mr. & Mrs. Wm. E. Chambers
1319 Mrs. Judith W. McGill

---

222 Mr. & Mrs. Frank L. Borton
Receiving day Tuesday
930 Mr. & Mrs. M. Foley
1130 Mr. & Mrs. William Howard
1206 Mr. & Mrs. Harry B. Judson
1300 Mr. & Mrs. M. W. McDonnell
1306 Mr. & Mrs. F. R. Carver
1306 Miss Bertha Langhenry
1310 Mr. & Mrs. James Lill
1428 Mrs. J. C. Waterbury

MADISON STREET.

819 Mr. & Mrs. Robt. K. Brown

---

730 Mr. & Mrs. F. D. Jackson
730 Mrs. Emily Jackson
732 Mr. & Mrs. Nicholas Traff &
dr.
826 Mr. & Mrs. Marshall Garrison
& dr.

830 Chas. W. Green & dr.
834 Mr. & Mrs. Thos. O. Moulton
834 Thos. T. Campbell & dr.
918 Mrs. D. A. Cutts & drs.

MAPLE AVENUE.

1023 Mr. & Mrs. John S. Metcalf &
drs.
1031 Mr. & Mrs. Lewis M. Sawyer
& drs.
1031 Ward B. Sawyer
1039 Dr. Abbie A. Hinkle
1039 Mrs. Elizabeth T. Hinkle
1039 Miss Maria R. Hinkle
1101 Mr. & Mrs. Geo. B. Bergen
1111 Mr. & Mrs. Edward W. Russell
1111 Frank H. Russell
1113 Mr. & Mrs. F. P. Judson
1203 Mrs. Mary A. Childs & dr.
1203 Frank A. Childs
1207 Mrs. Isabella Parkes & dr.
1209 Mr. & Mrs. Wm. F. Manson
1211 Mr. & Mrs. H. L. Duren
1213 Mr. & Mrs. Harry S. Stevens
1215 Mr. & Mrs. Frank W. Tuttle
1217 Mr. & Mrs. Wm. T. VanArsdale
1223 Mr. & Mrs. C. E. Morris
1223 Mrs. Mary E. Scranton
1227 Mr. & Mrs. C. B. Eyer
1231 Mr. & Mrs. J. A. Smith & dr.
1235 Dr. & Mrs. A. W. Cooper
1239 Mr. & Mrs. James Steele
1239 Mr. & Mrs. E. L. Scott
1305 Mr. & Mrs. M. Cochrane Armour
1313 Mr. & Mrs. Joseph K. Lewis
1319 Mr. & Mrs. J. A. Battle
1327 Mr. & Mrs. A. H. Lowden & drs.
1333 Mr. & Mrs. James K. Armsby jr.
1333 Richard L. Dakin
1403 Mr. & Mrs. Towner K. Webster & dr.
1403 Henry K. Webster
1403 Miss Laura Kitchell
1411 Mrs. M. L. Ridgway & dr.
1411 Mr. & Mrs. C. M. Knox
1415 Mr. & Mrs. Chas. H. Burkitt
1421 Mr. & Mrs. C. P. Spining
1421 N. G. Iglehart
1425 Mrs. Helen M. Ide & dr.
1425 William K. Ide
1425 Charles B. Ide
1433 Mrs. J. N. Hubbard
1453 Mr. & Mrs. Reuben Knox

1459 Mr. & Mrs. Frank A. Burgess
1463 Mr. & Mrs. Arthur W. Underwood
1501 Mr. & Mrs. Hópkins J. Hanford
Receiving day Monday
1501 Scott Hanford
1505 Mr. & Mrs. Albert G. Coe
1553 Mr. & Mrs. J. W. Thompson
1553 F. W. Hardman
1559 Mr. & Mrs. Charles Aikin
1561 Mr. & Mrs. Willard S. Pàden

930 Mr. & Mrs. John Evans
930 Mrs. J. E. Greaves
930 Wm. C. Evans
1014 Mr. & Mrs. E. L. Harphàm
1030 Mr. & Mrs. A. L. Fanning
1032 Mr. & Mrs. Wm. H. Cooley
1116 Mr. & Mrs. Stephen W. Wylie
1202 Mr. & Mrs. Albert F. McCarrell
1202 Mr. & Mrs. Francis S. Oliver
1208 Mr. & Mrs. Wm. Feiler
1214 Mrs. Fannie L. Larimer
1220 Mrs. James C. Connor
1224 Mr. & Mrs. Wm. Smith Mason
1232 Mr. & Mrs. N. Arthur Coblé
1232 J. H. Kellam
1236 Mr. & Mrs. John Handford
1242 C. O. Boring
1242 Mrs. M. Augusta Jones
1242 Walter B. Jones
1246 Mr. & Mrs. L. D. Parker
Receiving day Thursday
1246 Mr. & Mrs. E. H. Parker
1246 Harry M. Parker
1308 Mr. & Mrs. Andrew Házlehurst
1310 Mr. & Mrs. Wm. S. Candée
1312 Mr. & Mrs. Rivers McNeill
1316 Mr. & Mrs. Holmes Hoge & dr.
1416 Mr. & Mrs. Knowlton Ames
1422 Mr. & Mrs. Louis K. Goffe
1428 Mr. & Mrs. Thomas Bates
1428 Miss Rosa C. Bates
1432 Mr. & Mrs. H. A. Beidler
1454 Mr. & Mrs. E. H. Reed
1454 James H. Reed
1458 Mr. & Mrs. Wm. B. Parkes
1458 Dr. & Mrs. Wm. R. Parkes
1460 Mr. & Mrs. John R. Woodbridge
1500 Mr. & Mrs. F. A. Aplin
1500 Mrs. E. H. Miller
1500 Fred C. Miller
1506 Mrs. D. B. Dewey
1516 Mrs. James K. Armsby

1516 George N. Armsby
1516 E. R. Armsby
1516 Gordon Armsby
1516 Joseph D. Stubbs
1516 Miss Maria Anderson

MICHIGAN AVENUE.

649 Mr. & Mrs. Foster H. Biggs
705 Mr. & Mrs. Egbert S. Gaines
715 Mr. & Mrs. Wm. L. Steele
803 Mr. & Mrs. J. H. McConnell
803 Mrs. E. C. McConnell
815 Mr. & Mrs. J. T. Barker
915 Mr. & Mrs. Wm. Trater
943 Mr. & Mrs. C. Clarence Poole
1037 Mr. & Mrs. E. K. Boyd & drs.
1115 Mr. & Mrs. F. R. Bissell
1217 Mr. & Mrs. Wm. L. Wells & drs.
1225 Mr. & Mrs. Eugene E. Osborn

712 Mr. & Mrs. H. S. Knapp
712 Mrs. E. S. Waddell
716 Mr. & Mrs. Geo. A. Weston
720 Mr. & Mrs. Robert C. Knaggs & dr.
720 George B. Knaggs
724 Mr. & Mrs. B. T. Holcomb & dr.
746 Mr. & Mrs. Wm. I. Earhart
746 Mrs. M. A. Tibbils
840 Mr. & Mrs. Geo. W. Burchard
Receiving day Tuesday
840 Ernest F. Burchard
1040 Mr. & Mrs. Franklin Overbagh
1042 Mrs. E. O. Hills & dr.
1046 Mr. & Mrs. William E. Hills
1104 Mrs. C. Marion Hotchkin
1104 Paul M. Hotchkin
1110 Mr. & Mrs. Robert S. Clark
1110 Mrs. Theodosia Emory
1110 Mrs. W. L. Breckinridge
1116 Mr. & Mrs. J. S. Dickerson
1126 Mr. & Mrs. W. Findley Hypes
1130 Mr. & Mrs. Chas. P. Coffin
1134 Mrs. Anne W. Tower
1134 Mr. & Mrs. Arthur Tower
1144 Mr. & Mrs. Howard Tracy
1144 Leverett L. Hull
1210 Mr. & Mrs. Otto C. Ericson
& dr. *Receiving day Friday*
1210 Mrs. Cornelia Jóhnson
1210 Miss Matilda Gunderson
cor. Lincoln pl. Mr. & Mrs. O. M. Carson

MONROE STREET.

833 Mr. & Mrs. Geo. Timerman
903 Mr. & Mrs. Frank Sherman
913 Mr. & Mrs. W. S. Gates
913 William W. Gates
919 Mr. & Mrs. Arthur M. Morgan

---

726 Mr. & Mrs. Nicholas Kirschten
802 Mr. & Mrs. Peter Risch
806 Mr. & Mrs. John P. Risch
810 Mr. & Mrs. Max Hahn
828 Miss Anna Koob
828 M. L. Koob
828 Mr. & Mrs. Nicholas F. Kranz
834 Mr. & Mrs. Geo. G. Goble

OAK AVENUE.

1115 Mr. & Mrs. James Wigginton
1217 Mr. & Mrs. Thos. E. Connor
1219 Mr. & Mrs. J. M. Bond
1223 Mr. & Mrs. Daniel McCann
1229 Mr. & Mrs. Henry H. Kerr
1231 Mr. & Mrs. Frederick W. Smith
1235 Mr. & Mrs. Geo. H. Doran
1239 Mr. & Mrs. Howard Field
1505 Mr. & Mrs. Andrew J. Brown
1553 Mr. & Mrs. Rufus C. Dawes
1563 Mr. & Mrs. A. H. Childs
1567 Mr. & Mrs. E. C. Nelson
1571 Mr. & Mrs. George H. Iott & dr
1575 Mr. & Mrs. Alfred L. Sproule
1615 M. P. Aiken
1615 Miss Rose T. Aiken
1621 Mr. & Mrs. Simon S. Davis
1625 Mr. & Mrs. F. H. Walker & dr.
1625 Edwin F. Walker
1633 Mr. & Mrs. James M. Barnes

1120 John L. Connor
1134 Mr. & Mrs. Paul Tietjens
1238 Mr. & Mrs. Herbert I. Keen
1304 Mr. & Mrs. Allen R. Vinnedge
1456 C. George Lewis
1456 Martin O. Lewis
1456 Martin Lewis & dr.
1456 Thomas H. Lewis
1462 Mr. & Mrs. Geo. L. Harvey
1500 Mr. & Mrs. Wm. Holabird
1500 R. G. Holabird
1504 Mr. & Mrs. David R. Lewis
1504 J. William Kelly
1554 Mr. & Mrs. L. K. Gillson
1560 Mr. & Mrs. J. W. Low
1566 Mr. & Mrs. H. C. Hunt & drs.
1570 Mr. & Mrs. Theodore Reese & drs.

1614 Mr. & Mrs. Daniel W. Hess
1618 Mr. & Mrs. Morton Butler
1622 Mrs. J. R. VanArsdale & dr.
1622 John R. VanArsdale

ORRINGTON AVENUE.

1625 Dr. Mary F. McCrillis
1627 Mr. & Mrs. Edward S. Taylor
1631 Mr. & Mrs. George R. Kline & dr.
1631 Rolland R. Kline
1715 Mr. & Mrs. J. B. Huse
1715 Frank J. Huse
1723 Mrs. Margaret Tubman
1735 Dr. & Mrs. H. G. Miller & dr.
1807 Mrs. E. J. Hudson
1815 Mrs. Catharine S. Clow & drs.
1819 Alton Parkhurst
1819 Dr. Emogene Parkhurst
1823 Prof. & Mrs. Charles S. Farrar & dr.
1823 Mr. & Mrs. H. S. Dietrich & dr.
1827 Mr. & Mrs. Ernest L. Clark
1925 Mrs. F. A. Bradley
1925 F. O. Bradley
1931 Mr. & Mrs. R. R. McCabe & drs.
1943 Mr. & Mrs. Chas. W. Lasher
1945 Mr. & Mrs. Geo. A. Foster
1945 Mr. & Mrs. G. F. Foster
1945 Mrs. M. M. Scovil
2001 S. Wade Hunt
2001 Mrs. Nancy D. Hunt
2003 Mrs. Clara Root
2003 Theodore W. Chaffee
2103 Mr. & Mrs. Chas. P. Stevens & dr.
2103 Mr. & Mrs. C. Nelson Stevens
2131 Mr. & Mrs. Geo. H. Moore & dr.
2131 George A. Moore
2145 John W. Rodgers
2145 Mrs. Julia Rodgers
2145 Mr. & Mrs. Lester Price
2145 Miss Mary Fullagar
2203 Mr. & Mrs. John G. Orchard & dr.
2203 James G. S. Orchard
2243 Mr. & Mrs. Malcolm McDowell & dr.
2243 Hansen McDowell
2243 Irvin McDowell

1614 Mr. & Mrs. C. H. Mecum
1708 Mrs. Emily A. Woodson
1708 Mr. & Mrs. John J. Waldron
1740 Mrs. E. J. Towle & dr.

1800 Miss Mary Harriet Norris
1800 Miss Anna Patterson
1906 Mrs. A. B. Merrill
1914 Mrs. M. L. Hibbard & dr.
1922 Mr. & Mrs. Joseph A. Griffin
1922 John M. Curran
1930 Mr. & Mrs. Herbert S. Smith
1934 Mrs. J. J. Spalding & drs.
1934 Miss Catharine A. Pettis
1936 Mrs. Ellen E. Langlois
1942 Mr. & Mrs. G. A. Kittredge
2032 Mr. & Mrs. Chas. S. Raddin
2034 Mrs. H. A. Raddin & drs.
2102 Mr. & Mrs. George P. Mills
2106 Mr. & Mrs. Frank C. Lewis
    Receiving day Thursday
2106 James S. Lewis
2110 Mr. & Mrs. John A. Scott
2112 Mr. & Mrs. C. L. Whittemore
2112 Mrs. Elvira L. Wilson
2118 Mrs. Olive Beason & drs.
2118 Mr. & Mrs. Wm. S. Blair
2236 Frank H. McCulloch
2236 Mrs. Catharine Waugh Mc
    Culloch
    Receiving day Saturday
2306 Prof. & Mrs. A. F. Ericson &
    drs.
2422 Mrs. Julius F. Kellogg

PRAIRIE AVENUE.

2607 Dr. & Mrs. J. H. Burchmore
2675 Mr. & Mrs. Herman Hoff

REBA PLACE.

715 Rev. & Mrs. Joseph Rushton
    & dr.
715 Joseph A. Rushton
727 Mr. & Mrs. C. S. Redfield & dr.
819 Mr. & Mrs. Edwin C. Crawford
823 George Colling
823 Mr. & Mrs. Byron G. Ruedy
911 Mr. & Mrs. John R. Bowman

714 Mr. & Mrs. M. T. Lane & drs.
722 Mr. & Mrs. Jas. Moore & drs.
802 Mr. & Mrs. John G. Beazley & dr.
810 Mr. & Mrs. W. E. Brothers
814 Mr. & Mrs. Charles Lincoln
826 Mr. & Mrs. F. F. Lewis

RIDGE AVENUE.

319 Mr. & Mrs. Charles Husche
319 Mr. & Mrs. Chas. H. Meyer
365 Mr. & Mrs. Chas. G. Haskin

365 Mrs. J. S. Kirk
515 Henry Sontag & drs.
521 Mr. & Mrs. Joseph J. Berry
545 Mr. & Mrs. P. J. Kasper
707 Mrs. John W. Hoffman & drs.
707 Charles A. Hoffman
921 Dr. Alice B. Stockham & dr.
1139 Dr. & Mrs. N. R. Marshall
1205 Mrs. Osro A. Crain
1225 Judge & Mrs. Chas. G. Neely
1225 Rev. & Mrs. E. F. Fish
1247 Mrs. P. N. Fox & dr.
1307 Mr. & Mrs. David L. Zook
1309 Mrs. Hugh A. White
1407 Mr. & Mrs. L. G. Hallberg
1429 Mr. & Mrs. M. M. Kirkman &
    dr.
1429 Mr. & Mrs. Wm. Bruce Kirk-
    man
1429 A. T. Kirkman
1429 Marshall J. Kirkman
1453 Mr. & Mrs. Walter W. Ross
1461 Mr. & Mrs. Charles Raymond
    & drs.
1501 Mr. & Mrs. Frank P. Sheldon
1501 Miss Mae Dingee
1509 Mr. & Mrs. W. J. Fabian
1555 Mr. & Mrs. Chas. D. Irwin
1579 Dr. & Mrs. Isaac Poole & dr.
1579 Joshua O. Cook
1585 Mr. & Mrs. Wm. H. Warren
2237 Mr. & Mrs. S. C. Ingraham
2237 Mrs. Mary L. Mulford

826 Mr. & Mrs. Henry A. Hoffman
906 Mr. & Mrs. Jas. D. Tucker
930 Mr. & Mrs. F. C. Fargo
938 Mr. & Mrs. J. W. Hartshorn &
    drs.
1046 Mrs. Sarah Crain & dr.
1046 Mr. & Mrs. Wm. Crain
1100 Mr. & Mrs. Alfred H. Gross
1128 Mr. & Mrs. Henry C. Rew
1128 Irwin Rew
1142 Mr. & Mrs. E. P. Griswold &
    drs.
1142 Harold T. Griswold
1214 Mr. & Mrs. Francis A. Hardy
1220 Mr. & Mrs. David R. Forgan
    Receive Wednesday
1232 Mr. & Mrs. William H. Jones
1246 Mr. & Mrs. H. C. Tillinghast
1246 Clark Tillinghast
1246 Miss Jane E. Kitchell
1314 Mr. & Mrs. Augustine C. Buell
    & dr.

1326 Mrs.·Charles Comstock & dr.
1326 Alphonso S. Comstock
1408 Mrs. Julia M. Watson & dr.
1408 Mr. & Mrs. J. D. Hubbard
1426 Mr. & Mrs. Fred S. James
1426 Louis N. James
1426 Whitney P. James
1456 Mr. & Mrs. John B. Kirk
1456 James M. Kirk
1462 Mr. & Mrs. George W. Smith
1514 Mr. & Mrs. J. H. Kedzie & dr.
1514 John H. Kedzie jr.
1558 Mr. & Mrs. George S. Lord
Receiving day Wednesday
1572 H. B. Hurd
1572 Mrs. J. A. Comstock
1608 Mr. & Mrs. Royal Cooper Vilas
1608 Royal Cooper Vilas jr.
1620 Thomas Lord & drs.
1622 Mr. & Mrs. Louis Hertle
1628 Mr. & Mrs. D. F. Stearns
1632 Mr. & Mrs. Calvin F. Rice
1632 Miss May Louise Rice
1708 Richard C. Lake & drs.
1726 Rev. & Mrs. E. C. Ray

SEWARD AVENUE.

908 Mr. & Mrs. Wm. A. Illsley

SHERIDAN ROAD.

621 Mr. & Mrs. D. H. Lamberson
& dr.
621 Miss Josie M. Lamberson
621 Frank Lamberson
621 Mr. & Mrs. Wm. H. Webster
707 Mr. & Mrs. V. H. Troendle
707 Miss Lena E. Troendle
721 Dr. & Mrs. P. L. McKinnie & dr
721 Ralph R. McKinnie
721 Leonard G. McKinnie
1031 Mr. & Mrs. Chas. S. Hannan
2235 Prof. & Mrs. Geo. W. Hough
2235 George J. Hough
2235 William Hough
ne. cor. Milburn Mr. & Mrs. Edwin
F. Brown
2645 Mr. & Mrs. Chas. W. Deering
2703 Mr. & Mrs. E. G. Henderson
2703 Mrs. Catharine N. Barlow
2703 Miss Ida B. Brook

634 Mr. & Mrs. Ovington Ross
706 Mrs. A. K. Biggs
714 Mr. & Mrs. Frank L. Donaldson

926 Mr. & Mrs. Chas. R. Webster
928 Mr. & Mrs. E. G. Yates
Receiving day Friday
936 Albert D. Currier
1014 Mr. & Mrs. R. H. Buckingham
1014 Dr. & Mrs. Edward F. Baker
1124 Rev. & Mrs. G. W. Gray
1124 Edwin W. Gray
1124 Mrs. Mary B. Gray
1138 Mr. & Mrs. Herbert A. Thomas
1138 Mrs. D. H. Seavey
1204 Mr. & Mrs. W. R. Condict & dr.
1204 Wallace R. Condict jr.
1224 Mr. & Mrs. Wm. Hudson Harper
1430 Mr. & Mrs. W. J. Johnston
1430 Mrs. C. M. Walkup
1434 Mr. & Mrs. Gary G. Calkins
1632 Mr. & Mrs. W. H. Damsel
1632 Miss Jessamine Damsel
1632 Miss Ethel B. Damsel
1640 Mr. & Mrs. F. S. Martin
1640 Miss Lizzie A. Sands
1806 Mr. & Mrs. L. D. Norton & dr.
1818 Mr. & Mrs. Wm. B. Bogert
1830 Mr. & Mrs. Wm. E. Paddock
1830 Mrs. Wm. G. Paddock
1830 Miss Minnie A. Phelps
1834 Capt. & Mrs. L. O. Lawson
1882 Mrs. D. R. Dyche
1882 Mr. & Mrs. William A. Dyche
1882 Dr. George B. Dyche
1888 Mrs. E. Stanford & dr.
1888 Arthur L. Stanford
1888 George E. Stanford
1892 Mr. & Mrs. Francis B. Daniels
& drs.
1896 Mr. & Mrs. Frank B. Dyche
1896 Mrs. H. B. Dyche
1908 Mr. & Mrs. Wm. A. Jackson
1908 Mr. & Mrs. H. H. Robinson
1914 Mrs. George H. Foster
1930 Prof. C. W. Pearson
1930 Miss Margaret J. Pearson
1930 Mowbray F. Pearson
1936 Mr. & Mrs. Eugene E. Barnard
1936 Cornelius R. Barnard
1940 Mr. & Mrs. Leroy D. Thoman
1958 Mr. & Mrs. Henry Wade Rogers
Receiving day Saturday
2010 Mr. & Mrs. Frank W. Handy
2016 Rev. & Mrs. Chas. J. Little
2016 Charles G. Little
2238 Prof. & Mrs. Robert Baird & dr.

SHERIDAN SQUARE.

624 Mrs. John C. Bundy
624 Mr. & Mrs. Lewis W. Parker

SHERMAN AVENUE.

821 Mr. & Mrs. J. E. Paden
1403 Mr. & Mrs. J. C. Moore & dr.
1425 Mr. & Mrs. Allen Wass
1431 Rev. & Mrs. August Edgren
1853 Mr. & Mrs. Alex. McConnell & dr.
1853 Howard McConnell
1857 Mr. & Mrs. Eugene L. Stoker
1925 Mr. & Mrs. Russell M. Wing & drs.
1925 Frederick M. Wing
2011 Mr. & Mrs. E. B. Spear
2015 Mrs. Hester E. Walker & drs.
2031 Prof. & Mrs. Wm. A. Locy
2031 Prof. C. R. Robinson
2031 Prof. Otto H. Swezey
2043 Mr. & Mrs. Jas. Hartray
2043 William C. Hartray
2043 Mrs. N. Stewart
2111 Mr. & Mrs. J. A. Bellows
2119 Mr. & Mrs. Louis S. Rice
2119 Mrs. Emma L. S. Rice & dr.
2131 Rev. & Mrs. S. W. Siberts
2131 Paul R. Siberts
2137 Mr. & Mrs. J. W. Work
2137 Mr. & Mrs. Wm. H. Jakway
2137 Miss Isabel Jakway.
2147 Mrs. E. Hansen & drs.

822 Mr. & Mrs. Jos. J. Van Every
1202 Dr. & Mrs. I. M. Neely & dr.
1216 Mr. & Mrs. Chauncey B. Bradley
1216 Frank W. Bradley
1216 Mrs. Courtland P. Carr
1224 Mrs. S. S. Neal
1506 Mr. & Mrs. A. L. Currey
1508 Mr. & Mrs. Frank R. Grover
1716 Mr. & Mrs. Thomas T. Johnston
1716 Alexander C. Johnston
1810 Mr. & Mrs. Chas. Rosenberg
1900 Mr. & Mrs. A. J. Thayer & drs.
1910 Mrs. S. E. Bedell & drs.
1928 Mr. & Mrs. Jos. McCallum & dr.
1928 Miss Kittie Livingston
1928 Joseph N. McCallum
1930 Mr. & Mrs. John D. Terras
1938 Prof. & Mrs. Charles B. Atwell
1938 Mr. & Mrs. Henry H. Kellogg

1942 Mrs. Elizabeth Stuart & dr.
2012 William D. Murdock
2012 Mr. & Mrs. Wm. H. Murdoch & dr.
2040 Mr. & Mrs. F. M. Forrey
2112 Mr. & Mrs. W. L. Loveland
2112 Mrs. C. B. Abernathy
2122 Mr. & Mrs. H. W. Hubbard & drs.

SIMPSON PLACE.

561 Rev. & Mrs. Chas. H. Zimmerman & dr.
561 Cecil E. Zimmerman

SIMPSON STREET.

833 Rev. & Mrs. A. S. Brown

UNIVERSITY PLACE.

615 Mr. & Mrs. G. W. Cushing
619 Mrs. Harriette S. Kidder
619 Prof. & Mrs. H. S. White
625 Mr. & Mrs. E. B. Case
625 Rev. & Mrs. N. A. Prentiss
645 Mr. & Mrs. Chas. H. Aldrich

620 Prof. and Mrs. Geo. A. Coe
    Receive 1st Saturday in mo.
628 Rev. & Mrs. M. E. Eversz & drs.
628 Ernest H. Eversz
630 Mrs. Ida J. Shotwell
630 Mr. & Mrs. C. W. Moore
630 Mr. & Mrs. Walter F. Lewis

WASHINGTON STREET.

823 Mr. & Mrs. Elmer E. Billow
    Receiving day Thursday
823 Mrs. Susan Billow
827 Mr. & Mrs. L. M. Bernhisel
    Receiving day Thursday
903 Mr. & Mrs. Paul Mullmann
903 Frank Mullmann
915 Mr. & Mrs. F. S. Capron & drs.
927 Mr. & Mrs. Gerry H. Taylor

802 Mr. & Mrs. Mason B. Loomis
808 Mr. & Mrs. Wm. Whitfield
808 Joseph H. Whitfield
822 Mr. & Mrs. Albert Durham & dr.
834 Mr. & Mrs. John Furlong & dr.

1310 Mr. & Mrs. Axel Carlson
1330 Adelbert Hamilton
1330 Mrs. Catherine Hamilton

WESLEY AVENUE.

1413 Mr. & Mrs. J. P. Boutelle
1413 Clinton K. French
1427 Mr. & Mrs. H. W. Weaver
1427 Mrs. A. M. Linnell
1515 Mr. & Mrs. Geo. Ebeling
1613 Mr. & Mrs. A. S. Van Deusen
1627 Mr. & Mrs. Myron Hunt
1627 Mr.& Mrs.Edgar Stanton & dr.
1721 Mr. & Mrs. Frank E. Winans
     & dr.
1731 Mr. & Mrs. Edward Mendsen
1735 Mr. & Mrs. Chas. A.Wightman
1743 Rev. & Mrs. N. McGee Waters
1745 Mr. & Mrs. Geo. W. Lyle
1745 William T. Gascoigne
1745 Mrs. L. M. Gascoigne
1805 Mr. & Mrs. Wm. Stacey
1805 William A. Stacey

1811 Mrs. Maria J. Garland
1815 Jacob Bodine
1815 Mrs. Jacob Bodine jr.
1837 Mr. & Mrs. Geo. W. Paullin

1432 Mr. & Mrs. William C. Magill
     & dr.
1462 Mr. & Mrs. Percy L. Shuman
1584 Mr. & Mrs. Wm. D. Salisbury
1612 J. A. Comstock
1612 Mr. & Mrs. F. J. McCartney
1618 Mr. & Mrs. Frank R. McBerty
1622 Mr. & Mrs. Jason R. Prindle &
     dr.
1632 Mr. & Mrs. George R. Jenkins
     & dr.

1632 Miss Elizabeth A. Pratt
1702 Thos. Hutchinson & drs.
1710 Mr. & Mrs. Thos. H. Linsley
1720 Mr. & Mrs. Louis A. Ferguson
1802 Mr. & Mrs. J. E. Keelyn
1814 Mr. & Mrs. A. Balfour
1818 Mr. & Mrs. George H. Ellis
        Receiving day Thursday

FORT SHERIDAN.

Maj. George W. Adair
Capt. & Mrs. Frank B. Andrus
Lieut-Col. & Mrs. August H. Bain-
     bridge
Maj. Stephen Baker
Capt. & Mrs. H. P. Birmingham
Lieut. & Mrs. Wm. Brooke
Lieut. & Mrs. Austin H. Brown
Capt & Mrs. Edward H. Browne
Maj. & Mrs. John W. Bubb & drs.
Lieut. Halstead Dorey
Capt. & Mrs. Geo. B. Duncan
Lieut. & Mrs. Geo. E. French
Lieut. Frank Halstead
Lieut. Louis E. Hill
Lieut. & Mrs. Dwight E. Holley
Lieut. W. Howell

Lieut. J. H. Hughes
Lieut. F. G. Knabenhue
Maj. & Mrs. Henry Lippincott
Capt. Leonard A. Lovering
Capt. Charles W. Mason
Capt. & Mrs. Daniel E. McCarthy
Capt. & Mrs. Butler D. Price & dr.
Capt. & Mrs. Henry E. Robinson
Lieut. I. A. Saxton
Capt. Henry Seton
Lieut. & Mrs. John S. Switzer
Capt. & Mrs. Robt. P. P.Wainwright
Capt. & Mrs. Geo. O. Webster
Lieut. Mark Wheeler
Lieut. & Mrs. Paul A. Wolf
Capt. & Mrs. Silas A. Wolf

GLEN ELLYN.

Mr. & Mrs. R. G. Boyd
John Boyd jr.
Mr. & Mrs. W. E. Catlin
Mr. & Mrs. L. C. Cooper
Mr. & Mrs. O. D. Dodge
Mr. & Mrs. A. E. G. Goodridge
Mr. & Mrs. Newton F. Gordon
Mr. & Mrs. Thos. E. Hill
Mr. & Mrs. Alex J. Johnson
Mr. & Mrs. O. Kohnhurst

Mr. & Mrs. John LeMessurrier
John McNab
Mr. & Mrs. G. W. Meacham & dr.
George Meacham
Mr. & Mrs. C. L. Moulton
Mr. & Mrs. L. Q. Newton
Mr. & Mrs. Wm. Newton
Mr. & Mrs. R. W. Owen
Richard Owen
Mr. & Mrs. A. W. Rathbun

Mr. & Mrs. A. E. Riddle
Mr. & Mrs. P. W. Stacy & dr.
Mr. & Mrs. M. Strauss
W. H. Stubbings
Mr. & Mrs. Oscar Swan

Dr. & Mrs. Geo. B. Tope
Mr. & Mrs. F. M. Wagner
Mr. & Mrs. G. M. H. Wagner
Dr. & Mrs. Albert Winn
Mr. & Mrs. P. R. Youngs

GLENCOE.

Mr. & Mrs. C. W. Allison
Mr. & Mrs. F. A. Andrew
Mr. & Mrs. Otto Barnett
Mr. & Mrs. James P. Brewster
Miss Isabelle Brown
Mr. & Mrs. G. J. Case
Mr. & Mrs. John C. Clarke
Mr. & Mrs. J. E. Colburn
Mr. & Mrs. R. D. Coy
Alvin H. Culver
Mr. & Mrs. Morton Culver & drs.
Morton T. Culver
Mrs. Joseph Daggitt
Mr. & Mrs. Arthur H. Day
Mr. & Mrs. C. L. Day
Rev. & Mrs. Hiram Day
Mr. & Mrs. John L. Day
Mr. & Mrs. F. C. DeLang
Mrs. J. J. Dennis
James F. Dennis
Mrs. E. W. Dupee & dr.
C. F. Dupee
Mr. & Mrs. John Fanning
J. J. Flanders
Mr. & Mrs. Joseph F. Forsyth & drs.
Miss Grace Fuller
Mrs. Michael Gormully & dr.
Miss Helen R. Green
Walter H. Green
Mrs. F. D. Hall & dr.
Mr. & Mrs. G. D. Hall
Mr. & Mrs. F. L. Hankey
Mr. & Mrs. W. A. Hovey
Gen. & Mrs. C. H. Howard & dr.

O. McG. Howard
Mr. & Mrs. Frederick G. Howell
Mr. & Mrs. S. R. Hurford
Mr. & Mrs. W. H. Johnson
Prof. & Mrs. G. H. King
Mr. & Mrs. T. C. King
Mr. & Mrs. Ashbel G. Ligare
Mr. & Mrs. George G. Ligare
Mr. & Mrs. L. H. Lloyd
Mr. & Mrs. Andrew McLeish
Mr. & Mrs. Ralph Miller
Edward Murdow
Mr. & Mrs. Benjamin Newhall
Franklin Newhall
Mr. & Mrs. S. F. Newhall
Mr. & Mrs. George F. Orde
Mr. & Mrs. Markham B. Orde
Dr. & Mrs. John Nutt
Mr. & Mrs. John C. Parry
Mr. & Mrs. A. W. Plummer
Mr. & Mrs. J. P. Plummer
Mr. & Mrs. J. W. Plummer & dr.
Mr. & Mrs. W. C. Richmond
Mr. & Mrs. Jacob Schnur
Mrs. E. N. Sherwood
Mrs. P. N. Sherwood & dr.
Mrs. J. C. Starr
Herbert S. Stone
Mr. & Mrs. Melville E. Stone
Receiving day Monday
Melville E. Stone jr.
Dr. & Mrs. O. D. Swain
Mr. & Mrs. Harry B. Totten
Mr. & Mrs. J. H. Winslow

HIGHLAND PARK.

Mr. & Mrs. Wm. A. Alexander
Mrs. Anna M. Allen
Mr. & Mrs. Charles H. Baker
Mrs. M. H. Baker
Milton H. Baker jr.
Mr. & Mrs. Joseph L. Ball
A. A. Basye
Mr. & Mrs. H. C. Basye
Dr. & Mrs. Lloyd M. Bergen
Mr. & Mrs. G. D. Boulton & dr.
Kenneth B. Boulton

Mr. & Mrs. Arthur M. Boyington
Mr. & Mrs. George B. Boyington
Mrs. W. W. Boyington & drs.
Mr. & Mrs. Edgar S. Boynton
Frederick P. Boynton
Mr. & Mrs. Jacob J. Brand
Mr. & Mrs. Wm. E. Brand
Mr. & Mrs. Edward H. Brown
Mr. & Mrs. Francis C. Brown
Mr. & Mrs. T. Barbour Brown
Capt. & Mrs. George W. Burke

Dr. & Mrs. Chas. A. Canfield
Mrs. Henry C. Carver
R. G. Chandler
Mr. & Mrs. Chas. A. Chapman
Clarence C. Chapman
Walter A. Chapman
Theodore M. Clark
Mr. & Mrs. Daniel Cobb
John D. Cobb
Dr. & Mrs. J. E. Colburn
Mr. & Mrs. George S. Cole
Dr. & Mrs. Theodore H. Conger
Mr. & Mrs. Nathan Corwith
Mr. & Mrs. Washington R. Cregier
    Receiving day Thursday
Mr. & Mrs. Geo. B. Cummings
    Receiving day Thursday
Mr. & Mrs. Frederick W. Cushing
Mr. & Mrs. J. C. Cushman & dr.
Col. & Mrs. H. P. Davidson
Miss Alice S. Davidson
Maj. & Mrs. R. P. Davidson
Miss Belle Dickinson
Mr. & Mrs. Henry G. Dickinson
Mrs. Edwin Dyer
Mrs. Harry Eaton
Mrs. Anna G. Edwards & dr.
Mr. & Mrs. Wm. C. Egan & dr.
Mr. & Mrs. Leo Ernst
Mr. & Mrs. David M. Erskine jr.
Miss Emily L. Erskine
Mr. & Mrs. Filmore Evans
Mr. & Mrs. Robert G. Evans
Frank D. Everett & dr.
Charles F. Everett
Mr. & Mrs. G. S. Everingham
Mr. & Mrs. Benj. A. Fessenden
Mr. & Mrs. John Finney & drs.
Mr. & Mrs. Frederick Fischer
Mr. & Mrs. A. W. Fletcher
Mr. & Mrs. William W. Flinn
Mrs. F. F. Flint & drs.
Mrs. Helen C. Floyd & drs.
Mr. & Mrs. Charles W. Fullerton
Mr. & Mrs. Robert Gillette
Prof. & Mrs. Elisha Gray & drs.
Mr. & Mrs. Charles M. Green
Mr. & Mrs. F. B. Green
Mrs. H. R. Green
Mr. & Mrs. Cyrenius M. Greene
Mr. & Mrs. B. F. Gump
Mr. & Mrs. Ford P. Hall
Mrs. C. G. Hammond
Dr. & Mrs. Henry L. Haskin
Mr. & Mrs. Frank P. Hawkins
Richard W. Hawkins

Mr. & Mrs. Lewis B. Hibbard
Charles S. Hill
Judge Lysander Hill
Miss Mabel Hill
Mr. & Mrs. Russell D. Hill
Mr. & Mrs. W. O. Hipwell & dr.
M. E. Hodson
Mr. & Mrs. David Holmes & dr.
Mr. & Mrs. Thomas Hudson
Mr. & Mrs. Tracy D. Hull
Dr. & Mrs. Frank M. Ingalls
Mrs. David Inman
Mrs. W. A. James
Mrs. S. W. James
Mrs. Mary E. Jennings
John H. Jennings
Mrs. Ben C. Jones
Mr. & Mrs. W. R. Kenny
Mr. & Mrs. Chas. Wright Kirk
Mr. & Mrs. S. Fred Knox
Mr. & Mrs. William S. Lasher
Joseph F. Leaming
Tumley Lightner
Dr. Helen M. Lynch
Mrs. J. W. Lynch
Mr. & Mrs. G. A. Mason
Mr. & Mrs. James McDonald
W. A. McLaren
Rt. Rev. & Mrs. W. E. McLaren &
  drs.
Mr. & Mrs. J. D. Mersereau
Mr. & Mrs. W. D. Messinger
Mr. & Mrs. John Middleton & dr.
Mr. & Mrs. Merrick A. Mihills & dr.
    Receiving day Wednesday
Mr. & Mrs. S. M. Millard & dr.
Everett Lee Millard
Mr. & Mrs. William Millard
Mr. & Mrs. T. F. Miller
Mr. & Mrs. William H. Miller
Mr. & Mrs. P. A. Montgomery
Mr. & Mrs. J. H. Moore
A. C. Morgan
Elisha Morgan
Capt. & Mrs. O. H. Morgan & dr.
Mr. & Mrs. H. I. Morris
Mr. & Mrs. David Morrison
Mr. & Mrs. Carleton Moseley
Samuel M. Myers
Mr. & Mrs. John Wykopf & dr.
Dr. & Mrs. H. P. Newman
Mr. & Mrs. Edmund Norton
    Receiving day Wednesday
Miss Belle O'Brien
J. Gregg O'Brien
Mr. & Mrs. E. B. Palmer & dr.

Miss Sarah A. Patchen
Mr. & Mrs. Robert W. Patton
Rev. & Mrs. A. A. Pfanstiehl
Mr. & Mrs. C. G. Phillips
Mr. & Mrs. T. E. Pierson
Mr. & Mrs. J. S. Prall
Mrs. M. B. A. Pratt
Prof. & Mrs. G. W. Reddick
Mr. & Mrs. Harry L. Requa
Mr. & Mrs. C. B. Rice
Mr. & Mrs. G. W. Roberts
Capt. & Mrs. Daniel Robinson & dr
Mr. & Mrs. Emil Rudolph
Mr. & Mrs. W. H. Russell & dr.
Mr. & Mrs. H. C. Sampson
Mr. & Mrs. Chas. E. Schauffler
Mr. & Mrs. B. W. Schumacher
Mr. & Mrs. Fred Schumacher
Herbert E. Schwarz
Mr. & Mrs. Theodore Schwarz
Mr. & Mrs. James H. Shields
Charles J. Sine
Mr. & Mrs. G. L. Sites
Mr. & Mrs. Edward A. Small
Mrs. A. P. Smith
Mrs. C. R. Smith
Mr. & Mrs. K. R. Smoot
Receiving day Wednesday
Mr. & Mrs. Edgar M. Snow
Clinton J. Spencer
Mr. & Mrs. T. H. Spencer
Mrs. Jonas Steers
Mr. & Mrs. John L. Stockton
Mr. & Mrs. Henry C. Street

Mr. & Mrs. R. P. Street
Richard H. Street
Miss J. H. Street
Mr. & Mrs. R. J. Street
Mr. & Mrs. C. E. Stuart
Mr. & Mrs. Wm. C. Stubbs
Mr. & Mrs. Dale W. Sweetland
Dr. & Mrs. Warren M. Sweetland
Mr. & Mrs. Francis Thorn & dr.
Henry A. Towner & dr.
Henry A. Towner jr.
Mr. & Mrs. T. T. Watson
Dr. G. H. Townsend
Capt. & Mrs. B. E. Trask
Capt. & Mrs. Thomas G. Troxell
Col. & Mrs. P. T. Turnley & dr.
Mr. & Mrs. H. S. Vail
Mr. & Mrs. L. O. Van Riper
Mrs. A. G. VanSchaick & drs.
H. Van Schaick
Mr. & Mrs. J. Wallace Wakem
Mr. & Mrs. Chas. H. Warren
Mr. & Mrs. T. T. Watson
Miss Lyda E. Watson
Mr. & Mrs. T. Wheelwright
W. B. White
Mr. & Mrs. C. E. Wilcox & dr.
Prof. & Mrs. W. A. Wilson
F. C. Winchester
C. J. Winchester
Rev. & Mrs. P. C. Wolcott
Capt. Ernest G. Wood
Rev. & Mrs. George L. Wrenn
Mr. & Mrs. Chas. C. Yoe & drs.

HINSDALE.

Mr. & Mrs. C. A. Allen
F. G. Allen
Mrs. Sarah R. Andrews
Mrs. Anson Ayres
Frank E. Ayres
Mr. & Mrs. E. D. Baker
Mr. & Mrs. Wm. T. Barr
Mr. & Mrs. Jesse B. Barton
O. P. Bassett
Mr. & Mrs. George Beach
Dr. William Bebb
Mr. & Mrs. A. F. Beidler
James E. Bennett
Mr. & Mrs. Thos. Bennett
Mr. & Mrs. E. L. Benton
Mr. & Mrs. C. D. Bird
Mr. & Mrs. W. L. Blackman
Mr. & Mrs. J. A. Blood
Mr. & Mrs. G. M. Bogue

Elias Bogue
John Bohlander jr.
Alexander Boyd
Mr. & Mrs. Robert Boyd
Mr. & Mrs. W. P. Boyd
William S. Boyd
Mr. & Mrs. J. H. Bradley
Mrs. E. L. Bradley
J. C. F. Bradley
Ralph R. Bradley
Mr. & Mrs. Lafayette Briggs
Mr. & Mrs. A. C. Bryan
Walter J. Buffington
Dr. & Mrs. A. S. Burdick
Mr. & Mrs. John Burton
O. M. Burton
Mr. & Mrs. I. S. Bush
Mr. & Mrs. F. O. Butler
Mr. & Mrs. J. W. Butler

Mr. & Mrs. Fayette S. Cable
Miss Annie S. Cable
Mr. & Mrs. Fred J. Candee
Mr. & Mrs. Henry W. Candee
Mr. & Mrs. W. B. Carleton
Mr. & Mrs. Byron B. Carter
Mr. & Mrs. George P. Cary
Mrs. John W. Cary
Paul V. Cary
Mr. & Mrs. Robert A. Childs
   Receiving day Thursday
R. W. Clarke
Mr. & Mrs. William Coffeen
Mrs. S. A. Colburn & dr.
Harry Colburn
William Colburn
Mr. & Mrs. S. T. Collins
Mr. & Mrs. Lawrence P. Conover
Mrs. A. A. Convis
Mr. & Mrs. J. E. Convis
Mr. & Mrs. Owen D. Cook
Mr. & Mrs. W. P. Cortis
Mr. & Mrs. D. A. Courter
Mrs. W. H. Crocker
Mrs. W. D. Crooke
Mr. & Mrs. E. C. Crosby
Rev. & Mrs. W. R. Cross
Charles D. Crossette
Mr. & Mrs. C. H. Crossette
Mr. & Mrs. C. H. Cushing
Mr. & Mrs. Otis Cushing
Mr. & Mrs. Harry C. Dana
Mr. & Mrs. Jerome J. Danforth
Mr. & Mrs. Martin G. Danforth
Mr. & Mrs. Walter Davidson
Mr. & Mrs. Edgar F. Davis
Mr. & Mrs. Z. W. Davis
Mr. & Mrs. Harvey Dean
Robert L. Dean
Mr. & Mrs. R. M. Dean
Mr. & Mrs. C. G. Dennison
Mr. & Mrs. Eli H. Ditzler
Dr. & Mrs. John B. Doane
Mr. & Mrs. William Duncan
Mr. & Mrs. John E. Earle
Mr. & Mrs. B. G. Edgerton
Mr. & Mrs. Harry L. Edwards
Mr. & Mrs. Willard H. Edwards
Rev. & Mrs. C. F. Elliott
Mr. & Mrs. Truman W. Eustis
Mr. & Mrs. William Evernden
E. J. Fairchild
Mr. & Mrs. E. E. Fayerweather
Mrs. Charles Fox & dr.
Mr. & Mrs. Heman Fox
Mr. & Mrs. William O. Fox

Dr. & Mrs. A. B. Freeman
Mr. & Mrs. William H. Freeman
Mr. & Mrs. Adolph Froscher
Mr. & Mrs. J. M. Frost
Mr. & Mrs. George E. Fuller
Mr. & Mrs. H. A. Fulton
Mr. & Mrs. Henry A. Gardner
George C. Gardner
Mrs. S. P. Gardner
Mr. & Mrs. William D. Gates
Mr. & Mrs. F. O. Gear
Mrs. H. M. Gibbs
Mr. & Mrs. F. W. Godwin
Mr. & Mrs. Edward K. Gordon
Mrs. J. W. Gordon
Mr. & Mrs. William G. Gordon
Carl Groff
Miss Emily Gscheidlen
Mr. & Mrs. George W. Hall
Mr. & Mrs. S. B. Hamill
Dr. & Mrs. L. P. Haskell & dr.
Mr. & Mrs. F. W. Hawtin
Mr. & Mrs. A. T. Heaphy
Mr. & Mrs. Samuel Heineman
Dr. & Mrs. J. B. Hench
Charles H. Hess
Mr. & Mrs. Herbert G. Hetzler
Mr. & Mrs. C. F. Heyer
Mr. & Mrs. C. W. Higgins
Mr. & Mrs. L. K. Hildebrand
Mr. & Mrs. Charles E. Hinds
Mr. & Mrs. E. P. Hinds
E. P. Hinds jr.
Mr. & Mrs. George W. Hinckley
Mr. & Mrs. Wm. B. Hinckley
Mr. & Mrs. Wm. S. Hinckley
   Receiving day Thursday
Mr. & Mrs. A. G. Hines
Mr. & Mrs. Edward Hoar
Mr. & Mrs. Wm. H. Holcomb & dr.
Mr. & Mrs. Wm. H. Holcomb jr.
Herbert W. Holcomb
Mrs. Caroline Holverscheid
Mr. & Mrs. Henry Holverscheid
Mr. & Mrs. Wm. Hopkins
Mr. & Mrs. Chas. Hudson
Mr. & Mrs. Frank Hughes
Mrs. H. C. Irish
Mr. & Mrs. F. R. Irvine
Mr. & Mrs. Chas. C. Irwin
Mr. & Mrs. Horace Jackson
Mr. & Mrs. W. W. Jackson
Mr. & Mrs. John R. Jarrett & dr.
N. Jefferson
Rev. & Mrs. D. S. Johnson
Mr. & Mrs. P. C. Johnson

Mr. & Mrs. W. A. Johnson
Mr. & Mrs. A. S. Johnston
Mr. & Mrs. William Johnston
Mrs. Robert Jones
Mr. & Mrs. Thomas Jordan
Mr. & Mrs. James F. Joseph
Mr. & Mrs. A. E. Keith
Mr. & Mrs. C. B. Kimbell
Mr. & Mrs. H. M. Kimbell
Mr. & Mrs. S. T. Kimbell
Mr. & Mrs. E. B. Kittle
George Kline
Mr. & Mrs. W. H. Knight
Mr. & Mrs. Harry C. Knisely
Mr. & Mrs. Frank Krohn
John W. Landis
Roland R. Landis
Mr. & Mrs. William Landis
Dr. & Mrs. Thomas Lawton
Dr. & Mrs. T. F. Leech
Charles H. Leech
Walter Leslie
Mr. & Mrs. George F. Lewis
Mr. & Mrs. A. A. Lincoln
Mr. & Mrs. Chas. Linsley
Mrs. F. Linsley
Mr. & Mrs. T. H. Linsley
Mr. & Mrs. Henry C. Lockwood
Mr. & Mrs. Henry S. Loomis
Mr. & Mrs. John Mason
H. F. Maydwell
B. R. McClintock
Mr. & Mrs. J. McClintock
Rev. & Mrs. D. C. McCoy
Mr. & Mrs. Wm. McCredie & dr.
Mr. & Mrs. James McDonald
Mrs. Hugh F. McFarlane
Mr. & Mrs. W. E. McGee
Miss Emily McKinnie
Pascal P. Matthews
Mr. & Mrs. Arthur Meeker
Miss Hattie Merrill
J. C. F. Merrill
Mr. & Mrs. Charles T. Merritt
        Receiving day Thursday
Mr. & Mrs. H. C. Middaugh
George L. Miller
Miss Anna Belle Mitchell
Mr. & Mrs. D. J. Mitchell
Edward G. Mitchell
Mr. & Mrs. George H. Mitchell
Grant Mitchell
Miss N. Adelaide Mitchell
Mrs. Mary Mix
Mr. & Mrs. J. C. Mohor
Dr. & Mrs. A. W. Morrow

Mr. & Mrs. L. Muller
G. W. Munson
Mr. & Mrs. M. W. Murphy
Mr. & Mrs. James Murray
Mr. & Mrs. Thos. W. B. Murray
Mr. & Mrs. Myron A. Myers
Mr. & Mrs. E. B. Needham
Mr. & Mrs. Lester C. Newell
Mr. & Mrs. George W. Noble
Miss Eva Olney
Mr. & Mrs. R. H. Osgoodby
Mr. & Mrs. E. T. Pape
T. C. Pape
Mrs. Alfred Payne
Miss Ann Payne
Mr. & Mrs. Henry Payne
W. C. Payne
Mr. & Mrs. A. L. Pearsall
Mr. & Mrs. D. K. Pearsons
Mr. & Mrs. W. D. Perry
George L. Pollock
Mr. & Mrs. W. J. Pollock
Mr. & Mrs. D. H. Preston
Rev. & Mrs. M. N. Preston
Mrs. Frances L. Pulver
Miss C. Gertrude Pulver
Mr. & Mrs. M. L. Raftree
Mrs. C. A. Rawson
Miss Addie M. Raymond
Mr. & Mrs. Chas. E. Raymond
J. N. Redfern
Mr. & Mrs. J. Warner Reed
Mr. & Mrs. Bruce E. Richie
Mr. & Mrs. James V. Ridgway
Edwin S. Ripley
Mr. & Mrs. J. A. Ripley
Mr. & Mrs. George B. Robbins
Mr. & Mrs. Albert R. Robinson
Mr. & Mrs. John C. Ross
Mr. & Mrs. M. L. Roth
Mr. & Mrs. L. C. Ruth
Mr. & Mrs. Chauncey F. Ryder
Mr. & Mrs. Albert Sabin & drs.
Mr. & Mrs. H. N. Sager
Mr. & Mrs. F. J. Schuyler
Mr. & Mrs. F. E. Scotford
H. A. Scotford
Mr. & Mrs. J. S. Shannon
Mr. & Mrs. Edward E. Shaw
Miss E. M. Shaw
James W. Shaw
Mr. & Mrs. J. W. Shaw & dr.
Mr. & Mrs. Mark R. M. Sherry
Mrs. Susan C. Shewell
Mr. & Mrs. Dana Slade jr.
Mr. & Mrs. Donald Smith

Mr. & Mrs. Geo. E. Smith
Wyllys K. Smith
Mr. & Mrs. Chas. E. Spear
Mrs. E. Raymond Spear
W. T. Steward
Mrs. Abbie H. Stewart
Charles Stuart
Mr. & Mrs. J. F. Stuart & dr.
Mr. & Mrs. L. C. Tallman
Mr. & Mrs. C. H. Thayer
Herbert Thayer
Mr. & Mrs. H. R. Thayer
Mr. & Mrs. William Thayer
P. S. Townsend
Robert Treat
Mr. & Mrs. Fred VanInwagen
Mrs. Frederick VanLiew & drs.
Mr. & Mrs. L. C. VanLiew
Mr. & Mrs. John Wadington
Mr. & Mrs. Wm. W. Waite
Mrs. Athalia A. Walker
Mr. & Mrs. A. E. Walker
Mr. & Mrs. C. A. Walker

Mr. & Mrs. H. K. Walker
Miss Lizzie M. Walker
Miss E. L. Walton
Mr. & Mrs. C. C. Warren
Mr. & Mrs. C. T. Warren
Mr. & Mrs. Charles L. Washburn
N. H. Webster
Mr. & Mrs. J. W. Webster
Miss Edna Webster
Roy Webster
Mr. & Mrs. Horace S. Weeks & dr
Mr. & Mrs. Adolph Weidig
Mr. & Mrs. Henry W. Weiss
Mr. & Mrs. George H. Williams
Mr. & Mrs. George W. Wilson&drs.
S. C. Wilson
Mrs. Thos. J. Woodcock & drs.
Miss Frances E. A. Wright
George Wright
Mr. & Mrs. G. K. Wright
Mr. & Mrs. Edward Wylde
Mr. & Mrs. H. D. Wylie

IRVING PARK.

Dr. & Mrs. H. E. Adams
Dr. & Mrs. C. F. Barstow
Mrs. H. D. Barstow
A. V. Berry
Mr. & Mrs. D. W. Blair
Mr. & Mrs. G. C. Blair
Mr. & Mrs. S. A. Bobb
Rev. & Mrs. J. W. Brooks
Miss Emma E. Brown
Mr. & Mrs. F. I. Brown
Mr. & Mrs. D. L. Buzzell
Mrs. George Calhoun
Mrs. Sophia A. Christensen
S. J. Christensen
Mr. & Mrs. C. P. Coggeshall
James W. Converse
Mr. & Mrs. C. A. Cook
Mr. & Mrs. F. L. Cook
Dr. W. W. Cook
Mr. & Mrs. Theron W. Cookingham
   & dr.
Miss Marietta Coon
Mr. & Mrs. F. A. Crego
Mr. & Mrs. F. J. Cushing
Mr. & Mrs. T. W. Cushman
Mr. & Mrs. P. I. Davis
Mr. & Mrs. John De Vos
Mr. & Mrs. J. E. Dietz & drs.
Mr. & Mrs. J. M. Dietz
Mr. & Mrs. Thos. Edgar

Mr. & Mrs. C. W. Farr
Mrs. Wm. Florance
Mr. & Mrs. J. J. Fones
Mr. & Mrs. Mark Foote
Miss Mildred French
Mr. & Mrs. C. F. Gooding
Mr. & Mrs. A. G. Goodridge
Mrs. Margaret Goodwin
Dr. & Mrs. C. W. Gould
Mr. & Mrs. W. H. Gray
Dr. & Mrs. A. C. Hammett
Mr. & Mrs. F. L. Hand
Mr. & Mrs. Chas. H. Hadvard
Mr. & Mrs. J. S. Heath
Mr. & Mrs. George C. Hield
Mr. & Mrs. A. H. Hill
Mr. & Mrs. L. C. Humble
Mr. & Mrs. C. F. Hunting
Mr. & Mrs. J. Milton Johnston
Mr. & Mrs. W. C. Jordan
Mr. & Mrs. Joseph A. Kane
Mr. & Mrs. W. R. Kellogg
W. N. Ketcham
Mr. & Mrs. Benson Landon
Mr. & Mrs. Arthur M. Lane
F. E. Larson
Mrs. M. C. Lincoln
Mr. & Mrs. F. L. Lively
Mrs. Anna Livesey
Mr. & Mrs. Charles N. Loucks

Mr. & Mrs. J. A. MacBurney
Mrs. John R. Madison
Mr. & Mrs. J. T. Madison
Mr. & Mrs. George Mamerow
Mr. & Mrs. Chas. E. Martin
Mr. & Mrs. W. M. McEwen
Mr. & Mrs. C. S. McNett
Mr. & Mrs. J. F. Merchant & dr.
Mr. & Mrs. W. K. Millard
Mr. & Mrs. Charles R. Mitchell
Mr. & Mrs. J. S. Monk
Mr. & Mrs. A. J. Nowlen
Mrs. Margaret Nuveen
A. C. Osborn
F. W. Paige
Mr. & Mrs. T. G. Palmer
Mr. & Mrs. Lucius W. Parish
Dr. & Mrs. Wm. W. Parker
Mr. & Mrs. W. R. Parsons
Mr. & Mrs. W. H. Pentecost
Mr. & Mrs. J. A. Peterson
Dr. Kate B. Peterson
Mr. & Mrs. E. D. Pitcher
R. T. Race
Miss Ambrosia Race
Miss Jane M. Race
Ernest H. Rehwoldt
A. D. Richey
Mr. & Mrs. F. L. Richey
Silas Ropp
Mr. & Mrs. Albert R. Sabin
Mr. & Mrs. Walter Sayler

Mr. & Mrs. Chas. O. Sethness
Mr. & Mrs. H. V. Shepard
Mr. & Mrs. C. C. Sherman
Mr. & Mrs. Fred J. Sherman
Mrs. C. F. Smith
Dr. & Mrs. D. A. Smith
Mr. & Mrs. S. M. St. Clair
Mr. & Mrs. J. B. Tallman
Dr. & Mrs. E. J. Tanner
G. W. Thomas
Mr. & Mrs. Horatio Thomas
Mr. & Mrs. Leonidas Thomas
Mr. & Mrs. LeRoy C. Tryon
Mrs. Carrie VanNess
Gardiner VanNess
Mr. & Mrs. L. T. VanNess
Mr. & Mrs. A. E. VanOstrand
Mr. & Mrs. John A. Wadhams
Mr. & Mrs. William Wallace
Mr. & Mrs. A. H. Walmsley
Mr. & Mrs. J. B. Weeks
Mr. & Mrs. J. G. Wells
Dr. & Mrs. John A. Wheeler
Mr. & Mrs. J. R .Wickersham & dr.
Mrs. D. Lemoyne Wickersham
Mr. & Mrs. Wm. D. Wilcox
Mrs. W. L. Wilcox
Mr. & Mrs. J. W. Williams
F. J. Wilson
S. R. Wilson
Mr. & Mrs. H. G. Zander
Receiving day Wednesday

JEFFERSON PARK.

Rev. & Mrs. John Block
Mr. & Mrs. Hubert W. Butler
Mr. & Mrs. David S. Dunning
Mr. & Mrs. Edwin Dymond
Mr. & Mrs. John H. Dymond
Mr. & Mrs. Fred E. Eldred
Mr. & Mrs. Henry Esdohr
Mr. & Mrs. Herman H. Esdohr
Mr. & Mrs. Charles E. Farnsworth
Dr. David B. Fonda
Mr. & Mrs. Wm. P. Gray
Mr. & Mrs. Albert W. Holmes

Mr. & Mrs. Isaac N. Huestis
Mr. & Mrs. L. D. Lowell
Dr. & Mrs. Malcomb T. Moore
Mr. & Mrs. W. D. Price
Mr. & Mrs. Clark Roberts
Mr. & Mrs. C. N. Roberts
Roscoe L. Roberts
Mrs. M. D. Stevers
Rev. & Mrs. A. M. Thome
Mr. & Mrs. Peter F. Thomsen
Mr. & Mrs. Ewald Weber
Mr. & Mrs. Henry Wulff & dr.

KENILWORTH.

Dr. & Mrs. Charles Adams
Mr. & Mrs. Henry H. Babcock
Mrs. Mary Keys Babcock & drs.
Mr. & Mrs. E. G. Barratt
Mr. & Mrs. L. Brinckerhoff
Mr. & Mrs. Mortimer N. Burchard
  & drs.

Mr. & Mrs. S. B. Cadow
Mr. & Mrs. J. Y. Calahan
Mr. & Mrs. Orly Casper
Mr. & Mrs. Clarence C. Cheney
Mr. & Mrs. M. L. Coffeen
Mr. & Mrs. F. King Cook
Mr. &. Mrs. H. B. Cook

48

Mr. & Mrs. H. J. Cosgrove
Mr. & Mrs. J. A. Culbertson ·
Receive Friday
Mr. & Mrs. George Cutter
Mrs. E. C. Derickson
Mr. & Mrs. L. F. Dudley
Mr. & Mrs. J. L. Ferguson
Receiving day Wednesday
Prof. & Mrs. James Gill
Mr. & Mrs. T. S. Gordon
Mrs. & Mrs. Robert Hadley
Mr. & Mrs. Henry A. Hall
B. P. Hinman jr.
Mr. & Mrs. Horace E. Hurlbut
Mr. & Mrs. W. H. Isom
Mr. & Mrs. Rollin A. Keyes
Mr. & Mrs. George Kruse
Mr. & Mrs. George W. Maher
Mr. & Mrs. H. C. Mallory
Mr. & Mrs. A. V. Martin & dr.
Mr. & Mrs. Thomas J. Martin
Mr. & Mrs. J. L. McAfee
Mr. & Mrs. George A. McClellan
Mr. & Mrs. C. T. Morse
Mr. & Mrs. J. W. deCourcy O'Grady
Mr. & Mrs. Alex. Officer
Mr. & Mrs. E. D. Parmalee
Mr. & Mrs. J. W. Pease
Mrs. M. E. Pratt
Mrs. Mary Rew & drs.

George Campbell Rew
William Robinson & drs.
William F. Robinson
Mr. & Mrs. Frank K. Root
Mr. & Mrs. Walter R. Root
Mr. & Mrs. Harrison H. Rountree
Mr. & Mrs. Frederick Schramm
Mr. & Mrs. Joseph Sears
Joseph M. Sears
J. Barry Sears
Dr. & Mrs. Charles S. Smith
Mr. & Mrs. Howard H. Spaulding
Mr. & Mrs. Vive K. Spicer
Dr. & Mrs. W. M. Stearns
Dr. & Mrs. Rufus B. Stolp
Mr. & Mrs. Ullman Strong
C. H. Stumpoffski
Mrs. R. Stumpoffski
Mr. & Mrs. Charles I. Sturgis
Mr. & Mrs. Henry Taylor
Mr. & Mrs. Homer S. Taylor & dr.
Mr. & Mrs. William J. Taylor
Mr. & Mrs. E. C. Tracy
Mr. & Mrs. W. R. Trowbridge
Mr. & Mrs. Robert H. Van Schaack
Coles V. Veeder
Mr. & Mrs. Herbert B. Walker
Mr. & Mrs. Charles Ware
Mr. & Mrs. Burtin F. White
Mr. & Mrs. Russell Whitman

LAGRANGE.

Mr. & Mrs. Frank E. Abbott
Mr. & Mrs. Alex. C. Allen
Mr. & Mrs. Chas. A. Allen jr.
Mr. & Mrs. John T. Allison
Mr. & Mrs. F. W. Ambler
Mr. & Mrs. Llewellyn W. Arnold
Mr. & Mrs. A. B. Ashley & dr.
Mr. & Mrs. William Aspden
Mr. & Mrs. T. Fred Aspden
Mr. & Mrs. Clarence M. Babbitt
Mr. & Mrs. C. M. Babcock
Mr. & Mrs. J. G. Bailey
Mr. & Mrs. Foree Bain & drs.
Mr. & Mrs. Henry Baker
W. N. Bamant
Mr. & Mrs. J. C. Banks
Mr. & Mrs. H. Bearse
Mr. & Mrs. J. T. Beatty
Mr. & Mrs. W. R. Beatty
Mr. & Mrs. M. S. Beebe
Mr. & Mrs. Felix W. Beecroft
Theodore L. Bergen
Mr. & Mrs. S. H. Bingham

Mr. & Mrs. O. O. Bird
Mrs. Edwin R. Bishop & dr.
Mr. & Mrs. G. W. Blakelidge & dr.'
Mr. & Mrs. Levi Blakeslee & dr.
Mr. & Mrs. Albert E. Boerlin
Mr. & Mrs. August J. Boerlin
Henry T. Boerlin
Mr. & Mrs. Emile K. Boisot
Mr. & Mrs. Frank L. Borwell
Mr. & Mrs. Oscar T. Bourgeois
Mr. & Mrs. W. F. Brabook jr.
Mr. & Mrs. C. F. Braffette
Mr. & Mrs. H. F. Brainard
Mr. & Mrs. Charles L. Breed
George M. Briggs
Mr. & Mrs. N. E. Briggs
Mr. & Mrs. L. Cass Brown
Mr. & Mrs. Josiah M. Browne
Mr. & Mrs. Malcolm J. Browne
Mr. & Mrs. Willis W. Browne
Mr. & Mrs. J. A. Brydon
F. M. Bunch
R. H. Bunch

Mr. & Mrs. W. I. Bunker
Mr. & Mrs. Mark Burget
Mr. & Mrs. H. Burkholder & drs.
H. P. Burkholder
Mr. & Mrs. W. R. Burleigh
Dr. & Mrs. L. Bush
Mr. & Mrs. E. B. Bushnell
Rév. & Mrs. H. A. Bushnell
Mr. & Mrs. Fred H. Butler
Mr. & Mrs. W. L. Cadle
Mr. & Mrs. B. Cadwallader
Mrs. E. S. Cadwell
Mr. & Mrs. Colin C. Campbell
Mrs. E. Campbell
John D. Campbell
Dr. & Mrs. W. Carey
Mr. & Mrs. B. J. Carpenter
Mr. & Mrs. Miron J. Carpenter
Mr. & Mrs. Newton H. Carpenter
J. N. Carter
J. H. Cathrae
Mr. & Mrs. Theo. D. Christopher
J. Irving Christopher
Mr. & Mrs. F. H. Churchill
Mr. & Mrs. Egbert B. Clark
Mr. & Mrs. Jason E. Clark
Mr. & Mrs. P. M. Coates
Mr. & Mrs. L. H. Cohn
Prof. E. R. Cole
Mr. & Mrs. J. A. Connell
Mr. & Mrs. Edwin G. Cooley
Mr. & Mrs. Henry N. Cooper
Mr. & Mrs. W. D. Cornell
Mr. & Mrs. F. D. Cossitt
Mr. & Mrs. F. D. Cossitt jr.
Mr. & Mrs. Edward Coulter
Mr. & Mrs. M. C. Covell
E. Cowan
Mr. & Mrs. Frederick A. Crane
Mr. & Mrs. Albert E. Cross
Mr. & Mrs. John F. Daggett
Receiving day Thursday
Mr. & Mrs. F. J. Daly
Prof. J. F. Darby
Mr. & Mrs. Herbert Darlington
Mr. & Mrs. S. Frank Davidson
Alfred B. Davis
Frank B. Davis
George C. Davis
Dr. W. Crosbie Davis
Mr. & Mrs. H. E. DeCamp
Dr. & Mrs. E. S. Detweiler
Mr. & Mrs. Fred M. Dewey
Herbert C. Dewey
Mr. & Mrs. O. J. Dewey
Mr. & Mrs. F. L. DeWitt

Mr. & Mrs. J. C. F. Dick
Mr. & Mrs. Robert L. Dickey
Mr. & Mrs. John A. Dillon
Mr. & Mrs. M. D. Dimick & dr.
Mr. & Mrs. Chris Dirks
Mr. & Mrs. George E. Dixon
Mr. & Mrs. C. J. Dorr
Mrs. N. Doty
Mr. & Mrs. G. R. Dunne
Mr. & Mrs. W. S. Edes
Mr. & Mrs. Fred C. Edler
Mr. & Mrs. Charles Edwards
Mr. & Mrs. B. H. Eldridge
Mr. & Mrs. John Eldridge
W. S. Ellis
Edward S. Ely
Mr. & Mrs. H. B. Ely
John H. Esson
Miss Mabel Clare Estes
St. Louis A. Estes
Mr. & Mrs. P. S. Eustis
Mr. & Mrs. W. B. Ewing
Mrs. C. M. Farley & dr.
John W. Farley
R. L. Fellows
Mr. & Mrs. C. H. Field & dr.
Mr. & Mrs. Frank F. Fisher
Walter Foley
Mr. & Mrs. W. A. Follette
Mr. & Mrs. F. D. Ford
Mr. & Mrs. George D. Forrest
Mr. & Mrs. W. H. Fosner
Dr. G. M. Fox & dr.
F. P. Fredenhagen
Mr. & Mrs. L. H. Freer
Mr. & Mrs. John W. French
H. L. Fulton
Mr. & Mrs. P. G. Gardner
Mr. & Mrs. James R. Gilbert
C. F. Gillett
Mr. & Mrs. J. E. Gilmore
H. E. Goodwin
Mr. & Mrs. Sidney S. Gorham
Mr. & Mrs. F. L. Grant
Mr. & Mrs. J. R. Griffitts
Mr. & Mrs. W. F. Griffitts
Rev. James M. Hagan
Mr. & Mrs. Ferd Hall
Mr. & Mrs. Irving Hall
Mr. & Mrs. O. E. Haman
Receiving day Thursday
Mr. & Mrs. Edgar Hapeman
Mr. & Mrs. L. B. Harrington
Mrs. Henry S. Harrison
J. M. Hart
Mr. & Mrs. Edward P. Hatch

Mr. & Mrs. R. C. Haviland
Dr. & Mrs. Clark W. Hawley
Mr. & Mrs. F. A. S. Hayes
E. L. Hicks
James A. Hicks
Dr. & Mrs. A. E. Higgins
Mr. & Mrs. Fremont Hill
O. J. Holbrook
Mr. & Mrs. Joseph S. Holden
O. Q. Holman
Mr. & Mrs. L. H. Holmes
Receiving day Thursday
Ralph H. Holmes
C. H. Hood
Thomas W. Hoover
Richard Horton
Mr. & Mrs. John Hoskins
Mr. & Mrs. William Hoskins
Mrs. Geo. Howard
Mr. & Mrs. John C. Howell & dr.
Mr. & Mrs. H. M. Huff & drs.
Mr. & Mrs. A. H. Humphrey
A. O. Humphrey
Mr. & Mrs. W. C. Hunter
Mr. & Mrs. Abner Hurd & dr.
Mr. & Mrs. A. Haynes Hurd
Mr. & Mrs. F. D. Isham
Mr. & Mrs. C. L. Iverson
Mr. & Mrs. R. W. Iverson
Mr. & Mrs. N. E. Jennison
Mr. & Mrs. E. H. Johnson
Mr. & Mrs. Geo. A. Joyce
Mr. & Mrs. M. R. Kavanagh
Mr. & Mrs. H. D. Keeler
Mr. & Mrs. M. L. Kellogg
Mr. & Mrs. James Kidston
W. H. Kidston
Mr. & Mrs. Thomas Kimball
Charles H. Knapp
George S. Knapp
Mr. & Mrs. C. M. La Shelle
W. A. Lalor
W. A. Lantz
A. M. Langwill
Mr. & Mrs. G. H. Laubenstein
Mr. & Mrs. Archibald S. Leckie
P. W. Leffler
Dr. & Mrs. H. S. Llewellyn
Mr. & Mrs. Joseph C. Llewellyn
Mr. & Mrs. P. A. Lord
Mr. & Mrs. H. E. Loveday
Dr. & Mrs. R. F. Ludwig & dr.
Mr. & Mrs. Ayres D. Lundy
David Lyman
Mr. & Mrs. D. B. Lyman
Mr. & Mrs. O. S. Lyman

Mr. & Mrs. C. B. Lyon
Mr. & Mrs. J. M. Lyon
Mr. & Mrs. W. H. McClintock
George McCoy
Mr. & Mrs. G. H. McDonald
Mr. & Mrs. Harley C. McDonald
Walter McDonald
Mr. & Mrs. D. B. McGill
Mr. & Mrs. G. F. McGill
Mr. & Mrs. J. H. McGrew
Mr. & Mrs. P. D. McGregor
George H. McKay
Mrs. M. McKay
Mr. & Mrs. Albert McLaughlin
F. B. McLoraine
Mr. & Mrs. S. P. McMahon
Mrs. T. W. McMillan
Mr. & Mrs. James Mac Edward
Mr. & Mrs. Fred Mandell
Rev. J. W. Marcusson
Mr. & Mrs. H. H. Marcusson
Mr. & Mrs. Hiram C. Marsh
O. B. Marsh
Capt. Joseph A. Marshall
Mrs. Medora Estes Marshall
Receiving day Thursday 3 to 6 p. m.
Mr. & Mrs. Chester M. Marthens
Mr. & Mrs. H. S. Martin & dr.
Receiving day Thursday
Mr. & Mrs. C. A. Mather
Mr. & Mrs. John Mavor
Mr. & Mrs. J. E. A. Maxwell
Mr. & Mrs. L. Byron Mears & dr.
Mr. & Mrs. Charles W. Melcher
T. H. Merriam
Mr. & Mrs. J. K. Mettler
Dr. Ina M. Mighell
Mr. & Mrs. A. Minor
Mr. & Mrs. F. H. Mitchell
G. W. Mitchell
Mr. & Mrs. Harley B. Mitchell
Mr. & Mrs. H. S. Mitchell
Rev. & Mrs. J. A. Montgomery
Mr. & Mrs. S. B. Moody
John Morava
F. E. Morey
Geo. W. Morgan
Mr. & Mrs. J. W. Morrill
Charles A. Moses
Mr. & Mrs. Daniel W. Munn
Fred O. Munn
Mr. & Mrs. George L. Murchie
George L. Murchie jr.
Mr. & Mrs. John A. Murphy jr.
Mr. & Mrs. Donald Murray
Edward E. Naugle

Mr. & Mrs. E. R. Neely
Mr. & Mrs. E. R. Newcomb
Mr. & Mrs. J. C. Osborne
Rev. Alfred Ostrom
Mr. & Mrs. Henry A. Otis
Mr. & Mrs. J. F. Packer
Mr. & Mrs. Martin L. Paddock
F. P. Page
Mr. & Mrs. L. A. Pagin
Mr. & Mrs. H. B. Parker
Miss Jessie Paton
Mr. & Mrs. H. E. Patterson
Mr. & Mrs. A. S. Peck
Mr. & Mrs. Frank L. Peck
Mr. & Mrs. B. C. Perkins
Mr. & Mrs. B. W. Perkins
Mr. & Mrs. Francis V. Phillips
Mrs. E. B. Philo & drs.
C. M. Pitts
Mr. & Mrs. G. O. Pratt
Jacob C. Pratt
Edwin Pridham
Mr. & Mrs. Thomas C. Purves
Mr. & Mrs. Elmer A. Rich
C. D. Richmond
Mrs. C. W. Richmond & dr.
Dr. & Mrs. A. J. Roberts
Dr. & Mrs. Dwight J. Roberts
Mr. & Mrs. Jesse E. Roberts
J. W. R. Rogers
Mr. & Mrs. E. J. Rogerson
A. G. Rollo
Frank C. Rollo
Mr. & Mrs. L. E. Rollo
Mr. & Mrs. C. Rossman
Arnold S. Rothwell
Harry L. Rothwell
Mr. & Mrs. H. R. Rothwell
R. E. Rothwell
Mr. & Mrs. C. L. Sackett
Frank V. Sackett
Mr. & Mrs. W. B. Sale
Mr. & Mrs. V. C. Sanborn
Mr. & Mrs. Frank E. Sanford
Dr. & Mrs. F. W. Satterlee
Rev. & Mrs. Charles Scadding
Mr. & Mrs. W. A. Scott
Mr. & Mrs. S. G. Seaton
W. L. Shergold
Mr. & Mrs. E. W. Silsby
Mr. & Mrs. J. W. Simpson
T. J. C. Simpson
Mr. & Mrs. L. W. Slocum
David R. Smith jr.
Mr. & Mrs. E. B. Smith
Mr. & Mrs. F. C. Smith

Mr. & Mrs. Jesse E. Smith
Mr. & Mrs. Wm. Squirer
R. T. Stanton
Mr. & Mrs. Fred H. Stevens
Mr. & Mrs. C. L. Stiles
Luther C. Stiles
Mrs. M. M. Stone
Alexander M. Straiton
Mr. & Mrs. C. A. Street
Mr. & Mrs. Stephen G. Swisher
Mr. & Mrs. Ethan Taylor
Dr. Chester I. Thacher
H. S. Thompson
Mr. & Mrs. R. D. Thompson
S. C. Thompson
Mr. & Mrs. Edward C. Thornton
Mr. & Mrs. F. H. Thorp
Mr. & Mrs. J. Neal Tilton
Mrs. Margaret Timberlake & dr.
Thomas M. Timberlake
Mr. & Mrs. James A. Todd
J. B. Tower
Dr. & Mrs. F. M. Trask
Mr. & Mrs. J. W. Troeger
Mr. & Mrs. James W. Turner
Mr. & Mrs. Geo. D. Unold
Mr. & Mrs. John Unold
Mr. & Mrs. Geo. W. Updike
Mr. & Mrs. C. M. Upton
Mr. & Mrs. George M. Vial
Mr. & Mrs. Joseph Vial
Samuel Vial & dr.
Mrs. W. H. Walbridge
W. P. Walbridge
Mr. & Mrs. Chas. H. Walker & dr.
Charles N. Walker
Mr. & Mrs. C. Hayward Walker
Dudley Walker
J. R. Walker
Mr. & Mrs. Moses B. Walker & drs.
Mr. & Mrs. M. H. Walker
Mr. & Mrs. G. W. R. Wallace
Mr. & Mrs. Wm. Walmsley & drs.
Mr. & Mrs. R. F. Walton
Mr. & Mrs. James P. Weatherstone
Mr. & Mrs. Wm. W. Weatherstone
Mr. & Mrs. Arthur B. Wells
Mr. & Mrs. Henry Werno
C. L. Wheat
Mr. & Mrs. C. A. Whitney
Mr. & Mrs. Frank L. Wilder
Walter L. Wilder
Mr. & Mrs. T. D. Williams
Mr. & Mrs. R. C. Wilson
Charles J. Windsor
Joseph L. Windsor

Mr. & Mrs. J. E. Windsor
Rev. & Mrs. J. H. Windsor & dr.
Mr. & Mrs. E. Witte

Mr. & Mrs. James G. Wolcott
Mr. & Mrs. C. W. Wright
James Wyper

LAKE FOREST.

Mr. & Mrs. F. C. Aldrich
Mr. & Mrs. F. W. Alex
Mr. & Mrs. W. S. L. Anderson
Miss J. L. Axtell
Mr. & Mrs. Robert Bell
Mr. & Mrs. Samuel Blackler
Miss Annie E. Brearley
Prof. & Mrs. Walter R. Bridgeman
Miss Annie Brown
Miss Clara J. Brown
Mr. & Mrs. Edgar S. Calvert
Mr. & Mrs. Frank Calvert
Edward F. Chapin
Mr. & Mrs. H. C. Chatfield-Taylor
Mr. & Mrs. A. W. Cobb
Mr. & Mrs. Geo. W. Cobb
Mr. & Mrs. Ambrose Cramer
Mr. & Mrs. Claude Crippen
Miss Lillian S. Cushman
Mr. & Mrs. E. L. Davies
Prof. Arthur C. Dawson
Miss Annie L. Day
Miss Julia H. Day
Mr. & Mrs. James Dewey
Mr. & Mrs. Calvin Durand & dr.
    Receiving day Monday
Charles E. Durand
Mrs. Chas. E. Durand
Henry Z. Durand
Mr. & Mrs. Joseph B. Durand
Scott Durand
Mr. & Mrs. J. H. Dwight
Mr. & Mrs. David Fales
Miss Catherine Fales
David Fales jr.
Mr. & Mrs. Frank C. Farwell
Mr. & Mrs. Granger Farwell
Mr. & Mrs. John V. Farwell jr.
Mr. & Mrs. T. S. Fauntleroy
Mrs. Abbie F. Ferry
Dr. & Mrs. Geo. F. Fiske
Mr. & Mrs. Carter H. Fitz Hugh
Mr. & Mrs. George Finley
Dr. & Mrs. G. G. French
Mr. & Mrs. Chas. S. Frost
Miss Katherine Gardner
Mr. & Mrs. Charles K. Giles
Mr. & Mrs. Bernard J. Gilroy
Miss Lucia Goodwin
Mr. & Mrs. E. F. Gorton

Mr. & Mrs. John Gould
Mrs. S. P. Gould &.drs.
Mr. & Mrs. Alfred H. Granger
Clifford P. Hall
Mr. & Mrs. Frank G. Hall
Prof. & Mrs. J. J. Halsey
Dr. & Mrs. Alfred C. Haven
    Receiving day Friday
Mrs. F. H. Hewitt
Mr. & Mrs. D. R. Holt & dr.
Mr. & Mrs. Henry Horton & dr.
Mr. & Mrs. W. H. Hubbard
Miss Susie H. Hull
Mr. & Mrs. Alexander Kelly
Mr. & Mrs. Walter C. Larned
Miss Frances Greene Larned
Mr. & Mrs. Charles E. Latimer & dr.
E. J. Learned
Mrs. S. J. Learned & drs.
Miss Alice S. Leonard
Mrs. Sylvester Lind
Miss Fannie Belle Maxwell
Mrs. E. B. McClanahan
Rev. & Mrs. James G. K. McClure
Mr. & Mrs. H. R. McCullough
Prof. Malcolm McNeill
Miss Eliza J. McWilliams
Mr. & Mrs. James A. Miller
Mrs. Josiah Moore & dr.
Mr. & Mrs. Wm. A. Morgan
Mr. & Mrs. Jesse L. Moss
Miss Julia L. Moss
Mr. & Mrs. P. L. Mullen
William R. Nash
Mr. & Mrs. W. A. Nichols
Mr. & Mrs. E. A. Nordling.
Mr. & Mrs. Joseph O'Neil
S. C. Orr
Mr. & Mrs. Frank Parcells
Dr. & Mrs. Parmenter
L. C. Platt & drs.
Francis N. Pratt
Mr. & Mrs. N. D. Pratt & dr.
Wm. E. Pratt
Arthur S. Reid
Mrs. Simon S. Reid & drs.
Foster A. Rhea
Miss Carrie Ripley
Mr. & Mrs. Gilbert Rossiter
J. Franck Rumsey

Mr. & Mrs. 'Israel P. Rumsey & drs.
Miss Sabra L. Sargent
Miss Annie K. Sizer
Mr. & Mrs. E. S. Skinner & dr.
Delavan Smith
Miss Lucy M. Smith
Solomon A. Smith
Prof. & Mrs. Walter Smith
Mr. & Mrs. J. M. Snodgrass
Mr. & Mrs. L. H. Speidel
Mrs. Cornelia C. Stanley & drs.
Hiram M. Stanley
Mr. & Mrs. Edgar Stanton
Miss Edna Stanton
Miss Ida Maria Street
Prof. Louis Stuart
Mr. & Mrs. Louis F. Swift
Mr. & Mrs. Sydney R. Taber
Mrs. Louise M. Taylor & drs.
Miss Mary E. Taylor
Prof. & Mrs. M. B. Thomas
Miss Blanche E. Treat
Mr. & Mrs. Henry Tuttle
Dr. & Mrs. E. P. Ward
Mr. & Mrs. Ezra J. Warner & dr.
Mr. & Mrs. Richard G. Watson
Mr. & Mrs. Edwin S. Wells
Mr. & Mrs. L. W. Yaggy
Mr. & Mrs. T. A. Yaggy

LAKESIDE.

Rev. H. W. Arth
Dr. & Mrs. Coolidge
J. A. Cunningham jr.
John P. Dabney
Mr. & Mrs. Andrew Davis
Mr. & Mrs. W. L. Fisher
Mr. & Mrs. Frank Heinig
Mr. & Mrs. James L. High
Mr. & Mrs. Cyrus Kehr
Mr. & Mrs. John Merrilies & dr.
Mr. & Mrs. O. E. Poole
Mr. & Mrs. C. B. Powell
George Scott
Mr. & Mrs. Robert S. Scott
Miss Martha Scott
Mr. & Mrs. W. J. Watson
Mr. & Mrs. Robert Watt
Mr. & Mrs. James R. West & dr.
Mr. & Mrs. Frank Whitney
Miss Mary A. Witmer

LOMBARD.

Mrs. P. Albee & dr.
Mr. & Mrs. A. H. Andrews & drs.
Rev. & Mrs. James M. Campbell
Mr. & Mrs. Charles O. Chapin
Mrs. Isaac Claflin
Mr. & Mrs. W. Claflin
Mr. & Mrs. W. T. Claflin
Mrs. N. S. Cushing
Mr. & Mrs. George Hill
Dr. & Mrs. W. G. Leroy
Mr. & Mrs. S. J. Lumbard
Charles R. McKay
Miss Ellen A. Martin
Mrs. N. Matson
Dr. & Mrs. C. W. Oleson
Mr. & Mrs. R. B. Oleson
Mr. & Mrs. John H. Patterson
Mr. & Mrs. Henry Peck
V. H. Peck
Mr. & Mrs. H. W. Plum
Mr. & Mrs. W. R. Plum
Mr. & Mrs. H. S. Rand
Mrs. H. V. Rand & dr.
J. T. Reade & dr.
John Q. A. Reber
Mr. & Mrs. George H. Rogers
Mr. & Mrs. J. A. Sharp
Mrs. Jessie Thomas
Mr. & Mrs. S. R. Thurston
Mr. & Mrs. Walter Tod
Mrs. C. L. Towne & dr.
Miss Margaret Towne
Mr. & Mrs. T. H. Vance
Mr. & Mrs. A. B. Wrisley

LONGWOOD.

Mr. & Mrs. E. W. Bennett
Mr. & Mrs. N. W. Bliss
Rev. & Mrs. C. Bradford
Dr. & Mrs. C. S. Burr
Mr. & Mrs. Chas. P. Campbell
Mr. & Mrs. D. C. Campbell
Mr. & Mrs. Chas. W. Capper
Mr. & Mrs. F. S. Church
William T. Church
Mr. & Mrs. C. M. Clark
Dr. & Mrs. F. M. Clement
Mr. & Mrs. Henry B. Clement
Mr. & Mrs. C. J. Corse
Mr. & Mrs. T. A. Dent

Mrs. C. Nathan Dye
Mr. & Mrs. D. C. Franche
Mr. & Mrs. W. M. R. French
Mr. & Mrs. Wm. P. Hilliard
Mrs. Eugene S. Morse
Mrs. C. S. Nellis
Mr. & Mrs. John F. Phillips
Mrs. C. Ratledge
Mr. & Mrs. Jeremiah Ryan

Mrs. Leslie E. Snow
Mr. & Mrs. W. H. Stafford
Mr. & Mrs. Harry S. Stanton
Mr. & Mrs. Henry L. Stanton
Mr. & Mrs. Arthur W. Tobias
Mr. & Mrs. J. H. Vanderpoel
Mr. & Mrs. Clinton Weeks
Mr. & Mrs. Wm. Williamson
Mr. & Mrs. Edward C. Young

MAYFAIR.

Dr. & Mrs. Eisen Bockius
Dr. & Mrs. W. H. Colvin
Mr. & Mrs. Albert M. Cross
Rev. & Mrs. J. M. Cross
Mr. & Mrs. Ivar M. Doe
Mr. & Mrs. Ernest L. Farnsworth
Mr. & Mrs. J. B. Farnsworth
Mrs. K. V. Grinnell
Mr. & Mrs. J. G. Haberer
Mr. & Mrs. Theron L. Hiles
Mr. & Mrs. Everett S. Hotchkiss
Mr. & Mrs. John Houston
Mr. & Mrs. C. Fred Hunting
Miss S. Alice Judd
Mr. & Mrs. M. H. Kilgallen
Mr. & Mrs. C. L. Kingsley & dr.
Mr. & Mrs. Frank W. Kingsley

Mr. & Mrs. Robert Laurine
Rev. & Mrs. J. W. Lee
Mr. & Mrs. Arthur B. Lewis
Mr. & Mrs. E. W. Lewis
Mr. & Mrs. Evan J. Morton
Mr. & Mrs. A. C. Neff
Mr. & Mrs. H. V. Peters
Dr. & Mrs. E. L. Rivenburgh
Mr. & Mrs. George W. Savage
Mr. & Mrs. Fred Sedgwick
Mr. & Mrs. G. W. Smith
Mr. & Mrs. W. Frank Stickney
Mrs. Mary M. Strong & drs.
Mr. & Mrs. Grove E. Walter
Rev. & Mrs. C. D. Williams
Mr. & Mrs. H. H. Williams
Mr. & Mrs. John Yorty

MAYWOOD.

Mr. & Mrs. J. Porter Adams
Mrs. Abel Akin
Mr. & Mrs. H. F. Akin
Mr. & Mrs. Joseph R. Albertson
Mr. & Mrs. H. A. Armstrong
Mr. & Mrs. W. P. Ballard
Mr. & Mrs. J. Bohlander
Mr. & Mrs. E. S. Bryan
Mr. & Mrs. Charles W. Bullard
Mr. & Mrs. B. L. Chamberlain
Mrs. Elizabeth Clark
Dr. I. Clendenen & dr.
Dr. Irving B. Clendenen
Mr. & Mrs. Edwin C. K. Davies
Mr. & Mrs. C. E. Dobbins
Mr. & Mrs. S. H. Donaldson
Rev. & Mrs. S. B. Dunlap
Mr. & Mrs. L. Vernon Ferris
Mr. & Mrs. Wm. L. Gifford
Mr. & Mrs. C. B. Grimes
Allen Hatch
Mr. & Mrs. George Hatch
Mr. & Mrs. Eugene Heim
Mr. & Mrs. J. G. Hodson
Mrs. Sarah Hubbell

Mr. & Mrs. E. T. Hughes
Mr. & Mrs. Wm. M. Hulbert
Mr. & Mrs. Joel H. Hulburd
Mrs. Joseph Jennings
Mr. & Mrs. W. C. H. Keough
Mr. & Mrs. J. A. Lambert
Mr. & Mrs. Frederick P. Lancaster
Mr. & Mrs. B. H. Larkins
Dr. & Mrs. W. R. Livingston
Mr. & Mrs. Frank Lonas
Mr. & Mrs. Chas. W. Maynard
Mr. & Mrs. Stephen McEvoy
Dr. H. W. Merrill
Mr. & Mrs. James Munton
Mr. & Mrs. Charles A. Newcomb & dr.
Mr. & Mrs. Edward C. Nichols
Mr. & Mrs. Harry H. Nichols
Mr. & Mrs. H. P. Nichols
Mr. & Mrs. Edwin Norton
Mr. & Mrs. C. E. Pickard
Mr. & Mrs. Wilson J. Robb
Mr. & Mrs. F. E. Roberts
Mrs. Lydia Roberts
Mrs. Walter C. Roberts

Mrs. C. H. Robison
Mr. & Mrs. H. W. Small
Mr. & Mrs. W. S. Smith jr.
Gen. & Mrs. Wm. Sooy-Smith
C. W. Steines
Mr. & Mrs. James S. Stephens
Mr. & Mrs. James M. Stimpson

Mr. & Mrs. Charles Westcott
Mr. & Mrs. George T. Westcott
Mr. & Mrs. Oliver J. Westcott
Mr. & Mrs. Daniel Wing & dr.
Henry Wing
Mrs. Samuel Woodruff
Mr. & Mrs. Horace Zoellin

MORGAN PARK.

Rev. & Mrs. Galusha Anderson
Mr. & Mrs. Joseph Anderson
Miss Sarah B. Anderson
Mr. & Mrs. A. J. Atwater
Mr. & Mrs. Edgar Ayres
Mrs. John N. Babcock
Mr. & Mrs. J. D. Barnes
Dr. Lila Beers
Mr. & Mrs. I. S. Blackwelder
 Receiving day Friday
Mr. & Mrs. H. J. Bohn
 Receiving day Wednesday
Mr. & Mrs. J. J. Borland
Mr. & Mrs. R. B. Brigham
Frederick A. Brooks
Frederick W. Brookes
Rev. & Mrs. H. W. Brown
Mr. & Mrs. L. L. Brown
Mr. & Mrs. F. M. Brunson
Mr. & Mrs. I. S. Burgess
Mr. & Mrs. Ernest L. Caldwell
Prof. & Mrs. W. J. Chase
Mrs. George R. Clarke
Mr. & Mrs. H. R. Clissold
Mr. & Mrs. Geo. G. Coldwell
Mr. & Mrs. John T. Cowles
Mr. & Mrs. Henry Crossman
Mr. & Mrs. R. A. Dandliker
Mr. & Mrs. C. Dashiel
Dr. & Mrs. F. P. DeVries
Mr. & Mrs. G. H. Drew
Rev. & Mrs. W. A. Eisenhart
Mr. & Mrs. W. G. Ferguson
Mr. & Mrs. George E. Frazier
Rev. & Mrs. N. O. Freeman
Mrs. Mary T. Gage & dr.
Mr. & Mrs. I. W. Gantt
Dr. & Mrs. W. H. German
Mr. & Mrs. Chas. T. Gilbert
Mr. & Mrs. John Grainger
Mr. & Mrs. James R. Gray
Mr. & Mrs. W. L. Gregson
Prof. & Mrs. H. Gunderson
Dr. & Mrs. E. M. Harrison
Mr. & Mrs. John Harvey & drs.
Dr. M. C. Hawk

Mr. & Mrs. A. H. Hovey & drs.
Mr. & Mrs. F. T. Husted
Mr. & Mrs. C. A. Iglehart
Mrs. Elizabeth Iglehart & drs.
Mr. & Mrs. Samuel Job
Mr. & Mrs. E. D. Kenfield
Mr. & Mrs. M. H. King
Mr. & Mrs. Fred L. Kimmey
Prof. & Mrs. C. G. Lagergren
Mr. & Mrs. Chas. E. Leech
 Receiving day Monday
Mr. & Mrs. W. A. Lutrell
Mr. & Mrs. D. C. McKinnon
Mrs. C. W. Madeira
Mr. & Mrs. John Mansfield
Mr. & Mrs. R. Ivan Mansfield
Mr. & Mrs. G. A. Meech
Mr. & Mrs. J. B. Merrill
Mr. & Mrs. F. S. Moffat
Mr. & Mrs. D. B. Nichols & dr.
Mr. & Mrs. Fred D. Nichols
Fred C. Paulin
Mr. & Mrs. G. A. Pfuhl
Mrs. Eva M. Pierce
Mr. & Mrs. W. H. Poole
 Receiving day Tuesday
Mr. & Mrs. G. D. Prentiss
Prof. & Mrs. Ira M. Price
Mr. & Mrs. J. F. Price
Clement M. Regan
Mr. & Mrs. B. T. Roberts
Mr. & Mrs. Alfred Rushton
Mr. & Mrs. H. Clay Russell
 Receiving day Thursday
Miss Mary D. Russell
Mr. & Mrs. H. Schmitt & drs.
Henry I. Saxton
Dr. H. E. Sheldon
Mr. & Mrs. F. B. Sherwood
Mr. & Mrs. E. G. Short
Mr. & Mrs. F. J. Short
Mr. & Mrs. C. P. Silva
Mr. & Mrs. F. P. Silva
Henry R. Singler
Mrs. N. Singler & drs.

Mr. & Mrs. C. O. Ten Broeke
   Receiving day Wednesday
Mrs. Gilbert Thayer
Mrs. H. E. Thayer & dr.
H. W. Thayer
Mr. & Mrs. Robert B. Thomson
Rev. C. H. Thurber
Mr. & Mrs. I. H. Vail
Mr. & Mrs. Porter J. Walker
Mr. & Mrs. William W. Washburn

H. H. Watterman
Mrs. John Wayte
Rev. W. D. Westervelt
Mr. & Mrs. F. S. Wheaton
Mr. & Mrs. C. G. Wicker
Mr. & Mrs. F. N. Wilder
Mr. & Mrs. G. P. Williams
Mr. & Mrs. A. Wiswall & dr.
Rev. & Mrs. A. R. E. Wyant
Mr. & Mrs. C. Zeiss

MORTON PARK.

Mr. & Mrs. Lot Brown
Mr. & Mrs. Charles Bruce
Mr. & Mrs. George W. Bushnell & dr.
Mr. & Mrs. William H. Clarkson
Mr. & Mrs. H. W. Cottrell
Mrs May Day
Mrs. Nellie E. Dorr
Mr. & Mrs. Buell B. Dutton
D. G. Edgerly
Risley Edgerly
Mr. & Mrs. S. A. Flagler
Mr. & Mrs. William B. Flagler
Mr. & Mrs. J. E. Gardin
Mr. & Mrs. Ashley L. Gilbert
Mr. & Mrs. Robert Gorman
Mr. & Mrs. G. N. Gridley
Mr. & Mrs. Frank Hall
Mr. & Mrs. J. D. Hall
H. M. Hall
Mr. & Mrs. William Henzell
Mr. & Mrs. Edward B. Higgs
Herbert Hoffman
Mr. & Mrs. Wm. D. Hyslop
Mr. & Mrs. E. J. Meaney
George E. Moore

Mr. & Mrs. Joseph L. Moore
Mr. & Mrs. W. A. Moore
John H. Morley
Mr. & Mrs. John J. Murray
Mr. & Mrs. J. E. Naylor
Mr. & Mrs. William B. Porter
Mr. & Mrs. Miller Purvis
Mr. & Mrs. J. W. Radford
Mr. & Mrs. Hugh Richards
Mr. & Mrs. L. B. Richardson
Mrs. Barbara E. Rubins
Charles C. Rubins
Harry W. Rubins
Willis F. Rubins
Mr. & Mrs. L. M. Russell
Mr. & Mrs. O. M. Schantz
Mr. & Mrs. Harry W. Squire
Rev. J. M. Stevens
Mr. & Mrs. A. Van Dorn
Mr. & Mrs. Portus B. Weare
Mr. & Mrs. William W. Weare
Miss Ida M. Wolfe
Miss Lottie Wolfe
Mrs. Mary Wolfe
Oswald Wolfe

NORWOOD PARK.

Dr. & Mrs. S. F. Aby
Mr. & Mrs. Jean E. C. Agnass
Mr. & Mrs. B. L. Anderson
Mr. & Mrs. C. A. Baird
Mr. & Mrs. D. M. Ball
Dr. Mary E. Bennett
Mr. & Mrs. Edward W. Buss
Mrs. John P. Campbell
Mr. & Mrs. F. A. Cleaveland
Mr. & Mrs. F. B. Cleaveland
Mr. & Mrs. William E. Dankert
Mr. & Mrs. G. N. Davis
Mr. & Mrs. Charles J. DeBerard
Mr. & Mrs. A. F. Dodd

Mr. & Mrs. S. S. Dodge
Mrs. George J. Eckhoff
Mr. & Mrs. George H. Evans
Mr. & Mrs. H. A. Farnum
Mr. & Mrs. Frederick Finden
Mr. & Mrs. William E. Fisher
Mr. & Mrs. John B. Foote
Mr. & Mrs. F. W. Fox
Mr. & Mrs. James Guilbert
Mr. & Mrs. Emil Hoffman
Julius Hoffman
Mr. & Mrs. Otto E. H. Hoffman
Dr. & Mrs. J. O. Hughes & dr.
Rev. & Mrs. John N. Hutchison

Mr. & Mrs. Byron Mercer
Mr. & Mrs. Paul Ranier
Mr. & Mrs. Fred A. Rich
Mr. & Mrs. Nels Sampson
Lynden A. Seymour
Mr. & Mrs. T. H. Seymour
Mr. & Mrs. G. H. Thayer

Mr. & Mrs. Edward Trenah
Mrs. Martha Voorhees
Mr. & Mrs. James T. Walsh & dr.
Mr. & Mrs. H. G. Wells
Mr. & Mrs. F. A. Winchell
Rev. & Mrs. Eric Wingren

OAK PARK.

BELLEFORTE AVENUE.

719 Mr. & Mrs. A. Burgess
723 Mr. & Mrs. G. A. Metzgar

NORTH BOULEVARD.

323 Mr. & Mrs. B. L. Dodge & dr.
329 Wm. C. Hunter
329 Mr. & Mrs. D. W. Hunter
Receive Wednesday 2 to 5
355 Henry Lumbard
365 Mr. & Mrs. Duncan Garcelon & dr.
433 Mr. & Mrs. Charles Reifsnider

SOUTH BOULEVARD.

310 Dr. & Mrs. W. E. Kidd
340 Mr. & Mrs. F. J. Knott & dr.
412 Edward Van Keuren & drs.
412 C. W. Van Keuren
418 Mr. & Mrs. Oliver Hammond
424 William F. Barnard
518 Dr. & Mrs. Frank L. Howard
518 Mr. & Mrs. Thomas Wrigley
806 R. E. Dorsey
814 Mr. & Mrs. Norman C. Betts
814 Mr. & Mrs. John D. Suydam
818 Mr. & Mrs. F. W. Leach
820 Mr. & Mrs. Harry G. Bentley
1002 Frank S. Kipp
1002 Mrs. Mary E. Kipp
1240 Mr. & Mrs. Frank E. Hall
1324 Mr. & Mrs. F. H. Oriel & drs.

CHICAGO AVENUE.

117 Walter S. Smith
125 E. H. Eddie
209 Mr. & Mrs. Graves Holbrook
403 Mrs. Mary Hafner & dr.
409 Mr. & Mrs. C. F. Hafner
421 Mr. & Mrs. S. W. Briggs

302 Mr. & Mrs. Geo. Nordenholt
306 Mr. & Mrs. A. B. Melville

330 Mr. & Mrs. Robert P. Parker
330 Mrs. Sarah A. Devereux
424 Mrs. A. L. Wright & dr.

CLINTON AVENUE.

115 Mr. & Mrs. Geo. M. Black
117 Mr. & Mrs. J. B. Webb
207 Judge & Mrs. F. Q. Ball
Receiving day Friday
207 Farlin H. Ball
221 Mr. & Mrs. George H. Teter
237 Mr. & Mrs. W. A. Rice & dr
245 Mr. & Mrs. Fred Comley
251 Mr. & Mrs. Louis Olcese
309 Mr. & Mrs. J. Howard Jones
313 Mrs. S. Claflin & Dr.
313 M. A. Claflin
317 Mr. & Mrs. H. E. Vincent
325 Mr. & Mrs. W. J. Wallace
329 Mr. & Mrs. G. D. Webb
335 Mr. & Mrs. Frank H. June
339 Mr. & Mrs. S. C. Miller

————

100 Mr. & Mrs. W. J. VanKeuren
102 Mr. & Mrs. Wm. W. Macomber & dr.
110 Mr. & Mrs. L. S. VanVliet & drs.
112 Mrs. P. R. Lord & dr.
118 Mr. & Mrs. C. M. Morton
120 Mr. & Mrs. E. G. Case
126 Mr. & Mrs. W. A. Hutchinson
138 Mr. & Mrs. Hervey W. Booth
200 Mr. & Mrs. H. H. Hopkins
204 Mr. & Mrs. Neal Farnham
208 Mr. & Mrs. J. L. Tucker
210 Mr. & Mrs. Isaac N. Connard
210 Miss Lydia Mead
228 Mr. & Mrs. C. F. Walker
230 Mr. & Mrs. Miller Hall
230 Fred E. Hall
234 Mr. & Mrs. W. D. Hall
308 Mrs. T. C. Rounds
308 Mr. & Mrs. C. W. C. Chandler

CUYLER AVENUE.

221 Mr. & Mrs. F. H. Brown
317 Mr. & Mrs. John G. Raubold & dr.
319 Mr. & Mrs. David Keighin &dr.

---

220 N. G. Woodside
236 Mr. & Mrs. Frank Borwell
242 Mr. & Mrs. Hiram Coombs

NORTH EAST AVENUE.

234 Mr. & Mrs. Edward H. Pitkin & drs.
. *Receiving day Tuesday*
234 Frank L. Pitkin
330 Mr. & Mrs. Robert Erskine
618 Mr. & Mrs. Charles R. Erwin
704 Mr. & Mrs. Walter R. Corlett
720 Mrs. M. S. Fearing & drs.
720 Harry L. Fearing
720 Roy M. Fearing
722 Mr. & Mrs. Walter Ruan
722 Miss Jennie Ruan

SOUTH EAST AVENUE.

121 Mr. & Mrs. Joseph R. Noel
125 Mr. & Mrs. Chas. L. Bliss
131 Mr. & Mrs. J. R. Payson jr.
213 Mr. & Mrs. Albert C. Putnam
221 Mr. & Mrs. Wm. H. French & dr.
221 Mrs. A. K. Walter & dr.
315 Mr. & Mrs. W. R. Townsend&dr
323 Mrs. M. E. Putnam & dr.
323 Frank H. Putnam
323 Mr. & Mrs. J. W. Taylor & drs.
333 Mr. & Mrs. Geo. L. Wilson
339 Mr. & Mrs. James H. Gormley
423 Mr. & Mrs. Frank C. Wood

---

124 Mr. & Mrs. E. G. Corneau
124 Edwin N. Corneau
130 Mr. & Mrs. J. D. Caldwell
138 Mr. & Mrs. R. W. Sears
200 Mr. & Mrs. W. S. Gerts
332 Mr. & Mrs. W. A. Blanchard & dr.
332 Arthur S. Blanchard

ELIZABETH COURT.

1 Mr. & Mrs. Edward Payson
3 Mr. & Mrs. J. Fred Butler
5 Mr. & Mrs. H. S. Duncombe

---

4 Mr. & Mrs. A. C. Reed
4 Albert M. Reed
8 Rev. & Mrs. J. E. Roy

NORTH ELMWOOD AVENUE.

214 Mr. & Mrs. C. L. Ames & dr.
214 A. H. Frost
226 Mr. & Mrs. Geo. F. Whidden
234 Rev. & Mrs. Sydney Strong
Receiving day Tuesday
324 Rev. & Mrs. A. N. Hitchcock & dr. *Receiving day Tuesday*
506 Mr. & Mrs. B. W. Firman
514 Mr. & Mrs. E. Herrick Brown
522 Mr. & Mrs. Wm. G. Fricke

SOUTH ELMWOOD AVENUE.

109 Mr. & Mrs. Eugene C. Fisher
113 Mr. & Mrs. R. J. Kerr
121 Mrs. J. Sinclair
135 Mr. & Mrs. S. D. Attridge
139 Mr. & Mrs. Wm. Ritchie
139 Miss Mary L. Ritchie
311 Mr. & Mrs. John W. Langston
313 Mr. & Mrs. W. F. Hayes
421 Mr. & Mrs. George D. Griffith

ERIE STREET.

325 Mr. & Mrs. T. S. Swirles
325 Joseph J. Miller
331 Mr. & Mrs. A. W. Pebbles & drs.
331 H. R. Pebbles
331 Charles P. Miller
337 Mr. & Mrs. Frank M. Pebbles
337 Frank M. Pebbles jr.

NORTH EUCLID AVENUE.

239 Mr. & Mrs. Jacob Mortenson
305 Mr. & Mrs. Edwin Osgood & dr.
309 Mr. & Mrs. Geo. W. Melville
315 Alfred L. Bostedo & drs.
319 Mr. & Mrs. J. W. Ott
323 Mr. & Mrs. George Warren Furbeck
323 Mrs. Emma Harrington
405 Mr. & Mrs. M. G. Wallace
Receiving day Wednesday
413 Mr. & Mrs. T. S. Rattle
421 Mr. & Mrs. C. E. Roberts & dr.
Receive 1st & 3d Wednesday in mo.
433 Mr. & Mrs. Paul Blatchford
715 Mr. & Mrs. W. G. Adams
737 Mr. & Mrs. Sampson Rogers
823 Mr. & Mrs. C. H. King

823 Mrs. G. R. Means
837 Mr. & Mrs. Chas. G. Page
     Receiving day Friday
837 Harvey L. Page

---

308 Mr. & Mrs. C. A. Sharpe
308 N. M. Freer
422 Mr. & Mrs. P. E. Wilson
430 Mr. & Mrs. M. Dwight Johnson
     Receiving day Thursday
434 Mr. & Mrs. E. B. Bartlett

SOUTH EUCLID AVENUE.

111 Mr. & Mrs. John Nelson
115 Porter B. Coolidge ·
131 Mr. & Mrs. John B. Cooley
131 Mrs. M. M. Jones
139 Mr. & Mrs. G. B. Woodward &
     drs.
143 Mr. & Mrs. Henry M. Hollister
213 Mr. & Mrs. Geo. W. Woodbury
221 Mr. & Mrs. J. T. Ehrhart
301 Dr. L. H. Baker & drs.
317 Mr. & Mrs. Geo. M. Patch
321 Mr. & Mrs. D. R. Niver & dr.
321 Miss Lizzie Abbott
325 Mr. & Mrs. A. E. Walters

---

114 Mr. & Mrs. J. H. Howard & dr.
114 H. Benton Howard
210 Mr. & Mrs. Cholett Cady
210 Mr. & Mrs. Lewis B. Carpentei
230 Mr. & Mrs. Charles E. Jenkins
230 Miss B. D. Jenkins
330 Mr. & Mrs. W. H. Cribben

FOREST AVENUE.

403 Mr. & Mrs. R. K. Bickford & dr.
     Receiving day Wednesday
409 Mr. & Mrs. Jas. T. Hayden
415 Mr. & Mrs. Albert H. Vilas & drs.
419 Mr. & Mrs. J. D. Miller
423 Mr. & Mrs. M. B. Austin
427 Mr. & Mrs. F. D. Updike
505 Dr. & Mrs. A. J. Rosenberry
509 C. W. Seabury
513 Mr. & Mrs. D. L. McDaniel
513 Charles W. McDaniel
521 Dr. & Mrs. A. F. Storke
521 W. H. Rogers
529 Mr. & Mrs. N. G. Moore
529 Mrs. S. S. Walker
603 Mr. & Mrs. H. N. Norton

607 Dr. Emily M. Luff
623 Mr. & Mrs. R. L. Boyd & dr.
625 Mr. & Mrs. John Kirkpatrick
627 Mr. & Mrs. C. R. McHugh

---

214 Mr. & Mrs. Luther Hatch
220 Mr. & Mrs. N. H. Whittlesey & dr.
300 Mr. & Mrs. E. W. Carpe
302 Mr. & Mrs. Geo. W. Hayden
304 Mr. & Mrs. W. H. Hatch
306 Mrs. Mary E. Ingalls
306 Grant Ingalls
404 Mr. & Mrs. F. W. Cook
406 Mr. & Mrs. Lawrence Muther
412 Mr. & Mrs. E. A. Hartwell &
     drs.
412 Mrs. M. J. Earle & dr.
422 Mr. & Mrs. James L. Fargo
430 Mr. & Mrs. George Walker
430 G. Albert Walker
430 Seymour Ferris
508 Mr. & Mrs. C. A. Purcell
518 P. L. Hanscom
528 Mr. & Mrs. W. M. Harman & dr.
606 Mr. & Mrs. Edward King & dr.
612 Mr. & Mrs. Virgil E. Titus
616 Mr. & Mrs. A. J. Redmond ·
620 Mr. & Mrs. Frank L. Wright

NORTH GROVE AVENUE.

225 N. S. Patton
231 Mr. & Mrs. J. F. Cleveland
231 Augustus F. Cleveland
231 Miss Kate Bradley
237 Mr. & Mrs. Wm. Spooner
237 Harry S. Spooner
421 Mr. & Mrs. L. O. Stanton
421 Mrs. A. E. Stanton
427 Rev. & Mrs. Charles S. Hoyt
427 Mrs. S. C. Hoyt
431 Mr. & Mrs. G. H. Orr
443 Mr. & Mrs. Wm. H. Noakes
449 Mr. & Mrs. Albert H. Standish
455 Dr. & Mrs. Austin F. James
459 Mr. & Mrs. William R. Wagner
459 Mrs. L. F. Whittlesey
459 Charles E. Camp
503 Mr. & Mrs. Henry L. Millis ·
503 Mrs. Charles Russ

---

302 Mr. & Mrs. D. L. Goodwillie
316 Mr. & Mrs. A. J. Cheney
328 Mr. & Mrs. L. Scott & drs.
328 Lee C. Scott

328 F. B. Sherman
402 Mr. & Mrs. C. S. Yerkes
402 R. Archie Yerkes
422 Mrs. W. P. Smith & dr.
424 Mr. & Mrs. Benj. Lockyer
Receiving day Wednesday
426 Fred A. Sperry
426 Miss Grace Draper
440 Mr. & Mrs. Theron Durham
454 Mr. & Mrs. J. L. Pearson
472 Mr. & Mrs. Geo. D. Keefer
472 Harry H. Keefer
472 Frank H. Keefer
476 Mr. & Mrs. I. E. Brown

SOUTH GROVE AVENUE.

103 Mrs. F. H. Sturtevant
103 Chester D. Sturtevant
123 E. Wood Ratcliff
129 C. S. Pellet
133 Mr. & Mrs. Henry D. Pierce &
dr.
Receiving day Wednesday
139 Mr. & Mrs. Chas. H. Marshall
& dr.
209 Mr. & Mrs. John I. Jones
211 Mr. & Mrs. John A. Seaman
213 Mrs. Wilhelmine Juergens & dr.
219 Mrs. A. M. Draper
219 Mr. & Mrs. Herbert L. Draper
223 Mr. & Mrs. O. B. Barker
231 Mr. & Mrs. C. A. Weage & dr.
235 Mr. & Mrs. C.R.Blanchard&drs.
237 Mr. & Mrs. B. F. Crosby & drs.
237 David K. Crosby
237 Mr. & Mrs. J. C. Moore
239 Mr. & Mrs. David S. Baldwin
317 Mr. & Mrs. R. W. Patrick
321 Mr. & Mrs. W. R. Vosburgh
323 Mr. & Mrs. J. D. Andrews
325 Mr. & Mrs. Eli Anerson & dr.
331 Mr. & Mrs. H. A. Taylor
Receiving day Thursday

102 Mr. & Mrs. A. A. Adair & dr.
102 C. M. Adair
110 Mr. & Mrs. Carlos J. Ward
110 Mrs. C. T. Jones
110 Miss Mary Wardwell Marks
116 Mr. & Mrs. Chas. H. Wells
140 Mr. & Mrs. E. S. Tomlinson
212 Mr. & Mrs. S. F. Leonard
218 Mr. & Mrs. Frank B. Newell
222 Mr. & Mrs. G. A. Swartwout &
dr.

222 Leslie G. Swartwout
222 Mrs. N. E. Carpenter
230 Mr. & Mrs. Frank Durrie
234 Mr. & Mrs. I. G. Hatcher
324 Mr. & Mrs. N. A. McClary

NORTH HARVEY AVENUE.

227 Mr. & Mrs. Chas. C. Carr & dr.
231 Mr. & Mrs. John L. Lyon
Receiving day Tuesday
235 Mr. & Mrs. John A. Mallin
239 Mr. & Mrs. John Furlong
329 Mr. & Mrs. Thos. Quayle & drs.
333 Mr. & Mrs. Robt. Quayle

332 Mr. & Mrs. G. E. Allison

SOUTH HARVEY AVENUE.

121 Mr. & Mrs. W. H. Robinson
141 Mr. & Mrs. James T. Barbeau
201 Mr. & Mrs. G. W. Padelford
201 Mr. & Mrs. Herbert Templeton
205 Mrs. Fanny Murray
205 H. A. Murray
417 Mr. & Mrs. B. L. Bevington
Receiving day Thursday
425 Mr. & Mrs. S. H. Nichols
Receiving day Thursday

216 Mr. & Mrs. Geo. C. Sutphen

HOLLEY COURT.

107 Mr. & Mrs. J. S. Ingram & drs.
107 Mrs. I. M. Borwell
115 Mr. & Mrs. Robert Many
114 Mr. & Mrs. Wm. H. Thompson

HOME AVENUE.

113 Mr. & Mrs. R. C. Rogers
113 Horace W. Bingham
229 Mr. & Mrs. W. R. Harvey & dr.
241 Mr. & Mrs. Abraham Edmunds
& drs.
245 Mr. & Mrs. A. P. Holbrook
247 Mr. & Mrs. James Harvey
247 Sydney B. Harvey
249 Mr. & Mrs. S. H. Crounse &
drs.
305 Mr. & Mrs. J. C. Skeen
305 Miss Lillian Faulknor
317 Mr. & Mrs. W. H. Cotter
321 Mr. & Mrs. J. L. Worthington
325 Mr. & Mrs. W. G. Barfield

327 Mr. & Mrs. E. T. Johnson
337 Rev. & Mrs. J. W. Conley
341 Mr. & Mrs. John Hohmann
345 Mr. & Mrs. Dwight Jackson
401 Mrs. Mary A. Lenox
401 Mr. & Mrs. John P. Lenox
 Receive 1st & 3d Tuesday in mo.
409 Mr. & Mrs. Amza L. Fitch
421 Mr. & Mrs. Chas. S. Woodward
425 Mr. & Mrs. C. D. Smith

100 Dr. & Mrs. L. S. Ingman
100 J. I. Cooper
102 Mr. & Mrs. G. A. Barrows
104 Mr. & Mrs. J. H. Kiel
106 Mr. & Mrs. H. A. Angel
108 Mr. & Mrs. C. W. Castle
110 Mr. & Mrs. J. M. H. Burgett
112-114 The Kenton
 Mr. & Mrs. S. M. Delano
  Receiving day Tuesday
 Mr. & Mrs. Charles Godee
  Receiving day Monday
 Mrs. Hattie E. Hart
 W. P. Marseilles
 Mr. & Mrs. C. E. Marsh
 Mr. & Mrs. W. E. Morse
 Mrs. Esther M. Orton
 Ira J. Owen
 Mr. & Mrs. William R. Owen
 Mr. & Mrs. H. E. Patrick
 Mr. & Mrs. Frank B. Pettibone
 Mrs. George A. Shufeldt & dr.
 Mr. & Mrs. W. B. Sizer
 Mr. & Mrs. J. E. Turney & dr.
  Receiving day Tuesday
 Mrs. R. H. Ullman
 C. Orton Wetmore
 Mr. & Mrs. C. F. Willard
118 Mr. & Mrs. E. A. Roser
  Receiving day Monday
126 Mr. & Mrs. Warren F. Furbeck
  Receiving day Wednesday
126 J. Philip Furbeck
210 Mr. & Mrs. R. S. Thain & dr.
210 Miss Hattie Jenness
214 Mr. & Mrs. Arthur Gustorf
220 Mr. & Mrs. James Adams
248 Mr. & Mrs. W. H. Stearns
248 Miss A. Lee
250 Mr. & Mrs. C. R. White & drs.
252 Asahel F. Bennett
326 Mr. & Mrs. F. B. Gibbs
338 Mr. & Mrs. C. A. Blaurock & drs.
404 Mr. & Mrs. G. W. Smith
416 Mrs. E. A. Carr

416 Mrs. Aurora Bricker
416 R. F. Carr
416 W. S. Carr
420 Mr. & Mrs. R. N. Trimingham

NORTH HUMPHREY AVE-NUE.

223 Mr. & Mrs. W. C. Stephens
  Receiving day Thursday
227 Mr. & Mrs. John T. Bullen
253 Mr. & Mrs. Jerome A. Woodford
 & drs.

SOUTH HUMPHREY AVE-NUE.

229 Dr. & Mrs. J. C. Panter
301 Mr. & Mrs. Edward J. Kelly
307 Mr. & Mrs. J. Rice Brown
311 Mr. & Mrs. Wm. G. Newbury
  Receiving day Thursday
315 Mr. & Mrs. Fred L. Goss & drs.

228 Mr. & Mrs. George W. Wilson
228 Mr. & Mrs. C. G. Burlingame

NORTH KENILWORTH AVE-NUE.

109 Mr. & Mrs. Thos. H. Gale
111 Mr. & Mrs. George E. Hall
231 Mr. & Mrs. Stanley Carleton
239 Charles A. Schroyer & drs.
303 Mr. & Mrs. C. G. Marsh
303 Edward P. Marsh
309 F. W. Bicknell & drs.
309 Edwin D. Bicknell
309 William W. Bicknell
319 Dr. & Mrs. W. C. Gray.
327 Mr. & Mrs. J. M. Baker
331 Mr. & Mrs. W. H. Kirkhoff
345 Mr. & Mrs. John Rankin & drs.
345 George Rankin
409 Mr. & Mrs. D. J. Kennedy
417 W. A. Douglass
429 Mr. & Mrs. Lindsay T. Wood-cock
429 John Builder
435 Mr. & Mrs. J. K. Dunlop
435 Mrs. Juliette Davis & dr.
445 Mr. & Mrs. Simpson Dunlop
527 Mr. & Mrs. James R. McGregor
723 Prof. & Mrs. W. B. Chamberlain
723 Miss Florence B. Bardill
729 Mr. & Mrs. Frank B. White

729 Mr. & Mrs. John S. Draper
739 Prof. & Mrs. W. D. Mackenzie
739 Rev. Thomas S. Miller

234 Mr. & Mrs. Geo. L. Eastman
324 Mr. & Mrs N. M. Jones
400 Mr. & Mrs. W. J. MacDonald & dr.
Receiving day Wednesday
416 Mr. & Mrs. Maurice von Platen
422 Mr. & Mrs. H. B. Horton
422 Ben P. Horton
428 Mr. & Mrs. George Sharp
428 Louis H. Sharp
428 E W. McCready
434 Mr. & Mrs. H. P. Young
438 Mr.& Mrs.S. A. Rothermel & dr.
444 Mr. & Mrs. Wilton C. Smith
452 Mr. & Mrs. E. C. Glover & drs.
Receiving day Wednesday
482 Mr.& Mrs. Richard Beard & drs.

SOUTH KENILWORTH AVENUE.

125 Mr. & Mrs. F. H. Lumbard
203 Mr. & Mrs. A. W. Giles & drs.
203 Walter M. Giles
209 Mr. & Mrs. Austin Cruver
209 Mrs. Arthur L. Dobie
217 Mrs. A. M. Daniels
243 Mr. & Mrs. J. L. Freeman
313 Mr. & Mrs. F. G. Barnard
413 Mr. & Mrs. E. B. Morse
421 Guy M. Chase
425 Mr. & Mrs. J. F. Routledge
425 William McDonald

110 Mr. & Mrs. John C. McDonald
114 Mr. & Mrs. W. E. Hughes
114 Mrs. Mary W. Tompkins
122 Mr. & Mrs. Miles Crandall
138 Mr. & Mrs. E. S. Wheeler
142 Mr. & Mrs. J. H. Morrison
214 Mrs. F. Engelman
214 Wm. T. Engelman
232 Mr. & Mrs. Geo. F. Holloway
232 Mr. & Mrs. C. E. Fisher
234 Rev. & Mrs. R. F. Johonnot
238 Mr. & Mrs. Duke Nichelson

LAKE STREET.

cor. Kenilworth av. Mr. & Mrs. W. H. Gale
217 H. W. Austin

217 Mr. & Mrs. Gardner Morris
307 Mr. & Mrs. Herman Lieb jr.
309 Mrs. S. A. Holley
309 E. E. Giddings
333 Mr. & Mrs. G. E. Gerts & drs.
Receiving day Wednesday

200 L. M. Lovett
204 Silas E. McDonald
320 Mr. & Mrs. H. R. Hamilton
324 Dr. & Mrs. R. P. Johnson & dr.
332 Mr. & Mrs. Edward Hilton
350 Dr. & Mrs. John W. Tope & dr.
356 Dr. & Mrs. John D. Waller
358 Mr. & Mrs. C. E. Bolles
364 Mr. & Mrs. L. G. Holley
368 Mr. & Mrs. S. W. Packard
416 Mr. & Mrs. Luther Conant & dr.
416 William C. Conant
422 Mr. & Mrs. M. T. Cole & dr.
428 Mr. & Mrs. George J. Bliss & dr.
432 Mr. & Mrs. O. D. Allen & drs.
432 J. Thornton Gilbert
440 Mr. & Mrs. A. A. Stewart
Receiving day Tuesday
454 E. S. Watts
502 Mr. & Mrs. Charles A. Wright

LINDEN AVENUE.

303 Dr. W. H. Stennett
303 Mrs. M. Covert
317 Mr. & Mrs. George M. Davidson
335 Mr. & Mrs. Chas. B. Holdredge
409 Mr. & Mrs. Stephen E. Cate
715 Mr. & Mrs. Henry C. Todd
Receiving day Wednesday

302 Mrs. S. F. Wadsworth
302 Frank R. Wadsworth
320 Mr. & Mrs. O. L. Bicknell
334 Mr. & Mrs. T. F. Bliss
334 Theodore F. Bliss jr.

NORTH LOMBARD AVENUE.

241 Mr. & Mrs. E. A. Cummings&dr.
241 Mrs. E. Cummings
247 Dr. & Mrs. Francis B. Clarke

236 Mr. & Mrs. J. B. Willard & dr.
236 Edward O. Willard
244 Mr. & Mrs. J. E. Hammond
252 Mr. & Mrs. Edgar N. Goodwillie & dr.

SOUTH LOMBARD AVENUE.

217 Mr. & Mrs. Albert E. Livingston

MAPLE AVENUE.

117 Mrs. Elizabeth V. Port & dr. .
121 Mr. & Mrs. W. A. McConnell
201 Mr. & Mrs. Josiah Cratty
201 Mrs. Mary E. Haller
211 Mr. & Mrs. E. D. L. Sweet
211 Charles S. Sweet ·
217 Mr. & Mrs. T. G. Morris
227 Mr. & Mrs. Charles E. Roe & dr.
235 Mr. & Mrs. H. H. Wallis
237 Mr. & Mrs. C. Y. Knight
239 Mr. & Mrs. L. P. Sigsbee
239 Lincoln Richards
241 Gen. & Mrs. Milo S. Hascall
   Receiving day Thursday
243 Mr. & Mrs. T. J. Skillin & drs.
   Receiving day Thursday
309 Mr. & Mrs. James E. Tristram
   & dr.
315 Mrs. Jennie A. June & dr.
315 Paul S. June
315 Jesse D. June
317 Mr. & Mrs. Geo. R. Lewis
319 Mr. & Mrs. E. J. Skillin
337 Mrs. R. E. Payn
337 Mrs. A. M. Kingman & dr.
405 Mr. & Mrs. H. K. Smith & dr.
409 Mr. & Mrs. A. Austin
409 Mr. & Mrs. Clarence E. Fox
425 Mr. & Mrs. S. R. Ainslie & dr.

———

120 Mrs. M. J. Russell
120 Dr. & Mrs. W. R. Lewis
126 Mr. & Mrs. J. W. Middleton & dr.
126 Mr. & Mrs. B. F. Stout
200 Mr. & Mrs. S. S. Niles
210 Mr. & Mrs. G. A. Bodenschatz
216 Mr. & Mrs. A. F. Banks
226 Mr. & Mrs. E. S. Conway
226 E. E. Conway
234 Mr. & Mrs. A. W. Bryant .
242 Mrs. William Beye
252 Mr. & Mrs. C. B. Flinn
324 Mr. & Mrs. Thos. Pattison & dr.
344 Mr. & Mrs. Charles C. Todd
344 Mrs. E. B. Miller
400 Mr. & Mrs. G. W. Moser
400 Mrs. Jane Leslie
414 Mr. & Mrs. J. T. Ripley

49

MARION STREET.

103 Dr. & Mrs. A. S. Melvin jr.
111 Dr. Allan A. Mathews
111 Miss Anna M. Mathews
111 Miss Jessie Mathews
127 Mr. & Mrs. E. W. Hoard
127 Mrs. B. Congdon
127 Miss Ida B. Gurley
305 Dr. & Mrs. Arthur Loewy
509 Mr. & Mrs. L. M. Brochon
519 Mr. & Mrs. Channing Taylor
525 Mr. & Mrs. W. N. Kettlestrings
   & dr.
525 John W. Meier

———

122 Mr. & Mrs. K. Oaks & dr.
122 W. W. Oaks
228 Mr. & Mrs. C. Miller & dr.
238 Mr. & Mrs. John Kohn
246 Maurice Evans & drs.
516 Mr. & Mrs. Chas. F. Kannenberg & drs.
516 Baldwin H. Kannenberg
524 Mr. & Mrs. J. W. Johnston & drs.
604 Mr. & Mrs. August Einfeldt

NORTH OAK PARK AVENUE.

109 Dr. Clara A. Hendy
109 Mrs. A. Hendy & drs.
113 Dr. & Mrs. H. C. Worthington
307 Mr. & Mrs. O. W. Herrick & dr.
333 Mr. & Mrs. Henry S. Towle
333 Miss Helen M. Towle
405 Mr. & Mrs. E. W. Lyman & dr.
417 Mrs. H. N. Bishop & drs.
417 Chas. Nelson Bishop
425 Mr. & Mrs. George Eckart
433 Mr. & Mrs. C. B. Ayers & dr.
439 Ernest Hall
439 Leicester C. Hall
439 Dr. & Mrs. C. E. Hemingway
   Receiving day Thursday
443 Mr. & Mrs. R. H. Hennegen
443 Miss Martha Worthington
447 Mr. & Mrs. Geo. W. Ingersoll
447 Mrs. Mary J. Shawcross
507 Mrs. J. W. Kettlestrings
507 Dr. Fred. W. Kettlestrings
507 Joseph Kettlestrings
507 Wilbur Kettlestrings
507 Orrin R. Kettlestrings

519 Mr. & Mrs. Wm. J. Cooke & dr.
605 Mr. & Mrs. A. E. Morey
605 Mrs. Anna M. Morey
643 Mr. & Mrs. C. D. Paine
643 Mrs. M. A. Sinclair

---

224 Mr. & Mrs. Arthur Heurtley
224 Mr. & Mrs. Chas. H. Ackert
224 Mr. & Mrs. E. F. Nettleton
228 Mrs. Palmer S. Hulbert
238 Mr. & Mrs. John D. Ross & drs.
238 John F. Ross
308 Mr. & Mrs. Wm. H. Wood & dr.
308 Mrs. F. E. Ingraham
308 G. Foster Ingraham
324 Mr. & Mrs. H. J. Straight & drs.
332 Mr. & Mrs. Geo. Clapp & dr.
416 Mr. & Mrs. N. D. Crosby
416 Miss Bessie E. Crosby
420 Mr. & Mrs. W. S. Herrick
424 Mr. & Mrs. John Lewis
500 Mr. & Mrs. A. T. Hemingway
& dr.
Receiving day Wednesday
500 Willoughby A. Hemingway
516 Mr. & Mrs. George R. Hemingway
Receiving day Wednesday
606 Mr. & Mrs. John B. Richardson
& dr.
606 Donald Richardson
616 Mr. & Mrs. Walter O. Hill
616 Mr. & Mrs. S. S. Denniston
620 Capt. & Mrs. Edmund Luff & dr.
620 Henry E. Luff
732 Mr. & Mrs. Wm. C. Warner
736 Mr. & Mrs. D. C. Herrick & dr.
736 Harry Herrick

SOUTH OAK PARK AVENUE.

107 Mr. & Mrs. Henry Cribben
Receiving day Wednesday
107 Miss Laura M. Hyne
113 Mr. & Mrs. H. A. Potwin
117 Mr. & Mrs. Orrin W. Nash
117 Edwin N. Nash
117 Mr. & Mrs. Wilmar H. Nash
125 Dr. & Mrs. H. W. Bassett
133 Mr. & Mrs. C. B. S. Conyne
133 Wallace K. Conyne
141 Mrs. Margaret A. Elliott & dr.
141 Frank A. Elliott
203 Mr. & Mrs. E. T. Malone
209 Mr. & Mrs. Ernest S. Fowler
211 Mrs. Geo. Royal

235 Mr. & Mrs. O. L. Bailey
237 Mr. & Mrs. John Farson
333 Mr. & Mrs. John C. Clark

---

108 Dr. & Mrs. John Storer
112 Mr. & Mrs. Edward C. Porter
& dr.
118 Mr. & Mrs. Wm. A. Robertson
124 Mr. & Mrs. Walter S. Holden
132 Mr. & Mrs. W. E. Blackstone
132 Andrew P. Blackstone
136 Dr. & Mrs. John E. Nyman
136 Mr. & Mrs. John Sargent
144 Dr. & Mrs. T. E. Roberts
200 Mr. & Mrs. E. J. Hall
200 Rider Hall
210 Mr. & Mrs. A. S. Ray
210 Mrs. P. A. Ray
214 Mr. & Mrs. Geo. M. Clayberg
228 Mr. & Mrs. Melancthon Smith
234 Mr. & Mrs. R. H. Salter
308 Mr. & Mrs. James L. Ward
408 Mr. & Mrs. Frederick H. Wood

ONTARIO STREET.

115 Mr. & Mrs. Wm. Forbush
309 Mr. & Mrs. E. R. Blanchard
323 Mr. & Mrs. John G. Ingalls
325 Rowland S. Ludington
325 Mrs. M. K. Ludington.
325 Mr. & Mrs. W. H. Whittlesey

316 Mr. & Mrs. Herbert A. Dodge
328 Frank Rowley & dr.
328 Dr. Fanny M. Rowley

PARK AVENUE.

sw. cor. Lombard av. Mr. & Mrs.
Arthur R. Metcalfe

PARK PLACE.

121 Mrs. Mary L. Niles
121 William H. Shuey
121 Mrs. Hannah Gill & dr.
129 Mr. & Mrs. M. C. Niles & dr.

PEASE COURT.

331 Mr. & Mrs. C. W. Hawley

PLEASANT STREET.

323 Rev. & Mrs. James Tompkins
323 William C. Tompkins
329 Mrs. H. H. Hunt & dr.
329 Dr. Rodney Hunt

335 Mr. & Mrs. C. B. Albro
Receiving day Wednesday
337 Mr. & Mrs. Pierce Underwood
341 Mr. & Mrs. Jesse A. Baldwin
509 Mr. & Mrs. R. L. Crockett

314 Mr. & Mrs. J. H. Heald
314 James H. Heald jr.
510 Mr. & Mrs. George Lee
512 Mr. & Mrs. E. F. Burton
512 Mr. & Mrs. R. L. Crampton

NORTH SCOVILLE AVENUE.

221 Mr. & Mrs. Walter G. Bentley & dr.
229 Mr. & Mrs. George J. Charlton
607 Mr. & Mrs. J. L. Whaples & dr.
609 Mr. & Mrs. R. J. Furbeck
631 Mr. & Mrs. John Tucker
715 Mr. & Mrs. Harvey A. Higgins
719 Mr. & Mrs. W. N. Ketchum

214 Mr. & Mrs. E. P. Martin
220 Mr. & Mrs. Ryerson D. Gates
400 Mr. & Mrs. T. J. Hyman
Receiving day Tuesday
408 W. G. Prall & dr.
412 Mr. & Mrs. John E. Hunt
412 Miss Florence E. Bissell
632 Mr. & Mrs. W. Fred Van Bergen
632 Mrs. F. S. Van Bergen
710 Mr. & Mrs. Frank H. Clarke

SOUTH SCOVILLE AVENUE.

127 John S. Coffey
129 Mr. & Mrs. F. W. Pringle
129 George D. Hale
131 Mr. & Mrs. John S. McCready
135 Mr. & Mrs. H. Grenell
141 Mr. & Mrs. S. S. Rogers
213 Mr. & Mrs. Herbert H. Hewes
309 Mr. & Mrs. Ross C. Hall
311 Mr. & Mrs. John J. Cleary
311 Mrs. Katherine McAllister
315 Mr. & Mrs. Daniel L. Hall & drs.
323 Mr. & Mrs. James H. Wells
323 Mrs. N. E. Chandler
431 Mr. & Mrs. Chas. Russell Smith

112 Mr. & Mrs. M. L. Doty
Receiving day Thursday
114 Sig. & Mrs. A. A. Jannotta
138 Mr. & Mrs. Chas. L. Chenoweth

142 Mr. & Mrs. Henry C. Cooke & dr. *Receiving day Thursday*
312 Mr. & Mrs. Ernest Woltersdorf
Receive 1st Tuesday
316 Mr. & Mrs. Jos. M. Nockin & dr.

NORTH SIXTY-FOURTH AV.

223 Mrs. Hattie Randell
245 Mr. & Mrs. George Butters
301 Mr. & Mrs. F. G. Ensign & drs.
301 Frank G. Ensign
305 Mrs. Aubrey Warren
309 Mr. & Mrs. N. M. Keeney
325 Mr. & Mrs. E. E. Morrell
405 Dr. & Mrs. F. S. Buckley
411 Mr. & Mrs. H. F. Sayles
417 L. W. Ervine
611 Mr. & Mrs. Robt. Robinson
611 Robert C. Robinson

218 Mr. & Mrs. Samuel S. Pruyn
218 Chas. E. Pruyn
222 Mr. & Mrs. Chas. H. Wood
226 Mr. & Mrs. Albert Budde
324 Mr. & Mrs. Wm. C. Scott & drs.
520 Mr. & Mrs. J. W. Attridge

SOUTH SIXTY-FOURTH AV.

311 Mrs. Charles K. Ballard
311 Mr. & Mrs. F. E. Ballard
315 Mr. & Mrs. C. D. Vallette & dr.
421 Mr. & Mrs. Louis D. Taylor
421 Mr. & Mrs. Osborn J. Pierce & dr.

SUPERIOR STREET.

321 Mr. & Mrs. Francis J. Woolley
325 Mr. & Mrs. George W. Wilbur
325 Miss Susie W. Rice
329 Mr. & Mrs. John Hoggins
709 Dr. & Mrs. M. H. Aspinwall & dr.
721 Edward Cook & dr.

326 Rev. & Mrs. C. P. Anderson

TAYLOR AVENUE.

215 Mr. & Mrs. Robt. H. Lay & dr·
215 Mr. & Mrs. W. W. De Armond
219 Mr. & Mrs. D. E. Brink & dr.
233 Mr. & Mrs. Cookson M. Wright

218 Mr. & Mrs. T. H. Butler
218 Thomas G. Butler

WASHINGTON BOULEVARD.

622 Mr. & Mrs. Albert L. Weaver
1112 Mr. & Mrs. J. C. Griffith
1126 Mrs. Annie E. Preston
1126 Thomas C. Preston
1126 William N. Preston
1226 Mr. & Mrs. Charles D. Richards
s.e. cor. Elmwood av. Mr. & Mrs. Frank R. Lindop

WESLEY AVENUE.

103 Mr. & Mrs. Lewis D. Jones
115 Mr. & Mrs. James A. Lewis
115 Miss Fannie M. Evans
115 Jesse M. Evans
121 Mr. & Mrs. W. A. Sheridan
201 Mr. & Mrs. H. J. Ullmann
213 Mr. & Mrs. Thomas T. Bethell
  Receiving day Thursday
217 Mr. & Mrs. De Los Hull
  Receiving day Thursday
217 Mr. & Mrs. Geo. Sinden
225 Mr. & Mrs. A. H. Adams
231 Mr. & Mrs. F. P. Armbruster
301 Mrs. L. B. Castle & dr.
301 Mr. & Mrs. W. J. Nye
301 Harry B. Castle
305 Mr. & Mrs. Clyde J. McCary
309 Mr. & Mrs. Pliny I. Lawrence
315 Mr. & Mrs. J. E. Davis & dr.
319 Mr.& Mrs. Frederick W.Wilcox
319 Mr. & Mrs. Geo. H.Wilcox & dr.
321 Mr. & Mrs. Leigh H. Jackson
321 Mr. & Mrs. Abram Jackson
405 Mrs. Laura Ashleman & drs.
  Receiving day Saturday
405 John Ashleman
405 Paul Ashleman

118 Mr. & Mrs. Wm. P. Winslow
122 Mr. & Mrs. A. E. Branch
124 Mr. & Mrs. W. C. Curtis & dr.
218 Mr. & Mrs. Geo. H. Owen
218 Edwin G. Owen
218 Willis P. Owen
218 D. J. Pridham
234 Mr. & Mrs. E. E. Morrell
326 Mr. & Mrs. George Royal
332 Mr. & Mrs. S. C. Postlewait & dr.

WISCONSIN AVENUE.

117 Mr. & Mrs. J. P. Sharp
117 George P. Sharp

123 Hotel Plaza
  William T. Best
  W. G. Derbyshire
  Mr. & Mrs. Henry P. Harned
  Miss Bessie Otis Hinckley
  Dr. & Mrs. J. E. Keefe
203 Mr. & Mrs. James C. Rogers & drs.
223 Mr. & Mrs. R. S. Worthington
227 Mr.& Mrs. Harry B. Richardson
229 Mr. & Mrs. O. J. Rattle
235 Mrs. A. E. Howes & dr.
235 Mrs. H. C. Hazen
241 Mr. & Mrs. E. R. Haase
249 Mr. & Mrs. Louis Cook
317 Mr. & Mrs. Edmund B. Blinn
327 Mr. & Mrs. Edwin H. Cheney
329 Mr. & Mrs. Harry B. Noyes
337 Mr. & Mrs. F. C. S. Calhoun
341 Mr. & Mrs. Geo. F. Cook
341 Mrs. E. V. Bronson
401 Mr. & Mrs. L. E. Bailey
413 Mr. & Mrs. Judson M. Fuller
433 Mr. & Mrs. Elmer E. Pierce

116 Mr. & Mrs. Andrew O. Butler
116 Andrew O. Butler jr.
116 Frank M. Butler
116 Julian T. Butler
202 Mr. & Mrs. J. C. Rogers
308 Mr. & Mrs. Albert C. Childs
308 Mrs. O. A. Leonard
316 Mr. & Mrs. Fred Gustorf & drs.
324 Mr. & Mrs. Arthur N. Sullivan
328 Mr. & Mrs. Charles S. Burton
332 Mr. & Mrs. John W. Palmer
  Receiving day Thursday
340 Mr. & Mrs. W. P. Utley
402 Mr. & Mrs. J. Warren Faxon
410 Mrs. Mary Lovett
414 Mr. & Mrs. W. W. Wood
416 Mr. & Mrs. Raymond K. Maynard
420 Mr. & Mrs. John C. Miller
424 W. C. Brown
424 Mrs. Frank Prindle
428 Mr. & Mrs. John P. Breitling

WOODBINE AVENUE.

736 Mr. & Mrs. H. S. Eckart
736 Mrs. O. P. Melin
738 Mr. & Mrs. J. W. Hansel jr.
738 Miss Agnes M. Hansel
738 Mrs. A. Mowat
740 Dr.& Mrs. F. M. Reynolds & dr.
740 William J. Reynolds

PARK RIDGE.

Mr. & Mrs. John C. Ahrensfeld
Mr. & Mrs. H. M. Baker
Mr. & Mrs. A. C. Becker
Dr. & Mrs. E. E. Best
Mr. & Mrs. W. W. Burns
J. H. Butler
Mr. & Mrs. Robert Cade
Mr. & Mrs. A. J. Carstens
Mr. & Mrs. Geo. C. Chittendon
Mr. & Mrs. W. S. Chittendon
Mr. & Mrs. A. W. Cochran
Mr. & Mrs. Samuel Cochran
Mr. & Mrs. G. E. Clark
Mr. & Mrs. G. H. Cornell
Mr. & Mrs. Samuel Cummings & dr.
Mr. & Mrs. E. N. Darrow
Noble C. Darrow
Mr. & Mrs. E. T. Davis
Mr. & Mrs. S. L. Davis
Mrs. George Drake
Mr. & Mrs. I. F. Dunwiddie
Dr. & Mrs. G. H. Fricke
Mr. & Mrs. O. D. S. Gallup
Mr. & Mrs. H. H. Harries
Mr. & Mrs. Ira Harries
Mr. & Mrs. E. H. Hunt
Mr. & Mrs. F. C. Jorgesson
Mr. & Mrs. C. O. Lowman
Mr. & Mrs. Chas. H. Marsh

Mr. & Mrs. W. H. Martin
Mr. & Mrs. O. W. Mayer
Mrs. E. Millard
Mr. & Mrs. A. R. Mora
Mr. & Mrs. A. C. Orr
Mr. & Mrs. J. G. Orr
Mr. & Mrs. A. W. Penny
Mr. & Mrs. Joseph A. Phelps
Dr. & Mrs. W. H. Pontious
Mr. & Mrs. J. Ramsdell
Mr. & Mrs. S. W. Robinson
Mr. & Mrs. Z. D. Root
Mr. & Mrs. O. R. Shearman
Mr. & Mrs. J. C. Sinclair
Mr. & Mrs. Robert Stagg
Mr. & Mrs. Chas. W. Stansbury
Mr. & Mrs. C. E. Stebbings
Mr. & Mrs. R. F. Stockdale
Mr. & Mrs. Owen Stuart & drs.
Mr. & Mrs. W. P. Thornton
Mr. & Mrs. Hugo Von Doeming
G. S. Wells
Mr. & Mrs. A. J. Whitcomb
Mr. & Mrs. A. E. Whitlock
Mr. & Mrs. C. Whitlock
Miss Mary A. Wilson
Mr. & Mrs. J. C. Wood
Dr. & Mrs. S. A. Woodworth

PULLMAN.

ARCADE ROW.

4 Mr. & Mrs. Frank G. Secord
12 Mr. & Mrs. E. W. Henricks
12 John P. Hopkins

FLORENCE BOULEVARD.
(111th Street.)

1 Mr. & Mrs. H. H. Sessions
1 Mrs. H. S. Maxham
2 Mr. & Mrs. Arthur M. Parent
3 Dr. & Mrs. John McLean
4 Mr. & Mrs. Edward F. Bryant
7 Mr. & Mrs. A. Rapp

HOTEL FLORENCE.

Mr. & Mrs. Harry E. Carpenter
Mr. & Mrs. W. P. Kennard
Mr. & Mrs. James A. Ramsey
Mr. & Mrs. Henry A. Sanger
George W. Scott

MARKET CIRCLE.

11 Mr. & Mrs. Daniel R. Martin
20 Carlton C. Hewitt

WATT AVENUE.

248 Mr. & Mrs. Frederick Wild

RAVINIA.

Mr. & Mrs. Griffin Baker
O. F. Bentley
Mr. & Mrs. W. R. Boerner
John C. Coe
Mr. & Mrs. Levi M. Comstock
Mr. & Mrs. G. Denmark

Mr. & Mrs. John Dings
Mr. & Mrs. Peter Gehrity
Mr. & Mrs. James Ginty
Prof. & Mrs. D. W. Gross
Mr. & Mrs. Samuel Guilford
Mr. & Mrs. O. G. Kellogg

Mr. & Mrs. Charles Kollar
Mr. & Mrs. Alexander Lang
Mr. & Mrs. William Law
Mr. & Mrs. Samuel P. Lucas
Mr. & Mrs. W. C. McKenzie
Mr. & Mrs. W. L. McKenzie
Mr. & Mrs. A. Mitchell

Mr. & Mrs. Julius Neist
Mrs. Isaac Russell
Mr. & Mrs. Adolph Stark
Mr. & Mrs. Joseph Stype
Mr. & Mrs. Sebastian Stype
Miss Emma Vanduyn
Mrs. A. V. Willoughby

RIVER FOREST.

ASHLAND AVENUE.

319 Mr. & Mrs. S. E. Baker & dr.
339 Mr. & Mrs. Frank D. Butler

278 Rev. & Mrs. Elwood M. Wherry
   & drs.
278 William B. Wherry
316 Mr. & Mrs. O. M. Barr

AUVERGNE PLACE.

Mr. & Mrs. Edward C. Waller & dr·
   Receiving day Thursday
Henry Waller
Mr. & Mrs. W. H. Winslow
   Receiving day Thursday

CENTRAL AVENUE

56 Mr. & Mrs. Chas. M. Sturges
358 Mrs. H. L. McKallor
362 Mr.&Mrs. Felix J. Griffen & drs.

FOREST AVENUE.

239 Henry Struble
245 Mr. & Mrs. Wm. P. Crenshaw
   Receiving day Wednesday
245 John W. Nuckols
281 Mr. & Mrs. J. E. Adams
295 Mr. & Mrs. E. C. Moeller
337 Mr. & Mrs. Wm. C. Walsh
343 Mr. & Mrs. C. Juergens
347 Mr. & Mrs. F. Juergens
357 Mr. & Mrs. J. T. Hodgson & drs.

244 Geo. W. Homer
322 Mr. & Mrs. A. P. Grant
486 Mr. & Mrs. Henry E. Graves
492 Mr. & Mrs. F. J. Reichmann

FRANKLIN AVENUE.

279 Mr. & Mrs. Fred M. Homer
349 Mr. & Mrs. Frank L. Munroe

312 Mr. & Mrs. Brunot Bailey
312 Mrs. Sally G. Root

GALE AVENUE.

97 Mr. & Mrs. P. C. Porter
107 Mr. & Mrs. W. C. D. Gillespie
121 Mrs. W. M. Powell
121 Mr. & Mrs. H. E. Page

114 Mr. & Mrs. H. E. Parker
114 M. L. Parker
118 Mr. & Mrs. Charles Davis
130 Mrs. John Downey
130 Mr. & Mrs. Wm. H. Reedy
   Receiving day Wednesday
160 Mrs. D. D. O'Brien
172 Mr. & Mrs. L. E. Moore
172 Mr. & Mrs. Frank D. Thompson

GROVE STREET.

87 Mr. & Mrs. D. F. Disbrow
97 Mr. & Mrs. C. E. Marble
   Receiving day Thursday
113 Mr. & Mrs. E. F. Dunne
133 Mr. & Mrs. Morris M. Herriman
   Receiving day Wednesday
133 William N. Herriman
145 Mr. & Mrs. W. H. Chenoweth
   & drs.
145 W. H. Chenoweth jr.
187 Mr. & Mrs. John J. Ryan

32 Mr. & Mrs. Charles J. Barnard.
36 Mr. & Mrs. Herman Glaess
114 Mr. & Mrs. Wm. H. Hatch
148 Mr. & Mrs. Lewis B. Mayo

JOHN STREET.

cor. Madison av. Rev. & Mrs. Geo.
   B. Day & dr.
Elias V. Day

KEYSTONE AVENUE.

245 Mr. & Mrs. Frank Little
245 Mrs. Solomon Thatcher & dr.
245 Frederic S. Thatcher
253 Mr. & Mrs. C. C. Collins

281 D. W. Thatcher & dr.
281 Mrs. J. C. Mooar
315 Mr. & Mrs. Wm. T. Barbour
347 Mr. & Mrs. E. J. MacAdams
363 Mr. & Mrs. W. C. Freymuth
399 Mr. & Mrs. E. T. Converse
455 Mr. & Mrs. E. H. Duensing

254 Mr. & Mrs. R. S. Odell
254 Mrs. Mary A. Odell
296 Carl A. Wilmeroff
306 Mr. & Mrs. G. W. Clark
336 Mr. & Mrs. J. B. Blank
336 Mr. & Mrs. Thomas A. Cobb
340 Mr. & Mrs. Ralph J. Hirsch
344 Mr. & Mrs. Jacob A. Cost

LATHROP AVENUE.

279 Mr. & Mrs. Geo. T. Howser
317 Mr. & Mrs. L. G. Bostedo
333 Mr. & Mrs. John F. Barrett
333 Miss Emma De Gan
339 Mr. & Mrs. Anthony J. Barrett

MADISON AVENUE..

85 Mr. & Mrs. Frank H. Hillmer
89 Mr. & Mrs. C. J. Schoening
Receiving day Wednesday

OAK AVENUE.

257 Mr. & Mrs. C. L. Williams
261 Mr. & Mrs. John Humphrey & dr.
271 Mr. & Mrs. A. C. Kelsey
Receiving day Wednesday
299 Mr. & Mrs. Edw. Tracy

270 Mr. & Mrs. George L. Thatcher & dr.

PARK AVENUE.

305 Rev. & Mrs. Joseph N. Boyd
435 Mrs. Wm. E. Clarke

435 Mr. & Mrs. Glenn E. Plumb
445 Mrs. Isabel Plumb
445 Mr. & Mrs. Allan F. Millikan

334 Mr. & Mrs. Wm. O. Coleman
348 Mr. & Mrs. J. Sidney Hotton
348 Mrs. E. A. Hotton

QUICK AVENUE.

34 Mr. & Mrs. Wm. F. Quick

THATCHER AVENUE.

263 Mr. & Mrs. Ellison H. Ross
269 Mr. & Mrs. Walter J. Kelly
Receiving day Wednesday
273 Mr. & Mrs. Wm. H. Turner
273 Mrs. M. W. Prouty
275 Mr. & Mrs. Andrew Jaicks
277 Mr. & Mrs. F. B. Klock
281 Mr. & Mrs. James P. Luse
293 Mr. & Mrs. J. B. Miller

238 Rev. & Mrs. Wm. Fawcett
256 Mr. & Mrs. John W. Broughton
260 Mr. & Mrs. J. L. Jackson
272 Mr. & Mrs. D.A.Thatcher & dr.
278 Mr. & Mrs. Jas. S. Goodman
284 Mrs. Lucinda S. Lord
284 Fred W. Lord
284 Herbert J. Lord
290 Mr. & Mrs. R. C. Brown
304 Mr. & Mrs. H. W. Yalding & dr·
310 Mr. & Mrs. T. M. Jackson
334 Mr. & Mrs. Joseph D. Pickett & drs.
334 Mr. & Mrs. John D. Pickett
338 W. R. Patterson
338 Mr. & Mrs. John Coleman
sw. cor. Chicago av. Mr. & Mrs. Webster Hakes
sw. cor. Chicago av. Mr. & Mrs. M. W. Hakes & dr.

RIVERSIDE.

Rev. & Mrs. George Davis Adams
Mr. & Mrs. Charles E. Allen
Harry K. Allen
Mrs. Sarah C. Allen
Mr. & Mrs. A. F. Ames
Mr. & Mrs. James S. Andrews
Mr. & Mrs. H. M. Avers
Carlton S. Badger
Mr. & Mrs. H. H. Badger
Mr. & Mrs. Edward Badger

Harry A. Badger
Mr. & Mrs. John Balfour
Harry Balfour
Walter E. Balfour
Mr. & Mrs. Albert W. Barnum
Mr. & Mrs. W. H. Barnum
Receiving day Thursday
Mr. & Mrs. Walter N. Bates
Mr. & Mrs. C. B. Beach & drs.
Mr. & Mrs. M. H. E. Beckley

Mr. & Mrs. George W. Beisel
Mrs. Louise Blayney
Mr. & Mrs. Thomas C. Blayney
Mr. & Mrs. Edgar B. Bliss
Mr. & Mrs. Arthur P. Bowen
Mr. & Mrs. Charles C. Boyles & dr.
Charles D. Boyles
Thomas D. Boyles
Mr. & Mrs. Street Bradley
Dr. S. L. Breckenridge
Mr. & Mrs. John J. Bryant & dr.
John J. Bryant jr.
Mr. & Mrs. John M. Cameron
Miss H. S. Campbell
Mrs. William J. Campbell
Mr. & Mrs. Harry G. Chester
Dr. & Mrs. J. L. Congdon
Mr. & Mrs. Thomas M. Conpropst
Mr. & Mrs. A. D. Craig
Mr. & Mrs. Chauncey H. Crosby & dr.
Mrs. Amanda Crosby
Mr. & Mrs. C. L. Cross
Mrs. S. E. Dane
Asa Dearborn
Mr. & Mrs. Watts De Golyer & dr.
Receiving day Wednesday
W. A. Drake
Mr. & Mrs. E. A. Driver & dr.
Mr. & Mrs. J. S. Driver
E. Raymond Driver
Mr. & Mrs. L. F. Dyrenforth
Mr. & Mrs. Julius T. Edson
Miss Margaret Elliott
Jerome A. Ellis
Mr. & Mrs. James Forsyth
Frank Fredericks & drs.
Frank Fredericks jr.
Arthur C. Gehr
Herbert B. Gehr
Mrs. Phebe B. Gehr
S. Whipple Gehr
Mrs. Nellie Gettier
Mr. & Mrs. Stephen Gitterman
Mr. & Mrs. A. Gorique
Mr. & Mrs. Chas. H. Gould
Mrs. M. E. Graham
Mrs. Henry R. Green
Mr. & Mrs. Walter G. Greenleaf
Receiving day Wednesday
Mr. & Mrs. Charles O. Gregg
Mr. & Mrs. Seymour Guthrie
John W. Halliday & drs.
Mr. & Mrs. W. B. Hamblin
Mr. & Mrs. Thomas C. Hannah
Mr. & Mrs. George Hargreaves

S. H. Harrington & dr.
Mr. & Mrs. Jesse Hart
Mr. & Mrs. W. A. Havemeyer & dr.
W. A. Havemeyer jr.
Mr. & Mrs. F. Hellyer & dr.
Mr. & Mrs. E. E. Helmer
Mr. & Mrs. C. M. Higginson
Mr. & Mrs. Frank A. Hitchcock
Mr. & Mrs. Walter E. Hodges
Mr. & Mrs. Frank G. Holton
Mr. & Mrs. Freelon Hotchkiss
Dr. I. S. Hotchkiss
Miss Hariette Hotchkiss
Mr. & Mrs. L. A. Howland
Mrs. Gurdon S. Hubbard jr.
Mr. & Mrs. David J. Hull
Mr. & Mrs. George Hunt
Mrs. W. W. Hutchinson
Mrs. Sarah E. Jackson
Mr. & Mrs. Archibald Johnston & dr.
Mr. & Mrs. S. T. Johnston
Mr. & Mrs. Cyrus M. Jones
Mr. & Mrs. M. Helles Jordan
Mr. & Mrs. W. S. Kammerer
George Chandlin Kimbark
Mr. & Mrs. A. M. Kinzie
Mr. & Mrs. Edward L. Lalk
Mr. & Mrs. Charles Lange
Mr. & Mrs. Wm. E. Lawrence
J. Lewis Lee
Mr. & Mrs. Chas. G. Leison
Mr. & Mrs. A. Lipsey
Mr. & Mrs. James H. Lipsey
Mr. & Mrs. Archibald McArthur
Receive Tuesday & Sunday
Miss Florence B. McArthur
Mrs. H. J. McClintock
Mrs. E. C. McCloud
Frank N. Sheldon
Mr. & Mrs. Wm. T. Sheldon
Mr. & Mrs. George W. Sherlock
Mr. & Mrs. Charles D. Sherman & drs.
Mrs. Bessie W. Sherman
Mr. & Mrs. W. C. Shoemaker
Gen. & Mrs. M. D. L. Simpson
Receiving day Thursday
Jerome W. Simpson
Mr. & Mrs. E. E. Smith
Mr. & Mrs. George A. Smith
Mr. & Mrs. Herbert E. Smith
Mr. & Mrs. J. W. Smith & drs.
Rev. & Mrs. Charles C. Snyder & dr.
Karl F. Snyder

Mr. & Mrs. P. K. Solger
Mr. & Mrs. Robert Somerville
Mrs. James Soper
Mr. & Mrs. Edward Southwood&dr.
Mr. & Mrs. M. Standiford
Dr. & Mrs. Alexander Sterl
Mr. & Mrs. Edward H. Storey
Mr. & Mrs. Cornelius Sullivan&drs.
John E. Sullivan
Mr. & Mrs. George Tapper
Roy M. McCloud
Mrs. Anna Wood McDougal & dr.
James B. McLaughlin
Mr. & Mrs. David W. MacDonald
Mr. & Mrs. George A. Maclean
Receiving day Tuesday
Mr. & Mrs. Randolph Manning
Miss Vivia E. Mellor
Mr. & Mrs. Amos C. Miller
Miss Lula Miller
Mr. & Mrs. Thomas Miller & dr.
George B. Miner
Noyes B. Miner
Mr. & Mrs. James S. Moore
Mr. & Mrs. T. T. Morford
Mr. & Mrs. George Morton
Mr. & Mrs. Norris W. Mundy
Norris H. Mundy
Mrs. Leverett W. Murray
Mr. & Mrs. George P. Nichols
Mr. & Mrs. John F. Palmer
Dr. & Mrs. J. P. Palmer
Mrs. J. S. Pode
Mrs. Lucy G. Porter
Mr. & Mrs. John A. Post
Edwin R. Puffer
Mr. & Mrs. H. J. Racey
Mr. & Mrs. William Radford
Mr. & Mrs. Isham Randolph
Miss P. C. Randolph
Mr. & Mrs. J. N. Rawlings
Mr. & Mrs. James D. Raynolds
Mr. & Mrs. Frank F. Reed
Miss Mary Reed
Mrs. M. D. Reed
Mrs. Charles Reissig
Mr. & Mrs. August Repka

Mr. & Mrs. Benj. Reynolds
Mr. & Mrs. Myron B. Rice
Receiving day Thursday
Dr. & Mrs. Frederick W. Rich
Albert D. Rich
Mr. & Mrs. S. P. Richards & drs.
Mr. & Mrs. D. E. Richardson
Mr. & Mrs. L. E. Riggs
Mr. & Mrs. W. E. Riggs
Mr. & Mrs. Edward P. Ripley & drs
Mrs. J. S. Ross
Mrs. Kate Sanborn
George M. Scott
Mrs. Mary Scott
Mr. & Mrs. A. U. Scoville
Mr. & Mrs. Albert Seckel
Mrs. Elise Seckel
Mr. & Mrs. Louis A. Seeberger
Mr. & Mrs. Oscar M. Shannon
Mr. & Mrs. Charles Tarnow & dr.
Mrs. J. S. Taylor & drs.
Louis S. Taylor
Mr. & Mrs. Milton Thomas
Mr. & Mrs. W. A. Thompson
Mr. & Mrs. R. P. Travis
Dr. & Mrs. E. A. Van Tuyl
Miss Maggie Van Tuyl
Mr. & Mrs. H. C. Vilas
Prof. & Mrs. Joseph Vilim
Mr. & Mrs. C. M. L. Walker
Mr. & Mrs. Chas. A. Walter
Mr. & Mrs. Wm. H. Ward
Mr. & Mrs. C. F. Wardell
R. J. Wardell
Mr. & Mrs. Robert M. Ware
Mr. & Mrs. J. L. Warren
Mr. & Mrs. Alexander Watson
Mr. & Mrs. J. M. Weir & drs.
Silas Weir
Mrs. Jane Wesencraft
Mrs. Lotta Wesencraft
Mr. & Mrs. F. L. Whitcomb
Mr. & Mrs. Herbert T. Windsor
Mr. & Mrs. Charles A. Woodruff
Mr. & Mrs. Joseph G. Wurtele

TRACY.

Daniel Barnard
Mr. & Mrs. E. A. Barnard
Miss Alice L. Barnard
Daniel E. Barnard
Miss Elizabeth Barnard
Mr. & Mrs. Edwin Bebb

Mr. & Mrs. Robert Bebb
Mr. & Mrs. James L. Clark
Mr. & Mrs. Cornelius Cox & dr.
Mrs. A. S. Dittman
Mr. & Mrs. P. W. Dorn
Mr. & Mrs. Albert B. Fairfield

Albert B. Fairfield jr.
Frank M. Fairfield
Mr. & Mrs. Leonard Ficklin
Mr. & Mrs. G. M. French
Mr. & Mrs. Charles B. Goes
Mr. & Mrs. C. H. Gorton & dr.
Mrs. Edward Grady
Mrs. J. M. Griswold & drs.
Mr. & Mrs. A. C. Halliwell
Mr. & Mrs. John Hill jr.
Mr. & Mrs. W. I. Hitt
George T. Horton
Mr. & Mrs. H. E. Horton & dr.
Receiving day Tuesday
Rev. & Mrs. George E. Hunt
Mr. & Mrs. O. P. Laird
Mr. & Mrs. William Law
R. P. Layton & drs.
Mr. & Mrs. William Macklem
Mr. & Mrs. Alfred H. Marsh
E. P. Marsh & drs.

Mr. & Mrs. F. M. McClure
Mr. & Mrs. J. A. McKeever
Mr. & Mrs. G. F. Meader
Dr. Ada B. Morgan
Mr. & Mrs. George W. Murray
Mr. & Mrs. H. A. Parker & dr.
Mr. & Mrs. Sidney Parker
Mr. & Mrs. E. L. Roberts
Mr. & Mrs. W. H. Roberts
Mr. & Mrs. Frank Stewart
Mr. & Mrs. D. W. Sutherland
Mr. & Mrs. Grant Colfax Tullar
Mr. & Mrs. T. T. Verdier & dr.
Mr. & Mrs. D. C. Wagner
Mr. & Mrs. Edwin A. Warfield
Mr. & Mrs. Edwin A. Warfield jr
Mr. & Mrs. Robert Warfield
Mr. & Mrs. Samuel Wells
Mr. & Mrs. Frank White
Mr. & Mrs. James M. Young

WASHINGTON HEIGHTS.

Mr. & Mrs. C. H. L. Ahrens & dr.
Dr. H. B. Beegle
Rev. & Mrs. P. H. Budach
Mr. & Mrs. John W. Casey
Prof. John W. Clarke
Mr. & Mrs. J. B. Clarke
Mr. & Mrs. J. F. Clausson
Elliott De Land & dr.
Walter De Land
Mr. & Mrs. J. L. Dodd
Henry C. Ebel jr.
Mr. & Mrs. John Elmstedt
Mr. & Mrs. I. T. Greenacre

Mr. & Mrs. A. D. Heffron
Rev. & Mrs. D. S. Heffron & dr.
Mr. & Mrs. Chas. Holmberg
Mr. & Mrs. John H. Kistner
Mr. & Mrs. Gottlieb Klein
Dr. & Mrs. Louis Lowenthal
Mr. & Mrs. John H. Madigan
Mr. & Mrs. S. Edward Rumsey
Thomas C. Senn
Mr. & Mrs. Joseph A. Singler
Mr. & Mrs. A. B. Stevens & dr.
Mr. & Mrs. William Vear
Mr. & Mrs. H. H. Wilder

WILMETTE.

Mr. & Mrs. John Arndt
Mr. & Mrs. James A. Arthur
Rev. & Mrs. Hugh Atchinson
Mr. & Mrs. Harry M. Ayars
Mr. & Mrs. F. W. Barnes
Mr. & Mrs. George Barry & drs.
George F. Barry
Mr. & Mrs. Frank Berry
Mr. & Mrs. J. A. Bockius & drs.
Mr. & Mrs. R. Bodinghouse
Mr. & Mrs. S. E. Bradley
J. B. Breen
Mr. & Mrs. Leland Breese & drs.
Mr. & Mrs. C. H. Brethold
Edward A. Burge
George Cantlie
Mr. & Mrs. W. W. Carroll

Mr. & Mrs. M. T. Carter & drs.
E. J. Chalfant & dr.
Mr. & Mrs. R. W. Chappell & dr.
Dr. & Mrs. A. S. Childs & dr.
Ralph Childs
Mr. & Mrs. C. S. Clark
Mr. & Mrs. John B. Clay
Mr. & Mrs. Geo. A. Colton & drs.
Mrs. Alonzo P. Convis
Mr. & Mrs. C. D. Cramer
Mr. & Mrs. H. A. Crane & drs.
Mr. & Mrs. Willis E. Crane
Mr. & Mrs. C. W Crocker & dr.
Mr. & Mrs. P. O. Crocker
Mrs. Elizabeth Davenport
Rev. & Mrs. E. B. Dean
Mr. & Mrs. John De Haye

Mrs. Caroline De Zeng
Mr. & Mrs. Harvey M. Dibble
Mr. & Mrs. Albert Dietz
Mr. & Mrs. J. G. Dietz
Mr. & Mrs. S. M. Dingee & dr.
Mr. & Mrs. S. S. Dingee
Mr. & Mrs. Harry V. Donaldson
Mr. & Mrs. Edwin Drury & dr.
Mr. & Mrs. Frank Drury
Mr. & Mrs. H. G. Drury & dr.
Mr. & Mrs. A. C. Duncan
Mr. & Mrs. W. M. Egan & drs.
Dr. & Mrs. C. H. Eldred
Mr. & Mrs. Edgar Ellis
Mr. & Mrs. Edward F. Ernst
Mr. & Mrs. Walter Faraday
Miss Ann Farnsworth
Mr. & Mrs. Edward P. Fatch
Mr. & Mrs. G. E. Fernald
Miss Jeanie Furman
Miss Nettie Furman
Mr. & Mrs. A. N. Gage
Edward B. Gage
Mrs. Helen S. Gage
Mr. & Mrs. Henry H. Gage
Mr. & Mrs. John S. Gage
Mr. & Mrs. Henry B. Gates
Mr. & Mrs. L. A. Gearing
Mrs. I. A. Gooding & dr.
S. E. Gooding
W. S. Gooding
Mr. & Mrs. W. G. Groover
Dr. & Mrs. Geo. W. Haskin
George W. Hess
Mr. & Mrs. H. H. Hitchcock
Mr. & Mrs. W. J. Hosmer
Mr. & Mrs. J. M. Johnson
Mr. & Mrs. E. C. Jones
Mr. & Mrs. F. L. Joy
Mr. & Mrs. A. Kaynor & dr.
Miss Margaret Kearney
Mr. & Mrs. W. D. Ketchum & drs
Mr. & Mrs. W. G. King & drs.
Mrs. W. H. Kinney
Mr. & Mrs. G. G. Knox & dr.
Mr. & Mrs. Thomas M. Knox
Mr. & Mrs. Frank Kunz
Mr. & Mrs. Carl R. Latham
Mr. & Mrs. E. C. Latham
Miss Hattie Latham
Mr. & Mrs. Hubbard Latham
Mr. & Mrs. H. H. Latham
Francis B. Law
Miss Anna E. Law
Miss Ida I. Law
Mr. & Mrs. John Ling

Mr. & Mrs. Warren Lusted
Mr. & Mrs. A. J. Lyon
Mr. & Mrs. A. W. MacLean & dr.
Theophile Maher
Mr. & Mrs. Walter S. Maher
Mr. & Mrs. Alex. McDaniel
Mr. & Mrs. J. L. McKittrick
Mr. & Mrs. W. J. Merriam
Mr. & Mrs. Chas. J. Michelet
Dr. & Mrs. W. E. Michelet
Mrs. Mary J. Mills
Harry I. Mills
Mr. & Mrs. H. E. Moore
Mr. & Mrs. W. R. Morley
Mr. & Mrs. L. N. Moyer
Mr. & Mrs. C. S. Musson
Frederick Norman
Mr. & Mrs. F. S. Pallett
Mr. & Mrs. William Panushka & drs.
John W. Panushka
Mrs. Alexander Parr & dr.
E. S. Parr
George R. Parr
Mr. & Mrs. Edgar T. Paul
Mr. & Mrs. Frank M. Paul
Mr. & Mrs. F. C. Penniman
Mr. & Mrs. J. C. Pierson
Mr. & Mrs. L. J. Pierson
Mr. & Mrs. Mortimer Power
Mr. & Mrs. George W. Rogers & dr.
Miss Lena L. Russell
Mr. & Mrs. James C. Savage
Mr. & Mrs. B. F. Schlesinger
Mr. & Mrs. Carl S. Schroeder
Dr. & Mrs. John Segsworth
Mr. & Mrs. Samuel C. Sexauer
Mrs. Jane Shantz & dr.
Mr. & Mrs. W. C. Shurtleff
Dr. & Mrs. J. W. Slonaker
John J. Spear
G. W. Springer
Mr. & Mrs. L. B. Springer
Mrs. M. C. Springer & drs.
Mr. & Mrs. Geo. E. Spry
Dr. & Mrs. B. C. Stolp
Mr. & Mrs. Calvin A. Strong
Mr. & Mrs. W. W. Sutton
Mr. & Mrs. Charles Swartout
Mr. & Mrs. Wm. G. Sweetman
Mr. & Mrs. Albert H. Taylor
Mr. & Mrs. Cortland C. Taylor
Dr. & Mrs. W. M. Tomlinson
Mr. & Mrs. Howard N. Tyson
Mr. & Mrs. Frank C. Van Ness
Mr. & Mrs. Wm. Von Glahn
Mr. & Mrs. M. E. Walters

Mr. & Mrs. James Watson
Mr. & Mrs. Thomas Watson & dr.
Mr. & Mrs. Thomas W. Watson
Mr. & Mrs. E. R. Webber
Mr. & Mrs. E. B. Wheelock

Mr. & Mrs. S. A. Wheelock & dr.
Mr. & Mrs. James M. Willard
Mr. & Mrs. F. L. Wolf
Thomas Wright & dr.

WINDSOR PARK.

BOND AVENUE.

7301 Mr. & Mrs. Isaac T. Sutton
7305 Mr. & Mrs. Albert Mohr
     Receive Wednesday
7329 Mr. & Mrs. George T. Kessler
7339 Mr. & Mrs. George G. Barrows
7429 Mrs. Helen B. Stephens
7433 Mr. & Mrs. A. J. Simpson
7443 Mr. & Mrs. Samuel A. French
7443 Mr. & Mrs. Garrie S. French
7465 Mr. & Mrs. P. J. McDonagh
7565 Mr. & Mrs. George Nichols
    & dr.
7565 Jean O. Nichols

7300 Mr. & Mrs. Henry J. Hetherington
7306 Mr. & Mrs. Jno. T. Hetherington
7316 Mr. & Mrs. Hugh P. Walden
7318 Mr. & Mrs. Harry W. Mace
7330 Mr. & Mrs. Wm. Pettis
7334 Mrs. Caroline J. Baker
7346 Mr. & Mrs. Harry W. Darling
7400 Mr. & Mrs. Cyrus H. Howell
7408 Mr. & Mrs. W. E. McDermut
7432 Mrs. Chas. F. Lynn & dr.
7436 Mrs. Hattie S. Goodrich & dr.
7452 Mr. & Mrs. Wm. B. Jones
7456 Mr. & Mrs. Frederick J. Wagner
7554 Dr. & Mrs. U. B. Ferris
7554 Frederick M. Barnes
7620 Mr. & Mrs. Charles J. Johnson
7620 Mrs. S. J. Olds
7636 Mr. & Mrs. John H. Jones
7640 Mr. & Mrs. A. F. Middagh
7650 Mr. & Mrs. Wellington B. Stone

7734 Mr. & Mrs. T. C. Lutz
7750 Mr. & Mrs. Edward P. Skene

SAGINAW AVENUE.

7535 Mr. & Mrs. Leonard Holmboe
7641 Mrs. Winnifred Harvey
7657 Mr. & Mrs. Charles M. Steffens
7626 Mr. & Mrs. Chas. H. Brachvogel
7626 Mr. & Mrs. Robert J. Mertens

SEVENTY-THIRD STREET.

43 Mr. & Mrs. John A. Colby
138 Mr. & Mrs. Ernest M. Kimball

SEVENTY-FOURTH STREET.

80 Mr. & Mrs. John A. Kelly
83 Mr. & Mrs. Andrew Wallace jr.
87 Mr. & Mrs. Samuel M. Rowe
204 Mrs. R. H. Long & dr.
230 Mr. & Mrs. Jonathan Smith & drs.

SEVENTY-FOURTH PLACE.

225 Mr. & Mrs. Isaac A. Fleming

SEVENTY-FIFTH STREET.

107 Mr. & Mrs. F. Munson
107 Frank W. Munson

SEVENTY-SEVENTH ST.

47 Mr. & Mrs. H. W. Parkhurst
59 Mr. & Mrs. Charles H. Wilcox
59 Mr. & Mrs. David M. Deutsch

WINNETKA.

Mrs. John Alles
Mr. & Mrs. John Alles jr.
Mr. & Mrs. Charles C. Arnold
Mr. & Mrs. George Baker & dr.
Mr. & Mrs. J. H. Batchelder
Mr. & Mrs. Chas. Guy Bolte

Mr. & Mrs. J. Edwin Bradstreet
Miss Lizzie Brock
Col. & Mrs. J. E. Buckbee & dr.
Julian E. Buckbee jr.
Mr. & Mrs. Otto C. Butz
    Receiving day Monday

Mrs. H. E. Calrow
Mr. & Mrs. J. G. Calrow
Mr. & Mrs. A. B. Capron & dr.
Mr. & Mrs. Benj. Carpenter
Mr. & Mrs. William Warren Case
Mr. & Mrs. Arthur S. Coffin
E. F. Clifton
Mr. & Mrs. Charles W. Cole
Mr. & Mrs. Jirah D. Cole
Mr. & Mrs. F. K. Copeland
Lowell Copeland
Mr, & Mrs. Thomas Copelin
J. A. Cunningham
Mr. & Mrs. J. T. Dale
Miss Jane E. Dale
Mrs. J. A. Densmore & dr.
Mr. & Mrs. J. B. Densmore
Mr. & Mrs. H. A. de Windt
Rev. & Mrs. Q. L. Dowd
Mr. & Mrs. Charles Eastman
Edwin S. Fechheimer
Mr. & Mrs. Charles Graves
Mr. & Mrs. R. M. Graves & dr.
Mr. & Mrs. Frederick Greeley
Morris L. Greeley
Mrs. Morris L. Greeley
Samuel S. Greeley
Mrs. Thomas Hawkes & dr.
Mr. & Mrs. Samuel Hazlehurst
Mr. & Mrs. F. E. Herdman
Geo. Higginson jr.
Mr. & Mrs. G. C. Hoge
Mr. & Mrs. James L. Houghtéling
Mr.&Mrs. DeWitt P. Hubbard
Mr. & Mrs. Arthur B. Jones
Mr. & Mrs. William H. King
Mr. & Mrs. M. R. Kultchar
Mr. & Mrs. George H. Leslie
Mr. & Mrs. H. D. Lloyd
Mr. & Mrs. Francis O. Lyman
Mr. & Mrs. H. V. Mann
Mr. & Mrs. W. H. Martin
Mr. & Mrs. B. A. May & drs.
Alfred C. Maynard
Edwin Maynard
E. Percy Maynard
Mr. & Mrs. Howard McAllaster
Mr. & Mrs. G. M. McConnel & dr.
Mr. & Mrs. Robert B. McConnel
Receiving day Tuesday

Mr. & Mrs. Alfred E. McCordie
Mrs. John McFarlin
Mr. & Mrs. George McKinney
Mr. & Mrs. C. W. Merrilies
Mr. & Mrs. J. H. Monrad
Mr. & Mrs. Edwin W. Moore
Mr. & Mrs. James B. Moore
Mrs. G. H. Morrison
R. S. Moth
Mr. & Mrs. George Nethercott
Mr. & Mrs. G. W. Oldfather
Mr. & Mrs. H. I. Orwig
E. W. Osgood
Mr. & Mrs. S. W. Osgood
Mrs. B. Ostrander
Mr. & Mrs. Wm. A. Otis
Mr. & Mrs. J. O. Parker & drs.
James K. Parker
Mr. & Mrs. C. B. Powell
Mr. & Mrs. Carlton Prouty
Mr. & Mrs. M. F. Prouty
Mr. & Mrs. J. A. Pugh
Mrs. Nannie Reagan
Mr. & Mrs. G. H. Ruel
Mr. & Mrs. Jos. B. Sanborn
Mr. & Mrs. Samuel Schackford
Joseph Sherlock
Mr. & Mrs. F. C. Sherman
Miss Elizabeth O. Shibley
Mrs. E. W. Shippen
Mrs. C. J. Sloate & drs.
Mr. & Mrs. J. O. Smith
Mrs. Susan Smith & drs.
Mr. & Mrs. W. Smith
Mr. & Mrs. Merritt Starr
Mr. & Mrs. Oren Edwin Taft
Mr. & Mrs. C. S. Thorne & drs.
Mr. & Mrs. Clarence W. Tostiven
Mr. & Mrs. H. Totten
Mrs. Susan Totten & dr.
Harry Totten
Mr. & Mrs. H. A. Ware
Mr. & Mrs. J. G. Weart
Mr. & Mrs. Charles Wicks
A. J. Willard
Mr. & Mrs. J. H. S. Williams
Mr. & Mrs. Thomas G. Windes
Mr. & Mrs. Zell Windes
Mr. & Mrs. J. C. Winship
Mr. & Mrs. W. S. Worman

PART EIGHTH.

SHOPPING GUIDE.

THE BLUE BOOK.

*CONTAINING A SELECTED LIST OF PROMINENT
FIRMS AND INDIVIDUALS OF CHICAGO,
ARRANGED UNDER THEIR PROPER
PROFESSIONAL AND BUSI-
NESS HEADINGS.*

LADIES' SHOPPING GUIDE.

EMBRACING NAMES AND ADDRESSES OF RELIABLE AND PROMI-
NENT FIRMS AND INDIVIDUALS, CLASSIFIED UNDER
APPROPRIATE BUSINESS HEADINGS AND
PROFESSIONS.

The Only Antique Store in the West.

J. J. G. BURGHOFFER

584 N. CLARK ST.
Two Blocks South of Lincoln Park.

Original Antiques, Louis XV Furniture, Draperies, Silver,
Ivory Carvings, Japanese and Chinese Porcelains, Old Berlin,
Dresden and English Porcelains, Rare Etchings, Paintings,
Arms, Unset Precious Stones, Fine Opals.

Addressing and Mailing.

TELEPHONE 314-HARRISON
WARNE ADDRESSING COMPANY
334 DEARBORN STREET
Addressing, Enclosing, Delivering—Invitation,
Wedding and Society Work Our Specialty.

Antique Furniture.

D. Leve, Dealer in Antique Furniture.
Artistic Repairing. High Grade Furniture made to order. Fine Upholstering. Gilding and Enameling. Furniture Packed and Shipped.
4642 Cottage Grove Ave.

Art—High Class Works.

ABEL R. R. 772 W. Madison
ANDERSON ART CO. Wabash av. cor. Madison
HALLS ART STUDIO, 559 W. Madison
MOULTON J. G. 45 Jackson boul.
THURBER W. SCOTT, 210 Wabash av.

Art—China and Glass.

BURLEY & CO. 145-147 State

Art Galleries.

Art Institute (The) Lake Front opp. Adams st.

Artists.

Mrs. E. Van Osdel Gowan
·· Portraits
From Life Sittings
241 Wabash Ave.

Artists.
(Miniature.)

GILLETTE WILMARTH B. 300 Wabash av. No. 4 League Studio

M. Ellen Iglehart
Artist and *Teacher*
Studio: 100 Auditorium Bldg.
Oil, Water Color, China.

Artists.
(Photo-Colorist.)

FRANK E. BUTLER
- - - Water Color Artist - - -
Makes a specialty of coloring all kinds of Photographs. Photographs of Residences colored in good taste. Studio 815, 21 Quiney St. Opposite Great Northern Theatre.

Awnings, Canopies and Flags.

CARPENTER GEO. B. & CO. 202-208 South Water

775

Awnings for Rent.

**Awnings, Carpet Coverings,
Chairs, Tables, Step Carpets, Car-
riage Men and Calcium Lights
Furnished for Weddings,
Receptions, Etc.**

GEO. M. COOK,
3742 Cottage Grove Avenue.
TELEPHONE OAKLAND 1281.
Branch Office : 4612 Cottage Grove Av.

Badges and Pins.
(For Societies and Clubs.)
Winship Chas. A. & Co. 4th floor 78
State

Bakeries, Fancy.
ENGLE NEWTON W. 973 W. Madison and 259 Ogden av.

Banks.
WESTERN STATE BANK, s. w.
cor. Lasalle and Randolph

Baths.
(Mud. Steam, Electric.)
KERCHER TONY & SON, 1927-1929
Wabash av.

Bicycle Saddles.
(Manufacturers.)
PLEW JAMES E. 1446 Wabash av.

Bicycles and Athletic Goods.
SPALDING A. G. & BROS. 147 and
149 Wabash av.

Billiard and Pool Tables.
BRUNSWICK – BALKE – COLL-·
ENDER CO. 263 Wabash av.

Bird Hospitals.
Chicago Bird Hospital, 3711 Cottage
Grove av.

Birds.
Columbia Bird Store, 3711 Cottage
Grove av.
Kaempfer Fred, 88 State

Booksellers and Stationers.
BRENTANO'S, 218 Wabash av..

Bookbinders.
Ringer P. & Go. 108 and 110 Randolph

Bottlers.
(Beer.)
SCHLITZ JOS. BREWING CO.
Ohio cor. Union

Braiding, Beading and Embroid-
ery.
CHICAGO BRAIDING AND EM-
BROIDERY CO. Jos. Alexander
and Hans Schloetzer, props. 78 State
and 254 and 256 Franklin

Butter and Eggs.

CHARLES CREAMERY CO.
Sells Finer Butter than any other Dealer
AND GIVES FULL WEIGHT.
41 N. State St., 313, 35th Street,
Tel. Main-600. Tel. Oakland-1075.

H. G. NABER & CO.
Creamery and Dairy Butter
Fresh-Laid Eggs . . .
2327 Cottage Grove Ave., Chicago
TELEPHONE SO.-905

SPRINGBROOK TIOGA
CREAMERY CO.
81 Dearborn Ave.   Tel. North-1135
Purest Butter.   Freshest Eggs.

Butterine
(Manufacturers.)
BRAUN & FITTS, 187 to 193 North
Union

Chicago Rug Mfg. Co.
I. M. IRALSON, Manager.

Rug Weaving and Steam Carpet Cleaning Works

Carpets Sewed, Fitted
and Renovated.

Estimates Furnished on
Application.

Office and Works:
4524 Cottage Grove Ave.

Telephone:
Oakland-1031.

NOTICE—This is the only house in the city which cleans all Carpets by steam before weaving into rugs, free of charge. SEND FOR CIRCULARS.

...ROBERT ATKIN...
Carpet Cleaning and Renovating Works,
700-702 ROOT STREET.

Carpets Cleaned, Refitted and Relaid. New Carpets Made and Laid. Rugs a specialty.

All Mail Orders will Receive Prompt Attention.

Carpets Taken in Exchange for Work.

Cabinet Makers.
VISCONTI F. 2209 Michigan av.
Cameras.
YALE CAMERA CO. 35 Randolph
Carpet Cleaners.
ATKIN ROBERT CARPET CLEANING & RENOVATING WORKS, 700-702 Root
BEDELL GEORGE MRS. 265 N. Clark
BEECROFT & CO. 107 W. Monroe
Chicago Rug Mnfg. Co. 4524 Cottage Grove av.
50

COOK GEORGE M. 3742 Cottage Grove av.
EUREKA LAUNDRY CO. 155 to 159 W. Madison

Hoerlein Carpet Cleaning and Upholstering Co.

8146 Cottage Grove Ave.
Telephone South-647.

WILSON & CO. 403 N. Clark

CHAUNCEY J. BLAIR, President.   JOHN BENHAM, Vice-Pres't and Gen. Manager.
        GEORGE BARRY, Secretary and Treasurer.

THE CONSUMERS COMPANY

DEALERS IN

ANTHRACITE  BITUMINOUS

35th, Butler and 36th Streets   Telephone South-620

NORTH SIDE DEPOT: No. 416 Wells St., Telephone North-331.
WEST SIDE DEPOT: Nos. 1101-1111 W. Van Buren St., Telephone West-1350.
KENWOOD DEPOT: No. 4839 Cottage Grove Ave., Telephone Oakland-1236.
ENGLEWOOD DEPOT: Nos. 736 to 744 West 65th St., Telephone Wentworth-583.
WOODLAWN DEPOT: Nos. 301 and 303 East 62d St., Telephone Oakland-151.
EVANSTON BRANCH: Nos. 800 and 802 Davis St., Telephone Evanston-229.
CITY BRANCH OFFICE: No. 44 Randolph St., Telephone Main-1397.

Our coal is loaded in box cars at the mines, from these cars we transfer mechanically to our coal pockets which are entirely enclosed and fully protected from the weather.
From the pockets we load directly into the wagons by gravity, the coal passing over screens in loading, thus insuring clean coal.
Send your order, or write or telephone for prices.
We will send our men to carry the coal from the wagon in baskets and place same in your bins, for a slight additional charge.
Weight Guaranteed.

Coal Dealers.

CONSUMERS CO. (THE), 36th and Butler
BECKER J. E. 2013 W. Madison

Corsets.

EDISON CORSET CO.
Nora B. Fitzgerald, Mgr.

The Edison Kid Corset

**Famous for Beauty, Durability, etc.
Extra Long Corsets for Fleshy Ladies a Specialty.**

17 McVICKER'S THEATRE BLDG.

Corsets.
(Fine Custom Work.)
Stathem M. A. 16, 34 Monroe

Corsets.
(Manufacturers.)

ST. CLAIRE CORSET CO.
FINE CORSETS MADE TO ORDER
163 STATE ST., COR. MONROE,
4th Floor.
MME. O. M. ZUGSCHWERT

Cuckoo Clocks.
(Importer.)
KUEHL GEORGE, 184 Randolph, Tel. Main-1626

Curiosity Shop.
BURGHOFFER J. J. G. 584 N. Clark

Dancing Academies.
PETERSON MINNIE MISS, 477 Washington boul.

Decorators.
CRANDALL FRANK A. 2210 and 2212 Indiana av. Tel. South-1

ABRAM & SCHUELER,
Successors to HENRY G. EMMEL CO.
...Painting and Decorating...
PAPER HANGINGS.
500 WELLS ST.   Tel. North-901

JOHN L. NELSON & BRO.
Decorators and Painters.
4 MONROE. TEL. MAIN-2026.

:::W. P. NELSON COMPANY...
**Fine Paper Hangings
Painters and Decorators**
193 WABASH AVE.   Tel. Main-2716

OLIVER S. ROSS,
PAINTER AND DECORATOR
DEALER IN
Wall Paper, Paints, Oils, Glass, etc.
Tel Oakland-1056. } 4221 LAKE AVE.
and United-28.

Dentists.

DR. H. E. BLILER,
DENTIST.
Teeth Without Plate and Fine Gold Work a Specialty.
Suite 1319 Masonic Temple.

Telephone Main-3860.

DR. M. B. PINE,
...Dentist...

Hours:
9 A. M. to 5 P. M.
1102 Stewart Bldg.
N. W. Cor. Washington St.

92 State Street.

Dentists –continued.

Eagles A. E. 354 N. Clark

L. A. EDWARDS, D. D. S.
...DENTIST...
Cor. Michigan Ave. and Thirty-First St.

G. EDGAR EVERETT,
....DENTIST
1496 W. MADISON ST.
TEL. WEST-996.　COR. KEDZIE AVE.
Residence, 964 Warren Ave.

HAYES HAROLD H., D.D.S. 700, 96 State

Mrs. H. E. Lawrence,
...DENTIST...
100 State St.,　　　Chicago.
RELIANCE BUILDING, SUITE 1017,
OVER CARSON, PIRIE, SCOTT & CO.

MARSHALL JOHN S., M.D. 1013, 36 Washington. Tel. Main-4852
NOYES EDMUND, 1109, 92 State
NOYES FREDERICK B. 1109, 92 State

Adelbert H. Peck, M. D.
DENTIST
92 State St., N.W. Cor. Washington St.
　　Suite 1107—Tel. Main-3860

PINE M. B. 1102, 92 State
Rankine Clarence M. Dr. 699 Washington boul.

G. H. RICHARDSON,
...DENTIST...
Tel. Oakland-417.　**3505 Indiana Ave.**

SACKETT H. R., D.D.S. 804, 92 State. Hours 9 to 1, 2 to 5. Tel. Main-3860

DR. E. O. SARBER,
Dentist
291 THIRTY-FIRST STREET,
S. E. COR. WABASH AVENUE.
Telephone So -145.　　Open Evenings.

SWAIN EDGAR D. 1109, 92 State
WHITMORE CHARLES C. 1207 Champlain bldg.

Dermatologists.

BUTLER CORA A. MISS, 102 Auditorium bldg. Wabash av. entrance

Detective Agencies.

MOONEY & BOLAND AGENCY (THE) 418-420 Chicago Stock Exch. bldg.
THIEL'S DETECTIVE SERVICE CO. 701 Monadnock blk.

Diamonds.

CHAMBERS J. B. & CO. 128 Madison

Dramatic Schools.

Mortimer Edmund, Steinway Hall

Dress Pleating.

CASLER'S Dress Pleating Bazaar.
78 State, Room 33.
Accordeon Skirt, Buttons Covered, Button Holes Made, Shirring, Pinking, Fringing, Tucking, Cording, Braiding.

Dressmakers.

Bell Mattie, Steinway Hall
Cummings H. J. Miss, 633 W. Adams

Elocutionists.

COLUMBIA SCHOOL
OF ORATORY and PHYSICAL CULTURE,
STEINWAY HALL.
MARY A. BLOOD, Principal.
IDA MOREY RILEY, Associate Principal.
Send for illustrated catalogue or call and see the school.

SOPER SCHOOL OF ORATORY,
17 Vanburen

Embalmers.

Arntzen Bernard E. 245 N. Clark

Embroideries.

HOME NEEDLE WORK CO.
Corticelli Silks etc. 155 State

Embroideries, Stamping, Etc.

SCHRODER MINNIE MISS, 1329
W. Madison

Employment Agencies.

W. FELLER & CO.

The First German-American Female Employment Office. Ladies supplied with competent help of all nationalities in city and suburbs.

586 N. CLARK ST. Tel. North-455.

Employment Agency
Mrs. Alex Jacobs, Manager
All kinds of help furnished. Domestics a specialty. Character, Experience, and References Carefully Investigated.
385 E. 43d Street. - **Chicago**

MRS. C. OTTINGER
SUCCESSOR TO MRS. STORM,
EMPLOYMENT AGENCY.
Ladies supplied with competent help of all nationalities.
3110 Indiana Ave. Tel. South-15.

Reliable Employment Bureau
132 North Clark Street
Help of all kinds, Male or Female, promptly supplied for any locality.
Established 1889. Tel. North-869.

MISS JENNIE SQUIER
FIRST-CLASS EMPLOYMENT OFFICE
For Private Families Only.
Office References. **186 E. 53d Street.**
Domestics required to furnish best of references.

Engravers.

Wedding Invitations,
Announcements, At Home,
Visiting Cards, Etc.

Fountain & Co.

26 Randolph St. Tel. Main-2759

Stecher M. D. 70 Madison
WINTER ALBERT A. 701, 92 State

Engravers.

(Wedding Invitations, Announcements and Calling Cards.)

CHILDS S. D. & CO. 140 and 142
Monroe

Wedding and Reception
INVITATIONS

Correct Forms. Latest Styles.
Embossed Stationery.

WM. FREUND AND SONS
174-176 State St...CHICAGO

TEL. EX. 423. Opposite Palmer House Entrance

W. McDONALD.

Invitations and Announcements for Weddings. receptions and dinners, Business and Calling Cards, Stamping and Embossing.
Room 51-52, 163 State St.

Florists.

ANDERSON FLORAL CO. Wabash av. and Madison
BAY STATE FLORAL CO. 74 State

BEAUDRY W. E. 5411 Woodlawn av.

GARFIELD PARK FLOWER CO. 1688 W. Madison

LANGE A. 51 Monroe
MANGEL J. 92 State
MUIR SAMUEL, 3530 Michigan av.
WIENHOEBER ERNEST, 413 to 417 Elm. Tel. North-610

Furnaces.
(Warm Air.)
REYNOLDS STEEL PLATE HEATER, office 69 Dearborn

Funeral Director.
Arntzen Bernard E. 245 N. Clark

Furniture.
(High Class)

Furniture.
(Home, Library, etc.)
GLOBE COMPANY, THE 226 and 228 Wabash av.

Furniture and Piano Movers.
DECKER J. E. EXPRESS & VAN CO. 2013 W. Madison
HEBARD'S WAREHOUSE & VAN CO. Winchester and Ogden aves.

Furrier.
MINTZ SAMUEL J. 545 W. Adams

Genealogists.
CLAYPOOL EDWARD A. 219 Dearborn av.

Gloves.
PALAIS ROYAL, 147 State

Gloves.
(Cleaned, Dyed and Repaired.)
REED WM. A. & CO. 274 and 276 Winchester av.

Grocers, Fancy.
AHRENS H. 306 and 308 Ogden av.
EILERS PAUL C. 528 W. Vanburen
JEVNE C. & CO. 109 and 111 Wabash av. and 110 and 112 Madison, 8 Tels. Main-35
STANTON & CO. 54 Madison

Gymnasiums.
YOUNG MEN'S CHRISTIAN ASSOCIATION, 153 Lasalle

Hair.

Chauncey J. Blair, President.   John Benham, Vice-Pres. and Gen'l Mgr.
          George Barry, Secretary and Treasurer.

DISTILLED
WATER ICE Manufactured from Distilled Water. The Purest Product, Lasting Longest, and the Best Delivery.

Distillers of
..HYDROX..   **THE CONSUMERS COMPANY**   Double Distilled and Aerated
A Pure Water.   for Table Use.

BUTLER STREET, 35th to 36th

Give Us a Trial Order.   ✳✳✳✳   Telephone South-620.

NORTH SIDE DEPOT—No. 416 Wells Street. Telephone North-331.
WEST SIDE DEPOT—Nos. 1101-1111 W. Van Buren St. Telephone West-1350.
KENWOOD DEPOT—No. 4839 Cottage Grove Avenue. Telephone Oakland-1236.
ENGLEWOOD DEPOT—Nos. 736 to 744 West 65th St., Tel. Wentworth-583.
WOODLAWN DEPOT—Nos. 301 and 303 East 62d St. Telephone Oakland-151.
EVANSTON BRANCH—Nos. 800 and 802 Davis St. Telephone Evanston-229.
CITY BRANCH OFFICE—No. 44 Randolph Street. Telephone Main-1397.

Hair Dresser and Manicure.

MISS M. E. CONLAN,

Hair Dressing and Manicure.
Facial and Scalp Treatment a Specialty.

SUITE 26 OWINGS BUILDING
209 State Street, cor. Adams.

Hair Dressers.

HANNAH M. HART,

Ladies' Hair Dressing and Manicur-
ing Parlors.

242 Fifty-fifth Street.

PULLMAN BLOCK, HYDE PARK.

Telephone 510-Oakland.
Open Evenings till Eight.

Marshall Miss Carrie M. 19, 34 Monroe

Hair Dressers, Etc.
BURNHAM E. 71 and 73 State

Hair and Scalp Specialist.

MISS A. D. NORLSTANE
Scientific Swedish Facial Massage.
Facial Blemishes removed by Elec-
tricity. Manicuring.

408 VENETIAN BLDG. 34 WASHINGTON

Hardware, Stoves, Etc.

L. H. SCHMERTMAN
         (HARDWARE
Dealer in ⟨ STOVES
Tin and   (BICYCLES
Iron Work.   **588 W. Madison St.**

Hardware and Cutlery.
**ORR & LOCKETT HARDWARE
CO.** 50 State

Harness and Horse Clothing.
HARTFORD & HALL, 369 Wabash
av.
STUDEBAKER BROS. MFG. CO.
378 to 388 Wabash av.

Hay, Grain and Feed.
DECKER J. E. 2013 W. Madison

Hospitals.
**SPRAGUE HOT AIR TREAT-
MENT CO., THE** 5201 Drexel av.
and 663 W. Congress
STREETER HOSPITAL, 2646 Cal-
umet av.

Ice Dealers.
CONSUMERS COMPANY (THE),
36th and Butler

Insurance.
GERMANIA LIFE INS. CO. 416
Unity bldg. 79 Dearborn

Interior Decorators.
Nelson John L. & Bro. 4 Monroe

Iron Works.
Smith F. P. Wire and Iron Works, 100
and 102 Lake

Jewelers.
CHAMBERS J. B. & CO. 128 Madison

Jewelry.
(Actual Manufacturers.)
Winship Chas. A. & Co. 4th floor 78
State

Kindergarten Supplies.
CHARLES THOMAS CO. 195 and
197 Wabash av.

Livery, Boarding and Carriages.
DREXEL STABLES, 171-173, 43d

Livery and Boarding Stables.
CLEVELAND S. E. & SON, 1462 to
1470 W. Madison
KNICKERBOCKER & COST, 135
and 137 E. 35th
PERKINS A. D. 3153 and 3158 Cottage Grove av.
POSTLEWAIT'S LIVERY, 673 and
675 W. VanBuren

Loans on Real Estate.
CHANDLER MORTGAGE CO.
110 Dearborn

Magazines.
MUSIC MAGAZINE PUB. CO.
1402-1405 Auditorium Tower

Mandolin Orchestras.
VARALLO BROS. 85-86 Auditorium
bldg.

Manicures.
Elmore Miss Isabel C. 21, 34 Monroe
Marshall Carrie M. Miss, 34 Monroe

Massage.
ELROY LOTTIE, 182 State
OLDENBORG HUGO A. 18 Central Music hall

Men's Furnishing Goods.
BARTLETT LINCOLN CO. 46
Jackson
Lukey William, 511 Champlain bldg.

Milk Depots.
BOWMAN DAIRY CO. 169 to 173
Ontario, 3514 Rhodes av., 6939-41
Wentworth av., 943 and 945 W. Adams, 1245 and 1247 Belmont av., 214
and 216 Randolph st. Oak Park
MOSS RICHARD E. 3455 Prairie av.

Milliners.
Allison. E. J. 36 and 37, 34 Monroe
SEESE, 919 to 921 N. Clark

Mineral Spring Water.
CHIPPEWA SPRING CO. 14 to 18
Charles pl. Tel. Express-327

Mineral Waters.
Boro-Lithia Spring Water, 11 to 17
Michigan st.
DEER LICK MINERAL
WATER, 185 Dearborn

FRANK S. HANNAH,

Steinway Hall, Chicago,

....MANAGER FOR HIGH CLASS ARTISTS....

JENNY OSBORN, Exclusive Management.

Also authorized to book for prominent eastern managers all VISITING and NEW YORK ARTISTS. Complete entertainments furnished. Recitals given and ORATORIO ARTISTS selected. Anything in HIGH CLASS music given in the most pleasing form with the best available artists.

Music Teachers—continued.

MR. & MRS. E. CALAMARA
MANDOLIN, GUITAR,
AND BANJO . . .
Calamara's Mandolin Orchestra
3156 FOREST AVE.

Fleming Helen, voice culture, Steinway Hall
French Lillian, 810½ Steinway Hall

Miss Frances Frothingham,
**PIANO, ORGAN
AND HARMONY,**
STEINWAY HALL.
Residence: 527 Kenwood Ter., Bryn Mawr.

PROF. BERT. HANNA,
Conservatory of Music.
Teacher of Violin, Mandolin, Guitar, Banjo and Cornet. Also Band and Orchestra.
Music Furnished for all Occasions.
119 Thirty-Fifth St.,   CHICAGO.

HANNAH FRANK S. Steinway
Hall

Mr. W. Waugh Lauder,

...PIANIST...

Originator Musical "Lecture-Recital."

MRS. LAUDER, VOICE AND PIANO.

Studio,   1015 Steinway Hall.

MISS IDA LINN,
SOPRANO
Studio,   807 Steinway Hall
Residence, 8952 Houston Ave.

EDWARD J. NAPIER,
..Concert Organist and Accompanist..
Instruction in Organ, Piano, Sight-Reading and Church Music.
8131 Indiana Ave.

MISS MARY M. NEVIN,
- PIANO -
STEINWAY HALL.
Special advantages for advanced pupils

MRS. N. C. SAFFORD,
Concert Soprano and Teacher of Voice.
Receptions and Musicals a Specialty.
Studio: Room 302 Athenæum Bldg.,
26 E. Van Buren St. Residence: 427 Warren Ave.

MRS. NELLIE BANGS SKELTON,
**•• Pianist, Accompanist, ••
•• and Teacher of Piano. ••**
Studio, 909 Steinway Hall,
Residence, 51 Twenty-Second St.

Smith Nora, Steinway Hall.

MR. L. A. TORRENS,
..*TEACHER OF SINGING*...
Director of Musical Societies.
STEINWAY HALL.

William A. Wegener....
....*TENOR*
VOCAL INSTRUCTION
Suite 1105 Steinway Hall

Music and Musical Instruments.
NELSON & REARDON, 67 Wabash av.

FRANK F. WINTER'S

VIOLIN COLLEGE

642 WASHINGTON BOULEVARD
(Near Robey Street)

Musical Colleges.

AMERICAN CONSERVATORY,
KIMBALL HALL.
All branches of Music and Dramatic
Art. Catalogue mailed free.
JOHN J. HATTSTAEDT, - **Director.**

**CHICAGO CONSERVATORY OF
MUSIC AND DRAMATIC ART,**
BERNHARD ULRICH, MGR.
Auditorium Bldg.,
Wabash Ave., · Cor. Congress St.

CHICAGO NATIONAL COLLEGE OF MUSIC
26 Van Buren Street
DR. H. S. PERKINS, Director.

Musical Instruments.

CABLE PIANO CO. 258-260 Wabash av.
CHICAGO COTTAGE ORGAN CO. 258-260 Wabash av.
CHICKERING - CHASE BROS. CO. 259 Wabash av.
CHURCH JOHN CO. THE, 200 to 206 Wabash av.
CROWN PIANOS, 209 Wabash av.
LYON & HEALY, Wabash av. and Adams
SMITH & BARNES PIANO CO. 250 and 252 Wabash av.
SUMMY CLAYTON F. CO. 220 Wabash av.
VOSE & SONS PIANO CO. 248 Wabash av.
WEBER-WHEELOCK CO. 268 Wabash av.

Musical Schools.
VARALLO BROS. 85-86 Auditorium bldg.

Nurseries.
DUNDEE NURSERY THE, Porter & Hill, props. Garfield boul. bet. State and Mich. av. from 55th to 56th

Obesity Specialists.

SNYDER O. W. F. DR. McVickers Theater bldg.

Oculists and Aurists.

Buffum J. H. 905, 34 Washington, Venetian bldg; hours 9 to 12 a.m. and 3 to 5 p.m.; residence 366 Ontario

DR. W. B. HUNT,
Oculist and Aurist,
Tel. Main-3860. 92 State Street.
Hours: 9 a. m. to 5 p. m., 1102 Stewart Bldg.,
N. W. Cor. Washington Street.

Paul Ph.D., M.D. suite 1201, 103 State, hours 9 a.m. to 2 p.m.; suite 1008 Masonic Temple, hours 2 to 5 p. m.; residence 915 Chase av. Rogers Park, hours 6 to 7 and 9 to 10 p.m.
Walker Sidney, 78 State

Optical Goods.

CHAMBERS J. B. & CO. 128 Madison

L. MANASSE, OPTICIAN.

Eyes
Tested
Free

88
Madison.

Spectacles and Eyeglasses made to order

Orchestras.

FREIBERG BROS. ORCHESTRA
Schiller Bldg., 103-109 Randolph St.
. . . Room 606 . . .
RESIDENCE: 1217 MICHIGAN AVENUE.

KRELL ORCHESTRA
OFFICE:
Brainard Music Co., 298 Wabash Ave.
RESIDENCE:
"The Delmonte," 4257 Grand Boul.,
Cor. 43d St.

**TOMASO MANDOLIN OR-
CHESTRA & SCHOOL,** 21 Central Music Hall

VARALLO BROS. 85-86 Auditorium
bldg.

Organs.

KIMBALL W. W. CO. 243 to 253
Wabash av. south of Jackson
LYON & HEALY, Wabash av. and
Adams

Organs and Pianos.

**CHICAGO COTTAGE ORGAN
CO.** 258 and 260 Wabash av.
CROWN PIANOS, 209 Wabash av.

Painters.

CRANDALL FRANK A. 2210 and
2212 Indiana av. Tel. South-1

JOHN L. NELSON & BRO.
Decorators and Painters,
No. 4 Monroe St. · · Tel. Main-2026·

Painters and Decorators.
COLLISON BROS. 267 Rush
GALVEN & DAVIS, 1448 W. Madison

:::W. P. NELSON COMPANY:::
. Fine Paper Hangings
. Painters and Decorators
193 WABASH AVE. Tel. Main-2716

H. T. WHITE ☙ PAINTER and DECORATOR.
— DEALER · IN —
WALL PAPER, PAINTS, OILS, GLASS, Etc.,
No. 25 East Forty-Third St. .
Phones, Oakland-1252 and United-23.

MORGAN & CO. 477 W. Madison
Palms, Ferns, Etc.

BOTANICAL DECORATING CO.
Importers.
NATURAL PREPARED PALMS.
CYCAS LEAVES, GRASSES, ETC.
271 Wabash Av., 43 Van Buren, Room 7.

Parquet Floors.
CHICAGO FLOOR CO. 132 Wa-
bash av.
DUNFEE J. & CO. 106 Franklin

Photographers.
GEHRIG J. W. 337 W. Madison
Hoffman F. W. 1194 Washington boul.
MELLIN GEO. E. 96 5th av.

Photographic Developing and
Printing.
WARD GEO. B. & CO. 208 Wa-
bash av.

Pianoforte Tuners and Repairers.
BROWN JULIUS N. 269 Wabash
av. res. 3142 Groveland av.

CAMERAS and KODAKS

Largest and most select
line in the city.

DEVELOPING and
PRINTING

—for Amateurs.

YALE CAMERA CO.
35 Randolph Street

Catalogue on request

Pianos.

Bradbury Piano

255-257
WABASH·AVENUE· CHICAGO·
J·M·HAWXHURST manager.

CABLE PIANO CO. 258-260 Wabash av.
CHICKERING-CHASE BROS. CO. 259 Wabash av.
CHICKERING PIANOS, 220 Wabash av.
CROWN PIANOS, 209 Wabash av.

The Everett Piano.

THE JOHN CHURCH COMPANY
General Factors. 200-206 Wabash Ave.

KIMBALL W. W. CO. 243 to 253 Wabash av south of Jackson
LYON & HEALY, Wabash av. and Adams
NELSON & REARDON, 67 Wabash av.
SINGER PIANOS, 235 Wabash av.
SMITH & BARNES PIANO CO 250 and 252 Wabash av.
STEGER & CO. 235 Wabash av.
STORY & CLARK, 231 Wabash av.

SUMMY CLAYTON F. CO. 220 Wabash av.
VOSE & SONS PIANO CO. 248 Wabash av.
WEBER-WHEELOCK CO. 268 Wabash av.

Picture Frames.

W. W. ABBOTT,
PICTURE FRAMES AND MATS
TO ORDER.
Tel. Main-4395.   182 Wabash Ave.

F. A. BRYDEN & CO.,
Picture Frame Makers
255 and 257 Wabash Ave.

MUELLER BROS.
MAKERS OF ARTISTIC
PICTURE FRAMES, MATS AND
PASSEPARTOUTS.
No. 140 Wabash Ave.

SWIGART BROS. ART ROOMS
185 WABASH AVE.
Photographs of Celebrated Paintings,
Manufacturers of Framing.

Plumbers and Gasfitters.
LOESCHER MARTIN, 254 N. Clark, tel. North-484

Railroads.
CHICAGO, MILWAUKEE AND ST. PAUL RY. ticket office, 95 Adams
CHICAGO, ROCK ISLAND & PACIFIC RY. ticket office, 91 Adams

Refrigerators.
(Wickes' Patent.)
**BRUNSWICK - BALKE - COL-
LENDER CO.** 263 Wabash av.

Rheumatic Rings.
**KIMBALL'S ANTI-RHEU-
MATIC RING,** 167 and 169 Wabash
av.

Roofers.
POWELL M. W. CO. 926, 204 Dearborn

**Rugs Manufactured from Old
Carpets.**
CHICAGO RUG MNFG. CO. 4524
Cottage Grove av. tel. Oakland-1031

Safety Deposit Vaults.
**CENTRAL SAFETY DEPOSIT
VAULTS,** The Rookery
**ILLINOIS TRUST SAFETY DE-
POSIT CO.** Vaults, Lasalle st. ne.
cor. Jackson boul.
NATIONAL SAFE DEPOSIT CO.
160 Dearborn

Sanitariums.
**GARFIELD PARK SANITA-
RIUM,** Dr. H. P. Skiles, 900, 100
State
MILWAUKEE SANITARIUM,
Richard Dewey, M.D. 1113, 34 Wash-
ington
**SPRAGUE HOT-AIR TREAT-
MENT CO. THE,** 5201 Drexel av.
and 663 W. Congress

Schools and Academies.
ASSOCIATION COLLEGE, day
and evening departments, Central
Y. M. C. A. 153 Lasalle
**COLUMBIA SCHOOL OF ORA-
TORY AND PHYSICAL CUL-
TURE,** Steinway Hall, 17 Vanburen
SOPER SCHOOL OF ORATORY,
Steinway Hall, 17 Van Buren

Sewing Machines.

WHEELER & WILSON
No. 9
82 & 80 WABASH AVE. Tel. Express-624

Shirt Makers.
Lukey William, 511 Champlain bldg.
Stationers.
**THAYER & JACKSON STA-
TIONERY CO.** 71 Monroe

Steamship Agencies.
(Ocean.)
WHITE STAR LINE, S. Tenney
French, gen. west'n agt. 244 S. Clark

Steamship Agencies.
(Ocean Lines.)
CUNARD LINE, F. G. Whiting,
mngr. Western Dept. 67 Dearborn
cor. Randolph
DOMINION LINE, Gus Broberg,
gen. western pass. agt. 69 Dearborn
HAMBURG AMERICAN LINE,
C. Ramm, west'n agt. nw. cor. Ran-
dolph and Lasalle
**INTERNATIONAL NAVIGA-
TION CO.** F. C. Brown, W. G. P. A.
143 Lasalle
**NORTH GERMAN LLOYD
STEAMSHIP CO.** 90-92 Dearborn

Storage.
**HEBARD'S WAREHOUSE &
VAN CO.** Winchester and Ogden
avs.

The Palace Storage Co.
Lake Ave. and 42nd St.
Phone Oakland-1244.
**500 Moth-Proof Iron Rooms, Fire-Proof
Vaults and Steel Deposit Boxes.**

Tailors, Merchant.
McMILLAN JAMES & CO. 44 Jack-
son boul.
Stoffregen C. 112 N. Clark
SCHALL TAILORING CO., THE,
317 Dearborn

Tally-ho Coaches, Busses, etc.
(For Parties, Picnics and Parades.)
**HEBARD'S WAREHOUSE &
VAN CO.** Winchester and Ogden
avs.

Taxidermists.

RUD HAMAN,
ART TAXIDERMIST.
PRICES REASONABLE.
434 Wells Street.

KAEMPFER FRED, 88 State

Teas, Coffees and Spices,
CEYLON TEA COMPANY THE,
514 W. Madison

Teas and Coffees.

HENRY G. NABER & CO.

2327 Cottage Grove Avenue.

Tel. South-905.

Theatrical Agencies.

WESTERN THEATRICAL EX-CHANGE, Arthur Fabish, mngr., 20½ and 21, 81 S. Clark

Tires, Rubber.
(Carriages, Buggies, Etc.)

RUBBER TIRE WHEEL CO. THE, 447 Wabash av.

Umbrellas, Parasols, Etc.
(Made and Repaired.)

GUMM M. C. 83 Wabash av.

Undertakers.

Open Day and Night. Tel. North-615.

R. A. ALLEN & CO.
FUNERAL DIRECTORS

284 N. Clark St. Private Ambulance.

Office Never Closed. · Established 1880

Bernard E. Arntzen
Funeral Director
245 North Clark Street

Fine Furnishings
Private Ambulance Telephone North-56.

C. E. ELLSWORTH CO.
UNDERTAKERS

809 W. Madison St. Tel. West-1347.

Lady Attendant.

Furth & Co. 2931 Cottage Grove av.

POSTLEWAIT S. C. 310 and 312 Ogden av.

Underwear.

STRAUSS H. 258 E. Division and 152 Dearborn

Upholsterers.

A. G. AEPPLI,
ARTISTIC UPHOLSTERING,
Upholstered Furniture to order, Draperies and Shades.

3142 Cottage Grove Ave.
Factory Rear 3142-3144.

51

ANDERSON & EKSTROM,
UPHOLSTERERS,
CURTAINS AND CARPETS

Tel. South-1184. 232, 35th St.

WM. DRITLEY
Successor to John Nelson

Upholsterer and Decorator

268 31ST STREET

Telephone South-243

THEO. RAUSCHERT

UPHOLSTERER AND GENERAL REPAIRER
Mail orders receive attention

1406 MADISON ST.

Upholsterers and Drapers.

HOERLEIN CARPET CLEANING AND UPHOLSTERING CO.

3146 COTTAGE GROVE AVENUE
Telephone South 647.

Vocal Teachers.

MARIE BIRO DE MARION
VOCAL INSTRUCTIONS
Monday and Thursday, Steinway Hall, Room 614
Tuesday and Friday, at Academy of Our Lady,
Longwood, 5th year.
Wed. and Sat. at Residence 3407 Indiana Ave.
Applicants can hear my pupil Clara Bunte.

Dunn Mrs. L. M. Steinway Hall

Miss Rose A. Moore
- - - Soprano - - -

STEINWAY HALL Voice Culture

Wall Paper.

CRANDALL FRANK A. 2210 and 2212 Indiana av. Tel. South-1

MORGAN & CO. 477 W. Madison

JOHN L. NELSON & BRO.
INTERIOR DECORATION
WALL PAPER, PAINTING

4 Monroe Street Tel. Main-2026

:::W. P. NELSON COMPANY:::
Fine Paper Hangings
Painters and Decorators

193 WABASH AVE. Tel. Main-2716

HYDROX.

The most delicious, pure, twice-distilled aerated table water produced. Delivered in sealed glass bottles.

One case twelve half-gallon bottles............60 cents.
One five-gallon bottle.........................50 cents.

Hydrox Carbonated Waters and Sparkling Beverages, all of superior quality and made from distilled water.

THE CONSUMERS COMPANY

Telephone South-620.   35th, Butler and 36th Streets.

NORTH SIDE DEPOT, No. 416 Wells St.   . . . . . Tel. North-331
WEST SIDE DEPOT, Nos. 1101-1111 W. VanBuren St. Tel. West-1350
KENWOOD DEPOT, No. 4839 Cottage Grove Ave. . . Tel. Oakland-1236
ENGLEWOOD DEPOT, Nos. 736 to 744 West 65th St. Tel. Went'th -583
WOODLAWN DEPOT, Nos. 301 and 303 E. 62d St. . Tel. Oakland-151
EVANSTON BRANCH, Nos. 800 and 802 Davis St. . . Tel. Evanston-229
CITY BRANCH OFFICE, No. 44 Randolph St. . . . Tel. Main-1397

CHAUNCEY J. BLAIR, Pres.   JOHN BENHAM Vice-Pres and Gen. Mgr.
GEORGE BARRY, Secretary and Treasurer.

Watches.

CHAMBERS J. B. & CO. 128 Madison

Water.
(Distilled.)

CONSUMERS COMPANY THE, 36th and Butler

Water Stills.

PALATABLE WATER STILL CO. 518, 145 Lasalle

Waukesha Water.

SILURIAN MINERAL SPRING CO. 431 Wabash av. Tel. Harrison-401 Waukesha Hygeia Mineral Spring Water, 11 to 17 Michigan st.

White Rock Mineral Spring Co.

O. W. HINCKLEY, Manager.

...570 LOOMIS STREET...
Telephone Canal-212.

Window Shades.

CRANDALL FRANK A. 2210 and 2212 Indiana av. Tel. South-1
SMITH AMOS, 405 N. Clark

Wines.
(Unfermented.)

DR. A. B. RICE
PURE GRAPE JUICE

A delicious Nutrient for Invalids and Delicate Persons. Expressed from Clean, Selected Grapes.

Suite 60.   78 State Street

Wire and Iron Works.

SMITH F. P. WIRE AND IRON WORKS, 100 and 102 Lake

Wood Carpets.

CHICAGO FLOOR CO. 132 Wabash av.

796

PART NINE.

DIAGRAMS

OF

PLACES OF AMUSEMENT

SHOWING POSITION OF BOXES AND SEATS BY
NUMBER AND SECTION

ASSOCIATION AUDITORIUM

AUDITORIUM

CENTRAL MUSIC HALL

COLUMBIA THEATRE

GREAT NORTHERN THEATRE

POWER'S THEATRE

McVICKER'S THEATRE

Illinois Trust
Safety Deposit Company

Northeast Cor. La Salle St. and Jackson Blvd.

A SAFE PLACE AT SMALL COST

TO KEEP YOUR BANK BOOKS, TAX RECEIPTS, DEEDS, NOTES,
BONDS, AND OTHER VALUABLE PROPERTY.

The Storage Vaults are the most convenient and secure place in the city for storing
Silver Plate, Jewelry and all articles coveted by
burglars.

ROBERT BOYD,
Secretary and Manager.

Telephone

ASSOCIATION AUDITORIUM

153 and 155 La Salle St., corner Arcade Court.   *Seating Capacity, 1,000*

GENERAL OFFICE, 709 ASSOCIATION BLDG., 153. LA SALLE ST.

Telephone Express-359

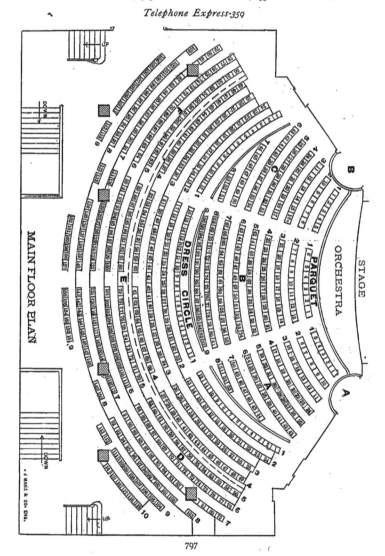

797

ABEL'S ART STUDIO

772 W. Madison Street.

Lewis Institute, corner Robey Street.

Permanent Exhibition of Free Hand
Portraits in Pastel, Oil and Crayon.

Portraits in Oil and Pastel a Specialty.
Work Guaranteed.

Artistic Picture Frames Made to Order.

Have you any kind of Pictures or Paintings needing Frames?
Call, Examine and get Prices.

TEL. WEST-22

MORGAN & CO.

R. MORGAN, MNGR.

PAINTERS AND DECORATORS

WALL PAPER, PAINTS
OILS AND GLASS . . .

ESTIMATES GIVEN FOR PAINTING, CALCIMINING
PAPER HANGING, ETC.

477 W. MADISON ST.

FOYER

■　　　■　　　■　　　■

■

MAIN BALCONY

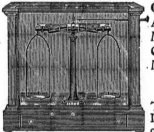

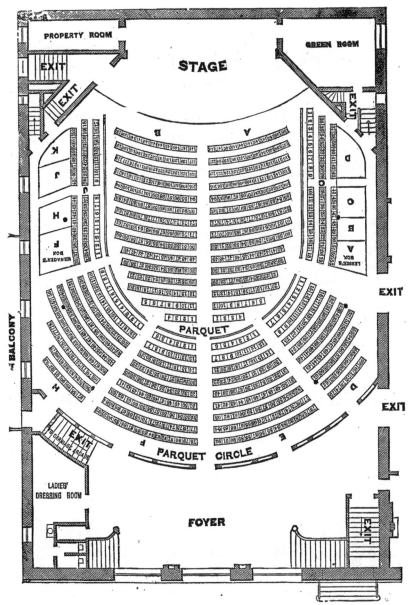

CENTRAL MUSIC HALL

803

804

The Columbia

The Leading Theatre of Chicago

AL. HAYMAN, New York
WILL DAVIS, Chicago
Proprietors and Managers

MONROE AND DEARBORN STS.

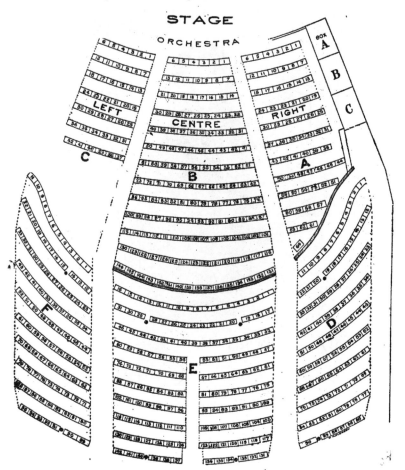

Presents only Highest Class Attractions

GREAT NORTHERN THEATRE

CHAS. P. SALISBURY AND FRANK R. TATE,
Managers.

*Entrances on Jackson Boulevard, and Quincy Street,
Between State and Dearborn Streets.*

THE SAFEST AND THE HANDSOMEST THEATRE
IN THE WORLD.

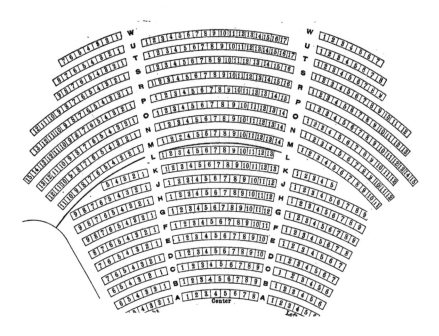

POWERS' THEATRE

Randolph and La Salle Streets

HARRY J. POWERS, Sole Lessee and Manager

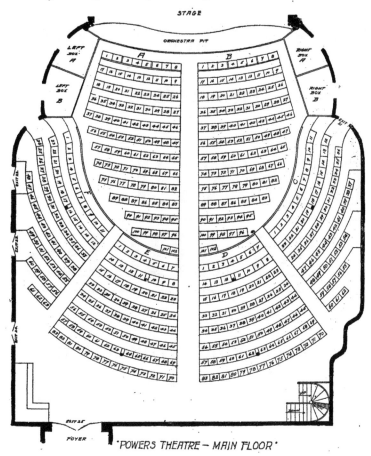

"POWERS THEATRE — MAIN FLOOR"

POWERS' THEATRE

Randolph and La Salle Streets

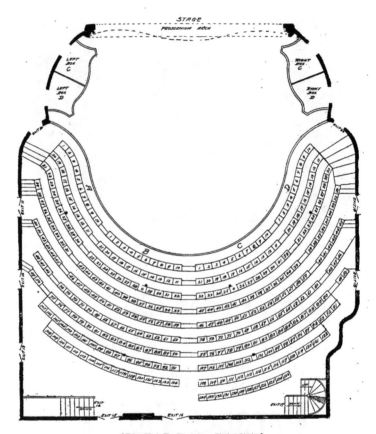

POWERS THEATRE - BALCONY

McVICKER'S THEATER

MADISON STREET, NEAR STATE STREET

JACOB LITT, LESSEE AND MANAGER
SOL LITT, BUSINESS MANAGER

Every Night and Saturday Matinee, 25c, 35c, 50c, 75c and $1.00
Wednesday Matinee, All Seats Reserved, 25c and 50c

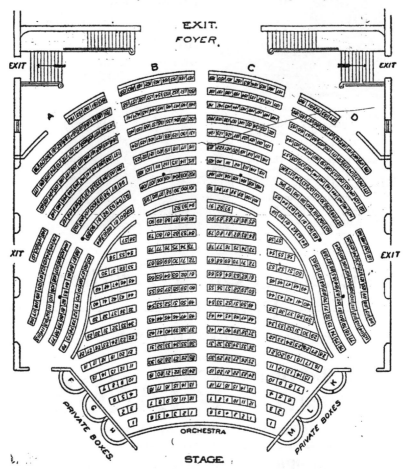

Telephone West-283 *100 Lake ℓℓ...*
cor Dearborn

HEBARD'S

WAREHOUSE AND VAN COMPANY

Offices and Warehouses:
Winchester and Ogden Avenues

Furniture and Pianos

Stored, Packed, Moved and Shipped

Private Locked Rooms
for Furniture

Trunks Stored for One
Cent Each Day

Winchester and Ogden Avenues

Lightning Source UK Ltd.
Milton Keynes UK
UKHW010628101218
333747UK00012B/491/P